VIRGINIA COURT RULES AND PROCEDURE

VOLUME I – STATE

2016

THOMSON REUTERS™

Mat #41608719

ISBN: 978–0–314–67496–8

PREFACE

Designed for use in the office or courtroom, this pamphlet contains the Virginia state rules.

WHAT'S NEW

Virginia Court Rules and Procedure, Volume I – State, 2016, includes rules and associated material governing practice before the Virginia state courts. It replaces the 2015 edition, and any accompanying supplements. It is current with amendments received through October 1, 2015.

CONTACT US

For additional information or research assistance, call the West reference attorneys at 1-800-REF-ATTY (1-800-733-2889). Contact our U.S. legal editorial department directly with your questions and suggestions by e-mail at editors.us-legal@thomsonreuters.com.

Thank you for subscribing to this product. Should you have any questions regarding this product please contact Customer Service at 1-800-328-4880 or by fax at 1-800-340-9378. If you would like to inquire about related publications, or to place an order, please contact us at 1-800-344-5009 or visit us online.

The Publisher

November 2015

THOMSON REUTERS PROVIEW™

TABLE OF CONTENTS

	Page
Rules of the Supreme Court of Virginia	1
Index to Supreme Court Rules	425
Civil Remedies and Procedure [Title 8.01, Code of Virginia]	459
Index	711
Criminal Procedure [Title 19.2, Code of Virginia]	795
Index	1009
Medical Malpractice Rules of Practice	1063
Rules of the Judicial Inquiry and Review Commission	1071
Rules of the Virginia Workers' Compensation Commission	1077
Bylaws of the Virginia State Bar and Council	1093
Mandatory Continuing Legal Education Regulations	1101
Clients' Protection Fund Rules	1127

RULES OF THE SUPREME COURT OF VIRGINIA

Including Amendments Received Through
October 15, 2015

Table of Rules

PART ONE. GENERAL RULES APPLICABLE TO ALL PROCEEDINGS

Rule
1:1. Finality of Judgments, Orders and Decrees.
1:1A. Recovery of Appellate Attorney's Fees in Circuit Court.
1:2. Venue in Criminal Cases [Repealed Effective March 1, 2007].
1:3. Reporters and Transcripts of Proceedings in Courts.
1:4. General Provisions as to Pleadings.
1:4A. A Special Rule for Pleadings in General District Courts [Repealed Effective July 1, 1982].
1:5. Counsel.
1:6. Res Judicata Claim Preclusion.
1:7. Computation of Time.
1:8. Amendments.
1:9. Discretion of Court.
1:10. Verification.
1:11. Striking the Evidence.
1:12. Service of Papers After the Initial Process.
1:13. Endorsements.
1:14. Preservation of the Record.
1:15. Local Rules of Court.
1:16. Filing Format and Procedure.
1:17. Electronic Filing and Service.
1:18. Pretrial Scheduling Order.
1:19. Pretrial Conferences.
1:20. Scheduling Civil Cases for Trial.
1:21. Preliminary Voir Dire Information.
1:22. Exercise of Challenges to Prospective Jurors.
1:23. Note Taking by Jurors.

APPENDIX OF FORMS

Form
1. Praecipe (Rule 1:15(b)).
2. Instructions (Rule 1:15(c)).
3. Uniform Pretrial Scheduling Order (Rule 1:18B).

PART ONE A. FOREIGN ATTORNEYS

Introduction.
Rule
1A:1. Admission to Practice in This Commonwealth Without Examination.
1A:2. Foreign Patent and Trademark Attorneys—When Admitted to Practice in the Courts of This State Limited to Patent and Trademark Law Without Examination.
1A:3. Revocation of Certificates Issued to Attorneys Admitted Pursuant to Rule 1A:2.
1A:4. Out–Of–State Lawyers—When Allowed by Comity to Participate in a Case Pro Hac Vice.
1A:5. Virginia Corporate Counsel & Corporate Counsel Registrants.
1A:6. Foreign Attorneys—Registered Military Legal Assistance Attorneys.
Rule
1A:7. Certification of Foreign Legal Consultants.
1A:8. Military Spouse Provisional Admission.

APPENDIX OF FORMS

Form
1. Application to Appear Pro Hac Vice Before a Virginia Tribunal.
2. Motion and Oath for Admission as Corporate Counsel.

PART TWO. VIRGINIA RULES OF EVIDENCE

ARTICLE I. GENERAL PROVISIONS

Rule
2:101. Title.
2:102. Scope and Construction of These Rules.
2:103. Objections and Proffers.
2:104. Preliminary Determinations.
2:105. Proof Admitted for Limited Purposes.
2:106. Remainder of a Writing or Recorded Statement (Rule 2:106(b) Derived from Code § 8.01–417.1).

ARTICLE II. JUDICIAL NOTICE

2:201. Judicial Notice of Adjudicative Facts.
2:202. Judicial Notice of Law (Derived from Code §§ 8.01–386 and 19.2–265.2).
2:203. Judicial Notice of Official Publications (Derived from Code § 8.01–388).

ARTICLE III. PRESUMPTIONS

2:301. Presumptions in General in Civil Actions and Proceedings.
2:302. Applicability of Federal Law in Civil Actions and Proceedings.

ARTICLE IV. RELEVANCY, POLICY, AND CHARACTER TRAIT PROOF

2:401. Definition of "Relevant Evidence".
2:402. Relevant Evidence Generally Admissible; Irrelevant Evidence Inadmissible.
2:403. Exclusion of Relevant Evidence on Grounds of Prejudice, Confusion, Misleading the Jury, or Needless Presentation of Cumulative Evidence.
2:404. Character Evidence Not Admissible to Prove Conduct; Exceptions; Other Crimes.
2:405. Methods of Proving Character Traits.
2:406. Habit and Routine Practice in Civil Cases (Derived from Code § 8.01–397.1).
2:407. Subsequent Remedial Measures (Derived from Code § 8.01–418.1).
2:408. Compromise and Offers to Compromise.
2:409. Evidence of Abuse Admissible in Certain Criminal Trials (Derived from Code § 19.2–270.6).
2:410. Withdrawn Pleas, Offers to Plead, and Related Statements.
2:411. Insurance.

Rule

2:412. Admissibility of Complaining Witness' Prior Sexual Conduct; Criminal Sexual Assault Cases; Relevance of Past Behavior (Derived from Code § 18.2–67.7).
2:413. Evidence of Similar Crimes in Child Sexual Offense Cases (Derived from Code § 18.2–67.7:1).

ARTICLE V. PRIVILEGES

2:501. Privileged Communications.
2:502. Attorney–Client Privilege.
2:503. Clergy and Communicant Privilege (Derived from Code §§ 8.01–400 and 19.2–271.3).
2:504. Spousal Testimony and Marital Communications Privileges (Rule 2:504(a) Derived from Code § 8.01–398; and Rule 2:504(b) Derived from Code § 19.2–271.2).
2:505. Healing Arts Practitioner and Patient Privilege (Derived from Code § 8.01–399).
2:506. Mental Health Professional and Client Privilege (Derived from Code § 8.01–400.2).
2:507. Privileged Communications Involving Interpreters (Derived from Code §§ 8.01–400.1, 19.2–164, and 19.2–164.1).

ARTICLE VI. WITNESS EXAMINATION

2:601. General Rule of Competency.
2:602. Lack of Personal Knowledge.
2:603. Oath or Affirmation.
2:604. Interpreters (Derived from Code § 8.01–406).
2:605. Competency of Court Personnel as Witnesses (Derived from Code) § 19.2–271.
2:606. Competency of Juror as Witness.
2:607. Impeachment of Witnesses (Rule 2:607(b) Derived from Code § 8.01–401(A); and Rule 2:607(c) Derived from Code § 8.01–403).
2:608. Impeachment by Evidence of Reputation for Truthtelling and Conduct of Witness.
2:609. Impeachment by Evidence of Conviction of Crime (Derived from Code § 19.2–269).
2:610. Bias or Prejudice of a Witness.
2:611. Mode and Order of Interrogation and Presentation (Rule 2:611(c) Derived from Code § 8.01–401(A)).
2:612. Writing or Object Used to Refresh Memory.
2:613. Prior Statements of Witness (Rule 2:613(a)(i) Derived from Code § 8.01–403; Rule 2:613(b)(i) Derived from Code §§ 8.01–404 and 19.2–268.1; and Rule 2:613(b)(ii) Derived from Code § 8.01–404).
2:614. Calling and Interrogation of Witnesses by Court.
2:615. Exclusion of Witnesses (Rule 2:615(a) Derived from Code §§ 8.01–375, 19.2–184, and 19.2–265.1; Rule 2:615(b) Derived from Code § 8.01–375; and Rule 2:615(c) Derived from Code § 19.2–265.1).

ARTICLE VII. OPINIONS AND EXPERT TESTIMONY

2:701. Opinion Testimony by Lay Witnesses (Derived from Code § 8.01–401.3(B)).
2:702. Testimony by Experts (Rule 2:702(a)(i) Derived from Code § 8.01–401.3(A)).
2:703. Basis of Expert Testimony (Rule 2:703(a) Derived from Code § 8.01–401.1).
2:704. Opinion on Ultimate Issue (Rule 2:704(a) Derived from Code § 8.01–401.3(B) and (C)).
2:705. Facts or Data Used in Testimony (Rule 2:705(a) Derived from Code § 8.01–401.1).
2:706. Use of Learned Treatises with Experts (Rule 2:706(a) Derived from Code § 8.01–401.1).

Rule

ARTICLE VIII. HEARSAY

2:801. Definitions.
2:802. Hearsay Rule.
2:803. Hearsay Exceptions Applicable Regardless of Availability of the Declarant (Rule 2:803(10)(a) Derived from Code § 8.01–390(C); Rule 2:803(10)(b) Derived from Code § 19.2–188.3; Rule 2:803(17) Derived from Code § 8.2–724; and Rule 2:803(23) Is Derived from Code § 19.2–268.2).
2:804. Hearsay Exceptions Applicable Where the Declarant Is Unavailable (Rule 2:804(b)(5) Derived from Code § 8.01–397).
2:805. Hearsay Within Hearsay.
2:806. Attacking and Supporting Credibility of Hearsay Declarant.

ARTICLE IX. AUTHENTICATION

2:901. Requirement of Authentication or Identification.
2:902. Self–Authentication (Rule 2:902(6) Derived from Code § 8.01–390.3 and Code § 8.01–391(D)).
2:903. Subscribing Witness Testimony Not Necessary.

ARTICLE X. BEST EVIDENCE

2:1001. Definitions.
2:1002. Requirement of Production of Original.
2:1003. Use of Substitute Checks (Derived from Code § 8.01–391.1(A) and (B)).
2:1004. Admissibility of Other Evidence of Contents.
2:1005. Admissibility of Copies (Derived from Code § 8.01–391).
2:1006. Summaries.
2:1007. Testimony or Written Admission of a Party.
2:1008. Functions of Court and Jury.

ARTICLE XI. APPLICABILITY

2:1101. Applicability of Evidentiary Rules.

PART TWO A. APPEALS PURSUANT TO THE ADMINISTRATIVE PROCESS ACT

2A:1. Authorization; Definitions; Application.
2A:2. Notice of Appeal.
2A:3. Record on Appeal.
2A:4. Petition for Appeal.
2A:5. Further Proceedings.
2A:6. Small Business Challenges.

PART THREE. PRACTICE AND PROCEDURE IN CIVIL ACTIONS

3:1. Scope.
3:2. Commencement of Civil Actions.
3:3. Filing of Pleadings; Return of Certain Writs.
3:4. Copies of Complaint.
3:5. The Summons.
3:6. Proof of Service.
3:7. Bills of Particulars.
3:8. Answers, Pleas, Demurrers and Motions.
3:9. Counterclaims.
3:10. Cross–Claims.
3:11. Reply.
3:12. Joinder of Additional Parties.
3:13. Third–Party Practice.
3:14. Intervention.
3:15. Statutory Interpleader.
3:16. New Parties.
3:17. Substitution of Parties.
3:18. General Provisions as to Pleadings.

Rule
3:19. Default.
3:20. Summary Judgment.
3:21. Jury Trial of Right.
3:22. Trial by Jury or by the Court.
3:22A. Examination of Prospective Trial Jurors (Voir Dire).
3:23. Use of and Proceedings Before a Commissioner in Chancery.
3:24. Appeal of Orders of Quarantine or Isolation Regarding Communicable Diseases of Public Health Threat.
3:25. Claims for Attorney's Fees.

PART THREE A. CRIMINAL PRACTICE AND PROCEDURE

3A:1. Scope.
3A:2. Purpose and Interpretation; Definitions.
3A:2.1. Venue in Criminal Cases.
3A:3. The Complaint.
3A:4. Arrest Warrant or Summons.
3A:5. The Grand Jury.
3A:6. The Indictment and the Information.
3A:7. Capias or Summons Upon Indictment or Information.
3A:8. Pleas.
3A:9. Pleadings and Motions for Trial; Defenses and Objections.
3A:10. Trial Together of More Than One Accused or More Than One Offense.
3A:11. Discovery and Inspection.
3A:12. Subpoena.
3A:13. Trial by Jury or by Court.
3A:14. Trial Jurors.
3A:14.1. Confidentiality of Juror Personal Information.
3A:15. Motion to Strike or to Set Aside Verdict; Judgment of Acquittal or New Trial.
3A:16. Instructions.
3A:17. Jury Verdicts.
3A:17.1. Proceedings in Bifurcated Jury Trials of Non–Capital Felonies and Class 1 Misdemeanors.
3A:18. Death Penalty.
3A:19. Appeals.
3A:20. Time.
3A:21. Service and Filing of Papers.
3A:22. Forms.
3A:23. Electronic Filing.
3A:24. Special Rule Applicable to Post–Conviction Proceedings: Circuit Court Orders Denying Petitions for Writs of Habeas Corpus.
3A:25. Special Rule Applicable to Post–Conviction Proceedings: Inmate Filings in the Trial Courts Under Code § 8.01–654.

APPENDIX OF FORMS

Form
1. Criminal Complaint (Rule 3A:3).
2. Statement of Witness for Arrest Warrant (Rule 3A:3).
3. Summons (Rule 3A:4(b)).
4. Indictments (Rule 3A:6).
5. Capias (Rule 3A:7).
6. Suggested Questions to Be Put by the Court to an Accused Who Has Pleaded Guilty (Rule 3A:8).
7. Suggested Questions to Be Put by the Court to an Accused Who Has Pleaded Not Guilty (Rule 3A:8).
8. Subpoena (Rule 3A:12(a)).
9. Subpoena Duces Tecum (Rule 3A:12(b)).

Form
10. Contents of Sentencing Orders.
11. Misdemeanor Proceedings in District and Circuit Courts (Rule 3A:8(b)(2); Rule 7C:6; and Rule 8:18).

PART THREE B. TRAFFIC INFRACTIONS AND UNIFORM FINE SCHEDULE

Rule
3B:1. Purpose.
3B:2. Uniform Fine Schedule.

PART THREE C. NON–TRAFFIC PREPAYABLE OFFENSES AND UNIFORM FINE SCHEDULE

3C:1. Purpose and Effective Date.
3C:2. Uniform Fine Schedule.

PART FOUR. PRETRIAL PROCEDURES, DEPOSITIONS AND PRODUCTION AT TRIAL

4:0. Application of Part Four.
4:1. General Provisions Governing Discovery.
4:2. Depositions Before Action or Pending Appeal.
4:3. Persons Before Whom Depositions May Be Taken.
4:4. Stipulations Regarding Discovery.
4:5. Depositions Upon Oral Examination.
4:6. Depositions Upon Written Questions.
4:6A. Number of Depositions.
4:7. Use of Depositions in Court Proceedings.
4:7A. Audio–Visual Depositions.
4:8. Interrogatories to Parties.
4:9. Production by Parties of Documents, Electronically Stored Information, and Things; Entry on Land for Inspection and Other Purposes; Production at Trial.
4:9A. Production from Non–Parties of Documents, Electronically Stored Information, and Things and Entry on Land for Inspection and Other Purposes; Production at Trial.
4:10. Physical and Mental Examination of Persons.
4:11. Requests for Admission.
4:12. Failure to Make Discovery; Sanctions.
4:13. Pretrial Procedure; Formulating Issues.
4:14. Disposition of Discovery Material.
4:15. Motions Practice.

PART FIVE. THE SUPREME COURT

A. GENERAL

5:1. Scope, Citation, Applicability, and General Provisions.
5:1A. Penalties for Non–Compliance; Show Cause; Dismissal.
5:2. Sessions and Divisions.
5:3. Convening of Court—When En Banc—When in Division.
5:4. Motions and Responses; Orders.
5:5. Filing Deadlines; Post Trial Proceedings Below; Timely Filing by Mail; Inmate Mailing; Extension of Time.
5:6. Forms of Briefs and Other Papers.
5:6A. Citation of Supplemental Authorities.

B. ORIGINAL JURISDICTION

5:7. Petitions for Writs of Habeas Corpus, Mandamus, and Prohibition.
5:7A. Petitions for Writs of Habeas Corpus in Cases in Which the Sentence of Death Has Been Imposed.
5:7B. Petition for a Writ of Actual Innocence.

Rule

C. Procedure For Filing An Appeal From A Trial Court

5:8. Applicability.
5:8A. Appeal from Partial Final Judgment in Multi–Party Cases.
5:9. Notice of Appeal.
5:10. Record on Appeal: Contents.
5:11. Record on Appeal: Transcript or Written Statement.
5:12. Judge Authorized to Act.
5:13. Record on Appeal: Preparation and Transmission.
5:13A. Digital Appellate Record: Preparation and Transmission.

D. Procedure For Filing An Appeal From the Court of Appeals

5:14. Notice of Appeal; Certification.
5:15. Record on Appeal from Court of Appeals or Certification for Review.
5:16. Disposition of Record.

E. Perfecting the Appeal

5:17. Petition for Appeal.
5:17A. Petition for Review Pursuant to Code § 8.01–626; Injunctions.
5:18. Brief in Opposition.
5:19. Reply Brief.
5:20. Petition for Rehearing After Refusal of Petition for Appeal, Refusal of Assignments of Cross–Error, or Disposition of an Original Jurisdiction Petition.
5:20A. Denial of Appeal: Petition for Rehearing [Deleted].

F. Special Rules

5:21. Special Rules Applicable to Certain Appeals of Right.
5:22. Special Rule for Appeals in Death Penalty Cases.

G. Procedure Following Perfection of Appeal

5:23. Perfection of Appeal; Docketing.
5:24. Security for Appeal.
5:25. Preservation of Issues for Appellate Review.
5:26. General Requirements for All Briefs.
5:27. Requirements for Opening Brief of Appellant.
5:28. Requirements for Brief of Appellee.
5:29. Requirements for Reply Brief.
5:30. Briefs Amicus Curiae.
5:31. Covers of Documents.
5:32. Appendix.
5:33. Oral Argument.

H. Decision, Costs, and Mandate

5:34. Notice of Decision.
5:35. Attorney's Fees, Costs, and Notarized Bill of Costs.
5:36. Mandate.
5:37. Petition for Rehearing After Consideration by the Full Court.

I. Settlement or Withdrawal

5:38. Settlement or Withdrawal of Pending Appeal.

J. Supreme Court of the United States

5:39. Delay in Issuing Mandate Upon Appeal or Petition to Supreme Court of the United States.

K. Certification of Questions of Law

5:40. Certification Procedures.

Rule

L. Appeals Relating to Quarantine or Isolation Orders

5:41. Appeal of Orders Relating to Quarantine or Isolation of Persons.

Appendix of Forms

Form

1. Bond for Costs Alone—Appeal of Right from Circuit Court to Court of Appeals (Including Further Appeal to the Supreme Court).
2. Bond for Costs and Suspension—Appeal from Circuit Court to Appellate Court.
3. Bond for Costs Alone Required by Appellate Court on Appeal from Circuit Court.
4. Bond for Suspension Alone Required by Appellate Court on Appeal from Circuit Court.
5. Bond for Costs and Suspension Required by Appellate Court on Appeal from Circuit Court.
6. Additional Bond Required by Appellate Court on Appeal from Circuit Court.
7. Bond for Costs Alone—Appeal of Right from Virginia Workers' Compensation Commission to Court of Appeals (Including Further Appeal to the Supreme Court).
8. Bond for Costs Alone—Required by Supreme Court on Appeal of Right from State Corporation Commission.
9. Bond for Costs and Suspension—Required by Supreme Court on Appeal of Right from State Corporation Commission.
10. Form for Execution and Acknowledgment of All Bonds.
11. Irrevocable Letters of Credit.
12. Petition for a Writ of Actual Innocence.

PART FIVE A. THE COURT OF APPEALS

A. General

Rule

5A:1. Scope, Citation, Applicability and General Provisions.
5A:1A. Penalties for Non–Compliance; Show Cause; Dismissal.
5A:2. Motions and Responses; Orders.
5A:3. Filing Deadlines; Post Trial Proceedings Below; Timely Filing by Mail; Inmate Filing; Extension of Time.
5A:4. Forms of Briefs and Other Papers.
5A:4A. Citation of Supplemental Authorities.

B. Original Jurisdiction

5A:5. Original Proceedings.

C. Procedure For Filing An Appeal From the Trial Court

5A:6. Notice of Appeal.
Form. Notice of Appeal From Trial Court (Rule 5A:6).
5A:7. Record on Appeal: Contents.
5A:8. Record on Appeal: Transcript or Written Statement.
5A:9. Judge Authorized to Act.
5A:10. Record on Appeal: Preparation and Transmission.
5A:10A. Digital Appellate Record: Preparation and Transmission.

D. Procedure for Filing An Appeal From the Workers' Compensation Commission

5A:11. Special Rule Applicable to Appeals from the Virginia Workers' Compensation Commission.

Rule

E. Procedure On Petition For Appeal In Criminal Cases and Traffic Infractions

5A:12. Petition for Appeal.
5A:13. Brief in Opposition.
5A:14. Reply Brief.
5A:15. Denial of Petition for Appeal; Petition for Rehearing.
5A:15A. Denial of Petition for Appeal; Petition for Rehearing Filed by Electronic Means.

F. Procedure Following Perfection of Appeal

5A:16. Perfection of Appeal; Docketing.
5A:17. Security for Appeal.
5A:18. Preservation of Issues for Appellate Review.
5A:19. General Requirements for All Briefs.
5A:20. Requirements for Opening Brief of Appellant.
5A:21. Requirements for Brief of Appellee or Guardian Ad Litem.
5A:22. Requirements for Reply Brief.
5A:23. Briefs Amicus Curiae.
5A:24. Covers of Documents.
5A:25. Appendix.
5A:26. Effect of Noncompliance with Rules Regarding Briefs.
5A:27. Summary Disposition.
5A:28. Oral Argument.

G. Decision, Costs, and Mandate

5A:29. Notice of Decision.
5A:30. Costs and Notarized Bill of Costs.
5A:31. Mandate.

H. Rehearing

5A:32. Scope.
5A:33. Rehearing—on Motion of a Party After Final Disposition of a Case.
5A:34. Rehearing En Banc After Final Disposition of Case.
5A:35. Procedure for Rehearing.

I. Settlement, Withdrawal, and Mediation

5A:36. Settlement or Withdrawal of Pending Appeal.
5A:37. Appellate Settlement Conference in the Court of Appeals.
5A:38. Petition for Review Pursuant to Code § 8.01–626; Injunctions.

Appendix of Forms

Form
1. Bond for Costs Alone—Appeal of Right from Circuit Court to Court of Appeals (Including Further Appeal to the Supreme Court).
2. Bond for Costs and Suspension—Appeal from Circuit Court to Appellate Court.
3. Bond for Costs Alone Required by Appellate Court on Appeal from Circuit Court.
4. Bond for Suspension Alone Required by Appellate Court on Appeal from Circuit Court.
5. Bond for Costs and Suspension Required by Appellate Court on Appeal from Circuit Court.
6. Additional Bond Required by Appellate Court on Appeal from Circuit Court.
7. Bond for Costs Alone—Appeal of Right from Virginia Workers' Compensation Commission to Court of Appeals (Including Further Appeal to the Supreme Court).
8. Bond for Costs Alone—Required by Supreme Court on Appeal of Right from State Corporation Commission.
9. Bond for Costs and Suspension—Required by Supreme Court on Appeal of Right from State Corporation Commission.
10. Form for Execution and Acknowledgment of All Bonds.
11. Irrevocable Letters of Credit.
12. Petition for a Writ of Actual Innocence Based on Nonbiological Evidence.

PART SIX. INTEGRATION OF THE STATE BAR

Section I. Unauthorized Practice Rules and Considerations

Introduction.
Practice of Law in the Commonwealth of Virginia.

Rule
1. Practice Before Tribunals.
2. Lay Adjusters.
3. Collection Agencies.
4. Estate Planning and Settlement.
5. Tax Practice.
6. Real Estate Practice.
7. Title Insurance.
8. Trade Associations.
9. Administrative Agency Practice.

Section II. Virginia Rules of Professional Conduct

Preamble: A Lawyer's Responsibilities.
Cross Reference Table: Virginia Rules of Professional Conduct to Code of Professional Responsibility.
Cross Reference Table: Virginia Code of Professional Responsibility to Rules of Professional Conduct.

CLIENT–LAWYER RELATIONSHIP

Rule
1.1. Competence.
1.2. Scope of Representation.
1.3. Diligence.
1.4. Communication.
1.5. Fees.
1.6. Confidentiality of Information.
1.7. Conflict of Interest: General Rule.
1.8. Conflict of Interest: Prohibited Transactions.
1.9. Conflict of Interest: Former Client.
1.10. Imputed Disqualification: General Rule.
1.11. Special Conflicts of Interest for Former and Current Government Officers and Employees.
1.12. Former Judge or Arbitrator.
1.13. Organization as Client.
1.14. Client with Impairment.
1.15. Safekeeping Property.
1.16. Declining or Terminating Representation.
1.17. Sale of Law Practice.
1.18. Duties to Prospective Client.

COUNSELOR AND THIRD–PARTY NEUTRAL

2.1. Advisor.
2.2. Intermediary [Deleted Effective January 1, 2004].
2.3. Evaluation for Use by Third Persons.
2.10. Third Party Neutral.
2.11. Mediator.

Rule

ADVOCATE

3.1. Meritorious Claims and Contentions.
3.3. Candor Toward the Tribunal.
3.4. Fairness to Opposing Party and Counsel.
3.5. Impartiality and Decorum of the Tribunal.
3.6. Trial Publicity.
3.7. Lawyer as Witness.
3.8. Additional Responsibilities of a Prosecutor.

TRANSACTIONS WITH PERSONS OTHER THAN CLIENTS

4.1. Truthfulness in Statements to Others.
4.2. Communication with Persons Represented by Counsel.
4.3. Dealing with Unrepresented Persons.
4.4. Respect for Rights of Third Persons.

LAW FIRMS AND ASSOCIATIONS

5.1. Responsibilities of Partners and Supervisory Lawyers.
5.3. Responsibilities Regarding Nonlawyer Assistants.
5.4. Professional Independence of a Lawyer.
5.5. Unauthorized Practice of Law; Multijurisdictional Practice of Law.
5.6. Restrictions on Right to Practice.
5.8. Procedures for Notification to Clients When a Lawyer Leaves a Law Firm or When a Law Firm Dissolves.

PUBLIC SERVICE

6.1. Voluntary Pro Bono Publico Service.
6.2. Accepting Appointments.
6.3. Membership in Legal Services Organization.
6.5. Nonprofit and Court–Annexed Limited Legal Services Programs.

INFORMATION ABOUT LEGAL SERVICES

7.1. Communications Concerning a Lawyer's Services.
7.2. Advertising [Deleted].
7.3. Direct Contact with Potential Clients.
7.4. Communication of Fields of Practice and Certification.
7.5. Lawyer and Firm Names and Letterheads.

MAINTAINING THE INTEGRITY OF THE PROFESSION

8.1. Bar Admission and Disciplinary Matters.
8.2. Judicial Officials.
8.3. Reporting Misconduct.
8.4. Misconduct.
8.5. Disciplinary Authority; Choice of Law.

SECTION III. CANONS OF JUDICIAL CONDUCT FOR THE COMMONWEALTH OF VIRGINIA

Preamble.

Canon

1. A Judge Shall Uphold the Integrity and Independence of the Judiciary.
2. A Judge Shall Avoid Impropriety and the Appearance of Impropriety in All of the Judge's Activities.
3. A Judge Shall Perform the Duties of Judicial Office Impartially and Diligently.
4. A Judge May Engage in Extra–Judicial Activities Designed to Improve the Law, the Legal System, and the Administration of Justice, and Shall Conduct Any Such Extra–Judicial Activities in a Manner That Minimizes the Risk of Conflict with Judicial Obligations.

Canon

5. A Judge Shall Refrain from Political Activity Inappropriate to the Judicial Office.
6. Judges Pro Tempore, Retired Judges, Substitute Judges and Persons Selected for Judgeship Are Required to Comply with the Canons.
7. Effective Date.

Supreme Court Order Judicial Ethics Advisory Committee.

SECTION IV. ORGANIZATION AND GOVERNMENT

Paragraph

1. Name.
2. Membership and Registration.
3. Classes of Membership.
4. Officers.
5. The Council.
6. Election of Council.
7. Meetings of the Council.
8. Annual Meeting of the Virginia State Bar.
9. Powers of the Council.
10. Promulgation of Legal Ethics, Unauthorized Practice of Law Opinions, and Rules of Court; Informal Staff Opinions of Ethics Counsel; and Complaints of Unauthorized Practice of Law.
11. Dues.
12. Disbursements.
13. Procedure for Disciplining, Suspending, and Disbarring Attorneys.
13.1. Suspension for Failure to Complete Professionalism Course.
13.2. Suspension for Failure to Complete Continuing Legal Education Requirement.
13.3. [Reserved Effective January 1, 1999].
13.4. Insurance Coverage Requirement for Respondents Under Va. Code § 54.1–335(D).
14. Professional Corporations, Professional Limited Liability Companies and Limited Liability Partnerships (Limited Liabilities Entities).
15. Third Year Student Practice Rule.
16. Clients' Protection Fund.
17. Mandatory Continuing Legal Education Rule.
18. Financial Responsibility.
19. Procedure for the Administrative Suspension of a Member.
20. Maintenance of Trust Accounts; Notice of Election Requirements.
21. Computerized Legal Research Services Rule.

SECTION V. BYLAWS OF THE COUNCIL OF THE VIRGINIA STATE BAR [DELETED]

SECTION VI. VIRGINIA STATE BAR BYLAWS [DELETED]

APPENDIX

App.

A. Virginia State Bar Approved Financial Institution Agreement.

PART SEVEN A. GENERAL DISTRICT COURTS—IN GENERAL

Rule

7A:1. Scope.
7A:2. Computation of Time.
7A:3. Counsel.
7A:4. Reporters and Transcripts of Proceedings in Court.
7A:5. Discretion of Court.
7A:6. Preservation of the Record.
7A:7. Filing Format and Procedure.

Rule
7A:8. General Provisions as to Pleadings.
7A:9. Amendments.
7A:10. Copies of Pleadings and Requests for Subpoenas Duces Tecum to Be Furnished.
7A:11. Endorsements.
7A:12. Requests for Subpoenas for Witnesses and Records.
7A:13. What Constitutes Noting an Appeal.
7A:14. Continuances.
7A:15. General Information Relating to Each Court.
7A:16. Isolation Proceedings Under Article 3.01 of Title 32.1 of the Code of Virginia; Communicable Diseases of Public Health Significance.

PART SEVEN B. GENERAL DISTRICT COURTS—CIVIL

7B:1. Scope.
7B:2. Specific Rule for Pleadings in General District Courts.
7B:3. General Provisions as to Pleadings.
7B:4. Trial of Action.
7B:5. Production of Written Agreement.
7B:6. Verification.
7B:7. Appearance by Plaintiff.
7B:8. Failure of Plaintiff to Appear.
7B:9. Failure of Defendant to Appear.
7B:10. Third–Party Practice and Consolidation of Actions.
7B:11. Motions to Transfer.

PART SEVEN C. GENERAL DISTRICT COURTS—CRIMINAL AND TRAFFIC

7C:1. Scope.
7C:2. Venue.
7C:3. The Complaint, Warrant, Summons and Capias.
7C:4. Trial Together of More Than One Accused or More Than One Offense and Joint Preliminary Hearings.

Rule
7C:5. Discovery.
7C:6. Pleas.
7C:7. Service and Filing of Papers.

PART EIGHT. JUVENILE AND DOMESTIC RELATIONS DISTRICT COURTS

8:1. Scope.
8:2. Definitions.
8:3. Contents of Petitions in Certain Proceedings.
8:4. Service of Process—Motion to Reduce Support Arrearages to Judgment.
8:5. Court–Ordered Reports.
8:6. The Roles of Counsel and of Guardians Ad Litem When Representing Children.
8:7. Format for Filing.
8:8. Pleadings.
8:9. Discretion of Court.
8:10. Motions to Transfer Venue.
8:11. Reporters and Transcripts of Proceedings in Court.
8:12. Preservation of the Record.
8:13. Requests for Subpoenas for Witnesses and Records.
8:14. Continuances.
8:15. Discovery.
8:16. Arraignment in Juvenile Delinquency Cases.
8:17. Notification and Waiver of Trial Rights of Parties.
8:18. Pleas.
8:19. Endorsements of Orders.
8:20. Appeals.
8:21. Deleted.
8:22. Judicial Consent.

PART NINE. JUDICIAL PERFORMANCE EVALUATION PROGRAM

9:1. Purpose and Operation.
9:2. Confidentiality.

PART ONE. GENERAL RULES APPLICABLE TO ALL PROCEEDINGS

Effective March 1, 1972

Including Amendments Received Through October 15, 2015

RULE 1:1. FINALITY OF JUDGMENTS, ORDERS AND DECREES

All final judgments, orders, and decrees, irrespective of terms of court, shall remain under the control of the trial court and subject to be modified, vacated, or suspended for twenty-one days after the date of entry, and no longer. But notwithstanding the finality of the judgment, in a criminal case the trial court may postpone execution of the sentence in order to give the accused an opportunity to apply for a writ of error and supersedeas; such postponement, however, shall not extend the time limits hereinafter prescribed for applying for a writ of error. The date of entry of any final judgment, order, or decree shall be the date it is signed by the judge either on paper or by electronic means in accord with Rule 1:17.

[Amended effective September 1, 1976; July 1, 1988; May 2, 2011.]

Source: Rule 1:9.

Comment: The first sentence is changed [under the 1976 amendment] to add authority for the trial court to suspend, by order entered within twenty-one days, a final judgment pending disposition of a motion for a new trial, a petition for rehearing, or a like pleading. The new material following the semicolon in the second sentence [under the 1976 amendment] is intended to eliminate misunderstanding concerning the effect of postponement of execution of sentence in a criminal case.

RULE 1:1A. RECOVERY OF APPELLATE ATTORNEY'S FEES IN CIRCUIT COURT

(a) Notwithstanding any provision of Rule 1:1, in any civil action in which an appeal lies from the circuit court to the Supreme Court and a petition for appeal is denied by the Supreme Court (and, if a petition for rehearing has been filed pursuant to Rule 5:20, such petition has been denied), an appellee who has recovered attorneys' fees, costs or both in the circuit court pursuant to a contract, statute or other applicable law may make application in the circuit court in which judgment was entered for attorneys' fees, costs or both incurred on appeal. The application must be filed within thirty (30) days after denial of the petition for appeal or of any petition for rehearing, whichever is later, and may be made in the same case from which the appeal was taken, which case shall be reinstated on the circuit court docket upon the filing of the application. The appellee shall not be required to file a separate suit or action to recover the fees and costs incurred on appeal, and the circuit court shall have continuing jurisdiction of the case for the purpose of adjudicating the application. The circuit court's order granting or refusing the application, in whole or in part, shall be a final order for purposes of Rule 1:1.

(b) Nothing in this Rule shall restrict or prohibit the exercise of any other right or remedy for the recovery of attorneys' fees or costs, by separate suit or action, or otherwise.

[Adopted effective April 1, 2005.]

RULE 1:2. VENUE IN CRIMINAL CASES [REPEALED EFFECTIVE MARCH 1, 2007]

RULE 1:3. REPORTERS AND TRANSCRIPTS OF PROCEEDINGS IN COURTS

Reporters shall be first duly sworn to take down and transcribe the proceedings faithfully and accurately to the best of their ability, and shall be subject to the control and discipline of the judge.

When a reporter takes down any proceeding in a court, any person interested shall be entitled to obtain a transcript of the proceedings or any part thereof upon terms and conditions to be fixed in each case by the judge.

The proceedings may be taken down by means of any recording device approved by the judge.

[Amended effective July 1, 1983.]

Source: Rule 1:10.

RULE 1:4. GENERAL PROVISIONS AS TO PLEADINGS

(a) Counsel tendering a pleading gives his assurance as an officer of the court that it is filed in good faith and not for delay.

(b) A pleading that is sworn to is an affidavit for all purposes for which an affidavit is required or permitted.

(c) Counsel or an unrepresented party who files a pleading shall sign it and state his address.

(d) Every pleading shall state the facts on which the party relies in numbered paragraphs, and it shall be sufficient if it clearly informs the opposite party of the true nature of the claim or defense.

(e) An allegation of fact in a pleading that is not denied by the adverse party's pleading, when the adverse party is required by these Rules to file such pleading, is deemed to be admitted. An allegation in a pleading that the party does not know whether a fact exists shall be treated as a denial that the fact exists.

(f) Requirements of pleadings applicable to instruments not under seal shall apply to instruments under seal.

(g) Requirements of pleadings applicable to legal defenses shall apply to equitable defenses.

(h) The clerk shall note and attest the filing date on every pleading. In an Electronically Filed Case, the procedures of Rule 1:17 shall be applicable to the notation by the clerk of the date of filing.

(i) The mention in a pleading of an accompanying exhibit shall, of itself and without more, make such exhibit a part of the pleading. Filing of such exhibits shall be governed by Rule 3:4.

(j) Brevity is enjoined as the outstanding characteristic of good pleading. In any pleading a simple statement, in numbered paragraphs, of the essential facts is sufficient.

(k) A party asserting either a claim, counterclaim, cross-claim, or third-party claim or a defense may plead alternative facts and theories of recovery against alternative parties, provided that such claims, defenses, or demands for relief so joined arise out of the same transaction or occurrence. When two or more statements are made in the alternative and one of them if made independently would be sufficient, the pleading is not made insufficient by the insufficiency of one or more of the alternative statements. A party may also state as many separate claims or defenses as he has regardless of consistency and whether based on legal or equitable grounds.

(l) Every pleading, motion or other paper served or filed shall contain at the foot the Virginia State Bar number, office address and telephone number of the counsel of record submitting it, along with any electronic mail (E–mail) address and facsimile number regularly used for business purposes by such counsel of record.

[Amended effective October 1, 1977; July 1, 1984; February 1, 1999; May 2, 2011; January 1, 2013.]

Source: Various rules in Parts Two and Three.

Comment: The October 1, 1977 amendment added paragraph (k) to conform to § 8.01–281.

RULE 1:4A. SPECIAL RULE FOR PLEADINGS IN GENERAL DISTRICT COURTS [REPEALED EFFECTIVE JULY 1, 1982]

RULE 1:5. COUNSEL

When used in these Rules, the word "counsel" includes a partnership, a professional corporation or an association of members of the Virginia State Bar practicing under a firm name.

When such firm name is signed to a pleading, notice or brief, the name of at least one individual member or associate of such firm must be signed to it. Papers filed electronically may be signed electronically or by inclusion of a digital image of the signature, as provided in Rule 1:17. Signatures to briefs and petitions for rehearing may be printed or typed and need not be in handwriting.

Service on one member or associate of such firm shall constitute service on the firm. Service is not required to be made on foreign attorneys.

"Counsel of record" includes a counsel or party who has signed a pleading in the case or who has notified the other parties and the clerk in writing that he appears in the case. Counsel of record shall not withdraw from a case except by leave of court after notice to the client of the time and place of a motion for leave to withdraw.

[Amended effective October 15, 1979; May 2, 2011.]

Source: Rule 1:13.

RULE 1:6. RES JUDICATA CLAIM PRECLUSION.

(a) Definition of Cause of Action. A party whose claim for relief arising from identified conduct, a transaction, or an occurrence, is decided on the merits by a final judgment, shall be forever barred from prosecuting any second or subsequent civil action against the same opposing party or parties on any claim or cause of action that arises from that same conduct, transaction or occurrence, whether or not the legal theory or rights asserted in the second or subsequent action were raised in the prior lawsuit, and regardless of the legal elements or the evidence upon which any claims in the prior proceeding depended, or the particular remedies sought. A claim for relief pursuant to this rule includes those set forth in a complaint, counterclaim, cross-claim or third-party pleading.

(b) Effective Date. This rule shall apply to all Virginia judgments entered in civil actions commenced after July 1, 2006.

(c) Exceptions. The provisions of this Rule shall not bar a party or a party's insurer from prosecuting separate personal injury and property damage suits arising out of the same conduct, transaction or occurrence, and shall not bar a party who has pursued mechanic's lien remedies pursuant to Virginia Code § 43–1 et seq. from prosecuting a subsequent claim against the same or different defendants for relief not recovered in the prior mechanic's lien proceedings, to the extent heretofore permitted by law.

(d) Privity. The law of privity as heretofore articulated in case law in the Commonwealth of Virginia is unaffected by this Rule and remains intact. For purposes of this Rule, party or parties shall include all named parties and those in privity.

[Adopted effective July 1, 2006.]

RULE 1:7. COMPUTATION OF TIME

Whenever a party is required or permitted under these Rules, or by direction of the court, to do an act within a prescribed time after service of a paper upon counsel of record, three (3) days shall be added to the prescribed time when the paper is served by mail, or one (1) day shall be added to the prescribed time when the paper is served by facsimile, electronic mail or commercial delivery service. With respect to Parts Five and Five A of the Rules, this Rule applies only to the time for filing a brief in opposition.

[Amended effective August 1, 1977; July 1, 1987; February 1, 1999; October 15, 2003.]

Source: New; Rule 5:3, § 5.

Comment: The August 1, 1977 amendment conforms the Rule to the 1977 amendment of § 1–13.3:1.

[Comment to the 1987 amendment:] The provisions of former subsection (a) are covered by Code § 1–13.3:1. The addition of the second sentence of the retained paragraph merely explicates the current application of the three-day rule.

RULE 1:8. AMENDMENTS

No amendments shall be made to any pleading after it is filed save by leave of court. Leave to amend shall be liberally granted in furtherance of the ends of justice. Unless otherwise provided by order of the court in a particular case, any written motion for leave to file an amended pleading shall be accompanied by a properly executed proposed amended pleading, in a form suitable for filing. If the motion is granted, the amended pleading accompanying the motion shall be deemed filed in the clerk's office as of the date of the court's order permitting such amendment. If the motion is granted in part, the court may provide for filing an amended pleading as the court may deem reasonable and proper. Where leave to amend is granted other than upon a written motion, whether on demurrer or oral motion or otherwise, the amended pleading shall be filed within 21 days after leave to amend is granted or in such time as the court may prescribe. In granting leave to amend, the court may make such provision for notice thereof and opportunity to make response as the court may deem reasonable and proper.

[Amended effective May 2, 2011.]

Source: Rules 2:12, 3:13.

RULE 1:9. DISCRETION OF COURT

All steps and procedures in the clerk's office touching the filing of pleadings and the maturing of suits or actions may be reviewed and corrected by the court.

The time allowed for filing pleadings may be extended by the court in its discretion and such extension may be granted although the time fixed already has expired; but the time fixed for the filing of a motion challenging the venue shall in no case be extended except to the extent permitted by § 8.01–264.

[Amended effective October 1, 1977.]

Source: Rules 2:23, 3:13.

Comment: Pleas in abatement have been abolished by § 8.01–276 and references to such pleas have been eliminated from the Rules by the amendments effective October 1, 1977. Matters formerly raised by a plea in abatement should be raised by written motion. The principal purpose of a plea in abatement is to challenge venue; that is now to be done by motion within the time limits established by § 8.01–264.

RULE 1:10. VERIFICATION

If a statute requires a pleading to be sworn to, and it is not, or requires a pleading to be accompanied by an affidavit, and it is not, but contains all the allegations required, objection on either ground must be made within seven days after the pleading is filed by a motion to strike; otherwise the objection is waived. At any time before the court passes on the motion or within such time thereafter as the court may prescribe, the pleading may be sworn to or the affidavit filed. In an Electronically Filed Case, verification shall be subject to the provisions of Rule 1:17.

[Amended effective May 2, 2011]

Source: Rules 2:20.1, 3:14.

RULE 1:11. STRIKING THE EVIDENCE

If the court sustains a motion to strike the evidence of either party in a civil case being tried before a jury, or the evidence of the Commonwealth in a criminal case being so tried, then the court shall enter summary judgment or partial summary judgment in conformity with its ruling on the motion to strike.

If the court overrules a motion to strike the evidence and there is a hung jury, the moving party may renew the motion immediately after the discharge of the jury, and, if the court is of opinion that it erred in denying the motion, it shall enter summary judgment or partial summary judgment in conformity with its ruling on the motion to strike.

[Amended effective July 1, 1988.]

Source: Rule 1:11.

RULE 1:12. SERVICE OF PAPERS AFTER THE INITIAL PROCESS

All pleadings, motions and other papers not required to be served otherwise and requests for subpoenas duces tecum shall be served by delivering, dispatching by commercial delivery service, transmitting by facsimile, delivering by electronic mail when Rule 1:17 so provides or when consented to in writing signed by the person to be served, or by mailing, a copy to each counsel of record on or before the day of filing.

Subject to the provisions of Rule 1:17, service pursuant to this Rule shall be effective upon such delivery, dispatch, transmission or mailing, except that papers served by facsimile transmission completed after 5:00 p.m. shall be deemed served on the next day that is not a Saturday, Sunday, or legal holiday. Service by electronic mail under this Rule is not effective if the party making service learns that the attempted service did not reach the person to be served.

At the foot of such pleadings and requests shall be appended either acceptance of service or a certificate of counsel that copies were served as this Rule requires, showing the date of delivery and method of service, dispatching, transmitting, or mailing. When service is made by electronic mail, a certificate of counsel that the document was served by electronic mail shall be served by mail or transmitted by facsimile to each counsel of record on or before the day of service.

[Amended effective September 1, 1976; February 1, 1999; October 15, 2003; May 2, 2011.]

Source: Rules 2:17, 3:15.

Comment: New language in this rule [under the 1976 amendment] requires service of requests for subpoenas duces tecum upon each counsel of record.

RULE 1:13. ENDORSEMENTS

Drafts of orders and decrees shall be endorsed by counsel of record, or reasonable notice of the time and place of presenting such drafts together with copies thereof shall be served pursuant to Rule 1:12 upon all counsel of record who have not endorsed them. Compliance with this Rule and with Rule 1:12 may be modified or dispensed with by the court in its discretion. In an Electronically Filed Case, endorsement and specification of any objections to the draft order shall be accomplished as provided in Rule 1:17.

[Amended effective February 1, 1999; October 15, 2003; May 2, 2011.]

Source: Rules 2:18, 3:16.

RULE 1:14. PRESERVATION OF THE RECORD

A court may authorize the use of electronic or photographic means for the preservation of the record or parts thereof.

[Amended effective October 15, 1979; June 16, 1987; July 1, 1989; July 1, 1990; July 1, 1992.]

RULE 1:15. LOCAL RULES OF COURT

(a) Whenever a local rule is prescribed by a circuit court it shall be spread upon the order book and a copy with the date of entry shall be forthwith posted in the clerk's office, filed with the Executive Secretary of the Supreme Court, and furnished to attorneys regularly practicing before that circuit court; and whenever an attorney becomes counsel of record in any proceedings in a circuit court in which he does not regularly practice, it shall be his responsibility to ascertain the rules of that court and abide thereby. The clerk shall, upon request, promptly furnish a copy of all rules then in force and effect.

(b) Whenever a local rule is prescribed by a circuit court providing for the orderly management of the civil docket by use of the praecipe system, the praecipe shall be substantially in the form appearing in the appendix of forms at the end of this Part One.

(c) Whenever a local rule is prescribed by a circuit court providing for the submission of instructions prior to trial, such local rule shall be substantially in the form appearing in the appendix of forms at the end of this Part One.

(d) The chief judges of the circuit and juvenile and domestic relations district courts shall, on or before December 31 of each year, furnish the Executive Secretary of the Supreme Court current general information relating to the management of the courts within each circuit and district. This information shall be assembled and published electronically by the Executive Secretary.

[Adopted effective May 1, 1972. Amended effective September 1, 1976; July 1, 1989; July 1, 2009.]

CIRCUIT	COUNTY OR CITY	TERM
First	Chesapeake	Criminal terms: First Tuesday of each month, 2:00 p.m. except when election date is Term Day, then Term Day will be held on Wednesday after the first Tuesday. Civil terms: First Tuesday in each month, 10:00 a.m. except when election date is Term Day, then Term Day will be held on Wednesday after the first Tuesday.
Second	Virginia Beach	First Monday in each month unless holiday, then following day.
	Accomack	First Monday in February, April, June, August, October and December.
	Northampton	Second Monday in January, March, May, July, September and November.
Third	Portsmouth	First Thursday in each month.
Fourth	Norfolk	Terms begin the first day of the month.
Fifth	Isle of Wight	Second Monday in January, March, May July, September and November.
	Southampton	Third Monday in January, March, May, July, September, and November.
	Suffolk	Fourth Monday in January, March, May, July, September and November.
Sixth	Hopewell	Second Tuesday in February, April, June, August, October and December.
	Prince George	Third Tuesday in January, March, May, July, September and November.
	Surry	Fourth Tuesday in January, March, May, July, September and November.
	Sussex	Second Tuesday in January, March, May, July, September and November.
	Greenville	First Tuesday in February, April, June, August, October and December.
	Brunswick	Fourth Tuesday in February, April, June, August, October, and December.
Seventh	Newport News	Criminal terms: Second Monday in each month. Civil terms: Second Monday in January, March, May, July, September and November.
Eighth	Hampton	First Monday in February, April, June, August, October and December. Criminal Term Grand Juries: First Monday of each month at 9:00 a.m.

CIRCUIT	COUNTY OR CITY	TERM
Ninth	James City County/Williamsburg	Third Wednesday in January, March, May, July, September and November.
	York County/ Poquson	Third Tuesday in January, March, May, July, September and November.
	Charles City	First Tuesday in January, March, May, July, and September; Nov. 1
	New Kent	Second Monday in January; third Monday in March, May, July, September and November.
	Gloucester	First Monday in January, March, May, July, September and November.
	Mathews	Third Monday in January, March, May, July, September and November.
	Middlesex	Fourth Monday in January, March, May, July, September and November.
	King William	First Monday in February, April, June, August, October and December.
	King and Queen	Second Monday in February, April, June, August, October and December.
Tenth	Halifax	Second Monday in January, March, May, July, September and November.
	Mecklenburg	Third Monday in February, April, June, August and October, and the second Monday in December.
	Lunenburg	First Monday in February, April, June, August, October and December.
	Charlotte	Wednesday after the first Monday in February, April, June, August, October and December.
	Prince Edward	Tuesday after the third Monday in January, April, June, September and November.
	Buckingham	Tuesday after the second Monday in January, April, June, September and November.
	Cumberland	Tuesday following the fourth Monday in January, April, June and September.
	Appomattox	Tuesday after the first Monday in April, June, October and December.
Eleventh	Powhatan	Second Tuesday in February, April, June, October and December.
	Dinwiddie	Third Tuesday in January, March, May, July, September and November.
	Nottoway	First Tuesday in January, March, May, July, September and November.
	Ameila	First Tuesday in February, April, June, October and December.
	Petersburg	Criminal terms: Third Thursday in each month. Civil terms: Third Thursday in each month.
Twelfth	Chesterfield	Criminal and Civil terms: Tuesday following third Monday in January, and third Monday in March, May, July, September and November.
	Colonial Heights	First Tuesday in January, March, July, September and November.

CIRCUIT	COUNTY OR CITY	TERM
Thirteenth	Richmond City	Criminal terms: First Monday in each month. Civil terms: Fourth Monday in January, April, July and October. Civil term days: First Monday in March, June and December and third Monday in September.
Fourteenth	Henrico	Criminal terms: Second Monday in January, March, May, July, September and November. Civil cases set second Monday in January, April, July and October at 2:00 p.m. or may be set by telephone. Criminal cases set when appealed or at preliminary hearing.
Fifteenth	Caroline	First Wednesday at 10:00 a.m. in January, April, July and October.
	Essex	Fourth Wednesday in January, April, July and October.
	Fredericksburg	Fourth Monday in January, April, July and October.
	Hanover	Third Tuesday in January, March, May, July, September and November. Criminal: 9:00 a.m.; Civil: 2:00 p.m.
	King George	Second Thursday in January, April, July and October at 10 a.m.
	Lancaster	Fourth Friday in January, April, July and October.
	Northumberland	Fourth Tuesday in January, April, July and October.
	Richmond County	Fourth Monday of January, April, July and October. All cases set by agreement with Commonwealth's Attorney at preliminary hearing, on Term Day, or by agreement of counsel and the Court. The latter may be done by a telephone call to the Judge's office @ 804-333-5568.
	Spotsylvania	Third Monday at 9:00 a.m. in January, April, July and October.
	Stafford	Criminal Term: First Monday in each month. Civil Terms: First Monday in January, April, July and October. Motion Days: First and third Mondays, Pendente Lite Second Friday of each month. If any Monday is a State holiday, Term/Motions will be held the following day.
	Westmoreland	Fourth Thursday in January, April, July and October.
Sixteenth	Charlottesville	Third Monday in April, June, August, October and December; third Tuesday in February (as third Monday is a holiday).
	Madison	First Monday in January, March, May, July, September and November.
	Louisa	Second Monday in January, March, May, July, September and November.
	Greene	Second Monday in February, April, June, August, October and December.
	Orange	Fourth Monday in January, March, May, July, September and November.

CIRCUIT	COUNTY OR CITY	TERM
Sixteenth (cont'd)	Albemarle	Criminal terms: First Monday in February, April, June, August, October and December. Civil terms: Last Thursday of each month except November and December (which is the third Thursday). Grand Juries: First day of Term.
	Goochland	Second Tuesday in February, April, June, August, October and December.
	Culpeper	Third Monday in February, April, June, August, October and December.
	Fluvanna	Fourth Monday in February, April, June, August and October; and third Tuesday in December.
Seventeenth	Arlington	Third Monday (or Tuesday, if holiday falls on Monday) in February, April, June, August, October and December.
Eighteenth	Alexandria	Second Monday in January, March, May, July, September and November; at 9:00 a.m.; cases may also be set for trial by telephone (703-838-4123).
Nineteenth	Fairfax	Criminal terms: Tuesday following third Monday in January, March, May, July, September and November. Civil terms: Fourth Monday in January, March, May, July, September and November.
Twentieth	Fauquier	Misdemeanor Appeal Days: Second Tuesday of each month. Terms: Fourth Monday in January, March, May, July, September and November.
	Loudoun	Second Monday in February, April, June, August and December; and Tuesday following second Monday in October.
	Rappahannock	Second Monday in January, March, May, July, September and November.
Twenty-First	Henry	Tuesday following Third Monday in January; third Monday in March, May, July, September and November at 9 a.m.
	Martinsville	Criminal terms: Second Monday in February; the first Monday in May; the fourth Monday in July; and the first Monday in November. Civil cases set by Pretrial Scheduling Order.
	Patrick	First Monday in March, June, September and December.
Twenty-Second	Danville	Grand Juries and Terms: Jan. 3, Feb. 26, April 23, June 25, Aug. 27 and Oct. 29.
	Pittsylvania	Third Monday in February, April, June, August, October and December.
	Franklin	First Monday in February, April, June, August, October and December. Criminal cases set the week following the preliminary hearing. Civil cases are set 90 days after filing.

CIRCUIT	COUNTY OR CITY	TERM
Twenty-Third	Roanoke County	Criminal terms: First Friday in February, April, June, October and December; and the second Friday in August. Civil terms: First Friday in January, February, April, June, October and December; and second Friday in August.
	Roanoke City	Criminal terms: First Monday in each month. Civil terms: Tuesday after first Monday in each month.
	Salem	Third Friday in February, May, July and September; and the second Friday in December.
Twenty-Fourth	Lynchburg	Criminal terms: First Monday in each month. Civil terms: First Monday in each month.
	Amherst	Second Tuesday in February, April, June, October and December.
	Bedford	First Tuesday in January, March, May, July, September and November.
	Campbell	Second Monday in January, March, May, July, September and November.
	Nelson	Fourth Tuesday in January, March, May, September and November.
Twenty-Fifth	Buena Vista	Fourth Wednesday in January and July; the first Monday in April; and the fourth Monday in September.
	Clifton Forge	* Consolidated with the County of Alleghany as of July 1, 2001.
	Staunton	Third Monday in January, April, July and October.
	Waynesboro	Second Monday in January, March, May, September and November.
	Alleghany	Second Monday in January, April and July, and the first Tuesday after second Monday in October.
	Augusta	Fourth Monday in January, April, July and October.
	Bath	Third Monday (or Tuesday, if holiday falls on Monday) in January, June and September; and the first Monday in April.
	Botetourt	First Monday in March, June, August, October and December.
	Craig	Last Monday in February; and the second Monday in May, September and November.
	Highland	Third Tuesday in March, June, September and December.
	Rockbridge	First Monday in February, May and November; second Monday in July; and Tuesday following Labor Day in September.
Twenty-Sixth	Clarke	Third Monday in January, April, July and October.
	Frederick	Thursday after the first Monday in January, April, July and October.
	Page	Fourth Monday in January, April, July and October.
	Shenandoah	Wednesday after the second Monday in January, April, July and October.

CIRCUIT	COUNTY OR CITY	TERM
Twenty-Sixth (cont'd)	Warren	First Monday in January, April, July and October.
	Winchester	Second Monday in January, April, July and October.
	Rockingham	Criminal terms: Third Monday in January, April, July and October. Civil terms: First Monday and Wednesday after third Monday each month except Wednesday after third Monday only in January and August.
Twenty-Seventh	Bland	Criminal terms: Second Monday in March, June, September and December. Civil terms: Immediately following end of criminal term.
	Carroll	Third Monday in March, June and September; and the second Monday in December.
	Floyd	First day of March, June, September and December.
	Giles	Second Tuesday in January, April, July and October.
	Grayson	Fourth Friday in January, April, July and October.
	Montgomery	Second Tuesday of January, April, July and October.
	Pulaski	Third Monday in February and November; the fourth Monday in May; and the second Monday in September.
	Radford	Second Friday in March, June, September and December.
	Wythe	Third Monday in January, April, July and October.
Twenty-Eighth	Washington	Fourth Tuesday in January, April, July and October.
	Smyth	Fourth Tuesday in March, June and September; and second Tuesday in December.
	Bristol	Tuesday in February, May, August and November.
Twenty-Ninth	Buchanan	Terms begin second Monday in January, April, July and October. Criminal terms: Fourth Monday in January, April, July and October. Civil terms: Second Tuesday in January, April, July and October.
	Dickenson	Criminal terms: Second Monday in March, June and September; and the first Monday in December. Civil terms: Tuesday, following Grand Jury (Grand Juries: Second Monday in March, June and September; first Monday in December).
	Russell	Second Monday in February, May, August and November.
	Tazewell	Second Tuesday in January, March, May, July, September and November.
Thirtieth	Wise	First Tuesday after the third Monday in January; and the third Monday in April, July and October.
	Scott	First Monday in February, May, August and November.
	Lee	First Monday in March, June and December; and second Monday in September.

CIRCUIT	COUNTY OR CITY	TERM
Thirty-First	Prince William	First Tuesday of every month, the next business day on which the Court is open if the Court is closed on the first Tuesday.

Comment: The only change [under the 1976 amendment] in paragraph (a) from the present rule is to require the filing of local rules with the executive secretary of the Supreme Court rather than with the executive director of the State Bar.

Paragraphs (b) and (c) are recommended to provide suggested forms for those circuits using the praecipe system in calling the civil docket and/or those courts requiring that instructions be submitted prior to trial. There is no requirement that circuit courts adopt such rules; however, should they do so, the procedure will be uniform in circuits having such rules.

Paragraph (d) provides for the publication as an appendix to the Rules of the Supreme Court of current information on each circuit and district court to meet the present problems confronting attorneys and litigants in ascertaining general information and local procedures. This information would include the name, location, and telephone number of the court and clerk's office; names of judges and clerk; terms of court, including when grand juries are convened and docket call procedures in civil and criminal cases; procedures including pretrial conferences and furnishing of instructions prior to trial; motion days, etc.

RULE 1:16. FILING FORMAT AND PROCEDURE

(a) Except as provided in Rules 1:17, 3:3, 3A:23, 7A:7(c), and 8:8(f) pertaining to Electronically Filed Cases,

(1) All pleadings, motions, briefs, depositions, requests for discovery and responses thereto, and all other documents filed in any clerk's office in any proceeding pursuant to these Rules shall be produced on pages 8 1/2 by 11 inches in size and all typed material shall be double spaced except for quotations.

(2) Subdivision (a)(1) of this Rule shall not apply to tables, charts, plats, photographs, and other material that cannot be reasonably reproduced on paper of that size.

(b) No paper shall be refused for failure to comply with the provisions of this Rule, but the clerk may require that the paper be redone in compliance with this Rule and substituted for the paper initially filed. Counsel shall certify that the substituted paper is identical in content to the paper initially filed.

[Amended effective January 1, 1984; May 2, 2011.]

RULE 1:17. ELECTRONIC FILING AND SERVICE

(a) Scope of Electronic Filing Rules. Pursuant to § 8.01–271.01 and Article 4.1 (§§ 17.1–258.2 et seq.) of Chapter 2 of Title 17.1 of the Code of Virginia, this Rule shall be applicable in any court that has established an electronic filing system under the standards and procedures set forth in subdivision (c) of this Rule, and applies in civil cases in circuit court as provided in Rule 3:3, in criminal cases in circuit court as provided in Rule 3A:23, in general district court proceedings as provided in Rule 7A:7(c), and in juvenile and domestic relations district court proceedings as provided in Rule 8:8(f).

(b) Definitions.

(1) "**Electronic Document**" means any defined set of textural matter, graphic content or other encoded information in an approved format, that can be read, printed, and stored or retained as electrical, magnetic or optically encoded signals in some medium and that can be transmitted by a data-link.

(2) "**Data-link**" refers to any means of electronic transmission of a document in a coded form such that the document can be received, read, printed, and stored by the recipient.

(3) "**E–Filing Portal**" means the electronic web site maintained by the Supreme Court of Virginia designated as the facility for electronically filing documents, or an alternative which meets the standards set forth in this Rule and is made available by individual circuit courts.

(4) "**Electronic filing**" means the official filing of an electronic document on the court's docket and case files in electronic form by transmission over a datalink.

(5) "**Electronically Filed Case**" means a case in which pleadings, motions, notices and other filings are made electronically in accordance with these rules.

(6) "**Hyperlink**" means an electronic connection or reference to another place in the document, such that when the hyperlink is selected the user is taken to the portion of the document to which the link refers. It is not in itself a part of the document.

(c) System Operational Standards. In addition to the obligations and procedures set forth in subdivision (d) of this Rule, electronic filing systems under this Rule shall meet these requirements:

(1) Electronic documents must be stored without loss of content or material alteration of appearance.

(2) Files capable of carrying viruses into court computers must be scanned for viruses prior to being written to disk in the clerk's office.

(3) The electronic filing system must be capable of securing the document upon receipt so that it is protected from alteration.

(4) The electronic filing system must be capable of establishing the identity of a sender of a document by means of a registered user identity and password, or by digitally encrypted electronic signatures, or by any other means reasonably calculated to ensure identification to a high degree of certainty.

(5) Remote electronic access to documents submitted in an electronically filed case and stored electronically shall be limited to judges, court personnel, any persons assisting such persons in the administration of the electronic filing system, and to active members of the Virginia State Bar and their authorized agents, who have complied with the registration requirements to use the electronic filing system.

(6) If the court accepts payment of fees by credit card, debit card, debit account, or electronic funds transfer, registration for the user identity shall include submission of all information required to effect the payment of fees. Electronic submission of this information shall be deemed a signature by the cardholder sender, authorizing the payment of document filing fees. This information shall be kept confidential. There shall be an electronic confirmation from the clerk of any charge to or the debit from the user's account.

(7) No unauthorized person shall be permitted access to other court networks, data or applications unrelated to electronic filing. Administrative access to computer equipment and networks handling electronic filing will be restricted to designated court employees or authorized maintenance personnel.

(8) Electronic filing systems must reasonably protect filed documents against system and security failures and must provide, at a minimum, for daily backup, periodic off-site backup storage if feasible, and prudent disaster recovery mechanisms.

(d) Electronic Service and Filing Practice and Procedures.

(1) In an Electronically Filed Case, all pleadings, motions, notices and other material filed with the court shall be in the form of Electronic Documents except where otherwise expressly provided by statute or the Rules of Court, or where the court orders otherwise in an individual case for good cause shown.

(2) Each attorney admitted to practice in the Commonwealth shall be entitled to a registered User ID and password issued by the clerk, or access using any comparable identification system approved by the Supreme Court, for the electronic filing and retrieval of documents.

(3) The clerk shall provide a means, in the courthouse or other designated location, for the parties, counsel and the public to review and copy electronic records from the electronic file during normal business hours.

(4) The format for electronically filed material shall be the Portable Document Format (PDF). Notice will be provided if any other format is approved.

(5) (i) Subject to the provisions of subsections (d)(6) and (7) of this Rule, an electronic document shall be filed by following the procedures of the applicable E–Filing Portal, and shall be deemed filed on the date that it is received in the E–Filing Portal without regard to whether the filing occurred within or outside of standard business hours. If the electronic document is received in the E–Filing Portal on a Saturday, Sunday, legal holiday, or any day or part of a day on which the clerk's office is closed as authorized by an act of the General Assembly, then such document shall be deemed filed on the next day that is not a Saturday/Sunday, legal holiday, or day or part of a day on which the clerk's office is closed.

(ii) Upon electronic filing of a document, an electronic confirmation shall be transmitted to the filing party indicating that the document has been successfully filed through the E–Filing Portal. In addition, the court to which the document is directed shall promptly transmit an electronic acknowledgement of its receipt of the electronically filed document, specifying the identity of the receiving court, the date the document was received by the court, and a court-assigned document reference or docketing number.

(6) A person who files a document electronically shall have the same responsibility as a person filing a document in paper form to ensure that the document is properly filed, complete, and readable. However,

(i) if technical problems at the E–Filing Portal result in a failure to timely file the electronic document, counsel shall provide to the clerk of the court on the next business day all documentation which exists demonstrating the attempt to file the document through the E–Filing Portal, any delivery failure notice received in response to the attempt, and a copy of the document, and

(ii) in the event that the E–Filing Portal was not available due to technical problems during the last filing hours of a business day, the office of the clerk of the court to which the document is directed shall be deemed to have been closed on that day solely with respect to that attempted filing and the provisions of Virginia Code § 1–210(B) and (C) shall apply to that particular attempted filing for purposes of computing the last day for performing any act in a judicial proceeding or the filing of any legal action.

(7) Clerk's Notice of Defects in a Filing; Striking Documents; Court Orders.

(i) Incorrect or Missing Fee. If the clerk of court determines that an electronically filed document is defective because of an incorrect or missing filing fee, and

(A) if the clerk has been provided by the filing party with a credit or payment account through which to obtain payment of fees, the clerk shall immediately process payment of the correct fee through such credit or payment account; or

(B) if processing by the clerk of the proper payment through a credit or payment account authorized by the filing party is not feasible, notice shall be sent by the clerk electronically to the filing party, and all other parties who have appeared in the case.

(ii) Document Filed in the Wrong Case by Counsel. If the clerk of court determines prior to acceptance that an electronic document has been filed by counsel under the wrong case or docket number, the clerk shall notify the filing party as soon as practicable, by notice through the E–Filing system, by telephone, or by other effective means.

(iii) A copy of all notices transmitted by the clerk under this subpart (d)(7) shall be retained in the permanent electronic case file maintained by the clerk. A copy of any document stricken shall be retained by the clerk with a designation clearly reflecting that it was stricken and the date of such striking, as a record of its content and disposition.

(8) The clerk's office must accommodate the submission of non-electronic documents in an Electronically Filed Case if filing in electronic form cannot, as a practical matter, be achieved. Such documents shall be imaged to facilitate the creation of a single electronic case file to the extent reasonably possible. An outsized document that is capable of being imaged shall be retained in the form submitted.

(9) When an order is entered, the electronic record will be updated to identify the judge who directed entry of the order and the date it was entered, and a notification shall be sent to counsel of record that the order has been entered, along with a copy of the order or an electronic link providing access to such order. If the entry of an order is done on a paper copy of the

order, a digital image of such order shall be made a part of the electronic record, and the endorsed original paper shall be retained for the record.

(10) Hyperlinks between two portions of a filed document or between two or more documents filed in the same case, are permissible, but hyperlinks to other documents, or to external websites, are prohibited. A hyperlink is not itself a part of the official filed document and each hyperlink must contain a text reference to the target of the link.

(e) Application of, and Compliance With, Other Rules. In an Electronically Filed Case:

(1) Unless otherwise agreed by all parties, or ordered by the court in an individual case for good cause shown, all documents required to be served—after the initial service of process—shall be served by electronic transmission. Such service shall be effective as provided in Rule 1:12.

(2) Annotation by the clerk as provided in Rule 1:4(h) is not required to be made physically upon the face of the pleading and—if it is made by a separate document—it shall specify the pleading to which such annotation pertains.

(3) An e-mail address of the counsel of record shall be included in the electronic documents filed as required by Rule 1:4(*l*).

(4) The approved electronic identification accompanying the document when filed shall constitute that person's signature on the document for purposes of Rule 1:5 and Virginia Code § 8.01–271.1.

(5) The provisions of Article 4.1 (§§ 17.1–258.2 et seq.) of Chapter 2 of Title 17.1 of the Code of Virginia shall be applicable where a document is to be notarized, sworn, attested, verified, or otherwise certified, or if any sworn signatures, stamps, seals or other authentications relating to the document are required by any statute or Rule, and an electronic or digitally imaged document with such accompanying entries shall be filed in the clerk's office. Electronic notarization in compliance with the Virginia Notary Act (§§ 47.1–1 et seq.) may also be employed with the filing.

(6) An acceptance of service or a certificate of counsel that electronic copies were served as this Rule requires, showing the date of delivery, shall electronically accompany the served papers and shall satisfy Rule 1:12.

(7) In compliance with Rule 1:13, drafts of orders, decrees and notices shall be served on each counsel of record. Such service may be by electronic transmission and shall make provision for electronic endorsement by multiple parties where applicable. Objections or other notations by the parties shall be entered upon the drafts so circulated, or appended to such drafts by specific cross-reference or other unambiguous association. Endorsed drafts shall be submitted electronically whenever possible, and shall be accompanied by proof of service or acceptance of service when required by the rules of court. If there is no practical means of submitting an electronic or digitally imaged endorsed draft, the manually endorsed document shall be filed in the clerk's office. The clerk shall accommodate the imaging of the document into electronic form and shall retain the original endorsed document.

[Adopted effective February 1, 2001. Amended effective October 1, 2001; May 2, 2011; January 1, 2013.]

RULE 1:18. PRETRIAL SCHEDULING ORDER

A. In any civil case the parties, by counsel of record, may agree and submit for approval and entry by the court a pretrial scheduling order. If the court determines that the submitted order is not consistent with the efficient and orderly administration of justice, then the court shall notify counsel and provide an opportunity to be heard.

B. In any civil case in which a pretrial scheduling order has not otherwise been entered pursuant to the court's normal scheduling procedure, the court may, upon request of counsel of record for any party, or in its own discretion, enter the pretrial scheduling order contained in Section 3 of the Appendix of Forms at the end of Part I of these Rules (Uniform Pretrial Scheduling Order). The court shall cause copies of the order so entered to forthwith be transmitted to counsel for all parties. If any party objects to or requests modification of that order, the court shall (a) hold a hearing to rule upon the objection or request or (b) with the consent of all parties and the approval of the court, enter an amended pretrial scheduling order.

C. With the exception of domestic relations cases, a court may not enter a scheduling order which deviates from the terms of the Uniform Pretrial Scheduling Order unless either (1) counsel of record for all parties agree to different provisions, or (2) the court, after providing an opportunity for counsel of record to be heard, makes a finding that the scheduling order contained in the Appendix is not consistent with the efficient and orderly administration of justice under the specific circumstances of that case.

[Adopted effective July 1, 2000. Amended effective May 1, 2014.]

RULE 1:19. PRETRIAL CONFERENCES

In addition to the pretrial scheduling conferences provided for by Rule 4:13, each trial court may, upon request of counsel of record, or in its own discretion, schedule a final pretrial conference within an appropriate time before the commencement of trial. At the final pretrial conference, the court and counsel of record may consider any of the following:

(a) settlement;

(b) a determination of the issues remaining for trial and whether any amendments to the pleadings are necessary;

(c) the possibility of obtaining stipulations of fact, including, but not limited to, the admissibility of documents;

(d) a limitation of the number of expert and/or lay witnesses;

(e) any pending motions including motions in limine;

(f) issues relating to proposed jury instructions; and

(g) such other matters as may aid in the disposition of the action.

[Adopted effective July 1, 2000.]

RULE 1:20. SCHEDULING CIVIL CASES FOR TRIAL

The circuit courts of the Commonwealth shall adopt one or a combination of the following procedures for scheduling civil cases for trial.

(a) Counsel of record may agree to a trial date and may secure approval of the court by telephone call or other electronic communication to the designated court official.

(b) Counsel of record may agree to a trial date as a part of a written plan prepared and submitted to the court for approval pursuant to Rule 1:18.

(c) The court may, at the request of counsel of record, or may in its own discretion, direct counsel of record to appear, in person or by telephone, for a conference to set a trial date and consider other matters set forth in Rule 1:19 or Rule 4:13.

(d) The court may set civil cases for trial at a docket call held on a day as provided by § 17.1–517.

(e) Following the submission of a praecipe, the court may set civil cases for trial at a docket call held on a day as provided by § 17.1–517.

The Executive Secretary shall make accessible these procedures on the Internet. The clerk of each district and circuit court shall make their respective procedures available in the office of the clerk of that court.

[Adopted effective July 1, 2000. Amended effective July 1, 2009.]

RULE 1:21. PRELIMINARY VOIR DIRE INFORMATION

At the outset of jury selection in any civil or criminal case, the court shall deliver preliminary instructions that: (1) explain the purpose of the voir dire examination, (2) explain the difference between peremptory challenges and removals for cause, (3) summarize the nature of the case, (4) estimate how long the trial may last, and (5) indicate whether it is anticipated that the jury will be sequestered.

[Adopted effective January 1, 2002.]

RULE 1:22. EXERCISE OF CHALLENGES TO PROSPECTIVE JURORS

Counsel shall be afforded the opportunity to challenge jurors for cause out of the presence of the panel.

[Adopted effective January 1, 2002.]

RULE 1:23. NOTE TAKING BY JURORS

A. The court, in the exercise of its discretion, may permit jurors to take notes during the trial.

B. If notes are taken by any of the jurors, at the conclusion of each day of a trial, the court shall collect juror notes and provide for their security until the trial resumes. Upon conclusion of the trial, the court shall collect and destroy all juror notes.

[Adopted effective January 1, 2002.]

Appendix of Forms

FORM 1. PRAECIPE (RULE 1:15(b))

VIRGINIA: IN THE CIRCUIT COURT OF THE

..................,

Plaintiff

AT LAW NO. ... ..

v. or

.... IN CHANCERY NO.....

Defendant

PRAECIPE

I certify that the above styled cause is matured for trial on its merits and request the Clerk to place it on the docket to be called on ....
date of next docket call

to be set for trial *with* ( ) or *without* ( ) a jury.

Dated this ....day of ...., 20....

....

Counsel for ....

CERTIFICATE OF SERVICE

I certify that on the .... day of ...., 20..... I mailed or delivered a true copy of the foregoing praecipe to all counsel of record herein pursuant to the provisions of Rule 1:12 of the Rules of the Supreme Court of Virginia, and served a true copy upon parties not represented by counsel, if any.

....

Counsel for ....

FORM 2. INSTRUCTIONS (RULE 1:15(c))

Counsel for all parties, unless compliance is waived by the court, shall, two days before a civil jury trial date, submit to the court a copy of all instructions such counsel proposes to request – in electronic or paper form as directed by the court – and noting thereon the authority or authorities relied upon for such instructions. Counsel may be required to exchange copies of proposed instructions. This rule shall not preclude the offering of additional instructions at the trial.

[Amended effective October 1, 1997; May 2, 2011.]

FORM 3. UNIFORM PRETRIAL SCHEDULING ORDER (RULE 1:18B)

I. Trial

The trial date is .... (with a jury) (without a jury).

The estimated length of trial is ....

II. Discovery

The parties shall complete discovery, including depositions, by 30 days before trial; however, depositions taken in lieu of live testimony at trial will be permitted until 15 days before trial. "Complete" means that all interrogatories, requests for production, requests for admissions and other discovery must be served sufficiently in advance of trial to allow a timely response at least 30 days before trial. Depositions may be taken after the specified time period by agreement of counsel of record or for good cause shown, provided however, that the taking of a deposition after the deadline established herein shall not provide a basis for continuance of the trial date or the scheduling of motions inconsistent with the normal procedures of the court. The parties have a duty to seasonably supplement and amend discovery responses pursuant to Rule 4:1(e) of the Rules of Supreme Court of Virginia. Seasonably means as soon as practical. No provision of this Order supersedes the Rules of Supreme Court of Virginia governing discovery. Any discovery motion filed shall contain a certification that counsel has made a good faith effort to resolve the matters set forth in the motion with opposing counsel.

III. Designation of Experts

If requested in discovery, plaintiff's, counter-claimant's, third party plaintiff's, and cross-claimant's experts shall be identified on or before 90 days before trial. If requested in discovery, defendant's and all other opposing experts shall be identified on or before 60 days before trial. If requested in discovery, experts or opinions responsive to new matters raised in the opposing parties, identification of experts shall be designated no later than 45 days before trial. If requested, all information discoverable under Rule 4:1(b)(4)(A)(i) of the Rules of Supreme Court of Virginia shall be provided or the expert will not ordinarily be permitted to express any nondisclosed opinions at trial. The foregoing deadlines shall not relieve a party of the obligation to respond to discovery requests within the time periods set forth in the Rules of Supreme Court of Virginia, including, in particular, the duty to supplement or amend prior responses pursuant to Rule 4:1(e).

IV. Dispositive Motions

All dispositive motions shall be presented to the court for hearing as far in advance of the trial date as practical. All counsel of record are encouraged to bring on for hearing all demurrers, special pleas, motions for summary judgment or other dispositive motions not more than 60 days after being filed.

V. Exhibit and Witness List

Counsel of record shall exchange 15 days before trial a list specifically identifying each exhibit to be introduced at trial, copies of any exhibits not previously supplied in discovery, and a list of witnesses proposed to be introduced at trial. The lists of exhibits and witnesses shall be filed with the Clerk of the Court simultaneously therewith but the exhibits shall not then be filed. Any exhibit or witness not so identified and filed will not be received in evidence, except in rebuttal or for impeachment or unless the admission of such exhibit or testimony of the witness would cause no surprise or prejudice to the opposing party and the failure to list the exhibit or witness was through inadvertence. Any objections to exhibits or witnesses shall state the legal reasons therefor except on relevancy grounds, and shall be filed with the Clerk of the Court and a copy delivered to opposing counsel at least five days before trial or the objections will be deemed waived absent leave of court for good cause shown.

VI. Pretrial Conferences

Pursuant to Rule 4:13 of the Rules of Supreme Court of Virginia, when requested by any party or upon its own motion, the court may order a pretrial conference wherein motions in limine, settlement discussions or other pretrial motions which may aid in the disposition of this action can be heard.

VII. Motions in Limine

Absent leave of court, any motion in limine which requires argument exceeding five minutes shall be duly noticed and heard before the day of trial.

VIII. Witness Subpoenas

Early filing of a request for witness subpoenas is encouraged so that such subpoenas may be served at least 10 days before trial.

IX. Continuances

Continuances will only be granted by the court for good cause shown.

X. Jury Instructions

Counsel of record, unless compliance is waived by the court, shall, two business days before a civil jury trial date, exchange proposed jury instructions. At the commencement of trial, counsel of record shall tender the court the originals of all agreed upon instructions and copies of all contested instructions with appropriate citations. This requirement shall not preclude the offering of additional instructions at the trial.

XI. Deposition Transcripts to be Used at Trial

Counsel of record shall confer and attempt to identify and resolve all issues regarding the use of depositions at trial. It is the obligation of the proponent of any deposition of any non-party witness who will not appear at trial to advise opposing counsel of record of counsel's intent to use all or a portion of the deposition at trial at the earliest reasonable opportunity. Other than trial depositions taken after completion of discovery under Paragraph II, designations of portions of non-party depositions, other than for rebuttal or impeachment, shall be exchanged no later than 15 days before trial, except for good cause shown or by agreement of counsel. It becomes the obligation of the opponent of any such deposition to bring any objection or other unresolved issues to the court for hearing before the day of trial, and to counter-designate any additional portions of designated depositions at least 5 days before such hearing.

XII. Waiver or Modification of Terms of Order

Upon motion, the time limits and prohibitions contained in this order may be waived or modified by leave of court for good cause shown.

[Adopted effective July 1, 2000. Amended February 26, 2010, effective May 3, 2010.]

PART ONE A. FOREIGN ATTORNEYS

Effective March 1, 1972

Including Amendments Received Through October 15, 2015

INTRODUCTION

Each person who has met the educational requirements and has proved that he or she satisfies the character and fitness requirements as established by the law of Virginia may seek admission to the Virginia Bar by taking the Virginia Bar Examination. A primary purpose of the Virginia Bar Examination is to determine whether an applicant is able to demonstrate his or her current minimum competency to engage in the general practice of law in Virginia.

In addition to admission to the Bar by examination, the Supreme Court of Virginia, in its discretion under Code § 54.1–3931, has determined that a person who has been admitted to practice law before the court of last resort of a state or territory of the United States or of the District of Columbia for a minimum of five years, who has been admitted to the bar of a Reciprocal Jurisdiction, hereinafter defined, and who has been engaged in the lawful practice of law on a full-time basis for at least three of the immediately preceding five years, may seek to demonstrate that he or she has made such progress in the practice of law that it would be unreasonable to require the person to take an examination to demonstrate current minimum competency. In other words, an applicant's experience in the practice of law may, at the discretion of the Court, be accepted as adequate evidence of current minimum competency in lieu of the bar examination.

The Supreme Court of Virginia has assigned to the Virginia Board of Bar Examiners (the "Board") the responsibility to assess the information furnished by an applicant for admission without examination and to determine, from the information so furnished, whether the applicant's experience in the practice of law is sufficient to demonstrate his or her current competence, good character, and fitness to practice law in Virginia.

In order to guide the Board in its determinations, the Court has adopted the following criteria to be applied by the Board in assessing applications for admission to the bar of Virginia without examination:

THRESHOLD REQUIREMENTS

1. Reciprocity. The Board shall consider an application for admission without examination only from a person who has been admitted to practice before the court of last resort of, a jurisdiction (i.e., a state or territory of the United States, or the District of Columbia) that permits lawyers licensed in Virginia to be admitted to practice without examination in such jurisdiction (a "Reciprocal Jurisdiction"). The purpose of the reciprocity requirement is to encourage other jurisdictions to grant the same privilege to Virginia lawyers.

2. Minimum Period of Bar Admission. Before being eligible to apply for admission without examination, the applicant must have been admitted to practice law before the court of last resort of a state or territory of the United States, or of the District of Columbia, for at least five (5) years.

3. Requirement of Minimum Current Practice. An applicant may apply for admission without examination only if the applicant has been engaged in the full-time practice of law for at least three (3) of the last five (5) years immediately preceding his or her application for admission to the Virginia Bar. The applicant must have been engaged in this practice in a jurisdiction other than Virginia. Only practice occurring subsequent to the applicant's having been issued a license to engage in the general practice of law in such other jurisdiction shall qualify. Practice from an office located in Virginia or in a foreign country shall not be accepted as qualifying practice. Persons holding a Virginia Corporate Counsel Certificate under Part I of Rule 1A:5 may receive credit as provided in such Rule.

4. Practice of Law. For purposes of admission without examination, "practice of law" ordinarily shall mean (i) private practice as a sole practitioner or for a law firm, legal services office, legal clinic, or similar entity; (ii) practice as an attorney for a corporation, limited liability company, partnership, trust, individual or other entity, provided such practice involved the primary duties of furnishing legal counsel, drafting legal documents and pleadings, interpreting and giving advice regarding the law, and preparing, trying or presenting cases before courts or administrative agencies; (iii) practice as an attorney for the federal or a state or local government with the same primary duties as described above regarding attorneys for a corporation; (iv) employment as a judge for the federal or a state government; (v) service as a judicial law clerk for a state or federal court; or (vi) service on active duty in a branch of the armed forces of the United States as a judge advocate or law specialist, as those terms are defined in the Uniform Code of Military Justice, 10 U.S.C. § 801, as amended, provided that such position requires a valid license to practice law and involves the same primary duties as described above regarding attorneys for a corporation. With the exception of the positions described in (iv) and (v) above, qualifying law practice must have involved an attorney-client relationship and, with the exception of the positions described in (v) and (vi) above, must have occurred subsequent to having been issued a license to engage in the general practice of law in the jurisdiction where the law practice was conducted.

5. Legal Education. The applicant must have received a J.D. degree from a law school that was approved by the American Bar Association at the time of such applicant's graduation.

6. Bar Examination History. The applicant must have failed no more than two bar examinations of any of the states or territories of the United States (including Virginia), or the District of Columbia, and must have failed no bar examination within the five years immediately preceding the application for admission to the Virginia Bar.

7. Instruction in Virginia Law. The applicant must have completed twelve (12) hours of instruction approved by the Virginia Continuing Legal Education Board on Virginia substantive and/or procedural law within six (6) months immediately prior to filing an application and must have read and be familiar with the Virginia Rules of Professional Conduct.

ASSESSMENT OF FITNESS AND PROGRESS

If an applicant provides satisfactory evidence that he or she meets all of the above threshold requirements, the Board shall thereafter determine from the evidence provided by the applicant and the results of any investigation conducted by the Board or its designee whether such applicant (i) is a person of honest demeanor and good moral character and possesses the requisite fitness to perform the obligations and responsibilities of a practicing attorney, and (ii) has made such progress in the practice of law that it would be unreasonable to require the applicant to take an examination to demonstrate current minimum competency. The applicant has the burden to prove by clear and convincing evidence that he or she is a person of honest demeanor and good moral character and possesses the requisite fitness to perform the obligations and responsibilities of a practicing attorney and thus is a proper person to practice law in Virginia. If an applicant fails to answer any question on the Character and Fitness Questionnaire or which is otherwise propounded by the Board, or to supply any requested documentary material, the Board may find that the applicant has not met the burden of proving his or her good moral character.

The primary purposes of character and fitness screening before admission to the Virginia Bar are to assure the protection of the public and safeguard the system of justice. An attorney should be one whose record of conduct justifies the trust of clients, adversaries, courts, and others with respect to the professional duties owed to them. A record manifesting a significant deficiency in the honesty, trustworthiness, diligence, or reliability of an applicant may constitute a basis for denial of admission. The revelation or discovery of any of the following may be treated as cause for further inquiry before the Board decides whether the applicant possesses the character and fitness to practice law:

A. commission or conviction of a crime;

B. violation of the honor code of the applicant's college or university, law school, or other academic misconduct;

C. making of false statements or omissions, including failing to provide complete and accurate information concerning the applicant's past;

D. misconduct in employment;

E. other than an honorable discharge from any branch of the armed services;

F. acts involving dishonesty, fraud, deceit or misrepresentation;

G. abuse of legal process;

H. neglect of financial responsibilities;

I. neglect of professional obligations;

J. violation of an order of a court;

K. denial of admission to the bar in another jurisdiction on character and fitness grounds;

L. disciplinary action by a lawyer disciplinary agency or other professional disciplinary agency of any jurisdiction, including pending, unresolved disciplinary complaints against the applicant;

M. commission of an act constituting the unauthorized practice of law, or unresolved complaints involving allegations of the unauthorized practice of law;

N. any other conduct which reflects adversely upon the character or fitness of an applicant.

The Board shall determine whether the present character and fitness of an applicant qualifies the applicant for admission to the practice of law. In making this determination, the following factors will be considered in assigning weight and significance to the applicant's prior conduct:

i. age of the applicant at the time of the conduct;

ii. recency of the conduct;

iii. reliability of the information concerning the conduct;

iv. seriousness of the conduct;

v. factors underlying the conduct;

vi. cumulative effect of the conduct or information;

vii. evidence of rehabilitation;

viii. positive social contributions of the applicant since the conduct;

ix. candor of the applicant in the admissions process; and

x. materiality of any omissions or misrepresentations.

The Board's obligation to the public requires the Board to address recent mental health and chemical or psychological dependency matters, which may affect, or if untreated could affect, an applicant's ability to perform any of the obligations and responsibilities of a practicing lawyer in a competent and professional manner. Accordingly, the Board will inquire concerning

i. mental or emotional instability, and

ii. existing and untreated drug or alcohol dependency.

The mere fact of treatment for mental health problems or chemical or psychological dependency is not, in itself, a basis on which an applicant is ordinarily denied admission in Virginia, and the Board of Bar Examiners regularly recommends the issuance of certificates to individuals who have demonstrated personal responsibility and maturity in dealing with mental health and chemical or psychological dependency issues. The Board encourages applicants who may benefit from treatment or counseling to seek it. A license or certificate may be denied or deferred when an applicant's ability to function is impaired in a manner relevant to the practice of law at the time the admission decision is made, or when an applicant demonstrates a lack of candor by his or her responses.

In addition, an application will not be approved unless the applicant is a member in good standing of the bar of the Reciprocal Jurisdiction at the time the Board receives the character report and conducts its review of that report. If the applicant's license has ever been suspended or revoked in any jurisdiction, it must be fully reinstated and in good standing (no pending disciplinary charges).

In evaluating whether an applicant has demonstrated satisfactory progress in the practice of law for admission to the practice of law in Virginia without examination, the Board considers whether the following requirements are evident from the information supplied by the applicant and from the investigative report:

1. Knowledge of the fundamental principles of law and the ability to recall that knowledge, to reason, to analyze, and to apply one's knowledge to relevant facts;

2. The ability to communicate clearly, candidly and civilly with clients, attorneys, courts, and others;

3. The ability to exercise good judgment in conducting one's professional business;

4. The ability to conduct oneself with a high degree of honesty, integrity, and trustworthiness in all professional relationships and with respect to all legal obligations;

5. The ability to conduct oneself with respect for and in accordance with the law and the Rules of Professional Conduct;

6. The ability to avoid acts that exhibit disregard for the health, safety and welfare of others;

7. The ability to conduct oneself diligently and reliably in fulfilling all obligations to clients, attorneys, courts, and others;

8. The ability to use honesty and good judgment in financial dealings on behalf of oneself, clients, and others;

9. The ability to comply with deadlines and time constraints; and

10. The ability to conduct oneself professionally and in a manner that engenders respect for the law and the profession.

[Effective February 1, 2014. Amended effective October 31, 2014.]

RULE 1A:1. ADMISSION TO PRACTICE IN THIS COMMONWEALTH WITHOUT EXAMINATION

(a) Reciprocity. Any person who has been admitted to practice law before the court of last resort of any state or territory of the United States or of the District of Columbia may file an application to be admitted to practice law in this Commonwealth without examination, if counsel licensed to practice law in this Commonwealth may be admitted in that jurisdiction without examination.

(b) Application. An applicant for admission to practice law without examination in this Commonwealth shall;

(1) File with the Secretary of the Virginia Board of Bar Examiners (the Board) an application under oath on a form furnished by the Board;

(2) Furnish a certificate, signed by the presiding judge of the court of last resort or other proper official for every jurisdiction in which the applicant is or has been licensed to practice law, stating:

i. that the applicant is in good standing, and if not the reasons why;

ii. the length of time the applicant has been or was licensed in that jurisdiction; and

iii. any restriction or condition placed on the applicant's license to practice law in that jurisdiction.

(3) Certify in writing under oath that the applicant has completed 12 hours of instruction approved by the Virginia Continuing Legal Education Board on Virginia substantive and/or procedural law within the preceding six-month period;

(4) Certify in writing under oath that the applicant has read and is familiar with the Virginia Rules of Professional Conduct;

(5) Complete the Applicant's Character and Fitness Questionnaire and furnish a report of the National Conference of Bar Examiners, or such other report as the Board may require, concerning the applicant's past practice and record, and pay the fee for such report; and

(6) Pay such filing fee as may be fixed from time to time by the Board.

(c) Board Review. Upon receipt of a completed application, the Board will determine in accordance with the regulations issued by the Supreme Court whether the applicant has established by satisfactory evidence that he or she:

(1) Is a proper person to practice law; and

(2) Pursuant to Code § 54.1–3931, has been admitted to practice law before the court of last resort of any state or territory of the United States or of the District of Columbia for at least five years; and

(3) Has practiced law for at least three of the immediately preceding five years and has made such progress in the practice of law that it would be unreasonable to require the applicant to take an examination.

The Board may require the applicant to appear personally before the Board, the Character and Fitness Committee (the Committee) of the Board, or a member of either the Board or the Committee, and furnish any such additional information as may be required. If the applicant's license to practice law in any other jurisdiction is subject to any restriction or condition, the Board shall determine whether the nature of such restriction or condition is inconsistent with the general practice of law and, if so, shall deny the application. If the Board determines that the applicant is qualified to be admitted to the practice of law in this Commonwealth without examination, the Board shall approve the application and shall notify the applicant of its decision.

(d) Admission. Upon notification by the Board that the applicant's application has been approved, the applicant may be issued a certificate, pursuant to Code § 54.1–3931, to practice law in this Commonwealth if:

(1) A member of the Virginia State Bar who is qualified to practice before the Supreme Court moves the applicant's admission to practice law in this Commonwealth in open court;

(2) The motion is granted; and

(3) The applicant takes and subscribes to the oath required of attorneys at law.

(e) Active Membership. Upon payment of applicable dues and completion of other membership obligations set forth in Part 6, Section IV of the Rules of the Supreme Court of Virginia, the applicant shall become an active member of the Virginia State Bar, An attorney admitted pursuant to this Rule shall be deemed subject to the same membership obligations as other active members of the Virginia State Bar, and all legal services provided in Virginia by an attorney admitted pursuant to this Rule shall be deemed the practice of law and shall subject the attorney to all rules governing the practice of law in Virginia, including the Virginia Rules of Professional Conduct. The rules set forth in Part 6, Section IV, governing how members may change their status to associate, judicial, disabled, retired or emeritus shall apply to attorneys admitted pursuant to this Rule.

(f) An attorney admitted to practice law in this Commonwealth without examination under prior versions of this Rule is no longer subject to the requirement that he or she intends to practice law full time as a member of the Virginia State Bar.

[Amended effective June 24, 1988; July 1, 1992; July 6, 1998; March 21, 2001; February 1, 2014; October 31, 2014.]

Source: Rule 1:5.

RULE 1A:2. FOREIGN PATENT AND TRADEMARK ATTORNEYS—WHEN ADMITTED TO PRACTICE IN THE COURTS OF THIS STATE LIMITED TO PATENT AND TRADEMARK LAW WITHOUT EXAMINATION

No lawyer admitted to practice limited to patent and trademark law as defined in § 54.1–3901(A) prior to July 1, 2000, pursuant to this Rule 1A:2 prior to July 1, 2000, shall hold himself or herself out as authorized to practice law generally in this Commonwealth.

[Amended effective July 1, 1982; June 24, 1988; January 23, 1995; July 6, 1998; July 1, 2000.]

Source: Rule 1:15.1.

Comment: The General Assembly in 1981 revised § 54–42.1 on which this rule is based. The [1982] revision conforms the rule to the amended statute.

RULE 1A:3. REVOCATION OF CERTIFICATES ISSUED TO ATTORNEYS ADMITTED PURSUANT TO RULE 1A:2

Following receipt of evidence that a person who was admitted to practice pursuant to Rule 1A:2 prior to July 1, 2000, has been disbarred pursuant to Part Six of the Rules, the Supreme Court will revoke the certificate issued to that person.

[Amended effective June 24, 1988; July 6, 1998; July 1, 2000; February 1, 2014.]

Source: Rule 1:5.2.

RULE 1A:4. OUT–OF–STATE LAWYERS—WHEN ALLOWED BY COMITY TO PARTICIPATE IN A CASE *PRO HAC VICE*

1. Introduction. A lawyer who is not a member of the Virginia State Bar, but is currently licensed and authorized to practice law in another state, territory, or possession of the United States of America (hereinafter called an "out-of-state lawyer") may apply to appear as counsel *pro hac vice* in a particular case before any court, board or administrative agency (hereinafter called "tribunal") in the Commonwealth of Virginia upon compliance with this rule.

2. Association of Local Counsel. No out-of-state lawyer may appear *pro hac vice* before any tribunal in Virginia unless the out-of-state lawyer has first associated in that case with a lawyer who is an active member in good standing of the Virginia State Bar (hereinafter called "local counsel"). The name of local counsel shall appear on all notices, orders, pleadings, and other documents filed in the case. Local counsel shall personally appear and participate in pretrial conferences, hearings, trials, or other proceedings actually conducted before the tribunal. Local counsel associating with an out-of-state lawyer in a particular case shall accept joint responsibility with the out-of-state lawyer to the client, other parties, witnesses, other counsel and to the tribunal in that particular case. Any pleading or other paper required to be served (whether relating to discovery or otherwise) shall be invalid unless it is signed by local counsel. The tribunal in which such case is pending shall have full authority to deal with local counsel exclusively in all matters connected with the pending case. If it becomes necessary to serve notice or process in the case, any notice or process served upon local counsel shall be deemed valid as if served on the out-of-state lawyer.

3. **Procedure for Applying.** Appearance *pro hac vice* in a case is subject to the discretion and approval of the tribunal where such case is pending. An out-of-state lawyer desiring to appear *pro hac vice* under this rule shall comply with the procedures set forth herein for each case in which *pro hac vice* status is requested. For good cause shown, a tribunal may permit an out-of-state lawyer to appear *pro hac vice* on a temporary basis prior to completion by the out-of-state lawyer of the application procedures set forth herein. At the time such temporary admission is granted, the tribunal shall specify a time limit within which the out-of-state lawyer must complete the application procedures, and any temporary *pro hac vice* admission shall be revoked in the event the out-of-state lawyer fails to complete the application procedure within the time limit.

(a) *Notarized Application.* In order to appear *pro hac vice* as counsel in any matter pending before a tribunal in the Commonwealth of Virginia, an out-of-state lawyer shall deliver to local counsel to file with the tribunal an original notarized application and a non-refundable application fee of $250.00 payable to the Clerk of the Supreme Court. *Pro hac vice* counsel must submit a notarized application with the non-refundable application fee of $250.00 for each separate case before a tribunal. The fee shall be paid to the Clerk of the Supreme Court of Virginia. The tribunal shall file a copy of the notarized application, as well as its order granting *pro hac vice* admission in the case and the $250.00 fee, with the Clerk of the Supreme Court of Virginia. Original, notarized applications and orders granting, denying or revoking applications to appear *pro hac vice* shall be retained in a separate file containing all applications. The clerk of the tribunal shall maintain the application for a period of three years after completion of the case and all appeals.

(b) *Motion to Associate Counsel Pro Hac Vice.* Local counsel shall file a motion to associate the out-of-state lawyer as counsel *pro hac vice* with the tribunal where the case is pending, together with proof of service on all parties in accordance with the Rules of the Supreme Court of Virginia. The motion of local counsel shall be accompanied by: (1) the original, notarized application of the out-of-state lawyer; (2) a proposed order granting or denying the motion; and (3) the required application fee.

(c) *Entry of Order.* The order granting or denying the motion to associate counsel *pro hac vice* shall be entered by the tribunal promptly and a copy of the order shall be forwarded to the Clerk of the Supreme Court. An out-of-state lawyer shall make no appearance in a case until the tribunal where the case is pending enters the order granting the motion to associate counsel *pro hac vice* unless temporary admission has been approved pursuant to this rule. The order granting *pro hac vice* status shall be valid until the case is concluded in the courts of this Commonwealth or a court revokes the *pro hac vice* admission.

4. **Notarized Application.** The notarized application required by this rule shall be on a form approved by the Supreme Court of Virginia and available at the office of the clerk of the tribunal where the case is pending.

5. **Discretion and Limitation on Number of Matters.** The grant or denial of a motion pursuant to this rule by the tribunal is discretionary. The tribunal shall deny the motion if the out-of-state lawyer has been previously admitted *pro hac vice* before any tribunal or tribunals in Virginia in twelve (12) cases within the last twelve (12) months preceding the date of the current application. In the enforcement of this limitation, the tribunal may consider whether the pending case is a related or consolidated matter for which the out-of-state lawyer has previously applied to appear *pro hac vice.* Before ruling on a *pro hac vice* motion, the tribunal shall verify with the Supreme Court of Virginia the number of cases during the preceding twelve (12) months in which the out-of-state lawyer was admitted in Virginia *pro hac vice.*

6. **Transfer of Venue and Appeal.** The out-of-state lawyer's *pro hac vice* admission shall be deemed to continue in the event the venue in the case or proceeding is transferred to another tribunal or is appealed; provided, however, that the tribunal having jurisdiction over such transferred or appealed case shall have the discretion to revoke the authority of the out-of-state lawyer to appear *pro hac vice.*

7. **Duty to Report Status.** An out-of-state lawyer admitted *pro hac vice* shall have a continuing obligation during the period of such admission to advise the tribunal promptly of any disposition made of pending disciplinary charges or the institution of any new disciplinary proceedings or investigations. The tribunal shall advise the Clerk of the Supreme Court of Virginia if the tribunal denies or revokes the out-of-state lawyer's permission to appear *pro hac vice.*

8. **Record–Keeping.** The Clerk of the Supreme Court of Virginia will maintain an electronic database

necessary for the administration and enforcement of this rule.

9. Disciplinary Jurisdiction of the Virginia State Bar. An out-of-state lawyer admitted *pro hac vice* pursuant to this rule shall be subject to the jurisdiction of all tribunals and agencies of the Commonwealth of Virginia, and the Virginia State Bar, with respect to the laws and rules of Virginia governing the conduct and discipline of out-of-state lawyers to the same extent as an active member of the Virginia State Bar. An applicant or out-of-state lawyer admitted *pro hac vice* may be disciplined in the same manner as a member of the Virginia State Bar.

10. In–State Services Related to Out–of–State Proceedings. Subject to the requirements and limitations of Rule 5.5 of the Virginia Rules of Professional Conduct, an out-of-state lawyer may provide the following services without the entry of a *pro hac vice* order:

(a) In connection with a proceeding pending outside of Virginia, an out-of-state lawyer admitted to appear in that proceeding may render legal services in Virginia pertaining to or in aid of such proceeding.

(b) In connection with a case in which an out-of-state lawyer reasonably believes he is eligible for admission *pro hac vice* under this rule: (1) the out-of-state lawyer may consult in Virginia with a member of the Virginia State Bar concerning a pending or potential proceeding in Virginia; (2) the out-of-state lawyer may, at the request of a person in Virginia contemplating or involved in a proceeding in Virginia, consult with that person about that person's retention of the out-of-state lawyer in connection with that proceeding; and (3) on behalf of a client residing in Virginia or elsewhere, the out-of-state lawyer may render legal services in Virginia in preparation for a potential case to be filed in Virginia.

(c) An out-of-state lawyer may render legal services to prepare for and participate in an ADR process, regardless of where the ADR process or proceeding is expected to take place or actually takes place.

[Amended effective July 1, 1986; July 1, 2007.]

Source: Rule 1:6.

RULE 1A:5. VIRGINIA CORPORATE COUNSEL & CORPORATE COUNSEL REGISTRANTS

Introduction

Notwithstanding any rule of this Court to the contrary, after July 1, 2004, any person employed in Virginia as a lawyer exclusively for a for-profit or a non-profit corporation, association, or other business entity, including its subsidiaries and affiliates, that is not a government entity, and the business of which consists solely of lawful activities other than the practice of law or the provisions of legal services ("Employer"), for the primary purpose of providing legal services to such Employer, including one who holds himself or herself out as "in-house counsel," "corporate counsel," "general counsel," or other similar title indicating that he or she is serving as legal counsel to such Employer, shall either (i) be a regularly admitted active member of the Virginia State Bar; (ii) be issued a Corporate Counsel Certificate as provided in Part I of this rule and thereby become an active member of the Virginia State Bar with his or her practice limited as provided therein; or (iii) register with the Virginia State Bar as provided in Part II of this rule; provided, however, no person who is or has been a member of the Virginia State Bar, and whose Virginia License, at the time of application, is revoked or suspended, shall be issued a Corporate Counsel Certificate or permitted to register under this Rule.

Part I

Virginia Corporate Counsel

(a) A lawyer admitted to the practice of law in a state (other than Virginia), or territory of the United States, or the District of Columbia may apply to the Virginia State Bar for a certificate as a Registered Virginia Corporate Counsel ("Corporate Counsel Certificate") to practice law as in-house counsel in this state when he or she is employed by an Employer in Virginia.

(b) Each applicant for a Corporate Counsel Certificate shall:

(1) File with the Virginia State Bar an application, under oath, upon a form furnished by the Virginia State Bar.

(2) Furnish a certificate, signed by the presiding judge of the court of last resort of a jurisdiction in which the applicant is admitted to practice law, stating that the applicant is licensed to practice law and is an active member in good standing of the bar of such jurisdiction.

(3) File an affidavit, upon a form furnished by the Virginia State Bar, from an officer of the applicant's Employer attesting to the fact that the applicant is employed as legal counsel to provide legal services exclusively to the Employer, including its subsidiaries and affiliates; that the nature of the applicant's employment conforms to the requirements of Part I of this rule; and that the Employer shall notify the Virginia State Bar immediately upon the termination of the applicant's employment.

(4) Certify that the applicant has read and is familiar with the Virginia Rules of Professional Conduct.

(5) Pay an application fee of one-hundred and fifty dollars.

(c) During the period in which an application for a Corporate Counsel Certificate is pending with the Virginia State Bar until the applicant is notified that either (i) his or her application is rejected; or (ii) he or she is eligible to practice pursuant to Part I of this rule, the applicant may be employed in Virginia as Certified Corporate Counsel on a provisional basis by an Employer furnishing the affidavit required by Part I(b)(3) of this rule.

(d) Upon a finding by the Virginia State Bar that the applicant has complied with the requirements of Part I(b) of this rule, the Virginia State Bar shall notify the applicant that he or she is eligible to be issued a Corporate Counsel Certificate. After the applicant has taken and subscribed to the oath required of attorneys at law, the applicant shall be issued a Corporate Counsel Certificate, which shall permit the applicant to practice law in Virginia solely as provided in Part I(f) of this rule. The applicant may take the required oath by appearing before the Justices of the Supreme Court of Virginia in Richmond at an appointed date and time or by appearing before a judge of a court of record in Virginia. The necessary motion and oath for an applicant who appears before a judge of a court of record can be found in the Appendix of Forms following Part One A of the Rules.

(e) A lawyer issued a Corporate Counsel Certificate shall immediately become an active member of the Virginia State Bar, with his or her practice limited as provided in Part I(f) of this rule, and shall pay to the Virginia State Bar the annual dues required of regularly admitted active members of the Virginia State Bar.

(f) The practice of a lawyer certified pursuant to Part I of this rule shall be limited to practice exclusively for the Employer furnishing the affidavit required by Part I(b)(3) of this rule, including its subsidiaries and affiliates, and may include appearing before a Virginia court or tribunal as counsel for the Employer. Except as specifically authorized under Part I(g) below, no lawyer certified pursuant to Part I of this rule shall (i) undertake to represent any person other than his or her Employer before a Virginia court or tribunal; (ii) offer or provide legal services to any person other than his or her Employer; (iii) undertake to provide legal services to any other person through his or her Employer; or (iv) hold himself or herself out to be authorized to provide legal services or advice to any person other than his or her Employer.

(g) Notwithstanding the restrictions set out in Part I(f) above on the scope of practice, a lawyer certified pursuant to Part I of this rule may, and is encouraged to, provide voluntary *pro bono publico* services in accordance with Rule 6.1 of the Virginia Rules of Professional Conduct.

(h) All legal services provided in Virginia by a lawyer certified pursuant to Part I of this rule shall be deemed the practice of law in Virginia and shall subject the lawyer to all rules governing the practice of law in Virginia, including the Virginia Rules of Professional Conduct and Part 6, Section IV, Paragraph 13 of the Rules of the Supreme Court of Virginia. Jurisdiction of the Virginia State Bar shall continue whether or not the lawyer retains the Corporate Counsel Certificate and irrespective of the lawyer's presence in Virginia.

(i) A lawyer certified pursuant to Part I of this rule shall be subject to the same membership obligations as other active members of the Virginia State Bar, including Mandatory Continuing Legal Education requirements. A lawyer certified pursuant to Part I of this rule shall use as his or her address of record with the Virginia State Bar a business address in Virginia of the Employer furnishing the affidavit required by Part I(b)(3) of this rule.

(j) A lawyer certified pursuant to Part I of this rule shall promptly report to the Virginia State Bar any change in employment, any change in bar membership status in any state, territory of the United States or the District of Columbia in which the lawyer has been admitted to the practice of law, or the imposition of any disciplinary sanction in a state, territory of the United States or the District of Columbia or by any federal court or agency before which the lawyer has been admitted to practice.

(k) A lawyer's authority to practice law which may be permitted pursuant to Part I of this rule shall be automatically suspended when (i) employment by the Employer furnishing the affidavit required by Part I(b)(3) of this rule is terminated, (ii) the lawyer fails to comply with any provision of Part I of this rule, or (iii) when the lawyer is suspended or disbarred for disciplinary reasons in any state, territory of the United States or the District of Columbia or by any federal court or agency before which the lawyer has been admitted to practice. Any lawyer whose authority to practice is suspended pursuant to (i) above shall be reinstated upon evidence satisfactory to the Virginia State Bar that the lawyer is in full compliance with the requirements of Part I of this rule, which shall include an affidavit furnished by the lawyer's new Employer. Any lawyer whose authority to practice is suspended pursuant to (ii) above may be reinstated by compliance with applicable provisions of Part 6, Section IV, Paragraph 19 of the Rules of the Supreme Court of Virginia. Any lawyer whose authority to practice is suspended or terminated under (iii) above shall petition for reinstatement pursuant to Part 6, Section IV, Paragraph 13 I.7. of the Rules of the Supreme Court of Virginia.

(*l*) The period of time a lawyer practices law is permitted by a Corporate Counsel Certificate issued pursuant to Part I of this rule shall be considered in determining whether the lawyer has fulfilled the requirements for admission to practice law in Virginia without examination pursuant to Rule 1A:1 and any guidelines approved by the Supreme Court of Virginia for review of applications for admission without examination.

(m) The Virginia State Bar may adopt regulations as needed to implement the requirements of Part I of this rule.

Part II

Corporate Counsel Registrants

(a) Notwithstanding the requirements of Part I of this rule, any lawyer as defined in the Introduction and Part I(a) of this rule may register with the Virginia State Bar as a "Corporate Counsel Registrant." A person admitted to the practice of law only in a country other than the United States, and who is a member in good standing of a recognized legal profession in that country, the members of which are admitted to practice law as lawyers, counselors at law, or the equivalent, and are subject to effective regulation and discipline by a duly constituted professional body or public authority, may also register under Part II of this rule.

(b) A registrant shall:

(1) Register with the Virginia State Bar upon a form, under oath, furnished by the Virginia State Bar, which shall include affirmations that (i) he or she will at no time undertake to represent his or her Employer or any other person, organization or business entity before a Virginia court or tribunal except as permitted pursuant to Rule 1A:4 of this Court, (ii) his or her work is limited to business and legal services related to issues confronting his or her Employer at a regional, national or international level with no specific nexus to Virginia, and (iii) he or she will not provide legal advice or services to any person other than his or her Employer.

(2) Furnish a certificate, signed by the presiding judge of the court of last resort of a jurisdiction in which the registrant is admitted to practice law, stating that the registrant is licensed to practice law and is an active member in good standing of the bar of such jurisdiction.

(3) File an affidavit, upon a form furnished by the Virginia State Bar, from an officer of the registrant's Employer attesting to the fact that the registrant is employed as legal counsel to provide legal services exclusively to the Employer, including its subsidiaries and affiliates; that the nature of the registrant's employment conforms to the requirements of Part II of this rule; and that the Employer shall notify the Virginia State Bar immediately upon the termination of the registrant's employment.

(4) Certify that the registrant has read and is familiar with the Virginia Rules of Professional Conduct.

(5) Pay a registration fee of one hundred and fifty dollars.

(c) During the period in which a corporate counsel registration is pending with the Virginia State Bar until the registrant is notified that either (i) his or her registration is rejected; or (ii) he or she is eligible to practice pursuant to Part II of this rule, the registrant may be employed in Virginia as a Corporate Counsel Registrant on a provisional basis by the Employer furnishing the affidavit required by Part II(b)(3) of this rule.

(d) Upon completion of the requirements of Part II(b) of this rule, the registrant shall immediately be recorded by the Virginia State Bar as a Corporate Counsel Registrant. Each registrant shall pay to the Virginia State Bar the annual dues required of regularly admitted active members of the Virginia State Bar. No lawyer registered pursuant to Part II of this rule shall (i) undertake to represent his or her Employer or any other person or entity before a Virginia court or tribunal except as permitted for lawyers licensed and in good standing in another United States jurisdiction pursuant to Rule 1A:4 of this Court; (ii) offer or provide legal services to any person other than his or her Employer; (iii) undertake to provide legal services to another through his or her Employer; or (iv) hold himself or herself out to be authorized to provide legal services or advice to any person other than his or her Employer.

(e) The provision of legal services to his or her Employer by a lawyer registered pursuant to Part II of this rule shall be deemed the practice of law in Virginia only for purposes of subjecting the lawyer to the Virginia Rules of Professional Conduct; the jurisdiction of the disciplinary system of the Virginia State Bar; and Part 6, Section IV, Paragraph 13 of the Rules of the Supreme Court of Virginia. Jurisdiction of the Virginia State Bar shall continue whether or not the lawyer maintains the registration and irrespective of the lawyer's presence in Virginia.

(f) A lawyer registered pursuant to Part II of this rule shall use as his or her address of record with the Virginia State Bar a business address in Virginia of the Employer furnishing the affidavit required by Part II(b) (3) of this rule.

(g) A lawyer registered pursuant to Part II of this rule shall promptly report to the Virginia State Bar any change in employment, any change in bar membership status in any state, territory of the United States, the District of Columbia, or other country in which the lawyer has been admitted to the practice of law, or the imposition of any disciplinary sanction in a state, territory of the United States, the District of Columbia, or other country, or by any federal court or agency before which the lawyer has been admitted to practice.

(h) A lawyer's authority to provide legal services which may be permitted pursuant to Part II of this rule shall be automatically suspended when (i) employment by the Employer furnishing the affidavit required by Part II(b)(3) of this rule is terminated, (ii) the lawyer fails to comply with any provision of Part II of this rule, or (iii) the lawyer is suspended or disbarred for disciplinary reasons in any state, territory of the United States, the District of Columbia, other country, or by any federal court or agency before which the lawyer has been admitted to practice. Any lawyer whose authority to practice is suspended pursuant to (i) above shall be reinstated upon evidence satisfactory to the Virginia State Bar that the lawyer is in full compliance with the requirements of Part II of this rule, which shall include an affidavit furnished by the lawyer's new Employer. Any lawyer whose authority to practice is suspended pursuant to (ii) above may be reinstated by compliance with applicable provisions of Part 6, Section IV, Paragraph 19 of the Rules of the Supreme Court of Virginia. Any lawyer whose authority to practice is suspended or terminated pursuant to (iii) above, shall petition for reinstatement pursuant to Part 6, Section IV, Paragraph 13 I.7. of the Rules of the Supreme Court of Virginia.

(i) No time spent as Corporate Counsel Registrant shall be considered in determining eligibility for admission to the Virginia Bar without examination.

(j) The Virginia State Bar may adopt regulations as needed to implement the requirements of Part II of this rule.

[Adopted effective September 1, 2003. Amended effective January 1, 2004; March 4, 2005; May 1, 2006; April 15, 2011; June 10, 2011.]

RULE 1A:6. FOREIGN ATTORNEYS—REGISTERED MILITARY LEGAL ASSISTANCE ATTORNEYS

(a) A lawyer admitted to the practice of law in a state or territory of the United States, other than Virginia, who is serving in or employed by the armed services and is authorized to provide legal assistance pursuant to 10 U.S. Code § 1044, may apply to the Board of Bar Examiners for a certificate as a Registered Military Legal Assistance Attorney in Virginia ("Military Legal Assistance Attorney Certificate") to represent clients eligible for legal assistance in the courts and tribunals of this Commonwealth while the lawyer is employed, stationed, or assigned within Virginia.

(b) Each applicant for a Military Legal Assistance Attorney Certificate shall:

(1) File with the secretary of the Virginia Board of Bar Examiners an application, under oath, upon a form furnished by the Board.

(2) Furnish a certificate, signed by the presiding judge of the court of last resort, or other appropriate official of the jurisdiction in which the applicant is admitted to practice law, stating that the applicant is licensed to practice law and is an active member in good standing of the bar of such jurisdiction.

(3) File an affidavit, upon a form furnished by the Board, from commanding officer, staff judge advocate or chief legal officer of the military base in Virginia where the applicant is employed, stationed, or assigned, attesting to the fact that the applicant is serving as a lawyer to provide legal services exclusively for the military, that the nature of the applicant's employment or service conforms to the requirements of this rule, and that the commanding officer, staff judge advocate or chief legal officer, or his or her successor, shall notify the Virginia State Bar immediately upon the termination of the applicant's employment or service at the military base.

(c) Upon a finding by the Board of Bar Examiners that the applicant has produced evidence sufficient to satisfy the Board that the applicant is a person of honest demeanor and good moral character who possesses the requisite fitness to perform the obligations and responsibilities of a practicing attorney at law and satisfies all other requirements of this rule, the Board shall notify the applicant that he or she is eligible to be issued a Military Legal Assistance Attorney Certificate. After the applicant has taken and subscribed to the oaths required of attorneys at law, the Board shall issue to the applicant a Military Legal Assistance Attorney Certificate, which shall entitle the applicant to represent clients eligible for legal assistance in the courts and tribunals of this Commonwealth solely as provided in this rule.

(d) Each lawyer issued a Military Legal Assistance Attorney Certificate shall immediately register as an active member of the Virginia State Bar, with his or her practice limited as provided in this rule, and pay to the Virginia State Bar the same dues required of regularly admitted active members. (The requirement to pay dues shall be waived for a lawyer during the first two years immediately following the initial issue of a Military Legal Assistance Attorney Certificate to that lawyer.)

(e) The practice of a lawyer registered under this rule shall be limited within this Commonwealth to practice exclusively pursuant to the laws, rules, and regulations governing the military services, and may include appearing before a court or tribunal of this Commonwealth as counsel for a client eligible for legal assistance on:

(1) Adoptions,

(2) Guardianships,

(3) Name changes,

(4) Divorces,

(5) Paternity,

(6) Child custody and visitation, and child and spousal support,

(7) Landlord–tenant disputes on behalf of tenants,

(8) Consumer advocacy cases involving alleged breaches of contracts or warranties, repossession, or fraud,

(9) Garnishment defense,

(10) Probate,

(11) Enforcement of rights under the Soldiers' and Sailors' Civil Relief Act of 1940 (50 U.S. Code App. §§ 501–548, 560–593),

(12) Enforcement of rights under the Uniformed Services Employment and Reemployment Rights Act of 1994 (38 U.S. Code §§ 4301–4333), and

(13) Such other cases within the discretion of the court or tribunal before which the matter is pending.

(f) Representation in proceedings before courts or tribunals of this Commonwealth shall be limited to low-income legal assistance clients for whom hiring a lawyer in private practice would entail a substantial financial hardship to themselves or their families. All pleadings filed by a legal assistance attorney will cite this rule, include the name, complete address, and telephone number of the military legal office representing the client and the name, rank or grade, and armed service of the lawyer registered under this rule providing representation.

(g) No lawyer registered under this rule shall (i) undertake to represent any person other than an eligible legal assistance client before a court or tribunal of this Commonwealth, (ii) offer to provide legal services in this Commonwealth to any person other than as authorized by his or her military service, (iii) undertake to provide legal services in this Commonwealth to any person other than as authorized by his or her military service, or (iv) hold himself or herself out in this Commonwealth to be authorized to provide legal services to any person other than as authorized by his or her military service.

(h) Representing clients eligible for legal assistance in the courts or tribunals of this Commonwealth under this rule shall be deemed the practice of law and shall subject the lawyer to all rules governing the practice of law in Virginia, including the Virginia Rules of Professional Conduct and the Rules of Procedure for Disciplining Lawyers (Rules of Court, Pt. 6, Section IV, Paragraph 13). Jurisdiction of the Virginia State Bar shall continue whether or not the lawyer retains the Military Legal Assistance Attorney Certificate and irrespective of the lawyer's presence in Virginia.

(i) Each person registered with the Virginia State Bar as an active member on the basis of a Military Legal Assistance Attorney Certificate shall be subject to the same membership obligations as other active members, including completion of the required Professionalism Course and annual Mandatory Continuing Education requirements. A lawyer registered under this rule shall use as his or her address of record with the Virginia State Bar the military address in Virginia of the commanding officer, staff judge advocate or chief legal officer which filed the affidavit on the lawyer's behalf.

(j) Each person issued a Military Legal Assistance Attorney Certificate shall promptly report to the Virginia State Bar any change in employment or military service, any change in bar membership status in any state or territory of the United States, or the District of Columbia where the applicant has been admitted to the practice of law, or the imposition of any disciplinary sanction in a state or territory of the United States or the District of Columbia or by any federal court or agency where the applicant has been admitted to the practice of law.

(k) The limited authority to practice law which may be granted under this rule shall be automatically terminated when (i) the lawyer is no longer employed, stationed, or assigned at the military base in Virginia from which affidavit required by this rule was filed, (ii) the lawyer has been admitted to the practice of law in this state by examination or pursuant to any other provision of part 1A of these Rules, (iii) the lawyer fails to comply with any provision of this rule, (iv) the lawyer fails to maintain current good standing as an active member of a bar in at least one state or territory of the United States, other than Virginia, or the District of Columbia, or (v) when suspended or disbarred for disciplinary reasons in any state or territory of the United States or the District of Columbia or by any federal court or agency where the lawyer has been admitted to the practice of law. If a lawyer is no longer employed, stationed, or assigned at the military base in Virginia from which affidavit required by this rule was filed, but the lawyer, within six months after the last day of employment or service, is re-employed by, or militarily reassigned to, the same military base or by another military base in Virginia filing the affidavit required by this rule, the Military Legal Assistance Attorney Certificate shall be reinstated upon evidence satisfactory to the Board that the lawyer remains in full compliance with all requirements of this rule.

(l) The period of time a lawyer practices law full time on the basis of a Military Legal Assistance Attorney Certificate issued pursuant to this rule shall be considered in determining whether such lawyer has fulfilled the requirements for admission to practice law in this Commonwealth without examination under Rule 1A:1 and any guidelines approved by the Supreme Court of Virginia for review of applications for admission without examination.

[Adopted effective January 14, 2003.]

RULE 1A:7. CERTIFICATION OF FOREIGN LEGAL CONSULTANTS

(a) General Requirements. A person admitted to practice law by the duly constituted and authorized professional body or governmental authority of any foreign nation may apply to the Virginia Board of Bar Examiners ("Board") for a certificate as a foreign legal consultant, provided the applicant:

(1) is a member in good standing of a recognized legal profession in a foreign nation, the members of which are admitted to practice as attorneys or counselors at law or the equivalent and are subject to effective regulation and discipline by a duly constituted professional body or a governmental authority;

(2) for at least five of the seven years immediately preceding his or her application has been a member in good standing of such legal profession and has actually been engaged in the authorized practice of law, substantially involving or relating to the rendering of

advice or the provision of legal services concerning the law of the said foreign nation;

(3) possesses the good moral character and general fitness requisite for a member of the bar of this Commonwealth;

(4) is at least twenty-six years of age; and

(5) intends to practice as a foreign legal consultant in this Commonwealth and maintain an office in this Commonwealth for that purpose.

(b) Proof Required. An applicant under this rule shall file with the secretary of the Board:

(1) an application for a foreign legal consultant certificate, on a form furnished by the Board,

(2) a certificate, for each foreign nation in which the applicant is admitted to practice, from the professional body or governmental authority in such foreign country having final jurisdiction over professional discipline, certifying as to the applicant's admission to practice and the date thereof, and as to his or her good standing as an attorney or counselor at law or the equivalent;

(3) a letter of recommendation, for each foreign nation in which the applicant is admitted to practice, from one of the members of the executive body of such professional body or governmental authority or from one of the judges of the highest law court or court of original jurisdiction of such foreign country;

(4) a duly authenticated English translation of each certificate and letter if, in either case, it is not in English;

(5) a copy or summary of the law, regulations, and customs of the foreign country that describes the opportunity afforded to a member of the Virginia State Bar ("the Bar") to establish an office to provide legal services to clients in such foreign country, together with an authenticated English translation if it is not in English;

(6) the requisite documentation establishing the applicant's compliance with the immigration laws of the United States; and

(7) such other evidence as to the applicant's educational and professional qualifications, good moral character and general fitness, and compliance with the requirements of paragraph (a) of this rule as the Board may require.

(c) Reciprocal Treatment of Members of the Bar of This Commonwealth. In considering whether to certify an applicant to practice as a foreign legal consultant, the Board may in its discretion take into account whether a member of the Bar would have a reasonable and practical opportunity to establish an office and give legal advice to clients in the applicant's country of admission. Any member of the Bar who is seeking or has sought to establish an office or give advice in that country may request the Board to consider the matter, or the Board may do so *sua sponte*.

(d) Scope of Practice. A person certified to practice as foreign legal consultant under this Rule may render legal services in the Commonwealth only with regard to matters involving the law of foreign nation(s) in which the person is admitted to practice or international law. For purposes of this paragraph, the term "international law" means a body of laws, rules or legal principles that are based on custom, treaties or legislation and that control or affect (1) the rights and duties of nations in relation to other nations or their citizens, or (2) the rights and obligations pertaining to international transactions.

The practice permitted under this rule does not authorize the foreign legal consultant to appear in court.

(e) Rights and Obligations. Subject to the scope of practice limitations set forth in paragraph (d) of this rule, a person certified as a foreign legal consultant under this rule shall be entitled and subject to:

(1) the rights and obligations contained in the Virginia Rules of Professional Conduct as set forth in Part 6, Section II of the Rules of the Supreme Court of Virginia; and the procedure for disciplining attorneys as set forth in Part 6, Section IV, Paragraph 13 of the Rules of the Supreme Court of Virginia

(2) the rights and obligations of a member of the Bar with respect to:

(i) affiliation in the same law firm with one or more members of the bar of this Commonwealth, including by:

(A) employing one or more members of the Bar;

(B) being employed by one or more members of the Bar or by any partnership or other limited liability entity authorized to practice law pursuant to Part 6, Section IV, Paragraph 14 of the Rules of the Supreme Court of Virginia, which such entity includes an active member of the Bar or which maintains an office in this Commonwealth;

(C) being a director, partner, member, manager or shareholder in any partnership or other professional limited liability entity authorized by Part 6, Section IV, Paragraph 14 to practice law in this Commonwealth which includes an active member of the Bar or which maintains an office in this Commonwealth;

(ii) employment as in-house counsel under Part II of Rule 1A:5; and

(iii) attorney-client privilege, work-product privilege and similar professional privileges.

(3) No time spent practicing as a foreign legal consultant shall be considered in determining eligibility for admission to the Virginia bar without examination.

(f) Disciplinary Provisions. A person certified to practice as a foreign legal consultant under this Rule shall be subject to professional discipline in the same manner and to the same extent as any member of the Bar and to this end:

(1) Every person certified to practice as a foreign legal consultant under these Rules:

(i) shall be subject to regulation by the Bar and to admonition, reprimand, suspension, removal or revocation of his or her certificate to practice in accordance with the rules of procedure for disciplinary proceedings set forth in Part 6, Section IV, Paragraph 13 of the Rules of the Supreme Court of Virginia; and

(ii) shall execute and file with the Bar, in such form and manner as the Bar may prescribe:

(A) his or her commitment to observe the Virginia Rules of Professional Conduct and any other rules of court governing members of the bar to the extent they may be applicable to the legal services authorized under paragraph (d) of this Rule;

(B) a written undertaking to notify the Bar of any change in such person's good standing as a member of any foreign legal profession referred to in paragraph (a)(1) of this rule and of any final action of any professional body or governmental authority referred to in paragraph (b)(2) of this rule imposing any disciplinary censure, suspension, or other sanction upon such person; and

(C) a duly acknowledged instrument, in writing, setting forth his or her address in this Commonwealth which shall be both his or her address of record with the Bar and such person's actual place of business for rendering services authorized by this rule. Such address shall be one where process can be served and the foreign legal consultant shall have a duty to promptly notify the Membership Department of the Bar in writing of any changes in his or her address of record.

(g) Application and Renewal Fees. An applicant for a certificate as a foreign legal consultant under this rule shall pay to the Virginia Board of Bar Examiners the application fee and costs as may be fixed from time to time by the Board. A person certified as a foreign legal consultant shall pay an annual fee to the Virginia State Bar which shall also be fixed by the Supreme Court of Virginia. A person certified as a foreign legal consultant who fails to complete and file the renewal form supplied by the Bar or pay the annual fee shall have his or her certificate as a foreign legal consultant administratively suspended in accordance with the procedures set out in Part 6, Section IV, Paragraph 19 of the Rules of the Supreme Court of Virginia.

(h) Revocation of Certificate for Non–Compliance. In the event that the Bar determines that a person certified as a foreign legal consultant under this rule no longer meets the requirements under this rule, it shall revoke the certificate granted to such person hereunder.

(i) Reinstatement. Any foreign legal consultant whose authority to practice is suspended shall be reinstated upon evidence satisfactory to the Bar that such person is in full compliance with this rule; however, a reinstatement of a foreign legal consultant's certificate following a suspension for non-compliance with paragraph (g) of this rule shall be governed by Part 6, Section IV, Paragraph 19 of the Rules of the Supreme Court of Virginia; and reinstatement of a foreign legal consultant's certificate following a disciplinary suspension or revocation shall be governed by Part Six, Section IV, Paragraph 13 of the Rules of the Supreme Court of Virginia.

(j) Admission to Bar. In the event that a person certified as a foreign legal consultant under this rule is subsequently admitted as a member of the Bar under the provisions of the rules governing such admission, the certificate granted to such person hereunder shall be deemed superseded by the admission of such person to the Bar.

(k) Regulations. The Bar and the Board may adopt regulations as needed to implement their respective responsibilities under this rule.

(*l*) Effective Date. This rule shall become effective on January 1, 2009.

[Adopted effective January 1, 2009. Amended effective January 1, 2009.]

RULE 1A:8. MILITARY SPOUSE PROVISIONAL ADMISSION

1. Requirements. A person who meets all requirements of subparagraphs (a) through (m) of paragraph 2 of this Rule 1A:8 may, upon motion, be provisionally admitted to the practice of law in Virginia.

2. Required Evidence. The applicant for provisional admission shall submit evidence satisfactory to the Virginia Board of Bar Examiners (the "Board") that he or she:

(a) has been admitted by examination to practice law before the court of last resort of any state or territory of the United States or of the District of Columbia;

(b) holds a Juris Doctor degree from a law school accredited by the American Bar Association at the time of such applicant's graduation;

(c) has achieved a passing score on the Multistate Professional Responsibility Examination as it is established in Virginia at the time of application;

(d) is currently an active member in good standing in at least one state or territory of the United States, or the District of Columbia, where the applicant is admitted to the unrestricted practice of law, and is a member in good standing in all jurisdictions where the applicant has been admitted;

(e) is not currently subject to lawyer discipline or the subject of a pending disciplinary matter in any other jurisdiction;

(f) possesses the good character and fitness to practice law in Virginia;

(g) is the dependent spouse of an active duty service member of the United States Uniformed Services as defined by the Department of Defense (or, for the Coast Guard when it is not operating as a service in the Navy, by the Department of Homeland Security) and that the service member is on military orders stationed in the Commonwealth of Virginia or the National Capitol region, as defined by the Department of Defense;

(h) is physically residing in Virginia;

(i) has submitted all requested character investigation information, in a manner and to the extent established by the Board, including all required supporting documents;

(j) has never failed the Virginia Bar Examination;

(k) has completed twelve (12) hours of instruction approved by the Virginia Continuing Legal Education Board on Virginia substantive and/or procedural law, including four (4) hours of ethics, within the six-month period immediately preceding or following the filing of the applicant's application;

(*l*) certifies that he or she has read and is familiar with the Virginia Rules of Professional Conduct; and

(m) has paid such fees as may be set by the Board to cover the costs of the character and fitness investigation and the processing of the application.

3. Issuance, Admission, Duration and Renewal.

(a) *Issuance.* The Board having certified that all prerequisites have been complied with, the applicant for provisional admission shall, upon payment of applicable dues and completion of the other membership obligations set forth in Part 6, Section IV of the Rules of the Supreme Court of Virginia, become an active member of the Virginia State Bar. An attorney provisionally admitted pursuant to this Rule shall be subject to the same membership obligations as other active members of the Virginia State Bar, and all legal services provided in Virginia by a lawyer admitted pursuant to this Rule shall be deemed the practice of law and shall subject the attorney to all rules governing the practice of law in Virginia, including the Virginia Rules of Professional Conduct.

(b) *Admission.* Upon notification by the Board that the applicant's application has been approved, the applicant shall take and subscribe to the oath required of attorneys at law. The applicant may take the required oath by appearing before the Justices of the Supreme Court of Virginia in Richmond at an appointed date and time or by appearing before a judge of a court of record in Virginia. Once the attorney has taken the oath, it shall remain effective until the attorney's provisional admission is terminated pursuant to paragraph 5 of this Rule,

(c) *Duration.* A provisional admission may be renewed by July 31 of each year, upon filing with the Virginia State Bar (i) a written request for renewal, (ii) an affidavit by supervising Local Counsel, who certifies to the provisionally admitted attorney's continuing employment by or association with Local Counsel and to Local Counsel's adherence to the supervision requirements as provided under this Rule, and (iii) compliance with the membership obligations of Part 6, Section IV of the Rules of the Supreme Court of Virginia applicable to active members of the Virginia State Bar.

(d) *Renewal.* When the active duty service member is assigned to an unaccompanied or remote follow-on assignment and the attorney continues to physically reside in Virginia, the provisional admission may be renewed until that unaccompanied or remote assignment ends, provided that the attorney complies with the other requirements for renewal.

4. Supervision of Local Counsel. A person provisionally admitted to practice under this Rule may engage in the practice of law in this jurisdiction only under the supervision and direction of Local Counsel.

(a) As used in this Rule, Local Counsel means an active member in good standing of the Virginia State Bar, whose office is in Virginia.

(b) Local Counsel must provide to the Virginia State Bar his or her Virginia State Bar number, physical office address, mailing address, email address, telephone number, and written consent to serve as Local Counsel, on the form provided by the Board.

(c) Unless specifically excused from attendance by the trial judge, Local Counsel shall personally appear with the provisionally admitted attorney on all matters before the court.

(d) Local Counsel will be responsible to the courts, the Virginia State Bar, the Supreme Court of Virginia, and the client for all services provided by the provisionally admitted attorney pursuant to this Rule.

(e) Local Counsel is obligated to notify the Executive Director of the Virginia State Bar when the supervising relationship between the provisionally admitted attorney and Local Counsel is terminated.

5. Events of Termination. An attorney's provisional admission to practice law pursuant to this Rule shall immediately terminate and the attorney shall immediately cease all activities under this Rule upon the occurrence of any of the following:

(a) The spouse's discharge, separation or retirement from active duty in the United States Uniformed Services, or the spouse's no longer being on military orders stationed in the Commonwealth of Virginia or the National Capitol region as defined by the Department of Defense, except as provided in section 3(c) of this Rule;

(b) Failure to meet the annual licensing requirements of an active member of the Virginia State Bar;

(c) The absence of supervision by Local Counsel;

(d) The attorney no longer physically residing within the Commonwealth of Virginia;

(e) The attorney ceasing to be a dependent as defined by the Department of Defense (or, for the Coast Guard when it is not operating as a service in the Navy, by the Department of Homeland Security) on the spouse's official military orders;

(f) The attorney being admitted to practice law in this Commonwealth under an admissions rule other than that of Provisional Admission;

(g) The attorney receiving a failing score on the Virginia Bar Examination;

(h) The attorney being suspended from the practice of law in Virginia; or

(i) Request by the attorney.

6. Notices Required.

(a) An attorney provisionally admitted under this Rule shall provide written notice to the Virginia State Bar of any Event of Termination within thirty (30) days of the occurrence thereof.

(b) Within thirty (30) days of the occurrence of any Event of Termination, the attorney shall:

(i) provide written notice to all his or her clients that he or she can no longer represent such clients and furnish proof to the Executive Director of the Virginia State Bar within sixty (60) days of such notification; and

(ii) file in each matter pending before any court or tribunal in this Commonwealth a notice that the attorney will no longer be involved in the matter, which shall include the substitution of the Local Counsel, or such other attorney licensed to practice law in Virginia selected by the client, as counsel in the place of the provisionally admitted attorney.

7. Benefits and Responsibilities. An attorney provisionally admitted under this Rule shall be entitled to the benefits and be subject to all responsibilities and obligations of active members of the Virginia State Bar, and shall be subject to the jurisdiction of the courts and agencies of the Commonwealth of Virginia and to the Virginia State Bar with respect to the laws and rules of this Commonwealth governing the conduct and discipline of attorneys to the same extent as an active member of the Virginia State Bar.

[Adopted effective July 1, 2014. Amended effective February 27, 2015.]

APPENDIX OF FORMS

FORM 1. APPLICATION TO APPEAR *PRO HAC VICE* BEFORE A VIRGINIA TRIBUNAL

[Note: *the following form may be submitted electronically pursuant to Rule 1:17 and related provisions of Virginia law.*]

I, ..., the undersigned attorney, hereby apply
NAME OF APPLICANT
to this tribunal of the Commonwealth of Virginia, ..., to appear as
NAME OF TRIBUNAL
Counsel pro hac vice pursuant to Rule 1A:4 of the Rules of the Supreme Court of Virginia. I further state the following:

1. The case in which I seek to appear pro hac vice is styled ...., has docket number .... and is pending in ....
This case [ ] is [ ] is not a related or consolidated matter for which I have previously applied to appear pro hac vice.

2. ....
APPLICANT'S RESIDENCE ADDRESS
....
APPLICANT'S OFFICE ADDRESS

3. ....
NAME OF LOCAL COUNSEL VSB NUMBER
....
STREET ADDRESS
....
....
FAX NUMBER EMAIL ADDRESS TELEPHONE NUMBER

4. ....
NAME OF PARTY TO CASE
....
NAME AND ADDRESS OF COUNSEL FOR PARTY
....
NAME OF PARTY TO CASE
....
NAME AND ADDRESS OF COUNSEL FOR PARTY
....
NAME OF PARTY TO CASE
....
NAME AND ADDRESS OF COUNSEL FOR PARTY

[ ] Additional Sheet attached.

5. ....
COURT TO WHICH APPLICANT IS ADMITTED DATE OF ADMISSION

....
COURT TO WHICH APPLICANT IS ADMITTED DATE OF ADMISSION

[ ] Additional Sheet attached.

6. I am a member in good standing and authorized to appear in the courts identified in paragraph 5.

7. I am not currently disbarred or suspended in any state, territory, United States possession or tribunal.

8. I [ ] am not [ ] am subject to a pending disciplinary investigation or proceeding by any court, agency or organization authorized to discipline me as a lawyer. (If such an investigation or proceeding is pending, attach to this application and incorporate by reference a statement specifying the jurisdiction, the nature of the matter under investigation or being prosecuted, and the name and address of the disciplinary authority investigating or prosecuting the matter.)

9. Within the past three (3) years, I [ ] have not [ ] have been disciplined by any court, agency or organization authorized to discipline me as a lawyer. (If so, attach to this application and incorporate by reference a statement specifying the name of the court, agency or organization imposing discipline, the date(s) of such discipline, the nature of the complaint or charge on which discipline was imposed, and the sanction.)

10. Within the last twelve (12) months preceding this application, I [ ] have not [ ] have sought admission pro hac vice under this rule. (If so, attach to this application and incorporate by reference a copy of the order of the tribunal granting or denying your previous application. Such order(s) must include the name of the tribunal, the style of case and the docket number for the case(s) in which you filed an application and whether the application was granted or denied.)

[ ] Order(s) attached and incorporated by reference.

11. I hereby consent to the jurisdiction of the courts and agencies of the Commonwealth of Virginia and of the Virginia State Bar and I further consent to service of process at any address(es) required by this Rule.

12. I agree to review and comply with appropriate rules of procedure as required in the case for which I am applying to appear pro hac vice.

13. I understand and I agree to comply with the rules and standards of professional conduct required of members of the Virginia State Bar.

....
DATE SIGNATURE OF APPLICANT

Commonwealth/State of ....

[ ] City [ ] County of ....

Subscribed and sworn to/affirmed before me on this date by the above-named person.

....
DATE NOTARY PUBLIC

My commission expires: ....

[Adopted effective July 1, 2007. Amended effective May 2, 2011.]

FORM 2. MOTION AND OATH FOR ADMISSION AS CORPORATE COUNSEL

ADMISSION ON MOTION
(CORPORATE COUNSEL)

MAY IT PLEASE THE COURT, I WISH TO PRESENT

____,

A MEMBER OF THE BAR OF THE STATE OF ________________

(OR THE DISTRICT OF COLUMBIA), WHO HAS FILED AN

APPLICATION TO BE ADMITTED TO PRACTICE LAW IN THE

COMMONWEALTH OF VIRGINIA AS CORPORATE COUNSEL.

______________________________________ HAS BEEN

NOTIFIED THAT HIS/HER APPLICATION HAS BEEN APPROVED,

AND I NOW MOVE HIS/HER ADMISSION AS A CORPORATE

COUNSEL TO THE BAR OF THE SUPREME COURT OF VIRGINIA.

____
Signature of Sponsor

________________________________ #________________
Printed Name of Sponsor Virginia Bar Number

ATTORNEY OATH (CORPORATE COUNSEL)

I do solemnly swear or affirm that I will support the Constitution of the United States and the Constitution of the Commonwealth of Virginia, and that I will faithfully, honestly, professionally, and courteously demean myself in the practice of law and execute my office of attorney at law to the best of my ability, so help me God.

(Print Full Name)____

(Signature)____

(Phone and email)____

____

Signature of Judge Administering Oath

____

Printed Name of Judge Administering Oath

____

Name of Court

____

Date

A Copy,

Teste:

Clerk

[Added effective June 10, 2011.]

PART TWO. VIRGINIA RULES OF EVIDENCE

Effective July 1, 2012

Including Amendments Received Through October 15, 2015

ARTICLE I

GENERAL PROVISIONS

RULE 2:101. TITLE

These Rules shall be known as Virginia Rules of Evidence.

[Adopted effective July 1, 2012.]

RULE 2:102. SCOPE AND CONSTRUCTION OF THESE RULES

These Rules state the law of evidence in Virginia. They are adopted to implement established principles under the common law and not to change any established case law rendered prior to the adoption of the Rules. Common law case authority, whether decided before or after the effective date of the Rules of Evidence, may be argued to the courts and considered in interpreting and applying the Rules of Evidence. As to matters not covered by these Rules, the existing law remains in effect. Where no rule is set out on a particular topic, adoption of the Rules shall have no effect on current law or practice on that topic.

[Adopted effective July 1, 2012.]

RULE 2:103. OBJECTIONS AND PROFFERS

(a) Admission or Exclusion of Evidence. Error may not be predicated upon admission or exclusion of evidence, unless:

(1) As to evidence admitted, a contemporaneous objection is stated with reasonable certainty as required in Rule 5:25 and 5A:18 or in any continuing objection on the record to a related series of questions, answers or exhibits if permitted by the trial court in order to avoid the necessity of repetitious objections; or

(2) As to evidence excluded, the substance of the evidence was made known to the court by proffer.

(b) Hearing of Jury. In jury cases, proceedings shall be conducted so as to prevent inadmissible evidence from being made known to the jury.

[Adopted effective July 1, 2012.]

RULE 2:104. PRELIMINARY DETERMINATIONS

(a) Determinations Made by the Court. The qualification of a person to be a witness, the existence of a privilege, or the admissibility of evidence shall be decided by the court, subject to the provisions of subdivision (b).

(b) Relevancy Conditioned on Proof of Connecting Facts. Whenever the relevancy of evidence depends upon proof of connecting facts, the court may admit the evidence upon or, in the court's discretion, subject to, the introduction of proof sufficient to support a finding of the connecting facts.

(c) Hearing of Jury. Hearings on the admissibility of confessions in all criminal cases shall be conducted out of the hearing of the jury. Hearings on other preliminary matters in all cases shall be so conducted whenever a statute, rule, case law or the interests of justice require, or when an accused is a witness and so requests.

(d) Testimony by Accused. The accused does not, by testifying upon a preliminary matter, become subject to cross-examination as to other issues in the case.

(e) Evidence of Weight or Credibility. This rule does not limit the right of any party to introduce before the jury evidence relevant to weight or credibility.

[Adopted effective July 1, 2012.]

RULE 2:105. PROOF ADMITTED FOR LIMITED PURPOSES

When evidence is admissible as to one party or for one purpose but not admissible as to another party or for another purpose, the court upon motion shall restrict such evidence to its proper scope and instruct the jury accordingly. The court may give such limiting instructions sua sponte, to which any party may object.

[Adopted effective July 1, 2012.]

RULE 2:106. REMAINDER OF A WRITING OR RECORDED STATEMENT (Rule 2:106(b) derived from Code § 8.01–417.1)

(a) Related Portions of a Writing in Civil and Criminal Cases. When part of a writing or recorded statement is introduced by a party, upon motion by another party the court may require the offering party to introduce any other part of the writing or recorded statement which ought in fairness to be considered contemporaneously with it, unless such additional portions are inadmissible under the Rules of Evidence.

(b) Lengthy Documents in Civil Cases. To expedite trials in civil cases, upon timely motion, the court may permit the reading to the jury, or the introduction into evidence, of relevant portions of lengthy and complex documents without the necessity of having the jury hear or receive the entire document. The court, in its discretion, may permit the entire document to be received by the jury, or may order the parties to edit from any such document admitted into evidence information that is irrelevant to the proceedings.

[Adopted effective July 1, 2012.]

ARTICLE II

JUDICIAL NOTICE

RULE 2:201. JUDICIAL NOTICE OF ADJUDICATIVE FACTS

(a) Notice. A court may take judicial notice of a factual matter not subject to reasonable dispute in that it is either (1) common knowledge or (2) capable of accurate and ready determination by resort to sources whose accuracy cannot reasonably be questioned.

(b) Time of Taking Notice. Judicial notice may be taken at any stage of the proceeding.

(c) Opportunity to Be Heard. A party is entitled upon timely motion to an opportunity to be heard as to the propriety of taking judicial notice.

[Adopted effective July 1, 2012.]

RULE 2:202. JUDICIAL NOTICE OF LAW (derived from Code §§ 8.01–386 and 19.2–265.2)

(a) Notice to Be Taken. Whenever, in any civil or criminal case it becomes necessary to ascertain what the law, statutory, administrative, or otherwise, of this Commonwealth, of another state, of the United States, of another country, or of any political subdivision or agency of the same, or under an applicable treaty or international convention is, or was, at any time, the court shall take judicial notice thereof whether specially pleaded or not.

(b) Sources of Information. The court, in taking such notice, shall in a criminal case and may in a civil case consult any book, record, register, journal, or other official document or publication purporting to contain, state, or explain such law, and may consider any evidence or other information or argument that is offered on the subject.

[Adopted effective July 1, 2012.]

RULE 2:203. JUDICIAL NOTICE OF OFFICIAL PUBLICATIONS (derived from Code § 8.01–388)

The court shall take judicial notice of the contents of all official publications of the Commonwealth and its political subdivisions and agencies required to be published pursuant to the laws thereof, and of all such official publications of other states, of the United States, of other countries, and of the political subdivisions and agencies of each published within those jurisdictions pursuant to the laws thereof.

[Adopted effective July 1, 2012.]

ARTICLE III

PRESUMPTIONS

RULE 2:301. PRESUMPTIONS IN GENERAL IN CIVIL ACTIONS AND PROCEEDINGS

Unless otherwise provided by Virginia common law or statute, in a civil action a rebuttable presumption imposes on the party against whom it is directed the burden of going forward with evidence to rebut or meet the presumption, but does not shift to such party the burden of proof, which remains throughout the trial upon the party on whom it originally rested.

[Adopted effective July 1, 2012.]

RULE 2:302. APPLICABILITY OF FEDERAL LAW IN CIVIL ACTIONS AND PROCEEDINGS

The effect of a presumption is determined by federal law in any civil action or proceeding as to which federal law supplies the rule of decision.

[Adopted effective July 1, 2012.]

ARTICLE IV

RELEVANCY, POLICY, AND CHARACTER TRAIT PROOF

RULE 2:401. DEFINITION OF "RELEVANT EVIDENCE"

"Relevant evidence" means evidence having any tendency to make the existence of any fact in issue more probable or less probable than it would be without the evidence.

[Adopted effective July 1, 2012.]

RULE 2:402. RELEVANT EVIDENCE GENERALLY ADMISSIBLE; IRRELEVANT EVIDENCE INADMISSIBLE

(a) General Principle. All relevant evidence is admissible, except as otherwise provided by the Constitution of the United States, the Constitution of Virginia, statute, Rules of the Supreme Court of Virginia, or other evidentiary principles. Evidence that is not relevant is not admissible.

(b) Results of Polygraph Examinations. The results of polygraph examinations are not admissible.

[Adopted effective July 1, 2012.]

RULE 2:403. EXCLUSION OF RELEVANT EVIDENCE ON GROUNDS OF PREJUDICE, CONFUSION, MISLEADING THE JURY, OR NEEDLESS PRESENTATION OF CUMULATIVE EVIDENCE

Relevant evidence may be excluded if:

(a) the probative value of the evidence is substantially outweighed by (i) the danger of unfair prejudice, or (ii) its likelihood of confusing or misleading the trier of fact; or

(b) the evidence is needlessly cumulative.

[Adopted effective July 1, 2012.]

RULE 2:404. CHARACTER EVIDENCE NOT ADMISSIBLE TO PROVE CONDUCT; EXCEPTIONS; OTHER CRIMES

(a) Character Evidence Generally. Evidence of a person's character or character trait is not admissible for the purpose of proving action in conformity therewith on a particular occasion, except:

(1) *Character Trait of Accused.* Evidence of a pertinent character trait of the accused offered by the accused, or by the prosecution to rebut the same;

(2) *Character Trait of Victim.* Except as provided in Rule 2:412, evidence of a pertinent character trait or acts of violence by the victim of the crime offered by an accused who has adduced evidence of self defense, or by the prosecution (i) to rebut defense evidence, or (ii) in a criminal case when relevant as circumstantial evidence to establish the death of the victim when other evidence is unavailable; or

(3) *Character Trait of Witness.* Evidence of the character trait of a witness, as provided in Rules 2:607, 2:608, and 2:609.

(b) Other Crimes, Wrongs, or Acts. Except as provided in Rule 2:413 or by statute, evidence of other crimes, wrongs, or acts is generally not admissible to prove the character trait of a person in order to show that the person acted in conformity therewith. However, if the legitimate probative value of such proof outweighs its incidental prejudice, such evidence is admissible if it tends to prove any relevant fact pertaining to the offense charged, such as where it is relevant to show motive, opportunity, intent, preparation, plan, knowledge, identity, absence of mistake, accident, or if they are part of a common scheme or plan.

[Adopted effective July 1, 2012. Amended effective July 1, 2014.]

RULE 2:405. METHODS OF PROVING CHARACTER TRAITS

(a) Reputation Proof. Where evidence of a person's character trait is admissible under these Rules, proof may be made by testimony as to reputation; but a witness may not give reputation testimony except upon personal knowledge of the reputation. On cross-examination, inquiry is allowable into relevant specific instances of conduct.

(b) Specific Instances of Conduct. In cases in which a character trait of a person is an essential element of a charge, claim, or defense, proof may also be made of specific instances of conduct of such person on direct or cross-examination.

[Adopted effective July 1, 2012.]

RULE 2:406. HABIT AND ROUTINE PRACTICE IN CIVIL CASES (derived from Code § 8.01–397.1)

(a) Admissibility. In a civil case, evidence of a person's habit or of an organization's routine practice, whether corroborated or not and regardless of the presence of eyewitnesses, is relevant to prove that the conduct of the person or organization on a particular occasion conformed with the habit or routine practice. Evidence of prior conduct may be relevant to rebut evidence of habit or routine practice.

(b) Habit and Routine Practice Defined. A "habit" is a person's regular response to repeated specific situations. A "routine practice" is a regular course of conduct of a group of persons or an organization in response to repeated specific situations.

[Adopted effective July 1, 2012.]

RULE 2:407. SUBSEQUENT REMEDIAL MEASURES (derived from Code § 8.01–418.1)

When, after the occurrence of an event, measures are taken which, if taken prior to the event, would have made the event less likely to occur, evidence of such subsequent measures is not admissible to prove negligence or culpable conduct as a cause of the occurrence of the event; provided that evidence of subsequent measures shall not be required to be excluded when offered for another purpose for which it may be admissible, including, but not limited to, proof of ownership, control, feasibility of precautionary measures if controverted, or for impeachment.

[Adopted effective July 1, 2012.]

RULE 2:408. COMPROMISE AND OFFERS TO COMPROMISE

Evidence of offers and responses concerning settlement or compromise of any claim which is disputed as to liability or amount is inadmissible regarding such issues. However, an express admission of liability, or an admission concerning an independent fact pertinent to a question in issue, is admissible even if made during settlement negotiations. Otherwise admissible evidence is not excludable merely because it was presented in the course of compromise negotiations. Nor is it required that evidence of settlement or compromise negotiations be excluded if the evidence is offered for another purpose, such as proving bias or prejudice of a witness or negating a contention of undue delay.

[Adopted effective July 1, 2012.]

RULE 2:409. EVIDENCE OF ABUSE ADMISSIBLE IN CERTAIN CRIMINAL TRIALS (derived from Code § 19.2–270.6)

In any criminal prosecution alleging personal injury or death, or the attempt to cause personal injury or death, relevant evidence of repeated physical and psychological abuse of the accused by the victim shall be admissible, subject to the general rules of evidence.

[Adopted effective July 1, 2012.]

RULE 2:410. WITHDRAWN PLEAS, OFFERS TO PLEAD, AND RELATED STATEMENTS

Admission of evidence concerning withdrawn pleas in criminal cases, offers to plead, and related statements shall be governed by Rule 3A:8(c)(5) of the Rules of Supreme Court of Virginia and by applicable provisions of the Code of Virginia.

[Adopted effective July 1, 2012.]

RULE 2:411. INSURANCE

Evidence that a person was or was not insured is not admissible on the question whether the person acted negligently or otherwise wrongfully, and not admissible on the issue of damages. But exclusion of evidence of insurance is not required when offered for another purpose, such as proof of agency, ownership, or control, or bias or prejudice of a witness.

[Adopted effective July 1, 2012.]

RULE 2:412. ADMISSIBILITY OF COMPLAINING WITNESS' PRIOR SEXUAL CONDUCT; CRIMINAL SEXUAL ASSAULT CASES; RELEVANCE OF PAST BEHAVIOR (derived from Code § 18.2–67.7)

(a) In prosecutions under Article 7, Chapter 4 of Title 18.2 of the Code of Virginia, under clause (iii) or (iv) of § 18.2–48, or under §§ 18.2–370, 18.2–370.01, or 18.2–370.1, general reputation or opinion evidence of the complaining witness' unchaste character or prior sexual conduct shall not be admitted. Unless the complaining witness voluntarily agrees otherwise, evidence of specific instances of his or her prior sexual conduct shall be admitted only if it is relevant and is:

1. Evidence offered to provide an alternative explanation for physical evidence of the offense charged which is introduced by the prosecution, limited to evidence designed to explain the presence of semen, pregnancy, disease, or physical injury to the complaining witness' intimate parts; or

2. Evidence of sexual conduct between the complaining witness and the accused offered to support a contention that the alleged offense was not accomplished by force, threat or intimidation or through the use of the complaining witness' mental incapacity or physical helplessness, provided that the sexual conduct occurred within a period of time reasonably proximate to the offense charged under the circumstances of this case; or

3. Evidence offered to rebut evidence of the complaining witness' prior sexual conduct introduced by the prosecution.

(b) Nothing contained in this Rule shall prohibit the accused from presenting evidence relevant to show that the complaining witness had a motive to fabricate the charge against the accused. If such evidence relates to the past sexual conduct of the complaining witness with a person other than the accused, it shall not be admitted and may not be referred to at any preliminary hearing or trial unless the party offering same files a written notice generally describing the evidence prior to the introduction of any evidence, or the opening statement of either counsel, whichever first occurs, at the preliminary hearing or trial at which the admission of the evidence may be sought.

(c) Evidence described in subdivisions (a) and (b) of this Rule shall not be admitted and may not be referred to at any preliminary hearing or trial until the court first determines the admissibility of that evidence at an evidentiary hearing to be held before the evidence is introduced at such preliminary hearing or trial. The court shall exclude from the evidentiary hearing all persons except the accused, the complaining witness, other necessary witnesses, and required court personnel. If the court determines that the evidence meets the requirements of subdivisions (a) and (b) of this Rule, it shall be admissible before the judge or jury trying the case in the ordinary course of the preliminary hearing or trial. If the court initially determines that the evidence is inadmissible, but new information is discovered during the course of the preliminary hearing or trial which may make such evidence admissible, the court shall determine in an evidentiary hearing whether such evidence is admissible.

[Adopted effective July 1, 2012.]

RULE 2:413. EVIDENCE OF SIMILAR CRIMES IN CHILD SEXUAL OFFENSE CASES (derived from Code § 18.2–67.7:1)

(a) In a criminal case in which the defendant is accused of a felony sexual offense involving a child victim, evidence of the defendant's conviction of another sexual offense or offenses is admissible and may be considered for its bearing on any matter to which it is relevant.

(b) The Commonwealth shall provide to the defendant 14 days prior to trial notice of its intention to introduce copies of final orders evidencing the defendant's qualifying prior criminal convictions. Such notice shall include (i) the date of each prior conviction, (ii) the name and jurisdiction of the court where each prior conviction was obtained, and (iii) each offense of which the defendant was convicted. Prior to commencement of the trial, the Commonwealth shall provide to the defendant photocopies of certified copies of the final orders that it intends to introduce.

(c) This Rule shall not be construed to limit the admission or consideration of evidence under any other rule of court or statute.

(d) For purposes of this Rule, "sexual offense" means any offense or any attempt or conspiracy to engage in any offense described in Article 7 (§ 18.2–61 et seq.) of Chapter 4 or § 18.2–370, 18.2–370.01, or 18.2–370.1 or any substantially similar offense under the laws of another state or territory of the United States, the District of Columbia, or the United States.

(e) Evidence offered in a criminal case pursuant to the provisions of this Rule shall be subject to exclusion in accordance with the Virginia Rules of Evidence, including but not limited to Rule 2:403.

[Adopted effective July 1, 2014.]

ARTICLE V

PRIVILEGES

RULE 2:501. PRIVILEGED COMMUNICATIONS

Except as otherwise required by the Constitutions of the United States or the Commonwealth of Virginia or provided by statute or these Rules, the privilege of a witness, person, government, State, or political subdivision thereof, shall be governed by the principles of common law as they may be interpreted by the courts of the Commonwealth in the light of reason and experience.

[Adopted July 1, 2012.]

RULE 2:502. ATTORNEY–CLIENT PRIVILEGE

Except as may be provided by statute, the existence and application of the attorney-client privilege in Virginia, and the exceptions thereto, shall be governed by the principles of common law as interpreted by the courts of the Commonwealth in the light of reason and experience.

[Adopted effective July 1, 2012.]

RULE 2:503. CLERGY AND COMMUNICANT PRIVILEGE (derived from Code §§ 8.01–400 and 19.2–271.3)

A *clergy member* means any regular minister, priest, rabbi, or accredited practitioner over the age of 18 years, of any religious organization or denomination usually referred to as a church. A clergy member shall not be required:

(a) in any civil action, to give testimony as a witness or to disclose in discovery proceedings the contents of notes, records or any written documentation made by the clergy member, where such testimony or disclosure would reveal any information communicated in a confidential manner, properly entrusted to such clergy member in a professional capacity and necessary to enable discharge of the functions of office according to the usual course of the clergy member's practice or discipline, wherein the person so communicating such information about himself or herself, or another, was seeking spiritual counsel and advice relating to and growing out of the information so imparted; and

(b) in any criminal action, in giving testimony as a witness to disclose any information communicated by the accused in a confidential manner, properly entrusted to the clergy member in a professional capacity and necessary to enable discharge of the functions of office according to the usual course of the clergy member's practice or discipline, where the person so communicating such information about himself or herself, or another, was seeking spiritual counsel and advice relating to and growing out of the information so imparted.

[Adopted effective July 1, 2012.]

RULE 2:504. SPOUSAL TESTIMONY AND MARITAL COMMUNICATIONS PRIVILEGES (Rule 2:504(a) derived from Code § 8.01–398; and Rule 2:504(b) derived from Code § 19.2–271.2)

(a) Privileged Marital Communications in Civil Cases.

1. Husband and wife shall be competent witnesses to testify for or against each other in all civil actions.

2. In any civil proceeding, a person has a privilege to refuse to disclose, and to prevent anyone else from disclosing, any confidential communication between such person and his or her spouse during their marriage, regardless of whether such person is married to that spouse at the time he or she objects to disclosure. This privilege may not be asserted in any proceeding in which the spouses are adverse parties, or in which either spouse is charged with a crime or tort against the person or property of the other or against the minor child of either spouse. For the purposes of this Rule, "confidential communication" means a communication made privately by a person to his or her spouse that is not intended for disclosure to any other person.

(b) Testimony of Husband and Wife in Criminal Cases.

1. In criminal cases husband and wife shall be allowed, and, subject to the Rules of Evidence governing other witnesses, may be compelled to testify in behalf of each other, but neither shall be compelled to be called as a witness against the other, except (i) in the case of a prosecution for an offense committed by one against the other, against a minor child of either, or against the property of either; (ii) in any case where either is charged with forgery of the name of the other or uttering or attempting to utter a writing bearing the allegedly forged signature of the other; or (iii) in any proceeding relating to a violation of the laws pertaining to criminal sexual assault (§§ 18.2–61 through 18.2–67.10), crimes against nature (§ 18.2–361) involving a minor as a victim and provided the defendant and the victim are not married to each other, incest (§ 18.2–366), or abuse of children (§§ 18.2–370 through 18.2–371). The failure of either husband or wife to testify, however, shall create no presumption against the accused, nor be the subject of any comment before the court or jury by any attorney.

2. Except in the prosecution for a criminal offense as set forth in subsections (B)(1)(i), (ii) and (iii) above, in any criminal proceeding, a person has a privilege to refuse to disclose, and to prevent anyone else from disclosing, any confidential communication between such person and his or her spouse during their marriage, regardless of whether the person is married to that spouse at the time the person objects to disclosure. For the purposes of this Rule, "confidential communication" means a communication made privately by a person to his or her spouse that is not intended for disclosure to any other person.

[Adopted effective July 1, 2012.]

RULE 2:505. HEALING ARTS PRACTITIONER AND PATIENT PRIVILEGE (derived from Code § 8.01–399)

The scope and application of the privilege between a patient and a physician or practitioner of the healing arts in a civil case shall be as set forth in any specific statutory provisions, including Code § 8.01–399, as amended from time to time, which presently provides:

A. Except at the request or with the consent of the patient, or as provided in this section, no duly licensed practitioner of any branch of the healing arts shall be permitted to testify in any civil action, respecting any information that he may have acquired in attending, examining or treating the patient in a professional capacity.

B. If the physical or mental condition of the patient is at issue in a civil action, the diagnoses, signs and symptoms, observations, evaluations, histories, or treatment plan of the practitioner, obtained or formulated as contemporaneously documented during the course of the practitioner's treatment, together with the facts communicated to, or otherwise learned by, such practitioner in connection with such attendance, examination or treatment shall be disclosed but only in discovery pursuant to the Rules of Court or through testimony at the trial of the action. In addition, disclosure may be ordered when a court, in the exercise of sound discretion, deems it necessary to the proper administration of justice. However, no order shall be entered compelling a party to sign a release for medical records from a health care provider unless the health care provider is not located in the Commonwealth or is a federal facility. If an order is issued pursuant to this section, it shall be restricted to the medical records that relate to the physical or mental conditions at issue in the case. No disclosure of diagnosis or treatment plan facts communicated to, or otherwise learned by, such practitioner shall occur if the court determines, upon the request of the patient, that such facts are not relevant to the subject matter involved in the pending action or do not appear to be reasonably calculated to lead to the discovery of admissible evidence. Only diagnosis offered to a reasonable degree of medical probability shall be admissible at trial.

C. This section shall not (i) be construed to repeal or otherwise affect the provisions of § 65.2–607 relating to privileged communications between physicians and surgeons and employees under the Workers' Compensation Act; (ii) apply to information communicated to any such practitioner in an effort unlawfully to procure a narcotic drug, or unlawfully to procure the administration of any such drug; or (iii) prohibit a duly licensed practitioner of the healing arts, or his agents, from disclosing information as required by state or federal law.

D. Neither a lawyer nor anyone acting on the lawyer's behalf shall obtain, in connection with pending or threatened litigation, information concerning a patient from a practitioner of any branch of the healing arts without the consent of the patient, except through discovery pursuant to the Rules of Supreme Court as herein provided. However, the prohibition of this subsection shall not apply to:

1. Communication between a lawyer retained to represent a practitioner of the healing arts, or that lawyer's agent, and that practitioner's employers, partners, agents, servants, employees, co-employees or others for whom, at law, the practitioner is or may be liable or who, at law, are or may be liable for the practitioner's acts or omissions;

2. Information about a patient provided to a lawyer or his agent by a practitioner of the healing arts employed by that lawyer to examine or evaluate the patient in accordance with Rule 4:10 of the Rules of Supreme Court; or

3. Contact between a lawyer or his agent and a nonphysician employee or agent of a practitioner of healing arts for any of the following purposes: (i) scheduling appearances, (ii) requesting a written recitation by the practitioner of handwritten records obtained by the lawyer or his agent from the practitioner, provided the request is made in writing and, if litigation is pending, a copy of the request and the practitioner's response is provided simultaneously to the patient or his attorney, (iii) obtaining information necessary to obtain service upon the practitioner in pending litigation, (iv) determining when records summoned will be provided by the practitioner or his agent, (v) determining what patient records the practitioner possesses in order to summons records in pending litigation, (vi) explaining any summons that the lawyer or his agent caused to be issued and served on the practitioner, (vii) verifying dates the practitioner treated the patient, provided that if litigation is pending the information obtained by the lawyer or his agent is promptly given, in writing, to the patient or his attorney, (viii) determining charges by the practitioner for appearance at a deposition or to testify before any tribunal or administrative body, or (ix) providing to or obtaining from the practitioner directions to a place to which he is or will be summoned to give testimony.

E. A clinical psychologist duly licensed under the provisions of Chapter 36 (§ 54.1–3600 et seq.) of Title 54.1 shall be considered a practitioner of a branch of the healing arts within the meaning of this section.

F. Nothing herein shall prevent a duly licensed practitioner of the healing arts, or his agents, from disclosing any information that he may have acquired in attending, examining or treating a patient in a professional capacity where such disclosure is necessary in connection with the care of the patient, the protection or enforcement of a practitioner's legal rights including such rights with respect to medical malpractice actions, or the operations of a health care facility or health maintenance organization or in order to comply with state or federal law.

[Adopted effective July 1, 2012.]

RULE 2:506. MENTAL HEALTH PROFESSIONAL AND CLIENT PRIVILEGE (derived from Code § 8.01–400.2)

Except at the request of or with the consent of the client, no licensed professional counselor, as defined in Code § 54.1–3500; licensed clinical social worker, as defined in Code § 54.1–3700; licensed psychologist, as defined in Code § 54.1–3600; or licensed marriage and family therapist, as defined in Code § 54.1–3500, shall be required in giving testimony as a witness in any civil action to disclose any information communicated in a confidential manner, properly entrusted to such person in a professional capacity and necessary to enable discharge of professional or occupational services according to the usual course of his or her practice or discipline, wherein the person so communicating such information about himself or herself, or another, is seeking professional counseling or treatment and advice relating to and growing out of the information so imparted; provided, however, that when the physical or mental condition of the client is at issue in such action, or when a court, in the exercise of sound discretion, deems such disclosure necessary to the proper administration of justice, no fact communicated to, or otherwise learned by, such practitioner in connection with such counseling, treatment or advice shall be privileged, and disclosure may be required. The privileges conferred by this Rule shall not extend to testimony in matters relating to child abuse and neglect nor serve to relieve any person from the reporting requirements set forth in § 63.2–1509.

[Adopted effective July 1, 2012.]

RULE 2:507. PRIVILEGED COMMUNICATIONS INVOLVING INTERPRETERS (derived from Code §§ 8.01–400.1, 19.2–164, and 19.2–164.1)

Whenever a deaf or non-English-speaking person communicates through an interpreter to any person under such circumstances that the communication would be privileged, and such person could not be compelled to testify as to the communications, the privilege shall also apply to the interpreter.

[Adopted effective July 1, 2012.]

ARTICLE VI

WITNESS EXAMINATION

RULE 2:601. GENERAL RULE OF COMPETENCY

(a) Generally. Every person is competent to be a witness except as otherwise provided in other evidentiary principles, Rules of Court, Virginia statutes, or common law.

(b) Rulings. A court may declare a person incompetent to testify if the court finds that the person does not have sufficient physical or mental capacity to testify truthfully, accurately, or understandably.

[Adopted effective July 1, 2012.]

RULE 2:602. LACK OF PERSONAL KNOWLEDGE

A witness may not testify to a matter unless evidence is introduced sufficient to support a finding that the witness has personal knowledge of the matter. Evidence to prove personal knowledge may, but need not, consist of the testimony of the witness. This Rule does not bar testimony admissible under Rules 2:701, 2–702 and 2:703.

[Adopted effective July 1, 2012.]

RULE 2:603. OATH OR AFFIRMATION

Before testifying, every witness shall be required to declare that he or she will testify truthfully, by oath or affirmation administered in a form calculated to awaken the conscience and impress the mind of the witness with the duty to do so.

[Adopted effective July 1, 2012.]

RULE 2:604. INTERPRETERS (derived from Code § 8.01–406)

An interpreter shall be qualified as competent and shall be placed under oath or affirmation to make a true translation.

[Adopted effective July 1, 2012.]

RULE 2:605. COMPETENCY OF COURT PERSONNEL AS WITNESSES (derived from Code) § 19.2–271

(a) No judge shall be competent to testify in any criminal or civil proceeding as to any matter which came before the judge in the course of official duties.

(b) Except as otherwise provided in this Rule, no clerk of any court, magistrate, or other person having the power to issue warrants, shall be competent to testify in any criminal or civil proceeding, as to any matter which came before him or her in the course of official duties. Such person shall be competent to testify in any criminal proceeding wherein the defendant is charged with perjury or pursuant to the provisions of § 18.2–460 or in any proceeding authorized pursuant to § 19.2–353.3. Notwithstanding any other provision of this section, any judge, clerk of any court, magistrate, or other person having the power to issue warrants, who is the victim of a crime, shall not be incompetent solely because of his or her office to testify in any criminal or civil proceeding arising out of the crime. Nothing in this subpart (b) shall preclude otherwise proper testimony by a clerk or deputy clerk concerning documents filed in the official records.

[Adopted effective July 1, 2012. Amended effective July 1, 2015.]

RULE 2:606. COMPETENCY OF JUROR AS WITNESS

Upon inquiry regarding the validity of a verdict or indictment, a juror is precluded from testifying as to any matter or statement occurring during the course of the jury's deliberations or to the effect of anything upon any juror's mind or emotions as influencing any juror to assent to or dissent from the verdict or indictment or concerning any juror's mental processes in connection therewith.

A juror may testify only as to questions regarding extraneous prejudicial information improperly brought to the jury's attention as a result of conduct outside the jury room, or whether any improper influence was brought to bear upon any juror from a source outside the jury room.

[Adopted effective July 1, 2012.]

RULE 2:607. IMPEACHMENT OF WITNESSES (Rule 2:607(b) derived from Code § 8.01–401(A); and Rule 2:607(c) derived from Code § 8.01–403)

(a) In General. Subject to the provisions of Rule 2:403, the credibility of a witness may be impeached by any party other than the one calling the witness, with any proof that is relevant to the witness's credibility. Impeachment may be undertaken, among other means, by:

(i) introduction of evidence of the witness's bad general reputation for the traits of truth and veracity, as provided in Rule 2:608(a) and (b);

(ii) evidence of prior conviction, as provided in Rule 2:609;

(iii) evidence of prior unadjudicated perjury, as provided in Rule 2:608(d);

(iv) evidence of prior false accusations of sexual misconduct, as provided in Rule 2:608(e);

(v) evidence of bias as provided in Rule 2:610;

(vi) prior inconsistent statements as provided in 2:613;

(vii) contradiction by other evidence; and

(viii) any other evidence which is probative on the issue of credibility because of a logical tendency to convince the trier of fact that the witness's perception, memory, or narration is defective or impaired, or that the sincerity or veracity of the witness is questionable.

Impeachment pursuant to subdivisions (a)(i) and (ii) of this Rule may not be undertaken by a party who has called an adverse witness.

(b) Witness With Adverse Interest. A witness having an adverse interest may be examined with leading questions by the party calling the witness. After such an adverse direct examination, the witness is subject to cross-examination.

(c) Witness Proving Adverse.

(i) If a witness proves adverse, the party who called the witness may, subject to the discretion of the court, prove that the witness has made at other times a statement inconsistent with the present testimony as provided in Rule 2:613.

(ii) In a jury case, if impeachment has been conducted pursuant to this subdivision (c), the court, on motion by either party, shall instruct the jury to consider the evidence of such inconsistent statements solely for the purpose of contradicting the witness.

[Adopted effective July 1, 2012.]

RULE 2:608. IMPEACHMENT BY EVIDENCE OF REPUTATION FOR TRUTHTELLING AND CONDUCT OF WITNESS

(a) Reputation Evidence of the Character Trait for Truthfulness or Untruthfulness. The credibility of a witness may be attacked or supported by evidence in the form of reputation, subject to these limitations: (1) the evidence may relate only to character trait for truthfulness or untruthfulness; (2) evidence of truthful character is admissible only after the character trait of the witness for truthfulness has been attacked by reputation evidence or otherwise; and (3) evidence is introduced that the person testifying has sufficient familiarity with the reputation to make the testimony probative.

(b) Specific Instances of Conduct; Extrinsic Proof. Except as otherwise provided in this Rule, by other principles of evidence, or by statute, (1) specific instances of the conduct of a witness may not be used to attack or support credibility; and (2) specific instances of the conduct of a witness may not be proved by extrinsic evidence.

(c) Cross–Examination of Character Witness. Specific instances of conduct may, if probative of truthfulness or untruthfulness, be inquired into on cross-examination of a character witness concerning the character trait for truthfulness or untruthfulness of another witness as to whose character trait the witness being cross-examined has testified.

(d) Unadjudicated Perjury. If the trial judge makes a threshold determination that a reasonable probability of falsity exists, any witness may be questioned about prior specific instances of unadjudicated perjury. Extrinsic proof of the unadjudicated perjury may not be shown.

(e) Prior False Accusations in Sexual Assault Cases. Except as otherwise provided by other evidentiary principles, statutes or Rules of Court, a complaining witness in a sexual assault case may be cross-examined about prior false accusations of sexual misconduct.

[Adopted effective July 1, 2012.]

RULE 2:609. IMPEACHMENT BY EVIDENCE OF CONVICTION OF CRIME (derived from Code § 19.2–269)

Evidence that a witness has been convicted of a crime may be admitted to impeach the credibility of that witness subject to the following limitations:

(a) Party in a Civil Case or Criminal Defendant.

(i) The fact that a party in a civil case or an accused who testifies has previously been convicted of a felony, or a misdemeanor involving moral turpitude, and the number of such convictions may be elicited during examination of the party or accused.

(ii) If a conviction raised under subdivision (a)(i) is denied, it may be proved by extrinsic evidence.

(iii) In any examination pursuant to this subdivision (a), the name or nature of any crime of which the party or accused was convicted, except for perjury, may not be shown, nor may the details of prior convictions be elicited, unless offered to rebut other evidence concerning prior convictions.

(b) Other Witnesses. The fact that any other witness has previously been convicted of a felony, or a misdemeanor involving moral turpitude, the number, and the name and nature, but not the details, of such convictions may be elicited during examination of the witness or, if denied, proved by extrinsic evidence.

(c) Juvenile Adjudications. Juvenile adjudications may not be used for impeachment of a witness on the subject of general credibility, but may be used to show bias of the witness if constitutionally required.

(d) Adverse Witnesses. A party who calls an adverse witness may not impeach that adverse witness with a prior conviction.

[Adopted effective July 1, 2012.]

RULE 2:610. BIAS OR PREJUDICE OF A WITNESS

A witness may be impeached by a showing that the witness is biased for or prejudiced against a party. Extrinsic evidence of such bias or prejudice may be admitted.

[Adopted effective July 1, 2012.]

RULE 2:611. MODE AND ORDER OF INTERROGATION AND PRESENTATION (Rule 2:611(c) derived from Code § 8.01–401(A))

(a) Presentation of Evidence. The mode and order of interrogating witnesses and presenting evidence may be determined by the court so as to (1) facilitate the ascertainment of the truth, (2) avoid needless consumption of time, and (3) protect witnesses from harassment or undue embarrassment.

(b) Scope of Cross–Examination.

(i) Cross-examination should be limited to the subject matter of the direct examination and matters affecting the credibility of the witness. The court may, in the exercise of discretion, permit inquiry into additional matters as if on direct examination.

(ii) In a criminal case, if a defendant testifies on his or her own behalf and denies guilt as to an offense charged, cross-examination of the defendant may be permitted in the discretion of the court into any matter relevant to the issue of guilt or innocence.

(c) Leading Questions. Leading questions should not be used on the direct examination of a witness except as may be permitted by the court in its discretion to allow a party to develop the testimony. Leading questions should be permitted on cross-examination. Whenever a party calls a hostile witness, an adverse party, a witness having an adverse interest, or a witness proving adverse, interrogation may be by leading questions.

[Adopted effective July 1, 2012.]

RULE 2:612. WRITING OR OBJECT USED TO REFRESH MEMORY

If while testifying, a witness uses a writing or object to refresh his memory, an adverse party is entitled to have the writing or object produced at the trial, hearing, or deposition in which the witness is testifying.

[Adopted effective July 1, 2012.]

RULE 2:613. PRIOR STATEMENTS OF WITNESS (Rule 2:613(a)(i) derived from Code § 8.01–403; Rule 2:613(b)(i) derived from Code §§ 8.01–404 and 19.2–268.1; and Rule 2:613(b)(ii) derived from Code § 8.01–404)

(a) Examining Witness Concerning Prior Oral Statement.

(i) *Prior Oral Statements of Witnesses.* In examining a witness in any civil or criminal case concerning a prior oral statement, the circumstances of the supposed statement, sufficient to designate the particular occasion, must be mentioned to the witness, and the witness must be asked whether the statement was made.

(ii) *Extrinsic Evidence of Prior Inconsistent Oral Statement of Witness.* Extrinsic evidence of a prior inconsistent oral statement by a witness is not admissible unless the witness is first given an opportunity to explain or deny the statement and the opposing party is given an opportunity to interrogate the witness thereon, or the interests of justice otherwise require. This provision does not apply to admissions of a party opponent.

Extrinsic evidence of a witness' prior inconsistent statement is not admissible unless the witness denies or does not remember the prior inconsistent statement. Extrinsic evidence of collateral statements is not admissible.

(b) Contradiction by Prior Inconsistent Writing.

(i) *General Rule.* In any civil or criminal case, a witness may be cross-examined as to previous statements made by the witness in writing or reduced to writing, relating to the subject matter of the action, without such writing being shown to the witness; but if the intent is to contradict such witness by the writing, his or her attention must, before such contradictory proof can be given, be called to the particular occasion on which the writing is supposed to have been made; the witness may be asked whether he or she made a writing of the purport of the one to be offered, and if the witness denies making it, or does not admit its execution, it shall then be shown to the witness, and if the witness admits its genuineness, the witness shall be allowed to make an explanation of it; but the court may, at any time during the trial, require the production of the writing for its inspection, and the court may then make such use of it for the purpose of the trial as it may think best.

(ii) *Personal Injury or Wrongful Death Cases.* Notwithstanding the general principles stated in this subpart (b), in an action to recover for personal injury or wrongful death, no ex parte affidavit or statement in writing other than a deposition, after due notice, of a witness and no extrajudicial recording made at any time other than simultaneously with the wrongful act or negligence at issue of the voice of such witness, or reproduction or transcript thereof, as to the facts or circumstances attending the wrongful act or neglect complained of, shall be used to contradict such witness in the case. Nothing in this subdivision shall be construed to prohibit the use of any such ex parte affidavit or statement in an action on an insurance policy based upon a judgment recovered in a personal injury or wrongful death case.

[Adopted effective July 1, 2012.]

RULE 2:614. CALLING AND INTERROGATION OF WITNESSES BY COURT

(a) Calling by the Court in Civil Cases. The court, on motion of a party or on its own motion, may call witnesses, and all parties are entitled to cross-examine. The calling of a witness by the court is a matter resting in the trial judge's sound discretion and should be exercised with great care.

(b) Interrogation by the Court. In a civil or criminal case, the court may question witnesses, whether called by itself or a party, subject to the applicable Rules of Evidence.

[Adopted effective July 1, 2012.]

RULE 2:615. EXCLUSION OF WITNESSES (Rule 2:615(a) derived from Code §§ 8.01–375, 19.2–184, and 19.2–265.1; Rule 2:615(b) derived from Code § 8.01–375; and Rule 2:615(c) derived from Code § 19.2–265.1)

(a) The court, in a civil or criminal case, may on its own motion and shall on the motion of any party, require the exclusion of every witness including, but not limited to, police officers or other investigators. The court may also order that each excluded witness be kept separate from all other witnesses. But each named party who is an individual, one officer or agent of each party which is a corporation, limited liability entity or association, and an attorney alleged in a habeas corpus proceeding to have acted ineffectively shall be exempt from the exclusion as a matter of right.

(b) Where expert witnesses are to testify in the case, the court may, at the request of all parties, allow one expert witness for each party to remain in the courtroom; however, in cases pertaining to the distribution of marital property pursuant to § 20–107.3 or the determination of child or spousal support pursuant to § 20–108.1, the court may, upon motion of any party, allow one expert witness for each party to remain in the courtroom throughout the hearing.

(c) Any victim as defined in Code § 19.2–11.01 who is to be called as a witness may remain in the courtroom and shall not be excluded unless pursuant to Code § 19.2–265.01 the court determines, in its discretion, that the presence of the victim would impair the conduct of a fair trial.

[Adopted effective July 1, 2012.]

ARTICLE VII

OPINIONS AND EXPERT TESTIMONY

RULE 2:701. OPINION TESTIMONY BY LAY WITNESSES (derived from Code § 8.01–401.3(B))

Opinion testimony by a lay witness is admissible if it is reasonably based upon the personal experience or observations of the witness and will aid the trier of fact in understanding the witness' perceptions. Lay opinion may relate to any matter, such as—but not limited to—sanity, capacity, physical condition or disability, speed of a vehicle, the value of property, identity, causation, time, the meaning of words, similarity of objects, handwriting, visibility or the general physical situation at a particular location. However, lay witness testimony that amounts only to an opinion of law is inadmissible.

[Adopted effective July 1, 2012.]

RULE 2:702. TESTIMONY BY EXPERTS (Rule 2:702(a)(i) derived from Code § 8.01–401.3(A))

(a) Use of Expert Testimony.

(i) In a civil proceeding, if scientific, technical, or other specialized knowledge will assist the trier of fact to understand the evidence or to determine a fact in issue, a witness qualified as an expert by knowledge, skill, experience, training, or education may testify thereto in the form of an opinion or otherwise.

(ii) In a criminal proceeding, expert testimony is admissible if the standards set forth in subdivision (a)(i) of this Rule are met and, in addition, the court finds that the subject matter is beyond the knowledge and experience of ordinary persons, such that the jury needs expert opinion in order to comprehend the subject matter, form an intelligent opinion, and draw its conclusions.

(b) Form of Opinion. Expert testimony may include opinions of the witness established with a reasonable degree of probability, or it may address empirical data from which such probability may be established in the mind of the finder of fact. Testimony that is speculative, or which opines on the credibility of another witness, is not admissible.

[Adopted effective July 1, 2012.]

RULE 2:703. BASIS OF EXPERT TESTIMONY (Rule 2:703(a) derived from Code § 8.01–401.1)

(a) Civil Cases. In a civil action an expert witness may give testimony and render an opinion or draw inferences from facts, circumstances, or data made known to or perceived by such witness at or before the hearing or trial during which the witness is called upon to testify. The facts, circumstances, or data relied upon by such witness in forming an opinion or drawing inferences, if of a type normally relied upon by others in the particular field of expertise in forming opinions and drawing inferences, need not be admissible in evidence.

(b) Criminal Cases. In criminal cases, the opinion of an expert is generally admissible if it is based upon facts personally known or observed by the expert, or based upon facts in evidence.

[Adopted effective July 1, 2012.]

RULE 2:704. OPINION ON ULTIMATE ISSUE (Rule 2:704(a) derived from Code § 8.01–401.3(B) and (C))

(a) Civil Cases. In civil cases, no expert or lay witness shall be prohibited from expressing an otherwise admissible opinion or conclusion as to any matter of fact solely because that fact is the ultimate issue or critical to the resolution of the case. But in no event shall such witness be permitted to express any opinion which constitutes a conclusion of law. Any other exceptions to the "ultimate fact in issue" rule recognized in the Commonwealth remain in full force.

(b) Criminal Cases. In criminal proceedings, opinion testimony on the ultimate issues of fact is not admissible. This Rule does not require exclusion of otherwise proper expert testimony concerning a witness' or the defendant's mental disorder and the hypothetical effect of that disorder on a person in the witness' or the defendant's situation.

[Adopted effective July 1, 2012.]

RULE 2:705. FACTS OR DATA USED IN TESTIMONY (Rule 2:705(a) derived from Code § 8.01–401.1)

(a) Civil Cases. In civil cases, an expert may testify in terms of opinion or inference and give reasons therefor without prior disclosure of the underlying facts or data, unless the court requires otherwise. The expert may in any event be required to disclose the underlying facts or data on cross-examination.

(b) Criminal Cases. In criminal cases, the facts on which an expert may give an opinion shall be disclosed in the expert's testimony, or set forth in a hypothetical question.

[Adopted effective July 1, 2012.]

RULE 2:706. USE OF LEARNED TREATISES WITH EXPERTS (Rule 2:706(a) derived from Code § 8.01–401.1)

(a) Civil Cases. To the extent called to the attention of an expert witness upon cross-examination or relied upon by the expert witness in direct examination, statements contained in published treatises, periodicals or pamphlets on a subject of history, medicine or other science or art, established as a reliable authority by testimony or by stipulation shall not be excluded as hearsay. If admitted, the statements may be read into evidence but may not be received as exhibits. If the statements are to be introduced through an expert witness upon direct examination, copies of the specific statements shall be designated as literature to be introduced during direct examination and provided to opposing parties 30 days prior to trial unless otherwise ordered by the court. If a statement has been designated by a party in accordance with and satisfies the requirements of this rule, the expert witness called by that party need not have relied on the statement at the time of forming his opinion in order to read the statement into evidence during direct examination at trial.

(b) Criminal Cases. Where an expert witness acknowledges on cross-examination that a published work is a standard authority in the field, an opposing party may ask whether the witness agrees or disagrees with statements in the work acknowledged. Such proof shall be received solely for impeachment purposes with respect to the expert's credibility.

[Adopted effective July 1, 2012. Amended effective July 1, 2013.]

ARTICLE VIII

HEARSAY

RULE 2:801. DEFINITIONS

The following definitions apply under this article:

(a) Statement. A "statement" is (1) an oral or written assertion or (2) nonverbal conduct of a person, if it is intended as an assertion.

(b) Declarant. A "declarant" is a person who makes a statement.

(c) Hearsay. "Hearsay" is a statement, other than one made by the declarant while testifying at the trial or hearing, offered in evidence to prove the truth of the matter asserted.

(d) Prior Statements. When a party or non-party witness testifies either live or by deposition, a prior statement (whether under oath or not) is hearsay if offered in evidence to prove the truth of the matters it asserts, but may be received in evidence for all purposes if the statement is admissible under any hearsay exception provided in Rules 2:803 or 2:804. In addition, if not excluded under another Rule of Evidence or a statute, a prior hearsay statement may also be admitted as follows:

(1) *Prior Inconsistent Statements.* A prior statement that is inconsistent with the hearing testimony of the witness is admissible for impeachment of the witness' credibility when offered in compliance with Rule 2:613.

(2) *Prior Consistent Statements.* A prior statement that is consistent with the hearing testimony of the witness is admissible for purposes of rehabilitating the witness' credibility, but only if

(A) the witness has been impeached using a prior inconsistent statement as provided in Rule 2:607, Rule 2:613 and/or subpart (d)(1) of this Rule 801, or

(B)(i) the witness has been impeached based on alleged improper influence, or a motive to falsify testimony, such as bias, interest, corruption or relationship to a party or a cause, or by an express or implied charge that the in-court testimony is a recent fabrication; and

(ii) the proponent of the prior statement shows that it was made before any litigation motive arose for the witness to make a false statement.

[Adopted effective July 1, 2012. Amended effective July 15, 2015.]

RULE 2:802. HEARSAY RULE

Hearsay is not admissible except as provided by these Rules, other Rules of the Supreme Court of Virginia, or by Virginia statutes or case law.

[Adopted effective July 1, 2012.]

RULE 2:803. HEARSAY EXCEPTIONS APPLICABLE REGARDLESS OF AVAILABILITY OF THE DECLARANT (Rule 2:803(10)(a) derived from Code § 8.01–390(C); Rule 2:803(10)(b) derived from Code § 19.2–188.3; Rule 2:803(17) derived from Code § 8.2–724; and Rule 2:803(23) is derived from Code § 19.2–268.2)

The following are not excluded by the hearsay rule, even though the declarant is available as a witness:

(0) Admission by Party—Opponent. A statement offered against a party that is (A) the party's own statement, in either an individual or a representative capacity, or (B) a statement of which the party has manifested adoption or belief in its truth, or (C) a statement by a person authorized by the party to make a statement concerning the subject, or (D) a statement by the party's agent or employee, made during the term of the agency or employment, concerning a matter within the scope of such agency or employment, or (E) a statement by a co-conspirator of a party during the course and in furtherance of the conspiracy.

(1) Present Sense Impression. A spontaneous statement describing or explaining an event or condition made contemporaneously with, or while, the declarant was perceiving the event or condition.

(2) Excited Utterance. A spontaneous or impulsive statement prompted by a startling event or condition and made by a declarant with firsthand knowledge at a time and under circumstances negating deliberation.

(3) Then Existing Mental, Emotional, or Physical Condition. A statement of the declarant's then existing state of mind, emotion, sensation, or physical condition (such as intent, plan, motive, design, mental feeling, pain, and bodily health), but not including a statement of memory or belief to prove the fact remembered or believed unless it relates to the execution, revocation, identification, or terms of the declarant's will.

(4) Statements for Purposes of Medical Treatment. Statements made for purposes of medical diagnosis or treatment and describing medical history, or past or present symptoms, pain, or sensations, or the inception or general character of the cause or external source thereof insofar as reasonably pertinent to diagnosis or treatment.

(5) Recorded Recollection. Except as provided by statute, a memorandum or record concerning a matter about which a witness once had firsthand knowledge made or adopted by the witness at or near the time of the event and while the witness had a clear and accurate memory of it, if the witness lacks a present recollection of the event, and the witness vouches for the accuracy of the written memorandum. If admitted, the memorandum or record may be read into evidence but may not itself be received as an exhibit unless offered by an adverse party.

(6) Records of a Regularly Conducted Activity. A record of acts, events, calculations, or conditions if:

(A) the record was made at or near the time of the acts, events, calculations, or conditions by—or from information transmitted by—someone with knowledge;

(B) the record was made and kept in the course of a regularly conducted activity of a business, organization, occupation, or calling, whether or not for profit;

(C) making and keeping the record was a regular practice of that activity;

(D) all these conditions are shown by the testimony of the custodian or another qualified witness, or by a certification that complies with Rule 2:902(6) or with a statute permitting certification; and

(E) neither the source of information nor the method or circumstances of preparation indicate a lack of trustworthiness.

(7) Reserved.

(8) Public Records and Reports. In addition to categories of government records made admissible by statute, records, reports, statements, or data compilations, in any form, prepared by public offices or agencies, setting forth (A) the activities of the office or agency, or (B) matters observed within the scope of the office or agency's duties, as to which the source of the recorded information could testify if called as a witness; generally excluding, however, in criminal cases matters observed by police officers and other law enforcement personnel when offered against a criminal defendant.

(9) Records of Vital Statistics. Records or data compilations, in any form, of births, fetal deaths, deaths, or marriages, if the report was made to a public office pursuant to requirements of law.

(10) Absence of Entries in Public Records and Reports.

(a) *Civil Cases.* An affidavit signed by an officer, or the deputy thereof, deemed to have custody of records of this Commonwealth, of another state, of the United States, of another country, or of any political subdivision or agency of the same, other than those located in a clerk's office of a court, stating that after a diligent search, no record or entry of such record is found to exist among the records in such office is admissible as evidence that the office has no such record or entry.

(b) *Criminal Cases.* In any criminal hearing or trial, an affidavit signed by a government official who is competent to testify, deemed to have custody of an official record, or signed by such official's designee, stating that after a diligent search, no record or entry of such record is found to exist among the records in such official's custody, is admissible as evidence that the office has no such record or entry, provided that if the hearing or trial is a proceeding other than a preliminary hearing the procedures set forth in subsection G of § 18.2–472.1 for admission of an affidavit have been satisfied, mutatis mutandis, and the accused has not objected to the admission of the affidavit pursuant to the procedures set forth in subsection H of § 18.2–472.1, mutatis mutandis. Nothing in this subsection (b) shall be construed to affect the admissibility of affidavits in civil cases under subsection (a) of this Rule.

(11) Records of Religious Organizations. Statements of births, marriages, divorces, deaths, legitimacy, ancestry, relationship by blood or marriage, or other similar facts of personal or family history, contained in a regularly kept record of a religious organization.

(12) Marriage, Baptismal, and Similar Certificates. Statements of fact contained in a certificate that the maker performed a marriage or other ceremony or administered a sacrament, made by a clergyman, public official, or other person authorized by the rules or practices of a religious organization or by law to perform the act certified, and purporting to have been issued at the time of the act or within a reasonable time thereafter.

(13) Family Records. Statements of fact concerning personal or family history contained in family bibles, genealogies, charts, engravings on rings, inscriptions on family portraits, engravings on urns, crypts, or tombstones, or the like.

(14) Records of Documents Affecting an Interest in Property. The record of a document purporting to establish or affect an interest in property, as proof of the content of the original recorded document and its execution, and delivery by each person by whom it purports to have been executed, if the record is a record of a public office and an applicable statute authorizes the recording of documents of that kind in that office.

(15) Statements in Documents Affecting an Interest in Property. A statement contained in a document purporting to establish or affect an interest in property if the matter stated was relevant to the purpose of the document, unless dealings with the property since the document was made have been inconsistent with the truth of the statement or the purport of the document.

(16) Statements in Ancient Documents. Statements generally acted upon as true by persons having an interest in the matter, and contained in a document in existence 30 years or more, the authenticity of which is established.

(17) Market Quotations. Whenever the prevailing price or value of any goods regularly bought and sold in any established commodity market is in issue, reports in official publications or trade journals or in newspapers or periodicals of general circulation published as the reports of such market shall be admissible in evidence. The circumstances of the preparation of such a report may be shown.

(18) Learned Treatises. *See* Rule 2:706.

(19) Reputation Concerning Boundaries. Reputation in a community, arising before the controversy, as to boundaries of lands in the community, where the reputation refers to monuments or other delineations on the ground and some evidence of title exists.

(20) Reputation as to a Character Trait. Reputation of a person's character trait among his or her associates or in the community.

(21) Judgment as to Personal, Family, or General History, or Boundaries. Judgments as proof of matters of personal, family or general history, or boundaries, essential to the judgment, if the same would be provable by evidence of reputation.

(22) Statement of Identification by Witness. The declarant testifies at the trial or hearing and is subject to cross-examination concerning the statement, and the statement is one of identification of a person.

(23) Recent Complaint of Sexual Assault. In any prosecution for criminal sexual assault under Article 7 (§ 18.2–61 *et seq.*) of Chapter 4 of Title 18.2, a violation of §§ 18.2–361, 18.2–366, 18.2–370 or § 18.2–370.1, the fact that the person injured made complaint of the offense recently after commission of the offense is admissible, not as independent evidence of the offense, but for the purpose of corroborating the testimony of the complaining witness.

(24) Price of Goods. In shoplifting cases, price tags regularly affixed to items of personalty offered for sale, or testimony concerning the amounts shown on such tags.

[Adopted effective July 1, 2012. Amended effective July 1, 2014; July 1, 2015.]

RULE 2:804. HEARSAY EXCEPTIONS APPLICABLE WHERE THE DECLARANT IS UNAVAILABLE (Rule 2:804(b)(5) derived from Code § 8.01–397)

(a) Applicability. The hearsay exceptions set forth in subpart (b) hereof are applicable where the declarant is dead or otherwise unavailable as a witness.

(b) Hearsay Exceptions. The following are not excluded by the hearsay rule:

(1) *Former Testimony.* Testimony given under oath or otherwise subject to penalties for perjury at a prior hearing, or in a deposition, if it is offered in reasonably accurate form and, if given in a different proceeding, the party against whom the evidence is now offered, or in a civil case a privy, was a party in that proceeding who examined the witness by direct examination or had the opportunity to cross-examine the witness, and the issue on which the testimony is offered is substantially the same in the two cases.

(2) *Statement Under Belief of Impending Death.* In a prosecution for homicide, a statement made by a declarant who believed when the statement was made that death was imminent and who had given up all hope of survival, concerning the cause or circumstances of declarant's impending death.

(3) *Statement Against Interest.* (A) A statement which the declarant knew at the time of its making to be contrary to the declarant's pecuniary or proprietary interest, or to tend to subject the declarant to civil liability. (B) A statement which the declarant knew at the time of its making would tend to subject the declarant to criminal liability, if the statement is shown to be reliable.

(4) *Statement of Personal or Family History.* If no better evidence is available, a statement made before the existence of the controversy, concerning family relationships or pedigree of a person, made by a member of the family or relative.

(5) *Statement by Party Incapable of Testifying.* Code § 8.01–397, entitled "Corroboration required and evidence receivable when one party incapable of testifying," presently provides:

In an action by or against a person who, from any cause, is incapable of testifying, or by or against the committee, trustee, executor, administrator, heir, or other representative of the person so incapable of testifying, no judgment or decree shall be rendered in favor of an adverse or interested party founded on his uncorroborated testimony. In any such action, whether such adverse party testifies or not, all entries, memoranda, and declarations by the party so incapable of testifying made while he was capable, relevant to the matter in issue, may be received as evidence in all proceedings including without limitation those to which a person under a disability is a party. The phrase "from any cause" as used in this section shall not include situations in which the party who is incapable of testifying has rendered himself unable to testify by an intentional self-inflicted injury.

For the purposes of this section, and in addition to corroboration by any other competent evidence, an entry authored by an adverse or interested party contained in a business record may be competent evidence for corroboration of the testimony of an adverse or interested party. If authentication of the business record is not admitted in a request for admission, such business record shall be authenticated by a person other than the author of the entry who is not an adverse or interested party whose conduct is at issue in the allegations of the complaint.

[Adopted effective July 1, 2012. Amended effective July 1, 2013.]

RULE 2:805. HEARSAY WITHIN HEARSAY

Hearsay included within hearsay is not excluded under the hearsay rule if each part of the combined statements conforms with an exception to the hearsay rule.

[Adopted effective July 1, 2012.]

RULE 2:806. ATTACKING AND SUPPORTING CREDIBILITY OF HEARSAY DECLARANT

When a hearsay statement has been admitted in evidence, the credibility of the declarant may be attacked, and if attacked may be supported, by any evidence which would be admissible for those purposes if the declarant had testified as a witness.

[Adopted effective July 1, 2012.]

ARTICLE IX

AUTHENTICATION

RULE 2:901. REQUIREMENT OF AUTHENTICATION OR IDENTIFICATION

The requirement of authentication or identification as a condition precedent to admissibility is satisfied by evidence sufficient to support a finding that the thing in question is what its proponent claims.

[Adopted effective July 1, 2012.]

RULE 2:902. SELF-AUTHENTICATION (Rule 2:902(6) derived from Code § 8.01–390.3 and Code § 8.01–391(D))

Additional proof of authenticity as a condition precedent to admissibility is not required with respect to the following:

(1) Domestic Public Records Offered in Compliance With Statute. Public records authenticated or certified as provided under a statute of the Commonwealth.

(2) Foreign Public Documents. A document purporting to be executed or attested in his official capacity by a person authorized by the laws of a foreign country to make the execution or attestation, and accompanied by a final certification as to the genuineness of the signature and official position (a) of the executing or attesting person, or (b) of any foreign official whose certificate of genuineness of signature and official position relates to the execution or attestation or is in a chain of certification of genuineness of signature and official position relating to the execution or attestation. A final certification may be made by a secretary of embassy or legation, consul general, consul, vice consul, or consular agent of the United States, or a diplomatic or consular official of the foreign country assigned or accredited to the United States. If reasonable opportunity has been given to all parties to investigate the authenticity and accuracy of official documents, the court may for good cause shown order that they be treated as presumptively authentic without final certification or permit them to be evidenced by an attested summary with or without final certification.

(3) Presumptions Created by Law. Any signature, document, or other matter declared by any law of the United States or of this Commonwealth, to be presumptively or prima facie genuine or authentic.

(4) Medical Records and Medical Bills in Particular Actions. Where authorized by statute, medical records and medical bills, offered upon the forms of authentication specified in the Code of Virginia.

(5) Specific Certificates of Analysis and Reports. Certificates of analysis and official reports prepared by designated persons or facilities, when authenticated in accordance with applicable statute.

(6) Certified Records of a Regularly Conducted Activity.

(a) In any civil proceeding where a business record is material and otherwise admissible, authentication of the record and the foundation required by subdivision (6) of Rule 2:803 may be laid by (i) witness testimony, (ii) a certification of the authenticity of and foundation for the record made by the custodian of such record or other qualified witness either by affidavit or by declaration pursuant to Code § 8.01–4.3, or (iii) a combination of witness testimony and a certification.

(b) The proponent of a business record shall (i) give written notice to all other parties if a certification under this section will be relied upon in whole or in part in authenticating and laying the foundation for admission of such record and (ii) provide a copy of the record and the certification to all other parties, so that all parties have a fair opportunity to challenge the record and certification. The notice and copy of the record and certification shall be provided no later than 15 days in advance of the trial or hearing, unless an order of the court specifies a different time. Objections shall be made within five days thereafter, unless an order of the court specifies a different time. If any party timely objects to reliance upon the certification, the authentication and foundation required by subdivision (6) of Rule 2:803 shall be made by witness testimony unless the objection is withdrawn.

(c) A certified business record that satisfies the requirements of this section shall be self-authenticating and requires no extrinsic evidence of authenticity.

(d) A copy of a business record may be offered in lieu of an original upon satisfaction of the requirements of Code § 8.01–391(D) by witness testimony, a certification, or a combination of testimony and a certification.

[Adopted effective July 1, 2012. Amended effective July 1, 2014.]

RULE 2:903. SUBSCRIBING WITNESS TESTIMONY NOT NECESSARY

The testimony of a subscribing witness is not necessary to authenticate a writing unless required by the laws of the jurisdiction whose laws govern the validity of the writing.

[Adopted effective July 1, 2012.]

Article X

BEST EVIDENCE

RULE 2:1001. DEFINITIONS

For purposes of this Article, the following definitions are applicable.

(1) Writings. "Writings" consist of letters, words, or numbers, or their equivalent, set down by handwriting, typewriting, printing, photostating, photographing, magnetic impulse, mechanical or electronic recording, or other form of data compilation or preservation.

(2) Original. An "original" of a writing is the writing itself or any other writing intended to have the same effect by a person executing or issuing it.

[Adopted effective July 1, 2012.]

RULE 2:1002. REQUIREMENT OF PRODUCTION OF ORIGINAL

To prove the content of a writing, the original writing is required, except as otherwise provided in these Rules, other Rules of the Supreme Court of Virginia, or in a Virginia statute.

[Adopted effective July 1, 2012.]

RULE 2:1003. USE OF SUBSTITUTE CHECKS (derived from Code § 8.01–391.1(A) and (B))

(a) Admissibility Generally. A substitute check created pursuant to the federal Check Clearing for the 21st Century Evidence Act, 12 U.S.C. § 5001 et seq., shall be admissible in evidence in any Virginia legal proceeding, civil or criminal, to the same extent the original check would be.

(b) Presumption From Designation and Legend. A document received from a banking institution that is designated as a "substitute check" and that bears the legend "This is a legal copy of your check. You can use it the same way you would use the original check" shall be presumed to be a substitute check created pursuant to the Act applicable under subdivision (a) of this Rule.

[Adopted effective July 1, 2012.]

RULE 2:1004. ADMISSIBILITY OF OTHER EVIDENCE OF CONTENTS

The original is not required, and other evidence of the contents of a writing is admissible if:

(a) Originals Lost or Destroyed. All originals are lost or have been destroyed, unless the proponent lost or destroyed them in bad faith; or

(b) Original Not Obtainable. No original can be obtained by any available judicial process or procedure, unless the proponent acted in bad faith to render the original unavailable; or

(c) Original in Possession of Opponent. At a time when an original was under the control of the party against whom offered, that party was put on notice, by the pleadings or otherwise, that the contents would be a subject of proof at the hearing, and that party does not produce the original at the hearing; or

(d) Collateral Matters. The writing is not closely related to a controlling issue.

[Adopted effective July 1, 2012.]

RULE 2:1005. ADMISSIBILITY OF COPIES (derived from Code § 8.01–391)

In addition to admissibility of copies of documents as provided in Rules 2:1002 and 2:1004, and by statute, copies may be used in lieu of original documents as follows:

(a) Whenever the original of any official publication or other record has been filed in an action or introduced as evidence, the court may order the original to be returned to its custodian, retaining in its stead a copy thereof. The court may make any order to prevent the improper use of the original.

(b) If any department, division, institution, agency, board, or commission of this Commonwealth, of another state or country, or of the United States, or of any political subdivision or agency of the same, acting pursuant to the law of the respective jurisdiction or other proper authority, has copied any record made in the performance of its official duties, such copy shall be as admissible into evidence as the original, whether the original is in existence or not, provided that such copy is authenticated as a true copy either by the custodian of said record or by the person to whom said custodian reports, if they are different, and is accompanied by a certificate that such person does in fact have the custody.

(c) If any court or clerk's office of a court of this Commonwealth, of another state or country, or of the United States, or of any political subdivision or agency of the same, has copied any record made in the performance of its official duties, such copy shall be admissible into evidence as the original, whether the original is in existence or not, provided that such copy is authenticated as a true copy by a clerk or deputy clerk of such court.

(d) If any business or member of a profession or calling in the regular course of business or activity has made any record or received or transmitted any document, and again in the regular course of business has caused any or all of such record or document to be copied, the copy shall be as admissible in evidence as the original, whether the original exists or not, provided that such copy is satisfactorily identified and authenticated as a true copy by a custodian of such record or by the person to whom said custodian reports, if they be different, and is accompanied by a certificate that said person does in fact have the custody. Copies in the regular course of business shall be deemed to include reproduction at a later time, if done in good faith and without intent to defraud. Copies in the regular course of business shall include items such as checks which are regularly copied before transmission to another person or bank, or records which are acted upon without receipt of the original when the original is retained by another party.

(e) The original of which a copy has been made may be destroyed unless its preservation is required by law, or its validity has been questioned.

(f) The introduction in an action of a copy under this Rule precludes neither the introduction or admission of the original nor the introduction of a copy or the original in another action.

(g) Copy, as used in these Rules, shall include photographs, microphotographs, photostats, microfilm, microcard, printouts or other reproductions of electronically stored data, or copies from optical disks, electronically transmitted facsimiles, or any other reproduction of an original from a process which forms a durable medium for its recording, storing, and reproducing.

[Adopted effective July 1, 2012.]

RULE 2:1006. SUMMARIES

The contents of voluminous writings that, although admissible, cannot conveniently be examined in court may be represented in the form of a chart, summary, or calculation. Reasonably in advance of the offer of such chart, summary, or calculation, the originals or duplicates shall be made available for examination or copying, or both, by other parties at a reasonable time and place. The court may order that they be produced in court.

[Adopted effective July 1, 2012.]

RULE 2:1007. TESTIMONY OR WRITTEN ADMISSION OF A PARTY

Contents of writings may be proved by the admission of the party against whom offered without accounting for the nonproduction of the original.

[Adopted effective July 1, 2012.]

RULE 2:1008. FUNCTIONS OF COURT AND JURY

Whenever the admissibility of other evidence of contents or writings under these provisions depends upon the fulfillment of a condition of fact, the question whether the condition has been fulfilled is ordinarily for the court to determine. However, when an issue is raised whether (1) the asserted writing ever existed, or (2) another writing produced at the trial is the original, or (3) other evidence of contents correctly reflects the contents, the issue is for the trier of fact to determine.

[Adopted effective July 1, 2012.]

ARTICLE XI

APPLICABILITY

RULE 2:1101. APPLICABILITY OF EVIDENTIARY RULES

(a) Proceedings to Which Applicable Generally. Evidentiary rules apply generally to (1) all civil actions and (2) proceedings in a criminal case (including preliminary hearings in criminal cases), and to contempt proceedings (except contempt proceedings in which the court may act summarily), in the Supreme Court of Virginia, the Court of Appeals of Virginia, the State Corporation Commission (when acting as a court of record), the circuit courts, the general district courts (except when acting as a small claims court as provided by statute), and the juvenile and domestic relations district courts.

(b) Law of Privilege. The law with respect to privileges applies at all stages of all actions, cases, and proceedings.

(c) Permissive Application. Except as otherwise provided by statute or rule, adherence to the Rules of Evidence (other than with respect to privileges) is permissive, not mandatory, in the following situations:

(1) Criminal proceedings other than (i) trial, (ii) preliminary hearings, (iii) sentencing proceedings before a jury, and (iv) capital murder sentencing hearings.

(2) Administrative proceedings.

[Adopted effective July 1, 2012.]

PART TWO A. APPEALS PURSUANT TO THE ADMINISTRATIVE PROCESS ACT

Effective July 1, 1977

Including Amendments Received Through October 15, 2015

RULE 2A:1. AUTHORIZATION; DEFINITIONS; APPLICATION

(a) These rules are promulgated pursuant to § 2.2–4026 of the Code of Virginia. They shall apply to the review of, by way of direct appeal from, the adoption of a regulation or the decision of a case by an agency.

(b) All terms used in this part that are defined in Chapter 40, Article 1 of Title 2.2 are used with the definitions therein contained. Every agency may designate some individual to perform the function of "agency secretary." If there is no designated "agency secretary," that term shall mean the executive officer of the agency.

(c) The term "party" means any person affected by and claiming the unlawfulness of a regulation, or a party aggrieved who asserts a case decision is unlawful or any other affected person or aggrieved person who appeared in person or by counsel at a hearing, as defined in § 2.2–4001, with respect to the regulation or case decision as well as the agency itself. Whenever a case decision disposes of an application for a license, permit or other benefit, the applicant, licensee or permittee shall be a necessary party to any proceeding under this part.

[Amended effective September 1, 1991; December 22, 2004; February 26, 2010, effective May 3, 2010.]

RULE 2A:2. NOTICE OF APPEAL

(a) Any party appealing from a regulation or case decision shall file with the agency secretary, within 30 days after adoption of the regulation or after service of the final order in the case decision, a notice of appeal signed by the appealing party or that party's counsel. With respect to appeal from a regulation, the date of adoption or readoption shall be the date of publication in the Register of Regulations. In the event that a case decision is required by § 2.2–4023 or by any other provision of law to be served by mail upon a party, 3 days shall be added to the 30–day period for that party. Service under this Rule shall be sufficient if sent by registered or certified mail to the party's last address known to the agency.

(b) The notice of appeal shall identify the regulation or case decision appealed from, shall state the names and addresses of the appellant and of all other parties and their counsel, if any, shall specify the circuit court to which the appeal is taken, and shall conclude with a certificate that a copy of the notice of appeal has been mailed to each of the parties. Any copy of a notice of appeal that is sent to a party's counsel or to a party's registered agent, if the party is a corporation, shall be deemed adequate and shall not be a cause for dismissal of the appeal; provided, however, sending a notice of appeal to an agency's counsel shall not satisfy the requirement that a notice of appeal be filed with the agency secretary. The omission of a party whose name and address cannot, after due diligence, be ascertained shall not be cause for dismissal of the appeal.

(c) Any final agency case decision as described in § 2.2–4023 shall advise the party of the time for filing a notice of appeal under this Rule.

[Amended effective September 1, 1991; December 22, 2004; February 26, 2010; May 3, 2010; July 2, 2014.]

RULE 2A:3. RECORD ON APPEAL

(a) If a formal hearing was held before the agency, the appellant shall deliver to the agency secretary with his notice of appeal, or within 30 days thereafter, a transcript of the testimony if it was taken down in writing, or if it was not taken down in writing, a statement of the testimony in narrative form. If the agency secretary deems the statement inaccurate, he may append a further statement specifying the inaccuracies.

(b) The agency secretary shall prepare and certify the record as soon as possible after the notice of appeal and transcript or statement of testimony is filed and served. Once the court has entered an order overruling any motions, demurrers and other pleas filed by the agency, or if none have been filed within the time provided by Rule 3:8 for the filing of a response to the process served under Rule 2A:4, the agency secretary shall, as soon as practicable or within such time as the court may order, transmit the record to the clerk of the court named in the notice of appeal. In the event of multiple appeals in the same proceeding, only one record need be prepared and it shall be transmitted to the clerk of the court named in the first notice of appeal filed. If there are multiple appeals to different courts from the same regulation or case decision, all such appeals shall be transferred to and heard by the court having jurisdiction that is named in the notice of appeal that is the first to be filed. The agency secretary shall notify all parties in writing when the record is transmitted, naming the court to which it is transmitted. Papers filed in any other clerk's office shall be forwarded by such clerk to the proper clerk's office.

(c) The record on appeal from an agency proceeding shall consist of all notices of appeal, any application or petition, all orders or regulations promulgated in the proceeding by the agency, the opinions, the transcript or statement of the testimony filed by appellant, and all exhibits accepted or rejected, together with such other material as may be certified by the agency secretary to be a part of the record.

(d) Upon the adoption of standards for the preparation of electronic or digital records for use in appeals, records under this Rule shall comply with such standards.

(e) In the event the agency secretary determines that the record is so voluminous that its certification and filing pursuant to part (b) of this Rule would be unduly burdensome upon the agency or upon the clerk of the court, the agency may, prior to and in lieu of filing the entire record, move the court for leave to file an index to such record. A party shall have the opportunity to respond to the agency's motion within 10 days of filing the motion. Thereafter, if the court grants the agency's motion, the record, or such parts thereof as the parties may agree upon or as the court may determine, shall be filed in the form of a joint appendix or in such other form as the court may direct. The agency shall nevertheless retain the entire record and make it available to the parties on reasonable request during the pendency of the appeal.

[Amended February 26, 2010, effective May 3, 2010.]

RULE 2A:4. PETITION FOR APPEAL

(a) Within 30 days after the filing of the notice of appeal, the appellant shall file a petition for appeal with the clerk of the circuit court named in the first notice of appeal to be filed. Such filing shall include within such 30–day period both the payment of all fees and the taking of all steps provided in Rules 3:2, 3:3 and 3:4 to cause a copy of the petition for appeal to be served (as in a civil action) on the agency secretary and on every other party. The petition may be filed electronically as provided under Rule 1:17.

(b) The petition for appeal shall designate the regulation or case decision appealed from, specify the errors assigned, state the reasons why the regulation or case decision is deemed to be unlawful and conclude with a specific statement of the relief requested.

[Amended effective September 1, 1991; January 1, 2006; February 26, 2010, effective May 3, 2010; May 2, 2011.]

RULE 2A:5. FURTHER PROCEEDINGS

Further proceedings in an appeal under this Part Two–A shall be governed by the rules contained in Part Three, where not in conflict with the Code of Virginia or this part, subject to the following:

(1) No appeal or issue under this Part Two–A shall be referred to a commissioner in chancery.

(2) Except for Rule 4:15 where applicable under this Rule, the provisions of Part Four shall not apply to appeals under this part and, unless ordered by the court, depositions shall not be taken.

(3) Once any motions, demurrers or other pleas filed by the agency have been overruled, or if none have been filed within the time provided by Rule 3:8 for the filing of a response to the process served under Rule 2A:4, the appeal shall be deemed submitted and no answer or further pleadings shall be required except as provided herein or by order of the court.

(4) When the case is submitted and the record has been filed as provided in Rule 2A:3, the court shall establish by order a schedule for briefing and argument of the issues raised in the petition for appeal.

(5) The court shall dispose of the appeal by an order consistent with its authority set forth in §§ 2.2–4029 and 2.2–4030 of the Code of Virginia.

[Amended February 26, 2010, effective May 3, 2010.]

RULE 2A:6. SMALL BUSINESS CHALLENGES

(a) In addition to the other remedies established in this Part Two–A, as provided by § 2.2–4027 of the Code of Virginia, a "small business" as defined in § 2.2–4007.1(A) of the Code of Virginia that is adversely affected or aggrieved by final agency regulatory action as described therein may seek judicial review for the limited purpose of appealing the issue of compliance with the requirements of §§ 2.2–4007.04 and 2.2–4007.1. Such appeal shall be initiated by filing a notice of appeal as described in Rule 2A:2 within one year of the date of such final agency action.

(b) In all other respects, the provisions of this Part Two–A shall apply to such appeals.

[Adopted February 26, 2010, effective May 3, 2010.]

PART THREE. PRACTICE AND PROCEDURE IN CIVIL ACTIONS

Effective March 1, 1972

Including Amendments Received Through October 15, 2015

RULE 3:1. SCOPE

There shall be one form of civil case, known as a civil action. These Rules apply to all civil actions, in the circuit courts, whether the claims involved arise under legal or equitable causes of action, unless otherwise provided by law. These rules apply in cases appealed or removed to such courts from inferior courts whenever applicable to such cases. These Rules shall not apply in petitions for a writ of habeas corpus. In matters not covered by these Rules, the established practices and procedures are continued. Whenever in this Part Three the words "action" or "suit" appear they shall refer to a civil action, which may include legal and equitable claims.

[Adopted effective January 1, 2006.]

A former Rule 3:1 was repealed effective January 1, 2006.

RULE 3:2. COMMENCEMENT OF CIVIL ACTIONS

(a) Commencement. A civil action shall be commenced by filing a complaint in the clerk's office. When a statute or established practice requires, a proceeding may be commenced by a pleading styled "Petition." Upon filing of the pleading, the action is then instituted and pending as to all parties defendant thereto. The statutory writ tax and clerk's fees shall be paid before the summons is issued.

(b) Caption. The complaint shall be captioned with the name of the court and the full style of the action, which shall include the names of all the parties. The requirements of Code § 8.01–290 may be met by giving the address or other data after the name of each defendant.

(c) Form and Content of the Complaint.

(i) It shall be sufficient for the complaint to ask for the specific relief sought. Without more it will be understood that all defendants mentioned in the caption are made parties defendant and required to answer the complaint; that proper process against them is requested; that answers under oath are waived, except when required by law, and that all relief authorized by law and demanded in the complaint may be granted. No formal conclusion is necessary.

(ii) Every complaint requesting an award of money damages shall contain an ad damnum clause stating the amount of damages sought. Leave to amend the ad damnum clause shall be available under Rule 1:8.

[Adopted effective January 1, 2006. Amended effective March 1, 2007.]

A former Rule 3:2 was repealed effective January 1, 2006.

RULE 3:3. FILING OF PLEADINGS; RETURN OF CERTAIN WRITS

(a) Filing Generally. The clerk shall receive and file all pleadings when tendered, without order of the court. The clerk shall note and attest the date of filing thereon. In an Electronically Filed Case, the procedures of Rule 1:17 shall be applicable to the notation by the clerk of the date of filing. Any controversy over whether a party who has filed a pleading has a right to file it shall be decided by the court.

(b) Electronic Filing. In any circuit court which has established an electronic filing system pursuant to Rule 1:17:

(1) Any civil action for which electronic filing is available in the circuit court may be designated as an Electronically Filed Case upon consent of all parties in the case. Such designation shall be made promptly, complying with all filing and procedural requirements for making such designations as may be prescribed by such circuit court.

(2) Except where service and/or filing of an original paper document is expressly required by these rules, all pleadings, motions, notices and other filings in an Electronically Filed Case shall be formatted, served and filed as specified in the requirements and procedures of Rule 1:17; provided, however, that when any document listed below is filed in the case, the filing party shall notify the clerk of court that the original document must be retained.

(i) Any pleading or affidavit required by statute or rule to be sworn, verified or certified as provided in Rule 1:17(d)(5).

(ii) Any last will and testament or other testamentary document, whether or not it is holographic.

(iii) Any contract or deed.

(iv) Any prenuptial agreement or written settlement agreement, including any property settlement agreement.

(v) Any check or other negotiable instrument.

(vi) Any handwritten statement, waiver, or consent by a defendant or witness in a criminal proceeding.

(vii) Any form signed by a defendant in a criminal proceeding, including any typed statements or a guilty plea form.

(viii) Any document that cannot be converted into an electronic document in such a way as to produce a clear and readable image.

(c) Return of Writs. No writ shall be returnable more than 90 days after its date unless a longer period is provided by statute.

[Adopted effective January 1, 2006. Amended effective May 2, 2011; January 1, 2013.]

A former Rule 3:3 was repealed effective January 1, 2006.

RULE 3:4. COPIES OF COMPLAINT

(a) Copies for Service. Except in cases where service is waived pursuant to Code § 8.01–286.1, the plaintiff shall furnish the clerk when the complaint is filed with as many paper copies thereof as there are defendants upon whom it is to be served. In an Electronically Filed Case, the plaintiff shall file the complaint electronically and furnish paper copies to the clerk as provided in this Rule.

(b) Exhibits. It is not required that physical copies of exhibits filed with the complaint be furnished or served. Unless an individual case is exempted by order of the court for good cause shown, an electronic or digitally imaged copy of all exhibits that are incorporated by reference in the pleading shall be filed with the complaint. Upon the adoption of standards for the preparation of electronic or digital records for use in appeals, exhibits under this Rule shall comply with such standards.

(c) Additional Copies. A deficiency in the number of copies of the complaint shall not affect the pendency of the action.

(1) If the plaintiff fails to furnish the required number of copies, the clerk shall request that additional copies be furnished by the plaintiff as needed, and if the plaintiff fails to do so promptly, the clerk shall bring the fact to the attention of the judge, who shall notify the plaintiff's counsel, or the plaintiff personally if no counsel has appeared for plaintiff, to furnish them by a specified date. If the required copies are not furnished on or before that date, the court may enter an order dismissing the suit.

(2) Additionally, in an Electronically Filed Case, if the clerk has been provided by the plaintiff with a credit or payment account through which to obtain payment of fees for duplication of required copies of filings, the clerk shall promptly prepare additional copies of the pleading as needed, and process payment through such credit or payment account; or, if processing by the clerk of the proper payment for duplication of additional copies of the pleading through a credit or payment account authorized by the filing party is not feasible, the clerk shall proceed as provided in subpart (c)(1) of this Rule.

[Adopted effective January 1, 2006. Amended effective May 1, 2006; May 2, 2011; January 1, 2013.]

A former Rule 3:4 was repealed effective January 1, 2006.

RULE 3:5. THE SUMMONS

(a) Form of Process. The process of the courts in civil actions shall be a summons in substantially this form:

Commonwealth of Virginia

In the .... Court of the .... of ....

SUMMONS

Civil Action No. . . .

The party upon whom this summons and the attached complaint are served is hereby notified that unless within 21 days after such service response is made by filing in the clerk's office of this court a pleading in writing, in proper legal form, the allegations and charges may be taken as admitted and the court may enter an order, judgment or decree against such party either by default or after hearing evidence.

Appearance in person is not required by this summons.

Done in the name of the Commonwealth of Virginia, this .... day of ...., 20 ....

.........., Clerk.

(b) Affixing Summons for Service; Voluntary Appearance. Upon the commencement of a civil action defendants may appear voluntarily and file responsive pleadings and may appear voluntarily and waive process, but in cases of divorce or annulment of marriage only in accordance with the provisions of the controlling statutes. With respect to defendants who do not appear voluntarily or file responsive pleadings or waive service of process, the clerk shall issue summonses and securely attach one to and upon the front of each copy of the complaint to be served. The copies of the complaint, with a summons so attached, shall be delivered by the clerk for service together as the plaintiff may direct.

(c) Defendant Under a Disability. Except when sued for divorce or annulment of marriage, or a judgment in personam is sought, a summons need not be issued for or served upon a defendant who is a person under a disability (except as otherwise provided in § 8.01–297), the procedure described in Code § 8.01–9 constituting due process as to such defendants.

(d) Additional Summonses. The clerk shall on request issue additional summonses, dating them as of the day of issuance.

(e) Service More Than One Year After Commencement of the Action. No order, judgment or decree shall be entered against a defendant who was served with process more than one year after the institution of the action against that defendant unless the court finds as a fact that the plaintiff exercised due diligence to have timely service on that defendant.

[Adopted effective January 1, 2006.]

A former Rule 3:5 was repealed effective January 1, 2006.

RULE 3:6. PROOF OF SERVICE

Returns shall be made on a paper styled "Proof of Service" which shall be substantially in this form:

Virginia:
In the .... Court of the .... of ....:

......................)
)
v. (short style)) Proof of Service
)
......................)

Returns shall be made hereon, showing service of the summons issued ...., 20 ..., with copy of the complaint filed ...., 20 ..., attached.

The clerk shall prepare as many as may be needed and deliver them with the summons and copies of the complaint.

The summons with copy of the complaint attached shall constitute and be served as one paper.

It shall be the duty of all persons eligible to serve process to make service within five days after receipt, and make return as to those served within 72 hours after the earliest service upon any party shown on each Proof of Service; but failure to make timely service and return shall not prejudice the rights of any party except as provided in Rule 3:5.

Additional copies of the Proof of Service may be obtained from the clerk and returns thereon made in similar manner.

[Adopted effective January 1, 2006.]

A former Rule 3:6 was repealed effective January 1, 2006.

RULE 3:7. BILLS OF PARTICULARS

(a) Timing and Grounds. On motion made promptly, a bill of particulars may be ordered to amplify any pleading that does not provide notice of a claim or defense adequate to permit the adversary a fair opportunity to respond or prepare the case.

(b) Striking of Insufficient Bills of Particulars. A bill of particulars that fails to inform the opposing party fairly of the true nature of the claim or defense may, on motion made promptly, be stricken and an amended bill of particulars ordered. If the amended bill of particulars fails to inform the opposite party fairly of the true nature of the claim or defense, the pleading not so amplified and the bills of particulars may be stricken.

(c) Date for Filing Bill of Particulars. An order requiring or permitting a bill of particulars or amended bill of particulars shall fix the time within which it must be filed.

(d) Date for Responding to Amplified Pleading. If the bill of particulars amplifies a complaint, a defendant shall respond to the amplified pleading within 21 days after the filing thereof, unless the defendant relies on pleadings already filed. If the bill of particulars amplifies any other pleading, any required response shall be filed within 21 days after the filing of the bill of particulars, or within such shorter or longer time as the court may prescribe.

[Adopted effective January 1, 2006.]

A former Rule 3:7 was repealed effective January 1, 2006.

RULE 3:8. ANSWERS, PLEAS, DEMURRERS AND MOTIONS

(a) Response Requirement. A defendant shall file pleadings in response within 21 days after service of the summons and complaint upon that defendant, or if service of the summons has been timely waived on request under Code § 8.01-286.1, within 60 days after the date when the request for waiver was sent, or within 90 days after that date if the defendant was addressed outside the Commonwealth. A demurrer, plea, motion to dismiss, and motion for a bill of particulars shall each be deemed a pleading in response for the count or counts addressed therein. If a defendant files no other pleading than the answer, it shall be filed within said time. An answer shall respond to the paragraphs of the complaint. A general denial of the entire complaint or plea of the general issue shall not be permitted.

(b) Response After Demurrer, Plea or Motion. When the court has entered its order overruling all motions, demurrers and other pleas filed by a defendant, such defendant shall, unless the defendant has already done so, file an answer within 21 days after the entry of such order, or within such shorter or longer time as the court may prescribe.

[Adopted effective January 1, 2006; amended effective May 1, 2006.]

A former Rule 3:8 was repealed effective January 1, 2006.

RULE 3:9. COUNTERCLAIMS

(a) Scope. A defendant may, at that defendant's option, plead as a counterclaim any cause of action that the defendant has against the plaintiff or all plaintiffs jointly, whether or not it grows out of any transaction mentioned in the complaint, whether or not it is for liquidated damages, whether it is in tort or contract, and whether or not the amount demanded in the counterclaim is greater than the amount demanded in the complaint.

(b) Time for Initiation.

(i) A counterclaim shall, subject to the provisions of Rule 1:9, be filed within 21 days after service of the summons and complaint upon the defendant asserting the counterclaim, or if service of the summons has been timely waived on request under Code § 8.01–286.1, within 60 days after the date when the request for waiver was sent, or within 90 days after that date if the defendant was addressed outside the Commonwealth.

(ii) If a demurrer, plea, motion to dismiss, or motion for a bill of particulars is filed within the period provided in subsection (b)(i) of this Rule, the defendant may file any counterclaim at any time up to 21 days after the entry of the court's order ruling upon all such motions, demurrers and other pleas, or within such shorter or longer time as the court may prescribe.

(c) Response to Counterclaim. The plaintiff shall file pleadings in response to such counterclaim within 21 days after it is served.

(d) Separate Trials. The court in its discretion may order a separate trial of any cause of action asserted in a counterclaim.

[Adopted effective January 1, 2006. Amended effective May 1, 2006; July 1, 2008.]

A former Rule 3:9 was repealed effective January 1, 2006.

RULE 3:9A. REPEALED EFFECTIVE JANUARY 1, 2006

RULE 3:10. CROSS–CLAIMS

(a) Scope. A defendant may, at that defendant's option, plead as a cross-claim any cause of action that such defendant has or may have against one or more other defendants growing out of any matter pled in the complaint. Such cross-claim may include a claim that the party against whom it is asserted is or may be liable to the cross-claimant for all or part of a claim asserted in the action against the cross-claimant.

(b) Time for Initiation. A cross-claim shall, subject to the provisions of Rule 1:9, be filed within 21 days after service of the summons and complaint on the defendant asserting the cross-claim, or if service of the summons has been timely waived on request under Code § 8.01–286.1, within 60 days after the date when the request for waiver was sent, or within 90 days after that date if the defendant was addressed outside the Commonwealth.

(c) Response to Cross–Claim. The cross-claim defendant shall file pleadings in response to such cross-claim within 21 days after it is served.

(d) Separate Trials. The court in its discretion may order a separate trial of any cause of action asserted in a cross-claim.

[Adopted effective January 1, 2006. Amended effective May 1, 2006.]

A former Rule 3:10 was repealed effective January 1, 2006.

Rule 3:11. REPLY

Responding to New Matter. If a pleading, motion or affirmative defense sets up new matter and contains words expressly requesting a reply, the adverse party shall within 21 days file a reply admitting or denying such new matter. If it does not contain such words, the allegation of new matter shall be taken as denied or avoided without further pleading. All allegations contained in a reply shall be taken as denied or avoided without further pleading.

[Adopted effective January 1, 2006.]

A former Rule 3:11 was repealed effective January 1, 2006.

RULE 3:12. JOINDER OF ADDITIONAL PARTIES

(a) Persons to Be Joined if Feasible. A person who is subject to service of process may be joined as a party in the action if (1) in the person's absence complete relief cannot be accorded among those already parties, or (2) the person claims an interest relating to the subject of the action and is so situated that the disposition of the action in the person's absence may (i) as a practical matter impair or impede the person's ability to protect that interest or (ii) leave any of the persons already parties subject to a substantial risk of incurring double, multiple, or otherwise inconsistent obligations by reason of the claimed interest of the person to be joined. If such a person should join as a plaintiff but refuses to do so, the person may be made a defendant, or, in a proper case, an involuntary plaintiff.

(b) Method of Joinder. A motion to join an additional party shall, subject to the provisions of Rule 1:9, be filed with the clerk within 21 days after service of the complaint and shall be served on the party sought to be joined who shall thereafter be subject to all provisions of these Rules, except the provisions requiring payment of writ tax and clerk's fees.

(c) Determination by Court Whenever Joinder Not Feasible. If a person as described in subdivision (a) hereof cannot be made a party, the court shall determine whether in equity and good conscience the action should proceed among the parties before it, or should be dismissed, the absent person being thus regarded as indispensable. The factors to be considered by the court include: first, to what extent a judgment rendered in the person's absence might be prejudicial to the absent person or those already parties; second, the extent to which, by protective provisions in the judgment, by the shaping of relief, or other measures, the prejudice can be lessened or avoided; third, whether a judgment rendered in the person's absence will be adequate; fourth, whether the plaintiff will have an adequate remedy if the action is dismissed for nonjoinder.

(d) Pleading Reasons for Nonjoinder. A pleading asserting a claim for relief shall state the names, if known to the pleader, of any persons as described in subdivision (a) hereof who are not joined, and the reasons why they are not joined.

[Adopted effective January 1, 2006.]

A former Rule 3:12 was repealed effective January 1, 2006.

RULE 3:13. THIRD–PARTY PRACTICE

(a) When Defendant May Bring in Third Party. At any time after commencement of the action a defending party, as a third-party plaintiff, may file and serve a third-party complaint upon a person not a party to the action who is or may be liable to the third-party plaintiff for all or part of the plaintiff's claim against the third-party plaintiff. The third-party plaintiff need not obtain leave therefore if the third-party complaint is filed not later than 21 days after the third-party plaintiff serves an original pleading in response. Otherwise the third-party plaintiff must obtain leave therefore on motion after notice to all parties to the action. The person served with the third-party complaint, hereinafter called the third-party defendant, shall make defenses to the third-party plaintiff's claim as provided in Rules 3:7 and 3:8. The third-party defendant may plead counterclaims against the third-party plaintiff and cross-claims against other third-party defendants as provided in Rules 3:9 and 3:10. The third-party defendant may assert against the plaintiff any defenses that the third-party plaintiff has to the plaintiff's claim. The third-party defendant may also assert any claim against the plaintiff arising out of the transaction or occurrence that is the subject matter of the plaintiff's claim against the third-party plaintiff. The plaintiff may, at plaintiff's option, within 21 days after service of the third-party complaint upon the third-party defendant, assert any claim against the third-party defendant arising out of the transaction or occurrence that is the subject matter of the plaintiff's claim against the third-party plaintiff, and the third-party defendant thereupon shall assert defenses as provided in Rules 3:7 and 3:8 and any counterclaims and cross-claims, including claims against the plaintiff, as provided in Rules 3:9 and 3:10. Any party may move to strike the third-party complaint, or for its severance or separate trial. A third-party defendant may proceed under this rule against any person not a party to the action who is or may be liable to the third-party defendant for all or part of the claim made in the action against the third-party defendant.

(b) When Plaintiff May Bring in Third Party. When a counterclaim is asserted against a plaintiff, the plaintiff may cause a third party to be brought in under circumstances that under this rule would entitle a defendant to do so.

[Adopted effective January 1, 2006.]

A former Rule 3:13 was repealed effective January 1, 2006.

RULE 3:14. INTERVENTION

A new party may by leave of court file a pleading to intervene as a plaintiff or defendant to assert any claim or defense germane to the subject matter of the proceeding.

All provisions of these Rules applicable to civil cases, except those provisions requiring payment of writ tax and clerk's fees, shall apply to such pleadings. The parties on whom such pleadings are served shall respond thereto as provided in these Rules.

[Adopted effective January 1, 2006.]

A former Rule 3:14 was repealed effective January 1, 2006.

RULE 3:15. STATUTORY INTERPLEADER

Proceedings brought pursuant to statutory provisions relating to interpleader shall, to the extent not inconsistent with the governing statutes, be conducted in accordance with the Rules contained in this Part Three.

[Adopted effective January 1, 2006.]

A former Rule 3:15 was repealed effective January 1, 2006.

RULE 3:16. NEW PARTIES

A new party may be added, on motion of the plaintiff, by order of the court at any stage of the case as the ends of justice may require. The motion, accompanied by a properly executed proposed amended complaint, shall be served on the existing parties as required by Rule 1:12. If the motion is granted, the amended pleading accompanying the motion shall be deemed filed in the clerk's office as of the date of the court's order permitting such amendment and all the provisions of Rule 3:4 shall apply as to the new parties, but no writ tax, clerk's fee, or deposit for costs is required. All defendants shall file pleadings in response thereto as required by these Rules unless otherwise ordered by the court.

[Adopted effective January 1. 2006. Amended effective May 2, 2011.]

A former Rule 3:16 was repealed effective January 1, 2006.

RULE 3:17. SUBSTITUTION OF PARTIES

(a) Substitution of a Successor. If a person becomes incapable of prosecuting or defending because of death, disability, conviction of felony, removal from office, or other cause, a successor in interest may be substituted as a party in such person's place.

(b) Motion, Consent, Procedure. Substitution shall be made on motion of the successor or of any party to the suit. If the successor does not make or consent to the motion, the party making the motion shall file the motion and a proposed amended pleading effecting the substitution in the clerk's office and serve a copy of the motion and the proposed amended pleading upon the party to be substituted in the manner prescribed by the Code of Virginia for serving original process upon such party. Unless the movant and the party to be substituted agree otherwise, or the court orders a different schedule, the party sought to be substituted shall file a written response to the motion for substitution within 21 days after service of the motion and proposed amended pleading upon the party sought to be substituted.

[Adopted effective January 1, 2006.]

A former Rule 3:17 was repealed effective January 1, 2006.

RULE 3:18. GENERAL PROVISIONS AS TO PLEADINGS

(a) Pleadings. All motions in writing, including a motion for a bill of particulars and a motion to dismiss, whether filed in paper document format or as electronic or digitally imaged filings, are pleadings.

(b) Allegation of Negligence. An allegation of negligence or contributory negligence is sufficient without specifying the particulars of the negligence.

(c) Contributory Negligence as a Defense. Contributory negligence shall not constitute a defense unless pleaded or shown by the plaintiff's evidence.

(d) Pleading the Statute of Limitations. An allegation that an action is barred by the statute of limitations is sufficient without specifying the particular statute relied on.

(e) Separate or Combined Filings. Answers, counterclaims, cross-claims, pleas, demurrers, affirmative defenses and motions may all be included in the same filing if they are separately identified in both the caption and the body of the filing.

[Adopted effective January 1, 2006. Amended effective May 2, 2011.]

A former Rule 3:18 was repealed effective January 1, 2006.

RULE 3:19. DEFAULT

(a) Failure Timely to Respond. A defendant who fails timely to file a responsive pleading as prescribed in Rule 3:8 is in default. A defendant in default is not entitled to notice of any further proceedings in the case, including notice to take depositions, except that written notice of any further proceedings shall be given to counsel of record, if any. The defendant in default is deemed to have waived any right to trial of issues by jury.

(b) Relief From Default. Prior to the entry of judgment, for good cause shown the court may grant leave to a defendant who is in default to file a late responsive pleading. Relief from default may be conditioned by the court upon such defendant reimbursing any extra costs and fees, including attorney's fees, incurred by the plaintiff solely as a result of the delay in the filing of a responsive pleading by the defendant.

(c) Default Judgment and Damages.

(1) Except in suits for divorce or annulling a marriage, the court shall, on motion of the plaintiff, enter judgment for the relief appearing to the court to be due. When service of process is effected by posting, no judgment by default shall be entered until the requirements of Code § 8.01–296(2)(b) have been satisfied.

(2) If the relief demanded is unliquidated damages, the court shall hear evidence and fix the amount thereof, unless the plaintiff demands trial by jury, in which event, a jury shall be impaneled to fix the amount of damages.

(3) If a defendant participates in the hearing to determine the amount of damages such defendant may not offer proof or argument on the issues of liability, but may (i) object to the plaintiff's evidence regarding damages, (ii) offer evidence regarding the quantum of damages, (iii) participate in jury selection if a jury will hear the damage inquiry, (iv) submit proposed jury instructions regarding damages, and (v) make oral argument on the issues of damages.

(d) Relief From Default Judgment.

(1) Within 21 Days. During the period provided by Rule 1:1 for the modification, vacation or suspension of a judgment, the court may by written order relieve a defendant of a default judgment after consideration of the extent and causes of the defendant's delay in tendering a responsive pleading, whether service of process and actual notice of the claim were timely provided to the defendant, and the effect of the delay upon the plaintiff. Relief from default may be conditioned by the court upon the defendant reimbursing any extra costs and fees, including attorney's fees, incurred by the plaintiff solely as a result of the delay in the filing of a responsive pleading by the defendant.

(2) After 21 Days. A final judgment no longer within the jurisdiction of the trial court under Rule 1:1 may not be vacated by that court except as provided in Virginia Code §§ 8.01–428 and 8.01–623.

[Adopted effective January 1, 2006.]

A former rule 3:19 was repealed effective January 1, 2006.

RULE 3:20. SUMMARY JUDGMENT

Any party may make a motion for summary judgment at any time after the parties are at issue, except in an action for divorce or for annulment of marriage. If it appears from the pleadings, the orders, if any, made at a pretrial conference, the admissions, if any, in the proceedings, or, upon sustaining a motion to strike the evidence, that the moving party is entitled to judgment, the court shall enter judgment in that party's favor. Summary judgment, interlocutory in nature, may be entered as to the undisputed portion of a contested claim or on the issue of liability alone although there is a genuine issue as to the amount of damages. Summary judgment shall not be entered if any material fact is genuinely in dispute. No motion for summary judgment or to strike the evidence shall be sustained when based in whole or in part upon any discovery depositions under Rule 4:5, unless all parties to the action shall agree that such deposition may be so used, or unless the motion is brought in accordance with the provisions of subsection B of § 8.01–420.

[Adopted effective January 1, 2006. Amended effective July 1, 2013.]

RULE 3:21. JURY TRIAL OF RIGHT

(a) Jury Trial Situations Unchanged. The right of trial by jury as declared by the Constitution of Virginia, or as given by an applicable statute or other authority, is unchanged by these rules, and shall be implemented as established law provides. Established practice for the trial and decision of equitable claims by the judge alone shall be continued.

(b) Demand. Any party may demand a trial by jury of any issue triable of right by a jury in the complaint or by (1) serving upon other parties a demand therefore in writing at any time after the commencement of the action and not later than 10 days after the service of the last pleading directed to the issue, and (2) filing the demand with the trial court. Such demand may be endorsed upon a pleading of the party. In an Electronically Filed Case, endorsement of such demand may be made as provided in Rule 1:17. The court may set a final date for service of jury demands. Leave to file amended pleadings shall not extend the time for serving and filing a jury demand unless the order granting leave to amend expressly so states.

(c) Specification of Issues. In the demand a party may specify the issues which the party wishes so tried; otherwise the party shall be deemed to have demanded trial by jury for all the issues so triable. If the party has demanded trial by jury for only some of the issues, any other party within 10 days after service of the demand or such lesser time as the court may order, may serve a demand for trial by jury of any other or all of the issues of fact in the action.

(d) Waiver. Absent leave of court for good cause shown, the failure of a party to serve and file a demand as required by this rule constitutes a waiver by the party of trial by jury.

[Adopted effective January 1, 2006. Amended effective March 1, 2007; July 1, 2008; May 2, 2011.]

RULE 3:22. TRIAL BY JURY OR BY THE COURT

(a) By Jury. When trial by jury has been demanded as provided in Rule 3:21, the action shall be designated upon the docket as a jury action. The trial of all issues so demanded shall be by jury, unless (1) the parties or their attorneys of record, by written stipulation filed with the court or by an oral stipulation made in open court and entered in the record, consent to trial by the court sitting without a jury; or (2) the court upon motion or of its own initiative finds that a right of trial by jury on some or all of those issues does not exist under applicable law.

(b) By the Court. Except as otherwise provided in this Rule, issues not demanded for trial by jury as provided in Rule 3:21, and issues as to which a right of trial by jury does not exist, shall be tried by the court.

(c) Statutory Jury Rights in Certain Equitable Claims.

(1) In an equitable claim where no right to a jury trial otherwise exists, where impaneling of an advisory jury pursuant to Code § 8.01–336(E) to hear an issue will be helpful to the court concerning disputed fact issues, such a jury may be seated. Decision on such claims and issues shall be made by the judge.

(2) Where a jury trial on a defendant's plea in an equitable claim is authorized under Code § 8.01–336(D), trial of the issues presented by the plea shall be by a jury whose verdict on those issues has the same effect as if trial by jury had been a matter of right.

(d) Party Consent to Jury. As to any claim not triable of right by a jury, the court, with the consent of the parties, may (i) order trial of any claim or issue with an advisory jury or, (ii) a trial with a jury whose verdict has the same effect as if trial by jury had been a matter of right.

(e) Trial by Mixed Jury and Non–Jury Claims. In any case when there are both jury and non-jury issues to be tried, the court shall adopt trial procedures and a sequence of proceedings to assure that all issues properly heard by the jury are decided by it, and applicable factual determinations by the jury shall be used by the judge in resolving the non-jury issues in the case.

[Adopted effective January 1, 2006. Amended effective March 1, 2007.]

RULE 3:22A. EXAMINATION OF PROSPECTIVE TRIAL JURORS (VOIR DIRE)

(a) Examination. After the prospective jurors are sworn on the voir dire, the court shall question them individually or collectively to determine whether anyone:

(1) Is related by blood, adoption, or marriage to the accused or to the Plaintiff or Defendant;

(2) Is an officer, director, agent or employee of the Plaintiff or Defendant;

(3) Has any interest in the trial or the outcome of the case,

(4) Has acquired any information about the case or the parties from the news media or other sources and, if so, whether such information would affect the juror's impartiality in the case;

(5) Has expressed or formed any opinion about the case;

(6) Has a bias or prejudice against the Plaintiff or Defendant; or

(7) Has any reason to believe the juror might not give a fair and impartial trial to the Plaintiff and Defendant based solely on the law and the evidence.

Thereafter, the court, and counsel as of right, may examine on oath the venire, and any prospective juror, and ask questions relevant to the qualifications as an impartial juror. A party objecting to a juror may introduce competent evidence in support of the objection.

(b) Challenge for Cause. The court, on its own motion or following a challenge for cause, may excuse a prospective juror if it appears the juror is not qualified, and another shall be drawn or called and placed in the juror's stead for the trial of that case.

[Adopted effective January 1, 2013.]

RULE 3:23. USE OF AND PROCEEDINGS BEFORE A COMMISSIONER IN CHANCERY

(a) Commissioners in chancery may be appointed in cases in circuit court, including uncontested divorce cases, only when (1) there is agreement by the parties with concurrence of the court or (2) upon motion of a party or the court on its own motion with a finding of good cause shown in each individual case.

(b) Upon entry of a decree by the court referring any matter to a commissioner in chancery, the clerk shall mail or deliver to the commissioner a copy of the decree of reference. Unless the decree prescribes otherwise, the commissioner shall promptly set a time and place for the first meeting of the parties or their attorneys, and shall notify the parties or their attorneys of the time and place so set. It shall be the duty of the commissioner to proceed with all reasonable diligence to execute the decree of reference.

(c) A commissioner may require the production of evidence upon all matters embraced in the decree of reference including the production of all books, papers, vouchers, documents and writings applicable thereto. The commissioner shall have the authority to call witnesses or the parties to the action to testify and may examine them upon oath. The commissioner may rule upon the admissibility of evidence unless otherwise directed by the decree of reference; but when a party so requests, the commissioner shall cause a record to be made of all proffered evidence which is excluded by the commissioner as inadmissible.

(d) The commissioner shall prepare a report stating his findings of fact and conclusions of law with respect to the matters submitted by the decree of reference. The commissioner shall file the report, together with all exhibits admitted in evidence and a transcript of the proceedings and of the testimony, with the clerk of the court. In an Electronically Filed Case, filing as required in this Rule shall be in accord with the requirements of Rule 1:17. The commissioner shall mail or deliver to counsel of record and to parties not represented by counsel, using the last address shown in the record, written notice of the filing of the report. Provided, however, that in divorce cases a copy of the report shall accompany the notice. Provided, further, that no such notice or copy shall be given parties who have not appeared in the proceeding.

[Adopted effective January 1, 2006. Amended effective May 2, 2011.]

RULE 3:24. APPEAL OF ORDERS OF QUARANTINE OR ISOLATION REGARDING COMMUNICABLE DISEASES OF PUBLIC HEALTH THREAT

A. Where an order of quarantine has been issued relating to a communicable disease of public health threat pursuant to § 32.1–48.09, the provisions of § 32.1–48.010, and related sections of Article 3.02 of Title 32.1 of the Code of Virginia, shall govern any appeal of such order to the appropriate circuit court.

B. Where an order of isolation has been issued relating to a communicable disease of public health threat pursuant to § 32.1–48.012, the provisions of § 32.1–48.013 and related sections of Article 3.02 of Title 32.1 of the Code of Virginia shall govern any appeal of such order to the appropriate circuit court.

C. The circuit court shall hold hearings under this rule in a manner to protect the health and safety of individuals subject to any such order or quarantine or isolation, court personnel, counsel, witnesses, and the general public. To this end, the circuit court may take measures including, but not limited to, ordering the hearing to be held by telephone or video conference or ordering those present to take appropriate precautions, including wearing personal protective equipment.

[Adopted effective May 1, 2006.]

RULE 3:25. CLAIMS FOR ATTORNEY'S FEES

A. Scope of Rule. This rule applies to claims for attorney's fees, excluding (i) attorney's fees under § 8.01–271.1 of the Code of Virginia, and (ii) attorney's fees in domestic relations cases.

B. Demand. A party seeking to recover attorney's fees shall include a demand therefor in the complaint filed pursuant to Rule 3:2, in a counterclaim filed pursuant to Rule 3:9, in a cross-claim filed pursuant to Rule 3:10, in a third-party pleading filed pursuant to Rule 3:13, or in a responsive pleading filed pursuant to Rule 3:8. The demand must identify the basis upon which the party relies in requesting attorney's fees.

C. Waiver. The failure of a party to file a demand as required by this rule constitutes a waiver by the party of the claim for attorney's fees, unless leave to file an amended pleading seeking attorney's fees is granted under Rule 1:8.

D. Procedure. Upon the motion of any party, the court shall, or upon its own motion, the court may, in advance of trial, establish a procedure to adjudicate any claim for attorney's fees.

[Adopted effective May 1, 2009.]

PART THREE A. CRIMINAL PRACTICE AND PROCEDURE

Revised Effective July 1, 1984

Including Amendments Received Through October 15, 2015

RULE 3A:1. SCOPE

These Rules govern criminal proceedings in circuit courts and juvenile and domestic relations district courts (except proceedings concerning a child in a juvenile and domestic relations district court) and before the magistrates defined in Rule 3A:2 except for cases which have been returned to the general district court. Special statutes applicable to practices and procedures in juvenile and domestic relations district courts are incorporated herein by this reference and in such cases shall prevail over the general rule set forth in Part 3A.

[Amended effective July 1, 1989.]

Source: Former Rule 3A:1.

Cross-reference: As to the criminal practice and procedure in the general district courts, see Rule 7C:1.

Rule 3A:2. PURPOSE AND INTERPRETATION; DEFINITIONS

(a) Purpose and Interpretation. These Rules are intended to provide for the just determination of criminal proceedings. They shall be interpreted so as to promote uniformity and simplicity in procedure, fairness in administration, and the elimination of unjustifiable expense and delay. Errors, defects, irregularities or variances that do not affect substantive rights shall not constitute reversible error.

(b) Definitions. Except as otherwise expressly provided in this Part Three A or unless the context otherwise requires:

(1) "Clerk" includes deputy clerk.

(2) "Commonwealth's attorney" includes assistant or acting Commonwealth's attorney.

(3) "Continuance" includes adjournment or recess.

(4) "Indictment" includes presentment and information filed upon presentment.

(5) "Magistrate" means a judicial or quasi-judicial officer authorized to issue arrest and search warrants, commit arrested persons to jail or admit them to bail, or conduct preliminary hearings.

(6) "Recognizance" means an undertaking, with or without surety or other security, made before a magistrate to perform one or more acts—for example, to appear in court. A recognizance may be written or oral but, if oral, shall be evidenced by a memorandum signed by the magistrate.

(7) Writings or memoranda under these Rules, and any required signatures or sworn verifications, shall be valid in the form of electronic files or digital images as provided in Rule 1:17.

[Amended effective May 2, 2011.]

Source: Former Rule 3A:2.

Comment: With respect to former Rule 3A:2, the [1984] amendment deletes the second sentence of subdivision (b)(5).

RULE 3A:2.1. VENUE IN CRIMINAL CASES

In criminal cases, questions of venue must be raised in the trial court and before the verdict in cases tried by a jury and before the finding of guilty in cases tried by a court.

[Adopted effective March 1, 2007.]

Source: Rule 1.2; Rule 1:8.

Cross-reference: As to the criminal practice and procedure in the general district courts, see Rule 7C:2.

[Cross-reference added effective July 1, 1989.]

RULE 3A:3. THE COMPLAINT

The complaint shall consist of sworn statements of a person or persons of facts relating to the commission of an alleged offense. The statements shall be made upon oath before a magistrate empowered to issue arrest warrants. The magistrate may require the sworn statements to be reduced to writing and signed if the complainant is a law-enforcement officer, but shall require the sworn statements to be reduced to writing if the complainant is not a law enforcement officer.

[Amended effective March 1, 2012.]

Source: Former Rule 3A:3.

Cross-reference: As to the criminal practice and procedure in the general district courts, see Rule 7C:3.

[Cross-reference added effective July 1, 1989.]

RULE 3A:4. ARREST WARRANT OR SUMMONS

(a) Issuance. More than one warrant or summons may issue on the same complaint. A warrant may be issued by a judicial officer if the accused fails to appear in response to a summons.

(b) Form of Summons. A summons, whether issued by a magistrate or a law-enforcement officer, shall command the accused to appear at a stated time and place before a court of appropriate jurisdiction in the county, city or town in which the summons is issued. It shall (i) state the name of the accused or, if his name is unknown, set forth a description by which he can be identified with reasonable certainty, (ii) describe the offense charged and state whether the offense is a violation of state, county, city or town law, and (iii) be signed by the magistrate or the law-enforcement office, as the case may be.

(c) Execution and Return. If a warrant has been issued but the officer does not have the warrant in his possession at the time of the arrest, he shall (i) inform the accused of the offense charged and that a warrant has been issued, and (ii) deliver a copy of the warrant to the accused as soon thereafter as practicable.

Source: Former Rule 3A:4.

Comment: With respect to former Rule 3A:4, the [1984] amendment deletes the words "by a magistrate" from the title to subsection (a), deletes the first two sentences of subsection (a), deletes subsection (b), redesignates subsection (c) as subsection (b) and alters its title, deletes former subdivision (c)(1), deletes former subsection (d) in its entirety and adds a new subsection (c).

Cross-reference: As to the criminal practice and procedure in the general district courts, see Rule 7C:3.

[Cross-reference added effective July 1, 1989.]

RULE 3A:5. THE GRAND JURY

(a) Who May Be Present. Only the grand jurors and the witness under examination and, if directed by the court, an interpreter shall be present during the hearing of evidence by a grand jury. Only the grand jurors shall be present during their deliberations and voting.

(b) Secrecy. No obligation of secrecy may be imposed upon any person except in accordance with law.

(c) Finding and Return of Indictment. The indictment shall be endorsed "A True Bill" or "Not a True Bill" and signed by the foreman. The indictment shall be returned by the grand jury in open court.

(d) Motion to Dismiss. A motion to dismiss the indictment may be based on constitutional objections to the array or on the lack of legal qualification of an individual juror.

Source: Former Rule 3A:6.

Comment: With respect to former Rule 3A:6, the [1984] amendment deletes subsection (a), deletes the second sentence of subsection (b), deletes the first sentence of subsection (c) and substitutes the word "law" for the words "this rule" at the end of the second sentence of subsection (c), deletes the second sentence of subsection (d), and deletes the second sentence of subsection (e).

RULE 3A:6. THE INDICTMENT AND THE INFORMATION

(a) Contents. The indictment or information, in describing the offense charged, shall cite the statute or ordinance that defines the offense or, if there is no defining statute or ordinance, prescribes the punishment for the offense. Error in the citation of the statute or ordinance that defines the offense or prescribes the punishments therefor, or omission of the citation, shall not be grounds for dismissal of an indictment or information, or for reversal of a conviction, unless the court finds that the error or omission prejudiced the accused in preparing his defense.

(b) Joinder of Offenses. Two or more offenses, any of which may be a felony or misdemeanor, may be charged in separate counts of an indictment or information if the offenses are based on the same act or transaction, or on two or more acts or transactions that are connected or constitute parts of a common scheme or plan.

(c) Joinder of Defendants. Two or more accused may be charged with a count(s) of an indictment, if they are charged with participating in contemporaneous and related acts or occurrences or in a series of acts or occurrences constituting an offense or offenses.

(d) Form. The indictment or information need not contain a formal commencement or conclusion. The return of an indictment shall be signed by the foreman of the grand jury, and the information shall be signed by the Commonwealth's attorney.

Source: Former Rule 3A:7.

Comment: With respect to former Rule 3A:7, the [1984] amendment deletes the first two sentences of subsection (a), and adds to subsection (a) the sentence beginning "The indictment or information, in describing the offense charged" and ending "prescribes the punishment for the offense."

Cross-reference: As to the criminal practice and procedure in the general district courts regarding joinder of offenses, see Rule 7C:4.

[Cross-reference added effective July 1, 1989; amended effective January 1, 1994.]

RULE 3A:7. CAPIAS OR SUMMONS UPON INDICTMENT OR INFORMATION

(a) Form.

(1) *Capias.* The form of the capias shall be the same as that provided for a warrant except that it shall be signed by the clerk and shall state that an indictment or information has been filed against the accused.

(2) *Summons.* The summons shall be in the same form as the capias except that it shall summons the accused to appear before the court at a stated time and place.

(b) Execution and Return.

(1) *Execution.* The capias shall be executed as provided in Rule 3A:4(c).

(2) *Return.* The officer executing a capias or summons shall endorse the date of execution thereon and make return thereof to the court that issued the capias or summons. At the request of the Commonwealth's attorney made at any time while the indictment or information is pending, a capias returned unexecuted and not cancelled or a summons returned unexecuted or a duplicate thereof may be delivered by the clerk to any authorized person for execution.

Source: Former Rule 3A:9.

Comment: With respect to former Rule 3A:9, the [1984] amendment deletes subsection (a) in its entirety, redesignates former subsection (b) as subsection (a), deletes the reference to Rule 3A:4(b)(1) in, and deletes the last two sentences of former subdivision (c)(1), changes the reference to Rule 3A:4(d) in former subdivision (c)(1) to Rule 3A:4(c), and redesignates former subsection (c) as subsection (b).

RULE 3A:8. PLEAS

(a) Pleas by a Corporation. A corporation, acting by counsel or through an agent, may enter the same pleas as an individual.

(b) Determining Voluntariness of Pleas of Guilty or Nolo Contendere.

(1) A circuit court shall not accept a plea of guilty or nolo contendere to a felony charge without first determining that the plea is made voluntarily with an understanding of the nature of the charge and the consequences of the plea.

(2) A circuit court shall not accept a plea of guilty or nolo contendere to a misdemeanor charge except in compliance with Rule 7C:6.

(c) Plea Agreement Procedure.

(1) The attorney for the Commonwealth and the attorney for the defendant or the defendant when acting pro se may engage in discussions with a view toward reaching an agreement that, upon entry by the defendant of a plea of guilty, or a plea of nolo contendere, to a charged offense, or to a lesser or related offense, the attorney for the Commonwealth will do any of the following:

(A) Move for nolle prosequi or dismissal of other charges;

(B) Make a recommendation, or agree not to oppose the defendant's request, for a particular sentence, with the understanding that such recommendation or request shall not be binding on the court;

(C) Agree that a specific sentence is the appropriate disposition of the case.

In any such discussions under this Rule, the court shall not participate.

(2) If a plea agreement has been reached by the parties, it shall, in every felony case, be reduced to writing, signed by the attorney for the Commonwealth, the defendant, and, in every case, his attorney, if any, and presented to the court. The court shall require the disclosure of the agreement in open court or, upon a showing of good cause, in camera, at the time the plea is offered. If the agreement is of the type specified in subdivision (c)(1)(A) or (C), the court may accept or reject the agreement, or may defer its decision as to the acceptance or rejection until there has been an opportunity to consider a presentence report. If the agreement is of the type specified in subdivision (c)(1)(B), the court shall advise the defendant that, if the court does not accept the recommendation or request, the defendant nevertheless has no right to withdraw his plea, unless the Commonwealth fails to perform its part of the agreement. In that event, the defendant shall have the right to withdraw his plea.

(3) If the court accepts the plea agreement, the court shall inform the defendant that it will embody in its judgment and sentence the disposition provided for in the agreement.

(4) If the agreement is of the type specified in subdivision (c)(1)(A) or (C) and if the court rejects the plea agreement, the court shall inform the parties of this fact, and advise the defendant personally in open court or, on a showing of good cause, in camera, that the court will not accept the plea agreement. Thereupon, neither party shall be bound by the plea agreement. The defendant shall have the right to withdraw his plea of guilty or plea of nolo contendere and the court shall advise the defendant that, if he does not withdraw his plea, the disposition of the case may be less favorable to him than that contemplated by the plea agreement; and the court shall further advise the defendant that, if he chooses to withdraw his plea of guilty or of nolo contendere, his case will be heard by another judge, unless the parties agree otherwise.

(5) Upon rejecting a plea agreement, a judge shall immediately recuse himself from any further proceedings on the same matter unless the parties agree otherwise.

(6) Except as otherwise provided by law, evidence of a plea of guilty later withdrawn, or a plea of nolo contendere! or of an offer to plead guilty or nolo contendere to the crime charged, or any other crime, or of statements made in connection with and relevant to any of the foregoing pleas or offers, is not admissible in the case-in-chief in any civil or criminal proceeding against the person who made the plea or offer. But evidence of a statement made in connection with and relevant to a plea of guilty, later withdrawn, a plea of nolo contendere, or any offer to plead guilty or nolo contendere to the crime charged or to any other crime, is admissible in any criminal proceeding for perjury or false statement, if the statement was made by the defendant under oath and on the record. In the event that a plea of guilty or a plea of nolo contendere is withdrawn in accordance with this Rule, the judge having received the plea shall take no further part in the trial of the case, unless the parties agree otherwise.

[Amended effective August 1, 1985; January 1, 2001; June 1, 2005; July 1, 2014.]

Source: Former Rule 3A:11.

Comment: With respect to former Rule 3A:11, the [1984] amendment deletes former subsections (a) and (b), adds a new subsection (a) regarding pleas by a corporation, redesignates former subsection (c) as subsection (b), and redesignates former subsection (d) as subsection (c) and changes the reference to a "court of record" in former subsection (c) to a "circuit court."

§ 19.2–153 was amended by Ch. 253 of the Acts of 1985.

Cross-reference: As to the criminal practice and procedure in the general district courts, see Rule 7C:6.

[Cross-reference added effective July 1, 1989.]

RULE 3A:9. PLEADINGS AND MOTIONS FOR TRIAL; DEFENSES AND OBJECTIONS

(a) Pleadings and Motions. Pleadings in a criminal proceeding shall be the indictment, information, warrant or summons on which the accused is to be tried and the plea of not guilty, guilty or nolo contendere. Defenses and objections made before trial that heretofore could have been made by other pleas or by demurrers and motions to quash shall be made only by motion to dismiss or to grant appropriate relief, as provided in these Rules.

(b) The Motion Raising Defenses and Objections.

(1) *Defenses and Objections That Must Be Raised Before Trial.* Defenses and objections based on defects in the institution of the prosecution or in the written charge upon which the accused is to be tried, other than that it fails to show jurisdiction in the court or to charge an offense, must be raised by motion made within the time prescribed by paragraph (c) of this Rule. The motion shall include all such defenses and objections then available to the accused. Failure to present any such defense or objection as herein provided shall constitute a waiver thereof. Lack of jurisdiction or the failure of the written charge upon which the accused is to be tried to state an offense shall be noticed by the court at any time during the pendency of the proceeding.

(2) *Defenses and Objections That May Be Raised Before Trial.* In addition to the defenses and objections specified in subparagraph (b)(1) of this Rule, any defense or objection that is capable of determination without the trial of the general issue may be raised by motion before trial. Failure to present any such defense or objection before the jury returns a verdict or the court finds the defendant guilty shall constitute a waiver thereof.

(3) *Form of Motion.* Any motion made before trial shall be in writing if made in a circuit court, unless the court for good cause shown permits an oral motion. A motion shall state with particularity the ground or grounds on which it is based.

(4) *Hearing on Motion.* A motion before trial raising defenses or objections shall be determined before the trial unless the court orders that it be deferred for determination at the trial of the general issue. An issue of fact shall be heard and determined by the court, unless a jury trial is required by constitution or statute.

(5) *Effect of Determination.* If a motion is determined adversely to the accused, his plea shall stand or he may plead over or, if the accused has not previously pleaded, he shall be permitted to plead. The motion need not be renewed if the accused properly saves the point for the purpose of appeal when the court first determines the motion.

(c) Time of Filing Notice or Making Motion. A motion referred to in subparagraph (b)(1) shall be filed or made before a plea is entered and, in a circuit court, at least 7 days before the day fixed for trial, or, if the motion raises speedy trial or Double Jeopardy grounds as specified in Code § 19.2–266.2A(ii), at such time prior to trial as the grounds for the motion or objection shall arise, whichever occurs last. A copy of such motion shall, at the time of filing, be submitted to the judge of the circuit court who will hear the case, if known.

(d) Relief From Waiver. For good cause shown the court may grant relief from any waiver provided for in this Rule.

[Amended effective August 29, 2005; October 31, 2006; May 2, 2011.]

Source: Former Rule 3A:12.

Comment: With respect to former Rule 3A:12, the [1984] amendment deletes the words "Notice of Insanity Defense" from the title of the Rule, deletes subsection (b), redesignates former subsections (c) and (d) and (e) as subsections (b) and (c) and (d), respectively, changes the references to a "court of record" in former subdivision (c)(3) and former subsection (d) to a "circuit court," and adds the language beginning "and a copy of such motion shall, at the time of filing" at the end of former subsection (d).

RULE 3A:10. TRIAL TOGETHER OF MORE THAN ONE ACCUSED OR MORE THAN ONE OFFENSE

(a) More Than One Accused—Joinder of Defendants. On motion of the Commonwealth, for good cause shown, the court shall order persons charged with participating in contemporaneous and related acts or occurrences or in a series of acts or occurrences constituting an offense or offenses to be tried jointly unless such joint trial would constitute prejudice to a defendant.

(b) More Than One Accused—Severance of Defendants. If the court finds that a joint trial would constitute prejudice to a defendant, the court shall order severance as to that defendant or provide such other relief as justice requires.

(c) An Accused Charged With More Than One Offense. The court may direct that an accused be tried at one time for all offenses then pending against him, if justice does not require separate trials and (i) the offenses meet the requirements of Rule 3A:6(b) or (ii) the accused and the Commonwealth's attorney consent thereto.

[Amended effective May 2, 2011.]

Source: Former Rule 3A:13.

Cross-reference: As to the criminal practice and procedure in the general district courts, see Rule 7C:4.

[Cross-reference added effective July 1, 1989; amended effective January 1, 1994.]

RULE 3A:11. DISCOVERY AND INSPECTION

(a) Application of Rule. This Rule applies to any prosecution for a felony in a circuit court and to any misdemeanor brought on direct indictment.

(b) Discovery by the Accused.

(1) Upon written motion of an accused a court shall order the Commonwealth's attorney to permit the accused to inspect and copy or photograph any relevant (i) written or recorded statements or confessions made by the accused, or copies thereof, or the substance of any oral statements or confessions made by the ac-

cused to any law enforcement officer, the existence of which is known to the attorney for the Commonwealth, and (ii) written reports of autopsies, ballistic tests, fingerprint analyses, handwriting analyses, blood, urine and breath tests, other scientific reports, and written reports of a physical or mental examination of the accused or the alleged victim made in connection with the particular case, or copies thereof, that are known by the Commonwealth's attorney to be within the possession, custody or control of the Commonwealth.

(2) Upon written motion of an accused a court shall order the Commonwealth's attorney to permit the accused to inspect and copy or photograph designated books, papers, documents, tangible objects, buildings or places, or copies or portions thereof, that are within the possession, custody, or control of the Commonwealth, upon a showing that the items sought may be material to the preparation of his defense and that the request is reasonable. This subparagraph does not authorize the discovery or inspection of statements made by Commonwealth witnesses or prospective Commonwealth witnesses to agents of the Commonwealth or of reports, memoranda or other internal Commonwealth documents made by agents in connection with the investigation or prosecution of the case, except as provided in clause (ii) of subparagraph (b)(1) of this Rule.

(c) Discovery by the Commonwealth. If the court grants relief sought by the accused under clause (ii) of subparagraph (b)(1) or under subparagraph (b)(2) of this Rule, it shall, upon motion of the Commonwealth, condition its order by requiring that:

(1) The accused shall permit the Commonwealth within a reasonable time but not less than ten (10) days before trial or sentencing, as the case may be, to inspect, copy or photograph any written reports of autopsy examinations, ballistic tests, fingerprint, blood, urine and breath analyses, and other scientific tests that may be within the accused's possession, custody or control and which the defense intends to proffer or introduce into evidence at trial or sentencing.

(2) The accused disclose whether he intends to introduce evidence to establish an alibi and, if so, that the accused disclose the place at which he claims to have been at the time of the commission of the alleged offense.

(3) If the accused intends to rely upon the defense of insanity or feeblemindedness, the accused shall permit the Commonwealth to inspect, copy or photograph any written reports of physical or mental examination of the accused made in connection with the particular case, provided, however, that no statement made by the accused in the course of an examination provided for by this Rule shall be used by the Commonwealth in its case-in-chief, whether the examination shall be with or without the consent of the accused.

(d) Time of Motion. A motion by the accused under this Rule must be made at least 10 days before the day fixed for trial. The motion shall include all relief sought under this Rule. A subsequent motion may be made only upon a showing of cause why such motion would be in the interest of justice.

(e) Time, Place and Manner of Discovery and Inspection. An order granting relief under this Rule shall specify the time, place and manner of making the discovery and inspection permitted and may prescribe such terms and conditions as are just.

(f) Protective Order. Upon a sufficient showing the court may at any time order that the discovery or inspection be denied, restricted or deferred, or make such other order as is appropriate. Upon motion by the Commonwealth the court may permit the Commonwealth to make such showing, in whole or in part, in the form of a written statement to be inspected by the court in camera. If the court denies discovery or inspection following a showing in camera, the entire text of the Commonwealth's statement shall be sealed and preserved in the records of the court to be made available to the appellate court in the event of an appeal by the accused.

(g) Continuing Duty to Disclose; Failure to Comply. If, after disposition of a motion filed under this Rule, and before or during trial, counsel or a party discovers additional material previously requested or falling within the scope of an order previously entered, that is subject to discovery or inspection under this Rule, he shall promptly notify the other party or his counsel or the court of the existence of the additional material. If at any time during the course of the proceedings, it is brought to the attention of the court that a party has failed to comply with this Rule or with an order issued pursuant to this Rule, the court shall order such party to permit the discovery or inspection of materials not previously disclosed, and may grant such other relief as it may deem appropriate.

[Amended effective April 1, 2004.]

Source: Former Rule 3A:14.

Comment: With respect to former Rule 3A:14, the [1984] amendment changes the reference to a "court of record" in subsection (a) to a "circuit court," and substantially rewrites subdivision (c)(1) to permit discovery by the Commonwealth of scientific reports that may be in the possession of the accused and which the defense intends to introduce into evidence at trial or at sentencing.

Cross references. As to criminal practice and procedure in the general district courts, see Rule 7C:5. As to discovery required by attorney for the Commonwealth in misdemeanors in circuit courts, see Va. Code § 19.2–265.4A and Rule 7C:5.

[Cross-reference added effective July 1, 1989; amended effective September 30, 2004.]

RULE 3A:12. SUBPOENA

(a) For Attendance of Witnesses. A subpoena for the attendance of a witness to testify before a court not of record shall be issued by the judge, clerk, magistrate, Commonwealth's Attorney or by the attorney for the defendant. A subpoena for the attendance of a witness to testify before a circuit court or a grand jury shall be issued by the clerk or Commonwealth's Attorney and, for the attendance of a witness to testify before a circuit court, by the attorney for the defendant as well. The subpoena shall (i) be directed to an appropriate officer or officers, (ii) name the witness to be summoned, (iii) state the name of the court and the title, if any, of the proceeding, (iv) command the officer to summon the witness to appear at the time and place specified in the subpoena for the purpose of giving testimony, and (v) state on whose application the subpoena was issued.

No subpoena or subpoena duces tecum shall be issued in any criminal case or proceeding, including any proceeding before any grand jury, which subpoena or subpoena duces tecum is (i) directed to a member of the bar of this Commonwealth or any other jurisdiction, and (ii) compels production or testimony concerning any present or former client of the member of the bar, unless the subpoena request has been approved in all specifics, in advance, by a judge of the circuit court wherein the subpoena is requested after reasonable notice to the attorney who is the subject of the proposed subpoena. The proceedings for approval may be conducted in camera, in the judge's discretion, and the judge may seal such proceedings. Such subpoena request shall be made by the Commonwealth's attorney for the jurisdiction involved, either on motion of the Commonwealth's attorney or upon request to the Commonwealth's attorney by the foreman of any grand jury.

(b) For Production of Documentary Evidence and of Objects Before a Circuit Court. Upon notice to the adverse party and on affidavit by the party applying for the subpoena that the requested writings or objects are material to the proceedings and are in the possession of a person not a party to the action, the judge or the clerk may issue a subpoena duces tecum for the production of writings or objects described in the subpoena. Such subpoena shall command either (1) that the person to whom it is addressed shall appear with the items described either before the court or the clerk or (2) that such person shall deliver the items described to the clerk. The subpoena may direct that the writing or object be produced at a time before the trial or before the time when it is to be offered in evidence.

Any subpoenaed writings and objects, regardless by whom requested, shall be available for examination and review by all parties and counsel. Subpoenaed writings or objects shall be received by the clerk and shall not be open for examination and review except by the parties and counsel unless otherwise directed by the court. The clerk shall adopt procedures to ensure compliance with this paragraph.

Where subpoenaed writings and objects are of such nature or content that disclosure to other parties would be unduly prejudicial, the court, upon written motion and notice to all parties, may grant such relief as it deems appropriate, including limiting disclosure, removal and copying.

If a subpoena requires the production of information that is stored in an electronic format, the person to whom it is addressed shall produce a tangible copy of the information. If a tangible copy cannot be reasonably produced, the subpoenaed person shall permit the parties to review the information on a computer or by electronic means during normal business hours, provided that the information can be accessed and isolated. If a tangible copy cannot reasonably be produced and the information is commingled with information other than that requested in the subpoena and cannot reasonably be isolated, the person to whom the subpoena is addressed may file a motion for a protective order or motion to quash.

(c) Service and Return. A subpoena may be executed anywhere in the State by an officer authorized by law to execute the subpoena in the place where it is executed. The officer executing a subpoena shall make return thereof to the court named in the subpoena.

(d) Contempt. Failure by any person without adequate excuse to obey a subpoena served upon him may be deemed a contempt of the court to which the subpoena is returnable.

(e) Recognizance of a Witness. If it appears that the testimony of a person is material in any criminal proceeding, a judicial officer may require him to give a recognizance for his appearance.

(f) Photocopying of Subpoenaed Documents. Subject to the provisions of subsection (b), removal and photocopying of subpoenaed documents by any party or counsel shall be permitted. The court shall direct a procedure for removal, photocopying and return of such documents.

[Amended effective September 1, 1987; September 1, 1990; July 1, 2000; January 1, 2003; July 1, 2008.]

Source: Former Rules 3A:15 and 3A:29(d).

Comment: With respect to Former Rule 3A:15, the [1984] amendment adds the word "magistrate" after the word "clerk" and before the words "or Commonwealth's attorney" in subsection (a), and adds the words "Before a Circuit Court" to the title of subsection (b).

The addition to subsection (a) conforms the Rule to § 19.2–45(4). The addition to subsection (b) is necessary because § 16.1–89 provides a different scheme for production of documentary evidence and of objects in general district court.

RULE 3A:13. TRIAL BY JURY OR BY COURT

(a) Right to Jury; Duty of Court in Nonjury Trial. The accused is entitled to a trial by jury only in a circuit court on a plea of not guilty.

(b) Waiver of Jury in Circuit Court. If an accused who has pleaded not guilty in a circuit court consents to trial without a jury, the court may, with the concurrence of the Commonwealth's attorney, try the case without a jury. The court shall determine before trial that the accused's consent was voluntarily and intelligently given, and his consent and the concurrence of the court and the Commonwealth's attorney shall be entered of record.

Source: Former Rule 3A:19.

Comment: With respect to former Rule 3A:19, the [1984] amendment deletes the second sentence of subsection (a), deletes the third sentence of subsection (b) and deletes subsection (c) and (d), and changes the former Rule's references to a "court of record" to a "circuit court."

RULE 3A:14. TRIAL JURORS

(a) Examination. After the prospective jurors are sworn on the voir dire, the court shall question them individually or collectively to determine whether anyone:

(1) Is related by blood, adoption, or marriage to the accused or to a person against whom the alleged offense was committed;

(2) Is an officer, director, agent or employee of the accused;

(3) Has any interest in the trial or the outcome of the case;

(4) Has acquired any information about the alleged offense or the accused from the news media or other sources and, if so, whether such information would affect his impartiality in the case;

(5) Has expressed or formed any opinion as to the guilt or innocence of the accused;

(6) Has a bias or prejudice against the Commonwealth or the accused; or

(7) Has any reason to believe the juror might not give a fair and impartial trial to the Commonwealth and the accused based solely on the law and the evidence.

Thereafter, the court, and counsel as of right, may examine on oath any prospective juror and ask any questions relevant to the qualifications as an impartial juror. A party objecting to a juror may introduce competent evidence in support of the objection.

(b) Challenge for Cause. The court, on its own motion or following a challenge for cause, may excuse a prospective juror if it appears the juror is not qualified, and another shall be drawn or called and placed in the juror's stead for the trial of that case.

[Amended effective January 1, 2013.]

Source: Former Rule 3A:20.

Comment: With respect to former Rule 3A:20, the [1984] amendment substitutes the word "and" for the word "or" between the words "court" and "counsel" in the second paragraph of subsection (a)(7), substitutes the words "as of right" for the words "with permission of the court," substitutes the word "and" for the words "may ask" in the same subsection, and deletes subsections (c), (d) and (e).

RULE 3A:14.1. CONFIDENTIALITY OF JUROR PERSONAL INFORMATION

(a) Motion for Order Regulating Disclosure of Jurors' Personal Information. As provided in Code § 19.2-263.3, on motion of any party or its own motion, and only upon a finding of good cause sufficient to warrant departure from the norm of open proceedings, the court may issue an order which may include provisions:

(1) regulating the disclosure of the personal information of jurors or prospective jurors in a criminal trial. The court may limit or preclude dissemination of such information to particular persons, but in no event shall such information be denied to counsel for either party; and/or

(2) requiring that during the course of the trial, counsel for the parties, and the jurors themselves, shall refer to jurors by number and not by name.

Under this Rule, a finding of "good cause" includes, but is not limited to, a determination by the court in a particular case that if personal information of jurors or prospective jurors is disclosed there is a reasonable possibility of bribery, tampering, physical injury, harassment, intimidation of a juror, or any other material interference with the proper discharge of the jury's functions, such as a reasonably perceived threat to the jury's safety, well-being, or capacity to properly focus upon and perform its trial and deliberative duties.

(b) Modification of Order. An order under this Rule regulating the disclosure of personal information of the jurors in a criminal case may be modified by the court in the exercise of its discretion and for good cause shown, and such information may be disseminated to a person having a legitimate interest or need for the information, with such restrictions upon its use and further dissemination as may be deemed appropriate by the court.

(c) Personal Information. For purposes of this Rule, "personal information" means any information collected by the court, clerk, or jury commissioner at any time, including but not limited to, a juror's name, age, occupation, home and business addresses, telephone numbers, email addresses, and any other identifying information that would assist another in locating or contacting the juror.

[Adopted effective May 2, 2011.]

RULE 3A:15. MOTION TO STRIKE OR TO SET ASIDE VERDICT; JUDGMENT OF ACQUITTAL OR NEW TRIAL

(a) Motion to Strike Evidence. After the Commonwealth has rested its case or at the conclusion of all the evidence, the court on motion of the accused may strike the Commonwealth's evidence if the evidence is insufficient as a matter of law to sustain a conviction. If the court overrules a motion to strike the evidence and there is a hung jury, the accused may renew the motion within the time specified in Rule 1:11 and the court may take the action authorized by the Rule.

(b) Motion to Set Aside Verdict. If the jury returns a verdict of guilty, the court may, on motion of the accused made not later than 21 days after entry of a final order, set aside the verdict for error committed during the trial or if the evidence is insufficient as a matter of law to sustain a conviction.

(c) Judgment of Acquittal or New Trial. The court shall enter a judgment of acquittal if it strikes the evidence or sets aside the verdict because the evidence is insufficient as a matter of law to sustain a conviction. The court shall grant a new trial if it sets aside the verdict for any other reason.

Source: Former Rule 3A:22.

RULE 3A:16. INSTRUCTIONS

(a) Giving of Instructions. In a felony case, the instructions shall be reduced to writing. In all cases the court shall instruct the jury before arguments of counsel to the jury.

(b) Proposed Instructions. If directed by the court the parties shall submit proposed instructions to the court at such reasonable time before or during the trial as the court may specify and, whether or not proposed instructions have been submitted earlier, the parties may submit proposed instructions at the conclusion of all the evidence.

(c) Objections. Before instructing the jury, the court shall advise counsel of the instructions to be given and shall give counsel the opportunity to make objections thereto. Objections shall be made out of the presence of the jury, and before the court instructs the jury unless the court grants leave to make objections at a later time.

(d) Alternative Forms of Verdicts; Separate Verdicts. The court may submit alternate forms of verdicts to the jury. The jury shall be instructed to return a separate verdict on each count of an indictment or presentment.

Source: Former Rule 3A:23.

RULE 3A:17. JURY VERDICTS

(a) Return. In all criminal prosecutions, the verdict shall be unanimous, in writing and signed by the foreman, and returned by the jury in open court.

(b) Several Accused. If there are two or more accused, the jury may return a verdict as to any of them as to whom it can agree.

(c) Conviction of Lesser Offense. The accused may be found not guilty of an offense charged but guilty of any offense, or of an attempt to commit any offense, that is substantially charged or necessarily included in the charge against the accused. When the offense charged is a felony, the accused may be found not guilty thereof, but guilty of being an accessory after the fact to that felony.

(d) Poll of Jury. When a verdict is returned, the jury shall be polled individually at the request of any party or upon the court's own motion. If upon the poll, all jurors do not agree, the jury may be directed to retire for further deliberations or may be discharged.

Source: Former Rule 3A:24.

RULE 3A:17.1. PROCEEDINGS IN BIFURCATED JURY TRIALS OF NON–CAPITAL FELONIES AND CLASS 1 MISDEMEANORS

(a) Application. This Rule applies in cases of trial by jury upon a finding that the defendant is guilty of a non-capital felony or a Class 1 misdemeanor.

(b) Bifurcated Proceedings. In any jury trial in which the jury returns a verdict of guilty to one or more non-capital felony offenses, or Class 1 misdemeanor a separate proceeding limited to the ascertainment of punishment shall be held as soon as practicable before the same jury.

(c) Instruction at Guilt Phase. At the conclusion of all of the evidence in the guilt phase of the trial, the court shall instruct the jury as to punishment with respect to any Class 2, 3 or 4 misdemeanor being tried in the same proceeding or any lesser-included Class 2, 3 or 4 misdemeanor of any charged felony offense which may be properly considered by the jury. The jury shall not be instructed until the punishment phase with reference to the punishment for any charged or lesser-included felony offense or Class 1 misdemeanor.

(d) Opening Statements at Penalty Phase. Both the Commonwealth and the defense shall be entitled if they choose, to make an opening statement prior to the presentation of any evidence to the jury relevant to the penalty to be imposed. The Commonwealth shall give its statement first.

(e) Presentation of Evidence at Penalty Phase. If the jury convicts the defendant of one or more non-capital felony offenses, or a Class 1 misdemeanor the penalty phase shall proceed in the following order:

(1) The Commonwealth may present any victim impact testimony pursuant to § 19.2–295.3 and shall present the defendant's prior criminal history, including prior convictions and the punishments imposed, by certified, attested, or exemplified copies of the final order(s) as provided by law. As a prerequisite to the introduction of such evidence, the Commonwealth shall have advised the defense, in accord with the requirements of law, of its intention to introduce such evidence.

(2) The defense may introduce relevant admissible evidence related to punishment. The defense shall have the opportunity to present such evidence irrespective of whether or not the Commonwealth presents evidence of previous criminal history.

(3) The Commonwealth may introduce relevant admissible evidence related to punishment in rebuttal.

(4) The defense may introduce relevant, admissible evidence related to punishment in rebuttal.

(f) Closing Arguments at Penalty Phase. Both the Commonwealth and defense shall be entitled to make a closing argument on the subject of punishment if they elect to do so. The Commonwealth shall be given the opportunity to argue first, followed by the defense. Rebuttal argument may be made by the Commonwealth.

(g) Change of Plea. The accused may enter a plea of guilty to the whole of the indictment at any time until the jury returns a verdict on the issue of the defendant's guilt or innocence.

(h) Non–Unanimous Jury at the Penalty Phase. Should the jury fail to reach unanimous agreement as to punishment on any charge for which it returned a verdict of guilty, the court shall impanel a different jury to ascertain punishment, unless the defendant, the attorney for the Commonwealth and the court agree that the court shall fix punishment in the manner provided in Section 19.2–257, for the offense upon which the jury unanimously returned a verdict of guilty.

[Adopted effective February 15, 1998. Amended effective January 1, 2003; July 1, 2008; November 1, 2012.]

RULE 3A:18. DEATH PENALTY

The trial of capital cases shall proceed in accordance with the provisions of Article 4.1 of Chapter 15 of Title 19.2 and, except to the extent conflicting therewith, the provisions of this Part Three A shall be applicable thereto.

Except for good cause shown, the separate proceeding provided for in Section 19.2–264.3 C shall commence as if it were a continuation of the original trial and continue from day to day until concluded.

Source: Former Rule 3A:25A.

RULE 3A:19. APPEALS

(a) Appeal From Conviction in a Circuit Court. See Part Five of these Rules.

(b) Appeal From Conviction in a Juvenile and Domestic Relations District Court. The accused or his counsel shall advise the judge or clerk of the juvenile and domestic relations district court, within 10 days after conviction, of his intention to appeal. The appeal shall be noted on the warrant or summons and, if the accused does not withdraw his appeal before the expiration of the 10–day period, the papers shall be filed with the circuit court at the end of such period. Paying a fine or beginning to serve a sentence does not impair the right to appeal.

[Amended effective July 1, 1989.]

Source: Former Rule 3A:26.

Comment: With respect to former Rule 3A:26, the [1984] amendment changes the reference to a "Court of Record" in the title of subsection (a) to a "Circuit Court," changes the references to a "Court Not of Record" in the title and in the first sentence of subsection (b) to a "District Court," deletes the portion of the first sentence of subdivision (b)(1) beginning "Upon conviction in a court not of record" and ending with "provided," adds the word "shall" before the word "advises" in former subdivision (b)(1), and deletes subdivisions (b)(2) and (b)(3).

Cross-reference: As to the practice and procedure in the general district courts, see Rule 7A:13.

RULE 3A:20. TIME

(a) Extension. When under this Part Three A an act is required or allowed to be done at or within a specified time, the court for cause shown may at any time in its discretion (1) with or without motion or notice, order the period extended if request therefor is made before the expiration of the period originally prescribed or as extended by a previous order, or (2) upon motion made after the expiration of the specified period, permit the act to be done if the failure to act was the result of excusable neglect; but the court may not extend the time for taking any action under Rules 3A:15 and 19; except to the extent and under the conditions stated in those Rules.

(b) Unaffected by Expiration of Term. The period of time specified in this Part Three A for taking any action is not affected or limited by the expiration of a term of court.

Source: Former Rule 3A:32.

Comment: With respect to former Rule 3A:32, the [1984] amendment changes the references to Rules 3A:22 and 26 to Rules 3A:15 and 19 respectively.

Cross-reference: As to the practice and procedure in the general district courts, see Rule 7A:2.

[Cross-reference added effective July 1, 1989.]

RULE 3A:21. SERVICE AND FILING OF PAPERS

(a) Copies of Written Motions to Be Furnished. All written motions and notices not required to be served as process shall be served otherwise on each counsel of record by delivering or mailing a copy to him on or before the day of filing. In any case where electronic service and filing is permitted under Rule 1:17, delivery of an electronic copy or digital image of a document shall satisfy this requirement. At the foot of such motions and notices shall be appended either acceptance of service or a certificate of counsel that copies were served as this Rule requires, showing the date of delivery or mailing.

(b) Filing. Motions, notices and other items required to be served shall be filed with the clerk.

[Amended effective May 2, 2011.]

Source: Former Rule 3A:33.

Cross-reference: As to the practice and procedure in the general district courts, see Rule 7A:10.

[Cross-reference added effective July 1, 1989.]

RULE 3A:22. FORMS

Forms 1 through 9 and 11 in the Appendix of Forms are illustrative and not mandatory; however, Form 10 requires substantial compliance.

[Amended effective January 1, 1997; February 28, 2006.]

Source: Former Rule 3A:35.

RULE 3A:23. ELECTRONIC FILING

In any circuit court which has established an electronic filing system for criminal cases pursuant to Rule 1:17:

(a) Any criminal proceeding may be designated as an Electronically Filed Case upon consent of the Commonwealth and all defendants in the case.

(b) Except where service and/or filing of an original paper document is expressly required by these rules, all pleadings, motions, notices and other instruments in an Electronically Filed Case shall be formatted, served and filed as specified in the requirements and procedures of Rule 1:17; provided, however, that when any document listed below is filed in the case, the filing party shall notify the clerk of court that the original document must be retained.

(1) Any pleading or affidavit required by statute or rule to be sworn, verified or certified as provided in Rule 1:17(e)(5).

(2) Any check or other negotiable instrument.

(3) Any handwritten statement, waiver, or consent by a defendant or witness in a criminal proceeding.

(4) Any form signed by a defendant in a criminal proceeding, including any typed statements or a guilty plea form.

(5) Any document that cannot be converted into an electronic document in such a way as to produce a clear and readable image.

[Adopted effective May 2, 2011.]

Source: Former Rule 3A:36.

RULE 3A:24. SPECIAL RULE APPLICABLE TO POST–CONVICTION PROCEEDINGS: CIRCUIT COURT ORDERS DENYING PETITIONS FOR WRITS OF HABEAS CORPUS

Any Order of a circuit court denying a petition for a writ of habeas corpus shall include findings of fact and conclusions of law as required by Code § 8.01–654(B)(5). The order shall identify the substance of the claims asserted in the petition, and state the specific reason for the denial of each claim. Any such order may adopt a trial court's written opinion explaining its decision or a transcribed explanation of the court's ruling from the bench; however, an order shall not deny the petition without explanation, or rely upon incorporation by reference of a pleading filed in the case.

[Adopted effective July 1, 2003.]

RULE 3A:25. SPECIAL RULE APPLICABLE TO POST–CONVICTION PROCEEDINGS: INMATE FILINGS IN THE TRIAL COURTS UNDER CODE § 8.01–654

In actions brought under Code § 8.01–654, filed by an inmate confined to an institution, a paper is timely filed if deposited in the institution's internal mail system, with first-class postage prepaid on or before the last day for filing. Timely filing of a paper by an inmate confined to an institution may be established by (1) an official stamp of the institution showing that the paper was deposited in the internal mail system on or before the last day for filing, (2) an official postmark dated on or before the last day for filing, or (3) a notarized statement signed by an official of the institution showing that the paper was deposited in the internal mail system on or before the last day for filing.

[Adopted effective September 1, 2004.]

APPENDIX OF FORMS

FORM 1. CRIMINAL COMPLAINT (RULE 3A:3)

CRIMINAL COMPLAINT RULES 3A:3 AND 7C:3
Commonwealth of Virginia

Print ALL information clearly:

[ ] General District Court
.... [ ] Juvenile and Domestic Relations District Court
CITY OR COUNTY

Under penalty of perjury, I, the undersigned Complainant swear or affirm that I have reason to believe that the Accused committed a criminal offense, on or about

.... in the [ ] City [ ] County [ ] Town
DATE OFFENSE OCCURRED

of ....

I base my belief on the following facts:

....
....
....
....
....
....

The statements above are true and accurate to the best of my knowledge and belief.

In making this complaint, I have read and fully understand the following:

- By swearing to these facts, I agree to appear in court and testify if a warrant or summons is issued.
- The charge in this warrant cannot be dismissed except by the court, even at my request.

....
NAME OF COMPLAINANT (LAST, FIRST, MIDDLE) (PRINT CLEARLY) SIGNATURE OF COMPLAINANT

Subscribed and sworn to before me this day.

....
DATE AND TIME [ ] CLERK [ ] MAGISTRATE [ ] JUDGE

FORM DC-311 10/97 PC

CRIMINAL COMPLAINT

ACCUSED: Name, Description, Address/Location

....
LAST NAME, FIRST NAME, MIDDLE NAME

....

....

COMPLETE DATA BELOW IF KNOWN

RACE	SEX	BORN			HT.		WGT.	EYES	HAIR
		MO.	DAY	YR	FT.	IN			

SSN

[Amended effective October 1997.]

FORM 2. STATEMENT OF WITNESS FOR ARREST WARRANT (RULE 3A:3)

Witness: (Name and address) ....

(County) (City) of ....

I, the undersigned witness, after being duly sworn, make oath that I have personal knowledge of the following facts: ....

....

____
(Signature of complainant and title, if any)

Subscribed and sworn to before me this day.

____________ ____________________________
(Date and time) (Signature and title).

FORM 3. SUMMONS (RULE 3A:4(b))

SUMMONS

COMMONWEALTH OF VIRGINIA Va. Code § 19.2-73; Rule 3A: 4

....
CITY OR COUNTY

[ ] General District Court [ ] Juvenile and Domestic Relations District Court

....
STREET ADDRESS OF COURT

[ ] Commonwealth of Virginia [ ] City [ ] County [ ] Town of ....

TO THE ACCUSED:

You are hereby commanded to appear before this Court on

.... to answer the charge that on or about ....,
DATE AND TIME OF HEARING DATE

within this [ ] Town of .... [ ] CITY [ ] COUNTY you did unlawfully

....

....

....

....

....

....

in violation of Section .... , [ ] Code of Virginia (OR)
[ ] Ordinances of this City, County or Town.

YOU MUST APPEAR in court at the time and place shown above and appear at all other times and places and before any court or judge to which this case may be rescheduled, continued, transferred or appealed

WARNING TO THE ACCUSED You may be tried and convicted in your absence if you fail to appear in response to this summons. Willful failure to appear for a misdemeanor charge is a separate offense.

I, the undersigned, have found probable cause to believe that the Accused committed the offense charged, based on the sworn statements of ...., Complainant.

.... ________________________________
DATE AND TIME ISSUED [ ] CLERK [ ] MAGISTRATE [ ] JUDGE

FORM DC-319 (MASTER, PAGE ONE OF TWO) 10/08

CASE NO.

ACCUSED:

....
LAST NAME, FIRST NAME, MIDDLE NAME

....
ADDRESS/LOCATION

....

To be completed upon service as Summons

Mailing address ☐ Same as above

☐ ....

....

RACE	SEX	BORN			HT.		WGT.	EYES	HAIR
		MO.	DAY	YR.	FT.	IN.			

SSN

DL# STATE

CLASS _____ MISDEMEANOR

☐ EXECUTED by delivering a true copy of this summons to the Accused in person today

☐ For legal entities other than individuals, service pursuant to Va. Code § 19.2-76.

☐ The Accused certified to me the above mailing address.

....
DATE AND TIME OF SERVICE

...., ARRESTING OFFICER

....
BADGE NO., AGENCY AND JURISDICTION

for ....
SHERIFF

Attorney for the Accused:

Short Offense Description (not a legal definition):

Offense Tracking Number:

FOR ADMINISTRATIVE USE ONLY
Virginia Crime Code.

S

Hearing Date/Time

____

____

____

____

____

____

____

SUMMONS

The Accused was this day:
[ ] tried in absence [ ] present

[ ] PROSECUTING ATTORNEY PRESENT (NAME)

[ ] DEFENDANT'S ATTORNEY PRESENT (NAME)

[ ] NO ATTORNEY [ ] ATTORNEY WAIVED
[ ] If convicted, no jail sentence will be imposed

[ ] INTERPRETER PRESENT

Plea of Accused:
[ ] not guilty [ ] Witnesses sworn
[ ] nolo contendere
[ ] guilty [ ] Plea voluntarily and intelligently entered after the defendant was apprised of his right against compulsory self-incrimination and his right to confront the witnesses against him.

[ ] Plea and Recommendation

And was TRIED and FOUND by me:
[ ] not guilty [ ] guilty as charged
[ ] guilty of ....
VCC ....
[ ] facts sufficient to find guilt but defer adjudication/disposition to .... (DATE AND TIME) and place accused on probation, §§ 4.1-305, 18.2-57.3, 18.2-251 or 19.2-303.2.
[ ] A separate order for First Offender is attached and incorporated in this order.
[ ] Costs imposed upon defendant.

.... DATE .... JUDGE

And was FOUND by me to be:
[ ] driving a commercial motor vehicle
[ ] carrying hazardous materials

[ ] I ORDER a nolle prosequi on prosecution's motion

[ ] I ORDER the charge dismissed [ ] with prejudice
[ ] conditioned upon payment of costs [ ] accord and satisfaction, § 19.2-151 [ ] compliance with law, § 46.2-104 or § 46.2-1157.
[ ] conditioned upon payment of costs and successful completion of traffic school, § 16.1-69.48:1.
[ ] under §§ 4.1-305, 18.2-57.3, 18.2-251 or 19.2-303.2.

FORM DC-319 (MASTER, PAGE TWO OF TWO) 01/10

I impose the following Disposition:
[ ] FINE [ ] CIVIL PENALTY of $ ....
with $ .... suspended
[ ] JAIL SENTENCE of ....
imposed, [ ] of which .... days mandatory minimum with .... suspended
for a period of ...., conditioned upon being of good behavior, keeping the peace, obeying this order and paying fines and costs.
Pursuant to § 53.1-187, credit is granted for pre-trial detention.
[ ] Serve jail sentence beginning ....
[ ] on weekends only
[ ] Work release [ ] authorized if eligible [ ] required
[ ] not authorized
[ ] Public work force [ ] authorized [ ] not authorized
[ ] on PROBATION for ....
[ ] VASAP [ ] local community-based probation agency
[ ] DRIVER'S LICENSE suspended for ....
[ ] Restricted Driver's License per attached order
[ ] Ignition Interlock for ....
[ ] RESTITUTION of $ ....
due by ....
payable to ....
with interest thereon from .... ([ ] DATE OF LOSS OR DAMAGE [ ] TODAY'S DATE)
[ ] as condition of suspended sentence
[ ] COMMUNITY SERVICE .... hours to be completed by ....
and supervised by ....
[ ] to be credited against fines and costs
[ ] Contact prohibited between defendant and victim/victim's family or household members
[ ] Reimburse Commonwealth for investigatory medical fees
[ ] Pay $50 fee to the Court for Trauma Center Fund
[ ] Other: ....

[ ] Bail on Appeal $ ....
[ ] Remanded for [ ] CCRE Report [ ] ....

DRIVER'S LICENSE/PRIVILEGE TO DRIVE IN VIRGINIA SUSPENDED EFFECTIVE IN 15 DAYS IF FINES, COSTS, FORFEITURES, PENALTIES OR RESTITUTION ARE NOT PAID. Va. Code § 46.2-395.

.... DATE .... JUDGE

Offense Tracking Number: ....

FINE

.... (LOCALITY) $ ....

COSTS

461	FIXED MISD FEE	
462	FIXED DRUG MISD FEE	
460	FIXED TRAFFIC INFRACTION FEE	
113	WITNESS FEE	
113	IGNITION INTERLOCK	
113	DUI FEE	
113		
120	CT. APPT. ATTY	
125	WEIGHING FEE	
133	BLOOD TEST FEE	
137	TIME TO PAY	
192	TRAUMA CENTER FEE	
223	LIQUIDATED DAMAGES	
228	COURTHOUSE CONSTRUCTION FEE	
234	JAIL ADMISSION FEE	
243	LOCAL TRAINING ACADEMY FEE	
244	COURTHOUSE SECURITY FEE	

OTHER (SPECIFY) ....

TOTAL $ ....

[ ] Stay of the proceedings pursuant to § 16.1-131.1

.... DATE .... JUDGE

[Amended effective February 1, 1992; February 1, 2000; December 1, 2008.]

FORM 4. INDICTMENTS (RULE 3A:6)

Murder

COMMONWEALTH OF VIRGINIA

.... Court

...................., 20 .....

The Grand Jury charges that:

On or about ...., 20 .... in the (County) (City) of ....

the accused ....
(Name of accused)

feloniously did kill and murder .... *
(Name of victim)

Va. Code §§ 18.2-31, 18.2-32, 19.2-221.

A True Bill.

....
(Foreman)

* Language charging other offenses follows.

Attempted Grand Larceny

On or about ...., 20 ..... in the (County) (City) of ....

the accused ....
(Name of accused)

feloniously attempted to steal property, namely ....
(Describe property)

having a value of ($5 or more from the person of ....)
(Name of victim)

($200 or more from the person of ....)
(Name of victim)

(firearm of any value) belonging to ....
(Name of victim)

Va. Code §§ 18.2-95 and 18.2-26.

Burglary (Common Law)

On or about ...., 20 ..... in the (County) (City) of ....

the accused ....
(Name of accused)

feloniously did break and enter in the nighttime

the dwelling house of ....
(Name of victim)

with intent to commit a (felony) (larceny) therein.

Va. Code § 18.2-89.

Statutory (Burglary, Murder, Rape, Robbery, Arson)

(Va. Code § 18.2-90)

On or about ...., 20 ..... in the (County) (City) of..

the accused ....
(Name of accused)

feloniously did (enter in the nighttime) (break and enter in the daytime)

(enter and conceal himself in the daytime)

.... , with intent to
(Place described in Va. Code § 18.2-90)

commit (murder)(rape)(robbery)(arson).

Va. Code § 18.2-90.

Statutory Burglary, Va. Code § 18.2-91

On or about ...., 20 ..... in the (County) (City) of...

the accused ....
(Name of accused)

feloniously did (enter in the nighttime) (break and enter in the daytime)

(enter and conceal himself in the daytime)

.... , with intent to
(Place described in Va. Code § 18.2-90)

commit (larceny) (...)

(Describe felony other than murder, rape, robbery or arson)

(assault and battery).

Va. Code § 18.2-91.

Driving While Intoxicated

On or about ...., 20 ..... in the (County) (City) of...

the accused ....
(Name of accused)

(feloniously and) unlawfully did operate a motor vehicle while under the influence of alcohol, narcotic drug, or other self-administered intoxicant or drug of whatever nature.

Va. Code § 18.2-266.

Forgery - Check

On or about ...., 20 ..... in the (County) (City) of..

the accused ....
(Name of accused)

feloniously forged with the intent to defraud a check of the following words

and figures:

...., 20 .....
(Bank) (Date)

Pay to the order of .... $ .... Dollars

(Endorsed ....)

Va. Code § 18.2-172.

Malicious or Unlawful Wounding

On or about ...., 20 ..... in the (County) (City) of ....

the accused ....
(Name of accused)

feloniously (maliciously) (unlawfully but not maliously) caused bodily injury

to ....
(Name of victim)

with intent to maim, disfigure, disable or kill.

Va. Code § 18.2-51.

Rape

On or about ...., 20 ..... in the (County) (City) of..

the accused ....
(Name of accused)

feloniously did rape ....
(Name of victim)

Va. Code § 18.2-61.

Rape (Statutory, of Female of Age 13 or 14)

On or about ...., 20 ..... in the (County) (City) of ....

the accused ....
(Name of accused)

feloniously had (sexual intercourse with) (carnal knowledge of)

....
(Name of victim)

age ....
(Age of victim at time of offense)

Va. Code § 18.2-63.

Robbery

On or about ...., 20 ..... in the (County) (City) of...

the accused ....
(Name of accused)

feloniously did rob ....
(Name of victim)

of ....
(Describe property)

Va. Code § 18.2-58.

Uttering - Check

On or about ...., 20 ..... in the (County) (City) of ....

the accused ....
(Name of accused)

feloniously uttered with the intent to defraud a forged check of the following

words and figures:

...., 20 .....
(Bank) (Date)

Pay to the order of .... $ .... Dollars

(Endorsed ....)

Va. Code § 18.2-172.

[Amended effective January 1, 2001.]

FORM 5. CAPIAS (RULE 3A:7)

.... Court

Accused: (Name, description, address/location) ....

TO: .... or any other authorized officer
(Designation of officer)

You are hereby commanded in the name of the Commonwealth to forthwith arrest the accused and to bring him (her) before this Court to answer a charge that he (she) committed an offense in the (County) (City) of ...., on or about ...., namely ....
(Describe offense)

.... as charged in an (indictment) (presentment) (information) dated ...., ...

....
(Date) (Clerk)

FORM 6. SUGGESTED QUESTIONS TO BE PUT BY THE COURT TO AN ACCUSED WHO HAS PLEADED GUILTY (RULE 3A:8)

Before accepting your plea of guilty. I will ask you certain questions. If you do not understand any question, please ask me to explain it to you.

1. (a) What is your full name? ....
   (b) What is your date of birth? ....
   (c) What was the last grade in school which you completed? ....
   (d) What other education have you received? ....

2. Are you the person charged in the (indictment) (presentment) (information) (warrant) with commission of the offense(s) of ....

3. Do you fully understand the charge(s) against you? .... Have you discussed the charge(s) and (its) (their) elements with your lawyer and do you understand what the Commonwealth must prove before you may be found guilty of (this) (these) charge(s)? ....

4. Have you had enough time to discuss with your lawyer any possible defenses which you may have to (this) (these) charge(s)? ....

5. Have you discussed with your lawyer whether you should plead not guilty or guilty? ....

6. After the discussion, did you decide for yourself that you should plead guilty? ....

7. Are you entering the plea of guilty freely and voluntarily? ....

8. Are you entering the plea of guilty because you are, in fact, guilty of the crime(s) charged? .... If the defendant answers "No,"

   (a) Have the Commonwealth summarize the evidence on the record.

   (b) Ask the defendant, "Are you pleading guilty because this is the Commonwealth's evidence, and you do not wish to take the risk that you will be found guilty beyond a reasonable doubt?" [

   (c) If the defendant answers "Yes," the court may, but need not, accept the plea; if the court accepts the plea, the court should note that there is substantial evidence against the defendant. Otherwise the court should not accept the plea. (See North Carolina v. Alford, 400 U.S. 25 (1970).]

9. Do you understand that, by pleading guilty, you are NOT entitled to a trial by jury? ....

10. Do you understand that, by pleading guilty, you waive your right not to incriminate yourself? ....

11. Do you understand that, by pleading guilty, you waive your right to confront and cross-examine your accusers? ....

12. Do you understand that, by pleading guilty, you waive your right to defend yourself? ....

13. [If the accused is in prison, on parole, or probation,] Do you understand that conviction may (affect your right to parole) (cause revocation of your parole/probation?)

14. [If the crime involves possession/distribution of drugs,] Have you discussed with your lawyer whether the defense of accommodation may apply in this case?

15. [If the accused may be sentenced under the habitual offender statute,] Have you discussed with your lawyer the possibility that there may be mitigating circumstances that permit this court not to impose the mandatory sentence?

16. Has anyone connected with your arrest and prosecution, such as the police or the Commonwealth's attorney, or any other person, in any manner threatened you or forced you to enter this plea of guilty? Have they made any promises concerning your plea of guilty?

17. Do you understand that the maximum punishment for this crime is ... years imprisonment and $ ... fine plus all court costs? (If a guilty plea involves more than one offense, substitute the following: Do you understand that if you are sentenced consecutively, the maximum punishment for these crimes is ... fine and $ ... plus all court costs? [If the crime has a mandatory punishment, also question accused on his understanding of the mandatory punishment.]

18. Are you entirely satisfied with the service (of the lawyer who was appointed to represent you) (of the lawyer representing you) in this matter? ....

19. Do you understand that, by pleading guilty, you may waive any right to appeal the decision of this court? [The judge may, but need not, inform the defendant that a guilty plea does not waive the right to appeal lack of jurisdiction or imposition of an impermissible sentence.]

20. [If a written guilty plea form is used,]
(a) Have you read the guilty plea form? ....
(b) Do you understand the guilty plea form? ....
(c) Are the statements in the guilty plea form true? ....

21. Have you entered into a plea agreement with the Commonwealth's attorney in this case? If the answer is in the affirmative, read or otherwise put the plea agreement into the record, then ask the following: Does it contain the full and complete agreement entered into among you, your lawyer, and the Commonwealth's attorney? Complete either (a) or (b), whichever is appropriate: (a) [To be asked if the Commonwealth's attorney has agreed that a particular sentence is appropriate.] Do you understand that:

(1) The court may accept the agreement, reject the agreement, or may defer any decision to either accept or reject until there has been an opportunity to consider a presentence report? ....

(2) If the court accepts the agreement, the court will include in its judgment and sentence the sentence provided for in the agreement? ....

(3) If the court rejects the agreement, you will not be bound by the agreement and you will be given an opportunity to withdraw your plea of guilty, and if you do, your trial may be conducted by another judge of this court? ....

(4) If you still plead guilty after the court rejects the plea agreement, the sentence in the case may be more severe than the disposition contained in the plea agreement? ....

(b) [To be used if the Commonwealth's attorney merely recommends, or agrees not to oppose a request for, a specific sentence.] Do you understand that this agreement only provides for the Commonwealth's attorney (to make a recommendation) (to agree not to oppose a request for) a particular sentence, that this recommendation or request is not binding on the court, and if the court does not accept the recommendation or does not go along with the request, you have no right to withdraw your plea of guilty unless the Commonwealth fails to perform its part of the agreement? Do you also understand that the sentence the court imposes may be more severe than the sentence (recommended) (requested)?

22. [If the defendant was a juvenile at the time of the offense,] Do you understand that if you were tried for this offense and found guilty, the court and not the jury would set the sentence? ....

23. Do you understand all of these questions? ....

24. Do you have any questions you wish to ask the court? ....

[Amended effective July 1, 1988; January 1, 1990.]

FORM 7. SUGGESTED QUESTIONS TO BE PUT BY THE COURT TO AN ACCUSED WHO HAS PLEADED NOT GUILTY (RULE 3A:8)

Before accepting your plea of not guilty, I will ask you certain questions. If you do not understand any question, please ask me to explain it to you.

1. What is your full name and what is your age? ______________________

2. Are you the person charged in the (indictment) (information) (warrant) with the commission of the offense(s)? ______________________

3. Do you fully understand the charge(s) against you? ______________________

4. Have you discussed the charge(s) with your lawyer? ______________________

5. Have you had enough time to discuss with your lawyer any possible defense you may have to (this) (these) charge(s)? ______________________

6. Have you given your lawyer the names of witnesses, and if so, are they present? ______________________

7. Are you entirely satisfied with the services of your lawyer? __________

8. Are you entering this plea of not guilty freely and voluntarily? __________

9. Are you ready for trial today? ______________________

10. Do you understand that you are entitled to a trial by jury, but that you can consent to trial by the judge without a jury? ______________________

Have you discussed with your lawyer the advisability of trial by a jury or by the judge without a jury? ______________________

Do you wish to be tried by a jury or by the judge without a jury? __________

11. Do you understand all of the questions I have asked you? __________

These questions were asked of the defendant in open court in the absence of a jury on ________, 20____

____

Signature of defendant

____

Signature of attorney representing defendant

FORM 8. SUBPOENA (RULE 3A:12(a))

.... Court

....

(Address of court)

TO: .... or any other authorized officer
(Designation of officer)

You are commanded to summon ....
(Name and address)

TO the person summoned:

You are commanded to appear in this Court on ...., 20....at ....a.m., to testify in the case of Commonwealth v. ....

This subpoena is issued on application of the (Commonwealth) (City) (County) (Town) (Defendant) (Juvenile) in the case of the Commonwealth v. ....

....

(Date) (Judge) (Clerk) (Commonwealth's Attorney)

FORM 9. SUBPOENA DUCES TECUM (RULE 3A:12(b))

.... Court

....
(Address of court)

TO: .... or any other authorized officer
(Designation of officer)

You are commanded to summon ....
(Name and address)

TO the person summoned:

[ ] You are commanded to appear in (this Court) (the Clerk's office of this Court) on ...., 20 .... at .... a.m./p.m., and to bring with you the following:

....

....

....

....

OR

[ ] You are commanded to deliver to the Clerk's office of this Court on or before ...., 20 .... at .... a.m./p.m. the following:

....

....

....

....

This subpoena is issued on application of the (Commonwealth) (City) (County) (Town) (Defendant) (Juvenile) in the case of the Commonwealth v. ....

....
(Date) (Judge) (Clerk)

[Amended effective September 1, 1990.]

FORM 10. CONTENTS OF SENTENCING ORDERS

(Pursuant to the provisions of Code § 19.2-307, all orders wherein an accused is sentenced for a criminal conviction shall conform substantially to the following form. In cases where no prior criminal conviction order has been entered of record, state the defendant's plea, the verdict or findings, the adjudication, whether or not the case was tried by a jury, and, if not, whether the consent of the accused was concurred in by the court and the attorney for the Commonwealth.)

SENTENCING ORDER

VIRGINIA: IN THE CIRCUIT COURT OF ....

FEDERAL INFORMATION PROCESSING STANDARDS CODE: ....

Hearing Date: ....

Judge: ....

COMMONWEALTH OF VIRGINIA

v.

...., DEFENDANT

This case came before the Court for sentencing of the defendant, who appeared in person with his attorney, ... The Commonwealth was represented by ....

On .... the defendant was found guilty of the following offenses:

CASE NUMBER	OFFENSE DESCRIPTION AND INDICATOR	OFFENSE DATE	VA. CODE SECTION	VIRGINIA CRIME CODE REFERENCE
....	....	....	....	....
....	....	....	....	....

The presentence report was considered and is ordered filed as a part of the record in this case in accordance with the provisions of Code § 19.2-299.

Pursuant to the provisions of Code § 19.2-298.01, the Court has considered and reviewed the applicable discretionary sentencing guidelines and the guidelines worksheets. The sentencing guidelines worksheets and the written explanation of any departure from the guidelines are ordered filed as a part of the record in this case.

Before pronouncing the sentence, the Court inquired if the defendant desired to make a statement and if the defendant desired to advance any reason why judgment should not be pronounced.

The Court SENTENCES the defendant to:

Incarceration with the Virginia Department of Corrections for the term of: .... for ...., and .... for .... The total sentence imposed is ....

This sentence shall run (concurrently/consecutively) with ....

The Court SUSPENDS .... of the .... sentence and .... of the .... sentence, for a period of ...., for a total suspension of ...., upon the following condition(s):

Good behavior. The defendant shall be of good behavior for ... from the defendant's release from confinement.

Supervised probation. .... of the sentence of incarceration is suspended. The defendant is placed on probation to commence .... under the supervision of a Probation Officer for .... or unless sooner released by the court or by the Probation Officer. The defendant shall comply with all the rules and requirements set by the Probation Officer. Probation shall include substance abuse counseling and/or testing as prescribed by the Probation Officer.

Community-based Corrections System Program pursuant to Virginia Code § 19.2-316.2 or 19.2-316.3. The defendant shall successfully complete the .... program. Successful program completion shall be followed by a period of intensive probation supervision of .... and followed by a period of supervised probation of (at least one year). (If applicable: The defendant shall remain in custody until program entry.)

Post-Incarceration supervision following felony conviction pursuant to Virginia Code § 18.2-10 and 19.2-295.2.

A. Post-Incarceration Supervised Probation: The court has imposed above a term of .... of incarceration and has suspended (at least 6 months) of the term of incarceration. The defendant is placed on supervised probation to commence upon release from incarceration for a period of (at least 6 months), unless released earlier by the court. The defendant shall comply with all the rules and requirements set by the Probation Officer.

OR

B. Post-Incarceration Post-release Supervision: In addition to the above sentence of incarceration, the court imposes an additional term of (not less than 6 months nor more than 3 years) of incarceration. This term is suspended and a period of post-release supervision of (not less than 6 months nor more than 3 years), which is to commence upon release from incarceration. The defendant shall comply with all the rules and requirements set by the Probation Officer.

Special Conditions. The defendant shall complete any substance abuse screening, assessment, testing and treatment as directed by the Probation Officer, as well as the following conditions:
....

Costs. The defendant shall pay costs of ....

Fine. A fine of $ .... for ....

Restitution. The defendant shall make restitution as follows: .... to ....

DNA and Fingerprints. The defendant shall provide a DNA sample and legible fingerprints as directed.

Credit for time served. The defendant shall be given credit for time spent in confinement while awaiting trial pursuant to Code § 53.1-187.

....
DATE

ENTER: ....
JUDGE

DEFENDANT IDENTIFICATION:

Name: ....

Alias: ....

SSN: .... DOB: .... Sex: ....

SENTENCING SUMMARY:

TOTAL INCARCERATION SENTENCE IMPOSED: ....

TOTAL SENTENCE SUSPENDED: ....

TOTAL SUPERVISED PROBATION TERM: ....

TOTAL POSTRELEASE TERM IMPOSED and SUSPENDED: ....

[Adopted effective January 1, 1997. Amended effective December 22, 2004; May 1, 2006.]

FORM 11. MISDEMEANOR PROCEEDINGS IN DISTRICT AND CIRCUIT COURTS (RULE 3A:8(b)(2); RULE 7C:6; AND RULE 8:18)

Suggested Questions to Be Asked When Taking Pleas of Guilty or Nolo Contendere

A. Pleas of Guilty or Nolo Contendere with Plea Agreements Requiring

Imposition of an Active or Suspended Sentence of Confinement in Jail

1. Do you understand the charge(s) against you?

2. When Defendant appears without counsel:

a) Do you understand you have the right to be represented by a lawyer?

b) Do you understand that if you do not have the financial ability to hire your own lawyer, and you want me to, I will have you interviewed to see if you qualify for court-appointed counsel and I will appoint an attorney to represent you if you qualify?

c) Do you want to hire an attorney to represent you, or be interviewed for court-appointed counsel or do you want to proceed today without a lawyer?

3. In Circuit Court:

a) Do you understand that you have the right to have your case heard by a jury?

b) Do you want your case to be heard by a judge without a jury or do you want a jury trial?

4. a) I understand that you have agreed to plead guilty (no contest) with the understanding that you will be sentenced to ______________________. Is that correct?

or

b) I understand that you have agreed to plead guilty (no contest) with the understanding that the prosecutor will recommend a sentence of

_______________. Do you understand that I do not have to accept the recommendation and that I can sentence you from ___________________ to _______________? (provide full sentence range allowed by law)

5. Have you been promised anything else to get you to plead guilty (no contest)?

6. Are you being forced or threatened into pleading guilty (no contest)?

7. Do you understand that by pleading guilty (no contest) you are giving up your right to a trial including the right to hear from and question the witnesses against you and the right to avoid being required to give evidence against yourself?

8. Do you have any questions before I accept your plea(s) of guilty (no contest)?

B. Pleas of Guilty or Nolo Contendere Without a Plea Agreement

1. Do you understand the charge(s) against you?

2. When Defendant appears without counsel:

a) Do you understand you have the right to be represented by a lawyer?

b) Do you understand that if you do not have the financial ability to hire your own lawyer, and you want me to, I will have you interviewed to see if you qualify for court-appointed counsel and I will appoint an attorney to represent you if you qualify?

c) Do you want to hire an attorney to represent you, or be interviewed for court-appointed counsel or do you want to proceed today without a lawyer?

3. In Circuit Court:

a) Do you understand that you have the right to have your case heard by a jury?

b) Do you want your case to be heard by a judge without a jury or do you want a jury trial?

4. Do you understand that based upon your plea of guilty (no contest) the possible range of punishment is __________________ to ________________?

5. Have you been promised anything else to get you to plead guilty (no contest)?

6. Are you being forced or threatened into pleading guilty (no contest)?

7. Do you understand that by pleading guilty (no contest) you are giving up your right to a trial including the right to hear from and question the witnesses against you and the right to avoid being required to give evidence against yourself?

8. Do you have any questions before I accept your plea(s) of guilty (no contest)?

Suggested Plea of Guilty to Misdemeanor Plea Form with Plea Agreement Requiring Imposition of an Active or Suspended Sentence of Confinement in Jail

1. I understand the charge(s) against me.

2. a) I understand that I have the right to be represented by an attorney.

b) I understand that if I do not have the financial ability to hire my own attorney, I could be interviewed to see if I qualify for court appointed counsel and if I did qualify the court would appoint an attorney to represent me.

c) I do not want to be represented by an attorney and I do not want to be interviewed to see if I qualify for court appointed counsel. It is my desire to give up my right to counsel and to proceed today without an attorney.

3. In Circuit Court:

a) I understand that I have the right to have my case heard by a jury.

b) I do not want my case to be heard by a jury and wish to proceed to have my case heard today by a judge without a jury.

4. a) I am pleading guilty (no contest) today based upon my understanding that I will be sentenced to ______________.

b) I am pleading guilty (no contest) today based upon my understanding that the prosecutor will recommend a sentence of ______________. I understand that the judge does not have to accept the recommendation and can sentence me from ________________ to ________________.

5. I have not been promised anything to get me to plead guilty (no contest).

6. I am not being forced or threatened to get me to plead guilty (no contest).

7. I understand that by pleading guilty (no contest) I am giving up my right to a trial including the right to hear from and question the witnesses against me and the right to avoid being required to give evidence against myself.

8. I do not have any questions to ask the court before the court decides whether to accept my plea of guilty (no contest).

______________________________ ______________________________

Counsel for Defendant Defendant

Suggested Plea of Guilty to Misdemeanor Plea Form without Plea Agreement

1. I understand the charge(s) against me.

2. a) I understand that I have the right to be represented by an attorney.

b) I understand that if I do not have the financial ability to hire my own attorney, I could be interviewed to see if I qualify for court appointed counsel and if I did qualify the court would appoint an attorney to represent me.

c) I do not want to be represented by an attorney and I do not want to be interviewed to see if I qualify for court appointed counsel. It is my desire to give up my right to counsel and to proceed today without an attorney.

3. In Circuit Court:

a) I understand that I have the right to have my case heard by a jury.

b) I do not want my case to be heard by a jury and wish to proceed to have my case heard today by a judge without a jury.

4. I am pleading guilty (no contest) today based upon my understanding that I could be sentenced from ________________ to ________________.

5. I have not been promised anything to get me to plead guilty (no contest).

6. I am not being forced or threatened to get me to plead guilty (no contest).

7. I understand that by pleading guilty (no contest) I am giving up my right to a trial including the right to hear from and question the witnesses against me and the right to avoid being required to give evidence against myself.

8. I do not have any questions to ask the court before the court decides to accept my plea of guilty (no contest).

____________________ ____________________

Counsel for Defendant Defendant

[Adopted effective June 1, 2005.]

PART THREE B. TRAFFIC INFRACTIONS AND UNIFORM FINE SCHEDULE

Revised Effective December 1, 1982

Including Amendments Received Through October 15, 2015

RULE 3B:1. PURPOSE

These Rules are promulgated by the Supreme Court of Virginia pursuant to § 16.1–69.40:1 of the Code of Virginia to carry out the provisions of Chapter 585 of the Acts of Assembly of 1977 and Chapter 605 of the Acts of Assembly of 1978.

[Amended effective July 1, 1988; October 1, 1989.]

RULE 3B:2. UNIFORM FINE SCHEDULE

For any offense listed below, whether prescribed by the specified State statute or by a parallel local ordinance adopted pursuant to the authority granted in Virginia Code § 46.2-1300, a driver may enter a written appearance, waiver of court hearing, plea of guilty, and pay fines and costs. For traffic offenses not listed below, a court hearing is required. Nothing in this Rule affects bonding procedures for those offenses not listed below. Likewise, nothing in this Rule shall be construed to alter the operation of or the penalties prescribed pursuant to §§ 46.2-1220 through 46.2-1230.

This schedule is applied uniformly throughout the Commonwealth, and a clerk or magistrate may not impose a fine different from the amounts shown here. Costs shall be paid in accordance with the provisions of the Code of Virginia or any rules or regulations promulgated thereunder. This schedule does not restrict the fine a judge may impose for an offense listed here in any case for which there is a court hearing.

Description of Offense*	Statute or Regulation	Fine	Processing** Fee***	Total
1. Speed Violations				
Exceeding the speed limit	46.2-870 to 46.2-872, 46.2-873.1 to 46.2-876	$ 6 per mile over speed limit	$51	
Exceeding the speed limit in a school crossing	46.2-873	$ 7 per mile over speed limit	$51	
Exceeding speed limits set by Transportation Commissioner	46.2-878	$ 6 per mile over speed limit	$51	
Exceeding the speed limit in a highway work zone	46.2-878.1	$ 7 per mile over speed limit	$51	
Exceeding the speed limit in a residence district	46.2-878.2	$200 plus $ 8 per mile over speed limit	$51	
Exceeding the speed limit in a 55 mph or 65 mph zone	46.2-870	$ 6 per mile over speed limit	$51	

Exceeding the speed limit on bridge	46.2-881	$ 6 per mile over speed limit	$51	
Impeding traffic by slow speed	46.2-877	$30	$51	$81
Failure to drive at approximate speed authorized for lane in which vehicle is moving, on highway where slow moving traffic" lane is designated	46.2-804(1)	$30	$51	$81

2. Other Moving Offenses

Moving violation committed in highway safety corridor	46.2-947	Double otherwise applicable fine	$51	
Failure to obey highway sign	46.2-830	$30	$51	$81
Coasting on downgrade with gears in neutral	46.2-811	$30	$51	$81
Driving more than 13 hours in a 24-hour period	46.2-812	$30	$51	$81
Causing or permitting vehicle to be driven more than 13 hours in a 24-hour period	46.2-812	$30	$51	$81
Improper failure to drive on right side of highway	46.2-802	$30	$51	$81
Failure to move in designated direction on one-way roadway	46.2-806	$30	$51	$81
Failure to drive to right of rotary traffic island	46.2-807	$30	$51	$81
Improper failure to keep right in crossing highway intersection	46.2-803	$30	$51	$81
Improper failure to keep right in crossing highway intersection by railroad right of way	46.2-803	$30	$51	$81
Improper failure to observe lanes marked for traffic:				
- failure of slow moving traffic to keep right	46.2-804(1)	$30	$51	$81
- improperly driving in center	46.2-804(2)	$30	$51	$81

- changing lane without first ascertaining safety of move	46.2-804(2)	$30	$51	$81
- improperly driving in center lane of 3-lane highway	46.2-804(3)	$30	$51	$81
- improperly crossing solid line driver's lane	46.2-804(5)	$30	$51	$81
- improperly crossing double solid line	46.2-804(6)	$30	$51	$81
Disregard of lane direction control signal.	46.2-805	$30	$51	$81
Failure to obey traffic lights	46.2-833	$100	$51	$151
Evasion of a traffic control device	46.2-833.1	$50	$51	$101
Illegal right turn on red	46.2-835	$50	$51	$101
Illegal left turn on red	46.2-836	$50	$51	$101
Improper passing:				
- failure to remain on right side of highway when meeting vehicle proceeding in opposite direction	46.2-837	$30	$51	$81
- driving too close to vehicle being overtaken in same direction	46.2-838	$30	$51	$81
- returning to right side of highway before safely clear of overtaken vehicle	46.2-838	$30	$51	$81
- improperly passing to the right of a vehicle proceeding in same direction	46.2-841	$30	$51	$81
- failure to give way to the right to overtaking vehicle	46.2-842	$30	$51	$81
- improperly increasing speed when passed by overtaking vehicle	46.2-842	$30	$51	$81
- failure to give way to overtaking vehicle when	46.2-842.1	$30	$51	$81

driving abreast on divided highway				
- passing when left lane is not clearly visible	46.2-843	$30	$51	$81
- passing on left when oncoming traffic is too near to permit it in safety	46.2-843	$30	$51	$81
- truck or tractor and trailer impeding passage of following traffic by passing another truck or tractor and trailer on upgrade	46.2-843	$30	$51	$81
Following too closely:				
- motor vehicle following a vehicle more closely than is reasonable or prudent	46.2-816	$30	$51	$81
Improper U turn:				
- within business district, city or town, U turn other than at intersection	46.2-845	$30	$51	$81
- U turn on a curve or approaching crest of hill where not visible to vehicles approaching in any direction within 500 feet	46.2-845	$30	$51	$81
Improper position or method of turning at intersection:				
- unauthorized right turn from other than right hand curb or edge of roadway	46.2-846(A)(1)	$30	$51	$81
- on a two-way roadway, unauthorized left turn from other than lane nearest center line	46.2-846(A)(2)	$30	$51	$81
- on other than two-way roadway, unauthorized left turn from other than left-most available lane	46.2-846(A)(3)	$30	$51	$81
- failure to follow traffic control device of local authority	46.2-846(B)	$30	$51	$81

Starting, backing, stopping or turning without first seeing that such a move can be made in safety	46.2-848	$30	$51	$81
Starting, backing, stopping or turning without giving required signal	46.2-848	$30	$51	$81
Improper signals	46.2-849	$30	$51	$81
Improper change of course after giving signal	46.2-850	$30	$51	$81
Failure to signal prior to moving standing vehicle into traffic	46.2-851	$30	$51	$81
Failure to yield right of way or reduce speed on highway when approaching stopped vehicle with flashing blue, red or amber lights (not applicable to second and subsequent violations with vehicles flashing blue or red lights)	46.2-921.1	$100	$51	$15
Failure to yield right of way:				
- failure of driver on left to yield to driver on right entering intersection at same time	46.2-820	$30	$51	$81
- failure to obey "yield right of way" sign at intersection	46.2-821	$30	$51	$81
- failure of driver approaching or entering circular intersection to yield to driver already in the circle	46.2-822	$30	$51	$81
- failure to yield at uncontrolled "T" intersection	46.2-824	$30	$51	$81
- failure of driver turning left to yield to oncoming vehicle	46.2-825	$30	$51	$81
- failure to stop and yield when entering public highway or sidewalk from private road, etc.	46.2-826	$30	$51	$81

- failure to yield to U.S. Armed Services, National Guard, etc.	46.2-827	$30	$51	$81
- failure to yield to funeral procession under police escort	46.2-828	$30	$51	$81
- failure to yield right of way to emergency vehicle	46.2-829	$30	$51	$81
- following too near fire apparatus	46.2-921	$30	$51	$81
- driving over fire hose	46.2-922	$30	$51	$81
- failure to yield to pedestrian in clearly marked crosswalk or at intersection	46.2-924	$30	$51	$81
- failure to yield to pedestrian boarding or alighting from a bus	46.2-927	$30	$51	$81
- failure to stop and yield when approaching intersection of highway controlled by stop sign	46.2-821	$30	$51	$81
- failure to slow down or stop and yield when approaching intersection on highway controlled by "yield right of way" sign	46.2-821	$30	$51	$81
Driving through pedestrian safety zone	46.2-814	$30	$51	$81
Failure to obey railroad warning signal	46.2-884	$30	$51	$81
Proceeding improperly at railroad grade crossing:				
- generally	46.2-885	$30	$51	$81
- vehicles carrying passengers for hire, school bus or truck with flammable or explosive cargo	46.2-886	$30	$51	$81
- tractor, steam shovel, etc.	46.2-887	$30	$51	$81

Stopping bus or truck on highway to unload passengers or cargo	46.2-893	$30	$51	$81
Unlawful use of all-terrain vehicle	46.2-915.1	$30	$51	$81
Failure to display headlights at night or during time of poor visibility	46.2-1030	$30	$51	$81
Driving with excessive lights for purpose of general illumination ahead of vehicle	46.2-1030	$30	$51	$81
Failure to display warning lights properly	46.2-1030	$30	$51	$81
Failure to dim headlights	46.2-1034	$30	$51	$81
Driving in violation of HOV Lane Restrictions	33.2-501(B)	$100	$51	$151
Driving in violation of HOV Lane Restrictions, Planning District Eight (first offense)	33.2-501(B)(1)	$125	$51	$176
Driving in violation of HOV Lane Restrictions, Planning District Eight (second offense within five years from a first offense)	33.2-501(B)(2)	$250	$51	$301
Driving in violation of HOV Lane Restrictions, Planning District Eight (third offense within five years from a first offense)	33.2-501(B)(3)	$500	$51	$551
Driving in violation of HOV Lane Restrictions, Planning District Eight (fourth offense within five years from a first offense)	33.2-501(B)(4)	$1,000	$51	$1,051
Driving vehicle in violation of HOT lane vehicle classification restrictions (first offense)	33.2-503(4)	$125	$51	$176
Driving vehicle in violation of HOT lane vehicle classification restrictions (second offense within five years from a first offense)	33.2-503(4)	$250	$51	$301

Driving vehicle in violation of HOT lane vehicle classification restrictions (third offense within five years from a first offense)	33.2-503(4)	$500	$51	$551
Driving vehicle in violation of HOT lane vehicle classification restrictions (fourth and subsequent offense within five years from a first offense)	33.2-503(4)	$1,000	$51	$1,051
3. Equipment Violations				
Insufficient lighting equipment:	46.2-1010	$30	$51	$81
- less than two proper headlights on autos, trucks, busses, etc.	46.2-1011	$30	$51	$81
- motorcycle without proper headlight	46.2-1012	$30	$51	$81
- motorcycle with more than two headlights	46.2-1012	$30	$51	$81
- improper rear lights	46.2-1013	$30	$51	$81
- improper brake lights	46.2-1014	$30	$51	$81
- improper lighting equipment on all other mobile equipment	46.2-1016	$30	$51	$81
Failure of car to be equipped with supplemental high mount stop light	46.2-1014.1	$30	$51	$81
Improper dimension or marker lights:				
- generally	46.2-1017	$30	$51	$81
- vehicles or loads exceeding 35 feet	46.2-1018	$30	$51	$81
Spotlights or ditchlights				
- more than two	46.2-1019	$30	$51	$81
- aimed left of highway center or more than 100 feet ahead of vehicle	46.2-1019	$30	$51	$81
- unapproved type	46.2-1019	$30	$51	$81

- use in conjunction with or in place of headlights, except in emergency	46.2-1019	$30	$51	$81
- improper use of auxiliary lamps on emergency vehicles	46.2-1028	$30	$51	$81
Headlights improperly aimed or of improper intensity:				
- single beam headlights	46.2-1031	$30	$51	$81
- multiple beam headlights	46.2-1032	$30	$51	$81
Failure of car to be equipped with windshield defroster or defogger	46.2-1055.1	$30	$51	$81
Inadequate brakes:				
- generally	46.2-1066	$30	$51	$81
- bicycles	46.2-1066	$15	$51	$66
- holding device	46.2-1068	$30	$51	$81
- motorcycles	46.2-1069	$30	$51	$81
- trailers or semitrailers	46.2-1070	$30	$51	$81
Improper alteration of suspension system	46.2-1063	$30	$51	$81
Inadequate steering gear	46.2-1065	$30	$51	$81
Inadequate horn	46.2-1059	$30	$51	$81
Illegal siren, whistle or horn	46.2-1060	$30	$51	$81
Use of speedometer not in good working order	46.2-1080	$30	$51	$81
Improper painting and lettering on school bus	46.2-1089	$30	$51	$81
Absence of or inadequate rear view mirrors:				
- generally	46.2-1082	$30	$51	$81
- vehicle registered for passenger vehicular transportation	46.2-1082	$30	$51	$81
Insufficient rear fenders, flags or guards on trucks	46.2-1083	$30	$51	$81

Improper signs on windshields, etc.	46.2-1052	$30	$51	$81
Driver's view obstructed because of suspended objects or altered vehicle	46.2-1054	$30	$51	$81
Inadequate windshield wipers	46.2-1055	$30	$51	$81
Absence of required safety glass	46.2-1056	$30	$51	$81
Absence of windshield	46.2-1057	$30	$51	$81
Improper replacement of glass in vehicle	46.2-1058	$30	$51	$81
Improper or inadequate tires:				
- violation of restrictions on solid rubber tires	46.2-1041	$30	$51	$81
- operation of vehicle with insufficient tire tread	46.2-1043	$30	$51	$81
- improper use of studded tires	46.2-1044	$30	$51	$81
Lack of or inadequate signal device	46.2-1038, 46.2-1039	$30	$51	$81
Failure to use flashing signals when stopped on highway	46.2-1040	$30	$51	$81
Inadequate exhaust system:				
- driver of vehicle	46.2-1049	$30	$51	$81
- owner permitting or allowing operation of vehicle	46.2-1049	$30	$51	$81
- vehicle without proper pollution control device	46.2-1048	$30	$51	$81
- muffler cutout, straight exhaust or gutted muffler	46.2-1047	$30	$51	$81
Operation of vehicle without securely affixed or properly located operator's seat	46.2-1084	$30	$51	$81
Improper motorcycle steering mechanism	46.2-1085	$30	$51	$81

Motorcycle without muffler	46.2-1050	$30	$51	$81
Improper cooling unit	46.2-1088	$30	$51	$81
Use of unapproved equipment	46.2-1002	$30	$51	$81
Use of defective or unsafe equipment	46.2-1003	$30	$51	$81
Operating vehicle not equipped with proper seat belts	46.2-1092	$30	$51	$81
Failure to have vehicle inspected	46.2-1158	$30	$51	$81
Failure to correct defects discovered by inspection	46.2-1158	$50	$51	$101
Driving after expiration of rejection inspection sticker	46.2-1158	$50	$51	$101

4. Parking or Stopping Violations

Parking too near fire apparatus	46.2-921	$20	$51	$71
Vehicle improperly stopped or parked on highway	46.2-888	$20	$51	$71
- parked or stopped at or near fire or accident so as to cause traffic hazard or interfere with emergency operations	46.2-890	$20	$51	$71
Failure to use proper warning device when vehicle disabled in highway:				
- bus, truck, trailer, house trailer, or mobile home	46.2-111	$20	$51	$71
- vehicle transporting inflammable liquids	46.2-111	$20	$51	$71
- failure to use red flags when vehicle disabled	46.2-111	$20	$51	$71
Vehicle improperly parked in a VDOT owned commuter parking lot	46.2-1219.2	$20	$51	$71
Parking in front of fire hydrant, or private driveway, near street corner, fire station, or rescue squad	46.2-1239	$20	$51	$71

building and too close to intersection				
Failure to dim headlights on parked vehicle	46.2-1035	$20	$51	$71
Vehicle parked or stopped on highway without lights at night or during low visibility	46.2-1037	$20	$51	$71
Failure to set handbrake and turn wheels to curb on parked car	46.2-1071	$20	$51	$71
Improper use of parking space reserved for persons with disabilities	46.2-1242	$150	$51	$201

5. Trucks and Hauling or Towing Vehicles

Absence of flag or light at end of load of four feet or more (excluding violation on a two-lane highway where passing is permitted)	46.2-1121	$30	$51	$81
Absence of flag or light at end of load of four feet or more on a two-lane highway where passing is permitted	46.2-1121	$250	$51	$301
Failure to fasten load of logs, barrels, etc.	46.2-1155	$30	$51	$81
Load extending too far beyond front (excluding violation on a two-lane highway where passing is permitted)	46.2-1120	$30	$51	$81
Load extending too far beyond front on a two-lane highway where passing is permitted	46.2-1120	$30	$51	$81
Load extending too far beyond sides	46.2-1111	$250	$51	$301
Improper towing				
- improperly towing more than one trailer, etc. (excluding violation on a two-lane highway where passing is permitted)	46.2-1116	$30	$51	$81
- towing without draw bar not exceeding 15 feet and emergency chain (excluding	46.2-1118	$30	$51	$81

violation on a two-lane highway where passing is permitted)				
- improperly towing more than one trailer, etc., on a two-lane highway where passing is permitted	46.2-1116	$250	$51	$301
- towing without draw bar not exceeding 15 feet and emergency chain on a two-lane highway where passing is permitted	46.2-1118	250	$51	$301
6. Pedestrian Violations				
Malicious or careless interference with vehicle passage	46.2-923	$15	$51	$66
Failure to observe pedestrian control signals	46.2-925	$15	$51	$66
Stepping into street where driver's vision obscured	46.2-926	$15	$51	$66
Soliciting rides	46.2-929	$15	$51	$66
Failure to walk on left edge of roadway where no sidewalk	46.2-928	$15	$51	$66
Unlawful loitering on bridge or highway right-of-way	46.2-930	$15	$51	$66
Playing on streets or highways	46.2-932	$15	$51	$66
7. Miscellaneous Offenses				
Unlawful riding of an animal at night	46.2-800.1	$30	$51	$81
Improper abandonment of motor vehicle	46.2-1209	$40	$51	$91
Failure to obtain registration	46.2-600	$25	$51	$76
Failure to carry license or registration	46.2-104	$10	$51	$61
Expiration of registration	46.2-613	$25	$51	$76
Operate vehicle which is unregistered, untitled, or without plates/decals or with expired registration/license/decals	46.2-613(1)	$25	$51	$76

Possess, lend or knowingly permit use of registration card, license plate, or decal by anyone not entitled to it	46.2-613(3)	$25	$51	$76
Expired registration	46.2-646	$25	$51	$76
Pedestrian, bicycle, animal, moped, prohibited vehicle on controlled access highway	46.2-808	$30	$51	$81
Operating motorcycle without headlight, horn or rearview mirror at certain times	46.2-912	$30	$51	$81
Operating or riding a motorcycle without helmet; operating motorcycle without face shield, goggles or safety windshield	46:2-910(A)	$25	$51	$76
Occupation of trailer being towed on highways	46.2-813	$30	$51	$81
Unlawful use of radar detection device	46.2-1079	$40	$51	$91
Unlawful use of radar jamming device	46.2-1079	$40	$51	$91
Unlawful use of earphones while operating vehicle	46.2-1078	$25	$51	$76
Failure to display slow moving vehicle emblem	46.2-1081	$15	$51	$66
Failure to display license plate	46.2-711	$25	$51	$76
Improper display of license plate	46.2-715	$25	$51	$76
License plate improperly fastened or obscured	46.2-716	$25	$51	$76
Vehicle exceeding width limitations	46.2-1105	$250	$51	$301
Vehicle exceeding height limitations (excluding offenses of driving in violation of tunnel height restrictions and failure to report overhead bridge or structure collision)	46.2-1110	$250	$51	$301

Description of Offense*	Regulation[1]	Fine	Processing** Fee***	Total
Vehicle exceeding length regulations (excluding violation on a two-lane highway where passing is permitted)	46.2-1112	$250	$51	$301
Vehicle exceeding length regulations on a two-lane highway where passing is permitted	46.2-1112	$250	$51	$301
8. Bicycle Violations				
Riding bicycle improperly on roadway	46.2-905	$15	$51	$66
Carrying articles improperly on bicycle	46.2-906	$15	$51	$66
Bicycle without proper headlight	46.2-1015	$15	$51	$66
Bicycle without rear reflector or light	46.2-1015	$15	$51	$66
Bicycle on highway without adequate brake	46.2-1066	$15	$51	$66

Description of Offense*	Regulation[1]	Fine	Processing** Fee***	Total
9. Motor Carrier Offenses[†]				
(a.) General Violations				
Marking of motor vehicle	49 C.F.R. § 390.21	$25	$51	$76
Railroad crossing/stopping	49 C.F.R. § 392.10	$100	$51	$151
(b.) Driver Violations				
No medical examiner's certificate	49 C.F.R. § 391.41	$50	$51	$101
Improper medical examiner's certificate	49 C.F.R. § 391.43	$50	$51	$101
Medical certificate invalid	49 C.F.R. § 391.43	$50	$51	$101
No medical waiver	49 C.F.R. § 391.49	$50	$51	$101

Ill/fatigued driver	49 C.F.R. § 392.3	$75	$51	$126
Possess alcoholic beverage	49 C.F.R. § 392.5	$100	$51	$151
Violate 10-hour rule, 15-hour rule	49 C.F.R. § 395.3	$100	$51	$151
Violate 60/70 hour rule	49 C.F.R. § 395.3	$100	$51	$151
Log book violation (general)	49 C.F.R. § 395.8	$100	$51	$151
No log book	49 C.F.R. § 395.8	$100	$51	$151
Log book not current	49 C.F.R. § 395.8	$100	$51	$151
Fail to retain previous seven days on log book	49 C.F.R. § 395.8	$100	$51	$151

(c.) <u>Equipment Violations</u>

Equipment - inspection/use	49 C.F.R. § 392.7	$50	$51	$101
Emergency equipment - inspection/use	49 C.F.R. § 392.8	$50	$51	$101
Safe loading (secured)	49 C.F.R. § 392.9	$100	$51	$151
Brakes - inoperative or missing	49 C.F.R. § 393.40 to § 393.52	$100	$51	$151
Fuel tank securement	49 C.F.R. § 393.65	$50	$51	$101
Fuel leak/cap	49 C.F.R. § 393.67	$25	$51	$76
Coupling/towing devices	49 C.F.R. §§ 393.70, 393.71	$50	$51	$101
Defective tires/tire exceeds weight limit	49 C.F.R. § 393.75	$50	$51	$101
Bus violations	49 C.F.R. §§ 393.89 to 393.92	$50	$51	$101

Front end structure	49 C.F.R. § 393.106	$50	$51	$101
Frame - cracked, loose, sagging, broken	49 C.F.R. § 393.201	$100	$51	$151
Cab/body components – defective	49 C.F.R. § 393.203	$50	$51	$101
Wheels/rims defective	49 C.F.R. § 393.205	$50	$51	$101
Suspension – defective	49 C.F.R. § 393.207	$50	$51	$101
Steering system – defective	49 C.F.R. § 393.209	$100	$51	$151
Vehicle maintenance (general)	49 C.F.R. § 396.3	$100	$51	$151
No driver vehicle inspection report	49 C.F.R. § 396.11	$25	$51	$76
No periodic inspection	49 C.F.R. §§396.17 to 396.25	$25	$51	$76

(d.) Hazardous Materials - Driving and Parking

Fail to attend Division 1.1, 1.2 or 1.3 material	49 C.F.R. §397.5	$100	$51	$151
Fail to attend other hazardous materials class	49 C.F.R. § 397.5	$100	$51	$151
Improper parking Division 1.1, 1.2 or 1.3 material	49 C.F.R. § 397.7, § 397.11	$100	$51	$151
Improper parking other hazardous materials	49 C.F.R. § 397.7, § 397.11	$100	$51	$151
Fail to have route plan	49 C.F.R. § 397.67	$100	$51	$151
Smoking violations	49 C.F.R. § 397.13	$100	$51	$151
Instructions and document violations	49 C.F.R. § 397.19	$100	$51	$151

* The description of offense is for reference and is not a legal definition.

** Unless otherwise provided by statute.
*** See §§ 9.1-106 and 53.1-120 of the Code.
I The category "regulation" refers to the section of the Code of Federal Regulations as incorporated by regulation at 19 VAC 30-20-80 of the Virginia Motor Carrier Safety Regulations. These regulations are included for identification and reference purposes only, since these violations are violations of Virginia regulations.
† These fines are imposed for violations of certain Virginia Motor Carrier Safety Regulations. The statutory authority to impose these fines is contained in § 52-8.4 of the code of Virginia and in 19 VAC 30-20-10, et seq., of the Virginia Motor Carrier Safety Regulations, incorporating by reference 49 C.F.R. Parts 390-397.

[Amended effective July 1, 1988; October 1, 1989; February 1, 1991; July 1, 1992; January 1, 1996; July 1, 1997; August 15, 1997; July 1, 1998; October 21, 1998; February 1, 1999; July 1, 2000; January 1, 2001; December 23, 2002; April 1, 2002; July 1, 2002; May 1, 2003; July 1, 2003; July 22, 2003; July 1, 2004; January 1, 2006; July 1, 2006; January 1, 2007; July 1, 2008; July 1, 2010; July 1, 2011; March 1, 2012; January 1, 2014; October 1, 2014; July 1, 2015.]

PART THREE C. NON–TRAFFIC PREPAYABLE OFFENSES AND UNIFORM FINE SCHEDULE

Revised Effective December 1, 1982

Including Amendments Received Through October 15, 2015

RULE 3C:1. PURPOSE AND EFFECTIVE DATE

These rules are promulgated by the Supreme Court of Virginia pursuant to § 16.1–69.40:2 of the Code of Virginia to carry out the provisions of Chapter 605 of the Acts of Assembly of 1978 and Chapter 421 of the Acts of Assembly of 1989.

[Amended effective July 1, 1988; April 1, 1990.]

RULE 3C:2. UNIFORM FINE SCHEDULE

Any person charged with any offense listed below may enter a written appearance, waiver of court hearing, plea of guilty, and pay fines and costs.

This schedule is applied uniformly throughout the Commonwealth, and a clerk or magistrate may not impose a fine different from the amounts shown here. Costs shall be paid in accordance with the provisions of the Code of Virginia or any rules or regulations promulgated thereunder. The schedule does not restrict the fine a judge may impose for an offense listed here in any case for which there is a court hearing.

Where injury to the person is involved, prepayment may not be made, even though the offense or violation appears on the list below. See Va. Code § 16.1-69.40:2(A).

A violation of a provision of Title 28.2 may be prepaid only if the person has not violated a provision of Title 28.2 within the past 12 months. See Va. Code § 28.2-903.

Description of Offense*	Statute or Regulation	Fine	Processing** Fee***	Total
Drinking or tendering alcoholic beverage in public place	4.1-308	$25	$61	$86
Failing to assist forest warden in fighting fire	10.1-1139	$30	$61	$91
Unlawful burning of brush, leaves, etc.	10.1-1142(A) 10.1-1142(D)	$40	$61	$101
Unlawful burning during restricted period	10.1-1142(B) 10.1-1142(D)	$40	$61	$101
Leaving certain fires unattended or failing to extinguish the same	10.1-1142(C) 10.1-1142(D)	$40	$61	$101
Hunting or trapping in state forests without special use permit	10.1-1151	$35	$61	$96
Hunting or trapping in state forests in violation of restrictions or conditions of special use permit	10.1-1153	$35	$61	$96
Failure to post signs regarding disposal of used motor oils	10.1-1422.6(D)	$25	$61	$86
Unlawful buying, selling or	18.2-102.2	$35	$61	$96

disposing of milk case or crate				
Unlawful refusal to return milk case or crate	18.2-102.2	$35	$61	$96
Unlawful defacing, cover up or removal of business identification on milk case or crate	18.2-102.2	$35	$61	$96
Bringing unleashed dog into Capitol Square	18.2-123	$10	$61	$71
Trespassing at night upon cemetery	18.2-125	$35	$61	$96
Trespassing at night upon church or school property	18.2-128(A)	$35	$61	$96
Trespassing upon lands to hunt, fish or trap without consent	18.2-132	$50	$61	$111
Computer invasion of privacy by intentionally examining personal information without authority	18.2-152.5	$50	$61	$111
Trespassing on railroad track	18.2-159	$35	$61	$96
Trespassing on railroad trains	18.2-160	$35	$61	$96
Boarding or riding train without lawful payment of fare	18.2-160.1(A) 18.2-160.1(B)	$100	$61	$161
Unlawfully intercepting or monitoring employee›telephone calls	18.2-167.1	$35	$61	$96
Failing to report removal, alteration of trademark or identification numbers on a business machine	18.2-214.1	$50	$61	$111
Using games, contests, lotteries to promote sale of products having both federal and state tax	18.2-242	$50	$61	$111
Expectorating in public	18.2-322	$15	$61	$76
Drinking alcoholic beverage while driving motor vehicle	18.2-323.1	$75	$61	$136
Gambling illegally	18.2-326	$35	$61	$96
Selling to, distributing to or purchasing for persons under age 18 tobacco products	18.2-371.2(A)	$75	-	$75
Purchasing or possessing tobacco products when under age 18	18.2-371.2(B)	$35	-	$35

Profanely cursing or swearing in public	18.2-388	$25	$61	$86
Being intoxicated in public	18.2-388	$25	$61	$86
Shooting pigeons for amusement or renting premises for such purposes	18.2-403.3(2) 3.2-6573	$35	$61	$96
Making false statement to secure dog license	18.2-403.3(8) 3.2-6587(A)(1)	$35	$61	$96
Failing to pay dog license tax	18.2-403.3(9) 3.2-6530 3.2-6587(A)	$25	$61	$86
Concealing unlicensed dog	18.2-403.3(10) 3.2-6587(A)	$35	$61	$96
Unlawfully removing dog collar or tag	18.2-403.3(11) 3.2-6587(A)	$35	$61	$96
Using abusive language	18.2-416	$60	$61	$121
Using recorded telephone solicitation calls for initial sales contacts	18.2-425.1(A)	$50	$61	$111
Using recorded telephone solicitation calls which do not disengage when party called attempts to do so	18.2-425.1(B)	$50	$61	$111
Unlawfully communicating with prisoners by persons outside any jail	18.2-473.1	$75	$61	$136
Unlawfully possessing or duplicating keys to public buildings	18.2-503	$50	$61	$111
Unlawfully changing name	18.2-504.1	$60	$61	$121
Campaigning at election registration location	24.2-1003	$50	$61	$111
Failing to obey chief or other fire officer answering an alarm or operating at an emergency incident	27-15.1	$50	$61	$111
Fishing without a saltwater license	28.2-302.1	$75	$61	$136
Unlawful setting of fishnets	28.2-309	$150	$61	$211
Taking fish or shellfish on or within 500 yards below	28.2-311	$60	$61	$121

Chickahominy Dam at Walker's on the Chickahominy River other than with rod and reel and hand line				
Buying, selling or possessing oysters under the prescribed size and undersized shells taken from the natural rocks, beds and shoals	28.2-510	$110	$61	$171
Having oysters or shells on culling board, deck, washboard or other receptacle above hold or in deckhouse when boat is oystering upon natural rocks, beds or shoals and not at anchor; when off the public rocks; when approaching a buy boat; or when approaching a landing	28.2-513	$150	$61	$211
Having more than one-half gallon of shucked oysters on board a boat harvesting on the public rocks	28.2-514	$60	$61	$121
Taking or catching oysters or shells for purpose of converting same into lime without permission from Commission	28.2-529	$110	$61	$171
Unlawful violation of regulations governing use of crab traps and pounds	28.2-701	$150	$61	$211
Taking or catching crabs from statutorily prohibited area from June 1 to Sept. 15, for purpose of resale	28.2-709	$150	$61	$211
Placing or maintaining any crab, eel, or fish pot in navigable channel which has navigation aids installed or approved by any agency of U.S. government	28.2-710	$60	$61	$121
Placing, setting or leaving crab pots in tidal tributaries between Jan. 1 and Jan. 31 or other time period specified by Marine Res. Comm.	28.2-711	$60	$61	$121
Possess Striped Bass less than 18 inches	4VAC20-252-30(C)	$50 per fish (Maximum fine not to exceed $500)	$61	
Possess Striped Bass larger than the maximum size	4VAC20-252-50(E)	$50.00 per fish (Maximum fine not to exceed $500)	$61	

Possess Striped Bass over creel limit	4VAC20-252-50(C)	$100.00 per fish (Maximum fine not to exceed $500)	$61	
Fail to purchase Striped Bass buyer's permit	4VAC20-252-130(D)	$100.00	$61	$161
Unlawfully set, place, or leave crab pots in tidal waters	4VAC20-270-40(C)	$100.00	$61	$161
Unlawful for any person to take, catch, or possess any speckled trout less than minimum size	4VAC20-280-30(A)	$50 per fish (Maximum fine not to exceed $500)	$61	
Unlawful for hook-and-line, rod-and-reel or hand-line to possess oversize speckled trout	4VAC20-280-30(B)	$50 per fish (Maximum fine not to exceed $500)	$61	
Unlawful to possess any red drum less than 18 or greater than 26 inches	4VAC20-280-30(C)	$50 per fish (Maximum fine not to exceed $500)	$61	
Unlawful to possess more than creel limit for speckled trout	4VAC20-280-40	$100 per fish (Maximum fine not to exceed $500)	$61	
Unlawful to take or catch more than 1 black drum	4VAC20-320-40	$100 per fish (Maximum fine not to exceed $500)	$61	
Unlawful to take, catch or possess any black drum less than 16 inches	4VAC20-320-60	$50 per fish (Maximum fine not to exceed $500)	$61	
Failure to cull crabs at harvest location	4VAC20-370-20	$100	$61	$161
Unlawful crab culling containers	4VAC20-370-20	$100	$61	$161
Unlawful to possess more than the maximum number of gray trout or under the minimum size	4VAC20-380-60	$50 per fish (Maximum fine not to exceed $500)	$61	
Drift and anchor gill nets not marked	4VAC20-430-20	$50	$61	$111
Staked gill net not marked	4VAC20-430-30	$50	$61	$111
Unlawful for any person to possess more than 10 bluefish	4VAC20-450-20	$100 per fish (Maximum fine not to exceed $500)	$61	
Fail to completely remove traps, leads, wire, poles and all other related gear of crab traps and pounds no later than December 31 of each year	4VAC20-460-30	$100	$61	$161

Unlawful to possess more than 2 amberjack or more than 1 cobia at any time	4VAC20-510-20	$100 per fish (Maximum fine not to exceed $500)	$61	
Unlawful to possess amberjack less than 32 inches or cobia less than 37 inches	4VAC20-510-30	$50 per fish (Maximum fine not to exceed $500)	$61	
Unlawful to catch and retain possession of American shad	4VAC20-530-30	$100 per fish (Maximum fine not to exceed $500)	$61	
Unlawful for any person to possess more than 15 Spanish mackerel or more than 3 king mackerel	4VAC20-540-30	$100 per fish (Maximum fine not to exceed $500)	$61	
Unlawful for any person to set any gill net or nonfixed finfishing device and let net or device remain unfished	4VAC20-550-20	$150	$61	$211
Unlawful to alter finfish such that the species cannot be determined	4VAC20-580-20(A)	$200	$61	$261
Unlawful to alter any finfish regulated by size such that total length cannot be determined	4VAC20-580-20(B)	$200	$61	$261
Unlawful to possess any summer flounder smaller than designated size limit	4VAC20-620-50(D)	$50 per fish (Maximum fine not to exceed $500)	$61	
Unlawfully possessing fish from recreational gill net	4VAC20-670-30(E)	$50	$61	$111
Unlawfully fishing recreational crab pots	4VAC20-670-30(I)	$75	$61	$136
Unlawful to place, set or fish any crab pot that does not contain at least two unobstructed cull ring of proper size and location	4VAC20-700-20	$150	$61	$211
Unlawful to catch and retain possession of any scup smaller than the minimum sizes	4VAC20-910-30	$50 per fish (Maximum fine not to exceed $500)	$61	
Unlawful to possess any black sea bass smaller than minimum size limits	4VAC20-950-30(C)	$50 per fish (Maximum fine not to exceed $500)	$61	
Possession of any quantity of	4VAC20-950-45	$100 per fish	$61	

black sea bass that exceeds possession limit		(Maximum fine not to exceed $500)		
Unlawful to possess tautog smaller than minimum size limit	4VAC20-960-30(C)	$50 per fish (Maximum fine not to exceed $500)	$61	
Unlawful to possess more than four tautog recreationally	4VAC20-960-45	$100 per fish (Maximum fine not to exceed $500)	$61	
Unlawful to possess more than four spadefish recreationally	4VAC20-970-30(A)	$100 per fish (Maximum fine not to exceed $500)	$61	
Unlawful to possess more than six spadefish by commercial hook and line	4VAC20-970-30(C)	$100 per fish (Maximum fine not to exceed $500)	$61	
Unlawful to harvest, land or possess more than four sheepshead recreationally	4VAC20-1110-30	$100 per fish (Maximum fine not to exceed $500)	$61	
Failure to use and maintain a certified scale to weigh those fish, shellfish and marine organisms regulated by a harvest quota, weight limit or landing weight	4VAC20-1170-10	$50	$61	$111
Unlawful to place a net within 300 yards of the side or end of a fixed fishing device	4VAC20-1220-30	$100	$61	$161
Unlawful to take or catch any marine or anadromous fish species recreationally without obtaining, annually, a Fisherman Identification Program (FIP) Registration	4VAC20-1240-30	$25	$61	$86
Unlawful to catch and retain possession of any river herring from Virginia tidal waters	4VAC20-1260-30	$100 per fish (Maximum fine not to exceed $500)	$61	
Unauthorized Transfer of License	PRF Reg I 1 a[1]		[2]	$250
Setting 1 to 5 More Crab Pots than Licensed	PRFC Reg I 2 d (1)[1]		[2]	$150
Setting 6 to 10 More Crab Pots than Licensed	PRFC Reg I 2 d (1)[1]		[2]	$250
Setting 11 to 15 More Crab Pots than Licensed	PRFC Reg I 2 d (1)[1]		[2]	$350

Setting 16 to 20 More Crab Pots than Licensed	PRFC Reg I 2 d (1)[1]	2	$450
Setting 21 or More Crab Pots than Licensed	PRF Reg I 2 d (1)[1]	2	$500
Improper Identification of Oyster Tong Vessel	PRFC Reg I 2 f (1)[1]	2	$125
Improper Identification of Hand Scrape Vessel	PRFC Reg I 2 f (3)[1]	2	$125
Gill Net Set in Water Depth More than 36' MLW	PRF Reg I 2 (i)(1)[1]	2	$250
Failure to Display Commercial Hook and Line Pennant	PRFC Reg I 2 l (2)[1]	2	$125
More Unlicensed Commercial Hook and Line Crew Members Than Allowed	PRF Reg I 2 l (2)[1]	2	$300
Improper Identification of Eel, Fish, or Bait Pots or Vessel	PRFC Reg I 2 m (4)[1]	2	$125
Improper Identification of Pound, Gill or Fyke Net	PRFC Reg I 2 n (8)[1]	2	$125
Failing to Maintain 1 to 5 Stakes or Buoys	PRFC Reg I 2 n (9)		$200
Failing to Maintain 6 to 10 Stakes or Buoys	PRFC Reg I 2 n (9)		$250
Failing to Maintain 11 to 15 Stakes or Buoys	PRFC Reg I 2 n (9)		$300
Failing to Maintain 16 to 20 Stakes or Buoys	PRF Reg I 2 n (9)		$350
Failing to Maintain 21 or more Stakes or Buoys	PRF Reg I 2 n (9)[1]	2	$500
Improper Identification of Fish Trot Line or Vessel	PRFC Reg I 2 q[1]	2	$125
Gill Net Set Out of Location	PRFC Reg I 2 s (1)[1]	2	$200
Failing to Remove 1 to 5 Stakes	PRFC Reg I 2 s (2)[1]	2	$200
Failing to Remove 6 to 10 Stakes	PRFC Reg I 2 s (2)[1]	2	$250

Failing to Remove 11 to 15 Stakes	PRFC Reg I 2 s (2)[1]		[2]	$300
Failing to Remove 16 to 20 Stakes	PRFC Reg I 2 s (2)[1]		[2]	$350
Failing to Remove 21 or more Stakes	PRF Reg I s (2)[1]	2	[2]	$500
No Reflective Material/Flags on Gill, Fyke or Pound Net	PRF Reg I s (3)[1]	2	[2]	$125
Gill Net Set Out of Location	PRF Reg I s[1]	2	[2]	$75
Operating Charter Boat without Sport Decal	PRF Reg I u[1]	2	[2]	$300
Commercial Fishing/Crabbing/ Oystering/Clamming without License	PRF Reg I b[1]	3	[2]	$300
Failure to Exhibit Commercial License	PRFC Reg I 3 b[1]		[2]	$125
Placing 1 to 10 Buoys, Gear or Pots in Marked Channel	PRFC Reg I 3 c			$150
Placing 11 to 15 Buoys, Gear or Pots in Marked Channel	PRFC Reg I 3 c			$200
Placing 16 or more Buoys, Gear or Pots in Marked Channel	PRFC Reg I 3 c			$250
Altering/Modifying Striped Bass ID Tags per tag	PRF Reg I e[1]	3	[2]	$250
Possessing Hand Scrape During Unlawful Time (note Order #)	PRF Reg II 2 b[1]		[2]	$150
Oystering Before or After Closed Hours (note Order #)	PRF Reg II 2 b[1]		[2]	$250
Oystering During Closed Season (note Order #)	PRF Reg II 2 b[1]		[2]	$500
Possessing Patent Tong or Dredging Equipment without Permit	PRCC Reg II 2 e[1]		[2]	$125
Possessing 6 to 10% Unculled Oysters	PRFC Reg II 2 f (1)			$200
Possessing 11 to 15% Unculled Oysters	PRF Reg II 2 f (1)			$350
Possessing 16% or more Unculled Oysters	PRF Reg II 2 f (1)[1]		[2]	$500

Not Culling on Oyster Bar	PRFC Reg II 2 f (2)[1]	[2]	$ 500
Possessing Oysters in Containers	PRFC Reg II 2 g		$200
Possessing Oysters in Baskets without Permit	PRFC Reg II 2 g[1]	[2]	$125
Oystering in Closed Area (Sanctuaries)	PRF Reg II 4 a[1]	[2]	$500
Exceeding Minimum or Maximum Mesh Size	PRF Reg III 8 b[1]	[2]	$500
Violation of Haul Seine Regulations	PRF Reg III 8 c (1-2)[1]	[2]	$200
Fishing During Closed Season (Commercial)	PRF Reg III 9 a (1-7)[1]	[2]	$250
Possessing Fish During Closed Season (note Order #) per fish	PRF Reg III 9 b[1]	[2]	$125
Exceeding Fish Catch/Creel Limits (note Order #) per fish	PRF Reg III 10 a[1]	[2]	$125
Possessing Striped Bass in Excess of Catch/Creel Limits (note Order #) per fish	PRF Reg III 10 a[1]	[2]	$150
Using Striped Bass ID Tags of Another	PRF Reg III 10 b[1]	[2]	$250
Failure to Tag Commercially Caught Striped Bass per fish	PRF Reg III 10 b[1]	[2]	$125
Unlawful Use of Striped Bass Tags (i.e. by gear type) (note Order #)	PRF Reg III 10 b[1]	[2]	$500
Possessing Undersize Fish (note Order #) $125 1st fish plus $10 each add'l fish	PRFC Reg III 11a	[2]	$125
Possess Oversize Striped Bass (note Order #) per fish	PRF Reg III 11 a[1]	[2]	$250
Improper Identification of Soft Clam Vessel	PRF Reg V 1 a[1]	[2]	$125
Possessing 6% or more Undersized Clams	PRF Reg V 3 a[1]	[2]	$150
Exceeding Clam Catch Limits per bushel	PRF Reg V 4 a[1]	[2]	$ 250

Clamming in Closed Area	PRF Reg V 6 d[1]	[2]	$500
Failure to Exhibit Sport Fishing License/ Improper Display of License	PRFC Reg VI 2 c[1]	[2]	$125
Exceeding Unlicensed Recreational Crabbing Gear or Catch Limits	PRFC Reg VI 4 a	[2]	$150
Sport Crabbing without License	PRFC Reg VI 4 b[1]	[2]	$150
Failure to Exhibit Sport Crabbing License	PRF Reg VI 4 b[1]	[2]	$125
Exceeding Licensed Sport Crabbing Gear Limits	PRF Reg VI 4 c[1]	[2]	$125
Improper Identification of Sport Crabbing Gear	PRF Reg VI 4 d[1]	[2]	$125
Exceeding Licensed Sport Crabbing Catch Limits	PRF Reg VI 4 e[1]	[2]	$125
Sport Fishing without License	PRF Reg VI 5 a[1]	[2]	$150
Fishing for Striped Bass During Closed Season without Barbless Hooks	PRF Reg VI 5 e[1]	[2]	$125
Failing to Remove Peeler Traps per trap	PRF Reg VII 1 d[1]	[2]	$200
Possessing Undersize Crabs			
#per Bushel / #per Barrel			
5 to 9 / 11 to 24	PRFC Reg VII 2 a[1]	[2]	$150
10 to 14 / 25 to 39	PRFC Reg VII 2 a[1]	[2]	$225
15 to 25 / 40 to 59	PRFC Reg VII 2 a[1]	[2]	$275
26 or more / 60 or more	PRFC Reg VII 2 a[1]	[2]	$400
Improper Identification of Crab Pot Vessel	PRFC Reg VII 3 a[1]	[2]	$125
Improper Identification of Crabbing Gear	PRFC Reg VII 3 b[1]	[2]	$125

Crab Pots without Decal/Tag – 300 Pot License			
<u># pots without decal/tag</u>			
1 to 15	PRFC Reg VII 3 b[1]	[2]	$250
16 to 30	PRFC Reg VII 3 b[1]	[2]	$500
Crab Pots without Decal/Tag – 400 Pot License			
<u># pots without decal/tag</u>			
1 to 20	PRFC Reg VII 3 b[1]	[2]	$250
21 to 40	PRFC Reg VII 3 b[1]	[2]	$500
Crab Pots without Decal/Tag – 500 Pot License			
<u># pots without decal/tag</u>			
1 to 25	PRFC Reg VII 3 b[1]	[2]	$250
26 to 50	PRFC Reg VII 3 b[1]	[2]	$500
Crabbing/Possession of Crabs During Closed Season	PRFC Reg VII 4 a[1]	[2]	$250
Crabbing at Night	PRFC Reg VII 5 b[1]	[2]	$200
No Culling Container on Board	PRFC Reg VII 6 a[1]	[2]	$200
Transporting Crabs not in Baskets or Barrels	PRFC Reg VII 6 a[1]	[2]	$200
No or Closed Cull Rings in 1 to 5 Pots	PRFC Reg VII 6 b[1]	[2]	$175
No or Closed Cull Rings in 6 to 10 Pots	PRFC Reg VII 6 b[1]	[2]	$275
No or Closed Cull Rings in 11 to 15 Pots	PRFC Reg VII 6 b[1]	[2]	$450
No or Closed Cull Rings in 16 to 20 Pots	PRFC Reg VII 6 b[1]	[2]	$500

Failure to Separate Crabs per container	PRFC Reg VII 6 c [1]		[2]	$150
Exceeding Crab Harvest Limit per bushel	PRFC Reg VII 7 a [1]		[2]	$150
Hunting, trapping, or fishing without license	29.1-335	$60 + fee equal to cost of License	$61	$121
Failing to carry hunting, trapping or fishing license	29.1-336	$35	$61	$96
Hunting bear or deer w/out special stamp	29.1-354	$35	$61	$96
Hunting, fishing or trapping in national forest w/out special permit	29.1-408	$35	$61	$96
Failing to obtain permit for taxidermy	29.1-415 29.1-412	$50	$61	$111
Failing to obtain permit for netting fish	29.1-416 29.1-412	$50	$61	$111
Failing to obtain permit for capturing, propagating and disposing of wildlife for authorized purposes	29.1-417 29.1-412	$50	$61	$111
Failing to obtain permit for collecting specimens	29.1-418 29.1-412	$50	$61	$111
Failing to obtain permit for taking, holding falcons, hawks and owls to use to hunt wild game	29.1-419 29.1-412	$50	$61	$111
Failing to secure permits required for field trials	29.1-422 18.2-403.3(6)	$50	$61	$111
Hunting with unauthorized weapons	29.1-519	$60	$61	$121
Violating hunting times	29.1-520	$60	$61	$121
Hunting on Sunday	29.1-521(A)(1)	$50	$61	$111
Hunting after obtaining daily or season limit	29.1-521(A)(3)	$50	$61	$111
Hunting over bait or occupying baited blind	29.1-521(A)(4)	$100	$61	$161
Providing no name or address on traps set on another's property	29.1-521(A)(7)	$25	$61	$86

Failing to visit traps daily and remove animals	29.1-521(A)(9)	$35	$61	$96
Unlawfully hunting, trapping, possessing, transporting animals or carcasses	29.1-521(A)(10)	$100	$61	$161
Violating blaze orange law	29.1-530.1	$25	$61	$86
Certain violations pertaining to sanctuaries, refuges, etc.	29.1-554	$60	$61	$121
Shooting, attempting to shoot, or taking game on preserve before complying with regulations	29.1-603	$35	$61	$96
Removing shot game from preserve without attaching seal	29.1-606	$35	$61	$96
Unregistered motorboat	29.1-702(A)	$75	$61	$136
No registration on board	29.1-702(B)	$25	$61	$86
Expired registration	29.1-703	$25	$61	$86
Failure to display registration	29.1-703	$25	$61	$86
Failure to display expiration decal	29.1-703	$25	$61	$86
Operating motorboat or manipulating skis in marked area	29.1-734	$35	$61	$96
Operation of vessel without proper safety equipment	29.1-735(C)	$35	$61	$96
Renting out a motorboat without safety equipment	29.1-736(A)	$35	$61	$96
Offering for rent other boats without sufficient life preservers	29.1-736(B)	$35	$61	$96
Violation of muffling device requirements for motorboats	29.1-737	$25	$61	$86
Absence of observer when towing water skier not wearing life preserver	29.1-742(A)	$35	$61	$96
Skiing before/after hours	29.1-742(B)	$75	$61	$136
Operating motorboat at excessive speed when within 50 feet of docks, piers, ramps, people in water	29.1-744.3	$50	$61	$111

Operating personal watercraft under age 14	29.1-748(A)(1)	$35	$61	$96
Operating personal watercraft without wearing personal flotation device	29.1-748(A)(3)	$35	$61	$96
Operating personal watercraft without a lanyard	29.1-748(A)(4)	$35	$61	$96
Operating personal watercraft between sunset and sunrise	29.1-748(A)(5)	$35	$61	$96
Exceeding capacity on personal watercraft	29.1-748(A)(6)	$35	$61	$96
Permitting operation of personal watercraft by person under age 14	29.1-749(A)	$75	$61	$136
Destruction of flowers, plants, minerals, etc. on a state park[3]	4 VAC 5-30-50[4]	$100	$61	$161
Destruction of buildings, signs, structures, etc. on a state park[3]	4 VAC 5-30-60[4]	$100	$61	$161
Disposal of refuse, garbage, etc. on a state park[3]	4 VAC 5-30-70[4]	$50	$61	$111
Pollution of waters on a state park[3]	4 VAC 5-30-80[4]	$100	$61	$161
Opening and closing hours of a state park[3]	4 VAC 5-30-120[4]	$50	$61	$111
Failure to pay fees in a fee area of a state park[3]	4 VAC 5-30-130[4]	$50	$61	$111
Picknicking in non-designated areas of a state park[3]	4 VAC 5-30-140[4]	$25	$61	$86
Camping in a state park[3] other than according to established rule	4 VAC 5-30-150[4]	$50	$61	$111
Swimming in unauthorized area or manner in a state park[3]	4 VAC 5-30-170[4]	$50	$61	$111
Boating in a state park[3] swimming area	4 VAC 5-30-190[4]	$50	$61	$111
Possession of firearms in a state park[3] by unauthorized persons	4 VAC 5-30-200[4]	$100	$61	$161
Fires in unauthorized areas of a state park[3]	4 VAC 5-30-220[4]	$100	$61	$161

Smoking in a prohibited area of a state park[3]	4 VAC 5-30-230[4]	$50	$61	$111
Unauthorized hunting in a state park[3]	4 VAC 5-30-240[4]	$100	$61	$161
Fishing in non-designated areas of a state park[3]	4 VAC 5-30-250[4]	$50	$61	$111
Allowing animals to run at large in a state park[3]	4 VAC 5-30-260[4]	$50	$61	$111
Games or athletic contests in non-designated areas of a state park[3]	4 VAC 5-30-270[4]	$50	$61	$111
Persons in non-designated areas of a state park[3] or failure to comply with a safety sign	4 VAC 5-30-274[4]	$50	$61	$111
Bicycle in non-designated areas of a state park[3] or failure to comply with a safety sign	4 VAC 5-30-276[4]	$50	$61	$111
Horses in non-designated areas of a state park[3]	4 VAC 5-30-280[4]	$50	$61	$111
Vehicles in a prohibited area of a state park[3]	4 VAC 5-30-290[4]	$50	$61	$111
Parking in an unauthorized area of a state park[3]	4 VAC 5-30-300[4]	$25	$61	$86
Obstructing traffic in a state park[3]	4 VAC 5-30-310[4]	$50	$61	$111
Operating an excessively loaded vehicle in a state park[3]	4 VAC 5-30-330[4]	$50	$61	$111
Engaging in commercial enterprise on a state park[3] without a permit	4 VAC 5-30-340[4]	$50	$61	$111
Operate a commercial vehicle on a state park[3] without a permit	4 VAC 5-30-360[4]	$50	$61	$111
Advertising within a state park[3] without a permit	4 VAC 5-30-370[4]	$50	$61	$111
Soliciting alms or contributions within a state park[3] without a permit	4 VAC 5-30-390[4]	$25	$61	$86
Landing an aircraft or parachute within a state park[3] without a permit	4 VAC 5-30-400[4]	$50	$61	$111
Importation of firewood into a state park[3] contrary to the limitations imposed by the DCR Director	4 VAC 5-30-410[4]	$100	$61	$161

Release of animals or wildlife captured or propagated elsewhere into a state park[3]	4 VAC 5-30-420[4]	$50	$61	$111
Feeding wildlife on a state park[3]	4 VAC 5-30-422[4]	$50	$61	$111
Constructing, maintaining or occupying unauthorized structures on department-owned lands or national forest lands	4 VAC 15-20-150[†]	$30	$61	$91
Using recorded or electronically amplified imitations of animal or bird calls or sounds to take wild animals and wild birds	4 VAC 15-40-30[†]	$50	$61	$111
Unlawfully possessing or using a bow or gun which is not unloaded and cased or dismantled on national forest lands statewide or on department-owned lands or on other department-managed lands west of the Blue Ridge Mountains during closed season	4 VAC 15-40-60(A)[†]	$75	$61	$136
Using a bow or firearm outside the established boundaries of an archery or shooting range or using a bow or firearm for other than target shooting at such archery or shooting range during closed season	4 VAC 15-40-60(D)[†]	$50	$61	$111
Chasing with a dog or training dogs on national forest lands or on department-owned lands outside authorized hunting, chasing or training seasons or during unauthorized raccoon hound field trials	4 VAC 15-40-60(E)[†]	$50	$61	$111
Failing to mark certain traps or snares with non-ferrous identity tags	4 VAC 15-40-170[††]	$25	$61	$86
Killing or crippling and knowingly allowing any nonmigratory game bird or game animal to be wasted without making a reasonable effort to retrieve and retain it	4 VAC 15-40-250[†]	$25	$61	$86

Unlawfully validate (notch) a bear license prior to killing a bear or after killing bear fail to validate a bear license tag before moving the carcass from the place of kill	4 VAC 15-50-81(A)†	$50	$61	$111
Failing to present bear carcass at an authorized checking station after having validated the appropriate bear license tag or failing to comply with procedure at such checking station	4 VAC 15-50-81(B)†	$50	$61	$111
Destroying the identity (sex) of bear before validating bear license tag and checking at an authorized checking station	4 VAC 15-50-81(C)†	$50	$61	$111
Unlawfully validate a deer license tag prior to killing a deer or after killing deer fail to validate a deer license tag before moving the carcass from the place of kill	4 VAC 15-90-231(A)†	$50	$61	$111
Failing to either present deer carcass at an authorized checking station after having validated the appropriate deer license tag or report the kill through automated reporting system	4 VAC 15-90-231(B)†	$50	$61	$111
Destroying the identity (sex) of deer before validating deer license tag and checking at an authorized checking station	4 VAC 15-90-231(C)†	$50	$61	$111
Unlawfully validate a turkey license tag prior to killing a turkey or after killing turkey failing to validate a turkey license tag before moving the carcass from the place of kill	4 VAC 15-240-81(A)†	$50	$61	$111
Failing to either present turkey carcass at an authorized checking station after having validated the appropriate turkey license tag or during the spring season only report the kill through automated reporting system	4 VAC 15-240-81(B)†	$50	$61	$111
Destroying the identity (sex) of turkey before validating turkey license tag and checking at an authorized checking system	4 VAC 15-240-81(C)†	$50	$61	$111

Failing to use nontoxic shot for waterfowl hunting	4 VAC 15-260-140[†]	$25	$61	$86
Using a rifle of a calibre less than 23 for hunting or killing of bear or deer[†††]	4 VAC 15-270-10	$100	$61	$161
Exceeding the creel limits for various species of fish on designated waters	4 VAC 15-320-25[†]	$60	$61	$121
Possessing illegal size game fish	4 VAC 15-320-25[†]	$25	$61	$86
Fishing in designated stocked trout waters or in waters specified in the regulations listed (during the period from May 16 through September 30) after obtaining the daily creel limit of trout	4 VAC 15-330-80[†]	$50	$61	$111
Feeding or baiting trout in designated stocked trout waters	4 VAC 15-330-90[†]	$10	$61	$71
Taking or attempting to take fish at any time by snagging, grabbing, snaring, gigging, with a striking iron, or with the use of SCUBA gear	4 VAC 15-350-10[†]	$50	$61	$111
Unlawfully using trot-line, jugline or set pole	4 VAC 15-350-60[†]	$25	$61	$86
Failure to display light while drifting or at anchor	4 VAC 15-420-100[††††]	$25	$61	$86
Vessel failing to obey regulatory markers; placing in, on or near the water unauthorized regulatory markers	4 VAC 15-370-50[†]	$30	$61	$91
Failure to keep to starboard when meeting head and head	4 VAC 15-390-20[††††]	$30	$61	$91
Failure to yield right-of-way when crossing	4 VAC 15-390-30[††††]	$30	$61	$91
Failure to keep clear when overtaking another vessel	4 VAC 15-390-40(A)[††††]	$30	$61	$91
Failure of motorboat to yield right of way to sailing vessel	4 VAC 15-390-50[††††]	$35	$61	$96
Failure to slacken speed to avoid endangerment of persons or	4 VAC 15-390-80[††††]	$30	$61	$91

property by wake				
Failure of person at least age 18 occupying front seat of vehicle to use safety belt system	46.2-1094(A) 46.2-1094(C)	$25	-	$25
Failure of driver to ensure that child up to age 8 is properly secured in approved child restraint device (first violation only)	46.2-1095(A) 46.2-1098	$50	-	$50
Failure of driver to ensure that another person 8 through 17 years of age is properly secured by safety belt system (first violation only)	46.2-1095(B) 46.2-1098	$50	-	$50
Failure of driver to carry written statement exempting child from use of child restraint device	46.2-1096 46.2-1098	$20	-	$20
Refusing officer's order to drive vehicle to weighing station	46.2-1137	$35	$61	$96
Driving in violation of HOT Lane Restrictions (first offense)	33.2-503(3)	$50	$61	$111
Driving in violation of HOT Lane Restrictions (second offense)	33.2-503(3)	$250	$61	$311
Driving in violation of HOT Lane Restrictions (third offense within two years of second offense)	33.2-503(3)	$500	$61	$561
Driving in violation of HOT Lane Restrictions (fourth and subsequent offense within three years of second offense)	33.2-503(3)	$1,000	$61	$1,061

* The description of offense is for reference and is not a legal definition.

** Unless otherwise provided by statute.

*** See §§ 9.1-106 and 53.1-120 of the Code.

[1] This designation "PRF Reg" refers to the Potomac River Fisheries Commission Regulations. The cite provides the regulation number, the section number and the subsection number.

[2] Subtract fees from total and post balance to fine.

[3] "Park" is defined pursuant to § 4 VAC 5-30-10 as and is intended for the purposes of this rule to mean all designated parks, parkways, historical and natural areas, sites and other recreational areas under the jurisdiction of the Virginia Department of Conservation and Recreation.

[4] Established pursuant to § 10.1-104 of the Code.

† These Regulations are promulgated pursuant to §§ 29.1-501 and 29.1-502 of the Code.

†† The Regulations are promulgated pursuant to §§ 29.1-103, 29.1-501 and 29.1-502 of the Code.

††† The Regulations are promulgated pursuant to § 29.1-501 of the Code.

†††† The Regulations are promulgated pursuant to §§ 29.1-701 and 29.1- and 29.1-802 of the Code.

[Amended effective July 1, 1988; April 1, 1990; February 1, 1991; July 1, 1992; February 1, 1993; September 1, 1994; December 1, 1994; January 1, 1996; July 1, 1997; August 15, 1997; October 21, 1998; February 1, 1999; July 1, 2000; July 1, 2001; May 1, 2002; July 1, 2002; April 1, 2003; May 1, 2003; July 1, 2003; February 6, 2004; July 1, 2004; December 27, 2004; July 1, 2007; April 9, 2008; July 1, 2008; July 13, 2009; January 11, 2010; July 1, 2010; March 1, 2012; January 1, 2013; January 1, 2014; October 1, 2014.]

PART FOUR. PRETRIAL PROCEDURES, DEPOSITIONS AND PRODUCTION AT TRIAL

Revised Effective October 1, 1977

Including Amendments Received Through October 15, 2015

RULE 4:0. APPLICATION OF PART FOUR

(a) The Rules in this Part Four shall apply in civil cases in the circuit courts. They also shall apply to proceedings for separate maintenance, divorce or annulment of marriage, for the exercise of the right of eminent domain, and for writs of habeas corpus or in the nature of coram nobis as provided in Rule 4:1(b)(5). Whenever in this Part Four the word "action" appears it shall mean a civil case, whether the claims arise at law or in equity.

(b) No provision of any of the Rules in this Part Four shall affect the practice of taking evidence at trial in any action; but such practice, including that of generally taking evidence ore tenus in actions upon claims arising at law and of generally taking evidence by deposition in equitable claims, shall continue unaffected hereby.

[Amended effective January 1, 2006.]

Comment: The distinction between discovery depositions and depositions de bene esse in suits in equity has substantially disappeared in practice and no longer serve a useful purpose. Any deposition taken in a suit in equity may be used to the extent permitted by Rule 4:7(a).

RULE 4:1. GENERAL PROVISIONS GOVERNING DISCOVERY

(a) Discovery Methods. Parties may obtain discovery by one or more of the following methods: depositions upon oral examination or written questions; written interrogatories; production of documents, electronically stored information, or things or permission to enter upon land or other property, for inspection and other purposes; physical and mental examinations; and requests for admission.

(b) Scope of Discovery. Unless otherwise limited by order of the court in accordance with these Rules, the scope of discovery is as follows:

(1) *In General.* Parties may obtain discovery regarding any matter, not privileged, which is relevant to the subject matter involved in the pending action, whether it relates to the claim or defense of the party seeking discovery or to the claim or defense of any other party, including the existence, description, nature, custody, condition and location of any books, documents, or other tangible things and the identity and location of persons having knowledge of any discoverable matter. It is not ground for objection that the information sought will be inadmissible at the trial if the information sought appears reasonably calculated to lead to the discovery of admissible evidence. Subject to the provisions of Rule 4:8 (g), the frequency or extent of use of the discovery methods set forth in subdivision (a) shall be limited by the court if it determines that: (i) the discovery sought is unreasonably cumulative or duplicative, or is obtainable from some other source that is more convenient, less burdensome, or less expensive; (ii) the party seeking discovery has had ample opportunity by discovery in the action to obtain the information sought; or (iii) the discovery is unduly burdensome or expensive, taking into account the needs of the case, the amount in controversy, limitations on the parties' resources, and the importance of the issues at stake in the litigation. The court may act upon its own initiative after reasonable notice to counsel of record or pursuant to a motion under subdivision (c).

(2) *Insurance Agreements.* A party may obtain discovery of the existence and contents of any insurance agreement under which any person (which includes any individual, corporation, partnership or other association) carrying on an insurance business may be liable to satisfy part or all of a judgment which may be entered in the action or to indemnify or reimburse for payments made to satisfy the judgment. Information concerning the insurance agreement is not by reason of disclosure admissible in evidence at trial. For purposes of this paragraph, an application for insurance shall not be treated as part of an insurance agreement.

(3) *Trial Preparation: Materials.* Subject to the provisions of subdivision (b)(4) of this Rule, a party may obtain discovery of documents and tangible things otherwise discoverable under subdivision (b)(1) of this Rule and prepared in anticipation of litigation or for trial by or for another party or by or for that other party's representative (including his attorney, consultant, surety, indemnitor, insurer, or agent) only upon a showing that the party seeking discovery has substantial need of the materials in the preparation of his case and that he is unable without undue hardship to obtain the substantial equivalent of the materials by other means. In ordering discovery of such materials when the required showing has been made, the court shall protect against disclosure of the mental impressions, conclusions, opinions, or legal theories of an attorney or other representative of a party concerning the litigation.

A party may obtain without the required showing a statement concerning the action or its subject matter previously made by that party. Upon request, a person not a party may obtain without the required showing a statement concerning the action or its subject matter previously made by that person. If the request is refused, the person may move for a court order. The provisions of Rule 4:12(a)(4) apply to the award of expenses incurred in relation to the motion. For purposes of this paragraph, a statement previously made is (A) a written statement signed or otherwise adopted or approved by the person making it, or (B) a stenographic, mechanical, electrical, or other recording, or a transcription thereof, which is a substantially verbatim recital of an oral statement by the person making it and contemporaneously recorded.

(4) *Trial Preparation: Experts; Costs—Special Provisions for Eminent Domain Proceedings.* Discovery of facts known and opinions held by experts, otherwise discoverable under the provisions of subdivision (b)(1) of this Rule and acquired or developed in anticipation of litigation or for trial, may be obtained only as follows:

(A)(i) A party may through interrogatories require any other party to identify each person whom the other party expects to call as an expert witness at trial, to state the subject matter on which the expert is expected to testify, and to state the substance of the facts and opinions to which the expert is expected to testify and a summary of the grounds for each opinion. (ii) A party may depose any person who has been identified as an expert whose opinion may be presented at trial, subject to the provisions of subdivision (b)(4)(C) of this Rule concerning fees and expenses. (iii) Upon motion, the court may order further discovery by other means, subject to such restrictions as to scope and such provisions, pursuant to subdivision (b)(4)(C) of this Rule, concerning fees and expenses as the court may deem appropriate.

(B) A party may discover facts known or opinions held by an expert who has been retained or specially employed by another party in anticipation of litigation or preparation for trial and who is not expected to be called as a witness at trial, only upon a showing of exceptional circumstances under which it is impracticable for the party seeking discovery to obtain facts or opinions on the same subject by other means.

(C) Unless manifest injustice would result, (i) the court shall require that the party seeking discovery pay the expert a reasonable fee for time spent and expenses incurred in responding to discovery under subdivisions (b)(4)(A)(ii), (b)(4)(A)(iii), and (b)(4)(B) of this Rule; and (ii) with respect to discovery obtained under subdivision (b)(4)(A)(iii) of this Rule the court may require, and with respect to discovery obtained under subdivision (b)(4)(B) of this Rule the court shall require, the party seeking discovery to pay the other party a fair portion of the fees and expenses reasonably incurred by the latter party in obtaining facts and opinions from the expert.

(D) Notwithstanding the provisions of subdivision (b)(4)(C) of this Rule, the condemnor in eminent domain proceedings, when it initiates discovery, shall pay all costs thereof, including without limitation the cost and expense of those experts discoverable under subdivision (b) of this Rule. The condemnor shall be deemed to have initiated discovery if it uses, or gives notice of the use of, any discovery method before the condemnee does so, even though the condemnee subsequently engages in discovery.

(5) *Limitations on Discovery in Certain Proceedings.* In any proceeding (1) for separate maintenance, divorce, or annulment of marriage, (2) for the exercise of the right of eminent domain, or (3) for a writ of habeas corpus or in the nature of coram nobis; (a) the scope of discovery shall extend only to matters which are relevant to the issues in the proceeding and which are not privileged; and (b) no discovery shall be allowed in any proceeding for a writ of habeas corpus or in the nature of coram nobis without prior leave of the court, which may deny or limit discovery in any such proceeding. In any proceeding for divorce or annulment of marriage, a notice to take depositions must be served in the Commonwealth by an officer authorized to serve the same, except that, in cases where such suits have been commenced and an appearance has been made on behalf of the defendant by counsel, notices to take depositions may be served in accordance with Rule 1:12.

(6) *Claims of Privilege or Protection of Trial Preparation Materials.*

(i) When a party withholds information otherwise discoverable under these rules by claiming that it is privileged or subject to protection as trial preparation material, the party shall make the claim expressly and shall describe the nature of the documents, communications, or things not produced or disclosed in a manner that, without revealing information itself privileged or protected, will enable other parties to assess the applicability of the privilege or protection.

(ii) If a party believes that a document or electronically stored information that has already been produced is privileged or its confidentiality is otherwise protected the producing party may notify any other party of such claim and the basis for the claimed privilege or protection. Upon receiving such notice, any party holding a copy of the designated material shall sequester or destroy its copies thereof, and shall not duplicate or disseminate such material pending disposition of the claim of privilege or protection by agreement, or upon motion by any party. If a receiving party has disclosed the information before being notified of the claim of privilege or other protection, that party must take reasonable steps to retrieve the designated material. The producing party must preserve the information until the claim of privilege or other protection is resolved.

(7) *Electronically Stored Information.* A party need not provide discovery of electronically stored information from sources that the party identifies as

not reasonably accessible because of undue burden or cost. On motion to compel discovery or for a protective order, the party from whom discovery is sought must show that the information is not reasonably accessible because of undue burden or cost. If that showing is made, the court may nonetheless order discovery from such sources if the requesting party shows good cause, considering the limitations of Rule 4:1(b)(1). The court may specify conditions for the discovery, including allocation of the reasonable costs thereof.

(8) *Pre–Motion Negotiation.* A motion under this Rule must be accompanied by a certification that the movant has in good faith conferred or attempted to confer with other affected parties in an effort to resolve the dispute without court action.

(c) Protective Orders. Upon motion by a party or by the person from whom discovery is sought, accompanied by a certification that the movant has in good faith conferred or attempted to confer with other affected parties in an effort to resolve the dispute without court action, and for good cause shown, the court in which the action is pending or alternatively, on matters relating to a deposition, the court in the county or city where the deposition is to be taken, may make any order which justice requires to protect a party or person from annoyance, embarrassment, oppression, or undue burden or expense, including one or more of the following: (1) that the discovery not be had; (2) that the discovery may be had only on specified terms and conditions, including a designation of the time or place; (3) that the discovery may be had only by a method of discovery other than that selected by the party seeking discovery; (4) that certain matters not be inquired into, or that the scope of the discovery be limited to certain matters; (5) that discovery be conducted with no one present except persons designated by the court; (6) that a deposition after being sealed be opened only by order of the court; (7) that a trade secret or other confidential research, development, or commercial information not be disclosed or be disclosed only in a designated way; (8) that the parties simultaneously file specified documents or information enclosed in sealed envelopes to be opened as directed by the court.

If the motion for a protective order is denied in whole or in part, the court may, on such terms and conditions as are just, order that any party or person provide or permit discovery. The provisions of Rule 4:12(a)(4) apply to the award of expenses incurred in relation to the motion.

(d) Sequence and Timing of Discovery.

(1) Unless the court upon motion, for the convenience of parties and witnesses and in the interests of justice, orders otherwise, methods of discovery may be used in any sequence and the fact that a party is conducting discovery, whether by deposition or otherwise, shall not operate to delay any other party's discovery.

(2) Discovery shall continue after a demurrer, plea or dispositive motion addressing one or more claims or counter-claims has been filed and while such motion is pending decision—unless the court in its discretion orders that discovery on some or all issues in the action should be suspended.

(e) Supplementation of Responses. A party who has responded to a request for discovery is under a duty to supplement or correct the response to include information thereafter acquired in the following circumstances.

(1) A party is under a duty promptly to amend and/or supplement all responses to discovery requests directly addressed to (A) the identity and location of persons having knowledge of discoverable matters, and (B) the identity of each person expected to be called as an expert witness at trial, the subject matter on which the expert is expected to testify, and the substance of the expert's testimony, when additional or corrective information becomes available.

(2) A party is under a duty promptly to amend and/or supplement all other prior responses to interrogatories, requests for production, or requests for admission if the party learns that any such response is in some material respect incomplete or incorrect and if the additional or corrective information has not otherwise been made known to the other parties during the discovery process or in writing.

(3) A court may order, or the parties may agree to provide, supplementation in addition to that required in subsections (1) and (2) of this subpart (e).

(4) A party may supplement a prior discovery response by filing an updated response labelled "Supplemental" or "Amended", or by otherwise notifying all other parties of the updated information in writing, signed by counsel of record.

(f) Service Under This Part. Except for the service of the notice required under Rule 4:2(a)(2), any notice or document required or permitted to be served under this Part Four shall be served as provided in Rule 1:12 except that any notice or document permitted to be served with the initial pleading shall be served (or accepted) in the same manner as such pleading.

(g) Signing of Discovery Requests, Responses, and Objections. Every request for discovery or response or objection thereto made by a party represented by an attorney shall be signed by at least one attorney of record in the attorney's individual name, whose address shall be stated. A party who is not represented by an attorney shall sign the request, response, or objection, and state the party's address. The signature of the attorney or party constitutes a certification that the signer has read the request, response, or objection, and that to the best of the signer's knowledge, information, and belief formed after a reasonable inquiry it is: (1) consistent with these Rules and warranted by existing law or a good faith argument for extension, modification, or reversal of existing law; (2) not interposed for any improper purpose, such as to harass or to cause unnecessary delay or needless increase in the cost of litigation; and (3) not unreasonable or unduly burdensome or expensive, given the needs of the case, the discovery already had in the case, the amount in controversy and the importance of the issues at stake in the litigation. If a request, response, or objection is not signed, it shall be stricken unless it is signed promptly after the omission is called to the attention of the party making the request, response, or objection, and a party shall not be obligated to take any action with respect to it until it is signed.

If a certification is made in violation of the rule, the court, upon motion or upon its own initiative, shall impose upon the person who made the certification, the party on whose behalf the request, response, or objection is made, or both, an appropriate sanction, which may include an order to pay the amount of the reasonable expenses incurred because of the violation, including a reasonable attorney's fee.

[Amended effective July 1, 1982; July 1, 1983; August 1, 1985; September 1, 1990; July 1, 1999; January 1, 2001; January 1, 2002; January 1, 2003; January 1, 2009; February 26, 2010, effective May 3, 2010.]

Comment: The Rules are confusing as to filing. Depositions are filed (Rules 4:2(a)(5); 4:5(f); 4:6(b)). The requirement of filing is not clear as to answers to interrogatories and admissions. [The 1983] amendment makes the filing requirement unmistakable.

Although the encompassing reference to "other papers" in § 8.01–271.1 literally includes discovery papers, the certification requirement in that context is governed by Rule 4:1(g) [as amended in 1990]. Discovery motions, however, fall within the ambit of § 8.01–271.1.

RULE 4:2. DEPOSITIONS BEFORE ACTION OR PENDING APPEAL

(a) Before Action.

(1) *Petition.* A person who desires to perpetuate his own testimony or that of another person regarding any matter that may be cognizable in any court of this Commonwealth may file a verified petition in the circuit court in the county or city of the residence of any expected adverse party. The petition shall be entitled in the name of the petitioner and shall show: (A) that the petitioner expects to be a party to an action cognizable in a court of this Commonwealth but is presently unable to bring it or cause it to be brought; (B) the subject matter of the expected action and his interest therein; (C) the facts which he desires to establish by the proposed testimony and his reasons for desiring to perpetuate it; (D) the names or a description of the persons he expects will be adverse parties and their addresses so far as known; and (E) the names and addresses of the persons to be examined and the substance of the testimony which he expects to elicit from each, and shall ask for an order authorizing the petitioner to take the depositions of the persons to be examined named in the petition, for the purpose of perpetuating their testimony.

(2) *Notice and Service.* The petitioner shall thereafter serve a notice upon each person named in the petition as an expected adverse party, together with a copy of the petition, stating that the petitioner will apply to the court, at a time and place named therein, for the order described in the petition. At least 21 days before the date of hearing the notice shall be served either within the Commonwealth in the manner provided for service of a complaint or without the Commonwealth in the manner provided by Code § 8.01–320; but if such service cannot with due diligence be made upon any expected adverse party named in the petition, the court may make such order as is just for service by publication or otherwise, and shall appoint, for persons not so served, an attorney who shall represent them, and, in case they are not otherwise represented, shall cross-examine the deponent. If any expected adverse party is a person under a disability, a guardian ad litem shall be appointed to attend on his behalf.

(3) *Order and Examination.* If the court is satisfied that the perpetuation of the testimony may prevent a failure or delay of justice, it shall make an order designating or describing the persons whose depositions may be taken and specifying the subject matter of the examination and whether the depositions shall be taken upon oral examination or written interrogatories. The depositions may then be taken in accordance with these Rules. The attendance of witnesses may be compelled by subpoena, and the court may make orders of the character provided for by Rules 4:9 and 4:10. For the purpose of applying these Rules to depositions for perpetuating testimony, each reference therein to the court in which the action is pending shall be deemed to refer to the court in which the petition for such deposition was filed.

(4) *Cost.* The cost of such depositions shall be paid by the petitioner, except that the other parties in interest who produce witnesses on their behalf or who make use of witnesses produced by others shall pay their proportionate part of the cost of the transcribed testimony and evidence taken or given on behalf of each of such parties.

(5) *Filing.* The depositions shall be certified as prescribed in Rule 4:5 and then returned to and filed by the clerk of the court which ordered its taking.

(6) *Use of Deposition.* If a deposition to perpetuate testimony is taken under these Rules or if, although not so taken, it would be admissible in evidence in the courts of the state in which it is taken, it may be used in any action involving the same subject matter subsequently brought in a court of this Commonwealth in accordance with the provisions of Rule 4:1.

(b) Pending Appeal. If an appeal has been taken from a judgment of a court of record or before the taking of an appeal if the time therefor has not expired, the court in which the judgment was rendered may allow the taking of the depositions of witnesses to perpetuate their testimony for use in the event of further proceedings in that court. In such case the party who desires to perpetuate the testimony may make a motion in the court in which the judgment was rendered for leave to take the depositions, upon the same notice and service thereof as if the action was pending therein. The motion shall show (1) the names and addresses of persons to be examined and the substance of the testimony which he expects to elicit from each; and (2) the reasons for perpetuating their testimony. If the court finds that the perpetuation of the testimony is proper to avoid a failure or delay of justice, it may make orders of the character provided for by Rules 4:9 and 4:10, and thereupon the depositions may be taken and used in the same manner and under the same conditions as are prescribed in these Rules for depositions taken in pending actions.

(c) Perpetuation of Testimony. This Rule provides the exclusive procedure to perpetuate testimony.

[Amended effective February 28, 2006.]

RULE 4:3. PERSONS BEFORE WHOM DEPOSITIONS MAY BE TAKEN

(a) Within This Commonwealth. Within this Commonwealth depositions may be taken before any person authorized by law to administer oaths, and if certified by his hand may be received without proof of the signature to such certificate.

(b) Within the United States. In any other State of the United States or within any territory or insular possession subject to the dominion of the United States, depositions may be taken before any officer authorized to take depositions in the jurisdiction wherein the witness may be, or before any commissioner appointed by the Governor of this Commonwealth.

(c) No Commission Necessary. No commission by the Governor of this Commonwealth shall be necessary to take a deposition whether within or without this Commonwealth.

(d) In Foreign Countries. In a foreign state or country depositions shall be taken (1) before any American minister plenipotentiary, charge d'affaires, secretary of embassy or legation, consul general, consul, vice-consul, or commercial agent of the United States in a foreign country, or any other representative of the United States therein, including commissioned officers of the armed services of the United States, or (2) before the mayor, or other magistrate of any city, town or corporation in such country, or any notary therein.

(e) Certificate When Deposition Taken Outside Commonwealth. Any person before whom a deposition is taken outside this Commonwealth shall certify the same with his official seal annexed; and, if he have none, the genuineness of his signature shall be authenticated by some officer of the same state or country, under his official seal, except that no seal shall be required of a commissioned officer of the armed services of the United States, but his signature shall be authenticated by the commanding officer of the military installation or ship to which he is assigned.

RULE 4:4. STIPULATIONS REGARDING DISCOVERY

Unless the court orders otherwise, the parties may by written stipulation (1) provide that depositions may be taken before any person, at any time or place, upon any notice, and in any manner and when so taken may be used like other depositions and (2) modify the procedures provided by these Rules for other methods of discovery, including discovery of electronically stored information. Stipulations may include agreements with non-party witnesses, consistent with Code § 8.01–420.4. Such stipulations shall be filed with the deposition or other discovery completed pursuant thereto.

[Amended effective August 29, 2005; January 1, 2009.]

RULE 4:5. DEPOSITIONS UPON ORAL EXAMINATION

(a) When Depositions May Be Taken. After commencement of the action, any party may take the testimony of any person, including a party, by deposition upon oral examination. Leave of court, granted with or without notice, must be obtained only if the plaintiff seeks to take a deposition before the expiration of the period within which a defendant may file a responsive pleading under Rule 3:8, except that leave is not required (1) if a defendant has served a notice of taking deposition, or (2) if special notice is given as provided in subdivision (b)(2) of this Rule. The attendance of witnesses may be compelled by subpoena. The deposition of a person confined in prison may be taken only by leave of court on such terms as the court prescribes.

(a1) Taking of Depositions.

(i) *Party Depositions.* A deposition of a party, or any witness designated under Rule 4:5(b)(6) to testify on behalf of a party, shall be taken in the county or city in which suit is pending, in an adjacent county or city, at a place upon which the parties agree, or at a place that the court in such suit may, for good cause, designate. Good cause may include the expense or inconvenience of a non-resident party defendant appearing in one of the locations specified in this subsection. The restrictions as to parties set forth in this subdivision (a1)(i) shall not apply where no responsive pleading has been filed or an appearance otherwise made.

(ii) *Non–Party Witness Depositions.* Unless otherwise provided by the law of the jurisdiction where a non-party witness resides, a deposition of a non-party witness shall be taken in the county or city where the non-party witness resides, is employed, or has a principal place of business; at a place upon which the witness and the parties to the litigation agree; or at a place that the court may, for good cause, designate.

(iii) *Taking Depositions Outside the State.* Within another state, or within a territory or insular possession subject to the dominion of the United States, or in a foreign country, depositions may be taken (1) on notice before a person authorized to administer oaths in the place in which the examination is held, either by the law thereof or, where applicable, the law of the United States, or (2) before a person appointed or commissioned by the court in which the action is pending, and such a person shall have the power by virtue of such appointment or commission to administer any necessary oath and take testimony, or (3) pursuant to a letter rogatory. A commission or letter rogatory shall be issued upon application and notice and on terms that are just and appropriate. It is not requisite to the issuance of a commission or a letter rogatory that the taking of the deposition in any other manner is impracticable or inconvenient. A notice or commission may designate the person before whom the deposition is to be taken either by name or descriptive title. A commission or letter rogatory may be addressed "To the Appropriate Authority in (here name the state, territory, or country)." Witnesses may be compelled to appear and testify at depositions taken outside this state by process issued and served in accordance with the law of the jurisdiction where the deposition is taken or, where applicable, the law of the United States. Upon motion, the courts of this State shall issue a commission or letter rogatory requesting the assistance of the courts or authorities of the foreign jurisdiction.

(iv) *Uniform Interstate Depositions and Discovery Act.* Depositions and related documentary production sought in Virginia pursuant to a subpoena issued under the authority of a foreign jurisdiction shall be subject to the provisions of the Uniform Interstate Depositions and Discovery Act, Virginia Code §§ 8.01–412.8 through 8.01–412.15.

(b) Notice of Examination: General Requirements; Special Notice; Production of Documents and Things; Deposition of Organization.

(1) A party desiring to take the deposition of any person upon oral examination shall give reasonable notice in writing to every other party to the action. The notice shall state the time and place for taking the deposition and the name and address of each person to be examined, if known, and, if the name is not known, a general description sufficient to identify him or the particular class or group to which he belongs. If a subpoena duces tecum is to be served on the person to be examined, the designation of the materials to be produced as set forth in the subpoena shall be attached to or included in the notice.

(2) Leave of court is not required for the taking of a deposition by plaintiff if the notice (A) states that the person to be examined is about to go out of the Commonwealth, or is about to go out of the United States, or is bound on a voyage to sea, and will be unavailable for examination unless his deposition is taken before expiration of the period for filing a responsive pleading under Rule 3:8, and (B) sets forth facts to support the statement. The plaintiff's attorney shall sign the notice, and his signature constitutes a certification by him that to the best of his knowledge, information, and belief the statement and supporting facts are true.

If a party shows that when he was served with notice under this subdivision (b)(2) he was unable through the exercise of diligence to obtain counsel to represent him at the taking of the deposition, the deposition may not be used against him.

(3) The court may for cause shown enlarge or shorten the time for taking the deposition.

(4) [Deleted.]

(5) The notice to a party deponent may be accompanied by a request made in compliance with Rule 4:9 for the production of documents and tangible things at the taking of the deposition. The procedure of Rule 4:9 shall apply to the request.

(6) A party may in his notice name as the deponent a public or private corporation or a partnership or association or governmental agency and designate with reasonable particularity the matters on which examination is requested. The organization so named shall designate one or more officers, directors, or managing agents, or other persons who consent to testify on its behalf, and may set forth, for each person designated, the matters on which he will testify. The persons so designated shall testify as to matters known or reasonably available to the organization. This subdivision (b)(6) does not preclude taking a deposition by any other procedure authorized in these Rules.

(7) Unless the court orders otherwise, a deposition may be taken by telephone, video conferencing, or teleconferencing. A deposition taken by telephone, video conferencing, or teleconferencing shall be taken before an appropriate officer in the locality where the deponent is present to answer questions propounded to him.

(c) Examination and Cross–Examination; Record of Examination; Oath; Objections. Examination and cross-examination of witnesses may proceed as permitted at the trial. The officer before whom the deposition is to be taken shall put the witness on oath and shall personally, or by someone acting under his direction and in his presence, record the testimony of the witness. If requested by one of the parties, the testimony shall be transcribed.

All objections made at time of the examination to the qualifications of the officer taking the deposition, or to the manner of taking it, or to the evidence presented, or to the conduct of any party, and any other objection to the proceedings, shall be noted by the officer upon the deposition. Any objection must be stated concisely in a nonargumentative and nonsuggestive manner. Evidence objected to shall be taken subject to the objections. In lieu of participating in the oral examination, parties may serve written questions in a sealed envelope on the party taking the deposition and he shall transmit them to the officer, who shall propound them to the witness and record the answers verbatim.

(d) Motion to Terminate or Limit Examination. At any time during the taking of the deposition, on motion of a party or of the deponent and upon a showing that the examination is being conducted in bad faith or in such manner as unreasonably to annoy, embarrass, or oppress the deponent or party, the court in which the action is pending or the court in the county or city where the deposition is being taken may order the officer conducting the examination to cease forthwith from taking the deposition, or may limit the scope and manner of the taking of the deposition as provided in Rule 4:1(c). If the order made terminates the examination, it shall be resumed thereafter only upon the order of the court in which the action is pending. Upon demand of the objecting party or deponent, the taking of the deposition shall be suspended for the time necessary to make a motion for an order. The provisions of Rule 4:12(a)(4) apply to the award of expenses incurred in relation to the motion.

(e) Submission to Witness; Changes; Signing. When the testimony is fully transcribed, the deposition shall be submitted to the witness for examination and shall be read to or by him, unless such examination and reading are waived by the witness and by the parties. Any changes in form or substance which the witness desires to make shall be entered upon the deposition by the officer with a statement of the reasons given by the witness for making them. The deposition shall then be signed by the witness, unless the parties by stipulation waive the signing or the witness is ill or cannot be found or refuses to sign. If the deposition is not signed by the witness within 21 days of its submission to him, the officer shall sign it and state on the record the fact of the waiver or of the illness or absence of the witness or the fact of the refusal to sign together with the reason, if any, given therefor; and the deposition may then be used as fully as though signed unless on a motion to suppress under Rule 4:7(d)(4) the court holds that the reasons given for the refusal to sign require rejection of the deposition in whole or in part.

(f) Certification and Filing by Officer; Exhibits; Copies; Notice of Filing.

(1) The officer shall prepare an electronic or digitally imaged copy of the deposition transcript, including signatures and any changes as provided in subsection (e) of this Rule, and shall certify on the deposition that the witness was duly sworn by him and that the deposition is a true record of the testimony given by the witness. In a divorce or annulment case, the officer shall then promptly file the electronic or digitally imaged deposition in the office of the clerk, notifying all other parties of such action. In all other cases, the officer shall then lodge the deposition with the attorney for the party who initiated the taking of the deposition, notifying the clerk and all parties of such action. Depositions taken pursuant to this Rule or Rule 4:6 (except depositions taken in divorce and annulment cases) shall not be filed with the clerk until the court so directs, either on its own initiative or upon the request of any party prior to or during the trial. Any such filing shall be made electronically unless otherwise ordered by the judge. Documents and things produced for inspection during the examination of the witness, shall, upon the request of a party, be marked for identification and annexed to and returned with the deposition, and may be inspected and copied by any party, except that (A) the person producing the materials may substitute copies to be marked for identification, if he affords to all parties fair opportunity to verify the copies by comparison with the originals, and (B) if the person producing the materials requests their return, the officer shall mark them, give each party an opportunity to inspect and copy them, and return them to the person producing them, and the materials may then be used in the same manner as if annexed to and returned with the deposition. Any party may move for an order that the original be annexed to and returned with the deposition to the court, pending final disposition of the case.

(2) Upon payment of reasonable charges therefor, the officer shall furnish a copy of the deposition to any party or to the deponent.

(3) The party taking the deposition shall give prompt notice of its filing to all other parties.

(g) Failure to Attend or to Serve Subpoena; Expenses.

(1) If the party giving the notice of the taking of a deposition fails to attend and proceed therewith and another party attends in person or by attorney pursuant to the notice, the court may order the party giving the notice to pay to such other party the reasonable expenses incurred by him and his attorney in attending, including reasonable attorney's fees.

(2) If the party giving the notice of the taking of a deposition of a witness fails to serve a subpoena upon him and the witness because of such failure does not attend, and if another party attends in person or by attorney because he expects the deposition of that witness to be taken, the court may order the party giving the notice to pay to such other party the reasonable expenses incurred by him and his attorney in attending, including reasonable attorney's fees.

[Amended effective July 1, 1983; July 1, 1984; August 1, 1985; July 1, 1986; December 1, 1987; January 1, 1990; September 1, 1991; January 1, 1994; January 1, 2001; August 29, 2005; January 1, 2006; July 1, 2008; July 1, 2009; May 2, 2011; Jan. 1, 2013.]

Comment: [The 1983] addition [of (b)(7)] is derived from Federal Rule 30(b)(7) as amended effective August 1, 1980.

[The 1984] change is designed to eliminate filing of discovery material in the clerk's office unless required for use at the trial. The burden of maintaining discovery material in clerk's offices has become quite substantial.

Depositions should be filed with the clerk [under the 1985 amendment] in all divorce and annulment cases since ore tenus hearings—at least in many areas—are rare in such cases.

See § 8.01–420.4.

RULE 4:6. DEPOSITIONS UPON WRITTEN QUESTIONS

(a) Serving Questions; Notice. After commencement of the action, any party may take the testimony of any person, including a party, by deposition upon written questions. The attendance of witnesses may be compelled by the use of subpoena. The deposition of a person confined in prison may be taken only by leave of court on such terms as the court prescribes.

A party desiring to take the deposition upon written questions shall serve them upon every other party with a notice stating (1) the name and address of the person who is to answer them, if known, and if the name is not known, a general description sufficient to identify him or the particular class or group to which he belongs, and (2) the name or descriptive title and address of the officer before whom the deposition is to be taken. A deposition upon written questions may be taken of a public or private corporation or a partnership or association or governmental agency in accordance with the provisions of Rule 4:5(b)(6).

Within 21 days after the notice and written questions are served, a party may serve cross questions upon all other parties. Within 10 days after being served with cross questions, a party may serve redirect questions upon all other parties. Within 10 days after being served with redirect questions, a party may serve recross questions upon all other parties. The court may for cause shown enlarge or shorten the time.

(b) Officer to Take Responses and Prepare Record. A copy of the notice and copies of all questions served shall be delivered by the party taking the deposition to the officer designated in the notice, who shall proceed promptly, in the manner provided by Rule 4:5(c), (e), and (f), to take the testimony of the witness in response to the questions and to prepare, certify, and file the electronic or digitally imaged deposition or lodge the deposition with the attorney for the party who initiated the taking of the deposition, attaching thereto the copy of the notice and the questions received.

(c) Notice of Filing. When the deposition is filed, the party taking it shall promptly give notice thereof to all other parties.

[Amended effective May 2, 2011.]

RULE 4:6A. NUMBER OF DEPOSITIONS

There shall be no limit on the number of witnesses whose depositions may be taken by a party except by order of the court for good cause shown.

[Adopted effective July 1, 1983. Amended effective October 1, 2001.]

Comment: This new rule, designed to limit discovery sharply, is taken from the rules of the United States District Court for the Eastern District of Virginia.

RULE 4:7. USE OF DEPOSITIONS IN COURT PROCEEDINGS

(a) Use of Depositions. At the trial or upon the hearing of a motion or an interlocutory proceeding, any part or all of a deposition, so far as admissible under the rules of evidence applied as though the witness were then present and testifying, may be used against any party who was present or represented at the taking of the deposition or who had reasonable notice thereof, in accordance with any of the following provisions:

(1) Any deposition taken in a civil action may be used for any purpose in supporting or opposing an equitable claim; provided, however, that such a deposition may be used on an issue heard by an advisory jury empaneled pursuant to Code § 8.01–336(E) or a hearing ore tenus only as provided by subdivision (a)(4) of this Rule.

(2) Any deposition may be used by any party for the purpose of contradicting or impeaching the testimony of deponent as a witness.

(3) The deposition of a party or of anyone who at the time of taking the deposition was an officer, director, or managing agent, or a person designated under Rule 4:5(b)(6) or 4:6(a) to testify on behalf of a public or private corporation, partnership or association or governmental agency which is a party may be used by an adverse party for any purpose.

(4) The deposition of a witness, whether or not a party, may be used by any party for any purpose in any action upon a claim arising at law, issue heard by an advisory jury empaneled pursuant to Code § 8.01–336(E), or hearing ore tenus upon an equitable claim if the court finds: (A) that the witness is dead; or (B) that the witness is at a greater distance than 100 miles from the place of trial or hearing, or is out of this Commonwealth, unless it appears that the absence of the witness was procured by the party offering the deposition; or (C) that the witness is unable to attend or testify because of age, illness, infirmity, or imprisonment; or (D) that the party offering the deposition has been unable to procure the attendance of the witness by subpoena; or (E) that the witness is a judge, or is a superintendent of a hospital for the insane more than 30 miles from the place of trial, or is a physician, surgeon, dentist, chiropractor, or registered nurse who, in the regular course of his profession, treated or examined any party to the proceeding, or is in any

public office or service the duties of which prevent his attending court provided, however, that if the deponent is subject to the jurisdiction of the court, the court may, upon a showing of good cause or sua sponte, order him to attend and to testify ore tenus; or (F) upon application and notice, that such exceptional circumstances exist as to make it desirable, in the interest of justice and with due regard to the importance of presenting the testimony of witnesses orally in open court, to allow the deposition to be used.

(5) If only part of a deposition is offered in evidence by a party, an adverse party may require him to introduce any other part which ought in fairness to be considered with the part introduced, and any party may introduce any other parts.

(6) No deposition shall be read in any action against a person under a disability unless it be taken in the presence of the guardian ad litem appointed or attorney serving pursuant to § 8.01–9, or upon questions agreed on by the guardian or attorney before the taking.

(7) In any action, the fact that a deposition has not been offered in evidence prior to an interlocutory decree or order shall not prevent its thereafter being so offered except as to matters ruled upon in such interlocutory decree or order; provided, however, that such deposition may be read as to matters ruled upon in such an interlocutory decree or order if the principles applicable to after-discovered evidence would permit its introduction.

Substitution of parties does not affect the right to use depositions previously taken; and when there are pending in the same court several actions or suits between the same parties, depending upon the same facts, or involving the same matter of controversy, in whole or in part, a deposition taken in one of such actions or suits, upon notice to the same party or parties, may be read in all, so far as it is applicable and relevant to the issue; and, when an action in any court of the United States or of this or any other state has been dismissed and another action involving the same subject matter is afterward brought between the same parties or their representatives or successors in interest, all depositions lawfully taken and duly filed in the one action may be used in the other as if originally taken therefor.

(b) Form of Presentation; Objections to Admissibility. A party may offer deposition testimony pursuant to this Rule in stenographic or non-stenographic form. Except as otherwise directed by the court, if all or part of a deposition is offered, the offering party shall provide the court with a transcript of the portions so offered in either form or in electronic or digitally imaged form. Except as provided in Rule 1:18 and subject to the provisions of subdivision (d)(3) of this Rule, objection may be made at the trial or hearing to receiving in evidence any deposition or part thereof for any reason which would require the exclusion of the evidence if the witness were then present and testifying.

(c) Effect of Taking or Using Depositions. A party does not make a person his own witness for any purpose by taking his deposition. The introduction in evidence of the deposition or any part thereof for any purpose other than that of contradicting or impeaching the deponent makes the deponent the witness of the party introducing the deposition, but this shall not apply to the use by an adverse party of a deposition under subdivision (a)(3) of this Rule. At the trial or hearing any party may rebut any relevant evidence contained in a deposition whether introduced by him or by any other party.

(d) Effect of Errors and Irregularities in Depositions.

(1) *As to Notice.* All errors and irregularities in the notice for taking a deposition are waived unless written objection is promptly served upon the party giving the notice.

(2) *As to Disqualification of Officer.* Objection to taking a deposition because of disqualification of the officer before whom it is to be taken is waived unless made before the taking of the deposition begins or as soon thereafter as the disqualification becomes known or could be discovered with reasonable diligence.

(3) *As to Taking of Deposition.*

(A) Objections to the competency of a witness or to the competency, relevancy, or materiality of testimony are not waived by failure to make them before or during the taking of the deposition, unless the ground of the objection is one which might have been obviated or removed if presented at that time.

(B) Errors and irregularities occurring at the oral examination in the manner of taking the deposition, in the form of the questions or answers, in the oath or affirmation, or in the conduct of parties, and errors of any kind which might be obviated, removed, or cured if promptly presented, are waived unless seasonable objection thereto is made at the taking of the deposition.

(C) Objections to the form of written questions submitted under Rule 4:6 are waived unless served in writing upon the party propounding them within the time allowed for serving the succeeding cross or other questions and within 5 days after service of the last questions authorized.

(4) *As to Completion and Return of Deposition.* Errors and irregularities in the manner in which the testimony is transcribed or the deposition is prepared, signed, certified, sealed, endorsed, transmitted, filed or otherwise dealt with by the officer under Rules 4:5 and 4:6 are waived unless a motion to suppress the deposition or some part thereof is made with reasonable promptness after such defect is, or with due diligence might have been, ascertained.

(e) Limitation on Use of Depositions. No motion for summary judgment or to strike the evidence shall be sustained when based in whole or in part upon any depositions under Rule 4:5, unless such use of depositions is permitted by § 8.01–420.

(f) Record. Depositions shall become a part of the record only to the extent that they are offered in evidence.

[Amended effective August 15, 1979; July 1, 1983; February 1, 1997; July 1, 2000; October 15, 2003; January 1, 2006; May 2, 2011; July 1, 2013.]

Cross-reference: As to depositions as basis for motion for summary judgment or to strike evidence, see § 8.01–420.

Comment [to 1983 amendment adding paragraph (f)]: The Rules are not clear as to when discovery material becomes a part of the record. Only Rule 4:11(c) relating to requests for admission and responses thereto makes the matter clear as to those documents. The record should not be cluttered with material not offered in evidence.

RULE 4:7A. AUDIO–VISUAL DEPOSITIONS

(a) When Depositions May Be Taken by Audio–Visual Means. Any depositions permitted under these Rules may be taken by audio-visual means including, but not limited to, videoconferencing and teleconferencing, as authorized by and when taken in compliance with law.

(b) Procedure.

(1) The deposition must begin with an oral or written statement on camera which includes (i) each operator's name and business address or, if applicable, the identity of the video conferencing or teleconferencing proprietor and locations participating in the video conference or teleconference; (ii) the name and business address of the operator's employer; (iii) the date, time and place of the deposition; (iv) the caption of the case; (v) the name of the witness; (vi) the party on whose behalf the deposition is being taken; (vii) with respect to video conferencing or teleconferencing, the identities of persons present at the deposition and the location of each such person; and (viii) any stipulations by the parties; and

(2) In addition, all counsel present on behalf of any party or witness shall identify themselves on camera. The oath for witnesses shall be administered on camera. If the length of a deposition requires the use of more than one recording unit, the end of each unit and the beginning of each succeeding unit shall be announced on camera. At the conclusion of a deposition, a statement shall be made on camera that the deposition is concluded. A statement may be made on camera setting forth any stipulations made by counsel concerning the custody of the audio-visual recording and exhibits or other pertinent matters; and

(3) All objections must be made as in the case of stenographic depositions.

(c) Editing. No audio-visual deposition shall be edited except pursuant to a stipulation of the parties or pursuant to order of the court and only as and to the extent directed in such stipulation and/or order. In any case where the parties stipulate or the court orders the audio-visual recording to be edited prior to its use, the original recording shall not be altered and the editing shall be done on a copy or copies.

(d) Recording and Transcription.

(1) Any deposition may be recorded by audio-visual means without a stenographic record. The audio-visual recording is an official record of the deposition. A transcript prepared by a court reporter shall also be deemed an official record of the deposition. Any party may make, at its own expense, a simultaneous stenographic or audio record of the deposition. Upon request and at his own expense, any party is entitled to an audio or audio-visual copy of the audio-visual recording.

(2) If an appeal is taken in the case, the appellant must cause to be prepared and filed with the clerk a written transcript of that portion of an audio-visual deposition made a part of the record in the trial court to the extent germane to an issue on appeal. The appellee may designate additional portions to be so prepared by the appellant and filed.

(e) Use. An audio-visual deposition may be used for any purpose and under any circumstances in which a stenographic deposition may be used.

(f) Submission to the Witness; Changes; Signing. The provisions of Rule 4:5(e) shall not apply to an audio-visual deposition. The other provisions of Rule 4:5 shall be applicable to the extent practicable.

(g) Filing. Unless otherwise stipulated by the parties or ordered by the court, the original audio-visual recording of a deposition, any copy edited pursuant to stipulation or an order of the court, and exhibits shall be filed only in accord with Rule 4:5(f)(1).

[Adopted effective July 1, 1984. Amended effective January 1, 1994; January 1, 2001.]

RULE 4:8. INTERROGATORIES TO PARTIES

(a) Availability; Procedures for Use. Any party may serve upon any other party written interrogatories to be answered by the party served or, if the party served is a public or private corporation or a partnership or association or governmental agency, by any officer or agent, who shall furnish such information as is available to the party. Interrogatories may, without leave of court, be served upon the plaintiff after commencement of the action and upon any other party with or after service of the complaint upon that party.

(b) Form. The party answering the interrogatories shall restate each question, by photocopying it or otherwise, then insert the word "Answer" and immediately thereafter state the response to that question. The answering party shall attach the necessary oath and certificate of service to the answers.

(c) Filing.

(1) Interrogatories and answers or objections thereto shall not be filed unless the court directs such filing on its own initiative or upon the request of any party prior to or during the trial.

(2) When the propriety or sufficiency of any interrogatory, answer or objection, or the service thereof, is challenged, or any other issue concerning such discovery is presented to the court for decision, copies of the relevant items, including any applicable certificates of service, shall be made available to the court by counsel.

(3) In an Electronically Filed Case, submission of interrogatories, answers, objections and certificates of service as provided in subdivisions (c)(1) and (c)(2) of this Rule shall be made by filing an electronic or digitally imaged copy thereof, unless the court directs otherwise.

(d) Answers. Each interrogatory shall be answered separately and fully in writing under oath, unless it is objected to, in which event the reasons for objection shall be stated in lieu of an answer. The answers are to be signed by the person making them, and the objections signed by the attorney making them. The party upon whom the interrogatories have been served shall serve a copy of the answers, and objections if any, within 21 days after the service of the interrogatories, except that a defendant may serve answers or objections within 28 days after service of the bill of complaint or motion for judgment upon that defendant. The court may allow a shorter or longer time. The party submitting the interrogatories may move for an order under Rule 4:12(a) with respect to any objection to or other failure to answer an interrogatory.

(e) Scope; Use. Interrogatories may relate to any matters which can be inquired into under Rule 4:1(b), and the answers may be used to the extent permitted by the rules of evidence and for the purposes of Rule 3:20. Only such interrogatories and the answers thereto as are offered in evidence shall become a part of the record.

An interrogatory otherwise proper is not necessarily objectionable merely because an answer to the interrogatory involves an opinion or contention that relates to fact or the application of law to fact, but the court may order that such an interrogatory need not be answered until after designated discovery has been completed or until a pre-trial conference or other later time.

(f) Option to Produce Business Records. Where the answer to an interrogatory may be derived or ascertained from the business records, including electronically stored information, of the party upon whom the interrogatory has been served or from an examination, audit or inspection of such business records, or from a compilation, abstract or summary based thereon, and the burden of deriving or ascertaining the answer is substantially the same for the party serving the interrogatory as for the party served, it is a sufficient answer to such interrogatory to specify the records from which the answer may be derived or ascertained and to afford to the party serving the interrogatory reasonable opportunity to examine, audit or inspect such records and to make copies, compilations, abstracts or summaries. A specification shall be in sufficient detail to permit the interrogating party to locate and to identify, as readily as can the party served, the records from which the answer may be ascertained. A specification of electronically stored information may be made under this Rule if the information will be made available in a reasonably usable form or forms.

(g) Limitation on Interrogatories. No party shall serve upon any other party, at any one time or cumulatively, more than thirty written interrogatories, including all parts and sub-parts, without leave of court for good cause shown.

[Amended effective July 1, 1983; July 1, 1984; August 1, 1985; September 1, 1991; July 1, 1999; January 1, 2001; January 1, 2006; February 28, 2006; January 1, 2009; May 2, 2011.]

Comment: Subsection (b) has been inserted (and the other paragraphs relettered) [in 1983] in order to facilitate responses to interrogatories, to avoid the necessity of reproducing them, and to produce a single cohesive document.

The [1983] change to subsection (d), like the addition to Rule 4:5, is designed to clarify the contents of the record.

The [1983] addition of subsection (f), like Rule 4:6A, is taken from the Rules of the United States District Court for the Eastern District of Virginia.

The [1984] establishment of new subsection (c) is intended to relieve the crowded condition of clerks' offices. The [1984] amendment to subsection (d) makes it clear that interrogatories and their answers may be used in connection with summary judgments in suits in equity.

The first [1985] change [paragraph (a)] eliminates an unnecessary act; the second [paragraph (c)] is clarifying.

RULE 4:9. PRODUCTION BY PARTIES OF DOCUMENTS, ELECTRONICALLY STORED INFORMATION, AND THINGS; ENTRY ON LAND FOR INSPECTION AND OTHER PURPOSES; PRODUCTION AT TRIAL

(a) Scope. Any party may serve on any other party a request (1) to produce and permit the party making the request, or someone acting on his behalf, to inspect, copy, test, or sample any designated documents or electronically stored information (including writings, drawings, graphs, charts, photographs, and other data or data compilations stored in any medium from which information can be obtained, translated, if necessary, by the respondent into reasonably usable form), or to inspect, copy, test, or sample any designated tangible things which constitute or contain matters within the scope of Rule 4:1(b) and which are in the possession, custody, or control of the party upon whom the request is served; or (2) to produce any such documents or electronically stored information to the court in which the proceeding is pending at the time of trial; or (3) to permit entry upon designated land or other property in the possession or control of the party upon whom the request is served for the purpose of inspection and measuring, surveying, photographing, testing, or sampling the property or any designated object or operation thereon, within the scope of Rule 4:1(b).

(b) Procedure.

(i) *Initiation of the Request.* The request may, without leave of court, be served upon the plaintiff after commencement of the action and upon any other party with or after service of the complaint upon that party. The request shall set forth the items to be inspected either by individual item or by category, and describe each item and category with reasonable particularity. The request shall specify a reasonable time, place, period and manner of making the inspection and performing the related acts. The request may specify the form or forms in which electronically stored information is to be produced.

(ii) *Response.* The party upon whom the request is served shall serve a written response within 21 days after the service of the request, except that a defendant may serve a response within 28 days after service of the complaint upon that defendant. The court may allow a shorter or longer time. The response shall state, with respect to each item or category, that inspection and related activities will be permitted as requested, unless the request is objected to, including an objection to the requested form or forms for producing electronically stored information, stating the reasons for the objection. If objection is made to part of an item or category, the part shall be specified and production shall be permitted as to the remaining parts. If objection is made to the requested form or forms for producing electronically stored information—or if no form was specified in the request—the responding party must state the form or forms it intends to use. The party submitting the request may move for an order under Rule 4:12(a) with respect to any objection to or other failure to respond to the request or any part thereof, or any failure to permit inspection as requested. A motion under this Rule must be accompanied by a certification that the movant has in good faith conferred or attempted to confer with other affected parties in an effort to resolve the dispute without court action.

(iii) *Organization, Reasonable Accessibility, and Forms of Production.* Unless the parties otherwise agree, or the court otherwise orders:

(A) Production of Documents. A party who produces documents for inspection either shall produce them as they are kept in the usual course of business or shall organize and label them to correspond with the categories in the request.

(B) Electronically Stored Information.

(1) Responses to a request for production of electronically stored information shall be subject to the provisions of Rules 4:1(b)(7) and 4:1(b)(8).

(2) If a request does not specify the form or forms for producing electronically stored information, or if a responding party objects to the requested form or forms of production, a responding party must produce the information as it is ordinarily maintained if it is reasonably usable in such form or forms, or must produce the information in another form or forms in which it is reasonably usable. A party need not produce the same electronically stored information in more than one form.

(iv) *Proceedings Under the Uniform Interstate Depositions and Discovery Act.* Production of documents and electronic records sought in Virginia pursuant to a subpoena issued under the authority of a foreign jurisdiction shall be subject to the provisions of the Uniform Interstate Depositions and Discovery Act, Virginia Code §§ 8.01–412.8 through 8.01–412.15.

(c) Proceedings on Failure or Refusal to Comply. If a party fails or refuses to obey an order made under section (b) of this Rule, the court may proceed as provided by Rule 4:12(b)(2).

(d) Filing. Requests to a party pursuant to this Rule and responses or objections shall be filed as provided in Rule 4:8(c).

[Amended effective August 1, 1985; July 1, 1987; July 1, 1988; February 1, 1990; February 1, 1999; July 1, 1999; July 1, 2000; October 15, 2003; April 1, 2004; January 1, 2005; February 28, 2006; January 1, 2009; July 1, 2009.]

Comment: Again, the purpose of the [1985] amendment is to reduce the clutter in the clerk's office.

RULE 4:9A. PRODUCTION FROM NON-PARTIES OF DOCUMENTS, ELECTRONICALLY STORED INFORMATION, AND THINGS AND ENTRY ON LAND FOR INSPECTION AND OTHER PURPOSES; PRODUCTION AT TRIAL

(a) Issuance of a Subpoena Duces Tecum. Except as provided in paragraph (d) of this Rule, a subpoena duces tecum may be issued:

(1) *By the Clerk of Court.* Upon written request therefor filed with the clerk of the court in which the action or suit is pending by counsel of record for any party or by a party having no counsel in any pending case, with a certificate that a copy thereof has been served pursuant to Rule 1:12 upon counsel of record and to parties having no counsel, the clerk shall issue to a person not a party therein a subpoena duces tecum subject to this Rule.

(2) *By an Attorney.* In a pending civil proceeding, a subpoena duces tecum may be issued by an attorney-at-law as an officer of the court if he or she is an active member of the Virginia State Bar at the time of issuance. An attorney may not issue a subpoena duces tecum in those civil proceedings excluded in Virginia Code § 8.01–407. An attorney-issued subpoena duces tecum must be signed as if a pleading and must contain the attorney's address, telephone number and Virginia State Bar identification number. A copy of any

attorney-issued subpoena duces tecum must be mailed or delivered to the clerk's office of the court in which the case is pending on the day of issuance with a certificate that a copy thereof has been served pursuant to Rule 1:12 upon counsel of record and to parties having no counsel. If time for compliance with an attorney-issued subpoena duces tecum is less than fourteen (14) days after service of the subpoena, the person to whom the subpoena is directed may serve on the party issuing the subpoena a written objection setting forth any grounds upon which such production, inspection, copying, sampling or testing should not be had. If an objection is made, the party issuing the subpoena shall not be entitled to the requested production, inspection, copying, sampling or testing, except pursuant to an order of the court in which the civil proceeding is pending. If an objection is made, the party issuing the subpoena may, upon notice to the person to whom the subpoena is directed, move for an order to compel the production, inspection, copying, sampling or testing. Upon a timely motion, the court may quash, modify or sustain the subpoena as provided above in subsection (c) of this Rule.

(b) Content of Subpoena Duces Tecum; Objections. Subject to paragraph (d) of this Rule, a subpoena duces tecum shall command the person to whom it is directed, or someone acting on his behalf, to produce the documents, electronically stored information, or designated tangible things (including writings, drawings, graphs, charts, photographs, and other data or data compilations stored in any medium from which information can be obtained, translated, if necessary, by the respondent into reasonably usable form) designated and described in said request, and to permit the party filing such request, or someone acting in his behalf, to inspect and copy, test, or sample any designated tangible things which constitute or contain matters within the scope of Rule 4:1(b) which are in the possession, custody or control of such person to whom the subpoena is directed, at a time and place and for the period specified in the subpoena. A subpoena may specify the form or forms in which electronically stored information is to be produced.

(c) Responding to a Subpoena; Objections; Production of Documents and Electronically Stored Information.

(1) *Production of Documents.* A person responding to a subpoena to produce documents shall produce them as they are kept in the usual course of business or shall organize and label them to correspond with the categories in the demand.

(2) *Electronically Stored Information.*

(A) A person responding to a subpoena need not provide discovery of electronically stored information from sources the responder identifies as not reasonably accessible because of undue burden or cost. On motion to compel production or to quash a subpoena, the person from whom production is sought under the subpoena must show that the information sought is not reasonably accessible because of undue burden or cost. If that showing is made, the court may nonetheless order production of responsive material from such sources if the subpoenaing party shows good cause, considering the limitations of Rule 4:1(b)(1). The court may specify conditions for the production of such information, including allocation of the reasonable costs thereof.

(B) If a subpoena does not specify the form or forms for producing electronically stored information, a person responding thereto must produce the information as it is ordinarily maintained if it is reasonably usable in such form or forms, or must produce the information in another form or forms in which it is reasonably usable. A person responding to a subpoena need not produce the same electronically stored information in more than one form.

(3) *Objections and Procedures.* The court, upon written motion promptly made by the person so required to produce, or by the party against whom such production is sought, may (1) quash or modify the subpoena, or the method or form for production of electronically stored information, if the subpoena would otherwise be unduly burdensome or expensive, (2) condition denial of the motion to quash or modify upon the advancement by the party in whose behalf the subpoena is issued of some or all of the reasonable cost of producing the documents, electronically stored information, and tangible things so designated and described or (3) direct that the documents and tangible things subpoenaed, including electronically stored information (unless another location for production is agreed upon by the requesting and producing parties), be returned only to the office of the clerk of the court through which such documents and tangible things are subpoenaed in which event, upon request of any party in interest, or his attorney, the clerk of such court shall permit the withdrawal of such documents and tangible things by such party or his attorney for such reasonable period of time as will permit his inspection, photographing, or copying thereof.

(4) *Pre-Motion Negotiation.* A motion under this Rule must be accompanied by a certification that the movant has in good faith conferred or attempted to confer with other affected parties in an effort to resolve the dispute without court action.

(d) Certain Officials. No request to produce made pursuant to paragraph (b) above shall be served, and no subpoena provided for in paragraph (c) above shall issue, until prior order of the court is obtained when the party upon whom the request is to be served or the person to whom the subpoena is to be directed is the Governor, Lieutenant Governor, or Attorney General of this Commonwealth, or a judge of any court thereof; the President or Vice President of the United States; any member of the President's Cabinet; any Ambassador or Consul; or any Military Officer on active duty holding the rank of Admiral or General.

(e) Certain Health Records. Patient health records protected by the privacy provisions of Code Section 32.1–127.1:03 shall be disclosed only in accordance with the provisions and procedures prescribed by that statute.

(f) Copies of Documents and Other Subpoenaed Information.

(1) *Documents.* When one party to a civil proceeding subpoenas documents, the subpoenaing party, upon receipt of the subpoenaed documents, shall, if requested, provide true and full copies of the same to any party or to the attorney for any other party in accordance with Code § 8.01–417(B).

(2) *Electronically Stored Information.* When one party to a civil proceeding subpoenas and obtains electronically stored information, the subpoenaing party shall, if requested, provide true and full copies of the same to any party or that party's attorney, in the form the subpoenaing party received the information, upon reimbursement of the proportionate cost of obtaining such materials.

(g) Proceedings on Failure or Refusal to Comply. If a non-party, after being served with a subpoena issued under the provisions of this Rule, fails or refuses to comply therewith, he may be proceeded against as for contempt of court as provided in § 18.2–456.

[Adopted effective January 1, 2009.]

RULE 4:10. PHYSICAL AND MENTAL EXAMINATION OF PERSONS

(a) Order for Examination. When the mental or physical condition (including the blood group) of a party, or of a person in the custody or under the legal control of a party, is in controversy, the court in which the action is pending, upon motion of an adverse party, may order the party to submit to a physical or mental examination by one or more health care providers, as defined in § 8.01–581.1, employed by the moving party or to produce for examination the person in the party's custody or legal control. The order may be made only on motion for good cause shown and upon notice to the person to be examined and to all parties, shall specify the time, place, manner, conditions, and scope of the examination and the person or persons by whom it is to be made, and shall fix the time for filing the report and furnishing the copies.

(b) Out–of–State of Examiners. Examiners named in such an order shall be licensed to practice in, and shall be residents of or have an office in, this Commonwealth. However, notwithstanding the reference to licensure by this Commonwealth in the definition of health care providers in § 8.01–581.1, the court may, in the exercise of its sound discretion and upon determining that the ends of justice will be served, order an examination by one who is not licensed to practice in, is not a resident of, and does not have an office in, this Commonwealth but who is duly licensed in his or her jurisdiction.

(c) Report of Examiner.

(1) A written report of the examination shall be made by the examiner to the court and filed with the clerk thereof before the trial and a copy furnished to each party. The report shall be detailed, setting out the findings of the examiner, including results of all tests made, diagnosis and conclusions, together with like reports of all earlier examinations of the same condition. In an Electronically Filed Case, the report of examination shall be filed in electronic or digital image form as provided in Rule 1:17.

(2) The written report of the examination so filed with the clerk may be read into evidence if offered by the party who submitted to the examination. A party examined who takes the deposition of any examiner who shall have conducted an examination ordered pursuant to this Rule, waives any privilege that might have been asserted in that action or in any other involving the same controversy, regarding the testimony of every other person who has examined or may thereafter examine the party in respect of the same mental or physical condition.

(3) This subdivision applies to examination made by agreement of the parties, unless the agreement expressly provides otherwise. This subdivision does not preclude discovery of a report of a health care examiner or the taking of a deposition of such examiner in accordance with the provisions of any other Rule.

[Amended effective February 1, 1992; January 1, 2001; May 2, 2011.]

Comment: Attention should also be given to § 8.01–413.

RULE 4:11. REQUESTS FOR ADMISSION

(a) Request for Admission. A party may serve upon any other party a written request for the admission, for purposes of the pending action only, of the truth of any matters within the scope of Rule 4:1(b) set forth in the request that relate to statements or opinions of fact or of the application of law to fact, including the genuineness of any documents described in the request. Copies of documents shall be served with the request unless they have been or are otherwise furnished or made available for inspection and copying. The request may, without leave of court, be served upon the plaintiff after commencement of the action and upon any other party with or after service of the complaint upon that party.

Each matter of which an admission is requested shall be separately set forth. The matter is admitted unless, within 21 days after service of the request, or within such shorter or longer time as the court may allow, the party to whom the request is directed serves upon the party requesting the admission a written answer or objection addressed to the matter, signed by the party or by his attorney, but, unless the court shortens the time, a defendant shall not be required to serve answers or objections before the expiration of 28 days after service of the complaint upon him. If objection is made, the reasons therefore shall be stated. The answer shall specifically deny the matter or set forth in detail the reasons why the answering party cannot truthfully admit or deny the matter. A denial shall fairly meet the substance of the requested admission, and when good faith requires that a party qualify his answer or deny only a part of the matter of which an admission is requested, he shall specify so much of it as is true and qualify or deny the remainder. An answering party may not give lack of information or knowledge as a reason for failure to admit or deny unless he states that he has made reasonable inquiry and that the information known or readily obtainable by him is insufficient to enable him to admit or deny. A party who considers that a matter of which an admission has been requested presents a genuine issue for trial may not, on that ground alone, object to the request; he may, subject to the provisions of Rule 4:12(c), deny the matter or set forth reasons why he cannot admit or deny it.

The party who has requested the admissions may move to determine the sufficiency of the answers or objections. Unless the court determines that an objection is justified, it shall order that an answer be served. If the court determines that an answer does not comply with the requirements of this Rule, it may order either that the matter is admitted or that an amended answer be served. The court may, in lieu of these orders, determine that final disposition of the request be made at a pretrial conference or at a designated time prior to trial. The provisions of Rule 4:12(a)(4) apply to the award of expenses incurred in relation to the motion.

(b) Effect of Admission. Any matter admitted under this Rule is conclusively established unless the court on motion permits withdrawal or amendment of the admission. Subject to the provisions of Rule 4:13 governing amendment of a pretrial order, the court may permit withdrawal or amendment when the presentation of the merits of the action will be subserved thereby and the party who obtained the admission fails to satisfy the court that withdrawal or amendment will prejudice him in maintaining his action or defense on the merits. Any admission made by a party under this Rule is for the purpose of the pending action only and is not an admission by him for any other purpose nor may it be used against him in any other proceeding.

(c) Filing. Except as provided in Rules 3:3 and 1:17, requests for admissions and answers or objections shall be served and filed as provided in Rule 4:8.

(d) Part of Record. Only such requests for admissions and the answers thereto as are offered in evidence shall become a part of the record.

(e) Limitation on Number of Requests.

(1) Requests for admission not related to genuineness of documents. Unless all parties agree, or the court grants leave for good cause shown, no party shall serve upon any other party, at any one time or cumulatively, more than 30 requests for admission, including all parts and subparts, that do not relate to the genuineness of documents. Leave to propound additional requests shall be liberally granted in the interests of justice.

(2) Requests for admission relating to the genuineness of documents. The number of requests for admissions relating to the genuineness of documents shall not be limited unless the court enters a protective order pursuant to the provisions of Rule 4:1(c) upon a finding that justice so requires in order to protect the responding party from unwarranted annoyance, embarrassment, oppression, or undue burden or expense.

[Amended effective October 15, 1979; July 1, 1984; August 1, 1985; February 28, 2006; May 2, 2011; May 1, 2015.]

Comment: [The 1984] change is intended to eliminate the clutter in clerks' offices.

Again, the [1985] change is designed to avoid clutter of the record.

RULE 4:12. FAILURE TO MAKE DISCOVERY; SANCTIONS

(a) Motion for Order Compelling Discovery. A party, upon reasonable notice to other parties and all persons affected thereby, may apply for an order compelling discovery as follows:

(1) *Appropriate Court.* An application for an order to a party may be made to the court in which the action is pending, or, on matters relating to a deposition, to the court in the county or city where the deposition is to be taken. An application for an order to a deponent who is not a party shall be made to the court in the county or city where the deposition is being taken.

(2) *Motion.* If a deponent fails to answer a question propounded or submitted under Rule 4:5 or 4:6, or a corporation or other entity fails to make a designation under Rule 4:5(b)(6) or 4:6(a), or a party fails to answer an interrogatory submitted under Rule 4:8, or if a party, in response to a request for inspection submitted under Rule 4:9, fails to respond that inspection will be permitted as requested or fails to permit inspection as requested, the discovering party may move for an order compelling an answer, or a designation, or an order compelling inspection in accordance with the request. When taking a deposition on oral examination, the proponent of the question may complete or adjourn the examination before he applies for an order.

A motion under subdivision (a) of this Rule must be accompanied by a certification that the movant has in good faith conferred or attempted to confer with other affected parties in an effort to resolve the dispute without court action.

If the court denies the motion in whole or in part, it may make such protective order as it would have been empowered to make on a motion made pursuant to Rule 4:1(c).

(3) *Evasive or Incomplete Answer.* For purposes of this subdivision an evasive or incomplete answer is to be treated as a failure to answer.

(4) *Award of Expenses of Motion.* If the motion is granted, the court shall, after opportunity for hearing,

require the party or deponent whose conduct necessitated the motion or the party or attorney advising such conduct or both of them to pay to the moving party the reasonable expenses incurred in obtaining the order, including attorney's fees, unless the court finds that the opposition to the motion was substantially justified or that other circumstances make an award of expenses unjust.

If the motion is denied, the court shall, after opportunity for hearing, require the moving party or the attorney advising the motion or both of them to pay to the party or deponent who opposed the motion the reasonable expenses incurred in opposing the motion, including attorney's fees, unless the court finds that the making of the motion was substantially justified or that other circumstances make an award of expenses unjust.

If the motion is granted in part and denied in part, the court may apportion the reasonable expenses incurred in relation to the motion among the parties and persons in a just manner.

(b) Failure to Comply With Order.

(1) *Sanctions by Court in County or City Where Deposition Is Taken.* If a deponent fails to be sworn or to answer a question after being directed to do so by the court in the county or city in which the deposition is being taken, the failure may be considered a contempt of that court.

(2) *Sanctions by Court in Which Action Is Pending.* If a party or an officer, director, or managing agent of a party or a person designated under Rule 4:5(b)(6) or 4:6(a) to testify on behalf of a party fails to obey an order to provide or permit discovery, including an order made under subdivision (a) of this Rule or Rule 4:10, the court in which the action is pending may make such orders in regard to the failure as are just, and among others the following:

(A) An order that the matters regarding which the order was made or any other designated facts shall be taken to be established for the purposes of the action in accordance with the claim of the party obtaining the order;

(B) An order refusing to allow the disobedient party to support or oppose designated claims or defenses, or prohibiting him from introducing designated matters in evidence;

(C) An order striking out pleadings or parts thereof, or staying further proceedings until the order is obeyed, or dismissing the action or proceeding or any part thereof, or rendering a judgment by default against the disobedient party;

(D) In lieu of any of the foregoing orders or in addition thereto, an order treating as a contempt of court the failure to obey any orders except an order to submit to a physical or mental examination;

(E) Where a party has failed to comply with an order under Rule 4:10(a) requiring him to produce another for examination, such orders as are listed in paragraphs (A), (B), and (C) of this subdivision, unless the party failing to comply shows that he is unable to produce such person for examination.

In lieu of any of the foregoing orders or in addition thereto, the court shall require the party failing to obey the order or the attorney advising him or both to pay the reasonable expenses, including attorney's fees, caused by the failure, unless the court finds that the failure was substantially justified or that other circumstances make an award of expenses unjust.

(c) Expenses on Failure to Admit. If a party fails to admit the genuineness of any document or the truth of any matter as requested under Rule 4:11, and if the party requesting the admissions thereafter proves the genuineness of the document or the truth of the matter, he may apply to the court for an order requiring the other party to pay him the reasonable expenses incurred in making that proof, including reasonable attorney's fees. The court shall make the order unless it finds that (1) the request was held objectionable pursuant to Rule 4:11(a), or (2) the admission sought was of no substantial importance, or (3) the party failing to admit had reasonable ground to believe that he might prevail on the matter, or (4) there was other good reason for the failure to admit.

(d) Failure of Party to Attend at Own Deposition or Serve Answers to Interrogatories or Respond to Request for Inspection. If a party or an officer, director, or managing agent of a party or a person designated under Rule 4:5(b)(6) or 4:6(a) to testify on behalf of a party fails (1) to appear before the officer who is to take his deposition, after being served with a proper notice, or (2) to serve answers or objections to interrogatories submitted under Rule 4:8, after proper service of the interrogatories, or (3) to serve a written response to a request for inspection submitted under Rule 4:9, after proper service of the request, the court in which the action is pending on motion may make such orders in regard to the failure as are just, and among others it may take any action authorized under paragraphs (A), (B), and (C) of subdivision (b)(2) of this Rule. In lieu of any order or in addition thereto, the court shall require the party failing to act or the attorney advising him or both to pay the reasonable expenses, including attorney's fees, caused by the failure, unless the court finds that the failure was substantially justified or that other circumstances make an award of expenses unjust.

The failure to act described in this subdivision may not be excused on the ground that the discovery sought is objectionable unless the party failing to act has applied for a protective order as provided by Rule 4:1(c).

[Amended effective January 1, 2003.]

RULE 4:13. PRETRIAL PROCEDURE; FORMULATING ISSUES

The court may in its discretion direct the attorneys for the parties to appear before it for a conference to consider:

(1) A determination of the issues;

(2) A plan and schedule of discovery;

(3) Any limitations on the scope and methods of discovery;

(4) The necessity or desirability of amendments to the pleadings;

(5) The possibility of obtaining admissions of fact and admissions regarding documents and information obtained through electronic discovery;

(6) The limitation of the number of expert witnesses;

(7) The advisability of a preliminary reference of issues to a master for findings to be used as evidence when the trial is to be by jury;

(8) issues relating to the preservation of potentially discoverable information, including electronically stored information and information that may be located in sources that are believed not reasonably accessible because of undue burden or cost;

(9) provisions for disclosure or discovery of electronically stored information;

(10) any agreements the parties reach for asserting claims of privilege or of protection as trial-preparation material after production;

(11) any provisions that will aid in the use of electronically stored or digitally imaged documents in the trial of the action; and

(12) Such other matters as may aid in the disposition of the action.

The court shall make an order which recites the action taken at the conference, the amendments allowed to the pleadings, the agreements made by the parties as to any of the matters considered, and which limits the issues for trial to those not disposed of by admissions or agreements of counsel; and such order when entered controls the subsequent course of the action, unless modified at the trial to prevent manifest injustice.

[Amended effective July 1, 1983; January 1, 2009; May 2, 2011.]

Comment: [The 1983] change is designed to give the court greater powers to limit discovery if it desires to exercise them.

RULE 4:14. DISPOSITION OF DISCOVERY MATERIAL

Any discovery material not admitted in evidence filed in a clerk's office may be destroyed by the clerk after one year after entry of the final judgment or decree. But if the action or suit is the subject of an appeal, such material shall not be destroyed until the lapse of one year after receipt of the mandate on appeal or the entry of any final judgment or decree thereafter.

[Amended effective July 1, 1983.]

Comment: [The 1984 amendment] is designed to benefit clerks of court who complain that storage space is not available.

RULE 4:15. MOTIONS PRACTICE

All civil case motions in circuit court shall be scheduled and heard using the following procedures:

(a) Scheduling. All civil case motions in circuit court shall be scheduled and heard using the following procedures:

(1) Presenting the motion on a day the court designates for motions hearings, or

(2) Contacting designated personnel in the office of the clerk of the court or the chambers of the judge or judges of the court.

(b) Notice. Reasonable notice of the presentation of a motion shall be served on all counsel of record. Absent leave of court, and except as provided in paragraph (c) of this Rule, reasonable notice shall be in writing and served at least seven days before the hearing. Counsel of record shall make a reasonable effort to confer before giving notice of a motion to resolve the subject of the motion and to determine a mutually agreeable hearing date and time. The notice shall be accompanied by a certification that the movant has in good faith conferred or attempted to confer with other affected parties in an effort to resolve the dispute without court action. In an Electronically Filed Case, the notice provisions of this paragraph and the filing and service requirements of paragraph (c) of this Rule shall be accomplished in accord with Rule 1:17.

(c) Filing and Service of Briefs. Counsel of record may elect or the court may require the parties to file briefs in support of or in opposition to a motion. Any such briefs should be filed with the court and served on all counsel of record sufficiently before the hearing to allow consideration of the issues involved. Absent leave of court, if a brief in support of a motion is five or fewer pages in length, the required notice and the brief shall be filed and served at least 14 days before the hearing and any brief in opposition to the motion shall be filed and served at least seven days before the hearing. If a brief will be more than five pages in length, an alternative hearing date, notice requirement, and briefing schedule may be determined by the court or its designee. Absent leave of court, the length of a brief shall not exceed 20 pages double spaced

(d) Hearing. Except as otherwise provided in this subparagraph, upon request of counsel of record for any party, or at the court's request, the court shall hear oral argument on a motion. Oral argument on a motion for reconsideration or any motion in any case where a pro se incarcerated person is counsel of record shall be heard orally only at the request of the court. A court may place reasonable limits on the length of oral argument. No party shall be deprived of the opportunity to present its position on the merits of a motion solely because of the unfamiliarity of counsel of record with the motions procedures of that court. A court, however, at the request of counsel of record, or in the judge's discretion, may postpone the hearing of the motion, or require the filing of briefs to assure fairness to all parties and the ability of the court to review all such briefs in advance of the hearing.

(e) Definition of Served. For purposes of this Rule, a pleading shall be deemed served when it is actually received by, or in the office of, counsel of record through delivery, mailing, facsimile transmission or electronic mail as provided in Rule 1:12.

[Adopted effective July 1, 2000. Amended effective January 1, 2003; November 1, 2005; May 2, 2011.]

PART FIVE. THE SUPREME COURT

Revised Effective August 1, 1985

Including Amendments Received Through October 15, 2015

A. General

RULE 5:1. SCOPE, CITATION, APPLICABILITY, AND GENERAL PROVISIONS

(a) Scope of Rules. Part Five governs all proceedings in the Supreme Court of Virginia.

(b) Citation. These Rules may be cited generally as the "Rules of the Supreme Court of Virginia" and specifically as "Rule 5: ___."

(c) Definitions.

(1) "clerk" means clerk of the court or commission from which an appeal is taken unless some other clerk is specified and, unless the context otherwise requires, includes a deputy clerk;

(2) "clerk of this Court" includes a deputy clerk;

(3) "counsel" has the definition given in Rule 1:5 and in this Part Five includes a party not represented by counsel;

(4) "counsel for the appellant" means one of the attorneys representing each appellant represented by an attorney and each appellant not represented by an attorney;

(5) "counsel for the appellee" means one of the attorneys representing each appellee represented by an attorney and each appellee not represented by an attorney. In an appeal from the State Corporation Commission, "counsel for the appellee" shall also include counsel for the Commission and, unless the Commonwealth is the appellant, the Attorney General;

(6) "Court of Appeals" means the Court of Appeals of Virginia;

(7) "opposing counsel" means, depending on the context, "counsel for the appellant" or "counsel for the appellee";

(8) "judge" means judge of the trial court, unless the context otherwise requires, or if the judge of the trial court is not available, any judge authorized to act under Rule 5:12;

(9) "judgment" includes an order or decree from which an appeal is taken;

(10) "trial court" means the circuit court from which an appeal is taken;

(11) the "date of entry" of any final judgment or other appealable order or decree shall be the date the judgment, order, or decree is signed by the judge.

(d) Service. Unless service or notice is otherwise specified in a given Rule, any paper or object filed with this Court must have included within it or appended to it a certificate of service or acceptance of service showing that a copy has been transmitted to all counsel and showing the date and manner of transmittal. If a word count is used, the certificate must also state the number of words (headings, footnotes, and quotations count towards the word limitation; the cover page, table of contents, table of authorities, and certificate do not count towards the word count).

(e) Notice of Change of Address and Other Contact Information. If an attorney has a change in mailing address, telephone number, facsimile number, or e-mail address any time after the filing of the notice of appeal, the attorney must immediately notify the clerk of this Court and all other counsel of record in writing. The notice must reference the style and record number of all cases pending before this Court.

(f) Citing Unpublished Judicial Dispositions. The citation of judicial opinions, orders, judgments, or other written dispositions that are not officially reported, whether designated as "unpublished," "not for publication," "non precedential," or the like, is permitted as informative, but shall not be received as binding authority. If the cited disposition is not available in a publicly accessible electronic database, a copy of that disposition must be filed with the brief or other paper in which it is cited.

[Amended effective July 1, 1988; July 1, 2010.]

Source: Rule 5A:1. Cf. Rule 5:1.

RULE 5:1A. PENALTIES FOR NON-COMPLIANCE; SHOW CAUSE; DISMISSAL

(a) Penalties; Show Cause; Dismissal. This Court may dismiss an appeal or impose such other penalty as it deems appropriate for non-compliance with these Rules. Except as provided in Rule 5:17(c)(1)(i) and (iii), regarding assignments of error, prior to the dismissal of an appeal for any defect in the filings related to formatting, curable failure to comply with other requirements, or the failure to meet non-mandatory filing deadlines, this Court may issue a show cause order to counsel or a party not represented by an attorney, prescribing a time in which to cure such defect or to otherwise show cause why the appeal should not be dismissed or other penalty imposed.

(b) Report to Virginia State Bar. If an attorney's failure to comply with these Rules results in the dismissal of an appeal, this Court may report the attorney to the Virginia State Bar in accordance with Rule 8.3 of the Virginia Rules of Professional Conduct.

[Added effective July 1, 2010. Amended effective May 16, 2014.]

RULE 5:2. SESSIONS AND DIVISIONS

Except as provided in Code § 17.1–304, sessions and divisions of this Court will be held at Richmond, or at such other locations as this Court may designate consistent with applicable law, and will continue for such length of time as this Court may determine.

[Amended effective October 31, 2006; July 1, 2010.]

Source: Rule 5:2.

RULE 5:3. CONVENING OF COURT—WHEN EN BANC—WHEN IN DIVISION

(a) This Court will sit en banc or in divisions.

(b) Whenever four or more of the Justices are convened, this Court shall be deemed to be sitting en banc and vested with all of the powers of this Court. Whenever three of the Justices are convened, this Court shall be deemed to be sitting as a division, and vested with all of the powers of a division of this Court.

(c) If the Justices composing any division shall differ as to the judgment to be rendered in any case, or if, within ten days after the decision is rendered by the division any Justice of such division shall file in the office of the clerk of this Court a certificate that, in the opinion of the Justice, such decision is in conflict with a prior decision of this Court or of one of the divisions thereof, or if this Court shall so determine, the case shall be reheard and decided by this Court sitting en banc.

[Amended effective July 1, 2010.]

Source: Rule 5:3.

RULE 5:4. MOTIONS AND RESPONSES; ORDERS

(a) Motions and Responses.

(1) *Motions.* All motions, except motions for the qualification of attorneys at law to practice in this Court, shall be in writing and filed with the clerk of this Court. All motions shall contain a statement by the movant that the other parties to the appeal have been informed of the intended filing of the motion. For all motions in cases in which all parties are represented by counsel—except motions to dismiss petitions for a writ of habeas corpus—the statement by the movant shall also indicate whether the other parties consent to the granting of the motion, or intend to file responses in opposition.

(2) *Responses.* Opposing counsel may have 10 days after such motion is filed to file with such clerk a response to such motion, but this Court may act before the 10 days expire, if necessary.

(3) *Number of Copies.* An original and three copies of all motions or responses must be filed.

(4) *Oral Argument.* No motion shall be argued orally except by leave of this Court.

(b) Orders. Promptly after this Court has entered an order, the clerk of this Court shall send a copy of the order to all counsel.

ADVISORY NOTE

This rule is not intended to limit the scope of motions that may be filed in the Supreme Court. Such motions may be filed in any pending or contemplated appeal, and may request from the Court any form of relief that is available to the movant. The practitioner should consult individual rules relating to the filing of motions in particular matters; for example, Rule 5:12 (trial judge authorized to act on matters pertaining to record); Rule 5:30(a)(3) (motion for leave to file brief amicus curiae). Rehearings are not within the scope of this rule, but are governed by Rules 5:20, 5:20A, and 5:37.

[Amended effective July 1, 2010.]

Source: Rule 5A:2. Cf. Rule 5:4.

RULE 5:5. FILING DEADLINES; POST TRIAL PROCEEDINGS BELOW; TIMELY FILING BY MAIL; INMATE MAILING; EXTENSION OF TIME

(a) Filing Deadlines. The times prescribed for filing the notice of appeal (Rules 5:9(a), 5:14(a) and 5:21(c)), a petition for appeal (Rules 5:17(a) and 5:21(g)), a petition for review pursuant to Code § 8.01–626 (Rule 5:17A) and a petition for rehearing (Rules 5:20 and 5:37), are mandatory. A single extension not to exceed thirty days may be granted if at least two Justices of the Supreme Court of Virginia concur in a finding that an extension for papers to be filed is warranted by a showing of good cause sufficient to excuse the delay.

(b) Post–Trial Proceedings Below and Their Effect on the Notice of Appeal. The time period for filing the notice of appeal is not extended by the filing of a motion for a new trial, a petition for rehearing, or a like pleading unless the final judgment is modified, vacated, or suspended by the trial court pursuant to Rule 1:1 or a timely petition for rehearing is filed in the Court of Appeals. In any such case, the time for filing the notice of appeal shall be computed from the date of final judgment entered following such modification, vacation, or suspension, or from the date the Court of Appeals refuses a timely petition for rehearing or enters final judgment following the granting of such a petition.

(c) How to File by Mail in a Timely Manner. Any document required to be filed with the clerk of this Court shall be deemed to be timely filed if (1) it is transmitted expense pre-paid to the clerk of this Court by priority, express, registered, or certified mail via the United States Postal Service, or by a third-party commercial carrier for next-day delivery, and (2) if the official receipt therefor be exhibited upon demand of the clerk of this Court or any party and it shows such transmission or mailing within the prescribed time limits. This rule does not apply to documents to be filed in the office of the clerk of the trial court or clerk of the Virginia Workers' Compensation Commission or clerk of the State Corporation Commission.

(d) Inmate Filing. A paper filed by an individual confined in an institution, including a prison, jail, or the Virginia Center for Behavioral Rehabilitation, is timely filed if deposited in the institution's internal mail system with first-class postage prepaid on or before the last day for filing. Timely filing of a paper by an individual confined in such an institution may be established by (1) an official stamp of the institution showing that the paper was deposited in the internal mail system on or before the last day for filing, (2) an official postmark dated on or before the last day for filing, or (3) a notarized statement signed by an official of the institution showing that the paper was deposited in the internal mail system on or before the last day for filing.

(e) Extensions Generally. Except as provided in paragraph (a) of this Rule, a motion for an extension of time is timely if filed either within the original filing deadline or within any extension period specified by the governing rule. Filing the motion within the original filing deadline or within the specified extension period does not toll the original filing deadline or further extend the period of extension.

[Amended effective July 1, 1988; February 1, 1992; February 1, 2000; September 1, 2000; July 1, 2010; May 2, 2011; January 1, 2013.]

Source: Rule 5A:3. Cf. Rules 5:1A and 5:7.

Comment: See also Rule 1:7 regarding computation of time.

RULE 5:6. FORMS OF BRIEFS AND OTHER PAPERS

(a) Paper Size, Line Spacing, Font, and Margins.

(1) *General Rules.* Briefs, appendices, motions, petitions, and other papers may be printed or produced on screen by any process that yields a clear black image on a white background and, when printed, must be on 8–½ × 11 inch paper. Margins must be at least one inch on all four sides of each page.

(2) *Specific Rules for Motions, Petitions, and Briefs.* Except by leave of Court, all motions, petitions, and briefs, including footnotes, must be in at least 14–point font, must use either Courier, Arial, or Verdana font, and must be printed on only one side of the page. Text shall not be reduced and must be double spaced except for headings, assignments of error, quotations, and footnotes, which must be single spaced. Page numbers are required and may appear in either the top or bottom margin, but no text, including footnotes, is permitted in the one inch margins. Page or word limits for motions, petitions, and briefs do not include the cover page, table of contents, table of authorities, or certificate.

(3) *Specific Rules for the Appendix.* The appendix may be printed using both sides of the page. Any transcript, including a deposition transcript, that is made a part of the appendix shall be in 12–point type or larger. Any transcript contained in the appendix that fails to conform to the 12–point type requirement may be returned to counsel, and counsel shall be required to promptly comply with this requirement in accordance with the instruction of this Court. The use of condensed or multi-page transcripts is prohibited. Page numbers are required and may appear in either the top or bottom margin.

(b) Binding and Cover. All briefs and appendices shall be bound on the left margin in such a manner as to produce a flat, smooth binding. Spiral binding, acco fasteners, and the like are not acceptable. The style of the case (with the name of the appellant stated first) and the record number of the case shall be stated on the front cover of all briefs and appendices and, in addition, the name, Virginia State Bar number, mailing address, telephone number (including any applicable extension), facsimile number (if any), and e-mail address of counsel submitting the brief shall be placed on the front cover of all briefs.

(c) Effect of Non–Compliance. No appeal shall be dismissed for failure to comply with the provisions of this Rule; the clerk of this Court may, however, require that a document be redone in compliance with this Rule. Failure to comply after notice of noncompliance, however, may result in the dismissal of the case.

[Amended effective May 15, 1996; February 1, 2008; July 1, 2010; July 1, 2015.]

Source: Rule 5A:4. Cf. Rule 5:33.

RULE 5:6A. CITATION OF SUPPLEMENTAL AUTHORITIES

If pertinent and significant authorities come to a party's attention after the party's petition for appeal, brief in opposition, or brief has been filed, or after oral argument but before decision, a party may promptly advise the clerk by letter, with a copy to all other parties, setting forth the citations. The letter must state the reasons for the supplemental citations, referring either to the page of the brief or to a point argued orally. The body of the letter must not exceed 350 words. Any response must be made promptly and shall not exceed 350 words. The Court, in its discretion, may refuse to consider the supplemental authorities if they unfairly expand the scope of the arguments on brief, raise matters that should have been previously briefed, appear to be untimely, or are otherwise inappropriate to consider.

[Adopted effective July 1, 2015.]

B. ORIGINAL JURISDICTION

RULE 5:7. PETITIONS FOR WRITS OF HABEAS CORPUS, MANDAMUS, AND PROHIBITION

(a) Petition for Writ of Habeas Corpus. An application to this Court for a writ of habeas corpus under its original jurisdiction shall be by petition filed in the office of the clerk of this Court.

(1) *When Petition Must Be Filed.* The petition for a writ of habeas corpus challenging a criminal conviction or sentence, except as provided in Rule 5:7A for cases in which the death penalty has been imposed, shall be filed within two years from the date of the final judgment in the trial court or within one year from either final disposition of the direct appeal in state court or the time for filing such appeal has expired, whichever is later. All other petitions for a writ of habeas corpus must be filed within one year after the cause of action accrues.

(2) *What the Petition Must Contain.* The petition must be notarized and must state whether the petitioner believes that the taking of evidence is necessary for the proper disposition of the petition. A memorandum of law citing relevant authorities must accompany each petition. All petitions must comply with the requirements of Code § 8.01–655.

(3) *Service of Petitions.* Except as provided herein, service of process must be accomplished in accordance with Chapter 8 of Title 8.01.

(i) Non–Public Officials. A petition must be accompanied by a return of service executed by the appropriate officer evidencing service of a copy thereof on the respondent or by an acceptance of service signed by the respondent.

(ii) Public Officials. When habeas corpus is directed to a public official, service shall be made on the respondent and shall also be made on or accepted by the Attorney General or an Assistant Attorney General. A petition must be accompanied by a return of service executed by the appropriate officer evidencing service of a copy thereof on the respondent or by an acceptance of service signed by the respondent.

(iii) Prisoners Pro Se. In cases brought by prisoners pro se, a copy of the petition shall be forwarded to the respondent by first class mail, and the application shall contain a certificate at the end stating as follows:

I hereby certify that on the ___ day of ________, 20___, I mailed a copy of the foregoing application to the respondent(s), ________, by first class mail.

Petitioner

(4) *When to Respond to a Petition.* No responsive pleading to a petition filed by a prisoner acting pro se shall be required except as ordered by this Court. For all other petitions, a responsive pleading must be filed with the clerk of this Court within forty days after service of the petition.

(5) *Contents of the Response.* In one responsive pleading, the respondent may move to dismiss on any appropriate ground, including the failure to state facts upon which relief should be granted, and, in the alternative, may set forth grounds of defense as in an action at law. The answer shall state whether, in the opinion of the respondent, the taking of evidence is necessary for the proper disposition of the petition. A memorandum of law citing the relevant authorities shall accompany each responsive pleading.

(6) *Length.* Except by permission of a Justice of this Court, no petition, including the accompanying memorandum of law, or a response thereto, including its accompanying memorandum of law, shall exceed the longer of 50 printed pages or 8,750 words. Page and word limits do not include appendices, exhibits, cover page, table of contents, table of authorities, and certificate.

(7) *Number of Copies.* Ten copies of the petition, responsive pleading, memoranda of law, and motions shall be filed in the office of the clerk of this Court. Prisoners filing pro se shall only be required to file three copies.

(8) *Calling Up the Record.* If this Court determines that any portion of the underlying trial or appellate record is necessary for a proper determination of the merits of the petition, the clerk of this Court is authorized to request the record and the clerk of the trial court, commission, or the Court of Appeals, as appropriate shall transmit it forthwith upon request without the necessity of an order.

(b) Petitions for Writs of Mandamus and Prohibition. An application for a writ of mandamus or a writ of prohibition under the original jurisdiction of this Court shall be by petition filed in the office of the clerk of this Court.

(1) *What the Petition Must Contain.* The petition must be notarized and must state whether the petitioner believes that the taking of evidence is necessary for the proper disposition of the petition. A memorandum of law citing relevant authorities must accompany each petition.

(2) *Service of Petitions.*

(i) Generally. A petition must be accompanied by a return of service executed by the appropriate officer evidencing service of a copy thereof on the respondent or by an acceptance of service signed by the respondent. Except in cases brought by prisoners acting pro se, service of process must be accomplished in accordance with Chapter 8 of Title 8.01.

(ii) Prisoners Pro Se. In cases brought by prisoners pro se, a copy of the petition shall be forwarded to the respondent by first class mail, and the application shall contain a certificate at the end stating as follows:

I hereby certify that on the ___ day of __________, 20___, I mailed a copy of the foregoing application to the respondent(s), __________, by first class mail.

Petitioner

(3) *Limitations for Petitions for Mandamus.* A petition for writ of mandamus filed by or on behalf of a person confined in a state correctional facility must be brought within one year after the cause of action accrues.

(4) *Petitions for Mandamus or Prohibition Against a Judge.* A petition for writ of mandamus or writ of prohibition against a judge shall not bear the name of the judge but shall be entitled, "In re, Petitioner." When the Attorney General determines, with the concurrence of the judge, that it is impracticable or unnecessary for the Attorney General to represent the judge, the judge may be represented pro forma by counsel for the party opposing the relief, who shall appear in the name of the party and not that of the judge. Or, in the alternative, the Attorney General may provide for the appointment of special counsel to represent the judge, in accordance with the provisions of Code §§ 2.2–507 or 2.2–510.

(5) *When to Respond to a Petition.* No responsive pleading shall be required for a petition filed by a prisoner acting pro se except as ordered by this Court. For all other petitions, a responsive pleading must be filed with the clerk of this Court within 21 days after service of the petition or the filing thereof, whichever date is later.

(6) *Contents of the Response.* In one responsive pleading, the respondent may move to dismiss on any appropriate ground, including the failure to state facts upon which relief should be granted, and, in the alternative, may set forth an answer as in an action at law. The answer shall state whether, in the opinion of the respondent, the taking of evidence is necessary for the proper disposition of the petition. A memorandum of law citing the relevant authorities should accompany each responsive pleading.

(7) *Length.* Except by permission of a Justice of this Court, no petition, including the accompanying memorandum of law, or a response thereto, including its accompanying memorandum of law, shall exceed the longer of 50 printed pages or 8,750 words. This page or word limit does not include appendices, exhibits, cover page, table of contents, table of authorities, and certificate.

(8) *Number of Copies.* Ten copies of the petition, responsive pleading, memoranda of law, and motions shall be filed in the office of the clerk of this Court. Prisoners filing pro se shall only be required to file three copies.

(c) When This Court May Act on a Petition. This Court may act on any petition for a writ of habeas corpus, mandamus, or prohibition before a responsive pleading is filed. This Court may by order shorten the period within which a responsive pleading must be filed.

(d) Further Proceedings on Petitions. Further proceedings shall be in accordance with the orders of this Court or a Justice thereof to whom this Court may delegate authority to determine all procedural matters. If this Court or the designated Justice determines that evidence is desirable, depositions shall be taken according to a schedule agreed upon by counsel and filed in the office of the clerk of this Court or, in the absence of agreement, according to a schedule determined by this Court or the designated Justice.

(e) Amendment of Petition. If the statute of limitations has not expired, a petitioner may move—at any time before a ruling is rendered on the merits of the petition as initially filed—for leave of this Court to substitute an amended petition. This amendment can include additional claims not presented in the petition as initially filed. Any such motion shall attach a copy of the proposed amended petition.

[Amended effective September 1, 1993; November 15, 1995; August 15, 1997; August 1, 2001; July 1, 2010; May 2, 2011.]

Source: Rule 5:5 and Rule 5A:5.

RULE 5:7A. PETITIONS FOR WRITS OF HABEAS CORPUS IN CASES IN WHICH THE SENTENCE OF DEATH HAS BEEN IMPOSED

In cases in which the sentence of death has been imposed:

(a) Petition for the Writ. A petition for a writ of habeas corpus shall be filed in the office of the clerk of this Court within 60 days after the earliest of: (i) the denial by the Supreme Court of the United States of a petition for a writ of certiorari to the judgment of this Court on direct appeal, (ii) an order of the Supreme Court of the United States affirming imposition of the sentence of death in a case in which that Court granted a writ of certiorari to review the judgment of this Court on direct appeal, or (iii) the expiration of the period for filing a petition for a writ of certiorari in the Supreme Court of the United States without such a petition being filed.

(b) Contents of Petition for Writ. Each petition for a writ of habeas corpus shall be verified and shall include an enumerated list of the grounds asserted for relief together with all supporting facts upon which the petitioner relies. The petition shall contain citation to the relevant legal authorities and an enumeration of all previous petitions and their disposition. The petition shall state whether, in the opinion of the petitioner, the taking of evidence is necessary for the proper disposition of the petition. The petition shall be accompanied by a return of service executed by the appropriate officer evidencing service of a copy thereof upon the Attorney General of Virginia or by an acceptance of service signed by the Attorney General or an Assistant Attorney General.

(c) Response. Within 30 days after service of the petition, the Attorney General shall file with the clerk of this Court a responsive pleading, which may include a motion to dismiss. The response shall include citation to the relevant legal authorities and shall state whether, in the opinion of the Attorney General, the taking of evidence is necessary for the proper disposition of the petition.

(d) Reply. Within 20 days after the Attorney General's responsive pleading is filed pursuant to subparagraph (c), the petitioner may file a reply.

(e) Copies to Be Filed. Ten copies of the petition, the Attorney General's responsive pleading, and the petitioner's reply shall be filed in the office of the clerk of this Court.

(f) Motions. Upon the filing of any motion other than a motion to dismiss included in a responsive pleading filed pursuant to subparagraph (c) of this Rule, or upon the filing of an objection pursuant to Code § 8.01–654(C)(3), the opposing party may file a response within ten days of the filing of the motion or objection, or within such time as this Court may order.

(g) Length. Except by permission of a justice of this Court, no petition for a writ of habeas corpus or a response thereto shall exceed the longer of 100 pages or 17,500 words, and no reply to a response shall exceed the longer of 50 pages or 8,750 words. Page or word limits under this Rule do not include appendices, the cover page, table of contents, table of authorities, and certificate. All petitions, responses, replies, motions, and other papers filed pursuant to this Rule shall conform to the provisions of Rule 5:6(a). If counsel wishes to file a petition or response in excess of the page or word limit prescribed in this paragraph, a motion to exceed the page or word limit must be filed with the clerk of this Court at least 10 days before the due date for the petition or response. If the motion is denied, or if no timely motion to exceed the page or word limit is filed, any pages in the petition or response that exceed the page or word limit, except the signature and certificate of service, shall be stricken and not considered by this Court.

(h) Further Proceedings by Order of This Court. Further proceedings shall be conducted in accordance with the orders of this Court. If it is determined that an evidentiary hearing is necessary for the proper disposition of the petition, this Court shall enter an order directing the circuit court that entered the judgment imposing the sentence of death to conduct such a hearing in accordance with the provisions of Code § 8.01–654(C)(1), (2), and (3).

(i) Amendment of Petition. If the statute of limitations has not expired, a petitioner may move—at any time before a ruling is rendered on the merits of the petition as initially filed—for leave of this Court to substitute an amended petition. This amendment can include additional claims not presented in the petition as initially filed. Any such motion shall attach a copy of the proposed amended petition.

[Adopted November 15, 1995. Amended effective May 15, 1996; March 1, 2007; July 1, 2010; May 2, 2011.]

RULE 5:7B. PETITION FOR A WRIT OF ACTUAL INNOCENCE

(a) Who May File a Petition. A petition for a writ of actual innocence based upon previously unknown or untested human biological evidence may be filed by any person who has been convicted of a felony upon a plea of not guilty, or who was adjudicated delinquent upon a plea of not guilty by a circuit court of an offense that would be a felony if committed by an adult, or by any person, regardless of plea, who has been sentenced to death, or convicted or adjudicated delinquent of a class 1 felony, a class 2 felony or any felony for which the maximum penalty is imprisonment for life.

(b) Time for Filing. A petition under this Rule shall be filed in the office of the Clerk of this Court within 60 days after the date upon which exculpatory test results are obtained by the petitioner or his counsel of record from the Department of Forensic Science for any tests conducted on human biological evidence pursuant to Code § 19.2–327.1.

(c) Contents of the Petition. Each petition for a writ of actual innocence shall be filed on a form provided by this Court and shall be verified under oath. The petition must state categorically and with specificity: (i) the offense or offenses for which petitioner was convicted or adjudicated delinquent, including all previous records, applications, petitions, and appeals relating to these convictions or adjudications of delinquency, and their dispositions; (ii) that the petitioner is actually innocent of the crime or crimes for which he was convicted or adjudicated delinquent; (iii) an exact description of the human biological evidence and the scientific testing supporting the allegation of innocence, attaching a copy of the test results; (iv) that the human biological evidence was not known or available to the petitioner or his attorney at trial, or if it was known, why it was not subject to scientific testing; (v) the earliest date the test results described in the petition became known to the petitioner or any attorney of record; (vi) that the petitioner or his attorney has filed the petition within 60 days of obtaining the test results; (vii) an explanation of the reason or reasons the evidence will prove that no rational trier of fact would have found the petitioner guilty or delinquent beyond a reasonable doubt of the offense or offenses for which the petitioner was convicted or adjudicated delinquent; and (viii) if the conviction or adjudication of delinquency became final in the circuit court after June 30, 1996, that the evidence was not available for testing under Code § 9.1–1104.

(d) Service of the Petition and Return of Service. Prior to filing a petition, the petitioner shall serve the petition, along with all attachments, on the Attorney General and on the Commonwealth's Attorney for the jurisdiction where the conviction or adjudication of delinquency occurred. The petitioner shall file with the petition either (i) a duly executed return of service in the form of a verification that a copy of the petition and all attachments have been served, or (ii) an acceptance of service signed by either or both of the parties to be served, or (iii) a combination of the two.

(e) Filing Fee. The petition must be accompanied by either (i) a check or money order for the filing fee required by statute, or (ii) an in forma pauperis affidavit demonstrating that the petitioner cannot afford the filing fee.

(f) Response. The Attorney General shall respond to the petition as follows:

(1) Within 30 days after service of the petition, the Attorney General shall file with the clerk of this Court a pleading in the form of a declaration stating, in the opinion of the Attorney General, with an explanation of the reasons therefor, whether the record of any trial or appellate proceedings involving the conviction or convictions, or adjudication or adjudications of delinquency, or of any proceedings under Code § 19.2–327.1, is necessary for preparation of a response to the petition. If the Attorney General asserts that the record, or any part thereof, of any trial or appellate court proceedings is necessary, the Attorney General shall request the production of such record by this Court, and shall describe with specificity, including the court, docket number and date of judgment, each and every record or part thereof which is requested.

(2) If the Attorney General asserts in the declaration required by subparagraph (f)(1) of this Rule that no trial or appellate court record, or any part thereof, is necessary for the preparation of a responsive pleading to the petition, the Attorney General shall file with the clerk of this Court within 30 days thereafter a pleading in response to the petition. Any pleading in response filed by the Attorney General may include a motion to dismiss. The response shall include citation to any relevant legal authorities, and may contain a proffer of any evidence pertaining to the guilt of the petitioner that is not included in the record of the case, including any evidence that was suppressed at trial.

(3) If the Attorney General asserts in the declaration required by subparagraph (f)(1) of this Rule that a trial or appellate court record, or any part thereof, is necessary for the preparation of a response to the petition, the court shall issue the writ of certiorari described in Code § 19.2–327.3(D) to the clerk of the respective court below for the production of the record forthwith to the clerk of this Court. Upon receipt of the record by the clerk of this Court, the clerk shall immediately notify in writing the petitioner, any attorney for the petitioner, the Attorney General, and the attorney for the Commonwealth of the jurisdiction where the conviction or convictions or adjudication or adjudications of delinquency occurred, of the date of receipt of the record. Within 30 days after receipt of the record by the clerk of this Court, the Attorney General shall file the responsive pleading described in subparagraph (f)(2) of this Rule.

(g) Reply. Within 20 days after the Attorney General's responsive pleading is filed pursuant to subparagraph (f) of this Rule, the petitioner may file a reply.

(h) Copies to Be Filed. Ten copies of the petition, and the Attorney General's responsive pleading, and the petitioner's reply, if any, shall be filed in the office of the clerk of this Court.

(i) Further Proceedings by Order of This Court. Further proceedings shall be conducted in accordance with the orders of this Court. If this Court determines that an evidentiary hearing is necessary for the proper disposition of the petition, this Court may order that the circuit court conduct a hearing within 90 days after the order has been issued to certify findings of fact with respect to such issues as this Court shall direct. The record and certified findings of fact of the circuit court shall be filed with the clerk of this Court within 30 days after the hearing is concluded.

(j) Appointment of Counsel. In any petition filed pursuant to and in compliance with this Rule, petitioner shall be entitled to the appointment of counsel subject to the provisions of Code § 19.2–157 *et seq.* Any request for counsel in this Court must be made on the form provided by this Court, entitled REQUEST FOR COUNSEL—PETITION FOR A WRIT OF ACTUAL INNOCENCE, and must include: (i) all the information required by the in forma pauperis affidavit attached to the request for appointment of counsel, and (ii) an attested copy of the order of the circuit court ordering that testing of human biological evidence on the petitioner's behalf be conducted by the Department of Forensic Science pursuant to Code § 19.2–327.1.

(k) Duty of Counsel. Any attorney(s) appointed to represent a petitioner pursuant to Code § 19.2–327.1 shall be deemed to be counsel of record for petitioner for all purposes and proceedings under this Rule until a final order of this Court is issued pursuant to Code § 19.2–327.5, or until counsel is relieved or replaced by other counsel by leave of this Court.

[Adopted effective January 15, 2003. Amended effective December 12, 2008; July 1, 2009; July 1, 2010; May 2, 2011; July 1, 2013.]

C. Procedure For Filing An Appeal From A Trial Court

RULE 5:8. APPLICABILITY

This Section C applies only to cases in which direct appeal to this Court from a trial court is authorized by law.

Source: New.

RULE 5:8A. APPEAL FROM PARTIAL FINAL JUDGMENT IN MULTI-PARTY CASES

(a) When Available. When claims for relief are presented in a civil action against multiple parties—whether in a complaint, counterclaim, cross-claim, or third-party claim—the trial court may enter final judgment as to one or more but fewer than all of the parties only by entering an order expressly labeled "Partial Final Judgment" which contains express findings that (i) the interests of such parties, and the grounds on which judgment is entered as to them, are separate and distinct from those raised by the issues in the claims against remaining parties, and (ii) the results of any appeal from the partial final judgment cannot affect decision of the claims against the remaining parties, and (iii) decision of the claims remaining in the trial court cannot affect the disposition of claims against the parties subject to the Partial Final Judgment if those parties are later restored to the case by reversal of the Partial Final Judgment on appeal.

(b) Time to Appeal. Entry of an order of Partial Final Judgment as provided in subparagraph (a) of this Rule commences the period for filing a notice of appeal from such Partial Final Judgment under Rule 5:9 and a petition for appeal under Rule 5:17, subject to the provisions of Rule 1:1 and these Rules.

(c) Refusal of Partial Final Judgment. No appeal shall lie from a refusal by the trial court to enter a Partial Final Judgment under this Rule.

(d) Other Dispositions Adjudicating Claims Against Fewer Than All Parties. In the absence of the entry of a Partial Final Judgment order as provided in subparagraph (a) of this Rule, any order which adjudicates fewer than all the claims or the rights and liabilities of fewer than all the parties in the action is not a final judgment.

[Added effective July 1, 2010.]

RULE 5:9. NOTICE OF APPEAL

(a) Filing Deadline; Where to File. No appeal shall be allowed unless, within 30 days after the entry of final judgment or other appealable order or decree, or within any specified extension thereof granted by this Court pursuant to Rule 5:5(a), counsel for the appellant files with the clerk of the trial court a notice of appeal and at the same time mails or delivers a copy of such notice to all opposing counsel. A notice of appeal filed after the court announces a decision or ruling—but before the entry of such judgment or order—is treated as filed on the date of and after the entry.

(b) Content. The notice of appeal shall contain a statement whether any transcript or statement of facts, testimony and other incidents of the case will be filed. In the event a transcript is to be filed, the notice of appeal shall certify that a copy of the transcript has been ordered from the court reporter who reported the case or is otherwise already in the possession of appellant, or was previously filed in the proceedings.

(c) Separate Cases. Whenever two or more cases were tried together in the trial court, one notice of appeal and one record may be used to bring all of such cases before this Court even though such cases were not consolidated by formal order.

(d) Special Provision for Cases Involving a Guardian Ad Litem. No appeal shall be dismissed because the notice of appeal fails to identify a guardian ad litem or to provide notice to a guardian ad litem. Upon motion for good cause shown or by sua sponte order of this Court, the notice of appeal may be amended to identify the guardian ad litem and to provide notice to such guardian.

[Amended effective December 1, 1990; January 1, 2009; July 1, 2010; July 1, 2015.]

Source: Rule 5A:6. Cf. Rules 5:6 and 5:16.

RULE 5:10. RECORD ON APPEAL: CONTENTS

(a) Contents. The following constitute the record on appeal from the trial court:

(1) the documents and exhibits filed or lodged in the office of the clerk of the trial court, including any report of a commissioner in chancery and the accompanying depositions and other papers;

(2) each instruction marked "given" or "refused" and initialed by the judge;

(3) each exhibit offered in evidence, whether admitted or not, and initialed by the trial judge (or any photograph thereof as authorized by § 19.2–270.4(A) and (C)). (All non-documentary exhibits shall be tagged or labeled in the trial court and the tag or label initialed by the judge.);

(4) the original draft or a copy of each order entered by the trial court;

(5) any opinion or memorandum decision rendered by the judge of the trial court;

(6) any deposition and any discovery material encompassed within Part Four offered in evidence (whether admitted or rejected) at any proceeding; and

(7) the transcript of any proceeding or a written statement of facts, testimony, and other incidents of the case when made a part of the record as provided in Rule 5:11, or the official videotape recording of any

proceeding in those circuit courts authorized by this Court to use videotape recordings. This Court may require that any videotape proceedings be transcribed, in whole or in part, and made a part of the record as provided in Rule 5:11, except that the transcript shall be filed within 60 days after the entry of the order requiring such transcript; and

(8) the notice of appeal.

(b) Disagreement on Contents. If disagreement arises as to the contents of any part of the record, the matter shall, in the first instance, be submitted to and decided by the trial court.

[Amended effective February 1, 1990; September 1, 1990; July 1, 2010; July 1, 2015.]

Source: Rule 5A:7. Cf. Rules 5:8 and 5:10.

RULE 5:11. RECORD ON APPEAL: TRANSCRIPT OR WRITTEN STATEMENT

(a) Effect of Non–Compliance.

(1) *Obligation of the Petitioner/Appellant.* It is the obligation of the petitioner/appellant to ensure that the record is sufficient to enable the Court to evaluate and resolve the assignments of error. When the appellant fails to ensure that the record contains transcripts or a written statement of facts necessary to permit resolution of appellate issues related to the assignments of error, any assignments of error affected by the omission shall not be considered.

(2) *Obligation of the Respondent/Appellee.* It is the obligation of the respondent/appellee to ensure that the record is sufficient to enable the Court to evaluate and resolve any assignments of cross-error. When the respondent/appellee who assigns cross-error fails to ensure that the record contains transcripts or a written statement of facts necessary to permit resolution of appellate issues related to the assignments of cross-error, any assignments of cross-error affected by the omission shall not be considered.

(b) Transcript. The transcript of any proceeding in the case that is necessary for the appeal shall be filed in the office of the clerk of the trial court within 60 days after entry of judgment.

(c) Notice of Filing Transcript.

(1) Within 10 days after the transcript is filed or, if the transcript is filed prior to the filing of the notice of appeal, within 10 days after the notice of appeal is filed, counsel for appellant shall (i) give written notice to all other counsel of the date on which the transcript was filed, and (ii) file a copy of the notice with the clerk of the trial court. There shall be appended to the notice either a certificate of counsel for appellant that a copy of the notice has been mailed to all other counsel or an acceptance of service of such notice by all other counsel.

(2) When multiple transcripts are filed, the 10 day period for filing the notice required by this Rule shall be calculated from the date on which the last transcript is filed, or from the date on which the notice of appeal is filed, whichever is later. The notice of filing transcripts shall identify all transcripts filed and the date upon which the last transcript was filed. If the notice of appeal states that no additional transcripts will be filed and identifies the transcripts that have been filed, if any, then no additional written notice of filing of transcripts is required and the notice of appeal will serve as the notice of filing transcripts for purposes of this Rule.

(3) Any failure to file the notice required by this Rule that materially prejudices an appellee will result in the affected transcripts being stricken from the record on appeal. For purposes of this Rule, material prejudice includes preventing the appellee from raising legitimate objections to the contents of the transcript or misleading the appellee about the contents of the record. The appellee shall have the burden of establishing such prejudice in the brief in opposition or, if no brief in opposition is filed, in a written statement filed with the clerk of this Court within the time fixed by these Rules for the filing of a brief in opposition.

(d) Supplementation, Correction, or Modification of Transcript. If anything material to any party is omitted from or misstated in the transcript, or if the transcript or any portion thereof is untimely filed, by omission, clerical error, or accident, the filing may be supplemented, corrected, or modified at any time within 70 days from the entry of judgment appealed from. Notice as provided in paragraph (c) of this Rule must be given for any such supplementation, correction, or modification. Thereafter, such supplementation, correction, or modification may be made, by order of this Court sua sponte or upon motion of any party, if at least two Justices of this Court concur in a finding that any such supplementation, correction, or modification is warranted by a showing of good cause sufficient to excuse the deficiency.

(e) Written Statement in Lieu of Transcript. A written statement of facts, testimony, and other incidents of the case, which may include or consist of a portion of the transcript, becomes a part of the record when:

(1) within 55 days after entry of judgment a copy of such statement is filed in the office of the clerk of the trial court. A copy must be mailed or delivered to opposing counsel on the same day that it is filed in the office of the clerk of the trial court, accompanied by notice that such statement will be presented to the trial judge no earlier than 15 days nor later than 20 days after such filing; and

(2) the statement is signed by the trial judge and filed in the office of the clerk of the trial court. The judge may sign the statement forthwith upon its presentation to him if it is signed by counsel for all parties, but if objection is made to the accuracy or

completeness of the statement, it shall be signed in accordance with paragraph (g) of this Rule.

(f) The term "other incidents of the case" in subsection (e) includes motions, proffers, objections, and rulings of the trial court regarding any issue that a party intends to assign as error or otherwise address on appeal.

(g) Objections. Any party may object to a transcript or written statement on the ground that it is erroneous or incomplete. Notice of such objection specifying the errors alleged or deficiencies asserted shall be filed with the clerk of the trial court within 15 days after the date the notice of filing the transcript (paragraph (c) of this Rule) or within 15 days after the date the notice of filing the written statement (paragraph (e) of this Rule) is filed in the office of the clerk of the trial court or, if the transcript or written statement is filed before the notice of appeal is filed, within 10 days after the notice of appeal has been filed with the clerk of the trial court. Counsel for the objecting party shall give the trial judge prompt notice of the filing of such objections. Within 10 days after the notice of objection is filed with the clerk of the trial court, the trial judge shall:

(1) overrule the objections; or

(2) make any corrections that the trial judge deems necessary; or

(3) include any accurate additions to make the record complete; or

(4) certify the manner in which the record is incomplete; and

(5) sign the transcript or written statement.

At any time while the record remains in the office of the clerk of the trial court, the trial judge may, after notice to counsel and hearing, correct the transcript or written statement.

The judge's signature on a transcript or written statement, without more, shall constitute certification that the procedural requirements of this Rule have been satisfied.

[Amended effective January 1, 1987; July 1, 1988; January 1, 1990; March 15, 1997; July 1, 2010.]

Source: Rule 5A:8. Cf. Rules 5:9 and 5:11.

RULE 5:12. JUDGE AUTHORIZED TO ACT

The judge authorized to act in all matters relating to the record on appeal shall be any judge having authority to enter orders in the case or in the court in which the case was heard or, in a case heard by three judges, any one of them.

[Amended effective July 1, 2010.]

Source: Rules 5A:9 and 5:12.

RULE 5:13. RECORD ON APPEAL: PREPARATION AND TRANSMISSION

(a) Preparation. The clerk of the trial court, disciplinary board, or commission in which the proceeding originated shall prepare the record as soon as possible after notice of appeal is filed. In the event of multiple appeals in the same case, or in cases tried together, only one record need be prepared and transmitted.

(b) Form of the Record.

(1) The record shall be compiled in the following order:

(i) a front cover setting forth the name of the court and the short style of the case;

(ii) a table of contents listing each paper included in the record and the page on which it begins;

(iii) each paper constituting a part of the record in chronological order; and

(iv) the certificate of the clerk of the trial court that the foregoing constitutes the true and complete record, except omitted exhibits as hereinafter provided.

(2) Each page of the record shall be numbered at the bottom.

(3) Transcripts, depositions, and reports of commissioners may be included in separate volumes identified by the clerk of the trial court if referred to in the table of contents and at the appropriate place in the record.

(4) Exhibits, other than those filed with pleadings, may be included in a separate volume or envelope certified by the clerk of the trial court, except that any exhibit that cannot be conveniently placed in a volume or envelope shall be identified by a tag. Each such volume or envelope shall include, on its cover or inside, a descriptive list of exhibits contained therein. Reference shall be made to exhibits in the table of contents and at the appropriate place in the record referred to in paragraph (b)(1) of this Rule. The clerk of the trial court shall not transmit the following types of exhibits, unless requested to do so by the clerk of this Court: drugs, guns and other weapons, ammunition, blood vials and other bio-hazard type materials, money, jewelry, articles of clothing, and bulky items such as large graphs and maps. The omission of any such exhibit shall be noted on the descriptive list of exhibits. Upon motion by counsel, this Court may order the trial court to transmit any of these prohibited exhibits.

(5) Any transcript or statement of facts that the clerk of the trial court deems not a part of the record because of untimely filing shall be certified as such and transmitted with the record.

(c) Transmission. The clerk of the trial court shall retain the record for 21 days after the notice of appeal has been filed with him pursuant to Rule 5:9. If the notice of appeal states that a transcript or statement will thereafter be filed, the clerk of the trial court shall retain the record for 21 days after the filing in his office of such transcript or statement or, if objection is made to the transcript or statement pursuant to Rule 5:11(g), the clerk of the trial court shall retain the record for 5 days after the objection is acted upon by the trial judge. The clerk of the trial court shall then forthwith transmit the record to the clerk of this Court; provided, however, that, notwithstanding that the foregoing periods of retention may not have expired, the clerk of the trial court shall transmit the record sooner if requested in writing by counsel for all parties to the appeal and shall, whether or not so requested, transmit the record in time for delivery to the clerk of this Court within three months after entry of the judgment appealed from. The failure of the clerk of the trial court to transmit the record as herein provided shall not be a ground for dismissal of the appeal by this Court.

(d) Record Returned to Trial Court. When the mandate is issued by this Court, the clerk of this Court shall return the record to the clerk of the trial court, disciplinary board, or commission in which the proceeding originated. The record shall be returned by that clerk upon the request of the clerk of this Court.

[Amended effective July 1, 2010; May 2, 2011.]

Source: Rule 5A:10. Cf. Rules 5:13, 5:14, 5:15, 5:16 and 5:17.

RULE 5:13A. DIGITAL APPELLATE RECORD: PREPARATION AND TRANSMISSION

(a) Preparation. For courts that utilize the Case Imaging System developed by the Office of the Executive Secretary, a Digital Appellate Record may be created instead of a paper record, with substantially the same content as its paper counterpart. The clerk of the court in which the proceeding originated shall be responsible for preparing the digital record, if the clerk chooses to transmit a digital record in place of the paper version.

(b) Form of Record. The digital record shall comply with the Digital Appellate Record Standards posted on the Supreme Court of Virginia intranet.

(c) Exhibits. Original exhibits should be imaged and retained by the clerk of the trial court. The omission of any exhibit that cannot be scanned or imaged must be noted in a descriptive list of exhibits. On motion or sua sponte, this Court may order the trial court to transmit any retained exhibit.

(d) Transmission. The clerk of the trial court shall transmit the record to the clerk of this Court, in a manner prescribed by the Digital Appellate Record Standards, using the Digital Records System created for this purpose. The same timing and dismissal rules apply to transmissions of digital records as apply to their paper counterparts in Rule 5:13.

(e) Disposition of Record. When the mandate is issued by this Court, the clerk of this Court shall return all tangible items, if any, to the clerk of the trial court in which the proceeding originated. The digital record will not be returned. If necessary, the record shall be re-sent by that clerk upon the request of the clerk of this Court.

(f) Public Record. The publicly available digital record shall be the digital document prepared by the trial court clerk with all information that is sealed or protected from public disclosure by law redacted or excluded.

[Adopted effective July 1, 2015.]

D. Procedure For Filing An Appeal From the Court of Appeals

RULE 5:14. NOTICE OF APPEAL; CERTIFICATION

(a) Notice of Appeal. No appeal from a judgment of the Court of Appeals which is subject to appeal to this Court shall be allowed unless, within 30 days after entry of final judgment or order denying a timely petition for rehearing, a notice of appeal is filed with the clerk of the Court of Appeals.

(b) Notice of Certification. Whenever this Court shall certify a case pending in the Court of Appeals for review by this Court, notice of certification shall be given by the clerk of this Court to all counsel and to the clerk of the Court of Appeals. A case certified for review by this Court shall proceed as if a petition for appeal had been granted by this Court on the date of the certification for review, except as otherwise ordered.

(c) Bail Pending Appeal in Criminal Cases. In criminal cases, either party may appeal an order of the Court of Appeals affirming, reversing, or modifying a circuit court order regarding bail pending appeal as provided by this Rule, Rule 5:15 and Rule 5:17.

[Amended effective March 15, 1997; July 1, 2010; March 1, 2012.]

Source: Rules 5:6(b) and 5:32.1.

RULE 5:15. RECORD ON APPEAL FROM COURT OF APPEALS OR CERTIFICATION FOR REVIEW

(a) Generally. In cases on appeal from the Court of Appeals and those certified for review, the record in this Court shall consist of the record as filed in the office of the clerk of the Court of Appeals and, in addition, all other documents relating to the case which have been filed in the office of the clerk of the Court of Appeals, including any opinion or memorandum decision in cases decided by the Court of Appeals. Pursuant to Rule 5:13 or Rule 5:13A, the clerk of the Court of Appeals shall transmit all such documents to the clerk of this Court within 10 days after the filing of the notice of appeal to this Court or the issuance of the certification for review. The clerk of the Court of Appeals shall certify that the documents so transmitted constitute the record in the Court of Appeals.

(b) Bail Pending Appeal in Criminal Cases. In criminal cases on appeal from a Court of Appeals' order affirming a trial court's order setting or denying bail pending appeal, the record shall consist of: (1) the sentencing order entered by the trial court; (2) a presentence report when available; (3) the trial court's order denying or setting bail; (4) the transcript of the bail hearing or a stipulation of facts between the parties regarding what evidence was introduced at the hearing and the reason(s) the trial judge gave for the bail decision; (5) appellant's motion for review in the Court of Appeals; and (6) the order of the Court of Appeals on the motion for review.

[Amended effective July 1, 1988; July 1, 2010; July 1, 2015.]

Source: Rule 5:16.1.

RULE 5:16. DISPOSITION OF RECORD

When there can be no further proceedings in this Court, the clerk of this Court shall return the record to the clerk of the trial court or commission in which the case originated. The record shall be returned by that clerk upon the request of the clerk of this Court.

[Amended effective July 1, 1986; July 1, 2010.]

Source: Rule 5:17.

E. PERFECTING THE APPEAL

RULE 5:17. PETITION FOR APPEAL

(a) When the Petition Must Be Filed. Unless otherwise provided by rule or statute, in every case in which the appellate jurisdiction of this Court is invoked, a petition for appeal must be filed with the clerk of this Court within the following time periods:

(1) in the case of an appeal direct from a trial court, not more than three months after entry of the order appealed from; or

(2) in the case of an appeal from the Court of Appeals, within 30 days after entry of the judgment appealed from or a denial of a timely petition for rehearing.

(b) Who Must Receive a Copy of the Petition. When the petition for appeal is filed with the clerk of this Court, a copy of the petition shall be served on opposing counsel.

(c) What the Petition Must Contain. A petition for appeal must contain the following:

(1) *Assignments of Error.* Under a heading entitled "Assignments of Error," the petition shall list, clearly and concisely and without extraneous argument, the specific errors in the rulings below upon which the party intends to rely, or the specific existing case law that should be overturned, extended, modified, or reversed. An exact reference to the page(s) of the transcript, written statement of facts, or record where the alleged error has been preserved in the trial court or other tribunal from which the appeal is taken shall be included with each assignment of error.

(i) Effect of Failure to Assign Error. Only assignments of error assigned in the petition for appeal will be noticed by this Court. If the petition for appeal does not contain assignments of error, the petition shall be dismissed.

(ii) Nature of Assignments of Error in Appeals From the Court of Appeals. When appeal is taken from a judgment of the Court of Appeals, only assignments of error relating to assignments of error presented in, and to actions taken by, the Court of Appeals may be included in the petition for appeal to this Court.

(iii) Insufficient Assignments of Error. An assignment of error that does not address the findings or rulings in the trial court or other tribunal from which an appeal is taken, or which merely states that the judgment or award is contrary to the law and the evidence, is not sufficient. An assignment of error in an appeal from the Court of Appeals to the Supreme Court which recites that "the trial court erred" and specifies the errors in the trial court, will be sufficient so long as the Court of Appeals ruled upon the specific merits of the alleged trial court error and the error assigned in this Court is identical to that assigned in the Court of Appeals. If the assignments of error are insufficient, the petition for appeal shall be dismissed.

(iv) Effect of Failure to Use Separate Heading or Include Preservation Reference. If the petition for appeal contains assignments of error, but the assignments of error are not set forth under a separate heading as provided in subparagraph (c)(1) of this Rule, a rule to show cause will issue pursuant to Rule 5:1A. If there is a deficiency in the reference to the page(s) of the transcript, written statement of facts, or record where the alleged error has been preserved in the trial court or other tribunal from which the appeal is taken, a rule to show cause will issue pursuant to Rule 5:1A.

(2) *Required Statements When the Appeal Is From the Court of Appeals.* When appeal is taken from a judgment of the Court of Appeals in a case in which judgment is made final under Code § 17.1–410, the petition for appeal shall contain a statement setting forth in what respect the decision of the Court of Appeals involves the following:

(i) a substantial constitutional question as a determinative issue, or

(ii) matters of significant precedential value. If the petition for appeal does not contain such a statement, the appeal will be dismissed.

(3) *Table of Contents and Table of Authorities.* A table of contents and table of authorities with cases alphabetically arranged. Citations of all authorities shall include the year thereof.

(4) *Nature of the Case and Material Proceedings Below.* A brief statement of the nature of the case and of the material proceedings in the trial court or commission in which the case originated. This statement shall omit references to any paper filed or action taken that does not relate to the assignments of error.

(5) *Statement of Facts.* A clear and concise statement of the facts that relate to the assignments of error, with references to the pages of the record, transcript, or written statement of facts. Any quotation from the record should be brief. When the facts are in dispute, the petition shall so state. The testimony of individual witnesses should not be summarized seriatim unless the facts are in dispute and such a summary is necessary to support the appellant's version of the facts.

(6) *Authorities and Argument.* With respect to each assignment of error, the standard of review and the argument—including principles of law and the authorities—shall be stated in one place and not scattered through the petition. At the option of counsel, the argument may be preceded by a short summary.

(7) *Conclusion.* A short conclusion stating the precise relief sought.

(d) Filing Fee Required With the Petition. When it is filed, the petition for appeal must be accompanied by a check or money order payable to the "Clerk of the Supreme Court of Virginia" for the amount required by statute. The clerk of this Court may file a petition for appeal that is not accompanied by such fee if the fee is received by the clerk within 10 days of the date the petition for appeal is filed. If the fee is not received within such time, the petition for appeal shall be dismissed.

(e) Number of Copies to File. Seven copies of the petition shall be filed with the clerk of this Court.

(f) Length. Except by leave of a Justice of this Court, a petition shall not exceed the longer of 35 pages or 6,125 words. The page or word limit does not include the cover page, table of contents, table of authorities, and certificate.

(g) Use of a Single Petition in Separate Cases. Whenever two or more cases were tried together in the court or commission below, one petition for appeal may be used to bring all such cases before this Court even though the cases were not consolidated below by formal order.

(h) Procedure for an *Anders* Appeal. If counsel for appellant finds appellant's appeal to be without merit, counsel must comply with the requirements of *Anders v. California*, 386 U.S. 738 (1967), and *Brown v. Warden of Virginia State Penitentiary*, 238 Va. 551, 385 S.E.2d 587 (1989). In compliance therewith, counsel is required to file (1) a petition for appeal which refers to anything in the record which might arguably support the appeal and which demonstrates to this Court counsel's conscientious examination of the merits of the appeal; (2) a motion for leave to withdraw as counsel; and (3) a motion for an extension of time to allow the appellant to file a supplemental petition for appeal. The petition for appeal and the motion for leave to withdraw as counsel should specifically cite to *Anders*. All three pleadings must be served on opposing counsel and upon the client and must contain a certificate providing evidence of such service. This Court will rule upon the motion for extension of time upon its receipt, but will not rule on the motion to withdraw until this Court considers the case in its entirety, including any supplemental petition for appeal that may be filed.

(i) What the Certificate Must Contain. The appellant shall include within the petition for appeal a certificate stating:

(1) the names of all appellants and appellees, the name, Virginia State Bar number, mailing address, telephone number (including any applicable extension), facsimile number (if any), and e-mail address (if any) of counsel for each party, and the mailing address, telephone number (including any applicable extension), facsimile number (if any), and e-mail address (if any) of any party not represented by counsel;

(2) that a copy of the petition for appeal has been mailed or delivered on the date stated therein to all opposing counsel and all parties not represented by counsel;

(3) if a word count is used, the number of words (headings, footnotes, and quotations count towards the word limitation; the cover page, table of contents, table of authorities, and certificate do not count towards the word count);

(4) in a criminal case or habeas corpus appeal, a statement whether counsel for defendant has been appointed or privately retained; and

(5) whether the appellant desires to state orally to a panel of this Court the reasons why the petition for appeal should be granted, and, if so, whether in person or by conference telephone call.

(j) Oral Argument.

(1) *Right to Oral Argument.* The appellant shall be entitled to state orally, in person or by telephone conference call, to a panel of this Court the reasons why the petition for appeal should be granted. The appellee shall not be entitled to oral argument, whether in person or by telephone conference call. Any lawyer not licensed in Virginia who seeks to appear pro hac

vice to present oral argument to the Court must comply with the requirements of Rule 1A:4.

(2) *Waiver of Right to Oral Argument.* The appellant may waive the right to oral argument on the petition for appeal before a panel by notifying the clerk of this Court and opposing counsel in writing, or by filing a reply brief.

(3) *No Oral Argument on Pro Se Inmate's Petition.* If an appellant is not represented by counsel and is incarcerated, the petition for appeal may be considered by this Court without oral argument.

(4) *Notice of Oral Argument.* If the appellant has requested oral argument, notice of the date and time of such argument shall be provided to counsel for the appellant or to any pro se appellant and to counsel for the appellee or any pro se appellee who has filed a Brief in Opposition or otherwise appeared in the appeal.

[Amended effective July 1, 1988; July 1, 1991; February 1, 1992; January 1, 1993; March 15, 1997; October 21, 1998; November 15, 2002; February 1, 2004; February 1, 2007; July 1, 2010; May 2, 2011; May 16, 2014; July 1, 2015.]

Source: Rule 5A:12. Cf. Rules 5:21, 5:22, 5:24 and 5:25.

RULE 5:17A. PETITION FOR REVIEW PURSUANT TO CODE § 8.01–626; INJUNCTIONS

(a) Time for Filing. In every case in which the jurisdiction of this Court is invoked pursuant to Code § 8.01–626, a petition for review must be filed with the clerk of this Court within 15 days of

(i) an order of a circuit court that grants an injunction, refuses an injunction, or dissolves or refuses to enlarge an existing injunction; or

(ii) an order of the Court of Appeals deciding a petition for review filed in that court pursuant to Code § 8.01–626.

(b) Copy to Opposing Counsel. At the time the petition for review is filed, a copy of the petition shall be served on counsel for the respondent. At the same time that the petition is served, a copy of the petition shall also be emailed to counsel for the respondent, unless said counsel does not have, or does not provide, an email address. With the agreement of the parties, the petition may be served on counsel for the respondent solely by email.

(c) Length and What the Petition for Review Must Contain.

(i) Except by permission of a Justice of this Court, a petition for review shall not exceed the longer of 15 pages or 2,625 words. The petition for review must otherwise comply with the requirements for a petition for appeal in Rule 5:17(c).

(ii) The petition shall be accompanied by a copy of the pertinent portions of the record of the lower tribunal(s), including the relevant portions of any transcripts filed in the circuit court and the order(s) entered by the lower tribunal(s) respecting the injunction (hereafter "the record"). The copy of the record shall constitute part of the petition for the purpose of paragraph (b), but shall not count against the petition size limit.

(iii) The petition for review shall contain a certificate:

(1) providing the names of all petitioners and respondents; the name, Virginia State Bar number, mailing address, telephone number, facsimile number (if any), and e-mail address of counsel for each party; and the mailing address, telephone number, facsimile number (if any), and e-mail address of any party not represented by counsel;

(2) certifying that a copy of the petition has been served on all opposing counsel and all parties not represented by counsel, and specifying the date and manner of service.

(3) if a word count is used, certifying the number of words (headings, footnotes, and quotations count towards the word limitation; the cover page, table of contents, table of authorities, and certificate do not count towards the word count);

(4) certifying that the copy of the record being filed is an accurate copy of the record of the lower tribunal(s) and contains everything therefrom necessary for a review of the petition.

(d) Number of Copies to File. Four copies of the petition, including the record of the lower tribunal(s), shall be filed. Only one copy of the record of the lower tribunal(s) need be filed if, upon filing the petition, counsel for the petitioner also files an electronic copy of the said record as an Adobe Acrobat Portable Document Format (PDF) document on a CD–ROM.

(e) Filing Fee. The petition must be accompanied by a check or money order payable to the clerk of this Court for the amount required by statute. The clerk of this Court may file a petition for review that is not accompanied by such fee if the fee is received by the clerk within 5 days of the date the petition for review is filed. If the fee is not received within such time, the petition for review shall be dismissed.

(f) Scope and Review.

(i) a petition for review may be considered by this Court whether the lower court's order, or that part of the order dealing with the injunction, is temporary or permanent. If review is sought from a final order that deals with injunctive relief and other issues, a petition for review must address only that part of the final order that actually addresses injunctive relief. All other issues shall be governed by the normal rules and timetables that apply to appeals. If both a petition for review under Code § 8.01–626 and an appeal under § 8.01–670 are filed to challenge the same final order, the clerk of this Court will assign separate record numbers to the two proceedings.

(ii) a petition for review may be considered by a single Justice of this Court, or by a panel of Justices.

(g) Responsive Pleading. A respondent may file a response to a petition for review within seven days of the date of service of same, unless the Court specifies a shorter time frame. For the purpose of this rule, a petition for review is considered served 3 days from the date on which it was mailed, or 1 day from the date on which the petition was faxed, emailed, or sent by commercial delivery service, to counsel for the respondent. Notwithstanding the foregoing, the Court may act on a petition for review without awaiting a response; however, absent exceptional circumstances, the Court shall not grant a petition for review without affording the respondent an opportunity to file a responsive pleading.

(h) Rehearing. The provisions of Rules 5:20 and 5:37 do not apply to proceedings under Code § 8.01–626.

[Adopted effective July 1, 1991. Amended effective July 1, 2010; May 2, 2011; July 1, 2015.]

RULE 5:18. BRIEF IN OPPOSITION

(a) Filing Time. A brief in opposition to granting the appeal may be filed with the clerk of this Court by the appellee within 21 days after petition for appeal is served on counsel for the appellee. Within the same time the counsel for appellee shall mail or deliver a copy to counsel for appellant. Seven copies shall be filed.

(b) Form and Content. The brief in opposition shall conform in all respects to the content requirements for the brief of appellee in Rule 5:28. However, the brief in opposition need not be bound or have a blue cover. Except by leave of a Justice of this Court, the brief shall not exceed the longer of 25 pages or 4,375 words. If the brief exceeds 10 pages or 1,750 words, it shall contain a table of contents and table of authorities with cases alphabetically arranged. The brief in opposition must be signed by at least one counsel of record.

(c) Assignments of Cross–Error. The brief in opposition may include assignments of cross-error. If the brief in opposition contains an assignment or assignments of cross-error, the cover of the brief must so indicate by being styled, "Brief in Opposition and Assignment of Cross–Error."

(1) A cross-error must be assigned in the brief in opposition in order to be noticed by this Court.

(2) The provisions of Rule 5:25 shall apply to limit the assignments of cross-error which will be heard on the appeal.

(3) A brief in opposition containing assignments of cross-error shall conform to the form, content, and maximum word requirements of paragraph (b) of this Rule.

(4) When an appellee assigns cross-error in the brief in opposition:

(i) this Court will not grant any assignment of cross-error unless it first decides to grant some or all of the assignments of error contained in the appellant's petition for appeal.

(ii) the appellee shall not be permitted to present oral argument to a writ panel.

(iii) if the appellant withdraws the petition for appeal, the appeal will be dismissed without consideration of the cross-error assigned by an appellee.

(d) Expedited Review. When it clearly appears that an appeal ought to be granted without further delay, an appeal may be granted before the filing of the brief in opposition.

[Amended effective February 1, 2004; July 1, 2010; May 2, 2011; July 1, 2015.]

Source: Rule 5A:13. Cf. Rule 5:27.

RULE 5:19. REPLY BRIEF

(a) When a brief in opposition to the petition for appeal has been filed, the appellant may, within 7 days thereafter, in lieu of oral argument, file with the clerk of this Court a reply brief not to exceed the longer of 15 pages or 2,625 words in length. Seven copies shall be filed.

(b) When cross-error is assigned in a brief in opposition, the appellant may, without waiving oral argument, file with the clerk of this Court within 14 days after filing of the brief in opposition a reply brief not in excess of 10 pages or 1,750 words which addresses only the cross-error. Seven copies shall be filed.

[Amended effective July 1, 1989; February 1, 2004; July 1, 2010; May 2, 2011; July 1, 2015.]

Source: Rule 5A:14. Cf. Rule 5:28.

RULE 5:20. PETITION FOR REHEARING AFTER REFUSAL OF PETITION FOR APPEAL, REFUSAL OF ASSIGNMENTS OF CROSS–ERROR, OR DISPOSITION OF AN ORIGINAL JURISDICTION PETITION

(a) Scope. This Rule governs requests for rehearing of the refusal or dismissal of a petition for appeal filed pursuant to Rule 5:17, the refusal of one or more assignments of cross-error, or the disposition of an original jurisdiction petition filed pursuant to Rule 5:7, Rule 5:7A, or Rule 5:7B.

(b) Time to File.

(1) *Petition for Rehearing After Refusal or Dismissal of Petition for Appeal.* When a petition for appeal is either refused or dismissed, in whole or in part, the clerk of this Court shall mail a copy of the order denying the appeal, in whole or in part, to counsel for the appellant and counsel for the appellee. Counsel for the appellant may, within 14 days after the

date of such order, file in the office of the clerk of this Court a petition for rehearing. If the petition for appeal is granted but one or more assignments of cross-error are refused, counsel for the appellee may, within 14 days after the date of that order, file in the office of the clerk of this Court a petition for rehearing.

(2) *Petition for Rehearing After Disposition of Original Jurisdiction Petition.* When a petition filed pursuant to this Court's original jurisdiction (habeas corpus, mandamus, prohibition, or actual innocence) is decided, the clerk of this Court shall mail a copy of the order to counsel for the petitioner and counsel for the respondent. Counsel for either party may, within 30 days after the date of this order, file in the office of the clerk of this Court a petition for rehearing.

(c) Filing Requirements. Except for petitions for rehearing filed by pro se prisoners or with leave of this Court, a petition for rehearing shall be filed electronically.

(1) Requirements for Electronic Filing.

(i) The petition for rehearing shall be filed as an Adobe Acrobat Portable Document Format (PDF) document attached to an e-mail addressed to scvpfr@courts.state.va.us and will be timely filed if received by the clerk's office on or before 11:59 p.m. on the date due.

(ii) The petition for rehearing must be formatted in compliance with the requirements of Rule 5:6(a) and must not exceed the greater of 10 pages or a word count of 1,750 words. The petition must include a certificate of service to counsel for the appellee and the certificate shall specify the manner of service and the date of service. The petition must also include a certificate of compliance with the word count limit. The petition will be considered filed on the date and time that it is received by scvpfr@courts.state.va.us. If the petition does not meet the requirements of this rule as to format, the clerk shall so notify counsel and provide a specific amount of time for a corrected copy of the petition to be filed.

(iii) A person who files a document electronically shall have the same responsibility as a person filing a document in paper form for ensuring that the document is properly filed, complete, and readable. However, if technical problems at the Supreme Court result in a failure to timely receive the electronically filed petition for rehearing, counsel shall provide to the clerk of this Court on the next business day all documentation which exists demonstrating the attempt to file the petition by email, any delivery failure notice received in response to the attempt, and a copy of the petition for rehearing.

(iv) The e-mail message to which the petition for rehearing is attached shall recite in the subject line the style of the case and the Supreme Court record number. The e-mail message shall contain a paragraph stating that a petition for rehearing is being filed, the style of the case, the Supreme Court record number, the name and Virginia State Bar number of counsel filing the petition, as well as the law firm name, mailing address, telephone number, facsimile number (if any), and e-mail address (if any) of counsel. The message shall also state whether a copy of the petition for rehearing has been served by e-mail or another means on opposing counsel and the date of such service. If opposing counsel has an e-mail address, that address shall also be included. Upon receipt of the petition for rehearing in the e-mail box of the clerk's office, an acknowledgment will automatically be forwarded to counsel seeking the rehearing.

(2) Requirements When Paper Filing is Allowed.

(i) The petition for rehearing shall not exceed the greater of 10 pages or 1,750 words in length and must be formatted in compliance with the requirements of Rule 5:6(a). The petition for rehearing shall state that a copy has been mailed or delivered to counsel for the appellee.

(ii) Ten copies shall be filed.

(d) Oral Argument and Responsive Brief. Oral argument on the petition for rehearing will not be allowed. No responsive brief shall be filed unless requested by this Court.

(e) Incorporation of Facts or Arguments. Attempts to incorporate facts or arguments from the petition for appeal or original jurisdiction petition are prohibited.

(f) Notification of Action on the Petition. The clerk of this Court shall notify counsel for all parties of the action taken by this Court on the petition for rehearing via e-mail, if e-mail addresses have been provided, or via U.S. Mail to any counsel or party who has not provided an email address.

(g) Attorney's Fees. Upon denial of a petition for appeal and any petition for rehearing, any appellee who has received attorney's fees and costs in the circuit court may make application in the circuit court for additional fees and costs incurred on appeal pursuant to Rule 1:1A.

[Amended effective December 1, 1990; April 1, 1995; January 1, 2005; April 1, 2005; January 1, 2006; July 1, 2010; May 2, 2011; November 1, 2013; July 1, 2015; October 7, 2015.]

RULE 5:20A. DENIAL OF APPEAL: PETITION FOR REHEARING [DELETED]

F. Special Rules

RULE 5:21. SPECIAL RULES APPLICABLE TO CERTAIN APPEALS OF RIGHT

(a) Appeals From the State Corporation Commission.

(1) *Applicability.* Paragraph (a) of this Rule applies to all appeals from the State Corporation Commission and supersedes all other Rules except as otherwise specified herein.

(2) *Party.* For the purposes of this Rule, the Commission, the Attorney General, the applicant or petitioner, and every person who made an appearance in person in a capacity other than as a witness or by counsel at any hearing in any proceeding before the Commission shall be the parties to such proceeding. Upon the request of any party, the clerk of the Commission shall prepare and certify a list of all parties (including their addresses and the names and addresses of their counsel) to a proceeding before the Commission. Initially, the parties to an appeal from an order in a proceeding shall be the parties to that proceeding, but the number of parties to an appeal may thereafter be limited as hereinafter provided. Service upon a party represented by counsel shall be made upon his counsel.

(3) *Notice of Appeal.* No appeal from an order of the Commission shall be allowed unless, within 30 days after entry of the order appealed from, counsel files in the office of the clerk of the Commission a notice of appeal. A copy of the notice of appeal shall be mailed or delivered to each party to the appeal, including the Attorney General of Virginia, and an acceptance of such service or a certificate showing the date of delivery or mailing shall be appended thereto. All petitions for appeal from the same order shall be deemed to be a consolidated case for the purpose of oral argument in this Court unless this Court shall order a severance for convenience of hearing.

(4) *Record.* The clerk of the Commission shall prepare and certify the record as soon as possible after the notice of appeal is filed and shall, as soon as it has been certified by him, transmit it to the clerk of this Court within 4 months after entry of the order appealed from. In the event of multiple appeals in the same case or in cases tried together below, only one record need be prepared and transmitted.

(5) *Contents of Record.* The record on appeal from the Commission shall consist of all notices of appeal, any application or petition, all orders entered in the case by the Commission, the opinions, the transcript of any testimony received, and all exhibits accepted or rejected, together with such other material as may be certified by the clerk of the Commission to be a part of the record. The record shall conform as nearly as practicable to the requirements of Rule 5:10.

(6) *Alignment of Parties.* Within 21 days after the notice of appeal shall have been filed in the office of the clerk of the Commission, each party who has not filed a notice of appeal and who intends to participate in the appeal shall file in the office of the clerk of the Commission and shall mail to every other party a notice that he intends to participate as an appellant or as an appellee. Every party who seeks reversal or modification of the order appealed from shall be deemed an appellant, and every party who seeks affirmance of the order appealed from shall be deemed an appellee. Every party who does not file such a notice and every party who, having filed such a notice as an appellant, does not thereafter file a petition for appeal shall be deemed no longer to be a party to the appeal, and no further papers need be served on him. Notwithstanding the foregoing provisions, (i) a necessary party who does not file such a notice or petition for appeal shall be deemed an appellee, and (ii) the Commission need not file such a notice and shall be deemed an appellee.

(7) *Petition for Appeal.* The petition(s) for appeal, accompanied by the prescribed filing fee, shall be filed in the office of the clerk of this Court within 4 months after entry of the final order, judgment or finding by the Commission. Each party deemed to be an appellant shall file a petition for appeal, as limited hereafter, and shall, before the petition is filed, mail or deliver a copy to every other party to the appeal. Except as provided herein, the provisions of Rule 5:17 do not apply to a petition filed pursuant to this paragraph. The petition for appeal need only identify the order appealed from, with its date, contain a prayer that the appeal be granted, and include the certificate required by Rule 5:17(i). Oral argument on the petition shall not be allowed nor will a brief in opposition be received. If the petition prays for a suspension of the effectiveness of the order appealed from, it shall contain such statements of the facts and argument as shall be necessary for an understanding of the assignments of error. In that event, a brief in opposition will be received and oral argument may be granted.

(8) *Award of Appeal.* When the notice of appeal, the record, and the petition(s) for appeal appear to have been filed in the manner provided herein and within the time provided herein and by law, the clerk of this Court shall forthwith enter an order docketing the appeal, requiring such bond as the clerk shall deem proper. The clerk's action shall be subject to review by this Court.

(9) *Assignments of Error.* Within 10 days after the issuance by the clerk of this Court of the certificate pursuant to Rule 5:23, each party appellant shall file assignments of error in the office of the clerk of this Court and mail a copy thereof to every other party to the appeal. Under a heading entitled "Assignments of

Error" shall be listed, clearly and concisely and without extraneous argument, the specific errors in the rulings below upon which the party intends to rely. A clear and exact reference to the pages of the transcript, written statement of facts, or record where the alleged error has been preserved shall be included with each assignment of error. Only errors so assigned will be noticed by this Court and no error not so assigned will be considered as grounds for reversal of the decision below. No ruling by the Commission will be considered as a basis for reversal unless an objection was stated with reasonable certainty at the time of the ruling, except for good cause shown or to enable this Court to attain the ends of justice. An assignment of error which merely states that the judgment is contrary to the law and the evidence is not sufficient.

(10) *Further Proceedings.* Further proceedings in this Court shall conform to Rules 5:23 through 5:38 provided that (i) the time within which the appellee may file with the clerk of this Court a designation of the additional parts of the record that the appellee wishes included in the appendix (Rule 5:32(b)) shall be extended to 30 days after the date of the certificate of the clerk of this Court pursuant to Rule 5:23 an appeal has been awarded; and (ii) the time within which the opening brief of the appellant shall be filed in the office of the clerk of this Court shall be extended to 50 days after such date.

(11) *Additional Brief.* An appellant who seeks relief different from that sought by another appellant may file an answering brief at the time prescribed for filing the brief of appellee.

(b) Appeals From the Virginia State Bar Disciplinary Board or a Three–Judge Circuit Court Determination.

(1) *Applicability.* Paragraph (b) of this Rule applies to appeals from the Virginia State Bar Disciplinary Board, pursuant to Part 6, § IV, Paragraph 13–26 of the Rules of the Supreme Court of Virginia, and to appeals from the decisions of a three-judge circuit court pursuant to Code § 54.1–3935. As used in this paragraph, "Respondent" is defined as the attorney who is appealing the decision of the disciplinary proceeding.

(2) *Perfecting the Appeal.*

(i) Provisions for Appeals From the Virginia State Bar Disciplinary Board. No appeal shall be allowed under this paragraph unless the Respondent files a notice of appeal and assignments of error with the clerk of the Disciplinary System within 30 days after the Memorandum Order is served on the attorney by certified mail, return receipt requested, at the attorney's last address on record for membership purposes with the Virginia State Bar. At the same time the Respondent files a notice of appeal and assignments of error, a copy of the notice of appeal and assignments of error must be sent to the counsel for the Bar and the Attorney General of Virginia. The Respondent is responsible for filing a transcript in compliance with Rule 5:11. The date of the Memorandum Order shall be the date from which the time limits contained in Rule 5:11 shall run. This action within the time prescribed is mandatory. Upon timely compliance with these rules, the Clerk of the Supreme Court shall docket the appeal as provided in Rule 5:23.

(ii) Provisions for Appeals From a Three–Judge Circuit Court. No appeal shall be allowed under this paragraph unless the Respondent files a notice of appeal and assignments of error with the clerk of the three-judge circuit court within 30 days after the entry of the final judgment and, at the same time, mails a copy of the notice of appeal and assignments of error to counsel for the Bar and the Attorney General of Virginia. The Respondent is responsible for filing a transcript in compliance with Rule 5:11. The date of the judgment shall be the date from which the time limits contained in Rule 5:11 shall run. This action within the time prescribed is mandatory. Upon timely compliance with these rules, the Clerk of the Supreme Court shall docket the appeal as provided in Rule 5:23.

(3) *Record on Appeal.* The clerk of the Disciplinary System or the clerk of the three-judge circuit court shall compile and transmit the record as set out in Rules 5:10, 5:11, and 5:13. The clerk shall immediately notify by certified mail the Respondent, and the Respondent's counsel, if any, and the Attorney General of the date the record is filed with the clerk of this Court. At the time the record is filed, the clerk shall also notify the clerk of this Court and the Respondent whether the Attorney General or Bar Counsel will represent the interests of the Commonwealth as appellee.

(4) *Time for Filing Briefs and Appendix.* The parties shall designate the contents of the appendix pursuant to the requirements of Rule 5:32 and the Respondent shall be responsible for filing the appendix pursuant to that Rule. The Respondent shall file the opening brief in the office of the clerk of this Court within 40 days after the date the record is filed. The opening brief shall contain assignments of error and references to the pages of the appendix, transcript, written statement, or record where each assignment of error was preserved. The brief of the appellee shall be filed in the office of the clerk of this Court within 25 days after the filing of the Respondent's opening brief. The Respondent may file a reply brief within 14 days after the filing of the appellee's brief. All briefs and the appendix shall conform to the provisions of Rules 5:26 through 5:32.

(5) *Stay Pending Appeal.* The Respondent may file a motion with the clerk of this Court requesting a stay pending appeal of an order suspending or revoking the Respondent's license. The Respondent must file four copies of the motion for stay along with a copy of the order imposing the suspension or revocation and a copy

of the Respondent's notice of appeal, which must contain the date stamp of the clerk showing the date the notice of appeal was filed. Any order of Admonition or Public Reprimand shall be automatically stayed prior to or during the pendency of an appeal of the order.

(6) *Procedure on Appeal.* Except as provided in this paragraph, further proceedings shall be as provided in this Court's procedure following the perfection of an appeal set out in Rules 5:23, 5:25, and Rules 5:33 through 5:38.

[Amended effective January 23, 1995; July 1, 2010; January 1, 2013; January 31, 2014.]

Source: Rule 5:18.

RULE 5:22. SPECIAL RULE FOR APPEALS IN DEATH PENALTY CASES

(a) Notice of Receipt of Record. Upon receipt of a record pursuant to § 17.1–313B, the clerk of this Court shall notify in writing counsel for the accused in the circuit court (who shall be deemed to be counsel for the appellant), the Attorney General (who shall be deemed to be counsel for the appellee), and the Director of the Department of Corrections of the date of its receipt. The date of the receipt of the record is the Filing Date and the case shall thereupon stand matured as if an appeal had been awarded to review the conviction and the sentence of death.

(b) Stay of Sentence of Death. Upon the Filing Date, the notice issued by the clerk of this Court shall be deemed to be the certificate of the clerk of this Court pursuant to Rule 5:23 that an appeal has been awarded, and the enforcement of the sentence of death shall thereby be stayed pending the final determination of the case by this Court.

(c) Filing of Assignments of Error and of the Appendix. Within 30 days after the Filing Date, counsel for the appellant shall file with the clerk of this Court assignments of error upon which the appellant intends to rely for reversal of the conviction or review of the sentence of death. Counsel for the appellant shall accompany the assignments of error with a designation of the parts of the record relevant to the review and to the assignments of error. Not more than 10 days after such assignments of error and designation are filed, counsel for the appellee may file with the clerk of this Court a designation of the additional parts of the record that he wishes included as germane to the review or to any assignments of error. Counsel for the appellant shall include in the appendix the parts so designated. The provisions of Rules 5:31 and 5:32 (except Rule 5:32(b)(1) and (b)(3)) shall apply to the appendix.

(d) Assigning Error to the Sentence of Death. With respect to the sentence of death, it shall be a sufficient assignment of error to state that the sentence was imposed under the influence of passion, prejudice, or other arbitrary factor or that the sentence is excessive or disproportionate to the penalty imposed in similar cases.

(e) Requirements for Briefs.

(1) *Brief of Appellant.* The appellant shall file the opening brief, which shall not exceed the longer of 100 pages or 17,500 words, in the office of the clerk of this Court within 60 days after the Filing Date.

(2) *Brief of the Appellee.* The appellee shall file its brief, which shall not exceed the longer of 100 pages or 17,500 words, in the office of the clerk of this Court within 120 days after the Filing Date.

(3) *Reply Brief of the Appellant.* The appellant shall file the reply brief, which shall not exceed the longer of 50 pages or 8,750 words, in the office of the clerk of this Court within 140 days after the Filing Date.

The page or word limits under this Rule do not include appendices, the cover page, table of contents, table of authorities, and certificate. There shall be no exception to these limits except by permission of this Court on motion for extension of the limits.

(f) Compliance With Rules for Perfected Appeals. Except to the extent that a conflict with this Rule may arise, in which case this Rule shall then be controlling, further proceedings in the case shall conform to the Rules relating to cases in which an appeal has been perfected.

(g) Varying Procedure to Attain the Ends of Justice. This Court may, on motion in a particular case, vary the procedure prescribed by this Rule in order to attain the ends of justice and the purpose of § 17.1–313.

[Amended effective October 21, 1998; December 22, 2004; July 1, 2010; May 2, 2011.]

Source: Rule 5:20.

G. PROCEDURE FOLLOWING PERFECTION OF APPEAL

RULE 5:23. PERFECTION OF APPEAL; DOCKETING

(a) Grant of Petition for Appeal. Promptly after a petition for appeal has been granted, the clerk of this Court shall certify this action to counsel for the appellant, counsel for the appellee, and the tribunal from which the appeal is taken. The case shall be considered mature for purposes of further proceedings from the date of such certificate.

(b) Docketing. Cases shall be placed on the docket when they mature. Precedence shall be given to the following cases:

(1) review of sentences of death;

(2) criminal cases;

(3) cases from the State Corporation Commission;

(4) cases of original jurisdiction;

(5) cases to be reheard; and

(6) any other cases required by statute to be given precedence.

This Court may, however, for good cause shown or for reasons appearing sufficient to the Court, give preference to other cases.

[Amended effective January 1, 1994; July 1, 2010.]

Source: Rule 5A:16. Cf. Rules 5:30 and 5:32.

RULE 5:24. SECURITY FOR APPEAL

(a) Compliance With Forms. All security for appeal required under Code § 8.01–676.1 shall substantially conform to the forms set forth in the Appendix to this Part Five.

(b) Procedure Concerning Defects. No appeal shall be dismissed because of a defect in any bond or irrevocable letter of credit unless an appellee, within 21 days after the issuance of the certificate pursuant to Rule 5:23, files with the clerk of this Court a statement in writing of the defects in the bond or irrevocable letter of credit, and unless the appellant fails to correct such defects, if any, within 21 days after such statement is filed. If the appellant fails to correct such defects within such period of 21 days, an appellee may move that the appeal be dismissed and it shall be dismissed unless the appellant satisfies this Court that the bond or irrevocable letter of credit, either as originally given or as amended, has been filed in the required form.

[Amended effective July 1, 1991; July 1, 2010.]

Source: Rule 5A:17. Cf. Rule 5:31.

RULE 5:25. PRESERVATION OF ISSUES FOR APPELLATE REVIEW

No ruling of the trial court, disciplinary board, or commission before which the case was initially heard will be considered as a basis for reversal unless an objection was stated with reasonable certainty at the time of the ruling, except for good cause shown or to enable this Court to attain the ends of justice. A mere statement that the judgment or award is contrary to the law and the evidence is not sufficient to preserve the issue for appellate review.

[Amended effective January 1, 1993; July 1, 2010.]

Source: Rule 5:21 and Rule 5A:18.

RULE 5:26. GENERAL REQUIREMENTS FOR ALL BRIEFS

(a) Applicability. This Rule, along with Rule 5:6, sets forth the general requirements for all briefs filed in this Court. Rule 5:22 sets forth the special rule for appeals in death penalty-cases.

(b) Length. Except by permission of a Justice of this Court, neither the opening brief of appellant, nor the brief of appellee, nor a brief amicus curiae shall exceed the longer of 50 pages or 8,750 words. No reply brief shall exceed the longer of 15 pages or 2,625 words. Briefs of amici curiae shall comply with the page limits that apply to briefs of the party being supported. The page or word limits under this Rule do not include appendices, the cover page, table of contents, table of authorities, and certificate. There shall be no exception to these limits except by permission of this Court on motion for extension of the limits.

(c) Filing Time. In cases in which a petition for appeal has been granted by this Court, briefs shall be filed subject to the provisions of Rule 5:1(d), as follows:

(1) The appellant shall file the opening brief in the office of the clerk of this Court within 4 0 days after the date of the certificate of appeal issued by the clerk of this Court pursuant to Rule 5:23.

(2) The brief of appellee shall be filed in the office of the clerk of this Court within 25 days after filing of the opening brief.

(3) The appellant may file a reply brief in the office of the clerk of this Court within 14 days after filing of the brief of appellee.

(d) Extension of Time. Upon motion and with permission of a Justice of this Court, the time for filing any brief in this Court may be altered.

(e) Copies for Filing. An electronic version, in Portable Document Format (PDF), must be filed with the clerk of this Court and served on opposing counsel, unless excused by this Court for good cause shown. An electronic version of a brief amicus curiae shall be filed with the clerk of this Court and served on counsel for all parties and on any other counsel amicus curiae. The electronic version must be filed in the manner prescribed by the VACES Guidelines and User's Manual, using the Virginia Appellate Courts eBriefs System (VACES). The Guidelines are located on the Court's website at www.courts.state.va.us/online/vaces/resources/guidelines.pdf. In addition, 10 printed copies of each brief (including a brief amicus curiae) shall be filed in the office of the clerk of this Court. All briefs shall contain a certificate evidencing the date and method of electronic transmission of the brief to opposing counsel.

(f) Reference to Parties. In their briefs, counsel should avoid reference to parties by such designations as "appellant" and "appellee." Clarity is promoted by the use of the names of the parties or descriptive terms such as "the employee," "the injured person," "the driver," "the wife," or the designations used in the lower court or commission.

(g) Arguments Made by Reference. Attempts to incorporate arguments made below by reference to pleadings, motions, memorandum, or other filings are prohibited.

(h) Signature and Certificate. All briefs shall contain the signature, which need not be in handwriting, of at least one counsel of record, counsel's Virginia State Bar number, address, telephone number, facsimile number (if any), and email address, and a certificate that there has been compliance with this Rule. If a word count is used, the certificate must also state the number of words (headings, footnotes, and quotations count towards the word limitation; the cover page, table of contents, table of authorities, and certificate do not count towards the word count).

(i) Failure to File Complying Brief. Any party who fails to file a brief in compliance with these Rules or otherwise fails to file a required brief may be subject to sanctions deemed reasonable by the Court, including, but not limited to, forfeiture of oral argument.

(j) Technical Problems With Electronic Filing of Brief or Appendix. A person who files a document electronically shall have the same responsibility as a person filing a document in paper form for ensuring that the document is properly filed, complete, and readable. However, if technical problems at the Supreme Court result in a failure to timely receive the electronically filed brief or appendix, counsel shall provide to the clerk of this Court on the next business day all documentation which exists demonstrating the attempt to electronically file the brief or appendix, any error message received in response to the attempt, documentation that the brief or appendix was later successfully resubmitted, and a motion requesting that the Court accept the resubmitted brief or appendix.

[Amended effective July 1, 1988; January 1, 2001; February 1, 2008; March 1, 2009; July 1, 2010; May 2, 2011; July 1, 2015.]

Source: Rule 5A:19. Cf. Rules 5:47, 5:48 and 5:49.

Comment: The time for filing the opening brief of the appellant in cases from the State Corporation Commission is stated in Rule 5:21(j).

RULE 5:27. REQUIREMENTS FOR OPENING BRIEF OF APPELLANT

The opening brief of the appellant shall comply with the requirements of Rules 5:6 and 5:26, and must contain the following:

(a) A table of contents and table of authorities with cases alphabetically arranged. Citations of all authorities shall include the year thereof.

(b) A statement of the case containing the material proceedings below and the facts, with references to the appendix.

(c) The assignments of error, with a clear and exact reference to the pages of the appendix where the alleged error has been preserved.

(d) The standard of review, the argument, and the authorities relating to each assignment of error. With respect to each assignment of error, the standard of review and the argument—including principles of law and the authorities—shall be stated in one place and not scattered through the brief. At the option of counsel, the argument may be preceded by a short summary.

(e) A short conclusion stating the precise relief sought.

[Amended effective January 1, 1993; February 1, 2008; July 1, 2010.]

Source: Rule 5A:20. Cf. Rule 5:42.

RULE 5:28. REQUIREMENTS FOR BRIEF OF APPELLEE

The brief of appellee shall comply with Rules 5:6 and 5:26, and must contain the following:

(a) A table of contents and table of authorities with cases alphabetically arranged. Citations of all authorities shall include the year thereof.

(b) A statement of the case if the appellee disagrees with the statement presented by the appellant. In an appeal of right to this Court from an order disciplining, suspending, or disbarring an attorney-at-law, the Virginia State Bar may include assignments of cross-error. In such cases, no cross-error not then assigned will be noticed by this Court.

(c) A statement of the facts necessary to correct or amplify the statement in the brief of appellant with appropriate references to the pages of the appendix. Any quotation from the record should be brief. The testimony of individual witnesses should not be summarized seriatim unless the facts are in dispute and such a summary is necessary to support the appellee's version of the facts.

(d) The standard of review, the argument, and the authorities relating to each assignment of error. With respect to each assignment of error, the standard of review and the argument—including principles of law and the authorities—shall be stated in one place and not scattered through the brief. At the option of counsel, the argument may be preceded by a short summary.

(e) With respect to the assignments of cross-error, if any:

(1) A statement of the assignment of cross-error, with a clear and exact reference to the pages of the appendix where the alleged cross-error has been preserved.

(2) The standard of review, the argument, and the authorities relating to each assignment of cross-error. With respect to each such assignment of cross-error, the standard of review and the argument—including principles of law and the authorities—shall be stated in one place and not scattered through the brief.

(3) A statement of the precise relief sought.

[Amended effective February 1, 2008; July 1, 2010.]

Source: Rule 5A:21. Cf. Rule 5:43.

RULE 5:29. REQUIREMENTS FOR REPLY BRIEF

The reply brief, if any, shall comply with the requirements of Rules 5:6 and 5:26 and shall contain only argument in reply to contentions made in the brief of appellee. No reply brief is necessary if the contentions have been adequately answered in the opening brief of appellant.

[Amended effective January 1, 1993; February 1, 2008; July 1, 2010.]

Source: Rule 5A:22. Cf. Rule 5:44.

RULE 5:30. BRIEFS AMICUS CURIAE

(a) Stage of Proceedings. Subject to the requirements outlined in this Rule, a brief amicus curiae may be filed during the petition, perfected appeal or rehearing stages of the appellate proceedings in this Court, and in proceedings invoking this Court's original jurisdiction.

(b) Who May File a Brief Amicus Curiae Without Leave of Court.

(1) The United States or the Commonwealth of Virginia; and

(2) Any other person whose filing is accompanied by the written consent of all counsel; and

(3) Any person requested by the Court to file a brief amicus curiae pursuant to paragraph (f) of this Rule.

(c) Who Needs Leave of Court to File a Brief Amicus Curiae. Any person or entity other than those described in paragraph (b) of this Rule.

(d) When a Brief Amicus Curiae Must Be Filed. A brief amicus curiae will be accepted only if filed on or before the date on which the brief of the party supported is required to be filed. A brief amicus curiae may be filed at the time of filing of the reply brief of the appellant only if an opening brief amicus curiae has been filed.

(e) What a Brief Amicus Curiae Must Contain. A brief amicus curiae shall comply with the rules applicable to the brief of the party supported.

(f) This Court's Authority to Request a Brief Amicus Curiae. Notwithstanding the provisions of this Rule, this Court may request that a brief amicus curiae be filed at any time.

[Amended effective July 1, 2010; July 1, 2015.]

Source: Rule 5A:23. Cf. Rule 5:45.

RULE 5:31. COVERS OF DOCUMENTS

(a) What Covers Must Be Used on Papers Filed With this Court. To facilitate identification, documents shall bear covers colored as follows:

Document	Color of Cover
Appendix	Red
Brief of the Appellant	White
Brief of the Appellee	Blue
Reply Brief of the Appellant	Green
Brief Amicus Curiae	Gray
Petition for Rehearing	Yellow

(b) Effect of Failure to Comply. No appeal shall be dismissed for failure to comply with the provisions of this Rule.

[Amended effective July 1, 2010.]

Source: Rules 5:34 and 5A:24.

RULE 5:32. APPENDIX

(a) Responsibility of the Appellant.

(1) *Contents of the Appendix.* The appellant must prepare and file an appendix. The appendix shall contain:

(i) the initial pleading (as finally amended), unless other versions are necessary to consider the assignments of error;

(ii) final judgments of all tribunals that have considered the case, including the judgment appealed from, and any opinion relating to such judgments;

(iii) testimony and other incidents of the case germane to the assignments of error;

(iv) exhibits necessary for an understanding of the case that can reasonably be reproduced;

(v) the granted assignments of error and cross-error;

(vi) other parts of the record to which the parties wish to direct this Court's attention; and

(vii) a table of contents as described in paragraph (d) below.

(2) *Assumptions and Excluded Material.* It will be assumed that the appendix contains everything germane to the granted assignments of error and, if any, assignments of cross-error. Memoranda of law in the trial court should not be included in the appendix unless they have independent relevance. Parts of the record may be relied on by this Court or the parties even though not included in the appendix.

(3) *Time to File; Number of Copies.*

(i) Generally. The appellant must file 3 printed copies and an electronic copy of the appendix with the appellant's brief, and must serve an electronic copy on counsel for each party separately represented. This Court may by order require the filing or service of a different number. The appendix shall be filed in the manner prescribed by the Guidelines and User's Manual, using the Virginia Appellate Courts eBriefs System (VACES). The Guidelines are located on the Court's website at www.courts.state.va.us/online/vaces/resources/guidelines.pdf.

(b) Responsibility of All Parties.

(1) *Determining the Contents of the Appendix.* The parties are encouraged to agree on the contents of the appendix. Within 15 days after the date of the certificate of the clerk of this Court issued pursuant to Rule 5:23, counsel for appellant shall file in the office of the clerk of this Court a written statement signed by all counsel setting forth an agreed designation of the parts of the record on appeal to be included in the appendix. In the absence of an agreement, the appellant must, within 15 days after the date of the certificate of appeal issued by the clerk of this Court pursuant to Rule 5:23, file with the clerk of this Court and serve on the appellee a designation of the parts of the record the appellant intends to include in the appendix. The appellee may, within 15 days after receiving the designation, file with the clerk of this Court and serve on the appellant a designation of additional parts of the record the appellee deems germane. The appellant must include the parts designated by the appellee in the appendix, together with any additional parts the appellant considers germane. The parties must not engage in an unnecessary designation of parts of the record, because the entire record is available to the Court.

(2) *Sealed Materials in the Appendix.* Appendices filed with this Court are a matter of public record. If counsel concludes it is necessary to include sealed material in the appendix, then, in order to maintain the confidentiality of the materials, counsel must designate the sealed material for inclusion in a supplemental appendix to be filed separately from the regular appendix, and must file a specific motion asking this Court to seal the supplemental appendix within the time stated for the designation of the appendix in paragraph (b)(1) of this Rule. A sealed volume of the appendix must be filed in the manner prescribed by the Guidelines and User's Manual. The Guidelines are located on the Court's website at www.courts.state.va.us/online/vaces/resources/guidelines.pdf.

(3) *Costs of Appendix.* Unless the parties agree otherwise, the appellant must initially pay the cost of the appendix, but if the appellant in good faith considers that parts of the record designated by the appellee for inclusion are unnecessary for the determination of the assignments of error, the appellant initially preparing the appendix may so advise the clerk of this Court and the appellee, and the appellee who designated the challenged material shall advance the cost of including such parts. The cost of producing the appendix shall be taxed as costs in the case, but if any party shall cause unnecessary material to be included in the appendix this Court sua sponte or upon motion may impose the cost of including such parts upon that party.

(c) Appeal on the Original Record Without an Appendix. This Court may, sua sponte or on motion, enter an order dispensing with the appendix and permitting an appeal to proceed on the original record with any copies of the record, or relevant parts, that the Court may order the parties to file. A motion may be made under this rule within 10 days of the issuance of a writ. The making of a motion under this paragraph does not excuse the filing of the proposed contents of an appendix under paragraph (b)(1).

(d) Table of Contents and Form of Presentation. The appendix must begin with a table of contents identifying the page at which each part begins. When the testimony of witnesses is included, the name of each witness who is testifying must be in the table of contents with a page number at which each portion of the testimony begins (direct, cross, redirect, etc.). Parts of the record should be in the appendix in chronological order. Omissions in the text of papers or of the transcript must be indicated by asterisks. The index for exhibits should include a description of the exhibit sufficient to inform this Court of its nature rather than merely an exhibit number.

(e) Effect of Non–Compliance With This Rule. An appeal will not be dismissed for failure to file an appendix in compliance with this Rule. If an appendix is not filed within the time prescribed, or on its face fails to comply with this Rule, this Court may direct the filing of a proper appendix within a specific time and may require a non-complying attorney or unrepresented party to advance all or part of the cost of printing the appendix. This Court may dismiss an appeal for non-compliance with an order entered under this paragraph.

[Amended effective July 1, 1988; November 15, 2002; July 1, 2010; May 2, 2011; July 1, 2015.]

Source: Rule 5A:25. Cf. Rules 5:35 through 5:40.

Comment: As to the time for designation of additional portions of the record on an appeal from the State Corporation Commission, see Rule 5:21(j).

RULE 5:33. ORAL ARGUMENT

(a) Notice. Whenever an appeal lies as a matter of right or a petition for appeal has been granted, the clerk of this Court, except in extraordinary circumstances, shall give at least 15 days notice to counsel of the date, approximate time, and location for oral argument.

(b) Length. Except as otherwise directed by this Court, argument for a party shall not exceed 15 minutes in length. Such time may be apportioned among counsel for the same side at their discretion.

(c) Appearance Pro Hac Vice. Any lawyer not licensed in Virginia who seeks to appear pro hac vice to present oral argument to the Court must comply with the requirements of Rule 1A:4.

(d) Amicus Curiae. No oral argument by amicus curiae is permitted except by leave of this Court. Leave may be granted upon the joint written request of amicus curiae and the party whose position amicus curiae supports. The request shall specify the amount of its allotted time the supported party is willing to yield to amicus curiae.

(e) **Waiver.** During oral argument, it shall not be necessary for any party to expressly reserve any argument made on brief, and the failure to raise any such argument shall not constitute a waiver. Any party may, without waiving the arguments made on brief, waive oral argument.

[Amended effective July 1, 2010.]

Source: Rules 5:50 and 5A:26.

H. Decision, Costs, and Mandate

RULE 5:34. NOTICE OF DECISION

Promptly after this Court has decided a case, the clerk of this Court shall send a copy of the decision to all counsel of record and to the court or commission from which the appeal proceeded.

[Amended effective July 1, 2010.]

Source: Rule 5:41.

RULE 5:35. ATTORNEY'S FEES, COSTS, AND NOTARIZED BILL OF COSTS

(a) To Whom Allowed. Except as otherwise provided by law, if an appeal is dismissed, costs shall be taxed against the appellant unless otherwise agreed by the parties or ordered by this Court; if a judgment is affirmed, costs shall be taxed against the appellant unless otherwise ordered; if a judgment is reversed, costs shall be taxed against the appellee unless otherwise ordered; if a judgment is affirmed in part or reversed in part, or is vacated, costs shall be allowed as ordered by this Court.

(b) Attorney's Fees. Upon refusal or dismissal of a petition for appeal and any petition for rehearing, any appellee who has received attorney's fees and costs in the circuit court may make application in the circuit court for additional fees and costs incurred on appeal pursuant to Rule 1:1A.

(c) Taxable Costs. Costs, including the filing fee and costs incurred in the printing or producing of necessary copies of briefs, appendices, and petitions for rehearing, shall be taxable in this Court. Costs incurred in the preparation of transcripts may be taxable in this Court. See, Code § 17.1–128.

(d) Notarized Bill of Costs. Counsel for a party who desires costs to be taxed shall itemize them in a notarized bill of costs, which shall be filed with the clerk of this Court within 14 days after the date of the decision in the case. Objections to the bill of costs must be filed with the clerk of this Court within 10 days after the date of filing the bill of costs.

(e) Award. The clerk of this Court shall prepare and certify an itemized statement of costs taxed in this Court for insertion in the mandate, but the issuance of the mandate shall not be delayed for taxation of costs. If the mandate has been issued before final determination of costs, the statement, or any amendment thereof, shall be added to the mandate on request by the clerk of this Court to the clerk of the tribunal in which the case originated.

[Amended effective July 1, 1987; July 1, 1988; March 1, 1998; February 1, 2007; July 1, 2010; January 1, 2013.]

Source: Rule 5A:28. Cf. Rules 5:51 and 5:52.

RULE 5:36. MANDATE

(a) Time. When there can be no further proceedings in this Court, the clerk of this Court shall forward its mandate promptly to the clerk of the circuit court or commission in which the case originated and to the clerk of the Court of Appeals if the case has been heard by that court.

(b) Opinions. If the judgment or order is supported by an opinion, a certified copy of the opinion shall accompany the mandate.

[Amended effective July 1, 2010.]

Source: Rule 5A:29.

RULE 5:37. PETITION FOR REHEARING AFTER CONSIDERATION BY THE FULL COURT

(a) Scope. This Rule does not apply to the refusal or dismissal of a petition for appeal, or the refusal or dismissal of an original jurisdiction petition. See Rules 5:20 and 5:20A.

(b) Notice of Intent. A party intending to apply for a rehearing shall file written notice with the clerk of this Court within 10 days after the date of the order or opinion of this Court deciding the case. If such notice is given, the clerk of this Court shall withhold certification of the mandate until time for filing the petition for rehearing has expired and, if the petition is filed, until it is disposed of.

(c) Requirements for Pro Se Prisoners or by Leave of Court. Unless the rehearing is abandoned, 20 copies of a petition for rehearing not to exceed the longer of 10 pages or 1,750 words in length shall be thereafter filed in the office of the clerk of this Court and 3 copies delivered or mailed to opposing counsel within 30 days after the date of the order of this Court deciding the case.

(d) Requirements for All Others.

(1) Except for petitions filed by pro se prisoners, or with leave of this Court, the petition for rehearing shall be filed as an Adobe Acrobat Portable Document Format (PDF) document attached to an e-mail addressed to scvpfr@courts.state.va.us and will be timely filed if received by the clerk's office on or before 11:59 p.m. within 30 days after the date of the order or

opinion of this Court deciding the case. The petition must be formatted to print on a page 8 1/2 × 11 inches, must be in 14–point font or larger, must be double-spaced, and must not exceed the longer of 10 pages or 1,750 words. The petition must include a certificate of service to opposing counsel and the certificate shall specify the manner of service and the date of service. The petition must also include a certificate of compliance with the word count limit. The petition will be considered filed on the date and time that it is received by scvpfr@courts.state.va.us. If the petition does not meet the requirements of this rule as to format, the clerk shall so notify counsel and provide a specific amount of time for a corrected copy of the petition to be filed. A person who files a document electronically shall have the same responsibility as a person filing a document in paper form for ensuring that the document is properly filed, complete, and readable. However, if technical problems at this Court result in a failure to timely receive the electronically filed petition for rehearing, counsel shall provide to the clerk of this Court on the next business day all documentation which exists demonstrating the attempt to email the petition, any delivery failure notice received in response to the attempt, and a copy of the petition for rehearing.

(2) The e-mail message to which the petition is attached shall recite in the subject line the style of the case and the Supreme Court record number. The e-mail message shall contain a paragraph stating that a petition for rehearing is being filed, the style of the case, the Supreme Court record number, the name and Virginia State Bar number of counsel filing the petition, as well as the law firm name, mailing address, telephone number, facsimile number (if any), and e-mail address (if any) of counsel. The message shall also state whether a copy of the petition has been served by e-mail or another means on opposing counsel and the date of such service. If the petition has been served on opposing counsel by e-mail, the e-mail address for opposing counsel shall also be included. Upon receipt of the petition for rehearing in the e-mail box of the clerk's office, an acknowledgment will automatically be sent to counsel seeking the rehearing.

(e) Grounds for Granting. No petition for rehearing shall be granted unless one of the Justices who decided the case adversely to the applicant determines that there is good cause for such rehearing. The proceedings upon such rehearing shall be in accordance with Code § 8.01–675.2. No oral argument will be permitted on applications for rehearing.

(f) When a Rehearing Is Granted. When a rehearing is granted, the Court will determine whether any additional briefing or argument is necessary. Thereafter, the Court may direct the respondent to electronically file a brief, in compliance with paragraph (d) of this Rule, that shall not exceed the longer of 15 pages in length or 2,625 words. After review of the petition for rehearing and the respondent's brief, if any is filed, the Court may set oral argument on the petition for rehearing at the next available session of the Court. Otherwise, the Court will issue a ruling on the rehearing without further briefing or oral argument.

[Amended effective July 1, 2010; May 2, 2011; June 13, 2012.]

Source: Rule 5A:30.

I. Settlement or Withdrawal

RULE 5:38. SETTLEMENT OR WITHDRAWAL OF PENDING APPEAL

When a case has been settled or the appeal withdrawn at any time after the notice of appeal has been filed, it shall be the duty of counsel to notify the clerk of this Court by filing a written notice that the case has been settled or the appeal withdrawn. If counsel certifies that the terms of the settlement or withdrawal require further proceedings in the trial court, a single Justice may approve entry of an order of remand.

[Amended effective July 1, 2010.]

Source: Rule 5A:31. Cf. Rule 5:54.

J. Supreme Court of the United States

RULE 5:39. DELAY IN ISSUING MANDATE UPON APPEAL OR PETITION TO SUPREME COURT OF THE UNITED STATES

If a party intends to file an appeal with the Supreme Court of the United States or seek a writ of certiorari from that court, this Court may, upon motion filed within 15 days after the date of the order of this Court deciding the case, and upon compliance with such conditions as this Court may impose, defer the issuance of its mandate until proceedings in the Supreme Court of the United States have been terminated. Thereupon, the mandate shall issue forthwith.

[Amended effective July 1, 1988; December 1, 1990; January 1, 2005; January 1, 2006; July 1, 2010.]

Source: Rule 5:53.

K. Certification of Questions of Law

RULE 5:40. CERTIFICATION PROCEDURES

(a) Power to Answer. This Court may in its discretion answer questions of law certified to it by the Supreme Court of the United States, a United States court of appeals for any circuit, a United States district court, or the highest appellate court of any state, territory, or the District of Columbia. Such answer may be furnished, when requested by the certifying court, if a question of Virginia law is determinative in any proceeding pending before the certifying court and it appears there is no controlling precedent on point in the decisions of this Court or the Court of Appeals of Virginia.

(b) Method of Invoking. This Rule may be invoked only by an order of one of the courts referred to in paragraph (a) of this Rule. No party litigant in the foregoing courts may file a petition or motion for certification in this Court.

(c) Contents of Certification Order. A certification order shall set forth:

(1) the nature of the controversy in which the question arises;

(2) the question of law to be answered;

(3) a statement of all facts relevant to the question certified;

(4) the names of each of the parties involved;

(5) the name, Virginia State Bar number, mailing address, telephone number (including any applicable extension), facsimile number (if any), and e-mail address (if any) of counsel for each of the parties involved;

(6) a brief statement explaining how the certified question of law is determinative of the proceeding in the certifying court; and

(7) a brief statement setting forth relevant decisions, if any, of this Court and the Court of Appeals of Virginia and the reasons why such decisions are not controlling.

(d) Preparation of Certification Order. The certification order shall be prepared by the certifying court, signed by the presiding justice or judge, and forwarded to this Court by the clerk of the certifying court under its official seal. This Court may require the original or copies of all or of any portion of the record before the certifying court to be filed, if, in the opinion of this Court, the record or portion thereof may be necessary in answering the certified question. This Court may in its discretion restate any question of law certified or may request from the certifying court additional clarification with respect to any question certified or with respect to any facts.

(e) Notification of Acceptance or Rejection. This Court, in its discretion, may decide whether to answer any certified question of law. This Court will notify the certifying court and counsel for the parties of its decision to accept or to reject any certified question of law. A notice accepting a question will include a briefing schedule and, if this Court permits oral argument, a tentative date and the length of time allowed for such argument.

(f) Revocation of Acceptance. This Court, in its discretion, may revoke its decision to answer a certified question of law at any time. This Court will notify the certifying court and counsel for the parties of any such action.

(g) Costs of Certification. Fees and costs shall be the same as in civil appeals docketed in this Court and shall be paid as ordered by the certifying court in its order of certification.

(h) Briefs. The form, length, and time for submission of briefs shall comply with Rules 5:26 through 5:32 mutatis mutandis.

(i) Opinion. A written opinion or order of this Court stating the law governing each question certified will be rendered as soon as practicable after the submission of briefs and after any oral argument. The opinion or order will be sent by the clerk under the seal of this Court to the certifying court and to counsel for the parties and shall, if this Court so directs, be published in the Virginia Reports.

[Amended effective July 1, 2010; February 24, 2012.]

Source: Rule 5:55.

L. Appeals Relating to Quarantine or Isolation Orders

RULE 5:41. APPEAL OF ORDERS RELATING TO QUARANTINE OR ISOLATION OF PERSONS

A. Quarantine Related Code Provisions. In proceedings involving circuit court orders of quarantine of a person or persons pursuant to Article 3.02 of Chapter 2 of Title 32.1 of the Code of Virginia, the provisions of Code § 32.1–48.010 shall apply with respect to appealability of such orders, the effect of an appeal upon any order of quarantine, availability of expedited review, stay of quarantine orders, and representation by counsel.

B. Isolation Order Code Provisions. In proceedings involving circuit court orders of isolation of a person or persons pursuant to Article 3.02 of Chapter 2 of Title 32.1 of the Code of Virginia, the provisions of Code § 32.1–48.013 shall apply with respect to appealability of such orders, the effect of an appeal upon any order of isolation, availability of expedited review, stay of isolation orders, and representation by counsel.

C. Transmission of Record. In all appeals under this rule, the clerk of the court from which an appeal is taken shall transmit the record to the Clerk of the Supreme Court immediately upon the filing of the notice of appeal.

D. Expedited Procedures. Unless otherwise ordered by the Supreme Court, after the filing of the petition for appeal under this Rule, 48 hours shall be allowed for the filing of the brief in opposition. However, the Supreme Court may employ the expedited review provision in Rule 5:18(c). The Supreme Court shall act upon the petition within 72 hours of its filing. Should the Supreme Court grant a writ, the Supreme Court may, in its discretion, permit oral argument within 48 hours of granting the writ. The Supreme Court will issue an order within 24 hours of the argument or of its review of the case without oral argument. The Supreme Court has the authority to alter these time frames in any case.

E. Oral Argument. The Court shall hold any oral argument in appeals under this rule in a manner so as to protect the health and safety of individuals subject to any such order or quarantine or isolation, court personnel, counsel, and the general public. To this end, the Court may take measures including, but not limited to, ordering any oral argument to be held by telephone or video conference or ordering those present to take appropriate precautions, including wearing personal protective equipment. If necessary, the Court may dispense with oral argument.

[Amended effective July 1, 2010; May 2, 2011.]

Source: Rule 5:56.

APPENDIX OF FORMS

FORM 1. BOND FOR COSTS ALONE—APPEAL OF RIGHT FROM CIRCUIT COURT TO COURT OF APPEALS (INCLUDING FURTHER APPEAL TO THE SUPREME COURT)

KNOW ALL MEN BY THESE PRESENTS, That we,

____ principal, and

____ surety, are held

and firmly bound unto ________________________________
appellee(s)

in the sum of ____________________________________
to the payment of which we bind ourselves, our heirs, successors, personal representatives and assigns, jointly and severally, firmly by these presents.

The condition of this obligation is such that:

Whereas judgment was rendered by the Circuit Court of ____________

on the __________ day of ________________________,

in the case of ______________________________________

____;

And whereas it is the intention of ________________________

________ to appeal said judgment to the Court of Appeals of Virginia;

Now, therefore, if ________________________________
appellant(s)
shall pay all damages, costs, and fees which may be awarded against (him) (her) (them) (it) in the Court of Appeals and Supreme Court if it takes cognizance of the claim, then this obligation shall be void, otherwise to remain in full force and virtue.

FORM 2. BOND FOR COSTS AND SUSPENSION—APPEAL FROM CIRCUIT COURT TO APPELLATE COURT

KNOW ALL MEN BY THESE PRESENTS, That we,

______________________________ principal, and

______________________________ surety, are held

and firmly bound unto ______________________________
appellee(s)

in the sum of ______________________________

to the payment of which we bind ourselves, our heirs, successors, personal representatives and assigns, jointly and severally, firmly by these presents.

The condition of this obligation is such that:

Whereas judgment was rendered by the Circuit Court of ______________

on the ______________ day of ______________________________,

in the case of ______________________________

______________________________;

And whereas it is the intention of ______________________________

to appeal said judgment to the (Supreme Court) (Court of Appeals) of Virginia,

and suspension of execution of the judgment is sought;

Now, therefore, if ______________________________
appellant(s)
shall perform and satisfy and said judgment or the part thereof proceedings on which are stayed, in case such judgment or such part be affirmed in whole or in part, or the appeal be dismissed, refused or not timely prosecuted, and shall pay all damages, costs, and fees which may be awarded against (him) (her) (them) (it) in the (Supreme Court) (Court of Appeals and Supreme Court if it takes cognizance of the claim) and all actual damages incurred in consequence of the suspension, then this obligation shall be void, otherwise to remain in full force and virtue.

FORM 3. BOND FOR COSTS ALONE REQUIRED BY APPELLATE COURT ON APPEAL FROM CIRCUIT COURT

KNOW ALL MEN BY THESE PRESENTS, That we,

________________________________ principal, and

________________________________ surety, are held

and firmly bound unto ____________________________
appellee(s)

in the sum of ____________________________

to the payment of which we bind ourselves, our heirs, successors, personal representatives and assigns, jointly and severally, firmly by these presents.

The condition of this obligation is such that:

Whereas the (Supreme Court of Virginia) (Court of Appeals of Virginia) on the

__________ day of ________________, _____, awarded an

appeal from a judgment rendered against ____________________ by
appellant(s)

the Circuit Court of ____________________, on the __________

day of ________________, _____, upon ________________

________________________ or some one for (him) (her) (them) (it),
appellant(s)

filing an appeal bond with sufficient security in the clerk's office of the

Circuit Court of, ____________________________

in the penalty of ________________________ within

fifteen (15) days of the date of the certificate of appeal, with condition as the law directs;

Now, therefore, if ____________________________
appellant(s)
shall pay all damages, costs, and fees which may be awarded against (him) (her) (them) (it) in the (Supreme Court) (Court of Appeals and Supreme Court if it takes cognizance of the claim), then this obligation shall be void, otherwise to remain in full force and virtue.

FORM 4. BOND FOR SUSPENSION ALONE REQUIRED BY APPELLATE COURT ON APPEAL FROM CIRCUIT COURT

KNOW ALL MEN BY THESE PRESENTS, That we,

____ principal, and

____ surety, are held

and firmly bound unto ____
appellee(s)

in the sum of ____

to the payment of which we bind ourselves, our heirs, successors, personal representatives and assigns, jointly and severally, firmly by these presents.

The condition of this obligation is such that:

Whereas the (Supreme Court of Virginia) (Court of Appeals of Virginia) on the ____________ day of ____________, ______, suspended execution of a judgment rendered against ______________________________ by the Circuit
appellant(s)

Court of __________, on the ________ day of ________, ______, upon ____________
____ or some one for
appellant(s)

for (him) (her) (them) (it), filing an appeal bond with sufficient security in the clerk's office of the Circuit Court of ______________, in the penalty of __________ within fifteen (15) days of the date of the certificate of appeal, with condition as the law directs;

Now, therefore, if ____
appellant(s)

shall perform and satisfy said judgment or the part thereof proceedings on which are stayed, in case such judgment or such part be affirmed in whole or in part, and shall pay all actual damages incurred in consequence of the suspension, then this obligation shall be void, otherwise to remain in full force and virtue.

FORM 5. BOND FOR COSTS AND SUSPENSION REQUIRED BY APPELLATE COURT ON APPEAL FROM CIRCUIT COURT

KNOW ALL MEN BY THESE PRESENTS, That we,

______________________________ principal, and

______________________________ surety, are held

and firmly bound unto ______________________________
appellee(s)

in the sum of ______________________________

to the payment of which we bind ourselves, our heirs, successors, personal representatives and assigns, jointly and severally, firmly by these presents.

The condition of this obligation is such that:

Whereas the (Supreme Court of Virginia) (Court of Appeals of Virginia) on the __________ day of __________, _____, awarded an appeal and (suspension of judgment) (supersedeas) from a judgment rendered against

______________________________ by the Circuit
appellant(s)

Court of __________, on the __________ day of __________, _____, upon __________

______________________________ or some one for
appellant(s)

(him)(her)(them)(it) filing an appeal bond with sufficient security in the clerk's office of the Circuit Court of __________, in the penalty of __________ within fifteen (15) days of the date of the certificate of appeal, with condition as the law directs;

Now, therefore, if ______________________________
appellant(s)

shall perform and satisfy said judgment or the part thereof proceedings on which are stayed, in case such judgment or such part be affirmed in whole or in part, and shall pay all damages, costs, and fees which may be awarded against (him) (her) (them) (it) in the (Supreme Court) (Court of Appeals and Supreme Court if it takes cognizance of the claim) and all actual damages incurred in consequence of the suspension, then this obligation shall be void, otherwise to remain in full force and virtue.

FORM 6. ADDITIONAL BOND REQUIRED BY APPELLATE COURT ON APPEAL FROM CIRCUIT COURT

KNOW ALL MEN BY THESE PRESENTS, That we,

______________________________ principal, and

______________________________ surety, are held

and firmly bound unto ______________________________
appellee(s)

in the sum of ______________________________

to the payment of which we bind ourselves, our heirs, successors, personal

representatives and assigns, jointly and severally, firmly by these presents.

The condition of this obligation is such that:

Whereas the (Supreme Court of Virginia) (Court of Appeals of Virginia) on the

______ day of ______________, ______, required additional bond on

this appeal from a judgment rendered against ______________ by the
appellant(s)

Circuit Court of ______, on the ______ day of ______________, ______, such

additional bond to be filed in the clerk's office of the Circuit Court of

______________________________ in the penalty of __________

______________________, and with the following additional

requirements: ______________________________

within fifteen (15) days of the date of the order requiring additional bond, with condition as the law directs;

Now, therefore, if ______________________________
appellant(s)

shall perform and satisfy said judgment or the part thereof proceedings on which are stayed, in case such judgment or such part be affirmed in whole or in part, and shall pay all actual damages incurred in consequence of the suspension, then this obligation shall be void, otherwise to remain in full force and virtue.

A Copy,

Teste:

Clerk

FORM 7. BOND FOR COSTS ALONE—APPEAL OF RIGHT FROM VIRGINIA WORKERS' COMPENSATION COMMISSION TO COURT OF APPEALS (INCLUDING FURTHER APPEAL TO THE SUPREME COURT)

KNOW ALL MEN BY THESE PRESENTS, That we,

______________________________ principal, and

______________________________ surety, are held

and firmly bound unto ______________________________
appellee(s)

in the sum of ______________________________

to the payment of which we bind ourselves, our heirs, successors, personal representatives and assigns, jointly and severally, firmly by these presents.

The condition of this obligation is such that:

Whereas an award was entered by the Virginia Workers' Compensation Commission on the ________ day of ______________, ______, in the case of ______________________________;

And whereas it is the intention of ______________________________ ________ to appeal said award to the Court of Appeals of Virginia;

Now, therefore, if ______________________________
appellant(s)
shall pay all damages, costs, and fees which may be awarded against (him) (her) (them) (it) in the Court of Appeals and Supreme Court if it takes cognizance of the claim, then this obligation shall be void, otherwise to remain in full force and virtue.

[Amended effective February 1, 1992.]

FORM 8. BOND FOR COSTS ALONE—REQUIRED BY SUPREME COURT ON APPEAL OF RIGHT FROM STATE CORPORATION COMMISSION

KNOW ALL MEN BY THESE PRESENTS, That we,

______________________________ principal, and

______________________________ surety, are held

and firmly bound unto ______________________________
appellee(s)

in the sum of ______________________________

to the payment of which we bind ourselves, our heirs, successors, personal representatives and assigns, jointly and severally, firmly by these presents.

The condition of this obligation is such that:

Whereas the Supreme Court of Virginia on the ____________ day of ____________, ______, awarded an appeal from a final order entered in Case No. ____________ under the style of ____________ by the State Corporation Commission of Virginia, on the ____________ day of ______________________________, on the condition that

____
appellant(s)

or someone for (him) (her) (them) (it), file an appeal bond with sufficient security in the clerk's office of the State Corporation Commission, in the penalty of ______________________________

______________________________ within fifteen (15) days of the date of the certificate of appeal, with condition as the law directs;

Now, therefore, if ______________________________
appellant(s)
shall pay all damages, costs, and fees which may be awarded against (him) (her) (them) (it) in the Supreme Court, then this obligation shall be void, otherwise to remain in full force and virtue.

FORM 9. BOND FOR COSTS AND SUSPENSION—REQUIRED BY SUPREME COURT ON APPEAL OF RIGHT FROM STATE CORPORATION COMMISSION

KNOW ALL MEN BY THESE PRESENTS, That we,

____ principal, and

____ surety, are held

and firmly bound unto ____________________________________
appellee(s)

in the sum of ____

to the payment of which we bind ourselves, our heirs, successors, personal representatives and assigns, jointly and severally, firmly by these presents.

The condition of this obligation is such that:

Whereas the Supreme Court of Virginia on the ______________ day of ______________, _____, awarded an appeal and suspension from a final order entered in Case No. ____________________ under the style of

____

by the State Corporation Commission of Virginia, on the __________________ day of ________________________________, on the condition that

__________________________ or some one for (him) (her) (them) (it), file an
appellant(s)

appeal bond with sufficient security in the clerk's office of the State Corporation Commission, in the penalty of ________________________________

within fifteen (15) days of the date of the certificate of appeal, with condition as the law directs;

Now, therefore, if ____________________________________
appellant(s)

shall perform and satisfy said order or the part thereof proceedings on which are stayed, in case such order or such part be affirmed in whole or in part, and shall pay all damages, costs, and fees which may be awarded against (him) (her) (them) (it) in the Supreme Court and all actual damages incurred in consequence of the suspension, then this obligation shall be void, otherwise to remain in full force and virtue.

FORM 10. FORM FOR EXECUTION AND ACKNOWLEDGMENT OF ALL BONDS

In witness whereof, the said ______________________________

______________________, principal, and ______________________

______________________________ surety, have hereunto set their

hands and seals, this ______ day of ______________, ______.

______________________________ (SEAL)

______________________________ (SEAL)

State of Virginia
City/County of ______________

The foregoing instrument was acknowledged before me this ______

day of ______________, ______, by ______________________

______________________________.

____
Notary Public

My commission expires: ______________________________

FORM 11. IRREVOCABLE LETTERS OF CREDIT

(Name and Address of Bank)

_______________, 20____

U.S. $____________

On all communications please refer to (No. of Letter of Credit)

(Name and address of appellee(s))

Dear______________:

We hereby establish our Irrevocable Letter of Credit No. ___________ in your favor, for the account of (name and address of appellant(s)), and hereby undertake to honor your draft at sight on us, not exceeding in the aggregate U.S. $ __(amount in words)__. A draft drawn under this letter of credit must be marked "Drawn under __(Name of Bank)__ Letter of Credit No. ______________ dated ______________, 20____." Funds under this letter of credit will be available to you in a single drawing by presentation of your sight draft drawn on us, accompanied by:

(For Costs Alone)

1. The original of this letter of credit.

2. Your verified statement that ___________________________(has)(have) failed to
appellant(s)
pay all damages, costs and fees assessed against (him)(her)(them)(it) in the Court of Appeals of Virginia in the case of ______________________________

3. A certified copy of an order or itemized statement of costs from the Court of Appeals assessing such damages, costs and fees against ____________________.
appellant(s)

(For Suspension Alone)

1. The original of this letter of credit.

2. Your verified statement that ______________________(has)(have) failed to
appellant(s)
perform and satisfy the judgment rendered against (him)(her)(them)(it) on

______________________ by the Circuit Court of ______________________ in

the case of ______________________, and (has)(have) failed to pay all actual damages incurred in consequence of the suspension of judgment.

3. A copy of the trial court judgment order, attested by its clerk.

4. A copy of an order of the Court of Appeals of Virginia, attested by its clerk, affirming said judgment or refusing, dismissing or allowing withdrawal of the appeal of said judgment, or certification by the clerk of the Court of Appeals that the appeal of said judgment was not prosecuted timely.

5. A copy of an order, if any, of the Court of Appeals or trial court, attested by the clerk, assessing actual damages in consequence of the suspension of judgment.

(For Costs and Suspension)

1. The original of this letter of credit.

2. Your verified statement that ______________________(has)(have) failed to
appellant(s)
perform and satisfy the judgment rendered against (him)(her)(them)(it) on

______________________ by the Circuit Court of ______________________ in

the case of ______________________, and (has)(have) failed to pay all damages, costs and fees assessed against (him)(her)(them)(it) in the Court of Appeals of Virginia, and all actual damages incurred in consequence of the suspension of judgment.

3. A copy of the trial court judgment order, attested by its clerk.

4. A copy of an order of the Court of Appeals, attested by its clerk, affirming said judgment or refusing, dismissing or allowing withdrawal of the appeal of said judgment, or certification by the clerk of the Court of Appeals

that the appeal of said judgment was not prosecuted timely.

5. A copy of an order, if any, of the Court of Appeals, attested by its clerk, assessing damages, costs and fees against ______________________.
appellant(s)

6. A copy of an order, if any, of the Court of Appeals or trial court, attested by the clerk, assessing actual damages in consequence of the suspension of judgment.

This letter of credit is valid until ____ p.m. local time ________, 20____, and a draft drawn hereunder, if accompanied by documents as specified above, will be honored if presented to (Presentation Address of Bank) on or before that date. However, this letter of credit automatically will be renewed for successive one (1) year periods from the initial expiration date or any renewal period expiration date hereunder, unless at least sixty (60) days prior to any such expiration date (Name of Bank) notifies you that it has elected not to renew this letter of credit for such additional one (1) year period. The notice required hereunder will be deemed to have been given when received by you.

In the event that (Name of Bank) elects not to renew this letter of credit as required above, the full amount of this letter of credit shall be payable to the Clerk of the Circuit Court of ____________ upon presentation of your verified statement that:

1. A final order of the Court of Appeals of Virginia has not been entered in

the case of ______________________________ (or, where there has been suspension of judgment, a final order has not been entered by the Court of Appeals or trial court assessing actual damages in consequence of the suspension).

2. Thirty (30) days have elapsed since notice of non-renewal was given and appellant(s) (has)(have) not filed acceptable substitute security.

In the event of non-renewal, within fifteen (15) days after payment to the clerk under the previous paragraph, the appellant(s) or someone for (him)(her)(them)(it) shall file with said clerk an appeal bond in substantial conformance with the appropriate form in the Appendix to Part Five A of the Rules of the Supreme Court of Virginia. The bond shall be in the penalty of the amount paid to said clerk under this letter of credit, and said funds shall be in lieu of surety.

Except as otherwise expressly stated herein, this letter of credit is subject to the Uniform Customs and Practice for Documentary Credits as most recently published by the International Chamber of Commerce.

Very truly yours,

______________________________ Bank

By ______________________________
Authorized Signature

[Adopted effective July 1, 1991.]

FORM 12. PETITION FOR A WRIT OF ACTUAL INNOCENCE

PETITION FOR A WRIT OF ACTUAL INNOCENCE

TO THE SUPREME COURT OF VIRGINIA

In re: ______________________________ Record No. ______________________________
(FULL NAME OF PETITIONER) (TO BE SUPPLIED BY THE CLERK OF THE SUPREME COURT)

______________________________ Circuit Court
(PRISONER NO., IF APPLICABLE) Case No.(s) ______________________________

______________________________ ______________________________
(PETITIONER'S ADDRESS)

______________________________ ______________________________

____

Pursuant to the provisions of Chapter 19.2 of Title 19.2 of the Code of Virginia, I,

____
NAME OF PETITIONER

hereby petition this Court for a writ of actual innocence. In support of this petition, I state under oath that the following information is true:

1. On ______________________________, I was convicted or adjudicated delinquent in the
DATE

______________________________ Circuit Court of the following offense(s):
NAME OF COURT

Description of Offense	Virginia Code	Class of Felony	Plea

[ ] ATTACHED ADDITIONAL SHEET(S)

2. I am innocent of the offense(s) for which I was convicted or adjudicated delinquent.

3. My claim of innocence is based upon the following human biological evidence and scientific testing:

____

____

[ ] ATTACHED ADDITIONAL SHEET(S)

4. Check one:

[ ] This evidence was not known or available to either me or my attorney at the time the conviction or adjudication of delinquency became final in the circuit court.

[ ] This evidence was known at the time the conviction or adjudication of delinquency became final in the circuit court, but was not tested because

____

[ ] ATTACHED ADDITIONAL SHEET(S)

5. This evidence was tested pursuant to the provisions of Virginia Code § 19.2-327.1 and the results were obtained by me or my attorney on ______________________.
DATE

This petition is filed within sixty days of obtaining those results and those test results are filed with this petition. Attached is a copy of the notice of the test results from the Department of Forensic Science.

6. The scientific evidence described in paragraph number 4 above will prove that no rational trier of fact would have found me to be guilty or delinquent beyond a reasonable doubt of the charge described above because

____

____

[ ] ATTACHED ADDITIONAL SHEET(S)

7. Check box if applicable and provide any additional information.

[ ] My conviction or adjudication of delinquency became final after June 30, 1996, and the scientific evidence described in paragraph number 4 above was not available for testing under Virginia Code § 9.1-1104 because:

____

____

[ ] ATTACHED ADDITIONAL SHEET(S)

8. This petition contains all relevant allegations of fact known to me at this time and all previous records, applications, petitions, appeals, and dispositions relating to this matter are attached. In support of this petition, the following documents are attached:

....

[ ] ATTACHED ADDITIONAL SHEET(S)

9. I understand that this petition must contain all relevant allegations of fact that are known to me at this time. I understand that it must include all previous records, applications, petitions, appeals, and their dispositions related to this conviction, as well as a copy of any test results of the scientific evidence described above. I understand that if this petition is not complete, this Court may dismiss the petition or return the petition to me pending the completion of such form. I understand that I am responsible for all statements contained in this petition. I understand that any knowingly or willfully made false statement shall be a ground for prosecution and conviction of perjury as provided in Virginia Code § 18.2-434. I understand that this Court shall not accept this petition unless it is accompanied by a duly executed return of service verifying that a copy of this petition and all attachments have been served on the attorney for the Commonwealth of the jurisdiction where the conviction occurred and on the Attorney General of Virginia.

10. Check box if claiming in forma pauperis status and seeking to file this petition without payment of fees.

[ ] I claim in forma pauperis status and I request that this Court accept this petition without the payment of filing fees. I affirm under oath that I am eligible for in forma pauperis status and I have attached the completed affidavit to this effect.

Based on the above, I petition this Court pursuant to the provisions of Chapter 19.2 of Title 19.2 of the Code of Virginia for a writ of actual innocence.

.... ____________________________________

DATE SIGNATURE OF PETITIONER

FOR NOTARY PUBLIC'S USE ONLY:

State of .... [ ] City [ ] County of ....

Acknowledged, subscribed and sworn to before me this .... day of ...., 20 ....

.... ____________________________________

NOTARY REGISTRATION NUMBER NOTARY PUBLIC

(My commission expires: ....)

AFFIDAVIT IN FORMA PAUPERIS

The petitioner, ______________________________, being duly sworn, says,

1. I am unable to pay for counsel to prosecute this action;

2. My assets amount to a total of $ ______________________

______________________ DATE

______________________ SIGNATURE OF PETITIONER

FOR NOTARY PUBLIC'S USE ONLY:

State of .... [ ] City [ ] County of ....

Acknowledged, subscribed and sworn to before me this .... day of ...., 20 ....

.... NOTARY REGISTRATION NUMBER

______________________ NOTARY PUBLIC
(My commission expires: ....)

[Adopted effective May 2, 2011. Amended effective July 1, 2013.]

PART FIVE A. THE COURT OF APPEALS

Revised Effective October 1, 1984

Including Amendments Received Through October 15, 2015

A. General

RULE 5A:1. SCOPE, CITATION, APPLICABILITY AND GENERAL PROVISIONS

(a) Scope of Rules. Part Five A governs all proceedings in the Court of Appeals of Virginia.

(b) Citation. These Rules may be cited generally as the "Rules of the Court of Appeals of Virginia" and specifically as "Rule 5A: __."

(c) Definitions.

(1) "clerk of the trial court" means clerk of the trial court from which an appeal is taken to the Court of Appeals, and shall include a deputy clerk and the clerk of the Virginia Workers' Compensation Commission when the context requires;

(2) "clerk of the Court of Appeals" includes a deputy clerk;

(3) "counsel" has the definition given in Rule 1:5 for Counsel of Record and in this Part Five A includes a party not represented by counsel and any attorney appointed as a guardian ad litem;

(4) "counsel for appellant" means one of the attorneys representing each appellant represented by an attorney, and each appellant not represented by an attorney;

(5) "counsel for appellee" means one of the attorneys representing each appellee represented by an attorney, and each appellee not represented by an attorney and shall include a guardian ad litem, unless the guardian ad litem is the appellant;

(6) "opposing counsel" means, depending on the context, "counsel for the appellant" or "counsel for the appellee";

(7) "judge" means judge of the trial court, unless the context otherwise requires, or if he be not available, any judge authorized to act under Rule 5A:9;

(8) "judgment" includes an order or decree from which an appeal is taken;

(9) "File with the clerk" or "files with the clerk" or "filed with the clerk" means deliver to the clerk specified a paper, a copy of which has been mailed or delivered to opposing counsel, and appended to which is either acceptance of service or a certificate showing the date of mailing or delivery. "File in the office of the clerk" or "files in the office of the clerk" or "filed in the office of the clerk" means, on the other hand, deliver a paper to the clerk specified;

(10) "trial court" means the circuit court from which an appeal is taken to the Court of Appeals;

(11) the "date of entry" of any final judgment or other appealable order or decree shall be the date the judgment, order, or decree is signed by the judge.

(d) Service. Unless service or notice is otherwise specified in a given Rule, any paper or object filed with this Court must have included within it or appended to it a certificate of service or acceptance of service showing that a copy has been transmitted to all counsel and showing the date and manner of transmittal. If a word count limitation is required, the certificate must also state the number of words (headings, footnotes, and quotations count towards the word limitation; the cover page, table of contents, table of authorities, and certificate do not count towards the word count).

(e) Notice of Change of Address and Other Contact Information. If an attorney has a change in mailing address, telephone number, facsimile number, or e-mail address any time after the filing of the notice of appeal, the attorney must immediately notify the clerk of this Court and all other counsel of record in writing. The notice must reference the style and record number of all cases pending before this Court.

(f) Citing Unpublished Judicial Dispositions. The citation of judicial opinions, orders, judgments, or other written dispositions that are not officially reported, whether designated as "unpublished," "not for publication," "non precedential," or the like, is permitted as informative, but shall not be received as binding authority. If the cited disposition is not available in a publicly accessible electronic database, a copy of that disposition must be filed with the brief or other paper in which it is cited.

[Amended effective July 1, 1988; February 1, 1992; September 1, 2004; July 1, 2010.]

RULE 5A:1A. PENALTIES FOR NON-COMPLIANCE; SHOW CAUSE; DISMISSAL

(a) Penalties; Show Cause; Dismissal. This Court may dismiss an appeal or impose such other penalty as it deems appropriate for non-compliance with these Rules. Except as provided in Rule 5A:12(c)(1)(i) and (ii) regarding assignments of error, prior to the dismissal of an appeal for any defect in the filings related to formatting, curable failure to comply with other requirements, or the failure to meet non-mandatory filing deadlines, this Court may issue a show cause order to counsel or a party not represented by an attorney, prescribing a time in which to cure such defect or to otherwise show cause why the appeal should not be dismissed or other penalty imposed.

(b) Report to Virginia State Bar. If an attorney's failure to comply with these Rules results in the dismissal of an appeal, this Court may report the attorney to the Virginia State Bar in accordance with Rule 8.3 of the Virginia Rules of Professional Conduct.

[Added effective May 16, 2014.]

RULE 5A:2. MOTIONS AND RESPONSES; ORDERS

(a) Motions and Responses.

(1) *Motions.* All motions shall be in writing and filed with the clerk of this Court. All motions shall contain a statement by the movant that the other parties to the appeal have been informed of the intended filing of the motion. For all motions in cases when all parties are represented by counsel—except motions to dismiss petitions for a writ of habeas corpus—the statement by the movant shall also indicate whether the other parties consent to the granting of the motion, or intend to file responses in opposition.

(2) *Responses.* Opposing counsel may have ten days after such motion is filed to file with such clerk a response to such motion, but this Court may act before the ten days expire, if necessary.

(3) *Number of Copies.* An original and three copies of all motions or responses must be filed.

(4) *Oral Argument.* No motion shall be argued orally except by leave of this Court.

(b) Motion for Review of Pre–Trial Bail Orders in Criminal Cases. When a circuit court has granted or denied pre-trial bail or set a bond or terms of recognizance or revoked bail, either party may move this Court to review the order. With the motion for review, the party seeking review shall submit copies of: (1) the warrant(s) or indictment(s) in the case; (2) the order granting, denying, or setting bond; and (3) a transcript of the bond hearing or a stipulation between counsel stating the evidence introduced at the bond hearing and the ruling of the circuit court. An order setting or denying bail or setting terms of a bond or recognizance shall be reviewable for abuse of discretion.

(c) Motion for Review of Post–Trial Bail Pending Appeal Orders in Criminal Cases. When a notice of appeal has been filed in a criminal case, an appellant other than the Commonwealth may move this Court to review the trial court's order denying bail pending appeal or setting an excessive bail pending appeal. With the motion for review, the appellant shall submit copies of: (1) the sentencing order entered by the trial court; (2) a pre-sentence report when available; (3) the trial court's decision setting or denying bail; and (4) a transcript of the bail hearing or a stipulation between counsel stating the evidence introduced at the bail hearing and the reason the trial court gave for the bail decision. An order setting or denying bail pending appeal in a criminal case shall be reviewable for abuse of discretion. If this Court overrules a trial court decision denying bail pending appeal, this Court shall set the amount of the bail pending appeal or remand the matter to the trial court with directions to set bail pending appeal.

(d) Orders. Promptly after this Court has entered an order, the clerk of this Court shall send a copy of the order to all counsel.

RULE 5A:3. FILING DEADLINES; POST TRIAL PROCEEDINGS BELOW; TIMELY FILING BY MAIL; INMATE FILING; EXTENSION OF TIME

(a) Filing Deadlines and Extensions. The times prescribed for filing the notice of appeal (Rules 5A:6 and 5A:11), a petition for appeal (Rule 5A:12), and a petition for rehearing (Rule 5A:33) and a request for rehearing en banc (Rule 5A:34) are mandatory. Except for the petition for appeal which is addressed in Rule 5A:12(a) and Code § 17.1–408, a single extension not to exceed thirty days may be granted if at least three judges of the Court of Appeals concur in a finding that an extension for papers to be filed is warranted upon a showing of good cause sufficient to excuse the delay. The time period for filing the notice of appeal is not extended by the filing of a motion for a new trial, a petition for rehearing, or a like pleading unless the final judgment is modified, vacated, or suspended by the trial court pursuant to Rule 1:1, in which case the time for filing shall be computed from the date of the final judgment entered following such modification, vacation, or suspension.

(b) Extensions Generally. Except as provided in paragraph (a) of this Rule, the times prescribed in these Rules for filing papers, except transcripts (Rule 5A:8(a)), may be extended by a judge of the court in which the papers are to be filed upon a showing of good cause sufficient to excuse the delay.

(c) Motions for Extension. A motion for extension of time is timely if filed:

(1) within the original filing deadline; or

(2) within the specified extension period—see Rules 5A:3(a) and 5A:12(a); or

(3) within any specific deadline governing motions to extend—see Rules 5A:8(a), 5A:13(a), 5A:14, 5A:19(b), and 5A:19(c).

Filing a motion for extension does not toll the applicable deadline or further extend the period of extension.

(d) How to File by Mail in a Timely Manner. Any document required to be filed with the clerk of this Court shall be deemed to be timely filed if (1) it is transmitted expense pre-paid to the clerk of this Court by priority, express, registered, or certified mail via the United States Postal Service, or by a third-party commercial carrier for next-day delivery, and (2) if the official receipt therefor be exhibited upon demand of the clerk or any party and it shows such transmission or mailing within the prescribed time limits. This Rule does not apply to documents to be filed in the office of the clerk of the trial court or clerk of the Virginia Workers' Compensation Commission.

(e) Inmate Filing. A paper filed by an inmate confined in an institution is timely filed if deposited in the institution's internal mail system with first-class postage prepaid on or before the last day for filing. Timely filing of a paper by an inmate confined in an institution may be established by (1) an official stamp of the institution showing that the paper was deposited in the internal mail system on or before the last day for filing, (2) an official postmark dated on or before the last day for filing, or (3) a notarized statement signed by an official of the institution showing that the paper was deposited in the internal mail system on or before the last day for filing.

[Amended effective April 1, 1991; February 1, 1992; August 1, 2000; January 1, 2003; July 1, 2010; May 2, 2011.]

Comment: See also Rule 1:7 regarding computation of time. See § 17–116.05:3, Virginia Code Ann., regarding extension of time to file petition for appeal.

RULE 5A:4. FORMS OF BRIEFS AND OTHER PAPERS

(a) Paper Size, Line Spacing, Font, and Margins. Briefs, appendices, motions, petitions, and other documents may be printed or produced on screen by any process that yields a clear black image on a white background and, when printed, must be on 8–½ × 11 inch paper. All briefs, appendices, motions, petitions, and other documents must be in at least 12–point font. Text shall not be reduced, and must be double-spaced except for headings, assignments of error, quotations, and footnotes. Margins must be at least one inch on all four sides of each page. The use of condensed or multi-page transcripts is prohibited.

(b) Binding and Cover. All briefs, appendices, petitions for rehearing, and petitions for rehearing en banc shall be bound on the left margin in such a manner as to produce a flat, smooth binding. Spiral binding, acco fasteners, and the like are not acceptable. The style of the case (with the name of the appellant stated first) and the record number of the case and the name, Virginia State Bar number, mailing address, telephone number (including any applicable extension), facsimile number (if any), and email address of counsel submitting the document shall be placed on the front cover.

(c) Effect of Non–Compliance. No appeal shall be dismissed for failure to comply with the provisions of this Rule; however, the clerk of this Court may require that a document be redone in compliance with this Rule, However, failure to comply after notice of noncompliance may result in the dismissal of the case.

(d) Certificate of Compliance With Word Count Limitation. Any brief, motion, petition, or other document that has a word count limitation in these Rules must include a certificate by the attorney, or unrepresented party, that the document complies with the applicable word count limitation. The person preparing the certificate may rely on the word count of the word-processing system used to prepare the document. The certificate must state the number of words the document contains, excluding those parts specifically exempted by these Rules.

[Amended effective January 1, 2001; April 1, 2005; July 1, 2010; July 1, 2015.]

RULE 5A:4A. CITATION OF SUPPLEMENTAL AUTHORITIES

If pertinent and significant authorities come to a party's attention after the party's petition for appeal brief in opposition, or brief has been filed or after oral argument but before decision, a party may promptly advise the clerk by letter, with a copy to all other parties, setting forth the citations. The letter must state the reasons for the supplemental citations, referring either to the page of the brief or to a point argued orally. The body of the letter must not exceed 350 words. Any response must be made within 14 days and shall not exceed 350 words. The Court, in its discretion, may refuse to consider the supplemental authorities if they unfairly expand the scope of the arguments on brief, raise matters that should have been previously briefed, appear to be untimely, or are otherwise inappropriate to consider.

[Adopted effective July 1, 2015.]

B. Original Jurisdiction

RULE 5A:5. ORIGINAL PROCEEDINGS

(a) Original Jurisdiction Proceedings Other Than Actual Innocence Petitions. With the exception of petitions for the issuance of writs of actual innocence under paragraph (b) of this Rule, all proceedings before the Court of Appeals pursuant to its original jurisdiction shall be conducted in accordance with the procedure prescribed by Rule 5:7 of the Rules of the Supreme Court.

(b) Petition for a Writ of Actual Innocence.

(1) *Scope.* Any person convicted of a felony upon a plea of not guilty or any person who was adjudicated delinquent, upon a plea of not guilty, by a circuit court of an offense that would be a felony if committed by an adult, may file in the Court of Appeals a petition under Code § 19.2–327.10 *et seq.* seeking a writ of actual innocence based on nonbiological evidence.

(2) *Form and Contents of Petition.* The petition must be filed using Form 12 in the Appendix of Forms following Part 5A and must include all allegations and documents required by subsections A and B of Code § 19.2–327.11. Under Code § 19.2–327.11(B) "relevant documents" shall include, but not be limited to, any orders of conviction, adjudication of delinquency, and sentencing orders being challenged, any appellate dispositions on direct review or any habeas corpus orders (issued by any federal or state court), and any prior petitions filed under Code § 19.2–327.10 *et seq.* in the Court of Appeals or under Code § 19.2–327.2 *et seq.* in the Supreme Court.

(3) *Parties.* All pleadings shall name as the petitioner the person convicted of a felony or adjudicated delinquent who is seeking relief. The pleadings shall identify the Commonwealth, represented by the Attorney General, as respondent.

(4) *Filing Fee.* The petition must be accompanied by either (i) a $25.00 check or money order for the filing fee, or (ii) an *in forma pauperis* affidavit demonstrating that the petitioner cannot afford the filing fee. An affidavit seeking *in forma pauperis* status shall list all assets and liabilities of petitioner, including the current balance of any inmate account maintained by correctional facility.

(5) *Appointment of Counsel.* If the Court does not summarily dismiss the petition, the Court shall appoint counsel for any indigent petitioner who requests the appointment of counsel and satisfies the indigency criteria of Code § 19.2–159. In the Court's discretion, counsel may be appointed at an earlier stage of the proceeding at the petitioner's request upon a showing of requisite indigency. All requests for the appointment of counsel shall be made on the form provided by the Court of Appeals.

(6) *Service of Petition and Return of Service.* Prior to filing a petition, the petitioner shall serve the petition, along with all attachments, on the Attorney General and on the Commonwealth's Attorney for the jurisdiction where the conviction or adjudication of delinquency occurred. When represented by counsel, the petitioner shall file with the petition either (i) a duly executed return of service in the form of a verification that a copy of the petition and all attachments have been served, or (ii) an acceptance of service signed by either or both of the parties to be served, or (iii) a combination of the two. When unrepresented by counsel, the petitioner shall file with the petition a certificate that a copy of the petition and all attachments have been sent, by certified mail, to the Attorney General and the Commonwealth's Attorney for the jurisdiction where the conviction or adjudication of delinquency occurred.

(7) *Response.* If the Court of Appeals does not summarily dismiss the petition, the court will provide written notice to all parties directing the Commonwealth, within 60 days after receipt of such notice, to file a response to the petition pursuant to Code § 19.2–327.11(C). For good cause shown, the 60–day deadline may be extended by the Court of Appeals. The Commonwealth's response may include any information pertinent to the petitioner's guilt, delinquency, or innocence, including proffers of evidence outside the trial court record and evidence previously suppressed at trial.

(8) *Reply.* The petitioner may file a reply to the Commonwealth's response only if directed to do so by the Court of Appeals.

(9) *Copies.* An original and four copies of the petition, the Commonwealth's response, and the petitioner's reply, if any, shall be filed with the Court of Appeals. Attachments shall be included with the original petition, response, or reply, but not with any copies of the same.

(10) *Evidentiary Hearing.* The Court of Appeals may order the circuit court that entered the conviction or adjudication of delinquency to conduct an evidentiary hearing and to certify factual findings pursuant to Code § 19.2–327.12. Such findings, however, shall be limited to the specific questions addressed by the Court of Appeals in its certification order. In the circuit court, the petitioner and the Commonwealth shall be afforded an opportunity to present evidence and to examine witnesses on matters relevant to the certified questions.

(11) *Oral Argument.* Unless otherwise directed by the Court of Appeals, oral argument shall only be allowed on the final decision whether to grant or deny the writ under Code § 19.2–327.13.

(12) *Appeal.* The petitioner or the Commonwealth may petition for appeal to the Supreme Court from any adverse final decision issued by the Court of Appeals under Code § 19.2–327.13 to issue or deny a writ of actual innocence. Such an appeal shall be initiated by the filing of a notice of appeal pursuant to Rule 5:14.

[Amended effective July 1, 1986; August 15, 2005; July 1, 2010; May 2, 2011; July 1, 2013.]

C. Procedure For Filing An Appeal From the Trial Court

RULE 5A:6. NOTICE OF APPEAL

(a) Filing Deadline; Where to File. No appeal shall be allowed unless, within 30 days after entry of final judgment or other appealable order or decree, or within any specified extension thereof granted by this Court under Rule 5A:3(a), counsel files with the clerk of the trial court a notice of appeal, and at the same time mails or delivers a copy of such notice to all opposing counsel. A notice of appeal filed after the court announces a decision or ruling—but before the entry of such judgment or order—is treated as filed on the date of and after the entry. A party filing a notice of an appeal of right to the Court of Appeals shall simultaneously file in the trial court an appeal bond in compliance with Code § 8.01–676.1.

(b) Content. The notice of appeal shall contain a statement whether any transcript or statement of facts, testimony, and other incidents of the case will be filed.

(c) Filing Fee. A copy of the notice of appeal shall be filed in the office of the clerk of the Court of Appeals and, except as otherwise provided by law, must be accompanied by a check or money order in the amount of $50 payable to the "Clerk of the Court of Appeals" for the filing fee required by statute. The fee shall be due at the time the notice of appeal is presented. The clerk of the Court of Appeals may file any notice of appeal that is not accompanied by such fee if the fee is received by the clerk within ten days of the date the notice of appeal is filed. If the fee is not received within such time, the appeal shall be dismissed.

(d) Certificate. The appellant shall include with the notice of appeal a certificate stating:

(1) the names and addresses of all appellants and appellees, the name, Virginia State Bar number, mailing address, telephone number (including any applicable extension), facsimile number (if any), and e-mail address (if any) of counsel for each party, and the mailing address, telephone number, facsimile number (if any), and e-mail address (if any) of any party not represented by counsel; and

(2) that a copy of the notice of appeal has been mailed or delivered to all opposing counsel; and

(3) in a criminal case, a statement whether counsel for defendant has been appointed or privately retained; and

(4) that in the event a transcript is to be filed a copy of the transcript has been ordered from the court reporter who reported the case or is otherwise already in the possession of appellant, or was previously filed in the proceedings.

(e) Separate Cases. Whenever two or more cases were tried together in the trial court, one notice of appeal and one record may be used to bring all of such cases before this Court even though such cases were not consolidated by formal order.

(f) Special Provision for Cases Involving a Guardian Ad Litem. No appeal shall be dismissed because the notice of appeal fails to identify a guardian ad litem or to provide notice to a guardian ad litem. Upon motion for good cause shown or by sua sponte order of this Court, the notice of appeal may be amended to identify the guardian ad litem and to provide notice to such guardian.

[Amended effective September 1, 1994; March 15, 1997; July 11, 2006; January 1, 2009; July 1, 2010; July 1, 2015.]

Cross-reference: As to time for filing notice of appeal, see also Va. Code §§ 8.01–675.3 and 17–116.05:3. For applicability of this rule to appeals from the Virginia Workers' Compensation Commission, see Rule 5A:11.

[Cross-reference amended effective February 1, 1992.]

Form. Notice of Appeal From Trial Court(Rule 5A:6)

VIRGINIA: IN THE CIRCUIT COURT OF ____________________

(The style of the case in the Circuit Court shall be used.)

NOTICE OF APPEAL

______________________________, (name(s) of party(ies))
______________________________ hereby (plaintiff, defendant or other designation in trial court)
appeals to the Court of Appeals of Virginia from the ______________________________ of this Court (final judgment or other appealable order or decree) entered on ________ (date).

[If applicable] A transcript or statement of facts, testimony, and other incidents of the case will be filed.

CERTIFICATE

The undersigned certifies as follows:

(1) The name(s) and address(es) of appellant(s) are:

(2) The name(s), address(es), and telephone number(s) of counsel for appellant(s) are:

(3) The name(s) and address(es) of appellee(s) are:

(4) The name(s), address(es), and telephone number(s) of counsel for appellee(s) are:

(5) [If applicable] Counsel for appellant has ordered from the court reporter who reported the case the transcript for filing as required by Rule 5A:8(a).

(6) [If applicable] __________ (name of party), __________ (appellant) __________ (appellee), is not represented by counsel. ______ (his) (her)

(7) [In criminal cases only] Counsel for defendant has been ______________ (appointed) (privately retained).

(8) A copy of this Notice of Appeal has been mailed or delivered to all opposing counsel [and/or to unrepresented parties, if applicable] and to the Clerk of the Court of Appeals this ___ day of ________, 19___.

____
(Signature of counsel or unrepresented party)

[Amended effective December 1, 1990.]

RULE 5A:7. RECORD ON APPEAL: CONTENTS

(a) Contents. The following constitute the record on appeal from the trial court:

(1) the documents and exhibits filed or lodged in the office of the clerk of the trial court including any report of a commissioner in chancery and the accompanying depositions and other papers;

(2) each instruction marked "given" or "refused" and initialed by the judge;

(3) each exhibit offered in evidence, whether admitted or not, and initialed by the trial judge (or any photograph thereof as authorized by § 19.2–270.4(A) and (C)). (All non-documentary exhibits shall be tagged or labeled in the trial court and the tag or label initialed by the judge.);

(4) each order entered by the trial court;

(5) any opinion or memorandum decision rendered by the judge of the trial court;

(6) any deposition and any discovery material encompassed within Part Four offered in evidence (whether admitted or rejected) at any proceeding; and

(7) the transcript of any proceeding or a written statement of facts, testimony, and other incidents of the case when made a part of the record as provided in Rule 5A:8, or the official videotape recording of any proceeding in those circuit courts authorized by the Supreme Court to use videotape recordings. This Court may require that any videotape proceedings be transcribed, in whole or in part, and made a part of the record as provided in Rule 5A:8, except that the transcript shall be filed within 60 days after the entry of the order requiring such transcript; and

(8) the notice of appeal.

(b) Disagreement on Contents. If disagreement arises as to the contents of any part of the record, the matter shall, in the first instance, be submitted to and decided by the trial court.

[Amended effective August 1, 1985; February 1, 1990; September 1, 1990; July 1, 2010; July 1, 2015.]

Cross-reference: For applicability of this rule to appeals from the Virginia Workers' Compensation Commission, see Rule 5A:11. As to inspection of record of former appeal where case has previously been in an appellate court, see Va. Code § 8.01–675.4. As to writ of certiorari to clerk of trial court for purpose of obtaining omitted part of record, see Va. Code § 8.01–675.4.

[Cross-reference amended effective February 1, 1992.]

RULE 5A:8. RECORD ON APPEAL: TRANSCRIPT OR WRITTEN STATEMENT

(a) Transcript. The transcript of any proceeding is a part of the record when it is filed in the office of the clerk of the trial court within 60 days after entry of the final judgment. This deadline may be extended by a Judge of the Court of Appeals only upon a written motion filed within 90 days after the entry of final judgment. Timely motions will be granted only upon a showing of good cause to excuse the delay.

(b) Notice of Filing Transcript.

(1) *Time for Filing.* Within 10 days after the transcript is filed or, if the transcript is filed prior to the filing of the notice of appeal, within 10 days after the notice of appeal is filed, counsel for appellant shall:

(i) give written notice to all other counsel of the date on which the transcript was filed, and

(ii) file a copy of the notice with the clerk of the trial court.

There shall be appended to the notice either a certificate of counsel for appellant that a copy of the notice has been mailed to all other counsel or an acceptance of service of such notice by all other counsel.

(2) *Multiple Transcripts.* When multiple transcripts are filed, the 10–day period for filing the notice required by this Rule shall be calculated from the date on which the last transcript is filed or from the date on which the notice of appeal is filed, whichever is later. The notice of filing transcripts shall identify all transcripts filed and the date upon which the last transcript was filed.

(3) *Notice of No Further Transcripts.* If the notice of appeal states that no additional transcripts will be filed and identifies the transcripts that have been filed, if any, then no additional written notice of filing transcripts is required and the notice of appeal will serve as the notice of filing transcripts for purposes of Rule 5A:8(b).

(4) *Effect of Non–Compliance.*

(i) Any failure to file the notice required by this Rule that materially prejudices an appellee will result in the affected transcripts being stricken from the record on appeal. For purposes of this Rule, material prejudice includes preventing the appellee from raising legitimate objections to the contents of the transcript or misleading the appellee about the contents of the record. The appellee shall have the burden of establishing such prejudice in the brief in opposition or, if no brief in opposition is filed, in a written statement filed with the clerk of this Court within twenty-one days after the record is received by the clerk.

(ii) When the appellant fails to ensure that the record contains transcripts or a written statement of facts necessary to permit resolution of appellate issues, any assignments of error affected by such omission shall not be considered.

(c) Written Statement in Lieu of Transcript. A written statement of facts, testimony, and other incidents of the case becomes a part of the record when:

(1) within 55 days after entry of judgment a copy of such statement is filed in the office of the clerk of the trial court. A copy must be mailed or delivered to opposing counsel on the same day that it is filed in the office of the clerk of the trial court, accompanied by notice that such statement will be presented to the trial judge no earlier than 15 days nor later than 20 days after such filing; and

(2) the statement is signed by the trial judge and filed in the office of the clerk of the trial court. The judge may sign the statement forthwith upon its presentation to him if it is signed by counsel for all parties, but if objection is made to the accuracy or completeness of the statement, it shall be signed in accordance with paragraph (d) of this Rule.

The term "other incidents of the case" in this subsection includes motions, proffers, objections, and rulings of the trial court regarding any issue that a party intends to assign as error or otherwise address on appeal.

(d) Objections. Any party may object to a transcript or written statement on the ground that it is erroneous or incomplete. Notice of such objection specifying the errors alleged or deficiencies asserted shall be filed with the clerk of the trial court within 15 days after the date the notice of filing the transcript (paragraph (b) of this Rule) or within 15 days after the date the notice of filing the written statement (paragraph (c) of this Rule) is filed in the office of the clerk of the trial court or, if the transcript or written statement is filed before the notice of appeal is filed, within 10 days after the notice of appeal has been filed with the clerk of the trial court. The clerk shall give prompt notice of the filing of such objections to the trial judge. Within 10 days after the notice of objection is filed with the clerk of the trial court, the judge shall:

(1) overrule the objection; or

(2) make any corrections that the trial judge deems necessary; or

(3) include any accurate additions to make the record complete; or

(4) certify the manner in which the record is incomplete; and

(5) sign the transcript or written statement.

At any time while the record remains in the office of the clerk of the trial court, the trial judge may, after notice to counsel and hearing, correct the transcript or written statement.

The judge's signature on a transcript or written statement, without more, shall constitute certification that the procedural requirements of this Rule have been satisfied.

[Amended effective July 1, 1988; January 1, 1990; July 1, 1990; April 1, 1991; March 15, 1997; January 1, 2003; July 1, 2010.]

Cross-reference: For applicability of this rule to appeals from the Virginia Workers' Compensation Commission, see Rule 5A:11.

[Cross-reference amended effective February 1, 1992.]

RULE 5A:9. JUDGE AUTHORIZED TO ACT

The judge authorized to act in all matters relating to the record on appeal shall be any judge having authority to enter orders in the case or in the court in which the case was heard or, in a case heard by three judges, any one of them.

[Amended effective July 1, 2010.]

Cross-reference: For applicability of this rule to appeals from the Virginia Workers' Compensation Commission, see Rule 5A:11.

[Cross-reference amended effective February 1, 1992.]

RULE 5A:10. RECORD ON APPEAL: PREPARATION AND TRANSMISSION

(a) Preparation. The clerk of the trial court shall prepare the record as soon as possible after notice of appeal is filed. In the event of multiple appeals in the same case, or in cases tried together, only one record need be prepared and transmitted.

(b) Form of the Record.

(1) The record shall be compiled in the following order:

(i) a front cover setting forth the name of the court and the short style of the case;

(ii) a table of contents listing each document included in the record and the page on which it Begins;

(iii) each document constituting a part of the record in chronological order; and

(iv) the certificate of the clerk of the trial court that the foregoing constitutes the true and complete record, except omitted exhibits as hereinafter provided.

(2) Each page of the record shall be numbered at the bottom.

(3) Transcripts, depositions, and reports of commissioners may be included in separate volumes identified by the clerk of the trial court if referred to in the table of contents and at the appropriate place in the record.

(4) Exhibits, other than those filed with pleadings, may be included in a separate volume or envelope certified by the clerk of the trial court, except that any exhibit that cannot be conveniently placed in a volume or envelope shall be identified by a tag. Each such volume or envelope shall include, on its cover or inside, a descriptive list of exhibits contained therein. Reference shall be made to exhibits in the table of contents and at the appropriate place in the record referred to in paragraph (b)(1) of this Rule. The clerk of the trial court shall not transmit the following types of exhibits, unless requested to do so by the clerk of this Court: drugs, guns and other weapons, ammunition, blood vials and other bio-hazard type materials, money, jewelry, articles of clothing, and bulky items such as large graphs and maps. The omission of any such exhibit shall be noted on the descriptive list of exhibits. Upon motion by counsel, this Court may order the trial court to transmit any of these prohibited exhibits.

(5) Any transcript or statement of facts that the clerk of the trial court deems not a part of the record because of untimely filing shall be certified as such and transmitted with the record.

(c) Abbreviated Record. When the assignments of error presented by an appeal can be determined without examination of all the pleadings, facts, testimony, and other incidents of the case, all counsel with the approval of the trial court may prepare for submission an abbreviated record, stating how the assignments of error in the case arose and were decided, and setting forth only so much of the pleadings, facts, testimony, and other incidents of the case as are essential to a determination of the issues on appeal. Such abbreviated record shall be signed by all counsel and the trial judge and filed in the office of the clerk of the trial court. It will be assumed that the abbreviated record contains everything germane to the assignments of error. The Court of Appeals may, however, consider other parts of the record to enable this Court to attain the ends of justice.

(d) Transmission. The clerk of the trial court shall retain the record for 21 days after the notice of appeal has been filed with him pursuant to Rule 5A:6. If the notice of appeal states that a transcript or statement will thereafter be filed, the clerk of the trial court shall retain the record for 21 days after the filing in his office of such transcript or statement or, if objection is made to the transcript or statement pursuant to Rule 5A:8(d), the clerk of the trial court shall retain the record for five days after the objection is acted upon by the trial judge. The clerk of the trial court shall then forthwith transmit the record to the clerk of this Court; provided, however, that, notwithstanding that the foregoing periods of retention may not have expired, the clerk of the trial court shall transmit the record sooner if requested in writing by counsel for all parties to the appeal and shall, whether or not so requested, transmit the record in time for delivery to the clerk of this Court within three months after entry of the judgment appealed from. The failure of the clerk of the trial court to transmit the record as herein provided shall not be a ground for dismissal of the appeal by this Court.

(e) Notice of Filing. The clerk of this Court shall promptly notify all counsel of the date on which the record is filed in the office of the clerk of the Court of Appeals.

(f) Disposition of Record. When the mandate is issued by this Court, the clerk of this Court shall return the record to the clerk of the trial court. The record shall be returned by that clerk upon the request of the clerk of this Court.

[Amended effective August 1, 1985; July 1, 2010; May 2, 2011; July 1, 2015.]

Cross-reference: For applicability of this rule to appeals from the Virginia Workers' Compensation Commission, see Rule 5A:11.

[Cross-reference amended effective February 1, 1992.]

RULE 5A:10A. DIGITAL APPELLATE RECORD: PREPARATION AND TRANSMISSION

(a) Preparation. For courts that utilize the Case Imaging System developed by the Office of the Executive Secretary, a Digital Appellate Record may be created instead of a paper record, with substantially the same content as its paper counterpart. The clerk of the court in which the proceeding originated shall be responsible for preparing the digital record, if the clerk chooses to transmit a digital record in place of the paper version.

(b) Form of Record. The digital record shall comply with the Digital Appellate Record Standards posted on the Court of Appeals of Virginia intranet.

(c) Exhibits. Original exhibits should be scanned or imaged and retained by the clerk of the trial court. The omission of any exhibit that cannot be scanned or imaged must be noted in a descriptive list of exhibits. On motion or sua sponte, this Court may order the trial court to transmit any retained exhibit.

(d) Transmission. The clerk of the trial court shall transmit the record to the clerk of this Court in the manner prescribed by the Digital Appellate Record Standards, using the Digital Records System created for this purpose. The same timing and dismissal rules apply to transmissions of digital records as apply to their paper counterparts in Rule 5A:10.

(e) Disposition of Record. When the mandate is issued by this Court, the clerk of this Court shall return all tangible items, if any, to the clerk of the trial court in which the proceeding originated. The digital record will not be returned. If necessary, the record shall be re-sent by that clerk upon the request of the clerk of this Court.

(f) Public Record. The publicly available digital record shall be the digital document prepared by the trial court clerk with all information that is sealed or protected from public disclosure by law redacted or excluded.

[Adopted effective July 1, 2015.]

D. Procedure for Filing An Appeal From the Workers' Compensation Commission

RULE 5A:11. SPECIAL RULE APPLICABLE TO APPEALS FROM THE VIRGINIA WORKERS' COMPENSATION COMMISSION

(a) Non–Application of Other Rules. Rules 5A:6 through 5A:10 do not apply to appeals from the Virginia Workers' Compensation Commission except as otherwise specified in this Part Five A.

(b) Notice of Appeal. No appeal from an order of the Commission shall be allowed unless, within 30 days after entry of the order appealed from, or within 30 days after receipt of notice by priority mail with delivery confirmation or equivalent mailing option of the order appealed from, counsel files with the clerk of the Virginia Workers' Compensation Commission a notice of appeal which shall state the names and addresses of all appellants and appellees, the name, Virginia State Bar number, mailing address, telephone number (including any applicable extension), facsimile number (if any), and e-mail address (if any) of counsel for each party, and the mailing address, telephone number, facsimile number (if any), and e-mail address (if any) of any party not represented by counsel, and whether the appellant challenges the sufficiency of the evidence to support the findings of the Commission. A copy of the notice of appeal also shall be filed in the office of the clerk of this Court, and except as otherwise provided by law, must be accompanied by a check or money order in the amount of $50 payable to the "Clerk of the Court of Appeals," for the filing fee required by statute. The fee shall be due at the time the notice of appeal is presented. The clerk of this Court may file any notice of appeal that is not accompanied by such fee if the fee is received by the clerk within ten days of the date the notice of appeal is filed. If the fee is not received within such time, the appeal shall be dismissed.

(c) Record on Appeal. The record on appeal from the Commission shall consist of the originals or copies of the notice of appeal, the employer's first report, medical reports, applications for hearings, the transcript of any hearing, depositions, interrogatories and answer to interrogatories, and opinions of a commissioner or deputy commissioner and opinions of the Commission, together with such other material as may be certified by the clerk of the Commission and shall conform as nearly as practicable to the requirements of Rule 5A:10 (b), provided, that, unless it is stated in the notice of appeal that the appellant challenges the sufficiency of the evidence to support the findings of the Commission, the clerk of the Commission need not prepare or certify the transcript of any hearing.

(d) Transmission of Record. The record shall, as soon as it is certified by the clerk of the Commission, be transmitted by him to the clerk of this Court. It shall be so transmitted within 30 days after filing of the notice of appeal.

(e) Notice of Filing. The clerk of this Court shall promptly notify all counsel of the date on which the record is filed in the office of the clerk of this Court.

(f) Separate Cases. Whenever two or more cases were tried together in the Virginia Workers' Compensation Commission, one notice of appeal and one record may be used to bring all such cases before this Court even though such cases were not consolidated by formal order.

(g) Record Returned to Commission. When the mandate is issued by this Court, the clerk of this Court shall return the record to the clerk of the Commission. The clerk of the Commission shall return the record upon request of the clerk of this Court.

[Amended effective November 1, 1984; February 1, 1992; July 1, 1999; April 1, 2004; July 11, 2006; July 1, 2010.]

E. Procedure On Petition For Appeal In Criminal Cases and Traffic Infractions

RULE 5A:12. PETITION FOR APPEAL

(a) When the Petition Must Be Filed. When an appeal to the Court of Appeals does not lie as a matter of right, a petition for appeal must be filed with the clerk of this Court not more than 40 days after the filing of the record with the Court of Appeals. An extension of 30 days may be granted on motion in the discretion of this Court upon a showing of good cause sufficient to excuse the delay.

(b) Copy to Opposing Counsel. At the time the petition for appeal is filed, a copy of the petition shall be mailed or delivered to the Commonwealth's attorney or the city, county, or town attorney, as the case may be.

(c) What the Petition Must Contain. A petition for appeal must contain the following:

(1) *Assignments of Error.* Under a heading entitled "Assignments of Error," the petition shall list, clearly and concisely and without extraneous argument, the specific errors in the rulings below upon which the party intends to rely, or the specific existing case law that should be overturned, extended, modified or reversed. An exact reference to the page(s) of the transcript, written statement of facts, or record where the alleged error has been preserved in the trial court or other tribunal from which the appeal is taken shall be included with each assignment of error.

(i) Effect of Failure to Assign Error. Only assignments of error assigned in the petition for appeal will be noticed by this Court. If the petition for appeal does not contain assignments of error, the petition shall be dismissed.

(ii) Insufficient Assignments of Error. An assignment of error which does not address the findings or rulings in the trial court or other tribunal from which an appeal is taken, or which merely states that the judgment or award is contrary to the law and the evidence, is not sufficient. If the assignments of error are insufficient, the petition for appeal shall be dismissed.

(iii) Effect of Failure to Use Separate Heading or Include Preservation Reference. If the petition for appeal contains assignments of error, but the assignments of error are not set forth under a separate heading as provided in subparagraph (c)(1) of this Rule, a rule to show cause will issue pursuant to Rule 5A:1A. If there is a deficiency in the reference to the page(s) of the transcript, written statement of facts, or record where the alleged error has been preserved in the trial court or other tribunal from which the appeal is taken, a rule to show cause will issue pursuant to Rule 5A:1A.

(2) *Table of Contents and Table of Authorities.* A table of contents and table of authorities with cases alphabetically arranged. Citations of all authorities shall include the year thereof.

(3) *Nature of the Case and Material Proceedings Below.* A brief statement of the nature of the case and of the material proceedings in the trial court or commission in which the case originated. This statement shall omit references to any paper filed or action taken that does not relate to the assignments of error.

(4) *Statement of Facts.* A clear and concise statement of the facts that relate to the assignments of error, with references to the pages of the record, transcript, or written statement of facts. Any quotation from the record should be brief. When the facts are in dispute, the petition shall so state. The testimony of individual witnesses should not be summarized seriatim unless the facts are in dispute and such a summary is necessary to support the appellant's version of the facts.

(5) *Authorities and Argument.* With respect to each assignment of error, the standard of review and the argument—including principles of law and the authorities—shall be stated in one place and not scattered through the petition. At the option of counsel, the argument may be preceded by a short summary.

(6) *Conclusion.* A short conclusion stating the precise relief sought.

(7) *Contact Information.* The signature of at least one counsel, counsel's name, Virginia State Bar number, mailing address, telephone number, facsimile number (if any), and email address (if any).

(8) *Certificate.* A certificate stating the date of mailing or delivery of the petition to opposing counsel and whether or not the appellant desires to state orally the reasons why the petition for appeal should be granted.

(d) Number of Copies to File. Four copies of the petition shall be filed with the clerk of this Court.

(e) Length. Except by leave of a Judge of this Court, a petition shall not exceed 12,300 words. The word limit does not include the cover page, table of contents, table of authorities, and certificate.

(f) Single Petition in Separate Cases. Whenever two or more cases were tried together in the trial court or commission below, one petition for appeal may be used to bring all such cases before the Court of Appeals even though the cases were not consolidated below by formal order.

(g) Oral Argument. When the appeal is not granted by the Judge of this Court to whom the petition for appeal is originally presented, the petitioner shall be entitled to state orally, in person or by conference telephone call, to a panel of this Court the reasons the petition for appeal should be granted. The appellant may waive the right to oral argument on the petition for appeal before a panel by notifying the clerk of this Court and opposing counsel in writing, or by filing a reply brief. Any lawyer not licensed to practice in Virginia who seeks to appear pro hac vice to present oral argument to this Court must comply with the requirements of Rule 1A:4.

(h) Procedure for an *Anders* Appeal. If counsel for appellant finds his client's appeal to be without merit, he must comply with the requirements of *Anders v. California*, 386 U.S. 738 (1967), and *Akbar v. Commonwealth*, 7 Va. App. 611, 376 S.E.2d 545 (1989). In compliance therewith, counsel is required to file (1) a petition for appeal which refers to anything in the record which might arguably support the appeal and which demonstrates to the Court of Appeals counsel's conscientious examination of the merits of the appeal; (2) a motion for leave to withdraw as counsel; and (3) a motion for an extension of time to allow the appellant to file a supplemental petition for appeal. The petition for appeal and the motion for leave to withdraw as counsel should specifically cite to *Anders*. All three pleadings must be served on opposing counsel and upon the client and must contain a certificate providing evidence of such service. The Court of Appeals will rule upon the motion for extension of time upon its receipt, but will not rule on the motion to withdraw as counsel until this Court considers the case in its entirety, including any supplemental petition for appeal that may be filed.

[Amended effective July 1, 1988; August 1, 2000; February 1, 2007; July 1, 2010; May 2, 2011; May 16, 2014; July 1, 2015.]

Cross-reference: See §§ 17–116.05:2 and 17–116.05:3, Virginia Code Ann.

RULE 5A:13. BRIEF IN OPPOSITION

(a) Filing Time. A brief in opposition to granting the appeal may be filed with the clerk of this Court by the appellee within 21 days after the petition for appeal is served on counsel for the appellee. Within the same time he shall mail or deliver a copy to counsel for appellant. Four copies shall be filed. Motions for an extension to this briefing deadline shall be filed no later than 10 days after the expiration of the deadline.

(b) Form and Content. The brief in opposition shall conform in all respects to the requirements of the brief of appellee (Rule 5A:21).

(1) *Length.* Except by leave of a Judge of this Court, the brief shall not exceed 8,800 words.

(2) *Table of Contents and Table of Authorities.* If the brief exceeds 3,500 words, it shall contain a table of contents and table of authorities with cases alphabetically arranged.

(3) *Criminal or Traffic Cases.* In a criminal or traffic case, a brief may be filed by the Commonwealth's attorney, city, county, or town attorney, as the case may be.

(c) Expedited Review. When it clearly appears that an appeal ought to be granted without further delay, an appeal may be granted before the filing of the brief in opposition.

[Amended effective December 1, 1987; July 1, 2010.]

Purpose [of 1987 amendment]: The change makes this Rule consistent with Rule 5:18.

RULE 5A:14. REPLY BRIEF

When a brief in opposition to the petition for appeal has been filed, the appellant may, within 14 days thereafter, in lieu of oral argument, file with the clerk of this Court a reply brief not to exceed 5,300 words in length. Four copies shall be filed. Motions for an extension to this briefing deadline shall be filed no later than 10 days after the expiration of the deadline.

[Amended effective July 1, 2010.]

RULE 5A:15. DENIAL OF PETITION FOR APPEAL; PETITION FOR REHEARING

(a) Denial by a Single Judge. When a petition for appeal is denied by a Judge of this Court pursuant to Code § 17.1–407(C), the clerk of this Court shall send a copy of the order denying the petition to counsel for the appellant and counsel for the appellee. Pro se prisoners and those with leave of this Court to proceed under this Rule may demand consideration of the petition by three-judge panel pursuant to Code § 17.1–

407(D). The demand shall be filed in writing. Four copies must be filed with the clerk of this Court within fourteen days after the date of the order by which the petition was denied. The demand, which shall include a statement identifying how the one-judge order is in error, shall not exceed 350 words. Oral argument shall not be permitted on consideration of a petition by a three-judge panel unless oral argument was requested in the petition for appeal pursuant to Rule 5A:12(c). A petitioner who has previously requested oral argument may waive oral argument by so stating in the demand for review. All petitioners other than pro se prisoners and those with leave of this Court to proceed under this Rule must follow the provisions of Rule 5A:15A(a) when filing a demand for three-judge review pursuant to Code § 17.1–407(D).

(b) Denial by a Three–Judge Panel. When a petition for appeal is denied by a three-judge panel, the clerk of this Court shall send a copy of the order or memorandum opinion denying the appeal to counsel for the appellant and counsel for the appellee. Pro se prisoners and those with leave of this Court to proceed under this Rule may, within 14 days after the date of this notice, file a petition for rehearing in writing in the office of the clerk of this Court unless the denial was by a three-Judge panel after its consideration of a petition denied by a Judge of this Court pursuant to Code § 17.1–407. The petition for rehearing shall not exceed 5,300 words in length. The petition shall state that a copy has been mailed or delivered to counsel for the appellee. Four copies shall be filed. Oral argument on the petition for rehearing will not be allowed. The petition for rehearing shall be referred to the panel of this Court that considered the petition for appeal. No responsive brief shall be filed unless requested by this Court. The clerk of this Court shall notify counsel for the appellant and counsel for the appellee of the action taken by this Court on the petition for rehearing. All petitioners other than pro se prisoners and those with leave of this Court to proceed under this Rule must follow the provisions of Rule 5A:15A(b) when filing a petition for a rehearing of an order of a three-judge panel denying a petition for appeal.

[Amended effective January 1, 1996; October 21, 1998; January 1, 2005; January 1, 2006; July 1, 2010.]

RULE 5A:15A. DENIAL OF PETITION FOR APPEAL; PETITION FOR REHEARING FILED BY ELECTRONIC MEANS

(a) Proceedings After Denial of Petition by Single Judge.

(1) When a petition for appeal is denied by a Judge of this Court pursuant to Code § 17.1–407(C), the clerk of this Court shall send a copy of the order denying the petition to counsel for the appellant and counsel for the appellee. The appellant may demand consideration of the petition by three-judge panel pursuant to Code § 17.1–407(D). Demands for three-judge review filed by pro se prisoners or by those with leave of this Court to proceed under Rule 5A:15(a) shall be filed in accordance with the provisions of Rule 5A:15(a).

(2) Except for demands for three-judge review filed by pro se prisoners or by those with leave of this Court to proceed under Rule 5A:15(a), the demand shall be filed as a single Adobe Acrobat Portable Document Format (PDF) document attached to an e-mail addressed to cavpfr@courts.state.va.us and will be timely filed if received by the clerk's office at or before 11:59 p.m. on the fourteenth day after the date of the order by which the petition was denied.

(3) The demand, which shall include a statement identifying how the one-judge order is in error, must be formatted to print on a page 8 1/2 × 11 inches, must be in 12–point font or larger, must be double-spaced, and must not exceed 350 words. The demand must include a certificate of service to opposing counsel and the certificate shall specify the manner of service and the date of service. If opposing counsel has an e-mail address, service on opposing counsel shall be by electronic means and such address shall be included in the certificate of service. The demand must also include a certificate of compliance with the word count limit. The demand will be considered filed on the date and time that it is received by cavpfr@courts.state.va.us. If the demand does not meet the requirements of this rule as to format, the clerk of this Court shall so notify counsel and provide a specific amount of time for a corrected copy of the demand to be filed. A person who files a document electronically shall have the same responsibility as a person filing a document in paper form for ensuring that the document is properly filed, complete, and readable. However, if technical problems at the Court of Appeals result in a failure to timely receive the electronically filed demand for three-judge review, counsel shall provide to the clerk of this Court on the next business day all documentation which exists demonstrating the attempt to file the demand by e-mail, any delivery failure notice received in response to the attempt, and a copy of the demand for three-judge review.

(4) The e-mail message to which the demand is attached shall recite in the subject line the style of the case and the Court of Appeals record number. The body of the e-mail message shall contain a paragraph stating that a demand for three-judge review is being filed, the style of the case, the Court of Appeals record number, the name and Virginia State Bar number of counsel filing the demand, as well as the law firm name, mailing address, telephone number, facsimile number (if any), and e-mail address (if any) of counsel filing the demand. The message shall also state whether a copy of the demand has been served by e-mail or another means on opposing counsel and the date of such service. If the demand has been served on opposing counsel by e-mail, the e-mail address for opposing counsel shall also be included. Upon receipt of the demand for three-judge review in the e-mail box of the

clerk's office, an acknowledgment will be forwarded by e-mail to counsel seeking the rehearing.

(5) Oral argument shall not be permitted on consideration of a petition by a three-judge panel unless oral argument was requested in the petition for appeal pursuant to Rule 5A:12(c). An appellant who has previously requested oral argument may waive oral argument by so stating in the demand for review.

(b) Proceedings After Denial of Petition by Three–Judge Panel.

(1) When a petition for appeal is denied by a three-judge panel, the clerk of this Court shall send a copy of the order or memorandum opinion denying the appeal to counsel for the appellant and counsel for the appellee. Counsel for the appellant may file a petition for rehearing in the office of the clerk of this Court unless the denial was by a three-judge panel after its consideration of a petition denied by a Judge of this Court pursuant to Code § 17.1–407. Petitions for rehearing filed by pro se prisoners or by those with leave of court to proceed under Rule 5A:15(b) shall be in accordance with the provisions of Rule 5A:15(b).

(2) Except for petitions for rehearing filed by pro se prisoners or by those with leave of this Court to proceed under Rule 5A:15(b), the petition shall be filed as a single PDF document attached to an email addressed to cavpfr@courts.state.va.us and will be timely filed if received by the clerk's office at or before 11:59 p.m. on the fourteenth day after the date of the order by which the petition was denied.

(3) The petition must be formatted to print on a page 8 1/2 × 11 inches, must be in 12–point font or larger, must be double-spaced, and must not exceed 5,300 words. The petition must include a certificate of service to opposing counsel and the certificate shall specify the manner of service and the date of service. If opposing counsel has an e-mail address, service on opposing counsel shall be by electronic means and such address shall be included in the certificate of service. The petition must also include a certificate of compliance with the word count limit. Petitions filed by e-mail will be considered filed on the date and time that it is received by cavpfr@courts.state.va.us. If the petition does not meet the requirements of this rule as to format, the clerk of this Court shall so notify counsel and provide a specific amount of time for a corrected copy of the petition to be filed. A person who files a document electronically shall have the same responsibility as a person filing a document in paper form for ensuring that the document is properly filed, complete, and readable. However, if technical problems at the Court of Appeals result in a failure to timely receive the electronically filed petition for rehearing, counsel shall provide to the clerk of this Court on the next business day all documentation which exists demonstrating the attempt to file the petition by e-mail, any delivery failure notice received in response to the attempt, and a copy of the petition for rehearing.

(4) The e-mail message to which the petition is attached shall recite in the subject line the style of the case and the Court of Appeals record number. The body of the e-mail message shall contain a paragraph stating that a petition for rehearing is being filed, the style of the case, the Court of Appeals record number, the name and Virginia State Bar number of counsel filing the petition, as well as the law firm name, mailing address, telephone number, facsimile number (if any), and e-mail address (if any) of counsel filing the petition. The message shall also state whether a copy of the petition has been served by e-mail or another means on opposing counsel and the date of such service. If the petition has been served on opposing counsel by e-mail, the e-mail address for opposing counsel shall also be included. Upon receipt of the petition for rehearing in the e-mail box of the clerk's office, an acknowledgment will be forwarded by e-mail to counsel seeking the rehearing.

(5) Oral argument on the petition for rehearing will not be allowed. The petition for rehearing shall be referred to the panel of this Court that considered the petition for appeal. No responsive brief shall be filed unless requested by this Court. The clerk of this Court shall notify counsel for the appellant and counsel for the appellee of the action taken by the Court of Appeals on the petition for rehearing via e-mail, if e-mail addresses for both counsel have been provided, or via U.S. Mail to any counsel or party who has not provided an e-mail address.

[Added effective January 1, 2005. Amended effective January 1, 2006; July 1, 2010.]

F. Procedure Following Perfection of Appeal

RULE 5A:16. PERFECTION OF APPEAL; DOCKETING

(a) Appeals as a Matter of Right. In cases when an appeal lies as a matter of right to the Court of Appeals, such appeal shall be perfected by the timely filing of a notice of appeal pursuant to Rule 5A:6. Such case shall be considered mature for purposes of further proceedings from the date the record is filed in the office of the clerk of the Court of Appeals. A party filing a notice of an appeal of right to the Court of Appeals shall simultaneously file in the trial court an appeal bond in compliance with Code § 8.01–676.1.

(b) Grant of Petition for Appeal. Promptly after a petition for appeal has been granted by the Court of Appeals, the clerk of the Court of Appeals shall certify this action to the trial court and all counsel. Such case shall be considered mature for purposes of further proceedings from the date of such certificate.

(c) Docketing. Cases shall be placed on the docket in the order in which they mature, provided that precedence shall be given to the following cases:

(1) criminal cases;

(2) cases from the Virginia Workers' Compensation Commission;

(3) cases involving termination of parental rights;

(4) cases of original jurisdiction;

(5) cases to be reheard; and

(6) any other cases required by statute to be given precedence.

The Court of Appeals may, however, for good cause shown or for reasons appearing sufficient to the Court, give preference to other cases.

[Amended effective July 1, 1987; February 1, 1992; September 1, 1994; July 1, 2010.]

RULE 5A:17. SECURITY FOR APPEAL

(a) Form for Security. All security for appeal required under Code § 8.01–676.1 shall substantially conform to the forms set forth in the Appendix to this Part Five A.

(b) Security for Appeal; Defects. Whenever an appellant files an appeal bond or irrevocable letter of credit, he shall contemporaneously give notice in writing of said filing to counsel for appellee. No appeal shall be dismissed because of defect in any bond or irrevocable letter of credit unless an appellee, within 21 days after the giving of such notice, files with the clerk of the Court of Appeals a statement in writing of the defects in the bond or irrevocable letter of credit, and unless the appellant fails to correct such defects, if any, within 21 days after such statement is filed. If the appellant fails to correct such defects within 21 days, an appellee may move that the appeal be dismissed and it shall be dismissed unless the appellant satisfies the Court of Appeals that the bond or irrevocable letter of credit, either as originally given or as amended, has been filed as required by law.

[Amended effective December 1, 1984; July 1, 1991; July 1, 2010.]

Cross-reference: See Virginia Code Ann. § 8.01–676 for appeal bonds.

RULE 5A:18. PRESERVATION OF ISSUES FOR APPELLATE REVIEW

No ruling of the trial court or the Virginia Workers' Compensation Commission will be considered as a basis for reversal unless an objection was stated with reasonable certainty at the time of the ruling, except for good cause shown or to enable the Court of Appeals to attain the ends of justice. A mere statement that the judgment or award is contrary to the law and the evidence is not sufficient to preserve the issue for appellate review.

[Amended effective August 1, 1985; February 1, 1992; July 1, 2010.]

Comment [on 1985 Amendment]: Inasmuch as assignments of error have been discarded, reference to error in this rule is archaic. Cf. proposed Rule 5:25.

RULE 5A:19. GENERAL REQUIREMENTS FOR ALL BRIEFS

(a) Length. Except by permission of a Judge of this Court, neither the opening brief of appellant, nor the brief of appellee shall exceed 12,300 words. No reply brief shall exceed 3,500 words. Briefs of amici curiae shall comply with the word limits that apply to briefs of the party being supported. Word limits under this Rule do not include appendices, or the cover page, table of contents, table of authorities, and certificate. There shall be no exception to these limits except by permission of this Court on motion for extension of the limits.

(b) Filing Time: Appeal as a Matter of Right. In cases when appeal lies as a matter of right to the Court of Appeals, briefs shall be filed as follows:

(1) The appellant shall file the opening brief in the office of the clerk of the Court of Appeals within 40 days after the date of the filing of the record in such office.

(2) The brief of appellee and the brief of the guardian ad litem shall be filed in the office of the clerk of the Court of Appeals within 25 days after filing of the opening brief.

(3) The appellant may file a reply brief in the office of the clerk of the Court of Appeals within 14 days after filing of the brief of appellee or guardian ad litem.

(4) Motions for extensions to these briefing deadlines shall be filed no later than 10 days after the expiration of the deadline.

(c) Filing Time: Grant of Petition for Appeal. In cases when a petition for appeal has been granted by the Court of Appeals, briefs shall be filed as follows:

(1) The appellant shall file the opening brief in the office of the clerk of the Court of Appeals within 40 days after the date of the certificate of appeal issued by the clerk of the Court of Appeals pursuant to Rule 5A:16(b).

(2) The brief of appellee shall be filed in the office of the clerk of the Court of Appeals within 25 days after filing of the opening brief.

(3) The appellant may file a reply brief in the office of the clerk of the Court of Appeals within 14 days after filing of the brief of appellee.

(4) Motions for extensions to these briefing deadlines shall be filed no later than 10 days after the expiration of the deadline.

(d) Participation by Guardian Ad Litem. If a guardian ad litem joins with either appellant or appellee, the guardian ad litem must notify the Clerk's Office, in writing, which side it joins. Thereafter, the guardian ad litem may rely on the brief of that party and is entitled to oral argument under Rule 5A:26.

(e) Arguments Made by Reference. Attempts to incorporate arguments made below by reference to pleadings, motions, memorandum, or other filings are prohibited.

(f) Copies. An electronic version, in Portable Document Format (PDF), must be filed with the clerk of this Court and served on opposing counsel at the time of filing the brief with the Court, unless excused by this Court for good cause shown. An electronic version of a brief amicus curiae shall be filed with the clerk of this Court and served on counsel for all parties and on any other counsel amicus curiae. For purposes of this Rule, service by email shall be governed by Rule 1:17, which allows electronic transmission without the need of consent by opposing counsel. The electronic version must be filed in the manner prescribed by the VACES Guidelines and User's Manual, using the Virginia Appellate Courts eBriefs System (VACES). The Guidelines are located on the Court's website at www.courts.state.va.us/online/vaces/resources/guidelines.pdf. In addition, four printed copies of each brief (including a brief amicus curiae) shall be filed in the office of the clerk of this Court. All briefs shall contain a certificate evidencing the date and method of electronic transmission of the brief to opposing counsel.

(g) Technical Problems With Electronic Filing of Brief or Appendix. A person who files a document electronically shall have the same responsibility as a person filing a document in paper form for ensuring that the document is properly filed, complete, and readable. However, if technical problems at the Court of Appeals result in a failure to timely receive the electronically filed brief or appendix, counsel shall provide to the clerk of this Court on the next business day all documentation which exists demonstrating the attempt to electronically file the brief or appendix, any error message received in response to the attempt, documentation that the brief or appendix was later successfully resubmitted, and a motion requesting that the Court accept the resubmitted brief or appendix.

[Amended effective May 1, 2004; September 1, 2004; July 1, 2010; July 1, 2015.]

Cross-reference: See Rules 5A:10 and 5A:11 regarding filing of the record.

RULE 5A:20. REQUIREMENTS FOR OPENING BRIEF OF APPELLANT

The opening brief of appellant shall contain:

(a) A table of contents and table of authorities with cases alphabetically arranged. Citations of all authorities shall include the year thereof,

(b) A brief statement of the nature of the case and of the material proceedings in the trial court, which shall omit references to any paper filed or action taken that does not relate to the assignments of error.

(c) A statement of the assignments of error with a clear and exact reference to the page(s) of the transcript, written statement, record, or appendix where each assignment of error was preserved in the trial court.

(d) A clear and concise statement of the facts that relate to the assignments of error, with references to the pages of the transcript, written statement, record, or appendix. Any quotation from the record should be brief. When the facts are in dispute, the brief shall so state. The testimony of individual witnesses should not be summarized seriatim unless the facts are in dispute and such a summary is necessary to support the appellant's version of the facts.

(e) The standard of review and the argument (including principles of law and authorities) relating to each assignment of error. When the assignment of error was not preserved in the trial court, counsel shall state why the good cause and/or ends of justice exceptions to Rule 5A:18 are applicable. With respect to each assignment of error, the standard of review and the argument—including principles of law and the authorities—shall be stated in one place and not scattered through the brief. At the option of counsel, the argument may be preceded by a short summary.

(f) A short conclusion stating the precise relief sought.

(g) The signature (which need not be in handwriting) of at least one counsel and counsel's Virginia State Bar number, address, telephone number, facsimile number (if any), and email address.

(h) A certificate (which need not be signed in handwriting) stating (1) that Rule 5A:19(f) has been complied with, and (2) whether counsel desires to waive oral argument. The certificate must also state the number of words (headings, footnotes, and quotations count towards the word limitation; the cover page, table of contents, table of authorities, and certificate do not count towards the word count). Additionally, any party may waive oral argument without leave of this Court by written notification to the clerk of this Court within 21 days after the date on which the appellee's brief is due to be filed or has been filed.

[Amended effective October 1, 1997; August 15, 2005; July 1, 2010; July 1, 2015.]

RULE 5A:21. REQUIREMENTS FOR BRIEF OF APPELLEE OR GUARDIAN AD LITEM

The brief of appellee or the brief of the guardian ad litem shall contain:

(a) A table of contents and table of authorities with cases alphabetically arranged. Citations of all authorities shall include the year thereof.

(b) A statement of the case if the appellee disagrees with the statement presented by the appellant and a statement of any additional assignments of error the appellee wishes to present with a clear and exact reference to the page(s) of the transcript, written statement, record, or appendix where each additional assignment of error was preserved in the trial court.

(c) A statement of the facts necessary to correct or amplify the statement in the brief of appellant with appropriate references to the pages of the transcript, written statement, record, or appendix. The testimony of individual witnesses should not be summarized seriatim unless the facts are in dispute and such a summary is necessary to support the appellee's version of the facts.

(d) The standard of review and the argument (including principles of law and authorities) relating to each assignment of error. For any additional assignment of error by appellee which was not preserved in the trial court, counsel shall state why the good cause and/or ends of justice exceptions to Rule 5A:18 are applicable. With respect to each assignment of error, the standard of review and the argument—including principles of law and the authorities—shall be stated in one place and not scattered through the brief. At the option of counsel, the argument may be preceded by a short summary.

(e) A statement of the precise relief sought, if any.

(f) The signature (which need not be in handwriting) of at least one counsel and counsel's Virginia State Bar number, address, telephone number, facsimile number (if any), and email address.

(g) A certificate (which need not be signed in handwriting) stating (1) that Rule 5A:19(f) has been complied with, and (2) whether counsel desires to waive oral argument. The certificate must also state the number of words (headings, footnotes, and quotations count towards the word limitation; the cover page, table of contents, table of authorities, and certificate do not count towards the word count). Additionally, any party may waive oral argument without leave of this Court by written notification to the clerk of this Court within 21 days after the date on which the appellee's brief is due to be filed or has been filed.

[Amended effective October 1, 1997; September 1, 2004; August 15, 2005; July 1, 2010; July 1, 2015.]

RULE 5A:22. REQUIREMENTS FOR REPLY BRIEF

The reply brief, if any, shall contain argument in reply to contentions made in the brief of appellee. No reply brief is necessary if the contentions have been adequately answered in the opening brief of appellant. The reply brief shall contain a certificate (which need not be signed in handwriting) that Rule 5A:19(f) has been complied with. The certificate must also state the number of words (headings, footnotes, and quotations count towards the word limitation; the cover page, table of contents, table of authorities, and certificate do not count towards the word count).

[Amended effective July 1, 2010.]

RULE 5A:23. BRIEFS AMICUS CURIAE

(a) A brief amicus curiae may be filed at the petition, perfected appeal and rehearing stages of the appellate proceedings, and in proceedings invoking this Court's original jurisdiction:

(1) on behalf of the United States or the Commonwealth of Virginia without the prior consent of this Court or counsel; and

(2) by any other person if it is accompanied by the written consent of all counsel; and

(3) otherwise only on motion (which may be accompanied by the proposed brief) and the consent of this Court.

(b) A brief amicus curiae will be accepted only if filed on or before the date on which the brief of the party supported is required to be filed. A brief amicus curiae may be filed at the time of filing of the reply brief of the appellant only if an opening brief amicus curiae has been filed.

(c) A brief amicus curiae shall comply with the rules applicable to the brief of the party supported.

(d) Notwithstanding the provisions of paragraphs (a) and (b) of this Rule, the Court of Appeals may request that a brief amicus curiae be filed at any time.

[Amended effective July 1, 2010; July 1, 2015.]

RULE 5A:24. COVERS OF DOCUMENTS

(a) To facilitate identification, documents shall bear covers colored as follows:

Document	Color of Cover
Appendix	Red
Brief of the Appellant	White
Brief of the Appellee	Blue
Brief of Guardian Ad Litem (if separate from appellant and appellee)	Brown
Reply Brief of the Appellant	Green
Brief Amicus Curiae	Gray
Petition for Rehearing	Yellow
Petition for Rehearing En Banc	Yellow

(b) No appeal shall be dismissed for failure to comply with the provisions of this rule; however, the clerk of the Court of Appeals may require that a document be redone in compliance with this Rule.

[Amended effective January 1, 2001; September 1, 2004; July 1, 2010.]

RULE 5A:25. APPENDIX

(a) When Required. An appendix shall be filed by the appellant in all cases no later than the time of filing his opening brief.

(b) Filing. If the combined lengths of the appendix and the opening brief of the appellant do not exceed the limitation prescribed in Rule 5A:19, the appendix may be filed as an addendum to the opening brief and within the same cover. If the combined lengths of the appendix and the opening brief exceed the limitation prescribed in Rule 5A:19, the appellant shall file the appendix as a separate volume. The appellant must file four printed copies and an electronic version in Portable Document Format (PDF) of the appendix and must serve an electronic copy on counsel for each party separately represented at the time of filing the appendix with the Court. For purposes of this Rule, service by email shall be governed by Rule 1:17, which allows electronic transmission without the need of consent by opposing counsel. This Court may by order require the filing or service of a different number. The appendix shall be filed in the manner prescribed by the VACES Guidelines and User's Manual, using the Virginia Appellate Courts eBriefs System (VACES). The Guidelines are located on the Court's website at www.courts.state.va.us/online/vaces/resources/guidelines.pdf.

(c) Contents. An appendix shall include:

(1) the basic initial pleading (as finally amended);

(2) the judgment appealed from, and any memorandum or opinion relating thereto;

(3) any testimony and other incidents of the case germane to the assignments of error;

(4) the title (but not the caption) of each paper contained in the appendix, and its filing date;

(5) the names of witnesses printed at the beginning of excerpts from their testimony and at the top of each page thereof; and

(6) exhibits necessary for an understanding of the case that can reasonably be reproduced.

(d) Determination of Contents. Within ten days after the filing of the record with the Court of Appeals or, in a case in which a petition for appeal has been granted, within ten days after the date of the certificate of appeal issued by the clerk of the Court of Appeals, counsel for appellant shall file in the office of the clerk of the Court of Appeals a written statement signed by all counsel setting forth an agreed designation of the parts of the record to be included in the appendix. In the absence of such an agreement, counsel for appellant shall file with the clerk of the Court of Appeals a statement of the assignments of error and a designation of the contents to be included in the appendix within fifteen days after the filing of the record or, in a case in which a petition for appeal has been granted, within fifteen days after the date of the certificate of appeal; not more than ten days after this designation is filed, counsel for appellee shall file with the clerk of the Court of Appeals a designation of any additional contents to be included in the appendix. The appellant shall include in the appendix the parts thus designated, together with any additional parts he considers germane.

(e) Table of Contents; Form of Presentation. At the beginning of the appendix there shall be a table of contents, which shall include the name of each witness whose testimony is included in the appendix and the page number of the appendix at which each portion of the testimony of the witness begins. Thereafter, the parts of the record to be reproduced shall be set out in chronological order. When matter contained in the transcript of proceedings is set out in the appendix, the page of the transcript or of the record at which such matter may be found shall be indicated in brackets immediately before the matter which is set out. Omissions in the text of papers or of the transcript must be indicated by asterisks. Immaterial matters (such as captions, subscriptions and acknowledgements) shall be omitted. A question and its answer may be contained in a single paragraph.

(f) Costs. Unless counsel otherwise agree, the cost of producing the appendix shall initially be paid by the appellant, but if the appellant considers that parts of the record designated by the appellee for inclusion are unnecessary for the determination of the issue presented, he may so advise the appellee, and the appellee shall advance the cost of including such parts. The cost of producing the appendix shall be taxed as costs in the case.

(g) Penalty. Nothing shall be included in the appendix that is not germane to an assignment of error. As examples, no pleadings (other than the basic initial pleading as finally amended) shall be included unless an assignment of error is presented relating to it, and then only the portion thereof to which the assignment relates; and testimony relating solely to the amount of damages shall not be included unless error is assigned relating to the amount of damages. If parts of the record are included in the appendix unnecessarily at the direction of a party, this Court may impose the cost of producing such parts on that party.

(h) Assumptions. It will be assumed that the appendix contains everything germane to the assignments of error. The Court of Appeals may, however, consider other parts of the record.

(i) Sealed Materials in the Appendix. Appendices filed with this Court are a matter of public record. If counsel concludes it is necessary to include sealed material in the appendix, then, in order to maintain the confidentiality of the materials, counsel must designate the sealed material for inclusion in a sealed supplemental appendix to be filed separately from the regular appendix. A sealed volume of the appendix must be filed in the manner prescribed by the VACES Guidelines and User's Manual. The Guidelines are located on the Court's website at www.courts.state.va.us/online/vaces/resources/guidelines.pdf.

[Amended effective July 1, 1988; July 1, 2010; July 1, 2015.]

RULE 5A:26. EFFECT OF NONCOMPLIANCE WITH RULES REGARDING BRIEFS

If an appellant fails to file a brief in compliance with these Rules, the Court of Appeals may dismiss the appeal. If an appellee fails to file a brief in compliance with these Rules, the Court of Appeals may disregard any additional assignments of error raised by the appellee. If one party has complied with the Rules governing briefs, but the other has not, the party in default will not be heard orally if the case proceeds to oral argument, except for good cause shown.

[Amended effective July 1, 2010.]

RULE 5A:27. SUMMARY DISPOSITION

In cases in which appeal lies as a matter of right, if all the Judges of the panel of the Court of Appeals to which a pending appeal has been referred conclude from a review of the record and the briefs of the parties that the appeal is without merit, the panel shall forthwith affirm the judgment of the trial court or commission.

[Amended effective July 1, 2010.]

RULE 5A:28. ORAL ARGUMENT

(a) Notice. Whenever appeal lies as a matter of right or a petition for appeal has been granted, oral argument shall be permitted except in those cases disposed of pursuant to Rule 5A:27. The Clerk of the Court of Appeals, except in extraordinary circumstances, shall give at least 15 days notice to counsel of the date, approximate time, and location for oral argument.

(b) Length. Except as otherwise directed by the Court of Appeals, argument for a party shall not exceed 15 minutes in length. Such time may be apportioned among counsel for the same side at their discretion, except that only one counsel may present the opening argument for the appellant. If a guardian ad litem joins with either appellant or appellee, the guardian ad litem shall share the time for oral argument with the party. If a guardian ad litem requests additional time to argue, the guardian ad litem must state that application in its brief, subject to approval of this Court.

(c) Appearance Pro Hac Vice. Any lawyer not licensed in Virginia who seeks to appear pro hac vice to present oral argument to the Court of Appeals must comply with the requirements of Rule 1A:4.

(d) Amicus Curiae. No oral argument is permitted by amicus curiae except by leave of this Court. Leave may be granted upon the joint written request of amicus curiae and the party whose position amicus curiae supports. The request shall specify the amount of its allotted time the supported party is willing to yield to amicus curiae.

(e) Waiver. During oral argument, it shall not be necessary for any party to expressly reserve any argument made on brief, and the failure to raise any such argument shall not constitute a waiver. Any party may, without waiving the arguments made on brief, waive oral argument. See Rules 5A:20(h) and 5A:21(g).

[Amended effective October 1, 1997; September 1, 2004; February 1, 2007; July 1, 2010.]

G. Decision, Costs, and Mandate

RULE 5A:29. NOTICE OF DECISION

Promptly after the Court of Appeals has decided a case, the clerk of the Court of Appeals shall send a copy of the decision to all counsel of record and to the court or commission from which the appeal proceeded.

[Amended effective February 1, 1992; July 1, 2010.]

RULE 5A:30. COSTS AND NOTARIZED BILL OF COSTS

(a) To Whom Allowed. Except as otherwise provided by law, if an appeal is dismissed, costs shall be taxed against the appellant unless otherwise agreed by the parties or ordered by the Court of Appeals; if a judgment is affirmed, costs shall be taxed against the appellant unless otherwise ordered; if a judgment is reversed, costs shall be taxed against the appellee unless otherwise ordered; if a judgment is affirmed in part or reversed in part, or is vacated, costs shall be allowed as ordered by the Court of Appeals.

(b) Taxable Costs. Costs, including the filing fee and costs incurred in the printing or producing of necessary copies of briefs, appendices, and petitions for rehearing, shall be taxable in this Court. Costs incurred in the preparation of transcripts may be taxable in this Court. See, Code § 17.1–128.

(c) Notarized Bill of Costs. Counsel for a party who desires costs to be taxed shall itemize them in a notarized bill of costs, which shall be filed with the clerk of this Court within 14 days after the date of the decision in the case. Objections to the bill of costs must be filed with the clerk of this Court within 10 days after the date of filing the bill of costs.

(d) Award. The clerk of this Court shall prepare and certify an itemized statement of costs taxed in this Court for insertion in the mandate, but the issuance of the mandate shall not be delayed for taxation of costs. If the mandate has been issued before final determination of costs, the statement, or any amendment thereof, shall be added to the mandate on request by the clerk

of this Court to the clerk of the trial court or the clerk of the Virginia Workers' Compensation Commission.
[Amended effective February 1, 1992; July 1, 2010; January 1, 2013.]

RULE 5A:31. MANDATE

(a) Time. When there can be no further proceedings in the Court of Appeals or in the Supreme Court with respect to a decision of the Court of Appeals, the clerk of the Court of Appeals shall forward its mandate promptly to the clerk of the court or commission from which the appeal proceeded.

(b) Opinions. If the judgment or order is supported by an opinion, a certified copy of the opinion shall accompany the mandate.
[Amended effective February 1, 1992; July 1, 2010.]

H. Rehearing

RULE 5A:32. SCOPE

The provisions of Rules 5A:33 through 5A:35 do not apply to the denial of a petition for appeal.
[Amended effective July 1, 2010.]

RULE 5A:33. REHEARING—ON MOTION OF A PARTY AFTER FINAL DISPOSITION OF A CASE

(a) Requirements for Pro Se Prisoners and by Leave of Court. Pro se prisoners and those with leave of Court to proceed under this paragraph of the Rule desiring a rehearing of a decision or order of the Court of Appeals finally disposing of a case shall within 14 days following such decision or order, file seven copies of a petition for rehearing with the clerk of the Court of Appeals. The petition for rehearing shall not exceed 5,300 words in length. All petitioners other than pro se prisoners and those with leave of Court to proceed under this paragraph of the Rule must follow the provisions of paragraph (b) of this Rule when filing a petition for rehearing.

(b) Requirements for All Others. Any party, other than pro se prisoners or those with leave of Court to proceed under paragraph (a) of this Rule, desiring a rehearing of a decision or order of the Court of Appeals finally disposing of a case shall, within 14 days following such decision, file a petition for rehearing with the clerk of the Court of Appeals.

(1) The petition shall be filed as a single Adobe Acrobat Portable Document Format (PDF) document attached to an e-mail addressed to cavpfr@courts.state.va.us and will be timely filed if received by the clerk's office at or before 11:59 p.m. on the fourteenth day after the date of the decision or order sought to be reheard.

(2) The petition must be formatted to print on a page 8 1/2 × 11 inches, must be in 12–point font or larger, must be double-spaced, and must not exceed 5,300 words. The petition must include a certificate of service to opposing counsel and the certificate shall specify the manner of service and the date of service. If opposing counsel has an e-mail address, service on opposing counsel shall be by electronic means and such address shall be included in the certificate of service. The petition must also include a certificate of compliance with the word count limit. The petition will be considered filed on the date and time that it is received by cavpfr@courts.state.va.us. If the petition does not meet the requirements of this rule as to format, the clerk of the Court of Appeals shall so notify counsel and provide a specific amount of time for a corrected copy of the petition to be filed. A person who files a document electronically shall have the same responsibility as a person filing a document in paper form for ensuring that the document is properly filed, complete, and readable. However, if technical problems at the Court of Appeals result in a failure to timely receive the electronically filed petition for rehearing, counsel shall provide to the clerk of this Court on the next business day all documentation which exists demonstrating the attempt to file e-mail the petition by e-mail, any delivery failure notice received in response to the attempt, and a copy of the petition for rehearing.

(3) The e-mail message to which the petition is attached shall recite in the subject line the style of the case and the Court of Appeals record number. The body of the e-mail message shall contain a paragraph stating that a petition for rehearing is being filed, the style of the case, the Court of Appeals record number, the name and Virginia State Bar number of counsel filing the petition, as well as the law firm name, mailing address, telephone number, facsimile number (if any), and e-mail address (if any) of counsel filing the petition. The message shall also state whether a copy of the petition has been served by e-mail or another means on opposing counsel and the date of such service. If the petition has been served on opposing counsel by e-mail, the e-mail address for opposing counsel shall also be included. Upon receipt of the petition for rehearing in the e-mail box of the clerk's office, an acknowledgment will be forwarded by e-mail to counsel filing the petition for rehearing.

(c) Response. No response to a petition for rehearing will be received unless requested by the Court of Appeals.

(d) No Oral Argument. No oral argument on the petition will be permitted.

(e) Grounds. No petition for rehearing will be granted unless one of the Judges who decided the case adversely to the petitioner determines that there is good cause for such rehearing. The clerk of the Court of Appeals shall notify counsel for the appellant and counsel for the appellee of the action taken by the Court of Appeals on the petition for rehearing via e-mail, if e-mail addresses for both counsel have been provided, or via U.S. Mail to any counsel or party who has not provided an e-mail address.

[Amended effective January 1, 2005; January 1, 2006; July 1, 2010.]

RULE 5A:34. REHEARING EN BANC AFTER FINAL DISPOSITION OF CASE

(a) Who May File. Any party wishing to raise any issue decided by a panel of this Court must file a petition for rehearing en banc pursuant to this Rule.

(b) Requirements for Pro Se Prisoners and by Leave of Court. A pro se prisoner or a party who has leave of Court to proceed under this paragraph of the Rule aggrieved by a decision of a panel of this Court may file a petition for rehearing en banc within 14 days after the date of the order sought to be reheard. Twelve copies of any such petition shall be filed with the clerk of the Court of Appeals. The petition for rehearing en banc shall not exceed 5,300 words in length. All petitioners other than pro se prisoners and those with leave of this Court to proceed under this paragraph of the Rule must follow the provisions of paragraph (c) of this Rule when filing a petition for rehearing en banc.

(c) Requirements for All Others.

(1) Except for petitions for rehearing en banc filed by pro se prisoners or by those with leave of Court to proceed under paragraph (b) of this Rule, the petition shall be filed as a single Adobe Acrobat Portable Document Format (PDF) document attached to an e-mail addressed to cavpfr@courts.state. va.us and will be timely filed if received by the clerk's office at or before 11:59 p.m. on the fourteenth day after the date of the decision or order sought to be reheard.

(2) The petition must be formatted to print on a page 8 1/2 × 12 inches, must be in 12–point font or larger, must be double-spaced, and must not exceed 5,300 words. The petition must include a certificate of service to opposing counsel and the certificate shall specify the manner of service and the date of service. If opposing counsel has an e-mail address, service on opposing counsel shall be by electronic means and such address shall be included in the certificate of service. The petition must also include a certificate of compliance with the word count limit. The petition will be considered filed on the date and time that it is received by cavpfr@courts.state.va.us. If the petition does not meet the requirements of this rule as to format, the clerk of the Court of Appeals shall so notify counsel and provide a specific amount of time for a corrected copy of the petition to be filed. A person who files a document electronically shall have the same responsibility as a person filing a document in paper form for ensuring that the document is properly filed, complete, and readable. However, if technical problems at the Court of Appeals result in a failure to timely receive the electronically filed petition for rehearing, counsel shall provide to the clerk of this Court on the next business day all documentation which exists demonstrating the attempt to file the petition by e-mail, any delivery failure notice received in response to the attempt, and a copy of the petition for rehearing.

(3) The e-mail message to which the petition is attached shall recite in the subject line the style of the case and the Court of Appeals record number. The body of the e-mail message shall contain a paragraph stating that a petition for rehearing en banc is being filed, the style of the case, the Court of Appeals record number, the name and Virginia State Bar number of counsel filing the petition, as well as the law firm name, mailing address, telephone number, facsimile number (if any), and e-mail address (if any) of counsel filing the petition. The message shall also state whether a copy of the petition has been served by e-mail or another means on opposing counsel and the date of such service. If the petition has been served on opposing counsel by e-mail, the e-mail address for opposing counsel shall also be included. Upon receipt of the petition for rehearing in the e-mail box of the clerk's office, an acknowledgment will be forwarded by e-mail to counsel filing the petition.

(d) Proceedings After Petition for Rehearing. No answer to a petition for a rehearing en banc will be received unless requested by the Court of Appeals. A rehearing en banc on motion of the Court of Appeals shall be ordered no later than 20 days after the date of rendition of the order to be reheard. The clerk of the Court of Appeals shall promptly notify counsel for both parties of the action taken by this Court on the petition for rehearing en banc via e-mail, if e-mail addresses for both counsel have been provided, or via U.S. Mail to any counsel or party who has not provided an e-mail address.

[Amended effective January 1, 2001; January 1, 2005; January 1, 2006; July 1, 2010.]

RULE 5A:35. PROCEDURE FOR REHEARING

(a) Rehearing by a Panel. When rehearing by a panel is granted on petition of a party, the clerk of the Court of Appeals shall notify all counsel promptly. No brief in addition to the petition may be filed by petitioner. Respondent may file in the office of the clerk seven copies of an answering brief, which shall not exceed 5,300 words in length, within 21 days following the date of the order of this Court granting a rehearing. Three copies of the respondent's answering brief shall be mailed or delivered to opposing counsel on or before the date the answering brief is filed. Respondent may be heard orally whether or not an answering brief is filed. The case will be placed on the docket for oral argument. When practicable, such a rehearing will be heard by the same panel that rendered the final decision in the case.

(b) Rehearing En Banc. When all or part of a petition for rehearing en banc is granted, the clerk of this Court shall notify all counsel promptly. The mandate entered is stayed as to all issues decided by the panel pending the decision of the Court en banc. The appeal is reinstated on the docket of the Court for oral argument only as to issues granted. Briefing and oral argument shall proceed in the same order as before the three judge panel. The Court of Appeals may require any party to whom rehearing en banc has been granted to file 20 copies of an appendix, prepared in conformity with the provisions of Rule 5A:25, with the clerk of the Court within such time as the Court of Appeals shall specify.

(1) *Issues Considered Upon Rehearing En Banc.* Only issues raised in the petition for rehearing en banc and granted for rehearing or included in the grant by the Court on its own motion are available for briefing, argument, and review by the en banc Court. The Court may grant a petition in whole or in part. Any issue decided by a panel of this Court not subject to a petition for rehearing en banc remains undisturbed by an en banc decision.

(2) *Appellant's Opening Brief Upon Rehearing En Banc.* The party who was the appellant before the panel of this Court shall file in the office of the clerk 20 copies of a brief, which shall not exceed 12,300 words in length. Such brief shall be filed within 21 days following the date of the order of this Court granting rehearing en banc, and shall be accompanied by a certificate that three copies were mailed or delivered to opposing counsel on or before the date of filing. The brief shall bear a white cover.

(3) *Appellee's Answering Brief Upon Rehearing En Banc.* The party who was the appellee before the panel of this Court may file in the office of the clerk 20 copies of an answering brief not to exceed 12,300 words in length, within 14 days after the opening brief has been filed. Three copies of appellee's answering brief shall be mailed or delivered to opposing counsel on or before the date the answering brief is filed. The brief shall bear a blue cover. Appellee may be heard orally whether or not the answering brief is filed.

(4) *Appellant's Reply Brief Upon Rehearing En Banc.* The party who was the appellant before the panel may file in the office of the clerk a reply brief, not to exceed 3,500 words, within 14 days after the answering brief has been filed. Twenty copies of the reply brief shall be filed. Three copies of such brief shall be mailed or delivered to opposing counsel on or before the date the answering brief is filed. The brief shall bear a green cover.

[Amended effective January 1, 2001; July 1, 2010; May 2, 2011.]

I. Settlement, Withdrawal, and Mediation

RULE 5A:36. SETTLEMENT OR WITHDRAWAL OF PENDING APPEAL

When a case has been settled or the appeal withdrawn at any time after the notice of appeal has been filed, it shall be the duty of counsel to notify the clerk of the Court of Appeals by filing a written notice that the case has been settled or the appeal withdrawn. If counsel certifies that the terms of the settlement or withdrawal require further proceedings in the trial court, a single Judge of the Court of Appeals may approve entry of an order of remand.

[Amended effective July 1, 2010.]

RULE 5A:37. APPELLATE SETTLEMENT CONFERENCE IN THE COURT OF APPEALS

(a) Settlement Conference. Upon motion or sua sponte, this Court may order counsel, and clients in appropriate cases, to participate in a settlement conference. An informal motion requesting a settlement conference may be filed at any time while the matter is on appeal and should state briefly why a settlement conference would be useful. The motion shall state whether all parties concur. If a party objects, that party shall file within 7 days a short response explaining the grounds for the objection. All motions and responses may be in letter format addressed to the clerk of this Court. If this Court orders a settlement conference, it will ordinarily be held by telephone conference call and, in the discretion of the settlement judge, may be held in person at a convenient location.

(b) Settlement Judge. A senior or retired appellate judge will conduct all settlement conferences at no cost to the litigants.

(c) Excluded Cases. No settlement conference shall be conducted in appeals of criminal judgments or orders terminating parental rights or in any other case arising under this Court's original jurisdiction.

(d) Conferences. Prior to participating in a settlement conference, all counsel shall consult with their respective clients about settlement options and ask for express authority to settle within any parameters acceptable to the client. The settlement judge may conduct more than one conference if, in his discretion, he deems it advisable. During a conference, the settlement judge may consult ex parte with counsel, or with counsel and that counsel's client, but shall not consult ex parte with any represented client without counsel's agreement.

(e) Conference Orders. A settlement conference, if ordered in a case, shall not automatically affect any time deadline otherwise applicable. The settlement judge, however, may direct the clerk of court to enter orders tolling any non-mandatory time deadline before or after the deadline has passed. If any party advises the settlement judge that all or part of an appeal has been settled, the settlement judge shall direct the parties to prepare and sign a settlement agreement setting forth all agreed-upon terms. Upon receiving a copy of the settlement agreement, the settlement judge shall thereafter direct the clerk of court to enter an order dismissing with prejudice all or part of the appeal subject to the agreement.

(f) Confidentiality. The provisions of the settlement agreement shall not be considered confidential except to the extent the agreement specifically requires it. No confidentiality provision, however, shall prejudice any party's ability to seek judicial enforcement of a settlement agreement. In any case in which a settlement conference does not result in a settlement agreement, no statement made during a settlement conference or in motions requesting a settlement conference or responses to such motions shall be disclosed by the settlement judge, the parties, or counsel to any (i) appellate judge who may be called upon to decide the merits of the appeal or any related appeal, or (ii) lower court judge who may be called upon to decide the merits of the case if remanded or the merits of any related case.

(g) Cross–Appeals and Related Appeals. Appeals and cross-appeals will ordinarily be addressed in a single settlement conference. At the discretion of the settlement judge, related appeals may be consolidated for settlement conference purposes.

[Added effective July 1, 2010.]

RULE 5A:38. PETITION FOR REVIEW PURSUANT TO CODE § 8.01–626; INJUNCTIONS

(a) Time for Filing. In every case in which the jurisdiction of this Court is invoked pursuant to Code § 8.01–626, a petition for review must be filed with the clerk of this Court within 15 days of an order of a circuit court that grants an injunction, refuses an injunction, or dissolves or refuses to enlarge an existing injunction.

(b) Copy to Opposing Counsel. At the time the petition for review is filed, a copy of the petition shall be served on counsel for the respondent. At the same time that the petition is served, a copy of the petition shall also be emailed to counsel for the respondent, unless said counsel does not have, or does not provide, an email address. With the agreement of the parties, the petition may be served on counsel for the respondent solely by email.

(c) Length and What the Petition for Review Must Contain.

(i) Except by permission of a Judge of this Court, a petition for review shall not exceed the longer of 15 pages or 2,625 words. The petition for review must otherwise comply with the requirements for a petition for appeal in Rule 5A:12(c).

(ii) The petition shall be accompanied by a copy of the pertinent portions of the record of the circuit court, including the relevant portions of any transcripts filed in the circuit court and the order(s) entered by the court respecting the injunction (hereafter "the record"). The copy of the record shall constitute part of the petition for the purpose of paragraph (b), but shall not count against the petition size limit.

(iii) The petition for review shall contain a certificate:

(1) providing the names of all petitioners and respondents; the name, Virginia State Bar number, mailing address, telephone number, facsimile number (if any), and e-mail address of counsel for each party; and the mailing address, telephone number, facsimile number (if any), and e-mail address of any party not represented by counsel;

(2) certifying that a copy of the petition has been served on all opposing counsel and all parties not represented by counsel, and specifying the date and manner of service.

(3) if a word count is used, certifying the number of words (headings, footnotes, and quotations count towards the word limitation; the cover page, table of contents, table of authorities, and certificate do not count towards the word count);

(4) certifying that the copy of the record being filed is an accurate copy of the record of the circuit court and contains everything therefrom necessary for a review of the petition.

(d) Number of Copies to File. Four copies of the petition, including the record of the circuit court, shall be filed. Only one copy of the record need be filed if, upon filing the petition, counsel for the petitioner also files an electronic copy of the said record as an Adobe Acrobat Portable Document Format (PDF) document on a CD–ROM.

(e) Filing Fee. The petition must be accompanied by a check or money order payable to the clerk of this Court for the amount required by statute. The clerk of this Court may file a petition for review that is not accompanied by such fee if the fee is received by the clerk within 5 days of the date the petition for review is filed. If the fee is not received within such time, the petition for review shall be dismissed.

(f) Scope and Review.

(i) a petition for review may be considered by this Court whether the circuit court's order, or that part of the order dealing with the injunction, is temporary or permanent. If review is sought from a final order that deals with injunctive relief and other issues, a petition for review must address only that part of the final order that actually addresses injunctive relief. All other issues shall be governed by the normal rules and timetables that apply to appeals. If both a petition for review under Code § 8.01–626 and an appeal under § 8.01–675.3 are filed to challenge the same final order, the clerk of this Court will assign separate record numbers to the two proceedings.

(ii) a petition for review may be considered by a single Judge of this Court, or by a three-judge panel.

(g) Responsive Pleading. A respondent may file a response to a petition for review within seven days of the date of service of same, unless the Court specifies a shorter time frame. For the purpose of this rule, a petition for review is considered served 3 days from the date on which it was mailed, or 1 day from the date on which the petition was faxed, emailed, or sent by commercial delivery service, to counsel for the respondent. Notwithstanding the foregoing, the Court may act on a petition for review without awaiting a response; however, absent exceptional circumstances, the Court shall not grant a petition for review without affording the respondent an opportunity to file a responsive pleading.

(h) Rehearing and Further Review. The provisions of Rules 5A:15, 5A:15A, and 5A:33 through 5A:35 do not apply to proceedings under Code § 8.01–626.
[Adopted effective July 1, 2015.]

APPENDIX OF FORMS

FORM 1. BOND FOR COSTS ALONE—APPEAL OF RIGHT FROM CIRCUIT COURT TO COURT OF APPEALS (INCLUDING FURTHER APPEAL TO THE SUPREME COURT)

KNOW ALL MEN BY THESE PRESENTS, That we,

______________________________ principal, and

______________________________ surety, are held

and firmly bound unto ______________________________
appellee(s)

in the sum of ______________________________
to the payment of which we bind ourselves, our heirs, successors, personal representatives and assigns, jointly and severally, firmly by these presents.

The condition of this obligation is such that:

Whereas judgment was rendered by the Circuit Court of ______________

on the ______________ day of ______________________________,

in the case of ______________________________

______________________________;

And whereas it is the intention of ______________________________

__________ to appeal said judgment to the Court of Appeals of Virginia;

Now, therefore, if ______________________________
appellant(s)
shall pay all damages, costs, and fees which may be awarded against (him) (her) (them) (it) in the Court of Appeals and Supreme Court if it takes cognizance of the claim, then this obligation shall be void, otherwise to remain in full force and virtue.

FORM 2. BOND FOR COSTS AND SUSPENSION—APPEAL FROM CIRCUIT COURT TO APPELLATE COURT

KNOW ALL MEN BY THESE PRESENTS, That we,

____ principal, and

____ surety, are held

and firmly bound unto __________________________________
appellee(s)

in the sum of ______________________________________

to the payment of which we bind ourselves, our heirs, successors, personal representatives and assigns, jointly and severally, firmly by these presents.

The condition of this obligation is such that:

Whereas judgment was rendered by the Circuit Court of ________________

on the ____________ day of __________________________,

in the case of ______________________________________

____;

And whereas it is the intention of ____________________________

to appeal said judgment to the (Supreme Court) (Court of Appeals) of Virginia,

and suspension of execution of the judgment is sought;

Now, therefore, if __________________________________
appellant(s)

shall perform and satisfy and said judgment or the part thereof proceedings on which are stayed, in case such judgment or such part be affirmed in whole or in part, or the appeal be dismissed, refused or not timely prosecuted, and shall pay all damages, costs, and fees which may be awarded against (him) (her) (them) (it) in the (Supreme Court) (Court of Appeals and Supreme Court if it takes cognizance of the claim) and all actual damages incurred in consequence of the suspension, then this obligation shall be void, otherwise to remain in full force and virtue.

FORM 3. BOND FOR COSTS ALONE REQUIRED BY APPELLATE COURT ON APPEAL FROM CIRCUIT COURT

KNOW ALL MEN BY THESE PRESENTS, That we,

______________________________ principal, and

______________________________ surety, are held

and firmly bound unto ______________________________
appellee(s)

in the sum of ______________________________

to the payment of which we bind ourselves, our heirs, successors, personal representatives and assigns, jointly and severally, firmly by these presents.

The condition of this obligation is such that:

Whereas the (Supreme Court of Virginia) (Court of Appeals of Virginia) on the

__________ day of ______________, ______, awarded an

appeal from a judgment rendered against ______________________ by
appellant(s)

the Circuit Court of ______________________, on the __________

day of ______________, ______, upon ______________________

______________________ or some one for (him) (her) (them) (it),
appellant(s)

filing an appeal bond with sufficient security in the clerk's office of the

Circuit Court of, ______________________________

in the penalty of ______________________________ within

fifteen (15) days of the date of the certificate of appeal, with condition as the law directs;

Now, therefore, if ______________________________
appellant(s)
shall pay all damages, costs, and fees which may be awarded against (him) (her) (them) (it) in the (Supreme Court) (Court of Appeals and Supreme Court if it takes cognizance of the claim), then this obligation shall be void, otherwise to remain in full force and virtue.

FORM 4. BOND FOR SUSPENSION ALONE REQUIRED BY APPELLATE COURT ON APPEAL FROM CIRCUIT COURT

KNOW ALL MEN BY THESE PRESENTS, That we,

______________________________ principal, and

______________________________ surety, are held

and firmly bound unto ______________________________
appellee(s)

in the sum of ______________________________

to the payment of which we bind ourselves, our heirs, successors, personal representatives and assigns, jointly and severally, firmly by these presents.

The condition of this obligation is such that:

Whereas the (Supreme Court of Virginia) (Court of Appeals of Virginia) on the

__________ day of __________, ______, suspended execution of a

judgment rendered against ______________________________ by the Circuit
appellant(s)

Court of __________, on the ______ day of ______, ______, upon __________

______________________________ or some one for
appellant(s)

for (him) (her) (them) (it), filing an appeal bond with sufficient security in the clerk's office of the Circuit Court of __________, in the penalty of __________ within fifteen (15) days of the date of the certificate of appeal, with condition as the law directs;

Now, therefore, if ______________________________
appellant(s)

shall perform and satisfy said judgment or the part thereof proceedings on which are stayed, in case such judgment or such part be affirmed in whole or in part, and shall pay all actual damages incurred in consequence of the suspension, then this obligation shall be void, otherwise to remain in full force and virtue.

FORM 5. BOND FOR COSTS AND SUSPENSION REQUIRED BY APPELLATE COURT ON APPEAL FROM CIRCUIT COURT

KNOW ALL MEN BY THESE PRESENTS, That we,

____ principal, and

____ surety, are held

and firmly bound unto ____
appellee(s)

in the sum of ____

to the payment of which we bind ourselves, our heirs, successors, personal representatives and assigns, jointly and severally, firmly by these presents.

The condition of this obligation is such that:

Whereas the (Supreme Court of Virginia) (Court of Appeals of Virginia) on the ________ day of ____________, ______, awarded an appeal and (suspension of judgment) (supersedeas) from a judgment rendered against

____ by the Circuit
appellant(s)

Court of ________, on the ______ day of ______, ______, upon ________

____ or some one for
appellant(s)

(him)(her)(them)(it) filing an appeal bond with sufficient security in the clerk's office of the Circuit Court of ____________, in the penalty of ________ within fifteen (15) days of the date of the certificate of

appeal, with condition as the law directs;

Now, therefore, if ____
appellant(s)

shall perform and satisfy said judgment or the part thereof proceedings on which are stayed, in case such judgment or such part be affirmed in whole or in part, and shall pay all damages, costs, and fees which may be awarded against (him) (her) (them) (it) in the (Supreme Court) (Court of Appeals and Supreme Court if it takes cognizance of the claim) and all actual damages incurred in consequence of the suspension, then this obligation shall be void, otherwise to remain in full force and virtue.

FORM 6. ADDITIONAL BOND REQUIRED BY APPELLATE COURT ON APPEAL FROM CIRCUIT COURT

KNOW ALL MEN BY THESE PRESENTS, That we,

______________________________ principal, and

______________________________ surety, are held

and firmly bound unto ______________________________
appellee(s)

in the sum of ______________________________

to the payment of which we bind ourselves, our heirs, successors, personal representatives and assigns, jointly and severally, firmly by these presents.

The condition of this obligation is such that:

Whereas the (Supreme Court of Virginia) (Court of Appeals of Virginia) on the ________ day of ________________, ______, required additional bond on this appeal from a judgment rendered against ______________________ by the
appellant(s)

Circuit Court of ________, on the ________ day of ____________, ______, such additional bond to be filed in the clerk's office of the Circuit Court of

______________________________ in the penalty of __________

______________________________, and with the following additional requirements: ______________________________

within fifteen (15) days of the date of the order requiring additional bond, with condition as the law directs;

Now, therefore, if ______________________________
appellant(s)

shall perform and satisfy said judgment or the part thereof proceedings on which are stayed, in case such judgment or such part be affirmed in whole or in part, and shall pay all actual damages incurred in consequence of the suspension, then this obligation shall be void, otherwise to remain in full force and virtue.

A Copy,

Teste:

Clerk

FORM 7. BOND FOR COSTS ALONE—APPEAL OF RIGHT FROM VIRGINIA WORKERS' COMPENSATION COMMISSION TO COURT OF APPEALS (INCLUDING FURTHER APPEAL TO THE SUPREME COURT)

KNOW ALL MEN BY THESE PRESENTS, That we,

______________________________ principal, and

______________________________ surety, are held

and firmly bound unto ______________________________
appellee(s)

in the sum of ______________________________

to the payment of which we bind ourselves, our heirs, successors, personal representatives and assigns, jointly and severally, firmly by these presents.

The condition of this obligation is such that:

Whereas an award was entered by the Virginia Workers' Compensation Commission on the ________ day of ______________, ______, in the case of ______________________________;

And whereas it is the intention of ______________________________ ________ to appeal said award to the Court of Appeals of Virginia;

Now, therefore, if ______________________________
appellant(s)
shall pay all damages, costs, and fees which may be awarded against (him) (her) (them) (it) in the Court of Appeals and Supreme Court if it takes cognizance of the claim, then this obligation shall be void, otherwise to remain in full force and virtue.

[Amended effective February 1, 1992.]

FORM 8. BOND FOR COSTS ALONE—REQUIRED BY SUPREME COURT ON APPEAL OF RIGHT FROM STATE CORPORATION COMMISSION

KNOW ALL MEN BY THESE PRESENTS, That we,

______________________________ principal, and

______________________________ surety, are held

and firmly bound unto ______________________________
appellee(s)

in the sum of ______________________________

to the payment of which we bind ourselves, our heirs, successors, personal representatives and assigns, jointly and severally, firmly by these presents.

The condition of this obligation is such that:

Whereas the Supreme Court of Virginia on the __________ day of __________, ____, awarded an appeal from a final order entered in Case No. __________ under the style of __________ by the State Corporation Commission of Virginia, on the __________ day of ______________________________, on the condition that

____
appellant(s)

or someone for (him) (her) (them) (it), file an appeal bond with sufficient security in the clerk's office of the State Corporation Commission, in the penalty of ______________________________

______________________________ within fifteen (15) days of the date of the certificate of appeal, with condition as the law directs;

Now, therefore, if ______________________________
appellant(s)
shall pay all damages, costs, and fees which may be awarded against (him) (her) (them) (it) in the Supreme Court, then this obligation shall be void, otherwise to remain in full force and virtue.

FORM 9. BOND FOR COSTS AND SUSPENSION—REQUIRED BY SUPREME COURT ON APPEAL OF RIGHT FROM STATE CORPORATION COMMISSION

KNOW ALL MEN BY THESE PRESENTS. That we,

______________________________ principal, and

______________________________ surety, are held

and firmly bound unto ______________________________
appellee(s)

in the sum of ______________________________

to the payment of which we bind ourselves, our heirs, successors, personal representatives and assigns, jointly and severally, firmly by these presents.

The condition of this obligation is such that:

Whereas the Supreme Court of Virginia on the ______________ day of

______________, ______, awarded an appeal and suspension from a final

order entered in Case No. ______________ under the style of

____

by the State Corporation Commission of Virginia, on the ______________

day of ______________________________, on the condition that

______________________________ or some one for (him) (her) (them) (it), file an
appellant(s)

appeal bond with sufficient security in the clerk's office of the State Corporation Commission, in the penalty of ______________________________

within fifteen (15) days of the date of the certificate of appeal, with condition as the law directs;

Now, therefore, if ______________________________
appellant(s)

shall perform and satisfy said order or the part thereof proceedings on which are stayed, in case such order or such part be affirmed in whole or in part, and shall pay all damages, costs, and fees which may be awarded against (him) (her) (them) (it) in the Supreme Court and all actual damages incurred in consequence of the suspension, then this obligation shall be void, otherwise to remain in full force and virtue.

FORM 10. FORM FOR EXECUTION AND ACKNOWLEDGMENT OF ALL BONDS

In witness whereof, the said ______________________________

______________________, principal, and ______________________

______________________________ surety, have hereunto set their

hands and seals, this ______ day of ____________________, ______.

______________________________ (SEAL)

______________________________ (SEAL)

State of Virginia
City/County of ______________________

The foregoing instrument was acknowledged before me this ______________

day of ______________, ______, by ______________________________

______________________________________.

____
Notary Public

My commission expires: ______________________________

FORM 11. IRREVOCABLE LETTERS OF CREDIT

(Name and Address of Bank)

__________, 20____

U.S. $__________

On all communications please refer to (No. of Letter of Credit)

(Name and address of appellee(s))

Dear __________:

We hereby establish our Irrevocable Letter of Credit No. __________ in your favor, for the account of (name and address of appellant(s)), and hereby undertake to honor your draft at sight on us, not exceeding in the aggregate U.S. $ (amount in words) . A draft drawn under this letter of credit must be marked "Drawn under (Name of Bank) Letter of Credit No. __________ dated __________, 20____." Funds under this letter of credit will be available to you in a single drawing by presentation of your sight draft drawn on us, accompanied by:

(For Costs Alone)

1. The original of this letter of credit.

2. Your verified statement that __________ (has)(have) failed to
appellant(s)
pay all damages, costs and fees assessed against (him)(her)(them)(it) in the Court of Appeals of Virginia in the case of __________

3. A certified copy of an order or itemized statement of costs from the Court of Appeals assessing such damages, costs and fees against __________.
appellant(s)

(For Suspension Alone)

1. The original of this letter of credit.

2. Your verified statement that ______________________ (has)(have) failed to
appellant(s)
perform and satisfy the judgment rendered against (him)(her)(them)(it) on

______________________ by the Circuit Court of ______________________ in

the case of ______________________, and (has)(have) failed to pay all actual damages incurred in consequence of the suspension of judgment.

3. A copy of the trial court judgment order, attested by its clerk.

4. A copy of an order of the Court of Appeals of Virginia, attested by its clerk, affirming said judgment or refusing, dismissing or allowing withdrawal of the appeal of said judgment, or certification by the clerk of the Court of Appeals that the appeal of said judgment was not prosecuted timely.

5. A copy of an order, if any, of the Court of Appeals or trial court, attested by the clerk, assessing actual damages in consequence of the suspension of judgment.

(For Costs and Suspension)

1. The original of this letter of credit.

2. Your verified statement that ______________________ (has)(have) failed to
appellant(s)
perform and satisfy the judgment rendered against (him)(her)(them)(it) on

______________________ by the Circuit Court of ______________________ in

the case of ______________________, and (has)(have) failed to pay all damages, costs and fees assessed against (him)(her)(them)(it) in the Court of Appeals of Virginia, and all actual damages incurred in consequence of the suspension of judgment.

3. A copy of the trial court judgment order, attested by its clerk.

4. A copy of an order of the Court of Appeals, attested by its clerk, affirming said judgment or refusing, dismissing or allowing withdrawal of the appeal of said judgment, or certification by the clerk of the Court of Appeals

that the appeal of said judgment was not prosecuted timely.

5. A copy of an order, if any, of the Court of Appeals, attested by its clerk, assessing damages, costs and fees against ______________.
appellant(s)

6. A copy of an order, if any, of the Court of Appeals or trial court, attested by the clerk, assessing actual damages in consequence of the suspension of judgment.

This letter of credit is valid until ____ p.m. local time ________, 20____. and a draft drawn hereunder, if accompanied by documents as specified above, will be honored if presented to (Presentation Address of Bank) on or before that date. However, this letter of credit automatically will be renewed for successive one (1) year periods from the initial expiration date or any renewal period expiration date hereunder, unless at least sixty (60) days prior to any such expiration date (Name of Bank) notifies you that it has elected not to renew this letter of credit for such additional one (1) year period. The notice required hereunder will be deemed to have been given when received by you.

In the event that (Name of Bank) elects not to renew this letter of credit as required above, the full amount of this letter of credit shall be payable to the Clerk of the Circuit Court of ____________ upon presentation of your verified statement that:

1. A final order of the Court of Appeals of Virginia has not been entered in

the case of ______________________________ (or, where there has been suspension of judgment, a final order has not been entered by the Court of Appeals or trial court assessing actual damages in consequence of the suspension).

2. Thirty (30) days have elapsed since notice of non-renewal was given and appellant(s) (has)(have) not filed acceptable substitute security.

In the event of non-renewal, within fifteen (15) days after payment to the clerk under the previous paragraph, the appellant(s) or someone for (him)(her)(them)(it) shall file with said clerk an appeal bond in substantial conformance with the appropriate form in the Appendix to Part Five A of the Rules of the Supreme Court of Virginia. The bond shall be in the penalty of the amount paid to said clerk under this letter of credit, and said funds shall be in lieu of surety.

Except as otherwise expressly stated herein, this letter of credit is subject to the Uniform Customs and Practice for Documentary Credits as most recently

published by the International Chamber of Commerce.

Very truly yours,

______________________ Bank

By ______________________
Authorized Signature

[Adopted effective July 1, 1991.]

FORM 12. PETITION FOR A WRIT OF ACTUAL INNOCENCE BASED ON NONBIOLOGICAL EVIDENCE

PETITION FOR A WRIT OF ACTUAL INNOCENCE BASED ON NONBIOLOGICAL EVIDENCE

THE COURT OF APPEALS OF VIRGINIA

______________________ Record No. ______________________

(FULL NAME OF PETITIONER AND PRISONER NO., IF APPLICABLE) (TO BE SUPPLIED BY THE CLERK OF THE COURT OF APPEALS)

v.

Commonwealth of Virginia
(RESPONDENT)

____

(PETITIONER'S ADDRESS)

____

____

Pursuant to the provisions of Chapter 19.3 of Title 19.2 of the Code of Virginia, I, ______________________________
NAME OF PETITIONER
hereby petition this Court for a WRIT OF ACTUAL INNOCENCE BASED ON NONBIOLOGICAL EVIDENCE. In support of this petition, I state under oath that the following information is true:

1. On ______________________, I was convicted or adjudicated delinquent in the
DATE
______________________ Circuit Court of the following offense(s):
JURISDICTION (CITY/COUNTY)

Description of Felony Offense	Virginia Code	Circuit Court Case No.	Plea

2. I am innocent of the offenses(s) that are the subject of this petition.

3. I understand that I can file only one petition for any felony (a) conviction or (b) adjudication of delinquency and I have not previously filed a Petition For A Writ Of Actual Innocence Based On Nonbiological Evidence with regard to the above conviction(s) or adjudication(s) of delinquency in the Court of Appeals of Virginia.

4. My claim of innocence is based upon the following evidence:

____

____

[ ] ATTACHED ADDITIONAL SHEET(S)

5. This evidence was previously unknown or unavailable to either me or my attorney at the time the conviction(s) or adjudication(s) of delinquency became final in the circuit court.

6. This evidence became known or available to me on ______________.
DATE

7. The circumstances under which the evidence was discovered were

____

____

[ ] ATTACHED ADDITIONAL SHEET(S)

8. This evidence could not have been discovered or obtained by the exercise of diligence before the expiration of 21 days following entry of the final order(s) of conviction or adjudication of delinquency by the court.

9. The evidence upon which I base my claim is material and when considered with all of the other evidence in the record, will prove that no rational trier of fact would have found me to be guilty or delinquent beyond a reasonable doubt of the charge(s) described above because

____

____

[ ] ATTACHED ADDITIONAL SHEET(S)

10. In support of this petition, I have attached the following documents:

____

____

[ ] ATTACHED ADDITIONAL SHEET(S)

11. I understand that this petition must contain all relevant allegations of facts that are known to me at this time.

12. I understand that it must include all previous records, applications, petitions, and appeals and their dispositions related to this/these conviction(s) or adjudication(s) of delinquency, as well as a copy of any documents or evidence in support of the facts that I assert above.

13. I understand that if this petition is not complete, this Court may dismiss the petition or return the petition to me pending the completion of such form.

14. I understand that I am responsible for all statements contained in this petition.

15. I understand that any knowingly or willfully made false statement shall be a ground for prosecution and conviction of perjury as provided for in Virginia Code § 18.2-434.

16. Counsel. Check the appropriate box.

[ ] I am being represented by an attorney on the filing of this petition. My attorney's name and address are

____

____

____

____

[ ] I am not being represented by an attorney on the filing of this petition.

17. Exemption from filing fee. Check box below if claiming in forma pauperis status and seeking to file this petition without payment of fees.

[ ] I claim *in forma pauperis* status and I request that this Court accept this petition without the payment of filing fees. I affirm under oath that I am eligible for *in forma pauperis* status. My assets amount to $__________ (which sum includes my institutional inmate account which has a balance of $__________), and my liabilities amount to $__________.

18. Request for counsel. Check box below if claiming eligibility for court-appointed counsel and requesting appointment of counsel.

[ ] I am requesting that the Court appoint counsel to represent me in this action. I affirm under oath that I am unable to pay for an attorney to represent me in this action, as set forth in item No. 17 above.

Based on the above, I petition this Court pursuant to the provisions of Chapter 19.3 of Title 19.2 of the Code of Virginia for a Writ of Actual Innocence Based on Nonbiological Evidence.

______________________________ ______________________________

DATE SIGNATURE OF PETITIONER

Commonwealth/State of ______________________

[ ] City [ ] County of ______________________

Subscribed and sworn to/affirmed before me on this date by the above-named person.

______________________ ______________________
DATE NOTARY PUBLIC

My commission expires: ______________

______________________ ______________________
DATE SIGNATURE OF ATTORNEY (IF APPLICABLE)

____
VIRGINIA STATE BAR NUMBER

Pro se (self-represented) petitioners: You are required to send copies of the PETITION FOR A WRIT OF ACTUAL INNOCENCE BASED ON NONBIOLOGICAL EVIDENCE and all attachments to the Commonwealth's Attorney of the jurisdiction where the conviction(s) or adjudication(s) of delinquency occurred and to the Attorney General of Virginia by certified mail. You must complete the form entitled Court of Appeals Form CAV-104, CERTIFICATE OF MAILING - PETITION FOR A WRIT OF ACTUAL INNOCENCE BASED ON NONBIOLOGICAL EVIDENCE.

Petitioners represented by counsel: You are required to serve copies of the PETITION FOR A WRIT OF ACTUAL INNOCENCE BASED ON NONBIOLOGICAL EVIDENCE and all attachments on the Commonwealth's Attorney of the jurisdiction where the conviction(s) or adjudication(s) of delinquency occurred and on the Attorney General of Virginia. You must include the forms entitled Court of Appeals Form CAV-103CA, ACCEPTANCE OF SERVICE OR RETURN OF SERVICE BY THE COMMONWEALTH'S ATTORNEY - PETITION FOR A WRIT OF ACTUAL INNOCENCE BASED ON NONBIOLOGICAL EVIDENCE Court of Appeals Form CAV-103AG, ACCEPTANCE OF SERVICE OR RETURN OF SERVICE BY THE ATTORNEY GENERAL - PETITION FOR A WRIT OF ACTUAL INNOCENCE BASED ON NONBIOLOGICAL EVIDENCE.

[Adopted effective August 15, 2005. Amended effective July 1, 2013.]

PART SIX. INTEGRATION OF THE STATE BAR

Including Amendments Received Through October 15, 2015

SECTION I. UNAUTHORIZED PRACTICE RULES AND CONSIDERATIONS

INTRODUCTION

The right of individuals to represent themselves is an inalienable right common to all natural persons. But no one has the right to represent another; it is a privilege to be granted and regulated by law for the protection of the public.

The Supreme Court of Virginia has the inherent power to make rules governing the practice of law in the Commonwealth of Virginia. The Court has promulgated the definition of the practice of law. See "PRACTICE OF LAW IN THE COMMONWEALTH OF VIRGINIA," infra.

The public is best served in legal matters by lawyers. A client is entitled to be served disinterestedly by a lawyer who is not motivated or influenced by any allegiance other than to the client and our system of justice.

The services of a lawyer are essential and in the public interest whenever the exercise of professional legal judgment is required. The essence of such judgment is the lawyer's educated ability to relate the general body and philosophy of law to a specific legal problem. The public is better served by those who have met rigorous educational requirements, have been certified of honest demeanor and good moral character, and are subject to high ethical standards and strict disciplinary rules in the conduct of their practice.

By statute, any person practicing law without being duly authorized or licensed is guilty of a misdemeanor. The Attorney General of Virginia may leave the prosecution to the local attorney for the Commonwealth, or he may in his discretion institute and conduct such proceedings.

The courts of the Commonwealth have the inherent power, apart from statute, to inquire into the conduct of any person to determine whether he is illegally engaged in the practice of law, and to enjoin such conduct. The State Corporation Commission of Virginia may order the dissolution of any corporation or revoke its certificate of authority to transact business in the Commonwealth upon a finding that any officer, member, agent or employee thereof has been engaged in the unauthorized practice of law.

Any fees charged by a person engaged in the unauthorized practice of law are not collectible in court.

Any lawyer who aids a non-lawyer in the unauthorized practice of law is subject to discipline and disbarment. A lawyer has an affirmative duty to report unprivileged knowledge of such misconduct by another lawyer to the appropriate District Committee, and to discontinue his representation of a client when he discovers that his employment furthers the unauthorized practice of law by the client. Advisory opinions on the unauthorized practice of law, therefore, are as much intended to assist lawyers in fulfilling their ethical responsibilities as to inform and deter those who are engaged, or would engage, in such practice in derogation of the public's interest in a trained and regulated legal profession.

With the increase in the complexity of our society and its laws, the independence and integrity of a strong legal profession, devoted disinterestedly to those requiring legal services, are crucial to a free and democratic society. Allegiance to this principle, rather than the preservation of economic benefits for lawyers, is the basis upon which the Virginia State Bar, as the administrative agency of the Supreme Court of Virginia, carries forward the responsibility for the discipline of lawyers and the investigation of persons practicing law in the Commonwealth without proper authority.

PRACTICE OF LAW IN THE COMMONWEALTH OF VIRGINIA

(A) No non-lawyer shall engage in the practice of law in the Commonwealth of Virginia or in any manner hold himself out as authorized or qualified to practice law in the Commonwealth of Virginia except as may be authorized by rule or statute.

(B) Definition of the Practice of Law. The principles underlying a definition of the practice of law have been developed through the years in social needs and have received recognition by the courts. It has been found necessary to protect the relation of attorney and client against abuses. Therefore, it is from the relation of attorney and client that any practice of law must be derived.

The relation of attorney and client is direct and personal, and a person, natural or artificial, who undertakes the duties and responsibilities of an attorney is nonetheless practicing law though such person may employ others to whom may be committed the actual performance of such duties.

The gravity of the consequences to society resulting from abuses of this relation demands that those assuming to advise or to represent others shall be properly trained and educated, and be subject to a peculiar discipline. That fact, and the necessity for protection of society in its affairs and in the ordered proceedings of its tribunals, have developed the principles which serve to define the practice of law.

Generally, the relation of attorney and client exists, and one is deemed to be practicing law whenever he furnishes to another advice or service under circumstances which imply his possession and use of legal knowledge or skill.

Specifically, the relation of attorney and client exists, and one is deemed to be practicing law whenever—

(1) One undertakes for compensation, direct or indirect, to advise another, not his regular employer, in any matter involving the application of legal principles to facts or purposes or desires.

(2) One, other than as a regular employee acting for his employer, undertakes, with or without compensation, to prepare for another legal instruments of any character, other than notices or contracts incident to the regular course of conducting a licensed business.

(3) One undertakes, with or without compensation, to represent the interest of another before any tribunal—judicial, administrative, or executive—otherwise than in the presentation of facts, figures, or factual conclusions, as distinguished from legal conclusions, by an employee regularly and bona fide employed on a salary basis, or by one specially employed as an expert in respect to such facts and figures when such representation by such employee or expert does not involve the examination of witnesses or preparation of pleadings.

(4) One holds himself or herself out to another as qualified or authorized to practice law in the Commonwealth of Virginia.

(C) Definition of "Non–Lawyer." The term "non-lawyer" means any person, firm, association or corporation not duly licensed or authorized to practice law in the Commonwealth of Virginia. However, any lawyer not licensed to practice law in Virginia, but licensed in any other state or territory of the United States or the District of Columbia, or a foreign nation, who provides legal advice or services to clients in Virginia, shall not be subject to these Unauthorized Practice rules but shall be subject to the laws, rules and regulations of the jurisdiction(s) in which he/she is licensed to practice, as well as otherwise applicable Virginia Law including the Virginia Rules of Professional Conduct.

(D) The Unauthorized Practice rules which follow represent a nonexclusive list of specific types of practice which would violate these rules.

[Amended effective September 1, 1987; September 18, 1996; November 22, 1999; January 11, 2010.]

UNAUTHORIZED PRACTICE RULE 1. PRACTICE BEFORE TRIBUNALS

Note: The unauthorized practice considerations and rules stated herein are derived from Va. Rules of Court Part Six, § I; 171 Va. xvii (1938); 216 Va. 1062 (1976), and the principles referred to in the Introduction, supra; and such authorities are hereby incorporated by reference herein.

UPR 1–101. Representation Before Tribunals.

(A) A non-lawyer, with or without compensation, shall not represent the interest of another before a tribunal, otherwise than in the presentation of facts, figures or factual conclusions, as distinguished from legal conclusions, except:

(1) A non-lawyer under the supervision of a lawyer who is a regular employee of a legal aid society approved by the Virginia State Bar in accordance with its rules and regulations adopted under § 54–52.1 of the Code of Virginia may represent an indigent patron of such society before such a tribunal when authorized to do so by the governing body of such society and when such representation is permitted by the rules of practice of such tribunal. The supervising attorney shall assume personal professional responsibility for any work undertaken by the non-lawyer.

(2) A law student may appear and represent others before such a tribunal in accordance with the third-year student practice rule.

(B) A non-lawyer regularly employed on a salary basis by a corporation appearing on behalf of his employer before a tribunal shall not engage in activities involving the examination of witnesses, the preparation and filing of briefs or pleadings or the presenting of legal conclusions.

(C) A non-lawyer regularly employed by a corporation or partnership may appear and file certain pleadings on behalf of his or her employer as authorized by Virginia Code § 16.1–88.03.

UNAUTHORIZED PRACTICE CONSIDERATIONS

UPC 1–1. The term "tribunal" shall include, in addition to the courts and judicial officers of Virginia or of the United States of America, the State Corporation Commission of Virginia and its various divisions, the Virginia Workers' Compensation Commission, and the Alcoholic Beverage Control Board, or any agency, authority, board, or commission when it determines the rights and obligations of parties to proceedings before it, as opposed to promulgating rules and regulations of general applicability. Such term does not include a tribunal established by virtue of the Constitution or laws of the United States, to the extent that the regulation of practice before such tribunal has been preempted by federal law, nor does it include a tribunal established under the Constitution or laws of Virginia before which the practice or appearance by a non-lawyer on behalf of another is authorized by statute.

UPC 1–2. A non-lawyer may represent himself, but not the interest of another, before any tribunal. A non-lawyer regularly employed on a salary basis or one specially retained as an expert (whether as an independent contractor or an employee of another) may present facts, figures, or factual conclusions, as distinguished from legal conclusions, when such presentation does not involve the examination of witnesses or preparation of briefs or pleadings.

UPC 1–3. A corporation (other than a duly registered law corporation) does not have the same right of appearance before a tribunal as an individual and may not be represented before a tribunal by its officers, employees or agents who are not duly authorized or licensed to practice law in Virginia. A corporation can be represented only by a lawyer before a tribunal, with respect to matters involving legal conclusions, examination of witnesses or preparation of briefs or pleadings.

UPC 1–4. A lawyer who is duly authorized or licensed to practice law in Virginia and who is also regularly employed on a salary basis by a corporation may represent such corporation before a tribunal as lawyer for the corporation, with the same privileges of a lawyer in private practice (including confidential communications with his employer when he is acting as a lawyer in connection with such communication).

UPC 1–5. A lawyer who is duly authorized or licensed to practice law in Virginia and who is regularly employed on a salary basis by a corporation may also represent before a tribunal the interest of a subsidiary or affiliated corporation when requested to do so by his employer and when not otherwise in conflict with the Virginia Code of Professional Responsibility. Such lawyer (unless a regular employee of a duly registered law corporation) in the course of his employment may not normally represent before a tribunal customers or patrons of his employer.

[Amended effective February 1, 1992; amended effective September 29, 1999.]

UNAUTHORIZED PRACTICE RULE 2. LAY ADJUSTERS

Note: The unauthorized practice considerations and rules stated herein are derived from Va. Rules of Court Part Six, § I; 171 Va. xvii (1938); 216 Va. 1062 (1976), and the principles referred to in the Introduction, supra; and such authorities are hereby incorporated by reference herein.

UPR 2–101. Definitions.

(A) "Lay adjuster" refers to a non-lawyer retained by a principal as an employee, independent contractor, or employee of an independent contractor, for the purposes of

(1) investigating facts and circumstances related to a personal injury and/or property claim;

(2) reporting such facts to his principal; or

(3) assisting his principal in the handling, negotiation and settlement of such claim.

(B) "Principal" refers to:

(1) an insurance company as defined in Title 38.2 of the Code of Virginia;

(2) a self-insured; or

(3) any insured individual, business entity or governmental organization asserting a right to payment under an insurance policy or insurance contract issued to such individual, business entity or governmental organization arising out of the occurrence of the contingency or loss covered by such policy or contract.

(C) A business entity shall include but not be limited to a sole proprietorship, firm, partnership, corporation, joint venture, association or unincorporated association engaged in a commercial, charitable or professional activity.

(D) "Self-insured" refers to any person, business entity (as defined hereinabove) or governmental organization which is potentially liable for claims and which does not elect to insure against loss or, to the extent such organization retains by way of a percentage or deductible, a portion of its risk.

UPR 2–102. Investigation.

(A) A non-lawyer shall not for compensation, direct or indirect, advise another as to the law governing the facts as disclosed by his investigation, except:

(1) A lay adjuster may investigate the facts relative to a claim, and make a report thereon and an estimate of its monetary value to his principal.

(2) A lay adjuster may give his opinion to his principal as to liability with respect to a claim investigated by him.

UPR 2–103. Negotiation of a Settlement.

(A) A non-lawyer shall not for compensation, direct or indirect, negotiate or settle a claim on behalf of another party not represented by a lawyer except:

(1) A lay adjuster may secure and convey factual data and information, transmit settlement offers made by either party, determine and express his opinion on the extent of damage or injury and its monetary value, deliver releases or other documents, and assist the lawyer for his principal in the efficient performance of ministerial acts arising out of the settlement negotiations.

(2) A lay adjuster may, in the course of negotiating a settlement for his principal, make statements to the claimant or others as to his principal's liability or as to the law governing the facts to the extent consistent with the principles enunciated in the Rules Governing Unfair Claim Settlement Practices as from time to time promulgated by the State Corporation Commission of Virginia, § 38.2–510 of the Code of Virginia, provided that

(a) the lay adjuster has informed the claimant or other person that his principal may be adversarial to the claimant or other person;

(b) it is clear that the claimant or other person recognizes the lay adjuster as an adversary; and

(c) it is apparent that the claimant or other person is otherwise competent to manage his own affairs.

(B) A non-lawyer shall not for compensation, direct or indirect, conduct negotiations to settle a claim pending in court except with the approval of the lawyer for his principal.

UPR 2–104. Preparation of Documents.

(A) A non-lawyer shall not, with or without compensation, direct or indirect, prepare or deliver legal instruments of any character except a lay adjuster may prepare a form of release or other document prepared or approved by his principal as to which the lay adjuster may fill in blanks supplying factual data.

UPR 2–105. Third Party Claims.

(A) The activities authorized under UPR 2–102, 2–103 and 2–104 are permitted only on behalf of a principal

(1) which is making a claim against its own insurance carrier; or

(2) which is subject to a claim which may be paid by the principal or its insurance carrier; or

(3) which is pursuing its subrogation rights.

(B) Except as permitted in (A)(3) above, neither a non-lawyer nor a lay adjuster may engage in any of the activities described in UPR 2–102, 2–103 and 2–104, on behalf of any principal or other party which is making or may make a claim against a third party or against an insurance carrier or other potential guarantor or payor of third party liability to the principal or other party. Claims against an insured's insurance carrier for Uninsured Motorists or Under Insured Motorists coverage shall be deemed to be third party claims.

UNAUTHORIZED PRACTICE CONSIDERATIONS

UPC 2–1. For example, the activities of a lay adjuster in claims may consist of acting on behalf of his principal in identifying the facts and parties, securing witness statements, estimating the costs of repair, and compiling other information about the claim. Statements are given by the lay adjuster to his principal from whom he receives instructions as to the disposition of the claim. The lay adjuster then may attempt to settle the claim at the monetary value his principal is willing to pay or accept.

UPC 2–2. As a part of his factual analysis, a lay adjuster may express his opinion on the extent of damage or injury and the monetary value of any claim investigated by him.

UPC 2–3. A lay adjuster may, incident to his investigation of the facts, give to his principal his opinion of liability as disclosed by his investigation. Such lay adjuster is authorized to make a settlement on behalf of his principal and, in the course of such negotiations, make statements as to his principal's liability or as to the law governing the facts to the extent consistent with the Rules Governing Unfair Claim Settlement Practices, as applicable. A lay adjuster not now covered by such Rules may make statements as to his principal's legal liability, or as to the law governing the facts to the extent consistent with the principles enunciated in such Rules, and with the requirements of UPR 2–103(A)(2).

UPC 2–4. In a claim pending in court, a lay adjuster may properly secure factual data and transmit settlement offers made on behalf of his principal when acting with the consent of the lawyers for both plaintiff and defendant. With such consent, he may also assist in the settlement negotiations with the approval of the lawyer for his principal.

UPC 2–5. A lawyer who is regularly employed on a salary basis as a lay adjuster is deemed to be acting on behalf of his employer and is subject to the same limitations with respect to representing his employer's customers or patrons as are imposed on his employer hereunder.

UPC 2–6. If a lay adjuster in any case attempts to draft legally binding settlement papers, he is engaged in the unauthorized practice of law. A lay adjuster may draft a receipt or fill in blanks supplying factual data in a form of release or other document prepared or approved by his principal, but he may not otherwise undertake to draft particular provisions intended to have legally binding effect in a specific case.

[Amended effective April 1, 1991.]

UNAUTHORIZED PRACTICE RULE 3. COLLECTION AGENCIES

Note: The unauthorized practice considerations and rules stated herein are derived from Va. Rules of Court Part Six, § I; 171 Va. xvii (1938); 216 Va. 1062 (1976), and the principles referred to in the Introduction, supra; and such authorities are hereby incorporated by reference herein.

UPR 3–101. Attorney–Client Relationship.

(A) An agency shall not disrupt the relationship of confidence and trust which must exist between a lawyer and his client.

(B) An agency shall not prevent a lawyer from exercising independent professional judgment on behalf of his client by attempting to fix the lawyer's compensation, or sharing in a percentage of his compensation, or prescribing the terms of his employment, or attempting in any way to control or direct his actions.

(C) An agency shall not place itself between the lawyer and the creditor in an attempt to act as the only conduit of information between the two, since this would prevent the establishment of the fundamental relationship of trust and direct personal responsibility which ought to exist between a lawyer and his client.

UPR 3–102. Referral and Control of Claims.

(A) An agency may refer claims to a lawyer on behalf of the creditor subject to the following:

(1) The creditor shall first have the opportunity to select a lawyer of his own choosing.

(2) If the creditor does not so select a lawyer, the agency shall submit a list of lawyers from which the creditor may make his selection, which list may include the customary fee of each attorney. The creditor may subsequently authorize the agency to refer his account to the lawyer so selected by the creditor.

(3) The lawyer shall be free at all times to communicate directly with the creditor; and, upon receipt of the initial referral, as well as upon receipt of any subsequent referral unacceptable to the lawyer on the basis of the prior fee arrangement, the lawyer shall communicate with the creditor for the purpose of establishing the fee arrangement, in which arrangement the agency shall not participate.

(4) The agency may thereafter, if authorized by the creditor, continue correspondence of a routine nature with the lawyer on behalf of the creditor.

(B) An agency shall not exercise or attempt to exercise any control or imply that it has any right to control the actions of the lawyer in the handling of the creditor's claim. All decisions are to be those of the lawyer acting on behalf of his client, the creditor.

UPR 3–103. Preparation of Documents.

(A) An agency may prepare statements of accounts and affidavits of facts relating to accounts and may file the same with personal representatives and trustees in bankruptcy.

(B) An agency shall not prepare a proof of claim or file such a claim as agent for the creditor with the bankruptcy court except to the extent it is permitted to do so by the Bankruptcy Rules.

(C) An agency shall not prepare for others any document which requires legal training or the application of legal principles to factual situations except as authorized under these Rules.

(D) An agency shall not use any letters or forms which threaten the institution of legal proceedings or simulate judicial process or notice of judicial process.

UNAUTHORIZED PRACTICE CONSIDERATIONS

UPC 3–1. A collection agency (herein referred to as "an agency") is a business involved in the collection of past-due accounts for its customer (herein referred to as "the creditor"). The efforts of an agency to collect such a claim through correspondence or personal contacts, or both, are not the unauthorized practice of law. It is, however, improper for an agency to refer an account to a lawyer in a manner which disrupts the fundamental lawyer-client relationship.

UPC 3–2. It is critical to the lawyer-client relationship that the lawyer remain in a position that will enable him to exercise independent judgment on behalf of his client, the creditor. A lawyer should not accept a claim from an agency under circumstances or pursuant to an arrangement that would render his judgment susceptible to control by the agency.

UPC 3–3. A referral by an agency which permits the agency to fix the lawyer's compensation, or share in a percentage of his compensation, or prescribe the terms of his employment, or control and direct his actions, is improper. The lawyer, while handling such a claim, would not be governed by his independent judgment of what would best benefit his client, the creditor, but would be influenced, if not controlled, by the provisions of the agreement by which the referral was made. Since an agency itself cannot directly provide the creditor with legal advice, it cannot be permitted to provide such advice indirectly by influencing the actions of the lawyer.

UPC 3–4. With regard to referrals by an agency to a lawyer, any arrangement or understanding requiring that communications between the lawyer and the creditor be handled only through the agency is improper. Such an arrangement could disrupt the relationship of trust and direct personal responsibility which ought to exist between a lawyer and his client. With direct communications, the lawyer can better perceive and analyze the individual needs of his client, and the creditor's direct contact with his lawyer lessens the possibility of misunderstanding and affords him the opportunity to determine for himself the quality of service that he is receiving. Furthermore, if the agency is the sole conduit of information, the lawyer is unable to preserve the confidences and secrets of his client. There can be no effective representation of a client if the client is reluctant to provide his lawyer with a complete and accurate statement of the facts because of his concern that this information might be divulged to some third party without his permission. It is the responsibility of both the lawyer and the agency to abide by these considerations and to avoid arrangements contrary thereto.

UPC 3–5. The decision to bring suit on a claim involves the application of legal principles to a factual situation. An agency threatening the institution of legal proceedings is engaged in the unauthorized practice of law, but the mere statement that the claim is being or will be referred to a lawyer, without more, is not deemed to be threatening the institution of legal proceedings as long as the lawyer remains free to exercise his independent professional judgment on behalf of the creditor. Likewise, the use by an agency of letters or forms that simulate or are intended to simulate judicial process or notice of judicial process is improper.

UPC 3–6. Statements of account and affidavits of facts relating to accounts and other matters are not legal instruments, and the preparation of the same by an agency is not the unauthorized practice of law. Such preparation does not require legal training or the application of legal principles; nor is the mere filing of such accounts or affidavits with personal representatives, trustees in bankruptcy and the like representing the interest of another before a tribunal.

UPC 3–7. A non-lawyer may properly act as a trustee in bankruptcy but may not prepare pleadings in the bankruptcy court except as authorized by the Bankruptcy Rules.

UNAUTHORIZED PRACTICE RULE 4. ESTATE PLANNING AND SETTLEMENT

Note: The unauthorized practice considerations and rules stated herein are derived from Va. Rules of Court Part Six, § I; 171 Va. xvii (1938); 216 Va. 1062 (1976), and the principles referred to in the Introduction, supra; and such authorities are hereby incorporated by reference herein.

UPR 4–101. Estate Planning Advice.

(A) A non-lawyer shall not advise another for compensation, direct or indirect, in any matter involving the application of legal principles to particular facts or purposes or desires, except:

(1) A non-lawyer may collect information and analyze the facts and assets of a particular estate in relation to its economic or investment needs.

(2) A non-lawyer may, incident to the sale or transfer of a particular investment asset, give information about the laws affecting the holding or disposition of such asset, such as making projections of possible tax effects arising from a transfer of ownership of a life insurance policy, security or other investment.

(3) A non-lawyer may specifically recommend dispositive provisions for a will or trust.

UPR 4–102. Holding Out With Regard to Estate Planning.

(A) Except to the extent estate planning advice is permitted under UPR 4–101, a non-lawyer shall not hold himself out as authorized to furnish another advice or service under circumstances which imply his possession of legal knowledge or skill in the application of any law, federal, state or local, to a specific set of facts for a particular person.

(B) A non-lawyer shall not be excused from any violation of these Rules by any disclaimer or other statement that his unauthorized advice or conduct should be reviewed by his customer's own lawyer.

UPR 4–103. Preparation of Documents.

(A) A non-lawyer shall not, with or without compensation, prepare or draft, or cause his own lawyer to prepare or draft, for another, legal instruments of any character, including the filling out of a form for any will or trust, except:

(1) A non-lawyer may prepare forms of wills or trusts of general application.

(2) A non-lawyer, as an incident to the regular course of conducting his business, may submit to his customer's lawyer specimen language for inclusion in a legal instrument to be prepared by such lawyer, subject to acceptance, modification or rejection by such lawyer.

(3) A non-lawyer, as an incident to the regular course of conducting his business, may furnish his customer with routine forms or contracts of generally accepted application which do not go beyond the legitimate interest of the non-lawyer and do not involve a selection by the customer as between alternative with materially different legal results not generally understood in the community. For example, the offering by a savings institution of a joint account with right of survivorship, a simple revocable trust account or a custodial account under the Virginia Uniform Gifts to Minors Act would normally not constitute the unauthorized practice of law.

UPR 4–104. Settlement of Estates.

(A) A non-lawyer shall not give legal advice with respect to a person's domicile.

(B) A non-lawyer shall not prepare or draft instruments, or give legal advice, with respect to the disclaimer of all or part of a person's interest in property, or a person's right to renounce all or part of any interest due under the will of such person's spouse.

(C) A non-lawyer shall not undertake in the settlement of an estate or trust to represent the interest of another before any tribunal, judicial, administrative or executive, otherwise than in the presentation of facts, figures or factual conclusions, except:

(1) A non-lawyer may offer to the proper clerk of court a will for probate or qualify as a fiduciary in any uncontested proceeding.

(2) A non-lawyer may prepare and file accountings and confer with the Commissioner of Accounts in any uncontested proceeding.

(3) With respect to tax matters, as set forth in Unauthorized Practice Rule 5, infra.

UNAUTHORIZED PRACTICE CONSIDERATIONS

UPC 4–1. "Estate planning," as that term is generally used and understood today, refers to the orderly arrangement of an individual's assets so as to provide most effectively for his economic needs while living, and for the personal and economic needs of those he may wish to benefit after his death. Estate planning necessarily involves, among other things, a knowledge and application of principles of the law relating to wills and descents and distribution, trusts and future interests, real and personal property, gifts, and taxation. In addition, effective postmortem estate planning requires an intimate familiarity with probate procedure and practice.

UPC 4–2. The proper planning of an individual's estate is often aided by the services of non-lawyers skilled in insurance, investments, accounting services, and the like. An analysis of the facts and assets of an estate in relation to its economic or investment needs, and the giving of general information as to the laws affecting the disposition of estates without any specific application thereof to a particular situation, other than mathematical computations to support a hypothetical analysis, is not the unauthorized practice of law.

UPC 4–3. The holding out to the public, directly or indirectly, overtly or subtly, by any non-lawyer of his willingness to give advice as to the legal consequences of a particular plan which goes beyond matters incident to the sale or transfer of a particular investment asset, such as a life insurance policy or security, in the regular course of the non-lawyer's business, or his willingness to perform legal services in the field of estate planning, is a holding out to engage in the unauthorized practice of law. A non-lawyer cannot solicit such services and then hire a lawyer to perform them. A non-lawyer consultant or adviser cannot offer the legal services of his own lawyer. Such practices are not purged or purified by an acknowledgment that the consultant or adviser is not authorized to give legal advice, or by any disclaimer or suggestion that such advice should be reviewed by the customer's own lawyer.

UPC 4–4. Activities geared to motivating an individual to give consideration to his estate, and to seek the advice of a lawyer of his own choosing as early as possible, preferably from the outset, with regard to the development of an overall estate plan, are in the public interest. Advice on matters of law with respect to the particular factual situation of the individual concerned, however, is the unauthorized practice of law whenever it goes beyond advice on matters incident to the sale or transfer of a particular investment asset, such as a life insurance policy or security, in the regular course of the non-lawyer's business.

UPC 4–5. The preparation of legal instruments such as wills, codicils and trusts by a non-lawyer for another, with or without compensation, goes beyond the area of permitted advice incident to the regular course of a non-lawyer's business. There is nothing improper, however, in the submission of suggested forms for various types of wills or trusts to lawyers for present or prospective customers of a non-lawyer. Distributing forms of separate administrative or dispositive provisions setting forth the proper name of a fiduciary, a charity or the like is not improper.

UPC 4–6. Selecting or filling out a form of will or trust for another is an exercise in legal judgment. As an aid to a customer's lawyer, a non-lawyer may submit to such lawyer, and only to him, specimen language for technical provisions to be included in his client's will, codicil or trust; but such non-lawyer is not entitled to hold himself out as the responsible draftsman of such provisions.

UPC 4–7. Advice by a non-lawyer as to the use of his "standard form trust," "plain English trust," "mini-trust," or the like constitutes the unauthorized practice of law when the provisions of such instrument go beyond the legitimate interest of the non-lawyer therein, seek to do more than the normal agency or deposit contract, or affect the legal rights of persons not parties to the contract. For example, the furnishing by a non-lawyer to his customer of a power of attorney which extends the authority of the attorney-in-fact to deal on behalf of his principal with all his principal's assets or accounts, whether or not maintained by that particular non-lawyer, goes beyond the area of that non-lawyer's legitimate interest.

UPC 4–8. The settlement of a decedent's estate invariably poses problems of a legal nature. Such settlement may involve the practice of law in such areas, among others, as the offering of writings for probate, the qualification of fiduciaries, the preparation of accountings, and the determination of legal rights and liabilities with respect to the assets of the estate. In administering and settling the affairs of an estate, a fiduciary is not acting primarily for himself; and the drafting of instruments and appearance at probate hearings by a non-lawyer, as contrasted to the preparation and filing of a list of heirs, inventory or accountings, whether in person or through lawyers who are salaried employees, ordinarily constitutes the unauthorized practice of law.

UNAUTHORIZED PRACTICE RULE 5. TAX PRACTICE

Note: The unauthorized practice considerations and rules stated herein are derived from Va. Rules of Court Part Six, § I; 171 Va. xvii (1938); 216 Va. 1062 (1976), and the principles referred to in the Introduction, supra; and such authorities are hereby incorporated by reference herein.

UPR 5–101. Holding Out as a Tax Expert.

(A) A non-lawyer shall not hold himself out as authorized to furnish to another advice or service under circumstances which imply his possession of legal knowledge or skill in the application of any law, federal, state or local, dealing with taxes, except:

(1) A non-lawyer may hold himself out as an expert in the preparation of tax returns.

(2) A certified public accountant or a person duly enrolled may hold himself out as authorized to practice before the Internal Revenue Service, as those terms are defined by the then applicable federal regulations and to the extent permitted therein.

(3) A person admitted to practice before the United States Tax Court may hold himself out as such to the extent permitted by the rules of such Court.

(4) As permitted by UPR 5–102.

UPR 5–102. Practicing Law in Tax Matters.

(A) A non-lawyer shall not furnish to another for compensation, direct or indirect, advice or service under circumstances which require his use of legal knowledge or skill in the application of any law, federal, state or local, dealing with taxes, except:

(1) A non-lawyer may prepare tax returns.

(2) A certified public accountant or a person duly enrolled may practice before the Internal Revenue Service, as those terms are defined by the then applicable federal regulations and to the extent permitted therein.

(3) A non-lawyer may render such advice or service in connection with his representation of his employer or others before a tribunal, judicial, administrative, or executive, (i) in the presentation of facts, figures or factual conclusions, (ii) as authorized before the Internal Revenue Service, in (2) above, or (iii) as permitted by the rules of practice of the United States Tax Court.

(4) A non-lawyer may render such advice or service incident to an engagement to provide products or services which he is otherwise authorized to provide, where such advice or service arises out of the providing of such other products or services and was not the principal purpose of the engagement.

(5) A non-lawyer may render such advice or service to his regular employer other than in aid of such employer's unauthorized rendition of legal advice or services to another.

UNAUTHORIZED PRACTICE CONSIDERATIONS

UPC 5–1. Taxation affects almost every phase of modern life. The giving of tax advice necessarily involves many branches of law and requires a familiarity with many nontax legal principles on which the tax issues depend. In addition, the legal and accounting phases of tax practice are often so interrelated and overlapping that they are difficult to distinguish.

UPC 5–2. The preparation of a tax return does not necessarily involve the practice of law. It may often be accomplished by one having only incidental legal knowledge.

UPC 5–3. A non-lawyer otherwise entitled to do so may hold himself out as a tax return preparer or as enrolled to practice before the Internal Revenue Service; but he may not hold himself out as qualified to deal with difficult and involved questions of tax law, wholly apart from any engagement to prepare tax returns or practice before the Internal Revenue Service.

UPC 5–4. In general, tax planning is not considered to be the unauthorized practice of law. Attempting to resolve uncertainties as to the interpretation or application of tax or general law to a particular transaction, however, involves the practice of law unless it is incidental to a tax return preparer's engagement or the regular course of conducting a licensed business, for example, an investment business, or is limited to an analysis of merely the facts and assets of an estate.

UPC 5–5. Only a lawyer may prepare legal instruments for others or take the necessary steps to create, amend or dissolve a partnership, corporation or other business entity. Suggesting that any such legal work should be reviewed by the taxpayer's lawyer will not cure any unauthorized practice. In general, a lawyer working for a corporation not engaged in the practice of law as a registered law corporation is not entitled in the course of his employment to provide such services for customers or patrons of his employer.

UPC 5–6. Non-lawyers authorized by statute or Treasury Department regulations to represent taxpayers may do so in accordance with the existing law, rules and regulations governing such practice.

UPC 5–7. When a taxpayer is being investigated for a possible criminal violation of the tax laws, he should be promptly advised to seek advice from a lawyer. The lawyer-client privilege is a unique relationship to which the taxpayer is entitled at the earliest stage of the investigation.

UPC 5–8. Nothing herein is intended to modify or limit the right of a certified public accountant to certify, attest or express an opinion that financial data comply with conditions established by law or contract. Certified public accountants are members of a profession regulated by law who must meet certain minimal education requirements and observe certain rules of professional conduct. As such, certified public accountants engaged in the practice of their profession are entitled to a greater degree of latitude in the resolution of issues involving overlapping legal and accounting principles.

UNAUTHORIZED PRACTICE RULE 6. REAL ESTATE PRACTICE

Note: The unauthorized practice considerations and rules stated herein are derived from Va. Rules of Court Part Six, § I; 171 Va. xvii (1938); 216 Va. 1062 (1976), and the principles referred to in the Introduction printed at 28 Va.Bar News No. 2, pp. 39–42 (Aug. 1979); and such authorities are hereby incorporated herein.

UPR 6–101. Giving Legal Advice.

(A) A non-lawyer shall not undertake for compensation, direct or indirect, to advise another in any matter involving the application of legal principles to the ownership, use, disposition or encumbrance of real estate, except that, incident to his investigation of factual matters, he may give advice to his regular employer, other than in aid of his employer's unauthorized practice of law, or to a lawyer upon request by the lawyer therefor.

(B) A non-lawyer or lay entity may not employ a lawyer, directly or indirectly, to advise a customer in any matter involving the application of legal principles to the ownership, use, disposition or encumbrance of real estate. A non-lawyer or lay entity may, however, refer its customer to a lawyer for legal services.

(C) If a non-lawyer or lay entity refers its customer to a lawyer for legal services involving the application of legal principles to the ownership, use, disposition or encumbrance of real estate, such a non-lawyer or lay entity shall not exercise or attempt to exercise any control over, or imply that the non-lawyer or lay entity has any right to control, the actions of the lawyer in the handling of the transaction. All decisions are to be those of the lawyer acting on behalf of his client.

UPR 6–102. Holding Out With Regard to Real Estate Services.

(A) Except as specifically provided in UPR 6–101(A), a non-lawyer shall not hold himself out as authorized to furnish to another advice or service with respect to real estate transactions under circumstances which imply his possession of legal knowledge or skill in the application of any law, federal, state or local, to a specific set of facts for a particular person.

(B) Notwithstanding any rule of this Court to the contrary, a settlement agent authorized by law to provide escrow, closing or settlement services for real estate transactions may hold himself out as authorized to provide such services in the purchase or financing of real estate in the Commonwealth of Virginia.

(C) A non-lawyer shall not be excused from any violation of these Rules by any disclaimer, admonition to seek the advice of an attorney, or waiver by the customer.

UPR 6–103. Preparation of Legal Instruments.

(A) Unless a party to the transaction, a non-lawyer shall not, with or without compensation, prepare for another legal instruments of any character affecting the title to or use of real estate.

(1) A non-lawyer may prepare a for any real estate owned by him. A non-lawyer may prepare a deed of trust or deed of trust note for any real estate owned by him or in connection with any transaction to which he is a party involving its purchase, sale, transfer or encumbrance.

(2) A regular employee may prepare legal instruments for use by his employer for which no separate charge shall be made. However, such employee may not assist his employer in the unauthorized practice of law.

(3) A real estate agent, or his regular employee, involved in the negotiation of a transaction and incident to the regular course of conducting his licensed business, may prepare a contract of sale, exchange, option or lease with respect to such transaction, for which no separate charge shall be made.

(4) A lending institution may in the regular course of conducting its business prepare a deed of trust or mortgage on real estate securing the payment of its loan, for which no separate charge shall be made.

(5) A settlement agent authorized to provide escrow, closing or settlement services for real estate transactions under the Consumer Real Estate Settlement Protection Act (CRESPA), Va. Code §§ 6.1–2.19, et seq. or the Real Estate Settlement Agent Registration Act (RESARA), Va. Code §§ 6.1–2.30, et seq. or any other Virginia statute now existing or hereafter enacted may complete form documents and instruments selected by and in accordance with the instructions of the parties to the transaction.

(B) A non-lawyer or lay entity may not employ a lawyer, directly or indirectly, for the purpose of drafting legal instruments affecting the title to or use of real estate for a customer of the non-lawyer or lay entity. A non-lawyer or lay entity may, however, refer its customer to a lawyer for legal services.

UPR 6–104. Real Estate Closings.

(A) In connection with a real estate closing, a non-lawyer shall not give legal advice to another, or prepare for or advise another in the preparation of legal instruments, for compensation, direct or indirect. A non-lawyer may:

(1) Act as a settlement agent if registered under and in compliance with CRESPA.

(2) Provide such services of a clerical or ministerial nature as may assist the parties in the settlement of a contract, commitment or other agreement with respect to the sale or encumbrance of property including administrative and clerical services as authorized under CRESPA and RESARA.

(3) Act as an agent or broker in connection with issuance of title insurance commitments, binders and policies.

(4) Perform searches of public land and related records, make abstracts of title (i.e., copy salient portions of what the public records show as distinguished from expressing an opinion on the legal consequences of such records, prepare title reports and, to the extent licensed to do so, underwrite for and prepare title insurance commitments or binders and policies.

UPR 6–105. Lawyer–Client Relationship.

(A) A real estate agent, closing agent, lender or other party interested in a real estate transaction shall not:

(1) Disrupt the relationship of confidence and trust which must exist between a lawyer and his client.

(2) Prevent a lawyer from exercising independent judgment on behalf of his client by attempting to fix the lawyer's compensation, or sharing in a percentage of his compensation, or prescribing the terms of his employment, or attempting in any way to control or direct his actions.

(3) Place himself between the lawyer and the owner or landlord in an attempt to act as the only conduit of information between the two, since this would prevent the establishment of the fundamental relationship of trust and direct personal responsibility which ought to exist between a lawyer and his client.

UPR 6–106. Referral of Business.

(A) A real estate agent, closing agent, lender or other party interested in a real estate transaction may refer its customer to a lawyer subject to the following:

(1) The customer shall first have the opportunity to select a lawyer of his own choosing.

(2) If the customer does not so select a lawyer, the agency shall submit a list of lawyers from which the customer may make his selection and subsequently authorize the agent to refer the representation of such customer to the lawyer so selected.

(3) The lawyer shall be free at all times to communicate directly with such customer, now his client; and, upon receipt of the initial referral, as well as upon the receipt of any subsequent business unacceptable to the lawyer on the basis of the prior fee arrangement, the lawyer shall communicate with his client for the purpose of establishing the fee arrangement, in which arrangement the agent shall not participate.

(B) A real estate agent, closing agent, lender or other party interested in a real estate transaction shall not exercise or attempt to exercise any control over or imply that he has any right to control the actions of the lawyer in the handling of the transaction. All decisions are to be those of the lawyer acting on behalf of his client.

UNAUTHORIZED PRACTICE CONSIDERATIONS

UPC 6–1. A non-lawyer may not express to any person, an opinion as to the validity or legal status of title to real estate or as to the legal effect of anything found in the chain of title such as, for example, a suit, will, judgment, release deed or extension agreement or as to the effect on title of matters not necessarily appearing of record such as, for example, adverse possession, the statute of limitations, or the disabilities of parties. A lawyer employed by a lay agency to render services for others is restricted to the doing of acts in the course of his employment that a non-lawyer can lawfully do. Nothing herein shall be construed to impair the right to practice of duly licensed house counsel, see Unauthorized Practice Rule 1, Practice Before Tribunals; or to impair rights guaranteed by the Constitution; or to impair the rights of a subscriber under a legal services plan licensed under Chapter 23 of Title 38.2 of the Code of Virginia.

UPC 6–2. A non-lawyer may not hold out to the public, directly or indirectly, his willingness to give legal advice or perform legal services, nor solicit such services and then hire a lawyer to perform them. Such practices are not validated by an acknowledgment that the non-lawyer is not authorized to give legal advice, or by any disclaimer or suggestion that such advice should be reviewed by the customer's own lawyer. A settlement agent registered under and in compliance with CRESPA or RESARA, may hold himself or herself out as providing escrow, closing or settlement services in the purchase or financing of real estate in the Commonwealth of Virginia.

UPC 6–3. A non-lawyer may compile and report factual information as disclosed by the public records, sometimes referred to as making an abstract of title; but he may not express an opinion or issue a certificate as to the legal consequences of what his investigation of the public records may show. Incident to his investigation of the facts, an abstracter may give to his regular employer or, upon request, to a lawyer his opinion as to the status of legal title as disclosed by his investigation; but neither he nor his employer, unless a lawyer or registered law corporation, may give a certificate of title or opinion to a third party, or otherwise hold themselves out as possessing legal knowledge or skill.

UPC 6–4. The drawing or preparation of deeds, deeds of trust, mortgages, deeds of release, and other instruments affecting title to real estate requires the possession and use of legal knowledge and skill. Such instruments are extraordinary contracts and muniments of title to real estate. This is nonetheless true where a form of deed or deed of trust prepared by a lawyer may be followed or filled in, and whether the instrument is deemed simple or complex. Legal knowledge and skill are required, in any event, in the selection and completion of the proper form to fit the facts of the particular case. Notwithstanding the foregoing, a settlement agent registered under and in compliance with CRESPA may complete form documents and instruments selected by and in accordance with the instructions of the parties to the transaction. However, a non-lawyer settlement agent may not draft the deed or deed of trust or select the form of the deed or deed of trust to be used for a particular transaction.

UPC 6–5. An individual, if he chooses to do so, may draw or attempt to draw legal instruments for himself or affecting his property. A corporation acting through its employees may do the same with respect to its own property.

UPC 6–6. A non-lawyer licensed real estate agent may, pursuant to Virginia Code § 54.1–2101.1, prepare for another contracts incident to the regular course of conducting a licensed real estate business. Whether in a particular case the preparation of a contract by a non-lawyer is incident to the regular course of conducting such licensed business must, of necessity, be determined on the facts of that particular case. Preparation, in this context, includes not only the drafting of a form but also the filling in of a previously prepared form. In making such a determination, the following facts, not necessarily listed in the order of their importance, are among those which should be considered:

A. Whether the preparer is a party to the contract;

B. Whether the object to be accomplished by the contract is essential to the regular conduct of the real estate business of the preparer or merely ancillary thereto or an indirect by-product;

C. Whether a separate charge is made for preparation of the contract;

D. Whether the implication of legal knowledge and skill on the part of the drafter is minimal;

E. Whether the reliance on such service as a legal service is minimal;

F. The extent to which the licensed purpose of the business would be frustrated if preparation of the contract were not permitted;

G. The likelihood that legal advice will in fact be given by a non-lawyer, in connection with the execution of the contract by the parties;

H. The extent to which preparation of the contract by a non-lawyer reduces costs, saves time and avoids inconvenience to the parties; and

I. The custom and practice in the industry.

UPC 6–7. In connection with a real estate closing, a non-lawyer settlement agent may not give legal advice to another, or prepare for or advise another in the preparation of legal instruments, for compensation, direct or indirect. A non-lawyer may, however:

A. Order a survey, but not give an opinion as to the adequacy of such survey or with respect to matters reflected therein.

B. Obtain copies of leases, easements, restrictions, building codes, zoning ordinances and the like, but not give an opinion as to the legal effects thereof or any party's legal obligation to comply therewith.

C. Order termite or other inspections, but not give an opinion as to a party's legal obligations with respect thereto.

D. Ascertain the status of utility services and assist in their transfer, but not give advice as to a party's legal obligation with respect thereto.

E. Arrange for the issuance of casualty insurance coverage, as requested by a party in interest.

F. Provide lien payoff figures as asserted by the lienholder, but not give advice as to a party's legal obligation to pay the amount claimed.

G. Make mathematical computations involving the proration of taxes, insurance, rents, interest and the like in accordance with the terms of the contract or local custom.

H. Obtain lien waivers from mechanics or materialmen in form acceptable to the party in interest.

I. Prepare settlement statements and complete form documents and instruments selected by and in accordance with the instructions of the parties to the transaction and prepare settlement statements, such as the HUD–1, and other form documents such as the Owner's/Seller's Affidavit, Notice of Availability(of Owner's Title Insurance), and tax reporting forms including FIRPTA, Form 1099, VA R–5, and VA R–5E.

J. Receive and disburse settlement funds, and serve as escrow agent, to the extent licensed to do so.

K. Prepare receipts and certificates of satisfaction, but not deeds, deeds of trust, deeds of trust notes, or deeds of release.

L. Create or prepare a title abstract or title report, and to the extent licensed to do so, underwrite for and prepare title insurance commitments or binders and policies.

The foregoing list of examples would not be considered to be the unauthorized practice of law; it is intended only to provide guidance and is thus non-exclusive.

UPC 6–8. While a lay agency may recommend to its customers the employment of a lawyer, the lawyer so employed should in all matters be employed, controlled and paid by his client, the customer. The lay agency may refer its customer to a lawyer and may consult with that lawyer or any other lawyer engaged by its customer. The lawyer, however, owes his undivided loyalty to his client, the customer, and not to the lay agency, and should be especially sensitive in real estate transactions to the ethical constraints governing conflicts of interest. To the extent the lawyer considers the lay agency to be his client and, in the preparation of legal instruments for the lay agency, he knows, or should know, that the lay agency intends to use such legal instruments in the closing of a real estate transaction for another, such lawyer is aiding such lay agency in the unauthorized practice of law. A lawyer may, however, in representing his or her lay agency client, advise the lay agency as to compliance with applicable law including the legal sufficiency and accuracy of legal documents or instruments. A direct and personal lawyer-client relationship must be established and preserved at all times; otherwise, through its own lawyer, such lay agency becomes engaged in the business of providing legal services to others.

UPC 6–9. If legal advice is requested by a party, the non-lawyer settlement agent should take care to refer the party to a lawyer. Defining what is legal advice is difficult; however, a non-lawyer acting as a settlement agent is engaged in the unauthorized practice of law if he or she:

A. Recommends or urges a course of action to a party to the transaction under circumstances which require the exercise of legal judgment;

B. Drafts a legal instrument for a party to the transaction, other than completing form documents selected by and in accordance with the instructions of the parties to the transaction; or selects or assists a party in selecting a form document, if such selection or assistance requires the exercise of legal judgment;

C. Assists a party to the transaction in the completion of a legal document, other than a form document selected by and in accordance with the instruction of the parties, if such assistance requires the exercise of legal judgment;

D. Advises or instructs a party to the transaction of which way to take title to the property or the legal consequences of taking title in a particular manner, except that providing a description of the various tenancies recognized under Virginia law shall be permitted;

E. Attempts to settle or resolve a dispute between the parties to the transaction which requires the exercise of legal judgment to a particular situation;

F. Explains the legal effect of an item reported as an exception in a title commitment except as necessary to underwrite a policy of insurance and except that a licensed title insurer, agency or agent may explain an underwriting decision to an insured or prospective insured including providing the reason for such decision;

G. Provides a legal opinion in response to inquiries regarding rights and obligations under legal documents provided that a layman's description of the purpose or intent of a document shall not constitute a legal opinion.

The foregoing list of examples would not be considered to be the unauthorized practice of law; it is intended only to provide guidance and is thus non-exclusive.
[Amended effective June 24, 2002.]

UNAUTHORIZED PRACTICE RULE 7. TITLE INSURANCE

Note: The unauthorized practice considerations and rules stated herein are derived from Va. Rules of Court Part Six, § I; 171 Va. xvii (1938); 216 Va. 1062 (1976), and the principles referred to in the Introduction printed at 28 Va.Bar News No. 2, pp. 39–42 (Aug. 1979); and such authorities are hereby incorporated herein.

UPR 7–101. Title Insurance Practice.

(A) A title insurance company, through its employees, agents or other representatives acting as such, shall not give legal advice or express an opinion to any person other than, upon request, to a lawyer, as to the status or marketability of title to real property in Virginia, or as to the legal effect of documents comprising the chain of title or matters revealed by a title search or examination.

(B) A title insurance commitment, binder or policy, or any of the provisions thereof, shall not be held out, directly or indirectly, by any person as constituting the equivalent of, or as tantamount to, a legal opinion based upon an examination of title.

(C) A title insurance company may in the regular course of conducting its business, issue directly to an insured or prospective insured its title insurance commitments, binders and policies, as otherwise permitted by law.

(D) A title insurance company, its employees, agents and other representatives are subject in all respects to the Rules set forth in Unauthorized Practice Rule 6, Real Estate Practice.

UNAUTHORIZED PRACTICE CONSIDERATIONS

UPC 7–1. Title insurance is insurance indemnifying the insured from loss if the status of title on a certain date is other than as stated in the policy, subject to the exclusions and exceptions from coverage set out in the policy.

UPC 7–2. The abstracting of title to real property located in Virginia by a non-lawyer from public records does not, standing alone, constitute the practice of law; but the interpretation of the meaning of documents comprising and affecting the chain of title, and the concepts attendant thereto, require a knowledge of statutes, general law in the field, and judicial decisions not generally possessed by non-lawyers. It is not improper, however, for an employee of a title insurance company to search the title records and report his findings to his employer, and express his conclusions to his employer or, upon request, to a lawyer as to which liens, encumbrances and the like relate to or affect the status of a particular title.

UPC 7–3. Although legal knowledge and skill may be utilized in the preparation and issuance of a title insurance policy, this does not make such policy a legal opinion. The policy is one of indemnity against loss issued in the regular course of its business by a title insurance company subject to inspection, supervision and regulation by the State Corporation Commission of Virginia.

UPC 7–4. If an employee, agent or other representative of a title insurance company attempts to advise another, other than such company or, upon request, a lawyer, on the legal effect of matters affecting the chain of title to real estate located in Virginia and the concepts attendant thereto, he then engages in the unauthorized practice of law since he would be furnishing to another advice or service under circumstances which imply his possession and use of legal knowledge and skill.

UNAUTHORIZED PRACTICE RULE 8. TRADE ASSOCIATIONS

Note: The unauthorized practice considerations and rules stated herein are derived from Va. Rules of Court Part Six, § I; 171 Va. xvii (1938); 216 Va. 1062 (1976), and the principles referred to in the Introduction, 29 Va.Bar News No. 2, pp. 10–12 (Aug. 1980); and such authorities are hereby incorporated by reference herein.

UPR 8–101. Giving Legal Advice.

(A) A trade association shall not give legal advice or provide legal services to its members, directly or through its employed or retained lawyer, except that a trade association may:

(1) Distribute to its members any legal opinion rendered to the trade association by its lawyer on a matter which affects or may affect the general membership of the association.

(2) Appear through its lawyer as an intervenor or amicus curiae in any case involving a member, to the extent otherwise permitted by the court.

(3) Refer one or more of its members to its lawyer with respect to any legal matter so long as such lawyer is recognized throughout by all concerned as representing solely the interest of such member or members, free of control by or interference from the trade association.

(4) Solicit the comments of its members on proposed legislation or regulations drafted by its lawyer which affect or may affect the general membership of the association.

(5) Provide legal advice and the services of its lawyer to one or more of its members preliminary to and in connection with any matter that may seek to:

(a) Further the political goals of the association;

(b) Obtain meaningful access to the courts; or

(c) Vindicate civil liberties guaranteed by the Constitutions of Virginia or the United States.

UPR 8–102. Holding Out With Regard to Legal Services.

(A) Except to the extent legal advice or services are permitted to be provided under UPR 8–101, a trade association shall not hold itself out as authorized to furnish its members legal advice or services.

UPR 8–103. Attorney–Client Relationship.

(A) A trade association shall not:

(1) Disrupt the relationship of confidence and trust which must exist between a lawyer and his client.

(2) Prevent a lawyer from exercising independent judgment on behalf of his client by attempting to fix the lawyer's compensation, or sharing in a percentage of his compensation, or prescribing the terms of his employment, or attempting in any way to control or direct his actions, except that in matters of collective interest a trade association may negotiate on behalf of its members with respect to the legal fees to be charged.

(3) Place itself between the lawyer and the member in an attempt to act as the only conduit of information between the two, since this would prevent the establishment of the fundamental relationship of trust and direct personal responsibility which ought to exist between a lawyer and his client.

UPR 8–104. Referral of Business.

(A) A trade association may refer its member to a lawyer subject to the following:

(1) The member shall first have the opportunity to select a lawyer of his own choosing.

(2) If the member does not so select a lawyer, the trade association shall submit a list of lawyers from which the member may make his selection, which list may include the customary fee of each lawyer on the list.

(3) The lawyer shall be free at all times to communicate directly with such member, now his client; and upon receipt of the initial referral, as well as upon the receipt of any subsequent business unacceptable to the lawyer on the basis of the prior fee arrangement, the lawyer shall communicate with his client for the purpose of establishing the fee arrangement, in which arrangement the trade association, in pursuit of its associational goals, may participate as a negotiator or contributor, or both.

(B) A trade association shall not exercise or attempt to exercise any control or imply that it has any right to control the action of the lawyer in the handling of the transaction. All decisions are to be those of the lawyer acting on behalf of his client.

UNAUTHORIZED PRACTICE CONSIDERATIONS

UPC 8–1. The term "trade association" as used herein means a nonprofit organization formed for the principal purpose of furthering the common business or professional interest of its members. Any organization that qualifies as a business league or chamber of commerce under § 501(c)(6) of the Internal Revenue Code shall be presumed to be a trade association for purposes of this Rule. The conduct of a prepaid legal services plan is not to be considered governed by this Rule.

UPC 8–2. A trade association may recommend to its members the services of a lawyer. A trade association should not interfere with the personal lawyer-client relationship that should exist between a member and such member's own lawyer.

UPC 8–3. If a trade association offers to provide or provides its members with the services of a lawyer subject to the trade association's direction and control, it is engaged in the unauthorized practice of law unless such services seek to further the political or ideological goals of their associational activity. For example, a trade association may provide its members with its views, including the legal opinions of its employed or retained lawyer, on legislative, administrative and judicial developments or other matters of general interest to some or all of its members, but may not advise, or hold itself out as permitted to advise, an individual member as to the application of a statute, regulation or decision to such member's particular set of facts, unless such advice is incident to or part of the association's collective activity undertaken to obtain meaningful access to the courts or other fundamental rights within the protection of Article I, § 12 of the Virginia Constitution or the First Amendment to the United States Constitution.

UPC 8–4. Incident to his normal duties as a lobbyist or otherwise, a non-lawyer representative of a trade association may discuss with a member of the trade association the possible application of a proposed or enacted statute, regulation or decision to a particular set of facts; provided that such discussion does not constitute the giving of legal advice.

UNAUTHORIZED PRACTICE RULE 9. ADMINISTRATIVE AGENCY PRACTICE

Note: The unauthorized practice considerations and rules stated herein are derived from Va. Rules of Court Part Six, § I; 171 Va. xvii (1938); 216 Va. 1062 (1976), and the principles referred to in the Introduction, 29 Va.Bar News No. 2, pp. 10–12 (Aug. 1980); and such authorities are hereby incorporated by reference herein.

UPR 9–101. Holding Out as an Expert.

(A) A non-lawyer shall not hold himself out as authorized to furnish to another advice or service under circumstances which imply his possession of legal knowledge or skill in the application of any law, federal, state or local, or administrative regulation or ruling applicable thereto, except that a person admitted to practice by an administrative agency may hold himself out as such to the extent permitted by such agency as long as he does not misrepresent the scope of his practice authorized by such agency.

(B) A person duly licensed or authorized to practice law in another state or before any administrative agency shall not use the descriptive term "law office" or its equivalent on any signs or listings in Virginia, unless he is an employee or member of a firm with one or more lawyers duly licensed to practice law in Virginia.

UPR 9–102. Agency Practice.

(A) A non-lawyer shall not furnish to another for compensation, direct or indirect, advice or service under circumstances which require his use of legal knowledge or skill in the application of any law, federal, state or local, or administrative regulation or ruling applicable thereto, except:

(1) As an employee to his regular employer.

(2) As permitted by the rules of such agency and reasonably within the scope of his practice authorized by such agency.

(B) A non-lawyer shall not undertake, with or without compensation, to prepare for another legal instruments of any character incident to his practice before an administrative agency, except:

(1) As an employee for his regular employer.

(2) In the regular course and reasonably within the scope of his practice authorized by such agency.

(C) As to representing the interest of another before an administrative tribunal, see Unauthorized Practice Rule 1, Practice Before Tribunals.

UPR 9–103. Immigration Practice.

(A) The preceding provisions of UPR 9 also apply to unauthorized nonlawyers who represent persons, with or without compensation, before federal administrative agencies in connection with petitions or applications for benefits under the Immigration and Nationality Act and other federal immigration and nationality statutes and regulations.

(B) For purposes of UPR 9–103(A):

(1) "Unauthorized" means unable to show specific authorization by the appropriate federal agency to practice before it. With respect to matters before the Immigration and Naturalization Service, this means unable to show recognition as an authorized nonlawyer representative pursuant to 8 CFR Part 292, to wit: providing for representation by law students, law graduates not yet admitted to the bar, "reputable individuals" appearing without direct or indirect remuneration, accredited representatives, accredited officials, and certain attorneys residing outside the United States.

(2) "Represent" means to engage in "practice" or "preparation" as those terms are defined, respectively, in 8 CFR §§ 1.1(i) and (k), to wit: "practice" means the act or acts of any person appearing in any case, either in person or through the preparation or filing of any brief or other document, paper, application, or petition on behalf of another person or client before or with the Service . . . ; "preparation" means the study of the facts of a case and the applicable laws, coupled with the giving of advice and auxiliary activities, including the incidental preparation of papers, but does not include the lawful functions of a notary public or service consisting solely of assistance in the completion of blank spaces on printed Service forms by one whose remuneration, if any, is nominal and who does not hold himself out as qualified in legal matters or in immigration and naturalization procedure or as 8 CFR Part 292 may be amended from time to time.

(C) The provisions of (A) and (B) above are not intended to prohibit an unauthorized nonlawyer from assisting an individual in the completion of forms which had been personally selected by the individual, to the extent that such assistance involves only the taking and transcription of dictation or the translation of such dictation into English. However, the referenced provisions are intended to prohibit such an unauthorized nonlawyer from selecting specific forms for completion or from advising the individual as to which forms are appropriate for completion and submission to the Service provided such activities require the use of legal knowledge and skill.

UNAUTHORIZED PRACTICE CONSIDERATIONS

UPC 9–1. Representing another before an administrative agency normally constitutes the practice of law.

UPC 9–2. Regulation of the practice of law before federal administrative agencies is the responsibility of Congress. When Congress grants authority to an agency to prescribe regulations governing the recognition and conduct of a person representing the interest of another before such agency, the State is preempted from enforcing its own rules of practice while such person is acting reasonably within the scope of the practice authorized by the agency. As to rules of practice before Virginia administrative agencies, see Unauthorized Practice Rule 1, Practice Before Tribunals.

UPC 9–3. Normally, a person authorized to practice before an administrative agency may give advice to others informing them of their rights and obligations as to matters pending before, to be presented to or otherwise within the jurisdiction of such agency; prepare applications, exhibits and other documents as required by such agency in the submission of matters to it and in the performance of its regulatory functions; appear before such agency at any hearing, formal or informal, within Virginia and, as otherwise permitted by such agency, represent the interests of others before such agency, including filing motions and briefs, cross-examining witnesses, and making oral arguments as to matters of law; and hold himself out as qualified to perform such services before such agency within the scope of his agency license.

UPC 9–4. A person authorized to practice before an administrative agency may not prepare for another, not his regular employer, legal instruments not reasonably within the scope of his agency practice. For example, the preparation of a lease or contract to be approved by an administrative agency may facially appear to be incident to the regular course of conducting an approved agency practice; but such a document normally creates substantive rights and obligations for the parties under state law, and to prepare such documents and give advice concerning their significance beyond their compliance with federal law or regulations may constitute the unauthorized practice of law.

UPC 9–5. The privilege of practicing before most federal administrative agencies is not restricted to lawyers. The federal Administrative Procedure Act grants to an individual who is a member in good standing of the Bar of the highest court of any state an initial right to represent others before any federal agency; but if such person is not duly licensed or authorized to practice law in Virginia or has not obtained the requisite revenue license required by § 58–371 of the Code of Virginia, he is subject to the same rules as a non-lawyer when his activities in Virginia extend beyond the scope of the practice authorized by the federal agency.

UPC 9–6. A person who is authorized to practice before an administrative agency and who is duly licensed or authorized to practice law in another state presumably has met certain minimal educational requirements and is subject to discipline for violations of a code of professional responsibility similar to that governing the conduct of lawyers licensed to practice in Virginia. As such, a person licensed or authorized to practice law in another state is entitled to a greater degree of latitude in the resolution of issues involving whether his activity is within the scope of the practice authorized by such agency and whether any legal instruments prepared by him are properly incident thereto.

UPC 9–7. Aliens are especially vulnerable to the unauthorized practice of law. Such unauthorized practice, which may include incompetent or fraudulent legal services, can cause serious economic harm, may result in the separation of families, and may even result in the death of an individual forcibly repatriated to another country if asylum is denied to him in the United States.

The Virginia State Bar recognizes that certain nonlawyers may be authorized to practice before a federal immigration agency. However, nonlawyers who are not so authorized are limited to providing assistance to an alien resident for such limited services as translation of documents, and assistance in the transcription of documents or answers provided by the alien, for a fee commensurate with such limited services. However, the selection of appropriate immigration forms, the assistance to the alien in the information to be provided on such forms, and other related services by an unauthorized nonlawyer may constitute the unauthorized practice of law.

Furthermore, in addition to engaging in the unauthorized practice of law, an individual who holds himself or herself out as qualified to render such legal services and performs such services, may also be subject to criminal prosecution, to civil remedies such as quo warranto actions, and to such discipline and sanctions as may be imposed under federal statutes and regulations.

[Amended effective October 1, 1993.]

SECTION II. VIRGINIA RULES OF PROFESSIONAL CONDUCT

Adopted Effective January 1, 2000

PREAMBLE: A LAWYER'S RESPONSIBILITIES

A lawyer is a representative of clients or a neutral third party, an officer of the legal system and a public citizen having special responsibility for the quality of justice.

A lawyer may perform various functions. As advisor, a lawyer provides a client with an informed understanding of the client's legal rights and obligations and explains their practical implications. As advocate, a lawyer zealously asserts the client's position under the rules of the adversary system. As negotiator, a lawyer seeks a result advantageous to the client but consistent with requirements of honest dealing with others. As intermediary between clients, a lawyer seeks to reconcile their divergent interests as an advisor and, to a limited extent, as a spokesperson for each client. As third party neutral, a lawyer represents neither party, but helps the parties arrive at their own solution. As evaluator, a lawyer examines a client's legal affairs and reports about them to the client or to others.

In all professional functions a lawyer should be competent, prompt and diligent. A lawyer should maintain communication with a client concerning the representation. A lawyer should keep in confidence information relating to representation of a client except so far as disclosure is required or permitted by the Rules of Professional Conduct or other law.

A lawyer's conduct should conform to the requirements of the law, both in professional service to clients and in the lawyer's business and personal affairs. A lawyer should use the law's procedures only for legitimate purposes and not to harass or intimidate others. A lawyer should demonstrate respect for the legal system and for those who serve it, including judges, other lawyers and public officials. While it is a lawyer's duty, when necessary, to challenge the rectitude of official action, it is also a lawyer's duty to uphold legal process.

As a public citizen, a lawyer should seek improvement of the law, the administration of justice and the quality of service rendered by the legal profession. As a member of a learned profession, a lawyer should cultivate knowledge of the law beyond its use for clients, employ that knowledge in reform of the law and work to strengthen legal education. A lawyer should be mindful of deficiencies in the administration of justice and of the fact that the poor, and sometimes persons who are not poor, cannot afford adequate legal assistance, and should therefore devote professional time and civic influence in their behalf. A lawyer should aid the legal profession in pursuing these objectives and should help the bar regulate itself in the public interest.

Many of a lawyer's professional responsibilities are prescribed in the Rules of Professional Conduct, as well as substantive and procedural law. However, a lawyer is also guided by personal conscience and the approbation of professional peers. A lawyer should strive to attain the highest level of skill, to improve the law and the legal profession, and to exemplify the legal profession's ideals of public service.

A lawyer's responsibilities as a representative of clients, an officer of the legal system and a public citizen are usually harmonious. Thus, when an opposing party is well represented, a lawyer can be a zealous advocate on behalf of a client and at the same time assume that justice is being done. So also, a lawyer can be sure that preserving client confidences ordinarily serves the public interest because people are more likely to seek legal advice, and thereby heed their legal obligations, when they know their communications will be private.

In the nature of law practice, however, conflicting responsibilities are encountered. Virtually all difficult ethical problems arise from conflict between a lawyer's responsibilities to clients, to the legal system and to the lawyer's own interest in remaining an upright person while earning a satisfactory living. The Rules of Professional Conduct prescribe terms for resolving such conflicts. Within the framework of these Rules, many difficult issues of professional discretion can arise. Such issues must be resolved through the exercise of sensitive professional and moral judgment guided by the basic principles underlying the Rules.

The legal profession is largely self-governing. Although other professions also have been granted powers of self-government, the legal profession is unique in this respect because of the close relationship between the profession and the processes of government and law enforcement. This connection is manifested in the fact that ultimate authority over the legal profession is vested largely in the courts.

To the extent that lawyers meet the obligations of their professional calling, the occasion for government regulation is obviated. Self-regulation also helps maintain the legal profession's independence from government domination. An independent legal profession is an important force in preserving government under law, for abuse of legal authority is more readily challenged by a profession whose members are not dependent on government for the right to practice.

The legal profession's relative autonomy carries with it special responsibilities of self-government. The profession has a responsibility to assure that its regulations are conceived in the public interest and not in furtherance of parochial or self-interested concerns of the bar. Every lawyer is responsible for observance of the Rules of Professional Conduct. A lawyer should also aid in securing their observance by other lawyers. Neglect of these responsibilities compromises the independence of the profession and the public interest which it serves.

Lawyers play a vital role in the preservation of society. The fulfillment of this role requires an understanding by lawyers of their relationship to our legal system. The Rules of Professional Conduct, when properly applied, serve to define that relationship.

Scope

The Rules of Professional Conduct are rules of reason. They should be interpreted with reference to the purposes of legal representation and of the law itself. Some of the Rules are imperatives, cast in the terms "shall" or "shall not." These define proper conduct for purposes of professional discipline. Others, generally cast in the term "may," are permissive and define areas under the Rules in which the lawyer has professional discretion. No disciplinary action should be taken when the lawyer chooses not to act or acts within the bounds of such discretion. Other Rules define the nature of relationships between the lawyer and others. The Rules are thus partly obligatory and disciplinary and partly constitutive and descriptive in that they define a lawyer's professional role. Many of the Comments use the term "should." Comments do not add obligations to the Rules but provide guidance for practicing in compliance with the Rules.

These Rules follow the same format as the current American Bar Association Model Rules of Professional Conduct ("*ABA Model Rules*"), rather than the former American Bar Association Model Code of Professional Responsibility ("*ABA Model Code*"), or the former Virginia Code of Professional Responsibility ("*Virginia Code*"). Although interpretation of similar language in the *ABA Model Rules* by other states' courts and bars might be helpful in understanding Virginia's Rules, those foreign interpretations should not be binding in Virginia.

The Rules presuppose a larger legal context shaping the lawyer's role. That context includes court rules and statutes relating to matters of licensure, laws defining specific obligations of lawyers and substantive and procedural law in general. Compliance with the Rules, as with all law in an open society, depends primarily upon understanding and voluntary compliance, secondarily upon reinforcement by peer and public opinion and finally, when necessary, upon enforcement through disciplinary proceedings. The Rules do not, however, exhaust the moral and ethical considerations that should inform a lawyer, for no worthwhile human activity can be completely defined by legal rules. The Rules simply provide a framework for the ethical practice of law.

Furthermore, for purposes of determining the lawyer's authority and responsibility, principles of substantive law external to these Rules determine whether a client-lawyer relationship exists. Most of the duties flowing from the client-lawyer relationship attach only after the client has requested the lawyer to render legal services and the lawyer has agreed to do so. But there are some duties, such as that of confidentiality under Rule 1.6, that may attach when the lawyer agrees to consider whether a client-lawyer relationship shall be established. Whether a client-lawyer relationship exists for any specific purpose can depend on the circumstances and may be a question of fact.

These Rules apply to all lawyers, whether practicing in the private or the public sector. However, under various legal provisions, including constitutional, statutory and common law, the responsibilities of government lawyers may include authority concerning legal matters that ordinarily reposes in the client in private client-lawyer relationships. For example, a lawyer for a government agency may have authority on behalf of the government to decide upon settlement or whether to appeal from an adverse judgment. Such authority in various respects is generally vested in the Attorney General and the commonwealth attorneys in state government, and their federal counterparts, and the same may be true of other government law officers. Also, lawyers under the supervision of these officers may be authorized to represent several government agencies in intragovernmental legal controversies in circumstances where a private lawyer could not represent multiple private clients. They also may have authority to represent the "public interest" in circumstances where a private lawyer would not be authorized to do so. These Rules do not abrogate any such authority.

Failure to comply with an obligation or prohibition imposed by a Rule is a basis for invoking the disciplinary process. The Rules presuppose that disciplinary assessment of a lawyer's conduct will be made on the basis of the facts and circumstances as they existed at the time of the conduct in question and in recognition of the fact that a lawyer often has to act upon uncertain or incomplete evidence of the situation. Moreover, the Rules presuppose that whether or not discipline should be imposed for a violation, and the severity of a sanction, depend on all the circumstances, such as the willfulness and seriousness of the violation, extenuating factors and whether there have been previous violations.

Violation of a Rule should not give rise to a cause of action nor should it create any presumption that a legal duty has been breached. The Rules are designed to provide guidance to lawyers and to provide a structure for regulating conduct through disciplinary agencies. They are not designed to be a basis for civil liability. Furthermore, the purpose of the Rules can be subverted when they are invoked by opposing parties as procedural weapons. The fact that a Rule is a just basis for a lawyer's self-assessment, or for sanctioning a lawyer under the administration of a disciplinary authority, does not imply that an antagonist in a collateral proceeding or transaction has standing to seek enforcement of the Rule. Accordingly, nothing in the Rules should be deemed to augment any substantive legal duty of lawyers or the extra-disciplinary consequences of violating such a duty.

Moreover, these Rules are not intended to govern or affect judicial application of either the attorney-client or work product privilege. Those privileges were developed to promote compliance with law and fairness in litigation. In reliance on the attorney-client privilege, clients are entitled to expect that communications within the scope of the privilege will be protected against compelled disclosure. The attorney-client privilege is that of the client and not of the lawyer. The fact that in exceptional situations the lawyer under the Rules has either a limited discretion or a limited obligation to disclose a client confidence does not vitiate the proposition that, as a general matter, the client has a reasonable expectation that information relating to the client will not be voluntarily disclosed and that disclosure of such information may be judicially compelled only in accordance with recognized exceptions to the attorney-client and work product privileges.

The lawyer's exercise of discretion not to disclose information under Rule 1.6 should not be subject to reexamination. Permitting such reexamination would be incompatible with the general policy of promoting compliance with law through assurances that communications will be protected against disclosure.

The Preamble and this note on Scope provide general orientation. The text of each Rule and the following Terminology section are authoritative and the Comments accompanying each Rule are interpretive.

Terminology

"Belief" or "believes" denotes that the person involved actually supposed the fact in question to be true. A person's belief may be inferred from circumstances.

"Consult" or "consultation" denotes communication of information reasonably sufficient to permit the client to appreciate the significance of the matter in question.

"Firm" or "law firm" denotes a professional entity, public or private, organized to deliver legal services, or a legal department of a corporation or other organization. See Comment, Rule 1.10.

"Fraud" or "fraudulent" denotes conduct having a purpose to deceive and not merely negligent misrepresentation or failure to apprise another of relevant information.

"Knowingly," "known," or "knows" denotes actual knowledge of the fact in question. A person's knowledge may be inferred from circumstances.

"Partner" denotes a member of a partnership or a shareholder or member of a professional entity, public or private, organized to deliver legal services, or a legal department of a corporation or other organization.

"Reasonable" or "reasonably" when used in relation to conduct by a lawyer denotes the conduct of a reasonably prudent and competent lawyer.

"Reasonable belief" or "reasonably believes" when used in reference to a lawyer denotes that the lawyer believes the matter in question and that the circumstances are such that the belief is reasonable.

"Reasonably should know" when used in reference to a lawyer denotes that a lawyer of reasonable prudence and competence would ascertain the matter in question.

"Should" when used in reference to a lawyer's action denotes an aspirational rather than a mandatory standard.

"Substantial" when used in reference to degree or extent denotes a material matter of clear and weighty importance.

[Adopted effective January 1, 2000.]

CROSS REFERENCE TABLE: VIRGINIA RULES OF PROFESSIONAL CONDUCT TO CODE OF PROFESSIONAL RESPONSIBILITY

NOTE: Please observe the symbol (***) for rules which have no direct counterpart in the Virginia Code of Professional Responsibility. While often the case, a cross-reference to a provision in the Code of Professional Responsibility does not necessarily mean that the cited provision is identical or even substantially similar to a particular rule. A citation may simply mean that a provision in the Code of Professional Responsibility applies to the same issue covered by the rule. In some instances, an area covered by a rule was addressed in an Ethical Consideration (EC), but not a Disciplinary Rule (DR), and, therefore, only the EC is cited.

Virginia Rules of Professional Conduct	Issue or Topic	Virginia Code of Professional Responsibility
1.1	Competence	DR 6–101(A)(2)
1.2(a)	Scope of Representation	*** EC 7–7; EC 7–8
1.2(b)	" " " "	DR 7–101(B)(1)
1.2(c)	" " " "	DR 7–102(A)(7); DR 7–102(A)(6); DR 7–105(A); EC 7–5
1.2(d)	" " " "	DR 2–108(A)(1)
1.3(a)	Diligence	DR 6–101(B)
1.3(b)	" " " "	DR 7–101(A)(2)
1.3(c)	" " " "	DR 7–101(A)(3)
1.4(a)	Communication	DR 6–101(C)
1.4(b)	" " " "	*** EC 7–8; EC 9–2
1.4(c)	" " " "	DR 6–101(D)
1.5(a)	Fees	DR 2–105(A); EC 2–20
1.5(b)	Contingent Fees	DR 2–105(C); EC 2–22
1.5(c)	Fee Splitting	DR 2–105(D)
1.6(a)	Confidentiality	DR 4–101(A), (B)
1.6(b)(1)	Disclosure Required By Law or Court Order	DR 4–101(C)(2)
1.6(b)(2)	Disclosure to Protect Lawyer's Legal Rights	DR 4–101(C)(4)
1.6(b)(3)	Disclosure of Client Fraud on Third Party	DR 4–101(C)(3)
1.6(b)(4)	Disclosure of Client Information for LOMAP	***
1.6(b)(5)	Disclosure of Client Information to Outside Auditor	*** EC 4–3
1.6(c)(1)	Disclosure of Client's Intent to Commit Crime	DR 4–101(D)
1.6(c)(2)	Disclosure of Client Fraud on Tribunal	DR 4–101(D)
1.6(c)(3)	Reporting Misconduct of another attorney	***
1.7(a), (b)	Conflict of Interest	DR 5–105(A), (C)
1.8(a)	Business Transaction With Client	DR 5–104(A)
1.8(b)	Improper Use of Client Confidences or Secrets	DR 4–101(B)(3)
1.8(c)	Preparing Instrument in Which Lawyer is Beneficiary	DR 5–104(B)
1.8(d)	Literary Rights in Subject Matter of Representation	*** EC 5–4
1.9(a)	Conflict of Interest: Former Client	DR 5–105(D)
1.9(b)	" " " "	***
1.9(c)	" " " "	***
1.10(a), (b)	Imputed Disqualification	*** DR 5–105(E)

Virginia Rules of Professional Conduct	Issue or Topic	Virginia Code of Professional Responsibility
1.11(a)	Public Officials: Successive Employment	DR 8–101(A)
1.11(b)	" " " "	DR 9–101(B)
1.11(c)	" " " "	***
1.11(d)	" " " "	***
1.11(e)	" " " "	***
1.11(f)	" " " "	***
1.12(a)	Former Judge, Arbitrator or Mediator	DR 9–101(A); EC 5–20
1.12(b)	" " " "	***
1.12(c)	" " " "	***
1.12(d)	" " " "	***
1.13	Organization as a Client	*** EC 5–18; EC 5–24
1.14	Client Under a Disability	*** EC 7–11: EC 7–12
1.15(a)	Safekeeping Property	DR 9–102(A)
1.15(b)	" " " "	***
1.15(c)	" " " "	DR 9–102(B)
1.15(d)	" " " "	***
1.15(e)(1)	Recordkeeping Requirements for Trust Accounts	DR 9–103
1.15(e)(2)	Recordkeeping Requirements for Lawyers Serving as Fiduciaries	***
1.16(a)	Terminating or Declining Representation	DR 2–108(A)
1.16(b)	" " " "	DR 2–108(B)
1.16(c)	" " " "	DR 2–108(C)
1.16(d)	" " " "	DR 2–108(D)
1.16(e)	Delivery of Former Client's File	***
1.17	Sale of a Law Practice	*** EC 4–6
2.1	Lawyer as Advisor	*** EC 7–8
2.2	Lawyer as Intermediary	*** EC 5–20
2.3	Lawyer as Evaluator	*** EC 5–20
2.10	Third Party Neutral	***
2.11	Mediator	***
3.1	Meritorious Claims	DR 7–102(A)(1), (2)
3.3(a)(1)	Candor Toward Tribunal	DR 7–102(A)(5)
3.3(a)(2)	" " " "	DR 7–102(A)(3)
3.3(a)(3)	Controlling Legal Authority	*** EC 7–20
3.3(a)(4)	False Evidence	DR 7–102(A)(4)
3.3(b)	" " " "	***
3.3(c)	Ex Parte Proceedings	***
3.3(d)	Reporting Third Party Fraud on Tribunal	DR 7–102(B)
3.4(a)	Fairness To Opposing Party & Counsel; Obstructing Access to Evidence	DR 7–108(A)
3.4(b)	Secreting Witnesses	DR 7–108(B)
3.4(c)	Compensating Witnesses	DR 7–108(C); EC 7–25
3.4(d)	Disregarding Court Rules or Orders	DR 7–105(A)
3.4(e)	Discovery Abuse	***
3.4(f)	Improper Trial Conduct	DR 7–105(C)(1)-(4)
3.4(g)	Discouraging Witnesses	***
3.4(h)	Threatening Criminal or Disciplinary Action	DR 7–104

Virginia Rules of Professional Conduct	Issue or Topic	Virginia Code of Professional Responsibility
3.5(a), (b), (c)	Communications With Jurors	DR 7–107(A)-(F)
3.5(d)	Influencing Judges	DR 7–109(A)
3.5(e)	Ex Parte Communication With Judge	DR 7–109(B)
3.5(f)	Disruptive Conduct Toward Tribunal	***
3.6(a), (b)	Trial Publicity	DR 7–106
3.7(a)	Lawyer as Witness	DR 5–101(B); DR 5–102(A)
3.7(b)	" " " "	DR 5–102(B)
3.7(c)	" " " "	***
3.8(a)	Additional Responsibilities of a Prosecutor	DR 8–102(A)(1)
3.8(b)	" " " "	DR 8–102(A)(1)
3.8(c)	" " " "	DR 8–102(A)(2)
3.8(d)	" " " "	DR 8–102(A)(3)
3.8(e)	" " " "	DR 7–106(B)
4.1(a)	Truthfulness in Statements to Others	DR 7–102(A)(5)
4.1(b)	" " " "	*** DR 7–102(A)(3); DR 7–102(A)(7)
4.2	Ex Parte Communication With Represented Person	DR 7–103(A)(1)
4.3(a)	Dealing With Unrepresented Persons	DR 7–103(B)
4.3(b)	" " " "	DR 7–103(A)(2)
4.4	Respect for Rights of Third Persons	*** DR 7–102(A)(1); DR 7–105(C)(2); DR 7–107(C); DR 7–107(D)
5.1	Responsibilities of a Supervising Lawyer	*** DR 1–103(A); DR 4–101(E); DR 7–106(B)
5.3(a), (b)	Nonlawyer Assistants	DR 3–104(C); DR 4–101(E)
5.3(c)	" " " "	***
5.4(a)	Sharing Fees With Nonlawyer	DR 3–102(A)
5.4(b)	Partnership with Nonlawyer	DR 3–103(A)
5.4(c)	Avoiding Influence By Non-clients	DR 5–106(B)
5.4(d)	Professional Corporations Owned by Nonlawyers	DR 5–106(C)
5.5(a)(1)	Unauthorized Practice of Law	*** EC 3–9
5.5(a)(2)	" " " "	DR 3–101(A)
5.5(b)	Employment of Suspended or Disbarred Lawyers	DR 3–101(B)
5.5(c)	" " " "	DR 3–101(C)
5.6(a), (b)	Agreements Restricting Practice of Law	DR 2–106
6.1	Voluntary Pro Bono Publico Service	*** ECs 2–26, 2–27, 2–28, 2–29, 2–30, 2–31, 2–32, 2–33, 2–34
6.2	Accepting Appointments	*** EC 2–38; EC 2–39
6.3	Membership in Legal Services Organization	***
7.1(a)	Publicity & Advertising Concerning a Lawyer's Services	DR 2–101(A)
7.1(b)	" " " "	DR 2–101(B)
7.1(c)	" " " "	DR 2–101(C)
7.1(d)	" " " "	DR 2–101(D)
7.1(e)	" " " "	***
7.3	Recommendation or Solicitation of Professional Employment	DR 2–103

Virginia Rules of Professional Conduct	Issue or Topic	Virginia Code of Professional Responsibility
7.4(a), (b)	Communication of Fields of Practice & Certification	DR 2–104(A), (B)
7.4(c)	" " " "	***
7.4(d)	" " " "	***
7.5	Firm Names & Letterheads	DR 2–102
8.1	Bar Admission & Disciplinary Matters	DR 1–101
8.2	Judicial Officials	*** EC 8–6
8.3(a)	Reporting Professional Misconduct	DR 1–103(A)
8.3(b)	" " " "	***
8.3(c)	" " " "	***
8.3(d)	" " " "	***
8.4(a)	Misconduct	DR 1–102(A)(1)
8.4(b)	" " " "	DR 1–102(A)(3)
8.4(c)	" " " "	DR 1–102(A)(4)
8.4(d)	" " " "	DR 9–101(C)
8.4(e)	" " " "	EC 7–31, EC 9–1
8.5(a)	Disciplinary Authority; Choice of Law	DR 1–102(B)
8.5(b)	" " " "	***

[Adopted effective January 1, 2000.]

CROSS REFERENCE TABLE: VIRGINIA CODE OF PROFESSIONAL RESPONSIBILITY TO RULES OF PROFESSIONAL CONDUCT

Virginia Code of Professional Responsibility (DR)	Issue or Topic	Virginia Rule of Professional Conduct
DR 1–101	Bar Admissions or Renewal	Rule 8.1
DR 1–102	Misconduct	Rule 8.4
DR 1–103	Reporting Professional Misconduct	Rule 8.3
DR 2–101	Publicity and Advertising	Rule 7.1
DR 2–102	Professional Letterheads, Offices, Notices	Rule 7.5
DR 2–103	Recommendation or Solicitation of Employment	Rule 7.3
DR 2–104	Specialists; Limitation of Practice	Rule 7.4
DR 2–105	Fees	Rule 1.5
DR 2–106	Agreements Restricting Practice of Law	Rule 5.6
DR 2–107	Acceptance of Employment	***
DR 2–108	Terminating Representation	Rule 1.16
DR 3–101	Aiding Unauthorized Practice of Law	Rule 5.5(a)(2)
DR 3–102	Dividing Fees With a Nonlawyer	Rule 5.4(a)
DR 3–103	Forming Partnership With a Nonlawyer	Rule 5.4(b), (d)
DR 3–104	Supervising Nonlawyer Personnel	Rule 5.3
DR 4–101	Preservation of Confidences & Secrets of a Client	Rule 1.6
DR 5–101(A)	Personal Interests Affecting Professional Judgment	Rule 1.7(b)
DR 5–101(B)	Lawyer as Witness	Rule 3.7
DR 5–102(A), (B)	" " " "	" " " "
DR 5–103(A)	Acquiring Proprietary Interest in Subject Matter of Litigation	Rule 1.8(d), Rule 1.8(j)
DR 5–103(B)	Financial Assistance to Client	Rule 1.8(e)
DR 5–104(A)	Business Transactions with Client	Rule 1.8(a)
DR 5–104(B)	Preparing Instrument in Which Lawyer Receives Gift	Rule 1.8(c)
DR 5–105	Representing Multiple Clients Whose Interests Conflict	Rule 1.7
DR 5–106	Avoiding Influence by Persons Other Than Client	Rule 1.8(f), Rule 5.4(c)
DR 5–107	Settling Similar Claims of Clients	Rule 1.8(g)
DR 6–101(A)	Competence	Rule 1.1
DR 6–101(B)	Promptness	Rule 1.3(a)
DR 6–101(C)	Communication	Rule 1.4(a), (b)
DR 6–101(D)	" " " "	Rule 1.4(c)
DR 6–102	Limiting Liability to Client	Rule 1.8(h)
DR 7–101(A)	Representing Client Zealously	Rule 1.3(b), (c)
DR 7–101(B)	Limitations on Zealous Representation	Rule 1.2(b), (c)
DR 7–102(A)	Representing Client Within Bounds of Law	Rule 3.1, Rule 3.3, Rule 4.4
DR 7–102(B)	Reporting Third Party Fraud on Tribunal	Rule 3.3(d)
DR 7–103(A)(1)	Communication with Persons Represented by Counsel	Rule 4.2
DR 7–103(A)(2)	Advising Unrepresented Persons	Rule 4.3
DR 7–103(B)	Dealing with Unrepresented Persons	Rule 4.3

Virginia Code of Professional Responsibility (DR)	Issue or Topic	Virginia Rule of Professional Conduct
DR 7–104	Threatening Criminal or Disciplinary Charges	Rule 3.4(h)
DR 7–105(A)	Trial Conduct: Disregarding Court Rule or Order	Rule 3.4(d)
DR 7–105(B)	Disclosing Representation to Court	***
DR 7–105(C)	Trial Conduct	Rule 3.4
DR 7–106	Trial Publicity	Rule 3.6
DR 7–107	Communication With or Investigation of Jurors	Rule 3.5(a)–(c)
DR 7–108	Contact with Witnesses	Rule 3.4
DR 7–109	Contact with Officials	Rule 3.5(d), (e)
DR 8–101	Action as Public Official	Rule 1.11(a)
DR 8–102	Special Responsibilities of a Prosecutor	Rule 3.8
DR 9–101	Avoiding Even the Appearance of Impropriety	Rule 1.11
DR 9–102	Preserving Identity of Funds and Property of Client	Rule 1.15
DR 9–103	Record Keeping Requirements	Rule 1.15

[Adopted effective January 1, 2000.]

CLIENT–LAWYER RELATIONSHIP

RULE 1.1 COMPETENCE

A lawyer shall provide competent representation to a client. Competent representation requires the legal knowledge, skill, thoroughness and preparation reasonably necessary for the representation.

[Adopted effective January 1, 2000.]

Comment

Legal Knowledge and Skill

[1] In determining whether a lawyer employs the requisite knowledge and skill in a particular matter, relevant factors include the relative complexity and specialized nature of the matter, the lawyer's general experience, the lawyer's training and experience in the field in question, the preparation and study the lawyer is able to give the matter and whether it is feasible to refer the matter to, or associate or consult with, a lawyer of established competence in the field in question. In many instances, the required proficiency is that of a general practitioner. Expertise in a particular field of law may be required in some circumstances.

[2] A lawyer need not necessarily have special training or prior experience to handle legal problems of a type with which the lawyer is unfamiliar. A newly admitted lawyer can be as competent as a practitioner with long experience. Some important legal skills, such as the analysis of precedent, the evaluation of evidence and legal drafting, are required in all legal problems. Perhaps the most fundamental legal skill consists of determining what kind of legal problems a situation may involve, a skill that necessarily transcends any particular specialized knowledge. A lawyer can provide adequate representation in a wholly novel field through necessary study. Competent representation can also be provided through the association of a lawyer of established competence in the field in question.

[2a] Another important skill is negotiating and, in particular, choosing and carrying out the appropriate negotiating strategy. Often it is possible to negotiate a solution which meets some of the needs and interests of all the parties to a transaction or dispute, i.e., a problem-solving strategy.

[3] In an emergency a lawyer may give advice or assistance in a matter in which the lawyer does not have the skill ordinarily required where referral to or consultation or association with another lawyer would be impractical. Even in an emergency, however, assistance should be limited to that reasonably necessary in the circumstances, for ill-considered action under emergency conditions can jeopardize the client's interest.

[4] A lawyer may accept representation where the requisite level of competence can be achieved by reasonable preparation. This applies as well to a lawyer who is appointed as counsel for an unrepresented person. *See* also Rule 6.2.

Thoroughness and Preparation

[5] Competent handling of a particular matter includes inquiry into and analysis of the factual and legal elements of the problem, and use of methods and procedures meeting the standards of competent practitioners. It also includes adequate preparation. The required attention and preparation are determined in part by what is at stake; major litigation and complex transactions ordinarily require more elaborate treatment than matters of lesser consequence.

Maintaining Competence

[6] To maintain the requisite knowledge and skill, a lawyer should engage in continuing study and education. The Mandatory Continuing Legal Education requirements of the Rules of the Supreme Court of Virginia set the minimum standard for continuing study and education which a lawyer licensed and practicing in Virginia must satisfy. If a system of peer review has been established, the lawyer should consider making use of it in appropriate circumstances.

Virginia Code Comparison

Rule 1.1 is substantially similar to DR 6–101(A). DR 6–101(A)(1) provided that a lawyer "shall undertake representation only in matters in which . . . [t]he lawyer can act with competence and demonstrate the specific legal knowledge, skill, efficiency, and thoroughness in preparation employed in acceptable practice by lawyers undertaking similar matters." DR 6–101(A)(2) also permitted representation in matters if a lawyer "associated with another lawyer who is competent in those matters."

Committee Commentary

The Committee adopted the *ABA Model Rule* verbatim, but added the third paragraph of the Comment to make it clear that legal representation, in which a lawyer is expected to be competent, involves not only litigation but also negotiation techniques and strategies.

In addition, the Committee added the second sentence under Maintaining Competence Comment section to note Virginia's Mandatory Continuing Legal Education requirements.

RULE 1.2 SCOPE OF REPRESENTATION

(a) A lawyer shall abide by a client's decisions concerning the objectives of representation, subject to paragraphs (b), (c), and (d), and shall consult with the client as to the means by which they are to be pursued. A lawyer shall abide by a client's decision, after consultation with the lawyer, whether to accept an offer of settlement of a matter. In a criminal case, the lawyer shall abide by the client's decision, after consultation with the lawyer, as to a plea to be entered, whether to waive jury trial and whether the client will testify.

(b) A lawyer may limit the objectives of the representation if the client consents after consultation.

(c) A lawyer shall not counsel a client to engage, or assist a client, in conduct that the lawyer knows is criminal or fraudulent, but a lawyer may discuss the legal consequences of any proposed course of conduct with a client and may counsel or assist a client to make a good faith effort to determine the validity, scope, meaning, or application of the law.

(d) A lawyer may take such action on behalf of the client as is impliedly authorized to carry out the representation.

(e) When a lawyer knows that a client expects assistance not permitted by the Rules of Professional Conduct or other law, the lawyer shall consult with the client regarding the relevant limitations on the lawyer's conduct.

[Adopted effective January 1, 2000. Amended effective January 1, 2004.]

Comment

Scope of Representation

[1] Both lawyer and client have authority and responsibility in the objectives and means of representation. The client has ultimate authority to determine the purposes to be served by legal representation, within the limits imposed by the law and the lawyer's professional obligations. Within those limits, a client also has a right to consult with the lawyer about the means to be used in pursuing those objectives. In that context, a lawyer shall advise the client about the advantages, disadvantages, and availability of dispute resolution processes that might be appropriate in pursuing these objectives. At the same time, a lawyer is not required to pursue objectives or employ means simply because a client may wish that the lawyer do so. A clear distinction between objectives and means sometimes cannot be drawn, and in many cases the client-lawyer relationship partakes of a joint undertaking. In questions of means, the lawyer should assume responsibility for technical and legal tactical issues, but should defer to the client regarding such questions as the expense to be incurred and concern for third persons who might be adversely affected. These Rules do not define the lawyer's scope of authority in litigation.

[2] In a case in which the client appears to be suffering mental disability, the lawyer's duty to abide by the client's decisions is to be guided by reference to Rule 1.14.

Independence from Client's Views or Activities

[3] Legal representation should not be denied to people who are unable to afford legal services, or whose cause is controversial or the subject of popular disapproval. By the same token, a lawyer's representation of a client, including representation by appointment, does not constitute an endorsement of the client's political, economic, social or moral views or activities.

Services Limited in Objectives or Means

[4] The objectives or scope of services provided by a lawyer may be limited by agreement with the client or by the terms under which the lawyer's services are made available to the client. For example, a retainer may be for a specifically defined purpose. Representation provided through a legal aid agency may be subject to limitations on the types of cases the agency handles. When a lawyer has been retained by an insurer to represent an insured, the representation may be limited to matters related to the insurance coverage. The terms upon which representation is undertaken may exclude specific objectives or means. Such limitations may exclude objectives or means that the lawyer regards as repugnant or imprudent.

[5] An agreement concerning the scope of representation must accord with the Rules of Professional Conduct and other law. Thus, the client may not be asked to agree to representation so limited in scope as to violate Rule 1. 1, or to surrender the right to terminate the lawyer's services or the right to settle litigation that the lawyer might wish to continue.

Criminal, Fraudulent and Prohibited Transactions

[6] A lawyer is required to give an honest opinion about the actual consequences that appear likely to result from a client's conduct. The fact that a client uses advice in a course of action that is criminal or fraudulent does not, of itself, make a lawyer a party to the course of action. However, a lawyer may not

knowingly assist a client in criminal or fraudulent conduct. There is a critical distinction between presenting an analysis of legal aspects of questionable conduct and recommending the means by which a crime or fraud might be committed with impunity.

[7] When the client's course of action has already begun and is continuing, the lawyer's responsibility is especially delicate. The lawyer is not permitted to reveal the client's wrongdoing, except where permitted or required by Rule 1.6. However, the lawyer is required to avoid furthering the purpose, for example, by suggesting how it might be concealed. A lawyer shall not continue assisting a client in conduct that the lawyer originally supposes is legally proper but then discovers is criminal or fraudulent. *See* Rule 1.16.

[8] Where the client is a fiduciary, the lawyer may be charged with special obligations in dealings with a beneficiary.

[9] Paragraph (c) applies whether or not the defrauded party is a party to the transaction. Hence, a lawyer should not participate in a sham transaction; for example, a transaction to effectuate criminal or fraudulent escape of tax liability. Paragraph (c) does not preclude undertaking a criminal defense incident to a general retainer for legal services to a lawful enterprise. The last clause of paragraph (c) recognizes that determining the validity or interpretation of a statute or regulation may require a course of action involving disobedience of the statute or regulation or of the interpretation placed upon it by governmental authorities. See also Rule 3.4(d).

Virginia Code Comparison

Paragraph (a) has no direct counterpart in the Disciplinary Rules of the *Virginia Code*. EC 7–7 stated: "In certain areas of legal representation not affecting the merits of the cause or substantially prejudicing the rights of a client, a lawyer is entitled to make decisions on his own. But otherwise the authority to make decisions is exclusively that of the client ...." EC 7–8 stated that "[I]n the final analysis, however, the ... decision whether to forego legally available objectives or methods because of nonlegal factors is ultimately for the client ... In the event that the client in a nonadjudicatory matter insists upon a course of conduct that is contrary to the judgment and advice of the lawyer but not prohibited by Disciplinary Rules, the lawyer may withdraw from the employment." DR 7–101(A)(1) provided that a lawyer "shall not intentionally ... [f]ail to seek the lawful objectives of his client through reasonably available means permitted by law .... A lawyer does not violate this Disciplinary Rule, however, by ... avoiding offensive tactics ...."

With regard to paragraph (b), DR 7–101(B)(1) provided that a lawyer may, "with the express or implied authority of his client, exercise his professional judgment to limit or vary his client's objectives and waive or fail to assert a right or position of his client."

With regard to paragraph (c), DR 7–102(A)(7) provided that a lawyer shall not "counsel or assist his client in conduct that the lawyer knows to be illegal or fraudulent." DR 7–102(A)(6) provided that a lawyer shall not "participate in the creation or preservation of evidence when he knows or it is obvious that the evidence is false." DR 7–105(A) provided that a lawyer shall not "advise his client to disregard a standing rule of a tribunal or a ruling of a tribunal ... but he may take appropriate steps in good faith to test the validity of such rule or ruling." EC 7–5 stated that a lawyer "should never encourage or aid his client to commit criminal acts or counsel his client on how to violate the law and avoid punishment therefor."

Paragraph (d) had no counterpart in the *Virginia Code*.

With regard to paragraph (e), DR 2–108(A)(1) provided that a lawyer shall withdraw from representation if "continuing the representation will result in a course of conduct by the lawyer that is illegal or inconsistent with the Disciplinary Rules." DR 9–101(C) provided that "[a] lawyer shall not state or imply that he is able to influence improperly ... any tribunal, legislative body or public official."

Committee Commentary

The Committee adopted this Rule as a more succinct and useful statement regarding the scope of the relationship between a lawyer and the client. However, the Committee moved the language of paragraph (b) of the *ABA Model Rule* to the Comment section styled "Independence from Client's Views or Activities" since it appears more appropriate as a Comment than a Rule. Subsequent paragraphs were redesignated accordingly.

The Committee added the fourth sentence in Comment [1] requiring lawyers to advise clients of dispute resolution processes that might be "appropriate."

In Comment [7], the Committee used the verb "shall" to match the mandatory standard of the *Virginia Code* and these Rules.

RULE 1.3 DILIGENCE

(a) A lawyer shall act with reasonable diligence and promptness in representing a client.

(b) A lawyer shall not intentionally fail to carry out a contract of employment entered into with a client for professional services, but may withdraw as permitted under Rule 1.16.

(c) A lawyer shall not intentionally prejudice or damage a client during the course of the professional relationship, except as required or permitted under Rule 1.6 and Rule 3.3.

[Adopted effective January 1, 2000. Amended effective January 1, 2004; February 28, 2006.]

Comment

[1] A lawyer should pursue a matter on behalf of a client despite opposition, obstruction or personal inconvenience to the lawyer, and may take whatever lawful and ethical measures are required to vindicate a client's cause or endeavor. A lawyer should act with commitment and dedication to the interests of the client and with zeal in advocacy upon the client's behalf. However, a lawyer is not bound to press for every advantage that might be realized for a client. A lawyer has professional discretion in determining the means by which a matter should be pursued. *See* Rule 1.2. A lawyer's work load should be controlled so that each matter can be handled adequately.

[1a] Additionally, lawyers have long recognized that a more collaborative, problem-solving approach is often preferable to an adversarial strategy in pursuing the client's needs and interests. Consequently, diligence includes not only an adversarial strategy but also the vigorous pursuit of the client's interest in reaching a solution that satisfies the interests of all parties. The client can be represented zealously in either setting.

[2] Perhaps no professional shortcoming is more widely resented than procrastination. A client's interests often can be adversely affected by the passage of time or the change of conditions; in extreme instances, as when a lawyer overlooks a statute of limitations, the client's legal position may be destroyed. Even when the client's interests are not affected in substance, however, unreasonable delay can cause a client needless anxiety and undermine confidence in the lawyer's trustworthiness.

[3] Unless the relationship is terminated as provided in Rule 1.16, a lawyer should carry through to conclusion all matters undertaken for a client. If a lawyer's employment is limited to a specific matter, the relationship terminates when the matter has been resolved. If a lawyer has served a client over a substantial period in a variety of matters, the client sometimes may assume that the lawyer will continue to serve on a continuing basis unless the lawyer gives notice of withdrawal. Doubt about whether a client-lawyer relationship still exists should be clarified by the lawyer, preferably in writing, so that the client will not mistakenly suppose the lawyer is looking after the client's affairs when the lawyer has ceased to do so. For example, if a lawyer has handled a judicial or administrative proceeding that produced a result adverse to the client but has not been specifically instructed concerning pursuit of an appeal, the lawyer should advise the client of the possibility of appeal before relinquishing responsibility for the matter.

[4] A lawyer should plan for client protection in the event of the lawyer's death, disability, impairment, or incapacity. The plan should be in writing and should designate a responsible attorney capable of making, and who has agreed to make, arrangements for the protection of client interests in the event of the lawyer's death, impairment, or incapacity.

Virginia Code Comparison

With regard to paragraph (a), DR 6–101(B) required that a lawyer "attend promptly to matters undertaken for a client until completed or until the lawyer has properly and completely withdrawn from representing the client." EC 6–4 stated that a lawyer should "give appropriate attention to his legal work." Canon 7 stated that "a lawyer should represent a client zealously within the bounds of the law."

Paragraphs (b) and (c) adopt the language of DR 7–101(A)(2) and DR 7–101(A)(3) of the *Virginia Code.*

Committee Commentary

The Committee added DR 7–101(A)(2) and DR 7–101(A)(3) from the *Virginia Code* as paragraphs (b) and (c) of this Rule in order to make it a more complete statement about fulfilling one's obligations to a client. Additionally, the Committee added the second paragraph to the Comment as a reminder to lawyers that there is often an appropriate collaborative component to zealous advocacy.

RULE 1.4 COMMUNICATION

(a) A lawyer shall keep a client reasonably informed about the status of a matter and promptly comply with reasonable requests for information.

(b) A lawyer shall explain a matter to the extent reasonably necessary to permit the client to make informed decisions regarding the representation.

(c) A lawyer shall inform the client of facts pertinent to the matter and of communications from another party that may significantly affect settlement or resolution of the matter.

[Adopted effective January 1, 2000.]

Comment

[1] The client should have sufficient information to participate intelligently in decisions concerning the objectives of the representation and the means by which they are to be pursued, to the extent the client is willing and able to do so. For example, a lawyer negotiating on behalf of a client should provide the client with facts relevant to the matter, inform the client of communications from another party and take other reasonable steps that permit the client to make a decision regarding an offer from another party. A lawyer who receives from opposing counsel an offer of settlement in a civil controversy or a proffered plea agreement in a criminal case should promptly inform the client of its substance unless prior discussions with the client have left it clear that the proposal will be unacceptable. *See* Rule 1.2(a). Even when a client delegates authority to the lawyer, the client should be kept advised of the status of the matter.

[1a] This continuing duty to keep the client informed includes a duty to advise the client about the availability of dispute resolution processes that might be more appropriate to the client's goals than the initial process chosen. For example, information obtained during a lawyer-to-lawyer negotiation may give rise to consideration of a process, such as mediation, where the parties themselves could be more directly involved in resolving the dispute.

[2] Adequacy of communication depends in part on the kind of advice or assistance involved. For example, in negotiations where there is time to explain a proposal, the lawyer should review all important provisions with the client before proceeding to an agreement. In litigation a lawyer should explain the general strategy and prospects of success and ordinarily should consult the client on tactics that might injure or coerce others. On the other hand, a lawyer ordinarily cannot be expected to describe trial or negotiation strategy in detail. The guiding principle is that the lawyer should fulfill reasonable client expectations for information consistent with the duty to act in the client's best interests, and the client's overall requirements as to the character of representation.

[3] Ordinarily, the information to be provided is that appropriate for a client who is a comprehending and responsible adult. However, fully informing the client according to this standard may be impracticable, for example, where the client is a child or suffers from mental disability. *See* Rule 1.14. When the client is an organization or group, it is often impossible or inappropriate to inform every one of its members about its legal affairs; ordinarily, the lawyer should address communications to the appropriate officials of the organization. *See* Rule 1.13. Where many routine matters are involved, a system of limited or occasional reporting may be arranged with the client. Practical exigency may also require a lawyer to act for a client without prior consultation.

Withholding Information

[4] In some circumstances, a lawyer may be justified in delaying transmission of information when the client would be likely to react imprudently to an immediate communication. Thus, a lawyer might withhold a psychiatric diagnosis of a client when the examining psychiatrist indicates that disclosure would harm the client. A lawyer may not withhold information to serve the lawyer's own interest or convenience. Rules or court orders governing litigation may provide that information supplied to a lawyer may not be disclosed to the client. Rule 3.4(d) directs compliance with such rules or orders.

Virginia Code Comparison

Rule 1.4(a) is substantially similar to DR 6–101(C) of the *Virginia Code* which stated: "A lawyer shall keep a client reasonably informed about matters in which the lawyer's services are being rendered."

Paragraph (b) has no direct counterpart in the *Virginia Code.* EC 7–8 stated that a lawyer "should exert his best efforts to insure that decisions of his client are made only after the client has been informed of relevant considerations." EC 9–2 stated that "a lawyer should fully and promptly inform his client of material developments in the matters being handled for the client."

Paragraph (c) is identical to DR 6–101(D) of the *Virginia Code.*

Committee Commentary

The *Virginia Code* had already substituted the essential notion of paragraph (a) as DR 6–101(C), thus specifically addressing a responsibility omitted from the *ABA Model Code.* The Committee believed that paragraph (b) specifically addressed a responsibility only implied in the *Virginia Code* and that adding DR 6–101(D) as paragraph (c) made the Rule a more complete statement regarding a lawyer's obligation to communicate with a client. Additionally, the Committee added a new second paragraph to the Comment to remind lawyers of their continuing duty to help clients choose the most appropriate settlement process.

RULE 1.5 FEES

(a) A lawyer's fee shall be reasonable. The factors to be considered in determining the reasonableness of a fee include the following:

(1) the time and labor required, the novelty and difficulty of the questions involved, and the skill requisite to perform the legal service properly;

(2) the likelihood, if apparent to the client, that the acceptance of the particular employment will preclude other employment by the lawyer;

(3) the fee customarily charged in the locality for similar legal services;

(4) the amount involved and the results obtained;

(5) the time limitations imposed by the client or by the circumstances;

(6) the nature and length of the professional relationship with the client;

(7) the experience, reputation, and ability of the lawyer or lawyers performing the services; and

(8) whether the fee is fixed or contingent.

(b) The lawyer's fee shall be adequately explained to the client. When the lawyer has not regularly represented the client, the amount, basis or rate of the fee shall be communicated to the client, preferably in writing, before or within a reasonable time after commencing the representation.

(c) A fee may be contingent on the outcome of the matter for which the service is rendered, except in a matter in which a contingent fee is prohibited by paragraph (d) or other law. A contingent fee agreement shall state in writing the method by which the fee is to be determined, including the percentage or percentages that shall accrue to the lawyer in the event of settlement, trial or appeal, litigation and other expenses to be deducted from the recovery, and whether such expenses are to be deducted before or after the contingent fee is calculated. Upon conclusion of a contingent fee matter, the lawyer shall provide the client with a written statement stating the outcome of the matter and, if there is a recovery, showing the remittance to the client and the method of its determination.

(d) A lawyer shall not enter into an arrangement for, charge, or collect a contingent fee:

(1) in a domestic relations matter, except in rare instances; or

(2) for representing a defendant in a criminal case.

(e) A division of a fee between lawyers who are not in the same firm may be made only if:

(1) the client is advised of and consents to the participation of all the lawyers involved;

(2) the terms of the division of the fee are disclosed to the client and the client consents thereto;

(3) the total fee is reasonable; and

(4) the division of fees and the client's consent is obtained in advance of the rendering of legal services, preferably in writing.

(f) Paragraph (e) does not prohibit or regulate the division of fees between attorneys who were previously associated in a law firm or between any successive attorneys in the same matter. In any such instance, the total fee must be reasonable.

[Adopted effective January 1, 2000. Amended effective January 1, 2004.]

Comment

Basis or Rate of Fee

[1] When the lawyer has regularly represented a client, they ordinarily will have evolved an understanding concerning the basis or rate of the fee. In a new client-lawyer relationship, however, an understanding as to the amount, basis, or rate of the fee should be promptly established. It is not necessary to recite all the factors that underlie the basis of the fee, but only those that are directly involved in its computation. It is sufficient, for example, to state that the basic rate is an hourly charge or a fixed amount or an estimated amount, or to identify the factors that may be taken into account in finally fixing the fee. A written statement concerning the fee reduces the possibility of misunderstanding. Furnishing the client with a simple letter, memorandum, receipt or a copy of the lawyer's customary fee schedule may be sufficient if the basis or rate of the fee is set forth.

Terms of Payment

[2] A lawyer may require advance payment of a fee, but is obliged to return any unearned portion. *See* Rule 1.16(d). A lawyer may accept property in payment for services, such as an ownership interest in an enterprise, providing this does not involve acquisition of a proprietary interest in the cause of action or subject matter of the litigation contrary to

Rule 1.8(j). However, a fee paid in property instead of money may be subject to special scrutiny because it involves questions concerning both the value of the services and the lawyer's special knowledge of the value of the property.

[3] An agreement may not be made whose terms might induce the lawyer improperly to curtail services for the client or perform them in a way contrary to the client's interest. For example, a lawyer should not enter into an agreement whereby services are to be provided only up to a stated amount when it is foreseeable that more extensive services probably will be required, unless the situation is adequately explained to the client. Otherwise, the client might have to bargain for further assistance in the midst of a proceeding or transaction. However, it is proper to define the extent of services in light of the client's ability to pay. A lawyer should not exploit a fee arrangement based primarily on hourly charges by using wasteful procedures. When considering whether a contingent fee is consistent with the client's best interest, the lawyer should offer the client alternative bases for the fee and explain their implications. Applicable law may impose limitations on contingent fees, such as a ceiling on the percentage. In any event, a fee should not be imposed upon a client, but should be the result of an informed decision concerning reasonable alternatives.

Contingent Fees in Domestic Relations Cases

[3a] An arrangement for a contingent fee in a domestic relations matter has been previously considered appropriate only in those rare instances where:

(a) the contingent fee is for the collection of, and is to be paid out of (i) accumulated arrearages in child or spousal support; (ii) an asset not previously viewed or contemplated as a marital asset by the parties or the court; (iii) a monetary award pursuant to equitable distribution or under a property settlement agreement;

(b) the parties are divorced and reconciliation is not a realistic prospect;

(c) the children of the marriage are or will soon achieve the age of maturity and the legal services rendered pursuant to the contingent fee arrangement are not likely to affect their relationship with the non-custodial parent;

(d) the client is indigent or could not otherwise obtain adequate counsel on an hourly fee basis; and

(e) the fee arrangement is fair and reasonable under the circumstances.

Division of Fee

[4] A division of fee refers to a single billing to a client covering the fee of two or more lawyers who are not in the same firm. A division of fee facilitates association of more than one lawyer in a matter in which neither alone could serve the client as well, and most often is used when the fee is contingent and the division is between a referring lawyer and a trial specialist.

Disputes over Fees

[5] If a procedure has been established for resolution of fee disputes, such as an arbitration or mediation procedure established by the bar, the lawyer should conscientiously consider submitting to it. Law may prescribe a procedure for determining a lawyer's fee, for example, in representation of an executor or administrator, a class or a person entitled to a reasonable fee as part of the measure of damages. The lawyer entitled to such a fee and a lawyer representing another party concerned with the fee should comply with the prescribed procedure.

Virginia Code Comparison

With regard to paragraph (a), DR 2–105(A) required that a "lawyer's fees . . . be reasonable and adequately explained to the client." The factors involved in assessing the reasonableness of a fee listed in Rule 1.5(a) are substantially similar to those listed in EC 2–20.

Paragraph (b) emphasizes the lawyer's duty to adequately explain fees (which appears in DR 2–105(A)) but stresses the lawyer's duty to disclose fee information to the client rather than merely responding to a client's request for information (as in DR 2–105(B)).

Paragraph (c) is substantially the same as DR 2–105(C). EC 2–22 provided that "[c]ontingent fee arrangements in civil cases have long been commonly accepted in the United States," but that "a lawyer generally should decline to accept employment on a contingent fee basis by one who is able to pay a reasonable fixed fee . . . ."

With regard to paragraph (d), DR 2–105(C) prohibited a contingent fee in a criminal case. EC 2–22 provided that "contingent fee arrangements in domestic relation cases are rarely justified."

With regard to paragraph (e), DR 2–105(D) permitted division of fees only if: "(1) The client consents to employment of additional counsel; (2) Both attorneys expressly assume responsibility to the client; and (3) The terms of the division of the fee are disclosed to the client and the client consents thereto."

There was no counterpart to paragraph (f) in the *Virginia Code.*

Committee Commentary

The Committee believes that DR 2–105 placed greater emphasis than the *ABA Model Rule* on the Full Disclosure of Fees and Fee Arrangements to Clients and therefore added language from DR 2–105(A) to paragraph (a) and from DR 2–105(D)(3) to paragraph (e). The Comment to paragraph (d)(1) reflects the Committee's conclusion that the public policy concerns which preclude contingent fee arrangements in certain domestic relations cases do not apply when property division, support matters or attorney's fee awards have been previously determined. Paragraph (e) eliminates the requirement in the *Virginia Code* that each lawyer involved in a fee-splitting arrangement assume full responsibility to the client, regardless of the degree of the lawyer's continuing participation. The requirement in the *Virginia Code* was deleted to encourage referrals under appropriate circumstances by not requiring the lawyer making the referral to automatically assume ethical responsibility for all of the activities of the other lawyers involved in the arrangement. However, such an arrangement is acceptable only if the client consents after full disclosure, which must include a delineation of each lawyer's responsibilities to the client.

RULE 1.6 CONFIDENTIALITY OF INFORMATION

(a) A lawyer shall not reveal information protected by the attorney-client privilege under applicable law or other information gained in the professional relationship that the client has requested be held inviolate or the disclosure of which would be embarrassing or would be likely to be detrimental to the client unless the client consents after consultation, except for disclosures that are impliedly authorized in order to carry out the representation, and except as stated in paragraphs (b) and (c).

(b) To the extent a lawyer reasonably believes necessary, the lawyer may reveal:

(1) such information to comply with law or a court order;

(2) such information to establish a claim or defense on behalf of the lawyer in a controversy between the lawyer and the client, to establish a defense to a criminal charge or civil claim against the lawyer based upon conduct in which the client was involved, or to respond to allegations in any proceeding concerning the lawyer's representation of the client;

(3) such information which clearly establishes that the client has, in the course of the representation, perpetrated upon a third party a fraud related to the subject matter of the representation;

(4) such information reasonably necessary to protect a client's interests in the event of the representing lawyer's death, disability, incapacity or incompetence;

(5) such information sufficient to participate in a law office management assistance program approved by the Virginia State Bar or other similar private program;

(6) information to an outside agency necessary for statistical, bookkeeping, accounting, data processing, printing, or other similar office management purposes, provided the lawyer exercises due care in the selection of the agency, advises the agency that the information must be kept confidential and reasonably believes that the information will be kept confidential.

(c) A lawyer shall promptly reveal:

(1) the intention of a client, as stated by the client, to commit a crime and the information necessary to prevent the crime, but before revealing such information, the attorney shall, where feasible, advise the client of the possible legal consequences of the action, urge the client not to commit the crime, and advise the client that the attorney must reveal the client's criminal intention unless thereupon abandoned, and, if the crime involves perjury by the client, that the attorney shall seek to withdraw as counsel;

(2) information which clearly establishes that the client has, in the course of the representation, perpetrated a fraud related to the subject matter of the representation upon a tribunal. Before revealing such information, however, the lawyer shall request that the client advise the tribunal of the fraud. For the purposes of this paragraph and paragraph (b)(3), information is clearly established when the client acknowledges to the attorney that the client has perpetrated a fraud; or

(3) information concerning the misconduct of another attorney to the appropriate professional authority under Rule 8.3. When the information necessary to report the misconduct is protected under this Rule, the attorney, after consultation, must obtain client consent. Consultation should include full disclosure of all reasonably foreseeable consequences of both disclosure and non-disclosure to the client.

[Adopted effective January 1, 2000. Amended effective January 1, 2004.]

Comment

[1] The lawyer is part of a judicial system charged with upholding the law. One of the lawyer's functions is to advise clients so that they avoid any violation of the law in the proper exercise of their rights.

[2] The common law recognizes that the client's confidences must be protected from

disclosure. The observance of the ethical obligation of a lawyer to hold inviolate confidential information of the client not only facilitates the full development of facts essential to proper representation of the client but also encourages people to seek early legal assistance.

[3] Almost without exception, clients come to lawyers in order to determine what their rights are and what is, in the maze of laws and regulations, deemed to be legal and correct. Based upon experience, lawyers know that clients usually follow the advice given, and the law is upheld.

[4] A fundamental principle in the client-lawyer relationship is that the lawyer maintain confidentiality of information relating to the representation. The client is thereby encouraged to communicate fully and frankly with the lawyer even as to embarrassing or legally damaging subject matter.

[5] The principle of confidentiality is given effect in two related bodies of law, the attorney-client privilege (which includes the work product doctrine) in the law of evidence and the rule of confidentiality established in professional ethics. The attorney-client privilege applies in judicial and other proceedings in which a lawyer may be called as a witness or otherwise required to produce evidence concerning a client. The rule of client-lawyer confidentiality applies in situations other than those where evidence is sought from the lawyer through compulsion of law. The confidentiality rule applies not merely to matters communicated in confidence by the client but also to all information protected by the attorney-client privilege under applicable law or other information gained in the professional relationship that the client has requested be held inviolate or the disclosure of which would be embarrassing or would be likely to be detrimental to the client, whatever its source. A lawyer may not disclose such information except as authorized or required by the Rules of Professional Conduct or other law.

[5a] The rules governing confidentiality of information apply to a lawyer who represents an organization of which the lawyer is an employee.

[6] The requirement of maintaining confidentiality of information relating to representation applies to government lawyers who may disagree with the policy goals that their representation is designed to advance.

Authorized Disclosure

[7] A lawyer is impliedly authorized to make disclosures about a client when appropriate in carrying out the representation, except to the extent that the client's instructions or special circumstances limit that authority. In litigation, for example, a lawyer may disclose information by admitting a fact that cannot properly be disputed, or in negotiation by making a disclosure that facilitates a satisfactory conclusion.

[7a] Lawyers frequently need to consult with colleagues or other attorneys in order to competently represent their clients' interests. An overly strict reading of the duty to protect client information would render it difficult for lawyers to consult with each other, which is an important means of continuing professional education and development. A lawyer should exercise great care in discussing a client's case with another attorney from whom advice is sought. Among other things, the lawyer should consider whether the communication risks a waiver of the attorney-client privilege or other applicable protections. The lawyer should endeavor when possible to discuss a case in strictly hypothetical or abstract terms. In addition, prior to seeking advice from another attorney, the attorney should take reasonable steps to determine whether the attorney from whom advice is sought has a conflict. The attorney from whom advice is sought must be careful to protect the confidentiality of the information given by the attorney seeking advice and must not use such information for the advantage of the lawyer or a third party.

[7b] Compliance with Rule 1.6(a) might include fulfilling duties under Rule 1.14, regarding a client with an impairment.

[7c] Compliance with Rule 1.6(b)(5) might require a written confidentiality agreement with the outside agency to which the lawyer discloses information.

[8] Lawyers in a firm may, in the course of the firm's practice, disclose to each other information relating to a client of the firm, unless the client has instructed that particular information be confined to specified lawyers.

[8a] Lawyers involved in insurance defense work that includes submission of detailed information regarding the client's case to an auditing firm must be extremely careful to gain consent from the client after full and adequate disclosure. Client consent to provision of information to the insurance carrier does not equate with consent to provide the information to an outside auditor. The lawyer must obtain specific consent to disclose the information to that auditor. Pursuant to the lawyer's duty of loyalty to the client, the lawyer should not recommend that the client

provide such consent if the disclosure to the auditor would in some way prejudice the client. *Legal Ethics Opinion #1723, approved by the Supreme Court of Virginia, September 29, 1999.*

Disclosure Adverse to Client

[9] The confidentiality rule is subject to limited exceptions. However, to the extent a lawyer is required or permitted to disclose a client's confidences, the client will be inhibited from revealing facts which would enable the lawyer to counsel against a wrongful course of action. The public is better protected if full and open communication by the client is encouraged than if it is inhibited.

[10] Several situations must be distinguished.

[11] First, the lawyer may not counsel or assist a client in conduct that is criminal or fraudulent. *See* Rule 1.2(c). Similarly, a lawyer has a duty under Rule 3.3(a)(4) not to use false evidence. This duty is essentially a special instance of the duty prescribed in Rule 1.2(c) to avoid assisting a client in criminal or fraudulent conduct.

[12] Second, the lawyer may have been innocently involved in past conduct by the client that was criminal or fraudulent. In such a situation the lawyer has not violated Rule 1.2(c), because to "counsel or assist" criminal or fraudulent conduct requires knowing that the conduct is of that character.

[13] Third, the lawyer may learn that a client intends prospective criminal conduct. As stated in paragraph (c)(1), the lawyer is obligated to reveal such information. Some discretion is involved as it is very difficult for a lawyer to "know" when proposed criminal conduct will actually be carried out, for the client may have a change of mind.

[14] The lawyer's exercise of discretion requires consideration of such factors as the nature of the lawyer's relationship with the client, the nature of the client's intended conduct, the lawyer's own involvement in the transaction, and factors that may extenuate the conduct in question. Where practical, the lawyer should seek to persuade the client to take appropriate action. In any case, a disclosure adverse to the client's interest should be no greater than the lawyer reasonably believes necessary to the purpose.

Withdrawal

[15] If the lawyer's services will be used by the client in materially furthering a course of criminal or fraudulent conduct, the lawyer must withdraw, as stated in Rule 1.16(a)(1).

[16] After withdrawal the lawyer is required to refrain from making disclosure of the client's confidences, except as otherwise provided in Rule 1.6. Neither this Rule nor Rule 1.8(b) nor Rule 1.16(d) prevents the lawyer from giving notice of the fact of withdrawal, and the lawyer may also withdraw or disaffirm any opinion, document, affirmation, or the like.

[17] Where the client is an organization, the lawyer may be in doubt whether contemplated conduct will actually be carried out by the organization. Where necessary to guide conduct in connection with this Rule, the lawyer may make inquiry within the organization as indicated in Rule 1.13(b).

Dispute Concerning a Lawyer's Conduct

[18] Where a legal claim or disciplinary charge alleges complicity of the lawyer in a client's conduct or other misconduct of the lawyer involving representation of the client, the lawyer may respond to the extent the lawyer reasonably believes necessary to establish a defense. The same is true with respect to a claim involving the conduct or representation of a former client. The lawyer's right to respond arises when an assertion of such complicity has been made. Paragraph (b)(2) does not require the lawyer to await the commencement of an action or proceeding that charges such complicity, so that the defense may be established by responding directly to a third party who has made such an assertion. The right to defend, of course, applies where a proceeding has been commenced. Where practicable and not prejudicial to the lawyer's ability to establish the defense, the lawyer should advise the client of the third party's assertion and request that the client respond appropriately. In any event, disclosure should be no greater than the lawyer reasonably believes is necessary to vindicate innocence, the disclosure should be made in a manner which limits access to the information to the tribunal or other persons having a need to know it, and appropriate protective orders or other arrangements should be sought by the lawyer to the fullest extent practicable.

[19] If the lawyer is charged with wrongdoing in which the client's conduct is implicated, the rule of confidentiality should not prevent the lawyer from defending against the charge. Such a charge can arise in a civil, criminal or professional disciplinary proceeding, and can be based on a wrong allegedly committed by the lawyer against the client, or on a wrong alleged by a third person; for example, a person claiming to have been defrauded by

the lawyer and client acting together. A lawyer entitled to a fee is permitted by paragraph (b)(2) to prove the services rendered in an action to collect it. This aspect of the Rule expresses the principle that the beneficiary of a fiduciary relationship may not exploit it to the detriment of the fiduciary. As stated above, the lawyer must make every effort practicable to avoid unnecessary disclosure of information relating to a representation, to limit disclosure to those having the need to know it, and to obtain protective orders or make other arrangements minimizing the risk of disclosure.

Disclosures Otherwise Required or Authorized

[20] If a lawyer is called as a witness to give testimony concerning a client, absent waiver by the client, paragraph (a) requires the lawyer to invoke the attorney-client privilege when it is applicable. Except as permitted by Rule 3.4(d), the lawyer must comply with the final orders of a court or other tribunal of competent jurisdiction requiring the lawyer to give information about the client.

[21] The Rules of Professional Conduct in various circumstances permit or require a lawyer to disclose information relating to the representation. *See* Rules 2.3, 3.3 and 4.1. In addition to these provisions, a lawyer may be obligated or permitted by other provisions of law to give information about a client. Whether another provision of law supersedes Rule 1.6 is a matter of interpretation beyond the scope of these Rules, but a presumption should exist against such a supersession.

Attorney Misconduct

[21a] Self-regulation of the legal profession occasionally places attorneys in awkward positions with respect to their obligations to clients and to the profession. Paragraph (c)(3) requires an attorney who has information indicating that another attorney has violated the Rules of Professional Conduct, learned during the course of representing a client and protected as a confidence or secret under Rule 1.6, to request the permission of the client to disclose the information necessary to report the misconduct to disciplinary authorities. In requesting consent, the attorney must inform the client of all reasonably foreseeable consequences of both disclosure and non-disclosure.

[21b] Although paragraph (c)(3) requires that authorized disclosure be made promptly, a lawyer does not violate this Rule by delaying in reporting attorney misconduct for the minimum period of time necessary to protect a client's interests. For example, a lawyer might choose to postpone reporting attorney misconduct until the end of litigation when reporting during litigation might harm the client's interests.

Former Client

[22] The duty of confidentiality continues after the client-lawyer relationship has terminated.

Virginia Code Comparison

Rule 1.6 retains the two-part definition of information subject to the lawyer's ethical duty of confidentiality. EC 4–4 added that the duty differed from the evidentiary privilege in that it existed "without regard to the nature or source of information or the fact that others share the knowledge." However, the definition of "client information" as set forth in the *ABA Model Rules*, which includes all information "relating to" the representation, was rejected as too broad.

Paragraph (a) permits a lawyer to disclose information where impliedly authorized to do so in order to carry out the representation. Under DR 4–101(B) and (C), a lawyer was not permitted to reveal "confidences" unless the client first consented after disclosure.

Paragraph (b)(1) is substantially the same as DR 4–101(C)(2).

Paragraph (b)(2) is substantially similar to DR 4–101(C)(4) which authorized disclosure by a lawyer of "[c]onfidences or secrets necessary to establish the reasonableness of his fee or to defend himself or his employees or associates against an accusation of wrongful conduct."

Paragraph (b)(3) is substantially the same as DR 4–101(C)(3).

Paragraph (b)(4) had no counterpart in the *Virginia Code.*

Paragraphs (c)(1) and (c)(2) are substantially the same as DR 4–101(D).

Paragraph (c)(3) had no counterpart in the *Virginia Code.*

Committee Commentary

The Committee added language to this Rule from DR 4–101 to make the disclosure provisions more consistent with current Virginia policy. The Committee specifically concluded that the provisions of DR 4–101(D) of the *Virginia Code,* which required broader disclosure than the *ABA Model Rule* even permitted, should be added as paragraph (c). Additionally, to promote the integrity of the legal profession, the Committee adopted new language as paragraph (c)(3) setting forth the circumstances under which a lawyer must report the misconduct of another lawyer when such a report may require disclosure of privileged information.

RULE 1.7 CONFLICT OF INTEREST: GENERAL RULE

(a) Except as provided in paragraph (b), a lawyer shall not represent a client if the representation involves a concurrent conflict of interest. A concurrent conflict of interest exists if:

(1) the representation of one client will be directly adverse to another client; or

(2) there is significant risk that the representation of one or more clients will be materially limited by the lawyer's responsibilities to another client, a former client or a third person or by a personal interest of the lawyer.

(b) Notwithstanding the existence of a concurrent conflict of interest under paragraph (a), a lawyer may represent a client if each affected client consents after consultation, and:

(1) the lawyer reasonably believes that the lawyer will be able to provide competent and diligent representation to each affected client;

(2) the representation is not prohibited by law;

(3) the representation does not involve the assertion of a claim by one client against another client represented by the lawyer in the same litigation or other proceeding before a tribunal; and

(4) the consent from the client is memorialized in writing.

[Adopted effective January 1, 2000. Amended effective June 30, 2005.]

COMMENT

Loyalty to a Client

[1] Loyalty and independent judgment are essential elements in the lawyer's relationship to a client. An impermissible conflict of interest may exist before representation is undertaken, in which event the representation should be declined. The lawyer should adopt reasonable procedures, appropriate for the size and type of firm and practice, to determine in both litigation and non-litigation matters the parties and issues involved and to determine whether there are actual or potential conflicts of interest.

[2] If such a conflict arises after representation has been undertaken, the lawyer should withdraw from the representation. *See* Rule 1.16. Where more than one client is involved and the lawyer withdraws because a conflict arises after representation, whether the lawyer may continue to represent any of the clients is determined by Rule 1.9. As to whether a client-lawyer relationship exists or, having once been established, is continuing, see Comment to Rule 1.3 and Scope.

[3] As a general proposition, loyalty to a client prohibits undertaking representation directly adverse to that client without that client's consent. Paragraph (a) expresses that general rule. Thus, a lawyer ordinarily may not act as advocate against a person the lawyer represents in some other matter, even if it is wholly unrelated. On the other hand, simultaneous representation in unrelated matters of clients whose interests are only generally adverse, such as competing economic enterprises, does not require consent of the respective clients.

[4] Loyalty to a client is also impaired when a lawyer cannot consider, recommend or carry out an appropriate course of action for the client because of the lawyer's other responsibilities or interests. The conflict in effect forecloses alternatives that would otherwise be available to the client. A possible conflict does not itself preclude the representation. The critical questions are the likelihood that a conflict will eventuate and, if it does, whether it will materially interfere with the lawyer's independent professional judgment in considering alternatives or foreclose courses of action that reasonably should be pursued on behalf of the client. Nevertheless, a lawyer can never adequately provide joint representation in certain matters relating to divorce, annulment or separation—specifically, child custody, child support, visitation, spousal support and maintenance or division of property.

Special Considerations in Common Representation

[5] In considering whether to represent multiple clients in the same matter, a lawyer should be mindful that if the common representation fails because the potentially adverse interests cannot be reconciled, the result can be additional cost, embarrassment and recrimination. Ordinarily, the lawyer will be forced to withdraw from representing all of the clients if the common representation fails. In some situations, the risk of failure is so great that multiple representation is plainly impossible. For example, a lawyer cannot undertake common representation of clients where contentious litigation or negotiations between them are imminent or contemplated. Moreover, because the lawyer is required to be impartial between commonly represented clients, representation of multiple clients is improper when it is unlikely that impartiality can be maintained. Generally, if the relationship between the parties has already assumed antagonism, the possibility that the client's interests can be adequately served by common representation is not very good. Other

relevant factors are whether the lawyer subsequently will represent both parties on a continuing basis and whether the situation involves creating or terminating a relationship between the parties.

[6] A particularly important factor in determining the appropriateness of common representation is the effect on client-lawyer confidentiality and the attorney-client privilege. With regard to the attorney-client privilege, the prevailing rule is that, as between commonly represented clients, the privilege does not attach. Hence, it must be assumed that if litigation eventuates between the clients, the privilege will not protect any such communications, and the clients should be so advised.

[7] As to the duty of confidentiality, continued common representation will almost certainly be inadequate if one client asks the lawyer not to disclose to the other client information relevant to the common representation. This is so because the lawyer has an equal duty of loyalty to each client, and each client has the right to be informed of anything bearing on the representation that might affect the client's interests and the right to expect that the lawyer will use that information to that client's benefit. *See* Rule 1.4. The lawyer should, at the outset of the common representation and as part of the process of obtaining each client's informed consent, advise each client that information will be shared and that the lawyer will have to withdraw if one client decides that some matter material to the representation should be kept from the other. In limited circumstances, it may be appropriate for the lawyer to proceed with the representation when the clients have agreed, after being properly informed, that the lawyer will keep certain information confidential. For example, the lawyer may reasonably conclude that failure to disclose one client's trade secrets to another client will not adversely affect representation involving a joint venture between the clients and agree to keep that information confidential with the informed consent of both clients.

[8] When seeking to establish or adjust a relationship between clients, the lawyer should make clear that the lawyer's role is not that of partisanship normally expected in other circumstances and, thus, that the clients may be required to assume greater responsibility for decisions than when each client is separately represented. Any limitations on the scope of the representation made necessary as a result of the common representation should be fully explained to the clients at the outset of the representation. *See* Rule 1.2(b).

[9] Subject to the above limitations, each client in the common representation has the right to loyal and diligent representation and the protection of Rule 1.9 concerning the obligations to a former client. The client also has the right to discharge the lawyer as stated in Rule 1.16.

Consultation and Consent

[10] A client may consent to representation notwithstanding a conflict. However, when a disinterested lawyer would conclude that the client should not agree to the representation under the circumstances, the lawyer involved cannot properly ask for such agreement or provide representation on the basis of the client's consent. When more than one client is involved, the question of conflict must be resolved as to each client. Moreover, there may be circumstances where it is impossible to make the disclosure necessary to obtain consent. For example, when the lawyer represents different clients in related matters and one of the clients refuses to consent to the disclosure necessary to permit the other client to make an informed decision, the lawyer cannot properly ask the latter to consent. A lawyer's obligations regarding conflicts of interest are not present solely at the onset of the attorney- client relationship; rather, such obligations are ongoing such that a change in circumstances may require a lawyer to obtain new consent from a client after additional, adequate disclosure regarding that change in circumstances.

Paragraph (b) requires that client consent be memorialized in writing. Preferably, the attorney should present the memorialization to the client for signature or acknowledgement; however, any writing will satisfy this requirement, including, but not limited to, an attorney's notes or memorandum, and such writing need not be signed by, reviewed with, or delivered to the client.

Lawyer's Interests

[11] A lawyer may not allow business or personal interests to affect representation of a client. For example, a lawyer's need for income should not lead the lawyer to undertake matters that cannot be handled competently and at a reasonable fee. *See* Rules 1.1 and 1.5. Similarly, a lawyer may not refer clients to an enterprise in which the lawyer has an undisclosed interest. A lawyer's romantic or other intimate personal relationship can also adversely affect representation of a client.

Conflicts in Litigation

[12] Paragraph (a)(1) prohibits representation of opposing parties in litigation. Simultaneous representation of parties whose interests in litigation may conflict, such as co-plaintiffs or co-defendants, is governed by paragraph (a)(2). An impermissible conflict may exist by reason of substantial discrepancy in the parties' testimony, incompatibility in positions in relation to an opposing party or the fact that there are substantially different possibilities of settlement of the claims or liabilities in question. Such conflicts can arise in criminal cases as well as civil. The potential for conflict of interest in representing multiple defendants in a criminal case is so grave that ordinarily a lawyer should decline to represent more than one co-defendant. On the other hand, common representation of persons having similar interests is proper if the risk of adverse effect is minimal and the requirements of paragraph (b) are met.

[13] Ordinarily, a lawyer may not act as advocate against a client the lawyer represents in some other matter, even if the other matter is wholly unrelated. However, there are circumstances in which a lawyer may act as advocate against a client. For example, a lawyer representing an enterprise with diverse operations may accept employment as an advocate against the enterprise in an unrelated matter if doing so will not adversely affect the lawyer's relationship with the enterprise or conduct of the suit and if both clients consent upon consultation. By the same token, government lawyers in some circumstances may represent government employees in proceedings in which a government agency is the opposing party. The propriety of concurrent representation can depend on the nature of the litigation. For example, a suit charging fraud entails conflict to a degree not involved in a suit for a declaratory judgment concerning statutory interpretation.

[14] A lawyer may represent parties having antagonistic positions on a legal question that has arisen in different cases, unless representation of either client would be materially limited. Thus, it is ordinarily not improper to assert such positions in cases pending in different trial courts, but it may be improper to do so in cases pending at the same time in an appellate court.

Interest of Person Paying for a Lawyer's Service

[15] A lawyer may be paid from a source other than the client if the client is informed of that fact and consents and the arrangement does not compromise the lawyer's duty of loyalty to the client. *See* Rule 1.8(f). For example, when an insurer and its insured have conflicting interests in a matter arising from a liability insurance agreement, and the insurer is required to provide special counsel for the insured, the arrangement should assure the special counsel's professional independence. So also, when a corporation and its directors or employees are involved in a controversy in which they have conflicting interests, the corporation may provide funds for separate legal representation of the directors or employees, if the clients consent after consultation and the arrangement ensures the lawyer's professional independence.

Other Conflict Situations

[16] Conflicts of interest in contexts other than litigation sometimes may be difficult to assess. Relevant factors in determining whether there is a potential conflict include the duration and intimacy of the lawyer's relationship with the client or clients involved, the functions being performed by the lawyer, the likelihood that actual conflict will arise and the likely prejudice to the client from the conflict if it does arise. The question is often one of proximity and degree.

[17] For example, a lawyer may not represent multiple parties to a negotiation whose interests are fundamentally antagonistic to each other, but common representation is permissible where the clients are generally aligned in interest even though there is some difference of interest among them.

[18] Conflict questions may also arise in estate planning and estate administration. A lawyer may be called upon to prepare wills for several family members, such as husband and wife, and, depending upon the circumstances, a conflict of interest may arise. The lawyer should make clear his relationship to the parties involved.

[19] A lawyer for a corporation or other organization who is also a member of its board of directors should determine whether the responsibilities of the two roles may conflict. The lawyer may be called on to advise the corporation in matters involving actions of the directors. Consideration should be given to the frequency with which such situations may arise, the potential intensity of the conflict, the effect of the lawyer's resignation from the board and the possibility of the corporation's obtaining legal advice from another lawyer in such situations. If there is material risk that the dual role will compromise the lawyer's independence of professional judgment, the lawyer should not serve as a director.

Conflict Charged by an Opposing Party

[20] Resolving questions of conflict of interest is primarily the responsibility of the lawyer undertaking the representation. In litigation, a court may raise the question when there is reason to infer that the lawyer has neglected the responsibility. In a criminal case, inquiry by the court is generally required when a lawyer represents multiple defendants. Where the conflict is such as clearly to call in question the fair or efficient administration of justice, opposing counsel may properly raise the question. Such an objection should be viewed with caution, however, for it can be misused as a technique of harassment.

Virginia Code Comparison

This Rule is similar to DR 5-101(A) and DR 5-105(C). DR 5-101(A) provided that "[a] lawyer shall not accept employment if the exercise of his professional judgment on behalf of his client may be affected by his own financial, business, property, or personal interests, except with the consent of his client after full and adequate disclosure under the circumstances." DR 5-105(C) provided that "a lawyer may represent multiple clients if it is obvious that he can adequately represent the interest of each and if each consents to the representation after full disclosure of the possible effect of such representation on the exercise of his independent professional judgment on behalf of each."

Rule 1.7(b) clarifies DR 5-105(A) by requiring that, when the lawyer's other interests are involved, not only must the client consent after consultation but also that, independent of such consent, the lawyer must believe that he can provide competent and diligent representation, that the representation must be lawful, and the representation must not involve asserting a claim on behalf of one client against another client in the same litigation or other proceeding before a tribunal. This requirement appears to be the intended meaning of the provision in DR 5-105(C) that "it [be] obvious that [the lawyer] can adequately represent" the client, and was implicit in EC 5-2, which stated that a lawyer "should not accept proffered employment if his personal interests or desires may affect adversely the advice to be given or services to be rendered the prospective client."

Committee Commentary

Although there are few substantive differences between this Rule and corresponding provisions in the Virginia Code, the Committee concluded that the ABA Model Rule provides a more succinct statement of a general conflicts rule.

RULE 1.8 CONFLICT OF INTEREST: PROHIBITED TRANSACTIONS

(a) A lawyer shall not enter into a business transaction with a client or knowingly acquire an ownership, possessory, security or other pecuniary interest adverse to a client unless:

(1) the transaction and terms on which the lawyer acquires the interest are fair and reasonable to the client and are fully disclosed and transmitted in writing to the client in a manner which can be reasonably understood by the client;

(2) the client is given a reasonable opportunity to seek the advice of independent counsel in the transaction; and

(3) the client consents in writing thereto.

(b) A lawyer shall not use information relating to representation of a client for the advantage of the lawyer or of a third person or to the disadvantage of the client unless the client consents after consultation, except as permitted or required by Rule 1.6 or Rule 3.3.

(c) A lawyer shall not solicit, for himself or a person related to the lawyer, any substantial gift from a client including a testamentary gift. A lawyer shall not accept any such gift if solicited at his request by a third party. A lawyer shall not prepare an instrument giving the lawyer or a person related to the lawyer any substantial gift from a client, including a testamentary gift, unless the lawyer or other recipient of the gift is related to the client. For purposes of this paragraph, a person related to a lawyer includes a spouse, child, grandchild, parent, or other relative or individual with whom the lawyer or the client maintains a close, familial relationship.

(d) Prior to the conclusion of all aspects of a matter giving rise to the representation of a client, a lawyer shall not make or negotiate an agreement giving the lawyer literary or media rights to a portrayal or account based in substantial part on information relating to the representation.

(e) A lawyer shall not provide financial assistance to a client in connection with pending or contemplated litigation, except that:

(1) a lawyer may advance court costs and expenses of litigation, provided the client remains ultimately liable for such costs and expenses; and

(2) a lawyer representing an indigent client may pay court costs and expenses of litigation on behalf of the client.

(f) A lawyer shall not accept compensation for representing a client from one other than the client unless:

(1) the client consents after consultation;

(2) there is no interference with the lawyer's independence of professional judgment or with the client-lawyer relationship; and

(3) information relating to representation of a client is protected as required by Rule 1.6.

(g) A lawyer who represents two or more clients shall not participate in making an aggregate settlement of the claims of or against the clients, or in a criminal case an aggregated agreement as to guilty or nolo contendere pleas, unless each client consents after consultation, including disclosure of the existence and nature of all the claims or pleas involved and of the participation of each person in the settlement.

(h) A lawyer shall not make an agreement prospectively limiting the lawyer's liability to a client for malpractice, except that a lawyer may make such an agreement with a client of which the lawyer is an employee as long as the client is independently represented in making the agreement.

(i) A lawyer related to another lawyer as parent, child, sibling or spouse, or who is intimately involved with another lawyer, shall not represent a client in a representation directly adverse to a person whom the lawyer knows is represented by the other lawyer except upon consent by the client after consultation regarding the relationship.

(j) A lawyer shall not acquire a proprietary interest in the cause of action or subject matter of litigation the lawyer is conducting for a client, except that the lawyer may:

(1) acquire a lien granted by law to secure the lawyer's fee or expenses; and

(2) contract with a client for a reasonable contingent fee in a civil case, unless prohibited by Rule 1.5.

(k) While lawyers are associated in a firm, none of them shall knowingly enter into any transaction or perform any activity when one of them practicing alone would be prohibited from doing so by paragraphs (a), (b), (c), (d), (e), (f), (g), (h), or (j) of this Rule.

[Adopted effective January 1, 2000. Amended effective January 1, 2004.]

Comment

Transactions Between Client and Lawyer

[1] As a general principle, all transactions between client and lawyer should be fair and reasonable to the client. In such transactions a review by independent counsel on behalf of the client is often advisable. Furthermore, a lawyer may not exploit information relating to the representation to the client's disadvantage. For example, a lawyer who has learned that the client is investing in specific real estate may not, without the client's consent, seek to acquire nearby property where doing so would adversely affect the client's plan for investment. Paragraph (a) does not, however, apply to standard commercial transactions between the lawyer and the client for products or services that the client generally markets to others, for example, banking or brokerage services, medical services, products manufactured or distributed by the client, and utilities services. In such transactions, the lawyer has no advantage in dealing with the client, and the restrictions in paragraph (a) are unnecessary and impracticable. Similarly, paragraph (b) does not limit an attorney's use of information obtained independently outside the attorney-client relationship.

[2] A lawyer may accept ordinary gifts from a client. For example, an ordinary gift such as a present given at a holiday or as a token of appreciation is permitted. If effectuation of a substantial gift requires preparing a legal instrument such as a will or conveyance, however, the client should have the detached advice that another lawyer can provide. Paragraph (c) recognizes an exception where the client is a relative of the donee or the gift is not substantial.

Literary Rights

[3] An agreement by which a lawyer acquires literary or media rights concerning the conduct of the representation creates a conflict between the interests of the client and the personal interests of the lawyer. Measures suitable in the representation of the client may detract from the publication value of an account of the representation. Paragraph (d) does not prohibit a lawyer representing a client in a transaction concerning literary property from agreeing that the lawyer's fee shall consist of a share in ownership in the property, if the arrangement conforms to Rule 1.5 and paragraph (j).

Person Paying for a Lawyer's Services

[4] Paragraph (f) requires disclosure of the fact that the lawyer's services are being paid for by a third party. Such an arrangement must also conform to the requirements of Rule 1.6 concerning confidentiality, Rule 1.7 concerning conflict of interest, and Rule 5.4(c) concerning the professional independence of a lawyer. Where the client is a class, consent may be obtained on behalf of the class by court-supervised procedure.

[5] *ABA Model Rule* Comment not adopted.

Family Relationships Between Lawyers

[6] Paragraph (i) applies to related lawyers who are in different firms. Related lawyers in the same firm are governed by Rules 1.7, 1.9, and 1.10. The disqualification stated in paragraph (i) is personal and is not imputed to

members of firms with whom the lawyers are associated.

Acquisition of Interest in Litigation

[7] Paragraph (j) states the traditional general rule that lawyers are prohibited from acquiring a proprietary interest in litigation. This general rule, which has its basis in common law champerty and maintenance, is subject to specific exceptions developed in decisional law and continued in these Rules, such as the exception for reasonable contingent fees set forth in Rule 1.5 and the exception for certain advances or payment of the costs of litigation set forth in paragraph (e).

Virginia Code Comparison

With regard to paragraph (a), DR 5–104(A) provided that a lawyer "shall not enter into a business transaction with a client if they have differing interests therein and if the client expects the lawyer to exercise his professional judgment therein for the protection of the client, unless the client has consented after full and adequate disclosure ...." EC 5–3 stated that a lawyer "should not seek to persuade his client to permit him to invest in an undertaking of his client nor make improper use of his professional relationship to influence his client to invest in an enterprise in which the lawyer is interested."

Paragraph (b) is substantially similar to DR 4–101(B)(3) which provided that a lawyer should not use "a confidence or secret of his client for the advantage of himself, or a third person, unless the client consents after full disclosure."

Paragraph (c) is substantially similar to DR 5–104(B) which stated that a lawyer "shall not prepare an instrument giving the lawyer or a member of the lawyer's family any gift from a client, including a testamentary gift, except where the client is a relative of the donee." EC 5–5 stated that a lawyer "should not suggest to his client that a gift be made to himself or for his benefit. If a lawyer accepts a gift from his client, he is peculiarly susceptible to the charge that he unduly influenced or overreached the client. If a client voluntarily offers to make a gift to his lawyer, the lawyer may accept the gift, but before doing so, he should urge that the client secure disinterested advice from an independent, competent person who is cognizant of all the circumstances. Except in those instances in which the client is related to the donee, a lawyer may not prepare an instrument by which the client gives a gift to the lawyer or to a member of his family."

Paragraph (d) has no direct counterpart in the *Virginia Code*. EC 5–4 stated that in order to avoid "potentially differing interests" a lawyer should "scrupulously avoid [literary arrangements with a client] prior to the termination of all aspects of the matter giving rise to the employment, even though [the lawyer's] employment has previously ended."

Paragraph (e)(1) incorporates the provisions of DR 5–103(B), including the requirement that the client remain "ultimately liable" for such advanced expenses.

Paragraph (e)(2) has no direct counterpart in the *Virginia Code*, although DR 5–103(B) allowed a lawyer to advance or guarantee expenses of litigation as long as the client remained ultimately liable.

Paragraph (f) is substantially similar to DR 5–106(A)(1) and DR 5–106(B). DR 5–106(A)(1) stated: "Except with the consent of his client after full and adequate disclosure under the circumstances, a lawyer shall not ... [a]ccept compensation for his legal services from one other than his client." DR 5–106(B) stated that "[a] lawyer shall not permit a person who recommends, employs, or pays him to render legal services for another to direct or regulate his professional judgment in rendering such legal services."

Paragraph (g) is substantially similar to DR 5–107, but also covers aggregated plea agreements in criminal cases.

The first portion of Paragraph (h) is essentially the same as DR 6–102(A), but the second portion of Paragraph (h) has no counterpart in the *Virginia Code*. The new provision allows in-house lawyers to arrange for the same indemnity available to other officers and employees, as long as their employers are independently represented in making the arrangement.

Paragraph (i) has no counterpart in the *Virginia Code*.

Paragraph (j) is substantially the same as DR 5–103(A).

Paragraph (k) had no counterpart in the *Virginia Code*.

Committee Commentary

The Committee added "for the advantage of himself or a third person" from DR 4–101(B)(3) to paragraph (b) as a further limitation on a lawyer's use of information relating to representation of a client.

The Committee added a further time limitation to paragraph (d)'s restriction. Borrowing language from EC 5–4, the restriction on agreements giving a lawyer literary or media rights extends through the conclusion of "all aspects of a matter giving rise to the representation."

In Rule 1.8(e)(1), the Committee retained the requirement in DR 5–103(B) that a client must "remain ultimately liable for [litigation] expenses." However, the Committee adopted the limited exception for indigent clients that appears in Rule 1.8(e)(2).

After lengthy debate, the Committee adopted 1.8(h), which retains the general prohibition on lawyers prospectively limiting their malpractice liability to clients (which appeared in *Virginia Code* DR 6–102). However, the Committee added a limited exception that allows in-house lawyers to arrange for the type of indemnity that other officers and employees of entities may obtain. The Committee voted to insist that the client be independently represented in agreeing to any such arrangement.

In 1.8(i), the Committee adopted the *ABA Model Rule* approach, which permits lawyers who are members of the same nuclear family to represent clients adverse to each other, as long as both clients consent after full disclosure. The *Virginia Code* was interpreted to create a non-waivable *per se* conflict of interest in these circumstances. *See* LEO 190 (April 1, 1985).

RULE 1.9 CONFLICT OF INTEREST: FORMER CLIENT

(a) A lawyer who has formerly represented a client in a matter shall not thereafter represent another person in the same or a substantially related matter in which that person's interests are materially adverse to the interests of the former client unless both the present and former client consent after consultation.

(b) A lawyer shall not knowingly represent a person in the same or a substantially related matter in which a firm with which the lawyer formerly was associated had previously represented a client

(1) whose interests are materially adverse to that person; and

(2) about whom the lawyer had acquired information protected by Rules 1.6 and 1.9(c) that is material to the matter; unless both the present and former client consent after consultation.

(c) A lawyer who has formerly represented a client in a matter or whose present or former firm has formerly represented a client in a matter shall not thereafter:

(1) use information relating to or gained in the course of the representation to the disadvantage of the former client except as Rule 1.6 or Rule 3.3 would permit or require with respect to a client, or when the information has become generally known; or

(2) reveal information relating to the representation except as Rule 1.6 or Rule 3.3 would permit or require with respect to a client.

[Adopted effective January 1, 2000. Amended effective January 4, 2010.]

Comment

[1] After termination of a client-lawyer relationship, a lawyer may not represent another client except in conformity with this Rule. The principles in Rule 1.7 determine whether the interests of the present and former client are adverse. Thus, a lawyer could not properly seek to rescind on behalf of a new client a contract drafted on behalf of the former client. So also a lawyer who has prosecuted an accused person could not properly represent the accused in a subsequent civil action against the government concerning the same transaction.

[2] The scope of a "matter" for purposes of this Rule may depend on the facts of a particular situation or transaction. The lawyer's involvement in a matter can also be a question of degree. When a lawyer has been directly involved in a specific transaction, subsequent representation of other clients with materially adverse interests clearly is prohibited. On the other hand, a lawyer who recurrently handled a type of problem for a former client is not precluded from later representing another client in a wholly distinct problem of that type even though the subsequent representation involves a position adverse to the prior client. Similar considerations can apply to the reassignment of military lawyers between defense and prosecution functions within the same military jurisdiction. The underlying question is whether the lawyer was so involved in the matter that the subsequent representation can be justly regarded as a changing of sides in the matter in question.

Lawyers Moving Between Firms

[3] When lawyers have been associated within a firm but then end their association, the question of whether a lawyer should undertake representation is more complicated. There are several competing considerations. First, the client previously represented by the former firm must be reasonably assured that the principle of loyalty to the client is not compromised. Second, the Rule should not be so broadly cast as to preclude other persons from having reasonable choice of legal counsel. Third, the Rule should not unreasonably hamper lawyers from forming

new associations and taking on new clients after having left a previous association. In this connection, it should be recognized that today many lawyers practice in firms, that many lawyers to some degree limit their practice to one field or another, and that many move from one association to another several times in their careers. If the concept of imputation were applied with unqualified rigor, the result would be radical curtailment of the opportunity of lawyers to move from one practice setting to another and of the opportunity of clients to change counsel.

[4] Reconciliation of these competing principles in the past has been attempted under two rubrics. One approach has been to seek *per se* rules of disqualification. For example, it has been held that a partner in a law firm is conclusively presumed to have access to all confidences concerning all clients of the firm. Under this analysis, if a lawyer has been a partner in one law firm and then becomes a partner in another law firm, there may be a presumption that all confidences known by the partner in the first firm are known to all partners in the second firm. This presumption might properly be applied in some circumstances, especially where the client has been extensively represented, but may be unrealistic where the client was represented only for limited purposes. Furthermore, such a rigid rule exaggerates the difference between a partner and an associate in modern law firms.

[5] Paragraph (b) operates to disqualify the lawyer only when the lawyer involved has actual knowledge of information protected by Rules 1.6 and 1.9(b). Thus, if a lawyer while with one firm acquired no knowledge or information relating to a particular client of the firm, and that lawyer later joined another firm, neither the lawyer individually nor the second firm is disqualified from representing another client in the same or a related matter even though the interests of the two clients conflict. *See* Rule 1.10(b) for the restrictions on a firm once a lawyer has terminated association with the firm; and Rule 1.11(d) for restrictions regarding a lawyer moving from private employment to public employment.

Confidentiality

[6] Preserving confidentiality is a question of access to information. Access to information, in turn, is essentially a question of fact in particular circumstances, aided by inferences, deductions or working presumptions that reasonably may be made about the way in which lawyers work together. A lawyer may have general access to files of all clients of a law firm and may regularly participate in discussions of their affairs; it should be inferred that such a lawyer in fact is privy to all information about all the firm's clients. In contrast, another lawyer may have access to the files of only a limited number of clients and participate in discussions of the affairs of no other clients; in the absence of information to the contrary, it should be inferred that such a lawyer in fact is privy to information about the clients actually served but not those of other clients.

[7] Application of paragraph (b) depends on a situation's particular facts. In such an inquiry, the burden of proof should rest upon the firm whose disqualification is sought.

[8] Paragraph (b) operates to disqualify the lawyer only when the lawyer involved has actual knowledge of information protected by Rules 1.6 and 1.9(b). Thus, if a lawyer while with one firm acquired no knowledge or information relating to a particular client of the firm, and that lawyer later joined another firm, neither the lawyer individually nor the second firm is disqualified from representing another client in the same or a related matter even though the interests of the two clients conflict. *See* Rule 1.10(b) for the restrictions on a firm once a lawyer has terminated association with the firm.

[9] Independent of the question of disqualification of a firm, a lawyer changing professional association has a continuing duty to preserve confidentiality of information about a client formerly represented. *See* Rules 1.6 and 1.9.

Adverse Positions

[10] The second aspect of loyalty to a client is the lawyer's obligation to decline subsequent representations involving positions adverse to a former client arising in substantially related matters. This obligation requires abstention from adverse representation by the individual lawyer involved and other lawyers may be subject to imputed disqualification under Rule 1.10. If a lawyer left one firm for another, the new affiliation would not preclude the firms involved from continuing to represent clients with adverse interests in the same or related matters, so long as the conditions of paragraphs 1.9 (b) and (c) concerning confidentiality have been met.

[11] Information acquired by the lawyer in the course of representing a client may not subsequently be used or revealed by the lawyer to the disadvantage of the client. However, the fact that a lawyer has once served a client does not preclude the lawyer

from using non-confidential information about that client when later representing another client.

[12] Disqualification from subsequent representation is primarily for the protection of former clients but may also affect current clients. This protection, however, can be waived by both. A waiver is effective only if there is full disclosure of the circumstances, including the lawyer's intended role in behalf of the new client.

[13] With regard to an opposing party's raising a question of conflict of interest, *see* Comment to Rule 1.7. With regard to disqualification of a firm with which a lawyer is or was formerly associated, *see* Rule 1.10.

Virginia Code Comparison

Paragraph (a) is substantially the same as DR 5–105(D), although the Rule requires waiver by both a lawyer's current and former client, rather than just the former client.

There was no direct counterpart to paragraph (b) in the *Virginia Code*. Representation by a lawyer adverse to a client of a law firm with which a lawyer was previously associated was sometimes dealt with under the rubric of Canon 9 of the *Virginia Code* which provided: "A lawyer should avoid even the appearance of impropriety."

There was no counterpart to paragraph (c) in the *Virginia Code*. The exception in the last clause of paragraph (c)(1) permits a lawyer to use information relating to a former client that is in the "public domain," a use that also was not prohibited by the *Virginia Code* which protected only "confidences and secrets." Since the scope of paragraphs (a) and (b) is much broader than "confidences and secrets," it is necessary to define when a lawyer may make use of information about a client after the client-lawyer relationship has terminated.

Committee Commentary

The Committee believed that, in an era when lawyers frequently move between firms, this Rule provided more specific guidance than the implicit provisions of the Disciplinary Rules. However, the Committee added language to paragraph (a) requiring consent of both present and former clients. Additionally, the Committee adopted broader language in paragraph (c) precluding the use of any information "relating to or gained in the course of" the representation of a former client, rather than precluding the use only of information "relating to" the former representation.

RULE 1.10 IMPUTED DISQUALIFICATION: GENERAL RULE

(a) While lawyers are associated in a firm, none of them shall represent a client when the lawyer knows or reasonably should know that anyone of them practicing alone would be prohibited from doing so by Rules 1.6, 1.7, 1.9, or 2.10(e).

(b) When a lawyer has terminated an association with a firm, the firm is not prohibited from thereafter representing a person with interests materially adverse to those of a client represented by the formerly associated lawyer and not currently represented by the firm, unless:

(1) the matter is the same or substantially related to that in which the formerly associated lawyer represented the client; and

(2) any lawyer remaining in the firm has information protected by Rules 1. 6 and 1.9(c) that is material to the matter.

(c) A disqualification prescribed by this Rule may be waived by the affected client under the conditions stated in Rule 1.7.

(d) The imputed prohibition of improper transactions is governed by Rule 1.8(k).

(e) The disqualification of lawyers associated in a firm with former or current government lawyers is governed by Rule 1.11.

[Adopted effective January 1, 2000. Amended effective January 1, 2004; July 31, 2015.]

Comment

Definition of "Firm"

[1] Whether two or more lawyers constitute a firm as defined in the Terminology section can depend on the specific facts. For example, two practitioners who share office space and occasionally consult or assist each other ordinarily would not be regarded as constituting a firm. However, if they present themselves to the public in a way suggesting that they are a firm or conduct themselves as a firm, they should be regarded as a firm for the purposes of the Rules. The terms of any formal agreement between associated lawyers are relevant in determining whether they are a firm, as is the fact that they have mutual access to information concerning the clients they serve. Furthermore, it is relevant in doubtful cases to consider the underlying purpose of the Rule that is involved. A group of lawyers could be regarded as a firm for purposes of the Rule that the same lawyer should not represent opposing parties in litigation, while it might not be so regarded for purposes of the Rule that information acquired by one lawyer is attributed to the other.

[2] With respect to the law department of an organization, there is ordinarily no question that the members of the department constitute a firm within the meaning of the Rules of Professional Conduct. However, there can be uncertainty as to the identity of the client. For example, it may not be clear whether the law department of a corporation represents a subsidiary or an affiliated corporation, as well as the corporation by which the members of the department are directly employed. A similar question can arise concerning an unincorporated association and its local affiliates.

[2a] A lawyer or firm should maintain and use an appropriate system for detecting conflicts of interest. The failure to maintain a system for identifying conflicts or to use that system when making a decision to undertake employment in a particular matter may be deemed a violation of Rule 1.10(a) if proper use of a system would have identified the conflict.

[3] Similar questions can also arise with respect to lawyers in legal aid. Lawyers employed in the same unit of a legal service organization constitute a firm, but not necessarily those employed in separate units. As in the case of independent practitioners, whether the lawyers should be treated as associated with each other can depend on the particular rule that is involved, and on the specific facts of the situation.

[4] Where a lawyer has joined a private firm after having represented the government, the situation is governed by Rule 1.11(b) and (c); where a lawyer represents the government after having served private clients, the situation is governed by Rule 1.11(d)(1). The individual lawyer involved is bound by the Rules generally, including Rules 1.6, 1.7 and 1.9.

[5] Different provisions are thus made for movement of a lawyer from one private firm to another and for movement of a lawyer between a private firm and the government. The government is entitled to protection of its client confidences and, therefore, to the protections provided in Rules 1.6, 1.9 and 1.11. However, if the more extensive disqualification in Rule 1.10 were applied to former government lawyers, the potential effect on the government would be unduly burdensome. The government deals with all private citizens and organizations and, thus, has a much wider circle of adverse legal interests than does any private law firm. In these circumstances, the government's recruitment of lawyers would be seriously impaired if Rule 1.10 were applied to the government. On balance, therefore, the government is better served in the long run by the protections stated in Rule 1.11.

Principles of Imputed Disqualification

[6] The rule of imputed disqualification stated in paragraph (a) gives effect to the principle of loyalty to the client as it applies to lawyers who practice in a law firm. Such situations can be considered from the premise that a firm of lawyers is essentially one lawyer for purposes of the rules governing loyalty to the client, or from the premise that each lawyer is vicariously bound by the obligation of loyalty owed by each lawyer with whom the lawyer is associated. Paragraph (a) operates only among the lawyers currently associated in a firm. When a lawyer moves from one firm to another, the situation is governed by Rules 1.9(b) and 1.10(b).

[7] Rule 1.10(b) operates to permit a law firm, under certain circumstances, to represent a person with interests directly adverse to those of a client represented by a lawyer who formerly was associated with the firm. The Rule applies regardless of when the formerly associated lawyer represented the client. However, the law firm may not represent a person with interests adverse to those of a present client of the firm, which would violate Rule 1.7. Moreover, the firm may not represent the person where the matter is the same or substantially related to that in which the formerly associated lawyer represented the client and any other lawyer currently in the firm has material information protected by Rules 1.6 and 1.9(c).

Virginia Code Comparison

There was no direct counterpart to this Rule in the *Virginia Code*. DR 5–105(E) provided that "[i]f a lawyer is required to decline employment or to withdraw from employment under DR 5–105, no partner of his or his firm may accept or continue such employment."

Committee Commentary

The *ABA Model Code* contained a broadly inclusive imputation rule, prohibiting representation by a partner, associate, or any affiliated lawyer when a lawyer would be required to decline employment under any Disciplinary Rule. *See ABA Model Code* DR 5–105(D). The *Virginia Code* limited imputation to disqualification under DR 5–105. *See Virginia Code* DR 5–105(E). The Committee concluded that the provisions of the *ABA Model Rule* struck the appropriate balance between the confidentiality needs of clients and the professional needs of lawyers.

RULE 1.11 SPECIAL CONFLICTS OF INTEREST FOR FORMER AND CURRENT GOVERNMENT OFFICERS AND EMPLOYEES

(a) A lawyer who holds public office shall not:

(1) use the public position to obtain, or attempt to obtain, a special advantage in legislative matters for the lawyer or for a client under circumstances where the lawyer knows or it is obvious that such action is not in the public interest;

(2) use the public position to influence, or attempt to influence, a tribunal to act in favor of the lawyer or of a client; or

(3) accept anything of value from any person when the lawyer knows or it is obvious that the offer is for the purpose of influencing the lawyer's action as a public official.

(b) Except as law may otherwise expressly permit, a lawyer shall not represent a private client in connection with a matter in which the lawyer participated personally and substantially as a public officer or employee, unless the private client and the appropriate government agency consent after consultation. No lawyer in a firm with which that lawyer is associated may knowingly undertake or continue representation in such a matter unless:

(1) the disqualified lawyer is screened from any participation in the matter and is apportioned no part of the fee therefrom; and

(2) written notice is promptly given to the appropriate government agency to enable it to ascertain compliance with the provisions of this Rule.

(c) Except as law may otherwise expressly permit, a lawyer having information that the lawyer knows is confidential government information about a person acquired when the lawyer was a public officer or employee, may not represent a private client whose interests are adverse to that person in a matter in which the information could be used to the material disadvantage of that person. As used in this Rule, the term "confidential government information" means information that has been obtained under governmental authority and that the government is prohibited by law from disclosing to the public or has a legal privilege not to disclose, and that is not otherwise available to the public. A firm with which that lawyer is associated may undertake or continue representation in the matter only if the disqualified lawyer is screened from any participation in the matter and is apportioned no part of the fee therefrom.

(d) Except as law may otherwise expressly permit, a lawyer serving as a public officer or employee shall not:

(1) participate in a matter in which the lawyer participated personally and substantially while in private practice or nongovernmental employment, unless under applicable law no one is, or by lawful delegation may be, authorized to act in the lawyer's stead in the matter or unless the private client and the appropriate government agency consent after consultation; or

(2) negotiate for private employment with any person who is involved as a party or as attorney for a party in a matter in which the lawyer is participating personally and substantially, except that a lawyer serving as a law clerk to a judge, other adjudicative officer, mediator or arbitrator may negotiate for private employment as permitted by Rule 1.12(b) and subject to the conditions stated in Rule 1.12(b).

(e) Paragraph (d) does not disqualify other lawyers in the disqualified lawyer's agency.

(f) As used in this Rule, the term "matter" includes:

(1) any judicial or other proceeding, application, request for a ruling or other determination, contract, claim, controversy, investigation, charge, accusation, arrest or other particular matter involving a specific party or parties; and

(2) any other matter covered by the conflict of interest rules of the appropriate government agency.

[Adopted effective January 1, 2000. Amended effective January 1, 2004; January 4, 2010; November 1, 2013.]

Comment

[1] This Rule prevents a lawyer from exploiting public office for the advantage of the lawyer or a private client, A lawyer who is a public officer should not engage in activities in which his personal or professional interests are or foreseeably may be in conflict with official duties or obligations to the public.

[2] A lawyer representing a government agency, whether employed or specially retained by the government, is subject to the Rules of Professional Conduct, including the prohibition against representing adverse interests stated in Rule 1.7 and the protections afforded former clients in Rule 1.9. In addition, such a lawyer is subject to Rule 1.11 and to statutes and government regulations regarding conflict of interest. Such statutes and regulations may circumscribe the extent to which the government agency may give consent under this Rule.

[3] Paragraphs (b) and (d) apply regardless of whether a lawyer is adverse to a former client and are thus designed not only to protect the former client, but also to prevent a lawyer from exploiting public office for the advantage of another client. For example, a lawyer who has pursued a claim on behalf of the government may not pursue the same claim on behalf of a later private client after the lawyer has left government service, except when authorized to do so by the govern-

ment agency under paragraph (b). Similarly, a lawyer who has pursued a claim on behalf of a private client may not pursue the claim on behalf of the government, except when authorized to do so by paragraph (d). Rule 1.10 is not applicable to the conflicts of interest addressed by these paragraphs.

[4] Where the successive clients are a public agency and a private client, the risk exists that power or discretion vested in public authority might be used for the special benefit of a private client. A lawyer should not be in a position where benefit to a private client might affect performance of the lawyer's professional functions on behalf of public authority. Also, unfair advantage could accrue to the private client by reason of access to confidential government information about the client's adversary obtainable only through the lawyer's government service. However, the rules governing lawyers presently or formerly employed by a government agency should not be so restrictive as to inhibit transfer of employment to and from the government. The government has a legitimate need to attract qualified lawyers as well as to maintain high ethical standards. The provisions for screening and waiver are necessary to prevent the disqualification rule from imposing too severe a deterrent against entering public service. The private client should be informed of the lawyer's prior relationship with a public agency at the time of engagement of the lawyer's services.

[5] When the client is an agency of one government, that agency should be treated as a private client for purposes of this Rule if the lawyer thereafter represents an agency of another government, as when a lawyer represents a city and subsequently is employed by a federal agency.

[6] Paragraphs (b)(1) and (c) do not prohibit a lawyer from receiving a salary or partnership share established by prior independent agreement. They prohibit directly relating the attorney's compensation to the fee in the matter in which the lawyer is disqualified.

[7] Paragraph (b)(2) does not require that a lawyer give notice to the government agency at a time when premature disclosure would injure the client; a requirement for premature disclosure might preclude engagement of the lawyer. Such notice is, however, required to be given as soon as practicable in order that the government agency will have a reasonable opportunity to ascertain that the lawyer is complying with Rule 1.11 and to take appropriate action if it believes the lawyer is not complying.

[8] Paragraph (c) operates only when the lawyer in question has knowledge of the information, which means actual knowledge; it does not operate with respect to information that merely could be imputed to the lawyer.

[9] Paragraphs (b) and (d) do not prohibit a lawyer from jointly representing a private party and a government agency when doing so is permitted by Rule 1.7 and is not otherwise prohibited by law.

Virginia Code Comparison

Paragraph (a) is identical to DR 8–101(A).

Paragraph (b) is substantially similar to DR 9–101(B), except that the latter used the terms "in which he had substantial responsibility while he was a public employee." The Rule also requires consent of both a current client and the former agency.

Paragraphs (c), (d), (e) and (f) have no counterparts in the *Virginia Code*.

Committee Commentary

The Committee believed that the *ABA Model Rule* provides more complete guidance regarding lawyers' movement between the public and private sectors. However, the Committee added the language of DR 8–101(A) as paragraph (a) in order to make this Rule a more complete statement regarding the particular responsibilities of lawyers who are public officials. Additionally, to make paragraph (b) consistent with similar provisions under Rule 1.9(a) and (b), the Committee modified the paragraph to require consent to representation by both the current client and the lawyer's former government agency.

The amendments effective January 1, 2004, rewrote the rule heading.

The amendments effective January 4, 2010, added present paragraph (e) and re-designated former paragraphs (e) and (f) as present paragraphs (f) and (g); deleted Comment [10].

Amendments effective November 1, 2013, moved the definition of "confidential government information" from paragraph (g) to paragraph (e), added a provision to paragraph (d) allowing the conflict to be waived with consent from the private client and the appropriate government agency, and adopted ABA Model Rule Comment 3, which explains why paragraph (b) and (d) apply even when a lawyer is not adverse to a former client.

RULE 1.12 FORMER JUDGE OR ARBITRATOR

(a) Except as stated in paragraph (d), a lawyer shall not represent anyone in connection with a matter in which the lawyer participated personally and substantially as a judge, other adjudicative officer, arbitrator or a law clerk to such a person, unless all parties to the proceeding consent after consultation.

(b) A lawyer shall not negotiate for employment with any person who is involved as a party or as attorney for a party in a matter in which the lawyer is participating personally and substantially as a judge, other adjudicative officer or arbitrator. A lawyer serving as a law clerk to a judge, other adjudicative officer, or arbitrator may negotiate for employment with a party or attorney involved in a matter in which the clerk is participating personally and substantially, but only after the lawyer has notified the judge, other adjudicative officer, or arbitrator.

(c) If a lawyer is disqualified by paragraph (a), no lawyer in a firm with which that lawyer is associated may knowingly undertake or continue representation in the matter unless:

(1) the disqualified lawyer is timely screened from any participation in the matter and is apportioned no part of the fee therefrom; and

(2) written notice is promptly given to the parties and any appropriate tribunal to enable them to ascertain compliance with the provisions of this Rule.

(d) An arbitrator selected as a partisan of a party in a multimember arbitration panel is not prohibited from subsequently representing that party.

[Adopted effective January 1, 2000. Amended effective January 1, 2004.]

Comment

[1] This Rule generally parallels Rule 1.11. The term "personally and substantially" signifies that a judge who was a member of a multimember court, and thereafter left judicial office to practice law, is not prohibited from representing a client in a matter pending in the court, but in which the former judge did not participate. So also the fact that a former judge exercised administrative responsibility in a court does not prevent the former judge from acting as a lawyer in a matter where the judge had previously exercised remote or incidental administrative responsibility that did not affect the merits. Compare the Comment to Rule 1.11. The term "adjudicative officer" includes such officials as judges pro tempore, referees, special masters, hearing officers and other parajudicial officers, and also lawyers who serve as part-time judges. Compliance Canons A(2), B(2) and C of the *Virginia Code of Judicial Conduct* provide that a part-time judge, judge pro tempore or retired judge recalled to active service, may not "act as a lawyer in any proceeding in which he served as a judge or in any other proceeding related thereto." Although phrased differently from this Rule, those rules correspond in meaning.

[2] Like former judges, lawyers who have served as arbitrators, may be asked to represent a client in a matter in which the lawyer participated personally and substantially. This Rule forbids such representation unless all of the parties to the proceedings give their consent after consultation. Other law or codes of ethics governing these roles may impose more stringent standards of personal or imputed disqualification.

[3] Although lawyers who serve as judges and arbitrators do not have information concerning the parties that is protected under Rule 1.6, they typically owe the parties an obligation of confidentiality under law or codes of ethics governing their roles. Thus, paragraph (c) provides that conflicts of the personally disqualified lawyer will be imputed to other lawyers in a law firm unless the conditions of paragraph (c) are met.

[4] Notice, including a description of the screened lawyer's representation and of the screening procedures employed, generally should be given as soon as practicable after the need for screening becomes apparent.

Virginia Code Comparison

Paragraph (a) is substantially similar to DR 9–101(A), which provided that a lawyer "shall not accept private employment in a matter upon the merits of which he has acted in a judicial capacity." Paragraph (a) differs, however, in that it is broader in scope and states more specifically the persons to whom it applies. There was no counterpart in the *Virginia Code* to paragraphs (b), (c) or (d).

With regard to arbitrators and mediators, EC 5–20 stated that "a lawyer [who] has undertaken to act as an impartial arbitrator or mediator ... should not thereafter represent in the dispute any of the parties involved." DR 9–101(A) did not permit a waiver of the disqualification applied to former judges by consent of the parties. However, DR 5–105(C) was similar in effect and could be construed to permit waiver.

Committee Commentary

The Committee adopted the *ABA Model Rule* essentially verbatim for former judges and arbitrators since it clearly provides more complete guidance to judicial officials than DR 9–101(A). However, the committee chose not to extend these provisions to mediators and other third-party neutrals, as those roles are distinguishable.

RULE 1.13 ORGANIZATION AS CLIENT

(a) A lawyer employed or retained by an organization represents the organization acting through its duly authorized constituents.

(b) If a lawyer for an organization knows that an officer, employee or other person associated with the organization is engaged in action, intends to act or refuses to act in a matter related to the representation that is a violation of a legal obligation to the organization, or a violation of law which reasonably might be imputed to the organization, and is likely to result in substantial injury to the organization, the lawyer shall proceed as is reasonably necessary in the best interest of the organization. In determining how to proceed, the lawyer shall give due consideration to the seriousness of the violation and its consequences, the scope and nature of the lawyer's representation, the responsibility in the organization and the apparent motivation of the person involved, the policies of the organization concerning such matters and any other relevant considerations. Any measures taken shall be designed to minimize disruption of the organization and the risk of revealing information relating to the representation to persons outside the organization. Such measures may include among others:

(1) asking for reconsideration of the matter;

(2) advising that a separate legal opinion on the matter be sought for presentation to appropriate authority in the organization;

(3) referring the matter to higher authority in the organization, including, if warranted by the seriousness of the matter, referral to the highest authority that can act in behalf of the organization as determined by applicable law.

(c) If, despite the lawyer's efforts in accordance with paragraph (b), the highest authority that can act on behalf of the organization insists upon action, or a refusal to act, that is clearly a violation of law and is likely to result in substantial injury to the organization, the lawyer may resign or may decline to represent the client in that matter in accordance with Rule 1.16.

(d) In dealing with an organization's directors, officers, employees, members, shareholders or other constituents, a lawyer shall explain the identity of the client when it is apparent that the organization's interests are adverse to those of the constituents with whom the lawyer is dealing.

(e) A lawyer representing an organization may also represent any of its directors, officers, employees, members, shareholders or other constituents, subject to the provisions of Rule 1.7. If the organization's consent to the dual representation is required by Rule 1.7, the consent shall be given by an appropriate official of the organization other than the individual who is to be represented, or by the shareholders.

[Adopted effective January 1, 2000. Amended effective January 1, 2004.]

Comment

The Entity as the Client

[1] An organizational client is a legal entity, but it cannot act except through its officers, directors, employees, shareholders and other constituents. These persons are referred to herein as the constituents of the corporate organizational client. The duties defined in this Comment apply equally to unincorporated associations. "Other constituents" as used in this Comment means the positions equivalent to officers, directors, employees and shareholders held by persons acting for organizational clients that are not corporations.

[2] When one of the constituents of an organizational client communicates with the organization's lawyer in that person's organizational capacity, the communication is protected by Rule 1.6. Thus, by way of example, if an organizational client requests its lawyer to investigate allegations of wrongdoing, interviews made in the course of that investigation between the lawyer and the client's employees or other constituents are covered by Rule 1.6. This does not mean, however, that constituents of an organizational client are the clients of the lawyer. The lawyer may not disclose to such constituents information relating to the representation except for disclosures explicitly or impliedly authorized by the organizational client in order to carry out the representation or as otherwise permitted by Rule 1.6.

[3] The decisions of constituents of the organization ordinarily must be accepted by the lawyer even if their utility or prudence is doubtful. Decisions concerning policy and operations, including ones entailing serious risk, are not as such in the lawyer's province. However, different considerations arise when the lawyer knows that the organization may be substantially injured by action of a constituent that is in violation of law. In such a circumstance, it may be reasonably necessary for the lawyer to ask the constituent to reconsider the matter. If that fails, or if the matter is of sufficient seriousness and importance to the organization, it may be reasonably necessary for the lawyer to take steps to have the matter reviewed by a higher authority in the organization. Substantial justification should exist for seeking review over the head of the constituent normally responsible for it. The stated policy of the organization may define circumstances and prescribe channels for such review, and a lawyer should encourage the formulation of such a policy. Even in the absence of organization policy, however, the lawyer may have an obligation

to refer a matter to higher authority, depending on the seriousness of the matter and whether the constituent in question has apparent motives to act at variance with the organization's interest. Review by the chief executive officer or by the board of directors may be required when the matter is of importance commensurate with their authority. At some point it may be useful or essential to obtain an independent legal opinion.

[4] In an extreme case, it may be reasonably necessary for the lawyer to refer the matter to the organization's highest authority. Ordinarily, that is the board of directors or similar governing body. However, applicable law may prescribe that under certain conditions highest authority reposes elsewhere; for example, in the independent directors of a corporation.

Relation to Other Rules

[5] The authority and responsibility provided in paragraph (b) are concurrent with the authority and responsibility provided in other Rules. In particular, this Rule does not limit or expand the lawyer's responsibility under Rules 1.6, 1.8, 1.16, 3.3 or 4.1. If the lawyer's services are being used by an organization to further a crime or fraud by the organization, Rule 1.2(c) can be applicable.

Government Agency

[6] The duty defined in this Rule applies to government organizations. However, when the client is a governmental organization, a different balance may be appropriate between maintaining confidentiality and assuring that the wrongful official act is prevented or rectified, for public business is involved. In addition, duties of lawyers employed by the government or lawyers in military service may be defined by statutes and regulation. Therefore, defining precisely the identity of the client and prescribing the resulting obligations of such lawyers may be more difficult in the government context. Government lawyers, in many situations, are asked to represent diverse client interests. The government lawyer may be authorized by the organization to represent subordinate, internal clients in the interest of the organization subject to the other Rules relating to conflicts.

Although in some circumstances the client may be a specific agency, it is generally the government as a whole. For example, if the action or failure to act involves the head of a bureau, either the department of which the bureau is a part or the government as a whole may be the client for purpose of this Rule. Moreover, in a matter involving the conduct of government officials, a government lawyer may have authority to question such conduct more extensively than that of a lawyer for a private organization in similar circumstances. This Rule does not limit that authority. *See* note on Scope.

Clarifying the Lawyer's Role

[7] When the organization's interest may be or become adverse to those of one or more of its constituents, the lawyer should advise any constituent, whose interest the lawyer finds adverse to that of the organization of the conflict or potential conflict of interest, that the lawyer cannot represent such constituent, and that such person may wish to obtain independent representation. Care must be taken to assure that the individual understands that, when there is such adversity of interest, the lawyer for the organization cannot provide legal representation for that constituent individual, and that discussions between the lawyer for the organization and the individual may not be privileged.

[8] Whether such a warning should be given by the lawyer for the organization to any constituent individual may turn on the facts of each case.

Dual Representation

[9] Paragraph (e) recognizes that a lawyer for an organization may also represent individuals within the organization. When an organization's lawyer is assigned or authorized to represent such an individual, the lawyer has an attorney-client relationship with both that individual and the organization. Accordingly, the lawyer's representation of both is controlled by the confidentiality and conflicts provisions of these Rules.

Derivative Actions

[10] Under generally prevailing law, the shareholders or members of a corporation may bring suit to compel the directors to perform their legal obligations in the supervision of the organization. Members of unincorporated associations have essentially the same right. Such an action may be brought nominally by the organization, but usually is, in fact, a legal controversy over management of the organization.

[11] The question can arise whether counsel for the organization may defend such an action. The proposition that the organization is the lawyer's client does not alone resolve the issue. Most derivative actions are a normal incident of an organization's affairs, to be defended by the organization's lawyer like any other suit. However, if the claim involves

serious charges of wrongdoing by those in control of the organization, a conflict may arise between the lawyer's duty to the organization and the lawyer's relationship with the board. In those circumstances, Rule 1.7 governs who should represent the directors and the organization.

Virginia Code Comparison

There was no direct counterpart to this Rule in the Disciplinary Rules of the *Virginia Code*. EC 5–18 stated that a "lawyer employed or retained by a corporation or similar entity owes his allegiance to the entity and not to a stockholder, director, officer, employee, representative, or other person connected with the entity. In advising the entity, a lawyer should keep paramount its interests and the lawyer's professional judgment should not be influenced by the personal desires of any person or organization. Occasionally, a lawyer for an entity is requested by a stockholder, director, officer, employee, representative, or other person connected with the entity to represent the individual in an individual capacity; in such case the lawyer may serve the individual only if the lawyer is convinced that differing interests are not present." EC 5–24 stated that although a lawyer "may be employed by a business corporation with non-lawyers serving as directors or officers, and they necessarily have the right to make decisions of business policy, a lawyer must decline to accept direction of his professional judgment from any layman." DR 5–106(B) provided that a lawyer "shall not permit a person who . . . employs . . . him to render legal services for another to direct or regulate his professional judgment in rendering such legal services."

Committee Commentary

The Committee adopted this Rule because it directly addresses matters only implicitly addressed in Ethical Considerations of the *Virginia Code*.

RULE 1.14 CLIENT WITH IMPAIRMENT

(a) When a client's capacity to make adequately considered decisions in connection with a representation is diminished, whether because of minority, mental impairment or some other reason, the lawyer shall, as far as reasonably possible, maintain a normal client-lawyer relationship with the client.

(b) When the lawyer reasonably believes that the client has diminished capacity, is at risk of substantial physical, financial or other harm unless action is taken and cannot adequately act in the client's own interest, the lawyer may take reasonably necessary protective action, including consulting with individuals or entities that have the ability to take action to protect the client and, in appropriate cases, seeking the appointment of a guardian ad litem, conservator or guardian.

(c) Information relating to the representation of a client with diminished capacity is protected by Rule 1.6. When taking protective action pursuant to paragraph (b), the lawyer is impliedly authorized under Rule 1.6(a) to reveal information about the client, but only to the extent reasonably necessary to protect the client's interests.

[Adopted effective January 1, 2000. Amended effective January 1, 2004.]

Comment

[1] The normal client-lawyer relationship is based on the assumption that the client, when properly advised and assisted, is capable of making decisions about important matters. When the client is a minor or suffers from a diminished mental capacity, however, maintaining the ordinary client-lawyer relationship may not be possible in all respects. In particular, an incapacitated person may have no power to make legally binding decisions. Nevertheless, a client with diminished capacities often has the ability to understand, deliberate upon, and reach conclusions about matters affecting the client's own well-being. For example, children as young as five or six years of age, and certainly those of ten or twelve, are regarded as having opinions that are entitled to weight in legal proceedings concerning their custody. So also, it is recognized that some persons of advanced age can be quite capable of handling routine financial matters while needing special legal protection concerning major transactions.

[2] The fact that a client suffers a disability does not diminish the lawyer's obligation to treat the client with attention and respect. If the person has no guardian or legal representative, the lawyer often must act as de facto guardian. Even if the person does have a legal representative, the lawyer should as far as possible accord the represented person the status of client, particularly in maintaining communication.

[3] If the client has a legal representative, the lawyer should ordinarily look to the representative for decisions on behalf of the client. If there is no legal representative, the lawyer should seek such an appointment where it would serve the client's best interests. Thus, if a disabled client has substantial property that should be sold for the client's benefit, effective completion of the transaction ordinarily requires appointment of a legal representative. In many circumstances, how-

ever, appointment of a legal representative may be expensive or traumatic for the client. Evaluation of these considerations is a matter of professional judgment on the lawyer's part.

[4] If the lawyer represents the guardian as distinct from the ward, and is aware that the guardian is acting adversely to the ward's interest, the lawyer may have an obligation to prevent or rectify the guardian's misconduct. *See* Rule 1.2(d).

Disclosure of the Client's Condition

[5] Court Rules generally provide that minors or persons suffering mental disability shall be represented by a guardian or next friend if they do not have a guardian. However, disclosure of the client's disability can adversely affect the client's interests. For example, raising the question of disability could, in some circumstances, lead to proceedings for involuntary commitment. The lawyer's position in such cases is an unavoidably difficult one. The lawyer may seek guidance from an appropriate diagnostician.

Virginia Code Comparison

There was no direct counterpart to this Rule in the Disciplinary Rules of the *Virginia Code*. EC 7–11 stated that the "responsibilities of a lawyer may vary according to the intelligence, experience, mental condition or age of a client ... Examples include the representation of an illiterate or an incompetent ...." EC 7–12 stated that "[a]ny mental or physical condition of a client that renders him incapable of making a considered judgment on his own behalf casts additional responsibilities upon his lawyer. Where an incompetent is acting through a guardian or other legal representative, a lawyer must look to such representative for those decisions which are normally the prerogative of the client to make. If a client under disability has no legal representative, his lawyer may be compelled in court proceedings to make decisions on behalf of the client. If the client is capable of understanding the matter in question or of contributing to the advancement of his interests, regardless of whether he is legally disqualified from performing certain acts, the lawyer should obtain from him all possible aid. If the disability of a client and the lack of a legal representative compel the lawyer to make decisions for his client, the lawyer should consider all circumstances then prevailing and act with care to safeguard and advance the interests of his client. But obviously a lawyer cannot perform any act or make any decision which the law requires his client to perform or make, either acting for himself if competent, or by a duly constituted representative if legally incompetent."

Committee Commentary

The Committee adopted this Rule because it directly addresses matters only implicitly addressed in Ethical Considerations of the *Virginia Code*.

RULE 1.15. SAFEKEEPING PROPERTY

(a) Depositing Funds.

(1) All funds received or held by a lawyer or law firm on behalf of a client or a third party, or held by a lawyer as a fiduciary, other than reimbursement of advances for costs and expenses, shall be deposited in one or more identifiable trust accounts; all other property held on behalf of a client should be placed in a safe deposit box or other place of safekeeping as soon as practicable.

(2) For lawyers or law firms located in Virginia, a lawyer trust account shall be maintained only at a financial institution approved by the Virginia State Bar, unless otherwise expressly directed in writing by the client for whom the funds are being held.

(3) No funds belonging to the lawyer or law firm shall be deposited or maintained therein except as follows:

(i) funds reasonably sufficient to pay service or other charges or fees imposed by the financial institution or to maintain a required minimum balance to avoid the imposition of service fees, provided the funds deposited are no more than necessary to do so; or

(ii) funds in which two or more persons (one of whom may be the lawyer) claim an interest shall be held in the trust account until the dispute is resolved and there is an accounting and severance of their interests. Any portion finally determined to belong to the lawyer or law firm shall be promptly withdrawn from the trust account.

(b) Specific Duties. A lawyer shall:

(1) promptly notify a client of the receipt of the client's funds, securities, or other properties;

(2) identify and label securities and properties of a client, or those held by a lawyer as a fiduciary, promptly upon receipt;

(3) maintain complete records of all funds, securities, and other properties of a client coming into the possession of the lawyer and render appropriate accountings to the client regarding them;

(4) promptly pay or deliver to the client or another as requested by such person the funds, securities, or other properties in the possession of the lawyer that such person is entitled to receive; and

(5) not disburse funds or use property of a client or of a third party with a valid lien or assignment without

their consent or convert funds or property of a client or third party, except as directed by a tribunal.

(c) Record–Keeping Requirements. A lawyer shall, at a minimum, maintain the following books and records demonstrating compliance with this Rule:

(1) Cash receipts and disbursements journals for each trust account, including entries for receipts, disbursements, and transfers, and also including, at a minimum: an identification of the client matter; the date of the transaction; the name of the payor or payee; and the manner in which trust funds were received, disbursed, or transferred from an account.

(2) A subsidiary ledger containing a separate entry for each client, other person, or entity from whom money has been received in trust.

The ledger should clearly identify:

(i) the client or matter, including the date of the transaction and the payor or payee and the means or methods by which trust funds were received, disbursed or transferred; and

(ii) any unexpended balance.

(3) In the case of funds or property held by a lawyer as a fiduciary, the required books and records shall include an annual summary of all receipts and disbursements and changes in assets comparable in detail to an accounting that would be required of a court-supervised fiduciary in the same or similar capacity, including all source documents sufficient to substantiate the annual summary.

(4) All records subject to this Rule shall be preserved for at least five calendar years after termination of the representation or fiduciary responsibility.

(d) Required Trust Accounting Procedures. In addition to the requirements set forth in Rule 1.15(a) through (c), the following minimum trust accounting procedures are applicable to all trust accounts:

(1) *Insufficient Fund Reporting.* All accounts are subject to the requirements governing insufficient fund check reporting as set forth in the Virginia State Bar Approved Financial Institution Agreement.

(2) *Deposits.* All trust funds received shall be deposited intact. Mixed trust and non-trust funds shall be deposited intact into the trust fund and the non-trust portion shall be withdrawn upon the clearing of the mixed fund deposit instrument. All such deposits should include a detailed deposit slip or record that sufficiently identifies each item.

(3) *Reconciliations.*

(i) At least quarterly, a reconciliation shall be made that reflects the trust account balance for each client, person or other entity.

(ii) A monthly reconciliation shall be made of the cash balance that is derived from the cash receipts journal, cash disbursements journal, the trust account checkbook balance, and the trust account bank statement balance.

(iii) At least quarterly, a reconciliation shall be made that reconciles the cash balance from (d)(3)(ii) above and the subsidiary ledger balance from (d)(3)(i).

(iv) Reconciliations must be approved by a lawyer in the law firm.

(4) The purpose of all receipts and disbursements of trust funds reported in the trust journals and ledgers shall be fully explained and supported by adequate records.

[Adopted effective January 1, 2000. Amended effective January 1, 2004; June 21, 2011; November 1, 2013.]

Comment

[1] A lawyer should hold property of others with the care required of a professional fiduciary. Securities should be kept in a safe deposit box, except when some other form of safekeeping is warranted by special circumstances. For purposes of this Rule, the term "fiduciary" includes personal representative, trustee, receiver, guardian, committee, custodian, and attorney-in-fact. All property that is the property of clients or third persons should be kept separate from the lawyer's business and personal property and, if funds, in one or more trust accounts. Separate trust accounts may be warranted when administering estate funds or acting in similar fiduciary capacities.

[2] Separation of the funds of a client from those of the lawyer not only serves to protect the client but also avoids even the appearance of impropriety and, therefore, commingling of such funds should be avoided.

[2a] In relation to (b)(5), consent can be inferred from the engagement agreement or any consequential agreement between the lawyer and the client regarding the disbursement of fees, i.e., when earned fees are routinely withdrawn from the lawyer's trust account upon an accounting to the client, when costs and expenses of litigation are routinely withdrawn, or when other fees/costs or expenses are agreed upon in advance.

[3] Lawyers often receive funds from third parties from which the lawyer's fee will be paid. If there is risk that the client may divert the funds without paying the fee, the lawyer is not required to remit the portion from which the fee is to be paid. However, a lawyer may not hold funds to coerce a client into accepting the lawyer's contention. The disputed portion of the funds should be kept in trust and the lawyer should suggest means for prompt resolution of the dispute, such as arbitration or mediation. The undisputed portion of the funds shall be promptly distributed.

[4] Paragraphs (b)(4) and (b)(5) do not impose an obligation upon the lawyer to protect funds on behalf of the client's general creditors who have no valid claim to an interest in the specific funds or property in the lawyer's possession. However, a lawyer may be in possession of property or funds claimed both by the lawyer's client and a third person; for example, a previous lawyer of the client claiming a lien on the client's recovery or a person claiming that the property deposited with the lawyer was taken or withheld unlawfully from that person. Additionally, a lawyer may have a duty under applicable law to protect such third-party claims against wrongful interference by the client, and accordingly may refuse to surrender the property to the client. For example, if a lawyer has actual knowledge of a third party's lawful claim to an interest in the specific funds held on behalf of a client, then by virtue of a statutory lien (e.g., medical, workers' compensation, attorneys' lien, a valid assignment executed by the client, or a lien on the subject property created by a recorded deed of trust) the lawyer has a duty to secure the funds claimed by the third party. Under the above-described circumstances, paragraphs (b)(4) and (b)(5) require the lawyer either to deliver the funds or property to the third party or, if a dispute to the third party's claim exists, to safeguard the contested property or funds until the dispute is resolved. If the client has a non-frivolous dispute with the third party's claim, then the lawyer cannot release those funds without the agreement of all parties involved or a court determination of who is entitled to receive them, such as an interpleader action. A lawyer does not violate paragraphs (b)(4) and (b)(5) if he has acted reasonably and in good faith to determine the validity of a third-party's claim or lien.

[5] The obligations of a lawyer under this Rule are independent of those arising from activity other than rendering legal services. For example, a lawyer who serves as an escrow agent is governed by the applicable law relating to fiduciaries even though the lawyer does not render legal services in the transaction.

[6] Nothing in this Rule is intended to prohibit an attorney from using electronic checking for his trust account so long as all requirements in this Rule are fulfilled. It is the lawyer's responsibility to assure that complete and accurate records of the receipt and disbursement of entrusted property are maintained in accordance with this Rule. Many businesses are now converting paper checks to automated clearinghouse (ACH) debits. Authorized ACH debits that are electronic transfers of funds (in which no checks are involved) are allowed provided the lawyer maintains a record of the transaction as required by this Rule. The record, whether consisting of the instructions or authorization to debit the account, a record or receipt from the financial institution, or the lawyer's independent record of the transaction, must show the amount, date, recipient of the transfer or disbursement, and the name of the client or other person to whom the funds belong.

Prior Rule Comparison

This rule is substantially the same as the original Rule 1.15 adopted January 1, 2000 except that the language has been substantially simplified for ease of understanding and the portions regarding the Financial Institutions duties redacted as they are appropriately incorporated into the "Trust Account Notification Agreement" signed by all Virginia-approved financial institutions.

Committee Commentary

The Committee chose to modify the rule for ease of understanding and enforcement with no substantive changes to a lawyer's safekeeping property and record-keeping requirements.

RULE 1.16 DECLINING OR TERMINATING REPRESENTATION

(a) Except as stated in paragraph (c), a lawyer shall not represent a client or, where representation has commenced, shall withdraw from the representation of a client if:

(1) the representation will result in violation of the Rules of Professional Conduct or other law;

(2) the lawyer's physical or mental condition materially impairs the lawyer's ability to represent the client; or

(3) the lawyer is discharged.

(b) Except as stated in paragraph (c), a lawyer may withdraw from representing a client if withdrawal can be accomplished without material adverse effect on the interests of the client, or if:

(1) the client persists in a course of action involving the lawyer's services that the lawyer reasonably believes is illegal or unjust;

(2) the client has used the lawyer's services to perpetrate a crime or fraud;

(3) a client insists upon pursuing an objective that the lawyer considers repugnant or imprudent;

(4) the client fails substantially to fulfill an obligation to the lawyer regarding the lawyer's services and has been given reasonable warning that the lawyer will withdraw unless the obligation is fulfilled;

(5) the representation will result in an unreasonable financial burden on the lawyer or has been rendered unreasonably difficult by the client; or

(6) other good cause for withdrawal exists.

(c) In any court proceeding, counsel of record shall not withdraw except by leave of court after compliance with notice requirements pursuant to applicable Rules of Court. In any other matter, a lawyer shall continue representation notwithstanding good cause for terminating the representation, when ordered to do so by a tribunal.

(d) Upon termination of representation, a lawyer shall take steps to the extent reasonably practicable to protect a client's interests, such as giving reasonable notice to the client, allowing time for employment of other counsel, refunding any advance payment of fee that has not been earned and handling records as indicated in paragraph (e).

(e) All original, client-furnished documents and any originals of legal instruments or official documents which are in the lawyer's possession (wills, corporate minutes, etc.) are the property of the client and, therefore, upon termination of the representation, those items shall be returned within a reasonable time to the client or the client's new counsel upon request, whether or not the client has paid the fees and costs owed the lawyer. If the lawyer wants to keep a copy of such original documents, the lawyer must incur the cost of duplication. Also upon termination, the client, upon request, must also be provided within a reasonable time copies of the following documents from the lawyer's file, whether or not the client has paid the fees and costs owed the lawyer: lawyer/client and lawyer/third–party communications; the lawyer's copies of client-furnished documents (unless the originals have been returned to the client pursuant to this paragraph); transcripts, pleadings and discovery responses; working and final drafts of legal instruments, official documents, investigative reports, legal memoranda, and other attorney work product documents prepared or collected for the client in the course of the representation; research materials; and bills previously submitted to the client. Although the lawyer may bill and seek to collect from the client the costs associated with making a copy of these materials, the lawyer may not use the client's refusal to pay for such materials as a basis to refuse the client's request. The lawyer, however, is not required under this Rule to provide the client copies of billing records and documents intended only for internal use, such as memoranda prepared by the lawyer discussing conflicts of interest, staffing considerations, or difficulties arising from the lawyer-client relationship. The lawyer has met his or her obligation under this paragraph by furnishing these items one time at client request upon termination; provision of multiple copies is not required. The lawyer has not met his or her obligation under this paragraph by the mere provision of copies of documents on an item-by-item basis during the course of the representation.

[Adopted effective January 1, 2000. Amended effective January 1, 2004.]

Comment

[1] A lawyer should not accept or continue representation in a matter unless it can be performed competently, promptly, without improper conflict of interest and to completion.

Mandatory Withdrawal

[2] A lawyer ordinarily must decline or withdraw from representation if the client demands that the lawyer engage in conduct that is illegal or violates the Rules of Professional Conduct or other law. The lawyer is not obliged to decline or withdraw simply because the client suggests such a course of conduct; a client may make such a suggestion in the hope that a lawyer will not be constrained by a professional obligation.

[3] When a lawyer has been appointed to represent a client, withdrawal ordinarily requires approval of the appointing authority. *See* also Rule 6.2. Difficulty may be encountered if withdrawal is based on the client's demand that the lawyer engage in unprofessional conduct. The court may wish an explanation for the withdrawal, while the lawyer may be bound to keep confidential the facts that would constitute such an explanation. The lawyer's statement that professional considerations require termination of the representation ordinarily should be accepted as sufficient.

Discharge

[4] A client has a right to discharge a lawyer at any time, with or without cause. Where future dispute about the withdrawal may be anticipated, it may be advisable to prepare a written statement reciting the circumstances.

[5] Whether a client can discharge appointed counsel may depend on applicable law. A client seeking to do so should be given a full explanation of the consequences. These consequences may include a decision by the appointing authority that appointment of successor counsel is unjustified, thus requiring the client to proceed *pro se*.

[6] If the client is mentally incompetent, the client may lack the legal capacity to discharge the lawyer, and in any event the discharge may be seriously adverse to the

client's interests. The lawyer should make special effort to help the client consider the consequences and, in an extreme case, may initiate proceedings for a conservatorship or similar protection of the client. *See* Rule 1.14.

Optional Withdrawal

[7] A lawyer may withdraw from representation in some circumstances. The lawyer has the option to withdraw if it can be accomplished without material adverse effect on the client's interests. Withdrawal is also justified if the client persists in a course of action that the lawyer reasonably believes is illegal or unjust, for a lawyer is not required to be associated with such conduct even if the lawyer does not further it. Withdrawal is also permitted if the lawyer's services were misused in the past even if that would materially prejudice the client. The lawyer also may withdraw where the client insists on a repugnant or imprudent objective.

[8] A lawyer may withdraw if the client refuses to abide by the terms of an agreement' relating to the representation, such as an agreement concerning fees or court costs or an agreement limiting the objectives of the representation.

Assisting the Client upon Withdrawal

[9] Even if the lawyer has been unfairly discharged by the client, a lawyer must take all reasonable steps to mitigate the consequences to the client. Whether or not a lawyer for an organization may under certain unusual circumstances have a legal obligation to the organization after withdrawing or being discharged by the organization's highest authority is beyond the scope of these Rules.

Retention of Client Papers or File When Client Fails or Refuses to Pay Fees/Expenses Owed to Lawyer

[10] Paragraph (e) eschews a "prejudice" standard in favor of a more objective and easily-applied rule governing specific kinds of documents in the lawyer's files.

[11] The requirements of paragraph (e) should not be interpreted to require disclosure of materials where the disclosure is prohibited by law.

Virginia Code Comparison

Paragraph (a) is substantially the same as DR 2–108(A).

Paragraph (b) is substantially similar to DR 2–108(B) which provided that a lawyer "may withdraw from representing a client if: (1) Withdrawal can be effected without material prejudice to the client; or (2) The client persists in a course of conduct involving the lawyer's services that the lawyer reasonably believes is illegal or unjust; or (3) The client fails to fulfill an obligation to the lawyer regarding the lawyer's services and such failure continues after reasonable notice to the client; or (4) The representation will result in an unreasonable financial burden on the lawyer or has been rendered unreasonably difficult by the client."

Paragraph (c) is identical to DR 2–108(C).

Paragraph (d) is based on DR 2–108(D), but does not address documents in the lawyer's files (which are handled under paragraph (e).

Paragraph (e) is new.

Committee Commentary

The provisions of DR 2–108 of the *Virginia Code* derived more from *ABA Model Rule* 1.16 than from its counterpart in the *ABA Model Code,* DR 2–110. Accordingly, the Committee generally adopted the *ABA Model Rule,* but substituted the "illegal or unjust" language from DR 2–108(B)(2) for the "criminal or fraudulent" language of the *ABA Model Rule.* Additionally, the Committee substituted the language of DR 2–108(C) for that of paragraph (c) of the *ABA Model Rule* to make it clear that a lawyer, in circumstances involving court proceedings, has an affirmative duty to request leave of court to withdraw. The Committee recommended paragraph (e) instead of a "prejudice" standard as being more easily understood and applied by lawyers.

RULE 1.17. SALE OF LAW PRACTICE

A lawyer or a law firm may sell or purchase a law practice, partially or in its entirety, including good will, if the following conditions are satisfied:

(a) The seller ceases to engage in the private practice of law, or in the area of practice that has been sold, in the geographic area in which the practice has been conducted, except the lawyer may practice law while on staff of a public agency or legal services entity which provides legal services to the poor, or as in-house counsel to a business.

(b) The entire practice, or the entire area of practice, is sold to one or more lawyers or law firms;

(c) Actual written notice is given by the seller to each of the seller's clients (as defined by the terms of the proposed sale) regarding:

(1) the proposed sale and the identity of the purchaser;

(2) any proposed change in the terms of the future representation including the fee arrangement;

(3) the client's right to consent or to refuse to consent to the transfer of the client's matter, and that said right must be exercised within ninety (90) days of receipt of the notice;

(4) the client's right to retain other counsel and/or take possession of the file; and

(5) the fact that the client's refusal to consent to the transfer of the client's matter will be presumed if the client does not take any action or does not otherwise consent within ninety (90) days of receipt of the notice.

(d) If a client involved in a pending matter cannot be given notice, the representation of that client may be transferred to the purchaser only upon entry of an order so authorizing by a court having jurisdiction. The seller may disclose to the court *in camera* information relating to the representation only to the extent necessary to obtain an order authorizing the transfer of a file.

(e) The fees charged clients shall not be increased by reason of the sale.

[Adopted effective January 1, 2000. Amended effective January 1, 2004; January 4, 2010.

COMMENT

[1] The practice of law is a profession, not merely a business. Clients are not commodities that can be purchased and sold at will. Pursuant to this Rule, when a lawyer or an entire firm ceases to practice and another lawyer or firm takes over the representation, the selling lawyer or firm may obtain compensation for the reasonable value of the practice as may withdrawing partners of law firms. *See* Rules 5.4 and 5.6.

Termination of Practice by Seller

[2] The fact that a number of the seller's clients decide not to be represented by the purchaser but take their matters elsewhere does not result in a violation. Neither does the seller's return to private practice after the sale as a result of an unanticipated change in circumstances result in a violation. For example, a lawyer who has sold the practice to accept an appointment to judicial office does not violate the requirement that the sale be attendant to cessation of practice if the lawyer later resumes private practice upon leaving the office.

[3] Comment [3] to *ABA Model Rule* 1.17 substantially appears in paragraph (a) of this Rule.

[4] The Rule permits a sale of an entire practice attendant upon retirement from the private practice of law within the jurisdiction.

[5] This Rule also permits a lawyer or law firm to sell an area of practice. If an area of practice is sold and the lawyer remains in the active practice of law, the lawyer must cease accepting any matters in the area of practice that has been sold, either as counsel or co-counsel or by assuming joint responsibility for a matter in connection with the division of a fee with another lawyer as would otherwise be permitted by Rule 1.5(e). For example, a lawyer with a substantial number of estate planning matters and a substantial number of probate administration cases may sell the estate planning portion of the practice but remain in the practice of law by concentrating on probate administration; however, that practitioner may not thereafter accept any estate planning matters. Although a lawyer who leaves a jurisdiction or geographical area typically would sell the entire practice, this Rule permits the lawyer to limit the sale to one or more areas of the practice, thereby preserving the lawyer's right to continue practice in the areas of the practice that were not sold.

Sale of Entire Practice or Entire Area of Practice

[6] The Rule requires that the seller's entire practice, or an entire area of practice, be sold. The prohibition against sale of less than an entire practice area protects those clients whose matters are less lucrative and who might find it difficult to secure other counsel if a sale could be limited to substantial fee-generating matters. The purchasers are required to undertake all client matters in the practice or practice area, subject to client consent. This requirement is satisfied, however, even if a purchaser is unable to undertake a particular client matter because of a conflict of interest.

Client Confidences, Consent and Notice

[7] Negotiations between seller and prospective purchaser prior to disclosure of information relating to a specific representation of an identifiable client no more violate the confidentiality provisions of Rule 1. 6 than do preliminary discussions concerning the possible association of any lawyer or mergers between firms, with respect to which client consent is not required. Providing the purchaser access to client-specific information relating to the representation and to the file, however, requires client consent. The Rule provides that before such information can be disclosed by the seller to the purchaser the client must be given actual written notice of the contemplated sale, including the identity of the purchaser and any proposed change in the terms of future representation, and must be told that the decision to consent or to make other arrangements must be made within 90 days. If nothing is heard from the client

within that time, the client's refusal to consent to the sale is presumed.

[8] A lawyer or law firm ceasing to practice cannot be required to remain in practice because some clients cannot be given actual notice of the proposed purchase. Since these clients cannot themselves consent to the purchase or direct any other disposition of their files, the Rule requires an order from a court having jurisdiction authorizing their transfer or other disposition. The Court can be expected to determine whether reasonable efforts to locate the client have been exhausted, and whether the absent client's legitimate interest will be served by authorizing the transfer of the file so that the purchaser may continue the representation. Preservation of client confidences requires that the petition for a court order be considered *in camera.*

[9] All the elements of client autonomy, including the client's absolute right to discharge a lawyer and transfer the representation to another, survive the sale of the practice.

Fee Arrangements Between Client and Purchaser

[10] The sale may not be financed by increases in fees charged the clients of the practice. Existing agreements between the seller and the client as to fees and the scope of work must be honored by the purchaser, unless the client consents after consultation.

Other Applicable Ethical Standards

[11] Lawyers participating in the sale of a law practice are subject to the ethical standards applicable to involving another lawyer in the representation of a client. These include, for example, the seller's obligation to assure that the purchaser is qualified to assume the practice and the purchaser's obligation to undertake the representation competently (*see* Rule 1.1); the obligation to avoid disqualifying conflicts, and to secure client consent after consultation for those conflicts which can be agreed to (*see* Rule 1.7); and the obligation to protect information relating to the representation (*see* Rules 1.6 and 1.9).

[12] If approval of the substitution of the purchasing attorney for the selling attorney is required by the rules of any tribunal in which a matter is pending, such approval must be obtained before the matter can be concluded in the sale (*see* Rule 1.16).

Applicability of the Rule

[13] This Rule applies to the sale of a law practice by representatives of a deceased, disabled or disappeared lawyer. Thus, the seller may be represented by a nonlawyer representative not subject to these Rules. Since, however, no lawyer may participate in a sale of a law practice which does not conform to the requirements of this Rule, the representatives of the seller as well as the purchasing lawyer shall see to it that they are met.

[14] Admission to or retirement from a law partnership or professional association, retirement plans and similar arrangements, and a sale of tangible assets of a law practice, do not constitute a sale or purchase governed by this Rule.

[15] This Rule does not apply to the transfers of legal representation between lawyers when such transfers are unrelated to the sale of a practice.

Virginia Code Comparison

Ethical Consideration 4–6 states that a lawyer should not attempt to sell a law practice as a going business because, among other things, to do so would involve the disclosure of confidences and secrets.

Committee Commentary

The Committee was persuaded to eliminate the prohibition of the sale of a law practice currently set forth in Ethical Consideration 4–6 by several arguments, the first being that sole practitioners and their clients are often unreasonably discriminated against when the attorney's practice is terminated. When lawyers who are members of firms retire, the transition for the client is usually smooth because another attorney of the firm normally takes over the matter. Such a transition is usually more difficult for the clients of a sole practitioner, who must employ another attorney or firm.

Another persuasive argument is that some attorneys leaving practice, firm members and sole practitioners alike, indirectly "sell" their practices, including its good will, by utilizing various arrangements. For example, firm members sometimes receive payments from their firm pursuant to retirement agreements that have the effect of rewarding the lawyer for the value of his/her practice. Sole practitioners contemplating leaving the practice of law may sell their tangible assets at an inflated price or bring in a partner prior to retirement, then allow the partner to take over the practice pursuant to a compensation agreement. Such arrangements do not always involve significant client participation or consent.

In addition, an attorney's practice has value that is recognized in the law. Under Virginia divorce law, for example, a professional's practice, including its good will, may be subject to equitable distribution. (*Russell v. Russell*, 11 Va. App. 411, 399 S.E.2d 166 (1990)). Therefore, under the *Virginia Code*, an attorney in a divorce proceeding may be required to compensate his/her spouse for the value of the practice, yet be forbidden to sell it.

The Committee recommended, after considering all of these factors, that adopting a carefully crafted rule allowing such sales without resort to these alternate methods would be preferable and would assure maximum protection of clients. This recommended Rule is based on the *ABA Model Rule* 1.17 with several significant changes, the chief ones relating to consent and fees.

Upon consideration whereof, it is ordered that the Rules for Integration of the Virginia State Bar, Part Six of the Rules of Court, be and the same hereby are amended in accordance with the prayer of the petition aforesaid, effective January 4, 2010.

RULE 1.18. DUTIES TO PROSPECTIVE CLIENT

(a) A person who discusses with a lawyer the possibility of forming a client-lawyer relationship with respect to a matter is a prospective client.

(b) Even when no client-lawyer relationship ensues, a lawyer who has had discussions with a prospective client shall not use or reveal information learned in the consultation, except as Rule 1.9 would permit with respect to information of a former client.

(c) A lawyer subject to paragraph (b) shall not represent a client with interests materially adverse to those of a prospective client in the same or a substantially related matter if the lawyer received information from the prospective client that could be significantly harmful to that person in the matter, except as provided in paragraph (d). If a lawyer is disqualified from representation under this paragraph, no lawyer in a firm with which that lawyer is associated may knowingly undertake or continue representation in such a matter, except as provided in paragraph (d).

(d) When the lawyer has received disqualifying information as defined in paragraph (c), representation is permissible if:

(1) both the affected client and the prospective client have given informed consent, confirmed in writing, or

(2) the lawyer who received the information took reasonable measures to avoid exposure to more disqualifying information than was reasonably necessary to determine whether to represent the prospective client; and

(i) the disqualified lawyer is timely screened from any participation in the matter; the disqualified lawyer reasonably believes that the screen would be effective to sufficiently protect information that could be significantly harmful to the prospective client; and

(ii) written notice that includes a general description of the subject matter about which the lawyer was consulted and the screening procedures employed is promptly given to the prospective client.

[Adopted effective June 21, 2011.]

COMMENT

[1] Prospective clients, like clients, may disclose information to a lawyer, place documents or other property in the lawyer's custody, or rely on the lawyer's advice. A lawyer's discussions with a prospective client usually are limited in time and depth and leave both the prospective client and the lawyer free (and sometimes required) to proceed no further. The principle of loyalty diminishes in importance if the sole reason for an individual lawyer's disqualification is the lawyer's initial consultation with a prospective new client with whom no client-lawyer relationship is formed, either because the lawyer detected a conflict of interest as a result of an initial consultation, or for some other reason (e.g., the prospective client decided not to retain the firm). Hence, prospective clients should receive some but not all of the protection afforded clients.

[2] Not all persons who communicate information to a lawyer are entitled to protection under this Rule. A person who unilaterally communicates information to a lawyer, without any reasonable expectation that the lawyer is willing to discuss the possibility of forming a client-lawyer relationship, is not a "prospective client" within the meaning of paragraph (a).

[3] It is often necessary for a prospective client to reveal information to the lawyer during an initial consultation prior to the decision about formation of a client-lawyer relationship. The client may disclose such information as part of the process of determining whether the client wishes to form a client-lawyer relationship. The lawyer often must learn such information to determine whether there is a conflict of interest with an existing client and whether the matter is one that the lawyer is willing to undertake. Paragraph (b) prohibits the lawyer from using or revealing that information, except as permitted by Rule 1.9, even if the client or lawyer decides not to proceed with the representation. The duty exists regardless of how brief the initial conference may be.

[4] In order to avoid acquiring disqualifying information from a prospective client, a lawyer considering whether or not to undertake a new matter should limit the initial interview to only such information as reasonably appears necessary for that purpose. Where the information indicates that a conflict of interest or other reason for non-representation exists, the lawyer should so inform the prospective client or decline the representation. If the prospective client wishes to retain the lawyer, and if consent is possible under Rule 1.7, then consent from all affected present or former clients must be obtained before accepting the representation.

[5] A lawyer may condition conversations with a prospective client on the person's informed consent that no information disclosed during the consultation will prohibit the lawyer from representing a different client in the matter. If the agreement expressly so provides, the prospective client may also consent to the lawyer's subsequent use of information received from the prospective client.

[6] Even in the absence of an agreement, under paragraph (c), the lawyer is not prohibited from representing a client with interests adverse to those of the prospective client in the same or a substantially related matter unless the lawyer has received from the prospective client information that could be significantly harmful if used in the matter and the lawyer believes that an effective screen could not be engaged to protect the prospective client.

[7] Under paragraph (c), the prohibition in this Rule is imputed to other lawyers as provided in Rule 1.10, but, under paragraph (d)(1), imputation may be avoided if the lawyer obtains the informed consent, confirmed in writing, of both the prospective and affected clients. In the alternative, imputation may be avoided if the conditions of paragraph (d)(2) are met and all disqualified lawyers are timely screened and written notice is promptly given to the prospective client and the lawyer reasonably believes that an effective screen will protect the confidential information of the prospective client.

[8] Notice, including a general description of the subject matter about which the lawyer was consulted, and of the screening procedures employed, generally should be given as soon as practicable after the need for screening becomes apparent.

[9] For the duty of competence of a lawyer who gives assistance on the merits of a matter to a prospective client, see Rule 1.1. For a lawyer's duties when a prospective client entrusts valuables or papers to the lawyer's care, see Rule 1.15.

COUNSELOR AND THIRD–PARTY NEUTRAL

RULE 2.1 ADVISOR

In representing a client, a lawyer shall exercise independent professional judgment and render candid advice. In rendering advice, a lawyer may refer not only to law but to other considerations such as moral, economic, social and political factors, that may be relevant to the client's situation.

[Adopted effective January 1, 2000.]

Comment

Scope of Advice

[1] A client is entitled to straightforward advice expressing the lawyer's honest assessment. Legal advice often involves unpleasant facts and alternatives that a client may be disinclined to confront. In presenting advice, a lawyer endeavors to sustain the client's morale and may put advice in as acceptable a form as honesty permits. However, a lawyer should not be deterred from giving candid advice by the prospect that the advice will be unpalatable to the client.

[2] Advice couched in narrowly legal terms may be of little value to a client, especially where practical considerations, such as cost or effects on other people, are predominant. Purely technical legal advice, therefore, can sometimes be inadequate. It could also ignore, to the client's disadvantage, the relational or emotional factors driving a dispute. In such a case, advice may include the advantages, disadvantages and availability of other dispute resolution processes that might be appropriate under the circumstances.

[2a] It is proper for a lawyer to refer to relevant moral and ethical considerations in giving advice. Although a lawyer is not a moral advisor as such, moral and ethical considerations impinge upon most legal questions and may decisively influence how the law will be applied.

[3] A client may expressly or impliedly ask the lawyer for purely technical advice. When such a request is made by a client experienced in legal matters, the lawyer may accept it at face value. When such a request is made by a client inexperienced in legal mat-

ters, however, the lawyer's responsibility as advisor may include indicating that more may be involved than strictly legal considerations.

[4] Matters that go beyond strictly legal questions may also be in the domain of another profession. Family matters can involve problems within the professional competence of psychiatry, clinical psychology or social work; business matters can involve problems within the competence of the accounting profession or of financial specialists. Where consultation with a professional in another field is itself something a competent lawyer would recommend, the lawyer should make such a recommendation. At the same time, a lawyer's advice at its best often consists of recommending a course of action in the face of conflicting recommendations of experts.

Offering Advice

[5] In general, a lawyer is not expected to give advice until asked by the client. However, when a lawyer knows that a client proposes a course of action that is likely to result in substantial adverse legal, moral or ethical consequences to the client or to others, duty to the client under Rule 1.4 may require that the lawyer act if the client's course of action is related to the representation. A lawyer ordinarily has no duty to initiate investigation of a client's affairs or to give advice that the client has indicated is unwanted, but a lawyer may initiate advice to a client when doing so appears to be in the client's interest.

Virginia Code Comparison

There was no direct counterpart to this Rule in the Disciplinary Rules of the *Virginia Code*. DR 5–106(B) provided that a lawyer "shall not permit a person who recommends, employs, or pays him to render legal services for another to direct or regulate his professional judgment in rendering such legal services." EC 7–8 stated that "[a]dvice of a lawyer to his client need not be confined to purely legal considerations. . . . In assisting his client to reach a proper decision, it is often desirable for a lawyer to point out those factors which may lead to a decision that is morally just as well as legally permissible. . . . In the final analysis, however, . . . the decision whether to forego legally available objectives or methods because of nonlegal factors is ultimately for the client. . . . "

Committee Commentary

The Committee adopted the *ABA Model Rule* verbatim because it sets forth more clearly than the Disciplinary Rules the scope of a lawyer's advisory role.

RULE 2.2 INTERMEDIARY [DELETED EFFECTIVE JANUARY 1, 2004]

RULE 2.3 EVALUATION FOR USE BY THIRD PERSONS

(a) A lawyer acts as evaluator by examining a client's legal affairs and reporting about them to the client or to others.

(b) A lawyer may undertake an evaluation of a matter affecting a client for the use of someone other than the client if:

(1) the lawyer reasonably believes that making the evaluation is compatible with other aspects of the lawyer's relationship with the client; and

(2) the client consents after consultation.

(c) Except as disclosure is required in connection with a report of an evaluation, information relating to the evaluation is otherwise protected by Rule 1.6.

[Adopted effective January 1, 2000.]

Comment

Definition

[1] An evaluation may be performed at the client's direction but for the primary purpose of establishing information for the benefit of third parties; for example, an opinion concerning the title of property rendered at the behest of a vendor for the information of a prospective purchaser, or at the behest of a borrower for the information of a prospective lender. In some situations, the evaluation may be required by a government agency; for example, an opinion concerning the legality of the securities registered for sale under the securities laws. In other instances, the evaluation may be required by a third person, such as a purchaser of a business.

[2] Lawyers for the government may be called upon to give a formal opinion on the legality of contemplated government agency action. In making such an evaluation, the government lawyer acts at the behest of the government as the client but for the purpose of establishing the limits of the agency's authorized activity. Such an opinion is to be distinguished from confidential legal advice given agency officials. The critical question is whether the opinion is to be made public.

[3] A legal evaluation should be distinguished from an investigation of a person with whom the lawyer does not have a client-lawyer relationship. For example, a lawyer retained by a purchaser to analyze a vendor's title to property does not have a client-lawyer relationship with the vendor. So also, an

investigation into a person's affairs by a government lawyer, or by special counsel employed by the government, is not an evaluation as that term is used in this Rule. The question is whether the lawyer is retained by the person whose affairs are being examined. When the lawyer is retained by that person, the general rules concerning loyalty to client and preservation of confidences apply, which is not the case if the lawyer is retained by someone else. For this reason, it is essential to identify the person by whom the lawyer is retained. This should be made clear not only to the person under examination, but also to others to whom the results are to be made available.

Duty to Third Person

[4] When the evaluation is intended for the information or use of a third person, a legal duty to that person may or may not arise. That legal question is beyond the scope of this Rule. However, since such an evaluation involves a departure from the normal client-lawyer relationship, careful analysis of the situation is required. The lawyer must be satisfied as a matter of professional judgment that making the evaluation is compatible with other functions undertaken in behalf of the client. For example, if the lawyer is acting as advocate in defending the client against charges of fraud, it would normally be incompatible with that responsibility for the lawyer to perform an evaluation for others concerning the same or a related transaction. Assuming no such impediment is apparent, however, the lawyer should advise the client of the implications of the evaluation, particularly the lawyer's responsibilities to third persons and the duty to disseminate the findings.

Access to and Disclosure of Information

[5] The quality of an evaluation depends on the freedom and extent of the investigation upon which it is based. Ordinarily a lawyer should have whatever latitude of investigation seems necessary as a matter of professional judgment. Under some circumstances, however, the terms of the evaluation may be limited. For example, certain issues or sources may be categorically excluded, or the scope of search may be limited by time constraints or the noncooperation of persons having relevant information. Any such limitations which are material to the evaluation should be described in the report. If after a lawyer has commenced an evaluation, the client refuses to comply with the terms upon which it was understood the evaluation was to have been made, the lawyer's obligations are determined by law, having reference to the terms of the client's agreement and the surrounding circumstances.

Financial Auditors' Requests for Information

[6] When a question concerning the legal situation of a client arises at the instance of the client's financial auditor and the question is referred to the lawyer, the lawyer's response may be made in accordance with procedures recognized in the legal profession. Such a procedure is set forth in the American Bar Association Statement of Policy Regarding Lawyers' Responses to Auditors' Requests for Information, adopted in 1975.

Virginia Code Comparison

There was no counterpart to this Rule in the *Virginia Code.*

Committee Commentary

The Committee adopted this Rule because it addressed matters not addressed in the *Virginia Code.* This Rule generally follows *ABA Model Rule* 2.3, but the Committee added subparagraph 2.3(c) in recognition of the statutory requirement of confidentiality in the dispute resolution process. *See Code of Virginia* Section 8.01–576.10.

RULE 2.10 THIRD PARTY NEUTRAL

(a) A third party neutral assists parties in reaching a voluntary settlement of a dispute through a structured process known as a dispute resolution proceeding. The third party neutral does not represent any party.

(b) A lawyer who serves as a third party neutral

(1) shall inform the parties of the difference between the lawyer's role as third party neutral and the lawyer's role as one who represents a client;

(2) shall encourage unrepresented parties to seek legal counsel before an agreement is executed; and

(3) may encourage and assist the parties in reaching a resolution of their dispute; but

(4) may not compel or coerce the parties to make an agreement.

(c) A lawyer may serve as a third party neutral only if the lawyer has not previously represented and is not currently representing one of the parties in connection with the subject matter of the dispute resolution proceeding.

(d) A lawyer may serve as a third party neutral in a dispute resolution proceeding involving a client whom the lawyer has represented or is representing in a matter unrelated to the dispute resolution proceeding, provided:

(1) there is full disclosure of the prior or present representation;

(2) in light of the disclosure, the third party neutral obtains the parties' informed consent;

(3) the third party neutral reasonably believes that a prior or present representation will not compromise or adversely affect the ability to act as a third party neutral; and

(4) there is no unauthorized disclosure of information in violation of Rule 1.6.

(e) A lawyer who serves or has served as a third party neutral may not serve as a lawyer on behalf of any party to the dispute, nor represent one such party against the other in any legal proceeding related to the subject of the dispute resolution proceeding.

(f) A lawyer shall withdraw as third party neutral if any of the requirements stated in this Rule is no longer satisfied or if any of the parties in the dispute resolution proceeding so requests. If the parties are participating pursuant to a court referral, the third party neutral shall report the withdrawal to the authority issuing the referral.

(g) A lawyer who serves as a third party neutral shall not charge a fee contingent on the outcome of the dispute resolution proceeding.

(h) This Rule does not apply to joint representation, which is covered by Rule 1.7.

[Adopted effective January 1, 2000. Amended effective January 1, 2004.]

Comment

[1] This Rule sets forth conflicts of interest and other ethical guidelines for a lawyer who serves as a third party neutral. Dispute resolution proceedings that are conducted by a third party neutral include mediation, conciliation, early neutral evaluation, non-binding arbitration and non-judicial settlement conferences.

[2] A lawyer who serves as a third party neutral under this Rule or as a mediator under Rule 2.11 is engaged in the provision of a law-related service that may involve the application of a lawyer's particular legal expertise and skills. The standards set forth in this Rule, however, do not amount to a determination that a lawyer who serves as a third party neutral pursuant to this Rule or as a mediator pursuant to Rule 2.11 is engaged in the practice of law. The determination of whether a particular activity constitutes the practice of law is beyond the scope and purpose of these Rules.

[3] A lawyer serving as third party neutral shall not offer any of the parties legal advice, which is a function of the lawyer who is representing a client (*See* Preamble: A Lawyer's Responsibilities). A third party neutral may, however, offer neutral evaluations, if requested by the parties. Special provisions under which a lawyer-mediator can offer certain neutral evaluations are contained in Rule 2.11.

[4] Confidentiality of information revealed in the dispute resolution process is governed by *Code of Virginia* Sections 8.01–576.9 and 8.01–576.10.

[5] A third party neutral as defined in these Rules does not include a lawyer providing binding arbitration services (*See Code of Virginia* Section 8.01–577 et seq.).

[6] The imputation of conflicts arising under paragraph (e) is addressed in Rule 1.10.

Virginia Code Comparison

There was no counterpart to this Rule in the *Virginia Code.*

Committee Commentary

The Committee adopted this Rule, not part of the *ABA Model Rules*, to provide guidelines for lawyers who serve as neutrals and who do not represent a party to a dispute or transaction. Following adoption of Virginia Rule 2.10, the ABA adopted Model Rule 2.4 governing third-party neutrals. The Virginia and ABA Rules are substantially different.

RULE 2.11 MEDIATOR

(a) A lawyer-mediator is a third party neutral (*See* Rule 2.10) who facilitates communication between the parties and, without deciding the issues or imposing a solution on the parties, enables them to understand and resolve their dispute.

(b) Prior to agreeing to mediate and throughout the mediation process a lawyer-mediator should reasonably determine that:

(1) mediation is an appropriate process for the parties;

(2) each party is able to participate effectively within the context of the mediation process; and

(3) each party is willing to enter and participate in the process in good faith.

(c) A lawyer-mediator may offer legal information if all parties are present or separately to the parties if they consent. The lawyer-mediator shall inform unrepresented parties or those parties who are not accompanied by legal counsel about the importance of reviewing the lawyer-mediator's legal information with legal counsel.

(d) A lawyer-mediator may offer evaluation of, for example, strengths and weaknesses of positions, assess the value and cost of alternatives to settlement or assess the barriers to settlement (collectively referred to as evaluation) only if such evaluation is incidental to the facilitative role and does not interfere with the lawyer-mediator's impartiality or the self-determination of the parties.

(e) Prior to the mediation session a lawyer-mediator shall:

(1) consult with prospective parties about

(i) the nature of the mediation process;

(ii) the limitations on the use of evaluation, as set forth in subparagraph (d) above;

(iii) the lawyer-mediator's approach, style and subject matter expertise; and

(iv) the parties' expectations regarding the mediation process; and

(2) enter into a written agreement to mediate which references the choice and expectations of the parties, including whether the parties have chosen, permit or expect the use of neutral evaluation or evaluative techniques during the course of the mediation.

(f) A lawyer-mediator shall conduct the mediation in a manner that is consistent with the parties' choice and expectations.

[Adopted effective January 1, 2000. Amended effective December 30, 2008.]

Comment

[1] Offering assessments, evaluations, and advice are traditional lawyering functions for the lawyer who represents a client. A lawyer-mediator, who does not represent any of the parties to the mediation, should not assume that these functions are appropriate. Although these functions are not specifically prohibited in the statutory definition of mediation which is set forth as subparagraph (a) of this Rule, an evaluative approach which interferes with the parties' self-determination and the mediator's impartiality would be inconsistent with this definition of mediation.

[2] Defining mediation to exclude an evaluative approach is difficult not only because practice varies widely but because no consensus exists as to what constitutes an evaluation. Also, the effects of an evaluation on the mediation process depend upon the attitude and style of the mediator and the context in which it is offered. Thus, a question by a lawyer-mediator to a party that might be considered by some as "reality testing" and facilitative, might be viewed by others as evaluative. On the other hand, an evaluation by a facilitative mediator could help free the parties from the narrowing effects of the law and help empower them to resolve their dispute.

Informed Consent to Mediator's Approach

[3] The Rule focuses on the informed consent of the prospective mediation clients to the particular approach, style and subject matter expertise of the lawyer-mediator. This begins with consultation about the nature of the mediation process, the limitations on evaluation, the lawyer-mediator's approach, style and subject matter expertise and the parties' expectations regarding the mediation process. If the parties request an evaluative approach, the lawyer-mediator shall explain the risk that evaluation might interfere with mediator impartiality and party self-determination. Following this consultation the lawyer-mediator and the parties shall sign a written agreement to mediate which reflects the choice and expectation of the parties. The lawyer-mediator shall then conduct the mediation in a manner that is consistent with the parties' choice and expectations. This is similar to the lawyer-client consultation about the means to be used in pursuing a client's objectives in Rule 1.2.

Continuing Responsibility to Examine Potential Impact of Evaluation

[4] If the parties choose a lawyer-mediator who is willing and able to offer evaluation during the mediation process and has met the requirements of paragraph (e), a lawyer-mediator has a continuing responsibility under paragraphs (b) and (d) to assess the situation and consult with the parties before offering or responding to a request for an evaluation. Consideration shall be given again to whether mediator impartiality and party self-determination are at risk. Consideration should also be given as to whether an evaluation could detract from the willingness of the parties to work at understanding their own and each other's situation and at considering a broader range of interests, issues and options. Also, with an evaluation the parties may miss out on opportunities to maintain or improve relationships or to create a higher quality and more satisfying result.

[5] On the other hand, the parties may expect the lawyer-mediator to offer an evaluation in helping the parties reach agreement, especially when the most important issues are the strengths or weaknesses of legal positions, or the significance of commercial or financial risks. This is particularly useful after parties have worked at possible solutions and have built up confidence in the mediator's impartiality or where widely divergent party evaluations are major barriers to settlement.

[6] The presence of attorneys for the parties offers additional protection in minimizing the risk of a poor quality evaluation and of too strong an influence on the parties' self-determination. An evaluation, coupled with a reminder to the parties that the

evaluation is but one of the factors to be considered as they deliberate on the outcome, may in certain cases be the most appropriate way to assure that the parties are making fully informed decisions.

Legal Advice, Legal Information and Neutral Evaluation

[7] A lawyer-mediator shall not offer any of the parties legal advice which is a function of the lawyer who is representing a client. However, a lawyer-mediator may offer legal information under the conditions outlined in paragraph (c). Offering legal information is an educational function which aids the parties in making informed decisions. Neutral evaluations in the mediation process consist of, for example, opining as to the strengths and weaknesses of positions, assessing the value and costs of alternatives to settlement or assessing the barriers to settlement.

[8] The lawyer-mediator shall not, however, make decisions for any party to the mediation process nor shall the lawyer-mediator use a neutral evaluation to coerce or influence the parties to settle their dispute or to accept a particular solution to their dispute. Paragraphs (d), (e), and (f) restrict the use of evaluative techniques by the lawyer-mediator to situations where the parties have given their informed consent to the use of such techniques and where a neutral evaluation will assist, rather than interfere with the ability of the parties to reach a mutually agreeable solution to their dispute.

Mediation

[9] While a lawyer is cautioned in Rule 1.7 regarding the special considerations in common representation, these should not deter a lawyer-mediator from accepting clients for mediation. In mediation, a lawyer-mediator represents none of the parties and should be trained to deal with strong emotions. In fact, mediation can be especially useful in a case where communication and relational breakdown have made negotiation or litigation of legal issues more difficult.

Confidentiality and Professional Responsibility Standards

[10] Confidentiality of information revealed in the mediation process is governed by *Code of Virginia* Sections 8.01–576.09 and 8.01–576.10 and Section 8.01–581.22.

Virginia Code Comparison

There was no counterpart to this Rule in the *Virginia Code.*

Committee Commentary

The Committee adopted this Rule, not part of the *ABA Model Rules,* to give further guidance to lawyers who serve as mediators. Although Legal Ethics Opinions (e.g., LEO 590 (May 17, 1985)) have approved of lawyers serving as mediators, different approaches to and styles of mediation ranging from pure facilitation to evaluation of positions are being offered. This Rule requires lawyer-mediators to consult with prospective parties about the lawyer-mediators' approach, style and subject matter expertise and to honor the parties' choice and expectations.

ADVOCATE

RULE 3.1 MERITORIOUS CLAIMS AND CONTENTIONS

A lawyer shall not bring or defend a proceeding, or assert or controvert an issue therein, unless there is a basis for doing so that is not frivolous, which includes a good faith argument for an extension, modification or reversal of existing law. A lawyer for the defendant in a criminal proceeding, or the respondent in a proceeding that could result in incarceration, may nevertheless so defend the proceeding as to require that every element of the case be established.

[Adopted effective January 1, 2000.]

Comment

[1] The advocate has a duty to use legal procedure for the fullest benefit of the client's cause, but also a duty not to abuse legal procedure. The law, both procedural and substantive, establishes the limits within which an advocate may proceed. However, the law is not always clear and is never static. Accordingly, in determining the proper scope of advocacy, account must be taken of the law's ambiguities and potential for change.

[2] The filing of an action or defense or similar action taken for a client is not frivolous merely because the facts have not first been fully substantiated or because the lawyer expects to develop vital evidence only by discovery. Such action is not frivolous even though the lawyer believes that the client's position ultimately will not prevail. The action is frivolous, however, if the client desires to have the action taken primarily for the purpose of harassing or maliciously injuring a person, or if the lawyer is unable either to make a good faith argument on the merits of the action taken or to support the action taken by a good faith argument for an extension, modification or reversal of existing law.

Virginia Code Comparison

Rule 3.1 is similar to DR 7–102(A)(1), but with three differences. First, the test of improper conduct is changed from "merely to harass or maliciously injure another" to the requirement that there be a basis for the litigation measure involved that is "not frivolous." This includes the concept stated in DR 7–102(A)(2) that a lawyer may advance a claim or defense unwarranted by existing law if "it can be supported by good faith argument for an extension, modification, or reversal of existing law." Second, the test in Rule 3.1 is an objective test, whereas DR 7–102(A)(1) applied only if the lawyer "knows or when it is obvious" that the litigation is frivolous. Third, Rule 3.1 has an exception that in a criminal case, or a case in which incarceration of the client may result (for example, certain juvenile proceedings), the lawyer may put the prosecution to its proof even if there is no nonfrivolous basis for defense.

Committee Commentary

Although Rule 3.1 is similar in substance to existing *Virginia Code* provisions, the Committee concluded that the objective standard of the *ABA Model Rule* was preferable and more closely paralleled Section 8.01–271.1 of the *Code of Virginia*, dealing with lawyer sanctions.

RULE 3.3 CANDOR TOWARD THE TRIBUNAL

(a) A lawyer shall not knowingly:

(1) make a false statement of fact or law to a tribunal;

(2) fail to disclose a fact to a tribunal when disclosure is necessary to avoid assisting a criminal or fraudulent act by the client, subject to Rule 1.6;

(3) fail to disclose to the tribunal controlling legal authority in the subject jurisdiction known to the lawyer to be adverse to the position of the client and not disclosed by opposing counsel; or

(4) offer evidence that the lawyer knows to be false. If a lawyer has offered material evidence and comes to know of its falsity, the lawyer shall take reasonable remedial measures.

(b) A lawyer may refuse to offer evidence that the lawyer reasonably believes is false.

(c) In an ex parte proceeding, a lawyer shall inform the tribunal of all material facts known to the lawyer which will enable the tribunal to make an informed decision, whether or not the facts are adverse.

(d) A lawyer who receives information clearly establishing that a person other than a client has perpetrated a fraud upon a tribunal shall promptly reveal the fraud to the tribunal.

[Adopted effective January 1, 2000.]

Comment

[1] The advocate's task is to present the client's case with persuasive force. Performance of that duty while maintaining confidences of the client is qualified by the advocate's duty of candor to the tribunal. However, an advocate does not vouch for the evidence submitted in a cause; the tribunal is responsible for assessing its probative value.

Representations by a Lawyer

[2] An advocate is responsible for pleadings and other documents prepared for litigation, but is usually not required to have personal knowledge of matters asserted therein, for litigation documents ordinarily present assertions by the client, or by someone on the client's behalf, and not assertions by the lawyer. Compare Rule 3.1. However, Section 8.01–271.1 of the *Code of Virginia* states that a lawyer's signature on a pleading constitutes a certification that the lawyer believes, after reasonable inquiry, that there is a factual and legal basis for the pleading. Additionally, an assertion purporting to be on the lawyer's own knowledge, as in an affidavit by the lawyer or in a statement in open court, may properly be made only when the lawyer knows the assertion is true or believes it to be true on the basis of a reasonably diligent inquiry. There are circumstances where failure to make a disclosure is the equivalent of an affirmative misrepresentation. The obligation prescribed in Rule 1.2(c) not to counsel a client to commit or assist the client in committing a fraud applies in litigation. Regarding compliance with Rule 1.2(c), *see* the Comment to that Rule. *See also* the Comment to Rule 8.4(b).

Misleading Legal Argument

[3] Legal argument based on a knowingly false representation of law constitutes dishonesty toward the tribunal. Furthermore, the complexity of law often makes it difficult for a tribunal to be fully informed unless pertinent law is presented by the lawyers in the cause. A tribunal that is fully informed on the applicable law is better able to make a fair and accurate determination of the matter before it. The underlying concept is that legal argument is a discussion seeking to determine the legal premises properly applicable to the case. A lawyer is not required to make a disinterested exposition of the law, but must recognize the existence of pertinent legal

authorities. Furthermore, as stated in paragraph (a)(3), an advocate has a duty to disclose controlling adverse authority in the subject jurisdiction which has not been disclosed by the opposing party.

False Evidence

[4] When evidence that a lawyer knows to be false is provided by a person who is not the client, the lawyer must refuse to offer it regardless of the client's wishes.

[5] When false evidence is offered by the client, however, a conflict may arise between the lawyer's duty to keep the client's revelations confidential and the duty of candor to the court. Upon ascertaining that material evidence is false, the lawyer should seek to persuade the client that the evidence should not be offered or, if it has been offered, that its false character should immediately be disclosed. If the persuasion is ineffective, the lawyer must take reasonable remedial measures.

[6] Except in the defense of a criminal accused, the rule generally recognized is that, if necessary to rectify the situation, an advocate must disclose the existence of the client's deception to the court or to the other party. Such a disclosure can result in grave consequences to the client, including not only a sense of betrayal but also loss of the case and perhaps a prosecution for perjury. But the alternative is that the lawyer cooperate in deceiving the court, thereby subverting the truth-finding process which the adversary system is designed to implement. *See* Rule 1.2(c). Furthermore, unless it is clearly understood that the lawyer will act upon the duty to disclose the existence of false evidence, the client can simply reject the lawyer's advice to reveal the false evidence and insist that the lawyer keep silent. Thus the client could in effect coerce the lawyer into being a party to fraud on the court.

Perjury by a Criminal Defendant

[7] Whether an advocate for a criminally accused has the same duty of disclosure has been intensely debated. While it is agreed that the lawyer should seek to persuade the client to refrain from perjurious testimony, there has been dispute concerning the lawyer's duty when that persuasion fails. If the confrontation with the client occurs before trial, the lawyer ordinarily can withdraw. Withdrawal before trial may not be possible, however, either because trial is imminent, or because the confrontation with the client does not take place until the trial itself, or because no other counsel is available.

[8] The most difficult situation, therefore, arises in a criminal case where the accused insists on testifying when the lawyer knows that the testimony is perjurious. The lawyer's effort to rectify the situation can increase the likelihood of the client's being convicted as well as opening the possibility of a prosecution for perjury. On the other hand, if the lawyer does not exercise control over the proof, the lawyer participates, although in a merely passive way, in deception of the court.

[9] Three resolutions of this dilemma have been proposed. One is to permit the accused to testify by a narrative without guidance through the lawyer's questioning. This compromises both contending principles; it exempts the lawyer from the duty to disclose false evidence but subjects the client to an implicit disclosure of information imparted to counsel. Another suggested resolution, of relatively recent origin, is that the advocate be entirely excused from the duty to reveal perjury if the perjury is that of the client. This is a coherent solution but makes the advocate a knowing instrument of perjury.

[10] The ultimate resolution of the dilemma, however, is that the lawyer must reveal the client's perjury if necessary to rectify the situation. A criminal accused has a right to the assistance of an advocate, a right to testify and a right of confidential communication with counsel. However, an accused should not have a right to assistance of counsel in committing perjury. Furthermore, an advocate has an obligation, not only in professional ethics but under the law as well, to avoid implication in the commission of perjury or other falsification of evidence. *See* Rule 1.2(c).

Remedial Measures

[11] *ABA Model Rule* Comment not adopted.

[12] *ABA Model Rule* Comment not adopted.

[13] *ABA Model Rule* Comment not adopted.

[14] *ABA Model Rule* Comment not adopted.

Ex Parte Proceedings

[15] Ordinarily, an advocate has the limited responsibility of presenting one side of the matters that a tribunal should consider in reaching a decision; the conflicting position is expected to be presented by the opposing party. However, in an ex parte proceeding, such as an application for a temporary restraining order, there is no balance of presentation by opposing advocates. The object of an ex parte proceeding is nevertheless to yield a

substantially just result. The judge has an affirmative responsibility to accord the absent party just consideration. The lawyer for the represented party has the correlative duty to make disclosures of material facts known to the lawyer and that the lawyer reasonably believes are necessary to an informed decision. For purposes of this Rule, *ex parte* proceedings do not include grand jury proceedings or proceedings which are non-adversarial, including various administrative proceedings in which a party chooses not to appear. However, a particular tribunal (including an administrative tribunal) may have an explicit rule or other controlling precedent which requires disclosure even in a non-adversarial proceeding. If so, the lawyer must comply with a disclosure demand by the tribunal or challenge the action by available legal means. The failure to disclose information as part of a legal challenge to a demand for disclosure will not constitute a violation of this Rule.

Virginia Code Comparison

Paragraph (a)(1) is substantially similar to DR 7–102(A)(5), which provided that "[i]n his representation of a client, a lawyer shall not knowingly make a false statement of law or fact."

With regard to paragraph (a)(2), DR 7–102(A)(3) provided that "[i]n his representation of a client, a lawyer shall not conceal or knowingly fail to disclose that which he is required by law to reveal."

Paragraph (a)(3) has no direct counterpart in the *Virginia Code*. EC 7–20 stated: "Where a lawyer knows of legal authority in the controlling jurisdiction directly adverse to the position of his client, he should inform the tribunal of its existence unless his adversary has done so; but, having made such disclosure, he may challenge its soundness in whole or in part."

With regard to paragraph (a)(4), the first sentence of this subparagraph is similar to DR 7–102(A)(4), which provided that a lawyer shall not "knowingly use perjured testimony or false evidence." DR 4–101(D)(2), adopted here as Rule 1.6(c)(2), made it clear that the "remedial measures" referred to in the second sentence of paragraph (a)(4) could include disclosure of the fraud to the tribunal.

Paragraph (b) confers discretion on the lawyer to refuse to offer evidence that the lawyer "reasonably believes" is false. This gives the lawyer more latitude than DR 7–102(A)(4), which prohibited the lawyer from offering evidence the lawyer "knows" is false.

There was no counterpart in the *Virginia Code* to paragraph (c).

Paragraph (d) is identical to DR 7–102(B).

Committee Commentary

The Committee generally adopted the *ABA Model Rule*, but it deleted the word "material" from paragraph (a)(1) to make it identical to DR 7–102(A)(5) and from paragraph (a)(2) because it appeared to be redundant. Additionally, the word "directly," preceding "adverse" was deleted from paragraph (a)(3).

With respect to paragraph (a)(3), the Committee believed it advisable to adopt a provision requiring the disclosure of controlling adverse legal authority. While there was no corresponding provision within the Disciplinary Rules of the *Virginia Code*, there is a corresponding provision within the *ABA Model Code*, DR 7–106(B)(1). However, the Committee deleted the word "directly" from the paragraph in the belief that the limiting effect of that term could seriously dilute the paragraph's meaning.

The Committee determined to retain the obligation to report a non-client's fraud on the tribunal, and therefore repeated the provisions of DR 7–102(B) in paragraph (d).

RULE 3.4 FAIRNESS TO OPPOSING PARTY AND COUNSEL

A lawyer shall not:

(a) Obstruct another party's access to evidence or alter, destroy or conceal a document or other material having potential evidentiary value for the purpose of obstructing a party's access to evidence. A lawyer shall not counsel or assist another person to do any such act.

(b) Advise or cause a person to secrete himself or herself or to leave the jurisdiction of a tribunal for the purpose of making that person unavailable as a witness therein.

(c) Falsify evidence, counsel or assist a witness to testify falsely, or offer an inducement to a witness that is prohibited by law. But a lawyer may advance, guarantee, or pay:

(1) reasonable expenses incurred by a witness in attending or testifying;

(2) reasonable compensation to a witness for lost earnings as a result of attending or testifying;

(3) a reasonable fee for the professional services of an expert witness.

(d) Knowingly disobey or advise a client to disregard a standing rule or a ruling of a tribunal made in the course of a proceeding, but the lawyer may take steps, in good faith, to test the validity of such rule or ruling.

(e) Make a frivolous discovery request or fail to make reasonably diligent effort to comply with a legally proper discovery request by an opposing party.

(e)* In trial, allude to any matter that the lawyer does not reasonably believe is relevant or that will not be supported by admissible evidence, assert personal knowledge of facts in issue except when testifying as a witness, or state a personal opinion as to the justness of a cause, the credibility of a witness, the culpability of a civil litigant or the guilt or innocence of an accused.

(g) Intentionally or habitually violate any established rule of procedure or of evidence, where such conduct is disruptive of the proceedings.

(h) Request a person other than a client to refrain from voluntarily giving relevant information to another party unless:

(1) the information is relevant in a pending civil matter;

(2) the person in a civil matter is a relative or a current or former employee or other agent of a client; and

(3) the lawyer reasonably believes that the person's interests will not be adversely affected by refraining from giving such information.

(i) Present or threaten to present criminal or disciplinary charges solely to obtain an advantage in a civil matter.

(j) File a suit, initiate criminal charges, assert a position, conduct a defense, delay a trial, or take other action on behalf of the client when the lawyer knows or when it is obvious that such action would serve merely to harass or maliciously injure another.

[Adopted effective January 1, 2000. Amended effective January 1, 2004.]

* So in original. Probably should read (f).

Comment

[1] The procedure of the adversary system contemplates that the evidence in a case is to be marshaled competitively by the contending parties. Fair competition in the adversary system is secured by prohibitions against destruction or concealment of evidence, improperly influencing witnesses, obstructive tactics in discovery procedure, and the like.

[2] Documents and other items of evidence are often essential to establish a claim or defense. Subject to evidentiary privileges, the right of an opposing party, including the government, to obtain evidence through discovery or subpoena is an important procedural right. The exercise of that right can be frustrated if relevant material is altered, concealed or destroyed. Applicable law makes it an offense to destroy material for purpose of impairing its availability in a pending proceeding or one whose commencement can be foreseen. Paragraph (a) applies to evidentiary material generally, including computerized information.

[3] With regard to paragraph (c), it is not improper to pay a witness's reasonable expenses or to pay a reasonable fee for the services of an expert witness. The common law rule is that it is improper to pay an occurrence witness any fee for testifying and that it is improper to pay an expert witness a contingent fee.

[3a] The legal system depends upon voluntary compliance with court rules and rulings in order to function effectively. Thus, a lawyer generally is not justified in consciously violating such rules or rulings. However, paragraph (d) allows a lawyer to take measures necessary to test the validity of a rule or ruling, including open disobedience. *See* also Rule 1.2(c).

[4] Paragraph (g) prohibits lawyers from requesting persons other than clients to refrain from voluntarily giving relevant information. The Rule contains an exception permitting lawyers to advise current or former employees or other agents of a client to refrain from giving information to another party, because such persons may identify their interests with those of the client. The exception is limited to civil matters because of concerns with allegations of obstruction of justice (including perceived intimidation of witnesses) that could be made in a criminal investigation and prosecution. *See* also Rule 4.2.

[5] Although a lawyer is prohibited by paragraph (h) from presenting or threatening to present criminal or disciplinary charges solely to obtain an advantage in a civil matter, a lawyer may offer advice about the possibility of criminal prosecution and the client's rights and responsibilities in connection with such prosecution.

[6] Paragraph (i) deals with conduct that could harass or maliciously injure another. Dilatory practices bring the administration of justice into disrepute. Delay should not be indulged merely for the convenience of the advocates, or solely for the purpose of frustrating an opposing party's attempt to obtain rightful redress or repose. It is not a justification that similar conduct is tolerated by the bench and the bar. The question is whether a competent lawyer acting in good faith would regard the course of action as having some substantial purpose other than delay.

[7] In the exercise of professional judgment on those decisions which are for the lawyer's determination in the handling of a

legal matter, a lawyer should always act in a manner consistent with the best interests of a client. However, when an action in the best interest of a client seems to the lawyer to be unjust, the lawyer may ask the client for permission to forego such action. The duty of lawyer to represent a client with zeal does not militate against his concurrent obligation to treat, with consideration, all persons involved in the legal process and to avoid the infliction of needless harm. Under this Rule, it would be improper to ask any question that the lawyer has no reasonable basis to believe is relevant to the case and that is intended to degrade any witness or other person.

[8] In adversary proceedings, clients are litigants and though ill feeling may exist between the clients, such ill feeling should not influence a lawyer's conduct, attitude or demeanor towards opposing counsel. A lawyer should not make unfair or derogatory personal reference to opposing counsel. Haranguing and offensive tactics by lawyers interfere with the orderly administration of justice and have no proper place in our legal system. A lawyer should be courteous to opposing counsel and should accede to reasonable requests regarding court proceedings, settings, continuances, waiver of procedural formalities, and similar matters which do not prejudice the rights of the client. A lawyer should follow the local customs of courtesy or practice, unless the lawyer gives timely notice to opposing counsel of the intention not to do so. A lawyer should be punctual in fulfilling all professional commitments.

Virginia Code Comparison

With regard to paragraph (a), DR 7–108(A) provided that a lawyer "shall not suppress any evidence that he or his client has a legal obligation to reveal or produce."

Paragraph (b) is identical to DR 7–108(B).

Paragraph (c) is substantially similar to DR 7–108(C) which provided that a lawyer "shall not pay, offer to pay, or acquiesce in the payment of compensation to a witness contingent upon the content of his testimony or the outcome of the case. But a lawyer may advance, guarantee or acquiesce in the payment of: (1) Expenses reasonably incurred by a witness in attending or testifying; (2) Reasonable compensation to a witness for his loss of time in attending or testifying; (or) (3) A reasonable fee for the professional services of an expert witness." EC 7–25 stated that witnesses "should always testify truthfully and should be free from any financial inducements that might tempt them to do otherwise."

Paragraph (d) is substantially the same as DR 7–105(A).

Paragraph (e) is new.

Paragraph (f) is substantially similar to DR 7–105(C)(1), (2), (3) and (4) which stated: In appearing in his professional capacity before a tribunal, a lawyer shall not: (1) State or allude to any matter that he has no reasonable basis to believe is relevant to the case or that will not be supported by admissible evidence. (2) Ask any question that he has no reasonable basis to believe is relevant to the case and that is intended to degrade a witness or other person. (3) Assert his personal knowledge of the facts in issue, except when testifying as a witness. (4) Assert his personal opinion as to the justness of a cause, as to the credibility of a witness, as to the culpability of a civil litigant, or as to the guilt or innocence of an accused, but he may argue, on his analysis of the evidence, for any position or conclusion with respect to the matters stated herein

Paragraph (g) is identical to DR 7–105 (C)(5).

Paragraph (h) is new.

Paragraph (i) is similar to DR 7–104, although a lawyer is no longer prohibited from "participat[ing] in presenting" criminal charges and therefore may freely offer advice to the client about the client's rights under the criminal law.

Paragraph (j) is identical to DR 7–102(A)(1).

Committee Commentary

The Committee attempted to join the best of both the *Virginia Code* and *ABA Model Rule* 3.4 in this Rule. For example, paragraph (a) was adopted because it appears to place a broader obligation on lawyers than DR 7–108(A), but DR 7–108(B) was added to the Rule as paragraph (b) because it states explicitly what is only implicit in paragraph (a).

Language from DR 7–108(C) was added to paragraph (c) to make it clear that certain witness compensation is permitted—something not clear from the language of the *ABA Model Rule*, although it is stated in the *ABA Model Rule's* Comment.

The language of DR 7–105(A) was adopted as paragraph (d) in lieu of the *ABA Model Rule* language because it states more clearly what is apparently intended by the Rule. However, the Committee deleted as unnecessary the word "appropriate" preceding "steps."

With respect to paragraph (e), the Committee saw no reason to limit the discovery request provisions to the pretrial period, as is explicitly the case in the *ABA Model Rule.*

Paragraph (f) parallels similar provisions in DR 7–105(C) and paragraph (h) covers a subject not addressed in the *Virginia Code.*

Paragraph (i) is similar to DR 7–104, although the Committee voted to delete the reference to "participate in presenting." This deletion allows a lawyer to offer advice to the client about the client's rights under the criminal law without violating this Rule.

The Committee determined that the existing language of DR 7–102(A)(1) should appear as paragraph (j), although the *ABA Model Rules* do not contain this section.

RULE 3.5 IMPARTIALITY AND DECORUM OF THE TRIBUNAL

(a) A lawyer shall not:

(1) before or during the trial of a case, directly or indirectly, communicate with a juror or anyone the lawyer knows to be a member of the venire from which the jury will be selected for the trial of the case, except as permitted by law;

(2) after discharge of the jury from further consideration of a case:

(i) ask questions of or make comments to a member of that jury that are calculated merely to harass or embarrass the juror or to influence the juror's actions in future jury service;

(ii) communicate with a member of that jury if the communication is prohibited by law or court order; or

(iii) communicate with a member of that jury if the juror has made known to the lawyer a desire not to communicate; or

(3) conduct or cause, by financial support or otherwise, another to conduct a vexatious or harassing investigation of either a juror or a member of a venire.

(b) All restrictions imposed by paragraph (a) upon a lawyer also apply to communications with or investigations of members of the immediate family or household of a juror or a member of a venire.

(c) A lawyer shall reveal promptly to the court improper conduct by a member of a venire or a juror, or by another toward a venireman or a juror or a member of the juror's family, of which the lawyer has knowledge.

(d) A lawyer shall not give or lend anything of value to a judge, official, or employee of a tribunal under circumstances which might give the appearance that the gift or loan is made to influence official action.

(e) In an adversary proceeding, a lawyer shall not communicate, or cause another to communicate, as to the merits of the cause with a judge or an official before whom the proceeding is pending, except:

(1) in the course of official proceedings in the cause;

(2) in writing if the lawyer promptly delivers a copy of the writing to opposing counsel or to the adverse party who is not represented by a lawyer;

(3) orally upon adequate notice to opposing counsel or to the adverse party who is not represented by a lawyer; or

(4) as otherwise authorized by law.

(f) A lawyer shall not engage in conduct intended to disrupt a tribunal.

[Adopted effective January 1, 2000; amended effective January 1, 2004.]

Comment

[1] *ABA Model Rule* Comment not adopted.

[1a] To safeguard the impartiality that is essential to the judicial process, veniremen and jurors should be protected against extraneous influences. When impartiality is present, public confidence in the judicial system is enhanced. There should be no extra-judicial communication with veniremen prior to trial or with jurors during trial by or on behalf of a lawyer connected with the case. Furthermore, a lawyer who is not connected with the case should not communicate with or cause another to communicate with a venireman or juror about the case. After the trial, communication by a lawyer with jurors is permitted so long as the lawyer refrains from asking questions or making comments that tend to harass or embarrass the juror or to influence actions of the juror in future cases. Were a lawyer to be prohibited from communicating after trial with a juror, the lawyer could not ascertain if the verdict might be subject to legal challenge, in which event the invalidity of a verdict might go undetected. When an extra-judicial communication by a lawyer with a juror is permitted by law, it should be made considerately and with deference to the personal feelings of the juror.

[1b] All litigants and lawyers should have access to tribunals on an equal basis. Generally, in adversary proceedings a lawyer should not communicate with a judge relative to a matter pending before, or which is to be brought before, a tribunal over which the judge presides in circumstances which might have the effect or give the appearance of granting undue advantage to one party. For example, a lawyer should not communicate with a tribunal by a writing unless a copy

thereof is promptly delivered to opposing counsel or to an adverse party proceeding *pro se*. Ordinarily an oral communication by a lawyer with a judge or hearing officer should be made only upon adequate notice to opposing counsel, or, if there is none, to the opposing party. A lawyer should not condone or lend himself or herself to private importunities by another with a judge or hearing officer on behalf of the lawyer or the client.

[2] The advocate's function is to present evidence and arguments so that the cause may be decided according to law. Refraining from abusive or obstreperous conduct is a corollary of the advocate's right to speak on behalf of litigants. A lawyer must stand firm against abuse by a judge but should avoid reciprocation; the judge's default is no justification for similar dereliction by an advocate. An advocate can present the cause, protect the record for subsequent review and preserve professional integrity by patient firmness no less effectively than by belligerence or theatrics. Rule 8.3(b) also requires a lawyer to report such conduct by a judge to the appropriate authority and with this duty and recourse there is no reason for a lawyer to reciprocate.

Virginia Code Comparison

Paragraphs (a)–(c) are substantially the same as DR 7–107(A)—7–107(F). Paragraph (a)(2)(ii) and (iii) are new.

Paragraph (d) is identical to DR 7–109(A).

Paragraph (e) is identical to DR 7–109(B).

Paragraph (f) is new.

Committee Commentary

The Committee believed that the adopted language of DR 7–107 and DR 7–109 provides better guidance to lawyers than that of paragraphs (a) and (b) of the *ABA Model Rule*. In paragraph (f) of this Rule, the Committee adopted the language of paragraph (d) of the *ABA Model Rule*, which prohibits "conduct intended to disrupt a tribunal," because the Committee considered the general admonition against "conduct prejudicial to the administration of justice" to be vague.

RULE 3.6 TRIAL PUBLICITY

(a) A lawyer participating in or associated with the investigation or the prosecution or the defense of a criminal matter that may be tried by a jury shall not make or participate in making an extrajudicial statement that a reasonable person would expect to be disseminated by means of public communication that the lawyer knows, or should know, will have a substantial likelihood of interfering with the fairness of the trial by a jury.

(b) A lawyer shall exercise reasonable care to prevent employees and associates from making an extrajudicial statement that the lawyer would be prohibited from making under this Rule.

[Adopted effective January 1, 2000.]

Comment

[1] It is difficult to strike a balance between protecting the right to a fair trial and safeguarding the right of free expression. In a criminal matter which may be tried by a jury, preserving the right to a fair trial necessarily entails some curtailment of the information that may be disseminated about a defendant or witnesses prior to trial. If there were no such limits, the result would be the practical nullification of the protective effect of the rules of forensic decorum and the exclusionary rules of evidence. On the other hand, there are vital social interests served by the free dissemination of information about events having legal consequences and about legal proceedings themselves. In addition to its legitimate interest in the conduct of judicial proceedings, the public has a right to know about threats to its safety and measures aimed at assuring its security.

Virginia Code Comparison

Rule 3.6 is substantially the same as DR 7–106, except that paragraph (a) adopts a "substantial likelihood of material prejudice" standard rather than the "clear and present danger" standard of DR 7–106(A).

Committee Commentary

The Committee believed that one lesson of *Hirschkop v. Snead*, 594 F.2d 356 (4th Cir. 1979) is that a rule, such as the *ABA Model Rule*, which sets forth a specific list of prohibited statements by lawyers in connection with a trial, is constitutionally suspect. Accordingly, the more succinct language of DR 7–106 was adopted. However, the Committee changed the standard to the arguably broader "substantial likelihood of material prejudice," in accord with the language approved by the Supreme Court of the United States in *Gentile v. State Bar*, 501 U.S. 1030 (1991).

RULE 3.7 LAWYER AS WITNESS

(a) A lawyer shall not act as an advocate in an adversarial proceeding in which the lawyer is likely to be a necessary witness except where:

(1) the testimony relates to an uncontested issue;

(2) the testimony relates to the nature and value of legal services rendered in the case; or

(3) disqualification of the lawyer would work substantial hardship on the client.

(b) If, after undertaking employment in contemplated or pending litigation, a lawyer learns or it is obvious that the lawyer may be called as a witness other than on behalf of the client, the lawyer may continue the representation until it is apparent that the testimony is or may be prejudicial to the client.

(c) A lawyer may act as advocate in an adversarial proceeding in which another lawyer in the lawyer's firm is likely to be called as witness unless precluded from doing so by Rule 1.7 or 1.9.

[Adopted effective January 1, 2000.]

Comment

[1] Combining the roles of advocate and witness can prejudice the opposing party and can involve a conflict of interest between the lawyer and client.

[2] The opposing party has proper objection where the combination of roles may prejudice that party's rights in the litigation. A witness is required to testify on the basis of personal knowledge, while an advocate is expected to explain and comment on evidence given by others. It may not be clear whether a statement by an advocate—witness should be taken as proof or as an analysis of the proof.

[3] Paragraph (a)(1) recognizes that if the testimony will be uncontested, the ambiguities in the dual role are purely theoretical. Paragraph (a)(2) recognizes that where the testimony concerns the extent and value of legal services rendered in the action in which the testimony is offered, permitting the lawyers to testify avoids the need for a second trial with new counsel to resolve that issue. Moreover, in such a situation the judge has firsthand knowledge of the matter in issue; hence, there is less dependence on the adversary process to test the credibility of the testimony.

[4] Apart from these two exceptions, paragraph (a)(3) recognizes that a balancing is required between the interests of the client and those of the opposing party. Whether the opposing party is likely to suffer prejudice depends on the nature of the case, the importance and probable tenor of the lawyer's testimony, and the probability that the lawyer's testimony will conflict with that of other witnesses. Even if there is risk of such prejudice, in determining whether the lawyer should be disqualified, due regard must be given to the effect of disqualification on the lawyer's client. It is relevant that one or both parties could reasonably foresee that the lawyer would probably be a witness. The principle of imputed disqualification stated in Rule 1.10 has no application to this aspect of the problem.

[5] Whether the combination of roles involves an improper conflict of interest with respect to the client is determined by Rule 1.7 or 1.9. For example, if there is likely to be substantial conflict between the testimony of the client and that of the lawyer or a member of the lawyer's firm, the representation is improper. The problem can arise whether the lawyer is called as a witness on behalf of the client or is called by the opposing party. Where a lawyer may be called as a witness other than on behalf of the client, paragraph (b) allows the lawyer to continue representation until it becomes apparent that the testimony may be prejudicial to the client. Determining whether or not such a conflict exists is primarily the responsibility of the lawyer involved. *See* Comment to Rule 1.7. If a lawyer who is a member of a firm may not act as both advocate and witness by reason of conflict of interest, Rule 1.10 disqualifies the firm also.

Virginia Code Comparison

With regard to paragraph (a), DR 5–101(B) prohibited a lawyer, or the lawyer's firm, from serving as advocate if the lawyer "knows or it is obvious that he or a lawyer in his firm ought to be called as a witness" unless "(1) . . . the testimony will relate solely to an uncontested matter or to a matter of formality and there is no reason to believe that substantial evidence will be offered in opposition to the testimony; (2) . . . the testimony will relate solely to the nature and value of legal services rendered in the case by the lawyer or his firm to the client; (3) . . . refusal would work a substantial hardship on the client because of the distinctive value of the lawyer or his firm as counsel in the particular case." Similarly, DR 5–102(A) stated: "If, after undertaking employment in contemplated or pending litigation, a lawyer learns or it is obvious that he or a lawyer in his firm ought to be called as a witness on behalf of his client, he shall withdraw from the conduct of the trial and his firm, if any, shall not continue representation in the trial, except that he may continue the representation and he or a lawyer in his firm may testify in the circumstances enumerated in DR 5–101(B)(1) through (3)," quoted above.

Paragraph (b) is substantially the same as DR 5–102(B).

Paragraph (c) had no counterpart in the *Virginia Code*.

Committee Commentary

The Committee concluded that the test in the *ABA Model Rule*, i.e., whether a lawyer "is likely to be a necessary witness," is more instructive than that in DR 5–101(B), i.e., whether the lawyer "knows or it is obvious that he . . . ought to be called as a witness." The Committee did, however, conclude that the *ABA Model Rule* should be modified to apply not just to trials but to any "adversarial proceeding." Additionally, the *ABA Model Rule* applies only to individual lawyers and not, in general, to an entire firm—providing a flexibility which the Committee believed is needed. Additionally, the Committee incorporated the language of DR 5–102(B) as paragraph (b) to give the Rule additional flexibility. With respect to paragraph (b), the Committee deleted the DR 5–102(B)'s reference to "a lawyer in his firm" since that situation is now addressed by paragraph (c) and the conflicts provisions of these Rules.

RULE 3.8 ADDITIONAL RESPONSIBILITIES OF A PROSECUTOR

A lawyer engaged in a prosecutorial function shall:

(a) not file or maintain a charge that the prosecutor knows is not supported by probable cause;

(b) not knowingly take advantage of an unrepresented defendant;

(c) not instruct or encourage a person to withhold information from the defense after a party has been charged with an offense;

(d) make timely disclosure to counsel for the defendant, or to the defendant if he has no counsel, of the existence of evidence which the prosecutor knows tends to negate the guilt of the accused, mitigate the degree of the offense, or reduce the punishment, except when disclosure is precluded or modified by order of a court; and

(e) not direct or encourage investigators, law enforcement personnel, employees or other persons assisting or associated with the prosecutor in a criminal case to make an extrajudicial statement that the prosecutor would be prohibited from making under Rule 3.6.

[Adopted effective January 1, 2000.]

Comment

[1] A prosecutor has the responsibility of a minister of justice and not simply that of an advocate. This responsibility carries with it specific obligations to see that the defendant is accorded procedural justice and that guilt is decided upon the basis of sufficient evidence.

[2] Paragraph (a) prohibits a prosecutor from initiating or maintaining a charge once he knows that the charge is not supported by even probable cause. The prohibition recognizes that charges are often filed before a criminal investigation is complete.

[3] Paragraph (b) is intended to protect the unrepresented defendant from the overzealous prosecutor who uses tactics that are intended to coerce or induce the defendant into taking action that is against the defendant's best interests, based on an objective analysis. For example, it would constitute a violation of the provision if a prosecutor, in order to obtain a plea of guilty to a charge or charges, falsely represented to an unrepresented defendant that the court's usual disposition of such charges is less harsh than is actually the case, e.g., that the court usually sentences a first-time offender for the simple possession of marijuana under the deferred prosecution provisions of *Code of Virginia* Section 18.2–251 when, in fact, the court has a standard policy of not utilizing such an option.

[4] At the same time, the prohibition does not apply to the knowing and voluntary waiver by an accused of constitutional rights such as the right to counsel and silence which are governed by controlling case law. Nor does (b) apply to an accused appearing pro se with the ultimate approval of the tribunal. Where an accused does appear pro se before a tribunal, paragraph (b) does not prohibit discussions between the prosecutor and the defendant regarding the nature of the charges and the prosecutor's intended actions with regard to those charges. It is permissible, therefore, for a prosecutor to state that he intends to reduce a charge in exchange for a guilty plea from a defendant if nothing in the manner of the offer suggests coercion and the tribunal ultimately finds that the defendant's waiver of his right to counsel and his guilty plea are knowingly made and voluntary.

[5] The qualifying language in paragraph (c), i.e., " . . . after a party has been charged with an offense," is intended to exempt the rule from application during the investigative phase (including grand jury) when a witness may be requested to maintain secrecy in order to protect the integrity of the investigation and support concerns for safety. The term "encourage" in paragraph (c) is intended to prevent a prosecutor from doing indirectly what cannot be done directly. The exception in paragraph (d) also recognizes that a prosecutor may seek a protective order from the tribunal if disclosure of information to the

defense could result in substantial harm to an individual or to the public interest.

[6] Paragraphs (d) and (e) address knowing violations of the respective provisions so as to allow for better understanding and easier enforcement by excluding situations (paragraph (d)), for example, where the lawyer/prosecutor does not know the theory of the defense so as to be able to assess the exculpatory nature of evidence or situations (paragraph (e)) where the lawyer/prosecutor does not have knowledge or control over the *ultra vires* actions of law enforcement personnel who may be only minimally involved in a case.

Virginia Code Comparison

With respect to paragraphs (a), DR 8–102(A)(1) provided that a "public prosecutor or other government lawyer shall . . . refrain from prosecuting a charge that [he] . . . knows is not supported by probable cause."

Paragraph (b) is derived from DR 8–102(A)(2) which prohibited prosecutors from inducing an unrepresented defendant to "surrender important procedural rights."

The counterpart to paragraph (c) is DR 8–102(A)(3) which proscribed "discouraging" a person from giving relevant information to the defendants.

Paragraph (d) is similar to DR 8–102(A)(4), but requires actual knowledge on the part of prosecuting lawyers that they are in possession of exculpatory evidence as opposed to simply being in knowing possession of evidence that may be determined to be of such a nature, although acknowledging that such disclosure may be affected by court orders.

Paragraph (e) has no direct counterpart in *Virginia Code*, but it generally parallels DR 7–106(B), now Rule 3.6(b), which directed that a lawyer "exercise reasonable care to prevent his employees and associates from making a [prohibited] extrajudicial statement."

Paragraph DR 8–102(A)(5), which prohibited the subpoena of an attorney as a witness in a criminal prosecution regarding a present or past client without prior judicial approval, has been deleted in light of prevailing case law.

Committee Commentary

The Committee retitled this Rule "Additional Responsibilities of a Prosecutor," rather than "Special Responsibilities of a Prosecutor," as in the *ABA Model Rule*, to make it clear that the Rule's provisions are in addition to the obligations of the attorney acting in a prosecutorial role as set forth in the remaining Rules. The Committee also thought it appropriate to address the proscriptions of the Rule to any "lawyer engaged in a prosecutorial function" as opposed to just a "prosecutor in a criminal case" so as to eliminate any confusion on the part of any lawyer (such as a County Attorney or assistant Attorney General) who may be acting in the role of a prosecutor without being a member of a Commonwealth's Attorney's office.

The Committee believed that paragraph (a) in which actual knowledge is required is more understandable and more susceptible to ready enforcement where any more subjective standard (such as "or it is obvious") is too vague. At the same time, the Committee wanted to strengthen the proscription set forth in the *Virginia Code* ("shall refrain") so as to make clear that the prosecutor should not even file a charge if it is not supported by "probable cause" and should certainly not pursue a charge to trial, even if initially supported by the minimum standard of "probable cause," if it cannot reasonably expected to survive a motion to strike the evidence or motion for judgment of acquittal. The original *ABA Model Rule* language only proscribed "prosecuting a charge that . . . is not supported by probable cause."

The Committee did not include the language of *ABA Model Rule* 3.8(b) in which the prosecutor is required to "make reasonable efforts to assure that the accused has been advised of the right to, and the procedure for obtaining, counsel and has been given reasonable opportunity to obtain counsel" because the Committee did not believe that such an obligation should formally be placed on the lawyer-prosecutor.

The Committee concluded that the language of proposed paragraph (b) more accurately focuses on the type of prosecutorial conduct that is prohibited, rather than the provision of the existing DR and *ABA Model Rule* 3.8(c) which address the waiver of important procedural rights which, in fact, can be knowingly waived as the Comment attempts to explain. In addition, the Committee felt that the example of the waiver of such a procedural right as that of a preliminary hearing as set forth in the existing DR and *ABA Model Rule* is misleading at best, since it is exceedingly rare that a defendant charged with a felony would insist on proceeding *pro se* and then agree to waive the hearing.

The Committee felt that it was appropriate to strengthen the provisions of DR 8–102(A)(3) to provide that the lawyer acting in a prosecutorial function shall not "instruct or encourage a person to withhold information from the defense" as opposed to the more subjective and less enforceable "shall not discourage". In addition, in recognition of the reality of the investigative stage of a matter in which a witness may be asked to "keep quiet" in order to protect the witness and the integrity of the investigation, the Committee felt it appropriate to restrict application of the prohibition to that point in the process after formal charge when the "person" becomes a "party."

The Committee felt a change from existing DR 8–102(A)(4) concerning the disclosure of exculpatory evidence to the defense was appropriate by clarifying that it would apply only to that evidence which the prosecutor knows is exculpatory as opposed to a more subjective analysis of evidence which may be in the knowing possession of the prosecutor but which he does not have reason to believe would be exculpatory.

The Committee felt that the language of the *ABA Model Rule* which speaks in terms of "exercising reasonable care" to prevent others involved in a prosecution from making prohibited extrajudicial statements placed an unreasonable affirmative duty on the attorney acting in a prosecutorial role whereby the attorney would be held responsible for attempting to control the conduct of others.

Finally, the Committee decided to recommend deletion of DR 8–102(5) prohibiting the subpoena of an attorney as a witness in a criminal matter involving a present or former client without prior judicial approval because of prevailing case law and judicial fiat (the United States District Court for the Eastern District of Virginia) which does not require same.

TRANSACTIONS WITH PERSONS OTHER THAN CLIENTS

RULE 4.1 TRUTHFULNESS IN STATEMENTS TO OTHERS

In the course of representing a client a lawyer shall not knowingly:

(a) Make a false statement of fact or law; or

(b) Fail to disclose a fact when disclosure is necessary to avoid assisting a criminal or fraudulent act by a client.

[Adopted effective January 1, 2000.]

Comment

Misrepresentation

[1] A lawyer is required to be truthful when dealing with others on a client's behalf, but generally has no affirmative duty to inform an opposing party of relevant facts. A misrepresentation can occur if the lawyer incorporates or affirms a statement of another person that the lawyer knows is false. Misrepresentations can also occur by failure to act or by knowingly failing to correct false statements made by the lawyer's client or someone acting on behalf of the client.

Statements of Fact

[2] This Rule refers to statements of fact. Whether a particular statement should be regarded as one of fact can depend on the circumstances. Under generally accepted conventions in negotiation, certain types of statements ordinarily are not taken as statements of material fact. Estimates of price or value placed on the subject of a transaction and a party's intentions as to an acceptable settlement of a claim are in this category, and so is the existence of an undisclosed principal except where nondisclosure of the principal would constitute fraud.

Fraud by Client

[3] Paragraph (b) recognizes that substantive law may require a lawyer to disclose certain information to avoid being deemed to have assisted the client's crime or fraud. The requirement of disclosure is governed by Rule 1.6.

Virginia Code Comparison

Paragraph (a) is substantially similar to DR 7–102(A)(5), which stated, "[I]n his representation of a client, a lawyer shall not ... [k]nowingly make a false statement of law or fact."

With regard to paragraph (b), DR 7–102(A)(3) provided, "In his representation of a client, a lawyer shall not ... [c]onceal or knowingly fail to disclose that which he is required by law to reveal."

Committee Commentary

The Committee deleted the *ABA Model Rule's* references to a "third person" in the belief that such language merely confused the Rule. Additionally, the Committee deleted the word "material" preceding "fact or law" from paragraph (a) to make it more closely parallel DR 7–102(A)(5). The word "material" was similarly deleted from paragraph (b) as it appears somewhat redundant. Finally, the modified Comment expands the coverage of the Rule to constructive misrepresentation—

i.e., the knowing failure of a lawyer to correct a material misrepresentation by the client or by someone on behalf of the client.

RULE 4.2 COMMUNICATION WITH PERSONS REPRESENTED BY COUNSEL

In representing a client, a lawyer shall not communicate about the subject of the representation with a person the lawyer knows to be represented by another lawyer in the matter, unless the lawyer has the consent of the other lawyer or is authorized by law to do so.
[Adopted effective January 1, 2000.]

Comment

[1–2] *ABA Model Rule* Comments not adopted.

[3] The Rule applies even though the represented person initiates or consents to the communication. A lawyer must immediately terminate communication with a person if, after commencing communication, the lawyer learns that the person is one with whom communication is not permitted by this Rule. A lawyer is permitted to communicate with a person represented by counsel without obtaining the consent of the lawyer currently representing that person, if that person is seeking a "second opinion" or replacement counsel.

[4] In the case of an organization, this Rule prohibits communications by a lawyer for one party concerning the matter in representation with persons in the organization's "control group" as defined in *Upjohn v. United States*, 449 U.S. 383 (1981) or persons who may be regarded as the "alter ego" of the organization. The "control group" test prohibits *ex parte* communications with any employee of an organization who, because of their status or position, have the authority to bind the corporation. Such employees may only be contacted with the consent of the organization's counsel, through formal discovery or as authorized by law. An officer or director of an organization is likely a member of that organization's "control group." The prohibition does not apply to former employees or agents of the organization, and an attorney may communicate *ex parte* with such former employee or agent even if he or she was a member of the organization's "control group." If an agent or employee of the organization is represented in the matter by separate counsel, the consent by that counsel to a communication will be sufficient for purposes of this Rule.

[5] This Rule covers any person, whether or not a party to a formal proceeding, who is represented by counsel concerning the matter in question. Neither the need to protect uncounselled persons against being taken advantage of by opposing counsel nor the importance of preserving the client-attorney relationship is limited to those circumstances where the represented person is a party to an adjudicative or other formal proceeding. The interests sought to be protected by the Rule may equally well be involved when litigation is merely under consideration, even though it has not actually been instituted, and the persons who are potentially parties to the litigation have retained counsel with respect to the matter in dispute.

[5a] Concerns regarding the need to protect uncounselled persons against the wiles of opposing counsel and preserving the attorney-client relationship may also be involved where a person is a target of a criminal investigation, knows this, and has retained counsel to receive advice with respect to the investigation. The same concerns may be involved where a "third-party" witness furnishes testimony in an investigation or proceeding, and although not a formal party, has decided to retain counsel to receive advice with respect thereto. Such concerns are equally applicable in a non-adjudicatory context, such as a commercial transaction involving a sale, a lease or some other form of contract.

Virginia Code Comparison

This Rule is substantially the same as DR 7–103(A)(1), except for the change of "party" to "person" to emphasize that the prohibition on certain communications with a represented person applies outside the litigation context.

Committee Commentary

The Committee believed that substituting "person" for "party" more accurately reflected the intent of the Rule, as shown in the last sentence of the Comment, and was preferable to the apparent limitation of DR 7–103(A)(1) which referred to "[c]ommunicat[ion] on the subject of the representation with a party. . . . "

RULE 4.3 DEALING WITH UNREPRESENTED PERSONS

(a) In dealing on behalf of a client with a person who is not represented by counsel, a lawyer shall not state or imply that the lawyer is disinterested. When the lawyer knows or reasonably should know that the unrepresented person misunderstands the lawyer's role in the matter, the lawyer shall make reasonable efforts to correct the misunderstanding.

(b) A lawyer shall not give advice to a person who is not represented by a lawyer, other than the advice to secure counsel, if the interests of such person are or have a reasonable possibility of being in conflict with the interest of the client.

[Adopted effective January 1, 2000.]

Comment

[1] An unrepresented person, particularly one not experienced in dealing with legal matters, might assume that a lawyer is disinterested in loyalties or is a disinterested authority on the law even when the lawyer represents a client. During the course of a lawyer's representation of a client, the lawyer should not give advice to an unrepresented person other than the advice to obtain counsel.

Virginia Code Comparison

Paragraph (a) is identical to DR 7–103(B) and paragraph (b) is similar to DR 7–103(A)(2).

Committee Commentary

The *Virginia Code* had deviated from the *ABA Model Code* by using the language of *ABA Model Rule* 4.3(a) as DR 7–103(B). This provision continues unchanged in Rule 4.3.

RULE 4.4 RESPECT FOR RIGHTS OF THIRD PERSONS

In representing a client, a lawyer shall not use means that have no purpose other than to embarrass, delay, or burden a third person, or use methods of obtaining evidence that violate the legal rights of such a person.

[Adopted effective January 1, 2000.]

Comment

[1] Responsibility to a client requires a lawyer to subordinate the interests of others to those of the client, but that responsibility does not imply that a lawyer may disregard the rights of third persons. It is impractical to catalogue all such rights, but they include legal restrictions on methods of obtaining evidence from third persons.

Virginia Code Comparison

Rule 4.4 has no direct counterpart in the *Virginia Code*. DR 7–105(C)(2) provided that a lawyer shall not "[a]sk any question that he has no reasonable basis to believe is relevant to the case and that is intended to degrade a witness or other person." DR 7–102(A)(1) provided that a lawyer shall not "take . . . action on behalf of his client when he knows or when it is obvious that such action would serve merely to harass or maliciously injure another." DR 7–107(C) provided that "[a]fter discharge of the jury . . . the lawyer shall not ask questions or make comments to a member of that jury that are calculated merely to harass or embarrass the juror. . . . " DR 7–107(D) provided that a lawyer "shall not conduct . . . a vexatious or harassing investigation of either a venireman or a juror."

Committee Commentary

The Committee adopted this Rule, for which there was no specific corresponding Disciplinary Rule, as a reminder that there is some limitation placed upon activities for which "zealous representation" might be offered as an excuse. For the same reason, the Committee deleted the word "substantial" from the *ABA Model Rules* provision.

LAW FIRMS AND ASSOCIATIONS

RULE 5.1 RESPONSIBILITIES OF PARTNERS AND SUPERVISORY LAWYERS

(a) A partner in a law firm, or a lawyer who individually or together with other lawyers possesses managerial authority, shall make reasonable efforts to ensure that the firm has in effect measures giving reasonable assurance that all lawyers in the firm conform to the Rules of Professional Conduct.

(b) A lawyer having direct supervisory authority over another lawyer shall make reasonable efforts to ensure that the other lawyer conforms to the Rules of Professional Conduct.

(c) A lawyer shall be responsible for another lawyer's violation of the Rules of Professional Conduct if:

(1) the lawyer orders or, with knowledge of the specific conduct, ratifies the conduct involved; or

(2) the lawyer is a partner or has managerial authority in the law firm in which the other lawyer practices, or has direct supervisory authority over the other lawyer, and knows of the conduct at a time when its consequences can be avoided or mitigated but fails to take reasonable remedial action.

[Adopted effective January 1, 2000. Amended effective January 1, 2004.]

Comment

[1] Paragraph (a) applies to lawyers who have managerial authority over the professional work of a firm. This includes members of a partnership and the shareholders in a law firm organized as a professional corporation; lawyers having managerial authority in the law department of an enterprise or government agency; and lawyers who have intermediate managerial responsibilities in a firm.

See the "partner" definition in the Terminology section at the beginning of these Rules. Paragraph (b) applies to lawyers who have supervisory authority over the work of other lawyers.

[2] Paragraph (a) requires lawyers with a managerial authority within a firm to make reasonable efforts to establish internal policies and procedures designed to provide reasonable assurance that all lawyers in the firm will conform to the Rules of Professional Conduct. Such policies and procedures include those designed to detect and resolve conflicts of interest, identify dates by which actions must be taken in pending matters, account for client funds and property and ensure that inexperienced lawyers are properly supervised.

[3] Other measures that may be required to fulfill the responsibility prescribed in paragraph (a) can depend on the firm's structure and the nature of its practice. In a small firm, informal supervision and periodic review ordinarily will suffice. In a large firm, or in practice situations in which difficult ethical problems frequently arise, more elaborate measures may be necessary. Firms, whether large or small, may also rely on continuing legal education in professional ethics. In any event, the ethical atmosphere of a firm can influence the conduct of all its members and the partners or those lawyers with managerial authority may not assume that all lawyers associated with the firm will inevitably conform to the Rules.

[4] Paragraph (c) expresses a general principle of personal responsibility for acts of another. *See* also Rule 8.4(a).

[5] Paragraph (c)(2) defines the duty of a lawyer having direct supervisory authority over performance of specific legal work by another lawyer. Whether a lawyer has such supervisory authority in particular circumstances is a question of fact. Partners of a private firm have at least indirect responsibility for all work being done by the firm, while a partner in charge of a particular matter ordinarily has responsibility for the work of other firm lawyers engaged in the matter. Appropriate remedial action by a partner would depend on the immediacy of the partner's involvement and the seriousness of the misconduct. The supervisor is required to intervene to prevent avoidable consequences of misconduct if the supervisor knows that the misconduct occurred. Thus, if a supervising lawyer knows that a subordinate misrepresented a matter to an opposing party in negotiation, the supervisor as well as the subordinate has a duty to correct the resulting misapprehension.

[6] Professional misconduct by a lawyer under supervision could reveal a violation of paragraph (b) on the part of the supervisory lawyer even though it does not entail a violation of paragraph (c) because there was no direction, ratification or knowledge of the violation.

[7] Apart from this Rule and Rule 8.4(a), a lawyer does not have disciplinary liability for the conduct of a partner, associate or subordinate. Whether a lawyer may be liable civilly or criminally for another lawyer's conduct is a question of law beyond the scope of these Rules.

Virginia Code Comparison

There was no direct counterpart to this Rule in the *Virginia Code.* DR 1–103(A) provided that "[a] lawyer having information indicating that another lawyer has committed a violation of the Disciplinary Rules that raises a substantial question as to that lawyer's honesty, trustworthiness, or fitness to practice law in other respects, shall report such information to the appropriate professional authority . . . ."

Committee Commentary

The Committee adopted the language of *ABA Model Rule* 5.1 because lawyers who practice in firms should have an affirmative obligation to assure adherence to the Rules of Professional Conduct by those with whom they professionally associate.

RULE 5.3 RESPONSIBILITIES REGARDING NONLAWYER ASSISTANTS

With respect to a nonlawyer employed or retained by or associated with a lawyer:

(a) a partner or a lawyer who individually or together with other lawyers possesses managerial authority in a law firm shall make reasonable efforts to ensure that the firm has in effect measures giving reasonable assurance that the person's conduct is compatible with the professional obligations of the lawyer;

(b) a lawyer having direct supervisory authority over the nonlawyer shall make reasonable efforts to ensure that the person's conduct is compatible with the professional obligations of the lawyer; and

(c) a lawyer shall be responsible for conduct of such a person that would be a violation of the Rules of Professional Conduct if engaged in by a lawyer if:

(1) the lawyer orders or, with the knowledge of the specific conduct, ratifies the conduct involved; or

(2) the lawyer is a partner or has managerial authority in the law firm in which the person is employed, or has direct supervisory authority over the person, and knows or should have known of the conduct at a time when its consequences can be avoided or mitigated but fails to take reasonable remedial action.

[Adopted effective January 1, 2000. Amended effective January 1, 2004.]

Comment

[1] Lawyers generally employ assistants in their practice, including secretaries, investigators, law student interns, and paraprofessionals. Such assistants, whether employees or independent contractors, act for the lawyer in rendition of the lawyer's professional services. A lawyer must give such assistants appropriate instruction and supervision concerning the ethical aspects of their employment, particularly regarding the obligation not to disclose information relating to representation of the client, and should be responsible for their work product. The measures employed in supervising nonlawyers should take account of the fact that they do not have legal training and are not subject to professional discipline. At the same time, however, the Rule is not intended to preclude traditionally permissible activity such as misrepresentation by a nonlawyer of one's role in a law enforcement investigation or a housing discrimination "test".

Virginia Code Comparison

Rule 5.3(a) and (b) are similar to DR 3–104(C). The *Virginia Code* also addressed a supervising lawyer's responsibilities in DR 4–101 (E) and DR 7–106(B). The *Virginia Code* did not contain any explanation of a lawyer's responsibility for a nonlawyer assistant's wrongdoing, which is addressed in Rule 5.3(c).

Committee Commentary

The Committee adopted this Rule as a parallel companion to Rule 5.1 which applies similar provisions to lawyers with supervisory authority over other lawyers. The Committee inserted the phrase "or should have known" in Rule 5.3(c)(2) to reflect a negligence standard. The Committee also deemed it appropriate to add the language in the last sentence of the Comment to cover such recognized and accepted activities as those described.

RULE 5.4. PROFESSIONAL INDEPENDENCE OF A LAWYER

(a) A lawyer or law firm shall not share legal fees with a nonlawyer, except that:

(1) an agreement by a lawyer with the lawyer's firm, partner, or associate may provide for the payment of money, over a reasonable period of time after the lawyer's death, to the lawyer's estate or to one or more specified persons;

(2) a lawyer who undertakes to complete unfinished legal business of a deceased, disabled, or disappeared lawyer may pay to the estate or other representative of that lawyer that portion of the total compensation that fairly represents the services rendered by the deceased, disabled or disappeared lawyer;

(3) a lawyer or law firm may include nonlawyer employees in a compensation or retirement plan, even though the plan is based in whole or in part on a profit-sharing arrangement; and

(4) a lawyer may accept discounted payment of his fee from a credit card company on behalf of a client.

(b) A lawyer shall not form a partnership with a nonlawyer if any of the activities of the partnership consist of the practice of law.

(c) A lawyer shall not permit a person who recommends, employs, or pays the lawyer to render legal services for another to direct or regulate the lawyer's professional judgment in rendering such legal services.

(d) A lawyer shall not practice with or in the form of a professional corporation or association authorized to practice law for a profit, if:

(1) a nonlawyer owns any interest therein, except as provided in (a)(3) above, or except that a fiduciary representative of the estate of a lawyer may hold the stock or interest of the lawyer for a reasonable time during administration;

(2) a nonlawyer is a corporate director or officer thereof, except as permitted by law; or

(3) a nonlawyer has the right to direct or control the professional judgment of a lawyer.

[Adopted effective January 1, 2000. Amended effective January 1, 2004; November 1, 2013.]

Comment

[1] The provisions of this Rule express traditional limitations on sharing fees. These limitations are to protect the lawyer's professional independence of judgment. Where someone other than the client pays the lawyer's fee or salary or recommends employment of the lawyer, that arrangement does not modify the lawyer's obligation to the client. As stated in paragraph (c), such arrangements should not interfere with the lawyer's professional judgment. *See also* Rule 1.8(f).

Virginia Code Comparison

Paragraph (a)(1) is identical to DR 3–102(A)(1).

Paragraph (a)(2) is substantially similar to DR 3-102(A)(2) which stated: "A lawyer who undertakes to complete unfinished legal business of a deceased lawyer may pay to the estate of the deceased lawyer that proportion of the total compensation that fairly represents the services rendered by the deceased lawyer."

Paragraph (a)(3) is substantially the same as DR 3-102(A)(3).

Paragraph (a)(4) had no counterpart in the *Virginia Code.*

Paragraph (b) is identical to DR 3-103(A).

Paragraph (c) is identical to DR 5-106(B).

Paragraph (d) is identical to DR 5-106(C).

Committee Commentary

Paragraph (d)(2) was amended to reflect Virginia Code § 54.1-3902(B)(1), which creates an exception to the general rule that a nonlawyer may not be a director or officer of a professional corporation, professional limited liability company, or registered limited liability partnership that provides legal services.

The *ABA Model Rule* generally paralleled various Disciplinary Rules.

RULE 5.5. UNAUTHORIZED PRACTICE OF LAW; MULTIJURISDICTIONAL PRACTICE OF LAW

(a) A lawyer, law firm or professional corporation shall not employ in any capacity a lawyer whose license has been suspended or revoked for professional misconduct, during such period of suspension or revocation, if the disciplined lawyer was associated with such lawyer, law firm, or professional corporation at any time on or after the date of the acts which resulted in suspension or revocation.

(b) A lawyer, law firm or professional corporation employing a lawyer as a consultant, law clerk, or legal assistant when that lawyer's license is suspended or revoked for professional misconduct shall not represent any client represented by the disciplined lawyer or by any lawyer with whom the disciplined lawyer practiced on or after the date of the acts which resulted in suspension or revocation.

(c) A lawyer shall not practice law in a jurisdiction in violation of the regulation of the legal profession in that jurisdiction, or assist another in doing so.

(d) Foreign Lawyers:

(1) "Foreign Lawyer" is a person authorized to practice law by the duly constituted and authorized governmental body of any State or Territory of the United States or the District of Columbia, or a foreign nation, but is neither licensed by the Supreme Court of Virginia or authorized under its rules to practice law generally in the Commonwealth of Virginia, nor disbarred or suspended from practice in any jurisdiction.

(2) A Foreign Lawyer shall not, except as authorized by these Rules or other law:

(i) establish an office or other systematic and continuous presence in Virginia for the practice of law, which may occur even if the Foreign Lawyer is not physically present in Virginia; or

(ii) hold out to the public or otherwise represent that the Foreign Lawyer is admitted to practice law in Virginia.

(3) A Foreign Lawyer shall inform the client and interested third parties in writing:

(i) that the lawyer is not admitted to practice law in Virginia;

(ii) the jurisdiction(s) in which the lawyer is licensed to practice; and

(iii) the lawyer's office address in the foreign jurisdiction.

(4) A Foreign Lawyer may, after informing the client as required in 3(i)-(iii) above, provide legal services on a temporary and occasional basis in Virginia that:

(i) are undertaken in association with a lawyer who is admitted to practice without limitation in Virginia or admitted under Part I of Rule 1A:5 of this Court and who actively participates in the matter;

(ii) are in or reasonably related to a pending or potential proceeding before a tribunal in Virginia or another jurisdiction, if the Foreign Lawyer, or a person the Foreign Lawyer is assisting, is authorized by law or order to appear in such proceeding or reasonably expects to be so authorized;

(iii) are in or reasonably related to a pending or potential arbitration, mediation, or other alternative dispute resolution proceeding in Virginia or another jurisdiction, if the services arise out of or are reasonably related to the Foreign Lawyer's practice in a jurisdiction in which the Foreign Lawyer is admitted to practice and are not services for which the forum requires pro hac vice admission; or

(iv) are not within paragraphs (4)(ii) or (4)(iii) and arise out of or are reasonably related to the representation of a client by the Foreign Lawyer in a jurisdiction in which the Foreign Lawyer is admitted to practice or, subject to the foregoing limitations, are governed primarily by international law.

(5) A foreign legal consultant practicing under Rule 1A:7 of this Court and a corporate counsel registrant practicing under Part II of Rule 1A:5 of this Court are not authorized to practice under this rule.

[Adopted effective January 1, 2000. Amended effective March 1, 2009; December 13, 2013.]

Comment

[1] A lawyer may practice law only in a jurisdiction in which the lawyer is authorized to practice. A lawyer may be admitted to practice law in a jurisdiction on a regular basis or may be authorized by court rule or order or by law to practice for a limited purpose or on a restricted basis. Paragraph (c) applies to unauthorized practice of law by a lawyer, whether through the lawyer's direct action or by the lawyer assisting another person.

[1a] For purposes of paragraphs (a), (b), and (c) "Lawyer," denotes a person authorized by the Supreme Court of Virginia or its Rules to practice law in the Commonwealth of Virginia including persons admitted to practice in this state pro hac vice.

[2] The definition of the practice of law is established by law and varies from one jurisdiction to another. Whatever the definition, limiting the practice of law to members of the bar protects the public against rendition of legal services by unauthorized persons. Paragraph (c) does not prohibit a lawyer from employing the services of paraprofessionals and delegating functions to them, so long as the lawyer supervises the delegated work and retains responsibility for their work. *See* Rule 5.3.

[3] Likewise, the definition of the practice of law does not prohibit lawyers from providing professional advice and instruction to nonlawyers whose employment requires knowledge of law—for example, claims adjusters, employees of financial or commercial institutions, social workers, accountants, and persons employed in government agencies.

[4] Other than as authorized by law or this Rule, a Foreign Lawyer violates paragraph (d)(2)(i) if the Foreign Lawyer establishes an office or other systematic and continuous presence in Virginia for the practice of law. Presence may be systematic and continuous even if the Foreign Lawyer is not physically present here. Such "non-physical" presence includes, but is not limited to, the regular interaction with residents of Virginia for delivery of legal services in Virginia through exchange of information over the Internet or other means. Such Foreign Lawyer must not hold out to the public or otherwise represent that the Foreign Lawyer is admitted to practice law in Virginia. *See also,* Rules 7.1(a) and 7.5(b). Despite the foregoing general prohibition, a Foreign Lawyer may establish an office or other systematic and continuous presence in Virginia if the Foreign Lawyer's practice is limited to areas which by state or federal law do not require admission to the Virginia State Bar. Examples of lawyers admitted in another United States jurisdiction include those lawyers whose practices are limited to federal tax practice before the IRS and Tax Court, patent law before the Patent and Trademark Office, or immigration law. A Foreign Lawyer admitted to practice in a jurisdiction outside the United States may be authorized to practice under Rule 1A:7 as a foreign legal consultant and may likewise establish an office or other systematic and continued presence in Virginia.

[5] Paragraph (d)(4) identifies circumstances in which a Foreign Lawyer may provide legal services on a temporary basis in Virginia that do not create an unreasonable risk to the interests of their clients, the public, or the courts. The fact that conduct is not so identified does not imply that the conduct is or is not authorized. Except as authorized by this rule or other law, a Foreign Lawyer may not establish an office or other systematic and continuous presence in Virginia without being admitted to practice generally here.

[6] There is no single test to determine whether a Foreign Lawyer's services are provided on a "temporary basis" in Virginia, and may therefore be permissible under paragraph (d)(4). Services may be "temporary" even though the Foreign Lawyer provides services in Virginia on a recurring basis, or for an extended period of time, as when the Foreign Lawyer is representing a client in a single lengthy negotiation or litigation. "Temporary" refers to the duration of the Foreign lawyer's presence and provision of services, while "occasional" refers to the frequency with which the Foreign lawyer comes into Virginia to provide legal services.

[7] Paragraph (d)(1) requires that the Foreign Lawyer be authorized to practice in the jurisdiction in which the Foreign Lawyer is admitted and excludes a Foreign Lawyer who, while technically admitted, is not authorized to practice because, for example, the Foreign Lawyer is on inactive status.

[8] Paragraph (d)(4)(i) recognizes that the interests of clients and the public are protected if a Foreign Lawyer associates with a lawyer licensed to practice Virginia. For this paragraph to apply, however, the lawyer admitted to practice in Virginia must actively participate in and share responsibility for the representation of the client.

[9] Foreign Lawyers not admitted to practice generally in this jurisdiction may be authorized by law or order of a tribunal or an administrative agency to appear before the

tribunal or agency. Under paragraph (d)(4)(ii), a Foreign Lawyer does not violate this Rule when the Foreign Lawyer appears before a tribunal or agency pursuant to such authority. To the extent that a court rule or other law of Virginia requires a Foreign Lawyer to obtain admission pro hac vice before appearing before a tribunal or administrative agency, this Rule requires the Foreign Lawyer to obtain that authority.

[10] Paragraph (d)(4)(ii) also provides that a Foreign Lawyer rendering services in Virginia on a temporary basis does not violate this Rule when the Foreign Lawyer engages in conduct in anticipation of a proceeding or hearing in a jurisdiction in which the Foreign Lawyer is authorized to practice law or in which the Foreign Lawyer reasonably expects to be admitted pro hac vice. Examples of such conduct include meetings with the client, interviews of potential witnesses, and the review of documents. Similarly, a Foreign Lawyer may engage in conduct temporarily in Virginia in connection with pending litigation in another jurisdiction in which the Foreign Lawyer is or reasonably expects to be authorized to appear, including taking depositions in Virginia.

[11] *ABA Model Rule* Comment not adopted.

[12] Paragraph (d)(4)(iii) permits a Foreign Lawyer to perform services on a temporary basis in Virginia if those services are in or reasonably related to a pending or potential arbitration, mediation, or other alternative dispute resolution proceeding in this or another jurisdiction, if the services arise out of or are reasonably related to the Foreign Lawyer's practice in a jurisdiction in which the Foreign Lawyer is admitted to practice. The Foreign Lawyer, however, must obtain admission pro hac vice in the case of a court-annexed arbitration or mediation or otherwise if court rules or law so require.

[13] Paragraph (d)(4)(iv) permits a Foreign Lawyer to provide certain legal services on a temporary basis in Virginia that arise out of or are reasonably related to that lawyer's practice in a jurisdiction in which the Foreign Lawyer is admitted but are not within paragraphs (d)(4)(ii) or (d)(4)(iii). These services include both legal services and services that nonlawyers may perform but that are considered the practice of law when performed by lawyers.

[14] Paragraphs (d)(4)(ii), (d)(4)(iii), and (d)(4)(iv) require that the services arise out of or be reasonably related to the Foreign Lawyer's practice in a jurisdiction in which the Foreign Lawyer is admitted to practice. A variety of factors evidence such a relationship. The Foreign Lawyer's client may have been previously represented by the Foreign Lawyer, or may be resident in or have substantial contacts with the jurisdiction in which the Foreign Lawyer is admitted. The matter, although involving other jurisdictions, may have a significant connection with that jurisdiction. In other cases, significant aspects of the Foreign Lawyer's work might be conducted in that jurisdiction or a significant aspect of the matter may involve the law of that jurisdiction. The necessary relationship might arise when the client's activities or the legal issues involve multiple jurisdictions, such as when the officers of a multinational corporation survey potential business sites and seek the services of their Foreign Lawyer in assessing the relative merits of each. In addition, the services may draw on the Foreign Lawyer's recognized expertise developed through the regular practice of law on behalf of clients in matters involving a particular body of federal, nationally-uniform, foreign, or international law.

[14a] Paragraph (d)(4)(iv) recognizes that a Foreign Lawyer may provide legal services when the services provided are governed by international law or the law of a foreign jurisdiction in which the Foreign Lawyer is admitted to practice.

[15–18] *ABA Model Rule* Comments not adopted.

[19] A Foreign Lawyer who practices law in Virginia pursuant to this Rule is subject to the disciplinary authority of Virginia. See Rule 8.5(a).

[20] *ABA Model Rule* Comment not adopted.

[21] Paragraph (d)(4) does not authorize communications advertising legal services to prospective clients in Virginia by Foreign Lawyers who are admitted to practice in other jurisdictions. Whether and how Foreign Lawyers may communicate the availability of their services to prospective clients in Virginia is governed by Rules 7.1 to 7.5.

Prior Rule Comparison

Neither former Rule 5.5 nor any other of the Virginia Rules of Professional Conduct provided any criteria for practice in Virginia by a foreign lawyer (non-Virginia or non-U.S.). Such practice was controlled by Part 6, § I(C) of the Rules of the Virginia Supreme Court which defined "non-lawyer" and set out the parameters for temporary practice in Virginia by a "foreign lawyer," defined only as admitted to practice and in good standing in any state in the U.S. There was no provision for practice by a foreign, non-U.S. lawyer. Enforcement of Part 6, § I(C) fell within the authority of the Virginia State Bar's Standing Committee on the Unauthorized Practice of Law. Rule 5.5 allows for temporary and occasional practice in Virginia by both non-Virginia and non-U.S. lawyers and places enforcement within the Virginia State Bar's disciplinary system.

Committee Commentary

The Committee adopted this Rule in light of the recommendation of the American Bar Association (ABA) that the states adopt more specific rules governing multi-jurisdictional practice. This rule adopts language similar to ABA Model Rule 5.5 allowing for circumstances of temporary and occasional practice by lawyers licensed in other U.S. jurisdictions, but expands such practice to include lawyers licensed in non-U.S. jurisdictions. Paragraphs (a) and (b) are identical to paragraphs (b) and (c) in former Virginia Rule 5.5.

RULE 5.6 RESTRICTIONS ON RIGHT TO PRACTICE

A lawyer shall not participate in offering or making:

(a) a partnership or employment agreement that restricts the right of a lawyer to practice after termination of the relationship, except an agreement concerning benefits upon retirement; or

(b) an agreement in which a restriction on the lawyer's right to practice is part of the settlement of a controversy, except where such a restriction is approved by a tribunal or a governmental entity.

[Adopted effective January 1, 2000. Amended effective January 1, 2004; September 1, 2006.]

Comment

[1] An agreement restricting the right of lawyers to practice after leaving a firm not only limits their professional autonomy but also limits the freedom of clients to choose a lawyer. Paragraph (a) prohibits such agreements except for restrictions incident to provisions concerning retirement benefits for service with the firm.

[2] Paragraph (b) prohibits lawyers from agreeing to a restriction on their right to practice, unless approved by a tribunal (in such situations as the settlement of mass tort cases) or a governmental entity. However, the lawyer must fully disclose the extent of any restriction to any future client and refer the client to another lawyer if requested to do so.

Virginia Code Comparison

This Rule is similar to DR 2–106, although it specifically permits a restriction if it is approved by a tribunal or a governmental entity.

Committee Commentary

After a lengthy debate about the merits of settlements and the public policy favoring clients' unrestricted choice of legal representation, the Committee decided to generally prohibit provisions in settlement agreements that restricted a lawyer's right to practice, but added an exception if a tribunal or a governmental entity approves the restriction. The Comment emphasizes that lawyers whose right to practice has been restricted by a court-approved settlement should advise all future clients of the restriction and refer them to other counsel, if necessary.

Originally, Rule 5.6(b) prohibited only *broad* restrictions on an attorney's right to practice in settlement agreements. However, in line with the recommendations of the Boyd–Graves Conference Report of August 2004, the prohibition in Rule 5.6(b) is now expanded to reach *all* restrictions on the right to practice in settlement agreements, other than those within the exception afforded for settlement agreements approved by a tribunal or governmental entity. The current more expansive prohibition is in line with both the ABA's Model Rule 5.6 and with provisions in other jurisdictions.

RULE 5.8. PROCEDURES FOR NOTIFICATION TO CLIENTS WHEN A LAWYER LEAVES A LAW FIRM OR WHEN A LAW FIRM DISSOLVES

(a) Absent a specific agreement otherwise:

(1) Neither a lawyer who is leaving a law firm nor other lawyers in the firm shall unilaterally contact clients of the law firm for purposes of notifying them about the anticipated departure or to solicit representation of the clients unless the lawyer and an authorized representative of the law firm have conferred or attempted to confer and have been unable to agree on a joint communication to the clients concerning the lawyer leaving the law firm; and

(2) A lawyer in a dissolving law firm shall not unilaterally contact clients of the law firm unless authorized members of the law firm have conferred or attempted to confer and have been unable to agree on a method to provide notice to clients.

(b) When no procedure for contacting clients has been agreed upon:

(1) Unilateral contact by a lawyer who is leaving a law firm or the law firm shall not contain false or misleading statements, and shall give notice to the clients that the lawyer is leaving the law firm and provide options to the clients to choose to remain a client of the law firm, to choose representation by the departing lawyer, or to choose representation by other lawyers or law firms; and

(2) Unilateral contact by members of a dissolving law firm shall not contain false or misleading statements, and shall give notice to clients that the firm is being dissolved and provide options to the clients to choose representation by any member of the dissolving law firm, or representation by other lawyers or law firms.

(c) Timely notice to the clients shall be given promptly either by agreement or unilaterally in accordance with Rule 5.8(a) or (b).

(d) In the event that a client of a departing lawyer fails to advise the lawyer and law firm of the client's intention with regard to who is to provide future legal services, the client shall be deemed a client of the law firm until the client advises otherwise or until the law firm terminates the engagement in writing.

(e) In the event that a client of a dissolving law firm fails to advise the lawyers of the client's intention with regard to who is to provide future legal services, the client shall be deemed to remain a client of the lawyer who is primarily responsible for the legal services to the client on behalf of the firm until the client advises otherwise.

[Adopted effective May 1, 2015.]

Source: New.

Comment

[1] Although there may also be significant business and legal issues involved when a lawyer leaves a law firm or a law firm dissolves, this rule addresses the rights of the clients to be fully informed and able to make decisions about their representation. Accordingly, the rule emphasizes both the timing and the content of the required notice to clients. Upon the departure of a lawyer or the dissolution of the law firm, the client is entitled to notice that clearly provides the contact information for the departing lawyer and information about the ability and willingness of the lawyer and/or firm to continue the representation, subject to Rule 1.16. Either the departing lawyer or the law firm shall take appropriate steps in accordance with Rule 1.16 regarding the client's file, and any other property, including advanced legal fees. Nothing in this rule or in the contract for representation may alter the ethical obligations that individual lawyers have to a client as provided elsewhere in these rules. Any client notification agreement, whether pursuant to this rule or otherwise, must also comport with Rule 5.6(a). Lawyers may also have fiduciary, contract, or other obligations to their firms that are outside the scope of these rules.

[2] While this rule requires the departing lawyer and the law firm to confer in order to make a joint communication to the departing lawyer's clients, the duty to communicate with clients and to avoid prejudicing the clients during the course of representation requires prompt communication when the lawyer primarily responsible for those clients is leaving the firm. See, e.g, Rules 1.3(c), 1.16(d) and 1.16(e). If continued representation by the departing lawyer and/or by the law firm is not possible, the communication shall clearly state that fact and advise the client of the remaining options for continued representation, including the client's right to choose other lawyers or law firms.

[3] For purposes of the notification required by this rule, "client" refers to clients for whose active matters the departing lawyer has primary responsibility.

[4] While clients have the right to choose counsel, such choice may implicate obligations. Those obligations may include a requirement to pay for legal services previously rendered and costs expended in connection with the representation as well as a reasonable fee for copying the client's file. See Rule 1.16(e). Some clients may be limited in their ability to choose counsel. For example, when the lawyer is appointed by a court to represent a client, the appointed lawyer is responsible for the representation until relieved or replaced by the court.

[5] Lawyers involved in either a change in law firm composition or a law firm dissolution may have duties to notify the court if they represent clients in litigation. In either case, a lawyer who is counsel of record before a court must file a motion to withdraw or a motion for substitution of counsel if he no longer represents the client. See Rule 1.16(c).

PUBLIC SERVICE

RULE 6.1 VOLUNTARY PRO BONO PUBLICO SERVICE

(a) A lawyer should render at least two percent per year of the lawyer's professional time to pro bono publico legal services. Pro bono publico services include poverty law, civil rights law, public interest law, and volunteer activities designed to increase availability of pro bono legal services.

(b) A law firm or other group of lawyers may satisfy their responsibility collectively under this Rule.

(c) Direct financial support of programs that provide direct delivery of legal services to meet the needs described in (a) above is an alternative method for fulfilling a lawyer's responsibility under this Rule.

[Adopted effective January 1, 2000.]

Comment

[1] Every lawyer, regardless of professional prominence or professional work load, has a personal responsibility to provide legal services to those unable to pay, and personal involvement in the problems of the disadvantaged can be one of the most rewarding experiences in the life of a lawyer. The Council for the Virginia State Bar urges all Virginia lawyers to contribute a minimum of two percent of their professional time annually to pro bono services. Pro bono legal services consist of any professional services for which the lawyer would ordinarily be compensated, including dispute resolution as a mediator or third party neutral.

[2] Pro bono services in poverty law consist of free or nominal fee professional services for people who do not have the financial resources to compensate a lawyer. Private attorneys participating in legal aid referral programs are typical examples of "poverty law." Legal services for persons whose incomes exceed legal aid guidelines, but who nevertheless have insufficient resources to compensate counsel, would also qualify as "poverty law," provided the free or nominal fee nature of any such legal work is established in advance.

[3] Pro bono publico legal services in civil rights law consists of free or nominal fee professional services to assert or protect rights of individuals in which society has an interest. Professional services to assert or protect for victims of discrimination based on race, sex, age or handicap would be typical examples of "civil rights law," provided the free or nominal nature of any such legal work is established in advance.

[4] Free or nominal fee provision of legal services to religious, charitable or civic groups in efforts such as setting up a shelter for the homeless, operating a hotline for battered spouses or providing public service information would be examples of "public interest law."

[5] Training and mentoring lawyers who have volunteered to take legal aid referrals or helping recruit lawyers for pro bono referral programs would be examples of "volunteer activities designed to increase availability of pro bono legal services."

[6] Service in any of the categories described is not pro bono publico if provided on a contingent fee basis. Because service must be provided without fee or expectation of fee, the intent of the lawyer to render free or nominal fee legal services is essential. Accordingly, services for which fees go uncollected would not qualify.

Collective Fulfillment of Pro Bono Publico Service

[7] Although every lawyer has an individual responsibility to provide pro bono publico services, some legal matters require the application of considerably greater effort and resources than a lawyer, acting alone, could reasonably provide on a pro bono basis. In fulfilling their obligation under this Rule, a group of two or more lawyers may pool their resources to ensure that individuals in need of such assistance, who would otherwise be unable to afford to compensate counsel, receive needed legal services. The designation of one or more lawyers to work on pro bono publico matters may be attributed to other lawyers within the firm or group who support the representation.

Financial Support in Lieu of Direct Pro Bono Publico Services

[8] The provision of free or nominally priced legal services to those unable to pay continues to be the obligation of each lawyer as well as the profession generally, but the efforts of individual lawyers are often not enough to meet the need Not only do these needs far exceed the capacity of the collective bar, the nature of legal practice for many lawyers places constraints on their ability to render pro bono publico legal services. For example, some lawyers (e.g., some government lawyers) are prohibited by the terms of their employment from engaging in any outside practice. Other lawyers lack the experience and access to resources necessary to provide competent legal assistance.

[9] To provide legal services beyond those available through the pro bono efforts of individual lawyers, the legal profession and government have established additional programs to provide such services. Lawyers who are unable to fulfill their pro bono publico obligation through direct, legal representation should support programs that provide legal services for the purposes described in (a) through financial contributions in proportion to their professional income.

Virginia Code Comparison

There was no direct counterpart to this Rule in the Disciplinary Rules of the *Virginia Code*. EC 2–27 stated that the "basic responsibility for providing legal services for those unable to pay ultimately rests upon the individual lawyer.... Every lawyer, regardless of professional prominence or professional work load, should find time to participate in serving the disadvantaged." EC 8–9 stated that "[t]he advancement of our legal system is of vital importance in maintaining the rule of law ... [and] lawyers should encourage, and should aid in making, needed changes and improvements." EC 8–3 stated that "[t]hose persons unable to pay for legal services should be provided needed services."

Committee Commentary

The subject matter of this Rule was not specifically addressed in the Disciplinary Rules of the *Virginia Code*. The Committee drafted language different from that of the *ABA Model Rule* to bring the Rule in line with Ethical Considerations approved by the Supreme Court of Virginia on June 17, 1994 (specifically EC 2–28 and 2–29). The Committee then adopted the new versions of EC 2–27 and EC 2–30, EC 2–31, and EC 2–32 as the Rule's Comment for section (a). Sections (b) and (c) permit greater flexibility in the manner in which lawyers fulfill their pro bono obligations.

RULE 6.2 ACCEPTING APPOINTMENTS

A lawyer should not seek to avoid appointment by a tribunal to represent a person except for good cause, such as:

(a) representing the client is likely to result in violation of the Rules of Professional Conduct or other law;

(b) representing the client is likely to result in an unreasonable financial burden on the lawyer; or

(c) the client or the cause is so repugnant to the lawyer as to be likely to impair the client-lawyer relationship or the lawyer's ability to represent the client.

[Adopted effective January 1, 2000.]

Comment

[1] A lawyer ordinarily is not obliged to accept a client whose character or cause the lawyer regards as repugnant. The lawyer's freedom to select clients is, however, qualified. All lawyers have a responsibility to assist in providing pro bono publico service. *See* Rule 6.1. An individual lawyer fulfills this responsibility by accepting a fair share of unpopular matters or indigent or unpopular clients. A lawyer may also be subject to appointment by a court to serve unpopular clients or persons unable to afford legal services.

Appointed Counsel

[2] For good cause a lawyer may seek to decline an appointment to represent a person who cannot afford to retain counsel or whose cause is unpopular. Good cause exists if the lawyer could not handle the matter competently, *see* Rule 1.1, or if undertaking the representation would result in an improper conflict of interest, for example, when the client or the cause is so repugnant to the lawyer as to be likely to impair the client-lawyer relationship or the lawyer's ability to represent the client. A lawyer may also seek to decline an appointment if acceptance would be unreasonably burdensome, for example, when it would impose a financial sacrifice so great as to be unjust.

[3] An appointed lawyer has the same obligations to the client as retained counsel, including the obligations of loyalty and confidentiality, and is subject to the same limitations on the client-lawyer relationship, such as the obligation to refrain from assisting the client in violation of the Rules.

Virginia Code Comparison

There was no counterpart to this Rule in the Disciplinary Rules of the *Virginia Code*. EC 2–38 stated that when a lawyer is "appointed by a court or requested by a bar association to undertake representation of a person unable to obtain counsel, whether for financial or other reasons, he should not seek to be excused from undertaking the representation except for compelling reasons. Compelling reasons do not include such factors as the repugnance of the subject matter of the proceeding, the identity or position of a person involved in the case, the belief of the lawyer that the defendant in a criminal proceeding is guilty, or the belief of the lawyer regarding the merits of the civil case." EC 2–39 stated that "a lawyer should decline employment if the intensity of his personal feelings, as distinguished from a community attitude, may impair his effective representation of a prospective client."

Committee Commentary

The Committee adopted this Rule as an appropriate companion to Rule 6.1 because it emphasizes the responsibility of lawyers to increase the availability of legal services by accepting court appointed clients.

RULE 6.3 MEMBERSHIP IN LEGAL SERVICES ORGANIZATION

A lawyer may serve as a director, officer or member of a legal services organization, apart from the law firm in which the lawyer practices, notwithstanding that the organization serves persons having interests adverse to a client of the lawyer. The lawyer shall not knowingly participate in a decision or action of the organization:

(a) if participating in the decision or action would be incompatible with the lawyer's obligations to a client under Rule 1.7; or

(b) where the decision or action could have a material adverse effect on the representation of a client of the organization whose interests are adverse to a client of the lawyer.

[Adopted effective January 1, 2000.]

Comment

[1] Lawyers should be encouraged to support and participate in legal service organizations. A lawyer who is an officer or a member of such an organization does not thereby have a client-lawyer relationship with persons served by the organization. However, there is potential conflict between the interests of such persons and the interests of the lawyer's clients. If the possibility of such conflict disqualified a lawyer from serving on the board of a legal services organization, the profession's involvement in such organizations would be severely curtailed.

[2] It may be necessary in appropriate cases to reassure a client of the organization that the representation will not be affected by conflicting loyalties of a member of the board. Established, written policies in this respect can enhance the credibility of such assurances.

Virginia Code Comparison

There was no counterpart to this Rule in the *Virginia Code*.

Committee Commentary

The Committee adopted this Rule to recognize and address the potential tension between private clients and participation by their lawyers in legal services organizations—which was not addressed by the *Virginia Code*.

RULE 6.5 NONPROFIT AND COURT–ANNEXED LIMITED LEGAL SERVICES PROGRAMS

(a) A lawyer who, under the auspices of a program sponsored by a nonprofit organization or court, provides short-term limited legal services to a client without expectation by either the lawyer or the client that the lawyer will provide continuing representation in the matter:

(1) is subject to Rules 1.7 and 1.9(a) only if the lawyer knows that the representation of the client involves a conflict of interest; and

(2) is subject to Rule 1.10 only if the lawyer knows that another lawyer associated with the lawyer in a law firm is disqualified by Rule 1.7 or 1.9(a) with respect to the matter.

(b) Except as provided in paragraph (a)(2), Rule 1.10 is inapplicable to a representation governed by this Rule.

[Adopted effective January 1, 2004.]

Comment

[1] Legal services organizations, courts and various nonprofit organizations have established programs through which lawyers provide short-term limited legal services—such as advice or the completion of legal forms—that will assist persons to address their legal problems without further representation by a lawyer. In these programs, such as legal-advice hotlines, advice-only clinics or pro se counseling programs, a client-lawyer relationship is established, but there is no expectation that the lawyer's representation of the client will continue beyond the limited consultation. Such programs are normally operated under circumstances in which it is not feasible for a lawyer to systematically screen for conflicts of interest as is generally required before undertaking a representation. *See,* e.g., Rules 1.7, 1.9 and 1.10.

[2] A lawyer who provides short-term limited legal services pursuant to this Rule must secure the client's informed consent to the limited scope of the representation. *See* Rule 1.2(b). If a short-term limited representation would not be reasonable under the circumstances, the lawyer may offer advice to the client but must also advise the client of the need for further assistance of counsel. Ex-

cept as provided in this Rule, the Rules of Professional Conduct, including Rules 1.6 and 1.9(c), are applicable to the limited representation.

[3] Because a lawyer who is representing a client in the circumstances addressed by this Rule ordinarily is not able to check systematically for conflicts of interest, paragraph (a) requires compliance with Rules 1.7 or 1. 9(a) only if the lawyer knows that the representation presents a conflict of interest for the lawyer, and with Rule 1.10 only if the lawyer knows that another lawyer in the lawyer's firm is disqualified by Rules 1.7 or 1.9(a) in the matter.

[4] Because the limited nature of the services significantly reduces the risk of conflicts of interest with other matters being handled by the lawyer's firm, paragraph (b) provides that Rule 1.10 is inapplicable to a representation governed by this Rule except as provided by paragraph (a)(2). Paragraph (a)(2) requires the participating lawyer to comply with Rule 1.10 when the lawyer knows that the lawyer's firm is disqualified by Rules 1.7 or 1.9(a). By virtue of paragraph (b), however, a lawyer's participation in a short-term limited legal services program will not preclude the lawyer's firm from undertaking or continuing the representation of a client with interests adverse to a client being represented under the program's auspices. Nor will the personal disqualification of a lawyer participating in the program be imputed to other lawyers participating in the program.

[5] If, after commencing a short-term limited representation in accordance with this Rule, a lawyer undertakes to represent the client in the matter on an ongoing basis, Rules 1.7, 1.9(a) and 1.10 become applicable.

Virginia Code Comparison

This Rule had no counterpart in the *Virginia Code.*

Committee Commentary

The committee adopted this specific conflicts of interest rule in recognition of the distinctive nature of services provided in this context.

INFORMATION ABOUT LEGAL SERVICES

RULE 7.1. COMMUNICATIONS CONCERNING A LAWYER'S SERVICES

(a) A lawyer shall not make a false or misleading communication about the lawyer or the lawyer's services. A communication is false or misleading if it contains a material misrepresentation of fact or law, or omits a fact when omission of such fact makes the statement materially false or misleading as a whole.

(b) A communication violates this rule if it advertises specific or cumulative case results, without a disclaimer that (i) puts the case results in a context that is not misleading; (ii) states that case results depend upon a variety of factors unique to each case; and (iii) further states that case results do not guarantee or predict a similar result in any future case undertaken by the lawyer. The disclaimer shall precede the communication of the case results. When the communication is in writing, the disclaimer shall be in bold type face and uppercase letters in a font size that is at least as large as the largest text used to advertise the specific or cumulative case results and in the same color and against the same colored background as the text used to advertise the specific or cumulative case results.

(c) Any advertising pursuant to this Rule shall include the name and office address of at least one lawyer responsible for its content; or, in the alternative, a law firm may file with the Virginia State Bar a current written statement identifying the lawyer responsible for the law firm's advertising and its office address. The law firm shall promptly update the written statement if there is any change in status.

(d) A lawyer shall timely respond to and fully cooperate with any requests for information by Ethics Counsel regarding the lawyer's advertising.

[Adopted effective January 1, 2000. Amended November 1, 2002; December 1, 2012 (order vacated November 29, 2012); July 1, 2013.]

Comment

[1] This Rule governs all communications about a lawyer's services, including advertising. The purpose of lawyer advertising is to promote or propose the hiring of the lawyer. Communications about a lawyer's services are statements or claims made about the lawyer or lawyer's services that are intended, in whole or in part, to inform others about the availability of the lawyer's services. Communications through public media as well as communications targeted to one or more persons are subject to this Rule. This Rule is not intended to regulate forms of non-commercial speech by lawyers such as political or religious commentary. Whatever means are used to communicate regarding a lawyer's services, statements about them must be truthful and not misleading. A statement or claim is misleading if it is likely to mislead the public or a prospective client. For example, a

statement that "you pay nothing unless we win" is false and misleading if the client is held responsible for payment or reimbursement of costs or expenses related to the client's case, as required by Rule 1.8(e). Similarly, a statement or claim that a lawyer handles a particular type of case, i.e., products liability, is false and misleading if the lawyer does not practice in that area of law and the lawyer's only involvement is to intake the client and then refer the client to another lawyer outside the firm.

[2] Advertisements and other communications about a lawyer or a lawyer's services that are not false or misleading will make it apparent that the necessity and advisability of legal action depends on variant factors that must be evaluated individually. Due to fee information that may frequently be incomplete and misleading to a layperson, a lawyer should exercise great care that fee information is complete and accurate. Due to the individuality of each legal problem, statements regarding average, minimum, or estimated fees may be misleading, as will commercial publicity conveying information as to results previously achieved, general or average solutions, or expected outcomes. It would be misleading to advertise a set fee for a specific type of case without adhering to the stated fee in charging clients. Advertisements or other claims that convey an impression that the ingenuity of the lawyer, rather than the justice of the claim is determinative are similarly likely to be misleading. Advertising and other communications stating specific or aggregate case results should disclose the impossibility of assuring any particular result. Not only must a communication be truthful, but its meaning must be capable of being understood by the reasonably prudent layperson.

[3] Truthful statements that are misleading are also prohibited by this Rule. A truthful statement is misleading if it omits a fact necessary to make the lawyer's communication considered as a whole not materially misleading. A truthful statement is also misleading if there is a substantial likelihood that it will lead a reasonable person to formulate a specific conclusion about the lawyer or the lawyer's services for which there is no reasonable factual foundation. A good example of a truthful statement that is misleading by omission of a material fact is the statement "We won a $2 million verdict in this case" when in fact the verdict had been overturned by the court. The omission of that key fact makes the statement itself misleading.

[4] A statement or claim that an outcome was not or will not be related to the facts or merits of the particular matter is false or misleading and, therefore, improper. An advertisement that truthfully reports a lawyer's achievements on behalf of clients or former clients may be misleading if presented so as to lead a reasonable person to form an unjustified expectation that the same results could be obtained for other clients in similar matters without reference to the specific factual and legal circumstances of each client's case. Further, any statement or claim that is likely to create an unjustified expectation about the results the lawyer can achieve is misleading. The inclusion of the disclaimer required by paragraph (b) of this Rule is necessary to avoid creating unjustified expectations or misleading a potential client. The required disclaimer must precede each and every statement of specific or cumulative case results.

[5] Similarly, an unsubstantiated comparison of the lawyer's services or fees with the services or fees of other lawyers may be misleading if presented with such specificity as would lead a reasonable person to conclude that the comparison can be substantiated.

[6] Statements or claims made by others about the lawyer's services are governed by this rule if the lawyer adopts them in his or her communications. See also Rule 8.4(a) regarding violations of the Rules of Professional Conduct through the agency of another.

[7] This Rule permits public dissemination of information concerning, for example, a lawyer's name or firm name, address, and telephone number; the kinds of services the lawyer will undertake; the basis on which the lawyer's fees are determined, including prices for specific services and payment and credit arrangements; a lawyer's foreign language ability; names of references and, with their consent, names of clients regularly represented; and other information that might invite the attention of those seeking legal assistance.

Committee Commentary

The Committee has revised Rules 7.1–7.5 in their entirety. Rule 7.2 has been eliminated and relevant parts of Rule 7.2 regarding lawyer advertising are incorporated within Rule 7.1 as that Rule covers all communications including lawyer advertising; relevant parts of Rule 7.2 regarding solicitation and paying others to recommend a lawyer have been incorporated within Rule 7.3.

RULE 7.2. ADVERTISING [DELETED]

RULE 7.3. DIRECT CONTACT WITH POTENTIAL CLIENTS

(a) A lawyer shall not solicit employment from a potential client if:

(1) the potential client has made known to the lawyer a desire not to be solicited by the lawyer; or

(2) the solicitation involves harassment, undue influence, coercion, duress, compulsion, intimidation, threats or unwarranted promises of benefits.

(b) A lawyer shall not give anything of value to a person for recommending the lawyer's services except that a lawyer may.

(1) pay the reasonable costs of advertisements or communications permitted by this Rule and Rule 7.1;

(2) pay the usual charges of a legal service plan or a not-for-profit qualified lawyer referral service;

(3) pay for a law practice in accordance with Rule 1.17; and

(4) give nominal gifts of gratitude that are neither intended nor reasonably expected to be a form of compensation for recommending a lawyer's services.

(c) Every written, recorded or electronic communication from a lawyer soliciting professional employment from a potential client known to be in need of legal services in a particular matter shall conspicuously display the words "ADVERTISING MATERIAL" on the outside envelope, if any, and at the beginning and ending of any recorded or electronic communication, unless the recipient of the communication:

(1) is a lawyer; or

(2) has a familial, personal, or prior professional relationship with the lawyer; or

(3) is one who has had prior contact with the lawyer.

[Adopted effective January 1, 2000. Amended November 1, 2002; December 1, 2012 (order vacated November 29, 2012); July 1, 2013.]

Comment

Direct Contact between Lawyers and Laypersons

[1] A solicitation is a targeted communication initiated by the lawyer that is directed to a specific potential client and that offers to provide, or can reasonably be understood as offering to provide, legal services. In contrast, a lawyer's communication typically does not constitute a solicitation if it is directed to the general public, such as through a billboard, an Internet banner advertisement, a website or a television commercial, or if it is in response to a request for information or is automatically generated in response to Internet searches.

[2] There is far less likelihood that a lawyer would engage in abusive practices against an individual who is a former client, or with whom the lawyer has a close personal or family relationship; nor is there a serious potential for abuse when the person contacted is a lawyer or when the person has already initiated contact with the lawyer. Consequently, the requirements of Rule 7.3(c) are not applicable in those situations.

[3] Even permitted forms of solicitation can be abused; thus, any solicitation that contains information that is false or misleading within the meaning of Rule 7.1, which involves coercion, duress or harassment within the meaning of Rule 7.3(a), or which involves contact with a potential client who has made known to the lawyer a desire not to be solicited by the lawyer within the meaning of Rule 7.3(a), is prohibited. Moreover, if after sending a letter or other communication to a potential client the lawyer receives no response, continued repeated efforts to communicate with the potential client may constitute harassment and therefore violate the provisions of Rule 7.3(a). Regardless of the form of the communication, its propriety will be judged by the totality of the circumstances under which it is made, including the potential client's sophistication and physical, emotional, and mental state, the nature and characterization of the legal matter, the parties' previous relationship, the lawyer's conduct, and the words spoken.

Paying Others to Recommend a Lawyer

[4] Lawyers are not permitted to pay others for channeling professional work. However, Paragraph (b)(1) allows a lawyer to pay for advertising and communications permitted by this Rule, including the costs of print directory listings, on-line directory listings, newspaper ads, television and radio airtime, domain-name registrations, sponsorship fees, banner ads, and group advertising. A lawyer may compensate employees, agents, and vendors who are engaged to provide marketing or client-development services, such as publicists, public-relations personnel, business-development staff, and website designers. See Rule 5.3 for the duties of lawyers and law firms with respect to the conduct of nonlawyers who prepare marketing materials for them.

[5] Selection of a lawyer by a layperson should be made on an informed basis. Advice and recommendation of third parties-relatives, friends, acquaintances, business associates, or other lawyers-and publicity and personal communications from lawyers may help to make this possible. A lawyer should not compensate another person for recommend-

ing him or her, for influencing a potential client to employ him or her, or to encourage future recommendations.

[6] A lawyer may pay the usual charges of a legal service plan or a not-for-profit lawyer referral service. A legal service plan is a prepaid or group legal service plan or a similar delivery system that assists potential clients to secure legal representation. Not-for-profit lawyer referral services are consumer-oriented organizations that provide unbiased referrals to lawyers with appropriate experience in the subject matter of the representation and afford other client protections, such as complaint procedures or malpractice insurance requirements. Consequently, this Rule permits a lawyer to pay only the usual charges of a not-for-profit lawyer referral service.

[7] A lawyer who accepts assignments or referrals from a legal service plan or referrals from a not-for-profit lawyer referral service must act reasonably to assure that the activities of the plan or service are compatible with the lawyer's professional obligations. See Rule 5.3. Legal service plans and not-for-profit lawyer referral services may communicate with potential clients, but such communication must be in conformity with these Rules. Thus, advertising must not be false or misleading, as would be the case if the communications of a group advertising program or a group legal services plan would mislead potential clients to think that it was a lawyer referral service sponsored by a state agency or bar association. Nor could the lawyer allow in-person, telephonic, or real-time contacts that would violate Rule 7.3.

[8] The requirement in Rule 7.3(c) that certain communications be marked "ADVERTISING MATERIAL" does not apply to communications sent in response to requests of potential clients or their spokespersons or sponsors; however, prior contact from the lawyer in the form of advertising material does not circumvent the need to include the words "ADVERTISING MATERIAL" in future contacts. General announcements by lawyers, including changes in personnel or office location, do not constitute communications soliciting professional employment from a potential client known to be in need of legal services within the meaning of this Rule.

Committee Commentary

The Committee changed the rule to refer to the "potential" client as a result of the recent adoption of Rule 1.18 which narrowly defines the "prospective" client.

RULE 7.4. COMMUNICATION OF FIELDS OF PRACTICE AND CERTIFICATION

Lawyers may state, announce or hold themselves out as limiting their practice in a particular area or field of law so long as the communication of such limitation of practice is in accordance with the standards of this Rule, Rule 7.1 and Rule 7.3, as appropriate. A lawyer shall not state or imply that the lawyer has been recognized or certified as a specialist in a particular field of law except as follows:

(a) A lawyer admitted to engage in patent practice before the United States Patent and Trademark Office may use the designation "Patent Attorney" or a substantially similar designation;

(b) A lawyer engaged in Admiralty practice may use as a designation "Admiralty," "Proctor in Admiralty" or a substantially similar designation;

(c) A lawyer who has been certified by the Supreme Court of Virginia as a specialist in some capacity may use the designation of being so certified, e.g., "certified mediator" or a substantially similar designation;

(d) A lawyer may communicate the fact that the lawyer has been certified as a specialist in a field of law by a named organization, provided that the communication clearly states that there is no procedure in the Commonwealth of Virginia for approving certifying organizations.

[Adopted effective January 1, 2000. Amended November 1, 2002; December 1, 2012 (order vacated November 29, 2012); July 1, 2013.]

Comment

[1] This Rule permits a lawyer to indicate areas of practice in communications about the lawyer's services. If a lawyer practices only in certain fields, or will not accept matters in a specified field or fields, the lawyer is permitted to so indicate. A lawyer is generally permitted to state that the lawyer is a "specialist," practices a "specialty," or "specializes in" particular fields, but such communications are subject to the "false and misleading" standard applied in Rule 7.1 to public communications concerning a lawyer's services.

[2] However, a lawyer may not communicate that the lawyer has been recognized or certified as a specialist in a particular field of law, except as provided by this Rule. Recognition of specialization in patent matters is a matter of long-established policy of the Patent and Trademark Office as reflected in paragraph (a). Paragraph (b) recognizes that designation of admiralty practice has a long historical tradition associated with maritime commerce and the federal courts.

[3] Because Virginia has no procedure for approving organizations granting certifications of other specialties, lawyers communicating the fact that they have been certified as

specialists in a field of law by a named organization (other than the Supreme Court of Virginia as provided in paragraph (c)) must clearly disclose that there is no procedure in Virginia for approving certifying organizations (paragraph (d)).

Virginia Code Comparison

Rule 7.4(a) and (b) are substantially the same as DR 2–104(A). Paragraph (c) is new, and paragraph (d) follows one of the two options in ABA Model Rule 7.4(c).

Committee Commentary

The Committee maintained the current DR 2–104(A) approach in the first two paragraphs of this Rule.

Because national organizations are increasingly certifying specialists in different areas of the law, the Committee determined to permit Virginia lawyers to describe such certifications. However, Virginia has no procedure for state approval of such certifications. For this reason, the Committee adopted the alternative ABA Model Rule 7.4(c) that requires lawyers communicating certified specializations to make the additional clear disclosure that Virginia has no procedure for approving certifying organizations. This additional disclosure balances Virginia clients' interest in receiving additional information about lawyers and the need to avoid misleading clients by implying some government-approved certification. At the same time, it was deemed that any certification process implemented by the Supreme Court of Virginia (under (d)) would obviously be reliable, so as to eliminate the necessity for any disclaimer.

RULE 7.5. LAWYER AND FIRM NAMES AND LETTERHEADS

(a) A lawyer shall not use a name, firm name, letterhead, or other professional designation that violates Rule 7.1. A trade name may be used by a lawyer in private practice if it does not imply a connection with a government agency or with a public or charitable legal services organization and is not otherwise in violation of Rule 7.1.

(b) A law firm with offices in more than one jurisdiction may use the same name or other professional designation in each jurisdiction, but identification of the lawyers in an office of the firm shall indicate the jurisdictions in which they are licensed to practice if they are not licensed to practice in the jurisdiction where the office is located.

(c) The name of a lawyer holding a public office shall not be used in the name of a law firm, or in communications on its behalf, during any substantial period in which the lawyer is not actively and regularly practicing with the firm.

(d) Lawyers may state or imply that they practice in a partnership or other organization only when that is the fact.

[Adopted effective January 1, 2000. Amended November 1, 2002; June 30, 2002; December 1, 2012 (order vacated November 29, 2012); July 1, 2013.]

Comment

[1] A firm may be designated by the names of all or some of its members, by the names of deceased members where there has been a continuing succession in the firm's identity or by a trade name such as the "ABC Legal Clinic." A lawyer or law firm may also be designated by a distinctive website address or comparable professional designation. Although the Supreme Court of the United States has held that legislation may prohibit the use of trade names in professional practice, use of such names in law practice is acceptable so long as it is not misleading. If a private firm uses a trade name that includes a geographical name such as "Springfield Legal Clinic," an express disclaimer that it is not a public legal aid agency may be required to avoid a misleading implication. It may be observed that any firm name including the name of a retired or deceased partner is, strictly speaking, a trade name. The use of such names to designate law firms has proven a useful means of identification. However, it is misleading to use the name of a lawyer not associated with the firm or a predecessor of the firm, or the name of a nonlawyer.

[2] With regard to paragraph (d), lawyers sharing office facilities, but who are not in fact partners associated with each other in a law firm, may not denominate themselves as, for example, "Smith and Jones," for that title suggests that they are practicing law together in a firm.

[3] Lawyers should practice using the official name under which they are licensed or seek an appropriate and legal change of name from the Supreme Court of Virginia. The lawyer's use of a name other than the lawyer's name on record with the Virginia State Bar may be a misleading communication about the lawyer's services to the public in violation of Rule 7.1.

MAINTAINING THE INTEGRITY OF THE PROFESSION

RULE 8.1 BAR ADMISSION AND DISCIPLINARY MATTERS

An applicant for admission to the bar, or a lawyer already admitted to the bar, in connection with a bar admission application, any certification required to be filed as a condition of maintaining or renewing a license to practice law, or in connection with a disciplinary matter, shall not:

(a) knowingly make a false statement of material fact;

(b) fail to disclose a fact necessary to correct a misapprehension known by the person to have arisen in the matter;

(c) fail to respond to a lawful demand for information from an admissions or disciplinary authority, except that this Rule does not require disclosure of information otherwise protected by Rule 1.6; or

(d) obstruct a lawful investigation by an admissions or disciplinary authority.

[Adopted effective January 1, 2000. Amended effective September 26, 2002; effective January 1, 2004.]

Comment

[1] The duty imposed by this Rule extends to persons seeking admission to the bar as well as to lawyers. Hence, if a person makes a materially false statement in connection with an application for admission or a certification necessary for license renewal, it may be the basis for disciplinary action once that person has been admitted to the Bar. The duty imposed by this Rule applies to a lawyer's own admission or discipline as well as that of others. Thus, it is a separate professional offense for a lawyer to knowingly make a misrepresentation or omission in connection with a disciplinary investigation of the lawyer's own conduct. This Rule also requires affirmative clarification of any material misstatement, of which the person involved becomes aware, that could lead to a misunderstanding on the part of the admissions or disciplinary authority.

[2] This Rule is subject to the provisions of the Fifth Amendment of the United States Constitution, corresponding provisions of state constitutions, or other lawfully recognized matters of privilege. A person relying on such a provision in response to a question should openly assert the basis for nondisclosure.

[3] A lawyer representing an applicant for admission to the bar, or representing a lawyer who is the subject of a disciplinary inquiry or proceeding, is governed by the Rules applicable to the attorney-client relationship.

[4] The Rule also prohibits the obstruction of either an admissions or disciplinary inquiry. "Obstruction" is used in the ordinary sense and includes, among other intentional acts, purposeful delay, attempts to improperly influence others who are requested to provide information, and the falsification or destruction of relevant documentation.

Virginia Code Comparison

Rule 8.1 is broader than DR 1–101 of the *Virginia Code*. DR 1–101(A) provided that a lawyer is "subject to discipline if he has made a materially false statement in, or if he has deliberately failed to disclose a material fact requested in connection with, his or another's application for admission to the bar." DR 1–101(B) provided that a lawyer is "subject to discipline if he has made a materially false statement in any certification required to be filed as a condition of maintaining or renewing his license to practice law."

Committee Commentary

The Committee preferred the broader coverage of the *ABA Model Rule* to that of DR 1–101 and made it even broader by adding language to the opening sentence covering required certifications and license renewal. Additionally, the Committee added paragraph (c) to impose an affirmative duty of cooperation with lawful demands for information, and added paragraph (d) to make it a separate violation to obstruct any investigation by a disciplinary or admissions authority.

RULE 8.2 JUDICIAL OFFICIALS

A lawyer shall not make a statement that the lawyer knows to be false or with reckless disregard as to its truth or falsity concerning the qualifications or integrity of a judge or other judicial officer.

[Adopted effective January 1, 2000.]

Comment

[1] False statements by a lawyer concerning the qualifications or integrity of a judge can unfairly undermine public confidence in the administration of justice. To maintain the fair and independent administration of justice, lawyers are encouraged to continue traditional efforts to defend judges and courts unjustly criticized.

Virginia Code Comparison

There was no direct counterpart to Rule 8.2 in the *Virginia Code*. EC 8–6 stated: "While a lawyer as a citizen has a right to criticize [judges and other judicial officers], he should be certain of the merit of his complaint, use appropriate language, and avoid petty criticisms, for unrestrained and intemperate statements tend to lessen public confidence in our legal system."

Committee Commentary

The Committee adopted this Rule because it addressed a subject not explicitly addressed by the *Virginia Code*. However, the Committee deleted *ABA Model Rule* language which brought candidates for judicial office under the protection of this Rule and which required such candidates to abide by applicable provisions of the *Virginia Code*—concluding that such requirements and protections were neither necessary nor advisable for lawyers who are being considered for judicial office. While the dignity of courts and the attendant requirement that judicial officials be treated with respect acts as a restraint on lawyer criticism of those officials, the Committee concluded that to extend this Rule to those being considered for judicial office might have a chilling effect on free discussion of judicial candidates' qualifications.

RULE 8.3 REPORTING MISCONDUCT

(a) A lawyer having reliable information that another lawyer has committed a violation of the Rules of Professional Conduct that raises a substantial question as to that lawyer's honesty, trustworthiness or fitness to practice law shall inform the appropriate professional authority.

(b) A lawyer having reliable information that a judge has committed a violation of applicable rules of judicial conduct that raises a substantial question as to the judge's fitness for office shall inform the appropriate authority.

(c) If a lawyer serving as a third party neutral receives reliable information during the dispute resolution process that another lawyer has engaged in misconduct which the lawyer would otherwise be required to report but for its confidential nature, the lawyer shall attempt to obtain the parties' written agreement to waive confidentiality and permit disclosure of such information to the appropriate professional authority.

(d) This Rule does not require disclosure of information otherwise protected by Rule 1.6 or information gained by a lawyer or judge who is a member of an approved lawyer's assistance program, or who is a trained intervenor or volunteer for such a program or committee, or who is otherwise cooperating in a particular assistance effort, when such information is obtained for the purposes of fulfilling the recognized objectives of the program.

(e) A lawyer shall inform the Virginia State Bar if:

(1) the lawyer has been disciplined by a state or federal disciplinary authority, agency or court in any state, U.S. territory, or the District of Columbia, for a violation of rules of professional conduct in that jurisdiction;

(2) the lawyer has been convicted of a felony in a state, U.S. territory, District of Columbia, or federal court;

(3) the lawyer has been convicted of either a crime involving theft, fraud, extortion, bribery or perjury, or an attempt, solicitation or conspiracy to commit any of the foregoing offenses, in a state, U.S. territory, District of Columbia, or federal court.

[Adopted effective January 1, 2000. Amended effective September 26, 2002.]

Comment

[1] Self–regulation of the legal profession requires that members of the profession initiate disciplinary investigation when they know of a violation of the Rules of Professional Conduct. Lawyers have a similar obligation with respect to judicial misconduct. An apparently isolated violation may indicate a pattern of misconduct that only a disciplinary investigation can uncover. Reporting a violation is especially important where the victim is unlikely to discover the offense.

[2] A report about misconduct is not required where it would involve violation of Rule 1.6. *See* Rule 1.6(c)(3).

[3] If a lawyer were obliged to report every violation of the Rules, the failure to report any violation would itself be a professional offense. Such a requirement existed in many jurisdictions but proved to be unenforceable. This Rule limits the reporting obligation to those offenses that a self-regulating profession must vigorously endeavor to prevent. A measure of judgment is, therefore, required in complying with the provisions of this Rule. The term "substantial" refers to the seriousness of the possible offense and not the quantum of evidence of which the lawyer is aware. A report should be made to the bar disciplinary agency unless some other agency, such as a peer review agency, is more appropriate in the circumstances. Similar considerations apply to the reporting of judicial misconduct.

[3a] In court-related dispute resolution proceedings, a third party neutral cannot disclose any information exchanged or observations regarding the conduct and demeanor of the parties and their counsel during the proceeding. Mediation sessions are covered by another statute, which is less restrictive, covering "any communication made in or in

connection with the mediation which relates to the controversy being mediated." Thus a lawyer serving as a mediator or third party neutral may not be able to discharge his or her obligation to report the misconduct of another lawyer if the reporting lawyer's information is based on information protected as confidential under the statutes. However, both statutes permit the parties to agree in writing to waive confidentiality.

[3b] The Rule requires a third party neutral lawyer to attempt to obtain the parties' written consent to waive confidentiality as to professional misconduct, so as to permit the lawyer to reveal information regarding another lawyer's misconduct which the lawyer would otherwise be required to report.

[4] The duty to report professional misconduct does not apply to a lawyer retained to represent a lawyer or judge whose professional conduct is in question. Such a situation is governed by the rules applicable to the client-lawyer relationship.

[5] Information about a lawyer's or judge's misconduct or fitness may be received by a lawyer in the course of that lawyer's participation in or cooperation with an approved lawyers or judges assistance program. In that circumstance, providing for the confidentiality of such information encourages lawyers and judges to seek treatment through such program. Conversely, without such confidentiality, lawyers and judges may hesitate to seek assistance from these programs, which may then result in additional harm to their professional careers and additional injury to the welfare of clients and the public. The duty to report, therefore, does not apply to a lawyer who is participating in or cooperating with an approved lawyer assistance program such as the Virginia Bar Association's Committee on Substance Abuse and who learns of the confidences and secrets of another lawyer who is the object of a particular assistance effort when such information is obtained for the purpose of fulfilling the recognized objectives of the program. Such confidences and secrets are to be protected to the same extent as the confidences and secrets of a lawyer's client in order to promote the purposes of the assistance program. On the other hand, a lawyer who receives such information would nevertheless be required to comply with the Rule 8.3 reporting provisions to report misconduct if the impaired lawyer or judge indicates an intent to engage in illegal activity, for example, the conversion of client funds to personal use.

[6] The duty of a lawyer to self-report a criminal conviction or professional discipline under paragraph (e) of this rule is triggered only after the conviction or decision has become final. Whether an offense is a felony shall be governed by the state, U.S. territory, District of Columbia or federal law under which the conviction is obtained. Thus, it is possible that an offense in another jurisdiction may be a misdemeanor crime for which there is no duty to self-report, even though under Virginia law the offense is a felony.

Virginia Code Comparison

Paragraph (a) is substantially similar to DR 1–103(A) when coupled with the reference to Rule 1.6 in paragraph (d). DR 1–103(A) stated: "A lawyer having information indicating that another lawyer has committed a violation of the Disciplinary Rules that raises a substantial question as to that lawyer's honesty, trustworthiness, or fitness to practice law in other respects, shall report such information to the appropriate professional authority, except as provided in DR 4–101."

Paragraph (c) has no counterpart in the *Virginia Code.*

With respect to paragraph (d), DR 1–103(B) effectively excluded from the disclosure requirements of DR 1–103(A) "any information gained in the performance of . . . duties" by "a lawyer who is a member of The Virginia Bar Association's Committee on Substance Abuse and/or who is a trained intervenor for the Committee."

Committee Commentary

These attorney misconduct reporting requirements do not differ substantially from those of the corresponding Disciplinary Rule, DR 1–103. Although paragraph (b), requiring the reporting of judicial misconduct, and paragraph (c), requiring reporting of lawyer misconduct by a third party neutral, have no counterpart in the *Virginia Code,* the Committee believed them to be appropriate additions. With respect to both paragraphs (a) and (b) and (c), the Committee believed that the phrase "reliable information" indicated more clearly than the *ABA Model Rule's* "knowledge" the sort of information which should support a report of attorney misconduct.

RULE 8.4 MISCONDUCT

It is professional misconduct for a lawyer to:

(a) violate or attempt to violate the Rules of Professional Conduct, knowingly assist or induce another to do so, or do so through the acts of another;

(b) commit a criminal or deliberately wrongful act that reflects adversely on the lawyer's honesty, trustworthiness or fitness to practice law;

(c) engage in conduct involving dishonesty, fraud, deceit or misrepresentation which reflects adversely on the lawyer's fitness to practice law;

(d) state or imply an ability to influence improperly or upon irrelevant grounds any tribunal, legislative body, or public official; or

(e) knowingly assist a judge or judicial officer in conduct that is a violation of applicable rules of judicial conduct or other law.

[Adopted effective January 1, 2000. Amended effective March 25, 2003.]

Comment

[1] Many kinds of illegal conduct reflect adversely on fitness to practice law, such as offenses involving fraud and the offense of willful failure to file an income tax return. However, some kinds of offense carry no such implication. Traditionally, the distinction was drawn in terms of offenses involving "moral turpitude." That concept can be construed to include offenses concerning some matters of personal morality, such as adultery and comparable offenses, that have no specific connection to fitness for the practice of law. Although a lawyer is personally answerable to the entire criminal law, a lawyer should be professionally answerable only for offenses that indicate lack of those characteristics relevant to law practice. Offenses involving violence, dishonesty, breach of trust, or serious interference with the administration of justice are in that category. A pattern of repeated offenses, even ones of minor significance when considered separately, can indicate indifference to legal obligation.

[2] A lawyer may refuse to comply with an obligation imposed by law upon a good faith belief that no valid obligation exists. The provisions of Rule 1.2(c) concerning a good faith challenge to the validity, scope, meaning or application of the law apply to challenges of legal regulation of the practice of law. *See* also Rule 3.1, Rule 3.4(d).

[3] Lawyers holding public office assume legal responsibilities going beyond those of other citizens. A lawyer's abuse of public office can suggest an inability to fulfill the professional role of attorney. The same is true of abuse of positions of private trust such as trustee, executor, administrator, guardian, agent and officer, director or manager of a corporation or other organization.

Virginia Code Comparison

With regard to paragraphs (a) through (c), DR 1–102(A) provided that a lawyer shall not:

"(1) Violate a Disciplinary Rule or knowingly aid another to do so.

(2) Circumvent a Disciplinary Rule through actions of another.

(3) Commit a crime or other deliberately wrongful act that reflects adversely on the lawyer's fitness to practice law.

(4) Engage in conduct involving dishonesty, fraud, deceit, or misrepresentation which reflects adversely on a lawyer's fitness to practice law."

Paragraph (d) is substantially the same as DR 9–101(C).

There was no direct counterpart to paragraph (e) in the Disciplinary Rules of the *Virginia Code*. EC 7–31 stated in part that "[a] lawyer . . . is never justified in making a gift or a loan to a [judicial officer] under circumstances which might give the appearance that the gift or loan is made to influence official action." EC 9–1 stated that a lawyer "should promote public confidence in our [legal] system and in the legal profession."

Committee Commentary

Much of this Rule parallels provisions of the Disciplinary Rules of the *Virginia Code*. Paragraph (e), however, sets forth a prohibition not in the *Virginia Code*, and the Committee believed it is an appropriate addition.

RULE 8.5 DISCIPLINARY AUTHORITY; CHOICE OF LAW

(a) Disciplinary Authority. A lawyer admitted to practice in this jurisdiction is subject to the disciplinary authority of Virginia, regardless of where the lawyer's conduct occurs. A lawyer not admitted in Virginia is also subject to the disciplinary authority of Virginia if the lawyer provides, holds himself out as providing, or offers to provide legal services in Virginia. By doing so, such lawyer consents to the appointment of the Clerk of the Supreme Court of Virginia as his or her agent for purposes of notices of any disciplinary action by the Virginia State Bar. A lawyer may be subject for the same conduct to the disciplinary authority of Virginia and any other jurisdiction where the lawyer is admitted.

(b) Choice of Law. In any exercise of the disciplinary authority of Virginia, the rules of professional conduct to be applied shall be as follows:

(1) for conduct in connection with a proceeding in a court, agency, or other tribunal before which a lawyer appears, the rules to be applied shall be the rules of the jurisdiction in which the court, agency, or other tribu-

nal sits, unless the rules of the court, agency, or other tribunal provide otherwise;

(2) for any other conduct, the rules of the jurisdiction in which the lawyer's conduct occurred; and

(3) notwithstanding subparagraphs (b)(1) and (b)(2), for conduct in the course of providing, holding out as providing, or offering to provide legal services in Virginia, the Virginia Rules of Professional Conduct shall apply.

[Adopted effective January 1, 2000; amended effective March 1, 2009.]

Comment

Disciplinary Authority

[1] In the past, a jurisdiction's authority to discipline a lawyer has been based upon whether the lawyer is admitted in that jurisdiction. Subparagraph (a) is a significant change in that a lawyer not admitted in Virginia is nonetheless subject to the disciplinary authority of Virginia for conduct occurring in the course of providing, holding himself out as providing, or offering to provide legal services in Virginia. Subparagraph (a) adopts the scope of jurisdiction recommended by the ABA Model Rules for Lawyer Disciplinary Enforcement, as amended in 1996, by extending Virginia's disciplinary authority to any lawyer who commits misconduct within Virginia.

It is longstanding law that the conduct of a lawyer admitted to practice in this jurisdiction is subject to the disciplinary authority of this jurisdiction. Extension of the disciplinary authority of this jurisdiction to other lawyers who provide or offer to provide legal services in this jurisdiction is for the protection of the citizens of this jurisdiction. Reciprocal enforcement of a jurisdiction's disciplinary findings and sanctions will further advance the purposes of this Rule. A lawyer who is subject to the disciplinary authority of this jurisdiction under Rule 8.5(a) appoints the Clerk of the Supreme Court of Virginia to receive service of process in this jurisdiction.

Choice of Law

[2—7] *ABA Model Rule* Comments not adopted.

[8] Subparagraph (b) seeks to resolve conflicts that may arise when a lawyer is subject to the rules of more than one jurisdiction. The rules of one jurisdiction may prohibit the questioned conduct while the rules of another jurisdiction may permit it. A lawyer admitted in only one jurisdiction may also be subject to the rules of another jurisdiction in which he is not admitted to practice for conduct occurring in the course of providing, holding himself out as providing, or offering to provide legal services in the non-admitting jurisdiction. Also, a lawyer admitted in one jurisdiction may be subject to the rules of another jurisdiction if he appears before a court, agency, or other tribunal in that jurisdiction.

[9] If the lawyer appears before a court, agency, or other tribunal in another jurisdiction, subparagraph (b)(1) applies the law of the jurisdiction in which the court, agency, or other tribunal sits. In some instances, the court, agency, or other tribunal may have its own lawyer conduct rules and disciplinary authority. For example, the United States Patent and Trademark Office ("PTO"), through the Office of Enrollment and Discipline, enforces its own rules of conduct and disciplines practitioners under its own procedures. A lawyer admitted in Virginia who engages in misconduct in connection with practice before the PTO is subject to the PTO rules, and in the event of a conflict between the rules of Virginia and the PTO rules with respect to the questioned conduct, the latter would control.

[10] As to other conduct, if jurisdictions have conflicting rules regarding the questioned conduct, subparagraph (b)(2) resolves the conflict by choosing the rules of the jurisdiction where the conduct occurred. The physical presence of the lawyer is not dispositive in determining where the questioned conduct occurred. Determining where the lawyer's conduct occurred in the context of transactional work may require the appropriate disciplinary tribunal to consider other factors, including the residence and place of business of any client, third person, or public institution such as a court, tribunal, public body, or administrative agency, the interests of which are materially affected by the lawyer's actions.

Prior Rule Comparison

Virginia Rule 8.5 made no provision for disciplinary authority over a lawyer not admitted to practice in Virginia. Rather, a nonlawyer who committed misconduct in Virginia was subject to Virginia's unauthorized practice of law rules and the authority of the Virginia State Bar's Standing Committee on the Unauthorized Practice of Law.

Under former Rule 8.5(b)(2), if a lawyer was subject to the rules of more than one jurisdiction, the rules of the jurisdiction in which the lawyer principally practiced applied unless the conduct had its predominant effect in another jurisdiction in which the lawyer was admitted to practice. The former rule, however, did not provide clear guidance if the lawyer's conduct occurred in a jurisdiction where the lawyer was not admitted.

Committee Commentary

The Committee adopted this Rule in light of the ABA recommendation that the states adopt more specific rules governing multi-jurisdictional practice. Like ABA Model Rule 8.5(a), this rule states that for conduct occurring in the course of providing, holding oneself out as providing, or offering to provide legal services in Virginia the Virginia State Bar may exercise disciplinary authority over a lawyer not admitted in Virginia. Consistent with ABA Model Rule 8.5, the Virginia rule adopts choice of law rules for circumstances in which the lawyer is subject to the professional conduct rules of more than one jurisdiction and they conflict. The Virginia rule adopts verbatim ABA Model Rule 8.5(b)(1), applying the rules of the jurisdiction in which the court, agency, or other tribunal sits. The Committee, however, did not adopt the "predominant effect" test used in ABA Model Rule 8.5(b)(2), favoring instead the application of the rules of the jurisdiction in which the lawyer's conduct occurred. Virginia Rule 8.5(b)(3) is new. The Committee did not adopt *ABA Model Rule* Comments 2–7.

SECTION III. CANONS OF JUDICIAL CONDUCT FOR THE COMMONWEALTH OF VIRGINIA

PREAMBLE

Our legal system is based on the principle that an independent, fair and competent judiciary will interpret and apply the laws that govern us. The role of the judiciary is central to American concepts of justice and the rule of law. Intrinsic to all sections of these Canons are the precepts that judges, individually and collectively, must respect and honor the judicial office as a public trust and strive to enhance and maintain confidence in our legal system. The judge is an arbiter of facts and law for the resolution of disputes and a highly visible symbol of government under the rule of law.

The Canons of Judicial Conduct are intended to establish standards for ethical conduct of judges. They consist of broad statements called Canons, specific rules set forth in Sections under each Canon and Commentary. The text of the Canons and the Sections is authoritative. Each Commentary, by explanation and example, is advisory and provides guidance with respect to the purpose and meaning of the Canons and Sections. The Commentary is not intended as a statement of additional rules. When the text uses "shall" or "shall not" or "must" or "must not" it is intended to impose binding obligations the violation of which can result in disciplinary action. When "should" or "should not" is used, the text is intended as a statement of what is or is not appropriate conduct but not as a binding rule under which a judge may be disciplined. When "may" is used, it denotes permissible discretion or, depending on the context, it refers to action that is not covered by specific proscriptions.

The Canons and Sections are rules of reason. They should be applied consistent with constitutional requirements, statutes, other court rules and decisional law and in the context of all relevant circumstances. The Canons are to be construed so as not to impinge on the essential independence of judges in making judicial decisions.

The Canons are designed to provide guidance to judges and candidates for judicial office and to provide a structure for regulating conduct through the Judicial Inquiry and Review Commission. They are not designed or intended as a basis for civil liability or criminal prosecution. Furthermore, the purpose of the Canons would be subverted if the Canons were invoked by lawyers for mere tactical advantage in a proceeding.

The text of the Canons and Sections is intended to govern conduct of judges and to be binding upon them. It is not intended, however, that every transgression will result in disciplinary action. Whether disciplinary action is appropriate, and the degree of discipline to be imposed, should be determined through a reasonable and reasoned application of the text and should depend on such factors as the seriousness of the transgression, whether there is a pattern of improper activity and the effect of the improper activity on others or on the judicial system.

These Canons apply to (1) all active Justices of the Supreme Court of Virginia, and Judges of the Court of Appeals of Virginia, Circuit Courts, General District Courts, Juvenile and Domestic Relations District Courts, Members of the State Corporation Commission and the Virginia Workers' Compensation Commission; (2) retired Judges and Members eligible for recall to judicial service; (3) substitute Judges and Special Justices; (4) persons selected for a full-time judgeship either by election by both houses of the General Assembly or appointment by the appropriate authority who are not already justices, judges or retired judges, but who have not taken the oath of office as a justice or judge; and (5) Judges pro tempore while acting as a Judge pro tempore. Magistrates are not bound by these Canons. However, Canons of Conduct for Virginia Magistrates were adopted by the Committee on District Courts effective January 1, 1980.

[Effective July 1, 1999. Amended effective July 1, 2001.]

CANON 1. A JUDGE SHALL UPHOLD THE INTEGRITY AND INDEPENDENCE OF THE JUDICIARY

A. An independent and honorable judiciary is indispensable to justice in our society. A judge should participate in establishing, maintaining and enforcing high standards of conduct, and shall personally observe those standards so that the integrity and independence of the judiciary will be preserved. The provisions of these Canons are to be construed and applied to further that objective.

Commentary

Deference to the judgments and rulings of courts depends upon public confidence in the integrity and independence of judges. The integrity and independence of judges depends in turn upon their acting without fear or favor. Although judges should be independent, they must comply with the law, including the provisions of these Canons. Public confidence in the impartiality of the judiciary is maintained by the adherence of each judge to this responsibility. Conversely, violation of this Canon diminishes public confidence in the judiciary and thereby does injury to the system of government under law.

[Effective July 1, 1999.]

CANON 2. A JUDGE SHALL AVOID IMPROPRIETY AND THE APPEARANCE OF IMPROPRIETY IN ALL OF THE JUDGE'S ACTIVITIES

A. A judge shall respect and comply with the law and shall act at all times in a manner that promotes public confidence in the integrity and impartiality of the judiciary.

Commentary

Public confidence in the judiciary is eroded by irresponsible or improper conduct by judges. A judge must avoid all impropriety and appearance of impropriety. A judge must expect to be the subject of constant public scrutiny. A judge must therefore accept restrictions on the judge's conduct that might be viewed as burdensome by the ordinary citizen and should do so freely and willingly.

The prohibition against behaving with impropriety or the appearance of impropriety applies to both the professional and personal conduct of a judge. Because it is not practicable to list all prohibited acts, the proscription is necessarily cast in general terms that extend to conduct by judges that is harmful although not specifically mentioned in the Canons. Actual improprieties under this standard include violations of law, court rules or other specific provisions of these Canons. The test for appearance of impropriety is whether the conduct would create in reasonable minds a perception that the judge's ability to carry out judicial responsibilities with integrity and impartiality is impaired.

See also Commentary under Section 2C.

A judge may vote in a primary election conducted by the State Board of Elections that is open to all registered voters qualified to vote pursuant to Code § 24.2–530. Voting in such a primary election does not constitute an act of partiality by a judge as prohibited by subdivision A. The act of a judge voting in a primary election is the discharge of an honorable civic duty, an obligation of responsible citizenship, and does not give the "appearance of impropriety."

The statutory requirements for voting in a primary election reflect voting in a primary election by a judge as an act of "impartiality" as used in subdivision A(1)(c) because there is no registration by political affiliation, no loyalty or political party oath required to vote, and no pledge of support for any person or political group. It is the impartial nature of such a primary election that enables judges to avoid an "appearance of impropriety."

See also Commentary under Canon 5A.

B. A judge shall not allow family, social, political or other relationships to influence the judge's judicial conduct or judgment. A judge shall not lend the prestige of judicial office to advance the private interests of the judge or others; nor shall a judge convey or permit others to convey the impression that they are in a special position to influence the judge. A judge shall not testify as a character witness.

Commentary

Maintaining the prestige of judicial office is essential to a system of government in which the judiciary functions independently of the executive and legislative branches. Respect for the judicial office facilitates the orderly conduct of legitimate judicial functions. Judges should distinguish between proper and improper use of the prestige of office in all of their activities. For example, it would be improper for a judge to allude to his or her judgeship to gain a personal advantage such as deferential treatment when stopped by a police officer for a traffic offense. Similarly, judicial letterhead must not be used for conducting a judge's personal business.

A judge must avoid lending the prestige of judicial office for the advancement of the private interests of others. For example, a judge must not use the judge's judicial position to gain advantage in a civil suit involving a member of the judge's family. As to the acceptance of awards, see Section 4D(5)(a) and Commentary.

In a criminal case, a judge may not approve a plea agreement or disposition that requires or permits the defendant to make a charitable contribution or donation, or any other monetary payment other than a statutorily authorized fine or restitution or payment in satisfaction of an injury pursuant to Code § 19.2–151, as a condition of a suspended sentence or the reduction or dismissal of charges.

Although a judge should be sensitive to possible abuse of the prestige of office, a judge may, based on the judge's personal knowledge, serve as a reference or provide a letter of recommendation. When using court stationery for letters of reference an indication should be made that the opinion expressed is personal and not an opinion of the court. However, a judge must not initiate the communication of information to a sentencing judge or a probation or corrections officer but may provide to such person information for the record in response to a formal request.

Judges may participate in the process of judicial selection by cooperating with appointing authorities and screening committees seeking names for consideration, and by responding to official inquiries concerning a person being considered for a judgeship.

C. A judge shall not hold membership in any organization that practices invidious discrimination on the basis of race, sex, religion or national origin.

Commentary

Membership of a judge in an organization that practices invidious discrimination gives rise to perceptions that the judge's impartiality is impaired. Section 2C refers to the current practices of the organization. Whether an organization practices invidious discrimination is often a complex question to which judges should be sensitive. The answer cannot be determined from a mere examination of an organization's current membership rolls but rather depends on how the organization selects members and other relevant factors, such as that the organization is dedicated to the preservation of religious, ethnic or cultural values of legitimate common interest to its members, or that it is in fact and effect an intimate, purely private organization whose membership limitations could not be constitutionally prohibited. Absent such factors, an organization is generally said to discriminate invidiously if it arbitrarily excludes from membership on the basis of race, religion, sex or national origin persons who would otherwise be admitted to membership.

Although Section 2C relates only to membership in organizations that invidiously discriminate on the basis of race, sex, religion or national origin, a judge's membership in an organization that engages in any discriminatory membership practices prohibited by the law of the jurisdiction also violates Canon 2 and Section 2A and gives the appearance of impropriety. In addition, it would be a violation of Canon 2 and Section 2A for a judge to arrange a meeting at a club that the judge knows practices invidious discrimination on the basis of race, sex, religion or national origin in its membership or other policies, or for the judge to regularly use such a club. Moreover, public manifestation by a judge of the judge's knowing approval of invidious discrimination on any basis gives the appearance of impropriety under Canon 2 and diminishes public confidence in the integrity and impartiality of the judiciary, in violation of Section 2A.

[Effective July 1, 1999. Amended effective February 6, 2004; November 2, 2004.]

CANON 3. A JUDGE SHALL PERFORM THE DUTIES OF JUDICIAL OFFICE IMPARTIALLY AND DILIGENTLY

A. Judicial Duties in General. The judicial duties of a judge take precedence over all the judge's other activities. The judge's judicial duties include all the duties of the judge's office prescribed by law. In the performance of these duties, the following standards apply.

B. Adjudicative Responsibilities.

(1) A judge shall hear and decide promptly matters assigned to the judge except those in which disqualification is required.

(2) A judge shall be faithful to the law and maintain professional competence in it. A judge shall not be swayed by partisan interests, public clamor or fear of criticism.

(3) A judge shall require order, decorum, and civility in proceedings before the judge.

Commentary

"Require." The rules prescribing that a judge "require" certain conduct of others are, like all of the rules in these Canons, rules of reason. The use of the term "require" in that context means a judge is to exercise reasonable direction and control over the conduct of those persons subject to the judge's direction and control.

In performing the duties of his or her judicial office, a judge may explain the judicial process, while maintaining impartiality. A judge may also inform unrepresented persons of free legal aid and similar assistance that is available.

(4) A judge shall be patient, dignified and courteous to litigants, jurors, witnesses, lawyers and others with whom the judge deals in an official capacity, and shall require similar conduct of lawyers, and of staff, court officials and others subject to the judge's direction and control.

Commentary

The duty to hear all proceedings fairly and with patience is not inconsistent with the duty to dispose promptly of the business of the court. Judges can be efficient and businesslike while being patient and deliberate.

(5) A judge shall perform judicial duties without bias or prejudice. A judge shall not, in the performance of judicial duties, by words or conduct manifest bias or prejudice, including but not limited to bias or prejudice based upon race, sex, religion, national origin, disability, age, sexual orientation or socioeconomic status, and shall not permit staff, court officials and others subject to the judge's direction and control to do so. This Section 3B(5) does not preclude proper judicial consid-

eration when race, sex, religion, national origin, disability, age, sexual orientation or socioeconomic status, or similar factors, are issues in the proceeding.

Commentary

A judge must refrain from speech, gestures or other conduct that could reasonably be perceived as sexual harassment and must require the same standard of conduct of others subject to the judge's direction and control.

A judge must perform judicial duties impartially and fairly. A judge who manifests bias on any basis in a proceeding impairs the fairness of the proceeding and brings the judiciary into disrepute. Facial expression and body language, in addition to oral communication, can give to parties or lawyers in the proceeding, jurors, the media and others an appearance of judicial bias. A judge must be alert to avoid behavior that may be perceived as prejudicial.

(6) A judge shall require all persons appearing in proceedings before the judge to refrain from manifesting, by words or conduct, bias or prejudice based upon race, sex, religion, national origin, disability, age, sexual orientation or socioeconomic status, against parties, witnesses, counsel or others. This Section 3B(6) does not preclude legitimate advocacy when race, sex, religion, national origin, disability, age, sexual orientation or socioeconomic status, or other similar factors, are issues in the proceeding.

(7) A judge shall accord to every person who has a legal interest in a proceeding, or that person's lawyer, the right to be heard according to law. A judge shall not initiate, permit, or consider ex parte communications, or consider other communications made to the judge outside the presence of the parties concerning a pending or impending proceeding except that:

(a) Where circumstances require, ex parte communications for scheduling, administrative purposes or emergencies that do not deal with substantive matters or issues on the merits are authorized; provided:

(i) The judge reasonably believes that no party will gain a procedural or tactical advantage as a result of the ex parte communication, and

(ii) The judge makes provision promptly to notify all other parties of the substance of the ex parte communication and allows an opportunity to respond.

(b) A judge may obtain the advice of a disinterested expert on the law applicable to a proceeding before the judge if the judge gives notice to the parties of the person consulted and the substance of the advice, and affords the parties reasonable opportunity to respond.

(c) A judge may consult with law clerks whose function is to aid the judge in carrying out the judge's adjudicative responsibilities or with other judges.

(d) A judge may, with the consent of the parties, confer separately with the parties and their lawyers in an effort to settle matters pending before the judge.

(e) A judge may initiate or consider any ex parte communications when expressly authorized by law to do so.

Commentary

The proscription against communications concerning a proceeding includes communications from lawyers, law teachers, and other persons who are not participants in the proceeding, except to the limited extent permitted.

To the extent reasonably possible, all parties or their lawyers shall be included in communications with a judge. A judge should always be cautious with regard to the possibility of prejudice or the appearance of such when communicating with a probation officer or a similarly situated person without the involvement of all parties.

Whenever presence of a party or notice to a party is required by Section 3B(7), it is the party's lawyer or if the party is unrepresented, the party who is to be present or to whom notice is to be given.

An appropriate and often desirable procedure for a court to obtain the advice of a disinterested expert on legal issues is to invite the expert to file a brief *amicus curiae*.

Certain ex parte communication is approved by Section 3B(7) to facilitate scheduling and other administrative purposes and to accommodate emergencies. In general, however, a judge must discourage ex parte communication and allow it only if all the criteria stated in Section 3B(7) are clearly met. A judge must disclose to all parties all ex parte communications described in Sections 3B(7)(a) and 3B(7)(b) regarding a proceeding pending or impending before the judge.

A judge must not independently investigate facts in a case and must consider only the evidence presented.

A judge may request a party to submit proposed findings of fact and conclusions of law, so long as the other parties are apprised of the request and are given an opportunity to respond to the proposed findings and conclusions.

A judge must make reasonable efforts, including the provision of appropriate supervision, to ensure that Section 3B(7) is not violated through law clerks or other personnel on the judge's staff.

A judge may consult with the Legal Research Assistance Project of the Supreme Court of Virginia for aid in carrying out the judge's adjudicative responsibilities.

If communication between the trial judge and the appellate court with respect to a proceeding is permitted, a copy of any written communication or the substance of any oral communication should be provided to all parties.

Judges have historically played an important role in providing instruction, advice and mentoring to lawyers as they begin and continue to develop their practice skills. Judges should insure that the instruction and advice they provide will not result in unfair advantage to the recipient or prejudice to other parties in a pending proceeding.

(8) A judge shall dispose promptly of the business of the court.

Commentary

In disposing of matters promptly, a judge must demonstrate due regard for the rights of the parties to be heard and to have issues resolved without unnecessary cost or delay. Containing costs while preserving fundamental rights of parties also protects the interests of witnesses and the general public.

Prompt disposition of the court's business requires a judge to devote adequate time to judicial duties, to be punctual in attending court and expeditious in determining matters under submission, and to insist that court officials, litigants and their lawyers cooperate with the judge to that end.

(9) A judge shall abstain from public comment about a pending or impending proceeding in any court, and should direct similar abstention on the part of court personnel subject to his direction and control. This subsection does not prohibit judges or court personnel from speaking on the legal system or the administration of justice or from explaining for public information the procedures of the court. This Section does not apply to proceedings in which the judge is a litigant in a personal capacity.

Commentary

The requirement that judges abstain from public comment regarding a pending or impending proceeding continues during any appellate process and until final disposition. This Section does not prohibit a judge from commenting on proceedings in which the judge is a litigant in a personal capacity, but in cases such as a writ of mandamus where the judge is a litigant in an official capacity, the judge must not comment publicly.

See also Commentary under Canon 6C.

(10) A judge shall not commend or criticize jurors for their verdict other than in a court order or opinion in a proceeding, but may express appreciation to jurors for their service to the judicial system and the community.

Commentary

Commending or criticizing jurors for their verdict may imply a judicial expectation in future cases and may impair a juror's ability to be fair and impartial in a subsequent case.

(11) A judge shall not disclose or use, for any purpose unrelated to judicial duties, nonpublic information acquired in a judicial capacity.

C. Administrative Responsibilities.

(1) A judge shall diligently discharge the judge's administrative responsibilities without bias or prejudice and maintain professional competence in judicial administration, and shall cooperate with other judges and court officials in the administration of court business.

(2) A judge shall require staff, court officials and others subject to the judge's direction and control to observe the standards of fidelity and diligence that apply to the judge and to refrain from manifesting bias or prejudice in the performance of their official duties.

(3) The chief judge shall take reasonable measures to assure the prompt disposition of matters before the court.

(4) A judge shall not make unnecessary appointments. A judge shall exercise the power of appointment impartially and on the basis of merit. A judge shall avoid nepotism and favoritism. A judge shall not approve compensation of appointees beyond the fair value of services rendered.

Commentary

Appointees of a judge include assigned counsel, officials such as commissioners, receivers and guardians and personnel such as clerks, and secretaries. Consent by the parties to an appointment or an award of compensation does not relieve the judge of the obligation prescribed by Section 3C(4).

D. Disciplinary Responsibilities.

(1) A judge who receives reliable information indicating a substantial likelihood that another judge has committed a violation of these Canons should take appropriate action. A judge having knowledge that another judge has committed a violation of these Canons that raises a substantial question as to the other judge's fitness for office should inform the Judicial Inquiry and Review Commission.

(2) A judge who receives reliable information indicating a substantial likelihood that a lawyer has committed a violation of the Code of Professional Responsibility should take appropriate action. A judge having knowledge that a lawyer has committed a violation of the Code of Professional Responsibility that raises a substantial question as to the lawyer's honesty, trustworthiness or fitness as a lawyer in other respects should inform the Virginia State Bar.

(3) A judge shall have absolute immunity from civil action with respect to the discharge of disciplinary responsibilities required or permitted by Sections 3D(1) and 3D(2).

Commentary

Appropriate action may include direct communication with the judge or lawyer who has committed the violation, other direct action if available, and reporting the violation to the appropriate authority or other agency or body.

E. Disqualification.

(1) A judge shall disqualify himself or herself in a proceeding in which the judge's impartiality might reasonably be questioned, including but not limited to instances where:

Commentary

Under this rule, a judge is disqualified whenever the judge's impartiality might reasonably be questioned, regardless whether any of the specific rules in Section 3E(1) apply.

A judge should disclose information that the judge believes the parties or their lawyers might consider relevant to the question of disqualification, even if the judge believes there is no real basis for disqualification.

By decisional law, the rule of necessity may override the rule of disqualification. For example, a judge might be required to participate in judicial review of a judicial salary statute, or might be the only judge available in a matter requiring immediate judicial action, such as a hearing on probable cause or a temporary restraining order. In the latter case, the judge must disclose the basis for possible disqualification and use reasonable efforts to transfer the matter to another judge as soon as practicable.

(a) The judge has a personal bias or prejudice concerning a party or a party's lawyer, or personal knowledge of disputed evidentiary facts concerning the proceeding;

(b) The judge served as a lawyer in the matter in controversy, or a lawyer with whom the judge previously practiced law served during such association as a lawyer concerning the matter, or the judge has been a material witness concerning it;

Commentary

A lawyer in a government agency does not ordinarily have an association with other lawyers employed by that agency within the meaning of Section 3E(1)(b); a judge formerly employed by a government agency, however, should disqualify himself or herself in a proceeding if the judge's impartiality might reasonably be questioned because of such association.

(c) The judge knows that he or she, individually or as a fiduciary, or the judge's spouse, parent, or child wherever residing, or any other member of the judge's family residing in the judge's household, has an economic interest in the subject matter in controversy or in a party to the proceeding or has more than a de minimis interest that could be substantially affected by the proceeding;

(d) The judge or the judge's spouse, or a person within the third degree of relationship to either of them, or the spouse of such a person:

Commentary

"Third degree of relationship." The following persons are relatives within the third degree of relationship: great-grandparent, grandparent, parent, uncle, aunt, brother, sister, child, grandchild, great-grandchild, nephew or niece.

(i) is a party to the proceeding, or an officer, director or trustee of a party;

(ii) is acting as a lawyer in the proceeding;

(iii) is known by the judge to have a more than de minimis interest that could be substantially affected by the proceeding;

(iv) is to the judge's knowledge likely to be a material witness in the proceeding.

Commentary

The fact that a lawyer in a proceeding is affiliated with a law firm or governmental agency with which a relative of the judge is affiliated does not of itself disqualify the judge. Under appropriate circumstances, the fact that "the judge's impartiality might reasonably be questioned" under Section 3E(1), or that the relative is known by the judge to have an interest in the law firm or governmental agency that could be "substantially affected by the outcome of the proceeding" under Section 3E(1)(d)(iii) may require the judge's disqualification.

(2) A judge shall keep informed about the judge's personal and fiduciary economic interests, and make a reasonable effort to keep informed about the personal

economic interests of the judge's spouse and minor children residing in the judge's household.

Commentary

"Economic interest" denotes ownership of a more than de minimis legal or equitable interest, or a relationship as officer, director, advisor or other active participant in the affairs of a party, except that:

(i) ownership of an interest in a mutual or common investment fund that holds securities is not an economic interest in such securities unless the judge participates in the management of the fund or a proceeding pending or impending before the judge could substantially affect the value of the interest;

(ii) service by a judge as an officer, director, advisor or other active participant in an educational, religious, charitable, fraternal or civic organization, or service by a judge's spouse, parent or child as an officer, director, advisor or other active participant in any organization does not create an economic interest in securities held by that organization.

(iii) a deposit in a financial institution, the proprietary interest of a policy holder in a mutual insurance company, of a depositor in a mutual savings association or of a member in a credit union, or a similar proprietary interest, is not an economic interest in the organization unless a proceeding pending or impending before the judge could substantially affect the value of the interest;

(iv) ownership of government securities is not an economic interest in the issuer unless a proceeding pending or impending before the judge could substantially affect the value of the securities.

"Member of the judge's family residing in the judge's household" denotes any relative of a judge by blood or marriage, or a person treated by a judge as a member of the judge's family, who resides in the judge's household.

F. Remittal of Disqualification. A judge who may be disqualified by the terms of Section 3E may ask, or have the clerk of court ask, the parties and their lawyers to consider, out of the presence of the judge, whether to waive disqualification. If following disclosure of any basis for disqualification other than personal bias or prejudice concerning a party, the parties and lawyers, without participation by the judge, all agree that the judge should not be disqualified, and the judge is then willing to participate, the judge may participate in the proceeding. Written evidence of the agreement shall be incorporated in the record of the proceeding.

Commentary

A remittal procedure provides the parties an opportunity to proceed without delay if they wish to waive the contemplated disqualification. To assure that consideration of the question of remittal is made independently of the judge, a judge may ask, or have the clerk of court ask, the parties and their lawyers to consider, out of the presence of the judge, whether to waive disqualification.

[Effective July 1, 1999; amended effective March 9, 2000; February 27, 2015.]

CANON 4. A JUDGE MAY ENGAGE IN EXTRA–JUDICIAL ACTIVITIES DESIGNED TO IMPROVE THE LAW, THE LEGAL SYSTEM, AND THE ADMINISTRATION OF JUSTICE, AND SHALL CONDUCT ANY SUCH EXTRA–JUDICIAL ACTIVITIES IN A MANNER THAT MINIMIZES THE RISK OF CONFLICT WITH JUDICIAL OBLIGATIONS

A. Extra Judicial Activities in General. A judge shall conduct all of the judge's extra judicial activities so that they do not:

(1) cast reasonable doubt on the judge's capacity to act impartially as a judge;

(2) demean the judicial office; or

(3) interfere with the proper performance of judicial duties.

Commentary

Complete separation of a judge from extra judicial activities is neither possible nor wise; a judge should not become isolated from the community in which the judge lives.

Expressions of bias or prejudice by a judge, even outside the judge's judicial activities, may cast reasonable doubt on the judge's capacity to act impartially as a judge. Expressions which may do so include jokes or other remarks demeaning individuals on the basis of their race, sex, religion, national origin, disability, age, sexual orientation or socioeconomic status.

See Section 2C and accompanying Commentary.

B. Avocational Activities. A judge may speak, write, lecture, teach and participate in other extra judicial activities concerning the law, the legal system, the administration of justice and non-legal subjects, subject to the requirements of these Canons.

Commentary

A judge may promote broader access to justice by encouraging lawyers to participate in pro bono public or legal services, if in doing so the judge does not employ coercion, or abuse the prestige of judicial office. Such encouragement may take many forms, including providing a list of available programs, training lawyers to do pro bono public service or legal work, and participating in events recognizing lawyers who have done pro bono public work.

As a judicial officer and person specially learned in the law, a judge is in a unique position to contribute to the improvement of the law, the legal system, and the administration of justice. To the extent that time permits, a judge is encouraged to do so, either independently or through a bar association, judicial conference or other organization dedicated to the improvement of the law. Judges may participate in efforts to promote the fair administration of justice, the independence of the judiciary and the integrity of the legal profession.

C. Governmental, Civic or Charitable Activities.

(1) A judge shall not appear at a public hearing before, or otherwise consult with, an executive or legislative body or official except on matters concerning the law, the legal system or the administration of justice or except when acting pro se in a matter involving the judge or the judge's interests.

Commentary

See Section 2B regarding the obligation to avoid improper influence.

(2) A judge shall not accept appointment to a governmental committee or commission or other governmental position that is concerned with issues of fact or policy on matters other than the improvement of the law, the legal system or the administration of justice. A judge may, however, represent a country, state or locality on ceremonial occasions or in connection with historical, educational or cultural activities.

Commentary

A judge may serve on a governmental committee or commission concerned with issues of fact or policy, provided the judge's role is limited to discussion of and voting on matters (i) which involve the improvement of the law, the legal system or the administration of justice, and (ii) that are not issues in specific cases pending before or likely to come before the judge. This may include serving on committees or task forces created by the executive and legislative branches of state government or by local governments to review policies affecting entities that interact with the judicial system.

(3) A judge may serve as an officer, director, trustee or non legal advisor of an organization or governmental agency devoted to the improvement of the law, the legal system or the administration of justice or of an educational, religious, charitable, fraternal or civic organization not conducted for profit, subject to the following limitations and the other requirements of this Code.

(a) A judge shall not serve as an officer, director, trustee or non legal advisor of a governmental, civic, or charitable organization if it is likely that the organization:

(i) will be engaged in proceedings that would ordinarily come before the judge, or

(ii) will be engaged frequently in adversary proceedings in the court of which the judge is a member or in any court subject to the appellate jurisdiction of the court of which the judge is a member.

Commentary

Nothing contained in these Canons shall be deemed to prohibit a judge from serving in a nonvoting capacity on the Board of Directors of Lawyers Helping Lawyers, or any committees of Lawyers Helping Lawyers.

(b) A judge as an officer, director, trustee or non legal advisor, or as a member or otherwise:

(i) may assist such an organization in planning fund raising and may participate in the management and investment of the organization's funds, but shall not personally participate in the solicitation of funds, except that a judge may solicit funds from other judges over whom the judge does not exercise supervisory or appellate authority;

(ii) may make recommendations to public and private fund granting organizations on projects and programs concerning the law, the legal system or the administration of justice so long as one organization is not favored over another;

(iii) shall not personally participate in membership solicitation if the solicitation might reasonably be perceived as coercive or, except as permitted in Section 4C(3)(b)(i), if the membership solicitation is essentially a fund raising mechanism;

(iv) shall not use or permit the use of the prestige of judicial office for fund raising or membership solicitation; and

(v) shall not be a speaker or guest of honor at an organization's fund raising events, but may attend such events.

Commentary

A judge may solicit membership or endorse or encourage membership efforts for an organization devoted to the improvement of the law, the legal system or the administration of justice or a nonprofit educational, religious, charitable, fraternal or civic organization as long as the solicitation cannot reasonably be perceived as coercive and is not essentially a fund raising mechanism. Solicitation of funds for an organization and solicitation of memberships similarly involve the danger that the person solicited will feel obligated to respond favorably to the solicitor if the solicitor is in a position of influence or control. A judge must not engage in direct, individual solicitation of funds or memberships in person, in writing or by telephone except in the following cases: 1) a judge may solicit funds or memberships from other judges over whom the judge does not exercise supervisory or appellate authority, 2) a judge may solicit other persons for membership in the organizations described above if neither those persons nor persons with whom they are affiliated are likely ever to appear before the court on which the judge serves and 3) a judge who is an officer of such an organization may send a general membership solicitation mailing over the judge's signature.

This Canon is not intended to prohibit judges from participating in all charitable events. Judges are encouraged to be involved in community activities so long as the judge does not participate in the solicitation of funds and the prestige of the office is not used for fund raising.

Use of an organization letterhead for fund raising or membership solicitation does not violate Section 4C(3)(b) provided the letterhead lists only the judge's name and office or other position in the organization, and, if comparable designations are listed for other persons, the judge's judicial designation. In addition, a judge must also make reasonable efforts to ensure that the judge's staff, court officials and others subject to the judge's direction and control do not solicit funds on the judge's behalf for any purpose, charitable or otherwise.

D. Financial Activities.

(1) A judge shall not engage in financial and business dealings that:

(a) may reasonably be perceived to exploit the judge's judicial position, or

(b) involve the judge in frequent transactions or continuing business relationships with those lawyers or other persons likely to come before the court on which the judge serves.

Commentary

A judge must avoid financial and business dealings that involve the judge in frequent transactions or continuing business relationships with persons likely to come either before the judge personally or before other judges on the judge's court. In addition, a judge should discourage members of the judge's family from engaging in dealings that would reasonably appear to exploit the judge's judicial position. This rule is necessary to avoid creating an appearance of exploitation of office or favoritism and to minimize the potential for disqualification.

(2) A judge may, subject to the requirements of this Canon, hold and manage investments of the judge and members of the judge's family, including real estate.

Commentary

This Section provides that, subject to the requirements of this Canon, a judge may hold and manage investments owned solely by the judge, investments owned solely by a member or members of the judge's family, and investments owned jointly by the judge and members of the judge's family. A judge may own real estate or other property with others, who are not family members, so long as the judge complies with Section 4D(1) and (2).

(3) A judge shall not serve as an officer, director, manager, general partner, advisor or employee of any business entity except that a judge may, subject to the requirements of this Canon, manage and participate in:

(a) a business closely held by the judge or members of the judge's family, or

(b) a business entity primarily engaged in investment of the financial resources of the judge or members of the judge's family.

Commentary

Subject to the requirements of this Canon, a judge may participate in a business in which at least fifty percent is held either by the judge alone, by members of the judge's family, or by the judge and members of the judge's family.

Although participation by a judge in a closely held family business might otherwise be permitted by Section 4D(3), a judge may be prohibited from participation by other provisions of these Canons when, for example, the business entity frequently appears before the judge's court or the participation requires significant time away from judicial duties. Similarly, a judge must avoid participating in a closely held family business if the judge's participation would involve misuse of the prestige of judicial office, subject the judge to public criticism or give the appearance of impropriety.

"Member of the judge's family" denotes a spouse, child, grandchild, parent, grandparent, or other relative or person with whom the judge maintains a close familial relationship.

(4) A judge shall manage the judge's investments and other financial interests to minimize the number of

cases in which the judge is disqualified. As soon as the judge can do so without serious financial detriment, the judge shall divest himself or herself of investments and other financial interests that might require frequent disqualification.

(5) A judge shall not accept, and shall urge members of the judge's family residing in the judge's household not to accept, a gift, favor or loan from anyone except for:

Commentary

Because a gift, favor or loan to a member of the judge's family residing in the judge's household might be viewed as intended to influence the judge, a judge must inform those family members of the relevant ethical constraints upon the judge in this regard and discourage those family members from violating them. A judge cannot, however, reasonably be expected to know or control all of the financial or business activities of all family members residing in the judge's household.

(a) a gift incident to a public testimonial, books, tapes and other resource materials supplied by publishers on a complimentary basis for official use, or an invitation to the judge and the judge's spouse or guest to attend a bar related function or an activity devoted to the improvement of the law, the legal system or the administration of justice;

Commentary

Acceptance of an invitation to a law related function is governed by Section 4D(5)(a).

(b) A gift, award or benefit incident to the business, profession or other separate activity of a spouse or other family member of a judge residing in the judge's household, including gifts, awards and benefits for the use of both the spouse or other family member and the judge (as spouse or family member), provided the gift, award or benefit could not reasonably be perceived as intended to influence the judge in the performance of judicial duties;

(c) ordinary social hospitality;

(d) a gift from a relative or friend, for a special occasion, such as a wedding, anniversary or birthday, if the gift is fairly commensurate with the occasion and the relationship;

Commentary

A gift to a judge, or to a member of the judge's family living in the judge's household, that is excessive in value raises questions about the judge's impartiality and the integrity of the judicial office and might require disqualification of the judge where disqualification would not otherwise be required. See, however, Section 4D(5)(e).

(e) a gift, favor or loan from a relative or close personal friend whose appearance or interest in a case would in any event require disqualification under Section 3E;

(f) a loan from a lending institution in its regular course of business on the same terms generally available to persons who are not judges;

(g) a scholarship or fellowship awarded on the same terms and based on the same criteria applied to other applicants.

E. Fiduciary Activities.

(1) A judge shall not serve as executor, administrator or other personal representative, trustee, guardian, attorney in fact or other fiduciary, except for the estate, trust or person of a member of the judge's family, and then only if such service will not interfere with the proper performance of judicial duties.

(2) A judge shall not serve as a fiduciary if it is likely that the judge as a fiduciary will be engaged in proceedings that would ordinarily come before the judge, or if the estate, trust or ward becomes involved in adversary proceedings in the court on which the judge serves or one under its appellate jurisdiction.

(3) The same restrictions on financial activities that apply to a judge personally also apply to the judge while acting in a fiduciary capacity.

Commentary

The restrictions imposed by this Canon may conflict with the judge's obligation as a fiduciary. For example, a judge should resign as trustee if detriment to the trust would result from divestiture of holdings the retention of which would place the judge in violation of Section 4D(4).

F. Service as Arbitrator or Mediator. A judge shall not act as an arbitrator or mediator or otherwise perform judicial functions in a private capacity.

Commentary

Section 4F does not prohibit a judge from participating in settlement conferences performed as part of judicial duties.

G. Practice of Law. A judge shall not practice law. Notwithstanding this prohibition, a judge may act pro se and may, without compensation, give legal advice to and draft or review documents for a member of the judge's family.

Commentary

This prohibition refers to the practice of law in a representative capacity and not in a pro se capacity. A judge may act for himself or herself in all legal matters, including matters involving litigation and matters involving appearances before or other dealings with legislative and other governmental bodies. However, in so doing, a judge must not abuse the prestige of office to advance the interests of the judge or the judge's family. See Section 2(B).

These Canons allow a judge to give legal advice to and draft legal documents for members of the judge's family, so long as the judge receives no compensation. A judge must not, however, act as an advocate or negotiator for a member of the judge's family in a legal matter.

Section 51.1–309 of the Virginia Code prohibits a retired judge who is receiving benefits under the Judicial Retirement System from appearing as counsel in any case in any court in the Commonwealth.

H. Compensation, Reimbursement and Reporting.

(1) *Compensation and Reimbursement.* A judge may receive compensation and reimbursement of expenses for the extra judicial activities permitted by these Canons, if the source of such payments does not give the appearance of influencing the judge's performance of judicial duties or otherwise give the appearance of impropriety.

(a) Compensation shall not exceed a reasonable amount nor shall it exceed what a person who is not a judge would receive for the same activity.

(b) Expense reimbursement shall be limited to the actual cost of travel, food and lodging reasonably incurred by the judge and, where appropriate to the occasion, by the judge's spouse or guest. Any payment in excess of such an amount is compensation.

(2) *Public Reports.* A Judge shall report compensation as required by § 2.2–3114 of the Code of Virginia.

Commentary

The Canons do not prohibit a judge from accepting honoraria or speaking fees provided that the compensation is reasonable and commensurate with the task performed. A judge should ensure, however, that no conflicts are created by the arrangement. A judge must not appear to trade on the judicial position for personal advantage. Nor should a judge spend significant time away from court duties to meet speaking or writing commitments for compensation. In addition, the source of the payment must not raise any question of undue influence or the judge's ability or willingness to be impartial.

[Effective July 1, 1999. Amended effective April 13, 2004; November 2, 2009; February 27, 2015; October 21, 2015.]

CANON 5. A JUDGE SHALL REFRAIN FROM POLITICAL ACTIVITY INAPPROPRIATE TO THE JUDICIAL OFFICE

A. Political Conduct in General.

(1) A judge shall not:

(a) act as a leader or hold any office in a political organization;

(b) make speeches for a political organization or candidate or publicly endorse or oppose a candidate for public office; or

(c) solicit funds for or pay an assessment or make a contribution to a political organization or candidate, attend political gatherings, or purchase tickets for political party dinners, or other political functions.

(2) A judge shall resign his office when he becomes a candidate either in a party primary or in a general election for a public office, except that he may continue to hold his judicial office while being a candidate for election to or serving as a delegate in a state constitutional convention, if he is otherwise permitted by law to do so.

(3) A judge shall not engage in any other political activity except in behalf of measures to improve the law, the legal system, or the administration of justice.

Commentary

A judge may vote in a primary election conducted by the State Board of Elections that is open to all registered voters qualified to vote pursuant to Code § 24.2–530. Voting in such a primary election does not constitute attending a "political gathering" as prohibited by subdivision A(1)(c) or constitute engaging "in any other political activity" as prohibited by subdivision A(3). The act of a judge voting in a primary election is the discharge of an honorable civic duty and an obligation of responsible citizenship.

The statutory requirements for voting in a primary election distinguish voting in a primary election by a judge from a "political gathering" as used in subdivision A(1)(c) because there is no registration by political affiliation, no loyalty or political party oath required to vote, and no pledge of support for any person or political group. For the same reasons, voting in a primary election by a judge is not engaging "in any other political activity" as used in subdivision A(3).

See also Commentary under Canon 2A.

[Effective July 1, 1999. Amended effective November 2, 2004.]

CANON 6. JUDGES PRO TEMPORE, RETIRED JUDGES, SUBSTITUTE JUDGES AND PERSONS SELECTED FOR JUDGESHIP ARE REQUIRED TO COMPLY WITH THE CANONS

A. Judge Pro Tempore. A judge pro tempore is a person who is appointed pursuant to §§ 17.1–109, 17.1–110, and 17.1–111 of the Code of Virginia to act temporarily as a judge.

(1) While acting as such, a judge pro tempore is required to comply with the Canons as they apply to the case before him.

(2) A person who has been a judge pro tempore shall not act as a lawyer in a proceeding in which he has served as a judge or in any proceeding related thereto.

B. Retired Judge, Senior Judge or Justice. The provisions of § 51.1–309 of the Code of Virginia and of these Canons shall apply to all retired judges. Such judges, however, are not required to comply with Canon 4C(2), D(3), E, F, G, and H(2).

C. Substitute Judge or Special Justice. A substitute judge or special justice shall not act as a lawyer in a proceeding in which he has served as a judge or in any other proceeding related thereto but otherwise may practice law in the court on which he serves. A substitute judge or special justice is not required to comply with 4C(*l*)(2) and (3) except that he shall not use or permit the use of the prestige of judicial office for fund raising or membership solicitation. A substitute judge or special justice is not required to comply with 4D(3), E, F, and G.

D. Person Selected for Judgeship. A person selected for a full-time position subject to the provisions of these Canons who is not already a justice or judge, from either election by both houses of the General Assembly or appointment by the appropriate authority until taking the oath of office as a justice or judge, is required to comply with Canons 1, 2, 2A, 2B, 4A, 4B, 4C(2), 4C(3)(b)(i, iii, and iv), 4D(1)(a), 4D(5), 4H(1), and 5. Such person shall arrange his or her affairs to be in compliance with the other appropriate parts of the Canons of Judicial Conduct at the time that he or she takes the oath of office.

Commentary

Comment on subdivision A. A judge pro tempore appointed under the provisions of Section 16.1–69.9:2 or 17–120 [17.1–509] of the Code shall be bound by the same Canons as a full time judge.

Comment on subdivision B. A retired judge who both receives retirement benefits and appears in Virginia courts violates Va. Code § 51.1–309 and subdivision B of this Canon.

Retired judges may be listed as such or be referred to as "Honorable" in materials distributed by alternative dispute resolution groups and they may list their judicial service on resumes distributed by such organizations. When the term "Honorable" is used, however, the materials shall make clear that the judge is a retired judge.

Comment on subdivision C. When sitting as a substitute judge or special justice, the substitute judge or special justice shall be bound by the Canons in the same manner as a full time judge. When a substitute judge or special justice is acting as a practicing attorney, he or she will not be precluded from those activities otherwise authorized as a practicing attorney.

Comment on subdivision D. A person who has been selected as a judge but who has not yet taken the oath of office is perceived by the public as a person who should adhere to the high standards of conduct applicable to a judge. However, such a person needs time to arrange his or her affairs to be in compliance with these Canons at the time of taking the oath of office, and to wind down his or her practice prior to taking the oath of office. This provision applies the rule of reason to this transition process. During this period, such person should act in a manner appropriate to, and should not take advantage of, his or her status of impending judicial position.

[Effective July 1, 1999. Amended effective July 1, 2001.]

CANON 7. EFFECTIVE DATE

These Canons shall become effective July 1, 1999.

[Effective July 1, 1999.]

SUPREME COURT ORDER JUDICIAL ETHICS ADVISORY COMMITTEE

January 5, 1999

A Judicial Ethics Advisory Committee is hereby established to render advisory opinions concerning the compliance of proposed future conduct with the Canons of Judicial Conduct. The committee shall have nine members. Five members shall be active or retired judges; two members shall be attorneys; and two members shall be lay persons. All members shall be appointed by the Chief Justice of the Virginia Supreme Court. Committee members shall serve for three-year terms from the date of appointment.

A request for an advisory opinion may be made by any judge or any person whose conduct is subject to the Canons of Judicial Conduct. The committee may not issue an opinion in response to a request where the facts are known to be the subject of a past or pending litigation or disciplinary proceeding or investigation. The committee may also issue opinions at its own initiative on matters of interest to the judiciary.

All opinions shall be advisory only, and no opinion shall be binding on the Judicial Inquiry and Review Commission or the Supreme Court in the exercise of its judicial discipline responsibilities. However, the Judicial Inquiry and Review Commission and the Supreme Court may in their discretion consider compliance with an advisory opinion by the requesting individual to be evidence of a good faith effort to comply with the Canons of Judicial Conduct provided that compliance with an opinion issued to one judge shall not be considered evidence of good faith of another judge unless the underlying facts are substantially the same.

Membership

1. The committee shall have nine members appointed by the Chief Justice of the Supreme Court. Members of the Judicial Inquiry and Review Commission may not serve simultaneously on the Judicial Ethics Advisory Committee.

2. Five members shall be either active or retired judges. One judge member shall be appointed from the Circuit, General District and Juvenile and Domestic Relations Courts and from the Court of Appeals. No member of the Supreme Court may be appointed to the Judicial Ethics Advisory Committee.

3. Two members shall be attorneys admitted to the practice of law in Virginia for at least ten years, who

shall not be judges nor ever have been judges. The attorney members shall not be employees or officers within any branch of government except that they may be employees of educational institutions.

4. Two members shall be citizens who are not admitted to practice law in any state and who are not employees or officers within any branch of government except that they may be employees of educational institutions.

5. Committee members shall serve for three-year terms from the date of appointment, except that, to achieve staggered terms, three of the members first appointed shall be appointed for one year, three shall be appointed for two years, and three shall be appointed for three years. Committee members may be reappointed, but no member shall serve for more than two full consecutive terms.

6. A vacancy shall occur when a committee member resigns, ceases to be a member of the category from which the member was appointed, or becomes unable to serve for any reason. Vacancies shall be filled in the same manner as the original appointment, and appointments to fill a vacancy shall be for the balance of the term vacated. A member whose term expires shall continue to serve until a successor is appointed.

General Provisions

7. Members should be reimbursed for expenses actually and necessarily incurred in the performance of their duties for the committee.

8. To encourage judges to seek advice from the committee, the judge members of the committee, when acting in their advisory capacity, shall be exempt from the provisions regarding disciplinary responsibilities in the Canons of Judicial Conduct. The attorney members of the committee, when acting in their advisory capacity shall be exempt from the provisions regarding reporting misconduct in the Code of Professional Responsibility.

9. By the concurrence of a majority of its members and subject to approval by the Supreme Court, the committee may promulgate additional rules of procedure not inconsistent with these rules.

10. The chair of the committee shall be elected by the members of the committee. The chair shall serve for a term of one year and shall not serve more than two successive terms. The chair is authorized to call meetings as needed, to preside over those meetings, and to coordinate the work of the committee. A vice chair shall be elected in the same manner.

11. No member of the committee shall participate in any request for advice in which he or she has a direct or indirect interest, including his or her personal inquiry.

12. The committee may submit to the Supreme Court recommendations for amendments to the Canons of Judicial Conduct.

13. Each year, the committee shall submit to the Supreme Court a report of its activities.

14. Counsel to the Judicial Inquiry and Review Commission shall provide administrative and research support sufficient to carry out the committee's functions.

Jurisdiction

15. Any judge or any person whose conduct is subject to the Canons of Judicial Conduct may request an advisory opinion about the propriety of his or her own conduct. The committee may decline to respond to an inquiry from someone who is not a member of the judiciary.

16. The committee shall not render opinions regarding the proposed conduct of someone other than the inquirer, except the committee may respond to requests from a judge about a person subject to the judge's direction and control, from a judge about the judge's relatives, or from a judge with supervisory responsibilities.

17. The committee shall only issue opinions that address contemplated or proposed future conduct and shall not issue opinions addressing past or current conduct unless the past or current conduct relates to future conduct or is continuing. The committee may not issue an opinion in response to a request when the facts are known to be the subject of a past or pending litigation or disciplinary investigation or proceeding.

18. The committee may in its discretion decline to respond to any inquiry where the committee determines that a response would be inappropriate or that an opinion will not aid the judge, benefit the judiciary as a whole, or serve the public interest.

19. The committee may not issue an advisory opinion that interprets any constitutional provision, statute, rule, or regulation that does not relate to judicial ethics.

20. Notwithstanding any other provision of these rules, the committee may also issue opinions at its own initiative on matters of interest to the judiciary.

Procedures

21. A request for an advisory opinion must be in writing, signed by the person requesting the opinion, and sent to Counsel for the Judicial Inquiry and Review Commission.

22. A request shall contain a statement describing in detail all relevant facts and circumstances pertaining to the conduct for which an opinion is being sought. The request shall also include a clear, concise statement of the question of judicial ethics for which an opinion is sought and include references to the relevant section(s) of the Canons of Judicial Conduct, advisory opinions, case law, and other authority that the inquirer has already consulted.

23. Counsel shall review the request for an advisory opinion and notify the inquirer if it does not comply with these rules.

24. If an existing opinion answers the question presented in a request, Counsel may send a copy of the opinion to the inquirer, and the committee need not issue a new advisory opinion.

25. If an existing opinion does not answer the question presented in a request, Counsel shall send the request and any accompanying documents to all members of the committee.

26. If the facts or circumstances provided by the requesting individual are unclear, vague, or insufficient in detail, the chair or any member of the committee shall request supplemental information. If the supplemental information provided is still insufficient or is not provided within a reasonable time, the chair shall inform the inquirer, and the committee shall not render an advisory opinion.

27. After discussion and consideration of the request, the chair shall assign the responsibility for drafting an opinion to members of the committee. The assigned member will have 30 days to prepare a proposed opinion and circulate it to the other members.

28. Committee members will have 15 days to indicate their approval or disapproval of a proposed opinion and to make comments. The failure to respond within 15 days shall be deemed an assent to the proposed opinion. Each committee member will send his or her response to all other committee members, including the chair, and to staff. Members will have an additional 15 days to respond to the comments of other members.

29. A telephone conference call may be arranged to discuss the proposed opinion and any comments.

30. A majority of the members shall be required to concur in any advisory opinion issued by the committee.

31. Any member of the committee may submit a minority opinion to be circulated for comment.

Formal Opinions

32. Formal opinions shall set forth the facts upon which the opinion is based and provide advice only with regard to those facts. Formal opinions shall cite the rules, cases, and other authorities that bear upon the advice rendered and shall quote the applicable provisions of the Canons of Judicial Conduct.

33. Formal opinions shall contain a discussion section that analyzes the issues and provides the rationale for the advice given by the committee. If the opinion responds to more than one issue, each issue shall be answered separately.

34. If the request raises issues under constitutional provisions, statutes, rules, or regulations other than the Canons of Judicial Conduct, the formal opinion may note the issues but shall indicate that the committee is not authorized to interpret a judge's obligations under any law other than the Canons of Judicial Conduct.

35. Formal opinions shall state the authority of the committee and explain the effect of compliance with the opinion in disciplinary proceedings.

Informal Opinions

36. Counsel for the Judicial Inquiry and Review Commission may issue informal opinions. An informal advisory opinion may be issued if the opinion is not inconsistent with prior formal opinions and Counsel finds that the subject is not of general substantial interest and continuing concern to the judiciary or the public.

37. If a request is made that requires only an informal opinion, Counsel may render an informal opinion at once or solicit the advice of the chair and other members before rendering an informal opinion.

38. Informal opinions may be oral. A written record shall be maintained by Counsel and a copy of the memorandum shall be promptly forwarded to the chair.

39. Counsel shall report in writing at the next meeting of the committee, on all informal opinions. If one-third of the members of the committee disagree with an informal opinion, that opinion shall be resubmitted for further study and issuance of a formal opinion.

40. Compliance with an informal opinion shall have the same effect as compliance with a formal opinion in judicial discipline proceedings.

41. Informal opinions will not be distributed or published in the same manner as formal opinions.

Distribution and Publication

42. The original formal opinion shall be mailed to the person requesting the opinion, and copies shall be mailed to all committee members.

43. The committee shall cause to be prepared an edited version of a formal opinion that omits the names of persons, courts, places, and any other information that might tend to identify either the person making the request or any other person. The edited opinion shall use neutral gender references. The chair shall review the edited opinion and add a heading.

44. Copies of edited opinions as they are prepared shall be sent to the Supreme Court, the Judicial Inquiry and Review Commission, the Executive Secretary of the Supreme Court, the Supreme Court Law Library, all law school libraries in Virginia, and the American Judicature Society.

45. Copies of edited opinions shall be published in a publication generally available to judges.

46. Copies of all edited opinions shall be sent by the Executive Secretary of the Supreme Court to all judges at least once a year. An index shall be distributed to all judges annually. A complete set of the committee's edited opinions shall be provided to each new judge.

47. A minority opinion shall be distributed and published in the same manner as the majority opinion of the committee.

48. The committee will release a copy of any edited opinion upon request.

Reconsideration and Modification

49. Any determination of the propriety of particular conduct by the Judicial Inquiry and Review Commission or the Supreme Court shall supersede any conflicting opinion of the committee. The committee shall examine and reconsider any of its opinions upon the request of the Judicial Inquiry and Review Commission or the Supreme Court.

50. At any time, a majority of the committee may modify or reverse any advisory opinion. The committee shall periodically review all of its opinions to determine if any are obsolete.

51. Within thirty days after the distribution of an edited opinion to all judges, any person, court, or agency authorized to request an opinion may petition the committee to reconsider the opinion by letter or memorandum explaining the basis for the request. The committee shall respond to the request by either reaffirming or revising the opinion. Revised opinions shall be distributed and published in the same manner as the original opinion.

SECTION IV. ORGANIZATION AND GOVERNMENT

PARAGRAPH 1. NAME

The name of the Organization shall be the Virginia State Bar.

[Amended effective January 4, 2010.]

PARAGRAPH 2. MEMBERSHIP AND REGISTRATION

(a) Every person licensed by the Virginia Board of Bar Examiners or admitted by the Supreme Court of Virginia is a member of the Virginia State Bar. Such persons shall register with the Virginia State Bar within one year after licensure or admission. Attorneys who are seeking active membership in the Virginia State Bar under Virginia Supreme Court Rule 1A:5, Part I (Virginia Corporate Counsel) must complete their registration requirements with the Virginia State Bar and their admission before the Supreme Court of Virginia within six months; otherwise such attorneys will be required to initiate a new application process.

(b) Every lawyer making application to the Virginia State Bar as a Corporate Counsel Registrant under Virginia Supreme Court Rule 1A:5 Part II, and every lawyer issued a certificate by the Virginia Board of Bar Examiners under Virginia Supreme Court Rules 1A:6 or 1A:7 must complete their registration requirements with the Virginia State Bar within six months; otherwise such attorneys will be required to initiate a new application process.

[Amended effective January 4, 2010.]

PARAGRAPH 3. CLASSES OF MEMBERSHIP

Members of the Virginia State Bar shall be divided into five classes, namely: (a) Active Members, (b) Associate Members, (c) Judicial Members, (d) Disabled and Retired Members; and (e) Emeritus Members. Each member shall submit in writing to the membership department of the Virginia State Bar an address of record which will be used for all membership and regulatory purposes, including official mailings and notices of disciplinary proceedings. If a member's address of record is not a physical address where process can be served, the member must submit in writing to the membership department an alternate address where process can be served. The alternate address is personal information and shall not be disclosed pursuant to Section 2.2–3704, *Code of Virginia.* Members have a duty promptly to notify the membership department in writing of any changes in either the address of record or any alternate address. Members, by request, may have their names and addresses removed from the Virginia State Bar's membership list when it is distributed for other than official purposes.

(a) Active Members. Those attorneys who are admitted to practice law in this state and who are engaged in the practice of law, either full-time or part-time, salaried or non-salaried, shall be active members of the Virginia State Bar. Those attorneys who are admitted to practice law in this state, but who are not presently so engaged, may acquire active status by paying the dues prescribed for active members and satisfying any other required membership obligations. Each active member's address of record will establish the judicial circuit in which the member is entitled to vote and hold office in the Virginia State Bar.

(b) Associate Members. Those attorneys who have been admitted to practice law in the courts of this state but who are not presently so engaged and all persons on the law faculties of any law schools of this state that have been approved by the American Bar Association may become associate members of the Virginia State Bar upon application to the secretary and payment of the required dues. Associate members shall be entitled to all the privileges of active members except that they may not practice law, vote or hold office (other than as members of committees) in the Virginia State Bar.

(c) Judicial Members. All full-time judges of the State (including federal judges), other officers qualified but forbidden by statute to practice law, and all retired judges who are receiving retirement benefits and are prohibited from appearing as counsel in any case in any court of the Commonwealth under section 51.1–309 of the *Code of Virginia* shall constitute the Judicial Membership of the Virginia State Bar. They shall pay no dues but shall be entitled to all of the privileges of active members except that they may not vote or hold office in the Virginia State Bar, and shall comply with any statutory limitations regulating their practice of law.

(d) Disabled and Retired Members. Any member of the Virginia State Bar, upon attaining the age of 70 or on the basis of a permanent disability, may submit to the executive director of the Virginia State Bar a written request to be transferred to the disabled and retired class of membership. Members who are electing this status based on a permanent disability must submit adequate medical and/or psychological documentation with the request. Members qualifying for transfer to the disabled and retired class shall not be entitled to practice law. Further, such members shall not be eligible to vote or hold office in the Virginia State Bar. Disabled and retired members may submit a petition to the executive director in writing for reinstatement to active or associate membership and state in the petition each circumstance that has changed since the member elected disabled or retired status. Adequate medical and/or psychological documentation must be submitted with the petition showing that the member is fit and capable of practicing law. If there are any misconduct complaints or proceedings pending when the executive director receives a petition for reinstatement, or if the member appears to suffer from a disability, the executive director shall defer consideration of the petition until the misconduct or disability issues are resolved. The Executive Committee of the Virginia State Bar shall consider and act on any such petition, taking into account the recommendation of the executive director. The Executive Committee may deny a petition for reinstatement if the member is publicly disciplined or is determined to have a disability raising a serious question as to the member's fitness or capacity to practice law. If the Executive Committee approves the petition, the member shall be returned to active or associate status upon payment of the appropriate dues, satisfaction of any other required membership obligations, and payment of any outstanding financial obligations to the bar. Medical and/or psychological information provided pursuant to this subparagraph (d) is confidential and shall not be disclosed by the bar.

(e) Emeritus Members. Those attorneys who are admitted to practice law in the Commonwealth of Virginia may, upon request to the Virginia State Bar with the supporting materials specified in this subparagraph, become emeritus members and provide *pro bono* legal services to the poor and working poor as emeritus members subject to the terms and conditions stated in this subparagraph. They shall pay no dues, may not practice law except in the limited manner specified in this subparagraph, and may not vote or hold office in the Virginia State Bar.

[Amended effective July 1, 1988; December 1, 1988; September 29, 1999; September 26, 2002; September 1, 2004; January 4, 2010.]

PARAGRAPH 4. OFFICERS

The officers of the Virginia State Bar shall be a President, a President-elect, an Immediate Past President and a Secretary–Treasurer. The President-elect shall be elected annually for a term to commence immediately upon the adjournment of the Annual Meeting of the Virginia State Bar and to continue until adjournment of the next Annual Meeting of the Virginia State Bar, at which time he or she shall take office as President. The President shall continue in office until adjournment of the next Annual Meeting, at which time he or she shall become the Immediate Past–President until adjournment of the following Annual Meeting.

To be eligible for nomination as President-elect, the candidate must, at the time of nomination, have been an active member of the Virginia State Bar for a period of seven years and must have served on the Council for a minimum of two years within the five-year period next preceding his or her election.

The method of election of the President-elect shall be in the manner prescribed by the Bylaws of the Council.

Vacancies in the office of President or President-elect shall be filled by the Council.

The President, the President-elect and the Immediate Past President shall be ex officio members of the Council; the President shall preside over the Council. In the absence of the President, the President-elect shall preside.

The Secretary–Treasurer shall also bear the title of Executive Director and Chief Operating Officer. The Council shall recommend its nominee as Secretary–Treasurer to the Supreme Court of Virginia which shall approve or reject the Council's recommendation. If the Supreme Court rejects Council's recommendation, Council shall submit another recommendation to the Court for its consideration. The Secretary–Treasurer shall keep all records of the Council and the Virginia State Bar. Accounts of the Secretary–Treasurer shall be audited annually.

The Secretary–Treasurer may be removed from office by the Council with the approval of the Supreme Court or by the Supreme Court, acting *sua sponte*.

[Amended effective February 1, 1988; February 6, 2004; January 1, 2006.]

PARAGRAPH 5. THE COUNCIL

The powers of the Virginia State Bar shall be exercised by a Council composed of at least thirty-seven members in addition to the President, President-elect and Immediate Past President, as ex officio members, elected and appointed as follows:

At least one active member from each of the thirty-one judicial circuits, elected for a term of three years by the members of the bar of each circuit, and nine members appointed by the Supreme Court of Virginia from the active members of the bar of the state at large. The Court shall appoint the at-large members to serve for a term of three years and, further, shall appoint in such a manner as to ensure that three members are appointed annually. A person who has served two successive full three-year terms as an elected or appointed member of Council shall not be eligible for election or appointment to a third successive term.

For each additional judicial circuit, whenever created, there shall be a member of the Council, who shall be an active member of the bar of that circuit. An election shall be held in such circuit within sixty (60) days after the creation of such circuit or as soon thereafter as may be feasible in the manner provided at Paragraph 6. The Council at its meeting next thereafter shall determine the length of the term of the first member from that circuit so that, as nearly as possible, the terms of one-third of the members of the Council expire each year.

Any circuit having as of the 1st day of February in any year more than 500 active members in good standing who are domiciled or principally practice their profession in such circuit shall be entitled to one additional member of the Council for each additional 500 members or major fraction thereof. In the event that the membership in a circuit as of February 1 is such that it is no longer entitled to one or more additional members, the term of such additional member[s] of the Council shall end at the expiration of the term for which the member[s] was elected. Provided, however, that the number of Council members from each circuit as of July 1, 2008, shall not be reduced unless the active membership in the circuit first increases to the number which will sustain its allocation of Council members as of July 1, 2008, under the above formula, and subsequently falls below that number.

Whenever a judicial circuit shall be abolished, the term of any member of the Council from that circuit shall end forthwith.

The President of the Young Lawyers Conference shall serve as an ex officio member of the Council.

The Chair of the Conference of Local Bar Associations shall serve as an ex officio member of the Council.

The Chair of the Senior Lawyers Conference shall serve as an ex officio member of the Council.

The Chair of the Diversity Conference shall serve as an ex officio member of the Council.

[Amended effective July 1, 1989; February 1, 1994; July 1, 1999; May 1, 2000; October 1, 2001; October 31, 2008; January 22, 2010.]

PARAGRAPH 6. ELECTION OF COUNCIL

Prior to the expiration of a term of a Council member from a circuit, or when it appears that such a position has otherwise become vacant, or the circuit becomes entitled to an additional Council member under other provisions of this section, the Executive Director shall initiate the election process for the election of a Council member in the manner prescribed by the Bylaws of the Council.

[Amended effective February 1, 1988.]

PARAGRAPH 7. MEETINGS OF THE COUNCIL

The Council shall hold meetings at such regular times and upon such call as it may specify. A quorum at any meeting shall consist of not less than twenty members. Between meetings of the Council its duties and functions may be performed by such Executive Committee of members or officers as the Council may designate.

PARAGRAPH 8. ANNUAL MEETING OF THE VIRGINIA STATE BAR

Annually, on or before July 1, there shall be held a meeting of the members of the Virginia State Bar at a time and place designated by the Council or Executive Committee and presided over by the President. All officers elected at the annual meeting or by the Council shall take office immediately upon adjournment of the annual meeting except in cases where vacancies are filled for an unexpired term. At such meeting there shall be a report from the officers and from the Council, and there shall be elected the President and President–Elect for the ensuing year.

A quorum at such meeting shall be those members of the Virginia State Bar present and voting.

There may be transacted also such other business as may come before the meeting.

A special meeting of the Virginia State Bar may be called by the Council.

PARAGRAPH 9. POWERS OF THE COUNCIL

The Council shall have general charge of the administration of the affairs of the Virginia State Bar, and shall have the power:

(a) To adopt Bylaws for the Council and the Virginia State Bar not in conflict with these rules.

(b) To elect the officers provided for by these rules.

(c) To fill vacancies in the Council for unexpired terms if there should be a failure for sixty days to elect as provided in Paragraph 6 and to fill vacancies in any office for unexpired terms.

(d) To appoint Committees and prescribe their duties.

(e) To employ such assistants as it deems necessary and to fix their duties and compensation and the compensation of the Secretary–Treasurer.

(f) To make allocations of funds within the amounts available.

(g) To conduct such investigations and make such reports as may be directed by the Supreme Court or by the Bar.

(h) To render advisory opinions as provided in Paragraph 10.

(i) To establish an Administration and Finance Fund from which expenses related to meetings of the Council, meetings of the Executive Committee, the Annual and Midyear Meetings, and other official functions of the Virginia State Bar may be paid. The Fund shall be composed of funds appropriated to it by Council, or otherwise received. Such funds may be held, managed and invested as authorized or directed by Council. Disbursements from the fund shall be made as authorized by Council to pay the necessary expenses related to official functions of the Virginia State Bar as authorized by these Rules including, but not limited to, those expenses resulting from the exercise of the Council's powers under these Rules.

(j) The Council may, at its discretion or upon a written request of the majority of the members of the Virginia State Bar or pursuant to a resolution duly adopted at a regular or called meeting, exercise the necessary powers:

To promote reforms in judicial procedure and the judicial system that are intended to improve the quality and fairness of the system;

To recommend to the Supreme Court procedures for the disciplining, suspending and disbarring of attorneys;

To recommend to the Supreme Court the adoption of, modifications to, amendments to or the repeal of any rule of the Rules of the Supreme Court of Virginia;

To regulate the legal profession;

To improve the quality of the legal services made available to the people of Virginia;

To investigate, evaluate or endorse judicial candidates on a nonpartisan, merit basis;

To uphold and elevate the standards of honor, of integrity and of courtesy in the legal profession;

To encourage higher and better education for membership in the profession;

To encourage and promote diversity in the profession and the judiciary; and

To perform all duties imposed by law.

[Amended effective September 1, 1987; April 1, 1991; January 22, 2010.]

PARAGRAPH 10. PROMULGATION OF LEGAL ETHICS, UNAUTHORIZED PRACTICE OF LAW OPINIONS, AND RULES OF COURT; INFORMAL STAFF OPINIONS OF ETHICS COUNSEL; AND COMPLAINTS OF UNAUTHORIZED PRACTICE OF LAW

10–1. Definitions.

As used in this Paragraph, the following terms shall have the meaning herein stated unless the context clearly requires otherwise:

"Advisory Opinion" means a written statement of the subject involved, the question presented, the Rule of Court or other precedents relied upon, the opinion reached, and the reasons therefore.

"Bar" means the Virginia State Bar.

"Committee" means the Standing Committee on Legal Ethics or the Standing Committee on Unauthorized Practice of Law.

"Council" means the Council of the Virginia State Bar.

"Court" means the Supreme Court of Virginia.

"Ethics Counsel" means the Ethics Counsel or an assistant ethics counsel of the Virginia State Bar.

"Member" means any active member of the Virginia State Bar or a Foreign Lawyer as defined under Rule 5.5(d)(1) of the *Rules of Professional Conduct.*

"Notice" means publishing in the *Virginia Lawyer Register* and at a minimum posting on the Virginia State Bar's website for at least 30 calendar days.

"Rule" means any proposed new Rule of Court or any modification, amendment, or proposed repeal of any existing Rule of Court promulgated by either the Standing Committee on Legal Ethics or the Standing Committee on Unauthorized Practice of Law.

10–2. Advisory Opinions or Rules.

A. *Request for Advisory Opinion.* Any Member may request a legal ethics opinion or unauthorized practice of law opinion. The request shall be submitted as a hypothetical on a form approved by the Committee. A request for an Advisory Opinion will be reviewed by Ethics Counsel and forwarded to the appropriate Committee for consideration. In its discretion, the Committee may decline to render an Advisory Opinion regarding a previously resolved issue, or any matter that is currently the subject of any disciplinary proceeding or litigation.

B. *Rules.* The Committee may propose a new Rule or propose amendments, modifications, or repeal of existing Rules at its discretion. For rule changes that declare conduct as the unauthorized practice of law, the Bar shall seek comment from the Attorney General's office analyzing any restraint on competition that might result from the adoption of the proposed change.

C. *Notice and Comments.* The Committee shall provide Notice and opportunity for public comment on proposed Advisory Opinions or proposed Rules. Public comments shall be directed to the Executive Director of the Virginia State Bar. For proposed Advisory Opinions, the Committee will consider any comments received and either publish the opinion as an Advisory Opinion or ask for Council review in accordance with section 10–3. Advisory Opinions express the judgment of the Committee and are not binding on any judicial or administrative tribunal. In the case of a Rule, the Committee will consider any comments received and then submit the Rule to Council for consideration in accordance with section 10–3.

D. *Appeal.* After the comment period, any party requesting an Advisory Opinion who disagrees with the result may appeal the opinion to Council for approval, modification, or disapproval.

E. *Unauthorized Practice of Law Advisory Opinions.* An unauthorized practice of law Advisory Opinion in which the Committee concludes that the conduct in question constitutes or would constitute the unauthorized practice of law shall be sent to Council in accordance with section 10–3. For these Advisory Opinions, the Bar shall seek comment from the Attorney General's office analyzing any restraint on competition that might result from the promulgation and implementation of the opinion.

F. *Confidentiality.* All Committee deliberations, memoranda, correspondence, and work product shall be confidential and privileged from discovery or subpoena and will not be provided to anyone absent a court order.

10–3. Advisory Opinion or Rule Consideration by Council.

A. *Review.* After considering all materials and written comments, Council may approve, modify, or disapprove any Advisory Opinion or Rule by a majority vote of those present and voting. If Council approves or modifies an Advisory Opinion it may be published as an Advisory Opinion of the Bar and have the same legal effect as a Committee-issued opinion. Council may determine to submit the Advisory Opinion or Rule to the Court for review along with copies of all public comments.

B. *Unauthorized Practice of Law Advisory Opinions.* If Council concurs by a majority vote of those present and voting that the proposed conduct in any unauthorized practice of law Advisory Opinion constitutes the unauthorized practice of law, the Advisory Opinion shall be sent to the Court for review along with copies of all public comments.

10–4. Advisory Opinion or Rule Review by the Supreme Court of Virginia.

A. *Review.* After considering all materials submitted to it, the Court shall approve, modify, or disapprove any Advisory Opinion or Rule.

10–5. Informal Staff Opinions of Ethics Counsel.

A. *Informal Advice.* At the request of a Member, Ethics Counsel shall provide informal advice or opinion based on the facts provided.

B. *Protection.* Ethics Counsel shall not be compelled to testify, via subpoena or otherwise, in any judicial or adjudicative proceeding, except on behalf of a respondent in disciplinary proceedings of the Virginia State Bar, regarding any advice or opinion provided to that attorney. Except as stated herein, Ethics Counsel shall not be subject to subpoena or otherwise compelled to testify or to produce any documents in any judicial or adjudicative proceeding or to testify as an expert witness regarding legal ethics or the practice of law. In a disciplinary proceeding, testimony of Ethics Counsel shall be limited to the substance of any communications by and between Ethics and the Member, where such communications are an issue in the proceeding.

C. *Confidentiality.* All communications between Ethics Counsel and any Member requesting advice or opinion shall be confidential. Ethics Counsel shall not disclose the content of any such discussion without the express written consent of the Member to whom Ethics Counsel provided such advice or opinion. No Member shall withhold consent if the Member is claiming, in the course of a disciplinary investigation or hearing, that the Member relied on the advice of Ethics Counsel.

D. *Use of Informal Advice in Collateral Litigation.* Informal advice of Ethics Counsel is advisory only and expresses the judgment of the Ethics Counsel and is not binding on the Court, Council, Committee or any judicial or administrative tribunal. Except as provided herein in connection with attorney disciplinary proceedings, informal advice of Ethics Counsel shall not be used, admitted, introduced, argued or cited in any litigation or before any judicial or administrative tribunal for the purpose of seeking disqualification of a lawyer or law firm.

10–6. Complaints of Unauthorized Practice of Law.

A. *Review of Complaints.* Any written complaint alleging the unauthorized practice of law shall be reviewed by Ethics Counsel and either dismissed or referred for investigation with full report to the Committee. After reviewing a report of investigation, the Committee may conduct a hearing to take testimony from witnesses and review evidence. By majority vote the Committee may dismiss the complaint due to insufficient evidence or other good cause, dismiss the complaint with cautionary language, or enter a finding of probable cause to believe there is unauthorized practice of law.

B. *Referral.* If a majority of the Committee finds probable cause to believe there is unauthorized practice of law, the Committee may dismiss the complaint by letter agreement in which the party against whom the complaint is pending agrees to cease the activity; or refer the complaint to the Attorney General, a Commonwealth's Attorney, or other appropriate agency for action.

C. *Summons or Subpoena.* If a summons or subpoena is necessary for investigation of a matter outlined in section 10–6.A., Ethics Counsel may issue such a summons or subpoena in the name of the Commonwealth. The Committee or a Virginia State Bar investigator may use a summons to examine a witness or to obtain statements from persons having knowledge about the subject of the complaint.

D. *Enforcement of Summons or Subpoena.* Every Circuit Court shall have power to enforce a summons or subpoena issued by the Ethics Counsel and to adjudge disobedience thereof as contempt.

Upon consideration whereof, it is ordered that the Rules for Integration of the Virginia State Bar, Part Six, Section IV, of the Rules of Court, be and the same hereby are amended in accordance with the prayer of the petition aforesaid, effective immediately.

[Amended effective January 1, 1990; May 1, 1991; February 1, 1993; July 1, 1995; January 27, 1998; September 29, 1999; January 1, 2005; January 22, 2010; March 19, 2010.]

PARAGRAPH 11. DUES

Each active member shall pay to the Treasurer of the Virginia State Bar, annual dues not to exceed $250, and each associate member shall pay to the Treasurer of the Virginia State Bar annual dues not to exceed $125, on or before the 31st day of July of each fiscal year, provided that persons admitted to practice by examination or under Rule 1A:1 of the Supreme Court of Virginia shall not be liable for dues in the year of admission if admitted during the last three months of any fiscal year. Persons admitted to practice under Rule 1A:1 at any other point during any fiscal year shall pay the full amount of dues as specified above at the time they register with the Virginia State Bar. Persons admitted to practice by examination at any other point during any fiscal year shall pay one-half the amount of dues as specified above at the time they register with the Virginia State Bar. On or before April 1st, the Bar shall report to the Court the annual dues amount proposed for the next fiscal year.

No increase in the annual dues above $250 for active members or $125 for associate members will be authorized by the Court whenever the total combined cash balances of the State Bar Fund and the Virginia State Bar's Administration and Finance Account shall exceed fifteen (15) percent of the total annual operating expenditures of the Virginia State Bar for the year preceding the year in which the dues increase is sought.

All monies collected hereunder shall be accounted for and paid into the State Treasury of Virginia.

Failure to comply with this Rule shall subject the member to penalties set forth in Paragraph 19 herein.

[Amended effective July 1, 1986; July 1, 1988; January 1, 1990; July 1, 1990; July 1, 1992; February 5, 1996; July 1, 1996; February 4, 2000; April 12, 2001; March 9, 2011.]

PARAGRAPH 12. DISBURSEMENTS

Disbursements shall be paid out of the State Treasury in accordance with allocations of the Council and on requisitions signed by the President, President–Elect, or Secretary–Treasurer, and upon the warrant of the State Comptroller. No member of the Council, and no member or officer of the Virginia State Bar except the Secretary–Treasurer, shall receive compensation for his or her services as such, nor shall any member of the Council or of the Virginia State Bar receive compensation for service on any Committee, but such Council member or Committeeman shall be reimbursed for his or her necessary and actual traveling and subsistence expenses incurred in the performance of his or her duties. The Council shall cause proper books of account to be kept, and have them audited annually. At each annual meeting of the Virginia State Bar, the Council shall cause to be presented a financial statement of the receipts and expenditures of the Virginia State Bar, which shall be published in the next volume of reports.

PARAGRAPH 13. PROCEDURE FOR DISCIPLINING, SUSPENDING, AND DISBARRING ATTORNEYS

13–1. Definitions.

As used in this Paragraph, the following terms shall have the meaning herein stated unless the context clearly requires otherwise:

"Adjudication of a Crime Proceeding" means the proceeding which follows the summary Suspension of an Attorney after receipt by the Clerk of the Disciplinary System of initial notification from any court of competent jurisdiction stating that an Attorney has been found guilty of a Crime, irrespective of whether sentencing has occurred.

"Admonition" means a private sanction imposed by a Subcommittee *sua sponte*, a private or public sanction based upon an Agreed Disposition approved by a Subcommittee, or a public sanction imposed by a District Committee or the Board upon a finding that Misconduct has been established, but that no substantial harm to the Complainant or the public has occurred, and that no further disciplinary action is necessary.

"Agreed Disposition" means the disposition of a Disciplinary Proceeding agreed to by Respondent and Bar Counsel and approved by a Subcommittee, District Committee, the Board or a Circuit Court.

"Attorney" means a member of the Bar, a Corporate Counsel Registrant, Foreign Lawyer, Foreign Legal Consultant, and any member of the bar of any other jurisdiction while engaged, *pro hac vice* or otherwise, in the practice of law in Virginia.

"Bar" means the Virginia State Bar.

"Bar Counsel" means the Attorney who is appointed as such by Council and who is approved by the Attorney General pursuant to Va. Code § 2.2–510, and such deputies, assistants, and Investigators as may be necessary to carry out the duties of the office, except where the duties must specifically be performed by the individual appointed pursuant to Va. Code § 2.2–510.

"Bar Official" means any Bar officer or any member, employee, or counsel of Council, the Board, a District Committee, or COLD.

"Board" means the Bar Disciplinary Board.

"Certification" means the document issued by a Subcommittee or a District Committee when it has elected to certify allegations of Misconduct to the Board for its consideration, which document shall include sufficient facts to reasonably notify Bar Counsel and Respondent of the basis for such Certification and the Disciplinary Rules alleged to have been violated.

"Certification for Sanction Determination" means the document issued by a District Committee to certify to the Board that a sanction within the power of the Board is in order where the District Committee has found that Respondent failed to fulfill the terms of a Public Reprimand with Terms issued either by a Subcommittee on the basis of an Agreed Disposition or by a District Committee.

"Chair," unless otherwise specified, means the Chair, Vice Chair, or Acting Chair of a District Committee, or a Section, Panel, or Subcommittee of a District Committee, or of the Board or any Panel of the Board.

"Charge of Misconduct" means the notice given by the Bar to a Respondent, setting forth generally the Misconduct alleged to have been committed by the Respondent, and identifying the specific Disciplinary Rule(s) alleged to have been violated by the Respondent. The Charge of Misconduct shall also include the date, time, and place of the hearing.

"Circuit Court" means a court designated as such by Va. Code § 17.1–500.

"Clerk of the Disciplinary System" means the employee of the Bar who, together with such assistants as may be required, provides administrative support to the disciplinary system and serves as official custodian of the Disciplinary Records.

"COLD" means the Standing Committee on Lawyer Discipline.

"Complainant" means the initiator of a Complaint.

"Complaint" means any written communication to the Bar alleging Misconduct or from which allegations of Misconduct reasonably may be inferred.

"Committee Counsel" means an Attorney District Committee member assigned to prosecute a Complaint.

"Corporate Counsel Registrant" means a person who has been recorded by the Virginia State Bar as a Corporate Counsel Registrant pursuant to Rule 1A:5.

"Costs" means reasonable costs paid by the Bar to outside experts or consultants; reasonable travel and out-of-pocket expenses for witnesses; Court Reporter and transcript fees; electronic and telephone conferencing and recording costs, if such procedures are requested by Respondent; copying, mailing, and required publication costs, translator fees and an administrative charge determined by Council.

"Council" means the Council of the Bar.

"Court Reporter" means a person who is qualified to transcribe proceedings in a Circuit Court.

"CRESPA" means the Virginia Consumer Real Estate Settlement Protection Act, Va. Code, Title 6.1, Chapter 1.3, and any regulations promulgated thereunder.

"Crime" means:

1. Any offense declared to be a felony by federal or state law;

2. Any other offense involving theft, fraud, forgery, extortion, bribery, or perjury;

3. An attempt, solicitation or conspiracy to commit any of the foregoing; or

4. Any of the foregoing found by a foreign jurisdiction.

"Disbarment" has the same meaning as Revocation.

"Disciplinary Proceeding" means any proceeding governed by this Paragraph.

"Disciplinary Record" means any tangible or electronic record of:

1. Any proceeding in which the Respondent has been found guilty of Misconduct, including those proceedings in which (a) the Board's or Court's finding of Misconduct has been appealed to this Court; (b) the Respondent's License has been revoked upon consent to revocation or Respondent has been found guilty of a Crime; or (c) the Respondent has received a sanction pursuant to this Paragraph; and

2. Any proceeding which has been resolved by (a) a *De Minimis* Dismissal; (b) a Dismissal for Exceptional Circumstances; or (c) an Admonition; and

3. Any proceeding in which the Respondent has been found guilty of a violation of CRESPA; and

4. Any proceeding which resulted in a sanction which created a disciplinary record at the time it was imposed.

"Disciplinary Rules" means:

1. the Virginia Rules of Professional Conduct and Virginia Code of Professional Responsibility, as applicable; and

2. the disciplinary rules of any other jurisdiction applicable under Rule 8.5 of the Virginia Rules of Professional Conduct.

"Dismissal" means the dismissal of a Complaint or Disciplinary Proceeding by Bar Counsel, a Subcommittee, a District Committee, the Board or a Circuit Court.

"Dismissal De Minimis" means a finding that the Respondent has engaged in Misconduct that is clearly not of sufficient magnitude to warrant disciplinary action, and Respondent has taken reasonable precautions against a recurrence of same.

"Dismissal for Exceptional Circumstances" means a finding that the Respondent has engaged in Misconduct but there exist exceptional circumstances mitigating against further proceedings, which circumstances shall be set forth in writing.

"District Committee" means one of the District Committees appointed as hereinafter provided or, where the context requires, a Panel, a Section, or a Subcommittee thereof.

"District Committee Determination" means the written decision of a District Committee or a Subcommittee of a District Committee, relating to a Complaint or Charge of Misconduct.

"Executive Committee" means the Executive Committee of the Bar.

"Executive Director" means the Executive Director of the Bar and any deputy or assistant designated by Council to act as Executive Director.

"Files" means those files maintained by the Clerk of the Disciplinary System, and office of Bar Counsel with respect to each Complaint.

"Foreign Lawyer" means a person authorized to practice law by the duly constituted and authorized governmental body of any State or Territory of the United States or the District of Columbia, or a foreign nation, but is neither licensed by the Court or authorized under its rules to practice law generally in the Commonwealth of Virginia, nor disbarred or suspended from practice in any jurisdiction.

"Foreign Legal Consultant" means a person who has been issued a foreign legal consultant certificate by the Virginia Board of Bar Examiners pursuant to Rule 1A:7.

"Impairment" means any physical or mental condition that materially impairs the fitness of an Attorney to practice law.

"Impairment Proceeding" means the proceeding:

1. Initiated by Bar Counsel to petition the Board to order the Respondent to undergo examination(s) and provide releases for records;
2. Initiated by Bar Counsel to determine whether an Attorney has an Impairment;
3. That follows the summary Suspension of an Attorney who may have an Impairment; or
4. That follows a request by Respondent to terminate an Impairment Suspension.

"Investigation" means any inquiry by Bar Counsel, Committee Counsel, or the Bar's designee concerning any alleged Misconduct or Crime committed by an Attorney or any Impairment of an Attorney.

"Investigative Report" means the report prepared as a result of an Investigation.

"Investigator" means a person designated by the Bar to conduct an Investigation.

"Judge" means a judge within the meaning of Va. Code § 2.1–37.1, and any judge appointed or elected under the laws of any other jurisdiction.

"License" means the license or authority to practice law granted by this Court.

"Memorandum Order" means the opinion and order of the Board entered following a Disciplinary Proceeding that shall contain a brief statement of the findings of fact; the nature of the Misconduct shown by such finding of facts; the Disciplinary Rules found to have been violated by clear and convincing evidence; the sanction imposed; the notice requirements, if any, imposed upon Respondent; the time in which Terms are required to be satisfied by Respondent, if Terms are imposed; the alternative sanction, if Respondent fails to comply with any Terms that are imposed; the name and address of the Court Reporter who served at the hearing; the names of the members of the Board that constituted the Panel; and that Costs shall be reimbursed by Respondent.

"Misconduct" means any:

1. Unlawful conduct described in Va. Code § 54.1–3935;
2. Violation of the Disciplinary Rules;
3. Conviction of a Crime;
4. Conviction of any other criminal offense or commission of a deliberately wrongful act that reflects adversely on the Attorney's honesty, trustworthiness, or fitness as an Attorney; or
5. Violation of CRESPA or any regulations adopted pursuant thereto.

"Panel" means a group of members of a Section, District Committee, or the Board hearing a disciplinary matter that constitutes the quorum required by this Paragraph.

"Paragraph" means Paragraph 13 of the Rules of this Court, Part Six, Section IV.

"Petitioner" means:

1. An Attorney seeking Reinstatement after a Revocation; or
2. An Attorney seeking termination of an Impairment Suspension; or
3. A Bar Counsel or District Committee Chair seeking an expedited hearing before the Board and alleging that an Attorney is engaging in Misconduct likely to result in injury to or loss of property of a client or other entity, or alleging an Attorney poses imminent danger to the public.

"Private Discipline" means an Admonition without Terms issued by a Subcommittee *sua sponte*, a Private Reprimand or any form of discipline which is not public.

"Private Reprimand" means a form of non-public discipline that declares privately the conduct of the Respondent improper but does not limit the Respondent's right to practice law.

"Proceeding" means the same as Disciplinary Proceeding.

"Public Reprimand" means a form of public discipline that declares publicly the conduct of the Respondent improper, but does not limit the Respondent's right to practice law.

"Receivership" means a receivership created pursuant to Va. Code § 54.1–3900.01 or § 54.1–3936.

"Reinstatement" means the restoration by this Court of an Attorney's License in the manner provided in this Paragraph.

"Reinstatement Proceeding" means the proceeding which takes place upon referral from this Court of a Petition for Reinstatement by an Attorney whose License was previously revoked.

"Respondent" means any Attorney:

1. Who is the subject of a Complaint;

2. Who is the subject of any proceeding under this Paragraph, Va. Code §§ 54.1–3900.01, 54.1–3935, 54.1–3936, or CRESPA; or

3. Who is the subject of an Adjudication of a Crime Proceeding, Proceedings upon Disbarment, Revocation or Suspension in another jurisdiction, Impairment Proceeding, or Reinstatement Proceeding.

"Revocation" means any revocation of an Attorney's License and, when applied to a lawyer not admitted or authorized to practice law in Virginia, means the exclusion from the admission to, or the exercise of any privilege to, practice law in Virginia.

"Section" means a subgroup of a District Committee that has the same powers, authority, and duties as the District Committee.

"Subcommittee" means a subgroup of a District Committee or any Section thereof, convened for the purpose of performing the functions of a Subcommittee as described in this Paragraph.

"Summary Order" means a bench order entered by the Chair following a Disciplinary Proceeding that outlines in summary form the findings as to the allegations of Misconduct, the sanctions to be imposed, the effective date of any sanctions imposed, and any notice requirements.

"Suspension" means the temporary suspension of an Attorney's License for either a fixed or indefinite period of time and, when applied to a lawyer not admitted or authorized to practice law in Virginia, means the temporary or indefinite exclusion from the admission to, or the exercise of any privilege to, practice law in Virginia.

"Terms" shall mean those conditions imposed on the Respondent by a Subcommittee, District Committee, Board, or Circuit Court, that require the Respondent to perform certain remedial actions as a necessary condition for the imposition of an Admonition, a Private or Public Reprimand, or a Suspension pursuant to this Paragraph.

"Va. Code" means the 1950 Code of Virginia, as amended.

13–2. Authority of the Courts.

Nothing in this Paragraph shall be interpreted so as to eliminate, restrict or impair the jurisdiction of the courts of this Commonwealth to deal with the disciplining of Attorneys as provided by law. Every Judge shall have authority to take such action as may be necessary or appropriate to protect the interests of clients of any Attorney whose License is subject to a Suspension or Revocation. Every Circuit Court shall have power to enforce any order, summons or subpoena issued by the Board, a District Committee or Bar Counsel and to adjudge disobedience thereof as contempt.

A. *Attorney for Respondent.* A Respondent may be represented by a member of the Bar, or any member of the bar of any other jurisdiction while engaged *pro hac vice* in the practice of law in Virginia, at any time with respect to a Complaint.

13–3. General Administrative Authority of Council.

Council shall have general administrative authority over and responsibility for the disciplinary system created pursuant to this Paragraph.

13–4. Establishment of District Committees.

A. *Creation of District Committees.* Council shall appoint a sufficient number of District Committees to carry out the purposes of this Paragraph. District Committees shall be established in geographical areas consisting of one or more judicial circuits. In creating the District Committee areas, Council shall give due consideration to Attorney population and the community of interest among different judicial circuits within a District Committee area. Each District Committee shall consist of ten, or in the discretion of Council, 20, 30 or 40 members. Three members of a ten-member District Committee, six members of a 20–member District Committee, nine members of a 30–member District Committee, and 12 members of a 40–member District Committee shall be nonlawyers. All other members shall be active members of the Bar. Former members of a District Committee may serve on a District Committee Subcommittee or participate in a District Committee hearing whenever the District Committee Chair determines that such service is necessary for the orderly administration of the District Committee's work.

B. *Panel Quorum.* A Panel quorum shall consist of five or more persons. One person assigned to a District Committee Panel shall be a present or former nonlawyer member of a District Committee. If the scheduled nonlawyer is unable to attend, and if an alternate nonlawyer is not reasonably available, participation by a nonlawyer member shall not be required in a proceeding if a quorum is otherwise present. The action of a majority of a quorum shall be the action of the District Committee Panel.

C. *Geographic Criteria.* Each member of a District Committee shall be a resident of or have his or her office in the District Committee area for which such member is appointed. Members shall, to the extent practicable, be appointed from different geographical sections of their districts.

D. *Term of Office.* Council shall appoint members of each District Committee for such terms of service as will allow for the retirement from the District Committee, or completion of the existing terms, of one-third of the District Committee membership at the end of each fiscal year. A District Committee member's term shall be for three years, and, upon completion of such term, such member is eligible for appointment to a second successive three-year term. A member who has served two full successive terms of three years each on a District Committee shall not be eligible to serve again until one year after the expiration of the second term.

E. *Qualification of Members.* Before nominating any individual for membership on a District Committee, the Council members making such recommendation shall first determine that the nominee is willing to serve on the District Committee and will conscientiously discharge the responsibility as a member of the District Committee. Council members making the nominations shall also obtain a statement from the nominees, in writing, that the nominees are willing to serve on the District Committee, if elected. In order to be considered as a potential appointee to a District Committee, each potential appointee shall execute the following: (1) a waiver of confidentiality with respect to his or her Disciplinary Record and any pending Complaints and a release allowing production of his or her Disciplinary Record and any pending Complaints from any jurisdiction for purposes of the appointment process; and (2) an authorization for the Bar to conduct a criminal records check of all jurisdictions for any conviction of a Crime and provide the results to the members of Council and the staff of the Bar for purposes of the appointment process. No member of Council shall be a member of a District Committee; however, this rule shall not apply to the chair or president of any conference of the Virginia State Bar, such as the Conference of Local Bar Associations, Diversity Conference, Senior Lawyers Conference, or Young Lawyers Conference, who are ex-officio members of Council. An ex-officio member of Council who is also a member of a District Committee shall not vote on the selection or confirmation of nominees for any District Committee.

F. *Persons Ineligible for Appointment.* Any potential appointee shall be ineligible for appointment to a District Committee if such potential appointee has: (1) ever been convicted in any jurisdiction of a Crime; (2) ever committed any criminal act that reflects adversely on the potential appointee's honesty, trustworthiness or fitness as a member of a District Committee; (3) a Disciplinary Record in any jurisdiction consisting of a Disbarment, Revocation, Suspension imposed at any time or Public Reprimand imposed within the ten years immediately preceding the proposed appointment date; or (4) a Disciplinary Record in any jurisdiction consisting of Private Discipline, except for a *de minimis* dismissal or a dismissal for exceptional circumstances, or an Admonition imposed within the five years immediately preceding the proposed appointment date. The Standing Committee on Lawyer Discipline shall have the sole discretion to determine whether a *de minimis* dismissal or a dismissal for exceptional circumstances shall disqualify a potential appointee.

G. *Interim Vacancies.* Whenever a vacancy occurs on a District Committee, the Executive Committee may fill the vacancy. Bar Counsel or a majority of the members of a District Committee may request the Executive Committee to declare that a District Committee position held by any particular District Committee member has become vacant when, in the judgment of Bar Counsel or the Committee majority, such member has become, or has been for any reason, unavailable for or delinquent in the conduct of the District Committee's business. Similarly, upon request of Bar Counsel, the Executive Committee shall have the power to declare such vacancy. Before such vacancy is declared, the particular District Committee member shall be afforded notice and a reasonable opportunity to be heard.

13–5. Authority and Duties of COLD.

All powers and duties of Council, with respect to the Disciplinary System, except the power to appoint District Committee members, may be exercised by COLD, subject to the direction and control of Council. Notwithstanding any rule to the contrary, any member of COLD may attend proceedings of the Subcommittees, District Committees or the Board. Service by an Attorney on COLD shall be deemed to be a professional relationship within the meaning of Disciplinary Rules 1.6, 1.7, 1.9, 1.10 and 3.7. Such service shall be deemed the holding of public office within the meaning of Disciplinary Rules 1.11 and 1.12. Consent under Disciplinary Rules 1.6, 1.7 and 1.9 shall be deemed to include Bar Counsel's consent on behalf of the Bar.

13–6. Disciplinary Board.

A. *Appointment of Members.* This Court shall appoint, upon recommendation of Council, 20 members of the Board, 16 of whom shall be active members of the Bar and four of whom shall be nonlawyers. One Attorney member shall be designated by the Court as Chair and two Attorney members as Vice Chairs, upon recommendations of Council. Before nominating any individual for membership on the Board, the Bar's nominating committee shall first determine that the nominee is willing to serve on the Board and will conscientiously discharge the responsibilities as a member of the Board. All nominees shall have previously served on a district committee. The Bar nominating committee shall also obtain a statement from the nominees, in writing, that the nominees are willing to serve on the Board, if elected and appointed. In order to be considered as a potential appointee to the Board, each potential appointee shall execute the following: (1) a waiver of confidentiality with respect to his or her Disciplinary Record and any pending Complaints and a release allowing production of his or her Disciplinary Record and pending Complaints from any jurisdiction for purposes of the appointment process; and (2) an authorization for the Bar to conduct a criminal records check of all jurisdictions for any conviction of a Crime and provide the results to the members of Council and the staff of the Bar for purposes of the appointment process.

B. *Persons Ineligible for Appointment.* Any potential appointee shall be ineligible for appointment to the Board if such potential appointee has (1) ever been convicted in any jurisdiction of a Crime; (2) ever committed any criminal act that reflects adversely on the potential appointee's honesty, trustworthiness, or fitness as a Board member; (3) a Disciplinary Record in any jurisdiction of a Disbarment, Revocation, Suspension or Public Reprimand imposed within the ten years immediately preceding the proposed appointment date; (4) a Disciplinary Record in any jurisdiction consisting of Private Discipline, except for a *de minimis* dismissal or a dismissal for exceptional circumstances, or an Admonition within the five years immediately preceding the proposed appointment date. The Standing Committee on Lawyer Discipline shall have the sole discretion to determine whether a *de minimis* dismissal or a dismissal for exceptional circumstances shall disqualify a potential appointee.

C. *Term of Office.* Members shall serve staggered terms of three years each. No member shall serve more than two consecutive three-year terms but shall be eligible for reappointment after the lapse of one or more years following expiration of the previous three-year term. At the expiration of the initial term of any member so appointed for less than a three-year term, such member shall be eligible for immediate reappointment to the Board for two additional consecutive three-year terms.

D. *Meetings and Quorum.* The Board shall meet on reasonable notice by the Chair or a Vice Chair. A Panel of five members shall constitute a quorum, and the action of a majority of a Panel shall constitute action of the Board. One of the five persons assigned to any Panel shall be a present or former nonlawyer member. If the scheduled nonlawyer is unable to attend and an alternate nonlawyer member or former member is not reasonably available, participation by a nonlawyer shall not be required in any Proceeding if a quorum is otherwise present.

E. *Roster.* The Clerk of the Disciplinary System shall establish a roster of Board members sufficient to constitute a quorum for action on the matter to which they are being assigned. Former members of the Board may serve on a Panel of the Board or participate in Board matters whenever the Chair, Vice Chair or Clerk of the Disciplinary System determines that such service is necessary for the orderly administration of the Board's work.

F. *Jurisdiction.* The Board shall have jurisdiction to consider: (1) Appeals from Public or Private Reprimands, with or without Terms, or Admonitions, with or without Terms, imposed by District Committees or Dismissals that otherwise create a Disciplinary Record; (2) Complaints and Certifications submitted to it by a Subcommittee or a District Committee; (3) Misconduct by reason of conviction of a Crime; (4) Impairment Proceedings; (5) Revocation or Suspension in another jurisdiction; (6) Petitions from Bar Counsel or the Chair of a District Committee seeking summary Suspension upon a belief that an Attorney is engaging in Misconduct likely to result in injury to or loss of property of a client or other entity or alleging an Attorney poses imminent danger to the public; (7) Petitions for Reinstatement referred to the Board for its recommendation to this Court; (8) Violations of CRESPA or any regulations adopted pursuant thereto; (9) Failure of Respondent to make a complete transcript part of the Record, as provided in this Paragraph; (10) Failure of an Attorney to comply with an order, summons or subpoena issued in connection with a Disciplinary Proceeding; and (11) Failure of Respondent to fulfill the terms of a Public Reprimand with Terms certified to it by a District Committee for sanction determination.

G. *Additional Board Powers.* The Board shall have the following powers in addition to all other powers granted to the Board:

1. To sanction a Respondent for failing to comply with an order issued by the Board. This sanction can include an interim Suspension. Before imposing an interim Suspension, the Board shall issue a notice to the Respondent advising the Respondent that he or she may petition the Board within ten days after service of the notice to withhold entry of an interim Suspension order and to hold an evidentiary hearing. If ten days after service of the notice the Respondent has not petitioned the Board to withhold entry of an interim Suspension order, the Board shall enter an Order suspending the Attorney's License until such time as the Attorney remedies the failure to comply or a determination is made as to whether the Attorney has violated any Disciplinary Rules. An Attorney suspended pursuant to this subparagraph G.1. is subject to the provisions of subparagraph 13–29;

2. On its own motion or upon request by Bar Counsel or the Respondent, to summon and examine witnesses under oath or affirmation administered by any member of the Board and to compel the attendance of witnesses and the production of documents necessary or material to any proceeding. Any summons or subpoena may be issued by any Board member or the Clerk of the Disciplinary System and shall have the force of and may be enforced as a summons or subpoena issued by a Circuit Court. A subpoena duces tecum which compels the Respondent to produce documents may be served upon the Respondent by certified mail at the Respondent's last address of record for membership purposes with the Bar or, if service cannot be effected at the Respondent's last address on record, and if the Respondent is a Foreign Lawyer, a lawyer engaged *pro hac vice* in the practice of law in Virginia, or a lawyer not admitted in Virginia, when mailed by first class mail to the Clerk of the Supreme Court of Virginia.

3. To impose an interim Suspension if an Attorney fails to comply with a summons or subpoena issued by any member of the Board, the Clerk of the

Disciplinary System, Bar Counsel or any lawyer member of a District Committee for trust account, estate account, fiduciary account, operating account or other records maintained by the Attorney or the Attorney's law firm. In the event of alleged noncompliance, Bar Counsel may file with the Board and serve on the Attorney a notice of noncompliance requesting the Board to suspend the Attorney's License. The noncompliance notice must advise the Attorney that he or she may petition the Board within 10 days of service of the notice to withhold entry of a Suspension order and to hold a hearing, at which time the Attorney shall have the burden of proving good cause for the alleged noncompliance. If 10 days after service of the notice of noncompliance the Attorney has not petitioned the Board to withhold entry of an interim Suspension order, the Board shall enter an Order suspending the Attorney's License until such time as the Attorney fully complies with the summons or subpoena or a determination is made as to whether the Attorney's noncompliance violated the Disciplinary Rules. An Attorney suspended pursuant to this subparagraph G.3. is subject to the provisions of subparagraph 13–29;

4. To rule on the admissibility of evidence, through a panel Chair, which rulings may be overruled by a majority of the Panel; and

5. To act through its Chair or one of the Vice Chairs (an officer) on any non-dispositive pre-hearing matters and on any dispositive matters where all parties are in agreement, subject to the following qualification and exception: (1) any pre-hearing ruling on a non-dispositive matter made by an officer of the Board shall be subject to being overruled by a majority vote of the Panel which actually hears the matter; and (2) Agreed Dispositions must be approved by a Panel.

H. *Agreed Disposition.* Whenever Bar Counsel and Respondent are in agreement as to the disposition of a Disciplinary Proceeding, the parties may submit a proposed Agreed Disposition to five members of the Board selected by the Chair. The five members so selected will constitute a Panel. If the proposed Agreed Disposition is accepted by a majority of the Panel so selected, the Agreed Disposition will be adopted by order of the Board. If the Agreed Disposition is not accepted by the Panel, the Disciplinary Proceeding will then be set for hearing before another Panel of the Board at the earliest possible date. No member of the Panel which considered the proposed Agreed Disposition shall be assigned to the Panel which hears the Disciplinary Proceeding.

13–7. District Committees.

A. *Powers.* Each District Committee and Section thereof shall have the power to:

1. Elect a Chair, Vice Chair and Secretary, and such other officers as it considers appropriate;

2. Conduct hearings and adjudicate Charges of Misconduct as provided in this Paragraph;

3. Summon and examine witnesses under oath to be administered by any member of the District Committee;

4. Issue, through any of its Attorney members or through Bar Counsel, any summons or subpoena necessary to compel the attendance of witnesses and the production of documents or evidence necessary or material to any Investigation or Disciplinary Proceeding. Any such summons or subpoena issued to a non–Attorney shall have the force of and be enforced as a summons or subpoena issued by a Circuit Court. A subpoena duces tecum which compels the Respondent to produce documents may be served upon the Respondent by certified mail at the Respondent's last address of record for membership purposes with the Bar or, if service cannot be effected at the Respondent's last address on record, and if the Respondent is a Foreign Lawyer, a lawyer engaged *pro hac vice* in the practice of law in Virginia, or a lawyer not admitted in Virginia, when mailed by first class mail to the Clerk of the Supreme Court of Virginia.

5. Direct Bar Counsel to file a notice of noncompliance requesting the Board to suspend an Attorney's License until such time as the Attorney fully complies with a subpoena requiring production of trust account, estate account, fiduciary account, operating account or other records maintained by the Attorney or the Attorney's law firm;

6. Rule on the admissibility of evidence and other matters relating to the conduct of a Disciplinary Proceeding;

7. Rule on motions to limit or quash any summons or subpoena;

8. Maintain order in all its proceedings through its Chair; and

9. Approve, through a Subcommittee acting by a unanimous vote, an Agreed Disposition of a Complaint or Charge of Misconduct submitted by Bar Counsel and the Respondent.

B. *Creation of Subcommittees.* The Chair shall appoint one or more Subcommittees of each District Committee. Where a District Committee is divided into two or more Sections, there shall be one or more Subcommittees of each Section, as determined by the respective District Committee Section Chair. Each Subcommittee shall consist of three members of that District Committee or that Section of the District Committee. Two members of a Subcommittee shall be members of the Bar, one of whom shall be appointed by the District Committee or Section Chair to act as Chair of that Subcommittee, and one member of the Subcommittee shall be a non-lawyer member.

C. *Subcommittee Quorums.* A quorum of a Subcommittee shall consist of three members, who may act in a meeting in person or through any means of communication by which all three members participating may simultaneously hear each other during the meeting.

D. *District Committee Jurisdiction.* A District Committee shall have jurisdiction over all Complaints referred to it.

E. *Limitation on Private Discipline.* Private Discipline shall be imposed only in cases of minor Misconduct, when there is little or no injury to any of the following: a client, the public, the legal system or the profession, and when there is little likelihood of repetition by the Respondent. When any Respondent has received two determinations of Private Discipline, excepting only *de minimis* Dismissals, during any ten-year period, it shall be presumed that further Private Discipline is not an appropriate disposition. Any Respondent who has received two determinations of Private Discipline within the ten-year period immediately preceding the Bar's receipt of the oldest Complaint that the Subcommittee is considering, shall receive public discipline for any violation of the Disciplinary Rules, unless there are sufficient facts and circumstances to rebut such presumption.

F. *Venue.* Venue shall not be jurisdictional, but venue shall lie with the District Committee, in the following order of preference, where:

1. Any portion of the alleged Misconduct occurred;
2. The Respondent resides;
3. The Respondent maintains an office;
4. The Respondent has an address on record with the Bar as the Respondent's address for membership purposes; or
5. The Complainant resides.

G. *Preferred Venue.* If preferred venue does not lie with any District Committee able to adjudicate the Complaint against a Respondent, such Complaint may be filed with and adjudicated by a District Committee designated by the Clerk of the Disciplinary System. In determining to which District Committee a Complaint should be referred, the Clerk of the Disciplinary System shall consider the volume of Complaints pending before the District Committee and the inconvenience imposed upon the Respondent and the witnesses by the location of the District Committee.

H. *Objections to Venue.* Either the Respondent or Bar Counsel may object to venue by filing a notice of objection with the Clerk of the Disciplinary System within ten days of notification of the referral of the Complaint to a District Committee. Objections to venue shall be deemed waived unless made within this ten-day time period. Upon receipt of a timely filed notice of objection, the Clerk of the Disciplinary System shall forward the notice of objection to the Chair of the Board for decision.

I. *Complaints Referred to District Committee or Subcommittee.* A District Committee or Subcommittee shall consider, adjudicate and dispose of Complaints referred to the District Committee pursuant to this Paragraph. Where appropriate, the District Committee or Subcommittee shall also counsel Respondents concerning their conduct. In addition, members of a District Committee, other than nonlawyer members, may participate in the Investigation of Complaints, provided that a member participating in such Investigation shall not participate in a District Committee's consideration, adjudication and disposition of such Complaint or Charge of Misconduct.

J. *Service by a Member of the Bar and Professional Relationship.* Service by a member of the Bar on a District Committee shall be deemed to be a professional relationship within the meaning of Disciplinary Rules 1.6, 1.7, 1.9, 1.10 and 3.7. Such service shall be deemed the holding of public office within the meaning of Disciplinary Rules 1.11 and 1.12.

K. *Consent by Bar Counsel.* Consent under Disciplinary Rules 1.6, 1.7 and 1.9 shall be deemed to include Bar Counsel's consent on behalf of the Bar.

L. *Recusal or Disqualification of District Committee Members.* In the event of recusal or disqualification of so many District Committee members that the District Committee is unable to discharge its responsibilities under this Rule, the District Committee may supplement its membership with members from other District Committees to achieve a quorum. If every member of a District Committee is recused or is disqualified from considering Charges of Misconduct, the Clerk of the Disciplinary System shall assign the Charges of Misconduct to another District Committee.

13–8. Bar Counsel.

A. *Authority.* Bar Counsel shall have the authority, to the extent provided in this Paragraph and subject to the general supervision of COLD, to:

1. Initiate, investigate, present or prosecute Complaints or other Proceedings before Subcommittees, District Committees, the Board and Circuit Courts. Bar Counsel may represent the Bar in matters pending in this Court. In the course of performing such functions, Bar Counsel shall act independently and exercise prosecutorial autonomy and discretion;
2. Examine criminal history record information relating to any Attorney or former Attorney from any state or federal law enforcement agency;
3. Examine financial books and records, once a Complaint has been filed, including, without limitation, any and all escrow accounts, trust accounts, estate accounts, fiduciary accounts and operating or other accounts, maintained by the Attorney, the Attorney's law firm or any other third party organization by whom the Attorney is employed or with whom the Attorney is associated;
4. Examine the accounts described in the preceding subparagraph A.3. at any time when Bar Counsel

reasonably believes that such accounts may not be in compliance with the Disciplinary Rules. In every instance in which Bar Counsel initiates examination of accounts or issues any summons or subpoena in the conduct of an examination or an Investigation concerning accounts, other than on the basis of a Complaint against the Attorney, Bar Counsel shall file a written statement as part of the record setting forth the reasons supporting the belief that the accounts may not comply with the Disciplinary Rules. A copy of this written statement shall be served upon the Attorney who is the subject of the Investigation when an examination has begun or any summons or subpoena has been issued;

5. Issue such summons for the attendance of witnesses and subpoenae for the production of documents necessary or material to any Investigation, District Committee or Board proceeding; and

6. File a notice of noncompliance requesting the Board to suspend the Attorney's License until such time as the Attorney fully complies with a subpoena issued by the Bar Counsel, a District Committee or the Board, for the production of trust account, estate account, fiduciary account, operating account or other records maintained by the Attorney or the Attorney's law firm.

B. *Acting Bar Counsel.* In the event of disqualification or recusal of Bar Counsel in any Proceeding, the allegation of Misconduct shall be prosecuted by a District Committee member designated by the District Committee Chair if the Proceeding is before a District Committee, or by the Attorney General or his designee if the Proceeding is before the Board or a three-judge Circuit Court.

13–9. Clerk of the Disciplinary System.

A. *Current Dockets.* The Clerk of the Disciplinary System shall maintain a docket of current Attorney discipline and CRESPA matters pending before the District Committees, the Board or courts of this Commonwealth.

B. *Records Retention.* The Clerk of the Disciplinary System shall retain all Files with respect to any Disciplinary Record for a period of at least five years from the date of the final Order in the Disciplinary Proceeding that created that Disciplinary Record. The Clerk may destroy all other Files upon the expiration of one year after the Dismissal.

C. *File Destruction.* Whenever a File is destroyed, the following information shall be preserved:

1. The name and Bar identification number of Respondent;

2. The name and last known address of the Complainant;

3. The date the matter was initially received by the Bar;

4. A summary of the Complaint or allegation of Misconduct;

5. The date of the Dismissal or any sanction(s) imposed; and

6. The disposition of the matter, including the basis for Dismissal or the sanction(s) imposed.

Such summary information shall be retained for at least five years whenever the Complaint or allegation of Misconduct is dismissed with no Disciplinary Record having been created, and for at least ten years whenever a Disciplinary Record has been created, an Impairment determined, a Reinstatement Proceeding held, or a finding of Misconduct involving a CRESPA violation made.

D. *Preservation of Determinations and Orders.* The Clerk of the Disciplinary System shall preserve a copy of all District Committee Determinations and Board or court orders in which an Attorney has been found to have engaged in Misconduct, to be impaired, to have committed a violation of CRESPA or requested Reinstatement.

E. *Costs.* The Clerk of the Disciplinary System shall assess Costs against the Respondent in the following cases:

1. All cases in which a final determination of Misconduct is made by a Subcommittee, District Committee, three-judge Circuit Court, the Board or this Court;

2. All cases against a Respondent who consents to revocation;

3. All proceedings under this Paragraph in which there is a finding that a Respondent has been found guilty of a Crime;

4. All reciprocal cases under this Paragraph in which a final determination imposing discipline is made;

5. All Reinstatement cases under this Paragraph; and

6. All cases before the Board in which sanctions were imposed for violations of CRESPA and/or the Bar's CRESPA regulations.

F. *Review of Costs Assessment.* If the Respondent disagrees with the amount of Costs as calculated by the Clerk, or if the Respondent asserts that the immediate payment thereof would constitute a hardship, the Respondent may petition the Board for review within ten days of the notice assessing Costs. The Chair, upon written request of Respondent, included with his petition, may grant Respondent a hearing on the Costs issue. The decision of the Chair shall be final and nonappealable. Interest at the judgment rate shall commence on the Costs assessed 30 days after the issuance of the notice of assessment, unless otherwise prescribed by the Board. If the Respondent fails to pay the Costs and interest so assessed within 30 days of the notice of assessment or within such other time as the Board may order, then the Costs assessed and interest shall be a debt subject to collection by the Bar, and the Board shall issue an order of Suspension against the

Respondent until such time as Respondent shall pay all of the Costs and accrued interest.

G. *Public Notification of Sanctions.* The Clerk shall issue a statement to the communications media summarizing each public Admonition, Public Reprimand, Suspension or Revocation. The Clerk shall notify the following individuals and entities of each public Admonition, Public Reprimand, Suspension or Revocation:

1. The Clerk of the Supreme Court;

2. Clerks of the Circuit and District Courts in each judicial circuit in the Commonwealth where the Attorney resides or maintains an office; and

3. Disciplinary authorities for jurisdictions, federal or state, wherein it is reasonable to expect that the Attorney may be licensed.

13–10. Processing of Complaints by Bar Counsel.

A. *Review.* Bar Counsel shall review all Complaints. If, following review of a Complaint, Bar Counsel determines that the conduct questioned or alleged does not present an issue under the Disciplinary Rules, Bar Counsel shall not open an Investigation, and the Complaint shall be dismissed.

B. *No Dismissal by Complainant.* No Complaint or allegation of Misconduct shall be dismissed at any stage of the process solely upon a request by a Complainant to withdraw his or her Complaint.

C. *Summary Resolution.* Bar Counsel shall decide whether a Complaint is appropriate for an informal or abbreviated Investigation. When a Complaint involves minor allegations of Misconduct susceptible to early resolution, Bar Counsel may assign the Complaint to a staff member, a District Committee member, or use any other means practicable to speedily investigate and resolve the allegations of Misconduct. If the Complaint is resolved through this process, Bar Counsel shall then dismiss the Complaint. Such dismissal shall not become a part of the Respondent's Disciplinary Record. If Bar Counsel chooses not to proceed under this subsection, or, having elected to proceed under this subsection, the Complaint is not resolved within 90 days from the date of filing, Bar Counsel shall proceed pursuant to the following subsections.

D. *Preliminary Investigation.* A preliminary Investigation may consist of obtaining a response, in writing, from the Respondent to the Complaint and sharing the response, if any, with the Complainant, so the Complainant may have an opportunity to provide additional information.

E. *Disposition by Bar Counsel after Preliminary Investigation.* Bar Counsel may conduct a preliminary Investigation of any Complaint to determine whether it should be referred to the District Committee. Bar Counsel shall not file a Complaint with a District Committee following a preliminary Investigation when, in Bar Counsel's judgment:

1. As a matter of law, the conduct questioned or alleged does not constitute Misconduct;

2. The evidence available shows that the Respondent did not engage in the Misconduct questioned or alleged;

3. There is no credible evidence to support any allegation of Misconduct by the Respondent; or

4. The evidence available could not reasonably be expected to support any allegation of Misconduct under a clear and convincing evidentiary standard.

F. *Referral to District Committee.* Bar Counsel shall notify the District Committee Chair that a Complaint has been referred to a District Committee for investigation. Thereafter, the Complaint shall be investigated and a report thereof made to a Subcommittee.

G. *Report to Subcommittee.* When submitting an Investigative Report to the Subcommittee, Bar Counsel or Committee Counsel may also send a recommendation as to the appropriate disposition of the Complaint.

13–11. Limited Right to Discovery.

There shall be no right to discovery in connection with disciplinary matters, including matters before three-judge Circuit Courts, except:

A. Issuance of such summonses and subpoenae as are authorized; and

B. Bar Counsel shall furnish to Respondent a copy of the Investigative Report considered by the Subcommittee when the Subcommittee set the Complaint for hearing before the District Committee or certified the Complaint to the Board, with the following limitations:

1. Bar Counsel shall not be required to produce any information or document obtained in confidence from any law enforcement or disciplinary agency, or any documents that are protected by the attorney-client privilege or work product doctrine, unless attached to or referenced in the Investigative Report;

2. Bar Counsel shall not be required to reveal other communications between the Investigator and Bar Counsel, or between Bar Counsel and the Subcommittee; and

3. Bar Counsel shall make a timely disclosure to the Respondent of all known evidence that tends to negate the Misconduct of the Respondent or mitigate its severity or which, upon a finding of Misconduct, would tend to support imposition of a lesser sanction than might be otherwise imposed.

13–12. Substantial Compliance, Notice and Evidentiary Rulings, and Address Notification.

A. *Substantial Compliance.* Except where this Paragraph provides specific time deadlines, substantial compliance with the provisions hereof shall be sufficient, and no allegation of Misconduct shall be dismissed on the sole ground that any such provision has not been strictly complied with.

B. *Time Deadlines.* Where specific time deadlines are provided, such deadlines shall be jurisdictional, except when the Clerk of the Disciplinary System, Bar Counsel, a District Committee or the Board is granted specific authority herein to extend or otherwise modify any such deadline.

C. *Service.* Whenever any notice or other writing directed to the Respondent is required or permitted under this Rule, such notice or other writing shall be deemed effective and served when mailed by certified mail to the Respondent at the Respondent's last address on record for membership purposes with the Bar or, if service cannot be effected at the Respondent's last address on record, and if the Respondent is a Foreign Lawyer, a lawyer engaged *pro hac vice* in the practice of law in Virginia, or a lawyer not admitted in Virginia, when mailed by first class mail to the Clerk of the Supreme Court of Virginia.

D. *Evidentiary Rulings.* In any Disciplinary Proceeding, evidentiary rulings shall be made favoring receipt into evidence of all reasonably probative evidence to satisfy the ends of justice. The weight given such evidence received shall be commensurate with its evidentiary foundation and likely reliability.

E. *Rights of Counsel for Complainant or Witness.* Neither counsel for the Complainant, if there is one, nor counsel for any witnesses, may examine or cross-examine any witness, introduce any evidence or present any argument.

F. *Notice of Impairment Evidence.* A Respondent who intends to rely upon evidence of an Impairment in mitigation of Misconduct shall, absent good cause excusing his or her failure to do so, provide notice not less than 14 days prior to the hearing to Bar Counsel and the District Committee or Board of his or her intention to do so.

G. *English Required.* All communication with the Bar, whether written or oral, shall be in English.

13–13. Participation and Disqualification of Counsel.

A. *Attorney for Respondent.* A Respondent may be represented by a member of the Bar, or any member of the bar of any other jurisdiction while engaged pro hac vice in the practice of law in Virginia, at any time with respect to a Complaint.

B. *Signature Required by Respondent.* A Respondent must sign his or her written response to any Complaint, Charge of Misconduct or Certification.

C. *Disqualification.* An Attorney shall not represent a Respondent with respect to a Complaint or allegation of Misconduct:

1. While such Attorney is a current employee or current officer of the Bar or is a member of Council, COLD, the Board, or a District Committee;

2. For 90 days after such Attorney ceases to be an employee or officer of the Bar or a member of Council, COLD, the Board, or a District Committee;

3. At any time, after such Attorney ceases to be an employee or officer of the Bar or a member of Council, COLD, the Board, or a District Committee, if such Attorney was personally involved in the subject matter of the Complaint, allegation of Misconduct or any related matter while acting as such employee, officer or member;

4. At any time after such Attorney ceased to be a liaison from COLD to a District Committee before which the Disciplinary Proceeding involving such Complaint or Charge of Misconduct was pending during the time such Attorney was such liaison; or

5. If such Attorney is a partner or an associate of, or is a member, shareholder or has a similar relationship with an Attorney who is a current member of COLD or an officer of the Bar, or who was a member of COLD or an officer of the Bar within the previous 90 days.

6. If such Attorney is a partner or an associate of, or is a member, shareholder or has a similar relationship with an Attorney who is a current member of the Board or was a member of the Board within the previous 90 days, unless the Attorney's representation of the Respondent with respect to a Complaint or allegation of Misconduct preceded the Board member's appointment to the Board. In such cases, the Attorney may continue to represent the Respondent as follows:

a. Before a Three Judge Court in proceedings conducted pursuant to Va. Code § 54.1–3935, or any appeal therefrom;

b. Before any District Committee.

7. If such Attorney is a partner or an associate of, or is a member, shareholder or has a similar relationship with an Attorney who is a member of a District Committee, before that District Committee, or if the District Committee is divided into sections, before the District Committee section of which the Attorney's partner or associate is a member.

D. *No Imputation of Conflict.* Except as set forth in subparagraph C, there shall be no imputation of conflict that disqualifies an Attorney from representing a Respondent with respect to a Complaint or Charge of Misconduct.

13–14. Disqualification of District Committee Member or Board Member.

A. *Personal or Financial Interest.* A member or former member of a District Committee or the Board shall be disqualified from adjudicating any matter with respect to which the member has any personal or financial interest that might affect or reasonably be perceived to affect the member's ability to be impartial. The Chair shall rule on the issue of disqualification, subject to being overruled by a majority of the Panel or Subcommittee.

B. *Complaint Against a Member.* Upon the referral of any Complaint against a member or former member of a District Committee or the Board to a District Committee for Investigation, the member shall be recused from any service on the District Committee or the Board until the Dismissal of the Complaint without the imposition of any form of discipline.

C. *Imposition of Discipline.* Upon the final imposition of a Private Reprimand, a Public Reprimand, an Admonition, a Suspension or a Revocation against a member or former member of a District Committee or the Board, the member shall automatically be terminated from membership or further service on the District Committee or Board. Upon the final imposition of any other form of Attorney discipline, COLD shall have sole discretion to determine whether the member shall be terminated from membership or further service on the District Committee or the Board.

D. *Interpretation.* Unless otherwise stated, all questions of interpretation under this subparagraph 13–14 shall be decided by the tribunal before which the proceeding is pending, except that COLD shall determine discretionary termination of membership or further service.

E. *Ineligibility.* Any member or former member of a District Committee or the Board shall be ineligible to serve in a Disciplinary Proceeding in which:

1. The District Committee or Board member or any member of his or her firm is involved in any significant way with the matter on which the District Committee or Board would act;

2. The Board member or any member of the Board member's firm was serving on the District Committee that certified the matter to the Board or has otherwise acted on the matter;

3. A Judge would be required to withdraw from consideration of, or presiding over, the matter under the Canons of Judicial Conduct adopted by this Court;

4. The District Committee or Board member previously represented the Respondent; or

5. The District Committee or Board member, upon reasonable notice to the Clerk of the Disciplinary System or to the Chair presiding over a matter, disqualifies himself or herself from participation in the matter, because such member believes that he or she is unable to participate objectively in consideration of the matter or for any other reason.

13–15. Subcommittee Action.

A. *Referral.* Following receipt of the report of Investigation and Bar Counsel's recommendation, the Subcommittee may refer the matter to Bar Counsel for further Investigation.

B. *Other Actions.* Once the Investigation is complete to the Subcommittee's satisfaction, it will take one of the following actions.

1. Dismiss. It shall dismiss the Complaint when:

a. As a matter of law the conduct questioned or alleged does not constitute Misconduct; or

b. The evidence available shows that the Respondent did not engage in the Misconduct questioned or alleged, or there is no credible evidence to support any allegation of Misconduct by Respondent, or the evidence available could not reasonably be expected to support any allegation of Misconduct under a clear and convincing evidentiary standard; or

c. The Subcommittee concludes that a Dismissal *De Minimis* should be imposed; or

d. The Subcommittee concludes that a Dismissal for Exceptional Circumstances should be imposed; or

e. The action alleged to be Misconduct is protected by superseding law.

In making the determination in the preceding subparagraphs B.1.c. and B.1. d., the Subcommittee shall have access to Respondent's prior Disciplinary Record. Respondent, within ten days after the issuance of a dismissal which creates a Disciplinary Record, may request a hearing before the District Committee.

2. Impose an Admonition without Terms. In making this determination, the Subcommittee shall have access to Respondent's prior Disciplinary Record. Respondent, within ten days after the issuance of an Admonition without Terms, may request a hearing before the District Committee.

3. Certify to the Board. Certify the Complaint to the Board pursuant to this Paragraph or file a complaint in a Circuit Court, pursuant to Va. Code § 54.1–3935. Certification shall be based on a reasonable belief that the Respondent has engaged or is engaging in Misconduct that, if proved, would justify a Suspension or Revocation. In making this determination, the Subcommittee shall have access to Respondent's prior Disciplinary Record.

4. Approve an Agreed Disposition. Approve an Agreed Disposition imposing one of the following conditions or sanctions:

a. Admonition, with or without Terms; or

b. Private Reprimand, with or without Terms; or

c. Public Reprimand, with or without Terms.

5. Set the Complaint for Hearing before the District Committee. In making this determination, the Subcommittee shall have access to Respondent's prior Disciplinary Record.

C. *Vote Required for Action.* All actions taken by Subcommittees, except for approval of Agreed Dispositions, shall be by majority vote.

D. *Report of the Subcommittee.* All decisions of the Subcommittee shall be reported to the District Committee in a timely fashion.

E. *Notice of Action of the Subcommittee.* If a Subcommittee has dismissed the Complaint, the Chair shall promptly provide written notice to the Complainant, the Respondent and Bar Counsel of such Dismissal and the factual and legal basis therefor. If a Subcommittee determines to issue an Admonition with or without Terms, or a Private or Public Reprimand with or without Terms, the Chair shall promptly send the Complainant, the Respondent and Bar Counsel a copy of the Subcommittee's determination. If a Subcommittee elects to certify a Complaint to the Board, the Subcommittee Chair shall promptly mail a copy of the Certification to the Clerk of the Disciplinary System, Bar Counsel, the Respondent and the Complainant.

F. *Procedure in All Terms Cases.* If a Subcommittee imposes Terms, the Subcommittee shall specify the time period within which compliance with the Terms shall be completed. If Terms have been imposed against a Respondent, that Respondent shall deliver a certification of compliance with such Terms to Bar Counsel within the time period specified by the Subcommittee. If a Subcommittee issues an Admonition with Terms, a Private Reprimand with Terms, or a Public Reprimand with Terms based on an Agreed Disposition, the Agreed Disposition shall specify the alternative disposition to be imposed if the Terms are not complied with or if the Respondent does not certify compliance with Terms to Bar Counsel. If the Respondent does not comply with the Terms imposed or does not certify compliance with Terms to Bar Counsel within the time period specified, Bar Counsel shall serve notice requiring the Respondent to show cause why the alternative disposition should not be imposed. Such show cause proceeding shall be set for hearing before the District Committee at its next available hearing date as determined in the discretion of the District Committee Chair. The burden of proof shall be on the Respondent to show timely compliance and timely certification by clear and convincing evidence. If the District Committee determines that the Respondent failed to comply with the Terms or failed to certify compliance within the stated time period, the alternative disposition shall be imposed. Bar Counsel shall be responsible for monitoring compliance with Terms and reporting any noncompliance to the District Committee.

G. *Alternative Disposition for Public Reprimand with Terms.* The alternative disposition for a Public Reprimand with Terms shall be a Certification For Sanction Determination unless the Respondent has entered into an Agreed Disposition for the imposition of an alternative disposition of a specific period of Suspension of License.

13–16. District Committee Proceedings.

A. *Charge of Misconduct.* If the Subcommittee determines that a hearing should be held before a District Committee, Bar Counsel shall, at least 42 days prior to the date fixed for the hearing, serve upon the Respondent by certified mail the Charge of Misconduct, a copy of the Investigative Report considered by the Subcommittee and any exculpatory materials in the possession of Bar Counsel.

B. *Response by Respondent Required.* After the Respondent has been served with the Charge of Misconduct, the Respondent shall, within 21 days after service of the Charge of Misconduct:

1. File an answer to the Charge of Misconduct, which answer shall be deemed consent to the jurisdiction of the District Committee; or

2. File an answer to the Charge of Misconduct and a demand with the Clerk of the Disciplinary System that the proceedings before the District Committee be terminated and that further proceedings be conducted pursuant to Va. Code § 54.1–3935; and simultaneously provide available dates for a hearing not less than 30 nor more than 120 days from the date of the demand. Upon such demand and provision of available dates as specified above, further proceedings before the District Committee shall terminate, and Bar Counsel shall file the complaint required by Va. Code § 54.1–3935. The hearing shall be scheduled as soon as practicable. However, the 30 to 120 day time frame shall not constitute a deadline for the hearing to be held.

C. *Failure of Respondent to Respond.* If the Respondent fails to file an answer, or an answer and a demand, and provide available dates, as specified above, the Respondent shall be deemed to have consented to the jurisdiction of the District Committee.

D. *Pre–Hearing Orders.* The Chair may, *sua sponte* or upon motion of the Respondent or Bar Counsel, enter such pre-hearing order as is necessary for the orderly conduct of the hearing before the District Committee. Such order may establish time limits and:

1. Direct Bar Counsel and Respondent to provide to each other, with a copy to the Chair, a list of and copies of all exhibits proposed to be introduced at the Misconduct stage of the hearing;

2. Encourage Bar Counsel and Respondent to confer and discuss stipulations; and

3. Direct Bar Counsel and Respondent to serve on each other, with a copy to the Chair, lists setting forth the name of each witness the party intends to call.

E. *Subpoenae, Summonses and Counsel.* The Respondent may be represented by counsel. The Respondent may request Bar Counsel or the Chair of the District Committee to issue summonses or subpoenae for witnesses and documents. Requests for summonses and subpoenae shall be granted, unless, in the judgment of the Chair of the District Committee, such request is unreasonable. Either Bar Counsel or Respondent may move the District Committee to quash such summonses or subpoenae.

F. *Continuances.* Once a District Committee has scheduled a hearing, no continuance shall be granted unless in the judgment of the Chair the continuance is necessary to prevent injustice.

G. *Public Hearings.* District Committee hearings, except deliberations, shall be open to the public.

H. *Public Docket.* The Clerk's Office shall maintain a public docket of all matters set for hearing before a District Committee or certified to the Board. For every matter before a District Committee for which a Charge of Misconduct has been mailed by the Office of the Bar Counsel, the Clerk shall place it on the docket 21 days after the date of the Charge of Misconduct. For every Complaint certified to the Board by a Subcommittee, the Clerk shall place it on the docket on receipt of the statement of the certified charges from the Subcommittee.

I. *Oral Testimony and Exhibits.* Oral testimony shall be taken and preserved by a Court Reporter. All exhibits or copies thereof received in evidence or marked refused by the District Committee shall be preserved in the District Committee file on the matter.

J. *Opening Remarks by the Chair.* After swearing the Court Reporter, who thereafter shall administer oaths or affirmations to witnesses, the Chair shall make opening remarks in the presence of the Respondent and the Complainant, if present. The Chair shall also inquire of the members present whether any member has any personal or financial interest that may affect, or be reasonably perceived to affect, his or her ability to be impartial. Any member answering in the affirmative shall be excused from participation in the matter.

K. *Motion to Exclude Witnesses.* Witnesses other than the Complainant and the Respondent shall be excluded until excused from a public hearing on motion of Bar Counsel, the Respondent or the District Committee.

L. *Presentation of the Bar's Evidence.* Bar Counsel or Committee Counsel shall present witnesses and other evidence supporting the Charge of Misconduct. Respondent shall be afforded the opportunity to cross-examine the Bar's witnesses and to challenge any evidence introduced on behalf of the Bar. District Committee members may also examine witnesses offered by Bar Counsel or Committee Counsel.

M. *Presentation of the Respondent's Evidence.* Respondent shall be afforded the opportunity to present witnesses and other evidence on behalf of Respondent. Bar Counsel or Committee's Counsel shall be afforded the opportunity to cross-examine Respondent's witnesses and to challenge any evidence introduced on behalf of Respondent. District Committee members may also examine witnesses offered on behalf of Respondent.

N. *No Participation by Other Counsel.* Neither counsel for the Complainant, if there be one, nor counsel for any witness, may examine or cross-examine any witness, introduce any other evidence, or present any argument.

O. *Depositions.* Depositions may be taken only when witnesses are unavailable, in accordance with Rule 4:7(a)(4) of the Rules of this Court.

P. *Testimony by Videoconferencing and Telephone.* Testimony by videoconferencing and/or telephonic means may be utilized, if in compliance with the Rules of this Court.

Q. *Admissibility of Evidence.* The Chair shall rule on the admissibility of evidence, which rulings may be overruled by a majority of the remaining District Committee members participating in the hearing.

R. *Motion to Strike.* At the conclusion of the Bar's evidence or at the conclusion of all of the evidence, the District Committee on its own motion, or the Respondent or the Respondent's counsel may move to strike the Bar's evidence as to one or more allegations of Misconduct contained in the Charge of Misconduct. A motion to strike an allegation of Misconduct shall be sustained if the Bar has failed to introduce sufficient evidence that would under any set of circumstances support the conclusion that the Respondent engaged in the alleged Misconduct that is the subject of the motion to strike. If the Chair sustains the motion to strike an allegation of Misconduct, subject to being overruled by a majority of the remaining members of the Committee, that allegation of Misconduct shall be dismissed.

S. *Argument.* The District Committee shall afford a reasonable opportunity for argument on behalf of the Respondent and Bar Counsel on the allegations of Misconduct.

T. *Deliberations.* The District Committee members shall deliberate in private on the allegations of Misconduct. After due deliberation and consideration, the District Committee shall vote on the allegations of Misconduct.

U. *Change in District Committee Composition.* When a hearing has been adjourned for any reason and any of the members initially constituting the quorum for the hearing cannot be present, the hearing of the matter may be completed by furnishing a transcript of the subsequent proceedings conducted in one or more member's absence to any such absent member or members; or substituting another District Committee member for any absent member or members and furnishing a transcript of the prior proceedings in the matter to such substituted member or members.

V. *Show Cause for Compliance With Terms.* Any show cause proceeding involving the question of compliance with Terms shall be deemed a new hearing and not a continuation of the hearing that resulted in the imposition of Terms.

W. *Dismissal.* After due deliberation and consideration, the District Committee may dismiss the Charge of Misconduct, or any allegation thereof, as not warranting further action when in the judgment of the District Committee:

1. As a matter of law the conduct questioned or alleged does not constitute Misconduct;

2. The evidence presented shows that the Respondent did not engage in the Misconduct alleged, or there is no credible evidence to support any allegation of Misconduct by Respondent, or the evidence does not reasonably support any allegation of Misconduct under a clear and convincing evidentiary standard;

3. The action alleged to be Misconduct is protected by superseding law; or

4. The District Committee is unable to reach a decision by a majority vote of those constituting the hearing panel, the Charge of Misconduct, or any allegation thereof, shall be dismissed on the basis that the evidence does not reasonably support the Charge of Misconduct, or one or more allegations thereof, under a clear and convincing evidentiary standard.

X. *Sanctions.* If the District Committee finds that Misconduct has been shown by clear and convincing evidence, then the District Committee shall, prior to determining the appropriate sanction to be imposed, inquire whether the Respondent has been the subject of any Disciplinary Proceedings in this or any other jurisdiction and shall give Bar Counsel and the Respondent an opportunity to present material evidence in aggravation or mitigation, as well as argument. In determining what disposition of the Charge of Misconduct is warranted, the District Committee shall consider the Respondent's Disciplinary Record. A District Committee may:

1. Conclude that a Dismissal *De Minimis* should be imposed;

2. Conclude that a Dismissal for Exceptional Circumstances should be imposed;

3. Conclude that an Admonition, with or without Terms, should be imposed;

4. Issue a Public Reprimand, with or without Terms; or

5. Certify the Charge of Misconduct to the Board or file a complaint in a Circuit Court, pursuant to Va. Code § 54.1–3935.

Y. *District Committee Determinations.* If the District Committee finds that the evidence shows the Respondent engaged in Misconduct by clear and convincing evidence, then the Chair shall issue the District Committee's Determination, in writing, setting forth the following:

1. Brief findings of the facts established by the evidence;

2. The nature of the Misconduct shown by the facts so established, including the Disciplinary Rules violated by the Respondent; and

3. The sanctions imposed, if any, by the District Committee.

Z. *Notices.*

If the District Committee:

1. Issues a Dismissal, the Chair shall promptly provide written notice to the Complainant, the Respondent and Bar Counsel of such Dismissal and the factual and legal basis therefor.

2. Issues a Public Reprimand, with or without Terms; an Admonition, with or without Terms; a Dismissal *De Minimis;* or a Dismissal for Exceptional Circumstances, the Chair shall promptly send the Complainant, the Respondent and Bar Counsel a copy of the District Committee's Determination.

3. Finds that the Respondent failed to comply with the Terms imposed by the District Committee, the Chair shall notify the Complainant, the Respondent and Bar Counsel of the imposition of the alternative disposition.

4. Has elected to certify the Complaint, the Chair of the District Committee shall promptly mail to the Clerk of the Disciplinary System a copy of the Certification. A copy of the Certification shall be sent to Bar Counsel, Respondent and the Complainant.

AA. *District Committee Determination Finality and Public Statement.* Upon the expiration of the ten-day period after service on the Respondent of a District Committee Determination, if either a notice of appeal or a notice of appeal and a written demand that further Proceedings be conducted before a three-judge Circuit Court pursuant to Va. Code § 54.1–3935 has not been filed by the Respondent, the District Committee Determination shall become final, and the Clerk of the Disciplinary System shall issue a public statement as provided for in this Paragraph for the dissemination of public disciplinary information.

BB. *Enforcement of Terms.* In all cases where Terms are included in the disposition, the District Committee shall specify the time period within which compliance shall be completed and, if required, the time period within which the Respondent shall deliver a written certification of compliance to Bar Counsel. The District Committee shall specify the alternative disposition if the Terms are not complied with or, if required, compliance is not certified to Bar Counsel. Bar Counsel shall be responsible for monitoring compliance and reporting any noncompliance to the District Committee. Whenever it appears that the Respondent has not complied with the Terms imposed, including written certification of compliance if required, Bar Counsel shall serve notice requiring the

Respondent to show cause why the alternative disposition should not be imposed. Such show cause proceeding shall be set for hearing before the District Committee at its next available hearing date as determined in the discretion of the District Committee Chair. The burden of proof shall be on the Respondent to show compliance by clear and convincing evidence. If the Respondent has failed to comply with the Terms, including written certification of compliance if required, within the stated time period as determined by the District Committee, the alternative disposition shall be imposed. Any show cause proceeding involving the question of compliance shall be deemed a new matter and not a continuation of the matter that resulted in the imposition of Terms.

CC. *Alternative Disposition and Procedure for Public Reprimand with Terms.* The alternative disposition for a Public Reprimand with Terms shall be a Certification for Sanction Determination. Upon a decision to issue a Certification for Sanction Determination, Bar Counsel shall order the transcript of the show cause hearing and file it and a true copy of the Public Reprimand with Terms determination with the Clerk of the Disciplinary System.

DD. *Reconsideration of Action by the District Committee.*

1. A Charge of Misconduct dismissed by a District Committee may be reconsidered only upon:

(a) A finding by a majority vote of the Panel that heard the matter originally that material evidence not known or available when the matter was originally presented has been discovered; or

(b) A unanimous vote of the Panel that heard the matter originally.

2. No action by a District Committee imposing a sanction or certifying a matter to the Board shall be reconsidered unless a majority of the Panel that heard the matter votes to reconsider the sanction.

3. No member shall vote to reconsider a District Committee action unless it appears to such member that reconsideration is necessary to prevent an injustice or warranted by specific exceptional circumstances militating against adherence to the initial action of the District Committee.

4. District Committee members may be polled on the issue of whether to reconsider an earlier District Committee action.

5. Any reconsideration of an earlier District Committee action must occur at a District Committee meeting, whether in person or by any means of communication which allows all members participating to simultaneously hear each other.

13–17. Perfecting an Appeal of a District Committee Determination by the Respondent.

A. *Notice of Appeal; Demand.* Within ten days after service on the Respondent of the District Committee Determination, the Respondent may file with the Clerk of the Disciplinary System either a notice of appeal to the Board or a notice of appeal and a written demand that further Proceedings be conducted pursuant to Va. Code § 54.1–3935. In either case, the Respondent shall send copies to the District Committee Chair and to Bar Counsel. Upon such demand, further proceedings before the Board shall terminate, and Bar Counsel shall file the complaint required by Va. Code § 54.1–3935. The hearing shall be scheduled as soon as practicable. If the Respondent fails to file a demand, as specified above, the Respondent shall be deemed to have consented to the jurisdiction of the Board.

B. *Staying of Discipline.* If the Clerk of the Disciplinary System receives a timely notice of appeal from a Public Reprimand, with or without Terms, or an Admonition, with or without Terms, the sanction shall be stayed during the pendency of the appeal.

C. *Filing the Transcript and Record on Appeal.* The Respondent shall certify in the notice of appeal or written demand that he or she has ordered from the Court Reporter a complete transcript of the proceedings before the District Committee, at the Respondent's cost. Upon receipt of the notice of appeal or written demand, Bar Counsel shall forward those portions of the record in his or her possession to the Clerk of the Disciplinary System. The transcript is a part of the record when it is received in the office of the Clerk of the Disciplinary System within 40 days after filing of the notice of appeal or written demand. The Clerk of the Disciplinary System shall retain the records until the transcript has been received or for 40 days after the notice of appeal or written demand has been received, whichever occurs first, and shall then dispose of the record as prescribed in the records retention policy set forth in this Paragraph. Failure of the Respondent to make the complete transcript a part of the Record as specified herein shall result in Dismissal of the appeal by the Board, whether initiated by notice of appeal or written demand, and affirmance of the sanction imposed by the District Committee. Bar Counsel shall initiate the three-judge Circuit Court process for the appeal only after receipt of the transcript by the Clerk of the Disciplinary System.

D. *Appeal to a Circuit Court.* An appeal to a Circuit Court pursuant to Va. Code § 54.1–3935 shall be conducted before a duly convened three-judge Circuit Court as an appeal on the record using the same procedure prescribed for an appeal of a District Committee Determination before the Board under this Paragraph. The Clerk of the Disciplinary System shall forward the record to the clerk of the designated Circuit Court only upon receipt of the transcript as provided in the preceding subparagraph C.

E. *Appeal From Agreed Sanction Prohibited.* No appeal shall lie from any sanction to which the Respondent has agreed.

13–18. Board Proceedings Upon Certification.

A. *Filing by Respondent.* After a Subcommittee or District Committee certifies a matter to the Board, and the Respondent has been served with the Certification, the Respondent shall, within 21 days after service of the Certification:

1. File an answer to the Certification with the Clerk of the Disciplinary System, which answer shall be deemed consent to the jurisdiction of the Board; or file an answer to the Certification and a demand with the Clerk of the Disciplinary System that the proceedings before the Board be terminated and that further proceedings be conducted pursuant to Va. Code § 54.1–3935; and simultaneously provide available dates for a hearing not less than 30 nor more than 120 days from the date of the demand.

2. Upon such demand and provision of available dates as specified above, further proceedings before the Board shall terminate, and Bar Counsel shall file the complaint required by Va. Code § 54.1–3935. The hearing shall be scheduled as soon as practicable. However, the 30 to 120 day time frame shall not constitute a deadline for the hearing to be held.

B. *No Filing by Respondent.* If the Respondent fails to file an answer, or an answer and a demand, and provide available dates, as specified above, the Respondent shall be deemed to have consented to the jurisdiction of the Board.

C. *Notice of Hearing.* The Board shall set a date, time, and place for the hearing, and shall serve notice of such hearing upon the Respondent at least 21 days prior to the date fixed for the hearing.

D. *Expedited Hearings.*

1. If Bar Counsel or a District Committee Chair has reasonable cause to believe that an Attorney is engaging in Misconduct which is likely to result in injury to, or loss of property of, one or more of the Attorney's clients or any other person, and that the continued practice of law by the Attorney poses an imminent danger to the public, Bar Counsel or the District Committee Chair may petition the Board to issue an order requiring the Attorney to appear before the Board for a hearing in accordance with the procedures set forth below.

2. The petition shall be under oath and shall set forth the nature of the alleged Misconduct, the factual basis for the belief that immediate action by the Board is reasonable and necessary and any other facts which may be relevant to the Board's consideration of the matter, including any prior Disciplinary Record of the Attorney.

3. Upon receipt of the petition, the Chair or Vice–Chair of the Board shall issue an order requiring the Respondent to appear before the Board not less than 14 nor more than 30 days from the date of the order for a hearing to determine whether the Misconduct has occurred and the imposition of sanctions is appropriate. The Board's order shall be served on the Respondent no fewer than ten days prior to the date set for hearing.

4. If the Respondent, at the time the petition is received by the Board, is the subject of an order then in effect by a Circuit Court pursuant to Va. Code § 54.1–3936 appointing a receiver for his accounts, the Board shall issue a further order summarily suspending the License of the Respondent until the Board enters its order following the expedited hearing.

5. At least five days prior to the date set for hearing, the Respondent shall either file an answer to the petition with the Clerk of the Disciplinary System, which answer shall be conclusively deemed consent to the jurisdiction of the Board; or file an answer and a demand with the Clerk of the Disciplinary System that proceedings before the Board be terminated and that further proceedings be conducted pursuant to Va. Code § 54.1–3935; and simultaneously provide available dates for a hearing not less than 30 days nor more than 120 days from the date of the Board order. Upon such demand and provision of available dates as specified above, further proceedings before the Board shall be terminated and Bar Counsel shall file the complaint required by Va. Code § 54.1–3935. The hearing shall be scheduled as soon as practicable. However, the 30 to 120 day time frame shall not constitute a deadline for the hearing to be held. If any order of summary Suspension has been entered, such Suspension shall remain in effect until the court designated under Va. Code § 54.1–3935 enters a final order disposing of the issue before it. If the Respondent fails to file an answer, or an answer and a demand, and provide available dates, as specified above, the Respondent shall be deemed to have consented to the jurisdiction of the Board.

E. *Pre–Hearing Orders.* The Chair may, *sua sponte* or upon motion of the Respondent or Bar Counsel, enter such pre-hearing order as is necessary for the orderly conduct of the hearing before the Board in Misconduct cases. Such order may establish time limits and:

1. Direct Bar Counsel and the Respondent to provide to each other, with a copy to the Clerk of the Disciplinary System, a list of and copies of all exhibits proposed to be introduced at the Misconduct stage of the hearing;

2. Encourage Bar Counsel and the Respondent to confer and discuss stipulations; and

3. Direct Bar Counsel and the Respondent to provide to each other, with a copy to the Clerk of the Disciplinary System, lists setting forth the name of each witness the party intends to call.

F. *Continuance of a Hearing.* Absent exceptional circumstances, once the Board has scheduled a hearing, no continuance shall be granted unless, in the judgment of the Chair, the continuance is necessary to prevent injustice. No continuance will be granted because of a conflict with the schedule of the Respondent or the Respondent's counsel unless such continuance is requested in writing by the Respondent or the Respondent's counsel within 14 days after mailing of a notice of hearing. Any request for a continuance shall be filed with the Clerk of the Disciplinary System.

G. *Preliminary Explanation.* The Chair shall state in the presence of the Respondent and the Complainant, if present, a summary of the alleged Misconduct, the nature and purpose of the hearing, the procedures to be followed during the hearing, and the dispositions available to the Board following the hearing. The Chair shall also inquire of the members present whether any member has any personal or financial interest that may affect, or be reasonably perceived to affect, his or her ability to be impartial. Any member answering in the affirmative shall be excused from participation in the matter.

H. *Attendance at Hearing.* Witnesses other than the Complainant and the Respondent shall be excluded until excused from a public hearing on motion of Bar Counsel, the Respondent or the Board.

I. *Order of Hearing.*

1. Brief opening statements by Bar Counsel and by the Respondent or the Respondent's counsel shall be permitted but are not required.

2. Bar Counsel shall present witnesses and other evidence supporting the Certification. The Respondent shall be afforded the opportunity to cross-examine the Bar's witnesses and to challenge any evidence introduced on behalf of the Bar. Board members may also examine witnesses offered by Bar Counsel.

3. Respondent shall be afforded the opportunity to present witnesses and other evidence. Bar Counsel shall be afforded the opportunity to cross-examine Respondent's witnesses and to challenge any evidence introduced on behalf of Respondent. Board members may also examine witnesses offered on behalf of a Respondent.

4. Bar Counsel may rebut the Respondent's evidence.

5. Bar Counsel may make the initial closing argument.

6. The Respondent or the Respondent's counsel may then make a closing argument.

7. Bar Counsel may then make a rebuttal closing argument.

J. *Motion to Strike.* At the conclusion of the Bar's evidence or at the conclusion of all the evidence, the Board on its own motion, or the Respondent or the Respondent's counsel, may move to strike the Bar's evidence as to one or more allegations of Misconduct contained in the Certification. A motion to strike an allegation of Misconduct shall be sustained if the Bar has failed to introduce sufficient evidence that would under any set of circumstances support the conclusion that the Respondent engaged in the alleged Misconduct that is the subject of the motion to strike. If the Chair sustains the motion to strike an allegation of Misconduct, subject to being overruled by a majority of the remaining members of the Board, that allegation of Misconduct shall be dismissed from the Certification.

K. *Deliberations.* As soon as practicable after the conclusion of the evidence and arguments as to the issue of Misconduct, the Board shall deliberate in private. If the Board finds by clear and convincing evidence that the Respondent has engaged in Misconduct, the Board shall, prior to determining the appropriate sanction to be imposed, inquire whether the Respondent has been the subject of any Disciplinary Proceeding in this or any other jurisdiction and shall give Bar Counsel and the Respondent an opportunity to present material evidence and arguments in aggravation or mitigation. The Board shall deliberate in private on the issue of sanctions. The Board may address any legal questions to the Office of the Attorney General.

L. *Dismissal for Failure of the Evidence.* If the Board concludes that the evidence fails to show under a clear and convincing evidentiary standard that the Respondent engaged in the Misconduct, the Board shall dismiss any allegation of Misconduct not so proven.

M. *Disposition Upon a Finding of Misconduct.* If the Board concludes that there has been presented clear and convincing evidence that the Respondent has engaged in Misconduct, after considering evidence and arguments in aggravation and mitigation, the Board shall impose one of the following sanctions and state the effective date of the sanction imposed:

1. Admonition, with or without Terms;
2. Public Reprimand, with or without Terms;
3. Suspension of the License of the Respondent for a stated period not exceeding five years; provided, however, if the Suspension is for more than one year, the Respondent must apply for Reinstatement as provided in this Paragraph; or
4. Revocation of the Respondent's License.

N. *Dismissal for Failure to Reach a Majority Decision.* If the Board is unable to reach a decision by a majority vote of those constituting the hearing panel, the Certification, or any allegation thereof, shall be dismissed on the basis that the evidence does not reasonably support the Certification, or one or more allegations thereof, under a clear and convincing evidentiary standard.

O. *Enforcement of Terms.* In all cases where Terms are included in the disposition, the Board shall specify the time period within which compliance shall be completed and, if required, the time period within which the Respondent shall deliver a written certification of compliance to Bar Counsel. The Board shall specify the alternative disposition if the Terms are not complied with or, if required, compliance is not certified to Bar Counsel. Bar Counsel shall be responsible for monitoring compliance and reporting any noncompliance to the Board. Whenever it appears that the Respondent has not complied with the Terms imposed, including written certification of compliance if required, Bar Counsel shall serve notice requiring the Respondent to show cause why the alternative disposition should not be imposed. Such show cause proceeding shall be set for hearing before the Board at its next available hearing date. The burden of proof shall be on the Respondent to show compliance by clear and convincing evidence. If the Respondent has failed to comply with the Terms, including written certification of compliance if required, within the stated time period, as determined by the Board, the alternative disposition shall be imposed. Any show cause proceeding involving the question of compliance shall be deemed a new matter and not a continuation of the matter that resulted in the imposition of Terms.

P. *Orders, Findings and Opinions.* Upon disposition of a matter, the Board shall issue the Summary Order. Thereafter, the Board shall issue the Memorandum Order. A Board member shall prepare the Summary Order and Memorandum Order for the signature of the Chair or the Chair's designee. Dissenting opinions may be filed.

Q. *Change in Composition of Board Hearing Panel.* Whenever a hearing has been adjourned for any reason and one or more of the members initially constituting the quorum for the hearing are unable to be present, the hearing of the matter may be completed by furnishing a transcript of the subsequent proceedings conducted in one or more member's absence to such absent member, or substituting another Board member for any absent member and furnishing a transcript of the prior proceedings in the matter to such substituted member(s).

R. *Reconsideration of Board Action.* No motion for reconsideration or modification of the Board's decision shall be considered unless it is filed with the Clerk of the Disciplinary System within 10 days after the hearing before the Board. The moving party shall file an original and six copies of both the motion and all supporting exhibits with the Clerk of the Disciplinary System. Such motion shall be granted only to prevent manifest injustice upon the ground of:

1. Illness, injury or accident which prevented the Respondent or a witness from attending the hearing and which could not have been made known to the Board within a reasonable time prior to the hearing; or

2. Evidence which was not known to the Respondent at the time of the hearing and could not have been discovered prior to, or produced at, the hearing in the exercise of due diligence and would have clearly produced a different result if the evidence had been introduced at the hearing.

3. If such a motion is timely filed, the Clerk of the Disciplinary System shall promptly forward copies to each member of the hearing panel. The panel may deny the motion without response from Bar Counsel. No relief shall be granted without allowing Bar Counsel an opportunity to oppose the motion in writing. If no relief is granted, the Board shall enter its order disposing of the case.

13–19. Board Proceedings Upon Appeal.

A. *Docketing an Appeal.* Upon receipt of notice from the Clerk of the Disciplinary System that a Respondent has filed an appeal from a District Committee Determination the Board shall place such matter on its docket for review.

B. *Notice to the Appellant.* The Clerk of the Disciplinary System shall notify the appellant when the entire record of the Proceeding before the District Committee has been received or when the time for appeal has expired.

C. *Record on Appeal.* The record shall consist of the Charge of Misconduct, the complete transcript of the Proceeding, any exhibits received or refused by the District Committee, the District Committee Determination, and all briefs, memoranda or other papers filed with the District Committee by the Respondent or the Bar. Upon petition of the Respondent, for good cause shown, the Board may permit the record to be supplemented to prevent injustice, such supplement to be in such form as the Board may deem appropriate.

D. *Briefing.* Thereafter, briefs shall be filed in the office of the Clerk of the Disciplinary System, as follows:

1. The appellant shall file an opening brief within 40 days after the mailing of the notice to the appellant regarding the record by the Clerk of the Disciplinary System. Failure of the appellant to file an opening brief within the time specified herein shall result in the Dismissal of the appeal and affirmance of the decision by the District Committee.

2. The appellee shall file its brief within 25 days after filing of the opening brief.

3. The appellant may file a reply brief within 14 days after filing of the appellee's brief.

E. *Standard of Review.* In reviewing a District Committee Determination, the Board shall ascertain whether there is substantial evidence in the record upon which the District Committee could reasonably have found as it did.

F. *Oral Argument.* Oral argument shall be granted, unless waived by the appellant.

G. *Imposition of Sanctions.* Upon review of the record in its entirety, the Board may:

1. Dismiss the Charge of Misconduct upon a finding that the District Committee Determination is

contrary to the law or is not supported by substantial evidence;

2. Affirm the District Committee Determination, in which instance the Board may impose the same or any lesser sanction as that imposed by the District Committee. In no case shall it increase the severity of the sanction imposed by the District Committee; or

3. Reverse the decision of the District Committee and remand the Charge of Misconduct to the District Committee for further proceedings.

13–20. Board Proceedings Upon Certification for Sanction Determination.

A. *Initiation of Proceedings.* Upon receipt of the Certification for Sanction Determination from a District Committee, the Clerk of the Disciplinary System shall issue a notice of hearing on the Certification for Sanction Determination giving Respondent the date, time and place of the Proceeding and a copy of the Certification for Sanction Determination.

B. *Proceedings Upon the Record.* The proceeding shall be conducted upon the record which shall consist of the Public Reprimand with Terms determination issued by either a Subcommittee or a District Committee, the transcript of the District Committee show cause hearing, and the Certification for Sanction Determination.

C. *Evidence.* Evidence only of mitigation and aggravation with respect to compliance or certification shall be permitted in the proceeding.

D. *Argument.* Argument shall be conducted as in the sanction phase of a Misconduct case.

E. *Sanctions.* The Board may impose a sanction of Suspension or Revocation of License.

13–21. Board Proceedings Upon a First Offender Plea.

A. *Action Upon Receipt of Notification.* Whenever the Clerk of the Disciplinary System receives written notification from any court of competent jurisdiction stating that an Attorney has entered a plea to a Crime under a first offender statute, and that the court has found facts that would justify a finding of guilt and ordered that the Attorney be put on probation, the Board shall forthwith enter an order requiring the Attorney to appear at a specified time and place for a hearing before the Board to determine whether the Attorney's License should be revoked or suspended or, if not, whether the Attorney should be required to give notice, by certified mail, of the plea and probation ordered by the court, including the terms and duration of the probation, to all clients for whom the Attorney is currently handling matters, and to all opposing attorneys and the presiding judges in pending litigation. A copy of the written notification from the court shall be served with the order fixing the time and place of the hearing. The hearing shall be set not less than 14 or more than 30 days after the date of the Board's order.

B. *Burden of Proof.* At the hearing, the Attorney shall have the burden of proving why his or her License should not be suspended or revoked and why he or she should not be required to give notice of the plea and probation ordered by the court.

C. *Demand for Three Judge Court.* If the Attorney elects to have further proceedings conducted pursuant to Va. Code § 54.1–3935, the Attorney shall file a demand with the Clerk of the Disciplinary System not later than ten days prior to the date set for the Board hearing, and simultaneously provide available dates for a hearing not less than 30 nor more than 120 days from the date of the demand. Upon such demand and provision of available dates as specified above, further proceedings before the Board shall be terminated and Bar Counsel shall file the complaint required by Va. Code § 54.1–3935. The hearing shall be scheduled as soon as practicable. However, the 30 to 120 day time frame shall not constitute a deadline for the hearing to be held. If the Respondent fails to file a demand, and provide available dates, as specified above, the Respondent shall be deemed to have consented to the jurisdiction of the Board.

D. *Attorney Compliance With Notice Requirements.* If the Board or court suspends or revokes the Attorney's License to practice law, the Attorney must comply with the notice requirements set out in subparagraph 13–29. If the Board or court orders the Attorney to give notice of the plea and court ordered probation, the Attorney shall give such notice within 14 days after the effective date of the Board's order and furnish proof to the Bar within 60 days of the effective date of the order that such notices have been timely given. Issues concerning the adequacy of the notice shall be determined by the Board, which may suspend or revoke the Attorney for failure to comply with the above notice requirements.

13–22. Board Proceedings Upon a Guilty Plea or an Adjudication of a Crime.

A. *Action Upon Receipt of Notification.* Whenever the Clerk of the Disciplinary System receives written notification from any court of competent jurisdiction stating that an Attorney (the "Respondent") has been found guilty or convicted of a Crime by a Judge or jury, pled guilty to a Crime or entered a plea wherein the facts found by a court would justify a finding of guilt, irrespective of whether sentencing has occurred, a member of the Board shall forthwith and summarily enter an order of Suspension requiring the Respondent to appear at a specified time and place for a hearing before the Board to show cause why the Respondent's License to practice law should not be further suspended or revoked. A copy of the written notification from the court shall be served upon the Respondent with the Board's order of Suspension.

B. *Time of Hearing, Continuance and Interim Hearing.* The hearing shall be set not less than 14 or more than 30 days after the date of the Board's order.

Upon written request of the Respondent, the hearing may be continued until any probation ordered by a court has ended or after sentencing has occurred. Upon receipt by the Board of a certified copy of a notice of appeal from the conviction, proceedings before the Board shall, upon request of the Respondent, be continued pending disposition of such appeal. The Board shall, upon request of the Respondent, hold an interim hearing and shall terminate such Suspension while the probation, sentencing, or appeal is pending, if the Board finds that such Suspension, if not terminated, would be likely to exceed the discipline imposed by the Board upon a hearing on the merits of the case.

C. *Reversal of Conviction.* Upon presentation to the Board of a certified copy of an order setting aside the verdict or reversing the conviction on appeal, any Suspension shall be automatically terminated and any Revocation shall be vacated, and the License shall be deemed automatically reinstated. Discharge or Dismissal of a guilty plea or termination of probation shall not result in the automatic termination of the Suspension or vacation of the Revocation. Nothing herein shall preclude further proceedings against the Respondent upon allegations of Misconduct arising from the facts leading to such conviction.

D. *Burden of Proof.* At the hearing, the Respondent shall have the burden of proving why his or her License should not be further suspended or revoked.

E. *Action by the Board and Notice to Respondent.* If the Board finds at the hearing that the Respondent has been found guilty or convicted of a Crime by a Judge or jury, pled guilty to a Crime or entered a plea wherein the facts found by a court would justify a finding of guilt, an order shall be issued, and a copy thereof served upon the Respondent in which the Board shall continue the Suspension or issue an order of Suspension against the Respondent for a stated period not in excess of five years; or issue an order of Revocation against the Respondent.

F. *Procedure.* The procedure applicable to Proceedings related to Misconduct shall apply to Proceedings relating to guilty pleas or Adjudication of a Crime. If the Respondent elects to have further Proceedings conducted pursuant to Va. Code § 54.1–3935, the Respondent shall file a demand with the Clerk of the Disciplinary System not later than ten days prior to the date set for the hearing before the Board, and simultaneously provide available dates for a hearing not less than 30 nor more than 120 days from the date of the demand. Upon such demand and provision of available dates as specified above, further proceedings before the Board shall be terminated and Bar Counsel shall file the complaint required by Va. Code § 54.1–3935. The hearing shall be scheduled as soon as practicable. However, the 30 to 120 day time frame shall not constitute a deadline for the hearing to be held. The order of Suspension issued by the Board shall remain in effect until the court designated under Va. Code § 54.1–3935 enters a final order disposing of the issue before it. If the Respondent fails to file a demand, and provide available dates, as specified above, the Respondent shall be deemed to have consented to the jurisdiction of the Board.

13–23. Board Proceedings Upon Impairment.

A. *Suspension for Impairment.* The Board shall have the power to issue an order of Suspension to a Respondent who has an Impairment. The term of such Suspension shall be indefinite and, except as provided below, shall be terminated only upon determination by the Board that Respondent no longer has the Impairment. A Respondent who intends to rely upon evidence of an Impairment in mitigation of Misconduct shall, absent good cause excusing his or her failure to do so, provide notice not less than 14 days prior to the hearing to Bar Counsel and the District Committee or Board of his or her intention to do so. A finding of Impairment may be utilized by Bar Counsel to dismiss any pending Complaints or allegations of Misconduct on the basis of the existence of exceptional circumstances militating against further proceedings, which circumstances of Impairment shall be set forth in the Dismissal.

B. *Burden of Proof.* Whenever the existence of an Impairment is alleged in a Proceeding under this Rule or in mitigation of allegations of Misconduct, the burden of proving such an Impairment shall rest with the party asserting its existence. The issue of the existence of an Attorney's Impairment may be raised by any person at any time, and if a District Committee or the Board, during the course of a hearing on allegations of Misconduct against a Respondent, believes that the Respondent may then have an Impairment, the District Committee or the Board may postpone the hearing and initiate an Impairment Proceeding under this Rule. In Proceedings to terminate a Suspension for Impairment, the burden of proving the termination of an Impairment shall be on the Respondent.

C. *Investigation.* Upon receipt of notice or evidence that an Attorney has or may have an Impairment, Bar Counsel shall cause an Investigation to be made to determine whether there is reason to believe that the Respondent has the Impairment. As a part of the Investigation of whether an Impairment exists, and for good cause shown in the interest of public protection Bar Counsel may petition the Board to order the Respondent:

1. To undergo a psychiatric, physical or other medical examination by qualified physicians or other health care provider selected by the Board; and

2. To provide appropriate releases to health care providers authorizing the release of Respondent's psychiatric, physical or other medical records to Bar Counsel and the Board for purposes of the Investigation and any subsequent Impairment proceedings.

Upon notice to the Respondent, the Board shall hold a hearing to determine whether any such examination or release is appropriate.

D. *Summary Suspension.* Upon receipt of a notice from the Clerk of the Disciplinary System with supporting documentary evidence that an Attorney has been adjudicated by a court of competent jurisdiction to have an Impairment, or that an Attorney has been involuntarily admitted to a hospital (as defined in Va. Code § 37.1–1) for treatment of any addiction, inebriety, insanity or mental illness, any member of the Board shall summarily issue on behalf of the Board an order of Suspension against the Respondent and cause the order to be served on such Respondent.

E. *Action by Board after a Hearing.*

1. If Bar Counsel determines that there is reason to believe that an Attorney has an Impairment, Bar Counsel shall file a petition with the Board, and the Board shall promptly hold a hearing to determine whether such Impairment exists. A copy of the petition shall be served on the Respondent. If the Board determines that an Impairment exists, it shall enter an order of Suspension.

2. The Board shall hold a hearing upon petition of a Respondent who is subject to a Suspension for Impairment that alleges that the Impairment no longer exists. Evidence that the Respondent is no longer hospitalized shall not be conclusive to the Board's determination of the Respondent's ability to resume the practice of law.

F. *Procedure.* Such hearing shall be conducted substantially in accordance with the procedures established in proceedings related to Misconduct, except that the public and witnesses, other than the Complainant and the Respondent, shall be excluded throughout an Impairment Proceeding when not testifying.

G. *Guardian Ad Litem.* The notice of any hearing to determine whether the Respondent has an Impairment shall order Respondent to advise the Board whether Respondent has retained counsel for the hearing. Unless counsel for such Respondent enters an appearance with the Board within ten days of the date of the notice, the Board shall appoint a guardian *ad litem* to represent such Respondent at the hearing.

H. *Examination.* Following a psychiatric, physical or other medical examination, written reports of the results of such examination, along with written reports from other qualified physicians or other health care providers who have examined Respondent, may be considered as evidence by the Board. Such reports shall be filed with the Clerk of the Disciplinary System.

I. *Termination of Suspension.* In cases where a Suspension is based upon an adjudication of an Impairment by a court, upon receipt of documentary evidence of adjudication by a court of competent jurisdiction that the Respondent's Impairment has terminated, the Board shall promptly enter an order terminating such Suspension.

J. *Enforcement.* The Board shall have the power to sanction an Attorney for failure to comply with its orders and subpoenae issued in connection with an Impairment Proceeding. The sanction can include a summary Suspension in a case where it is determined that the public and/or the clients of the Attorney are in jeopardy; such action can be *sua sponte* or on motion by Bar Counsel, with appropriate notice to the Attorney and the Attorney's counsel or guardian *ad litem*.

13–24. Board Proceedings Upon Disbarment, Revocation or Suspension in Another Jurisdiction.

A. *Initiation of Proceedings.* Upon receipt of a notice from the Clerk of the Disciplinary System that another jurisdiction has suspended or revoked the License of the Respondent and that such action has become final (the "Suspension or Revocation Notice"), any Board member shall enter on behalf of the Board an order of Suspension against such Respondent to show cause why the same discipline imposed in the other jurisdiction should not be imposed by the Board. The Board shall serve upon such Respondent by certified mail: a copy of the Suspension or Revocation Notice; a copy of the Board's order; and a notice fixing the date, time and place of the hearing before the Board to determine what action should be taken in response to the Suspension or Revocation Notice and stating that the purpose of the hearing is to provide Respondent an opportunity to show cause why the same discipline that was imposed in the other jurisdiction should not be imposed by the Board.

B. *Opportunity for Response.* Within 14 days of the date of mailing of the Board order, via certified mail, return receipt requested, to the last address of record of the Respondent with the Bar, Respondent shall file with the Clerk of the Disciplinary System an original and six copies of any written response and any communications or other materials, which shall be confined to allegations that:

1. The record of the proceeding in the other jurisdiction would clearly show that such proceeding was so lacking in notice or opportunity to be heard as to constitute a denial of due process;

2. The imposition by the Board of the same discipline upon the same proof would result in a grave injustice; or

3. The same conduct would not be grounds for disciplinary action or for the same discipline in Virginia.

C. *Scheduling and Continuance of Hearing.* Unless continued by the Board for good cause, the hearing shall be set not less than 21 nor more than 30 days after the date of the Board's order of Suspension.

D. *Provision of Copies.* The Clerk of the Disciplinary System shall furnish to the Board members designated for the hearing and make available to

Respondent copies of the Suspension or Revocation Notice, the Board's order of Suspension against the Respondent, the notice of hearing, any notice of continuance of the hearing, and any response or materials filed by Respondent.

E. *Hearing Procedures.* Insofar as applicable, the procedures for Proceedings on allegations of Misconduct shall govern Proceedings under this subparagraph 13–24.

F. *Burden of Proof.* The Respondent shall have the burden of proof, by a clear and convincing evidentiary standard, and the burden of producing the Record upon which the Respondent relies to support the Respondent's contentions, and shall be limited at the hearing to proof of the specific contentions raised in any written response. Except to the extent the allegations of the written response are established, the findings in the other jurisdiction shall be conclusive of all matters for purposes of the Proceeding before the Board.

G. *Action by the Board.* If Respondent has not filed a timely written response, or does not appear at the hearing or if the Board, after a hearing, determines that the Respondent has failed to establish the contentions of the written response by clear and convincing evidence, the Board shall impose the same discipline as was imposed in the other jurisdiction. If the Board determines that the Respondent has established such contentions by clear and convincing evidence, the Board may dismiss the proceeding or impose a lesser discipline than was imposed in the other jurisdiction. A copy of any order imposing discipline shall be served upon the Respondent via certified mail, return receipt requested. Any such order shall be final and binding, subject only to appeal as provided in this Paragraph.

13–25. Board Proceedings for Reinstatement.

A. *Waiver of Confidentiality.* The filing by a former Attorney of a petition for Reinstatement shall constitute a waiver of all confidentiality relating to the petition, and to the Complaint or Complaints that resulted in, or were pending at, the time the former Attorney resigned or his or her License was revoked.

B. *Readmission After Resignation.* If after resigning from the Bar, a former Attorney wishes to resume practicing law in the Commonwealth of Virginia, the former Attorney must apply to the Board of Bar Examiners, satisfy the character and fitness requirements and pass the Bar examination. Before being readmitted to the Bar, the former Attorney must also satisfy any membership obligations that were delinquent when the former Attorney resigned.

C. *Petition for Reinstatement After Revocation.* After a Revocation, a Petitioner may petition this Court for Reinstatement, setting forth in that petition the reasons why his or her License should be reinstated. The following requirements shall apply: the petition shall be filed under oath or affirmation with penalty of perjury; no petition may be filed sooner than five years from the effective date of the Revocation; and the Petitioner must certify in the petition that he or she has met the requirements of the following subparagraph D. This Court may deny the petition or refer it to the Board for recommendation, together with the record before the clerk of this Court. The Board may recommend approval or disapproval of the petition. Final action on the petition shall be taken by this Court.

D. *Evidence Required for Reinstatement After Revocation.* After a Revocation, Petitioner's License shall not be reinstated unless the Petitioner proves by clear and convincing evidence that Petitioner:

1. Within five years prior to filing the petition has attended 60 hours of continuing legal education, of which at least ten hours shall be in the area of legal ethics or professionalism;

2. Has taken the Multistate Professional Responsibility Examination and received a scaled score of 85 or higher;

3. Has reimbursed the Bar's Clients' Protection Fund for any sums of money it may have paid as a result of Petitioner's Misconduct;

4. Has paid the Bar all Costs that have been previously assessed against Petitioner, together with any interest due thereon at the judgment rate;

5. Has reimbursed the Bar for any sums of money it may have paid as a result of a receivership involving Petitioner's law practice; and

6. Is a person of honest demeanor and good moral character and possesses the requisite fitness to practice law.

Upon consideration whereof, it is ordered that the Rules for Integration of the Virginia State Bar, Part Six of the Rules of Court, be and the same hereby are amended in accordance with the prayer of the petition aforesaid, effective immediately.

E. *Bond Required for Reinstatement After Revocation.* The Petitioner shall post with his or her petition for Reinstatement a $5,000 cash bond for payment of Costs resulting from the Reinstatement Proceedings.

F. *Determination of Costs for Reinstatement After Revocation.* At the conclusion of the Reinstatement Proceeding, the Board or the Clerk of the Disciplinary System shall determine the Costs associated with such proceeding and submit that determination to the clerk of this Court as part of the Board's findings of fact.

G. *Additional Requirements After Approval of Petition.* Upon approval of a petition by this Court, the Petitioner shall meet the following requirements prior to and as a condition of his or her Reinstatement:

1. Pay to the Bar any Costs assessed in connection with the Reinstatement Proceeding;

2. Take and pass the written portion of the Virginia State Bar examination;

3. If required by the Board, obtain and maintain a professional liability insurance policy issued by a company authorized to write such insurance in Virginia at the cost of the Petitioner in an amount and for such term as set by the Board; and

4. If required by the Board, obtain and maintain a blanket fidelity bond or dishonesty insurance policy issued by a company authorized to write such bonds or insurance in Virginia at the Petitioner's cost in an amount and for such term as set by the Board.

H. *Reinstatement After Disciplinary Suspension for More than One Year.* After a Suspension for more than one year, the License of the Attorney subject to the Suspension shall not be reinstated unless the Attorney demonstrates to the Board that he or she has:

1. Attended 12 hours of continuing legal education, of which at least two hours shall be in the area of legal ethics or professionalism, for every year or fraction thereof of the Suspension;

2. Taken the Multistate Professional Responsibility Examination since imposition of discipline and received a scaled score of 85 or higher;

3. Reimbursed the Bar's Clients' Protection Fund for any sums of money it may have paid as a result of the Attorney's Misconduct;

4. Paid to the Bar all Costs that have been assessed against him or her, together with any interest due thereon at the judgment rate at the time the Costs are paid; and

5. Reimbursed the Bar for any sums of money it may have paid as a result of a receivership involving Petitioner's law practice.

I. *Investigation of Impairment in Reinstatement Matters.* Upon receipt of notice or evidence that an individual seeking Reinstatement has or may have an Impairment, Bar Counsel shall cause an Investigation to be made to determine whether there is reason to believe that the Impairment exists. As part of the Investigation of whether an Impairment exists, and for good cause shown in the interest of public protection, Bar Counsel may petition the Board to order the individual:

1. To undergo at his or her expense a psychiatric, physical or other medical examination by a qualified physician or other health care provider selected by the Board; and

2. To provide appropriate releases to health care providers authorizing the release of his or her psychiatric, physical or other medical records to Bar Counsel and the Board for purposes of the Investigation and any subsequent Reinstatement Proceedings.

The Board shall hold a hearing to determine whether such examination(s) and releases(s) are appropriate, upon notice to the individual petitioning for Reinstatement.

J. *Reinstatement Hearings.* The Clerk of the Disciplinary System shall advise the Petitioner in writing upon receipt of a petition for Reinstatement from the clerk of this Court and arrange a hearing date with the Petitioner and Bar Counsel.

1. **Quorum.** A quorum shall be five members of the Board.

2. **Powers of the Board in Reinstatement Cases.** The Board is empowered to hold a hearing and make its recommendation to this Court either to approve or disapprove the petition.

3. **Hearing Date.** The date of the hearing shall be determined by the Chair. Upon the scheduling of a hearing date, the Clerk of the Disciplinary System shall file six copies of the available transcript, exhibits, pleadings, and orders from the original Disciplinary Proceeding.

4. **Investigation.** Bar Counsel shall conduct such Investigation and make such inquiry as it deems appropriate. On request of Bar Counsel, the Petitioner shall promptly sign such forms and give such permission as are necessary to permit inquiry of the Petitioner's background through the Internal Revenue Service, the National Criminal Information Center, the National Criminal Information Network and any other similar information network or system.

5. **Notice.** Reasonable notice of filing of the petition and the date of the hearing shall be mailed by the Clerk of the Disciplinary System to all members of the Bar of the circuit in the jurisdictions in which the Petitioner resided, and of the circuit in which the Petitioner maintained a principal office, at the time of the Revocation or Suspension. The Clerk of the Disciplinary System shall also mail the notice to the members of the District Committee who heard the original Complaint, to members of the Board who heard the original Complaint, to the members of the District Committee for the judicial circuit in which the Petitioner currently resides, to the complaining witness or witnesses on all Complaints pending against the Petitioner before the Board, a District Committee or a court at the date of the Revocation or Suspension and to such other individuals as the Clerk of the Disciplinary System deems appropriate. The Clerk of the Disciplinary System shall publish a synopsis of the petition in the Virginia Lawyer Register and in a newspaper of general circulation in the judicial circuit where the Petitioner currently resides and where the Petitioner maintained a principal office at the time of the Revocation or Suspension. The entire petition and exhibits together with the documents referred to in subparagraph 13–25.D. above, shall be available for inspection and copying by interested persons at the office of the Bar on reasonable notice and on payment of costs incurred to make the copies.

6. **Bill of Particulars.** On written request by Bar Counsel, served by certified mail, return receipt requested, a Petitioner seeking Reinstatement shall file with the Clerk of the Disciplinary System within 21 days after service of the request, an original and six copies of a bill of particulars setting forth the grounds for Reinstatement.

7. **Hearing.** On the date set for the hearing, the Petitioner shall have the right to representation by counsel, to examine and cross-examine witnesses and to present evidence. The testimony and other incidents of the hearing shall be transcribed and preserved, together with all exhibits (or copies thereof) received into evidence or refused. Bar Counsel shall appear and represent the Commonwealth and its citizens. Bar Counsel shall have the right to cross-examine, call witnesses and present evidence in opposition to the petition. Board members may examine witnesses called by either party. Legal advice to the Board, if required, shall be rendered by the Office of the Attorney General.

8. **Factors to Be Considered.** In considering the matter prior to making a recommendation to this Court the Board may consider, but is not bound by, the factors spelled out *In the Matter of Alfred Lee Hiss*, VSB Docket No. 83–26 (Va. Sup. Ct. July 2, 1984).

9. **Character Witnesses.** Up to five character witnesses supporting and up to five character witnesses opposing the petition shall be heard. In addition, the Board may consider any letters submitted regarding the Petitioner's character and fitness.

10. **Determination by the Board.** The Board shall, within 60 days after the receipt of the transcript, forward the record and its recommendations to this Court with a copy to the Petitioner and Bar Counsel. A recommendation of approval may be conditioned upon Petitioner obtaining malpractice insurance coverage and/or a blanket fidelity bond or dishonesty insurance coverage in amount(s) set by the Board from an approved professional insurance carrier for a definite term or on an ongoing basis.

13–26. Appeal From Board Determinations.

A. *Right of Appeal.* As a matter of right any Respondent may appeal to this Court from an order of Admonition, Public Reprimand, Suspension, or Disbarment imposed by the Board using the procedures outlined in Rule 5:21(b) of the Rules of the Supreme Court of Virginia. An appeal shall lie once the Memorandum Order described in this Paragraph has been served on the Respondent. No appeal shall lie from a Summary Order. If a Respondent appeals to the Supreme Court, then the Bar may file assignments of cross-error pursuant to Rule 5:28 of the Rules of the Supreme Court of Virginia.

B. *Determination.* This Court shall hear the case and make such determination in connection therewith as it shall deem right and proper.

C. *Office of the Attorney General.* In all appeals to this Court, the Office of the Attorney General, or the Bar Counsel, if so requested by the Attorney General, shall represent the interests of the Commonwealth and its citizens as appellees.

13–27. Resignation.

A. *Application.* A sworn and notarized application to resign from the practice of law shall be submitted to the Clerk of the Disciplinary System. The application shall state that the resignation is not being offered to avoid disciplinary action and that the Attorney has no knowledge of any complaint, investigation, action, or proceeding in any jurisdiction involving allegations of Misconduct by the Attorney. An application to resign will not prevent or preclude any disciplinary proceeding or action against an Attorney.

B. *Procedure.* The Clerk of the Disciplinary System shall submit applications for resignation to Bar Counsel, who shall investigate each application and determine whether, based upon the information available, the statements in the sworn application appear to be true and complete. If Bar Counsel files a written objection to the application with the Clerk of the Disciplinary System, the Board shall hold a hearing on whether the application should be accepted. If Bar Counsel does not file an objection, the Board may enter an order accepting the Attorney's resignation without a hearing. A resignation shall be effective only upon entry of an order accepting it. Upon entry of an order accepting an Attorney's resignation, the former Attorney shall immediately cease the practice of law and make appropriate arrangements for the disposition of matters in the Attorney's care in conformity with the wishes of the Attorney's clients.

C. *When Not Permitted.* An Attorney may not resign while the Attorney is the subject of a disciplinary complaint, investigation, action, or proceeding involving allegations of Misconduct.

13–28. Consent to Revocation.

A. *When Permitted.* An Attorney who is the subject of a disciplinary complaint, investigation or Proceeding involving allegations of Misconduct may consent to Revocation, but only by delivering to the Clerk of the Disciplinary System an affidavit declaring the Attorney's consent to Revocation and stating that:

1. The consent is freely and voluntarily rendered, that the Attorney is not being subjected to coercion or duress, and that the Attorney is fully aware of the implications of consenting to Revocation;

2. The Attorney is aware that there is currently pending a complaint, an investigation into, or a Proceeding involving, allegations of Misconduct, the nature of which shall be specifically set forth in the affidavit;

3. The Attorney acknowledges that the material facts upon which the allegations of Misconduct are predicated are true; and

4. The Attorney submits the consent to Revocation because the Attorney knows that if disciplinary Proceedings based on the alleged Misconduct were brought or prosecuted to a conclusion, the Attorney could not successfully defend them.

B. *Admissions.* The admissions offered in the affidavit consenting to Revocation shall not be deemed an admission in any proceeding except one relating to the status of the Attorney as a member of the Bar.

C. *Procedure.* The Clerk of the Disciplinary System shall submit the affidavit to Bar Counsel, who shall investigate the affidavit and determine whether, based upon the information available, the statements in the sworn application appear to be true and complete. If Bar Counsel files a written objection to the affidavit with the Clerk of the Disciplinary System, the Board shall hold a hearing on whether the affidavit and consent to Revocation should be accepted. If Bar Counsel does not file an objection, the Board shall enter an order revoking the Attorney's License by consent without a hearing.

D. *Attorney Action Required Upon Revocation.* Upon entry of such an order of Revocation by consent, the revoked Attorney shall immediately cease the practice of law and shall comply with the notice requirements set forth in subparagraph 13–29.

E. *Dismissal of Complaints or Allegations of Misconduct.* When an Attorney's License is revoked by consent, Bar Counsel, in his or her discretion, may dismiss without prejudice any and all Complaints or allegations of Misconduct then pending by notifying the Clerk of the Disciplinary System and the District Committee, Board or court wherein the matter or matters lie.

13–29. Duties of Disbarred or Suspended Respondent.

After a Suspension against a Respondent is imposed by either a Summary or Memorandum Order and no stay of the Suspension has been granted by this Court, or after a Revocation against a Respondent is imposed by either a Summary Order or Memorandum Order, that Respondent shall forthwith give notice, by certified mail, of his or her Revocation or Suspension to all clients for whom he or she is currently handling matters and to all opposing Attorneys and the presiding Judges in pending litigation. The Respondent shall also make appropriate arrangements for the disposition of matters then in his or her care in conformity with the wishes of his or her clients. The Respondent shall give such notice within 14 days of the effective date of the Revocation or Suspension, and make such arrangements as are required herein within 45 days of the effective date of the Revocation or Suspension. The Respondent shall also furnish proof to the Bar within 60 days of the effective date of the Revocation or Suspension that such notices have been timely given and such arrangements made for the disposition of matters. The Board shall decide all issues concerning the adequacy of the notice and arrangements required herein, and the Board may impose a sanction of Revocation or additional Suspension for failure to comply with the requirements of this subparagraph 13–29.

13–30. Confidentiality of Disciplinary Records and Proceedings.

A. *Confidential Matters.* Except as otherwise provided in this subparagraph 13–30, the following Disciplinary Proceedings, records, and information are confidential and shall not be disclosed:

1. Complaints, unless introduced at a public hearing or incorporated in a pending Charge of Misconduct, when the matter is placed on the public District Committee hearing docket, or a Certification;

2. Investigations, except that Investigative Reports admitted as exhibits at a public hearing are public;

3. Impairment proceedings, except that final orders are public;

4. Notes, memoranda, research, and all other work product of Bar Counsel;

5. Records, communications, and information protected by Disciplinary Rule 1.6;

6. Subcommittee records and proceedings, except determinations imposing public discipline; and

7. Deliberations and working papers of District Committees, the Board or a three-judge Circuit Court.

B. *Timing of Disclosure of Disciplinary Record in Sanctions Proceedings.* If an Attorney has a Disciplinary Record and is subsequently found by a Subcommittee, a District Committee, the Board or a three-judge Circuit Court empaneled under Va. Code § 54.1–3935 to have engaged in Misconduct, the facts and circumstances giving rise to such Disciplinary Record may be disclosed (i) to the Subcommittee, District Committee, Board or three-judge Circuit Court prior to the imposition of any sanction and (ii) by the Subcommittee, District Committee, Board or three-judge Circuit Court in its findings of fact set forth in its order. The facts and circumstances giving rise to such Disciplinary Record may also be disclosed to the Board during a hearing concerning whether an affidavit and consent to Revocation should be accepted.

C. *Timing of Public Access to Disciplinary Information.* All records of a matter set for public hearing remain confidential until the matter is dismissed or a public sanction is imposed except:

1. A Charge of Misconduct is public when the matter is placed on the public District Committee hearing docket; and

2. A Certification is public when filed with the Clerk of the Disciplinary System.

D. *Public Statements Concerning Disciplinary Information.* To the extent necessary to exercise their official duties, Bar Officials have access to all confidential information; however, except for Bar Counsel, no Bar Official shall communicate with a member of the media or the public concerning a matter that is confidential under this Paragraph. If an inquiry is made about a matter that, although confidential under this Paragraph, has become a matter of public record or has become known to the public, Bar Counsel may confirm whether the Bar is conducting an Investigation or if an Investigation resulted in a determination that further proceedings were not warranted.

E. *Protection of the Public.* Bar Counsel may transmit confidential information to persons or agencies outside of the disciplinary system if such disclosure is necessary to protect the public or the administration of justice.

F. *Disclosure to Other Jurisdictions.* Bar Counsel may share information regarding an Investigation with his or her counterparts in other jurisdictions provided that such jurisdiction agrees to maintain the confidentiality of the information as provided in this Paragraph.

G. *Disclosure of Criminal Activity.* If Bar Counsel or a Chair of the Board or a Chair of a District Committee discovers evidence of criminal activity by an Attorney, Bar Counsel, the Chair of the Board or a Chair of a District Committee shall forward such evidence to the appropriate Commonwealth's Attorney, United States Attorney or other law enforcement agency. The Attorney concerned shall be notified whenever this information is transmitted pursuant to this subparagraph 13–30 unless Bar Counsel decides that giving such notice will prejudice a disciplinary investigation.

H. *Disclosure of Information to Government Entities.* By order of this Court, confidential information may be disclosed to the Joint Legislative Audit and Review Commission or other governmental entities incident to their discharge of official duties, provided the entity is required or agrees to maintain the confidentiality of the information provided.

I. *Waiver of Confidentiality.* Confidential information, excluding notes, memoranda, research, and all other work product of Bar Counsel, may upon written request be disclosed when and to the extent confidentiality is waived by the Respondent, by the Complainant, and, if protected by Disciplinary Rule 1.6, by Respondent's client.

J. *Testimony About Disciplinary Proceedings.*

1. In no case shall Bar Counsel, a member of COLD, a member of a District Committee, a member of the Board, or a Committee Counsel be subject to a subpoena or otherwise compelled to testify in any proceeding regarding any matter investigated or considered in such person's official capacity, except that an Investigator may be compelled to testify in a Disciplinary Proceeding, subject to rulings of the court or Chair.

2. In no case shall the Clerk of the Disciplinary System be subject to a subpoena or otherwise compelled to testify regarding any matter investigated or considered in the disciplinary system, or the records of any such matter, dealt with by the Clerk of the Disciplinary System in his or her official capacity, except that the Clerk of the Disciplinary System may be compelled to testify in a Disciplinary Proceeding in order to authenticate records of the Clerk of the Disciplinary System.

K. *Records of the Disciplinary System.* In no case shall confidential records of the attorney disciplinary system be subject to subpoena.

L. *Virginia Lawyer Referral Service.* Bar Counsel shall notify the Virginia Lawyer Referral Service when a Complaint involving any Attorney member of the service is referred to a District Committee for Investigation or when any Attorney member of the service is disciplined. Bar Counsel shall also notify the Virginia Lawyer Referral Service when any Complaint involving an Attorney member of the service is dismissed following Investigation or when any Attorney member of the service complies with Terms imposed.

13–31. Dismissal of Complaints and Charges of Misconduct Upon Revocation Without Consent, or Upon Death.

When an Attorney's License is revoked without consent, or upon the death of an Attorney, Bar Counsel, in his or her discretion, may dismiss without prejudice any and all Complaints or allegations of Misconduct then pending against said Attorney by notifying the Clerk of the Disciplinary System, the Complainant(s) and the District Committee, Board or court wherein the matter(s) lies.

[Amended effective July 1, 1986; December 1, 1987; February 1, 1988; December 1, 1988; July 1, 1989; April 1, 1990; July 1, 1990; April 1, 1991; May 1, 1991; December 1, 1991; July 1, 1992; April 1, 1993; October 1, 1993; July 1, 1994; November 16, 1994; September 28, 1994; November 16, 1994; January 23, 1995; May 4, 1995; July 1, 1995; September 15, 1995; April 24, 1996; January 13, 1997; July 1, 1997; July 30, 1997; January 27, 1998; September 23, 1998; July 1, 1999; September 29, 1999; February 4, 2000; March 29, 2000; May 1, 2000; July 1, 2000; December 18, 2000; January 1, 2001; June 5, 2001; October 1, 2001; November 2, 2001; January 1, 2002; September 18, 2002; January 1, 2004; April 15, 2004; November 1, 2004; January 1, 2005; July 1, 2005; September 1, 2005; January 1, 2006; January 1, 2007; March 1, 2007; February 29, 2008; May 1, 2008; March 1, 2009; May 1, 2009; August 1, 2009; March 19, 2010; February 17, 2011; July 29, 2011; April 13, 2012; December 14, 2012; January 31, 2014; August 21, 2015.]

PARAGRAPH 13.1 SUSPENSION FOR FAILURE TO COMPLETE PROFESSIONALISM COURSE

Each person admitted to the Virginia State Bar on or after July 1, 1988, as an active member shall complete the course of study prescribed by the Executive Committee of the Virginia State Bar and approved by the Supreme Court of Virginia on the Rules of

Professional Conduct and the lawyer's broader professional obligations, and any active member who fails to complete the course shall be suspended unless a waiver is obtained for good cause shown. Such course of study shall be funded by attendance fees paid by those attending the course.

Any active member licensed after June 30, 1988, and any other member who changes his or her membership to active status shall complete the required course within twelve months of becoming an active member. Failure to comply with this Rule shall subject the active member to the penalties set forth in Paragraph 19 herein.

"Good cause shown" as used herein shall include illness, hospitalization or such other cause as may be determined by the Executive Committee, whose determination shall be final. Any determination by the Executive Committee may be reviewed by the Supreme Court on request of the member seeking a waiver.

[Amended effective December 1, 1987; January 1, 1990; February 4, 2000.]

PARAGRAPH 13.2 SUSPENSION FOR FAILURE TO COMPLETE CONTINUING LEGAL EDUCATION REQUIREMENT

Each active member of the Virginia State Bar shall complete the Continuing Legal Education requirement prescribed by Paragraph 17 of these Rules, and any active member who fails to complete the requirement shall be suspended unless a waiver is obtained for good cause shown. Any active member licensed on or after July 1, 1986, shall thereafter annually file prior to, but no later than, December 15, certifications that he or she has completed the mandatory continuing legal education programs required by Paragraph 17, or obtain a waiver for good cause shown; provided, however, the next certification deadline following July 31, 2001, shall be December 15, 2002. Failure to comply with this Rule shall subject the active member to the penalties set forth in Paragraph 19 herein.

"Good cause shown" as used herein shall include illness, hospitalization, or such other cause as may be determined by the Continuing Legal Education Board whose determination shall be final. Any determination by the Continuing Legal Education Board may be reviewed by the Supreme Court upon request of the member seeking a waiver.

[Amended effective December 1, 1987; January 1, 1990; October 1, 2001.]

PARAGRAPH 13.3 [RESERVED EFFECTIVE JANUARY 1, 1999]

13.4 INSURANCE COVERAGE REQUIREMENT FOR RESPONDENTS UNDER VA. CODE § 54.1–3935(D)

Pursuant to Va. Code § 54.1–3935(D), when an attorney who has been found guilty of engaging in criminal activity that violates the Rules of Professional Conduct and results in the loss of property of one or more of the attorney's clients and has been required by a three-judge court to maintain professional malpractice insurance during the time he or she is licensed to practice law in the Commonwealth of Virginia, that attorney shall carry such coverage in the minimum amount of $500,000 per claim and $1 million in the aggregate with a maximum $10,000 deductible, with a Virginia licensed insurer, eligible surplus line insurer or registered risk retention group. The coverage provider must have an A.M. Best minimum rating of A-.

The attorney shall require the insurer to include language in the policy specifying that the VSB be given notice of cancellation or nonrenewal. The attorney shall certify such coverage and the notice requirement to the VSB on a yearly basis with a certificate of insurance provided to the VSB by an agent or broker licensed in Virginia. This certificate must be received initially within 10 days after inception or reinstatement of the policy.

[Adopted effective August 21, 2015.]

PARAGRAPH 14. PROFESSIONAL CORPORATIONS, PROFESSIONAL LIMITED LIABILITY COMPANIES AND LIMITED LIABILITY PARTNERSHIPS (LIMITED LIABILITIES ENTITIES)

The rules and regulations in the following provisions of this Paragraph 14 shall constitute a Code of Ethics governing the professional conduct of the practice of law through professional law corporations, professional limited liability companies and registered limited liability partnerships in Virginia.

(a) Scope. All applications, reports and other documents required to be filed with the Virginia State Bar by this Paragraph 14 shall be signed and verified by an officer, director, partner, or manager of the applicant who is a duly licensed, active member of the Virginia State Bar or who is otherwise legally authorized to practice law in Virginia and filed at the office of the Virginia State Bar.

(b) Certificate of Registration. An applicant for registration as a limited liability entity shall file with the Virginia State Bar an application for a Certificate of Registration, on a form furnished by the Virginia State Bar, and pay a fee of $100. The term "limited liability entity," as used in this Paragraph 14 shall include a professional law corporation, professional limited liability company, and a registered limited liability partnership.

(i) The Executive Director of the Virginia State Bar, or a person or persons designated by him, shall review such application for registration and, within 15 days after receipt of such application, approve the application and issue a Certificate of Registration provided the application conforms to the requirements of law and this Paragraph 14. If the application fails to include the information required in subparagraphs (c)(i) through (c)(v) of this Paragraph 14, the Executive Director shall refuse to approve the application and notify the applicant of the reasons therefore. A request by the Executive Director for further information to comply with the requirement of said subparagraph (c) of this Paragraph 14, or a request that the application be amended, may be deemed by the applicant to be a refusal to approve the application for purposes of initiating review under subparagraph (b)(iii) of this Paragraph 14.

(ii) The effective date of the Certificate of Registration shall be the date on which the applicant has filed with the Virginia State Bar all material required for approval of the application; provided, however, that (1) a later effective date may be granted if requested by the applicant prior to the issuance of the Certificate of Registration, or (2) in the discretion of the Executive Director an earlier effective date may be granted if good cause appears therefore.

(iii) An applicant may request a review of a refusal to approve its application within sixty days after the date of the notice of such refusal. Such request shall be heard by the Executive Committee of the Virginia State Bar. Upon completion of review, which may include examination of all information submitted by the applicant and a hearing, the Committee shall either (1) approve the application and order the issuance of a Certificate of Registration, or (2) request further information required by subparagraph (c) of this Paragraph 14 or amendments not theretofore supplied by the applicant, or (3) refuse to approve the application in any case where the applicant fails or refuses to supply the required information or has made a material misrepresentation of fact. The Committee shall report in writing its findings of fact and the reasons for its order, whether approving or refusing to approve the application. Notice of the order and a copy of the report shall be mailed to the applicant.

(iv) Insofar as applicable, the rules of procedure of the Virginia State Bar shall apply to the procedure in (b)(iii) above. An aggrieved applicant may proceed in a court of competent jurisdiction by motion for declaratory judgment for review of matters relating to its application.

(c) Application for Certificates. A Certificate of Registration as a limited liability entity shall be issued if the application shows:

(i) The applicant is organized and qualified under the provisions of Chapter 7 (Section 13.1–542 et seq.) of Title 13.1 of the *Code of Virginia* (the Virginia Professional Corporations Act), organized and qualified under the provisions of Chapter 13 (Section 13.1–1100 et seq.) of Title 13.1 of the *Code of Virginia* (the Virginia Professional Limited Liability Company Act), organized and qualified under the provisions of Article 9 (Section 50–73.132 et seq.) of Chapter 2.2 of Title 50 (the Virginia Registered Limited Liability Partnership Act), or organized and qualified under the laws of a jurisdiction other than the Commonwealth of Virginia to perform a professional service of the type defined in Section 13. 1–543(A) of the *Code of Virginia*.

(ii) All of the applicant's shareholders, directors, officers, partners, members or managers and their names and addresses are set forth in full in the application.

(iii) Each member, manager, partner, employee or agent of the applicant who will practice law in Virginia, the names and addresses of whom are set forth in full in the application, whether or not a director, officer, shareholder, partner, member or manager of the applicant, is an active member of the Virginia State Bar or otherwise legally authorized to practice law in Virginia. Nothing in this Paragraph 14(c)(iii) shall be deemed to prohibit a non-licensed individual from serving as secretary, treasurer, office manager or business manager of any limited liability entity, provided, however, that such individual shall not be held out to be qualified or otherwise authorized to practice law or give advice on a legal or related matter to the clients of the entity. Any employee or agent of the applicant who is duly licensed to practice law in Virginia and who is not held out to the public to be so authorized shall be deemed for the purposes of these Rules to be a non-licensed individual.

(iv) A trade name may be used by a limited liability entity if it does not imply a connection with a government agency or with a public or charitable organization and is not otherwise in violation of Virginia Rules of Professional Conduct 7.1(a). The name of a lawyer holding a public office shall not be used in the name of the entity, or in communications on its behalf, during any substantial period in which the lawyer is not actively and regularly practicing with the entity.

(v) The applicant has advised or intends to advise the clients of any predecessor organization, and the clients of any shareholder, director, officer, member, partner, manager, employee or agent of the applicant who will practice law, of the transfer of such organization's or lawyer's practice to a limited liability entity.

(d) Ownership. An interest in or shares of a professional law corporation or professional limited liability company may be owned only in accordance with the provisions of Chapter 7 or Chapter 13 of Title 13.1. Ownership of shares of a professional law corporation or professional limited liability company for the purpose of construing this subparagraph (d) shall mean both legal and beneficial ownership. All the trustees of any voting trust which may be entered into by any shareholder shall be duly licensed or otherwise legally authorized to practice law in Virginia, and no proxy to vote any of such shares shall be valid unless granted to and voted by an individual or individuals duly licensed or otherwise legally authorized to practice law in Virginia.

(e) Control Over and Rendition of Legal Services; Letterhead. No person not a member of the Virginia State Bar and duly licensed to practice law in Virginia shall have the right to direct or control the professional judgment of any employee of a limited liability entity or the conduct of employees of the entity with respect to the practice of law in Virginia. Any limited liability entity practicing law in a foreign jurisdiction and which enumerates its employees on its letterhead and in other permissible listings shall do so in a manner which will make clear the jurisdictional limitations on those employees and agents of the entity not licensed to practice in all listed jurisdictions.

(f) Correspondence, Pleadings and Documents. Correspondence, pleadings and other documents, the execution of which constitutes the practice of law in Virginia, shall be executed on behalf of a limited liability entity by an employee who is an active member of the Virginia State Bar and duly licensed to practice law in Virginia. Corporate documents, the execution of which does not constitute the practice of law, may be executed on behalf of a limited liability entity by any authorized employee, whether or not licensed to practice law.

(g) Division of Fees. It shall be lawful, ethical and proper for a lawyer employed by a limited liability entity, as part of the terms of his employment, to agree to turn over to the entity by which he is employed all fees, compensation or reimbursement which he may be entitled to receive for his professional services, regardless of where such professional services are rendered. No limited liability entity with a Certificate of Registration in effect shall be deemed a lay agency, nor shall any employee of such entity be deemed to be practicing law through an intermediary during any period for which such entity maintains a Certificate of Registration in effect.

(h) Professional Responsibility. Nothing in this Paragraph 14 shall be deemed to diminish or change the obligation of any lawyer employed by a limited liability entity to conduct the practice of law in accordance with any specific standards promulgated by the Supreme Court of Virginia. Any lawyer who by act or omission causes the entity by which he is employed to act or fail to act in a manner which violates any applicable standard of professional conduct, including any of the provisions of this Paragraph 14, shall be personally responsible for such act or omission and subject to discipline therefore.

(i) Attorney–Client Privilege. Nothing in this Paragraph 14 shall be deemed to modify, abrogate or reduce the attorney-client privilege or any comparable privilege or relationship, whether derived by statute or from common law.

(j) Discipline. A Certificate of Registration shall continue in effect until it is suspended or revoked as provided herein. Such certificate may be suspended or revoked if a limited liability entity fails at any time to comply fully with the provisions of this Paragraph 14, the Rules of Professional Conduct, the Code of Professional Responsibility, the applicable Virginia Professional Corporation Act, the Virginia Professional Limited Liability Company Act, or the Virginia Registered Limited Liability Partnership Act, after notice and an opportunity to be heard as provided in 14(j)(ii) below; provided that, if the violation be such as can be corrected upon notice to the entity of its violation, or if the violation be that of one or several persons only, suspension or revocation of the certificate need not be invoked if the interest of justice and the protection of the public can be fairly served by appropriate disciplinary proceedings against the individual(s) involved.

(i) Upon receipt of a resolution of the board of directors or the written statement of the manager(s) or partner(s) of a limited liability entity requesting the cancellation of the Certificate of Registration of that entity, such certificate shall be cancelled by the Executive Director of the Virginia State Bar, or by a person or persons designated by him. The cancellation of a Certificate of Registration at the request of a limited liability entity shall be effective as of the date such request is received at the office of the Virginia State Bar, except that a later effective date shall be granted upon request of the entity or, in the discretion of the Executive Director of the Virginia State Bar, an earlier effective date may be granted if good cause appears therefore.

(ii) Where a limited liability entity has violated or is about to violate any pertinent statute, rule or any provision of this Paragraph 14, the Executive Director of the Virginia State Bar, or a person or persons designated by him, may issue a notice directing Bar Counsel to investigate the alleged violation. Bar Counsel may issue such summons and subpoenas, and/or compel the production of such documents as he/she may reasonably deem necessary or material for the effective conduct of an investigation. Every Circuit Court shall have power to enforce any summons or subpoena issued by Bar Counsel and to adjudge disobedience thereof as contempt. If the report of Bar Counsel concludes either that the allegation is without merit or that specific corrective action has been or will be taken, the Executive Director shall dismiss the matter forthwith. If Bar Counsel concludes that the allegation has merit warranting court action, Bar Counsel shall file with the Circuit Court having jurisdiction in the premises a verified complaint. The court shall issue a rule against the limited liability entity concerned and conduct further proceedings in the matter in accordance with Section 54.1–3937 of the *Code of Virginia*, as amended, which is incorporated herein by reference. In addition to or in lieu of a

Circuit Court complaint against the entity, Bar Counsel may refer the matter to the appropriate District Committee pursuant to Part 6, Section IV, Para. 13, B.(5)(a) et seq. of these Rules. After the court has held its hearing pursuant to its rule, it shall enter an order reprimanding the entity or revoking or suspending its Certificate of Registration if it finds that the circumstances of the violation warrant such action; otherwise the court shall dismiss the matter.

(k) Certificate Renewal. On the date two years after the effective date of its initial Certificate of Registration and biennially thereafter, each limited liability entity shall pay a fee of $50 whereupon its Certificate of Registration shall be automatically renewed.

(*l*) Annual Report; Corporate or Partnership Changes. Each limited liability entity shall file with the Virginia State Bar a copy of any document or report required to be filed with the State Corporation Commission. In addition, each such entity shall file a special report on a form provided by the Virginia State Bar within thirty days after any change in its shareholders, directors, officers, members, managers, partners, employees or agents duly licensed to practice law. Each such change in personnel of a limited liability entity shall be brought to the attention of each of its clients, so that such client may know by whom he is represented or may be represented and with whom his confidences may be shared, in the same manner as is customary with partnerships.

(m) Effective Dates. This Paragraph 14 shall become effective on [to be effective after the proposed statutory change goes into effect] and shall apply in like manner to professional corporations theretofore or thereafter organized under the provisions of Chapter 7 (Section 13.1–542 et seq.) of Title 13.1 of the *Code of Virginia* to practice law, and to professional limited liability companies theretofore or thereafter organized under the provisions of Chapter 13 (Section 13.1–1100 et. seq.) of Title 13.1 of the *Code of Virginia* to practice law, and to registered limited liability partnerships theretofore or thereafter organized under the provisions of Article 9 (Section 50–73.132 et seq.) of Chapter 2.2 of Title 50 of the *Code of Virginia* to practice law, except where inconsistent with the provisions of such laws.

[Amended effective February 1, 1993; July 1, 1995; February 4, 2000; March 29, 2000; January 1, 2005; July 1, 2006.]

PARAGRAPH 15. THIRD YEAR STUDENT PRACTICE RULE

(a) Activities.

(i) An eligible law student may, in the presence of a supervising lawyer, appear in any court or before any administrative tribunal in this Commonwealth in any civil, criminal or administrative matter on behalf of any person if the person on whose behalf he is appearing has indicated in writing his consent to that appearance. The eligible law student must obtain written approval from the court or administrative tribunal prior to any appearance before the court or administrative tribunal.

(ii) An eligible law student may also, in the presence of a supervising lawyer, appear in any criminal matter on behalf of the Commonwealth with the written approval of the prosecuting attorney or his authorized representative, provided the student obtains the written authorization from the court or administrative tribunal prescribed in paragraph (a)(i) of this Rule.

(iii) The written consent and approval of the person or entity on whose behalf the student appears shall be filed in the record of the case and shall be brought to the attention of the judge of the court or the presiding officer of the administrative tribunal.

(b) Requirements and Limitations. In order to qualify pursuant to this Rule, the law student must:

(i) a. Be duly enrolled and in good standing in a law school that is approved by the American Bar Association, but if such school is located in another state that permits law student practice, only if such other state permits a student of a law school in this State to engage in such practice; or

b. Be duly enrolled in a program of study in the office of an attorney as authorized in subdivision 2. of § 54.1–3926, Code of Virginia, and in accordance with the Rules of the Virginia Board of Bar Examiners.

(ii) a. Have completed satisfactorily legal studies amounting to at least four semesters, or the equivalent if the school is on a basis other than a semester basis; or

b. Be certified by the Virginia Board of Bar Examiners as being in the final year of a program of study in the office of an attorney as authorized in subdivision 2. of § 54.1–3926, Code of Virginia, and in accordance with the Rules of the Virginia Board of Bar Examiners.

(iii) Be certified by the dean of his law school, or by the attorney under whom he is studying in the case of a law reader, as being of good character and competent ability, and as having completed satisfactorily a course or program of study in each of the following: criminal law, professional ethics, evidence and procedure.

(iv) Be introduced to the court or agency in which he is appearing by an attorney admitted to practice in that court or agency.

(v) Neither ask for nor receive any compensation or remuneration of any kind for his services from the person on whose behalf he renders services but this shall not prevent a lawyer or law firm, legal aid bureau, public defender agency, or the Commonwealth from paying compensation to the eligible law student, nor shall it prevent charges by a lawyer or law firm for such services as may otherwise be proper.

(c) Certification. The certification of a student by the Virginia Board of Bar Examiners, the law school dean, or the attorney under whom the student is studying in compliance with Paragraph 15 (b)(ii) and (iii) above:

(i) Shall be filed with the Executive Director of the Virginia State Bar and, unless it is sooner withdrawn, shall remain in effect until the expiration of eighteen months after it is filed, or until the announcement of the results of the first examination given by the Virginia Board of Bar Examiners following the student's graduation or completion of the program of study, whichever date is earlier. Thereafter, the certification shall lapse and be of no further force or effect.

(ii) May be withdrawn by the Board, dean or attorney under whom the student is studying at any time by mailing a notice to that effect to the Executive Director of the Virginia State Bar. It is not necessary that the notice state the cause for withdrawal.

(d) Supervision. The supervising attorney under whose supervision an eligible law student performs any of the activities permitted by this Rule (Paragraph 15) shall:

(i) Be an active member of the Virginia State Bar who practices before, and whose service as a supervising lawyer for this program is approved by, each court or administrative body in which the eligible law student engages in limited practice.

(ii) Assume personal professional responsibility for the student's guidance in any work undertaken and for supervising the quality of the student's work.

(iii) Assist the student in his preparation to the extent the supervising lawyer considers it necessary.

(iv) The approval of the court designated in (a)(i) or (d)(i) may be withdrawn at any time without stating the cause for withdrawal.

(e) Miscellaneous. Nothing contained in this Rule (Paragraph) shall affect the right of any person who is not admitted to practice law to do anything that he might lawfully do before the adoption of this Rule (Paragraph).

[Amended effective July 1, 1994; July 1, 1999; October 1, 2001; October 26, 2007.]

PARAGRAPH 16. CLIENTS' PROTECTION FUND

The Council may establish a Clients' Protection Fund for the purposes of reimbursing all or part of losses sustained by a client or other person or entity to whom a fiduciary duty is owed as a result of dishonest conduct of a member of the Virginia State Bar. The Board shall be appointed by Council, and shall receive, hold, manage, invest and distribute funds appropriated to it by Council or otherwise received, in accordance with procedures established by Council.

Effective July 1, 2007, each active member of the Virginia State Bar shall be assessed a required fee of $25 for the Clients' Protection Fund on the bar's annual dues statement. The fee shall be in addition to each member's annual dues as prescribed in Part 6, Section IV, Paragraph 11 of these rules, and it shall be paid on or before the 31st day of July each fiscal year.

All monies collected under this Paragraph 16 shall be accounted for and paid into the State Treasury of Virginia and transferred by the bar from the Treasury to the Clients' Protection Fund. The bar shall report annually on or about January 15 to the Supreme Court of Virginia on the financial condition of the Clients' Protection Fund, and the assessment will be reduced or discontinued whenever directed by the Court.

Failure to comply with the requirements of this Paragraph 16 shall subject the active member to penalties set forth in Part 6, Section IV, Paragraph 19 of these rules.

[Amended effective July 1, 2007.]

PARAGRAPH 17. MANDATORY CONTINUING LEGAL EDUCATION RULE

The Virginia Supreme Court hereby establishes a Mandatory Continuing Legal Education Program in the Commonwealth of Virginia.

A. Purpose. Continuing professional education of lawyers serves to improve the administration of justice and benefit the public interest. Regular participation in Continuing Legal Education programs will enhance the professional skills of practicing lawyers, afford them periodic opportunities for professional self-evaluation and improve the quality of legal services rendered to the public. All active members of the Virginia State Bar shall participate in an additional amount of further legal study throughout the period of their active practice of law, and failure to do so shall result in their suspension from membership in the Virginia State Bar.

B. Continuing Legal Education Board. A Continuing Legal Education Board shall be established for the purpose of administering the program.

(1) *Appointment.* The Chief Justice of the Supreme Court shall appoint, after consultation with the Council, the members of the board who shall be members of the Bar and twelve in number. One member shall be designated by the Chief Justice as Chair and another as Vice-chair. Members shall serve terms of three years each, except that, initially, four members shall be appointed for terms of one year, four for terms of two years, and four for terms of three years. No member shall serve more than two consecutive terms but shall be eligible for reappointment after the lapse of one or more years following expiration of the previous term. The Executive Director of the Virginia State Bar shall be an ex-officio member of the board.

(2) *Notice of Meetings/Quorum.* The board shall meet on reasonable notice by the Chair, Vice-chair or the Executive Director. Five members shall constitute a quorum and the action of a majority of a quorum shall

constitute action of the board; however, new regulations or amendments shall be approved by a majority of the full membership of the board.

(3) *Powers.* The board shall have those general administrative and supervisory powers necessary to effectuate the purposes of this Rule, including the power to adopt, following the advice and comment of Council, reasonable and necessary regulations consistent with this Rule. The effective date of any regulations or amendments to the regulations adopted by the board shall be as prescribed by the board, but in no event earlier than one hundred twenty (120) days following such adoption. The Council may reject any regulations or amendments to the regulations adopted by the board on or after July 1, 2010, by a 2/3 vote of those members of Council present and voting. Council's rejection of any regulations or amendments to the regulations shall have the effect of suspending the regulation or amendment until the Supreme Court has reviewed and approved, rejected, or modified the proposed regulation or amendment. The Virginia State Bar shall have the responsibility for funding the board and for enforcing Mandatory Continuing Legal Education requirements. The board may delegate to the Virginia State Bar staff as it deems appropriate to carry out its responsibilities under this new Rule. The board shall specifically have the following powers and duties:

(a) To approve CLE programs and sponsors;

(b) To establish procedures for the approval of Continuing Legal Education courses, whether those courses are offered within the Commonwealth or elsewhere. These procedures should include the method by which CLE sponsors could make application to the board for approval, and if necessary, make amendments to their application;

(c) To authorize sponsors of Continuing Legal Education programs to advertise that participation in their program fulfills the CLE requirements of this Rule;

(d) To formulate and distribute to all members of the Virginia State Bar appropriate information regarding the requirements of this Rule, including the distribution of a certification form to be filed annually by each active member.

C. Continuing Legal Education Requirements.

(1) All active members of the Virginia State Bar shall annually complete and certify attendance at a minimum of twelve (12) credit hours of approved Continuing Legal Education courses of which at least two (2) hours shall be in the area of legal ethics or professionalism, except those lawyers expressly exempted from the requirement by this Rule or by decision of the Continuing Legal Education Board; provided, however, that for the period July 1, 2001 through October 31, 2002, active members shall complete and certify attendance at a minimum of fifteen (15) credit hours of approved Continuing Legal Education courses of which at least two (2) hours shall be in the area of legal ethics or professionalism, except those lawyers expressly exempted from the requirement by this rule or by decision of the Continuing Legal Education Board. Each active member shall complete the required Continuing Legal Education courses each year during the period November 1 through October 31 of the following year; provided, however, the next completion period following June 30, 2001, shall be July 1, 2001 through October 31, 2002.

(2) In order to provide flexibility in fulfilling the annual requirement, a one-year carryover of credit hours is permitted, so that accrued credit hours in excess of one year's requirement may be carried forward from one year to meet the requirement for the next year. A member may carry forward a maximum of twelve (12) credit hours, two (2) of which, if earned in legal ethics or professionalism, may be counted toward the two (2) hours required in legal ethics or professionalism.

(3) Each active member of the Virginia State Bar shall be responsible for ascertaining whether or not a particular course satisfies the requirements of this Rule. Each member should exercise discretion in choosing those approved programs which are most likely to enhance professional skills and improve delivery of legal services.

D. Certificate of Attendance.

(1) Each active member of the Virginia State Bar shall certify prior to December 15 each year that such lawyer attended approved Mandatory Continuing Legal Education programs for the minimum number of hours required during the previous calendar year ending October 31; provided, however, the next certification deadline following July 31, 2001, shall be December 15, 2002. The failure to certify shall cause suspension of such lawyer's license to practice law. An untruthful certification shall subject the lawyer to appropriate disciplinary action.

E. Exemptions. Each active member of the Virginia State Bar shall comply with this Rule except as follows:

(1) A newly admitted member shall be exempted from filing a certification for the completion period in which he or she is first admitted.

(2) A member who has obtained a waiver for good cause shown, as may be determined by the board, shall be exempted from filing a certification for the completion period for which the waiver is granted.

F. Activation or Reactivation. A member of any category who wishes to become an active member of the Virginia State Bar shall furnish to the Secretary an affidavit stating that he or she has completed twelve (12) hours of Continuing Legal Education, including two (2) hours in legal ethics or professionalism within the previous twelve months. Thereafter, that member shall have the same completion period and certification deadline as other active members.

G. Credits.

(1) Credit will be given only for Continuing Legal Education courses or activities approved by the board.

(2) Hours in excess of the minimum requirements defined in this Rule may not be carried forward for credit beyond the one year provided for in the Rule.

(3) Credit will not be given for Continuing Legal Education hours accumulated prior to admission to the Virginia State Bar.

(4) Credit shall be given to active members of the Virginia State Bar who prepare course materials and who personally participate as instructors. The credit, as determined by the Board, will reflect the time reasonably required for preparation of materials, as well as the actual time spent instructing.

H. Standards. In evaluating specific programs for approval, consideration shall be given to the following factors:

(1) Whether the course tends to increase the participant's professional competence as a lawyer.

(2) The number of hours of actual presentation, lecture, or participation, so that the appropriate number of credit hours can be identified and published.

(3) The usage of written educational materials which reflect a thorough preparation by the provider of the course, and which assist course participants in improving their legal competence.

(4) To qualify for mandatory legal education credit, a course is not required to have a component on legal ethics or professionalism, although such components are encouraged. When topics on legal ethics or professionalism are offered, either as an entire course or component thereof, they must be clearly identified as such.

[Amended effective December 1, 1987; July 1, 1991; November 16, 1994; February 4, 2000; December 18, 2000; October 1, 2001; January 7, 2011; May 1, 2014.]

PARAGRAPH 18. FINANCIAL RESPONSIBILITY

In order to make available to the public information about the financial responsibility of each active member of the Virginia State Bar for professional liability claims, each such member shall, upon admission to the Bar, and with each application for renewal thereof, submit the certification required herein or obtain a waiver for good cause shown. The active member shall certify to the Bar on or before July 31 of each year: a) whether or not such member is currently covered by professional liability insurance, other than an extended reporting endorsement; b) whether or not such member is engaged in the private practice of law involving representation of clients drawn from the public, and, if so, whether the member intends to maintain professional liability insurance coverage during the period of time the member remains engaged in the private practice of law; and c) the date, amount, and court where rendered, of any unsatisfied final judgment(s) against such member, or any firm or professional corporation in which he or she has practiced, for acts, errors, or omissions (including, but not limited to, acts of dishonesty, fraud, or intentional wrongdoing) arising out of the performance of legal services by such member.

The foregoing shall be certified by each active member of the Virginia State Bar in such form as may be prescribed by the Virginia State Bar and shall be made available to the public by such means as may be designated by the Virginia State Bar.

Each active member who certifies to the Bar that such member is covered by professional liability insurance shall notify the Bar in writing within thirty (30) days if the insurance policy providing coverage lapses, is no longer in effect or terminates for any reason, unless the policy is replaced with another policy and no lapse in coverage occurs.

Failure to comply with this Rule shall subject the active member to the penalties set forth in Paragraph 19 herein. An untruthful certification or unjustified failure to notify the Bar of a lapse or termination of coverage shall subject the member to appropriate disciplinary action.

"Good cause shown" as used herein shall include illness, absence from the Commonwealth of Virginia, or such cause as may be determined by the Executive Committee of the Virginia State Bar whose determination shall be final. Any determination by the Executive Committee may be reviewed by the Supreme Court upon request of the member seeking a waiver.

[Amended effective July 1, 1989; January 1, 1990; April 1, 1990; July 1, 2005.]

PARAGRAPH 19. PROCEDURE FOR THE ADMINISTRATIVE SUSPENSION OF A MEMBER

Whenever it appears that a member of the Virginia State Bar has failed to comply with any of the Rules of Court relating to such person's membership in the bar, the Secretary–Treasurer shall mail a notice to the member advising of the member's noncompliance and demanding (1) compliance within sixty (60) days of the date of such notice and (2) payment of a delinquency fee of $50, for each Rule violated, provided, however, that the delinquency fee for an attorney who does not comply with the timely completion requirements of Paragraphs 13.2 and 17(C) of these rules shall be $100, and the delinquency fee for an attorney who does not comply with the certification requirements of Paragraphs 13.2 and 17(D) of these rules shall be $100, and shall increase by $100 on February 1 for noncompliance with the certification requirements. The notice shall be mailed to the member at his last address on file at the Virginia State Bar.

In the event the member fails to comply with the directive of the Secretary–Treasurer within the time allowed, the Secretary–Treasurer will then mail a notice to the member by certified mail to advise (1) that the attorney's membership in the bar has been suspended and (2) that the attorney may no longer practice law in the Commonwealth of Virginia or in any way hold himself or herself out as a member of the Virginia State Bar. Thereafter the attorney's membership in the Virginia State Bar may be reinstated only upon showing to the Secretary–Treasurer (1) that the attorney has complied with all the Court's rules relating to his or her membership in the bar and (2) upon payment of a reinstatement fee of $150 for each Rule violated, provided, however, that the reinstatement fee for an attorney who was suspended for noncompliance with Paragraphs 13.2 and 17 of these rules shall be $250, and shall increase by $50 for each subsequent such suspension, not to exceed a maximum of $500.

Whenever the Secretary–Treasurer notifies a member that his or her membership in the bar has been administratively suspended, the Secretary–Treasurer shall also (1) advise the Chief Judges of the circuit and district in which the attorney has his or her office, as well as the clerks of those courts and the Clerk of the Supreme Court of Virginia, of such suspension and (2) publish notice of the suspension in the next issue of the *Virginia Lawyer Register*.

An administrative suspension shall not relieve the delinquent member of his or her annual responsibility to attend continuing legal education programs or to pay his or her dues to the Virginia State Bar.

[Adopted effective January 1, 1990. Amended effective July 1, 1993; February 4, 2000; July 1, 2007; August 1, 2009.]

PARAGRAPH 20. MAINTENANCE OF TRUST ACCOUNTS; NOTICE OF ELECTION REQUIREMENTS

Every trust account maintained by an active member of the VSB under Rules of Professional Conduct 1.15 shall also be maintained at a "financial institution approved by the Virginia State Bar" and maintained in accordance with this paragraph and Rule 1.15. A "financial institution approved by the Virginia State Bar" includes regulated state or federal chartered banks, savings institutions, and credit unions that are properly licensed and authorized to do business, have federal insurance on deposits, and have entered into and agreed to abide by a Virginia State Bar Approved Financial Institution Agreement. (See Appendix A which the Virginia State Bar reserves the right to amend or modify upon notice to all approved financial institutions.) The Virginia State Bar shall maintain and publish from time to time a list of approved financial institutions.

(A) Interest–Bearing Trust Accounts. A lawyer may maintain funds of clients in one or more interest-bearing accounts in one or more financial institutions, whenever the lawyer has established and follows record-keeping, accounting, clerical, and administrative procedures to compute and credit or pay periodically, but at least quarterly, pro rata to each client the interest on such client's funds less fees, costs, or expenses charged by the lawyer for the record-keeping, accounting, clerical, and administrative procedures associated with computing and crediting or paying such amounts.

(B) IOLTA Accounts. A lawyer may deposit funds of a client in an identifiable interest-bearing trust (IOLTA) account for which the lawyer has not established procedures to compute and credit or pay pro rata net earnings to such client whenever:

(1) At the time of such deposit the lawyer reasonably expects that the fees, costs, or expenses which the lawyer would be entitled to charge under Paragraph 20(A) would equal or exceed the pro rata interest on such client's funds (the determination of whether the funds of a client or third person can earn income in excess of fees, costs or expenses the lawyer would be entitled to charge under paragraph 20(A) shall rest in the sound judgment of the lawyer or law firm, and no lawyer shall be charged with an ethical impropriety or breach of professional conduct based on the good faith exercise of such judgment); and

(2) The financial institution has agreed to:

(a) Periodically, but at least quarterly, remit to the Legal Services Corporation of Virginia (LSCV) interest or dividends on the average monthly balance of each such account or as otherwise computed in accordance with such bank's standard accounting practice, provided that such rate of interest shall not be less than the rate paid by such bank to regular, non-attorney depositors;

(b) Transmit with each remittance to LSCV a statement identifying the name of the lawyer or law firm from whose account the remittance is sent, the rate of interest applied, the period for which the remittance is made, the total amount of interest earned, the service charges or other fees assessed against the account, if any, and the net amount of interest remitted;

(c) Transmit to the depositing lawyer or law firm at the same time a report showing the amount paid to LSCV from such interest-bearing account, the rate of interest applied, the fees assessed, if any, and the average account balance for the period for which the report is made;

(d) Charge no fees against an IOLTA trust account that are greater than the fees charged to non-attorney depositors, except that an IOLTA remittance fee may be charged to defray the depository institution's administrative costs attributable to calculating and remitting the interest to LSCV; other allowable fees are per check charges, per deposit charges, a fee in lieu of a minimum balance and sweep fees. Allowable, reasonable fees may be deducted from interest or dividends earned on an IOLTA account, provided that such charges or fees shall be calculated in accordance with the Financial Institutions' standard practice for non-IOLTA customers. Fees or charges in excess of the interest or dividends earned on the IOLTA account, for any month or quarter, shall not be taken from the interest or dividends of any other IOLTA account. Fees for wire transfers, insufficient funds, bad checks, stop payment, account reconciliation, negative collected balances, and check printing are not considered customary account maintenance charges and are not deductible from the interest or dividends earned on the IOLTA account. All other fees including those non-customary fees just listed are the responsibility of the lawyer or law firm, who in turn may absorb these specific costs or pass along those fees to the client(s) being served by the transaction in accordance with attorney/client agreements. Financial Institutions may elect to waive any or all fees on IOLTA accounts in recognition of their charitable nature;

(e) Collect no fees from the principal deposited in the IOLTA trust account;

(f) Pay all or part of the funds deposited in such interest-bearing trust account upon demand or order. An IOLTA account may be an interest-bearing check account, a money market account with or tied to check-writing, a sweep account which is a government money market fund or daily overnight financial institution repurchase agreement invested solely in or fully collateralized by United States government securities, or an open-end money market fund solely invested in or fully collateralized by the United States government securities; and

(g) Agree and abide by all provisions in the Virginia State Bar Approved Financial Institution Agreement.

(3) Interest accruing on such accounts and paid by the financial institution to LSCV shall be used for funding 1) civil legal services to the poor in Virginia, 2) LSCV's administrative expenses, and 3) the creation and augmentation of a reserve fund for the same purposes.

(C) Non–Interest–Bearing Trust Accounts. A lawyer may deposit funds of a client in an identifiable non-interest-bearing trust account for which the account accrues no interest or dividends so long as the attorney or law firm receives no consideration or benefit from the Financial Institution for opening a non-interest bearing trust account or for converting from an IOLTA account to a non-interest bearing trust account. A lawyer who elects not to participate in the maintenance of an interest-bearing trust account as described in Paragraph 20(B) must submit such an election in accordance with the procedures set forth in Paragraph 20(F) of this rule.

(D) Reporting to Client. A lawyer who elects to deposit funds of a client in an account pursuant to Paragraph 20(B) or (C) shall not be required to seek permission from such client in making the election. As to funds deposited in accordance with Paragraph 20(B), a lawyer shall not be required to compute or report to such client any payment to LSCV of interest or dividends by the banking institution on funds in any such account wherein the client's funds have been deposited by the lawyer.

(E) Law Firm Trust Accounts. A law firm of which any participating lawyer is a member may maintain the account(s) on behalf of any or all lawyers in the firm.

(F) Opt–Out of IOLTA Account. A lawyer who elects to open an IOLTA account shall obtain a "Request to Establish IOLTA Account" form from LSCV. A lawyer who elects not to maintain an IOLTA account shall make such election on a "Request to Opt–Out" form provided by LSCV.

[Adopted effective October 1, 1993. Amended effective July 1, 1995; February 4, 2000; June 21, 2011.]

PARAGRAPH 21. COMPUTERIZED LEGAL RESEARCH SERVICES RULE

The Supreme Court of Virginia hereby authorizes and directs the Virginia State Bar to contract to provide online computerized legal research services to its members.

(A) Purpose It is the policy and objective of the Commonwealth of Virginia to improve the quality and reduce the costs of legal services available to the citizens of Virginia. It is also the policy of this Commonwealth to enhance the availability of legal services to poor litigants and indigent criminal defendants. The provision of online computerized legal research tools to all Virginia lawyers will further these policies by increasing and improving the available knowledge and information base for attorneys, enhancing the quality of legal research and advice, making legal research more efficient for many attorneys, reducing the costs of legal services to the poor, and providing additional resources to lawyers who are appointed by courts to represent indigent criminal defendants. The provision of online computerized legal research services to all lawyers in Virginia will reduce the time spent and costs incurred in performing legal research, which will decrease the costs of legal services to consumers in Virginia and thereby increase access to attorneys. In addition, the provision of online computerized legal research will enable more lawyers to provide pro bono services since this research tool will lower their costs and reduce the amount of research time required.

(B) Procedure For these reasons, the Virginia State Bar, through its governing body, is authorized to contract to provide online computerized legal research services to its members. In connection therewith, the Virginia State Bar is authorized and directed to solicit proposals from providers of online computerized legal research services, enter into contracts for those services, and expend funds for the purchase of online computerized legal research services for its members. The Virginia State Bar shall supervise and periodically review the provision of online computerized legal research services to its members to ensure the continued quality of those services and that the policies and objectives of the Commonwealth are being met. The Virginia State Bar also shall submit to the Supreme Court of Virginia an annual report that describes and analyzes the status of the Bar's contracts for online computerized legal research services, the online computerized legal research services that are being provided, and the utilization of those services.

[Adopted effective July 13, 2005.]

SECTION V. BYLAWS OF THE COUNCIL OF THE VIRGINIA STATE BAR [DELETED]

[Deleted effective December 1, 1983.]

SECTION VI. VIRGINIA STATE BAR BYLAWS [DELETED]

[Deleted effective December 1, 1983.]

APPENDIX

APPENDIX A. VIRGINIA STATE BAR APPROVED FINANCIAL INSTITUTION AGREEMENT

This Virginia State Bar Financial Institution Agreement ("Agreement") is made this ___ day of _________, by and between the Virginia State Bar and _________, ("Financial Institution").

WITNESS:

The undersigned, an officer of the Financial Institution executing this Agreement, being duly authorized to bind said institution by this Agreement, hereby applies to be approved as a depository to receive escrow, trust, or client funds, as defined in Part 6, § IV, Para. 20, of the Rules of the Supreme Court of Virginia, or any successor provision(s), from attorneys for deposit in what are hereinafter referred to as "Trust Accounts." The Financial Institution agrees to comply with the following requirements, or any successor provisions:

1. **Notification to Attorneys or Law Firm.** To promptly notify the attorney or law firm of an overdraft in any Trust Account or the dishonor for insufficient funds of any instrument drawn on any Trust Account held by it.
2. **Notification to Bar Counsel.** To report the overdraft or dishonor to Bar Counsel of the Virginia State Bar, as set forth in Paragraph 5 of this Agreement.
3. **Audit of Trust Account.** To provide reasonable access to the Virginia State Bar of all records of the Trust Account if an audit of such account is ordered pursuant to court order, or upon receipt of a subpoena therefor. The financial institution may charge for the reasonable costs of producing these records.
4. **Interest Calculation.** The financial institution shall not engage in the practice of "negative netting" as to IOLTA trust accounts.
5. **Form of Report.** That all such reports shall be substantially in the following format:

   In either case of a dishonored instrument or an instrument presented against insufficient funds in a Trust Account, but honored by the financial institution, the report shall be identical to the notice customarily forwarded to the depositor and shall include the name and address of the depositor notified, including the name of the lawyer responsible for the account, as well as a copy of the dishonored instrument, if such copy is normally provided to the depositor. In addition, the report shall identify the financial institution reporting the overdraft, the account number, the date of the overdraft, the name of the person making the report, their address and telephone number and date. The report shall be made simultaneously with and within the time provided by law for notice of dishonor to the depositor or, in the case of instruments that are honored by the financial institution, within five (5) banking days after the date of presentation for payment against insufficient funds.
6. **Consent of Attorneys or Law Firms.** The Financial Institution may require, as a condition to opening an attorney Trust Account, the written consent of the attorney or law firm opening such account to the notification to Bar Counsel of the Virginia State Bar as set forth in Paragraph 2 of this Agreement.
7. **Change of Name or Corporate Form.** If a Financial Institution changes its name, merges or otherwise affiliates with, or is acquired by another entity, the successor Financial Institution shall promptly notify Bar Counsel of the change and whether the successor institution wishes to serve as a financial institution approved by the Virginia State Bar for attorney Trust Accounts and enter into an Agreement.
8. **Termination of Agreement.** This Agreement may terminate upon thirty (30) days notice from the Financial Institution in writing to Bar Counsel that the institution intends to terminate the Agreement on a stated date and that copies of the termination notice have been mailed to all attorneys and law firms that maintain Trust Accounts with the Financial Institution or any branch thereof. Notice to the Bar Counsel shall be sent by certified mail to the Virginia State Bar, Attention: Bar Counsel, 707 E. Main Street, Suite 1500, Richmond, Virginia 23219–2800. This agreement may also be canceled without prior notice by Bar Counsel of the Virginia State Bar if the financial institution fails to abide by the terms of the agreement.
9. **Binding Effect.** This Agreement shall be binding upon the Financial Institution and any branch thereof receiving Trust Accounts.
10. **Definitions.** For purposes of this agreement the following definitions will apply:
    a. "Notice of Dishonor" refers to the notice which, pursuant to Uniform Commercial Code Section 3–508(2), must be given by a drawee bank before its midnight deadline.
    b. "Insufficient funds" refers to a state of affairs in which there is an insufficient collected balance in an account as reflected in the financial institu-

tion's accounting records, so that an otherwise properly payable item presented for payment cannot be paid without creating an overdraft in the account.

c. "Dishonored" shall refer to instruments that have been dishonored because of insufficient funds as defined above.

d. "Negative Netting" refers to the practice of a financial institution collecting some part or all of the fees assessed during a stated period of time against any IOLTA account that has failed to generate enough interest to pay assessed fees from the positive interest generated by other IOLTA accounts and deducting those fees from the total interest remitted to the Legal Services Corporation of Virginia for that time period.

IN WITNESS WHEREOF, the Financial Institution has executed this Agreement on the date and year written above.

ATTEST:

____
Name of Financial Institution

____
Address of Financial Institution

____

By ____________________________
Officer's Name
(Please print)

____
Officer's Signature

____
Corporate Office Held

[Adopted effective June 21, 2011.]

PART SEVEN A. GENERAL DISTRICT COURTS—IN GENERAL

Adopted Effective July 1, 1989

Including Amendments Received Through October 15, 2015

RULE 7A:1. SCOPE

Part Seven A of the Rules shall apply to all proceedings in the General District Courts.

[Adopted effective July 1, 1989.]

Cf: Former Rule 3D:1; § 8.01–3

RULE 7A:2. COMPUTATION OF TIME

Whenever a party is required or permitted under these Rules to do an act within a prescribed time after receipt or delivery of a paper and the paper is sent by mail, three days shall be added to the prescribed period.

[Adopted effective July 1, 1989.]

Cf: Rule 1:7; Rule 3A:20

RULE 7A:3. COUNSEL

When used in these Rules, the word "counsel" or "attorney" includes a partnership, a professional corporation or an association of members of the Virginia State Bar practicing under a firm name.

"Counsel of record" in any case includes an attorney who has signed a pleading in the case or who has notified the clerk or judge that the attorney appears in the case and shall also include a party who appears in court pro se. Except as provided in § 16.1–69.32:1, counsel of record shall not withdraw from a case except by leave of court with such notice as the court may require to the client of the time and place of a motion for leave to withdraw.

[Adopted effective July 1, 1989.]

Cf: This is present Rule 3D:2, moved to Section A so that it will be applicable to civil, criminal and traffic cases. Rule 1:5; § 8.01–314; § 16.1–69.32:1

RULE 7A:4. REPORTERS AND TRANSCRIPTS OF PROCEEDINGS IN COURT

Reporters, when present, shall be first duly sworn to take down and transcribe the proceedings faithfully and accurately to the best of their ability and shall be subject to the control and discipline of the judge.

When a reporter is present and takes down any proceeding in a court, any person interested shall be entitled to obtain a transcript of the proceedings or any part thereof upon terms and conditions to be fixed in each case by the judge.

The proceedings may be taken down by means of any recording device approved by the judge.

[Adopted effective July 1, 1989.]

Cf: § 16.1–69.35:2; Rule 1:3

RULE 7A:5. DISCRETION OF COURT

All steps and procedures in the clerk's office touching the filing of pleadings and the maturing of suits or actions may be reviewed and corrected by the court.

The time allowed for filing pleadings may be extended by the court in its discretion and such extension may be granted although the time fixed already has expired.

[Adopted effective July 1, 1989.]

Cf: Rule 1:9; § 8.01–428B

RULE 7A:6. PRESERVATION OF THE RECORD

A court may authorize the use of electronic or photographic means for the preservation of the record or parts thereof.

[Adopted effective July 1, 1989; amended effective July 1, 1992.]

Cf: Rule 1:14; § 16.1–69.35:2; Canons of Judicial Conduct Canon 3A.(7); § 19.2–266

RULE 7A:7. FILING FORMAT AND PROCEDURE

(a) Except as provided in subdivision (c) of this Rule and Rule 1:17 pertaining to Electronically Filed Cases,

(1) All pleadings, motions, briefs and all other documents filed in any clerk's office in any proceeding pursuant to the Rules or statutes shall be 8–1/2 by 11 inches in size. All typed material shall be double spaced except for quotations.

(2) Subdivision (a)(1) of this Rule shall not apply to tables, charts, plats, photographs, and other material that cannot be reasonably reproduced on paper of that size.

(b) No paper shall be refused for failure to comply with the provisions of this Rule, but the clerk or judge may require that the paper be redone in compliance with this Rule and substituted for the paper initially filed. Counsel shall certify that the substituted paper is identical in content to the paper initially filed.

(c) Electronic Filing. In any general district court which has established an electronic filing system pursuant to Rule 1:17:

(1) Any proceeding may be designated as an Electronically Filed Case upon consent of all parties in the case.

(2) Except where service and/or filing of an original paper document is expressly required by these rules, all pleadings, motions, notices and other instruments in an Electronically Filed Case shall be formatted, served and filed as specified in the requirements and procedures of Rule 1:17; provided, however, that when any

document listed below is filed in the case, the filing party shall notify the clerk of court that the original document must be retained.

(i) Any pleading or affidavit required by statute or rule to be sworn, verified or certified as provided in Rule 1:17(e)(5).

(ii) Any contract or deed.

(iii) Any prenuptial agreement or written settlement agreement, including any property settlement agreement.

(iv) Any check or other negotiable instrument.

(v) Any handwritten statement, waiver, or consent by a defendant or witness in a criminal proceeding.

(vi) Any form signed by a defendant in a criminal proceeding, including any typed statements or a guilty plea form.

(vii) Any document that cannot be converted into an electronic document in such a way as to produce a clear and readable image.

[Adopted effective July 1, 1989. Amended effective May 2, 2011.]

Cf: Rule 1:16

RULE 7A:8. GENERAL PROVISIONS AS TO PLEADINGS

(a) Counsel of Record tendering a pleading gives assurances that it is filed in good faith and not for delay.

(b) A pleading that is sworn to is an affidavit for all purposes for which an affidavit is required or permitted.

(c) Counsel of Record who files a pleading shall sign it and state counsel's address and phone number.

(d) The mention in a pleading of an accompanying exhibit shall, of itself and without more, make such exhibit a part of the pleading.

[Adopted effective July 1, 1989.]

Cf: Rule 1:4; § 8.01–271.1

RULE 7A:9. AMENDMENTS

No amendment shall be made to any pleading after it is filed with the clerk, except by leave of court. Leave to amend shall be liberally granted in furtherance of the ends of justice.

In granting leave to amend, the court may make such provision for notice thereof and opportunity to make response as the court may deem reasonable and proper.

[Adopted effective July 1, 1989.]

Cf: Rule 1:8; § 16.1–86.1

RULE 7A:10. COPIES OF PLEADINGS AND REQUESTS FOR SUBPOENAS DUCES TECUM TO BE FURNISHED

All pleadings not otherwise required to be served and requests for subpoenas duces tecum shall be served on each counsel of record by delivering, dispatching by commercial delivery service, transmitting by facsimile, or mailing a copy to each on or before the day of filing.

At the foot of such pleadings and requests shall be appended either acceptance of service or a certificate of counsel that copies were served as this rule requires, showing the date of delivery, dispatching, transmitting, or mailing.

[Adopted effective July 1, 1989. Amended effective February 1, 1999.]

Cf: Rule 1:12; Rule 3A:21(a); § 16.1–89; § 16.1–131

RULE 7A:11. ENDORSEMENTS

Drafts of orders shall be endorsed by counsel of record, or reasonable notice of the time and place of presenting such drafts together with copies thereof shall be served by delivering, dispatching by commercial delivery service, transmitting by facsimile or mailing to all counsel of record who have not endorsed them. Compliance with this rule and with Rule 7A:10 may be modified or dispensed with by the court in its discretion. In an Electronically Filed Case, endorsement and specification of any objections to the draft order shall be accomplished as provided in Rule 1:17.

[Adopted effective July 1, 1989. Amended effective February 1, 1999; May 2, 2011.]

Cf: Rule 1:13

RULE 7A:12. REQUESTS FOR SUBPOENAS FOR WITNESSES AND RECORDS

(a) Subpoenas for Witnesses.

(1) Requests for subpoenas for witnesses should be filed at least ten days prior to trial.

(2) Requests for subpoenas for witnesses not timely filed should not be honored except when authorized by the court for good cause.

(b) Subpoenas Duces Tecum.

(1) Requests for subpoenas duces tecum should be filed at least 15 days prior to trial.

(2) Requests for subpoenas duces tecum not timely filed should not be honored except when authorized by a judge for good cause.

(c) Meaning of Filed. The term filed as used in this Rule means received in the appropriate clerk's office or by an appropriate magistrate.

(d) Exception. This Rule does not apply to subpoenas for witnesses and subpoenas duces tecum issued by attorneys in civil cases as authorized by Virginia Code §§ 8.01–407 and 16.1–89.

[Adopted effective July 1, 1989. Amended effective July 1, 2000.]

Cf: Rule 3A:12(a); Rule 4:9(c); § 16.1–69.25; § 16.1–89; § 16.1–131; § 8.01–407; § 8.01–506.1

RULE 7A:13. WHAT CONSTITUTES NOTING AN APPEAL

All appeals shall be noted in writing. An appeal is noted only upon timely receipt in the clerk's office of the writing. An appeal may be noted by a party or by the attorney for such party. In addition, in civil cases, an appeal may be noted by a party's regular and bona fide employee or by a person entitled to ask for judgment under any statute.

[Adopted effective July 1, 1989.]

Cf: Forms are available in the clerk's office for noting an appeal. DC–370, Notice of Appeal (Criminal) and DC–475 Civil Appeal Notice. Rule 3A:19(b); § 16.1–106; § 16.1–107; § 8.01–129; § 16.1–132; § 16.1–135

RULE 7A:14. CONTINUANCES

(a) Continuances Granted for Good Cause. Continuances should not be granted except by, and at the discretion of, a judge for good cause shown, or unless otherwise provided by law. The judge may, by order, delegate to the clerk the power to grant continuances consented to by all parties under such circumstances as are set forth in the order. Such an order of delegation should be reasonably disseminated and posted so as to inform the bar and the general public.

(b) All Parties Agree to Continuance. If all parties to a proceeding agree to seek a continuance, the request may be made orally by one party as long as that party certifies to the judge that all other parties know of the request and concur. Such a request should be made as far in advance of the scheduled hearing or trial as is practicable. If granted, the moving party shall be responsible for assuring that notice of the continuance is given to all subpoenaed witnesses and that they are provided with the new court date. This obligation may be met by (i) an agreement between the parties that each side will notify its own witnesses; or (ii) any other arrangement that is reasonably calculated to get prompt notice to all witnesses.

(c) All Parties Do Not Agree to Continuance. If a request for continuance is not agreed to by all parties, such request should be made to the court prior to the time originally scheduled for the hearing or trial. If the court determines that a hearing on the request should be conducted prior to the time originally scheduled for the trial, all parties shall be given notice of such hearing by the requesting party.

(d) Continuances Requested at the Time of Hearing. Where a request for a continuance has not been made prior to the hearing or trial and other parties or witnesses are present and prepared for trial, a continuance should be granted only upon a showing that to proceed with the trial would not be in the best interest of justice.

(e) Parties. For purposes of this Rule, the term "parties" shall mean all plaintiffs, defendants and third party defendants in a civil case and the prosecution and the defendant in a criminal or traffic infraction case.

[Adopted effective July 1, 1989.]

Cf: Former Rule 3D:7

RULE 7A:15. GENERAL INFORMATION RELATING TO EACH COURT

The chief judges of the general district courts shall, on or before December 31 of each year, furnish the Executive Secretary of the Supreme Court current general information relating to the management of the courts within each district. This information shall be assembled and published electronically by the Executive Secretary.

[Adopted effective July 1, 1989. Amended effective July 1, 2009.]

Cf: Rule 1:15

RULE 7A:16. ISOLATION PROCEEDINGS UNDER ARTICLE 3.01 OF TITLE 32.1 OF THE CODE OF VIRGINIA; COMMUNICABLE DISEASES OF PUBLIC HEALTH SIGNIFICANCE.

A. Upon any petition by the State Health Commissioner, or that official's designee, for an order that a person or persons appear before the court to determine whether isolation is necessary to protect the public health from the risk of infection with a communicable disease of public health significance, the provisions of §§ 32.1–48.03, 32.1–48.04, and related sections of Article 3.01 of Title 32.1 of the Code of Virginia shall be followed.

B. The court shall hold hearings under this rule in a manner to protect the health and safety of individuals subject to any such order or quarantine or isolation, court personnel, counsel, witnesses, and the general public. To this end, the court may take measures including, but not limited to, ordering the hearing to be held by telephone or video conference or ordering those present to take appropriate precautions, including wearing personal protective equipment.

[Adopted effective May 1, 2006.]

PART SEVEN B. GENERAL DISTRICT COURTS—CIVIL

Adopted Effective July 1, 1989

Including Amendments Received Through October 15, 2015

RULE 7B:1. SCOPE

These Rules apply to all civil cases in the General District Courts.

[Adopted effective July 1, 1989.]

Cf: Former Rule 3D:1; § 8.01–3

RULE 7B:2. SPECIFIC RULE FOR PLEADINGS IN GENERAL DISTRICT COURTS

The judge of any General District Court may require the plaintiff to file and serve a written bill of particulars and the defendant to file and serve a written grounds of defense within the periods of time specified in the order so requiring; the failure of either party to comply may be grounds for awarding summary judgment in favor of the adverse party. Upon trial, the judge may exclude evidence as to matters not described in any such pleading.

[Adopted effective July 1, 1989.]

Cf: Former Rule 3D:4; § 16.1–69.25:1

RULE 7B:3. GENERAL PROVISIONS AS TO PLEADINGS

(a) A party asserting either a claim, counterclaim, cross-claim or a defense may plead alternative facts and theories of recovery against alternative parties, provided that such claims, defenses, or demands for relief so joined arise out of the same transaction or occurrence. Subject to the jurisdictional limits of the General District Court, a party may also state separate related claims or defenses regardless of consistency and whether based on legal or equitable grounds.

(b) The warrant, summons or complaint or an attachment thereto shall contain a statement, approved by the Committee on District Courts, explaining how any party may object to venue.

(c) The warrant, summons or complaint, or an attachment thereto shall contain a statement, approved by the Committee on District Courts, explaining that if the case is contested, how a trial date will be set.

(d) All civil warrants and complaints shall contain on their face language in substantially the following form: "The defendant is not required to appear pursuant to this document, but if the defendant does not appear, judgment may be granted in favor of the plaintiff."

[Adopted effective July 1, 1989. Amended effective February 28, 2006; July 1, 2008.]

Cf: Rule 1:4; Former Rule 3D:3(b); Former Rule 3D:6; § 8.01–271 et seq.; § 8.01–281; § 16.1–88.01 and § 16.1–88.02

RULE 7B:4. TRIAL OF ACTION

(a) Method of Bringing Action. A civil action in a general district court may be brought by warrant, summons or complaint directed to the sheriff or to any other person authorized to serve process, requiring such individual to summon the person against whom the claim is asserted to appear before the court on a certain day to answer the complaint of the plaintiff set out in the warrant, summons or complaint.

(b) When Action Heard. If all parties appear and are ready for trial on the return date of the warrant, summons or complaint, the court may proceed with the trial of the case.

[Adopted effective July 1, 1989. Amended effective February 28, 2006.]

Cf: Former Rule 3D:3; § 16.1–79—§ 16.1–83; § 16.1–86; § 16.1–93

RULE 7B:5. PRODUCTION OF WRITTEN AGREEMENT

When a suit is brought on a written contract, note or other instrument, the original document shall be tendered to the court for entry of judgment thereon unless the production of the original is excused by the court for good cause or by statute.

[Adopted effective July 1, 1989.]

Cf: Former Rule 3D:8; § 16.1–94; § 8.01–32

RULE 7B:6. VERIFICATION

If a statute requires a pleading to be sworn to, and it is not, or requires a pleading to be accompanied by an affidavit, and it is not, but contains all the allegations required, objection on either ground must be made within seven days after the pleading is filed by a motion to strike; otherwise the objection is waived. At any time before the court passes on the motion or within such time thereafter as the court may prescribe, the pleading may be sworn to or the affidavit filed. In an Electronically Filed Case, verification shall be subject to the provisions of Rule 1:17.

[Adopted effective July 1, 1989. Amended effective May 2, 2011.]

Cf: Rule 1:10; § 16.1–88; § 16.1–88.2; § 8.01–279; § 8.3–307

RULE 7B:7. APPEARANCE BY PLAINTIFF

Except as may be permitted by statute, no judgment for plaintiff shall be granted in any case except on request made in person in court by the plaintiff,

plaintiff's attorney, or plaintiff's regular and bona fide employee.

[Adopted effective July 1, 1989.]

Cf: Former Rule 3D:5; § 55–246.1

RULE 7B:8. FAILURE OF PLAINTIFF TO APPEAR

(a) If neither the plaintiff nor the defendant appears, the Court shall dismiss the action without prejudice to the right of the plaintiff to refile.

(b) If the defendant, but not the plaintiff, appears on the return date and the case is not before the Court for trial, the Court shall dismiss the action without prejudice to the right of the plaintiff to refile.

(c) If the defendant, but not the plaintiff, appears on the trial date and:

(1) The defendant admits owing all or some portion of the claim, the Court shall dismiss the action without prejudice to the right of the plaintiff to refile; but if

(2) The defendant denies under oath owing anything to the plaintiff, the Court shall enter judgment for the defendant with prejudice to the right of the plaintiff to refile.

[Adopted effective July 1, 1989. Amended effective March 1, 1998.]

Cf: § 16.1–97.1 granting the Court the authority to grant a rehearing.

RULE 7B:9. FAILURE OF DEFENDANT TO APPEAR

Except as may be provided by statute, a defendant who fails to appear in person or by counsel is in default and:

(a) Waives all objections to the admissibility of evidence; and

(b) Is not entitled to notice of any further proceeding in the case, except that when service is by posting pursuant to § 8.01–296(2)(b), the ten day notice required by that section shall be complied with; and

(c) On request made in person in court by the plaintiff, plaintiff's attorney, plaintiff's regular and bona fide employee, or any other person authorized by law, judgment shall be entered for the amount appearing to the judge to be due. If the relief demanded is unliquidated damages, the court shall hear evidence and fix the amount thereof.

[Adopted effective July 1, 1989.]

Cf: Former Rule 3D:6; § 16.1–97.1 granting the Court authority to grant a rehearing.

Cross references. See also § 16.1–97.1, granting the Court authority to grant a rehearing.

[Cross-reference added effective September 30, 2004.]

See Title II of the Servicemembers Civil Relief Act, 50 U.S.C. Appx. § 520 et seq. (as affecting the validity of default judgments entered against defendants in military service). Also see, Va. Code § 8.01–15.2.

[Cross-reference added effective July 30, 1996; amended September 30, 2004.]

RULE 7B:10. THIRD–PARTY PRACTICE AND CONSOLIDATION OF ACTIONS

(a) When Defendant May Bring in Third Party. Whenever a party is served with a warrant, summons, complaint, counterclaim or cross-claim, such party may within 10 days after service or up to the trial date, whichever is sooner, file a third-party civil warrant or complaint on a person not a party to the action who is or may be liable to the party for all or part of the claim being asserted against such party. After such time period, such third-party claim may be asserted only with leave of court.

Any party may move to strike the third-party warrant or complaint, or move for its severance for a separate trial. A third-party defendant may proceed under this rule against any person not a party to the action who is or may be liable to him for all or part of the claim made in the action against the third-party defendant.

(b) Consolidation of Actions. The Court may, in its discretion, consolidate for trial separate suits which could be treated as counter-claims, cross-claims, and third-party claims. The judge may enter such orders as may be appropriate to effect a prompt and fair disposition of such cases.

[Adopted effective July 1, 1989. Amended effective February 28, 2006.]

RULE 7B:11. MOTIONS TO TRANSFER

(a) When a written motion to transfer objecting to venue is filed by any party, the party objecting shall mail a copy of such motion to all counsel of record. Failure to comply with this requirement shall not be a ground for denying the motion, but the court may grant a deferral of any hearing on the motion to transfer if it finds that the interest of justice would be served by such deferral.

(b) If any party who has filed a motion to transfer objecting to venue is not present when the court rules on such motion:

(1) If the motion is granted, the Clerk shall transmit the files in accordance with such order and shall send a copy of the letter of transmittal or order of transfer to all parties along with information as to any costs awarded under § 8.01–266; or

(2) If the motion is denied, the court shall set a date for the trial of the case and the Clerk shall notify the absent objecting party by first class mail of such date and of any costs awarded any other party under § 8.01–266.

[Adopted effective July 1, 1989. Amended effective January 1, 2002; July 1, 2008; May 2, 2011.]

Cf: § 16.1–76; § 8.01–257 et seq.

PART SEVEN C. GENERAL DISTRICT COURTS—CRIMINAL AND TRAFFIC

Adopted Effective July 1, 1989

Including Amendments Received Through October 15, 2015

RULE 7C:1. SCOPE

These rules shall apply to all criminal and traffic cases [infractions and others] in the General District Courts.

[Adopted effective July 1, 1989.]

Cf: Rule 3A:1; § 8.01–3

RULE 7C:2. VENUE

Questions of venue must be raised before a finding of guilty or venue shall be deemed waived.

[Adopted effective July 1, 1989.]

Cf: Rule 3A:2.1; § 19.2–244 et seq.

RULE 7C:3. THE COMPLAINT, WARRANT, SUMMONS AND CAPIAS

(a) The complaint shall consist of sworn statements of a person or persons of facts relating to the commission of an alleged offense. The statements shall be made upon oath before a judicial officer empowered to issue arrest warrants. The judicial officer may require the sworn statements to be reduced to writing if the complainant is not a law-enforcement officer.

(b) More than one warrant, summons or capias may issue on the same complaint. A warrant may be issued by a judicial officer if the accused fails to appear in response to a summons.

(c) A separate warrant, summons or capias shall be issued for each charge.

(d) A summons, whether issued by a judicial officer or a law-enforcement officer, shall command the accused to appear at a stated time and place before a court of appropriate jurisdiction. It shall (i) state the name of the accused or, if this name is unknown, set forth a description by which he can be identified with reasonable certainty, (ii) describe the offense charged and state whether the offense is a violation of state, county, city or town law, and (iii) be signed by the magistrate or the law-enforcement officer, as the case may be.

(e) If the warrant has been issued but the officer does not have the warrant in his possession at the time of the arrest, he shall (i) inform the accused of the offense charged and that a warrant has been issued, and (ii) deliver a copy of the warrant to the accused as soon thereafter as practicable.

[Amended effective March 1, 2012.]

Cf: Rule 3A:3; Rule 3A:4; § 16.1–129.1; § 16.1–129.2

RULE 7C:4. TRIAL TOGETHER OF MORE THAN ONE ACCUSED OR MORE THAN ONE OFFENSE AND JOINT PRELIMINARY HEARINGS

(a) More Than One Accused—Joinder of Defendants. On motion of the Commonwealth, for good cause shown, the court, in its discretion, may order persons charged with participation in related acts or occurrences or in a series of acts or occurrences constituting an offense or offenses to be tried jointly unless such joint trial would constitute prejudice to a defendant.

(b) More Than One Accused—Severance of Defendants. If the court finds that a joint trial would constitute prejudice to a defendant, the court shall order severance as to that defendant or provide such other relief as justice requires.

(c) An Accused Charged With More Than One Offense. The Court may direct that an accused be tried at one time for all offenses then pending against him, if justice does not require separate trials and (a) the offenses are based on the same act or transaction, or on two or more acts or transactions that are connected or constitute parts of a common scheme or plan, or (b) the accused and the Commonwealth's Attorney consent thereto.

(d) Joint Preliminary Hearing. Upon motion of the Commonwealth's Attorney, preliminary hearings for persons alleged to have participated in contemporaneous and related acts or occurrences or in a series of such acts or occurrences constituting an offense or offenses may be heard jointly, if jurisdiction over each person and offense lies in the same court, unless the court finds that such joint preliminary hearing would constitute prejudice to a defendant.

[Adopted effective July 1, 1989. Amended effective January 1, 1994.]

Cf: Rule 3A:6(b); Rule 3A:10

RULE 7C:5. DISCOVERY

(a) Application of Rule. This Rule applies only to the prosecution for a misdemeanor which may be punished by confinement in jail and to a preliminary hearing for a felony.

(b) Definitions. For purposes of discovery under this Rule 1) the prosecuting attorney is the attorney for the Commonwealth or the city attorney, county attorney, or town attorney, who is responsible for prosecuting the case; 2) if no prosecuting attorney prosecutes the case, the representative of the Commonwealth shall be the law enforcement officer, or, if none, such person who appears on behalf of the Commonwealth, county, city or town in the case.

(c) Discovery by the Accused. Upon motion of an accused, the court shall order the prosecuting attorney or representative of the Commonwealth to permit the accused to hear, inspect and copy or photograph the following information or material when the existence of such is known or becomes known to the prosecuting attorney or representative of the Commonwealth and such material or information is to be offered in evidence against the accused in a General District Court:

(1) any relevant written or recorded statements or confessions made by the accused, or copies thereof and the substance of any oral statements and confessions made by the accused to any law enforcement officer; and

(2) any criminal record of the accused.

(d) Time of Motion. A motion by the accused under this Rule shall be made in writing and filed with the Court and a copy thereof mailed, faxed, or otherwise delivered to the prosecuting attorney and, if applicable, to the representative of the Commonwealth at least 10 days before the day fixed for trial or preliminary hearing. The motion shall include the specific information or material sought under this Rule.

(e) Time, Place and Manner of Discovery and Inspection. An order granting relief under this Rule shall specify the time, place and manner of making the discovery and inspection permitted and may prescribe such terms and conditions as are just.

(f) Failure to Comply. If at any time during the course of the proceedings, it is brought to the attention of the court that the prosecuting attorney or representative of the Commonwealth has failed to comply with this Rule or with an order issued pursuant to this Rule, the court shall order the prosecuting attorney or representative of the Commonwealth to permit the discovery or inspection of the material not previously disclosed, and may grant such continuance to the accused as it deems appropriate.

[Adopted effective July 1, 1989. Amended effective February 1, 1991; July 1, 2000.]

Cf: Rule 3A:11; § 16.1–131; § 16.1–69.25:1

RULE 7C:6. PLEAS

(a) A court shall not accept a plea of guilty or nolo contendere to any misdemeanor charge punishable by confinement in jail without first determining that the plea is made voluntarily with an understanding of the nature of the charge and the consequences of the plea. Before accepting a plea to such a charge, the court shall inform the accused that such a plea constitutes a waiver of the right to confront one's accusers and the right against compulsory self-incrimination.

(b) Upon rejecting a plea agreement, a judge shall immediately recuse himself from any further proceedings on the same matter unless the parties agree otherwise.

(c) A corporation, acting by counsel or through an agent, may enter the same pleas as an individual.

[Adopted effective July 1, 1989. Amended effective June 1, 2005; July 1, 2014.]

Cf: Rule 3A:8

RULE 7C:7. SERVICE AND FILING OF PAPERS

(a) **Copies of Written Motions to Be Furnished.** All written motions and notices not required to be served otherwise shall be served on each counsel of record by delivering, dispatching by commercial delivery service, transmitting by facsimile, or mailing, a copy to him on or before the day of filing.

Service pursuant to this Rule shall be effective upon such delivery, dispatch, transmission or mailing, except that papers served by facsimile transmission completed after 5:00 p.m. shall be deemed served on the next day that is not a Saturday, Sunday, or legal holiday.

At the foot of such pleadings and requests shall be appended either acceptance of service or a certificate of counsel that copies were served as this Rule requires, showing the date of delivery and method of service, dispatching, transmitting, or mailing.

(b) Filing. Pleadings, motions, notices, and other materials required to be served shall be filed with the clerk. In an Electronically Filed Case, the provisions of Rule 1:17 shall be applicable.

[Adopted effective July 1, 2008. Amended effective May 2, 2011.]

PART EIGHT. JUVENILE AND DOMESTIC RELATIONS DISTRICT COURTS

Adopted Effective July 1, 1992

Including Amendments Received Through October 15, 2015

RULE 8:1. SCOPE

Part Eight of the Rules shall apply to all proceedings in the Juvenile and Domestic Relations District Courts.

[Adopted effective July 1, 1992.]

Comment

The Juvenile and Domestic Relations District Courts Rules of Court Subcommittee, at the suggestion of the juvenile judges, recommends that there be a separate part to avoid confusion with the Rules for General District Courts.

RULE 8:2. DEFINITIONS

(a) Statutory Definitions. The definitions stated in § 16.1–228 are applicable to this Part.

(b) Additional Definitions. The following words and phrases used in this Part are defined as follows:

(1) "Counsel" or "attorney" includes a partnership, a professional corporation or an association of members of the Virginia State Bar practicing under a firm name or governmental agency name.

(2) "Counsel of Record" in any pending case includes an attorney who has signed a pleading in the case or who has notified the clerk or judge that the attorney appears in the case and shall also include a guardian ad litem and a party who appears in court pro se. Except as provided by statute, counsel of record shall not withdraw from a case except by leave of court with such notice as the court may require to the client of the time and place of a motion for leave to withdraw.

[Adopted effective July 1, 1992.]

Comment

This Rule largely tracks Rule 7A:3 with some slight modifications to reflect situations unique to the juvenile and domestic relations district court.

RULE 8:3. CONTENTS OF PETITIONS IN CERTAIN PROCEEDINGS

(a) Proceedings for the Ordering of Services.

(1) *Motion or Petition.* When a party to a matter pending before the court, or a petition filed for the purpose, proposes that the court enter an order pursuant to § 16.1–278, directing that a governmental officer, employee, agency, or institution render information, assistance, services or cooperation, the petition or motion shall contain:

a) The information, assistance, services, or cooperation sought;

b) The state or federal law or regulation or city, county, or town ordinance that provides for the rendering of such information, assistance, services, or cooperation sought; and

c) The officer, employee, agency, or institution to whom the order should be directed.

(2) *Notice.* The motion or petition prescribed in paragraph (a)(1) of this Rule shall be served on the governmental officer, employee, agency, or institution in question pursuant to § 16.1–264.

(3) *Hearing.* The governmental officer, employee, agency, or institution against whom an order is sought shall be entitled to a hearing on the issues raised by the petition or motion. The hearing may be held at such time as the court deems appropriate.

(b) Proceedings for Judicial Consent to Emergency Surgical or Medical Treatment for a Juvenile. When a petition is filed for the purpose of seeking judicial consent for emergency surgical or medical treatment of a juvenile, the petition shall contain:

(1) The juvenile's name, date of birth, residence, and a statement as to whether or not the juvenile has ever been married;

(2) The names and residence of the juvenile's parents, guardian or legal custodian;

(3) The name and residence of the nearest known relative if no parent or guardian can be found;

(4) The name and address of the physician petitioning the court for authorization of surgical or medical treatment for the juvenile;

(5) The name and address of the hospital or medical facility petitioning for authorization of surgical or medical treatment for the juvenile;

(6) A statement of the diagnosis of the juvenile's physical condition, and the recommended medical, surgical, and nursing care; and

(7) A statement of the willingness of the physician and the hospital or medical facility to provide the necessary medical, surgical, and nursing care if judicial consent is given as requested.

(c) **Proceedings for Support**. Except for temporary child support orders issued pursuant to Va. Code § 16.1–279.1, when a petition is filed seeking a court order for support of a spouse or child, the petition shall contain:

(1) The name and residential address of the person seeking support;

(2) The name and residential address of the person from whom support is sought;

(3) The name, date of birth, and residential address of the person or persons for whom support is sought and the relationship of that person or those persons to the respondent;

(4) A statement whether the Division of Child Support Enforcement is involved in the case;

(5) If child support is at issue, a statement whether or not the petitioner and respondent are presently or have ever been married to each other and, if not, whether paternity has ever been adjudicated;

(6) If child support is at issue, a statement whether the child's custody has been adjudicated;

(7) If known, the name, date of birth, and social security number of each parent or spouse and, if different and if known, the name, date of birth, and social security number of the person responsible for support and, unless otherwise ordered, the residential and, if different, mailing address, residential and employer telephone number, driver's license number, and the name and address of the employer of each such parent or responsible person;

(8) As an attachment, a copy of the most recent court order, if any, concerning support of the person for whom support is sought in this petition; and

(9) A statement whether either or both parents hold a license, certificate, registration, or other authorization to engage in a profession, trade, business, occupation or recreational activity issued by the Commonwealth and, if so, the type of authorization held.

In the case of a petition for support, if a protective order has been issued or if a party asserts that the party is at risk of physical or emotional harm from the other party, information other than the name of the party at risk shall not be required on the petition; however, the information shall be provided to the court and shall not be disclosed except by order of the court.

[Adopted effective July 1, 1992; amended effective January 1, 1995; March 1, 1998; September 30, 2004; July 1, 2009.]

Comment

A. Section 16.1–278 is the so-called mandamus statute which gives the Juvenile and Domestic Relations District Court the power to order services, etc., that are required by law to be provided by a governmental agency. The statute provides for notice and an opportunity to be heard, but it is silent on all other procedural matters. This proposal fleshes out the statute by detailing the statements required in the petition, the type of notice to be given and the right to a hearing.

B. Section 16.1–24D gives jurisdiction to the Juvenile and Domestic Relations District Courts to authorize emergency medical treatment in certain circumstances. Section 16.1–262 specifies the form and content of petitions. The latter section is, however, very general and does not cover the specifics of an emergency medical situation. Further, there usually are no hearings in these cases as the court, by telephone, has already given authorization. The petition and order follow by several days the permission to treat. Without the statements under this rule, the record, at best, is very skimpy regarding the particulars of the child's condition and the reason for the request (see Rule 8:22 for time requirement).

C. There is a statutory requirement for the content of support orders (§ 20–60.3), but there is no requirement that these items be in the support petition. This rule corrects this deficiency and further includes other important items of which the court should be aware such as prior support orders, etc.

[Comment amended effective March 1, 1998.]

RULE 8:4. SERVICE OF PROCESS—MOTION TO REDUCE SUPPORT ARREARAGES TO JUDGMENT

Any motion to enter judgment for support arrearages pursuant to § 16.1–278.18 shall be served upon the respondent in accordance with the provisions of §§ 8.01–296, 8.01–327, 8.01–329, or by (1) certified mail, return receipt requested, and (2) first class mail. Upon sufficient showing that a diligent effort was made to ascertain the location of a party, that party may be served with any required notice by delivery of the written notice to that party's residential or business address as filed with the court pursuant to Code § 20–60.3 or the Department of Social Services, or if changed, as shown in the records of the Department of Social Services.

[Adopted effective July 1, 1992. Amended effective March 1, 1998.]

Comment

This rule corrects a serious problem under § 16.1–279(O) (see now § 16.1–278.18) relating to monetary judgments for support arrearages. The statute provided for notice "in accordance with the applicable provisions of law relating to notice when proceedings are reopened." The problem is that judges and attorneys cannot agree on what this means. Guidance is necessary (see Garrity and Sheffield cases).

[Comment amended effective March 1, 1998.]

RULE 8:5. COURT-ORDERED REPORTS

Copies of all studies and reports pursuant to §§ 16.1–269.2, 16.1–273, 16. 1–274, 16.1–275 and 63.2–1524, when received by the court shall be furnished by the court to counsel of record, and upon request shall be mailed to such counsel. Counsel of record shall return such reports to the clerk upon the conclusion of the hearing and shall not make copies of such report or amended report or any portion of either.

[Adopted effective July 1, 1992. Amended effective January 1, 1995; May 2, 2011.]

Comment

The statutes cited in the Rule refer to reports for transfer hearings; social history reports; custody, visitation, or support reports; and reports of physical and mental evaluations. Section 16.1–274 specifies time limits for the filing of reports and directs that "The clerk shall furnish a copy of such report to all attorneys representing parties in the matter before the court" but the statute does not specify whether the clerk has an affirmative obligation to mail copies of the report to all attorneys. Due to the heavy workload in many clerk's offices, it was felt that mailing of reports should not be required in every case, but the proposed Rule would require mailing upon request.

The term "counsel of record" in the Rule includes parties appearing pro se (see Rule 8:2(b)(2)). This would satisfy the requirement in § 16.1–305(B) that all records or reports which are presented to the judge shall also be made available to the parties and their attorneys.

RULE 8:6. THE ROLES OF COUNSEL AND OF GUARDIANS AD LITEM WHEN REPRESENTING CHILDREN

The role of counsel for a child is the representation of the child's legitimate interests.

When appointed for a child, the guardian ad litem shall vigorously represent the child fully protecting the child's interest and welfare. The guardian ad litem shall advise the court of the wishes of the child in any case where the wishes of the child conflict with the opinion of the guardian ad litem as to what is in the child's interest and welfare.

[Adopted effective July 1, 1992.]

Comment

This is an effort to satisfy concerns of the Judicial Council of the original proposal. The Rule has been narrowed in scope, i.e., the role is merely defined with a caveat of the duty of the guardian ad litem when the child's wishes run counter to what the guardian ad litem deems to be in the interest or welfare of the child. The language defining the two roles has been modified to track that of the ABA Standards and Virginia case law.

RULE 8:7. FORMAT FOR FILING

(a) Except as provided in Rule 8:8(f) and Rule 1:17 pertaining to Electronically Filed Cases,

(1) All pleadings, motions, briefs and all other documents filed in any clerk's office in any proceeding pursuant to the Rules or statutes shall be 8–1/2 by 11 inches in size. All typed material shall be double spaced except for quotations.

(2) Subdivision (a)(1) of this Rule shall not apply to tables, charts, plats, photographs, and other material that cannot be reasonably reproduced on paper of that size.

(b) No paper shall be refused for failure to comply with the provisions of this Rule, but the clerk or judge may require that the paper be redone in compliance with this Rule and substituted for the paper initially filed. Counsel shall certify that the substituted paper is identical in content to the paper initially filed.

[Adopted effective July 1, 1992. Amended effective May 2, 2011.]

Comment

This Rule is identical to Rules 1:16 and 7A:7.

RULE 8:8. PLEADINGS

(a) General. Counsel of record tendering a pleading gives assurances that it is filed in good faith and not for delay, and counsel of record who files a pleading shall sign it and state counsel's address and telephone number. A pleading that is sworn to is an affidavit for all purposes for which an affidavit is required or permitted. The mention in a pleading of an accompanying exhibit shall, of itself and without more, make such an exhibit a part of the pleading.

(b) Denial, Admission, Objection. A party respondent need not file a pleading or may file a pleading denying or admitting all or any facts alleged in the petition, motion, or summons, or the respondent may file a motion raising objections. Any allegation not admitted is deemed denied. If a respondent fails to file a pleading, the failure will be taken as a denial of the allegations in the petition, motion, or summons.

(c) Amendment of Written Pleading. Except as hereinafter provided, or as provided pursuant to §§ 16.1–129.2, 16.1–93 and 16.1–259, no amendment shall be made to any pleading after it is filed with the clerk, except by leave of court. Leave to amend a pleading shall be liberally granted in furtherance of the ends of justice. In granting leave to amend, the court may make such provision for notice thereof and opportunity to make response as the court may deem reasonable and proper.

In delinquency, child in need of services, child in need of supervision, and status offense proceedings, the court may permit amendment of the written pleading at any time before adjudication, provided that the amendment does not change the nature or character of the matter alleged. If the amendment is made after the respondent pleads or is made after any evidence is heard, the amended pleading shall be read to him and he shall be allowed to change his plea. If the court finds that the amendment operates as a surprise to the respondent, it shall upon request grant a continuance for a reasonable time.

(d) Bill of Particulars. The court may direct the filing of a bill of particulars at any time before trial.

(e) Copies of Pleadings to Be Furnished. Except as provided in subdivision (f) of this Rule, all pleadings not otherwise required to be served shall be served on each counsel of record by delivering, dispatching by commercial delivery service, transmitting by facsimile or mailing a copy to each on or before the day of filing. At the foot of such pleadings shall be appended either acceptances of service or a certificate that copies were served as this Rule requires, showing the date of delivery, dispatching, transmitting or mailing.

(f) Electronic Filing. In any juvenile and domestic relations district court which has established an electronic filing system pursuant to Rule 1:17:

(1) Any proceeding may be designated as an Electronically Filed Case upon consent of all parties in the case.

(2) Except where service and/or filing of an original paper document is expressly required by these rules, all pleadings, motions, notices and other instruments in an Electronically Filed Case shall be formatted, served and filed as specified in the requirements and procedures of Rule 1:17; provided, however, that when any document listed below is filed in the case, the filing party shall notify the clerk of court that the original document must be retained.

(i) Any pleading or affidavit required by statute or rule to be sworn, verified or certified as provided in Rule 1:17(e)(5).

(ii) Any contract or deed.

(iii) Any prenuptial agreement or written settlement agreement, including any property settlement agreement.

(iv) Any check or other negotiable instrument.

(v) Any handwritten statement, waiver, or consent by a defendant or witness in a criminal proceeding.

(vi) Any form signed by a defendant in a criminal proceeding, including any typed statements or a guilty plea form.

(vii) Any document that cannot be converted into an electronic document in such a way as to produce a clear and readable image.

[Adopted effective July 1, 1992. Amended effective February 1, 1999; May 2, 2011.]

Comment

Paragraph (a) is virtually identical to Rule 7A:8 of the Rules for General District Courts.

Paragraph (b) provides that any allegation of a pleading which is not admitted is deemed denied. This is the converse of the Rule applied in circuit courts (see Rule 1:42) because responsive pleadings are generally not required or filed in juvenile and domestic relations district courts.

The first paragraph under (c) is substantially identical to Rule 1:8 and Rule 7A:9 but adds statutory references. The second paragraph under (c) pertains to certain proceedings that are unique to the juvenile and domestic relations district court.

Paragraph (d) (Bill of Particulars) is adapted from § 16.1–69.25:1.

Paragraph (e) is patterned after Rules 1:12 and 7A:10 with minor modifications.

RULE 8:9. DISCRETION OF COURT

All steps and procedures in the clerk's office touching the filing of pleadings and the maturing of suits or actions may be reviewed and corrected by the court.

The time allowed for filing pleadings may be extended by the court in its discretion, and such extension may be granted although the time fixed already has expired.

[Adopted effective July 1, 1992.]

Comment

This Rule tracks Rules 1:9 and 7A:5.

RULE 8:10. MOTIONS TO TRANSFER VENUE

A motion to transfer venue shall be made in writing or in court with the parties present. When a written motion is filed, it shall be set for hearing, and the motion and notice of hearing shall be served on all other parties or on counsel of record, if any.

[Adopted effective July 1, 1992.]

Comment

Section 16.1–243 specifies the proper venue for various types of cases in the juvenile and domestic relations district court but does not specify the procedure for transfer. There is a lack of uniformity among the various courts in transferring venue. For example, some courts require a hearing to decide whether venue should be transferred while others do not; some courts will only transfer active cases, while others will transfer inactive or closed cases.

The proposed Rule would apply to both pending and inactive cases and would make it clear that proper notice must be given and a hearing held in every case.

RULE 8:11. REPORTERS AND TRANSCRIPTS OF PROCEEDINGS IN COURT

Any party shall have the right to have a court reporter present to take down or record the proceedings. In all proceedings not open to the public it shall be within the sound discretion of the judge as to whether a court reporter may take down or record the proceedings on behalf of a person not a party. In all other proceedings, any person not a party may bring a court reporter to take down the proceedings. Court reporters, when present, shall be first duly sworn to take down and transcribe the proceedings faithfully and accurately to the best of their ability and shall be subject to the control and discipline of the judge.

In proceedings open to the public, when a court reporter is present and takes down or records the proceeding, any interested person shall be entitled to obtain a transcript, unless the court records remain confidential pursuant to § 16.1–305. In proceedings not open to the public, when a court reporter is present and takes down or records the proceeding, a party shall be entitled to obtain a transcript without prior court order, but the court may limit the circulation of the transcript by a party. In such proceedings not open to the public, other than (i) proceedings closed for good cause pursuant to subsection C of § 16.1–302 and which result in an adjudication of delinquency of a juvenile, who was fourteen years or older at the time of the offense, on the basis of an act which would be a felony if committed by an adult or (ii) proceedings resulting in a subsequent adjudication of delinquency as described in subsection B1 of § 16.1–305, all other interested persons shall only be entitled to a transcript by order of court which shall state for whom such transcript shall be prepared and what restrictions, if any, are imposed on the use and distribution of the transcript, its contents or any part. In delinquency proceedings which are closed for good cause pursuant to subsection C of § 16.1–302 and which result in an adjudication of delinquency of a juvenile, who was fourteen years or older at the time of the offense, on the basis of an act which would be a felony if committed by an adult, when a court reporter is present and takes down or records the proceeding, any interested person shall be entitled to a transcript, except for those transcripts or portions of transcripts which the judge has ordered shall remain confidential pursuant to subsection B1 of § 16.1–305. In proceedings resulting in an adjudication of delinquency which is subsequent to a prior adjudication of delinquency of a juvenile who was fourteen years or older at the time of the prior offense and whose prior adjudication was on the basis of an act which would be a felony if committed by an adult, when a court reporter is present and takes down or records the proceeding, any interested person shall be entitled to obtain a transcript, except for those transcripts or portions of transcripts which the judge has ordered shall remain confidential pursuant to subsection B1 of § 16.1–305.

The proceedings may be taken down by means of any recording device approved by the court.

[Adopted effective July 1, 1992. Amended effective March 15, 1997.]

Comment

This language tracks Rule 7A:4 with modifications that relate to the confidentiality of proceedings not open to the public as set forth in § 16.1–302 and § 16.1–305.

[Comment amended effective March 15, 1997.]

RULE 8:12. PRESERVATION OF THE RECORD

A court may authorize the use of electronic or photographic means for the preservation of the record or parts thereof.

[Adopted effective July 1, 1992.]

Comment

This Rule is identical to Rule 7A:6.

RULE 8:13. REQUESTS FOR SUBPOENAS FOR WITNESSES AND RECORDS

(a) Subpoenas for Witnesses.

(1) Requests for subpoenas for witnesses should be filed at least ten days prior to hearing.

(2) Requests for subpoenas for witnesses not timely filed should not be honored except when authorized by the court for good cause.

(b) Subpoenas Duces Tecum.

(1) Requests for subpoenas duces tecum should be filed at least 15 days prior to hearing.

(2) Requests for subpoenas duces tecum not timely filed should not be honored except when authorized by a judge for good cause.

(c) Meaning of Filed. The term "filed" as used in this Rule means received in the appropriate clerk's office or by an appropriate magistrate.

(d) Copies of Requests for Subpoenas Duces Tecum. All requests for subpoenas duces tecum shall be served on each counsel of record by delivering, dispatching by commercial delivery service, transmitting by facsimile or mailing a copy to each on or before the day of filing. At the foot of such requests shall be appended either acceptance of service or a certificate that copies were served as this Rule requires, showing the date of delivery, dispatching, transmitting or mailing.

(e) Exception. This Rule does not apply to subpoenas for witnesses and subpoenas duces tecum issued by attorneys in civil cases as authorized by Virginia Code §§ 8.01–407 and 16.1–265.

[Adopted effective July 1, 1992. Amended effective February 1, 1999; July 1, 2000.]

Comment

This tracks Rules 7A:10 and 7A:12 with the substitution of "hearing" for "trial" to recognize the multiplicity of pre- and post-trial hearings in the juvenile and domestic relations district court.

RULE 8:14. CONTINUANCES

(a) Continuance Granted for Good Cause. Continuances should not be granted except by, and at the discretion of, a judge for good cause shown, or unless otherwise provided by law. The judge may, by order, delegate to the clerk the power to grant continuances consented to by all parties under such circumstances as are set forth in the order. Such an order of delegation should be reasonably disseminated and posted so as to inform the bar and the general public.

(b) All Parties Agree to Continuance. If all parties to a proceeding agree to seek a continuance, the request may be made orally by one party as long as that party certifies to the judge that all other parties know of the request and concur. Such a request should be made as far in advance of the scheduled hearing or trial as is practicable. If granted, the moving party shall be responsible for assuring that notice of the continuance is given to all subpoenaed witnesses and that they are provided with the new court date. This obligation may be met by (i) an agreement between the parties that each side will notify its own witnesses; or (ii) any other arrangement that is reasonably calculated to get prompt notice to all witnesses.

(c) All Parties Do Not Agree to Continuance. If a request for continuance is not agreed to by all parties to a proceeding, such request should be made to the court prior to the time originally scheduled for the hearing or trial. If the court determines that a hearing on the request should be conducted prior to the time originally scheduled for the trial, all parties shall be given notice of such hearing by the requesting party.

(d) Continuances Requested at the Time of Hearing. Where a request for a continuance has not been made prior to the hearing or trial and other parties or witnesses are present and prepared for trial, a continuance should be granted only upon a showing that to proceed with the trial would not be in the best interest of justice.

(e) Parties. For purposes of this Rule, the term "parties" shall mean all plaintiffs, petitioners, the prosecution, defendants, respondents and any person who is the subject of the proceeding.

[Adopted effective July 1, 1992.]

Comment

This tracks Rule 7A:14 except in paragraph (e) which has been expanded to include the greater multiplicity of parties in juvenile and domestic relations district courts.

RULE 8:15. DISCOVERY

(a) Adult Criminal Case. In any cases involving adults charged with crime, the provisions of Rule 7C:5 shall govern discovery.

(b) Juvenile Delinquency Cases. In juvenile delinquency cases, when the juvenile is charged with an act that would be a felony if committed by an adult, or in a transfer hearing or a preliminary hearing to certify charges pursuant to § 16.1–269.1, the court shall, upon motion timely made by the juvenile or the Commonwealth's Attorney, and for good cause, enter such orders in aid of discovery and inspection of evidence as provided under Rule 3A:11.

In juvenile delinquency cases when the juvenile is charged with an act that would be a misdemeanor if committed by an adult, the court shall, upon motion timely made and for good cause, enter such orders for discovery as provided under Rule 7C:5.

(c) Other Cases. In all other proceedings, the court may, upon motion timely made and for good cause, enter such orders in aid of discovery and inspection of evidence as permitted under Part Four of the Rules, except that no depositions may be taken.

(d) In proceedings concerning civil support, the judge may require parties to file a statement of gross income together with documentation in support of the statement.

[Adopted effective July 1, 1992. Amended effective March 15, 1997.]

Comment

The rule covers discovery in all types of cases in Juvenile and Domestic Relations District Court.

With regard to adult criminal cases, the rule would allow the same discovery that is allowed in the general district courts under Rule 7C:5. This would also be consistent with § 16.1–259(A).

With respect to juvenile delinquency cases, where the juvenile is charged with a felony or is the subject of a transfer hearing, the subcommittee believes that the juvenile should be afforded the same discovery rights as an adult under Rule 3A:11 in view of the potentially serious loss of liberty in such cases. To require less might result in a claim of denial of equal protection of law. However, in misdemeanor cases juveniles would be granted the same, more limited discovery as adults under Rule 7C:5.

In civil cases (c), the subcommittee recommends that all of the forms of discovery authorized by Part Four of the Rules be permitted in Juvenile and Domestic Relations District Court except for the taking of depositions. The subcommittee did not recommend depositions because of the cost involved. However, the other types of discovery, such as interrogatories and motions for production, are already commonly used by many attorneys in Juvenile and Domestic Relations District Court and should be officially sanctioned in order to promote uniform procedure among the courts.

Chapters 755 and 914 of the 1996 Acts of the General Assembly amended § 16.1–269.1 to provide that a juvenile may be tried in circuit court subsequent to either a transfer hearing or a preliminary hearing and certification. The first paragraph of subsection (b) has been amended to reflect these provisions.

[Comment amended effective March 15, 1997.]

RULE 8:16. ARRAIGNMENT IN JUVENILE DELINQUENCY CASES

Arraignment in a delinquency proceeding shall consist of reading to the juvenile the charge on which the juvenile will be tried and calling on the juvenile to plead thereto, and it shall be conducted in court. Arraignment may be waived by the juvenile in court, or by counsel.

[Adopted effective July 1, 1992.]

Comment

The Code is silent on this phase of a juvenile proceeding. It is felt that this gap in the Code should be filled in to have the Rules more closely track an actual delinquency case. See Rule 8:18 on the types of pleas by the juvenile.

RULE 8:17. NOTIFICATION AND WAIVER OF TRIAL RIGHTS OF PARTIES

Upon a juvenile's first appearance in court in a delinquency case, the juvenile shall be advised by the judge of the following trial rights: the right to counsel, to a public hearing, to the privilege against self-incrimination, to confront and cross-examine witnesses, to present evidence, and the right to appeal a final decision of the court. In determining whether a waiver of the right to counsel, of the right to a public hearing, and of the privilege against self-incrimination, is knowingly, voluntarily, and intelligently made, the court must find after a thorough inquiry that the juvenile is capable of making an intelligent and understanding decision in light of the child's age, mental condition, education, and experience, considering the nature and complexity of the case. Such waiver of trial rights shall be made orally in open court, and the waiver of the right to counsel shall also be reduced to writing, signed by the juvenile and filed with the court records of the case.

[Adopted effective July 1, 1992.]

Comment

This Rule deals with a crucial problem in the juvenile and domestic relations district court where a juvenile, presumptively incapable of having and exercising significant legal rights, is called on to waive some very basic Constitutional rights defined by the Supreme Court in *In re Gault,* 387 U.S. 1 (1967), and reaffirmed by the juvenile code. Such waivers should be surrounded by procedural protections to ensure that they are voluntarily, knowingly and intelligently made.

Since the Judicial Council last met and approved this Rule in its original form, we have received comments that some judges may interpret the Rule to require in all cases a suppression-type hearing for rights waived before the child ever appeared before a judge. To clarify the intent of the Rule, we suggest that it be amended to reflect "trial" rights. Note that the word "trial" has been inserted at appropriate places.

RULE 8:18. PLEAS

(a) Permissible Pleas by Child. A child may admit the allegations of the petition or summons by pleading guilty, or the child may plead not guilty, nolo contendere, or enter no plea. If the child enters no plea, the court will proceed as if a denial were entered to the allegations of the petition or summons.

(b) Determining Voluntariness, Understanding, and Intelligence of a Plea of Guilty by a Juvenile. The court shall not accept a plea of guilty or nolo contendere to a charge of delinquency by a child without first determining that the plea is made voluntarily with an understanding of the nature of the allegations in the petition or summons and the consequences of the plea, including that such a plea constitutes a waiver of the right to confront one's accusers and the right against compulsory self-incrimination.

(c) Determining Voluntariness, Understanding, and Intelligence of a Plea of Guilty by an Adult. In any case involving an adult charged with a crime, the court shall not accept a plea of guilty or nolo contendere to a misdemeanor charge except in compliance with Rule 7C:6.

(d) Upon rejecting a plea agreement in any criminal or delinquency matter, a judge shall immediately recuse himself from any further proceedings on the same matter unless the parties agree otherwise.

[Adopted effective July 1, 1992. Amended effective June 1, 2005; July 1, 2014.]

Comment

There is no statute covering the types of pleas of a child. There is also considerable variance in the Commonwealth on the types of pleas allowed, e.g., "guilty," "within the purview" and "not innocent." This will insure uniform procedure throughout the Commonwealth.

RULE 8:19. ENDORSEMENTS OF ORDERS

Drafts of orders prepared by counsel of record shall be endorsed by all counsel of record, or reasonable notice of the time and place of presenting such drafts together with copies thereof shall be served by delivering, dispatching by commercial delivery service, transmitting by facsimile or mailing to all counsel of record who have not endorsed them. Compliance with this Rule may be modified or dispensed with by the court in its discretion. In an Electronically Filed Case, endorsement and specification of any objections to the draft order shall be accomplished as provided in Rule 1:17.

[Adopted effective July 1, 1992. Amended effective February 1, 1999; May 2, 2011.]

Comment

This Rule tracks Rule 7A:11, with a minor amendment to acknowledge that many orders in juvenile and domestic relations district court are form orders prepared by the court, rather than counsel.

RULE 8:20. APPEALS

All appeals shall be noted in writing. An appeal is noted only upon timely receipt in the clerk's office of the writing. An appeal may be noted by a party or by the attorney for such party.

[Adopted effective July 1, 1992.]

Comment

Rule 8:20 tracks the relevant language of Rule 7A:13.

RULE 8:21. DELETED

[Deleted effective May 2, 2011.]

RULE 8:22. JUDICIAL CONSENT

In any instance where the court is called upon in an emergency situation to give judicial consent as provided for by statute, the request and court consent may be oral, but a written request shall be filed in the clerk's office within five days of such consent, and the consent of the court shall also be reduced to a written order as soon as reasonably possible.

[Adopted effective July 1, 1992.]

Comment

This Rule applies primarily to requests for emergency medical or surgical treatment of juveniles under § 16.1–241(d). Rule 8:3(b) covers the content of a petition filed for this purpose.

PART NINE. JUDICIAL PERFORMANCE EVALUATION PROGRAM

RULE 9:1. PURPOSE AND OPERATION

As provided by § 17.1–100 of the Code of Virginia, the Supreme Court of Virginia hereby establishes a judicial performance evaluation program that will provide both a self-improvement mechanism for judges and a source of information for the reelection process. The Program shall be maintained by the Office of the Executive Secretary who may engage a third party contractor to conduct surveys and prepare evaluations.

[Adopted effective October 31, 2014.]

RULE 9:2. CONFIDENTIALITY

All surveys, responses, evaluations, and other records created or maintained by or on behalf of the judicial performance evaluation program related to an evaluation of any individual justice or judge are confidential and may only be shared with the subject judge, or a facilitator judge assigned by the program to assist with the evaluation, and shall not be disclosed to any third party; except that any report provided to the General Assembly pursuant to this section shall be a public record that is open to inspection as provided in § 17.1–100.

[Adopted effective October 31, 2014.]

INDEX TO SUPREME COURT RULES

ABUSE
Evidence, **Rule 2:409**

ACTIONS AND PROCEEDINGS
Generally, **Rule 3:1 et seq.**
Administrative Law and Procedure, generally, this index
Appeal and Review, generally, this index
Attorney Fees, generally, this index
Chancery commissioners, proceedings before, **Rule 3:23**
Commencement, **Rule 3:2**
Compromise and Settlement, generally, this index
Counterclaims, **Rule 3:9**
Cross claims, **Rule 3:10**
Definitions, **Rule 3:1**
Attorney discipline, **BOG 13**
Disciplinary actions and proceedings. Attorneys, this index
Dismissal, generally, this index
Judgments and Decrees, generally, this index
Petitions, commencement, **Rule 3:2**
Res judicata, **Rule 1:6**
Venue, criminal cases, **Rule 3A:2.1**

ACTUAL INNOCENCE
Writs, petitions, **Rules 5:7B, 5A:5; Forms 12 (app. foll. Rule 5:41), 12 (app. foll. Rule 5A:37)**

AD DAMNUM CLAUSES
Money damages, complaints, **Rule 3:2**

ADJUDICATION OF A CRIME PROCEEDING
Definitions, attorney discipline, **BOG 13**

ADJUDICATIVE FACTS
Judicial notice, **Rule 2:201**

ADMINISTRATIVE LAW AND PROCEDURE
Appeal and review, **Rule 2A:1 et seq.**
Notice, appeal, **Rule 2A:2**
Petition for appeal, **Rule 2A:4**
Record on appeal, **Rule 2A:3**
Small businesses, appeal and review, **Rule 2A:6**
Unauthorized practice of law, **UPR 9–101 et seq.**

ADMISSIONS
Best evidence, **Rule 2:1007**
Hearsay evidence, exceptions, **Rule 2:803**
Juvenile and domestic relations district courts, **Rule 8:8**
Request for admissions, **Rule 4:11**

ADMONITION
Definitions, attorney discipline, **BOG 13**

ADVERSE OR PECUNIARY INTEREST
Conflict of Interest, generally, this index

ADVERTISEMENTS
Attorneys, this index

ADVISORY OPINIONS
Definitions, legal ethics, **BOG 10**
Unauthorized practice of law, **BOG 10**

AFFIRMATIONS AND OATHS
Oaths and Affirmations, generally, this index

AGENCY SECRETARY
Definitions, Administrative Process Act appeals, **Rule 2A:1**

AGREED DISPOSITION
Definitions, attorney discipline, **BOG 13**

AMENDMENTS
Pleadings, **Rule 1:8**
Juvenile and domestic relations district courts, **Rule 8:8**

AMICUS CURIAE
Briefs, **Rules 5:30, 5A:23**
Oral argument,
Court of appeals, **Rule 5A:28**
Supreme court appeals, **Rule 5:33**

ANCIENT DOCUMENTS
Statements, hearsay evidence, exceptions, **Rule 2:803**

ANDERS APPEALS
Petitions, **Rule 5A:12**

ANSWER
Generally, **Rule 3:8**

APPEAL AND REVIEW
Actual innocence, writs, **Rules 5:7B, 5A:5; Forms 12 (app. foll. Rule 5:41), 12 (app. foll. Rule 5A:37)**
Anders appeals, petitions, **Rule 5A:12**
Attorney discipline, **Rule 5:21; BOG 13**
Attorney fees, **Rule 1:1A**
Denial of appeal, petition for rehearing, **Rule 5:20**
Corporation commission, appeals to supreme court, **Rule 5:21**
Costs, **Rule 1:1A**
Denial of appeal, petition for rehearing, **Rule 5:20**
Criminal proceedings, **Rule 3A:19**
Depositions, **Rule 4:2**

APPEAL AND REVIEW—Cont'd
District courts, noting, **Rule 7A:13**
Guardians ad litem, notice, **Rule 5A:6**
Juvenile and domestic relations district courts, **Rule 8:20**
Multiparty cases, partial final judgment, **Rule 5:8A**
Notice, filing, time, **Rules 5:9, 5A:6**
Preservation of issues, supreme court proceedings, **Rule 5:25**
Pro hac vice, out of state attorneys,
Oral argument,
Court of appeals, **Rules 5A:12, 5A:28**
Supreme court, **Rule 5:33**
Participation in trial, **Rule 1A:4**
Forms, **Form 1 (app. foll. Rule 1A:7)**
Quarantine, isolation, communicable disease, public health threats, **Rules 3:24, 5:41**
Small businesses, administrative law and procedure, **Rule 2A:6**
State corporation commission, appeals to supreme court, **Rule 5:21**
Three judge circuit court panels, **Rule 5:21**

APPEAL BOND
Court of appeals, **Rule 5A:17**
Supreme court, **Rule 5:24**

APPEALS COURT
Court of Appeals, generally, this index

APPENDICES
Court of appeals, **Rule 5A:25**
Supreme court appeals, **Rule 5:32**

ARRAIGNMENT
Juvenile and domestic relations district courts, **Rule 8:16**

ARREST
Statement of witness for warrant, **Form 2 (app. foll. Rule 3A:25)**
Warrant or summons, **Rule 3A:4**

ASSIGNMENT OF ERROR
Generally, **Rule 5:17**

ATTORNEY CLIENT PRIVILEGE
Generally, **Rule 2:502**

ATTORNEY FEES
Generally, **Rule 3:25; RPC 1.5; DR 2–105**
Appeal and review, **Rule 1:1A**
Denial of appeal, petition for rehearing, **Rule 5:20**
Claims, demand, **Rule 3:25**
Credit cards, discounts, payment, **RPC 5.4**
Division, **RPC 1.5**
With nonlawyer, **RPC 5.4; DR 3–102**
Financial assistance, **RPC 1.8**
Limited liability entities, division, **BOG 14**
Pro bono services, **RPC 6.1**
Prohibited transactions, financial assistance, **RPC 1.8**

ATTORNEY FEES—Cont'd
Supreme court proceedings, **Rule 5:35**
Waiver, **Rule 3:25**

ATTORNEYS
Generally, **Rule 1:5**
Abbreviated or informal investigation, discipline, **BOG 13**
Acceptance of employment, **DR 2–107**
Action as public official, **RPC 1.11; DR 8–101**
Activation, continuing legal education, **BOG 17**
Address, advertising, attorney responsible, **RPC 7.1**
Administrative agency practice, unauthorized practice of law, **UPR 9–101 et seq.**
Administrative suspension, procedure, **BOG 19**
Admission to practice, foreign attorneys,
Admission without examination, **Rule 1A:1**
Corporations, certificates and certification, **Rule 1A:5**
Forms, **Form 2 (app. foll. Rule 1A:7)**
Foreign legal consultants, certificates and certification, **Rule 1A:7**
Military forces,
Legal assistance, **Rule 1A:6**
Spouses, provisional admission, **Rule 1A:8**
Patents and trademarks, **Rule 1A:2**
Certificates, revocation, **Rule 1A:3**
Pro hac vice, generally, post
Admonition, orders, **BOG 13**
Stay pending appeal, **Rule 5:21**
Adverse or pecuniary interest. Conflict of interest, generally, post
Advertisements, **RPC 7.1 et seq.; DR 2–101**
Names and letterheads, **RPC 7.5; DR 2–102**
Attorney responsible, **RPC 7.1**
Notice, **RPC 7.3**
Specialists, **RPC 7.4; DR 2–104**
Advice,
Scope, **RPC 2.1**
Unrepresented persons, **RPC 4.3**
Advisory opinions, legal ethics and unauthorized practice of law, **BOG 10**
Agreements restricting practice of lawyer, **RPC 5.6; DR 2–106**
Aiding unauthorized practice of law, **RPC 5.5; DR 3–101**
Alternative disposition, public reprimand with terms, **BOG 13**
Annual meeting, state bar, **BOG 8**
Appeal and review,
Advisory opinions, legal ethics and unauthorized practice of law, **BOG 10**
Discipline, **Rule 5:21; BOG 13**
Appearance of impropriety, avoiding, **DR 9–101**
Appointments, **RPC 6.2**
Actual innocence, writs, **Rules 5:7B, 5A:5; Forms 12 (app. foll. Rule 5:41), 12 (app. foll. Rule 5A:37)**
Assistants,
Professional misconduct, liability, nonlawyer assistants, **RPC 5.3**

ATTORNEYS—Cont'd
Assistants—Cont'd
Supervised attorneys, **RPC 5.1**
Attorney client privilege, **RPC 1.6**
Avoiding acquisition of interest in litigation, **DR 5–103**
Avoiding influence by others than client, **RPC 1.8, 5.4; DR 5–106**
Bar, organization and government, **BOG 1 et seq.**
Bar counsel, discipline, powers and duties, **BOG 13**
Board, discipline, powers and duties, **BOG 13**
Appeals, **Rule 5:21**
Bonds (officers and fiduciaries), reinstatement, **BOG 13**
Burden of proof, discipline, **BOG 13**
Business relations with client, **DR 5–104**
Candor, **RPC 3.3**
Case results, advertising, **RPC 7.1**
Certificates and certification,
Continuing legal education, attendance, **BOG 17**
Corporations, foreign states, **Rule 1A:5**
Forms, **Form 2 (app. foll. Rule 1A:7)**
Disciplinary proceedings, **BOG 13**
Foreign attorneys, **Rule 1A:1 et seq.**
Foreign legal consultants, admission to practice, **Rule 1A:7**
Limited liability entities, **BOG 14**
Malpractice insurance, crimes and offenses, **BOG 13.4**
Military forces, foreign states, legal assistance, **Rule 1A:6**
Sanction determination, **BOG 13**
Specialists, **RPC 7.4; DR 2–104**
Third year student practice, **BOG 15**
Change of address,
Court of appeals proceedings, **Rule 5A:1**
Supreme court proceedings, **Rule 5:1**
Children and minors, juvenile and domestic relations district courts, **Rule 8:6**
Classes, membership, state bar, **BOG 3**
Clerks, disciplinary system, powers and duties, discipline, **BOG 13**
Clients,
Corporate clients, **RPC 1.13**
Former clients, **RPC 1.9**
Funds and property, preserving identity, **DR 9–102; BOG 20**
Impairment, clients with, **RPC 1.14**
Nonprofit, court annexed limited legal services programs, **RPC 6.5**
Notice, departing attorneys, dissolving firms, **RPC 5.8**
Organizations, **RPC 1.13**
Prospective clients, duties, **RPC 1.18**
COLD, discipline, powers and duties, **BOG 13**
Collection agencies, unauthorized practice of law, **UPR 3–101 et seq.**
Communication, **RPC 7.1 et seq.**
Adverse interest, **DR 7–103**
Clients, **RPC 1.4**

ATTORNEYS—Cont'd
Communication—Cont'd
False or misleading communications, **RPC 7.1**
Fees, **RPC 1.5**
Jurors, **RPC 3.5; DR 7–107**
Persons represented by counsel, **RPC 4.2**
Prospective clients, **RPC 1.18**
Unrepresented persons, **RPC 4.3**
Competence and promptness, **RPC 1.1, 1.3; DR 6–101**
Complaints,
Disciplinary proceedings, **BOG 13**
Unauthorized practice of law, **BOG 10**
Compromise and settlement,
Mediator, **RPC 2.11**
Negotiation, lay adjusters, unauthorized practice of law, **UPR 2–103**
Third party neutral, **RPC 2.10**
Computerized legal research services, contracts, **BOG 21**
Conduct of trial, **DR 7–105**
Confidential or privileged information, **RPC 1.6; DR 4–101**
Disciplinary proceedings, **BOG 13**
Prospective clients, duties, **RPC 1.18**
Public employment, **RPC 1.11**
Conflict of interest, **RPC 1.7, 1.8; DR 5–101 et seq.**
Communication, **RPC 4.3; DR 7–103**
District committees, discipline, **BOG 13**
Former clients, **RPC 1.9**
Legal services organizations, membership, **RPC 6.3**
Nonprofit, court annexed limited legal services programs, **RPC 6.5**
Prohibited transactions, **RPC 1.8**
Prospective clients, duties, **RPC 1.18**
Consent,
Conflict of interest, representation, **RPC 1.7**
Licenses and permits, revocation or suspension, discipline, **BOG 13**
Consultants, foreign legal consultants, certificates and certification, **Rule 1A:7**
Contacts,
Court of appeals proceedings, change of information, **Rule 5A:1**
Officials, **RPC 3.5; DR 7–109**
Supreme court proceedings, change of information, **Rule 5:1**
Witnesses, **RPC 3.5; DR 7–108**
Continuance, disciplinary proceedings, **BOG 13**
Continuing legal education, **BOG 17**
Failure to complete requirement, suspension, **BOG 13.2**
Corporate clients, **RPC 1.13**
Costs, attorney discipline, **BOG 13**
Council,
Discipline, powers and duties, **BOG 13**
State bar, **BOG 5 et seq.**
Courts, discipline, powers and duties, **BOG 13**

ATTORNEYS—Cont'd
Crimes and offenses,
Discipline, **BOG 13**
Malpractice insurance, **BOG 13.4**
Criminal prosecution, threatening, **DR 7–104**
Declining representation, **RPC 1.16**
Definitions,
Discipline, **BOG 13**
Juvenile and domestic relations district courts, **Rule 8:2**
Departing attorneys, law firms, notice, **RPC 5.8**
Diligence, **RPC 1.3**
Direct contact with potential clients, **RPC 7.3**
Disbarment, **BOG 13**
Disbursements, state bar, **BOG 12**
Disciplinary actions and proceedings, **DR 1–101 et seq.; BOG 13**
Jurisdiction, **RPC 8.5**
Liability for professional misconduct of another, **RPC 5.1, 5.3**
Limited liability entities, **BOG 14**
Disclaimer, case results, advertising, **RPC 7.1**
Disclosure,
Attorney client privilege, **RPC 1.6**
Conflict of interest, **RPC 1.7, 1.8**
Former clients, **RPC 1.9**
Disciplinary proceedings, **BOG 13**
Prohibited transactions, **RPC 1.8**
Prospective clients, duties, **RPC 1.18**
Discovery,
Discipline, **BOG 13**
Work product, **Rule 4:1**
Dismissal, disciplinary proceedings, **BOG 13**
Dispute resolution,
Mediator, **RPC 2.11**
Third party neutral, **RPC 2.10**
Disqualification, **RPC 1.10 et seq.**
Disciplinary proceedings, **BOG 13**
Former or concurrent employment,
Judges and arbitrators, **RPC 1.12**
Public officers, **RPC 1.11**
Imputed, **RPC 1.10**
Prospective clients, **RPC 1.18**
Successive government and private employment, **RPC 1.11**
Disrupting proceedings, **RPC 3.4**
Dissolution, law firms, notice, **RPC 5.8**
District committees, discipline, **BOG 13**
District courts, **Rule 7A:3**
Dividing fees with nonlawyer, **RPC 5.4; DR 3–102**
Docket, disciplinary proceedings, **BOG 13**
Dues, state bar, **BOG 11**
Clients protection fund, **BOG 16**
Emeritus members, classes, state bar membership, **BOG 3**
English language, communications, disciplinary proceedings, **BOG 13**
Estate planning and settlement, unauthorized practice of law, **UPR 4–101 et seq.**

ATTORNEYS—Cont'd
Ethics, **DR 1–101 et seq.**
Promulgation, **BOG 10**
Evaluation for third party, **RPC 2.3**
Evidence,
Attorney client privilege, **Rule 2:502**
Discipline, **BOG 13**
Examinations,
Foreign attorneys, admission without examination, **Rule 1A:1**
Patents and trademarks, **Rule 1A:2**
Certificates, revocation, **Rule 1A:3**
Exemptions, continuing legal education, **BOG 17**
Failure to complete continuing legal education requirement, suspension, **BOG 13.2**
Failure to complete professionalism course, suspension, **BOG 13.1**
Fairness, **RPC 3.4**
False or misleading communications, **RPC 7.1**
False or misleading statements of law or fact, **RPC 3.3, 4.1, 8.1 et seq.**
False or unjust criticism of judges, **RPC 8.2**
Fees. Attorney Fees, generally, this index
Financial responsibility, **BOG 18**
Fines and penalties,
Clients protection fund, **BOG 16**
Disciplinary proceedings, **BOG 13**
First offender pleas, disciplinary proceedings, **BOG 13**
Foreign attorneys, **Rule 1A:1 et seq.**
Definitions,
Discipline, **BOG 13**
Unauthorized practice of law, **RPC 5.5**
Foreign legal consultants, certificates and certification, **Rule 1A:7**
Military forces, spouses, provisional admission, **Rule 1A:8**
Pro hac vice, generally, post
Unauthorized practice, **UPR**
Foreign states,
Disciplinary proceedings, **BOG 13**
Military forces, post
Former or concurrent employment,
Judges and arbitrators, **RPC 1.12**
Public officers, **RPC 1.11**
Forms,
Corporations, admission to practice, **Form 2 (app. foll. Rule 1A:7)**
Financial institutions, trust accounts, **Appendix A (foll. BOG 20)**
Pro hac vice, out of state attorneys, participation in trial, **Form 1 (app. foll. Rule 1A:7)**
Frivolous claims and contentions, **RPC 3.1**
Funds and property of client,
Preserving identity, **DR 9–102; BOG 20**
Protection fund, **BOG 16**
Safekeeping, **RPC 1.15**
Security fund, **BOG 16**
Gifts, prohibited transactions, **RPC 1.8**

ATTORNEYS—Cont'd
Government and organization, **BOG 1 et seq.**
Government lawyers, special responsibilities, **RPC 3.8; DR 8–102**
Hearings, disciplinary proceedings, **BOG 13**
Impairment, **BOG 13**
Clients with, **RPC 1.14**
Impropriety, avoiding appearance, **DR 9–101**
Indigents,
Appointments, **RPC 6.2**
Legal services organizations, membership, **RPC 6.3**
Pro bono services, **RPC 6.1**
Influence by others than client, **RPC 1.8, 5.4; DR 5–106**
Informal advisory opinions, legal ethics and unauthorized practice of law, **BOG 10**
Informal or abbreviated investigation, discipline, **BOG 13**
Interest,
Judgments, discipline, **BOG 13**
Trust accounts, client funds, **BOG 20**
Interest in litigation, avoiding acquisition, **DR 5–103**
Investigations,
Disciplinary proceedings, **BOG 13**
Jurors, **RPC 3.5; DR 7–107**
Lay adjusters, unauthorized practice of law, **UPR 2–102**
IOLTA accounts, client funds, **BOG 20**
Judicial officers, false or unjust criticism by attorneys, **RPC 8.2**
Jurisdiction, disciplinary authority, **RPC 8.5; BOG 13**
Jurors, communication with or investigation of, **RPC 3.5; DR 7–107**
Juvenile and domestic relations district courts, court-ordered reports, **Rule 8:5**
Law lists, **DR 2–102**
Lay adjusters, unauthorized practice of law, **UPR 2–101 et seq.**
Legal ethics,
Advisory opinions, **BOG 10**
Promulgation, **BOG 10**
Legal research services, online, contracts, **BOG 21**
Legal services organizations, membership, **RPC 6.3**
Letterheads and names, **RPC 7.5; DR 2–102**
Advertising, attorney responsible, **RPC 7.1**
Limited liability entities, **BOG 14**
Licenses and permits,
Foreign attorneys, **Rule 1A:1 et seq.**
Impairment, **BOG 13**
Resignation, **BOG 13**
Revocation or suspension, generally, post
Limitation of practice, **DR 2–104**
Emeritus members, state bar, **BOG 3**
Limited liability entities, **BOG 14**
Limiting business relations with client, **DR 5–104**
Limiting liability to client, **DR 6–102**
Maintaining integrity and competence of legal profession, **RPC 8.1 et seq.; DR 1–101**

ATTORNEYS—Cont'd
Malpractice insurance, crimes and offenses, **BOG 13.4**
Mandatory continuing legal education, **BOG 17**
Mediators, **RPC 2.11**
Meetings, state bar, **BOG 8**
Membership, state bar, **BOG 2, 3**
Military forces, foreign states,
Husband and wife, provisional admission, **Rule 1A:8**
Legal assistance, registration, **Rule 1A:6**
Misconduct, **RPC 8.4; DR 1–102; BOG 13**
Reports, **RPC 8.3; DR 1–103**
Supervisory liability,
Nonlawyer assistants, **RPC 5.3**
Supervised attorneys, **RPC 5.1**
Misleading communications, **RPC 7.1**
Mitigation, impairment, **BOG 13**
Names and letterheads, **RPC 7.5; DR 2–102**
Advertising, attorney responsible, **RPC 7.1**
Limited liability entities, **BOG 14**
Negotiation of settlement, lay adjusters, unauthorized practice of law, **UPR 2–103**
Nonlawyer personnel, **DR 3–104**
Professional misconduct, liability, **RPC 5.3**
Nonprofit, court annexed limited legal services programs, **RPC 6.5**
Notice,
Advertising materials, **RPC 7.3**
Advisory opinions, legal ethics and unauthorized practice of law, **BOG 10**
Discipline, **BOG 13**
Impairment, misconduct, mitigation, **BOG 13**
Law firms, leaving firm, dissolution, **RPC 5.8**
Prospective clients, duties, **RPC 1.18**
Officers, state bar, **BOG 4**
Offices, **DR 2–102**
Officials, contacts, **RPC 3.5; DR 7–109**
Online computerized legal research services, contracts, **BOG 21**
Organization and government, **BOG 1 et seq.**
Out of state attorneys. Foreign attorneys, generally, ante
Partners, professional conduct, responsibilities, **RPC 5.1**
Partnership with nonlawyer, **RPC 5.4; DR 3–103**
Patents, foreign attorneys,
Admission to practice without examination, **Rule 1A:2**
Certificates, revocation, **Rule 1A:3**
Pooled accounts, client funds, **BOG 20**
Practice before tribunals, unauthorized practice of law, **UPR 1–101**
Preliminary investigation, discipline, **BOG 13**
Preparation of documents,
Collection agencies, unauthorized practice of law, **UPR 3–103**
Lay adjusters, unauthorized practice of law, **UPR 2–104**
Preserving identity of funds and property of client, **DR 9–102**

ATTORNEYS—Cont'd
Press releases, advisory opinions, legal ethics and unauthorized practice of law, **BOG 10**
Private discipline, **BOG 13**
Privileged information. Confidential or privileged information, generally, ante
Privileges and immunities,
  Attorney client privilege, **Rule 2:502**
  Limited liability entities, **BOG 14**
Pro bono services, **RPC 6.1**
Pro hac vice,
  Appeal and Review, this index
  Disciplinary proceedings, representation, **BOG 13**
  Oral argument,
    Court of appeals, **Rules 5A:12, 5A:28**
    Supreme court, **Rule 5:33**
  Participation in trial, **Rule 1A:4**
    Forms, **Form 1 (app. foll. Rule 1A:7)**
Procedure for disciplining, suspending and disbarring attorneys, **BOG 13**
Professional corporations, professional limited liability companies, limited liability partnerships, **BOG 14**
Professional notices, letterheads, offices, and law lists, **DR 2–102**
Professional responsibility, **RPC 1.1 et seq.; DR 1–101 et seq.**
  Limited liability entities, **BOG 14**
Professionalism course, failure to complete, suspension, **BOG 13.1**
Prohibited acts and transactions, **RPC 1.2, 3.4; DR 7–102**
  Conflict of interest, **RPC 1.8**
  False or misleading statements of law or fact, **RPC 3.3, 4.1**
  Frivolous claims and contentions, **RPC 3.1**
  Jurors, contact and investigation, **RPC 3.5**
Promptness, **RPC 1.3; DR 6–101**
Property of client. Funds and property of client, generally, ante
Prosecutors, special responsibilities, **RPC 3.8; DR 8–102**
Prospective clients, duties, **RPC 1.18**
Protection fund, **BOG 16**
Public officials, actions, **RPC 1.11; DR 8–101**
Public reprimand, **BOG 13**
  Stay pending appeal, **Rule 5:21**
Publicity, **RPC 3.6, 7.1 et seq.; DR 2–101, 7–106**
Reactivation, continuing legal education, **BOG 17**
Real estate practice, unauthorized practice of law, **UPR 6–101 et seq.**
Recommendation or solicitation of professional employment, **RPC 7.3; DR 2–103**
Records and recordation, **RPC 1.15; DR 9–103**
  Discipline, **BOG 13**
Referral and control of claims, collection agencies, unauthorized practice of law, **UPR 3–102**
Referrals and recommendations, **RPC 7.3**
Refusing employment when interests of lawyer may impair independent professional judgment, **RPC 1.7; DR 5–101**

ATTORNEYS—Cont'd
Refusing to accept or continue employment if interest of another client may impair professional judgment, **RPC 1.7 et seq.; DR 5–105**
Registration, military forces, foreign states, legal assistance, **Rule 1A:6**
Reinstatement, **BOG 13**
Replacement counsel, communications, persons represented by counsel, **RPC 4.2**
Reports,
  Clients protection fund, **BOG 16**
  Investigations, discipline, **BOG 13**
  Limited liability entities, **BOG 14**
  Misconduct, **RPC 5.1, 8.3; DR 1–103**
  Trust accounts, client funds, **BOG 20**
Representation,
  Actual innocence, writs, petitions, **Rules 5:7B, 5A:5; Forms 12 (app. foll. Rule 5:41), 12 (app. foll. Rule 5A:37)**
  Candor, **RPC 3.3**
  Communication, **RPC 1.4**
  Conflict of interest, **RPC 1.7, 1.8**
    Nonprofit, court annexed limited legal services programs, **RPC 6.5**
  Corporate clients, **RPC 1.13**
  Corporations, foreign states, **Rule 1A:5**
    Forms, **Form 2 (app. foll. Rule 1A:7)**
  Declining representation, **RPC 1.16**
  Diligence, **RPC 1.3**
  Discipline, **BOG 13**
  Disqualification, **RPC 1.10 et seq.**
    Judges and arbitrators, **RPC 1.12**
    Public officers, **RPC 1.11**
  Evaluation for third party, **RPC 2.3**
  Fairness, **RPC 3.4**
  False or misleading statements of law or fact, **RPC 3.3, 4.1**
  Former clients, **RPC 1.9**
  Frivolous claims and contentions, **RPC 3.1**
  Impairment, clients with, **RPC 1.14**
  Joint representation, **RPC 1.7**
  Nonprofit, court annexed limited legal services programs, **RPC 6.5**
  Organizations, **RPC 1.13**
  Pro bono, **RPC 6.1**
  Promptness, **RPC 1.3; DR 6–101**
  Prospective clients, **RPC 1.18**
  Respect, third person rights, **RPC 4.4**
  Scope, **RPC 1.2; DR 7–102**
  Terminating representation, **RPC 1.16; DR 2–108**
  Third party neutral, **RPC 2.10**
  Tribunals, unauthorized practice of law, **UPR 1–101**
  Withdrawal, **RPC 1.16; DR 2–108**
Reprimand, **BOG 13**
Requirements, continuing legal education, **BOG 17**
Resignation, **BOG 13**
Respect, third person rights, **RPC 4.4**
Responsibilities of partners, professional conduct, **RPC 5.1**

ATTORNEYS—Cont'd
Revocation or suspension, **BOG 13**
Administrative suspension of member, procedure, **BOG 19**
Continuing legal education requirement, failure to complete, **BOG 13.2**
Foreign attorneys, **Rule 1A:3**
Professionalism course, failure to complete, **BOG 13.1**
Reinstatement, **BOG 13**
Safekeeping, funds and property of client, **RPC 1.15**
Sale of practice, **RPC 1.17**
Scope of advice, **RPC 2.1**
Scope of representation, **RPC 1.2; DR 7–102**
Second opinion, communications, persons represented by counsel, **RPC 4.2**
Security fund, **BOG 16**
Settlement negotiation, lay adjusters, unauthorized practice of law, **UPR 2–103**
Solicitation of professional employment, **RPC 7.3; DR 2–103**
Special responsibilities of prosecutor or government lawyer, **RPC 3.8; DR 8–102**
Specialists, **RPC 7.4; DR 2–104**
Standards, continuing legal education, **BOG 17**
Standing committee, limited liability entities, **BOG 14**
State bar, organization and government, **BOG 1 et seq.**
Stay pending appeal, disciplinary proceedings, **Rule 5:21; BOG 13**
Striking evidence, disciplinary proceedings, **BOG 13**
Subcommittees, discipline, **BOG 13**
Subpoenas,
Disciplinary proceedings, **BOG 13**
Unauthorized practice of law, **BOG 10**
Summary resolution, complaints, discipline, **BOG 13**
Summons, disciplinary proceedings, **BOG 13**
Supervision,
Professional conduct, **RPC 5.1**
Third year student practice, **BOG 15**
Suspension. Revocation or suspension, generally, ante
Tax practice, unauthorized practice of law, **UPR 5–101 et seq.**
Terminating representation, **RPC 1.16; DR 2–108**
Terms, discipline, **BOG 13**
Third party claims, lay adjusters, **UPR 2–105**
Third party neutral, **RPC 2.10**
Third year student practice, **BOG 15**
Threatening criminal prosecution, **DR 7–104**
Title insurance, unauthorized practice of law, **UPR 7–101**
Trade associations, unauthorized practice of law, **UPR 8–101 et seq.**
Trademarks and trade names, foreign attorneys, admission to practice without examination, **Rule 1A:2**
Certificates, revocation, **Rule 1A:3**

ATTORNEYS—Cont'd
Trial conduct, **DR 7–105**
Trial publicity, **RPC 3.6; DR 7–106**
Trust accounts, client funds, **RPC 1.15; BOG 20**
Unauthorized Practice of Law, generally, this index
Unlawful representation, **RPC 1.2; DR 7–102**
False or misleading statements of law or fact, **RPC 3.3, 4.1**
Frivolous claims and contentions, **RPC 3.1**
Wills, prohibited transactions, **RPC 1.8**
Withdrawal, **RPC 1.16; DR 2–108**
Witnesses,
Attorney as witness, **RPC 3.7; DR 5–102**
Contact, **DR 7–108**
False testimony, **RPC 3.4**
Work product, discovery, **Rule 4:1**
Zealous representation, **DR 7–101**

AUDIOVISUAL DEPOSITIONS
Generally, **Rule 4:7A**
Video and teleconferences, **Rule 4:5**

AUTHENTICATION
Evidence, requirement, **Rule 2:901 et seq.**

BAPTISM
Certificates and certification, hearsay evidence, exceptions, **Rule 2:803**

BAR
Generally, **BOG 1 et seq.**
Definitions,
Attorney discipline, **BOG 13**
Legal ethics, **BOG 10**

BAR COUNSEL
Definitions, attorney discipline, **BOG 13**

BAR OFFICIALS
Definitions, attorney discipline, **BOG 13**

BEHAVIORAL REHABILITATION CENTER
Supreme court, filing, **Rule 5:5**

BEST EVIDENCE
Generally, **Rule 2:1001 et seq.**

BIAS OR PREJUDICE
Jury, voir dire examination, **Rule 3:22A**
Witnesses, impeachment, **Rule 2:610**

BIFURCATED JURY TRIALS
Noncapital felonies, class 1 misdemeanors, **Rule 3A:17.1**

BILL OF PARTICULARS
Generally, **Rules 3:7, 8:8**

BOARDS AND COMMISSIONS
Continuing legal education board, **BOG 17**
Definitions, attorney discipline, **BOG 13**

BONDS
Additional bond, appeal from circuit court to appellate court, **Forms 6 (app. foll. Rule 5:41), 6 (app. foll. Rule 5A:37)**

BONDS—Cont'd
Appeal bond, supreme court, **Rules 5:24, 5A:17**
Attorneys, reinstatement, **BOG 13**
Costs alone,
Appeal from circuit court to appellate court, **Form 3 (app. foll. Rule 5A:37)**
Appeal of right from circuit court to court of appeals, **Forms 1 (app. foll. Rule 5:41), 1 (app. foll. Rule 5A:37)**
Appeal of right from state corporation commission to supreme court, **Forms 8 (app. foll. Rule 5:41), 8 (app. foll. Rule 5A:37)**
Appeal of right from workers compensation commission to court of appeals, **Forms 7 (app. foll. Rule 5:41), 7 (app. foll. Rule 5A:37)**
Required costs on appeal from circuit court to appellate court, **Form 3 (app. foll. Rule 5:41)**
Costs and suspension,
Appeal from circuit court to appellate court, **Forms 2 (app. foll. Rule 5:41), 5 (app. foll. Rule 5:41), 5 (app. foll. Rule 5A:37)**
Appeal of right from state corporation commission to supreme court, **Forms 9 (app. foll. Rule 5:41), 9 (app. foll. Rule 5A:37)**
Court of appeals, **Rule 5A:17**
Appeal as of right, filing, **Rules 5A:6, 5A:16**
Execution and acknowledgment, **Forms 10 (app. foll. Rule 5:41), 10 (app. foll. Rule 5A:37)**
Supreme court, appeal bond, **Rule 5:24**
Suspension alone, appeal from circuit court to appellate court, **Forms 4 (app. foll. Rule 5:41), 4 (app. foll. Rule 5A:37)**

BOOKS AND PAPERS
Juvenile and domestic relations district courts, size of paper, **Rule 8:7**
Subpoenas, production, criminal proceedings, **Rule 3A:12**

BOUNDARIES
Reputation, hearsay evidence, exceptions, **Rule 2:803**

BRIEFS
Amicus curiae, appeals to supreme court, **Rule 5:30**
Corporation commission, appeals to supreme court, **Rule 5:21**
Court of Appeals, this index
Electronic filing, **Rule 1:17**
Juvenile and domestic relations district courts, size of paper, **Rule 8:7**
Motions, **Rule 4:15**
Paper, size, **Rule 1:16**
Reply briefs, court of appeals, **Rule 5A:14**
Size of paper, **Rule 1:16**
State bar disciplinary board, appeals to supreme court, **Rule 5:21**
Supreme Court, this index
Three judge circuit court panels, appeals to supreme court, **Rule 5:21**

BUSINESS ENTITY
Definitions, lay adjusters, **UPR 2–101**

BUSINESS RECORDS
Hearsay evidence, exceptions, **Rules 2:803, 2:804**
Interrogatories, **Rule 4:8**
Regularly conducted activity, certified records, self-authentication, **Rule 2:902**

CAPIAS
Forms, **Form 5 (app. foll. Rule 3A:25)**
Indictment and information, **Rule 3A:7**

CAPITAL PUNISHMENT
Generally, **Rule 3A:18**
Habeas corpus petitions, **Rule 5:7A**
Supreme court, appeals, **Rule 5:22**

CASE RESULTS
Attorneys, advertising, **RPC 7.1**

CERTIFICATES AND CERTIFICATION
Attorneys, this index
Definitions, attorney discipline, **BOG 13**
Depositions, **Rules 4:3, 4:5**
Foreign attorneys, **Rule 1A:1 et seq.**
Foreign legal consultants, **Rule 1A:7**
Notice of appeal, court of appeals, **Rule 5A:6**
Supreme Court, this index
Third year student practice, attorneys, **BOG 15**

CERTIFICATES OF ANALYSIS
Authentication, **Rule 2:902**

CERTIFICATION FOR SANCTION DETERMINATION
Definitions, attorney discipline, **BOG 13**

CHAIR
Definitions, attorney discipline, **BOG 13**

CHALLENGES
Jurors, criminal proceedings, **Rule 3A:14**

CHANCERY COMMISSIONER
Proceedings before, **Rule 3:23**

CHARACTER EVIDENCE
Conduct, exclusion, **Rule 2:404**
Impeachment, witnesses, **Rule 2:608**
Proof, **Rule 2:405**

CHARGE OF MISCONDUCT
Definitions, attorney discipline, **BOG 13**

CHECKS
Best evidence, **Rule 2:1003**

CHILD SUPPORT
Support, generally, this index

CHILDREN AND MINORS
Attorneys,
Juvenile and domestic relations district courts, **Rule 8:6**
Representing persons with impairment, **RPC 1.14**

CHILDREN AND MINORS—Cont'd
Emergency surgical or medical treatment, judicial consent proceedings, petitions, **Rule 8:3**
Juvenile and Domestic Relations District Courts, generally, this index
Sex offenses, similar crimes, evidence, **Rule 2:413**

CIRCUIT COURTS
Boundaries and location, **Appendix**
Definitions, attorney discipline, **BOG 13**
List of judges, **Appendix**
Three judge panels, appeals from, **Rule 5:21**

CLERGY AND COMMUNICANT PRIVILEGE
Generally, **Rule 2:503**

CLERK OF THE COURT OF APPEALS
Definitions, **Rule 5A:1**

CLERK OF THE DISCIPLINARY SYSTEM
Definitions, attorneys, **BOG 13**

CLERK OF THE TRIAL COURT
Definitions, court of appeals, **Rule 5A:1**

CLERKS
Definitions,
Criminal practice and procedure, **Rule 3A:2**
Supreme court proceedings, **Rule 5:1**

CLERKS OF COURTS
Definitions, supreme court proceedings, **Rule 5:1**
Witnesses, competency, **Rule 2:605**

CLIENT FUNDS
Trust accounts, **BOG 20**

CLIENTS PROTECTION FUND
Generally, **BOG 16**

CLIENTS SECURITY FUND
Generally, **BOG 16**

COLD
Definitions, attorney discipline, **BOG 13**

COLLECTION AGENCIES
Unauthorized practice of law, **UPR 3–101 et seq.**

COMMISSIONER IN CHANCERY
Proceedings before, **Rule 3:23**

COMMITTEE COUNSEL
Definitions, attorney discipline, **BOG 13**

COMMITTEES
Definitions, legal ethics, **BOG 10**

COMMON LAW
Privileges and immunities, **Rule 2:501**

COMMONWEALTH ATTORNEY
Definitions, criminal practice and procedure, **Rule 3A:2**

COMMUNICABLE DISEASE
Quarantine, isolation, public health threats, **Rule 7A:16**
Appeal and review, **Rules 3:24, 5:41**

COMPLAINANT
Definitions, attorney discipline, **BOG 13**

COMPLAINTS
Attorney discipline, **BOG 13**
Attorney fees, demand, **Rule 3:25**
Copies, **Rule 3:4**
Crimes and offenses, **Rule 3A:3; Form 1 (app. foll. Rule 3A:25)**
Form, content, **Rule 3:2**
Money damages, ad damnum clauses, **Rule 3:2**
Unauthorized practice of law, **BOG 10**

COMPROMISE AND SETTLEMENT
Evidence, **Rule 2:408**
Lay adjusters, unauthorized practice of law, **UPR 2–103**
Pending appeal, court of appeals, **Rule 5A:36**
Settlement conferences, **Rule 5A:37**
Supreme court appeals, **Rule 5:38**

COMPUTERS
Subpoenas, production, criminal proceedings, **Rule 3A:12**

CONDUCT
Character evidence, proof, **Rule 2:405**

CONFERENCES
Civil actions, **Rule 1:19**
Depositions, video and teleconferences, **Rule 4:5**

CONFIDENTIAL OR PRIVILEGED INFORMATION
Attorney-client relationship, **RPC 1.6**
Judicial performance evaluation program, **Rule 9:2**
Jury, criminal proceedings, **Rule 3A:14.1**
Juvenile proceedings, transcripts, **Rule 8:11**

CONFLICT OF INTEREST
Attorneys, this index
Judges, extrajudicial activities, **CJC 4**
Jury, voir dire examination, **Rule 3:22A**

CONSENT
Attorneys, licenses and permits, revocation or suspension, discipline, **BOG 13**
Children and minors, emergency surgical or medical treatment, petitions, **Rule 8:3**
Jury, this index
Juvenile and domestic relations district courts, judicial consent, **Rule 8:22**
Substitution of parties, **Rule 3:17**

CONSISTENT PRIOR STATEMENTS
Witnesses, hearsay, **Rule 2:801**

CONSOLIDATION OF ACTIONS
District courts, civil cases, **Rule 7B:10**

CONTEMPT
Subpoenas, criminal proceedings, failure to obey, **Rule 3A:12**

CONTENTS
Best evidence, **Rule 2:1004**

CONTINUANCE
Attorneys, disciplinary proceedings, **BOG 13**
Definitions, criminal practice and procedure, **Rule 3A:2**
District courts, **Rule 7A:14**
Juvenile and domestic relations district courts, **Rule 8:14**

CONTINUING LEGAL EDUCATION
Generally, **BOG 17**
Suspension of attorneys, failure to complete, **BOG 13.2**

CONTRIBUTORY NEGLIGENCE
Pleadings, **Rule 3:18**

COPIES
Best evidence, **Rule 2:1005**
Complaints, **Rule 3:4**
Juvenile and domestic relations district courts, pleadings, **Rule 8:8**

CORPORATE COUNSEL REGISTRANTS
Definitions, attorneys, disciplinary proceedings, **BOG 13**

CORPORATION COMMISSION
Appeals to supreme court, **Rule 5:21**

CORPORATIONS
Attorneys, admission to practice, certificates and certification, **Rule 1A:5**
Forms, **Form 2 (app. foll. Rule 1A:7)**
Pleas,
Criminal proceedings, **Rule 3A:8**
District courts, **Rule 7C:6**
Practice of law, nonlawyers, limited exceptions, **UPR 1–101**
Unauthorized practice of law, limited exceptions, **UPR 1–101**

CORRECTIONAL INSTITUTIONS
Inmates,
Court of appeals, filing, extension of time, **Rule 5A:3**
Habeas corpus, filings, timeliness, **Rule 3A:25**
Supreme court, filing, **Rule 5:5**

COSTS
Appeal and review, **Rule 1:1A**
Denial of appeal, petition for rehearing, **Rule 5:20**
Appendices, court of appeals, **Rule 5A:25**
Attorney discipline, **BOG 13**
Definitions, attorney discipline, **BOG 13**
Depositions, **Rule 4:2**
Supreme Court, this index

COUNCIL OF STATE BAR
Generally, **BOG 5 et seq.**
Attorney discipline, **BOG 13 et seq.**
Disbursements, **BOG 12**
Dues, **BOG 11**
Elections, **BOG 6**

COUNCIL OF STATE BAR—Cont'd
Meetings, **BOG 7**
Opinions, **BOG 10**
Powers, **BOG 9**

COUNSEL
Attorneys, generally, this index
Definitions, **Rule 1:5**
Court of appeals, **Rule 5A:1**
Juvenile and domestic relations district courts, **Rule 8:2**
Supreme court proceedings, **Rule 5:1**

COUNSEL FOR APPELLANT
Definitions,
Court of appeals, **Rule 5A:1**
Supreme court proceedings, **Rule 5:1**

COUNSEL FOR APPELLEE
Definitions,
Court of appeals, **Rule 5A:1**
Supreme court proceedings, **Rule 5:1**

COUNSEL OF RECORD
Definitions, **Rule 1:5**
Juvenile and domestic relations district courts, **Rule 8:2**

COUNTERCLAIMS
Generally, **Rule 3:9**
Attorney fees, demand, **Rule 3:25**

COURT OF APPEALS
Abbreviated record, **Rule 5A:10**
Amicus curiae,
Briefs, **Rule 5A:23**
Oral argument, **Rule 5A:28**
Answering brief, rehearing, **Rule 5A:35**
Appeals as matter of right, perfection, **Rule 5A:16**
Appellants, opening brief, **Rule 5A:20**
Appellees brief, **Rule 5A:21**
Appendices, **Rule 5A:25**
Assignment of errors, appeal to supreme court, **Rule 5:17**
Attorneys, contact information, change, **Rule 5A:1**
Award, costs, **Rule 5A:30**
Bonds, **Rule 5A:17**
Appeal as of right, filing, **Rules 5A:6, 5A:16**
Briefs, **Rule 5A:19**
Amicus curiae, **Rule 5A:23**
Answering brief, rehearing, **Rule 5A:35**
Appellee, **Rule 5A:21**
Effect of noncompliance with rules, **Rule 5A:26**
Forms, **Rule 5A:4**
Guardians ad litem, **Rule 5A:21**
Notice, **Rule 5A:19**
Opening brief of appellant, **Rule 5A:20**
Opposing briefs, petition for appeal, criminal cases and traffic infractions, **Rule 5A:12**
Reply briefs, **Rule 5A:22**
Rehearing, **Rule 5A:35**
Supplemental authorities, citation, **Rule 5A:4A**

COURT OF APPEALS—Cont'd
Certificates and certification, notice of appeal, **Rule 5A:6**
Citation, supplemental authorities, **Rule 5A:4A**
Compromise and settlement, pending appeal, **Rule 5A:36**
Settlement conferences, **Rule 5A:37**
Contents, appendices, **Rule 5A:25**
Copies of briefs, **Rule 5A:19**
Correctional institutions, inmates, filing, extension of time, **Rule 5A:3**
Costs, **Rule 5A:30**
Appendices, **Rule 5A:25**
Covers of documents, **Rule 5A:24**
Crimes and offenses, practice and procedure, **Rule 5A:12 et seq.**
Definitions, supreme court proceedings, **Rule 5:1**
Denial of appeal, petition for rehearing, criminal cases and traffic infractions, **Rule 5A:12**
Digital appellate record, **Rule 5A:10A**
Dismissal of appeal,
Noncompliance, **Rule 5A:1A**
Nonpayment of fee, **Rule 5A:6**
Disposition of record, **Rule 5A:10**
Dockets and docketing, **Rule 5A:16**
Documents, covers, **Rule 5A:24**
Effect of noncompliance with rules regarding briefs, **Rule 5A:26**
Electronic filing,
Appendices, **Rule 5A:25**
Briefs, **Rule 5A:19**
Digital appellate record, **Rule 5A:10A**
Expedited review, **Rule 5A:13**
Extension of time, **Rule 5A:3**
Filing of briefs, **Rule 5A:19**
Petition for appeal, **Rule 5A:12**
Fees, petition for review, **Rule 5A:38**
Filing fee,
Notice of appeal, **Rule 5A:6**
Petition for review, **Rule 5A:38**
Filing time,
Briefs, **Rule 5A:19**
Extension of time, **Rule 5A:3**
Fines and penalties,
Appendices, **Rule 5A:25**
Noncompliance, **Rule 5A:1A**
Form of briefs, **Rule 5A:4**
Form of record, **Rule 5A:10**
Guardians ad litem, **Rule 5A:21**
Notice, **Rule 5A:19**
Injunctions, **Rule 5A:38**
Inmates, filing, extension of time, **Rule 5A:3**
Judge authorized act, record on appeal, **Rule 5A:9**
Judges, list, **Appendix**
Jurisdiction, original proceedings, **Rule 5A:5**
Length of briefs, **Rule 5A:19**
Letters of credit, security for appeal, **Rule 5A:17**
Mandate, **Rule 5A:31**
Motions, **Rule 5A:2**

COURT OF APPEALS—Cont'd
Multiple transcripts, time for filing notice of appeal, **Rule 5A:8**
Notarized bill for costs, **Rule 5A:30**
Notice, **Rule 5A:6**
Decision, **Rule 5A:29**
Oral argument, **Rule 5A:28**
Supplemental authorities, citation, **Rule 5A:4A**
Transcript, filing, **Rule 5A:8**
Workers compensation commission appeals, **Rule 5A:11**
Objections, transcript or written statement, **Rule 5A:8**
Opening brief of appellant, **Rule 5A:20**
Opinions, **Rule 5A:31**
Oral argument,
Petition for appeal, criminal cases and traffic infractions, **Rule 5A:12**
Rehearing, **Rules 5A:33, 5A:35**
Orders of court, **Rule 5A:2**
Original proceedings, **Rule 5A:5**
Penalties,
Appendices, **Rule 5A:25**
Noncompliance, **Rule 5A:1A**
Perfection of appeal, **Rule 5A:16**
Questions to be considered, **Rule 5A:18**
Petitions,
Appeal to supreme court, **Rule 5:17**
Criminal cases and traffic infractions, **Rule 5A:12**
Perfection of appeal, grant, **Rule 5A:16**
Rehearing, **Rule 5A:33**
Denial of appeal, **Rules 5A:15, 5A:15A**
Review, **Rule 5A:38**
Practice and procedure, **Rule 5A:1 et seq.**
Preservation of issues for review, **Rule 5A:18**
Pro hac vice, oral argument, **Rules 5A:12, 5A:28**
Records and recordation, **Rule 5A:7**
Judge authorized to act, **Rule 5A:9**
Preparation and transmission, **Rule 5A:10**
Digital appellate record, **Rule 5A:10A**
Transcript or written statement, **Rule 5A:8**
Workers compensation commission appeals, **Rule 5A:11**
Rehearing, **Rule 5A:32 et seq.**
Denial of appeal, **Rules 5A:15, 15:15A**
En banc, **Rules 5A:34, 5A:34A**
Reply briefs, **Rule 5A:22**
Criminal cases and traffic infractions, **Rule 5A:12**
Rehearing, **Rule 5A:35**
Responses, motions, **Rule 5A:2**
Security for appeal, **Rule 5A:17**
Separate cases, notice of appeal, **Rule 5A:6**
Service, **Rule 5A:1**
Settlement of pending appeal, **Rule 5A:36**
Settlement conferences, **Rule 5A:37**
Show cause orders, **Rule 5A:1A**
Striking transcripts, failure to file notice of appeal, **Rule 5A:8**

COURT OF APPEALS—Cont'd
Summary disposition, **Rule 5A:27**
Supplemental authorities, citation, **Rule 5A:4A**
Table of contents, appendices, **Rule 5A:25**
Taxable costs, **Rule 5A:30**
Time,
Brief in opposition, petition for appeal, criminal cases and traffic infractions, **Rule 5A:13**
Extension, **Rule 5A:3**
Petition for appeal, **Rule 5A:12**
Filing of briefs, **Rule 5A:19**
Mandate, **Rule 5A:31**
Notice of appeal, **Rule 5A:6**
Petition for review, filing, **Rule 5A:38**
Traffic rules and regulations, practice and procedure, **Rule 5A:12**
Transcripts, **Rule 5A:8**
Transmission of record, **Rule 5A:10**
Digital appellate record, **Rule 5A:10A**
Workers compensation commission appeals, **Rule 5A:11**
Unpublished opinions, citing, **Rule 5A:1**
Waiver, oral argument, **Rule 5A:28**
Withdrawal of pending appeal, **Rule 5A:36**
Workers compensation commission, appeals, practice and procedure, **Rule 5A:11**
Written statement, **Rule 5A:8**

COURT ORDERS
Orders of Court, generally, this index

COURT REPORTERS
Generally, **Rule 1:3**
Definitions, attorney discipline, **BOG 13**
Juvenile and domestic relations district courts, **Rule 8:11**

COURTS
Definitions, legal ethics, **BOG 10**
District Courts, generally, this index
Judges, generally, this index
Juvenile and Domestic Relations District Courts, generally, this index
Local rules, **Rule 1:15**
Orders of Court, generally, this index
Pleadings, discretion, **Rule 1:9**
Trial by, **Rule 3:22**

CREDIBILITY
Hearsay declarants, attacking, supporting, **Rule 2:806**

CREDIT CARDS
Discounts, payment, **RPC 5.4**

CRESPA
Definitions, attorney discipline, **BOG 13**

CRIME VICTIMS
Witnesses, exclusion, **Rule 2:615**

CRIMES AND OFFENSES
See, also, Fines and Penalties, generally, this index

CRIMES AND OFFENSES—Cont'd
Acquittal, judgment, **Rule 3A:15**
Actual innocence, writs, petitions, **Rules 5:7B, 5A:5; Forms 12 (app. foll. Rule 5:41), 12 (app. foll. Rule 5A:37)**
Appeal and review, **Rule 3A:19**
Appeals court, practice and procedure, **Rule 5A:12**
Arrest warrant or summons, **Rule 3A:4**
Attorneys, malpractice insurance, **BOG 13.4**
Bifurcated jury trials, noncapital felonies, class 1 misdemeanors, **Rule 3A:17.1**
Clergy and communicant privilege, **Rule 2:503**
Complaint, **Rule 3A:3**
Confessions, evidence, jury, **Rule 2:104**
Confidential or privileged information, jury, **Rule 3A:14.1**
Consent, jury trial, waiver, **Rule 3A:13**
Conviction of crime, witnesses, impeachment, **Rule 2:609**
Corporations, pleas, **Rule 3A:8**
Court of appeals, practice and procedure, **Rule 5A:12**
Death penalty, **Rule 3A:18**
Appeals to supreme court, **Rule 5:22**
Definitions, attorney discipline, **BOG 13**
Discovery, **Rule 3A:11**
Juvenile and domestic relations district courts, **Rule 8:15**
District courts, practice and procedure, **Rule 7C:1 et seq.**
DNA evidence, actual innocence, writs, petitions, **Rules 5:7, 5A:5; Form 12 (app. foll. Rule 5:41)**
Electronic filing, **Rule 3A:23**
Extension of time, **Rule 3A:20**
Filing of papers, **Rule 3A:21**
District courts, practice and procedure, **Rule 7C:7**
Electronic filing, **Rule 3A:23**
Fine schedule, nontraffic prepayable offenses, **Rule 3C:2**
Grand jury, **Rule 3A:5**
Guilty Pleas, generally, this index
Husband and wife, spousal privilege, **Rule 2:504**
Included offenses, jury verdicts, **Rule 3A:17**
Indictment and Information, generally, this index
Inspections and inspectors, **Rule 3A:11**
Instructions to jury, **Rule 3A:16**
Joinder, **Rule 3A:10**
Indictment and information, **Rule 3A:6**
Judgment of acquittal, **Rule 3A:15**
Jury, generally, this index
Lesser included offenses, jury verdicts, **Rule 3A:17**
Malpractice insurance, attorneys, **BOG 13.4**
New trial, **Rule 3A:15**
Nolo Contendere Pleas, generally, this index
Nontraffic prepayable offenses, fine schedule, **Rule 3C:2**
Opinion and expert testimony,
Basis, **Rule 2:703**

CRIMES AND OFFENSES—Cont'd
Opinion and expert testimony—Cont'd
Facts, data, basis, **Rule 2:705**
Learned treatises, use, **Rule 2:706**
Ultimate issues, **Rule 2:704**
Use, **Rule 2:702**
Plea bargaining, **Rule 3A:8**
Pleas, **Rule 3A:8**
Polling of jury, **Rule 3A:17**
Practice and procedure, **Rule 3A:1 et seq.**
Prepayable nontraffic offenses, fine schedule, **Rule 3C:2**
Prior sexual conduct, complaining witnesses, evidence, **Rule 2:412**
Schedule of fines, nontraffic prepayable offenses, **Rule 3C:2**
Sentencing orders, **Form 10 (app. foll. Rule 3A:25)**
Service and filing of papers, **Rule 3A:21**
District courts, practice and procedure, **Rule 7C:7**
Setting aside verdicts, motions, **Rule 3A:15**
Severance, trial of defendants, **Rule 3A:10**
District courts, **Rule 7C:4**
Spousal privilege, **Rule 2:504**
Subpoenas, **Rule 3A:12**
Time, extension, **Rule 3A:20**
Traffic Rules and Regulations, generally, this index
Uniform fine schedule, nontraffic prepayable offenses, **Rule 3C:2**
Venue, **Rule 3A:2.1**
Verdicts, **Rule 3A:17**
Motions to set aside, **Rule 3A:15**
Waiver, jury trial, **Rule 3A:13**
Warrant, arrest, **Rule 3A:4**
Withdrawn pleas, evidence, **Rule 2:410**
Witnesses, subpoenas, **Rule 3A:12**

CROSS EXAMINATION
Witnesses, this index

CROSSCLAIMS
Generally, **Rule 3:10**
Attorney fees, demand, **Rule 3:25**

CUMULATIVE EVIDENCE
Needless, exclusion, **Rule 2:403**

DATE OF ENTRY
Definitions,
Court of appeals, **Rule 5A:1**
Supreme court proceedings, **Rule 5:1**

DE MINIMIS DISMISSAL
Definitions, attorney discipline, **BOG 13**

DEATH PENALTY
Capital Punishment, generally, this index

DECLARANTS
Definitions, hearsay evidence, **Rule 2:801**

DECREES AND JUDGMENTS
Judgments and Decrees, generally, this index

DEFAULTS
Generally, **Rule 3:19**
Failure of defendant to appear, civil cases, **Rule 7B:9**

DEFENDANT IN ERROR
Definitions, court of appeals, **Rule 5A:1**

DEFENSES
Contributory negligence, pleadings, **Rule 3:18**
Crimes and offenses, motions, **Rule 3A:9**

DEMURRERS
Responses, **Rule 3:8**

DEPARTING ATTORNEYS
Law firms, notice, **RPC 5.8**

DEPOSITIONS
Generally, **Rule 4:1 et seq.**
Audiovisual, **Rules 4:5, 4:7A**
Certificates and certification, **Rule 4:5**
Foreign state, **Rule 4:3**
Copies, **Rule 4:5**
Court proceedings, use, **Rule 4:7**
Cross examination, **Rule 4:5**
Errors and irregularities, effect, **Rule 4:7**
Exhibits, **Rule 4:5**
Expenses, failure to attend, **Rules 4:5, 4:12**
Foreign states, **Rule 4:5**
Persons before whom taken, **Rule 4:3**
Uniform Interstate Depositions and Discovery Act, application of law, **Rule 4:5**
Form, presentation, **Rule 4:7**
Limitation on use, **Rule 4:7**
Limiting examination, motion, **Rule 4:5**
Nonparty witnesses, **Rule 4:5**
Notice, **Rules 4:2, 4:5**
Written questions, **Rule 4:6**
Number, limitation, **Rule 4:6A**
Oaths, **Rule 4:5**
Objections to admissibility, **Rule 4:7**
Oral examination, **Rule 4:5**
Order of court, **Rule 4:2**
Paper, size, **Rule 1:16**
Persons before whom taken, **Rule 4:3**
Petition, **Rule 4:2**
Production of documents and things, **Rule 4:5**
Record, **Rules 4:5, 4:7**
Service, **Rule 4:2**
Written questions, **Rule 4:6**
Signature, **Rule 4:5**
Size of paper, **Rule 1:16**
Stipulations, **Rule 4:4**
Submission to witness, **Rule 4:5**
Teleconferences, **Rules 4:5, 4:7A**
Terminating examination, motion, **Rule 4:5**
Time,
Audiovisual depositions, **Rule 4:7A**
Oral examinations, **Rule 4:5**
Transcripts,
Audiovisual depositions, **Rule 4:7A**

DEPOSITIONS—Cont'd
Transcripts—Cont'd
Supreme court, appendices, **Rule 5:32**
Uniform Interstate Depositions and Discovery Act, application of law, **Rule 4:5**
Use in court proceedings, **Rule 4:7**
Video and teleconferences, **Rules 4:5, 4:7A**
Written questions, **Rule 4:6**

DIGITAL APPELLATE RECORD
Court of appeals, **Rule 5A:10A**
Supreme court, **Rule 5:13A**

DISBARMENT
Definitions, attorney discipline, **BOG 13**

DISCIPLINARY PROCEEDINGS
Definitions, attorney discipline, **BOG 13**

DISCIPLINARY RECORD
Definitions, attorney discipline, **BOG 13**

DISCIPLINARY RULES
Definitions, attorney discipline, **BOG 13**

DISCLOSURE
Attorneys, this index
Jury, confidential or privileged information, criminal proceedings, **Rule 3A:14.1**

DISCOUNTS
Credit cards, payment, **RPC 5.4**

DISCOVERY
Generally, **Rule 4:0 et seq.**
Amendment of responses, **Rule 4:1**
Attorneys,
Discipline, **BOG 13**
Work product, **Rule 4:1**
Compelling, **Rule 4:12**
Conferences, civil actions, **Rule 1:19**
Crimes and offenses, **Rule 3A:11**
Dispositions, **Rule 4:1 et seq.**
Electronically stored information, **Rules 4:1, 4:9, 4:9A**
Eminent domain proceedings, expert witnesses, **Rule 4:1**
Entry on land, **Rules 4:9, 4:9A**
Evasive or incomplete answers, motion for order compelling discovery, **Rule 4:12**
Experts, trial preparation, **Rule 4:1**
Insurance agreements, **Rule 4:1**
Interrogatories, **Rule 4:8**
Juvenile and domestic relations district courts, **Rule 8:15**
Negotiation, pre-motion, certificates and certification, **Rules 4:1, 4:9A**
Nonparties, **Rule 4:9A**
Orders of court, compelling discovery, **Rule 4:12**
Pretrial conferences, **Rule 4:13**
Privileged materials, **Rule 4:1**
Production of documents and things, **Rules 4:9, 4:9A**

DISCOVERY—Cont'd
Protective orders, **Rule 4:1**
Sanctions, **Rule 4:12**
Scheduling, civil actions, **Rule 1:18**
Scope, **Rule 4:1**
Stipulations, **Rule 4:4**
Supplementation of responses, **Rule 4:1**
Time, **Rule 1:18**

DISMISSAL
Attorney discipline, **BOG 13**
Definitions, attorney discipline, **BOG 13**
Notice of appeal, court of appeals, nonpayment of fee, **Rule 5A:6**
Petition for appeal, supreme court, omission of assignments of error or nonpayment of fee, **Rule 5:17**

DISMISSAL DE MINIMIS
Definitions, attorney discipline, **BOG 13**

DISMISSAL FOR EXCEPTIONAL CIRCUMSTANCES
Definitions, attorney discipline, **BOG 13**

DISSOLUTION
Law firms, notice, **RPC 5.8**

DISTRICT COMMITTEE
Definitions, attorney discipline, **BOG 13**

DISTRICT COURT DETERMINATION
Definitions, attorney discipline, **BOG 13**

DISTRICT COURTS
Generally, **Rule 7A:1 et seq.**
Amendments, pleadings, **Rule 7A:9**
Appeal and review, noting, **Rule 7A:13**
Appearance by defendant, failure, civil cases, **Rule 7B:9**
Appearance by plaintiff, civil cases, **Rule 7B:7**
Failure to appear, **Rule 7B:8**
Boundaries and location, **Appendix**
Briefs, size of paper, **Rule 7A:7**
Capias, traffic and criminal cases, **Rule 7C:3**
Chief magistrates, **Appendix**
Civil cases, practice and procedure, **Rule 7B:1 et seq.**
Complaints, criminal and traffic cases, **Rule 7C:3**
Consolidation,
Civil cases, **Rule 7B:10**
Criminal and traffic cases, **Rule 7C:4**
Continuances, **Rule 7A:14**
Contracts, production, civil cases, **Rule 7B:5**
Copies of pleadings, furnishing, **Rule 7A:10**
Corporations, pleas, **Rule 7C:6**
Counsel, **Rule 7A:3**
Criminal cases, practice and procedure, **Rule 7C:1 et seq.**
Defaults, failure of defendant to appear, civil cases, **Rule 7B:9**
Discovery, criminal and traffic cases, **Rule 7C:5**
Discretion, **Rule 7A:5**

DISTRICT COURTS—Cont'd
Dismissal, failure of plaintiff to appear, civil cases, **Rule 7B:8**
Endorsements, **Rule 7A:11**
Failure of defendant to appear, civil cases, **Rule 7B:9**
Isolation, quarantine, communicable disease, public health threats, **Rule 7A:16**
Juvenile and Domestic Relations District Courts, generally, this index
List of judges, **Appendix**
Motions, transfer, civil cases, **Rule 7B:11**
Noting appeals, **Rule 7A:13**
Paper, size, **Rule 7A:7**
Plaintiffs, appearance, civil cases, **Rule 7B:7**
Pleadings, **Rule 7A:8**
  Amendments, **Rule 7A:9**
  Civil cases, **Rules 7B:2, 7B:3**
  Copies, furnishing, **Rule 7A:10**
  Size of paper, **Rule 7A:7**
  Verification, civil cases, **Rule 7B:6**
Pleas, corporations, **Rule 7C:6**
Preliminary hearings, joint criminal defendants, **Rule 7C:4**
Preservation of record, electronic or photographic means, **Rule 7A:6**
Production of written agreement, civil cases, **Rule 7B:5**
Quarantine, isolation, communicable disease, public health threats, **Rule 7A:16**
Records and recordation,
  Electronic or photographic preservation, **Rule 7A:6**
  Subpoenas duces tecum, **Rule 7A:12**
Reporters, **Rule 7A:4**
Severance, trials of joint defendants, **Rule 7C:4**
Size of paper, **Rule 7A:7**
Subpoenas, witnesses, **Rule 7A:12**
Subpoenas duces tecum, **Rule 7A:12**
  Furnishing requests, **Rule 7A:10**
Summons, criminal and traffic cases, **Rule 7C:3**
Third party practice, civil cases, **Rule 7B:10**
Time, computation, **Rule 7A:2**
Traffic cases, practice and procedure, **Rule 7C:1 et seq.**
Transcripts, **Rule 7A:4**
Transfers, motions, civil cases, **Rule 7B:11**
Trial of action, civil cases, **Rule 7B:4**
Trial together of more than one accused or more than one offense, criminal and traffic cases, **Rule 7C:4**
Venue,
  Criminal and traffic cases, **Rule 7C:2**
  Motions to transfer, civil cases, **Rule 7B:11**
Verification, pleadings, civil cases, **Rule 7B:6**
Warrants, criminal and traffic cases, **Rule 7C:3**
Witnesses, subpoenas, **Rule 7A:12**
Written agreement, production, civil cases, **Rule 7B:5**

DIVISIONS
Supreme court, **Rule 5:2**

DIVORCE
Juvenile and Domestic Relations District Courts, generally, this index

DNA EVIDENCE
Actual innocence, writs, petitions, **Rules 5:7B, 5A:5; Form 12 (app. foll. Rule 5:41)**

DOCKETS AND DOCKETING
Attorneys, disciplinary proceedings, **BOG 13**
Court of appeals, **Rule 5A:16**
Supreme court, **Rule 5:23**

DOCUMENTS
Authentication, **Rule 2:902**
Best evidence, **Rule 2:1001 et seq.**
Electronic filing, **Rule 1:17**
Subpoenas, production, criminal proceedings, **Rule 3A:12**
Supreme court, appeals, covers of documents, **Rule 5:31**

DOMESTIC RELATIONS DISTRICT COURT
Juvenile and Domestic Relations District Courts, generally, this index

DOMICILE AND RESIDENCE
Health care providers, physical and mental examinations of persons, **Rule 4:10**

DUES
Attorneys, state bar, **BOG 11**
  Clients protection fund, **BOG 16**

ELECTRONIC FILING
  Generally, **Rule 1:17**
Court of appeals,
  Appendices, **Rule 5A:25**
  Briefs, **Rule 5A:19**
  Digital appellate record, **Rule 5A:10A**
Crimes and offenses, **Rule 3A:23**
Supreme court,
  Briefs, **Rule 5:26**
    Appendix, **Rule 5:32**
  Digital appellate record, **Rule 5:13A**

ELECTRONIC RECORDATION
  Generally, **Rule 1:14**
Juvenile and domestic relations district courts, preservation of record, **Rule 8:12**

ELECTRONICALLY STORED INFORMATION
Discovery, **Rules 4:1, 4:9, 4:9A**

EMAIL
Service, **Rule 1:12**

EMERGENCIES
Children and minors, medical care and treatment, judicial consent proceedings, petitions, **Rule 8:3**
Juvenile and domestic relations district courts, judicial consent, **Rule 8:22**

EMERITUS ATTORNEYS
State bar, membership, **BOG 3**

EMINENT DOMAIN
Expert witnesses, discovery, **Rule 4:1**

EMOTIONAL CONDITION
Statements, hearsay evidence, exceptions, **Rule 2:803**

ENDORSEMENTS
District courts, **Rule 7A:11**
Juvenile and domestic relations district courts, orders, **Rule 8:19**
Orders and decrees, **Rule 1:13**

ENGLISH LANGUAGE
Communications, attorney discipline, **BOG 13**
Interpreters,
Competency, witnesses, **Rule 2:604**
Privileged communications, **Rule 2:507**

ENTRY ON LAND
Generally, **Rules 4:9, 4:9A**
Expenses, failure of party to respond to requests for inspection, **Rule 4:12**

ETHICS
Attorneys, **RPC 8.1; DR 1–101 et seq.**

EVIDENCE
Generally, **Rule 2:101 et seq.**
Abuse, **Rule 2:409**
Adjudicative facts, judicial notice, **Rule 2:201**
Admissions,
Best evidence, **Rule 2:1007**
Hearsay evidence, exceptions, **Rule 2:803**
Ancient documents, statements, hearsay evidence, exceptions, **Rule 2:803**
Application of rules, **Rule 2:1101**
Attorney client privilege, **Rule 2:502**
Attorneys, discipline, **BOG 13**
Authentication, requirement, **Rule 2:901 et seq.**
Baptism, certificates and certification, hearsay evidence, exceptions, **Rule 2:803**
Best evidence, **Rule 2:1001 et seq.**
Boundaries, reputation, hearsay evidence, exceptions, **Rule 2:803**
Business records,
Hearsay evidence, exceptions, **Rules 2:803, 2:804**
Regularly conducted activity, certified records, self-authentication, **Rule 2:902**
Certificates of analysis, authentication, **Rule 2:902**
Character Evidence, generally, this index
Checks, best evidence, **Rule 2:1003**
Child sex offenses, other crimes, **Rule 2:413**
Clergy and communicant privilege, **Rule 2:503**
Common law, privileges and immunities, **Rule 2:501**
Compromise and settlement, **Rule 2:408**
Conduct, character evidence, proof, **Rule 2:405**
Confessions, jury, **Rule 2:104**
Consistent prior statements, hearsay, **Rule 2:801**
Construction, rules, **Rule 2:102**
Contents, best evidence, **Rule 2:1004**

EVIDENCE—Cont'd
Copies, best evidence, **Rule 2:1005**
Credibility,
Hearsay declarants, attacking, supporting, **Rule 2:806**
Jury, **Rule 2:104**
Cumulative evidence, needless, exclusion, **Rule 2:403**
Documents,
Authentication, **Rule 2:902**
Best evidence, **Rule 2:1001 et seq.**
Emotional condition, statements, hearsay evidence, exceptions, **Rule 2:803**
English language, interpreters,
Competency, witnesses, **Rule 2:604**
Privileged communications, **Rule 2:507**
Exceptions, hearsay evidence, **Rule 2:803 et seq.**
Excited utterances, hearsay evidence, exceptions, **Rule 2:803**
Family records, hearsay evidence, exceptions, **Rule 2:803**
Foreign countries, public records, authentication, **Rule 2:902**
Habit, **Rule 2:406**
Healing arts practitioner and patient privilege, **Rule 2:505**
Hearing impaired persons, interpreters,
Competency, witnesses, **Rule 2:604**
Privileged communications, **Rule 2:507**
Hearsay evidence, **Rule 2:801 et seq.**
Hearsay within hearsay, **Rule 2:805**
Identity and identification,
Requirement, **Rule 2:901**
Witnesses, hearsay evidence, exceptions, **Rule 2:803**
Inconsistent prior statements, hearsay, **Rule 2:801**
Insurance, **Rule 2:411**
Interpreters,
Competency, witnesses, **Rule 2:604**
Privileged communications, **Rule 2:507**
Judicial notice, **Rule 2:201 et seq.**
Jury, generally, this index
Law, judicial notice, **Rule 2:202**
Lengthy documents, portions, **Rule 2:106**
Limited purposes, scope, **Rule 2:105**
Lost or destroyed documents, contents, best evidence, **Rule 2:1004**
Marital privilege, **Rule 2:504**
Market quotes, hearsay evidence, exceptions, **Rule 2:803**
Marriage, certificates and certification, hearsay evidence, exceptions, **Rule 2:803**
Medical bills, authentication, **Rule 2:902**
Medical care and treatment, statements, hearsay evidence, exceptions, **Rule 2:803**
Medical records, authentication, **Rule 2:902**
Mental condition, statements, hearsay evidence, exceptions, **Rule 2:803**
Mental health professional and client privilege, **Rule 2:506**

EVIDENCE—Cont'd
Negligence,
  Insurance, **Rule 2:411**
  Remedial measures, **Rule 2:407**
Negotiable instruments, checks, best evidence, **Rule 2:1003**
Objections and exceptions, **Rule 2:103**
Offers to compromise, **Rule 2:408**
Offers to plead, crimes and offenses, **Rule 2:410**
Official publications, judicial notice, **Rule 2:203**
Opinion and expert testimony. Witnesses, this index
Original in possession of party opponent, best evidence, **Rule 2:1004**
Other crimes, character, exclusion, **Rule 2:404**
  Child sex offenses, exception, **Rule 2:413**
Physical condition, statements, hearsay evidence, exceptions, **Rule 2:803**
Polygraph examinations, admissibility, **Rule 2:402**
Preliminary determinations, **Rule 2:104**
Present sense impressions, hearsay evidence, exceptions, **Rule 2:803**
Presumptions, **Rules 2:301, 2:302**
  Created by law, authentication, **Rule 2:902**
Prior sexual conduct, complaining witnesses, **Rule 2:412**
Prior statements, hearsay, **Rule 2:801**
Privileges and immunities, **Rule 2:501 et seq.**
  Preliminary determinations, **Rule 2:104**
Proffers, **Rule 2:103**
Public records,
  Authentication, **Rule 2:902**
  Reports, hearsay evidence, exceptions, **Rule 2:803**
Real estate, records and recordation, hearsay evidence, exceptions, **Rule 2:803**
Recorded recollection, hearsay evidence, exceptions, **Rule 2:803**
Recorded statements, related parts, **Rule 2:106**
Regularly conducted activity,
  Certified records, self-authentication, **Rule 2:902**
  Records and recordation, hearsay evidence, exceptions, **Rule 2:803**
Relevant Evidence, generally, this index
Religious organizations and societies, records and recordation, hearsay evidence, exceptions, **Rule 2:803**
Remedial measures, **Rule 2:407**
Reputation,
  Character evidence, proof, **Rule 2:405**
  Hearsay evidence, exceptions, **Rule 2:803**
Routine practices, **Rule 2:406**
Scope,
  Limited purposes, **Rule 2:105**
  Rules, **Rule 2:102**
Self authentication, **Rule 2:902**
Sex offenses, prior sexual conduct, complaining witnesses, **Rule 2:412**
Sexual assault, complaints, hearsay evidence, exceptions, **Rule 2:803**

EVIDENCE—Cont'd
Signatures, authentication, **Rule 2:902**
  Subscribing witnesses, **Rule 2:903**
Spousal privilege, **Rule 2:504**
Striking, **Rule 1:11**
  Attorney discipline, **BOG 13**
  Motions, criminal proceedings, **Rule 3A:15**
Subpoenas, production, criminal proceedings, **Rule 3A:12**
Subsequent remedial measures, **Rule 2:407**
Summaries, best evidence, **Rule 2:1006**
Unavailable declarants, hearsay evidence, exceptions, **Rule 2:804**
Vital statistics, hearsay evidence, exceptions, **Rule 2:803**
Weight, jury, **Rule 2:104**
Withdrawn pleas, crimes and offenses, **Rule 2:410**
Witnesses, generally, this index
Writings,
  Best evidence, **Rule 2:1001 et seq.**
  Related parts, **Rule 2:106**

EXCEPTIONS AND OBJECTIONS
Objections and Exceptions, generally, this index

EXCITED UTTERANCES
Hearsay evidence, exceptions, **Rule 2:803**

EXCLUDING WITNESSES
Generally, **Rule 2:615**

EXECUTION
Capias, indictment or information, **Rule 3A:7**

EXECUTIVE COMMITTEES
Definitions, attorney discipline, **BOG 13**

EXECUTIVE DIRECTOR
Definitions, attorney discipline, **BOG 13**

EXHIBITS
Depositions, **Rule 4:5**

EXPERT TESTIMONY
Witnesses, opinion and expert testimony. Witnesses, this index

FAMILY RECORDS
Hearsay evidence, exceptions, **Rule 2:803**

FEES
Attorney Fees, generally, this index
Filing, this index

FILES
Definitions, attorney discipline, **BOG 13**

FILING
Correctional institutions, habeas corpus, timeliness, **Rule 3A:25**
Crimes and offenses, district courts, practice and procedure, **Rule 7C:7**
Electronic filing, **Rule 1:17**
  Crimes and offenses, **Rule 3A:23**
Extension of time, supreme court, **Rule 5:5**

FILING—Cont'd
Fees,
Actual innocence, writs, **Rules 5:7B, 5A:5; Forms 12 (app. foll. Rule 5:41), 12 (app. foll. Rule 5A:37)**
Appeals court, notice of appeal, **Rule 5A:6**
Court of appeals, petitions, review, **Rule 5A:38**
Supreme court, petitions,
Appeals, **Rule 5:17**
Review, **Rule 5:17A**
Mail and mailing,
Correctional institutions, timeliness, **Rule 3A:25**
Supreme court, **Rule 5:5**
Motions, **Rule 4:15**
Notice of appeal,
Appeals court, **Rule 5A:6**
Supreme court, **Rules 5:9, 5:14, 5:22**
Petitions, supreme court,
Appeals, **Rules 5:17, 5:21**
Rehearings, **Rules 5:20, 5:37**
Pleadings, **Rule 3:1**
Traffic rules and regulations, district courts, practice and procedure, **Rule 7C:7**
Transcript, **Rule 5:11**

FINANCIAL RESPONSIBILITY
Attorneys, **BOG 18**

FINES AND PENALTIES
See, also, Crimes and Offenses, generally, this index
Appendices, court of appeals, **Rule 5A:25**
Attorneys,
Clients protection fund, **BOG 16**
Disciplinary proceedings, **BOG 13**
Nontraffic prepayable offenses, **Rule 3C:2**
Traffic infractions, **Rule 3B:2**

FOREIGN ATTORNEYS
Attorneys, this index

FOREIGN COUNTRIES
Depositions, **Rule 4:5**
Persons before whom taken, **Rule 4:3**
Foreign legal consultants, certificates and certification, **Rule 1A:7**
Public records, authentication, **Rule 2:902**

FOREIGN LEGAL CONSULTANTS
Definitions, attorneys, disciplinary proceedings, **BOG 13**

FOREIGN STATES
Attorneys, disciplinary proceedings, **BOG 13**
Depositions, **Rule 4:5**
Persons before whom taken, **Rule 4:3**
Foreign states, disciplinary proceedings, **BOG 13**

FORMS
Additional bond, appeal from circuit court to appellate court, **Forms 6 (app. foll. Rule 5:41), 6 (app. foll. Rule 5A:37)**
Arrest warrant, statement of witness, **Form 2 (app. foll. Rule 3A:25)**

FORMS—Cont'd
Attorneys, this index
Bonds,
Costs alone,
Appeal from circuit court to appellate court, **Forms 3 (app. foll. Rule 5:41), 3 (app. foll. Rule 5A:37)**
Appeal of right from circuit court to court of appeals, **Forms 1 (app. foll. Rule 5:41), 1 (app. foll. Rule 5A:37)**
Appeal of right from state corporation commission to supreme court, **Forms 8 (app. foll. Rule 5:41), 8 (app. foll. Rule 5A:37)**
Appeal of right from workers compensation commission to court of appeals, **Forms 7 (app. foll. Rule 5:41), 7 (app. foll. Rule 5A:37)**
Costs and suspension,
Appeal from circuit court to appellate court, **Forms 2 (app. foll. Rule 5:41), 2 (app. foll. Rule 5A:37), 5 (app. foll. Rule 5:41), 5 (app. foll. Rule 5A:37)**
Appeal of right from state corporation commission to supreme court, **Forms 9 (app. foll. Rule 5:41), 9 (app. foll. Rule 5A:37)**
Execution and acknowledgment, **Form 10 (app. foll. Rule 5:41)**
Suspension alone, appeal from circuit court to appellate court, **Forms 4 (app. foll. Rule 5:41), 4 (app. foll. Rule 5A:37)**
Capias, **Form 5 (app. foll. Rule 3A:25)**
Criminal complaints, **Form 1 (app. foll. Rule 3A:25)**
Execution and acknowledgment of all bonds, **Form 10 (app. foll. Rule 5A:37)**
Guilty plea, questions to be put by court to accused, **Forms 6 (app. foll. Rule 3A:25), 11 (app. foll. Rule 3A:25)**
Instructions, **Form 2 (app. foll. Rule 1:16)**
Irrevocable letters of credit,
Court of appeals, **Form 11 (app. foll. Rule 5A:37)**
Supreme court, **Form 11 (app. foll. Rule 5:41)**
Notice of appeal from trial court, **Rule 5A:6**
Plea of not guilty, suggested questions to be put by court to accused, **Form 7 (app. foll. Rule 3A:25)**
Praecipe, **Form 1 (app. foll. Rule 1:16)**
Pretrial scheduling, civil actions, **Rule 1:18B**
Pro hac vice, out of state attorneys, participation in trial, **Form 1 (app. foll. Rule 1A:7)**
Sentencing orders, **Form 10 (app. foll. Rule 3A:25)**
Subpoena, **Form 8 (app. foll. Rule 3A:25)**
Subpoena duces tecum, **Form 9 (app. foll. Rule 3A:25)**
Summons, **Rule 3:5**
Criminal proceedings, **Form 3 (app. foll. Rule 3A:25)**

FUNDS
Clients protection fund, **BOG 16**

FUNDS—Cont'd
Clients security fund, **BOG 16**
Safekeeping funds and property of client, **RPC 1.15**

GENERAL DISTRICT COURTS
District Courts, generally, this index

GRAND JURY
Generally, **Rule 3A:5**

GUARDIANS AD LITEM
Appeal and review, notice, **Rule 5A:6**
Court of appeals, briefs, **Rule 5A:21**
Notice, **Rule 5A:19**
Juvenile and domestic relations district courts, **Rule 8:6**

GUILTY PLEAS
Generally, **Rules 3A:8, 8:18**
Suggested questions to be put by court to accused, **Forms 6 (app. foll. Rule 3A:25, 11 (app. foll. Rule 3A:25)**
Voluntariness, **Rules 3A:8, 7C:6, 8:18**

HABEAS CORPUS
Capital punishment cases, petitions, **Rule 5:7A**
Denial, findings of fact, conclusions of law, **Rule 3A:24**
Inmate filings, timeliness, **Rule 3A:25**
Original jurisdiction, **Rule 5:7**

HABIT
Definitions, evidence, **Rule 2:406**
Evidence, **Rule 2:406**

HANDICAPPED PERSONS
Witnesses, competency, **Rule 2:601**

HEALING ARTS PRACTITIONER AND PATIENT PRIVILEGE
Generally, **Rule 2:505**

HEALTH CARE PROVIDERS
Physical and mental examinations of persons, **Rule 4:10**

HEALTH RECORDS
Production of documents and things, **Rules 4:9, 4:9A**

HEARING IMPAIRED PERSONS
Interpreters,
Competency, witnesses, **Rule 2:604**
Privileged communications, **Rule 2:507**

HEARINGS
Actual innocence, writs, **Rules 5:7B, 5A:5**
Attorneys, disciplinary proceedings, **BOG 13**
Crimes and offenses, defenses and objections, **Rule 3A:9**
Rehearing, generally, this index

HEARSAY EVIDENCE
Generally, **Rule 2:801 et seq.**
Definitions, **Rule 2:801**

HEARSAY WITHIN HEARSAY
Generally, **Rule 2:805**

HIGHWAYS AND ROADS
Traffic Rules and Regulations, generally, this index

HUSBAND AND WIFE
See, also, Marriage, generally, this index
Marriage certificates, hearsay evidence, exceptions, **Rule 2:803**
Military forces, attorneys, provisional admission to practice, **Rule 1A:8**
Spousal privilege, **Rule 2:504**

IDENTITY AND IDENTIFICATION
Requirement, evidence, **Rule 2:901**
Witnesses, hearsay evidence, exceptions, **Rule 2:803**

IMMIGRATION
Unauthorized practice of law, **UPR 9–103**

IMMUNITIES
Privileges and Immunities, generally, this index

IMPAIRMENT
Definitions, attorney discipline, **BOG 13**

IMPAIRMENT PROCEEDINGS
Definitions, attorney discipline, **BOG 13**

INCONSISTENT PRIOR STATEMENTS
Witnesses, **Rule 2:613**
Hearsay, **Rule 2:801**

INDICTMENT AND INFORMATION
Generally, **Rule 3A:6**
Capias or summons, **Rule 3A:7**
Definitions, criminal practice and procedure, **Rule 3A:2**
Forms, **Form 4 (app. foll. Rule 3A:25)**
Grand jury, **Rule 3A:5**

INFORMATION AND INDICTMENT
Indictment and Information, generally, this index

INJUNCTIONS
Court of appeals proceedings, **Rule 5A:38**
Supreme court proceedings, **Rule 5:17A**

INSPECTIONS AND INSPECTORS
Crimes and offenses, **Rule 3A:11**
Entry on land, **Rules 4:9, 4:9A**

INSTRUCTIONS TO JURY
Generally, **Rule 3A:16**
Form, **Form 2 (app. foll. Rule 1:16)**
Preliminary voir dire examination, **Rule 1:21**

INSURANCE
Attorneys, crimes and offenses, malpractice insurance, **BOG 13.4**
Discovery, insurance agreements, **Rule 4:1**
Evidence, **Rule 2:411**
Title insurance, unauthorized practice of law, **UPR 7–101**

INTEREST
Attorneys,
  Discipline, judgments, **BOG 13**
  Trust accounts, client funds, **BOG 20**

INTERNATIONAL LAW
Foreign legal consultants, **Rule 1A:7**

INTERPLEADER
Generally, **Rule 3:15**

INTERPRETERS
Competency, witnesses, **Rule 2:604**
Privileged communications, **Rule 2:507**

INTERROGATORIES
  Generally, **Rule 4:8**
Expenses, failure of party to serve answers, **Rule 4:12**

INTERVENTION
Generally, **Rule 3:14**

INVESTIGATIONS AND INVESTIGATORS
Attorney disciplinary proceedings, **BOG 13**
Definitions, attorney discipline, **BOG 13**
Lay adjusters, unauthorized practice of law, **UPR 2–102**

INVESTIGATIVE REPORTS
Definitions, attorney discipline, **BOG 13**

IOLTA ACCOUNTS
Attorneys, client funds, **BOG 20**

ISOLATION
Communicable disease, public health threats, **Rule 7A:16**
  Appeal and review, **Rules 3:24, 5:41**

JAILS
Supreme court, filing, **Rule 5:5**

JOINDER
  Generally, **Rule 3:12**
Crimes and offenses, **Rule 3A:10**
Indictment and information, **Rule 3A:6**

JUDGES
Activities to improve law, legal system, administration of justice, **CJC 4**
Avoiding impropriety, **CJC 2**
Bar membership, **BOG 3**
Best evidence, powers and duties, **Rule 2:1008**
Canons of judicial conduct, **CJC 1 et seq.**
Compensation and salaries, quasijudicial activities, reports, **CJC 5**
Confidential or privileged information, judicial performance evaluation program, **Rule 9:2**
Conflict of interest, extra-judicial activities, **CJC 4**
Definitions,
  Attorney discipline, **BOG 13**
  Court of appeals, **Rule 5A:1**
  Supreme court proceedings, **Rule 5:1**
Diligent performance, duties of office, **CJC 3**

JUDGES—Cont'd
Disciplinary responsibilities, **CJC 3**
Disqualification, **CJC 3**
Effective date, canons of judicial conduct, **CJC 7**
Ethics, **CJC 1 et seq.**
Extrajudicial activities, **CJC 4**
False or unjust criticism by attorneys, **RPC 8.2**
Impartial and diligent performance, duties of office, **CJC 3**
Impropriety, **CJC 2**
Improving law, legal system and administration of justice, **CJC 4**
Integrity and independence, **CJC 1**
Judicial conduct canons, **CJC 1 et seq.**
Judicial performance evaluation program, **Rules 9:1, 9:2**
Lists, **Appendix**
Notice, judicial notice, **Rule 2:201 et seq.**
Performance evaluation program, **Rules 9:1, 9:2**
Persons selected for judgeship, canons of judicial conduct, **CJC 6**
Political activity, **CJC 5**
Pro tempore judges, canons of judicial conduct, **CJC 6**
Public comment, pending proceedings, **CJC 5**
Quasijudicial activities, **CJC 5**
Reports, compensation, extrajudicial activities, **CJC 5**
Retired judges, canons of judicial conduct, **CJC 6**
Substitute judges, canons of judicial conduct, **CJC 6**
Witnesses,
  Calling, interrogating, **Rule 2:614**
  Competency, **Rule 2:605**

JUDGMENTS AND DECREES
Acquittal, **Rule 3A:15**
Defaults, generally, this index
Definitions,
  Court of appeals, **Rule 5A:1**
  Supreme court proceedings, **Rule 5:1**
Endorsements, **Rule 1:13**
Finality, **Rule 1:1**
Res judicata, **Rule 1:6**
Summary Judgment, generally, this index
Support arrearages, motion to enter judgment, service of process, **Rule 8:4**

JUDICIAL NOTICE
Generally, **Rule 2:201 et seq.**

JUDICIAL PERFORMANCE EVALUATION PROGRAM
Generally, **Rules 9:1, 9:2**

JURISDICTION
Attorney discipline, **RPC 8.5; BOG 13**
Original jurisdiction,
  Court of appeals, **Rule 5A:5**
  Supreme court, **Rules 5:7, 5:7A**

JURY
  Generally, **Rules 3:21, 3:22**

JURY—Cont'd
As of right, **Rule 3:21**
Best evidence, powers and duties, **Rule 2:1008**
Challenges, for cause, **Rule 1:22**
Excusing, **Rule 3:22A**
Confessions, evidence, **Rule 2:104**
Consent, **Rule 3:22**
Waiver, **Rule 3:21**
Criminal proceedings, **Rule 3A:13**
Criminal proceedings, **Rule 3A:13**
Bifurcated jury trials, noncapital felonies, class 1 misdemeanors, **Rule 3A:17.1**
Confidential or privileged information, **Rule 3A:14.1**
Examination, **Rule 3A:14**
Demand, **Rule 3:21**
Grand jury, **Rule 3A:5**
Misleading, relevant evidence, exclusion, **Rule 2:403**
Mixed jury, nonjury claims, **Rule 3:22**
Note taking, **Rule 1:23**
Polling, criminal proceedings, **Rule 3A:17**
Voir dire examination, **Rule 3:22A**
Criminal proceedings, **Rule 3A:14**
Preliminary information, **Rule 1:21**
Witnesses, competency, **Rule 2:606**

JUVENILE AND DOMESTIC RELATIONS DISTRICT COURTS
Generally, **Rule 8:1 et seq.**
Appeal from convictions, **Rule 3A:19**

JUVENILE DELINQUENTS AND DEPENDENTS
Witnesses, conviction of crime, impeachment, **Rule 2:609**

LABOR AND EMPLOYMENT
Jury, voir dire examination, **Rule 3:22A**

LAW
Judicial notice, **Rule 2:202**

LAWYERS
Attorneys, generally, this index

LAY ADJUSTERS
Definitions, unauthorized practice, **UPR 2–101**
Unauthorized practice of law, **UPR 2–101 et seq.**

LAY WITNESSES
Opinion and expert testimony, **Rule 2:701**

LEADING QUESTIONS
Witnesses, **Rule 2:611**

LEARNED TREATISES
Witnesses, opinion and expert testimony, use, **Rule 2:706**

LEAVE OF COURT
Amendment of pleadings, **Rule 1:8**

LEGAL ASSISTANCE
Emeritus members, state bar, **BOG 3**

LEGAL ASSISTANCE—Cont'd
Military forces, foreign states, registration, **Rule 1A:6**

LENGTHY DOCUMENTS
Portions, evidence, **Rule 2:106**

LETTERS OF CREDIT
Forms, irrevocable letters of credit,
Court of appeals, **Form 11 (app. foll. Rule 5A:37)**
Supreme court, **Form 11 (app. foll. Rule 5:41)**
Security for appeal,
Court of appeals, **Rule 5A:17**
Supreme court, **Rule 5:24**

LICENSES AND PERMITS
Attorneys, this index
Definitions, attorney discipline, **BOG 13**

LIMITATION OF ACTIONS
Pleadings, **Rule 3:18**

LIMITED LIABILITY ENTITIES
Attorneys, **BOG 14**

LOST OR DESTROYED DOCUMENTS
Contents, best evidence, **Rule 2:1004**

MAGISTRATES
Definitions, criminal practice and procedure, **Rule 3A:2**
Witnesses, competency, **Rule 2:605**

MAIL AND MAILING
Computation of time, **Rule 1:7**
Habeas corpus, inmate filings, **Rule 3A:25**
Support arrearages, motion to enter judgment, service of process, **Rule 8:4**
Supreme court, filing, **Rule 5:5**

MALPRACTICE INSURANCE
Attorneys, crimes and offenses, **BOG 13.4**

MANDAMUS
Original jurisdiction, **Rule 5:7**

MANDATE
Court of appeals, **Rule 5A:31**
Supreme court, **Rule 5:36**

MARITAL PRIVILEGE
Generally, **Rule 2:504**

MARKET QUOTES
Hearsay evidence, exceptions, **Rule 2:803**

MARRIAGE
See, also, Husband and Wife, generally, this index
Certificates and certification, hearsay evidence, exceptions, **Rule 2:803**
Jury, voir dire examination, **Rule 3:22A**
Privileges and immunities, **Rule 2:504**

MECHANICS LIENS
Res judicata, **Rule 1:6**

MEDICAL BILLS
Authentication, **Rule 2:902**

MEDICAL CARE AND TREATMENT
Children and minors, emergencies, judicial consent proceedings, petitions, **Rule 8:3**
Healing arts practitioner and patient privilege, **Rule 2:505**
Juvenile and domestic relations district courts, judicial consent, **Rule 8:22**
Statements, hearsay evidence, exceptions, **Rule 2:803**

MEDICAL EXAMINATIONS
Generally, **Rule 4:10**

MEDICAL RECORDS
Authentication, **Rule 2:902**

MEMBER
Definitions, legal ethics, **BOG 10**

MEMORANDUM ORDERS
Definitions, attorney discipline, **BOG 13**

MENTAL CONDITION
Statements, hearsay evidence, exceptions, **Rule 2:803**

MENTAL EXAMINATIONS
Generally, **Rule 4:10**

MENTAL HEALTH PROFESSIONAL AND CLIENT PRIVILEGE
Generally, **Rule 2:506**

MILITARY FORCES
Attorneys, foreign states,
  Legal assistance, registration, **Rule 1A:6**
  Spouses, provisional admission, **Rule 1A:8**

MISCONDUCT
Definitions, attorney discipline, **BOG 13**

MONEY DAMAGES
Complaints, ad damnum clauses, **Rule 3:2**

MOTIONS
  Generally, **Rule 4:15**
Counsel of record, **Rule 1:4**
Court of appeals, **Rule 5A:2**
Criminal proceedings, **Rule 3A:9**
  Furnishing copies of written motions, **Rule 3A:21**
Depositions, terminating or limiting examination, **Rule 4:5**
Discovery, criminal proceedings, **Rule 3A:11**
Electronic filing, **Rule 1:17**
Filing, **Rule 4:15**
Hearing, **Rule 4:15**
Juvenile and domestic relations district courts,
  Contents, **Rule 8:3**
  Size of paper, **Rule 8:7**
Paper, size, **Rule 1:16**
Responses, **Rule 3:8**

MOTIONS—Cont'd
Scheduling, **Rule 4:15**
Service, **Rules 1:12, 4:15**
Setting aside verdict, criminal proceedings, **Rule 3A:15**
Substitution of parties, **Rule 3:17**
Summary judgment, **Rule 3:20**
Supreme Court, this index

MOTOR VEHICLES
Traffic Rules and Regulations, generally, this index

MULTIPARTY CASES
Partial final judgment, appeals, **Rule 5:8A**

NEGLIGENCE
Insurance, evidence, **Rule 2:411**
Pleadings, **Rule 3:18**
Remedial measures, evidence, **Rule 2:407**

NEGOTIABLE INSTRUMENTS
Checks, best evidence, **Rule 2:1003**

NEGOTIATION
Discovery, pre-motion, certificates and certification, **Rule 4:1**

NEW PARTIES
Generally, **Rule 3:16**

NEW TRIALS
Criminal proceedings, **Rule 3A:15**

NOLO CONTENDERE PLEAS
Suggested questions to be put by court to accused, **Form 11 (app. foll. Rule 3A:25)**
Voluntariness, **Rules 3A:8, 7C:6, 8:18**

NONBIOLOGICAL EVIDENCE
Actual innocence, writs, petitions, **Rule 5A:5; Form 12 (app. foll. Rule 5A:37)**

NOT GUILTY PLEA
Suggested questions to be put by court to accused, **Form 7 (app. foll. Rule 3A:25)**

NOTES
Jury, taking, **Rule 1:23**

NOTICE
Administrative Process Act appeals, **Rule 2A:2**
Appeal and review, time, filing, **Rules 5:9, 5A:6**
Attorneys,
  Discipline, **BOG 13**
  Trust accounts, election not to maintain, **BOG 20**
Corporation commission, appeals to supreme court, **Rule 5:21**
Court of Appeals, this index
Definitions, legal ethics, **BOG 10**
Depositions, this index
Electronic filing, **Rule 1:17**
Guardians ad litem, appeal and review, **Rule 5A:6**
Judicial notice, **Rule 2:201 et seq.**
Juvenile and domestic relations district courts,
  Ordering of services, motion or petition, **Rule 8:3**

NOTICE—Cont'd
Juvenile and domestic relations district courts —Cont'd
Trial rights, **Rule 8:17**
State bar disciplinary board, appeals to supreme court, **Rule 5:21**
Supreme Court, this index
Three judge circuit court panels, appeals to supreme court, **Rule 5:21**

OATHS AND AFFIRMATIONS
Complaints, criminal proceedings, **Rule 3A:3**
Depositions, **Rule 4:5**
Witnesses, **Rule 2:603**

OBJECTIONS AND EXCEPTIONS
Court of appeals, transcript or written statement, **Rule 5A:8**
Crimes and offenses, motions, **Rule 3A:9**
Depositions, admissibility, **Rule 4:7**
Evidence, **Rule 2:103**
Instructions to jury, criminal proceedings, **Rule 3A:16**
Juvenile and domestic relations district courts, pleadings, **Rule 8:8**
Supreme court, transcript or written statement, **Rule 5:11**

OBJECTS
Witnesses, refreshing memory, **Rule 2:612**

OFFENSES AND CRIMES
Crimes and Offenses, generally, this index

OFFERS TO COMPROMISE
Evidence, **Rule 2:408**

OFFERS TO PLEAD
Evidence, crimes and offenses, **Rule 2:410**

OFFICIAL PUBLICATIONS
Judicial notice, **Rule 2:203**

OPINION AND EXPERT TESTIMONY
Witnesses, this index

OPINIONS
Advisory Opinions, generally, this index
Court of appeals, **Rule 5A:31**
Jury, voir dire examination, **Rule 3:22A**
Supreme court, **Rule 5:36**

OPPOSING COUNSEL
Definitions,
Court of appeals, **Rule 5A:1**
Supreme court proceedings, **Rule 5:1**

ORAL ARGUMENT
Actual innocence, writs, **Rule 5A:5**
Court of appeals, **Rule 5A:28**
Petition for appeal, criminal cases and traffic infractions, **Rule 5A:12**
Supreme court, **Rule 5:33**
Petition for appeal, **Rule 5:17**

ORDERS OF COURT
Depositions, **Rule 4:2**
Endorsements, **Rule 1:13**
Juvenile and domestic relations district courts, **Rule 8:19**
Finality, **Rule 1:1**
Habeas corpus, denial, findings of fact, conclusions of law, **Rule 3A:24**
Physical and mental examinations of persons, **Rule 4:10**
Protective orders, discovery, **Rule 4:1**
Criminal proceedings, **Rule 3A:11**
Scheduling, civil actions, **Rules 1:18, 1:20**
Sentencing in criminal cases, **Form 10 (app. foll. Rule 3A:25)**
Supreme Court, this index

ORIGINAL IN POSSESSION OF PARTY OPPONENT
Best evidence, **Rule 2:1004**

ORIGINAL JURISDICTION
Court of appeals, **Rule 5A:5**
Supreme court, **Rules 5:7, 5:7A**

ORIGINALS
Definitions, best evidence, **Rule 2:1001**

PANELS
Definitions, attorney discipline, **BOG 13**

PAPERS AND BOOKS
Juvenile and domestic relations district courts, size of papers, **Rule 8:7**

PARAGRAPHS
Definitions, attorney discipline, **BOG 13**

PARTIES
Actual innocence, writs, **Rule 5A:5**
Corporation commission, appeals to supreme court, **Rule 5:21**
Definitions,
Administrative Process Act appeals, **Rule 2A:1**
Juvenile and domestic relations district courts, continuances, **Rule 8:14**
Interpleader, **Rule 3:15**
Intervention, **Rule 3:14**
Joinder, generally, this index
Multi party cases, partial final judgment, appeals, **Rule 5:8A**
New parties, **Rule 3:16**
Substitution, **Rule 3:17**
Third Party Practice, generally, this index

PARTNERS AND PARTNERSHIPS
Attorneys, forming with nonlawyer, **RPC 5.4; DR 3–103**
Unauthorized practice of law, limited exceptions, **UPR 1–101**

PATENTS
Foreign attorneys, admission to practice without examination, **Rule 1A:2**
Certificates, revocation, **Rule 1A:3**

PENALTIES AND FINES
Fines and Penalties, generally, this index

PERSONAL INFORMATION
Definitions, jury, disclosure, criminal proceedings, **Rule 3A:14.1**

PERSONAL INJURIES
Res judicata, **Rule 1:6**
Witnesses, prior inconsistent statements, **Rule 2:613**

PERSONAL KNOWLEDGE
Witnesses, **Rule 2:602**

PERSONS SELECTED FOR JUDGESHIPS
Canons of judicial conduct, **CJC 6**

PETITIONERS
Definitions, attorney discipline, **BOG 13**

PETITIONS
Actual innocence, writs, petitions, **Rules 5:7B, 5A:5; Forms 12 (app. foll. Rule 5:41), 12 (app. foll. Rule 5A:37)**
Administrative Process Act appeals, **Rule 2A:4**
Commencement of actions, **Rule 3:2**
Corporation commission, appeals to supreme court, **Rule 5:21**
Court of Appeals, this index
Habeas corpus,
  Capital punishment cases, **Rule 5:7A**
  Denial, findings of fact, conclusions of law, **Rule 3A:24**
Juvenile and domestic relations district courts, contents, **Rule 8:3**
Reinstatement, attorney discipline, **BOG 13**
Supreme Court, this index

PHOTOGRAPHS AND PICTURES
Preservation of record, **Rule 1:14**
  District courts, **Rule 7A:6**
  Juvenile and domestic relations district courts, **Rule 8:12**

PHYSICAL CONDITION
Statements, hearsay evidence, exceptions, **Rule 2:803**

PHYSICAL EXAMINATIONS
Generally, **Rule 4:10**

PHYSICIANS AND SURGEONS
Healing arts practitioner and patient privilege, **Rule 2:505**
Physical and mental examinations of persons, **Rule 4:10**

PICTURES AND PHOTOGRAPHS
Photographs and Pictures, generally, this index

PLAINTIFF IN ERROR
Definitions, court of appeals, **Rule 5A:1**

PLEA BARGAINING
Generally, **Rule 3A:8**

PLEADINGS
  Generally, **Rules 1:4, 3:1, 3:18**
Amendments, **Rule 1:8**
  District courts, **Rule 7A:9**
Bills of particulars, **Rule 3:7**
Contributory negligence, **Rule 3:18**
Copies of pleadings, furnishing, district courts, **Rule 7A:10**
Counterclaims, generally, this index
Crimes and offenses, **Rule 3A:9**
Crossclaims, generally, this index
Discretion of court, **Rule 1:9**
District Courts, this index
Electronic filing, **Rule 1:17**
Juvenile and domestic relations district courts, **Rule 8:8**
  Size of paper, **Rule 8:7**
Limitation of actions, **Rule 3:18**
Negligence, **Rule 3:18**
Paper, size, **Rule 1:16**
Reply, **Rule 3:11**
Service, **Rule 1:12**
Verification, **Rule 1:10**

PLEAS
  Generally, **Rule 3A:8**
District court, corporations, **Rule 7C:6**
Juvenile and domestic relations district courts, **Rule 8:18**
Responses, **Rule 3:8**

POLICE
Witnesses, exclusion, **Rule 2:615**

POLYGRAPH EXAMINATIONS
Admissibility, **Rule 2:402**

POOLED ACCOUNTS
Attorneys, client funds, **BOG 20**

PRAECIPE
Form, **Form 1 (app. foll. Rule 1:16)**

PREJUDICE
Relevant evidence, exclusion, **Rule 2:403**
Witnesses, impeachment, **Rule 2:610**

PRELIMINARY HEARING
Joint defendants, district courts, **Rule 7C:4**

PRESENT SENSE IMPRESSIONS
Hearsay evidence, exceptions, **Rule 2:803**

PRESUMPTIONS
Created by law, authentication, **Rule 2:902**
Evidence, **Rules 2:301, 2:302**

PRETRIAL PROCEDURE
  Generally, **Rule 4:0 et seq.**
Conferences,
  Civil actions, **Rule 1:19**
  Discovery, **Rule 4:13**
Depositions, **Rule 4:0 et seq.**

PRETRIAL PROCEDURE—Cont'd
Scheduling, civil actions, **Rules 1:18, 1:20**
Forms, **Rule 1:18B**

PRINCIPAL
Definitions, lay adjusters, **UPR 2–101**

PRIOR SEXUAL CONDUCT
Complaining witnesses, evidence, **Rule 2:412**

PRIOR STATEMENTS
Witnesses, **Rule 2:613**
Hearsay, **Rule 2:801**

PRISONS
Inmates,
Court of appeals, filing, extension of time, **Rule 5A:3**
Habeas corpus, filings, timeliness, **Rule 3A:25**
Supreme court, filing, **Rule 5:5**

PRIVATE DISCIPLINE
Definitions, attorney discipline, **BOG 13**

PRIVATE REPRIMAND
Definitions, attorney discipline, **BOG 13**

PRIVILEGES AND IMMUNITIES
Discovery, **Rule 4:1**
Evidence, **Rule 2:501 et seq.**
Preliminary determinations, **Rule 2:104**

PRIVITY
Res judicata, **Rule 1:6**

PRO HAC VICE
Attorneys, this index

PRO TEMPORE JUDGES
Canons of judicial conduct, **CJC 6**

PROCESS
Service, generally, this index

PRODUCTION OF DOCUMENTS AND THINGS
Generally, **Rules 4:9, 4:9A**
Depositions, **Rule 4:5**
Uniform Interstate Depositions and Discovery Act, application of law, **Rule 4:5**

PROFESSIONAL CORPORATIONS
Attorneys, **BOG 14**

PROFESSIONAL RESPONSIBILITY
Attorneys, **DR 1–101 et seq.**

PROFFERS
Evidence, **Rule 2:103**

PROHIBITION
Original jurisdiction, **Rule 5:7**

PROOF OF SERVICE
Generally, **Rule 3:6**

PROPERTY
Real Estate, generally, this index

PROPERTY—Cont'd
Safekeeping funds and property of client, **RPC 1.15**

PROPERTY DAMAGE
Res judicata, **Rule 1:6**

PROSECUTING ATTORNEYS
Generally, **RPC 3.8; DR 8–102**

PROSPECTIVE CLIENTS
Attorneys, duties, **RPC 1.18**

PROTECTIVE ORDERS
Discovery, **Rule 4:1**
Criminal proceedings, **Rule 3A:11**

PUBLIC HEALTH THREATS
Quarantine, isolation, communicable disease, **Rule 7A:16**
Appeal and review, **Rules 3:24, 5:41**

PUBLIC RECORDS
Authentication, evidence, **Rule 2:902**
Hearsay evidence, exceptions, **Rule 2:803**

QUARANTINE
Communicable disease, public health threats, **Rule 7A:16**
Appeal and review, **Rules 3:24, 5:41**

RADIO AND TELEVISION
Television and Radio, generally, this index

REAL ESTATE
Entry on land, discovery, **Rules 4:9, 4:9A**
Records and recordation, hearsay evidence, exceptions, **Rule 2:803**
Unauthorized practice of law, **UPR 6–101 et seq.**

RECEIVERS AND RECEIVERSHIPS
Definitions, attorney discipline, **BOG 13**

RECOGNIZANCE
Appearance of witness, criminal proceedings, **Rule 3A:12**
Definitions, criminal practice and procedure, **Rule 3A:2**

RECORDED RECOLLECTION
Hearsay evidence, exceptions, **Rule 2:803**

RECORDED STATEMENTS
Related parts, evidence, **Rule 2:106**

RECORDS AND RECORDATION
Administrative Process Act appeals, **Rule 2A:3**
Attorneys, **RPC 1.15; DR 9–103**
Discipline, **BOG 13**
Business Records, generally, this index
Corporation commission, appeals to supreme court, **Rule 5:21**
Court of Appeals, this index
Depositions, **Rules 4:5, 4:7**
District courts, electronic or photographic preservation, **Rule 7A:6**
Interrogatories, business records, **Rule 4:8**

RECORDS AND RECORDATION—Cont'd
Juvenile and domestic relations district courts, **Rule 8:11**
Subpoenas, **Rule 8:13**
Preservation of record, electronic or photographic means, **Rule 1:14**
Juvenile and domestic relations district courts, **Rule 8:12**
State bar disciplinary board, appeals to supreme court, **Rule 5:21**
Supreme Court, this index
Three judge circuit court panel, appeals to supreme court, **Rule 5:21**

REFRESHING MEMORY
Witnesses, writings, objects, **Rule 2:612**

REGULARLY CONDUCTED ACTIVITY
Records and recordation, hearsay evidence, exceptions, **Rule 2:803**

REHEARING
Court of Appeals, this index
Supreme court, **Rule 5:37**
Denial of appeal, **Rule 5:20**

REINSTATEMENT
Definitions, attorney discipline, **BOG 13**

REINSTATEMENT PROCEEDINGS
Definitions, attorney discipline, **BOG 13**

RELATIVES
Jury, voir dire examination, **Rule 3:22A**

RELEVANT EVIDENCE
Generally, **Rule 2:401 et seq.**
Connecting facts, preliminary determinations, **Rule 2:104**
Definitions, **Rule 2:401**

RELIGIOUS ORGANIZATIONS AND SOCIETIES
Clergy and communicant privilege, **Rule 2:503**
Records and recordation, hearsay evidence, exceptions, **Rule 2:803**

REMEDIAL MEASURES
Evidence, **Rule 2:407**

REPLY
Generally, **Rule 3:11**

REPLY BRIEFS
Court of Appeals, this index
Supreme court, **Rule 5:19**

REPORTERS
Generally, **Rule 1:3**
District courts, **Rule 7A:4**
Juvenile and domestic relations district courts, **Rule 8:11**

REPORTS
Attorneys, this index
Chancery commissioners, proceedings before, **Rule 3:23**

REPORTS—Cont'd
Health care providers, physical and mental examinations of persons, **Rule 4:10**
Juvenile and domestic relations district courts, court-ordered reports, counsel of record, **Rule 8:5**

REPUTATION
Character evidence, proof, **Rule 2:405**
Hearsay evidence, exceptions, **Rule 2:803**

REQUEST FOR ADMISSIONS
Generally, **Rule 4:11**
Expenses, failure to admit, **Rule 4:12**

RES JUDICATA
Generally, **Rule 1:6**

RESIDENCE AND DOMICILE
Health care providers, physical and mental examinations of persons, **Rule 4:10**

RESPONDENT
Definitions, attorney discipline, **BOG 13**

RETIRED JUDGES
Canons of judicial conduct, **CJC 6**

RETURNS
Arrest warrants, **Rule 3A:4**
Summons, indictment and information, **Rule 3A:7**
Writs, **Rule 3:3**

REVIEW AND APPEAL
Appeal and Review, generally, this index

ROUTINE PRACTICES
Definitions, evidence, **Rule 2:406**
Evidence, **Rule 2:406**

RULES AND REGULATIONS
Definitions, legal ethics, **BOG 10**
Traffic Rules and Regulations, generally, this index

SANCTIONS
Discovery, **Rule 4:12**

SCHEDULING
Civil actions, **Rules 1:18, 1:20**
Motions, **Rule 4:15**

SECTIONS
Definitions, attorney discipline, **BOG 13**

SELF AUTHENTICATION
Evidence, **Rule 2:902**

SELF INSURED
Definitions, lay adjusters, **UPR 2–101**

SENTENCE AND PUNISHMENT
Crimes and Offenses, generally, this index

SEPARATE TRIALS
Counterclaims, **Rule 3:9**
Crossclaims, **Rule 3:10**

SERVICE
Court of appeals proceedings, **Rule 5A:1**

SERVICE—Cont'd
Crimes and offenses, district courts, practice and procedure, **Rule 7C:7**
Discovery, **Rule 4:1**
Electronic filing, **Rule 1:17**
Email, **Rule 1:12**
Motions, **Rule 4:15**
Pleadings, **Rule 1:12**
Proof of service, **Rule 3:6**
Subpoenas, criminal proceedings, **Rule 3A:12**
Support arrearages, motion to enter judgment, **Rule 8:4**
Supreme court proceedings, **Rule 5:1**
Third party practice, **Rule 3:13**
Traffic rules and regulations, district courts, practice and procedure, **Rule 7C:7**

SESSIONS
Supreme court, **Rule 5:2**

SETTLEMENT AND COMPROMISE
Compromise and Settlement, generally, this index

SEVERANCE
Criminal defendants, trial, **Rule 3A:10**
District courts, **Rule 7C:4**

SEX OFFENSES
Children and minors, similar crimes, evidence, **Rule 2:413**
Prior sexual conduct, complaining witnesses, evidence, **Rule 2:412**

SEXUAL ASSAULT
Complaints, hearsay evidence, exceptions, **Rule 2:803**
Witnesses, false accusations, cross examination, **Rule 2:608**

SIGNATURES
Authentication, **Rule 2:902**
Subscribing witnesses, **Rule 2:903**

SMALL BUSINESSES
Administrative law and procedure, appeal and review, **Rule 2A:6**

SOUND RECORDINGS
Tape Recordings, generally, this index

SPOUSAL PRIVILEGE
Generally, **Rule 2:504**

SPOUSAL SUPPORT
Support, generally, this index

STANDARDS
Electronic filing, **Rule 1:17**

STATE BAR
Generally, **BOG 1 et seq.**

STATEMENTS
Definitions, hearsay evidence, **Rule 2:801**

STATUTES
Indictment and information, citation, **Rule 3A:6**

STAY PENDING APPEAL
Attorney disciplinary proceedings, **Rule 5:21; BOG 13**

STIPULATIONS
Discovery, **Rule 4:4**

SUBCOMMITTEE
Definitions, attorney discipline, **BOG 13**

SUBPOENAS
Attorneys,
Disciplinary proceedings, **BOG 13**
Unauthorized practice of law, **BOG 10**
Criminal proceedings, **Rule 3A:12**
District courts, witnesses, **Rule 7A:12**
Forms, **Form 8 (app. foll. Rule 3A:25)**
Juvenile and domestic relations district courts, **Rule 8:13**
Service, **Rule 1:12**

SUBPOENAS DUCES TECUM
District courts, **Rule 7A:12**
Furnishing requests, **Rule 7A:10**
Forms, **Form 9 (app. foll. Rule 3A:25)**
Juvenile and domestic relations district courts, **Rule 8:13**
Nonparties, discovery, **Rule 4:9A**

SUBSEQUENT REMEDIAL MEASURES
Evidence, **Rule 2:407**

SUBSTITUTE JUDGES
Canons of judicial conduct, **CJC 6**

SUBSTITUTION OF PARTIES
Generally, **Rule 3:17**

SUMMARIES
Best evidence, **Rule 2:1006**

SUMMARY DISPOSITION
Court of appeals, **Rule 5A:27**

SUMMARY JUDGMENT
Generally, **Rule 3:20**
Striking evidence, **Rule 1:11**

SUMMARY ORDERS
Definitions, attorney discipline, **BOG 13**

SUMMONS
Generally, **Rule 3:5**
Arrest, **Rule 3A:4**
Attorneys, disciplinary proceedings, **BOG 13**
Indictment or information, **Rule 3A:7**

SUPPORT
Arrearages, motion to enter judgment, service of process, **Rule 8:4**
Juvenile and domestic relations district courts, petitions, **Rule 8:3**

SUPREME COURT
Amicus curiae,
Briefs, **Rule 5:30**

SUPREME COURT—Cont'd
Amicus curiae—Cont'd
  Oral argument, **Rule 5:33**
Answers, certified questions of law, **Rule 5:40**
Appendix, briefs, **Rule 5:32**
Assignment of error, **Rule 5:17**
Attorney fees, awards, **Rule 5:35**
Attorneys,
  Contact information, change, **Rule 5:1**
  State bar disciplinary board, **Rule 5:21**
Awards, attorney fees, costs, **Rule 5:35**
Bonds, **Rule 5:24**
Briefs, **Rules 5:6, 5:26**
  Amicus curiae, **Rule 5:30**
  Appellant, opening brief, **Rule 5:27**
  Appellees, **Rule 5:28**
  Appendix, **Rule 5:32**
  Certified questions of law, **Rule 5:40**
  Petition for appeal, brief in opposition, **Rule 5:18**
  Reply brief, **Rules 5:19, 5:29**
  Supplemental authorities, citation, **Rule 5:6A**
Capital punishment, **Rule 5:22**
  Habeas corpus petitions, **Rule 5:7A**
Certificates and certification,
  Court of appeals, **Rules 5:14, 5:15**
  Law questions, **Rule 5:40**
  Petition for appeal, **Rule 5:17**
Citation, supplemental authorities, **Rule 5:6A**
Convening of court, **Rule 5:3**
Copies, briefs, **Rule 5:26**
Corporation commission, appeals, **Rule 5:21**
Correctional institutions, inmates, filing, **Rule 5:5**
Costs, **Rule 5:35**
  Appendix, briefs, **Rule 5:32**
  Certification of questions of law, **Rule 5:40**
Death penalty, **Rule 5:22**
Decisions, notice, **Rule 5:34**
Deferral of issuance of mandate, appeal or petition to United States Supreme Court, **Rule 5:39**
Denial of appeal, petition for rehearing, **Rule 5:20**
Depositions, transcripts, appendices, **Rule 5:32**
Digital appellate record, **Rule 5:13A**
Dismissal of appeal,
  Assignments of error omitted from petition or nonpayment of fee, **Rule 5:17**
  Noncompliance, **Rule 5:1A**
Disposition of record, **Rule 5:16**
Divisions, **Rule 5:2**
Dockets and docketing, **Rule 5:23**
Documents, covers, **Rule 5:31**
Electronic filing, **Rule 1:17**
  Briefs, **Rule 5:26**
    Appendix, **Rule 5:32**
  Digital appellate record, **Rule 5:13A**
En banc, convening, **Rule 5:3**
Error, assignment, **Rule 5:17**
Expedited review, **Rule 5:18**
Extension of time, **Rule 5:5**
  Briefs, **Rule 5:26**

SUPREME COURT—Cont'd
Fees, petition for review, **Rule 5:17A**
Filing, time, **Rule 5:5**
Filing fee,
  Petition for appeal, **Rule 5:17**
  Petition for review, **Rule 5:17A**
Fines and penalties,
  Appendix, briefs, **Rule 5:32**
  Noncompliance, **Rule 5:1A**
Form of record, **Rule 5:13**
  Digital appellate record, **Rule 5:13A**
Habeas corpus petitions, **Rules 5:7, 5:7A**
In division, convening, **Rule 5:3**
Injunctions, **Rule 5:17A**
Isolation, quarantine, communicable disease, public health threats, **Rule 5:41**
Issuance of mandate, deferral, appeal or petition to United States Supreme Court, **Rule 5:39**
Judge authorized to act, record on appeal, **Rule 5:12**
Justices, list, **Appendix**
Law questions, certification, **Rule 5:40**
Letters of credit, security for appeal, **Rule 5:24**
Mail and mailing, filing, **Rule 5:5**
Mandamus, petitions, **Rule 5:7**
Mandate, **Rule 5:36**
  Deferral of issuance, appeal or petition to United State Supreme Court, **Rule 5:39**
Motions, **Rule 5:4**
Multiparty cases, partial final judgment, appeals, **Rule 5:8A**
Multiple transcripts, time for filing notice of appeal, **Rule 5:11**
Notarized bills, costs, **Rule 5:35**
Notice,
  Appeal, **Rule 5:9**
    Court of appeals, **Rule 5:14**
  Certified questions of law, acceptance or rejection, **Rule 5:40**
  Decisions, **Rule 5:34**
  Oral argument, **Rule 5:33**
  Supplemental authorities, citation, **Rule 5:6A**
  Transcript, **Rule 5:11**
Objections, transcript or written statement, **Rule 5:11**
Opening brief of appellant, **Rule 5:27**
Opinions, **Rule 5:36**
  Certified questions of law, **Rule 5:40**
Oral argument, **Rule 5:33**
  Motions, **Rule 5:4**
  Petition for appeal, **Rule 5:17**
Orders of court, **Rule 5:4**
  Certification order, questions of law, **Rule 5:40**
Original jurisdiction, **Rules 5:7, 5:7A**
Parties,
  Briefs, reference to parties, **Rule 5:26**
  Oral argument, reference to parties, **Rule 5:33**
Penalties,
  Appendix, briefs, **Rule 5:32**

SUPREME COURT—Cont'd
Penalties—Cont'd
  Noncompliance, **Rule 5:1A**
Pending appeal, settlement, withdrawal, **Rule 5:38**
Perfection of appeal, **Rule 5:23**
Petitions,
  Appeal, **Rule 5:17**
    Brief in opposition, **Rule 5:18**
    Perfection, **Rule 5:23**
  Rehearing, post
  Review, **Rule 5:17A**
Practice and procedure, **Rule 5:1 et seq.**
Preparation of record, **Rule 5:13**
  Digital appellate record, **Rule 5:13A**
Preservation of issues, **Rule 5:25**
Priorities and preferences, docketing, **Rule 5:23**
Pro hac vice, oral argument, **Rule 5:33**
Prohibitions, petitions, **Rule 5:7**
Punishment and sentence, death penalty, **Rule 5:22**
Quarantine, isolation, communicable disease, public health threats, **Rule 5:41**
Questions of law, certification, **Rule 5:40**
Questions to be considered, **Rule 5:25**
Records and recordation,
  Appeal,
    Contents, **Rule 5:10**
    Judge authorized to act, **Rule 5:12**
    Preparation and transmission, **Rule 5:13**
      Digital appellate record, **Rule 5:13A**
    Transcript or written statement, **Rule 5:11**
  Court of appeals, **Rule 5:15**
  Disposition, **Rule 5:16**
  Return to trial court, **Rule 5:13**
Rehearing, **Rule 5:37**
  Petitions, denial of appeal, **Rule 5:20**
Reply brief, **Rules 5:19, 5:29**
Responses, motions, **Rule 5:4**
Revocation of acceptance, certified questions of law, **Rule 5:40**
Sealed appendix, briefs, **Rule 5:32**
Security for appeal, **Rule 5:24**
Sentence and punishment, death penalty, **Rule 5:22**
Service, **Rule 5:1**
Sessions, **Rule 5:2**
Settlement, pending appeal, **Rule 5:38**
Show cause orders, **Rule 5:1A**
State corporation commission, appeals, **Rule 5:21**
Supplemental authorities, citation, **Rule 5:6A**
Table of contents, appendix, briefs, **Rule 5:32**
Taxable costs, **Rule 5:35**
Three judge circuit court panels, appeals from, **Rule 5:21**
Time,
  Briefs, filing, **Rule 5:26**
    Opposing briefs, **Rule 5:18**
  Extension, **Rule 5:5**
  Mandate, **Rule 5:36**

SUPREME COURT—Cont'd
Time—Cont'd
  Notice of appeal, **Rule 5:9**
  Oral argument, **Rule 5:33**
  Petition for appeal, filing, **Rule 5:17**
  Petition for review, filing, **Rule 5:17A**
Transcript, **Rule 5:11**
  Appendices, **Rule 5:32**
Transmission of record, **Rule 5:13**
  Digital appellate record, **Rule 5:13A**
United States Supreme Court,
  Certified questions of law, **Rule 5:40**
  Deferral of issuance of mandate, **Rule 5:39**
Unpublished opinions, citing, **Rule 5:1**
Waiver, oral argument, **Rule 5:33**
Withdrawal, pending appeal, **Rule 5:38**
Written statement, **Rule 5:11**

SUSPENSION
Definitions, attorney discipline, **BOG 13**

TAPE RECORDINGS
Juvenile and domestic relations district courts, preservation of record, **Rule 8:12**
Preservation of record, **Rule 1:14**
  District courts, **Rule 7A:6**

TAXATION
Unauthorized practice of law, **UPR 5–101 et seq.**

TELECOMMUNICATIONS
Depositions, video and teleconferences, **Rules 4:5, 4:7A**

TELEVISION AND RADIO
Preservation of record, **Rule 1:14**
  District courts, **Rule 7A:6**
  Juvenile and domestic relations district courts, **Rule 8:12**

TERMS
Definitions, attorney discipline, **BOG 13**

THIRD PARTY CLAIMS
Lay adjusters, unauthorized practice of law, **UPR 2–105**

THIRD PARTY PRACTICE
  Generally, **Rule 3:13**
District courts, civil cases, **Rule 7B:10**

TIME
Bills of particulars, **Rule 3:7**
Computation, **Rule 1:7**
Counterclaims, **Rule 3:9**
Court of Appeals, this index
Criminal proceedings, extension, **Rule 3A:20**
Crossclaims, **Rule 3:10**
Default judgments, relief, **Rule 3:19**
Depositions, oral examination, **Rule 4:5**
Discovery, civil actions, **Rule 1:18**
District courts, computation, **Rule 7A:2**
Electronic filing, **Rule 1:17**

TIME—Cont'd
Extension of time, supreme court, **Rule 5:5**
Motions and pleadings,
Criminal, **Rule 3A:9**
Service, **Rule 1:12**
Responses, pleadings, **Rule 3:8**
Scheduling, civil actions, **Rules 1:18, 1:20**
Supreme Court, this index
Trial dates, scheduling, civil actions, **Rules 1:18, 1:20**

TITLE INSURANCE
Unauthorized practice of law, **UPR 7–101**

TRADE ASSOCIATIONS
Unauthorized practice of law, **UPR 8–101 et seq.**

TRADEMARKS AND TRADE NAMES
Foreign attorneys, admission to practice without examination, **Rule 1A:2**
Certificates, revocation, **Rule 1A:3**

TRAFFIC RULES AND REGULATIONS
Court of appeals, practice and procedure, **Rule 5A:12**
District courts, practice and procedure, **Rule 7C:1 et seq.**
Filing, district courts, practice and procedure, **Rule 7C:7**
Fines and penalties, **Rule 3B:2**
Service, district courts, practice and procedure, **Rule 7C:7**

TRANSCRIPTS
Generally, **Rule 1:3**
Audiovisual depositions, **Rule 4:7A**
Court of appeals, **Rule 5A:8**
District courts, **Rule 7A:4**
Juvenile and domestic relations district courts, **Rule 8:11**
Striking, failure to give notice, **Rule 5:11**
Supreme court, **Rule 5:11**
Appendices, **Rule 5:32**

TRANSFER OF VENUE
Juvenile and domestic relations district courts, **Rule 8:10**

TREATISES
Witnesses, opinion and expert testimony, use, **Rule 2:706**

TRIAL
Juvenile and domestic relations district courts, notification and waiver of trial rights, **Rule 8:17**
Mixed jury, nonjury claims, **Rule 3:22**
Pro hac vice, out of state attorneys, participation in trial, **Rule 1A:4**
Forms, **Form 1 (app. foll. Rule 1A:7)**
Scheduling, civil actions, **Rules 1:18, 1:20**

TRUST ACCOUNTS
Attorneys, client funds, **RPC 1.15; BOG 20**

UNAUTHORIZED PRACTICE OF LAW
Generally, **UPR 1–101 et seq.; RPC 5.5**
Advisory opinions, **BOG 10**
Aiding, **DR 3–101**
Complaints, **BOG 10**
Corporations, limited exceptions, **UPR 1–101**
Foreign attorneys, **RPC 5.5**
Subpoenas, summons, **BOG 10**

UNAVAILABLE DECLARANTS
Hearsay evidence, exceptions, **Rule 2:804**

UNIFORM FINE SCHEDULE
Nontraffic prepayable offenses, **Rule 3C:2**
Traffic infractions, **Rule 3B:2**

UNIFORM INTERSTATE DEPOSITIONS AND DISCOVERY ACT
Application of law, **Rule 4:5**

UNITED STATES SUPREME COURT
Certified questions of law, **Rule 5:40**

VA CODE
Definitions, attorney discipline, **BOG 13**

VENUE
Criminal cases, **Rule 3A:2.1**
District courts, motions to transfer, civil cases, **Rule 7B:11**
Juvenile and domestic relations district courts, transfer, **Rule 8:10**
Pro hac vice, out of state attorneys, participation in trial, **Rule 1A:4**

VERDICTS
Bifurcated jury trials, noncapital felonies, class 1 misdemeanors, **Rule 3A:17.1**
Separate verdicts, criminal proceedings, **Rule 3A:16**
Setting aside, motions, criminal proceedings, **Rule 3A:15**

VERIFICATION
Pleadings, **Rule 1:10**

VITAL STATISTICS
Hearsay evidence, exceptions, **Rule 2:803**

VOIR DIRE
Criminal proceedings, **Rule 3A:14**

WAIVER
Attorney fees, **Rule 3:25**
Jury trial, criminal proceedings, **Rule 3A:13**
Juvenile and domestic relations district courts, trial rights of parties, **Rule 8:17**
Oral argument, court of appeals, **Rule 5A:28**

WARRANT
Arrest, **Rule 3A:4**

WILLS AND DECEDENTS ESTATES
Attorneys, prohibited transactions, **RPC 1.8**

WITHDRAWN PLEAS
Crimes and offenses, evidence, **Rule 2:410**

WITNESSES
Generally, **Rule 2:601 et seq.**
Accused, preliminary matters, cross examination, **Rule 2:104**
Adverse witnesses, conviction of crime, impeachment, **Rule 2:609**
Basis, opinion and expert testimony, **Rule 2:703**
Facts, data, **Rule 2:705**
Bias, impeachment, **Rule 2:610**
Character evidence, impeachment, **Rule 2:608**
Clerks of courts, competency, **Rule 2:605**
Competency, **Rule 2:601**
Consistent prior statements, hearsay, **Rule 2:801**
Conviction of crime, impeachment, **Rule 2:609**
Crime victims, exclusion, **Rule 2:615**
Cross examination,
Accused, preliminary matters, **Rule 2:104**
Character evidence, **Rule 2:608**
Court, calling, interrogating, **Rule 2:614**
Depositions, **Rule 4:5**
Scope, **Rule 2:611**
Depositions, generally, this index
Exclusion, **Rule 2:615**
Expert testimony. Opinion and expert testimony, generally, post
Handicapped persons, competency, **Rule 2:601**
Hearsay evidence, **Rule 2:801 et seq.**
Identity and identification, hearsay evidence, exceptions, **Rule 2:803**
Impeachment, **Rule 2:607 et seq.**
Inconsistent prior statements, **Rule 2:613**
Hearsay, **Rule 2:801**
Judges,
Calling, interrogating, **Rule 2:614**
Competency, **Rule 2:605**
Jury, competency, **Rule 2:606**
Juvenile delinquents and dependents, conviction of crime, impeachment, **Rule 2:609**
Lay witnesses, opinion and expert testimony, **Rule 2:701**
Leading questions, **Rule 2:611**
Learned treatises, opinion and expert testimony, use, **Rule 2:706**
Magistrates, competency, **Rule 2:605**
Mental capacity, competency, **Rule 2:601**
Mode, interrogation, presentation, **Rule 2:611**
Oaths and affirmations, **Rule 2:603**
Opinion and expert testimony, **Rule 2:701 et seq.**
Crimes and Offenses, this index
Discovery, **Rule 4:1**
Exclusion, **Rule 2:615**
Personal injuries, prior inconsistent statements, **Rule 2:613**
Personal knowledge, **Rule 2:602**
Police, exclusion, **Rule 2:615**
Prejudice, impeachment, **Rule 2:610**
Prior statements, **Rule 2:613**
Hearsay, **Rule 2:801**
Qualification, preliminary determinations, **Rule 2:104**

WITNESSES—Cont'd
Refreshing memory, writings, objects, **Rule 2:611**
Reputation, character evidence, proof, **Rule 2:405**
Sexual assault, false accusations, cross examination, **Rule 2:608**
Stipulations, discovery, **Rule 4:4**
Subpoenas,
Criminal proceedings, **Rule 3A:12**
Juvenile and domestic relations district courts, **Rule 8:13**
Treatises, opinion and expert testimony, use, **Rule 2:706**
Truth telling, character evidence, impeachment, **Rule 2:608**
Ultimate issues, opinion and expert testimony, **Rule 2:704**
Writings, prior inconsistent statements, **Rule 2:613**
Hearsay, **Rule 2:801**
Wrongful death, prior inconsistent statements, **Rule 2:613**

WORDS AND PHRASES
Actions, **Rule 3:1**
Adjudication of a crime proceeding, attorney discipline, **BOG 13**
Admonition, attorney discipline, **BOG 13**
Advisory opinion, legal ethics, **BOG 10**
Agency secretary, Administrative Process Act appeals, **Rule 2A:1**
Agreed disposition, attorney discipline, **BOG 13**
Attorney,
Discipline, **BOG 13**
Juvenile and domestic relations district courts, **Rule 8:2**
Bar,
Attorney discipline, **BOG 13**
Legal ethics, **BOG 10**
Bar counsel, attorney discipline, **BOG 13**
Bar official, attorney discipline, **BOG 13**
Board, attorney discipline, **BOG 13**
Business entity, lay adjusters, **UPR 2–101**
Certification, attorney discipline, **BOG 13**
Certification for sanction determination, attorney discipline, **BOG 13**
Chair, attorney discipline, **BOG 13**
Charge of misconduct, attorney discipline, **BOG 13**
Circuit courts, attorney discipline, **BOG 13**
Clerk,
Criminal practice and procedure, **Rule 3A:2**
Supreme court proceedings, **Rule 5:1**
Clerk of the court of appeals, **Rule 5A:1**
Clerk of the disciplinary system, attorneys, **BOG 13**
Clerk of the trial court, court of appeals, **Rule 5A:1**
Clerk of this court, supreme court proceedings, **Rule 5:1**
COLD, attorney discipline, **BOG 13**
Committee, legal ethics, **BOG 10**
Committee counsel, attorney discipline, **BOG 13**
Commonwealth attorney, criminal practice and procedure, **Rule 3A:2**

WORDS AND PHRASES—Cont'd
Complainant, attorney discipline, **BOG 13**
Complaint, attorney discipline, **BOG 13**
Continuance, criminal practice and procedure, **Rule 3A:2**
Corporate counsel registrants, attorney discipline, **BOG 13**
Costs, attorney discipline, **BOG 13**
Council,
  Attorney discipline, **BOG 13**
  Legal ethics, **BOG 10**
Counsel, **Rule 1:5**
  Court of appeals, **Rule 5A:1**
  Juvenile and domestic relations district courts, **Rule 8:2**
  Supreme court proceedings, **Rule 5:1**
Counsel for appellant,
  Court of appeals, **Rule 5A:1**
  Supreme court proceedings, **Rule 5:1**
Counsel for appellee,
  Court of appeals, **Rule 5A:1**
  Supreme court proceedings, **Rule 5:1**
Counsel of record, **Rule 1:5**
  Juvenile and domestic relations district courts, **Rule 8:2**
Court, legal ethics, **BOG 10**
Court of appeals, supreme court proceedings, **Rule 5:1**
Court reporters, attorney discipline, **BOG 13**
CRESPA, attorney discipline, **BOG 13**
Crime, attorney discipline, **BOG 13**
Data link, electronic filing, **Rule 1:17**
Date of entry,
  Court of appeals, **Rule 5A:1**
  Supreme court proceedings, **Rule 5:1**
De minimis dismissal, attorney discipline, **BOG 13**
Declarants, hearsay evidence, **Rule 2:801**
Defendant in error, court of appeals, **Rule 5A:1**
Disbarment, attorney discipline, **BOG 13**
Disciplinary proceedings, attorney discipline, **BOG 13**
Disciplinary record, attorney discipline, **BOG 13**
Disciplinary rules, attorney discipline, **BOG 13**
Dismissal, attorney discipline, **BOG 13**
Dismissal de minimis, attorney discipline, **BOG 13**
Dismissal for exceptional circumstances, attorney discipline, **BOG 13**
District committee, attorney discipline, **BOG 13**
District court determination, attorney discipline, **BOG 13**
E filing portal, electronic filing, **Rule 1:17**
Electronic document, **Rule 1:17**
Electronic filing, **Rule 1:17**
Electronically filed case, **Rule 1:17**
Ethics counsel, legal ethics, **BOG 10**
Executive committees, attorney discipline, **BOG 13**
Executive director, attorney discipline, **BOG 13**
File with the clerk, court of appeals, **Rule 5A:1**

WORDS AND PHRASES—Cont'd
Filed,
  Juvenile and domestic relations district courts, subpoenas for good cause shown, attorney discipline, **BOG 13.1**
  Witnesses and records, **Rule 8:13**
Files, attorney discipline, **BOG 13**
Foreign lawyers,
  Attorney discipline, **BOG 13**
  Unauthorized practice of law, **RPC 5.5**
Foreign legal consultants, attorney discipline, **BOG 13**
Habit, evidence, **Rule 2:406**
Hearsay evidence, **Rule 2:801**
Hyperlink, electronic filing, **Rule 1:17**
Identification, electronic filing, **Rule 1:17**
Impairment, attorney discipline, **BOG 13**
Impairment proceedings, attorney discipline, **BOG 13**
Indictment, criminal practice and procedure, **Rule 3A:2**
International law, foreign legal consultants, **Rule 1A:7**
Investigations, attorney discipline, **BOG 13**
Investigative reports, attorney discipline, **BOG 13**
Investigators, attorney discipline, **BOG 13**
Judge,
  Attorney discipline, **BOG 13**
  Court of appeals, **Rule 5A:1**
  Supreme court proceedings, **Rule 5:1**
Judgment,
  Court of appeals, **Rule 5A:1**
  Supreme court proceedings, **Rule 5:1**
Lay adjuster, unauthorized practice, **UPR 2–101**
Licenses, attorney discipline, **BOG 13**
Magistrate, criminal practice and procedure, **Rule 3A:2**
Member, legal ethics, **BOG 10**
Memorandum orders, attorney discipline, **BOG 13**
Misconduct, attorney discipline, **BOG 13**
Nonlawyer, unauthorized practice, **UPR Introduction**
Notice, legal ethics, **BOG 10**
Opposing counsel,
  Court of appeals, **Rule 5A:1**
  Supreme court proceedings, **Rule 5:1**
Originals, best evidence, **Rule 2:1001**
Panels, attorney discipline, **BOG 13**
Paragraphs, attorney discipline, **BOG 13**
Party,
  Administrative Process Act appeals, **Rule 2A:1**
  Juvenile and domestic relations district courts, continuances, **Rule 8:14**
Personal information, jury, disclosure, criminal proceedings, **Rule 5A:14.1**
Petitioners, attorney discipline, **BOG 13**
Plaintiff in error, court of appeals, **Rule 5A:1**
Practice, unauthorized practice of law, **UPR 9–103**
Practice of law, **UPR Introduction**

WORDS AND PHRASES—Cont'd
Preparation, unauthorized practice of law, **UPR 9–103**
Principal, lay adjusters, **UPR 2–101**
Private discipline, attorney discipline, **BOG 13**
Private reprimand, attorney discipline, **BOG 13**
Proceedings, attorney discipline, **BOG 13**
Prospective clients, attorneys, duties, **RPC 1.18**
Public reprimand, attorney discipline, **BOG 13**
Receiverships, attorney discipline, **BOG 13**
Recognizance, criminal practice and procedure, **Rule 3A:2**
Reinstatement, attorney discipline, **BOG 13**
Reinstatement proceedings, attorney discipline, **BOG 13**
Relevant evidence, **Rule 2:401**
Represent, unauthorized practice of law, **UPR 9–103**
Respondent, attorney discipline, **BOG 13**
Revocation, attorney discipline, **BOG 13**
Routine practices, evidence, **Rule 2:406**
Rules, legal ethics, **BOG 10**
Sections, attorney discipline, **BOG 13**
Self insured, lay adjusters, **UPR 2–101**
Sexual offense, children and minors, similar crimes, evidence, **Rule 2:413**
Statements, hearsay evidence, **Rule 2:801**
Subcommittee, attorney discipline, **BOG 13**
Suits, actions, **Rule 3:1**
Summary orders, attorney discipline, **BOG 13**
Suspension, attorney discipline, **BOG 13**
Terms, attorney discipline, **BOG 13**

WORDS AND PHRASES—Cont'd
Trial court,
  Court of appeals, **Rule 5A:1**
  Supreme court proceedings, **Rule 5:1**
Unauthorized, practice of law, **UPR 9–103**
VA Code, attorney discipline, **BOG 13**
Writ of error, court of appeals, **Rule 5A:1**
Writings, best evidence, **Rule 2:1001**

WRIT OF ERROR
Definitions, court of appeals, **Rule 5A:1**

WRITINGS
Best evidence, **Rule 2:1001 et seq.**
Definitions, best evidence, **Rule 2:1001**
Related parts, evidence, **Rule 2:106**
Witnesses,
  Prior inconsistent statements, **Rule 2:613**
    Hearsay, **Rule 2:801**
  Refreshing memory, **Rule 2:612**

WRITS
Actual innocence, petitions, **Rules 5:7B, 5A:5; Forms 12 (app. foll. Rule 5:41), 12 (app. foll. Rule 5A:37)**
Habeas corpus,
  Capital punishment cases, **Rule 5:7A**
  Denial, findings of fact, conclusions of law, **Rule 3A:24**
Original jurisdiction, **Rule 5:7**
Returns, **Rule 3:3**

WRONGFUL DEATH
Witnesses, prior inconsistent statements, **Rule 2:613**

CIVIL REMEDIES AND PROCEDURE

[Title 8.01, Code of Virginia]

Including Amendments Enacted Through the End of the 2015 Regular Session

Table of Sections

CHAPTER 1. GENERAL PROVISIONS AS TO CIVIL CASES

Section

8.01–1. How Proceedings May Be in Actions Pending When Title Takes Effect.
8.01–1.1. References to Former Sections, Articles and Chapters of Title 8 and Other Titles.
8.01–2. General Definitions for This Title.
8.01–3. Supreme Court May Prescribe Rules; Effective Date and Availability; Indexed, and Annotated; Effect of Subsequent Enactments of General Assembly.
8.01–4. District Courts and Circuit Courts May Prescribe Certain Rules.
8.01–4.1. How Jurisdiction Determined When Proceeding Is on Penal Bond.
8.01–4.2. Who May Execute Bond for Obtaining Writ or Order.
8.01–4.3. Unsworn Declarations Under Penalty of Perjury; Penalty.

CHAPTER 2. PARTIES

ARTICLE 1. GENERAL PROVISIONS

8.01–5. Effect of Nonjoinder or Misjoinder; Limitation on Joinder of Insurance Company.
8.01–6. Amending Pleading; Relation Back to Original Pleading.
8.01–6.1. Amendment of Pleading Changing or Adding a Claim or Defense; Relation Back.
8.01–6.2. Amendment of Pleading; Relation Back to Original Pleading; Confusion in Trade Name.
8.01–6.3. Actions or Suits Against Fiduciaries; Style of the Case; Amendment of Pleading.
8.01–7. When Court May Add New Parties to Suit.

ARTICLE 2. SPECIAL PROVISIONS

8.01–8. How Minors May Sue.
8.01–9. Guardian Ad Litem for Persons Under Disability; When Guardian Ad Litem Need Not Be Appointed for Person Under Disability.
8.01–10. Joinder of Tenants in Common.
8.01–11. Proceedings on Writing Binding Deceased Person.
8.01–12. Suit by Beneficial Owner When Legal Title in Another.
8.01–13. Assignee or Beneficial Owner May Sue in Own Name; Certain Discounts Allowed.
8.01–14. Suit Against Assignor.
8.01–15. Suits by and Against Unincorporated Associations or Orders.

Section

8.01–15.1. Anonymous Plaintiff; Motion for Identification; Factors to Be Considered by Court.
8.01–15.2. Servicemembers Civil Relief Act; Default Judgment.

ARTICLE 3. DEATH OR CHANGE OF PARTIES

8.01–16. New Parties May Have Continuance.
8.01–17. When Party Whose Powers Cease Is Defendant.
8.01–18. When Suit Discontinued Unless Revived.
8.01–19. Effect of Marriage or Change of Name of Party.
8.01–20. Effect of Marriage, Change of Name or Death on Appeal.
8.01–20.1. Certification of Expert Witness Opinion at Time of Service of Process.
8.01–21. Judgment When Death or Disability Occurs After Verdict But Before Judgment.
8.01–22. When Death or Disability Occurs as to Any of Several Plaintiffs or Defendants.
8.01–23. Decree in Suit When Number of Parties Exceeds 30 and One of Them Dies.

ARTICLE 4. WRIT OF SCIRE FACIAS ABOLISHED

8.01–24. Writ of Scire Facias Abolished; Substitutes Therefor.

CHAPTER 3. ACTIONS

ARTICLE 1. SURVIVAL AND ASSIGNMENT OF CAUSES OF ACTIONS

8.01–25. Survival of Causes of Action.
8.01–26. Assignment of Causes of Action.

ARTICLE 2. ACTIONS ON CONTRACTS GENERALLY

8.01–27. Civil Action on Note or Writing Promising to Pay Money.
8.01–27.1. Additional Recovery in Certain Civil Actions Concerning Checks or Rejected Electronic Funds Transfers.
8.01–27.2. Civil Recovery for Giving Bad Check.
8.01–27.3. Evidence in Actions Regarding Issuance of Bad Check.
8.01–27.4. Civil Recovery for Professional Services.
8.01–27.5. Duty of In-Network Providers to Submit Claims to Health Insurers; Liability of Covered Patients for Unbilled Health Care Services.
8.01–28. When Judgment to Be Given in Action Upon Contract or Note Unless Defendant Appears and Denies Claim Under Oath.
8.01–29. Procedure in Actions on Annuity and Installment Bonds, and Other Actions for Penalties for Nonperformance.

Section
8.01-30. Procedure in Actions on Contracts Made by Several Persons.
8.01-31. Accounting in Equity.
8.01-32. Action on Lost Evidences of Debt.
8.01-33. Equitable Relief in Certain Cases.

ARTICLE 3. INJURY TO PERSON OR PROPERTY

8.01-34. When Contribution Among Wrongdoers Enforced.
8.01-35. Damages for Loss of Income Not Diminished by Reimbursement.
8.01-35.1. Effect of Release or Covenant Not to Sue in Respect to Liability and Contribution.
8.01-36. Joinder of Action of Tort to Infant with Action for Recovery of Expenses Incurred Thereby and Claim for Recovery of Expenses by Infant.
8.01-37. Recovery of Lost Wages in Action for Injuries to Emancipated Infant.
8.01-37.1. Claims for Medical Services Provided by United States; Proof of Reasonable Value.
8.01-38. Tort Liability of Hospitals.
8.01-38.1. Limitation on Recovery of Punitive Damages.
8.01-39. Completion or Acceptance of Work Not Bar to Action Against Independent Contractor for Personal Injury, Wrongful Death or Damage to Property.
8.01-40. Unauthorized Use of Name or Picture of Any Person; Punitive Damages; Statute of Limitations.
8.01-40.1. Action for Injury Resulting from Violation of Computer Crimes Act; Limitations.
8.01-40.2. Unsolicited Transmission of Advertising Materials by Facsimile Machine.
8.01-40.3. Unauthorized Dissemination, Etc., of Criminal History Record Information; Civil Action.
8.01-41. Wrongful Distraint, Attachment.
8.01-42. Loss or Injury to Clothing in Dyeing, Dry Cleaning, or Laundering.
8.01-42.1. Civil Action for Racial, Religious, or Ethnic Harassment, Violence or Vandalism.
8.01-42.2. Liability of Guest for Hotel Damage.
8.01-42.3. Civil Action for Stalking.
8.01-43. Action Against Parent for Damage to Public Property by Minor.
8.01-44. Action Against Parent for Damage to Private Property by Minor.
8.01-44.1. Immunity from Civil Liability of Members of Certain Committees, Etc.
8.01-44.2. Action Against Physician for Vaccine-Related Injury or Death.
8.01-44.3. Divulgence of Communications by Qualified Interpreters and Communications Assistants.
8.01-44.4. Action for Shoplifting and Employee Theft.
8.01-44.5. Punitive Damages for Persons Injured by Intoxicated Drivers.
8.01-44.6. Action for Injury to Cemetery Property.
8.01-44.7. Action for Tampering with Metering Device and Diverting Service.

ARTICLE 4. DEFAMATION

8.01-45. Action for Insulting Words.
8.01-46. Justification and Mitigation of Damages.
8.01-46.1. Disclosure of Employment-Related Information; Presumptions; Causes of Action; Definitions.
8.01-47. Immunity of Persons Investigating or Reporting Certain Incidents at Schools.
8.01-48. Mitigation in Actions Against Newspapers, Etc.

Section
8.01-49. Defamatory Statements in Radio and Television Broadcasts.
8.01-49.1. Liability for Defamatory Material on the Internet.

ARTICLE 5. DEATH BY WRONGFUL ACT

8.01-50. Action for Death by Wrongful Act; How and When to Be Brought.
8.01-50.1. Certification of Expert Witness Opinion at Time of Service of Process.
8.01-51. No Action When Deceased Has Compromised Claim.
8.01-52. Amount of Damages.
8.01-52.1. Admissibility of Expressions of Sympathy.
8.01-53. Class and Beneficiaries; When Determined.
8.01-54. Judgment to Distribute Recovery When Verdict Fails to Do So.
8.01-55. Compromise of Claim for Death by Wrongful Act.
8.01-56. When Right of Action Not to Determine Nor Action to Abate.

ARTICLE 6. INJURIES TO RAILROAD EMPLOYEES

8.01-57. Liability of Railroads for Injury to Certain Employees.
8.01-58. Contributory Negligence No Bar to Recovery; Violation of Safety Appliance Acts.
8.01-59. Assumption of Risk; Violation of Safety Appliance Acts.
8.01-60. Contracts Exempting from Liability Void; Set-Off of Insurance.
8.01-61. Definition of "Common Carrier" as Used in Article.
8.01-62. Action May Embrace Liability Under Both State and Federal Acts.

ARTICLE 7. MOTOR VEHICLE ACCIDENTS

8.01-63. Liability for Death or Injury to Guest in Motor Vehicle.
8.01-64. Liability for Negligence of Minor.
8.01-65. Defense of Lack of Consent of Owner.
8.01-66. Recovery of Damages for Loss of Use of Vehicle.
8.01-66.1. Remedy for Arbitrary Refusal of Motor Vehicle Insurance Claim.
8.01-66.1:1. Subrogation Claims by Underinsured Motorist Benefits Insurer.

ARTICLE 7.1. LIEN FOR HOSPITAL, MEDICAL AND NURSING SERVICES

8.01-66.2. Lien Against Person Whose Negligence Causes Injury.
8.01-66.3. Lien Inferior to Claim of Attorney or Personal Representative.
8.01-66.4. Subrogation.
8.01-66.5. Written Notice Required.
8.01-66.6. Liability for Reasonable Charges for Services.
8.01-66.7. Hearing and Disposal of Claim of Unreasonableness.
8.01-66.8. Petition to Enforce Lien.
8.01-66.9. Lien in Favor of Commonwealth, Its Programs, Institutions or Departments on Claim for Personal Injuries.
8.01-66.9:1. Lien Against Recovery for Medical Treatment Provided to Prisoner.
8.01-66.10. Death Claims Settled by Compromise or Suit.
8.01-66.11. Necessity for Settlement or Judgment.
8.01-66.12. Term Physician to Include Chiropractor.

Section

ARTICLE 8. ACTIONS FOR THE SALE, LEASE, EXCHANGE, REDEMPTION AND OTHER DISPOSITION OF LANDS OF PERSONS UNDER A DISABILITY

8.01–67. Definitions; Persons Under a Disability; Fiduciary.
8.01–68. Jurisdiction.
8.01–69. Commencement of Suit; Parties.
8.01–70, 8.01–71. Repealed by Acts 1990, c. 831, Eff. Jan. 1, 1991.
8.01–72. When Death to Abate Such Suit.
8.01–73. Guardian Ad Litem to Be Appointed.
8.01–74. Leases on Behalf of Persons Under Disability; New Leases.
8.01–75. Who Not to Be Purchaser.
8.01–76. How Proceeds from Disposition to Be Secured and Applied; When Same May Be Paid Over.
8.01–77. What Proceeds of Sale to Pass as Real Estate.
8.01–78. Alternate Procedure for Sale of Real Estate of Person Under Disability.
8.01–79. Same; Reference of Petition to Commissioner.
8.01–80. Same; Action of Court on Report; Application of Proceeds of Transaction.

ARTICLE 9. PARTITION

8.01–81. Who May Compel Partition of Land; Jurisdiction; Validation of Certain Partitions of Mineral Rights.
8.01–82. When Shares of Two or More Laid Off Together.
8.01–83. Allotment to One or More Parties, or Sale, in Lieu of Partition.
8.01–84. Application of Proceeds of Sale to Payment of Lien.
8.01–85. Disposition of Share in Proceeds of Person Under Disability.
8.01–86. Repealed by Acts 1990, c. 831, Eff. Jan. 1, 1991.
8.01–87. Validation of Certain Partitions Prior to Act of 1922.
8.01–88. Decree of Partition to Vest Legal Title.
8.01–89. When Proceeds of Sale Deemed Personal Estate.
8.01–90. When Name or Share of Parties Unknown.
8.01–91. Effect of Partition or Sale on Lessee's Rights.
8.01–92. Allowance of Attorneys' Fees Out of Unrepresented Shares.
8.01–93. Partition of Goods, Etc., by Sale, If Necessary.

ARTICLE 10. SALE, LEASE, OR EXCHANGE OF CERTAIN ESTATES IN PROPERTY

8.01–94. When Sold, Leased or Exchanged.
8.01–95. Procedure in Such Case.

ARTICLE 11. GENERAL PROVISIONS FOR JUDICIAL SALES

8.01–96. Decree for Sale; How Made; Bond of Commissioner.
8.01–97. Delinquent Taxes to Be Ascertained.
8.01–98. Sales of Land When Purchase Price Insufficient to Pay Taxes, Etc.
8.01–99. Bond Required of Special Commissioner for Sale.
8.01–100. Liability of Clerk for False Certificate or Failure to Give Bond.
8.01–101. Purchasers Relieved of Liability for Purchase Money Paid to Such Commissioner.
8.01–102. Purchasers Not Required to See to Application of Purchase Money.
8.01–103. Special Commissioner or Other Person Appointed to Do So to Receive Purchase Money, Etc.; Liability of Clerk for Failure to Give Notice of Appointment.

Section

8.01–104. Repealed by Acts 1978, c. 718.
8.01–105. Rule Against Special Commissioner, Purchaser, Etc., for Judgment for Amounts Due.
8.01–106. How Cause Heard Upon Rule and Judgment Rendered.
8.01–107. Trial by Jury of Issues Made Upon Rule.
8.01–108. When Sureties of Commissioner, Purchaser, Etc., Proceeded Against by Rule.
8.01–109. Commission for Selling, Collecting, Etc.; Each Piece of Property to Constitute Separate Sale.
8.01–110. Appointment of Special Commissioner to Execute Deed, Etc.; Effect of Deed.
8.01–111. What Such Deed to Show.
8.01–112. Reinstatement of Cause to Appoint Special Commissioner to Make Deed.
8.01–113. When Title of Purchaser at Judicial Sale Not to Be Disturbed.

ARTICLE 12. DETINUE

8.01–114. When Property to Be Taken by Officer; Summary of Evidence, Affidavits and Report to Be Filed.
8.01–115. Bond Required as Prerequisite.
8.01–116. Return of Property to Defendant or Other Claimant.
8.01–117. Exceptions to Sufficiency of Bonds.
8.01–118. Repealed by Acts 1986, c. 341.
8.01–119. Hearing to Review Issuance of Order or Process Under § 8.01–114 or to Consider Request for Such Order or Process.
8.01–120. No Verdict as to Some Items; Omission of Price or Value.
8.01–121. Final Judgment.
8.01–122. Charges for Keeping Property.
8.01–123. Recovery of Damages Sustained for Property Withheld During Appeal.

ARTICLE 13. UNLAWFUL ENTRY AND DETAINER

8.01–124. Motion for Judgment in Circuit Court for Unlawful Entry or Detainer.
8.01–125. When Summons Returnable to Circuit Court; Jury.
8.01–126. Summons for Unlawful Detainer Issued by Magistrate or Clerk or Judge of a General District Court.
8.01–127, 8.01–127.1. Repealed by Acts 2007, c. 869.
8.01–128. Verdict and Judgment; Damages.
8.01–129. Appeal from Judgment of General District Court.
8.01–130. Judgment Not to Bar Action of Trespass or Ejectment.

ARTICLE 14. EJECTMENT

8.01–131. Action of Ejectment Retained; When and by Whom Brought.
8.01–132. What Interest and Right Plaintiff Must Have.
8.01–133. Who Shall Be Defendants; When and How Landlord May Defend.
8.01–134. How Action Commenced and Prosecuted.
8.01–135. What Is to Be Stated in Motion for Judgment.
8.01–136. How Premises Described.
8.01–137. Plaintiff to State How He Claims.
8.01–138. There May Be Several Counts and Several Plaintiffs.
8.01–139. What Proof by Plaintiff Is Sufficient.
8.01–140. Effect of Reservation in Deed; Burden of Proof.
8.01–141. When Action by Cotenants, Etc., Against Cotenants, What Plaintiff to Prove.

Section

8.01–142. Verdict When Action Against Several Defendants.
8.01–143. When There May Be Several Judgments Against Defendants.
8.01–144. Recovery of Part of Premises Claimed.
8.01–145. When Possession of Part Not Possession of Whole.
8.01–146. When Vendee, Etc., Entitled to Conveyance of Legal Title, Vendor Cannot Recover.
8.01–147. When Mortgagee or Trustee Not to Recover.
8.01–148. Right of Defendant to Resort to Equity Not Affected.
8.01–149. Verdict When Jury Finds for Plaintiffs or Any of Them.
8.01–150. Verdict When Any Plaintiff Has No Right.
8.01–151. How Verdict to Specify Premises Recovered.
8.01–152. How Verdict to Specify Undivided Interest or Share.
8.01–153. Verdict to Specify Estate of Plaintiff.
8.01–154. When Right of Plaintiff Expires Before Trial, What Judgment Entered.
8.01–155. How Judgment for Plaintiff Entered.
8.01–156. Authority of Sheriffs, Etc., to Store and Sell Personal Property Removed from Premises; Recovery of Possession by Owner; Disposition or Sale.
8.01–157. Repealed by Acts 1990, c. 831, Eff. Jan. 1, 1991.
8.01–158. How Claim of Plaintiff for Profits and Damages Assessed.
8.01–159. When Court to Assess Damages.
8.01–160. Defendant to Give Notice of Claim for Improvements.
8.01–161. How Allowed.
8.01–162. Postponement of Assessment and Allowance.
8.01–163. Judgment to Be Conclusive.
8.01–164. Recovery of Mesne Profits, Etc., Not Affected.
8.01–165. Writ of Right, Etc., Abolished.

ARTICLE 15. IMPROVEMENTS

8.01–166. How Defendant May Apply Therefor, and Have Judgment Suspended.
8.01–167. How Damages of Plaintiff Assessed.
8.01–168. For What Time.
8.01–169. How Value of Improvements Determined in Favor of Defendant.
8.01–170. If Allowance for Improvements Exceed Damages, What to Be Done.
8.01–171. Verdict for Balance, After Offsetting Damages Against Improvements.
8.01–172. Balance for Defendant a Lien on the Land.
8.01–173. How Tenant for Life, Paying for Improvements, Reimbursed.
8.01–174. Exception as to Mortgagees and Trustees.
8.01–175. When Plaintiff May Require His Estate Only to Be Valued; How Determined; How He May Elect to Relinquish His Title to Defendant.
8.01–176. How Payment of Such Value to Be Made by Defendant; When Land Sold Therefor.
8.01–177. When Such Value to Be Deemed Real Estate.
8.01–178. When and How Defendant, If Evicted, May Recover from Plaintiff Amount Paid.

ARTICLE 16. ESTABLISHING BOUNDARIES TO LAND

8.01–179. Motion for Judgment to Establish Boundary Lines.
8.01–180. Parties Defendant; Pleadings.
8.01–181. Surveys.
8.01–182. Claims to Rents, Etc., Not Considered.
8.01–183. Recordation and Effect of Judgment.

Section

ARTICLE 17. DECLARATORY JUDGMENTS

8.01–184. Power to Issue Declaratory Judgments.
8.01–184.1. Declaratory Judgment to Adjudicate Constitutional Nexus.
8.01–185. Venue.
8.01–186. Further Relief.
8.01–187. Commissioners or Condemnation Jurors to Determine Compensation for Property Taken or Damaged.
8.01–188. Jury Trial.
8.01–189. Injunction.
8.01–190. Costs.
8.01–191. Construction of Article.

ARTICLE 18. RECOVERY OF CLAIMS AGAINST THE COMMONWEALTH OF VIRGINIA

8.01–192. How Claims to Be Prosecuted.
8.01–193. Defense and Hearing.
8.01–194. Jury May Be Impaneled; Judgment.
8.01–195. No Judgment to Be Paid Without Special Appropriation.

ARTICLE 18.1. TORT CLAIMS AGAINST THE COMMONWEALTH OF VIRGINIA

8.01–195.1. Short Title.
8.01–195.2. Definitions.
8.01–195.3. Commonwealth, Transportation District or Locality Liable for Damages in Certain Cases.
8.01–195.4. Jurisdiction of Claims Under This Article; Right to Jury Trial; Service on Commonwealth or Locality.
8.01–195.5. Settlement of Certain Cases.
8.01–195.6. Notice of Claim.
8.01–195.7. Statute of Limitations.
8.01–195.8. Release of Further Claims.
8.01–195.9. Claims Evaluation Program.

ARTICLE 18.2. COMPENSATION FOR WRONGFUL INCARCERATION FOR A FELONY CONVICTION

8.01–195.10. Purpose; Action by the General Assembly Required; Definitions.
8.01–195.11. Compensation for Wrongful Incarceration.
8.01–195.12. Conditions for Continued Compensation.

ARTICLE 19. ACTIONS BY THE COMMONWEALTH

8.01–196. Comptroller to Institute Proceedings.
8.01–197. In What Name; When Not to Abate.
8.01–198. Action, Against Whom Instituted.
8.01–199. Judgment, Nature Of.
8.01–200. Mistakes Against State Corrected.
8.01–201. Execution; Real Estate to Be Sold.
8.01–202. Execution, to Whom Issued.
8.01–203. Goods and Chattels Liable Before Real Estate.
8.01–204. Notice of Sale of Real Estate; When Sale to Be Made.
8.01–205. How Sale Made.
8.01–206. Terms of Sale.
8.01–207. Who to Collect Purchase Money and Make Deed; Disposition of Proceeds of Sale.
8.01–208. When Successor of Officer to Make Deed.
8.01–209. Bond for Purchase Money to Have Force of Judgment.
8.01–210. Judgment Against Deceased Obligors.
8.01–211. When Venditioni Exponas Issued to Sheriff of Adjacent County; What to Contain.

Section
8.01–212. Officer to Deliver to Sheriff Goods and Chattels Levied On.
8.01–213. Where Same to Be Sold.
8.01–214. Where Real Estate to Be Sold.
8.01–215. Return of Officer When Sale Not Made Because of Prior Encumbrance.
8.01–216. Comptroller's Power to Adjust Old Claims.

ARTICLE 19.1. VIRGINIA FRAUD AGAINST TAXPAYERS ACT

8.01–216.1. Citation.
8.01–216.2. Definitions.
8.01–216.3. False Claims; Civil Penalty.
8.01–216.4. Attorney General; Investigation, Civil Action.
8.01–216.5. Civil Actions Filed by Private Persons; Commonwealth May Intervene.
8.01–216.6. Rights of Private Plaintiff and Commonwealth.
8.01–216.7. Award to Private Plaintiff.
8.01–216.8. Certain Actions Barred; relief from Employment Discrimination; Waiver of Sovereign Immunity.
8.01–216.9. Procedure; Statute of Limitations.
8.01–216.10. Civil Investigative Demands; Issuance; Sharing Information.
8.01–216.11. Civil Investigative Demands; Contents and Deadlines.
8.01–216.12. Civil Investigative Demands; Protected Material or Information.
8.01–216.13. Civil Investigative Demands; Service and Jurisdiction.
8.01–216.14. Civil Investigative Demands; Documentary Material.
8.01–216.15. Civil Investigative Demands; Interrogatories.
8.01–216.16. Civil Investigative Demands; Oral Examinations.
8.01–216.17. Civil Investigative Demands; Custodian of Documents; Answers.
8.01–216.18. Civil Investigative Demands; Judicial Proceedings for Noncompliance.
8.01–216.19. Application of the Rules of the Supreme Court.

ARTICLE 20. CHANGE OF NAME

8.01–217. How Name of Person May Be Changed.

ARTICLE 21. MISCELLANEOUS PROVISIONS

8.01–218. Replevin Abolished.
8.01–219. Effect of Judgment in Trover.
8.01–219.1. Responsibility of Possessor of Real Property for Harm to Trespasser.
8.01–220. Action for Alienation of Affection, Breach of Promise, Criminal Conversation and Seduction Abolished.
8.01–220.1. Defense of Interspousal Immunity Abolished as to Certain Causes of Action Arising on or After July 1, 1981.
8.01–220.1:1. Civil Immunity for Officers, Partners, Members, Managers, Trustees and Directors of Certain Tax Exempt Organizations.
8.01–220.1:2. Civil Immunity for Teachers Under Certain Circumstances.
8.01–220.1:3. Immunity for Members of Church, Synagogue or religious Body.
8.01–220.1:4. Civil Immunity for Officers and Directors of Certain Nonprofit Organizations.
8.01–220.2. Spousal Liability for Medical Care.
8.01–221. Damages from Violation of Statute, Remedy Therefor and Penalty.

Section
8.01–221.1. Unestablished Business Damages; Lost Profits.
8.01–221.2. Rescission; Undue Influence; Attorney Fees.
8.01–222. Repealed by Acts 2007, c. 368.
8.01–223. Lack of Privity No Defense in Certain Cases.
8.01–223.1. Use of Constitutional Rights.
8.01–223.2. Immunity of Persons at Public Hearing.
8.01–224. Defense of Governmental Immunity Not Available to Certain Persons in Actions for Damages from Blasting, Etc.
8.01–225. Persons Rendering Emergency Care, Obstetrical Services Exempt from Liability.
8.01–225.01. Certain Immunity for Health Care Providers During Disasters Under Specific Circumstances.
8.01–225.02. Certain Liability Protection for Health Care Providers During Disasters.
8.01–225.1. Immunity for Team Physicians.
8.01–225.2. Immunity for Those Rendering Emergency Care to Animals.
8.01–225.3. Immunity for Volunteer First Responders En Route to an Emergency.
8.01–226. Duty of Care to Law-Enforcement Officers and Firefighters, Etc.
8.01–226.1. Civil Immunity When Participating in Lawyers Helping Lawyers.
8.01–226.2. Civil Immunity for Licensed Professional Engineers and Licensed Architects Participating in Rescue or relief Assistance.
8.01–226.3. Civil Immunity for Officers, Directors and Members of Certain Crime Information-Gathering Organizations.
8.01–226.4. Civil Immunity for Hospice Volunteers.
8.01–226.5. Immunity for Installers and Inspectors of Child Restraint Devices.
8.01–226.5:1. Civil Immunity for School Board Employees Supervising Self-Administration of Certain Medication.
8.01–226.5:2. Immunity of Hospital and Emergency Medical Services Agency Personnel for the Acceptance of Certain Infants.
8.01–226.6. Repealed by Acts 2007, c. 250.
8.01–226.7. Owner and Agent Compliance with Residential Lead-Based Paint Notification; Maintenance Immunity.
8.01–226.8. Civil Immunity for Public Officials and Private Volunteers Participating in Certain Programs for Probationers.
8.01–226.9. Exemption from Civil Liability in Connection with Arrest or Detention of Person Suspected of Shoplifting.
8.01–226.10. Civil Immunity for Causing the Arrest of a Person for a Bad Check.
8.01–226.11. Civil Immunity for Operation of Victim Notification Program.
8.01–226.12. Duty of Landlord and Managing Agent with Respect to Visible Mold.
8.01–227. Remedy by Motion on Certain Bonds Given or Taken by Officers; Notice.

ARTICLE 22. YEAR 2000 LIABILITY AND DAMAGES

8.01–227.1. To 8.01–227.3. Repealed by Acts 2007, c. 250.

ARTICLE 23. DRUG DEALER LIABILITY ACT

8.01–227.4. Definitions.

Section

8.01–227.5. Persons Who May Bring Action; Persons Against Whom Actions May Be Brought; Damages Recoverable.

8.01–227.6. Law-Enforcement Officer or Agency; Health Care Provider Not Liable Under Certain Conditions.

8.01–227.7. Statute of Limitations.

ARTICLE 24. SPACE FLIGHT LIABILITY AND IMMUNITY ACT

8.01–227.8. Definitions.

8.01–227.9. Civil Immunity for Space Flight Entities.

8.01–227.10. Warning Required.

ARTICLE 25. WINTER SPORTS SAFETY ACT

8.01–227.11. Definitions.

8.01–227.12. Warnings and Other Winter Sports Area Operator Requirements.

8.01–227.13. Winter Sports Area Trail Maps.

8.01–227.14. Freestyle Terrain.

8.01–227.15. Winter Sports Area Vehicles.

8.01–227.16. Passenger Tramways.

8.01–227.17. Duties and Responsibilities of Winter Sports Participants and Certain Other Individuals.

8.01–227.18. Helmets.

8.01–227.19. Assumption of Risks.

8.01–227.20. Liability of Winter Sports Area Operator.

8.01–227.21. Common Law Regarding Minors.

8.01–227.22. Failure to Fulfill Duty or Responsibility Not Negligence Per Se.

8.01–227.23. Applicability of Article.

CHAPTER 4. LIMITATIONS OF ACTIONS

ARTICLE 1. IN GENERAL

8.01–228. Scope of Limitations; "Personal Action" Defined.

8.01–229. Suspension or Tolling of Statute of Limitations; Effect of Disabilities; Death; Injunction; Prevention of Service by Defendant; Dismissal, Nonsuit or Abatement; Devise for Payment of Debts; New Promises; Debts Proved in Creditors' Suits.

8.01–230. Accrual of Right of Action.

8.01–231. Commonwealth Not Within Statute of Limitations.

8.01–232. Effect of Promises Not to Plead Statute.

8.01–233. When Action Deemed Brought on Counterclaim or Cross-Claim; When Statute of Limitations Tolled; Defendant's Consent Required for Dismissal.

8.01–234. Repeal of Limitation Not to Remove Bar of Statute.

8.01–235. Bar of Expiration of Limitation Period Raised Only as Affirmative Defense in Responsive Pleading.

ARTICLE 2. LIMITATIONS ON RECOVERY OF REALTY AND ENFORCEMENT OF CERTAIN LIENS RELATING TO REALTY

8.01–236. Limitation of Entry on or Action for Land.

8.01–237. Effect of Disabilities Upon Right of Entry On, or Action For, Land.

8.01–238. To Repeal Grant.

8.01–239. Ground Rents.

8.01–240. Liens for Water, Sewer, or Sidewalk Assessments.

Section

8.01–241. Limitation of Enforcement of Deeds of Trust, Mortgages and Liens for Unpaid Purchase Money.

8.01–241.1. Permissible Form for Certificate.

8.01–242. Same; When No Maturity Date Is Given; Credit Line Deeds of Trust.

ARTICLE 3. PERSONAL ACTIONS GENERALLY

8.01–243. Personal Action for Injury to Person or Property Generally; Extension in Actions for Malpractice Against Health Care Provider.

8.01–243.1. Actions for Medical Malpractice; Minors.

8.01–243.2. Limitations of Actions by Confined Persons; Exhaustion.

8.01–244. Actions for Wrongful Death; Limitation.

8.01–245. Limitation on Actions Upon the Bond of Any Fiduciaries or as to Suits Against Fiduciaries Themselves; Accrual of Cause of Action Where Execution Sustained.

8.01–246. Personal Actions Based on Contracts.

8.01–247. When Action on Contract Governed by the Law of Another State or Country Barred in Virginia.

8.01–247.1. Limitation on Action for Defamation, Etc.

8.01–248. Personal Actions for Which No Other Limitation Is Specified.

8.01–249. When Cause of Action Shall Be Deemed to Accrue in Certain Personal Actions.

8.01–250. Limitation on Certain Actions for Damages Arising Out of Defective or Unsafe Condition of Improvements to Real Property.

8.01–250.1. Limitation on Actions Involving Removal of Asbestos.

ARTICLE 4. LIMITATIONS ON ENFORCEMENT OF JUDGMENTS AND DECREES

8.01–251. Limitations on Enforcement of Judgments.

8.01–252. Repealed by Acts 2005, cc. 139 and 203.

ARTICLE 5. MISCELLANEOUS LIMITATIONS PROVISIONS

8.01–253. Limitation of Suits to Avoid Voluntary Conveyances, Etc.

8.01–254. Limitation on Enforcement of Bequests and Legacies.

8.01–255. Time for Presenting Claim Against Commonwealth.

8.01–255.1. Limitation of Action for Breach of Condition Subsequent or Termination of Determinable Fee Simple Estate.

8.01–255.2. Limitation on Motion for New Execution After Loss of Property Sold Under Indemnity Bond.

8.01–256. As to Rights and Remedies Existing When This Chapter Takes Effect.

CHAPTER 5. VENUE

8.01–257. Venue Generally.

8.01–258. Venue Not Jurisdictional.

8.01–259. Application.

8.01–260. Proper Venue; Preferred Forum in Certain Actions; Permissible Forums for Other Actions.

8.01–261. Category a or Preferred Venue.

8.01–262. Category B or Permissible Venue.

8.01–262.1. Place for Bringing Action Under a Contract Related to Construction.

8.01–263. Multiple Parties.

Section
8.01–264. Venue Improperly Laid; Objection.
8.01–265. Change of Venue by Court.
8.01–266. Costs.
8.01–267. Discretion of Judge.

CHAPTER 5.1. MULTIPLE CLAIMANT LITIGATION ACT

8.01–267.1. Standards Governing Consolidation, Etc., and Transfer.
8.01–267.2. When Actions Pending in Same Court.
8.01–267.3. Consolidation and Other Combined Proceedings.
8.01–267.4. Transfer.
8.01–267.5. Joinder and Severance.
8.01–267.6. Separate Trials; Special Interrogatories.
8.01–267.7. Later-Filed Actions.
8.01–267.8. Interlocutory Appeal.
8.01–267.9. Effect on Other Law.

CHAPTER 6. NOTICE OF LIS PENDENS OR ATTACHMENT

8.01–268. When and How Docketed and Indexed.
8.01–269. Dismissal or Satisfaction of Same.

CHAPTER 7. CIVIL ACTIONS; COMMENCEMENT, PLEADINGS, AND MOTIONS

ARTICLE 1. CIVIL ACTIONS GENERALLY

8.01–270. Repealed by Acts 2005, c. 681, Eff. Jan. 1, 2006.

ARTICLE 2. PLEADINGS GENERALLY

8.01–271. Compliance with Rules of Supreme Court.
8.01–271.01. Electronic Filings in Civil Actions in Circuit Court.
8.01–271.1. Signing of Pleadings, Motions, and Other Papers; Oral Motions; Sanctions.
8.01–272. Pleading Several Matters; Joining Tort and Contract Claims; Separate Trial in Discretion of Court; Counterclaims.
8.01–273. Demurrer; Form; Grounds to Be Stated; Amendment.
8.01–273.1. Motion for Judgment; Motion to Refer; Virginia Birth–Related Neurological Injury Compensation Act.
8.01–274. Motion to Strike Defensive Pleading in Equity and at Law; Exceptions Abolished.
8.01–275. When Action or Suit Not to Abate for Want of Form; What Defects Not to Be Regarded.
8.01–275.1. When Service of Process Is Timely.
8.01–276. Demurrer to Evidence and Plea in Abatement Abolished; Motion to Strike Evidence and Written Motion, Respectively, to Be Used in Lieu Thereof.
8.01–277. Defective Process; Motion to Quash; Untimely Service; Motion to Dismiss.
8.01–277.1. Objections to Personal Jurisdiction or Defective Process; What Constitutes Waiver.
8.01–278. When Plea of Infancy Not Allowed; Liability of Infants for Debts as Traders; Liability of Infants on Loans to Defray Expenses of Education.
8.01–279. When Proof Is Unnecessary Unless Affidavit Filed; Handwriting; Ownership; Partnership or Incorporation.
8.01–280. Pleadings May Be Sworn to Before Clerk; Affidavit of Belief Sufficient.

Section
8.01–281. Pleading in Alternative; Separate Trial on Motion of Party.

ARTICLE 3. PARTICULAR EQUITY PROVISIONS

8.01–282. Motion to Strike Evidence.
8.01–283. Answer in Equity Proceeding.
8.01–284. Repealed by Acts 2005, c. 681, Eff. Jan. 1, 2006.

CHAPTER 8. PROCESS

ARTICLE 1. IN GENERAL

8.01–285. Definition of Certain Terms for Purposes of This Chapter; Process, Return, Statutory Agent.
8.01–286. Forms of Writs.
8.01–286.1. Service of Process; Waiver, Duty to Save Costs, Request to Waive, How Served.
8.01–287. How Process to Be Served.
8.01–288. Process Received in Time Good Though Neither Served Nor Accepted.
8.01–289. No Service of Process on Sunday; Exceptions.

ARTICLE 2. HOW PROCESS IS ISSUED

8.01–290. Plaintiffs Required to Furnish Full Name and Last Known Address of Defendants, Etc.
8.01–291. Copies to Be Made.
8.01–292. To Whom Process Directed and Where Executed.

ARTICLE 3. WHO AND WHERE TO SERVE PROCESS

8.01–293. Authorization to Serve Process, Capias or Show Cause Order; Execute Writ of Possession and Levy Upon Property.
8.01–294. Sheriff to Get from Clerk's Office Process and Other Papers; Return of Papers; Effect of Late Return.
8.01–295. Territorial Limits Within Which Sheriff May Serve Process in His Official Capacity; Process Appearing to Be Duly Served.

ARTICLE 4. WHO TO BE SERVED

8.01–296. Manner of Serving Process Upon Natural Persons.
8.01–297. Process on Convict Defendant.
8.01–298. How Summons for Witness or Juror Served.
8.01–299. How Process Served on Domestic Corporations Generally.
8.01–300. How Process Served on Municipal and County Governments and on Quasi-Governmental Entities.
8.01–301. How Process Served on Foreign Corporations Generally.
8.01–302. Repealed by Acts 2002, c. 702.
8.01–303. On Whom Process Served When Corporation Operated by Trustee or Receiver.
8.01–304. How Process Served on Copartner or Partnership.
8.01–305. Process Against Unincorporated Associations or Orders, or Unincorporated Common Carriers.
8.01–306. Process Against Unincorporated Associations or Orders, or Unincorporated Common Carriers; Principal Office Outside Virginia and Business Transactions in Virginia.
8.01–307. Definition of Terms "Motor Vehicle" and "Nonresident" in Motor Vehicle and Aircraft Accident Cases.
8.01–308. Service on Commissioner of the Department of Motor Vehicles as Agent for Nonresident Motor Vehicle Operator.

Section

8.01–309. Service on Secretary of Commonwealth as Agent of Nonresident Operator or Owner of Aircraft.
8.01–310. How Service Made on Commissioner and Secretary; Appointment Binding.
8.01–311. Continuance of Action Where Service Made on Commissioner or Secretary.
8.01–312. Effect of Service on Statutory Agent; Duties of Such Agent.
8.01–313. Specific Addresses for Mailing by Statutory Agent.
8.01–314. Service on Attorney After Entry of General Appearance by Such Attorney.
8.01–315. Notice to Be Mailed Defendant When Service Accepted by Another.
8.01–316. Service by Publication; When Available.
8.01–317. What Order of Publication to State; How Published; When Publication in Newspaper Dispensed With.
8.01–318. Within What Time After Publication Case Tried or Heard; No Subsequent Publication Required.
8.01–319. Publication of Interim Notice.
8.01–320. Personal Service Outside of Virginia.
8.01–321. Orders of Publication in Proceedings to Enforce Liens for Taxes Assessed Upon Real Estate.
8.01–322. Within What Time Case Reheard on Petition of Party Served by Publication, and Any Injustice Corrected.
8.01–323. In What Counties City Newspapers Deemed Published for Purpose of Legal Advertisements.
8.01–324. Newspapers Which May Be Used for Legal Notices and Publications.
8.01–325. Return by Person Serving Process.
8.01–326. Return as Proof of Service.
8.01–326.1. Service of Process or Notice on Statutory Agent; Copy to Be Sent to Defendant and Certificate Filed with Court; Effective Date of Service.
8.01–327. Acceptance of Service of Process.

ARTICLE 5. PRIVILEGE FROM CIVIL ARREST

8.01–327.1. Definition of "Arrest Under Civil Process".
8.01–327.2. Who Are Privileged from Arrest Under Civil Process.

CHAPTER 9. PERSONAL JURISDICTION IN CERTAIN ACTIONS

8.01–328. Person Defined.
8.01–328.1. When Personal Jurisdiction Over Person May Be Exercised.
8.01–329. Service of Process or Notice; Service on Secretary of Commonwealth.
8.01–330. Jurisdiction on Any Other Basis Authorized.

CHAPTER 10. DOCKETS

8.01–331. Entry of Cases on Current Dockets.
8.01–332. Calling Current Docket.
8.01–333. Reserved.
8.01–334. Repealed by Acts 1983, c. 293.
8.01–335. Certain Cases Struck from Dockets After Certain Period; Reinstatement.

Section

CHAPTER 11. JURIES

ARTICLE 1. WHEN JURY TRIAL MAY BE HAD

8.01–336. Jury Trial of Right; Waiver of Jury Trial; Court-Ordered Jury Trial; Trial by Jury of Plea in Equity; Equitable Claim.

ARTICLE 2. JURORS

8.01–337. Who Liable to Serve as Jurors.
8.01–338. Who Disqualified.
8.01–339. No Person Eligible for Whom Request Is Made.
8.01–340. No Person to Serve Who Has Case at That Term.
8.01–341. Who Are Exempt from Jury Service.
8.01–341.1. Exemptions from Jury Service Upon Request.
8.01–341.2. Deferral or Limitation of Jury Service for Particular Occupational Inconvenience.
8.01–342. Restrictions on Amount of Jury Service Permitted.

ARTICLE 3. SELECTION OF JURORS

8.01–343. Appointment of Jury Commissioners.
8.01–344. Notification of Jury Commissioners; Their Oath.
8.01–345. Lists of Qualified Persons to Be Prepared by Jury Commissioners; Random Selection Process.
8.01–346. Lists to Be Delivered to Clerk and Safely Kept by Him; Addition and Removal of Names.
8.01–347. How Names Put in Jury Box.
8.01–348. How Names of Jurors Drawn from Box.
8.01–349. Notations on Ballots Drawn; Return to Box; When Such Ballots May Be Drawn Again.
8.01–350. Repealed by Acts 1977, c. 451.
8.01–350.1. Selection of Jurors by Mechanical or Electronic Techniques for the Term of Court.
8.01–351. Preparation and Disposition of List of Jurors Drawn.
8.01–352. Objections to Irregularities in Jury Lists or for Legal Disability; Effect Thereof.

ARTICLE 4. JURY SERVICE

8.01–353. Notice to Jurors; Making Copy of Jury Panel Available to Counsel; Objection to Notice.
8.01–353.1. Jurors to Provide Identification.
8.01–354. "Writ of Venire Facias" Defined.
8.01–355. Jurors on List to Be Used for Trial of Cases During Term; Discharge or Dispensing with Attendance of Jurors; Drawing Additional Jurors.
8.01–356. Failure of Juror to Appear.
8.01–357. Selection of Jury Panel.
8.01–358. Voir Dire Examination of Persons Called as Jurors.
8.01–359. Trial; Numbers of Jurors in Civil Cases; How Jurors Selected from Panel.
8.01–360. Additional Jurors When Trial Likely to Be Protracted.
8.01–361. New Juror May Be Sworn in Place of One Disabled; When Court May Discharge Jury.
8.01–362. Special Juries.
8.01–363. When Impartial Jury Cannot Be Obtained Locally.

CHAPTER 12. INTERPLEADER; CLAIMS OF THIRD PARTIES TO PROPERTY DISTRAINED OR LEVIED ON, ETC.

ARTICLE 1. INTERPLEADER

8.01–364. Interpleader.

Section

ARTICLE 2. CLAIMS OF THIRD PARTIES TO PROPERTY DISTRAINED OR LEVIED ON

8.01–365. How Claim of Third Party Tried.
8.01–366. Sale of Property When No Forthcoming Bond Is Given.
8.01–367. Indemnifying Bond to Officer.
8.01–368. Return of Such Bond to Clerk's Office.
8.01–369. Effect of Such Bond.
8.01–370. Claimant May Give Suspending Bond; Proceedings to Have Title Settled; Action on Indemnifying or Suspending Bond.
8.01–371. How Forthcoming Bond Taken of Claimant of Property the Sale Whereof Has Been Suspended.
8.01–372. Sale Despite Bond When Property Perishable, Etc.
8.01–373. When Property Sells for More Than Claim, How Surplus Paid.

CHAPTER 13. CERTAIN INCIDENTS OF TRIAL

8.01–374. Procedure When Original Papers in Cause Are Lost.
8.01–374.1. Consolidation or Bifurcation of Issues or Claims in Certain Cases; Appeal.
8.01–375. Exclusion of Witnesses in Civil Cases (Subsection (a) of Supreme Court Rule 2:615 Derived in Part from This Section and Subsection (b) of Supreme Court Rule 2:615 Derived from This Section).
8.01–376. Views by Juries.
8.01–377. Remedy When Variance Appears Between Evidence and Allegations.
8.01–377.1. Summary Judgment.
8.01–378. Trial Judge Not to Direct Verdicts.
8.01–379. Argument Before Jury.
8.01–379.1. Informing Jury of Amounts Sued For.
8.01–379.2. Jury Instructions.
8.01–379.3. General Verdict Accompanied by Answer to Interrogatories.
8.01–380. Dismissal of Action by Nonsuit; Fees and Costs.
8.01–381. What Jury May Carry Out.
8.01–382. Verdict, Judgment or Decree to Fix Period at Which Interest Begins; Final Order; Judgment or Decree for Interest.
8.01–383. Power to Grant New Trial; How Often.
8.01–383.1. Appeal When Verdict Reduced and Accepted Under Protest; New Trial for Inadequate Damages.
8.01–384. Formal Exceptions to Rulings or Orders of Court Unnecessary; Motion for New Trial Unnecessary in Certain Cases.
8.01–384.1. Interpreters for Deaf in Civil Proceedings.
8.01–384.1:1. Interpreters for Non-English-Speaking Persons in Civil Cases.
8.01–384.2. Waiver of Discovery Time Limitations by Parties.

CHAPTER 14. EVIDENCE

ARTICLE 1. JUDICIAL NOTICE

8.01–385. Definitions.
8.01–386. Judicial Notice of Laws (Supreme Court Rule 2:202 Derived in Part from This Section).
8.01–387. Notice by Courts and Officers of Signatures of Judges and Governor.

Section

8.01–388. Judicial Notice of Official Publications (Supreme Court Rule 2:203 Derived from This Section).

ARTICLE 2. LAWS, PUBLIC RECORDS, AND COPIES OF ORIGINAL RECORDS AS EVIDENCE

8.01–389. Judicial Records as Evidence; Full Faith and Credit; Recitals in Deeds, Deeds of Trust, and Mortgages; "Records" Defined; Certification.
8.01–390. Nonjudicial Records as Evidence (Subdivision (10)(a) of Supreme Court Rule 2:803 Derived from Subsection C of This Section).
8.01–390.1. School Records as Evidence.
8.01–390.2. Reports by Chief Medical Examiner Received as Evidence.
8.01–390.3. Business Records as Evidence.
8.01–391. Copies of Originals as Evidence (Supreme Court Rule 2:1005 Derived from This Section).

ARTICLE 2.1. CHECK CLEARING FOR THE 21ST CENTURY EVIDENCE ACT

8.01–391.1. Substitute Checks as Evidence (Supreme Court Rule 2:1003 Derived from Subsections a and B of This Section).

ARTICLE 3. ESTABLISHING LOST RECORDS, ETC.

8.01–392. When Court Order Book or Equivalent Is Lost or Illegible, What Matters May Be Reentered.
8.01–393. When Book or Paper or Equivalent in Clerk's Office Lost, Destroyed, or Illegible to Be Again Recorded.
8.01–394. How Contents of Any Such Lost Record, Etc., Proved.
8.01–395. Validating Certain Proceedings Under § 8.01–394.

ARTICLE 4. WITNESSES GENERALLY

8.01–396. No Person Incompetent to Testify by Reason of Interest, or Because a Party.
8.01–396.1. Competency of Witness.
8.01–397. Corroboration Required and Evidence Receivable When One Party Incapable of Testifying (Subdivision (b)(5) of Supreme Court Rule 2:804 Derived from This Section).
8.01–397.1. Evidence of Habit or Routine Practice; Defined (Supreme Court Rule 2:406 Derived from This Section).
8.01–398. Privileged Marital Communications (Subsection (a) of Supreme Court Rule 2:504 Derived from This Section).
8.01–399. Communications Between Physicians and Patients (Supreme Court Rule 2:505 Derived from This Section).
8.01–400. Communications Between Ministers of Religion and Persons They Counsel or Advise (Supreme Court Rule 2:503 Derived in Part from This Section).
8.01–400.1. Privileged Communications by Interpreters for the Deaf (Supreme Court Rule 2:507 Derived in Part from This Section).
8.01–400.2. Communications Between Certain Mental Health Professionals and Clients (Supreme Court Rule 2:506 Derived from This Section).
8.01–401. How Adverse Party May Be Examined; Effect of Refusal to Testify (Subsection (b) of Supreme Court Rule 2:607 and Subsection (c) of

Section
Supreme Court Rule 2:611 Derived from Subsection a of This Section).
8.01–401.1. Opinion Testimony by Experts; Hearsay Exception (Subsection (a) of Supreme Court Rule 2:703, Subsection (a) of Supreme Court Rule 2:705, and Subsection (a) of Supreme Court Rule 2:706 Derived from This Section).
8.01–401.2. Chiropractor, Nurse Practitioner, or Physician Assistant as Expert Witness.
8.01–401.2:1. Podiatrist as an Expert Witness.
8.01–401.3. Opinion Testimony and Conclusions as to Facts Critical to Civil Case Resolution (Supreme Court Rule 2:701 Derived from Subsection B of This Section, Subdivision (a)(i) of Supreme Court Rule 2:702 Derived from Subsection a of This Section, and Subsection (a) of Supreme Court Rule 2:704 Derived from Subsections B and
8.01–402. Members of Department of Motor Vehicles' Crash Investigation Team Not to Be Required to Give Evidence in Certain Cases.
8.01–403. Witness Proving Adverse; Contradiction; Prior Inconsistent Statement (Subsection (c) of Supreme Court Rule 2:607 and Subdivision (a)(i) of Supreme Court Rule 2:613 Derived from This Section).
8.01–404. Contradiction by Prior Inconsistent Writing (Subdivision (b)(i) of Supreme Court Rule 2:613 Derived in Part from This Section and Subdivision (b)(ii) of Supreme Court Rule 2:613 Derived from This Section).
8.01–405. Who May Administer Oath to Witness.
8.01–406. Interpreters; Recording Testimony of Deaf Witness (Supreme Court Rule 2:604 Derived from This Section).

ARTICLE 5. COMPELLING ATTENDANCE OF WITNESSES, ETC.

8.01–407. How Summons for Witness Issued, and to Whom Directed; Prior Permission of Court to Summon Certain Officials and Judges; Attendance Before Commissioner of Other State; Attorney-Issued Summons.
8.01–407.1. Identity of Persons Communicating Anonymously Over the Internet.
8.01–408. Recognizance Taken Upon Continuance of Case.
8.01–409. When Court May Have Process for Witness Executed by Its Own Officer in Another County or City.
8.01–410. Inmates as Witnesses in Civil Actions.

ARTICLE 6. UNIFORM FOREIGN DEPOSITIONS ACT

8.01–411. To 8.01–412.1. Repealed by Acts 2009, c. 701.

ARTICLE 6.1. UNIFORM AUDIO-VISUAL DEPOSITION ACT

8.01–412.2. Authorization of Audio-Visual Deposition; Official Record; Uses.
8.01–412.3. Notice of Audio-Visual Deposition.
8.01–412.4. Procedure.
8.01–412.5. Costs.
8.01–412.6. Promulgation of Rules for Standards and Guidelines.
8.01–412.7. Short Title.

ARTICLE 6.2. UNIFORM INTERSTATE DEPOSITIONS AND DISCOVERY ACT

8.01–412.8. Short Title.

Section
8.01–412.9. Definitions.
8.01–412.10. Issuance of Subpoena.
8.01–412.11. Service of Subpoena.
8.01–412.12. Deposition, Production, and Inspection.
8.01–412.13. Application to Court.
8.01–412.14. Uniformity of Application and Construction; Reciprocal Privileges.
8.01–412.15. Application to Pending Actions.

ARTICLE 7. MEDICAL EVIDENCE

8.01–413. Certain Copies of Health Care Provider's Records or Papers of Patient Admissible; Right of Patient, His Attorney and Authorized Insurer to Copies of Such Records or Papers; Subpoena; Damages, Costs and Attorneys' Fees.
8.01–413.01. Authenticity and Reasonableness of Medical Bills; Presumption.
8.01–413.02. Admissibility of Written Reports or Records of Blood Alcohol Tests Conducted in the Regular Course of Providing Emergency Medical Treatment.

ARTICLE 7.1. EMPLOYMENT EVIDENCE

8.01–413.1. Certain Copies of Employment Records or Papers Admissible; Right of Employee or His Attorney to Copies of Such Records or Papers; Subpoena; Damages, Costs and Attorney's Fees.

ARTICLE 8. CERTAIN AFFIDAVITS

8.01–414. Affidavit Prima Facie Evidence of Nonresidence.
8.01–415. Affidavit Evidence of Publication.
8.01–416. Affidavit re Damages to Motor Vehicle.

ARTICLE 9. MISCELLANEOUS PROVISIONS

8.01–417. Copies of Written Statements or Transcriptions of Verbal Statements by Injured Person to Be Delivered to Him; Copies of Subpoenaed Documents to Be Provided to Other Party; Disclosure of Insurance Policy Limits.
8.01–417.1. Use of Portions of Documents in Evidence (Subsection (b) of Supreme Court Rule 2:106 Derived from This Section).
8.01–418. When Plea of Guilty or Nolo Contendere or Forfeiture in Criminal Prosecution or Traffic Case Admissible in Civil Action; Proof of Such Plea.
8.01–418.1. Evidence of Subsequent Measures Taken Not Admissible to Prove Negligence (Supreme Court Rule 2:407 Derived from This Section).
8.01–418.2. Evidence of Polygraph Examination Inadmissible in Any Proceeding.
8.01–418.3. Repealed by Acts 2007, c. 250.
8.01–419. Table of Life Expectancy.
8.01–419.1. Motor Vehicle Value.
8.01–420. Depositions as Basis for Motion for Summary Judgment or to Strike Evidence.
8.01–420.01. Limiting Further Disclosure of Discoverable Materials and Information; Protective Order.
8.01–420.1. Abolition of Common-Law Perpetuation of Testimony.
8.01–420.2. Limitation on Use of Recorded Conversations as Evidence.

Section
8.01–420.3. Court Reporters to Provide Transcripts; When Recording May Be Stopped; Use of Transcript as Evidence.
8.01–420.4. Taking of Depositions.
8.01–420.5. Estoppel Effect of Judicial Determination of Employment Status.
8.01–420.6. Number of Witnesses Whose Depositions May Be Taken.
8.01–420.7. Attorney-Client Privilege and Work Product Protection; Limitations on Waiver.
8.01–420.8. Protection of Confidential Information in Court Files.

CHAPTER 15. PAYMENT AND SETOFF

8.01–421. Payment May Be Pleaded; Payment Into Court of Part of Claim; Procedure Upon Such Payment.
8.01–422. Pleading Equitable Defenses.
8.01–423. When Plaintiff Claims as Assignee or Transferee.

CHAPTER 16. COMPROMISES

8.01–424. Approval of Compromises on Behalf of Persons Under a Disability in Suits or Actions to Which They Are Parties.
8.01–424.1. Settlement of Third—Party Action; Deemed Consent by Employer.
8.01–425. How Fiduciaries May Compromise Liabilities Due to or from Them.
8.01–425.1. Release of Liability; Right of Rescission.

CHAPTER 17. JUDGMENTS AND DECREES GENERALLY

ARTICLE 1. IN GENERAL

8.01–426. "Judgment" Includes Decree.
8.01–427. Persons Entitled Under Decree Deemed Judgment Creditors; Execution on Decree.
8.01–427.1. Repealed by Acts 1978, c. 426.
8.01–428. Setting Aside Default Judgments; Clerical Mistakes; Independent Actions to relieve Party from Judgment or Proceedings; Grounds and Time Limitations.
8.01–429. Action of Appellate Court When There Might Be Redress Under § 8.01–428.
8.01–430. When Final Judgment to Be Entered After Verdict Set Aside.

ARTICLE 2. JUDGMENTS BY CONFESSION

8.01–431. Judgment or Decree by Confession in Pending Suit.
8.01–432. Confession of Judgment Irrespective of Suit Pending.
8.01–433. Setting Aside Judgments Confessed Under § 8.01–432.
8.01–433.1. Notice of Confession of Judgment Provision.
8.01–434. Lien of Such Judgments.
8.01–435. Who May Confess Judgment.
8.01–436. Form of Confession of Judgment.
8.01–437. Endorsement of Clerk Thereon.
8.01–438. When Judgment Confessed by Attorney-In-Fact Copy to Be Served on Judgment Debtor.
8.01–439. Filing of Records by Clerk.
8.01–440. Docketing and Execution.
8.01–441. When Judgment Confessed by Virtue of Power of Attorney Invalid.

Section

ARTICLE 3. WHEN THERE ARE SEVERAL DEFENDANTS

8.01–442. In Joint Actions on Contract Plaintiff, Though Barred as to Some, May Have Judgment Against Others.
8.01–443. Joint Wrongdoers; Effect of Judgment Against One.
8.01–444. Where New Parties Added; If Some Not Liable, How Judgment Entered.

ARTICLE 4. DISTINCTION BETWEEN TERM AND VACATION ABOLISHED

8.01–445. Distinction Between Term and Vacation Abolished; Effect of Time.

ARTICLE 5. KEEPING OF DOCKET BOOKS; EXECUTION THEREON; DISPOSAL OF EXHIBITS

8.01–446. Clerks to Keep Judgment Dockets; What Judgments to Be Docketed Therein.
8.01–446.1. Keeping of Docket Books by Clerk of Court Using Micrographic Process; Form.
8.01–447. Docketing of Judgments and Decrees of United States Courts.
8.01–448. Attorney General, Etc., to Have Judgments in Favor of Commonwealth Docketed.
8.01–449. How Judgments Are Docketed.
8.01–450. How Indexed.
8.01–451. Judgments to Be Docketed and Indexed in New Names of Judgment Debtors; How Execution May Thereafter Issue.
8.01–452. Entry of Assignment of Judgment on Judgment Lien Docket.
8.01–452.1. Disposal of Exhibits in Civil Cases.

ARTICLE 6. SATISFACTION

8.01–453. When and How Payment or Discharge Entered on Judgment Docket.
8.01–454. Judgment, When Satisfied, to Be So Noted by Creditor.
8.01–455. Court, on Motion of Defendant, Etc., May Have Payment of Judgment Entered.
8.01–456. Satisfaction of Judgment When Judgment Creditor Cannot Be Located.
8.01–457. Marking Satisfied Judgments for Commonwealth; Payment by Third Parties releasing Recognizances.

ARTICLE 7. LIEN AND ENFORCEMENT THEREOF

8.01–458. From What Time Judgment to Be a Lien on Real Estate; Docketing Revived Judgment.
8.01–459. Priority of Judgments.
8.01–460. Decree for Support and Maintenance of Spouse or Infant Children of Parties as Lien on Real Estate.
8.01–461. Abstracts of Judgments.
8.01–462. Jurisdiction of Equity to Enforce Lien of Judgment; When It May Decree Sale.
8.01–463. Enforcement of Lien When Judgment Does Not Exceed Twenty Dollars.
8.01–464. Order of Liability Between Alienees of Different Parts of Estate.
8.01–465. Chapter Embraces Recognizances and Bonds Having Force of Judgment.

Section

CHAPTER 17.1. UNIFORM ENFORCEMENT OF FOREIGN JUDGMENTS ACT

8.01–465.1. Application of Chapter.
8.01–465.2. Filing and Status of Foreign Judgments.
8.01–465.3. Notice of Filing.
8.01–465.4. Stay of Enforcement.
8.01–465.5. Optional Procedure.

CHAPTER 17.2. UNIFORM FOREIGN–COUNTRY MONEY JUDGMENTS RECOGNITION ACT

8.01–465.6. to 8.01–465.13. Repealed by Acts 2014, c. 462.
8.01–465.13:1. Definitions.
8.01–465.13:2. Applicability.
8.01–465.13:3. Standards for Recognition of Foreign-Country Judgment.
8.01–465.13:4. Personal Jurisdiction.
8.01–465.13:5. Procedure for Recognition of Foreign-Country Judgment.
8.01–465.13:6. Effect of Recognition of Foreign-Country Judgment.
8.01–465.13:7. Stay of Proceedings Pending Appeal of Foreign-Country Judgment.
8.01–465.13:8. Statute of Limitations.
8.01–465.13:9. Uniformity of Interpretation.
8.01–465.13:10. Saving Clause.
8.01–465.13:11. Effective Date.

CHAPTER 17.3. UNIFORM FOREIGN–MONEY CLAIMS ACT

8.01–465.14. Definitions.
8.01–465.15. Scope.
8.01–465.16. Variation by Agreement.
8.01–465.17. Determining Money of the Claim.
8.01–465.18. Determining Amount of the Money of Certain Contract Claims.
8.01–465.19. Asserting and Defending Foreign-Money Claim.
8.01–465.20. Judgments and Awards on Foreign-Money Claims; Times of Money Conversion; Form of Judgment.
8.01–465.21. Conversions of Foreign Money in Distribution Proceeding.
8.01–465.22. Prejudgment and Judgment Interest.
8.01–465.23. Enforcement of Foreign Judgments.
8.01–465.24. Determining United States Dollar Value of Foreign-Money Claims for Limited Purposes.
8.01–465.25. Effect of Substitution of Currency by Issuing Authority.

CHAPTER 18. EXECUTIONS AND OTHER MEANS OF RECOVERY

ARTICLE 1. ISSUE AND FORM; MOTION TO QUASH

8.01–466. Clerk to Issue Fieri Facias on Judgment for Money.
8.01–467. What Writs May Not Issue.
8.01–468. Executions Against Corporations.
8.01–469. Executions on Joint Judgments.
8.01–470. Writs on Judgments for Specific Property.
8.01–471. Time Period for Issuing Writs of Possession in Unlawful Entry and Detainer; When Returnable.
8.01–472. Writs on Judgments for Personal Property.

Section

8.01–473. Judgment for Benefit of Other Person Than Plaintiff; Remedies of Such Person.
8.01–474. What Writ of Fieri Facias to Command.
8.01–475. Subsequent Executions.
8.01–476. New Execution After Loss of Property Sold Under Indemnifying Bond.
8.01–477. When Executions May Be Quashed; How Proceedings Thereon Stayed.
8.01–477.1. Claims of Exemption from Execution.

ARTICLE 2. LIEN IN GENERAL

8.01–478. On What Property Writ of Fieri Facias Levied; When Lien Commences.
8.01–479. Time for Enforcement.
8.01–480. Prior Security Interest on Property Levied On.
8.01–481. Territorial Extent of Lien.
8.01–482. If Levy Be on Coin or Currency, How Accounted For.

ARTICLE 3. RETURN AND VENDITIONI EXPONAS

8.01–483. Return of Officer on Fieri Facias; Statement Filed Therewith.
8.01–484. When Writ May Be Destroyed.
8.01–485. When Venditioni Exponas May Issue; Proceedings Thereon.
8.01–486. Procedure When Officer Taking Property Under Execution Dies Before Sale.

ARTICLE 4. ENFORCEMENT GENERALLY

8.01–487. Officer to Endorse on Fieri Facias Time of Receiving It.
8.01–487.1. Officer to Leave Copy of Writ Where Levy Made.
8.01–488. When Several Writs of Fieri Facias, How Satisfied.
8.01–489. Growing Crops, Not Severed, Not Liable to Distress or Levy.
8.01–490. No Unreasonable Distress or Levy; Sustenance Provided for Livestock; Removal of Property.
8.01–491. Officer May Break Open Dwelling House and Levy on Property in Personal Possession of Debtor.
8.01–492. Sale of Property.
8.01–493. Adjournment of Sale.
8.01–494. Resale of Property If Purchaser Fails to Comply; Remedy Against Such Purchaser.
8.01–495. When Money Received by Officer Under Execution to Be Repaid to Debtor.
8.01–496. Officer Not Required to Go Out of His Jurisdiction to Pay Over Money.
8.01–497. Suit by Officer to Recover Estate on Which Fieri Facias Is Lien.
8.01–498. Selling Officers and Employees Not to Bid or to Purchase.
8.01–499. Officer Receiving Money to Make Return Thereof and Pay Net Proceeds; Commission, Etc.
8.01–500. Officer Receiving Money to Notify Person Entitled to Receive It.

ARTICLE 5. LIEN ON PROPERTY NOT CAPABLE OF BEING LEVIED ON

8.01–501. Lien of Fieri Facias on Estate of Debtor Not Capable of Being Levied On.
8.01–502. Person Paying Debtor Not Affected by Lien Unless Notice Given.
8.01–502.1. Serving Notice of Lien on Financial Institution.

Section
8.01–503. Withholding of Wages or Salary Not Required by Preceding Sections Unless Garnishment Process Served.
8.01–504. Penalty for Service of Notice of Lien When No Judgment Exists.
8.01–505. When Lien Acquired on Intangibles Under § 8.01–501 Ceases.

ARTICLE 6. INTERROGATORIES

8.01–506. Proceedings by Interrogatories to Ascertain Estate of Debtor; Summons; Proviso; Objections by Judgment Debtor.
8.01–506.1. Production of Book Accounts or Other Writing Compelled.
8.01–506.2. Proceedings in Court of County or City Where Execution Debtor Resides.
8.01–507. Conveyance or Delivery of Property Disclosed by Interrogatories.
8.01–507.1. Interrogatories, Answers, Etc., to Be Returned to Court.
8.01–508. How Debtor May Be Arrested and Held to Answer.
8.01–509. Order for Sale and Application of Debtor's Estate.
8.01–510. Sale, Collection and Disposition of Debtor's Estate by Officer.

ARTICLE 7. GARNISHMENT

8.01–511. Institution of Garnishment Proceedings.
8.01–511.1. Garnishee Inability to Determine Whether It Holds Property of Judgment Debtor.
8.01–512, 8.01–512.1. Repealed by Acts 1983, c. 399.
8.01–512.2. Fee for Garnishee-Employers.
8.01–512.3. Form of Garnishment Summons.
8.01–512.4. Notice of Exemptions from Garnishment and Lien.
8.01–512.5. Hearing on Claim of Exemption from Garnishment.
8.01–513. Service Upon Corporation or Limited Liability Company.
8.01–514. When Garnishment Summons Returnable.
8.01–515. How Garnishee Examined; Determining Exemption from Employee's Withholding Certificate; Amount Due Pursuant to Exemptions in § 34–29(A).
8.01–516. Repealed by Acts 1983, c. 399.
8.01–516.1. Garnishment Dispositions.
8.01–517. Exemption of Portion of Wages; Payment of Excess Into Court.
8.01–518. When Garnishee Is Personal Representative of Decedent.
8.01–519. Proceedings Where Garnishee Fails to Appear or Answer, or to Disclose His Liability.
8.01–520. Payment, Etc., by Garnishee Before Return of Summons.
8.01–521. Judgments as to Costs.
8.01–522. Wages and Salaries of State Employees.
8.01–523. Service Upon Federal Government.
8.01–524. Wages and Salaries of City, Town and County Officials, Clerks and Employees.
8.01–525. Who Are Officers and Employees of Cities, Towns and Counties.

CHAPTER 19. FORTHCOMING BONDS

8.01–526. When Forthcoming Bond Taken; Property Remains in Debtor's Possession.

Section
8.01–527. If Bond Forfeited, Where Returned; Its Effect; Clerk to Endorse Time of Return.
8.01–528. Liability of Obligors; How Recovery on Bond Is Had.
8.01–529. When Bond Returned, How Endorsed and Recorded by Clerk; Lien.
8.01–530. Remedy of Creditor If Bond Quashed.
8.01–531. In What Cases Forthcoming Bond Not to Be Taken.
8.01–532. How Bond Withdrawn from Clerk's Office.

CHAPTER 20. ATTACHMENTS AND BAIL IN CIVIL CASES

ARTICLE 1. ATTACHMENTS GENERALLY

8.01–533. Who May Sue Out Attachment.
8.01–534. Grounds of Action for Pretrial Levy or Seizure of Attachment.
8.01–535. Jurisdiction of Attachments; Trial or Hearing of Issues.
8.01–536. Pleadings in Attachment.
8.01–537. Petition for Attachment; Costs, Fees and Taxes.
8.01–537.1. Plaintiff to File Bond.
8.01–538. Attachment of Ships, Boats and Other Vessels of More Than Twenty Tons.
8.01–539. Who Made Defendants.
8.01–540. Issuance of Attachment; Against What Attachment to Issue.
8.01–541. To Whom Attachments Directed; When and Where Returned.
8.01–542. Issue and Execution of Attachment on Any Day.
8.01–543. Issue of Other Attachments on Original Petition.
8.01–544. When Attachment Not Served Other Attachments May Issue; Order of Publication.
8.01–545. Amendments; Formal Defects.

ARTICLE 2. SUMMONS; LEVY; LIEN; BONDS, ETC.

8.01–546. What Attachment to Command; Summons.
8.01–546.1. Exemption Claims Form.
8.01–546.2. Hearing on Claim of Exemption from Levy or Seizure.
8.01–547. Attachment Against Remainders.
8.01–548. Who May Levy Attachment and on What.
8.01–549. Restraining Order or Receiver.
8.01–550. How Attachment Levied.
8.01–551. When Officer to Take Possession of Property.
8.01–552. Repealed by Acts 1984, c. 646.
8.01–553. Bonds for Retention of Property or Release of Attachment; Revising Bonds Mentioned in This and § 8.01–551.
8.01–554. Where Bond Returned and Filed; Exceptions to Bond.
8.01–555. When Appeal Bond Given Property to Be Delivered to Owner.
8.01–556. Bonds May Be Given by Any Person.
8.01–557. Lien of Attachment; Priority of Holder in Due Course.
8.01–558. Attachment Lien on Effects Already in Hands of Officer.
8.01–559. Return by Officer.

ARTICLE 3. SUBSEQUENT PROCEEDINGS GENERALLY

8.01–560. How Interest and Profits of Property Applied in Certain Cases.
8.01–561. How Property to Be Kept; How Sold, When Expensive to Keep or Perishable.

Section
8.01-562. Examination on Oath of Codefendant; Order and Bond.
8.01-563. Principal Defendant May Claim Exemption.
8.01-564. Procedure When Codefendant Fails to Appear.
8.01-565. Suggestion That Codefendant Has Not Made Full Disclosure.
8.01-566. Who May Make Defense to Attachment.
8.01-567. What Defense May Be Made to Attachments.
8.01-568. Quashing Attachment or Rendering Judgment for Defendant.
8.01-569. When Petition Dismissed; When Retained and Cause Tried.
8.01-570. Judgment, Etc., of Court When Claim of Plaintiff Established.
8.01-571. When Defendant Not Served Fails to Appear Plaintiff Required to Give Bond.
8.01-572. Sale of Real Estate Attached.
8.01-573. How and When Claims of Other Persons to Property Tried.
8.01-574. Attachments in Connection with Pending Suits or Actions.
8.01-575. Rehearing Permitted When Judgment Rendered on Publication.
8.01-576. Order of Court on Rehearing or New Trial; Restitution to Defendant.

CHAPTER 20.1. SUMMARY JURY TRIAL

8.01-576.1. Election by Parties; Order of Court.
8.01-576.2. Summary Jury Trial; Selection of Jury; Fees.
8.01-576.3. Procedures; Verdict Not Binding Unless Otherwise Agreed.

CHAPTER 20.2. COURT-REFERRED DISPUTE RESOLUTION PROCEEDINGS

8.01-576.4. Scope and Definitions.
8.01-576.5. Referral of Disputes to Dispute Resolution Proceedings.
8.01-576.6. Notice and Opportunity to Object.
8.01-576.7. Costs.
8.01-576.8. Qualifications of Neutrals; Referral.
8.01-576.9. Standards and Duties of Neutrals; Confidentiality; Liability.
8.01-576.10. Confidentiality of Dispute Resolution Proceeding.
8.01-576.11. Effect of Written Settlement Agreement.
8.01-576.12. Vacating Orders and Agreements.

CHAPTER 21. ARBITRATION AND AWARD

ARTICLE 1. GENERAL PROVISIONS

8.01-577. Submission of Controversy; Agreement to Arbitrate; Condition Precedent to Action.
8.01-578. to 8.01-580. Repealed by Acts 1986, c. 614.
8.01-581. Fiduciary May Submit to Arbitration.

ARTICLE 2. UNIFORM ARBITRATION ACT

8.01-581.01. Validity of Arbitration Agreement.
8.01-581.02. Proceedings to Compel or Stay Arbitration.
8.01-581.03. Appointment of Arbitrators by Court; Powers of Arbitrators.
8.01-581.04. Hearing.
8.01-581.05. Representation by Attorney.
8.01-581.06. Witnesses, Subpoenas, Depositions.
8.01-581.07. Award; Fees and Expenses to Be Fixed.
8.01-581.08. Change of Award by Arbitrators.
8.01-581.09. Confirmation of an Award.

Section
8.01-581.010. Vacating an Award.
8.01-581.011. Modification or Correction of Award.
8.01-581.012. Judgment or Decree on Award.
8.01-581.013. Applications to Court.
8.01-581.014. Court;, Jurisdiction.
8.01-581.015. Venue.
8.01-581.016. Appeals.

CHAPTER 21.1. MEDICAL MALPRACTICE

ARTICLE 1. MEDICAL MALPRACTICE REVIEW PANELS; ARBITRATION OF MALPRACTICE CLAIMS

8.01-581.1. Definitions.
8.01-581.2. Request for Review by Medical Malpractice Review Panel; Rescission of Request; Determination on Request.
8.01-581.2:1. Additional Parties.
8.01-581.3. Composition, Selection, Etc., of Panel.
8.01-581.3:1. Completion of Discovery; Hearing Date; Notification to Parties and Panel Members; Oath of Panel Members.
8.01-581.4. Submission of Evidence to Panel; Depositions and Discovery; Duties of Chairman; Access to Material.
8.01-581.4:1. Assembly of Record.
8.01-581.4:2. Removal of Record for Inspection and Copying; Notice.
8.01-581.5. When Hearing to Be Held; Notice to Parties.
8.01-581.6. Conduct of Proceedings.
8.01-581.7. Opinion of Panel.
8.01-581.7:1. Limitation on Panel Opinion.
8.01-581.8. Admissibility of Opinion as Evidence; Appearance of Panel Members as Witnesses; Immunity from Civil Liability.
8.01-581.9. Repealed by Acts 1993, c. 928.
8.01-581.10. Per Diem and Expenses of Panel.
8.01-581.11. Rules and Regulations.
8.01-581.11:1. Objections Not Waived by Participation.
8.01-581.12. Arbitration of Medical Malpractice Claims.
8.01-581.12:1. Repealed by Acts 1979, c. 325.
8.01-581.12:2. Article Not Applicable to Actions Arising Prior to July 1, 1976.

ARTICLE 2. MISCELLANEOUS PROVISIONS

8.01-581.13. Civil Immunity for Certain Health Professionals and Health Profession Students Serving as Members of Certain Entities.
8.01-581.14. Repealed by Acts 2003, c. 397.
8.01-581.15. Limitation on Recovery in Certain Medical Malpractice Actions.
8.01-581.16. Civil Immunity for Members of or Consultants to Certain Boards or Committees.
8.01-581.17. Privileged Communications of Certain Committees and Entities.
8.01-581.18. Delivery of Results of Laboratory Tests and Other Examinations Not Authorized by Physician.
8.01-581.18:1. Immunity of Physicians for Laboratory Results and Examinations.
8.01-581.19. Civil Immunity for Physicians, Psychologists, Podiatrists, Optometrists, Veterinarians, Nursing Home Administrators, and Certified Emergency Medical Services Providers While Members of Certain Committees.
8.01-581.19:1. Civil Immunity for Persons Providing Information to Certain Committees.

Section

8.01–581.20. Standard of Care in Proceeding Before Medical Malpractice Review Panel; Expert Testimony; Determination of Standard in Action for Damages.

8.01–581.20:1. Admissibility of Expressions of Sympathy.

CHAPTER 21.2. MEDIATION

8.01–581.21. Definitions.

8.01–581.22. Confidentiality; Exceptions.

8.01–581.23. Civil Immunity.

8.01–581.24. Standards and Duties of Mediators; Confidentiality; Liability.

8.01–581.25. Effect of Written Settlement Agreement.

8.01–581.26. Vacating Orders and Agreements.

CHAPTER 22. RECEIVERS, GENERAL AND SPECIAL

ARTICLE 1. GENERAL RECEIVERS

8.01–582. Appointment of General Receivers; Their Duties; Audit of Funds.

8.01–583. How Securities Taken and Kept; Power of Receivers Over Same.

8.01–584. How Dividends and Interest Collected and Invested.

8.01–585. How Accounts Kept by Receivers.

8.01–586. Inquiry as to Unknown Owners of Funds.

8.01–587. Liability of General Receivers.

8.01–588. Bonds Generally.

8.01–588.1. Bonds Apportioned to Funds Under Control; Annual Reports.

8.01–589. Compensation and Fees; When None Allowed.

8.01–590. Penalty for Failure of Duty.

ARTICLE 2. SPECIAL RECEIVERS

8.01–591. Notice Required Prior to Appointment of Receiver.

8.01–592. Notice Not Required in Emergencies.

8.01–593. Subsequent Proceedings After Emergency Appointment.

8.01–594. Notice Not Required to Parties Served with Process.

8.01–595. Preparation of List of Creditors; Notice to Them.

8.01–596. No Sale Prior to Such Notification; Exceptions.

8.01–597. Suits Against Receivers in Certain Cases.

8.01–598. Effect of Judgment Against Receiver.

8.01–599. Warrant or Motion for Judgment Against Receiver in General District Court, When to Be Tried.

ARTICLE 3. GENERAL PROVISIONS FOR MONEYS UNDER CONTROL OF COURT

8.01–600. How Money Under Control of Court Deposited; Record Kept; Liability of Clerk.

8.01–600.1. Repealed by Acts 1993, c. 939.

8.01–601. Deposit with General Receiver of Certain Funds Under Supervision of Fiduciary and Belonging to Person Under Disability.

8.01–602. Proceedings When Owner of Money Under Control of Court Unknown.

8.01–603. Repealed by Acts 1982, c. 155.

8.01–604. How State Treasurer to Keep Account of Such Money.

8.01–605. How Person Entitled to Money Paid Into State Treasury May Recover It.

8.01–606. Payment of Small Amounts to Certain Persons Through Court Without Intervention of Fiduciary; Authority of Commissioners of Accounts; Certain Fiduciaries Exempt from Accountings.

CHAPTER 23. COMMISSIONERS IN CHANCERY

8.01–607. Appointment and Removal.

8.01–608. How Accounts Referred.

8.01–609. Duties; Procedure Generally.

8.01–609.1. Commissioners in Chancery.

8.01–610. Weight to Be Given Commissioner's Report.

8.01–611. Notice of Time and Place of Taking Account.

8.01–612. Commissioner May Summons Witnesses.

8.01–613. Commissioner May Ask Instructions of Court.

8.01–614. His Power to Adjourn His Proceedings.

8.01–615. When Cause Heard on Report; Time for Filing Exceptions.

8.01–616. Delivery of Original Papers of Suit by Clerk to Commissioner.

8.01–617. Settlement of Accounts of Special Receivers and Special Commissioners.

8.01–618. Reports of Such Settlements; When New Bond Required.

8.01–618.1. Fees of Special Receivers and Commissioners for Reports.

8.01–619. Recordation of Reports of Such Settlements.

CHAPTER 24. INJUNCTIONS

8.01–620. General Jurisdiction of Circuit Court to Award Injunctions.

8.01–621. Repealed by Acts 1987, c. 567.

8.01–622. Injunction to Protect Plaintiff in Suit for Specific Property.

8.01–622.1. Injunction Against Assisted Suicide; Damages; Professional Sanctions.

8.01–623. Injunction Against Decree Subject to Bill of Review; Limitations to Bill of Review.

8.01–624. Duration of Temporary Injunctions to Be Fixed Therein.

8.01–625. Dissolution of Injunctions.

8.01–626. When Court Grants or Refuses Injunction, Justice of Supreme Court or Judge of Court of Appeals May Review It.

8.01–627. To What Clerk Order for Injunction Directed.

8.01–628. Equity of Prayer for Temporary Injunction to Be Shown by Affidavit or Otherwise.

8.01–629. Notice Required.

8.01–630. Forthcoming Bond in Connection with Injunction Against Removal of Property.

8.01–631. Injunction Bond.

8.01–631.1. Environmental Injunction; Financial Capacity.

8.01–632. How Surety in Forthcoming Bond May Obtain Additional Security.

8.01–633. Damages on Dissolution.

8.01–634. Dismissal of Injunction Bill.

CHAPTER 25. EXTRAORDINARY WRITS

ARTICLE 1. WRIT OF QUO WARRANTO

8.01–635. Common-Law Writ of Quo Warranto and Information in the Nature of Writ of Quo Warranto Abolished; Statutory Writ of Quo Warranto Established.

8.01–636. In What Cases Writ Issued.

8.01–637. By Whom Filed; When Leave Granted and Writ Issued.

8.01–638. Repealed by Acts 1987, c. 567.

8.01–639. How Summons Directed and Served.

Section
8.01–640. Judgment When Defendant Fails to Appear.
8.01–641. Reopening Same When Made on Service by Publication.
8.01–642. Pleading When Defendant Appears.
8.01–643. Trial; Verdict; Judgment; Costs; Attorney's Fee.

ARTICLE 2. MANDAMUS AND PROHIBITION

8.01–644. Application for Mandamus or Prohibition.
8.01–644.1. Limitations of Actions for Petition for Mandamus.
8.01–645. What Petition to State; Where Presented.
8.01–646. When Writ Awarded If No Defense Made.
8.01–647. Defense; How Made.
8.01–648. What Judgment to Be Rendered.
8.01–649. Proceedings When Application Is to Supreme Court or Court of Appeals.
8.01–650. Suspension of Proceedings, Where Prohibition Applied For.
8.01–651. Suspension of Proceedings by Justice of Supreme Court or Judge of Court of Appeals.
8.01–652. Service of Writ; How Obedience Enforced.
8.01–653. Mandamus to Secure Construction of Act Directing Payment Out of Treasury of the Commonwealth.
8.01–653.1. Mandamus to Secure Construction of Act Granting Power to Incur Certain Obligations for Transportation Needs.

ARTICLE 3. HABEAS CORPUS

8.01–654. When and by Whom Writ Granted; What Petition to Contain.
8.01–654.1. Limitation on Consideration of Petition Filed by Prisoner Sentenced to Death.
8.01–654.2. Presentation of Claim of Mental Retardation by Person Sentenced to Death Before April 29, 2003.
8.01–655. Form and Contents of Petition Filed by Prisoner.
8.01–656. Bond May Be Required of Petitioner.
8.01–657. How Directed and Returnable.
8.01–658. How Writ Served; Dismissal of Habeas Petition Without Prejudice.
8.01–659. Penalty for Disobeying It.
8.01–660. When Affidavits May Be Read.
8.01–661. Facts Proved May Be Made Part of Record.
8.01–662. Judgment of Court or Judge Trying It; Payment of Costs and Expenses When Petition Denied.
8.01–663. Judgment Conclusive.
8.01–664. How and When Supreme Court Summoned to Try Appeal Therefrom.
8.01–665. When Execution of Judgment Suspended; When Prisoner Admitted to Bail.
8.01–666. When and by Whom Writs of Habeas Corpus Ad Testificandum Granted.
8.01–667. Transmission of Records to Federal Court.
8.01–668. Writ De Homine Abolished.

CHAPTER 26. APPEALS TO THE SUPREME COURT

ARTICLE 1. DEFINITIONS

8.01–669. Definitions.

ARTICLE 2. WHEN GRANTED

Section
8.01–670. In What Cases Awarded.
8.01–670.1. Appeal of Interlocutory Orders and Decrees by Permission.

Section
8.01–671. Time Within Which Petition Must Be Presented.
8.01–672. Jurisdictional Amount.

ARTICLE 3. THE RECORD

8.01–673. Inspection and Return of Records; Certiorari When Part of Record Is Omitted; Binding or Retention of Records.

ARTICLE 4. THE PETITION

Section
8.01–674. With Whom Filed; Endorsement Thereon; Reference to Justice or Justices; When Deemed to Be Filed.
8.01–675. Repealed by Acts 1984, c. 703, Eff. Oct. 1, 1984.
8.01–675.1. When Dismissal Final; When Reinstated.
8.01–675.2. Rehearing.

CHAPTER 26.1. APPEALS TO THE COURT OF APPEALS

8.01–675.3. Time Within Which Appeal Must Be Taken; Notice.
8.01–675.4. Inspection and Return of Records; Certiorari When Part of Record Is Omitted; Retention of Records.

CHAPTER 26.2. APPEALS GENERALLY

ARTICLE 1. APPEAL BOND

8.01–676. Repealed by Acts 1984, c. 703.
8.01–676.1. Security for Appeal.

ARTICLE 2. ERRORS INSUFFICIENT IN THE APPELLATE COURT

8.01–677. Errors Corrected on Motion Instead of Writ of Error Coram Vobis.
8.01–677.1. Appeals Filed in Inappropriate Appellate Court.
8.01–678. For What a Judgment Not to Be Reversed.

ARTICLE 3. LIMITATIONS; HEARING AND DECISION

8.01–679. Failure of Trial Court Clerk to Deliver Record to Appellate Court.
8.01–679.1. Arguments Made on Brief Not Waived by Oral Argument.
8.01–680. When Judgment of Trial Court Not to Be Set Aside Unless Plainly Wrong, Etc.
8.01–681. Decision of Appellate Court.
8.01–682. What Damages Awarded Appellee.
8.01–683. When Clerk of Supreme Court to Transmit Its Decisions.
8.01–684. Copies of Court's Opinions to Be Furnished to Counsel.
8.01–685. Entry of Decision in Lower Court; Issue of Execution Thereon.
8.01–686, 8.01–687. Repealed by Acts 1984, c. 703.

ARTICLE 4. MISCELLANEOUS PROVISIONS

8.01–688. Order Books, Etc., of Former District Courts in Custody of Clerk of Supreme Court, Etc.

CHAPTER 27. VIRGINIA PRISONER LITIGATION REFORM ACT

8.01–689. Short Title.
8.01–690. Applicability Provisions.
8.01–691. Payment of Filing Fees and Costs by Prisoners; When in Forma Pauperis Status Granted.
8.01–692. When in Forma Pauperis Status Denied.
8.01–693. Venue of Prisoner Actions.

Section
8.01–694. Service of Process; Time for Response.
8.01–695. When Argument Held; When Discovery Permitted.
8.01–696. Summary Judgment; Pro Se Prisoner Civil Action.
8.01–697. Access to Department of Corrections Records.

CRIMINAL PROCEDURE. [Title 19.2, Code of Virginia]

CHAPTER 1

GENERAL PROVISIONS AS TO CIVIL CASES

§ 8.01–1. How proceedings may be in actions pending when title takes effect

Except as may be otherwise provided in § 8.01–256 of Chapter 4 (§ 8.01–228 et seq.) (Limitations of Actions), all provisions of this title shall apply to causes of action which arose prior to the effective date of any such provisions; provided, however, that the applicable law in effect on the day before the effective date of the particular provisions shall apply if in the opinion of the court any particular provision (i) may materially change the substantive rights of a party (as distinguished from the procedural aspects of the remedy) or (ii) may cause the miscarriage of justice.

Acts 1977, c. 617.

§ 8.01–1.1. References to former sections, articles and chapters of Title 8 and other titles

Whenever in this title any of the conditions, requirements, provisions or contents of any section, article or chapter of Title 8 or any other title of this Code as such titles existed prior to October 2, 1977, are transferred in the same or in modified form to a new section, article or chapter of this title or any other title of this Code and whenever any such former section, article or chapter is given a new number in this or any other title, all references to any such former section, article or chapter of Title 8 or such other title appearing elsewhere in this Code than in this title shall be construed to apply to the new or renumbered section, article or chapter containing such conditions, requirements, provisions or contents or portions thereof.

Acts 1978, c. 422.

§ 8.01–2. General definitions for this title

As used in this title, unless the context otherwise requires, the term:

1. "Action" and "suit" may be used interchangeably and shall include all civil proceedings whether upon claims at law, in equity, or statutory in nature and whether in circuit courts or district courts;

2. "Decree" and "judgment" may be used interchangeably and shall include orders or awards;

3. "Fiduciary" shall include any one or more of the following:

a. guardian,

b. committee,

c. trustee,

d. executor,

e. administrator, and administrator with the will annexed,

f. curator of the will of any decedent, or

g. conservator;

4. "Rendition of a judgment" means the time at which the judgment is signed and dated;

5. "Person" shall include individuals, a trust, an estate, a partnership, an association, an order, a corporation, or any other legal or commercial entity;

6. "Person under a disability" shall include:

a. a person convicted of a felony during the period he is confined;

b. an infant;

c. an incapacitated person as defined in § 64.2–2000;

d. an incapacitated ex-service person under § 64.2–2016; or

e. any other person who, upon motion to the court by any party to an action or suit or by any person in interest, is determined to be (i) incapable of taking proper care of his person, or (ii) incapable of properly handling and managing his estate, or (iii) otherwise unable to defend his property or legal rights either because of age or temporary or permanent impairment, whether physical, mental, or both. Such impairment may also include substance abuse as defined in § 37.2–100;

7. "Sheriff" shall include deputy sheriffs and such other persons designated in § 15.2–1603;

8. "Summons" and "subpoena" may be used interchangeably and shall include a subpoena duces tecum for the production of documents and tangible things;

9. "Court of equity," "law and equity court," "law and chancery court," "chancery court," "corporation court," "the chancery side," "court exercising powers in chancery," "court with equitable jurisdiction," and "receivership court" shall mean the circuit court when entertaining equitable claims;

10. A "motion for judgment," "bill," "bill of complaint," or "bill in equity" shall mean a complaint in a civil action, as provided in the Rules of Supreme Court of Virginia;

11. "Equity practice," "equity procedure," "chancery practice," and "chancery procedure" shall mean practice and procedure in a civil action as prescribed by this Code and the Rules of Supreme Court of Virginia.

Acts 1977, c. 617; Acts 1988, c. 37; Acts 1997, c. 921, eff. Jan. 1, 1998. Amended by Acts 2005, c. 681, eff. Jan. 1, 2006; Acts 2005, c. 716, eff. Oct. 1, 2005.

§ 8.01–3. Supreme Court may prescribe rules; effective date and availability; indexed, and annotated; effect of subsequent enactments of General Assembly

A. The Supreme Court, subject to §§ 17.1–503 and 16.1–69.32, may, from time to time, prescribe the forms of writs and make general regulations for the practice in all courts of the Commonwealth; and may prepare a system of rules of practice and a system of pleading and the forms of process and may prepare rules of evidence to be used in all such courts. This section shall be liberally construed so as to eliminate unnecessary delays and expenses.

B. New rules and amendments to rules shall not become effective until 60 days from adoption by the Supreme Court, and shall be made available to all courts, members of the bar, and the public.

C. The Virginia Code Commission shall publish and cause to be properly indexed and annotated the rules adopted by the Supreme Court, and all amendments thereof by the Court, and all changes made therein pursuant to subsection D.

D. The General Assembly may, from time to time, by the enactment of a general law, modify or annul any rules adopted or amended pursuant to this section. In the case of any variance between a rule and an enactment of the General Assembly such variance shall be construed so as to give effect to such enactment.

E. Any amendment or addition to the rules of evidence shall be adopted by the Supreme Court on or before November 15 of any year and shall become effective on July 1 of the following year unless the General Assembly modifies or annuls any such amendment or addition by enactment of a general law. Notwithstanding the foregoing, the Supreme Court, at any time, may amend the rules to conform with any enactment of the General Assembly and correct unmistakable printer's errors, misspellings, unmistakable errors to statutory cross-references, and other unmistakable errors in the rules of evidence.

F. When any rule contained in the rules of evidence is derived from one or more sections of the Code of Virginia, the Supreme Court shall include a citation to such section or sections in the title of the rule.

Acts 1977, c. 617; Acts 1979, c. 658; Acts 1984, c. 524; Acts 2003, c. 280. Amended by Acts 2012, c. 688; Acts 2012, c. 708.

§ 8.01–4. District courts and circuit courts may prescribe certain rules

The district courts and circuit courts may, from time to time, prescribe rules for their respective districts and circuits. Such rules shall be limited to those rules necessary to promote proper order and decorum and the efficient and safe use of courthouse facilities and clerks' offices. No rule of any such court shall be prescribed or enforced which is inconsistent with this statute or any other statutory provision, or the Rules of Supreme Court or contrary to the decided cases, or which has the effect of abridging substantive rights of persons before such court. Any rule of court which violates the provisions of this section shall be invalid.

The courts may prescribe certain docket control procedures which shall not abridge the substantive rights of the parties nor deprive any party the opportunity to present its position as to the merits of a case solely due to the unfamiliarity of counsel of record with any such docket control procedures. No civil matter shall be dismissed with prejudice by any district or circuit court for failure to comply with any rule created under this section.

Acts 1977, c. 617; Acts 1999, c. 839, eff. July 1, 2000; Acts 2000, c. 803. Amended by Acts 2014, c. 348.

§ 8.01–4.1. How jurisdiction determined when proceeding is on penal bond

When a proceeding before a court is on a penal bond, with condition for the payment of money, the jurisdiction shall be determined as if the undertaking to pay such money had been without a penalty. And when jurisdiction depends on the amount of a judgment, if it be on such a bond, the jurisdiction shall be determined by the sum, payment whereof will discharge the judgment.

Acts 1977, c. 617.

§ 8.01–4.2. Who may execute bond for obtaining writ or order

A bond for obtaining any writ or order may be executed by any person with sufficient surety, though neither be a party to the case.

Acts 1977, c. 617.

§ 8.01–4.3. Unsworn declarations under penalty of perjury; penalty

If a matter in any judicial proceeding or administrative hearing is required or permitted to be established by a sworn written declaration, verification, certificate, statement, oath, or affidavit, such matter may, with like force and effect, be evidenced, by the unsworn written declaration, certificate, verification, or statement, which is subscribed by the maker as true under penalty of perjury, and dated, in substantially the following form:

"I declare (or certify, verify or state) under penalty of perjury that the foregoing is true and correct."

This section shall not apply to a deposition, an oath of office, or an oath required to be taken before a specified official other than a notary public.

Added by Acts 2005, c. 423.

CHAPTER 2

PARTIES

ARTICLE 1

GENERAL PROVISIONS

§ 8.01–5. Effect of nonjoinder or misjoinder; limitation on joinder of insurance company

A. No action or suit shall abate or be defeated by the nonjoinder or misjoinder of parties, plaintiff or defendant, but whenever such nonjoinder or misjoinder shall be made to appear by affidavit or otherwise, new parties may be added and parties misjoined may be dropped by order of the court at any time as the ends of justice may require.

B. Nothing in this section shall be construed to permit the joinder of any insurance company on account of the issuance to any party to a cause of any policy or contract of liability insurance, or on account of the issuance by any such company of any policy or contract of liability insurance for the benefit of or that will inure to the benefit of any party to any cause.

Acts 1977, c. 617.

§ 8.01–6. Amending pleading; relation back to original pleading

A misnomer in any pleading may, on the motion of any party, and on affidavit of the right name, be amended by inserting the right name. An amendment changing the party against whom a claim is asserted, whether to correct a misnomer or otherwise, relates back to the date of the original pleading if (i) the claim asserted in the amended pleading arose out of the conduct, transaction, or occurrence set forth in the original pleading, (ii) within the limitations period prescribed for commencing the action against the party to be brought in by the amendment, that party or its agent received notice of the institution of the action, (iii) that party will not be prejudiced in maintaining a defense on the merits, and (iv) that party knew or should have known that but for a mistake concerning the identity of the proper party, the action would have been brought against that party.

Acts 1977, c. 617; Acts 1990, c. 80; Acts 1996, c. 693. Amended by Acts 2004, c. 141; Acts 2004, c. 326.

§ 8.01–6.1. Amendment of pleading changing or adding a claim or defense; relation back

Subject to any other applicable provisions of law, an amendment of a pleading changing or adding a claim or defense against a party relates back to the date of the original pleadings for purposes of the statute of limitations if the court finds (i) the claim or defense asserted in the amended pleading arose out of the conduct, transaction or occurrence set forth in the original pleading, (ii) the amending party was reasonably diligent in asserting the amended claim or defense, and (iii) parties opposing the amendment will not be substantially prejudiced in litigating on the merits as a result of the timing of the amendment. In connection with such an amendment, the trial court may grant a continuance or other relief to protect the parties. This section shall not apply to eminent domain or mechanics' lien claims or defenses.

Acts 1996, c. 693.

§ 8.01–6.2. Amendment of pleading; relation back to original pleading; confusion in trade name

A. A pleading which states a claim against a party whose trade name or corporate name is substantially similar to the trade name or corporate name of another entity may be amended at any time by inserting the correct party's name, if such party or its agent had actual notice of the claim prior to the expiration of the statute of limitations for filing the claim.

B. In the event that suit is filed against the estate of a decedent, and filed within the applicable statute of limitations, naming the proper name of estate of the deceased and service is effected or attempted on an individual or individuals as executor, administrator or other officers of the estate, such filing tolls the statute of limitations for said claim in the event the executor, administrator or other officers of the estate are unable to legally receive service at the time service was attempted, or defend suit because their authority as executor, administrator or other officer of the estate excludes defending said actions, or their duties as executor, administrator or other officer of the estate had expired at the time of service or during the time of defending said action.

Acts 1999, c. 686.

§ 8.01–6.3. Actions or suits against fiduciaries; style of the case; amendment of pleading

A. In any action or suit required to be prosecuted or defended by or in the name of a fiduciary, including a personal representative, trustee, conservator, or guardian, the style of the case in regard to the fiduciary shall be substantially in the following form: "(Name of fiduciary), (type of fiduciary relationship), (Name of the subject of the fiduciary relationship)."

B. Any pleading filed that does not conform to the requirements of subsection A but otherwise identifies the proper parties shall be amended on the motion of any party or by the court on its own motion. Such amendment relates back to the date of the original pleading.

Added by Acts 2010, c. 437.

§ 8.01–7. When court may add new parties to suit

In any case in which full justice cannot be done, or the whole controversy ended, without the presence of new parties to the suit, the court, by order, may direct the clerk to issue the proper process against such new parties, and, upon the maturing of the case as to them, proceed to make such orders or decrees as would have been proper if the new parties had been made parties at the commencement of the suit.

Acts 1977, c. 617.

Article 2

Special Provisions

§ 8.01–8. How minors may sue

Any minor entitled to sue may do so by his next friend. Either or both parents may sue on behalf of a minor as his next friend.

Acts 1977, c. 617; Acts 1998, c. 402.

§ 8.01–9. Guardian ad litem for persons under disability; when guardian ad litem need not be appointed for person under disability

A. A suit wherein a person under a disability is a party defendant shall not be stayed because of such disability, but the court in which the suit is pending, or the clerk thereof, shall appoint a discreet and competent attorney-at-law as guardian ad litem to such defendant, whether the defendant has been served with process or not. If no such attorney is found willing to act, the court shall appoint some other discreet and proper person as guardian ad litem. Any guardian ad litem so appointed shall not be liable for costs. Every guardian ad litem shall faithfully represent the estate or other interest of the person under a disability for whom he is appointed, and it shall be the duty of the court to see that the interest of the defendant is so represented and protected. Whenever the court is of the opinion that the interest of the defendant so requires, it shall remove any guardian ad litem and appoint another in his stead. When, in any case, the court is satisfied that the guardian ad litem has rendered substantial service in representing the interest of the person under a disability, it may allow the guardian reasonable compensation therefor, and his actual expenses, if any, to be paid out of the estate of the defendant. However, if the defendant's estate is inadequate for the purpose of paying compensation and expenses, all, or any part thereof, may be taxed as costs in the proceeding or, in the case of proceedings to adjudicate a person under a disability as an habitual offender pursuant to former § 46.2–351.2 or former § 46.2–352, shall be paid by the Commonwealth out of the state treasury from the appropriation for criminal charges. In a civil action against an incarcerated felon for damages arising out of a criminal act, the compensation and expenses of the guardian ad litem shall be paid by the Commonwealth out of the state treasury from the appropriation for criminal charges. If judgment is against the incarcerated felon, the amount allowed by the court to the guardian ad litem shall be taxed against the incarcerated felon as part of the costs of the proceeding, and if collected, the same shall be paid to the Commonwealth. By order of the court, in a civil action for divorce from an incarcerated felon, the compensation and expenses of the guardian ad litem shall be paid by the Commonwealth out of the state treasury from the appropriation for criminal charges if the crime (i) for which the felon is incarcerated occurred after the date of the marriage for which the divorce is sought, (ii) for which the felon is incarcerated was committed against the felon's spouse, child, or stepchild and involved physical injury, sexual assault, or sexual abuse, and (iii) resulted in incarceration subsequent to conviction and the felon was sentenced to confinement for more than one year. The amount allowed by the court to the guardian ad litem shall be taxed against the incarcerated felon as part of the costs of the proceeding, and if collected, the same shall be paid to the Commonwealth.

B. Notwithstanding the provisions of subsection A or the provisions of any other law to the contrary, in any suit wherein a person under a disability is a party and is represented by an attorney-at-law duly licensed to practice in this Commonwealth, who shall have entered of record an appearance for such person, no guardian ad litem need be appointed for such person unless the court determines that the interests of justice require such appointment; or unless a statute applicable to such suit expressly requires that the person under a disability be represented by a guardian ad litem. The court may, in its discretion, appoint the attorney of record for the person under a disability as his guardian ad litem, in which event the attorney shall perform all the duties and functions of guardian ad litem.

Any judgment or decree rendered by any court against a person under a disability without a guardian ad litem, but in compliance with the provisions of this subsection B, shall be as valid as if the guardian ad litem had been appointed.

Acts 1977, c. 617; Acts 1996, c. 887; Acts 1999, c. 945; Acts 1999, c. 955; Acts 1999, c. 987; Acts 2001, c. 127; Acts 2003, c. 563.

§ 8.01–10. Joinder of tenants in common

Tenants in common may join or be joined as plaintiffs or defendants.

Acts 1977, c. 617.

§ 8.01–11. Proceedings on writing binding deceased person

A. A bond, note, or other written obligation to a person or persons who, or some of whom, are dead at the time of its execution may be proceeded on in the name of the personal representative of such person, or the survivors or survivor, or of the representative of the last survivor of such persons.

B. If one person bound either jointly or as a partner with another by a judgment, bond, note, or otherwise for the payment of a debt, or the performance or forbearance of an act, or for any other thing, die in the lifetime of such other, the representative of the decedent may be charged in the same manner as the decedent might have been charged, if those bound jointly or as partners, had been bound severally as well as jointly, otherwise than as partners.

Acts 1977, c. 617.

§ 8.01–12. Suit by beneficial owner when legal title in another

When the legal title to any claim or chose in action, for the enforcement of the collection of which a court of equity has jurisdiction, is in one person and the beneficial equitable title thereto is in another, the latter may either maintain a suit in the name of the holder of the legal title for his use and benefit or in his own name to enforce collection of the same. In either case the beneficial equitable owner shall be deemed the real plaintiff and shall be liable for costs.

Acts 1977, c. 617.

§ 8.01–13. Assignee or beneficial owner may sue in own name; certain discounts allowed

The assignee or beneficial owner of any bond, note, writing or other chose in action, not negotiable may maintain thereon in his own name any action which the original obligee, payee, or contracting party might have brought, but, except as provided in § 8.9A–403, shall allow all just discounts, not only against himself, but against such obligee, payee, or contracting party, before the defendant had notice of the assignment or transfer by such obligee, payee, or contracting party, and shall also allow all such discounts against any intermediate assignor or transferor, the right to which was acquired on the faith of the assignment or transfer to him and before the defendant had notice of the assignment or transfer by such assignor or transferor to another.

Acts 1977, c. 617.

§ 8.01–14. Suit against assignor

Any assignee or beneficial owner may recover from any assignor of a writing; but only joint assignors shall be joined as defendants in one action. A remote assignor shall have the benefit of the same defense as if the suit had been instituted by his immediate assignee.

Acts 1977, c. 617.

§ 8.01–15. Suits by and against unincorporated associations or orders

All unincorporated associations or orders may sue and be sued under the name by which they are commonly known and called, or under which they do business, and judgments and executions against any such association or order shall bind its real and personal property in like manner as if it were incorporated.

Acts 1977, c. 617.

§ 8.01–15.1. Anonymous plaintiff; motion for identification; factors to be considered by court

A. In any legal proceeding commenced anonymously, any party may move for an order concerning the propriety of anonymous participation in the proceeding. The trial court may allow maintenance of the proceeding under a pseudonym if the anonymous litigant discharges the burden of showing special circumstances such that the need for anonymity outweighs the public's interest in knowing the party's identity and outweighs any prejudice to any other party. The court may consider whether the requested anonymity is intended merely to avoid the annoyance and criticism that may attend any litigation or is to preserve privacy in a sensitive and highly personal matter; whether identification poses a risk of retaliatory physical or mental harm to the requesting party or to innocent nonparties; the ages of the persons whose privacy interests are sought to be protected; whether the action is against a governmental or private party; and the risk of unfairness to other parties if anonymity is maintained.

B. If the court initially permits a party to proceed anonymously, the issue of the propriety of continued anonymous participation in the proceedings may be raised at any stage of the litigation when circumstances warrant a reconsideration of the issue. In all cases, all parties have the right to know the true identities of all other parties under such provisions of confidentiality as the court may deem appropriate.

C. If the court orders that the anonymous litigant be identified, the pleadings and any relevant dockets shall be reformed to reflect the party's true name, and the identification shall be deemed to relate back to the date of filing of the proceeding by the anonymous party.

D. In any legal proceeding in which a party is proceeding anonymously, the court shall enter appropriate orders to afford all parties the rights, procedures and discovery to which they are otherwise entitled.

Added by Acts 2003, c. 572.

§ 8.01-15.2. Servicemembers Civil Relief Act; default judgment

A. Notwithstanding the provisions of § 8.01-428, in any civil action or proceeding in which the defendant does not make an appearance, the court shall not enter a judgment by default until the plaintiff files with the court an affidavit (i) stating whether or not the defendant is in military service and showing necessary facts to support the affidavit; or (ii) if the plaintiff is unable to determine whether or not the defendant is in military service, stating that the plaintiff is unable to determine whether or not the defendant is in military service. Subject to the provisions of § 8.01-3, the Supreme Court shall prescribe the form of such affidavit, or the requirement for an affidavit may be satisfied by a written statement, declaration, verification or certificate, subscribed and certified or declared to be true under penalty of perjury. Any judgment by default entered by any court in any civil action or proceeding in violation of Article 2 of the Servicemembers Civil Relief Act (50 U.S.C. app. § 527 et seq.) may be set aside as provided by the Act. Failure to file an affidavit shall not constitute grounds to set aside an otherwise valid default judgment against a defendant who was not, at the time of service of process or entry of default judgment, a servicemember for the purposes of 50 U.S.C. app. § 502.

B. Where appointment of counsel is required pursuant to 50 U.S.C. app. § 521 or 522, the court may assess attorneys' fees and costs against any party as the court deems appropriate, and shall direct in its order which of the parties to the case shall pay such fees and costs. Such fees and costs shall not be assessed against the Commonwealth unless it is the party that obtains the judgment.

Added by Acts 2004, c. 381. Amended by Acts 2005, c. 909.

Article 3

Death or Change of Parties

§ 8.01-16. New parties may have continuance

Except in the Supreme Court any new party to a case, whether he be joined or substituted, may in the discretion of the court have a continuance; and the court may allow him to plead anew or amend the pleadings so far as it deems reasonable, but in other respects the case shall proceed to final judgment or decree for or against him, in like manner as if he had been an original party to the case.

Acts 1977, c. 617.

§ 8.01-17. When party whose powers cease is defendant

When the party whose powers cease is defendant, the plaintiff may continue his suit against him to final judgment or decree; provided that a successor in interest may be substituted in accordance with the Rules of Court; and provided further that upon motion the court may order that the suit proceed against the former party as well as the successor.

Acts 1977, c. 617.

§ 8.01-18. When suit discontinued unless revived

If the committee, personal representative, heir, or devisee of the plaintiff or appellant who was a party, or of the decedent whose personal representative was plaintiff or appellant, shall not make a motion for substitution of parties under the applicable Rules of Court within a reasonable time after there may have been a suggestion on the record of the fact making such motion proper, the suit of such plaintiff or appellant shall be discontinued, unless good cause be shown to the contrary.

Acts 1977, c. 617.

§ 8.01-19. Effect of marriage or change of name of party

The marriage of a party shall not cause a suit or action to abate. If a party changes his name, upon affidavit or other proof of the fact, the suit or action shall proceed in the new name, but if the change of name be not suggested before judgment, the judgment shall be as valid, and may be enforced in like manner, as if no such change of name had taken place.

Acts 1977, c. 617.

§ 8.01-20. Effect of marriage, change of name or death on appeal

If at any time after verdict or judgment in the trial court during the pendency of an appeal or before the appeal is granted, the marriage, change of name or death of a party, or any other fact which might otherwise be relied on in abatement occurs, and such fact is suggested or relied on in abatement in the Court of Appeals or the Supreme Court, the court may, in its discretion, take or retain jurisdiction and enter judgment or decree in the case as if such event had not occurred.

Acts 1977, c. 617; Acts 1984, c. 703.

§ 8.01–20.1. Certification of expert witness opinion at time of service of process

Every motion for judgment, counter claim, or third party claim in a medical malpractice action, at the time the plaintiff requests service of process upon a defendant, or requests a defendant to accept service of process, shall be deemed a certification that the plaintiff has obtained from an expert witness whom the plaintiff reasonably believes would qualify as an expert witness pursuant to subsection A of § 8.01–581.20 a written opinion signed by the expert witness that, based upon a reasonable understanding of the facts, the defendant for whom service of process has been requested deviated from the applicable standard of care and the deviation was a proximate cause of the injuries claimed. This certification is not necessary if the plaintiff, in good faith, alleges a medical malpractice action that asserts a theory of liability where expert testimony is unnecessary because the alleged act of negligence clearly lies within the range of the jury's common knowledge and experience.

The certifying expert shall not be required to be an expert witness expected to testify at trial nor shall any defendant be entitled to discover the identity or qualifications of the certifying expert or the nature of the certifying expert's opinions. Should the certifying expert be identified as an expert expected to testify at trial, the opinions and bases therefor shall be discoverable pursuant to Rule 4:1 of the Rules of Supreme Court of Virginia with the exception of the expert's status as a certifying expert.

Upon written request of any defendant, the plaintiff shall, within 10 business days after receipt of such request, provide the defendant with a certification form that affirms that the plaintiff had obtained the necessary certifying expert opinion at the time service was requested or affirms that the plaintiff did not need to obtain a certifying expert witness opinion. The court, upon good cause shown, may conduct an in camera review of the certifying expert opinion obtained by the plaintiff as the court may deem appropriate. If the plaintiff did not obtain a necessary certifying expert opinion at the time the plaintiff requested service of process on a defendant as required under this section, the court shall impose sanctions according to the provisions of § 8.01–271.1 and may dismiss the case with prejudice.

Added by Acts 2005, c. 649; Acts 2005, c. 692. Amended by Acts 2007, c. 489; Acts 2013, c. 65; Acts 2013, c. 610.

§ 8.01–21. Judgment when death or disability occurs after verdict but before judgment

When a party dies, or becomes convicted of a felony or insane, or the powers of a party who is a personal representative or committee cease, if such fact occurs after verdict, judgment may be entered as if it had not occurred.

Acts 1977, c. 617.

§ 8.01–22. When death or disability occurs as to any of several plaintiffs or defendants

If a party plaintiff or defendant becomes incapable of prosecuting or defending because of death, insanity, conviction of felony, removal from office, or other reason and there are one or more co-plaintiffs or co-defendants, the court on motion may in its discretion either (i) suspend the case until a successor in interest is appointed in accordance with the Rules of Court, or (ii) sever the action or suit so that the case shall proceed against the remaining parties without delay, with the case as to the former party being continued and tried separately against the successor in interest when he is substituted as provided by the Rules of Court.

Acts 1977, c. 617.

§ 8.01–23. Decree in suit when number of parties exceeds 30 and one of them dies

When, in any suit involving a decedent's estate or a trust, the number of parties exceeds 30, and any one of the parties jointly interested with others in any question arising therein, dies, the court may, notwithstanding, if in its opinion all classes of interests are represented and no one will be prejudiced thereby, proceed to render a decree in such suit as if such party were alive; decreeing to the heirs, devisees, legatees, distributees, or personal representatives, as the case may be, such interest as the deceased person, if alive, would be entitled to. The provisions of § 8.01–322 shall apply to decrees entered hereunder.

Acts 1977, c. 617. Amended by Acts 2005, c. 681, eff. Jan. 1, 2006.

ARTICLE 4

WRIT OF SCIRE FACIAS ABOLISHED

§ 8.01–24. Writ of scire facias abolished; substitutes therefor

The writ of scire facias is hereby abolished. Relief heretofore available by scire facias may be obtained by appropriate action or motion pursuant to applicable statutes and Rules of Court.

Acts 1977, c. 617.

CHAPTER 3

ACTIONS

ARTICLE 1

SURVIVAL AND ASSIGNMENT OF CAUSES OF ACTIONS

§ 8.01–25. Survival of causes of action

Every cause of action whether legal or equitable, which is cognizable in the Commonwealth of Virginia, shall survive either the death of the person against whom the cause of action is or may be asserted, or the death of the person in whose favor the cause of action existed, or the death of both such persons. Provided that in such an action punitive damages shall not be awarded after the death of the party liable for the injury. Provided, further, that if the cause of action asserted by the decedent in his lifetime was for a personal injury and such decedent dies as a result of the injury complained of with a timely action for damages arising from such injury pending, the action shall be amended in accordance with the provisions of § 8.01–56.

As used in this section, the term "death" shall include the death of an individual or the termination or dissolution of any other entity.

Acts 1977, c. 617.

§ 8.01–26. Assignment of causes of action

Only those causes of action for damage to real or personal property, whether such damage be direct or indirect, and causes of action ex contractu are assignable. The provisions of this section shall not prohibit any injured party or his estate from making a voluntary assignment of the proceeds or anticipated proceeds of any court award or settlement as security for new value given in consideration of such voluntary assignment.

Acts 1977, c. 617; Acts 1991, c. 256.

ARTICLE 2

ACTIONS ON CONTRACTS GENERALLY

§ 8.01–27. Civil action on note or writing promising to pay money

A civil action may be maintained upon any note or writing by which there is a promise, undertaking, or obligation to pay money, if the same be signed by the party who is to be charged thereby, or his agent. The action may also be maintained on any such note or writing for any past due installment on a debt payable in installments, although other installments thereof be not due.

Acts 1977, c. 617.

§ 8.01–27.1. Additional recovery in certain civil actions concerning checks or rejected electronic funds transfers

A. Except as otherwise provided in Chapter 13 (§ 55–217 et seq.) or Chapter 13.2 (§ 55–248.2 et seq.) of Title 55, in any civil claim or action made or brought against the drawer of a check, draft or order, payment of which has been refused by the drawee depository because of lack of funds in or credit with such drawee depository, or because such check, draft or order was returned because of a stop-payment order placed in bad faith on the check, draft or order by the drawer, the holder or his agent shall be entitled to claim, in addition to the face amount of the check (i) legal interest from the date of the check, (ii) the protest or bad check return fee, if any, charged to the holder by his bank or other depository, (iii) a processing charge of $50, and (iv) reasonable attorney's fees if awarded by the court.

B. Except as otherwise provided in Chapter 13 (§ 55–217 et seq.) or Chapter 13.2 (§ 55–248.2 et seq.) of Title 55, any holder of a check, draft or order, payment of which has been refused by the drawee for insufficient funds or credit or because of a stop-payment order placed in bad faith, who charges the drawer amounts in excess of those authorized in subsection A on account of payment being so refused shall, upon demand, be liable to the drawer for the lesser of (i) $50 plus the excess of the authorized amount or (ii) twice the amount charged in excess of the authorized amount.

C. If an electronic funds transfer has been rejected because of insufficient funds or a stop-payment order has been placed in bad faith by the authorizing party, the authorizing party and the payee shall have the same rights and remedies as if the drawer had issued a bad check under subsection B. For purposes of this subsection, "electronic funds transfer" has the same meaning as provided in 15 U.S.C. § 1693(a).

Acts 1981, c. 230; Acts 1992, c. 238; Acts 1996, c. 334; Acts 2003, c. 233. Amended by Acts 2008, c. 489; Acts 2009, c. 182; Acts 2013, c. 63.

§ 8.01–27.2. Civil recovery for giving bad check

A. Except as otherwise provided in Chapter 13 (§ 55–217 et seq.) or Chapter 13.2 (§ 55–248.2 et seq.) of Title 55, in the event a check, draft or order, the payment of which has been refused by the drawee because of lack of funds in or credit with such drawee, is not paid in full within thirty days after receipt by the drawer of (i) written notice by registered, certified, or regular mail with the sender retaining an affidavit of service of mailing or other sufficient proof of mailing, which may be a U.S. Postal Certificate of Mailing or (ii) if for nonpayment of rent under § 55–225 or 55–248.31, written notice in accordance therewith, from the payee that the check, draft or order has been returned unpaid, the payee may recover from the drawer in a civil action brought by the filing of a warrant in debt, the lesser of $250 or three times the amount of the check, draft or order. The amount recovered as authorized by this section shall be in addition to the amounts authorized for recovery under § 8.01–27.1. No action may be initiated under this section if any action has been initiated under § 18.2–181. The drawer shall be obligated to pay the cost of service and the cost of mailing, as applicable.

B. If an electronic funds transfer has been rejected because of insufficient funds or a stop-payment order has been placed in bad faith by the authorizing party, the authorizing party and the payee shall have the same rights and remedies as if the drawer had issued a bad check under § 8.01–27.1. For purposes of this subsection, "electronic funds transfer" has the same meaning as provided in 15 U.S.C. § 1693(a).

Acts 1985, c. 579; Acts 1988, c. 433; Acts 1992, c. 501; Acts 2002, c. 763. Amended by Acts 2008, c. 489; Acts 2013, c. 63.

§ 8.01–27.3. Evidence in actions regarding issuance of bad check

In any civil action growing out of an arrest under § 18.2–181 or § 18.2–182, no evidence of statements or representations as to the status of the check, draft, order or deposit involved, or of any collateral agreement with reference to the check, draft, or order, shall be admissible unless such statement, or representation, or collateral agreement, is written upon the instrument at the time it is given by the drawer.

Added by Acts 2004, c. 462.

§ 8.01–27.4. Civil recovery for professional services

In the event any insured or enrollee of an accident and sickness insurance policy, health services plan or health maintenance organization receives payment from the insurance company, health services plan or health maintenance organization licensed under Title 38.2, pursuant to a claim that involves the provision of services to the insured or enrollee by a professional licensed under Title 54.1, and within 30 days of receipt of the payment does not forward the payment with the necessary endorsement to the professional for application towards the unpaid balance on the professional services subject to the claim, the professional may in a civil action brought by the filing of a warrant in debt recover from the insured or enrollee the lesser of $250 or three times the amount of the payment, together with the amount of the payment. The amount recovered as authorized by this section shall be in addition to the amounts authorized for recovery under § 8.01–27.1. No action may be initiated under this section unless the professional, prior to receipt of payment by the insured or enrollee, forwards to the insured or enrollee via first class mail an invoice for services rendered.

Added by Acts 2004, c. 909. Amended by Acts 2005, c. 141.

§ 8.01–27.5. Duty of in-network providers to submit claims to health insurers; liability of covered patients for unbilled health care services

A. As used in this section:

"Covered patient" means a patient whose health care services are covered under terms of a health care policy.

"Health care policy" means any health care plan, subscription contract, evidence of coverage, certificate, health services plan, medical or hospital services plan, accident and sickness insurance policy or certificate, or other similar certificate, policy, contract, or arrangement, and any endorsement or rider thereto, offered, arranged, issued, or administered by a health insurer to an individual or a group contract holder to cover all or a portion of the cost of individuals, or their eligible dependents, receiving covered health care services. "Health care policy" includes coverages issued pursuant to (i) Chapter 28 (§ 2.2–2800 et seq.) of Title 2.2 (state employees); (ii) § 2.2–1204 (local choice); (iii) 5 U.S.C. § 8901 et seq. (federal employees); and (iv) an employee welfare benefit plan as defined in 29 U.S.C. § 1002(1) of the Employee Retirement Income Security Act of 1974 (ERISA) that is self-insured or self-funded. "Health care policy" does not include (a) coverages issued pursuant to Title XVIII of the Social Security Act, 42 U.S.C. § 1395 et seq. (Medicare), Title XIX of the Social Security Act, 42 U.S.C. § 1396 et seq. (Medicaid), or Title XXI of the Social Security Act, 42 U.S.C. § 1397aa et seq. (CHIP), or Chapter 55 of Title 10 of the United States Code, 10 U.S.C. § 1071 et seq. (TRICARE); (b) subscription contracts for one or more dental or optometric services plans that are subject to Chapter 45 (§ 38.2–4500 et seq.) of Title 38.2; (c) insurance policies that provide coverage, singly or in combination, for death, dismemberment, disability, or hospital and medical care caused by or necessitated as a result of accident or specified kinds of accidents, including student accident, sports accident, blanket accident, specific accident, and accidental death and dismemberment policies; (d) credit life insurance and credit accident and sickness insurance issued pursuant to Chapter 37.1 (§ 38.2–3717 et seq.) of Title 38.2; (e) insurance policies that provide payments when an insured is disabled or unable to work because of illness, disease, or injury, including incidental benefits; (f) long-term care insurance as defined in § 38.2–5200; (g) plans providing only limited health care services under § 38.2–4300 unless offered by endorsement or rider to a group health benefit plan; (h) TRICARE supplement, Medicare supplement, or workers' compensation coverages; or (i) medical expense coverage issued pursuant to § 38.2–2201.

"Health care provider" has the same meaning ascribed to the term in § 8.01–581.1.

"Health care services" means items or services furnished to any individual for the purpose of preventing, alleviating, curing, or healing human illness, injury, or physical disability.

"Health insurer" means any entity that is the issuer or sponsor of a health care policy.

"In-network provider" means a health care provider that is employed by or has entered into a provider agreement with the health insurer that has issued the health care policy, under which agreement the health care provider has agreed to provide health care services to covered patients.

"Patient" means an individual who receives health care services from a health care provider, or any person authorized by law to consent on behalf of the individual incapable of making an informed decision, or, in the case of a minor child, the parent or parents having custody of the child or the child's legal guardian, or as otherwise provided by law.

"Provider agreement" means a contract, agreement, or arrangement between a health care provider and a health insurer, or a health insurer's network, provider panel, intermediary, or representative, under which the health care provider has agreed to provide health care services to patients with coverage under a health care policy issued by the health insurer and to accept payment from the health insurer for the health care services provided.

B. An in-network provider that provides health care services to a covered patient shall submit its claim to the health insurer for the health care services in accordance with the terms of the applicable provider agreement, provided that the covered patient provides the in-network provider with information required by the terms of the covered patient's health care policy's plan documents, including the information that is required to verify the individual's coverage under the health care policy, within not fewer than 21 business days before the deadline for the in-network provider to submit its claim to the health insurer as required by the terms of the provider agreement. If an in-network provider does not submit its claim to the health insurer in accordance with the requirements of this subsection, then (i) the covered patient shall have no obligation to pay for health care services for which the in-network provider was required to submit its claim, (ii) the in-network provider shall not have the benefit of the liens provided by §§ 8.01–66.2 and 8.01–66.9 with regard to health care services for which the in-network provider was required to submit its claim, and (iii) the in-network provider shall be prohibited from recovering payment for any of the health care services for which it was required to submit its claim from an insurer providing medical expense benefits to the covered patient under a policy of motor vehicle liability insurance pursuant to § 38.2–2201, by exercising an assignment of the covered patient's rights to the medical expense benefits or by other means. If the in-network provider submits its claim to the health insurer in accordance with the requirements of this subsection, the covered patient or the health insurer shall be obligated to pay for the health care services in accordance with the terms of the provider agreement or health care policy's plan documents. To the extent that self-insured or self-funded plans governed by ERISA provide otherwise, health care providers shall be permitted to submit claims and coordinate benefits as provided for in the provider agreements or plan documents.

Added by Acts 2013, c. 700. Amended by Acts 2014, c. 157; Acts 2014, c. 417.

§ 8.01–28. When judgment to be given in action upon contract or note unless defendant appears and denies claim under oath

In any action at law on a note or contract, express or implied, for the payment of money, or unlawful detainer pursuant to § 55–225 or 55–248.31 for the payment of money or possession of the premises, or both, if (i) the plaintiff files with his motion for judgment or civil warrant an affidavit made by himself or his agent, stating therein to the best of the affiant's belief the amount of the plaintiff's claim, that such amount is justly due, and the time from which plaintiff claims interest, and (ii) a copy of the affidavit together with a copy of any account filed with the motion for judgment or warrant and, in actions pursuant to § 55–225 or 55–248.31, proof of required notices is served on the defendant as provided in § 8.01-296 at the time a copy of the motion for judgment or warrant is so served, the plaintiff shall be entitled to a judgment on the affidavit and statement of account without further evidence unless the defendant either appears and pleads under oath or files with the court before the return date an affidavit or responsive pleading denying that the plaintiff is entitled to recover from the defendant on the claim. A denial by the defendant in general district court need not be in writing. The plaintiff or defendant shall, on motion, be granted a continuance whenever the defendant appears and pleads. If the defendant's pleading or affidavit admits that the plaintiff is entitled to recover from the defendant a sum certain less than that stated in the affidavit filed by the plaintiff, judgment may be taken by the plaintiff for the sum so admitted to be due, and the case will be tried as to the residue.

In the event of a defect in the affidavit, the plaintiff shall be entitled to a continuance.

Acts 1977, c. 617; Acts 1983, c. 136; Acts 1991, c. 56; Acts 1991, c. 503. Amended by Acts 2014, c. 688.

§ 8.01-29. Procedure in actions on annuity and installment bonds, and other actions for penalties for nonperformance

In an action on an annuity bond, or a bond for money payable by installments, when there are further payments of the annuity, or further installments to become due after the commencement of the action, or in any other action for a penalty for the nonperformance of any condition, covenant, or agreement, the plaintiff may assign as many breaches as he may think fit, and shall, in his motion for judgment assign the specific breaches for which the action is brought. The jury impaneled in any such action shall ascertain the damages sustained, or the sum due, by reason of the breaches assigned, and judgment shall be entered for the penalty, to be discharged by the payment of what is so ascertained, and such further sums as may be afterwards assessed. Motion may be made by any person injured against the defendant and, for what may be assessed or found due upon the new breach or breaches assigned, execution may be awarded.

Acts 1977, c. 617.

§ 8.01-30. Procedure in actions on contracts made by several persons

Upon all contracts hereafter made by more than one person, whether joint only or joint and several, an action may be maintained and judgment rendered against all liable thereon, or any one or any intermediate number, and if, in an action on any contract heretofore or hereafter made, more than one person be sued and process be served on only a part of them, the plaintiff may dismiss or proceed to judgment as to any so served, and either discontinue as to the others, or from time to time as the process is served, proceed to judgment against them until judgment be obtained against all. Such dismissal or discontinuance of the action as to any defendant shall not operate as a bar to any subsequent action which may be brought against him for the same cause.

Acts 1977, c. 617.

§ 8.01-31. Accounting in equity

An accounting in equity may be had against any fiduciary or by one joint tenant, tenant in common, or coparcener for receiving more than comes to his just share or proportion, or against the personal representative of any such party.

Acts 1977, c. 617.

§ 8.01-32. Action on lost evidences of debt

A. A civil action may be maintained on any past-due lost bond, note, contract, open account agreement, or other written evidence of debt, provided the plaintiff verifies under oath either in open court or by affidavit that said bond, note, contract, open account agreement, or other written evidence of debt has been lost or destroyed.

B. Where a true and accurate copy of the written evidence of debt exists, which copy was produced in the normal course of business, the court shall accept such copy into evidence and shall give effect to its terms as if the original had been placed into evidence.

C. In the event of any inconsistency between this section and any applicable provisions of § 8.3A-309, the provisions of that section shall control.

Acts 1977, c. 617; Acts 2000, c. 245; Acts 2003, c. 125.

§ 8.01-33. Equitable relief in certain cases

A court shall not grant equitable relief in a suit upon a bond, note, or writing, by an assignee or holder thereof, unless it appears that the plaintiff had no adequate remedy thereon at law.

Acts 1977, c. 617. Amended by Acts 2005, c. 681, eff. Jan. 1, 2006.

Article 3

Injury to Person or Property

§ 8.01–34. When contribution among wrongdoers enforced

Contribution among wrongdoers may be enforced when the wrong results from negligence and involves no moral turpitude.

Acts 1977, c. 617.

§ 8.01–35. Damages for loss of income not diminished by reimbursement

In any suit brought for personal injury or death, provable damages for loss of income due to such injury or death shall not be diminished because of reimbursement of income to the plaintiff or decedent from any other source, nor shall the fact of any such reimbursement be admitted into evidence.

Acts 1977, c. 617.

§ 8.01–35.1. Effect of release or covenant not to sue in respect to liability and contribution

A. When a release or a covenant not to sue is given in good faith to one of two or more persons liable for the same injury to a person or property, or the same wrongful death:

1. It shall not discharge any other person from liability for the injury, property damage or wrongful death unless its terms so provide; but any amount recovered against the other person or any one of them shall be reduced by any amount stipulated by the covenant or the release, or in the amount of the consideration paid for it, whichever is the greater. In determining the amount of consideration given for a covenant not to sue or release for a settlement which consists in whole or in part of future payment or payments, the court shall consider expert or other evidence as to the present value of the settlement consisting in whole or in part of future payment or payments. A release or covenant not to sue given pursuant to this section shall not be admitted into evidence in the trial of the matter but shall be considered by the court in determining the amount for which judgment shall be entered; and

2. It shall discharge the person to whom it is given from all liability for contribution to any other person liable for the same injury to person or property or the same wrongful death.

B. A person who enters into a release or covenant not to sue with a claimant is not entitled to recover by way of contribution from another person whose liability for the injury, property damage or wrongful death is not extinguished by the release or covenant not to sue, nor in respect to any amount paid by the person which is in excess of what was reasonable.

C. For the purposes of this section, a covenant not to sue shall include any "high-low" agreement whereby a party seeking damages for injury to a person or property, or for wrongful death, agrees to accept as full satisfaction for any judgment no more than one sum certain and the party or parties from whom the damages are sought agree to pay no less than another sum certain regardless of whether any judgment rendered at trial is higher or lower than the respective sums certain set forth in the agreement and whereby such party provides notice to all of the other parties of the terms of such "high-low" agreement immediately after such agreement is reached.

D. A release or covenant not to sue given pursuant to this section shall be subject to the provisions of §§ 8.01–55 and 8.01–424.

E. This section shall apply to all such covenants not to sue executed on or after July 1, 1979, and to all releases executed on or after July 1, 1980. This section shall also apply to all oral covenants not to sue and oral releases agreed to on or after July 1, 1989, provided that any cause of action affected thereby accrues on or after July 1, 1989. A release or covenant not to sue need not be in writing where parties to a pending action state in open court that they have agreed to enter into such release or covenant not to sue and have agreed further to subsequently memorialize the same in writing.

Acts 1979, c. 697; Acts 1980, c. 411; Acts 1982, c. 196; Acts 1983, c. 181; Acts 1985, c. 330; Acts 1989, c. 681; Acts 2000, c. 351. Amended by Acts 2007, c. 443.

§ 8.01–36. Joinder of action of tort to infant with action for recovery of expenses incurred thereby and claim for recovery of expenses by infant

A. Where there is pending any action by an infant plaintiff against a tort-feasor for a personal injury, where the cause of action accrued prior to July 1, 2013, any parent or guardian of such infant, who is entitled to recover from the same tort-feasor the expenses of curing or attempting to cure such infant from the result of such personal injury, may bring an action against such tort-feasor for such expenses, in the same court where such infant's case is pending, either in the action filed in behalf of the infant or in a separate action. If the claim for expenses be by separate action, upon motion of any party to either case, made to the court at least one week before the trial, both cases shall be tried together at the same time as parts of the same transaction. But separate verdicts when there is a jury trial shall be rendered, and the judgment shall distinctly separate the decision and judgment in the separate causes of action.

In the event of the cases being carried to the Supreme Court, which may be done if there be the jurisdictional amount in either case, they shall both be carried together as one case and record, but the Supreme Court shall clearly specify the decision in each case, separating them in the decision to the extent necessary to do justice among the parties.

B. For causes of action that accrue on or after July 1, 2013, the past and future expenses of curing or attempting to cure an infant of personal injuries proximately caused by a tort-feasor are damages recoverable by an infant in a cause of action against the tort-feasor and, if applicable to the infant's cause of action, are subject to the limitation on damages in § 8.01–581.15. Any parent or guardian of such infant who has paid for or is personally obligated to pay for past or future expenses to cure or attempt to cure the infant shall have a lien and right of reimbursement against any recovery by the infant up to the amount the parent or guardian has actually paid or is personally obligated to pay. The right to reimbursement of any parent or guardian shall accrue upon the first tender of funds of any recovery from a tort-feasor to the infant. Court approval of the infant settlement shall release party defendants from all claims for past or future expenses of curing or attempting to cure the infant.

Nothing in this section shall relieve a parent of the obligation to pay for the medical expenses of curing or attempting to cure the infant as such obligation exists under current law.

Acts 1977, c. 617. Amended by Acts 2013, c. 551; Acts 2013, c. 689.

§ 8.01–37. Recovery of lost wages in action for injuries to emancipated infant

In any suit for personal injuries brought on behalf of an emancipated infant, when such infant has sustained lost wages as a result of such injuries, he shall be entitled to recover such lost wages as a part of his damages. Where recovery is made hereunder or where recovery is attempted to be made and a decision on the merits adverse to said infant results, no other person may recover such lost wages.

Acts 1977, c. 617.

§ 8.01–37.1. Claims for medical services provided by United States; proof of reasonable value

Whenever any person sustains personal injuries caused by the alleged negligence of another, and a claim against any person alleged to be liable is created in favor of the United States under federal law (42 U.S.C. § 2651 et seq.) for the reasonable value of medical, surgical or dental care and treatment provided, the injured party may, on behalf of the United States, claim the reasonable value of the medical services provided as an element of damages in a civil action against the person alleged to be liable. It shall not be required that the United States intervene in the action or be made a party in order to establish its claim. A sworn written statement of the authorized representative of the department or agency providing such services prepared in accordance with the regulations promulgated pursuant to 42 U.S.C. § 2652 shall be admissible as evidence of the reasonable value of the care and treatment provided.

Acts 1984, c. 42; Acts 1985, c. 205.

§ 8.01–38. Tort liability of hospitals

Hospital as referred to in this section shall include any institution within the definition of hospital in § 32.1–123.

No hospital, as defined in this section, shall be immune from liability for negligence or any other tort on the ground that it is a charitable institution unless (i) such hospital renders exclusively charitable medical services for which service no bill for service is rendered to, nor any charge is ever made to the patient or (ii) the party alleging such negligence or other tort was accepted as a patient by such institution under an express written agreement executed by the hospital and delivered at the time of admission to the patient or the person admitting such patient providing that all medical services furnished such patient are to be supplied on a charitable basis without financial liability to the patient. However, notwithstanding the provisions of § 8.01–581.15 a hospital which is exempt from taxation pursuant to § 501 (c) (3) of Title 26 of the United States Code (Internal Revenue Code of 1954) and which is insured against liability for negligence or other tort in an amount not less than $500,000 for each occurrence shall not be liable for damage in excess of the limits of such insurance, or in actions for medical malpractice pursuant to Chapter 21.1 (§ 8.01–581.1 et seq.) for damages in excess of the amount set forth in § 8.01–581.15.

Acts 1977, c. 617; Acts 1983, c. 496; Acts 1986, c. 389; Acts 1986, c. 454; Acts 2000, c. 464.

§ 8.01–38.1. Limitation on recovery of punitive damages

In any action accruing on or after July 1, 1988, including an action for medical malpractice under Chapter 21.1 (§ 8.01–581.1 et seq.), the total amount awarded for punitive damages against all defendants found to be liable shall be determined by the trier of fact. In no event shall the total amount awarded for punitive damages exceed $350,000. The jury shall not be advised of the limitation prescribed by this section. However, if a jury returns a verdict for punitive damages in excess of the maximum amount specified in this section, the judge shall reduce the award and enter judgment for such damages in the maximum amount provided by this section.

Acts 1987, c. 255.

§ 8.01-39. Completion or acceptance of work not bar to action against independent contractor for personal injury, wrongful death or damage to property

In any civil action in which it is alleged that personal injury, death by wrongful act or damage to property has resulted from the negligence of or breach of warranty by an independent contractor, it shall not be a defense by such contractor to such action that such contractor has completed such work or that such work has been accepted as satisfactory by the owner of the property upon which the work was done or by the person hiring such contractor.

Nothing contained herein shall be construed to limit, modify or otherwise affect the provisions of § 8.01-250.

Acts 1977, c. 617.

§ 8.01-40. Unauthorized use of name or picture of any person; punitive damages; statute of limitations

A. Any person whose name, portrait, or picture is used without having first obtained the written consent of such person, or if dead, of the surviving consort and if none, of the next of kin, or if a minor, the written consent of his or her parent or guardian, for advertising purposes or for the purposes of trade, such persons may maintain a suit in equity against the person, firm, or corporation so using such person's name, portrait, or picture to prevent and restrain the use thereof; and may also sue and recover damages for any injuries sustained by reason of such use. And if the defendant shall have knowingly used such person's name, portrait or picture in such manner as is forbidden or declared to be unlawful by this chapter, the jury, in its discretion, may award punitive damages.

B. No action shall be commenced under this section more than 20 years after the death of such person.

Acts 1977, c. 617. Amended by Acts 2015, c. 710.

§ 8.01-40.1. Action for injury resulting from violation of Computer Crimes Act; limitations

Any person whose property or person is injured by reason of a violation of the provisions of the Virginia Computer Crimes Act (§ 18.2-152.1 et seq.) may sue and recover damages as provided in § 18.2-152.12. An action shall be commenced before the earlier of (i) five years after the last act in the course of conduct constituting a violation of the Computer Crimes Act or (ii) two years after the plaintiff discovers or reasonably should have discovered the last act in the course of conduct constituting a violation of the Computer Crimes Act.

Acts 1985, c. 92.

§ 8.01-40.2. Unsolicited transmission of advertising materials by facsimile machine

A. Any person aggrieved by the intentional electronic or telephonic transmission to a facsimile device of unsolicited advertising material may bring an action against the person responsible for the transmission to enjoin further violations and to recover the greater of (i) actual damages sustained, together with costs and reasonable attorneys' fees, or (ii) $500. Carriers or other companies which provide facsimile transmission services shall not be responsible for transmissions of unsolicited advertising materials by their customers. An action brought pursuant to this section shall be commenced within two years of the transmission.

B. Any intentional transmission to a facsimile device of any unsolicited advertising material shall be a violation of the Virginia Consumer Protection Act (§ 59.1-196 et seq.).

Acts 1990, c. 246; Acts 2003, c. 800.

§ 8.01-40.3. Unauthorized dissemination, etc., of criminal history record information; civil action

A. Any person who disseminates, publishes, or maintains or causes to be disseminated, published, or maintained the criminal history record information as defined in § 9.1-101 of an individual pertaining to that individual's charge or arrest for a criminal offense and solicits, requests, or accepts money or other thing of value for removing such criminal history record information shall be liable to the individual who is the subject of the information for actual damages or $500, whichever is greater, in addition to reasonable attorney fees and costs.

B. Nothing in this section shall be construed to impose liability on:

1. An interactive computer service, as defined in 47 U.S.C. § 230(f), for content provided by another person.

2. Any speech protected by Article I, Section 12 of the Constitution of Virginia.

C. As used in this section, "criminal history record information" means the same as that term is defined in § 9.1-101.

Added by Acts 2015, c. 414; Acts 2015, c. 415.

§ 8.01-41. Wrongful distraint, attachment

If property be distrained for any rent not due, or attached for any rent not accruing, or taken under any attachment sued out without good cause, the owner of such property may, in an action against the party suing out the warrant of distress or attachment, recover damages for the wrongful distraint, seizure, or sale.

Acts 1977, c. 617.

§ 8.01–42. Loss or injury to clothing in dyeing, dry cleaning, or laundering

No person engaged in the business of dyeing, dry cleaning, or laundering wearing apparel, cloth or other articles, shall be liable, or in any action or suit against him be held liable, for the loss of, or injury to, any wearing apparel, cloth or other articles delivered to him to be dyed, dry cleaned, or laundered, in an amount greater than the purchase price minus depreciation of such wearing apparel, cloth or other articles, unless at the time of the delivery to him of any such wearing apparel, cloth or other articles, the value of the same, and when there is more than one piece or article the value of each piece or article, be agreed upon and evidenced by a writing stating such value, or separate values when there is more than one piece or article, signed by him; provided, however, that:

1. Nothing in this section contained shall be construed as requiring of any such person more than the exercise of such degree of care as is now imposed by existing law;

2. In no event shall any such person be held liable in any suit or action involving any such loss or injury for any sum greater than the damages suffered, and proved, by the plaintiff therein when such damages would not under the rules of law existing prior to June 18, 1920, exceed the purchase price minus depreciation of such wearing apparel, cloth, or other article;

3. Nothing in this section shall be construed as interfering with or inhibiting, or impairing the obligation of, any written contract between any hotel, railroad company, steamboat company or other patron and any person engaged in the business of dyeing, dry cleaning, or laundering of wearing apparel, cloth or other article, in relation to such work;

4. No liability shall rest upon or be borne by any hotel for any loss of or damage to wearing apparel, cloth or other article, the property of any guest of such hotel who shall have delivered, or caused the same to have been delivered, for dyeing, dry cleaning, or laundering to any person engaged in the business of dyeing, dry cleaning, or laundering.

5. Repealed.

Acts 1977, c. 192; Acts 1977, c. 617.

§ 8.01–42.1. Civil action for racial, religious, or ethnic harassment, violence or vandalism

A. An action for injunctive relief or civil damages, or both, shall lie for any person who is subjected to acts of (i) intimidation or harassment or (ii) violence directed against his person; or (iii) vandalism directed against his real or personal property, where such acts are motivated by racial, religious, or ethnic animosity.

B. Any aggrieved party who initiates and prevails in an action authorized by this section shall be entitled to damages, including punitive damages, and in the discretion of the court to an award of the cost of the litigation and reasonable attorneys' fees in an amount to be fixed by the court.

C. The provisions of this section shall not apply to any actions between an employee and his employer, or between or among employees of the same employer, for damages arising out of incidents occurring in the workplace or arising out of the employee-employer relationship.

Acts 1988, c. 492.

§ 8.01–42.2. Liability of guest for hotel damage

Any registered guest in a hotel, motel, inn or other place offering to the public transitory lodging or sleeping accommodations for compensation shall be civilly liable to the innkeeper for all property damage to such accommodation or its furnishings which occurs during the period of such person's occupancy when such damage results (i) from the negligence of the guest or of any person for whom he is legally responsible or (ii) from the failure of the guest to comply with reasonable rules and regulations of which he is given actual notice by the innkeeper.

Acts 1989, c. 426.

§ 8.01–42.3. Civil action for stalking

A. A victim has a civil cause of action against an individual who engaged in conduct that is prohibited under § 18.2–60.3, whether or not the individual has been charged or convicted for the alleged violation, for the compensatory damages incurred by the victim as a result of that conduct, in addition to the costs for bringing the action. If compensatory damages are awarded, a victim may also be awarded punitive damages.

B. As used in this section:

"Compensatory damages" includes damages for all of the defendant's acts prohibited by § 18.2–60.3.

"Victim" means a person who, because of the conduct of the defendant that is prohibited under § 18.2–60.3, was placed in reasonable fear of death, criminal sexual assault, or bodily injury to himself or to a minor child of whom the person is a parent or legal guardian.

C. No action shall be commenced under this section more than two years after the most recent conduct prohibited under § 18.2–60.3.

Acts 2001, c. 444.

§ 8.01–43. Action against parent for damage to public property by minor

The Commonwealth, acting through the officers having charge of the public property involved, or the governing body of a county, city, town, or other political subdivision, or a school board may institute an action and recover from the parents or either of them of any minor living with such parents or either of them for damages suffered by reason of the willful or

malicious destruction of, or damage to, public property by such minor. No more than $2,500 may be recovered from such parents or either of them as a result of any incident or occurrence on which such action is based.
Acts 1977, c. 617; Acts 1983, c. 330; Acts 1987, c. 193; Acts 1994, c. 508; Acts 1994, c. 552; Acts 1996, c. 698.

§ 8.01-44. Action against parent for damage to private property by minor

The owner of any property may institute an action and recover from the parents, or either of them, of any minor living with such parents, or either of them, for damages suffered by reason of the willful or malicious destruction of, or damage to, such property by such minor. No more than $2,500 may be recovered from such parents, or either of them, as a result of any incident or occurrence on which such action is based. Any recovery from the parent or parents of such minor shall not preclude full recovery from such minor except to the amount of the recovery from such parent or parents. The provisions of this statute shall be in addition to, and not in lieu of, any other law imposing upon a parent liability for the acts of his minor child.
Acts 1977, c. 617; Acts 1984, c. 48; Acts 1987, c. 193; Acts 1994, c. 508; Acts 1994, c. 552; Acts 1996, c. 698.

§ 8.01-44.1. Immunity from civil liability of members of certain committees, etc.

Every member of any committee, board, group, commission, or other entity established pursuant to federal or state law or regulation which functions to authorize, review, evaluate, or make recommendations on the nature, conduct, activities, or procedures involved in or related to programs or research protocols conducted under the supervision of members of the faculty or staff of any hospital, college, or university, including but not limited to the design or conduct of experiments involving human subjects, shall be immune from civil liability for any act, decision, omission, or utterance done or made in performance of such duties as a member of such committee, board, group, commission, or other entity, unless such act, decision, omission, or utterance is done or made in bad faith or with malicious intent or unless the member, when acting to authorize the nature, conduct, activities, or procedures involved in or related to a program or research protocol, knows or reasonably should know that the program or research protocol is being or will be conducted in violation of Chapter 5.1 (§ 32.1-162.16 et seq.) of Title 32.1. However, the immunity created herein shall not apply to those persons engaged in the actual conduct of the programs or research protocols.
Acts 1980, c. 479; Acts 1981, c. 40; Acts 1992, c. 603.

§ 8.01-44.2. Action against physician for vaccine-related injury or death

In any case where a person could file or could have filed a petition for compensation pursuant to Subtitle 2 of Title XXI of the Public Health Services Act of the United States (42 U.S.C. § 300aa-10 et seq.) for the vaccine-related injury or death associated with the administration of a vaccine in the Commonwealth by or under the supervision of a physician licensed to practice medicine in Virginia, no civil action shall lie against such physician, or any person administering such vaccine on behalf of such physician for injury or death resulting from an adverse reaction to such vaccine, except where such injury or death was caused by gross negligence of the physician, his agents or employees, in the administration of such vaccine.
Acts 1987, c. 664.

§ 8.01-44.3. Divulgence of communications by qualified interpreters and communications assistants

If the content of any communication which is facilitated for compensation in the professional capacity of a qualified interpreter, as defined in § 51.5-113, or in the professional capacity of any communications assistant employed by the statewide dual party relay service established under Article 5 (§ 56-484.4 et seq.) of Chapter 15 of Title 56, is divulged by such interpreter or assistant, any such party to the communication aggrieved by such divulgence may recover from such interpreter or assistant the greater of (i) actual damages sustained, together with costs and reasonable attorneys' fees, or (ii) $100. No such recovery shall be permitted if the interpreter or assistant and the parties to the communication have agreed that the interpreter or assistant may divulge the content of the communication.
Acts 1992, c. 614.

§ 8.01-44.4. Action for shoplifting and employee theft

A. A merchant may recover a civil judgment against any adult or emancipated minor who shoplifts from that merchant for two times the unpaid retail value of the merchandise, but in no event an amount less than $50. However, if the merchant recovers the merchandise in merchantable condition, he shall be entitled to liquidated damages of no more than $350.

B. A merchant may recover a civil judgment against any person who commits employee theft for two times the unpaid retail value of the merchandise, but in no event an amount less than $50. However, if the merchant recovers the merchandise in merchantable condition, he shall be entitled to liquidated damages of no more than $350.

C. The prevailing party in any action brought pursuant to this section shall be entitled to reasonable attorneys' fees and costs not to exceed $150.

D. A conviction of or a plea of guilty to a violation of any other statute is not a prerequisite to commencement of a civil action pursuant to this section or enforcement of a judgment. No action may be initiated under this section during the pendency of a criminal prosecution based on the same allegations of fact; however the initiation of any criminal action against the perpetrator for the alleged offense under § 18.2–95, 18.2–96, 18.2–102.1, or 18.2–103 or any other criminal offense defined under subsection F does not preclude a merchant from initiating or maintaining an action under this section once the prosecution has been concluded. A merchant may not recover more than the retail value of the merchandise, or more than the unpaid retail value of the merchandise if the merchandise is not recovered in a merchantable condition, for the same loss if both criminal and civil actions are initiated. However, nothing herein shall preclude a merchant from recovering damages in excess of the retail value of the merchandise, or the unpaid retail value of the merchandise if the merchandise is not recovered in a merchantable condition, if a criminal action is initiated. Nothing herein shall preclude a merchant from nonsuiting the civil action brought pursuant to this section and proceeding criminally under § 18.2–95, 18.2–96, 18.2–102.1, or 18.2–103 or any other criminal offense defined under subsection F.

E. Prior to the commencement of any action under this section, a merchant may demand, in writing, that an individual who may be civilly liable under this section make appropriate payment to the merchant in consideration for the merchant's agreement not to commence any legal action under this section.

F. For purposes of this section:

"Employee theft" means the removal of any merchandise or cash from the premises of the merchant's establishment or the concealment of any merchandise or cash by a person employed by a merchant without the consent of the merchant and with the purpose or intent of appropriating the merchandise or cash to the employee's own or another's use without full payment.

"Shoplift" means any one or more of the following acts committed by a person without the consent of the merchant and with the purpose or intent of appropriating merchandise to that person's own or another's use without payment, obtaining merchandise at less than its stated sales price, or otherwise depriving a merchant of all or any part of the value or use of merchandise: (i) removing any merchandise from the premises of the merchant's establishment; (ii) concealing any merchandise; (iii) substituting, altering, removing, or disfiguring any label or price tag; (iv) transferring any merchandise from a container in which that merchandise is displayed or packaged to any other container; (v) disarming any alarm tag attached to any merchandise; or (vi) obtaining or attempting to obtain possession of any merchandise by charging that merchandise to another person without the authority of that person or by charging that merchandise to a fictitious person.

Acts 1992, c. 721. Amended by Acts 2005, c. 142; Acts 2005, c. 234; Acts 2012, c. 526.

§ 8.01–44.5. Punitive damages for persons injured by intoxicated drivers

In any action for personal injury or death arising from the operation of a motor vehicle, engine or train, the finder of fact may, in its discretion, award punitive damages to the plaintiff if the evidence proves that the defendant acted with malice toward the plaintiff or the defendant's conduct was so willful or wanton as to show a conscious disregard for the rights of others.

A defendant's conduct shall be deemed sufficiently willful or wanton as to show a conscious disregard for the rights of others when the evidence proves that (i) when the incident causing the injury or death occurred, the defendant had a blood alcohol concentration of 0.15 percent or more by weight by volume or 0.15 grams or more per 210 liters of breath; (ii) at the time the defendant began drinking alcohol, or during the time he was drinking alcohol, he knew or should have known that his ability to operate a motor vehicle, engine or train would be impaired, or when he was operating a motor vehicle he knew or should have known that his ability to operate a motor vehicle was impaired; and (iii) the defendant's intoxication was a proximate cause of the injury to or death of the plaintiff. For the purposes of clause (i), it shall be rebuttably presumed that the blood alcohol concentration at the time of the incident causing injury or death was at least as high as the test result as shown in a certificate issued pursuant to § 18.2–268.9 or in a certificate of analysis for a blood test administered pursuant to § 18.2–268.7, provided that the test was administered within three hours of the incident causing injury or death. In addition to any other forms of proof, a party may submit a copy of a certificate issued pursuant to § 18.2–268.9 or a certificate of analysis for a blood test administered pursuant to § 18.2–268.7, which shall be prima facie evidence of the facts contained therein.

However, when a defendant has unreasonably refused to submit to a test of his blood alcohol content as required by § 18.2–268.2, a defendant's conduct shall be deemed sufficiently willful or wanton as to show a conscious disregard for the rights of others when the evidence proves that (a) when the incident causing the injury or death occurred the defendant was intoxicated, which may be established by evidence concerning the conduct or condition of the defendant; (b) at the time the defendant began drinking alcohol, or during the time he was drinking alcohol, he knew or should have known that his ability to operate a motor vehicle was impaired; and (c) the defendant's intoxication was a proximate cause of the injury to the plaintiff or death of the plaintiff's decedent. In addition to any other forms of proof, a party may submit a certified copy of a court's determination of unreasonable refusal pursuant to § 18.2–268.3, which shall be prima facie evidence that the defendant unreasonably refused to submit to the test.

Acts 1994, c. 570; Acts 1998, c. 722; Acts 1999, c. 324; Acts 2002, c. 879. Amended by Acts 2013, c. 636; Acts 2015, c. 710.

§ 8.01–44.6. Action for injury to cemetery property

The owner or operator of a cemetery company may bring an action to recover damages sustained, together with costs and reasonable attorneys' fees, against any person who willfully or maliciously destroys, mutilates, defaces, injures, or removes any tomb, monument, gravestone, or other structure placed within any cemetery, graveyard, or place of burial, or within any lot belonging to any memorial or monumental association, or any fence, railing, or other work for the protection or ornament of any tomb, monument, gravestone, or other structure aforesaid, or of any cemetery lot within any cemetery. The cemetery owner or operator may recover, as part of damages sustained, the cost of repair or replacement of damaged property, including any labor costs, regardless of whether the property damaged is owned by the cemetery or by another person.

Added by Acts 2004, c. 203.

§ 8.01–44.7. Action for tampering with metering device and diverting service

Any provider of services that have been tampered with or diverted in violation of § 18.2–163 may seek both injunctive and equitable relief, and an award of damages, including reasonable attorney fees and costs. In addition to any other remedy provided by law, the party aggrieved may recover an award of actual damages or $500 whichever is greater for each action.

Added by Acts 2006, c. 350.

ARTICLE 4

DEFAMATION

§ 8.01–45. Action for insulting words

All words shall be actionable which from their usual construction and common acceptance are construed as insults and tend to violence and breach of the peace.

Acts 1977, c. 617.

§ 8.01–46. Justification and mitigation of damages

In any action for defamation, the defendant may justify by alleging and proving that the words spoken or written were true, and, after notice in writing of his intention to do so, given to the plaintiff at the time of, or for, pleading to such action, may give in evidence, in mitigation of damages, that he made or offered an apology to the plaintiff for such defamation before the commencement of the action, or as soon afterwards as he had an opportunity of doing so in case the action shall have been commenced before there was an opportunity of making or offering such apology.

Acts 1977, c. 617.

§ 8.01–46.1. Disclosure of employment-related information; presumptions; causes of action; definitions

A. Any employer who, upon request by a person's prospective or current employer, furnishes information about that person's professional conduct, reasons for separation or job performance, including, but not limited to, information contained in any written performance evaluations, shall be immune from civil liability for furnishing such information, provided that the employer is not acting in bad faith. An employer shall be presumed to be acting in good faith. The presumption of good faith shall be rebutted if it is shown by clear and convincing evidence that the employer disclosed such information with knowledge that it was false, or with reckless disregard for whether it is false or not, or with the intent to deliberately mislead.

B. In a civil action brought against an employer for disclosing the information described in subsection A, if the trier of fact determines the employer acted in bad faith, punitive damages may be awarded, as provided by § 8.01–38.1.

C. As used in this section, the following words and phrases shall have the following meanings:

"Employee" means any person, paid or unpaid, in the service of an employer.

"Employer" means any person, firm or corporation, including the Commonwealth of Virginia and its political subdivisions, and their agents, who has one or more employees or individuals performing services under any contract of hire or service, express or implied, oral or written.

"Information" includes, but is not limited to, facts, data and opinions.

"Job performance" includes, but is not limited to, ability, attendance, awards, demotions, duties, effort, evaluations, knowledge, skills, promotions, productivity and disciplinary actions.

"Professional conduct" includes, but is not limited to, the ethical standards which govern the employee's profession, or lawful conduct which is expected of the employee by the employer.

"Prospective employer" means any employer who is considering a person for employment.

Acts 2000, c. 1005.

§ 8.01–47. Immunity of persons investigating or reporting certain incidents at schools

In addition to any other immunity he may have, any person who, in good faith with reasonable cause and without malice, acts to report, investigate or cause any investigation to be made into the activities of any student or students or any other person or persons as they relate to conduct involving bomb threats, firebombs, explosive materials or other similar devices as described in clauses (vi) and (vii) of subsection A of § 22.1–279.3:1, alcohol or drug use or abuse in or related to the school or institution or in connection with any school or institution activity, or information that an individual poses any credible danger of serious bodily injury or death to one or more students, school personnel, or others on school property shall be immune from all civil liability that might otherwise be incurred or imposed as the result of the making of such a report, investigation or disclosure.

Acts 1977, c. 617; Acts 1982, c. 259; Acts 1988, c. 159; Acts 1995, c. 759; Acts 2000, c. 79; Acts 2001, c. 688; Acts 2001, c. 820; Acts 2003, c. 954. Amended by Acts 2013, c. 665.

§ 8.01–48. Mitigation in actions against newspapers, etc.

In any civil action against the publisher, owner, editor, reporter or employee of any newspaper, magazine or periodical under § 8.01–45, or for libel or defamation, because of any article, statement or other matter contained in any such newspaper, magazine or periodical, the defendant, whether punitive damages be sought or not, may introduce in evidence in mitigation of general and punitive damages, or either, but not of actual pecuniary damages, all the circumstances of the publication, including the source of the information, its character as affording reasonable ground of reliance, any prior publication elsewhere of similar purport, the lack of negligence or malice on the part of the defendant, the good faith of the defendant in such publication, or that apology or retraction, if any, was made with reasonable promptness and fairness; provided that the defendant may introduce in evidence only such circumstances and to the extent set forth in his or its grounds of defense.

Acts 1977, c. 617.

§ 8.01–49. Defamatory statements in radio and television broadcasts

The owner, licensee or operator of a radio and television broadcasting station or network of stations, and the agents or employees of any such owner, licensee or operator, shall not be liable for any damages for any defamatory statement published or uttered in or as a part of any such broadcast, by one other than such owner, licensee or operator, or agent or employee thereof, unless it shall be alleged and proved by the complaining party, that such owner, licensee, operator, such agent or employee, failed to exercise due care to prevent the publication or utterance of such statement in such broadcast; provided, however, that in no event shall any owner, licensee or operator, or the agents or employees of any such owner, licensee or operator of such a station or network of stations be held liable for damages for any defamatory statement broadcast over the facilities of such station or network by or on behalf of any candidate for public office.

Acts 1977, c. 617.

§ 8.01–49.1. Liability for defamatory material on the Internet

A. No provider or user of an interactive computer service on the Internet shall be treated as the publisher or speaker of any information provided to it by another information content provider. No provider or user of an interactive computer service shall be liable for (i) any action voluntarily taken by it in good faith to restrict access to, or availability of, material that the provider or user considers to be obscene, lewd, lascivious, excessively violent, harassing, or intended to incite hatred on the basis of race, religious conviction, color, or national origin, whether or not such material is constitutionally protected, or (ii) any action taken to enable, or make available to information content providers or others, the technical means to restrict access to information provided by another information content provider.

B. Definitions. As used in this section:

"Information content provider" means any person or entity that is responsible, in whole or in part, for the creation or development of information provided through the Internet or any other interactive computer service.

"Interactive computer service" means any information service, system, or access software provider that provides or enables computer access by multiple users to a computer server, including specifically a service or system that provides access to the Internet and such systems operated or services offered by libraries or educational institutions.

"Internet" means the international computer network of interoperable packet-switched data networks.

Acts 2000, c. 930.

Article 5

Death by Wrongful Act

§ 8.01–50. Action for death by wrongful act; how and when to be brought

A. Whenever the death of a person shall be caused by the wrongful act, neglect, or default of any person or corporation, or of any ship or vessel, and the act, neglect, or default is such as would, if death had not ensued, have entitled the party injured to maintain an action, or to proceed in rem against such ship or vessel or in personam against the owners thereof or those having control of her, and to recover damages in respect thereof, then, and in every such case, the person who, or corporation or ship or vessel which, would have been liable, if death had not ensued, shall be liable to an action for damages, or, if a ship or vessel, to a libel in rem, and her owners or those responsible for her acts or defaults or negligence to a libel in personam, notwithstanding the death of the person injured, and although the death shall have been caused under such circumstances, as amount in law to a felony.

B. Whenever a fetal death, as defined in § 32.1–249, is caused by the wrongful act, neglect, or default of any person, ship, vessel, or corporation, the natural mother of the fetus may bring an action pursuant to this section against such tortfeasor. Nothing in this section shall be construed to create a cause of action for a fetal death against the natural mother of the fetus.

C. Every such action under subsection A shall be brought by and in the name of the personal representative of such deceased person. Actions for fetal death under subsection B shall be brought by and in the name of the natural mother; provided, however, if the natural mother dies, or is or becomes a person under a disability as defined in § 8.01–2, such action may be initiated or maintained by the administrator of the natural mother's estate, her guardian, or her personal representative qualified to bring such action. In an action for fetal death under subsection B brought under Chapter 21.1 (§ 8.01–581.1 et seq.) where the wrongful act that resulted in a fetal death also resulted in the death of another fetus of the natural mother or in the death or injury of the natural mother, recovery for all damages sustained as a result of such wrongful act shall not exceed the limitations on the total amount recoverable for a single patient for any injury under § 8.01–581.15. The person bringing an action under subsection B shall have the power to compromise a claim pursuant to § 8.01–55 and any damages recovered shall be distributed pursuant to this article. Every such action under this section shall be brought within the time limits specified in § 8.01–244.

D. If the deceased person was an infant who was in the custody of a parent pursuant to an order of court or written agreement with the other parent, administration shall be granted first to the parent having custody; however, that parent may waive his right to qualify in favor of any other person designated by him. If no such parent or his designee applies for administration within 30 days from the death of the infant, administration shall be granted as in other cases.

E. For purposes of this section, "natural mother" means the woman carrying the child.

Acts 1977, c. 617; Acts 1981, c. 115. Amended by Acts 2012, c. 725.

§ 8.01–50.1. Certification of expert witness opinion at time of service of process

Every motion for judgment, counter claim, or third party claim in any action pursuant to § 8.01–50 for wrongful death against a health care provider, at the time the plaintiff requests service of process upon a defendant, or requests a defendant to accept service of process, shall be deemed a certification that the plaintiff has obtained from an expert witness whom the plaintiff reasonably believes would qualify as an expert witness pursuant to subsection A of § 8.01–581.20 a written opinion signed by the expert witness that, based upon a reasonable understanding of the facts, the defendant for whom service of process has been requested deviated from the applicable standard of care and the deviation was a proximate cause of the injuries claimed. This certification is not necessary if the plaintiff, in good faith, alleges in his wrongful death action a medical malpractice theory of liability where expert testimony is unnecessary because the alleged act of negligence clearly lies within the range of the jury's common knowledge and experience.

The certifying expert shall not be required to be an expert expected to testify at trial nor shall any defendant be entitled to discover the identity or qualifications of the certifying expert or the nature of the certifying expert's opinions. Should the certifying expert be identified as an expert expected to testify at trial, the opinions and bases therefor shall be discoverable pursuant to Rule 4:1 of the Rules of Supreme Court of Virginia with the exception of the expert's status as a certifying expert.

Upon written request of any defendant, the plaintiff shall, within 10 business days after receipt of such request, provide the defendant with a certification form which affirms that the plaintiff had obtained the necessary certifying expert opinion at the time service was requested or affirms that the plaintiff did not need to obtain a certifying expert opinion. The court, upon good cause shown, may conduct an in camera review of the certifying expert opinion obtained by the plaintiff as the court may deem appropriate. If the plaintiff did not obtain a necessary certifying expert opinion at the time the plaintiff requested service of process on a defendant, the court shall impose sanctions according to the provisions of § 8.01–271.1 and may dismiss the case with prejudice.

Added by Acts 2005, c. 649; Acts 2005, c. 692. Amended by Acts 2007, c. 489; Acts 2013, c. 65; Acts 2013, c. 610.

§ 8.01–51. No action when deceased has compromised claim

No action shall be maintained by the personal representative of one who, after injury, has compromised for such injury and accepted satisfaction therefor previous to his death.

Acts 1977, c. 617.

§ 8.01–52. Amount of damages

The jury or the court, as the case may be, in any such action under § 8.01–50 may award such damages as to it may seem fair and just. The verdict or judgment of the court trying the case without a jury shall include, but may not be limited to, damages for the following:

1. Sorrow, mental anguish, and solace which may include society, companionship, comfort, guidance, kindly offices and advice of the decedent;

2. Compensation for reasonably expected loss of (i) income of the decedent and (ii) services, protection, care and assistance provided by the decedent;

3. Expenses for the care, treatment and hospitalization of the decedent incident to the injury resulting in death;

4. Reasonable funeral expenses; and

5. Punitive damages may be recovered for willful or wanton conduct, or such recklessness as evinces a conscious disregard for the safety of others.

Damages recoverable under 3, 4 and 5 above shall be specifically stated by the jury or the court, as the case may be. Damages recoverable under 3 and 4 above shall be apportioned among the creditors who rendered such services, as their respective interests may appear. Competent expert testimony shall be admissible in proving damages recoverable under 2 above.

The court shall apportion the costs of the action as it shall deem proper.

Acts 1977, c. 460; Acts 1977, c. 617; Acts 1982, c. 441.

§ 8.01–52.1. Admissibility of expressions of sympathy

In any wrongful death action brought pursuant to § 8.01–50 against a health care provider, or in any arbitration or medical malpractice review panel proceeding related to such wrongful death action, the portion of statements, writings, affirmations, benevolent conduct, or benevolent gestures expressing sympathy, commiseration, condolence, compassion, or a general sense of benevolence, together with apologies that are made by a health care provider or an agent of a health care provider to a relative of the patient, or a representative of the patient about the death of the patient as a result of the unanticipated outcome of health care, shall be inadmissible as evidence of an admission of liability or as evidence of an admission against interest. A statement of fault that is part of or in addition to any of the above shall not be made inadmissible by this section.

For purposes of this section, unless the context otherwise requires:

"Health care" has the same definition as provided in § 8.01–581.1.

"Health care provider" has the same definition as provided in § 8.01–581.1.

"Relative" means a decedent's spouse, parent, grandparent, stepfather, stepmother, child, grandchild, brother, sister, half-brother, half-sister, or spouse's parents. In addition, "relative" includes any person who had a family-type relationship with the decedent.

"Representative" means a legal guardian, attorney, person designated to make decisions on behalf of a patient under a medical power of attorney, or any person recognized in law or custom as a patient's agent.

"Unanticipated outcome" means the outcome of the delivery of health care that differs from an expected result.

Added by Acts 2005, c. 649; Acts 2005, c. 692. Amended by Acts 2009, c. 414.

§ 8.01–53. Class and beneficiaries; when determined

A. The damages awarded pursuant to § 8.01–52 shall be distributed as specified under § 8.01–54 to (i) the surviving spouse, children of the deceased and children of any deceased child of the deceased or (ii) if there be none such, then to the parents, brothers and sisters of the deceased, and to any other relative who is primarily dependent on the decedent for support or services and is also a member of the same household as the decedent or (iii) if the decedent has left both surviving spouse and parent or parents, but no child or grandchild, the award shall be distributed to the surviving spouse and such parent or parents or (iv) if there are survivors under clause (i) or clause (iii), the award shall be distributed to those beneficiaries and to any other relative who is primarily dependent on the decedent for support or services and is also a member of the same household as the decedent or (v) if no survivors exist under clause (i), (ii), (iii), or (iv), the award shall be distributed in the course of descents as provided for in § 64.2–200. Provided, however, no parent whose parental rights and responsibilities have been terminated by a court of competent jurisdiction or pursuant to a permanent entrustment agreement with a child welfare agency shall be eligible as a beneficiary under this section. For purposes of this section, a relative is any person related to the decedent by blood, marriage, or adoption and also includes a stepchild of the decedent.

B. The class and beneficiaries thereof eligible to receive such distribution shall be fixed (i) at the time the verdict is entered if the jury makes the specification, or (ii) at the time the judgment is rendered if the court specifies the distribution.

C. A beneficiary may renounce his interest in any claim brought pursuant to § 8.01-50 and, in such event, the damages shall be distributed to the beneficiaries in the same class as the renouncing beneficiary or, if there are none, to the beneficiaries in any subsequent class in the order of priority set forth in subsection A.

Acts 1977, c. 460; Acts 1977, c. 617; Acts 1979, c. 356; Acts 1992, c. 74; Acts 1994, c. 515; Acts 2003, c. 632.

§ 8.01-54. Judgment to distribute recovery when verdict fails to do so

A. The verdict may and the judgment of the court shall in all cases specify the amount or the proportion to be received by each of the beneficiaries, if there be any. No verdict shall be set aside for failure to make such specification.

B. If either party shall so request the case shall be submitted to the jury with instructions to specify the distribution of the award, if any. If the jury be unable to agree upon or fail to make such distribution, the court shall specify the distribution and enter judgment accordingly. For the purpose of distribution the court may hear additional evidence.

C. The amount recovered in any such action shall be paid to the personal representative who shall first pay the costs and reasonable attorney's fees and then distribute the amount specifically allocated to the payment of hospital, medical, and funeral expenses. The remainder of the amount recovered shall thereafter be distributed by the personal representative, as specified in subsections A and B above, to the beneficiaries set forth in § 8.01-53; provided that any distribution made to any such beneficiaries shall be free from all debts and liabilities of the decedent. If there be no such beneficiaries, the amount so recovered shall be assets in the hands of the personal representative to be disposed of according to law.

Acts 1977, c. 617.

§ 8.01-55. Compromise of claim for death by wrongful act

The personal representative of the deceased may compromise any claim to damages arising under or by virtue of § 8.01-50, including claims under the provision of a liability insurance policy, before or after an action is brought, with the approval of the court in which the action was brought, or if an action has not been brought, with the consent of any circuit court. Such approval may be applied for on petition to such court, by the personal representative, or by any potential defendant, or by any interested insurance carrier. If a potential defendant or any insurance carrier petitions the court for approval, the personal representative shall be made a party to the proceeding. The petition shall state the compromise, its terms and the reason therefor. The court shall require the convening of the parties in interest in person or by their authorized representative, but it shall not be necessary to convene grandchildren whose living parents are made parties to the proceeding. The parties in interest shall be deemed to be convened if each such party (i) endorses the order by which the court approves the compromise or (ii) is given notice of the hearing and proposed compromise as provided in § 8.01-296 if a resident of the Commonwealth or as provided in § 8.01-320 if a nonresident, or is otherwise given reasonable notice of the hearing and proposed compromise as may be required by the court.

If the court approves the compromise, and the parties in interest do not agree upon the distribution to be made of what has been or may be received by the personal representative under such compromise, or if any of them are incapable of making a valid agreement, the court shall direct such distribution as a jury might direct under § 8.01-52 as to damages awarded by them. In other respects, what is received by the personal representative under the compromise shall be treated as if recovered by him in an action under § 8.01-52.

Acts 1977, c. 617; Acts 1981, c. 286; Acts 1991, c. 97; Acts 1995, c. 366.

§ 8.01-56. When right of action not to determine nor action to abate

The right of action under § 8.01-50 shall not determine, nor the action, when brought, abate by the death, dissolution, or other termination of a defendant; and when a person who has brought an action for personal injury dies pending the action, such action may be revived in the name of his personal representative. If death resulted from the injury for which the action was originally brought, a motion for judgment and other pleadings shall be amended so as to conform to an action under § 8.01-50, and the case proceeded with as if the action had been brought under such section. In such cases, however, there shall be but one recovery for the same injury.

Acts 1977, c. 617.

ARTICLE 6

INJURIES TO RAILROAD EMPLOYEES

§ 8.01–57. Liability of railroads for injury to certain employees

Every common carrier by railroad engaged in intrastate commerce shall be liable in damages to any of its employees suffering injury while employed by such carrier or, in the case of the death of any such employee, to his personal representative, for such injury or death, resulting in whole or in part from the wrongful act or neglect of any of its officers, agents, servants, or employees, or by reason of any defect, or insufficiency due to its neglect in its cars, engines, appliances, machinery, track, roadbed, works, boats, wharves or other equipment, except when such employee is injured while engaged in interstate commerce, and except when such employee is injured in the course of his regular employment and such regular employment does not expose such employee to the hazards incident to the maintenance, use and operation of such railroad. If the action be for the death of an employee, §§ 8.01–50 through 8.01–56 shall apply thereto.

Acts 1977, c. 617.

§ 8.01–58. Contributory negligence no bar to recovery; violation of safety appliance acts

In all actions brought against any such common carrier to recover damages for personal injuries to any employee or when such injuries have resulted in his death, the fact that such employee may have been guilty of contributory negligence shall not bar a recovery, but the damages shall be diminished by the jury in proportion to the amount of negligence attributable to such employee; and no such employee, who may be injured or killed, shall be held to have been guilty of contributory negligence in any case when the violation by such common carrier of any statute enacted for the safety of employees contributed to the injury or death of such employee.

Acts 1977, c. 617.

§ 8.01–59. Assumption of risk; violation of safety appliance acts

In any action brought against any common carrier, under or by virtue of § 8.01–57, to recover damages for injuries to, or death of, any of its employees, the knowledge of any employee injured or killed of the defective or unsafe character or condition of any machinery, ways, appliances, or structures of such carrier shall not of itself be a bar to recovery for an injury or death caused thereby, nor shall such employee be held to have assumed the risk of his employment in any case in which the violation by such common carrier of any statute enacted for the safety of employees contributed to the injury, or death of such employee.

Acts 1977, c. 617.

§ 8.01–60. Contracts exempting from liability void; set-off of insurance

Any contract, rule, regulation or device whatsoever the purpose or intent of which shall be to enable any common carrier to exempt itself from any liability created by § 8.01–57, shall to that extent be void; but in any action brought against any such common carrier under or by virtue of such section, such common carrier may set off therein any sum it has contributed or paid to any insurance, relief, benefit or indemnity company that may have been paid to the injured employee or the person entitled thereto on account of the injury or death for which such action was brought.

Acts 1977, c. 617.

§ 8.01–61. Definition of "common carrier" as used in article

The term "common carrier" as used in §§ 8.01–57 to 8.01–60 shall include the receivers or other persons or corporations charged with the duty of the management or operation of the business of a common carrier by railroad; but shall not include persons, firms or corporations owning or operating railroads when such railroads are primarily and chiefly used as incidental to the operation of coal, gypsum or iron mines or saw mills, nor shall it apply to any railroad owned or operated by any county.

Acts 1977, c. 617.

§ 8.01–62. Action may embrace liability under both State and federal acts

The motion for judgment or other pleading in any such action may embrace a cause of action growing out of any statute of the United States or this Commonwealth for such injury or death, without being demurrable on this account, and without the plaintiff being required to elect under which statute he claims. Sections 8.01–57 through 8.01–61 shall not apply to electric railways operated wholly within this Commonwealth.

Acts 1977, c. 617.

Article 7

Motor Vehicle Accidents

§ 8.01–63. Liability for death or injury to guest in motor vehicle

Any person transported by the owner or operator of any motor vehicle as a guest without payment for such transportation and any personal representative of any such guest so transported shall be entitled to recover damages against such owner or operator for death or injuries to the person or property of such guest resulting from the negligent operation of such motor vehicle. However, this statute does not limit any defense otherwise available to the owner or operator.

Acts 1977, c. 617.

§ 8.01–64. Liability for negligence of minor

Every owner of a motor vehicle causing or knowingly permitting a minor under the age of sixteen years who is not permitted under the provisions of § 46.2–335 to drive such a vehicle upon a highway, and any person who gives or furnishes a motor vehicle to such minor, shall be jointly or severally liable with such minor for any damages caused by the negligence of such minor in driving such vehicle.

Acts 1977, c. 617.

§ 8.01–65. Defense of lack of consent of owner

It shall be a valid defense to any action brought for the negligent operation of a motor vehicle for the owner of such vehicle to prove that the same was being driven or used without his knowledge or consent, express or implied, but the burden of proof thereof shall be on such owner.

Acts 1977, c. 617.

§ 8.01–66. Recovery of damages for loss of use of vehicle

A. Whenever any person is entitled to recover for damage to or destruction of a motor vehicle, he shall, in addition to any other damages to which he may be legally entitled, be entitled to recover the reasonable cost which was actually incurred in hiring a comparable substitute vehicle for the period of time during which such person is deprived of the use of his motor vehicle. However, such rental period shall not exceed a reasonable period of time for such repairs to be made or if the original vehicle is a total loss, a reasonable time to purchase a new vehicle. Nothing herein contained shall relieve the claimant of the duty to mitigate damages.

B. Whenever any insurance company licensed in this Commonwealth to write insurance as defined in § 38.2–124 or any self-insured company refuses or fails to provide a comparable temporary substitute vehicle to any person entitled to recover the actual cost of hiring a substitute vehicle as set forth in subsection A, and if the trial judge of a court of proper jurisdiction subsequently finds that such refusal or failure was not made in good faith, such company shall be liable to that person in the amount of $500 or double the amount of the rental cost he is entitled to recover under subsection A, whichever amount is greater. If the trial court finds that an action brought against an insurance company or any self-insured company under subsection B is frivolous, or not to have been brought in good faith, the court may in its discretion require the plaintiff to pay the reasonable attorney's fees, not to exceed $350, incurred by the defendant in defending the action. This section shall in no way preclude any party from seeking such additional common law remedies as might otherwise be available.

Acts 1977, c. 617; Acts 1979, c. 499; Acts 1986, c. 296; Acts 1987, c. 116; Acts 1989, c. 348. Amended by Acts 2010, c. 343.

§ 8.01–66.1. Remedy for arbitrary refusal of motor vehicle insurance claim

A. Whenever any insurance company licensed in this Commonwealth to write insurance as defined in § 38.2–124 denies, refuses or fails to pay to its insured a claim of $3,500 or less in excess of the deductible, if any, under the provisions of a policy of motor vehicle insurance issued by such company to the insured and it is subsequently found by the judge of a court of proper jurisdiction that such denial, refusal or failure to pay was not made in good faith, the company shall be liable to the insured in an amount double the amount otherwise due and payable under the provisions of the insured's policy of motor vehicle insurance, together with reasonable attorney's fees and expenses.

The provisions of this subsection shall be construed to include an insurance company's refusal or failure to pay medical expenses to persons covered under the terms of any medical payments coverage extended under a policy of motor vehicle insurance, when the amount of the claim therefor is $3,500 or less and the refusal was not made in good faith.

B. Notwithstanding the provisions of subsection A, whenever any insurance company licensed in this Commonwealth to write insurance as defined in § 38.2–124 denies, refuses or fails to pay to a third party claimant, on behalf of an insured to whom such company has issued a policy of motor vehicle liability insurance, a claim of $3,500 or less made by such third party claimant and if the judge of a court of proper jurisdiction finds that the insured is liable for the claim, the third party claimant shall have a cause of action against the insurance company. If the judge finds that such denial, refusal or failure to pay was not made in good faith, the company, in addition to the liability assumed by the company under the provisions of the insured's policy of motor vehicle liability insurance, shall be liable to the third party claimant in an amount double the amount of the judgment awarded the third party claimant, together with reasonable attorney's fees and expenses.

C. Notwithstanding the provisions of subsections A and B whenever any person who has paid a fee to the Department of Motor Vehicles to register an uninsured motor vehicle pursuant to § 46.2–706 or any person who has furnished proof of financial responsibility in lieu of obtaining a policy or policies of motor vehicle liability insurance pursuant to the provisions of Title 46.2 or any person who is required and has failed either to pay such fee or to furnish such proof pursuant to the provisions of Title 46.2 denies, refuses or fails to pay to a claimant a claim of $3,500 or less made by such claimant as a result of a motor vehicle accident; and if the trial judge of a court of proper jurisdiction finds that such denial, refusal or failure to pay was not made in good faith, such person shall be liable to the claimant in an amount double the amount otherwise due and payable together with reasonable attorney's fees and expenses.

For the purposes of this subsection C "person" shall mean and include any natural person, firm, partnership, association or corporation.

D. 1. Whenever a court of proper jurisdiction finds that an insurance company licensed in this Commonwealth to write insurance as defined in § 38.2–124 denies, refuses or fails to pay to its insured a claim of more than $3,500 in excess of the deductible, if any, under the provisions of a policy of motor vehicle insurance issued by such company to the insured and it is subsequently found by the judge of a court of proper jurisdiction that such denial, refusal or failure to pay was not made in good faith, the company shall be liable to the insured in the amount otherwise due and payable under the provisions of the insured's policy of motor vehicle insurance, plus interest on the amount due at double the rate provided in § 6.2–301 from the date that the claim was submitted to the insurer or its authorized agent, together with reasonable attorney's fees and expenses.

2. The provisions of this subsection shall be construed to include an insurance company's refusal or failure to pay medical expenses to persons covered under the terms of any medical payments coverage extended under a policy of motor vehicle insurance when the refusal was not made in good faith.

Acts 1977, c. 621; Acts 1979, c. 521; Acts 1980, c. 437; Acts 1989, c. 698; Acts 1991, c. 155; Acts 1997, c. 401; Acts 2002, c. 631.

§ 8.01–66.1:1. Subrogation claims by underinsured motorist benefits insurer

Section becomes applicable to policies issued or renewed on or after January 1, 2016

A. Any underinsured motorist benefits insurer paying such benefits to an insured, by way of settlement or payment pursuant to a judgment, shall have no right of subrogation against any individual or entity who settled with the underinsured motorist benefits insurer's insured pursuant to subsection K of § 38.2–2206 unless the underinsured motorist failed to reasonably cooperate in the defense of any lawsuit brought against him. An underinsured motorist shall be presumed to have failed to reasonably cooperate if he fails or refuses:

1. To attend his deposition or trial if subpoenaed to appear at least 21 days in advance of either event;

2. To assist in responding to written discovery;

3. To meet with defense counsel for a reasonable period of time after reasonable notice, by phone or in person, within 21 days of being served with any lawsuit and again prior to his deposition and trial; or

4. To notify counsel for the underinsured motorist benefits insurer of any change in address.

The underinsured motorist may rebut the presumption that he failed to reasonably cooperate. If the court finds that the underinsured motorist's failure to cooperate was not unreasonable or that the underinsured motorist otherwise acted in good faith in attempting to comply with his duty to reasonably cooperate with the underinsured motorist benefits insurer, then the underinsured motorist benefits insurer will not regain its right of subrogation.

B. The underinsured motorist benefits insurer seeking the cooperation of the underinsured motorist shall pay the reasonable costs and expenses related to procuring such cooperation, including any travel costs if the underinsured motorist resides more than 100 miles from the location of his deposition or trial. Travel costs may be considered by the court in determining whether the underinsured motorist's failure to cooperate was unreasonable or not.

C. If the court finds that the underinsured motorist satisfied his duty to cooperate with the underinsured motorist benefits insurer or that his failure to do so was not unreasonable, then the court may award him his costs in defending such subrogation action, including reasonable attorney fees.

Added by Acts 2015, c. 584; Acts 2015, c. 585.

ARTICLE 7.1

LIEN FOR HOSPITAL, MEDICAL AND NURSING SERVICES

§ 8.01–66.2. Lien against person whose negligence causes injury

Whenever any person sustains personal injuries caused by the alleged negligence of another and receives treatment in any hospital, public or private, or nursing home, or receives medical attention or treatment from any physician, or receives nursing service or care from any registered nurse, or receives physical therapy treatment from any registered physical therapist in this Commonwealth, or receives medicine from a pharmacy, or receives any emergency medical services and transportation provided by an emergency medical services vehicle, such hospital, nursing home, physician, nurse, physical therapist, pharmacy or emergency medical services and transportation provided by an emergency medical services vehicle shall each have a lien for the amount of a just and reasonable charge for the service rendered, but not exceeding $2,500 in the case of a hospital or nursing home, $750 for each physician, nurse, physical therapist, or pharmacy, and $200 for each emergency medical services agency providing emergency medical services or emergency medical services vehicle transportation on the claim of such injured person or of his personal representative against the person, firm, or corporation whose negligence is alleged to have caused such injuries.

Acts 1979, c. 722; Acts 1981, c. 313; Acts 1988, c. 505; Acts 1988, c. 544; Acts 1995, c. 470; Acts 1995, c. 550; Acts 1995, c. 669; Acts 2003, c. 455; Acts 2003, c. 525. Amended by Acts 2010, c. 343; Acts 2015, c. 502; Acts 2015, c. 503.

§ 8.01–66.3. Lien inferior to claim of attorney or personal representative

The lien provided for in § 8.01–66.2 shall be of inferior dignity to the claim or lien of the attorney of such injured person or of his personal representative for professional services for representing such injured person or his personal representative in his claim or suit for damages for such personal injuries.

Acts 1979, c. 722.

§ 8.01–66.4. Subrogation

Any municipal corporation or any person, firm or corporation who may pay the charges for which a lien is provided in § 8.01–66.2 shall be subrogated to such lien.

Acts 1979, c. 722.

§ 8.01–66.5. Written notice required

A. No lien provided for in § 8.01–66.2, 8.01–66.9, or 19.2–368.15 shall be created or become effective in favor of the Commonwealth, an institution thereof, or a hospital, nursing home, physician, nurse, or physical therapist, or emergency medical services and transportation provided by an emergency medical services vehicle, unless and until a written notice of lien setting forth the name of the Commonwealth or the institution, hospital, nursing home, physician, nurse, physical therapist, or emergency medical services agency that provided emergency medical services or emergency medical services vehicle transportation and the name of the injured person has been served upon or given to the person, firm, or corporation whose negligence is alleged to have caused such injuries, or to the attorney for the injured party, or to the injured party. Such written notice of lien shall not be required if the attorney for the injured party knew that medical services were either provided or paid for by the Commonwealth.

B. In any action for personal injuries or wrongful death against a nursing home or its agents, if the Department of Medical Assistance Services has paid for any health care services provided to the injured party or decedent relating to the action, the injured party or personal representative shall, within 60 days of filing a lawsuit or 21 days of determining that the Department of Medical Assistance Services has paid for such health care services, whichever is later, give written notice to the Department of Medical Assistance Services that the lawsuit has been filed. The Department of Medical Assistance Services shall provide a written response, stating the amount of the lien as of the date of their response, within 60 days of receiving a request for that information from the injured party or personal representative.

Acts 1979, c. 722; Acts 1980, c. 623; Acts 1983, c. 263; Acts 1988, c. 544; Acts 1998, c. 183; Acts 2003, c. 455; Acts 2003, c. 525. Amended by Acts 2013, c. 273; Acts 2015, c. 502; Acts 2015, c. 503.

§ 8.01–66.6. Liability for reasonable charges for services

The notice set forth in subsection A of § 8.01–66.5, when served upon or given to the person, firm or corporation whose negligence is alleged to have caused injuries or to the attorney for the injured party, shall have the effect of making such person, firm, corporation or attorney liable for the reasonable charges for the services rendered the injured person to the extent of the amount paid to or received by such injured party or his personal representative exclusive of attorney's fees, but, except in liens created under § 8.01–66.9 or 19.2–368.15, not in excess of the maximum amounts prescribed in § 8.01–66.2.

Acts 1979, c. 722; Acts 1980, c. 623; Acts 2003, c. 525. Amended by Acts 2013, c. 273.

§ 8.01–66.7. Hearing and disposal of claim of unreasonableness

If the injured person questions the reasonableness of the charges made by a hospital, nurse, physician, or

emergency medical services agency that provided emergency medical services or emergency medical services vehicle transportation claiming a lien pursuant to § 8.01–66.2, the injured person or the hospital, physician, nurse, or emergency medical services agency that provided emergency medical services or emergency medical services vehicle transportation may file, in the court that would have jurisdiction of such claim if such claim were asserted against the injured person by such hospital, physician, nurse, or emergency medical services agency that provided emergency medical services or emergency medical services vehicle transportation, a petition setting forth the facts. The court shall hear and dispose of the matter in a summary way after five days' notice to the other party in interest.
Acts 1979, c. 722; Acts 2003, c. 455. Amended by Acts 2015, c. 502; Acts 2015, c. 503.

§ 8.01–66.8. Petition to enforce lien

If suit is instituted by an injured person or his personal representative against the person, firm, or corporation allegedly causing the person's injuries, a hospital, nursing home, physician, nurse, or emergency medical services agency that provided emergency medical services or emergency medical services vehicle transportation, in lieu of proceeding according to §§ 8.01–66.5 to 8.01–66.7, may file in the court wherein such suit is pending a petition to enforce the lien provided for in § 8.01–66.2 or 8.01–66.9. Such petition shall be heard and disposed of in a summary way.
Acts 1979, c. 722; Acts 1980, c. 623; Acts 2003, c. 455; Acts 2003, c. 525. Amended by Acts 2015, c. 502; Acts 2015, c. 503.

§ 8.01–66.9. Lien in favor of Commonwealth, its programs, institutions or departments on claim for personal injuries

Whenever any person sustains personal injuries and receives treatment in any hospital, public or private, or nursing home, or receives medical attention or treatment from any physician, or receives nursing services or care from any registered nurse in this Commonwealth, or receives pharmaceutical goods or any type of medical or rehabilitative device, apparatus, or treatment which is paid for pursuant to the Virginia Medical Assistance Program, the State/Local Hospitalization Program and other programs of the Department of Medical Assistance Services, the Maternal and Child Health Program, or the Children's Specialty Services Program, or provided at or paid for by any hospital or rehabilitation center operated by the Commonwealth, the Department for Aging and Rehabilitative Services or any state institution of higher education, the Commonwealth shall have a lien for the total amount paid pursuant to such program, and the Commonwealth or such Department or institution shall have a lien for the total amount due for the services, equipment or devices provided at or paid for by such hospital or center operated by the Commonwealth or such Department or institution, or any portion thereof compromised pursuant to the authority granted under § 2.2–514, on the claim of such injured person or of his personal representative against the person, firm, or corporation who is alleged to have caused such injuries.

The Commonwealth or such Department or institution shall also have a lien on the claim of the injured person or his personal representative for any funds which may be due him from insurance moneys received for such medical services under the injured party's own insurance coverage or through an uninsured or underinsured motorist insurance coverage endorsement. The lien granted to the Commonwealth for the total amounts paid pursuant to the Virginia Medical Assistance Program, the State/Local Hospitalization Program and other programs of the Department of Medical Assistance Services, the Maternal and Child Health Program, or the Children's Specialty Services Program shall have priority over the lien for the amounts due for services, equipment or devices provided at a hospital or center operated by the Commonwealth. The Commonwealth's or such Department's or institution's lien shall be inferior to any lien for payment of reasonable attorney's fees and costs, but shall be superior to all other liens created by the provisions of this chapter and otherwise. Expenses for reasonable legal fees and costs shall be deducted from the total amount recovered. The amount of the lien may be compromised pursuant to § 2.2–514.

The court in which a suit by an injured person or his personal representative has been filed against the person, firm or corporation alleged to have caused such injuries or in which such suit may properly be filed, may, upon motion or petition by the injured person, his personal representative or his attorney, and after written notice is given to all those holding liens attaching to the recovery, reduce the amount of the liens and apportion the recovery, whether by verdict or negotiated settlement, between the plaintiff, the plaintiff's attorney, and the Commonwealth or such Department or institution as the equities of the case may appear, provided that the injured person, his personal representative or attorney has made a good faith effort to negotiate a compromise pursuant to § 2.2–514. The court shall set forth the basis for any such reduction in a written order.
Acts 1979, c. 722; Acts 1981, c. 562; Acts 1982, c. 491; Acts 1983, c. 263; Acts 1984, c. 767; Acts 1985, c. 580; Acts 1986, c. 238; Acts 1988, c. 544; Acts 1989, c. 624; Acts 1992, c. 104; Acts 2003, c. 525. Amended by Acts 2012, c. 803; Acts 2012, c. 835.

§ 8.01–66.9:1. Lien against recovery for medical treatment provided to prisoner

In any civil action brought for injuries or death suffered by any person while confined in a state or local correctional facility, the Commonwealth or the locality, as the case may be, shall have a lien against any recovery by settlement or verdict for all actual expenses incurred by the Commonwealth or the locality for medical, surgical and hospital treatment and supplies for the prisoner, whether provided by public or private health care providers, as a result of the injury. Such lien shall be subject to the payment of reasonable attorneys' fees and costs.

Acts 1984, c. 519.

§ 8.01–66.10. Death claims settled by compromise or suit

In case of personal injuries resulting in death and settlement therefor by compromise or suit under the provisions of §§ 8.01–50 to 8.01–56, the liens provided for in this article may be asserted against the recovery, or against the estate of the decedent, but not both. If asserted against the recovery and paid, such liens shall attach pro rata to the amounts received respectively by such beneficiaries as are designated to receive the moneys distributed and in their respective amounts; and such beneficiaries, or the personal representative for their benefit, shall be subrogated to the liens against the estate of such decedent provided for by § 64.2–528.

Acts 1979, c. 722.

§ 8.01–66.11. Necessity for settlement or judgment

Nothing contained in this article shall be construed as imposing liability on any person, firm or corporation whose negligence is alleged to have caused injuries or on the attorney for the injured party where no settlement is made, or, in case of an attorney, where no funds come into his hands, or where no judgment is obtained in favor of such injured party or his personal representative.

Acts 1979, c. 722.

§ 8.01–66.12. Term physician to include chiropractor

Wherever the term physician is used in this article, it shall include chiropractor.

Acts 1993, c. 702.

Article 8

Actions for the Sale, Lease, Exchange, Redemption and Other Disposition of Lands of Persons Under a Disability

§ 8.01–67. Definitions; persons under a disability; fiduciary

The terms "fiduciary" and "person under a disability" as used in this article shall have the meanings ascribed to them in § 8.01–2.

Acts 1977, c. 617.

§ 8.01–68. Jurisdiction

Circuit courts in the exercise of their equity jurisdiction, upon being satisfied by competent evidence independent of the admissions in the pleadings or elsewhere in the proceedings, that one or more of the types of relief hereinafter specified will promote the interest of an owner of land, or any interest therein, who is a person under a disability as defined in this chapter for whom a conservator has not been appointed pursuant to Chapter 20 (§ 64.2–2000 et seq.) of Title 64.2, and taking into consideration the rights of any other party interested in such land, may order the sale, exchange, lease, encumbrance, redemption, or other disposition of such real estate as to the court may seem just and equitable.

In the case of the sales of such lands or interest therein, the court shall be governed by the established practices for judicial sales generally except as they may be specifically modified by provisions of this article.

Acts 1977, c. 617; Acts 1997, c. 921, eff. Jan. 1, 1998.

§ 8.01–69. Commencement of suit; parties

Any of the relief specified in this article may be sought by bill in equity filed by a fiduciary, as defined in this article, or by any other person having an interest in the subject matter of the proceedings. A person under a disability, fiduciary, all those who would be the heirs or distributees of the defendant person under disability if he had died at the time of the commencement of this proceeding, except as provided in § 8.01–78, and all other persons interested in the subject matter of the proceeding, shall be made parties defendant when not parties plaintiff.

Acts 1977, c. 617; Acts 1983, c. 459.

§§ 8.01–70, 8.01–71. Repealed by Acts 1990, c. 831, eff. Jan. 1, 1991

§ 8.01–72. When death to abate such suit

A suit instituted under this article shall abate by reason of the death of the person under a disability unless a sale, exchange, lease, encumbrance, redemption, or other disposition of real estate has been confirmed by a decree in such suit.

Acts 1977, c. 617.

§ 8.01–73. Guardian ad litem to be appointed

In every suit brought under this article, a guardian ad litem shall be appointed for any person under a disability not otherwise represented by a guardian or committee, or trustee appointed pursuant to § 64.2–2003, and for all persons proceeded against by an order or publication under the designation of "parties un-

known" as provided for in § 8.01–316. The guardian ad litem shall file an answer as such.
Acts 1977, c. 617; Acts 1997, c. 540.

§ 8.01–74. Leases on behalf of persons under disability; new leases

A. Leases on behalf of persons under a disability.—When a person under a disability is entitled to or bound to renew any lease, any fiduciary on behalf of such person under a disability or any other interested person may apply by motion after reasonable notice to parties having a present interest in the property to be leased, to the circuit court as prescribed in subdivision 3 of § 8.01–261, and by the order of the court any person appointed by it may, from time to time, surrender or accept a surrender of such lease, or take or make a new lease of the same premises for such term and with such provisions as the court directs. Such reasonable sums as are incurred to renew any such lease shall, with interest thereon, be paid out of the profits of the leasehold premises, and be a charge thereon until payment.

B. New leases.—When it shall appear to a circuit court that the interests of a person under a disability will be promoted by the execution of a new lease, where no prior lease exists, any fiduciary or any other person interested in the subject matter may apply in like summary fashion as stated in subsection A of this section and upon showing to the satisfaction of the court that the provisions therein were complied with, including reasonable notice to parties having a present interest to the property to be leased, the circuit court upon the consideration of the probable length of the disability and the duration of the proposed lease, may order such lease to be executed. Such lease may be renewed or surrendered at any time pursuant to subsection A of this section and under such conditions as the court may direct.
Acts 1977, c. 617.

§ 8.01–75. Who not to be purchaser

At any sale under this article neither a fiduciary for a person under a disability, as defined under this article, nor the guardian ad litem shall be a purchaser directly or indirectly; provided, however, such fiduciary may be a purchaser if the court finds that such a purchase by the fiduciary is in the best interests of the person under a disability.
Acts 1977, c. 617; Acts 1980, c. 346.

§ 8.01–76. How proceeds from disposition to be secured and applied; when same may be paid over

The proceeds of sale, or rents, income, or royalties, arising from the sale or lease, or other disposition, of lands of persons under a disability, whether in a suit for sale or lease thereof, or in a suit for partition, or in condemnation proceedings, shall be invested under the direction of the court for the use and benefit of the persons entitled to the estate; and in case of a trust estate subject to the uses, limitations, and conditions, contained in the writing creating the trust. The court shall take ample security for all investments so made, and from time to time require additional security, if necessary, and make any proper order for the faithful application and safe investment of the fund, and for the management and preservation of any properties or securities in which the same has been invested, and for the protection of the rights of all persons interested therein, whether such rights be vested or contingent, but nothing hereinbefore contained shall prevent the court having charge thereof from directing such funds to be paid over to the legally appointed and qualified fiduciary (as defined in § 8.01–67) of the person under a disability, whenever the court is satisfied that such fiduciary has executed sufficient bond; or from applying at any time all or any portion thereof to the proper needs and requirements of the person under a disability. Provided, however, that if such funds do not exceed $4,000, the court, in its discretion and without the intervention of a fiduciary, may pay such funds to any person deemed appropriate by the court for the use and benefit of a person under a disability, whether such person resides within or without the Commonwealth. Such funds not in excess of $4,000 shall, when paid over to such person deemed appropriate, be treated as personal property.
Acts 1977, c. 617; Acts 1978, c. 419; Acts 1981, c. 129.

§ 8.01–77. What proceeds of sale to pass as real estate

The proceeds received under the preceding provisions of this article or under Article 9 (§ 8.01–81 et seq.) of this chapter, from the sale or division of real estate of a person under a disability or so much thereof as may remain at such person's death, if such person continue until death incapable from any cause of making a will, shall pass to those who would have been entitled to the land if it had not been sold or divided.
Acts 1977, c. 617.

§ 8.01–78. Alternate procedure for sale of real estate of person under disability

If the personal estate of any person under a disability for whom a fiduciary has been appointed under any of the provisions of Title 37.2, be insufficient for the discharge of his debts or if the personal estate or residue thereof after payment of debts and the rents and profits of his real estate be insufficient for his maintenance and that of his family, if any, the fiduciary of his estate may petition a circuit court for authority to mortgage, lease or sell so much of the real estate of such person as may be necessary for the purposes aforesaid, or any of them, setting forth in the petition the particulars and amount of the estate, real and personal, and a statement of the application of any personal estate, and debts and demands existing against the estate. Those persons who would be heirs or distributees of the person under a disability if he had died at the time of commencement of the proceeding need not be made parties defendant to a proceeding pursuant to this section.

Acts 1977, c. 617; Acts 1983, c. 459.

§ 8.01-79. Same; reference of petition to commissioner

On the presenting of such petition it may be referred to a commissioner in chancery or to a special commissioner appointed by the court, to inquire into and report upon the matters therein contained, whose duty it shall be to make such inquiry, to give notice to and hear all parties interested in such real estate and to report thereon with all convenient speed.

Acts 1977, c. 617.

§ 8.01-80. Same; action of court on report; application of proceeds of transaction

If upon the filing of the report and examination of the matter it shall appear to the court to be proper, an order shall be entered for the mortgaging, leasing, or sale, on such terms and conditions as the court may deem proper, of so much of such real estate as may be necessary; but no conveyance shall be executed until such shall have been confirmed by the court. The proceeds of such transactions shall be secured and applied under the order of the court.

Acts 1977, c. 617.

Article 9

Partition

§ 8.01-81. Who may compel partition of land; jurisdiction; validation of certain partitions of mineral rights

Tenants in common, joint tenants, executors with the power to sell, and coparceners of real property, including mineral rights east and south of the Clinch River, shall be compellable to make partition and may compel partition, but in the case of an executor only if the power of sale is properly exercisable at that time under the circumstances; and a lien creditor or any owner of undivided estate in real estate may also compel partition for the purpose of subjecting the estate of his debtor or the rents and profits thereof to the satisfaction of his lien. Any court having general equity jurisdiction shall have jurisdiction in cases of partition; and in the exercise of such jurisdiction may take cognizance of all questions of law affecting the legal title that may arise in any proceedings, between such tenants in common, joint tenants, executors with the power to sell, coparceners and lien creditors.

All partitions of mineral rights heretofore had, are hereby validated.

Acts 1977, c. 617; Acts 1984, c. 226.

§ 8.01-82. When shares of two or more laid off together

Any two or more of the parties, if they so elect, may have their shares laid off together when partition can be conveniently made in that way.

Acts 1977, c. 617.

§ 8.01-83. Allotment to one or more parties, or sale, in lieu of partition

When partition cannot be conveniently made, the entire subject may be allotted to any one or more of the parties who will accept it and pay therefor to the other parties such sums of money as their interest therein may entitle them to; or in any case in which partition cannot be conveniently made, if the interest of those who are entitled to the subject, or its proceeds, will be promoted by a sale of the entire subject, or allotment of part and sale of the residue, the court, notwithstanding any of those entitled may be a person under a disability, may order such sale, or an allotment of a part thereof to any one or more of the parties who will accept it and pay therefor to the other parties such sums of money as their interest therein may entitle them to, and a sale of the residue, and make distribution of the proceeds of sale, according to the respective rights of those entitled, taking care, when there are creditors of any deceased person who was a tenant in common, joint tenant, or coparcener, to have the proceeds of such deceased person's part applied according to the rights of such creditors.

Acts 1977, c. 617.

§ 8.01-84. Application of proceeds of sale to payment of lien

When there are liens on the interest of any party in the subject so sold, the court may, on the petition of any person holding a lien, ascertain the liens, and apply the dividend of such party in the proceeds of sale to the discharge thereof, so far as the same may be necessary.

Acts 1977, c. 617.

§ 8.01-85. Disposition of share in proceeds of person under disability

The court making an order for sale shall, when the dividend of a party exceeds $2500, if such party be a person under a disability, order the same to be disposed as the proceeds of a sale under the provisions of § 8.01-76 are required to be invested.

Acts 1977, c. 617.

§ 8.01–86. Repealed by Acts 1990, c. 831, eff. Jan. 1, 1991

§ 8.01–87. Validation of certain partitions prior to act of 1922

All partitions heretofore had, when the proceedings conformed to the law as it existed prior to the amendment of § 5281 of the Code of 1919 by an act approved March 27, 1922, although they did not conform to such section as it read under the amendment of 1922, as aforesaid, are hereby validated; but nothing in this validating section shall be construed as intended to affect vested rights.

Acts 1977, c. 617.

§ 8.01–88. Decree of partition to vest legal title

A decree heretofore or hereafter made, confirming any partition or allotment in a suit for partition, shall vest in the respective co-owners, between or to whom the partition or allotment is made, the title to their shares under the partition or allotment, in like manner and to the same extent, as if such decree direct such title be conveyed to them and the conveyance was made accordingly.

Acts 1977, c. 617.

§ 8.01–89. When proceeds of sale deemed personal estate

The proceeds of any sale made under § 8.01–83 shall, except as provided in § 8.01–77, be deemed personal estate from the time of the confirmation of such sale by the court.

Acts 1977, c. 617.

§ 8.01–90. When name or share of parties unknown

If the name or share of any person interested in the subject of the partition be unknown, so much as is known in relation thereto shall be stated in the bill.

Acts 1977, c. 617.

§ 8.01–91. Effect of partition or sale on lessee's rights

Any person who, before the partition or sale, was lessee of any of the lands divided or sold, shall hold the same of him to whom such land is allotted or sold on the same term on which by his lease he held it before the partition.

Acts 1977, c. 617.

§ 8.01–92. Allowance of attorneys' fees out of unrepresented shares

In any partition suit when there are unrepresented shares, the court shall allow reasonable fees to the attorney or attorneys bringing the action on account of the services rendered to the parceners unrepresented by counsel.

Acts 1977, c. 617.

§ 8.01–93. Partition of goods, etc., by sale, if necessary

When an equal division of goods or chattels cannot be made in kind among those entitled, a court of equity may direct the sale of the same, and the distribution of the proceeds according to the rights of the parties.

Acts 1977, c. 617.

Article 10

Sale, Lease, or Exchange of Certain Estates in Property

§ 8.01–94. When sold, leased or exchanged

Whenever an interest in property, real or personal, is held by a person, natural or artificial, with remainder or limitation over contingent upon any event, or for his life or for the life of another, and there is limited thereon any other estate, vested or contingent, to any other such person, whether in being or to be thereafter born or created in any manner whatsoever, such person holding an interest in the property so subject to remainder or limitation over or for his own life, or his committee, guardian, if a minor, or conservator, or, if the estate so held be for the life of another, then his heir or personal representative, as the case may be, may for the purpose of obtaining a sale or leasing or exchange of the fee simple interest or absolute estate in such property, if the sale or leasing or exchange thereof is not prohibited by the instrument creating the estate, and the remaindermen, or any of them, whether in being or hereafter to be born or created, are from any cause incapable at the time of filing the bill as herein provided or of giving their assent, or the remainder or limitation over is contingent or defeasible, file a bill in equity in the circuit court stating plainly the property to be sold or leased or exchanged and all facts calculated to show the propriety of such sale or lease or exchange. A like bill may be filed for the sale or leasing or exchange of the remainder in such estate by a remainderman, his guardian, conservator or committee. All persons interested in the property presently or contingently, other than the plaintiff, shall be made defendants, and if such remaindermen be not born or created at such time of filing such bill, such suit shall not for such cause abate, but such unborn person or uncreated artificial person shall be made defendant and subject to the decree of the court by the name of "person unknown or person yet to be born or created," and the court shall upon the filing of such bill appoint a guardian ad litem to defend the interest of such unborn person or uncreated artificial person. If it be clearly shown independently of any admissions in the pleadings that the interest of the plaintiff will be promoted and the rights of no other person will be violated thereby, the court may decree a sale or lease or exchange of the property or any part thereof, or of the remainder therein. In case of a sale on credit, the court shall take ample security. If such sale on credit be of real estate, a lien thereon shall be reserved. The title to any land acquired in any exchange herein provided for shall be held and owned by the same persons in the same way, to the same extent and subject to the same conditions that they owned the land given in such exchange.

Acts 1977, c. 617; Acts 1997, c. 801, eff. Jan. 1, 1998.

§ 8.01–95. Procedure in such case

The procedure in such suit and the investment of the proceeds of sale shall be in accordance with §§ 8.01–73, 8.01–75 and 8.01–76, so far as the same can be made applicable, and the court may, in its discretion, commute the life estate according to § 55–269.1. In the case of a lease, however, the rents may be made payable direct to the person or persons entitled thereto, for the time being.

Acts 1977, c. 617.

ARTICLE 11

GENERAL PROVISIONS FOR JUDICIAL SALES

§ 8.01–96. Decree for sale; how made; bond of commissioner

In decreeing a sale under any provisions of law, the court may provide for the sale of property in any part of the Commonwealth, and may direct the sale to be for cash, or on such credit and terms as it may deem best, and it may appoint one or more special commissioners to make such sale. No special commissioner, appointed by a court, shall receive money under a decree, until he gives bond, with approved security, before such court or its clerk, in a penalty to be prescribed by the court, conditioned upon the faithful discharge of his duties as such commissioner and to account for and pay over as the court may direct all money that may come into his hands as such commissioner.

Acts 1977, c. 617.

§ 8.01–97. Delinquent taxes to be ascertained

In every suit brought in this Commonwealth for the sale of lands for the payment of debts or to subject lands to the payment of liens binding thereon, it shall be the duty of the court, or any commissioner to whom the cause is referred, to ascertain all delinquent taxes on such land together with interest and penalties if any.

Acts 1977, c. 617.

§ 8.01–98. Sales of land when purchase price insufficient to pay taxes, etc.

In any proceedings for the sale of real estate or to subject real estate to the payment of debts, it appears to the court that the real estate cannot be sold for enough to pay off the liens of taxes, levies, and assessments returned delinquent against it, and it further appears that the purchase price offered is adequate and reasonable, such sale shall be confirmed, and the court shall decree the payment and distribution of the proceeds of such sale pro rata to the taxes, levies, and assessments due the Commonwealth or any political subdivision thereof, after having first deducted the cost of such proceedings in court. Such decree shall be certified to the clerk of the appropriate court who has charge of the delinquent tax books, and such clerk shall cause the lien of such taxes, levies, and assessments to be marked satisfied upon the list of delinquent lands regardless of whether the same shall have been paid in full.

Acts 1977, c. 617.

§ 8.01–99. Bond required of special commissioner for sale

Except as hereinafter provided, no special commissioner shall advertise the property for sale or renting, or sell or rent the same, until he shall have given bond in a penalty to be prescribed by the court sufficient to cover at least the probable amount of the whole purchase money or such portion of the rent the court deems appropriate, and shall have obtained from such clerk a certificate that such bond has been given. The certificate or a copy thereof shall be appended to the advertisement; provided, however, that in any case of such sale or rental, the court may direct all the cash proceeds thereof to be deposited by the purchaser or lessee to the credit of such court in some bank to be designated by it, and may direct that all evidences of indebtedness arising from such transaction or rent be deposited for safekeeping with such bank or the clerk of such court and the court may in its discretion thereafter dispense with the bond.

The clerk shall make the certificate whenever the bond has been given and note the same in the proceedings in the cause. The certificate or a copy thereof shall be returned with the report of the sale or renting.

Acts 1977, c. 617.

§ 8.01–100. Liability of clerk for false certificate or failure to give bond

If any clerk make a certificate as to the bond, which is untrue, he and the sureties on his official bond shall be liable to any person injured thereby.

Acts 1977, c. 617; Acts 1978, c. 718.

§ 8.01–101. Purchasers relieved of liability for purchase money paid to such commissioner

When the certificate pursuant to the provisions in § 8.01–99 shall have been published with an advertisement of the sale or renting of property, or when such bond shall have been given prior to a sale or renting not publicly advertised, any person purchasing or renting such property in pursuance of such advertisement or in pursuance of the decree or order of sale or renting, shall be relieved of all liability for the purchase money or rent, or any part thereof, which he may pay to any special commissioner, as to whom the proper certificate shall have been appended to such advertisement, or who shall have given the bond aforesaid.

Acts 1977, c. 617.

§ 8.01–102. Purchasers not required to see to application of purchase money

No purchaser or renter at a duly authorized sale or renting made by a receiver, personal representative, trustee, or other fiduciary shall be required to see to the application of the purchase money.

Acts 1977, c. 617.

§ 8.01–103. Special commissioner or other person appointed to do so to receive purchase money, etc.; liability of clerk for failure to give notice of appointment

The special commissioner, who makes the sale or renting, shall receive and collect all the purchase money or rent, unless some other person be appointed to collect the same and in such case the court shall require of such person bond with surety in such penalty as to it may seem fit. When such appointment is made, it shall be the duty of the clerk to give notice thereof, in writing, to the purchaser or lessee, to be served as other notices are required by law to be served; but no payment shall be made to the person so appointed, until he shall have given the bond required by the decree or order; provided, however, that if, before the purchaser or lessee has received notice of such appointment, he shall have made any payment on account of the purchase money or rent to the special commissioner, or any person appointed for the purpose, who made the sale or renting, such special commissioner, or other person, who made the sale or renting, and the sureties on his bond, shall be responsible for the money so paid, and the purchaser or lessee, who made the payment, shall not be responsible therefor.

If any clerk fail to give the notice hereinbefore required to be given by him, he and the sureties on his official bond shall be liable to any person injured by such failure.

Acts 1977, c. 617; Acts 1978, c. 718.

§ 8.01–104. Repealed by Acts 1978, c. 718

§ 8.01–105. Rule against special commissioner, purchaser, etc., for judgment for amounts due

Any court of this Commonwealth, may, at the instance of any party in interest, award a rule against any special commissioner or receiver appointed by or acting under the authority of such court, and against the surety of such commissioner or receiver, or against a purchaser at a judicial sale under a decree of such court, and against the surety or sureties of such purchaser, returnable to such date as the court may fix, to show cause why judgment shall not be entered against them for any amount which the court may ascertain to be due from such commissioner, receiver, or purchaser. A rule issued under this section shall be executed at least fifteen days before the return day thereof.

Acts 1977, c. 617.

§ 8.01–106. How cause heard upon rule and judgment rendered

Upon the return of a rule executed under § 8.01–105 upon any of the parties thereto, the court may if neither party demand a jury, proceed to hear and determine all questions raised by such rule, and shall enter a judgment against such special commissioner, receiver, or purchaser, as the case may be, and his surety or sureties, for the amount appearing to be due by such commissioner, receiver or purchaser, or may enter judgment against such of them as have been summoned to answer such rule. If it appears in such proceeding that such commissioner, receiver, purchaser, or any of them, or their sureties is dead, or under a disability, then such rule shall be awarded against the personal representative of those dead, and the fiduciary of those who are under a disability, and judgment may be rendered jointly and severally against such personal representative, fiduciary and those laboring under no disability in the same proceeding.

Acts 1977, c. 617.

§ 8.01–107. Trial by jury of issues made upon rule

If, upon the return of such rule, any party thereto demand a trial by jury, the court shall order a trial by jury to ascertain what liability, if any, exists against any such special commissioner, receiver, or purchaser, and their sureties; and the court shall enter judgment on the verdict awarded by the jury. New trials may be granted as in other cases; and notwithstanding such rules be awarded and judgment be rendered against part only of the persons liable thereto, the court may award new rules and proceed to judgment against all the parties who are liable thereto. The provisions of this section, and §§ 8.01–105 and 8.01–106, shall apply to any officers and their sureties, acting under the decree of the court.

Acts 1977, c. 617.

§ 8.01-108. When sureties of commissioner, purchaser, etc., proceeded against by rule

Whenever a special commissioner, a receiver, purchaser at a judicial sale, or his personal representative, or any of them, can be proceeded against by rule for the recovery of money under §§ 8.01-105, 8.01-106 and 8.01-107, the surety of such commissioner, receiver, or purchaser, and the personal representatives of such sureties, may also be proceeded against under such sections.

Acts 1977, c. 617.

§ 8.01-109. Commission for selling, collecting, etc.; each piece of property to constitute separate sale

For the services of commissioners or officers under any decree for a sale, including the collection and paying over of the proceeds, there may be allowed a commission of five percent on amounts up to and including $100,000, and two percent on all amounts above $100,000. If the sale is made by one commissioner or officer and the proceeds collected by another, the court under whose decree they acted shall apportion the commission between them as may be just.

For the purposes of this section, each piece of property so sold shall constitute a separate sale, even though more than one piece of property is sold under the same decree.

Acts 1977, c. 617; Acts 1993, c. 311.

§ 8.01-110. Appointment of special commissioner to execute deed, etc.; effect of deed

A court in a suit wherein it is proper to decree the execution of any deed or writing may appoint a special commissioner to execute the same on behalf of any party in interest and such instrument shall be as valid as if executed by the party on whose behalf it is so executed.

Acts 1977, c. 617.

§ 8.01-111. What such deed to show

Every deed executed by any such commissioner pursuant to the provisions of § 8.01-110 shall specifically set out as nearly as practicable the name of the person on whose behalf the same is executed; provided, that when such deed conveys the right, title or interest of the heirs of a person who is dead it shall be sufficient for such deed to set out that the same is executed on behalf of the heirs of such decedent. But a failure to comply with the provisions of this section shall not affect or invalidate any such deed; and all deeds heretofore executed by any such commissioner in which such persons or heirs are not specifically set out are hereby validated.

Acts 1977, c. 617.

§ 8.01-112. Reinstatement of cause to appoint special commissioner to make deed

Any ended cause may be reinstated for the purpose of entering a decree directing a deed to be made to any party clearly shown by the record to be entitled thereto, or for the purpose of substituting a new commissioner to make a deed in the place of one previously appointed for that purpose, but who has died or become incapacitated to act before making such deed.

Acts 1977, c. 617.

§ 8.01-113. When title of purchaser at judicial sale not to be disturbed

If a sale of property is made under a decree of a court, and such sale is confirmed, the title of the purchaser at such sale shall not be disturbed unless within twelve months from such confirmation the sale is set aside by the trial court or an appeal is taken to the Court of Appeals or allowed by the Supreme Court, and a decree is therein afterwards entered requiring such sale to be set aside. This limitation shall not affect any right of restitution of the proceeds of sale.

Acts 1977, c. 617; Acts 1984, c. 703.

Article 12

Detinue

§ 8.01-114. When property to be taken by officer; summary of evidence, affidavits and report to be filed

A. A proceeding in detinue to recover personal property unlawfully withheld from the plaintiff may be brought on a warrant or motion for judgment if pretrial seizure is not sought at the time of filing.

A petition in detinue for pretrial seizure pursuant to this article may be filed either to commence the detinue proceeding or may be filed during the pendency of a detinue proceeding which commenced on a warrant or motion for judgment. If a petition is filed, it shall:

1. Describe the kind, quantity and estimated fair market value of the specific personal property as to which plaintiff seeks possession;

2. Describe the basis of the plaintiff's claim of entitlement to recover the property, with such certainty as will give the adverse party reasonable notice of the true nature of the claim and the particulars thereof and, if based on a contract to secure the payment of money, the amount due on such contract; and

3. Allege one or more of the grounds mentioned in § 8.01–534 and set forth specific facts in support of such allegation. Further, if a petition is filed, a judge, or a magistrate appointed pursuant to Article 3 (§ 19.2–33 et seq.) of Chapter 3 of Title 19.2, may issue an order or other process directed to the sheriff or other proper officer, as the case may be, commanding him to seize the property for the recovery of which such action or warrant is brought, or a specified portion thereof, and deliver same to the plaintiff pendente lite under the circumstances hereinafter set forth.

B. The judge or the magistrate may issue such an order or other process in accordance with the prayer of the petition after an ex parte review of the petition only upon a determination that: (i) the petition conforms with subsection A and (ii) there is reasonable cause to believe that the grounds for detinue seizure described in the petition exist. The plaintiff praying for an order shall, at the time that he files his petition, pay the proper costs, fees and taxes, and in the event of his failure to do so, the order shall not be issued.

C. The judge or magistrate, as the case may be, may receive evidence only in the form of a sworn petition which shall be filed with the papers in the cause.

D. The order commanding the seizure of property shall be issued and served together with the form for requesting a hearing on a claim of exemption from seizure as provided in § 8.01–546.1. The order shall be issued and returned as provided in § 8.01–541 and may be issued or executed on any day, including a Saturday, Sunday or other legal holiday. Service shall be in accordance with the methods described in § 8.01–487.1. The provisions of § 8.01–546.2 shall govern claims for exemption.

Acts 1977, c. 617; Acts 1978, c. 403; Acts 1986, c. 341; Acts 1993, c. 841.

§ 8.01–115. Bond required as prerequisite

No such order or process, however, shall be issued until a bond, conforming with the requirements of § 8.01–537.1, is posted with the judge or magistrate, in a penalty at least double the estimated fair market value of the property claimed, payable to the defendant, with the additional condition to redeliver the property so seized to the defendant, or to the person from whose possession it was taken, if the right to the possession shall be adjudged against the plaintiff.

Acts 1977, c. 230; Acts 1977, c. 617; Acts 1986, c. 341; Acts 1993, c. 841.

§ 8.01–116. Return of property to defendant or other claimant

A. Subject to the provisions of subsection B below, the defendant in any such proceeding, or any other person claiming title to the property so seized and taken possession of by the officer, may have such property returned to him at any time after such seizure upon executing a bond, with sufficient surety, to be approved by the officer, payable to the plaintiff, in a penalty at least double the estimated value of the property. The bond shall contain a condition to (i) pay all costs and damages which may be awarded against the defendant in the proceeding and all damages which may accrue to any person by reason of the return of the property to the defendant or the claimant and (ii) have the property forthcoming to answer any judgment or order of the court or judge respecting the same. The bond shall be delivered to the officer and returned by him to the office of the clerk. The officer, on receiving the bond, shall forthwith return the property taken by him to the defendant or any other person claiming title thereto or from whose possession it was taken.

B. In any such proceeding, upon application of the defendant after reasonable notice to the plaintiff or his attorney, the judge of the court in which the proceeding is pending may order the property returned to the defendant upon such lesser security and upon such terms as in the nature of the case may be just and reasonable.

C. If no bond or security is delivered to the officer after his seizing and taking possession of such property, the property, if in the hands of the officer, shall be kept by him. However, if the property is perishable or expensive to keep, it may be sold by order of the court in the same manner as if it were a sale under execution.

Acts 1977, c. 617; Acts 1993, c. 841.

§ 8.01–117. Exceptions to sufficiency of bonds

Either party may file exceptions to the sufficiency of the bond of the other or of the claimant of the property, if he has given bond, or such claimant may file exceptions to the sufficiency of the bond of either party. The court before whom the proceeding is pending, may, on the motion of either party or of the claimant, after reasonable notice to the others, pass upon such exceptions and make such order thereupon as may be just and reasonable.

Acts 1977, c. 617; Acts 1993, c. 841.

§ 8.01–118. Repealed by Acts 1986, c. 341

§ 8.01–119. Hearing to review issuance of order or process under § 8.01–114 or to consider request for such order or process

A. Within thirty days after the issuance of any ex parte order or process pursuant to § 8.01–114, or promptly upon application of either party, and in either event after reasonable notice, the court in which such proceeding is pending shall conduct a hearing to review the decision to issue the order or other process described in § 8.01–114, or to consider the request of the plaintiff for issuance of such order or other process, whether or not the plaintiff has attempted to previously obtain an order pursuant to § 8.01–114. The hearing may be combined with a prompt hearing held pursuant to § 8.01–546.2 on an exemption claimed or a trial on the merits or both. If combined with a hearing on an exemption claim, the hearing shall be conducted within ten business days of the filing of the request for a hearing. If the plaintiff gives reasonable notice of his intention to apply for such an order or process before the court, such hearing may be on the return day of the warrant. Evidence may be presented in the same manner as in subsection B of § 8.01–114.

B. At the conclusion of the hearing, if the evidence establishes the facts set forth in subdivision 1 of subsection A of § 8.01–114, and the court is satisfied from the evidence that (i) one or more of the grounds set forth in § 8.01–534 exist, (ii) there is good reason to believe that the defendant is insolvent, so that any recovery against him for the alternate value of the property and for damages and costs will probably prove unavailing, or (iii) the plaintiff may suffer other irreparable harm if his request is denied, and if it further appears to the court that there is a substantial likelihood that the plaintiff's allegations will be sustained at the trial, then the court shall issue the order or other process requested by the plaintiff, or let stand an order issued in the cause pursuant to § 8.01–114.

If the decision of the court is in favor of the defendant, the former order or process issued in the cause shall be abated and the property returned to the possession of the person from whom it was taken to abide the final trial of the action or warrant. Proof of insolvency as grounds for possession of goods by the plaintiff shall not be introduced for purposes of affirming a prior ex parte order, but only upon an initial application for possession after reasonable notice.

C. Issuance of any order or process pursuant to this section shall be subject to the provisions of §§ 8.01–115 and 8.01–116.

Acts 1977, c. 617; Acts 1986, c. 341; Acts 1993, c. 841.

§ 8.01–120. No verdict as to some items; omission of price or value

If in such detinue action, on an issue concerning several things, in one or more counts, no verdict be found for part of them, it shall not be error, but the plaintiff shall be barred of his title to the things omitted; and if the verdict omit the price or value, the court may at any time have a jury impaneled to ascertain the same.

Acts 1977, c. 617.

§ 8.01–121. Final judgment

When final judgment is rendered on the trial of such detinue proceeding, the court shall dispose of the property or proceeds according to the rights of those entitled. When, in any such proceeding, the plaintiff prevails under a contract which, regardless of its form or express terms, was in fact made to secure the payment of money to the plaintiff or his assignor, judgment shall be for the recovery of the amount due the plaintiff thereunder or for the specific property, and costs. The defendant shall have the election of paying the amount of such judgment or surrendering the specific property. The court may grant the defendant a reasonable time not exceeding thirty days, within which to make the election upon such security being given as the court may deem sufficient. When the property involves an animal as defined in § 3.2–6500, the court may order the return of the animal to the prevailing plaintiff without regard to any alternative method of recovery.

If the defendant elects to surrender the property as aforesaid, upon delivery of the property to the plaintiff or repossession thereof by him, the plaintiff may proceed to sell the property in accordance with the applicable provisions of the Uniform Commercial Code (Part 6 (§§ 8.9A–601 et seq.) of Title 8.9A) with all the rights and responsibilities therein provided.

Acts 1977, c. 617; Acts 1987, c. 1; Acts 1993, c. 841.

§ 8.01–122. Charges for keeping property

The legal charges, if any, for keeping any such property, while in the possession of the officer, shall be paid by the plaintiff and certified by the officer to the court who, in case such order or process be not abated and final judgment be rendered for the plaintiff, shall tax the same along with the other costs of the suit.

Acts 1977, c. 617.

§ 8.01–123. Recovery of damages sustained for property withheld during appeal

When a judgment for specific personal property is affirmed by an appellate court, or an injunction to such judgment is dissolved, the person who is entitled to execution of such judgment, or who would be entitled if execution had not been had, may, on motion to the court from which such execution has issued, or might issue, after fifteen days' notice to the defendant or his personal representative, have a jury impaneled to ascertain the damages sustained by reason of the detention of such property, subsequent to such judgment, or if it was on a verdict, subsequent to such verdict; and judgment shall be rendered for the damages, if any, so ascertained.

Acts 1977, c. 617.

Article 13

Unlawful Entry and Detainer

§ 8.01–124. Motion for judgment in circuit court for unlawful entry or detainer

If any forcible or unlawful entry be made upon lands, or if, when the entry is lawful and peaceable, the tenant shall detain the possession of land after the right has expired, without the consent of him who is entitled to the possession, the party so turned out of possession, no matter what right of title he had thereto, or the party against whom such possession is unlawfully detained may file a motion for judgment in the circuit court alleging that the defendant is in possession and unlawfully withholds from the plaintiff the premises in question.

Acts 1977, c. 617.

§ 8.01–125. When summons returnable to circuit court; jury

When the action is commenced in the circuit court, the summons is returnable thereto and, upon application of either party trial by jury shall be had.

Acts 1977, c. 617.

§ 8.01–126. Summons for unlawful detainer issued by magistrate or clerk or judge of a general district court

A. In any case when possession of any house, land or tenement is unlawfully detained by the person in possession thereof, the landlord, his agent, attorney, or other person, entitled to the possession may present to a magistrate or a clerk or judge of a general district court a statement under oath of the facts which authorize the removal of the tenant or other person in possession, describing such premises; and thereupon such magistrate, clerk or judge shall issue his summons against the person or persons named in such affidavit. The process issued upon any such summons issued by a magistrate, clerk or judge may be served as provided in § 8.01–293, 8.01–296, or 8.01–299. When issued by a magistrate it may be returned to and the case heard and determined by the judge of a general district court. If the summons for unlawful detainer is filed to terminate a tenancy pursuant to the Virginia Residential Landlord Tenant Act (§ 55–248.2 et seq.), the initial hearing on such summons shall occur as soon as practicable, but not more than 21 days from the date of filing. If the case cannot be heard within 21 days from the date of filing, the initial hearing shall be held as soon as practicable. If the plaintiff requests that the initial hearing be set on a date later than 21 days from the date of filing, the initial hearing shall be set on a date the plaintiff is available that is also available for the court. Such summons shall be served at least 10 days before the return day thereof.

B. Notwithstanding any other rule of court or provision of law to the contrary, the plaintiff in an unlawful detainer case may submit into evidence a photocopy of a properly executed paper document or paper printout of an electronically stored document including a copy of the original lease or other documents, provided that the plaintiff provides an affidavit or sworn testimony that the copy of such document is a true and accurate copy of the original lease. An attorney or agent of the landlord or managing agent may present such affidavit into evidence.

C. 1. Notwithstanding any other rule of court or provision of law to the contrary, when the defendant does not make an appearance in court, the plaintiff or the plaintiff's attorney or agent may submit into evidence by an affidavit or sworn testimony a statement of the amount of outstanding rent, late charges, attorney fees, and any other charges or damages due as of the date of the hearing. The plaintiff or the plaintiff's attorney or agent shall advise the court of any payments by the defendant that result in a variance reducing the amount due the plaintiff as of the day of the hearing.

2. If the unlawful detainer summons served upon the defendant requests judgment for all amounts due as of the date of the hearing, the court shall permit amendment of the amount requested on the summons for unlawful detainer filed in court in accordance with the evidence and shall enter a judgment for such amount due as of the date of the hearing in addition to entering an order of possession for the premises.

3. In determining the amount due the plaintiff as of the date of the hearing, if the rental agreement or lease provides that rent is due and payable on the first of the month in advance for the entire month, at the request of the plaintiff or the plaintiff's attorney or agent, the amount due as of the date of the hearing shall include the rent due for the entire month in which the hearing is held, and rent shall not be prorated as of the actual court date. Otherwise, the rent shall be prorated as of the date of the hearing. However, nothing herein shall be construed to permit a landlord to collect rent in excess of the amount stated in such rental agreement or lease. If a money judgment has been granted for the amount due for the month of the hearing pursuant to this section and the landlord re-rents such dwelling unit and receives rent from a new tenant prior to the end of such month, the landlord is required to reflect the applicable portion of the judgment as satisfied pursuant to § 16.1–94.01.

Acts 1977, c. 617; Acts 1978, c. 344; Acts 1980, c. 502; Acts 2000, c. 1055. Amended by Acts 2008, c. 551; Acts 2008, c. 691; Acts 2012, c. 788; Acts 2013, c. 63; Acts 2014, c. 168; Acts 2015, c. 547.

§§ 8.01–127, 8.01–127.1. Repealed by Acts 2007, c. 869

§ 8.01–128. Verdict and judgment; damages

A. If it appears that the plaintiff was forcibly or unlawfully turned out of possession, or that it was unlawfully detained from him, the verdict or judgment shall be for the plaintiff for the premises, or such part thereof as may be found to have been so held or detained. The verdict or judgment shall also be for such damages as the plaintiff may prove to have been sustained by him by reason of such forcible or unlawful entry, or unlawful detention, of such premises, and such rent as he may prove to have been owing to him.

B. The plaintiff may, alternatively, receive a final, appealable judgment for possession of the property unlawfully entered or unlawfully detained and be issued a writ of possession, and continue the case for up to 90 days to establish final rent and damages. If the plaintiff elects to proceed under this section, the judge shall hear evidence as to the issue of possession on the initial court date and shall hear evidence on the final rent and damages at the hearing set on the continuance date, unless the plaintiff requests otherwise or the judge rules otherwise. Nothing in this section shall preclude a defendant who appears in court at the initial court date from contesting an unlawful detainer action as otherwise provided by law.

If under this section an appeal is taken as to possession, the entire case shall be considered appealed. The plaintiff shall, in the instance of a continuance taken under this section, mail to the defendant at the defendant's last known address at least 15 days prior to the continuance date a notice advising of (i) the continuance date; (ii) the amounts of final rent and damages; and (iii) that the plaintiff is seeking judgment for additional sums. A copy of such notice shall be filed with the court.

C. No verdict or judgment rendered under this section shall bar any separate concurrent or future action for any such damages or rent as may not be so claimed.

Acts 1977, c. 617. Amended by Acts 2005, c. 779; Acts 2010, c. 550; Acts 2011, c. 76.

§ 8.01–129. Appeal from judgment of general district court

An appeal shall lie from the judgment of a general district court, in any proceeding under this article, to the circuit court in the same manner and with like effect and upon like security as appeals taken under the provisions of § 16.1–106 et seq. except as specifically provided in this section. The appeal shall be taken within 10 days and the security approved by the court from which the appeal is taken. Notwithstanding the provisions of § 16.1–106 et seq. the bond shall be posted and the writ tax paid within 10 days of the date of the judgment. Unless otherwise specifically provided in the court's order, no writ of execution shall issue on a judgment for possession until the expiration of this 10–day period, except in cases of judgment of default (i) wherein the case arises out of a trustee's deed following foreclosure, (ii) for the nonpayment of rent where the writ of execution shall issue immediately upon entry of judgment for possession, if requested by the plaintiff, or (iii) for immediate nonremediable terminations where the writ of execution shall issue immediately upon entry of judgment for possession, if requested by the plaintiff. When the appeal is taken by the defendant, he shall be required to give security also for all rent which has accrued and may accrue upon the premises, but for not more than one year's rent, and also for all damages that have accrued or may accrue from the unlawful use and occupation of the premises for a period not exceeding three months. Trial by jury shall be had upon application of any party.

Acts 1977, c. 617; Acts 1984, c. 565; Acts 1998, c. 750. Amended by Acts 2004, c. 343; Acts 2008, c. 489.

§ 8.01–130. Judgment not to bar action of trespass or ejectment

No judgment in an action brought under the provisions of this article shall bar any action of trespass or ejectment between the same parties, nor shall any such judgment or verdict be conclusive, in any such future action, of the facts therein found.

Acts 1977, c. 617.

Article 14

Ejectment

§ 8.01–131. Action of ejectment retained; when and by whom brought

A. The action of ejectment is retained, subject to the provisions hereinafter contained, and to the applicable Rules of Court.

B. Such action may be brought in the same cases in which a writ of right might have been brought prior to the first day of July, 1850, and by any person claiming real estate in fee or for life or for years, either as heir, devisee or purchaser, or otherwise.

Acts 1977, c. 617.

§ 8.01–132. What interest and right plaintiff must have

No person shall bring such ejectment action unless he has, at the time of commencing it, a subsisting interest in the premises claimed and a right to recover the same, or to recover the possession thereof, or some share, interest or portion thereof.

Acts 1977, c. 617.

§ 8.01–133. Who shall be defendants; when and how landlord may defend

The person actually occupying the premises and any person claiming title thereto or claiming any interest therein adversely to the plaintiff may also, at the discretion of the plaintiff, be named defendants in the action. If there be no person actually occupying the premises adversely to the plaintiff, then the action must be against some person exercising ownership thereon or claiming title thereto or some interest therein at the commencement of suit. If a lessee be made defendant at the suit of a party claiming against the title of his landlord such landlord may appear and be made a defendant with or in place of his lessee.

Acts 1977, c. 617.

§ 8.01–134. How action commenced and prosecuted

The action shall be commenced and prosecuted as other actions at law. The name of the real claimant shall be inserted as plaintiff, and all the provisions of law concerning a lessor of a plaintiff shall apply to such plaintiff.

Acts 1977, c. 617.

§ 8.01–135. What is to be stated in motion for judgment

It shall be sufficient for the plaintiff to aver in his motion for judgment that on some day specified therein, which shall be after his title accrued, he was possessed of the premises claimed, and, being so possessed thereof, the defendant afterwards, on some day likewise specified, entered into such premises or exercised acts of ownership thereon or claimed title thereto or some interest therein, to the damage of the plaintiff in such sum as he shall state in his motion for judgment.

Acts 1977, c. 617.

§ 8.01–136. How premises described

The premises claimed shall be described in the motion for judgment with convenient certainty, so that, from such description, with the aid of information derived from the plaintiff, possession thereof may be delivered.

Acts 1977, c. 617.

§ 8.01–137. Plaintiff to state how he claims

The plaintiff shall also state whether he claims in fee or for his life, or the life of another, or for years, specifying such lives or the duration of such term, and when he claims an undivided share or interest he shall state the same.

Acts 1977, c. 617.

§ 8.01–138. There may be several counts and several plaintiffs

The motion for judgment may contain several counts, and several parties may be named as plaintiffs jointly in one count and separately in others.

Acts 1977, c. 617.

§ 8.01–139. What proof by plaintiff is sufficient

The consent rule, formerly used, remains abolished. The plaintiff need not prove an actual entry on, or possession of, the premises demanded, or receipt of any profits thereof, or any lease, entry, or ouster, except as hereinafter provided. But it shall be sufficient for him to show a right to the possession of the premises at the time of the commencement of the suit.

Acts 1977, c. 617.

§ 8.01–140. Effect of reservation in deed; burden of proof

In any action, suit or other judicial proceeding involving the title to land embraced in the exterior boundaries of any patent, deed or other writing, which reserves one or more parcels of land from the operation of such patent, deed or other writing, if there be no claim made by a party to the proceedings that the land in controversy, or any part thereof, lies within such reservation, such patent, deed or other writing shall be construed, and shall have the same effect, as if it contained no such reservation; and if any party to such proceeding claims that the land in controversy, or any part thereof, lies within such reservation, the burden shall be upon him to prove the fact, and all land not shown by a preponderance of the evidence to lie within such reservation shall be deemed to lie without the same.

This section shall apply in cases involving the right to the proceeds of any such land when condemned or sold, as well as in cases where the title to land is directly involved, and shall apply in any case in which the title to any part of the land, or its proceeds, but for this section, would or might be in this Commonwealth.

Acts 1977, c. 617.

§ 8.01–141. When action by cotenants, etc., against cotenants, what plaintiff to prove

If the action be by one or more tenants in common, joint tenants or coparceners against their cotenants, the plaintiff shall be bound to prove actual ouster or some other act amounting to total denial of the plaintiff's right as cotenant.

Acts 1977, c. 617.

§ 8.01–142. Verdict when action against several defendants

If the action be against several defendants, and a joint possession of all be proved, and the plaintiff be entitled to a verdict, it shall be against all, whether they pleaded separately or jointly.

Acts 1977, c. 617.

§ 8.01-143. When there may be several judgments against defendants

If the action be against several defendants, and it appear on the trial that any of them occupy distinct parcels in severalty or jointly, and that other defendants possess other parcels in severalty or jointly, the plaintiff may recover several judgments against them, for the parcels so held by one or more of the defendants, separately from others.

Acts 1977, c. 617.

§ 8.01-144. Recovery of part of premises claimed

The plaintiff may recover any specific or any undivided part or share of the premises, though it be less than he claimed in the motion for judgment.

Acts 1977, c. 617.

§ 8.01-145. When possession of part not possession of whole

In a controversy affecting real estate, possession of part shall not be construed as possession of the whole when an actual adverse possession can be proved.

Acts 1977, c. 617.

§ 8.01-146. When vendee, etc., entitled to conveyance of legal title, vendor cannot recover

A vendor, or any claiming under him, shall not, at law any more than in equity, recover against a vendee, or those claiming under him, lands sold by such vendor to such vendee, when there is a writing, stating the purchase and the terms thereof, signed by the vendor or his agent and there has been such payment or performance of what was contracted to be paid or performed on the part of the vendee, as would in equity entitle him, or those claiming under him, to a conveyance of the legal title of such land from the vendor, or those claiming under him, without condition.

Acts 1977, c. 617.

§ 8.01-147. When mortgagee or trustee not to recover

The payment of the whole sum, or the performance of the whole duty, or the accomplishment of the whole purpose, which any mortgage or deed of trust may have been made to secure or effect, shall prevent the grantee, or his heirs, from recovering at law, by virtue of such mortgage or deed of trust, property thereby conveyed, whenever the defendant would in equity be entitled to a decree, revesting the legal title in him without condition.

Acts 1977, c. 617.

§ 8.01-148. Right of defendant to resort to equity not affected

Whether the defendant shall or shall not make or attempt a defense under §§ 8.01-146 and 8.01-147, he shall not be precluded from resorting to equity for any relief to which he would have been entitled if such sections had not been enacted.

Acts 1977, c. 617.

§ 8.01-149. Verdict when jury finds for plaintiffs or any of them

If the jury be of opinion for the plaintiffs, or any of them, the verdict shall be for the plaintiffs, or such of them as appear to have right to the possession of the premises, or any part thereof, and against such of the defendants as were in possession thereof or claimed title thereto at the commencement of the action.

Acts 1977, c. 617.

§ 8.01-150. Verdict when any plaintiff has no right

When any plaintiff appears to have no such right, the verdict as to such plaintiff shall be for the defendants.

Acts 1977, c. 617.

§ 8.01-151. How verdict to specify premises recovered

When the right of the plaintiff is proved to all the premises claimed, the verdict shall be for the premises generally as specified in the motion for judgment, but if it be proved to only a part or share of the premises, the verdict shall specify such part particularly as the same is proved, and with the same certainty of description as is required in the motion for judgment.

Acts 1977, c. 617.

§ 8.01-152. How verdict to specify undivided interest or share

If the verdict be for an undivided share or interest in the premises claimed, it shall specify the same, and if for an undivided share or interest of a part of the premises, it shall specify such share or interest, and describe such part as before required.

Acts 1977, c. 617.

§ 8.01-153. Verdict to specify estate of plaintiff

The verdict shall also specify the estate found in the plaintiff, whether it be in fee or for life, stating for whose life, or whether it be a term of years, and specifying the duration of such term.

Acts 1977, c. 617.

§ 8.01-154. When right of plaintiff expires before trial, what judgment entered

If the right or title of a plaintiff in ejectment expire after the commencement of the suit, but before trial, the verdict shall be according to the fact, and judgment shall be entered for his damages sustained from the withholding of the premises by the defendant, and as to the premises claimed, the judgment shall be for the defendant.

Acts 1977, c. 617.

§ 8.01–155. How judgment for plaintiff entered

The judgment for the plaintiff shall be, that he recover the possession of the premises, according to the verdict of the jury, if there be a verdict, or if the judgment be by default, or on demurrer, according to the description thereof in the motion for judgment.

Acts 1977, c. 617.

§ 8.01–156. Authority of sheriffs, etc., to store and sell personal property removed from premises; recovery of possession by owner; disposition or sale

In any county or city, when personal property is removed from premises pursuant to an action of unlawful detainer or ejectment, or pursuant to any other action in which personal property is removed from premises in order to restore such premises to the person entitled thereto, the sheriff shall oversee the removal of such personal property and it shall be placed in a storage area designated by the governing body of the county or city if such an area has been so designated, or, in the case of a manufactured home, at the request of the owner of the real property, to be placed into a storage area designated by the owner of the real property which may be the manufactured home lot or other location within the manufactured home park, unless the owner of such personal property then and there removes it from the public way. The sheriff and the owner of the real property shall not have any liability for the loss of any such manufactured home remaining on the manufactured home lot, nor shall they have any liability for the loss of any removed personal property.

The owner, before obtaining possession of such personal property so placed in a storage area shall pay to the parties entitled thereto the reasonable and necessary costs incidental to such removal and storage. Should such owner fail or refuse to pay such costs within 30 days from the date of placing the property in storage, the sheriff shall, after due notice to the owner and holders of liens of record, dispose of the property by publicly advertised public sale. The proceeds from such sale shall be used to pay all costs of removal, storage, and sale, all fees and liens, and the balance of such funds shall be paid to the person entitled thereto. Should the cost of removal and storage exceed the proceeds realized from such sale the county or city shall reimburse the sheriff for such excess, except that any such excess costs related to the disposal of a manufactured home shall be paid by the owner of the real property from which the manufactured home was removed. The sheriff, in his discretion, may refuse to remove or dispose of such manufactured home until the owner of the real property pays to the sheriff the estimated cost of such removal and disposition. Subsequent to disposition, the sheriff shall reimburse the owner to the extent the actual cost is less than the estimated cost, or shall request additional payment to the extent the actual cost exceeds the estimated cost.

Acts 1977, c. 617; Acts 1992, c. 454; Acts 1993, c. 16. Amended by Acts 2005, c. 791; Acts 2006, c. 129.

§ 8.01–157. Repealed by Acts 1990, c. 831, eff. Jan. 1, 1991

§ 8.01–158. How claim of plaintiff for profits and damages assessed

If the plaintiff file with his motion for judgment a statement of the profits and other damages which he means to demand, and the jury find in his favor, they shall, at the same time, unless the court otherwise order, assess the damages for mesne profits of the land for any period not exceeding five years previously to the commencement of the suit until the verdict, and also the damages for any destruction or waste of the buildings or other property during the same time for which the defendant is chargeable.

Acts 1977, c. 617.

§ 8.01–159. When court to assess damages

If there be no issue of fact tried in the cause, and judgment is to be rendered for the plaintiff on demurrer, or otherwise, such damages shall be assessed by the court, unless either party shall move to have them assessed by a jury, or the court shall think proper to have them so assessed, in which case a jury shall be impaneled to assess them. If the defendant is in default the court shall proceed to render judgment and assess damages as provided in Rule of Court 3:19.

Acts 1977, c. 617.

§ 8.01–160. Defendant to give notice of claim for improvements

If the defendant intends to claim allowance for improvements made upon the premises by himself or those under whom he claims, he shall file with his pleading a statement of his claim therefor, in case judgment be rendered for the plaintiff.

Acts 1977, c. 617.

§ 8.01–161. How allowed

In such case, the damages of the plaintiff, and the allowance to the defendant for improvements, shall be estimated, and the balance ascertained, and judgment therefor rendered, as prescribed in Article 15 (§ 8.01–166 et seq.) of this chapter.

Acts 1977, c. 617.

§ 8.01–162. Postponement of assessment and allowance

On the motion of either party, the court may order the assessment of such damages and allowance to be postponed until after the verdict on the title is recorded.

Acts 1977, c. 617.

§ 8.01–163. Judgment to be conclusive

Any such judgment in an action of ejectment shall be conclusive as to the title or right of possession established in such action, upon the party against whom it is rendered, and against all persons claiming from, through, or under such party, by title accruing after the commencement of such action, except as hereinafter mentioned.

Acts 1977, c. 617.

§ 8.01–164. Recovery of mesne profits, etc., not affected

Nothing in this chapter shall prevent the plaintiff from recovering mesne profits, or damages done to the premises, from any person other than the defendant, who may be liable to such action.

Acts 1977, c. 617.

§ 8.01–165. Writ of right, etc., abolished

No writ of right, writ of entry, or writ of formedon, shall be hereafter brought.

Acts 1977, c. 617.

Article 15

Improvements

§ 8.01–166. How defendant may apply therefor, and have judgment suspended

Any defendant against whom a decree or judgment shall be rendered for land, when no assessment of damages has been made under Article 14 (§ 8.01–131 et seq.) of this chapter, may, at any time before the execution of the decree or judgment, present a pleading to the court rendering such decree or judgment, stating that he, or those under whom he claims while holding the premises under a title believed by him or them to have been good, have made permanent improvements thereon, and moving that he should have an allowance for the same which are over and above the value of the use and occupation of such land; and thereupon the court may, if satisfied of the probable truth of the allegation, suspend the execution of the judgment or decree, and impanel a jury to assess the damages of the plaintiff, and the allowances to the defendant for such improvements.

Acts 1977, c. 617.

§ 8.01–167. How damages of plaintiff assessed

The jury, in assessing such damages, either under this article or under Article 14 (§ 8.01–131 et seq.) of this chapter, shall determine the annual value of the premises during the time the defendant was in possession thereof, exclusive of the use by the tenant of the improvements thereon made by himself or those under whom he claims, and also the damages for waste or other injury to the premises committed by the defendant.

Acts 1977, c. 617.

§ 8.01–168. For what time

The defendant shall not be liable for such annual value for any longer time than five years before the suit, or for damages for any such waste or other injury done before such five years, except when he claims for improvements as aforesaid.

Acts 1977, c. 617.

§ 8.01–169. How value of improvements determined in favor of defendant

If the jury shall be satisfied that the defendant, or those under whom he claims, made on the premises, at a time when there was reason to believe the title good under which he or they were holding the same, permanent and valuable improvements, they shall determine the value of such improvements as were so made before receipt by the person making the same of notice in writing of the title under which the plaintiff claims, not exceeding the amount actually expended in making them, and not exceeding the amount to which the value of the premises is actually increased thereby at the time of such determination.

Acts 1977, c. 617.

§ 8.01–170. If allowance for improvements exceed damages, what to be done

If the sum determined for the improvements exceed the damages determined by the jury against the defendant as aforesaid, they shall then determine against him, for any time before such five years, the rents and profits accrued against, or damage for waste or other injury done by him, or those under whom he claims, so far as may be necessary to balance his claim for improvements, but in such case he shall not be liable for the excess, if any, of such rents and profits, or damages, beyond the value of the improvements.

Acts 1977, c. 617.

§ 8.01–171. Verdict for balance, after offsetting damages against improvements

After offsetting the damages assessed for the plaintiff and the allowances to the defendant for improvements, if any, the jury shall find a verdict for the balance for the plaintiff or defendant, as the case may be, and judgment or decree shall be entered therefor according to the verdict.

Acts 1977, c. 617.

§ 8.01–172. Balance for defendant a lien on the land

Any such balance due to the defendant shall constitute a lien upon the land recovered by the plaintiff, until the same shall be paid.

Acts 1977, c. 617.

§ 8.01–173. How tenant for life, paying for improvements, reimbursed

If the plaintiff claim only an estate for life in the land recovered, and pay any sum allowed to the defendant for improvements, he, or his personal representative at the determination of his estate, may recover from the remainderman or reversioner, the value of such improvements as they then exist, not exceeding the amount so paid by him, and shall have a lien therefor on the premises, in like manner as if they had been mortgaged for the payment thereof, and may keep possession of such premises until the same be paid.

Acts 1977, c. 617.

§ 8.01–174. Exception as to mortgagees and trustees

Nothing in this article, nor anything concerning rents, profits, and improvements, in Article 14 (§ 8.01–131 et seq.) of this chapter, shall extend or apply to any suit brought by a mortgagee, or trustee in a deed of trust to secure creditors, his heirs, or assigns, against a mortgagor or grantor in such deed of trust, his heirs, or assigns, for the recovery of the mortgaged premises or of the land conveyed by such deed of trust.

Acts 1977, c. 617.

§ 8.01–175. When plaintiff may require his estate only to be valued; how determined; how he may elect to relinquish his title to defendant

A. When the defendant shall claim allowance for improvements, the plaintiff may, by an entry on the record, require that the value of his estate in the premises, without the improvements, shall also be ascertained.

B. The value of the premises in such case shall be determined as it would have been at the time of the inquiry, if no such improvements had been made, and shall be ascertained in the manner hereinbefore provided for determining the value of improvements.

C. The plaintiff in such case, if judgment is rendered for him, may at any time, enter on the record his election to relinquish his estate in the premises to the defendant at the value so ascertained under this section, and the defendant shall thenceforth hold all the estate that the plaintiff had therein at the commencement of the suit, provided he pay therefor such value, with interest, in the manner in which the court may direct.

Acts 1977, c. 617.

§ 8.01–176. How payment of such value to be made by defendant; when land sold therefor

The payments shall be made to the plaintiff, or into court for his use, and the land shall be bound therefor, and if the defendant fail to make such payments within or at the times limited therefor respectively, the court may order the land to be sold and the proceeds applied to the payment of such value and interest, and the surplus, if any, to be paid to the defendant; but if the net proceeds be insufficient to satisfy such value and interest, the defendant shall not be bound for the deficiency.

Acts 1977, c. 617.

§ 8.01–177. When such value to be deemed real estate

If the party by or for whom the land is claimed in the suit be a person under a disability, such value shall be deemed to be real estate, and be disposed of as the court may consider proper for the benefit of the persons interested therein.

Acts 1977, c. 617.

§ 8.01–178. When and how defendant, if evicted, may recover from plaintiff amount paid

If the defendant or his heirs or assigns shall, after the premises are so relinquished to him, be evicted thereof by force of any better title than that of the original plaintiff, the person so evicted may recover from such plaintiff or his representative the amount so paid for the premises, as so much money had and received by such plaintiff in his lifetime for the use of such person, with lawful interest thereon from the time of such payment.

Acts 1977, c. 617.

ARTICLE 16

ESTABLISHING BOUNDARIES TO LAND

§ 8.01–179. Motion for judgment to establish boundary lines

Any person having a subsisting interest in real estate and a right to its possession, or to the possession of some share, interest or portion thereof, may file a motion for judgment to ascertain and designate the true boundary line or lines to such real estate as to one or more of the coterminous landowners. Plaintiff in stating his interest shall conform to the requirements of § 8.01-137, and shall describe with reasonable certainty such real estate and the boundary line or lines thereof which he seeks to establish.

Acts 1977, c. 617.

§ 8.01–180. Parties defendant; pleadings

The plaintiff shall make defendants to such motion for judgment all persons having a present interest in the boundary line or lines sought to be ascertained and designated.

Acts 1977, c. 617.

§ 8.01–181. Surveys

The court may appoint a surveyor and direct such surveys to be made as it deems necessary, and the costs thereof shall be assessed as the court may direct.

Acts 1977, c. 617.

§ 8.01–182. Claims to rents, etc., not considered

In a proceeding under this article, no claim of the plaintiff for rents, profits or damages shall be considered.

Acts 1977, c. 617.

§ 8.01–183. Recordation and effect of judgment

The judgment of the court shall be recorded in the current deed book of the court. The judgment shall forever settle, determine, and designate the true boundary line or lines in question, between the parties, their heirs, devisees, and assigns. The judgment may be enforced in the same manner as a judgment in an action of ejectment.

Acts 1977, c. 617.

ARTICLE 17

DECLARATORY JUDGMENTS

§ 8.01–184. Power to issue declaratory judgments

In cases of actual controversy, circuit courts within the scope of their respective jurisdictions shall have power to make binding adjudications of right, whether or not consequential relief is, or at the time could be, claimed and no action or proceeding shall be open to objection on the ground that a judgment order or decree merely declaratory of right is prayed for. Controversies involving the interpretation of deeds, wills, and other instruments of writing, statutes, municipal ordinances and other governmental regulations, may be so determined, and this enumeration does not exclude other instances of actual antagonistic assertion and denial of right.

Acts 1977, c. 617.

§ 8.01–184.1. Declaratory judgment to adjudicate constitutional nexus

A. Circuit courts shall have original jurisdiction over civil actions seeking declaratory judgment where:

1. The party seeking declaratory relief is a business that (i) is organized under the laws of the Commonwealth or a sole proprietorship owned by a Commonwealth domiciliary, or (ii) has qualified to do business in the Commonwealth; and

2. The responding party is a government official of another state, or political subdivision of another state, who asserts that the business in question is or was in the past obliged to collect sales or use taxes for such state or political subdivision based upon conduct of the business occurring wholly or partially within the Commonwealth.

B. Any business meeting the requirements and facing the circumstances described in subsection A shall be entitled to declaratory relief on the issue of whether the requirement of another state, or political subdivision of another state, that the business collect and remit sales or use taxes to that state, or political subdivision, in the factual circumstances of the business' operations giving rise to the demand, constitutes an undue burden on interstate commerce within the meaning of Article I, Section 8, Clause 3 of the United States Constitution.

C. Any government official meeting the requirements of subdivision A 2 shall be subject to the personal jurisdiction of Virginia circuit courts to the extent permitted by the Constitution of the United

States. This subsection shall govern personal jurisdiction in actions under this section, and shall constitute authorization for purposes of § 8.01–330.

Added by Acts 2004, c. 609; Acts 2004, c. 647. Amended by Acts 2005, c. 736; Acts 2005, c. 800.

§ 8.01–185. Venue

The venue of actions seeking declarations of right with or without consequential relief shall be determined in accordance with provisions of Chapter 5 (§ 8.01–257 et seq.) of this title.

Acts 1977, c. 617.

§ 8.01–186. Further relief

Further relief based on a declaratory judgment order or decree may be granted whenever necessary or proper. The application shall be by motion to a court having jurisdiction to grant the relief. If the application is deemed sufficient the court shall, on reasonable notice, require an adverse party whose rights have been adjudicated by the declaration of right to show cause why further relief should not be granted forthwith.

Acts 1977, c. 617.

§ 8.01–187. Commissioners or condemnation jurors to determine compensation for property taken or damaged

Whenever it is determined in a declaratory judgment proceeding that a person's property has been taken or damaged within the meaning of Article I, Section 11 of the Constitution of Virginia and compensation has not been paid or any action taken to determine the compensation within 60 days following the entry of such judgment order or decree, the court which entered the order or decree may, upon motion of such person after reasonable notice to the adverse party, enter a further order appointing commissioners or condemnation jurors to determine the compensation. The appointment of commissioners or condemnation jurors and all proceedings thereafter shall be governed by the procedure prescribed for the condemning authority. Notwithstanding the provisions of § 25.1–100, the date of valuation in actions pursuant to this section shall be the date determined by the court to be the date the property was taken or damaged.

Acts 1977, c. 617. Amended by Acts 2007, c. 450; Acts 2007, c. 720; Acts 2010, c. 835; Acts 2014, c. 618.

§ 8.01–188. Jury trial

When a declaration of right or the granting of further relief based thereon shall involve the determination of issues of fact triable by a jury, such issues may be submitted to a jury in the form of interrogatories, with proper instructions by the court, whether a general verdict be required or not.

Acts 1977, c. 617.

§ 8.01–189. Injunction

The pendency of any action at law or suit in equity brought merely to obtain a declaration of rights or a determination of a question of construction shall not be sufficient grounds for the granting of any injunction.

Acts 1977, c. 617.

§ 8.01–190. Costs

The costs, or such part thereof as the court may deem proper and just in view of the particular circumstances of the case, may be awarded to any party.

Acts 1977, c. 617.

§ 8.01–191. Construction of article

This article is declared to be remedial. Its purpose is to afford relief from the uncertainty and insecurity attendant upon controversies over legal rights, without requiring one of the parties interested so to invade the rights asserted by the other as to entitle him to maintain an ordinary action therefor. It is to be liberally interpreted and administered with a view to making the courts more serviceable to the people.

Acts 1977, c. 617.

Article 18

Recovery of Claims Against the Commonwealth of Virginia

§ 8.01–192. How claims to be prosecuted

When the Comptroller or other authorized person shall disallow, either in whole or in part, any such claim against the Commonwealth as is provided for by §§ 2.2–814, 2.2–815 or 8.01–605 at which time a right of action under this section shall be deemed to accrue, the person presenting such claim may petition an appropriate circuit court for redress.

Acts 1977, c. 617.

§ 8.01–193. Defense and hearing

In every such case, the Comptroller shall be a defendant. He shall file an answer stating the objections to the claim. The cause shall be heard upon the petition, answer, and the evidence.

Acts 1977, c. 617.

§ 8.01–194. Jury may be impaneled; judgment

The court may, and on the motion of any party shall, cause a jury to be impaneled to ascertain any facts which are disputed, or the amount of any claim which is unliquidated.

Acts 1977, c. 617.

§ 8.01-195. No judgment to be paid without special appropriation

No judgment against the Commonwealth, unless otherwise expressly provided, shall be paid without a special appropriation therefor by law.

Acts 1977, c. 617.

ARTICLE 18.1

TORT CLAIMS AGAINST THE COMMONWEALTH OF VIRGINIA

§ 8.01-195.1. Short title

This article shall be known and may be cited as the "Virginia Tort Claims Act."

Acts 1981, c. 449.

§ 8.01-195.2. Definitions

As used in this article:

"Agency" means any department, institution, authority, instrumentality, board or other administrative agency of the government of the Commonwealth of Virginia and any transportation district created pursuant to the Transportation District Act of 1964 (§ 33.2-1900 et seq.) of Title 33.2 and Chapter 630 of the 1964 Acts of Assembly[1].

"Employee" means any officer, employee or agent of any agency, or any person acting on behalf of an agency in an official capacity, temporarily or permanently in the service of the Commonwealth, or any transportation district, whether with or without compensation.

"School boards" as defined in § 22.1-1 are not state agencies nor are employees of school boards state employees.

"Transportation district" shall be limited to any transportation district or districts which have entered into an agreement in which the Northern Virginia Transportation District is a party with any firm or corporation as an agent to provide passenger rail services for such district or districts while such firm or corporation is performing in accordance with such agreement.

Acts 1981, c. 449; Acts 1986, c. 534; Acts 1986, c. 584; Acts 1991, c. 23.

[1] Acts 2004, c. 1000, in the third enactment provided for the repeal of Acts 1964, c. 630.

§ 8.01-195.3. Commonwealth, transportation district or locality liable for damages in certain cases

Subject to the provisions of this article, the Commonwealth shall be liable for claims for money only accruing on or after July 1, 1982, and any transportation district shall be liable for claims for money only accruing on or after July 1, 1986, on account of damage to or loss of property or personal injury or death caused by the negligent or wrongful act or omission of any employee while acting within the scope of his employment under circumstances where the Commonwealth or transportation district, if a private person, would be liable to the claimant for such damage, loss, injury or death. However, except to the extent that a transportation district contracts to do so pursuant to § 33.2-1919, neither the Commonwealth nor any transportation district shall be liable for interest prior to judgment or for punitive damages. The amount recoverable by any claimant shall not exceed (i) $25,000 for causes of action accruing prior to July 1, 1988, $75,000 for causes of action accruing on or after July 1, 1988, or $100,000 for causes of action accruing on or after July 1, 1993, or (ii) the maximum limits of any liability policy maintained to insure against such negligence or other tort, if such policy is in force at the time of the act or omission complained of, whichever is greater, exclusive of interest and costs.

Notwithstanding any provision hereof, the individual immunity of judges, the Attorney General, attorneys for the Commonwealth, and other public officers, their agents and employees from tort claims for damages is hereby preserved to the extent and degree that such persons presently are immunized. Any recovery based on the following claims are hereby excluded from the provisions of this article:

1. Any claim against the Commonwealth based upon an act or omission which occurred prior to July 1, 1982.

1a. Any claim against a transportation district based upon an act or omission which occurred prior to July 1, 1986.

2. Any claim based upon an act or omission of the General Assembly or district commission of any transportation district, or any member or staff thereof acting in his official capacity, or to the legislative function of any agency subject to the provisions of this article.

3. Any claim based upon an act or omission of any court of the Commonwealth, or any member thereof acting in his official capacity, or to the judicial functions of any agency subject to the provisions of this article.

4. Any claim based upon an act or omission of an officer, agent or employee of any agency of government in the execution of a lawful order of any court.

5. Any claim arising in connection with the assessment or collection of taxes.

6. Any claim arising out of the institution or prosecution of any judicial or administrative proceeding, even if without probable cause.

7. Any claim by an inmate of a state correctional facility, as defined in § 53.1–1, unless the claimant verifies under oath, by affidavit, that he has exhausted his remedies under the adult institutional inmate grievance procedures promulgated by the Department of Corrections. The time for filing the notice of tort claim shall be tolled during the pendency of the grievance procedure.

Nothing contained herein shall operate to reduce or limit the extent to which the Commonwealth or any transportation district, agency or employee was deemed liable for negligence as of July 1, 1982, nor shall any provision of this article be applicable to any county, city or town in the Commonwealth or be so construed as to remove or in any way diminish the sovereign immunity of any county, city or town in the Commonwealth.

Acts 1981, c. 449; Acts 1982, c. 397; Acts 1986, c. 584; Acts 1988, c. 884; Acts 1989, c. 446; Acts 1993, c. 481; Acts 1998, c. 203; Acts 1998, c. 820. Amended by Acts 2007, c. 250.

§ 8.01–195.4. Jurisdiction of claims under this article; right to jury trial; service on Commonwealth or locality

The general district courts shall have exclusive original jurisdiction to hear, determine, and render judgment on any claim against the Commonwealth or any transportation district cognizable under this article when the amount of the claim does not exceed $4,500, exclusive of interest and any attorneys' fees. Jurisdiction shall be concurrent with the circuit courts when the amount of the claim exceeds $4,500 but does not exceed $25,000, exclusive of interest and such attorneys' fees. Jurisdiction of claims when the amount exceeds $25,000 shall be limited to the circuit courts of the Commonwealth. The parties to any such action in the circuit courts shall be entitled to a trial by jury.

In all actions against the Commonwealth commenced pursuant to this article, the Commonwealth shall be a proper party defendant, and service of process shall be made on the Attorney General. The notice of claim shall be filed pursuant to § 8.01–195.6 on the Director of the Division of Risk Management or the Attorney General. In all such actions against a transportation district, the district shall be a proper party and service of process and notices shall be made on the chairman of the commission of the transportation district.

Acts 1981, c. 449; Acts 1984, c. 698; Acts 1986, c. 584; Acts 1987, c. 567; Acts 1987, c. 674; Acts 1989, c. 121; Acts 1989, c. 337; Acts 1991, c. 23; Acts 1992, c. 111; Acts 1992, c. 796; Acts 2002, c. 645. Amended by Acts 2005, c. 144; Acts 2011, c. 14; Acts 2011, c. 702.

§ 8.01–195.5. Settlement of certain cases

The Attorney General shall have authority in accordance with § 2.2–514 to compromise and settle claims against the Commonwealth cognizable under this article.

The chairman of the commission for a transportation district against which a claim was filed pursuant to this article, or such other person as may be designated by the commission, shall have the authority to compromise, settle and discharge the claim provided (i) the proposed settlement and reasons therefor are submitted to the commission in writing and approved by its members or (ii) the settlement is made in accordance with a written policy approved by the transportation district commission for such settlements. The Director of the Division of Risk Management may adjust, compromise and settle claims against the Commonwealth cognizable under this article prior to the commencement of suit unless otherwise directed by the Attorney General.

Acts 1981, c. 449; Acts 1986, c. 584; Acts 1991, c. 23; Acts 1992, c. 796.

§ 8.01–195.6. Notice of claim

A. Every claim cognizable against the Commonwealth or a transportation district shall be forever barred unless the claimant or his agent, attorney or representative has filed a written statement of the nature of the claim, which includes the time and place at which the injury is alleged to have occurred and the agency or agencies alleged to be liable, within one year after such cause of action accrued. However, if the claimant was under a disability at the time the cause of action accrued, the tolling provisions of § 8.01–229 shall apply.

B. If the claim is against the Commonwealth, the statement shall be filed with the Director of the Division of Risk Management or the Attorney General. If the claim is against a transportation district the statement shall be filed with the chairman of the commission of the transportation district.

C. The notice is deemed filed when it is received in the office of the official to whom the notice is directed. The notice may be delivered by hand, by any form of United States mail service (including regular, certified, registered or overnight mail), or by commercial delivery service.

D. In any action contesting the filing of the notice of claim, the burden of proof shall be on the claimant to establish receipt of the notice in conformity with this section. A signed United States mail return receipt indicating the date of delivery, or any other form of signed and dated acknowledgment of delivery given by authorized personnel in the office of the official with whom the statement is filed, shall be prima facie evidence of filing of the notice under this section.

E. Claims against the Commonwealth involving medical malpractice shall be subject to the provisions of this article and to the provisions of Chapter 21.1

(§ 8.01–581.1 et seq.) of this title. However, the recovery in such a claim involving medical malpractice shall not exceed the limits imposed by § 8.01–195.3.

Acts 1981, c. 449; Acts 1984, c. 638; Acts 1984, c. 698; Acts 1986, c. 584; Acts 1991, c. 23; Acts 1992, c. 796; Acts 2002, c. 207. Amended by Acts 2007, c. 368.

§ 8.01–195.7. Statute of limitations

Every claim cognizable against the Commonwealth or a transportation district under this article shall be forever barred, unless within one year after the cause of action accrues to the claimant the notice of claim required by § 8.01–195.6 is properly filed. An action may be commenced pursuant to § 8.01–195.4 (i) upon denial of the claim by the Attorney General or the Director of the Division of Risk Management or, in the case of a transportation district, by the chairman of the commission of that district or (ii) after the expiration of six months from the date of filing the notice of claim unless, within that period, the claim has been compromised and discharged pursuant to § 8.01–195.5. All claims against the Commonwealth or a transportation district under this article shall be forever barred unless such action is commenced within eighteen months of the filing of the notice of claim.

The limitations periods prescribed by this section and § 8.01–195.6 shall be subject to the tolling provision of § 8.01–229 and the pleading provision of § 8.01–235. Additionally, claims involving medical malpractice in which the notice required by this section and § 8.01–195.6 has been given shall be subject to the provisions of § 8.01–581.9. Notwithstanding the provisions of this section, if notice of claim against the Commonwealth was filed prior to July 1, 1984, any claimant so filing shall have two years from the date such notice was filed within which to commence an action pursuant to § 8.01–195.4.

Acts 1981, c. 449; Acts 1984, c. 638; Acts 1984, c. 698; Acts 1985, c. 514; Acts 1986, c. 584; Acts 1988, c. 778; Acts 1988, c. 801; Acts 1992, c. 796.

§ 8.01–195.8. Release of further claims

Notwithstanding any provision of this article, the liability for any claim or judgment cognizable under this article shall be conditioned upon the execution by the claimant of a release of all claims against the Commonwealth, its political subdivisions, agencies, and instrumentalities or against the transportation district, and against any officer or employee of the Commonwealth or the transportation district in connection with, or arising out of, the occurrence complained of.

Acts 1981, c. 449; Acts 1986, c. 584; Acts 1991, c. 23.

§ 8.01–195.9. Claims evaluation program

The Division of Risk Management of the Department of the Treasury and the Attorney General shall develop cooperatively an actuarially sound program for identifying, evaluating and setting reserves for the payment of claims cognizable under this article.

Acts 1988, c. 644; Acts 2000, c. 618; Acts 2000, c. 632.

Article 18.2

Compensation for Wrongful Incarceration for a Felony Conviction

§ 8.01–195.10. Purpose; action by the General Assembly required; definitions

A. The purpose of this article is to provide directions and guidelines for the compensation of persons who have been wrongfully incarcerated in the Commonwealth. Compensation for wrongful incarceration is governed by Article IV, Section 14 of the Constitution of Virginia, which prohibits the General Assembly from granting relief in cases in which the courts or other tribunals may have jurisdiction and any individual seeking payment of state funds for wrongful incarceration shall be deemed to have waived all other claims. The payment and receipt of any compensation for wrongful incarceration shall be contingent upon the General Assembly appropriating funds for that purpose. This article shall not provide an entitlement to compensation for persons wrongfully incarcerated or require the General Assembly to appropriate funds for the payment of such compensation. No estate of or personal representative for a decedent shall be entitled to seek a claim for compensation for wrongful incarceration.

B. As used in this article:

"Incarceration" or "incarcerated" means confinement in a local or regional correctional facility, juvenile correctional center, state correctional facility, residential detention center, or facility operated pursuant to the Corrections Private Management Act (§ 53.1–261 et seq.).

"Wrongful incarceration" or "wrongfully incarcerated" means incarceration for a felony conviction for which (i) the conviction has been vacated pursuant to Chapter 19.2 (§ 19.2–327.2 et seq.) or 19.3 (§ 19.2–327.10 et seq.) of Title 19.2, or the person incarcerated has been granted an absolute pardon for the commission of a crime that he did not commit, (ii) the person incarcerated must have entered a final plea of not guilty, or regardless of the plea, any person sentenced to death, or convicted of a Class 1 felony, a Class 2 felony, or any felony for which the maximum penalty is imprisonment for life, and (iii) the person incarcerated did not by any act or omission on his part intentionally contribute to his conviction for the felony for which he was incarcerated.

Added by Acts 2004, c. 818; Acts 2004, c. 840. Amended by Acts 2010, c. 496; Acts 2010, c. 557.

§ 8.01–195.11. Compensation for wrongful incarceration

A. Any person who is convicted of a felony by a county or city circuit court of the Commonwealth and is wrongfully incarcerated for such felony may be awarded compensation in an amount equal to 90 percent of the inflation adjusted Virginia per capita personal income as reported by the Bureau of Economic Analysis of the United States Department of Commerce for each year of incarceration, or portion thereof.

B. Any compensation computed pursuant to subsection A and approved by the General Assembly shall be paid by the Comptroller by his warrant on the State Treasurer in favor of the person found to have been wrongfully incarcerated. The person wrongfully incarcerated shall be paid an initial lump sum equal to 20 percent of the compensation award with the remaining 80 percent of the principal of the compensation award to be used by the State Treasurer to purchase an annuity from any A+ rated company, including any A+ rated company from which the Virginia Lottery may purchase an annuity, to provide equal monthly payments to such person for a period certain of 25 years commencing no later than one year after the effective date of the appropriation. The annuity shall provide that it shall not be sold, discounted, or used as securitization for loans and mortgages by the person awarded compensation. The annuity shall, however, contain beneficiary provisions providing for the annuity's continued disbursement in the event of the death of the person awarded compensation. All payments or costs of annuities under this section shall be made by check issued by the State Treasurer on warrant of the Comptroller.

C. Any person who is convicted of a felony by a county or city circuit court of the Commonwealth and is wrongfully incarcerated for such felony shall receive a transition assistance grant of $15,000 to be paid from the Criminal Fund, which amount shall be deducted from any award received pursuant to subsection B. In addition, such person shall be entitled to receive reimbursement up to $10,000 for tuition for career and technical training within the Virginia community college system contingent upon successful completion of the training. Reimbursement for tuition shall be provided by the community college at which the career or technical training was completed.

Added by Acts 2004, c. 818; Acts 2004, c. 840. Amended by Acts 2010, c. 557; Acts 2012, c. 675; Acts 2014, c. 225.

§ 8.01–195.12. Conditions for continued compensation

A. Any person awarded compensation under this article who is subsequently convicted of a felony shall, immediately upon such conviction, not be eligible to receive any unpaid amounts from any compensation awarded and his beneficiaries shall not be eligible to receive any payments under an annuity purchased pursuant to subsection B of § 8.01–195.11. Any unpaid amounts remaining under any annuity shall become the property of the Commonwealth and shall be deposited into the general fund of the state treasury.

A1. Any person awarded compensation under this article who is subsequently incarcerated upon the revocation of parole or probation resulting from the commission of an act that constitutes a crime shall, during the period of such incarceration, forfeit any payments under an annuity purchased pursuant to subsection B of § 8.01–195.11. Any forfeited amounts under any annuity shall become the property of the Commonwealth and shall be deposited into the general fund of the state treasury.

B. As a condition of receiving any compensation under this article, a person shall execute a release and waiver forever releasing (i) the Commonwealth or any agency, instrumentality, officer, employee, or political subdivision thereof, (ii) any legal counsel appointed pursuant to § 19.2–159, and (iii) all other parties of interest, from any present or future claims the person receiving compensation may have against such enumerated parties and arising out of the factual situation in connection with the conviction for which compensation is being sought under this article. In addition, the person receiving compensation shall not have been awarded a finally adjudicated judgment in a court of law against or received any funds pursuant to a settlement agreement with any person or entity described in this subsection for compensation or damages arising out of the factual situation in connection with the conviction.

Added by Acts 2004, c. 818; Acts 2004, c. 840. Amended by Acts 2010, c. 557.

ARTICLE 19

ACTIONS BY THE COMMONWEALTH

§ 8.01–196. Comptroller to institute proceedings

The Comptroller shall institute and prosecute all proceedings proper to enforce payment of money to the Commonwealth.

Acts 1977, c. 617.

§ 8.01–197. In what name; when not to abate

Any such action shall be in the name of the Commonwealth of Virginia except when it is on a bond payable to, or a contract made with, the Governor or some other person. And then it may be in the name of such

Governor or other person for the use of the Commonwealth, notwithstanding such Governor or other person may have died, resigned, or been removed from office before the commencement of the action. And there shall be no abatement thereof, by reason of the death, resignation, or removal from office of any such plaintiff pending the action.

Acts 1977, c. 617.

§ 8.01-198. Action, against whom instituted

Any such action may be instituted against any person indebted or liable to the Commonwealth in any way whatever, and against his sureties, and against his and their personal representatives. And it may be made when the debt or liability is created or secured by a bond or other instrument, whether the same be payable to the Commonwealth or to any person acting in a public character on behalf of the Commonwealth, or be for the payment of money or the performance of other duties. Every judgment on any such motion shall be in the name of the Commonwealth.

Acts 1977, c. 617.

§ 8.01-199. Judgment, nature of

On any such motion, the judgment shall be for so much principal and interest as would be recoverable by action. It may be also for fifteen per centum damages in addition thereto when the proceeding is against a treasurer, sheriff, or other collector, or his sureties, or his or their personal representatives, for taxes or other public money which ought to have been paid into the state treasury. In such proceeding, the court, in pronouncing judgment, may consider all the circumstances, and give judgment for the damages or not, or for such part of the damages, as it may deem proper.

Acts 1977, c. 617.

§ 8.01-200. Mistakes against State corrected

After a debt to the Commonwealth shall have been paid, if it appear that an error or mistake has been committed to its prejudice, whether before or after the issuing of execution, a motion may be made on ten days' notice against any person liable for the debt, for the amount of such error or mistake, and judgment may be given therefor, without interest or damages thereon.

Acts 1977, c. 617.

§ 8.01-201. Execution; real estate to be sold

In a writ of fieri facias upon a judgment or decree against any person indebted or liable to the Commonwealth, or against any surety of his, after the words "we command you that of the," the clerk shall insert the words "goods, chattels, and real estate," and conform the subsequent part of such writ thereto. And under any writ so issued, real estate may be taken and sold.

Acts 1977, c. 617.

§ 8.01-202. Execution, to whom issued

An execution on behalf of the Commonwealth from the Circuit Court of the City of Richmond may, if the Comptroller see fit, be directed to any sheriff, of any political subdivision, and shall be served by any of such officers in whose hands the Comptroller may cause it to be placed.

Acts 1977, c. 617.

§ 8.01-203. Goods and chattels liable before real estate

Every writ of fieri facias, issued according to § 8.01-201, shall be levied first on the goods and chattels of the person against whose estate such writ issued. If, in the political subdivision, the residence of such person, there are no goods and chattels liable thereto, or not a sufficiency thereof, then the officer having such writ shall levy it on the real estate of such person.

Acts 1977, c. 617.

§ 8.01-204. Notice of sale of real estate; when sale to be made

When a levy is so made upon real estate, the officer making it shall post notice thereof, and of the time and place of sale, at such public places as may seem to him expedient, and at the front door of the courthouse of the political subdivision in which the real estate is, on a court day. The time of selling real estate shall be not less than sixty nor more than ninety days from the time of posting the notice at the courthouse door. And the sale shall take place at the premises or at the door of the courthouse, as the officer may deem most advisable.

Acts 1977, c. 617.

§ 8.01-205. How sale made

If the amount of the execution be not sooner paid, such officer shall proceed, on the day mentioned in the notice, to sell at public auction the interest of the party against whom the execution issued in the real estate or so much thereof as the officer may deem sufficient; and if a part only be sold it shall be laid off in one parcel in such place and manner as the debtor or his agent may direct or, if he give no direction, as the officer may deem best.

Acts 1977, c. 617.

§ 8.01-206. Terms of sale

The sale shall be upon six months' credit; and if the land be not purchased for the Commonwealth, the officer shall take bond of the purchaser, with sureties, for the payment of the purchase money to the Commonwealth. Every such bond shall mention on what occasion the same was taken, and be returned to the office of the court from which the execution issued, and the clerk shall endorse thereon the date of its return.

Acts 1977, c. 617.

§ 8.01–207. Who to collect purchase money and make deed; disposition of proceeds of sale

On or before the maturity of such bond the sheriff or other officer who made the sale shall withdraw the bond from the clerk's office, leaving his receipt therefor and an attested copy thereof, and collect the same. So soon as the purchase money has been paid, the sheriff or other principal officer, or the deputy who acted in making the sale, shall, as commissioner, and in the name of the Commonwealth, convey the land to the purchaser by deed executed at his costs, reciting the execution, the sale and the price of the land. Such deed shall pass to the purchaser all the interest which the party against whom the execution issued had in the land at the date of the judgment or decree. Out of the money so collected the sheriff or officer who made the sale shall pay all costs attending such execution and sale, the costs of a survey, if there was one, all delinquent and unpaid taxes and levies on such land and the debt due the Commonwealth, and the residue, if any, he shall pay to the judgment debtor.

Acts 1977, c. 617.

§ 8.01–208. When successor of officer to make deed

When the officer and his deputy who acted in making the sale have both died or removed from the Commonwealth before making such deed, the same may be executed by any successor of such officer.

Acts 1977, c. 617.

§ 8.01–209. Bond for purchase money to have force of judgment

When any bond taken under § 8.01–206 becomes payable and is returned to the office of the court from which the execution issued, it shall have the force of a judgment against such of the obligors therein as may be then alive. Execution may be issued thereon against them. And the same shall be proceeded under in like manner as an execution issued on such a judgment or decree as is mentioned in § 8.01–201, save only that the clerk shall endorse "no security is to be taken," and the officer shall govern himself accordingly and sell for ready money any real estate which he may levy on under the same.

Acts 1977, c. 617.

§ 8.01–210. Judgment against deceased obligors

A judgment may be obtained against the survivors of a deceased obligor of a bond taken under the provisions of § 8.01–206 by an action at law against the personal representative of such obligor.

Acts 1977, c. 617.

§ 8.01–211. When venditioni exponas issued to sheriff of adjacent county; what to contain

When return is made on any execution on behalf of the Commonwealth that goods, chattels or real estate remain unsold for want of bidders, or to that effect, the clerk of the court from which such execution issued shall, when required by the Comptroller, issue a writ of venditioni exponas, directed to the sheriff of any county adjacent to that in which the levy was made that the Comptroller may designate. Such writ shall recite the execution under which the levy was made, the nature of such levy and return that the property remains unsold for the want of bidders and shall command the sheriff of such adjacent county, if the property remaining unsold be goods or chattels, to go into the county in which the levy was made and receive the same from the officer that made the levy and, whether the property be goods, chattels, or real estate, to sell the same.

Acts 1977, c. 617.

§ 8.01–212. Officer to deliver to sheriff goods and chattels levied on

The officer who made the levy shall deliver the goods and chattels to the sheriff to whom such writ of venditioni exponas may be directed, upon such sheriff's producing to him such writ and executing a receipt for such goods and chattels. If the officer shall fail to deliver the same and return be made on such writ to that effect, the court from which it issued, upon motion, may give judgment against him and his sureties for the whole sum that the execution amounted to at the time of such failure, with interest thereon from that time.

Acts 1977, c. 617.

§ 8.01–213. Where same to be sold

The sheriff to whom such writ of venditioni exponas is directed, shall sell the goods and chattels in the county where received, if they can be sold therein, and if not he shall cause them to be removed to the courthouse of his own county and there sold. The removal shall be at the costs of the party against whom the execution issued, and the sale under the execution shall be to raise the cost of removal, in addition to the amount which it would otherwise have been necessary to raise.

Acts 1977, c. 617.

§ 8.01–214. Where real estate to be sold

Such sheriff shall also sell the real estate levied on in the county wherein the levy was made, if it can be done, and if it cannot he shall make the sale at the courthouse of his own county.

Acts 1977, c. 617.

§ 8.01–215. Return of officer when sale not made because of prior encumbrance

In any case in which an officer, having an execution on behalf of the Commonwealth, shall decline levying it because of any previous conveyance, execution, or encumbrance, a return shall be made setting forth the nature of such conveyance, execution or encumbrance, in whose favor, and for what amount, and the court in which the conveyance or encumbrance is recorded, or from which the execution issued.

Acts 1977, c. 617.

§ 8.01-216. Comptroller's power to adjust old claims

The Comptroller, with the advice of the Attorney General, may adjust and settle upon equitable principles, without regard to strict legal rules, any doubtful or disputed account or claim in favor of the Commonwealth which may have been standing on the books of his office not less than two years, and may, with the like advice, dismiss any proceedings instituted by him; but before such adjustment or settlement can in any wise affect the rights of the Commonwealth it shall be approved and endorsed by the Attorney General and shall then be submitted to the supervision of the judge of the Circuit Court of the City of Richmond, accompanied by a written statement signed by the Comptroller of the facts and reasons which, in his opinion, render such adjustment or settlement just and proper. When such judge endorses the same with his written approval, signed in his official character, it shall be considered and treated as valid and binding.

Acts 1977, c. 617.

ARTICLE 19.1

VIRGINIA FRAUD AGAINST TAXPAYERS ACT

§ 8.01-216.1. Citation

This article may be cited as the Virginia Fraud Against Taxpayers Act.

Added by Acts 2002, c. 842, eff. Jan. 1, 2003.

§ 8.01-216.2. Definitions

As used in this article, unless the context requires otherwise:

"Attorney General" means the Attorney General of Virginia, the Chief Deputy, other deputies, counsels or assistant attorneys general employed by the Office of the Attorney General and designated by the Attorney General to act pursuant to this article.

"Claim" means any request or demand, whether under a contract or otherwise, for money or property, regardless of whether the Commonwealth has title to the money or property, that (i) is presented to an officer, employee, or agent of the Commonwealth or (ii) is made to a contractor, grantee, or other recipient (a) if the money or property is to be spent or used on the Commonwealth's behalf or to advance a governmental program or interest and (b) if the Commonwealth provides or has provided any portion of the money or property requested or demanded or will reimburse such contractor, grantee, or other recipient for any portion of the money or property that is requested or demanded. For purposes of this article, "claim" does not include requests or demands for money or property that the Commonwealth has paid to an individual as compensation for employment with the Commonwealth or as income subsidy with no restriction on that individual's use of the money or property.

"Commonwealth" means the Commonwealth of Virginia, any agency of state government, and any political subdivision of the Commonwealth.

"Documentary material" means the original or any copy of any book, record, report, memorandum, paper, communication, tabulation, chart, or other document, or data compilations stored in or accessible through computer or other information retrieval systems, together with instructions and all other materials necessary to use or interpret such data compilations, and any product of discovery.

"Employee" includes an employee or officer of the Commonwealth.

"Employer" includes the Commonwealth.

"Investigation" means any inquiry conducted by an investigator for the purpose of ascertaining whether any person is or has been engaged in any violation of this article.

"Material" means having a natural tendency to influence, or be capable of influencing, the payment or receipt of money or property.

"Obligation" means an established duty, whether or not fixed, arising from (i) an express or implied contractual, grantor-grantee, or licensor-licensee relationship; (ii) a fee-based or similar relationship; (iii) a statute or regulation; or (iv) the retention of any overpayment.

"Official use" means any use that is consistent with the law, regulations, and policies of the Commonwealth, including use in connection with (i) internal memoranda and reports of the Office of the Attorney General; (ii) communications between the Office of the Attorney General and a federal, state, or local government agency, or a contractor of a federal, state, or local government agency, undertaken in furtherance of an Office of the Attorney General investigation or prosecution of a case; (iii) interviews of any qui tam relator or other witness; (iv) oral examinations; (v) depositions; (vi) the preparation for and response to civil discovery requests; (vii) the introduction into the record of a case or proceeding; (viii) applications, motions, memoranda, and briefs submitted to a court or other tribunal; and (ix) communications with government investigators, auditors, consultants, experts, the counsel of other parties, arbitrators, and mediators, concerning an investigation, case, or proceeding.

"Person" includes any natural person, corporation, firm, association, organization, partnership, limited liability company, business or trust.

"Product of discovery" means (i) the original or duplicate of any deposition, interrogatory, document, thing, result of the inspection of land or other property, examination, or admission, which is obtained by any method of discovery in any judicial or administrative proceeding of an adversarial nature; (ii) any digest, analysis, selection, compilation, or derivation of any item listed in clause (i); and (iii) any index or other manner of access to any item listed in clause (i).

Added by Acts 2002, c. 842, eff. Jan. 1, 2003. Amended by Acts 2011, c. 651; Acts 2011, c. 676.

§ 8.01-216.3. False claims; civil penalty

A. Any person who:

1. Knowingly presents, or causes to be presented, a false or fraudulent claim for payment or approval;

2. Knowingly makes, uses, or causes to be made or used, a false record or statement material to a false or fraudulent claim;

3. Conspires to commit a violation of subdivision 1, 2, 4, 5, 6, or 7;

4. Has possession, custody, or control of property or money used, or to be used, by the Commonwealth and knowingly delivers, or causes to be delivered, less than all such money or property;

5. Is authorized to make or deliver a document certifying receipt of property used, or to be used, by the Commonwealth and, intending to defraud the Commonwealth, makes or delivers the receipt without completely knowing that the information on the receipt is true;

6. Knowingly buys or receives as a pledge of an obligation or debt, public property from an officer or employee of the Commonwealth who lawfully may not sell or pledge the property; or

7. Knowingly makes, uses, or causes to be made or used, a false record or statement material to an obligation to pay or transmit money or property to the Commonwealth or knowingly conceals or knowingly and improperly avoids or decreases an obligation to pay or transmit money or property to the Commonwealth;

shall be liable to the Commonwealth for a civil penalty of not less than $5,500 and not more than $11,000, plus three times the amount of damages sustained by the Commonwealth.

A person violating this section shall be liable to the Commonwealth for reasonable attorney fees and costs of a civil action brought to recover any such penalties or damages. All such fees and costs shall be paid to the Attorney General's Office by the defendant and shall not be included in any damages or civil penalties recovered in a civil action based on a violation of this section.

B. If the court finds that (i) the person committing the violation of this section furnished officials of the Commonwealth responsible for investigating false claims violations with all information known to the person about the violation within 30 days after the date on which the defendant first obtained the information; (ii) such person fully cooperated with any Commonwealth investigation of such violation; (iii) at the time such person furnished the Commonwealth with the information about the violation, no criminal prosecution, civil action, or administrative action had commenced with respect to such violation; and (iv) the person did not have actual knowledge of the existence of an investigation into such violation, the court may assess not less than two times the amount of damages that the Commonwealth sustains because of the act of that person. A person violating this section shall also be liable to the Commonwealth for the costs of a civil action brought to recover any such penalty or damages.

C. For purposes of this section, the terms "knowing" and "knowingly" mean that a person, with respect to information, (i) has actual knowledge of the information; (ii) acts in deliberate ignorance of the truth or falsity of the information; or (iii) acts in reckless disregard of the truth or falsity of the information and require no proof of specific intent to defraud.

D. This section shall not apply to claims, records or statements relating to state or local taxes.

Added by Acts 2002, c. 842, eff. Jan. 1, 2003. Amended by Acts 2004, c. 589; Acts 2007, c. 569; Acts 2011, c. 676.

§ 8.01-216.4. Attorney General; investigation, civil action

The Attorney General shall investigate any violation of § 8.01-216.3. If the Attorney General finds that a person has violated or is violating § 8.01-216.3, the Attorney General may bring a civil action under this section.

Added by Acts 2002, c. 842, eff. Jan. 1, 2003.

§ 8.01-216.5. Civil actions filed by private persons; Commonwealth may intervene

A. A person may bring a civil action for a violation of § 8.01-216.3 for the person and for the Commonwealth. The action shall be brought in the name of the Commonwealth. The action may be dismissed only if the court and the Attorney General give written consent to the dismissal and their reasons for consenting.

B. A copy of the complaint and written disclosure of substantially all material evidence and information the person possesses shall be served on the Commonwealth. The complaint shall be filed in camera, shall remain under seal for at least 120 days, and shall not be served on the defendant until the court so orders. The

Commonwealth may elect to intervene and proceed with the action within 120 days after it receives both the complaint and the material evidence and information.

C. The Commonwealth may, for good cause shown, move the court for extensions of the time during which the complaint remains under seal. Any such motions may be supported by affidavits or other submissions in camera. The defendant shall not be required to respond to any motion for judgment filed under this section until twenty-one days after the complaint is unsealed and served upon the defendant.

D. Before the expiration of the 120–day period or any extensions obtained under subsection C, the Commonwealth shall proceed with the action, in which case the action shall be conducted by the Commonwealth, or notify the court that it declines to take over the action, in which case the person bringing the action shall have the right to prosecute the action.

E. When a person brings an action under this section, no person other than the Commonwealth may intervene or bring a related action based on the facts underlying the pending action.

Added by Acts 2002, c. 842, eff. Jan. 1, 2003. Amended by Acts 2007, c. 569.

§ 8.01–216.6. Rights of private plaintiff and Commonwealth

A. If the Commonwealth proceeds with the action, it shall have the primary responsibility for prosecuting the action, and shall not be bound by an act of the person bringing the action. Such person shall have the right to continue as a party to the action, subject to the limitations of this section.

B. The Commonwealth may dismiss the action notwithstanding the objections of the person initiating the action if the person has been notified by the Commonwealth of the filing of the complaint and the court has provided the person with an opportunity for a hearing on the complaint.

C. The Commonwealth may settle the action with the defendant notwithstanding the objections of the person initiating the action if the court determines, after a hearing, that the proposed settlement is fair, adequate, and reasonable under all the circumstances. Upon a showing of good cause, such hearing may be held in camera. The Commonwealth may, for good cause shown, move the court for a partial lifting of the seal to facilitate the investigative process or settlement.

D. Upon a showing by the Commonwealth that unrestricted participation during the course of the litigation by the person initiating the action would interfere with or unduly delay the Commonwealth's prosecution of the case, or would be repetitious, irrelevant, or for purposes of harassment, the court may, in its discretion, impose limitations on the person's participation, such as (i) limiting the number of witnesses the person may call; (ii) limiting the length of the testimony of such witnesses; (iii) limiting the person's cross-examination of witnesses; and (iv) otherwise limiting the participation by the person in the litigation.

E. Upon a showing by the defendant that unrestricted participation during the course of the litigation by the person initiating the action would be for purposes of harassment or would cause the defendant undue burden or unnecessary expense, the court may limit the participation by the person in the litigation.

F. If the Commonwealth elects not to proceed with the action, the person who initiated the action shall have the right to conduct the action. If the Commonwealth so requests, it shall be served with copies of all pleadings filed in the action and shall be supplied with copies of all deposition transcripts at the Commonwealth's expense. When a person proceeds with the action, the court, without limiting the status and rights of the person initiating the action, may nevertheless permit the Commonwealth to intervene at a later date upon a showing of good cause.

G. Whether or not the Commonwealth proceeds with the action, upon a showing by the Commonwealth that certain actions of discovery by the person initiating the action would interfere with the Commonwealth's investigation or prosecution of a criminal or civil matter arising out of the same facts, the court may stay such discovery for a period of not more than sixty days. Such a showing shall be conducted in camera. The court may extend the sixty-day period upon a further showing in camera that the Commonwealth has pursued the criminal or civil investigation or proceedings with reasonable diligence and any proposed discovery in the civil action will interfere with the ongoing criminal or civil investigation or proceedings.

H. Notwithstanding the provisions of subsection B of § 8.01–216.5, the Commonwealth may elect to pursue its claim through any alternate remedy available to the Commonwealth, including any administrative proceeding to determine a civil money penalty. If any such alternate remedy is pursued in another proceeding, the person initiating the action shall have the same rights in such proceeding as such person would have had if the action had continued under this section. Any finding of fact or conclusion of law made in such other proceeding that has become final shall be conclusive on all parties to an action under this article. For purposes of this subsection, a finding or conclusion is final if it has been finally determined on appeal to a court of competent jurisdiction of the Commonwealth, if the time for filing an appeal with respect to the finding or conclusion has expired, or if the finding or conclusion is not subject to judicial review.

Added by Acts 2002, c. 842, eff. Jan. 1, 2003. Amended by Acts 2007, c. 569.

§ 8.01–216.7. Award to private plaintiff

A. Except as hereinafter provided, if the Commonwealth proceeds with an action brought by a person under § 8.01–216.5, such person shall receive at least fifteen percent but not more than twenty-five percent of the proceeds of the action or settlement of the claim, depending upon the extent to which the person substantially contributed to the prosecution of the action. Where the action is one that the court finds to be based primarily on disclosures of specific information, other than information provided by the person bringing the action, relating to allegations or transactions in a criminal, civil, or administrative hearing, in a legislative, administrative, or Auditor of Public Accounts' report, hearing, audit, or investigation, or from the news media, the court may award such sums as it considers appropriate, but in no case more than ten percent of the proceeds, taking into account the significance of the information and the role of the person bringing the action in advancing the case to litigation. Any payment to a person under this section shall be made from the proceeds of the award. Any such person shall also receive an amount for reasonable expenses that the court finds to have been necessarily incurred, plus reasonable attorneys' fees and costs. All such expenses, fees, and costs shall be awarded against the defendant.

B. If the Commonwealth does not proceed with an action, the person bringing the action or settling the claim shall receive an amount that the court decides is reasonable for collecting the civil penalty and damages. The amount shall be not less than twenty-five percent and not more than thirty percent of the proceeds of the award or settlement and shall be paid out of the proceeds. Such person shall also receive an amount for reasonable expenses that the court finds to have been necessarily incurred, plus reasonable attorneys' fees and costs. All such expenses, fees, and costs shall be awarded against the defendant.

C. Whether or not the Commonwealth proceeds with the action, if the court finds that the action was brought by a person who planned and initiated the violation of § 8.01–216.3 upon which the action was brought, or if the person bringing the action is convicted of criminal conduct arising from his role in the violation of § 8.01–216.3, that person shall be dismissed from the civil action and shall not receive any share of the proceeds of the action. Such dismissal shall not prejudice the right of the Commonwealth to continue the action.

D. If the Commonwealth does not proceed with the action and the person bringing the action conducts the action, the court may award to the defendant its reasonable attorneys' fees and expenses if the defendant prevails in the action and the court finds that the claim of the person bringing the action was clearly frivolous, clearly vexatious, or brought primarily for purposes of harassment.

Added by Acts 2002, c. 842, eff. Jan. 1, 2003.

§ 8.01–216.8. Certain actions barred; relief from employment discrimination; waiver of sovereign immunity

No court shall have jurisdiction over any action brought under this article by an inmate incarcerated within a state or local correctional facility as defined in § 53.1–1.

No court shall have jurisdiction over an action brought under this article against any department, authority, board, bureau, commission, or agency of the Commonwealth, any political subdivision of the Commonwealth, a member of the General Assembly, a member of the judiciary, or an exempt official if the action is based on evidence or information known to the Commonwealth when the action was brought. For purposes of this section, "exempt official" means the Governor, Lieutenant Governor, Attorney General and the directors or members of any department, authority, board, bureau, commission or agency of the Commonwealth or any political subdivision of the Commonwealth.

In no event may a person bring an action under this article that is based upon allegations or transactions that are the subject of a civil suit or an administrative proceeding in which the Commonwealth is already a party.

The court shall dismiss an action or claim under § 8.01–216.5 unless opposed by the Commonwealth if substantially the same allegations or transactions as alleged in the action or claim were publicly disclosed in a criminal, civil or administrative hearing in which the Commonwealth or its agent is a party, in a Virginia legislative, administrative, or Auditor of Public Accounts' report, hearing, audit, or investigation, or from the news media, unless the action is brought by the Attorney General or the person bringing the action is an original source of the information. For purposes of this section, "original source" means an individual (i) who either prior to a public disclosure has voluntarily disclosed to the Commonwealth the information on which the allegations or transactions in a claim are based or (ii) who has knowledge that is independent of and materially adds to the publicly disclosed allegations or transactions and who has voluntarily provided the information to the Commonwealth before filing an action under this article.

Except as otherwise provided in this section, the Commonwealth shall not be liable for expenses a person incurs in bringing an action under this article.

Any employee, contractor, or agent shall be entitled to all relief necessary to make that employee, contractor, or agent whole, if that employee, contractor, or agent is discharged, demoted, suspended, threatened, harassed, or in any other manner discriminated against in the terms and conditions of employment because of lawful acts done by the employee, contractor, agent, or associated others in furtherance of an action under this article or other efforts to stop one or more violations of this article. Relief shall include reinstatement with the same seniority status that employee, contractor, or agent would have had but for the discrimination, two times the amount of back pay, interest on the back pay, and compensation for any special damages sustained as a result of the discrimination, including litigation costs and reasonable attorney fees. Any relief awarded to an employee under this section shall be reduced by any amount awarded to the employee through a state or local grievance process. An action under this section may be brought in a court of competent jurisdiction for the relief provided in this section, but may not be brought more than three years after the date the discrimination occurred. This paragraph shall constitute a waiver of sovereign immunity and creates a cause of action by an employee against the Commonwealth if the Commonwealth is the employer responsible for the adverse employment action that would entitle the employee to the relief set forth in this paragraph.

Added by Acts 2002, c. 842, eff. Jan. 1, 2003. Amended by Acts 2011, c. 651; Acts 2011, c. 676; Acts 2012, c. 479; Acts 2014, c. 403.

§ 8.01–216.9. Procedure; statute of limitations

A subpoena requiring the attendance of a witness at a trial or hearing conducted under this article may be served at any place in the Commonwealth.

A civil action under § 8.01–216.4 or 8.01–216.5 may not be brought (i) more than six years after the date on which the violation is committed or (ii) more than three years after the date when facts material to the right of action are known or reasonably should have been known by the official of the Commonwealth charged with responsibility to act in the circumstances, but in that event no more than ten years after the date on which the violation is committed, whichever occurs last.

If the Commonwealth elects to intervene and proceed with an action brought under § 8.01–216.5, the Commonwealth may file its own complaint or amend the complaint of a person who has brought an action under § 8.01–216.5 to clarify or add detail to any claim in which the Commonwealth is intervening and to add any additional claim for which the Commonwealth contends it is entitled to relief. Any complaint filed by the Commonwealth pursuant to this paragraph shall relate back to the filing date of the complaint of the person who originally brought the action, to the extent that the claim of the Commonwealth arises out of the conduct, transactions, or occurrences set forth, or attempted to be set forth, in such person's complaint.

In any action brought under § 8.01–216.4 or 8.01–216.5, the Commonwealth shall be required to prove all essential elements of the cause of action, including damages, by a preponderance of the evidence.

Notwithstanding any other provision of law, a final judgment rendered in favor of the Commonwealth in any criminal proceeding charging fraud or false statements, whether upon a verdict after trial or upon a plea of guilty or nolo contendere, shall estop the defendant from denying the essential elements of the offense in any action that involves the same transaction as in the criminal proceeding and which is brought under § 8.01–216.4 or 8.01–216.5.

Added by Acts 2002, c. 842, eff. Jan. 1, 2003. Amended by Acts 2007, c. 569; Acts 2011, c. 676.

§ 8.01–216.10. Civil investigative demands; issuance; sharing information

A. Whenever the Attorney General or his designee has reason to believe that any person may be in possession, custody, or control of any documentary material or information relevant to a false claims law investigation, the Attorney General or his designee may, before commencing a civil proceeding or making an election under this article, issue in writing and cause to be served upon such person, a civil investigative demand requiring such person (i) to produce such documentary material for inspection and copying, (ii) to answer in writing written interrogatories with respect to such documentary material or information, (iii) to give oral testimony concerning such documentary material or information, or (iv) to furnish any combination of such material, answers, or testimony.

B. Whenever a civil investigative demand is an express demand for any product of discovery, the Attorney General shall cause to be served, in any manner authorized by this article, a copy of such demand upon the person from whom the discovery was obtained and shall notify the person to whom such demand is issued of the date on which such copy was served.

C. Any information obtained by the Attorney General or his designee pursuant to this section may be shared with any qui tam relator and any state or federal governmental entity if the Attorney General or his designee determines that such information is necessary as part of any false claims investigation.

Added by Acts 2002, c. 842, eff. Jan. 1, 2003. Amended by Acts 2011, c. 676; Acts 2012, c. 479.

§ 8.01–216.11. Civil investigative demands; contents and deadlines

Each civil investigative demand issued under this article shall state the nature of the conduct constituting the alleged violation of a false claims law that is under investigation, and the applicable provision of law alleged to be violated.

If such demand is for the production of documentary material, the demand shall (i) describe each class of documentary material to be produced with such definiteness and certainty as to permit such material to be fairly identified; (ii) prescribe a return date for each such class that will provide a reasonable period of time within which the material so demanded may be assembled and made available for inspection and copying; and (iii) identify the false claims law investigator to whom such material shall be made available.

If such demand is for answers to written interrogatories, the demand shall (i) set forth with specificity the written interrogatories to be answered; (ii) prescribe dates at which time answers to written interrogatories shall be submitted; and (iii) identify the false claims law investigator to whom such answers shall be submitted.

If such demand is for the giving of oral testimony, the demand shall (i) prescribe a date, time, and place at which oral testimony shall be commenced; (ii) identify a false claims law investigator who shall conduct the examination and the custodian to whom the transcript of such examination shall be submitted; (iii) specify that such attendance and testimony are necessary to the conduct of the investigation; (iv) notify the person receiving the demand of the right to be accompanied by an attorney and any other representative; and (v) describe the general purpose for which the demand is being issued and the general nature of the testimony, including the primary areas of inquiry that will be taken pursuant to the demand.

Any civil investigative demand that is an express demand for any product of discovery shall not be returned or returnable until twenty–one days after a copy of such demand has been served upon the person from whom the discovery was obtained.

The date prescribed for the commencement of oral testimony pursuant to a civil investigative demand issued under this article shall be a date that is not less than seven days after the date on which the demand is received, unless the Attorney General determines that exceptional circumstances are present that warrant the commencement of such testimony within a lesser period of time.

The Attorney General shall not authorize the issuance of more than one civil investigative demand for oral testimony by the same person unless the person requests otherwise or unless the Attorney General, after investigation, notifies that person in writing that an additional demand for oral testimony is necessary.

Added by Acts 2002, c. 842, eff. Jan. 1, 2003.

§ 8.01–216.12. Civil investigative demands; protected material or information

A civil investigative demand issued under this article shall not require the production of any documentary material, the submission of any answers to written interrogatories, or the giving of any oral testimony if such material, answers, or testimony would be protected from disclosure under (i) the standards applicable to subpoenas or subpoenas duces tecum issued by a court of this Commonwealth to aid in a grand jury investigation or (ii) the standards applicable to discovery requests under the Rules of the Supreme Court of Virginia, to the extent that the application of such standards to any such demand is appropriate and consistent with the provisions and purposes of this article.

Any such demand that is an express demand for any product of discovery supersedes any inconsistent order, rule, or provision of law, other than this section, preventing or restraining disclosure of such product of discovery to any person. Disclosure of any product of discovery pursuant to any such express demand does not constitute a waiver of any right or privilege that the person making such disclosure may be entitled to invoke to resist discovery of trial preparation materials.

Added by Acts 2002, c. 842, eff. Jan. 1, 2003.

§ 8.01–216.13. Civil investigative demands; service and jurisdiction

Any civil investigative demand issued under this article may be served by an investigator, or by any person authorized to serve process on individuals in the Commonwealth.

Any such demand or any petition filed under this article may be served upon any person who is not found within Virginia in such manner as the Rules of the Supreme Court of Virginia or the Code of Virginia prescribe for service of process outside Virginia. To the extent that the courts of this Commonwealth can assert jurisdiction over any such person consistent with due process, the courts of this Commonwealth shall have the same jurisdiction to take any action respecting compliance with the provisions of this article by any such person that the court would have if such person were personally within the jurisdiction of the court.

Service of any civil investigative demand issued under this article or of any petition filed under this article may be made upon a partnership, corporation, association, or other legal entity by (i) delivering an executed copy of such demand or petition to any partner, executive officer, managing agent, or general agent of the partnership, corporation, association, or entity, or to any agent authorized by appointment or by law to receive service of process on behalf of such partnership, corporation, association, or entity; (ii) delivering an executed copy of such demand or petition to the principal office or place of business of the partnership, corporation, association, or entity; or (iii) depositing an executed copy of such demand or petition in the United States mail by registered or certified mail, with a return receipt requested, addressed to such partnership, corporation, association, or entity at its principal office or place of business.

Service of any such demand or petition may be made upon any natural person by (i) delivering an executed copy of such demand or petition to the person, or (ii) depositing an executed copy of such demand or petition in the United States mail by registered or certified mail, with a return receipt requested, addressed to the person at the person's residence or principal office or place of business.

A verified return by the individual serving any civil investigative demand issued under this article or any petition filed under this article setting forth the manner of such service shall be proof of service. In the case of service by registered or certified mail, such return shall be accompanied by the return post office receipt of delivery of such demand.

Added by Acts 2002, c. 842, eff. Jan. 1, 2003.

§ 8.01-216.14. Civil investigative demands; documentary material

The production of documentary material in response to a civil investigative demand served under this article shall be made under a sworn certificate, in such form as the demand designates, by (i) in the case of a natural person, the person to whom the demand is directed, or (ii) in the case of a person other than a natural person, a person having knowledge of the facts and circumstances relating to such production and authorized to act on behalf of such person. The certificate shall state that all of the documentary material required by the demand and in the possession, custody, or control of the person to whom the demand is directed has been produced and made available to the investigator identified in the demand.

Any person upon whom any civil investigative demand for the production of documentary material has been served shall make such material available for inspection and copying to the investigator identified in such demand at the principal place of business of such person, or at such other place as the investigator and the person thereafter may agree and prescribe in writing, or as the court may direct. Such material shall be made available on the return date specified in such demand, or on such later date as the investigator may prescribe in writing. Such person may, upon written agreement between the person and the investigator, substitute copies for originals of all or any part of such material.

Added by Acts 2002, c. 842, eff. Jan. 1, 2003.

§ 8.01-216.15. Civil investigative demands; interrogatories

Each inquiry in a civil investigative demand served under this article shall be answered separately and fully in writing under oath and shall be submitted under a sworn certificate, in such form as the demand designates, by (i) in the case of a natural person, the person to whom the demand is directed, or (ii) in the case of a person other than a natural person, the person or persons responsible for answering each inquiry. If any inquiry is objected to, the reasons for the objection shall be stated in the certificate instead of an answer. The certificate shall state that all information required by the demand and in the possession, custody, control, or knowledge of the person to whom the demand is directed has been submitted. To the extent that any information is not furnished, the information shall be identified and reasons set forth with particularity regarding the reasons why the information was not furnished.

Added by Acts 2002, c. 842, eff. Jan. 1, 2003.

§ 8.01-216.16. Civil investigative demands; oral examinations

A. The examination of any person pursuant to a civil investigative demand for oral testimony served under this article shall be taken before an officer authorized to administer oaths under the laws of this Commonwealth or of the place where the examination is held. The officer before whom the testimony is to be taken shall put the witness on oath and shall, personally or by someone acting under the direction of the officer and in the officer's presence, record the testimony of the witness. The testimony shall be taken stenographically and shall be transcribed. When the testimony is fully transcribed, the officer before whom the testimony is taken shall promptly transmit a copy of the transcript of the testimony to the Attorney General. This section shall not preclude the taking of testimony by any means authorized by and in a manner consistent with the Rules of the Supreme Court of Virginia.

B. The investigator conducting the examination shall exclude from the place where the examination is held all persons except the person giving the testimony, the attorney for and any other representative of the person giving the testimony, the attorney for the Commonwealth, any person who may be agreed upon by the attorney for the Commonwealth and the person giving the testimony, the officer before whom the testimony is to be taken, and any court reporter taking such testimony.

C. The oral testimony of any person taken pursuant to a civil investigative demand served under this article shall be taken in the county or city within which such person resides, is found, or transacts business or in such other place as may be agreed upon by the investigator conducting the examination and such person.

D. When the testimony is fully transcribed, the investigator or the officer before whom the testimony is taken shall afford the witness, who may be accompanied by counsel, a reasonable opportunity to examine and read the transcript, unless such examination and reading are waived by the witness. Any changes in form or substance that the witness desires to make shall be entered and identified upon the transcript by the officer or the investigator, with a statement of the reasons given by the witness for making such changes. The transcript shall then be signed by the witness, unless the witness in writing waives the signing, is ill, cannot be found, or refuses to sign. If the transcript is not signed by the witness within thirty days after being afforded a reasonable opportunity to examine it, the officer or the investigator shall sign it and state on the record the fact of the waiver, illness, absence of the witness, or the refusal to sign, together with the reasons, if any, given therefor.

E. The officer before whom the testimony is taken shall certify on the transcript that the witness was sworn by the officer and that the transcript is a true record of the testimony given by the witness, and the officer or investigator shall promptly deliver the transcript, or send the transcript by registered or certified mail, to the Attorney General.

F. Upon payment of reasonable charges therefor, the investigator shall furnish a copy of the transcript to the witness only, except that the Attorney General may, for good cause, limit such witness to inspection of the official transcript of the witness' testimony.

G. Any person compelled to appear for oral testimony under a civil investigative demand may be accompanied, represented, and advised by counsel. Counsel may advise such person, in confidence, with respect to any question asked of such person. Such person or counsel may object on the record to any question, in whole or in part, and shall briefly state for the record the reason for the objection. An objection may be made, received, and entered upon the record when it is claimed that such person is entitled to refuse to answer the question on the grounds of any constitutional or other legal right or privilege. Such person may not otherwise object to or refuse to answer any question, and may not directly or through counsel otherwise interrupt the oral examination. If such person refuses to answer any question, a petition may be filed in the circuit court for an order compelling such person to answer such question. If such person refuses to answer any question on the grounds of the privilege against self-incrimination, the testimony of such person may be compelled in accordance with applicable law.

H. Any person appearing for oral testimony under a civil investigative demand issued under this article shall be entitled to the same fees and allowances paid to witnesses in the circuit court.

Added by Acts 2002, c. 842, eff. Jan. 1, 2003.

§ 8.01–216.17. Civil investigative demands; custodian of documents; answers

A. The Attorney General shall serve as custodian of documentary material, answers to interrogatories, and transcripts of oral testimony received under this article.

B. An investigator who receives any documentary material, answers to interrogatories, or transcripts of oral testimony under this section shall transmit them to the Attorney General. The Attorney General shall take physical possession of such material, answers, or transcripts and shall be responsible for the use made of them and for the return of documentary material.

C. The Attorney General may cause the preparation of such copies of documentary material, answers to interrogatories, or transcripts of oral testimony as may be required for official use by any investigator, or other officer or employee of the Attorney General or employee of the Department of State Police. Such material, answers, and transcripts may be used by any authorized investigator or other officer or employee in connection with the taking of oral testimony under this article.

D. Except as otherwise provided in this section, no documentary material, answers to interrogatories, or transcripts of oral testimony, or copies thereof, while in the possession of the Attorney General, shall be available for examination by any individual other than an investigator or other officer or employee of the Attorney General or employee of the Department of State Police authorized by the Attorney General. The prohibition on the availability of material, answers, or transcripts shall not apply if consent is given by the person who produced such material, answers, or transcripts, or, in the case of any product of discovery produced pursuant to an express demand for such material, consent is given by the person from whom the discovery was obtained. Nothing in this subsection is intended to prevent disclosure to the General Assembly, including any committee or subcommittee of the General Assembly, or to any other state agency for use by such agency in furtherance of its statutory responsibilities.

E. While in the possession of the Attorney General and under such reasonable terms and conditions as the Attorney General shall prescribe, (i) documentary material and answers to interrogatories shall be available for examination by the person who produced such material or answers, or by a representative of that person authorized by that person to examine such material and answers, and (ii) transcripts of oral testimony shall be available for examination by the person who produced such testimony or by a representative of that person authorized by that person to examine such transcripts.

F. Any attorney employed by the Office of the Attorney General designated to appear before any court, grand jury, or state agency in any case or proceeding may use any documentary material, answers to interrogatories, or transcripts of oral testimony in connection with any such case or proceeding as such attorney determines to be required. Upon the completion of any such case or proceeding, such attorney shall return to the custodian any such material, answers, or transcripts so delivered that have not passed into the control of the court, grand jury, or agency through introduction into the record of such case or proceeding.

G. If any documentary material has been produced by any person in the course of any investigation pursuant to a civil investigative demand under this article, and (i) any case or proceeding before the court or grand jury arising out of such investigation, or any proceeding before any state agency involving such material, has been completed, or (ii) no case or proceeding in which such material may be used has been commenced within a reasonable time after completion of the examination and analysis of all documentary material and other information assembled in the course of such investigation, the Attorney General shall, upon written request of the person who produced such material, return to such person any material, other than copies furnished to the investigator, or made for the Attorney General that has not passed into the control of any court, grand jury, or agency through introduction into the record of such case or proceeding.

Added by Acts 2002, c. 842, eff. Jan. 1, 2003. Amended by Acts 2011, c. 676.

§ 8.01–216.18. Civil investigative demands; judicial proceedings for noncompliance

A. Whenever any person fails to comply with any civil investigative demand issued under this article, or whenever satisfactory copying or reproduction of any material requested in such demand cannot be done and such person refuses to surrender the material, the Attorney General may file in the appropriate circuit court for the county or city in which such person resides, is found, or transacts business, and serve upon such person a petition for a court order for the enforcement of the civil investigative demand.

B. Any person who has received a civil investigative demand issued under this article may file, in the circuit court of any county or city within which such person resides, is found, or transacts business, and serve upon the investigator identified in such demand a petition for an order of the court to modify or set aside the demand. In the case of a petition addressed to an express demand for any product of discovery, a petition to modify or set aside such demand may be brought only in the circuit court of the county or city in which the proceeding in which such discovery was obtained is or was last pending. Any petition under this section shall be filed (i) within twenty–one days after the date of service of the civil investigative demand, or at any time before the return date specified in the demand, whichever date is earlier, or (ii) within such longer period as may be prescribed in writing by any investigator identified in the demand.

C. The petition shall specify each ground upon which the petitioner relies in seeking relief, and may be based upon any failure of the demand to comply with the provisions of this article or upon any constitutional or other legal right or privilege of such person. During the pendency of the petition in the court, the court may stay, as it deems proper, the running of the time allowed for compliance with the demand, in whole or in part, except that the person filing the petition shall comply with any portions of the demand not sought to be modified or set aside.

D. In the case of any civil investigative demand issued under this article that is an express demand for any product of discovery, the person from whom such discovery was obtained may file, in the circuit court of the county or city in which the proceeding in which such discovery was obtained is or was last pending, and serve upon any investigator identified in the demand and upon the recipient of the demand a petition for a court order to modify or set aside those portions of the demand requiring production of any such product of discovery. Any petition under this subsection shall be filed (i) within twenty–one days after the date of service of the civil investigative demand or at any time before the return date specified in the demand, whichever date is earlier, or (ii) within such longer period as may be prescribed in writing by any investigator identified in the demand.

E. The petition shall specify each ground upon which the petitioner relies in seeking relief and may be based upon any failure of the demand from which relief is sought to comply with the provisions of this article, or upon any constitutional or other legal right or privilege of the petitioner. During the pendency of the petition, the court may stay, as it deems proper, compliance with the demand and the running of the time allowed for compliance with the demand.

F. At any time during which any custodian is in custody or control of any documentary material or answers to interrogatories produced, or transcripts of oral testimony given by any person in compliance with any civil investigative demand issued under this article, such person, and in the case of an express demand for any product of discovery, the person from whom such discovery was obtained, may file, in the circuit court of the county or city within which the office of such custodian is situated, and serve upon such custodian a petition for a court order to require the performance by the custodian of any duty imposed upon the custodian by this section. Whenever any petition is filed in any circuit court under this section, the court shall have jurisdiction to hear and determine the matter so presented, and to enter such order or orders as may be required to carry out the provisions of this section. Any final order so entered shall be subject to appeal in the same manner as appeals of other final orders in civil matters. Any disobedience of any final order entered under this section by any court shall be punished as contempt of the court.

G. Any documentary material, answers to written interrogatories, or oral testimony provided under any civil investigative demand issued under this article shall be exempt from disclosure under the Virginia Administrative Process Act (§ 2.2–4000 et seq.).

Added by Acts 2002, c. 842, eff. Jan. 1, 2003.

§ 8.01–216.19. Application of the Rules of the Supreme Court

The Rules of the Supreme Court of Virginia shall apply to all proceedings under this article, except when those Rules are inconsistent with this article.

Added by Acts 2002, c. 842, eff. Jan. 1, 2003.

Article 20

Change of Name

§ 8.01–217. How name of person may be changed

A. Any person desiring to change his own name, or that of his child or ward, may apply therefor to the circuit court of the county or city in which the person whose name is to be changed resides, or if no place of abode exists, such person may apply to any circuit court which shall consider such application if it finds that good cause exists therefor under the circumstances alleged. An incarcerated person may apply to the circuit court of the county or city in which such person is incarcerated. In case of a minor who has no living parent or guardian, the application may be made by his next friend. In case of a minor who has both parents living, the parent who does not join in the application shall be served with reasonable notice of the application pursuant to § 8.01–296 and, should such parent object to the change of name, a hearing shall be held to determine whether the change of name is in the best interest of the minor. It shall not be necessary to effect service upon any parent who files an answer to the application. If, after application is made on behalf of a minor and an ex parte hearing is held thereon, the court finds by clear and convincing evidence that such notice would present a serious threat to the health and safety of the applicant, the court may waive such notice.

B. Every application shall be under oath and shall include the place of residence of the applicant, the names of both parents, including the maiden name of his mother, the date and place of birth of the applicant, the applicant's felony conviction record, if any, whether the applicant is a person for whom registration with the Sex Offender and Crimes Against Minors Registry is required pursuant to Chapter 9 (§ 9.1–900 et seq.) of Title 9.1, whether the applicant is presently incarcerated or a probationer with any court, and if the applicant has previously changed his name, his former name or names.

C. On any such application and hearing, if such be demanded, the court, shall, unless the evidence shows that the change of name is sought for a fraudulent purpose or would otherwise infringe upon the rights of others or, in a case involving a minor, that the change of name is not in the best interest of the minor, order a change of name.

D. No application shall be accepted by a court for a change of name of a probationer, person for whom registration with the Sex Offender and Crimes Against Minors Registry is required pursuant to Chapter 9 (§ 9.1–900 et seq.) of Title 9.1, or incarcerated person unless the court finds that good cause exists for consideration of such application under the reasons alleged in the application for the requested change of name. If the court accepts the application, the court shall mail or deliver a copy of the application to the attorney for the Commonwealth for the jurisdiction where the application was filed and the attorney for the Commonwealth for any jurisdiction in the Commonwealth where a conviction occurred that resulted in the applicant's probation, registration with the Sex Offender and Crimes Against Minors Registry pursuant to Chapter 9 (§ 9.1–900 et seq.) of Title 9.1, or incarceration. The attorney for the Commonwealth where the application was filed shall be entitled to respond and represent the interests of the Commonwealth by filing a response within 30 days after the mailing or delivery of a copy of the application. The court shall conduct a hearing on the application and may order a change of name if, after receiving and considering evidence concerning the circumstances regarding the requested change of name, the court determines that the change of name (i) would not frustrate a legitimate law-enforcement purpose, (ii) is not sought for a fraudulent purpose, and (iii) would not otherwise infringe upon the rights of others. Such order shall contain written findings stating the court's basis for granting the order.

E. The provisions of subsection D are jurisdictional and any order granting a change of name pursuant to subsection D that fails to comply with any provision of subsection D is void ab initio. The attorney for the Commonwealth for the jurisdiction where such an application was filed has the authority to bring an independent action at any time to have such order declared void. If the attorney for the Commonwealth brings an independent action to have the order declared void, notice of the action shall be served upon the person who was granted a change of name who shall have 30 days after service to respond. If the person whose name was changed files a response objecting to having the order declared void, the court shall hold a hearing. If an order granting a change of name is declared void pursuant to this subsection, or if a person is convicted of perjury pursuant to § 18.2–434 for unlawfully changing his name pursuant to § 18.2–504.1 based on conduct that violates this section, the clerk of the court entering the order or the order of conviction shall transmit a certified copy of the order to (i) the State Registrar of Vital Records, (ii) the Department of Motor Vehicles, (iii) the State Board of Elections, (iv) the Central Criminal Records Exchange, and (v) any agency or department of the Commonwealth that has issued a license to the person where such license utilizes the person's changed name, if known to the court and identified in the court order.

F. The order shall contain no identifying information other than the applicant's former name or names, new name, and current address. The clerk of the court shall spread the order upon the current deed book in his office, index it in both the old and new names, and transmit a certified copy of the order and the application to the State Registrar of Vital Records and the Central Criminal Records Exchange. Transmittal of a copy of the order and the application to the State Registrar of Vital Records and the Central Criminal Records Exchange shall not be required of a person who changed his or her former name by reason of marriage and who makes application to resume a former name pursuant to § 20-121.4.

G. If the applicant shall show cause to believe that in the event his change of name should become a public record, a serious threat to the health or safety of the applicant or his immediate family would exist, the chief judge of the circuit court may waive the requirement that the application be under oath or the court may order the record sealed and direct the clerk not to spread and index any orders entered in the cause, and a certified copy shall not be transmitted to the State Registrar of Vital Records or the Central Criminal Records Exchange. At such time as a name change order is received by the State Registrar of Vital Records, for a person born in the Commonwealth, together with a proper request and payment of required fees, the Registrar shall issue certifications of the amended birth record which do not reveal the former name or names of the applicant unless so ordered by a court of competent jurisdiction. Such certifications shall not be marked "amended" and show the effective date as provided in § 32.1-272. Such order shall set forth the date and place of birth of the person whose name is changed, the full names of his parents, including the maiden name of the mother and, if such person has previously changed his name, his former name or names.

Acts 1977, c. 457; Acts 1977, c. 617; Acts 1979, c. 599; Acts 1979, c. 603; Acts 1979, c. 612; Acts 1980, c. 448; Acts 1980, c. 455; Acts 1981, c. 297; Acts 1983, c. 355; Acts 1985, c. 483; Acts 1991, c. 144; Acts 2003, c. 258. Amended by Acts 2005, c. 579; Acts 2014, c. 232; Acts 2015, c. 631.

ARTICLE 21

MISCELLANEOUS PROVISIONS

§ 8.01-218. Replevin abolished

No action of replevin shall be hereafter brought.

Acts 1977, c. 617.

§ 8.01-219. Effect of judgment in trover

A judgment for the plaintiff in an action of trover shall not operate to transfer the title to the property converted unless and until such judgment has been satisfied.

Acts 1977, c. 617.

§ 8.01-219.1. Responsibility of possessor of real property for harm to trespasser

A. A possessor of real property, including an owner, lessee, or other lawful occupant, owes no duty of care to a trespasser except in those circumstances where a common-law right of action, statutory right of action, or judicial exception existed as of July 1, 2013.

B. This section does not affect any immunities from or defenses to liability established by another section of the Code or available at common law to which a possessor of real property may be entitled.

Added by Acts 2013, c. 217.

§ 8.01-220. Action for alienation of affection, breach of promise, criminal conversation and seduction abolished

A. Notwithstanding any other provision of law to the contrary, no civil action shall lie or be maintained in this Commonwealth for alienation of affection, breach of promise to marry, or criminal conversation upon which a cause of action arose or occurred on or after June 28, 1968.

B. No civil action for seduction shall lie or be maintained where the cause of action arose or accrued on or after July 1, 1974.

Acts 1977, c. 617.

§ 8.01-220.1. Defense of interspousal immunity abolished as to certain causes of action arising on or after July 1, 1981

The common-law defense of interspousal immunity in tort is abolished and shall not constitute a valid defense to any such cause of action arising on or after July 1, 1981.

Acts 1981, c. 451.

§ 8.01-220.1:1. Civil immunity for officers, partners, members, managers, trustees and directors of certain tax exempt organizations

A. Directors, partners, members, managers, trustees and officers of organizations exempt from income taxation under § 501 (c) or § 528 of the Internal Revenue Code who serve without compensation shall be immune from civil liability for acts taken in their capacities as officers, partners, members, managers, trustees or directors of such organizations.

B. In any proceeding against a director, partner, member, manager, trustee or officer of an organization exempt from income taxation under § 501 (c) or § 528 of the Internal Revenue Code who receives compensation, the damages assessed for acts taken in his capacity as an officer, partner, member, manager, trustee or director and arising out of a single transaction, occurrence or course of conduct shall not exceed the amount of compensation received by the officer, partner, member, manager, trustee or director during the 12 months immediately preceding the act or omission for which liability was imposed. As used herein "compensation" shall mean payment for services over and above per diem and expenses.

C. The liability of an officer, partner, member, manager, trustee or director shall not be limited as provided in this section if the officer, partner, member, manager, trustee or director engaged in willful misconduct or a knowing violation of the criminal law or if liability derives from the operation of a motor vehicle, or from the violation of a fiduciary obligation imposed during the period of declarant control by § 55–79.74.

D. The immunity provided by this section shall survive any termination, cancellation, or other discontinuance of the organization.

Acts 1987, c. 637; Acts 1988, c. 566. Amended by Acts 2005, c. 255; Acts 2011, c. 693; Acts 2011, c. 704.

§ 8.01–220.1:2. Civil immunity for teachers under certain circumstances

A. Any teacher employed by a local school board in the Commonwealth shall not be liable for any civil damages for any acts or omissions resulting from the supervision, care or discipline of students when such acts or omissions are within such teacher's scope of employment and are taken in good faith in the course of supervision, care or discipline of students, unless such acts or omissions were the result of gross negligence or willful misconduct.

B. No school employee or school volunteer shall be liable for any civil damages arising from the prompt good faith reporting of alleged acts of bullying or crimes against others to the appropriate school official in compliance with §§ 22.1–279.6 and 22.1–291.4 and specified procedures.

C. This section shall not be construed to limit, withdraw, or overturn any defense or immunity already existing in statutory or common law, to affect any claim occurring prior to the effective date of this law, or to prohibit any person subject to bullying or a criminal act from seeking redress under any other provision of law.

Acts 1997, c. 349, eff. April 2, 1997; Acts 1997, c. 879, eff. April 2, 1997. Amended by Acts 2005, c. 462; Acts 2013, c. 575.

§ 8.01–220.1:3. Immunity for members of church, synagogue or religious body

No member of any church, synagogue or religious body shall be liable in tort or contract for the actions of any officer, employee, leader, or other member of such church, synagogue or religious body solely because of his membership in such church, synagogue or religious body. Nothing in this section shall prevent any person from being held liable for his own actions.

Acts 1997, c. 480.

§ 8.01–220.1:4. Civil immunity for officers and directors of certain nonprofit organizations

A. Directors and officers of any entity created to ensure the implementation in the Commonwealth of a national tobacco trust established to provide payments to tobacco growers and tobacco quota owners to ameliorate adverse economic consequences resulting from a national settlement of states' claims against tobacco manufacturers shall be immune from civil liability for acts taken in their capacities as officers or directors of such entities.

B. The liability of an officer or director shall not be limited as provided in this section if the officer or director was grossly negligent or engaged in willful misconduct or a knowing violation of the criminal law.

Acts 2000, c. 1048.

§ 8.01–220.2. Spousal liability for medical care

Each spouse shall be jointly and severally liable for all emergency medical care furnished to the other spouse by a physician licensed to practice medicine in the Commonwealth or by a hospital located in the Commonwealth, including all follow-up inpatient care provided during the initial emergency admission to any such hospital, which is furnished while the spouses are living together. For the purposes of this section, emergency medical care shall mean any care the physician or other health care professional deems necessary to preserve the patient's life or health and which, if not rendered timely, can be reasonably anticipated to adversely affect the patient's recovery or imperil his life or health.

Acts 1984, c. 482. Amended by Acts 2009, c. 797.

§ 8.01–221. Damages from violation of statute, remedy therefor and penalty

Any person injured by the violation of any statute may recover from the offender such damages as he may sustain by reason of the violation, even though a penalty or forfeiture for such violation be thereby imposed, unless such penalty or forfeiture be expressly mentioned to be in lieu of such damages. And the damages so sustained together with any penalty or forfeiture imposed for the violation of the statute may be recovered in a single action when the same person is entitled to both damages and penalty; but nothing herein contained shall affect the existing statutes of limitation applicable to the foregoing causes of action respectively.

Acts 1977, c. 617.

§ 8.01-221.1. Unestablished business damages; lost profits

Damages for lost profits of a new or unestablished business may be recoverable upon proper proof. A party shall not be deemed to have failed to prove lost profits because the new or unestablished business has no history of profits. Such damages for a new or unestablished business shall not be recoverable in wrongful death or personal injury actions other than actions for defamation.

Added by Acts 2002, c. 624.

§ 8.01-221.2. Rescission; undue influence; attorney fees

In any civil action to rescind a deed, contract, or other instrument, the court may award to the plaintiff reasonable attorney fees and costs associated with bringing such action where the court finds, by clear and convincing evidence, that the deed, contract, or other instrument was obtained by fraud or undue influence on the part of the defendant.

Added by Acts 2014, c. 164.

§ 8.01-222. Repealed by Acts 2007, c. 368

§ 8.01-223. Lack of privity no defense in certain cases

In cases not provided for in § 8.2-318 where recovery of damages for injury to person, including death, or to property resulting from negligence is sought, lack of privity between the parties shall be no defense.

Acts 1977, c. 617.

§ 8.01-223.1. Use of constitutional rights

In any civil action the exercise by a party of any constitutional protection shall not be used against him.

Acts 1985, c. 192.

§ 8.01-223.2. Immunity of persons at public hearing

A person shall be immune from civil liability for a violation of § 18.2-499 or a claim of tortious interference with an existing contract or a business or contractual expectancy based solely on statements made by that person at a public hearing before the governing body of any locality or other political subdivision, or the boards, commissions, agencies and authorities thereof, and other governing bodies of any local governmental entity concerning matters properly before such body. The immunity provided by this section shall not apply to any statements made with knowledge that they are false, or reckless disregard for whether they are false.

Added by Acts 2007, c. 798.

§ 8.01-224. Defense of governmental immunity not available to certain persons in actions for damages from blasting, etc.

The defense of governmental immunity shall not be available to any person, firm or corporation in any cause of action for damages to the property of others proximately or directly resulting from blasting or the use of explosives in the performance of work for or on behalf of any governmental agency.

Acts 1977, c. 617.

§ 8.01-225. Persons rendering emergency care, obstetrical services exempt from liability

A. Any person who:

1. In good faith, renders emergency care or assistance, without compensation, to any ill or injured person (i) at the scene of an accident, fire, or any life-threatening emergency; (ii) at a location for screening or stabilization of an emergency medical condition arising from an accident, fire, or any life-threatening emergency; or (iii) en route to any hospital, medical clinic, or doctor's office, shall not be liable for any civil damages for acts or omissions resulting from the rendering of such care or assistance. For purposes of this subdivision, emergency care or assistance includes the forcible entry of a motor vehicle in order to remove an unattended minor at risk of serious bodily injury or death, provided the person has attempted to contact a law-enforcement officer, as defined in § 9.1-101, a firefighter, as defined in § 65.2-102, emergency medical services personnel, as defined in § 32.1-111.1, or an emergency 911 system, if feasible under the circumstances.

2. In the absence of gross negligence, renders emergency obstetrical care or assistance to a female in active labor who has not previously been cared for in connection with the pregnancy by such person or by another professionally associated with such person and whose medical records are not reasonably available to such person shall not be liable for any civil damages for acts or omissions resulting from the rendering of such emergency care or assistance. The immunity herein granted shall apply only to the emergency medical care provided.

3. In good faith and without compensation, including any emergency medical services provider who holds a valid certificate issued by the Commissioner of Health, administers epinephrine in an emergency to an individual shall not be liable for any civil damages for ordinary negligence in acts or omissions resulting from the rendering of such treatment if such person has reason to believe that the individual receiving the injection is suffering or is about to suffer a life-threatening anaphylactic reaction.

4. Provides assistance upon request of any police agency, fire department, emergency medical services agency, or governmental agency in the event of an accident or other emergency involving the use, handling, transportation, transmission, or storage of liquefied petroleum gas, liquefied natural gas, hazardous material, or hazardous waste as defined in § 10.1-1400 or regulations of the Virginia Waste Management

Board shall not be liable for any civil damages resulting from any act of commission or omission on his part in the course of his rendering such assistance in good faith.

5. Is an emergency medical services provider possessing a valid certificate issued by authority of the State Board of Health who in good faith renders emergency care or assistance, whether in person or by telephone or other means of communication, without compensation, to any injured or ill person, whether at the scene of an accident, fire, or any other place, or while transporting such injured or ill person to, from, or between any hospital, medical facility, medical clinic, doctor's office, or other similar or related medical facility, shall not be liable for any civil damages for acts or omissions resulting from the rendering of such emergency care, treatment, or assistance, including but in no way limited to acts or omissions which involve violations of State Department of Health regulations or any other state regulations in the rendering of such emergency care or assistance.

6. In good faith and without compensation, renders or administers emergency cardiopulmonary resuscitation (CPR); cardiac defibrillation, including, but not limited to, the use of an automated external defibrillator (AED); or other emergency life-sustaining or resuscitative treatments or procedures which have been approved by the State Board of Health to any sick or injured person, whether at the scene of a fire, an accident, or any other place, or while transporting such person to or from any hospital, clinic, doctor's office, or other medical facility, shall be deemed qualified to administer such emergency treatments and procedures and shall not be liable for acts or omissions resulting from the rendering of such emergency resuscitative treatments or procedures.

7. Operates an AED at the scene of an emergency, trains individuals to be operators of AEDs, or orders AEDs, shall be immune from civil liability for any personal injury that results from any act or omission in the use of an AED in an emergency where the person performing the defibrillation acts as an ordinary, reasonably prudent person would have acted under the same or similar circumstances, unless such personal injury results from gross negligence or willful or wanton misconduct of the person rendering such emergency care.

8. Maintains an AED located on real property owned or controlled by such person shall be immune from civil liability for any personal injury that results from any act or omission in the use in an emergency of an AED located on such property unless such personal injury results from gross negligence or willful or wanton misconduct of the person who maintains the AED or his agent or employee.

9. Is an employee of a school board or of a local health department approved by the local governing body to provide health services pursuant to § 22.1-274 who, while on school property or at a school-sponsored event, (i) renders emergency care or assistance to any sick or injured person; (ii) renders or administers emergency cardiopulmonary resuscitation (CPR); cardiac defibrillation, including, but not limited to, the use of an automated external defibrillator (AED); or other emergency life-sustaining or resuscitative treatments or procedures that have been approved by the State Board of Health to any sick or injured person; (iii) operates an AED, trains individuals to be operators of AEDs, or orders AEDs; or (iv) maintains an AED, shall not be liable for civil damages for ordinary negligence in acts or omissions on the part of such employee while engaged in the acts described in this subdivision.

10. Is a volunteer in good standing and certified to render emergency care by the National Ski Patrol System, Inc., who, in good faith and without compensation, renders emergency care or assistance to any injured or ill person, whether at the scene of a ski resort rescue, outdoor emergency rescue, or any other place or while transporting such injured or ill person to a place accessible for transfer to any available emergency medical system unit, or any resort owner voluntarily providing a ski patroller employed by him to engage in rescue or recovery work at a resort not owned or operated by him, shall not be liable for any civil damages for acts or omissions resulting from the rendering of such emergency care, treatment, or assistance, including but not limited to acts or omissions which involve violations of any state regulation or any standard of the National Ski Patrol System, Inc., in the rendering of such emergency care or assistance, unless such act or omission was the result of gross negligence or willful misconduct.

11. Is an employee of a school board, authorized by a prescriber and trained in the administration of insulin and glucagon, who, upon the written request of the parents as defined in § 22.1-1, assists with the administration of insulin or administers glucagon to a student diagnosed as having diabetes who requires insulin injections during the school day or for whom glucagon has been prescribed for the emergency treatment of hypoglycemia shall not be liable for any civil damages for ordinary negligence in acts or omissions resulting from the rendering of such treatment if the insulin is administered according to the child's medication schedule or such employee has reason to believe that the individual receiving the glucagon is suffering or is about to suffer life-threatening hypoglycemia. Whenever any employee of a school board is covered by the immunity granted herein, the school board employing him shall not be liable for any civil damages for ordinary negligence in acts or omissions resulting from the rendering of such insulin or glucagon treatment.

12. Is a school nurse, an employee of a school board, an employee of a local governing body, or an employee of a local health department who is authorized by a prescriber and trained in the administration

of epinephrine and who provides, administers, or assists in the administration of epinephrine to a student believed in good faith to be having an anaphylactic reaction, or is the prescriber of the epinephrine, shall not be liable for any civil damages for ordinary negligence in acts or omissions resulting from the rendering of such treatment.

13. Is an employee of a school for students with disabilities, as defined in § 22.1–319 and licensed by the Board of Education, or an employee of a private school that complies with the accreditation requirements set forth in § 22.1–19 and is accredited by the Virginia Council for Private Education who is authorized by a prescriber and trained in the administration of epinephrine and who administers or assists in the administration of epinephrine to a student believed in good faith to be having an anaphylactic reaction, or is the prescriber of the epinephrine, shall not be liable for any civil damages for ordinary negligence in acts or omissions resulting from the rendering of such treatment. Whenever any employee is covered by the immunity granted in this subdivision, the school shall not be liable for any civil damages for ordinary negligence in acts or omissions resulting from such administration or assistance.

14. Is an employee of a provider licensed by the Department of Behavioral Health and Developmental Services, or provides services pursuant to a contract with a provider licensed by the Department of Behavioral Health and Developmental Services, who has been trained in the administration of insulin and glucagon and who administers or assists with the administration of insulin or administers glucagon to a person diagnosed as having diabetes who requires insulin injections or for whom glucagon has been prescribed for the emergency treatment of hypoglycemia in accordance with § 54.1–3408 shall not be liable for any civil damages for ordinary negligence in acts or omissions resulting from the rendering of such treatment if the insulin is administered in accordance with the prescriber's instructions or such person has reason to believe that the individual receiving the glucagon is suffering or is about to suffer life-threatening hypoglycemia. Whenever any employee of a provider licensed by the Department of Behavioral Health and Developmental Services or a person who provides services pursuant to a contract with a provider licensed by the Department of Behavioral Health and Developmental Services is covered by the immunity granted herein, the provider shall not be liable for any civil damages for ordinary negligence in acts or omissions resulting from the rendering of such insulin or glucagon treatment.

15. Is an employee of a provider licensed by the Department of Behavioral Health and Developmental Services, or provides services pursuant to a contract with a provider licensed by the Department of Behavioral Health and Developmental Services, who has been trained in the administration of epinephrine and who administers or assists in the administration of epinephrine to a person believed in good faith to be having an anaphylactic reaction in accordance with the prescriber's instructions shall not be liable for any civil damages for ordinary negligence in acts or omissions resulting from the rendering of such treatment.

16. In good faith prescribes, dispenses, or administers naloxone or other opioid antagonist used for overdose reversal in an emergency to an individual who is believed to be experiencing or about to experience a life-threatening opiate overdose shall not be liable for any civil damages for ordinary negligence in acts or omissions resulting from the rendering of such treatment if acting in accordance with the provisions of subsection X of § 54.1–3408 or in his role as a member of an emergency medical services agency.

B. Any licensed physician serving without compensation as the operational medical director for an emergency medical services agency that holds a valid license as an emergency medical services agency issued by the Commissioner of Health shall not be liable for any civil damages for any act or omission resulting from the rendering of emergency medical services in good faith by the personnel of such licensed agency unless such act or omission was the result of such physician's gross negligence or willful misconduct.

Any person serving without compensation as a dispatcher for any licensed public or nonprofit emergency medical services agency in the Commonwealth shall not be liable for any civil damages for any act or omission resulting from the rendering of emergency services in good faith by the personnel of such licensed agency unless such act or omission was the result of such dispatcher's gross negligence or willful misconduct.

Any individual, certified by the State Office of Emergency Medical Services as an emergency medical services instructor and pursuant to a written agreement with such office, who, in good faith and in the performance of his duties, provides instruction to persons for certification or recertification as a certified basic life support or advanced life support emergency medical services provider shall not be liable for any civil damages for acts or omissions on his part directly relating to his activities on behalf of such office unless such act or omission was the result of such emergency medical services instructor's gross negligence or willful misconduct.

Any licensed physician serving without compensation as a medical advisor to an E–911 system in the Commonwealth shall not be liable for any civil damages for any act or omission resulting from rendering medical advice in good faith to establish protocols to be used by the personnel of the E–911 service, as defined in § 58.1–1730, when answering emergency calls unless such act or omission was the result of such physician's gross negligence or willful misconduct.

Any licensed physician who directs the provision of emergency medical services, as authorized by the State

Board of Health, through a communications device shall not be liable for any civil damages for any act or omission resulting from the rendering of such emergency medical services unless such act or omission was the result of such physician's gross negligence or willful misconduct.

Any licensed physician serving without compensation as a supervisor of an AED in the Commonwealth shall not be liable for any civil damages for any act or omission resulting from rendering medical advice in good faith to the owner of the AED relating to personnel training, local emergency medical services coordination, protocol approval, AED deployment strategies, and equipment maintenance plans and records unless such act or omission was the result of such physician's gross negligence or willful misconduct.

C. Any communications services provider, as defined in § 58.1–647, including mobile service, and any provider of Voice-over-Internet Protocol service, in the Commonwealth shall not be liable for any civil damages for any act or omission resulting from rendering such service with or without charge related to emergency calls unless such act or omission was the result of such service provider's gross negligence or willful misconduct.

Any volunteer engaging in rescue or recovery work at a mine, or any mine operator voluntarily providing personnel to engage in rescue or recovery work at a mine not owned or operated by such operator, shall not be liable for civil damages for acts or omissions resulting from the rendering of such rescue or recovery work in good faith unless such act or omission was the result of gross negligence or willful misconduct. For purposes of this subsection, "Voice-over-Internet Protocol service" or "VoIP service" means any Internet protocol-enabled services utilizing a broadband connection, actually originating or terminating in Internet Protocol from either or both ends of a channel of communication offering real time, multidirectional voice functionality, including, but not limited to, services similar to traditional telephone service.

D. Nothing contained in this section shall be construed to provide immunity from liability arising out of the operation of a motor vehicle.

E. For the purposes of this section, "compensation" shall not be construed to include (i) the salaries of police, fire, or other public officials or personnel who render such emergency assistance; (ii) the salaries or wages of employees of a coal producer engaging in emergency medical services or first aid services pursuant to the provisions of § 45.1–161.38, 45.1–161.101, 45.1–161.199, or 45.1–161.263; (iii) complimentary lift tickets, food, lodging, or other gifts provided as a gratuity to volunteer members of the National Ski Patrol System, Inc., by any resort, group, or agency; (iv) the salary of any person who (a) owns an AED for the use at the scene of an emergency, (b) trains individuals, in courses approved by the Board of Health, to operate AEDs at the scene of emergencies, (c) orders AEDs for use at the scene of emergencies, or (d) operates an AED at the scene of an emergency; or (v) expenses reimbursed to any person providing care or assistance pursuant to this section.

For the purposes of this section, "emergency medical services provider" shall include a person licensed or certified as such or its equivalent by any other state when he is performing services that he is licensed or certified to perform by such other state in caring for a patient in transit in the Commonwealth, which care originated in such other state.

Further, the public shall be urged to receive training on how to use CPR and an AED in order to acquire the skills and confidence to respond to emergencies using both CPR and an AED.

Acts 1977, c. 441; Acts 1978, c. 94; Acts 1978, c. 707; Acts 1979, c. 713; Acts 1979, c. 729; Acts 1980, c. 419; Acts 1983, c. 72; Acts 1984, c. 493; Acts 1984, c. 577; Acts 1987, c. 260; Acts 1987, c. 382; Acts 1990, c. 898; Acts 1996, c. 899; Acts 1997, c. 334; Acts 1997, c. 809; Acts 1998, c. 493; Acts 1998, c. 500; Acts 1999, c. 570; Acts 1999, c. 1000; Acts 2000, c. 928; Acts 2000, c. 1064; Acts 2003, c. 18, eff. March 5, 2003; Acts 2003, c. 978, eff. April 2, 2003; Acts 2003, c. 1020. Amended by Acts 2005, c. 426; Acts 2006, c. 780, eff. Jan. 1, 2007; Acts 2008, c. 229; Acts 2012, c. 787; Acts 2012, c. 833; Acts 2013, c. 183; Acts 2013, c. 267; Acts 2013, c. 300; Acts 2013, c. 336, eff. March 14, 2013; Acts 2013, c. 617, eff. March 20, 2013; Acts 2014, c. 468; Acts 2015, c. 340; Acts 2015, c. 387; Acts 2015, c. 502; Acts 2015, c. 503; Acts 2015, c. 725, eff. April 15, 2015; Acts 2015, c. 732, eff. April 15, 2015; Acts 2015, c. 752, eff. April 15, 2015.

§ 8.01–225.01. Certain immunity for health care providers during disasters under specific circumstances

A. In the absence of gross negligence or willful misconduct, any health care provider who responds to a disaster by delivering health care to persons injured in such disaster shall be immune from civil liability for any injury or wrongful death arising from abandonment by such health care provider of any person to whom such health care provider owes a duty to provide health care when (i) a state or local emergency has been or is subsequently declared; and (ii) the provider was unable to provide the requisite health care to the person to whom he owed such duty of care as a result of the provider's voluntary or mandatory response to the relevant disaster.

B. In the absence of gross negligence or willful misconduct, any hospital or other entity credentialing health care providers to deliver health care in response to a disaster shall be immune from civil liability for any cause of action arising out of such credentialing or granting of practice privileges if (i) a state or local emergency has been or is subsequently declared and (ii) the hospital has followed procedures for such credentialing and granting of practice privileges that are consistent with the applicable standards of an approved national accrediting organization for granting emergency practice privileges.

C. For the purposes of this section:

"Approved national accrediting organization" means an organization granted authority by the Centers for Medicare and Medicaid Services to ensure compliance with Medicare conditions of participation pursuant to § 1865 of Title XVIII of the Social Security Act (42 U.S.C. § 1395bb).

"Disaster" means any "disaster," "emergency," or "major disaster" as those terms are used and defined in § 44–146.16; and

"Health care provider" means those professions defined as such in § 8.01–581.1.

D. The immunity provided by this section shall be in addition to, and shall not be in lieu of, any immunities provided in other state or federal law, including, but not limited to, §§ 8.01–225 and 44–146.23.

Added by Acts 2003, c. 507. Amended by Acts 2008, c. 121; Acts 2008, c. 157; Acts 2014, c. 320.

§ 8.01–225.02. Certain liability protection for health care providers during disasters

A. In the absence of gross negligence or willful misconduct, any health care provider who responds to a disaster shall not be liable for any injury or wrongful death of any person arising from the delivery or withholding of health care when (i) a state or local emergency has been or is subsequently declared in response to such disaster, and (ii) the emergency and subsequent conditions caused a lack of resources, attributable to the disaster, rendering the health care provider unable to provide the level or manner of care that otherwise would have been required in the absence of the emergency and which resulted in the injury or wrongful death at issue.

B. For purposes of this section:

"Disaster" means any "disaster," "emergency," or "major disaster" as those terms are used and defined in § 44–146.16; and

"Health care provider" has the same definition as provided in § 8.01–581.1.

Added by Acts 2008, c. 121; Acts 2008, c. 157.

§ 8.01–225.1. Immunity for team physicians

Any physician, surgeon or chiropractor licensed to practice by the Board of Medicine in the Commonwealth who, in the absence of gross negligence or willful misconduct, renders emergency medical care or emergency treatment to a participant in an athletic event sponsored by a public, private or religious elementary, middle or high school while acting without compensation as a team physician, shall not be liable for civil damages resulting from any act or omission related to such care or treatment.

Acts 1989, c. 436; Acts 1993, c. 702. Amended by Acts 2005, c. 928.

§ 8.01–225.2. Immunity for those rendering emergency care to animals

Any person, including a person licensed to practice veterinary medicine, who in good faith and without compensation renders emergency care or treatment to an injured animal at the scene of an emergency or accident shall not be liable for any injuries to such animals resulting from the rendering of such care or treatment.

Acts 1998, c. 669.

§ 8.01–225.3. Immunity for volunteer first responders en route to an emergency

Notwithstanding any other provision of law, no volunteer firefighter or volunteer emergency medical services personnel shall be liable for any injury to persons or property arising out of the operation of an emergency vehicle as defined in § 46.2–920 when such volunteer is en route to respond to a fire or to render emergency care or assistance to any ill or injured person at the scene of an accident, fire, or life-threatening emergency and the emergency vehicle displays warning lights as provided in § 46.2–1022 or 46.2–1023 and sounds a siren, exhaust whistle, or air horn, unless such injury results from gross negligence or willful or wanton misconduct. The immunity provided by this section shall be in addition to, not in lieu of, any other applicable immunity provided by state or federal law, including § 2.2–3605 or 27–6.02.

Added by Acts 2015, c. 417.

§ 8.01–226. Duty of care to law-enforcement officers and firefighters, etc.

An owner or occupant of real property containing premises normally open to the public shall, with respect to such premises, owe to firefighters, Department of Emergency Management hazardous materials officers, nonfirefighter regional hazardous materials emergency response team members, and law-enforcement officers who in the performance of their duties come upon that portion of the premises normally open to the public the duty to maintain the same in a reasonably safe condition or to warn of dangers thereon of which he knows or has reason to know, whether or not such premises are at the time open to the public.

An owner or occupant of real property containing premises not normally open to the public shall, with respect to such premises, owe the same duty to firefighters, Department of Emergency Management hazardous materials officers, nonfirefighter regional hazardous materials emergency response team members, and law-enforcement officers who he knows or has reason to know are upon, about to come upon or imminently likely to come upon that portion of the premises not normally open to the public.

While otherwise engaged in the performance of his duties, a law-enforcement officer, Department of Emergency Management hazardous materials officer, nonfirefighter regional hazardous materials emergency response team member, or firefighter shall be owed a duty of ordinary care.

For purposes of this section, the term "law-enforcement officers" shall mean only police officers, sheriffs and deputy sheriffs and the term "firefighter" includes (i) emergency medical personnel and (ii) special forest wardens designated pursuant to § 10.1–1135.

Acts 1987, c. 442; Acts 1992, c. 731; Acts 1996, c. 646; Acts 1996, c. 660; Acts 2000, c. 962.

§ 8.01–226.1. Civil immunity when participating in Lawyers Helping Lawyers

Any person shall be immune from civil liability for, or resulting from, any act, decision, omission, communication, finding, opinion or conclusion made or conducted in connection with the investigation, intervention, counseling or monitoring of a lawyer, judge, paralegal, or other member of the legal profession by "Lawyers Helping Lawyers," a Virginia nonprofit, nonstock corporation dedicated to assisting members of the legal profession engaged in substance abuse or suffering from mental illness, if such act, decision, omission, communication, finding, opinion or conclusion is made or conducted in good faith and without malicious intent.

Nothing in this section shall be construed to grant immunity to any claim by a client against a person licensed to practice law.

Acts 1987, c. 527; Acts 1992, c. 534; Acts 2003, c. 571.

§ 8.01–226.2. Civil immunity for licensed professional engineers and licensed architects participating in rescue or relief assistance

Any licensed professional engineer or licensed architect who, in good faith and without charge or compensation, utilizes his professional skills in providing rescue or relief assistance at the scene of or in connection with a natural or man-made disaster or other life-threatening emergency, shall not be liable for any civil damages for acts or omissions on his part resulting from the rendering of such assistance or professional services in the absence of gross negligence or willful misconduct.

Acts 1992, c. 702; Acts 1997, c. 866.

§ 8.01–226.3. Civil immunity for officers, directors and members of certain crime information-gathering organizations

Any officer, director or member of a nonprofit organization which, pursuant to a written agreement with a local government or a law-enforcement agency, regularly assists law-enforcement agencies by (i) publicly soliciting information from anonymous informants concerning criminal activity; (ii) gathering such information from informants; (iii) offering and paying rewards to informants for such information; and (iv) communicating such information to law-enforcement agencies, shall not be liable for any civil damages for acts or omissions on his part directly relating to his activities on behalf of such organization but only in the absence of gross negligence or willful misconduct.

Acts 1993, c. 769.

§ 8.01–226.4. Civil immunity for hospice volunteers

Any individual who, in good faith, without compensation, and in the absence of gross negligence or willful misconduct, renders care to a terminally ill patient pursuant to a hospice program whose sole purpose is to provide care and treatment to terminally ill patients and whose services are equally available to all members of the community, shall not be liable for any civil damages for acts or omissions resulting from the rendering of such care.

Acts 1994, c. 738.

§ 8.01–226.5. Immunity for installers and inspectors of child restraint devices

Any person who has successfully met the minimum required training standards for installation of child restraint devices established by the National Highway Traffic Safety Administration of the United States Department of Transportation, who in good faith and without compensation installs, or inspects the installation of, a child restraint device shall not be liable for any damages resulting from an act or omission related to such installation or inspection, unless such act or omission was the result of the person's gross negligence or willful misconduct.

Acts 1999, c. 293.

§ 8.01–226.5:1. Civil immunity for school board employees supervising self-administration of certain medication

A. Any school principal or other employee of a school board who, in good faith, without compensation, and in the absence of gross negligence or willful misconduct, supervises the self-administration of inhaled asthma medications or auto-injectable epinephrine by a student, pursuant to § 22.1–274.2, shall not be liable for any civil damages for acts or omissions resulting from the supervision of self-administration of inhaled asthma medications or auto-injectable epinephrine by such student. Further, no such principal or school board employee shall be liable for any civil damages for any injuries or deaths resulting from the misuse of such auto-injectable epinephrine.

B. For the purposes of this section, "employee" shall include any person employed by a local health department who is assigned to a public school pursuant to an agreement between a local health department and a school board.

Acts 2000, c. 871. Amended by Acts 2005, c. 785.

§ 8.01–226.5:2. Immunity of hospital and emergency medical services agency personnel for the acceptance of certain infants

Any personnel of a hospital or emergency medical services agency receiving a child under the circumstances described in the second paragraph of § 18.2–371, subdivision B 2 of § 18.2–371.1, or subsection B of § 40.1–103 shall be immune from civil liability or criminal prosecution for injury or other damage to the child unless such injury or other damage is the result of gross negligence or willful misconduct by such personnel.

Added by Acts 2003, c. 816; Acts 2003, c. 822. Amended by Acts 2015, c. 502; Acts 2015, c. 503.

§ 8.01–226.6. Repealed by Acts 2007, c. 250

§ 8.01–226.7. Owner and agent compliance with residential lead-based paint notification; maintenance immunity

A. As used in this section, the following definitions apply:

"Agent" means any party who enters into a contract with a seller or lessor, including any party who enters into a contract with a representative of the seller or lessor, for the purpose of selling or leasing a residential dwelling. This term includes all persons licensed under Chapter 21 (§ 54.1–2100 et seq.) of Title 54.1. This term does not apply to purchasers or any purchaser's representative who receives compensation from the purchaser.

"Lead-based paint" means paint or other surface coatings that contain lead equal to or in excess of 1.0 milligram per square centimeter or 0.5 percent by weight.

"Lead-based paint hazard" means any condition that causes exposure to lead from lead-contaminated dust, lead-contaminated soil, or lead-contaminated paint that is deteriorated or present in accessible surfaces, friction surfaces, or impact surfaces that would result in adverse human health effects as established by the appropriate federal or state agency.

"Lead-based paint maintenance" means ensuring that the painted surfaces are maintained in accordance with the provisions of the International Property Maintenance Code adopted as part of the Uniform Statewide Building Code.

"Residential dwelling" means a structure or part of a structure that is used as a home or residence by one or more persons who maintain a household, whether single family or multifamily.

B. Any agent who has complied with the requirements of the United States Residential Lead–Based Paint Hazard Reduction Act of 1992 (42 U.S.C. § 4851 et seq.) shall not be liable for civil damages in any personal injury or wrongful death action for lead poisoning arising from the condition of a residential dwelling, provided that before the purchaser signs any contract to purchase the residential dwelling or the tenant signs any lease for an initial term to rent the residential dwelling:

1. An EPA-approved lead hazard information pamphlet was provided to the purchaser or lessee;

2. The agent disclosed to the lessee the presence of any known lead-based paint and/or lead-based paint hazards and any additional information or reports about which the agent had actual knowledge concerning the known lead-based paint or lead-based paint hazards;

3. The purchaser or tenant signed a written statement acknowledging the disclosure and receipt of the literature;

4. If the agent is a public housing authority, it has complied with all applicable federal laws and regulations. Nothing in this subdivision shall be construed to require compliance with the federal laws and regulations that are applicable to federal housing authorities by owners or agents who are not a public housing authority; and

5. The disclosure requirements in subsection B shall continue during the term of the tenancy for any new information in the possession of the agent or about which the agent has actual knowledge concerning the presence of lead-based paint or lead-based paint hazards. The agent shall make a written disclosure of any new information and provide the tenant with a copy of a summary thereof, advising the tenant that the full package of information and any report is available for inspection and copying if requested by the tenant.

However, if the agent is responsible for lead-based paint maintenance on the residential dwelling, the agent shall not be entitled to immunity unless the agent has also met the requirements of subsection C of this section. For purposes of subsection B, an agent is responsible for lead-based paint maintenance if the agent is a party to a written agreement that requires the agent to be responsible for the maintenance of the painted surfaces in accordance with the International Property Maintenance Code adopted as part of the Uniform Statewide Building Code.

C. An owner of a residential dwelling, or agent responsible for the lead-based paint maintenance of a residential dwelling, who has complied with the requirements of the United States Residential Lead–Based Paint Hazard Reduction Act of 1992 (42 U.S.C. § 4851 et seq.) shall not be liable for civil damages in a personal injury or wrongful death action for lead poisoning arising from the condition of the residential dwelling, provided that before the purchaser signs any contract to purchase the residential dwelling, or the tenant signs any lease for an initial term to rent the residential dwelling:

1. An EPA-approved lead hazard information pamphlet was provided to the purchaser or lessee;

2. The owner or agent responsible for the lead-based paint maintenance of a residential dwelling disclosed to the lessee the presence of any known lead-based paint and/or lead-based paint hazards and any additional information or reports about which the owner or such agent had of their own actual knowledge concerning the known lead-based paint or lead-based paint hazards;

3. The purchaser or tenant signed a written statement acknowledging the disclosure and receipt of the literature;

4. With regards to lead-based paint and lead-based paint hazards, the painted surfaces of the residential dwelling were maintained in compliance with the International Property Maintenance Code of the Uniform Statewide Building Code; and

5. The disclosure requirements in subsection C shall continue during the term of the tenancy for any new information in the possession of the owner or about which the owner has actual knowledge concerning the presence of lead-based paint or lead-based paint hazards. Further, the disclosure requirements in subsection C shall continue during the term of the tenancy for any new information in the possession of such agent or about which such agent has actual knowledge concerning the presence of lead-based paint or lead-based paint hazards. The agent shall make a written disclosure of any new information and provide the tenant with a copy of a summary thereof, advising the tenant that the full package of information and any report is available for inspection and copying if requested by the tenant.

D. An owner or agent claiming immunity under this section may assert such immunity in responsive pleadings and request a hearing, after discovery on issues related to immunity, before the court to determine entitlement to such immunity prior to further proceedings in the case.

Acts 2000, c. 1071. Amended by Acts 2006, c. 855; Acts 2007, c. 255.

§ 8.01–226.8. Civil immunity for public officials and private volunteers participating in certain programs for probationers

Probation officers; court personnel; county, city and town personnel; any other public officials; and private volunteers who participate in a program where persons on probation or community service are ordered as a condition of probation or community service to pick up litter along a section of public roadway or waterway, to perform recycling duties at landfills, garbage transfer sites, and other waste disposal systems, to mow rights-of-way or to perform other landscaping maintenance tasks shall not be liable for any civil damages to a probationer or person on community service, or the property of such person, for acts or omissions resulting from such participation, unless such act or omission is the result of willful misconduct. The provisions of this section shall not be interpreted to grant any immunity to a driver transporting the persons on probation or community service or a motorist who, by his negligence, may injure such probationer or person on community service.

Added by Acts 2004, c. 387; Acts 2004, c. 434. Amended by Acts 2007, c. 182; Acts 2008, c. 688.

§ 8.01–226.9. Exemption from civil liability in connection with arrest or detention of person suspected of shoplifting

A merchant, agent or employee of the merchant, who causes the arrest or detention of any person pursuant to the provisions of §§ 18.2–95, 18.2–96 or § 18.2–103, shall not be held civilly liable for unlawful detention, if such detention does not exceed one hour, slander, malicious prosecution, false imprisonment, false arrest, or assault and battery of the person so arrested or detained, whether such arrest or detention takes place on the premises of the merchant, or after close pursuit from such premises by such merchant, his agent or employee, provided that, in causing the arrest or detention of such person, the merchant, agent or employee of the merchant, had at the time of such arrest or detention probable cause to believe that the person had shoplifted or committed willful concealment of goods or merchandise. The activation of an electronic article surveillance device as a result of a person exiting the premises or an area within the premises of a merchant where an electronic article surveillance device is located shall constitute probable cause for the detention of such person by such merchant, his agent or employee, provided such person is detained only in a reasonable manner and only for such time as is necessary for an inquiry into the circumstances surrounding the activation of the device, and provided that clear and visible notice is posted at each exit and location within the premises where such a device is located indicating the presence of an antishoplifting or inventory control device. For purposes of this section, "electronic article surveillance device" means an electronic device designed and operated for the purpose of detecting the removal from the premises, or a protected area within such premises, of specially marked or tagged merchandise.

Added by Acts 2004, c. 462.

§ 8.01–226.10. Civil immunity for causing the arrest of a person for a bad check

If payment of any check, draft, or order for the payment of money is refused by the financial institution, trust company or other depository upon which such instrument is drawn, and the person who drew or uttered such instrument is arrested or prosecuted under the provisions of § 18.2–181 or § 18.2–182, for failure or refusal to pay such instrument, the one who arrested or caused such person to be arrested and prosecuted, or either, shall be conclusively deemed to have acted with reasonable or probable cause in any suit for damages that may be brought by the person who drew or uttered such instrument, if the one who arrested or caused such person to be arrested and prosecuted, or either, shall have, before doing so, presented or caused such instrument to be presented to the depository on which it was drawn where it was refused, and then waited five days after notice, as provided in § 18.2–183, without the amount due under the provisions of such instrument being paid.

Added by Acts 2004, c. 462.

§ 8.01–226.11. Civil immunity for operation of victim notification program

The Virginia Sheriffs' Association and the Virginia Community Policing Institute, and the directors, managers, members, officers and employees of such entities shall be immune from civil liability for their acts or omissions relating to the establishment and operation of an automated victim notification system unless such act or omission was the result of gross negligence or willful misconduct.

Added by Acts 2006, c. 267.

§ 8.01–226.12. Duty of landlord and managing agent with respect to visible mold

A. As used in this section, the following definitions apply:

"Authorized occupant" means a person entitled to occupy a dwelling unit with the consent of the landlord, but who has not signed the rental agreement and therefore does not have the rights and obligations as a tenant under the rental agreement.

"Dwelling unit" means a structure or part of a structure that is used as a home or residence by one or more persons who maintain a household, whether single family or multifamily, including, but not limited to, a manufactured home.

"Guest or invitee" means a person, other than the tenant or person authorized by the landlord to occupy the dwelling unit, who has the permission of the tenant to visit but not to occupy the premises.

"Interior of the dwelling unit" means the inside of the dwelling unit, consisting of interior walls, floor, and ceiling that enclose the dwelling unit as conditioned space from the outside air.

"Landlord" means the owner or lessor of the dwelling unit or the building of which such residential dwelling unit is a part. "Landlord" also includes a managing agent of the premises who fails to disclose the name of such owner, lessor, or sublessor. Such managing agent shall be subject to the provisions of § 16.1–88.03.

"Managing agent" means a person authorized by the landlord to act on behalf of the landlord under an agreement.

"Mold remediation in accordance with professional standards" means mold remediation of that portion of the dwelling unit or premises affected by mold, or any personal property of the tenant affected by mold, performed consistent with guidance documents published by the United States Environmental Protection Agency, the United States Department of Housing and Urban Development, the American Conference of Governmental Industrial Hygienists (the Bioaerosols Manual), Standard Reference Guides of the Institute of Inspection, Cleaning and Restoration for Water Damage Restoration and Professional Mold Remediation, or any protocol for mold remediation prepared by an industrial hygienist consistent with said guidance documents.

"Notice" means notice given in writing by either regular mail or hand delivery, with sender retaining sufficient proof of having given such notice, which may be either a United States postal certificate of mailing or a certificate of service confirming such mailing prepared by the sender. However, a person shall be deemed to have notice of a fact if he has actual knowledge of it, or he received a verbal notice of it. A person "notifies" or "gives" a notice or notification to another by taking steps reasonably calculated to inform another person whether or not the other person actually comes to know of it. If a notice given is not in writing, the person giving the notice has the burden of proof to show that the notice was given to the recipient of the notice.

"Readily accessible" means areas within the interior of the dwelling unit available for observation at the time of the move-in inspection that do not require removal of materials, personal property, equipment, or similar items.

"Tenant" means a person entitled under a rental agreement to occupy a dwelling unit to the exclusion of others. Tenant shall not include (i) an authorized occupant, (ii) a guest or invitee, or (iii) any person who guarantees or cosigns the payment of the financial obligations of a rental agreement but has no right to occupy a dwelling unit.

"Visible evidence of mold" means the existence of mold in the residential dwelling unit that is visible to the naked eye of the landlord or tenant at the time of the move-in inspection.

Any term not expressly defined herein shall have the same meaning as those defined in § 55–248.4.

B. Neither the landlord nor the managing agent shall be liable for civil damages in any personal injury or wrongful death action brought by a tenant, authorized occupant, or guest or invitee for exposure to mold arising from the condition within the interior of a dwelling unit, or for any property damage claims arising out of the landlord-tenant relationship, if the mold condition is caused solely by the negligence of the tenant.

C. A managing agent with no maintenance responsibilities shall not be liable for civil damages in any personal injury or wrongful death action brought by the tenant, authorized occupant, or guest or invitee for exposure to mold, or for any property damage claims arising out of the residential landlord-tenant relationship, unless the managing agent fails to disclose the existence of a mold condition of which the managing agent has actual knowledge to the landlord and any prospective or actual tenants.

D. If the written move-in inspection report authorized under Chapter 13 (§ 55–217 et seq.) or 13.2 (§ 55–248.2 et seq.) of Title 55 reflects that there is no visible evidence of mold in areas readily accessible within the interior of the dwelling unit, and the tenant does not object thereto in writing within five days after receiving the report, there shall be a rebuttable presumption that no mold existed at the time of the move-in inspection.

E. If visible evidence of mold occurs within the dwelling unit, the landlord or managing agent with the maintenance responsibilities shall, exercising ordinary care, perform mold remediation in accordance with professional standards.

F. The landlord or managing agent with maintenance responsibilities shall comply with any other applicable provisions of law.

Added by Acts 2008, c. 162; Acts 2008, c. 341.

§ 8.01–227. Remedy by motion on certain bonds given or taken by officers; notice

The court in which any bond given or taken by an officer is required to be returned, filed or recorded, may, on motion of any person protected by such bond, give judgment in favor of such person for such amount as he would be entitled by virtue of the bond to recover in an action at law. Any such motion shall be made after reasonable notice, not less than ten days, to the obligors on the bond. Service may be in any manner sufficient to support a judgment in personam.

Acts 1977, c. 617.

ARTICLE 22

YEAR 2000 LIABILITY AND DAMAGES

§§ 8.01–227.1 to 8.01–227.3. Repealed by Acts 2007, c. 250

ARTICLE 23

DRUG DEALER LIABILITY ACT

§ 8.01–227.4. Definitions

As used in this article:

"Controlled substance" means a controlled substance as defined in Article 1 (§ 18.2–247 et seq.) of Chapter 7 of Title 18.2.

"Health care provider" means a health care provider as defined in § 8.01–581.1.

Added by Acts 2002, c. 863.

§ 8.01–227.5. Persons who may bring action; persons against whom actions may be brought; damages recoverable

A. A parent or legal custodian may bring an action for damages incurred because of his child's unlawful use of a controlled substance while under the age of eighteen against a natural person age eighteen years or older who sold, administered, furnished or knowingly participated in the unlawful distribution of a controlled substance to the child.

B. A parent or legal custodian entitled to bring an action under this article may recover damages limited to physical and emotional pain and suffering, the cost of treatment and rehabilitation and medical expenses, proximately caused to the parent or legal custodian by the child's unlawful use of a controlled substance.

Added by Acts 2002, c. 863.

§ 8.01–227.6. Law-enforcement officer or agency; health care provider not liable under certain conditions

A law-enforcement officer or agency shall not be liable under this article if acting in furtherance of an official investigation. A health care provider who in good faith and in compliance with state or federal law, sells, administers, furnishes or distributes a controlled substance shall not be liable under this article.

Added by Acts 2002, c. 863.

§ 8.01–227.7. Statute of limitations

Every action brought pursuant to this article shall be commenced no later than two years after the child's eighteenth birthday.

Added by Acts 2002, c. 863.

Article 24

Space Flight Liability and Immunity Act

§ 8.01–227.8. Definitions

For purposes of this section:

"Participant" means any space flight participant as that term is defined in 49 U.S.C. § 70102.

"Participant Injury" means any bodily injury, including death; emotional injury; or property damage sustained by the participant.

"Space flight activities" means launch services or reentry services as those terms are defined in 49 U.S.C. § 70102.

"Space flight entity" means any public or private entity holding, either directly or through a corporate subsidiary or parent, a license, permit, or other authorization issued by the United States Federal Aviation Administration pursuant to the Federal Space Launch Amendments Act (49 U.S.C. § 70101 et seq.), including, but not limited to, a safety approval and a payload determination. "Space flight entity" shall also include any manufacturer or supplier of components, services, or vehicles that have been reviewed by the United States Federal Aviation Administration as part of issuing such a license, permit, or authorization.

Added by Acts 2007, c. 893.

§ 8.01–227.9. Civil immunity for space flight entities

A. Except as provided in subsection B, a space flight entity is not liable for a participant injury resulting from the risks of space flight activities, provided that the participant has been informed of the risks of space flight activities as required by federal law pursuant to federal law and this article, and the participant has given his informed consent that he is voluntarily participating in space flight activities after having been informed of the risks of those activities as required by federal law and this article. Except as provided in subsection B, no (i) participant, (ii) participant's representative, including the heirs, administrators, executors, assignees, next of kin, and estate of the participant, or (iii) any person who attempts to bring a claim on behalf of the participant for a participant injury, is authorized to maintain an action against or recover from a space flight entity for a participant injury that resulted from the risks of space flight activities.

B. Nothing in subsection A shall prevent or limit the liability of a space flight entity if the space flight entity does either of the following:

1. Commits an act or omission that constitutes gross negligence evidencing willful or wanton disregard for the safety of the participant, and that act or omission proximately causes a participant injury; or

2. Intentionally causes a participant injury.

C. Any limitation on legal liability afforded by this section to a space flight entity is in addition to any other limitations of legal liability otherwise provided by law.

Added by Acts 2007, c. 893.

§ 8.01–227.10. Warning required

A. Every space flight entity providing space flight activities to a participant shall have each participant sign the warning statement specified in subsection B.

B. The warning statement described in subsection A shall contain, at a minimum and in addition to any language required by federal law, the following statement:

"WARNING AND ACKNOWLEDGEMENT: I understand and acknowledge that, under Virginia law, there is no civil liability for bodily injury, including death, emotional injury, or property damage sustained by a participant in space flight activities provided by a space flight entity if such injury or damage results from the risks of the space flight activity. I have given my informed consent to participate in space flight activities after receiving a description of the risks of space flight activities as required by federal law pursuant to 49 U.S.C. § 70105 and 14 C.F.R. § 460.45. The consent that I have given acknowledges that the risks of space flight activities include, but are not limited to, risks of bodily injury, including death, emotional injury, and property damage. I understand and acknowledge that I am participating in space flight activities at my own risk. I have been given the opportunity to consult with an attorney before signing this statement."

C. Failure to comply with the requirements concerning the warning statement provided in this section shall prevent a space flight entity from invoking the privileges of immunity provided by this article.

Added by Acts 2007, c. 893.

ARTICLE 25

WINTER SPORTS SAFETY ACT

§ 8.01–227.11. Definitions

As used in this article, unless the context requires a different meaning:

"ANSI Ski Lift Code" means the American National Standard (B77.1–2006): Passenger Ropeways—Aerial Tramways, Aerial Lifts, Surface Lifts, Tows and Conveyors—Safety Requirements, as published by the American National Standards Institute, including any supplements thereto or revisions thereof.

"Competition" means any contest or event operated by a winter sports area operator or any other party authorized by the operator at a winter sports area involving comparison of skills, including, but not limited to, a ski race, mogul contest, jumping event, freestyle event, snowcross contest, or other similar contest or event. "Competition" includes training sessions or practice for a contest or event.

"Competition terrain" means any part of a winter sports area in which an operator has authorized a competition to take place.

"Competitor" means a winter sports participant who actually is engaged in a competition in any portion of a winter sports area made available by the winter sports area operator.

"Designated trail" means a winter sports area trail on which a participant is permitted by the operator to participate in a winter sport.

"Freestyle terrain" and "freestyle terrain park" means any portion of a winter sports area that has been designated as such by the operator for freestyle skiing, freestyle snowboarding, or similar freestyle winter sports and includes, but is not limited to, the terrain park itself and features such as rails, boxes, jumps, hits, jibs, tabletops, spines, ramps, banks, pipes, half-pipes, quarter-pipes, tables, logs, or other man-made features such as buses and other vehicles, propane tanks, and tractor tires; snowcross terrain and features; and other constructed or natural features, but does not include moguls, bumps, or rollers or jumps not built by the operator, unless they are within a designated freestyle terrain park.

"Freestyler" means a winter sports participant utilizing freestyle terrain or a freestyle terrain park.

"Helmet" means a type of molded headgear equipped with a neck or chin strap specifically designed by the manufacturer to be used while engaged in the winter sport of alpine skiing or snowboarding.

"Inherent risks of winter sports" or "inherent risks of the winter sport" include:

1. Existing and changing weather conditions and visibility;

2. Hazards associated with varying surface or subsurface conditions on a single trail or from one trail to another, including but not limited to hazards such as participant use, snow in any condition and changing snow conditions, man-made snow, synthetic snow, ice, synthetic ice, snow or ice falling from a tree or natural or man-made structure, crust, slush, soft spots, ridges, rollers, knobs, holes, grooves, tracks from winter sports area vehicles, bare spots, rocks, boulders, stumps, logs, and brush or other forest growth or debris, or piles thereof;

3. Variations in difficulty of terrain, whether natural or as a result of slope use, slope design, or both;

4. Trails that have, or fall away or drop off toward, natural or man-made obstacles or hazards, including but not limited to sharp corners, ridges, jumps, bumps, rollers, moguls, valleys, dips, compressions, cliffs, ravines, drop-offs, streams, rivers, ponds, lakes, stream beds, open water or water with thin ice, holes, steep, flat, and uphill sections, and all variants and combinations thereof;

5. The potential for collision with other participants or other individuals, including with winter sports area personnel, whether or not those personnel are on duty or off duty; with wild or domestic animals; or with equipment or objects such as winter sports area infrastructure, snowmaking equipment, buildings and posts, and stationary and moving lit or flagged winter sports area vehicles;

6. The potential for a participant to act in a negligent or reckless manner that may cause or contribute to the injury or death of the participant or other individuals or damage to property;

7. The location, construction, design, layout, configuration, and condition of trails, freestyle terrain, and competition terrain;

8. The fact that use of trails, freestyle terrain, and competition terrain and participation in or being near races or other competitions or events, including but not limited to as a participant, employee at a winter sports area, spectator, or observer, involves the risk of serious injury or death or damage to property;

9. The fact that a helmet may not afford protection in all instances and that failure to wear a helmet that is properly sized, fitted, and secured may increase the risk of injury or death or the risk of more severe injury; and

10. The fact that the use of passenger tramways may be hazardous to passengers, including but not limited to risks resulting from loading or unloading a tramway and the potential for a passenger to fall from a tramway.

"Operator" or "winter sports area operator" means any person who has responsibility for the operations of a winter sports area, including its officers, directors, and employees and agents acting within the scope of their employment.

"Participant" or "winter sports participant" means an individual of any age or physical or mental ability who is an amateur or professional invitee of the operator or a trespasser and who participates in a winter sport at the winter sports area, whether or not consideration is paid to participate in the winter sport and whether or not the participant holds a valid admission ticket for all or a portion of the winter sports area, and any employee of the operator who participates in a winter sport either as part of his employment duties or as recreation.

"Participates in a winter sport" or "participating in a winter sport" means:

1. Using a trail or other terrain at a winter sports area to engage in a winter sport;

2. Participating in training or lessons for a winter sport as either an instructor or a student;

3. Being a spectator, observer, bystander, or pedestrian of or to any activity on a trail or other terrain at or near a winter sports area; or

4. Being a passenger on a passenger tramway.

"Passenger" means any individual, including a winter sports participant, while being transported or conveyed by a passenger tramway, while waiting in the immediate vicinity for such transportation or conveyance, while moving away from the disembarkation or unloading point of a passenger tramway to clear the way for the following passengers, or while boarding or embarking upon or unloading or disembarking from a passenger tramway.

"Passenger tramway" means any ski lift, chairlift, gondola, tramway, cable car, or other aerial lift and any rope tow, conveyor, t-bar, j-bar, handle tow, or other surface lift used by an operator to transport participants, spectators, observers, or pedestrians at a winter sports area, and any associated components including, but not limited to, lift towers, concrete tower foundations, tower bolts, tower ladders, lift terminals, chairs, gondolas, t-bars, j-bars, conveyors, and other structures relating to passenger tramways.

"Person" means any individual, corporation, partnership, association, cooperative, limited liability company, trust, joint venture, government, political subdivision, or any other legal or commercial entity and any successor, representative, agent, agency, or instrumentality thereof.

"Snowmaking equipment" means any machine used to make snow, including but not limited to snow guns and any associated towers, components, pipe, hydrant, hose, or other structures or equipment, including electrical equipment.

"Trail" or "winter sports area trail" means any slope, trail, run, freestyle terrain, or competition terrain located in a winter sports area. "Trail" includes edges and transition areas to other terrain, but does not include a tubing park.

"Tubing" means sliding on inflatable tubes, minibobs, sleds, toboggans, or any other comparable devices down a prepared course or lanes at a winter sports area.

"Tubing park" means an area designated by an operator for tubing.

"Winter sport" means a recreational or sporting activity, including sliding, jumping, walking, or traveling on a winter sports area trail for alpine skiing; Nordic skiing; telemark skiing; freestyle skiing; snowboarding; freestyle snowboarding; snowshoeing; tobogganing; sledding; or use of a snowmobile, minibob, snowbike, or comparable device; or any similar activity or use of a device that takes place at any time of the year on natural snow, man-made snow, ice, synthetic snow, synthetic ice, or any other synthetic surface, including a competition or the use of any device by a disabled or adaptive participant for a winter sport. "Winter sport" does not include ice skating or tubing.

"Winter sports area" means all the real and personal property under control of the operator or on the premises of such property that is being occupied by the operator by fee simple, lease, license, easement, permission, or otherwise, including but not limited to any and all trails, freestyle terrain, competition terrain, passenger tramways, or other areas of real property. "Winter sports area" does not include a tubing park except for any passenger tramway serving a tubing park and the immediate vicinity of such a passenger tramway in which individuals embark upon or disembark from the passenger tramway.

"Winter sports area infrastructure" means:

1. Passenger tramways;

2. Snowmaking equipment;

3. Towers, buildings, shacks, fixtures, furniture, and other structures, including utility infrastructure, located on the winter sports area property; and

4. Signs, fences, ropes, flags, posts, poles, and any other materials or structures used for posting signs or to manage or direct winter sports participants, spectators, observers, or pedestrians or any combination thereof.

"Winter sports area vehicle" means a vehicle used on a winter sports area trail in the operation and maintenance of winter sports areas and competitions and includes, but is not limited to, snowmobiles, all-terrain vehicles, and any other similarly sized vehicles as well as larger maintenance vehicles such as snow grooming equipment.

Added by Acts 2012, c. 713.

§ 8.01–227.12. Warnings and other winter sports area operator requirements

A. Each winter sports area operator shall include the following warning on each ticket, season pass, and written contract for professional services, instruction, or the rental of equipment to a winter sports participant and on each sign required by this subsection:

"WARNING: Under Virginia law, a ski area operator or other winter sports area operator is not liable for an injury to or death of a winter sports participant in a winter sport conducted at this location, or for damage to property, if such injury, death, or damage results from the inherent risks of the winter sport or from the participant's own negligence. The inherent risks of a winter sport include, among others, risks associated with the land, equipment, other participants, and animals, as well as the potential for you or another participant to act in a negligent manner that may contribute to the injury, death, or damage. You are assuming the inherent risks of participating in a winter sport at this location. Complete copies of the applicable Virginia law and the participant responsibility code published by the National Ski Areas Association are available for review at each ticket sales office of this winter sports area and online at [insert website for winter sports area]."

Every ticket, season pass, and written contract for professional services, instruction, or the rental of equipment to a participant shall contain the warning required by this subsection in clearly readable print. Every sign required by this section shall contain the warning required by this subsection in black letters, with each letter to be a minimum of one inch in height. An operator also may print on a ticket; season pass; written contract for professional services, instruction, or rental of equipment to a participant; or any sign required by this section any additional warning it deems appropriate. The warning required by this section does not constitute a preinjury contractual release and nothing in this section alters the common law of Virginia with regard to preinjury contractual releases.

B. Each operator shall install and maintain a sign containing the warning set forth in subsection A (i) at each designated ticketing office, (ii) at each front desk at each building or facility at which guests check in, (iii) at or near each ticket sales office of the winter sports area, and (iv) at, near, or en route to the loading area of each passenger tramway.

C. Each operator shall install and maintain at or near the beginning of each designated trail a sign that contains the name of the trail and any of the applicable difficulty-level words and emblems contained in this subsection, as determined by the operator. Directional arrows may be included on any sign, but shall be included if the sign is located at such a distance or position relative to the beginning of a trail that it would not be understandable by a reasonably prudent participant without directional arrows. As applicable, the signs shall indicate: (i) "Easiest" and include a green circle emblem, (ii) "More Difficult" and include a blue square emblem, (iii) "Most Difficult" and include a black diamond emblem, (iv) "Expert" or "Extreme Terrain" and include a two black diamond emblem, (v) "Freestyle Terrain" and include an orange oval emblem, or (vi) "Closed" and include a border around a black figure in the shape of a skier inside with a band running diagonally across the sign.

D. Each operator shall install and maintain at, near, or en route to the loading area for each passenger tramway that does not service trails that are designated by the operator as "Easiest" a sign that includes the following warning:

"WARNING. This lift does not service any trails that are designated Easiest (green circle emblem). All of the trails serviced by this lift are designated [as applicable, More Difficult (blue square emblem), Most Difficult (black diamond emblem), Expert (two black diamond emblem), or Freestyle Terrain (orange oval emblem)]."

E. Each operator shall install and maintain at, near, or en route to the entrance to each trail containing freestyle terrain a sign that indicates the location of the freestyle terrain. Each sign shall be denoted by an orange oval emblem, a stop sign emblem, and the statements "Freestyle skills required" and "Helmets are recommended." Each sign also may include any other freestyle warning the operator deems appropriate.

F. Whenever trail grooming or snowmaking operations are being undertaken, or trail grooming equipment is being operated, on a trail that is at that time open to the public, the operator shall place or cause to be placed a sign to that effect at the top or beginning of the trail.

G. An operator may vary from the specific location requirements required by this section provided that the location is substantially the same as the location required by this section and that the sign is plainly visible to a reasonably prudent winter sports participant abiding by all of the participant's duties and responsibilities.

H. Each operator shall make available, by oral or written report or otherwise, information concerning the daily conditions of its trails.

I. Each operator that offers a winter sport at nighttime shall meet the lighting standards for that winter sport provided by Illuminating Engineering Society of North America RP–6–01, Sports and Recreational Area Lighting § 6.24, including any supplements thereto or revisions thereof.

J. Each operator shall, upon request, provide (i) a freestyler who holds a valid admission ticket to the winter sports area's freestyle terrain a reasonable opportunity to view the freestyle terrain and (ii) a competitor who has properly registered for the competition a reasonable opportunity to visually inspect the portion of the winter sports area designated by the operator for the competition.

K. Each operator shall provide a ski patrol and first-aid services.

L. Each operator shall make available on the winter sports area's website and at each ticket sales office of the winter sports area for review by any winter sports participant, upon request, a copy of the participant responsibility code posted and available at each winter sports area and a copy of this article.

Added by Acts 2012, c. 713.

§ 8.01–227.13. Winter sports area trail maps

Each operator, upon request, shall provide to a participant a trail map of all trails located in the operator's winter sports area. The maps shall be available at each ticket sales office and at other locations at the winter sports area such that the maps are easily accessible to participants. All trail maps shall indicate the skill-level designation for each trail at the winter sports area as designated in subsection C of § 8.01–227.12.

Added by Acts 2012, c. 713.

§ 8.01–227.14. Freestyle terrain

In addition to providing the signage and warnings set forth in subsections C and E of § 8.01–227.12, an operator shall construct a barricade through use of fencing, flagging, or similar means at the entrance to any trail containing freestyle terrain. The barricade shall contain an entrance opening not wider than 30 feet.

Added by Acts 2012, c. 713.

§ 8.01–227.15. Winter sports area vehicles

An operator shall install and maintain on or near the top of each winter sports area vehicle that is present on any designated trail of a winter sports area during the operating hours of any passenger tramway serving that trail a flashing or rotating light that flashes or rotates whenever the vehicle is on any such trail. An operator also shall install and maintain on any snowmobile, all-terrain vehicle, or any other similarly sized vehicle that is present on any designated trail during the operating hours of any passenger tramway serving that trail a red or orange flag that is at least 40 square inches in size and is mounted at least five feet from the bottom of the vehicle's tracks or tires.

Added by Acts 2012, c. 713.

§ 8.01–227.16. Passenger tramways

A. Each operator shall be responsible for the safe operation and maintenance of each passenger tramway in its winter sports area whenever the tramway is in use, and for the safe construction of any passenger tramway that the operator constructed. At least once during each calendar year, each operator shall have all passenger tramways within the operator's winter sports area inspected by an individual who is qualified pursuant to Virginia law to inspect passenger tramways for compliance with the requirements of the ANSI Ski Lift Code and shall not operate a passenger tramway that is not in compliance until that passenger tramway is certified by such an individual as being in compliance. An operator's compliance with this inspection requirement does not by itself preclude potential liability on the part of the operator for any failure to operate or maintain a passenger tramway safely.

B. If a participant or a passenger using a passenger tramway at a winter sports area with the permission of the operator is unfamiliar with the use of a passenger tramway and asks for instruction on its use, the operator shall provide a reasonable opportunity for such instruction. In addition to the signs required by subsections A, B, and D of § 8.01–227.12, an operator shall install and maintain at or near the loading area for each passenger tramway in the winter sports area a sign stating that if a participant or other passenger is unfamiliar with the use of the passenger tramway and asks for instruction for its use, the operator will provide a reasonable opportunity for such instruction.

Added by Acts 2012, c. 713.

§ 8.01–227.17. Duties and responsibilities of winter sports participants and certain other individuals

A. A winter sports participant has a duty and responsibility to:

1. Exercise reasonable care in engaging in winter sports at the winter sports area, including, but not limited to, the exercise of reasonable care in:

a. Participating in a winter sport at a winter sports area only on designated trails that are not marked "closed" and refraining from participating in a winter sport in any portion of a winter sports area that is not a designated trail or is marked "closed";

b. Knowing the range of his ability to participate in the winter sport in which he is participating and acting within the limits of that ability;

c. Being the sole judge of his knowledge of and ability to successfully negotiate any trail or passenger tramway and refraining from negotiating any trail or passenger tramway until obtaining sufficient knowledge and ability to do so;

d. Heeding and obeying all warnings, notices, and signs provided by an operator and not altering, defacing, removing, or destroying any such warning, notice, or sign;

e. Maintaining control of his speed and course at all times and maintaining a proper lookout so as to be able to avoid other participants and objects;

f. Staying clear of any winter sports area vehicle or infrastructure, other than when embarking on or disembarking from a passenger tramway or when present at or in a residential building or other building that is open to the public;

g. Wearing retention straps, ski brakes, or other devices to prevent runaway equipment;

h. Making a visual inspection of any winter sports area competition terrain and viewing any freestyle terrain the participant intends to use;

i. Acting in a safe manner that will avoid contributing to the injury or death of himself or others or the damage to property, including refraining from participating in a winter sport when the participant's ability to do so safely is impaired by the consumption of alcohol or by the use of any narcotic or other drug or while under the influence of alcohol or any narcotic or other drug, or placing, fabricating, or shaping any object in a trail;

j. Embarking on a passenger tramway only with the authority of the operator;

k. Boarding or dismounting from a passenger tramway only at a designated area;

l. Acting in a manner while riding a passenger tramway that is consistent with posted rules and that will not interfere with the proper and safe operation of the passenger tramway;

m. Refraining from throwing or expelling any object while riding on a passenger tramway, and from placing an object on or about the uphill track, the entry area, or the exit area of any passenger tramway;

n. Crossing the uphill track of a passenger tramway only at designated locations; and

o. When involved in a winter sports collision or other accident involving another individual who the participant knows or reasonably should know is in need of medical or other assistance, obtaining assistance for that individual, notifying the proper authorities, and not leaving the scene of the collision or accident without giving the participant's personal identification, including his name and local and permanent address, to an employee or representative of the operator or to someone providing assistance to the individual, except for the purpose of obtaining assistance for the individual, in which case the participant shall give his personal identification to an employee or representative of the operator or to someone providing assistance to the individual after obtaining such assistance; and

2. When requested, provide his personal identification to an employee or representative of the winter sports area or operator.

B. Each passenger using a passenger tramway with the permission of an operator shall abide by and fulfill each duty and responsibility set forth in subsection A that is applicable to use of a passenger tramway.

C. Each participant, and each passenger using a passenger tramway with the permission of an operator, shall be deemed as a matter of law to have seen and understood all postings, signs, and other warnings provided by the winter sports area operator as required by this article.

D. An operator is entitled to assume that each passenger who boards a passenger tramway has sufficient knowledge, ability, and physical dexterity to embark upon, disembark from, and negotiate the passenger tramway. Any passenger who is unfamiliar with the use of a passenger tramway or who believes he does not have sufficient knowledge to embark upon, disembark from, and negotiate a passenger tramway shall ask the operator for instruction on such use or to provide such knowledge. Nothing in this article shall be construed to extend liability to an operator for injury to or death of a participant or other individual or damage to property resulting from a passenger who is unfamiliar with the use of a passenger tramway or believes he does not have sufficient knowledge to embark, disembark from, or negotiate a passenger tramway and does not ask the operator for instruction on such use or to provide such knowledge, or who does not have the ability or physical dexterity to embark upon, disembark from, or negotiate a passenger tramway.

E. Any individual who is not authorized by the operator to use or be present at the winter sports area shall be deemed a trespasser.

Added by Acts 2012, c. 713.

§ 8.01–227.18. Helmets

Each winter sports participant, or the parent or legal guardian of, or adult acting in a supervisory position over, a participant under the age of 18, shall be responsible for determining whether the participant will wear a helmet and whether the helmet is sufficiently protective and properly sized, fitted, and secured.

Nothing in this article shall be construed to extend liability to an operator for injury to or death of a participant or other individual or damage to property resulting from a participant not wearing a helmet while participating in a winter sport.

Added by Acts 2012, c. 713.

§ 8.01–227.19. Assumption of risks

A. A winter sports participant shall be presumed to have known the inherent risks of the winter sport in which he participates, to have fully appreciated the nature and extent of such risks, and to have voluntarily exposed himself to such risks, even if a particular risk was not specifically presented or stated to the participant by the operator. A passenger who uses a passenger tramway with the permission of an operator shall be presumed to have known the risks of winter sports that are applicable to the use of passenger tramways, to have fully appreciated the nature and extent of such risks, and to have voluntarily exposed himself to such risks, even if a particular risk was not specifically presented or stated to the individual by the operator. Such presumption may be rebutted by the participant or passenger by proving that the participant or passenger did not know the particular inherent risk of winter sports that proximately caused the injury or death or damage to property at issue, did not fully appreciate the nature and extent of such risk, or did not voluntarily expose himself to such risk.

B. An operator's negligence is not an inherent risk of winter sports, and a participant or passenger is not presumed to have accepted the risk of such negligence and the injuries proximately caused therefrom.

C. In determining if the presumption set forth in subsection A applies in a particular case, whether a particular circumstance or set of circumstances constitutes an inherent risk of winter sports shall be a question of law, and whether the participant or passenger assumed the particular inherent risk of winter sports shall be a question of fact.

D. Nothing herein shall prevent a participant or passenger from offering evidence that he did not know the particular inherent risk of winter sports that proximately caused the injury or death or damage to property at issue, did not fully appreciate the nature and extent of such risk, or did not voluntarily expose himself to such risk.

Added by Acts 2012, c. 713.

§ 8.01–227.20. Liability of winter sports area operator

A. A winter sports area operator shall be liable if the operator does any of the following:

1. Commits an act or omission related to a winter sport that constitutes negligence or gross negligence regarding the safety of an individual, or of property, and that act or omission proximately causes injury to or the death of the individual or damage to property; or

2. Recklessly, knowingly, or intentionally commits an act or omission related to a winter sport that proximately causes injury to or the death of a winter sports participant or other individual or damage to property.

B. No operator shall be liable and no individual or individual's representative may recover from an operator under subdivision A 1 or subsection C if the individual is found to have assumed the risk of his injury or death, or damage to property, pursuant to § 8.01–227.19 or if a proximate cause of the injury, death, or damage was his own negligence, provided that in any action for damages against an operator pursuant to subdivision A 1 or subsection C, the operator shall plead, as appropriate, the affirmative defense of (i) assumption of the risk by the individual, (ii) contributory negligence by the individual, or (iii) both assumption of the risk and contributory negligence.

C. A winter sports area operator shall not be considered a common carrier under Virginia law but shall be liable for any injury to or death of an individual or damage to property caused by the operator's failure to operate a passenger tramway in a reasonable manner or to comply with any mandatory provision of the ANSI Ski Lift Code.

D. The liability of a winter sports area operator to another individual who is not authorized by the operator to use or be present at the winter sports area shall be only the liability for the duty owed under Virginia law to a trespasser.

Added by Acts 2012, c. 713.

§ 8.01–227.21. Common law regarding minors

Nothing in this article shall abrogate Virginia common law regarding either (i) the capacity of a minor to be contributorily negligent or to assume a risk or (ii) the standard for measuring the conduct of a minor.

Added by Acts 2012, c. 713.

§ 8.01–227.22. Failure to fulfill duty or responsibility not negligence per se

An operator's or participant's failure to abide by or fulfill a duty or responsibility under this article shall not constitute negligence per se.

Added by Acts 2012, c. 713.

§ 8.01–227.23. Applicability of article

Any liabilities and presumptions pursuant to this article apply only with regard to actions or potential actions between an operator and a participant or passenger. This article has no applicability to actions between a participant or passenger and any other person.

Added by Acts 2012, c. 713.

CHAPTER 4

LIMITATIONS OF ACTIONS

ARTICLE 1

IN GENERAL

§ 8.01–228. Scope of limitations; "personal action" defined

Every action for which a limitation period is prescribed by law must be commenced within the period prescribed in this chapter unless otherwise specifically provided in this Code. As used in this chapter, the term "personal action" shall include an action wherein a judgment for money is sought, whether for damages to person or property.

Acts 1977, c. 617.

§ 8.01–229. Suspension or tolling of statute of limitations; effect of disabilities; death; injunction; prevention of service by defendant; dismissal, nonsuit or abatement; devise for payment of debts; new promises; debts proved in creditors' suits

A. Disabilities which toll the statute of limitations.—Except as otherwise specifically provided in §§ 8.01–237, 8.01–241, 8.01–242, 8.01–243, 8.01–243.1 and other provisions of this Code,

1. If a person entitled to bring any action is at the time the cause of action accrues an infant, except if such infant has been emancipated pursuant to Article 15 (§ 16.1–331 et seq.) of Chapter 11 of Title 16.1, or incapacitated, such person may bring it within the prescribed limitation period after such disability is removed; or

2. After a cause of action accrues,

a. If an infant becomes entitled to bring such action, the time during which he is within the age of minority shall not be counted as any part of the period within which the action must be brought except as to any such period during which the infant has been judicially declared emancipated; or

b. If a person entitled to bring such action becomes incapacitated, the time during which he is incapacitated shall not be computed as any part of the period within which the action must be brought, except where a conservator, guardian or committee is appointed for such person in which case an action may be commenced by such conservator, committee or guardian before the expiration of the applicable period of limitation or within one year after his qualification as such, whichever occurs later.

For the purposes of subdivisions 1 and 2 of this subsection, a person shall be deemed incapacitated if he is so adjudged by a court of competent jurisdiction, or if it shall otherwise appear to the court or jury determining the issue that such person is or was incapacitated within the prescribed limitation period.

3. If a convict is or becomes entitled to bring an action against his committee, the time during which he is incarcerated shall not be counted as any part of the period within which the action must be brought.

B. Effect of death of a party.—The death of a person entitled to bring an action or of a person against whom an action may be brought shall toll the statute of limitations as follows:

1. Death of person entitled to bring a personal action.—If a person entitled to bring a personal action dies with no such action pending before the expiration of the limitation period for commencement thereof, then an action may be commenced by the decedent's personal representative before the expiration of the limitation period including the limitation period as provided by subdivision E 3 or within one year after his qualification as personal representative, whichever occurs later.

2. Death of person against whom personal action may be brought.—a. If a person against whom a personal action may be brought dies before the commencement of such action and before the expiration of the limitation period for commencement thereof then a claim may be filed against the decedent's estate or an action may be commenced against the decedent's personal representative before the expiration of the applicable limitation period or within one year after the qualification of such personal representative, whichever occurs later.

b. If a person against whom a personal action may be brought dies before suit papers naming such person as defendant have been filed with the court, then such suit papers may be amended to substitute the decedent's personal representative as party defendant before the expiration of the applicable limitation period or within two years after the date such suit papers were filed with the court, whichever occurs later, and such suit papers shall be taken as properly filed.

3. Effect of death on actions for recovery of realty, or a proceeding for enforcement of certain liens relating to realty.—Upon the death of any person in whose favor or against whom an action for recovery of realty, or a proceeding for enforcement of certain liens relating to realty, may be brought, such right of action shall accrue to or against his successors in interest as provided in Article 2 (§ 8.01–236 et seq.) of this chapter.

4. Accrual of a personal cause of action against the estate of any person subsequent to such person's death.—If a personal cause of action against a decedent accrues subsequent to his death, an action may be brought against the decedent's personal representative or a claim thereon may be filed against the estate of such decedent before the expiration of the applicable limitation period or within two years after the qualification of the decedent's personal representative, whichever occurs later.

5. Accrual of a personal cause of action in favor of decedent.—If a person dies before a personal cause of action which survives would have accrued to him, if he had continued to live, then an action may be commenced by such decedent's personal representative before the expiration of the applicable limitation period or within one year after the qualification of such personal representative, whichever occurs later.

6. Delayed qualification of personal representative.—If there is an interval of more than two years between the death of any person in whose favor or against whom a cause of action has accrued or shall subsequently accrue and the qualification of such person's personal representative, such personal representative shall, for the purposes of this chapter, be deemed to have qualified on the last day of such two-year period.

C. Suspension during injunctions.—When the commencement of any action is stayed by injunction, the time of the continuance of the injunction shall not be computed as any part of the period within which the action must be brought.

D. Obstruction of filing by defendant.—When the filing of an action is obstructed by a defendant's (i) filing a petition in bankruptcy or filing a petition for an extension or arrangement under the United States Bankruptcy Act or (ii) using any other direct or indirect means to obstruct the filing of an action, then the time that such obstruction has continued shall not be counted as any part of the period within which the action must be brought.

E. Dismissal, abatement, or nonsuit.—

1. Except as provided in subdivision 3 of this subsection, if any action is commenced within the prescribed limitation period and for any cause abates or is dismissed without determining the merits, the time such action is pending shall not be computed as part of the period within which such action may be brought, and another action may be brought within the remaining period.

2. If a judgment or decree is rendered for the plaintiff in any action commenced within the prescribed limitation period and such judgment or decree is arrested or reversed upon a ground which does not preclude a new action for the same cause, or if there is occasion to bring a new action by reason of the loss or destruction of any of the papers or records in a former action which was commenced within the prescribed limitation period, then a new action may be brought within one year after such arrest or reversal or such loss or destruction, but not after.

3. If a plaintiff suffers a voluntary nonsuit as prescribed in § 8.01–380, the statute of limitations with respect to such action shall be tolled by the commencement of the nonsuited action, and the plaintiff may recommence his action within six months from the date of the order entered by the court, or within the original period of limitation, or within the limitation period as provided by subdivision B 1, whichever period is longer. This tolling provision shall apply irrespective of whether the action is originally filed in a federal or a state court and recommenced in any other court, and shall apply to all actions irrespective of whether they arise under common law or statute.

F. Effect of devise for payment of debts.—No provision in the will of any testator devising his real estate, or any part thereof, subject to the payment of his debts or charging the same therewith, or containing any other provision for the payment of debts, shall prevent this chapter from operating against such debts, unless it plainly appears to be the testator's intent that it shall not so operate.

G. Effect of new promise in writing.—

1. If any person against whom a right of action has accrued on any contract, other than a judgment or recognizance, promises, by writing signed by him or his agent, payment of money on such contract, the person to whom the right has accrued may maintain an action for the money so promised, within such number of years after such promise as it might be maintained if such promise were the original cause of action. An acknowledgment in writing, from which a promise of payment may be implied, shall be deemed to be such promise within the meaning of this subsection.

2. The plaintiff may sue on the new promise described in subdivision 1 of this subsection or on the original cause of action, except that when the new promise is of such a nature as to merge the original cause of action then the action shall be only on the new promise.

H. Suspension of limitations in creditors' suits.—When an action is commenced as a general creditors' action, or as a general lien creditors' action, or as an action to enforce a mechanics' lien, the running of the statute of limitations shall be suspended as to debts provable in such action from the commencement of the action, provided they are brought in before the commissioner in chancery under the first reference for an account of debts; but as to claims not so brought in the statute shall continue to run, without interruption by reason either of the commencement of the action or of the order for an account, until a later order for an account, under which they do come in, or they are asserted by petition or independent action.

In actions not instituted originally either as general creditors' actions, or as general lien creditors' actions, but which become such by subsequent proceedings, the statute of limitations shall be suspended by an order of reference for an account of debts or of liens only as to those creditors who come in and prove their claims under the order. As to creditors who come in afterwards by petition or under an order of recommittal, or a later order of reference for an account, the statute shall continue to run without interruption by reason of previous orders until filing of the petition, or until the date of the reference under which they prove their claims, as the case may be.

I. When an action is commenced within a period of thirty days prior to the expiration of the limitation period for commencement thereof and the defending party or parties desire to institute an action as third-party plaintiff against one or more persons not party to the original action, the running of the period of limitation against such action shall be suspended as to such new party for a period of sixty days from the expiration of the applicable limitation period.

J. If any award of compensation by the Workers' Compensation Commission pursuant to Chapter 5 (§ 65.2–500 et seq.) of Title 65.2 is subsequently found void ab initio, other than an award voided for fraudulent procurement of the award by the claimant, the statute of limitations applicable to any civil action upon the same claim or cause of action in a court of this Commonwealth shall be tolled for that period of time during which compensation payments were made.

K. Suspension of limitations during criminal proceedings.—In any personal action for damages, if a criminal prosecution arising out of the same facts is commenced, the time such prosecution is pending shall not be computed as part of the period within which such a civil action may be brought. For purposes of this subsection, the time during which a prosecution is pending shall be calculated from the date of the issuance of a warrant, summons or capias, the return or filing of an indictment or information, or the defendant's first appearance in any court as an accused in such a prosecution, whichever date occurs first, until the date of the final judgment or order in the trial court, the date of the final disposition of any direct appeal in state court, or the date on which the time for noting an appeal has expired, whichever date occurs last. Thereafter, the civil action may be brought within the remaining period of the statute or within one year, whichever is longer.

If a criminal prosecution is commenced and a grand jury indictment is returned or a grand jury indictment is waived after the period within which a civil action arising out of the same set of facts may be brought, a civil action may be brought within one year of the date of the final judgment or order in the trial court, the date of the final disposition of any direct appeal in state court, or the date on which the time for noting an appeal has expired, whichever date occurs last, but no more than ten years after the date of the crime or two years after the cause of action shall have accrued under § 8.01–249, whichever date occurs last.

Acts 1977, c. 617; Acts 1978, c. 65; Acts 1978, c. 767; Acts 1983, c. 404; Acts 1983, c. 437; Acts 1986, c. 506; Acts 1987, c. 294; Acts 1987, c. 645; Acts 1988, c. 711; Acts 1989, c. 588; Acts 1990, c. 280; Acts 1991, c. 693; Acts 1991, c. 722; Acts 1993, c. 844; Acts 1997, c. 801, eff. Jan. 1, 1998; Acts 2000, c. 531; Acts 2001, c. 773; Acts 2001, c. 781.

§ 8.01–230. Accrual of right of action

In every action for which a limitation period is prescribed, the right of action shall be deemed to accrue and the prescribed limitation period shall begin to run from the date the injury is sustained in the case of injury to the person or damage to property, when the breach of contract occurs in actions ex contractu and not when the resulting damage is discovered, except where the relief sought is solely equitable or where otherwise provided under § 8.01–233, subsection C of § 8.01–245, §§ 8.01–249, 8.01–250 or other statute.

Acts 1977, c. 617; Acts 1996, c. 328.

§ 8.01–231. Commonwealth not within statute of limitations

No statute of limitations which shall not in express terms apply to the Commonwealth shall be deemed a bar to any proceeding by or on behalf of the same.

Acts 1977, c. 617; Acts 1988, c. 544.

§ 8.01–232. Effect of promises not to plead statute

A. Whenever the failure to enforce a promise, written or unwritten, not to plead the statute of limitations would operate as a fraud on the promisee, the promisor shall be estopped to plead the statute. In all other cases, an unwritten promise not to plead the statute shall be void, and a written promise not to plead such statute shall be valid when (i) it is made to avoid or defer litigation pending settlement of any case, (ii) it is not made contemporaneously with any other contract, and (iii) it is made for an additional term not longer than the applicable limitations period. No provision of this subsection shall operate contrary to subsections B and C of this section.

B. No acknowledgment or promise by any personal representative of a decedent shall charge the estate of the decedent, revive a cause of action otherwise barred, or relieve the personal representative of his duty to defend under § 64.2–1415 in any case in which but for such acknowledgment or promise, the decedent's estate could have been protected under a statute of limitations.

C. No acknowledgment or promise by one of two or more joint contractors shall charge any of such contractors in any case in which but for such acknowledgment another contractor would have been protected under a statute of limitations.

Acts 1977, c. 617. Amended by Acts 2006, c. 278.

§ 8.01-233. When action deemed brought on counterclaim or cross-claim; when statute of limitations tolled; defendant's consent required for dismissal

A. A defendant who pleads a counterclaim or cross-claim shall be deemed to have brought an action at the time he files such pleading.

B. If the subject matter of the counterclaim or cross-claim arises out of the same transaction or occurrence upon which the plaintiff's claim is based, the statute of limitations with respect to such pleading shall be tolled by the commencement of the plaintiff's action.

Acts 1977, c. 617.

§ 8.01-234. Repeal of limitation not to remove bar of statute

If, after a right of action or remedy is barred by a statute of limitations, the statute be repealed, the bar of the statute as to such right or remedy shall not be deemed to be removed by such repeal.

Acts 1977, c. 617.

§ 8.01-235. Bar of expiration of limitation period raised only as affirmative defense in responsive pleading

The objection that an action is not commenced within the limitation period prescribed by law can only be raised as an affirmative defense specifically set forth in a responsive pleading. No statutory limitation period shall have jurisdictional effects and the defense that the statutory limitation period has expired cannot be set up by demurrer. This section shall apply to all limitation periods, without regard to whether or not the statute prescribing such limitation period shall create a new right.

Acts 1977, c. 617.

ARTICLE 2

LIMITATIONS ON RECOVERY OF REALTY AND ENFORCEMENT OF CERTAIN LIENS RELATING TO REALTY

§ 8.01-236. Limitation of entry on or action for land

No person shall make an entry on, or bring an action to recover, any land unless within fifteen years next after the time at which the right to make such entry or bring such action shall have first accrued to such person or to some other person through whom he claims; provided that an action for unlawful entry or detainer under § 8.01-124 shall be brought within three years after such entry or detainer.

Acts 1977, c. 617; Acts 1978, c. 471.

§ 8.01-237. Effect of disabilities upon right of entry on, or action for, land

Notwithstanding the provisions of subsection A of § 8.01-229, no disabilities or tacking of disabilities shall preserve to any person or his successors a right to make entry on or bring an action to recover land for more than twenty-five years after such right first accrued, although such person or persons shall have been disabled during the whole of such twenty-five years.

Acts 1977, c. 617.

§ 8.01-238. To repeal grant

A bill in equity to repeal, in whole or in part, any grant of land by the Commonwealth, shall be brought within ten years next after the date of such grant.

Acts 1977, c. 617.

§ 8.01-239. Ground rents

No action shall be brought for the recovery of any ground rent reserved upon real estate after the expiration of ten years from the time such ground rent becomes due and payable.

Acts 1977, c. 617.

§ 8.01-240. Liens for water, sewer, or sidewalk assessments

No suit shall be brought to enforce the lien of any water, sewer, or sidewalk assessment, heretofore or hereafter made, against lands which have been conveyed by the person owning them at the time of such assessment to a grantee for value unless the same be brought within ten years from the due recordation of the deed from such person to grantee and within twenty years from the due docketing of such assessment.

Acts 1977, c. 617.

§ 8.01-241. Limitation of enforcement of deeds of trust, mortgages and liens for unpaid purchase money

A. No deed of trust or mortgage heretofore or hereafter given to secure the payment of money, and no lien heretofore or hereafter reserved to secure the payment of unpaid purchase money, shall be enforced after 10 years from the time when the original obligation last maturing thereby secured shall have become due and payable according to its terms and without regard to any provision for the acceleration of such date; provided that the period of one year from the death of any party in interest shall be excluded from the computation of time.

B. Notwithstanding the limitations prescribed by subsection A, a deed of trust or mortgage given, and a lien reserved to secure the payment of money, for which the original obligation last maturing thereby secured became due and payable according to its terms between July 1, 1988, and July 1, 2000, without regard to any provision for the acceleration of the date such obligation became due and payable, shall not be enforced after July 1, 2010. However, the provisions of this subsection shall have no effect on the rights of a person who (i) acquired an interest in the real property securing such deed of trust or mortgage between July 1, 2008, and the date of enactment of this subsection and (ii) would otherwise have priority over or take free of such deed of trust or mortgage under the laws of the Commonwealth at that time.

C. The limitations prescribed by this section may be extended by the recordation of a certificate in the form provided in § 8.01–241.1 prior to the expiration of the limitation period prescribed herein in the clerk's office in which such lien is recorded and executed either by the party in whom the beneficial title to the property so encumbered is vested at the time of such recordation or by his duly authorized attorney-in-fact, or agent. Recordation of the certificate shall extend the limitations of the right to enforce the lien for 10 years from the date of the recordation of the certificate. The clerk of the court shall index the certificate in both names in the index of the deed book and give reference to the book and page in which the original writing is recorded. Unless the deed or deeds executed pursuant to the foreclosure of any mortgage or to the execution of or sale under any deed of trust is recorded in the county or city where the land is situated within one year after the time the right to enforce the mortgage or deed of trust shall have expired as hereinabove provided, such deed or deeds shall be void as to all purchasers for valuable consideration without notice and lien creditors who make any purchase of or acquire any lien on the land conveyed by any such deed prior to the time such deed is so recorded.

Acts 1977, c. 617; Acts 1980, c. 499; Acts 1994, c. 547; Acts 1999, c. 788. Amended by Acts 2008, c. 226; Acts 2009, c. 163, eff. July 1, 2008.

§ 8.01–241.1. Permissible form for certificate

Any extension of the limitations of the right to enforce the lien of a deed of trust or mortgage shall conform substantially with the following form:

CERTIFICATE OF EXTENSION OF LIMITATION OF
RIGHT TO ENFORCE DEED OF TRUST OR MORTGAGE

Place of Record ....
Date of Deed of Trust/Mortgage ....
Deed Book .... Book Page .....
Name of Guarantor(s) ....
Name of Trustee(s) ....
Maker(s) of Note ....
Date of Note(s) ....

I/we, the beneficial title holder(s) of the property encumbered by the above mentioned deed of trust do hereby certify that the lien of the same is hereby extended 10 years from the date of my/our endorsement upon this certificate.

....
Beneficial Titleholder/Attorney-in-Fact/Agent

Commonwealth of Virginia County/City of ....:
Subscribed, sworn to and acknowledged before me by ...., this .... day of ...., 20 ...
My Commission expires: ....
Notary Public

Acts 1994, c. 547. Amended by Acts 2008, c. 226.

§ 8.01–242. Same; when no maturity date is given; credit line deeds of trust

No deed of trust or mortgage given to secure the payment of money, other than credit line deeds of trust described in § 55–58.2, and no lien reserved to secure the payment of unpaid purchase money, in which no date is fixed for the maturity of the debt secured by such deed of trust, mortgage, or lien, shall be enforced after twenty years from the date of the deed of trust, mortgage, or other lien; provided that the period of one year from the death of any party in interest shall be excluded from the computation of time, and provided further that the limitation may be extended by recordation of a certificate within the twenty-year period in the manner set forth in § 8.01–241. No credit line deed of trust described in § 55–58.2 in which no date is fixed for the maturity of the debt secured thereby shall be enforced after forty years from the date of the credit line deed of trust; provided that the period of one year from the death of any party in interest shall be excluded from the computation of time.

Acts 1977, c. 617; Acts 1994, c. 547; Acts 1999, c. 788.

Article 3

Personal Actions Generally

§ 8.01–243. Personal action for injury to person or property generally; extension in actions for malpractice against health care provider

A. Unless otherwise provided in this section or by other statute, every action for personal injuries, whatever the theory of recovery, and every action for damages resulting from fraud, shall be brought within two years after the cause of action accrues.

B. Every action for injury to property, including actions by a parent or guardian of an infant against a tort-feasor for expenses of curing or attempting to cure such infant from the result of a personal injury or loss of services of such infant, shall be brought within five years after the cause of action accrues. An infant's claim for medical expenses pursuant to subsection B of § 8.01-36 accruing on or after July 1, 2013, shall be governed by the applicable statute of limitations that applies to the infant's cause of action.

C. The two-year limitations period specified in subsection A shall be extended in actions for malpractice against a health care provider as follows:

1. In cases arising out of a foreign object having no therapeutic or diagnostic effect being left in a patient's body, for a period of one year from the date the object is discovered or reasonably should have been discovered;

2. In cases in which fraud, concealment or intentional misrepresentation prevented discovery of the injury within the two-year period, for one year from the date the injury is discovered or, by the exercise of due diligence, reasonably should have been discovered; and

3. In a claim for the negligent failure to diagnose a malignant tumor or cancer, for a period of one year from the date the diagnosis of a malignant tumor or cancer is communicated to the patient by a health care provider, provided the health care provider's underlying act or omission was on or after July 1, 2008. Claims under this section for the negligent failure to diagnose a malignant tumor or cancer, where the health care provider's underlying act or omission occurred prior to July 1, 2008, shall be governed by the statute of limitations that existed prior to July 1, 2008.

However, the provisions of this subsection shall not apply to extend the limitations period beyond ten years from the date the cause of action accrues, except that the provisions of subdivision A 2 of § 8.01-229 shall apply to toll the statute of limitations in actions brought by or on behalf of a person under a disability.

D. Every action for injury to the person, whatever the theory of recovery, resulting from sexual abuse occurring during the infancy or incapacity of the person as set forth in subdivision 6 of § 8.01-249 shall be brought within 20 years after the cause of action accrues.

E. Every action for injury to property brought by the Commonwealth against a tort-feasor for expenses arising out of the negligent operation of a motor vehicle shall be brought within five years after the cause of action accrues.

Acts 1977, c. 617; Acts 1986, c. 389; Acts 1986, c. 454; Acts 1987, c. 294; Acts 1987, c. 645; Acts 1987, c. 679. Amended by Acts 2008, c. 175; Acts 2011, c. 617; Acts 2011, c. 641; Acts 2013, c. 551; Acts 2013, c. 689; Acts 2014, c. 586.

§ 8.01-243.1. Actions for medical malpractice; minors

Notwithstanding the provisions of § 8.01-229 A and except as provided in subsection C of § 8.01-243, any cause of action accruing on or after July 1, 1987, on behalf of a person who was a minor at the time the cause of action accrued for personal injury or death against a health care provider pursuant to Chapter 21.1 (§ 8.01-581.1 et seq.) shall be commenced within two years of the date of the last act or omission giving rise to the cause of action except that if the minor was less than eight years of age at the time of the occurrence of the malpractice, he shall have until his tenth birthday to commence an action. Any minor who is ten years of age or older on or before July 1, 1987, shall have no less than two years from that date within which to commence such an action.

Acts 1987, c. 294; Acts 1987, c. 645.

§ 8.01-243.2. Limitations of actions by confined persons; exhaustion

No person confined in a state or local correctional facility shall bring or have brought on his behalf any personal action relating to the conditions of his confinement until all available administrative remedies are exhausted. Such action shall be brought by or on behalf of such person within one year after cause of action accrues or within six months after all administrative remedies are exhausted, whichever occurs later.

Acts 1998, c. 596; Acts 1999, c. 47.

§ 8.01-244. Actions for wrongful death; limitation

A. Notwithstanding the provisions of § 8.01-229 B, if a person entitled to bring an action for personal injury dies as a result of such injury with no such action pending before the expiration of the limitations period set forth in § 8.01-243, then an action under § 8.01-50 may be commenced within the time limits specified in subsection B of this section.

B. Every action under § 8.01-50 shall be brought by the personal representative of the decedent within two years after the death of the injured person. If any such action is brought within such period of two years after such person's death and for any cause abates or is dismissed without determining the merits of such action, the time such action is pending shall not be counted as any part of such period of two years and another action may be brought within the remaining period of such two years as if such former action had not been instituted. However, if a plaintiff suffers a voluntary nonsuit pursuant to § 8.01-380, the nonsuit shall not be deemed an abatement nor a dismissal pursuant to this subsection, and the provisions of subdivision E 3 of § 8.01-229 shall apply to such a nonsuited action.

Acts 1977, c. 617; Acts 1991, c. 722. Amended by Acts 2008, c. 175.

§ 8.01-245. Limitation on actions upon the bond of any fiduciaries or as to suits against fiduciaries themselves; accrual of cause of action where execution sustained

A. No action shall be brought upon the bond of any fiduciary except within ten years next after the right to bring such action shall have first accrued.

B. When any fiduciary has settled an account under the provisions of Part A (§ 64.2–1200 et seq.) of Subtitle IV of Title 64.2, and whether or not he has given bond, a suit to surcharge or falsify such account, or to hold such fiduciary or his sureties liable for any balance stated in such account, to be in his hands, shall be brought within ten years after the account has been confirmed.

C. In actions upon the bond of any personal representative of a decedent or fiduciary of a person under a disability against whom an execution has been obtained or where a court acting upon the account of such representative or committee shall order payment or delivery of estate in the hands of such committee and representative, the cause of action shall be deemed to accrue from the return day of such execution or from the time of the right to require payment or delivery upon such order, whichever shall happen first.

Acts 1977, c. 617.

§ 8.01–246. Personal actions based on contracts

Subject to the provisions of § 8.01–243 regarding injuries to person and property and of § 8.01–245 regarding the application of limitations to fiduciaries, and their bonds, actions founded upon a contract, other than actions on a judgment or decree, shall be brought within the following number of years next after the cause of action shall have accrued:

1. In actions or upon a recognizance, except recognizance of bail in a civil suit, within ten years; and in actions or motions upon a recognizance of bail in a civil suit, within three years, omitting from the computation of such three years such time as the right to sue out such execution shall have been suspended by injunction, supersedeas or other process;

2. In actions on any contract which is not otherwise specified and which is in writing and signed by the party to be charged thereby, or by his agent, within five years whether such writing be under seal or not;

3. In actions by a partner against another for settlement of the partnership account or in actions upon accounts concerning the trade of merchandise between merchant and merchant, their factors, or servants, within five years from the cessation of the dealings in which they are interested together;

4. In actions upon any unwritten contract, express or implied, within three years.

Provided that as to any action to which § 8.2–725 of the Uniform Commercial Code is applicable, that section shall be controlling except that in products liability actions for injury to person and for injury to property, other than the property subject to contract, the limitation prescribed in § 8.01–243 shall apply.

Acts 1977, c. 617.

§ 8.01–247. When action on contract governed by the law of another state or country barred in Virginia

No action shall be maintained on any contract which is governed by the law of another state or country if the right of action thereon is barred either by the laws of such state or country or of this Commonwealth.

Acts 1977, c. 617.

§ 8.01–247.1. Limitation on action for defamation, etc.

Every action for injury resulting from libel, slander, insulting words, or defamation shall be brought within one year after the cause of action accrues.

If a publisher of statements actionable under this section publishes anonymously or under a false identity on the Internet, an action may be filed under this section and the statute of limitations shall be tolled until the identity of the publisher is discovered or, by the exercise of due diligence, reasonably should have been discovered.

Acts 1995, c. 9. Amended by Acts 2015, c. 128.

§ 8.01–248. Personal actions for which no other limitation is specified

Every personal action accruing on or after July 1, 1995, for which no limitation is otherwise prescribed, shall be brought within two years after the right to bring such action has accrued.

Acts 1977, c. 617; Acts 1995, c. 9.

§ 8.01–249. When cause of action shall be deemed to accrue in certain personal actions

The cause of action in the actions herein listed shall be deemed to accrue as follows:

1. In actions for fraud or mistake, in actions for violations of the Consumer Protection Act (§ 59.1–196 et seq.) based upon any misrepresentation, deception, or fraud, and in actions for rescission of contract for undue influence, when such fraud, mistake, misrepresentation, deception, or undue influence is discovered or by the exercise of due diligence reasonably should have been discovered;

2. In actions or other proceedings for money on deposit with a bank or any person or corporation doing a banking business, when a request in writing be made therefor by check, order, or otherwise;

3. In actions for malicious prosecution or abuse of process, when the relevant criminal or civil action is terminated;

4. In actions for injury to the person resulting from exposure to asbestos or products containing asbestos, when a diagnosis of asbestosis, interstitial fibrosis, mesothelioma, or other disabling asbestos-related injury or disease is first communicated to the person or his agent by a physician. However, no such action may be

brought more than two years after the death of such person;

5. In actions for contribution or for indemnification, when the contributee or the indemnitee has paid or discharged the obligation. A third-party claim permitted by subsection A of § 8.01–281 and the Rules of Court may be asserted before such cause of action is deemed to accrue hereunder;

6. In actions for injury to the person, whatever the theory of recovery, resulting from sexual abuse occurring during the infancy or incapacity of the person, upon the later of the removal of the disability of infancy or incapacity as provided in § 8.01–229 or when the fact of the injury and its causal connection to the sexual abuse is first communicated to the person by a licensed physician, psychologist, or clinical psychologist. As used in this subdivision, "sexual abuse" means sexual abuse as defined in subdivision 6 of § 18.2–67.10 and acts constituting rape, sodomy, object sexual penetration or sexual battery as defined in Article 7 (§ 18.2–61 et seq.) of Chapter 4 of Title 18.2;

7. In products liability actions against parties other than health care providers as defined in § 8.01–581.1 for injury to the person resulting from or arising as a result of the implantation of any prosthetic device for breast augmentation or reconstruction, when the fact of the injury and its causal connection to the implantation is first communicated to the person by a physician;

8. In actions on an open account, from the later of the last payment or last charge for goods or services rendered on the account.

Acts 1977, c. 617; Acts 1985, c. 459; Acts 1986, c. 601; Acts 1991, c. 674; Acts 1992, c. 817; Acts 1993, c. 523; Acts 1995, c. 268; Acts 1997, c. 565; Acts 1997, c. 801, eff. Jan. 1, 1998. Amended by Acts 2005, c. 213; Acts 2013, c. 292.

§ 8.01–250. Limitation on certain actions for damages arising out of defective or unsafe condition of improvements to real property

No action to recover for any injury to property, real or personal, or for bodily injury or wrongful death, arising out of the defective and unsafe condition of an improvement to real property, nor any action for contribution or indemnity for damages sustained as a result of such injury, shall be brought against any person performing or furnishing the design, planning, surveying, supervision of construction, or construction of such improvement to real property more than five years after the performance or furnishing of such services and construction.

The limitation prescribed in this section shall not apply to the manufacturer or supplier of any equipment or machinery or other articles installed in a structure upon real property, nor to any person in actual possession and in control of the improvement as owner, tenant or otherwise at the time the defective or unsafe condition of such improvement constitutes the proximate cause of the injury or damage for which the action is brought; rather each such action shall be brought within the time next after such injury occurs as provided in §§ 8.01–243 and 8.01–246.

Acts 1977, c. 617.

§ 8.01–250.1. Limitation on actions involving removal of asbestos

Notwithstanding the provisions of § 8.01–234 or any other section in this chapter, every action against a manufacturer or supplier of asbestos or material containing asbestos brought by or on behalf of any agency of the Commonwealth incorporated for charitable or educational purposes; counties, cities or towns; or school boards, to recover for (i) removal of asbestos or materials containing asbestos from any building owned or used by such entity, (ii) other measures taken to correct or ameliorate any problem related to asbestos in such building or (iii) reimbursement for such removal, correction or amelioration which would otherwise be barred prior to July 1, 1990, as a result of expiration of the applicable period of limitation, is hereby revived or extended. Any action thereon may be commenced prior to July 1, 1990.

Acts 1985, c. 262; Acts 1986, c. 458.

Article 4

Limitations on Enforcement of Judgments and Decrees

§ 8.01–251. Limitations on enforcement of judgments

A. No execution shall be issued and no action brought on a judgment, including a judgment in favor of the Commonwealth and a judgment rendered in another state or country, after 20 years from the date of such judgment or domestication of such judgment, unless the period is extended as provided in this section.

B. The limitation prescribed in subsection A may be extended on motion of the judgment creditor or his assignee with notice to the judgment debtor, and an order of the circuit court of the jurisdiction in which the judgment was entered to show cause why the period for issuance of execution or bringing of an action should not be extended. Any such motion shall be filed within the 20–year period from the date of the original judgment or from the date of the latest extension thereof. If upon the hearing of the motion the court decides that there is no good cause shown for not extending the period of limitation, the order shall so state and the period of limitation mentioned in subsection A shall be extended for an additional 20 years from the date of filing of the motion to extend. Additional extensions may be granted upon the same procedure, subject in each case to the recording provisions prescribed in § 8.01–458. This extension procedure is subject to the exception that if the action is against a personal representative of a decedent, the motion shall be within two years from the date of his qualification, the extension may be for only two years from the time of the filing of the motion, and there may be only one such extension.

C. No suit shall be brought to enforce the lien of any judgment, including judgments in favor of the Commonwealth, upon which the right to issue an execution or bring an action is barred by other subsections of this section, nor shall any suit be brought to enforce the lien of any judgment against the lands which have been conveyed by the judgment debtor to a grantee for value, unless the same be brought within 10 years from the due recordation of the deed from such judgment debtor to such grantee and unless a notice of lis pendens shall have been recorded in the manner provided by § 8.01–268 before the expiration of such 10–year period.

D. In computing the time, any time during which the right to sue out execution on the judgment is suspended by the terms thereof, or by legal process, shall be omitted. Sections 8.01–230 et seq., 8.01–247 and 8.01–256 shall apply to the right to bring such action in like manner as to any right.

E. The provisions of this section apply to judgments obtained after June 29, 1948, and to judgments obtained prior to such date which are not then barred by the statute of limitations, but nothing herein shall have the effect of reducing the time for enforcement of any judgment the limitation upon which has been extended prior to such date by compliance with the provisions of law theretofore in effect.

F. This section shall not be construed to impair the right of subrogation to which any person may become entitled while the lien is in force, provided he institutes proceedings to enforce such right within five years after the same accrued, nor shall the lien of a judgment be impaired by the recovery of another judgment thereon, or by a forthcoming bond taken on an execution thereon, such bond having the force of a judgment.

G. Limitations on enforcement of judgments entered in the general district courts shall be governed by § 16.1–94.1, unless an abstract of such judgment is docketed in the judgment book of a circuit court. Upon the docketing of such judgment, the limitation for the enforcement of a district court judgment is the same as for a judgment of the circuit court.

Acts 1977, c. 617; Acts 1983, c. 449; Acts 2002, c. 394. Amended by Acts 2005, c. 139; Acts 2005, c. 203.

§ 8.01–252. Repealed by Acts 2005, cc. 139 and 203

Article 5

Miscellaneous Limitations Provisions

§ 8.01–253. Limitation of suits to avoid voluntary conveyances, etc.

No gift, conveyance, assignment, transfer, or charge, which is not on consideration deemed valuable in law, or which is upon consideration of marriage, shall be avoided in whole or in part for that cause only, unless within five years from its recordation, and if not so recorded within five years from the time the same was or should have been discovered, suit be brought for that purpose, or the subject thereof, or some part of it, be distrained or levied on by or at the suit of a creditor, as to whom such gift, conveyance, assignment, transfer, or charge, is declared to be void by § 55–81.

Acts 1977, c. 617.

§ 8.01–254. Limitation on enforcement of bequests and legacies

Wherever by any will, the testator devises any real estate to some person and requires such person to pay some other person a specified sum of money, or provides a legacy for some person which constitutes a charge against the real estate of the testator, or any part thereof, no suit or action shall be brought to subject such real estate to the payment of such specified sum of money or such legacy, as the case may be, after twenty years from the time when the same shall have been payable, and if the will specifies no time for the payment thereof, it shall be deemed to have been payable immediately upon death of the testator.

Acts 1977, c. 617.

§ 8.01–255. Time for presenting claim against Commonwealth

Any pecuniary claim authorized to be presented under §§ 2.2–814 and 2.2–815 shall be barred unless presented in writing to the comptroller or other authorized person no later than five years after the right to such claim shall arise. If such claim be not thus barred, any action thereon against the Commonwealth must be brought no later than three years after disallowance of such claim in whole or in part.

Acts 1977, c. 617.

§ 8.01–255.1. Limitation of action for breach of condition subsequent or termination of determinable fee simple estate

No person shall commence an action for the recovery of lands, nor make an entry thereon, by reason of a breach of a condition subsequent, or by reason of the termination of an estate of fee simple determinable, unless the action is commenced or entry is made within ten years after breach of the condition or within ten years from the time when the estate of fee simple determinable has been terminated. Where there has been a breach of a condition subsequent or termination of an estate fee simple determinable which occurred prior to July 1, 1965, recovery of the lands, or an entry may be made thereon by the owner of a right of entry or possibility of reverter, by July 1, 1977. Possession of land after breach of a condition subsequent or after termination of an estate of fee simple determinable shall be deemed adverse and hostile from the first breach of a condition subsequent or from the occurrence of the event terminating an estate of fee simple determinable.

Acts 1977, c. 617.

§ 8.01–255.2. Limitation on motion for new execution after loss of property sold under indemnity bond

A motion made pursuant to § 8.01–476 shall be made within five years after the right to make the same shall have accrued.

Acts 1977, c. 617.

§ 8.01–256. As to rights and remedies existing when this chapter takes effect

No action, suit, scire facias, or other proceeding which is pending before October 1, 1977, shall be barred by this chapter, and any action, suit, scire facias or other proceeding so pending shall be subject to the same limitation, if any, which would have been applied if this chapter had not been enacted. If a cause of action, as to which no action, suit, scire facias, or other proceeding is pending, exists before October 1, 1977, then this chapter shall not apply and the limitation as to such cause of action shall be the same, if any, as would apply had this chapter not been enacted. Any new limitation period imposed by this chapter, where no limitation previously existed or which is different from the limitation existing before this chapter was enacted, shall apply only to causes or rights of action accruing on or after October 1, 1977.

Acts 1977, c. 617.

CHAPTER 5

VENUE

§ 8.01–257. Venue generally

It is the intent of this chapter that every action shall be commenced and tried in a forum convenient to the parties and witnesses, where justice can be administered without prejudice or delay. Except where specifically provided otherwise, whenever the word "action(s)" is used in this chapter, it shall mean all actions at law, suits in equity, and statutory proceedings, whether in circuit courts or district courts.

Acts 1977, c. 617.

§ 8.01–258. Venue not jurisdictional

The provisions of this chapter relate to venue - the place of trial - and are not jurisdictional. No order, judgment, or decree shall be voidable, avoided, or subject to collateral attack solely on the ground that there was improper venue; however, nothing herein shall affect the right to appeal an error of court concerning venue.

Acts 1977, c. 617.

§ 8.01–259. Application

Nothing in this chapter shall apply to venue in the following proceedings:

(1), (2) Repealed.

(3) Habeas corpus;

(4) Tax proceedings, other than those in Title 58.1;

(5) Juvenile and domestic relations district courts proceedings concerning children; or

(6) Repealed.

(7) Adoptions.

(8) Repealed.

In all other actions, venue shall be in accordance with the provisions of this chapter, and, with respect to such actions, in case of conflict between the provisions of this chapter and other provisions outside this chapter relating to venue, all such other provisions are hereby superseded.

Acts 1977, c. 617; Acts 1987, c. 567; Acts 1989, c. 556.

§ 8.01–260. Proper venue; preferred forum in certain actions; permissible forums for other actions

Except for those actions expressly excluded from the operation of this chapter, and subject to the provisions of §§ 8.01–264 and 8.01–265, the venue for any action shall be deemed proper only if laid in accordance with the provisions of §§ 8.01–261 and 8.01–262.

Acts 1977, c. 617.

§ 8.01–261. Category A or preferred venue

In the actions listed in this section, the forums enumerated shall be deemed preferred places of venue and may be referred to as "Category A" in this title. Venue laid in any other forum shall be subject to objection; however, if more than one preferred place of venue applies, any such place shall be a proper forum. The following forums are designated as places of preferred venue for the action specified:

1. In actions for review of, appeal from, or enforcement of state administrative regulations, decisions, or other orders:

a. If the moving or aggrieved party is other than the Commonwealth or an agency thereof, then the county or city wherein such party:

(1) Resides;

(2) Regularly or systematically conducts affairs or business activity; or

(3) Wherein such party's property affected by the administrative action is located.

b. If the moving or aggrieved party is the Commonwealth or an agency thereof, then the county or city wherein the respondent or a party defendant:

(1) Resides;

(2) Regularly or systematically conducts affairs or business activity; or

(3) Has any property affected by the administrative action.

c. If subdivisions 1 a and 1 b do not apply, then the county or city wherein the alleged violation of the administrative regulation, decision, or other order occurred.

2. Except as provided in subdivision 1 of this section, where the action is against one or more officers of the Commonwealth in an official capacity, the county or city where any such person has his official office.

3. The county or city wherein the subject land, or a part thereof, is situated in the following actions:

a. To recover or partition land;

b. To subject land to a debt;

c. To sell, lease, or encumber the land of persons under disabilities;

d. Repealed.

e. To sell wastelands;

f. To establish boundaries;

g. For unlawful entry or detainer;

h. For ejectment; or

i. To remove clouds on title.

4. Reserved.

5. In actions for writs of mandamus, prohibition, or certiorari, except such as may be issued by the Supreme Court, the county or city wherein is the record or proceeding to which the writ relates.

6. In actions on bonds required for public contract, the county or city in which the public project, or any part thereof, is situated.

7. In actions to impeach or establish a will, the county or city wherein the will was probated, or, if not probated at the time of the action, where the will may be properly offered for probate.

8., 9. Repealed.

10. In actions on any contract between a transportation district and a component government, any county or city any part of which is within such transportation district.

11. In attachments,

a. With reference to the principal defendant and those liable with or to him, venue shall be determined as if the principal defendant were the sole defendant; or

b. In the county or city in which the principal defendant has estate or has debts owing to him.

12. Repealed.

13. a. In any action for the collection of state, county, or municipal taxes, any one of the following counties or cities shall be deemed preferred places of venue:

(1) Wherein the taxpayer resides;

(2) Wherein the taxpayer owns real or personal property;

(3) Wherein the taxpayer has a registered office, or regularly or systematically conducts business; or

(4) In case of withdrawal from the Commonwealth by a delinquent taxpayer, wherein venue was proper at the time the taxes in question were assessed or at the time of such withdrawal.

b. In any action for the correction of an erroneous assessment of state taxes and tax refunds, any one of the following counties or cities shall be deemed preferred places of venue:

(1) Wherein the taxpayer resides;

(2) Wherein the taxpayer has a registered office or regularly or systematically conducts business;

(3) Wherein the taxpayer's real or personal property involved in such a proceeding is located; or

(4) The Circuit Court of the City of Richmond.

14. In proceedings by writ of quo warranto:

a. The city or county wherein any of the defendants reside;

b. If the defendant is a corporation, the city or county where its registered office is or where its mayor, rector, president, or other chief officer resides; or

c. If there is no officer or none of the defendants reside in the Commonwealth, venue shall be in the City of Richmond.

15. In proceedings to award an injunction:

a. To any judgment or judicial proceeding of a circuit court, venue shall be in the court in the county or city in which the judgment was rendered or such proceeding is pending;

b. To any judgment or judicial proceeding of a district court, venue shall be in the circuit court of the county or city in which the judgment was rendered or such proceeding is pending; or

c. To any other act or proceeding, venue shall be in the circuit court of the county or city in which the act is to be done, or being done, or is apprehended to be done or the proceeding is pending.

16. Repealed.

17. In disbarment or suspension proceedings against any attorney-at-law, in the county or city where the defendant:

a. Resides;

b. Has his principal office or place of practice when the proceeding is commenced;

c. Resided or had such principal office or place of practice when any misconduct complained of occurred; or

d. Has any pending case as to which any misconduct took place.

18. In actions under the Virginia Tort Claims Act, Article 18.1 (§ 8.01-195.1 et seq.) of Chapter 3 of this title:

a. The county or city where the claimant resides;

b. The county or city where the act or omission complained of occurred; or

c. If the claimant resides outside the Commonwealth and the act or omission complained of occurred outside the Commonwealth, the City of Richmond.

19. In suits for annulment, affirmance, or divorce, the county or city in which the parties last cohabited, or at the option of the plaintiff, in the county or city in which the defendant resides, if a resident of this Commonwealth, and in cases in which an order of publication may be issued against the defendant under § 8.01-316, venue may also be in the county or city in which the plaintiff resides.

20. In distress actions, in the county or city when the premises yielding the rent, or some part thereof, may be or where goods liable to distress may be found.

Acts 1977, c. 617; Acts 1978, c. 334; Acts 1979, c. 331; Acts 1985, c. 433; Acts 1987, c. 567; Acts 1988, c. 766; Acts 1989, c. 556; Acts 1990, c. 831; Acts 1993, c. 841.

§ 8.01-262. Category B or permissible venue

In any actions to which this chapter applies except those actions enumerated in Category A where preferred venue is specified, one or more of the following counties or cities shall be permissible forums, such forums being sometimes referred to as "Category B" in this title:

1. Wherein the defendant resides or has his principal place of employment or, if the defendant is not an individual, wherein its principal office or principal place of business is located;

2. Wherein the defendant has a registered office, has appointed an agent to receive process, or such agent has been appointed by operation of the law; or, in case of withdrawal from the Commonwealth by such defendant, wherein venue herein was proper at the time of such withdrawal;

3. Provided there exists any practical nexus to the forum including, but not limited to, the location of fact witnesses, plaintiffs, or other evidence to the action, wherein the defendant regularly conducts substantial business activity, or in the case of withdrawal from the Commonwealth by such defendant, wherein venue herein was proper at the time of such withdrawal;

4. Wherein the cause of action, or any part thereof, arose;

5. In actions to recover or partition personal property, whether tangible or intangible, the county or city:

a. Wherein such property is physically located; or

b. Wherein the evidence of such property is located;

c. And if subdivisions a and b do not apply, wherein the plaintiff resides.

6. In actions against a fiduciary as defined in § 8.01-2 appointed under court authority, the county or city wherein such fiduciary qualified;

7. In actions for improper message transmission or misdelivery wherein the message was transmitted or delivered or wherein the message was accepted for delivery or was misdelivered;

8. In actions arising based on delivery of goods, wherein the goods were received;

9. If there is no other forum available in subdivisions 1 through 8 of this category, then the county or city where the defendant has property or debts owing to him subject to seizure by any civil process; or

10. Wherein any of the plaintiffs reside if (i) all of the defendants are unknown or are nonresidents of the Commonwealth or if (ii) there is no other forum available under any other provisions of § 8.01-261 or this section.

Acts 1977, c. 617; Acts 1978, c. 414; Acts 1979, c. 331; Acts 1985, c. 213; Acts 1999, c. 73. Amended by Acts 2004, c. 979; Acts 2013, c. 71; Acts 2013, c. 103.

§ 8.01-262.1. Place for bringing action under a contract related to construction

A. Where a party whose principal place of business is in the Commonwealth enters into a contract on or after July 1, 1997, to design, manage construction of, construct, alter, repair, maintain, move, demolish, or excavate, or supply goods, equipment, or materials for the construction, alteration, repair, maintenance, movement, demolition, or excavation of a building, structure, appurtenance, road, bridge, or tunnel which is physically located in the Commonwealth, any cause of action arising under such contract may be brought in the jurisdiction where the construction project is located, or such other jurisdiction where the venue is proper under the provisions of this chapter. Any provision in the contract mandating that such action be brought in a location outside the Commonwealth shall be unenforceable.

B. The forum for any arbitration proceedings required in such a contract entered into on or after July 1, 1991, shall be in this Commonwealth. If the contract provides for arbitration proceedings outside the Commonwealth, such provision is unenforceable and arbitration proceedings shall be in the county or city where the work is to be performed, unless the parties agree to conduct the proceedings elsewhere within the Commonwealth. The enforceability of the remaining provisions of the arbitration agreement and the method of selecting a forum for the conduct of the arbitration proceedings are as provided in this Code, the Federal Arbitration Act, and any applicable rules of arbitration.

Acts 1991, c. 489; Acts 1997, c. 424; Acts 1999, c. 130.

§ 8.01–263. Multiple parties

In actions involving multiple parties, venue shall not be subject to objection:

1. If one or more of the parties is entitled to preferred venue, and such action is commenced in any such forum; provided that in any action where there are one or more residents and one or more nonresidents or parties unknown, venue shall be proper (preferred or permissible, as the case may be) as to at least one resident defendant;

2. In all other cases, if the venue is proper as to any party.

Acts 1977, c. 617.

§ 8.01–264. Venue improperly laid; objection

A. Venue laid in forums other than those designated by this chapter shall be subject to objection, but no action shall be dismissed solely on the basis of venue if there be a forum in the Commonwealth where venue is proper. In actions where venue is subject to objection, the action may nevertheless be tried where it is commenced, and the venue irregularity shall be deemed to have been waived unless the defendant objects to venue by motion filed, as to actions in circuit courts, within twenty-one days after service of process commencing the action, or within the period of any extension of time for filing responsive pleadings fixed by order of the court. As to actions in general district courts, a motion objecting to venue, which may be in the form of a letter or other written communication, shall be filed with or received by the court on or before the day of trial. Waiver by any defendant shall not constitute waiver for any other defendant entitled to object to venue. Such motion shall set forth where the defendant believes venue to be proper, may be in writing, and shall be promptly heard by the court upon reasonable notice by any party. The court shall hear the motion only on the basis of the action as commenced against the original defendant and not on the basis of subsequent joinder or intervention of any other party. If such motion is sustained, the court shall order the venue transferred to a proper forum under the appropriate provisions of §§ 8.01–195.4, 8.01–260, 8.01–261 and 8.01–262 and shall so notify each party.

B. In the event a party defendant whose presence created venue is dismissed after the parties are at issue, then the remaining parties defendant may object to venue within ten days after such dismissal if the remaining defendants can demonstrate that the dismissed defendant was not properly joined or was added as a party defendant for the purpose of creating venue. However, nothing in this section shall impair the right of the court under § 8.01–265 to retain the action for trial on motion of a plaintiff and for good cause shown.

C. The initial pleading, in any action brought in a general district court, shall inform the defendant of his right to object to venue if the action is brought in any forum other than that specified in §§ 8.01–261, 8.01–262, or § 8.01–263. The information to the defendant shall be stated in clear, nontechnical language reasonably calculated to accomplish the purpose of this subsection.

D. Where a suit described in subdivision 19 of § 8.01–261 is filed in a venue that is not described therein, the court, on its own motion and upon notice to all parties, may transfer the suit to a venue described in such subdivision provided the transfer is implemented within sixty days after service of process upon all parties.

Acts 1977, c. 617; Acts 1982, c. 601; Acts 1985, c. 433; Acts 1985, c. 492; Acts 1986, c. 396; Acts 1986, c. 403; Acts 1987, c. 709; Acts 1991, c. 692.

§ 8.01–265. Change of venue by court

In addition to the provisions of § 8.01–264 and notwithstanding the provisions of §§ 8.01–195.4, 8.01–260, 8.01–261 and 8.01–262, the court wherein an action is commenced may, upon motion by any party and for good cause shown, (i) dismiss an action brought by a person who is not a resident of the Commonwealth without prejudice under such conditions as the court deems appropriate if the cause of action arose outside of the Commonwealth and if the court determines that a more convenient forum which has jurisdiction over all parties is available in a jurisdiction other than the Commonwealth or (ii) transfer the action to any fair and convenient forum having jurisdiction within the Commonwealth. Such conditions as the court deems appropriate shall include, but not be limited to, a requirement that the defendant agree not to assert the statute of limitations as a defense if the action is brought in a more convenient forum within a time specified by the court. The court, on motion of any party and for good cause shown, may retain the action for trial. Except by agreement of all parties, no action enumerated in Category A, § 8.01-261, shall be transferred to or retained by a forum not enumerated in such category. Good cause shall be deemed to include, but not to be limited to, the agreement of the parties or the avoidance of substantial inconvenience to the parties or the witnesses, or complying with the law of any other state or the United States.

The provisions of (i) of this section shall not apply to causes of action which accrue under § 8.01-249(4).

Acts 1979, c. 662; Acts 1982, c. 601; Acts 1991, c. 530. Amended by Acts 2007, c. 105.

§ 8.01-266. Costs

In any action which is transferred or retained for trial pursuant to this chapter, the court in which the action is initially brought may award an amount necessary to compensate a party for such inconvenience, expense, and delay as he may have been caused by the commencement of the suit in a forum to which an objection, pursuant to § 8.01-264, is sustained or by the bringing of a frivolous motion to transfer. In addition, the court may award those attorney's fees deemed just and reasonable which are occasioned by such commencement of a suit or by such motion to transfer. The awarding of such costs by the transferor court shall not preclude the assessment of costs by the clerk of the transferee court.

Acts 1977, c. 617; Acts 1994, c. 32.

§ 8.01-267. Discretion of judge

Both the decision of the court transferring or refusing to transfer an action under § 8.01-265 and the decision of the court as to amount of costs awarded under § 8.01-266 shall be within the sound discretion of the trial judge. However, nothing herein shall affect the right to assign as error a court's decision concerning venue.

Acts 1977, c. 617.

CHAPTER 5.1

MULTIPLE CLAIMANT LITIGATION ACT

§ 8.01-267.1. Standards governing consolidation, etc., and transfer

On motion of any party, a circuit court may enter an order joining, coordinating, consolidating or transferring civil actions as provided in this chapter upon finding that:

1. Separate civil actions brought by six or more plaintiffs involve common questions of law or fact and arise out of the same transaction, occurrence or series of transactions or occurrences;

2. The common questions of law or fact predominate and are significant to the actions; and

3. The order (i) will promote the ends of justice and the just and efficient conduct and disposition of the actions, and (ii) is consistent with each party's right to due process of law, and (iii) does not prejudice each individual party's right to a fair and impartial resolution of each action.

Factors to be considered by the court include, but are not limited to, (i) the nature of the common questions of law or fact; (ii) the convenience of the parties, witnesses and counsel; (iii) the relative stages of the actions and the work of counsel; (iv) the efficient utilization of judicial facilities and personnel; (v) the calendar of the courts; (vi) the likelihood and disadvantages of duplicative and inconsistent rulings, orders or judgments; (vii) the likelihood of prompt settlement of the actions without the entry of the order; and (viii) as to joint trials by jury, the likelihood of prejudice or confusion.

The court may organize and manage the combined litigation and enter further orders consistent with the right of each party to a fair trial as may be appropriate to avoid unnecessary costs, duplicative litigation or delay and to assure fair and efficient conduct and resolution of the litigation, including but not limited to orders which organize the parties into groups with like interest; appoint counsel to have lead responsibility for certain matters; allocate costs and fees to separate issues into common questions that require treatment on a consolidated basis and individual cases that do not; and to stay discovery on the issues that are not consolidated.

Acts 1995, c. 555.

§ 8.01-267.2. When actions pending in same court

For purposes of this chapter, actions shall be considered pending in the same circuit court when they have been (i) filed in that court, regardless of whether the defendant has been served with process, or (ii) properly transferred to that court.

Acts 1995, c. 555.

§ 8.01-267.3. Consolidation and other combined proceedings

On motion of any party, a circuit court in which separate civil actions are pending which were brought by six or more plaintiffs may enter an order coordinating, consolidating or joining any or all of the proceedings in the actions upon making the findings required by § 8.01-267.1. The order may provide for any or all of the following:

1. Coordinated or consolidated pretrial proceedings;

2. A joint hearing or, if requested by any party, trial by jury with respect to any or all common questions at issue in the actions; or

3. Consolidation of the actions.

Acts 1995, c. 555.

§ 8.01–267.4. Transfer

A. Whenever there are pending in different circuit courts of the Commonwealth civil actions brought by six or more plaintiffs which involve common issues of law or fact and arise out of the same transaction, occurrence or the same series of transactions or occurrences, any party may apply to a panel of circuit court judges designated by the Supreme Court for an order of transfer. Upon such application and upon making the findings required by § 8.01–267.1, the panel may order some or all of the actions transferred to a circuit court in which one or more of the actions are pending for purposes of coordinated or consolidated pretrial proceedings. The circuit court to which actions are transferred may enter further orders as provided in § 8.01–267.3. Any subsequent application for further transfer shall be made to the circuit court to which the actions were transferred. Upon completion of pretrial proceedings and any joint hearings or trials, the circuit court may remand the actions to the circuit courts in which they were originally filed or may retain them for final disposition.

B. Any party who files an application for transfer shall at the same time give notice of such application to all parties and to the clerk of each circuit court in which an action that is the subject of the application is pending. Upon receipt of the notice, a circuit court shall not enter any further orders under § 8.01–267.3 until after the panel has entered an order granting or denying an application for transfer pursuant to subsection A.

Acts 1995, c. 555.

§ 8.01–267.5. Joinder and severance

Six or more parties may be joined initially as plaintiffs in a single action if their claims involve common issues of fact and arise out of the same transaction or occurrence or the same series of transactions or occurrences. On motion of a defendant, the actions so joined shall be severed unless the court finds that the claims of the plaintiffs were ones which, if they had been filed separately, would have met the standards of § 8.01–267.1 and would have been consolidated under § 8.01–267.3. If the court orders severance, the claims may proceed separately upon payment of any appropriate filing fees due in the separate circuit courts within sixty days of entry of the order. The date of the original filing shall be the date of filing for each of the severed actions for purposes of applying the statutes of limitations.

Acts 1995, c. 555.

§ 8.01–267.6. Separate trials; special interrogatories

In any combined action under this chapter, the court, on motion of any party, may order separate or bifurcated trials of any one or more claims, cross-claims, counterclaims, third-party claims, or separate issues, always preserving the right of trial by jury.

Additionally, the court may submit special interrogatories to the jury to resolve specific issues of fact.

Acts 1995, c. 555.

§ 8.01–267.7. Later-filed actions

Later-filed actions may be joined with ongoing litigation in accordance with the procedures of § 8.01–267.3 or § 8.01–267.4 and the standards of § 8.01–267.1. Parties in later-filed actions joined with ongoing multiple claimant litigation may, in the discretion of the court, be bound to prior proceedings but only to the extent permitted by law and only to the extent that the court finds that the interests of such parties were adequately and fairly represented. Consistent with the language of this section and the standards of § 8.01–267.1, the parties may utilize all prior discovery taken by any party in on-going multiple party litigation as if the parties in the later-filed actions had been parties at the time the discovery was taken. On motion of any party or by the person from whom discovery is sought, the court may limit or prohibit discovery by parties in later-filed actions if the court finds that the matters on which the discovery is sought have been covered adequately by prior discovery.

Acts 1995, c. 555.

§ 8.01–267.8. Interlocutory appeal

A. The Supreme Court or the Court of Appeals, in its discretion, may permit an appeal to be taken from an order of a circuit court although the order is not a final order where the circuit court has ordered a consolidated trial of claims joined or consolidated pursuant to this chapter.

B. The Supreme Court or the Court of Appeals, in its discretion, may permit an appeal to be taken from any other order of a circuit court in an action combined pursuant to this chapter although the order is not a final order provided the written order of the circuit court states that the order involves a controlling question of law as to which there is substantial ground for difference of opinion and that an immediate appeal from the order may materially advance the ultimate termination of the litigation.

C. Application for an appeal pursuant to this section shall be made within ten days after the entry of the order and shall not stay proceedings in the circuit court unless the circuit court or the appellate court shall so order.

Acts 1995, c. 555.

§ 8.01–267.9. Effect on other law

The procedures set out in this chapter are in addition to procedures otherwise available by statute, rule or common law and do not limit in any way the availability of such procedures, but shall not apply to any action against a manufacturer or supplier of asbestos or product for industrial use that contains asbestos to which the provisions of § 8.01–374.1 may apply.

Acts 1995, c. 555.

CHAPTER 6

NOTICE OF LIS PENDENS OR ATTACHMENT

§ 8.01–268. When and how docketed and indexed

A. No lis pendens or attachment shall bind or affect a subsequent bona fide purchaser of real or personal estate for valuable consideration and without actual notice of such lis pendens or attachment, until and except from the time a memorandum setting forth the title of the cause or attachment, the general object thereof, the court wherein it is pending, the amount of the claim asserted by the plaintiff, a description of the property, the name of the person whose estate is intended to be affected thereby, and in an action to enforce a zoning ordinance a description of the alleged violation, shall be admitted to record in the clerk's office of the circuit court of the county or the city wherein the property is located; or if it be in that part of the City of Richmond lying north of the south bank of the James River and including the islands in such river, in the clerk's office of the Circuit Court, Division I, of such city, or if it be in the part of the City of Richmond lying south of the south bank of the James River, in the clerk's office of the Circuit Court, Division II, of such city. Clerks of circuit courts are authorized and directed to admit to record memoranda of lis pendens or attachment for actions pending in any court of this Commonwealth, or in any other state, federal, or territorial court. The provisions of this section shall not be construed to mean that any such memoranda heretofore recorded are not properly of record. Such memorandum shall not be deemed to have been recorded unless and until indexed as required by law. A memorandum of lis pendens admitted to record in an action to enforce a zoning ordinance shall expire after 180 days.

B. No memorandum of lis pendens shall be filed unless the action on which the lis pendens is based seeks to establish an interest by the filing party in the real property described in the memorandum, or unless the action on which the lis pendens is based seeks to enforce a zoning ordinance.

Acts 1977, c. 617; Acts 1988, c. 503. Amended by Acts 2008, c. 60; Acts 2008, c. 204.

§ 8.01–269. Dismissal or satisfaction of same

If such attachment or lis pendens is quashed or dismissed or such cause is dismissed, or judgment or final decree in such attachment or cause is for the defendant or defendants, the court shall direct in its order (i) that the names of all interested parties thereto, as found in the recorded attachment or lis pendens be listed for the clerk, and (ii) that the attachment or lis pendens be released and, the court may, in an appropriate case, impose sanctions as provided in § 8.01–271.1. It shall then become the duty of the clerk in whose office such attachment or lis pendens is recorded to record the order in the order book together with a separate instrument or order releasing such lien and referencing the deed book and page where the original lien is recorded. However, in any case in which an appeal or writ of error from such judgment or decree or dismissal would lie, the clerk shall not record the order or make the entry until after the expiration of the time in which such appeal or writ of error may be applied for, or if applied for after refusal thereof, or if granted, after final judgment or decree is entered by the appellate court.

In any case in which the debt for which such attachment is issued, or suit is brought and notice of lis pendens recorded is satisfied by payment, it shall be the duty of the creditor, within 10 days after payment of same, to provide the clerk with a separate instrument or order for recordation releasing such lis pendens and referencing the order book and page where the original lis pendens is recorded.

Acts 1977, c. 617; Acts 1985, c. 310; Acts 1986, c. 278; Acts 1989, c. 450. Amended by Acts 2014, c. 330.

CHAPTER 7

CIVIL ACTIONS; COMMENCEMENT, PLEADINGS, AND MOTIONS

ARTICLE 1

CIVIL ACTIONS GENERALLY

§ 8.01–270. Repealed by Acts 2005, c. 681, eff. Jan. 1, 2006

ARTICLE 2

PLEADINGS GENERALLY

§ 8.01–271. Compliance with Rules of Supreme Court

Subject to the provisions of this title, pleadings shall be in accordance with Rules of the Supreme Court.

Acts 1977, c. 617.

§ 8.01–271.01. Electronic filings in civil actions in circuit court

Electronic filings in civil actions and proceedings in the circuit court shall be governed by Article 4.1 (§ 17.1–258.2 et. seq.) of Chapter 2 of Title 17.1 and applicable Rules of the Supreme Court of Virginia.

Added by Acts 2010, c. 717; Acts 2010, c. 760.

§ 8.01–271.1. Signing of pleadings, motions, and other papers; oral motions; sanctions

Except as otherwise provided in §§ 16.1–260 and 63.2–1901, every pleading, written motion, and other paper of a party represented by an attorney shall be signed by at least one attorney of record in his individual name, and the attorney's address shall be stated on the first pleading filed by that attorney in the action. A party who is not represented by an attorney, including a person confined in a state or local correctional facility proceeding pro se, shall sign his pleading, motion, or other paper and state his address.

The signature of an attorney or party constitutes a certificate by him that (i) he has read the pleading, motion, or other paper, (ii) to the best of his knowledge, information and belief, formed after reasonable inquiry, it is well grounded in fact and is warranted by existing law or a good faith argument for the extension, modification, or reversal of existing law, and (iii) it is not interposed for any improper purpose, such as to harass or to cause unnecessary delay or needless increase in the cost of litigation. If a pleading, written motion, or other paper is not signed, it shall be stricken unless it is signed promptly after the omission is called to the attention of the pleader or movant.

An oral motion made by an attorney or party in any court of the Commonwealth constitutes a representation by him that (i) to the best of his knowledge, information and belief formed after reasonable inquiry it is well grounded in fact and is warranted by existing law or a good faith argument for the extension, modification or reversal of existing law, and (ii) it is not interposed for any improper purpose, such as to harass or to cause unnecessary delay or needless increase in the cost of litigation.

If a pleading, motion, or other paper is signed or made in violation of this rule, the court, upon motion or upon its own initiative, shall impose upon the person who signed the paper or made the motion, a represented party, or both, an appropriate sanction, which may include an order to pay to the other party or parties the amount of the reasonable expenses incurred because of the filing of the pleading, motion, or other paper or making of the motion, including a reasonable attorney's fee.

Acts 1987, c. 259; Acts 1987, c. 682; Acts 1998, c. 596. Amended by Acts 2008, c. 136; Acts 2008, c. 845.

§ 8.01–272. Pleading several matters; joining tort and contract claims; separate trial in discretion of court; counterclaims

In any civil action, a party may plead as many matters, whether of law or fact, as he shall think necessary. A party may join a claim in tort with one in contract provided that all claims so joined arise out of the same transaction or occurrence. The court, in its discretion, may order a separate trial for any claim. Any counterclaim shall be governed by the Rules of the Supreme Court of Virginia.

Acts 1977, c. 617; Acts 1979, c. 367. Amended by Acts 2005, c. 681, eff. Jan. 1, 2006.

§ 8.01–273. Demurrer; form; grounds to be stated; amendment

A. In any suit in equity or action at law, the contention that a pleading does not state a cause of action or that such pleading fails to state facts upon which the relief demanded can be granted may be made by demurrer. All demurrers shall be in writing and shall state specifically the grounds on which the demurrant concludes that the pleading is insufficient at law. No grounds other than those stated specifically in the demurrer shall be considered by the court. A demurrer may be amended as other pleadings are amended.

B. Wherever a demurrer to any pleading has been sustained, and as a result thereof the demurree has amended his pleading, he shall not be deemed to have waived his right to stand upon his pleading before the amendment, provided the order of the court shows that he objected to the ruling of the court sustaining the demurrer. On any appeal of such a case the demurree may insist upon his original pleading, and if the same be held to be good, he shall not be prejudiced by having made the amendment.

Acts 1977, c. 617.

§ 8.01–273.1. Motion for judgment; motion to refer; Virginia Birth–Related Neurological Injury Compensation Act

A. In any civil action, where a party, who is a participating hospital or physician as defined in § 38.2–5001, moves to refer a cause of action to the Workers' Compensation Commission for the purposes of determining whether the cause of action satisfies the requirements of the Virginia Birth–Related Neurological Injury Compensation Act (§ 38.2–5000 et seq.), the court shall forward the motion to refer together with a copy of the motion for judgment to the Commission and stay all proceedings on the cause of action pending an award and notification by the Commission of its disposition; provided, however, that the motion to refer the cause of action to the Workers' Compensation Commission shall be filed no later than 120 days after the date of filing a grounds of defense by the party seeking the referral.

B. Upon entry of the order of referral by the court, the clerk of the circuit court shall file with the Workers' Compensation Commission within thirty days a copy of the motion for judgment and the responsive pleadings of all the parties to the action. The clerk shall copy all counsel of record in the civil action on the transmittal letter accompanying the materials being filed with the Workers' Compensation Commission. All parties to the civil action shall be entitled to participate before the Commission upon filing a notice of appearance with the Clerk of the Commission within twenty-one days after receipt of the transmittal letter to the clerk of the circuit court. Notwithstanding the provisions of § 32.1–127.1:03, the moving party shall provide the Commission with an original and five copies of the following: appropriate assessments, evaluations, and prognoses and such other records obtained during discovery and are reasonably necessary for the determination of whether the infant has suffered a birth-related neurological injury. The medical records and the pleadings referenced in this subsection shall constitute a petition as referenced in § 38.2–5004. The moving party shall be reimbursed for all copying costs upon entry of an award of benefits as referenced in § 38.2–5009.

Acts 1999, c. 822; Acts 2000, c. 207, eff. April 1, 2000.

§ 8.01–274. Motion to strike defensive pleading in equity and at law; exceptions abolished

Exceptions to answers for insufficiency are abolished. The test of the sufficiency of any defensive pleading in any suit in equity or action at law shall be made by a motion to strike; if found insufficient, but amendable, the court may allow amendment on terms. If a second pleading is adjudged insufficient, the court may enter such judgment or decree or take such other action that it deems appropriate.

Acts 1977, c. 617; Acts 1978, c. 336.

§ 8.01–275. When action or suit not to abate for want of form; what defects not to be regarded

No action or suit shall abate for want of form where the motion for judgment or bill of complaint sets forth sufficient matter of substance for the court to proceed upon the merits of the cause. The court shall not regard any defect or imperfection in the pleading, whether it has been heretofore deemed mispleading or insufficient pleading or not, unless there be omitted something so essential to the action or defense that judgment, according to law and the very right of the cause, cannot be given.

Acts 1977, c. 617.

§ 8.01–275.1. When service of process is timely

Service of process in an action or suit within twelve months of commencement of the action or suit against a defendant shall be timely as to that defendant. Service of process on a defendant more than twelve months after the suit or action was commenced shall be timely upon a finding by the court that the plaintiff exercised due diligence to have timely service made on the defendant.

Acts 1994, c. 519.

§ 8.01–276. Demurrer to evidence and plea in abatement abolished; motion to strike evidence and written motion, respectively, to be used in lieu thereof

Demurrers to the evidence and pleas in abatement are hereby abolished.

Any matter that heretofore could be reached by a demurrer to the evidence may hereafter be subject to a motion to strike the evidence.

Any defense heretofore required or permitted to be made by plea in abatement may be made by written motion stating specifically the relief demanded and the grounds therefor. Except when the ground of such motion is the lack of the court's jurisdiction over the person of an indispensable party, or of the subject matter of the litigation, such motion shall be made within the time prescribed by Rules of the Supreme Court.

If the motion challenges the venue of the action, the movant shall state therein why venue is improperly laid and what place or places within the Commonwealth would constitute proper venue for the action.

Acts 1977, c. 617.

§ 8.01–277. Defective process; motion to quash; untimely service; motion to dismiss

A. A person, upon whom process to answer any action has been served, may take advantage of any defect in the issuance, service or return thereof by a motion to quash filed prior to or simultaneously with the filing of any pleading to the merits. Upon sustaining the motion, the court may strike the proof of service or permit amendment of the process or its return as may seem just.

B. A person, upon whom process has not been served within one year of commencement of the action against him, may make a special appearance, which does not constitute a general appearance, to file a motion to dismiss. Upon finding that the plaintiff did not exercise due diligence to have timely service and sustaining the motion to dismiss, the court shall dismiss the action with prejudice. Upon finding that the plaintiff did exercise due diligence to have timely service and denying the motion to dismiss, the court shall require the person filing such motion to file a responsive pleading within 21 days of such ruling. Nothing herein shall prevent the plaintiff from filing a nonsuit under § 8.01–380 before the entry of an order granting a motion to dismiss pursuant to the provisions of this section. Nothing in this subsection shall pertain to cases involving asbestos.

Acts 1977, c. 617; Acts 1994, c. 37. Amended by Acts 2006, c. 151.

§ 8.01–277.1. Objections to personal jurisdiction or defective process; what constitutes waiver

A. Except as provided in § 8.01–277, a person waives any objection to personal jurisdiction or defective process if he engages in conduct related to adjudicating the merits of the case, including, but not limited to:

1. Filing a demurrer, plea in bar, answer, counterclaim, cross-claim, or third-party claim;

2. Conducting discovery, except as provided in subsection B;

3. Seeking a ruling on the merits of the case; or

4. Actively participating in proceedings related to determining the merits of the case.

B. A person does not waive any objection to personal jurisdiction or defective process if he engages in conduct unrelated to adjudicating the merits of the case, including, but not limited to:

1. Requesting or agreeing to an extension of time;

2. Agreeing to a scheduling order;

3. Conducting discovery authorized by the court related to adjudicating the objection;

4. Observing or attending proceedings in the case;

5. Filing a motion to transfer venue pursuant to § 8.01–264 when such motion is filed contemporaneously with the objection; or

6. Removing the case to federal court.

Added by Acts 2011, c. 710.

§ 8.01–278. When plea of infancy not allowed; liability of infants for debts as traders; liability of infants on loans to defray expenses of education

A. If any minor now transacting business or who may hereafter transact business as a trader fails to disclose (i) by a sign in letters easy to be read, kept conspicuously posted at the place wherein such business is transacted and (ii) also by a notice published for two weeks in a newspaper meeting the requirements of § 8.01–324, the fact that he is a minor, all property, stock, and choses in action acquired or used in such business shall as to the creditors of any such person be liable for the debts of such person, and no plea of infancy shall be allowed.

B. If any minor shall procure a loan upon the representation in writing that the proceeds thereof are to be expended by such minor to defray any or all expenses incurred by reason of attendance at an institution of higher education, which has been approved by any regional accrediting association which is approved by the United States Office of Education, or by reason of attendance at any school eligible for the guarantee of the State Education Assistance Authority, such minor shall be liable for the repayment thereof as though he were an adult, and no plea of infancy shall be allowed.

Acts 1977, c. 617.

§ 8.01–279. When proof is unnecessary unless affidavit filed; handwriting; ownership; partnership or incorporation

A. Except as otherwise provided by § 8.3A–308, when any pleading alleges that any person made, endorsed, assigned, or accepted any writing, no proof of the handwriting shall be required, unless it be denied by an affidavit accompanying the plea putting it in issue.

B. When any pleading alleges that any person, partnership, corporation, or unincorporated association at a stated time, owned, operated, or controlled any property or instrumentality, no proof of the fact alleged shall be required unless an affidavit be filed with the pleading putting it in issue, denying specifically and with particularity that such property or instrumentality was, at the time alleged, so owned, operated, or controlled.

C. When parties sue or are sued as partners, and their names are set forth in the pleading, or when parties sue or are sued as a corporation, it shall not be necessary to prove the fact of the partnership or incorporation unless with the pleading which puts the matter in issue there be filed an affidavit denying such partnership or incorporation.

Acts 1977, c. 617.

§ 8.01–280. Pleadings may be sworn to before clerk; affidavit of belief sufficient

Any pleading to be filed in any court may be sworn to before the clerk or any officer authorized to administer oath thereof; and when an affidavit is required in support of any pleading or as a prerequisite to the issuance thereof, it shall be sufficient if the affiant swear that he believes it to be true.

Acts 1977, c. 617.

§ 8.01–281. Pleading in alternative; separate trial on motion of party

A. A party asserting either a claim, counterclaim, cross-claim, or third-party claim or a defense may plead alternative facts and theories of recovery against alternative parties, provided that such claims, defenses, or demands for relief so joined arise out of the same transaction or occurrence. Such claim, counterclaim, cross-claim, or third-party claim may be for contribution, indemnity, subrogation, or contract, express or implied; it may be based on future potential liability, and it shall be no defense thereto that the party asserting such claim, counterclaim, cross-claim, or third-party claim has made no payment or otherwise discharged any claim as to him arising out of the transaction or occurrence.

B. The court may, upon motion of any party, order a separate trial of any claim, counterclaim, cross-claim, or third-party claim, and of any separate issue or of any number of such claims; however, in any action wherein a defendant files a third-party motion for judgment alleging that damages to the person or property of the plaintiff were caused by the negligence of the third-party defendant in the operation of a motor vehicle, the court shall, upon motion of the plaintiff made at least five days in advance of trial, order a separate trial of such third-party claim.

Acts 1977, c. 617; Acts 1981, c. 426; Acts 1983, c. 183.

Article 3

Particular Equity Provisions

§ 8.01–282. Motion to strike evidence

When a defendant moves the court to strike out all of the evidence, upon any grounds, and such motion is overruled by the court, such defendant shall not thereafter be precluded from introducing evidence in his behalf.

Acts 1977, c. 617. Amended by Acts 2005, c. 681, eff. Jan. 1, 2006.

§ 8.01–283. Answer in equity proceeding

There shall be no requirement that a sworn answer in a proceeding on an equitable claim be rebutted by the testimony of two witnesses.

Acts 1977, c. 617. Amended by Acts 2005, c. 681, eff. Jan. 1, 2006.

§ 8.01–284. Repealed by Acts 2005, c. 681, eff. Jan. 1, 2006

CHAPTER 8

PROCESS

Article 1

In General

§ 8.01–285. Definition of certain terms for purposes of this chapter; process, return, statutory agent

For the purposes of this chapter:

1. The term "process" shall be deemed to include notice;

2. The term "return" shall be deemed to include the term "proof of service";

3. The term "statutory agent" means the Commissioner of the Department of Motor Vehicles and the Secretary of the Commonwealth, and the successors of either, when appointed pursuant to law for the purpose of service of process on the nonresident defined in subdivision 2 of § 8.01–307; and

4. The term "person" includes an individual, his executor, administrator, or other personal representative, or a corporation, partnership, association or any other legal or commercial entity, whether or not a

citizen or domiciliary of the Commonwealth and whether or not organized under the laws of the Commonwealth.

Acts 1977, c. 617; Acts 1991, c. 672. Amended by Acts 2005, c. 866.

§ 8.01–286. Forms of writs

Subject to the provisions of § 8.01–3, the Supreme Court may prescribe the forms of writs, and where no such prescription is made, the forms of writs shall be the same as heretofore used.

Acts 1977, c. 617.

§ 8.01–286.1. Service of process; waiver, duty to save costs, request to waive, how served

A. In an action pending in general district court or circuit court, the plaintiff may notify a defendant of the commencement of the action and request that the defendant waive service of process as provided in subsection B. Any person subject to service as set forth in § 8.01–296, 8.01–299, §§ 8.01–301 through 8.01–306 or § 8.01–320, with the exception of the Secretary of the Commonwealth and the Clerk of the State Corporation Commission, who receives actual notice of an action in the manner provided in this section, has a duty to avoid any unnecessary costs of serving process.

B. The notice and request shall incorporate the request for waiver and shall:

1. Be in writing and shall be addressed directly to the defendant, if an individual, or else to an officer, director or registered agent authorized by appointment or law to receive service of process of a defendant subject to service under § 8.01–299, §§ 8.01–301 through 8.01–306 or § 8.01–320;

2. Be dispatched through first-class mail or other reliable means;

3. Be accompanied by a copy of the motion for judgment, bill of complaint or other such initial pleading and identify the court in which it has been filed;

4. Inform the defendant, by means of a form provided by Executive Secretary of the Supreme Court, of the consequences of compliance and failure to comply with the request;

5. Set forth the date on which the request is sent;

6. Allow the defendant a reasonable time to return the waiver, which shall be no more than 30 days from the date on which the request is sent, or 60 days from that date if the defendant's address is outside the Commonwealth; and

7. Provide the defendant with an extra copy of the notice and request, as well as a prepaid means of compliance in writing.

If a defendant fails to comply with a request for waiver made by a plaintiff, the court shall impose the costs subsequently incurred in effecting service on the defendant unless good cause for the failure is shown.

C. A defendant that, before being served with process, timely returns a waiver so requested is not required to serve a grounds of defense or other responsive pleading to the motion for judgment or other initial pleading until 60 days after the date on which the request for waiver of service was sent, or 90 days after that date if the defendant's address was outside the Commonwealth.

D. When the plaintiff files a waiver of service with the court, the action shall proceed as if a notice and motion for judgment or other initial pleading had been served at the time of filing the waiver, and no proof of service shall be required.

E. The costs to be imposed on a defendant for failure to comply with a request to waive service of a summons shall include the costs subsequently incurred in effecting service under § 8.01–299, §§ 8.01–301 through 8.01–306 or § 8.01–320, together with the costs, including reasonable attorneys' fees, of any motion required to collect the costs of service. This provision does not apply to the Commissioner of the Department of Motor Vehicles, the Secretary of the Commonwealth or the Clerk of the State Corporation Commission.

F. A defendant who waives service of process pursuant to this section does not thereby waive any objection to the venue or to the jurisdiction of the court over the person of that defendant, or to any other defense or objection other than objections based on inadequacy of process or service of process.

Added by Acts 2005, c. 866. Amended by Acts 2011, c. 766.

§ 8.01–287. How process to be served

Upon commencement of an action, process shall be served in the manner set forth in this chapter and by the Rules of the Supreme Court.

Acts 1977, c. 617.

§ 8.01–288. Process received in time good though neither served nor accepted

Except for process commencing actions for divorce or annulment of marriage or other actions wherein service of process is specifically prescribed by statute, process which has reached the person to whom it is directed within the time prescribed by law, if any, shall be sufficient although not served or accepted as provided in this chapter.

Acts 1977, c. 617; Acts 1987, c. 594; Acts 1988, c. 583.

§ 8.01–289. No service of process on Sunday; exceptions

No civil process shall be served on Sunday, except in cases of persons escaping out of custody, or where it is otherwise expressly provided by law.

Acts 1977, c. 617.

Article 2

How Process Is Issued

§ 8.01-290. Plaintiffs required to furnish full name and last known address of defendants, etc.

Upon the commencement of every action, the plaintiff shall furnish in writing to the clerk or other issuing officer the full name and last known address of each defendant and if unable to furnish such name and address, he shall furnish such salient facts as are calculated to identify with reasonable certainty such defendant. The clerk or other official whose function it is to issue any such process shall note in the record or in the papers the address or other identifying facts furnished. Failure to comply with the requirements of this section shall not affect the validity of any judgment.

Acts 1977, c. 617.

§ 8.01-291. Copies to be made

The clerk issuing any such process unless otherwise directed shall deliver or transmit therewith as many copies thereof as there are persons named therein on whom it is to be served.

Acts 1977, c. 617.

§ 8.01-292. To whom process directed and where executed

Process from any court, whether original, mesne, or final, may be directed to the sheriff of, and may be executed in, any county, city, or town in the Commonwealth.

Acts 1977, c. 617.

Article 3

Who and Where to Serve Process

§ 8.01-293. Authorization to serve process, capias or show cause order; execute writ of possession and levy upon property

A. The following persons are authorized to serve process:

1. The sheriff within such territorial bounds as described in § 8.01-295;

2. Any person of age 18 years or older and who is not a party or otherwise interested in the subject matter in controversy. However, in any case in which custody or visitation of a minor child or children is at issue and a summons is issued for the attendance and testimony of a teacher or other school personnel who is not a party to the proceeding, if such summons is served on school property, it shall be served only by a sheriff or his deputy; or

3. A private process server. For purposes of this section, "private process server" means any person 18 years of age or older and who is not a party or otherwise interested in the subject matter in controversy, and who charges a fee for service of process.

Whenever in this Code the term "officer" or "sheriff" is used to refer to persons authorized to make, return or do any other act relating to service of process, such term shall be deemed to refer to any person authorized by this section to serve process.

B. Notwithstanding any other provision of law (i) only a sheriff or high constable may execute an order or writ of possession for personal, real or mixed property, including an order or writ of possession arising out of an action in unlawful entry and detainer or ejectment; (ii) any sheriff, high constable or law-enforcement officer as defined in § 9.1-101 of the Code of Virginia may serve any capias or show cause order; and (iii) only a sheriff, the high constable for the City of Norfolk or Virginia Beach or a treasurer may levy upon property.

Acts 1977, c. 617; Acts 1981, c. 110; Acts 1986, c. 275; Acts 1996, c. 501; Acts 1996, c. 608; Acts 1997, c. 820; Acts 2002, c. 342. Amended by Acts 2004, c. 210; Acts 2004, c. 588; Acts 2011, c. 766.

§ 8.01-294. Sheriff to get from clerk's office process and other papers; return of papers; effect of late return

Every sheriff who attends a court shall, every day when the clerk's office is open for business, go to such office and receive all process, and other papers to be served by him, and give receipts therefor, unless he has received notice from a regular employee of the clerk's office that there are no such papers requiring service and shall return all papers within 72 hours of service, except when such returns would be due on a Saturday, Sunday, or legal holiday. In such case, the return is due on the next day following such Saturday, Sunday, or legal holiday.

Failure to make return of service of process by anyone authorized to serve process under § 8.01-293 within the time specified in this section shall not invalidate any service of process or any judgment based thereon. In the event a late return prejudices a party or interferes with the court's administration of a case, the court may, in its discretion, continue the case, require additional or substitute service of process, or take such other action or enter such order as the court deems appropriate under the circumstances.

Acts 1977, c. 617; Acts 1978, c. 831; Acts 2002, c. 65. Amended by Acts 2004, c. 627.

§ 8.01-295. Territorial limits within which sheriff may serve process in his official capacity; process appearing to be duly served

The sheriff may execute such process throughout the political subdivision in which he serves and in any contiguous county or city. If the process appears to be duly served, and is good in other respects, it shall be deemed valid although not directed to an officer, or if directed to any officer, though executed by some other person. This section shall not be construed to require the sheriff to serve such process in any jurisdiction other than in his own.

Acts 1977, c. 617; Acts 1982, c. 674.

ARTICLE 4

WHO TO BE SERVED

§ 8.01-296. Manner of serving process upon natural persons

Subject to the provisions of § 8.01-286.1, in any action at law or in equity or any other civil proceeding in any court, process, for which no particular mode of service is prescribed, may be served upon natural persons as follows:

1. By delivering a copy thereof in writing to the party in person; or

2. By substituted service in the following manner:

a. If the party to be served is not found at his usual place of abode, by delivering a copy of such process and giving information of its purport to any person found there, who is a member of his family, other than a temporary sojourner or guest, and who is of the age of 16 years or older; or

b. If such service cannot be effected under subdivision 2 a, then by posting a copy of such process at the front door or at such other door as appears to be the main entrance of such place of abode, provided that not less than 10 days before judgment by default may be entered, the party causing service or his attorney or agent mails to the party served a copy of such process and thereafter files in the office of the clerk of the court a certificate of such mailing. In any civil action brought in a general district court, the mailing of the application for a warrant in debt or affidavit for summons in unlawful detainer or other civil pleading or a copy of such pleading, whether yet issued by the court or not, which contains the date, time and place of the return, prior to or after filing such pleading in the general district court, shall satisfy the mailing requirements of this section. In any civil action brought in a circuit court, the mailing of a copy of the pleadings with a notice that the proceedings are pending in the court indicated and that upon the expiration of 10 days after the giving of the notice and the expiration of the statutory period within which to respond, without further notice, the entry of a judgment by default as prayed for in the pleadings may be requested, shall satisfy the mailing requirements of this section and any notice requirement of the Rules of Court. Any judgment by default entered after July 1, 1989, upon posted service in which proceedings a copy of the pleadings was mailed as provided for in this section prior to July 1, 1989, is validated.

c. The person executing such service shall note the manner and the date of such service on the original and the copy of the process so delivered or posted under this subdivision and shall effect the return of process as provided in §§ 8.01-294 and 8.01-325.

3. If service cannot be effected under subdivisions 1 and 2, then by order of publication in appropriate cases under the provisions of §§ 8.01-316 through 8.01-320.

4. The landlord or his duly authorized agent or representative may serve notices required by the rental agreement or by law upon the tenant or occupant under a rental agreement that is within the purview of Chapter 13 (§ 55-217 et seq.) of Title 55.

Acts 1977, c. 617; Acts 1989, c. 518; Acts 1989, c. 524; Acts 1990, c. 729; Acts 1990, c. 767; Acts 1996, c. 538. Amended by Acts 2005, c. 866; Acts 2008, c. 489.

§ 8.01-297. Process on convict defendant

In all actions against one who has been convicted of a felony and is confined in a local or regional jail or State correctional institution, process shall be served on such convict and, subject to § 8.01-9, a guardian ad litem shall be appointed for him. Such service may be effected by delivery to the officer in charge of such jail or institution whose duty it shall be to deliver forthwith such process to the convict.

Acts 1977, c. 617.

§ 8.01-298. How summons for witness or juror served

In addition to the manner of service on natural persons prescribed in § 8.01-296, a summons for a witness or for a juror may be served:

1. At his or her usual place of business or employment during business hours, by delivering a copy thereof and giving information of its purport to the person found there in charge of such business or place of employment; or

2. In the case of a juror, by mailing a summons to the person being served, at least seven days prior to the day he is summoned to appear.

Acts 1977, c. 617; Acts 1979, c. 444.

§ 8.01–299. How process served on domestic corporations generally

Except as prescribed in § 8.01–300 as to municipal and quasi-governmental corporations, and subject to § 8.01–286.1, process may be served on a corporation created by the laws of the Commonwealth as follows:

1. By personal service on any officer, director, or registered agent of such corporation; or

2. By substituted service on stock corporations in accordance with § 13.1–637 and on nonstock corporations in accordance with § 13.1–836.

Acts 1977, c. 617; Acts 1991, c. 672. Amended by Acts 2005, c. 866.

§ 8.01–300. How process served on municipal and county governments and on quasi-governmental entities

Notwithstanding the provisions of § 8.01–299 for service of process on other domestic corporations, process shall be served on municipal and county governments and quasi-governmental bodies or agencies in the following manner:

1. If the case be against a city or a town, on its city or town attorney in those cities or towns which have created such a position, otherwise on its mayor, manager or trustee of such town or city; and

2. If the case be against a county, on its county attorney in those counties which have created such a position, otherwise on its attorney for the Commonwealth; and

3. If the case be against any political subdivision, or any other public governmental entity created by the laws of the Commonwealth and subject to suit as an entity separate from the Commonwealth, then on the director, commissioner, chief administrative officer, attorney, or any member of the governing body of such entity; and

4. If the case be against a supervisor, county officer, employee or agent of the county board, arising out of official actions of such supervisor, officer, employee or agent, then, in addition to the person named defendant in the case, on each supervisor and the county attorney, if the county has a county attorney, and if there be no county attorney, on the clerk of the county board.

Service under this section may be made by leaving a copy with the person in charge of the office of any officer designated in subdivisions 1 through 4.

Acts 1977, c. 617; Acts 1980, c. 732; Acts 1985, c. 416.

§ 8.01–301. How process served on foreign corporations generally

Subject to § 8.01–286.1, service of process on a foreign corporation may be effected in the following manner:

1. By personal service on any officer, director or on the registered agent of a foreign corporation which is authorized to do business in the Commonwealth, and by personal service on any agent of a foreign corporation transacting business in the Commonwealth without such authorization, wherever any such officer, director, or agents be found within the Commonwealth;

2. By substituted service on a foreign corporation in accordance with §§ 13.1–766 and 13.1–928, if such corporation is authorized to transact business or affairs within the Commonwealth;

3. By substituted service on a foreign corporation in accordance with § 8.01–329 or by service in accordance with § 8.01–320, where jurisdiction is authorized under § 8.01–328.1, regardless of whether such foreign corporation is authorized to transact business within the Commonwealth; or

4. By order of publication in accordance with §§ 8.01–316 and 8.01–317 where jurisdiction in rem or quasi in rem is authorized, regardless of whether the foreign corporation so served is authorized to transact business within the Commonwealth.

This section does not prescribe the only means, or necessarily the required means, of serving a foreign corporation.

Acts 1977, c. 617; Acts 1991, c. 672. Amended by Acts 2005, c. 866; Acts 2013, c. 113.

§ 8.01–302. Repealed by Acts 2002, c. 702

§ 8.01–303. On whom process served when corporation operated by trustee or receiver

Subject to § 8.01–286.1, when any corporation is operated by a trustee or by a receiver appointed by any court, in any action against such corporation, process may be served on its trustee or receiver; and if there is more than one such trustee or receiver, then service may be on any one of them. In the event that no service of process may be had on any such trustee or receiver, then process may be served by any other mode of service upon corporations authorized by this chapter.

Acts 1977, c. 617. Amended by Acts 2005, c. 866.

§ 8.01–304. How process served on copartner or partnership

Subject to § 8.01–286.1, process against a copartner or partnership may be served upon a general partner, and it shall be deemed service upon the partnership and upon each partner individually named in the action, provided the person served is not a plaintiff in the suit and provided the matter in suit is a partnership matter.

Provided further that process may be served upon a limited partner in any proceeding to enforce a limited partner's liability to the partnership.

Acts 1977, c. 617. Amended by Acts 2005, c. 866.

§ 8.01-305. Process against unincorporated associations or orders, or unincorporated common carriers

Subject to § 8.01-286.1, process against an unincorporated (i) association, (ii) order, or (iii) common carrier, may be served on any officer, trustee, director, staff member or other agent.

Acts 1977, c. 617. Amended by Acts 2005, c. 866.

§ 8.01-306. Process against unincorporated associations or orders, or unincorporated common carriers; principal office outside Virginia and business transactions in Virginia

Subject to § 8.01-286.1, if an unincorporated (i) association, (ii) order, or (iii) common carrier has its principal office outside Virginia and transacts business or affairs in the Commonwealth, process may be served on any officer, trustee, director, staff member, or agent of such association, order, or carrier in the city or county in which he may be found or on the clerk of the State Corporation Commission, who shall be deemed by virtue of such transaction of business or affairs in the Commonwealth to have been appointed statutory agent of such association, order, or carrier upon whom may be made service of process in accordance with § 12.1-19.1. Service, when duly made, shall constitute sufficient foundation for a personal judgment against such association, order or carrier. If service may not be had as aforesaid, then on affidavit of that fact an order of publication may be awarded as provided by §§ 8.01-316 and 8.01-317.

Acts 1977, c. 617; Acts 1991, c. 672. Amended by Acts 2005, c. 866.

§ 8.01-307. Definition of terms "motor vehicle" and "nonresident" in motor vehicle and aircraft accident cases

For the purpose of §§ 8.01-308 through 8.01-313:

1. The term "motor vehicle" shall mean every vehicle which is self-propelled or designed for self-propulsion and every vehicle drawn by or designed to be drawn by a motor vehicle and includes every device in, upon, or by which any person or property is or can be transported or drawn upon a highway, except devices moved by human or animal power and devices used exclusively upon stationary rails or tracks.

2. The term "nonresident" includes any person who, though a resident of the Commonwealth when the accident or collision specified in § 8.01-308 or § 8.01-309 occurred, has been continuously outside the Commonwealth for at least sixty days next preceding the date when process is left with the Commissioner of the Department of Motor Vehicles or the Secretary of the Commonwealth and includes any person against whom an order of publication may be issued under the provisions of § 8.01-316.

Acts 1977, c. 617.

§ 8.01-308. Service on Commissioner of the Department of Motor Vehicles as agent for nonresident motor vehicle operator

Any operation in the Commonwealth of a motor vehicle by a nonresident, including those nonresidents defined in subdivision 2 of § 8.01-307, either in person or by an agent or employee, shall be deemed equivalent to an appointment by such nonresident of the Commissioner of the Department of Motor Vehicles, and his successors in office, to be the attorney or statutory agent of such nonresident for the purpose of service of process in any action against him growing out of any accident or collision in which such nonresident, his agent, or his employee may be involved while operating motor vehicles in this Commonwealth. Acceptance by a nonresident of the rights and privileges conferred by Article 5 (§ 46.2-655 et seq.) of Chapter 6 of Title 46.2 shall have the same effect under this section as the operation of such motor vehicle, by such nonresident, his agent, or his employee.

Acts 1977, c. 617.

§ 8.01-309. Service on Secretary of Commonwealth as agent of nonresident operator or owner of aircraft

Any nonresident owner or operator of any aircraft that is operated over and above the land and waters of the Commonwealth or uses aviation facilities within the Commonwealth, shall by such operation and use appoint the Secretary of the Commonwealth as his statutory agent for the service of process in any action against him growing out of any accident or collision occurring within or above the Commonwealth in which such aircraft is involved.

Acts 1977, c. 617.

§ 8.01-310. How service made on Commissioner and Secretary; appointment binding

A. Service of process on either the Commissioner of the Department of Motor Vehicles as authorized under § 8.01-308 or on the Secretary of the Commonwealth as authorized under § 8.01-309 shall be made by the plaintiff or his agent or the sheriff leaving a copy of such process together with the fee for service of process on parties, in the amount prescribed in § 2.2-409, for each party to be thus served, in the hands, or in the office, of the Commissioner or the Secretary, and such service shall be sufficient upon the nonresident and shall be effective on the date when service is made on the Commissioner or the Secretary. All fees collected by the Commissioner pursuant to the provisions of this section shall be paid into the state treasury and shall be set aside as a special fund to be used to meet the expenses of the Department of Motor Vehicles.

B. Appointment of the Commissioner or Secretary as attorney or agent for the service of process on a nonresident under § 8.01-308 or 8.01-309 shall be irrevocable and binding upon the executor or other personal representative of such nonresident:

1. Where a nonresident has died before the commencement of an action against him regarding an accident or collision under § 8.01-308 or 8.01-309 shall be irrevocable and binding upon the executor or other personal representative of such nonresident; or

2. Where a nonresident dies after the commencement of an action against him regarding an accident or collision under § 8.01-308 or 8.01-309, the action shall continue and shall be irrevocable and binding upon his executor, administrator, or other personal representative with such additional notice of the pendency of the action as the court deems proper.

Acts 1977, c. 617; Acts 1987, c. 696; Acts 1992, c. 459; Acts 2000, c. 579. Amended by Acts 2013, c. 113.

§ 8.01-311. Continuance of action where service made on Commissioner or Secretary

The court, in which an action is pending against a nonresident growing out of an accident or collision as specified in §§ 8.01-308 and 8.01-309, may order such continuances as necessary to afford such nonresident reasonable opportunity to defend the action.

Acts 1977, c. 617.

§ 8.01-312. Effect of service on statutory agent; duties of such agent

A. Service of process on the statutory agent shall have the same legal force and validity as if served within the Commonwealth personally upon the person for whom it is intended. It shall be the duty of the statutory agent to:

1. Provide a receipt to a party seeking service who serves process on the statutory agent by hand delivery or any other method that does not provide a return of service or other means showing the date on which service on the statutory agent was accomplished. The party seeking service shall be responsible for filing such receipt in the office of the clerk of court in which the action is pending;

2. Forthwith send by registered or certified mail, with return receipt requested, a copy of the process to the person named therein and for whom the statutory agent is receiving the process; and

3. File an affidavit of compliance with this section with the papers in the action; this filing shall be made in the office of the clerk of the court in which the action is pending.

B. Unless otherwise provided by § 8.01-313 and subject to the provisions of § 8.01-316, the address for the mailing of the process required by this section shall be that as provided by the party seeking service.

C. The time for a nonresident to respond to process sent by the statutory agent shall run from the date when the affidavit of compliance is filed in the office of the clerk of the court in which the action is pending.

Acts 1977, c. 617. Amended by Acts 2013, c. 113.

§ 8.01-313. Specific addresses for mailing by statutory agent

A. For the statutory agent appointed pursuant to §§ 8.01-308 and 8.01-309, the address for the mailing of the process as required by § 8.01-312 shall be the last known address of the nonresident or, where appropriate under subdivision 1 or 2 of § 8.01-310 B, of the executor, administrator, or other personal representative of the nonresident. However, upon the filing of an affidavit by the plaintiff that he does not know and is unable with due diligence to ascertain any post-office address of such nonresident, service of process on the statutory agent shall be sufficient without the mailing otherwise required by this section. Provided further that:

1. In the case of a nonresident defendant licensed by the Commonwealth to operate a motor vehicle, the last address reported by such defendant to the Department of Motor Vehicles as his address on an application for or renewal of a driver's license shall be deemed to be the address of the defendant for the purpose of the mailing required by this section if no other address is known, and, in any case in which the affidavit provided for in § 8.01-316 of this chapter is filed, such a defendant, by so notifying the Department of such an address, and by failing to notify the Department of any change therein, shall be deemed to have appointed the Commissioner of the Department of Motor Vehicles his statutory agent for service of process in an action arising out of operation of a motor vehicle by him in the Commonwealth, and to have accepted as valid service such mailing to such address; or

2. In the case of a nonresident defendant not licensed by the Commonwealth to operate a motor vehicle, the address shown on the copy of the report of accident required by § 46.2-372 filed by or for him with the Department, and on file at the office of the Department, or the address reported by such a defendant to any state or local police officer, or sheriff investigating the accident sued on, if no other address is known, shall be conclusively presumed to be a valid address of such defendant for the purpose of the mailing provided for in this section, and his so reporting of an incorrect address, or his moving from the address so reported without making provision for forwarding to him of mail directed thereto, shall be deemed to be a waiver of notice and a consent to and acceptance of service of process served upon the Commissioner of the Department of Motor Vehicles as provided in this section.

B. For the statutory agent appointed pursuant to § 64.2-1426, the address for the mailing of process as required by § 8.01-312 shall be the address of the fiduciary's statutory agent as contained in the written consent most recently filed with the clerk of the circuit court wherein the qualification of such fiduciary was had or, in the event of the death, removal, resignation or absence from the Commonwealth of such statutory agent, or in the event that such statutory agent cannot with due diligence be found at such address, the address of the clerk of such circuit court.

Acts 1977, c. 617; Acts 1983, c. 467; Acts 1984, c. 780; Acts 1991, c. 672.

§ 8.01–314. Service on attorney after entry of general appearance by such attorney

When an attorney authorized to practice law in this Commonwealth has entered a general appearance for any party, any process, order or other legal papers to be used in the proceeding may be served on such attorney of record. Such service shall have the same effect as if service had been made upon such party personally; provided, however, that in any proceeding in which a final decree or order has been entered, service on an attorney as provided herein shall not be sufficient to constitute personal jurisdiction over a party in any proceeding citing that party for contempt, either civil or criminal, unless personal service is also made on the party.

Provided, further, that if such attorney objects by motion within five days after such legal paper has been so served upon him, the court shall enter an order in the proceeding directing the manner of service of such legal paper.

Acts 1977, c. 617; Acts 1981, c. 495.

§ 8.01–315. Notice to be mailed defendant when service accepted by another

No judgment shall be rendered upon, or by virtue of, any instrument in writing authorizing the acceptance of service of process by another on behalf of any person who is obligated upon such instrument, when such service is accepted as therein authorized, unless the person accepting service shall have made and filed with the court an affidavit showing that he mailed or caused to be mailed to the defendant at his last known post-office address at least ten days before such judgment is to be rendered a notice stating the time when and place where the entry of such judgment would be requested.

Acts 1977, c. 617.

§ 8.01–316. Service by publication; when available

A. Except in condemnation actions, an order of publication may be entered against a defendant in the following manner:

1. An affidavit by a party seeking service stating one or more of the following grounds:

a. That the party to be served is (i) a foreign corporation, (ii) a foreign unincorporated association, order, or a foreign unincorporated common carrier, or (iii) a nonresident individual, other than a nonresident individual fiduciary who has appointed a statutory agent under § 64.2–1426; or

b. That diligence has been used without effect to ascertain the location of the party to be served; or

c. That the last known residence of the party to be served was in the county or city in which service is sought and that a return has been filed by the sheriff that the process has been in his hands for twenty-one days and that he has been unable to make service; or

2. In any action, when a pleading (i) states that there are or may be persons, whose names are unknown, interested in the subject to be divided or disposed of; (ii) briefly describes the nature of such interest; and (iii) makes such persons defendants by the general description of "parties unknown"; or

3. In any action, when (i) the number of defendants upon whom process has been served exceeds ten and (ii) it appears by a pleading, or exhibit filed, that such defendants represent like interests with the parties not served with process.

Under subdivisions 1 and 2 of this subsection, the order of publication may be entered by the clerk of the court. Under this subdivision such order may be entered only by the court. However, any orders not properly entered, but processed by a clerk prior to July 1, 2010, shall be deemed to have been properly entered.

Every affidavit for an order of publication shall state the last known post office address of the party against whom publication is asked, or if such address is unknown, the affidavit shall state that fact.

B. The cost of such publication shall be paid initially by the party seeking service; however, such costs ultimately may be recoverable pursuant to § 17.1–601.

Acts 1977, c. 617; Acts 1982, c. 384; Acts 1983, c. 467; Acts 1996, c. 352; Acts 1999, c. 353. Amended by Acts 2010, c. 827.

§ 8.01–317. What order of publication to state; how published; when publication in newspaper dispensed with

Except in condemnation actions, every order of publication shall give the abbreviated style of the suit, state briefly its object, and require the defendants, or unknown parties, against whom it is entered to appear and protect their interests on or before the date stated in the order which shall be no sooner than fifty days after entry of the order of publication. Such order of publication shall be published once each week for four successive weeks in such newspaper as the court may prescribe, or, if none be so prescribed, as the clerk may direct, and shall be posted at the front door of the courthouse wherein the court is held; also a copy of such order of publication shall be mailed to each of the defendants at the post office address given in the affidavit required by § 8.01–316. The clerk shall cause copies of the order to be so posted, mailed, and transmitted to the designated newspaper within twenty days after the entry of the order of publication. Upon completion of such publication, the clerk shall file a certificate in the papers of the case that the requirements of this section have been complied with. Provided, the court may, in any case where deemed proper, dispense with such publication in a newspaper. The cost of such publication shall be paid by the petitioner or applicant.

Acts 1977, c. 617; Acts 1982, c. 384; Acts 1996, c. 352; Acts 1996, c. 710.

§ 8.01–318. Within what time after publication case tried or heard; no subsequent publication required

If after an order of publication has been executed, the defendants or unknown parties against whom it is entered shall not appear on or before the date specified in such order, the case may be tried or heard as to them. When the provisions of § 8.01–317, or, if applicable, the provisions of § 8.01–321, have been complied with, no other publication or notice shall thereafter be required in any proceeding in court, or before a commissioner, or for the purpose of taking depositions, unless specifically ordered by the court as to such defendants or unknown parties.

Acts 1977, c. 617.

§ 8.01–319. Publication of interim notice

A. In any case in which a nonresident party or party originally served by publication has been served as provided by law, and notice of further proceedings in the case is required but no method of service thereof is prescribed either by statute or by order or rule of court, such notice may be served by publication thereof once each week for two successive weeks in a newspaper published or circulated in the city or county in which the original proceedings are pending. If the original proceedings were instituted by order of publication, then the publication of such notice of additional or further proceedings shall be made in the same newspaper. A party, who appears pro se in an action, shall file with the clerk of the court in which the action is pending a written statement of his place of residence and mailing address, and shall inform the clerk in writing of any changes of residence and mailing address during the pendency of the action. The clerk and all parties to the action may rely on the last written statement filed as aforesaid. The court in which the action is pending may dispense with such notice for failure of the party to file the statement herein provided for or may require notice to be given in such manner as the court may determine.

B. Notwithstanding any provision to the contrary in paragraph A hereof, depositions may be taken, testimony heard and orders and decrees entered without an order of publication, when the defendant has been legally served with or has accepted service of process to commence a suit for divorce or for annulling or affirming a marriage, and he or she or the plaintiff:

1. Shall thereafter become a nonresident; or

2. Shall remove from the county or city in which the suit is pending, if a resident thereof, or in which he or she resided at the time of the institution of the suit, or was served with process, without having filed with the clerk of the court where the suit is pending a written statement of his or her intended future place of residence, and a like statement of subsequent changes of residence; or

3. When after such written statement has been filed with the clerk, notice shall have been served upon him or her at the last place of residence given in the written statement as provided by law; or

4. Could not be found by the sheriff of the county or city for the service of the notice, and the party sending the service makes affidavit that he has used due diligence to find the adverse party without success. If such absent party has an attorney of record in such suit, notice shall be served on such attorney, as provided by § 8.01–314.

C. This section shall not apply to orders of publication in condemnation actions.

Acts 1977, c. 617; Acts 1978, c. 676; Acts 1979, c. 464; Acts 1982, c. 384.

§ 8.01–320. Personal service outside of Virginia

A. Subject to § 8.01–286.1, service of a process on a nonresident person outside the Commonwealth may be made by: (i) any person authorized to serve process in the jurisdiction where the party to be served is located; or (ii) any person 18 years of age or older who is not a party or otherwise interested in the subject matter of the controversy and notwithstanding any other provision of law to the contrary, such person need not be authorized by the circuit court to serve process which commences divorce or annulment actions. When the court can exercise jurisdiction over the nonresident pursuant to § 8.01–328.1, such service shall have the same effect as personal service on the nonresident within Virginia. Such service when no jurisdiction can be exercised pursuant to § 8.01–328.1, or service in accordance with the provisions of subdivision 2 a of § 8.01–296 shall have the same effect, and no other, as an order of publication duly executed, or the publication of a copy of process under this chapter, as the case may be; however, depositions may be taken at any time after 21 days' notice of the taking of the depositions has been personally served. The person so served shall be in default upon his failure to file a pleading in response to original process within 21 days after such service. If no responsive pleading is filed within the time allowed by law, the case may proceed without service of any additional pleadings, including the notice of the taking of depositions.

B. Any personal service of process outside of this Commonwealth executed in such manner as is provided for in this section prior or subsequent to October 1, 1977, in a divorce or annulment action is hereby validated. Personal service of process outside this

Commonwealth in a divorce or annulment action may be executed as provided in this section.

Acts 1977, c. 617; Acts 1978, c. 90; Acts 1981, c. 6; Acts 1983, c. 402; Acts 1984, c. 18; Acts 1985, c. 177; Acts 1986, c. 263; Acts 1987, c. 594; Acts 1997, c. 754. Amended by Acts 2005, c. 866.

§ 8.01–321. Orders of publication in proceedings to enforce liens for taxes assessed upon real estate

Whenever an order of publication is entered in any proceeding brought by any county, city or town to enforce a lien for taxes assessed upon real estate, such order need not be published more than once a week for two successive weeks. The party served by publication shall be required to appear and protect his interest by the date stated in the order of publication which shall be not less than twenty-four days after entry of such order. The publication shall in other respects conform to § 8.01–317, and when such publication so conforms, the provisions of § 8.01–318 shall apply.

Acts 1977, c. 617.

§ 8.01–322. Within what time case reheard on petition of party served by publication, and any injustice corrected

If a party against whom service by publication is had under this chapter did not appear before the date of judgment against him, then such party or his representative may petition to have the case reheard, may plead or answer, and may have any injustice in the proceeding corrected within the following time and not after:

1. Within two years after the rendition of such judgment, decree or order; but

2. If the party has been served with a copy of such judgment, decree, or order more than a year before the end of such two-year period, then within one year of such service.

For the purpose of subdivision 2 of this section, service may be made in any manner provided in this chapter except by order of publication, but including personal or substituted service on the party to be served, and personal service out of the Commonwealth by any person of eighteen years or older and who is not a party or otherwise interested in the subject matter in controversy.

Acts 1977, c. 617.

§ 8.01–323. In what counties city newspapers deemed published for purpose of legal advertisements

Any newspaper published in a city adjoining or wholly or partly within the geographical limits of any county shall be deemed to be published in such county or counties as well as in such city, for the purpose of legal advertisements.

Acts 1977, c. 617.

§ 8.01–324. Newspapers which may be used for legal notices and publications

A. Whenever any ordinance, resolution, notice, or advertisement is required by law to be published in a newspaper, such newspaper, in addition to any qualifications otherwise required by law, shall:

1. Have a bona fide list of paying subscribers;

2. Have been published and circulated at least once a week for twenty-four consecutive weeks without interruption for the dissemination of news of a general or legal character;

3. Have a general circulation in the area in which the notice is required to be published;

4. Be printed in the English language; and

5. Have a second-class mailing permit issued by the United States Postal Service.

B. However, a newspaper which does not have a second-class mailing permit may petition the circuit court for the jurisdiction in which the newspaper is located for authority to publish ordinances, resolutions, notices or advertisements. Prior to filing the petition, the newspaper shall publish a notice of intention to file a petition pursuant to this section in a newspaper published or having general circulation in the jurisdiction in which the petition will be filed. The court shall grant the authority for a period of one year upon finding that the newspaper (i) meets the requirements of subdivisions A 2, A 3, and A 4; (ii) has been continually published for at least one year, employs a full-time news staff, reports local current events and governmental meetings, has an editorial page, accepts letters to the editor and is, in general, a news forum for the community in which it is circulated; (iii) has a circulation within the community to which the publication is directed and maintains permanent records of the fact and substance of the publication; and (iv) has an audit of circulation certified by an independent auditing firm or a business recognized in the newspaper industry as a circulation auditor. The authority shall be continued for successive one-year periods upon the filing of an affidavit certifying that the newspaper continues to meet the requirements of this subsection.

C. If a county with a population of less than 15,000 had regularly advertised its ordinances, resolutions, notices in a newspaper published in the county which had a general circulation in the county, a bona fide list of paying subscribers, a second class mailing permit and the newspaper continued to be published in the county and continued to have a general circulation in the county but failed to maintain its bona fide list of paying subscribers and its second class mailing permit, any advertisement of ordinances, resolutions, notices in the newspaper by the county shall be deemed to have been in compliance with this section.

Acts 1977, c. 617; Acts 1983, c. 297; Acts 1989, c. 611; Acts 1992, c. 392; Acts 1992, c. 537; Acts 1992, c. 719. Amended by Acts 2007, c. 183; Acts 2007, c. 603.

§ 8.01-325. Return by person serving process

Unless otherwise directed by the court, the person serving process shall make return thereof to the clerk's office within seventy-two hours of service, except when such return would be due on a Saturday, Sunday, or legal holiday. In such case, the return is due on the next day following such Saturday, Sunday, or legal holiday. The process shall state thereon the date and manner of service and the name of the party served.

Proof of service shall be in the following manner:

1. If service by sheriff, the form of the return of such sheriff as provided by the Rules of the Supreme Court; or

2. If service by any other person qualified under § 8.01-293, whether service made in or out of the Commonwealth, his affidavit of such qualifications; the date and manner of service and the name of the party served; and stamped, typed, or printed on the return of process, an annotation that the service was by a private server, and the name, address, and telephone number of the server; or

3. In case of service by publication, the affidavit of the publisher or his agent giving the dates of publication and an accompanying copy of the published order.

Acts 1977, c. 617; Acts 1996, c. 538.

§ 8.01-326. Return as proof of service

No return shall be conclusive proof as to service of process. The return of a sheriff shall be prima facie evidence of the facts therein stated, and the return of a qualified individual under subdivision 2 of § 8.01-293 shall be evidence of the facts stated therein.

Acts 1977, c. 617.

§ 8.01-326.1. Service of process or notice on statutory agent; copy to be sent to defendant and certificate filed with court; effective date of service

Any statutory agent who has been served with process or notice shall forthwith mail a copy of such process or notice to the person or persons to be served at the last known post office address of such person and file a certificate of compliance with the papers in the action. Service of process or notice on a statutory agent shall be effective as of the date the certificate of compliance is filed with the clerk of the court in which the action or suit is pending.

Acts 1990, c. 741.

§ 8.01-327. Acceptance of service of process

Service of process may be accepted by the person for whom it is intended by signing the proof of service and indicating the jurisdiction and state in which it was accepted. However, service of process in divorce or annulment actions may be accepted only as provided in § 20-99.1:1.

Acts 1977, c. 617; Acts 1987, c. 594; Acts 1988, c. 583; Acts 1988, c. 642.

Article 5

Privilege From Civil Arrest

§ 8.01-327.1. Definition of "arrest under civil process"

The terms "arrest under civil process" and "civil arrest" shall be synonymous and shall be the apprehending and detaining of a person pursuant to specific provisions of this title to achieve the following:

1. A full and proper answer or response to interrogatories under § 8.01-506;

2. His obedience to the orders, judgments, and decrees of any court.

Acts 1977, c. 617; Acts 1984, c. 93.

§ 8.01-327.2. Who are privileged from arrest under civil process

In addition to the exemptions made by §§ 30-4, 30-6, 30-7, 30-8, 19.2-280, and 44-97, the following persons shall not be arrested, apprehended, or detained under any civil process during the times respectively herein set forth, but shall not otherwise be privileged from service of civil process by this section:

1. The President of the United States, and the Governor of the Commonwealth at all times during their terms of office;

2. The Lieutenant Governor of the Commonwealth during attendance at sessions of the General Assembly and while going to and from such sessions;

3. Members of either house of the Congress of the United States during the session of Congress and for fifteen days next before the beginning and after the ending of any session, and during any time that they are serving on any committee or performing any other service under an order or request of either house of Congress;

4. A judge, grand juror or witness, required by lawful authority to attend any court or place, during such attendance and while going to and from such court or place;

5. Members of the National Guard while going to, attending at, or returning from, any muster or court-martial;

6. Ministers of the gospel while engaged in performing religious services in a place where a congregation is assembled and while going to and returning from such place; and

7. Voters going to, attending at, or returning from an election. Such privilege shall only be on the days of such attendance.

Acts 1977, c. 617. Amended by Acts 2015, c. 221.

CHAPTER 9

PERSONAL JURISDICTION IN CERTAIN ACTIONS

§ 8.01–328. Person defined

As used in this chapter, "person" includes an individual, his executor, administrator, or other personal representative, or a corporation, partnership, association or any other legal or commercial entity, whether or not a citizen or domiciliary of this Commonwealth and whether or not organized under the laws of this Commonwealth.

Acts 1977, c. 617.

§ 8.01–328.1. When personal jurisdiction over person may be exercised

A. A court may exercise personal jurisdiction over a person, who acts directly or by an agent, as to a cause of action arising from the person's:

1. Transacting any business in this Commonwealth;

2. Contracting to supply services or things in this Commonwealth;

3. Causing tortious injury by an act or omission in this Commonwealth;

4. Causing tortious injury in this Commonwealth by an act or omission outside this Commonwealth if he regularly does or solicits business, or engages in any other persistent course of conduct, or derives substantial revenue from goods used or consumed or services rendered, in this Commonwealth;

5. Causing injury in this Commonwealth to any person by breach of warranty expressly or impliedly made in the sale of goods outside this Commonwealth when he might reasonably have expected such person to use, consume, or be affected by the goods in this Commonwealth, provided that he also regularly does or solicits business, or engages in any other persistent course of conduct, or derives substantial revenue from goods used or consumed or services rendered in this Commonwealth;

6. Having an interest in, using, or possessing real property in this Commonwealth;

7. Contracting to insure any person, property, or risk located within this Commonwealth at the time of contracting;

8. Having (i) executed an agreement in this Commonwealth which obligates the person to pay spousal support or child support to a domiciliary of this Commonwealth, or to a person who has satisfied the residency requirements in suits for annulments or divorce for members of the armed forces or foreign service officers of the United States pursuant to § 20–97 provided proof of service of process on a nonresident party is made by a law-enforcement officer or other person authorized to serve process in the jurisdiction where the nonresident party is located, (ii) been ordered to pay spousal support or child support pursuant to an order entered by any court of competent jurisdiction in this Commonwealth having in personam jurisdiction over such person, or (iii) shown by personal conduct in this Commonwealth, as alleged by affidavit, that the person conceived or fathered a child in this Commonwealth;

9. Having maintained within this Commonwealth a matrimonial domicile at the time of separation of the parties upon which grounds for divorce or separate maintenance is based, or at the time a cause of action arose for divorce or separate maintenance or at the time of commencement of such suit, if the other party to the matrimonial relationship resides herein; or

10. Having incurred a liability for taxes, fines, penalties, interest, or other charges to any political subdivision of the Commonwealth.

Jurisdiction in subdivision 9 is valid only upon proof of service of process pursuant to § 8.01–296 on the nonresident party by a person authorized under the provisions of § 8.01–320. Jurisdiction under subdivision 8 (iii) of this subsection is valid only upon proof of personal service on a nonresident pursuant to § 8.01–320.

B. Using a computer or computer network located in the Commonwealth shall constitute an act in the Commonwealth. For purposes of this subsection, "use" and "computer network" shall have the same meanings as those contained in § 18.2–152.2.

C. When jurisdiction over a person is based solely upon this section, only a cause of action arising from acts enumerated in this section may be asserted against him; however, nothing contained in this chapter shall limit, restrict or otherwise affect the jurisdiction of any court of this Commonwealth over foreign corporations which are subject to service of process pursuant to the provisions of any other statute.

Acts 1977, c. 617; Acts 1978, c. 132; Acts 1981, c. 6; Acts 1982, c. 313; Acts 1983, c. 428; Acts 1984, c. 609; Acts 1986, c. 275; Acts 1987, c. 594; Acts 1988, c. 866; Acts 1988, c. 878; Acts 1992, c. 571; Acts 1999, c. 886; Acts 1999, c. 904; Acts 1999, c. 905; Acts 2001, c. 221. Amended by Acts 2007, c. 533; Acts 2009, c. 582.

§ 8.01–329. Service of process or notice; service on Secretary of Commonwealth

A. When the exercise of personal jurisdiction is authorized by this chapter, service of process or notice may be made in the same manner as is provided for in Chapter 8 (§ 8.01–285 et seq.) in any other case in which personal jurisdiction is exercised over such a party, or process or notice may be served on any agent of such person in the county or city in the Commonwealth in which that agent resides or on the Secretary of the Commonwealth of Virginia, hereinafter referred to in this section as the "Secretary," who, for this purpose, shall be deemed to be the statutory agent of such person.

B. When service is to be made on the Secretary, the party or his agent or attorney seeking service shall file an affidavit with the court, stating either (i) that the person to be served is a nonresident or (ii) that, after exercising due diligence, the party seeking service has been unable to locate the person to be served. In either case, such affidavit shall set forth the last known address of the person to be served. For the mailing, by the clerk to the party or his agent or attorney, in accordance with subsection C, of verification of the effective date of service of process, the person filing an affidavit may leave a self-addressed, stamped envelope with the clerk.

When the person to be served is a resident, the signature of an attorney, party or agent of the person seeking service on such affidavit shall constitute a certificate by him that process has been delivered to the sheriff or to a disinterested person as permitted by § 8.01–293 for execution and, if the sheriff or disinterested person was unable to execute such service, that the person seeking service has made a bona fide attempt to determine the actual place of abode or location of the person to be served.

C. Service of such process or notice on the Secretary shall be made by the plaintiff's, his agent's or the sheriff's leaving a copy of the process or notice, together with a copy of the affidavit called for in subsection B and the fee prescribed in § 2.2–409 in the office of the Secretary in the City of Richmond, Virginia. Service of process or notice on the Secretary may be made by mail if such service otherwise meets the requirements of this section. Such service shall be sufficient upon the person to be served and shall be effective on the date when service is made on the Secretary. It shall be the duty of the Secretary to:

1. Provide a receipt to a party seeking service who serves process on the Secretary by hand delivery or any other method that does not provide a return of service or other means showing the date on which service on the Secretary was accomplished. The party seeking service shall be responsible for filing such receipt in the office of the clerk of the court in which the action is pending;

2. Forthwith send by certified mail, return receipt requested, to the person or persons to be served at the last known post-office address of such person notice of such service, a copy of the process or notice, and a copy of the affidavit; and

3. Forthwith file with the papers in the action a certificate of compliance herewith by the Secretary or someone designated by him for that purpose and having knowledge of such compliance.

Upon receipt of the certificate of compliance, the clerk of the court shall mail verification of the date the certificate of compliance was filed with the court to the person who filed the affidavit required by subsection B, in the self-addressed, stamped envelope, if any, provided to the clerk at the time of filing of the affidavit. The clerk shall not be required to mail verification unless the self-addressed, stamped envelope has been provided. The time for the person to be served to respond to process sent by the Secretary shall run from the date when the certificate of compliance is filed in the office of the clerk of the court in which the action is pending.

D. Service of process in actions brought on a warrant or motion for judgment pursuant to § 16.1–79 or 16.1–81 shall be void and of no effect when such service of process is received by the Secretary within ten days of any return day set by the warrant. In such cases, the Secretary shall return the process or notice, the copy of the affidavit, and the prescribed fee to the plaintiff or his agent. A copy of the notice of the rejection shall be sent to the clerk of the court in which the action was filed.

E. The Secretary shall maintain a record of each notice of service sent to a person for a period of two years. The record maintained by the Secretary shall include the name of the plaintiff or the person seeking service, the name of the person to be served, the date service was received by the Secretary, the date notice of service was forwarded to the person to be served, and the date the certificate of compliance was sent by the Secretary to the appropriate court. The Secretary shall not be required to maintain any other records pursuant to this section.

Acts 1977, c. 617; Acts 1979, c. 31; Acts 1986, c. 388; Acts 1987, c. 449; Acts 1987, c. 450; Acts 1987, c. 459; Acts 1990, c. 741; Acts 1998, c. 259; Acts 2001, c. 29. Amended by Acts 2013, c. 113.

§ 8.01–330. Jurisdiction on any other basis authorized

A court of this State may exercise jurisdiction on any other basis authorized by law.

Acts 1977, c. 617.

CHAPTER 10

DOCKETS

§ 8.01–331. Entry of cases on current dockets

When any civil action is commenced in a circuit court, or any such action is removed to such court and the required writ tax and fees thereon paid, the clerk shall enter the same in the civil docket. These dockets may be either (i) a substantial, well-bound loose-leaf book, (ii) a visible card index or (iii) automated data processing media. Each case shall be entered on the civil docket, on which shall be entered:

1. The short style of the suit or action,
2. The names of the attorneys,
3. The nature of the suit or action, and
4. The date filed and case file number.

In addition the docket may contain the following information applicable in an individual case as deemed appropriate:

1. The names of the parties,
2. The date of the issuance of process,
3. A memorandum of the service of process,
4. A memorandum of the orders and proceedings in the case, and
5. The hearing date(s) and type(s) of hearing(s) conducted on such date(s).

The clerk may enter the clerk's fees in the case on such docket instead of in the fee book.

Cases appealed from the juvenile and domestic relations district courts shall be docketed as provided in this section and, to the extent inconsistent with this section, § 16.1–302.

Acts 1977, c. 617; Acts 1983, c. 293; Acts 1990, c. 258. Amended by Acts 2005, c. 681, eff. Jan. 1, 2006.

§ 8.01–332. Calling current docket

The current docket may be called for the purpose of fixing cases for trial, on such days or at such intervals as may be directed by order of court.

Acts 1977, c. 617.

§ 8.01–333. Reserved

§ 8.01–334. Repealed by Acts 1983, c. 293

§ 8.01–335. Certain cases struck from dockets after certain period; reinstatement

A. Except as provided in subsection C, any court in which is pending an action, wherein for more than two years there has been no order or proceeding, except to continue it, may, in its discretion, order it to be struck from its docket and the action shall thereby be discontinued. However, no case shall be discontinued if either party requests that it be continued. The court shall thereafter enter a pretrial order pursuant to Rule 4:13 [1] controlling the subsequent course of the case to ensure a timely resolution of that case. If the court thereafter finds that the case has not been timely prosecuted pursuant to its pretrial order, it may strike the case from its docket. The clerk of the court shall notify the parties in interest if known, or their counsel of record at his last known address, at least fifteen days before the entry of such order of discontinuance so that all parties may have an opportunity to be heard on it. Any case discontinued under the provisions of this subsection may be reinstated, on motion, after notice to the parties in interest if known or their counsel of record, within one year from the date of such order but not after.

B. Any court in which is pending a case wherein for more than three years there has been no order or proceeding, except to continue it, may, in its discretion, order it to be struck from its docket and the action shall thereby be discontinued. The court may dismiss cases under this subsection without any notice to the parties. The clerk shall provide the parties with a copy of the final order discontinuing or dismissing the case. Any case discontinued or dismissed under the provisions of this subsection may be reinstated, on motion, after notice to the parties in interest, if known, or their counsel of record within one year from the date of such order but not after.

C. If a civil action is pending in a circuit court on appeal from a general district court and (i) an appeal bond has been furnished by or on behalf of any party against whom judgment has been rendered for money or property and (ii) for more than one year there has been no order or proceeding, except to continue the matter, the action may, upon notice to the parties in accordance with subsection A, be dismissed and struck from the docket of the court. Upon dismissal pursuant to this subsection, the judgment of the general district court shall stand and the appeal bond shall be forfeited after application of any funds needed to satisfy the judgment.

D. Any court in which is pending a case wherein process has not been served within one year of the commencement of the case may, in its discretion, order it to be struck from the docket, and the action shall thereby be discontinued. The clerk of the court shall notify the plaintiff or his counsel of record at his last known address at least 30 days before the entry of an order of discontinuance so that the plaintiff may have an opportunity to show that service has been timely effected on the defendant or that due diligence has been exercised to have service timely effected on the defendant. Upon finding that service has been timely effected or that due diligence has been exercised to have service timely effected, the court shall maintain the action on the docket and, if service has not been timely effected but due diligence to effect service has been exercised, shall require the plaintiff to attempt service in any manner permitted under Chapter 8 (§ 8.01–285 et seq.) of this title. Nothing herein shall prevent the plaintiff from filing a nonsuit under § 8.01–380 before the entry of a discontinuance order pursuant to the provisions of this subsection. Nothing in this subsection shall apply to asbestos litigation.

Acts 1977, c. 617; Acts 1990, c. 730; Acts 1992, c. 532; Acts 1992, c. 792; Acts 1992, c. 803; Acts 1992, c. 835; Acts 1994, c. 517; Acts 1997, c. 680; Acts 1999, c. 652. Amended by Acts 2007, c. 498.

1 Supreme Court Rule 4:13.

CHAPTER 11

JURIES

ARTICLE 1

WHEN JURY TRIAL MAY BE HAD

§ 8.01–336. Jury trial of right; waiver of jury trial; court-ordered jury trial; trial by jury of plea in equity; equitable claim

A. The right of trial by jury as declared in Article I, Section 11 of the Constitution of Virginia and by statutes thereof shall be preserved inviolate to the parties. Unless waived, any demand for a trial by jury in a civil case made in compliance with the Rules of Supreme Court of Virginia shall be sufficient, with no further notice, hearing, or order, to proceed thereon.

B. Waiver of jury trial.—In any action at law in which the recovery sought is greater than $20, exclusive of interest, unless one of the parties demands that the case or any issue thereof be tried by a jury, or in a criminal action in which trial by jury is dispensed with as provided by law, the whole matter of law and fact may be heard and judgment given by the court.

C. Court-ordered jury trial.—Notwithstanding any provision in this Code to the contrary, in any action asserting a claim at law in which there has been no demand for trial by jury by any party, a circuit court may on its own motion direct one or more issues, including an issue of damages, to be tried by a jury.

D. Trial by jury of plea in equity.—In any action in which a plea has been filed to an equitable claim, and the allegations of such plea are denied by the plaintiff, either party may have the issue tried by jury.

E. Suit on equitable claim.—In any suit on an equitable claim, the court may, of its own motion or upon motion of any party, supported by such party's affidavit that the case will be rendered doubtful by conflicting evidence of another party, direct an issue to be tried before an advisory jury.

Acts 1977, c. 617. Amended by Acts 2005, c. 681, eff. Jan. 1, 2006; Acts 2014, c. 172.

ARTICLE 2

JURORS

§ 8.01–337. Who liable to serve as jurors

All citizens over 18 years of age who have been residents of the Commonwealth one year, and of the county, city, or town in which they reside six months next preceding their being summoned to serve as such, and competent in other respects, except as hereinafter provided, shall be liable to serve as jurors. No person shall be deemed incompetent to serve on any jury because of blindness or partial blindness. Military personnel of the United States Army, Air Force, Marine Corps, Coast Guard, or Navy shall not be considered residents of this Commonwealth by reason of their being stationed herein.

Acts 1977, c. 617; Acts 1987, c. 189. Amended by Acts 2014, c. 595.

§ 8.01–338. Who disqualified

The following persons shall be disqualified from serving as jurors:

1. Persons adjudicated incapacitated;

2. Persons convicted of treason or a felony; or

3. Any other person under a disability as defined in § 8.01–2 and not included in subdivisions 1 or 2 above.

Acts 1977, c. 617; Acts 1997, c. 801, eff. Jan. 1, 1998.

§ 8.01–339. No person eligible for whom request is made

No person shall be eligible to serve on any jury when he, or any person for him, solicits or requests a jury commissioner to place his name in a jury box or in any way designate such person as a juror.

Acts 1977, c. 617.

§ 8.01–340. No person to serve who has case at that term

No person shall be admitted to serve as a juror at a term of a court during which he has any matter of

controversy which has been or is expected to be tried by a jury during the same term.
Acts 1977, c. 617.

§ 8.01–341. Who are exempt from jury service

The following shall be exempt from serving on juries in civil and criminal cases:

1. The President and Vice President of the United States,

2. The Governor, Lieutenant Governor and Attorney General of the Commonwealth,

3. The members of both houses of Congress,

4. The members of the General Assembly, while in session or during a period when the member would be entitled to a legislative continuance as a matter of right under § 30–5,

5. Licensed practicing attorneys,

6. The judge of any court, members of the State Corporation Commission, members of the Virginia Workers' Compensation Commission, and magistrates,

7. Sheriffs, deputy sheriffs, state police, and police in counties, cities and towns,

8. The superintendent of the penitentiary and his assistants and the persons composing the guard,

9. Superintendents and jail officers, as defined in § 53.1–1, of regional jails.

Acts 1977, c. 458; Acts 1977, c. 617; Acts 1978, c. 176; Acts 1978, c. 340; Acts 1980, c. 535; Acts 1982, c. 315; Acts 1987, c. 256; Acts 1990, c. 758; Acts 1993, c. 572; Acts 1998, c. 83.

§ 8.01–341.1. Exemptions from jury service upon request

Any of the following persons may serve on juries in civil and criminal cases but shall be exempt from jury service upon his request:

1. through 3. Repealed.

4. A mariner actually employed in maritime service;

5. through 7. Repealed.

8. A person who has legal custody of and is necessarily and personally responsible for a child or children 16 years of age or younger requiring continuous care by him during normal court hours, or any mother who is breast-feeding a child;

9. A person who is necessarily and personally responsible for a person having a physical or mental impairment requiring continuous care by him during normal court hours;

10. Any person over 70 years of age;

11. Any person whose spouse is summoned to serve on the same jury panel;

12. Any person who is the only person performing services for a business, commercial or agricultural enterprise and whose services are so essential to the operations of the business, commercial or agricultural enterprise that such enterprise must close or cease to function if such person is required to perform jury duty;

13. Any person who is the only person performing services for a political subdivision as a firefighter, as defined in § 65.2–102, and whose services are so essential to the operations of the political subdivision that such political subdivision will suffer an undue hardship in carrying out such services if such person is required to perform jury duty;

14. Any person employed by the Office of the Clerk of the House of Delegates, the Office of the Clerk of the Senate, the Division of Legislative Services, and the Division of Legislative Automated Systems ; however, this exemption shall apply only to jury service starting (i) during the period beginning 60 days prior to the day any regular session commences and ending 30 days after the day of adjournment of such session and (ii) during the period beginning seven days prior to the day any reconvened or special session commences and ending seven days after the day of adjournment of such session;

15. Any general registrar, member of a local electoral board, or person appointed or employed by either the general registrar or the local electoral board, except officers of election appointed pursuant to Article 5 (§ 24.2–115 et seq.) of Chapter 1 of Title 24.2; however, this exemption shall apply only to jury service starting (i) during the period beginning 90 days prior to any election and continuing through election day, (ii) during the period to ascertain the results of the election and continuing for 10 days after the local electoral board certifies the results of the election under § 24.2–671 or the State Board of Elections certifies the results of the election under § 24.2–679, or (iii) during the period of an election recount or contested election pursuant to Chapter 8 (§ 24.2–800 et seq.) of Title 24.2. Any officer of election shall be exempt from jury service only on election day and during the periods set forth in clauses (ii) and (iii); and

16. Any member of the armed services of the United States or the diplomatic service of the United States appointed under the Foreign Service Act (22 U.S.C. § 3901 et seq.) who will be serving outside of the United States at the time of such jury service.

Acts 1977, c. 458; Acts 1987, c. 256; Acts 1997, c. 693; Acts 1999, c. 153. Amended by Acts 2004, c. 106; Acts 2005, c. 195; Acts 2011, c. 389; Acts 2011, c. 708; Acts 2012, c. 98.

§ 8.01–341.2. Deferral or limitation of jury service for particular occupational inconvenience

The court, on its own motion, may exempt any person from jury service for a particular term of court, or limit that person's service to particular dates of that term, if serving on a jury during that term or certain dates of that term of court would cause such person a particular occupational inconvenience. Any such person who is selected for jury service, and who is exempted under the provisions of this section, shall not be discharged from his obligation to serve on a jury, but such obligation shall only be deferred until the term of court next after such particular occupational inconvenience shall end.

Acts 1981, c. 108; Acts 1987, c. 155.

§ 8.01–342. Restrictions on amount of jury service permitted

A. The jury commissioners shall not include on the jury list provided for in § 8.01–345 the name of any person who has been called and reported to any state court for jury duty at any time during the period of three years next preceding the date of completion of such jury list.

B. If such person has been called and reported for jury duty in the trial of any case, either civil or criminal, at any one term of a court, he shall not be permitted to serve as a juror in any civil or criminal case, at any other term of that court during the three-year period set forth in subsection A of this section, unless all the persons whose names are in the jury box have been drawn to serve during such three-year period; however, such person shall be permitted to serve on any special jury ordered pursuant to § 8.01–362 and on any grand jury.

Acts 1977, c. 451; Acts 1977, c. 617; Acts 1984, c. 165; Acts 1992, c. 312; Acts 1994, c. 27.

Article 3

Selection of Jurors

§ 8.01–343. Appointment of jury commissioners

The judge of each circuit court in which juries are impaneled shall, prior to the first day of July in each year, appoint for the next ensuing year ending on the following first day of July not less than two nor more than fifteen persons as jury commissioners, who shall be competent to serve as jurors under the provisions of this chapter, and shall be citizens of intelligence, morality, and integrity. The judge of the circuit court of a county having the urban county executive form of government may appoint jury commissioners at any time prior to the first day of November in each year. Any one judge of the judicial circuit may make such appointment under this section. No practicing attorney-at-law, however, shall be appointed as a jury commissioner. Such appointment shall be certified by the judge to the clerk of the court for which the appointment is made, who shall enter the same on the civil order book of such court. No jury commissioner shall be eligible to reappointment for at least three years after the expiration of the year for which he was appointed. For the purpose of this section, the two divisions of the Circuit Court of the City of Richmond shall be deemed to be separate courts.

Acts 1977, c. 617; Acts 1979, c. 269; Acts 1996, c. 332; Acts 1999, c. 221; Acts 2000, c. 251. Amended by Acts 2006, c. 306; Acts 2009, c. 790.

§ 8.01–344. Notification of jury commissioners; their oath

Such commissioners shall be immediately notified of their appointment by the clerk, and before entering upon the discharge of their duties shall take and subscribe an oath or affirmation before the clerk of such court in the following form: "I do solemnly swear (or affirm) that I will honestly, without favor or prejudice, perform the duties of jury commissioner during the year; that in selecting persons to be drawn as jurors, I will not select any person I believe to be disqualified or exempt from serving as a juror; that I will select none whom I have been requested to select; and that in all my selections I will endeavor to promote only the impartial administration of justice."

Acts 1977, c. 617.

§ 8.01–345. Lists of qualified persons to be prepared by jury commissioners; random selection process

The commissioners shall, not later than December 1 following their appointment, submit a list showing the names, addresses, freeholder status and, if available, the occupations of such of the inhabitants of their respective counties or cities as are well qualified under § 8.01–337 to serve as jurors and are not excluded or exempt by §§ 8.01–338 to 8.01–341 and 8.01–342. Such master jury list shall be used in selecting jurors for a twelve-month period beginning on the first day of the first term of court in the calendar year next succeeding December 1. The number of persons selected for each court shall be as specified in the order appointing the commissioners.

The jury commissioners shall utilize random selection techniques, either manual, mechanical or electronic, using a current voter registration list and, where feasible, a list of persons issued a driver's license as defined in § 46.2–100 from the Department of Motor Vehicles, city or county directories, telephone books, personal property tax rolls, and other such lists as may be designated and approved by the chief judge of the circuit, to select the jurors representative of the broad community interests, to be placed on the master jury list. The commissioners shall make reasonable effort to exclude the names of deceased persons and unqualified persons from the master jury list. After such random selection, the commissioners shall apply such statutory exceptions and exemptions as may be applicable to the names so selected. The chief judge shall promulgate such procedural rules as are necessary to ensure the integrity of the random selection process and to ensure compliance with other provisions of law with respect to jury selection and service.

Where a city and county adjoin, in whole or in part, the names of the inhabitants of a city shall not be placed upon the county list, nor those of a county upon the city list except in those cases in which the circuit court of the county and the circuit court of the city have concurrent jurisdiction of both civil and criminal cases arising within the territorial limits of such county or city. However, in the case of the City of Franklin and the County of Southampton, the number of jurors selected from Southampton County shall be proportionate to the number of jurors selected from the City of Franklin based upon the respective populations of the county and city.

Acts 1977, c. 617; Acts 1977, c. 451; Acts 1978, c. 209; Acts 1979, c. 665; Acts 1983, c. 107; Acts 1984, c. 50; Acts 1989, c. 616; Acts 1989, c. 632; Acts 1990, c. 758; Acts 2000, c. 828. Amended by Acts 2007, c. 450; Acts 2007, c. 720.

§ 8.01–346. Lists to be delivered to clerk and safely kept by him; addition and removal of names

The list so prepared shall be delivered to the clerk of the court to be safely kept by him. The list shall include a notation indicating those persons who are freeholders. The judge may from time to time order the commissioners to add to the list such additional number of jurors as the court shall direct and to strike therefrom any who have become disqualified or exempt.

Acts 1977, c. 617. Amended by Acts 2007, c. 450; Acts 2007, c. 720.

§ 8.01–347. How names put in jury box

When such list is made out, the commissioners shall cause all the names thereon to be fairly written, each on a separate paper or ballot, and shall so fold or roll up the ballots that they will resemble each other as nearly as may be and the names written thereon will not be visible on the outside, and shall deposit the ballots with the list in a secure box prepared for that purpose. Such box shall be locked and safely kept by the clerk of such court and opened only by the direction of the judge thereof.

Acts 1977, c. 617.

§ 8.01–348. How names of jurors drawn from box

Prior to or during any term of court at which a jury may be necessary, the clerk or deputy clerk, in the presence of the judge or, in his absence, a commissioner in chancery appointed for the purpose by the judge, shall, after thoroughly mixing the ballots in the box, openly draw therefrom such number of ballots as are necessary for the trial of all cases during the term or as the judge shall direct. However, a commissioner shall not be eligible to witness the drawing of a jury to be used in the trial of any case in which he will be interested as attorney or otherwise.

Acts 1977, c. 617; Acts 1983, c. 425.

§ 8.01–349. Notations on ballots drawn; return to box; when such ballots may be drawn again

If any ballot drawn from the box shall bear the name of a person known by the clerk or other person attending the drawing to be deceased, exempt or disqualified by law, not a resident of the county or city, or physically or mentally incapacitated for jury service, an appropriate notation on the ballot, as well as opposite the name of such person on the jury list, shall be made and the ballot shall be placed by the clerk in an envelope kept for that purpose. The other ballots, marked "drawn," shall be placed in a separate envelope and a notation of the date of the drawing shall be made on the jury list opposite the name of each juror drawn. The envelope shall be kept in the box. After all ballots have been drawn from the box, the ballots marked "drawn" may be again drawn subject to the provisions hereof applying to the original drawing.

Acts 1977, c. 617.

§ 8.01–350. Repealed by Acts 1977, c. 451

§ 8.01–350.1. Selection of jurors by mechanical or electronic techniques for the term of court

Notwithstanding the provisions of §§ 8.01–347 through 8.01–349, the chief judge may order that selection of the list of jurors necessary for the trial of all cases during any term of court for that year be made by the use of random selection techniques, either mechanically or electronically, from the list submitted pursuant to § 8.01–345.

Acts 1978, c. 400.

§ 8.01–351. Preparation and disposition of list of jurors drawn

The clerk shall make and sign a list of the names on the ballots in alphabetical order showing the name, age, address, occupation and employer of each juror, and shall deliver an attested copy of the list to the sheriff. The list shall be signed also by the judge or the commissioner in chancery appointed by the judge. The list shall be available in the clerk's office for inspection by counsel in any case to be tried by a jury during the term.

Acts 1977, c. 617; Acts 1988, c. 818.

§ 8.01–352. Objections to irregularities in jury lists or for legal disability; effect thereof

A. Prior to the jury being sworn, the following objections may be made without leave of court: (i) an objection specifically pointing out the irregularity in any list or lists of jurors made by the clerk from names drawn from the jury box, or in the drawing, summoning, returning or impaneling of jurors or in copying or signing or failing to sign the list, and (ii) an objection to any juror on account of any legal disability; after the jury is sworn such objection shall be made only with leave of court.

B. Unless objection to such irregularity or disability is made pursuant to subsection A herein and unless it appears that the irregularity was intentional or that the irregularity or disability be such as to probably cause injustice in a criminal case to the Commonwealth or to the accused and in a civil case to the party making the objection, then such irregularity or disability shall not be cause for summoning a new panel or juror or for setting aside a verdict or granting a new trial.

Acts 1977, c. 617.

ARTICLE 4

JURY SERVICE

§ 8.01–353. Notice to jurors; making copy of jury panel available to counsel; objection to notice

A. The sheriff shall notify the jurors on the list, or such number of them as the judge may direct to appear in court on such day as the court may direct. Such notice shall be given a juror as provided by § 8.01–298. Verbal direction given by the judge, or at his direction, to a juror who has been given notice as hereinbefore provided that he appear at a later specified date, shall be a sufficient notice. Any notice given as provided herein shall have the effect of an order of court. No particular time in advance of the required appearance date shall be necessary for verbal notice hereunder, but the court may, in its discretion, excuse from service a juror who claims lack of sufficient notice. Upon request, the clerk or sheriff or other officer responsible for notifying jurors to appear in court for the trial of a case shall make available to all counsel of record in that case, a copy of the jury panel to be used for the trial of the case at least three full business days before the trial. Such copy of the jury panel shall show the name, age, address, occupation and employer of each person on the panel. Any error in the information shown on such copy of the jury panel shall not be grounds for a mistrial or assignable as error on appeal, and the parties in the case shall be responsible for verifying the accuracy of such information.

B. No judgment shall be arrested or reversed for the failure of the record to show that there was service upon a juror of notice to appear in court unless made a ground of exception in the trial before the jury is sworn.

Acts 1977, c. 617; Acts 1980, c. 452; Acts 1981, c. 150; Acts 1988, c. 350. Amended by Acts 2010, c. 799.

§ 8.01–353.1. Jurors to provide identification

At the time of assembly for the purpose of juror selection, the identity of each member of the jury venire shall be verified as provided in this section. Prior to being selected from the jury venire, a potential juror shall verify his identity by presenting to the person taking jury attendance any of the following forms of identification: his Commonwealth of Virginia voter registration card; his social security card; his valid Virginia driver's license or any other identification card issued by a government agency of the Commonwealth, one of its political subdivisions, or the United States; or any valid employee identification card containing a photograph of the juror and issued by an employer of the juror in the ordinary course of the employer's business. If the juror is unable to present one of these forms of identification, he shall sign a statement affirming, under penalty of perjury, that he is the named juror.

Added by Acts 2010, c. 765. Amended by Acts 2011, c. 470.

§ 8.01–354. "Writ of venire facias" defined

The term "writ of venire facias" for the purpose of this chapter shall be construed as referring to the list or lists of jurors made by the clerk from names drawn from the jury box and notice to appear in court served or mailed as provided herein shall be equivalent to summoning such juror in execution of a writ of venire facias.

Acts 1977, c. 617.

§ 8.01–355. Jurors on list to be used for trial of cases during term; discharge or dispensing with attendance of jurors; drawing additional jurors

Jurors whose names appear in the list provided for under §§ 8.01–348 and 8.01–351 shall be used for the trial of cases, civil and criminal, to be tried during the term. The judge shall direct the selection of as many jurors as may be necessary to appear for the trial of any case. Any court shall have power to discharge persons summoned as jurors therein, or to dispense with their attendance on any day of its sitting. When by reason of challenge or otherwise a sufficient number of jurors summoned cannot be obtained for the trial of any case, the judge may select from the names on the jury list provided for by § 8.01–345 the names of as many persons as he deems necessary and cause them to be summoned to appear forthwith for the trial.

Acts 1977, c. 617.

§ 8.01–356. Failure of juror to appear

If any juror who has been given due notice to appear in court shall fail to do so without sufficient excuse, he shall be fined not less than $50 nor more than $200.

Acts 1977, c. 617. Amended by Acts 2004, c. 116.

§ 8.01–357. Selection of jury panel

On the day on which jurors have been notified to appear, jurors not excused by the court shall be called in such manner as the judge may direct to be sworn on their voir dire until a panel free from exceptions shall be obtained. The jurors shall be selected randomly. The remaining jurors may be discharged or excused subject to such orders as the court shall make.
Acts 1977, c. 617; Acts 1999, c. 3.

§ 8.01–358. Voir dire examination of persons called as jurors

The court and counsel for either party shall have the right to examine under oath any person who is called as a juror therein and shall have the right to ask such person or juror directly any relevant question to ascertain whether he is related to either party, or has any interest in the cause, or has expressed or formed any opinion, or is sensible of any bias or prejudice therein; and the party objecting to any juror may introduce any competent evidence in support of the objection; and if it shall appear to the court that the juror does not stand indifferent in the cause, another shall be drawn or called and placed in his stead for the trial of that case.

A juror, knowing anything relative to a fact in issue, shall disclose the same in open court.
Acts 1977, c. 617; Acts 1981, c. 280.

§ 8.01–359. Trial; numbers of jurors in civil cases; how jurors selected from panel

A. Five persons from a panel of not less than 11 shall constitute a jury in a civil case when the amount involved exclusive of interest and costs does not exceed the maximum jurisdictional limits as provided in § 16.1–77 (1). Seven persons from a panel of not less than 13 shall constitute a jury in all other civil cases except that when a special jury is allowed, 12 persons from a panel of not less than 20 shall constitute the jury.

B. The parties or their counsel, beginning with the plaintiff, shall alternately strike off one name from the panel until the number remaining shall be reduced to the number required for a jury. Where there are more than two parties, all plaintiffs shall share three strikes between them and all defendants and third-party defendants shall share three strikes between them.

C. In any case in which there are two or more parties on the same side, if counsel or the parties are unable to agree on the full number to be stricken, or, if for any other reason a party or his counsel fails or refuses to strike off the full number of jurors allowed such party, the clerk shall place in a box ballots bearing the names of the jurors whose names have not been stricken and shall cause to be drawn from the box such number of ballots as may be necessary to complete the number of strikes allowed the party or parties failing or refusing to strike. Thereafter, if the opposing side is entitled to further strikes, they shall be made in the usual manner.

D. In any civil case in which the consent of the plaintiff and defendant shall be entered of record, it shall be lawful for the plaintiff to select one person who is eligible as a juror and for the defendant to select another, and for the two so selected to select a third of like qualifications, and the three so selected shall constitute a jury in the case. They shall take the oath required of jurors, and hear and determine the issue, and any two concurring shall render a verdict in like manner and with like effect as a jury of seven.
Acts 1977, c. 617; Acts 1985, c. 188. Amended by Acts 2005, c. 356.

§ 8.01–360. Additional jurors when trial likely to be protracted

Whenever in the opinion of the court the trial of any criminal or civil case is likely to be a protracted one, the court may direct the selection of additional jurors who shall be drawn from the same source, in the same manner and at the same time as the regular jurors. These additional jurors shall have the same qualifications, and be considered and treated in every respect as regular jurors and be subject to examination and challenge as such jurors. When one additional juror is desired, there shall be drawn three veniremen, and the plaintiff and defendant in a civil case or the Commonwealth and accused in a criminal case shall each be allowed one peremptory challenge. When two or more additional jurors are desired there shall be drawn twice as many venireman as the number of additional jurors desired. The plaintiff and defendant in a civil case or the Commonwealth and accused in a criminal case shall each be allowed one additional peremptory challenge for every two additional jurors. The court shall select, by lot, those jurors to be designated additional jurors. The plaintiff and defendant in a civil case or the Commonwealth and accused in a criminal case shall be advised by the court which jurors are additional jurors at the time the jury is impaneled; however, in no event, shall any juror be made aware of his status as a regular or additional juror until he is excused as a juror. Before final submission of the case, the court shall excuse any additional jurors in order to reduce the number of jurors to that required by §§ 8.01–359 and 19.2–262.
Acts 1977, c. 617; Acts 1992, c. 536; Acts 1998, c. 279.

§ 8.01–361. New juror may be sworn in place of one disabled; when court may discharge jury

If a juror, after he is sworn, be unable from any cause to perform his duty, the court may, in its discretion, cause another qualified juror to be sworn in his place, and in any case, the court may discharge the jury when it appears that they cannot agree on a verdict or that there is a manifest necessity for such discharge.
Acts 1977, c. 617.

§ 8.01–362. Special juries

Any court in a civil case in which a jury is required may allow a special jury, in which event the court shall order such jurors to be summoned as it shall designate, and from those summoned, a jury shall be made in accordance with the provisions of § 8.01–359 A. The court may, in its discretion, cause the entire cost of such jury to be taxed as a part of the cost in such action, and to be paid by the plaintiff or defendant as the court shall direct.

Acts 1977, c. 617.

§ 8.01–363. When impartial jury cannot be obtained locally

In any case in which qualified jurors who are not exempt from serving and who the judge is satisfied can render a fair and impartial trial cannot be conveniently found in the county or city in which the trial is to be, the court may cause so many jurors as may be necessary to be summoned from any other county or city by the sheriff thereof, or by its own officer, from a list prepared pursuant to Article 3 (§ 8.01–343 et seq.) of this chapter and furnished by the circuit court of the county or city from which the jurors are to be summoned.

Acts 1977, c. 617.

CHAPTER 12

INTERPLEADER; CLAIMS OF THIRD PARTIES TO PROPERTY DISTRAINED OR LEVIED ON, ETC.

Article 1

Interpleader

§ 8.01–364. Interpleader

A. Whenever any person is or may be exposed to multiple liability through the existence of claims by others to the same property or fund held by him or on his behalf, such person may file a pleading and require such parties to interplead their claims. It is not ground for objection to the joinder that the claims of the several claimants or the titles on which their claims depend do not have a common origin or are not identical but are adverse to and independent of one another, or that the plaintiff avers that he is not liable in whole or in part to any or all of the claimants. A defendant in an action who is exposed to similar liability may likewise obtain such interpleader. The provisions of this rule supplement and do not in any way limit the joinder of parties permitted in § 8.01–5.

B. The remedy herein provided is in addition to and in no way supersedes or limits the remedy provided by any other section of this Code.

C. In any action of interpleader, the court may enter its order restraining all claimants from instituting or prosecuting any proceeding in any court of the Commonwealth affecting the property involved in the interpleader action until further order of the court.

Such court shall hear and determine the case and may discharge the appropriate party from further liability, make the injunction permanent, and make all appropriate orders to enforce its judgment.

D. A person interpleading may voluntarily pay or tender into court the property claimed, or may be ordered to do so by the court; and the court may thereupon order such party discharged from all or part of any liability as between the claimants of such property.

Acts 1977, c. 617; Acts 1978, c. 415.

Article 2

Claims of Third Parties to Property Distrained or Levied On

§ 8.01–365. How claim of third party tried

When a writ of fieri facias issued from a circuit court, or a warrant of distress, is levied on property, or when a lien is acquired on money or other personal estate by virtue of § 8.01–501, and when some other person than the one against whom the process issued claims the property, money, other personal estate, or some part or the proceeds thereof, then either (i) the claimant, if such suspending bond as is hereinafter mentioned has been given, (ii) the officer having such process, if no indemnifying bond has been given, or (iii) the party who had the process issued, may apply to try the claim, by motion to the adverse party, to the circuit court of the county or city wherein the property, money, or other personal estate is located.

Acts 1977, c. 617.

§ 8.01–366. Sale of property when no forthcoming bond is given

In such case as is mentioned in § 8.01–365, when no bond is given for the forthcoming of the property, the court may, before a decision of the rights of the parties, make an order for the sale of the property, or any part thereof, on such terms as the court may deem advisable, and for the proper application of the proceeds. The court may make such orders and enter such judgment as to costs and all other matters as may be just and proper.

Acts 1977, c. 617.

§ 8.01–367. Indemnifying bond to officer

A. If any officer levies or is required to levy a fieri facias, an attachment, or a warrant of distress on property, and the officer doubts whether such property is liable to such levy, he may give the plaintiff, his agent or attorney-at-law, notice that an indemnifying bond is required in the case; bond may thereupon be given by any person, with good security, payable to the officer in a penalty equal to the value of the property in the case of a fieri facias or a warrant of distress on property and equal to double the value of the property in case of an attachment, with condition to indemnify him against all damage which he may sustain in consequence of the seizure or sale of such property and to pay to any claimant of such property all damage which he may sustain in consequence of such seizure or sale, and also to warrant and defend to any purchaser of the property such estate or interest therein as is sold. If the officer has performed more than one levy for a single plaintiff, the officer may permit the plaintiff to give a single indemnifying bond for such levies, provided that any such bond shall be in a penalty amount not less than the aggregate sum of the penalty amounts of the bonds required had the levies been bonded individually.

Provided, however, that when the property claimed to be liable by virtue of the process aforesaid is in the possession of any of the parties against whom such process was issued but is claimed by any other person or is claimed to belong to any other person, the officer having such process in his hands to be executed shall proceed to execute the same notwithstanding such claim unless the claimant of the property or someone for him shall give a suspending bond as provided by § 8.01–370 and shall within 30 days after such bond is given proceed to have the title to the property settled in accordance with the provisions of this chapter. And in case such claimant or someone for him fails to give such suspending bond, or having given such bond fails to have such proceedings instituted to settle the title thereto, the claimant shall be barred from asserting such claim to the property and the officer shall proceed to execute the process, and the officer who executes such process shall not be liable to any such claimant for any damages resulting from the proper execution of such process as is required by this section. If an indemnifying bond is not given within a reasonable time after such notice, the officer may refuse to levy on such property, or may restore it to the person from whose possession it was taken. If such bond is given, the officer shall proceed to levy (i) if he has not already done so, or (ii) if necessary to restore a levy previously released.

B. The Commonwealth shall not be required to give an indemnifying bond under the provisions of this section.

Acts 1977, c. 617. Amended by Acts 2005, c. 690; Acts 2012, c. 206.

§ 8.01–368. Return of such bond to clerk's office

Any indemnifying bond taken by an officer under the preceding section shall be returned by him within twenty-one days to the clerk's office of the circuit court of the county or city wherein the property levied on, or to be levied on, is located.

Acts 1977, c. 617.

§ 8.01–369. Effect of such bond

The claimant or purchaser of such property shall, after such bond is so returned, be barred from any action against the officer levying thereon, provided the security therein be good at the time of taking it.

Acts 1977, c. 617.

§ 8.01–370. Claimant may give suspending bond; proceedings to have title settled; action on indemnifying or suspending bond

The sale of any property levied on under a fieri facias or distress warrant shall be suspended at the instance of any claimant thereof who will deliver to the officer a suspending bond, with good security, in a penalty equal to double the value thereof, payable to such officer, with condition to pay to all persons who may be injured by suspending the sale thereof, until the claim thereto is adjudicated or otherwise adjusted, such damage as they may sustain by such suspension. If the property claimed to be liable by virtue of such process is in the possession of any of the parties against whom such process was issued, but is claimed by any other person, or is claimed to belong to any other person, the officer having such process in his hands to be executed shall, whether an indemnifying bond has been given or not, after notice to the claimant, or his agent, proceed to execute the same notwithstanding such claim, unless the claimant of such property or someone for him shall give the suspending bond aforesaid, and shall within thirty days after such bond is given proceed to have the title to such property settled in accordance with the provisions of this chapter. And in case such claimant or someone for him fails to give a suspending bond, or having given such bond fails to have such proceedings instituted to settle the title thereto, the claimant shall be barred from asserting such claim to the property and the sale of the property shall proceed. For the purpose of this section, a person making a claim of ownership of property on behalf of another shall be deemed to be the latter's agent, and the notice required by this section may be verbal or in writing. Upon any such indemnifying or suspending bond as is mentioned

in this section or § 8.01–369 an action may be prosecuted in the name of the officer for the benefit of the claimant, creditor, purchaser, or other person injured, and such damages recovered in such action as a jury may assess. The action may be prosecuted and a writ of fieri facias had in the name of such officer when he is dead in like manner as if he were alive.
Acts 1977, c. 617.

§ 8.01–371. How forthcoming bond taken of claimant of property the sale whereof has been suspended

The sheriff or other officer levying a writ of fieri facias or distress warrant on property, the sale of which is suspended under this chapter at the instance of a claimant thereof, may, if such claimant desires the property to remain in such possession as it was immediately before the levy, and if the case be one in which a bond for the forthcoming of the property is not prohibited from being taken from the debtor by § 8.01–531, take from the claimant a bond, with sufficient surety, in a penalty equal to double the value of the property, payable to the creditor, with such recital as is required in a forthcoming bond taken from the debtor, and with condition that the property shall be forthcoming at such day and place of sale as may be thereafter lawfully appointed. Such property may then be permitted to remain, at the risk of such claimant, in such possession as it was immediately before the levy; and §§ 8.01–527, 8.01–528, 8.01–530, 8.01–531 and 55–232 shall apply to such forthcoming bond in like manner as to a forthcoming bond taken from the debtor.
Acts 1977, c. 617.

§ 8.01–372. Sale despite bond when property perishable, etc.

In such case as is mentioned in § 8.01–371 and whether a forthcoming bond is given or not, if the property be expensive to keep or perishable, the court in which proceedings in the case under § 8.01–365 are pending or may be had, may, before a decision of the rights of the parties under such proceedings, on the application of such claimant or of the surety in such suspending or forthcoming bond, after reasonable notice of the intended application has been given by such claimant or the surety to the other parties in the case, order a sale of the property, or any part thereof, on such terms as the court may deem advisable. The court shall apply the proceeds according to the rights of the parties when determined.
Acts 1977, c. 617.

§ 8.01–373. When property sells for more than claim, how surplus paid

When property, the sale of which is indemnified, sells for more than enough to satisfy the execution, attachment, or distress warrant under which it is taken, the surplus shall be paid by the officer into the court where the indemnifying bond is required to be returned, or as such court may direct. The court wherein the surplus is held may make such order for the disposition thereof, either temporarily until the question as to the title of the property sold is determined, or absolutely, as in respect to the rights of those interested may seem to it proper.
Acts 1977, c. 617.

CHAPTER 13

CERTAIN INCIDENTS OF TRIAL

§ 8.01–374. Procedure when original papers in cause are lost

If in any case the original papers therein, or any of them, or the record for or in an appellate court, or any paper filed or connected with such record, be lost or destroyed, any party to such case may present to the court wherein the case is, or in which it would or ought to be, but for such loss or destruction, a petition verified by affidavit stating such loss or destruction, and praying that such case be heard and determined or tried on the reproduction of such record or papers, or satisfactory proof of their contents. Upon such petition and an authenticated copy of what is lost or destroyed, the court may hear and determine the case, or proceed to a trial thereof, if before a jury. The court may also hear and determine the case, or proceed to the trial thereof, if before a jury, upon proof, after reasonable notice to the parties interested, of the contents of such record or papers, or so much thereof, as may be necessary for a decision by the court, or by a jury, and may make such order or decree as if the papers or any of them had not been lost or destroyed.

The court may in its discretion, require new pleadings to be made up in whole or in part.

A plaintiff instead of proceeding under this section may commence and prosecute a new suit for the same matter; and no certified copy of any deed, will, account, or other original paper required by law to be recorded shall be used by any party as evidence for him, in any case when the original deed, will, account, or other original paper or record thereof has been destroyed, until such copy has been properly admitted to record, according to law. This section shall not apply to criminal cases.
Acts 1977, c. 617.

§ 8.01–374.1. Consolidation or bifurcation of issues or claims in certain cases; appeal

A. In any circuit court in which there are pending more than forty civil actions against manufacturers or suppliers of asbestos or products for industrial use that contain asbestos in which recovery is sought for personal injury or wrongful death alleged to have been caused by exposure to asbestos or products for industrial use that contain asbestos, the court may order a joint hearing or trial by jury of any or all common questions of law or fact which are at issue in those actions. The court may order any or all the actions consolidated, unless the court finds consolidation would adversely affect the rights of the parties to a fair trial. The court may submit special interrogatories to the jury to resolve specific issues of fact, and may make such orders concerning proceedings therein consistent with the right of each of the parties to a fair trial as may be appropriate to avoid unnecessary costs, duplicative litigation or delay.

B. To further convenience or avoid prejudice in such consolidated hearings, when separate or bifurcated trials will be conducive to judicial economy, the court may order a separate or bifurcated trial of any claim, or any number of claims, cross-claims, counterclaims, third-party claims, or separate issues, always preserving the right of trial by jury. However, in any such bifurcated proceeding, the entitlement of an individual plaintiff to an award of punitive damages against any defendant shall not be determined unless compensatory damages have been awarded to that individual.

C. Any order entered pursuant to this section shall, for purposes of appeal, be an interlocutory order. Any findings of the court or jury in any bifurcated trial shall not be appealable until a final order adjudicating all issues on a specific claim or consolidated group of claims has been entered.

D. This section shall not apply to actions arising under Article 6 (§ 8.01–57 et seq.) of Chapter 3 of this title or the Federal Employers Liability Act (45 U.S.C. § 51 et seq.). In addition, this section shall not apply to any party defendant unless that defendant was a manufacturer of, or a supplier of, asbestos or products for industrial use that contain asbestos, at any of the times alleged in the motion for judgment.

Acts 1992, c. 615.

§ 8.01–375. Exclusion of witnesses in civil cases (Subsection (a) of Supreme Court Rule 2:615 derived in part from this section and subsection (b) of Supreme Court Rule 2:615 derived from this section)

The court trying any civil case may upon its own motion and shall upon the motion of any party, require the exclusion of every witness. However, each named party who is an individual, one officer or agent of each party which is a corporation or association and an attorney alleged in a habeas corpus proceeding to have acted ineffectively shall be exempt from the rule of this section as a matter of right.

Where expert witnesses are to testify in the case, the court may, at the request of all parties, allow one expert witness for each party to remain in the courtroom; however, in cases pertaining to the distribution of marital property pursuant to § 20–107.3 or the determination of child or spousal support pursuant to § 20–108.1, the court may, upon motion of any party, allow one expert witness for each party to remain in the courtroom throughout the hearing.

Acts 1977, c. 617; Acts 1986, c. 36; Acts 1987, c. 70; Acts 2001, c. 348. Amended by Acts 2006, c. 757.

§ 8.01–376. Views by juries

The jury may, in any civil case, at the request of either party, be taken to view the premises or place in question, or any property, matter or thing relating to the controversy between the parties, when it shall appear to the court that such view is necessary to a just decision; provided that the expenses of the jury and the officers who attend them in taking the view shall be afterwards taxed like other legal costs.

Acts 1977, c. 617; Acts 1978, c. 367.

§ 8.01–377. Remedy when variance appears between evidence and allegations

If, at the trial of any action, there appears to be a variance between the evidence and the allegations or recitals, the court, if it consider that substantial justice will be promoted and that the opposite party cannot be prejudiced thereby, may allow the pleadings to be amended, on such terms as to the payment of costs or postponement of the trial, or both, as it may deem reasonable. Or, instead of the pleadings being amended, the court may direct the jury to find the facts, and, after such finding, if it consider the variance such as could not have prejudiced the opposite party, shall give judgment according to the right of the case.

Acts 1977, c. 617.

§ 8.01–377.1. Summary judgment

In any action at law or equity at the close of all the evidence, any party may move for a summary judgment upon the entire case or upon any severable issue including the issue of liability alone although there is a genuine issue as to damages.

Acts 1990, c. 628.

§ 8.01–378. Trial judge not to direct verdicts

In no action tried before a jury shall the trial judge give to the jury a peremptory instruction directing what verdict the jury shall render. If the trial judge has granted a motion to strike the evidence of the plaintiff or the defendant, the judge shall enter summary judgment or partial summary judgment in conformity with his ruling on the motion to strike.

Acts 1977, c. 617; Acts 1985, c. 214; Acts 1986, c. 253.

§ 8.01–379. Argument before jury

Counsel's right to argument before a jury is preserved.

Acts 1977, c. 617.

§ 8.01–379.1. Informing jury of amounts sued for

Notwithstanding any other provision of law, any party in any civil action may inform the jury of the amount of damages sought by the plaintiff in the opening statement or closing argument, or both. The plaintiff may request an amount which is less than the ad damnum in the motion for judgment.

Acts 1988, c. 321; Acts 1993, c. 615.

§ 8.01–379.2. Jury instructions

A proposed jury instruction submitted by a party, which constitutes an accurate statement of the law applicable to the case, shall not be withheld from the jury solely for its nonconformance with the model jury instructions.

Acts 1992, c. 522.

§ 8.01–379.3. General verdict accompanied by answer to interrogatories

Except in actions for negligence resulting in injury to person or death by wrongful act, in civil actions when the court determines that the complexity of the issues warrant, the court may submit to the jury, together with appropriate forms for a general verdict, written interrogatories upon one or more issues of fact the decision of which is necessary to a verdict. In actions for negligence resulting in injury to person or death by wrongful act, the court shall submit to the jury a general verdict form only, provided that the court may submit interrogatories to the jury if otherwise specifically authorized by law, if under substantive law governing the case comparative negligence applies, or if all parties to the action agree that interrogatories may be submitted to the jury. The court shall give such explanation or instruction as may be necessary to enable the jury both to make answers to the interrogatories and to render a general verdict, and the court shall direct the jury both to make written answers and to render a general verdict. When the general verdict and the answers are consistent, the appropriate judgment upon the verdict and answers shall be entered by the court. When the answers are consistent with each other but one or more is inconsistent with the general verdict, or when the answers are inconsistent with each other and one or more is likewise inconsistent with the general verdict, judgment shall not be entered and the court shall either order the jury to further consider its answers and verdict or order a new trial.

Added by Acts 2005, c. 499.

§ 8.01–380. Dismissal of action by nonsuit; fees and costs

A. A party shall not be allowed to suffer a nonsuit as to any cause of action or claim, or any other party to the proceeding, unless he does so before a motion to strike the evidence has been sustained or before the jury retires from the bar or before the action has been submitted to the court for decision. After a nonsuit no new proceeding on the same cause of action or against the same party shall be had in any court other than that in which the nonsuit was taken, unless that court is without jurisdiction, or not a proper venue, or other good cause is shown for proceeding in another court, or when such new proceeding is instituted in a federal court. If after a nonsuit an improper venue is chosen, the court shall not dismiss the matter but shall transfer it to the proper venue upon motion of any party.

B. Only one nonsuit may be taken to a cause of action or against the same party to the proceeding, as a matter of right, although the court may allow additional nonsuits upon reasonable notice to counsel of record for all defendants and upon a reasonable attempt to notify any party not represented by counsel, or counsel may stipulate to additional nonsuits. The court, in the event additional nonsuits are allowed, may assess costs and reasonable attorney fees against the nonsuiting party. When suffering a nonsuit, a party shall inform the court if the cause of action has been previously nonsuited. Any order effecting a subsequent nonsuit shall reflect all prior nonsuits and shall include language that reflects the date of any previous nonsuit together with the court in which any previous nonsuit was taken.

C. If notice to take a nonsuit of right is given to the opposing party within seven days of trial or during trial, the court in its discretion may assess against the nonsuiting party reasonable witness fees and travel costs of expert witnesses scheduled to appear at trial, which are actually incurred by the opposing party, solely by reason of the failure to give notice at least seven days prior to trial. The court shall have the authority to determine the reasonableness of expert witness fees and travel costs. Invoices, receipts, or confirmation of payment shall be admissible to prove reasonableness without the need to offer testimony to support the authenticity or reasonableness of such documents, and may, in the court's discretion, satisfy the reasonableness requirement under this subsection. Nothing herein shall preclude any party from offering additional evidence or testimony to support or rebut the reasonableness requirement.

D. A party shall not be allowed to nonsuit a cause of action, without the consent of the adverse party who has filed a counterclaim, cross claim or third-party claim which arises out of the same transaction or occurrence as the claim of the party desiring to nonsuit unless the counterclaim, cross claim or third-party claim can remain pending for independent adjudication by the court.

E. A voluntary nonsuit taken pursuant to this section is subject to the tolling provisions of subdivision E 3 of § 8.01-229.

Acts 1977, c. 617; Acts 1983, c. 404; Acts 1991, c. 19; Acts 2001, c. 825. Amended by Acts 2004, c. 362; Acts 2007, c. 179; Acts 2007, c. 367; Acts 2013, c. 274; Acts 2013, c. 366; Acts 2014, c. 86.

§ 8.01-381. What jury may carry out

No pleadings may be carried from the bar by the jury. Exhibits may, by leave of court, be so carried by the jury. Upon request of any party, the court shall instruct the jury that they may request exhibits for use during deliberations. Exhibits requested by the jury shall be sent to the jury room or may otherwise be made available to the jury.

Acts 1977, c. 617; Acts 1992, c. 495.

§ 8.01-382. Verdict, judgment or decree to fix period at which interest begins; final order; judgment or decree for interest

In any Administrative Process Act (§ 2.2-4000 et seq.) action or action at law or suit in equity, the final order, verdict of the jury, or if no jury the judgment or decree of the court, may provide for interest on any principal sum awarded, or any part thereof, and fix the period at which the interest shall commence. The final order, judgment or decree entered shall provide for such interest until such principal sum be paid. If a final order, judgment or decree be rendered which does not provide for interest, the final order, judgment or decree awarded or jury verdict shall bear interest at the judgment rate of interest as provided for in § 6.2-302 from its date of entry or from the date that the jury verdict was rendered. Notwithstanding the provisions of this section, any judgment entered for a sum due under a negotiable instrument, as defined by § 8.3A-104, shall provide for interest on the principal sum in accordance with § 8.3A-112 at the rate specified in the instrument. If no such rate is specified, interest on the principal sum shall be at the judgment rate provided in § 6.2-302. Final orders may be recorded, enforced, and satisfied as orders or decrees of a circuit court upon certification of such orders by the agency head or his designee.

Acts 1977, c. 617; Acts 1979, c. 501; Acts 1997, c. 551. Amended by Acts 2004, c. 646; Acts 2008, c. 219; Acts 2009, c. 797.

§ 8.01-383. Power to grant new trial; how often

In any civil case or proceeding, the court before which a trial by jury is had, may grant a new trial, unless it be otherwise specially provided. A new trial may be granted as well where the damages awarded are too small as where they are excessive. Not more than two new trials shall be granted to the same party in the same cause on the ground that the verdict is contrary to the evidence, either by the trial court or the appellate court, or both.

Acts 1977, c. 617.

§ 8.01-383.1. Appeal when verdict reduced and accepted under protest; new trial for inadequate damages

A. In any action at law in which the trial court shall require a plaintiff to remit a part of his recovery, as ascertained by the verdict of a jury, or else submit to a new trial, such plaintiff may remit and accept judgment of the court thereon for the reduced sum under protest, but, notwithstanding such remittitur and acceptance, if under protest, the judgment of the court in requiring him to remit may be reviewed by the Supreme Court upon an appeal awarded the plaintiff as in other actions at law; and in any such case in which an appeal is awarded the defendant, the judgment of the court in requiring such remittitur may be the subject of review by the Supreme Court, regardless of the amount.

B. In any action at law when the court finds as a matter of law that the damages awarded by the jury are inadequate, the trial court may (i) award a new trial or (ii) require the defendant to pay an amount in excess of the recovery of the plaintiff found in the verdict. If either the plaintiff or the defendant declines to accept such additional award, the trial court shall award a new trial.

If additur pursuant to this subsection is accepted by either party under protest, it may be reviewed on appeal.

Acts 1977, c. 617; Acts 1994, c. 807; Acts 1998, c. 861.

§ 8.01-384. Formal exceptions to rulings or orders of court unnecessary; motion for new trial unnecessary in certain cases

A. Formal exceptions to rulings or orders of the court shall be unnecessary; but for all purposes for which an exception has heretofore been necessary, it shall be sufficient that a party, at the time the ruling or order of the court is made or sought, makes known to the court the action which he desires the court to take or his objections to the action of the court and his grounds therefor; and, if a party has no opportunity to object to a ruling or order at the time it is made, the absence of an objection shall not thereafter prejudice him on motion for a new trial or on appeal. No party, after having made an objection or motion known to the court, shall be required to make such objection or motion again in order to preserve his right to appeal, challenge, or move for reconsideration of, a ruling, order, or action of the court. No party shall be deemed to have agreed to, or acquiesced in, any written order of a trial court so as to forfeit his right to contest such order on appeal except by express written agreement in his endorsement of the order. Arguments made at trial via written pleading, memorandum, recital of objections in a final order, oral argument reduced to transcript, or agreed written statements of facts shall, unless expressly withdrawn or waived, be deemed preserved therein for assertion on appeal.

B. The failure to make a motion for a new trial in any case in which an appeal, writ of error, or supersedeas lies to or from a higher court shall not be deemed a waiver of any objection made during the trial if such objection be properly made a part of the record.
Acts 1977, c. 617; Acts 1992, c. 564.

§ 8.01–384.1. Interpreters for deaf in civil proceedings

In any civil proceeding in which a speech-impaired or hearing-impaired person is a party or witness, the court may appoint a qualified interpreter to assist such person in the proceeding. The court shall appoint an interpreter for any speech-impaired or hearing-impaired person who requests this assistance.

Interpreters for the deaf in these proceedings shall be procured through the Department for the Deaf and Hard-of-Hearing.

Any person who is eligible for an interpreter pursuant to this section may waive the use of an interpreter appointed by the court for all or a portion of the proceedings. A person who waives his right to an interpreter may provide his own interpreter at his own expense without regard to whether the interpreter is qualified under this section.

The compensation of interpreters appointed pursuant to this section shall be fixed by the court and paid from the general fund of the state treasury or may, in the discretion of the court, be assessed as a part of the cost of the proceedings.

The provisions of this section shall apply in both circuit courts and district courts.
Acts 1982, c. 444.

§ 8.01–384.1:1. Interpreters for non-English-speaking persons in civil cases

A. In any trial, hearing or other proceeding before a judge in a civil case in which a non-English-speaking person is a party or witness, an interpreter for the non-English-speaking person may be appointed by the court. A qualified English-speaking person fluent in the language of the non-English-speaking person may be appointed by the judge of the court in which the case is to be heard unless the non-English-speaking person shall obtain a qualified interpreter of his own choosing who is approved by the court as being competent.

B. To the extent of available appropriations, the compensation of such interpreter shall be fixed by the court in accordance with guidelines set by the Judicial Council of Virginia and shall be paid from the general fund of the state treasury as part of the expense of trial. The amount allowed by the court to the interpreter may, in the discretion of the court, be assessed against either party as a part of the cost of the case and, if collected, the same shall be paid to the Commonwealth.

C. Whenever a person communicates through an interpreter to any person under such circumstances that the communications would be privileged, and such persons could not be compelled to testify as to the communications, this privilege shall also apply to the interpreter. The provisions of this section shall apply in circuit courts and district courts.
Acts 1996, c. 559; Acts 2003, c. 1011.

§ 8.01–384.2. Waiver of discovery time limitations by parties

Parties involved in any civil litigation may, without court order and upon agreement of all of them or their counsel, waive any time limitations established by the Rules of the Virginia Supreme Court relating to any response to a motion or request for discovery or the scheduling of any discovery proceedings. The court shall allow any such waiver unless an order establishing discovery or filing deadlines has been entered previously by the court in the action.
Acts 1991, c. 75.

CHAPTER 14

EVIDENCE

Article 1

Judicial Notice

§ 8.01–385. Definitions

As used in this chapter:

1. The term "United States" shall be deemed to refer to the United States of America and to include any of its territories, commonwealths, insular possessions, the District of Columbia, and any of its other political subdivisions other than states.

2. The term "court" shall be deemed to include the courts of this Commonwealth, any other person or body appointed by it or acting under its process or authority in a judicial or quasi-judicial capacity, and any other judicial, quasi-judicial, or fact-finding body acting pursuant to the laws of the Commonwealth, including without limitation, the State Corporation

Commission and the Virginia Workers' Compensation Commission.

3. The term "political subdivision" shall: (i) as applied to the United States, include any other political subdivision other than states and including without limitation the District of Columbia and the Commonwealth of Puerto Rico; (ii) as applied to other countries, include without limitation states, counties, cities, towns, boroughs, and any division thereof recognized and vested with the authority to enact or promulgate ordinances, rules, and regulations having the force or effect of law; (iii) as applied to this Commonwealth and other states of the United States, include without limitation counties, cities, towns, boroughs, and any other division thereof recognized and vested with the authority to enact or promulgate ordinances, rules, and regulations having the force or effect of law.

4. The term "agency" shall be deemed to include without limitation any department, division, commission, association, board, or other administrative body established pursuant to the laws of a jurisdiction.

5. The term "official publication" includes any registry or listing of licenses, permits, or registrations posted on the official website of an agency or political subdivision.

6. The term "publish" includes posting by an agency or political subdivision on its official website.

7. The term "required to be published pursuant to the laws thereof" includes being subject to disclosure under § 54.1–108.

Acts 1977, c. 617. Amended by Acts 2011, c. 81.

§ 8.01–386. Judicial notice of laws (Supreme Court Rule 2:202 derived in part from this section)

A. Whenever, in any civil action it becomes necessary to ascertain what the law, statutory or otherwise, of this Commonwealth, of another state, of the United States, of another country, or of any political subdivision or agency of the same is, or was, at any time, the court shall take judicial notice thereof whether specially pleaded or not.

B. The court, in taking such notice, may consult any book, record, register, journal, or other official document or publication purporting to contain, state, or explain such law, and may consider any evidence or other information or argument that is offered on the subject.

Acts 1977, c. 617.

§ 8.01–387. Notice by courts and officers of signatures of judges and Governor

All courts and officers shall take notice of the signature of any of the judges, or of the Governor of this Commonwealth, to any judicial or official document.

Acts 1977, c. 617.

§ 8.01–388. Judicial notice of official publications (Supreme Court Rule 2:203 derived from this section)

The court shall take judicial notice of the contents of all official publications of this Commonwealth and its political subdivisions and agencies required to be published pursuant to the laws thereof, and of all such official publications of other states, of the United States, of other countries, and of the political subdivisions and agencies of each published within those jurisdictions pursuant to the laws thereof.

Acts 1977, c. 617.

Article 2

Laws, Public Records, and Copies of Original Records as Evidence

§ 8.01–389. Judicial records as evidence; full faith and credit; recitals in deeds, deeds of trust, and mortgages; "records" defined; certification

A. The records of any judicial proceeding and any other official records of any court of this Commonwealth shall be received as prima facie evidence provided that such records are certified by the clerk of the court where preserved to be a true record. For the purposes of this section, judicial proceeding shall include the review of a petition and issuance of a temporary detention order under § 16.1–340.1 or 37.2–809.

A1. The records of any judicial proceeding and any other official record of any court of another state or country, or of the United States, shall be received as prima facie evidence provided that such records are certified by the clerk of the court where preserved to be a true record.

B. Every court of this Commonwealth shall give such records of courts not of this Commonwealth the full faith and credit given to them in the courts of the jurisdiction from whence they come.

B1. In any instance in which a court not of this Commonwealth shall have entered an order of injunction limiting or preventing access by any person to the courts of this Commonwealth without that person having had notice and an opportunity for a hearing prior to the entry of such foreign order, that foreign order is not required to be given full faith and credit in any Virginia court. The Virginia court may, in its discretion, hold a hearing to determine the adequacy of notice and opportunity for hearing in the foreign court.

C. Specifically, recitals of any fact in a deed or deed of trust of record conveying any interest in real property shall be prima facie evidence of that fact.

D. "Records" as used in this article, shall be deemed to include any memorandum, report, paper, data compilation, or other record in any form, or any combination thereof.

E. The use of the term "copy teste," "true copy," or "certified copy" or a substantially similar term on a certification affixed or annexed to a copy of an official record maintained by a clerk of court that bears the signature of the clerk or any deputy clerk, and that has the name of the court where such record is preserved on the document or on the certification, shall be prima facie proof that such record is certified by such clerk to be a true copy of the official record kept in the office of the clerk. Nothing herein shall be construed to require or prevent a clerk from using an official seal or prevent a clerk from using any other acceptable method of certification for a court record.

F. The certification of any record pursuant to this section shall automatically authenticate such record for the purpose of its admission into evidence in any trial, hearing, or proceeding.

Acts 1977, c. 617; Acts 1980, c. 453; Acts 1995, c. 594; Acts 1996, c. 417. Amended by Acts 2008, c. 786; Acts 2010, c. 778; Acts 2010, c. 825; Acts 2013, c. 263.

§ 8.01-390. Nonjudicial records as evidence (Subdivision (10)(a) of Supreme Court Rule 2:803 derived from subsection C of this section)

A. Copies of records of this Commonwealth, of another state, of the United States, of another country, or of any political subdivision or agency of the same, other than those located in a clerk's office of a court, shall be received as prima facie evidence provided that such copies are authenticated to be true copies either by the custodian thereof or by the person to whom the custodian reports, if they are different.

B. Records and recordings of 911 emergency service calls shall be deemed authentic transcriptions or recordings of the original statements if they are accompanied by a certificate that meets the provisions of subsection A and the certificate contains the date and time of the incoming call and the incoming phone number, if available, associated with the call.

C. An affidavit signed by an officer deemed to have custody of such an official record, or by his deputy, stating that after a diligent search, no record or entry of such record is found to exist among the records in his office is admissible as evidence that his office has no such record or entry.

Acts 1977, c. 617; Acts 1996, c. 668; Acts 2000, c. 334. Amended by Acts 2014, c. 353.

§ 8.01-390.1. School records as evidence

In a proceeding where a minor's school records are material and otherwise admissible, copies of such school records shall be received as evidence in any matter, provided that such copies are authenticated to be true and accurate copies by the custodian thereof, or by the person to whom the custodian reports if they are different. An affidavit signed by the custodian of such records, or by the person to whom the custodian reports if they are different, stating that such records are true and accurate copies of such records shall be valid authentication for the purposes of this section. Except for copies of report cards and letters previously sent to parents, subjective information, including observations, comments or opinions shall be redacted, by the court, from any records prior to admittance of the records into evidence pursuant to this section. Any party seeking to introduce records authenticated by affidavit under this section shall deliver notice and a copy of such records to the other parties so that they are received not less than seven days prior to the introduction of such records.

Acts 2000, c. 558. Amended by Acts 2009, c. 212; Acts 2012, c. 499.

§ 8.01-390.2. Reports by Chief Medical Examiner received as evidence

Reports of investigations made by the Chief Medical Examiner, his assistants or medical examiners, and the records and certified reports of autopsies made under the authority of Title 32.1, shall be received as evidence in any court or other proceeding, and copies of photographs, laboratory findings and reports in the office of the Chief Medical Examiner or any medical examiner, when duly attested by the Chief Medical Examiner or an Assistant Chief Medical Examiner, shall be received as evidence in any court or other proceeding for any purpose for which the original could be received without proof of the official character or the person whose name is signed thereto.

Added by Acts 2003, c. 459.

§ 8.01-390.3. Business records as evidence

A. In any civil proceeding where a business record is material and otherwise admissible, authentication of the record and the foundation required by subdivision (6) of Rule 2:803 of the Rules of Supreme Court of Virginia may be laid by (i) witness testimony, (ii) a certification of the authenticity of and foundation for the record made by the custodian of such record or other qualified witness either by affidavit or by declaration pursuant to § 8.01-4.3, or (iii) a combination of witness testimony and a certification.

B. The proponent of a business record shall (i) give written notice to all other parties if a certification under this section will be relied upon in whole or in part in authenticating and laying the foundation for admission of such record and (ii) provide a copy of the record and the certification to all other parties, so that all parties have a fair opportunity to challenge the record and certification. The notice and copy of the record and certification shall be provided no later than 15 days in advance of the trial or hearing, unless an order of the court specifies a different time. Objections shall be made within five days thereafter, unless an order of the court specifies a different time. If any party timely objects to reliance upon the certification, the authentication and foundation required by subdivision (6) of Rule 2:803 of the Rules of Supreme Court of Virginia shall be made by witness testimony unless the objection is withdrawn.

C. A certified business record that satisfies the requirements of this section shall be self-authenticating and requires no extrinsic evidence of authenticity.

D. A copy of a business record may be offered in lieu of an original upon satisfaction of the requirements of subsection D of § 8.01–391 by witness testimony, a certification, or a combination of testimony and a certification.

Added by Acts 2014, c. 398.

§ 8.01–391. Copies of originals as evidence (Supreme Court Rule 2:1005 derived from this section)

A. Whenever the original of any official publication or other record has been filed in an action or introduced as evidence, the court may order the original to be returned to its custodian, retaining in its stead a copy thereof. The court may make any order to prevent the improper use of the original.

B. If any department, division, institution, agency, board, or commission of this Commonwealth, of another state or country, or of the United States, or of any political subdivision or agency of the same, acting pursuant to the law of the respective jurisdiction or other proper authority, has copied any record made in the performance of its official duties, such copy shall be as admissible into evidence as the original, whether the original is in existence or not, provided that such copy is authenticated as a true copy either by the custodian of said record or by the person to whom said custodian reports, if they are different, and is accompanied by a certificate that such person does in fact have the custody.

C. If any court or clerk's office of a court of this Commonwealth, of another state or country, or of the United States, or of any political subdivision or agency of the same, has copied any record made in the performance of its official duties, such copy shall be admissible into evidence as the original, whether the original is in existence or not, provided that such copy is authenticated as a true copy by a clerk or deputy clerk of such court.

D. If any business or member of a profession or calling in the regular course of business or activity has made any record or received or transmitted any document, and again in the regular course of business has caused any or all of such record or document to be copied, the copy shall be as admissible in evidence as the original, whether the original exists or not, provided that such copy is satisfactorily identified and authenticated as a true copy by a custodian of such record or by the person to whom said custodian reports, if they be different, and is accompanied by a certificate that said person does in fact have the custody. Such identification and authentication may be made through witness testimony or a certificate by affidavit or by declaration pursuant to § 8.01–4.3, or a combination of witness testimony and a certificate. Copies in the regular course of business shall be deemed to include reproduction at a later time, if done in good faith and without intent to defraud. Copies in the regular course of business shall include items such as checks which are regularly copied before transmission to another person or bank, or records which are acted upon without receipt of the original when the original is retained by another party.

E. The original of which a copy has been made may be destroyed unless its preservation is required by law or its validity has been questioned.

F. The introduction in an action of a copy under this section precludes neither the introduction or admission of the original nor the introduction of a copy or the original in another action.

G. Copy, as used in this section, shall include photographs, microphotographs, photostats, microfilm, microcard, printouts or other reproductions of electronically stored data, or copies from optical disks, electronically transmitted facsimiles, or any other reproduction of an original from a process which forms a durable medium for its recording, storing, and reproducing.

Acts 1977, c. 532; Acts 1977, c. 617; Acts 1978, c. 75; Acts 1979, c. 447; Acts 1989, c. 212; Acts 1990, c. 355; Acts 1991, c. 145; Acts 1992, c. 393; Acts 2000, c. 334. Amended by Acts 2012, c. 802; Acts 2014, c. 398.

Article 2.1

Check Clearing for the 21st Century Evidence Act

§ 8.01-391.1. Substitute checks as evidence (Supreme Court Rule 2:1003 derived from subsections A and B of this section)

A. A substitute check created pursuant to the federal Check Clearing for the 21st Century Evidence Act (Check 21 Act), 12 U.S.C. § 5001 et seq., shall be admissible in evidence in any legal proceeding, civil or criminal, to the same extent the original check would be.

B. A document received from a banking institution that is designated as a "substitute check" and that bears the legend "This is a legal copy of your check. You can use it the same way you would use the original check" shall be presumed to be a substitute check created pursuant to the Check 21 Act.

C. Any person who shall forge a substitute check or utter or attempt to employ as true any forged substitute check shall be punished as provided in § 18.2-172.

Added by Acts 2006, c. 127.

Article 3

Establishing Lost Records, etc.

§ 8.01-392. When court order book or equivalent is lost or illegible, what matters may be reentered

When any book, microfilm record, or record in other form containing judgments, decrees, orders or proceedings of a court is lost, destroyed, or illegible, and there can be again entered correctly, by means of any writing, any matters which were in such book, such court may cause its clerk to have such matters reentered, and such reentries shall have the same effect as the original entries.

Acts 1977, c. 617.

§ 8.01-393. When book or paper or equivalent in clerk's office lost, destroyed, or illegible to be again recorded

When any such book, or any book, microfilm record, or record in other form containing the record of wills, deeds, or other papers, or any other paper filed in a clerk's office, is lost, destroyed, or is illegible, the clerk in whose office such book or paper was, upon the production to him of any original paper which was recorded in such book, or of an attested copy of the record thereof, or of anything else in such book, or of any paper so filed, shall, on application, record the same anew. The record shall show whether it is made from an original or a copy, and how the paper from which it was made was authenticated or attested. Such record shall have, as far as may be, the same effect that the record or paper for which it is substituted would have had.

Acts 1977, c. 617.

§ 8.01-394. How contents of any such lost record, etc., proved

A. Any person desirous of proving the contents of any such book, record, or other paper as is mentioned in either § 8.01-392 or § 8.01-393, may file before the circuit court of the county or city in which such record, book, or other paper was a petition in writing, stating the nature of the record, book, or paper, the contents of which he desires to prove, and what persons may be affected by such proof. Thereupon the court shall appoint a time and place for proceeding on such petition, of which reasonable notice shall be given by him to all parties named in such petition, or interested in the proceedings, and to any others who shall be known to the court, or who shall claim to be so interested. If any party interested other than the petitioner, or who may be affected by the proof, be a person under a disability, the court shall appoint a guardian ad litem to represent his interest in the proceeding.

B. The evidence upon said petition shall be in writing and filed, and the court shall make such order in respect to such record, book, or other paper, or anything therein, as may be necessary to secure the benefits thereof to the parties interested, or such other order as may be proper in the case.

Before such court shall make such order, the petitioner shall cause to be served on the persons interested a notice in writing that he will apply for such order, in the manner provided by § 8.01-296, at least ten days before such order is to be made; but if such persons, or any of them, do not reside in this Commonwealth, or after due diligence cannot be found therein, an order of publication may be issued as provided by §§ 8.01-316 and 8.01-317.

Acts 1977, c. 617.

§ 8.01-395. Validating certain proceedings under § 8.01-394

All proceedings had in any case, under the provisions of § 8.01-394, wherein a final judgment or decree has stood unimpeached for more than twenty years are declared to be valid and binding in all respects.

Acts 1977, c. 617.

ARTICLE 4

WITNESSES GENERALLY

§ 8.01–396. No person incompetent to testify by reason of interest, or because a party

No person shall be incompetent to testify because of interest, or because of his being a party to any civil action; but he shall, if otherwise competent to testify, and subject to the rules of evidence and practice applicable to other witnesses, be competent to give evidence in his own behalf and be competent and compellable to attend and give evidence on behalf of any other party to such action; but, in any case, the court, for good cause shown, may require any such person to attend and testify ore tenus and, upon his failure to so attend and testify, may exclude his deposition.

Acts 1977, c. 617.

§ 8.01–396.1. Competency of witness

No child shall be deemed incompetent to testify solely because of age.

Acts 1993, c. 441; Acts 1993, c. 605.

§ 8.01–397. Corroboration required and evidence receivable when one party incapable of testifying (subdivision (b)(5) of Supreme Court Rule 2:804 derived from this section)

In an action by or against a person who, from any cause, is incapable of testifying, or by or against the committee, trustee, executor, administrator, heir, or other representative of the person so incapable of testifying, no judgment or decree shall be rendered in favor of an adverse or interested party founded on his uncorroborated testimony. In any such action, whether such adverse party testifies or not, all entries, memoranda, and declarations by the party so incapable of testifying made while he was capable, relevant to the matter in issue, may be received as evidence in all proceedings including without limitation those to which a person under a disability is a party. The phrase "from any cause" as used in this section shall not include situations in which the party who is incapable of testifying has rendered himself unable to testify by an intentional self-inflicted injury.

For the purposes of this section, and in addition to corroboration by any other competent evidence, an entry authored by an adverse or interested party contained in a business record may be competent evidence for corroboration of the testimony of an adverse or interested party. If authentication of the business record is not admitted in a request for admission, such business record shall be authenticated by a person other than the author of the entry who is not an adverse or interested party whose conduct is at issue in the allegations of the complaint.

Acts 1977, c. 617; Acts 1988, c. 426. Amended by Acts 2013, c. 61; Acts 2013, c. 637.

§ 8.01–397.1. Evidence of habit or routine practice; defined (Supreme Court Rule 2:406 derived from this section)

A. Admissibility. Evidence of the habit of a person or of the routine practice of an organization, whether corroborated or not and regardless of the presence of eye witnesses, is relevant to prove that the conduct of the person or organization on a particular occasion was in conformity with the habit or routine practice. Evidence of prior conduct may be relevant to rebut evidence of habit or routine practice.

B. Habit and routine practice defined. A "habit" is a person's regular response to repeated specific situations. A "routine practice" is a regular course of conduct of a group of persons or an organization in response to repeated specific situations.

C. The provisions of this section are applicable only in civil proceedings.

Acts 2000, c. 1026, eff. April 19, 2000.

§ 8.01–398. Privileged marital communications (Subsection (a) of Supreme Court Rule 2:504 derived from this section)

Husband and wife shall be competent witnesses to testify for or against each other in all civil actions.

In any civil proceeding, a person has a privilege to refuse to disclose, and to prevent anyone else from disclosing, any confidential communication between his spouse and him during their marriage, regardless of whether he is married to that spouse at the time he objects to disclosure. This privilege may not be asserted in any proceeding in which the spouses are adverse parties, or in which either spouse is charged with a crime or tort against the person or property of the other or against the minor child of either spouse. For the purposes of this section, "confidential communication" means a communication made privately by a person to his spouse that is not intended for disclosure to any other person.

Acts 1977, c. 617. Amended by Acts 2005, c. 809.

§ 8.01–399. Communications between physicians and patients (Supreme Court Rule 2:505 derived from this section)

A. Except at the request or with the consent of the patient, or as provided in this section, no duly licensed practitioner of any branch of the healing arts shall be permitted to testify in any civil action, respecting any information that he may have acquired in attending, examining or treating the patient in a professional capacity.

B. If the physical or mental condition of the patient is at issue in a civil action, the diagnoses, signs and symptoms, observations, evaluations, histories, or treatment plan of the practitioner, obtained or formulated as contemporaneously documented during the course of the practitioner's treatment, together with the facts communicated to, or otherwise learned by, such practitioner in connection with such attendance, examination or treatment shall be disclosed but only in discovery pursuant to the Rules of Court or through testimony at the trial of the action. In addition, disclosure may be ordered when a court, in the exercise of sound discretion, deems it necessary to the proper administration of justice. However, no order shall be entered compelling a party to sign a release for medical records from a health care provider unless the health care provider is not located in the Commonwealth or is a federal facility. If an order is issued pursuant to this section, it shall be restricted to the medical records that relate to the physical or mental conditions at issue in the case. No disclosure of diagnosis or treatment plan facts communicated to, or otherwise learned by, such practitioner shall occur if the court determines, upon the request of the patient, that such facts are not relevant to the subject matter involved in the pending action or do not appear to be reasonably calculated to lead to the discovery of admissible evidence. Only diagnosis offered to a reasonable degree of medical probability shall be admissible at trial.

C. This section shall not (i) be construed to repeal or otherwise affect the provisions of § 65.2-607 relating to privileged communications between physicians and surgeons and employees under the Workers' Compensation Act; (ii) apply to information communicated to any such practitioner in an effort unlawfully to procure a narcotic drug, or unlawfully to procure the administration of any such drug; or (iii) prohibit a duly licensed practitioner of the healing arts, or his agents, from disclosing information as required by state or federal law.

D. Neither a lawyer nor anyone acting on the lawyer's behalf shall obtain, in connection with pending or threatened litigation, information concerning a patient from a practitioner of any branch of the healing arts without the consent of the patient, except through discovery pursuant to the Rules of Supreme Court as herein provided. However, the prohibition of this subsection shall not apply to:

1. Communication between a lawyer retained to represent a practitioner of the healing arts, or that lawyer's agent, and that practitioner's employers, partners, agents, servants, employees, co-employees or others for whom, at law, the practitioner is or may be liable or who, at law, are or may be liable for the practitioner's acts or omissions;

2. Information about a patient provided to a lawyer or his agent by a practitioner of the healing arts employed by that lawyer to examine or evaluate the patient in accordance with Rule 4:10 of the Rules of Supreme Court; or

3. Contact between a lawyer or his agent and a nonphysician employee or agent of a practitioner of healing arts for any of the following purposes: (i) scheduling appearances, (ii) requesting a written recitation by the practitioner of handwritten records obtained by the lawyer or his agent from the practitioner, provided the request is made in writing and, if litigation is pending, a copy of the request and the practitioner's response is provided simultaneously to the patient or his attorney, (iii) obtaining information necessary to obtain service upon the practitioner in pending litigation, (iv) determining when records summoned will be provided by the practitioner or his agent, (v) determining what patient records the practitioner possesses in order to summons records in pending litigation, (vi) explaining any summons that the lawyer or his agent caused to be issued and served on the practitioner, (vii) verifying dates the practitioner treated the patient, provided that if litigation is pending the information obtained by the lawyer or his agent is promptly given, in writing, to the patient or his attorney, (viii) determining charges by the practitioner for appearance at a deposition or to testify before any tribunal or administrative body, or (ix) providing to or obtaining from the practitioner directions to a place to which he is or will be summoned to give testimony.

E. A clinical psychologist duly licensed under the provisions of Chapter 36 (§ 54.1-3600 et seq.) of Title 54.1 shall be considered a practitioner of a branch of the healing arts within the meaning of this section.

F. Nothing herein shall prevent a duly licensed practitioner of the healing arts, or his agents, from disclosing any information that he may have acquired in attending, examining or treating a patient in a professional capacity where such disclosure is necessary in connection with the care of the patient, the protection or enforcement of a practitioner's legal rights including such rights with respect to medical malpractice actions, or the operations of a health care facility or health maintenance organization or in order to comply with state or federal law.

Acts 1977, c. 617; Acts 1993, c. 556; Acts 1996, c. 937; Acts 1996, c. 980; Acts 1998, c. 314; Acts 2002, c. 308; Acts 2002, c. 723. Amended by Acts 2005, c. 649; Acts 2005, c. 692; Acts 2009, c. 714.

§ 8.01-400. Communications between ministers of religion and persons they counsel or advise (Supreme Court Rule 2:503 derived in part from this section)

No regular minister, priest, rabbi, or accredited practitioner over the age of eighteen years, of any religious organization or denomination usually referred to as a church, shall be required to give testimony as a witness or to relinquish notes, records or any written documentation made by such person, or disclose the contents of any such notes, records or written documentation, in discovery proceedings in any civil action which would disclose any information communicated to him in a confidential manner, properly entrusted to him in his professional capacity and necessary to enable him to discharge the functions of his office according to the usual course of his practice or discipline, wherein such person so communicating such information about himself or another is seeking spiritual counsel and advice relative to and growing out of the information so imparted.

Acts 1977, c. 617; Acts 1979, c. 3; Acts 1994, c. 198.

§ 8.01–400.1. Privileged communications by interpreters for the deaf (Supreme Court Rule 2:507 derived in part from this section)

Whenever a deaf person communicates through an interpreter to any person under such circumstances that the communication would be privileged, and such person could not be compelled to testify as to the communications, this privilege shall also apply to the interpreter.

Acts 1978, c. 601.

§ 8.01–400.2. Communications between certain mental health professionals and clients (Supreme Court Rule 2:506 derived from this section)

Except at the request of or with the consent of the client, no licensed professional counselor, as defined in § 54.1–3500; licensed clinical social worker, as defined in § 54.1–3700; licensed psychologist, as defined in § 54.1–3600; or licensed marriage and family therapist, as defined in § 54.1–3500, shall be required in giving testimony as a witness in any civil action to disclose any information communicated to him in a confidential manner, properly entrusted to him in his professional capacity and necessary to enable him to discharge his professional or occupational services according to the usual course of his practice or discipline, wherein such person so communicating such information about himself or another is seeking professional counseling or treatment and advice relative to and growing out of the information so imparted; provided, however, that when the physical or mental condition of the client is at issue in such action, or when a court, in the exercise of sound discretion, deems such disclosure necessary to the proper administration of justice, no fact communicated to, or otherwise learned by, such practitioner in connection with such counseling, treatment or advice shall be privileged, and disclosure may be required. The privileges conferred by this section shall not extend to testimony in matters relating to child abuse and neglect nor serve to relieve any person from the reporting requirements set forth in § 63.2–1509.

Acts 1982, c. 537. Amended by Acts 2005, c. 110.

§ 8.01–401. How adverse party may be examined; effect of refusal to testify (subsection (b) of Supreme Court Rule 2:607 and subsection (c) of Supreme Court Rule 2:611 derived from subsection A of this section)

A. A party called to testify for another, having an adverse interest, may be examined by such other party according to the rules applicable to cross-examination.

B. If any party, required by another to testify on his behalf, refuses to testify, the court, officer, or person before whom the proceeding is pending, may, in addition to punishing said party as for contempt, dismiss the action, or other proceeding of the party so refusing, as to the whole or any part thereof, or may strike out and disregard the plea, answer, or other defense of such party, or any part thereof, as justice may require.

Acts 1977, c. 617.

§ 8.01–401.1. Opinion testimony by experts; hearsay exception (subsection (a) of Supreme Court Rule 2:703, subsection (a) of Supreme Court Rule 2:705, and subsection (a) of Supreme Court Rule 2:706 derived from this section)

In any civil action any expert witness may give testimony and render an opinion or draw inferences from facts, circumstances or data made known to or perceived by such witness at or before the hearing or trial during which he is called upon to testify. The facts, circumstances or data relied upon by such witness in forming an opinion or drawing inferences, if of a type normally relied upon by others in the particular field of expertise in forming opinions and drawing inferences, need not be admissible in evidence.

The expert may testify in terms of opinion or inference and give his reasons therefor without prior disclosure of the underlying facts or data, unless the court requires otherwise. The expert may in any event be required to disclose the underlying facts or data on cross-examination.

To the extent called to the attention of an expert witness upon cross-examination or relied upon by the expert witness in direct examination, statements contained in published treatises, periodicals or pamphlets on a subject of history, medicine or other science or art, established as a reliable authority by testimony or by stipulation, shall not be excluded as hearsay. If admitted, the statements may be read into evidence but may not be received as exhibits. If the statements are to be introduced through an expert witness upon direct examination, copies of the specific statements shall be designated as literature to be introduced during direct examination and provided to opposing parties 30 days prior to trial unless otherwise ordered by the court.

If a statement has been designated by a party in accordance with and satisfies the requirements of this section, the expert witness called by that party need not have relied on the statement at the time of forming his opinion in order to read the statement into evidence during direct examination at trial.

Acts 1982, c. 392; Acts 1994, c. 328. Amended by Acts 2013, c. 379.

§ 8.01–401.2. Chiropractor, nurse practitioner, or physician assistant as expert witness

A. A doctor of chiropractic, when properly qualified, may testify as an expert witness in a court of law as to etiology, diagnosis, prognosis, treatment, treatment plan, and disability, including anatomical, physiological, and pathological considerations within the scope of the practice of chiropractic as defined in § 54.1–2900.

B. A physician assistant or nurse practitioner, when properly qualified, may testify as an expert witness in a court of law as to etiology, diagnosis, prognosis, treatment, treatment plan, and disability, including anatomical, physiological, and pathological considerations within the scope of his activities as authorized pursuant to § 54.1–2952. However, no physician assistant or nurse practitioner shall be permitted to testify as an expert witness for or against (i) a defendant doctor of medicine or osteopathic medicine in a medical malpractice action regarding the standard of care of a doctor of medicine or osteopathic medicine or (ii) a defendant health care provider in a medical malpractice action regarding causation.

Acts 1984, c. 569. Amended by Acts 2014, c. 361; Acts 2014, c. 391; Acts 2015, c. 295; Acts 2015, c. 306.

§ 8.01–401.2:1. Podiatrist as an expert witness

A podiatrist shall not be permitted to testify as an expert witness against a doctor of medicine or osteopathic medicine in connection with a medical malpractice civil court proceeding or a medical malpractice review panel in any case where the doctor or osteopath is a defendant in such proceeding.

Added by Acts 2010, c. 715, eff. April 13, 2010; Acts 2010, c. 725, eff. April 13, 2010.

§ 8.01–401.3. Opinion testimony and conclusions as to facts critical to civil case resolution (Supreme Court Rule 2:701 derived from subsection B of this section, subdivision (a)(i) of Supreme Court Rule 2:702 derived from subsection A of this section, and subsection (a) of Supreme Court Rule 2:704 derived from subsections B and C of this section)

A. In a civil proceeding, if scientific, technical, or other specialized knowledge will assist the trier of fact to understand the evidence or to determine a fact in issue, a witness qualified as an expert by knowledge, skill, experience, training, or education may testify thereto in the form of an opinion or otherwise.

B. No expert or lay witness while testifying in a civil proceeding shall be prohibited from expressing an otherwise admissible opinion or conclusion as to any matter of fact solely because that fact is the ultimate issue or critical to the resolution of the case. However, in no event shall such witness be permitted to express any opinion which constitutes a conclusion of law.

C. Except as provided by the provisions of this section, the exceptions to the "ultimate fact in issue" rule recognized in the Commonwealth prior to enactment of this section shall remain in full force.

Acts 1993, c. 909.

§ 8.01–402. Members of Department of Motor Vehicles' Crash Investigation Team not to be required to give evidence in certain cases

No member of the Department of Motor Vehicles' Crash Investigation Team shall be required to give evidence concerning any statements made to him in the course of such investigation before any court or grand jury in any case involving a motor vehicle crash on the highways of the Commonwealth in which any member or members of such Crash Investigation Team made or took part in any investigation pursuant to a directive from the Commissioner of the Department of Motor Vehicles for purposes of research and evaluation of the Commonwealth's highway safety program.

Acts 1977, c. 617; Acts 1992, c. 108.

§ 8.01–403. Witness proving adverse; contradiction; prior inconsistent statement (Subsection (c) of Supreme Court Rule 2:607 and subdivision (a)(i) of Supreme Court Rule 2:613 derived from this section)

A party producing a witness shall not be allowed to impeach his credit by general evidence of bad character, but he may, in case the witness shall in the opinion of the court prove adverse, by leave of the court, prove that he has made at other times a statement inconsistent with his present testimony; but before such last mentioned proof can be given the circumstances of the supposed statement, sufficient to designate the particular occasion, must be mentioned to the witness, and he must be asked whether or not he has made such statement. In every such case the court, if requested by either party, shall instruct the jury not to consider the evidence of such inconsistent statements, except for the purpose of contradicting the witness.

Acts 1977, c. 617.

§ 8.01–404. Contradiction by prior inconsistent writing (Subdivision (b)(i) of Supreme Court Rule 2:613 derived in part from this section and subdivision (b)(ii) of Supreme Court Rule 2:613 derived from this section)

A witness may be cross-examined as to previous statements made by him in writing or reduced into writing, relative to the subject matter of the civil action, without such writing being shown to him; but if it is intended to contradict such witness by the writing, his attention must, before such contradictory proof can be given, be called to the particular occasion on which the writing is supposed to have been made, and he may be asked if he did not make a writing of the purport of the one to be offered to contradict him, and if he denies making it, or does not admit its execution, it shall then be shown to him, and if he admits its genuineness, he shall be allowed to make his own explanation of it; but it shall be competent for the court at any time during the trial to require the production of the writing for its inspection, and the court may thereupon make such use of it for the purpose of the trial as it may think best. This section is subject to the qualification, that in an action to recover for a personal injury or death by wrongful act or neglect, no ex parte affidavit or statement in writing other than a deposition, after due notice, of a witness and no extrajudicial recording made at any time other than simultaneously with the wrongful act or negligence at issue of the voice of such witness, or reproduction or transcript thereof, as to the facts or circumstances attending the wrongful act or neglect complained of, shall be used to contradict him as a witness in the case. Nothing in this section shall be construed to prohibit the use of any such ex parte affidavit or statement in an action on an insurance policy based upon a judgment recovered in a personal injury or death by wrongful act case.

Acts 1977, c. 617. Amended by Acts 2007, c. 598.

§ 8.01–405. Who may administer oath to witness

Any person before whom a witness is to be examined may administer an oath to such witness. In addition, a clerk or deputy clerk may administer an oath to a witness in the presence and at the direction of a judge before whom the witness is to be examined.

Acts 1977, c. 617; Acts 1984, c. 536.

§ 8.01–406. Interpreters; recording testimony of deaf witness (Supreme Court Rule 2:604 derived from this section)

Interpreters shall be sworn truly so to do. In any judicial proceeding, the judge on his own motion or on the motion of a party to the proceeding may order all of the testimony of a deaf individual and the interpretation thereof to be visually electronically recorded for use in verification of the official transcript of the proceedings.

Acts 1977, c. 617; Acts 1978, c. 601.

ARTICLE 5

COMPELLING ATTENDANCE OF WITNESSES, ETC.

§ 8.01–407. How summons for witness issued, and to whom directed; prior permission of court to summon certain officials and judges; attendance before commissioner of other state; attorney-issued summons

A. A summons may be issued, directed as prescribed in § 8.01–292, commanding the officer to summon any person to attend on the day and at the place that such attendance is desired, to give evidence before a court, grand jury, arbitrators, magistrate, notary, or any commissioner or other person appointed by a court or acting under its process or authority in a judicial or quasi-judicial capacity. The summons may be issued by the clerk of the court if the attendance is desired at a court or in a proceeding pending in a court. The clerk shall not impose any time restrictions limiting the right to properly request a summons up to and including the date of the proceeding:

If attendance is desired before a commissioner in chancery or other commissioner of a court, the summons may be issued by the clerk of the court in which the matter is pending, or by such commissioner in chancery or other commissioner;

If attendance is desired before a notary or other officer taking a deposition, the summons may be issued by such notary or other officer at the instance of the attorney desiring the attendance of the person sought;

If attendance is sought before a grand jury, the summons may be issued by the attorney for the Commonwealth, or the clerk of the court, at the instance of the attorney for the Commonwealth.

Except as otherwise provided in this subsection, if attendance is desired in a civil proceeding pending in a court or at a deposition in connection with such proceeding, including medical malpractice review panels, and a claim before the Workers' Compensation Commission, a summons may be issued by an attorney-at-law who is an active member of the Virginia State Bar at the time of issuance, as an officer of the court. An attorney-issued summons shall be on a form approved by the Supreme Court, signed by the attorney and shall include the attorney's address. The summons and any transmittal sheet shall be deemed to be a pleading to which the provisions of § 8.01–271.1 shall apply. A copy of the summons and, if served by a sheriff, all service of process fees, shall be mailed or delivered to the clerk's office of the court in which the case is pending or the Workers' Compensation Commission, as applicable, on the day of issuance by the attorney. The law governing summonses issued by a clerk shall apply mutatis mutandis. When an attorney-at-law transmits one or more attorney-issued subpoenas to a sheriff to be served in his jurisdiction, such subpoenas shall be accompanied by a transmittal sheet. The transmittal sheet, which may be in the form of a letter, shall contain for each subpoena: (i) the person to be served, (ii) the name of the city or county in which the subpoena is to be served, in parentheses, (iii) the style of the case in which the subpoena was issued, (iv) the court in which the case is pending, and (v) the amount of fees tendered or paid to each clerk in whose court the case is pending together with a photocopy of the payment instrument or clerk's receipt. If copies of the same transmittal sheet are used to send subpoenas to more than one sheriff for service of process, then subpoenas shall be grouped by the jurisdiction in which they are to be served. For each person to be served, an original subpoena and copy thereof shall be included. If the attorney desires a return copy of the transmittal sheet as proof of receipt, he shall also enclose an additional copy of the transmittal sheet together with an envelope addressed to the attorney with sufficient first class postage affixed. Upon receipt of such transmittal, the transmittal sheet shall be date-stamped and, if the extra copy and above-described envelope are provided, the copy shall also be date-stamped and returned to the attorney-at-law in the above-described envelope.

However, when such transmittal does not comply with the provisions of this section, the sheriff may promptly return such transmittal if accompanied by a short description of such noncompliance. An attorney may not issue a summons in any of the following civil proceedings: (i) habeas corpus under Article 3 (§ 8.01–654 et seq.) of Chapter 25 of this title, (ii) delinquency or abuse and neglect proceedings under Article 3 (§ 16.1–241 et seq.) of Chapter 11 of Title 16.1, (iii) civil forfeiture proceedings, (iv) habitual offender proceedings under Article 9 (§ 46.2–351 et seq.) of Chapter 3 of Title 46.2, (v) administrative license suspension pursuant to § 46.2–391.2, and (vi) petition for writs of mandamus or prohibition in connection with criminal proceedings. A sheriff shall not be required to serve an attorney-issued subpoena that is not issued at least five business days prior to the date that attendance is desired.

In other cases, if attendance is desired, the summons may be issued by the clerk of the circuit court of the county or city in which the attendance is desired.

A summons shall express on whose behalf, and in what case or about what matter, the witness is to attend. Failure to respond to any such summons shall be punishable by the court in which the proceeding is pending as for contempt. When any subpoena is served less than five calendar days before appearance is required, the court may, after considering all of the circumstances, refuse to enforce the subpoena for lack of adequate notice. If any subpoena is served less than five calendar days before appearance is required upon any judicial officer generally incompetent to testify pursuant to § 19.2–271, such subpoena shall be without legal force or effect unless the subpoena has been issued by a judge.

B. No subpoena shall, without permission of the court first obtained, issue for the attendance of the Governor, Lieutenant Governor, or Attorney General of this Commonwealth, a judge of any court thereof; the President or Vice President of the United States; any member of the President's Cabinet; any ambassador or consul; or any military officer on active duty holding the rank of admiral or general.

C. This section shall be deemed to authorize a summons to compel attendance of a citizen of the Commonwealth before commissioners or other persons appointed by authority of another state when the summons requires the attendance of such witness at a place not out of his county or city.

Acts 1977, c. 617; Acts 1992, c. 506; Acts 2000, c. 813; Acts 2002, c. 463. Amended by Acts 2004, c. 335; Acts 2007, c. 199; Acts 2010, c. 302; Acts 2010, c. 486.

§ 8.01–407.1. Identity of persons communicating anonymously over the Internet

A. In civil proceedings where it is alleged that an anonymous individual has engaged in Internet communications that are tortious, any subpoena seeking information held by a nongovernmental person or entity that would identify the tortfeasor shall be governed by the following procedure unless more expedited scheduling directions have been ordered by the court upon consideration of the interests of each person affected thereby:

1. At least thirty days prior to the date on which disclosure is sought, a party seeking information identifying an anonymous communicator shall file with the appropriate circuit court a complete copy of the subpoena and all items annexed or incorporated therein, along with supporting material showing:

a. That one or more communications that are or may be tortious or illegal have been made by the anonymous communicator, or that the party requesting the subpoena has a legitimate, good faith basis to contend that such party is the victim of conduct actionable in the jurisdiction where the suit was filed. A copy of the communications that are the subject of the action or subpoena shall be submitted.

b. That other reasonable efforts to identify the anonymous communicator have proven fruitless.

c. That the identity of the anonymous communicator is important, is centrally needed to advance the claim, relates to a core claim or defense, or is directly and materially relevant to that claim or defense.

d. That no motion to dismiss, motion for judgment on the pleadings, or judgment as a matter of law, demurrer or summary judgment-type motion challenging the viability of the lawsuit of the underlying plaintiff is pending. The pendency of such a motion may be considered by the court in determining whether to enforce, suspend or strike the proposed disclosure obligation under the subpoena.

e. That the individuals or entities to whom the subpoena is addressed are likely to have responsive information.

f. If the subpoena sought relates to an action pending in another jurisdiction, the application shall contain a copy of the pleadings in such action, along with the mandate, writ or commission of the court where the action is pending that authorizes the discovery of the information sought in the Commonwealth.

2. Two copies of the subpoena and supporting materials set forth in subdivision A. 1. a. through f. shall be served upon the person to whom it is addressed along with payment sufficient to cover postage for mailing one copy of the application within the United States by registered mail, return receipt requested.

3. Except where the anonymous communicator has consented to disclosure in advance, within five business days after receipt of a subpoena and supporting materials calling for disclosure of identifying information concerning an anonymous communicator, the individual or entity to whom the subpoena is addressed shall (i) send an electronic mail notification to the anonymous communicator reporting that the subpoena has been received if an e-mail address is available and (ii) dispatch one copy thereof, by registered mail or commercial delivery service, return receipt requested, to the anonymous communicator at his last known address, if any is on file with the person to whom the subpoena is addressed.

4. At least seven business days prior to the date on which disclosure is sought under the subpoena, any interested person may file a detailed written objection, motion to quash, or motion for protective order. Any such papers filed by the anonymous communicator shall be served on or before the date of filing upon the party seeking the subpoena and the party to whom the subpoena is addressed. Any such papers filed by the party to whom the subpoena is addressed shall be served on or before the date of filing upon the party seeking the subpoena and the anonymous communicator whose identifying information is sought. Service is effective when it has been mailed, dispatched by commercial delivery service, transmitted by facsimile, or delivered to counsel of record and to parties having no counsel.

5. Any written objection, motion to quash, or motion for protective order shall set forth all grounds relied upon for denying the disclosure sought in the subpoena and shall also address to the extent feasible (i) whether the identity of the anonymous communicator has been disclosed in any way beyond its recordation in the account records of the party to whom the subpoena is addressed, (ii) whether the subpoena fails to allow a reasonable time for compliance, (iii) whether it requires disclosure of privileged or other protected matter and no exception or waiver applies, or (iv) whether it subjects a person to undue burden.

6. The party to whom the subpoena is addressed shall not comply with the subpoena earlier than three business days before the date on which disclosure is due, to allow the anonymous communicator the opportunity to object. If any person files a written objection, motion to quash, or motion for protective order, compliance with the subpoena shall be deferred until the appropriate court rules on the obligation to comply. If an objection or motion is made, the party serving the subpoena shall not be entitled to inspect or copy the materials except pursuant to an order of the court on behalf of which the subpoena was issued. If an objection or motion has been filed, any interested person may notice the matter for a hearing. Two copies of any such notice shall be served upon the subpoenaed party, who shall mail one copy thereof, by registered mail or commercial delivery service, return receipt requested, to the anonymous communicator whose identifying information is the subject of the subpoena at that person's last known address.

B. The party requesting or issuing a subpoena for information identifying an anonymous Internet communicator shall serve along with each copy of such subpoena notices in boldface capital letters in substantially this form:

NOTICE TO INTERNET SERVICE PROVIDER

WITHIN FIVE BUSINESS DAYS AFTER RECEIPT OF THIS SUBPOENA CALLING FOR IDENTIFYING INFORMATION CONCERNING YOUR CLIENT, SUBSCRIBER OR CUSTOMER, EXCEPT WHERE CONSENT TO DISCLOSURE HAS BEEN GIVEN IN ADVANCE, YOU ARE REQUIRED BY § 8.01–407.1 OF THE CODE OF VIRGINIA TO MAIL ONE COPY THEREOF, BY REGISTERED MAIL OR COMMERCIAL DELIVERY SERVICE, RETURN RECEIPT REQUESTED, TO THE CLIENT, SUBSCRIBER OR CUSTOMER WHOSE IDENTIFYING INFORMATION IS THE SUBJECT OF THE SUBPOENA. AT LEAST SEVEN BUSINESS DAYS PRIOR TO THE DATE ON WHICH DISCLOSURE IS SOUGHT YOU MAY, BUT ARE NOT REQUIRED TO, FILE A DETAILED WRITTEN OBJECTION, MOTION TO QUASH OR MOTION FOR PROTECTIVE OR-

DER. ANY SUCH OBJECTION OR MOTION SHALL BE SERVED UPON THE PARTY INITIATING THE SUBPOENA AND UPON THE CLIENT, SUBSCRIBER OR CUSTOMER WHOSE IDENTIFYING INFORMATION IS SOUGHT.

IF YOU CHOOSE NOT TO OBJECT TO THE SUBPOENA, YOU MUST ALLOW TIME FOR YOUR CLIENT, SUBSCRIBER OR CUSTOMER TO FILE HIS OWN OBJECTION, THEREFORE YOU MUST NOT RESPOND TO THE SUBPOENA ANY EARLIER THAN THREE BUSINESS DAYS BEFORE THE DISCLOSURE IS DUE.

IF YOU RECEIVE NOTICE THAT YOUR CLIENT, SUBSCRIBER OR CUSTOMER HAS FILED A WRITTEN OBJECTION, MOTION TO QUASH OR MOTION FOR PROTECTIVE ORDER REGARDING THIS SUBPOENA, OR IF YOU FILE A MOTION TO QUASH THIS SUBPOENA, NO DISCLOSURE PURSUANT TO THE SUBPOENA SHALL BE MADE EXCEPT PURSUANT TO AN ORDER OF THE COURT ON BEHALF OF WHICH THE SUBPOENA WAS ISSUED.

NOTICE TO INTERNET USER

THE ATTACHED PAPERS MEAN THAT ______

____

(INSERT NAME OF PARTY REQUESTING OR CAUSING ISSUANCE OF THE SUBPOENA) HAS EITHER ASKED THE COURT TO ISSUE A SUBPOENA, OR A SUBPOENA HAS BEEN ISSUED, TO YOUR INTERNET SERVICE PROVIDER ___

____

(INSERT NAME OF INTERNET SERVICE PROVIDER) REQUIRING PRODUCTION OF INFORMATION REGARDING YOUR IDENTITY. UNLESS A DETAILED WRITTEN OBJECTION IS FILED WITH THE COURT, THE SERVICE PROVIDER WILL BE REQUIRED BY LAW TO RESPOND BY PROVIDING THE REQUIRED INFORMATION. IF YOU BELIEVE YOUR IDENTIFYING INFORMATION SHOULD NOT BE DISCLOSED AND OBJECT TO SUCH DISCLOSURE, YOU HAVE THE RIGHT TO FILE WITH THE CLERK OF COURT A DETAILED WRITTEN OBJECTION, MOTION TO QUASH THE SUBPOENA OR MOTION TO OBTAIN A PROTECTIVE ORDER. YOU MAY ELECT TO CONTACT AN ATTORNEY TO REPRESENT YOUR INTERESTS. IF YOU ELECT TO FILE A WRITTEN OBJECTION, MOTION TO QUASH, OR MOTION FOR PROTECTIVE ORDER, IT SHOULD BE FILED AS SOON AS POSSIBLE, AND MUST IN ALL INSTANCES BE FILED NO LESS THAN SEVEN BUSINESS DAYS BEFORE THE DATE ON WHICH DISCLOSURE IS DUE (LISTED IN THE SUBPOENA). IF YOU ELECT TO FILE A WRITTEN OBJECTION OR MOTION AGAINST THIS SUBPOENA, YOU MUST AT THE SAME TIME SEND A COPY OF THAT OBJECTION OR MOTION TO BOTH YOUR INTERNET SERVICE PROVIDER AND THE PARTY WHO REQUESTED THE SUBPOENA. IF YOU WISH TO OPPOSE THE ATTACHED SUBPOENA, IN WHOLE OR IN PART, YOU OR YOUR ATTORNEY MAY FILE A WRITTEN OBJECTION, A MOTION TO QUASH THE SUBPOENA, OR A MOTION FOR A PROTECTIVE ORDER OR YOU MAY USE THE FORM BELOW, WHICH MUST BE FILED WITH THE COURT AND SERVED UPON THE PARTY REQUESTING THE SUBPOENA AND THE INTERNET SERVICE PROVIDER BY MAILING AT LEAST SEVEN BUSINESS DAYS PRIOR TO THE DATE SET IN THE SUBPOENA FOR DISCLOSURE:

____

Name of Court Listed on Subpoena

____

Name of Party Seeking Information
Case No. __________

OBJECTION TO SUBPOENA DUCES TECUM

I object to the Subpoena Duces Tecum addressed to

____

for the following reasons:

[Name of Internet Service Provider to Whom the Subpoena is Addressed]

(Please PRINT. Set forth, in detail, all reasons why the subpoena should not be complied with, and in addition, state (i) whether the identity of the anonymous communicator has been disclosed in any fashion, (ii) whether the subpoena fails to allow a reasonable time for compliance, (iii) whether it requires disclosure of privileged or other protected matter and no exception or waiver applies, or (iv) whether it subjects a person to undue burden.)

____
____
____
____
____
____
____
____

(attach additional sheets if needed)

____

Respectfully Submitted,

____

John Doe ______________________________

____

Enter e-mail nickname or other alias used in communicating via the Internet service provider to whom the subpoena is addressed. ______________

CERTIFICATE

I hereby certify that a true copy of the above Objection to Subpoena Duces Tecum was mailed this _____ day of __________, (month, year), to

____

(Name and address of party seeking information) and

____

(Name and address of Internet Service Provider)

John Doe ______________

Enter e-mail nickname or other alias used in communicating via the Internet service provider to whom the subpoena is addressed. ______________

Added by Acts 2002, c. 875.

§ 8.01–408. Recognizance taken upon continuance of case

Upon the continuance of any civil case in a court, the court shall at the request of any party litigant require such party's witnesses then present to enter into recognizance in such penalty as the court may deem proper, either with or without security, for their appearance to give evidence in such case on such day as may then be fixed for the trial thereof, such recognizance to be taken, conditioned, and entered of record in the same manner provided in §§ 19.2–135 to 19.2–137, for taking recognizance.

Acts 1977, c. 617.

§ 8.01–409. When court may have process for witness executed by its own officer in another county or city

Whenever on the calling or during the trial of a civil case in any court it appears to the court that it is necessary to have a witness from a county or city other than that of trial, the summons, rule, or attachment issued for such witness from the trial court may, when the court so orders, be executed by its officers in any county or city of the Commonwealth, for which services the officer shall be allowed a reasonable compensation by the court.

Acts 1977, c. 617.

§ 8.01–410. Inmates as witnesses in civil actions

Whenever any party in a civil action in any circuit court in this Commonwealth requires as a witness in his behalf, an inmate in a state or local correctional facility as defined in § 53.1–1, the court, on the application of such party or his attorney may, in its discretion and upon consideration of the importance of the personal appearance of the witness and the nature of the offense for which he is imprisoned, issue an order to the Director of the Department of Corrections to deliver such witness to the sheriff of the jurisdiction of the court issuing the order. If authorized by the court, the clerk of the circuit court or a deputy clerk may issue these orders on behalf of the court. The sheriff shall transport the inmate to the court to testify as such witness, and after he has testified and been released as such witness, the sheriff shall return the witness to the custody of the Department.

If necessary the sheriff may confine the inmate for the night in any convenient local correctional facility.

Under such rules and regulations as the superintendent of such an institution may prescribe, any party to a civil action in any circuit court in this Commonwealth may take the deposition of an inmate in the facility, which deposition, when taken, may be admissible in evidence as other depositions in civil actions.

The party seeking the testimony of such inmate shall advance a sum sufficient to defray the expenses and compensation of the correctional officers and sheriff, which the court shall tax as other costs.

For the purposes of this section, "correctional officers" shall have the same meaning as provided in § 53.1–1.

Acts 1977, c. 617; Acts 1998, c. 596; Acts 2001, c. 513; Acts 2002, c. 515; Acts 2002, c. 544.

ARTICLE 6

UNIFORM FOREIGN DEPOSITIONS ACT

§§ 8.01–411 to 8.01–412.1. Repealed by Acts 2009, c. 701

ARTICLE 6.1

UNIFORM AUDIO-VISUAL DEPOSITION ACT

§ 8.01–412.2. Authorization of audio-visual deposition; official record; uses

Any deposition may be recorded by audio-visual means without a stenographic record. Any party may make, at his own expense, a simultaneous stenographic or audio record of the deposition. Upon request and at his own expense, any party is entitled to an audio or audio-visual copy of the audio-visual recording.

The audio-visual recording is an official record of the deposition. A transcript prepared by a court reporter shall also be deemed an official record of the deposition. An audio-visual deposition may be used for any purpose and under any circumstances in which a stenographic deposition may be used.

For purposes of this article, "audio-visual" shall include video conferencing and teleconferencing.

Acts 1983, c. 305; Acts 2000, c. 821.

§ 8.01–412.3. Notice of audio-visual deposition

The notice for taking an audio-visual deposition and the subpoena for attendance at that deposition shall state that the deposition will be recorded by audio-visual means.

Acts 1983, c. 305.

§ 8.01–412.4. Procedure

The taking of audio-visual depositions shall be in accordance with the rules of the Supreme Court generally applicable to depositions. However, the following procedure shall be observed in recording an audio-visual deposition:

The deposition must begin with an oral or written statement on camera which includes (i) each operator's name and business address or, if applicable, the identity of the video conferencing or teleconferencing proprietor and locations participating in the video conference or teleconference; (ii) the name and business address of the operator's employer; (iii) the date, time and place of the deposition; (iv) the caption of the case; (v) the name of the witness; (vi) the party on whose behalf the deposition is being taken; (vii) with respect to video conferencing or teleconferencing, the identities of persons present at the deposition and the location of each such person; and (viii) any stipulations by the parties.

In addition, all counsel present on behalf of any party or witness shall identify themselves on camera. The oath for witnesses shall be administered on camera. If the length of a deposition requires the use of more than one recording unit, the end of each unit and the beginning of each succeeding unit shall be announced on camera. At the conclusion of a deposition, a statement shall be made on camera that the deposition is concluded. A statement may be made on camera setting forth any stipulations made by counsel concerning the custody of the audio-visual recording and exhibits or other pertinent matters.

All objections must be made as in the case of stenographic depositions. In any case where the court orders the audio-visual recording to be edited prior to its use, the original recording shall not be altered but shall be maintained as is.

Unless otherwise stipulated by the parties, the original audio-visual recording of a deposition, any copy edited pursuant to an order of the court, and exhibits shall be filed with the clerk of the court in accordance with the rules of the Supreme Court.

Acts 1983, c. 305; Acts 1993, c. 208; Acts 2000, c. 821.

§ 8.01–412.5. Costs

In any case where a deposition taken pursuant to this article does not conform to the requirements for use of such deposition as provided in the rules of the Supreme Court, the expense of conforming the recording shall be borne by the proponent of the deposition.

Acts 1983, c. 305; Acts 1984, c. 95.

§ 8.01–412.6. Promulgation of rules for standards and guidelines

The Supreme Court may promulgate rules establishing standards for audio-visual equipment and guidelines for taking and using audio-visual depositions.

Acts 1983, c. 305.

§ 8.01–412.7. Short title

This article may be cited as the "Uniform Audio–Visual Deposition Act."

Acts 1983, c. 305.

ARTICLE 6.2

UNIFORM INTERSTATE DEPOSITIONS AND DISCOVERY ACT

For text of Uniform Act and variation notes and annotation materials for adopting jurisdictions, see Uniform Laws Annotated, Master Edition, Volume 13, Pt. II.

§ 8.01–412.8. Short title

This article may be cited as the Uniform Interstate Depositions and Discovery Act.

Added by Acts 2009, c. 701.

§ 8.01–412.9. Definitions

For purposes of this article, unless the context requires otherwise:

"Foreign jurisdiction" means a state other than the Commonwealth.

"Foreign subpoena" means a subpoena issued under authority of a court of record of a foreign jurisdiction.

"Person" means an individual, corporation, business trust, estate, trust, partnership, limited liability company, association, joint venture, public corporation, government, or governmental subdivision, agency or instrumentality, or any other legal or commercial entity.

"State" means a state of the United States, the District of Columbia, Puerto Rico, the United States Virgin Islands, or any territory or insular possession subject to the jurisdiction of the United States.

"Subpoena" means a document, however denominated, issued under the authority of a court of record requiring a person to:

1. Attend and give testimony at a deposition;

2. Produce and permit inspection and copying of designated books, documents, records, electronically stored information, or tangible things in the possession, custody, or control of the person; or

3. Permit inspection of premises under the control of the person.

Added by Acts 2009, c. 701.

§ 8.01–412.10. Issuance of subpoena

A. To request the issuance of a subpoena under this article, a party shall submit to the clerk of court in the circuit in which discovery is sought to be conducted in the Commonwealth (i) a foreign subpoena and (ii) a written statement that the law of the foreign jurisdiction grants reciprocal privileges to citizens of the Commonwealth for taking discovery in the jurisdiction that issued the foreign subpoena.

B. When a party submits a foreign subpoena to a clerk of court in the Commonwealth, the clerk, in accordance with that court's procedure, shall promptly issue a subpoena for service upon the person to which the foreign subpoena is directed.

C. A subpoena under subsection B shall:

1. Incorporate the terms used in the foreign subpoena; and

2. Contain or be accompanied by the names, addresses, and telephone numbers of all counsel of record in the proceeding to which the subpoena relates and of any party not represented by counsel.

D. A request for the issuance of a subpoena under this article does not constitute an appearance in the courts of the Commonwealth, and no civil action need be filed in the circuit court of the Commonwealth.

E. The provisions of this article shall be in addition to other procedures authorized in the Code of Virginia and the rules of court for obtaining discovery.

Added by Acts 2009, c. 701.

§ 8.01–412.11. Service of subpoena

A subpoena issued by a clerk of court under this article shall be served in compliance with the applicable statutes of the Commonwealth for service of a subpoena.

Added by Acts 2009, c. 701.

§ 8.01–412.12. Deposition, production, and inspection

Statutes and rules applicable in actions pending in the circuit courts of the Commonwealth with respect to compliance with subpoenas to attend and give testimony, produce designated books, documents, records, electronically stored information, or tangible things, or permit inspection of premises, shall apply to subpoenas issued under § 8.01–412.10.

Added by Acts 2009, c. 701.

§ 8.01–412.13. Application to court

An application to the court for a protective order or to enforce, quash, or modify a subpoena issued by a clerk of court under § 8.01–412.10 shall comply with the statutes and rules of court of the Commonwealth and be submitted to the court in the circuit in which discovery is to be conducted. A separate civil action need not be filed.

Added by Acts 2009, c. 701.

§ 8.01–412.14. Uniformity of application and construction; reciprocal privileges

In applying and construing this uniform act, consideration shall be given to the need to promote uniformity of the law with respect to its subject matter among states that enact it. The privilege extended to persons in other states for discovery under this article shall only apply if the jurisdiction where the action is pending has extended a similar privilege to persons in the Commonwealth, by that jurisdiction's enactment of the Uniform Interstate Depositions and Discovery Act, a predecessor uniform act, or another comparable law or rule of court providing substantially similar mechanisms for use by out-of-state parties.

Added by Acts 2009, c. 701.

§ 8.01–412.15. Application to pending actions

This article applies to requests for discovery submitted on or after July 1, 2009.

Added by Acts 2009, c. 701.

ARTICLE 7

MEDICAL EVIDENCE

§ 8.01–413. Certain copies of health care provider's records or papers of patient admissible; right of patient, his attorney and authorized insurer to copies of such records or papers; subpoena; damages, costs and attorneys' fees

A. In any case where the hospital, nursing facility, physician's, or other health care provider's original records or papers of any patient in a hospital or institution for the treatment of physical or mental illness are admissible or would be admissible as evidence, any typewritten copy, photograph, photostatted copy, or microphotograph or printout or other hard copy generated from computerized or other electronic storage, microfilm, or other photographic, mechanical, electronic or chemical storage process thereof shall be admissible as evidence in any court of this Commonwealth in like manner as the original, if the printout or hard copy or microphotograph or photograph is properly authenticated by the employees having authority to release or produce the original records.

Any hospital, nursing facility, physician, or other health care provider whose records or papers relating to any such patient are subpoenaed for production as provided by law may comply with the subpoena by a timely mailing to the clerk issuing the subpoena or in whose court the action is pending properly authenticated copies, photographs or microphotographs in lieu of the originals. The court whose clerk issued the subpoena or, in the case of an attorney-issued subpoena, in which the action is pending, may, after notice to such hospital, nursing facility, physician, or other health care provider, enter an order requiring production of the originals, if available, of any stored records or papers whose copies, photographs or microphotographs are not sufficiently legible.

Except as provided in subsection G, the party requesting the subpoena duces tecum or on whose behalf an attorney-issued subpoena duces tecum was issued shall be liable for the reasonable charges of the hospital, nursing facility, physician, or other health care provider for the service of maintaining, retrieving, reviewing, preparing, copying and mailing the items produced. Except for copies of X-ray photographs, however, such charges shall not exceed $0.50 for each page up to 50 pages and $0.25 a page thereafter for copies from paper or other hard copy generated from computerized or other electronic storage, or other photographic, mechanical, electronic, imaging or chemical storage process and $1 per page for copies from microfilm or other micrographic process, plus all postage and shipping costs and a search and handling fee not to exceed $10.

Upon request, a patient's account balance or itemized listing of charges maintained by a health care provider shall be supplied at no cost up to three times every twelve months to either the patient or the patient's attorney.

B. Copies of hospital, nursing facility, physician's, or other health care provider's records or papers shall be furnished within 15 days of receipt of such request to the patient, his attorney, his executor or administrator, or an authorized insurer upon such patient's, attorney's, executor's, administrator's, or authorized insurer's written request, which request shall comply with the requirements of subsection E of § 32.1–127.1:03.

However, copies of a patient's records shall not be furnished to such patient when the patient's treating physician or clinical psychologist, in the exercise of professional judgment, has made a part of the patient's records a written statement that in his opinion the furnishing to or review by the patient of such records would be reasonably likely to endanger the life or physical safety of the patient or another person, or that such health records make reference to a person, other than a health care provider, and the access requested would be reasonably likely to cause substantial harm to such referenced person. In any such case, if requested by the patient or his attorney or authorized insurer, such records shall be furnished within 15 days of the date of such request to the patient's attorney or authorized insurer, rather than to the patient.

If the records are not provided to the patient in accordance with this section, then, if requested by the patient, the hospital, nursing facility, physician, or other health care provider denying the request shall comply with the patient's request to either (i) provide a copy of the records to a physician or clinical psychologist of the patient's choice whose licensure, training, and experience, relative to the patient's condition, are at least equivalent to that of the treating physician or clinical psychologist upon whose opinion the denial is based, who shall, at the patient's expense, make a judgment as to whether to make the records available to the patient or (ii) designate a physician or clinical psychologist, whose licensure, training, and experience, relative to the patient's condition, are at least equivalent to that of the treating physician or clinical psychologist upon whose opinion the denial is based and who did not participate in the original decision to deny the patient's request for his records, who shall, at the expense of the provider denying access to the patient, review the records and make a judgment as to whether to make the records available to the patient. In either such event, the hospital, nursing facility, physician, or other health care provider denying the request shall comply with the judgment of the reviewing physician or clinical psychologist.

Except as provided in subsection G, a reasonable charge may be made by the hospital, nursing facility, physician or other health care provider maintaining the records for the cost of the services relating to the maintenance, retrieval, review, and preparation of the copies of the records. Except for copies of X-ray photographs, however, such charges shall not exceed $0.50 per page for up to 50 pages and $0.25 a page thereafter for copies from paper or other hard copy generated from computerized or other electronic storage, or other photographic, mechanical, electronic, imaging or chemical storage process and $1 per page for copies from microfilm or other micrographic process, a fee for search and handling, not to exceed $10, and all postage and shipping costs. Any hospital, nursing facility, physician, or other health care provider receiving such a request from a patient's attorney or authorized insurer shall require a writing signed by the patient confirming the attorney's or authorized insurer's authority to make the request and shall accept a photocopy, facsimile, or other copy of the original signed by the patient as if it were an original.

Upon request, a patient's account balance or itemized listing of charges maintained by a health care provider shall be supplied at no cost up to three times every twelve months to either the patient or the patient's attorney.

C. Upon the failure of any hospital, nursing facility, physician, or other health care provider to comply with any written request made in accordance with subsection B within the period of time specified in that subsection and within the manner specified in subsections E and F of § 32.1–127.1:03, the patient, his attorney, his executor or administrator, or authorized insurer may cause a subpoena duces tecum to be issued. The subpoena may be issued (i) upon filing a request therefor with the clerk of the circuit court wherein any eventual suit would be required to be filed, and upon payment of the fees required by subdivision A 18 of § 17.1–275, and fees for service or (ii) by the patient's attorney in a pending civil case in accordance with § 8.01–407 without payment of the fees established in subdivision A 23 of § 17.1–275. A sheriff shall not be required to serve an attorney-issued subpoena that is not issued at least five business days prior to the date production of the record is desired. The subpoena shall be returnable within 20 days of proper service, directing the hospital, nursing facility, physician, or other health care provider to produce and furnish copies of the reports and papers to the clerk who shall then make the same available to the patient, his attorney or authorized insurer. If the court finds that a hospital, nursing facility, physician, or other health care provider willfully refused to comply with a written request made in accordance with subsection B, either by willfully or arbitrarily refusing or by imposing a charge in excess of the reasonable expense of making the copies and processing the request for records, the court may award damages for all expenses incurred by the patient or authorized insurer to obtain such copies, including court costs and reasonable attorney's fees.

D. The provisions of subsections A, B, and C hereof shall apply to any health care provider whose office is located within or without the Commonwealth if the records pertain to any patient who is a party to a cause of action in any court in the Commonwealth of Virginia, and shall apply only to requests made by the patient, his attorney, his executor or administrator, or any authorized insurer, in anticipation of litigation or in the course of litigation.

E. Health care provider, as used in this section, shall have the same meaning as provided in § 32.1–127.1:03 and shall also include an independent medical copy retrieval service contracted to provide the service of retrieving, reviewing, and preparing such copies for distribution.

F. Notwithstanding the authorization to admit as evidence patient records in the form of microphotographs, prescription dispensing records maintained in or on behalf of any pharmacy registered or permitted in Virginia shall only be stored in compliance with §§ 54.1–3410, 54.1–3411 and 54.1–3412.

G. The provisions of this section governing fees that may be charged by a health care provider whose records are subpoenaed or requested pursuant to this section shall not apply in the case of any request by a patient for his own records, which shall be governed by subsection J of § 32.1–127.1:03. This subsection shall not be construed to affect other provisions of state or federal statute, regulation or any case decision relating to charges by health care providers for copies of records requested by any person other than a patient when requesting his own records pursuant to subsection J of § 32.1–127.1:03.

Acts 1977, c. 208; Acts 1977, c. 617; Acts 1981, c. 457; Acts 1982, c. 378; Acts 1990, c. 99; Acts 1990, c. 320; Acts 1992, c. 696; Acts 1994, c. 390; Acts 1994, c. 572; Acts 1995, c. 586; Acts 1997, c. 682; Acts 1998, c. 470; Acts 2000, c. 813; Acts 2002, c. 463; Acts 2002, c. 654. Amended by Acts 2004, c. 65; Acts 2004, c. 335; Acts 2004, c. 742; Acts 2004, c. 1014; Acts 2005, c. 642; Acts 2005, c. 697; Acts 2009, c. 270.

§ 8.01–413.01. Authenticity and reasonableness of medical bills; presumption

A. In any action for personal injuries, wrongful death, or for medical expense benefits payable under a motor vehicle insurance policy issued pursuant to § 38.2–124 or § 38.2–2201, the authenticity of bills for medical services provided and the reasonableness of the charges of the health care provider shall be rebuttably presumed upon identification by the plaintiff of the original bill or a duly authenticated copy and the plaintiff's testimony (i) identifying the health care provider, (ii) explaining the circumstances surrounding his receipt of the bill, (iii) describing the services rendered and (iv) stating that the services were rendered in connection with treatment for the injuries received in the event giving rise to the action. The presumption herein shall not apply unless the opposing party or his attorney has been furnished such medical records at least twenty-one days prior to the trial.

B. Where no medical bill is rendered or specific charge made by a health care provider to the insured, an insurer, or any other person, the usual and customary fee charged for the service rendered may be established by the testimony or the affidavit of an expert having knowledge of the usual and customary fees charged for the services rendered. If the fee is to be established by affidavit, the affidavit shall be submitted to the opposing party or his attorney at least twenty-one days prior to trial. The testimony or the affidavit is subject to rebuttal and may be admitted in the same manner as an original bill or authenticated copy described in subsection A of this section.

Acts 1993, c. 610; Acts 1996, c. 516; Acts 1997, c. 503.

§ 8.01–413.02. Admissibility of written reports or records of blood alcohol tests conducted in the regular course of providing emergency medical treatment

A. Notwithstanding any other provision of law, the written reports or records of blood alcohol tests conducted upon persons receiving medical treatment in a hospital or emergency room are admissible in evidence as a business records exception to the hearsay rule in any civil proceeding.

B. The provisions of law pertaining to confidentiality of medical records and medical treatment shall not be applicable to reports or records of blood alcohol tests sought or admitted as evidence under the provisions of this section. Owners or custodians of such reports or records may disclose them, in accordance with regulations concerning patient privacy promulgated by the U.S. Department of Health and Human Services, without obtaining consent or authorization for such disclosure. No person who is involved in taking blood or conducting blood alcohol tests shall be liable for civil damages for breach of confidentiality or unauthorized release of medical records because of the evidentiary use of blood alcohol test results under this section, or as a result of that person's testimony given pursuant to this section.

Added by Acts 2005, c. 801.

Article 7.1

Employment Evidence

§ 8.01–413.1. Certain copies of employment records or papers admissible; right of employee or his attorney to copies of such records or papers; subpoena; damages, costs and attorney's fees

In any case where the original wage or salary records or papers of any employee are admissible or would be admissible as evidence, any typewritten copy, photograph, photostatic copy, or microphotograph thereof shall be admissible as evidence in any court of this Commonwealth in like manner as the original, provided the typewritten copy, photograph, photostatic copy or microphotograph is properly authenticated by the individual who would have authority to release or produce in court the original records. Any employer whose records or papers relating to any such employee are subpoenaed for production may comply with the subpoena by a timely mailing to the clerk issuing the subpoena properly authenticated copies, photographs or microphotographs in lieu of the originals. The court whose clerk issued the subpoena may, after notice to such employer, enter an order requiring production of the originals, if available, of any records or papers whose copies, photographs or microphotographs are not sufficiently legible. The party requesting the subpoena shall be liable for the reasonable charges of the employer for copying and mailing the items produced.

Acts 1987, c. 503.

Article 8

Certain Affidavits

§ 8.01–414. Affidavit prima facie evidence of nonresidence

In any action, an affidavit that a witness or party resides out of this Commonwealth, or is out of it, shall be prima facie evidence of the fact, although such affidavit be made by a party, and without previous notice.

Acts 1977, c. 617.

§ 8.01–415. Affidavit evidence of publication

When anything is authorized or required by law to be published in a newspaper, the certificate of the editor, publisher, business manager or assistant business manager, or the affidavit of any other person, shall be admitted as evidence of what is stated herein as to the publication.

Acts 1977, c. 617.

§ 8.01–416. Affidavit re damages to motor vehicle

A. In a civil action in any court, whether sounding in contract or tort, to recover for damages to a motor vehicle in excess of $2,500, evidence as to such damages may be presented by an itemized estimate or appraisal sworn to by a person who also makes oath (i) that he is a motor vehicle repairman, estimator or appraiser qualified to determine the amount of such damage or diminution in value; (ii) as to the approximate length of time that he has engaged in such work; and (iii) as to the trade name and address of his business and employer. Such estimate shall not be admitted unless by consent of the adverse party or his counsel, or unless a true copy thereof is mailed or delivered to the adverse party or his counsel not less than seven days prior to the date fixed for trial.

B. In a civil action in any court, whether sounding in contract or tort, to recover for damages to a motor vehicle of $2,500 or less, evidence as to such damages may be presented by an itemized estimate or appraisal sworn to by a person who also makes oath (i) that he is a motor vehicle repairman, estimator or appraiser qualified to determine the amount of such damage or diminution in value; (ii) as to the approximate length of time that he has engaged in such work; and (iii) as to the trade name and address of his business and employer.

Acts 1977, c. 617; Acts 1980, c. 183; Acts 1990, c. 724. Amended by Acts 2010, c. 343.

ARTICLE 9

MISCELLANEOUS PROVISIONS

§ 8.01–417. Copies of written statements or transcriptions of verbal statements by injured person to be delivered to him; copies of subpoenaed documents to be provided to other party; disclosure of insurance policy limits

A. Any person who takes from a person who has sustained a personal injury a signed written statement or voice recording of any statement relative to such injury shall deliver to such injured person a copy of such written statement forthwith or a verified typed transcription of such recording within 30 days from the date such statement was given or recording made, when and if the statement or recording is transcribed or in all cases when requested by the injured person or his attorney.

B. Unless otherwise ordered for good cause shown, when one party to a civil proceeding subpoenas documents, the subpoenaing party, upon receipt of the subpoenaed documents, shall, if requested in writing, provide true and full copies of the same to any other party or to the attorney for any other party, provided the other party or attorney for the other party pays the reasonable cost of copying or reproducing the subpoenaed documents. This provision does not apply where the subpoenaed documents are returnable to and maintained by the clerk of court in which the action is pending.

C. After he gives written notice that he represents an injured person, an attorney, or an individual injured in a motor vehicle accident if he is not represented by counsel, may, prior to the filing of a civil action for personal injuries sustained as a result of a motor vehicle accident, request in writing that the insurer disclose (i) the limits of liability of any motor vehicle liability or any personal injury liability insurance policy that may be applicable to the claim and (ii) the address of the alleged tortfeasor who is insured by the insurer, if not previously reported to the requesting party. The requesting party shall provide the insurer with the date of the motor vehicle accident, the name and last known address of the alleged tortfeasor if it has been reported to the requesting party, a copy of the accident report, if any, and the claim number, if available. The requesting party shall also submit to the insurer the injured person's medical records, medical bills, and wage-loss documentation, if applicable, pertaining to the claimed injury. If the total of the medical bills and wage losses submitted equals or exceeds $12,500, the insurer shall respond in writing within 30 days of receipt of the request and shall disclose the limits of liability at the time of the accident of all such policies, regardless of whether the insurer contests the applicability of the policy to the injured person's claim, and the insured's address. Disclosure of the policy limits under this section shall not constitute an admission that the alleged injury or damage is subject to the policy. Information concerning the insurance policy is not by reason of disclosure pursuant to this subsection admissible as evidence at trial.

D. After he gives written notice that he represents the personal representative of the estate of a decedent who died as a result of a motor vehicle accident, an attorney, or the personal representative of the estate of the decedent who died as a result of a motor vehicle accident if he is not represented by counsel, may, prior to the filing of a civil action for wrongful death as a result of a motor vehicle accident, request in writing that the insurer disclose (i) the limits of liability of any motor vehicle liability insurance policy or any personal injury liability insurance policy that may be applicable to the claim and (ii) the address of the alleged tortfeasor who is insured by the insurer, if not previously reported to the requesting party. The requesting party shall provide the insurer with the date of the motor vehicle accident, the name and last known address of the alleged tortfeasor if it has been reported to the requesting party, a copy of the accident report, if any, and the claim number, if available. The requesting party shall submit to the insurer the death certificate of the decedent; the certificate of qualification of the personal representative of the decedent's estate; the names and relationships of the statutory beneficiaries of the decedent; medical bills, if any, supporting a claim for damages under subdivision 3 of § 8.01–52; and, if at the time the request is made a claim for damages under clause (i) of subdivision 2 of § 8.01–52 is anticipated, a description of the source, amount, and payment history of the claimed income loss for each beneficiary. The insurer shall respond in writing within 30 days of receipt of the request and shall disclose the limits of liability at the time of the accident of all such policies, regardless of whether the insurer contests the applicability of the policy to the personal representative's claim, and the insured's address. Disclosure of the policy limits under this section shall not constitute an admission that the alleged death or other damage is subject to the policy. Information concerning the insurance policy is not by reason of disclosure pursuant to this subsection admissible as evidence at trial.

E. For purposes of subsections C and D, if the alleged tortfeasor has insurance coverage from a self-insured locality for a motor vehicle accident, as described in this section, and the locality is authorized by the alleged tortfeasor to accept service of process on behalf of the alleged tortfeasor and agrees to do so, the locality, in its discretion and instead of disclosing the alleged tortfeasor's home address, may disclose the insured's work address and the name and address of the person who shall accept service of process on behalf of the alleged tortfeasor. If the locality makes such a disclosure, the locality shall not be required to disclose the alleged tortfeasor's home address.

F. As used in subsections C and D, "insurer" does not include the insurance agency or the insurance agent representing the alleged tortfeasor as the authorized representative or agent with respect to the alleged tortfeasor's motor vehicle insurance policy.

Acts 1977, c. 617. Amended by Acts 2004, c. 345; Acts 2005, c. 211; Acts 2008, c. 819; Acts 2010, c. 354; Acts 2010, c. 435; Acts 2015, c. 711.

§ 8.01–417.1. Use of portions of documents in evidence (Subsection (b) of Supreme Court Rule 2:106 derived from this section)

To expedite trial proceedings in civil cases, upon appropriate and timely motion by counsel, the court may permit the reading to the jury, or the introduction into evidence, of relevant portions of lengthy and complex documents without the necessity of having the jury read or receive the entire document. The court, in its discretion, may permit the entire document to be received by the jury, or may order the parties to edit from any such document admitted into evidence information that is irrelevant to the proceedings.

Acts 1992, c. 720.

§ 8.01–418. When plea of guilty or nolo contendere or forfeiture in criminal prosecution or traffic case admissible in civil action; proof of such plea

Whenever, in any civil action, it is contended that any party thereto pled guilty or nolo contendere or suffered a forfeiture in a prosecution for a criminal offense or traffic infraction which arose out of the same occurrence upon which the civil action is based, evidence of said plea or forfeiture as shown by the records of the criminal court shall be admissible. Where the records of the court in which such prosecution was had are silent or ambiguous as to whether or not such plea was made or forfeiture occurred the court hearing the civil case shall admit such evidence on the question of such plea or forfeiture as may be relevant, and the question of whether such plea was made or forfeiture suffered shall be a question for the court to determine.

Acts 1977, c. 617; Acts 1986, c. 46.

§ 8.01–418.1. Evidence of subsequent measures taken not admissible to prove negligence (Supreme Court Rule 2:407 derived from this section)

When, after the occurrence of an event, measures are taken which, if taken prior to the event would have made the event less likely to occur, evidence of such subsequently taken measures is not admissible to prove negligence or culpable conduct as a cause of the occurrence of the event; provided, that evidence of subsequent measures taken shall not be required to be excluded when offered for another purpose for which it may be admissible, including, but not limited to, proof of ownership, control, feasibility of precautionary measures if controverted, or for impeachment.

Acts 1978, c. 165.

§ 8.01–418.2. Evidence of polygraph examination inadmissible in any proceeding

The analysis of any polygraph test charts produced during any polygraph examination administered to a party or witness shall not be admissible in any proceeding conducted pursuant to § 2.2–1202.1 or conducted by any county, city or town over the objection of any party except as to disciplinary or other actions taken against a polygrapher.

Acts 1993, c. 570; Acts 1995, c. 770; Acts 1995, c. 818; Acts 2012, c. 803; Acts 2012, c. 835.

§ 8.01–418.3. Repealed by Acts 2007, c. 250

§ 8.01–419. Table of life expectancy

Whenever, in any case not otherwise specifically provided for, it is necessary to establish the expectancy of continued life of any person from any period of such person's life, whether he be living at the time or not, the following table shall be received in all courts and by all persons having power to determine litigation as evidence, with other evidence as to the health, constitution and habits of such person, of such expectancy represented by the figures in the following columns:

AGE	BOTH SEXES	MALE	FEMALE
0	77.4	74.7	80
1	77	74.3	79.5
2	76	73.3	78.5
3	75	72.4	77.6
4	74	71.4	76.6
5	73.1	70.4	75.6
6	72.1	69.4	74.6
7	71.1	68.4	73.6
8	70.1	67.4	72.6
9	69.1	66.5	71.6
10	68.1	65.5	70.6
11	67.1	64.5	69.6
12	66.1	63.5	68.7
13	65.1	62.5	67.7
14	64.2	61.5	66.7
15	63.2	60.5	65.7
16	62.2	59.6	64.7
17	61.2	58.6	63.7
18	60.3	57.7	62.8
19	59.3	56.7	61.8
20	58.4	55.8	60.8
21	57.4	54.9	59.8
22	56.5	54	58.9
23	55.5	53	57.9
24	54.6	52.1	56.9
25	53.6	51.2	56
26	52.7	50.3	55
27	51.7	49.3	54
28	50.8	48.4	53
29	49.8	47.4	52.1
30	48.9	46.5	51.1
31	47.9	45.6	50.1
32	47	44.6	49.2
33	46	43.7	48.2
34	45.1	42.8	47.2
35	44.1	41.8	46.3
36	43.2	40.9	45.3
37	42.3	40	44.4
38	41.3	39.1	43.4
39	40.4	38.1	42.5
40	39.5	37.2	41.5
41	38.6	36.3	40.6
42	37.6	35.4	39.7
43	36.7	34.5	38.7
44	35.8	33.6	37.8
45	34.9	32.8	36.9
46	34	31.9	36
47	33.1	31	35.1
48	32.3	30.2	34.1
49	31.4	29.3	33.2
50	30.5	28.5	32.3

AGE	BOTH SEXES	MALE	FEMALE
51	29.6	27.6	31.4
52	28.8	26.8	30.6
53	27.9	26	29.7
54	27.1	25.1	28.8
55	26.2	24.3	27.9
56	25.4	23.5	27
57	24.6	22.7	26.2
58	23.8	21.9	25.3
59	23	21.2	24.5
60	22.2	20.4	23.7
61	21.4	19.6	22.8
62	20.6	18.9	22
63	19.8	18.2	21.2
64	19.1	17.5	20.4
65	18.4	16.8	19.7
66	17.6	16.1	18.9
67	16.9	15.4	18.1
68	16.2	14.7	17.4
69	15.5	14.1	16.7
70	14.8	13.4	15.9
71	14.2	12.8	15.2
72	13.5	12.2	14.5
73	12.9	11.6	13.8
74	12.3	11	13.2
75	11.7	10.5	12.5
76	11.1	9.9	11.9
77	10.5	9.4	11.3
78	10	8.9	10.7
79	9.4	8.4	10.1
80	8.9	7.9	9.5
81	8.4	7.5	9
82	7.9	7	8.4
83	7.5	6.6	7.9
84	7	6.3	7.4
85	6.6	5.9	7
86	6.2	5.5	6.6
87	5.8	5.2	6.1
88	5.5	4.9	5.7
89	5.1	4.6	5.4
90	4.8	4.3	5
91	4.5	4	4.7
92	4.2	3.8	4.4
93	4	3.5	4.1
94	3.7	3.3	3.8
95	3.5	3.1	3.5
96	3.2	2.9	3.3
97	3	2.7	3.1
98	2.8	2.5	2.9
99	2.6	2.4	2.7
100+	2.5	2.2	2.5

Acts 1977, c. 617; Acts 1986, c. 317; Acts 1996, c. 394. Amended by Acts 2009, c. 454.

§ 8.01–419.1. Motor vehicle value

Whenever in any case not otherwise specifically provided for the value of an automobile is in issue, either civilly or criminally, the tabulated retail values set forth in the National Automobile Dealers' Association (NADA) "yellow" or "black" books or any vehicle valuation service regularly used and recognized in the automobile industry that is in effect on the relevant date, shall be admissible as evidence of fair market value on the relevant date.

The determination of value shall be subject to such other creditable evidence as any party may offer to demonstrate that the value as set forth in the NADA publication or any vehicle valuation service utilized by another party fails to reflect the actual condition of the vehicle and that therefore the value may be greater or less than that shown by the NADA publication or any vehicle valuation service.

Acts 1993, c. 759. Amended by Acts 2006, c. 402.

§ 8.01–420. Depositions as basis for motion for summary judgment or to strike evidence

A. Except as provided in subsection B, no motion for summary judgment or to strike the evidence shall be sustained when based in whole or in part upon any discovery depositions under Rule 4:5, unless all parties to the suit or action shall agree that such deposition may be so used. Notwithstanding the foregoing, requests for admissions for which the responses are submitted in support of a motion for summary judgment may be based in whole or in part upon any discovery depositions under Rule 4:5 and may include admitted facts learned or referenced in such a deposition, provided that any such request for admission shall not reference the deposition or require the party to admit that the deponent gave specific testimony.

B. Notwithstanding the provisions of subsection A, a motion for summary judgment seeking dismissal of any claim or demand for punitive damages may be sustained, as to the punitive damages claim or demand only, when based in whole or in part upon any discovery depositions under Rule 4:5. However, such a motion may not be based upon discovery depositions under Rule 4:5 with respect to any claim or demand for punitive damages based on the operation of a motor vehicle by a person while under the influence of alcohol, any narcotic drug, or any other self-administered intoxicant or drug.

Acts 1977, c. 617; Acts 1978, c. 417. Amended by Acts 2013, c. 76.

§ 8.01–420.01. Limiting further disclosure of discoverable materials and information; protective order

A. A protective order issued to prevent disclosure of materials or information related to a personal injury action or action for wrongful death produced in discovery in any cause shall not prohibit an attorney from voluntarily sharing such materials or information with an attorney involved in a similar or related matter, with the permission of the court, after notice and an opportunity to be heard to any party or person protected by the protective order, and provided the attorney who receives the material or information agrees, in writing, to be bound by the terms of the protective order.

B. The provisions of this section shall apply only to protective orders issued on or after July 1, 1989.

Acts 1989, c. 702.

§ 8.01–420.1. Abolition of common-law perpetuation of testimony

The common-law proceeding to perpetuate testimony is abolished.

Acts 1977, c. 617.

§ 8.01–420.2. Limitation on use of recorded conversations as evidence

No mechanical recording, electronic or otherwise, of a telephone conversation shall be admitted into evidence in any civil proceeding unless (i) all parties to the conversation were aware the conversation was being recorded or (ii) the portion of the recording to be admitted contains admissions that, if true, would constitute criminal conduct which is the basis for the civil action, and one of the parties was aware of the recording and the proceeding is not one for divorce, separate maintenance or annulment of a marriage. The parties' knowledge of the recording pursuant to clause (i) shall be demonstrated by a declaration at the beginning of the recorded portion of the conversation to be admitted into evidence that the conversation is being recorded. This section shall not apply to emergency reporting systems operated by police and fire departments and by emergency medical services agencies, nor to any communications common carrier utilizing service observing or random monitoring pursuant to § 19.2–62.

Acts 1983, c. 503; Acts 1992, c. 567. Amended by Acts 2015, c. 502; Acts 2015, c. 503.

§ 8.01–420.3. Court reporters to provide transcripts; when recording may be stopped; use of transcript as evidence

Upon the request of any counsel of record, or of any party not represented by counsel, and upon payment of the reasonable cost thereof, the court reporter covering any proceeding shall provide the requesting party with a copy of the transcript of such proceeding or any requested portion thereof.

The court shall not direct the court reporter to cease recording any portion of the proceeding without the consent of all parties or of their counsel of record.

Whenever a party seeks to introduce the transcript or record of the testimony of a witness at an earlier trial, hearing or deposition, it shall not be necessary for the reporter to be present to prove the transcript or record, provided the reporter duly certifies, in writing, the accuracy of the transcript or record.

Acts 1983, c. 505; Acts 1990, c. 77.

§ 8.01–420.4. Taking of depositions

A. Party Depositions.— A deposition of a party, or any witness designated under Rule 4:5(b)(6) [1] to testify on behalf of a party, shall be taken in the county or city in which suit is pending, in an adjacent county or city, at a place upon which the parties agree, or at a place that the court may, for good cause, designate. Good cause may include the expense or inconvenience of a non-resident party defendant appearing in one of the locations specified in this subsection. The restrictions as to parties set forth in this subsection shall not apply where no responsive pleading has been filed or an appearance otherwise made.

B. Non–party Witness Depositions.— Unless otherwise provided by the law of the jurisdiction where a non-party witness resides, a deposition of a non-party witness shall be taken in the county or city where the non-party witness resides, is employed, or has his principal place of business; at a place upon which the witness and the parties to the litigation agree; or at a place that the court may, for good cause, designate.

Acts 1989, c. 209; Acts 1991, c. 81; Acts 1993, c. 428; Acts 1993, c. 940. Amended by Acts 2005, c. 597.

1 See Supreme Court Rule 4:5(b)(6).

§ 8.01–420.5. Estoppel effect of judicial determination of employment status

A final, unappealed order entered by a circuit court of this Commonwealth that a person is or is not an employee of another for the purpose of obtaining jurisdiction shall estop either of said parties from asserting otherwise in any subsequent action between such parties upon the same claim or cause of action before a court of this Commonwealth or the Virginia Workers' Compensation Commission.

Acts 1997, c. 333.

§ 8.01–420.6. Number of witnesses whose depositions may be taken

Notwithstanding any other provision of law or rule of court, there shall be no limit on the number of witnesses whose depositions may be taken by a party except by order of the court for good cause shown.

Acts 2001, c. 595.

§ 8.01–420.7. Attorney-client privilege and work product protection; limitations on waiver

A. When disclosure of a communication or information covered by the attorney-client privilege or work product protection made in a proceeding or to any public body as defined in § 2.2–3701 operates as a waiver of the privilege or protection, the waiver extends to an undisclosed communication or information only if:

1. The waiver is intentional;

2. The disclosed and undisclosed communications or information concern the same subject matter; and

3. The disclosed and undisclosed communications or information ought in fairness be considered together.

B. Disclosure of a communication or information covered by the attorney-client privilege or work product protection made in a proceeding or to any public body as defined in § 2.2–3701 does not operate as a waiver of the privilege or protection if:

1. The disclosure is inadvertent;

2. The holder of the privilege or protection took reasonable steps to prevent disclosure; and

3. The holder promptly took reasonable steps to rectify the error, including, if applicable, complying with the provisions of subdivision (b)(6)(ii) of Rule 4:1 of the Rules of the Supreme Court.

C. A court may order that the privilege or protection is not waived by the disclosure connected with the litigation pending before the court, in which case the disclosure does not operate as a waiver in any other proceeding.

D. An agreement on the effect of the disclosure in a proceeding is binding only on the parties to the agreement, unless it is incorporated into a court order.

E. This section shall not limit any otherwise applicable waiver of attorney-client privilege or work product protection by an inmate who files an action challenging his conviction or sentence.

Added by Acts 2010, c. 350.

§ 8.01–420.8. Protection of confidential information in court files

A. Whenever a party files, or causes to be filed, with the court a motion, pleading, subpoena, exhibit, or other document containing a social security number or other identification number appearing on a driver's license, credit card, debit card, bank account, or other electronic billing and payment system, the party shall make reasonable efforts to redact all but the last four digits of the identification number.

B. The provisions of subsection A apply to all civil actions in circuit and district court, unless there is a specific statute to the contrary that applies to the particular type of proceeding in which the party is involved.

C. Nothing in this section shall create a private cause of action against the party or lawyer who filed the document or any court personnel, the clerk, or any employees of the clerk's office who received it for filing.

Added by Acts 2014, c. 427.

CHAPTER 15

PAYMENT AND SETOFF

§ 8.01–421. Payment may be pleaded; payment into court of part of claim; procedure upon such payment

A. In any action for recovery of a debt the defendant may plead payment of the debt or any part thereof prior to the commencement of the action.

B. In any personal action, the defendant may pay into court a sum of money on account of what is claimed, or by way of compensation or amends, and plead that he is not indebted to the plaintiff, or that the plaintiff has not sustained damages, to a greater amount than such sum. The plaintiff may accept such sum either in full satisfaction, and then have judgment for his costs, or in part satisfaction, and reply to the allegations of the defendant's pleadings, and, if issue thereon be found for the defendant, judgment shall be given for the defendant, and he shall recover his costs. The payment of such sum into court shall not be admissible in evidence.

Acts 1977, c. 617; Acts 1978, c. 416.

§ 8.01–422. Pleading equitable defenses

In any action on a contract, the defendant may file a pleading, alleging any matter which would entitle him to relief in equity, in whole or in part, against the obligation of the contract; or, if the contract be by deed, alleging any such matter arising under the contract, existing before its execution, or any such mistake therein, or in the execution thereof, or any such other matter as would entitle him to such relief in equity; and in either case alleging the amount to which he is entitled by reason of the matters contained in the pleading. If the amount claimed by the defendant exceed the amount of the plaintiff's claim the court may, in a proper case, give judgment in favor of the defendant for such excess.

Acts 1977, c. 617.

§ 8.01–423. When plaintiff claims as assignee or transferee

If the plaintiff claims as assignee or transferee under a person with whom the contract sued on was originally made, and the defendant's claim exceeds the plaintiff's demand, the defendant:

1. In his counterclaim, may waive the benefit of his claim as to any excess beyond the plaintiff's claim, whereupon, the further proceedings shall be upon the plaintiff's claim and the defendant's counterclaim as a defense thereto; or

2. Instead of such waiver such defendant may, by rule issued by the court, to which rule shall be attached a copy of the counterclaim and served on the person, under whom plaintiff claims as aforesaid, make such person a party to the action; and, on the trial of the case, the jury shall ascertain and apply, the amount and interest to which the defendant is entitled; and, for any excess beyond the plaintiff's demand for which such person under whom the plaintiff claims as aforesaid is liable, with such interest as the court or jury allows, judgment shall be rendered for the defendant against such person.

Acts 1977, c. 617.

CHAPTER 16

COMPROMISES

§ 8.01–424. Approval of compromises on behalf of persons under a disability in suits or actions to which they are parties

A. In any action or suit wherein a person under a disability is a party, the court in which the matter is pending shall have the power to approve and confirm a compromise of the matters in controversy on behalf of such party, including claims under the provisions of any liability insurance policy, if such compromise is deemed to be to the interest of the party. Any order or decree approving and confirming the compromise shall be binding upon such party, except that the same may be set aside for fraud.

B. In case of damage to the person or property of a person under a disability, caused by the wrongful act, neglect or default of any person, when death did not ensue therefrom, any person or insurer interested in compromise of any claim for such damages, including any claim under the provisions of any liability insurance policy, may, upon motion to the court in which the action is pending for the recovery of damages on account of such injury, or if no such action is pending, then to any circuit court, move the court to approve the compromise. The court shall require the movant to give reasonable notice of such motion to all parties and to any person found by the court to be interested in the compromise.

C. A compromise action involving a claim for wrongful death shall be in accordance with the applicable provisions of § 8.01–55. Nothing in this section shall be construed to affect the provisions of § 8.01–76.

D. In any compromise action the court shall direct the payment of the proceeds of the compromise agreement, when approved, as follows:

1. Payment of the sum into court as provided by § 8.01–600 or to the general receiver of such court;

2. To a duly qualified fiduciary of the person under a disability, after due inquiry as to the adequacy of the bond of such fiduciary;

3. As provided in § 8.01–606; or

4. Where the agreement of settlement provides for payments to be made over a period of time in the future, whether such payments are lump sum, periodic, or a combination of both, the court shall approve the settlement only if it finds that all payments which are due to be made are (i) secured by a bond issued by an insurance company authorized to write such bonds in this Commonwealth or (ii) to be made or irrevocably guaranteed by an insurance company or companies authorized to do business in this Commonwealth and rated "A plus" (A+) or better by Best's Insurance Reports. Payments made under this subdivision totaling not more than $4,000 in any calendar year may be paid in accordance with § 8.01–606. Payments made under this subdivision, totaling more than $4,000 in any calendar year while the recipient is under a disability, shall be paid to a duly qualified fiduciary after due inquiry as to adequacy of the bond of such fiduciary.

E. Payments made under this section, in the case of damage to the person or property of a minor, may be made payable in the discretion of the court to the parent or guardian of the minor to be held in trust for the benefit of the minor. Any such trust shall be subject to court approval and the court may provide for the termination of such trust at any time following attainment of majority which the court deems to be in the best interest of the minor. In an order authorizing the trust or additions to an existing trust the court may order that the trustee thereof be subject to the same duty to qualify in the clerk's office and to file an inventory and annual accountings with the commissioner of accounts as would apply to a testamentary trustee.

Acts 1977, c. 617; Acts 1985, c. 499; Acts 1988, c. 409; Acts 1991, c. 97; Acts 1991, c. 257; Acts 1993, c. 945; Acts 1994, c. 39; Acts 1998, c. 584; Acts 1998, c. 607; Acts 1998, c. 610. Amended by Acts 2009, c. 688.

§ 8.01–424.1. Settlement of third—party action; deemed consent by employer

In any action or claim for damages by an employee, his personal representative, or other person against any person other than the employer, in which the employer has an interest pursuant to § 65.2–309, where the employer fails to consent to an offer of settlement acceptable to the employee, his personal representative or other person, such person may petition the court where the action is pending for approval of the settlement. Where no action is pending, or such action is pending in a state other than Virginia, the petition may be filed in any circuit court in which venue will lie as to the employee pursuant to § 8.01–262. The petition shall state the compromise, its terms, and the reason therefor. The court in which such petition is filed shall require the convening of the parties in interest in person or by an authorized representative. The parties in interest shall be deemed convened if twenty–one days notice of the hearing and proposed compromise was served pursuant to §§ 8.01–296, 8.01–299, 8.01–300, 8.01–301, or Rule 1:12 of the Rules of the Supreme Court of Virginia, as applicable. In the case of an insured employer, service shall also be made on the workers compensation insurer's registered agent or counsel. During the twenty–one day notice period, the person making the settlement offer to the employee shall make himself reasonably available to answer questions under oath by the employee, employer, or employer's workers compensation insurer concerning matters relating to such person's financial condition that are known or reasonably available to such person.

If the court determines that the settlement is fair and just to the parties in interest, it shall approve such settlement. In no event shall the court have jurisdiction to reduce or otherwise compromise the subrogation interest created pursuant to § 65.2–309. The employer, if aggrieved by the court's decision, may appeal. Should the employer's appeal be denied or decided adversely to the employer, the employer shall pay interest at the judgment rate on the full settlement amount until the date of the denial of the appeal or date the final adverse decision is rendered against the employer. Should the settlement include periodic payments into the future, the value of the settlement amount, discounted to present value, shall be determined in calculating interest due from the employer. Once the decision is final and all appeals, if any, have been exhausted, and because the employer's subrogation interest has not been compromised, the decision approving the settlement shall be deemed consent to the settlement by the employer.

Added by Acts 2002, c. 751.

§ 8.01–425. How fiduciaries may compromise liabilities due to or from them

Any fiduciary may compromise any liability due to or from him, provided that such compromise be ratified and approved by a court of competent jurisdiction, all parties in interest being before such court by proper process. When such compromise shall have been so ratified and approved, it shall be binding on all parties in interest before such court. Nothing contained in this section shall affect the right of indemnity or of contribution among the parties.

Acts 1977, c. 617.

§ 8.01–425.1. Release of liability; right of rescission

When a claimant or plaintiff executes a release of liability as a condition of settlement in a claim or action for personal injury within thirty days of the incident

giving rise to such claim, such claimant or plaintiff shall have a right of rescission until midnight of the third business day after the day on which the release was executed, provided that he was not represented by counsel when the release was executed, the rescission was made in writing to the person or persons being released, their representative or insurance carrier, and the claimant returns to the person or persons being released any check or settlement proceeds received by the claimant prior to the rescission. A release of liability executed within thirty days of the incident giving rise to the claim for personal injury by a person who is not represented by counsel shall contain a notice of the claimant's or the plaintiff's right to rescind conspicuously and separately stated on the release.
Acts 1999, c. 326; Acts 2000, c. 839.

CHAPTER 17

JUDGMENTS AND DECREES GENERALLY

ARTICLE 1

IN GENERAL

§ 8.01–426. "Judgment" includes decree

A decree for land or specific personal property, and a decree or order requiring the payment of money, shall have the effect of a judgment for such land, property, or money, and be embraced by the word "judgment," where used in this chapter or in Chapters 18, 19 or 20 [1] of this title or in Title 43; but a party may proceed to carry into execution a decree or order other than for the payment of money, as he might have done if this and the following section had not been enacted.
Acts 1977, c. 617. Amended by Acts 2005, c. 681, eff. Jan. 1, 2006.

[1] See § 8.01–466 et seq.

§ 8.01–427. Persons entitled under decree deemed judgment creditors; execution on decree

The persons entitled to the benefit of any decree or order requiring the payment of money shall be deemed judgment creditors, although the money be required to be paid into a court, or a bank, or other place of deposit. In such case, an execution on the decree or order shall make such recital thereof, and of the parties to it, as may be necessary to identify the case; and if a time be specified in the decree or order within which the payment is to be made, the execution shall not issue until the expiration of that time.
Acts 1977, c. 617.

§ 8.01–427.1. Repealed by Acts 1978, c. 426

§ 8.01–428. Setting aside default judgments; clerical mistakes; independent actions to relieve party from judgment or proceedings; grounds and time limitations

A. Default judgments and decrees pro confesso; summary procedure.—Upon motion of the plaintiff or judgment debtor and after reasonable notice to the opposite party, his attorney of record or other agent, the court may set aside a judgment by default or a decree pro confesso upon the following grounds: (i) fraud on the court, (ii) a void judgment, (iii) on proof of an accord and satisfaction, or (iv) on proof that the defendant was, at the time of service of process or entry of judgment, a person in the military service of the United States for purposes of 50 U.S.C. app. § 502. Such motion on the ground of fraud on the court shall be made within two years from the date of the judgment or decree.

B. Clerical mistakes.—Clerical mistakes in all judgments or other parts of the record and errors therein arising from oversight or from an inadvertent omission may be corrected by the court at any time on its own initiative or upon the motion of any party and after such notice, as the court may order. During the pendency of an appeal, such mistakes may be corrected before the appeal is docketed in the appellate court, and thereafter while the appeal is pending such mistakes may be corrected with leave of the appellate court.

C. Failure to notify party or counsel of final order.—If counsel, or a party not represented by counsel, who is not in default in a circuit court is not notified by any means of the entry of a final order and the circuit court is satisfied that such lack of notice (i) did not result from a failure to exercise due diligence on the part of that party and (ii) denied that party an opportunity to pursue post-trial relief in the circuit court or to file an appeal therefrom, the circuit court may, within 60 days of the entry of such order, modify, vacate, or suspend the order or grant the party leave to appeal. Where the circuit court grants the party leave to appeal, the computation of time for noting and perfecting an appeal shall run from the entry of such order, and such order shall have no other effect.

D. Other judgments or proceedings.—This section does not limit the power of the court to entertain at any time an independent action to relieve a party from any judgment or proceeding, or to grant relief to a defendant not served with process as provided in § 8.01–322, or to set aside a judgment or decree for fraud upon the court.

E. Nothing in this section shall constitute grounds to set aside an otherwise valid default judgment against a defendant who was not, at the time of service of process or entry of judgment, a servicemember for purposes of 50 U.S.C. app. § 502.

Acts 1977, c. 617; Acts 1991, c. 39; Acts 1993, c. 951. Amended by Acts 2005, c. 333; Acts 2005, c. 909.

§ 8.01–429. Action of appellate court when there might be redress under § 8.01–428

No appeal shall be allowed by the Court of Appeals or the Supreme Court or any judge or justice thereof for any matter for which a judgment or decree is liable to be reversed or amended, on motion as aforesaid, by the court which rendered it, or the judge thereof, until such motion is made and overruled in whole or in part. And when the Court of Appeals or the Supreme Court hears a case on appeal, if it appears that, either before or since the appeal, the judgment or decree has been so amended, the Court of Appeals or the Supreme Court shall affirm the judgment or decree, unless there is other error. If it appears that the amendment ought to be, and has not been made, the Court of Appeals or the Supreme Court may make such amendment, and affirm in like manner the judgment or decree, unless there is other error.

Acts 1977, c. 617; Acts 1984, c. 703.

§ 8.01–430. When final judgment to be entered after verdict set aside

When the verdict of a jury in a civil action is set aside by a trial court upon the ground that it is contrary to the evidence, or without evidence to support it, a new trial shall not be granted if there is sufficient evidence before the court to enable it to decide the case upon its merits, but such final judgment shall be entered as to the court shall seem right and proper. If necessary to assess damages which have not been assessed, the court may empanel a jury at its bar to make such assessment, and then enter such final judgment.

Nothing in this section contained shall be construed to give to trial courts any greater power over verdicts than they now have under existing rules of procedure, nor to impair the right to move for a new trial on the ground of after-discovered evidence.

Acts 1977, c. 617.

Article 2

Judgments by Confession

§ 8.01–431. Judgment or decree by confession in pending suit

In any suit a defendant may, whether the suit is on the court docket or not, confess a judgment in the clerk's office for so much principal and interest as the plaintiff may be willing to accept a judgment or decree for. The same shall be entered of record by the clerk in the order book and be as final and as valid as if entered in court on the day of such confession. The clerk shall record such judgment or decree and the date and time of the day at which the same was confessed. The lien of such judgment or decree shall run from the time such judgment is recorded on the judgment lien docket of the clerk's office of the county or city in which land of the defendant lies.

Acts 1977, c. 617. Amended by Acts 2012, c. 802; Acts 2014, c. 330.

§ 8.01–432. Confession of judgment irrespective of suit pending

Any person being indebted to another person, or any attorney-in-fact pursuant to a power of attorney, may at any time confess judgment in the clerk's office of any circuit court in this Commonwealth, whether a suit, motion or action be pending therefor or not, for only such principal and interest as his creditor may be willing to accept a judgment for, which judgment, when so confessed, shall be forthwith entered of record by the clerk in whose office it is confessed, in the proper order book of his court. Such judgment shall be as final and as binding as though confessed in open court or rendered by the court, subject to the control of the court in the clerk's office of which the same shall have been confessed.

Acts 1977, c. 617.

§ 8.01–433. Setting aside judgments confessed under § 8.01–432

Any judgment confessed under the provisions of § 8.01–432 may be set aside or reduced upon motion of the judgment debtor made within twenty-one days following notice to him that such judgment has been entered against him, and after twenty-one days notice to the judgment creditor or creditors for whom the judgment was confessed, on any ground which would have been an adequate defense or setoff in an action at law instituted upon the judgment creditor's note, bond or other evidence of debt upon which such judgment was confessed. Whenever any such judgment is set aside or modified the case shall be placed on the trial docket of the court, and the proceedings thereon shall thereafter be the same as if an action at law had been instituted upon the bond, note or other evidence of debt upon which judgment was confessed. After such case is so docketed the court shall make such order as to the pleadings, future proceedings and costs as to the court may seem just.

Acts 1977, c. 617.

§ 8.01–433.1. Notice of confession of judgment provision

No judgment shall be confessed upon a note, bond, or other evidence of debt pursuant to a confession of judgment provision contained therein which does not contain a statement typed in boldface print of not less than eight point type on its face:

IMPORTANT NOTICE

THIS INSTRUMENT CONTAINS A CONFESSION OF JUDGMENT PROVISION WHICH CONSTITUTES A WAIVER OF IMPORTANT RIGHTS YOU MAY HAVE AS A DEBTOR AND ALLOWS THE CREDITOR TO OBTAIN A JUDGMENT AGAINST YOU WITHOUT ANY FURTHER NOTICE.

This section shall only apply to notes, bonds, or other evidences of debt containing confession of judgment provisions entered into after January 1, 1993.

Acts 1992, c. 396.

§ 8.01–434. Lien of such judgments

The clerk shall record in the proper book any judgment confessed under the provisions of § 8.01–432 and the day and hour when the same was confessed, and the lien thereof shall attach and be binding from the time such judgment is recorded on the judgment lien docket of the clerk's office of the county or city in which land of the defendant lies. If the credit was extended for personal, family or household purposes, the judgment shall not be a lien against the real estate of the obligor or the basis of obtaining execution against his personal property until the expiration of the 21–day period allowed the judgment debtor as set forth in § 8.01–433. In the event the judgment debtor files a motion or other pleading within such 21–day period, the judgment shall not be a lien against such real estate or its basis of execution against personal property until an order to that effect is entered by the court. It will be presumed that the obligation is for personal, family or household purposes if the debtor is a natural person, unless the plaintiff or someone on his behalf makes oath or makes out and files an affidavit that the obligation was not for such purposes, or the obligation for which judgment is confessed recites that it is for other purposes.

Acts 1977, c. 617; Acts 1986, c. 523. Amended by Acts 2014, c. 330.

§ 8.01–435. Who may confess judgment

Confession of judgment under the provisions of § 8.01–432 may be made either by the debtor himself or by his duly constituted attorney-in-fact, acting under and by virtue of a power of attorney duly executed and acknowledged by him as deeds are required to be acknowledged, before any officer or person authorized to take acknowledgments of writings to be recorded in this Commonwealth, provided, however, that any power of attorney incorporated in, and made part of, any note or bond authorizing the confession of judgment thereon against the makers and endorsers in the event of default in the payment thereof at maturity need not be acknowledged, but shall specifically name therein the attorney or attorneys or other person or persons authorized to confess such judgment and the clerk's office in which the judgment is to be confessed.

The payee, obligee, or person otherwise entitled to payment under any note or bond may appoint a substitute for any attorney-in-fact authorized to confess judgment that is specifically named in such note or bond, by specifically naming the substitute attorney-in-fact in an instrument appointing the substitute attorney-in-fact. Such instrument shall be recorded and indexed according to law in the clerk's office where judgment is to be confessed by the terms of such note or bond, and a clerk's fee for such recording shall be paid as set out in § 17.1–275. If such note or bond does not contain a notice informing the debtor that a substitute attorney-in-fact may be appointed by the payee, obligee, or person otherwise entitled to payment under the note or bond, then within 10 days after the instrument appointing the substitute attorney-in-fact is recorded, the person appointing the substitute attorney-in-fact shall send notice of the appointment by certified mail to the debtor's last known address as it appears in the records of the person appointing the substitute attorney-in-fact.

Acts 1977, c. 617. Amended by Acts 2012, c. 31; Acts 2012, c. 118.

§ 8.01–436. Form of confession of judgment

On the presentation of any such power of attorney as is mentioned in § 8.01–435 by any of the persons therein named as attorney-in-fact, or on the personal appearance of the debtor and the expression by him of his desire to confess such judgment, the clerk of the court mentioned in such power of attorney, or before whom such debtor shall so appear, shall draw and require the attorney-in-fact so appearing, or the debtor, as the case may be, to sign a confession of judgment, which shall be in form substantially as follows:

"Virginia: In the clerk's office of the .... court of the .... of ...., I, (or we) A.B., (or A.B. and C.D., etc.) hereby acknowledged myself (or ourselves) to be justly indebted to, and do hereby confess judgment in favor of (name of creditor) in the sum of .... dollars ($.......) with interest thereon from the .... day of ...., two thousand ...., until paid, and the cost of this proceeding (including the attorney's fees and collection fees provided for in the instrument on which the proceeding is based) hereby waiving the benefit of my (or our) homestead exemptions as to the same, provided the instrument on which the proceeding is based carries such homestead waiver.

Given under my (or our) hand, this .... day of ...., two thousand and ....

(Signatures)

or, if by an attorney-in-fact, signatures and seals of debtors,

By ....
his (or their) attorney-in-fact."

Acts 1977, c. 617.

§ 8.01–437. Endorsement of clerk thereon

When a judgment is so confessed, the clerk shall endorse upon such confession, or attach thereto, his certificate in manner and form substantially as follows:

"Virginia: In the clerk's office of the .... court of the .... of ....

The foregoing (or attached) judgment was duly confessed before me in my said office on the .... day of ...., two thousand and ...., at .... o'clock ....a.m., p.m. and has been duly entered of record in common-law order book number ...., page ....

Teste:
.... clerk."

Acts 1977, c. 617.

§ 8.01–438. When judgment confessed by attorney-in-fact copy to be served on judgment debtor

If a judgment is confessed by an attorney-in-fact, it shall be the duty of the clerk within ten days from the entry thereof to cause to be served upon the judgment debtor a certified copy of the order so entered in the common-law order book, to which order shall be appended a notice setting forth the provisions of § 8.01–433. The officer who serves the order shall make return thereof within ten days after service to the clerk. The clerk shall promptly file the order with the papers in the case. The failure to serve a copy of the order within sixty days from the date of entry thereof shall render the judgment void as to any debtor not so served.

Service of a copy of the order on a nonresident judgment debtor by an officer of the county or city of his residence, authorized by law to serve processes therein, or by the clerk of the court sending a copy of the order by registered or certified mail to such nonresident judgment debtor at his last known post-office address and the filing of a certificate with the papers in the case showing that such has been done or of a receipt showing the receipt of such letter by such nonresident judgment debtor, shall be deemed sufficient service thereof for the purposes of this section.

Acts 1977, c. 617; Acts 1988, c. 420.

§ 8.01–439. Filing of records by clerk

Such confession and clerk's certificate, together with the power of attorney if the confession be by an attorney-in-fact, and the note, bond or other obligation, if there be such, on which the judgment is based, shall be securely attached together by the clerk and filed by him among the records in his office.

Acts 1977, c. 617.

§ 8.01–440. Docketing and execution

The clerk shall forthwith docket such judgment in the current judgment lien docket in his office and shall issue execution thereon as he may be directed by the creditor therein named, or his assigns, in the manner prescribed by law.

Acts 1977, c. 617.

§ 8.01–441. When judgment confessed by virtue of power of attorney invalid

No judgment confessed in the office of the clerk of any circuit court in this Commonwealth, by virtue of a power of attorney, shall be valid, unless such power of attorney be in conformity with the provisions of this article.

Acts 1977, c. 617.

Article 3

When There Are Several Defendants

§ 8.01–442. In joint actions on contract plaintiff, though barred as to some, may have judgment against others

In an action or motion, founded on contract, against two or more defendants, although the plaintiff may be barred as to one or more of them, yet he may have judgment against any other or others of the defendants, against whom he is not so barred.

Acts 1977, c. 617.

§ 8.01–443. Joint wrongdoers; effect of judgment against one

A judgment against one of several joint wrongdoers shall not bar the prosecution of an action against any or all the others, but the injured party may bring separate actions against the wrongdoers and proceed to judgment in each, or, if sued jointly, he may proceed to judgment against them successively until judgment has been rendered against, or the cause has been otherwise disposed of as to, all of the defendants, and no bar shall arise as to any of them by reason of a judgment against another, or others, until the judgment has been satisfied. If there be a judgment against one or more joint wrongdoers, the full satisfaction of such judgment accepted as such by the plaintiff shall be a discharge of all joint wrongdoers, except as to the costs; provided, however, this section shall have no effect on the right of contribution between joint wrongdoers as set out in § 8.01–34.

Acts 1977, c. 617.

§ 8.01–444. Where new parties added; if some not liable, how judgment entered

If it shall appear at the trial that all the original defendants are liable, but that one or more of the other persons added under the provisions of § 8.01–5 are not liable, the plaintiff shall be entitled to judgment, or to verdict and judgment, as the case may be, against the defendants who appear liable, and such as are not liable shall have judgment and recover costs as against the plaintiff, who shall be allowed the same as costs against the defendants who cause them to be made parties.

Acts 1977, c. 617.

Article 4

Distinction Between Term and Vacation Abolished

§ 8.01–445. Distinction between term and vacation abolished; effect of time

The distinction of what a court may do in term as opposed to vacation is hereby abolished. The period of time provided for the doing of any act or the taking of any proceeding is not affected or limited by the continued existence or expiration of a term of court. The continued existence or expiration of a term of court in no way affects the power of a court to do any act or take any proceeding in any civil action which has been pending before it.

Acts 1977, c. 617.

Article 5

Keeping of Docket Books; Execution Thereon; Disposal of Exhibits

§ 8.01–446. Clerks to keep judgment dockets; what judgments to be docketed therein

The clerk of each court of every circuit shall keep in his office, in a well-bound book, or by microphotographic or electronic process allowed by § 17.1–240, a judgment docket, in which he shall docket, without delay, any judgment for a specific amount of money rendered in his court, and shall likewise docket without delay any judgment for a specific amount of money rendered in this Commonwealth by any other court of this Commonwealth or federal court, when he shall be required so to do by any person interested, on such person delivering to him an authenticated legible abstract of it and also upon the request of any person interested therein, any such judgment rendered by a district court judge whose book has been filed in his office under the provisions of Title 16.1 or of which a legible abstract is delivered to him certified by the district court judge who rendered it; provided, that judgments docketed in the clerk's office of the Circuit Court of the City of Williamsburg and the County of James City shall be docketed and indexed in one book. A specific judgment for money shall state that it is a judgment for money in a specific amount in favor of a named party, against a named party, with that party's address, if known, and it shall further state the time from which the judgment bears interest. An order of restitution docketed pursuant to § 19.2–305.2 shall have the same force and effect as a specific judgment for money and shall state that it is an order of restitution in a specific amount in favor of a named party, against a named party, with that party's address, if known, and it shall further state the time from which the judgment bears interest. If the clerk determines that an abstract is not legible, the clerk shall refuse to record it and shall return it to the person who tendered the abstract for recording. No judgment for assessments described in subsection A of § 17.1–275.5 or for the fees provided for by § 17.1–275.1, 17.1–275.2, 17.1–275.3, 17.1–275.4, 17.1–275.7, 17.1–275.8, 17.1–275.9, 17.1–275.10, 17.1–275.11, 17.1–275.11:1, or 17.1–275.12 or for all other fines and costs shall be recorded as a judgment in favor of the Commonwealth if such fees, assessments, fines, or costs have been fully paid by the defendant by the date of sentencing by the court.

Acts 1977, c. 617; Acts 1993, c. 412; Acts 1994, c. 538; Acts 1995, c. 434; Acts 1997, c. 579. Amended by Acts 2008, c. 823; Acts 2008, c. 833; Acts 2013, c. 263; Acts 2015, c. 641.

§ 8.01–446.1. Keeping of docket books by clerk of court using micrographic process; form

Whenever judgments are docketed in the judgment lien book in the office of the clerk of the circuit court and are recorded by a procedural micrographic process as provided in § 17.1–240, or by any other method or process which renders impractical or impossible the subsequent entry of notations upon the docketed judgment, an appropriate certificate of assignment, release, partial release, certified copy of any order, or other separate instrument setting forth the necessary information as provided in this section shall be recorded and indexed according to law. Such instrument shall conform substantially with the following form:

TYPE OF FILING (Check One)

( ) Assignment ORIGINAL BOOK # .... PAGE ....
( ) Release (or instrument no)
( ) Partial Release ORIGINAL DATE DOCKETED: ....
( ) Credit(s)
( ) Additional Debtor(s)
( ) New Name of Debtor

Date of Judgment:
Amount of Judgment:
Plaintiff(s):
Defendant(s):
Assignee (If assignment): ....
Payments (If credits): AMOUNT .... DATE PAID ......
(Complete below if additional debtor or change of name of debtor)
Debtor:
Social Security Number of Debtor (Last Four Digits) (If known):
Given under my hand this ...... day of ...., ...
....
(Plaintiff) (Attorney for Plaintiff)
(Authorized Agent for Plaintiff)

Any judgment creditor who knowingly gives false information upon such certificate made under this section shall be guilty of a Class 1 misdemeanor.

Acts 1985, c. 48. Amended by Acts 2008, c. 823; Acts 2008, c. 833.

§ 8.01–447. Docketing of judgments and decrees of United States courts

Judgments and decrees rendered in the circuit court of appeals or a district court of the United States within this Commonwealth may be docketed and indexed in the clerks' offices of courts of this Commonwealth in the same manner and under the same rules and requirements of law as judgments and decrees of courts in this Commonwealth.

Acts 1977, c. 617.

§ 8.01–448. Attorney General, etc., to have judgments in favor of Commonwealth docketed

Whenever a judgment is recovered in favor of the Commonwealth, it shall be the duty of the Attorney General or other attorney representing the Commonwealth, to cause such judgment to be docketed in all counties and cities wherein there is any real estate owned by any person against whom the judgment is recovered.

Acts 1977, c. 617.

§ 8.01–449. How judgments are docketed

A. The judgment docket required by § 8.01–446 may be kept in a well-bound book, or any other media permitted by § 17.1–240. The date and time of docketing shall be recorded with each judgment docketed. The clerk of the circuit court of any county using card files on July 1, 1975, may continue to use the card file system. The docketing may be done by copying the wording of the judgment order verbatim or by abstracting the information therefrom into a book or into fixed fields of an electronic data storage system. Where a procedural microphotographic system is used, the docketing may be done by recording and storing a retrievable image of the judgment order, judgment abstract, or other source document such as a certificate of assignment or release. Where an electronic imaging system is used, the document image shall be stored in a data format which permits recall of the image. Any judgment docketed pursuant to this subsection shall contain the information required by subsection B.

B. Where a well-bound book is used for the judgment docket there shall be stated in separate columns (i) the date and amount of the judgment, (ii) the time from which it bears interest, (iii) the costs, (iv) the full names of all the parties thereto, including the address, date of birth and the last four digits of the social security number, if known, of each party against whom judgment is rendered, (v) the alternative value of any specific property recovered by it, (vi) the date and the time of docketing it, (vii) the amount and date of any credits thereon, (viii) the court by which it was rendered and the case number, and (ix) when paid off or discharged in whole or in part, the time of payment or discharge and by whom made when there is more than one defendant. And in case of a judgment or decree by confession, the clerk shall also enter in such docket the time of day at which the same was confessed, or at which the same was received in his office to be entered of record. There shall also be shown on such book the name of the plaintiff's attorney, if any.

C. Error or omission in the entry of the address or addresses or the social security number or numbers of each party against whom judgment is rendered shall in no way affect the validity, finality or priority of the judgment docketed.

D. Beginning July 1, 2012, any judgment made available to subscribers via secure remote access pursuant to § 17.1–294 shall contain only the last four digits of the social security number of any party. However, the information otherwise required in the judgment docket pursuant to this section shall be provided.

E. The attorney or party who prepares or submits the judgment for recordation has the responsibility for ensuring that only the last four digits of the social security number are included in the judgment prior to the instrument's being submitted for recordation. The clerk has the authority to reject any judgment that does not comply with the provisions of this section.

Acts 1977, c. 617; Acts 1982, c. 405; Acts 1985, c. 171; Acts 1988, c. 420; Acts 1996, c. 427; Acts 1997, c. 579. Amended by Acts 2007, c. 548; Acts 2007, c. 626; Acts 2008, c. 823; Acts 2008, c. 833; Acts 2010, c. 430.

§ 8.01–450. How indexed

Every judgment shall, as soon as it is docketed, be indexed by the clerk in the name of each defendant, as required by § 17.1–249, and shall not be regarded as docketed as to any defendant in whose name it is not so indexed. The clerk may maintain such index on computer, word processor, microfilm, microfiche, or other micrographic process.

Acts 1977, c. 617; Acts 1985, c. 171.

§ 8.01–451. Judgments to be docketed and indexed in new names of judgment debtors; how execution may thereafter issue

Whenever there is a judgment docketed and indexed, as required by § 17.1–249, and thereafter a judgment debtor whose name is so recorded changes his name, whether by marriage, court order, by a voluntary assumption of a new name or otherwise, the clerk of the court in which the judgment was obtained, upon satisfactory proof that the judgment debtor has acquired a new name, shall docket and index the judgment in the new name. Execution may thereafter issue against the judgment debtor in the prior name, the new name, or both. The clerk may require the submission by any party interested in the judgment or by his duly authorized attorney or agent of a form similar to that set out in § 8.01–446.1 indicating that the judgment debtor has acquired a new name, and stating the new name. Such form shall constitute satisfactory proof of the new name. This section shall apply to all judgments obtained prior or subsequent to the enactment hereof.

Acts 1977, c. 617; Acts 1998, c. 639.

§ 8.01–452. Entry of assignment of judgment on judgment lien docket

Whenever there shall be an assignment of a judgment, such assignment must be in writing, showing the date thereof, the name of the assignor and assignee, the amount of the judgment, and when and by what court granted, and either acknowledged as are deeds for recordation in the clerks' offices of circuit courts in the Commonwealth, or signed by the assignor, attested by two witnesses. Such assignment shall be recorded in a separate instrument referencing the page of the book where same is docketed, by the judgment creditor or his attorney of record. When such assignment is docketed as herein provided, further executions shall be issued in the name of the assignee as the plaintiff in the case.

Acts 1977, c. 617. Amended by Acts 2014, c. 330.

§ 8.01–452.1. Disposal of exhibits in civil cases

A clerk of court, after sixty days have elapsed from the entry of judgment in a civil case or, if the civil case is appealed or notice of appeal is pending or the case is being reheard, when the appeal or rehearing is concluded, may dispose of or donate any exhibits filed in the case and in his possession after notifying the owner or his attorney by first-class mail and after twenty-one days from the mailing of the notice to the owner or attorney unless the owner or attorney requests the return of the exhibits.

Acts 1981, c. 312; Acts 1992, c. 57; Acts 1995, c. 13; Acts 1997, c. 135; Acts 1998, c. 886.

Article 6

Satisfaction

§ 8.01–453. When and how payment or discharge entered on judgment docket

The fact of satisfaction of any judgment so docketed, and if there is more than one defendant, by which defendant it was satisfied, shall be entered by the clerk in whose office the judgment is docketed whenever it appears from a certificate of the clerk of the court in which the judgment was rendered that the judgment has been satisfied or upon the direction, in writing, of the judgment creditor or his duly authorized attorney or other agent.

Acts 1977, c. 617; Acts 1979, c. 192; Acts 1986, c. 276; Acts 1988, c. 420. Amended by Acts 2015, c. 631.

§ 8.01–454. Judgment, when satisfied, to be so noted by creditor

In all cases in which satisfaction of any judgment so docketed is made, which is not required to be certified to the clerk under § 8.01–455, it shall be the duty of the judgment creditor, himself, or by his agent or attorney, to cause such satisfaction by the defendant, and if there is more than one defendant, by which defendant it was satisfied, to be entered within 30 days after the same is made, on such judgment docket. If the judgment has not been docketed, then the entry shall be made on the execution book in the office of the clerk from which the execution issued. For any failure to do so within 90 days, or after 10 days' notice to do so by the judgment debtor or his agent or attorney, the judgment creditor shall be liable to a fine of $100 and shall pay the filing cost of the release. The entry of satisfaction shall be signed by the creditor or his duly authorized attorney or other agent and be attested by the clerk in whose office the judgment is docketed, or when not docketed, by the clerk from whose office the execution issued; however, the cost of the release shall be paid by the judgment debtor. For any money judgment marked as satisfied pursuant to this section, nothing herein shall satisfy an unexecuted order of possession entered pursuant to § 8.01–126.

Acts 1977, c. 617; Acts 1988, c. 420. Amended by Acts 2014, c. 274; Acts 2015, c. 547; Acts 2015, c. 553; Acts 2015, c. 631.

§ 8.01–455. Court, on motion of defendant, etc., may have payment of judgment entered

A. A defendant in any judgment, his heirs or personal representatives, may, on motion, after ten days' notice thereof to the plaintiff in such judgment, or his assignee, or if he be dead, to his personal representative, or if he be a nonresident, to his attorney, if he have one, apply to the court in which the judgment was rendered, to have the same marked satisfied, and upon proof that the judgment has been paid off or discharged, such court shall order such satisfaction to be recorded in the judgment docket book together with a separate instrument or order discharging the judgment and referencing the judgment docket book and page where the original judgment was entered, and a certificate of such order to be made to the clerk of the court in which such judgment is required by § 8.01–446 to be docketed, and the clerk of such court shall immediately, upon the receipt of such certificate, enter the same in the judgment docket book where such judgment is docketed. If the plaintiff be a nonresident and have no attorney of record residing in this Commonwealth, the notice may be published and posted as an order of publication is required to be published and posted under §§ 8.01–316 and 8.01–317. Upon a like motion and similar proceeding, the court may order that a separate instrument or order be recorded to reflect that a judgment has been "discharged in bankruptcy" for any judgment that may be shown to have been so discharged.

B. The cost of such proceedings, including reasonable attorney fees, may be ordered to be paid by the plaintiff.

Acts 1977, c. 617. Amended by Acts 2014, c. 330.

§ 8.01–456. Satisfaction of judgment when judgment creditor cannot be located

Whenever a judgment debtor or anyone for him or any party liable on the judgment wishes to pay off and discharge a judgment, of record in any clerk's office in this Commonwealth, when the judgment creditor cannot be located, he may do so by paying into the court having jurisdiction over such judgment an amount sufficient to pay the principal, interest, and all costs due thereupon, together with the cost of entering necessary orders, and other service attendant upon the proceeding herein provided for, and satisfaction upon such judgment. Upon such payment, the court, by an order entered of record shall direct the clerk to deposit the same at interest in any bank which is a member of the Federal Deposit Insurance Corporation and is designated in such order; to file evidence of such deposit in the office of the clerk in an appropriate file and shall be payable to the court entering the order for the benefit of the judgment creditor; and to enter upon the judgment docket, where the judgment is docketed, the date of such deposit, the date of the entry of the order of the court receiving same, referring to the number and page of the order book in which it is entered.

The judgment creditor or his attorney may have the money, so paid, to which he is entitled, upon application to the court therefor whenever it may appear to the court that it should be paid to him.

From and after the time of such payment, into the court, as aforesaid, the property of the defendant shall be free and clear of any lien created by any such judgment, or any execution issued thereupon.

Acts 1977, c. 617.

§ 8.01–457. Marking satisfied judgments for Commonwealth; payment by third parties releasing recognizances

It shall be the duty of the clerks of the circuit courts of this Commonwealth, upon the payment of any judgment in favor of the Commonwealth by any person or upon the release of any recognizance by court order, to mark the same satisfied upon the judgment lien docket at every place such judgment or recognizance, as the case may be, shall have been recorded upon such lien docket. In marking such recognizance satisfied it shall be the duty of such clerk to refer by marginal reference to the court order, if any, releasing or discharging such recognizance.

Acts 1977, c. 617; Acts 1986, c. 132.

Article 7

Lien and Enforcement Thereof

§ 8.01–458. From what time judgment to be a lien on real estate; docketing revived judgment

Every judgment for money rendered in this Commonwealth by any state or federal court or by confession of judgment, as provided by law, shall be a lien on all the real estate of or to which the defendant in the judgment is or becomes possessed or entitled, from the time such judgment is recorded on the judgment lien docket of the clerk's office of the county or city where such land is situated; provided, however, when a judgment is revived under the provisions of § 8.01–251, that such revived judgment shall not be a lien as prescribed in this section unless and until such judgment is again docketed as provided herein. In such event the lien shall be effective from the date of the original docketing. Any judgment or decree properly docketed under the provisions of this section shall, if the real estate subject to the lien of such judgment has been annexed to or merged with an adjoining city subsequent to such docketing, be deemed to have been docketed in the proper clerk's office of such city.

Acts 1977, c. 617.

§ 8.01–459. Priority of judgments

Judgments against the same person shall, as among themselves, attach to his real estate, and be payable thereout in the order of the priority of the lien of such judgments, respectively.

Acts 1977, c. 617.

§ 8.01–460. Decree for support and maintenance of spouse or infant children of parties as lien on real estate

A decree, order or judgment for support and maintenance of a spouse or of infant children of the parties payable in future installments or a monetary award for future installments as provided for in § 20–107.3, shall be a lien upon such real estate of the obligor as the court shall, from time to time, designate by order or decree. An order after reasonable notice to the obligor adjudicating that the obligor is delinquent, shall be a lien on the obligor's real estate. Liens under this section shall arise when duly docketed in the manner prescribed for the docketing of other judgments for money; however, no such decree, order or judgment for support and maintenance or for a monetary award in accordance with § 20–107.3 shall be docketed unless so ordered by the court in such decree, order or judgment. On petition by any interested person and after reasonable notice to the obligee, the court in which the obligor was adjudicated delinquent may order the release or other modification of such lien.

The lien may also be released upon agreement of all persons for whom support and maintenance is ordered under the decree, order or judgment, provided all such persons are sui juris. The clerk shall note the release on the record upon receipt of an affidavit from all the obligees stating that (i) all the obligees are sui juris and (ii) they agreed to the release of the lien on specified real property. Any lien created pursuant to this section shall expire upon the support obligation being paid in full by the obligor. The clerk may release such liens upon receipt of an affidavit of all the obligees that such support obligation has been paid in full, or upon an order or decree of a court of competent jurisdiction.

Acts 1977, c. 617; Acts 1979, c. 496; Acts 1985, c. 529; Acts 1989, c. 8.

§ 8.01–461. Abstracts of judgments

An abstract of any judgment shall, upon request to the clerk of the court wherein the judgment is rendered, be granted to any person interested immediately upon its rendition, subject to the future action of the court rendering the same.

Acts 1977, c. 617; Acts 1982, c. 105.

§ 8.01–462. Jurisdiction of equity to enforce lien of judgment; when it may decree sale

Jurisdiction to enforce the lien of a judgment shall be in equity. If it appear to the court that the rents and profits of all real estate subject to the lien will not satisfy the judgment in five years, the court may decree such real estate, or any part thereof, to be sold, and the proceeds applied to the discharge of the judgment.

Acts 1977, c. 617.

§ 8.01–463. Enforcement of lien when judgment does not exceed twenty dollars

If the amount of the judgment does not exceed twenty dollars, exclusive of interest and costs, no bill to enforce the lien thereof shall be entertained, unless it appear that thirty days before the institution of the suit, the judgment debtor or his personal representative, and the owner of the real estate on which the judgment is a lien, or, in case of a nonresident, his agent or attorney, if he had one in this Commonwealth, had notice that the suit would be instituted, if the judgment was not paid within that time.

Acts 1977, c. 617.

§ 8.01–464. Order of liability between alienees of different parts of estate

When the real estate liable to the lien of a judgment is more than sufficient to satisfy the same, and it, or any part of it, has been aliened, as among the alienees for value, that which was aliened last, shall, in equity, be first liable, and so on with other successive alienations, until the whole judgment is satisfied. And as among alienees who are volunteers under such judgment debtor, the same rule as to the order of liability shall prevail; but as among alienees for value and volunteers, the lands aliened to the latter shall be subjected before the lands aliened to the former are resorted to; and, in either case, any part of such real estate retained by the debtor shall be first liable to the satisfaction of the judgment. An alienee for value, however, from a volunteer shall occupy the same position that he would have occupied had he purchased from the debtor at the time he purchased from the voluntary donee.

Acts 1977, c. 617.

§ 8.01-465. Chapter embraces recognizances and bonds having force of judgment

The foregoing sections of this chapter, so far as they relate to the docketing of judgments, the entering of satisfaction thereof, and the liens of judgments and enforcement of such liens, shall be construed as embracing recognizances, and bonds having the force of a judgment.

Acts 1977, c. 617.

CHAPTER 17.1

UNIFORM ENFORCEMENT OF FOREIGN JUDGMENTS ACT

§ 8.01-465.1. Application of chapter

As used in this chapter "foreign judgment" means any judgment, decree, or order of a court of the United States or of any other court which is entitled to full faith and credit in this state.

Acts 1988, c. 539.

§ 8.01-465.2. Filing and status of foreign judgments

A copy of any foreign judgment authenticated in accordance with the act of Congress or the statutes of this Commonwealth may be filed in the office of the clerk of any circuit court of any city or county of this Commonwealth upon payment of the fee prescribed in subdivision A 17 of § 17.1-275. The clerk shall treat the foreign judgment in the same manner as a judgment of the circuit court of any city or county of this Commonwealth. A judgment so filed has the same effect and is subject to the same procedures, defenses and proceedings for reopening, vacating, or staying as a judgment of a circuit court of any city or county of this Commonwealth and may be enforced or satisfied in like manner.

Acts 1988, c. 539; Acts 1990, c. 738.

§ 8.01-465.3. Notice of filing

At the time of the filing of the foreign judgment, the judgment creditor or his lawyer shall make and file with the clerk of court an affidavit setting forth the name and last known post office address of the judgment debtor, and the judgment creditor.

Promptly upon the filing of the foreign judgment and the affidavit, the clerk shall mail notice of the filing of the foreign judgment to the judgment debtor at the address given and shall make a note of the mailing in the docket. The notice shall include the name and post office address of the judgment creditor and the judgment creditor's lawyer, if any, in the Commonwealth. In addition, the judgment creditor may mail a notice of the filing of the judgment to the judgment debtor and may file proof of mailing with the clerk. Lack of mailing notice of filing by the clerk shall not affect the enforcement proceedings if proof of mailing by the judgment creditor has been filed.

Acts 1988, c. 539.

§ 8.01-465.4. Stay of enforcement

If the judgment debtor shows the circuit court that an appeal from the foreign judgment is pending or will be taken, or that a stay of execution has been granted, the court shall stay enforcement of the foreign judgment until the appeal is concluded, the time for appeal expires, or the stay of execution expires or is vacated, upon proof that the judgment debtor has furnished the security for the satisfaction of the judgment required by the state in which it was rendered.

If the judgment debtor shows the circuit court any ground upon which enforcement of a judgment of any court of this Commonwealth would be stayed, including the ground that an appeal from the foreign judgment is pending or will be taken, or that the time for taking such an appeal has not expired, the court shall stay enforcement of the foreign judgment for an appropriate period until all available appeals are concluded or the time for taking all appeals has expired, upon requiring the same security for satisfaction of the judgment which is required in this Commonwealth, subject to the provisions of subsections J and K of § 8.01-676.1.

Acts 1988, c. 539; Acts 2000, c. 100.

§ 8.01-465.5. Optional procedure

The right of a judgment creditor to bring an action to enforce his judgment instead of proceeding under this chapter remains unimpaired.

Acts 1988, c. 539.

CHAPTER 17.2

UNIFORM FOREIGN–COUNTRY MONEY JUDGMENTS RECOGNITION ACT

§§ 8.01–465.6 to 8.01–465.13. Repealed by Acts 2014, c. 462

§ 8.01–465.13:1. Definitions

As used in this chapter:

"Foreign country" means a government other than any of the following: the United States; a state, district, commonwealth, territory, or insular possession of the United States; or a government with regard to which the decision in the Commonwealth as to whether to recognize a judgment of that government's courts is initially subject to determination under the Full Faith and Credit Clause of the United States Constitution.

"Foreign-country judgment" means a judgment of a court of a foreign country.

Added by Acts 2014, c. 462.

§ 8.01–465.13:2. Applicability

A. Except as otherwise provided in subsection B, this chapter applies to a foreign-country judgment to the extent that the judgment:

1. Grants or denies recovery of a sum of money; and

2. Under the law of the foreign country where rendered, is final, conclusive, and enforceable.

B. This chapter does not apply to a foreign-country judgment, even if the judgment grants or denies recovery of a sum of money, to the extent that the judgment is:

1. A judgment for taxes;

2. A fine or other penalty; or

3. A judgment for divorce, support, or maintenance, or other judgment rendered in connection with domestic relations.

C. A party seeking recognition of a foreign-country judgment has the burden of establishing that this chapter applies to the foreign-country judgment.

Added by Acts 2014, c. 462.

§ 8.01–465.13:3. Standards for recognition of foreign-country judgment

A. Except as otherwise provided in subsections B and C, a court of the Commonwealth shall recognize a foreign-country judgment to which this chapter applies.

B. A court of the Commonwealth shall not recognize a foreign-country judgment if:

1. The judgment was rendered under a judicial system that does not provide impartial tribunals or procedures compatible with the requirements of due process of law;

2. The foreign court did not have personal jurisdiction over the defendant; or

3. The foreign court did not have jurisdiction over the subject matter.

C. A court of the Commonwealth need not recognize a foreign-country judgment if:

1. The defendant in the proceeding in the foreign court did not receive notice of the proceeding in sufficient time to enable the defendant to defend;

2. The judgment was obtained by fraud that deprived the losing party of an adequate opportunity to present its case;

3. The judgment or the cause of action on which the judgment is based is repugnant to the public policy of the Commonwealth or of the United States;

4. The judgment conflicts with another final and conclusive judgment;

5. The proceeding in the foreign court was contrary to an agreement between the parties under which the dispute in question was to be determined otherwise than by proceedings in that foreign court;

6. In the case of jurisdiction based only on personal service, the foreign court was a seriously inconvenient forum for the trial of the action;

7. The judgment was rendered in circumstances that raise substantial doubt about the integrity of the rendering court with respect to the judgment; or

8. The specific proceeding in the foreign court leading to the judgment was not compatible with the requirements of due process of law.

D. A party resisting recognition of a foreign-country judgment has the burden of establishing that a ground for nonrecognition stated in subsection B or C exists.

Added by Acts 2014, c. 462.

§ 8.01–465.13:4. Personal jurisdiction

A. A foreign-country judgment may not be refused recognition for lack of personal jurisdiction if:

1. The defendant was served with process personally in the foreign country;

2. The defendant voluntarily appeared in the proceeding, other than for the purpose of protecting property seized or threatened with seizure in the proceeding or of contesting the jurisdiction of the court over the defendant;

3. The defendant, before the commencement of the proceeding, had agreed to submit to the jurisdiction of the foreign court with respect to the subject matter involved;

4. The defendant was domiciled in the foreign country when the proceeding was instituted or was a corporation or other form of business organization that had its principal place of business in, or was organized under the laws of, the foreign country;

5. The defendant had a business office in the foreign country and the proceeding in the foreign court involved a cause of action arising out of business done by the defendant through that office in the foreign country; or

6. The defendant operated a motor vehicle or airplane in the foreign country and the proceeding involved a cause of action arising out of that operation.

B. The list of bases for personal jurisdiction in subsection A is not exclusive. The courts of the Commonwealth may recognize bases of personal jurisdiction other than those listed in subsection A as sufficient to support a foreign-country judgment.

Added by Acts 2014, c. 462.

§ 8.01–465.13:5. Procedure for recognition of foreign-country judgment

A. If recognition of a foreign-country judgment is sought as an original matter, the issue of recognition shall be raised by filing an action seeking recognition of the foreign-country judgment.

B. If recognition of a foreign-country judgment is sought in a pending action, the issue of recognition may be raised by counterclaim, cross-claim, or affirmative defense.

Added by Acts 2014, c. 462.

§ 8.01–465.13:6. Effect of recognition of foreign-country judgment

If the court in a proceeding under § 8.01–465.13:5 finds that the foreign-country judgment is entitled to recognition under this chapter then, to the extent that the foreign-country judgment grants or denies recovery of a sum of money, the foreign-country judgment is:

1. Conclusive between the parties to the same extent as the judgment of a sister state entitled to full faith and credit in the Commonwealth would be conclusive; and

2. Enforceable in the same manner and to the same extent as a judgment rendered in the Commonwealth.

Added by Acts 2014, c. 462.

§ 8.01–465.13:7. Stay of proceedings pending appeal of foreign-country judgment

If a party establishes that an appeal from a foreign-country judgment is pending or will be taken, the court may stay any proceedings with regard to the foreign-country judgment until the appeal is concluded, the time for appeal expires, or the appellant has had sufficient time to prosecute the appeal and has failed to do so.

Added by Acts 2014, c. 462.

§ 8.01–465.13:8. Statute of limitations

An action to recognize a foreign-country judgment must be commenced within the earlier of the time during which the foreign-country judgment is effective in the foreign country or 15 years from the date that the foreign-country judgment became effective in the foreign country.

Added by Acts 2014, c. 462.

§ 8.01–465.13:9. Uniformity of interpretation

In applying and construing this uniform act, consideration must be given to the need to promote uniformity of the law with respect to its subject matter among states that enact it.

Added by Acts 2014, c. 462.

§ 8.01–465.13:10. Saving clause

This chapter does not prevent the recognition under principles of comity or otherwise of a foreign-country judgment not within the scope of this chapter.

Added by Acts 2014, c. 462.

§ 8.01–465.13:11. Effective date

This chapter applies to all actions commenced on or after July 1, 2014, in which the issue of recognition of a foreign-country judgment is raised.

Added by Acts 2014, c. 462.

CHAPTER 17.3

UNIFORM FOREIGN–MONEY CLAIMS ACT

§ 8.01–465.14. Definitions

As used in this chapter:

"Action" means a judicial proceeding or arbitration in which a payment in money may be awarded or enforced with respect to a foreign-money claim.

"Bank-offered spot rate" means the spot rate of exchange at which a bank will sell foreign money at a spot rate.

"Conversion date" means the banking day next preceding the date on which money, in accordance with this chapter, is (i) paid to a claimant in an action or distribution proceeding; (ii) paid to the official designated by law to enforce a judgment or award on behalf of a claimant; or (iii) used to recoup, set off, or counterclaim in different moneys in an action or distribution proceeding.

"Distribution proceeding" means a judicial or nonjudicial proceeding for the distribution of a fund in which one or more foreign-money claims are asserted and includes an accounting, an assignment for the benefit of creditors, a foreclosure, the liquidation or rehabilitation of a corporation or other entity, and the distribution of an estate, trust, or other fund.

"Foreign money" means money other than money of the United States of America.

"Foreign-money claim" means a claim upon an obligation to pay, or a claim for recovery of a loss, expressed in or measured by a foreign money.

"Money" means a medium of exchange for the payment of obligations or a store of value authorized or adopted by a government or by intergovernmental agreement.

"Money of the claim" means the money determined as proper pursuant to § 8.01–465.17.

"Person" means an individual, a corporation, government or governmental subdivision or agency, business trust, estate, trust, joint venture, partnership, association, two or more persons having a joint or common interest, or any other legal or commercial entity.

"Rate of exchange" means the rate at which money of one country may be converted into money of another country in a free financial market convenient to or reasonably usable by a person obligated to pay or to state a rate of conversion. If separate rates of exchange apply to different kinds of transactions, the term means the rate applicable to the particular transaction giving rise to the foreign-money claim.

"Spot rate" means the rate of exchange at which foreign money is sold by a bank or other dealer in foreign exchange for immediate or next day availability or for settlement by immediate payment in cash or equivalent, by charge to an account, or by an agreed delayed settlement not exceeding two days.

"State" means a state of the United States, the District of Columbia, the Commonwealth of Puerto Rico, or a territory or insular possession subject to the jurisdiction of the United States.

Acts 1991, c. 24.

§ 8.01–465.15. Scope

This chapter applies only to a foreign-money claim in an action or distribution proceeding and applies to foreign-money issues even if other law under the conflict-of-laws rules of the Commonwealth applies to other issues in the action or distribution proceeding.

Acts 1991, c. 24.

§ 8.01–465.16. Variation by agreement

The effect of this chapter may be varied by agreement of the parties made before or after commencement of an action or distribution proceeding or the entry of judgment.

Parties to a transaction may agree upon the money to be used in a transaction giving rise to a foreign-money claim and may agree to use different moneys for different aspects of the transaction. Stating the price in a foreign money for one aspect of a transaction does not alone require the use of that money for other aspects of the transaction.

Acts 1991, c. 24.

§ 8.01–465.17. Determining money of the claim

The money in which the parties to a transaction have agreed that payment is to be made is the proper money of the claim for payment. If the parties to a transaction have not otherwise agreed, the proper money of the claim is the money (i) regularly used between the parties as a matter of usage or course of dealing; (ii) used at the time of a transaction in international trade, by trade usage or common practice, for valuing or settling transactions in the particular commodity or service involved; or (iii) in which the loss was ultimately felt or will be incurred by the party claimant.

Acts 1991, c. 24.

§ 8.01–465.18. Determining amount of the money of certain contract claims

A. If an amount contracted to be paid in a foreign money is measured by a specified amount of a different money, the amount to be paid is determined on the conversion date.

B. If an amount contracted to be paid in a foreign money is to be measured by a different money at the rate of exchange prevailing on a date before default, that rate of exchange applies only to payments made within a reasonable time after default, not exceeding thirty days. Thereafter, conversion is made at the bank-offered spot rate on the conversion date.

C. A monetary claim is neither usurious nor unconscionable because the agreement on which it is based provides that the amount of the debtor's obligation to be paid in the debtor's money, when received by the creditor, must equal a special amount of the foreign money of the country of the creditor. If, because of unexcused delay in payment of a judgment or award, the amount received by the creditor does not equal the amount of the foreign money specified in the agreement, the court or arbitrator shall amend the judgment or award accordingly.

Acts 1991, c. 24.

§ 8.01–465.19. Asserting and defending foreign-money claim

A person may assert a claim in a specified foreign money. If a foreign-money claim is not asserted, the claimant makes the claim in United States dollars.

An opposing party may allege and shall prove that all or part of a claim is in a different money than that asserted by the claimant. A person may assert a defense, setoff, recoupment, or counterclaim in any money without regard to the money of other claims.

The determination of the proper money of the claim is a question of law.

Acts 1991, c. 24.

§ 8.01–465.20. Judgments and awards on foreign-money claims; times of money conversion; form of judgment

A. A judgment or award on a foreign-money claim must be stated in an amount of the money of the claim. However, assessed costs must be entered in United States dollars. A judgment in substantially the following form complies with this subsection: [IT IS ADJUDGED AND ORDERED, that Defendant (insert name) pay to Plaintiff (insert name) the sum of (insert amount in the foreign money) plus interest on that sum at the rate of (insert rate—see § 8.01–465.22) percent a year or, at the option of the judgment debtor, the number of United States dollars which will purchase the (insert name of foreign money) with interest due, at a bank-offered spot rate at or near the close of business on the banking day next before the day of payment, together with assessed costs of (insert amount) United States dollars.]

B. A judgment or award on a foreign-money claim is payable in that foreign money or, at the option of the debtor, in the amount of United States dollars which will purchase that foreign money on the conversion date at a bank-offered spot rate.

Each payment in United States dollars must be accepted and credited on a judgment or award on a foreign-money claim in the amount of the foreign money that could be purchased by the dollars at a bank-offered spot rate of exchange at or near the close of business on the conversion date for that payment.

C. A judgment or award made in an action or distribution proceeding on both a defense, setoff, recoupment, or counterclaim and the adverse party's claim, must be netted by converting the money of the smaller into the money of the larger, and by subtracting the smaller from the larger, and shall specify the rates of exchange used.

D. If a contract claim is of the type covered by § 8.01–465.18 A or B, the judgment or award must be entered for the amount of money stated to measure the obligation to be paid in the money specified for payment or, at the option of the debtor, the number of United States dollars which will purchase the computed amount of the money of payment on the conversion date at a bank-offered spot rate.

E. A judgment shall be docketed and indexed in foreign money in the same manner, and has the same effect as a lien, as other judgments. It may be discharged by payment.

Acts 1991, c. 24.

§ 8.01–465.21. Conversions of foreign money in distribution proceeding

The rate of exchange prevailing at or near the close of business on the day the distribution proceeding is initiated governs all exchanges of foreign money in a distribution proceeding. A foreign-money claimant in a distribution proceeding shall assert its claim in the named foreign money and show the amount of United States dollars resulting from a conversion as of the date the proceeding was initiated.

Acts 1991, c. 24.

§ 8.01–465.22. Prejudgment and judgment interest

With respect to a foreign-money claim, recovery of prejudgment or preaward interest and the rate of interest to be applied in the action or distribution proceeding are matters of the substantive law governing the right to recovery under the conflict-of-laws rules of the Commonwealth.

However, the court or arbitrator shall increase or decrease the amount of prejudgment or preaward interest otherwise payable in a judgment or award in foreign money to the extent required by the law of the Commonwealth.

A judgment or award on a foreign-money claim bears interest at the rate applicable to judgments of the Commonwealth.

Acts 1991, c. 24.

§ 8.01–465.23. Enforcement of foreign judgments

If an action is brought to enforce a judgment of another jurisdiction expressed in a foreign money and the judgment is enforceable in the Commonwealth, the enforcing judgment must be entered as provided in § 8.01–465.20, whether or not the foreign judgment confers an option to pay in an equivalent amount of United States dollars.

A foreign judgment may be filed in accordance with Chapter 17.1 (§ 8.01–465.1 et seq.) or Chapter 17.2 (§ 8.01–465.13:1 et seq.).

A satisfaction or partial payment made upon the foreign judgment, on proof thereof, must be credited against the amount of foreign money specified in the judgment, notwithstanding the entry of judgment in the Commonwealth.

A judgment entered on a foreign-money claim only in United States dollars in another state shall be enforced in United States dollars only.

Acts 1991, c. 24. Amended by Acts 2014, c. 462.

§ 8.01–465.24. Determining United States dollar value of foreign-money claims for limited purposes

For the limited purpose of facilitating the enforcement of provisional remedies in an action, (i) the value in United States dollars of assets to be seized or restrained pursuant to a writ of attachment, garnishment, execution, or other legal process, (ii) the amount of United States dollars at issue for assessing costs, or (iii) the amount of United States dollars involved for a surety bond or other court-required undertaking shall be ascertained by a party seeking the process, costs, bond or other undertaking as follows:

1. The amount of the foreign money claimed shall be computed from a bank-offered spot rate prevailing at or near the close of business on the banking day next preceding the filing of (i) a request or application for the issuance of process or for the determination of costs, or (ii) an application for a bond or other court-required undertaking.

2. An affidavit or certificate executed in good faith by the party's counsel or a bank officer shall be filed with each request or application, stating the market quotation used and how it was obtained, and setting forth the calculation. Affected court officials incur no liability, after a filing of the affidavit or certificate, for acting as if the judgment were in the amount of United States dollars stated in the affidavit or certificate.

Computations under this section are for the limited purposes of the section and do not affect computation of the United States dollar equivalent of the money of the judgment for the purpose of payment.

Acts 1991, c. 24.

§ 8.01–465.25. Effect of substitution of currency by issuing authority

If, after an obligation is expressed or a loss is incurred in a foreign money, the country issuing or adopting that money substitutes a new money in place of that money, the obligation or the loss is treated as if expressed or incurred in the new money at the rate of conversion the issuing country establishes for the payment of like obligations or losses denominated in the former money. If such substitution occurs after a judgment or award is entered on a foreign-money claim, the court or arbitrator shall amend the judgment or award by a like conversion of the former money.

Acts 1991, c. 24.

CHAPTER 18

EXECUTIONS AND OTHER MEANS OF RECOVERY

ARTICLE 1

ISSUE AND FORM; MOTION TO QUASH

§ 8.01–466. Clerk to issue fieri facias on judgment for money

On a judgment for money, it shall be the duty of the clerk of the court in which such judgment was rendered, upon request of the judgment creditor, his assignee or his attorney, to issue a writ of fieri facias at the expiration of twenty-one days from the date of the entry of the judgment and place the same in the hands of a proper person to be executed and take his receipt therefor. The writ shall be issued together with the form for requesting a hearing on a claim of exemption from levy as provided in § 8.01–546.1. For good cause the court may order an execution to issue on judgments and decrees at an earlier period.

Acts 1977, c. 617; Acts 1986, c. 341; Acts 1996, c. 501; Acts 1996, c. 608.

§ 8.01–467. What writs may not issue

No writ of levari facias, writ of extendi facias, writ of elegit, writ of capias ad satisfaciendum, or writ of distringas shall be issued hereafter.

Acts 1977, c. 617; Acts 1984, c. 94.

§ 8.01–468. Executions against corporations

Such executions as may issue against a natural person may issue against a corporation.

Acts 1977, c. 617.

§ 8.01–469. Executions on joint judgments

When a judgment is against several persons jointly, executions thereon may be joint against all of them.

Acts 1977, c. 617.

§ 8.01–470. Writs on judgments for specific property

On a judgment for the recovery of specific property, real or personal, a writ of possession may issue for the specific property, which shall conform to the judgment as to the description of the property and the estate, title and interest recovered, and there may also be issued a writ of fieri facias for the damages or profits and costs. In cases of unlawful entry and detainer and of ejectment, the officer to whom a writ of possession has been delivered to be executed shall, at least 72 hours before execution, serve notice of intent to execute, including the date and time of execution, as well as the rights afforded to tenants in §§ 55–237.1 and 55–248.38:2, together with a copy of the writ attached, on the defendant in person or, if the party to be served is not found at the specific property for which a writ of possession has been issued, then service shall be effected by posting a copy of such process at the front door or at such other door as appears to be the main entrance of such property. The execution of the writ of possession by the sheriff should occur within 15 calendar days from the date the writ of possession is received by the sheriff, or as soon as practicable thereafter, but in no event later than 30 days from the date the writ of possession is issued. In cases of unlawful entry and detainer and of ejectment, whenever the officer to whom a writ of possession has been delivered to be executed finds the premises locked, he may, after declaring at the door the cause of his coming and demanding to have the door opened, employ reasonable and necessary force to break and enter the door and put the plaintiff in possession. The execution of the writ of possession shall be effective against the tenants named in the writ of possession and their authorized occupants, guests or invitees, and any trespassers in the premises. And an officer having a writ of possession for specific personal property, if he finds locked or fastened the building or place wherein he has reasonable cause to believe the property specified in the writ is located, may in the daytime, after notice to the defendant, his agent or bailee, break and enter such building or place for the purpose of executing such writ.

Acts 1977, c. 617; Acts 1991, c. 503; Acts 2000, c. 640; Acts 2001, c. 222; Acts 2003, c. 259. Amended by Acts 2007, c. 128.

§ 8.01-471. Time period for issuing writs of possession in unlawful entry and detainer; when returnable

Writs of possession, in case of unlawful entry and detainer, shall be issued within one year from the date of judgment for possession and shall be made returnable within 30 days from the date of issuing the writ. No writ shall issue, however, in cases under the Virginia Residential Landlord and Tenant Act (§ 55-248.2 et seq.) if, following the entry of judgment, the landlord has accepted rent payments without reservation, as described in § 55-248.34:1. A writ of possession may be requested by the plaintiff or the plaintiff's attorney or agent.

Acts 1977, c. 617; Acts 1999, c. 683; Acts 2003, c. 427. Amended by Acts 2006, c. 667; Acts 2013, c. 63.

§ 8.01-472. Writs on judgments for personal property

When the judgment is for personal property, the plaintiff may, at his option, have a fieri facias for the alternative value, instead of a writ of possession, and the damages and costs.

Acts 1977, c. 617.

§ 8.01-473. Judgment for benefit of other person than plaintiff; remedies of such person

When an execution issues on a judgment, for the benefit, in whole or in part, of any person other than the plaintiff, if the fact appears by the record, the clerk shall, in the execution, or by an endorsement thereon, state the extent of the interest therein of such person; and such person, either in his own name or that of the plaintiff, may, as a party injured, prosecute a suit or motion against the officer.

Acts 1977, c. 617.

§ 8.01-474. What writ of fieri facias to command

By a writ of fieri facias, the officer shall be commanded to make the money therein mentioned out of the goods and chattels of the person against whom the judgment is.

Acts 1977, c. 617.

§ 8.01-475. Subsequent executions

Subject to the limitations prescribed by Chapter 17 (§ 8.01-426 et seq.) of this title, a party obtaining an execution may sue out other executions at his own costs, though the return day of a former execution has not arrived; and may sue out other executions at the defendant's costs, when on a former execution there is a return by which it appears that the writ has not been executed, or that it or any part of the amount thereof is not levied, or that property levied on has been discharged by legal process which does not prevent a new execution on the judgment. In no case shall there be more than one satisfaction for the same money or thing.

And the fact that a judgment creditor may have availed himself of the benefit of any other remedies under this chapter, shall not prevent him from issuing, from time to time, without impairing his lien under it, other executions upon his judgment until the same is satisfied.

Acts 1977, c. 617.

§ 8.01-476. New execution after loss of property sold under indemnifying bond

When property sold under an execution, or its value, is recovered from an obligor on an indemnifying bond given before such sale, or from a purchaser having a right of action on such bond, the person having such execution, or his personal representative, may, by motion, after reasonable notice to the person, or the personal representative of the person, against whom the execution was, obtain a new execution against him, without credit for the amount for which the property was sold under the former execution. Such motion shall be made within the period of time prescribed by § 8.01-255.2.

Acts 1977, c. 617.

§ 8.01-477. When executions may be quashed; how proceedings thereon stayed

A motion to quash an execution may, after reasonable notice to the adverse party, be heard and decided by the court which issued the execution. Such court, on the application of the plaintiff in the motion, may make an order staying the proceedings on the execution until the motion be heard and determined, the order not to be effectual until bond be given in such penalty and with such condition, and either with or without surety, as the court may prescribe. The clerk from whose office the execution issued, shall take the bond and make as many copies of the order as may be necessary and endorse thereon that the bond required has been given; and a copy shall be served on the plaintiff in the execution and on the officer in whose hands the execution is placed.

Acts 1977, c. 617.

§ 8.01–477.1. Claims of exemption from execution

The procedures specified in § 8.01–546.2 shall govern further proceedings regarding claims of exemption from levy.

Acts 1986, c. 341.

ARTICLE 2

LIEN IN GENERAL

§ 8.01–478. On what property writ of fieri facias levied; when lien commences

The writ of fieri facias may be levied as well on the current money and bank notes, as on the goods and chattels of the judgment debtor, except such as are exempt from levy under Title 34, and shall bind what is capable of being levied on only from the time it is actually levied by the officer to whom it has been delivered to be executed.

Acts 1977, c. 617.

§ 8.01–479. Time for enforcement

Property levied on, on or before the return day, may be advertised and sold within a reasonable time thereafter, and the lien given by this section may also be enforced after the return day of the writ by proceedings under § 8.01–506 and following of this chapter, if such proceedings be commenced before that day.

Acts 1977, c. 617; Acts 1984, c. 557.

§ 8.01–480. Prior security interest on property levied on

Tangible personal property subject to a prior security interest, or in which the execution debtor has only an equitable interest, may nevertheless be levied on for the satisfaction of a fieri facias. If the prior security interest is due and payable, the officer levying the fieri facias may sell the property free of such security interest, and apply the proceeds first to the payment of such security interest, and the residue, so far as necessary, to the satisfaction of the fieri facias. In the event the property is to be sold free of such prior security interest, the judgment creditor shall give written notice by certified mail to each secured party of record as hereafter specified, as his name and address shall appear on record, of the proposed sale, or to any secured party of whom the judgment creditor shall have actual knowledge. Such notice shall be given to each secured party who is of record at the State Corporation Commission, at the Department of Motor Vehicles, at the Department of Game and Inland Fisheries, or in the clerk's office in the city or county in Virginia, where the debtor has resided to the knowledge of the judgment creditor at any time during a one-year period prior to the sale. Certification of such notice shall be delivered to the sheriff or other officer conducting the sale pursuant to execution of the judgment, who shall announce that except as to such person so notified, the sale is subject to any prior security interest of record, other than one of record at a place where the debtor may have resided more than one year previously. If such prior security interest is not due and payable at the time of sale, such officer shall sell the property levied on subject to such security interest.

Acts 1977, c. 617; Acts 1979, c. 491; Acts 1990, c. 553.

§ 8.01–481. Territorial extent of lien

The lien given by this chapter on personal property by levy shall, as to property capable of being levied on, be restricted to the bailiwick of the officer into whose hands the execution is placed to be executed, but as to property not capable of being levied on the lien shall extend throughout the limits of the Commonwealth.

Acts 1977, c. 617.

§ 8.01–482. If levy be on coin or currency, how accounted for

If the levy be on coin or currency (including notes) made a legal tender for the payment of debts, the same shall be accounted for at its par value as so much money made under the execution. If it be upon coin or currency (including notes) not a legal tender for the payment of debts, and the creditor will not take them at their nominal value, they shall be sold and accounted for as any other property taken under execution.

Acts 1977, c. 617.

ARTICLE 3

RETURN AND VENDITIONI EXPONAS

§ 8.01–483. Return of officer on fieri facias; statement filed therewith

Upon a writ of fieri facias, the officer shall return whether the money therein mentioned has been or cannot be made. If there is only part thereof which is or cannot be made, he shall return the amount of such part. With every execution under which money is recovered, he shall return a statement of the amount received, including his fees and other charges, and shall pay such amount, except such fees and charges, to the person entitled. In his return upon every execution, the officer shall also state in what manner a copy of the writ was served in accordance with § 8.01–487.1, whether or not he made a levy of the same, the date and time of such levy, the date when he received such payment or obtained such satisfaction upon such execution and, if there is more than one defendant, from which defendant he received the same.

Acts 1977, c. 617; Acts 1986, c. 341.

§ 8.01–484. When writ may be destroyed

A writ of fieri facias returned by the officer to the clerk's office with a notation that the money cannot be made may be destroyed after two years from the date of the return.

Acts 1977, c. 617; Acts 1988, c. 420.

§ 8.01–485. When venditioni exponas may issue; proceedings thereon

When it appears by the return on an execution that property taken to satisfy it remains unsold, a writ of venditioni exponas may issue, whereupon the like proceedings shall be had as might have been had on the first execution; except, that if it issue upon a return of no sale for want of bidders, or of a sufficient bid, the advertisement shall state the fact, and that the sale will be made peremptorily.

Acts 1977, c. 617.

§ 8.01–486. Procedure when officer taking property under execution dies before sale

If an officer taking property under execution die before the sale thereof, and there be no deputies of such officer acting in the case, upon a suggestion of the fact a writ of venditioni exponas may be directed to the sheriff or other officer of the county or city wherein the property was taken. Whereupon the officer to whom the writ is directed shall take possession of the property previously levied upon, whether the same be in possession of the representatives of the deceased officer or the execution debtor, and proceed to advertise and sell it and account for the proceeds thereof in like manner as if the levy had been made by himself.

Acts 1977, c. 617.

ARTICLE 4

ENFORCEMENT GENERALLY

§ 8.01–487. Officer to endorse on fieri facias time of receiving it

Every officer shall endorse on each writ of fieri facias the date and time he receives the same and also when he levies upon tangible personal property of the debtor.

Acts 1977, c. 617. Amended by Acts 2009, c. 443.

§ 8.01–487.1. Officer to leave copy of writ where levy made

An officer into whose hands a writ of fieri facias is placed to be levied, when making a levy shall serve a copy of the writ and any attachments thereto on the judgment debtor or other responsible person at the premises where the levy is made. If no such person is present, a copy of the writ and any attachments thereto shall be posted on the front door of such premises.

Acts 1986, c. 341.

§ 8.01–488. When several writs of fieri facias, how satisfied

Of writs of fieri facias, that which was first delivered to the officer, though two or more be delivered on the same day, shall be first levied and satisfied, and when several such executions are delivered to the officer at the same time they shall be satisfied ratably. But if an indemnifying bond be required by the officer as a prerequisite to a sale, and the same to be given by some of the creditors and not by others, and the officer sells under the protection of such bond, the proceeds of the sale shall be paid to the creditors giving the bond in the order in which their liens attached.

Acts 1977, c. 617.

§ 8.01–489. Growing crops, not severed, not liable to distress or levy

No growing crop of any kind, not severed, shall be liable to distress or levy.

Acts 1977, c. 617.

§ 8.01–490. No unreasonable distress or levy; sustenance provided for livestock; removal of property

Officers shall in no case make an unreasonable distress or levy. For horses, or any livestock distrained or levied on, the officer shall provide sufficient sustenance while they remain in his possession. Nothing distrained or levied on shall be removed by him out of his county or city, unless when it is otherwise specially provided.

Acts 1977, c. 617.

§ 8.01–491. Officer may break open dwelling house and levy on property in personal possession of debtor

An officer into whose hands an execution is placed to be levied, may, if need be, break open the outer doors of a dwelling house in the daytime, after having first demanded admittance of the occupant, in order to make a levy, and may also levy on property in the personal possession of the debtor if the same be open to observation.

Acts 1977, c. 617.

§ 8.01–492. Sale of property

In any case of goods and chattels which an officer shall distrain or levy on, otherwise than under an attachment, or which he may be directed to sell by an order of a court, unless such order prescribe a different course, the officer shall fix upon a time and place for the sale thereof and post notice of the same at least ten days before the day of sale at some place near the residence of the owner if he reside in the county or city and at two or more public places in the officer's county or city. If the goods and chattels be expensive to keep or perishable, the court from whose clerk's office the writ of fieri facias or the distress warrant was issued under which the seizure is made, or if the distress warrant was issued by a clerk, the court of which he is a clerk, may order a sale of the property seized under fieri facias or distress warrant to be made upon such notice less than ten days as to such court may seem proper. At the time and place so appointed, such officer shall sell to the highest bidder, for cash, such goods and chattels, or so much thereof as may be necessary.

Acts 1977, c. 617.

§ 8.01–493. Adjournment of sale

When there is not time, on the day appointed for any such sale, to complete the same, the sale may be adjourned from day to day until completed.

Acts 1977, c. 617.

§ 8.01–494. Resale of property if purchaser fails to comply; remedy against such purchaser

If, at any sale by an officer, the purchaser does not comply with the terms of sale, the officer may sell the property, either forthwith or under a new advertisement, or return that the property was not sold for want of bidders. If, on a resale, the property be sold for less than it sold for before, the first purchaser shall be liable for the difference to the creditor, so far as is required to satisfy him, and to the debtor for the balance. This section shall not prevent the creditor from proceeding as he might have done if it had not been enacted.

Acts 1977, c. 617.

§ 8.01–495. When money received by officer under execution to be repaid to debtor

When an officer has received money under execution, if any surplus remain in his hands after satisfying the execution, such surplus shall be repaid to the debtor; and if the debtor, or his personal representative, obtain an injunction or supersedeas to an execution, in whole or in part, before money received under it, or any part of it, is paid over to the creditor, the officer shall repay such debtor the money so received and not so paid over, or so much thereof as the injunction or supersedeas may extend to, unless such process otherwise direct.

Acts 1977, c. 617.

§ 8.01–496. Officer not required to go out of his jurisdiction to pay over money

No officer receiving money under execution, when the person to whom it is payable resides in a different county or city from that in which the officer resides, shall be liable to have any judgment rendered against him or his sureties for the nonpayment thereof, until a demand of payment be made of such officer in his county or city, by such creditor or his attorney-at-law, or some person having a written order from the creditor.

Acts 1977, c. 617.

§ 8.01–497. Suit by officer to recover estate on which fieri facias is lien

For the recovery of any estate on which a writ of fieri facias is a lien under this chapter, or on which the judgment on which such writ issues is a lien under Chapter 17 (§ 8.01–426 et seq.) of this title, or for the enforcement of any liability in respect to any such estate, a suit may be maintained, at law or in equity, as the case may require, in the name of the officer to whom such writ was delivered, or in the name of any other officer who may be designated for the purpose by an order of the court in which the judgment is entered. No officer shall be bound to bring such suit unless bond, with sufficient surety, be given him to indemnify him against all expenses and costs which he may incur or become liable for by reason thereof. But any person interested may bring such suit at his own costs in the officer's name.

Acts 1977, c. 617.

§ 8.01-498. Selling officers and employees not to bid or to purchase

No officer of any city, town, county or constitutional officer or employee of any such city, town, county or constitutional office shall, directly or indirectly, bid on or purchase effects sold under a writ by such officer. Anyone violating this section shall be guilty of a Class 1 misdemeanor.

Acts 1977, c. 617; Acts 1988, c. 674.

§ 8.01-499. Officer receiving money to make return thereof and pay net proceeds; commission, etc.

An officer receiving money under this chapter shall make return thereof forthwith to the court or the clerk's office of the court in which the judgment is entered. For failing to do so, the officer shall be liable as if he had acted under an order of such court. After deducting from such money a commission of 10 percent and his necessary expenses and costs, including reasonable fees to sheriff's counsel, he shall pay the net proceeds, and he and his sureties and their representatives shall be liable therefor, in like manner as if the same had been made under a writ of fieri facias on the judgment.

Acts 1977, c. 617. Amended by Acts 2004, c. 198; Acts 2004, c. 211.

§ 8.01-500. Officer receiving money to notify person entitled to receive it

Every officer collecting or receiving money to be applied on any execution or other legal process, or on any claim, whether judgment has been rendered thereon or not, shall notify in writing by mail or otherwise, within thirty days after such money is received, the person entitled to receive such money, if known. Any officer failing without good cause to comply with this section within the time prescribed shall be fined not less than twenty dollars nor more than fifty dollars for each offense.

Acts 1977, c. 617.

Article 5

Lien on Property Not Capable of Being Levied on

§ 8.01-501. Lien of fieri facias on estate of debtor not capable of being levied on

Every writ of fieri facias shall, in addition to the lien it has under §§ 8.01-478 and 8.01-479 on what is capable of being levied on under those sections, be a lien from the time it is delivered to a sheriff or other officer, or any person authorized to serve process pursuant to § 8.01-293, to be executed, on all the personal estate of or to which the judgment debtor is, or may afterwards and on or before the return day of such writ or before the return day of any wage garnishment to enforce the same, become, possessed or entitled, in which, from its nature is not capable of being levied on under such sections, except such as is exempt under the provisions of Title 34, and except that, as against an assignee of any such estate for valuable consideration, the lien by virtue of this section shall not affect him unless he had notice thereof at the time of the assignment.

Acts 1977, c. 617; Acts 1996, c. 1002. Amended by Acts 2006, c. 575.

§ 8.01-502. Person paying debtor not affected by lien unless notice given

As against a person making a payment to the judgment debtor, the lien referred to in § 8.01-501 shall not affect him, unless and until he be given written notice thereof setting forth (i) the name of the person against whom obtained, (ii) by whom obtained, (iii) the amount and costs of the judgment, (iv) the date recovered, (v) the date of the issuance or renewal of execution thereon, (vi) the return day of execution, and (vii) the date of placing of the execution in the hands of the officer or other person authorized to serve process pursuant to § 8.01-293, and unless such notice shall be personally signed by the plaintiff or his attorney and shall have been duly served upon the person making payment and the judgment debtor by an officer authorized to serve civil process.

Acts 1977, c. 617; Acts 1996, c. 1002.

§ 8.01-502.1. Serving notice of lien on financial institution

A. No judgment creditor or attorney for a judgment creditor shall have a notice of lien served on a financial institution under § 8.01-502 unless such judgment creditor or attorney has a reasonable basis for believing that the judgment debtor is entitled to a payment from such institution. The fact that a financial institution is doing business in a geographic area where the judgment debtor resides, works or has a place of business is not, by itself, a reasonable basis for believing that the judgment debtor is entitled to a payment from a financial institution. Any person violating this section shall be liable to a financial institution for the sum of $100 for each notice of lien wrongfully served on such institution. In any action at law to recover an amount due hereunder, the judgment creditor or attorney for the judgment creditor causing the notice of lien to be served on the financial institution shall have the burden of showing a reasonable basis for believing that the judgment debtor was entitled to a payment from such institution.

B. Any judgment creditor serving a notice of lien on a financial institution shall, within five business days of such service, mail to the judgment debtor at his last known address a copy of the notice of lien along with a notice of exemptions and claim for exemption form in accordance with § 8.01-512.4. The judgment creditor or attorney for the judgment creditor shall file a certification with the court affirming that he has mailed the judgment debtor these notices. In the event that the judgment creditor fails to comply with the requirements of this subsection, he shall be liable to the judgment debtor for no more than $100 in damages, unless he proves by a preponderance of the evidence that the failure was not willful.

C. A financial institution served with a valid notice of lien shall provide a written response to the judgment creditor or attorney for the judgment creditor within twenty-one days after being served with such notice of lien indicating the amount of money held by the financial institution pursuant to the notice of lien.

Acts 1997, c. 750; Acts 1999, c. 48. Amended by Acts 2010, c. 673.

§ 8.01-503. Withholding of wages or salary not required by preceding sections unless garnishment process served

Nothing contained in §§ 8.01-501 and 8.01-502 shall have the effect of requiring any employer paying wages or salary to an employee to withhold any part of such wages or salary unless and until such employer is duly served with process in garnishment.

Acts 1977, c. 617.

§ 8.01-504. Penalty for service of notice of lien when no judgment exists

Whoever causes to be served a notice of lien of a writ of fieri facias without there being a judgment against the defendant named therein, shall pay to him the sum of $350, and whoever serves a notice of lien of a writ of fieri facias before the issuance of a writ of fieri facias, or after the return day thereof, or serves or in any way gives a notice of a lien of fieri facias by means other than by service by an officer authorized to serve civil process, shall pay to the named defendant the sum of $350, to be recoverable as damages in an action at law, in addition to whatever damages may be alleged and proven.

Acts 1977, c. 617. Amended by Acts 2010, c. 343.

§ 8.01-505. When lien acquired on intangibles under § 8.01-501 ceases

The lien acquired under § 8.01-501 on intangibles shall cease whenever the right of the judgment creditor to enforce the judgment by execution or by action, or to extend the right by motion, ceases or is suspended by a forthcoming bond being given and forfeited or by other legal process. Furthermore, as to all such intangibles the lien shall cease upon the expiration of the following periods whichever is the longer: (i) one year from the return day of the execution pursuant to which the lien arose, or (ii) if the intangible is a debt due from, or a claim upon, a third person in favor of the judgment debtor or the estate of such third person, one year from the final determination of the amount owed to the judgment debtor.

Acts 1977, c. 617.

Article 6

Interrogatories

§ 8.01-506. Proceedings by interrogatories to ascertain estate of debtor; summons; proviso; objections by judgment debtor

A. To ascertain the personal estate of a judgment debtor, and to ascertain any real estate, in or out of this Commonwealth, to which the debtor named in a judgment and fieri facias is entitled, upon the application of the execution creditor, the clerk of the court from which such fieri facias issued shall issue a summons against (i) the execution debtor, (ii) any officer of the corporation if such execution debtor is a corporation having an office in this Commonwealth, (iii) any employee of a corporation if such execution debtor is a corporation having an office but no officers in the Commonwealth provided that a copy of the summons shall also be served upon the registered agent of the corporation, or (iv) any debtor to, or bailee of, the execution debtor.

B. The summons shall require him to appear before the court from which the fieri facias issued or a commissioner of the county or city in which such court is located, or a like court or a commissioner of a county or city contiguous thereto, or upon request of the execution creditor, before a like court or a commissioner of the county or city in which the execution debtor resides, or of a county or city contiguous thereto, to answer such interrogatories as may be propounded to him by the execution creditor or his attorney, or the court, or the commissioner, as the case may be. If the execution creditor requests that the summons require the execution debtor to appear before a like court of the county or city in which the execution debtor resides, or of a county or city contiguous thereto, the case may be filed or docketed in accordance with the requirements of § 8.01-506.2 prior to issuance of the summons.

C. Provided, however, that as a condition precedent to proceeding under this section, the execution creditor has furnished to the court a certificate setting forth that he has not proceeded against the execution debtor under this section within the six months last preceding the date of such certificate. Except that for good cause shown, the court may, on motion of the execution creditor, issue an order allowing further proceedings before a commissioner by interrogatories during the six-month period. Any judgment creditor who knowingly gives false information upon any such certificate made under this article shall be guilty of a Class 1 misdemeanor. The issuance of a summons that is not served shall not constitute the act of proceeding against an execution debtor for purposes of making the certificate required by this subsection.

D. The debtor or other person served with such summons shall appear at the time and place mentioned and make answer to such interrogatories. The commissioner shall, at the request of either of the parties, enter in his proceedings and report to the court mentioned in § 8.01-507.1, any and all objections taken by such debtor against answering such interrogatories, or any or either of them, and if the court afterwards sustains any one or more of such objections, the answers given to such interrogatories as to which objections are sustained shall be held for naught in that or any other case.

E. Notwithstanding the foregoing provisions of this section, the court from which a writ of fieri facias issued, upon motion by the execution debtor and for good cause shown, shall transfer debtor interrogatory proceedings to a forum more convenient to the execution debtor.

Acts 1977, c. 617; Acts 1978, c. 66; Acts 1979, c. 225; Acts 1985, c. 433; Acts 1987, c. 182; Acts 1991, c. 463. Amended by Acts 2005, c. 726; Acts 2009, c. 622.

§ 8.01-506.1. Production of book accounts or other writing compelled

In any proceeding under the provisions of § 8.01-506, a subpoena duces tecum may be issued for a book of accounts or other writing containing material evidence pursuant to Rule 4:9A of the Rules of the Supreme Court. However, notwithstanding the provisions of Rule 4:9A, a subpoena duces tecum issued pursuant to this section may (i) be directed to a party to the case and (ii) be issued by a commissioner and may direct that evidence and any custodians subpoenaed be produced before the commissioner. If the subpoena duces tecum is against a party who is not a resident of the Commonwealth, but who has appeared in the case or been served with process in this Commonwealth, the service may be on his attorney of record.

The provisions of Rule 4:1 (c) of the Supreme Court as to protective orders shall be applicable to proceedings under this section.

Acts 1978, c. 339; Acts 1986, c. 249; Acts 1993, c. 267.

§ 8.01-506.2. Proceedings in court of county or city where execution debtor resides

When pursuant to subsection B of § 8.01-506, a summons requires the execution debtor to appear before a court of the county or city in which the execution debtor resides, or of a county or city contiguous thereto, the execution creditor may have the case filed or docketed in that court as follows:

1. The execution creditor shall file with that court an abstract of the judgment rendered.

2. The execution creditor shall pay a fee to that court in accordance with the provisions of § 16.1-69.48:2 or subdivision 17 of § 17.1-275.

3. After docketing or filing the abstract of judgment and payment of any fees, the court shall issue the summons and any subsequent executions on the filed or docketed judgment, including a subpoena duces tecum pursuant to § 8.01-506.1, and shall conduct such hearings and enter such orders pursuant to §§ 8.01-507, 8.01-507.1, 8.01-508, 8.01-509, and 8.01-510 as may be required.

4. The execution creditor shall file in both courts any releases or satisfactions of judgment.

Added by Acts 2005, c. 726.

§ 8.01-507. Conveyance or delivery of property disclosed by interrogatories

Any real estate out of this Commonwealth to which it may appear by such answer that the debtor is entitled shall, upon order of the court or commissioner, be forthwith conveyed by him to the officer to whom was delivered such fieri facias, and any money, bank notes, securities, evidences of debt, or other personal estate, tangible or intangible, which it may appear by such answers are in possession of or under the control of the debtor or his debtor or bailee, shall be delivered by him or them, as far as practicable, to such officer, or to some other, or in such manner as may be ordered by the commissioner or court.

Acts 1977, c. 617.

§ 8.01-507.1. Interrogatories, answers, etc., to be returned to court

The commissioner shall, at the request of either of the parties, return the interrogatories and answers filed with him, and a report of the proceedings under §§ 8.01-506 and 8.01-507, to the court in which the judgment is rendered.

Acts 1977, c. 617.

§ 8.01-508. How debtor may be arrested and held to answer

If any person summoned under § 8.01-506 fails to appear and answer, or makes any answers which are deemed by the commissioner or court to be evasive, or if, having answered, fails to make such conveyance and delivery as is required by § 8.01-507, the commissioner or court shall issue (i) a capias directed to any sheriff requiring such sheriff to take the person in default and deliver him to the commissioner or court so that he may be compelled to make proper answers, or such conveyance or delivery, as the case may be or (ii) a rule to show cause why the person summoned should not appear and make proper answer or make conveyance and delivery. If the person in default fails to answer or convey and deliver he may be incarcerated until he makes such answers or conveyance and delivery. Where a capias is issued, the person in default shall be admitted to bail as provided in Article 1 (§ 19.2–119 et seq.) of Chapter 9 of Title 19.2 if he cannot be brought promptly before the commissioner or court in the county or city to which the capias is returnable. Upon making such answers, or such conveyance and delivery, he shall be discharged by the commissioner or the court. He may also be discharged by the court from whose clerk's office the capias issued in any case where the court is of the opinion that he was improperly committed or is improperly or unlawfully detained in custody. If the person in default appeals the decision of the commissioner or court, he shall be admitted to bail as provided in Article 1 (§ 19.2–119 et seq.) of Chapter 9 of Title 19.2.

If the person held for failure to appear and answer interrogatories is detained in a jurisdiction other than that where the summons is issued, the sheriff in the requesting jurisdiction shall have the duty to transport such person to the place where interrogatories are to be taken.

Acts 1977, c. 617; Acts 1983, c. 278; Acts 1985, c. 290; Acts 1986, c. 326; Acts 1999, c. 829; Acts 1999, c. 846.

§ 8.01–509. Order for sale and application of debtor's estate

The court to which the commissioner returns his report may make any order it may deem right, as to the sale and proper application of the estate conveyed and delivered under §§ 8.01–506 and 8.01–507.

Acts 1977, c. 617.

§ 8.01–510. Sale, collection and disposition of debtor's estate by officer

Real estate, conveyed to an officer under this chapter, shall, unless the court otherwise direct, be sold as other property levied on is required to be sold under § 8.01–492 and be conveyed to the purchaser by the officer. An officer to whom there is delivery under this chapter, when the delivery is of money, bank notes, or any goods or chattels, shall dispose of the same as if levied on by him under a fieri facias; and when the delivery is of evidences of debts, other than such bank notes, may receive payment of such debts within sixty days after such delivery. Any evidence of debt or other security, remaining in his hands at the end of such sixty days, shall be returned by him to the clerk's office of such court, and collection thereof may be enforced as prescribed by § 8.01–497. For a failure to make such return, he may be proceeded against as if an express order of the court for such return had been disobeyed.

Acts 1977, c. 617.

Article 7

Garnishment

§ 8.01–511. Institution of garnishment proceedings

A. On a suggestion by the judgment creditor that, by reason of the lien of his writ of fieri facias, there is a liability on any person other than the judgment debtor or that there is in the hands of some person in his capacity as personal representative of some decedent a sum of money to which a judgment debtor is or may be entitled as creditor or distributee of such decedent, upon which sum when determined such writ of fieri facias is a lien, a summons in the form prescribed by § 8.01–512.3 may (i) be sued out of the clerk's office of the court from which an execution on the judgment is issued so long as the judgment shall remain enforceable as provided in § 8.01–251, (ii) be sued out of the clerk's office to which an execution issued thereon has been returned as provided in § 16.1–99 against such person, or (iii) be sued out of the clerk's office from which an execution issued as provided in § 16.1–278.18. If the judgment debtor does not reside in the city or county where the judgment was entered, the judgment creditor may have the case filed or docketed in the court of the city or county where the judgment debtor resides and such court may issue an execution on the judgment, provided that the judgment creditor (a) files with the court an abstract of the judgment rendered, (b) pays fees to the court in accordance with § 16.1–69.48:2 or subdivision 17 of § 17.1–275, and (c) files in both courts any release or satisfaction of judgment. The summons and the notice and claim for exemption form required pursuant to § 8.01–512.4 shall be served on the garnishee, and shall be served on the judgment debtor promptly after service on the garnishee. Service on the judgment debtor and the garnishee shall be made pursuant to subdivision 1 or 2 of § 8.01–296. When making an application for garnishment, the judgment creditor shall set forth on the suggestion for summons in garnishment the last known address of the judgment debtor, and shall furnish the clerk, if service is to be made by the sheriff, or shall furnish any other person making service with an envelope, with first-class postage attached, addressed to such address. A copy of the summons and the notice and claim for exemptions form required under § 8.01–512.4 shall be sent by the clerk to the sheriff or provided by the judgment creditor to the person making service, with the process to be served. Promptly after service on the garnishee, the person making service shall mail such envelope by first-class mail to the judgment debtor at his last known address. If the person making service is unable to serve the judgment debtor pursuant to subdivision 1 of § 8.01–296, such mailing shall satisfy the mailing requirements of subdivision 2 b of § 8.01–296. The person making service shall note on his return the date of such mailing which, with the notation "copy mailed to judgment debtor," shall be sufficient proof of the mailing of such envelope with the required copy of the summons and the notice and claim for exemption form with no examination of such contents being required nor separate certification by the clerk or judgment creditor that the appropriate documents have been so inserted. If the person making service is unable to serve the judgment debtor pursuant to subdivision 1 or 2 of § 8.01–296, such mailing shall constitute service of process on the judgment debtor. The judgment creditor shall furnish the social security number of the judgment debtor to the clerk, except as hereinafter provided.

B. The judgment creditor may require the judgment debtor to furnish his correct social security number by the use of interrogatories. However, use of such interrogatories shall not be a required condition of a judgment creditor's diligent good faith effort to secure the judgment debtor's social security number. Such remedy shall be in addition to all other lawful remedies available to the judgment creditor. Upon a representation by the judgment creditor, or his agent or attorney, that he has made a diligent good faith effort to secure the social security number of the judgment debtor and has been unable to do so, the garnishment shall be issued without the necessity for such number.

C. Except as provided herein, no summons shall be issued pursuant to this section for the garnishment of wages, salaries, commissions, or other earnings unless it: (i) is in the form prescribed by § 8.01–512.3; (ii) is directed to only one garnishee for the garnishment of only one judgment debtor; (iii) contains both the "TOTAL BALANCE DUE" and the social security number of the judgment debtor in the proper places as provided on the summons; and (iv) specifies that it is a garnishment against (a) the judgment debtor's wages, salary, or other compensation or (b) some other debt due or property of the judgment debtor. The garnishee shall not be liable to the judgment creditor for any property not specified in the summons as provided in (iv) above. Upon receipt of a summons not in compliance with this provision, the garnishee shall file a written answer to that effect and shall have no liability to the judgment creditor, such summons being void upon transmission of the answer.

D. The judgment creditor shall, in the suggestion, specify the amount of interest, if any, that is claimed to be due upon the judgment, calculated to the return day of the summons. He shall also set out such credits as may have been made upon the judgment.

All costs incurred by the judgment creditor after entry of the judgment, in aid of execution of the judgment and paid to a clerk of court, sheriff, or process server are chargeable against the judgment debtor, unless such costs are chargeable against the judgment creditor pursuant to § 8.01–475. Regardless of the actual amount of the fee paid by the judgment creditor, the fee for a process server chargeable against the judgment debtor shall not exceed the fee authorized for service by the sheriff. All such previous costs chargeable against the judgment debtor may be included by the judgment creditor as judgment costs in the garnishment summons form prescribed in § 8.01–512.3. This paragraph shall not be construed to limit any cost assessed by a court as part of the judgment.

E. In addition, the suggestion shall contain an allegation that:

1. The summons is based upon a judgment upon which a prior summons has been issued but not fully satisfied; or

2. No summons has been issued upon his suggestion against the same judgment debtor within a period of 18 months, other than under the provisions of subdivision 1; or

3. The summons is based upon a judgment granted against a debtor upon a debt due or made for necessary food, rent or shelter, public utilities including telephone service, drugs, or medical care supplied the debtor by the judgment creditor or to one of his lawful dependents, and that it was not for luxuries or nonessentials; or

4. The summons is based upon a judgment for a debt due the judgment creditor to refinance a lawful loan made by an authorized lending institution; or

5. The summons is based upon a judgment on an obligation incurred as an endorser or comaker upon a lawful note; or

6. The summons is based upon a judgment for a debt or debts reaffirmed after bankruptcy.

F. Any judgment creditor who knowingly gives false information upon any such suggestion or certificate made under this chapter shall be guilty of a Class 1 misdemeanor.

Acts 1977, c. 454; Acts 1977, c. 617; Acts 1978, c. 321; Acts 1978, c. 506; Acts 1979, c. 242; Acts 1979, c. 345; Acts 1980, c. 537; Acts 1983, c. 399; Acts 1983, c. 468; Acts 1984, c. 1; Acts 1985, c. 524; Acts 1991, c. 534; Acts 1996, c. 501; Acts 1996, c. 608. Amended by Acts 2006, c. 55; Acts 2012, c. 127; Acts 2012, c. 129; Acts 2012, c. 251; Acts 2012, c. 409.

§ 8.01–511.1. Garnishee inability to determine whether it holds property of judgment debtor

If a summons for the garnishment of property other than wages, salaries, commissions or other earnings does not contain sufficient or accurate information to enable the garnishee to reasonably identify the judgment debtor, the garnishee shall have no liability to the judgment creditor for failing to deliver the judgment debtor's property in response to the summons. If the summons contains either the social security number or taxpayer identification number of the judgment debtor as it appears in the records of the garnishee, or the name and address of the judgment debtor as they appear in the records of the garnishee, the summons shall be deemed to contain information sufficient to enable the garnishee to reasonably identify the judgment debtor.

If the summons contains sufficient or accurate information to enable the garnishee to reasonably identify the judgment debtor, the garnishee shall (i) answer to the summoning court and further state what the garnishee's records show as the last known address for the judgment debtor and any other information the garnishee deems relevant and (ii) send to the judgment debtor at the last known address a copy of its answer to the court.

No garnishee or creditor who proceeds under the terms of this statute in good faith shall be liable to any person therefor.

Added by Acts 2002, c. 688.

§§ 8.01–512, 8.01–512.1. Repealed by Acts 1983, c. 399

§ 8.01–512.2. Fee for garnishee-employers

Garnishee-employers may charge and collect a fee of up to ten dollars from a judgment-debtor employee on account of such employers' expense in processing each garnishment summons served on such employers on account of the judgment-debtor employee.

Acts 1980, c. 537; Acts 1994, c. 664.

§ 8.01–512.3. Form of garnishment summons

Any garnishment issued pursuant to § 8.01–511 shall be in the following form:

(a) Front side of summons:

GARNISHMENT SUMMONS

(Court Name)

(Name, address and telephone number of judgment creditor except that when the judgment creditor's attorney's name, address and telephone number appear on the summons, only the creditor's name shall be used.)

(Name, address and telephone number of judgment creditor's attorney)

(Name, street address and social security number of judgment debtor)

(Name and street address of garnishee)

.... Hearing Date and Time

This is a garnishment against (check only one of the designations below):

☐ wages, salary, or other compensation. ☐ some other debt due or property of the judgment debtor.

MAXIMUM PORTION OF DISPOSABLE EARNINGS SUBJECT TO GARNISHMENT	STATEMENT	
	Judgment Principal	$ .....
	Credits	$ .....
	Interest	$ .....
[ ] Support	Judgment Costs	$ .....
[ ] 50% [ ] 55% [ ] 60% [ ] 65% (if not specified, then 50%)	Attorney's Fees	$ .....
[ ] state taxes, 100%	Garnishment Costs	$ .....
If none of the above is checked, then § 34–29 (a) applies.	TOTAL BALANCE DUE The garnishee shall rely on this amount.	$ .....

....

Date of Judgment

TO ANY AUTHORIZED OFFICER: You are hereby commanded to serve this summons on the judgment debtor and the garnishee.

TO THE GARNISHEE: You are hereby commanded to

(1) File a written answer with this court, or

(2) Deliver payment to this court, or

(3) Appear before this court on the return date and time shown on this summons to answer the Suggestion for Summons in Garnishment of the judgment creditor that, by reason of the lien of writ of fieri facias, there is a liability as shown in the statement upon the garnishee.

As garnishee, you shall withhold from the judgment debtor any sums of money to which the judgment debtor is or may be entitled from you during the period between the date of service of this summons on you and the date for your appearance in court, subject to the following limitations:

(1) The maximum amount which may be garnished is the "TOTAL BALANCE DUE" as shown on this summons.

(2) If the sums of money being garnished are earnings of the judgment debtor, then the provision of "MAXIMUM PORTION OF DISPOSABLE EARNINGS SUBJECT TO GARNISHMENT" shall apply.

If a garnishment summons is served on an employer having 1,000 or more employees, then money to which the judgment debtor is or may be entitled from his or her employer shall be considered those wages, salaries, commissions, or other earnings which, following service on the garnishee-employer, are determined and are payable to the judgment debtor under the garnishee-employer's normal payroll procedure with a reasonable time allowance for making a timely return by mail to this court.

....
Date of Issuance of Summons Clerk

....
Date of delivery of writ of fieri facias to sheriff if different from date of issuance of this summons.

(b) A plain language interpretation of § 34–29 shall appear on the reverse side of the summons as follows:

"The following statement is not the law but is an interpretation of the law which is intended to assist those who must respond to this garnishment. You may rely on this only for general guidance because the law itself is the final word. (Read the law, § 34–29 of the Code of Virginia, for a full explanation. A copy of § 34–29 is available at the clerk's office. If you do not understand the law, call a lawyer for help.)

An employer may take as much as 25 percent of an employee's disposable earnings to satisfy this garnishment. But if an employee makes the minimum wage or less for his week's earnings, the employee will ordinarily get to keep 30 times the minimum hourly wage."

But an employer may withhold a different amount of money from that above if:

(1) The employee must pay child support or spousal support and was ordered to do so by a court procedure or other legal procedure. No more than 65 percent of an employee's earnings may be withheld for support;

(2) Money is withheld by order of a bankruptcy court; or

(3) Money is withheld for a tax debt.

"Disposable earnings" means the money an employee makes after taxes and after other amounts required by law to be withheld are satisfied. Earnings can be salary, hourly wages, commissions, bonuses, or otherwise, whether paid directly to the employee or not. After those earnings are in the bank for 30 days, they are not considered earnings any more.

If an employee tries to transfer, assign, or in any way give his earnings to another person to avoid the garnishment, it will not be legal; earnings are still earnings.

An employee cannot be fired because he is garnished for one debt.

Financial institutions that receive an employee's paycheck by direct deposit do not have to determine what part of a person's earnings can be garnished.
Acts 1983, c. 399; Acts 1994, c. 40; Acts 1995, c. 379; Acts 1996, c. 1051. Amended by Acts 2006, c. 55.

§ 8.01–512.4. Notice of exemptions from garnishment and lien

No summons in garnishment shall be issued or served, nor shall any notice of lien be served on a financial institution pursuant to § 8.01–502.1, unless a notice of exemptions and claim for exemption form are attached. The notice shall contain the following statement:

NOTICE TO JUDGMENT DEBTOR

HOW TO CLAIM EXEMPTIONS FROM GARNISHMENT AND LIEN

The attached Summons in Garnishment or Notice of Lien has been issued on request of a creditor who holds a judgment against you. The Summons may cause your property or wages to be held or taken to pay the judgment.

The law provides that certain property and wages cannot be taken in garnishment. Such property is said to be exempted. A summary of some of the major exemptions is set forth in the request for hearing form. There is no exemption solely because you are having difficulty paying your debts.

If you claim an exemption, you should (i) fill out the claim for exemption form and (ii) deliver or mail the form to the clerk's office of this court. You have a right to a hearing within seven business days from the date you file your claim with the court. If the creditor is asking that your wages be withheld, the method of computing the amount of wages which are exempt from garnishment by law is indicated on the Summons in Garnishment attached. You do not need to file a claim for exemption to receive this exemption, but if you believe the wrong amount is being withheld you may file a claim for exemption.

On the day of the hearing you should come to court ready to explain why your property is exempted, and you should bring any documents which may help you prove your case. If you do not come to court at the designated time and prove that your property is exempt, you may lose some of your rights.

It may be helpful to you to seek the advice of an attorney in this matter.

REQUEST FOR HEARING–GARNISHMENT/LIEN EXEMPTION CLAIM

I claim that the exemption(s) from garnishment or lien which are checked below apply in this case:

MAJOR EXEMPTIONS UNDER FEDERAL AND STATE LAW

.... 1. Social Security benefits and Supplemental Security Income (SSI)(42 U.S.C. § 407).

.... 2. Veterans' benefits (38 U.S.C. § 5301).

.... 3. Federal civil service retirement benefits (5 U.S.C. § 8346).

.... 4. Annuities to survivors of federal judges (28 U.S.C. § 376(n)).

.... 5. Longshore and Harbor Workers' Compensation Act (33 U.S.C. § 916).

.... 6. Black lung benefits.

Exemptions listed under 1 through 6 above may not be applicable in child support and alimony cases (42 U.S.C. § 659).

.... 7. Seaman's, master's or fisherman's wages, except for child support or spousal support and maintenance (46 U.S.C. § 11109).

.... 8. Unemployment compensation benefits (§ 60.2–600, Code of Virginia). This exemption may not be applicable in child support cases (§ 60.2–608, Code of Virginia).

.... 9. Portions or amounts of wages subject to garnishment (§ 34–29, Code of Virginia).

.... 10. Public assistance payments (§ 63.2–506, Code of Virginia).

.... 11. Homestead exemption of $5,000, or $10,000 if the debtor is 65 years of age or older, in cash (§ 34–4, Code of Virginia). This exemption may not be claimed in certain cases, such as payment of spousal or child support (§ 34–5, Code of Virginia).

.... 12. Property of disabled veterans—additional $10,000 cash (§ 34–4.1, Code of Virginia).

.... 13. Workers' Compensation benefits (§ 65.2–531, Code of Virginia).

.... 14. Growing crops (§ 8.01–489, Code of Virginia).

.... 15. Benefits from group life insurance policies (§ 38.2–3339, Code of Virginia).

.... 16. Proceeds from industrial sick benefits insurance (§ 38.2–3549, Code of Virginia).

.... 17. Assignments of certain salary and wages (§ 55–165, Code of Virginia).

.... 18. Benefits for victims of crime (§ 19.2–368.12, Code of Virginia).

.... 19. Preneed funeral trusts (§ 54.1–2823, Code of Virginia).

.... 20. Certain retirement benefits (§ 34–34, Code of Virginia).

.... 21. Child support payments (§ 20–108.1, Code of Virginia).

.... 22. Support for dependent minor children (§ 34–4.2, Code of Virginia). To claim this exemption, the debtor shall attach to the claim for exemption form an affidavit that complies with the requirements of subsection B of § 34–4.2 and two items of proof showing that the debtor is entitled to this exemption.

.... 23. Other (describe exemption): $............

I request a court hearing to decide the validity of my claim. Notice of the hearing should be given me at:

....
(address) (telephone no.)

The statements made in this request are true to the best of my knowledge and belief.

....
(date) (signature of judgment debtor)

Acts 1984, c. 1; Acts 1986, c. 489; Acts 1989, c. 684; Acts 1994, c. 40. Amended by Acts 2007, c. 872; Acts 2009, c. 332; Acts 2009, c. 387; Acts 2009, c. 388; Acts 2010, c. 673; Acts 2012, c. 23; Acts 2012, c. 79.

§ 8.01–512.5. Hearing on claim of exemption from garnishment

A judgment debtor shall have the right to a hearing on his claim of exemption from garnishment no later than seven business days from the date that the claim is filed with the court.

The clerk shall notify the parties of the date, time and place of the hearing and the exemption being claimed. The garnishee shall comply with the garnishment summons unless and until ordered otherwise in writing by the court. The order shall take effect upon receipt by the garnishee. The clerk is required to provide a copy of the order or other hearing disposition to the garnishee only if the garnishment summons is dismissed or is modified by the judge.

Acts 1984, c. 1.

§ 8.01–513. Service upon corporation or limited liability company

A. If the person upon whom there is a suggestion of liability as provided in § 8.01–511 is a corporation, the summons shall be served upon an officer, an employee designated by the corporation other than an officer of the corporation, or, if there is no designated employee or the designated employee cannot be found, upon a managing employee of the corporation other than an officer of the corporation. If the judgment creditor or his attorney files with the court a certificate that he has used due diligence and that (i) no such officer or employee or other person authorized to accept such service can be found within the Commonwealth or (ii) such designated or managing employee found is also the judgment debtor, then such summons shall be served on the registered agent of the corporation or upon the clerk of the State Corporation Commission as provided in §§ 13.1–637, 13.1–766, 13.1–836 and 13.1–928. However, service on the corporation shall not be made upon a designated or managing employee who is also the judgment debtor. If the corporation intends to designate an employee for service, the corporation shall file a designation with the State Corporation Commission.

B. If the person upon whom there is a suggestion of liability as provided in § 8.01–511 is a limited liability company, the summons shall be served upon a member, manager, or employee designated by the limited liability company for the purpose of such service or, if there is no designated member, manager, or employee, or the designated member, manager, or employee cannot be found, upon a managing employee of the limited liability company. If the judgment creditor or his attorney files with the court a certificate that he has used due diligence and that (i) no such member, manager, or employee or other person authorized to accept such service can be found within the Commonwealth or (ii) such designated member, manager, employee, or managing employee found is also the judgment debtor, then such summons shall be served on the registered agent of the limited liability company or upon the clerk of the State Corporation Commission as provided in § 13.1–1018. However, service on the limited liability company shall not be made upon a designated member, manager, employee, or managing employee who is also the judgment debtor. If the limited liability company intends to designate a member, manager, or employee for service, the limited liability company shall file a designation with the State Corporation Commission.

C. For the purposes of this section, "managing employee" means an employee charged by the corporation or the limited liability company, as applicable, with the control of operations and supervision of employees at the business location of such corporation or limited liability company where process is sought to be served.

Acts 1977, c. 617; Acts 1980, c. 514; Acts 1997, c. 395; Acts 1998, c. 723; Acts 1998, c. 737. Amended by Acts 2004, c. 231; Acts 2006, c. 912.

§ 8.01–514. When garnishment summons returnable

The summons in garnishment, whether issued by a circuit court or a district court, may be directed to a sheriff of any county or city wherein the judgment debtor resides or where the garnishment defendant resides or where either may be found and shall be made returnable to the court that issued it within 90 days from the writ's issuance, except that, in the case of a wage garnishment, the summons shall be returnable not more than 180 days after such issuance.

Acts 1977, c. 454; Acts 1977, c. 617; Acts 1979, c. 36; Acts 2003, c. 234. Amended by Acts 2006, c. 575.

§ 8.01–515. How garnishee examined; determining exemption from employee's withholding certificate; amount due pursuant to exemptions in § 34–29(a)

A person so summoned shall appear in person and be examined on oath or he may file a statement. A corporation so summoned shall appear by an authorized agent who shall be examined on oath or may file a statement, not under seal of such authorized agent. Such statement shall show the amount the garnishee is indebted to the judgment debtor, if any, or what property or effects, if any, the garnishee has or holds which belongs to the judgment debtor, or in which he has an interest. Payment to the court of any amount by the garnishee shall have the same force and effect as a statement which contains the information required by this section. If the judgment debtor or judgment creditor disputes the verity or accuracy of such statement or amount and so desires, then summons shall issue requiring the appearance of such person or authorized agent for examination on oath, and requiring him to produce such books and papers as may be necessary to determine the fact.

In determining the exemption to which the employee is entitled, the employer may until otherwise ordered by the court rely upon the information contained in the employee's withholding exemption certificate filed by the employee for federal income tax purposes, and any person showing more than one exemption thereon shall be considered by him to be a householder or head of a family.

The employer may apply the exemptions provided in § 34–29 (a) unless otherwise specified on the summons, or unless otherwise ordered by the court.

Acts 1977, c. 617; Acts 1979, c. 242; Acts 1983, c. 399.

§ 8.01–516. Repealed by Acts 1983, c. 399

§ 8.01–516.1. Garnishment dispositions

A. If the amount of liability is not disputed and the garnishee admits liability to the court either by (i) examination on the return date of the summons, or (ii) written statement as provided by § 8.01–515 on or before the return date of the summons, the court shall order the delivery of such estate or payment of the value of such estate into court without entering judgment against the garnishee. Should a garnishee fail to comply with the order within thirty days after service of such order on the garnishee, then judgment may be entered against the garnishee.

B. Upon certification by the judgment creditor, its bona fide employee, or its attorney that its claim has been satisfied or that it desires its action against the garnishee to be dismissed for any other reason, the court, or clerk thereof, where the action has been filed, shall, by written order, which may be served by the sheriff, notify the garnishee to cease withholding assets of the judgment debtor, and to treat any funds previously withheld as if the original garnishment action had not been filed. The court in which the garnishment action was filed shall then dismiss the action on or before the return date.

Acts 1983, c. 399; Acts 1993, c. 385.

§ 8.01–517. Exemption of portion of wages; payment of excess into court

Notwithstanding the provisions of §§ 8.01–515 and 8.01–516.1, any employer against whom any garnishment is served in connection with an action or judgment against an employee may pay to such employee when due wages or salary not exceeding the amount exempted by § 34–29 unless such exemptions shall have been specifically disallowed by the court and shall answer such garnishment summons by a written statement verified by affidavit, showing the amount of wages or salary due on the return date of the garnishment summons and the amount of wages or salary so exempted, and if there shall be an excess of wages or salary so due over the amount of the exemptions, the employer may pay the amount of such excess into the court where the garnishment summons is returnable, which payment when determined by the court to be correct will constitute a discharge of any liability of the employer to the employee for the wages or salary so withheld.

Acts 1977, c. 617.

§ 8.01–518. When garnishee is personal representative of decedent

If the person so summoned be the personal representative of a decedent, he shall answer in writing whether or not there is in his hands in his fiduciary capacity, any sum of money owing to the judgment debtor, and if so, the amount thereof, if the same has been definitely determined, and when it will be payable by him; and if such amount has not been definitely ascertained, the court shall continue the case, with direction to him to thereafter, and as soon as such amount has been definitely determined, report the same to the court, and say when it will be payable by him. In either event, and when the amount so owing to the judgment debtor has been definitely fixed and determined, the court shall direct the disposition of such fund to the creditor of such other person or persons according as their rights may be determined.

Acts 1977, c. 617.

§ 8.01–519. Proceedings where garnishee fails to appear or answer, or to disclose his liability

If the garnishee, after being served with the summons, fail to appear or answer personally, or if it be suggested that he has not fully disclosed his liability, the proceedings shall be according to §§ 8.01–564 and 8.01–565, mutatis mutandis, except that when the summons is before a general district court, the court shall proceed without a jury.

Acts 1977, c. 617.

§ 8.01–520. Payment, etc., by garnishee before return of summons

Any person, summoned under § 8.01–511, before the return day of the summons, may pay what he is liable for to the clerk of the court issuing the summons and such clerk shall give a receipt, upon request, for what is so paid.

Acts 1977, c. 617; Acts 1983, c. 399.

§ 8.01–521. Judgments as to costs

Unless the garnishee appear to be liable for more than is so delivered and paid, there shall be no judgment against him for costs. In other cases, judgment under §§ 8.01–516.1 and 8.01–519 may be for such costs, and against such party, as the court may deem just.

Acts 1977, c. 617.

§ 8.01–522. Wages and salaries of State employees

Unless otherwise exempted, the wages and salaries of all employees of this Commonwealth, other than State officers, shall be subject to garnishment or execution upon any judgment rendered against them. Whenever the salary or wages of such employees as above mentioned shall be garnished under this section, the process shall be such as is usual in other cases of garnishment and shall be served on the judgment debtor and on the officer or supervisor who is head of the department, agency, or institution where the employee is employed, or other officer through whom the judgment debtor's salary or wages is paid, provided that process shall not be served upon the State Treasurer or the State Comptroller except as to employees of their respective departments, and upon such service the officer or supervisor shall, on or before the return day of process, transmit to the clerk of the court issuing the process a certificate showing the amount due from the Commonwealth to such judgment debtor, up to the return day of the process, which amount the officer or supervisor shall hold subject to order of the court issuing the process. Such certificate shall be evidence of all facts therein stated, unless the court direct that the deposition of the officer or supervisor, or such other officer through whom the judgment debtor's salary or wages be paid, be taken, in which event the deposition of the officer or supervisor shall be taken in his office and returned to the clerk of the court in which the garnishment is, just as other depositions are returned, and in no such case shall the officer or supervisor be required to leave his office to testify. In all proceedings under this section, if the judgment be for the plaintiff, the amount found to be due the judgment debtor by the Commonwealth shall be paid as directed by the court.

Acts 1977, c. 617.

§ 8.01–523. Service upon federal government

A. If the suggestion of liability as provided in § 8.01–511 is against the United States of America, the summons shall be served upon the managing employee of the agency of the federal government which is alleged to be liable, or, if the judgment debtor is a member of the armed forces of the United States, upon the chief fiscal officer of the military post to which the judgment debtor was last assigned.

B. If service on the agents identified in subsection A for service of process on the United States cannot be made, then service may be made on a United States attorney or other agent in the manner set forth in Rule 4 (d) (4) of the Federal Rules of Civil Procedure, as from time to time amended.

Acts 1977, c. 617.

§ 8.01-524. Wages and salaries of city, town and county officials, clerks and employees

Unless otherwise exempt, the wages and salaries of all officials, clerks and employees of any city, town or county shall be subject to garnishment or execution upon any judgment rendered against them.

Acts 1977, c. 617.

§ 8.01-525. Who are officers and employees of cities, towns and counties

All officers, clerks and employees who hold their office by virtue of authority from the General Assembly or by virtue of city, town or county authority whether by election or appointment and who receive compensation for their services from the moneys of such city, town or county shall, for the purposes of garnishment, be deemed to be, and are, officers, clerks or employees of such city, town or county.

Acts 1977, c. 617.

CHAPTER 19

FORTHCOMING BONDS

§ 8.01-526. When forthcoming bond taken; property remains in debtor's possession

The sheriff or other officer levying a writ of fieri facias, or distress warrant, may take from the debtor a bond, with sufficient surety, payable to the creditor, reciting the service of such writ or warrant, and the amount due thereon, including the officer's fee for taking the bond, commissions, and other lawful charges, if any, with condition that the property shall be forthcoming at the day and place of sale; whereupon, such property may be permitted to remain in the possession and at the risk of the debtor.

Acts 1977, c. 617.

§ 8.01-527. If bond forfeited, where returned; its effect; clerk to endorse time of return

If the condition of such forthcoming bond be not performed, the officer, unless payment be made of the amount due on the execution or warrant, including his fee, commission, and charges as aforesaid, shall, after the bond is forfeited, return it forthwith, with the execution or warrant, to such court, or the clerk's office of such court as is prescribed by § 15.1-80.[1] The clerk shall endorse on the bond the date of its return; and against such of the obligors therein as may be alive when it is forfeited and so returned, it shall have the force of a judgment. But no execution shall issue thereon under this section.

Acts 1977, c. 617.

[1] Section 15.1-80, referred to in the first sentence, was repealed by Acts 1997, c. 587, eff. Dec. 1, 1997.

§ 8.01-528. Liability of obligors; how recovery on bond is had

The obligors in such forfeited bond shall be liable for the money therein mentioned, with interest thereon from the date of the bond till paid, and the costs. The obligee or his personal representative shall be entitled to recover the same by action or motion.

Acts 1977, c. 617.

§ 8.01-529. When bond returned, how endorsed and recorded by clerk; lien

Upon the return of a forthcoming bond to the clerk's office in the manner prescribed by § 8.01-527, it shall be the duty of the clerk to endorse thereon the date of such return, and his fee as provided by law for recordation of items specified herein, and to record in a book to be kept by him for the purpose, the date of such bond and of the return endorsed thereon, the amount of the penalty thereof, the amount, the payment whereof will discharge such penalty, and the names of the obligee and obligor to such bond. Such bond, when so returned to the clerk's office aforesaid, shall constitute a lien on the real estate of the obligor.

Acts 1977, c. 617.

§ 8.01-530. Remedy of creditor if bond quashed

If any forthcoming bond be at any time quashed, the obligee, besides his remedy against the officer, may have such execution on his judgment, or issue such distress warrant, as would have been lawful if such bond had not been taken.

Acts 1977, c. 617.

§ 8.01-531. In what cases forthcoming bond not to be taken

No bond for the forthcoming of property shall be taken:

1. On an execution on a forthcoming bond;

2. On an execution on a judgment against (i) a treasurer, sheriff, or a deputy of either of them, or a surety or personal representative of either such officer or deputy, for money received by any such officer or deputy, by virtue of his office, (ii) any such officer or his personal representative, in favor of a surety of such officer for money paid or a judgment rendered for a default in office, or (iii) a deputy of any such officer, or his surety or personal representative, in favor of his principal or the personal representative of such principal, for money paid or a judgment rendered for a default in office; or

3. On any other execution on which the clerk is required by law or by order of court to endorse that "no security is to be taken."

Acts 1977, c. 617.

§ 8.01–532. How bond withdrawn from clerk's office

The obligee in a forthcoming bond, or his agent, may, at any time after the record of such bond is made by the clerk, required by § 8.01–529, withdraw the same from the clerk's office, leaving a copy thereof attested by the clerk.

Acts 1977, c. 617.

CHAPTER 20

ATTACHMENTS AND BAIL IN CIVIL CASES

ARTICLE 1

ATTACHMENTS GENERALLY

§ 8.01–533. Who may sue out attachment

If any person has a claim, legal or equitable, to (i) any specific personal property, (ii) any debt, including rent, whether the debt is due and payable or not, (iii) damages for breach of any contract, express or implied, or (iv) damages for a wrong, or for a judgment for which no supersedeas or other appeal bond has been posted, he may sue out an attachment therefor on any one or more of the grounds stated in § 8.01–534. However, if the claim is for a debt not due and payable, no attachment shall be sued out when the only ground for the attachment is that the defendant or one of the defendants is a foreign corporation, or is not a resident of this Commonwealth, and has estate or debts owing to him within this Commonwealth.

Acts 1977, c. 617; Acts 1986, c. 341; Acts 1993, c. 841.

§ 8.01–534. Grounds of action for pretrial levy or seizure of attachment

A. It shall be sufficient ground for an action for pretrial levy or seizure or an attachment that the principal defendant or one of the principal defendants:

1. Is a foreign corporation, or is not a resident of this Commonwealth, and has estate or has debts owing to such defendant within the county or city in which the attachment is, or that such defendant being a nonresident of this Commonwealth, is entitled to the benefit of any lien, legal or equitable, on property, real or personal, within the county or city in which the attachment is. The word "estate," as herein used, includes all rights or interests of a pecuniary nature which can be protected, enforced, or proceeded against in courts of law or equity;

2. Is removing or is about to remove himself out of this Commonwealth with intent to change his domicile;

3. Intends to remove, or is removing, or has removed the specific property sued for, or his own estate, or the proceeds of the sale of his property, or a material part of such estate or proceeds, out of this Commonwealth so that there will probably not be therein effects of such debtor sufficient to satisfy the claim when judgment is obtained therefor should only the ordinary process of law be used to obtain the judgment;

4. Is converting, is about to convert or has converted his property of whatever kind, or some part thereof, into money, securities or evidences of debt with intent to hinder, delay, or defraud his creditors;

5. Has assigned or disposed of or is about to assign or dispose of his estate, or some part thereof, with intent to hinder, delay or defraud his creditors;

6. Has absconded or is about to abscond or has concealed or is about to conceal himself or his property to the injury of his creditors, or is a fugitive from justice.

The intent mentioned in subdivisions 4 and 5 above may be stated either in the alternative or conjunctive.

B. It shall be sufficient ground for an action for pretrial levy or seizure or an attachment if the specific personal property sought to be levied or seized:

1. Will be sold, removed, secreted or otherwise disposed of by the defendant, in violation of an obligation to the plaintiff, so as not to be forthcoming to answer the final judgment of the court respecting the same; or

2. Will be destroyed, or materially damaged or injured if permitted to remain in the possession of the principal defendant or one of the principal defendants or other person or persons claiming under them.

C. In an action for rent, it also shall be a sufficient ground if there is an immediate danger that the property subject to the landlord's lien for rent will be destroyed or concealed.

Acts 1977, c. 617; Acts 1993, c. 841.

§ 8.01-535. Jurisdiction of attachments; trial or hearing of issues

Except as provided in § 16.1-77 the jurisdiction of attachments under this chapter shall be in the circuit courts. The trial or hearing of the issues, except as otherwise provided, shall be the same, as near as may be, as in actions in personam.

Acts 1977, c. 617.

§ 8.01-536. Pleadings in attachment

No pleading on behalf of the plaintiff shall be necessary except the petition mentioned in § 8.01-537. The principal defendant, and any other defendant who seeks to defeat the petitioner's attachment, may demur to the petition, issue on which demurrer shall be deemed to be joined; but if such demurrer be overruled, such defendant shall answer the petition in writing. No replication shall be necessary to such answer. The answer shall be sworn to by such defendant, or his agent. Any other defendant may answer the petition, under oath, and the cause shall be deemed at issue as to him, if he denies any of the allegations of the petition, without any replication. Answers under this section shall not have the effect of evidence for the defendant.

Acts 1977, c. 617.

§ 8.01-537. Petition for attachment; costs, fees and taxes

A. Every attachment shall be commenced by a petition filed before a clerk of a circuit or general district court of, or magistrate serving, the county or city in which venue is given by subdivision 11 of § 8.01-261. If it is sought to recover specific personal property, the petition shall state (i) the kind, quantity, and estimated fair market value thereof, (ii) the character of estate therein claimed by the plaintiff, (iii) the plaintiff's claim with such certainty as will give the adverse party reasonable notice of the true nature of the claim and the particulars thereof and (iv) what sum, if any, the plaintiff claims an entitlement to recover for its detention. If it is sought to recover a debt or damages for a breach of contract, express or implied, or damages for a wrong, the petition shall set forth (i) the plaintiff's claim with such certainty as will give the adverse party reasonable notice of the true nature of the claim and the particulars thereof, (ii) a sum certain which, at the least, the plaintiff is entitled to, or ought to recover, and (iii) if based on a contract and if the claim is for a debt not then due and payable, at what time or times the same will become due and payable. The petition shall also allege the existence of one or more of the grounds mentioned in § 8.01-534, and shall set forth specific facts in support of the allegation. The petition shall ask for an attachment against the specific personal property mentioned in the petition, or against the estate, real and personal, of one or more of the principal defendants, or against the estate, real and personal, of one or more of the principal defendants, or against both the specific personal property and the estate of such defendants, real or personal. The petition shall state whether the officer is requested to take possession of the attached tangible personal property. The petition shall be sworn to by the plaintiff or the plaintiff's agent, or some other person cognizant of the facts therein stated.

B. The plaintiff praying for an attachment shall, at the time the petition is filed, pay to the magistrate or clerk of the court to which the return is made the proper costs, fees and taxes, and in the event the plaintiff fails to do so, the attachment shall not be issued.

Acts 1977, c. 617; Acts 1978, c. 418; Acts 1984, c. 646; Acts 1993, c. 841. Amended by Acts 2008, c. 551; Acts 2008, c. 691; Acts 2015, c. 639.

§ 8.01-537.1. Plaintiff to file bond

A. The plaintiff or someone for him shall, at the time of suing out an attachment or other pretrial levy or seizure, give bond. The fact that bond has been given shall be endorsed on the process, or certified by the clerk to the serving officer. If certified by the clerk, the serving officer shall return the certificate with the process. The bond shall be a bond with approved surety, a cash bond or a property bond.

B. If the plaintiff seeks only pretrial levy on property and a bond with approved surety or cash bond is posted, the amount of the bond shall be at least the estimated fair market value of the property to be levied. If a property bond is posted, the amount of the bond shall be at least double the estimated fair market value of the property to be levied.

C. If the plaintiff seeks pretrial seizure of property, the amount of the bond shall be at least double the estimated fair market value of the property to be seized.

D. The bond shall contain a condition to pay all costs and damages which may be awarded against the plaintiff, or sustained by any person, by reason of a wrongful levy or seizure.

Acts 1984, c. 646; Acts 1993, c. 841.

§ 8.01-538. Attachment of ships, boats and other vessels of more than twenty tons

No attachment against any ship, boat, or other vessel of more than twenty tons, shall issue unless the plaintiff or someone in his behalf, shall first establish, to the satisfaction of the court in which he files his petition for attachment that he has a reasonable expectation of recovering an amount exclusive of all costs, equal to at least one-half the damages demanded in the petition for attachment. Reasonable notice of appearance before the court shall be given the owner, agent or master of said vessel, and at the time of the appearance the court shall determine the amount of such reasonable expectation of recovery and the amount of bond necessary to secure the release of the vessel if and when a writ be levied in accordance with this section.

No attachment issued in violation of the provisions of this section shall create a valid lien upon the property sought to be attached, and no levy made under authority thereof shall be of any effect.

Acts 1977, c. 617.

§ 8.01–539. Who made defendants

A person against whom the plaintiff is asserting the claim shall be made a defendant to the petition, and shall be known as a principal defendant. There shall also be made a defendant any person indebted to or having in his possession property, real or personal, belonging to a principal defendant, which is sought to be attached. There may also be made a defendant any person claiming title to, and interest in, or a lien upon the property sought to be attached. A defendant, other than a principal defendant, shall be known as a codefendant.

Acts 1977, c. 617.

§ 8.01–540. Issuance of attachment; against what attachment to issue

A judge of, or a magistrate serving, the court in which a petition for attachment is filed shall make an ex parte review of the petition. The judge or magistrate shall issue an attachment in accordance with the prayer of the petition only upon a determination that (i) there is reasonable cause to believe that grounds for attachment may exist and (ii) the petition complies with §§ 8.01–534, 8.01–537, and 8.01–538. The judge or magistrate may receive evidence only in the form of a sworn petition which shall be filed in the office of the clerk of the court. If the plaintiff seeks the recovery of specific personal property, the attachment may be (i) against such property and against the principal defendant's estate for so much as is sufficient to satisfy the probable damages for its detention or (ii) at the option of the plaintiff, against the principal defendant's estate for the value of the specific property and the damages for its detention. If the plaintiff seeks to recover a debt or damages for the breach of a contract, express or implied, or damages for a wrong, the attachment shall be against the principal defendant's estate for the amount specified in the petition as that which the plaintiff at the least is entitled to or ought to recover.

If the attachment is issued by a magistrate, it shall be returnable as prescribed by § 8.01–541. The magistrate shall promptly return to the clerk's office of the court to which the attachment is returnable the petition and the bond, if any, filed before him. The proceedings thereafter shall be the same as if the attachment had been issued by a judge.

Acts 1977, c. 617; Acts 1984, c. 646; Acts 1993, c. 841. Amended by Acts 2008, c. 551; Acts 2008, c. 691.

§ 8.01–541. To whom attachments directed; when and where returned

Any attachment issued under this chapter may be directed to the sheriff of any county or city. Except when otherwise provided, it shall be returnable to the office of the clerk of court wherein the petition has been filed not more than thirty days from its date of issuance.

Acts 1977, c. 617; Acts 1993, c. 841.

§ 8.01–542. Issue and execution of attachment on any day

Such attachment may be issued or executed on any day, including a Sunday or holiday.

Acts 1977, c. 617.

§ 8.01–543. Issue of other attachments on original petition

Upon the written application of the plaintiff, his agent or attorney, other attachments founded on the original petition may be issued from time to time by the clerk of the court in which the original attachment is pending, and the same may be directed, executed, and returned in like manner as an original attachment. However, the clerk shall not issue an attachment where new or additional grounds of attachment are relied upon or where any ship, boat or vessel of more than twenty tons is sought to be attached.

If new or additional grounds of attachment are relied on, the plaintiff may amend his petition in accordance with Rule of Court 1:8 according to the facts and swear to the same. Except as otherwise provided in this section, an additional attachment as prayed for shall be issued by a judge or magistrate only upon his determination that (i) there is reasonable cause to believe that the grounds for attachment may exist and (ii) that the amended petition complies with §§ 8.01–534 and 8.01–537. Where any ship, boat, or other vessel of more than twenty tons is sought to be attached, a judge or magistrate shall issue the additional attachment only on his determination that § 8.01–538 has been complied with. The cause shall proceed, under the provisions of this chapter, upon the petition as amended.

The court shall adjudge the costs of such attachments as it deems proper.

The following, or its equivalent, shall be a sufficient form of application for an additional attachment:

To A.B., clerk of the .... court of .... county (or city): In the case of .... v. ...., on an attachment, an additional attachment and summons is requested to be issued against

.... X.Y. (or X.Y. by H., attorney or agent, as the case may be).

Acts 1977, c. 617; Acts 1984, c. 646.

§ 8.01-544. When attachment not served other attachments may issue; order of publication

When an attachment is returned not served on a principal defendant, whether levied on property or not, further attachments and summonses may be issued until service is obtained on him, if he be a resident of the Commonwealth. If for any cause service cannot be had in the Commonwealth, upon affidavit of that fact, an order of publication shall be made against him.

Acts 1977, c. 617.

§ 8.01-545. Amendments; formal defects

Such amendments shall be allowed of the petition, answer and of any of the other proceedings in the attachment as shall be conducive to the attainment of the ends of substantial justice, and upon such terms as to continuance and costs as may seem proper. An amendment when made shall as against the principal defendant and as to claims against him existing at the time the attachment was issued relate back to the time of the levy of the attachment, unless otherwise directed. No attachment shall be quashed or dismissed for mere formal defects.

Acts 1977, c. 617.

Article 2

Summons; Levy; Lien; Bonds, etc.

§ 8.01-546. What attachment to command; summons

Every attachment sued out against specific personal property shall command the sheriff or other officer to whom it may be directed to attach the specific property claimed in the petition, and so much more of the real and personal property of the principal defendant as shall be necessary to cover the damages for the detention of the specific property sued for and the costs of the attachment. Every other attachment shall command the sheriff or other officer to whom it may be directed to attach the property mentioned and sought to be attached in the petition, if any, and so much of the lands, tenements, goods, chattels, moneys and effects of the principal defendant not exempt from execution as will be sufficient to satisfy the plaintiff's demand, and, in case of tangible personal property, taken possession of under § 8.01-551, to keep the same safely in his possession to satisfy any judgment that may be recovered by the plaintiff in such attachment.

Every attachment sued out under this section shall also command the sheriff or other officer to summon the defendant or defendants, if he or they are found within his county or city, or any county or city wherein he may have seized property under and by virtue of such writ, to appear and answer the petition for the attachment.

Each copy of the summons shall be issued together with a form for requesting a hearing on a claim of exemption from levy or seizure as provided in § 8.01-546.1. Both documents shall be served on each defendant.

Acts 1977, c. 617; Acts 1986, c. 341.

§ 8.01-546.1. Exemption claims form

The form for requesting a hearing or a claim for exemption from levy or seizure shall be designed by the Supreme Court and provided to all courts which may issue attachments and to all magistrates.

Acts 1986, c. 341.

§ 8.01-546.2. Hearing on claim of exemption from levy or seizure

A judgment debtor shall have the right to a hearing on his claim of exemption from levy or seizure. If a defendant files a request for a hearing, the clerk shall (i) schedule a hearing no later than ten business days from the date that the request is filed with the court, and (ii) notify the parties of the date, time and place of hearing and the exemption being claimed. This hearing may be combined with a hearing pursuant to § 8.01-119 or § 8.01-568 or with a trial on the merits if held within the ten-business day limitation.

The clerk shall notify the parties and the sheriff of the date, time and place of hearing and the exemption being claimed. The court may stay the sale pending this hearing by interlocutory order. The sheriff shall comply with the writ unless and until ordered otherwise in writing by the court. The order shall take effect upon receipt by the sheriff. The clerk is required to provide a copy of the order or the hearing disposition to the sheriff only if the writ or levy is dismissed or is modified by the judge. The court shall release all exempt property from the judgment creditor's lien and order the sheriff to return such exempt property to the judgment debtor.

Acts 1986, c. 341.

§ 8.01-547. Attachment against remainders

If the attachment be against a principal defendant who is a nonresident or an absconding debtor, the attachment may also direct the sheriff or other officer to levy the same on any remainder, vested or contingent, of the principal defendant, or so much thereof as may be sufficient to pay the amount for which it issues. But no such remainder shall be sold until it becomes vested. A judgment, however, ascertaining the amount due the plaintiff may be docketed as other judgments are docketed, but unless it be a personal judgment, it shall be a lien only on the property levied on.

Acts 1977, c. 617.

§ 8.01–548. Who may levy attachment and on what

An attachment may be levied upon any estate of the defendant, whether the same be in the county or city in which the attachment issued, or in any other, either by the officer of the county or city wherein the attachment issued, or by the officer of the county or city where the estate is.

Acts 1977, c. 617.

§ 8.01–549. Restraining order or receiver

The court may interpose by a restraining order, or the appointment of a receiver, or otherwise, to secure the forthcoming of the specific property sued for, and so much other estate as will probably be required to satisfy any further order that may be made in the proceedings.

Acts 1977, c. 617.

§ 8.01–550. How attachment levied

An attachment may be levied as follows:

On tangible personal property in possession of a principal defendant, whether such possession be actual or constructive, it may be levied as at common law or by delivering a copy of the attachment to such principal defendant or, if possession is requested in the petition, then by taking possession of such personal property;

On choses in action or on tangible personal property in possession of any defendant other than the principal defendant, it may be levied by delivering a copy of the attachment to the person indebted to the principal defendant or having possession of the property belonging to him; and

On real estate, it may be levied by such estate being mentioned and described in an endorsement on the attachment by the officer to whom it is delivered for service to the following effect:

"Levied on the following real estate of the defendant A. (or defendants A. and B.), to-wit: (here describe the real estate) this the .... day of .... at .... o'clock. E.F., sheriff (or other officer)," and by service of the attachment on the person, if any, in possession of such real estate.

Wherever a copy of an attachment is required or allowed to be served on any person, natural or artificial, it may be served as a notice is served under §§ 8.01–296, 8.01–299, 8.01–300 or 8.01–301, as the case may be.

Acts 1977, c. 617; Acts 1984, c. 646.

§ 8.01–551. When officer to take possession of property

If so requested by the plaintiff in his petition, the officer to whom the attachment is directed shall take possession of the property specified in the attachment, or when no such property is specified, of any estate or effects of the defendant, or so much thereof as is sufficient to pay the plaintiff's claim. But the officer levying the attachment shall, before taking possession of any property as aforesaid, make his certificate of the estimated fair market value of the property on which the attachment is levied, and he shall not take possession of the same unless and until bond in conformance with § 8.01–537.1 based on the estimated fair market value of the property as so stated in his certificate is posted. The certificate shall be filed in the clerk's office of the court to which the attachment is returnable and the value so certified shall be subject to review by the court to which the attachment is returnable.

Acts 1977, c. 617; Acts 1984, c. 646; Acts 1993, c. 841.

§ 8.01–552. Repealed by Acts 1984, c. 646

§ 8.01–553. Bonds for retention of property or release of attachment; revising bonds mentioned in this and § 8.01–551

Any property levied on or seized as aforesaid, under any attachment, may be retained by or returned to the defendant or other person in whose possession it was on his giving bond, with condition to have the same forthcoming at such time and place as the court may require. In the alternative, the principal defendant may, by giving bond with condition to perform the judgment of the court, release from any attachment the whole of any estate attached. The bond in either case shall be taken by the officer serving the attachment, with surety, payable to the plaintiff, and in a penalty in the latter case either double the amount or value for which the attachment issued or double the value of the property on which the attachment was levied, at the option of the person giving it, and in the former, either double the amount of value for which the attachment issued or double the value of the property retained or returned, at the option of the person giving it. However, in the event the court shall consider that the amount of any bond required by this section or § 8.01–551 is excessive or inadequate, such court may, upon motion of any party in interest after reasonable notice to the opposite party if he can be found in the jurisdiction of the court or to his attorney of record, if any, fix the amount of such bond to conform to the equities of the case.

Acts 1977, c. 617; Acts 1984, c. 646.

§ 8.01–554. Where bond returned and filed; exceptions to bond

Every such bond shall be returned by the officer to and filed by the clerk of the court in which the attachment is pending, or to which the attachment is returnable, and the plaintiff may, within thirty days after the return thereof, file exceptions to the same, or to the sufficiency of the surety therein. If such exception be sustained, the court shall order the officer to file a good bond, with sufficient surety, to be approved by it, on or before a certain day to be fixed by the court. If he fail to do so, he and his sureties in his official bond shall be liable to the plaintiff as for a breach of such bond; but the officer shall have the same rights and remedies against the parties to any bonds so adjudged bad as if he were a surety for them.

Acts 1977, c. 617.

§ 8.01–555. When appeal bond given property to be delivered to owner

When judgment in favor of the plaintiff is rendered by a general district court in any case in which an attachment is issued and on appeal therefrom to a circuit court an appeal bond is given, with condition to prosecute the appeal with effect or pay the debt, interest, costs and damages, as well as the costs of the appeal, the officer, in whose custody any attached property is, shall deliver the same to the owner thereof. When an appeal is from a circuit court to the Supreme Court and an appeal bond is given pursuant to § 8.01–676.1, the officer having custody shall proceed in like manner.

Acts 1977, c. 617.

§ 8.01–556. Bonds may be given by any person

Any bond authorized or required by any section of this chapter may be given either by the party himself or by any other person.

Acts 1977, c. 617.

§ 8.01–557. Lien of attachment; priority of holder in due course

The plaintiff shall have a lien from the time of the levying of such attachment, or serving a copy thereof as aforesaid, upon the personal property of the principal defendant, when the same is in his possession, actual or constructive, and upon the personal property, choses in action, and other securities of such defendant in the hands of, or owing by a codefendant on whom it is so served; and on any real estate mentioned in such an endorsement by the officer on the attachment or summons as is prescribed by § 8.01–550, from the time of levy and service pursuant to such section. But a holder in due course of negotiable paper shall have priority over an attachment levied thereon.

Acts 1977, c. 617.

§ 8.01–558. Attachment lien on effects already in hands of officer

When an officer has in his possession or custody money or effects of the defendant held under an attachment executed, or other legal process, a delivery to such officer of an attachment under this chapter shall be deemed a levy thereof as to such money or effects, and constitute a lien thereon from the time of such delivery.

Acts 1977, c. 617.

§ 8.01–559. Return by officer

The officer levying the attachment shall show in his return the time, date and manner of the service, or execution thereof, on each person and parcel of property, and also give a list and description of the property, if any, levied on under the attachment.

Acts 1977, c. 617.

Article 3

Subsequent Proceedings Generally

§ 8.01–560. How interest and profits of property applied in certain cases

When any attachment is sued out, although the property or estate attached be not seized, the interest and profits thereof pending the attachment and before judgment may be paid to the defendant, if the court deem it proper.

Acts 1977, c. 617.

§ 8.01–561. How property to be kept; how sold, when expensive to keep or perishable

Any property seized under any attachment and not sold before judgment shall be kept in the same manner as similar property taken under execution. But such as is expensive to keep or perishable may be sold by order of the court upon such terms as the court may direct. If the court directs that the sale may be made on credit, the court may order the sheriff to take a bond with sufficient surety, payable to the sheriff, for the benefit of the party entitled. Such bond shall be returned forthwith by the officer to the court.

Acts 1977, c. 617.

§ 8.01–562. Examination on oath of codefendant; order and bond

A defendant who at the time of service of the attachment was alleged to be indebted to a principal defendant, or had in his possession personal property belonging to such principal defendant, shall appear in person and submit to an examination on oath touching such debt or personal property, or he may, with the consent of the court, after reasonable notice to the plaintiff, file an answer in writing under oath, stating whether or not he was so indebted, and if so, the amount thereof and the time of maturity, or whether he had in his possession any personal property belonging to such principal defendant and, if so, the nature and value thereof. If it appear on such examination or by his answer that at the time of the service of the attachment, he was indebted to the principal defendant, or had in his possession or control any goods, chattels, money, securities or other effects belonging to such defendant, the court may order him to pay the amount so owing by him, or to deliver such effects to the sheriff, or other person designated by the court to receive the same; or such defendant may, with the leave of the court, give bond with sufficient security, payable to such person and in such penalty as the court shall prescribe, with condition to pay the amount owing by him, and have such effects forthcoming, at such time and place as the court may thereafter require. An answer under oath under this section shall be deemed prima facie to be true.

Acts 1977, c. 617.

§ 8.01–563. Principal defendant may claim exemption

The principal defendant, if a householder or head of a family, may claim that the amount so found owing from his codefendant, or the personal property in his possession, shall be exempt from liability for the plaintiff's claim; and if it shall appear that the principal defendant is entitled to such exemption, then the court shall render a judgment against the defendant only for the excess, if any, beyond the exemption to which the principal defendant is entitled.

Acts 1977, c. 617.

§ 8.01–564. Procedure when codefendant fails to appear

If the attachment be served on a defendant who the petition alleges is indebted to, or has in his possession effects of, the principal defendant, and he fail to appear, the court may either compel him to appear, or hear proof of any debt owing by him, or of effects in his hands belonging to a principal defendant in such attachment, and make such orders in relation thereto as if what is so proved had appeared on his examination.

Acts 1977, c. 617.

§ 8.01–565. Suggestion that codefendant has not made full disclosure

When it is suggested by the plaintiff in any attachment that a codefendant has not fully disclosed the debts owing by him, or effects in his hands belonging to the principal defendant in such attachment, the court, without any formal pleading, shall inquire as to such debts and effects, or, if either party demand, it shall cause a jury to be impaneled for that purpose, and proceed in respect to any such debts or effects found by the court or the jury in the same manner as if they had been confessed by such codefendant. If the judgment of the court or verdict of the jury be in favor of such codefendant, he shall have judgment for his costs against the plaintiff.

Acts 1977, c. 617.

§ 8.01–566. Who may make defense to attachment

Any of the defendants in any such attachment, or any party to any forthcoming bond given as aforesaid, or the officer who may be liable to the plaintiff by reason of such bond being adjudged bad, or any person authorized by § 8.01–573 to file a petition, may make defense to such attachment, but the attachment shall not thereby be discharged, or the property levied on released.

Acts 1977, c. 617.

§ 8.01–567. What defense may be made to attachments

Any party in interest may show that the court is without jurisdiction to hear and determine the controversy.

The principal defendant, if not served with process, may appear specially and show that the attachment was issued on false suggestion or without sufficient cause, in which event the attachment shall be quashed.

Any person claiming title to, an interest in, or a lien upon the property attached, or any part thereof, after being admitted as a party defendant, if not already a defendant, and the principal defendant, may contest the liability of the principal defendant for the plaintiff's claim, in whole or in part, by proof of any manner which would constitute a good defense by the principal defendant to an action at law on such claim, and may also show that the attachment was not issued on any of the grounds set forth in § 8.01–534, or that the plaintiff is not likely to succeed on the merits of his underlying claim. The principal defendant may also file counterclaims or defenses available under § 8.01–422 as in an action at law.

Other defendants shall be limited to defenses personal to themselves, or which may prevent a liability upon them or their property.

Acts 1977, c. 617.

§ 8.01–568. Quashing attachment or rendering judgment for defendant

The court in which an attachment is pending shall, on motion of the principal defendant, or any defendant claiming title to, an interest in, or a lien upon the property attached, or any part thereof, after reasonable notice to the plaintiff, hear testimony and quash the attachment, if of opinion that (i) the attachment is invalid on its face, (ii) none of the grounds for attachment in § 8.01–534 exist, or (iii) the plaintiff is not likely to succeed on the merits of his underlying claim. The hearing shall be held not later than ten business days following the defendant's motion. When the attachment is properly sued out, and the case is heard upon its merits, if the court is of opinion that the claim of the plaintiff is not established, final judgment shall be given for the defendant. In either case, he shall recover his costs, and damages for loss of the use of his property, and there shall be an order for the restoration of the attached effects. The plaintiff shall have the burden of proof in proceedings pursuant to this section.

Acts 1977, c. 617; Acts 1984, c. 646.

§ 8.01-569. When petition dismissed; when retained and cause tried

If the principal defendant has not appeared generally, nor been served with process, and the sole ground of jurisdiction of the court is the right to sue out the attachment, and this right be decided against the plaintiff, the petition shall be dismissed at the cost of the plaintiff; but if the plaintiff's claim be due at the hearing, and the court would otherwise have jurisdiction of an action against such defendant for the cause set forth in the petition, and such defendant has appeared generally, or been served with process, it shall retain the cause and proceed to final judgment as in other actions at law.

Acts 1977, c. 617.

§ 8.01-570. Judgment, etc., of court when claim of plaintiff established

If the claim of the plaintiff be established, judgment shall be rendered for him, and the court shall dispose of the specific property levied on, as may be right, and order the sale of any other effects or real estate which shall not have been previously released or sold under this chapter, and direct the proceeds of sale, and whatever else is subject to the attachment, including what is embraced by such forthcoming bond, to be applied in satisfaction of the judgment.

Acts 1977, c. 617.

§ 8.01-571. When defendant not served fails to appear plaintiff required to give bond

If the principal defendant has not appeared or been served with a copy of the attachment ten days before the judgment therein mentioned, the plaintiff shall not have the benefit of § 8.01-570 unless and until he shall have given bond with sufficient surety in such penalty as the court shall approve, with condition to perform such future order as may be made upon the appearance of such defendant and his making defense. If the plaintiff fail to give such bond in a reasonable time, the court shall dispose of the estate attached, or the proceeds thereof, as to it shall seem just.

Acts 1977, c. 617.

§ 8.01-572. Sale of real estate attached

No real estate shall be sold until all other property and money subject to the attachment have been exhausted, and then only so much thereof as is necessary to pay the judgment. Upon a sale of real estate, under an attachment the court shall have the same powers and jurisdiction, and like proceedings thereon may be had, as if it were a sale of real estate by a court of equity exercising general equity powers.

Acts 1977, c. 617.

§ 8.01-573. How and when claims of other persons to property tried

Any person may file his petition at any time before the property attached as the estate of a defendant is sold or the proceeds of sale paid to the plaintiff under the judgment, disputing the validity of the plaintiff's attachment thereon, or stating a claim thereto, or an interest in or lien on the same, under any other attachment or otherwise, and its nature, and upon giving security for cost, the court, without any other pleading, shall inquire into such claim, or, if either party demand it, impanel a jury for that purpose. If it be found that the petitioner has title to, or a lien on, or any interest in, such property, or its proceeds, the court shall make such order as may be necessary to protect his rights. The costs of such inquiry shall be paid by either party, at the discretion of the court.

Acts 1977, c. 617.

§ 8.01-574. Attachments in connection with pending suits or actions

If an attachment be desired in connection with a pending suit or action, a petition for an attachment may be filed in the same court in which such suit or action is pending, and the procedure thereon shall be the same as if no suit or action were pending; but the attachment may be heard along with any suit in equity relating to the same subject so far as may be necessary for the convenient administration of justice. The suing out of an attachment in connection with a pending suit or action shall not be deemed the prosecution of a second action for the same cause.

Acts 1977, c. 617.

§ 8.01-575. Rehearing permitted when judgment rendered on publication

If a defendant, against whom, on publication, judgment is rendered under any attachment, or his personal representative, shall return to or appear openly in this Commonwealth, he may, within one year after a copy of such judgment shall be served on him at the instance of the plaintiff, or within two years from the date of the judgment, if he be not so served, petition to have the proceedings reheard. On giving security for costs he shall be admitted to make defense against such judgment, as if he had appeared in the case before the same was rendered, except that the title of any bona fide purchaser to any property, real or personal, sold under such attachment, shall not be brought in question or impeached. But this section shall not apply to any case in which the petitioner, or his decedent, was served with a copy of the attachment more than ten days before the date of the judgment, or to any case in which he appeared and made defense.

Acts 1977, c. 617.

§ 8.01–576. Order of court on rehearing or new trial; restitution to defendant

On any rehearing or new trial had under § 8.01–575, the court may order the plaintiff in the original attachment to restore any money paid to him under such judgment to such defendant if living, or if dead to the heir or personal representative of such defendant, as the same may be, the proceeds of real or personal estate, and enter a judgment therefor against him; or it may confirm the former judgment. In either case it shall adjudge the costs of the prevailing party.

Acts 1977, c. 617.

CHAPTER 20.1

SUMMARY JURY TRIAL

§ 8.01–576.1. Election by parties; order of court

In any civil action pending before a circuit court, the parties may, by agreement in writing submitted to the court at any time prior to trial, elect to have a summary jury trial of the issues in the case in accordance with this chapter. However, where the court determines that the election is made for the purpose of delaying a trial on the merits, a summary jury trial shall not be had.

Acts 1988, c. 759.

§ 8.01–576.2. Summary jury trial; selection of jury; fees

Upon election of the parties, the court shall schedule a summary jury trial to be held as soon as convenient. Notice shall be given to the parties by means adequate to ensure their presence at the time and place of the trial. Seven jurors shall be randomly selected in accordance with the procedures specified in Chapter 11 (§ 8.01–336 et seq.). Fees shall be allowed to jurors selected for a summary jury trial as provided in § 17.1–618.

Acts 1988, c. 759.

§ 8.01–576.3. Procedures; verdict not binding unless otherwise agreed

A judge of the court having jurisdiction over the case shall preside over a summary jury trial. Counsel for the parties or, if a party is not represented by counsel, a party shall verbally present a summary of the issues in the case and the evidence on behalf of each party. Evidence for the plaintiff shall be presented first. Each party shall be given the opportunity to rebut the evidence of another party upon request. The testimony of witnesses and the submission of documentary evidence shall not be allowed except as stipulated or agreed to by the parties.

Upon conclusion of the presentations of the summary evidence, the court shall instruct the jury on the law applicable to the cause. The jury shall advise the court of its verdict upon conclusion of the deliberations.

Unless otherwise agreed by the parties in writing submitted to the court prior to a jury being impanelled pursuant to this chapter, the verdict of a summary jury shall not be binding on either party and shall not be admissible on any subsequent trial of the case. If the parties have agreed to be bound by the verdict, judgment shall be entered by the court in accordance with the verdict.

Acts 1988, c. 759.

CHAPTER 20.2

COURT–REFERRED DISPUTE RESOLUTION PROCEEDINGS

§ 8.01–576.4. Scope and definitions

The provisions of this chapter apply only to court-referred dispute resolution services.

As used in this chapter:

"Conciliation" means a process in which a neutral facilitates settlement by clarifying issues and serving as an intermediary for negotiations in a manner which is generally more informal and less structured than mediation.

"Court" means any juvenile and domestic relations district court, general district court, circuit court, or appellate court, and includes the judges and any intake specialist to whom the judge has delegated specific authority under this chapter.

"Dispute resolution proceeding" means any structured process in which a neutral assists disputants in reaching a voluntary settlement by means of dispute resolution techniques such as mediation, conciliation, early neutral evaluation, nonjudicial settlement conferences or any other proceeding leading to a voluntary settlement conducted consistent with the requirements of this chapter. The term includes the orientation session.

"Dispute resolution program" means a program that offers dispute resolution services to the public, which is run by the Commonwealth or any private for–profit or not–for–profit organization, political subdivision, or public corporation, or a combination of these.

"Dispute resolution services" includes screening and intake of disputants, conducting dispute resolution proceedings, drafting agreements and providing information or referral services.

"Intake specialist" means an individual who is trained in analyzing and screening cases to assist in determining whether a case is appropriate for referral to a dispute resolution proceeding.

"Mediation" means a process in which a neutral facilitates communication between the parties and, without deciding the issues or imposing a solution on the parties, enables them to understand and to reach a mutually agreeable resolution to their dispute.

"Neutral" means an individual who is trained or experienced in conducting dispute resolution proceedings and in providing dispute resolution services.

"Orientation session" means a preliminary meeting during which the dispute resolution proceeding is explained to the parties and the parties and the neutral assess the case and decide whether to continue with a dispute resolution proceeding or adjudication.

Acts 1993, c. 905; Acts 2002, c. 718.

§ 8.01–576.5. Referral of disputes to dispute resolution proceedings

While protecting the right to trial by jury, a court, on its own motion or on motion of one of the parties, may refer any contested civil matter, or selected issues in a civil matter, to an orientation session in order to encourage the early resolution of disputes through the use of procedures that facilitate (i) open communication between the parties about the issues in the dispute, (ii) full exploration of the range of options to resolve the dispute, (iii) improvement in the relationship between the parties, and (iv) control by the parties over the outcome of the dispute. The neutral or intake specialist conducting the orientation session shall provide information regarding dispute resolution options available to the parties, screen for factors that would make the case inappropriate for a dispute resolution proceeding, and assist the parties in determining whether their case is suitable for a dispute resolution process such as mediation. The court shall set a date for the parties to return to court in accordance with its regular docket and procedure, irrespective of the referral to an orientation session. The parties shall notify the court, in writing, if the dispute is resolved prior to the return date.

Upon such referral, the parties shall attend one orientation session unless excused pursuant to § 8.01–576.6. Further participation in a dispute resolution proceeding shall be by consent of all parties. Attorneys for any party may participate in a dispute resolution proceeding.

Acts 1993, c. 905; Acts 2002, c. 718.

§ 8.01–576.6. Notice and opportunity to object

When a court has determined that referral to an orientation session is appropriate, an order of referral to a neutral or to a dispute resolution program shall be entered and the parties shall be so notified as expeditiously as possible. The court shall excuse the parties from participation in an orientation session if, within fourteen days after entry of the order, a written statement signed by any party is filed with the court, stating that the dispute resolution process has been explained to the party and he objects to the referral.

Acts 1993, c. 905; Acts 2002, c. 718.

§ 8.01–576.7. Costs

The orientation session shall be conducted at no cost to the parties. Unless otherwise provided by law, the cost of any subsequent dispute resolution proceeding shall be as agreed to by the parties and the neutral.

Acts 1993, c. 905; Acts 2002, c. 718.

§ 8.01–576.8. Qualifications of neutrals; referral

A neutral who provides dispute resolution services other than mediation pursuant to this chapter shall provide the court with a written statement of qualifications, describing the neutral's background and relevant training and experience in the field. A dispute resolution program may satisfy the requirements of this section on behalf of its neutrals by providing the court with a written statement of the background, training, experience, and certification, as appropriate, of any neutral who participates in its program. A neutral who desires to provide mediation and receive referrals from the court shall be certified pursuant to guidelines promulgated by the Judicial Council of Virginia. The court shall maintain a list of mediators certified pursuant to guidelines promulgated by the Judicial Council and may maintain a list of neutrals and dispute resolution programs which have met the requirements of this section. The list may be divided among the areas of specialization or expertise of the neutrals.

At the conclusion of the orientation session, or no later than ten days thereafter, parties electing to continue with the dispute resolution proceeding may: (i) continue with the neutral who conducted the orientation session, (ii) select any neutral or dispute resolution program from the list maintained by the court to conduct such proceedings, or (iii) pursue any other alternative for voluntarily resolving the dispute to which the parties agree. If the parties choose to proceed with the dispute resolution proceeding but are unable to agree on a neutral or dispute resolution program during that period, the court shall refer the case to a neutral or dispute resolution program who accepts such referrals, on the list maintained by the court on the basis of a fair and equitable rotation, taking into account the subject matter of the dispute and the expertise of the neutral, as appropriate. If one or more of the parties is indigent or no agreement as to payment is reached between the parties and a neutral, the court shall set a reasonable fee for the service of any neutral who accepts such referral pursuant to this paragraph.

Acts 1993, c. 905; Acts 2002, c. 718.

§ 8.01–576.9. Standards and duties of neutrals; confidentiality; liability

A neutral selected to conduct a dispute resolution proceeding under this chapter may encourage and assist the parties in reaching a resolution of their dispute, but may not compel or coerce the parties into entering into a settlement agreement. A neutral has an obligation to remain impartial and free from conflict of interests in each case, and to decline to participate further in a case should such partiality or conflict arise. Unless expressly authorized by the disclosing party, the neutral may not disclose to either party information relating to the subject matter of the dispute resolution proceeding provided to him in confidence by the other. In reporting on the outcome of the dispute resolution proceeding to the referring court, the neutral shall indicate whether an agreement was reached, the terms of the agreement if authorized by the parties, the fact that no agreement was reached, or the fact that the orientation session or mediation did not occur. The neutral shall not disclose information exchanged or observations regarding the conduct and demeanor of the parties and their counsel during the dispute resolution proceeding, unless the parties otherwise agree.

However, where the dispute involves the support of minor children of the parties, the parties shall disclose to each other and to the neutral the information to be used in completing the child support guidelines worksheet required by § 20–108.2. The guidelines computations and any reasons for deviation shall be incorporated in any written agreement between the parties.

With respect to liability, when mediation is provided by a mediator who is certified pursuant to guidelines promulgated by the Judicial Council of Virginia, then the mediator, mediation program for which the certified mediator is providing services, and a mediator co-mediating with a certified mediator shall be immune from civil liability for, or resulting from, any act or omission done or made while engaged in efforts to assist or conduct a mediation, unless the act or omission was made or done in bad faith, with malicious intent or in a manner exhibiting a willful, wanton disregard of the rights, safety or property of another. This language is not intended to abrogate any other immunity that may be applicable to a mediator.

Acts 1993, c. 905; Acts 1994, c. 687; Acts 2002, c. 718.

§ 8.01–576.10. Confidentiality of dispute resolution proceeding

All memoranda, work products and other materials contained in the case files of a neutral or dispute resolution program are confidential. Any communication made in or in connection with the dispute resolution proceeding that relates to the controversy, including screening, intake and scheduling a dispute resolution proceeding, whether made to the neutral or dispute resolution program staff or to a party, or to any other person, is confidential. However, a written settlement agreement signed by the parties shall not be confidential, unless the parties otherwise agree in writing.

Confidential materials and communications are not subject to disclosure in discovery or in any judicial or administrative proceeding except (i) where all parties to the dispute resolution proceeding agree, in writing, to waive the confidentiality, (ii) in a subsequent action between the neutral or dispute resolution program and a party to the dispute resolution proceeding for damages arising out of the dispute resolution proceeding, (iii) statements, memoranda, materials and other tangible evidence, otherwise subject to discovery, that were not prepared specifically for use in and actually used in the dispute resolution proceeding, (iv) where a threat to inflict bodily injury is made, (v) where communications are intentionally used to plan, attempt to commit, or commit a crime or conceal an ongoing crime, (vi) where an ethics complaint is made against the neutral by a party to the dispute resolution proceeding to the extent necessary for the complainant to prove misconduct and the neutral to defend against such complaint, (vii) where communications are sought or offered to prove or disprove a claim or complaint of misconduct or malpractice filed against a party's legal representative based on conduct occurring during a mediation, (viii) where communications are sought or offered to prove or disprove any of the grounds listed in § 8.01–576.12 in a proceeding to vacate a mediated agreement, or (ix) as provided by law or rule. The use of attorney work product in a dispute resolution proceeding shall not result in a waiver of the attorney work product privilege.

Acts 1993, c. 905; Acts 1994, c. 687; Acts 2002, c. 718. Amended by Acts 2013, c. 283; Acts 2013, c. 383.

§ 8.01–576.11. Effect of written settlement agreement

If the parties reach a settlement and execute a written agreement disposing of the dispute, the agreement is enforceable in the same manner as any other

written contract. Upon request of all parties and consistent with law and public policy, the court shall incorporate the written agreement into the terms of its final decree disposing of a case. In cases in which the dispute involves support for the minor children of the parties, an order incorporating a written agreement shall also include the child support guidelines worksheet and, if applicable, the written reasons for any deviation from the guidelines. The child support guidelines worksheet shall be attached to the order.
Acts 1993, c. 905; Acts 1994, c. 687.

§ 8.01-576.12. Vacating orders and agreements

Upon the filing of an independent action by a party, the court shall vacate a mediated agreement reached in a dispute resolution proceeding pursuant to this chapter, or vacate an order incorporating or resulting from such agreement, where:

1. The agreement was procured by fraud or duress, or is unconscionable;

2. If property or financial matters in domestic relations cases involving divorce, property, support or the welfare of a child are in dispute, the parties failed to provide substantial full disclosure of all relevant property and financial information; or

3. There was evident partiality or misconduct by the neutral, prejudicing the rights of any party.

For purposes of this section, "misconduct" includes failure of the neutral to inform the parties in writing at the commencement of the mediation process that: (i) the neutral does not provide legal advice, (ii) any mediated agreement may affect the legal rights of the parties, (iii) each party to the mediation has the opportunity to consult with independent legal counsel at any time and is encouraged to do so, and (iv) each party to the mediation should have any draft agreement reviewed by independent counsel prior to signing the agreement.

The fact that any provisions of a mediated agreement were such that they could not or would not be granted by a court of law or equity is not, in and of itself, grounds for vacating an agreement.

A motion to vacate under this section shall be made within two years after the mediated agreement is entered into, except that, if predicated upon fraud, it shall be made within two years after these grounds are discovered or reasonably should have been discovered.
Acts 1993, c. 905; Acts 2002, c. 718.

CHAPTER 21

ARBITRATION AND AWARD

Article 1

General Provisions

§ 8.01-577. Submission of controversy; agreement to arbitrate; condition precedent to action

A. Persons desiring to end any controversy, whether there is a suit pending therefor or not, may submit the same to arbitration, and agree that such submission may be entered of record in any court. Upon proof of such agreement out of court, or by consent of the parties given in court in person or by counsel, it shall be entered in the proceedings of such court. Thereupon a rule shall be made, that the parties shall submit to the award which shall be made in accordance with such agreement and the provisions of this chapter.

B. Neither party shall have the right to revoke an agreement to arbitrate except on a ground which would be good for revoking or annulling other agreements. Submission of any claim or controversy to arbitration pursuant to such agreement shall be a condition precedent to institution of suit or action thereon, and the agreement to arbitrate shall be enforceable, unless the agreement also provides that submission to arbitration shall not be a condition precedent to suit or action.
Acts 1977, c. 617; Acts 1983, c. 485; Acts 1986, c. 614.

§§ 8.01-578 to 8.01-580. Repealed by Acts 1986, c. 614

§ 8.01-581. Fiduciary may submit to arbitration

Any personal representative of a decedent, fiduciary of a person under a disability, or other fiduciary may submit to arbitration any suit or matter of controversy touching the estate or property of such decedent, or person under a disability or in respect to which he is trustee. And any submission so made in good faith, and the award made thereupon, shall be binding and entered as the judgment of a court, if so required by the agreement, in the same manner as other submissions and awards. No such fiduciary shall be responsible for any loss sustained by an award adverse to the interests of the person under a disability or beneficiary under any such trust, unless it was caused by his fault or neglect.
Acts 1977, c. 617.

ARTICLE 2

UNIFORM ARBITRATION ACT

§ 8.01–581.01. Validity of arbitration agreement

A written agreement to submit any existing controversy to arbitration or a provision in a written contract to submit to arbitration any controversy thereafter arising between the parties is valid, enforceable and irrevocable, except upon such grounds as exist at law or in equity for the revocation of any contract. This article also applies to arbitration agreements between employers and employees or between their respective representatives unless otherwise provided in the agreement; provided, however, that nothing in this chapter shall be construed to create any right to arbitration with respect to any controversy regarding the employment or terms and conditions of employment of any officer or employee of the Commonwealth.

Acts 1986, c. 614.

§ 8.01–581.02. Proceedings to compel or stay arbitration

A. On application of a party showing an agreement described in § 8.01–581.01, and the opposing party's refusal to arbitrate, the court shall order the parties to proceed with arbitration. However, if the opposing party denies the existence of the agreement to arbitrate, the court shall proceed summarily to the determination of the issue of the existence of an agreement and shall order arbitration only if found for the moving party.

B. On application, the court may stay an arbitration proceeding commenced or threatened on a showing that there is no agreement to arbitrate. Such an issue, when in substantial and bona fide dispute, shall be forthwith and summarily tried and the stay ordered if found for the moving party. If found for the opposing party, the court shall order the parties to proceed to arbitration.

C. If an issue referable to arbitration under the alleged agreement is involved in an action or proceeding pending in a court having jurisdiction to hear applications under subsection A of this section, the application shall be made therein. Otherwise, subject to § 8.01–581.015, the application may be made in any court of competent jurisdiction.

D. Any action or proceeding involving an issue subject to arbitration shall be stayed if an order for arbitration or an application therefor has been made under this section. However, if the issue is severable, the stay may be with respect thereto only. When the application is made in such action or proceeding, the order for arbitration shall include the stay.

E. An order for arbitration shall not be refused on the ground that the claim in issue lacks merit or bona fides or because any fault or grounds for the claim sought to be arbitrated have not been shown.

Acts 1986, c. 614.

§ 8.01–581.03. Appointment of arbitrators by court; powers of arbitrators

If the arbitration agreement provides a method of appointment of arbitrators, this method shall be followed. In the absence thereof, or if the agreed method fails or for any reason cannot be followed, or when an arbitrator appointed fails or is unable to act and his successor has not been duly appointed, the court on application of a party shall appoint one or more arbitrators. An arbitrator so appointed has all the powers of one specifically named in the agreement.

The powers of the arbitrators may be exercised by a majority, unless otherwise provided by the agreement or by this article.

Acts 1986, c. 614.

§ 8.01–581.04. Hearing

Unless otherwise provided by the agreement:

1. The arbitrators shall appoint a time and place for the hearing and cause notification to the parties to be served personally or by registered mail not less than five days before the hearing. Appearance at the hearing waives such notice. The arbitrators may adjourn the hearing from time to time as necessary and, on request of a party for good cause, or upon their own motion may postpone the hearing to a time not later than the date fixed by the agreement for making the award unless the parties consent to a later date. The arbitrators may hear and determine the controversy upon the evidence produced notwithstanding the failure of a party duly notified to appear. The court on application may direct the arbitrators to proceed promptly with the hearing and determination of the controversy.

2. The parties are entitled to be heard, to present evidence material to the controversy and to cross-examine witnesses appearing at the hearing.

3. The hearing shall be conducted by all the arbitrators, but a majority may determine any question and render a final award. If, during the course of the hearing, an arbitrator for any reason ceases to act, the remaining arbitrator or arbitrators appointed to act as neutrals may continue with the hearing and determination of the controversy.

Acts 1986, c. 614.

§ 8.01–581.05. Representation by attorney

A party has the right to be represented by an attorney at any proceeding or hearing under this article. A waiver thereof prior to the proceeding or hearing is ineffective.

Acts 1986, c. 227.

§ 8.01–581.06. Witnesses, subpoenas, depositions

The arbitrators may issue subpoenas for the attendance of witnesses and for the production of books, records, documents and other evidence, and shall have the power to administer oaths. Subpoenas so issued shall be served, and upon application to the court by a party or the arbitrators, enforced, in the manner provided by law for the service and enforcement of subpoenas in a civil action. All provisions of law compelling a person under subpoena to testify are applicable.

On application of a party and for use as evidence, the arbitrators may permit a deposition to be taken of a witness who cannot be subpoenaed or is unable to attend the hearing, in the manner and upon the terms designated by the arbitrators.

Fees for attendance as a witness shall be the same as for a witness in the circuit court.

Acts 1986, c. 614.

§ 8.01–581.07. Award; fees and expenses to be fixed

The award shall be in writing and signed by the arbitrators joining in the award. The arbitrators shall deliver a copy to each party personally or by registered mail, or as provided in the agreement.

An award shall be made within the time fixed therefor by the agreement or, if not so fixed, within such time as the court orders on application of a party. The parties may extend the time in writing either before or after the expiration thereof. A party waives the objection that an award was not made within the time required unless he notifies the arbitrators of his objection prior to the delivery of the award to him. Unless otherwise provided in the agreement to arbitrate, the arbitrators' expenses and fees incurred in the conduct of the arbitration, and all other expenses, not including counsel fees, shall be paid as provided in the award.

Acts 1986, c. 614.

§ 8.01–581.08. Change of award by arbitrators

On application of a party or, if an application to the court is pending under §§ 8.01–581.09, 8.01–581.010 or § 8.01–581.011, on submission to the arbitrators by the court under such conditions as the court may order, the arbitrators may modify or correct the award upon the grounds stated in subdivisions 1 and 3 of § 8.01–581.011, or for the purpose of clarifying the award. The application shall be made within twenty days after delivery of the award to the applicant. Written notice thereof shall be given forthwith to the opposing party, stating that he must serve his objections thereto, if any, within ten days from the notice. The award as modified or corrected is subject to the provisions of §§ 8.01–581.09, 8.01–581.010 or § 8.01–581.011.

Acts 1986, c. 614.

§ 8.01–581.09. Confirmation of an award

Upon application of a party any time after an award is made, the court shall confirm an award, unless within the time limits hereinafter imposed grounds are urged for vacating or modifying or correcting the award, in which case the court shall proceed as provided in §§ 8.01–581.010 and 8.01–581.011.

Acts 1986, c. 614; Acts 1998, c. 303.

§ 8.01–581.010. Vacating an award

Upon application of a party, the court shall vacate an award where:

1. The award was procured by corruption, fraud or other undue means;

2. There was evident partiality by an arbitrator appointed as a neutral, corruption in any of the arbitrators, or misconduct prejudicing the rights of any party;

3. The arbitrators exceeded their powers;

4. The arbitrators refused to postpone the hearing upon sufficient cause being shown therefor or refused to hear evidence material to the controversy or otherwise so conducted the hearing, contrary to the provisions of § 8.01–581.04, in such a way as to substantially prejudice the rights of a party; or

5. There was no arbitration agreement and the issue was not adversely determined in proceedings under § 8.01–581.02 and the party did not participate in the arbitration hearing without raising the objection.

The fact that the relief was such that it could not or would not be granted by a court of law or equity is not grounds for vacating or refusing to confirm the award.

An application under this section shall be made within ninety days after delivery of a copy of the award to the applicant, except that, if predicated upon corruption, fraud or other undue means, it shall be made within ninety days after such grounds are known or reasonably should have been known. An application shall be made by filing a petition with the appropriate court within the prescribed time limits of this section, or by raising reasons supporting vacation in response to another party's petition to confirm the award, provided that such response is filed within the prescribed time limits of this section.

In vacating the award on grounds other than that stated in subdivision 5, the court may order a rehearing before new arbitrators chosen as provided in the agreement, or in the absence thereof, by the court in accordance with § 8.01–581.03. If the award is vacated on grounds set forth in subdivisions 3 and 4 the court may order a rehearing before the arbitrators who made the award or their successors appointed in accordance with § 8.01–581.03. The time within which the agreement requires the award to be made is applicable to the rehearing and commences from the date of the order.

If the application to vacate is denied and no motion to modify or correct the award is pending, the court shall confirm the award.

Acts 1986, c. 614; Acts 1998, c. 303.

§ 8.01–581.011. Modification or correction of award

Upon application made within ninety days after delivery of a copy of the award to the applicant, the court shall modify or correct the award where:

1. There was an evident miscalculation of figures or an evident mistake in the description of any person, thing or property referred to in the award;

2. The arbitrators have awarded upon a matter not submitted to them and the award may be corrected without affecting the merits of the decision upon the issues submitted; or

3. The award is imperfect in a matter of form, not affecting the merits of the controversy.

If the application is granted, the court shall modify and correct the award so as to effect its intent and shall confirm the award as so modified and corrected. Otherwise, the court shall confirm the award as made.

An application to modify or correct an award may be joined in the alternative with an application to vacate the award.

Acts 1986, c. 614.

§ 8.01–581.012. Judgment or decree on award

Upon granting an order confirming, modifying or correcting an award, a judgment or decree shall be entered in conformity therewith and be docketed and enforced as any other judgment or decree. Costs of the application and of the proceedings subsequent thereto, and disbursements may be awarded by the court.

Acts 1986, c. 614.

§ 8.01–581.013. Applications to court

An application to the court under this article shall be by motion and shall be heard in the manner and upon the notice provided by law or rule of court for the making and hearing of motions. Unless the parties have agreed otherwise, notice of an initial application for an order shall be served in the manner provided by law for the service of a summons in an action.

Acts 1986, c. 614.

§ 8.01–581.014. Court; jurisdiction

The term "court" means a court of this Commonwealth having jurisdiction over the subject matter of the controversy.

Acts 1986, c. 614; Acts 1995, c. 342.

§ 8.01–581.015. Venue

Except as provided in subsection B of § 8.01–262.1, an initial application shall be made to the court of the county or city in which the agreement provides the arbitration hearing shall be held or, if the hearing has been held, in the county or city in which it was held. Otherwise, venue of the application shall be as provided in Chapter 5 (§ 8.01–257 et seq.) of this title. All subsequent applications shall be made to the court hearing the initial application unless the court otherwise directs.

Acts 1986, c. 614; Acts 1991, c. 489.

§ 8.01–581.016. Appeals

An appeal may be taken from:

1. An order denying an application to compel arbitration made under § 8.01–581.02;

2. An order granting an application to stay arbitration made under subsection B of § 8.01–581.02;

3. An order confirming or denying an award;

4. An order modifying or correcting an award;

5. An order vacating an award without directing a rehearing; or

6. A judgment or decree entered pursuant to the provisions of this article.

The appeal shall be taken in the manner and to the same extent as from orders or judgments in a civil action.

Acts 1986, c. 614.

CHAPTER 21.1

MEDICAL MALPRACTICE

ARTICLE 1

MEDICAL MALPRACTICE REVIEW PANELS; ARBITRATION OF MALPRACTICE CLAIMS

§ 8.01–581.1. Definitions

As used in this chapter:

"Health care" means any act, professional services in nursing homes, or treatment performed or furnished, or which should have been performed or furnished, by any health care provider for, to, or on behalf of a patient during the patient's medical diagnosis, care, treatment or confinement.

"Health care provider" means (i) a person, corporation, facility or institution licensed by this Commonwealth to provide health care or professional services as a physician or hospital, dentist, pharmacist, registered nurse or licensed practical nurse or a person who holds a multistate privilege to practice such nursing under the Nurse Licensure Compact, nurse practitioner, optometrist, podiatrist, physician assistant, chiropractor, physical therapist, physical therapy assistant, clinical psychologist, clinical social worker, professional counselor, licensed marriage and family therapist, licensed dental hygienist, health maintenance organization, or emergency medical care attendant or technician who provides services on a fee basis; (ii) a professional corporation, all of whose shareholders or members are so licensed; (iii) a partnership, all of whose partners are so licensed; (iv) a nursing home as defined in § 54.1–3100 except those nursing institutions conducted by and for those who rely upon treatment by spiritual means alone through prayer in accordance with a recognized church or religious denomination; (v) a professional limited liability company comprised of members as described in subdivision A 2 of § 13.1–1102; (vi) a corporation, partnership, limited liability company or any other entity, except a state-operated facility, which employs or engages a licensed health care provider and which primarily renders health care services; or (vii) a director, officer, employee, independent contractor, or agent of the persons or entities referenced herein, acting within the course and scope of his employment or engagement as related to health care or professional services.

"Health maintenance organization" means any person licensed pursuant to Chapter 43 (§ 38.2–4300 et seq.) of Title 38.2 who undertakes to provide or arrange for one or more health care plans.

"Hospital" means a public or private institution licensed pursuant to Chapter 5 (§ 32.1–123 et seq.) of Title 32.1 or Article 2 (§ 37.2–403 et seq.) of Chapter 4 of Title 37.2.

"Impartial attorney" means an attorney who has not represented (i) the claimant, his family, his partners, co-proprietors or his other business interests; or (ii) the health care provider, his family, his partners, coproprietors or his other business interests.

"Impartial health care provider" means a health care provider who (i) has not examined, treated or been consulted regarding the claimant or his family; (ii) does not anticipate examining, treating, or being consulted regarding the claimant or his family; or (iii) has not been an employee, partner or co-proprietor of the health care provider against whom the claim is asserted.

"Malpractice" means any tort action or breach of contract action for personal injuries or wrongful death, based on health care or professional services rendered, or which should have been rendered, by a health care provider, to a patient.

"Patient" means any natural person who receives or should have received health care from a licensed health care provider except those persons who are given health care in an emergency situation which exempts the health care provider from liability for his emergency services in accordance with § 8.01–225 or 44–146.23.

"Physician" means a person licensed to practice medicine or osteopathy in this Commonwealth pursuant to Chapter 29 (§ 54.1–2900 et seq.) of Title 54.1.

"Professional services in nursing homes" means services provided in a nursing home, as that term is defined in clause (iv) of the definition of health care provider in this section, by a health care provider related to health care, staffing to provide patient care, psycho-social services, personal hygiene, hydration, nutrition, fall assessments or interventions, patient monitoring, prevention and treatment of medical conditions, diagnosis or therapy.

Acts 1977, c. 617; Acts 1981, c. 305; Acts 1986, c. 227; Acts 1986, c. 511; Acts 1989, c. 146; Acts 1989, c. 730; Acts 1991, c. 455; Acts 1991, c. 464; Acts 1993, c. 268; Acts 1994, c. 114; Acts 1994. c. 616; Acts 1994, c. 651; Acts 2001, c. 98; Acts 2003, c. 487; Acts 2003, c. 492. Amended by Acts 2005, c. 482; Acts 2005, c. 649; Acts 2005, c. 692; Acts 2006, c. 638; Acts 2008, c. 121; Acts 2008, c. 157; Acts 2008, c. 169; Acts 2008, c. 205; Acts 2014, c. 89; Acts 2015, c. 295; Acts 2015, c. 306.

§ 8.01–581.2. Request for review by medical malpractice review panel; rescission of request; determination on request

A. At any time within thirty days from the filing of the responsive pleading in any action brought for malpractice against a health care provider, the plaintiff or defendant may request a review by a medical malpractice review panel established as provided in § 8.01–581.3. The request shall be forwarded by the party making the request to the Clerk of the Supreme Court of Virginia with a copy of the Motion for Judgment and a copy of all responsive pleadings. A copy of the request shall be filed with the clerk of the circuit court, and a copy shall be sent to all counsel of record. The request shall include the name of the judge to whom the case is assigned, if any. Upon receipt of such request, the Supreme Court shall select the panel members as provided in § 8.01–581.3:1 and shall designate a panel within sixty days after receipt of the request. If a panel is requested, proceedings on the action based on the alleged malpractice shall be stayed during the period of review by the medical review panel, except that the judge may rule on any motions, demurrers, or pleas that can be disposed of as a matter of law, set the trial date after the panel has been designated and, prior to the designation of the panel, shall rule on any motions to transfer venue.

B. After the selection of the members of the review panel, the requesting party may rescind a request for review by the panel only with the consent of all parties or with leave of the judge presiding over the panel.

C. Any health care provider named as a defendant shall have the right to request a panel and, in that event, shall give notice of its request to the other health care providers named in the motion for judgment as well as to the plaintiff and his counsel of record. When a request for a medical review panel is made by any party, a single panel shall be designated and all health care providers against whom a claim is asserted shall be subject to the jurisdiction of such panel. The provisions of this subsection shall not prohibit the addition of parties pursuant to § 8.01–581.2:1.

Acts 1977, c. 617; Acts 1982, c. 151; Acts 1984, c. 443; Acts 1984, c. 777; Acts 1986, c. 227; Acts 1989, c. 561; Acts 1993, c. 928; Acts 1994, c. 38; Acts 1995, c. 367; Acts 2000, c. 213; Acts 2001, c. 252.

§ 8.01–581.2:1. Additional parties

The judge of the circuit court hearing the case may grant leave to amend the request for a review panel to add additional parties or causes of action in furtherance of the ends of justice except where (i) the request for leave to amend is made less than ten days before the date set for the review panel to convene or for the hearing or (ii) the judge finds that the request for leave to amend is without merit. If leave to amend is granted, the judge may, upon motion of either party, stay the review panel proceedings or continue the trial, extend the time for completion of discovery, filing of pleadings and other procedural limitations periods, or enter such other orders as are appropriate to avoid prejudice to the parties and to avoid unnecessary delay and duplication in the proceedings.

The statute of limitations as to any party added shall be tolled from the date of the request until completion of the panel proceedings. Leave to add additional parties to the review panel proceeding shall not be granted if the judge finds that the applicable statute of limitations has expired with respect to the new or additional parties or causes of action.

Acts 1986, c. 614; Acts 1993, c. 928.

§ 8.01–581.3. Composition, selection, etc., of panel

The medical review panel shall consist of (i) two impartial attorneys and two impartial health care providers, licensed and actively practicing their professions in the Commonwealth and (ii) the judge of a circuit court in which the action was filed, who shall preside over the panel. The judge shall have no vote and need not attend or participate in the deliberations. The medical review panel shall be selected by the Supreme Court from a list of health care providers submitted by the Board of Medicine and a list of attorneys submitted by the Virginia State Bar. In the selection of the health care provider members, the Court shall give due regard to the nature of the claim and the nature of the practice of the health care provider.

Acts 1977, c. 202; Acts 1977, c. 617; Acts 1983, c. 208; Acts 1984, c. 777; Acts 1986, c. 227; Acts 1993, c. 928; Acts 1994, c. 384.

§ 8.01–581.3:1. Completion of discovery; hearing date; notification to parties and panel members; oath of panel members

At the time that the panel is designated, the Supreme Court shall advise the clerk of the circuit court in which the matter was filed of the names of the panel members.

Except for good cause shown, the date for completion of discovery shall not be set beyond 120 days from the date on which the panel was requested. Within the period set for the taking of discovery and upon consultation with the panel members, the judge shall notify the parties of the date set for a hearing by the review panel, if any, or the date on which the panel will convene. Such date shall not be set sooner than ten days after the date for completion of discovery. Upon completion of discovery, the clerk of the circuit court shall notify the parties of the name, address and professional practice of each panel member and shall also notify the panel members, in writing, of their appointment.

The written notification to the panel members shall include the definitions of "impartial attorney" and "impartial health care provider" as contained in § 8.01–581.1 and a copy of the oath to which the panel members will be required to subscribe when the panel convenes. The oath shall be as follows:

"I do solemnly swear (or affirm) that I have no past or present relationship with the parties nor am I aware of anything that would prevent me from being impartial in my deliberations. I further swear (or affirm) that I will render an opinion faithfully and fairly on the basis of the evidence presented, applying any professional expertise I may have, giving due regard to the nature of the claim and the nature of the practice of the health care provider." A panel member who, for any reason, could not take the oath of impartiality shall promptly notify the judge presiding over the panel, in writing, of such inability. The judge shall notify the Supreme Court, which shall then select and notify another panel member in place of and practicing the same profession as the disqualified member.

Acts 1986, c. 227; Acts 1993, c. 928.

§ 8.01–581.4. Submission of evidence to panel; depositions and discovery; duties of chairman; access to material

The evidence to be considered by the medical review panel shall be promptly submitted by the respective parties, upon appointment of the panel, to each member of the panel in written form. Either party, upon request, shall be granted a hearing before the panel. The evidence may consist of medical charts, X-rays, laboratory tests, excerpts of treatises, and depositions of witnesses, including parties, and, when a hearing is held, oral testimony before the panel. The parties shall submit to the panel members only those portions of deposition transcripts, medical records, treatises and other documents which are relevant to the claim. However, upon request of the judge, a party shall produce all or part of any such document submitted. At the discretion of the judge, additional depositions of parties and witnesses may be taken, or other additional discovery may be had, at any time prior to hearing by any party. The judge shall rule on the admissibility of all or any part of a deposition offered as evidence at the hearing. Either party may have discovery pursuant to procedures set out in Part Four of the Rules of the Supreme Court of Virginia prior to appointment of the panel or thereafter in the discretion of the judge.

Process shall be returnable to the office of the clerk where the action was filed and shall issue under the style of the case as filed. Process for discovery shall issue upon application to the clerk. Any such discovery and any depositions taken for purposes of discovery or otherwise, under this section, may be used in the action filed for any purpose otherwise proper under Part Four of the Rules of Court. The judge of the panel shall advise the panel relative to any legal question involved in the review proceeding and shall prepare the opinion of the panel as provided in § 8.01–581.7. All parties shall have full access to any material submitted to the panel.

Acts 1977, c. 617; Acts 1979, c. 261; Acts 1984, c. 777; Acts 1986, c. 227; Acts 1993, c. 928.

§ 8.01–581.4:1. Assembly of record

Upon conclusion of deliberations and rendering of an opinion by the panel, all documentary evidence submitted to the panel, a transcript of the ore tenus hearing, if any, and a copy of the written opinion of the panel shall be filed in the office of the clerk. The record shall be maintained until the action is completed in the circuit court. Upon completion of the action, the clerk of the trial court shall include a copy of the panel record along with the record of the case.

Acts 1986, c. 227; Acts 1993, c. 928.

§ 8.01–581.4:2. Removal of record for inspection and copying; notice

Any party may, upon notice to all other parties or their counsel, remove any book, record or document which has been filed with the clerk or has become a part of the permanent record filed with the Executive Secretary for purposes of inspection and copying. The party removing the documents shall give an appropriate receipt to the clerk or Executive Secretary and shall be responsible for the return of the materials within ten days.

Acts 1986, c. 227.

§ 8.01–581.5. When hearing to be held; notice to parties

The plaintiff or defendant may request the medical review panel to hold a hearing on any claim referred to the medical review panel, in which case the medical review panel shall conduct a hearing thereon in accordance with § 8.01–581.6 after notice to the parties by means adequate to ensure their presence at the time and place of the hearing.

Acts 1977, c. 617; Acts 1979, c. 261; Acts 1984, c. 777; Acts 1993, c. 928.

§ 8.01–581.6. Conduct of proceedings

In the conduct of its proceedings:

1. The testimony of the witnesses shall be given under oath. Members of the medical review panel, once sworn, shall have the power to administer oaths.

2. In the event a hearing is held, the parties are entitled to be heard, to present relevant evidence, and to cross-examine witnesses to the extent necessary to enable the panel to render an opinion as specified in § 8.01–581.7. The rules of evidence need not be observed. The medical review panel may proceed with the hearing and shall render an opinion upon the evidence produced, notwithstanding the failure of a party duly notified to appear.

3. The medical review panel may issue or cause to be issued, on its own motion or on application of any party, subpoenas for the attendance of witnesses and for the production of books, records, documents, and other evidence. Subpoenas so issued shall be served and, upon application by a party or the panel to a court of proper venue having jurisdiction over a motion for judgment based on such claim, enforced in the manner provided for the service and enforcement of subpoenas in a civil action. All provisions of law compelling a person under subpoena to testify are applicable.

4. Repealed.

5. The hearing shall be conducted by all members of the medical review panel unless the parties otherwise agree. A majority of the members present may determine any question and may render an opinion.

6. The medical review panel members may apply their expertise in evaluating the evidence giving due regard to the nature of the claim and the nature of the practice of the health care provider, whether expert medical opinions are presented by the parties or not.

Acts 1977, c. 617; Acts 1979, c. 261; Acts 1984, c. 777; Acts 1986, c. 227.

§ 8.01–581.7. Opinion of panel

A. Within thirty days, after receiving all the evidence, the panel shall have the duty, after joint deliberation, to render one or more of the following opinions:

1. The evidence does not support a conclusion that the health care provider failed to comply with the appropriate standard of care;

2. The evidence supports a conclusion that the health care provider failed to comply with the appropriate standard of care and that such failure is a proximate cause in the alleged damages;

3. The evidence supports a conclusion that the health care provider failed to comply with the appropriate standard of care and that such failure is not a proximate cause in the alleged damages; or

4. The evidence indicates that there is a material issue of fact, not requiring an expert opinion, bearing on liability for consideration by a court or jury.

B. If the review panel's finding is that set forth in subdivision 2 of subsection A of this section, the panel may determine whether the plaintiff suffered any disability or impairment and the degree and extent thereof.

C. The opinion shall be in writing and shall be signed by all panelists who agree therewith. Any member of the panel may note his dissent. All such opinions shall be filed with the clerk of the court in which the action is pending and mailed to the plaintiff and the defendant within five days of the date of their rendering. However, this subsection shall not be construed to preclude the panel from announcing the opinion in the presence of the parties or their counsel, provided a signed written opinion is subsequently mailed as provided in this subsection.

Acts 1977, c. 617; Acts 1986, c. 227; Acts 1993, c. 928.

§ 8.01–581.7:1. Limitation on panel opinion

Unless the parties otherwise agree, any opinion of the panel shall be rendered no later than six months from the designation of the panel unless the judge shall extend the period one time, not to exceed ninety days, upon a showing of extraordinary circumstances. If the opinion of the panel is not rendered within the time provided, any panel opinion rendered subsequently shall be inadmissible as evidence unless the failure of the panel to render a decision within the time provided was caused by delay on the plaintiff's part.

Acts 1981, c. 327; Acts 1993, c. 928.

§ 8.01–581.8. Admissibility of opinion as evidence; appearance of panel members as witnesses; immunity from civil liability

An opinion of the medical review panel shall be admissible as evidence in the action brought by the plaintiff, but shall not be conclusive. Either party shall have the right to call, at his cost, any member of the panel, except the judge, as a witness. If called, each witness shall be required to appear and testify. The panelist shall have absolute immunity from civil liability for all communications, findings, opinions and conclusions made in the course and scope of duties prescribed by this chapter.

Acts 1977, c. 617; Acts 1978, c. 406; Acts 1993, c. 928.

§ 8.01–581.9. Repealed by Acts 1993, c. 928

§ 8.01–581.10. Per diem and expenses of panel

Each member of the medical review panel shall be reimbursed for his actual and necessary expenses and shall be paid at a rate of fifty dollars per diem for work performed as a member of the panel exclusive of time involved if called as a witness to testify in court. Per diem and expenses of the panel shall be borne by the parties in such proportions as may be determined by the chairman in his discretion.

Acts 1977, c. 617; Acts 1984, c. 777.

§ 8.01–581.11. Rules and regulations

The Chief Justice of the Supreme Court of Virginia shall promulgate all necessary rules and regulations to carry out the provisions of this chapter.

Acts 1977, c. 617.

§ 8.01–581.11:1. Objections not waived by participation

Participation in any medical malpractice review panel proceeding pursuant to this article shall not constitute a waiver by a party to the proceedings of any objections to the review panel procedure.

Acts 1986, c. 227.

§ 8.01–581.12. Arbitration of medical malpractice claims

A. Persons desiring to enter into an agreement to arbitrate medical malpractice claims which have then arisen or may thereafter arise may submit such matters to arbitration under the provisions of Chapter 21 (§ 8.01–577 et seq.) of this title and an agreement to submit such matters shall be binding upon the parties if the patient or claimant or his guardian, conservator, committee or personal representative is allowed by the terms of the agreement to withdraw therefrom, and to decline to submit any matter then or thereafter in controversy, within a period of at least sixty days after the termination of health care or, if the patient is under disability by reason of age and at the time of termination without a guardian who could take such action for him, or if he is incapacitated and without a guardian or conservator who could take such action for him, or if such termination is by death or if death occurs within sixty days after termination, then within a period of at least sixty days after the appointment and qualification of the guardian, conservator or committee or personal representative.

B. Proof of agreement to arbitrate and submission of a medical malpractice claim pursuant thereto shall be in accordance with Chapter 21 of this title, and a medical malpractice panel appointed under this article may be designated to arbitrate the matter, either by the arbitration agreement or by the parties to the agreement.

C. An insurer of a health care provider shall be bound by the award of an arbitration panel or arbitrators acting pursuant to a good faith submission hereunder to the extent to which it would have been obligated by a judgment entered in an action at law with respect to the matter submitted; provided, that such insurer has agreed prior to the submission to be bound by the award of such arbitration panel or arbitrators.

Acts 1977, c. 617; Acts 1997, c. 801, eff. Jan. 1, 1998.

§ 8.01–581.12:1. Repealed by Acts 1979, c. 325

§ 8.01–581.12:2. Article not applicable to actions arising prior to July 1, 1976

(a) The provisions of this article shall not apply to any cause of action which arose prior to July 1, 1976, and as to which the statute of limitations had not run prior to that date, regardless of the date any suit brought thereon is filed. Notwithstanding the foregoing, in actions which accrued prior to July 1, 1976, if a claimant has filed notice under § 8.01–581.2 of this article, his cause of action and any defense thereto shall be governed by this article.

(b) The term "has filed," as used in this section, is deemed to include the filing of notice under § 8.01–581.2 (or under repealed § 8–912) of this article where such filing occurred prior to the expiration of any applicable statute of limitation when the cause of action arose prior to July 1, 1976. This subsection (b) shall be applied retroactively to such causes of action.

Acts 1977, c. 422; Acts 1978, c. 262.

Article 2

Miscellaneous Provisions

§ 8.01–581.13. Civil immunity for certain health professionals and health profession students serving as members of certain entities

A. For the purposes of this subsection, "health professional" means any clinical psychologist, applied psychologist, school psychologist, dentist, certified emergency medical services provider, licensed professional counselor, licensed substance abuse treatment practitioner, certified substance abuse counselor, certified substance abuse counseling assistant, licensed marriage and family therapist, nurse, optometrist, pharmacist, physician, chiropractor, podiatrist, or veterinarian who is actively engaged in the practice of his profession or any member of the Health Practitioners' Monitoring Program Committee pursuant to Chapter 25.1 (§ 54.1–2515 et seq.) of Title 54.1.

Unless such act, decision, or omission resulted from such health professional's bad faith or malicious intent, any health professional, as defined in this subsection, shall be immune from civil liability for any act, decision or omission resulting from his duties as a member or agent of any entity which functions primarily (i) to investigate any complaint that a physical or mental impairment, including alcoholism or drug addiction, has impaired the ability of any such health professional to practice his profession and (ii) to encourage, recommend and arrange for a course of treatment or intervention, if deemed appropriate, or (iii) to review or monitor the duration of patient stays in health facilities, delivery of professional services, or the quality of care delivered in the statewide emergency medical services system for the purpose of promoting the most efficient use of available health facilities and services, the adequacy and quality of professional services, or the reasonableness or appropriateness of charges made by or on behalf of such health professionals. Such entity shall have been established pursuant to a federal or state law, or by one or more public or licensed private hospitals, or a relevant health professional society, academy or association affiliated with the American Medical Association, the American Dental Association, the American Pharmaceutical Association, the American Psychological Association, the American Podiatric Medical Association, the American Society of Hospitals and Pharmacies, the American Veterinary Medical Association, the American Association for Counseling and Development, the American Optometric Association, International Chiropractic Association, the American Chiropractic Association, the NAADAC: the Association for Addiction Professionals, the American Association for Marriage and Family Therapy or a governmental agency.

B. For the purposes of this subsection, "health profession student" means a student in good standing who is enrolled in an accredited school, program, or curriculum in clinical psychology, counseling, dentistry, medicine, nursing, pharmacy, chiropractic, marriage and family therapy, substance abuse treatment, or veterinary medicine and has received training relating to substance abuse.

Unless such act, decision, or omission resulted from such health profession student's bad faith or malicious intent, any health profession student, as defined in this subsection, shall be immune from civil liability for any act, decision, or omission resulting from his duties as a member of an entity established by the institution of higher education in which he is enrolled or a professional student's organization affiliated with such institution which functions primarily (i) to investigate any complaint of a physical or mental impairment, including alcoholism or drug addiction, of any health profession student and (ii) to encourage, recommend, and arrange for a course of treatment, if deemed appropriate.

C. The immunity provided hereunder shall not extend to any person with respect to actions, decisions or omissions, liability for which is limited under the provisions of the federal Social Security Act or amendments thereto.

Acts 1977, c. 617; Acts 1983, c. 567; Acts 1984, c. 494; Acts 1987, c. 713; Acts 1989, c. 729; Acts 1992, c. 590; Acts 1993, c. 702; Acts 1995, c. 636; Acts 1996, c. 937; Acts 1996, c. 980; Acts 1997, c. 439; Acts 1997, c. 901; Acts 2001, c. 460. Amended by Acts 2006, c. 412; Acts 2006, c. 638; Acts 2009, c. 472; Acts 2015, c. 502; Acts 2015, c. 503.

§ 8.01–581.14. Repealed by Acts 2003, c. 397

§ 8.01–581.15. Limitation on recovery in certain medical malpractice actions

In any verdict returned against a health care provider in an action for malpractice where the act or acts of malpractice occurred on or after August 1, 1999, which is tried by a jury or in any judgment entered against a health care provider in such an action which is tried without a jury, the total amount recoverable for any injury to, or death of, a patient shall not exceed the following, corresponding amount:

August 1, 1999, through June 30, 2000	$1.50 million
July 1, 2000, through June 30, 2001	$1.55 million
July 1, 2001, through June 30, 2002	$1.60 million
July 1, 2002, through June 30, 2003	$1.65 million
July 1, 2003, through June 30, 2004	$1.70 million
July 1, 2004, through June 30, 2005	$1.75 million
July 1, 2005, through June 30, 2006	$1.80 million
July 1, 2006, through June 30, 2007	$1.85 million
July 1, 2007, through June 30, 2008	$1.925 million
July 1, 2008, through June 30, 2012	$2.00 million
July 1, 2012, through June 30, 2013	$2.05 million
July 1, 2013, through June 30, 2014	$2.10 million
July 1, 2014, through June 30, 2015	$2.15 million
July 1, 2015, through June 30, 2016	$2.20 million
July 1, 2016, through June 30, 2017	$2.25 million
July 1, 2017, through June 30, 2018	$2.30 million
July 1, 2018, through June 30, 2019	$2.35 million
July 1, 2019, through June 30, 2020	$2.40 million
July 1, 2020, through June 30, 2021	$2.45 million
July 1, 2021, through June 30, 2022	$2.50 million
July 1, 2022, through June 30, 2023	$2.55 million
July 1, 2023, through June 30, 2024	$2.60 million
July 1, 2024, through June 30, 2025	$2.65 million
July 1, 2025, through June 30, 2026	$2.70 million
July 1, 2026, through June 30, 2027	$2.75 million
July 1, 2027, through June 30, 2028	$2.80 million
July 1, 2028, through June 30, 2029	$2.85 million
July 1, 2029, through June 30, 2030	$2.90 million
July 1, 2030, through June 30, 2031	$2.95 million

In any verdict returned against a health care provider in an action for malpractice where the act or acts of malpractice occurred on or after July 1, 2031, which is tried by a jury or in any judgment entered against a health care provider in such an action which is tried without a jury, the total amount recoverable for any injury to, or death of, a patient shall not exceed $3 million. Each annual increase shall apply to the act or acts of malpractice occurring on or after the effective date of the increase.

Where the act or acts of malpractice occurred prior to August 1, 1999, the total amount recoverable for any injury to, or death of, a patient shall not exceed the limitation on recovery set forth in this statute as it was in effect when the act or acts of malpractice occurred.

In interpreting this section, the definitions found in § 8.01–581.1 shall be applicable.

Acts 1977, c. 617; Acts 1983, c. 496; Acts 1999, c. 711, eff. Aug. 1, 1999; Acts 2001, c. 211. Amended by Acts 2011, c. 758; Acts 2011, c. 759.

§ 8.01–581.16. Civil immunity for members of or consultants to certain boards or committees

Every member of, or health care professional consultant to, any committee, board, group, commission or other entity shall be immune from civil liability for any act, decision, omission, or utterance done or made in performance of his duties while serving as a member of or consultant to such committee, board, group, commission or other entity, which functions primarily to review, evaluate, or make recommendations on (i) the duration of patient stays in health care facilities, (ii) the professional services furnished with respect to the medical, dental, psychological, podiatric, chiropractic, veterinary or optometric necessity for such services, (iii) the purpose of promoting the most efficient use or monitoring the quality of care of available health care facilities and services, or of emergency medical services agencies and services, (iv) the adequacy or quality of professional services, (v) the competency and qualifications for professional staff privileges, (vi) the reasonableness or appropriateness of charges made by or on behalf of health care facilities or (vii) patient safety, including entering into contracts with patient safety organizations, provided that such committee, board, group, commission or other entity has been established pursuant to federal or state law or regulation, the requirements of a national accrediting organization granted authority by the Centers for Medicare and Medicaid Services to assure compliance with Medicare conditions of participation pursuant to § 1865 of Title XVIII of the Social Security Act (42 U.S.C. § 1395bb), or guidelines approved or adopted by a statewide or local association representing health care providers licensed in the Commonwealth pursuant to clause (iii) (f) of subsection B of § 8.01–581.17, or established and duly constituted by one or more public or licensed private hospitals, health systems, community services boards, or behavioral health authorities, or with a governmental agency and provided further that such act, decision, omission, or utterance is not done or made in bad faith or with malicious intent.

Acts 1977, c. 617; Acts 1981, c. 174; Acts 1987, c. 713; Acts 1989, c.729; Acts 1993, c. 702; Acts 2001, c. 381; Acts 2002, c. 675. Amended by Acts 2006, c. 412; Acts 2014, c. 17; Acts 2014, c. 320; Acts 2014, c. 363.

§ 8.01–581.17. Privileged communications of certain committees and entities

A. For the purposes of this section:

"Centralized credentialing service" means (i) gathering information relating to applications for professional staff privileges at any public or licensed private hospital or for participation as a provider in any health maintenance organization, preferred provider organization or any similar organization and (ii) providing such information to those hospitals and organizations that utilize the service.

"Patient safety data" means reports made to patient safety organizations together with all health care data, interviews, memoranda, analyses, root cause analyses, products of quality assurance or quality improvement processes, corrective action plans or information collected or created by a health care provider as a result of an occurrence related to the provision of health care services.

"Patient safety organization" means any organization, group, or other entity that collects and analyzes patient safety data for the purpose of improving patient safety and health care outcomes and that is independent and not under the control of the entity that reports patient safety data.

B. The proceedings, minutes, records, and reports of any (i) medical staff committee, utilization review committee, or other committee, board, group, commission or other entity as specified in § 8.01–581.16; (ii) nonprofit entity that provides a centralized credentialing service; or (iii) quality assurance, quality of care, or peer review committee established pursuant to guidelines approved or adopted by (a) a national or state physician peer review entity, (b) a national or state physician accreditation entity, (c) a national professional association of health care providers or Virginia chapter of a national professional association of health care providers, (d) a licensee of a managed care health insurance plan (MCHIP) as defined in § 38.2–5800, (e) the Office of Emergency Medical Services or any regional emergency medical services council, or (f) a statewide or local association representing health care providers licensed in the Commonwealth, together with all communications, both oral and written, originating in or provided to such committees or entities, are privileged communications which may not be disclosed or obtained by legal discovery proceedings unless a circuit court, after a hearing and for good cause arising from extraordinary circumstances being shown, orders the disclosure of such proceedings, minutes, records, reports, or communications. Additionally, for the purposes of this section, accreditation and peer review records of the American College of Radiology and the Medical Society of Virginia are considered privileged communications. Oral communications regarding a specific medical incident involving patient care, made to a quality assurance, quality of care, or peer review committee established pursuant to clause (iii), shall be privileged only to the extent made more than 24 hours after the occurrence of the medical incident. Nothing in this section shall be construed as providing any privilege to any health care provider, emergency medical services agency, community services board, or behavioral health authority with respect to any factual information regarding specific patient health care or treatment, including patient health care incidents, whether oral, electronic, or written. However, the analysis, findings, conclusions, recommendations, and the deliberative process of any medical staff committee, utilization review committee, or other committee, board, group, commission, or other entity specified in § 8.01–581.16, as well as the proceedings, minutes, records, and reports, including the opinions and reports of experts, of such entities shall be privileged in their entirety under this section. Information known by a witness with knowledge of the facts or treating health care provider is not privileged or protected from discovery merely because it is provided to a committee, board, group, commission, or other entity specified in § 8.01–581.16, and may be discovered by deposition or otherwise in the course of discovery. A person involved in the work of the entities referenced in this subsection shall not be made a witness with knowledge of the facts by virtue of his involvement in the quality assurance, peer review, or credentialing process.

C. Nothing in this section shall be construed as providing any privilege to health care provider, emergency medical services agency, community services board, or behavioral health authority medical records kept with respect to a patient, whose treatment is at issue, in the ordinary course of business of operating a hospital, emergency medical services agency, community services board, or behavioral health authority nor to any facts or information contained in medical records, nor shall this section preclude or affect discovery of or production of evidence relating to hospitalization or treatment of such patient in the ordinary course of the patient's hospitalization or treatment. However, the proceedings, minutes, records, reports, analysis, findings, conclusions, recommendations, and the deliberative process, including opinions and reports of experts, of any medical staff committee, utilization review committee, or other committee, board, group, commission, or other entity specified in § 8.01–581.16 shall not constitute medical records, are privileged in their entirety, and are not discoverable.

D. Notwithstanding any other provision of this section, reports or patient safety data in possession of a patient safety organization, together with the identity of the reporter and all related correspondence, documentation, analysis, results or recommendations, shall be privileged and confidential and shall not be subject to a civil, criminal, or administrative subpoena or admitted as evidence in any civil, criminal, or administrative proceeding. Nothing in this subsection shall affect the discoverability or admissibility of facts, information or records referenced in subsection C as related to patient care from a source other than a patient safety organization.

E. Any patient safety organization shall promptly remove all patient-identifying information after receipt of a complete patient safety data report unless such organization is otherwise permitted by state or federal law to maintain such information. Patient safety organizations shall maintain the confidentiality of all patient-identifying information and shall not disseminate such information except as permitted by state or federal law.

F. Exchange of (i) patient safety data among health care providers or patient safety organizations that does not identify any patient or (ii) information privileged pursuant to subsection B between committees, boards, groups, commissions, or other entities specified in § 8.01–581.16 shall not constitute a waiver of any privilege established in this section.

G. Reports of patient safety data to patient safety organizations shall not abrogate obligations to make reports to health regulatory boards or other agencies as required by state or federal law.

H. No employer shall take retaliatory action against an employee who in good faith makes a report of patient safety data to a patient safety organization.

I. Reports produced solely for purposes of self-assessment of compliance with requirements or standards of a national accrediting organization granted authority by the Centers for Medicare and Medicaid Services to ensure compliance with Medicare conditions of participation pursuant to § 1865 of Title XVIII of the Social Security Act (42 U.S.C. § 1395bb) shall be privileged and confidential and shall not be subject to subpoena or admitted as evidence in a civil or administrative proceeding. Nothing in this subsection shall affect the discoverability or admissibility of facts, information, or records referenced in subsection C as related to patient care from a source other than such accreditation body. A health care provider's release of such reports to such accreditation body shall not constitute a waiver of any privilege provided under this section.

Acts 1977, c. 617; Acts 1995, c. 500; Acts 1997, c. 292; Acts 2001, c. 381; Acts 2002, c. 675. Amended by Acts 2004, c. 250; Acts 2006, c. 412; Acts 2006, c. 678; Acts 2007, c. 530; Acts 2010, c. 196; Acts 2011, c. 15; Acts 2011, c. 753; Acts 2014, c. 320.

§ 8.01–581.18. Delivery of results of laboratory tests and other examinations not authorized by physician

A. Whenever a laboratory test or other examination of the physical or mental condition of any person is conducted by or under the supervision of a person other than a physician and not at the request or with the authorization of a physician, any report of the results of such test or examination shall be provided by the person conducting such test or examination to the person who was the subject of such test or examination. Such report shall state in bold type that it is the responsibility of the person so examined or tested to arrange with his physician for consultation and interpretation of the results of such test or examination. The provisions of this subsection shall not apply to any test or examination conducted under the auspices of the State Department of Health.

B. As used in this section and § 8.01–581.18:1, "physician" means a person licensed to practice medicine, podiatry, chiropractic or osteopathy in this Commonwealth pursuant to Chapter 29 (§ 54.1–2900 et seq.) of Title 54.1.

Acts 1977, c. 527; Acts 1993, c. 702. Amended by Acts 2006, c. 684; Acts 2006, c. 877.

§ 8.01–581.18:1. Immunity of physicians for laboratory results and examinations

A. No physician shall be liable for the failure to review or act on the results of laboratory tests or examinations of the physical or mental condition of any patient, which tests or examinations the physician neither requested nor authorized, unless (i) the report of such results is provided directly to the physician by the patient so examined or tested with a request for consultation; (ii) the physician assumes responsibility to review or act on the results; or (iii) the physician has reason to know that in order to manage the specific mental or physical condition of the patient, review of or action on the pending results is needed. However, no physician shall be immune under this section unless the physician establishes that (a) no physician-patient relationship existed when the results were received or accessed; or (b) the physician received or accessed the results without a request for consultation and without responsibility for management of the specific mental or physical condition of the patient relating to the results or (c) the physician consulted on a specific mental or physical condition, the results were not part of that physician's management of the patient and the physician had no reason to know that he was to inform the patient of the results or refer the patient to another physician; or (d) the physician received or accessed results, the interpretation of which would exceed the physician's scope of practice and the physician had no reason to know that he was to inform the patient of the results or refer the patient to another physician.

B. As used in this section, "physician" means a person licensed to practice medicine, chiropractic, or osteopathy in the Commonwealth pursuant to Chapter 29 (§ 54.1–2900 et. seq.) of Title 54.1.

Added by Acts 2006, c. 684.

§ 8.01–581.19. Civil immunity for physicians, psychologists, podiatrists, optometrists, veterinarians, nursing home administrators, and certified emergency medical services providers while members of certain committees

A. Any physician, chiropractor, psychologist, podiatrist, veterinarian, or optometrist licensed to practice in the Commonwealth shall be immune from civil liability for any communication, finding, opinion, or conclusion made in performance of his duties while serving as a member of any committee, board, group, commission, or other entity that is responsible for resolving questions concerning the admission of any physician, psychologist, podiatrist, veterinarian, or optometrist to, or the taking of disciplinary action against any member of, any medical society, academy, or association affiliated with the American Medical Association, the Virginia Academy of Clinical Psychologists, the American Psychological Association, the Virginia Applied Psychology Academy, the Virginia Academy of School Psychologists, the American Podiatric Medical Association, the American Veterinary Medical Association, the International Chiropractic Association, the American Chiropractic Association, the Virginia Chiropractic Association, or the American Optometric Association, provided that such communication, finding, opinion, or conclusion is not made in bad faith or with malicious intent.

B. Any nursing home administrator licensed under the laws of the Commonwealth shall be immune from civil liability for any communication, finding, opinion, decision, or conclusion made in performance of his duties while serving as a member of any committee, board, group, commission, or other entity that is responsible for resolving questions concerning the admission of any health care facility to, or the taking of disciplinary action against any member of, the Virginia Health Care Association, provided that such communication, finding, opinion, decision, or conclusion is not made in bad faith or with malicious intent.

C. Any emergency medical services provider who holds a valid certificate issued by the Commissioner of Health shall be immune from civil liability for any communication, finding, opinion, decision, or conclusion made in performance of his duties while serving as a member of any regional council, committee, board, group, commission, or other entity that is responsible for resolving questions concerning the quality of care, including triage, interfacility transfer, and other components of emergency medical services care, unless such communication, finding, opinion, decision, or conclusion is made in bad faith or with malicious intent.

Acts 1978, c. 541; Acts 1987, c. 713; Acts 1989, c.729; Acts 1993, c. 702; Acts 1996, c. 937; Acts 1996, c. 980. Amended by Acts 2006, c. 412; Acts 2015, c. 502; Acts 2015, c. 503.

§ 8.01–581.19:1. Civil immunity for persons providing information to certain committees

Any person who provides information to any committee, board, group, commission, or other entity which is authorized to investigate any complaint of physical or mental impairment, that may show that any practitioner of medicine, osteopathy, optometry, chiropractic, podiatry, clinical psychology, physical therapy, veterinary medicine or any physical therapist assistant is unable to practice his profession with reasonable skill and safety, by reason of the use of alcohol, drugs, or other substances, or as a result of any mental or physical condition, shall be immune from civil liability for any act done for, or any utterance or communication made to, such entity in the course of providing such information. However, this section shall not apply if the act, utterance, or communication is done or made in bad faith or with malicious intent or if such disclosure is prohibited by federal law or regulations promulgated thereunder.

The provisions of this section shall apply only to such entities described in this section as are (i) established pursuant to a federal or state law, (ii) established and duly constituted by one or more public or licensed private hospitals, (iii) a medical or chiropractic society that is operating its health care provider impairment program in cooperation with the Board of Medicine, or another governmental agency, (iv) an optometric society or association that is operating its optometric impairment program in cooperation with the Virginia Board of Optometry, (v) a veterinary medical association that is operating its veterinarian impairment program in cooperation with the Virginia Board of Veterinary Medicine, or (vi) a clinical psychology academy that is operating its clinical psychology impairment program in cooperation with the Board of Psychology.

Acts 1986, c. 604; Acts 1987, c. 713; Acts 1989, c.729; Acts 1993, c. 702; Acts 1996, c. 937; Acts 1996, c. 980.

§ 8.01–581.20. Standard of care in proceeding before medical malpractice review panel; expert testimony; determination of standard in action for damages

A. In any proceeding before a medical malpractice review panel or in any action against a physician, clinical psychologist, podiatrist, dentist, nurse, hospital or other health care provider to recover damages alleged to have been caused by medical malpractice where the acts or omissions so complained of are alleged to have occurred in this Commonwealth, the standard of care by which the acts or omissions are to be judged shall be that degree of skill and diligence practiced by a reasonably prudent practitioner in the field of practice or specialty in this Commonwealth and the testimony of an expert witness, otherwise qualified, as to such standard of care, shall be admitted; provided, however, that the standard of care in the locality or in similar localities in which the alleged act or omission occurred shall be applied if any party shall prove by a preponderance of the evidence that the health care services and health care facilities available in the locality and the customary practices in such locality or similar localities give rise to a standard of care which is more appropriate than a statewide standard. Any health care provider who is licensed to practice in Virginia shall be presumed to know the statewide standard of care in the specialty or field of practice in which he is qualified and certified. This presumption shall also apply to any person who, but for the lack of a Virginia license, would be defined as a health care provider under this chapter, provided that such person is licensed in some other state of the United States and meets the educational and examination requirements for licensure in Virginia. An expert witness who is familiar with the statewide standard of care shall not have his testimony excluded on the ground that he does not practice in this Commonwealth. A witness shall be qualified to testify as an expert on the standard of care if he demonstrates expert knowledge of the standards of the defendant's specialty and of what conduct conforms or fails to conform to those standards and if he has had active clinical practice in either the defendant's specialty or a related field of medicine within one year of the date of the alleged act or omission forming the basis of the action.

The provisions of this section shall apply to expert witnesses testifying on the standard of care as it relates to professional services in nursing homes.

B. In any action for damages resulting from medical malpractice, any issue as to the standard of care to be applied shall be determined by the jury, or the court trying the case without a jury.

C. In any action described in this section, each party may designate, identify or call to testify at trial no more than two expert witnesses per medical discipline on any issue presented. The court may permit a party, for good cause shown, to designate, identify, or call to testify at trial additional expert witnesses. The number of treating health care providers who may serve as expert witnesses pursuant to § 8.01–399 shall not be limited pursuant to this subsection, except for good cause shown. If the court permits a party to designate, identify, or call additional experts, the court may order that party to pay all costs incurred in the discovery of such additional experts. For good cause shown, pursuant to the Rules of Supreme Court of Virginia, the court may limit the number of expert witnesses other than those identified in this subsection whom a party may designate, identify, or call to testify at trial.

Acts 1979, c. 325; Acts 1980, c. 164; Acts 1989, c. 146; Acts 1989, c. 729; Acts 1992, c. 240; Acts 2003, c. 251. Amended by Acts 2008, c. 125; Acts 2008, c. 169; Acts 2008, c. 205; Acts 2015, c. 310; Acts 2015, c. 361.

§ 8.01–581.20:1. Admissibility of expressions of sympathy

In any civil action brought by an alleged victim of an unanticipated outcome of health care, or in any arbitration or medical malpractice review panel proceeding related to such civil action, the portion of statements, writings, affirmations, benevolent conduct, or benevolent gestures expressing sympathy, commiseration, condolence, compassion, or a general sense of benevolence, together with apologies that are made by a health care provider or an agent of a health care provider to the patient, a relative of the patient, or a representative of the patient, shall be inadmissible as evidence of an admission of liability or as evidence of an admission against interest. A statement of fault that is part of or in addition to any of the above shall not be made inadmissible by this section.

For purposes of this section, unless the context otherwise requires:

"Health care" has the same definition as provided in § 8.01–581.1.

"Health care provider" has the same definition as provided in § 8.01–581.1.

"Relative" means a patient's spouse, parent, grandparent, stepfather, stepmother, child, grandchild, brother, sister, half-brother, half-sister, or spouse's parents. In addition, "relative" includes any person who has a family-type relationship with the patient.

"Representative" means a legal guardian, attorney, person designated to make decisions on behalf of a patient under a medical power of attorney, or any person recognized in law or custom as a patient's agent.

"Unanticipated outcome" means the outcome of the delivery of health care that differs from an expected result.

Added by Acts 2005, c. 649; Acts 2005, c. 692. Amended by Acts 2009, c. 414.

CHAPTER 21.2

MEDIATION

§ 8.01–581.21. Definitions

As used in this chapter:

"Mediation" means a process in which a mediator facilitates communication between the parties and, without deciding the issues or imposing a solution on the parties, enables them to understand and to reach a mutually agreeable resolution to their dispute.

"Mediation program" means a program through which mediators or mediation is made available and includes the director, agents and employees of the program.

"Mediator" means an impartial third party selected by agreement of the parties to a controversy to assist them in mediation.

Acts 1988, c. 623; Acts 1988, c. 857; Acts 2002, c. 718.

§ 8.01–581.22. Confidentiality; exceptions

All memoranda, work products and other materials contained in the case files of a mediator or mediation program are confidential. Any communication made in or in connection with the mediation, which relates to the controversy being mediated, including screening, intake, and scheduling a mediation, whether made to the mediator, mediation program staff, to a party, or to any other person, is confidential. However, a written mediated agreement signed by the parties shall not be confidential, unless the parties otherwise agree in writing.

Confidential materials and communications are not subject to disclosure in discovery or in any judicial or administrative proceeding except (i) where all parties to the mediation agree, in writing, to waive the confidentiality, (ii) in a subsequent action between the mediator or mediation program and a party to the mediation for damages arising out of the mediation, (iii) statements, memoranda, materials and other tangible evidence, otherwise subject to discovery, which were not prepared specifically for use in and actually used in the mediation, (iv) where a threat to inflict bodily injury is made, (v) where communications are intentionally used to plan, attempt to commit, or commit a crime or conceal an ongoing crime, (vi) where an ethics complaint is made against the mediator by a party to the mediation to the extent necessary for the complainant to prove misconduct and the mediator to defend against such complaint, (vii) where communications are sought or offered to prove or disprove a claim or complaint of misconduct or malpractice filed against a party's legal representative based on conduct occurring during a mediation, (viii) where communications are sought or offered to prove or disprove any of the grounds listed in § 8.01–581.26 in a proceeding to vacate a mediated agreement, or (ix) as provided by law or rule. The use of attorney work product in a mediation shall not result in a waiver of the attorney work product privilege.

Acts 1988, c. 623; Acts 1988, c.857; Acts 2002, c. 718. Amended by Acts 2013, c. 283; Acts 2013, c. 383.

§ 8.01–581.23. Civil immunity

When a mediation is provided by a mediator who is certified pursuant to guidelines promulgated by the Judicial Council of Virginia, or who is trained and serves as a mediator through the statewide mediation program established pursuant to § 2.2–1202.1, then that mediator, mediation programs for which that mediator is providing services, and a mediator co-mediating with that mediator shall be immune from civil liability for, or resulting from, any act or omission done or made while engaged in efforts to assist or conduct a mediation, unless the act or omission was made or done in bad faith, with malicious intent or in a manner exhibiting a willful, wanton disregard of the rights, safety or property of another. This language is not intended to abrogate any other immunity that may be applicable to a mediator.

Acts 1988, c. 623; Acts 1988, c.857; Acts 2002, c. 718; Acts 2012, c. 803; Acts 2012, c. 835.

§ 8.01–581.24. Standards and duties of mediators; confidentiality; liability

A mediator selected to conduct a mediation under this chapter may encourage and assist the parties in reaching a resolution of their dispute, but may not compel or coerce the parties into entering into a settlement agreement. A mediator has an obligation to remain impartial and free from conflicts of interest in each case, and to decline to participate further in a case should such partiality or conflict arise. Unless expressly authorized by the disclosing party, the mediator may not disclose to either party information relating to the subject matter of the mediation provided to him in confidence by the other. A mediator shall not disclose information exchanged or observations regarding the conduct and demeanor of the parties and their counsel during the mediation, unless the parties otherwise agree.

However, where the dispute involves the support of minor children of the parties, the parties shall disclose to each other and to the mediator the information to be used in completing the child support guidelines worksheet required by § 20–108.2. The guidelines computations and any reasons for deviation shall be incorporated in any written agreement by the parties.

Added by Acts 2002, c. 718.

§ 8.01–581.25. Effect of written settlement agreement

If the parties reach a settlement and execute a written agreement disposing of the dispute, the agreement is enforceable in the same manner as any other written contract. If the mediation involves a case that is filed in court, upon request of all parties and consistent with law and public policy, the court shall incorporate the written agreement into the terms of its final decree disposing of a case. In cases in which the dispute involves support for the minor children of the parties, an order incorporating a written agreement shall also include the child support guidelines worksheet and, if applicable, the written reasons for any deviation from the guidelines. The child support guidelines worksheet shall be attached to the order.

Added by Acts 2002, c. 718.

§ 8.01–581.26. Vacating orders and agreements

Upon the filing of an independent action by a party, the court shall vacate a mediated agreement reached in a mediation pursuant to this chapter, or vacate an order incorporating or resulting from such agreement, where:

1. The agreement was procured by fraud or duress, or is unconscionable;

2. If property or financial matters in domestic relations cases involving divorce, property, support or the welfare of a child are in dispute, the parties failed to provide substantial full disclosure of all relevant property and financial information; or

3. There was evident partiality or misconduct by the mediator, prejudicing the rights of any party.

For purposes of this section, "misconduct" includes failure of the mediator to inform the parties at the commencement of the mediation process that: (i) the mediator does not provide legal advice, (ii) any mediated agreement may affect the legal rights of the parties, (iii) each party to the mediation has the opportunity to consult with independent legal counsel at any time and is encouraged to do so, and (iv) each party to the mediation should have any draft agreement reviewed by independent counsel prior to signing the agreement.

Added by Acts 2002, c. 718.

CHAPTER 22

RECEIVERS, GENERAL AND SPECIAL

ARTICLE 1

GENERAL RECEIVERS

§ 8.01–582. Appointment of general receivers; their duties; audit of funds

Any circuit court may appoint a general receiver of the court, who may be the clerk of the court, and who shall hold his office at its pleasure. The general receiver's duty shall be, unless it is otherwise specially ordered, to receive, take charge of and hold all moneys paid under any judgment, order or decree of the court, and also to pay out or dispose of same as the court orders or decrees. Moneys held pursuant to this section shall be deemed public deposits as set forth in Chapter 44 (§ 2.2–4400 et seq.) of Title 2.2 and shall be invested in certificates of deposit or time deposits, and in accordance with the provisions of Chapter 45 (§ 2.2–4500 et seq.) of Title 2.2, as ordered by the court. Prior to or at the time of entry of any judgment, order or decree placing moneys under the control of the general receiver for the benefit of any specifically identified beneficiary, the general receiver shall file an affidavit with the court providing the beneficiary's name, date of birth, and social security number, as well as the proposed dates of final and periodic disbursements. Such affidavit shall be maintained under seal by the clerk unless otherwise ordered by the court, and the information therein shall be used solely for the purposes of financial management and reporting. Orders creating funds pursuant to this section shall include information necessary to make prudent investment and disbursement decisions but shall not include the personal identifying information set forth in the general receiver's affidavit.

Unless otherwise ordered by the court, the provisions of this section shall not apply to:

1. Cash or other money received in lieu of surety on any bond posted in any civil or criminal case, including but not limited to, bail bonds, appeal bonds in appeals from a district court or circuit court, bonds posted in connection with the filing of an attachment, detinue seizure or distress, suspending bonds, and performance bonds;

2. Cash or other money paid or deposited in the clerk's office prior to final disposition of the case, including but not limited to interpleaders or eminent domain; or

3. Cash or other money deposits in lieu of surety on any bond posted in the clerk's office which is not posted in connection with any civil or criminal case, including bonds posted by executors or administrators.

To this end, the general receiver is authorized to verify, receive, and give acquittances for all such moneys, as the court may direct. Any interest which accrues on the funds, minus allowable fees and bond costs, shall be credited and payable to the person or persons entitled to receive such funds.

All moneys received under this section are subject to audit by the Auditor of Public Accounts. The Auditor of Public Accounts shall prescribe mandatory record keeping and accounting standards for general receivers.

Acts 1977, c. 617; Acts 1979, c. 498; Acts 1988, c. 553; Acts 1990, c. 414; Acts 1991, c. 635; Acts 1999, c. 198; Acts 2003, c. 97.

§ 8.01-583. How securities taken and kept; power of receivers over same

The securities in which under the orders of the court such investments may be made shall be taken in the name of the general receiver and be kept by him, unless otherwise specially ordered. He shall have power to sell, transfer or collect the same, only upon order of the court; and in case of his death, resignation or removal his successor, or any person specially appointed by the court for that purpose, shall have like power.

Notwithstanding the foregoing paragraph, when a general receiver places funds in a security or investment which is insured by the Federal Deposit Insurance Corporation or other federal insurance agency, the general receiver shall to the extent practicable invest these funds so that insurance coverage is provided by the Federal Deposit Insurance Corporation or other federal insurance agency.

Acts 1977, c. 617; Acts 1988, c. 553; Acts 1990, c. 3.

§ 8.01-584. How dividends and interest collected and invested

The general receiver shall collect the dividends and interest on all the securities in which investments have been or may be made, under the orders or decrees of his court, or under the provisions of § 8.01-582, when and as often as the same may become due and payable thereon, and shall invest the same in like securities, unless the court has ordered or decreed some other investment or disposition to be made thereof; and in such case he shall invest or dispose of the same as the court shall have ordered or decreed.

Acts 1977, c. 617.

§ 8.01-585. How accounts kept by receivers

Each such general receiver shall keep an accurate and particular account of all moneys received, invested and paid out by him, showing the respective amounts to the credit of each case in the court and designating in the items the judgments, orders or decrees of court under which the respective sums have been received, invested or paid out. No later than October 1 of each year, he shall make a report to his court showing the balance to the credit of each case in the court in which money has been received by him, the manner of each case in the court in which money has been received by him, the manner in which it is invested, the amounts received, invested or paid out during the year ending June 30 of the current year, the approximate date on which the moneys held for the beneficiaries will become payable, and the whole amount then invested and subject to the future order of the court. A copy of the annual report shall be recorded in the trust fund order book. He shall, at any time when required by the court or the Auditor of Public Accounts so to do, furnish a statement of the amount subject to the order of the court in any case pending therein and any other information required by the court or the Auditor of Public Accounts as to any money or other property under his control. He shall annually make formal settlement of his accounts before the court or before the commissioner mentioned in § 8.01-617 which settlement shall be recorded as provided in § 8.01-619.

Acts 1977, c. 617; Acts 1988, c. 553; Acts 1989, c. 69.

§ 8.01-586. Inquiry as to unknown owners of funds

When funds are held because of inability to find the person to whom payable, such receiver may be ordered by the court to make inquiry and due diligence to ascertain such person in order that payment may be made; and for this purpose, and to secure any other relevant information, he shall have power to summon witnesses and take evidence; and he shall report specifically to the court in each annual report, and at any other time when so ordered by the court, the details and results of his efforts.

Acts 1977, c. 617; Acts 1988, c. 553.

§ 8.01-587. Liability of general receivers

Except as otherwise ordered by the court, for good cause shown, a general receiver shall be liable for any loss of income which results from his (i) failure to invest any money held by him pursuant to §§ 8.01-582 through 8.01-586 within sixty days of his receipt of the funds or (ii) failure to pay out any money so ordered by the court within sixty days of the court order. He shall be charged with interest from the date of the court order until such investment or payment is made.

Acts 1977, c. 617; Acts 1988, c. 841.

§ 8.01-588. Bonds generally

A general receiver shall annually give before the court a bond with surety to be approved by it, in such penalty as the court directs, sufficient at least to cover the probable amount under his control in any one year.

This section shall apply to the clerk if the clerk is appointed such receiver, and his official bond as clerk shall not cover money or property under his control as general receiver.

Acts 1977, c. 617; Acts 1988, c. 841.

§ 8.01–588.1. Bonds apportioned to funds under control; annual reports

The general receiver shall obtain bond through the Department of the Treasury's Division of Risk Management. No later than October 1 of each year, he shall report to the Division the amount of moneys under his control pursuant to § 8.01–582 as of June 30 of the current year and shall report the amount he expects to come under his control for the year ending on June 30 of the following year. He shall also report any other information reasonably required by the Division concerning bond coverage of moneys under his control. The cost of the bond shall be apportioned among the funds under his control as of the billing date based on the amount of each owner's or beneficiary's moneys. This section shall not apply to any financial institution fulfilling the requirements set out in § 6.2–1003 or § 6.2–1085.

Acts 1988, c. 841; Acts 2000, c. 618; Acts 2000, c. 632.

§ 8.01–589. Compensation and fees; when none allowed

A. A general receiver may retain from moneys received and held pursuant to § 8.01–582, compensation for his services in such amount as the court deems reasonable, but not exceeding:

1. Ten dollars at receipt of the originating court order to receive funds, deposit funds, and establish files and accounting records with respect to those funds;

2. Ten dollars when all funds held for a beneficiary or beneficiaries are disbursed;

3. Ten dollars per draft or check for periodic and final disbursements;

4. Five percent of the interest income earned;

5. Ten dollars for remitting funds to the State Treasurer and up to ten dollars per draft for remitting those funds; and

6. Fifty dollars for conducting a hearing to ascertain the identity or location of trust fund beneficiaries pursuant to § 8.01–586 as the court directs and $50 per hour for an appearance in court.

B. When direct out-of-pocket expenses are necessary to carry out an order of the court, a general receiver may receive reimbursement for such expenses as the court deems reasonable.

C. Notwithstanding the foregoing subsections, general receivers shall not deduct fees or otherwise be compensated for services with respect to those funds which should have been reported and then remitted to the State Treasurer in accordance with § 8.01–602 or 55–210.9:1.

A general receiver shall promptly report to the court the execution of the bond or bonds required in § 8.01–588 and make the reports and perform the duties required of him. No compensation shall be allowed him until he has performed the duties aforesaid.

If such receiver is the clerk of court and if compensation is allowed, it shall be fee and commission income to the office of such clerk in accordance with § 17.1–287.

Acts 1977, c. 617; Acts 1979, c. 498; Acts 1988, c. 841. Amended by Acts 2014, c. 65.

§ 8.01–590. Penalty for failure of duty

If a general receiver fail to keep the account, or to make out and return the statements required by § 8.01–585, he shall be subject to a fine of not less than $100 nor more than $1,000 to be imposed by the court at its discretion; and the condition of his official bond shall be taken to embrace the liability of himself and his sureties for any such fine.

Acts 1977, c. 617.

ARTICLE 2

SPECIAL RECEIVERS

§ 8.01–591. Notice required prior to appointment of receiver

Whenever the pleadings in any suit make out a proper case for the appointment of a receiver and application is made therefor to any court, such court shall designate the time and place for hearing such application, and shall require reasonable notice thereof to be given to the defendant and to all other parties having a substantial interest, either as owners of or lienors of record and lienors known to the plaintiff, in the subject matter. The court to whom such application is made shall inquire particularly of the applicant as to the parties so substantially interested in the subject matter, and such applicant, for any intentional or wilful failure to disclose fully all material information relating to such inquiry, may be adjudged in contempt of court.

Acts 1977, c. 617.

§ 8.01–592. Notice not required in emergencies

Section 8.01–591 shall not apply to those cases in which an emergency exists and it is necessary that a receiver be immediately appointed to preserve the subject matter. In such emergency cases a receiver may be appointed and the order of appointment shall state the emergency and necessity for immediate action, and shall require bond in proper amount of the applicant or someone for him with sufficient surety conditioned to protect and save harmless the owners, lienors and creditors, lien or general, in the subject matter taken over by the receiver, from all damages and injury properly and naturally flowing from such emergency appointment of a receiver.

Acts 1977, c. 617.

§ 8.01–593. Subsequent proceedings after emergency appointment

Such emergency appointment shall be limited to a period of not longer than thirty days, during which period notice shall be given by the applicant to all parties having a substantial interest, either as owner of or lienor in the subject matter, of any motion to extend such receivership; and upon the hearing on such motion, the court shall hear the matter de novo, and shall discharge such receiver, or shall appoint the same receiver, or other receivers to act with him, or new receivers as to the court may seem right. Unless such receivership shall be so extended, all the rights and powers of such emergency receiver over the subject matter, at the end of such period for which he shall have been appointed, shall cease and determine, and such receiver shall forthwith file with such court an account of his dealing with such estate. The notices required to be given under this section and §§ 8.01–591 and 8.01–592 shall be served, as to residents of this Commonwealth, in any of the modes prescribed by § 8.01–296, and as to nonresidents of this Commonwealth, or persons unknown, or in any case in which the number of persons to be given notice exceeds thirty, in the manner prescribed by § 8.01–319.

Acts 1977, c. 617.

§ 8.01–594. Notice not required to parties served with process

In any suit matured and docketed in which the bill or petition prays for the appointment of a receiver, no notice shall be required under this article to be given to any defendant upon whom process to answer such bill or petition shall have been served.

Acts 1977, c. 617.

§ 8.01–595. Preparation of list of creditors; notice to them

When a receiver has been appointed he shall immediately prepare or cause to be prepared a list of all creditors, lien and general, of the person, firm, corporation or of any other legal or commercial entity for which he is a receiver; and the court may by proper order compel any defendant for whom a receiver is appointed, or any officer of the corporation or of any other legal or commercial entity for whom the receiver is appointed, to furnish or deliver to the receiver a list, duly sworn to, of all creditors, lien or general, together with their addresses if known. The receiver shall then promptly notify by mail each creditor whose name and address has been ascertained of the appointment of the receiver.

When a permanent receiver is appointed he shall not be required to make a new list of creditors if a temporary receiver or a prior receiver appointed in the same proceedings has already prepared one which is adequate, nor shall he be required to mail other notices to creditors if the prior receiver has given proper notice to the parties entitled thereto.

Acts 1977, c. 617.

§ 8.01–596. No sale prior to such notification; exceptions

No court shall order the sale of any assets of the receivership until a receiver has reported to the court in writing that he has mailed such notices to such creditors at least five days prior to the filing of such report, except that the court may at any time permit the sale of perishable or seasonable goods when necessary to preserve the estate, or may permit the receiver to conduct the business for which he is a receiver as a going business and to sell in the usual course of such business.

Acts 1977, c. 617.

§ 8.01–597. Suits against receivers in certain cases

Any receiver of any property appointed by the courts of this Commonwealth may be sued in respect of any act or transaction of his in carrying on the business connected with such property, without the previous leave of the court in which such receiver was appointed; but the institution or pendency of such suit shall not interfere with or delay a sale by trustees under a deed of trust or a decree of sale for foreclosure of any mortgage upon such property.

Acts 1977, c. 617.

§ 8.01–598. Effect of judgment against receiver

A judgment against a receiver under § 8.01–597 shall not be a lien on the property or funds under the control of the court, nor shall any execution issue thereon, but upon filing a certified copy of such judgment in the cause in which the receiver was appointed, the court shall direct payment of such judgment in the same manner as if the claim upon which the judgment is based had been proved and allowed in such cause.

Acts 1977, c. 617.

§ 8.01–599. Warrant or motion for judgment against receiver in general district court, when to be tried

A warrant or motion for judgment before a general district court under §§ 8.01–597 and 8.01–598 may be tried not less than ten days after service of process.

Acts 1977, c. 617.

Article 3

General Provisions for Moneys Under Control of Court

§ 8.01-600. How money under control of court deposited; record kept; liability of clerk

A. This section pertains only to money held by the clerk of the circuit court, when the court orders moneys to be held by the clerk pursuant to this section. Where judgment is taken in the circuit court, upon motion of a party for good cause shown, the court may enter an order directing the clerk to hold moneys pursuant to this section. The clerk shall have the duty, unless it is otherwise specially ordered, to receive, take charge of, hold or invest in such manner as the court orders and also to pay out or dispose of these moneys as the court orders or decrees. To this end, the clerk is authorized to verify, receive, and give acquittances for all such moneys as the court may direct.

B. Orders creating funds pursuant to this section or § 8.01-582 shall include information necessary to make prudent investment and disbursement decisions. The orders shall include, except when it is unreasonable, the proposed dates of periodic and final disbursements. Prior to the entry of the order, the beneficiary or his representative shall file an affidavit with the court providing the beneficiary's name, date of birth, address and social security number. The affidavit shall be maintained under seal by the clerk unless otherwise ordered by the court, and the information therein shall be used solely for the purposes of financial management and reporting.

Unless otherwise ordered by the court, the provisions of this section shall not apply to:

1. Cash or other money received in lieu of surety on any bond posted in any civil or criminal case, including but not limited to bail bonds, appeal bonds in appeals from a district court or circuit court, bonds posted in connection with the filing of an attachment, detinue seizure or distress, suspending bonds, and performance bonds;

2. Cash or other money paid or deposited in the clerk's office prior to final disposition of the case, including but not limited to interpleaders or eminent domain; or

3. Cash or other money deposited in lieu of surety on any bond posted in the clerk's office which is not posted in connection with any civil or criminal case, including bonds posted by executors or administrators.

C. All deposits under this section shall be secured in accordance with the Virginia Security for Public Deposits Act (§ 2.2-4400 et seq.).

D. Moneys held pursuant to this section shall be invested in certificates of deposit and time deposits, and in accordance with the provisions of Chapter 45 (§ 2.2-4500 et seq.) of Title 2.2 as ordered by the court.

E. Any interest which accrues on the funds, minus allowable fees and bond costs, shall be credited and payable to the person or persons entitled to receive such funds. The court may order the clerk to consolidate for investment purposes money received under this section, with income received hereunder to be apportioned among the several accounts.

F. Except as otherwise ordered by the court, for good cause shown, the clerk shall be liable for any loss of income which results from his (i) failure to invest the money within sixty days of the court order creating the fund or (ii) failure to pay out any money so ordered by the court within sixty days of the court order. He shall be charged with interest from the date of the court order until such investment or payment is made.

G. The clerk shall keep an accurate and particular account of all moneys received, invested, and paid out by him, showing the respective amounts to the credit of each case in the court and designating in the items the judgments, orders or decrees of court under which the respective sums have been received, invested or paid out. At least annually and no later than October 1 of each year, the clerk shall make a report to the court showing the balance to the credit of each case in the court in which money has been received by him, the manner in which money has been received by him, the manner in which it is invested, the amounts received, invested or paid out during the year ending June 30 of the current year, the approximate date on which the moneys held for the beneficiaries will become payable, and the whole amount then invested and subject to the future order of the court. A copy of this report shall be recorded in the trust fund order book. The clerk shall, at any time when required by the court or the Auditor of Public Accounts to do so, furnish a statement of the amount subject to the order of the court in any case pending therein and any other information required by the court or the Auditor of Public Accounts as to any money or other property under his control before the court. When the clerk receives funds under this section, he shall be entitled to receive fees in accordance with § 17.1-287 in the amounts as specified for general receivers in § 8.01-589.

H. All moneys received under this section are subject to audit by the Auditor of Public Accounts.
Acts 1977, c. 617; Acts 1986, c. 644; Acts 1988, c. 841; Acts 1990, c. 3; Acts 1990, c. 414; Acts 1991, c. 635; Acts 2002, c. 832. Amended by Acts 2015, c. 633.

§ 8.01-600.1. Repealed by Acts 1993, c. 939

§ 8.01-601. Deposit with general receiver of certain funds under supervision of fiduciary and belonging to person under disability

Whenever it appears to any fiduciary as defined in § 8.01-2 that a person under a disability as defined in

§ 8.01–2 is not represented by a fiduciary as defined above and is entitled to funds not exceeding $3,000 under the supervision and control of the fiduciary in charge of such funds, he may report such fact to the commissioner of accounts of the court in which he was admitted to qualify. With the approval of such commissioner of accounts, the fiduciary in charge of such funds may deposit such funds with the general receiver of the court in which he was admitted to qualify. The general receiver shall issue a receipt to such fiduciary which shall show the source of such fund, the amount and to whom it belongs and shall enter the amount and such facts in his accounts.

Acts 1977, c. 617.

§ 8.01–602. Proceedings when owner of money under control of court unknown

Whenever any money has remained payable or distributable for one year in the custody or under the control of any court of this Commonwealth without anyone known to the court claiming the same, except funds deposited as compensation and damages in condemnation proceedings pursuant to § 25.1–237 pending a final order or pursuant to § 33.2–1019, the court shall cause such money to be reported and then remitted to the State Treasurer pursuant to §§ 55–210.9:1, 55–210.12 and 55–210.14.

The general receiver, if one has been appointed, and the clerk of the circuit court shall be responsible for identifying such money held by them in their respective control pursuant to §§ 8.01–582 and 8.01–600 and for petitioning the court to remit as provided in this section.

Acts 1977, c. 617; Acts 1982, c. 155; Acts 1984, c. 121; Acts 1987, c. 708; Acts 1988, c. 841.

§ 8.01–603. Repealed by Acts 1982, c. 155

§ 8.01–604. How State Treasurer to keep account of such money

The State Treasurer shall keep an account of all money thus paid to him, showing the amount thereof, when, by whom, and under what order it was paid, and the name of the court, and, as far as practicable, a description of the suit or proceeding in which the order was made, and, as far as known, the names of the parties thereto.

Acts 1977, c. 617; Acts 1981, c. 514; Acts 1982, c. 155.

§ 8.01–605. How person entitled to money paid into state treasury may recover it

Money paid into the state treasury under the provisions of this article shall be accounted for and disbursed under the procedures provided for in Article 4 of Chapter 11.1 of Title 55 (§ 55–210.12 et seq.).

Acts 1977, c. 617; Acts 1981, c. 514; Acts 1982, c. 155.

§ 8.01–606. Payment of small amounts to certain persons through court without intervention of fiduciary; authority of commissioners of accounts; certain fiduciaries exempt from accountings

A. Whenever there is due to any person, any sum of money from any source, not exceeding $25,000, the fund may be paid into the circuit court of the county or city in which the fund became due or such person resides. The court may, by an order entered of record, (i) pay the fund to the person to whom it is due, if the person is considered by the court competent to expend and use the same in his behalf, or (ii) pay the fund to some other person who is considered competent to administer it, for the benefit of the person entitled to the fund, without the intervention of a fiduciary, whether the other person resides within or without this Commonwealth. The clerk of the court shall take a receipt from the person to whom the money is paid, which shall show the source from which it was derived, the amount, to whom it belongs, and when and to whom it was paid. The receipt shall be signed and acknowledged by the person receiving the money, and entered of record in the book in the clerk's office in which the current fiduciary accounts are entered and indexed. Upon the payment into court the person owing the money shall be discharged of such obligation. No bond shall be required of the party to whom the money is paid by the court.

B. Whenever (i) it appears to the court having control of a fund, tangible personal property or intangible personal property or supervision of its administration, whether a suit is pending therefor or not, that a person under a disability who has no fiduciary, is entitled to a fund arising from the sale of lands for a division or otherwise, or a fund, tangible personal property or intangible personal property as distributee of any estate, or from any other source, (ii) a judgment, decree, or order for the payment of a sum of money or for delivery of tangible personal property or intangible personal property to a person under a disability who has no fiduciary is rendered by any court, and the amount to which such person is entitled or the value of the tangible personal property or intangible personal property is not more than $25,000, or (iii) a person under a disability is entitled to receive payments of income, tangible personal property or intangible personal property and the amount of the income payments is not more than $25,000 in any one year, or the value of the tangible personal property is not more than $25,000, or the current market value of the intangible personal property is not more than $25,000, the court may, without the intervention of a fiduciary, cause such fund, property or income to be paid or delivered to any person deemed by the court capable of properly handling it, to be used solely for the education, maintenance and support of the person under a disability. In any case in which an infant is entitled to such fund, property or income, the court may, upon its being made to appear that the infant is of sufficient age and discretion to use the fund, property or income judiciously, cause the fund to be paid or delivered directly to the infant.

C. Where judgment is taken in the general district court, upon motion of a party for good cause shown, the general district court judge may enter an order directing the clerk of the general district court to hold such funds in escrow for a period not to exceed 180 days to enable such party to file a petition pursuant to § 8.01–600 requesting that such funds be received and held by the clerk of the circuit court upon payment of fees in accordance with § 17.1–275. The party petitioning the circuit court shall provide the clerk of the general district court a certified copy of any order entered by the circuit court directing that such funds held by the clerk of the general district court be transferred to the clerk of the circuit court. If no such order is received by the clerk of the general district court within the 180–day period, the clerk of the general district court shall give notice to the parties that such funds shall be disbursed to the plaintiff for which judgment was entered in the general district court within 30 days after such notice.

D. Whenever a person is entitled to a fund or such property distributable by a fiduciary settling his accounts before the commissioner of accounts of the court in which the fiduciary qualified, and the amount or value of the fund or property, or the value of any combination thereof, is not more than $25,000, the commissioner of accounts may approve distribution thereof in the same manner and to the extent of the authority herein conferred upon a court including exemption from filing further accounts where the value of the fund being administered is less than $25,000.

E. Whenever an incapacitated person or infant is entitled to a fund or such property distributable by a fiduciary settling accounts before the commissioner of accounts of the court in which the fiduciary qualified and the will or trust instrument under which the fiduciary serves, authorizes the fiduciary to distribute the property or fund to the incapacitated person or infant without the intervention of a guardian, conservator or committee, and the amount or value of such fund or property, or the value of any combination thereof, is not more than $25,000, the commissioner of accounts may approve distribution thereof in the same manner and to the extent of the authority hereinabove conferred upon a court or judge thereof.

F. Whenever a fiduciary is administering funds not exceeding $25,000, the circuit court of the county or city in which the fund is being administered by order entered of record may authorize the fiduciary, when considered competent to administer the funds, to continue to administer the funds for the benefit of the person entitled to the fund without the necessity of filing any further accounts, whether such person resides within or without this Commonwealth. The clerk of the court shall take a receipt from the fiduciary, which shall show the amount of the fund remaining, to whom it belongs, and the date the court entered the order exempting the filing of further accounts. The receipt shall be signed and acknowledged by the fiduciary, and entered of record in the book in the clerk's office in which the current fiduciary accounts are entered and indexed. No surety shall be required on the bond of a fiduciary granted an exemption from filing any further accounts.

G. Whenever a fiduciary qualifies pursuant to § 64.2–454 for the sole purpose of prosecuting or defending an action, the court in which the fiduciary qualifies or the commissioner of accounts for such court may exempt the fiduciary from filing further accounts where the fiduciary is not administering any funds and has no power of sale over any real estate the decedent owned.

Acts 1977, c. 462; Acts 1977, c. 617; Acts 1978, c. 525; Acts 1980, c. 544; Acts 1985, c. 216; Acts 1987, c. 378; Acts 1995, c. 405; Acts 1997, c. 801, eff. Jan. 1, 1998; Acts 2003, c. 195. Amended by Acts 2012, c. 43; Acts 2015, c. 129; Acts 2015, c. 130; Acts 2015, c. 633.

CHAPTER 23

COMMISSIONERS IN CHANCERY

§ 8.01–607. Appointment and removal

A. Each circuit court may, from time to time, appoint such commissioners in chancery as may be deemed necessary for the convenient dispatch of the business of such court. Such commissioners shall be removable at pleasure.

B. Commissioners in chancery may be appointed in cases in circuit court, including uncontested divorce cases, only when:

1. There is agreement by the parties with the concurrence of the court; or

2. Upon (i) motion of a party, or (ii) upon motion of the court, sua sponte. The court shall make a finding of good cause shown in each individual case.

Acts 1977, c. 617. Amended by Acts 2005, c. 885.

§ 8.01–608. How accounts referred

Accounts to be taken in any case shall be referred to a commissioner appointed pursuant to § 8.01–607, unless the parties interested agree, or the court shall deem it proper, that they be referred to some other person.

Acts 1977, c. 617.

§ 8.01–609. Duties; procedure generally

Every commissioner shall examine, and report upon, any matters as may be referred to him by any court. The proceedings before a commissioner in chancery shall be conducted as set forth in this chapter and the Rules of Court.

Acts 1977, c. 617; Acts 1981, c. 613; Acts 1992, c. 297.

§ 8.01–609.1. Commissioners in chancery

A commissioner in chancery may, for services rendered by virtue of his office, charge the following fees, to wit:

For services which might be performed by notaries, the fees for such services and for any other service such fees as the court by which the commissioner is appointed may from time to time prescribe.

A commissioner shall not be compelled to make out or return a report until his fees therefor are paid or security given him to pay so much as may be adjudged appropriate by the court to which the report is to be returned or by the judge thereof in vacation, unless the court finds cause to order it to be made out and returned without such payment or security.

Acts 1998, c. 872, eff. Oct. 1, 1998.

§ 8.01–610. Weight to be given commissioner's report

The report of a commissioner in chancery shall not have the weight given to the verdict of a jury on conflicting evidence, but the court shall confirm or reject such report in whole or in part, according to the view which it entertains of the law and the evidence.

Acts 1977, c. 617.

§ 8.01–611. Notice of time and place of taking account

The court, ordering an account to be taken, may direct that notice of the time and place of taking it be published once a week for two successive weeks in a newspaper meeting the requirements of § 8.01–324, and may also require notice to be served on the parties in the manner set forth in the Rules of Court for the taking of depositions.

Acts 1977, c. 617.

§ 8.01–612. Commissioner may summons witnesses

A commissioner in chancery, to whom has been referred any matter, may compel the attendance of all needed witnesses by summons. A summonsed witness who fails to attend shall be reported to the court for appropriate contempt proceedings.

Acts 1977, c. 617.

§ 8.01–613. Commissioner may ask instructions of court

A commissioner, who has doubts as to any point which arises before him, may, in writing, submit the point to the court, who may instruct him thereon.

Acts 1977, c. 617.

§ 8.01–614. His power to adjourn his proceedings

A commissioner in chancery may adjourn his proceedings from time to time, after the day to which notice was given, without any new notice, until his report is completed; and, when it is completed, it may be filed in the clerk's office at any time thereafter. The commissioner may, if it shall appear to him necessary, adjourn such proceedings, to any place within the Commonwealth, and there continue such proceedings and take depositions and other evidence in like manner and with like force and effect as if the same were done in the place where he was appointed, and the commissioner shall have the power to compel the attendance of witnesses before him in the manner prescribed by § 8.01–612.

Acts 1977, c. 617.

§ 8.01–615. When cause heard on report; time for filing exceptions

A cause may be heard by the court upon a commissioner's report. Subject to the Rules of Court regarding dispensing with notice of taking proofs and other proceedings, reasonable notice of such hearing shall be given to counsel of record and to parties not represented by counsel. Exceptions to the commissioner's report shall be filed within ten days after the report has been filed with the court, or for good cause shown, at a later time specified by the court.

This section shall not apply to the report of a commissioner appointed to sell property; in such cases the report of such commissioner, when filed in the clerk's office, shall be either confirmed, modified, or rejected forthwith.

Acts 1977, c. 617; Acts 1978, c. 237; Acts 1981, c. 500; Acts 1982, c. 339.

§ 8.01–616. Delivery of original papers of suit by clerk to commissioner

The clerk of a court shall, upon the request of any commissioner in chancery who has before him for execution an order made in such action, deliver to him the original papers thereof; and it shall not be necessary for the clerk to copy such papers, nor shall he charge any fee for copies of any of them, unless the same be specially ordered. The commissioner to whom such papers may be delivered, shall give his receipt therefor, and return the papers as speedily as possible to the office of the clerk of the court.

Acts 1977, c. 617.

§ 8.01–617. Settlement of accounts of special receivers and special commissioners

Every circuit court, by an order entered of record, shall appoint one of its commissioners in chancery, who shall hold office at its pleasure, to state and settle the accounts of all special receivers and of all special commissioners holding funds or evidences of debt subject to the order of the court.

All special receivers and special commissioners shall, unless their accounts have been previously verified and approved by the court, and ordered to be recorded, with reasonable promptness, and not longer than four months after any money in their hands should be distributed or at other intervals specified by the court, present to such commissioner in chancery an accurate statement of all receipts and disbursements, duly signed and supported by proper vouchers; and the commissioner in chancery shall examine and verify the same, and attach his certificate thereto approving it, if it is correct, or stating any errors or inaccuracies therein, and file same in the cause in which the special receiver or special commissioner was appointed, and present the same to the court.

The court may at any time appoint any of its other commissioners in chancery to perform the duties herein required in any case in which the regular commissioner in chancery appointed hereunder is himself the special receiver or special commissioner whose accounts are to be settled.

For his services performed hereunder the commissioner in chancery shall receive such compensation as the court allows, to be paid out of the fund in the hands of the special receiver or special commissioner.

If any special receiver or special commissioner fails to make settlement as herein required within the time herein provided, he shall forfeit his compensation, or so much thereof as the court orders.

The court may order its general receiver also to state and settle his accounts in the manner herein provided. When a general receiver settles his accounts before a commissioner of accounts or commissioner in chancery, fees charged by the commissioner are to be reasonable but may not exceed $100 per general receiver settlement or $1 per disbursement made by the general receiver as reflected in the settlement, whichever is greater.

Acts 1977, c. 617; Acts 1988, c. 553.

§ 8.01–618. Reports of such settlements; when new bond required

The court shall examine the reports required by § 8.01–617, when the same are made to it; and, if satisfied of the correctness thereof, shall order them to be recorded. If it appears from the report of the commissioner that any bond of a receiver, or any bond or other security given by any person to whom money has been loaned under its order, is insufficient, the court shall order additional security to be given, or a new bond to be executed before it, in such penalty as may seem right, and with sufficient sureties. But the execution of such new bond shall not discharge the sureties in any prior bond for their liability for acts of the principal obligor done previous to the execution of such new bond.

Acts 1977, c. 617.

§ 8.01–618.1. Fees of special receivers and commissioners for reports

Special receivers and commissioners may charge, for the reports made under § 8.01–617, the same fees allowed by law to commissioners in chancery for other reports, to be paid out of the fund in court, and charged to the respective cases therein, in such proportions as the court deems appropriate.

Acts 1977, c. 624, § 14.1-133.1; Acts 1998, c. 872, eff. Oct. 1, 1998.

§ 8.01–619. Recordation of reports of such settlements

The circuit court clerk shall record reports of receivers and commissioners when approved by the court, in a fiduciary book and properly index same to show the name of the receiver or commissioner and also the style of the suit in which the report is made; and such book shall be kept as a public record in the office of the clerk.

Acts 1977, c. 617.

CHAPTER 24

INJUNCTIONS

§ 8.01–620. General jurisdiction of circuit court to award injunctions

Every circuit court shall have jurisdiction to award injunctions, including cases involving violations of the Uniform Statewide Building Code, [1] whether the judgment or proceeding enjoined be in or out of the circuit, or the party against whose proceedings the injunction be asked resides in or out of the circuit.

Acts 1977, c. 617; Acts 1995, c. 310.

[1] See § 39–97 et seq.

§ 8.01–621. Repealed by Acts 1987, c. 567

§ 8.01–622. Injunction to protect plaintiff in suit for specific property

An injunction may be awarded to protect any plaintiff in a suit for specific property, pending either at law or in equity, against injury from the sale, removal, or concealment of such property.

Acts 1977, c. 617.

§ 8.01–622.1. Injunction against assisted suicide; damages; professional sanctions

A. Any person who knowingly and intentionally, with the purpose of assisting another person to commit or attempt to commit suicide, (i) provides the physical means by which another person commits or attempts to commit suicide or (ii) participates in a physical act by which another person commits or attempts to commit suicide shall be liable for damages as provided in this section and may be enjoined from such acts.

B. A cause of action for injunctive relief against any person who is reasonably expected to assist or attempt to assist a suicide may be maintained by any person who is the spouse, parent, child, sibling or guardian of, or a current or former licensed health care provider of, the person who would commit suicide; by an attorney for the Commonwealth with appropriate jurisdiction; or by the Attorney General. The injunction shall prevent the person from assisting any suicide in the Commonwealth.

C. A spouse, parent, child or sibling of a person who commits or attempts to commit suicide may recover compensatory and punitive damages in a civil action from any person who provided the physical means for the suicide or attempted suicide or who participated in a physical act by which the other person committed or attempted to commit suicide.

D. A licensed health care provider who assists or attempts to assist a suicide shall be considered to have engaged in unprofessional conduct for which his certificate or license to provide health care services in the Commonwealth shall be suspended or revoked by the licensing authority.

E. Nothing in this section shall be construed to limit or conflict with § 54.1–2971.01 or the Health Care Decisions Act (§ 54.1–2981 et seq.). This section shall not apply to a licensed health care provider who (i) administers, prescribes or dispenses medications or procedures to relieve another person's pain or discomfort and without intent to cause death, even if the medication or procedure may hasten or increase the risk of death, or (ii) withholds or withdraws life-prolonging procedures as defined in § 54.1–2982. This section shall not apply to any person who properly administers a legally prescribed medication without intent to cause death, even if the medication may hasten or increase the risk of death.

F. For purposes of this section:

"Licensed health care provider" means a physician, surgeon, podiatrist, osteopath, osteopathic physician and surgeon, physician assistant, nurse, dentist or pharmacist licensed under the laws of this Commonwealth.

"Suicide" means the act or instance of taking one's own life voluntarily and intentionally.

Acts 1998, c. 624. Amended by Acts 2015, c. 710.

§ 8.01–623. Injunction against decree subject to bill of review; limitations to bill of review

A court allowing a bill of review may award an injunction to the decree to be reviewed. But no bill of review shall be allowed to a final decree, unless it be exhibited within six months next after such decree, except that a person under a disability as defined in § 8.01–2 may exhibit the same within six months after the removal of his or her disability. In no case shall such a bill be filed without the leave of court first obtained, unless it be for error of law apparent upon the face of the record.

Acts 1977, c. 617.

§ 8.01–624. Duration of temporary injunctions to be fixed therein

When any court authorized to award injunctions shall grant a temporary injunction, either with or without notice to the adverse party, such court shall prescribe in the injunction order the time during which such injunction shall be effective and at the expiration of that time such injunction shall stand dissolved unless, before the expiration thereof, it be enlarged. Such injunction may be enlarged or a further injunction granted by the court in which the cause is pending or by the court to whom the bill is addressed in the event the cause be not matured, after reasonable notice to the adverse party, or to his attorney of record of the time and place of moving for the same.

Acts 1977, c. 617.

§ 8.01–625. Dissolution of injunctions

Any court wherein an injunction has been awarded may at any time when such injunction is in force dissolve the same after reasonable notice to the adverse party, or to his attorney of record, in which notice shall be set forth the grounds upon which such dissolution will be asked, unless such grounds be set forth in an answer previously filed in the case by the party giving such notice.

Acts 1977, c. 617.

§ 8.01–626. When court grants or refuses injunction, justice of Supreme Court or judge of Court of Appeals may review it

Wherein a circuit court (i) grants an injunction or (ii) refuses an injunction or (iii) having granted an injunction, dissolves or refuses to enlarge it, an aggrieved party may, within 15 days of the court's order, present a petition for review to a justice of the Supreme Court; however, if the issue concerning the injunction arose in a case over which the Court of Appeals would have appellate jurisdiction under § 17.1–405 or 17.1–406, the petition for review shall be initially presented to a judge of the Court of Appeals within 15 days of the court's order. The aggrieved party shall serve a copy of the petition for review on the counsel for the opposing party, which may file a response within seven days from the date of service unless the court determines a shorter time frame. The petition for review shall be accompanied by a copy of the proceedings, including the original papers and the court's order respecting the injunction. The justice or judge may take such action thereon as he considers appropriate under the circumstances of the case.

When a judge of the Court of Appeals has initially acted upon a petition for review of an order of a circuit court respecting an injunction, a party aggrieved by such action of the judge of the Court of Appeals may, within 15 days of the order of the judge of the Court of Appeals, present a petition for review of such order to a justice of the Supreme Court if the case would otherwise be appealable to the Supreme Court in accordance with § 17.1–410. The aggrieved party shall serve a copy of the petition for review on the counsel for the opposing party, which may file a response within seven days from the date of service unless the court determines a shorter time frame. The petition for review shall be accompanied by a copy of the proceedings before the circuit court, including the original papers and the circuit court's order respecting the injunction, and a copy of the order of the judge of the Court of Appeals from which review is sought. The justice may take such action thereon as he considers appropriate under the circumstances of the case.

Acts 1977, c. 617; Acts 1984, c. 703. Amended by Acts 2014, c. 526.

§ 8.01–627. To what clerk order for injunction directed

Every order, awarding an injunction made under § 8.01–620 or § 8.01–626, shall be directed to the clerk of the court which has venue under § 8.01–261 and the proceedings thereupon shall be as if the order has been made by such court.

Acts 1977, c. 617.

§ 8.01–628. Equity of prayer for temporary injunction to be shown by affidavit or otherwise

No temporary injunction shall be awarded unless the court shall be satisfied of the plaintiff's equity. An application for a temporary injunction may be supported or opposed by an affidavit or verified pleading.

Acts 1977, c. 617. Amended by Acts 2015, c. 125.

§ 8.01–629. Notice required

Any court may require that reasonable notice be given to the adverse party, or to his attorney of record, of the time and place of moving for it, before the injunction is granted, if, in the opinion of the court, it be proper that such notice be given.

Acts 1977, c. 617.

§ 8.01–630. Forthcoming bond in connection with injunction against removal of property

A court awarding a temporary injunction to restrain the removal of property out of this Commonwealth may require bond with security to be given before such officer and in such penalty as the court may direct, with condition to have the property forthcoming to abide the future order or decree of the court and, unless such bond be given, may order the officer serving its process to take possession of the property and keep it until the bond be given or until further order of the court.

Acts 1977, c. 617. Amended by Acts 2012, c. 8; Acts 2012, c. 77.

§ 8.01–631. Injunction bond

A. Except in the case of a fiduciary or any other person from whom in the opinion of the court awarding an injunction it may be improper or unnecessary to require bond, no temporary injunction shall take effect until the movant gives bond with security in an amount that the trial court considers proper to pay the costs and damages sustained by any party found to have been incorrectly enjoined, with such conditions as the trial court may prescribe.

B. When an appeal is taken from an interlocutory order or final judgment granting, dissolving, or denying a permanent injunction, and while the appeal is pending, the trial court in its discretion may suspend, modify, restore, or grant an injunction during the pendency of the appeal upon such terms as to bond or otherwise as it considers proper for the security of the rights of the adverse party.

C. The bond shall be given before the clerk of the court in which the injunction is awarded.

D. An order by the trial court under subsection A or B may be modified or vacated by the appellate court having jurisdiction over the appeal in accordance with § 8.01–676.1.

E. For any temporary or permanent injunction sought by, or awarded to, the Commonwealth, or any of its officers or agencies, no bond shall be required.

Acts 1977, c. 617. Amended by Acts 2012, c. 8; Acts 2012, c. 77.

§ 8.01–631.1. Environmental injunction; financial capacity

A court awarding a temporary or permanent injunction to the Commonwealth, or any of its officers or agencies, requiring any party to (i) abate, control, prevent, remove, or contain any substantial or imminent threat to public health or the environment, or (ii) develop a closure plan to address any substantial or imminent threat to public health or the environment that may result when a business ceases operation, shall require the defendant to demonstrate its financial capability to comply with the injunction. Financial capability may be demonstrated, at the court's discretion, by the establishment of an escrow account, the creation of a trust fund, the submission of a bond, or such other instruments as the court may deem appropriate.

For the purposes of this section "ceases operation" means to cease conducting the normal operation of a business in the Commonwealth where it would be reasonable to expect that such operation will not be resumed by the owner. The term shall not include the ordinary sale or transfer of a business.

Acts 1991, c. 236.

§ 8.01–632. How surety in forthcoming bond may obtain additional security

Any surety in the forthcoming bond described in §§ 8.01–630 and 8.01–631, or his personal representative, may move for and obtain an order for other or additional security, in the same manner as the defendant in an injunction.

Acts 1977, c. 617.

§ 8.01–633. Damages on dissolution

When an injunction to stay proceedings on a judgment or decree for money is dissolved wholly or in part there shall be paid to the party having such judgment or decree damages at the rate of ten per centum per annum from the time the injunction took effect until the dissolution, on such sum as appears to be due, including the costs; but the court wherein the injunction is may direct that no such damages be paid, or that there be paid only such portion thereof as it may deem just. In a case wherein a forthcoming bond was forfeited, and no execution was had thereon before the injunction took effect, a court awarding such execution shall include in its judgment or decree damages as aforesaid. In other cases damages may be included in the execution on the judgment or decree to which the injunction was awarded.

Acts 1977, c. 617.

§ 8.01–634. Dismissal of injunction bill

When an injunction is wholly dissolved the bill shall stand dismissed with costs, unless sufficient cause be shown against such dismissal.

Acts 1977, c. 617.

CHAPTER 25

EXTRAORDINARY WRITS

ARTICLE 1

WRIT OF QUO WARRANTO

§ 8.01–635. Common-law writ of quo warranto and information in the nature of writ of quo warranto abolished; statutory writ of quo warranto established

The common-law writ of quo warranto and information in the nature of writ of quo warranto is hereby abolished and superseded by the statutory writ of quo warranto.

Acts 1977, c. 617.

§ 8.01–636. In what cases writ issued

A writ of quo warranto may be issued and prosecuted in the name of the Commonwealth in any of the following cases:

1. Against a domestic corporation, other than a municipal corporation, for the misuse or nonuse of its corporate privileges and franchises, or for the exercise of a privilege or franchise not conferred upon it by law, or when a charter of incorporation has been obtained by it for a fraudulent purpose, or for a purpose not authorized by law;

2. Against a person for the misuse or nonuse of any privilege conferred upon him by law;

2a. Against a person engaged in the practice of any profession without being duly authorized or licensed to do so;

3. Against any person or persons acting as a corporation, other than a municipal corporation, without authority of law; and

4. Against any person who intrudes into or usurps any public office. But no writ shall be issued or prosecuted against any person now in office for any cause which would have been available in support of a proceeding to contest his election.

Provided that nothing herein shall be construed to give jurisdiction to any court to judge the election, qualifications, or returns of the members of either house of the General Assembly.

Acts 1977, c. 617; Acts 1980, c. 705.

§ 8.01–637. By whom filed; when leave granted and writ issued

A. The Attorney General or attorney for the Commonwealth of any county or city of which the circuit court has jurisdiction of the proceeding, at his own instance or at the relation of any interested person, or any interested person, may apply to such court by petition verified by oath for a writ of quo warranto. In case of an application under § 8.01–636 2a the term "any interested person" shall include any attorney licensed to practice law in this Commonwealth and qualified to practice before the Supreme Court of Virginia, or the circuit court in which the petition is filed.

B. If, in the opinion of the court, the matters stated in the petition are sufficient in law to authorize the issuance of such writ, a writ shall issue thereon, commanding the sheriff to summon the defendant to appear at a date set forth in the writ.

C. If the petition is filed on the relation of any person or by any person at his own instance, before the clerk shall issue the writ the court shall require the relator or person to give bond with sufficient surety, to be approved by the clerk, to indemnify the Commonwealth against all costs and expenses of the proceedings, in case the same shall not be recovered from and paid by the defendant.

Acts 1977, c. 617; Acts 1980, c. 705.

§ 8.01–638. Repealed by Acts 1987, c. 567

§ 8.01–639. How summons directed and served

The writ and a copy of the petition attached thereto may be directed to the sheriff of any county or city and shall be served as in other actions.

Acts 1977, c. 617.

§ 8.01–640. Judgment when defendant fails to appear

If the defendant fails to appear in accordance with the writ, the court may hear proof of the allegations of the petition, and if the allegations are sustained, shall give judgment accordingly.

Acts 1977, c. 617.

§ 8.01–641. Reopening same when made on service by publication

But if service is made by publication, the defendant against whom the judgment is rendered may file a motion within thirty days from the rendition of judgment to have such judgment set aside, upon giving bond with good security as prescribed by the court, with condition to pay all such costs as shall be awarded in the cause against the defendant. The defendant may then make such defense to the petition as he might have made, and in the same manner, before the judgment was rendered.

Acts 1977, c. 617.

§ 8.01–642. Pleading when defendant appears

The defendant against whom the writ was issued may plead, demur or answer the petition within the time set forth in the writ for his appearance.

Acts 1977, c. 617.

§ 8.01–643. Trial; verdict; judgment; costs; attorney's fee

Unless the defendant shall ask for a trial by jury, the court shall hear the same. If the case is tried by jury and the defendant is found guilty as to only a part of the charges, the verdict shall be guilty as to such part and shall particularly specify the same. As to the residue of such charges, the verdict shall be not guilty.

If the defendant appears and is found guilty the court shall give such judgment as is appropriate and authorized by law and for costs incurred in the prosecution of the information, including a reasonable attorney's fee to be prescribed by the court.

Acts 1977, c. 617.

Article 2

Mandamus and Prohibition

§ 8.01–644. Application for mandamus or prohibition

Except as provided in § 2.2–3713, application for a writ of mandamus or a writ of prohibition shall be on petition verified by oath, after the party against whom the writ is prayed has been served with a copy of the petition and notice of the intended application a reasonable time before such application is made.

Acts 1977, c. 617. Amended by Acts 2009, c. 634.

§ 8.01–644.1. Limitations of actions for petition for mandamus

A petition for extraordinary writ of mandamus, filed by or on behalf of a person confined in a state correctional facility, shall be brought within one year after the cause of action accrues.

Acts 1998, c. 596.

§ 8.01–645. What petition to state; where presented

The petition shall state plainly and concisely the grounds of the application, concluding with a prayer for the writ, and shall be presented to the court having jurisdiction, unless the application is to the Court of Appeals or the Supreme Court.

Acts 1977, c. 617; Acts 1984, c. 703.

§ 8.01-646. When writ awarded if no defense made

When the application is made, on proof of notice and service of the copy of the petition as aforesaid, if the defendant fails to appear, or appearing fails to make defense, and the petition states a proper case for the writ, a peremptory writ shall be awarded with costs.

Acts 1977, c. 617.

§ 8.01-647. Defense; how made

The defendant may file a demurrer or answer on oath to the petition, or both. The court may permit amendments of the pleadings as in other cases.

Acts 1977, c. 617.

§ 8.01-648. What judgment to be rendered

The court shall award or deny the writ according to the law and facts of the case, with or without costs.

Acts 1977, c. 617.

§ 8.01-649. Proceedings when application is to Supreme Court or Court of Appeals

If the application is to the Court of Appeals or the Supreme Court, the procedure shall be in accordance with the provisions of Rules of Court.

Acts 1977, c. 617; Acts 1984, c. 703.

§ 8.01-650. Suspension of proceedings, where prohibition applied for

On petition for a writ of prohibition, the court may, at any time before or after the application for the writ is made, make an order, a copy of which shall be served on the defendant, suspending the proceedings sought to be prohibited until the final decision of the cause.

Acts 1977, c. 617.

§ 8.01-651. Suspension of proceedings by justice of Supreme Court or judge of Court of Appeals

Whenever a court having jurisdiction refuses to suspend proceedings as provided in § 8.01-650 of this chapter, a copy of the proceedings in court, with any orders entered in the proceedings, may be presented to a judge of the Court of Appeals, if an application for a writ of prohibition is pending in that court, or to a justice of the Supreme Court if the application for a writ is pending there. Such judge or justice may thereupon award a suspension of the proceedings sought to be prohibited until the final decision of the cause.

Acts 1977, c. 617; Acts 1984, c. 703.

§ 8.01-652. Service of writ; how obedience enforced

Service of a copy of the order awarding the writ shall be equivalent to service of the writ, and obedience to the writ or order may be enforced by process of contempt.

Acts 1977, c. 617.

§ 8.01-653. Mandamus to secure construction of act directing payment out of treasury of the Commonwealth

Whenever the Comptroller or the Treasurer of the Commonwealth shall notify the Attorney General, in writing, that they, or either of them, entertain such doubt respecting the proper construction or interpretation of any act of the General Assembly which appropriates or directs the payment of money out of the treasury of the Commonwealth, or respecting the constitutionality of any such act, that they, or either of them, do not feel that it would be proper or safe to pay such money until there has been a final adjudication by the Supreme Court determining any and all such questions, and that, for such reason, they will not make payments pursuant to such act until such adjudication has been made, the Attorney General may file in such court a petition for a writ of mandamus directing or requiring the Comptroller or Treasurer of the Commonwealth, or both, to pay such money as provided by any such act at such time in the future as may be proper. In order to avoid delays in payments after the time for making them has arrived, any such petition may be filed at any time after the passage of any such act although the time for making such payments has not arrived and no demand for such payments has been made. In any such proceeding the court shall consider and determine all questions raised by the Attorney General's petition pertaining to the constitutionality or interpretation of any such act, even though some of such questions may not be necessary to the decision of the question of the duty of such Comptroller and Treasurer of the Commonwealth to make payment of the moneys appropriated or directed to be paid.

The Comptroller and the Treasurer of the Commonwealth, or either of them, as the case may be, shall be made a party or parties defendant to any such petition and the court may, in its discretion, cause such other officers or persons to be made parties defendant as it may deem proper, and may make such order respecting the employment of an attorney or attorneys for any officer of the Commonwealth who is a party defendant as may be appropriate. The compensation of any such attorney shall be fixed by such court and upon its order paid out of the appropriation to the office or department of any such public officer represented by any such attorney in such proceeding.

Acts 1977, c. 617.

§ 8.01-653.1. Mandamus to secure construction of act granting power to incur certain obligations for transportation needs

Whenever the Comptroller notifies the Attorney General in writing that he entertains doubt respecting the constitutionality of any act of the General Assembly granting an agency of the Commonwealth or other governmental board or entity of the Commonwealth general powers to incur obligations for transportation needs where such obligations are subject to authorization by the General Assembly, the Attorney General shall file in the Supreme Court a petition for a writ of mandamus directing or requiring the Comptroller to pay the money as provided by any such act at such time in the future as may be proper. In order to expedite long-term planning by such an agency of the Commonwealth or other governmental board or entity of the Commonwealth and expedite its advice to the Governor and the General Assembly on possible alternative means of financing Virginia's transportation needs, the petition may be filed after the enactment date of any such act, although (i) the General Assembly may not have enacted legislation specifically authorizing such an agency of the Commonwealth or other governmental board or entity of the Commonwealth to enter into specific obligations under its general authority or (ii) if such specific obligations have been authorized, the time for making payments has not arrived and no demand for payment has been made. The court shall consider and determine all questions raised by the Attorney General's petition pertaining to the constitutionality or interpretation of any such act, even though some of the questions may not be necessary to the decision regarding the duty of the Comptroller to make payment of the moneys appropriated or directed to be paid.

The Comptroller shall be made a party defendant to the petition. The court may, in its discretion, cause other officers or persons to be made parties defendant as it may deem proper, and may make such order respecting the employment of an attorney or attorneys for any officer of the Commonwealth who is a party defendant as may be appropriate. The compensation of any attorney so employed shall be fixed by the court and upon its order paid out of the appropriation to the office or department of the public officer represented by the attorney in the proceeding.

Acts 1986 Sp.Sess., c.14; Acts 1986 Sp.Sess., c. 16.

Article 3

Habeas Corpus

§ 8.01–654. When and by whom writ granted; what petition to contain

A. 1. The writ of habeas corpus ad subjiciendum shall be granted forthwith by the Supreme Court or any circuit court, to any person who shall apply for the same by petition, showing by affidavits or other evidence probable cause to believe that he is detained without lawful authority.

2. A petition for writ of habeas corpus ad subjiciendum, other than a petition challenging a criminal conviction or sentence, shall be brought within one year after the cause of action accrues. A habeas corpus petition attacking a criminal conviction or sentence, except as provided in § 8.01–654.1 for cases in which a death sentence has been imposed, shall be filed within two years from the date of final judgment in the trial court or within one year from either final disposition of the direct appeal in state court or the time for filing such appeal has expired, whichever is later.

B. 1. With respect to any such petition filed by a petitioner held under criminal process, and subject to the provisions of subsection C of this section and of § 17.1–310, only the circuit court which entered the original judgment order of conviction or convictions complained of in the petition shall have authority to issue writs of habeas corpus. If a district court entered the original judgment order of conviction or convictions complained of in the petition, only the circuit court for the city or county wherein the district court sits shall have authority to issue writs of habeas corpus. Hearings on such petition, where granted in the circuit court, may be held at any circuit court within the same circuit as the circuit court in which the petition was filed, as designated by the judge thereof.

2. Such petition shall contain all allegations the facts of which are known to petitioner at the time of filing and such petition shall enumerate all previous applications and their disposition. No writ shall be granted on the basis of any allegation the facts of which petitioner had knowledge at the time of filing any previous petition. The provisions of this section shall not apply to a petitioner's first petition for a writ of habeas corpus when the sole allegation of such petition is that the petitioner was deprived of the right to pursue an appeal from a final judgment of conviction or probation revocation, except that such petition shall contain all facts pertinent to the denial of appeal that are known to the petitioner at the time of the filing, and such petition shall certify that the petitioner has filed no prior habeas corpus petitions attacking the conviction or probation revocation.

3. Such petition may allege detention without lawful authority through challenge to a conviction, although the sentence imposed for such conviction is suspended or is to be served subsequently to the sentence currently being served by petitioner.

4. In the event the allegations of illegality of the petitioner's detention can be fully determined on the basis of recorded matters, the court may make its determination whether such writ should issue on the basis of the record.

5. The court shall give findings of fact and conclusions of law following a determination on the record or after hearing, to be made a part of the record and transcribed.

6. If petitioner alleges as a ground for illegality of his detention the inadequacy of counsel, he shall be deemed to waive his privilege with respect to communications between such counsel and himself to the extent necessary to permit a full and fair hearing for the alleged ground.

C. 1. With respect to any such petition filed by a petitioner held under the sentence of death, and subject to the provisions of this subsection, the Supreme Court shall have exclusive jurisdiction to consider and award writs of habeas corpus. The circuit court which entered the judgment order setting the sentence of death shall have authority to conduct an evidentiary hearing on such a petition only if directed to do so by order of the Supreme Court.

2. Hearings conducted in a circuit court pursuant to an order issued under the provisions of subdivision 1 of this subsection shall be limited in subject matter to the issues enumerated in the order.

3. The circuit court shall conduct such a hearing within 90 days after the order of the Supreme Court has been received and shall report its findings of fact and recommend conclusions of law to the Supreme Court within 60 days after the conclusion of the hearing. Any objection to the report of the circuit court must be filed in the Supreme Court within 30 days after the report is filed.

Acts 1977, c. 617; Acts 1978, c. 124; Acts 1995, c. 503; Acts 1998, c. 577. Amended by Acts 2005, c. 836.

§ 8.01–654.1. Limitation on consideration of petition filed by prisoner sentenced to death

No petition for a writ of habeas corpus filed by a prisoner held under a sentence of death shall be considered unless it is filed within sixty days after the earliest of: (i) denial by the United States Supreme Court of a petition for a writ of certiorari to the judgment of the Supreme Court of Virginia on direct appeal, (ii) a decision by the United States Supreme Court affirming imposition of the sentence of death when such decision is in a case resulting from a granted writ of certiorari to the judgment of the Supreme Court of Virginia on direct appeal, or (iii) the expiration of the period for filing a timely petition for certiorari without a petition being filed.

However, notwithstanding the time restrictions otherwise applicable to the filing of a petition for a writ of habeas corpus, an indigent prisoner may file such a petition within 120 days following appointment, made under § 19.2–163.7, of counsel to represent him.

Acts 1995, c. 503; Acts 1998, c. 199.

§ 8.01–654.2. Presentation of claim of mental retardation by person sentenced to death before April 29, 2003

Notwithstanding any other provision of law, any person under sentence of death whose sentence became final in the circuit court before April 29, 2003, and who desires to have a claim of his mental retardation presented to the Supreme Court, shall do so by one of the following methods: (i) if the person has not commenced a direct appeal, he shall present his claim of mental retardation by assignment of error and in his brief in that appeal, or if his direct appeal is pending in the Supreme Court, he shall file a supplemental assignment of error and brief containing his claim of mental retardation, or (ii) if the person has not filed a petition for a writ of habeas corpus under subsection C of § 8.01–654, he shall present his claim of mental retardation in a petition for a writ of habeas corpus under such subsection, or if such a petition is pending in the Supreme Court, he shall file an amended petition containing his claim of mental retardation. A person proceeding under this section shall allege the factual basis for his claim of mental retardation. The Supreme Court shall consider a claim raised under this section and if it determines that the claim is not frivolous, it shall remand the claim to the circuit court for a determination of mental retardation; otherwise the Supreme Court shall dismiss the petition. The provisions of §§ 19.2–264.3:1.1 and 19.2–264.3:1.2 shall govern a determination of mental retardation made pursuant to this section. If the claim is before the Supreme Court on direct appeal and is remanded to the circuit court and the case wherein the sentence of death was imposed was tried by a jury, the circuit court shall empanel a new jury for the sole purpose of making a determination of mental retardation.

If the person has completed both a direct appeal and a habeas corpus proceeding under subsection C of § 8.01–654, he shall not be entitled to file any further habeas petitions in the Supreme Court and his sole remedy shall lie in federal court.

Added by Acts 2003, c. 1031, eff. April 29, 2003; Acts 2003, c. 1040, eff. May 1, 2003.

§ 8.01–655. Form and contents of petition filed by prisoner

A. Every petition filed by a prisoner seeking a writ of habeas corpus must be filed on the form set forth in subsection B. The failure to use such form and to comply substantially with such form shall entitle the court to which such petition is directed to return such petition to the prisoner pending the use of and substantial compliance with such form. The petitioner shall be responsible for all statements contained in the petition and any false statement contained therein, if the same be knowingly or wilfully made, shall be a ground for prosecution and conviction of perjury as provided for in § 18.2–434.

B. Every petition filed by a prisoner seeking a writ of habeas corpus shall be filed on a form to be approved and provided by the office of the Attorney General, the contents of which shall be substantially as follows:

IN THE .... COURT

....

Full name and prisoner number (if any) of Petitioner
-vs-

Case No. .... (To be supplied by the Clerk of the Court)

....
....

Name and Title of Respondent

PETITION FOR WRIT OF HABEAS CORPUS

Instructions—Read Carefully

In order for this petition to receive consideration by the Court, it must be legibly handwritten or typewritten, signed by the petitioner and verified before a notary or other officer authorized to administer oaths. It must set forth in concise form the answers to each applicable question. If necessary, petitioner may finish his answer to a particular question on an additional page. Petitioner must make it clear to which question any such continued answer refers. The petitioner may also submit exhibits.

Since every petition for habeas corpus must be sworn to under oath, any false statement of a material fact therein may serve as the basis of prosecution and conviction for perjury under § 18.2–434. Petitioners should, therefore, exercise care to assure that all answers are true and correct.

When the petition is completed, the original and two copies (total of three) should be mailed to the clerk of the court. The petitioner shall keep one copy.

NOTICE

The granting of a writ of habeas corpus does not entitle the petitioner to dismissal of the charges for conviction of which he is being detained, but may gain him no more than a new trial.

....

Place of detention: ....

A. Criminal Trial

1. Name and location of court which imposed the sentence from which you seek relief:

....
....

2. The offense or offenses for which sentence was imposed (include indictment number or numbers if known):

a. ....
b. ....
c. ....

3. The date upon which sentence was imposed and the terms of the sentence:

a. ....
b. ....
c. ....

4. Check which plea you made and whether trial by jury: Plea of guilty: ...; Plea of not guilty: ...; Trial by jury: ...; Trial by judge without jury: ...

5. The name and address of each attorney, if any, who represented you at your criminal trial:

....
....

6. Did you appeal the conviction? ....

7. If you answered "yes" to 6, state: the result and the date in your appeal or petition for certiorari:

a. ....
b. ....

citations of the appellate court opinions or orders:

a. ....
b. ....

8. List the name and address of each attorney, if any, who represented you on your appeal:

....
....

B. Habeas Corpus

9. Before this petition did you file with respect to this conviction any other petition for habeas corpus in either a State or federal court? ....

10. If you answered "yes" to 9, list with respect to each petition: the name and location of the court in which each was filed:

a. ....
b. ....

the disposition and the date:

a. ....
b. ....

the name and address of each attorney, if any, who represented you on your habeas corpus:

a. ....
b. ....

11. Did you appeal from the disposition of your petition for habeas corpus?

12. If you answered "yes" to 11, state: the result and the date of each petition:

a. ....
b. ....

citations of court opinions or orders on your habeas corpus petition:

a. ....

b. ....

the name and address of each attorney, if any, who represented you on appeal of your habeas corpus:

a. ....

b. ....

C. Other Petitions, Motions or Applications

13. List all other petitions, motions or applications filed with any court following a final order of conviction and not set out in A or B. Include the nature of the motion, the name and location of the court, the result, the date, and citations to opinions or orders. Give the name and address of each attorney, if any, who represented you.

a. ....

b. ....

c. ....

D. Present Petition

14. State the grounds which make your detention unlawful, including the facts on which you intend to rely:

a. ....

b. ....

c. ....

15. List each ground set forth in 14, which has been presented in any other proceeding:

a. ....

b. ....

c. ....

List the proceedings in which each ground was raised:

a. ....

b. ....

c. ....

16. If any ground set forth in 14 has not been presented to a court, list each ground and the reason why it was not:

a. ....

b. ....

c. ....

....

Signature of Petitioner

....

Address of Petitioner

STATE OF VIRGINIA

CITY/COUNTY OF ....

The petitioner being first duly sworn, says:

1. He signed the foregoing petition;

2. The facts stated in the petition are true to the best of his information and belief.

....

Signature of Petitioner

Subscribed and sworn to before me

this .... day of ...., 20....

....

Notary Public

My commission expires: ....

The petition will not be filed without payment of court costs unless the petitioner is entitled to proceed in forma pauperis and has executed the affidavit in forma pauperis.

The petitioner who proceeds in forma pauperis shall be furnished, without cost, certified copies of the arrest warrants, indictment and order of his conviction at his criminal trial in order to comply with the instructions of this petition.

AFFIDAVIT IN FORMA PAUPERIS

STATE OF VIRGINIA

CITY/COUNTY OF ....

The petitioner being duly sworn, says:

1. He is unable to pay the costs of this action or give security therefor;

2. His assets amount to a total of $ ....

....

Signature of Petitioner

Subscribed and sworn to before me

this .... day of ...., 20 ....

....

Notary Public

My commission expires: ....

Acts 1977, c. 617.

§ 8.01-656. Bond may be required of petitioner

Before granting the writ, the court may require the petitioner to give bond with surety in a reasonable amount for the payment of such costs and charges as may be awarded against him.

Such bond shall be made payable to the person to whom the writ is directed, with condition that the petitioner will not escape, and shall be filed with the other proceedings on the writ, and may be sued on for the benefit of any person injured by the breach of its condition.

Acts 1977, c. 617.

§ 8.01-657. How directed and returnable

The writ shall be directed to the person in whose custody the petitioner is detained and shall be made returnable as soon as may be before the court ordering the same, or any other of such courts.

Provided that in the event the allegations of illegality of the petitioner's detention present a case for the determination of unrecorded matters of fact relating to any previous judicial proceeding, such writ shall be made returnable before the court in which such judicial proceeding occurred.

Acts 1977, c. 617.

§ 8.01-658. How writ served; dismissal of habeas petition without prejudice

A. The writ shall be served on the person to whom it is directed or, in his absence from the place where the petitioner is confined, on the person having the immediate or potential custody of him.

1. If the petitioner is in jail, prison, or other actual physical restraint due to the conviction or sentence he is attacking, the named respondent shall be (i) the Director of the Department of Corrections or the warden or superintendent of the state correctional facility where the petitioner is detained if the sentence is one year or more or (ii) the sheriff or superintendent of a local or regional jail facility if the sentence is less than one year.

2. If the petitioner is on probation or parole due to the conviction or sentence he is attacking, the named respondent shall be the probation or parole officer responsible for supervising the applicant or the official in charge of the parole or probation agency.

3. If a petitioner has a suspended sentence and is not under supervision by a probation or parole officer, the respondent shall be (i) the local sheriff if the judgment of conviction the petitioner challenges has a suspended sentence of less than one year or (ii) the Director of the Department of Corrections if the judgment of conviction the petitioner challenges has a suspended sentence of one year or more.

B. The petitioner shall name a proper party respondent, and if he fails to do so, the court shall allow amendment of the petition. If the petitioner fails to amend the petition by naming a proper party respondent in the time provided by the court, the court in which the petition is filed shall dismiss the habeas petition without prejudice.

Acts 1977, c. 617. Amended by Acts 2015, c. 554.

§ 8.01-659. Penalty for disobeying it

If the person on whom such writ is served shall, in disobedience to the writ, fail to bring the petitioner, with a return of the cause of his detention, before a court before which the writ is returnable, he shall forfeit to the petitioner $300.

Acts 1977, c. 617.

§ 8.01-660. When affidavits may be read

In the discretion of the court or judge before whom the petitioner is brought, the affidavits of witnesses taken by either party, on reasonable notice to the other, may be read as evidence.

Acts 1977, c. 617.

§ 8.01-661. Facts proved may be made part of record

All the material facts proved shall, when it is required by either party, be made a part of the proceedings and entered by the clerk among the records of the court.

Acts 1977, c. 617.

§ 8.01-662. Judgment of court or judge trying it; payment of costs and expenses when petition denied

After hearing the matter both upon the return and any other evidence, the court before whom the petitioner is brought shall either discharge or remand him, or admit him to bail and adjudge the cost of the proceeding, including the charge for transporting the prisoner.

Provided, however, that if the petition is denied, the costs and expenses of the proceeding and the attorney's fees of any attorney appointed to represent the petitioner shall be assessed against the petitioner. If such cost, expenses and fees are collected, they shall be paid to the Commonwealth.

Acts 1977, c. 617.

§ 8.01-663. Judgment conclusive

Any such judgment entered of record shall be conclusive, unless the same be reversed, except that the petitioner shall not be precluded from bringing the same matter in question in an action for false imprisonment.

Acts 1977, c. 617.

§ 8.01-664. How and when Supreme Court summoned to try appeal therefrom

If, during the recess of the Supreme Court, the Governor or the Chief Justice of the Court should think the immediate revision of any such judgment to be proper, he may summon the Court for that purpose, to meet on any day to be fixed by him.

Acts 1977, c. 617.

§ 8.01-665. When execution of judgment suspended; when prisoner admitted to bail

When the prisoner is remanded, the execution of the judgment shall not be suspended by a petition for appeal or by a writ of error, or for the purpose of applying for such writ. When he is ordered to be discharged, and the execution of the judgment is suspended for the purpose of petitioning for appeal to the Court of Appeals or applying for a writ of error from the Supreme Court, the court making such suspending order may admit the prisoner to bail until the expiration of the time allowed for filing a petition for appeal or applying for the writ of error, or, in case

the petition for appeal is filed or the writ of error is allowed, until the decision of the Court of Appeals or the Supreme Court thereon is duly certified.
Acts 1977, c. 617; Acts 1984, c. 703.

§ 8.01–666. When and by whom writs of habeas corpus ad testificandum granted

Writs of habeas corpus ad testificandum may be granted by any circuit court in the same manner and under the same conditions and provisions as are prescribed by this chapter as to granting the writ of habeas corpus ad subjiciendum so far as the same are applicable.
Acts 1977, c. 617.

§ 8.01–667. Transmission of records to federal court

Whenever any habeas corpus case is pending in a federal court, upon written request of the Attorney General or any assistant attorney general, a court of this Commonwealth shall transmit to such federal court such records as may be requested.
Acts 1977, c. 617.

§ 8.01–668. Writ de homine abolished

The writ de homine replegiando is abolished.
Acts 1977, c. 617.

CHAPTER 26

APPEALS TO THE SUPREME COURT

Article 1

Definitions

§ 8.01–669. Definitions

As used in Chapters 26, 26.1 and 26.2, unless the context otherwise requires, the term:

"Judgment" includes a decree, order, finding, or award.

"Petitioner" means a party who petitions to the Court of Appeals or the Supreme Court for an appeal.

"Appellant" means any aggrieved party who has an appeal of right or who has been granted an appeal by the Court of Appeals or the Supreme Court.

"Appellate court" means either the Court of Appeals or the Supreme Court, or both as the context may indicate.
Acts 1977, c. 617; Acts 1984, c. 703.

Article 2

When Granted

§ 8.01–670. In what cases awarded

A. Except as provided by § 17.1–405, any person may present a petition for an appeal to the Supreme Court if he believes himself aggrieved:

1. By any judgment in a controversy concerning:

a. The title to or boundaries of land,

b. The condemnation of property,

c. The probate of a will,

d. The appointment or qualification of a personal representative, guardian, conservator, committee, or curator,

e. A mill, roadway, ferry, wharf, or landing,

f. The right of the Commonwealth, or a county, or municipal corporation to levy tolls or taxes, or

g. The construction of any statute, ordinance, or county proceeding imposing taxes; or

2. By the order of a court refusing a writ of quo warranto or by the final judgment on any such writ; or

3. By a final judgment in any other civil case.

B. Except as provided by § 17.1–405, any party may present a petition for an appeal to the Supreme Court in any case on an equitable claim wherein there is an interlocutory decree or order:

1. Granting, dissolving or denying an injunction; or

2. Requiring money to be paid or the possession or title of property to be changed; or

3. Adjudicating the principles of a cause.

C. Except in cases where appeal from a final judgment lies in the Court of Appeals, as provided in § 17.1–405, any party may present a petition pursuant to § 8.01–670.1 for appeal to the Supreme Court.
Acts 1977, c. 617; Acts 1984, c. 703; Acts 1997, c. 801, eff. Jan. 1, 1998; Acts 2002, c. 107. Amended by Acts 2005, c. 681, eff. Jan. 1, 2006.

§ 8.01–670.1. Appeal of interlocutory orders and decrees by permission

When, prior to the commencement of trial, the circuit court has entered in any pending civil action, except any matters appealable to the Court of Appeals pursuant to § 17.1–405, an order or decree that is not otherwise appealable, any party may file in the circuit court a statement of the reasons why an immediate interlocutory appeal should be permitted.

The statement shall include a concise analysis of the statutes, rules or cases believed to be determinative of the issues and request that the court certify in writing that the order or decree involves a question of law as to which (i) there is substantial ground for difference of opinion, (ii) there is no clear, controlling precedent on point in the decisions of the Supreme Court of Virginia or the Court of Appeals of Virginia, (iii) determination of the issues will be dispositive of a material aspect of the proceeding currently pending before the court, and (iv) the court and the parties agree it is in the parties' best interest to seek an interlocutory appeal.

Within ten days of such certification by the circuit court, a petition for appeal may be filed with the appellate court that would have jurisdiction in an appeal from a final judgment in the proceeding. If the appellate court determines that the certification by the circuit court has sufficient merit, it may, in its discretion, permit an appeal to be taken from the interlocutory order or decree and shall notify the certifying circuit court and counsel for the parties of its decision. No petitions or appeals under this section shall stay proceedings in the circuit court unless the circuit court or appellate court so orders.

The consideration of any petition and appeal by the appellate court shall be in accordance with the applicable provisions of the Rules of the Supreme Court and shall not take precedence on the docket unless the court so orders.

Added by Acts 2002, c. 107.

§ 8.01–671. Time within which petition must be presented

A. In cases where an appeal is permitted from the trial court to the Supreme Court, no petition shall be presented for an appeal to the Supreme Court from any final judgment whether the Commonwealth be a party or not, (i) which shall have been rendered more than three months before the petition is presented, provided, that in criminal cases, a thirty-day extension may be granted, in the discretion of the court, in order to attain the ends of justice, or (ii) if it be an appeal from a final decree refusing a bill of review to a decree rendered more than four months prior thereto, unless the petition is presented within three months from the date of such decree.

B. When an appeal from an interlocutory decree or order is permitted, the petition for appeal shall be presented within the appropriate time limitation set forth in subsection A hereof.

C. No appeal to the Supreme Court from a decision of the Court of Appeals shall be granted unless a petition for appeal is filed within thirty days after the date of the decision appealed from.

Acts 1977, c. 2; Acts 1977, c. 617; Acts 1984, c. 703.

§ 8.01–672. Jurisdictional amount

No petition shall be presented for an appeal from any judgment of a circuit court except in cases in which the controversy is for a matter of $500 or more in value or amount, and except in cases in which it is otherwise expressly provided; nor to a judgment of any circuit court when the controversy is for a matter less in value or amount than $500, exclusive of costs, unless there be drawn in question a freehold or franchise or the title or bounds of land, or some other matter not merely pecuniary.

Acts 1977, c. 617.

Article 3

The Record

§ 8.01–673. Inspection and return of records; certiorari when part of record is omitted; binding or retention of records

A. The Supreme Court may, when a case has before been in an appellate court, inspect the record upon the former appeal; and the court may, in any case, after reasonable notice to counsel in the appellate court, award a writ of certiorari to the clerk of the court below, and have brought before it, when part of a record is omitted, the whole or any part of such record.

B. When an appeal is refused or after it has been allowed and decided, the Clerk of the Supreme Court shall return the record to the clerk of the circuit court or other tribunal. The clerk of such court or tribunal shall return the record upon the request of the Clerk of the Supreme Court. As soon as a case is decided, the Clerk of the Supreme Court shall cause the appendix and the briefs of counsel to be recorded and preserved in any manner which meets archival standards as recommended by the Archives and Records Division of The Library of Virginia.

The manuscript of the record in a case in which an opinion was delivered prior to 1950 by the Supreme Court upon refusal of an appeal shall not be destroyed and shall be retained by the clerk of such court in his files.

Acts 1977, c. 449; Acts 1977, c. 617; Acts 1984, c. 703; Acts 1988, c. 324; Acts 1994, c. 64.

ARTICLE 4

THE PETITION

§ 8.01–674. With whom filed; endorsement thereon; reference to justice or justices; when deemed to be filed

The petition for appeal to the Supreme Court shall be filed with the Clerk of the Supreme Court. The Clerk shall endorse thereon the day and year he received it and shall refer it to one or more justices of the Supreme Court as the Court shall direct. A petition shall, for the purposes of § 8.01–671, be deemed to be timely filed if it is mailed postage prepaid to the Clerk by registered or certified mail and if the official postal receipt therefor is exhibited upon the demand of the Clerk or any party and it shows mailing within the prescribed time limits.

Acts 1977, c. 617; Acts 1984, c. 703.

§ 8.01–675. Repealed by Acts 1984, c. 703, eff. Oct. 1, 1984

§ 8.01–675.1. When dismissal final; when reinstated

After the dismissal of an appeal by the Supreme Court, no other appeal shall be allowed to or from the same judgment. When an appeal is dismissed by reason of the nonpayment of the writ tax within the time required by law, the Court at its first session after such dismissal may on motion of any party for good cause shown and upon payment of such tax set aside the dismissal; and thereupon the appeal may be perfected as though no such dismissal had taken place. A motion under this section shall be made only after reasonable notice to the adverse party or his counsel.

Acts 1984, c. 703.

§ 8.01–675.2. Rehearing

The Supreme Court, on the petition of a party, shall rehear and review any case decided by such court if one of the justices who decides the case adversely to the petitioner certifies that in his opinion there is good cause for such rehearing. However, a notice of a petition for rehearing shall be filed as provided by the Rules of Court and the petition for rehearing shall be filed within thirty days after the entry of the judgment with the clerk, who shall note the date of such filing on the order book. The judgment resulting from any such rehearing shall be entered forthwith by the clerk who shall transmit a certified copy thereof to the clerk of the court below, to be entered by him as provided by § 8.01–685.

Acts 1984, c. 703.

CHAPTER 26.1

APPEALS TO THE COURT OF APPEALS

§ 8.01–675.3. Time within which appeal must be taken; notice

Except as provided in § 19.2–400 for pretrial appeals by the Commonwealth in criminal cases and in § 19.2–401 for cross appeals by the defendant in such pretrial appeals a notice of appeal to the Court of Appeals in any case within the jurisdiction of the court shall be filed within 30 days from the date of any final judgment order, decree or conviction. When an appeal from an interlocutory decree or order is permitted, the appeal shall be filed within 30 days from the date of such decree or order, except for pretrial appeals pursuant to § 19.2–398.

For purposes of this section, § 17.1–408, and an appeal pursuant to § 19.2–398, a petition for appeal in a criminal case or a notice of appeal to the Court of Appeals, shall be deemed to be timely filed if (i) it is mailed postage prepaid by registered or certified mail and (ii) the official postal receipt, showing mailing within the prescribed time limits, is exhibited upon demand of the clerk or any party.

Acts 1984, c. 703; Acts 1987, c. 710; Acts 2003, c. 109.

§ 8.01–675.4. Inspection and return of records; certiorari when part of record is omitted; retention of records

When a case has previously been in an appellate court, the Court of Appeals may inspect the record of the former appeal. The court may, in any case, after reasonable notice to counsel in the appellate court, award a writ of certiorari to the clerk of the trial court and have brought before it, when part of a record is omitted, the whole or any part of such record. As soon as a case is decided, the clerk of the Court of Appeals shall cause the appendix, if any, and briefs of counsel to be recorded and preserved in any manner which meets archival standards as recommended by the Archives and Records Division of The Library of Virginia.

Acts 1984, c. 703; Acts 1988, c. 197; Acts 1994, c. 64.

CHAPTER 26.2

APPEALS GENERALLY

ARTICLE 1

APPEAL BOND

§ 8.01–676. Repealed by Acts 1984, c. 703

§ 8.01–676.1. Security for appeal

A. Security for costs of appeal of right to Court of Appeals.—A party filing a notice of an appeal of right to the Court of Appeals shall simultaneously file an appeal bond or irrevocable letter of credit in the penalty of $500, or such sum as the trial court may require, subject to subsection E, conditioned upon paying all costs and fees incurred in the Court of Appeals and the Supreme Court if it takes cognizance of the claim. If the appellant wishes suspension of execution, the security shall also be conditioned and shall be in such sum as the trial court may require as provided in subsection C.

B. Security for costs on petition for appeal to Court of Appeals or Supreme Court.—An appellant whose petition for appeal is granted by the Court of Appeals or the Supreme Court shall (if he has not done so) within 15 days from the date of the Certificate of Appeal file an appeal bond or irrevocable letter of credit in the same penalty as provided in subsection A, conditioned on the payment of all damages, costs, and fees incurred in the Court of Appeals and in the Supreme Court.

C. Security for suspension of execution.—An appellant who wishes execution of the judgment or award from which an appeal is sought to be suspended during the appeal shall, subject to the provisions of subsection J, file an appeal bond or irrevocable letter of credit conditioned upon the performance or satisfaction of the judgment and payment of all damages incurred in consequence of such suspension, and except as provided in subsection D, execution shall be suspended upon the filing of such security and the timely prosecution of such appeal. Such security shall be continuing and additional security shall not be necessary except as to any additional amount which may be added or to any additional requirement which may be imposed by the courts.

D. Suspension of execution in decrees for support and custody; injunctions.—The court from which an appeal is sought may refuse to suspend the execution of decrees for support and custody, and may also refuse suspension when a judgment refuses, grants, modifies, or dissolves an injunction.

E. Increase or decrease in penalty or other modification of security.—The Court of Appeals or the Supreme Court, when it considers a petition for appeal, may order that the penalty or any other terms or requirements of the security for the appeal or of the security for the suspension of execution of a judgment be modified for good cause shown if such request is made in the brief of any party filed in the Court of Appeals, or in the Petition for Appeal or the appellee's Brief in Opposition filed in the Supreme Court or the Court of Appeals. Affidavits and counter-affidavits may be filed by the parties containing facts pertinent to such request. Any increase or decrease in the amount of or other modification of the security so ordered shall be effected in the clerk's office of the trial court within 15 days of the order of the Court of Appeals or the Supreme Court. If an increase so ordered is not effected within 15 days, the appeal shall be dismissed, in the case of the security required under subsection A, or the suspension of execution of a judgment shall be discontinued, in the case of the security required under subsection C. Such increase or decrease in the penalty of or other modification of the security may also be considered and ordered by the trial court for good cause shown, on motion of either party, at any time until the Court of Appeals or the Supreme Court acts upon any similar motion, and failure to increase such penalty as hereinabove provided shall also cause the appeal to be dismissed, in the case of the security required under subsection A, or the suspension of execution of a judgment to be discontinued, in the case of the security required under subsection C.

F. By whom executed.—Each bond filed shall be executed by a party or another on his behalf, and by surety approved by the clerk of the court from which appeal is sought, or by the clerk of the Supreme Court or the clerk of the Court of Appeals if the bond is ordered by such Court. Any letter of credit posted as security for an appeal shall be in a form acceptable to the clerk of the court from which appeal is sought, or by the clerk of the Supreme Court or the Court of Appeals if the security is ordered by such court. The letter of credit shall be from a bank incorporated or authorized to conduct banking business under the laws of this Commonwealth or authorized to do business in this Commonwealth under the banking laws of the United States, or a federally insured savings institution located in this Commonwealth.

G. Appeal from State Corporation Commission; security for costs.—When an appeal of right is entered from the State Corporation Commission to the Supreme Court, and no suspension of the order, judgment, or decree appealed from is requested, such appeal bond or letter of credit shall be filed when and in the amount required by the clerk of the Supreme

Court, whose action shall be subject to review by the Supreme Court.

H. Appeal from State Corporation Commission; suspension.—Any judgment, order, or decree of the State Corporation Commission subject to appeal to the Supreme Court may be suspended by the Commission or by the Supreme Court pending decision of the appeal if the Commission or the Supreme Court deems such suspension necessary for the proper administration of justice but only upon the written application of an appellant after reasonable notice to all other parties in interest and the filing of a suspending bond or irrevocable letter of credit with such conditions, in such penalty, and with such surety thereon as the Commission or the Supreme Court may deem sufficient. But no surety shall be required if the appellant is any county, city or town of this Commonwealth, or the Commonwealth.

I. Forms of bonds; letters of credit; where filed.—The Clerk of the Supreme Court shall prescribe separate forms for appeal bonds, one for costs alone, one for suspension of execution, and one for both and a form for irrevocable letters of credit, to which the bond or bonds or irrevocable letters of credit given shall substantially conform. The forms for each bond and the letter of credit shall be published in the Rules of Court. It shall be sufficient if the bond or letter of credit, when executed as required, is filed with the trial court, clerk of the Virginia Workers' Compensation Commission, or the clerk of the State Corporation Commission, whichever is applicable, and no personal appearance in the trial court, Virginia Workers' Compensation Commission, or State Corporation Commission by the principal, the surety on the bond or the bank issuing the letter of credit shall be required as a condition precedent to its filing.

J. In any civil litigation under any legal theory, the amount of the appeal bond or irrevocable letter of credit to be furnished during the pendency of all appeals or discretionary reviews of any judgment granting legal, equitable, or any other form of relief in order to stay the execution thereon during the entire course of appellate review by any courts shall be set in accordance with applicable laws or court rules, except that the total appeal bond or irrevocable letter of credit that is required of an appellant and all of its affiliates shall not exceed $25 million, regardless of the value of the judgment.

J1. Any objection to or motion for modification of the form, amount, or issuer of any letter of credit or bond may be made to, and decided by, the Court of Appeals or the Supreme Court. Any objection to or motion for modification of the form, amount, or issuer of any letter of credit or bond may also be made to, and decided by, the court or commission whose decision is being appealed at any time until the Court of Appeals or the Supreme Court acts upon any similar motion.

K. Dissipation of assets.—If the appellee proves by a preponderance of the evidence that a party bringing an appeal, for whom the appeal bond or irrevocable letter of credit requirement has been limited or waived pursuant to subsection J, is purposefully dissipating its assets or diverting assets outside the jurisdiction of the United States courts for the purpose of evading the judgment, the limitation or waiver granted pursuant to subsection J shall be rescinded and a court may require the appellant to post a bond or irrevocable letter of credit in an amount up to the full amount of the judgment. Dissipation of assets shall not include those ongoing expenditures made from assets of the kind that the appellant made in the regular course of business prior to the judgment being appealed, such as the payment of stock dividends and other financial incentives to the shareholders of publicly owned companies, continued participation in charitable and civic activities, and other expenditures consistent with the exercise of good business judgment.

L. For good cause shown, a court may otherwise waive the filing of an appeal bond or irrevocable letter of credit as to the damages in excess of, or other than, the compensatory damages.

M. Exemption.—When an appeal is proper to protect the estate of a decedent or person under disability, or to protect the interest of the Commonwealth or any county, city, or town of this Commonwealth, no security for appeal shall be required.

N. Indigents.—No person who is an indigent shall be required to post security for an appeal bond.

O. Virginia Workers' Compensation Commission.—No claimant who files an appeal from a final decision of the Virginia Workers' Compensation Commission with the Court of Appeals shall be required to post security for costs as provided in subsection A or B if such claimant has not returned to his employment or by reason of his disability is unemployed. Such claimant shall file an affidavit describing his disability and employment status with the Court of Appeals together with a motion to waive the filing of the security under subsection A or B.

P. Time for filing security for appeal.—The appeal bond or letter of credit prescribed in subsections A and B is not jurisdictional and the time for filing such security in cases before the Court of Appeals or the Supreme Court may be extended by a judge or justice of the court before which the case is pending on motion for good cause shown and to attain the ends of justice.

Q. Consideration of appeal bond or letter of credit by Court of Appeals or Supreme Court.—A determination on an issue affecting an appeal bond or letter of credit in a case before the Court of Appeals or the Supreme Court may be considered by an individual judge of such court rather than by a panel of judges.

R. This section applies to injunction bonds required pursuant to § 8.01–631.

Acts 1984, c. 703; Acts 1986, c. 89; Acts 1987, c. 460; Acts 1987, c. 684; Acts 1988, c. 883; Acts 1996, c. 77; Acts 2000, c. 100. Amended by Acts 2004, c. 328; Acts 2004, c. 356; Acts 2010, c. 494; Acts 2012, c. 8; Acts 2012, c. 77.

ARTICLE 2

ERRORS INSUFFICIENT IN THE APPELLATE COURT

§ 8.01–677. Errors corrected on motion instead of writ of error coram vobis

For any clerical error or error in fact for which a judgment may be reversed or corrected on writ of error coram vobis, the same may be reversed or corrected on motion, after reasonable notice, by the court.

Acts 1977, c. 617.

§ 8.01–677.1. Appeals filed in inappropriate appellate court

Notwithstanding any other provisions of this Code, no appeal which was otherwise properly and timely filed shall be dismissed for want of jurisdiction solely because it was filed in either the Supreme Court or the Court of Appeals and the appellate court in which it was filed thereafter rules that it should have been filed in the other court. In such event, the appellate court so ruling shall transfer the appeal to the appellate court having appropriate jurisdiction for further proceedings in accordance with the rules of the latter court. The parties shall be allowed a reasonable time to file such additional or amended pleadings as may be appropriate to proceed with the appeal in the appellate court to which the appeal is transferred.

Acts 1988, c. 382.

§ 8.01–678. For what a judgment not to be reversed

When it plainly appears from the record and the evidence given at the trial that the parties have had a fair trial on the merits and substantial justice has been reached, no judgment shall be arrested or reversed:

1. For the appearance of either party, being under the age of eighteen years, by attorney, if the verdict, where there is one, or the judgment be for him and not to his prejudice; or

2. For any other defect, imperfection, or omission in the record, or for any error committed on the trial.

Acts 1977, c. 617.

ARTICLE 3

LIMITATIONS; HEARING AND DECISION

§ 8.01–679. Failure of trial court clerk to deliver record to appellate court

Notwithstanding any provision of law to the contrary, no appeal shall be refused or dismissed for failure to deliver the record within the required time if it shall appear from evidence satisfactory to the appellate court that the clerk of the court below failed to deliver to the clerk of the appellate court the record on appeal within the required time.

Acts 1977, c. 617; Acts 1984, c. 703.

§ 8.01–679.1. Arguments made on brief not waived by oral argument

It shall not be necessary for any party to expressly reserve in oral argument any argument made on brief before an appellate court and failure to raise any such argument on oral argument shall not constitute a waiver.

Acts 1986, c. 268.

§ 8.01–680. When judgment of trial court not to be set aside unless plainly wrong, etc.

When a case, civil or criminal, is tried by a jury and a party objects to the judgment or action of the court in granting or refusing to grant a new trial on a motion to set aside the verdict of a jury on the ground that it is contrary to the evidence, or when a case is decided by a court without the intervention of a jury and a party objects to the decision on the ground that it is contrary to the evidence, the judgment of the trial court shall not be set aside unless it appears from the evidence that such judgment is plainly wrong or without evidence to support it.

Acts 1977, c. 617.

§ 8.01–681. Decision of appellate court

The appellate court shall affirm the judgment if there is no error therein, and reverse the same, in whole or in part, if erroneous, and enter such judgment as to the court shall seem right and proper and shall render final judgment upon the merits whenever, in the opinion of the court, the facts before it are such as to enable the court to attain the ends of justice. A civil case shall not be remanded for a trial de novo except when the ends of justice require it, but the appellate court shall, in the order remanding the case, if it be remanded, designate upon what questions or points a new trial is to be had.

Acts 1977, c. 617; Acts 1984, c. 703.

§ 8.01-682. What damages awarded appellee

When any judgment is affirmed, damages shall be awarded to the appellee. When the judgment is for the payment of money, the damages shall be the interest to which the party is legally entitled from the date of filing the notice of appeal until the date the appellate court issues its mandate. Such interest shall be computed upon the whole amount of the recovery, including interest and costs, and such damages shall be in satisfaction of all interest during such period of time. When the judgment is not for the payment of any money, except costs, the damages shall be such specific sum as the appellate court may deem reasonable, not being more than $2,500 nor less than $150.

Acts 1977, c. 617; Acts 1984, c. 703. Amended by Acts 2010, c. 343; Acts 2012, c. 58.

§ 8.01-683. When Clerk of Supreme Court to transmit its decisions

When any term of the Supreme Court is ended, or sooner if the court so direct, the Clerk thereof shall certify and transmit its decision to the clerk of the court or tribunal below, as the case may be, except that it shall not be his duty to certify or transmit a copy of a judgment of affirmance unless the appellee shall have paid all fees due from him in the case, or shall endorse on such copy so much of the judgment, for the benefit of the clerk, as the unpaid fees shall amount to. If any clerk fail to comply with this section for twenty days, except as aforesaid, he shall forfeit fifty dollars to any person aggrieved thereby.

Acts 1977, c. 617.

§ 8.01-684. Copies of Court's opinions to be furnished to counsel

When a case is decided by an appellate court the clerk shall furnish a copy of the opinion rendered by the court thereon to each counsel of record without making any charge therefor.

Acts 1977, c. 617; Acts 1984, c. 703.

§ 8.01-685. Entry of decision in lower court; issue of execution thereon

The court or other tribunal from which any case may have come to an appellate court shall enter the decision of the appellate court as its own, and execution or other appropriate process may issue thereon accordingly. When that decision is received by the clerk or secretary of the court or tribunal below, he shall enter it of record in his order book, and thereupon such execution may issue and such proceedings be had in the case as would have been proper if the decision had been entered in court or by such tribunal.

If the judgment of the lower court or tribunal is affirmed, in whole or in part, by the decision of an appellate court, execution or other appropriate process may issue thereon against the principal and surety on any appeal bond which may have been given, for the amount of such judgment, including the interest and cost and the damages awarded by the appellate court, not exceeding, however, the penalty of such bond.

Acts 1977, c. 617; Acts 1984, c. 703.

§§ 8.01-686, 8.01-687. Repealed by Acts 1984, c. 703

Article 4

Miscellaneous Provisions

§ 8.01-688. Order books, etc., of former district courts in custody of Clerk of Supreme Court, etc.

The order books, dockets and other office books formerly belonging to the several former district courts shall remain in the custody of the Clerk of the Supreme Court. Said Clerk shall furnish transcripts of the records and proceedings of such district courts when required, and perform all other duties in respect to records and proceedings of such district courts as might have been performed by the clerks of such district courts if such courts had continued to exist. All printed and manuscript orders, and other papers pertaining to cases decided in such district courts, shall remain in the custody of the clerks of the circuit courts at the several places where such district courts held their sessions, who shall be charged with the same duties in respect to such records and papers as might have been performed by the clerks of such district courts respectively, if such courts had continued to exist, and who shall receive for any such service fees similar to those charged by the clerks of district courts for such services.

Acts 1977, c. 617.

CHAPTER 27

VIRGINIA PRISONER LITIGATION REFORM ACT

§ 8.01–689. Short title

This chapter shall be known and may be cited as the "Virginia Prisoner Litigation Reform Act."

Added by Acts 2002, c. 871.

§ 8.01–690. Applicability provisions

The provisions of this chapter shall apply to all pro se civil actions for money damages brought under the laws of this Commonwealth, or for injunctive, declaratory or mandamus relief, brought by prisoners incarcerated in any state or local correctional facility, or operated pursuant to the Corrections Private Management Act (§ 53.1–261 et seq.).

Added by Acts 2002, c. 871.

§ 8.01–691. Payment of filing fees and costs by prisoners; when in forma pauperis status granted

A prisoner seeking in forma pauperis status shall provide the court with a certified copy of his inmate trust account for the preceding twelve months. Any prisoner granted leave to proceed in forma pauperis shall nonetheless make payments, in equal installments as the court directs, towards satisfaction of the filing fee and costs. If the court determines the prisoner has had no deposits in his inmate trust account for the preceding six months, the court shall permit the prisoner to proceed without paying the filing fee and costs. However, the filing fee and costs shall be taxed as costs at the end of the case. Any prisoner failing to make any payment when due shall have his case dismissed without prejudice.

Added by Acts 2002, c. 871.

§ 8.01–692. When in forma pauperis status denied

The court shall deny in forma pauperis status to any prisoner who has had three or more cases or appeals dismissed by any federal or state court for being frivolous, malicious, or for failure to state a claim, unless the prisoner shows that he is in imminent danger of serious physical injury at the time of filing his motion for judgment or the court determines that it would be manifest injustice to deny in forma pauperis status.

Added by Acts 2002, c. 871.

§ 8.01–693. Venue of prisoner actions

Notwithstanding any other provision of law, no prisoner action shall be filed except in the city or county in which the prison is located where the prisoner was housed when his cause of action arose. When an action is filed in an improper venue, upon motion of the defendant or the court sua sponte, the court shall transfer the case to the proper venue.

Added by Acts 2002, c. 871.

§ 8.01–694. Service of process; time for response

In any action in which any defendant is the Commonwealth or one of its officers, employees, or agents, upon the grant of in forma pauperis status or receipt of the filing fee and costs, the court shall serve the Office of the Attorney General with a copy of the motion for judgment and all necessary supporting papers. The Office of the Attorney General shall have no fewer than thirty days from receipt in which to file responsive pleadings. The prisoner's failure to state his claims in a written motion for judgment plainly stating facts sufficient to support his cause of action, accompanied by all necessary supporting documentation, may be grounds for dismissal of the action.

Added by Acts 2002, c. 871. Amended by Acts 2009, c. 372.

§ 8.01–695. When argument held; when discovery permitted

Oral argument on any motion in any prisoner civil action shall be heard orally only at the request of the court; whenever possible, the court shall rule upon the record before it. No prisoner shall be permitted to request subpoenas for witnesses or documents, or file discovery requests, until the court has ruled upon any demurrer, plea or motion to dismiss. Where a case proceeds past the initial dispositive motions, the court shall require the prisoner seeking discovery to demonstrate that his requests are relevant and material to the issues in the case. No subpoena for witnesses or documents shall issue unless a judge of the court has reviewed the subpoena request and specifically authorized a subpoena to issue. The court shall exercise its discretion in determining the scope of the subpoena and may condition its issuance on such terms as the court finds appropriate. The court shall take into account the burden placed upon the object of the subpoena in relation to the needs of the case, the amount in controversy, and the importance of the issues at stake in the litigation.

Added by Acts 2002, c. 871. Amended by Acts 2006, c. 435.

§ 8.01–696. Summary judgment; pro se prisoner civil action

Notwithstanding the provisions of § 8.01–420, any time after commencement of a pro se prisoner civil action, a party may move for summary judgment on all issues based upon the pleadings, any admissions, and supporting affidavits. The adverse party may serve supporting affidavits within 10 days after service of the motion. The judgment sought shall be rendered forthwith if the pleadings, admissions, and affidavits show that there is no genuine issue of material fact and that the moving party is entitled to a judgment as a matter of law.

Added by Acts 2006, c. 435.

§ 8.01–697. Access to Department of Corrections records

All records maintained by the Department of Corrections in the name of individual prisoners, including prisoner medical records, shall be the property of the Department. Notwithstanding the provisions of § 32.1–127.1:03, in any civil suit subject to this chapter, where the Commonwealth, an agency of the Commonwealth, an employee of the Commonwealth, or a private contractor providing services to the Department of Corrections is named as a defendant, the Director of the Department may share any records maintained by the Department in the name of the prisoner filing suit with counsel representing the above-named defendants.

Added by Acts 2006, c. 435.

INDEX TO CIVIL REMEDIES AND PROCEDURE

ABANDONED OR UNCLAIMED PROPERTY
Forcible Entry and Detainer, generally, this index

ABODE
Domicile and Residence, generally, this index

ACCIDENT INSURANCE
Health Insurance, generally, this index

ACCIDENTS
Motor Vehicle Insurance, this index
Motor Vehicles, this index
Personal Injuries, generally, this index
Traffic Rules and Regulations, this index
Wrongful Death, generally, this index

ACCORD AND SATISFACTION
Generally, **8.01–453 et seq.**
Attachment, **8.01–269**
Attorney fees, certificates and certification, **8.01–455**
Certificates and certification, **8.01–455**
Costs, certificates and certification, **8.01–455**
Debtors and creditors, **8.01–421**
Default judgments, vacating or setting aside, **8.01–428**
Dockets and docketing, **8.01–454**
Fines and penalties, dockets and docketing, **8.01–454**
Foreign countries, money, claims, **8.01–465.23**
Garnishment, **8.01–516.1**

ACCOUNTS AND ACCOUNTING
Circuit Courts, this index
Executions, coins, currency, **8.01–482**
Funds Transfers, generally, this index
Joint tenants, **8.01–31**
Tenants in common, **8.01–31**

ACTIONS AND PROCEEDINGS
Generally, **8.01–1 et seq.**
Alienation of affection, abolishment, **8.01–220**
Annuities, **8.01–29**
Anonymous plaintiffs, **8.01–15.1**
Appeal and Review, generally, this index
Appeals in Criminal Prosecutions, generally, this index
Application of law, **8.01–1**
Arbitration and Award, generally, this index
Arrest, civil arrest, **8.01–327.1, 8.01–327.2**
Asbestos, this index
Assignments, **8.01–26**
Beneficial owners, **8.01–14**
Associations and societies, **8.01–15**

ACTIONS AND PROCEEDINGS—Cont'd
Attachment, generally, this index
Bad checks, evidence, writing, **8.01–27.3**
Beneficial owners, **8.01–12 et seq.**
Bifurcated trials, **8.01–267.6**
Bonds, this index
Bonds (Officers and Fiduciaries), this index
Boundaries, **8.01–179 et seq.**
Breach of promise, abolishment, **8.01–220**
Children and Minors, this index
Clergy, privileges and immunities, **8.01–220.1:3**
Commencement of actions. Limitation of Actions, generally, this index
Compromise and Settlement, generally, this index
Constitution, rights, **8.01–223.1**
Construction, contracts, venue, **8.01–262.1**
Contracts, this index
Conviction of crime, severance of cause, **8.01–22**
Correctional Institutions, this index
Costs, generally, this index
Counterclaim. Setoff and Counterclaim, generally, this index
Covenant not to sue, **8.01–35.1**
Crimes and offenses, personal injuries, **8.01–221**
Criminal conversation, abolishment, **8.01–220**
Criminal history record information, disclosure, damages, **8.01–40.3**
Damages, generally, this index
Death, this index
Debtors and Creditors, this index
Declaratory Judgments, generally, this index
Decrees. Judgments and Decrees, generally, this index
Default Judgments, generally, this index
Depositions, generally, this index
Directed verdicts, **8.01–378**
Discontinuance, substitution, parties, **8.01–18**
Discovery, generally, this index
Dismissal and Nonsuit, generally, this index
District Courts, generally, this index
Divorce. Marriage, this index
Dockets and Docketing, generally, this index
Drug dealers, liability, **8.01–227.4 et seq.**
Ejectment, generally, this index
Emergency medical services, privileges and immunities, **8.01–225**
Equity, generally, this index
Evidence, generally, this index
Executions, generally, this index
Facsimile transmissions, unsolicited transmissions, damages, **8.01–40.2**

ACTIONS AND PROCEEDINGS—Cont'd
Fetal death, wrongful death, **8.01–50**
Fiduciaries, pleadings, style, **8.01–6.3**
Forcible Entry and Detainer, generally, this index
Fraud against taxpayers, **8.01–216.4 et seq.**
Garnishment, generally, this index
Guardian Ad Litem, generally, this index
Habeas Corpus, generally, this index
Handicapped Persons, this index
Hate crimes, **8.01–42.1**
Injunctions, generally, this index
Internet, torts, identity and identification, subpoenas, **8.01–407.1**
Interpleader, **8.01–364**
Interrogatories, generally, this index
Judgments and Decrees, generally, this index
Jury, generally, this index
Later filed actions, joinder, **8.01–267.7**
Libel and Slander, generally, this index
Limitation of Actions, generally, this index
Mandamus, generally, this index
Mediation. Arbitration and Award, generally, this index
Medical Malpractice, generally, this index
Misjoinder, **8.01–5**
Names, anonymous plaintiffs, **8.01–15.1**
Negligence, generally, this index
New trial. Trial De Novo, generally, this index
Nonjoinder, **8.01–5**
Nonprofit organizations, privileges and immunities, **8.01–220.1:1**
Parties, generally, this index
Partition, generally, this index
Pending Actions, generally, this index
Personal property, detinue, **8.01–114 et seq.**
Photography and pictures, unauthorized use, **8.01–40**
Pleadings, generally, this index
Prisoner litigation reform, **8.01–689 et seq.**
Probate Proceedings, generally, this index
Process, generally, this index
Production of Books and Papers, generally, this index
Prohibition, writ of, **8.01–650, 8.01–651**
Real Estate, this index
Receivers and Receivership, generally, this index
Release, **8.01–35.1**
Removal or Transfer of Causes, generally, this index
Schoolteachers, privileges and immunities, **8.01–220.1:2**
Scire facias, abolishment, **8.01–24**
Seduction, abolishment, **8.01–220**
Setoff and Counterclaim, generally, this index
Settlement. Compromise and Settlement, generally, this index
Severance, **8.01–267.5**
Shoplifting, **8.01–44.4**
Slander. Libel and Slander, generally, this index

ACTIONS AND PROCEEDINGS—Cont'd
Stalking, **8.01–42.3**
State, this index
Statute of limitations. Limitation of Actions, generally, this index
Stay. Supersedeas or Stay, generally, this index
Subpoenas, generally, this index
Subrogation, generally, this index
Summary judgment, **8.01–377.1, 8.01–378**
Summons, generally, this index
Supersedeas or Stay, generally, this index
Surveys and surveyors, boundaries, **8.01–181**
Survival, **8.01–25**
Third Parties, generally, this index
Time. Limitation of Actions, generally, this index
Title to Property, this index
Transfers. Removal or Transfer of Causes, generally, this index
Trial, generally, this index
Trial De Novo, generally, this index
Vacating or Setting Aside, generally, this index
Vandalism, children and minors, parental liability, **8.01–43, 8.01–44**
Venue, generally, this index
Witnesses, generally, this index
Wrongful Death, generally, this index

ACTS OF LEGISLATURE
Statutes, generally, this index

AD LITEM
Guardian Ad Litem, generally, this index

AD VALOREM TAXES
Real Property Taxation, generally, this index

ADDRESS
Garnishment, identity and identification, **8.01–511.1**

ADMINISTRATION OF ESTATES
Personal representatives. Probate Proceedings, this index

ADMINISTRATIVE LAW AND PROCEDURE
Fraud against taxpayers, alternative remedy, **8.01–216.6**
Interest, judgments and decrees, **8.01–382**
Judgments and decrees, interest, **8.01–382**
Judicial notice, publications, **8.01–388**
Publication, judicial notice, **8.01–388**
Venue, **8.01–261**

ADMINISTRATIVE REVIEW
Administrative Law and Procedure, generally, this index

ADMINISTRATIVE RULES AND REGULATIONS
Administrative Law and Procedure, generally, this index

ADMINISTRATORS
Personal representatives. Probate Proceedings, this index

ADMISSIONS
Summary judgment, requests for admissions, depositions, basis, **8.01–420**

ADOPTION
Venue, application of law, **8.01–259**

ADVERSE OR PECUNIARY INTEREST
Arbitration and Award, this index
Guardian ad litem, real estate, sales, **8.01–75**
Jury, removal, **8.01–358**
Witnesses, this index

ADVERSE POSSESSION
Limitation of actions, **8.01–236**

ADVERTISEMENTS
Facsimile transmissions, damages, **8.01–40.2**
Legal advertisements. Notice, generally, this index
Publication, generally, this index

ADVOCATES
Attorneys, generally, this index

AERONAUTICS
Aircraft, generally, this index
Privileges and immunities, space, flight, **8.01–227.8 et seq.**

AFFIDAVITS
Generally, **8.01–414 et seq.**
Domicile and residence, witnesses, **8.01–414**
Habeas corpus, **8.01–654**
Witnesses, **8.01–660**
Lost or destroyed documents, actions and proceedings, **8.01–32**
Motor vehicles, damages, **8.01–416**
Parties, domicile and residence, **8.01–414**
Pleadings, **8.01–279**
Publication, **8.01–415**
Unsworn written declarations, **8.01–4.3**
Witnesses, domicile and residence, **8.01–414**

AFFIRMATIONS
Oaths and Affirmations, generally, this index

AFFIRMATIVE DEFENSES
Winter sports safety, **8.01–227.20**

AGE
Jury, **8.01–337**
Exemptions, **8.01–341.1**

AGED PERSONS
Actions and proceedings, compromise and settlement, **8.01–424 et seq.**
Compromise and settlement, **8.01–424 et seq.**
Conservators and Conservatorship, generally, this index
Deeds and conveyances, **8.01–67 et seq.**
Exemptions, jury, **8.01–341.1**
Guardian and Ward, generally, this index
Indebtedness, real estate, sales, **8.01–78 et seq.**
Investments, real estate, proceeds, **8.01–76**

AGED PERSONS—Cont'd
Jury, exemptions, **8.01–341.1**
Leases, **8.01–67 et seq.**
Mortgages, **8.01–67 et seq.**
Nursing Homes, generally, this index
Real estate, **8.01–67 et seq.**
Sales, real estate, **8.01–67 et seq.**
Settlement, **8.01–424 et seq.**
Social Security, generally, this index
Title to property, **8.01–67 et seq.**

AGENCIES
Agents and Agencies, generally, this index

AGENTS AND AGENCIES
Actions and proceedings, venue, **8.01–262**
Forcible entry and detainer, affidavits, evidence, **8.01–126**
Foreign Corporations, this index
Notice, service of process, **8.01–315**
Service of process, **8.01–312, 8.01–326.1**
Notice, **8.01–315**
State Agencies, generally, this index
Trusts and Trustees, generally, this index
Venue, **8.01–262**

AGREEMENTS
Contracts, generally, this index

AGRICULTURAL PRODUCTS
Animals, generally, this index
Executions, exemptions, **8.01–489**
Exemptions, executions, **8.01–489**
Livestock. Animals, generally, this index

AGRICULTURE
Animals, generally, this index
Cattle. Animals, generally, this index
Livestock. Animals, generally, this index

AIR CARRIERS
Aircraft, generally, this index

AIR FORCE
Military Forces, generally, this index

AIRCRAFT
Accidents, service of process, nonresidents, **8.01–309 et seq.**
Nonresidents, accidents, service of process, **8.01–309 et seq.**
Service of process, nonresidents, accidents, **8.01–309 et seq.**

AIRLINES
Aircraft, generally, this index

AIRPLANES
Aircraft, generally, this index

ALCOHOLIC BEVERAGES
Driving under influence of alcohol or drugs. Traffic Rules and Regulations, this index

ALCOHOLICS AND INTOXICATED PERSONS
Driving under influence of alcohol or drugs. Traffic Rules and Regulations, this index

ALIEN CORPORATIONS
Foreign Corporations, generally, this index

ALTERNATIVE DISPUTE RESOLUTION
Arbitration and Award, generally, this index

ALZHEIMERS DISEASE
Conservators and Conservatorship, generally, this index
Guardian and Ward, generally, this index

AMBASSADORS AND CONSULS
Jury, exemptions, **8.01–341.1**

AMBULANCES
Emergency Medical Services, generally, this index

AMOUNT IN CONTROVERSY
Jurisdiction, generally, this index

ANAPHYLAXIS
Schools and school districts, drugs and medicine, privileges and immunities, **8.01–226.5:1**

ANIMALS
Care and maintenance, emergencies, emergency medical services, privileges and immunities, **8.01–225.2**
Detinue, **8.01–121**
Emergency medical services, privileges and immunities, **8.01–225.2**
Privileges and immunities, emergency medical services, **8.01–225.2**

ANNUITIES
Actions and proceedings, **8.01–29**
Wrongful incarceration, compensation and salaries, **8.01–195.11**

ANONYMOUS PLAINTIFFS
Generally, **8.01–15.1**

ANTISLAPP LAW
Strategic lawsuits against public participation, hearings, privileges and immunities, **8.01–223.2**

APARTMENT HOUSES
See, also, Landlord and Tenant, generally, this index
Forcible Entry and Detainer, generally, this index
Lead, privileges and immunities, **8.01–226.7**
Privileges and immunities, lead, **8.01–226.7**

APOLOGIES
Medical malpractice, evidence, **8.01–52.1, 8.01–581.20:1**

APOTHECARY
Pharmacists, generally, this index

APPEAL AND REVIEW
Generally, **8.01–676.1 et seq.**

APPEAL AND REVIEW—Cont'd
Affirmation, **8.01–681 et seq.**
Amount in controversy, **8.01–672**
Arbitration and award, **8.01–581.016**
Asbestos, consolidation, bifurcation, **8.01–374.1**
Attachment, bonds (officers and fiduciaries), **8.01–555**
Bifurcation, asbestos, **8.01–374.1**
Bonds (officers and fiduciaries), **8.01–676.1**
Boundaries, **8.01–670**
Briefs, arguments, **8.01–679.1**
Certificates and certification, interlocutory appeals, permission, **8.01–670.1**
Change of names, effect, **8.01–20**
Conservators and conservatorship, **8.01–670**
Copies, records and recordation, **8.01–684**
Court of Appeals, generally, this index
Criminal prosecutions. Appeals in Criminal Prosecutions, generally, this index
Death, **8.01–20**
Dismissal and nonsuit, **8.01–675.1**
Dockets and docketing, **8.01–331**
  Dismissal and nonsuit, **8.01–335**
Equity, **8.01–670**
Errors and omissions,
  Correction, **8.01–677**
  Fair trial, **8.01–678**
Evidence, **8.01–384**
Exhaustion of remedies, **8.01–429**
Forms, bonds (officers and fiduciaries), **8.01–676.1**
Fraud against taxpayers, actions and proceedings,
  Civil investigative demands, **8.01–216.18**
  Res judicata, **8.01–216.6**
Habeas corpus, **8.01–664**
Harmless error, **8.01–678**
Indigent persons, bonds (officers and fiduciaries), **8.01–676.1**
Injunctions, **8.01–626, 8.01–670**
Interest, **8.01–682**
Interlocutory appeals, permission, **8.01–670.1**
Joinder, **8.01–267.8**
  Asbestos, **8.01–374.1**
Jurisdiction, transfers, **8.01–677.1**
Letters of credit, **8.01–676.1**
Limitation of actions, **8.01–671**
  Court of appeals, **8.01–675.3**
Marriage, change of names, **8.01–20**
New trial. Trial De Novo, generally, this index
Notice, judgments and decrees, **8.01–428**
Objections and exceptions, **8.01–384**
  Letters of credit, bonds (officers and fiduciaries), **8.01–676.1**
Orders of court, **8.01–384**
Petitions, **8.01–674 et seq.**
Quo warranto, **8.01–670**
Records and Recordation, this index
Rehearings, **8.01–675.2**
Remand, **8.01–681**
Reversal, **8.01–681**
  Judgments and decrees, **8.01–678**

APPEAL AND REVIEW—Cont'd
Standards, **8.01–680**
Statements, interlocutory appeals, permission, **8.01–670.1**
Statutes, **8.01–670**
Stay of proceedings. Supersedeas or Stay, generally, this index
Supersedeas or Stay, generally, this index
Title to property, **8.01–670**
Transfers, **8.01–677.1**
Trial De Novo, generally, this index
Venue, **8.01–258**
Waiver, bonds (officers and fiduciaries), **8.01–676.1**

APPEALS COURT
Court of Appeals, generally, this index

APPEALS IN CRIMINAL PROSECUTIONS
Briefs, capital punishment, mentally retarded and developmentally disabled persons, claims, **8.01–654.2**
Errors, fair trial, **8.01–678**
Harmless error, conviction of crime, **8.01–678**
Reversal, **8.01–678**
Supersedeas or Stay, generally, this index

APPEARANCE
Special appearance, service of process, dismissal and nonsuit, motions, **8.01–277**
Subpoenas, generally, this index
Summons, generally, this index

ARBITRATION AND AWARD
Generally, **8.01–576.4 et seq., 8.01–577 et seq., 8.01–581.21 et seq.**
Adverse or pecuniary interest, **8.01–576.9**
Mediators, **8.01–581.24**
Vacating or setting aside, **8.01–581.26**
Appeal and review, **8.01–581.016**
Applications, **8.01–581.013**
Appointments, **8.01–581.03**
Attorneys, **8.01–576.5, 8.01–581.05**
Notice, misconduct, vacating or setting aside, **8.01–581.26**
Bias or prejudice, vacating or setting aside, **8.01–581.26**
Certificates and certification, training, **8.01–576.8**
Children and minors, vacating or setting aside, **8.01–576.12**
Compelling arbitration, orders of court, **8.01–581.02**
Confidential or privileged information, **8.01–576.9, 8.01–576.10, 8.01–581.22, 8.01–581.24**
Mediation, **8.01–581.22**
Confirmation, **8.01–581.09**
Contracts, **8.01–581.01 et seq.**
Written agreement, compromise and settlement, **8.01–581.25**
Correction, awards, **8.01–581.08, 8.01–581.011**
Costs, **8.01–576.7**
Depositions, **8.01–581.06**

ARBITRATION AND AWARD—Cont'd
Disclosure, **8.01–576.9**
Confidential or privileged information, **8.01–581.24**
Vacating or setting aside, **8.01–581.26**
Duress or coercion, mediators, **8.01–581.24**
Education, **8.01–576.8**
Enforcement, **8.01–577, 8.01–581.01**
Evidence, hearings, **8.01–581.04**
Fees, **8.01–581.07**
Fiduciaries, **8.01–581**
Fraud, **8.01–576.12, 8.01–581.010**
Taxation, **8.01–216.7**
Vacating or setting aside, **8.01–581.26**
Hearings, **8.01–581.04 et seq.**
Judgments and decrees, **8.01–581.012**
Written agreement, compromise and settlement, **8.01–581.25**
Jurisdiction, **8.01–581.014**
Medical malpractice, **8.01–581.12**
Misconduct, vacating or setting aside, **8.01–581.26**
Mistake, **8.01–581.010**
Modifications, **8.01–581.08, 8.01–581.011**
Notice, **8.01–576.6**
Attorneys, misconduct, vacating or setting aside, **8.01–581.26**
Hearings, **8.01–581.04**
Oaths and affirmations, **8.01–581.06**
Orders of court, compelling arbitration, **8.01–581.02**
Personal representatives, **8.01–581**
Powers and duties, mediators, **8.01–581.24**
Privileges and immunities, mediators, **8.01–576.9, 8.01–581.23**
Production of books and papers, **8.01–581.06**
Referrals, **8.01–576.5**
Revocation or suspension, **8.01–577**
Standards, mediators, **8.01–581.24**
Submission, controversy, **8.01–577**
Subpoenas, **8.01–581.06**
Supersedeas or stay, **8.01–581.02**
Support, this index
Training, **8.01–576.8**
Vacating or setting aside, **8.01–576.12, 8.01–581.010, 8.01–581.26**
Venue, **8.01–581.015**
Construction, contracts, **8.01–262.1**
Witnesses, **8.01–581.04, 8.01–581.06**
Written agreement, compromise and settlement, **8.01–581.25**

ARCHITECTS AND ARCHITECTURE
Actions and proceedings, limitation of actions, **8.01–250**
Disasters, privileges and immunities, rescue, **8.01–226.2**
Limitation of actions, **8.01–250**
Privileges and immunities, disasters, rescue, **8.01–226.2**
Rescue, disasters, privileges and immunities, **8.01–226.2**

ARMED FORCES
Military Forces, generally, this index

ARMY
Military Forces, generally, this index

ARREST
Actions and proceedings, civil arrest, **8.01–327.1, 8.01–327.2**
Bad checks, privileges and immunities, **8.01–226.10**
Civil arrest, **8.01–327.1, 8.01–327.2**
Clergy, privileges and immunities, **8.01–327.2**
Executions, interrogatories, failure to answer, **8.01–508**
Governor, privileges and immunities, **8.01–327.2**
Habeas Corpus, generally, this index
Interrogatories, privileges and immunities, **8.01–327.1**
Judges, privileges and immunities, **8.01–327.2**
Judgments and decrees, privileges and immunities, **8.01–327.1**
Jury, privileges and immunities, **8.01–327.2**
National guard, privileges and immunities, **8.01–327.2**
Negotiable instruments, bad checks, privileges and immunities, **8.01–226.10**
President of United States, privileges and immunities, **8.01–327.2**
Privileges and immunities, **8.01–327.1, 8.01–327.2**
  Bad checks, **8.01–226.10**
Searches and Seizures, generally, this index
Shoplifting, privileges and immunities, **8.01–226.9**
Voters and voting, privileges and immunities, **8.01–327.2**
Witnesses, privileges and immunities, **8.01–327.2**

ASBESTOS
Actions and proceedings,
  Consolidation or bifurcation, **8.01–374.1**
  Limitation of actions, **8.01–249**
    Removal, **8.01–250.1**
Joinder, **8.01–374.1**
Limitation of actions, **8.01–249**
  Removal, **8.01–250.1**
Statute of limitations, **8.01–249**
  Removal, **8.01–250.1**

ASSAULT AND BATTERY
Forcible Entry and Detainer, generally, this index
Shoplifting, arrest, detention, privileges and immunities, **8.01–226.9**

ASSIGNMENTS
Actions and proceedings, **8.01–26**
  Beneficial owners, **8.01–14**
Beneficial owners, actions and proceedings, **8.01–14**
Debtors and creditors, **8.01–14**
Dockets and docketing, **8.01–452**
Limitation of actions, **8.01–253**
Subrogation, generally, this index

ASSISTANCE
Social Services, generally, this index

ASSISTED LIVING FACILITIES
Conservators and Conservatorship, generally, this index
Guardian and Ward, generally, this index

ASSISTED SUICIDE
Injunctions, **8.01–622.1**

ASSOCIATIONS AND SOCIETIES
Actions and proceedings, **8.01–15**
Corporations, generally, this index
Executions, **8.01–15**
Foreign Corporations, generally, this index
Judgments and decrees, **8.01–15**
Nonprofit Organizations, generally, this index
Service of process, **8.01–305**
  Foreign states, **8.01–306**
  Fraud against taxpayers, actions and proceedings, civil investigative demands, **8.01–216.13**

ASSUMPTION OF RISK
Railroads, officers and employees, **8.01–59**
Winter sports safety, **8.01–227.19**

ATHLETICS
Winter sports safety, **8.01–227.11 et seq.**

ATTACHMENT
  Generally, **8.01–268, 8.01–269, 8.01–533 et seq.**
Additional property, **8.01–543**
Adverse or pecuniary interest, third parties, **8.01–573**
Amendments, **8.01–543, 8.01–545**
Appeal and review, bonds (officers and fiduciaries), **8.01–555**
Assignments, pretrial procedures, **8.01–534**
Boats and boating, **8.01–538**
Bonds (officers and fiduciaries), **8.01–537.1, 8.01–553 et seq.**
  Appeal and review, **8.01–555**
  Returns, **8.01–554**
  Service of process, failure, **8.01–571**
Certificates and certification, valuation, **8.01–551**
Conversion, pretrial procedures, **8.01–534**
Damages, **8.01–41**
Defenses, subsequent proceedings, **8.01–566, 8.01–567**
Dismissal and nonsuit, **8.01–269, 8.01–569**
Evidence, **8.01–540**
Examinations and examiners, subsequent proceedings, **8.01–562**
Executions, **8.01–546, 8.01–550**
  Sales, **8.01–570**
Exemptions,
  Forms, **8.01–546.1**
  Hearings, **8.01–546.2**
  Subsequent proceedings, **8.01–563**
Fees, petitions, **8.01–537**
Foreign corporations, pretrial procedures, **8.01–534**
Forms, exemptions, **8.01–546.1**
Fraud, pretrial procedures, **8.01–534**

ATTACHMENT—Cont'd
Grounds, pretrial procedures, **8.01–534**
Hearings,
Exemptions, **8.01–546.2**
Service by publication, rehearing, **8.01–575, 8.01–576**
Holidays, **8.01–542**
Injunctions, **8.01–549**
Joint and several liability, subsequent proceedings, **8.01–564, 8.01–565**
Judgments and decrees, **8.01–570**
Service by publication, rehearing, **8.01–575**
Jurisdiction, **8.01–535**
Liens and incumbrances, **8.01–557**
Nonresidents, pretrial procedures, **8.01–534**
Parties, **8.01–539**
Pending actions, **8.01–574**
Perishable goods, subsequent proceedings, **8.01–561**
Petitions, **8.01–537**
Dismissal and nonsuit, **8.01–569**
Pleadings, **8.01–536**
Possession, **8.01–551**
Pretrial procedures, **8.01–534**
Priorities and preferences, **8.01–557**
Real estate, sales, **8.01–572**
Property subject to attachment, **8.01–548, 8.01–550**
Publication, **8.01–544**
Rehearing, **8.01–575, 8.01–576**
Quashing, subsequent proceedings, **8.01–567, 8.01–568**
Real Estate, this index
Receivers and receivership, **8.01–549**
Records and recordation, **8.01–268**
Release, **8.01–269**
Bonds (officers and fiduciaries), **8.01–553**
Remainders, **8.01–547**
Removal, pretrial procedures, **8.01–534**
Retaining possession, bonds (officers and fiduciaries), **8.01–553**
Returns, **8.01–541, 8.01–559**
Bonds (officers and fiduciaries), **8.01–554**
Sales, **8.01–570**
Real estate, **8.01–572**
Service of process, **8.01–544, 8.01–550**
Failure, bonds (officers and fiduciaries), **8.01–571**
Ships and shipping, **8.01–538**
Subsequent proceedings, **8.01–560 et seq.**
Summons, **8.01–546**
Supersedeas or stay, exemptions, **8.01–546.2**
Third parties, **8.01–365 et seq., 8.01–539**
Adverse or pecuniary interest, **8.01–573**
Time, subsequent proceedings, **8.01–560 et seq.**
Valuation, possession, **8.01–551**
Zoning and planning, records and recordation, **8.01–268**

ATTESTATION
Oaths and Affirmations, generally, this index

ATTORNEY FEES
Cemeteries, destruction, damages, **8.01–44.6**

ATTORNEY FEES—Cont'd
Contracts, rescission, fraud, undue influence, **8.01–221.2**
Criminal history record information, disclosure, **8.01–40.3**
Deeds and conveyances, rescission, fraud, undue influence, **8.01–221.2**
Dismissal and nonsuit, **8.01–380**
Evidence, dismissal and nonsuit, reasonableness, **8.01–380**
Facsimile transmissions, advertisements, **8.01–40.2**
Fraud against taxpayers, actions and proceedings, **8.01–216.7**
Habeas corpus, **8.01–662**
Hate crimes, **8.01–42.1**
Interpreters, confidential or privileged information, disclosure, **8.01–44.3**
Military forces, Servicemembers Civil Relief Act, default judgments, **8.01–15.2**
Motor vehicle insurance,
See, also, Motor Vehicle Insurance, this index
Underinsured motorists, cooperation, subrogation, **8.01–66.1:1**
Natural gas, meters, tampering, **8.01–44.7**
Negotiable instruments, bad checks, actions and proceedings, **8.01–27.1**
Nonsuit, **8.01–380**
Partition, **8.01–92**
Pleadings, **8.01–271.1**
Process, service of process, waiver, **8.01–286.1**
Public utilities, meters, tampering, **8.01–44.7**
Quo warranto, **8.01–643**
Servicemembers Civil Relief Act, default judgments, **8.01–15.2**
Shoplifting, **8.01–44.4**
State agencies, fraud against taxpayers, **8.01–216.3**
State departments, fraud against taxpayers, **8.01–216.3**
Venue, objections and exceptions, **8.01–266**
Water supply, meters, tampering, **8.01–44.7**
Wrongful death, **8.01–54**

ATTORNEY GENERAL
Dockets and docketing, **8.01–448**
Fraud against taxpayers, actions and proceedings, civil investigative demands, **8.01–216.10 et seq., 8.01–216.17**
Jury, exemptions, **8.01–341**
Powers and duties, fraud against taxpayers, actions and proceedings, civil investigative demands, **8.01–216.10 et seq., 8.01–216.17**
Privileges and immunities, torts, **8.01–195.3**

ATTORNEYS
Alcoholics or intoxicated persons, privileges and immunities, counselors and counseling, **8.01–226.1**
Appearance, service of process, **8.01–314**
Arbitration and award, **8.01–576.5, 8.01–581.05**
Notice, misconduct, vacating or setting aside, **8.01–581.26**

ATTORNEYS—Cont'd
Argument, jury, **8.01–379**
Chemically dependent persons, privileges and immunities, counselors and counseling, **8.01–226.1**
Compensation and salaries. Attorney Fees, generally, this index
Confession of judgment, **8.01–435**
Confidential or privileged information, attorney client privilege, undisclosed information, waiver, **8.01–420.7**
Counselors and counseling, chemically dependent persons, privileges and immunities, **8.01–226.1**
Disbarment, venue, **8.01–261**
Dockets and docketing, **8.01–331**
Evidence, attorney client privilege, undisclosed information, waiver, **8.01–420.7**
Fees. Attorney Fees, generally, this index
Forcible entry and detainer, affidavits, evidence, **8.01–126**
Guardian Ad Litem, generally, this index
Habeas corpus, inadequate counsel, **8.01–654**
Intervention, Lawyers Helping Lawyers, privileges and immunities, **8.01–226.1**
Jury, this index
Lawyers Helping Lawyers, privileges and immunities, **8.01–226.1**
Monitoring, Lawyers Helping Lawyers, privileges and immunities, **8.01–226.1**
Motions, generally, this index
Orders of Court, generally, this index
Pleadings, generally, this index
Privileges and immunities,
  Attorney client privilege, undisclosed information, waiver, **8.01–420.7**
  Chemically dependent persons, counselors and counseling, **8.01–226.1**
Release, wrongful incarceration, compensation and salaries, **8.01–195.12**
Service of process, **8.01–314**
State. Attorney General, generally, this index
Substance abuse, privileges and immunities, counselors and counseling, **8.01–226.1**
Venue, disbarment, **8.01–261**
Waiver,
  Attorney client privilege, undisclosed information, waiver, **8.01–420.7**
  Wrongful incarceration, compensation and salaries, **8.01–195.12**

AUDIO VISUAL DEPOSITION ACT
Generally, **8.01–412.2 et seq.**

AUTHORITIES
Hearings, privileges and immunities, strategic lawsuits against public participation, **8.01–223.2**
Privileges and immunities, hearings, strategic lawsuits against public participation, **8.01–223.2**

AUTO INJECTABLE EPINEPHRINE
Schools and school districts, privileges and immunities, **8.01–226.5:1**

AUTOMATED EXTERNAL DEFIBRILLATORS
Privileges and immunities, **8.01–225**

AUTOMOBILE INSURANCE
Motor Vehicle Insurance, generally, this index

AUTOMOBILES
Motor Vehicles, generally, this index

AVIATION
Aircraft, generally, this index

AWARD
Arbitration and Award, generally, this index

BABIES
Children and Minors, generally, this index

BACKGROUND INVESTIGATIONS
Criminal History Record Information, generally, this index

BAD CHECKS
Negotiable Instruments, this index

BAIL
Habeas corpus, **8.01–665**
Limitation of actions, **8.01–246**

BANK DEPOSITS AND COLLECTIONS
Actions and proceedings, limitation of actions, **8.01–249**
Bad faith, stop payment, damages, **8.01–27.1**
Funds Transfers, generally, this index
Investments, generally, this index
Limitation of actions, **8.01–249**
Numbers and numbering, courts, records and recordation, redacting, **8.01–420.8**
Stop payment, bad faith, damages, **8.01–27.1**
Transfers. Funds Transfers, generally, this index

BANKS AND BANKING
Bank Deposits and Collections, generally, this index
Checks. Negotiable Instruments, this index
Collections. Bank Deposits and Collections, generally, this index
Deposits. Bank Deposits and Collections, generally, this index
Funds, transfers. Funds Transfers, generally, this index
Transfers. Funds Transfers, generally, this index

BAR
Attorneys, generally, this index

BARRISTER
Attorneys, generally, this index

BENEVOLENT ORGANIZATIONS
Insurance, generally, this index
Nonprofit Organizations, generally, this index

BEQUESTS
Probate Proceedings, generally, this index
Wills, generally, this index

BIAS AND PREJUDICE
Arbitration and award, vacating or setting aside, **8.01-581.010, 8.01-581.26**
Jury, removal, **8.01-358**

BILLS
Courts, records and recordation, identification numbers, redacting, **8.01-420.8**

BILLS OF REVIEW
Injunctions, **8.01-623**

BIOTERRORISM
Terrorism, generally, this index

BIRTH
Childbirth, generally, this index

BIRTH RELATED NEUROLOGICAL INJURY COMPENSATION ACT
Removal or transfer of causes, workers compensation, **8.01-273.1**

BLASTING
Explosives, generally, this index

BLIND PERSONS
Jury, **8.01-337**

BLOOD TESTS
Emergency medical services, evidence, admissibility, **8.01-413.02**

BOARDS AND COMMISSIONS
Administrative Law and Procedure, generally, this index
Hearings, privileges and immunities, strategic lawsuits against public participation, **8.01-223.2**
Privileges and immunities, **8.01-44.1**
  Hearings, strategic lawsuits against public participation, **8.01-223.2**

BOATS AND BOATING
Attachment, **8.01-538**

BOMBS
Explosives, generally, this index

BONDS
Actions and proceedings, **8.01-29**
  Death, **8.01-11**
  Lost or destroyed documents, **8.01-32**
Affidavits, lost or destroyed documents, actions and proceedings, **8.01-32**
Beneficial owners, actions and proceedings, **8.01-13**
Bonds (Officers and Fiduciaries), generally, this index
Copies, lost or destroyed documents, actions and proceedings, evidence, **8.01-32**
Evidence, lost or destroyed documents, actions and proceedings, copies, **8.01-32**
Lost or destroyed documents, actions and proceedings, **8.01-32**
Oaths and affirmations, lost or destroyed documents, actions and proceedings, **8.01-32**

BONDS (OFFICERS AND FIDUCIARIES)
Actions and proceedings, **8.01-227**
  Equity, relief, **8.01-33**
  Limitation of actions, **8.01-245**
  Lost or destroyed documents, **8.01-32**
  Venue, **8.01-261**
Attachment, this index
Detinue, personal property, **8.01-115 et seq.**
Equity, relief, **8.01-33**
Executions, this index
Habeas corpus, **8.01-656**
Injunctions, **8.01-630, 8.01-631**
Judgments and decrees, **8.01-227**
  Liens and incumbrances, **8.01-465**
Judicial sales, **8.01-96**
  Certificates and certification, **8.01-99**
  Claims against, **8.01-105 et seq.**
  Fraud, **8.01-100**
Jurisdiction, **8.01-4.1**
Limitation of actions, **8.01-245**
  Executions, loss of property sold, new execution, **8.01-255.2**
Lost or destroyed documents, actions and proceedings, **8.01-32**
Motions, judgments and decrees, **8.01-227**
Oaths and affirmations, lost or destroyed documents, actions and proceedings, **8.01-32**
Personal property, detinue, **8.01-115 et seq.**
Statute of limitations, **8.01-245**
Third parties, liens and incumbrances, **8.01-366 et seq.**
Venue, **8.01-261**
Witnesses, continuance, compelling attendance, **8.01-408**

BOOKS AND PAPERS
Evidence, generally, this index
Lost or Destroyed Documents, generally, this index
Production of Books and Papers, generally, this index
Records and Recordation, generally, this index
Searches and Seizures, generally, this index
Subpoena duces tecum. Production of Books and Papers, generally, this index

BORDERS
Boundaries, generally, this index

BOUNDARIES
Actions and proceedings, **8.01-179 et seq.**
  Venue, **8.01-261**
Appeal and review, **8.01-670**
Damages, **8.01-182**
Judgments and decrees, **8.01-183**
Motions, establishing, **8.01-179**
Parties, **8.01-180**
Profits, actions and proceedings, **8.01-182**
Records and recordation, judgments and decrees, **8.01-183**
Rents, actions and proceedings, **8.01-182**
Venue, **8.01-261**

BREAKING AND ENTERING
Executions, **8.01–491**

BREAST FEEDING
Jury, exemptions, **8.01–341.1**

BRIBERY AND CORRUPTION
Arbitration and award, vacating or setting aside, **8.01–581.010**

BUILDINGS
Architects and Architecture, generally, this index
Contractors, generally, this index
Entry on Property, generally, this index
Housing, generally, this index
Searches and Seizures, generally, this index
Vandalism, generally, this index

BURIAL
Cemeteries, generally, this index

BUSINESS AND COMMERCE
Contracts, generally, this index
Corporations, generally, this index
Damages, lost profits, new business, unestablished business, **8.01–221.1**
Evidence, records and recordation, **8.01–390.3, 8.01–391**
  Witnesses, corroboration, **8.01–397**
Hearings, privileges and immunities, strategic lawsuits against public participation, **8.01–223.2**
Interference, privileges and immunities, hearings, strategic lawsuits against public participation, **8.01–223.2**
Jurisdiction, **8.01–328 et seq.**
Lost profits, damages, new business, unestablished business, **8.01–221.1**
New business, lost profits, damages, **8.01–221.1**
Partnerships, generally, this index
Privileges and immunities, hearings, strategic lawsuits against public participation, **8.01–223.2**
Real Property Taxation, generally, this index
Records and recordation, witnesses, corroboration, **8.01–397**
Sales, generally, this index
Unestablished business, lost profits, damages, **8.01–221.1**
Venue, **8.01–262**
Witnesses, records and recordation, corroboration, **8.01–397**

BUSINESS CORPORATIONS
Corporations, generally, this index

CABLE CARS
Winter sports areas, safety, **8.01–227.11 et seq.**

CAMERAS
Photography and Pictures, generally, this index

CANADA
Foreign Countries, generally, this index

CAPITAL PUNISHMENT
Actions and proceedings, mentally retarded and developmentally disabled persons, claims, **8.01–654.2**
Appeals in criminal prosecutions, mentally retarded and developmentally disabled persons, **8.01–654.2**
Dismissal and nonsuit, mentally retarded and developmentally disabled persons, actions and proceedings, claims, **8.01–654.2**
Habeas corpus, **8.01–654, 8.01–654.1**
  Mentally retarded and developmentally disabled persons, **8.01–654.2**
Indigent persons, habeas corpus, limitation of actions, **8.01–654.1**
Jurisdiction, habeas corpus, **8.01–654**
Limitation of actions, habeas corpus, **8.01–654, 8.01–654.1**
Mentally retarded and developmentally disabled persons, actions and proceedings, claims, **8.01–654.2**
Petitions, mentally retarded and developmentally disabled persons, claims, **8.01–654.2**

CAR INSURANCE
Motor Vehicle Insurance, generally, this index

CARDIOPULMONARY RESUSCITATION
Privileges and immunities, **8.01–225**

CARRIERS
  See, also, Public Utilities, generally, this index
Aircraft, generally, this index
Process, service of process, foreign states, **8.01–306**
Railroads, generally, this index
Service of process, **8.01–305**
  Foreign states, **8.01–306**

CARS
Motor Vehicles, generally, this index

CATASTROPHES
Civil Defense, generally, this index
Disasters, generally, this index

CATS
Animals, generally, this index

CATTLE
Animals, generally, this index

CAUSES OF ACTION
Actions and Proceedings, generally, this index

CEMETERIES
Actions and proceedings, destruction, damages, **8.01–44.6**
Attorney fees, destruction, damages, **8.01–44.6**
Costs, destruction, damages, **8.01–44.6**
Damages, destruction, **8.01–44.6**
Destruction, damages, **8.01–44.6**
Vandalism, destruction, damages, **8.01–44.6**

CERTIFICATES AND CERTIFICATION
Accord and satisfaction, **8.01–455**

CERTIFICATES AND CERTIFICATION —Cont'd
Arbitration and award, training, **8.01–576.8**
Attachment, valuation, **8.01–551**
Executions, financial institutions, notice, **8.01–502.1**
Wrongful death, standard of care, medical malpractice, expert witnesses, **8.01–50.1**

CHAIRLIFTS
Winter sports areas, safety, **8.01–227.11 et seq.**

CHANCERY
Equity, generally, this index

CHANCERY COMMISSIONERS
Generally, **8.01–607 et seq.**

CHARACTER AND REPUTATION
Libel and Slander, generally, this index

CHATTELS
Personal Property, generally, this index

CHEATING
Fraud, generally, this index

CHECK CLEARING FOR THE 21ST CENTURY EVIDENCE ACT
Generally, **8.01–391.1**

CHECKS
Negotiable Instruments, this index

CHEMICALLY DEPENDENT PERSONS
Mentally Ill Persons, generally, this index

CHEMICALS, CHEMISTRY AND CHEMISTS
Hazardous Substances and Waste, generally, this index

CHILD ABUSE
Guardian Ad Litem, generally, this index
Limitation of actions, **8.01–243**

CHILD SUPPORT
Support, generally, this index

CHILDBIRTH
Birth related neurological injuries, workers compensation, **8.01–273.1**
Fetal death, wrongful death, **8.01–50**
Newborns. Children and Minors, this index
Wrongful death, fetal death, **8.01–50**

CHILDREN AND MINORS
Actions and proceedings, **8.01–8**
  Compromise and settlement, **8.01–424 et seq.**
  Drug dealers, liability, **8.01–227.4 et seq.**
  Guardian ad litem, **8.01–9**
  Joinder, personal injuries, **8.01–36**
  Limitation of actions, **8.01–229**
  Personal injuries,
    Joinder, **8.01–36**
    Limitation of actions, **8.01–243**
  Property damages, **8.01–43, 8.01–44**

CHILDREN AND MINORS—Cont'd
Actions and proceedings—Cont'd
  Reimbursement, personal injuries, parents and guardians, **8.01–36**
Arbitration and award, vacating or setting aside, **8.01–576.12**
Birth. Childbirth, generally, this index
Change of names, **8.01–217**
Compensation and salaries, personal injuries, lost income, **8.01–37**
Compromise and settlement, **8.01–424 et seq.**
Controlled substances, drug dealers, liability, **8.01–227.4 et seq.**
Crimes and offenses. Delinquent Children, generally, this index
Damages, personal injuries,
  Liens and incumbrances, reimbursement, **8.01–36**
  Limitation of actions, **8.01–243**
Debtors and creditors, liability, **8.01–278**
Delinquent Children, generally, this index
Drug dealers, liability, **8.01–227.4 et seq.**
Drugs and medicine, drug dealers, liability, **8.01–227.4 et seq.**
Emancipation, personal injuries, lost income, **8.01–37**
Emergencies, motor vehicles, forcible entry, privileges and immunities, **8.01–225**
Emergency medical services, newborns, accepting, privileges and immunities, **8.01–226.5:2**
Forcible entry, motor vehicles, emergencies, privileges and immunities, **8.01–225**
Guardian Ad Litem, generally, this index
Guardian and Ward, generally, this index
Hospitals, newborns, accepting, privileges and immunities, **8.01–226.5:2**
Indebtedness, real estate, sales, **8.01–78 et seq.**
Investments, real estate, proceeds, **8.01–76**
Joinder, torts, **8.01–36**
Joint and several liability, motor vehicles, accidents, **8.01–64**
Jurisdiction, real estate, **8.01–68**
Jury, exemptions, **8.01–341.1**
Juvenile delinquents. Delinquent Children, generally, this index
Leases, **8.01–67 et seq.**
Liens and incumbrances, personal injuries, parents, guardian and ward, **8.01–36**
Limitation of actions, **8.01–229**
  Medical malpractice, **8.01–243.1**
  Personal injuries, medical care and treatment, **8.01–243**
Loans, liability, **8.01–278**
Maintenance. Support, generally, this index
Medical care and treatment, personal injuries,
  Liens and incumbrances, reimbursement, **8.01–36**
  Limitation of actions, **8.01–243**
Medical malpractice, limitation of actions, **8.01–243.1**

CHILDREN AND MINORS—Cont'd
Mortgages, **8.01–67 et seq.**
Motor Vehicles, this index
Names, change of names, **8.01–217**
Newborns,
  Abandonment, accepting, privileges and immunities, **8.01–226.5:2**
  Emergency medical services, accepting, privileges and immunities, **8.01–226.5:2**
  Medical care and treatment, accepting, privileges and immunities, **8.01–226.5:2**
Next friend, actions and proceedings, **8.01–8**
Notice, change of names, **8.01–217**
Pain and suffering, drug dealers, liability, **8.01–227.4 et seq.**
Partition, **8.01–85**
Personal injuries,
  Drug dealers, liability, **8.01–227.4 et seq.**
  Joinder, **8.01–36**
  Limitation of actions, **8.01–243**
  Lost income, **8.01–37**
Pleadings, debtors and creditors, **8.01–278**
Privileges and immunities, motor vehicles, forcible entry, emergencies, **8.01–225**
Public buildings and grounds, property damages, **8.01–43**
Real estate, **8.01–67 et seq.**
Reimbursement, personal injuries, parents, guardian and ward, **8.01–36**
Sales, real estate, **8.01–67 et seq.**
Schools and School Districts, generally, this index
Settlement, **8.01–424 et seq.**
Skiing, winter sports safety, powers and duties, **8.01–227.21**
Support, generally, this index
Title to property, **8.01–67 et seq.**
Torts,
  Joinder, **8.01–36**
  Limitation of actions, personal injuries, **8.01–243**
Vandalism, parental liability, **8.01–43, 8.01–44**
Winter sports safety, powers and duties, **8.01–227.21**
Wrongful death, **8.01–50**

CHIROPODISTS AND CHIROPODY
Podiatrists, generally, this index

CHIROPRACTORS
  See, also, Health Care Professionals, generally, this index
Actions and proceedings. Medical Malpractice, generally, this index
Athletics, schools and school districts, privileges and immunities, **8.01–225.1**
Disasters, privileges and immunities, **8.01–225.01, 8.01–225.02**
Emergencies, privileges and immunities, **8.01–225.01, 8.01–225.02**
Evidence, opinions and expert testimony, **8.01–401.2**
Liens and incumbrances, personal injuries, claims, **8.01–66.2 et seq.**

CHIROPRACTORS—Cont'd
Malpractice. Medical Malpractice, generally, this index
Medical Malpractice, generally, this index
Opinions and expert testimony, **8.01–401.2**
Payments, liens and incumbrances, personal injuries, claims, **8.01–66.2 et seq.**
Privileges and immunities, disasters, **8.01–225.01, 8.01–225.02**
Schools and school districts, athletics, privileges and immunities, **8.01–225.1**
Witnesses, opinions and expert testimony, **8.01–401.2**

CHOICE OF LAW
Conflict of Laws, generally, this index

CHURCHES
Religion, generally, this index

CIRCUIT COURTS
Accounts and accounting, **8.01–600, 8.01–604**
  Chancery commissioners, **8.01–608**
  Receivers and receivership, **8.01–585**
Adjournment, chancery commissioners, **8.01–614**
Appointments, receivers and receivership, **8.01–582**
Audits and auditors, **8.01–600**
  Receivers and receivership, **8.01–582**
Chancery commissioners, **8.01–607 et seq.**
Clerks of court,
  Dockets and docketing, judgment dockets, **8.01–446 et seq.**
  Judgment dockets, **8.01–446 et seq.**
Compensation and salaries, receivers and receivership, **8.01–589**
Compromise and settlement, chancery commissioners, **8.01–617 et seq.**
Declaratory Judgments, generally, this index
Deeds and Conveyances, generally, this index
Deposits, **8.01–600 et seq.**
  Receivers and receivership, **8.01–582 et seq.**
Electronic filing,
  Application of law, **8.01–271.01**
  Judgment dockets, **8.01–446**
Escrows and escrow agents, payments, **8.01–606**
Executions, generally, this index
Fees, chancery commissioners, **8.01–609.1**
Financial statements and reports, **8.01–600**
  Receivers and receivership, **8.01–585, 8.01–588.1**
Funds, **8.01–600 et seq.**
  Receivers and receivership, **8.01–582 et seq.**
Interest, **8.01–600**
  Receivers and receivership, **8.01–584**
Investments, **8.01–600**
  Receivers and receivership, **8.01–584**
Judgment dockets, **8.01–446 et seq.**
Microfilms, judgment dockets, **8.01–446**
Notice, service of process, waiver, **8.01–286.1**
Officers and employees, chancery commissioners, **8.01–607 et seq.**
Payment, **8.01–606**

CIRCUIT COURTS—Cont'd
Powers and duties, chancery commissioners, **8.01–609**
Process, service of process, waiver, **8.01–286.1**
Receipts, funds, **8.01–601**
Receivers and Receivership, generally, this index
Reports, chancery commissioners, **8.01–610**
Rules and regulations, **8.01–4**
Securities, receivers and receivership, **8.01–583**
Service of process, process, waiver, **8.01–286.1**
State treasury, funds, **8.01–604, 8.01–605**
Waiver, service of process, **8.01–286.1**
Witnesses, chancery commissioners, **8.01–612**

CITIES AND TOWNS
Municipalities, generally, this index

CITIZENS AND CITIZENSHIP
Jury, **8.01–337**

CIVIL ACTIONS
Actions and Proceedings, generally, this index

CIVIL ARREST
Generally, **8.01–327.1, 8.01–327.2**

CIVIL DEFENSE
Health care professionals, privileges and immunities, **8.01–225.01, 8.01–225.02**
Privileges and immunities, health care professionals, **8.01–225.01, 8.01–225.02**
Terrorism, generally, this index

CIVIL INVESTIGATIVE DEMANDS
Fraud against taxpayers, actions and proceedings, **8.01–216.10 et seq.**

CIVIL PENALTIES
Fines and Penalties, generally, this index

CIVIL PRACTICE AND PROCEDURE
Actions and Proceedings, generally, this index

CIVIL PROCESS
Process, generally, this index

CLASS ACTIONS
Parties, death, **8.01–23**

CLEANING, DYEING AND PRESSING
Damages, privileges and immunities, **8.01–42**
Privileges and immunities, damages, **8.01–42**

CLERGY
Actions and proceedings, privileges and immunities, **8.01–220.1:3**
Confidential or privileged information, witnesses, **8.01–400**
Contracts, privileges and immunities, **8.01–220.1:3**
Evidence, confidential or privileged information, witnesses, **8.01–400**
Privileges and immunities, **8.01–220.1:3**
  Witnesses, **8.01–400**
Torts, privileges and immunities, **8.01–220.1:3**
Witnesses, confidential or privileged information, **8.01–400**

CLERKS OF COURT
Injunctions, **8.01–627**
Lost or destroyed documents, **8.01–393**

CLINICAL LABORATORIES
Laboratories, generally, this index

CLINICS
Medical Malpractice, generally, this index

COAST GUARD
Military Forces, generally, this index

CODE OF VIRGINIA
Statutes, generally, this index

CODES
Statutes, generally, this index

COERCION
Duress or Coercion, generally, this index

COINS
Money, generally, this index

COLLATERAL ESTOPPEL
Fraud against taxpayers, actions and proceedings, **8.01–216.9**

COLLEGES AND UNIVERSITIES
Community colleges,
  Tuition, wrongful incarceration, compensation and salaries, **8.01–195.11**
  Wrongful incarceration, compensation and salaries, **8.01–195.11**
Investigations and investigators, libel and slander, privileges and immunities, **8.01–47**
Libel and slander, investigations and investigators, privileges and immunities, **8.01–47**
Privileges and immunities, libel and slander, investigations and investigators, **8.01–47**
Reports, libel and slander, privileges and immunities, **8.01–47**

COLLUSION
Fraud, generally, this index

COMBUSTIBLES
Explosives, generally, this index

COMMERCE
Business and Commerce, generally, this index

COMMERCIAL CODE
Bank Deposits and Collections, generally, this index
Funds Transfers, generally, this index
Sales, generally, this index

COMMERCIAL PAPER
Negotiable Instruments, generally, this index

COMMISERATION
Medical malpractice, evidence, **8.01–52.1, 8.01–581.20:1**

COMMISSIONS AND COMMISSIONERS
Boards and Commissions, generally, this index

COMMITTEES
Administrative Law and Procedure, generally, this index
Medical malpractice, privileges and immunities, **8.01–581.19, 8.01–581.19:1**
Privileges and immunities, **8.01–44.1**

COMMON CARRIERS
Carriers, generally, this index

COMMONWEALTH
State, generally, this index

COMMUNICATION MEDIA
Newspapers, generally, this index

COMMUNICATIONS
Confidential or Privileged Information, generally, this index
Telecommunications, generally, this index

COMMUNITY POLICING INSTITUTE
Crime victims, notice, privileges and immunities, **8.01–226.11**

COMMUNITY SERVICE
Littering, pick up programs, privileges and immunities, **8.01–226.8**

COMPANIES
Corporations, generally, this index

COMPARATIVE NEGLIGENCE
Interrogatories, jury, general verdicts, **8.01–379.3**

COMPASSION
Medical malpractice, evidence, **8.01–52.1, 8.01–581.20:1**

COMPENSATION AND SALARIES
Actions and proceedings, lost income, reimbursement, **8.01–35**
Attachment, generally, this index
Attorney Fees, generally, this index
Delinquent children, wrongful incarceration, **8.01–195.10 et seq.**
Evidence, records and recordation, **8.01–413.01**
Garnishment, generally, this index
Records and recordation, evidence, **8.01–413.01**
Workers Compensation, generally, this index
Wrongful incarceration, **8.01–195.10 et seq.**

COMPILATION
Statutes, generally, this index

COMPLAINT
Pleadings, generally, this index

COMPROMISE AND SETTLEMENT
Generally, **8.01–424 et seq.**
Aged persons, **8.01–424 et seq.**
Arbitration and Award, generally, this index
Children and minors, **8.01–424 et seq.**
Covenant not to sue, **8.01–35.1**
Fraud against taxpayers, actions and proceedings, **8.01–216.6**

COMPROMISE AND SETTLEMENT—Cont'd
Handicapped persons, **8.01–424 et seq.**
Joinder, **8.01–267.1**
Labor and employment, third parties, actions and proceedings, consent, **8.01–424.1**
Mandatory arbitration. Arbitration and Award, generally, this index
Mentally ill persons, **8.01–424 et seq.**
Mentally retarded and developmentally disabled persons, **8.01–424 et seq.**
Motor vehicle insurance, underinsured motorists, subrogation, **8.01–66.1:1**
Personal Injuries, this index
Release, liability, rescission, **8.01–425.1**
Rescission, release, **8.01–425.1**
State, this index
Wrongful Death, this index

COMPUTERS
Actions and proceedings, damages, **8.01–40.1**
Crimes and offenses, damages, **8.01–40.1**
Damages, crimes and offenses, **8.01–40.1**
Funds Transfers, generally, this index
Internet, generally, this index
Limitation of actions, damages, crimes and offenses, **8.01–40.1**

CONCEALMENT
Shoplifting, generally, this index

CONCILIATION
Arbitration and Award, generally, this index

CONDOLENCES
Medical malpractice, evidence, **8.01–52.1, 8.01–581.20:1**

CONFESSION OF JUDGMENT
Generally, **8.01–431 et seq.**

CONFIDENTIAL OR PRIVILEGED INFORMATION
See, also, Disclosure, generally, this index
Anonymous plaintiffs, **8.01–15.1**
Arbitration and Award, this index
Attorneys, attorney client privilege, undisclosed information, waiver, **8.01–420.7**
Courts, identification numbers, redacting, **8.01–420.8**
Damages, interpreters, disclosure, **8.01–44.3**
Internet, torts, identity and identification, subpoenas, **8.01–407.1**
Mediation, **8.01–581.22**
Medical malpractice, **8.01–581.17**
Witnesses, this index

CONFLICT OF LAWS
Foreign currency, claims, **8.01–465.19**
Limitation of actions, **8.01–247**
Money, foreign currency, claims, **8.01–465.19**

CONFLICT RESOLUTION
Arbitration and Award, generally, this index

CONGRESS
Jury, exemptions, **8.01–341**

CONSERVATION
Recycling, generally, this index

CONSERVATORS AND CONSERVATORSHIP
See, also, Fiduciaries, generally, this index
Actions and proceedings, pleadings, style, **8.01–6.3**
Appeal and review, **8.01–670**
Names, pleadings, style, **8.01–6.3**
Pleadings, style, **8.01–6.3**

CONSOLIDATION OF ACTIONS
Joinder, generally, this index

CONSTITUTIONAL OFFICERS
Attorney General, generally, this index
Governor, generally, this index

CONSTRUCTION
Actions and proceedings, contracts, venue, **8.01–262.1**
Arbitration and award, contracts, venue, **8.01–262.1**
Contractors, generally, this index
Contracts, venue, **8.01–262.1**
Venue, contracts, **8.01–262.1**

CONSUMER PROTECTION
Facsimile transmissions, advertisements, unsolicited, **8.01–40.2**
Limitation of actions, **8.01–249**

CONSUMERS
Sales, generally, this index

CONTAINERS
Recycling, generally, this index

CONTEMPT
Fraud against taxpayers, actions and proceedings, civil investigative demands, **8.01–216.18**
Mandamus, **8.01–652**

CONTINUANCE
Service of process, late return, **8.01–294**

CONTRACTORS
Actions and proceedings, privileges and immunities, **8.01–39**
Privileges and immunities, actions and proceedings, **8.01–39**
Wrongful death, privileges and immunities, **8.01–39**

CONTRACTS
Actions and proceedings, **8.01–27 et seq.**
  Assignments, **8.01–423**
  Counterclaims, assignee, **8.01–423**
  Default judgments, **8.01–28**
  Defenses, equity, **8.01–422**
  Dismissal and nonsuit, joint and several liability, **8.01–30**
  Limitation of actions, **8.01–230**

CONTRACTS—Cont'd
Actions and proceedings—Cont'd
  Rescission, fraud, undue influence, **8.01–221.2**
Affidavits, lost or destroyed documents, actions and proceedings, **8.01–32**
Appearance, default judgments, **8.01–28**
Arbitration and award, **8.01–581.01 et seq.**
  Written agreement, compromise and settlement, **8.01–581.25**
Assignments, actions and proceedings, **8.01–423**
Breach of contract, limitation of actions, **8.01–230**
Clergy, privileges and immunities, **8.01–220.1:3**
Copies, lost or destroyed documents, actions and proceedings, evidence, **8.01–32**
Costs, rescission, fraud, undue influence, **8.01–221.2**
Counterclaims, assignee, **8.01–423**
Damages, equity, **8.01–422**
Deeds and Conveyances, generally, this index
Default judgments, **8.01–28**
Defenses, equity, **8.01–422**
Dismissal and nonsuit, joint and several liability, **8.01–30**
Equity, defenses, **8.01–422**
Evidence, lost or destroyed documents, actions and proceedings, copies, **8.01–32**
Fraud,
  Attorney fees, costs, **8.01–221.2**
  Equitable defense, **8.01–422**
Hearings, privileges and immunities, strategic lawsuits against public participation, **8.01–223.2**
Interference, privileges and immunities, hearings, strategic lawsuits against public participation, **8.01–223.2**
Joint and several liability, **8.01–30, 8.01–442**
Judgments and decrees, default judgments, **8.01–28**
Jurisdiction, **8.01–328 et seq.**
Leases, generally, this index
Limitation of actions, **8.01–230, 8.01–246**
  Foreign states, **8.01–247**
  Rescission, **8.01–249**
Oaths and affirmations, lost or destroyed documents, actions and proceedings, **8.01–32**
Pleadings, joinder, torts, **8.01–272**
Privileges and immunities, hearings, strategic lawsuits against public participation, **8.01–223.2**
Recoupment, equitable defense, **8.01–422**
Rescission,
  Attorney fees, costs, **8.01–221.2**
  Limitation of actions, **8.01–249**
Transfers, actions and proceedings, **8.01–423**
Undue influence, attorney fees, costs, **8.01–221.2**

CONTRIBUTORY NEGLIGENCE
Winter sports safety, **8.01–227.20**

CONTROLLED SUBSTANCES
  See, also, Drugs and Medicine, generally, this index

CONTROLLED SUBSTANCES—Cont'd
Actions and proceedings, drug dealers, liability, **8.01–227.4 et seq.**
Driving under influence of alcohol or drugs. Traffic Rules and Regulations, this index
Drug dealers, liability, **8.01–227.4 et seq.**
Liability, drug dealers, **8.01–227.4 et seq.**
Limitation of actions, drug dealers, liability, **8.01–227.7**
Naloxone, emergency medical services, administration, **8.01–225**
Opioid antagonists, administration, privileges and immunities, **8.01–225**
Overdose, naloxone, emergency medical services, administration, **8.01–225**

CONVALESCENT HOMES
Nursing Homes, generally, this index

CONVEYANCES
Deeds and Conveyances, generally, this index

CONVICTION OF CRIME
Crimes and Offenses, this index

CONVICTS
Correctional Institutions, generally, this index
Jails, generally, this index

COOPERATION
Motor vehicle insurance, underinsured motorists, subrogation, **8.01–66.1:1**

COPARTNERSHIP
Partnerships, generally, this index

CORPORATIONS
Actions and proceedings, venue, **8.01–262**
Executions, **8.01–468**
Foreign Corporations, generally, this index
Garnishment, **8.01–513**
Insurance companies. Insurance, generally, this index
Jurisdiction, **8.01–328.1**
Long Arm Statute, **8.01–328.1**
Pleadings, affidavits, **8.01–279**
Public Utilities, generally, this index
Quo warranto, **8.01–635 et seq.**
Service of process, **8.01–299**
  Fraud against taxpayers, actions and proceedings, civil investigative demands, **8.01–216.13**
  Garnishment, **8.01–513**
  Receivers and receivership, **8.01–303**
Trusts and trustees, service of process, **8.01–303**
Venue, **8.01–262**
Writs, quo warranto, **8.01–635 et seq.**

CORRECTIONAL INSTITUTIONS
  See, also, Jails, generally, this index
Actions and proceedings,
  Divorce, guardian ad litem, costs, **8.01–9**
  Fraud against taxpayers, application of law, **8.01–216.8**

CORRECTIONAL INSTITUTIONS—Cont'd
Actions and proceedings—Cont'd
  Limitation of actions, **8.01–243.2**
  Prisoner litigation reform, **8.01–689 et seq.**
Annuities, wrongful incarceration, compensation and salaries, **8.01–195.11**
Bonds (officers and fiduciaries), habeas corpus, **8.01–656**
Capital Punishment, generally, this index
Change of names, **8.01–217**
Community colleges, tuition, wrongful incarceration, compensation and salaries, **8.01–195.11**
Compensation and salaries, wrongful incarceration, **8.01–195.10 et seq.**
Costs,
  Actions and proceedings, prisoner litigation reform, **8.01–691**
  Divorce, guardian ad litem, **8.01–9**
Damages,
  Prisoner litigation reform, **8.01–689 et seq.**
  Wrongful incarceration, compensation and salaries, **8.01–195.10 et seq.**
Death penalty. Capital Punishment, generally, this index
Depositions, **8.01–410**
Discovery, prisoner litigation reform, **8.01–695**
Dismissal and nonsuit, prisoner litigation reform, **8.01–694**
Divorce, inmates, guardian ad litem, costs, **8.01–9**
Executions. Capital Punishment, generally, this index
Exhaustion of remedies, limitation of actions, **8.01–243.2**
Fraud against taxpayers, actions and proceedings, application of law, **8.01–216.8**
Grants, wrongful incarceration, compensation and salaries, **8.01–195.11**
Guardian ad litem,
  Inmates, divorce, **8.01–9**
  Service of process, **8.01–297**
Habeas Corpus, generally, this index
In forma pauperis, actions and proceedings, prisoner litigation reform, **8.01–691, 8.01–692**
Indigent persons, actions and proceedings, prisoner litigation reform, **8.01–691, 8.01–692**
Injunctions, prisoner litigation reform, **8.01–689 et seq.**
Jails, generally, this index
Jury, exemptions, **8.01–341**
Limitation of actions, **8.01–243.2**
Local correctional facilities. Jails, generally, this index
Local detention facilities. Jails, generally, this index
Mandamus, prisoner litigation reform, **8.01–689 et seq.**
Medical care and treatment, personal injuries, liens and incumbrances, **8.01–66.9:1**
Oral argument, prisoner litigation reform, **8.01–695**
Personal injuries, medical care and treatment, liens and incumbrances, **8.01–66.9:1**

CORRECTIONAL INSTITUTIONS—Cont'd
Postrelease supervision. Probation, generally, this index
Prisoner litigation reform, **8.01–689 et seq.**
Probation, generally, this index
Records and recordation, prisoner litigation reform, **8.01–697**
Release,
Habeas Corpus, generally, this index
Probation, generally, this index
Residential facilities, wrongful incarceration, compensation and salaries, **8.01–195.10 et seq.**
Service of process, **8.01–297**
Habeas corpus, **8.01–658**
Prisoner litigation reform, **8.01–694**
Statute of limitations, **8.01–243.2**
Subpoenas, prisoner litigation reform, **8.01–695**
Summary judgment, prisoner litigation reform, **8.01–696**
Superintendents, service of process, habeas corpus, **8.01–658**
Transition assistance grants, wrongful incarceration, compensation and salaries, **8.01–195.11**
Venue, prisoner litigation reform, **8.01–693**
Witnesses, compelling attendance, **8.01–410**
Wrongful incarceration, compensation and salaries, **8.01–195.10 et seq.**

CORROBORATION
Witnesses, incapacity, **8.01–397**

COSTS
Arbitration and award, **8.01–576.7**
Cemeteries, destruction, damages, **8.01–44.6**
Contracts, rescission, fraud, undue influence, **8.01–221.2**
Criminal history record information, disclosure, **8.01–40.3**
Declaratory judgments, **8.01–190**
Deeds and conveyances, rescission, fraud, undue influence, **8.01–221.2**
Dismissal and nonsuit, **8.01–380**
Evidence, dismissal and nonsuit, reasonableness, **8.01–380**
Fraud against taxpayers, actions and proceedings, **8.01–216.7**
Garnishment, **8.01–511, 8.01–521**
Habeas corpus, **8.01–662**
Interpreters, confidential or privileged information, disclosure, **8.01–44.3**
Military forces, Servicemembers Civil Relief Act, default judgments, **8.01–15.2**
Motor vehicle insurance, underinsured motorists, cooperation, subrogation, **8.01–66.1:1**
Process, service of process, waiver, **8.01–286.1**
Production of books and papers, copies, **8.01–417**
Servicemembers Civil Relief Act, default judgments, **8.01–15.2**
State, this index
State agencies, fraud against taxpayers, **8.01–216.3**
State departments, fraud against taxpayers, **8.01–216.3**

COUNSEL
Attorneys, generally, this index

COUNSELORS AND COUNSELING
Attorneys, chemically dependent persons, privileges and immunities, **8.01–226.1**
Confidential or privileged information, witnesses, **8.01–400.2**
Disasters, privileges and immunities, **8.01–225.01, 8.01–225.02**
Emergencies, privileges and immunities, **8.01–225.01, 8.01–225.02**
Evidence, confidential or privileged information, witnesses, **8.01–400.2**
Marriage and Family Therapists, generally, this index
Privileges and immunities,
Confidential or privileged information, witnesses, **8.01–400.2**
Disasters, **8.01–225.01, 8.01–225.02**
Psychologists and Psychology, generally, this index
Witnesses, confidential or privileged information, **8.01–400.2**

COUNTERCLAIM
Setoff and Counterclaim, generally, this index

COUNTIES
Circuit Courts, generally, this index
Correctional institutions. Jails, generally, this index
Delinquent Children, generally, this index
District Courts, generally, this index
Employees. County Officers and Employees, generally, this index
Evidence, records and recordation, **8.01–390**
Firefighters and Fire Departments, generally, this index
Garnishment, officers and employees, **8.01–524, 8.01–525**
Health department, officers and employees, emergency medical care, privileges and immunities, **8.01–225**
Hearings, privileges and immunities, strategic lawsuits against public participation, **8.01–223.2**
Jails, generally, this index
Jurisdiction, tax collection, Long Arm Statute, **8.01–328.1**
Labor and employment. County Officers and Employees, generally, this index
Officers and employees. County Officers and Employees, generally, this index
Prisons and prisoners. Jails, generally, this index
Privileges and immunities, hearings, strategic lawsuits against public participation, **8.01–223.2**
Process, service of process, **8.01–300**
Real Property Taxation, generally, this index
Records and recordation, evidence, **8.01–390**
Service of process, **8.01–300**
Tax collection, Long Arm Statute, **8.01–328.1**

COUNTIES—Cont'd
Taxation. Real Property Taxation, generally, this index

COUNTRIES
Foreign Countries, generally, this index

COUNTY ELECTORAL BOARDS
Jury, exemptions, **8.01–341.1**

COUNTY JAILS
Jails, generally, this index

COUNTY OFFICERS AND EMPLOYEES
Compensation and salaries, garnishment, **8.01–524, 8.01–525**
Emergency medical care, health department, privileges and immunities, **8.01–225**
Garnishment, **8.01–524, 8.01–525**
Littering, pick up programs, privileges and immunities, **8.01–226.8**
Privileges and immunities,
  Emergency medical care, health department, **8.01–225**
  Littering, pick up programs, **8.01–226.8**

COURT COSTS
Costs, generally, this index

COURT OF APPEALS
  Generally, **8.01–669 et seq.**
Appeals in Criminal Prosecutions, generally, this index
Bonds (officers and fiduciaries), appeal and review, **8.01–676.1**
Crimes and offenses. Appeals in Criminal Prosecutions, generally, this index
Limitation of actions, appeal and review, **8.01–671, 8.01–675.3**
Records and recordation, appeal and review, **8.01–675.4**

COURT OFFICERS AND EMPLOYEES
Attorneys, generally, this index
Littering, pick up programs, privileges and immunities, **8.01–226.8**
Privileges and immunities, littering, pick up programs, **8.01–226.8**

COURT ORDERS
Orders of Court, generally, this index

COURT REPORTERS
Certificates and certification, transcripts, **8.01–420.3**
Transcripts, **8.01–420.3**

COURTS
Appeal and Review, generally, this index
Attachment, generally, this index
Attorneys, generally, this index
Bank deposits and collections, records and recordation, numbers and numbering, redacting, **8.01–420.8**
Bonds (officers and fiduciaries), receivers and receivership, **8.01–588**

COURTS—Cont'd
Certificates and certification, records and recordation, evidence, **8.01–389**
Circuit Courts, generally, this index
Confidential or privileged information, identification numbers, redacting, **8.01–420.8**
Costs, generally, this index
Court of Appeals, generally, this index
Courts not of record. District Courts, generally, this index
District Courts, generally, this index
Dockets and Docketing, generally, this index
Garnishment, generally, this index
Habeas Corpus, generally, this index
Identification numbers, records and recordation, redacting, **8.01–420.8**
Judges, generally, this index
Judgments and Decrees, generally, this index
Jurisdiction, generally, this index
Jury, generally, this index
Lost or destroyed documents, **8.01–392 et seq.**
Not of record. District Courts, generally, this index
Orders of Court, generally, this index
Receivers and Receivership, generally, this index
Records and recordation,
  Certificates and certification, evidence, **8.01–389**
  Evidence, **8.01–389**
  Identification numbers, redacting, **8.01–420.8**
Removal or Transfer of Causes, generally, this index
Seals, records and recordation, evidence, **8.01–389**
Signatures, judicial notice, **8.01–387**
Supreme Court, generally, this index
Terms, **8.01–445**

COURTS NOT OF RECORD
District Courts, generally, this index

COURTS OF RECORD
Courts, generally, this index

CREDIT
Attachment, generally, this index
Garnishment, generally, this index
Judicial sales, **8.01–96**

CREDIT CARDS
Courts, records and recordation, numbers and numbering, redacting, **8.01–420.8**
Numbers and numbering, courts, records and recordation, redacting, **8.01–420.8**

CREDIT UNIONS
Funds Transfers, generally, this index

CREDITORS
Debtors and Creditors, generally, this index

CRIME LABORATORIES
Laboratories, generally, this index

CRIME VICTIMS
Actions and proceedings, personal injuries, **8.01–221**

CRIME VICTIMS—Cont'd
Damages, stalking, **8.01–42.3**
Notice, privileges and immunities, **8.01–226.11**
Personal injuries, actions and proceedings, **8.01–221**
Privileges and immunities, notice, **8.01–226.11**
Stalking, damages, **8.01–42.3**

CRIMES AND OFFENSES
Actions and proceedings, personal injuries, **8.01–221**
Appeals in Criminal Prosecutions, generally, this index
Arrest, generally, this index
Capital Punishment, generally, this index
Coercion. Duress or Coercion, generally, this index
Conviction of crime,
  Actions and proceedings, severance of cause, **8.01–22**
  Appeals in Criminal Prosecutions, generally, this index
  Contrary to evidence, setting aside, **8.01–680**
  Habeas corpus, **8.01–654**
  Harmless error, **8.01–678**
  Judgments and decrees, **8.01–21**
  Reversal, **8.01–678**
  Setting aside, contrary to evidence, **8.01–680**
  Severance of cause, **8.01–22**
  Successors in interest, **8.01–22**
County jails. Jails, generally, this index
Crime Victims, generally, this index
Damages, personal injuries, **8.01–221**
Death penalty. Capital Punishment, generally, this index
Delinquent Children, generally, this index
Driving under influence of alcohol or drugs. Traffic Rules and Regulations, this index
Duress or Coercion, generally, this index
Evidence, polygraph tests, **8.01–418.2**
Execution. Capital Punishment, generally, this index
False pretenses. Fraud, generally, this index
Fines and Penalties, generally, this index
Fraud, generally, this index
Habeas Corpus, generally, this index
Harmless error, conviction of crime, **8.01–678**
History record information. Criminal History Record Information, generally, this index
Informants, rewards, nonprofit organizations, **8.01–226.3**
Intimidation. Duress or Coercion, generally, this index
Jails, generally, this index
Libel and Slander, generally, this index
Nolo contendere, evidence, actions and proceedings, **8.01–418**
Penal institutions. Correctional Institutions, generally, this index
Penalties. Fines and Penalties, generally, this index

CRIMES AND OFFENSES—Cont'd
Polygraph tests, **8.01–418.2**
Prisons and prisoners. Correctional Institutions, generally, this index
Probation, generally, this index
Records and recordation. Criminal History Record Information, generally, this index
Reversal, **8.01–678**
Rewards, informants, privileges and immunities, **8.01–226.3**
Searches and Seizures, generally, this index
Second and subsequent offenses, wrongful incarceration, compensation and salaries, eligibility, **8.01–195.12**
Shoplifting, generally, this index
Slander. Libel and Slander, generally, this index
Supersedeas or Stay, generally, this index
Terrorism, generally, this index
Trial de novo, verdict contrary to evidence, **8.01–680**
Vandalism, generally, this index
Victims. Crime Victims, generally, this index
Writ of error. Appeals in Criminal Prosecutions, generally, this index
Wrongful incarceration, compensation and salaries, **8.01–195.10 et seq.**

CRIMINAL APPEALS
Appeals in Criminal Prosecutions, generally, this index

CRIMINAL HISTORY RECORD INFORMATION
Actions and proceedings, disclosure, damages, **8.01–40.3**
Attorney fees, disclosure, **8.01–40.3**
Costs, disclosure, **8.01–40.3**
Damages, disclosure, **8.01–40.3**
Disclosure, damages, **8.01–40.3**

CRIMINAL INJURIES COMPENSATION FUND
Liens and incumbrances, notice, **8.01–66.5, 8.01–66.6**

CRIMINAL JUSTICE
Crimes and Offenses, generally, this index

CRIPPLED PERSONS
Handicapped Persons, generally, this index

CROSS EXAMINATION
Witnesses, this index

CURRENCY
Money, generally, this index

DAMAGES
Additur, **8.01–383, 8.01–383.1**
Amount,
  Jury, **8.01–379.1**
  New trial, **8.01–383, 8.01–383.1**
Appeal and review, **8.01–383.1, 8.01–682**

DAMAGES—Cont'd
Arbitration and Award, generally, this index
Assignments, **8.01–26**
Assisted suicide, **8.01–622.1**
Bonds (officers and fiduciaries), appeal and review, **8.01–676.1**
Boundaries, **8.01–182**
Cemeteries, destruction, **8.01–44.6**
Compensation and salaries, reimbursement, **8.01–35**
Correctional institutions,
Prisoner litigation reform, **8.01–689 et seq.**
Wrongful incarceration, compensation and salaries, **8.01–195.10 et seq.**
Counterclaim. Setoff and Counterclaim, generally, this index
Crime victims, stalking, **8.01–42.3**
Criminal history record information, disclosure, **8.01–40.3**
Declaratory judgments, **8.01–186**
Property, **8.01–187**
Defamation, **8.01–45 et seq.**
Drug dealers, liability, **8.01–227.4 et seq.**
Ejectment, this index
Evidence, lost profits, new business, unestablished business, **8.01–221.1**
Excessive, new trial, **8.01–383, 8.01–383.1**
Executions, financial institutions, notice, certificates and certification, **8.01–502.1**
Exemplary damages,
Driving under influence of alcohol or drugs, **8.01–44.5**
Hate crimes, **8.01–42.1**
Libel and slander, labor and employment, **8.01–46.1**
Limitations, **8.01–38.1**
State, fraud against taxpayers, **8.01–216.3**
Summary judgment, depositions, basis, **8.01–420**
Torts, state, **8.01–195.3**
Wrongful death, **8.01–52**
Fraud against taxpayers, actions and proceedings, **8.01–216.7**
Hate crimes, **8.01–42.1**
Health care professionals, insurance, payment, actions and proceedings, **8.01–27.4**
Hotels and motels, **8.01–42.2**
Inadequate damages, new trial, **8.01–383, 8.01–383.1**
Interest, **8.01–382**
Interpreters, disclosure, **8.01–44.3**
Intimidation, hate crimes, **8.01–42.1**
Jails,
Prisoner litigation reform, **8.01–689 et seq.**
Wrongful incarceration, compensation and salaries, **8.01–195.10 et seq.**
Landlord and Tenant, this index
Laundries and dry cleaners, privileges and immunities, **8.01–42**
Libel and slander, **8.01–45 et seq.**
Limitation of actions, **8.01–230**
Suspension, **8.01–229**

DAMAGES—Cont'd
Limitations, punitive damages, **8.01–38.1**
Lost profits, new business, unestablished business, **8.01–221.1**
Medical malpractice,
Amount, limitations, **8.01–581.15**
Punitive damages, **8.01–38.1**
Mitigation, libel and slander, **8.01–46**
Motor Vehicles, this index
Natural gas, meters, tampering, **8.01–44.7**
New business, lost profits, **8.01–221.1**
New trial, **8.01–383, 8.01–383.1**
Personal Injuries, this index
Physicians and surgeons, insurance, payment, actions and proceedings, **8.01–27.4**
Reduction, appeal and review, **8.01–383.1**
Remittitur, new trial, **8.01–383, 8.01–383.1**
Setoff and Counterclaim, generally, this index
Shoplifting, **8.01–44.4**
Space, flight, privileges and immunities, **8.01–227.8 et seq.**
Stalking, crime victims, **8.01–42.3**
State, this index
Suicide, assisted suicide, **8.01–622.1**
Treble damages, health care professionals, insurance, payment, **8.01–27.4**
Unestablished business, lost profits, **8.01–221.1**
Water supply, meters, tampering, **8.01–44.7**
Wrongful death, **8.01–50 et seq.**
Wrongful incarceration, compensation and salaries, **8.01–195.10 et seq.**

DATA PROCESSING
Computers, generally, this index

DEAD BODIES
Cemeteries, generally, this index

DEAD MANS STATUTE
Witnesses, **8.01–397**

DEAF AND MUTE PERSONS
Hearing Impaired Persons, generally, this index

DEATH
Actions and proceedings,
Debtors and creditors, **8.01–11**
Limitation of actions, **8.01–229**
Severance of cause, **8.01–22**
Survival, **8.01–25**
Appeal and review, **8.01–20**
Capital Punishment, generally, this index
Cemeteries, generally, this index
Compromise and settlement, medical care and treatment, expenses, **8.01–66.10**
Debtors and creditors, actions and proceedings, **8.01–11**
Judgments and decrees, **8.01–21**
Limitation of actions, **8.01–229**
Motor vehicle insurance, policies, limits, disclosure, **8.01–417**
Negligence. Wrongful Death, generally, this index

DEATH—Cont'd
Parties, this index
Severance of cause, **8.01–22**
Space, flight, privileges and immunities, **8.01–227.8 et seq.**
Statute of limitations, **8.01–229**
Successors in interest, **8.01–22**
Survival, actions and proceedings, **8.01–25**
Wills, generally, this index
Winter sports safety, **8.01–227.11 et seq.**
Wrongful Death, generally, this index

DEATH PENALTY
Capital Punishment, generally, this index

DEBIT CARDS
Courts, records and recordation, numbers and numbering, redacting, **8.01–420.8**
Numbers and numbering, courts, records and recordation, redacting, **8.01–420.8**

DEBT
Debtors and Creditors, generally, this index
Indebtedness, generally, this index

DEBTORS AND CREDITORS
See, also, Indebtedness, generally, this index
Actions and proceedings, **8.01–27.1 et seq.**
Assignments, **8.01–14**
Beneficial owners, **8.01–13**
Death, **8.01–11**
Equity, relief, **8.01–33**
Limitation of actions, **8.01–229**
Lost or destroyed documents, **8.01–32**
Pleadings, payment, **8.01–421**
Affidavits, lost or destroyed documents, actions and proceedings, **8.01–32**
Assignments, actions and proceedings, **8.01–14**
Attachment, generally, this index
Beneficial owners, actions and proceedings, **8.01–13**
Children and minors, liability, **8.01–278**
Confession of judgment, **8.01–431 et seq.**
Copies, lost or destroyed documents, actions and proceedings, evidence, **8.01–32**
Death, actions and proceedings, **8.01–11**
Dockets and docketing, confession of judgment, **8.01–440**
Endorsements, confession of judgment, **8.01–437**
Equity, relief, **8.01–33**
Evidence, lost or destroyed documents, actions and proceedings, copies, **8.01–32**
Evidences of Indebtedness, generally, this index
Executions, **8.01–446 et seq.**
Third parties, **8.01–365 et seq.**
Forms, confession of judgment, **8.01–436**
Garnishment, generally, this index
Judgments and decrees, **8.01–427**
Liens and Incumbrances, generally, this index
Limitation of actions, **8.01–229**
Lost or destroyed documents, actions and proceedings, **8.01–32**

DEBTORS AND CREDITORS—Cont'd
Oaths and affirmations, lost or destroyed documents, actions and proceedings, **8.01–32**
Partition, **8.01–81**
Payment, pleadings, **8.01–421**
Personal property, executions, **8.01–446 et seq.**
Third parties, **8.01–365 et seq.**
Pleadings, payment, **8.01–421**
Receivers and Receivership, generally, this index
Records and recordation, confession of judgment, **8.01–439**
Statute of limitations, **8.01–229**
Writ of fieri facias, **8.01–446 et seq.**

DECEDENTS ESTATES
Probate Proceedings, generally, this index

DECEIT
Fraud, generally, this index

DECEPTION
Fraud, generally, this index

DECISIONS
Judgments and Decrees, generally, this index

DECLARATIONS
Unsworn written declarations, **8.01–4.3**

DECLARATORY JUDGMENTS
Generally, **8.01–184 et seq.**
Costs, **8.01–190**
Damages, **8.01–186**
Property, **8.01–187**
Injunctions, **8.01–189**
Interrogatories, jury, **8.01–188**
Jurisdiction, **8.01–184**
Jury, **8.01–188**
Property, compensation and salaries, **8.01–187**
Sales and use tax, foreign states, jurisdiction, **8.01–184.1**
Venue, **8.01–185**

DECREES
Judgments and Decrees, generally, this index

DEEDS AND CONVEYANCES
See, also, Title to Property, generally, this index
Aged persons, **8.01–67 et seq.**
Attorney fees, rescission, fraud, undue influence, **8.01–221.2**
Children and minors, **8.01–67 et seq.**
Costs, rescission, fraud, undue influence, **8.01–221.2**
Defenses, equity, **8.01–422**
Equity, defenses, **8.01–422**
Evidence, **8.01–389**
Lost or destroyed documents, **8.01–394**
Handicapped persons, **8.01–67 et seq.**
Judicial sales, **8.01–110 et seq.**
Limitation of actions, **8.01–253**
Lost or destroyed documents, **8.01–393**
Proof, **8.01–394**

DEEDS AND CONVEYANCES—Cont'd
Mentally ill persons, **8.01–67 et seq.**
Mentally retarded and developmentally disabled persons, **8.01–67 et seq.**
Rescission, attorney fees, fraud, undue influence, **8.01–221.2**
Undue influence, attorney fees, costs, **8.01–221.2**

DEEDS OF TRUST
Limitation of actions, **8.01–241 et seq.**

DEFAMATION
Libel and Slander, generally, this index

DEFAULT JUDGMENTS
Contracts, **8.01–28**
Forcible entry and detainer, **8.01–28**
Fraud, vacating or setting aside, **8.01–428**
Garnishment, **8.01–519**
Servicemembers Civil Relief Act, affidavits, **8.01–15.2**
Vacating or setting aside, **8.01–428**
Servicemembers Civil Relief Act, **8.01–15.2**

DEFENDANTS
Parties, generally, this index

DEFIBRILLATION
Privileges and immunities, **8.01–225**

DEFINITIONS
Words and Phrases, generally, this index

DELINQUENT CHILDREN
Annuities, wrongful incarceration, compensation and salaries, **8.01–195.11**
Community colleges, tuition, wrongful incarceration, compensation and salaries, **8.01–195.11**
Compensation and salaries, wrongful incarceration, **8.01–195.10 et seq.**
Facilities, wrongful incarceration, compensation and salaries, **8.01–195.10 et seq.**
Grants, wrongful incarceration, compensation and salaries, **8.01–195.11**
Transition assistance grants, wrongful incarceration, compensation and salaries, **8.01–195.11**
Venue, application of law, **8.01–259**
Wrongful incarceration, compensation and salaries, **8.01–195.10 et seq.**

DEMURRER
Pleadings, **8.01–273**
Evidence, abolishment, **8.01–276**

DENTAL LABORATORIES
Laboratories, generally, this index

DENTISTS AND DENTISTRY
Dental hygienists, privileges and immunities, disasters, **8.01–225.01, 8.01–225.02**
Disasters, privileges and immunities, **8.01–225.01, 8.01–225.02**
Emergencies, privileges and immunities, **8.01–225.01, 8.01–225.02**

DENTISTS AND DENTISTRY—Cont'd
Malpractice. Medical Malpractice, generally, this index
Medical Malpractice, generally, this index
Privileges and immunities, disasters, **8.01–225.01, 8.01–225.02**

DEPARTMENTS
State Departments, generally, this index

DEPENDENT OR NEGLECTED CHILDREN
See, also, Delinquent Children, generally, this index
Guardian Ad Litem, generally, this index
Juvenile delinquents. Delinquent Children, generally, this index

DEPOSITIONS
Arbitration and award, **8.01–581.06**
Correctional institutions, inmates, **8.01–410**
Costs, video tape, **8.01–412.5**
Cross examination, **8.01–404**
Foreign states, interstate depositions and discovery, **8.01–412.8 et seq.**
Fraud against taxpayers, actions and proceedings,
Civil investigative demands, **8.01–216.10 et seq.**
State, copies, **8.01–216.6**
Identity and identification, video tape, **8.01–412.4**
Impeachment, **8.01–404**
Inconsistent statements, **8.01–404**
Interstate depositions and discovery, **8.01–412.8 et seq.**
Limitations, numbers and numbering, witnesses, **8.01–420.6**
Location, **8.01–420.4**
Medical malpractice, review panel, **8.01–581.4**
Nonparty witnesses, **8.01–420.4**
Nonresidents, location, **8.01–420.4**
Notice, video tape, **8.01–412.3**
Numbers and numbering, witnesses, limitations, **8.01–420.6**
Oaths and affirmations, video tape, **8.01–412.4**
Objections and exceptions, video tape, **8.01–412.4**
Reciprocity, interstate depositions and discovery, **8.01–412.14**
Rules and regulations, video tape, **8.01–412.4, 8.01–412.6**
Service of process, publication, dissolution of marriage, **8.01–319**
State, this index
Subpoenas,
Interstate depositions and discovery, **8.01–412.8 et seq.**
Video tape, **8.01–412.3**
Summary judgment, **8.01–420**
Transcripts, video tape, **8.01–412.2 et seq.**
Video tape, **8.01–412.2 et seq.**

DEPOSITS
Bank Deposits and Collections, generally, this index

DESTITUTE PERSONS
Indigent Persons, generally, this index

DESTROYED DOCUMENTS
Lost or Destroyed Documents, generally, this index

DETAINER
Forcible Entry and Detainer, generally, this index

DETENTION
Arrest, generally, this index
Jails, generally, this index
Shoplifting, merchants, privileges and immunities, **8.01–226.9**

DETENTION FACILITIES
Correctional Institutions, generally, this index
Jails, generally, this index

DETINUE
Generally, **8.01–114 et seq.**

DETONATORS
Explosives, generally, this index

DEVELOPMENTALLY DISABLED PERSONS
Mentally Retarded and Developmentally Disabled Persons, generally, this index

DEVISES AND BEQUESTS
Probate Proceedings, generally, this index
Wills, generally, this index

DIABETES
Schools and school districts, drugs and medicine, privileges and immunities, **8.01–225**

DIRECTED VERDICTS
Generally, **8.01–378**

DISABILITIES
Handicapped Persons, generally, this index

DISABILITY INSURANCE
Health Insurance, generally, this index

DISABLED PERSONS
Handicapped Persons, generally, this index

DISASTERS
See, also, Emergencies, generally, this index
Architects and architecture, privileges and immunities, rescue, **8.01–226.2**
Civil Defense, generally, this index
Engineers, privileges and immunities, rescue, **8.01–226.2**
Health care professionals, privileges and immunities, **8.01–225.01, 8.01–225.02**
Privileges and immunities,
Health care professionals, **8.01–225.01, 8.01–225.02**
Rescue, **8.01–226.2**
Rescue, privileges and immunities, **8.01–226.2**

DISCLOSURE
See, also, Confidential or Privileged Information, generally, this index
Anonymous plaintiffs, **8.01–15.1**
Arbitration and Award, this index

DISCLOSURE—Cont'd
Discovery, generally, this index
Evidence, protective orders, **8.01–420.01**
Executions, interrogatories, **8.01–506**
Internet, torts, identity and identification, subpoenas, **8.01–407.1**
Interpreters, damages, **8.01–44.3**
Lead based paint, privileges and immunities, **8.01–226.7**

DISCOVERY
Correctional institutions, prisoner litigation reform, **8.01–695**
Depositions, generally, this index
Entry on Property, generally, this index
Executions, interrogatories, **8.01–506**
Foreign states, interstate depositions and discovery, **8.01–412.8 et seq.**
Fraud against taxpayers, actions and proceedings,
Civil investigative demands, **8.01–216.10 et seq.**
Supersedeas or stay, **8.01–216.6**
Interrogatories, generally, this index
Interstate depositions and discovery, **8.01–412.8 et seq.**
Jails, prisoner litigation reform, **8.01–695**
Joinder, **8.01–267.1**
Jurisdiction, personal jurisdiction, objections and exceptions, waiver, **8.01–277.1**
Limitation of actions, waiver, **8.01–384.2**
Process, defects, objections and exceptions, waiver, **8.01–277.1**
Production of Books and Papers, generally, this index
Protective orders, **8.01–420.01**
Reciprocity, interstate depositions and discovery, **8.01–412.14**
State, fraud against taxpayers, actions and proceedings, supersedeas or stay, **8.01–216.6**
Statute of limitations, waiver, **8.01–384.2**
Subpoenas, interstate depositions and discovery, **8.01–412.8 et seq.**
Waiver, limitation of actions, **8.01–384.2**

DISCRIMINATION
See, also, Bias and Prejudice, generally, this index
Hate crimes, actions and proceedings, **8.01–42.1**

DISMISSAL AND NONSUIT
Generally, **8.01–380**
Attachment, **8.01–269, 8.01–569**
Attorney fees, **8.01–380**
Capital punishment, mentally retarded and developmentally disabled persons, actions and proceedings, claims, **8.01–654.2**
Contracts, joint and several liability, **8.01–30**
Correctional institutions, prisoner litigation reform, **8.01–694**
Counterclaims, **8.01–380**
Dockets and docketing, **8.01–335**
Fraud against taxpayers, actions and proceedings, **8.01–216.6**
Consent, **8.01–216.5**

DISMISSAL AND NONSUIT—Cont'd
Garnishment, **8.01–516.1**
Injunctions, **8.01–634**
Jails, prisoner litigation reform, **8.01–694**
Limitation of actions, **8.01–229**
Lis pendens, **8.01–269**
Notice, previous nonsuits, **8.01–380**
Orders of court, previous nonsuits, **8.01–380**
Service of process, special appearance, motions, **8.01–277**
Special appearance, service of process, motions, **8.01–277**
State, this index
Statute of limitations, **8.01–229**
Third parties, **8.01–380**

DISPUTE RESOLUTION
Arbitration and Award, generally, this index

DISSOLUTION
Injunctions, this index

DISSOLUTION OF MARRIAGE
Divorce. Marriage, this index

DISTRESS
Forcible Entry and Detainer, generally, this index

DISTRICT COURTS
Executions, generally, this index
Judgments and Decrees, generally, this index
Records and recordation, **8.01–688**
Rules and regulations, **8.01–4**
Transcripts, **8.01–688**
Trial, generally, this index

DISTRICTS
Real Property Taxation, generally, this index

DIVISION OF PROPERTY
Partition, generally, this index

DIVORCE
Marriage, this index

DOCKETS AND DOCKETING
Generally, **8.01–331 et seq., 8.01–446 et seq.**
Accord and satisfaction, **8.01–453 et seq.**
Anonymous plaintiffs, **8.01–15.1**
Assignments, **8.01–452**
Attorney general, **8.01–448**
Attorneys, **8.01–331**
Calling, **8.01–332**
Confession of judgment, **8.01–440**
Control, **8.01–4**
Discontinuance, **8.01–335**
Dismissal and nonsuit, **8.01–335**
Indexes, judgments and decrees, **8.01–450, 8.01–451**
Judgment dockets, **8.01–446 et seq.**
Notice, discontinuance, **8.01–335**
Parties, **8.01–331**
Payment, judgments and decrees, **8.01–453 et seq.**

DOCKETS AND DOCKETING—Cont'd
Reinstatement, **8.01–335**
Service of process, **8.01–331**
Discontinuance, **8.01–335**
State, judgments and decrees, **8.01–448**
United States, **8.01–447**

DOCTORS
Physicians and Surgeons, generally, this index

DOMESTIC ANIMALS
Animals, generally, this index

DOMESTIC CORPORATIONS
Corporations, generally, this index

DOMESTIC INSURANCE
Insurance, generally, this index

DOMICILE AND RESIDENCE
See, also, Nonresidents, generally, this index
Affidavits, **8.01–414**
Executions, debtor, venue, **8.01–506.2**
Forcible Entry and Detainer, generally, this index
Nonresidents, generally, this index
Venue, generally, this index
Witnesses, compelling attendance, **8.01–409**

DOUBLE DAMAGES
Exemplary damages. Damages, this index

DRAINS AND DRAINAGE
Sewers and Sewer Systems, generally, this index
Stormwater. Sewers and Sewer Systems, generally, this index

DRINKING WATER
Water Supply, generally, this index

DRIVING RULES
Traffic Rules and Regulations, generally, this index

DRIVING UNDER INFLUENCE OF ALCOHOL OR DRUGS
Traffic Rules and Regulations, this index

DRUGGISTS
Pharmacists, generally, this index

DRUGS AND MEDICINE
See, also, Controlled Substances, generally, this index
Actions and proceedings, drug dealers, liability, **8.01–227.4 et seq.**
Controlled Substances, generally, this index
Driving under influence of alcohol or drugs. Traffic Rules and Regulations, this index
Drug dealers, liability, **8.01–227.4 et seq.**
Emergency medical services, privileges and immunities, **8.01–225**
Glucagon, emergency medical services, privileges and immunities, **8.01–225**
Liability, drug dealers, **8.01–227.4 et seq.**
Limitation of actions, drug dealers, liability, **8.01–227.7**

DRUGS AND MEDICINE—Cont'd
Naloxone, emergency medical services, administration, privileges and immunities, **8.01–225**
Narcotics. Controlled Substances, generally, this index
Opioid antagonists, administration, privileges and immunities, **8.01–225**
Pharmacists, generally, this index
Privileges and immunities, emergency medical services, **8.01–225**
School Officers and Employees, this index
Schools and School Districts, this index

DRUNKEN DRIVING
Driving under influence of alcohol or drugs. Traffic Rules and Regulations, this index

DURESS OR COERCION
Arbitration and award, mediators, **8.01–581.24**
Contracts, limitation of actions, **8.01–249**
Limitation of actions, contracts, **8.01–249**
Terrorism, generally, this index

DWELLINGS
Housing, generally, this index

DWI
Driving under influence of alcohol or drugs. Traffic Rules and Regulations, this index

DYNAMITE
Explosives, generally, this index

EARNINGS
Compensation and Salaries, generally, this index

EDUCATION
Arbitration and award, **8.01–576.8**
Colleges and Universities, generally, this index
High Schools or Secondary Schools, generally, this index
Schools and School Districts, generally, this index
Schoolteachers, generally, this index

EDUCATIONAL INSTITUTIONS
Colleges and Universities, generally, this index
Schools and School Districts, generally, this index

EJECTMENT
See, also, Forcible Entry and Detainer, generally, this index
Generally, **8.01–131 et seq.**
Allowances, improvements, **8.01–166 et seq.**
Burden of proof, **8.01–139 et seq.**
Claims, **8.01–137**
Commencement, **8.01–134**
Costs, personal property, removal, **8.01–156**
Damages, **8.01–158, 8.01–159**
Improvements, **8.01–166 et seq.**
Deeds of trust, **8.01–147**
Improvements, exemptions, **8.01–174**
Defendants, **8.01–133**
Equity, **8.01–148**
Evidence, burden of proof, **8.01–139 et seq.**

EJECTMENT—Cont'd
Improvements, **8.01–160, 8.01–161, 8.01–166 et seq.**
Joint and several liability, **8.01–138, 8.01–142, 8.01–143**
Joint tenants, **8.01–141**
Judgments and decrees, **8.01–149 et seq.**
Improvements, **8.01–166 et seq., 8.01–171**
Mortgages, **8.01–147**
Improvements, exemptions, **8.01–174**
Motions, **8.01–135 et seq.**
Parties, **8.01–131, 8.01–133**
Personal property, storage, **8.01–156**
Possession,
Recovery, **8.01–149 et seq.**
Undivided part, **8.01–145**
Profits, **8.01–158, 8.01–164**
Recovery, possession, **8.01–149 et seq.**
Reservations, deeds and conveyances, **8.01–140**
Sales,
Improvements, **8.01–176**
Personal property, **8.01–156**
Storage, personal property, **8.01–156**
Tenants for life, improvements, **8.01–173**
Tenants in common, **8.01–141**
Title to property, claims, **8.01–137**
Undivided part, possession, **8.01–145**
Valuation, improvements, **8.01–167**
Vendee in possession, **8.01–146**
Verdicts, **8.01–149 et seq.**
Waste, **8.01–158**
Writs, **8.01–165**

ELDERLY PERSONS
Aged Persons, generally, this index

ELECTIONS
Officers of election, jury, exemptions, **8.01–341.1**
Registrars, jury, exemptions, **8.01–341.1**

ELECTRICITY
See, also, Public Utilities, generally, this index
Attorney fees, meters, tampering, **8.01–44.7**
Costs, meters, tampering, **8.01–44.7**
Damages, meters, tampering, **8.01–44.7**
Injunctions, meters, tampering, **8.01–44.7**
Meters, tampering, damages, **8.01–44.7**

ELECTRONIC DATA PROCESSING
Computers, generally, this index

ELECTRONIC FUNDS TRANSFERS
Funds Transfers, generally, this index

ELECTRONIC TRANSACTIONS
Court records, identification numbers, redacting, **8.01–420.8**

ELEEMOSYNARY ORGANIZATIONS
Nonprofit Organizations, generally, this index

ELEMENTARY SCHOOLS
Schools and School Districts, generally, this index

EMERGENCIES
See, also, Disasters, generally, this index
Civil Defense, generally, this index
Disasters, generally, this index
Health care professionals, privileges and immunities, **8.01–225.01, 8.01–225.02**
Privileges and immunities, health care professionals, **8.01–225.01, 8.01–225.02**

EMERGENCY MEDICAL SERVICES
See, also, Firefighters and Fire Departments, generally, this index
Actions and proceedings, privileges and immunities, **8.01–225**
Blood tests, evidence, admissibility, **8.01–413.02**
Entry on property, **8.01–226**
Epinephrine, privileges and immunities, **8.01–225**
Glucagon, privileges and immunities, **8.01–225**
Good samaritan doctrine, privileges and immunities, **8.01–225**
Hypoglycemia, privileges and immunities, **8.01–225**
Joint and several liability, husband and wife, **8.01–220.2**
Liens and incumbrances, personal injuries, claims, **8.01–66.2 et seq.**
Medical records, blood alcohol tests, evidence, admissibility, **8.01–413.02**
Motor vehicles,
  Blood alcohol tests, evidence, admissibility, **8.01–413.02**
  Volunteers, privileges and immunities, **8.01–225.3**
Naloxone, administration, privileges and immunities, **8.01–225**
Newborns, accepting, privileges and immunities, **8.01–226.5:2**
Opioid antagonists, administration, privileges and immunities, **8.01–225**
Privileges and immunities, **8.01–225**
  Blood alcohol tests, evidence, admissibility, **8.01–413.02**
  Motor vehicles, volunteers, **8.01–225.3**
  Newborns, accepting, **8.01–226.5:2**
Reports, blood alcohol tests, evidence, admissibility, **8.01–413.02**
Schools and school districts, epinephrine, administration, privileges and immunities, **8.01–225**

EMERGENCY MEDICAL TECHNICIANS
Privileges and immunities, motor vehicles, volunteers, **8.01–225.3**

EMINENT DOMAIN
Appeal and review, **8.01–670**

EMPLOYMENT
Labor and Employment, generally, this index

ENCUMBRANCES
Liens and Incumbrances, generally, this index

ENEMY ATTACK
Civil Defense, generally, this index

ENERGY
Electricity, generally, this index
Public Utilities, generally, this index

ENGINEERS
Actions and proceedings, limitation of actions, **8.01–250**
Disasters, privileges and immunities, rescue, **8.01–226.2**
Limitation of actions, **8.01–250**
Privileges and immunities, disasters, rescue, **8.01–226.2**
Rescue, disasters, privileges and immunities, **8.01–226.2**

ENLISTED MEN
Military Forces, generally, this index

ENTRY OF JUDGMENT
Executions, generally, this index

ENTRY ON PROPERTY
Actions and proceedings, limitation of actions, **8.01–236**
Emergency medical services, **8.01–226**
Firefighters and fire departments, **8.01–226**
Forcible Entry and Detainer, generally, this index
Limitation of actions, **8.01–236**
  Handicapped persons, **8.01–237**
Statute of limitations, **8.01–236**

ENVIRONMENTAL PROTECTION
Hazardous Substances and Waste, generally, this index
Injunctions, **8.01–631.1**

EPINEPHRINE
Emergency medical services, privileges and immunities, **8.01–225**

EQUINE LIVESTOCK
Animals, generally, this index

EQUITY
Advisory jury, **8.01–336**
Answers, evidence, rebuttal, **8.01–283**
Appeal and review, **8.01–670**
Defensive pleadings, sufficiency, **8.01–274**
Demurrer, **8.01–273**
Evidence, answers, rebuttal, **8.01–283**
Failure to state, cause of action, **8.01–273**
Injunctions, generally, this index
Jury, advisory jury, **8.01–336**
Pleadings, **8.01–273**
  Answers, evidence, rebuttal, **8.01–283**
  Sufficiency, **8.01–274**
Sufficiency, pleadings, **8.01–274**
Supersedeas or Stay, generally, this index

ERROR CORAM VOBIS
Writ, **8.01–677**

ERRORS AND APPEALS
Appeal and Review, generally, this index

ESCROWS AND ESCROW AGENTS
Circuit courts, payments, **8.01–606**

ESTATES
Leases, generally, this index
Probate Proceedings, generally, this index
Trusts and Trustees, generally, this index
Wills, generally, this index

ESTOPPEL
Labor and employment, judgments and decrees, **8.01–420.5**
Limitation of actions, **8.01–232**

EVICTION
Ejectment, generally, this index
Forcible Entry and Detainer, generally, this index

EVIDENCE
Affidavits, generally, this index
Arbitration and award, hearings, **8.01–581.04**
Attachment, **8.01–540**
Attorneys, attorney client privilege, undisclosed information, waiver, **8.01–420.7**
Autopsies, reports, **8.01–390.2**
Bonds, lost or destroyed documents, actions and proceedings, copies, **8.01–32**
Burden of proof,
  Anonymous plaintiffs, **8.01–15.1**
  Ejectment, **8.01–139 et seq.**
Business and commerce, records and recordation, **8.01–390.3, 8.01–391**
  Witnesses, corroboration, **8.01–397**
Certificates and certification,
  Business and commerce, records and recordation, **8.01–390.3**
  Unsworn written declarations, **8.01–4.3**
Checks, substitute checks, **8.01–391.1**
Chiropractors, opinions and expert testimony, **8.01–401.2**
Clergy, confidential or privileged information, witnesses, **8.01–400**
Common law, perpetuation of testimony, abolishment, **8.01–420.1**
Compensation and salaries, reimbursement, personal injuries, **8.01–35**
Confidential or Privileged Information, generally, this index
Contracts, lost or destroyed documents, actions and proceedings, copies, **8.01–32**
Copies, **8.01–391**
  Medical examiners, reports, **8.01–390.2**
Cross examination. Witnesses, this index
Damages, lost profits, new business, unestablished business, **8.01–221.1**
Debtors and creditors,
  Lost or destroyed documents, actions and proceedings, copies, **8.01–32**
  Payment, **8.01–421**
Declarations, unsworn written declarations, **8.01–4.3**
Depositions, generally, this index

EVIDENCE—Cont'd
Discovery, generally, this index
Disposal, **8.01–452.1**
Documents, portions, **8.01–417.1**
Ejectment, burden of proof, **8.01–139 et seq.**
Emergency medical services, blood alcohol tests, admissibility, **8.01–413.02**
Exhibits, disposal, **8.01–452.1**
Forcible entry and detainer, documents, copies, **8.01–126**
Foreign judgments and decrees, **8.01–389**
Forfeitures, actions and proceedings, **8.01–418**
Fraud against taxpayers, actions and proceedings, **8.01–216.9**
Guilty pleas, actions and proceedings, **8.01–418**
Habit, **8.01–397.1**
Health care providers, records and recordation, **8.01–413**
Hearsay, exceptions,
  Blood alcohol tests, emergency medical services, **8.01–413.02**
  Opinions and expert testimony, **8.01–401.1**
Hospitals, records and recordation, **8.01–413**
Impeachment, witnesses, **8.01–403**
Inconsistent statements, **8.01–403**
  Writings, **8.01–404**
Indebtedness. Evidences of Indebtedness, generally, this index
Interpreters, generally, this index
Interrogatories, generally, this index
Jury, exhibits, **8.01–381**
Landlord and tenant, ejectment, burden of proof, **8.01–139 et seq.**
Life expectancy tables, **8.01–419**
Lost or destroyed documents, **8.01–374**
Lost profits, new business, unestablished business, damages, **8.01–221.1**
Medical Care and Treatment, this index
Medical examiners, reports, **8.01–390.2**
Medical Malpractice, this index
Mortality tables, **8.01–419**
Motion to strike, **8.01–276, 8.01–282**
  Depositions, basis, **8.01–420**
Negligence, subsequent measures, **8.01–418.1**
Nine one one (911), certificates and certification, **8.01–390**
Notice, business and commerce, records and recordation, certificates and certification, **8.01–390.3**
Nurse practitioners, opinions and expert testimony, **8.01–401.2**
Oaths and affirmations, unsworn written declarations, **8.01–4.3**
Objections and exceptions, business and commerce, records and recordation, certificates and certification, **8.01–390.3**
Opinions and expert testimony. Witnesses, this index
Perjury, unsworn written declarations, **8.01–4.3**
Perpetuation of testimony, common law, abolishment, **8.01–420.1**

EVIDENCE—Cont'd
Pharmacists, records and recordation, **8.01–413**
Physicians assistants, opinions and expert testimony, **8.01–401.2**
Pleadings, amendments, **8.01–377**
Podiatrists, medical malpractice, witnesses, **8.01–401.2:1**
Polygraph tests, **8.01–418.2**
Presumptions,
  Landlord and tenant, mold, **8.01–226.12**
  Winter sports safety, **8.01–227.19**
Prior conduct, **8.01–397.1**
Privileged communications. Confidential or Privileged Information, generally, this index
Production of Books and Papers, generally, this index
Protective orders, disclosure, **8.01–420.01**
Psychologists and Psychology, this index
Records and recordation, courts, **8.01–389**
Reports, medical examiners, **8.01–390.2**
Routine practice, **8.01–397.1**
Rules of evidence, **8.01–3**
Schools and school districts, records and recordation, **8.01–390.1**
Signatures, judicial notice, **8.01–387**
Subsequent measures, negligence, **8.01–418.1**
Summary jury trial, **8.01–576.3**
Sympathy, medical malpractice, **8.01–52.1, 8.01–581.20:1**
Tape and sound recordings, telecommunications, **8.01–420.2**
Telecommunications, tape and sound recordings, **8.01–420.2**
Unsworn written declarations, **8.01–4.3**
Venue, location, **8.01–262**
Verification, unsworn written declarations, **8.01–4.3**
Witnesses, generally, this index
Wrongful Death, this index

EVIDENCES OF INDEBTEDNESS
Copies, lost or destroyed documents, actions and proceedings, evidence, **8.01–32**
Lost or destroyed documents, actions and proceedings, **8.01–32**
Oaths and affirmations, lost or destroyed documents, actions and proceedings, **8.01–32**

EXCHANGE, BILLS OF
Negotiable Instruments, generally, this index

EXECUTIONS
  Generally, **8.01–292, 8.01–466 et seq.**
Accounts and accounting, coin or currency, **8.01–482**
Adjournment, sales, **8.01–493**
Adverse or pecuniary interest, sales, **8.01–498**
Agricultural products, exemptions, **8.01–489**
Alternative value, personal property, **8.01–472**
Animals, **8.01–490**
Assets, disclosure, interrogatories, **8.01–506**
Associations and societies, **8.01–15**

EXECUTIONS—Cont'd
Attachment, this index
Bonds (officers and fiduciaries), **8.01–4.2, 8.01–526 et seq.**
  Appeal and review, **8.01–676.1**
  Loss of property sold, new execution, limitation of actions, **8.01–255.2**
  Motions, quashing, **8.01–477**
  Property sold under bond, new execution, **8.01–476**
Boundaries, **8.01–481**
Breaking and entering, **8.01–491**
Certificates and certification, financial institutions, notice, **8.01–502.1**
Coin or currency, **8.01–482**
Compensation and salaries, sales, **8.01–499**
Confession of judgment, **8.01–440**
Damages, financial institutions, notice, certificates and certification, **8.01–502.1**
Disclosure, interrogatories, **8.01–506**
Discovery, interrogatories, **8.01–506**
Domicile and residence, debtor, venue, **8.01–506.2**
Endorsements, **8.01–487**
Exemptions, **8.01–477.1, 8.01–501 et seq.**
  Agricultural products, **8.01–489**
  Third parties, **8.01–365 et seq.**
Extensions, limitation of actions, **8.01–251**
Foreign countries, limitation of actions, **8.01–251**
Foreign states, limitation of actions, **8.01–251**
Forfeitures, bonds (officers and fiduciaries), **8.01–527**
Fraud, **8.01–504**
Horses, **8.01–490**
Intangibles, exemptions, **8.01–501 et seq.**
Interest, bonds (officers and fiduciaries), **8.01–528**
Interrogatories, **8.01–506**
Issuance, **8.01–466**
Joint and several liability, **8.01–469**
Liens and Incumbrances, this index
Limitation of actions, **8.01–251**
  Bonds (officers and fiduciaries), loss of property sold, **8.01–255.2**
Livestock, **8.01–490**
Lost or destroyed documents, **8.01–484**
Motions, quashing, **8.01–477**
Nonresidents, production of books and papers, **8.01–506.1**
Notice,
  Financial institutions, **8.01–502.1**
  Sales, **8.01–492**
    Proceeds, **8.01–500**
  Third parties, exemptions, **8.01–502**
Perishable goods, sales, **8.01–492**
Priorities and preferences, **8.01–488**
Production of books and papers, **8.01–506.1**
Quashing, **8.01–477**
  Bonds (officers and fiduciaries), **8.01–530**
Records and recordation,
  Bonds (officers and fiduciaries), **8.01–529**

EXECUTIONS—Cont'd
Records and recordation—Cont'd
Maintaining, **8.01–484**
Resale, **8.01–494**
Returns, **8.01–483 et seq.**
Bonds (officers and fiduciaries), **8.01–529**
Interrogatories, **8.01–507.1**
Sales, **8.01–492, 8.01–510**
Adjournment, **8.01–493**
Orders of court, **8.01–509**
Resale, **8.01–494**
Surplus, **8.01–495**
Secured transactions, prior security interest, **8.01–480**
Service of process, **8.01–292, 8.01–293, 8.01–487.1**
Specific property, **8.01–470**
Subpoena duces tecum, **8.01–506.1**
Subsequent executions, **8.01–475**
Supersedeas or stay, motion to quash, **8.01–477**
Surplus, **8.01–495**
Surrender, assets, **8.01–507**
Termination, intangibles, **8.01–505**
Third parties, **8.01–365 et seq.**
Beneficiaries, **8.01–473**
Time,
Extensions, **8.01–251**
Liens and incumbrances, **8.01–478 et seq.**
Subsequent executions, **8.01–475**
Value, alternative value, personal property, **8.01–472**
Venditioni exponas, writ, **8.01–485, 8.01–486**
Venue, debtor, domicile and residence, **8.01–506.2**
Withdrawal, bonds (officers and fiduciaries), **8.01–532**

EXECUTIVE DEPARTMENT
Governor, generally, this index

EXECUTORS AND ADMINISTRATORS
Personal representatives. Probate Proceedings, this index

EXEMPTIONS
Attachment, this index
Executions, this index
Garnishment, this index

EXHAUSTION OF REMEDIES
Generally, **8.01–429**

EXHIBITS
Identification numbers, redacting, **8.01–420.8**

EXPERT WITNESSES
Opinions and expert testimony. Witnesses, this index

EXPLOSIVES
Actions and proceedings, privileges and immunities, governmental immunity, **8.01–224**
Damages, privileges and immunities, governmental immunity, **8.01–224**
Privileges and immunities, governmental immunity, **8.01–224**

EXPRESS COMPANIES
Carriers, generally, this index

EXTRAORDINARY WRITS
Habeas Corpus, generally, this index
Mandamus, generally, this index
Quo Warranto, generally, this index

EYES AND EYESIGHT
Optometrists, generally, this index

FACSIMILE TRANSMISSIONS
Actions and proceedings, unsolicited transmissions, damages, **8.01–40.2**
Advertisements, damages, **8.01–40.2**
Attorney fees, unsolicited transmissions, damages, **8.01–40.2**
Consumer protection, advertisements, unsolicited, **8.01–40.2**
Damages, unsolicited transmissions, **8.01–40.2**
Injunctions, advertisements, **8.01–40.2**
Limitation of actions, advertisements, damages, **8.01–40.2**

FALSE IMPRISONMENT
Habeas Corpus, generally, this index
Shoplifting, arrest, detention, privileges and immunities, **8.01–226.9**

FALSE PERSONATION
Libel and slander, Internet, limitation of actions, tolling, **8.01–247.1**

FALSE STATEMENTS
Fraud, generally, this index

FAMILY THERAPISTS
Marriage and Family Therapists, generally, this index

FAULT
Negligence, generally, this index

FAX
Facsimile Transmissions, generally, this index

FEAR
Duress or Coercion, generally, this index

FEDERAL OLD AGE, SURVIVORS AND DISABILITY INSURANCE
Social Security, generally, this index

FEDERAL SOCIAL SECURITY ACT
Social Security, generally, this index

FEEBLE MINDED PERSONS
Mentally Retarded and Developmentally Disabled Persons, generally, this index

FEET
Podiatrists, generally, this index

FELONIES
Crimes and Offenses, generally, this index

FETAL DEATH
Wrongful death, **8.01–50**

FIDELITY BONDS
Bonds (Officers and Fiduciaries), generally, this index

FIDUCIARIES
Accounts and accounting, **8.01–31**
Actions and proceedings, pleadings, style, **8.01–6.3**
Adverse or pecuniary interest, real estate, sales, **8.01–75**
Arbitration and award, **8.01–581**
Attorneys, generally, this index
Bonds (Officers and Fiduciaries), generally, this index
Compromise and settlement, **8.01–424 et seq.**
Conservators and Conservatorship, generally, this index
Equity, accounts and accounting, **8.01–31**
Guardian and Ward, generally, this index
Names, pleadings, style, **8.01–6.3**
Personal representatives. Probate Proceedings, this index
Pleadings, style, **8.01–6.3**
Receivers and Receivership, generally, this index
Settlement, **8.01–424 et seq.**
Trusts and Trustees, generally, this index
Venue, **8.01–262**

FIERI FACIAS
Executions, generally, this index

FINAL PROCESS
Executions, generally, this index

FINANCIAL INSTITUTIONS
Bank Deposits and Collections, generally, this index
Checks. Negotiable Instruments, this index
Deposits. Bank Deposits and Collections, generally, this index
Executions, notice, **8.01–502.1**
Funds Transfers, generally, this index
Notice, executions, **8.01–502.1**

FINES AND PENALTIES
See, also, Crimes and Offenses, generally, this index
Capital Punishment, generally, this index
Death sentence. Capital Punishment, generally, this index
State, fraud against taxpayers, **8.01–216.3**
State agencies, fraud against taxpayers, **8.01–216.3**
State departments, fraud against taxpayers, **8.01–216.3**

FIRE DEPARTMENTS
Firefighters and Fire Departments, generally, this index

FIREFIGHTERS AND FIRE DEPARTMENTS
See, also, Emergency Medical Services, generally, this index
Entry on property, **8.01–226**
Jury, exemptions, **8.01–341.1**

FIREFIGHTERS AND FIRE DEPARTMENTS —Cont'd
Privileges and immunities, motor vehicles, volunteer firefighters, **8.01–225.3**
Volunteer firefighters,
Motor vehicles, privileges and immunities, **8.01–225.3**
Privileges and immunities, motor vehicles, **8.01–225.3**

FIRST AID
Emergency Medical Services, generally, this index

FLOODS AND FLOOD CONTROL
Civil Defense, generally, this index

FORCE AND VIOLENCE
Damages, hate crimes, **8.01–42.1**
Duress or Coercion, generally, this index
Hate crimes, actions and proceedings, **8.01–42.1**
Terrorism, generally, this index

FORCED SALES
Judicial Sales, generally, this index

FORCIBLE ENTRY AND DETAINER
Generally, **8.01–124 et seq.**
Affidavits, evidence, attorneys, agents and agencies, **8.01–126**
Agents and agencies, affidavits, evidence, **8.01–126**
Appeal and review, **8.01–129**
Appearance, default judgments, **8.01–28**
Attorney fees, affidavits, evidence, **8.01–126**
Attorneys, affidavits, evidence, **8.01–126**
Bonds (officers and fiduciaries), appeal and review, **8.01–129**
Continuance, possession, damages, **8.01–128**
Copies, documents, evidence, **8.01–126**
Damages, **8.01–128**
Affidavits, evidence, **8.01–126**
Default judgments, **8.01–28**
Documents, evidence, copies, **8.01–126**
Evidence, documents, copies, **8.01–126**
Executions, **8.01–470, 8.01–471**
Judgments and decrees, **8.01–128**
Appeal and review, **8.01–129**
Default judgments, **8.01–28**
Jury, **8.01–125**
Limitation of actions, **8.01–236**
Motions, **8.01–124**
Process, service of process, **8.01–293**
Summons, **8.01–126**
Statute of limitations, **8.01–236**
Summons, **8.01–126**
Venue, **8.01–261**

FORECLOSURE
Judicial Sales, generally, this index

FOREIGN CORPORATIONS
See, also, Corporations, generally, this index
Actions and proceedings, Long Arm Statute, **8.01–328.1**

FOREIGN CORPORATIONS—Cont'd
Agents and agencies,
Secretary of state, service of process, **8.01–329**
Service of process, **8.01–301**
Secretary of state, **8.01–329**
Jurisdiction, **8.01–328.1**
Long Arm Statute, **8.01–328.1**
Publication, service of process, **8.01–316 et seq.**
Secretary of state, service of process, **8.01–329**
Service of process, **8.01–301**
Publication, **8.01–316 et seq.**
Transacting business, Long Arm Statute, **8.01–328.1**

FOREIGN COUNTRIES
Accord and satisfaction, money, claims, **8.01–465.23**
Actions and proceedings, currency, **8.01–465.14 et seq.**
Application of law,
Judgments and decrees, **8.01–465.13:2**
Money, claims, **8.01–465.15**
Claims, money, **8.01–465.14 et seq.**
Conflict of Laws, generally, this index
Contracts,
Limitation of actions, **8.01–247**
Money, claims, **8.01–465.16**
Conversion rates, foreign currency, judgments and decrees, **8.01–465.20, 8.01–465.21**
Dockets and docketing, money, claims, **8.01–465.20**
Due process, judgments and decrees, **8.01–465.13:3**
Executions, limitation of actions, **8.01–251**
Fraud, judgments and decrees, **8.01–465.13:3**
Garnishment, **8.01–465.24**
Inconvenient forum, judgments and decrees, **8.01–465.13:3**
Judgments and decrees. Foreign Judgments and Decrees, generally, this index
Judicial notice, **8.01–385 et seq.**
Jurisdiction, judgments and decrees, **8.01–465.13:3, 8.01–465.13:4**
Limitation of actions,
Contracts, **8.01–247**
Foreign country money judgments, recognition, **8.01–465.13:8**
Judgments and decrees, **8.01–251**
Money, foreign country money judgments, recognition, **8.01–465.13:1 et seq.**

FOREIGN COUNTRY MONEY JUDGMENTS RECOGNITION ACT
Generally, **8.01–465.13:1 et seq.**

FOREIGN CURRENCY
Claims, **8.01–465.14 et seq.**

FOREIGN JUDGMENTS AND DECREES
Generally, **8.01–465.1 et seq.**
Conversion rates, foreign currency, **8.01–465.20, 8.01–465.21**
Due process, **8.01–465.13:3**

FOREIGN JUDGMENTS AND DECREES—Cont'd
Evidence, **8.01–389**
Filing, **8.01–465.2**
Fraud, **8.01–465.13:3**
Inconvenient forum, **8.01–465.13:3**
Limitation of actions, **8.01–251**
Money,
Foreign country money judgments, recognition, **8.01–465.13:1 et seq.**
Foreign currency, **8.01–465.14 et seq.**
Notice, **8.01–465.3**
Recognition, foreign country money judgments, **8.01–465.13:1 et seq.**
Supersedeas or stay, **8.01–465.4**

FOREIGN LANGUAGES
Trial, interpreters, **8.01–384.1:1**

FOREIGN NATIONS
Foreign Countries, generally, this index

FOREIGN STATES
Conflict of Laws, generally, this index
Contracts, limitation of actions, **8.01–247**
Depositions, interstate depositions and discovery, **8.01–412.8 et seq.**
Discovery, interstate depositions and discovery, **8.01–412.8 et seq.**
Domicile and Residence, generally, this index
Evidence, records and recordation, **8.01–389, 8.01–390**
Executions, limitation of actions, **8.01–251**
Foreign Judgments and Decrees, generally, this index
Internet, torts, identity and identification, subpoenas, **8.01–407.1**
Interstate depositions and discovery, **8.01–412.8 et seq.**
Judgments and decrees. Foreign Judgments and Decrees, generally, this index
Judicial notice, **8.01–385 et seq.**
Limitation of actions,
Contracts, **8.01–247**
Judgments and decrees, **8.01–251**
Public officers and employees, jurisdiction, sales and use tax, declaratory judgments, **8.01–184.1**
Records and recordation, evidence, **8.01–389, 8.01–390**

FORFEITURES
Evidence, actions and proceedings, **8.01–418**
Executions, bonds (officers and fiduciaries), **8.01–527**

FORMS
Attachment, exemptions, **8.01–546.1**
Garnishment, **8.01–512.3**
Writs, **8.01–286**

FRAUD
Actions and proceedings, limitation of actions, **8.01–243, 8.01–249**

FRAUD—Cont'd
Arbitration and Award, this index
Attachment, pretrial procedures, **8.01–534**
Default judgments, vacating or setting aside, **8.01–428**
Garnishment, **8.01–511**
Judgments and decrees, default judgments, vacating or setting aside, **8.01–428**
Limitation of actions, **8.01–243, 8.01–249**
State, fraud against taxpayers, **8.01–216.1 et seq.**
Statute of limitations, **8.01–243, 8.01–249**
Taxation, **8.01–216.1 et seq.**

FRAUDULENT CONVEYANCES
Rescission, attorney fees, costs, **8.01–221.2**

FREEDOM OF SPEECH AND PRESS
Hearings, privileges and immunities, strategic lawsuits against public participation, **8.01–223.2**

FULL FAITH AND CREDIT
Judicial records, **8.01–389**

FUND TRANSFERS
Funds Transfers, generally, this index

FUNDS
Investments, generally, this index
Receivers and Receivership, generally, this index
State Funds, generally, this index
Trusts and Trustees, generally, this index

FUNDS TRANSFERS
Court records, identification numbers, redacting, **8.01–420.8**
Insufficient funds, stop payment, damages, **8.01–27.1, 8.01–27.2**

GARNISHMENT
See, also, Attachment, generally, this index
Generally, **8.01–511 et seq.**
Accord and satisfaction, **8.01–516.1**
Address, identity and identification, **8.01–511.1**
Corporations, **8.01–513**
Costs, **8.01–511, 8.01–521**
County officers and employees, **8.01–524, 8.01–525**
Default judgments, **8.01–519**
Dismissal and nonsuit, **8.01–516.1**
Examinations and examiners, **8.01–515**
Exemptions,
Hearings, **8.01–512.5**
Notice, **8.01–512.4**
Payment, employee, **8.01–517**
Failure to appear, **8.01–519**
Fees, **8.01–512.2**
Foreign countries, **8.01–465.24**
Forms, **8.01–512.3**
Fraud, **8.01–511**
Hearings, exemptions, **8.01–512.5**
Identity and identification, summons, **8.01–511.1**
Interest, **8.01–511**

GARNISHMENT—Cont'd
Interrogatories, **8.01–511**
Limited liability companies, **8.01–513**
Municipal officers and employees, **8.01–524, 8.01–525**
Notice, **8.01–503**
Exemptions, **8.01–512.4**
Payments, **8.01–517**
Personal representatives, **8.01–518**
Probate proceedings, personal representatives, **8.01–518**
Returns, **8.01–514**
Service of process, **8.01–511**
Corporations, **8.01–513**
Limited liability companies, **8.01–513**
United States, **8.01–523**
Social security numbers, **8.01–511**
Identity and identification, **8.01–511.1**
State officers and employees, **8.01–522**
Summons, **8.01–511**
Identity and identification, **8.01–511.1**
Sufficiency, **8.01–511.1**
Taxpayer identification numbers, identity and identification, **8.01–511.1**
United States, **8.01–523**
Venue, **8.01–511**

GENERAL ASSEMBLY
House of delegates, clerks, jury, exemptions, **8.01–341.1**
Jury, exemptions, **8.01–341**
Officers and employees, **8.01–341.1**
Legislative automated systems division, officers and employees, jury, exemptions, **8.01–341.1**
Legislative services division, officers and employees, jury, exemptions, **8.01–341.1**
Officers and employees, jury, exemptions, **8.01–341.1**
Senate, clerks, jury, exemptions, **8.01–341.1**
Statutes, generally, this index

GENERAL DISTRICT COURTS
District Courts, generally, this index

GENERAL LAWS
Statutes, generally, this index

GENERAL PARTNER
Partnerships, generally, this index

GIFTS
Limitation of actions, **8.01–253**

GLASSES
Optometrists, generally, this index

GLUCAGON
Emergency medical services, privileges and immunities, **8.01–225**

GONDOLAS
Winter sports areas, safety, **8.01–227.11 et seq.**

GOOD SAMARITAN DOCTRINE
Privileges and immunities, **8.01–225**

GOODS, WARES AND MERCHANDISE
Attachment, generally, this index
Sales, generally, this index
Shoplifting, generally, this index

GOVERNING LAW
Conflict of Laws, generally, this index

GOVERNOR
Arrest, privileges and immunities, **8.01–327.2**
Jury, exemptions, **8.01–341**
Signatures, judicial notice, **8.01–387**

GRANTS
Deeds and Conveyances, generally, this index
Wrongful incarceration, compensation and salaries, **8.01–195.11**

GRAVES
Cemeteries, generally, this index

GRAVEYARDS
Cemeteries, generally, this index

GROSS NEGLIGENCE
Space, flight, privileges and immunities, **8.01–227.9**
Winter sports safety, **8.01–227.11 et seq.**

GUARDIAN AD LITEM
Adverse or pecuniary interest, real estate, sales, **8.01–75**
Appointment,
  Real estate, actions and proceedings, **8.01–73**
  Title to property, **8.01–73**
Compensation and salaries, actions and proceedings, **8.01–9**
Deeds and conveyances, **8.01–73**
Process, service of process, correctional institutions, **8.01–297**
Real estate, actions and proceedings, **8.01–73**
Removal, **8.01–9**
Sales, real estate, **8.01–73**
Service of process, correctional institutions, **8.01–297**
Title to property, **8.01–73**

GUARDIAN AND WARD
  See, also,
    Conservators and Conservatorship, generally, this index
    Fiduciaries, generally, this index
Actions and proceedings,
  Compromise and settlement, **8.01–424 et seq.**
  Pleadings, style, **8.01–6.3**
Ad litem. Guardian Ad Litem, generally, this index
Appeal and review, **8.01–670**
Compromise and settlement, **8.01–424 et seq.**
Names, pleadings, style, **8.01–6.3**
Pleadings, style, **8.01–6.3**

GUILTY PLEAS
Actions and proceedings, evidence, **8.01–418**
Evidence, actions and proceedings, **8.01–418**

HABEAS CORPUS
  Generally, **8.01–654 et seq.**
Affidavits, **8.01–654**
  Witnesses, **8.01–660**
Appeal and review, **8.01–664**
Attorney fees, **8.01–662**
Bail, **8.01–665**
Bonds (officers and fiduciaries), **8.01–656**
Capital Punishment, this index
Costs, **8.01–662**
Forms, **8.01–655**
Hearings, **8.01–654**
Inadequate counsel, **8.01–654**
Indigent persons, capital punishment, limitation of actions, **8.01–654.1**
Judgments and decrees, **8.01–662 et seq.**
Jurisdiction, **8.01–654**
Limitation of actions, **8.01–654, 8.01–654.1**
Records and recordation, **8.01–661, 8.01–667**
Service of process, **8.01–658**
Venue, application of law, **8.01–259**
Witnesses, affidavits, **8.01–660**

HABIT
Evidence, **8.01–397.1**

HABITATION
Housing, generally, this index

HANDICAPPED PERSONS
Actions and proceedings,
  Compromise and settlement, **8.01–424 et seq.**
  Guardian ad litem, **8.01–9**
  Limitation of actions, **8.01–229**
Compromise and settlement, **8.01–424 et seq.**
Deaf and mute persons. Hearing Impaired Persons, generally, this index
Deeds and conveyances, **8.01–67 et seq.**
Disposition, property, **8.01–67 et seq.**
Guardian Ad Litem, generally, this index
Guardian and Ward, generally, this index
Hearing Impaired Persons, generally, this index
Indebtedness, real estate, sales, **8.01–78 et seq.**
Interpreters, generally, this index
Investments, real estate, proceeds, **8.01–76**
Jurisdiction, real estate, **8.01–68**
Jury,
  Disqualification, **8.01–338**
  Exemptions, **8.01–341.1**
  Objections and exceptions, **8.01–352**
Leases, **8.01–67 et seq.**
Limitation of actions, **8.01–229**
Mentally Ill Persons, generally, this index
Mentally Retarded and Developmentally Disabled Persons, generally, this index
Mortgages, **8.01–67 et seq.**
Notice, indebtedness, mortgages, **8.01–79**
Partition, **8.01–85**
Property, disposition, **8.01–67 et seq.**
Real estate, **8.01–67 et seq.**

HANDICAPPED PERSONS—Cont'd
Sales, real estate, **8.01–67 et seq.**
Settlement, **8.01–424 et seq.**
Statute of limitations, **8.01–229**
Title to property, **8.01–67 et seq.**

HARASSMENT
Damages, hate crimes, **8.01–42.1**

HATE CRIMES
See, also, Terrorism, generally, this index
Actions and proceedings, **8.01–42.1**

HAZARDOUS MATERIALS
Hazardous Substances and Waste, generally, this index

HAZARDOUS SUBSTANCES AND WASTE
Emergencies, medical services, privileges and immunities, **8.01–225**
Entry on property, response teams, **8.01–226**
Explosives, generally, this index
Privileges and immunities, emergency medical services, **8.01–225**
Response teams, entry on property, **8.01–226**

HAZARDOUS WASTE
Hazardous Substances and Waste, generally, this index

HEALTH
Medical Care and Treatment, generally, this index

HEALTH AND SANITATION
Cemeteries, generally, this index
Drugs and Medicine, generally, this index
Hospitals, generally, this index
Injunctions, **8.01–631.1**
Medical Care and Treatment, generally, this index
Pharmacists, generally, this index
Sewers and Sewer Systems, generally, this index

HEALTH CARE AND TREATMENT
Medical Care and Treatment, generally, this index

HEALTH CARE DIRECTIVES
Conservators and Conservatorship, generally, this index
Guardian and Ward, generally, this index

HEALTH CARE FACILITIES
Disasters, privileges and immunities, **8.01–225.01, 8.01–225.02**
Emergencies, privileges and immunities, **8.01–225.01, 8.01–225.02**
Hospitals, generally, this index
Medical Malpractice, generally, this index
Nursing Homes, generally, this index
Privileges and immunities, disasters, **8.01–225.01, 8.01–225.02**

HEALTH CARE PROFESSIONALS
Actions and proceedings, insurance, payment, **8.01–27.4**
Assisted suicide, **8.01–622.1**

HEALTH CARE PROFESSIONALS—Cont'd
Bills, submission, in network providers, powers and duties, **8.01–27.5**
Boards and commissions, confidential or privileged information, **8.01–581.17**
Confidential or privileged information, boards and commissions, **8.01–581.17**
Damages, insurance, payment, actions and proceedings, **8.01–27.4**
Dentists and Dentistry, generally, this index
Disasters, privileges and immunities, **8.01–225.01, 8.01–225.02**
Emergencies, privileges and immunities, **8.01–225.01, 8.01–225.02**
Evidence, records and recordation, **8.01–413**
Good samaritan doctrine, **8.01–225**
Liens and incumbrances, personal injuries, claims, **8.01–66.2 et seq.**
Nurses, generally, this index
Optometrists, generally, this index
Payment,
- Insurance, actions and proceedings, **8.01–27.4**
- Liens and incumbrances, personal injuries, claims, **8.01–66.2 et seq.**

Pharmacists, generally, this index
Physical Therapists, generally, this index
Physicians and Surgeons, generally, this index
Privileges and immunities,
- Bills, submission, in network providers, **8.01–27.5**
- Boards and commissions, **8.01–581.16**
- Disasters, **8.01–225.01, 8.01–225.02**
- Emergency medical services, **8.01–225**

Records and recordation, evidence, **8.01–413**
Subpoenas, records and recordation, **8.01–413**
Suicide, assisted suicide, **8.01–622.1**
Time, bills, submission, in network providers, **8.01–27.5**

HEALTH FACILITIES
Health Care Facilities, generally, this index

HEALTH INSURANCE
Bills, submission, in network providers, powers and duties, **8.01–27.5**
Claims, bills, in network providers, powers and duties, **8.01–27.5**
Coverage, bills, in network providers, powers and duties, **8.01–27.5**
Group insurance. Health Maintenance Organizations, generally, this index
HMO. Health Maintenance Organizations, generally, this index
In network providers, bills, submission, time, **8.01–27.5**
Privileges and immunities, bills, submission, in network providers, **8.01–27.5**
Time, bills, submission, in network providers, **8.01–27.5**

HEALTH MAINTENANCE ORGANIZATIONS
Disasters, privileges and immunities, **8.01–225.01, 8.01–225.02**

HEALTH MAINTENANCE ORGANIZATIONS —Cont'd
Emergencies, privileges and immunities, **8.01–225.01, 8.01–225.02**
Medical Malpractice, generally, this index
Privileges and immunities, disasters, **8.01–225.01, 8.01–225.02**

HEALTH RECORDS
Medical Records, generally, this index

HEARING IMPAIRED PERSONS
Interpreters, witnesses, **8.01–406**
Confidential or privileged information, **8.01–400.1**
Trial, interpreters, **8.01–384.1**
Witnesses, interpreters, **8.01–406**

HEAT AND HEATING COMPANIES
Public Utilities, generally, this index

HELMETS
Winter sports safety, **8.01–227.18**

HIGH SCHOOLS OR SECONDARY SCHOOLS
See, also, Schools and School Districts, generally, this index
Athletics, physicians and surgeons, privileges and immunities, **8.01–225.1**
Libel and slander, investigations and investigators, privileges and immunities, **8.01–47**
Physicians and surgeons, athletics, privileges and immunities, **8.01–225.1**
Privileges and immunities, physicians and surgeons, athletics, **8.01–225.1**
Reports, libel and slander, privileges and immunities, **8.01–47**

HIGHER EDUCATION
Colleges and Universities, generally, this index

HIGHWAYS AND ROADS
Law of the road. Traffic Rules and Regulations, generally, this index
Littering, pick up programs, privileges and immunities, **8.01–226.8**
Rules of the road. Traffic Rules and Regulations, generally, this index
Traffic Rules and Regulations, generally, this index
Volunteers, littering, pick up programs, privileges and immunities, **8.01–226.8**

HMO
Health Maintenance Organizations, generally, this index

HOGS
Animals, generally, this index

HOLIDAYS
Attachment, **8.01–542**

HOME
Housing, generally, this index

HOME HEALTH SERVICES
Medical assistance. Social Services, this index

HOMELAND SECURITY
Terrorism, generally, this index

HORSES
See, also, Animals, generally, this index
Executions, **8.01–490**

HOSPICES
Privileges and immunities, volunteers, **8.01–226.4**
Volunteers, privileges and immunities, **8.01–226.4**

HOSPITALS
See, also, Health Care Facilities, generally, this index
Actions and proceedings, privileges and immunities, **8.01–38**
Conservators and Conservatorship, generally, this index
Disasters, privileges and immunities, **8.01–225.01, 8.01–225.02**
Emergencies, privileges and immunities, **8.01–225.01, 8.01–225.02**
Evidence, records and recordation, **8.01–413**
Guardian and Ward, generally, this index
Health Insurance, generally, this index
Health Maintenance Organizations, generally, this index
Insurance. Health Insurance, generally, this index
Liens and incumbrances, personal injuries, claims, **8.01–66.2 et seq.**
Malpractice. Medical Malpractice, generally, this index
Medical assistance. Social Services, this index
Medical Malpractice, generally, this index
Medical records, evidence, **8.01–413**
Negligence. Medical Malpractice, generally, this index
Newborns, accepting, privileges and immunities, **8.01–226.5:2**
Payments, liens and incumbrances, personal injuries, claims, **8.01–66.2 et seq.**
Physicians and Surgeons, generally, this index
Privileges and immunities,
Bills, submission, in network providers, **8.01–27.5**
Disasters, **8.01–225.01, 8.01–225.02**
Newborns, accepting, **8.01–226.5:2**
Torts, **8.01–38**
Subpoenas, records and recordation, **8.01–413**
Time, bills, submission, in network providers, **8.01–27.5**
Torts, privileges and immunities, **8.01–38**

HOTELS AND MOTELS
Actions and proceedings, guests, damages, **8.01–42.2**
Damages, **8.01–42.2**
Laundries and dry cleaners, privileges and immunities, **8.01–42**
Guests, damages, **8.01–42.2**
Laundries and dry cleaners, privileges and immunities, **8.01–42**

HOTELS AND MOTELS—Cont'd
Privileges and immunities, laundries and dry cleaners, damages, **8.01–42**

HOUSING
Contractors, generally, this index
Deeds and Conveyances, generally, this index
Disclosure, lead based paint, **8.01–226.7**
Landlord and Tenant, generally, this index
Lead paint, disclosure, **8.01–226.7**
Manufactured Housing, generally, this index
Mortgages, generally, this index
Nursing Homes, generally, this index
Privileges and immunities, lead based paint, **8.01–226.7**
Real Property Taxation, generally, this index
Rent, generally, this index
Searches and Seizures, generally, this index

HUSBAND AND WIFE
See, also, Marriage, generally, this index
Actions and proceedings, privileges and immunities, torts, abolishment, **8.01–220.1**
Confidential or privileged information, witnesses, **8.01–398**
Divorce. Marriage, this index
Emergency medical services, joint and several liability, **8.01–220.2**
Evidence, **8.01–398**
Joint and several liability, emergency medical services, **8.01–220.2**
Jury, exemptions, **8.01–341.1**
Maintenance. Support, generally, this index
Medical care and treatment, joint and several liability, emergency medical services, **8.01–220.2**
Privileges and immunities,
Torts, abolishment, **8.01–220.1**
Witnesses, **8.01–398**
Support, generally, this index
Torts, privileges and immunities, abolishment, **8.01–220.1**
Witnesses, **8.01–398**

HYPOGLYCEMIA
Emergency medical services, privileges and immunities, **8.01–225**

ICE AND SNOW
Winter sports safety, **8.01–227.11 et seq.**

IDENTITY AND IDENTIFICATION
Anonymous plaintiffs, **8.01–15.1**
Courts, records and recordation, numbers and numbering, redacting, **8.01–420.8**
Exhibits, identification numbers, redacting, **8.01–420.8**
Garnishment, summons, **8.01–511.1**
Internet, torts, subpoenas, **8.01–407.1**
Jury, **8.01–353.1**
Motions, identification numbers, redacting, **8.01–420.8**

IDENTITY AND IDENTIFICATION—Cont'd
Parties, anonymous plaintiffs, **8.01–15.1**
Pleadings, identification numbers, redacting, **8.01–420.8**
Subpoenas, identification numbers, redacting, **8.01–420.8**

ILLNESS
Health Insurance, generally, this index
Mentally Ill Persons, generally, this index

IMMUNITIES
Privileges and Immunities, generally, this index

IMMUNIZATION
Privileges and immunities, **8.01–44.2**

IMPLEADER
Third Parties, generally, this index

IMPRISONMENT
Correctional Institutions, generally, this index
Jails, generally, this index

IMPROVEMENTS
Defective conditions, limitation of actions, **8.01–250**

IN CAMERA PROCEEDINGS
Fraud against taxpayers,
Compromise and settlement, **8.01–216.6**
Judgments and decrees, evidence, **8.01–216.5**

INCENDIARY DEVICES
Explosives, generally, this index

INCOME
Compensation and Salaries, generally, this index

INCOME TAX—STATE
Fraud, fraud against taxpayers, application of law, **8.01–216.3**

INCONVENIENT FORUM
Change of venue, **8.01–265**

INCUMBRANCES
Liens and Incumbrances, generally, this index

INDEBTEDNESS
See, also, Debtors and Creditors, generally, this index
Attachment, generally, this index
Bonds, generally, this index
Children and minors, real estate, sales, **8.01–78 et seq.**
Confession of judgment, **8.01–432**
Evidences of Indebtedness, generally, this index
Garnishment, generally, this index
Mentally ill persons, real estate, sales, **8.01–78 et seq.**

INDEMNITY AND INDEMNIFICATION
Limitation of actions, third parties, **8.01–249**
Subrogation, generally, this index

INDEPENDENT CONTRACTORS
Contractors, generally, this index

INDIGENT PERSONS
Appeal and review, bonds (officers and fiduciaries), **8.01–676.1**
Habeas corpus, capital punishment, limitation of actions, **8.01–654.1**
Jails, actions and proceedings, prisoner litigation reform, **8.01–691, 8.01–692**
Medical assistance. Social Services, this index
Social Services, generally, this index

INFANTS
Children and Minors, generally, this index

INFORMATION
Confidential or Privileged Information, generally, this index
Criminal History Record Information, generally, this index
Disclosure, generally, this index

INFORMED CONSENT
Space, flight, privileges and immunities, **8.01–227.9**

INJUNCTIONS
Generally, **8.01–620 et seq.**
Affidavits, temporary injunctions, support, **8.01–628**
Appeal and review, **8.01–626, 8.01–670**
Assisted suicide, **8.01–622.1**
Attachment, **8.01–549**
Bills of review, **8.01–623**
Clerks of court, **8.01–627**
Correctional institutions, prisoner litigation reform, **8.01–689 et seq.**
Damages, dissolution, **8.01–633**
Declaratory judgments, **8.01–189**
Dismissal and nonsuit, **8.01–634**
Dissolution, **8.01–625**
Damages, **8.01–633**
Dismissal and nonsuit, **8.01–634**
Environmental protection, **8.01–631.1**
Exemptions, bonds (officers and fiduciaries), **8.01–631**
Facsimile transmissions, advertisements, **8.01–40.2**
Hate crimes, **8.01–42.1**
Interest, dissolution, **8.01–633**
Interpleader, **8.01–364**
Intimidation, hate crimes, **8.01–42.1**
Jurisdiction, **8.01–620**
Limitation of actions, **8.01–229**
Notice, **8.01–629**
Personal property, **8.01–622**
Pleadings, verified, temporary injunctions, support, **8.01–628**
Preliminary injunctions, equity, **8.01–628**
Removal of property, bonds (officers and fiduciaries), **8.01–630, 8.01–631**
Specific performance, **8.01–622**
Statute of limitations, **8.01–229**
Suicide, **8.01–622.1**
Time, temporary injunctions, **8.01–624**

INJUNCTIONS—Cont'd
Venue, **8.01–261**

INJURIES
Personal Injuries, generally, this index

INNS AND INNKEEPERS
Hotels and Motels, generally, this index

INSANITY
Mentally Ill Persons, generally, this index

INSTRUCTIONAL STAFF
Schoolteachers, generally, this index

INSTRUCTORS
Schoolteachers, generally, this index

INSULIN
Emergency medical services, privileges and immunities, **8.01–225**

INSURANCE
Accidents. Health Insurance, generally, this index
Actions and proceedings, joinder, **8.01–5**
Automobile insurance. Motor Vehicle Insurance, generally, this index
Disability insurance. Health Insurance, generally, this index
Group insurance. Health Maintenance Organizations, generally, this index
Health Insurance, generally, this index
Health Maintenance Organizations, generally, this index
HMO. Health Maintenance Organizations, generally, this index
Hospitals. Health Insurance, generally, this index
Illness. Health Insurance, generally, this index
Joinder, **8.01–5**
Jurisdiction, **8.01–328 et seq.**
Lines of insurance. Health Insurance, generally, this index
Medical care and treatment. Health Insurance, generally, this index
Medical records, access, **8.01–413**
Motor Vehicle Insurance, generally, this index
Sickness. Health Insurance, generally, this index
Surgical insurance. Health Insurance, generally, this index

INTANGIBLE PERSONAL PROPERTY
Personal Property, generally, this index

INTELLECTUAL DISABILITIES
Mentally Retarded and Developmentally Disabled Persons, generally, this index

INTENTIONAL TORTS
Torts, generally, this index

INTER VIVOS TRUSTS
Trusts and Trustees, generally, this index

INTEREST
Administrative law and procedure, judgments and decrees, **8.01–382**

INTEREST—Cont'd
Appeal and review, **8.01–682**
Executions, bonds (officers and fiduciaries), **8.01–528**
Garnishment, **8.01–511**
Injunctions, dissolution, **8.01–633**
Judgments and decrees, **8.01–382**
Labor and employment, third parties, compromise and settlement, consent, **8.01–424.1**
Rates and charges, judgments and decrees, **8.01–382**
Workers compensation, third parties, compromise and settlement, consent, **8.01–424.1**

INTERFERENCE
Business and commerce, privileges and immunities, hearings, strategic lawsuits against public participation, **8.01–223.2**

INTERLOCUTORY APPEALS
Permission, **8.01–670.1**

INTERLOCUTORY DECREES
Limitation of actions, appeal and review, **8.01–671**

INTERMEDIATE CARE FACILITIES
Nursing Homes, generally, this index

INTERMENT
Cemeteries, generally, this index

INTERNATIONAL COMPUTER NETWORK
Internet, generally, this index

INTERNET
Libel and slander,
False personation, limitation of actions, tolling, **8.01–247.1**
Privileges and immunities, **8.01–49.1**
Privileges and immunities, libel and slander, **8.01–49.1**
Subpoenas, torts, identity and identification, **8.01–407.1**

INTERPLEADER
Generally, **8.01–364**

INTERPRETERS
Confidential or privileged information,
Disclosure, damages, **8.01–44.3**
Trial, **8.01–384.1:1**
Trial, **8.01–384.1, 8.01–384.1:1**
Witnesses,
Confidential or privileged information, **8.01–400.1**
Hearing impaired persons, **8.01–406**
Oaths and affirmations, **8.01–406**

INTERROGATORIES
Arrest, privileges and immunities, **8.01–327.1**
Bifurcated trials, **8.01–267.6**
Fraud against taxpayers, actions and proceedings, civil investigative demands, **8.01–216.10 et seq., 8.01–216.15**

INTERROGATORIES—Cont'd
Garnishment, **8.01–511**
Jury, general verdicts, **8.01–379.3**

INTERSTATE DEPOSITIONS AND DISCOVERY ACT
Generally, **8.01–412.8 et seq.**

INTERVENTION
Attorneys, Lawyers Helping Lawyers, privileges and immunities, **8.01–226.1**
Fraud against taxpayers, actions and proceedings, **8.01–216.5, 8.01–216.6**
State, fraud against taxpayers, actions and proceedings, **8.01–216.5, 8.01–216.6, 8.01–216.9**

INTESTATE SUCCESSION
See, also,
Probate Proceedings, generally, this index
Wills, generally, this index
Personal representatives. Probate Proceedings, this index

INTIMIDATION
Duress or Coercion, generally, this index
Forcible Entry and Detainer, generally, this index

INTRASTATE TELECOMMUNICATIONS
Telecommunications, generally, this index

INVASIONS
Civil Defense, generally, this index

INVESTMENTS
Aged persons, real estate, proceeds, **8.01–76**
Children and minors, real estate, proceeds, **8.01–76**
Mentally ill persons, real estate, proceeds, **8.01–76**

IRON ORE
Mines and Minerals, generally, this index

ISSUE
Children and Minors, generally, this index

ISSUES, PROOF AND VARIANCE
Evidence, generally, this index

JAILS
See, also, Correctional Institutions, generally, this index
Actions and proceedings,
Fraud against taxpayers, application of law, **8.01–216.8**
Prisoner litigation reform, **8.01–689 et seq.**
Annuities, wrongful incarceration, compensation and salaries, **8.01–195.11**
Community colleges, tuition, wrongful incarceration, compensation and salaries, **8.01–195.11**
Compensation and salaries, wrongful incarceration, **8.01–195.10 et seq.**
Costs, actions and proceedings, prisoner litigation reform, **8.01–691**
Damages,
Prisoner litigation reform, **8.01–689 et seq.**

JAILS—Cont'd
Damages—Cont'd
Wrongful incarceration, compensation and salaries, **8.01–195.10 et seq.**
Discovery, prisoner litigation reform, **8.01–695**
Dismissal and nonsuit, prisoner litigation reform, **8.01–694**
Fraud against taxpayers, actions and proceedings, application of law, **8.01–216.8**
Grants, wrongful incarceration, compensation and salaries, **8.01–195.11**
Guardian ad litem, service of process, **8.01–297**
Habeas Corpus, generally, this index
In forma pauperis, actions and proceedings, prisoner litigation reform, **8.01–691, 8.01–692**
Indigent persons, actions and proceedings, prisoner litigation reform, **8.01–691, 8.01–692**
Injunctions, prisoner litigation reform, **8.01–689 et seq.**
Jury, exemptions, **8.01–341**
Mandamus, prisoner litigation reform, **8.01–689 et seq.**
Oral argument, prisoner litigation reform, **8.01–695**
Prisoner litigation reform, **8.01–689 et seq.**
Service of process, **8.01–297**
Habeas corpus, **8.01–658**
Prisoner litigation reform, **8.01–694**
Sheriffs, service of process, habeas corpus, **8.01–658**
Subpoenas, prisoner litigation reform, **8.01–695**
Superintendents, service of process, habeas corpus, **8.01–658**
Transition assistance grants, wrongful incarceration, compensation and salaries, **8.01–195.11**
Venue, prisoner litigation reform, **8.01–693**
Wrongful incarceration, compensation and salaries, **8.01–195.10 et seq.**

JOINDER
Generally, **8.01–267.1 et seq.**
Appeal and review, **8.01–267.8**
Asbestos, **8.01–374.1**
Asbestos, **8.01–374.1**
Assignments, beneficial owners, **8.01–14**
Beneficial owners, assignments, **8.01–14**
Bifurcated trials, **8.01–267.6**
Insurance, **8.01–5**
Interpleader, **8.01–364**
Landlord and tenant, tenants in common, **8.01–10**
Later filed actions, **8.01–267.7**
Misjoinder, **8.01–5**
Nonjoinder, **8.01–5**
Pleadings, **8.01–272**
Separate or bifurcated trials, **8.01–267.6**
Severance, **8.01–267.5**
Tenants in common, **8.01–10**
Third Parties, generally, this index
Torts, children and minors, **8.01–36**

JOINT AND SEVERAL LIABILITY
Generally, **8.01–442 et seq.**

JOINT AND SEVERAL LIABILITY—Cont'd
Contracts, **8.01–30**
Contribution, negligence, **8.01–34**
Covenant not to sue, **8.01–35.1**
Discharge, **8.01–443**
Ejectment, this index
Executions, **8.01–469**
Landlord and tenant, ejectment, **8.01–138**
Release, **8.01–35.1**
Torts, **8.01–443**

JOINT OWNERSHIP
Partnerships, generally, this index

JOINT TENANTS
Accounts and accounting, **8.01–31**
Ejectment, **8.01–141**
Partition, generally, this index

JUDGES
Arrest, privileges and immunities, **8.01–327.2**
Directed verdicts, **8.01–378**
Jury, exemptions, **8.01–341**
Privileges and immunities, torts, claims, **8.01–195.3**
Signatures, judicial notice, **8.01–387**

JUDGMENT CREDITORS AND DEBTORS
Debtors and Creditors, generally, this index

JUDGMENTS AND DECREES
See, also, Orders of Court, generally, this index
Generally, **8.01–426 et seq.**
Abstracts, **8.01–461**
Accord and Satisfaction, generally, this index
Affirmation, appeal and review, **8.01–681 et seq.**
Amendments, appeal and review, **8.01–429**
Appeal and Review, generally, this index
Application of law, foreign countries, **8.01–465.13:2**
Arbitration and award, **8.01–581.012**
Written agreement, compromise and settlement, **8.01–581.25**
Arrest, privileges and immunities, **8.01–327.1**
Associations and societies, **8.01–15**
Bills of review, injunctions, **8.01–623**
Boundaries, **8.01–183**
Clerical errors, error coram vobis writs, **8.01–677**
Clerical mistakes, corrections, **8.01–428**
Contrary to evidence, setting aside, **8.01–680**
Conviction of crime, **8.01–21**
Corrections, **8.01–428**
Damages, generally, this index
Death, **8.01–21**
Declaratory Judgments, generally, this index
Default Judgments, generally, this index
Detinue, **8.01–121**
Discharge, **8.01–453 et seq.**
Dismissal and Nonsuit, generally, this index
Dockets and docketing, **8.01–446 et seq.**
Due process, foreign countries, **8.01–465.13:3**
Ejectment, this index

JUDGMENTS AND DECREES—Cont'd
Entry of judgment. Executions, generally, this index
Error coram vobis writs, **8.01–677**
Evidence, **8.01–389**
Setting aside, contrary to evidence, **8.01–680**
Executions, generally, this index
Exhaustion of remedies, appeal and review, **8.01–429**
Extensions, limitation of actions, **8.01–251**
Federal courts, **8.01–465.1 et seq.**
Filing, foreign judgments and decrees, **8.01–465.2**
Fines and Penalties, generally, this index
Forcible Entry and Detainer, this index
Foreign countries,
Limitation of actions, **8.01–251**
Money, foreign country money judgments, recognition, **8.01–465.13:1 et seq.**
Foreign Judgments and Decrees, generally, this index
Foreign states, limitation of actions, **8.01–251**
Fraud,
Foreign countries, **8.01–465.13:3**
Vacating or setting aside, **8.01–428**
Garnishment, generally, this index
Habeas corpus, **8.01–662 et seq.**
Inconvenient forum, foreign countries, **8.01–465.13:3**
Indexes, dockets and docketing, **8.01–450, 8.01–451**
Injunctions, generally, this index
Interest, **8.01–382**
Appeal and review, **8.01–682**
Joint and several liability, **8.01–442 et seq.**
Jurisdiction, foreign countries, **8.01–465.13:3, 8.01–465.13:4**
Limitation of actions, **8.01–251**
Lost or destroyed documents, **8.01–392**
Proof, **8.01–394**
Mentally ill persons, **8.01–21**
Modification, confession of judgment, **8.01–433**
Money, foreign country money judgments, recognition, **8.01–465.13:1 et seq.**
Mortgages, generally, this index
Notice,
Appeal and review, **8.01–428**
Confession of judgment, **8.01–433.1**
Foreign judgments and decrees, **8.01–465.3**
Nunc pro tunc orders, **8.01–428**
Payment, **8.01–427, 8.01–453 et seq.**
Records and recordation, judgment dockets, **8.01–446 et seq.**
Reversal, **8.01–678**
Appeal and review, **8.01–429**
Review. Appeal and Review, generally, this index
Satisfaction. Accord and Satisfaction, generally, this index
State, indebtedness, collection, **8.01–199 et seq.**
Summary Judgment, generally, this index
Supersedeas or Stay, generally, this index

JUDGMENTS AND DECREES—Cont'd
Trover, title to property, **8.01–219**
Vacating or setting aside,
Confession of judgment, **8.01–433**
Default judgments, **8.01–428**
Servicemembers Civil Relief Act, **8.01–15.2**
Verdicts, **8.01–430**

JUDICIAL DEPARTMENT
Courts, generally, this index
Judges, generally, this index

JUDICIAL NOTICE
Generally, **8.01–385 et seq.**

JUDICIAL REVIEW
Appeal and Review, generally, this index

JUDICIAL SALES
Generally, **8.01–96 et seq.**
Accord and satisfaction, **8.01–98**
Appointments, special commissioners, **8.01–103**
Bonds (Officers and Fiduciaries), this index
Certificates and certification, bonds (officers and fiduciaries), **8.01–99**
Collection, **8.01–103**
Compensation and salaries, **8.01–109**
Credit, **8.01–96**
Deeds and conveyances, **8.01–110 et seq.**
Default, purchasers, claims against, **8.01–105 et seq.**
Delinquencies, real property taxation, **8.01–97, 8.01–98**
Distribution of proceeds, **8.01–98**
Executions, generally, this index
Fraud, bonds (officers and fiduciaries), **8.01–100**
Insufficient proceeds, real estate, **8.01–98**
Liens and incumbrances, **8.01–462**
Names, deeds and conveyances, **8.01–111**
Payments, **8.01–103 et seq.**
Privileges and immunities, purchasers, **8.01–101, 8.01–102**
Purchasers,
Claims against, **8.01–105 et seq.**
Liability, purchase money paid, **8.01–101, 8.01–102**
Real estate, insufficient proceeds, **8.01–98**
Real property taxation, delinquencies, **8.01–97, 8.01–98**
Special commissioners,
Appointments, **8.01–103**
Bonds (officers and fiduciaries), **8.01–99**
Claims against, **8.01–105 et seq.**
Compensation and salaries, **8.01–109**
Deeds and conveyances, executions, **8.01–110**
Title to property, **8.01–110 et seq.**

JUNIOR HIGH SCHOOLS
High Schools or Secondary Schools, generally, this index

JURISDICTION
Generally, **8.01–328 et seq.**

JURISDICTION—Cont'd
Arbitration and award, **8.01–581.014**
Attachment, **8.01–535**
Business and commerce, **8.01–328 et seq.**
Contracts, **8.01–328 et seq.**
Declaratory judgments, **8.01–184**
Discovery, personal jurisdiction, objections and exceptions, waiver, **8.01–277.1**
Foreign corporations, **8.01–328.1**
Foreign country money judgments, personal jurisdiction, recognition, **8.01–465.13:4**
Fraud against taxpayers, actions and proceedings, civil investigative demands, **8.01–216.13**
Insurance, **8.01–328 et seq.**
Liens and incumbrances, **8.01–462**
Long Arm Statute, **8.01–328.1**
Mandamus, **8.01–645**
Nonresidents, Long Arm Statute, **8.01–328.1**
Objections and exceptions,
  Personal jurisdiction, waiver, **8.01–277.1**
  Service of process, waiver, **8.01–286.1**
Partition, **8.01–81**
Personal jurisdiction, **8.01–328 et seq.**
  Objections and exceptions, waiver, **8.01–277.1**
Pleadings, personal jurisdiction, objections and exceptions, waiver, **8.01–277.1**
Removal or Transfer of Causes, generally, this index
Sales and use tax, declaratory judgments, foreign states, **8.01–184.1**
Tax collection, Long Arm Statute, **8.01–328.1**
Venue, generally, this index
Waiver, personal jurisdiction, objections and exceptions, **8.01–277.1**

JURY
  Generally, **8.01–336 et seq.**
Additional jurors, **8.01–360, 8.01–361**
Additions, lists, **8.01–346**
Adverse or pecuniary interest, removal, **8.01–358**
Age, **8.01–337**
  Exemptions, **8.01–341.1**
Aged persons, exemptions, **8.01–341.1**
Ambassadors and consuls, exemptions, **8.01–341.1**
Appearance, failure to appear, **8.01–356**
Argument, **8.01–379**
Arrest, privileges and immunities, **8.01–327.2**
Attorney general, exemptions, **8.01–341**
Attorneys,
  Argument, **8.01–379**
  Exemptions, **8.01–341**
  Jury panel, copy, providing, **8.01–353**
  Voir dire, **8.01–358**
Ballots, names, **8.01–347**
Bias and prejudice, removal, **8.01–358**
Blind persons, **8.01–337**
Breast feeding, exemptions, **8.01–341.1**
Calling, **8.01–357**
Challenges,
  Cause, **8.01–358**

JURY—Cont'd
Challenges—Cont'd
  Peremptory challenges, **8.01–360**
Children and minors, exemptions, **8.01–341.1**
Citizens and citizenship, **8.01–337**
Clerks of court, lists, maintaining, **8.01–346**
Commissioners, **8.01–343 et seq.**
Competency, objections and exceptions, **8.01–352**
Computers, random selection, **8.01–350.1**
Congress, exemptions, **8.01–341**
Correctional institutions, exemptions, **8.01–341**
Crimes and offenses, disqualification, **8.01–338**
Damages, amounts, **8.01–379.1**
  Vacating or setting aside, new trial, **8.01–383**
Declaratory judgments, **8.01–188**
Deferral, **8.01–341.2**
Directed verdicts, **8.01–378**
Discharge, **8.01–355**
  Hung jury, **8.01–361**
Disclosure, voir dire, **8.01–358**
Disqualification, **8.01–338**
  Ballots, removal, **8.01–349**
Domicile and residence, **8.01–337**
Drawing, names, **8.01–348**
Drivers licenses, lists, **8.01–345**
Elections, registrars, electoral boards, exemptions, **8.01–341.1**
Electronic selection, **8.01–350.1**
Equity, advisory jury, **8.01–336**
Evidence,
  Exhibits, **8.01–381**
  Summary jury trial, **8.01–576.3**
Examination, **8.01–358**
Exemptions, **8.01–341 et seq.**
  Ballots, removal, **8.01–349**
Exhibits, **8.01–381**
Failure to appear, **8.01–356**
Fines and penalties, failure to appear, **8.01–356**
Firefighters and fire departments, exemptions, **8.01–341.1**
Freeholder status, lists, **8.01–345, 8.01–346**
General assembly, exemptions, **8.01–341**
  Officers and employees, **8.01–341.1**
General verdicts, interrogatories, **8.01–379.3**
Governor, exemptions, **8.01–341**
Handicapped Persons, this index
Hung jury, **8.01–361**
Husband and wife, exemptions, **8.01–341.1**
Identity and identification, **8.01–353.1**
Impaneling, **8.01–357**
Impartial jury,
  Nonresidents, **8.01–363**
  Removal, cause, **8.01–358**
Instructions to jury, **8.01–379.2**
Interrogatories,
  Declaratory judgments, **8.01–188**
  General verdicts, **8.01–379.3**
Irregularities, objections and exceptions, **8.01–352**
Jails, exemptions, **8.01–341**

JURY—Cont'd
Joinder, **8.01-267.3**
Judges, exemptions, **8.01-341**
Labor and employment, exemption, **8.01-341.2**
Mentally ill persons, objections and exceptions, **8.01-352**
Military forces, **8.01-337**
Exemptions, **8.01-341.1**
Names, jury box, **8.01-347**
Nonresidents, impartial jury, **8.01-363**
Notice, **8.01-353**
Commissioners, **8.01-344**
Summary jury trial, **8.01-576.2**
Numbers and numbering, **8.01-359**
Oaths and affirmations, commissioners, **8.01-344**
Objections and exceptions, **8.01-352**
Notice, **8.01-353**
Removal, cause, **8.01-358**
Peremptory challenges, **8.01-360**
Pleadings, **8.01-381**
Police, exemptions, **8.01-341**
Prejudice, removal, **8.01-358**
Premises in question, viewing, **8.01-376**
President of United States, exemptions, **8.01-341**
Process, service of process, **8.01-298**
Questions, **8.01-358**
Quo warranto, **8.01-643**
Random selection, **8.01-345 et seq.**
Registration of voters, lists, **8.01-345**
Removal,
Cause, **8.01-358**
Disability, new juror, **8.01-361**
Peremptory challenges, **8.01-360**
Selection, **8.01-345 et seq.**
Summary jury trial, **8.01-576.2**
Service of process, **8.01-298, 8.01-353**
Sheriffs, exemptions, **8.01-341**
Special jury, **8.01-362**
Strikes, **8.01-359**
Summary jury trial, **8.01-576.1 et seq.**
Treason, disqualification, **8.01-338**
Vacating or setting aside,
New trial, **8.01-383**
Verdicts, **8.01-430**
Venire facias, **8.01-354**
Verdicts. Trial, this index
Viewing, premises in question, **8.01-376**
Voir dire, **8.01-358**
Waiver, **8.01-336**
Witnesses, summary jury trial, **8.01-576.3**
Writ of venire facias, **8.01-354**

JUSTICES
Judges, generally, this index

JUVENILE AND DOMESTIC RELATIONS DISTRICT COURTS
District Courts, generally, this index

JUVENILE DELINQUENTS AND DEPENDENTS
Delinquent Children, generally, this index

KNOWLEDGE
Notice, generally, this index

LABOR AND EMPLOYMENT
Actions and proceedings,
Libel and slander, **8.01-46.1**
Third parties, compromise and settlement, consent, **8.01-424.1**
Appeal and review, third parties, compromise and settlement, consent, **8.01-424.1**
Compensation and Salaries, generally, this index
Compromise and settlement, third parties, actions and proceedings, consent, **8.01-424.1**
Damages,
Libel and slander, **8.01-46.1**
Third parties, compromise and settlement, consent, **8.01-424.1**
Estoppel, workers compensation, **8.01-420.5**
Evidence, records and recordation, **8.01-413.1**
Exemplary damages, libel and slander, **8.01-46.1**
Garnishment, generally, this index
Hearings, third parties, actions and proceedings, compromise and settlement, **8.01-424.1**
Insurance, third parties, actions and proceedings, compromise and settlement, **8.01-424.1**
Interest, third parties, compromise and settlement, consent, **8.01-424.1**
Judgments and decrees, employment, estoppel, **8.01-420.5**
Jury, exemptions, **8.01-341.2**
Libel and slander, damages, **8.01-46.1**
Notice, third parties, actions and proceedings, compromise and settlement, **8.01-424.1**
Petitions, third parties, actions and proceedings, compromise and settlement, **8.01-424.1**
Privileges and immunities, libel and slander, **8.01-46.1**
Punitive damages, libel and slander, **8.01-46.1**
Records and recordation, evidence, **8.01-413.1**
Salaries. Compensation and Salaries, generally, this index
Third parties, actions and proceedings, compromise and settlement, consent, **8.01-424.1**
Volunteers, generally, this index
Workers Compensation, generally, this index

LABORATORIES
Delivery, results, **8.01-581.18**
Medical malpractice,
Privileges and immunities, **8.01-581.18:1**
Results, delivery, **8.01-581.18**

LACHES
Limitation of Actions, generally, this index

LAND
Real Estate, generally, this index

LANDLORD AND TENANT
See, also, Leases, generally, this index
Accounts and accounting, **8.01-31**
Actions and proceedings,
Attachment, **8.01-41**

LANDLORD AND TENANT—Cont'd
Actions and proceedings—Cont'd
Ejectment, generally, this index
Forcible Entry and Detainer, generally, this index
Attachment, damages, **8.01–41**
Attorney fees, bad checks, **8.01–27.1**
Costs, bad checks, **8.01–27.1**
Damages,
Attachment, **8.01–41**
Ejectment proceedings, **8.01–158, 8.01–159**
Mold, privileges and immunities, **8.01–226.12**
Disclosure,
Lead based paint, **8.01–226.7**
Mold, **8.01–226.12**
Distraint, damages, **8.01–41**
Distress. Forcible Entry and Detainer, generally, this index
Ejectment, generally, this index
Eviction,
Ejectment, generally, this index
Forcible Entry and Detainer, generally, this index
Evidence, ejectment, burden of proof, **8.01–139 et seq.**
Holdover tenants. Ejectment, generally, this index
Improvements, ejectment proceedings, **8.01–160, 8.01–161, 8.01–166 et seq.**
Inspection and inspectors,
Commencement, occupancy, mold, **8.01–226.12**
Mold, **8.01–226.12**
Joinder, tenants in common, **8.01–10**
Joint and several liability, ejectment, **8.01–138, 8.01–142, 8.01–143**
Judgments and decrees, ejectment, **8.01–149 et seq.**
Improvements, **8.01–166 et seq.**
Lead based paint, disclosure, **8.01–226.7**
Mold,
Disclosure, **8.01–226.12**
Maintenance and repairs, **8.01–226.12**
Privileges and immunities, **8.01–226.12**
Motions, ejectment, **8.01–135 et seq.**
Parties, ejectment, **8.01–131, 8.01–133**
Personal injuries, mold, privileges and immunities, **8.01–226.12**
Personal property, ejectment, storage, **8.01–156**
Possession. Forcible Entry and Detainer, generally, this index
Presumptions, mold, **8.01–226.12**
Privileges and immunities, mold, **8.01–226.12**
Process, service of process, **8.01–296**
Rent, generally, this index
Reports, inspection and inspectors, commencement, occupancy, **8.01–226.12**
Searches and seizures, damages, **8.01–41**
Service of process, **8.01–296**
Surrender of property by lessee. Ejectment, generally, this index
Tenants in Common, generally, this index

LANDLORD AND TENANT—Cont'd
Wrongful death, mold, privileges and immunities, **8.01–226.12**

LAW ENFORCEMENT OFFICERS
Arrest, generally, this index
Entry on property, **8.01–226**
Privileges and immunities, drug dealers, liability, **8.01–227.6**

LAW GOVERNING
Conflict of Laws, generally, this index

LAW OF THE ROAD
Traffic Rules and Regulations, generally, this index

LAWS
Statutes, generally, this index
Uniform Laws, generally, this index

LAWSUITS
Actions and Proceedings, generally, this index

LAWYERS
Attorneys, generally, this index

LAWYERS HELPING LAWYERS
Privileges and immunities, **8.01–226.1**

LEAD
Hazardous Substances and Waste, generally, this index

LEAD BASED PAINT
See, also, Hazardous Substances and Waste, generally, this index
Housing, disclosure, **8.01–226.7**

LEASE OF GOODS
Rent, generally, this index

LEASES
See, also,
Landlord and Tenant, generally, this index
Rent, generally, this index
Aged persons, **8.01–67 et seq.**
Children and minors, **8.01–67 et seq.**
Disclosure, lead based paint, **8.01–226.7**
Distress. Forcible Entry and Detainer, generally, this index
Ejectment, generally, this index
Forcible Entry and Detainer, generally, this index
Handicapped persons, **8.01–67 et seq.**
Lead based paint, disclosure, **8.01–226.7**
Life estates, **8.01–94, 8.01–95**
Mentally ill persons, **8.01–67 et seq.**
Partition, **8.01–91**
Termination of lease. Ejectment, generally, this index

LEGACIES
Probate Proceedings, generally, this index
Wills, generally, this index

LEGATEES
Wills, generally, this index

LEGISLATION
Statutes, generally, this index

LEGISLATURE
General Assembly, generally, this index

LESSEES AND LESSORS
Landlord and Tenant, generally, this index
Leases, generally, this index

LETTERS OF CREDIT
Appeal and review, **8.01–676.1**

LEVY
Executions, generally, this index

LIABILITY INSURANCE
Compromise and settlement, **8.01–424**
Motor Vehicle Insurance, generally, this index

LIBEL AND SLANDER
Generally, **8.01–45 et seq.**
Damages, **8.01–45 et seq.**
Lost profits, new business, unestablished business, **8.01–221.1**
Defenses, **8.01–46**
Exemplary damages, labor and employment, **8.01–46.1**
Internet,
False personation, limitation of actions, tolling, **8.01–247.1**
Privileges and immunities, **8.01–49.1**
Labor and employment, **8.01–46.1**
Limitation of actions, **8.01–247.1**
Mitigation,
Damages, **8.01–46**
Newspapers, **8.01–48**
Privileges and immunities, television and radio, **8.01–49**
Schoolteachers, privileges and immunities, investigations and investigators, **8.01–47**
Shoplifting, arrest, detention, privileges and immunities, **8.01–226.9**
Television and radio, privileges and immunities, **8.01–49**
Truth, defense, **8.01–46**

LICENSES AND PERMITS
Quo warranto, **8.01–635 et seq.**
Writs, quo warranto, **8.01–635 et seq.**

LIENS AND INCUMBRANCES
Generally, **8.01–458 et seq., 8.01–478 et seq.**
Abstracts, **8.01–461**
Aliened land, priorities and preferences, **8.01–464**
Amount, **8.01–463**
Assignments, dockets and docketing, **8.01–452**
Attachment, **8.01–458, 8.01–557**
Bonds (officers and fiduciaries), **8.01–465**
Third parties, **8.01–366 et seq.**
Boundaries, **8.01–481**
Certificates and certification, dockets and docketing, **8.01–446.1**

LIENS AND INCUMBRANCES—Cont'd
Children and minors, personal injuries, parents, guardian and ward, **8.01–36**
Confession of judgment, **8.01–431, 8.01–434**
Criminal injuries compensation fund, notice, **8.01–66.5, 8.01–66.6**
Death, limitation of actions, **8.01–229**
Dockets and docketing, certificates and certification, **8.01–446.1**
Emergency medical services, personal injuries, claims, **8.01–66.2 et seq.**
Equity, **8.01–462**
Executions, **8.01–478 et seq.**
Exemptions, **8.01–501 et seq.**
Perishable property, third parties, claims, **8.01–372**
Surplus, third parties, **8.01–373**
Third parties, claims, **8.01–365 et seq.**
Fraud, dockets and docketing, **8.01–446.1**
Hospitals, personal injuries, claims, **8.01–66.2 et seq.**
Judgments and decrees, **8.01–458 et seq.**
Records and recordation, **8.01–446.1**
Jurisdiction, **8.01–462**
Limitation of actions, **8.01–241**
Death, **8.01–229**
Medical care and treatment, personal injuries, claims, **8.01–66.2 et seq.**
Nursing homes, personal injuries,
Claims, **8.01–66.2 et seq.**
Medical assistance, **8.01–66.9**
Partition, **8.01–84**
Perishable property, sales, third parties, **8.01–372**
Personal injuries, medical care and treatment, **8.01–66.2 et seq.**
Priorities and preferences, **8.01–459**
Aliened land, **8.01–464**
Attachment, **8.01–557**
Public utilities, limitation of actions, **8.01–240**
Records and recordation, judgments and decrees, **8.01–446.1**
Revival, **8.01–458**
Sales, this index
Sidewalks, limitation of actions, **8.01–240**
State, executions, **8.01–202 et seq.**
Statute of limitations, death, **8.01–229**
Surplus, sales, third parties, **8.01–373**
Third parties, claims, **8.01–365 et seq.**
Venue, **8.01–261**

LIFE INSURANCE
See, also, Insurance, generally, this index
Mortality tables, evidence, **8.01–419**

LIGHT AND POWER COMPANIES
Electricity, generally, this index

LIMITATION OF ACTIONS
Generally, **8.01–228 et seq.**
Abatement of actions and proceedings, **8.01–229**
Wrongful death, **8.01–244**

LIMITATION OF ACTIONS—Cont'd
Abuse of process, **8.01–249**
Affirmative defenses, **8.01–235**
Appeal and review, court of appeals, **8.01–675.3**
Application of law, **8.01–256**
Arbitration and award, **8.01–581.010**
Asbestos, **8.01–249**
Removal, **8.01–250.1**
Assignments, **8.01–253**
Bail, **8.01–246**
Breach of condition subsequent, real estate, **8.01–255.1**
Certificates and certification, mortgages, extensions, **8.01–241.1**
Child abuse, **8.01–243**
Children and Minors, this index
Concealment, **8.01–243**
Conflict of laws, **8.01–247**
Contracts, this index
Correctional institutions, **8.01–229, 8.01–243.2**
Counterclaims, **8.01–233**
Cross claims, **8.01–233**
Damages, **8.01–230**
Suspension, **8.01–229**
Death, **8.01–229**
Debtors and creditors, **8.01–229**
Deeds and conveyances, **8.01–253**
Deeds of trust, **8.01–241 et seq.**
Defamation, **8.01–247.1**
Defense, pleadings, **8.01–235**
Discovery, waiver, **8.01–384.2**
Dismissal and nonsuit, **8.01–229**
Wrongful death, **8.01–244**
Drug dealers, liability, **8.01–227.7**
Duress or coercion, contracts, **8.01–249**
Estoppel, **8.01–232**
Extensions,
Judgments and decrees, **8.01–251**
Mortgages, **8.01–241 et seq.**
Facsimile transmissions, advertisements, damages, **8.01–40.2**
Fee simple, termination, **8.01–255.1**
Foreign Countries, this index
Fraud, **8.01–243, 8.01–249**
Taxation, **8.01–216.9**
Gifts, **8.01–253**
Habeas corpus, **8.01–654, 8.01–654.1**
Handicapped persons, **8.01–229**
Indemnity, third parties, **8.01–249**
Injunctions, **8.01–229**
Libel and slander, **8.01–247.1**
Liens and incumbrances, **8.01–241**
Death, **8.01–229**
Malicious prosecution, **8.01–249**
Mandamus, **8.01–644.1**
Mortgages, **8.01–241 et seq.**
Obstruction, **8.01–229**
Partnerships, **8.01–246**
Pending actions, **8.01–256**

LIMITATION OF ACTIONS—Cont'd
Personal injuries, **8.01–243 et seq.**
Pleadings, affirmative defense, **8.01–235**
Prisons and prisoners, **8.01–243.2**
Probate Proceedings, this index
Product liability, **8.01–249**
Property, damages, **8.01–243**
Public lands, grants, **8.01–238**
Public utilities, liens and incumbrances, **8.01–240**
Real Estate, this index
Rents, **8.01–239**
Repeal, **8.01–234**
Service of process, **8.01–275.1**
Publication, **8.01–322**
Sewers and sewer systems, liens and incumbrances, **8.01–240**
Sidewalks, liens and incumbrances, **8.01–240**
Slander, **8.01–247.1**
State, this index
Subrogation, judgments and decrees, **8.01–251**
Suspension, crimes and offenses, **8.01–229**
Third parties, **8.01–229**
Indemnity, **8.01–249**
Title to property, **8.01–236**
Tolling, libel and slander, false personation, Internet, **8.01–247.1**
Waiver, **8.01–232**
Discovery, **8.01–384.2**
Water supply, liens and incumbrances, **8.01–240**
Wills, **8.01–254**
Wrongful death, **8.01–50, 8.01–244**

LIMITED LIABILITY COMPANIES
Garnishment, **8.01–513**
Service of process, garnishment, **8.01–513**

LIQUEFIED PETROLEUM GAS
Natural Gas, generally, this index

LIS PENDENS
Pending Actions, generally, this index

LITTERING
Pick up programs, privileges and immunities, **8.01–226.8**
Volunteers, highways and roads, pick up programs, privileges and immunities, **8.01–226.8**

LIVESTOCK
Animals, generally, this index

LOANS
Children and minors, liability, **8.01–278**
Mortgages, generally, this index

LOCAL AGENCIES
Political Subdivisions, generally, this index

LOCAL DETENTION FACILITIES
Jails, generally, this index

LOCAL GOVERNMENT
Political Subdivisions, generally, this index

LODGING HOUSES
Hotels and Motels, generally, this index

LONG ARM STATUTE
Generally, **8.01–328.1**

LONG TERM CARE
Nursing Homes, generally, this index

LOST OR DESTROYED DOCUMENTS
Actions and proceedings, debtors and creditors, **8.01–32**
Affidavits, actions and proceedings, **8.01–32**
Bonds, actions and proceedings, **8.01–32**
Contracts, actions and proceedings, **8.01–32**
Courts, **8.01–392 et seq.**
Debtors and creditors, actions and proceedings, **8.01–32**
Evidences of indebtedness, actions and proceedings, **8.01–32**
Executions, **8.01–484**
Oaths and affirmations, actions and proceedings, **8.01–32**

LOST PROFITS
Damages, new business, unestablished business, **8.01–221.1**

LOTS
Real Estate, generally, this index

LOW INCOME PERSONS
Indigent Persons, generally, this index

MAGAZINES
See, also, Newspapers, generally, this index
Libel and Slander, generally, this index

MAIL AND MAILING
Certified or registered mail, torts, claims against state, notice, **8.01–195.6**
Service of process, **8.01–296**

MALICIOUS PROSECUTION
Limitation of actions, **8.01–249**
Shoplifting, arrest, detention, privileges and immunities, **8.01–226.9**

MALPRACTICE
Medical Malpractice, generally, this index

MANAGED CARE
Health Maintenance Organizations, generally, this index

MANAGERS AND MANAGEMENT
Nonprofit organizations, privileges and immunities, **8.01–220.1:1**

MANDAMUS
Generally, **8.01–644 et seq.**
Appropriations, payment, **8.01–653**
Contempt, **8.01–652**
Correctional institutions, prisoner litigation reform, **8.01–689 et seq.**
Defenses, **8.01–647**

MANDAMUS—Cont'd
Jails, prisoner litigation reform, **8.01–689 et seq.**
Jurisdiction, **8.01–645**
Limitation of actions, **8.01–644.1**
Oaths and affirmations, **8.01–644**
Payment, state treasury, **8.01–653**
Service of process, **8.01–644, 8.01–652**
State treasury, payments, **8.01–653**
Transportation, costs, **8.01–653.1**
Venue, **8.01–261**

MANDATORY ARBITRATION
Arbitration and Award, generally, this index

MANUFACTURED HOUSING
Disposal, ejectment, costs, **8.01–156**
Ejectment, **8.01–156**
Personal property, ejectment, **8.01–156**

MANUFACTURERS AND MANUFACTURING
Housing. Manufactured Housing, generally, this index
Manufactured Housing, generally, this index

MAPS AND PLATS
Boundaries, generally, this index
Winter sports areas, trails, **8.01–227.13**

MARINE CORPS
Military Forces, generally, this index

MARRIAGE
See, also, Husband and Wife, generally, this index
Breach of promise, abolishment, **8.01–220**
Change of names,
- Actions and proceedings, effect, **8.01–19**
- Appeal and review, **8.01–20**

Child support. Support, generally, this index
Divorce,
- Arbitration and award, vacating or setting aside, **8.01–576.12, 8.01–581.26**
- Chancery commissioners, appointment, **8.01–607**
- Children and minors. Support, generally, this index
- Correctional institutions, inmates, guardian ad litem, **8.01–9**
- Guardian ad litem, correctional institutions, inmates, **8.01–9**
- Publication, service of process, **8.01–319**
- Service of process, **8.01–288**
  - Nonresidents, **8.01–320**
  - Publication, **8.01–319**
- Support, generally, this index
- Venue, **8.01–261**

Marriage and Family Therapists, generally, this index
Parties, **8.01–19**
Support, generally, this index
Therapists. Marriage and Family Therapists, generally, this index
Venue, dissolution of marriage, **8.01–261**

MARRIAGE AND FAMILY THERAPISTS
Confidential or privileged information, witnesses, **8.01–400.2**
Evidence, confidential or privileged information, witnesses, **8.01–400.2**
Privileges and immunities, witnesses, **8.01–400.2**
Witnesses, confidential or privileged information, **8.01–400.2**

MASS MEDIA AND COMMUNICATIONS
Newspapers, generally, this index
Telecommunications, generally, this index

MASS TRANSPORTATION
Railroads, generally, this index

MASTER AND SERVANT
Labor and Employment, generally, this index

MEDIATION
Arbitration and Award, generally, this index

MEDICAL ASSISTANCE
Social Services, this index

MEDICAL CARE AND TREATMENT
Actions and proceedings. Medical Malpractice, generally, this index
Bills,
  Evidence, **8.01–413.01**
  Submission, in network providers, powers and duties, **8.01–27.5**
Blood alcohol tests, evidence, admissibility, **8.01–413.02**
Boards and commissions,
  Confidential or privileged information, **8.01–581.17**
  Privileges and immunities, **8.01–581.16**
Compromise and settlement, personal injuries, liens and incumbrances, **8.01–66.10**
Confidential or privileged information, boards and commissions, **8.01–581.17**
Conservators and Conservatorship, generally, this index
Consultants, boards and commissions, privileges and immunities, **8.01–581.16**
Emergency Medical Services, generally, this index
Epinephrine, emergency medical services, privileges and immunities, **8.01–225**
Evidence,
  Bills and billing, **8.01–413.01**
  Blood alcohol tests, emergency medical services, admissibility, **8.01–413.02**
  Records and recordation, **8.01–413**
Glucagon, emergency medical services, privileges and immunities, **8.01–225**
Good samaritan doctrine, privileges and immunities, **8.01–225**
Health Care Facilities, generally, this index
Health Care Professionals, generally, this index
Health Insurance, generally, this index
Health Maintenance Organizations, generally, this index

MEDICAL CARE AND TREATMENT—Cont'd
Hospitals, generally, this index
Husband and wife, joint and several liability, emergency medical services, **8.01–220.2**
Indigent persons, medical assistance. Social Services, this index
Insurance. Health Insurance, generally, this index
Joint and several liability, husband and wife, emergency medical services, **8.01–220.2**
Liens and incumbrances, personal injuries, claims, **8.01–66.2 et seq.**
Malpractice. Medical Malpractice, generally, this index
Medical assistance. Social Services, this index
Medical Malpractice, generally, this index
Naloxone, administration, privileges and immunities, **8.01–225**
Negligence. Medical Malpractice, generally, this index
Notice, liens and incumbrances, personal injuries, **8.01–66.5, 8.01–66.6**
Nurses, generally, this index
Payments, liens and incumbrances, personal injuries, claims, **8.01–66.2 et seq.**
Physical Therapists, generally, this index
Physicians and Surgeons, generally, this index
Pregnancy, generally, this index
Privileges and immunities,
  Bills, submission, in network providers, **8.01–27.5**
  Blood alcohol tests, emergency medical services, evidence, **8.01–413.02**
  Good samaritan doctrine, **8.01–225**
Records and recordation. Medical Records, generally, this index
Reports. Medical Records, generally, this index
Subpoenas, records and recordation, **8.01–413**

MEDICAL EXAMINERS
Autopsies, reports, evidence, **8.01–390.2**
Reports, evidence, **8.01–390.2**

MEDICAL MALPRACTICE
  Generally, **8.01–581.1 et seq.**
Additional parties, review panel, **8.01–581.2:1**
Amendment, pleadings, review panel, **8.01–581.2:1**
Amount of recovery, limitations, **8.01–581.15**
Apologies, evidence, **8.01–52.1, 8.01–581.20:1**
Appeal and review, medical malpractice review panel, **8.01–581.1 et seq.**
Application of law, **8.01–581.12:2**
Arbitration and award, **8.01–581.1 et seq., 8.01–581.12**
Boards and commissions, privileges and immunities, **8.01–581.16**
Certificates and certification, standard of care, expert witnesses, **8.01–20.1, 8.01–50.1**
Children and minors, limitation of actions, **8.01–243.1**
Commiseration, evidence, **8.01–52.1, 8.01–581.20:1**
Committees, privileges and immunities, **8.01–581.19, 8.01–581.19:1**

MEDICAL MALPRACTICE—Cont'd
Compassion, evidence, **8.01–52.1, 8.01–581.20:1**
Condolences, evidence, **8.01–52.1, 8.01–581.20:1**
Confidential or privileged information, **8.01–581.17**
Damages,
  Amount, limitations, **8.01–581.15**
  Punitive damages, **8.01–38.1**
Depositions, review panel, **8.01–581.4**
Discovery, review panel hearings, **8.01–581.3:1**
Evidence,
  Podiatrists, witnesses, **8.01–401.2:1**
  Review panel hearings, **8.01–581.3 et seq.**
  Sympathy, **8.01–52.1, 8.01–581.20:1**
Exemplary damages, **8.01–38.1**
Hearings, medical malpractice review panel, **8.01–581.5 et seq.**
Inspection and inspectors, records and recordation, **8.01–581.4:2**
Investigations and investigators, privileges and immunities, **8.01–581.19:1**
Laboratories,
  Privileges and immunities, **8.01–581.18:1**
  Results, delivery, **8.01–581.18**
Limitation of actions, **8.01–243**
  Children and minors, **8.01–243.1**
Limitations, punitive damages, **8.01–38.1**
Nurse practitioners, opinions and expert testimony, **8.01–401.2**
Oaths and affirmations, review panels, **8.01–581.3:1**
Opinions and expert testimony,
  Certificates and certification, standard of care, **8.01–20.1, 8.01–50.1**
  Physicians assistants, **8.01–401.2**
  Standard of care, **8.01–581.20**
Parties, review panel, **8.01–581.2:1**
Physicians assistants, opinions and expert testimony, **8.01–401.2**
Pleadings, amendment, review panel, **8.01–581.2:1**
Podiatrists, witnesses, evidence, **8.01–401.2:1**
Privileges and immunities, **8.01–581.13**
  Boards and commissions, **8.01–581.16**
  Committees, **8.01–581.19, 8.01–581.19:1**
  Laboratories, **8.01–581.18:1**
Production of books and papers, review panel, **8.01–581.6**
Punitive damages, **8.01–38.1**
Records and recordation, **8.01–581.4:1, 8.01–581.4:2**
Review panel, **8.01–581.1 et seq.**
Rules and regulations, review panel, **8.01–581.11**
Standard of care, **8.01–581.20**
  Expert witnesses, certificates and certification, **8.01–20.1, 8.01–50.1**
Statute of limitations, **8.01–243**
  Children and minors, **8.01–243.1**
Subpoenas, review panel, **8.01–581.6**
Summons, witnesses, review panel, **8.01–407**
Supersedeas or stay, review panel, **8.01–581.2**

MEDICAL MALPRACTICE—Cont'd
Sympathy, evidence, **8.01–52.1, 8.01–581.20:1**
Witnesses,
  Podiatrists, **8.01–401.2:1**
  Review panels, **8.01–581.6, 8.01–581.8**
    Summons, **8.01–407**

MEDICAL RECORDS
Blood alcohol tests, evidence, admissibility, **8.01–413.02**
Evidence, **8.01–413**
Privileges and immunities, blood alcohol tests, evidence, admissibility, **8.01–413.02**

MEDICAL TREATMENT
Medical Care and Treatment, generally, this index

MEDICINE
Drugs and Medicine, generally, this index

MENTAL CONDITION OR CAPACITY
Mentally Ill Persons, generally, this index
Mentally Retarded and Developmentally Disabled Persons, generally, this index

MENTAL INSTITUTIONS
See,
  Mentally Ill Persons, generally, this index
  Mentally Retarded and Developmentally Disabled Persons, generally, this index

MENTALLY ILL PERSONS
  See, also, Mentally Retarded and Developmentally Disabled Persons, generally, this index
Actions and proceedings,
  Compromise and settlement, **8.01–424 et seq.**
  Severance of cause, **8.01–22**
Attorneys, Lawyers Helping Lawyers, privileges and immunities, **8.01–226.1**
Compromise and settlement, **8.01–424 et seq.**
Conservators and Conservatorship, generally, this index
Deeds and conveyances, **8.01–67 et seq.**
Guardian Ad Litem, generally, this index
Guardian and Ward, generally, this index
Indebtedness, real estate, sales, **8.01–78 et seq.**
Investments, real estate, proceeds, **8.01–76**
Judgments and decrees, **8.01–21**
Jurisdiction, real estate, **8.01–68**
Leases, **8.01–67 et seq.**
Partition, **8.01–85**
Psychologists and Psychology, generally, this index
Real estate, **8.01–67 et seq.**
Sales, real estate, **8.01–67 et seq.**
Settlement, **8.01–424 et seq.**
Severance of cause, **8.01–22**
Successors in interest, **8.01–22**
Title to property, **8.01–67 et seq.**

MENTALLY RETARDED AND DEVELOPMENTALLY DISABLED PERSONS
See, also, Mentally Ill Persons, generally, this index
Actions and proceedings,
Compromise and settlement, **8.01–424 et seq.**
Guardian ad litem, **8.01–9**
Compromise and settlement, **8.01–424 et seq.**
Conservators and Conservatorship, generally, this index
Deeds and conveyances, **8.01–67 et seq.**
Guardian Ad Litem, generally, this index
Guardian and Ward, generally, this index
Indebtedness, real estate, sales, **8.01–78 et seq.**
Investments, real estate, proceeds, **8.01–76**
Jurisdiction, real estate, **8.01–68**
Jury, objections and exceptions, **8.01–352**
Leases, **8.01–67 et seq.**
Mortgages, **8.01–67 et seq.**
Partition, **8.01–85**
Real estate, **8.01–67 et seq.**
Sales, real estate, **8.01–67 et seq.**
Settlement, **8.01–424 et seq.**
Title to property, **8.01–67 et seq.**

METALS
Mines and Minerals, generally, this index

MILITARY FORCES
Affidavits, default judgments, Servicemembers Civil Relief Act, **8.01–15.2**
Attorney fees, Servicemembers Civil Relief Act, default judgments, **8.01–15.2**
Costs, Servicemembers Civil Relief Act, default judgments, **8.01–15.2**
Default judgments, Servicemembers Civil Relief Act, affidavits, **8.01–15.2**
Jury, **8.01–337**
Exemptions, **8.01–341.1**
Servicemembers Civil Relief Act, default judgments, affidavits, **8.01–15.2**

MINES AND MINERALS
Partition, **8.01–81**
Privileges and immunities, rescue, **8.01–225**
Rescue, privileges and immunities, **8.01–225**

MINING
Mines and Minerals, generally, this index

MINISTERS
Clergy, generally, this index

MINORS
Children and Minors, generally, this index

MISDEMEANORS
Crimes and Offenses, generally, this index

MISREPRESENTATION
Fraud, generally, this index

MOBILEHOMES AND MOBILEHOME PARKS
Manufactured Housing, generally, this index

MOLD
Landlord and Tenant, this index

MONEY
Conversion rates, foreign currency, judgments and decrees, **8.01–465.20, 8.01–465.21**
Foreign country money judgments, recognition, **8.01–465.13:1 et seq.**
Investments, generally, this index
Judgments and decrees, foreign country money judgments, recognition, **8.01–465.13:1 et seq.**

MORTGAGES
Actions and proceedings, limitation of actions, **8.01–241 et seq.**
Aged persons, **8.01–67 et seq.**
Children and minors, **8.01–67 et seq.**
Foreclosure, limitation of actions, **8.01–241 et seq.**
Handicapped persons, **8.01–67 et seq.**
Judicial Sales, generally, this index
Limitation of actions, **8.01–241 et seq.**
Mentally ill persons, **8.01–67 et seq.**
Statute of limitations, **8.01–241 et seq.**

MOTELS AND MOTOR COURTS
Hotels and Motels, generally, this index

MOTIONS
Anonymous plaintiffs, disclosure, **8.01–15.1**
Bonds (officers and fiduciaries), judgments and decrees, **8.01–227**
Boundaries, establishing, **8.01–179**
Ejectment, **8.01–135 et seq.**
Evidence, motion to strike, **8.01–276, 8.01–282**
Depositions, basis, **8.01–420**
Forcible entry and detainer, **8.01–124**
Identification numbers, redacting, **8.01–420.8**
Landlord and tenant, ejectment, **8.01–135 et seq.**
Process, service of process, defects, **8.01–277**
Service of process, defects, **8.01–277**
Summary Judgment, generally, this index
Venue, change of venue, **8.01–265**

MOTOR CARRIERS
See, also, Carriers, generally, this index
Railroads, generally, this index

MOTOR COURTS
Hotels and Motels, generally, this index

MOTOR LODGES
Hotels and Motels, generally, this index

MOTOR VEHICLE INSURANCE
Accidents,
Address, service of process, disclosure, **8.01–417**
Death, policy limits, disclosure, **8.01–417**
Policies, limits, disclosure, **8.01–417**
Rental vehicles, coverage, **8.01–66**
Address, accidents, service of process, disclosure, **8.01–417**
Attorney fees,
Denial, claims, **8.01–66.1**

MOTOR VEHICLE INSURANCE—Cont'd
Attorney fees—Cont'd
Rental vehicles, **8.01–66**
Underinsured motorists, cooperation, subrogation, **8.01–66.1:1**
Compromise and settlement, underinsured motorists, subrogation, **8.01–66.1:1**
Cooperation, underinsured motorists, subrogation, **8.01–66.1:1**
Costs, underinsured motorists, cooperation, subrogation, **8.01–66.1:1**
Coverage,
Denial, claims, **8.01–66.1**
Rental vehicles, **8.01–66**
Death, policies, limits, disclosure, **8.01–417**
Denial, claims, **8.01–66.1**
Disclosure, policies, limits, accidents, **8.01–417**
Evidence, accidents, medical care and treatment, fees, **8.01–413.01**
Limits, policies, accidents, disclosure, **8.01–417**
Medical care and treatment, fees, evidence, **8.01–413.01**
Policies, limits, accidents, disclosure, **8.01–417**
Rental vehicles, coverage, **8.01–66**
Service of process, accidents, address, disclosure, **8.01–417**
Settlement, underinsured motorists, subrogation, **8.01–66.1:1**
Subrogation, underinsured motorists, **8.01–66.1:1**
Third parties, denial, claims, **8.01–66.1**
Traveling expenses, underinsured motorists, cooperation, subrogation, **8.01–66.1:1**
Underinsured motorists, subrogation, **8.01–66.1:1**

MOTOR VEHICLES
See, also, Traffic Rules and Regulations, generally, this index
Accidents,
Address, service of process, disclosure, **8.01–417**
Children and minors, damages, **8.01–64**
Damages,
Children and minors, **8.01–64**
Driving under influence of alcohol or drugs, exemplary damages, **8.01–44.5**
Property, limitation of actions, **8.01–243**
Disclosure, motor vehicle insurance, policy limits, **8.01–417**
Driving under influence of alcohol or drugs, exemplary damages, **8.01–44.5**
Motor Vehicle Insurance, this index
Personal injuries, driving under influence of alcohol or drugs, exemplary damages, **8.01–44.5**
Property, damages, limitation of actions, **8.01–243**
Traffic Rules and Regulations, this index
Actions and proceedings, accidents, **8.01–63 et seq.**
Affidavits, damages, **8.01–416**
Alcoholic beverages, driving under influence of alcohol or drugs. Traffic Rules and Regulations, this index

MOTOR VEHICLES—Cont'd
Attorney fees, accidents, rental vehicles, coverage, **8.01–66**
Children and minors,
Accidents, damages, **8.01–64**
Forcible entry, privileges and immunities, **8.01–225**
Restraint devices, privileges and immunities, installation, **8.01–226.5**
Seat belts, privileges and immunities, installation, **8.01–226.5**
Confidential or privileged information, crash investigation team, **8.01–402**
Crash investigation team, witnesses, privileges and immunities, **8.01–402**
Damages,
Affidavits, **8.01–416**
Children and minors, forcible entry, privileges and immunities, **8.01–225**
Property, limitation of actions, **8.01–243**
Drivers licenses,
Court records, numbers and numbering, redacting, **8.01–420.8**
Numbers and numbering, court records, redacting, **8.01–420.8**
Driving rules. Traffic Rules and Regulations, generally, this index
Driving under influence of alcohol or drugs. Traffic Rules and Regulations, this index
Emergencies, children and minors, forcible entry, privileges and immunities, **8.01–225**
Evidence, valuation, **8.01–419.1**
Forcible entry, children and minors, privileges and immunities, **8.01–225**
Insurance. Motor Vehicle Insurance, generally, this index
Joint and several liability, accidents, children and minors, **8.01–64**
Law of the road. Traffic Rules and Regulations, generally, this index
Limitation of actions, property, damages, **8.01–243**
Motels and motor courts. Hotels and Motels, generally, this index
Motor Vehicle Insurance, generally, this index
NADA, valuation, **8.01–419.1**
Nonresidents, service of process, **8.01–307 et seq.**
Personal Injuries, this index
Privileges and immunities,
Children and minors, forcible entry, damages, **8.01–225**
Restraint devices, children and minors, installation, **8.01–226.5**
Property, damages, limitation of actions, **8.01–243**
Rental vehicles, accidents, insurance coverage, **8.01–66**
Rules of the road. Traffic Rules and Regulations, generally, this index
Seat belts, children and minors, privileges and immunities, installation, **8.01–226.5**
Service of process,
Accidents, address, disclosure, **8.01–417**

MOTOR VEHICLES—Cont'd
Service of process—Cont'd
Nonresidents, **8.01–307 et seq.**
Theft, accidents, defense, **8.01–65**
Traffic Rules and Regulations, generally, this index
Valuation, evidence, **8.01–419.1**
Winter sports areas, safety, **8.01–227.15**

MOTORCYCLES
Insurance. Motor Vehicle Insurance, generally, this index
Motor Vehicle Insurance, generally, this index
Rules of the road. Traffic Rules and Regulations, generally, this index

MULES
Animals, generally, this index

MUNICIPAL CORPORATIONS
Municipalities, generally, this index

MUNICIPAL ELECTIONS
Municipal electoral boards, jury, exemptions, **8.01–341.1**

MUNICIPAL OFFICERS AND EMPLOYEES
Compensation and salaries, garnishment, **8.01–524, 8.01–525**
Garnishment, **8.01–524, 8.01–525**
Littering, pick up programs, privileges and immunities, **8.01–226.8**
Privileges and immunities, littering, pick up programs, **8.01–226.8**

MUNICIPALITIES
See, also, Political Subdivisions, generally, this index
Courts. District Courts, generally, this index
District Courts, generally, this index
Employees. Municipal Officers and Employees, generally, this index
Evidence, records and recordation, **8.01–390**
Firefighters and Fire Departments, generally, this index
Hearings, privileges and immunities, strategic lawsuits against public participation, **8.01–223.2**
Jails, generally, this index
Jurisdiction, tax collection, Long Arm Statute, **8.01–328.1**
Labor and employment. Municipal Officers and Employees, generally, this index
Officers and employees. Municipal Officers and Employees, generally, this index
Privileges and immunities, hearings, strategic lawsuits against public participation, **8.01–223.2**
Process, service of process, **8.01–300**
Real Property Taxation, generally, this index
Records and recordation, evidence, **8.01–390**
Schools and School Districts, generally, this index
Service, **8.01–300**
Sewers and Sewer Systems, generally, this index

MUNICIPALITIES—Cont'd
Tax collection, Long Arm Statute, **8.01–328.1**
Taxation,
Long Arm Statute, tax collection, **8.01–328.1**
Real Property Taxation, generally, this index
Water Supply, generally, this index

MUTE PERSONS
Hearing Impaired Persons, generally, this index

NALOXONE
Emergency medical services, administration, privileges and immunities, **8.01–225**

NAMES
Actions and proceedings, unauthorized use, **8.01–40**
Advertisements, consent, damages, **8.01–40**
Anonymous plaintiffs, **8.01–15.1**
Change of name, **8.01–217**
Judgments and decrees, debtors and creditors, **8.01–451**
Children and minors, change of names, **8.01–217**
Consent, advertisements, damages, **8.01–40**
Conservators and conservatorship, pleadings, style, **8.01–6.3**
Correctional institutions, change of names, **8.01–217**
Fiduciaries, pleadings, style, **8.01–6.3**
Guardian and ward, pleadings, style, **8.01–6.3**
Hearings, change of name, **8.01–217**
Libel and Slander, generally, this index
Limitation of actions, advertisements, damages, **8.01–40**
Notice, change of names, **8.01–217**
Oaths and affirmations, change of names, **8.01–217**
Personal representatives, pleadings, style, **8.01–6.3**
Probation, change of name, **8.01–217**
Sex offenders and crimes against minors registry, change of name, **8.01–217**
Trusts and trustees, pleadings, style, **8.01–6.3**
Venue, change of names, **8.01–217**
Vital statistics, change of names, **8.01–217**

NARCOTICS
Controlled Substances, generally, this index

NATIONAL DEFENSE
Civil Defense, generally, this index

NATURAL DISASTERS
Disasters, generally, this index

NATURAL GAS
See, also, Public Utilities, generally, this index
Attorney fees, meters, tampering, **8.01–44.7**
Costs, meters, tampering, **8.01–44.7**
Damages, meters, tampering, **8.01–44.7**
Injunctions, meters, tampering, **8.01–44.7**
Meters, tampering, damages, **8.01–44.7**

NAVY
Military Forces, generally, this index

NEGLIGENCE
See, also, Torts, generally, this index

NEGLIGENCE—Cont'd
Contribution, **8.01–34**
Contributory negligence, railroads, officers and employees, **8.01–58**
Covenant not to sue, **8.01–35.1**
Evidence, subsequent measures, **8.01–418.1**
Health care practitioners. Medical Malpractice, generally, this index
Interrogatories, jury, general verdicts, **8.01–379.3**
Medical Malpractice, generally, this index
Privileges and immunities, hospitals, **8.01–38**
Privity, **8.01–223**
Railroads, personal injuries, officers and employees, **8.01–57 et seq.**
Remedial measures, evidence, **8.01–418.1**
Skiing, winter sports safety, **8.01–227.11 et seq.**
Subsequent measures, evidence, **8.01–418.1**
Trespass, privileges and immunities, harm to trespasser, **8.01–219.1**
Winter sports safety, **8.01–227.11 et seq.**
Wrongful Death, generally, this index

NEGOTIABLE INSTRUMENTS
Actions and proceedings, **8.01–27.1 et seq.**
Arrest, bad checks, privileges and immunities, **8.01–226.10**
Attorney fees, bad checks, actions and proceedings, **8.01–27.1**
Bad checks,
  Actions and proceedings, **8.01–27.1, 8.01–27.2**
    Evidence, writing, **8.01–27.3**
  Arrest, privileges and immunities, **8.01–226.10**
  Attorney fees, actions and proceedings, **8.01–27.1**
  Evidence, notations, **8.01–27.3**
  Privileges and immunities, arrest, **8.01–226.10**
  Writing, evidence, **8.01–27.3**
Bad faith, stop payment, damages, **8.01–27.1**
Checks,
  Actions and proceedings, **8.01–27.1, 8.01–27.2**
  Evidence, substitute checks, **8.01–391.1**
  Substitute checks, evidence, **8.01–391.1**
Crimes and offenses, arrest, bad checks, privileges and immunities, **8.01–226.10**
Evidence, substitute checks, **8.01–391.1**
Forgery, substitute checks, **8.01–391.1**
Privileges and immunities, bad checks, arrest, **8.01–226.10**
Probable cause, bad checks, arrest, **8.01–226.10**
Stop payment, bad faith, damages, **8.01–27.1**
Substitute checks, evidence, **8.01–391.1**
Writing, bad checks, evidence, **8.01–27.3**

NETWORK (COMPUTERS)
Internet, generally, this index

NEW BUSINESS
Damages, lost profits, **8.01–221.1**

NEW TRIAL
Trial De Novo, generally, this index

NEWBORNS
Children and Minors, this index

NEWSPAPERS
Defamation. Libel and Slander, generally, this index
Legal advertising. Notice, generally, this index
Libel and slander, mitigation, **8.01–48**
Notice, generally, this index
Publication, generally, this index
Service of process, publication, **8.01–323, 8.01–324**

NINE ONE ONE (911)
Evidence, certificates and certification, **8.01–390**
Privileges and immunities, **8.01–225**

NITROGLYCERINE
Explosives, generally, this index

NON COMPOS MENTIS
Mentally Ill Persons, generally, this index

NONCRIMINAL VIOLATIONS
Fines and Penalties, generally, this index

NONPROFIT CORPORATIONS
Nonprofit Organizations, generally, this index

NONPROFIT ORGANIZATIONS
Actions and proceedings, privileges and immunities, **8.01–220.1:1**
  Tobacco trust, **8.01–220.1:4**
Crimes and offenses, informants, privileges and immunities, **8.01–226.3**
Damages, privileges and immunities, **8.01–220.1:1**
  Tobacco trust, **8.01–220.1:4**
Managers and management, privileges and immunities, **8.01–220.1:1**
Members, privileges and immunities, **8.01–220.1:1**
Officers and employees, privileges and immunities, **8.01–220.1:1**
  Tobacco trust, **8.01–220.1:4**
Partnerships, privileges and immunities, **8.01–220.1:1**
Privileges and immunities, **8.01–220.1:1**
  Crimes and offenses, informants, **8.01–226.3**
  Tobacco trust, **8.01–220.1:4**

NONRESIDENTS
  See, also, Domicile and Residence, generally, this index
Aircraft, accidents, service of process, **8.01–309 et seq.**
Foreign States, generally, this index
Jurisdiction, Long Arm Statute, **8.01–328.1**
Long Arm Statute, **8.01–328.1**
Process, service of process, **8.01–320**
Service of process, **8.01–320**

NONSTOCK CORPORATIONS
Corporations, generally, this index

NONSUIT
Dismissal and Nonsuit, generally, this index

NORTH CAROLINA
Foreign States, generally, this index

NOTICE
Arbitration and Award, this index
Confession of judgment, **8.01–433.1**
Criminal injuries compensation fund, liens and incumbrances, **8.01–66.5, 8.01–66.6**
Executions, this index
Foreign judgments and decrees, **8.01–465.3**
Injunctions, **8.01–629**
Internet, torts, identity and identification, subpoenas, **8.01–407.1**
Judgments and Decrees, this index
Jury, this index
Receivers and receivership, **8.01–591 et seq.**
State, this index
Winter sports safety, warnings, **8.01–227.12, 8.01–227.14**

NUCLEAR ENERGY
Disasters, generally, this index

NURSE PRACTITIONERS
Evidence, opinions and expert testimony, **8.01–401.2**
Opinions and expert testimony, **8.01–401.2**
Witnesses, opinions and expert testimony, **8.01–401.2**

NURSES
Actions and proceedings. Medical Malpractice, generally, this index
Disasters, privileges and immunities, **8.01–225.01, 8.01–225.02**
Emergencies, privileges and immunities, **8.01–225.01, 8.01–225.02**
Liens and incumbrances, personal injuries, claims, **8.01–66.2 et seq.**
Malpractice. Medical Malpractice, generally, this index
Medical Malpractice, generally, this index
Nurse Practitioners, generally, this index
Practitioners. Nurse Practitioners, generally, this index
Privileges and immunities, disasters, **8.01–225.01, 8.01–225.02**

NURSING FACILITIES
Nursing Homes, generally, this index

NURSING HOMES
Conservators and Conservatorship, generally, this index
Disasters, privileges and immunities, **8.01–225.01, 8.01–225.02**
Emergencies, privileges and immunities, **8.01–225.01, 8.01–225.02**
Guardian and Ward, generally, this index
Liens and incumbrances, personal injuries,
Claims, **8.01–66.2 et seq.**
Medical assistance, **8.01–66.9**
Medical Malpractice, generally, this index
Notice, medical assistance, personal injuries, wrongful death, **8.01–66.5**

NURSING HOMES—Cont'd
Payment, personal injuries, claims, **8.01–66.2 et seq.**
Personal injuries,
Claims, payment, **8.01–66.2 et seq.**
Medical assistance, notice, **8.01–66.5**
Privileges and immunities, disasters, **8.01–225.01, 8.01–225.02**
Wrongful death, medical assistance, notice, **8.01–66.5**

OATHS AND AFFIRMATIONS
Affidavits, generally, this index
Arbitration and award, **8.01–581.06**
Change of names, **8.01–217**
Debtors and creditors, lost or destroyed documents, actions and proceedings, **8.01–32**
Depositions, video tape, **8.01–412.4**
Evidence, unsworn written declarations, **8.01–4.3**
Evidences of indebtedness, lost or destroyed documents, actions and proceedings, **8.01–32**
Jury, commissioners, **8.01–344**
Mandamus, **8.01–644**
Medical malpractice, review panels, **8.01–581.3:1**
Pleadings, **8.01–280**
Witnesses, this index

OBSTETRICIANS
Physicians and Surgeons, generally, this index

OCULISTS
Optometrists, generally, this index

OFFENSES
Crimes and Offenses, generally, this index

OFFICIAL BONDS
Bonds (Officers and Fiduciaries), generally, this index

OIL AND GAS
See, also,
Mines and Minerals, generally, this index
Public Utilities, generally, this index
Natural Gas, generally, this index

OLD AGE
Aged Persons, generally, this index

OLD AGE AND SURVIVORS INSURANCE
Social Security, generally, this index

OPEN PITS
Mines and Minerals, generally, this index

OPHTHALMOLOGY AND OPHTHALMOLOGISTS
Physicians and Surgeons, generally, this index

OPINIONS AND EXPERT TESTIMONY
Witnesses, this index

OPIOID ANTAGONISTS
Administration, privileges and immunities, **8.01–225**

OPPRESSION
Duress or Coercion, generally, this index

OPTOMETRISTS
See, also, Physicians and Surgeons, generally, this index
Actions and proceedings. Medical Malpractice, generally, this index
Disasters, privileges and immunities, **8.01–225.01, 8.01–225.02**
Emergencies, privileges and immunities, **8.01–225.01, 8.01–225.02**
Malpractice. Medical Malpractice, generally, this index
Medical Malpractice, generally, this index
Privileges and immunities, disasters, **8.01–225.01, 8.01–225.02**

ORAL ARGUMENT
Correctional institutions, prisoner litigation reform, **8.01–695**
Jails, prisoner litigation reform, **8.01–695**

ORDERS
Judgments and Decrees, generally, this index
Restraining orders. Injunctions, generally, this index

ORDERS OF COURT
See, also, Judgments and Decrees, generally, this index
Appeal and review, **8.01–384**
Arbitration and award, compelling arbitration, **8.01–581.02**
Dismissal and nonsuit, previous nonsuits, **8.01–380**
Fraud against taxpayers, actions and proceedings, civil investigative demands, **8.01–216.18**
Injunctions, generally, this index
Objections and exceptions, **8.01–384**
Restraining orders. Injunctions, generally, this index
Subpoenas, generally, this index
Summons, generally, this index

ORE
Mines and Minerals, generally, this index

OSTEOPATHS
See, also, Physicians and Surgeons, generally, this index
Medical Malpractice, generally, this index
Negligence. Medical Malpractice, generally, this index

OTHER STATES
Foreign States, generally, this index

OWNERS AND OWNERSHIP
Title to Property, generally, this index

PAIN AND SUFFERING
Children and minors, drug dealers, liability, **8.01–227.4 et seq.**

PANEL TRUCKS
Motor Vehicles, generally, this index

PAPERS
Newspapers, generally, this index
Production of Books and Papers, generally, this index

PARAMEDICS
Emergency Medical Services, generally, this index

PARDONS AND REPRIEVES
Wrongful incarceration, compensation and salaries, **8.01–195.10**

PARENT AND CHILD
Children and Minors, generally, this index

PAROLE
See, also, Probation, generally, this index
Habeas corpus, service of process, **8.01–658**
Service of process, habeas corpus, **8.01–658**

PARTIES
Additional parties, **8.01–7**
  Continuance, **8.01–16**
Affidavits, domicile and residence, **8.01–414**
Anonymous plaintiffs, **8.01–15.1**
Arbitration and Award, generally, this index
Attachment, **8.01–539**
Beneficial owners, **8.01–12**
Bifurcated trials, **8.01–267.6**
Children and minors, wrongful death, **8.01–50**
Class actions, death, **8.01–23**
Confidential or privileged information, anonymous plaintiffs, **8.01–15.1**
Consolidation of actions, **8.01–267.1 et seq.**
Continuance, additional parties, **8.01–16**
Conviction of crime, successors in interest, **8.01–22**
Costs, generally, this index
Death,
  Class actions, **8.01–23**
  Severance of cause, **8.01–22**
  Successors in interest, **8.01–22**
  Survival, **8.01–25**
Depositions, generally, this index
Disclosure, anonymous plaintiffs, **8.01–15.1**
Discontinuance, substitution, **8.01–18**
Dockets and docketing, **8.01–331**
Domicile and residence, affidavits, **8.01–414**
Ejectment, **8.01–131, 8.01–133**
Identity and identification, anonymous plaintiffs, **8.01–15.1**
Impleader. Third Parties, generally, this index
Joinder, generally, this index
Joint and Several Liability, generally, this index
Marriage, **8.01–19**
Mentally ill persons, successors in interest, **8.01–22**
Misjoinder, **8.01–5**
Multiple parties, venue, **8.01–263**
Names,
  Amendments, **8.01–6**
  Anonymous plaintiffs, **8.01–15.1**
Nonjoinder, **8.01–5, 8.01–5 et seq.**

PARTIES—Cont'd
Orders of Court, generally, this index
Pleadings, generally, this index
Process, generally, this index
Publication, service of process, **8.01–316 et seq.**
Quo warranto, **8.01–637**
Removal or transfer of causes, **8.01–267.1 et seq.**
Service of process. Process, this index
Severance, **8.01–267.5**
Substitution,
  Motions, discontinuance, **8.01–18**
  Successors in interest, **8.01–17**
Successors in interest, **8.01–17**
Summons, generally, this index
Third Parties, generally, this index
Title to property, beneficial owners, **8.01–12 et seq.**
Transfer of causes, **8.01–267.1 et seq.**
United States, personal injuries, **8.01–37.1**
Venue, location, **8.01–262**
Wrongful death, children and minors, **8.01–50**

PARTITION
  Generally, **8.01–81 et seq.**
Allotment, **8.01–83**
Attorney fees, **8.01–92**
Handicapped persons, **8.01–85**
Jurisdiction, **8.01–81**
Leases, **8.01–91**
Liens and incumbrances, **8.01–84**
Mines and minerals, **8.01–81**
Personal property, **8.01–93**
Sales, **8.01–83**
  Handicapped persons, proceeds, **8.01–85**
  Liens and incumbrances, **8.01–84**
Unknown parties, **8.01–90**
Venue, **8.01–261, 8.01–262**

PARTNERSHIPS
Actions and proceedings, limitation of actions, **8.01–246**
Limitation of actions, **8.01–246**
Nonprofit organizations, privileges and immunities, **8.01–220.1:1**
Pleadings, affidavits, **8.01–279**
Service of process, **8.01–304**
  Fraud against taxpayers, actions and proceedings, civil investigative demands, **8.01–216.13**
Statute of limitations, **8.01–246**

PASTORS
Clergy, generally, this index

PATENT MEDICINES
Drugs and Medicine, generally, this index

PAUPERS
Indigent Persons, generally, this index

PAY
Compensation and Salaries, generally, this index

PAYMENT
Health care professionals, insurance, actions and proceedings, **8.01–27.4**

PAYROLLS
Compensation and Salaries, generally, this index

PENAL INSTITUTIONS
Correctional Institutions, generally, this index

PENALTIES
Fines and Penalties, generally, this index

PENDING ACTIONS
  Generally, **8.01–268, 8.01–269**
Application of law, **8.01–1**
Attachment, **8.01–574**
Limitation of actions, **8.01–256**
Shoplifting, damages, **8.01–44.4**
Zoning and planning, records and recordation, **8.01–268**

PENITENTIARIES
Correctional Institutions, generally, this index

PER DIEM
Compensation and Salaries, generally, this index

PERFORMANCE BONDS
Bonds (Officers and Fiduciaries), generally, this index

PERISHABLE PROPERTY
Liens and incumbrances, sales, third parties, claims, **8.01–372**

PERJURY
Unsworn written declarations, **8.01–4.3**

PERSONAL INJURIES
Amendments, wrongful death, **8.01–56**
Asbestos, joinder, **8.01–374.1**
Children and Minors, this index
Compensation and salaries, lost income, reimbursement, **8.01–35**
Compromise and settlement,
  Medical care and treatment, expenses, **8.01–66.10**
  Rescission, release, **8.01–425.1**
  Wrongful death, **8.01–51**
Contractors, privileges and immunities, **8.01–39**
Crime victims, actions and proceedings, **8.01–221**
Crimes and offenses, actions and proceedings, **8.01–221**
Damages,
  Compensation and salaries, reimbursement, **8.01–35**
  Lost profits, new business, unestablished business, **8.01–221.1**
  Medical care and treatment, liens and incumbrances, **8.01–66.2 et seq.**
  Subrogation, medical care and treatment, **8.01–66.4**
Death, generally, this index

PERSONAL INJURIES—Cont'd
Emancipated minors, compensation and salaries, **8.01–37**
Evidence,
Compensation and salaries, reimbursement, **8.01–35**
Motor vehicles, medical care and treatment, **8.01–413.01**
Health care professionals, liens and incumbrances, **8.01–66.2 et seq.**
Interrogatories, jury, general verdicts, **8.01–379.3**
Intervention, United States, **8.01–37.1**
Joinder, children and minors, **8.01–36**
Jurisdiction, **8.01–328 et seq.**
Landlord and tenant, mold, privileges and immunities, **8.01–226.12**
Liens and incumbrances, medical care and treatment, **8.01–66.2 et seq.**
Limitation of actions, **8.01–243 et seq.**
Long Arm Statute, **8.01–328.1**
Medical care and treatment,
Fees, evidence, **8.01–413.01**
Liens and incumbrances, **8.01–66.2 et seq.**
Medical Malpractice, generally, this index
Motor vehicles,
Accidents, **8.01–63 et seq.**
Driving under influence of alcohol or drugs, exemplary damages, **8.01–44.5**
Medical care and treatment, evidence, **8.01–413.01**
Negligence, generally, this index
Notice, medical care and treatment, liens and incumbrances, **8.01–66.5, 8.01–66.6**
Nursing homes,
Liens and incumbrances, claims, **8.01–66.2 et seq.**
Medical assistance, notice, **8.01–66.5**
Pleadings, amendments, wrongful death, **8.01–56**
Privity, **8.01–223**
Release, compromise and settlement, rescission, **8.01–425.1**
Skiing, winter sports safety, **8.01–227.11 et seq.**
Social services, liens and incumbrances, reimbursement, **8.01–66.9**
Space, flight, privileges and immunities, **8.01–227.8 et seq.**
Statements, transcripts, **8.01–417**
Statute of limitations, **8.01–243 et seq.**
Subrogation, medical care and treatment, expenses, **8.01–66.4**
Survival, **8.01–25**
Transcripts, statements, **8.01–417**
United States, intervention, **8.01–37.1**
Winter sports safety, **8.01–227.11 et seq.**
Wrongful Death, generally, this index

PERSONAL PROPERTY
See, also, Property, generally, this index
Appeal and review, detinue, damages, **8.01–123**
Attachment, generally, this index

PERSONAL PROPERTY—Cont'd
Bonds (officers and fiduciaries), detinue, **8.01–115 et seq.**
Costs, detinue, **8.01–122**
Damages, detinue, **8.01–123**
Detinue, **8.01–114 et seq.**
Ejectment, storage, **8.01–156**
Evidence, detinue, **8.01–114**
Executions, generally, this index
Expenses and expenditures, detinue, **8.01–122**
Garnishment, generally, this index
Hearings, detinue, **8.01–119**
Injunctions, **8.01–622**
Judgments and decrees, detinue, **8.01–121**
Levy of execution. Executions, generally, this index
Life estates, **8.01–94, 8.01–95**
Motions, detinue, **8.01–114 et seq.**
Petitions, detinue, **8.01–114**
Pretrial seizures, detinue, **8.01–114 et seq.**
Recovery, detinue, **8.01–114 et seq.**
Replevin, abolishment, **8.01–218**
Sales, detinue, **8.01–116**
Sales and Use Tax, generally, this index
Searches and Seizures, generally, this index
Third parties, executions, **8.01–365 et seq.**
Title to Property, generally, this index
Use taxes. Sales and Use Tax, generally, this index
Valuation, detinue, **8.01–120**
Vandalism, generally, this index
Warrants, detinue, **8.01–114 et seq.**

PERSONAL REPRESENTATIVES
Probate Proceedings, this index

PERSONAL SERVICE
Service of process. Process, this index

PERSONNEL
Labor and Employment, generally, this index

PETITIONS
Fraud against taxpayers, actions and proceedings, civil investigative demands, **8.01–216.18**

PETS
Animals, generally, this index

PHARMACISTS
Controlled Substances, generally, this index
Disasters, privileges and immunities, **8.01–225.01, 8.01–225.02**
Emergencies, privileges and immunities, **8.01–225.01, 8.01–225.02**
Evidence, records and recordation, **8.01–413**
Liens and incumbrances, personal injuries, claims, **8.01–66.2 et seq.**
Malpractice. Medical Malpractice, generally, this index
Medical Malpractice, generally, this index
Privileges and immunities, disasters, **8.01–225.01, 8.01–225.02**
Records and recordation, evidence, **8.01–413**

PHOTOGRAPHY AND PICTURES
Actions and proceedings, unauthorized use, **8.01–40**
Advertisements, consent, damages, **8.01–40**
Consent, advertisements, damages, **8.01–40**
Limitation of actions, advertisements, damages, **8.01–40**

PHRASES
Words and Phrases, generally, this index

PHYSICAL THERAPISTS
Disasters, privileges and immunities, **8.01–225.01, 8.01–225.02**
Emergencies, privileges and immunities, **8.01–225.01, 8.01–225.02**
Liens and incumbrances, personal injuries, claims, **8.01–66.2 et seq.**
Malpractice. Medical Malpractice, generally, this index
Medical Malpractice, generally, this index
Privileges and immunities, disasters, **8.01–225.01, 8.01–225.02**

PHYSICALLY HANDICAPPED PERSONS
Handicapped Persons, generally, this index

PHYSICALLY INCAPACITATED
Handicapped Persons, generally, this index

PHYSICIANS AND SURGEONS
Actions and proceedings,
  Medical Malpractice, generally, this index
  Payment, insurance, **8.01–27.4**
Athletics, schools and school districts, privileges and immunities, **8.01–225.1**
Bills, submission, in network providers, powers and duties, **8.01–27.5**
Boards and commissions, confidential or privileged information, **8.01–581.17**
Committees, privileges and immunities, **8.01–581.19, 8.01–581.19:1**
Confidential or privileged information,
  Boards and commissions, **8.01–581.17**
  Witnesses, **8.01–399**
Controlled Substances, generally, this index
Damages, insurance, payment, actions and proceedings, **8.01–27.4**
Disasters, privileges and immunities, **8.01–225.01, 8.01–225.02**
Drugs and Medicine, generally, this index
Emergencies, privileges and immunities, **8.01–225.01, 8.01–225.02**
Evidence,
  Confidential or privileged information, witnesses, **8.01–399**
  Records and recordation, **8.01–413**
Good samaritan doctrine, privileges and immunities, **8.01–225**
Health Insurance, generally, this index
Health Maintenance Organizations, generally, this index
Immunization, privileges and immunities, **8.01–44.2**

PHYSICIANS AND SURGEONS—Cont'd
Insurance. Health Insurance, generally, this index
Laboratories, privileges and immunities, medical malpractice, **8.01–581.18:1**
Liens and incumbrances, personal injuries, claims, **8.01–66.2 et seq.**
Malpractice. Medical Malpractice, generally, this index
Medical assistance. Social Services, this index
Medical Malpractice, generally, this index
Negligence. Medical Malpractice, generally, this index
Payment,
  Insurance, actions and proceedings, **8.01–27.4**
  Liens and incumbrances, personal injuries, claims, **8.01–66.2 et seq.**
Physical Therapists, generally, this index
Podiatrists, generally, this index
Privileges and immunities,
  Athletics, schools and school districts, **8.01–225.1**
  Bills, submission, in network providers, **8.01–27.5**
  Committees, **8.01–581.19, 8.01–581.19:1**
  Disasters, **8.01–225.01, 8.01–225.02**
  Emergency medical services, **8.01–225**
  Immunization, **8.01–44.2**
  Laboratories, medical malpractice, **8.01–581.18:1**
  Witnesses, **8.01–399**
Psychologists and Psychology, generally, this index
Records and recordation, evidence, **8.01–413**
Subpoenas, records and recordation, **8.01–413**
Time, bills, submission, in network providers, **8.01–27.5**
Treble damages, insurance, payment, actions and proceedings, **8.01–27.4**
Witnesses, confidential or privileged information, **8.01–399**

PHYSICIANS ASSISTANTS
Evidence, opinions and expert testimony, **8.01–401.2**
Witnesses, opinions and expert testimony, **8.01–401.2**

PICKUP TRUCKS
Motor Vehicles, generally, this index

PICTURES
Photography and Pictures, generally, this index

PIPES AND PIPELINES
Public Utilities, generally, this index

PLAINTIFFS
Parties, generally, this index

PLANES
Aircraft, generally, this index

PLEADINGS
  Generally, **8.01–271 et seq.**
Abolishment, **8.01–276**
Affidavits, **8.01–279**

PLEADINGS—Cont'd
Alternative parties, counterclaims, **8.01–281**
Amendments, **8.01–6 et seq., 8.01–274**
  Evidence, **8.01–377**
  Fiduciaries, style, **8.01–6.3**
Anonymous plaintiffs, **8.01–15.1**
Answers, evidence, equity, rebuttal, **8.01–283**
Attachment, **8.01–536**
Attorney fees, **8.01–271.1**
Change of venue, **8.01–276**
Children and minors, debtors and creditors, **8.01–278**
Claims, amendments, **8.01–6.1**
Conservators and conservatorship, style, **8.01–6.3**
Continuance, amendments, **8.01–6.1**
Contracts, joinder, torts, **8.01–272**
Corporations, affidavits, **8.01–279**
Defects, **8.01–275**
  Service of process, **8.01–277**
Defenses, amendments, **8.01–6.1**
Demurrer, **8.01–273**
  Evidence, abolishment, **8.01–276**
Equity, this index
Evidence,
  Amendments, **8.01–377**
  Answers, equity, rebuttal, **8.01–283**
Failure to state cause of action, **8.01–273**
Fiduciaries, style, **8.01–6.3**
Form, defects, **8.01–275**
Guardian and ward, style, **8.01–6.3**
Handwriting, affidavits, **8.01–279**
Identification numbers, redacting, **8.01–420.8**
Joinder, **8.01–272**
Jurisdiction, personal jurisdiction, objections and exceptions, waiver, **8.01–277.1**
Jury, **8.01–381**
Limitation of actions, affirmative defense, **8.01–235**
Lost or destroyed documents, **8.01–374**
Medical malpractice, amendment, review panel, **8.01–581.2:1**
Motions, generally, this index
Names, amendments, **8.01–6**
Oaths and affirmations, **8.01–280**
Partnerships, affidavits, **8.01–279**
Personal representatives, style, **8.01–6.3**
Probate proceedings, **8.01–6.2**
Process, defects, objections and exceptions, waiver, **8.01–277.1**
Rules and regulations, **8.01–3, 8.01–271**
Sanctions, **8.01–271.1**
Service of process, defects, **8.01–277**
Signatures, **8.01–271.1**
Sufficiency, **8.01–274; 8.01–275**
Third parties, **8.01–281**
Torts, joinder, contracts, **8.01–272**
Trademarks and trade names, amendments, **8.01–6.2**
Trusts and trustees, style, **8.01–6.3**
Variance, evidence, **8.01–377**

PODIATRISTS
  See, also, Physicians and Surgeons, generally, this index
Actions and proceedings. Medical Malpractice, generally, this index
Disasters, privileges and immunities, **8.01–225.01, 8.01–225.02**
Emergencies, privileges and immunities, **8.01–225.01, 8.01–225.02**
Evidence, medical malpractice, witnesses, **8.01–401.2:1**
Medical malpractice, witnesses, evidence, **8.01–401.2:1**
Privileges and immunities, disasters, **8.01–225.01, 8.01–225.02**
Witnesses, medical malpractice, evidence, **8.01–401.2:1**

POLICE
Arrest, generally, this index
Jury, exemptions, **8.01–341**
Privileges and immunities, drug dealers, liability, **8.01–227.6**
Searches and Seizures, generally, this index
Traffic Rules and Regulations, generally, this index

POLITICAL SUBDIVISIONS
Administrative Law and Procedure, generally, this index
Counties, generally, this index
Evidence, records and recordation, **8.01–390**
Hearings, privileges and immunities, strategic lawsuits against public participation, **8.01–223.2**
Judicial notice, **8.01–385 et seq.**
Municipalities, generally, this index
Privileges and immunities, hearings, strategic lawsuits against public participation, **8.01–223.2**
Real Property Taxation, generally, this index
Records and recordation, evidence, **8.01–390**
Taxation. Real Property Taxation, generally, this index

POLLUTION
Asbestos, generally, this index
Hazardous Substances and Waste, generally, this index

POLYGRAPH TESTS
Evidence, **8.01–418.2**

POOR PERSONS
Indigent Persons, generally, this index

POPULAR NAME LAWS
AntiSLAPP Law, strategic lawsuits against public participation, hearings, privileges and immunities, **8.01–223.2**
Audio Visual Deposition Act, **8.01–412.2 et seq.**
Check Clearing for the 21st Century Evidence Act, **8.01–391.1**
Dead Mans Statute, **8.01–397**

POPULAR NAME LAWS—Cont'd
Depositions, Audio Visual Deposition Act, **8.01–412.2 et seq.**
Foreign Country Money Judgments Recognition Act, **8.01–465.13:1 et seq.**
Fraud Against Taxpayers Act, **8.01–216.1 et seq.**
Interstate Depositions and Discovery Act, **8.01–412.8 et seq.**
Long Arm Statute, **8.01–328.1**
Prisoner Litigation Reform Act, **8.01–689 et seq.**
Tort Claims Act, **8.01–195.1 et seq.**
Uniform Enforcement of Foreign Judgments Act, **8.01–465.1 et seq.**
Uniform Interstate Depositions and Discovery Act, **8.01–412.8 et seq.**
Winter Sports Safety Act, **8.01–227.11 et seq.**

POSTSECONDARY EDUCATION
Colleges and Universities, generally, this index

POWER COMPANIES
Electricity, generally, this index

POWER OF ATTORNEY
Confession of judgment, **8.01–435**
Substitutes, confession of judgment, **8.01–435**

PRACTICE OF LAW
Attorneys, generally, this index

PREACHERS
Clergy, generally, this index

PREFERENCES
Priorities and Preferences, generally, this index

PREGNANCY
Childbirth, generally, this index
Fetal death, wrongful death, **8.01–50**
Privileges and immunities, medical care and treatment, **8.01–225**
Wrongful death, fetal death, **8.01–50**

PREJUDICE
Bias and Prejudice, generally, this index

PRESS
Newspapers, generally, this index

PRIESTS
Clergy, generally, this index

PRIMA FACIE EVIDENCE
Evidence, generally, this index

PRINCIPAL AND AGENT
Agents and Agencies, generally, this index

PRINTING
Libel and Slander, generally, this index
Newspapers, generally, this index

PRIORITIES AND PREFERENCES
Attachment, **8.01–557**
  Real estate, sales, **8.01–572**
Executions, **8.01–488**

PRIORITIES AND PREFERENCES—Cont'd
Liens and Incumbrances, this index
Wrongful death, distribution, damages, **8.01–53, 8.01–54**

PRISONS AND PRISONERS
Correctional Institutions, generally, this index
Jails, generally, this index

PRIVACY
Confidential or Privileged Information, generally, this index

PRIVATE SCHOOLS
Epinephrine, administration, privileges and immunities, **8.01–225**

PRIVILEGED COMMUNICATIONS
Confidential or Privileged Information, generally, this index

PRIVILEGED INFORMATION
Confidential or Privileged Information, generally, this index

PRIVILEGES AND IMMUNITIES
Arbitration and award, mediators, **8.01–576.9, 8.01–581.23**
Arrest, **8.01–327.1, 8.01–327.2**
Automated external defibrillators, **8.01–225**
Bad checks, arrest, **8.01–226.10**
Boards and commissions, **8.01–44.1**
Cardiopulmonary resuscitation, **8.01–225**
Clergy, **8.01–220.1:3**
Committees, **8.01–44.1**
Confidential or Privileged Information, generally, this index
Consultants, boards and commissions, medical care and treatment, **8.01–581.16**
Contractors, actions and proceedings, **8.01–39**
Contracts, hearings, strategic lawsuits against public participation, **8.01–223.2**
Court officers and employees, littering, pick up programs, **8.01–226.8**
Covenant not to sue, **8.01–35.1**
Crime victims, notice, **8.01–226.11**
Defibrillation, **8.01–225**
Disasters, this index
Emergency management, health care professionals, **8.01–225.01, 8.01–225.02**
Emergency Medical Services, this index
Fraud against taxpayers, actions and proceedings, civil investigative demands, **8.01–216.12**
Good samaritan doctrine, **8.01–225**
Health Care Professionals, this index
Hearings, strategic lawsuits against public participation, **8.01–223.2**
Hospices, volunteers, **8.01–226.4**
Hospitals, this index
Judicial sales, purchasers, **8.01–101, 8.01–102**
Landlord and tenant, mold, **8.01–226.12**
Laundries and dry cleaners, damages, **8.01–42**
Littering, pick up programs, **8.01–226.8**

PRIVILEGES AND IMMUNITIES—Cont'd
Medical Care and Treatment, this index
Medical Malpractice, this index
Municipal officers and employees, littering, pick up programs, **8.01–226.8**
Naloxone, emergency medical services, administration, **8.01–225**
Negotiable instruments, bad checks, arrest, **8.01–226.10**
Nonprofit Organizations, this index
Physicians and Surgeons, this index
Probation officers, littering, pick up programs, **8.01–226.8**
Psychologists and Psychology, this index
Recycling, littering, pick up programs, **8.01–226.8**
Schools and School Districts, this index
Shoplifting, arrest, **8.01–226.9**
Skiing, winter sports safety, **8.01–227.20**
Space, flight, **8.01–227.8 et seq.**
Strategic lawsuits against public participation, hearings, **8.01–223.2**
Torts, hearings, strategic lawsuits against public participation, **8.01–223.2**
Trespass, harm to trespasser, **8.01–219.1**
Volunteers, highways and roads, littering, pick up programs, **8.01–226.8**
Winter sports safety, **8.01–227.20**
Witnesses, this index
Wrongful incarceration, compensation and salaries, release, waiver, **8.01–195.12**

PRIVITY
Negligence, **8.01–223**

PROBABLE CAUSE
Bad checks, arrest, **8.01–226.10**
Shoplifting, arrest, detention, privileges and immunities, **8.01–226.9**

PROBATE PROCEEDINGS
Appeal and review, **8.01–670**
Claims against estate,
  Limitation of actions, **8.01–229, 8.01–254**
    Pleadings, **8.01–6.2**
  Pleadings, **8.01–6.2**
Class actions, parties, death, **8.01–23**
Correctional institutions, wrongful incarceration, compensation and salaries, **8.01–195.10**
Debtors and creditors, real estate, limitation of actions, **8.01–254**
Delinquent children, wrongful incarceration, compensation and salaries, **8.01–195.10**
Garnishment, personal representatives, **8.01–518**
Guardian Ad Litem, generally, this index
Jails, wrongful incarceration, compensation and salaries, **8.01–195.10**
Limitation of actions, **8.01–6.2, 8.01–229, 8.01–254**
  Claims against estate, **8.01–229**
  Personal representatives, bonds (officers and fiduciaries), **8.01–245**
Medical records, access, **8.01–413**

PROBATE PROCEEDINGS—Cont'd
Parties, class actions, death, **8.01–23**
Personal representatives,
  Actions and proceedings, pleadings, style, **8.01–6.3**
  Arbitration and award, **8.01–581**
  Bonds (officers and fiduciaries), limitation of actions, **8.01–245**
  Garnishment, **8.01–518**
  Limitation of actions, bonds (officers and fiduciaries), **8.01–245**
  Names, pleadings, style, **8.01–6.3**
  Pleadings, style, **8.01–6.3**
  Witnesses, corroboration, **8.01–397**
Pleadings, limitation of actions, **8.01–6.2**
Process, service of process, limitation of actions, **8.01–6.2**
Real estate,
  Debtors and creditors, limitation of actions, **8.01–254**
  Limitation of actions, **8.01–254**
Trusts and Trustees, generally, this index
Venue, **8.01–261**
Wills, generally, this index
Witnesses, corroboration, **8.01–397**
Wrongful incarceration, compensation and salaries, **8.01–195.10**

PROBATION
Habeas corpus, service of process, **8.01–658**
Littering, pick up programs, privileges and immunities, **8.01–226.8**
Names, change of name, **8.01–217**
Service of process, habeas corpus, **8.01–658**

PROBATION OFFICERS
Privileges and immunities, littering, pick up programs, **8.01–226.8**

PROCEEDINGS
Actions and Proceedings, generally, this index

PROCESS
  Generally, **8.01–285 et seq.**
Actual notice, service of process, waiver, **8.01–286.1**
Address, **8.01–290**
Associations and societies, service of process, **8.01–305**
  Foreign states, **8.01–306**
Attachment, generally, this index
Attorney fees, service of process, waiver, **8.01–286.1**
Copies, **8.01–291**
Correctional institutions, service of process, **8.01–297**
Costs, service of process, waiver, **8.01–286.1**
Counties, service of process, **8.01–300**
Defects, service of process, **8.01–277**
  Objections and exceptions, waiver, **8.01–277.1**
Defenses, service of process, waiver, **8.01–286.1**
Discovery, defects, objections and exceptions, waiver, **8.01–277.1**

PROCESS—Cont'd
Executions, generally, this index
Garnishment, generally, this index
Identity and identification, **8.01–290**
Injunctions, generally, this index
Jurisdiction, service of process, waiver, objections and exceptions, **8.01–286.1**
Jury, service of process, **8.01–298**
Mail and mailing, **8.01–296**
  Service of process, waiver, **8.01–286.1**
Municipalities, service of process, **8.01–300**
Names, **8.01–290**
Nonresidents, service of process, **8.01–320**
Objections and exceptions, defects, waiver, **8.01–277.1**
Pleadings, defects, objections and exceptions, waiver, **8.01–277.1**
Private process servers, **8.01–293**
Publication, service of process, **8.01–296, 8.01–316 et seq.**
Receivers and receivership, service of process, corporations, **8.01–303**
Returns, **8.01–294**
Secretary of state, service of process, **8.01–329**
Service of process, **8.01–287 et seq., 8.01–292 et seq.**
  Acceptance, **8.01–327**
  Actual notice, waiver, **8.01–286.1**
  Address, agents and agencies, **8.01–313**
  Affidavits, returns, **8.01–325**
  Agents and Agencies, this index
  Aircraft, accidents, nonresidents, **8.01–309 et seq.**
  Associations and societies, **8.01–305**
    Foreign states, **8.01–306**
  Attachment, this index
  Attorney fees, waiver, **8.01–286.1**
  Attorneys, **8.01–314**
  Boundaries, **8.01–295**
  Carriers, **8.01–305**
    Foreign states, **8.01–306**
  Continuance, late return, **8.01–294**
  Corporations, this index
  Correctional Institutions, this index
  Costs, waiver, **8.01–286.1**
  Counties, **8.01–300**
  Default, **8.01–296**
  Defects, **8.01–277**
    Objections and exceptions, waiver, **8.01–277.1**
  Defenses, waiver, **8.01–286.1**
  Depositions, dissolution of marriage, publication, **8.01–319**
  Dockets and docketing, **8.01–331**
    Discontinuance, **8.01–335**
  Executions, **8.01–487.1**
  Fraud against taxpayers, actions and proceedings, civil investigative demands, **8.01–216.10, 8.01–216.13**
  Garnishment, this index

PROCESS—Cont'd
Service of process—Cont'd
  Habeas corpus, **8.01–658**
  Internet, identity and identification, subpoenas, **8.01–407.1**
  Interstate depositions and discovery, subpoenas, **8.01–412.11**
  Jails, this index
  Jurisdiction, **8.01–329**
    Waiver, objections and exceptions, **8.01–286.1**
  Jury, **8.01–298, 8.01–353**
  Landlord and tenant, **8.01–296**
  Late return, prejudice, **8.01–294**
  Limitation of actions, **8.01–275.1**
    Publication, **8.01–322**
  Mail and mailing, **8.01–296**
    Waiver, **8.01–286.1**
  Mandamus, **8.01–644, 8.01–652**
  Manner of service, **8.01–296**
  Motions, defects, **8.01–277**
  Municipalities, **8.01–300**
  Newspapers, publication, **8.01–323, 8.01–324**
  Nonresidents, **8.01–320**
    Motor vehicles, accidents, **8.01–307 et seq.**
  Notice,
    Agents and agencies, **8.01–315**
    Statutory agents, **8.01–326.1**
    Waiver, **8.01–286.1**
  Objections and exceptions, defects, waiver, **8.01–277.1**
  Private process servers, **8.01–293**
  Publication, **8.01–296, 8.01–316 et seq.**
  Quash, motion to quash, **8.01–277**
  Quo warranto, **8.01–639**
  Real property taxation, liens and incumbrances, publication, **8.01–321**
  Receivers and receivership, corporations, **8.01–303**
  Returns, **8.01–294, 8.01–325, 8.01–326**
    Waiver, **8.01–286.1**
  Secretary of state, **8.01–329**
  Special appearance, dismissal and nonsuit, motions, **8.01–277**
  State, this index
  Statutory agents, **8.01–312, 8.01–326.1**
    Notice, **8.01–326.1**
  Substituted service, **8.01–296**
    Late return, **8.01–294**
  Sundays, **8.01–289**
  Territorial limits, **8.01–295**
  Time, waiver, **8.01–286.1**
  Venue, waiver, objections and exceptions, **8.01–286.1**
  Waiver, **8.01–286.1**
    Defects, objections and exceptions, **8.01–277.1**
  Witnesses, **8.01–298**
State, torts, claims against, **8.01–195.4**
Statutory agents, service of process, **8.01–312, 8.01–326.1**

PROCESS—Cont'd
Subpoenas, generally, this index
Summons, generally, this index
Time, service of process, waiver, **8.01–286.1**
Venue, service of process, waiver, objections and exceptions, **8.01–286.1**
Waiver,
Defects, objections and exceptions, **8.01–277.1**
Service of process, **8.01–286.1**
Witnesses, service of process, **8.01–298**
Writs, **8.01–286**

PRODUCTION OF BOOKS AND PAPERS
See, also, Discovery, generally, this index
Arbitration and award, **8.01–581.06**
Copies, costs, **8.01–417**
Executions, **8.01–506.1**
Foreign states, interstate depositions and discovery, **8.01–412.8 et seq.**
Fraud against taxpayers, actions and proceedings, civil investigative demands, **8.01–216.10 et seq., 8.01–216.14**
Internet, torts, identity and identification, subpoenas, **8.01–407.1**
Interstate depositions and discovery, **8.01–412.8 et seq.**
Medical malpractice, review panel, **8.01–581.6**

PRODUCTS LIABILITY
Limitation of actions, **8.01–249**
Statute of limitations, **8.01–249**

PROFESSIONS AND OCCUPATIONS
Architects and Architecture, generally, this index
Attorneys, generally, this index
Chiropractors, generally, this index
Contractors, generally, this index
Counselors and Counseling, generally, this index
Dentists and Dentistry, generally, this index
Engineers, generally, this index
Health Care Professionals, generally, this index
Licenses and permits, quo warranto, **8.01–635 et seq.**
Nurse Practitioners, generally, this index
Nurses, generally, this index
Optometrists, generally, this index
Pharmacists, generally, this index
Physical Therapists, generally, this index
Physicians and Surgeons, generally, this index
Podiatrists, generally, this index
Psychologists and Psychology, generally, this index
Receivers and Receivership, generally, this index
Social Workers, generally, this index
Surgeons. Physicians and Surgeons, generally, this index
Writs, quo warranto, **8.01–635 et seq.**

PROFITS
Damages, evidence, new business, unestablished business, **8.01–221.1**

PROMISSORY NOTES
Negotiable Instruments, generally, this index

PROOF
Evidence, generally, this index

PROPERTY
Attachment, generally, this index
Boundaries, generally, this index
Deeds and Conveyances, generally, this index
Distraint, damages, **8.01–41**
Entry on Property, generally, this index
Executions, generally, this index
Limitation of actions, damages, **8.01–243**
Partition, generally, this index
Perishable property, liens and incumbrances, sales, third parties, claims, **8.01–372**
Personal Property, generally, this index
Real Estate, generally, this index
Tenants in Common, generally, this index
Title to Property, generally, this index

PROSECUTION
Crimes and Offenses, generally, this index

PROTECTIVE ORDERS
Internet, torts, identity and identification, subpoenas, **8.01–407.1**

PSYCHIATRISTS AND PSYCHIATRY
Medical Malpractice, generally, this index

PSYCHOLOGISTS AND PSYCHOLOGY
Confidential or privileged information, witnesses, **8.01–399, 8.01–400.2**
Disasters, privileges and immunities, **8.01–225.01, 8.01–225.02**
Emergencies, privileges and immunities, **8.01–225.01, 8.01–225.02**
Evidence,
Confidential or privileged information, witnesses, **8.01–399, 8.01–400.2**
Records and recordation, **8.01–413**
Medical Malpractice, generally, this index
Privileges and immunities,
Disasters, **8.01–225.01, 8.01–225.02**
Witnesses, **8.01–399, 8.01–400.2**
Records and recordation, evidence, **8.01–413**
Witnesses, confidential or privileged information, **8.01–399, 8.01–400.2**

PUBLIC ACCOMMODATIONS
Hotels and Motels, generally, this index

PUBLIC AGENCIES
State Agencies, generally, this index

PUBLIC ASSISTANCE
Social Services, generally, this index

PUBLIC BUILDINGS
Children and minors, property damages, **8.01–43**
Property damages, parental liability, **8.01–43**

PUBLIC EMPLOYEES
Public Officers and Employees, generally, this index

PUBLIC LANDS
Grants, limitation of actions, **8.01–238**
Limitation of actions, grants, **8.01–238**

PUBLIC OFFICERS AND EMPLOYEES
Bonds (Officers and Fiduciaries), generally, this index
County Officers and Employees, generally, this index
Foreign states, sales and use tax, declaratory judgments, jurisdiction, **8.01–184.1**
Mandamus, generally, this index
Municipal Officers and Employees, generally, this index
Quo warranto, **8.01–635 et seq.**
School Officers and Employees, generally, this index
State Officers and Employees, generally, this index
Writs, quo warranto, **8.01–635 et seq.**

PUBLIC POLICY
Automated external defibrillators, training, **8.01–225**
Cardiopulmonary resuscitation, training, **8.01–225**

PUBLIC RECORDS
Records and Recordation, generally, this index

PUBLIC SCHOOLS
Schools and School Districts, generally, this index

PUBLIC SERVICE CORPORATIONS
Public Utilities, generally, this index

PUBLIC UTILITIES
Actions and proceedings, liens and incumbrances, limitation of actions, **8.01–240**
Attorney fees, meters, tampering, **8.01–44.7**
Carriers, generally, this index
Costs, meters, tampering, **8.01–44.7**
Damages, meters, tampering, **8.01–44.7**
Electricity, generally, this index
Injunctions, meters, tampering, **8.01–44.7**
Limitation of actions, liens and incumbrances, **8.01–240**
Meters, tampering, damages, **8.01–44.7**
Natural Gas, generally, this index
Railroads, generally, this index
Statute of limitations, liens and incumbrances, **8.01–240**
Telecommunications, generally, this index
Water Supply, generally, this index

PUBLIC WELFARE
Social Services, generally, this index

PUBLICATION
Administrative law and procedure, judicial notice, **8.01–388**
Affidavits, **8.01–415**
Attachment, rehearing, **8.01–575, 8.01–576**
Foreign corporations, service of process, **8.01–316 et seq.**

PUBLICATION—Cont'd
Judicial notice, **8.01–388**
Libel and Slander, generally, this index
Quo warranto, **8.01–641**
Real property taxation, liens and incumbrances, service of process, **8.01–321**
Service of process, **8.01–296, 8.01–316 et seq.**

PUNITIVE DAMAGES
Exemplary damages. Damages, this index

PUPILS
Schools and School Districts, generally, this index

QUESTIONS OF LAW AND FACT
Jury, generally, this index
Trial, generally, this index

QUO WARRANTO
Generally, **8.01–635 et seq.**
Appeal and review, **8.01–670**
Venue, **8.01–261**

RABBIS
Clergy, generally, this index

RAILROADS
See, also,
Carriers, generally, this index
Public Utilities, generally, this index
Actions and proceedings, personal injuries, officers and employees, **8.01–57 et seq.**
Application of law, personal injuries, officers and employees, **8.01–62**
Assumption of risk, officers and employees, personal injuries, **8.01–59**
Contracts, officers and employees, personal injuries, exemptions, **8.01–60**
Contributory negligence, officers and employees, personal injuries, **8.01–58**
Damages, officers and employees, personal injuries, **8.01–57 et seq.**
Death, officers and employees, **8.01–57 et seq.**
Negligence, personal injuries, officers and employees, **8.01–57 et seq.**
Officers and employees, personal injuries, **8.01–57 et seq.**
Personal injuries, officers and employees, **8.01–57 et seq.**
Setoff and counterclaim, officers and employees, personal injuries, **8.01–60**
Taxation. Real Property Taxation, generally, this index

REAL ESTATE
Actions and proceedings,
Boundaries, **8.01–179 et seq.**
Personal injuries, limitation of actions, **8.01–250**
Venue, **8.01–261**
Aged persons, **8.01–67 et seq.**
Attachment, **8.01–548, 8.01–550**
Levy, **8.01–550**
Sales, **8.01–572**

REAL ESTATE—Cont'd
Boundaries, generally, this index
Breach of condition subsequent, limitation of actions, **8.01–255.1**
Cemeteries, generally, this index
Children and minors, **8.01–67 et seq.**
Contracts for sale of land. Deeds and Conveyances, generally, this index
Conveyances. Deeds and Conveyances, generally, this index
Deeds and Conveyances, generally, this index
Ejectment, generally, this index
Entry on Property, generally, this index
Fee simple, termination, limitation of actions, **8.01–255.1**
Guardian ad litem, actions and proceedings, **8.01–73**
Handicapped persons, limitation of actions, **8.01–237**
Jurisdiction, **8.01–328 et seq.**
Landlord and Tenant, generally, this index
Leases, generally, this index
Liens and Incumbrances, generally, this index
Life estates, **8.01–94, 8.01–95**
Limitation of actions, **8.01–236 et seq.**
  Breach of condition subsequent, **8.01–255.1**
  Defective conditions, **8.01–250**
  Wills, **8.01–254**
Loans. Mortgages, generally, this index
Mentally ill persons, **8.01–67 et seq.**
Mentally retarded and developmentally disabled persons, **8.01–67 et seq.**
Mortgages, generally, this index
Partition, generally, this index
Personal injuries, limitation of actions, **8.01–250**
Privileges and immunities, trespass, harm to trespasser, **8.01–219.1**
Remainder, life estates, **8.01–94**
Taxation. Real Property Taxation, generally, this index
Tenants in Common, generally, this index
Title to Property, generally, this index
Vandalism, generally, this index
Venue, **8.01–261**

REAL PROPERTY TAXATION
Appeal and review, **8.01–670**
Assessments, venue, **8.01–261**
Collections, venue, **8.01–261**
Delinquencies, judicial sales, **8.01–97, 8.01–98**
Judicial sales, delinquencies, **8.01–97, 8.01–98**
Liens and incumbrances, service of process, publication, **8.01–321**
Process, service of process, liens and incumbrances, publication, **8.01–321**
Publication, service of process, liens and incumbrances, **8.01–321**
Service of process, liens and incumbrances, publication, **8.01–321**
Venue, **8.01–261**
  Application of law, **8.01–259**

RECEIVERS AND RECEIVERSHIP
  See, also, Fiduciaries, generally, this index
  Generally, **8.01–582 et seq., 8.01–591 et seq.**
Accounts and accounting, circuit courts, **8.01–585**
Appointments, **8.01–582, 8.01–591**
  Emergencies, **8.01–592**
Attachment, **8.01–549**
Audits and auditors, **8.01–582**
Bonds (officers and fiduciaries), **8.01–588**
  Emergencies, **8.01–592**
Compensation and salaries, circuit courts, **8.01–589**
Compromise and settlement, chancery commissioners, **8.01–617 et seq.**
Corporations, service of process, **8.01–303**
Damages, **8.01–587**
Emergencies, **8.01–592, 8.01–593**
Financial statements and reports, circuit courts, **8.01–585, 8.01–588.1**
Fines and penalties, circuit courts, **8.01–590**
Hearings, emergencies, **8.01–593**
Interest, circuit courts, **8.01–584**
Investments, circuit courts, **8.01–584**
Judgments and decrees, **8.01–598**
Lists, debtors and creditors, **8.01–595**
Notice, **8.01–591 et seq.**
Records and recordation, compromise and settlement, **8.01–619**
Reports, compromise and settlement, **8.01–618**
Sales, **8.01–596**
Securities, **8.01–583**
Service of process, **8.01–594**

RECIPROCITY
Interstate depositions and discovery, **8.01–412.14**

RECORDS AND RECORDATION
Appeal and review, **8.01–673, 8.01–679**
  Copies, **8.01–684**
  Court of appeals, **8.01–675.4**
  Failure to deliver record, **8.01–679**
Attachment, **8.01–268**
Confidential or Privileged Information, generally, this index
Courts, this index
Criminal History Record Information, generally, this index
Documentary evidence. Evidence, generally, this index
Habeas corpus, **8.01–661, 8.01–667**
Lis pendens, **8.01–268**
Lost or Destroyed Documents, generally, this index
Medical malpractice, **8.01–581.4:1, 8.01–581.4:2**
Medical Records, generally, this index
Production of Books and Papers, generally, this index
Receivers and receivership, compromise and settlement, **8.01–619**
Transcripts, generally, this index

RECREATION AND RECREATIONAL AREAS
Winter sports safety, **8.01–227.11 et seq.**

RECREATIONAL TRAILS
Winter sports areas, safety, **8.01–227.11 et seq.**

RECYCLING
Littering, pick up programs, privileges and immunities, **8.01–226.8**
Privileges and immunities, littering, pick up programs, **8.01–226.8**
Volunteers, littering, pick up programs, privileges and immunities, **8.01–226.8**

REFORMATORIES
Correctional Institutions, generally, this index

RELEASE
Wrongful incarceration, compensation and salaries, **8.01–195.12**

RELIGION
Actions and proceedings, hate crimes, **8.01–42.1**
Clergy, generally, this index
Crimes and offenses, hate crimes, damages, **8.01–42.1**
Damages, hate crimes, **8.01–42.1**
Hate crimes, damages, **8.01–42.1**

RELIGIOUS ORGANIZATIONS AND SOCIETIES
Clergy, generally, this index

REMEDIES
Actions and Proceedings, generally, this index

REMOVAL OR TRANSFER OF CAUSES
See, also, Venue, generally, this index
Generally, **8.01–267.1 et seq.**
Birth related neurological injuries, workers compensation, **8.01–273.1**
Workers compensation, birth related neurological injuries, **8.01–273.1**

REMUNERATION
Compensation and Salaries, generally, this index

RENT
See, also, Leases, generally, this index
Attachment, damages, **8.01–41**
Distraint, damages, **8.01–41**
Ejectment, generally, this index
Limitation of actions, **8.01–239**
Nonpayment of rent. Ejectment, generally, this index
Sales and Use Tax, generally, this index
Searches and seizures, damages, **8.01–41**

REPLEVIN
Abolishment, **8.01–218**

REPORTS
Landlord and tenant, inspection and inspectors, commencement, occupancy, **8.01–226.12**
Receivers and receivership, compromise and settlement, **8.01–618**

RES JUDICATA
Fraud against taxpayers, actions and proceedings, **8.01–216.6**

RESCUE SQUADS
Emergency Medical Services, generally, this index

RESEARCH
Boards and commissions, privileges and immunities, **8.01–44.1**
Privileges and immunities, boards and commissions, **8.01–44.1**

RESIDENCE
Domicile and Residence, generally, this index

RESIDENTIAL CARE FACILITIES
Nursing Homes, generally, this index

RESIDENTIAL SCHOOLS FOR STUDENTS WITH DISABILITIES
Epinephrine, administration, privileges and immunities, **8.01–225**

RESOURCES AUTHORITY
Sewers and Sewer Systems, generally, this index

RESPONDENTS
Parties, generally, this index

RESTITUTION
Dockets and docketing, **8.01–446**

RESTRAINING ORDERS
Injunctions, generally, this index

RESTROOMS AND TOILETS
Sewers and Sewer Systems, generally, this index

RETAIL SALES
Sales, generally, this index

RETAIL SALES TAX
Sales and Use Tax, generally, this index

RETARDED PERSONS
Mentally Retarded and Developmentally Disabled Persons, generally, this index

RETIREMENT AND PENSIONS
Social Security, generally, this index

RETURNS
Executions, this index

REVENUE BONDS
Bonds, generally, this index

REVIEW
Appeal and Review, generally, this index

REVISED STATUTES
Statutes, generally, this index

ROPE TOWS
Winter sports areas, safety, **8.01–227.11 et seq.**

RULES OF EVIDENCE
Generally, **8.01–3**

SABOTAGE
Civil Defense, generally, this index

SAFE DRINKING WATER
Water Supply, generally, this index

SAFETY
Civil Defense, generally, this index
Winter sports, **8.01–227.11 et seq.**

SAILORS
Military Forces, generally, this index

SALARIES
Compensation and Salaries, generally, this index

SALES
Aged persons, real estate, **8.01–67 et seq.**
Attachment, **8.01–570**
Crimes and offenses. Fraud, generally, this index
Executions, this index
Guardian ad litem, real estate, **8.01–73**
Judicial Sales, generally, this index
Jurisdiction, **8.01–328 et seq.**
Liens and incumbrances, **8.01–462**
  Perishable property, third parties, claims, **8.01–372**
  Surplus, third parties, **8.01–373**
Life estates, **8.01–94, 8.01–95**
Partition, this index
Third parties, liens and incumbrances, personal property, **8.01–365 et seq.**

SALES AND USE TAX
Declaratory judgments, foreign states, jurisdiction, **8.01–184.1**
Foreign states, declaratory judgments, jurisdiction, **8.01–184.1**
Jurisdiction, declaratory judgments, foreign states, **8.01–184.1**
Nexus, declaratory judgments, foreign states, **8.01–184.1**
Planes. Aircraft, generally, this index
Public officers and employees, foreign states, declaratory judgments, jurisdiction, **8.01–184.1**

SATISFACTION
Accord and Satisfaction, generally, this index

SAVINGS AND LOAN ASSOCIATIONS
Bank Deposits and Collections, generally, this index
Funds Transfers, generally, this index

SCHEMES
Fraud, generally, this index

SCHIZOPHRENIA
Mentally Ill Persons, generally, this index

SCHOOL BUILDINGS AND GROUNDS
Threats, investigations and investigators, libel and slander, privileges and immunities, **8.01–47**
Weapons, investigations and investigators, libel and slander, privileges and immunities, **8.01–47**

SCHOOL OFFICERS AND EMPLOYEES
Anaphylaxis, drugs and medicine, privileges and immunities, **8.01–226.5:1**
Asthma, drugs and medicine, privileges and immunities, **8.01–226.5:1**
Auto injectable epinephrine, privileges and immunities, **8.01–226.5:1**
Bullying, privileges and immunities, **8.01–220.1:2**
Drugs and medicine, privileges and immunities,
  Anaphylaxis, **8.01–226.5:1**
  Asthma, **8.01–226.5:1**
  Epinephrine, administration, **8.01–225**
Emergency medical care, privileges and immunities, **8.01–225**
Epinephrine, administration, privileges and immunities, **8.01–225**
Instructional personnel. Schoolteachers, generally, this index
Libel and slander, privileges and immunities, investigations and investigators, **8.01–47**
Privileges and immunities,
  Bullying, **8.01–220.1:2**
  Emergency medical care, **8.01–225**
Schoolteachers, generally, this index
Teachers. Schoolteachers, generally, this index

SCHOOLS AND SCHOOL DISTRICTS
Alcoholics and intoxicated persons, libel and slander, privileges and immunities, **8.01–47**
Anaphylaxis, drugs and medicine, privileges and immunities, **8.01–226.5:1**
Asthma, drugs and medicine, privileges and immunities, **8.01–226.5:1**
Athletics, physicians and surgeons, privileges and immunities, **8.01–225.1**
Auto injectable epinephrine, privileges and immunities, **8.01–226.5:1**
Bullying,
  Privileges and immunities, **8.01–220.1:2**
  Reports, privileges and immunities, **8.01–220.1:2**
Chemically dependent persons, libel and slander, privileges and immunities, **8.01–47**
Chiropractors, athletics, privileges and immunities, **8.01–225.1**
Colleges and Universities, generally, this index
Diabetes, drugs and medicine, privileges and immunities, **8.01–225**
Disclosure, libel and slander, privileges and immunities, **8.01–47**
Drugs and medicine,
  Anaphylaxis, privileges and immunities, **8.01–226.5:1**
  Asthma, privileges and immunities, **8.01–226.5:1**
  Diabetes, privileges and immunities, **8.01–225**
Emergency medical services, epinephrine, administration, privileges and immunities, **8.01–225**
Employees. School Officers and Employees, generally, this index
Epinephrine, administration, privileges and immunities, **8.01–225, 8.01–226.5:1**

SCHOOLS AND SCHOOL DISTRICTS—Cont'd
Evidence, records and recordation, **8.01–390.1**
High Schools or Secondary Schools, generally, this index
Instructional personnel. Schoolteachers, generally, this index
Investigations and investigators, libel and slander, privileges and immunities, **8.01–47**
Labor and employment. School Officers and Employees, generally, this index
Libel and slander, privileges and immunities, investigations and investigators, **8.01–47**
Medical care and treatment, epinephrine, administration, privileges and immunities, **8.01–225**
Nurses, epinephrine, administration, privileges and immunities, **8.01–225**
Officers and employees. School Officers and Employees, generally, this index
Physicians and surgeons, privileges and immunities, athletics, **8.01–225.1**
Privileges and immunities,
  Bullying, **8.01–220.1:2**
  Diabetes, drugs and medicine, **8.01–225**
  Drugs and medicine,
    Anaphylaxis, **8.01–226.5:1**
    Asthma, **8.01–226.5:1**
  Libel and slander, investigations and investigators, **8.01–47**
Records and recordation, evidence, **8.01–390.1**
Reports,
  Crimes and offenses, privileges and immunities, **8.01–220.1:2**
  Libel and slander, privileges and immunities, **8.01–47**
Schoolteachers, generally, this index
Secondary schools. High Schools or Secondary Schools, generally, this index
Teachers. Schoolteachers, generally, this index
Threats, libel and slander, privileges and immunities, **8.01–47**
Volunteers, bullying, privileges and immunities, **8.01–220.1:2**
Weapons, libel and slander, privileges and immunities, **8.01–47**

SCHOOLTEACHERS
Actions and proceedings, privileges and immunities, **8.01–220.1:2**
Bullying, privileges and immunities, **8.01–220.1:2**
Damages, privileges and immunities, **8.01–220.1:2**
Discipline, privileges and immunities, **8.01–220.1:2**
Libel and slander, privileges and immunities, **8.01–47**
Privileges and immunities, **8.01–220.1:2**
  Bullying, **8.01–220.1:2**

SCIRE FACIAS
Abolishment, **8.01–24**

SEALS
Courts, records and recordation, evidence, **8.01–389**

SEARCHES AND SEIZURES
Bonds (officers and fiduciaries), detinue, **8.01–115 et seq.**
Detinue, **8.01–114 et seq.**
Hearings, detinue, **8.01–119**
Landlord and tenant, damages, **8.01–41**
Pretrial seizures, detinue, **8.01–114 et seq.**
Return, bonds (officers and fiduciaries), detinue, **8.01–116**

SECONDARY SCHOOLS
High Schools or Secondary Schools, generally, this index

SECRETARY OF THE COMMONWEALTH
Foreign corporations, service of process, **8.01–329**
Service of process, **8.01–329**

SECRETS AND SECRECY
Confidential or Privileged Information, generally, this index

SECURED TRANSACTIONS
Executions, prior security interest, **8.01–480**
Real estate. Mortgages, generally, this index

SECURITIES
Bonds, generally, this index

SECURITY
  See, also, Bonds (Officers and Fiduciaries), generally, this index
Mortgages, generally, this index

SEIZURES
Searches and Seizures, generally, this index

SENIOR CITIZENS
Aged Persons, generally, this index

SENIOR HIGH SCHOOLS
High Schools or Secondary Schools, generally, this index

SENTENCE AND PUNISHMENT
Crimes and Offenses, generally, this index

SEPTEMBER 11 TERRORIST ATTACK
Terrorism, generally, this index

SERVICE OF PROCESS
Process, this index

SETOFF AND COUNTERCLAIM
  Generally, **8.01–281**
Bifurcated trials, **8.01–267.6**
Covenant not to sue, **8.01–35.1**
Dismissal and nonsuit, **8.01–380**
Limitation of actions, **8.01–233**
Nonsuit, **8.01–380**
Pleadings, **8.01–281**
Railroads, officers and employees, personal injuries, **8.01–60**
Statute of limitations, **8.01–233**

SETTING ASIDE
Vacating or Setting Aside, generally, this index

SETTLEMENT
Compromise and Settlement, generally, this index

SETTLOR
Trusts and Trustees, generally, this index

SEVERAL LIABILITY
Joint and Several Liability, generally, this index

SEVERANCE
Actions and proceedings, **8.01–267.5**

SEWERS AND SEWER SYSTEMS
Actions and proceedings, liens and incumbrances, limitation of actions, **8.01–240**
Liens and incumbrances, limitation of actions, **8.01–240**
Limitation of actions, liens and incumbrances, **8.01–240**
Statute of limitations, liens and incumbrances, **8.01–240**

SEX OFFENDERS AND CRIMES AGAINST MINORS REGISTRY
Names, change of name, **8.01–217**

SEX OFFENSES
Limitation of actions, **8.01–249**
Registration, names, change of name, **8.01–217**

SHERIFFS
Arrest, generally, this index
Attachment, generally, this index
Executions, generally, this index
Garnishment, generally, this index
Habeas corpus, service of process, **8.01–658**
Jails, generally, this index
Jury, exemptions, **8.01–341**
Process, generally, this index
Searches and Seizures, generally, this index
Service of process. Process, this index

SHERIFFS ASSOCIATION
Crime victims, notice, privileges and immunities, **8.01–226.11**

SHIPMENTS
Carriers, generally, this index

SHIPS AND SHIPPING
Attachment, **8.01–538**

SHOPLIFTING
Arrest, privileges and immunities, **8.01–226.9**
Attorney fees, **8.01–44.4**
Damages, **8.01–44.4**
Detention, merchants, privileges and immunities, **8.01–226.9**
Pending actions, damages, **8.01–44.4**

SHORT TITLES
Popular Name Laws, generally, this index

SICKNESS
Health Insurance, generally, this index

SIGNATURES
Judicial notice, **8.01–387**
Pleadings, **8.01–271.1**

SIGNS AND SIGNALS
Winter sports safety, warnings, **8.01–227.12, 8.01–227.14**

SKI LIFTS
Winter sports areas, safety, **8.01–227.11 et seq.**

SKIING
Emergency medical services, privileges and immunities, **8.01–225**
Winter sports safety, **8.01–227.11 et seq.**

SLANDER
Libel and Slander, generally, this index

SLEDS
Winter sports safety, **8.01–227.11 et seq.**

SNOW BOARDING
Winter sports safety, **8.01–227.11 et seq.**

SNOWMOBILES
Winter sports safety, **8.01–227.11 et seq.**

SNOWSHOEING
Winter sports safety, **8.01–227.11 et seq.**

SOCIAL MEDIA
See,
  Internet, generally, this index
  Telecommunications, generally, this index

SOCIAL SECURITY
Garnishment, numbers and numbering, identity and identification, **8.01–511.1**
Numbers and numbering,
  Courts, records and recordation, redacting, **8.01–420.8**
  Garnishment, identity and identification, **8.01–511.1**

SOCIAL SERVICES
Medical assistance,
  Liens and incumbrances,
    Nursing homes, personal injuries, **8.01–66.9**
    Personal injuries, **8.01–66.9**
  Nursing homes,
    Liens and incumbrances, personal injuries, **8.01–66.9**
    Personal injuries, wrongful death, **8.01–66.5**
  Personal injuries, liens and incumbrances, **8.01–66.9**
Personal injuries, liens and incumbrances, reimbursement, **8.01–66.9**
Social Workers, generally, this index

SOCIAL WORKERS
Confidential or privileged information, witnesses, **8.01–400.2**
Disasters, privileges and immunities, **8.01–225.01, 8.01–225.02**

SOCIAL WORKERS—Cont'd
Emergencies, privileges and immunities, **8.01–225.01, 8.01–225.02**
Privileges and immunities,
Disasters, **8.01–225.01, 8.01–225.02**
Witnesses, **8.01–400.2**
Witnesses, confidential or privileged information, **8.01–400.2**

SOCIETIES
Associations and Societies, generally, this index

SOFTWARE AND ELECTRONIC DATA
Computers, generally, this index
Internet, generally, this index

SOLDIERS AND SAILORS
Military Forces, generally, this index

SOLICITATION
Sales, generally, this index

SOLICITORS
Attorneys, generally, this index

SOLID WASTE
Hazardous Substances and Waste, generally, this index
Recycling, generally, this index

SOVEREIGN IMMUNITY
State, this index

SPACE FLIGHT
Privileges and immunities, **8.01–227.8 et seq.**

SPECIAL APPEARANCE
Service of process, dismissal and nonsuit, motions, **8.01–277**

SPOUSES
Husband and Wife, generally, this index

STALKING
Damages, **8.01–42.3**

STANDARDS
Foreign country money judgments, recognition, **8.01–465.13:3**
Medical Malpractice, this index

STATE
Actions and proceedings, **8.01–196 et seq.**
Fraud against taxpayers, **8.01–216.4 et seq.**
Torts, **8.01–195.1 et seq.**
Venue, **8.01–261**
Administrative Law and Procedure, generally, this index
Agencies. State Agencies, generally, this index
Answers, claims against, **8.01–193**
Appeal and review, fraud against taxpayers, actions and proceedings, civil investigative demands, **8.01–216.18**
Arbitration and award, fraud against taxpayers, actions and proceedings, **8.01–216.7**
Attorney fees, fraud against taxpayers, **8.01–216.3**
Actions and proceedings, **8.01–216.7**

STATE—Cont'd
Attorney General, generally, this index
Attorneys. Attorney General, generally, this index
Boards and Commissions, generally, this index
Civil investigative demands, fraud against taxpayers, actions and proceedings, **8.01–216.10 et seq.**
Claims against, **8.01–192 et seq.**
Appropriations, **8.01–195**
Fraud against taxpayers, **8.01–216.1 et seq.**
Jury, torts, **8.01–195.4**
Limitation of actions, **8.01–195.6, 8.01–255**
Torts, **8.01–195.1 et seq.**
Venue, **8.01–261**
Collections, judgments and decrees, indebtedness, **8.01–199 et seq.**
Commissions. Boards and Commissions, generally, this index
Compromise and settlement,
Fraud against taxpayers, actions and proceedings, **8.01–216.6**
Indebtedness, **8.01–216**
Torts, claims against, **8.01–195.5**
Contempt, fraud against taxpayers, actions and proceedings, civil investigative demands, **8.01–216.18**
Correctional Institutions, generally, this index
Costs,
Fraud against taxpayers, **8.01–216.3**
Actions and proceedings, **8.01–216.7**
Sales, indebtedness, **8.01–207**
Damages,
Exemplary damages, torts, **8.01–195.3**
Fraud against taxpayers, **8.01–216.3**
Actions and proceedings, **8.01–216.7**
Indebtedness, collection, **8.01–199 et seq.**
Torts,
Compromise and settlement, **8.01–195.5**
Exemplary damages, **8.01–195.3**
Debtors and creditors, actions and proceedings, **8.01–196 et seq.**
Deeds and conveyances, indebtedness, collection, **8.01–207**
Defenses, claims against, **8.01–193**
Departments. State Departments, generally, this index
Depositions, fraud against taxpayers, actions and proceedings,
Civil investigative demands, **8.01–216.10 et seq., 8.01–216.16**
Copies, **8.01–216.6**
Discovery, fraud against taxpayers, actions and proceedings,
Civil investigative demands, **8.01–216.10 et seq.**
Supersedeas or stay, **8.01–216.6**
Dismissal and nonsuit,
Fraud against taxpayers, actions and proceedings, **8.01–216.6**
Consent, **8.01–216.5**
Indebtedness, **8.01–216**

STATE—Cont'd
Dockets and docketing, judgments and decrees, **8.01–448**
Employees. State Officers and Employees, generally, this index
Evidence,
  Fraud against taxpayers, actions and proceedings, **8.01–216.9**
  Records and recordation, **8.01–390**
Executions, indebtedness, **8.01–201 et seq.**
Exemplary damages,
  Fraud against taxpayers, **8.01–216.3**
  Torts, **8.01–195.3**
Explosives, sovereign immunity, **8.01–224**
Fines and penalties, fraud against taxpayers, **8.01–216.3**
Foreign States, generally, this index
Fraud against taxpayers, **8.01–216.1 et seq.**
Funds. State Funds, generally, this index
Governor, generally, this index
Indebtedness, actions and proceedings, **8.01–196 et seq.**
Interest, actions and proceedings, **8.01–199**
Interrogatories, fraud against taxpayers, actions and proceedings, civil investigative demands, **8.01–216.10 et seq., 8.01–216.15**
Intervention, fraud against taxpayers, actions and proceedings, **8.01–216.5, 8.01–216.6, 8.01–216.9**
Judgments and decrees, indebtedness, collection, **8.01–199 et seq.**
Judicial notice, publications, **8.01–388**
Jurisdiction,
  Fraud against taxpayers, actions and proceedings, civil investigative demands, **8.01–216.13**
  Torts, **8.01–195.4**
Jury, claims against, **8.01–194**
  Torts, **8.01–195.4**
Liens and incumbrances, executions, **8.01–202 et seq.**
Limitation of actions, **8.01–231**
  Claims against, **8.01–195.6, 8.01–255**
  Fraud against taxpayers, **8.01–216.9**
  Torts, **8.01–195.7**
Notice,
  Dismissal and nonsuit, fraud against taxpayers, motions, **8.01–216.6**
  Executions, indebtedness, **8.01–204**
  Torts, claims against, **8.01–195.6**
Officers and employees. State Officers and Employees, generally, this index
Orders of court, fraud against taxpayers, actions and proceedings, civil investigative demands, **8.01–216.18**
Parties, actions and proceedings, **8.01–197**
Petitions, fraud against taxpayers, actions and proceedings, civil investigative demands, **8.01–216.18**
Political Subdivisions, generally, this index

STATE—Cont'd
Privileges and immunities, fraud against taxpayers, actions and proceedings, civil investigative demands, **8.01–216.12**
Production of books and papers, fraud against taxpayers, actions and proceedings, civil investigative demands, **8.01–216.10 et seq., 8.01–216.14**
Publications, judicial notice, **8.01–388**
Punitive damages, torts, **8.01–195.3**
Records and recordation, evidence, **8.01–390**
Release, torts, claims against, **8.01–195.8**
Sales, real estate, indebtedness, **8.01–204 et seq.**
Service of process,
  Fraud against taxpayers, actions and proceedings, civil investigative demands, **8.01–216.10, 8.01–216.13**
  Torts, claims against, **8.01–195.4**
Social Services, generally, this index
Sovereign immunity,
  Explosives, **8.01–224**
  Fraud against taxpayers, state officers and employees, waiver, **8.01–216.8**
  Torts, limited waiver, **8.01–195.3**
  Waiver, torts, limited waiver, **8.01–195.3**
Subpoenas, fraud against taxpayers, actions and proceedings, **8.01–216.9**
Supersedeas or stay, fraud against taxpayers, actions and proceedings, discovery, **8.01–216.6**
Torts,
  Claims against, **8.01–195.1 et seq.**
  Sovereign immunity, limited waiver, **8.01–195.3**
Venditioni exponas, **8.01–211 et seq.**
Venue, **8.01–261**
Witnesses, fraud against taxpayers, actions and proceedings, limitation, **8.01–216.6**
Writs, venditioni exponas, **8.01–211 et seq.**

STATE AGENCIES
  See, also, State Departments, generally, this index
Actions and proceedings, fraud against taxpayers, **8.01–216.4 et seq.**
Administrative Law and Procedure, generally, this index
Attorney fees, fraud against taxpayers, **8.01–216.3**
Claims against. State, this index
Costs, fraud against taxpayers, **8.01–216.3**
Damages, fraud against taxpayers, **8.01–216.3**
Employees. State Officers and Employees, generally, this index
Evidence, records and recordation, **8.01–390**
Exemplary damages, fraud against taxpayers, **8.01–216.3**
Fines and penalties, fraud against taxpayers, **8.01–216.3**
Fraud, taxation, **8.01–216.1 et seq.**
Funds. State Funds, generally, this index
Intervention, fraud against taxpayers, actions and proceedings, **8.01–216.5, 8.01–216.6**
Judicial notice, **8.01–385 et seq.**

STATE AGENCIES—Cont'd
Officers and employees. State Officers and Employees, generally, this index
Torts, **8.01–195.1 et seq.**
Venue, **8.01–261**

STATE BOARDS
Boards and Commissions, generally, this index

STATE BONDS
Bonds, generally, this index

STATE DEPARTMENTS
Actions and proceedings, fraud against taxpayers, **8.01–216.4 et seq.**
Administrative Law and Procedure, generally, this index
Agencies. State Agencies, generally, this index
Attorney fees, fraud against taxpayers, **8.01–216.3**
Claims against. State, this index
Costs, fraud against taxpayers, **8.01–216.3**
Damages, fraud against taxpayers, **8.01–216.3**
Employees. State Officers and Employees, generally, this index
Exemplary damages, fraud against taxpayers, **8.01–216.3**
Fines and penalties, fraud against taxpayers, **8.01–216.3**
Fraud against taxpayers, **8.01–216.1 et seq.**
Funds. State Funds, generally, this index
Intervention, fraud against taxpayers, actions and proceedings, **8.01–216.5, 8.01–216.6**
Officers and employees. State Officers and Employees, generally, this index
Torts, **8.01–195.1 et seq.**

STATE FUNDS
Circuit courts, funds, **8.01–604, 8.01–605**
Mandamus, payments, **8.01–653**
Payment, mandamus, **8.01–653**

STATE OFFICERS AND EMPLOYEES
Actions and proceedings,
  Fraud against taxpayers, sovereign immunity, waiver, **8.01–216.8**
  Torts, **8.01–195.3**
Administrative Law and Procedure, generally, this index
Attorney fees, fraud against taxpayers, actions and proceedings, **8.01–216.8**
Attorney General, generally, this index
Compensation and salaries, garnishment, **8.01–522**
Costs, fraud against taxpayers, actions and proceedings, **8.01–216.8**
Fraud against taxpayers, actions and proceedings, application of law, **8.01–216.8**
Garnishment, **8.01–522**
Governor, generally, this index
Privileges and immunities, torts, **8.01–195.3**
Torts, **8.01–195.3**
Venue, **8.01–261**
Whistleblowing, fraud against taxpayers, actions and proceedings, **8.01–216.8**

STATE TREASURY
State Funds, generally, this index

STATUTE OF LIMITATIONS
Limitation of Actions, generally, this index

STATUTES
  See, also, Popular Name Laws, generally, this index
Appeal and review, **8.01–670**
Conflict of Laws, generally, this index
Construction of laws,
  Foreign country money judgments, recognition, **8.01–465.13:9**
  Interstate depositions and discovery, **8.01–412.14**
Judicial notice, **8.01–386**

STATUTORY LIENS
Liens and Incumbrances, generally, this index

STAY
Supersedeas or Stay, generally, this index

STORAGE
Sales and Use Tax, generally, this index
Searches and seizures, detinue, expenses and expenditures, **8.01–122**

STORES
Sales, generally, this index
Shoplifting, generally, this index

STORM SEWERS
Sewers and Sewer Systems, generally, this index

STORMWATER
Sewers and Sewer Systems, generally, this index

STRATEGIC LAWSUITS AGAINST PUBLIC PARTICIPATION
Hearings, privileges and immunities, **8.01–223.2**

STREETS AND ALLEYS
Traffic Rules and Regulations, generally, this index

STUDENTS
Colleges and Universities, generally, this index
Schools and School Districts, generally, this index

SUBPOENA DUCES TECUM
Production of Books and Papers, generally, this index

SUBPOENAS
Arbitration and award, **8.01–581.06**
Books and papers. Production of Books and Papers, generally, this index
Correctional institutions, prisoner litigation reform, **8.01–695**
Documents. Production of Books and Papers, generally, this index
Fraud against taxpayers, actions and proceedings, **8.01–216.9**
Identification numbers, redacting, **8.01–420.8**
Internet, torts, identity and identification, **8.01–407.1**

SUBPOENAS—Cont'd
Interstate depositions and discovery, **8.01–412.8 et seq.**
Jails, prisoner litigation reform, **8.01–695**
Medical care and treatment, records and recordation, **8.01–413**
Medical malpractice, review panel, **8.01–581.6**
Physicians and surgeons, records and recordation, **8.01–413**
Production of Books and Papers, generally, this index
Service of process, interstate depositions and discovery, **8.01–412.11**

SUBROGATION
Medical care and treatment, personal injuries, expenses, **8.01–66.4**
Motor vehicle insurance, underinsured motorists, **8.01–66.1:1**
Personal injuries, medical care and treatment, expenses, **8.01–66.4**

SUBSTANCE ABUSE
Controlled Substances, generally, this index

SUICIDE
Assisted suicide, injunctions, **8.01–622.1**

SUITS
Actions and Proceedings, generally, this index

SUMMARY JUDGMENT
Generally, **8.01–377.1, 8.01–378**
Admissions, requests for admissions, depositions, basis, **8.01–420**
Correctional institutions, prisoner litigation reform, **8.01–696**
Depositions, **8.01–420**
Exemplary damages, depositions, basis, **8.01–420**

SUMMARY PROCEEDINGS
Injunctions, generally, this index
Jury, summary jury trial, **8.01–576.1 et seq.**

SUMMONS
Attachment, **8.01–546**
Forcible entry and detainer, **8.01–126**
Garnishment, this index
Identity and identification, garnishment, **8.01–511.1**
Medical malpractice, witnesses, review panel, **8.01–407**
Workers compensation, witnesses, **8.01–407**

SUNDAYS
Service of process, **8.01–289**

SUPERSEDEAS OR STAY
Arbitration and award, **8.01–581.02**
Attachment, exemptions, **8.01–546.2**
Executions, motion to quash, **8.01–477**
Foreign country money judgments, recognition, **8.01–465.13:7**
Foreign judgments and decrees, **8.01–465.4**

SUPERSEDEAS OR STAY—Cont'd
Fraud against taxpayers, actions and proceedings, discovery, **8.01–216.6**
Interlocutory appeals, permission, **8.01–670.1**
State, fraud against taxpayers, actions and proceedings, discovery, **8.01–216.6**

SUPPORT
Arbitration and award, **8.01–576.9**
- Confidential or privileged information, disclosure, **8.01–581.24**
- Vacating or setting aside, **8.01–576.12, 8.01–581.26**
- Written agreement, compromise and settlement, **8.01–581.25**

Collections, liens and incumbrances, **8.01–460**
Guidelines, arbitration and award, written agreement, compromise and settlement, **8.01–581.25**
Jurisdiction, **8.01–328 et seq.**
Liens and incumbrances, **8.01–460**
Orders, arbitration and award, written agreement, compromise and settlement, **8.01–581.25**
Release, liens and incumbrances, **8.01–460**
Witnesses, opinions and expert testimony, exclusion, **8.01–375**

SUPREME COURT
Generally, **8.01–669 et seq.**
Bonds (officers and fiduciaries), appeal and review, **8.01–676.1**
Certificates and certification, judgments and decrees, **8.01–683**
Dismissal and nonsuit, appeal and review, **8.01–675.1**
Jurisdiction, **8.01–670**
Limitation of actions, appeal and review, **8.01–671**
Petitions, appeal and review, **8.01–674**
Probate proceedings, appeal and review, **8.01–670**
Real property taxation, appeal and review, **8.01–670**
Records and recordation, appeal and review, **8.01–673**
Rehearings, appeal and review, **8.01–675.2**
Statutes, appeal and review, **8.01–670**
Title to property, appeal and review, **8.01–670**

SURETIES AND SURETYSHIP
Bonds (Officers and Fiduciaries), generally, this index
Official bonds. Bonds (Officers and Fiduciaries), generally, this index

SURGEONS
Physicians and Surgeons, generally, this index

SURGICAL INSURANCE
Health Insurance, generally, this index

SURVEYS AND SURVEYORS
Actions and proceedings, boundaries, **8.01–181**

SWEARING
Oaths and Affirmations, generally, this index

SWINDLING
Fraud, generally, this index

SWORN STATEMENTS
Oaths and Affirmations, generally, this index

SYMPATHY
Medical malpractice, evidence, **8.01–52.1, 8.01–581.20:1**

SYNAGOGUES
Religion, generally, this index

TANGIBLE PERSONAL PROPERTY
Personal Property, generally, this index

TAPE AND SOUND RECORDINGS
Evidence, telecommunications, **8.01–420.2**
Telecommunications, evidence, **8.01–420.2**

TAX COLLECTION
Jurisdiction, Long Arm Statute, **8.01–328.1**
Long Arm Statute, **8.01–328.1**

TAXATION
Real Property Taxation, generally, this index
Sales and Use Tax, generally, this index

TEACHERS
Schoolteachers, generally, this index

TEETH
Dentists and Dentistry, generally, this index

TELECOMMUNICATIONS
See, also, Public Utilities, generally, this index
Computers, generally, this index
Evidence, tape and sound recordings, **8.01–420.2**
Facsimile Transmissions, generally, this index
Funds Transfers, generally, this index
Internet, generally, this index
Privileges and immunities, nine one one (911), **8.01–225**
Records and recordation, tape and sound recordings, evidence, **8.01–420.2**
Tape and sound recordings, evidence, **8.01–420.2**

TELEPHONES
Telecommunications, generally, this index

TELEVISION AND RADIO
Libel and slander, privileges and immunities, **8.01–49**
Privileges and immunities, **8.01–49**

TEMPORARY INJUNCTIONS
Injunctions, generally, this index

TENANTS
Landlord and Tenant, generally, this index

TENANTS IN COMMON
Accounts and accounting, **8.01–31**
Ejectment, **8.01–141**
Joinder, **8.01–10**
Partition, generally, this index

TERRORISM
Health care professionals, privileges and immunities, **8.01–225.01, 8.01–225.02**
Privileges and immunities, health care professionals, **8.01–225.01, 8.01–225.02**

TESTAMENTS
Wills, generally, this index

TESTIMONY
Evidence, generally, this index
Witnesses, generally, this index

THEFT
Attorney fees, officers and employees, **8.01–44.4**
Fraud, generally, this index
Officers and employees, damages, **8.01–44.4**
Shoplifting, generally, this index

THERAPISTS
Counselors and Counseling, generally, this index
Marriage and Family Therapists, generally, this index
Physical Therapists, generally, this index
Psychologists and Psychology, generally, this index

THIRD PARTIES
Attachment, **8.01–365 et seq., 8.01–539**
  Adverse or pecuniary interest, **8.01–573**
Bifurcated trials, **8.01–267.6**
Bonds (officers and fiduciaries), liens and incumbrances, **8.01–366 et seq.**
Dismissal and nonsuit, **8.01–380**
Fieri facias, **8.01–365 et seq.**
Liens and incumbrances, executions, **8.01–365 et seq.**
Limitation of actions, **8.01–229**
  Indemnity, **8.01–249**
Nonsuit, **8.01–380**
Pleadings, **8.01–281**
Statute of limitations, **8.01–229**
  Indemnity, **8.01–249**
Subrogation, generally, this index
Title to property, liens and incumbrances, **8.01–370, 8.01–371**
Writs, fieri facias, **8.01–365 et seq.**

THREATS
See, also, Duress or Coercion, generally, this index
Terrorism, generally, this index

TIN
Mines and Minerals, generally, this index

TITLE TO PROPERTY
See, also, Deeds and Conveyances, generally, this index
Actions and proceedings,
  Beneficial owners, **8.01–12 et seq.**
  Limitation of actions, **8.01–236**
  Venue, **8.01–261**
Adverse possession, limitation of actions, **8.01–236**

TITLE TO PROPERTY—Cont'd
Aged persons, **8.01–67 et seq.**
Appeal and review, **8.01–670**
Beneficial owners, actions and proceedings, **8.01–12**
Boundaries, generally, this index
Children and minors, **8.01–67 et seq.**
Ejectment, claims, **8.01–137**
Guardian ad litem, **8.01–73**
Judicial sales, **8.01–110 et seq.**
Liens and incumbrances, third parties, **8.01–370, 8.01–371**
Limitation of actions, **8.01–236**
Mentally retarded and developmentally disabled persons, **8.01–67 et seq.**
Mortgages, generally, this index
Partition, generally, this index
Possession, adverse possession, limitation of actions, **8.01–236**
Statute of limitations, **8.01–236**
Third parties, liens and incumbrances, **8.01–370, 8.01–371**
Trespass, privileges and immunities, harm to trespasser, **8.01–219.1**
Trover, judgments and decrees, **8.01–219**
Venue, **8.01–261**

TITLES OF ACTS
Popular Name Laws, generally, this index

TNT
Explosives, generally, this index

TOBACCO AND TOBACCO PRODUCTS
Trust funds, nonprofit organizations, privileges and immunities, **8.01–220.1:4**

TOBOGGANS
Winter sports safety, **8.01–227.11 et seq.**

TOMBS
Cemeteries, generally, this index

TORT CLAIMS ACT
Generally, **8.01–195.1 et seq.**

TORTS
Clergy, privileges and immunities, **8.01–220.1:3**
Contribution, **8.01–34**
Covenant not to sue, **8.01–35.1**
Hearings, privileges and immunities, strategic lawsuits against public participation, **8.01–223.2**
Hospitals, privileges and immunities, **8.01–38**
Husband and wife, privileges and immunities, abolishment, **8.01–220.1**
Internet, identity and identification, subpoenas, **8.01–407.1**
Joinder, children and minors, **8.01–36**
Joint and several liability, **8.01–443**
Jurisdiction, **8.01–328 et seq.**
  State, claims against, **8.01–195.4**
Libel and Slander, generally, this index
Negligence, generally, this index

TORTS—Cont'd
Personal Injuries, generally, this index
Pleadings, joinder, contracts, **8.01–272**
Privileges and immunities,
  Hearings, strategic lawsuits against public participation, **8.01–223.2**
  Hospitals, **8.01–38**
Release, **8.01–35.1**
Space, flight, privileges and immunities, **8.01–227.8 et seq.**
State, claims against, **8.01–195.1 et seq.**
Trespass, privileges and immunities, harm to trespasser, **8.01–219.1**
Venue, **8.01–261**
Winter sports safety, **8.01–227.11 et seq.**
Wrongful Death, generally, this index

TOWNS
Municipalities, generally, this index

TOXIC SUBSTANCES
Hazardous Substances and Waste, generally, this index

TRACKS
Railroads, generally, this index

TRADE
Business and Commerce, generally, this index

TRADEMARKS AND TRADE NAMES
Actions and proceedings, pleadings, amendments, **8.01–6.2**
Pleadings, amendments, **8.01–6.2**

TRAFFIC RULES AND REGULATIONS
  See, also, Motor Vehicles, generally, this index
Accidents,
  Affidavits, damages, **8.01–416**
  Children and minors, damages, **8.01–64**
  Damages,
    Children and minors, **8.01–64**
    Personal injuries, **8.01–63 et seq.**
  Driving under influence of alcohol or drugs, exemplary damages, **8.01–44.5**
  Medical care and treatment, evidence, **8.01–413.01**
  Nonresidents, service of process, **8.01–307 et seq.**
  Personal injuries, **8.01–63 et seq.**
  Process, service of process, nonresidents, **8.01–307 et seq.**
  Rental vehicles, insurance coverage, **8.01–66**
  Service of process, nonresidents, **8.01–307 et seq.**
  Theft, defense, **8.01–65**
Actions and proceedings, accidents, **8.01–63 et seq.**
Children and minors, accidents, damages, **8.01–64**
Damages,
  Accidents, personal injuries, **8.01–63 et seq.**
  Driving under influence of alcohol or drugs, **8.01–44.5**

TRAFFIC RULES AND REGULATIONS —Cont'd
Driving under influence of alcohol or drugs,
Accidents, exemplary damages, **8.01–44.5**
Blood tests,
Emergency medical services, evidence, **8.01–413.02**
Evidence, emergency medical services, **8.01–413.02**
Damages, **8.01–44.5**
Emergency medical services, blood tests, evidence, **8.01–413.02**
Evidence, blood tests, emergency medical services, **8.01–413.02**
Exemplary damages, **8.01–44.5**
Motor carriers, blood tests, emergency medical services, **8.01–413.02**
Personal injuries, exemplary damages, **8.01–44.5**
Emergency vehicles, privileges and immunities, volunteers, **8.01–225.3**
Joint and several liability, accidents, children and minors, **8.01–64**
Nonresidents, accidents, service of process, **8.01–307 et seq.**
Personal injuries,
Accidents, **8.01–63 et seq.**
Driving under influence of alcohol or drugs, exemplary damages, **8.01–44.5**
Service of process, accidents, nonresidents, **8.01–307 et seq.**
Theft, accidents, defense, **8.01–65**

TRAINING
Arbitration and award, **8.01–576.8**

TRAINS
Railroads, generally, this index

TRAMWAYS
Winter sports areas, safety, **8.01–227.11 et seq.**

TRANSCRIPTS
Generally, **8.01–420.3**
District courts, **8.01–688**
Evidence, **8.01–389, 8.01–420.3**
Lost or destroyed documents, **8.01–374**

TRANSFER OF CAUSES
Removal or Transfer of Causes, generally, this index

TRANSPORTATION
Carriers, generally, this index
Mandamus, costs, **8.01–653.1**
Railroads, generally, this index

TRANSPORTATION DISTRICTS
Torts, **8.01–195.1 et seq.**

TRAVELING EXPENSES
Motor vehicle insurance, underinsured motorists, cooperation, subrogation, **8.01–66.1:1**

TREATMENT
Medical Care and Treatment, generally, this index

TRESPASS
See, also, Entry on Property, generally, this index
Privileges and immunities, harm to trespasser, **8.01–219.1**
Winter sports safety, powers and duties, **8.01–227.20**

TRIAL
See, also, Jury, generally, this index
Generally, **8.01–374 et seq.**
Bifurcated trials, **8.01–267.6**
Bifurcation, asbestos, **8.01–374.1**
Compensation and salaries, interpreters, **8.01–384.1, 8.01–384.1:1**
Confidential or privileged information, interpreters, **8.01–384.1:1**
Consolidation and merger, asbestos, **8.01–374.1**
Costs, generally, this index
Counterclaim. Setoff and Counterclaim, generally, this index
Damages, new trial, **8.01–383, 8.01–383.1**
Depositions, generally, this index
Directed verdicts, **8.01–378**
Discovery, generally, this index
Dismissal and Nonsuit, generally, this index
Dockets and Docketing, generally, this index
Evidence, generally, this index
Exhibits, identification numbers, redacting, **8.01–420.8**
Foreign languages, interpreters, **8.01–384.1:1**
Hearing impaired persons, interpreters, **8.01–384.1**
Hung jury, **8.01–361**
Interpreters, **8.01–384.1, 8.01–384.1:1**
Judgments and Decrees, generally, this index
Jury, generally, this index
Lost or destroyed documents, **8.01–374**
Motions, generally, this index
New trial. Trial De Novo, generally, this index
Notice, summary jury trial, **8.01–576.2**
Objections and exceptions, **8.01–384**
Place of trial. Venue, generally, this index
Pleadings, generally, this index
Process, generally, this index
Quo warranto, **8.01–643**
Records and recordation,
Lost or destroyed documents, **8.01–374**
Transcripts, generally, this index
Remand, **8.01–681**
Setoff and Counterclaim, generally, this index
Setting aside, verdicts, **8.01–430**
Summary jury trial, **8.01–576.1 et seq.**
Supersedeas or Stay, generally, this index
Trial De Novo, generally, this index
Vacating or setting aside, verdicts, **8.01–430**
Venue, generally, this index
Verdicts,
Contrary to evidence, setting aside verdict, **8.01–680**
Directed verdicts, **8.01–378**

TRIAL—Cont'd
Verdicts—Cont'd
Interest, **8.01–382**
Jury, interrogatories, **8.01–379.3**
Set aside, **8.01–680**
Summary jury trial, **8.01–576.3**
Vacating or setting aside, **8.01–430**
New trial, **8.01–383**
Witnesses, generally, this index

TRIAL DE NOVO
Damages, **8.01–383 et seq.**
Interrogatories, jury, general verdicts, **8.01–379.3**
Remand, **8.01–681**
Verdict contrary to evidence, **8.01–680**

TRICK
Fraud, generally, this index

TRUST COMPANIES
Bank Deposits and Collections, generally, this index
Funds Transfers, generally, this index

TRUST FUNDS
See, also, Trusts and Trustees, generally, this index
Tobacco and tobacco products, nonprofit organizations, privileges and immunities, **8.01–220.1:4**

TRUSTS AND TRUSTEES
See, also, Fiduciaries, generally, this index
Actions and proceedings, pleadings, style, **8.01–6.3**
Class actions, parties, death, **8.01–23**
Names, pleadings, style, **8.01–6.3**
Parties, class actions, death, **8.01–23**
Personal representatives, pleadings, style, **8.01–6.3**
Pleadings, style, **8.01–6.3**
Service of process, corporations, **8.01–303**

UNDERINSURED MOTORISTS
Motor vehicle insurance, subrogation, **8.01–66.1:1**

UNDERTAKINGS
Bonds (Officers and Fiduciaries), generally, this index
Liens and Incumbrances, generally, this index

UNESTABLISHED BUSINESS
Damages, lost profits, **8.01–221.1**

UNIFORM COMMERCIAL CODE
Bank Deposits and Collections, generally, this index
Funds Transfers, generally, this index
Negotiable Instruments, generally, this index

UNIFORM ENFORCEMENT OF FOREIGN JUDGMENTS ACT
Generally, **8.01–465.1 et seq.**

UNIFORM INTERSTATE DEPOSITIONS AND DISCOVERY ACT
Generally, **8.01–412.8 et seq.**

UNIFORM LAWS
Audio Visual Deposition Act, **8.01–412.2 et seq.**
Foreign Country Money Judgments Recognition Act, **8.01–465.13:1 et seq.**
Interstate Depositions and Discovery Act, **8.01–412.8 et seq.**

UNITED STATES
Dockets and docketing, **8.01–447**
Evidence, records and recordation, **8.01–390**
Garnishment, **8.01–523**
Parties, personal injuries, **8.01–37.1**
Personal injuries, intervention, **8.01–37.1**
Records and recordation, evidence, **8.01–390**
Social Security, generally, this index

UNIVERSITIES
Colleges and Universities, generally, this index

UNSOUND MIND
Mentally Ill Persons, generally, this index

USE TAX
Sales and Use Tax, generally, this index

USES AND TRUSTS
Trusts and Trustees, generally, this index

UTILITIES
Public Utilities, generally, this index

VACATING OR SETTING ASIDE
Arbitration and award, **8.01–576.12, 8.01–581.010, 8.01–581.26**
Contrary to evidence, **8.01–680**
Default judgments, **8.01–428**
Servicemembers Civil Relief Act, **8.01–15.2**
Judgments and Decrees, this index
Verdicts, **8.01–430**
New trial, **8.01–383**

VANDALISM
Cemeteries, destruction, damages, **8.01–44.6**
Children and minors, parental liability, **8.01–43, 8.01–44**
Hate crimes, actions and proceedings, **8.01–42.1**

VANS
Motor Vehicles, generally, this index

VEHICLES
Motor Vehicles, generally, this index

VENDOR AND PURCHASER
Deeds and Conveyances, generally, this index

VENUE
Generally, **8.01–257 et seq.**
Administrative law and procedure, **8.01–261**
Agents and agencies, **8.01–262**
Appeal and review, **8.01–258**
Application of law, **8.01–259**
Arbitration and award, **8.01–581.015**
Construction, contracts, **8.01–262.1**

VENUE—Cont'd
Attachment, **8.01–261**
Attorney fees, objections and exceptions, **8.01–266**
Attorneys, disbarment, **8.01–261**
Bonds (officers and fiduciaries), **8.01–261**
Boundaries, **8.01–261**
Business and commerce, **8.01–262**
Certiorari, **8.01–261**
Change of venue, **8.01–265 et seq.**
  Pleadings, **8.01–276**
Conflict of laws, **8.01–259**
Construction, contracts, **8.01–262.1**
Correctional institutions, prisoner litigation reform, **8.01–693**
Costs, objections and exceptions, **8.01–266**
Dismissal and nonsuit, **8.01–264**
Dissolution of marriage, **8.01–261**
Distress, **8.01–261**
Ejectment, **8.01–261**
Evidence, location, **8.01–262**
Executions, debtor, domicile and residence, **8.01–506.2**
Fiduciaries, **8.01–262**
Forcible entry and detainer, **8.01–261**
Garnishment, **8.01–511**
Habeas corpus, application of law, **8.01–259**
Injunctions, **8.01–261**
Jails, prisoner litigation reform, **8.01–693**
Judges, discretion, change of venue, **8.01–267**
Juvenile delinquents and dependents, application of law, **8.01–259**
Liens and incumbrances, **8.01–261**
Mandamus, **8.01–261**
Motions, change of venue, **8.01–265**
Multiple parties, **8.01–263**
Objections and exceptions, **8.01–261, 8.01–264**
  Service of process, waiver, **8.01–286.1**
Parties, **8.01–263**
  Location, **8.01–262**
Partition, **8.01–261, 8.01–262**
Permissible venue, **8.01–261, 8.01–262**
Personal property, partition, **8.01–262**
Pleadings, change of venue, **8.01–276**
Priorities and preferences, **8.01–261**
Probate proceedings, **8.01–261**
Quo warranto, **8.01–261**
Real estate, **8.01–261**
State, **8.01–261**
State agencies, **8.01–261**
State officers and employees, **8.01–261**
Title to property, **8.01–261**
Torts, **8.01–261**
Transfers, **8.01–264**
Waiver, **8.01–264**
Wills, **8.01–261**
Witnesses, location, **8.01–262**
Writs of prohibition, **8.01–261**

VERDICTS
Trial, this index

VETERINARIANS
Emergencies, privileges and immunities, **8.01–225.2**
Privileges and immunities, emergency care, **8.01–225.2**

VICTIMS
Crime Victims, generally, this index

VIDEO IMAGES
Depositions, **8.01–412.2 et seq.**
Witnesses, audio visual depositions, **8.01–412.2 et seq.**

VILLAGES
Municipalities, generally, this index

VIOLENT CRIMES
Crimes and Offenses, generally, this index

VITAL STATISTICS
Birth certificates, change of names, **8.01–217**
Change of names, **8.01–217**

VOLUNTEERS
Highways and roads, littering, pick up programs, privileges and immunities, **8.01–226.8**
Hospices, privileges and immunities, **8.01–226.4**
Privileges and immunities,
  Highways and roads, littering, pick up programs, **8.01–226.8**
  Hospices, **8.01–226.4**

VULNERABLE ADULTS
Aged Persons, generally, this index
Handicapped Persons, generally, this index
Mentally Ill Persons, generally, this index
Mentally Retarded and Developmentally Disabled Persons, generally, this index

WAGES
Compensation and Salaries, generally, this index

WARDS
Guardian and Ward, generally, this index

WARNINGS
Space, flight, privileges and immunities, **8.01–227.10**
Winter sports safety, **8.01–227.12, 8.01–227.14**

WASTE
Hazardous Substances and Waste, generally, this index

WATER SUPPLY
  See, also, Public Utilities, generally, this index
Actions and proceedings, liens and incumbrances, limitation of actions, **8.01–240**
Attorney fees, meters, tampering, **8.01–44.7**
Costs, meters, tampering, **8.01–44.7**
Damages, meters, tampering, **8.01–44.7**
Injunctions, meters, tampering, **8.01–44.7**
Liens and incumbrances, limitation of actions, **8.01–240**

WATER SUPPLY—Cont'd
Limitation of actions, liens and incumbrances, **8.01–240**
Meters, tampering, **8.01–44.7**
Statute of limitations, liens and incumbrances, **8.01–240**

WATERS AND WATERCOURSES
Water Supply, generally, this index

WATERWORKS
Water Supply, generally, this index

WEAPONS
Explosives, generally, this index

WELFARE
Social Services, generally, this index

WHISTLEBLOWING
Taxation, fraud, **8.01–216.8**

WIFE
Husband and Wife, generally, this index

WILLS
See, also, Probate Proceedings, generally, this index
Evidence, lost or destroyed documents, **8.01–394**
Limitation of actions, **8.01–254**
Lost or destroyed documents, **8.01–393**
Proof, **8.01–394**
Venue, **8.01–261**

WINTER SPORTS
Safety, **8.01–227.11 et seq.**

WITNESSES
Generally, **8.01–396 et seq.**
Adverse or pecuniary interest, **8.01–396**
Corroboration, **8.01–397**
Cross examination, **8.01–401**
Affidavits, domicile and residence, **8.01–414**
Appearance,
Compelling attendance, **8.01–407 et seq.**
Subpoenas, generally, this index
Arbitration and award, **8.01–581.04, 8.01–581.06**
Arrest, privileges and immunities, **8.01–327.2**
Attendance, compelling attendance, **8.01–407 et seq.**
Audio visual depositions, **8.01–412.2 et seq.**
Bonds (officers and fiduciaries), continuance, compelling attendance, **8.01–408**
Business and commerce, records and recordation,
Corroboration, **8.01–397**
Evidence, **8.01–390.3**
Children and minors, **8.01–396.1**
Chiropractors, opinions and expert testimony, **8.01–401.2**
Clergy, confidential or privileged information, **8.01–400**
Compelling attendance, **8.01–407 et seq.**
Confidential or privileged information,
Clergy, **8.01–400**

WITNESSES—Cont'd
Confidential or privileged information—Cont'd
Counselors and counseling, **8.01–400.2**
Husband and wife, **8.01–398**
Interpreters, **8.01–400.1**
Marriage and family therapists, **8.01–400.2**
Motor vehicles, crash investigation team, **8.01–402**
Physicians and surgeons, **8.01–399**
Psychologists and psychology, **8.01–399, 8.01–400.2**
Social workers, **8.01–400.2**
Continuance, compelling attendance, bonds (officers and fiduciaries), **8.01–408**
Corroboration, incapacity, **8.01–397**
Counselors and counseling, confidential or privileged information, **8.01–400.2**
Cross examination, **8.01–401**
Depositions, **8.01–404**
Fraud against taxpayers, actions and proceedings, limitation, **8.01–216.6**
Impeachment, **8.01–403**
Dead Mans Statute, **8.01–397**
Death, corroboration, **8.01–397**
Depositions, generally, this index
Domicile and residence, compelling attendance, **8.01–409**
Exclusion, courtroom, **8.01–375**
Fees, dismissal and nonsuit, evidence, reasonableness, **8.01–380**
Fraud against taxpayers, actions and proceedings, limitation, **8.01–216.6**
Habeas corpus, affidavits, **8.01–660**
Habit, **8.01–397.1**
Hearing impaired persons, interpreters, **8.01–406**
Confidential or privileged information, **8.01–400.1**
Hearsay, exceptions, opinions and expert testimony, **8.01–401.1**
Impeachment, **8.01–403**
Writings, **8.01–404**
Incapacity, corroboration, **8.01–397**
Inconsistent statements, **8.01–403**
Writings, **8.01–404**
Interpreters, this index
Joinder, **8.01–267.1**
Marriage and family therapists, confidential or privileged information, **8.01–400.2**
Medical Malpractice, this index
Motor vehicles, crash investigation team, privileges and immunities, **8.01–402**
Nurse practitioners, opinions and expert testimony, **8.01–401.2**
Oaths and affirmations, **8.01–405**
Depositions, video tape, **8.01–412.4**
Interpreters, **8.01–406**
Opinions and expert testimony, **8.01–401.1 et seq.**
Medical Malpractice, this index
Physicians assistants, **8.01–401.2**
Support, exclusion, **8.01–375**

WITNESSES—Cont'd
Opinions and expert testimony—Cont'd
Wrongful death, standard of care, certificates and certification, **8.01–50.1**
Orders of court, compelling attendance, **8.01–407**
Personal representatives, corroboration, **8.01–397**
Physicians assistants, opinions and expert testimony, **8.01–401.2**
Podiatrists, medical malpractice, evidence, **8.01–401.2:1**
Privileges and immunities,
Clergy, **8.01–400**
Husband and wife, **8.01–398**
Interpreters, **8.01–400.1**
Motor vehicles, crash investigation team, **8.01–402**
Physicians and surgeons, **8.01–399**
Psychologists and psychology, **8.01–399, 8.01–400.2**
Process, service of process, **8.01–298**
Psychologists and psychology, confidential or privileged information, **8.01–399, 8.01–400.2**
Removal, courtroom, **8.01–375**
Residence, compelling attendance, **8.01–409**
Service of process, **8.01–298**
Social workers, confidential or privileged information, **8.01–400.2**
Subpoenas, generally, this index
Summary jury trial, **8.01–576.3**
Summons, compelling attendance, **8.01–407**
Support, opinions and expert testimony, exclusion, **8.01–375**
Time, subpoenas, effective, **8.01–407**
Traveling expenses, dismissal and nonsuit, evidence, reasonableness, **8.01–380**
Venue, location, **8.01–262**
Video tapes, audio visual depositions, **8.01–412.2 et seq.**
Writings, inconsistent statements, **8.01–404**

WIVES
Husband and Wife, generally, this index

WOMEN
Fetal death, wrongful death, **8.01–50**
Husband and Wife, generally, this index
Pregnancy, generally, this index
Wrongful death, fetal death, **8.01–50**

WORDS AND PHRASES
Action, **8.01–2**
Foreign countries, money, claims, **8.01–465.14**
Venue, **8.01–257**
Agency,
Judicial notice, **8.01–385**
Torts, **8.01–195.2**
Agents, lead based paint, **8.01–226.7**
ANSI Ski Lift Code, winter sports safety, **8.01–227.11**
Appellant, supreme court, **8.01–669**
Appellate court, supreme court, **8.01–669**

WORDS AND PHRASES—Cont'd
Approved national accrediting organizations, disasters, privileges and immunities, **8.01–225.01**
Arrest under civil process, privileges and immunities, **8.01–327.1**
Assisted suicide, injunctions, **8.01–622.1**
Attorney general, fraud against taxpayers, **8.01–216.2**
Authorized occupants, landlord and tenant, mold, **8.01–226.12**
Bank offered spot rate, foreign countries, money, claims, **8.01–465.14**
Bills, actions and proceedings, **8.01–2**
Bills in equity, actions and proceedings, **8.01–2**
Bills of complaint, actions and proceedings, **8.01–2**
Centralized credentialing service,
Health care professionals, privileges and immunities, **8.01–581.17**
Medical malpractice, **8.01–581.17**
Chancery courts, actions and proceedings, **8.01–2**
Chancery practice, actions and proceedings, **8.01–2**
Chancery procedure, actions and proceedings, **8.01–2**
Chancery side, actions and proceedings, **8.01–2**
Civil arrest, privileges and immunities, **8.01–327.1**
Claim, fraud against taxpayers, **8.01–216.2**
Common carrier, officers and employees, personal injuries, **8.01–61**
Commonwealth, fraud against taxpayers, **8.01–216.2**
Compensatory damages, stalking, **8.01–42.3**
Competition, winter sports safety, **8.01–227.11**
Competition terrain, winter sports safety, **8.01–227.11**
Competitors, winter sports safety, **8.01–227.11**
Computer network, jurisdiction, **8.01–328.1**
Conciliation, arbitration and award, **8.01–576.4**
Confidential communications, husband and wife, privileges and immunities, **8.01–398**
Controlled substances, drug dealers, liability, **8.01–227.4**
Conversion date, foreign countries, money, claims, **8.01–465.14**
Corporation courts, actions and proceedings, **8.01–2**
Court,
Arbitration and award, **8.01–576.4**
Judicial notice, **8.01–385**
Courts exercising powers in chancery, actions and proceedings, **8.01–2**
Courts of equity, actions and proceedings, **8.01–2**
Courts with equitable jurisdiction, actions and proceedings, **8.01–2**
Covered patients, health insurance, bills, submission, **8.01–27.5**
Decree, **8.01–2**
Designated trails, winter sports safety, **8.01–227.11**
Disposable earnings, garnishment, **8.01–512.3**
Dispute resolution proceeding, **8.01–576.4**
Dispute resolution program, **8.01–576.4**

WORDS AND PHRASES—Cont'd
Dispute resolution services, **8.01–576.4**
Distribution proceeding, foreign countries, money, claims, **8.01–465.14**
Documentary material, fraud against taxpayers, **8.01–216.2**
Dwelling units, landlord and tenant, mold, **8.01–226.12**
Electronic article surveillance device, shoplifting, arrest, detention, **8.01–226.9**
Electronic funds transfers, insufficient funds, stop payment, damages, **8.01–27.1, 8.01–27.2**
Employee theft, actions and proceedings, **8.01–44.4**
Employees,
  Fraud against taxpayers, **8.01–216.2**
  Libel and slander, **8.01–46.1**
  State, torts, **8.01–195.2**
Employer,
  Fraud against taxpayers, **8.01–216.2**
  Libel and slander, **8.01–46.1**
Equity practice, actions and proceedings, **8.01–2**
Equity procedure, actions and proceedings, **8.01–2**
Exempt official, fraud against taxpayers, **8.01–216.8**
Fiduciary,
  Actions and proceedings, **8.01–2**
  Handicapped persons, **8.01–67**
First responders, privileges and immunities, **8.01–225**
Foreign countries, judgments and decrees, **8.01–465.13:1**
Foreign country money judgment, **8.01–465.13:1**
Foreign judgment, **8.01–465.1**
Foreign jurisdictions, interstate depositions and discovery, **8.01–412.9**
Foreign money, claims, **8.01–465.14**
Foreign subpoenas, interstate depositions and discovery, **8.01–412.9**
Freestyle terrain, winter sports safety, **8.01–227.11**
Freestyle terrain park, winter sports safety, **8.01–227.11**
Freestyler, winter sports safety, **8.01–227.11**
Give notice, landlord and tenant, mold, **8.01–226.12**
Guests, landlord and tenant, mold, **8.01–226.12**
Habit, evidence, **8.01–397.1**
Health care, medical malpractice, **8.01–581.1**
  Sympathy, evidence, **8.01–52.1, 8.01–581.20:1**
Health care policies, medical care and treatment, bills, submission, **8.01–27.5**
Health care providers,
  Bills, submission, time, **8.01–27.5**
  Drug dealers, liability, **8.01–227.4**
  Medical malpractice, **8.01–581.1**
    Sympathy, evidence, **8.01–52.1, 8.01–581.20:1**
  Privileges and immunities, disasters, **8.01–225.01**
Health care services, bills, submission, time, **8.01–27.5**
Health insurers, bills, submission, time, **8.01–27.5**
Health maintenance organizations, medical malpractice, **8.01–581.1**

WORDS AND PHRASES—Cont'd
Health profession student, medical malpractice, privileges and immunities, **8.01–581.13**
Health professional, medical malpractice, privileges and immunities, **8.01–581.13**
Helmets, winter sports safety, **8.01–227.11**
Hospital, medical malpractice, **8.01–581.1**
Impartial attorney, medical malpractice, **8.01–581.1**
Impartial health care provider, medical malpractice, **8.01–581.1**
In network providers, medical care and treatment, bills, submission, **8.01–27.5**
Incarceration, wrongful incarceration, compensation and salaries, **8.01–195.10**
Information, libel and slander, labor and employment, **8.01–46.1**
Information content provider, libel and slander, **8.01–49.1**
Inherent risks of winter sports, winter sports safety, **8.01–227.11**
Intake specialist, arbitration and award, **8.01–576.4**
Interactive computer service, libel and slander, **8.01–49.1**
Interior of the dwelling unit, landlord and tenant, mold, **8.01–226.12**
Internet, libel and slander, **8.01–49.1**
Investigation, fraud against taxpayers, **8.01–216.2**
Invitees, landlord and tenant, mold, **8.01–226.12**
Job performance, libel and slander, **8.01–46.1**
Judgment, **8.01–2, 8.01–426**
  Appeal and review, supreme court, **8.01–669**
Knowing, fraud against taxpayers, **8.01–216.3**
Knowingly, fraud against taxpayers, **8.01–216.3**
Landlord, mold, **8.01–226.12**
Law and chancery courts, actions and proceedings, **8.01–2**
Law and equity courts, actions and proceedings, **8.01–2**
Lead based paint, **8.01–226.7**
Lead based paint hazard, **8.01–226.7**
Lead based paint maintenance, **8.01–226.7**
Licensed health care provider, assisted suicide, **8.01–622.1**
Malpractice, medical malpractice, **8.01–581.1**
Managing agent, landlord and tenant, mold, **8.01–226.12**
Managing employees, garnishment, service of process, **8.01–513**
Material, fraud against taxpayers, **8.01–216.2**
Mediation, **8.01–576.4, 8.01–581.21**
Mediation program, **8.01–581.21**
Mediator, **8.01–581.21**
Misconduct, arbitration and award, vacating or setting aside, **8.01–581.26**
Mold remediation in accordance with professional standards, landlord and tenant, **8.01–226.12**
Money, foreign countries, claims, **8.01–465.14**
Money of the claim, foreign countries, **8.01–465.14**

WORDS AND PHRASES—Cont'd
Motions for judgment, actions and proceedings, **8.01–2**
Motor vehicles, process, **8.01–307**
Neutral, arbitration and award, **8.01–576.4**
Nonresident, motor vehicles, process, **8.01–307**
Notice, landlord and tenant, mold, **8.01–226.12**
Notifies, landlord and tenant, mold, **8.01–226.12**
Obligation, fraud against taxpayers, **8.01–216.2**
Official publications, judicial notice, **8.01–385**
Official use, fraud against taxpayers, **8.01–216.2**
Operator, winter sports safety, **8.01–227.11**
Orientation session, arbitration and award, **8.01–576.4**
Original source, fraud against taxpayers, **8.01–216.8**
Participant,
  Space, flight, privileges and immunities, **8.01–227.8**
  Winter sports safety, **8.01–227.11**
Participant injuries, space, flight, privileges and immunities, **8.01–227.8**
Participates in a winter sport, winter sports safety, **8.01–227.11**
Participating in a winter sport, winter sports safety, **8.01–227.11**
Passenger tramways, winter sports safety, **8.01–227.11**
Passengers, winter sports safety, **8.01–227.11**
Patient,
  Medical care and treatment, bills, submission, **8.01–27.5**
  Medical malpractice, **8.01–581.1**
Patient safety data, health care professionals, privileges and immunities, **8.01–581.17**
Patient safety organization, health care professionals, privileges and immunities, **8.01–581.17**
Person,
  Foreign countries, money, claims, **8.01–465.14**
  Fraud against taxpayers, **8.01–216.2**
  Interstate depositions and discovery, **8.01–412.9**
  Jurisdiction, **8.01–328**
  Process, **8.01–285**
  Winter sports safety, **8.01–227.11**
Person under a disability,
  Actions and proceedings, **8.01–2**
  Property, **8.01–67**
Personal action, limitation of actions, **8.01–228**
Petitioner, appeal and review, supreme court, **8.01–669**
Physician,
  Laboratories, medical malpractice, privileges and immunities, **8.01–581.18:1**
  Medical malpractice, **8.01–581.1**
Political subdivision, judicial notice, **8.01–385**
Private process servers, **8.01–293**
Process, **8.01–285**
Product of discovery, fraud against taxpayers, **8.01–216.2**
Professional conduct, libel and slander, labor and employment, **8.01–46.1**

WORDS AND PHRASES—Cont'd
Professional services in nursing homes, medical malpractice, **8.01–581.1**
Prospective employer, libel and slander, labor and employment, **8.01–46.1**
Provider agreements, medical care and treatment, bills, submission, **8.01–27.5**
Publish, judicial notice, **8.01–385**
Rate of exchange, foreign countries, money, claims, **8.01–465.14**
Readily accessible, landlord and tenant, mold, **8.01–226.12**
Receivership courts, actions and proceedings, **8.01–2**
Record, courts, evidence, **8.01–389**
Relative, medical malpractice, sympathy, evidence, **8.01–52.1, 8.01–581.20:1**
Rendition of a judgment, actions and proceedings, **8.01–2**
Representatives, medical malpractice, sympathy, evidence, **8.01–52.1, 8.01–581.20:1**
Required, judicial notice, **8.01–385**
Residential dwelling, lead based paint, **8.01–226.7**
Return, process, **8.01–285**
Routine practice, evidence, **8.01–397.1**
School board, torts, **8.01–195.2**
Sheriff, actions and proceedings, **8.01–2**
Shoplift, actions and proceedings, **8.01–44.4**
Snowmaking equipment, winter sports safety, **8.01–227.11**
Space flight activities, privileges and immunities, **8.01–227.8**
Space flight entities, privileges and immunities, **8.01–227.8**
Spot rate, foreign countries, money, claims, **8.01–465.14**
State,
  Foreign countries, money, claims, **8.01–465.14**
  Interstate depositions and discovery, **8.01–412.9**
Statutory agent, process, **8.01–285**
Subpoena,
  Actions and proceedings, **8.01–2**
  Interstate depositions and discovery, **8.01–412.9**
Suit, **8.01–2**
Summons, actions and proceedings, **8.01–2**
Tenant, mold, **8.01–226.12**
Trails, winter sports safety, **8.01–227.11**
Transportation district, torts, **8.01–195.2**
Tubing, winter sports safety, **8.01–227.11**
Unanticipated outcome, medical malpractice, sympathy, evidence, **8.01–52.1, 8.01–581.20:1**
United States, judicial notice, **8.01–385**
Use, jurisdiction, **8.01–328.1**
Victim, stalking, **8.01–42.3**
Visible evidence of mold, landlord and tenant, **8.01–226.12**
Voice over Internet protocol service, nine one one (911), privileges and immunities, **8.01–225**
VoIP service, nine one one (911), privileges and immunities, **8.01–225**

WORDS AND PHRASES—Cont'd
Winter sports, safety, **8.01–227.11**
Winter sports area, winter sports safety, **8.01–227.11**
Winter sports area infrastructure, winter sports safety, **8.01–227.11**
Winter sports area operators, winter sports safety, **8.01–227.11**
Winter sports area trails, winter sports safety, **8.01–227.11**
Winter sports area vehicles, winter sports safety, **8.01–227.11**
Winter sports participants, winter sports safety, **8.01–227.11**
Writ of venire facias, jury, **8.01–354**
Wrongful incarceration, compensation and salaries, **8.01–195.10**

WORK
Labor and Employment, generally, this index

WORKERS COMPENSATION
Actions and proceedings,
 Birth related neurological injuries, removal or transfer of causes, **8.01–273.1**
 Third parties, compromise and settlement, consent, **8.01–424.1**
Appeal and review,
 Bonds (officers and fiduciaries), **8.01–676.1**
 Third parties, compromise and settlement, consent, **8.01–424.1**
Birth related neurological injuries, removal or transfer of causes, **8.01–273.1**
Children and minors, birth related neurological injuries, **8.01–273.1**
Compromise and settlement, third parties, actions and proceedings, consent, **8.01–424.1**
Consent, third parties, actions and proceedings, compromise and settlement, **8.01–424.1**
Estoppel, judgments and decrees, **8.01–420.5**
Interest, third parties, compromise and settlement, consent, **8.01–424.1**
Judgments and decrees, employment, estoppel, **8.01–420.5**
Limitation of actions, **8.01–229**
Petitions, third parties, actions and proceedings, compromise and settlement, **8.01–424.1**
Removal or transfer of causes, birth related neurological injuries, **8.01–273.1**
Summons, witnesses, boards and commissions, **8.01–407**
Third parties, actions and proceedings, compromise and settlement, consent, **8.01–424.1**
Witnesses, summons, **8.01–407**

WORLD WIDE WEB
Internet, generally, this index

WORSHIP
Religion, generally, this index

WRITS
Attachment, generally, this index

WRITS—Cont'd
Error coram vobis, **8.01–677**
Executions, generally, this index
Fieri facias. Executions, generally, this index
Forms, **8.01–3, 8.01–286**
Garnishment, generally, this index
Habeas Corpus, generally, this index
Injunctions, generally, this index
Mandamus, generally, this index
Quo warranto, **8.01–635 et seq.**
Venditioni exponas,
 Executions, **8.01–485, 8.01–486**
 State, **8.01–211 et seq.**
Venire facias, jury, **8.01–354**

WRONGFUL DEATH
 Generally, **8.01–50 et seq.**
Asbestos, joinder, **8.01–374.1**
Attorney fees, **8.01–54**
Beneficiaries, **8.01–53**
Certificates and certification, standard of care, medical malpractice, expert witnesses, **8.01–50.1**
Children and minors, **8.01–50**
Compensation and salaries, lost income, **8.01–52**
Compromise and settlement, **8.01–55**
 Fiduciaries, **8.01–424**
 Personal injuries, **8.01–51**
Contractors, privileges and immunities, **8.01–39**
Covenant not to sue, **8.01–35.1**
Damages, lost profits, new business, unestablished business, **8.01–221.1**
Distribution, damages, **8.01–53, 8.01–54**
Evidence,
 Distribution, damages, **8.01–54**
 Motor vehicles, medical care and treatment, **8.01–413.01**
 Standard of care, expert witnesses, certificates and certification, **8.01–50.1**
 Sympathy, medical malpractice, **8.01–52.1**
Exemplary damages, **8.01–52**
Expert witnesses, standard of care, medical malpractice, certificates and certification, **8.01–50.1**
Fetal death, **8.01–50**
Funeral expenses, **8.01–52**
Interrogatories, jury, general verdicts, **8.01–379.3**
Landlord and tenant, mold, privileges and immunities, **8.01–226.12**
Limitation of actions, **8.01–50, 8.01–244**
Medical care and treatment, expenses, **8.01–52, 8.01–54**
Mental anguish, damages, **8.01–52**
Motor vehicles, medical care and treatment, fees, **8.01–413.01**
Notice, compromise and settlement, **8.01–55**
Nursing homes, medical assistance, notice, **8.01–66.5**
Parties, **8.01–50**
Priorities and preferences, distribution, damages, **8.01–53, 8.01–54**

WRONGFUL DEATH—Cont'd
Privity, **8.01–223**
Punitive damages, **8.01–52**
Release, **8.01–35.1**
Standard of care, expert witnesses, medical malpractice, certificates and certification, **8.01–50.1**
Statute of limitations, **8.01–244**
Sympathy, evidence, medical malpractice, **8.01–52.1**
Time, limitation of actions, **8.01–244**
Witnesses, expert witnesses, standard of care, certificates and certification, **8.01–50.1**

WRONGFUL INCARCERATION
Compensation and salaries, **8.01–195.10 et seq.**

ZINC
Mines and Minerals, generally, this index

ZONING AND PLANNING
Attachment, records and recordation, **8.01–268**
Pending actions, records and recordation, **8.01–268**

CRIMINAL PROCEDURE

[Title 19.2, Code of Virginia]

Including Amendments Enacted Through the End of the 2015 Regular Session.

Table of Sections

CHAPTER 1. GENERAL PROVISIONS

Section

19.2–1. Repealing Clause.

19.2–2. Effect of Repeal of Title 19.1 and Enactment of This Title.

19.2–3. Certain Notices, Recognizances and Processes Validated.

19.2–3.1. Personal Appearance by Two-Way Electronic Video and Audio Communication; Standards.

19.2–4. References to Former Sections, Articles or Chapters of Titles 18.1 and 19.1.

19.2–5. Meaning of Certain Terms.

19.2–6. Appointive Power of Circuit Courts.

19.2–7. Rewards for Arrest of Persons Convicted of or Charged with Offenses; Rewards for Conviction of Unknown Offenders.

19.2–8. Limitation of Prosecutions.

19.2–8.1. Prosecution for Murder or Manslaughter; Passage of Time Not a Limitation.

19.2–9. Prosecution of Certain Criminal Cases Removed from State to Federal Courts; Costs.

19.2–9.1. Written Notice Required for Complaining Witness Who Is Requested to Take Polygraph Test.

19.2–10. Outlawry Abolished.

19.2–10.1. Subpoena Duces Tecum for Obtaining Records Concerning Banking and Credit Cards.

19.2–10.2. Administrative Subpoena Issued for Record from Provider of Electronic Communication Service or Remote Computing Service.

19.2–10.3. Reasonable Suspicion Required to Stop, Board, or Inspect a Noncommercial Vessel on Navigable Waters of the Commonwealth.

19.2–11. Procedure in Contempt Cases.

CHAPTER 1.1. CRIME VICTIM AND WITNESS RIGHTS ACT

19.2–11.01. Crime Victim and Witness Rights.

19.2–11.1. Establishment of Crime Victim-Witness Assistance Programs; Funding; Minimum Standards.

19.2–11.2. Crime Victim's Right to Nondisclosure of Certain Information; Exceptions; Testimonial Privilege.

19.2–11.3. Virginia Crime Victim–Witness Fund.

19.2–11.4. Establishment of Victim-Offender Reconciliation Program.

Section

CHAPTER 2. CONSERVATORS OF THE PEACE AND SPECIAL POLICEMEN

ARTICLE 1. APPOINTMENT

19.2–12. Who Are Conservators of the Peace.

19.2–13. Special Conservators of the Peace; Authority; Jurisdiction; Registration; Bond; Liability of Employers; Penalty; Report.

19.2–14. Conservators of the Peace for Fairgrounds and Cemeteries; Bond Required.

19.2–15. When Conservator Appointed Under § 19.2–13 Need Not Be a Citizen.

19.2–16. Repealed by Acts 1994, c. 205.

19.2–17. Repealed by Acts 1996, c. 850.

ARTICLE 2. POWERS AND DUTIES

19.2–18. Powers and Duties Generally.

19.2–19. Recognizance to Keep the Peace; When Required.

19.2–20. Same; Complaint and Issuance of Warrant Therefor.

19.2–21. Same; Procedure When Accused Appears.

19.2–22. Same; Arrest Without a Warrant.

19.2–23. Payment of Fees or Mileage Allowances Into County or City Treasury.

ARTICLE 3. APPEALS

19.2–24. When Appeal May Be Taken; Witnesses Recognized; Bail.

19.2–25. Power of Court on Appeal.

CHAPTER 3. MAGISTRATES

ARTICLE 1. TRANSITION PROVISIONS

19.2–26. Repeal of Inconsistent Statutes, Municipal Charters, Etc.

19.2–27. Effect of Repeal of Title 39.1 on Prior Acts, Offenses, Etc.

19.2–28. Certain Notices, Recognizances and Processes Validated.

19.2–29. References to Former Sections, Articles and Chapters in Title 39.1.

ARTICLE 2. ABOLITION OF JUSTICE OF THE PEACE SYSTEM

19.2–30. Repealed by Acts 2008, cc. 551 and 691.

19.2–31. Abolition of Office of Issuing Justice.

19.2–32. References to Justices of the Peace.

ARTICLE 3. THE MAGISTRATE SYSTEM

19.2–33. Office of Magistrate.

19.2–34. Number of Magistrates.

Section
19.2–35. Appointment; Supervision Generally.
19.2–36. Chief Magistrates.
19.2–37. Magistrates; Eligibility for Appointment; Restrictions on Activities.
19.2–38. Probationary Period; Compensation and Benefits; Vacancies; Revocation of Appointment.
19.2–38.1. Training Standards; Training Prerequisite to Reappointment; Waiver.
19.2–39. Bond.
19.2–40. Repealed by Acts 1980, c. 758.

ARTICLE 4. SUPERVISION

19.2–41. Repealed by Acts 2008, cc. 551 and 691.
19.2–42. Repealed by Acts 2004, c. 327.
19.2–43. Duty of Executive Secretary of Supreme Court.

ARTICLE 5. JURISDICTION AND POWERS

19.2–44. Territorial Jurisdiction.
19.2–44.1. Repealed by Acts 1976, c. 138.
19.2–45. Powers Enumerated.

ARTICLE 6. COMPENSATION AND FEES

19.2–46. Compensation.
19.2–46.1. Salaries to Be Fixed by the Executive Secretary; Limitations; Mileage Allowance.
19.2–46.2. Full-Time Magistrates; Certification for Retirement Coverage.
19.2–47. Magistrate Not to Receive Claims or Evidence of Debt for Collection.
19.2–47.1. Disposition of Funds.
19.2–48. Audits.
19.2–48.1. Quarters for Magistrates.

CHAPTER 4. SPECIAL MAGISTRATES

19.2–49. to 19.2–51. Repealed by Acts 1980, c. 758.

CHAPTER 5. SEARCH WARRANTS

19.2–52. When Search Warrant May Issue.
19.2–53. What May Be Searched and Seized.
19.2–53.1. Taking Blood Samples Pursuant to Search Warrant; Immunity.
19.2–54. Affidavit Preliminary to Issuance of Search Warrant; General Search Warrant Prohibited; Effect of Failure to File Affidavit.
19.2–55. Issuing General Search Warrant or Search Warrant Without Affidavit Deemed Malfeasance.
19.2–56. To Whom Search Warrant Directed; What It Shall Command; Warrant to Show Date and Time of Issuance; Copy of Affidavit to Be Part of Warrant and Served Therewith; Warrants Not Executed Within 15 Days.
19.2–56.1. Warrant Issued for Search of Attorney's Office.
19.2–56.2. Application for and Issuance of Search Warrant for a Tracking Device; Installation and Use.
19.2–57. Execution and Return of Warrant; List of Property Seized.
19.2–58. Disposition of Property Seized.
19.2–59. Search Without Warrant Prohibited; When Search Without Warrant Lawful.
19.2–59.1. Strip Searches Prohibited; Exceptions; How Strip Searches Conducted.

Section
19.2–60. Motion for Return of Seized Property and to Suppress.
19.2–60.1. Use of Unmanned Aircraft Systems by Public Bodies; Search Warrant Required.

CHAPTER 6. INTERCEPTION OF WIRE, ELECTRONIC OR ORAL COMMUNICATIONS

19.2–61. Definitions.
19.2–62. Interception, Disclosure, Etc., of Wire, Electronic or Oral Communications Unlawful; Penalties; Exceptions.
19.2–63. Manufacture, Possession, Sale or Advertising of Certain Devices Unlawful; Penalties; Exceptions.
19.2–63.1. Supervision and Control of Devices; Unauthorized Possession.
19.2–64. Forfeiture of Unlawful Devices.
19.2–65. When Intercepted Communications and Evidence Derived Therefrom Not to Be Received in Evidence.
19.2–66. When Attorney General or Chief Deputy Attorney General May Apply for Order Authorizing Interception of Communications.
19.2–67. Disclosure of Information Obtained by Authorized Means.
19.2–68. Application for and Issuance of Order Authorizing Interception; Contents of Order; Recording and Retention of Intercepted Communications, Applications and Orders; Notice to Parties; Introduction in Evidence of Information Obtained.
19.2–69. Civil Action for Unlawful Interception, Disclosure or Use.
19.2–70. Reports to Be Filed by Courts and Attorney General.
19.2–70.1. General Prohibition on Pen Register and Trap and Trace Device Use; Exceptions.
19.2–70.2. Application for and Issuance of Order for a Pen Register or Trap and Trace Device; Assistance in Installation and Use.
19.2–70.3. Obtaining Records Concerning Electronic Communication Service or Remote Computing Service.

CHAPTER 7. ARREST

19.2–71. Who May Issue Process of Arrest.
19.2–72. When It May Issue; What to Recite and Require.
19.2–73. Issuance of Summons Instead of Warrant in Certain Cases.
19.2–73.1. Notice of Issuance of Warrant or Summons; Appearance; Failure to Appear.
19.2–73.2. Law-Enforcement Officers to Issue Subpoenas; Penalty.
19.2–74. Issuance and Service of Summons in Place of Warrant in Misdemeanor Case; Issuance of Summons by Special Conservators of the Peace.
19.2–74.1. Repealed by Acts 1981, c. 382.
19.2–75. Copy of Process to Be Left with Accused; Exception.

Section
19.2–76. Execution and Return of Warrant, Capias or Summons; Arrest Outside County or City Where Charge Is to Be Tried.
19.2–76.1. Submission of Quarterly Reports Concerning Unexecuted Felony and Misdemeanor Warrants and Other Criminal Process; Destruction; Dismissal.
19.2–76.2. Mailing of Summons in Certain Cases.
19.2–76.3. Failure to Appear on Return Date for Summons Issued Under § 19.2–76.2.
19.2–77. Escape, Flight and Pursuit; Arrest Anywhere in Commonwealth.
19.2–78. Uniform of Officer Making Arrest.
19.2–79. Arrest by Officers of Other States of United States.
19.2–80. Duty of Arresting Officer; Bail.
19.2–80.1. When Arrested Person Operating Motor Vehicle; How Vehicle Removed from Scene of Arrest.
19.2–80.2. Duty of Arresting Officer; Providing Magistrate or Court with Criminal History Information.
19.2–81. Arrest Without Warrant Authorized in Certain Cases.
19.2–81.1. Arrest Without Warrant by Correctional Officers in Certain Cases.
19.2–81.2. Power of Correctional Officers and Designated Noncustodial Employees to Detain.
19.2–81.3. Arrest Without a Warrant Authorized in Cases of Assault and Battery Against a Family or Household Member and Stalking and for Violations of Protective Orders; Procedure, Etc.
19.2–81.4. Repealed by Acts 2008, cc. 600 and 771.
19.2–81.5. Cooperation with a Law-Enforcement Officer.
19.2–81.6. Authority of Law-Enforcement Officers to Arrest Illegal Aliens.
19.2–82. Procedure Upon Arrest Without Warrant.
19.2–82.1. Giving False Identity to Law-Enforcement Officer; Penalty.
19.2–83. Repealed by Acts 1994, c. 273.
19.2–83.1. Report of Arrest of School Employees and Adult Students for Certain Offenses.
19.2–83.2. Jail Officer to Ascertain Citizenship of Inmate.

CHAPTER 8. EXTRADITION OF CRIMINALS

Article 1. Fugitives From Foreign Nations

19.2–84. Governor to Surrender on Requisition of President.

Article 2. Uniform Criminal Extradition Act

19.2–85. Definitions.
19.2–86. Fugitives from Justice; Duty of Governor.
19.2–87. Form of Demand.
19.2–88. Governor May Investigate Case.
19.2–89. Extradition of Persons Imprisoned or Awaiting Trial in Another State.
19.2–90. Extradition of Persons Who Have Left Demanding State Involuntarily.
19.2–91. Extradition of Persons Not in Demanding State at Time of Commission of Crime.
19.2–92. Issuance of Governor's Warrant of Arrest; Its Recitals.
19.2–93. Manner and Place of Execution of Warrant.
Section
19.2–94. Assistance to Arresting Officer.
19.2–95. Rights of Accused Persons; Application for Writ of Habeas Corpus.
19.2–96. Penalty for Noncompliance with Preceding Section.
19.2–97. Confinement in Jail When Necessary.
19.2–98. Same; for Prisoners Being Taken Through Commonwealth.
19.2–99. Arrest Prior to Requisition.
19.2–100. Arrest Without Warrant.
19.2–101. Confinement to Await Requisition; Bail.
19.2–102. In What Cases Bail Allowed; Conditions of Bond.
19.2–103. Discharge, Recommitment or Renewal of Bail.
19.2–104. Forfeiture of Bail.
19.2–105. Persons Under Criminal Prosecution in This Commonwealth at Time of Requisition.
19.2–106. When Guilt or Innocence of Accused Inquired Into.
19.2–107. Governor May Recall Warrant or Issue Alias.
19.2–108. Fugitives from This Commonwealth; Duty of Governor.
19.2–109. Application for Requisition for Return of Person Charged with Crime.
19.2–110. Application for Requisition for Return of Escaped Convict, Etc.
19.2–111. Form of Such Applications; Copies, Etc.
19.2–112. Costs and Expenses of Extradition.
19.2–113. Immunity from Service of Process in Certain Civil Actions.
19.2–114. Written Waiver of Extradition Proceedings.
19.2–115. Nonwaiver by This Commonwealth.
19.2–116. No Right of Asylum; No Immunity from Other Criminal Prosecutions While in This Commonwealth.
19.2–117. Interpretation of Article.
19.2–118. Short Title.

CHAPTER 9. BAIL AND RECOGNIZANCES

Article 1. Bail

19.2–119. Definitions.
19.2–120. Admission to Bail.
19.2–120.1. Presumption of No Bail for Illegal Aliens Charged with Certain Crimes.
19.2–121. Fixing Terms of Bail.
19.2–122. Repealed by Acts 1986, c. 327.
19.2–123. Release of Accused on Secured or Unsecured Bond or Promise to Appear; Conditions of Release.
19.2–124. Appeal from Bail, Bond, or Recognizance Order.
19.2–125. Release Pending Appeal from Conviction in Court Not of Record.
19.2–126. Repealed by Acts 1999, cc. 829 and 846.
19.2–127. Conditions of Release of Material Witness.
19.2–128. Penalties for Failure to Appear.
19.2–129. Power of Court to Punish for Contempt.
19.2–130. Bail in Subsequent Proceeding Arising Out of Initial Arrest.
19.2–130.1. Bail Terms Set by Court on a Capias to Be Honored by Magistrate.
19.2–131. Bail for Person Held in Jurisdiction Other Than That of Trial.

Section

19.2–132. Motion to Increase Amount of Bond Fixed by Judicial Officer; When Bond May Be Increased.
19.2–132.1, 19.2–133. Repealed by Acts 1991, c. 581.
19.2–134. When Bail Piece to Be Delivered to Accused; Form of Bail Piece.

ARTICLE 2. RECOGNIZANCES

19.2–135. Commitment for Trial; Recognizance; Notice to Attorney for Commonwealth; Remand on Violation of Condition.
19.2–136. How Bonds in Recognizances Payable; Penalty.
19.2–137. Order of Court on Recognizance.
19.2–138. To 19.2–140. Repealed by Acts 1987, c. 670.
19.2–141. How Recognizance Taken for Incapacitated or Insane Person or One Under Disability.
19.2–142. Where Recognizance Taken Out of Court to Be Sent.
19.2–143. Where Default Recorded; Process on Recognizance; Forfeiture on Recognizance; When Copy May Be Used; Cash Bond.
19.2–144. Forfeiture of Recognizance While in Military or Naval Service.
19.2–145. How Penalty Remitted.
19.2–146. Defects in Form of Recognizance Not to Defeat Action or Judgment.
19.2–147. Docketing Judgment on Forfeited Recognizance or Bond.
19.2–148. Surety Discharged on Payment of Amount, Etc., Into Court.
19.2–149. How Surety on a Bond in Recognizance May Surrender Principal and Be Discharged from Liability.
19.2–150. Proceeding When Surety Surrenders Principal.

ARTICLE 3. SATISFACTION AND DISCHARGE

19.2–151. Satisfaction and Discharge of Assault and Similar Charges.
19.2–152. Order Discharging Recognizance or Superseding Commitment; Judgment for Costs.

ARTICLE 4. BAIL BONDSMEN

19.2–152.1. to 19.2–152.1:7. Repealed by Acts 2004, c. 460, Eff. July 1, 2005.

ARTICLE 5. PRETRIAL SERVICES ACT

19.2–152.2. Purpose; Establishment of Pretrial Services and Services Agencies.
19.2–152.3. Department of Criminal Justice Services to Prescribe Standards; Biennial Plan.
19.2–152.4. Mandated Services.
19.2–152.4:1. Form of Oath of Office for Local Pretrial Services Officer; Authorization to Seek Capias.
19.2–152.4:2. Confidentiality of Records of and Reports on Adult Persons Under Investigation by or in the Custody or Supervision of a Local Pretrial Services Agency.
19.2–152.4:3. Duties and Responsibilities of Local Pretrial Services Officers.
19.2–152.5. Community Criminal Justice Boards.
19.2–152.6. Withdrawal from Pretrial Services.

Section

19.2–152.7. Funding; Failure to Comply.
19.2–152.7:1. Definitions.

CHAPTER 9.1. PROTECTIVE ORDERS

19.2–152.8. Emergency Protective Orders Authorized.
19.2–152.9. Preliminary Protective Orders.
19.2–152.10. Protective Order.
19.2–152.11. Venue for Protective Orders.
19.2–152.12. Compensation for Required Representation of Respondents.

CHAPTER 10. DISABILITY OF JUDGE OR ATTORNEY FOR COMMONWEALTH; COURT-APPOINTED COUNSEL; INTERPRETERS; TRANSCRIPTS

ARTICLE 1. DISABILITY OF JUDGE

19.2–153. When Judge Cannot Sit on Trial; How Another Judge Procured to Try the Case.
19.2–154. Death or Disability of Judge During Trial; How Another Judge Procured to Continue with Trial.

ARTICLE 2. DISABILITY OF ATTORNEY FOR COMMONWEALTH

19.2–155. Disqualification or Temporary Disability of Attorney for Commonwealth; Appointment of Substitute; Powers, Duties and Compensation of Such Appointee.
19.2–156. Prolonged Absence of Attorney for Commonwealth.

ARTICLE 3. APPOINTMENT OF ATTORNEY FOR ACCUSED

19.2–157. Duty of Court When Accused Appears Without Counsel.
19.2–158. When Person Not Free on Bail Shall Be Informed of Right to Counsel and Amount of Bail.
19.2–159. Determination of Indigency; Guidelines; Statement of Indigence; Appointment of Counsel.
19.2–159.1. Interrogation by Court; Filing; Change in Circumstances; Investigation by Attorney for Commonwealth.
19.2–160. Appointment of Counsel or Waiver of Right.
19.2–161. Penalty for False Swearing with Regard to Statement of Indigence.
19.2–162. Continuances to Be Granted If Necessary.
19.2–163. Compensation of Court-Appointed Counsel.

ARTICLE 3.1. INDIGENT DEFENSE

19.2–163.01. Virginia Indigent Defense Commission Established; Powers and Duties.
19.2–163.01:1. Supplementing Compensation of Public Defender.
19.2–163.02. Membership of Indigent Defense Commission; Expenses.
19.2–163.03. Qualifications for Court-Appointed Counsel.
19.2–163.04. Public Defender Offices.

ARTICLE 4. PUBLIC DEFENDERS

19.2–163.1, 19.2–163.2. Repealed by Acts 2004, cc. 884 and 921.
19.2–163.3. Duties of Public Defenders.
19.2–163.4. Inapplicability of §§ 17.1–606 and 19.2–163 Where Public Defender Offices Established; Exception.

Section

19.2–163.4:1. Repayment of Representation Costs by Convicted Persons.
19.2–163.5. Legal Services to Public Defenders And/or Assistant Public Defenders.
19.2–163.6. Repealed by Acts 2004, cc. 884 and 921.

ARTICLE 4.1. COUNSEL IN CAPITAL CASES

19.2–163.7. Counsel in Capital Cases.
19.2–163.8. List of Qualified Attorneys.

ARTICLE 5. INTERPRETERS

19.2–164. Interpreters for Non-English-Speaking Persons (Supreme Court Rule 2:507 Derived in Part from This Section).
19.2–164.1. Interpreters for the Deaf (Supreme Court Rule 2:507 Derived in Part from This Section).

ARTICLE 6. RECORDING EVIDENCE AND INCIDENTS OF TRIAL

19.2–165. Recording Evidence and Incidents of Trial in Felony Cases; Cost of Recording; Cost of Transcripts; Certified Transcript Deemed Prima Facie Correct; Request for Copy of Transcript.
19.2–165.1. Payment of Medical Fees in Certain Criminal Cases; Reimbursement.
19.2–166. Court Reporters.

CHAPTER 11. PROCEEDINGS ON QUESTION OF INSANITY

19.2–167. Accused Not to Be Tried While Insane or Feebleminded.
19.2–168. Notice to Commonwealth of Intention to Present Evidence of Insanity; Continuance If Notice Not Given.
19.2–168.1. Evaluation on Motion of the Commonwealth After Notice.
19.2–169. Repealed by Acts 1982, c. 653.
19.2–169.1. Raising Question of Competency to Stand Trial or Plead; Evaluation and Determination of Competency.
19.2–169.2. Disposition When Defendant Found Incompetent.
19.2–169.3. Disposition of the Unrestorably Incompetent Defendant; Capital Murder Charge; Sexually Violent Offense Charge.
19.2–169.4. Litigating Certain Issues When the Defendant Is Incompetent.
19.2–169.5. Evaluation of Sanity at the Time of the Offense; Disclosure of Evaluation Results.
19.2–169.6. Inpatient Psychiatric Hospital Admission from Local Correctional Facility.
19.2–169.7. Disclosure by Defendant During Evaluation or Treatment; Use at Guilt Phase of Trial.
19.2–170. to 19.2–174. Repealed by Acts 1982, c. 653.
19.2–174.1. Information Required Prior to Admission to a Mental Health Facility.
19.2–175. Compensation of Experts.
19.2–176. Repealed by Acts 2010, cc. 340 and 406.
19.2–177. Repealed by Acts 1988, c. 787; Acts 1988, c. 873.
19.2–177.1. Repealed by Acts 2010, cc. 340 and 406.
19.2–178. Where Prisoner Kept When No Vacancy in Facility or Hospital.
19.2–179. Repealed by Acts 1981, c. 310.

Section

19.2–180. Sentence or Trial of Prisoner When Restored to Sanity.
19.2–181. Repealed by Acts 1991, c. 427.
19.2–182. Representation by Counsel in Proceeding for Commitment.
19.2–182.1. Repealed by Acts 1982, c. 653.

CHAPTER 11.1. DISPOSITION OF PERSONS ACQUITTED BY REASON OF INSANITY

19.2–182.2. Verdict of Acquittal by Reason of Insanity to State the Fact; Temporary Custody and Evaluation.
19.2–182.3. Commitment; Civil Proceedings.
19.2–182.4. Confinement and Treatment; Interfacility Transfers; Out–Of–Hospital Visits; Notice of Change in Treatment.
19.2–182.5. Review of Continuation of Confinement Hearing; Procedure and Reports; Disposition.
19.2–182.6. Petition for Release; Conditional Release Hearing; Notice; Disposition.
19.2–182.7. Conditional Release; Criteria; Conditions; Reports.
19.2–182.8. Revocation of Conditional Release.
19.2–182.9. Emergency Custody of Conditionally Released Acquittee.
19.2–182.10. Release of Person Whose Conditional Release Was Revoked.
19.2–182.11. Modification or Removal of Conditions; Notice; Objections; Review.
19.2–182.12. Representation of Commonwealth and Acquittee.
19.2–182.13. Authority of Commissioner; Delegation to Board; Liability.
19.2–182.14. Escape of Persons Placed or Committed; Penalty.
19.2–182.15. Escape of Persons Placed on Conditional Release; Penalty.
19.2–182.16. Copies of Orders to Commissioner.

CHAPTER 12. PRELIMINARY HEARING

19.2–183. Examination of Witnesses; Assistance of Counsel; Evidentiary Matters and Remedies; Power to Adjourn Case.
19.2–183.1. Joint Preliminary Hearings.
19.2–184. Witnesses May Be Separated (Subsection (a) of Supreme Court Rule 2:615 Derived in Part from This Section).
19.2–185. Testimony May Be Reduced to Writing and Subscribed.
19.2–186. When Accused to Be Discharged, Tried, Committed or Bailed by Judge.
19.2–187. Admission Into Evidence of Certain Certificates of Analysis.
19.2–187.01. Certificate of Analysis as Evidence of Chain of Custody of Material Described Therein.
19.2–187.02. Admissibility of Written Reports or Records of Blood Alcohol Tests Conducted in the Regular Course of Providing Emergency Medical Treatment.
19.2–187.1. Procedures for Notifying Accused of Certificate of Analysis; Waiver; Continuances.
19.2–187.2. Procedure for Subpoena Duces Tecum of Analysis Evidence.
19.2–188. Reports by Chief Medical Examiner Received as Evidence.

Section

19.2–188.1. Testimony Regarding Identification of Controlled Substances.
19.2–188.2. Certificate of Surgeon as Evidence.
19.2–188.3. Admissibility of Affidavits by Government Officials Regarding a Search of Government Records (Subdivision (10)(b) of Supreme Court Rule 2:803 Derived from This Section).
19.2–189. Commitment of Accused for Further Examination.
19.2–190. To Whom, and When, Examination and Recognizance to Be Certified.
19.2–190.1. Certification of Ancillary Misdemeanor Offenses.

CHAPTER 13. GRAND JURIES

ARTICLE 1. IN GENERAL

19.2–191. Functions of a Grand Jury.
19.2–192. Secrecy in Grand Jury Proceedings.
19.2–192.1. Sealing of Indictment.

ARTICLE 2. REGULAR GRAND JURIES

19.2–193. Number of Regular Grand Juries.
19.2–194. When and How Grand Jurors to Be Selected and Summoned; Lists to Be Delivered to Clerk.
19.2–195. Number and Qualifications of Grand Jurors.
19.2–196. How Deficiency of Jurors Supplied.
19.2–197. Foreman of Grand Jury; Oaths of Jurors and Witnesses.
19.2–198. When New Foreman or Juror May Be Sworn In.
19.2–199. Judge to Charge Grand Jury.
19.2–200. Duties of Grand Jury.
19.2–201. Officers to Give Information of Violation of Penal Laws to Attorney for Commonwealth.
19.2–202. How Indictments Found and Presentment Made.
19.2–203. Indictments Ignored May Be Sent to Another Grand Jury; What Irregularities Not to Vitiate Indictment, Etc.
19.2–204. Penalties on Officers and Jurors for Failure of Duty.
19.2–205. Pay and Mileage of Grand Jurors.

ARTICLE 3. SPECIAL GRAND JURIES

19.2–206. When Impanelled.
19.2–207. Composition of a Special Grand Jury.
19.2–208. Subpoena Power of Special Grand Jury.
19.2–209. Presence of Counsel for a Witness.
19.2–210. Presence of Attorney for the Commonwealth.
19.2–211. Provision for Special Counsel and Other Personnel.
19.2–212. Provision for Court Reporter; Use and Disposition of Notes, Tapes and Transcriptions.
19.2–213. Report by Special Grand Jury; Return of True Bill.
19.2–213.1. Discharge of Special Grand Jury.
19.2–214. Prosecutions Resulting from Report.
19.2–215. Costs of Special Grand Jury.

ARTICLE 4. MULTI-JURISDICTION GRAND JURIES

19.2–215.1. Functions of a Multijurisdiction Grand Jury.

Section

19.2–215.2. Application for Such Grand Jury.
19.2–215.3. When Impaneled; Impaneling Order.
19.2–215.4. Number and Qualifications of Jurors; Grand Jury List; When Convened; Compensation of Jurors.
19.2–215.5. Subpoena Power; Counsel for Witness; Oath.
19.2–215.6. Role and Presence of Special Counsel; Examination of Witnesses; Sworn Investigators.
19.2–215.7. Warnings Given to Witnesses; When Witness in Contempt; Use of Testimony Compelled After Witness Invokes Right Against Self-Incrimination.
19.2–215.8. Returning a "True Bill" of Indictment; Jurisdiction to Be Set Out.
19.2–215.9. Court Reporter Provided; Safekeeping of Transcripts, Notes, Etc.; When Disclosure Permitted; Access to Record of Testimony and Evidence.
19.2–215.10. Participation by Office of Attorney General; Assistance of Special Counsel Permitted in Certain Prosecutions.
19.2–215.11. Discharge of Grand Jury.

CHAPTER 14. PRESENTMENTS, INDICTMENTS AND INFORMATIONS

ARTICLE 1. NECESSITY FOR INDICTMENT, ETC.

19.2–216. Definition of Indictment, Presentment and Information.
19.2–217. When Information Filed; Prosecution for Felony to Be by Indictment or Presentment; Waiver; Process to Compel Appearance of Accused.
19.2–217.1. Central File of Capital Murder Indictments.
19.2–218. Preliminary Hearing Required for Person Arrested on Charge of Felony; Waiver.
19.2–218.1. Preliminary Hearings Involving Certain Sexual Crimes Against Spouses.
19.2–218.2. Hearing Before Juvenile and Domestic Relations District Court Required for Persons Accused of Certain Violations Against Their Spouses.
19.2–219. When Capias Need Not Be Issued; Summons; Judgment.

ARTICLE 2. FORM AND REQUISITES

19.2–220. Contents of Indictment in General.
19.2–221. Form of Prosecutions Generally; Murder and Manslaughter.
19.2–222. Repealed by Acts 1996, c. 676.
19.2–223. Charging Several Acts of Embezzlement; Description of Money.
19.2–224. In Prosecution for Forgery, Unnecessary to Set Forth Copy of Forged Instrument.
19.2–225. Allegation of Intent.
19.2–226. What Defects in Indictments Not to Vitiate Them.
19.2–227. When Judgment Not to Be Arrested or Reversed.
19.2–228. Name and Address of Complaining Witness to Be Written on Indictment, Etc., for Misdemeanor.
19.2–229. When Complaining Witness Required to Give Security for Costs.
19.2–230. Bill of Particulars.

Section

ARTICLE 3. AMENDMENTS

19.2–231. Amendment of Indictment, Presentment or Information.

ARTICLE 4. PROCESS

19.2–232. What Process to Be Awarded Against Accused on Indictment, Etc.
19.2–233. How Awarded, Directed, Returnable and Executed.
19.2–234. Procedure When Person Arrested Under Capias.
19.2–235. Clerks to Mail Process to Officers in Other Counties, Etc.
19.2–236. Where Process of Arrest May Be Executed.
19.2–237. Process on Indictment or Presentment for Misdemeanor.
19.2–238. Summons Against Corporation; Proceedings; Expense of Publication.

CHAPTER 15. TRIAL AND ITS INCIDENTS

ARTICLE 1. JURISDICTION

19.2–239. Jurisdiction in Criminal Cases.
19.2–240. Clerks Shall Make Out Criminal Docket.
19.2–241. Time Within Which Court to Set Criminal Cases for Trial.
19.2–242. Accused Discharged from Jail If Not Indicted in Time.
19.2–243. Limitation on Prosecution of Felony Due to Lapse of Time After Finding of Probable Cause; Misdemeanors; Exceptions.

ARTICLE 2. VENUE

19.2–244. Venue in General.
19.2–245. Offenses Committed Without and Made Punishable Within Commonwealth; Embezzlement or Larceny Committed Within Commonwealth; Where Prosecuted.
19.2–245.01. Offenses Involving Reports or Statements Concerning Cigarette Sales or Stamping.
19.2–245.1. Forgery; Where Prosecuted.
19.2–245.2. Tax Offenses; Where Prosecuted.
19.2–246. Injury Inflicted by Person Within Commonwealth Upon One Outside Commonwealth.
19.2–247. Venue in Certain Homicide Cases.
19.2–248. Venue When Mortal Wound, Etc., Inflicted in One County and Death Ensues in Another.
19.2–249. Offenses Committed on Boundary of Two Counties, Two Cities, or County and City, Etc.; Where Prosecuted.
19.2–249.1. Offenses Committed Within Towns Situated in Two or More Counties; Where Prosecuted.
19.2–249.2. Venue for Prosecution of Computer and Other Crimes.
19.2–250. How Far Jurisdiction of Corporate Authorities Extends.
19.2–251. When and How Venue May Be Changed.
19.2–252. Court Ordering Change of Venue May Admit Accused to Bail and Recognize Witnesses; Remand of Accused Not Admitted to Bail.
19.2–253. Procedure Upon and After Change of Venue.

Section

ARTICLE 3. ARRAIGNMENT; PLEAS; TRIAL WITHOUT JURY

19.2–254. Arraignment; Pleas; When Court May Refuse to Accept Plea; Rejection of Plea Agreement; Recusal.
19.2–254.1. Procedure in Traffic Infraction Cases.
19.2–254.2. Procedure in Nontraffic Offenses for Which Prepayment Is Authorized.
19.2–255. Defendant Allowed to Plead Several Matters of Law or Fact.
19.2–256. Approvers.
19.2–257. Trial Without Jury in Felony Cases.
19.2–258. Trial of Misdemeanors by Court Without Jury; Failure to Appear Deemed Waiver of Jury.
19.2–258.1. Trial of Traffic Infractions; Measure of Proof; Failure to Appear.
19.2–259. On Trial for Felony, Accused to Be Present; When Court May Enter Plea for Him, and Trial Go On.

ARTICLE 4. TRIAL BY JURY

19.2–260. Provisions of Title 8.01 Apply Except as Provided in This Article.
19.2–261. Charging Grand Jury in Presence of Person Selected as Juror.
19.2–262. Waiver of Jury Trial; Numbers of Jurors in Criminal Cases; How Jurors Selected from Panel.
19.2–262.1. Joinder of Defendants.
19.2–263. Repealed by Acts 1993, cc. 462 and 489.
19.2–263.1. Contact Between Judge and Juror Prohibited.
19.2–263.2. Jury Instructions.
19.2–263.3. Juror Information Confidential.
19.2–264. When Jury Need Not Be Kept Together in Felony Case; Sufficient Compliance with Requirement That Jury Be Kept Together.
19.2–264.1. Views by Juries.

ARTICLE 4.1. TRIAL OF CAPITAL CASES

19.2–264.2. Conditions for Imposition of Death Sentence.
19.2–264.3. Procedure for Trial by Jury.
19.2–264.3:1. Expert Assistance When Defendant's Mental Condition Relevant to Capital Sentencing.
19.2–264.3:1.1. Capital Cases; Determination of Mental Retardation.
19.2–264.3:1.2. Expert Assistance When Issue of Defendant's Mental Retardation Relevant to Capital Sentencing.
19.2–264.3:1.3. Expert Assistance for Indigent Defendants in Capital Cases.
19.2–264.3:2. Notice to the Defendant of Intention to Present Evidence of Unadjudicated Criminal Conduct.
19.2–264.3:3. Limitations on Use of Statements or Disclosure by Defendant During Evaluations.
19.2–264.3:4. Notice of Expert Testimony in Capital Case.
19.2–264.4. Sentence Proceeding.
19.2–264.5. Post-Sentence Reports.

ARTICLE 5. MISCELLANEOUS PROVISIONS

19.2–265. Opening Statement of Counsel.
19.2–265.01. Victims, Certain Members of the Family and Support Persons Not to Be Excluded.
19.2–265.1. Exclusion of Witnesses (Subsection (a) of Supreme Court Rule 2:615 Derived in Part from This Section and Subsection (c) of

Section

Supreme Court Rule 2:615 Derived from This Section).
19.2–265.2. Judicial Notice of Laws (Supreme Court Rule 2:202 Derived in Part from This Section).
19.2–265.3. Nolle Prosequi; Discretion of Court Upon Good Cause Shown.
19.2–265.4. Failure to Provide Discovery.
19.2–265.5. Prosecuting Misdemeanor Cases Without Attorney.
19.2–265.6. Effect of Dismissal of Criminal Charges.
19.2–266. Exclusion of Persons from Trial; Photographs and Broadcasting Permitted Under Designated Guidelines; Exceptions.
19.2–266.1. Conviction of Lesser Offense on Indictment for Homicide.
19.2–266.2. Defense Objections to Be Raised Before Trial; Hearing; Bill of Particulars.
19.2–266.3. Continuances; Appearances of Parties.

CHAPTER 16. EVIDENCE AND WITNESSES

ARTICLE 1. IN GENERAL

19.2–267. Provisions Applicable to Witnesses in Criminal as Well as Civil Cases; Obligation to Attend; Summons.
19.2–267.1. Authority of Law-Enforcement Officer to Issue Summons to Witness; Failure to Appear.
19.2–267.2. Response to Subpoena for Information Stored in Electronic Format.
19.2–268. Right of Accused to Testify.
19.2–268.1. Contradiction by Prior Inconsistent Writing (Subdivision (b)(i) of Supreme Court Rule 2:613 Derived in Part from This Section).
19.2–268.2. Recent Complaint Hearsay Exception (Subdivision (23) of Supreme Court Rule 2:803 Derived from This Section).
19.2–269. Convicts as Witnesses (Supreme Court Rule 2:609 Derived from This Section).
19.2–269.1. Inmates as Witnesses in Criminal Cases.
19.2–269.2. Nondisclosure of Addresses or Telephone Numbers of Crime Victims and Witnesses.
19.2–270. When Statement by Accused as Witness Not Received as Evidence.
19.2–270.1. Use of Photographs as Evidence in Certain Larceny and Burglary Prosecutions.
19.2–270.1:1. Computer and Electronic Data in Obscenity, Etc. Cases; Access to Defendant.
19.2–270.2. Disposition of Money, Securities or Documents Seized Upon Arrest, Etc., and Pertinent as Evidence.
19.2–270.3. Admissible Evidence as to Identity of Party Presenting Bad Check, Draft or Order.
19.2–270.4. When Donation, Destruction, or Return of Exhibits Received in Evidence Authorized.
19.2–270.4:1. Storage, Preservation and Retention of Human Biological Evidence in Felony Cases.
19.2–270.5. DNA Profile Admissible in Criminal Proceeding.
19.2–270.6. Evidence of Abuse Admissible in Certain Criminal Trials (Supreme Court Rule 2:409 Derived from This Section).
19.2–270.7. Determining Decibel Level of Sound with Proper Equipment; Certificate as to Accuracy of Equipment.

Section

19.2–271. Certain Judicial Officers Incompetent to Testify Under Certain Circumstances; Exceptions (Supreme Court Rule 2:605 Derived from This Section).
19.2–271.1. Competency of Husband and Wife to Testify.
19.2–271.2. Testimony of Husband and Wife in Criminal Cases (Subsection (b) of Supreme Court Rule 2:504 Derived from This Section).
19.2–271.3. Communications Between Ministers of religion and Persons They Counsel or Advise (Supreme Court Rule 2:503 Derived in Part from This Section).
19.2–271.4. Privileged Communications by Certain Public Safety Personnel.

ARTICLE 2. WITNESSES FROM OR FOR ANOTHER STATE

19.2–272. Definitions.
19.2–273. Certificate That Witness Is Needed in Another State; Hearing.
19.2–274. When Court to Order Witness to Attend.
19.2–275. Arrest of Witness.
19.2–276. Penalty for Failure to Attend and Testify.
19.2–277. Summoning Witnesses in Another State to Testify in This Commonwealth.
19.2–278. Reimbursement for Daily Mileage to Such Witnesses; Issuance of Warrant Necessary to Make Tender.
19.2–279. Penalty for Failure of Such Witnesses to Testify.
19.2–280. Exemption of Such Witnesses from Arrest or Service of Process.
19.2–281. Construction of Article.
19.2–282. How Article Cited.

CHAPTER 17. CONVICTIONS; EFFECT THEREOF

ARTICLE 1. PROOF AND VERDICTS

19.2–283. How Accused May Be Convicted of Felony.
19.2–284. Proof of Ownership in Offense relating to Property.
19.2–285. Accused Guilty of Part of Offense Charged; Sentence; on New Trial What Tried.
19.2–286. Conviction of Attempt or as Accessory on Indictment for Felony; Effect of General Verdict of Not Guilty.
19.2–287. Verdict and Judgment, When Jury Agree as to Some and Disagree as to Others.
19.2–288. Verdict When Accused Found Guilty of Punishable Homicide.
19.2–289. Conviction of Petit Larceny.
19.2–290. Conviction of Petit Larceny Though Thing Stolen Worth More Than $200.
19.2–291. Faulty Counts; Motion to Strike; General Verdict of Guilty.
19.2–291.1. Report of Conviction of School Employees for Certain Offenses.

ARTICLE 2. FORMER JEOPARDY

19.2–292. Acquittal by Jury on Merits Bar to Further Prosecution for Same Offense.
19.2–293. When Acquittal Not a Bar to Further Prosecution for Same Offense.
19.2–294. Offense Against Two or More Statutes or Ordinances.

Section

19.2–294.1. Dismissal of One of Dual Charges for Driving While Intoxicated and Reckless Driving Upon Conviction of Other Charge.

ARTICLE 3. CONVICTION OF ALIENS

19.2–294.2. Procedure When Aliens Convicted of Certain Felonies; Duties of Probation and Parole Officer.

CHAPTER 18. SENTENCE; JUDGMENT; EXECUTION OF SENTENCE

ARTICLE 1. GENERAL PROVISIONS

19.2–295. Ascertainment of Punishment.
19.2–295.1. Sentencing Proceeding by the Jury After Conviction.
19.2–295.2. Postrelease Supervision of Felons Sentenced for Offenses Committed on and After January 1, 1995, and on and After July 1, 2000.
19.2–295.2:1. Postrelease Supervision of Felons Sentenced for Certain Offenses Committed on or After July 1, 2006.
19.2–295.3. Admission of Victim Impact Testimony.
19.2–296. Withdrawal of Plea of Guilty.
19.2–297. Repealed by Acts 1994, c. 706.
19.2–297.1. Sentence of Person Twice Previously Convicted of Certain Violent Felonies.
19.2–298. Pronouncement of Sentence.
19.2–298.01. Use of Discretionary Sentencing Guidelines.
19.2–298.1. to 19.2–298.4. Repealed by Acts 2003, c. 584.
19.2–299. Investigations and Reports by Probation Officers in Certain Cases.
19.2–299.1. When Victim Impact Statement Required; Contents; Uses.
19.2–299.2. Alcohol and Substance Abuse Screening and Assessment for Designated Class 1 Misdemeanor Convictions.
19.2–300. Deferring for Mental Examination Sentence of Person Convicted of Offense Indicating Sexual Abnormality.
19.2–301. Judge Shall Require Examination Under § 19.2–300; by Whom Made; Report; Expenses of Psychiatrist.
19.2–302. Construction and Administration of §§ 19.2–300 and 19.2–301.
19.2–303. Suspension or Modification of Sentence; Probation; Taking of Fingerprints and Blood, Saliva, or Tissue Sample as Condition of Probation.
19.2–303.1. Fixing Period of Suspension of Sentence.
19.2–303.2. Persons Charged with First Offense May Be Placed on Probation.
19.2–303.3. Sentence to Local Community-Based Probation Services; Services Agency; Requirements for Participation; Sentencing; and Removal from Probation; Payment of Costs Towards Supervision and Services.
19.2–303.4. Payment of Costs When Proceedings Deferred and Defendant Placed on Probation.
19.2–303.5. Immediate Sanction Probation Programs.
19.2–304. Increasing or Decreasing Probation Period and Modification of Conditions.
19.2–305. Requiring Fines, Costs, Restitution for Damages, Support or Community Services from Probationer.

Section

19.2–305.1. Restitution for Property Damage or Loss; Community Service.
19.2–305.2. Amount of Restitution; Enforcement.
19.2–305.3. Repealed by Acts 1997, c. 140.
19.2–305.4. When Interest to Be Paid on Award of Restitution.
19.2–306. Revocation of Suspension of Sentence and Probation.
19.2–307. Contents of Judgment Order.
19.2–308. When Two or More Sentences Run Concurrently.
19.2–308.1. When Sentence May Run Concurrently with Sentence in Another Jurisdiction.
19.2–309. Sentence of Confinement for Conviction of a Combination of Felony and Misdemeanor Offenses.
19.2–309.1. Sentence of Confinement to Jail Farms Maintained by the Cities of Danville, Martinsville and Newport News.
19.2–310. Transfer of Prisoners to Custody of Director of Department of Corrections.
19.2–310.01. Transmission of Sentencing Documents.
19.2–310.1. Repealed by Acts 1982, c. 636.

ARTICLE 1.1. DNA ANALYSIS AND DATA BANK

19.2–310.2. Blood, Saliva, or Tissue Sample Required for DNA Analysis Upon Conviction of Certain Crimes; Fee.
19.2–310.2:1. Saliva or Tissue Sample Required for DNA Analysis After Arrest for a Violent Felony.
19.2–310.3. Procedures for Withdrawal of Blood, Saliva or Tissue Sample for DNA Analysis.
19.2–310.3:1. Procedures for Taking Saliva or Tissue Sample for DNA Analysis.
19.2–310.4. Procedures for Conducting DNA Analysis of Blood, Saliva or Tissue Sample.
19.2–310.5. DNA Data Bank.
19.2–310.6. Unauthorized Uses of DNA Data Bank; Forensic Samples; Penalties.
19.2–310.7. Expungement When DNA Taken for a Conviction.

ARTICLE 2. INDETERMINATE COMMITMENT

19.2–311. Indeterminate Commitment to Department of Corrections in Certain Cases; Duration and Character of Commitment; Concurrence by Department.
19.2–312. Repealed by Acts 1990, c. 701.
19.2–313. Eligibility for Release.
19.2–314. Supervision of Persons Released.
19.2–315. Compliance With Terms and Conditions of Parole; Time on Parole Not Counted as Part of Commitment Period.
19.2–316. Evaluation and Report Prior to Determining Punishment.

ARTICLE 3. BOOT CAMP INCARCERATION PROGRAM

19.2–316.1. Eligibility for Participation; Evaluation; Sentencing; Withdrawal or Removal from Program.

ARTICLE 4. DETENTION CENTER INCARCERATION PROGRAM

19.2–316.2. Eligibility for Participation in Detention Center Incarceration Program; Evaluation; Sentencing; Withdrawal or Removal from Program.

Section

ARTICLE 5. DIVERSION CENTER INCARCERATION PROGRAM

19.2–316.3. Eligibility for Participation in Diversion Center Incarceration Program; Evaluation; Sentencing; Withdrawal or Removal from Program; Payment for Costs.

CHAPTER 19. EXCEPTIONS AND WRITS OF ERROR

19.2–317. When Writ of Error Lies in Criminal Case for Accused; When for Commonwealth; When for County, City or Town.
19.2–317.1. Repealed by Acts 1990, c. 74.
19.2–318. Appeal on Writ of Error to Judgment for Contempt.
19.2–319. When Execution of Sentence to Be Suspended; Bail; Appeal from Denial.
19.2–320. Petitioner for Writ of Error to Comply with Rules of Court.
19.2–321. With Whom Petition for Writ of Error Filed.
19.2–321.1. Motion in the Court of Appeals for Delayed Appeal in Criminal Cases.
19.2–321.2. Motion in the Supreme Court for Delayed Appeal in Criminal Cases.
19.2–322. Repealed by Acts 1984, c. 703.
19.2–322.1. Suspension of Execution of Judgment on Appeal.
19.2–323. Denial by Judge or Justice No Bar to Allowance by Court.
19.2–324. Decision of Appellate Court.
19.2–324.1. Erroneously Admitted Evidence; Appeal.
19.2–325. Provisions Which Apply to Criminal as Well as Civil Cases; When Plaintiff in Error Unable to Pay Printing Costs.
19.2–326. Payment of Expenses of Appeals of Indigent Defendants.
19.2–327. How Judgment of Appellate Court Certified and Entered.
19.2–327.01. Repealed by Acts 2004, c. 337.

CHAPTER 19.1. SCIENTIFIC ANALYSIS OF NEWLY DISCOVERED OR UNTESTED SCIENTIFIC EVIDENCE

19.2–327.1. Motion by a Convicted Felon or Person Adjudicated Delinquent for Scientific Analysis of Newly Discovered or Previously Untested Scientific Evidence; Procedure.

CHAPTER 19.2. ISSUANCE OF WRIT OF ACTUAL INNOCENCE

19.2–327.2. Issuance of Writ of Actual Innocence Based on Biological Evidence.
19.2–327.2:1. Petition for Writ of Actual Innocence Joined by Attorney General; Release of Prisoner; Bond Hearing.
19.2–327.3. Contents and Form of the Petition Based on Previously Unknown or Untested Human Biological Evidence of Actual Innocence.
19.2–327.4. Determination by the Supreme Court for Findings of Fact by the Circuit Court.
19.2–327.5. Relief Under Writ.
19.2–327.6. Claims of Relief.

Section

CHAPTER 19.3. ISSUANCE OF WRIT OF ACTUAL INNOCENCE BASED ON NONBIOLOGICAL EVIDENCE

19.2–327.10. Issuance of Writ of Actual Innocence Based on Nonbiological Evidence.
19.2–327.10:1. Petition for Writ of Actual Innocence Joined by Attorney General; release of Prisoner; Bond Hearing.
19.2–327.11. Contents and Form of the Petition Based on Previously Unknown or Unavailable Evidence of Actual Innocence.
19.2–327.12. Determination by Court of Appeals for Findings of Fact by the Circuit Court.
19.2–327.13. Relief Under Writ.
19.2–327.14. Claims of Relief.

CHAPTER 20. TAXATION AND ALLOWANCE OF COSTS

19.2–328. When Jailers and Sheriffs to Summon or Employ Guards and Other Persons; Allowances Therefor.
19.2–329. Allowance to Witnesses.
19.2–330. Compensation to Witnesses from Out of Commonwealth.
19.2–331. When Commonwealth Pays Witnesses in Case of Misdemeanor.
19.2–332. Compensation to Officer or Other Person for Services Not Otherwise Compensable.
19.2–333. No State Fees to Attorney for the Commonwealth.
19.2–334. By Whom Certificate of Allowance to Be Made; Vouchers to Accompany It; Proof of Correctness; What Entry to State.
19.2–335. Judge of District Court to Certify to Clerk of Circuit Court Costs of Proceedings in Criminal Cases Before Him.
19.2–336. Clerk to Make Up Statement of Whole Cost, and Issue Execution Therefor.
19.2–337. Claims Not Presented in Time to Be Disallowed.
19.2–338. Collection by Town of Cost of Transporting Prisoners.

CHAPTER 21. RECOVERY OF FINES AND PENALTIES

ARTICLE 1. PROCEEDINGS TO RECOVER

19.2–339. Word "Fine" Construed.
19.2–340. Fines; How Recovered; in What Name.
19.2–340.1. Disposition of Fines in Criminal Cases.
19.2–341. Penalties Other Than Fines; How Recovered; in What Name; Limitation of Actions.
19.2–342. Where and in What Court Proceeding to Be.
19.2–343, 19.2–344. Reserved.

ARTICLE 2. REPORTS, ETC., OF FINES AND COSTS

19.2–345, 19.2–346. Repealed by Acts 1988, c. 509.
19.2–347. Repealed by Acts 1983, c. 499.

ARTICLE 3. COLLECTION AND DISPOSITION OF FINES

19.2–348. Attorneys for Commonwealth or Clerks to Superintend Issue of Executions, Etc.
19.2–349. Responsibility for Collections; Clerks to Report Unsatisfied Fines, Etc.; Duty of At-

Section

torneys for Commonwealth; Duties of Department of Taxation.
19.2–349.1. Receipt of Unpaid Fines, Costs, Forfeitures, Penalties, or Restitution by Department of Motor Vehicles.
19.2–350. When Sheriff Not to Receive Fines.
19.2–351. How Fines Disposed Of; Informer.
19.2–352. Officers to Pay Fines to Clerks; Default; Forfeiture, Etc.
19.2–353. Certain Fines Paid Into Literary Fund.
19.2–353.1. Fieri Facias and Proceedings Thereon.
19.2–353.2. Repealed by Acts 1988, cc. 770 and 852.
19.2–353.3. Acceptance of Checks and Credit or Debit Cards in Lieu of Money; Additional Fee.
19.2–353.4. Repealed by Acts 1988, cc. 770 and 852.
19.2–353.5. Interest on Fines and Costs.

ARTICLE 4. PAYMENT OF FINES AND COSTS ON INSTALLMENT BASIS, ETC.

19.2–354. Authority of Court to Order Payment of Fine, Costs, Forfeitures, Penalties or Restitution in Installments or Upon Other Terms and Conditions; Community Work in Lieu of Payment.
19.2–355. Petition of Defendant.
19.2–356. Payment of Fine or Costs as Condition of Probation or Suspension of Sentence.
19.2–357. Requiring That Defendant Be of Peace and Good Behavior Until Fine and Costs Are Paid.
19.2–358. Procedure on Default in Deferred Payment or Installment Payment of Fine, Costs, Forfeiture, Restitution or Penalty.

ARTICLE 5. RECEIPTS FOR FINES

19.2–359. Official Receipts to Be Given for Fines.
19.2–360. Forms of Receipts; Distribution; Record of Disposition.
19.2–361. Misuse, Misappropriation or Willful Failure to Account for Fines Is Embezzlement.

ARTICLE 6. RELIEF FROM FINES AND PENALTIES

19.2–362. Court Not to Remit Fine or Penalty, Other Than Fine for Contempt, Except as Provided in § 19.2–358.
19.2–363. Authority of Governor to Grant Relief From Fines and Penalties.
19.2–364. Petition for Relief; in What Court Filed; Notice to Attorney for Commonwealth.
19.2–365. Duties of Attorney for Commonwealth Upon Filing of Such Petition.
19.2–366. Duty of Court in Which Petition Filed; Certificate and Opinion.
19.2–367. Proceedings to Be According to Common Law.
19.2–368. Course of Proceeding When Relief Asked of the Governor.

CHAPTER 21.1. COMPENSATING VICTIMS OF CRIME

19.2–368.1. Findings; Legislative Intent.
19.2–368.2. Definitions.
19.2–368.3. Powers and Duties of Commission.
19.2–368.3:1. Crime Victims' Ombudsman.
19.2–368.4. Persons Eligible for Awards.

Section

19.2–368.5. Filing of Claims; Deferral of Proceedings; Restitution.
19.2–368.5:1. Failure to Perfect Claim; Denial.
19.2–368.5:2. Effect of Filing a Claim; Stay of Debt Collection Activities by Health Care Providers.
19.2–368.6. Assignment of Claims; Investigation; Hearing; Confidentiality of Records; Decisions.
19.2–368.7. Review by Commission.
19.2–368.8. Reinvestigation of Decision; Reconsideration of Award; Judicial Review.
19.2–368.9. Emergency Awards.
19.2–368.10. When Awards to Be Made; Reporting Crime and Cooperation with Law Enforcement.
19.2–368.11. Repealed by Acts 1986, c. 457.
19.2–368.11:1. Amount of Award.
19.2–368.12. Awards Not Subject to Execution or Attachment; Apportionment; Reductions.
19.2–368.13. Repealed by Acts 1984, c. 619.
19.2–368.14. Public Record; Exception.
19.2–368.15. Subrogation of Commonwealth to Claimant's Right of Action; Lien in Favor of the Commonwealth; Disposition of Funds Collected.
19.2–368.16. Claims to Be Made Under Oath.
19.2–368.17. Public Information Program.
19.2–368.18. Criminal Injuries Compensation Fund.

CHAPTER 21.2. PROFITS FROM CRIME

19.2–368.19. Definitions.
19.2–368.20. Special Order of Escrow.
19.2–368.21. Distribution.
19.2–368.22. Actions to Defeat Chapter Void.

CHAPTER 22. ENFORCEMENT OF FORFEITURES

19.2–369. to 19.2–386. Repealed by Acts 2012, cc. 283 and 756.

CHAPTER 22.1. ENFORCEMENT OF FORFEITURES

19.2–386.1. Commencing an Action of Forfeiture.
19.2–386.2. Seizure of Named Property.
19.2–386.2:1. Notice to Commissioner of Department of Motor Vehicles; Duties of Commissioner.
19.2–386.3. Notice of Seizure for Forfeiture and Notice of Motion for Judgment.
19.2–386.4. Records and Handling of Seized Property.
19.2–386.5. Release of Seized Property.
19.2–386.6. Bond to Secure Possession.
19.2–386.7. Sale of Property Liable to Deterioration.
19.2–386.8. Exemptions.
19.2–386.9. Appearance by Owner or Lien Holder.
19.2–386.10. Trial.
19.2–386.11. Judgment of Condemnation; Destruction.
19.2–386.12. Sale of Forfeited Property.
19.2–386.13. Writ of Error and Supersedeas.
19.2–386.14. Sharing of Forfeited Assets.

CHAPTER 22.2. MISCELLANEOUS FORFEITURE PROVISIONS

19.2–386.15. Seizure of Property Used in Connection with or Derived from Terrorism.
19.2–386.16. Forfeiture of Motor Vehicles Used in Commission of Certain Crimes.
19.2–386.17. Forfeitures for Computer Crimes.
19.2–386.18. Forfeiture of Unlawful Electronic Communication Devices.

Section
19.2–386.19. Seizure of Property Used in Connection with Money Laundering.
19.2–386.20. Forfeiture of Cigarettes Sold or Attempted to Be Sold in an Unlawful Delivery Sale.
19.2–386.21. Forfeiture of Counterfeit and Contraband Cigarettes.
19.2–386.21. Forfeiture of Counterfeit and Contraband Cigarettes.
19.2–386.22. Seizure of Property Used in Connection with or Derived from Illegal Drug Transactions.
19.2–386.23. Disposal of Seized Controlled Substances, Marijuana, and Paraphernalia.
19.2–386.24. Destruction of Seized Controlled Substances or Marijuana Prior to Trial.
19.2–386.25. Judge May Order Law-Enforcement Agency to Maintain Custody of Controlled Substances, Etc.
19.2–386.26. Seizure and Forfeiture of Drug Paraphernalia.
19.2–386.27. Forfeiture of Firearms Carried in Violation of Article 6.1 (§ 18.2–307.1 Et Seq.).
19.2–386.28. Forfeiture of Weapons That Are Concealed, Possessed, Transported or Carried in Violation of Law.
19.2–386.29. Forfeiture of Certain Weapons Used in Commission of Criminal Offense.
19.2–386.30. Forfeiture of Money, Gambling Devices, Etc., Seized from Illegal Gambling Enterprise; Innocent Owners or Lienors.
19.2–386.31. Seizure and Forfeiture of Property Used in Connection with the Exploitation and Solicitation of Children.
19.2–386.32. Seizure and Forfeiture of Property Used in Connection with the Abduction of Children.
19.2–386.33. Forfeiture of Money, Etc., Derived from Violation of §§ 2.2–3103 Through 2.2–3112.
19.2–386.34. Forfeiture of Vehicle Used in a Felony Violation of § 18.2–266.
19.2–386.35. Seizure of Property Used in Connection with Certain Offenses.

CHAPTER 23. CENTRAL CRIMINAL RECORDS EXCHANGE

19.2–387. Exchange to Operate as a Division of Department of State Police; Authority of Superintendent of State Police.
19.2–387.1. Protective Order Registry; Maintenance; Access.
19.2–388. Duties and Authority of Exchange.
19.2–389. Dissemination of Criminal History Record Information.
19.2–389.1. Dissemination of Juvenile Record Information.
19.2–389.2. Background Checks of Applicants of the Metropolitan Washington Airports Authority.
19.2–390. Reports to Be Made by Local Law-Enforcement Officers, Conservators of the Peace, Clerks of Court, Secretary of the Commonwealth and Corrections Officials to State Police; Material Submitted by Other Agencies.
19.2–390.01. Use of Virginia Crime Code References Required.

Section
19.2–390.02. Policies and Procedures for Law Enforcement to Conduct In-Person and Photo Lineups.
19.2–390.1. Sex Offender and Crimes Against Minors Registry; Maintenance; Access.
19.2–390.2. Repealed by Acts 2003, c. 584.
19.2–390.3. Child Pornography Images Registry; Maintenance; Access.
19.2–391. Records to Be Made Available to Exchange by State Officials and Agencies; Duplication of Records.
19.2–392. Fingerprints and Photographs by Police Authorities.
19.2–392.01. Judges May Require Taking of Fingerprints and Photographs in Certain Misdemeanor Cases.
19.2–392.02. National Criminal Background Checks by Businesses and Organizations Regarding Employees or Volunteers Providing Care to Children, or the Elderly or Disabled.

CHAPTER 23.1. EXPUNGEMENT OF CRIMINAL RECORDS

19.2–392.1. Statement of Policy.
19.2–392.2. Expungement of Police and Court Records.
19.2–392.3. Disclosure of Expunged Records.
19.2–392.4. Prohibited Practices by Employers, Educational Institutions, Agencies, Etc., of State and Local Governments.

CHAPTER 24. INSPECTION WARRANTS

19.2–393. Definitions.
19.2–394. Issuance of Warrant.
19.2–395. Duration of Warrant.
19.2–396. Conduct of Inspection, Testing or Collection of Samples for Testing; Special Procedure for Dwelling.
19.2–397. Refusal to Permit Authorized Inspection; Penalty.

CHAPTER 25. APPEALS BY THE COMMONWEALTH

19.2–398. When Appeal by the Commonwealth Allowed.
19.2–399. Renumbered as § 19.2–266.2.
19.2–400. Appeal Lies to the Court of Appeals; Time for Filing Notice.
19.2–401. Cross Appeal; When Allowed; Time for Filing.
19.2–402. Petition for Appeal; Brief in Opposition; Time for Filing.
19.2–403. Procedures on Petition for Pretrial Appeal.
19.2–404. Procedures on Awarded Pretrial Appeal.
19.2–405. Pretrial Appeals; Record on Appeal; Transcript; Written Statement of Facts; Time for Filing.
19.2–406. Bail Pending Pretrial Appeal.
19.2–407. Review by the Supreme Court.
19.2–408. Finality of Decision of the Court of Appeals in Pretrial Appeals.
19.2–409. Exclusion of Pretrial Appeal Period from Time Within Which Accused Must Be Tried; Reconsideration of Issues After Conviction.

CHAPTER 1

GENERAL PROVISIONS

§ 19.2–1. Repealing clause

All acts and parts of acts, all sections of this Code, and all provisions of municipal charters, inconsistent with the provisions of this title, are, except as herein otherwise provided, repealed to the extent of such inconsistency.

Acts 1975, c. 495.

§ 19.2–2. Effect of repeal of Title 19.1 and enactment of this title

The repeal of Title 19.1 effective as of October 1, 1975, shall not affect any act or offense done or committed, or any penalty or forfeiture incurred, or any right established, accrued, or accruing on or before such date, or any prosecution, suit or action pending on that day. Except as herein otherwise provided, neither the repeal of Title 19.1 nor the enactment of this title shall apply to offenses committed prior to October 1, 1975, and prosecutions for such offenses shall be governed by the prior law, which is continued in effect for that purpose. For the purposes of this section, an offense was committed prior to October 1, 1975, if any of the essential elements of the offense occurred prior thereto.

Acts 1975, c. 495.

§ 19.2–3. Certain notices, recognizances and processes validated

Any notice given, recognizance taken, or process or writ issued before October 1, 1975, shall be valid although given, taken or to be returned to a day after such date, in like manner as if this title had been effective before the same was given, taken or issued.

Acts 1975, c. 495.

§ 19.2–3.1. Personal appearance by two-way electronic video and audio communication; standards

A. Where an appearance is required or permitted before a magistrate, intake officer or, prior to trial, before a judge, the appearance may be by (i) personal appearance before the magistrate, intake officer or judge or (ii) use of two-way electronic video and audio communication. If two-way electronic video and audio communication is used, a magistrate, intake officer or judge may exercise all powers conferred by law and all communications and proceedings shall be conducted in the same manner as if the appearance were in person. If two-way electronic video and audio communication is available for use by a district court for the conduct of a hearing to determine bail or to determine representation by counsel, the court shall use such communication in any such proceeding that would otherwise require the transportation of a person from outside the jurisdiction of the court in order to appear in person before the court. Any documents transmitted between the magistrate, intake officer, or judge and the person appearing before the magistrate, intake officer, or judge may be transmitted by electronically transmitted facsimile process or other electronic method. The facsimile or other electronically generated document may be served or executed by the officer or person to whom sent, and returned in the same manner, and with the same force, effect, authority, and liability as an original document. All signatures thereon shall be treated as original signatures.

B. Any two-way electronic video and audio communication system used for an appearance shall meet the following standards:

1. The persons communicating must simultaneously see and speak to one another;

2. The signal transmission must be live, real time;

3. The signal transmission must be secure from interception through lawful means by anyone other than the persons communicating; and

4. Any other specifications as may be promulgated by the Chief Justice of the Supreme Court.

Acts 1991, c. 41; Acts 1996, c. 755; Acts 1996, c. 914; Acts 2006, c. 285. Amended by Acts 2009, c. 94; Acts 2009, c. 623; Acts 2010, c. 800.

§ 19.2–4. References to former sections, articles or chapters of Titles 18.1 and 19.1

Whenever in this title any of the conditions, requirements, provisions or contents of any section, article or chapter of Titles 18.1 and 19.1, as such titles existed prior to October 1, 1975, are transferred in the same or in modified form to a new section, article or chapter of this title or of Title 18.2, and whenever any such former section, article or chapter is given a new number in this title or in Title 18.2, all references to any such former section, article or chapter of Title 19.1 or of Title 18.1 appearing elsewhere in this Code than in this title or in Title 18.2, shall be construed to apply to the new or renumbered section, article or chapter containing such conditions, requirements, provisions or contents or portions thereof.

Acts 1975, c. 495.

§ 19.2–5. Meaning of certain terms

As used in this title, unless otherwise clearly indicated by the context in which it appears:

"Court" means any court vested with appropriate jurisdiction under the Constitution and laws of the Commonwealth.

"Court not of record" and "district court" shall have the respective meanings assigned to them in Chapter 4.1 (§ 16.1–69.1 et seq.) of Title 16.1.

"Judge" means any judge, associate judge or substitute judge of any court or any magistrate.

Acts 1975, c. 495; Acts 2005, c. 839, eff. Oct. 1, 2005. Amended by Acts 2008, c. 551; Acts 2008, c. 691.

§ 19.2–6. Appointive power of circuit courts

Unless otherwise specifically provided, whenever an appointive power is given to the judge of a circuit court, that power shall be exercised by a majority of the judges of the circuit. In case of a tie, such fact shall be communicated to the Chief Justice of the Supreme Court, who shall appoint a circuit judge from another circuit who shall act as a tie breaker. Where the power of appointment is to be exercised by a majority of the judges of the Second Judicial Circuit and such appointment is to a local post, board or commission in Accomack or Northampton County, the resident judge or judges of the County of Accomack or Northampton shall exercise such appointment power as if he or they comprise the majority of the judges of the Circuit.

Acts 1975, c. 495; Acts 1977, c. 288; Acts 1994, c. 407.

§ 19.2–7. Rewards for arrest of persons convicted of or charged with offenses; rewards for conviction of unknown offenders

The Governor may offer a reward for apprehending and securing any person convicted of an offense or charged therewith, who shall have escaped from lawful custody or confinement, or for apprehending and securing any person charged with an offense, who, there is reason to fear, cannot be arrested in the common course of proceeding. The Governor may also offer a reward for the detection and conviction of the person guilty of an offense when such offense has been committed but the person guilty thereof is unknown.

Any sheriff, deputy sheriff, sergeant, deputy sergeant or any other officer may claim and receive any reward which may be offered for the arrest and detention of any offender against the criminal laws of this or any other state or nation.

Acts 1975, c. 495.

§ 19.2–8. Limitation of prosecutions

A prosecution for a misdemeanor, or any pecuniary fine, forfeiture, penalty or amercement, shall be commenced within one year next after there was cause therefor, except that a prosecution for petit larceny may be commenced within five years, and for an attempt to produce abortion, within two years after commission of the offense.

A prosecution for any misdemeanor violation of § 54.1–3904 shall be commenced within two years of the discovery of the offense.

A prosecution for violation of laws governing the placement of children for adoption without a license pursuant to § 63.2–1701 shall be commenced within one year from the date of the filing of the petition for adoption.

A prosecution for making a false statement or representation of a material fact knowing it to be false or knowingly failing to disclose a material fact, to obtain or increase any benefit or other payment under the Virginia Unemployment Compensation Act (§ 60.2–100 et seq.) shall be commenced within three years next after the commission of the offense.

A prosecution for any violation of § 10.1–1320, 62.1–44.32 (b), 62.1–194.1, or Article 11 (§ 62.1–44.34:14 et seq.) of Chapter 3.1 of Title 62.1 that involves the discharge, dumping or emission of any toxic substance as defined in § 32.1–239 shall be commenced within three years next after the commission of the offense.

Prosecution of Building Code violations under § 36–106 shall commence within one year of discovery of the offense by the building official, provided that such discovery occurs within two years of the date of initial occupancy or use after construction of the building or structure, or the issuance of a certificate of use and occupancy for the building or structure, whichever is later. However, prosecutions under § 36–106 relating to the maintenance of existing buildings or structures as contained in the Uniform Statewide Building Code shall commence within one year of the issuance of a notice of violation for the offense by the building official.

Prosecution of any misdemeanor violation of § 54.1–111 shall commence within one year of the discovery of the offense by the complainant, but in no case later than five years from occurrence of the offense.

Prosecution of any misdemeanor violation of any professional licensure requirement imposed by a locality shall commence within one year of the discovery of the offense by the complainant, but in no case later than five years from occurrence of the offense.

Prosecution of nonfelonious offenses which constitute malfeasance in office shall commence within two years next after the commission of the offense.

Prosecution of any violation of § 55–79.87, 55–79.88, 55–79.89, 55–79.90, 55–79.93, 55–79.94, 55–79.95, 55–79.103, or any rule adopted under or order issued pursuant to § 55–79.98, shall commence within three years next after the commission of the offense.

Prosecution of illegal sales or purchases of wild birds, wild animals and freshwater fish under § 29.1–553 shall commence within three years after commission of the offense.

Prosecution of violations under Title 58.1 for offenses involving false or fraudulent statements, documents or returns, or for the offense of willfully attempting in any manner to evade or defeat any tax or the payment thereof, or for the offense of willfully failing to pay any tax, or willfully failing to make any return at the time or times required by law or regulations shall commence within three years next after the commission of the offense, unless a longer period is otherwise prescribed.

Prosecution of violations of subsection A or B of § 3.2–6570 shall commence within five years of the commission of the offense, except violations regarding agricultural animals shall commence within one year of the commission of the offense.

A prosecution for a violation of § 18.2–386.1 shall be commenced within five years of the commission of the offense.

A prosecution for any violation of the Campaign Finance Disclosure Act, Chapter 9.3 (§ 24.2–945 et seq.) of Title 24.2, shall commence within one year of the discovery of the offense but in no case more than three years after the date of the commission of the offense.

A prosecution of a crime that is punishable as a misdemeanor pursuant to the Virginia Computer Crimes Act (§ 18.2–152.1 et seq.) or pursuant to § 18.2–186.3 for identity theft shall be commenced before the earlier of (i) five years after the commission of the last act in the course of conduct constituting a violation of the article or (ii) one year after the existence of the illegal act and the identity of the offender are discovered by the Commonwealth, by the owner, or by anyone else who is damaged by such violation.

A prosecution for a violation of § 18.2–260.1 shall be commenced within three years of the commission of the offense.

Nothing in this section shall be construed to apply to any person fleeing from justice or concealing himself within or without the Commonwealth to avoid arrest or be construed to limit the time within which any prosecution may be commenced for desertion of a spouse or child or for neglect or refusal or failure to provide for the support and maintenance of a spouse or child.

Acts 1975, c. 495; Acts 1976, c. 114; Acts 1976, c. 620; Acts 1977, c. 108; Acts 1978, c. 730; Acts 1979, c. 243; Acts 1980, c. 496; Acts 1981, c. 31; Acts 1984, c. 601; Acts 1987, c. 488; Acts 1990, c. 575; Acts 1990, c. 976; Acts 1992, c. 177; Acts 1992, c. 435; Acts 1992, c. 650; Acts 1996, c. 484; Acts 1998, c. 566; Acts 1999, c. 620; Acts 2005, c. 746; Acts 2005, c. 761; Acts 2005, c. 827; Acts 2006, c. 193; Acts 2006, c. 787; Acts 2006, c. 892. Amended by Acts 2008, c. 769; Acts 2011, c. 118; Acts 2011, c. 143; Acts 2011, c. 494; Acts 2011, c. 553; Acts 2014, c. 169; Acts 2015, c. 176.

§ 19.2–8.1. Prosecution for murder or manslaughter; passage of time not a limitation

A prosecution for murder or manslaughter, whether at common law or under the Code of Virginia, may be instituted regardless of the time elapsed between the act or omission causing the death of the victim and the death of the victim.

Added by Acts 2009, c. 278.

§ 19.2–9. Prosecution of certain criminal cases removed from state to federal courts; costs

When any person indicted in the courts of this Commonwealth for a violation of its laws, has his case removed to the district court of the United States under 28 U.S.C. § 1442, it shall be the duty of the attorney for the Commonwealth for the county or city in which any such indictment is found to prosecute any such case in the United States district court to which the same shall be so removed, and for his services in this behalf he shall be paid a fee of $100 for each case tried by him in such United States district court, and mileage at the rate now allowed by law to the members of the General Assembly for all necessary travel in going to and returning from such court, to be paid on his account when approved by the Attorney General.

A per diem of one dollar and fifty cents for each day of actual attendance upon such United States district court and mileage at a rate as provided by law for every mile of necessary travel in going to and returning from such court shall be paid out of the state treasury to each witness for the Commonwealth in every such case upon accounts therefor against the Commonwealth, certified by the attorney for the Commonwealth prosecuting such case and approved by the Attorney General.

It shall not be the duty of the Attorney General to appear for the Commonwealth in such cases unless he can do so without interfering with the efficient discharge of the duties imposed upon him by law; but he may appear with the attorney for the Commonwealth prosecuting such case in any case when the interests of the Commonwealth may in his judgment require his presence.

The Comptroller shall from time to time draw his warrants upon the state treasury in favor of the parties entitled to be paid the above compensation and expenses, or their assigns, upon bills certified and approved as above prescribed.

Acts 1975, c. 495.

§ 19.2–9.1. Written notice required for complaining witness who is requested to take polygraph test

A. For offenses not specified in subsection B, if a complaining witness is requested to submit to a polygraph examination during the course of a criminal investigation, such witness shall be informed in writing prior to the examination that (i) the examination is voluntary, (ii) the results thereof are inadmissible as evidence and (iii) the agreement of the complaining witness to submit thereto shall not be the sole condition for initiating or continuing the criminal investigation.

B. No law-enforcement officer, attorney for the Commonwealth, or other government official shall ask or require a victim of an alleged sex offense to submit to a polygraph examination or other truth-telling device as a condition for proceeding with the investigation of such an offense. If a victim is requested to submit to a polygraph examination during the course of a criminal investigation, such victim shall be informed in writing of the provisions of subsection A and that the refusal of a victim to submit to such an examination shall not prevent the investigation, charging, or prosecution of the offense.

C. A "sex offense," for the purposes of this section, shall mean any offense set forth in Article 7 (§ 18.2–61 et seq.) of Chapter 4 of Title 18.2.

Acts 1994, c. 336. Amended by Acts 2008, c. 512; Acts 2008, c. 748.

§ 19.2–10. Outlawry abolished

No proceeding of outlawry shall hereafter be instituted or prosecuted.

Acts 1975, c. 495.

§ 19.2–10.1. Subpoena duces tecum for obtaining records concerning banking and credit cards

A. A financial institution as defined in § 6.2–604, money transmitter as defined in § 6.2–1900, or commercial businesses providing credit history or credit reports; or an issuer as defined in § 6.2–424 shall disclose a record or other information pertaining to a customer, to a law-enforcement officer pursuant to a subpoena duces tecum issued pursuant to this section.

1. In order to obtain such records, the law-enforcement official shall provide a statement of the facts documenting the reasons that the records or other information sought are relevant to a legitimate law-enforcement inquiry, relating to a named person or persons, to the attorney for the Commonwealth. A court shall issue a subpoena duces tecum upon motion of the Commonwealth only if the court finds that there is probable cause to believe that a crime has been committed and to believe the records sought or other information sought, including electronic data and electronic communications, are relevant to a legitimate law-enforcement inquiry into that offense. The court may issue a subpoena duces tecum under this section regardless of whether any criminal charges have been filed.

2. A court issuing an order pursuant to this section, on a motion made promptly by the financial institution or credit card issuer, or enterprise may quash or modify the subpoena duces tecum, if the information or records requested are unusually voluminous in nature or compliance with such subpoena duces tecum would otherwise cause an undue burden on such provider.

B. No cause of action shall lie in any court against a financial institution or credit card issuer, or enterprise, its officers, employees, agents, or other specified persons for providing information, facilities, or assistance in accordance with the terms of a subpoena duces tecum under this section.

C. Upon issuance of a subpoena duces tecum under this section, the statement shall be temporarily sealed by the court upon application of the attorney for the Commonwealth for good cause shown in an ex parte proceeding. Any individual arrested and claiming to be aggrieved by the order may move the court for the unsealing of the statement, and the burden of proof with respect to continued sealing shall be upon the Commonwealth.

D. Any and all records received by law enforcement pursuant to this section shall be utilized only for a reasonable amount of time and only for a legitimate law-enforcement purpose. Upon the completion of the investigation the records shall be submitted to the court by the attorney for the Commonwealth along with a proposed order requiring the records to be sealed. Upon entry of such order, the court shall seal the records in accordance with the requirements contained in subsection C.

Acts 2003, c. 223; Acts 2003, c. 541; Acts 2003, c. 549; Acts 2004, c. 883; Acts 2004, c. 996. Amended by Acts 2010, c. 702; Acts 2010, c. 794, eff. Oct. 1, 2010.

§ 19.2–10.2. Administrative subpoena issued for record from provider of electronic communication service or remote computing service

A. A provider of electronic communication service or remote computing service that is transacting or has transacted any business in the Commonwealth shall disclose a record or other information pertaining to a subscriber to or customer of such service, excluding the contents of electronic communications as required by § 19.2–70.3, to an attorney for the Commonwealth or the Attorney General pursuant to an administrative subpoena issued under this section.

1. In order to obtain such records or other information, the attorney for the Commonwealth or the Attorney General shall certify on the face of the subpoena that there is reason to believe that the records or other information being sought are relevant to a legitimate law-enforcement investigation concerning violations of §§ 18.2–47, 18.2–48, 18.2–49, 18.2–346, 18.2–347, 18.2–348, 18.2–349, 18.2–355, 18.2–356, 18.2–357, 18.2–374.1, and 18.2–374.1:1, former § 18.2–374.1:2,[1] and § 18.2–374.3.

2. Upon written certification by the attorney for the Commonwealth or the Attorney General that there is a reason to believe that the victim is under the age of 18 and that notification or disclosure of the existence of the subpoena will endanger the life or physical safety of an individual, or lead to flight from prosecution, the destruction of or tampering with evidence, the intimidation of potential witnesses, or otherwise seriously jeopardize an investigation, the subpoena shall include a provision ordering the service provider not to notify or disclose the existence of the subpoena to another person, other than an attorney to obtain legal advice,

for a period of 30 days after the date on which the service provider responds to the subpoena.

3. On a motion made promptly by the electronic communication service or remote computing service provider, a court of competent jurisdiction may quash or modify the administrative subpoena if the records or other information requested are unusually voluminous in nature or if compliance with the subpoena would otherwise cause an undue burden on the service provider.

B. All records or other information received by an attorney for the Commonwealth or the Attorney General pursuant to an administrative subpoena issued under this section shall be used only for a reasonable length of time not to exceed 30 days and only for a legitimate law-enforcement purpose. Upon completion of the investigation, the records or other information held by the attorney for the Commonwealth or the Attorney General shall be destroyed if no prosecution is initiated. The existence of such a subpoena shall be disclosed upon motion of an accused.

C. No cause of action shall lie in any court against an electronic communication service or remote computing service provider, its officers, employees, agents, or other specified persons for providing information, facilities, or assistance in accordance with the terms of an administrative subpoena issued under this section.

D. Records or other information pertaining to a subscriber to or customer of such service means name, address, local and long distance telephone connection records, or records of session times and durations, length of service, including start date, and types of service utilized, telephone or instrument number or other subscriber number or identity, including any temporarily assigned network address, and means and source of payment for such service.

E. Nothing in this section shall require the disclosure of information in violation of any federal law.

Acts 2007, c. 802; Acts 2007, c. 814. Amended by Acts 2014, c. 166; Acts 2015, c. 544; Acts 2015, c. 625.

1 Section 18.2–374.1:2 was repealed by Acts 2007, cc. 759 and 823.

§ 19.2–10.3. Reasonable suspicion required to stop, board, or inspect a noncommercial vessel on navigable waters of the Commonwealth

A. Notwithstanding any other provision of law, no law-enforcement officer charged with enforcing laws or regulations on the navigable waters of the Commonwealth shall stop, board, or inspect any noncommercial vessel on the navigable waters of the Commonwealth unless such officer has reasonable suspicion that a violation of law or regulation exists.

B. The provisions of subsection A shall not apply to lawful stops, boardings, or inspections conducted by conservation police officers, as defined in § 29.1–100, or the Virginia Marine Police for the purposes of inspecting hunting, fishing, and trapping licenses pursuant to §§ 28.2–231 and 29.1–337 or creel and bag limit inspections pursuant to § 29.1–209, nor shall it prohibit lawful boating safety checkpoints conducted by conservation police officers and Virginia Marine Police in accordance with established agency policy.

Added by Acts 2015, c. 484.

§ 19.2–11. Procedure in contempt cases

No court or judge shall impose a fine upon a juror, witness or other person for disobedience of its process or any contempt, unless he either be present in court at the time, or shall have been served with a rule, returnable to a certain time, requiring him to show cause why the fine should not be imposed and shall have failed to appear and show cause.

Acts 1975, c. 495.

CHAPTER 1.1

CRIME VICTIM AND WITNESS RIGHTS ACT

§ 19.2–11.01. Crime victim and witness rights

A. In recognition of the Commonwealth's concern for the victims and witnesses of crime, it is the purpose of this chapter to ensure that the full impact of crime is brought to the attention of the courts of the Commonwealth; that crime victims and witnesses are treated with dignity, respect and sensitivity; and that their privacy is protected to the extent permissible under law. It is the further purpose of this chapter to ensure that victims and witnesses are informed of the rights provided to them under the laws of the Commonwealth; that they receive authorized services as appropriate; and that they have the opportunity to be heard by law-enforcement agencies, attorneys for the Commonwealth, corrections agencies and the judiciary at all critical stages of the criminal justice process to the extent permissible under law. Unless otherwise stated and subject to the provisions of § 19.2–11.1, it shall be the responsibility of a locality's crime victim and witness assistance program to provide the information and assistance required by this chapter, including verification that the standardized form listing the specific rights afforded to crime victims has been received by the victim.

As soon as practicable after identifying a victim of a crime, the investigating law-enforcement agency shall provide the victim with a standardized form listing the specific rights afforded to crime victims. The form shall include a telephone number by which the victim can receive further information and assistance in securing the rights afforded crime victims, the name, address and telephone number of the office of the attorney for the Commonwealth, the name, address and telephone number of the investigating law-enforcement agency, and a summary of the victim's rights under § 40.1–28.7:2.

1. Victim and witness protection and law-enforcement contacts.

a. In order that victims and witnesses receive protection from harm and threats of harm arising out of their cooperation with law-enforcement, or prosecution efforts, they shall be provided with information as to the level of protection which may be available pursuant to § 52–35 or to any other federal, state or local program providing protection, and shall be assisted in obtaining this protection from the appropriate authorities.

b. Victims and witnesses shall be provided, where available, a separate waiting area during court proceedings that affords them privacy and protection from intimidation, and that does not place the victim in close proximity to the defendant or the defendant's family.

2. Financial assistance.

a. Victims shall be informed of financial assistance and social services available to them as victims of a crime, including information on their possible right to file a claim for compensation from the Crime Victims' Compensation Fund pursuant to Chapter 21.1 (§ 19.2–368.1 et seq.) of this title and on other available assistance and services.

b. Victims shall be assisted in having any property held by law-enforcement agencies for evidentiary purposes returned promptly in accordance with §§ 19.2–270.1 and 19.2–270.2.

c. Victims shall be advised that restitution is available for damages or loss resulting from an offense and shall be assisted in seeking restitution in accordance with §§ 19.2–305, 19.2–305.1, Chapter 21.1 (§ 19.2–368.1 et seq.) of this title, Article 21 (§ 58.1–520 et seq.) of Chapter 3 of Title 58.1, and other applicable laws of the Commonwealth.

3. Notices.

a. Victims and witnesses shall be (i) provided with appropriate employer intercession services to ensure that employers of victims and witnesses will cooperate with the criminal justice process in order to minimize an employee's loss of pay and other benefits resulting from court appearances and (ii) advised that pursuant to § 18.2–465.1 it is unlawful for an employer to penalize an employee for appearing in court pursuant to a summons or subpoena.

b. Victims shall receive advance notification when practicable from the attorney for the Commonwealth of judicial proceedings relating to their case and shall be notified when practicable of any change in court dates in accordance with § 19.2–265.01 if they have provided their names, current addresses and telephone numbers.

c. Victims shall receive notification, if requested, subject to such reasonable procedures as the Attorney General may require pursuant to § 2.2–511, from the Attorney General of the filing and disposition of any appeal or habeas corpus proceeding involving their case.

d. Victims shall be notified by the Department of Corrections or a sheriff or jail superintendent (i) in whose custody an escape, change of name, transfer, release or discharge of a prisoner occurs pursuant to the provisions of §§ 53.1–133.02 and 53.1–160 or (ii) when an accused is released on bail, if they have provided their names, current addresses and telephone numbers in writing. Such notification may be provided through the Virginia Statewide VINE (Victim Information and Notification Everyday) System or other similar electronic or automated system.

e. Victims shall be advised that, in order to protect their right to receive notices and offer input, all agencies and persons having such duties must have current victim addresses and telephone numbers given by the victims. Victims shall also be advised that any such information given shall be confidential as provided by § 19.2–11.2.

4. Victim input.

a. Victims shall be given the opportunity, pursuant to § 19.2–299.1, to prepare a written victim impact statement prior to sentencing of a defendant and may provide information to any individual or agency charged with investigating the social history of a person or preparing a victim impact statement under the provisions of §§ 16.1–273 and 53.1–155 or any other applicable law.

b. Victims shall have the right to remain in the courtroom during a criminal trial or proceeding pursuant to the provisions of § 19.2–265.01.

c. On motion of the attorney for the Commonwealth, victims shall be given the opportunity, pursuant to §§ 19.2–264.4 and 19.2–295.3, to testify prior to sentencing of a defendant regarding the impact of the offense.

d. In a felony case, the attorney for the Commonwealth, upon the victim's written request, shall consult with the victim either verbally or in writing (i) to inform the victim of the contents of a proposed plea agreement and (ii) to obtain the victim's views about the disposition of the case, including the victim's views concerning dismissal, pleas, plea negotiations and sentencing. However, nothing in this section shall limit the ability of the attorney for the Commonwealth to exercise his discretion on behalf of the citizens of the Commonwealth in the disposition of any criminal case. The court shall not accept the plea agreement unless it finds that, except for good cause shown, the Commonwealth has complied with clauses (i) and (ii). Good cause shown shall include, but not be limited to, the unavailability of the victim due to incarceration, hospitalization, failure to appear at trial when subpoenaed, or change of address without notice.

Upon the victim's written request, the victim shall be notified in accordance with subdivision A 3 b of any proceeding in which the plea agreement will be tendered to the court.

The responsibility to consult with the victim under this subdivision shall not confer upon the defendant any substantive or procedural rights and shall not affect the validity of any plea entered by the defendant.

5. Courtroom assistance.

a. Victims and witnesses shall be informed that their addresses and telephone numbers may not be disclosed, pursuant to the provisions of §§ 19.2–11.2 and 19.2–269.2, except when necessary for the conduct of the criminal proceeding.

b. Victims and witnesses shall be advised that they have the right to the services of an interpreter in accordance with §§ 19.2–164 and 19.2–164.1.

c. Victims and witnesses of certain sexual offenses shall be advised that there may be a closed preliminary hearing in accordance with § 18.2–67.8 and, if a victim was 14 years of age or younger on the date of the offense and is 16 or under at the time of the trial, or a witness to the offense is 14 years of age or younger at the time of the trial, that two-way closed-circuit television may be used in the taking of testimony in accordance with § 18.2–67.9.

6. Post trial assistance.

a. Within 30 days of receipt of a victim's written request after the final trial court proceeding in the case, the attorney for the Commonwealth shall notify the victim in writing, of (i) the disposition of the case, (ii) the crimes of which the defendant was convicted, (iii) the defendant's right to appeal, if known, and (iv) the telephone number of offices to contact in the event of nonpayment of restitution by the defendant.

b. If the defendant has been released on bail pending the outcome of an appeal, the agency that had custody of the defendant immediately prior to his release shall notify the victim as soon as practicable that the defendant has been released.

c. If the defendant's conviction is overturned, and the attorney for the Commonwealth decides to retry the case or the case is remanded for a new trial, the victim shall be entitled to the same rights as if the first trial did not take place.

B. For purposes of this chapter, "victim" means (i) a person who has suffered physical, psychological, or economic harm as a direct result of the commission of (a) a felony, (b) assault and battery in violation of § 18.2–57 or 18.2–57.2, stalking in violation of § 18.2–60.3, a violation of a protective order in violation of § 16.1–253.2 or 18.2–60.4, sexual battery in violation of § 18.2–67.4, attempted sexual battery in violation of § 18.2–67.5, or maiming or driving while intoxicated in violation of § 18.2–51.4 or 18.2–266, or (c) a delinquent act that would be a felony or a misdemeanor violation of any offense enumerated in clause (b) if committed by an adult; (ii) a spouse or child of such a person; (iii) a parent or legal guardian of such a person who is a minor; (iv) for the purposes of subdivision A 4 only, a current or former foster parent or other person who has or has had physical custody of such a person who is a minor, for six months or more or for the majority of the minor's life; or (v) a spouse, parent, sibling, or legal guardian of such a person who is physically or mentally incapacitated or was the victim of a homicide; however, "victim" does not mean a parent, child, spouse, sibling, or legal guardian who commits a felony or other enumerated criminal offense against a victim as defined in clause (i).

C. Officials and employees of the judiciary, including court services units, law-enforcement agencies, the Department of Corrections, attorneys for the Commonwealth and public defenders, shall be provided with copies of this chapter by the Department of Criminal Justice Services or a crime victim and witness assistance program. Each agency, officer or employee who has a responsibility or responsibilities to victims under this chapter or other applicable law shall make reasonable efforts to become informed about these responsibilities and to ensure that victims and witnesses receive such information and services to which they may be entitled under applicable law, provided that no liability or cause of action shall arise from the failure to make such efforts or from the failure of such victims or witnesses to receive any such information or services.

Acts 1995, c. 687; Acts 1996, c. 546; Acts 1997, c. 691; Acts 1998, c. 485; Acts 1999, c. 668; Acts 1999, c. 702; Acts 1999, c. 844; Acts 2000, c. 272; Acts 2000, c. 827; Acts 2001, c. 410; Acts 2001, c. 530; Acts 2001, c. 549; Acts 2002, c. 310; Acts 2002, c. 810; Acts 2002, c. 818; Acts 2003, c. 103; Acts 2003, c. 751; Acts 2003, c. 764; Acts 2006, c. 241; Acts 2007, c. 94; Acts 2007, c. 109; Acts 2007, c. 423. Amended by Acts 2014, c. 230.

§ 19.2–11.1. Establishment of crime victim-witness assistance programs; funding; minimum standards

Any local governmental body which establishes, operates and maintains a crime victim and witness assistance program, whose funding is provided in whole or part by grants administered by the Department of Criminal Justice Services pursuant to § 9.1–104, shall operate the program in accordance with guidelines which shall be established by the Department to implement the provisions of this chapter and other applicable laws establishing victims' rights.

Acts 1998, c. 542; Acts 1994, c. 361; Acts 1994, c. 598; Acts 1995, c. 687; Acts 1996, c. 545.

§ 19.2–11.2. Crime victim's right to nondisclosure of certain information; exceptions; testimonial privilege

Upon request of any witness in a criminal prosecution under § 18.2–46.2, 18.2–46.3, or 18.2–248 or of any violent felony as defined by subsection C of § 17.1-805, or any crime victim, neither a law-enforcement agency, the attorney for the Commonwealth, the counsel for a defendant, a court nor the Department of Corrections, nor any employee of any of them, may disclose, except among themselves, the residential address, telephone number, or place of employment of the witness or victim or a member of the witness' or victim's family, except to the extent that disclosure is (i) of the site of the crime, (ii) required by law or Rules of the Supreme Court, (iii) necessary for law-enforcement purposes or preparation for court proceedings, or (iv) permitted by the court for good cause.

Except with the written consent of the victim, a law-enforcement agency may not disclose to the public information which directly or indirectly identifies the victim of a crime involving any sexual assault, sexual abuse or family abuse, except to the extent that disclosure is (i) of the site of the crime, (ii) required by law, (iii) necessary for law-enforcement purposes, or (iv) permitted by the court for good cause. In addition, at the request of the victim to the Court of Appeals of Virginia or the Supreme Court of Virginia hearing, on or after July 1, 2007, the case of a crime involving any sexual assault or sexual abuse, no appellate decision shall contain the first or last name of the victim.

Nothing herein shall limit the right to examine witnesses in a court of law or otherwise affect the conduct of any criminal proceeding.

Acts 1994, c. 845; Acts 1994, c. 931; Acts 2002, c. 810; Acts 2002, c. 818; Acts 2005, c. 764; Acts 2005, c. 813; Acts 2007, c. 503. Amended by Acts 2014, c. 744.

§ 19.2-11.3. Virginia Crime Victim-Witness Fund

There is hereby established the Virginia Crime Victim-Witness Fund as a special nonreverting fund to be administered by the Department of Criminal Justice Services to support victim and witness services that meet the minimum standards prescribed for such programs under § 19.2-11.1. A portion of the sum collected pursuant to §§ 16.1-69.48:1, 17.1-275.1, 17.1-275.2, 17.1-275.3, 17.1-275.4, 17.1-275.7, 17.1-275.8, and 17.1-275.9, as specified in these sections, shall be deposited into the state treasury to the credit of this Fund. The Fund shall be distributed according to grant procedures adopted pursuant to § 9.1-104 and shall be established on the books of the Comptroller. Any funds remaining in such Fund at the end of the biennium shall not revert to the general fund, but shall remain in the Fund. Interest earned on the Fund shall be credited to the Fund.

Acts 1995, c. 371; Acts 2002, c. 831, eff. July 1, 2003.

§ 19.2-11.4. Establishment of victim-offender reconciliation program

A. Any Crime Victim and Witness Assistance Program may establish a victim-offender reconciliation program to provide an opportunity after conviction for a victim, at his request and upon the subsequent agreement of the offender, to:

1. Meet with the offender in a safe, controlled environment in accordance with the policies established pursuant to subsection B of § 53.1-30;

2. Give to the offender, either orally or in writing, a summary of the financial, emotional, and physical effects of the offense on the victim or the victim's family; and

3. Discuss a proposed restitution agreement which may be submitted for consideration by the sentencing court for damages incurred by the victim as a result of the offense.

B. If the victim chooses to participate in a victim-offender reconciliation program under this section, the victim shall execute a waiver releasing the Crime Victim and Witness Assistance Program, attorney for the offender and the attorney for the Commonwealth from civil and criminal liability for actions taken by the victim or offender as a result of participation by the victim or the offender in a victim-offender reconciliation program.

C. A victim shall not be required to participate in a victim-offender reconciliation program under this section.

D. The failure of any person to participate in a reconciliation program pursuant to this section shall not be used directly or indirectly at sentencing.

Acts 1995, c. 628. Amended by Acts 2010, c. 844.

CHAPTER 2

CONSERVATORS OF THE PEACE AND SPECIAL POLICEMEN

Article 1

Appointment

§ 19.2-12. Who are conservators of the peace

Every judge and attorney for the Commonwealth throughout the Commonwealth and every magistrate within the geographical area for which he is appointed or elected, shall be a conservator of the peace. In addition, every commissioner in chancery, while sitting as such commissioner; any special agent or law-enforcement officer of the United States Department of Justice, National Marine Fisheries Service of the United States Department of Commerce, Department of Treasury, Department of Agriculture, Department of Defense, Department of State, Office of the Inspector General of the Department of Transportation, Department of Homeland Security, and Department of Interior; any inspector, law-enforcement official or police personnel of the United States Postal Service; any United States marshal or deputy United States marshal whose duties involve the enforcement of the criminal laws of the United States; any officer of the Virginia Marine Police; any criminal investigator of the Department of Professional and Occupational Regulation, who meets the minimum law-enforcement training requirements established by the Department of Criminal Justice Services for in-service training; any criminal investigator of the United States Department of Labor; any special agent of the United States Naval Criminal Investigative Service, any special agent of the National Aeronautics and Space Administration, and any sworn municipal park ranger, who has completed all requirements under § 15.2-1706, shall be a conservator of the peace, while engaged in the performance of their official duties.

Acts 1975, c. 495; Acts 1978, c. 697; Acts 1981, c. 572; Acts 1981, c. 587; Acts 1990, c. 558; Acts 1991, c. 74; Acts 1991, c. 338; Acts 1994, c. 375; Acts 1994, c. 569; Acts 1994, c. 626; Acts 1997, c. 34; Acts 2001, c. 3; Acts 2001, c. 31; Acts 2002, c. 86; Acts 2002, c. 605, eff. July 1, 2003; Acts 2002, c. 789; Acts 2004, c. 1009, eff. April 21, 2004; Acts 2005, c. 372; Acts 2006, c. 88; Acts 2007, c. 224. Amended by Acts 2015, c. 75; Acts 2015, c. 126.

§ 19.2-13. Special conservators of the peace; authority; jurisdiction; registration; bond; liability of employers; penalty; report

A. Upon the submission of an application, which shall include the results of a background investigation, from (i) any sheriff or chief of police of any county, city, or town; (ii) any corporation authorized to do business in the Commonwealth; (iii) the owner, proprietor, or authorized custodian of any place within the Commonwealth; or (iv) any museum owned and managed by the Commonwealth, a circuit court judge of any county or city shall appoint special conservators of the peace who shall serve as such for such length of time as the court may designate, but not exceeding four years under any one appointment, during which time the court shall retain jurisdiction over the appointment order, upon a showing by the applicant of a necessity for the security of property or the peace and presentation of evidence that the person or persons to be appointed as a special conservator of the peace possess a valid registration issued by the Department of Criminal Justice Services in accordance with the provisions of subsection C. Upon an application made pursuant to clause (ii), (iii), or (iv), the court shall, prior to entering the order of appointment, transmit a copy of the application to the local attorney for the Commonwealth and the local sheriff or chief of police who may submit to the court a sworn, written statement indicating whether the order of appointment should be granted. However, a judge may deny the appointment for good cause, and shall state the specific reasons for the denial in writing in the order denying the appointment. A judge also may revoke the appointment order for good cause shown, upon the filing of a sworn petition by the attorney for the Commonwealth, sheriff, or chief of police for any locality in which the special conservator of the peace is authorized to serve or by the Department of Criminal Justice Services. Prior to revocation, a hearing shall be set and the special conservator of the peace shall be given notice and the opportunity to be heard. The judge may temporarily suspend the appointment pending the hearing for good cause shown. A hearing on the petition shall be heard by the court as soon as practicable. If the appointment order is suspended or revoked, the clerk of court shall notify the Department of Criminal Justice Services, the Department of State Police, the applicable local law-enforcement agencies in all cities and counties where the special conservator of the peace is authorized to serve, and the employer of the special conservator of the peace.

The order of appointment may provide that a special conservator of the peace shall have all the powers, functions, duties, responsibilities and authority of any other conservator of the peace within such geographical limitations as the court may deem appropriate within the confines of the county, city or town that makes application or on the real property where the corporate applicant is located, or any real property contiguous to such real property, limited, except as provided in subsection F, to the city or county wherein application has been made, whenever such special conservator of the peace is engaged in the performance of his duties as such. The order may provide that the special conservator of the peace shall have the authority to make an arrest outside of such geographical limitations if the arrest results from a close pursuit that was initiated when the special conservator of the peace was within the confines of the area wherein he has been authorized to have the powers and authority of a special conservator of the peace; the order may further delineate a geographical limitation or distance beyond which the special conservator of the peace may not effectuate such an arrest that follows from a close pursuit. The order shall require the special conservator of the peace to comply with the provisions of the United States Constitution and the Constitution of Virginia. The order shall not identify the special conservator of the peace as a law-enforcement officer pursuant to § 9.1-101. The order may provide, however, that the special conservator of the peace is a "law-enforcement officer" for the purposes of Article 4 (§ 37.2-808 et seq.) of Chapter 8 of Title 37.2 or Article 16 (§ 16.1-335 et seq.) of Chapter 11 of Title 16.1, but such designation shall not qualify the special conservator of the peace as a "qualified law-enforcement officer" or "qualified retired law-enforcement officer" within the meaning of the federal Law Enforcement

Officer Safety Act, 18 U.S.C. § 926(B) et seq., and the order of appointment shall specifically state this. Upon request and for good cause shown, the order may also provide that the special conservator of the peace is authorized to use the seal of the Commonwealth in a badge or other credential of office as the court may deem appropriate. Upon request and for good cause shown, the order may also provide that the special conservator of the peace may use the title "police" on any badge or uniform worn in the performance of his duties as such. The order may also provide that a special conservator of the peace who has completed the minimum training standards established by the Criminal Justice Services Board, has the authority to affect arrests, using up to the same amount of force as would be allowed to a law-enforcement officer employed by the Commonwealth or any of its political subdivisions when making a lawful arrest. The order shall prohibit blue flashing lights, but upon request and for good cause shown may provide that the special conservator of the peace may use flashing lights and sirens on any vehicle used by the special conservator of the peace when he is in the performance of his duties. Prior to granting an application for appointment, the circuit court shall ensure that the applicant has met the registration requirements established by the Criminal Justice Services Board.

B. All applications and orders for appointments of special conservators of the peace shall be submitted on forms developed by the Office of the Executive Secretary of the Supreme Court of Virginia in consultation with the Department of Criminal Justice Services and shall specify the duties for which the applicant is qualified. The applications and orders shall specify the geographic limitations consistent with subsection A.

C. No person shall seek appointment as a special conservator of the peace from a circuit court judge without possessing a valid registration issued by the Department of Criminal Justice Services, except as provided in this section. Applicants for registration may submit an application on or after January 1, 2004. A temporary registration may be issued in accordance with regulations established by the Criminal Justice Services Board while awaiting the results of a state and national fingerprint search. However, no person shall be issued a temporary registration until he has (i) complied with, or been exempted from the compulsory minimum training standards as set forth in this section; (ii) submitted his fingerprints on a form provided by the Department to be used for the conduct of a national criminal records search and a Virginia criminal history records search; (iii) submitted the results of a background investigation, performed by any state or local law-enforcement agency, which may, at its discretion, charge a reasonable fee to the applicant and which may include a review of the applicant's school records, employment records, or interviews with persons possessing general knowledge of the applicant's character and fitness for such appointment; and (iv) met all other requirements of this article and Board regulations. No person with a criminal conviction for a misdemeanor involving (a) moral turpitude, (b) assault and battery, (c) damage to real or personal property, (d) controlled substances or imitation controlled substances as defined in Article 1 (§ 18.2–247 et seq.) of Chapter 7 of Title 18.2, (e) prohibited sexual behavior as described in Article 7 (§ 18.2–61 et seq.) of Chapter 4 of Title 18.2, or (f) firearms, or any felony or who is required to register with the Sex Offender and Crimes Against Minors Registry pursuant to Chapter 9 (§ 9.1–900 et seq.) of Title 9.1 shall be eligible for registration or appointment as a special conservator of the peace. A special conservator of the peace shall report if he is arrested for, charged with, or convicted of any misdemeanor or felony offense to the Department of Criminal Justice Services and the chief law-enforcement officer of all localities in which he is authorized to serve within 3 days of such arrest. Any appointment for a special conservator of the peace shall be eligible for suspension and revocation after a hearing pursuant to subsection A if the special conservator of the peace is convicted of any offense listed in clauses (a) through (f) or of any felony. All appointments for special conservators of the peace shall become void on September 15, 2004, unless they have obtained a valid registration issued by the Department of Criminal Justice Services.

D. Each person registered as or seeking registration as a special conservator of the peace shall be covered by evidence of a policy of liability insurance or self-insurance in an amount and with coverage as fixed by the Board. Any person who is aggrieved by the misconduct of any person registered as a special conservator of the peace and recovers a judgment against the registrant, which is unsatisfied in whole or in part, may bring an action in his own name against the bond or insurance policy of the registrant.

E. Effective July 1, 2015, all persons currently appointed or seeking appointment or reappointment as a special conservator of the peace are required to register with the Department of Criminal Justice Services, regardless of any other standing the person may have as a law-enforcement officer or other position requiring registration or licensure by the Department. The employer of any special conservator of the peace shall notify the circuit court, the Department of Criminal Justice Services, the Department of State Police, and the chief law-enforcement officer of all localities in which the special conservator of the peace is authorized to serve within 30 days after the date such individual has left employment and all powers of the special conservator of the peace shall be void. Failure to provide such notification shall be punishable by a fine of $250 plus an additional $50 per day for each day such notice is not provided.

F. When the application is made by any sheriff or chief of police, the circuit court shall specify in the order of appointment the name of the applicant authorized under subsection A and the geographic jurisdiction of the special conservator of the peace. Such appointments shall be limited to the city or county wherein application has been made. When the application is made by any corporation authorized to do business in the Commonwealth, any owner, proprietor, or authorized custodian of any place within the Commonwealth, or any museum owned and managed by the Commonwealth, the circuit court shall specify in the order of appointment the name of the applicant authorized under subsection A and the specific real property where the special conservator of the peace is authorized to serve. Such appointments shall be limited to the specific real property within the county, city, or town wherein application has been made. In the case of a corporation or other business, the court appointment may also include, for good cause shown, any real property owned or leased by the corporation or business, including any subsidiaries, in other specifically named cities and counties, but shall provide that the powers of the special conservator of the peace do not extend beyond the boundaries of such real property. The clerk of the appointing circuit court shall transmit to the Department of State Police, the clerk of the circuit court of each locality where the special conservator of the peace is authorized to serve, and the sheriff or chief of police of each such locality a copy of the order of appointment that shall specify the following information: the person's complete name, address, date of birth, social security number, gender, race, height, weight, color of hair, color of eyes, firearm authority or limitation as set forth in subsection G, date of the order, and other information as may be required by the Department of State Police. The Department of State Police shall enter the person's name and other information into the Virginia Criminal Information Network established and maintained by the Department pursuant to Chapter 2 (§ 52–12 et seq.) of Title 52. The Department of State Police may charge a fee not to exceed $10 to cover its costs associated with processing these orders. Each special conservator of the peace so appointed on application shall present his credentials to the chief of police or sheriff or his designee of all jurisdictions where he has conservator powers. If his powers are limited to certain areas of real property owned or leased by a corporation or business, he shall also provide notice of the exact physical addresses of those areas. Each special conservator shall provide to the circuit court a temporary registration letter issued by the Department of Criminal Justice Services to include the results of the background check prior to seeking an appointment by the circuit court. Once the applicant receives the appointment from the circuit court the applicant shall file the appointment order and a copy of the application with the Department of Criminal Justice Services in order to receive his special conservator of the peace registration document. If the court appointment includes any real property owned or leased by the corporation or business in other specifically named cities and counties not within the city or county wherein application has been made, the clerk of the appointing court shall transmit a copy of the order of appointment to (i) the clerk of the circuit court for each jurisdiction where the special conservator of the peace is authorized to serve and (ii) the sheriff or chief of police of each jurisdiction where the special conservator of the peace is authorized to serve.

If any such special conservator of the peace is the employee, agent or servant of another, his appointment as special conservator of the peace shall not relieve his employer, principal or master from civil liability to another arising out of any wrongful action or conduct committed by such special conservator of the peace while within the scope of his employment.

Effective July 1, 2002, no person employed by a local school board as a school security officer, as defined in § 9.1–101, shall be eligible for appointment as a conservator for purposes of maintaining safety in a public school in the Commonwealth. All appointments of special conservators of the peace granted to school security officers as defined in § 9.1–101 prior to July 1, 2002 are void.

G. The court may limit or prohibit the carrying of weapons by any special conservator of the peace initially appointed on or after July 1, 1996, while the appointee is within the scope of his employment as such.

H. The governing body of any locality or the sheriff of a county where no police department has been established may enter into mutual aid agreements with any entity employing special conservators of the peace that is located in such locality for the use of their joint forces and their equipment and materials to maintain peace and good order. Any law-enforcement officer or special conservator of the peace, while performing his duty under any such agreement, shall have the same authority as lawfully conferred on him within his own jurisdiction.

Acts 1975, c. 495; Acts 1976, c. 220; Acts 1982, c. 523; Acts 1989, c. 455; Acts 1996, c. 850; Acts 1996, c. 956; Acts 2001, c. 249; Acts 2002, c. 605, eff. July 1, 2003; Acts 2002, c. 836; Acts 2002, c. 868; Acts 2003, c. 922; Acts 2004, c. 401; Acts 2005, c. 498; Acts 2006, c. 290; Acts 2007, c. 380; Acts 2007, c. 481. Amended by Acts 2008, c. 795; Acts 2010, c. 530; Acts 2010, c. 778; Acts 2010, c. 825; Acts 2013, c. 105; Acts 2013, c. 122; Acts 2015, c. 602; Acts 2015, c. 766; Acts 2015, c. 772.

§ 19.2–14. Conservators of the peace for fairgrounds and cemeteries; bond required

The superintendent or other person in charge of any fairgrounds or any public or private cemetery shall, for the purpose of maintaining order and enforcing the criminal and police laws of the Commonwealth, or the county or city in which such fairgrounds or cemetery is situated, have all the powers, functions, duties, responsibilities and authority of a conservator of the peace within the fairgrounds or cemetery over which he may have charge and within one-half of a mile around the same.

The provisions of § 19.2–13 relative to the giving of bond and the liability of an employer, principal or master, shall be applicable to every person exercising any powers of a conservator of the peace under this section.

Acts 1975, c. 495.

§ 19.2–15. When conservator appointed under § 19.2–13 need not be a citizen

Any such conservator appointed under the provisions of § 19.2–13 whose jurisdiction is limited to the grounds attached to an airport, need not be a citizen of the Commonwealth if the proprietors of such airport shall, before any such conservator shall enter upon the duties of the office, enter into bond with approved surety before the clerk of the circuit court having jurisdiction over such airport in the penalty of $1,000 for each conservator so appointed, with condition for the faithful discharge of his official duties.

Acts 1975, c. 495.

§ 19.2–16. Repealed by Acts 1994, c. 205

§ 19.2–17. Repealed by Acts 1996, c. 850

Article 2

Powers and Duties

§ 19.2–18. Powers and duties generally

Every conservator of the peace shall have authority to arrest without a warrant in such instances as are set out in §§ 19.2–19 and 19.2–81. Upon making an arrest without a warrant, the conservator of the peace shall proceed in accordance with the provisions of § 19.2–22 or § 19.2–82 as the case may be.

Acts 1975, c. 495.

§ 19.2–19. Recognizance to keep the peace; when required

If any person threatens to kill or injure another or to commit violence or injury against his person or property, or to unlawfully trespass upon his property, he shall be required to give a recognizance to keep the peace for such period not to exceed one year as the court hearing the complaint may determine.

Acts 1975, c. 495; Acts 1978, c. 500.

§ 19.2–20. Same; complaint and issuance of warrant therefor

If complaint be made to any magistrate or judge that a person should be required to give a recognizance to keep the peace due to any of the reasons set forth in § 19.2–19, such magistrate or judge shall examine on oath the complainant, and any witness who may be produced, reduce the complaint to writing, and cause it to be signed by the complainant; and if probable cause is established, such magistrate or judge shall issue a warrant, reciting the complaint, and requiring the person complained of forthwith to be apprehended and brought before the district court having appropriate jurisdiction.

Acts 1975, c. 495; Acts 1978, c. 500; Acts 1979, c. 708.

§ 19.2–21. Same; procedure when accused appears

When such person appears, if the judge, on hearing the parties, considers that there is not good cause for the complaint, he shall discharge such person, and may give judgment in his favor against the complainant for his costs. If he considers that there is good cause therefor, he may require a recognizance of the person against whom it is, and give judgment against him for the costs of the prosecution, or any part thereof; and, unless such recognizance be given, he shall commit him to jail by a warrant, stating the sum and time in and for which the recognizance is directed. The person given judgment under this section for costs may issue a writ of fieri facias thereon, if an appeal be not allowed; and proceedings thereupon may be according to §§ 16.1–99 through 16.1–101.

Acts 1975, c. 495; Acts 1978, c. 500.

§ 19.2–22. Same; arrest without a warrant

A person arrested without a warrant by any conservator of the peace or other law-enforcement officer for any of the acts set forth in § 19.2–19 committed in the presence of such conservator of the peace or law-enforcement officer, shall be brought forthwith before a magistrate or judge, and proceedings shall be had in accordance with §§ 19.2–20 and 19.2–21.

Acts 1975, c. 495.

§ 19.2–23. Payment of fees or mileage allowances into county or city treasury

Any conservator or policeman appointed under the provisions of this chapter shall not be entitled to fees or mileage for performance of his duties as such conservator or policeman.

Acts 1975, c. 495.

ARTICLE 3

APPEALS

§ 19.2–24. When appeal may be taken; witnesses recognized; bail

Any person from whom a recognizance is required under the provisions of this chapter or who has been committed to jail for failure to give security therefor, may appeal to the circuit court of the county or city, and, in such case, the judge from whose judgment the appeal is taken shall recognize such of the witnesses as he thinks proper; provided, however, that the person taking the appeal may be required to give bail, with good security, for his appearance at the circuit court of the county or city.

Acts 1975, c. 495; Acts 1978, c. 500.

§ 19.2–25. Power of court on appeal

The court may dismiss the complaint or affirm the judgment, and make what order it sees fit as to the costs. If it award costs against the appellant, the recognizance which he may have given shall stand as security therefor. When there is a failure to prosecute the appeal, such recognizance shall remain in force, although there be no order of affirmance. On any appeal the court may require of the appellant a new recognizance if it see fit.

Any person committed to jail under this chapter may be discharged by the circuit court of the county or city on such terms as it may deem reasonable.

Acts 1975, c. 495.

CHAPTER 3

MAGISTRATES

ARTICLE 1

TRANSITION PROVISIONS

§ 19.2–26. Repeal of inconsistent statutes, municipal charters, etc.

All acts and parts of acts, all sections of this Code, and all provisions of municipal charters, inconsistent with the provisions of this title, are, except as herein otherwise provided, repealed to the extent of such inconsistency.

Acts 1975, c. 495.

§ 19.2–27. Effect of repeal of Title 39.1 on prior acts, offenses, etc.

The repeal of Title 39.1 effective as of January 1, 1974, shall not affect any act or offense done or committed or any penalty or forfeiture incurred, or any right established, accrued, or accruing on or before such date, or any prosecution, suit or action pending on that day.

Acts 1975, c. 495.

§ 19.2–28. Certain notices, recognizances and processes validated

Any notice given, recognizance taken, or process or writ issued, before January 1, 1974, shall be valid although given, taken or to be returned to a day after such date, in like manner as if this title had been effective before the same was given, taken or issued.

Acts 1975, c. 495.

§ 19.2–29. References to former sections, articles and chapters in Title 39.1

Whenever in Chapter 3 (§ 19.2–26 et seq.) of this title any of the conditions, requirements, provisions or contents of any section, article or chapter of Title 39.1, as such title existed prior to January 1, 1974, are transferred in the same or modified form to a new section, article or chapter, and whenever any such former section, article or chapter is given a new number in Chapter 3 of this title all references to any such former section, article or chapter of Title 39.1 appearing elsewhere in this Code than in Chapter 3 of this title shall be construed to apply to the new or renumbered section, article or chapter containing such conditions, requirements, provisions or contents or portions thereof.

Acts 1975, c. 495; Acts 2002, c. 310.

Article 2

Abolition of Justice of the Peace System

§ 19.2-30. Repealed by Acts 2008, cc. 551 and 691

§ 19.2-31. Abolition of office of issuing justice

Effective January 1, 1974, the office of issuing justice as provided for in Chapter 2 (§ 39.1-20 et seq.) of Title 39.1 having been abolished, nevertheless, any such special justice of the peace in office December 31, 1973, and elected by the town council for a specific term to expire after that date, may continue in office for the remainder of that term. If he continues in office as provided herein, such justice shall exercise the same powers, perform the same duties, and receive such compensation as he was receiving as of December 31, 1973.

Acts 1975, c. 495.

§ 19.2-32. References to justices of the peace

References in law to justices of the peace shall be deemed to apply to magistrates unless the provisions of Chapter 3 (§ 19.2-26 et seq.) of this title shall render such reference inapplicable.

Acts 1975, c. 495; Acts 2002, c. 310.

Article 3

The Magistrate System

§ 19.2-33. Office of magistrate

The office of magistrate shall be vested with all the authority, duties and obligations previously vested in the office of justice of the peace prior to January 1, 1974.

Acts 1975, c. 495.

§ 19.2-34. Number of magistrates

There shall be appointed as many magistrates as are necessary for the effective administration of justice. The positions of all employees of the magistrate system shall be authorized by the Committee on District Courts established pursuant to § 16.1-69.33.

Acts 1975, c. 495; Acts 1976, c. 138; Acts 1977, c. 198; Acts 1981, c. 4; Acts 1992, c. 55. Amended by Acts 2008, c. 551; Acts 2008, c. 691.

§ 19.2-35. Appointment; supervision generally

Magistrates and any other personnel in the office of the magistrate shall be appointed by the Executive Secretary of the Supreme Court of Virginia in consultation with the chief judges of the circuit courts having jurisdiction within the region. Each magistrate shall be appointed to serve one or more of the magisterial regions created by the Executive Secretary. Each magisterial region shall be comprised of one or more judicial districts. The Executive Secretary shall have full supervisory authority over the magistrates so appointed. Notwithstanding any other provision of law, the only methods for the selection of magistrates shall be as set out in this section.

No person shall be appointed under this section until he has submitted his fingerprints to be used for the conduct of a national criminal records search and a Virginia criminal history records search. No person with a criminal conviction for a felony shall be appointed as a magistrate.

Acts 1975, c. 495; Acts 1976, c. 138; Acts 1981, c. 4; Acts 1988, c. 511; Acts 2002, c. 310; Acts 2004, c. 370; Acts 2004, c. 452. Amended by Acts 2008, c. 551; Acts 2008, c. 691.

§ 19.2-36. Chief magistrates

A. The Executive Secretary of the Supreme Court of Virginia may appoint chief magistrates, for the purpose of assisting in the training of the magistrates and being responsible to the Executive Secretary for the conduct of the magistrates and to further assist the Office of the Executive Secretary in the operation of one or more of the magisterial regions. The chief magistrate shall exercise direct daily supervision over the magistrates he supervises and shall have the power to suspend without pay a magistrate after consultation and with the concurrence of the Executive Secretary.

B. To be eligible for appointment as chief magistrate, a person shall meet all of the qualifications of a magistrate under § 19.2-37 and must be a member in good standing of the Virginia State Bar. His appointment as chief magistrate shall terminate effective on the date on which his membership in good standing ceases. The requirements of this subsection relating to membership in the Virginia State Bar shall not apply to any person appointed as a chief magistrate before July 1, 2008, who continues in that capacity without a break in service.

Acts 1975, c. 495; Acts 1984, c. 37; Acts 2004, c. 370. Amended by Acts 2008, c. 551; Acts 2008, c. 691.

§ 19.2-37. Magistrates; eligibility for appointment; restrictions on activities

A. Any person who is a United States citizen and resident of the Commonwealth may be appointed to the office of magistrate under this title subject to the limitations of Chapter 28 (§ 2.2–2800 et seq.) of Title 2.2 and of this section.

B. Every person appointed as a magistrate on and after July 1, 2008, shall be required to have a bachelor's degree from an accredited institution of higher education. A person initially appointed as a magistrate prior to July 1, 2008, who continues in office without a break in service is not required to have a bachelor's degree from an accredited institution of higher education.

C. A person shall not be eligible for appointment as a magistrate under the provisions of this title: (a) if such person is a law-enforcement officer; (b) if such person or his spouse is a clerk, deputy or assistant clerk, or employee of any such clerk of a district or circuit court, provided that the Committee on District Courts may authorize a magistrate to assist in the district court clerk's office on a part-time basis; (c) if the parent, child, spouse, or sibling of such person is a district or circuit court judge in the magisterial region where he will serve; or (d) if such person is the chief executive officer, or a member of the board of supervisors, town or city council, or other governing body for any political subdivision of the Commonwealth.

D. No magistrate shall issue any warrant or process in complaint of his spouse, child, grandchild, parent, grandparent, parent-in-law, child-in-law, brother, sister, brother-in-law or sister-in-law, nephew, niece, uncle, aunt, first cousin, guardian or ward.

E. A magistrate may not engage in any other activity for financial gain during the hours that he is serving on duty as a magistrate. A magistrate may not be employed outside his duty hours without the prior written approval of the Executive Secretary.

F. No person appointed as a magistrate on or after July 1, 2008, may engage in the practice of law.

G. A magistrate who is designated as a marriage celebrant under § 20–25 may not accept a fee, a gratuity, or any other thing of value for exercise of authority as a marriage celebrant.

Acts 1975, c. 495; Acts 1976, c. 138; Acts 1978, c. 463; Acts 1978, c. 760; Acts 1984, c. 41; Acts 1985, c. 45; Acts 1986, c. 202; Acts 1996, c. 112; Acts 1999, c. 267; Acts 2004, c. 830. Amended by Acts 2008, c. 551; Acts 2008, c. 691.

§ 19.2–38. Probationary period; compensation and benefits; vacancies; revocation of appointment

Persons appointed as magistrates under the provisions of this chapter shall serve at the pleasure of the Executive Secretary. Upon appointment by the Executive Secretary, every magistrate shall serve initially for a nine-month probationary period during which the magistrate must complete the minimum training program as established by the Committee on District Courts and satisfactorily complete a certification examination. Any magistrate who fails to successfully pass the certification examination shall not serve beyond the nine-month probationary period. The probationary period described in this section shall not apply to any magistrate serving on July 1, 2008, who has successfully completed the minimum training program and passed the certification examination, provided there is no break in service after July 1, 2008. Magistrates shall be entitled to compensation and other benefits only from the time they take office.

Acts 1975, c. 495; Acts 1980, c. 505; Acts 2004, c. 370. Amended by Acts 2008, c. 551; Acts 2008, c. 691.

§ 19.2–38.1. Training standards; training prerequisite to reappointment; waiver

The Committee on District Courts shall establish minimum training and certification standards for magistrates in accordance with such rules and regulations as may be established by the Committee. Every magistrate shall comply with these standards and shall complete the minimum training standards as a prerequisite for continuing to serve as magistrate beyond the nine-month probationary period as established by § 19.2–38. The Committee on District Courts upon request may waive any portion of the minimum training standards for an individual magistrate.

Acts 1980, c. 505; Acts 1985, c. 132; Acts 1995, c. 611. Amended by Acts 2008, c. 551; Acts 2008, c. 691.

§ 19.2–39. Bond

Every magistrate appointed under the provisions of this chapter shall enter into bond in the sum of $5,000, made payable to the Commonwealth, before a clerk of a circuit court, for the faithful performance of his duties. The premium for such bond shall be paid by the Commonwealth. Provided, however, that in lieu of specific bonds, the Committee on District Courts may in its discretion procure faithful performance of duty blanket bonds for all magistrates and for the penalty contained in this section, unless in the discretion of the Committee, bonds with a larger penalty should be obtained. Such blanket bonds shall be made payable to the Commonwealth and shall cover all funds handled by a magistrate whether such funds belong to the Commonwealth or any political subdivision thereof. Provided further, that in those instances where specific bonds for magistrates are in effect, the Committee on District Courts may, whenever it deems it advisable, terminate such specific bonds upon obtaining a blanket bond covering such magistrates with appropriate refunds or credit being made for the unearned premiums on the specific bonds terminated. A copy of any such blanket bond so procured shall be filed with the State Comptroller and with the clerk of the respective circuit courts. The premiums for such blanket bonds shall be paid by the Commonwealth.

Acts 1975, c. 495. Amended by Acts 2008, c. 551; Acts 2008, c. 691.

§ 19.2–40. Repealed by Acts 1980, c. 758

Article 4

Supervision

§ 19.2–41. Repealed by Acts 2008, cc. 551 and 691

§ 19.2–42. Repealed by Acts 2004, c. 327

§ 19.2–43. Duty of Executive Secretary of Supreme Court

It shall be the duty of the Executive Secretary of the Supreme Court to exercise general supervisory power over the administration of magistrates and adopt such policies as are deemed necessary to supplement or clarify the provisions of this chapter with respect to such magistrates, to include fixing the time and place such magistrates shall serve. The Executive Secretary shall conduct training sessions and meetings for magistrates and provide information and materials for their use. He may appoint one or more magistrates to assist him and, in addition, require annual reports to be filed by the magistrates on their work as such, fees associated therewith and other information pertinent to their office, on forms to be furnished by him. The Executive Secretary may appoint and employ such personnel as are needed to manage the magistrate system and carry out the duties and responsibilities conferred upon the Executive Secretary by this chapter.

Acts 1975, c. 495. Amended by Acts 2008, c. 551; Acts 2008, c. 691.

Article 5

Jurisdiction and Powers

§ 19.2–44. Territorial jurisdiction

A magistrate shall be authorized to exercise the powers conferred on magistrates by this title only in the magisterial region or regions for which he is appointed, except that a magistrate may issue search warrants in accordance with the provisions of Chapter 5 (§ 19.2–52 et seq.) throughout the Commonwealth. A magistrate may exercise all powers conferred on magistrates by this title throughout the Commonwealth when so authorized by the Executive Secretary upon a determination that such assistance is necessary.

Acts 1975, c. 495; Acts 1976, c. 138; Acts 1995, c. 551. Amended by Acts 2008, c. 551; Acts 2008, c. 691; Acts 2014, c. 305; Acts 2014, c. 310.

§ 19.2–44.1. Repealed by Acts 1976, c. 138

§ 19.2–45. Powers enumerated

A magistrate shall have the following powers only:

(1) To issue process of arrest in accord with the provisions of §§ 19.2–71 to 19.2–82 of the Code;

(2) To issue search warrants in accord with the provisions of §§ 19.2–52 to 19.2–60 of the Code;

(3) To admit to bail or commit to jail all persons charged with offenses subject to the limitations of and in accord with general laws on bail;

(4) The same power to issue warrants and subpoenas as is conferred upon district courts and as limited by the provisions of §§ 19.2–71 through 19.2–82. A copy of all felony warrants issued at the request of a citizen shall be promptly delivered to the attorney for the Commonwealth for the county or city in which the warrant is returnable. Upon the request of the attorney for the Commonwealth, a copy of any misdemeanor warrant issued at the request of a citizen shall be delivered to the attorney for the Commonwealth for such county or city. All attachments, warrants and subpoenas shall be returnable before a district court or any court of limited jurisdiction continued in operation pursuant to § 16.1–70.1;

(5) To issue civil warrants directed to the sheriff or constable of the county or city wherein the defendant resides, together with a copy thereof, requiring him to summon the person against whom the claim is, to appear before a district court on a certain day, not exceeding 30 days from the date thereof to answer such claim. If there be two or more defendants and any defendant resides outside the jurisdiction in which the warrant is issued, the summons for such defendant residing outside the jurisdiction may be directed to the sheriff of the county or city of his residence, and such warrant may be served and returned as provided in § 16.1–80;

(6) To administer oaths and take acknowledgments;

(7) To act as conservators of the peace;

(8), (9) Repealed.

(10) To perform such other acts or functions specifically authorized by law.

Acts 1975, c. 495; Acts 1976, c. 471; Acts 1977, c. 332; Acts 1978, c. 500; Acts 1978, c. 605; Acts 1985, c. 77; Acts 2007, c. 122; Acts 2007, c. 373. Amended by Acts 2008, c. 551; Acts 2008, c. 691; Acts 2009, c. 291; Acts 2009, c. 344.

Article 6

Compensation and Fees

§ 19.2–46. Compensation

The salaries of all magistrates shall be fixed and paid as provided in § 19.2–46.1. The salaries referred to herein shall be in lieu of all fees which may accrue to the recipient by virtue of his office.

Acts 1975, c. 495; Acts 1980, c. 139. Amended by Acts 2008, c. 551; Acts 2008, c. 691.

§ 19.2–46.1. Salaries to be fixed by the Executive Secretary; limitations; mileage allowance

Salaries of magistrates and any other personnel in the office of the magistrate shall be fixed by the Executive Secretary of the Supreme Court. Such salaries shall be fixed by the Executive Secretary at least annually at such time as he deems proper and as soon as practicable thereafter certified to the Comptroller.

In determining the salary of any magistrate, the Executive Secretary shall consider the work load of and territory and population served by the magistrate and such other factors he deems relevant.

The governing body of any county or city may add to the fixed compensation of magistrates such amount as the governing body may appropriate with the total amount not to exceed 50 percent of the amount paid by the Commonwealth to magistrates provided such additional compensation was in effect on June 30, 2008, for such magistrates and any magistrate receiving such additional compensation continues in office without a break in service. However, the total amount of additional compensation may not be increased after June 30, 2008. No additional amount paid by a local governing body shall be chargeable to the Executive Secretary of the Supreme Court, nor shall it remove or supersede any authority, control or supervision of the Executive Secretary or Committee on District Courts.

Acts 1975, c. 334; Acts 1981, c. 4; Acts 1995, c. 331; Acts 1995, c. 378; Acts 1998, c. 872, eff. Oct. 1, 1998. Amended by Acts 2008, c. 551; Acts 2008, c. 691.

§ 19.2–46.2. Full-time magistrates; certification for retirement coverage

The Committee on District Courts shall certify to the director of the Virginia Retirement System the names of those magistrates serving on a regular full-time basis. Certification by the Committee shall qualify a magistrate as a state employee, for purposes of §§ 51.1–124.3 and 51.1–152 of the Virginia Retirement System (§ 51.1–124.1 et seq.), effective on the date given in the certificate as the date on which such magistrate first served on a regular full-time basis on or after January 1, 1974.

Acts 1998, c. 872, eff. Oct. 1, 1998.

§ 19.2–47. Magistrate not to receive claims or evidence of debt for collection

No magistrate shall receive claims or evidence of debt for collection; and it shall be unlawful for any magistrate to receive claims of any kind for collection, or to accept or receive money or any other things of value by way of commission or compensation for or on account of any collection made by or through him on any such claim, either before or after judgment. Any magistrate violating this section shall be guilty of a Class 1 misdemeanor.

Acts 1975, c. 495.

§ 19.2–47.1. Disposition of funds

All funds paid to and collected by or on behalf of a magistrate shall be paid promptly to the appropriate district court clerk, circuit court clerk, commissioner in chancery, department of the Commonwealth, federal agency or as otherwise authorized by statute.

Acts 1998, c. 872, eff. Oct. 1, 1998.

§ 19.2–48. Audits

The Auditor of Public Accounts shall audit the records of all magistrates who serve any county or city when auditing the records of the district courts of such county or city or upon request of the chief district judge of the district in which such county or city is located.

Acts 1975, c. 495; Acts 1980, c. 195. Amended by Acts 2008, c. 551; Acts 2008, c. 691.

§ 19.2–48.1. Quarters for magistrates

A. The counties and cities served by a magistrate or magistrates shall provide suitable quarters for such magistrates, including a site for any videoconferencing equipment necessary to provide remote access to such magistrates. Insofar as possible, such quarters should be located in a public facility and should be appropriate to conduct the affairs of a judicial officer as well as provide convenient access to the public and law-enforcement officers. The county or city shall also provide all furniture and other equipment necessary for the efficient operation of the office.

B. Wherever practical, the office of magistrate shall be located at the county seat. However, offices may be located at other locations in the county, or city adjacent thereto, whenever such additional offices are necessary to effect the efficient administration of justice.

Acts 1975, c. 495; Acts 1981, c. 5; Acts 1988, c. 510. Amended by Acts 2008, c. 551; Acts 2008, c. 691.

CHAPTER 4

SPECIAL MAGISTRATES

§§ 19.2–49 to 19.2–51. Repealed by Acts 1980, c. 758

CHAPTER 5

SEARCH WARRANTS

§ 19.2–52. When search warrant may issue

Except as provided in § 19.2–56.1, search warrants, based upon complaint on oath supported by an affidavit as required in § 19.2–54, may be issued by any judge, magistrate or other person having authority to issue criminal warrants, if he be satisfied from such complaint and affidavit that there is reasonable and probable cause for the issuance of such search warrant.

Acts 1975, c. 495; Acts 1986, c. 636.

§ 19.2–53. What may be searched and seized

A. Search warrants may be issued for the search of or for specified places, things or persons, and seizure therefrom of the following things as specified in the warrant:

1. Weapons or other objects used in the commission of crime;

2. Articles or things the sale or possession of which is unlawful;

3. Stolen property or the fruits of any crime;

4. Any object, thing, or person, including without limitation, documents, books, papers, records or body fluids, constituting evidence of the commission of crime.

Notwithstanding any other provision in this chapter to the contrary, no search warrant may be issued as a substitute for a witness subpoena.

B. Any search warrant issued for the search and seizure of a computer, computer network, or other device containing electronic or digital information shall be deemed to include the search and seizure of the physical components and the electronic or digital information contained in any such computer, computer network, or other device.

C. Any search, including the search of the contents of any computer, computer network, or other device conducted pursuant to subsection B, may be conducted in any location and is not limited to the location where the evidence was seized.

Acts 1975, c. 495; Acts 1981, c. 559. Amended by Acts 2015, c. 501.

§ 19.2–53.1. Taking blood samples pursuant to search warrant; immunity

No cause of action shall lie in any court against any person authorized by law to withdraw blood pursuant to a search warrant issued in accordance with § 19.2–53 when that person is acting in accordance with such warrant, except in cases of negligence in the withdrawing of blood or willful misconduct.

Added by Acts 2015, c. 425.

§ 19.2–54. Affidavit preliminary to issuance of search warrant; general search warrant prohibited; effect of failure to file affidavit

No search warrant shall be issued until there is filed with the officer authorized to issue the same an affidavit of some person reasonably describing the place, thing, or person to be searched, the things or persons to be searched for thereunder, alleging briefly material facts, constituting the probable cause for the issuance of such warrant and alleging substantially the offense in relation to which such search is to be made and that the object, thing, or person searched for constitutes evidence of the commission of such offense. The affidavit may be filed by electronically transmitted (i) facsimile process or (ii) electronic record as defined in § 59.1–480. Such affidavit shall be certified by the officer who issues such warrant and delivered in person ; mailed by certified mail, return receipt requested ; or delivered by electronically transmitted facsimile process or by use of filing and security procedures as defined in the Uniform Electronic Transactions Act (§ 59.1–479 et seq.) for transmitting signed documents, by such officer or his designee or agent, to the clerk of the circuit court of the county or city wherein the search is made, with a copy of the affidavit also being delivered to the clerk of the circuit court of the county or city where the warrant is issued, if in a different county or city, within seven days after the issuance of such warrant and shall by such clerks be preserved as a record and shall at all times be subject to inspection by the public after the warrant that is the subject of the affidavit has been executed or 15 days after issuance of the warrant, whichever is earlier; however, such affidavit, any warrant issued pursuant thereto, any return made thereon, and any order sealing the affidavit, warrant, or return may be temporarily sealed for a specific period of time by the appropriate court upon application of the attorney for the Commonwealth for good cause shown in an ex parte hearing. Any individual arrested and claiming to be aggrieved by such search and seizure or any person who claims to be entitled to lawful possession of such property seized may move the appropriate court for the unsealing of such affidavit, warrant, and return. The burden of proof with respect to continued sealing shall be upon the Commonwealth. Each such clerk shall maintain an index of all such affidavits filed in his office in order to facilitate inspection. No such warrant shall be issued on an affidavit omitting such essentials, and no general warrant for the search of a house, place, compartment, vehicle or baggage shall be issued. The term "affidavit" as used in this section, means statements made under oath or affirmation and preserved verbatim.

Failure of the officer issuing such warrant to file the required affidavit shall not invalidate any search made under the warrant unless such failure shall continue for a period of 30 days. If the affidavit is filed prior to the expiration of the 30–day period, nevertheless, evidence obtained in any such search shall not be admissible until a reasonable time after the filing of the required affidavit.

Acts 1975, c. 495; Acts 1976, c. 552; Acts 1977, c. 109; Acts 1979, c. 583; Acts 1980, c. 362: Acts 1981, c. 559; Acts 1989, c. 719; Acts 2006, c. 285; Acts 2007, c. 212. Amended by Acts 2008, c. 147; Acts 2008, c. 183; Acts 2011, c. 196; Acts 2011, c. 219; Acts 2012, c. 5.

§ 19.2–55. Issuing general search warrant or search warrant without affidavit deemed malfeasance

Any person having authority to issue criminal warrants who wilfully and knowingly issues a general search warrant or a search warrant without the affidavit required by § 19.2–54 shall be deemed guilty of a malfeasance.

Acts 1975, c. 495.

§ 19.2–56. To whom search warrant directed; what it shall command; warrant to show date and time of issuance; copy of affidavit to be part of warrant and served therewith; warrants not executed within 15 days

The judge, magistrate or other official authorized to issue criminal warrants, shall issue a search warrant if he finds from the facts or circumstances recited in the affidavit that there is probable cause for the issuance thereof.

Every search warrant shall be directed to (i) the sheriff, sergeant, or any policeman of the county, city or town in which the place to be searched is located, (ii) any law-enforcement officer or agent employed by the Commonwealth and vested with the powers of sheriffs and police, or (iii) jointly to any such sheriff, sergeant, policeman or law-enforcement officer or agent and an agent, special agent or officer of the Federal Bureau of Investigation, the Bureau of Alcohol, Tobacco and Firearms of the United States Treasury, the United States Naval Criminal Investigative Service, the United States Department of Homeland Security, any inspector, law-enforcement official or police personnel of the United States Postal Service, or the Drug Enforcement Administration. The warrant shall (i) name the affiant, (ii) recite the offense in relation to which the search is to be made, (iii) name or describe the place to be searched, (iv) describe the property or person to be searched for, and (v) recite that the magistrate has found probable cause to believe that the property or person constitutes evidence of a crime (identified in the warrant) or tends to show that a person (named or described therein) has committed or is committing a crime.

The warrant shall command that the place be forthwith searched, either in day or night, and that the objects or persons described in the warrant, if found there, be seized. An inventory shall be produced before a court having jurisdiction of the offense in relation to which the warrant was issued as provided in § 19.2–57.

Any such warrant as provided in this section shall be executed by the policeman or other law-enforcement officer or agent into whose hands it shall come or be delivered. If the warrant is directed jointly to a sheriff, sergeant, policeman or law-enforcement officer or agent of the Commonwealth and a federal agent or officer as otherwise provided in this section, the warrant may be executed jointly or by the policeman, law-enforcement officer or agent into whose hands it is delivered. No other person may be permitted to be present during or participate in the execution of a warrant to search a place except (i) the owners and occupants of the place to be searched when permitted to be present by the officer in charge of the conduct of the search and (ii) persons designated by the officer in charge of the conduct of the search to assist or provide expertise in the conduct of the search.

Any search warrant for records or other information pertaining to a subscriber to, or customer of, an electronic communication service or remote computing service, whether a domestic corporation or foreign corporation, that is transacting or has transacted any business in the Commonwealth, to be executed upon such service provider may be executed within or without the Commonwealth by hand, United States mail, commercial delivery service, facsimile, or other electronic means upon the service provider. Notwithstanding the provisions of § 19.2–57, the officer executing a warrant pursuant to this paragraph shall endorse the date of execution thereon and shall file the warrant, with the inventory attached (or a notation that no property was seized) and the accompanying affidavit, unless such affidavit was made by voice or videotape recording, within three days after the materials ordered to be produced are received by the officer from the service provider. The return shall be made in the circuit court clerk's office for the jurisdiction wherein the warrant was issued. Saturdays, Sundays, or any federal or state legal holiday shall not be used in computing the three-day filing period.

Electronic communication service or remote computing service providers, whether a foreign or domestic corporation, shall also provide the contents of electronic communications pursuant to a search warrant issued under this section and § 19.2–70.3 using the same process described in the preceding paragraph.

Every search warrant shall contain the date and time it was issued. However, the failure of any such search warrant to contain the date and time it was issued shall not render the warrant void, provided that the date and time of issuing of said warrant is established by competent evidence.

The judge, magistrate, or other official authorized to issue criminal warrants shall attach a copy of the affidavit required by § 19.2–54, which shall become a part of the search warrant and served therewith. However, this provision shall not be applicable in any case in which the affidavit is made by means of a voice or videotape recording or where the affidavit has been sealed pursuant to § 19.2–54.

Any search warrant not executed within 15 days after issuance thereof shall be returned to, and voided by, the officer who issued such search warrant.

For the purposes of this section:

"Foreign corporation" means any corporation or other entity, whose primary place of business is located outside of the boundaries of the Commonwealth, that makes a contract or engages in a terms of service agreement with a resident of the Commonwealth to be performed in whole or in part by either party in the Commonwealth, or a corporation that has been issued a certificate of authority pursuant to § 13.1–759 to transact business in the Commonwealth. The making of the contract or terms of service agreement or the issuance of a certificate of authority shall be considered to be the agreement of the foreign corporation or entity that a search warrant or subpoena, which has been properly served on it, has the same legal force and effect as if served personally within the Commonwealth.

"Properly served" means delivery of a search warrant or subpoena by hand, by United States mail, by commercial delivery service, by facsimile or by any other manner to any officer of a corporation or its general manager in the Commonwealth, to any natural person designated by it as agent for the service of process, or if such corporation has designated a corporate agent, to any person named in the latest annual report filed pursuant to § 13.1–775.

Acts 1975, c. 495; Acts 1977, c. 289; Acts 1979, c. 584; Acts 1980, c. 573; Acts 1981, c. 559; Acts 1984, c. 491; Acts 1984, c. 598; Acts 1988, c. 50; Acts 1989, c. 719; Acts 2000, c. 783; Acts 2001, c. 183; Acts 2001, c. 205; Acts 2007, c. 416. Amended by Acts 2009, c. 725; Acts 2015, c. 75; Acts 2015, c. 126.

§ 19.2–56.1. Warrant issued for search of attorney's office

A. Any warrant sought for the search of a premises or the contents thereof belonging to or under the control of any licensed attorney-at-law to search for evidence of any crime solely involving a client of such attorney shall be issued only by a circuit court judge. Any evidence seized pursuant to this section shall be inventoried forthwith by the clerk of the issuing court and sealed by the issuing judge. As soon thereafter as is practicable, the issuing judge shall conduct an in camera inspection of the seized evidence in the presence of the attorney from whom the evidence was seized. Following such inspection the issuing judge shall return any evidence so seized which is determined to be within the scope of the attorney-client privilege and not otherwise subject to seizure.

B. Nothing herein shall bar the standing of the client to challenge the admissibility of any evidence seized pursuant to this section in any trial or proceeding.

Acts 1986, c. 636.

§ 19.2–56.2. Application for and issuance of search warrant for a tracking device; installation and use

A. As used in this section, unless the context requires a different meaning:

"Judicial officer" means a judge, magistrate, or other person authorized to issue criminal warrants.

"Law-enforcement officer" shall have the same meaning as in § 9.1–101.

"Tracking device" means an electronic or mechanical device that permits a person to remotely determine or track the position or movement of a person or object. "Tracking device" includes devices that store geographic data for subsequent access or analysis and devices that allow for the real-time monitoring of movement.

"Use of a tracking device" includes the installation, maintenance, and monitoring of a tracking device but does not include the interception of wire, electronic, or oral communications or the capture, collection, monitoring, or viewing of images.

B. A law-enforcement officer may apply for a search warrant from a judicial officer to permit the use of a tracking device. Each application for a search warrant authorizing the use of a tracking device shall be made in writing, upon oath or affirmation, to a judicial officer for the circuit in which the tracking device is to be installed, or where there is probable cause to believe the offense for which the tracking device is sought has been committed, is being committed, or will be committed.

The law-enforcement officer shall submit an affidavit, which may be filed by electronically transmitted (i) facsimile process or (ii) electronic record as defined in § 59.1–480, and shall include:

1. The identity of the applicant and the identity of the law-enforcement agency conducting the investigation;

2. The identity of the vehicle, container, item, or object to which, in which, or on which the tracking device is to be attached, placed, or otherwise installed; the name of the owner or possessor of the vehicle, container, item, or object described, if known; and the jurisdictional area in which the vehicle, container, item, or object described is expected to be found, if known;

3. Material facts constituting the probable cause for the issuance of the search warrant and alleging substantially the offense in relation to which such tracking device is to be used and a showing that probable cause exists that the information likely to be obtained will be evidence of the commission of such offense; and

4. The name of the county or city where there is probable cause to believe the offense for which the tracking device is sought has been committed, is being committed, or will be committed.

C. 1. If the judicial officer finds, based on the affidavit submitted, that there is probable cause to believe that a crime has been committed, is being committed, or will be committed and that there is probable cause to believe the information likely to be obtained from the use of the tracking device will be evidence of the commission of such offense, the judicial officer shall issue a search warrant authorizing the use of the tracking device. The search warrant shall authorize the use of the tracking device from within the Commonwealth to track a person or property for a reasonable period of time, not to exceed 30 days from the issuance of the search warrant. The search warrant shall authorize the collection of the tracking data contained in or obtained from the tracking device but shall not authorize the interception of wire, electronic, or oral communications or the capture, collection, monitoring, or viewing of images.

2. The affidavit shall be certified by the judicial officer who issues the search warrant and shall be delivered to and preserved as a record by the clerk of the circuit court of the county or city where there is probable cause to believe the offense for which the tracking device has been sought has been committed, is being committed, or will be committed. The affidavit shall be delivered by the judicial officer in person; mailed by certified mail, return receipt requested; or delivered by electronically transmitted facsimile process or by use of filing and security procedures as defined in the Uniform Electronic Transactions Act (§ 59.1–479 et seq.) for transmitting signed documents.

3. By operation of law, the affidavit, search warrant, return, and any other related materials or pleadings shall be sealed. Upon motion of the Commonwealth or the owner or possessor of the vehicle, container, item, or object that was tracked, the circuit court may unseal such documents if it appears that the unsealing is consistent with the ends of justice or is necessary to reasonably inform such person of the nature of the evidence to be presented against him or to adequately prepare for his defense.

4. The circuit court may, for good cause shown, grant one or more extensions, not to exceed 30 days each.

D. 1. The search warrant shall command the law-enforcement officer to complete the installation authorized by the search warrant within 15 days after issuance of the search warrant.

2. The law-enforcement officer executing the search warrant shall enter on it the exact date and time the device was installed and the period during which it was used.

3. Law-enforcement officers shall be permitted to monitor the tracking device during the period authorized in the search warrant, unless the period is extended as provided for in this section.

4. Law-enforcement officers shall remove the tracking device as soon as practical, but not later than 10 days after the use of the tracking device has ended. Upon request, and for good cause shown, the circuit court may grant one or more extensions for such removal for a period not to exceed 10 days each.

5. In the event that law-enforcement officers are unable to remove the tracking device as required by subdivision 4, the law-enforcement officers shall disable the device, if possible, and all use of the tracking device shall cease.

6. Within 10 days after the use of the tracking device has ended, the executed search warrant shall be returned to the circuit court of the county or city where there is probable cause to believe the offense for which the tracking device has been sought has been committed, is being committed, or will be committed, as designated in the search warrant, where it shall be preserved as a record by the clerk of the circuit court.

E. Within 10 days after the use of the tracking device has ended, a copy of the executed search warrant shall be served on the person who was tracked and the person whose property was tracked. Service may be accomplished by delivering a copy to the person who, or whose property, was tracked or by leaving a copy with any individual found at the person's usual place of abode who is a member of the person's family, other than a temporary sojourner or guest, and who is 16 years of age or older and by mailing a copy to the person's last known address. Upon request, and for good cause shown, the circuit court may grant one or more extensions for such service for a period not to exceed 30 days each. Good cause shall include, but not be limited to, a continuing criminal investigation, the potential for intimidation, the endangerment of an individual, or the preservation of evidence.

F. The disclosure or publication, without authorization of a circuit court, by a court officer, law-enforcement officer, or other person responsible for the administration of this section of the existence of a search warrant issued pursuant to this section, application for such search warrant, any affidavit filed in support of such warrant, or any return or data obtained as a result of such search warrant that is sealed by operation of law is punishable as a Class 1 misdemeanor.

Added by Acts 2012, c. 636, eff. April 5, 2012; Acts 2012, c. 679, eff. April 6, 2012.

§ 19.2–57. Execution and return of warrant; list of property seized

The warrant shall be executed by the search of the place described in the warrant and, if property described in the warrant is found there, by the seizure of the property. The officer who seizes any property shall prepare an inventory thereof, under oath. An inventory of any seized property shall be produced before the circuit court of the county or city where the search was conducted. The officer executing the warrant shall endorse the date of execution thereon and the officer or his designee shall file the warrant, with the inventory attached (or a notation that no property was seized) and the accompanying affidavit, unless such affidavit was made by voice or videotape recording, within three days after the execution of such search warrant in the circuit court clerk's office, wherein the search was made, as provided in § 19.2–54. Saturdays, Sundays, or any federal or state legal holiday shall not be used in computing the three-day filing period. The officer, or his designee or agent, may file the warrant, inventory, and accompanying affidavit by delivering them in person, or by mailing them certified mail, return receipt requested, or delivering them by electronically transmitted facsimile process.

Acts 1975, c. 495; Acts 1976, c. 142; Acts 1976, c. 552; Acts 1977, c. 109; Acts 1980, c. 573; Acts 1984, c. 491. Amended by Acts 2008, c. 147; Acts 2008, c. 183.

§ 19.2–58. Disposition of property seized

If any such warrant be executed by the seizure of property, or of any other of the things aforesaid, the same shall be safely kept by the direction of such judge or court, to be used as evidence, and thereafter be disposed of as provided by law; provided, however, that any such property seized under such warrant which is not used in evidence and any property which is stolen or embezzled property shall be restored to its owner, and the things mentioned in § 19.2–53 may be burnt or otherwise destroyed, under such direction, as soon as there is no further need for its use as evidence unless it is otherwise expressly provided by law.

Acts 1975, c. 495.

§ 19.2–59. Search without warrant prohibited; when search without warrant lawful

No officer of the law or any other person shall search any place, thing or person, except by virtue of and under a warrant issued by a proper officer. Any officer or other person searching any place, thing or person otherwise than by virtue of and under a search warrant, shall be guilty of malfeasance in office. Any officer or person violating the provisions of this section shall be liable to any person aggrieved thereby in both compensatory and punitive damages. Any officer found guilty of a second offense under this section shall, upon conviction thereof, immediately forfeit his office, and such finding shall be deemed to create a vacancy in such office to be filled according to law.

Provided, however, that any officer empowered to enforce the game laws or marine fisheries laws as set forth in Title 28.2 may without a search warrant enter for the purpose of enforcing such laws, any freight yard or room, passenger depot, baggage room or warehouse, storage room or warehouse, train, baggage car, passenger car, express car, Pullman car or freight car of any common carrier, or any boat, automobile or other vehicle; but nothing in this proviso contained shall be construed to permit a search of any occupied berth or compartment on any passenger car or boat or any baggage, bag, trunk, box or other closed container without a search warrant.

Acts 1975, c. 495; Acts 1976, c. 293; Acts 1978, c. 721; Acts 1997, c. 147.

§ 19.2–59.1. Strip searches prohibited; exceptions; how strip searches conducted

A. No person in custodial arrest for a traffic infraction, Class 3 or Class 4 misdemeanor, or a violation of a city, county, or town ordinance, which is punishable by no more than thirty days in jail shall be strip searched unless there is reasonable cause to believe on the part of a law-enforcement officer authorizing the search that the individual is concealing a weapon. All strip searches conducted under this section shall be performed by persons of the same sex as the person arrested and on premises where the search cannot be observed by persons not physically conducting the search.

B. A regional jail superintendent or the chief of police or the sheriff of the county or city shall develop a written policy regarding strip searches.

C. A search of any body cavity must be performed under sanitary conditions and a search of any body cavity, other than the mouth, shall be conducted either by or under the supervision of medically trained personnel.

D. Strip searches authorized pursuant to the exceptions stated in subsection A of this section shall be conducted by a law-enforcement officer as defined in § 9.1–101.

E. The provisions of this section shall not apply when the person is taken into custody by or remanded to a law-enforcement officer pursuant to a circuit or district court order.

F. For purposes of this section, "strip search" shall mean having an arrested person remove or arrange some or all of his clothing so as to permit a visual inspection of the genitals, buttocks, anus, female breasts, or undergarments of such person.

G. Nothing in this section shall prohibit a sheriff or a regional jail superintendent from requiring that inmates take hot water and soap showers and be subjected to visual inspection upon assignment to the general population area of the jail or upon determination by the sheriff or regional jail superintendent that the inmate must be held at the jail by reason of his inability to post bond after reasonable opportunity to do so.

Acts 1981, c. 608; Acts 1995, c. 112.

§ 19.2–60. Motion for return of seized property and to suppress

A person aggrieved by an allegedly unlawful search or seizure may move the court to return any seized property and to suppress it for use as evidence. The court shall receive evidence on any issue of fact necessary to the decision of the motion. If the motion is granted by a court of record, any seized property shall be restored as soon as practicable unless otherwise subject to lawful detention, and such property shall not be admissible in evidence at any hearing or trial. If the motion is granted by a court not of record, such property shall not be admissible in evidence at any hearing or trial before that court, but the ruling shall have no effect on any hearing or trial in a court of record.

Acts 1975, c. 495.

§ 19.2–60.1. Use of unmanned aircraft systems by public bodies; search warrant required

A. As used in this section, unless the context requires a different meaning:

"Unmanned aircraft" means an aircraft that is operated without the possibility of human intervention from within or on the aircraft.

"Unmanned aircraft system" means an unmanned aircraft and associated elements, including communication links, sensing devices, and the components that control the unmanned aircraft.

B. No state or local government department, agency, or instrumentality having jurisdiction over criminal law enforcement or regulatory violations, including but not limited to the Department of State Police, and no department of law enforcement as defined in § 15.2–836 of any county, city, or town shall utilize an unmanned aircraft system except during the execution of a search warrant issued pursuant to this chapter or an administrative or inspection warrant issued pursuant to law.

C. Notwithstanding the prohibition in this section, an unmanned aircraft system may be deployed without a warrant (i) when an Amber Alert is activated pursuant to § 52–34.3, (ii) when a Senior Alert is activated pursuant to § 52–34.6, (iii) when a Blue Alert is activated pursuant to § 52–34.9, (iv) where use of an unmanned aircraft system is determined to be necessary to alleviate an immediate danger to any person, (v) for training exercises related to such uses, or (vi) if a person with legal authority consents to the warrantless search.

D. The warrant requirements of this section shall not apply when such systems are utilized to support the Commonwealth for purposes other than law enforcement, including damage assessment, traffic assessment, flood stage assessment, and wildfire assessment. Nothing herein shall prohibit use of unmanned aircraft systems for private, commercial, or recreational use or solely for research and development purposes by institutions of higher education and other research organizations or institutions.

E. Evidence obtained through the utilization of an unmanned aircraft system in violation of this section is not admissible in any criminal or civil proceeding.

F. In no case may a weaponized unmanned aircraft system be deployed in the Commonwealth or its use facilitated in the Commonwealth by a state or local government department, agency, or instrumentality or department of law enforcement in the Commonwealth except in operations at the Space Port and Naval/Aegis facilities at Wallops Island.

G. Nothing herein shall apply to the Armed Forces of the United States or the Virginia National Guard while utilizing unmanned aircraft systems during training required to maintain readiness for its federal mission or when facilitating training for other U.S. Department of Defense units.

Added by Acts 2015, c. 764; Acts 2015, c. 774.

CHAPTER 6

INTERCEPTION OF WIRE, ELECTRONIC OR ORAL COMMUNICATIONS

§ 19.2-61. Definitions

As used in this chapter:

"Aggrieved person" means a person who was a party to any intercepted wire, electronic or oral communication or a person against whom the interception was directed;

"Aural transfer" means a transfer containing the human voice at any point between and including the point of origin and the point of reception;

"Communications common carrier" means any person engaged as a common carrier for hire in communication by wire or radio or in radio transmission of energy;

"Contents" when used with respect to any wire, electronic or oral communication, includes any information concerning the substance, purport or meaning of that communication;

"Electronic, mechanical or other device" means any device or apparatus that can be used to intercept a wire, electronic or oral communication other than:

(a) Any telephone or telegraph instrument, equipment or facility, or any component thereof, (i) furnished to the subscriber or user by a provider of wire or electronic communication service in the ordinary course of its business and being used by the subscriber or user in the ordinary course of its business or furnished by the subscriber or user for connection to the facilities of such service and used in the ordinary course of the subscriber's or user's business; or (ii) being used by a communications common carrier in the ordinary course of its business, or by an investigative or law-enforcement officer in the ordinary course of his duties;

(b) A hearing aid or similar device being used to correct subnormal hearing to not better than normal;

"Electronic communication" means any transfer of signs, signals, writing, images, sounds, data, or intelligence of any nature transmitted in whole or in part by a wire, radio, electromagnetic, photoelectronic or photooptical system. The term does not include:

1. Any wire communication or oral communication as defined herein;

2. Any communication made through a tone-only paging device;

3. Any communication from an electronic or mechanical device which permits the tracking of the movement of a person or object; or

4. Any electronic funds transfer information stored by a financial institution in a communications system used for the electronic storage and transfer of funds;

"Electronic communication service" means any service which provides to users thereof the ability to send or receive wire or electronic communications;

"Electronic communication system" means any wire, radio, electromagnetic, photooptical or photoelectronic facilities for the transmission of wire or electronic communications, and any computer facilities or related electronic equipment for the electronic storage of such communications;

"Electronic storage" means any temporary, intermediate storage of a wire or electronic communication incidental to the electronic transmission thereof and any storage of such communication by an electronic communication service for purposes of backup protection of such communication;

"Intercept" means any aural or other means of acquisition of the contents of any wire, electronic or oral communication through the use of any electronic, mechanical or other device;

"Investigative or law-enforcement officer" means any officer of the United States or of a state or political subdivision thereof, who is empowered by law to conduct investigations of or to make arrests for offenses enumerated in this chapter, and any attorney authorized by law to prosecute or participate in the prosecution of such offenses;

"Judge of competent jurisdiction" means a judge of any circuit court of the Commonwealth with general criminal jurisdiction;

"Monitor" or "monitoring" means the actual auditory or visual acquisition of an intercepted communication by any means;

"Oral communication" means any oral communication uttered by a person exhibiting an expectation that such communication is not subject to interception under circumstances justifying such expectations but does not include any electronic communication;

"Pen register" means a device or process that records or decodes dialing, routing, addressing or signaling information transmitted by an instrument or facility from which a wire or electronic communication is transmitted; however, such information shall not include the contents of any communication. The term does not include any device or process used by a provider or customer of a wire or electronic communication service for billing, or recording as an incident to billing, for communications services provided by such provider or any device or process used by a provider or customer of a wire communication service for cost accounting or other like purposes in the ordinary course of the provider's or customer's business;

"Person" means any employee or agent of the Commonwealth or a political subdivision thereof, and any individual, partnership, association, joint stock company, trust or corporation;

"Readily accessible to the general public" means, with respect to a radio communication, that such communication is not (i) scrambled or encrypted; (ii) transmitted using modulation techniques whose essential parameters have been withheld from the public with the intention of preserving the privacy of such communication; (iii) carried on a subcarrier or other signal subsidiary to a radio transmission; (iv) transmitted over a communication system provided by a communications common carrier, unless the communication is a tone-only paging system communication; or (v) transmitted on frequencies allocated under Part 25, subpart D, E, or F of Part 74, or Part 94 of the Rules of the Federal Communications Commission, unless, in the case of a communication transmitted on a frequency allocated under Part 74 that is not exclusively allocated to broadcast auxiliary services, the communication is a two-way voice communication by radio;

"Remote computing service" means the provision to the public of computer storage or processing services by means of an electronic communications system;

"Trap and trace device" means a device or process that captures the incoming electronic or other impulses that identify the originating number or other dialing, routing, addressing and signaling information reasonably likely to identify the source of a wire or electronic communication; however, such information shall not include the contents of any communication;

"User" means any person or entity who uses an electronic communication service and is duly authorized by the provider of such service to engage in such use;

"Wire communication" means any aural transfer made in whole or in part through the use of facilities for the transmission of communications by the aid of wire, cable, or other like connection, including the use of such connection in a switching station, furnished or operated by any person engaged in providing or operating such facilities for the transmission of communications.

Acts 1975, c. 495; Acts 1988, c. 889; Acts 2002, c. 588; Acts 2002, c. 623; Acts 2005, c. 934.

§ 19.2–62. Interception, disclosure, etc., of wire, electronic or oral communications unlawful; penalties; exceptions

A. Except as otherwise specifically provided in this chapter any person who:

1. Intentionally intercepts, endeavors to intercept or procures any other person to intercept or endeavor to intercept, any wire, electronic or oral communication;

2. Intentionally uses, endeavors to use, or procures any other person to use or endeavor to use any electronic, mechanical or other device to intercept any oral communication;

3. Intentionally discloses, or endeavors to disclose, to any other person the contents of any wire, electronic or oral communication knowing or having reason to know that the information was obtained through the interception of a wire, electronic or oral communication; or

4. Intentionally uses, or endeavors to use, the contents of any wire, electronic or oral communication, knowing or having reason to know that the information was obtained through the interception of a wire, electronic or oral communication; shall be guilty of a Class 6 felony.

B. 1. It shall not be unlawful under this chapter for an operator of a switchboard, or an officer, employee or agent of a provider of wire or electronic communications service, whose facilities are used in the transmission of a wire communication, to intercept, disclose or use that communication in the normal course of his employment while engaged in any activity which is a necessary incident to the rendition of his service or to the protection of the rights or property of the provider of that service. However, a provider of wire communication service to the public shall not utilize service observing or random monitoring except for mechanical or service quality control checks. It shall not be a criminal offense under this chapter for providers of wire or electronic communications service, their officers, employees and agents, landlords, custodians, or other persons pursuant to a court order under this chapter, to provide information facilities or technical assistance to an investigative or law-enforcement officer, who, pursuant to this chapter, is authorized to intercept a wire, electronic or oral communication.

2. It shall not be a criminal offense under this chapter for a person to intercept a wire, electronic or oral communication, where such person is a party to the communication or one of the parties to the communication has given prior consent to such interception.

3. It shall not be a criminal offense under this chapter for any person:

(a) To intercept or access an electronic communication made through an electronic communication system that is configured so that such electronic communication is readily accessible to the general public;

(b) To intercept any radio communication which is transmitted (i) by any station for the use of the general public, or that relates to ships, aircraft, vehicles, or persons in distress, (ii) by any governmental, law-enforcement, civil defense, private land mobile, or public safety communications system, including police and fire, readily accessible to the general public, (iii) by a station operating on an authorized frequency within the bands allocated to the amateur, citizens band, or general mobile radio services; or (iv) by any marine or aeronautical communications system;

(c) To intercept any wire or electronic communication the transmission of which is causing harmful interference to any lawfully operating station or consumer electronic equipment, to the extent necessary to identify the source of such interference;

(d) Using the same frequency to intercept any radio communication made through a system that utilizes frequencies monitored by individuals engaged in the provision or the use of such system, if such communication is not scrambled or encrypted;

(e) To use a pen register or a trap and trace device pursuant to §§ 19.2–70.1 and 19.2–70.2; or

(f) Who is a provider of electronic communication service to record the fact that a wire or electronic communication was initiated or completed in order to protect such provider, another provider furnishing service toward the completion of the wire or electronic communication, or a user of that service, from fraudulent, unlawful or abusive use of such service.

C. A person or entity providing an electronic communication service to the public shall not intentionally divulge the contents of any communication, other than one to such person or entity or an agent thereof, while in transmission on that service to any person or entity other than an addressee or intended recipient of such communication or an agent of the addressee or intended recipient. However, a person or entity providing electronic communication service to the public may divulge the contents of any such communication:

1. As authorized in subdivision B 1 of this section or § 19.2–67;

2. With the lawful consent of the originator or any addressee or intended recipient of such communication;

3. To a person employed or authorized, or whose facilities are used, to forward such communication to its destination; or

4. Which were inadvertently obtained by the service provider and which appear to pertain to the commission of a crime, to a law-enforcement agency.

Conduct otherwise an offense under this subsection that consists of or relates to the interception of a satellite transmission that is not encrypted or scrambled and that is transmitted (i) to a broadcasting station for purposes of retransmission to the general public, or (ii) as an audio subcarrier intended for redistribution to facilities open to the public, but not including data transmissions or telephone calls, is not an offense under this section unless the conduct is for the purposes of direct or indirect commercial advantage or private financial gain. Further, private viewing of a satellite video communication that is not scrambled or encrypted and interception of a radio communication that is transmitted on frequencies allocated under subpart D of Part 74 of the Rules of the Federal Communications Commission that is not scrambled or encrypted when the viewing or interception is not done for a tortious or illegal purpose or for purposes of direct or indirect commercial advantage or private commercial gain, shall not be offenses under this chapter.

Violation of this subsection shall be punishable as a Class 1 misdemeanor.

Acts 1975, c. 495; Acts 1988, c. 889; Acts 2004, c. 149.

§ 19.2–63. Manufacture, possession, sale or advertising of certain devices unlawful; penalties; exceptions

A. Except as otherwise specifically provided in this chapter, any person who intentionally:

1. Manufactures, assembles, possesses, or sells any electronic, mechanical, or other device, knowing or having reason to know that the design of such device renders it primarily useful for the purpose of the surreptitious interception of wire, electronic or oral communications; or

2. Places in any newspaper, magazine, handbill, or other publication any advertisement of:

(a) Any electronic, mechanical, or other device knowing or having reason to know that the design of such device renders it primarily useful for the purpose of the surreptitious interception of wire, electronic or oral communications, or

(b) Any other electronic, mechanical, or other device where such advertisement promotes the use of such device for the purpose of the surreptitious interception of wire, electronic or oral communications; shall be guilty of a Class 6 felony.

B. It shall not be unlawful under this section for:

1. A provider of wire or electronic communication service or an officer, agent, or employee of, or a person under contract with, such provider in the normal course of the provider's business, or

2. An officer, agent, or employee of, or a person under contract with the United States, the Commonwealth or a political subdivision thereof, in the normal course of the activities of the United States, the Commonwealth, or a political subdivision thereof, to manufacture, assemble, possess, or sell any electronic, mechanical, or other device knowing or having reason to know that the design of such device renders it primarily useful for the purpose of the surreptitious interception of wire, electronic or oral communications.

Acts 1975, c. 495; Acts 1988, c. 889.

§ 19.2–63.1. Supervision and control of devices; unauthorized possession

Any electronic, mechanical or other device as defined in this chapter which is in the possession of any sheriff's office or police department of a county, city or town, or in the possession of any employee of such office, shall be under the direct control and supervision of the sheriff or chief of police of the office or department or his designee who is an employee of the office or department. Unauthorized possession of any such device under the provisions of this section by any such employee is unlawful, notwithstanding the provisions of subdivision B 2 of § 19.2–63, and a Class 1 misdemeanor.

Acts 1975, c. 495; Acts 1988, c. 889. Amended by Acts 2011, c. 193.

§ 19.2–64. Forfeiture of unlawful devices

Any electronic, mechanical or other device used, manufactured, assembled, possessed, sold, or advertised in violation of § 19.2–62 or § 19.2–63 may be seized and forfeited to the Commonwealth, and turned over to the court of record in the city or county in which it was seized and such property shall be disposed of in such manner as the court may direct.

Acts 1975, c. 495.

§ 19.2–65. When intercepted communications and evidence derived therefrom not to be received in evidence

Whenever any wire or oral communication has been intercepted, no part of the contents of such communication and no evidence derived therefrom may be received in evidence in any trial, hearing or other proceeding in or before any court, grand jury, department, officer, commission, regulatory body, legislative committee or other agency of this Commonwealth or a political subdivision thereof if the disclosure of that information would be in violation of this chapter.

Acts 1975, c. 495.

§ 19.2–66. When Attorney General or Chief Deputy Attorney General may apply for order authorizing interception of communications

A. The Attorney General or Chief Deputy Attorney General, if the Attorney General so designates in writing, in any case where the Attorney General is authorized by law to prosecute or pursuant to a request in his official capacity of an attorney for the Commonwealth in any city or county, may apply to a judge of competent jurisdiction for an order authorizing the interception of wire, electronic or oral communications by the Department of State Police, when such interception may reasonably be expected to provide evidence of the commission of a felonious offense of extortion, bribery, kidnapping, murder, any felony violation of § 18.2–248 or 18.2–248.1, any felony violation of Chapter 29 (§ 59.1–364 et seq.) of Title 59.1, any felony violation of Article 2 (§ 18.2–38 et seq.), Article 2.1 (§ 18.2–46.1 et seq.), Article 2.2 (§ 18.2–46.4 et seq.), Article 5 (§ 18.2–58 et seq.), Article 6 (§ 18.2–59 et seq.) or any felonies that are not Class 6 felonies in Article 7 (§ 18.2–61 et seq.) of Chapter 4 of Title 18.2, or any conspiracy to commit any of the foregoing offenses. The Attorney General or Chief Deputy Attorney General may apply for authorization for the observation or monitoring of the interception by a police department of a county or city, by a sheriff's office, or by law-enforcement officers of the United States. Such application shall be made, and such order may be granted, in conformity with the provisions of § 19.2–68.

B. The application for an order under subsection B of § 19.2–68 shall be made as follows:

1. In the case of an application for a wire or electronic interception, a judge of competent jurisdiction shall have the authority to issue an order under subsection B of § 19.2–68 if there is probable cause to believe that an offense was committed, is being committed, or will be committed or the person or persons whose communications are to be intercepted live, work, subscribe to a wire or electronic communication system, maintain an address or a post office box, or are making the communication within the territorial jurisdiction of the court.

2. In the case of an application for an oral intercept, a judge of competent jurisdiction shall have the authority to issue an order under subsection B of § 19.2–68 if there is probable cause to believe that an offense was committed, is being committed, or will be committed or the physical location of the oral communication to be intercepted is within the territorial jurisdiction of the court.

C. For the purposes of an order entered pursuant to subsection B of § 19.2–68 for the interception of a wire or electronic communication, such communication shall be deemed to be intercepted in the jurisdiction where the order is entered, regardless of the physical location or the method by which the communication is captured or routed to the monitoring location.

Acts 1975, c. 495; Acts 1976, c. 271; Acts 1979, c. 602; Acts 1982, c. 40; Acts 1982, c. 274; Acts 1988, c. 855; Acts 1988, c. 889; Acts 2002, c. 588; Acts 2002, c. 623; Acts 2004, c. 122; Acts 2005, c. 934. Amended by Acts 2011, c. 403; Acts 2011, c. 414; Acts 2013, c. 448; Acts 2013, c. 664.

§ 19.2–67. Disclosure of information obtained by authorized means

A. Any investigative or law-enforcement officer, or police officer of a county or city, who, by any means authorized by this chapter, has obtained knowledge of the contents of any wire, electronic or oral communication, or evidence derived therefrom, may disclose such contents to another investigative or law-enforcement officer, or police officer of a county or city, to the extent that such disclosure is appropriate to the proper performance of the official duties of the officer making or receiving the disclosure.

B. Any investigative or law-enforcement officer or police officer of a county or city, who, by any means authorized by this chapter, has obtained knowledge of the contents of any wire, electronic or oral communication or evidence derived therefrom may use such contents to the extent such use is appropriate to the proper performance of his official duties.

C. Any person who has received, by any means authorized by this chapter, any information concerning a wire, electronic or oral communication, or evidence derived therefrom intercepted in accordance with the provisions of this chapter may disclose the contents of that communication or such derivative evidence while giving testimony under oath or affirmation in any criminal proceeding for an offense specified in § 19.2–66, or any conspiracy or attempt to commit the same, in any court of the United States or of any state or in any federal or state grand jury proceeding.

D. No wire, electronic or oral communication which is a privileged communication between the parties to the conversation which is intercepted in accordance with, or in violation of, the provisions of this chapter shall lose its privileged character, nor shall it be disclosed or used in any way.

E. When an investigative or law-enforcement officer, or police officer of a county or city, while engaged in intercepting wire, electronic or oral communications in the manner authorized herein, or observing or monitoring such interception intercepts, observes or monitors wire, electronic or oral communications relating to offenses other than those specified in the order of authorization, the contents thereof, and evidence derived therefrom, shall not be disclosed or used as provided in subsections A, B and C of this section, unless such communications or derivative evidence relates to a felony, in which case use or disclosure may be made as provided in subsections A, B and C of this section. Such use and disclosure pursuant to subsection C of this section shall be permitted only when approved by a judge of competent jurisdiction where such judge finds, on subsequent application, that such communications were otherwise intercepted in accordance with the provisions of this chapter. Violations of this subsection E shall be punishable as provided in § 19.2–62.

Acts 1975, c. 495; Acts 1976, c. 231; Acts 1979, c. 602; Acts 1983, c. 536; Acts 1988, c. 889.

§ 19.2–68. Application for and issuance of order authorizing interception; contents of order; recording and retention of intercepted communications, applications and orders; notice to parties; introduction in evidence of information obtained

A. Each application for an order authorizing the interception of a wire, electronic or oral communication shall be made in writing upon oath or affirmation to the appropriate judge of competent jurisdiction and shall state the applicant's authority to make such application. Each application shall be verified by the Attorney General to the best of his knowledge and belief and shall include the following information:

1. The identity of the attorney for the Commonwealth and law-enforcement officer who requested the Attorney General to apply for such order;

2. A full and complete statement of the facts and circumstances relied upon by the applicant to justify his belief that an order should be issued, including (i) details as to the particular offense that has been, is being or is about to be committed, (ii) except as provided in subsection I, a particular description of the nature and location of the facilities from which or the place where the communication is to be intercepted, (iii) a particular description of the type of communications sought to be intercepted, (iv) the identity of the person, if known, committing the offense and whose communications are to be intercepted;

3. A full and complete statement as to whether or not other investigative procedures have been tried and failed or why they reasonably appear to be unlikely to succeed if tried or to be too dangerous;

4. A statement of the period of time for which the interception is required to be maintained. If the nature of the investigation is such that the authorization for interception should not automatically terminate when the described type of communication has been first obtained, a particular description of facts establishing probable cause to believe that additional communications of the same type will occur thereafter;

5. A full and complete statement of the facts concerning all previous applications known to the individual authorizing and making the application, made to any judge for authorization to intercept wire, electronic or oral communications involving any of the same persons, facilities or places specified in the application, and the action taken by the judge on each such application;

6. Where the application is for the extension of an order, a statement setting forth the results thus far obtained from the interception, or a reasonable explanation of the failure to obtain such results; and

7. If authorization is requested for observation or monitoring by a police department of a county or city, by a sheriff's office, or by law-enforcement officers of the United States, a statement containing the name of the police department, sheriff's office, or United States agency and an explanation of the reasons such observation or monitoring is necessary.

The judge may require the applicant to furnish additional testimony or documentary evidence in support of the application.

B. Upon such application the judge may enter an ex parte order, as requested or as modified, authorizing interception of wire, electronic or oral communications if the judge determines on the basis of the facts submitted by the applicant that:

1. There is probable cause for belief that an individual is committing, has committed or is about to commit an offense enumerated in § 19.2–66 of this chapter;

2. There is probable cause for belief that particular communications concerning that offense will be obtained through such interception;

3. Normal investigative procedures have been tried and have failed, or reasonably appear to be unlikely to succeed if tried, or to be too dangerous; and intercep-

tion under this chapter is the only alternative investigative procedure available;

4. Except as provided in subsection I, there is probable cause for belief that the facilities from which, or the place where, the wire, electronic or oral communications are to be intercepted are being used, or are about to be used, in connection with the commission of such offense, or are leased to, listed in the name of, or commonly used by such person;

5. A wire, electronic or oral communication authorized to be intercepted pursuant to this section may be monitored at any location within the Commonwealth of Virginia.

C. Each order authorizing the interception of any wire, electronic or oral communication shall specify:

1. The identity of the person, if known, whose communications are to be intercepted;

2. The nature and location of the communications facilities as to which, or the place where, authority to intercept is granted;

3. A particular description of the type of communication sought to be intercepted, and a statement of the particular offense enumerated in § 19.2–66 to which it relates;

4. That such interception is to be conducted only by the Department of State Police;

5. If observation or monitoring by the police department of a county or city, by a sheriff's office, or by law-enforcement officers of the United States is authorized, only that police department, sheriff's office, or agency or the officers from any police department of a town which originated the investigation leading to the application shall observe or monitor the interception; and

6. The period of time during which such interception is authorized, including a statement as to whether or not the interception shall automatically terminate when the described communication has been first obtained.

An order authorizing the interception of a wire, electronic or oral communication shall, upon request of the applicant, direct that a provider of wire or electronic communications service, landlord, custodian or other person shall furnish the Department of State Police forthwith all information, facilities and technical assistance necessary to accomplish the interception unobtrusively and with a minimum of interference with the services that such service provider, landlord, custodian or person is providing the person whose communications are to be intercepted. Any provider of wire or electronic communications service, landlord, custodian or other person furnishing such facilities or technical assistance shall be compensated therefor by the Commonwealth for reasonable and actual expenses incurred in providing such facilities or assistance, to be paid out of the criminal fund.

D. No order entered under this section may authorize the interception of any wire, electronic or oral communication for any period longer than is necessary to achieve the objective of the authorization, nor in any event longer than 30 days which period begins to run on the earlier of the day on which the investigative or law-enforcement officer begins to conduct an interception under the order or 10 days after the date of entry of the order. Extensions of an order may be granted, but only upon application for an extension made in accordance with subsection A of this section and the court's making the findings required by subsection B of this section. The period of extension shall be no longer than the authorizing judge deems necessary to achieve the purposes for which it was granted and in no event for longer than 30 days. Every order and extension thereof shall contain a provision that the authorization to intercept shall be executed as soon as practicable, shall be conducted in such a way as to minimize the interception of communications not otherwise subject to interception under this chapter, and must terminate upon attainment of the authorized objective, or in any event in 30 days. In the event the intercepted communication is in a code or foreign language, and an expert in that foreign language or code is not reasonably available during the interception period, minimization may be accomplished as soon as practicable after such interception.

E. Whenever an order authorizing interception is entered pursuant to this chapter, the order shall require reports to be made to the judge who issued the order showing what progress has been made toward achievement of the authorized objective and the need for continued interception. Such reports shall be made at such intervals as the judge shall require.

F. 1. The contents of any wire, electronic or oral communication intercepted by any means authorized by this chapter shall, if possible, be recorded on tape or wire or other comparable device. Should it not be possible to record the intercepted communication, a detailed resume of such communication shall forthwith be reduced to writing and filed with the court. The recording of the contents of any wire, electronic or oral communication under this subsection shall be done in such way as will protect the recording from editing or other alterations and shall not be duplicated except upon order of the court as hereafter provided. Immediately upon the expiration of the period of the order, or extensions thereof, such recording or detailed resume shall be made available to the judge issuing such order and sealed under his directions. Custody of any recordings or detailed resumes shall be vested with the court and shall not be destroyed for a period of 10 years from the date of the order and then only by direction of the court; provided, however, should any interception fail to reveal any information related to the offense or offenses for which it was authorized, such recording or resume shall be destroyed after the expiration of 60 days after the notice required by subdivision 4 of this subsection is served. Duplicate recordings may be made for use or disclosure pursuant to the provisions of subsections A and B of § 19.2–67 for investigations. The presence of the seal provided for by this subsection, or a satisfactory explanation for the absence thereof, shall be a prerequisite for the use or disclosure of the contents of any wire, electronic or oral communication or evidence derived therefrom under subsection C of § 19.2–67.

2. Applications made and orders granted or denied under this chapter shall be sealed by the judge. Custody of the applications and orders shall be wherever the judge directs. Such applications and orders shall be disclosed only upon a showing of good cause before a judge of competent jurisdiction and shall not be destroyed except on order of the issuing or denying judge, and in any event shall be kept for 10 years.

3. Any violation of the provisions of this subsection may be punished as contempt of the issuing or denying court.

4. Within a reasonable time but not later than 90 days after the filing of an application for an order of authorization which is denied or the termination of the period of an order or extensions thereof, the issuing or denying judge shall cause to be served, on the persons named in the order or the application, and such other parties to intercepted communications as the judge may determine in his discretion that is in the interest of justice, an inventory which shall include notice of:

(a) The fact of the entry of the order or the application;

(b) The date of the entry and the period of authorized interception, or the denial of the application;

(c) The fact that during the period wire, electronic or oral communications were or were not intercepted; and

(d) The fact that unless he files a motion with the court within 60 days after the service of notice upon him, the recordation or resume may be destroyed in accordance with subdivision 1 of this subsection.

The judge, upon the filing of a motion, shall make available to such person or his counsel for inspection the intercepted communications, applications and orders. The serving of the inventory required by this subsection may be postponed for additional periods, not to exceed 30 days each, upon the ex parte showing of good cause to a judge of competent jurisdiction.

G. The contents of any intercepted wire, electronic or oral communication or evidence derived therefrom shall not be received in evidence or otherwise disclosed in any trial, hearing or other proceeding in a state court unless each party to the communication and to such proceeding, not less than 10 days before the trial, hearing or proceeding, has been furnished with a copy of the court order, accompanying application under which the interception was authorized and the contents of any intercepted wire, electronic or oral communication that is to be used in any trial, hearing or other proceeding in a state court. This 10–day period may be waived by the judge if he finds that it was not possible to furnish the party with the above information 10 days before the trial, hearing or proceeding and that the party will not be prejudiced by the delay in receiving such information; provided that such information in any event shall be given prior to the day of the trial, and the inability to comply with such 10–day period shall be grounds for the granting of a continuance to either party.

The judge who considers an application for an interception under this chapter, whether issuing or denying the order, shall be disqualified from presiding at any trial resulting from or in any manner connected with such interception, regardless of whether the evidence acquired thereby is used in such trial.

H. Any aggrieved person in any trial, hearing or proceeding in or before any court, department, officer, agency, regulatory body or other authority of the Commonwealth, or a political subdivision thereof, may move to suppress the contents of any intercepted wire, electronic or oral communication, or evidence derived therefrom, on the grounds that:

1. The communication was unlawfully intercepted, or was not intercepted in compliance with this chapter; or

2. The order of the authorization or approval under which it was intercepted is insufficient on its face; or

3. The interception was not made in conformity with the order of authorization or approval; or

4. The interception is not admissible into evidence in any trial, proceeding or hearing in a state court under the applicable rules of evidence.

Such motion shall be made before the trial, hearing or proceeding unless there was no opportunity to make such motion or the person was not aware of the grounds of the motion. If the motion is granted pursuant to subdivision 1, 2 or 3 of this subsection, the contents of the intercepted wire, electronic or oral communication or evidence derived therefrom shall be treated as having been obtained in violation of this chapter. The judge, upon the filing of such motion by the aggrieved person, shall make available to the aggrieved person, or his counsel, for inspection the intercepted communication.

I. The requirements of subdivision 2 of subsection A and subdivision 4 of subsection B of this section relating to the specification of the facilities from which, or the place where, the communication is to be intercepted do not apply if:

1. In the case of an application with respect to the interception of an oral communication:

(a) The application contains a full and complete statement as to why such specification is not practical and identifies the person committing the offense and whose communications are to be intercepted; and

(b) The judge finds that such specification is not practical; or

2. In the case of an application with respect to a wire or electronic communication:

(a) the application identifies the person believed to be committing the offense and whose communications are to be intercepted and the applicant makes a showing of a purpose, on the part of that person, to thwart interception by changing facilities; and

(b) the judge finds that such purpose has been adequately shown.

The interception of a communication under an order issued pursuant to this subsection shall not begin until the facilities from which, or the place where, the communication is to be intercepted is ascertained by the person implementing the interception order. A provider of wire or electronic communications service that has received an order issued pursuant to this subdivision 2 may move the court to modify or quash the order on the ground that its assistance with respect to the interception cannot be performed in a timely or reasonable fashion. The court, upon notice to the Attorney General, shall decide the motion expeditiously.

Acts 1975, c. 495; Acts 1976, c. 163; Acts 1977, c. 335; Acts 1979, c. 602; Acts 1980, c. 244; Acts 1988, c. 889; Acts 2002, c. 91; Acts 2005, c. 934. Amended by Acts 2013, c. 448; Acts 2013, c. 664.

§ 19.2–69. Civil action for unlawful interception, disclosure or use

Any person whose wire, electronic or oral communication is intercepted, disclosed or used in violation of this chapter shall (i) have a civil cause of action against any person who intercepts, discloses or uses, or procures any other person to intercept, disclose or use such communications, and (ii) be entitled to recover from any such person:

1. Actual damages but not less than liquidated damages computed at the rate of $400 a day for each day of violation or $4,000, whichever is higher, provided that liquidated damages shall be computed at the rate of $800 a day for each day of violation or $8,000, whichever is higher, if the wire, electronic, or oral communication intercepted, disclosed, or used is between (i) a husband and wife; (ii) an attorney and client; (iii) a licensed practitioner of the healing arts and patient; (iv) a licensed professional counselor, licensed clinical social worker, licensed psychologist, or licensed marriage and family therapist and client; or (v) a clergy member and person seeking spiritual counsel or advice;

2. Punitive damages; and

3. A reasonable attorney's fee and other litigation costs reasonably incurred.

A good faith reliance on a court order or legislative authorization shall constitute a complete defense to any civil or criminal action brought under this chapter or under any other law.

Acts 1975, c. 495; Acts 1988, c. 889. Amended by Acts 2010, c. 343; Acts 2015, c. 672.

§ 19.2–70. Reports to be filed by courts and Attorney General

All courts of the Commonwealth and the Attorney General shall file all reports required by 18 U.S.C.A. § 2519. The Attorney General shall file a written report with the Clerks of the Senate and House of Delegates on or before December 31 of each year setting forth the number of applications made pursuant to this chapter, the number of interceptions authorized, the number of arrests resulting from each application, the number of convictions including a breakdown by offense, the cost of each application granted and the number of requests denied. Such information shall be made available by such Clerks to any member of the General Assembly upon request. However, notwithstanding the above requirements, no report shall be made concerning a granted application until after all inventories associated with such application are served pursuant to subdivision F 4 of § 19.2–68.

Acts 1975, c. 495. Amended by Acts 2011, c. 403; Acts 2011, c. 414.

§ 19.2–70.1. General prohibition on pen register and trap and trace device use; exceptions

Except as provided in this section, no person may install or use a pen register or a trap and trace device without first obtaining a court order under § 19.2–70.2.

However, a court order shall not be required for use of a pen register or trap and trace device by a provider of electronic or wire communication service (i) relating to the operation, maintenance, and testing of a wire or electronic communication service or to the protection of the rights or property of the provider, or to the protection of users of that service from abuse of service or unlawful use of service; (ii) to record the fact that a wire or electronic communication was initiated or completed in order to protect such provider, another provider furnishing service toward the completion of the wire communication, or a user of that service, from fraudulent, unlawful or abusive use of service; or (iii) where the consent of the user of that service has been obtained.

Any person who knowingly violates this section shall be guilty of a Class 1 misdemeanor.

Acts 1988, c. 889.

§ 19.2–70.2. Application for and issuance of order for a pen register or trap and trace device; assistance in installation and use

A. An investigative or law-enforcement officer may make application for an order or an extension of an order authorizing or approving the installation and use of a pen register or a trap and trace device, in writing under oath or equivalent affirmation, to a court of competent jurisdiction. The application shall include:

1. The identity of the officer making the application and the identity of the law-enforcement agency conducting the investigation; and

2. A certification by the applicant that the information likely to be obtained is relevant to an ongoing criminal investigation being conducted by that agency.

The application may include a request that the order require information, facilities and technical assistance necessary to accomplish the installation be furnished.

B. An application for an ex parte order authorizing the installation and use of a pen register or trap and trace device may be filed in the jurisdiction where the person or persons who subscribe to the wire or electronic communication system live, work, or maintain an address or a post office box. For the purposes of an order entered pursuant to this section for the installation and use of a pen register or trap and trace device, such installation shall be deemed to occur in the jurisdiction where the order is entered, regardless of the physical location or the method by which the information is captured or routed to the law-enforcement officer that made the application. Upon application, the court shall enter an ex parte order authorizing the installation and use of a pen register or a trap and trace device if the court finds that the investigative or law-enforcement officer has certified to the court that the information likely to be obtained by such installation and use is relevant to an ongoing criminal investigation.

The order shall specify:

1. The identity, if known, of the person in whose name the telephone line or other facility to which the pen register or trap and trace device is to be attached or applied is listed or to whom the line or other facility is leased;

2. The identity, if known, of the person who is the subject of the criminal investigation;

3. The attributes of the communications to which the order applies, including the number or other identifier and, if known, the location of the telephone line or other facility to which the pen register or trap and trace device is to be attached or applied; and

4. A statement of the offense to which the information likely to be obtained by the pen register or trap and trace device relates.

C. Installation and use of a pen register or a trap and trace device shall be authorized for a period not to exceed 60 days. Extensions of the order may be granted, but only upon application made and order issued in accordance with this section. The period of an extension shall not exceed 60 days.

D. An order authorizing or approving the installation and use of a pen register or a trap and trace device shall direct that:

1. The order and application be sealed until otherwise ordered by the court;

2. Information, facilities and technical assistance necessary to accomplish the installation be furnished if requested in the application; and

3. The person owning or leasing the line or other facility to which the pen register or trap and trace device is attached or applied, or who is obligated by the order to provide assistance to the applicant, not disclose the existence of the pen register or trap and trace device or the existence of the investigation to the listed subscriber, or to any other person, unless or until otherwise ordered by the court.

E. Upon request of an investigative or a law-enforcement officer authorized by the court to install and use a pen register, a provider of wire or electronic communication service, a landlord, custodian or any other person so ordered by the court shall, as soon as practicable, furnish the officer with all information, facilities, and technical assistance necessary to accomplish the installation of the pen register unobtrusively and with a minimum of interference with the services that the person so ordered by the court accords the party with respect to whom the installation and use is to take place.

F. Upon request of an investigative or law-enforcement officer authorized by the court to receive the results of a trap and trace device under this section, a provider of wire or electronic communication service, a landlord, custodian or any other person so ordered by the court shall, as soon as practicable, install the device on the appropriate line and furnish the officer with all additional information, facilities and technical assistance, including installation and operation of the device, unobtrusively and with a minimum of interference with the services that the person so ordered by the court accords the party with respect to whom the installation and use is to take place. Unless otherwise ordered by the court, the results of the trap and trace device shall be furnished to the investigative or law-enforcement officer designated by the court at reasonable intervals during regular business hours for the duration of the order. Where the law-enforcement agency implementing an ex parte order under this subsection seeks to do so by installing and using its own pen register or trap and trace device on a packet-switched data network of a provider of electronic communication service to the public, the agency shall ensure that a record will be maintained that will identify (i) any officer or officers who installed the device and any officer or officers who accessed the device to obtain information from the network; (ii) the date and time the device was installed, the date and time the device was uninstalled, and the date, time, and duration of each time the device is accessed to obtain information; (iii) the configuration of the device at the time of its installation and any subsequent modification thereof; and (iv) any information that has been collected by the device. To the extent that the pen register or trap and trace device can be set automatically to record this information electronically, the record shall be maintained electronically throughout the installation and use of such device. The record maintained hereunder shall be provided ex parte and under seal of the court that entered the ex parte order authorizing the installation and use of the device within 30 days after termination of the order, including any extensions thereof.

G. A provider of a wire or electronic communication service, a landlord, custodian or other person who furnishes facilities or technical assistance pursuant to this section shall be reasonably compensated for reasonable and actual expenses incurred in providing such facilities and assistance. The expenses shall be paid out of the criminal fund.

H. No cause of action shall lie in any court against a provider of a wire or electronic communication service, its officers, employees, agents or other specified persons for providing information, facilities, or assistance in accordance with the terms of a court order issued pursuant to this section. Good faith reliance on a court order, a legislative authorization or a statutory authorization is a complete defense against any civil or criminal action based upon a violation of this chapter.

Acts 1988, c. 889; Acts 2002, c. 588; Acts 2002, c. 623; Acts 2005, c. 934.

§ 19.2–70.3. Obtaining records concerning electronic communication service or remote computing service

A. A provider of electronic communication service or remote computing service, which, for purposes of subdivisions 2 through 4, includes a foreign corporation that provides such services, shall disclose a record or other information pertaining to a subscriber to or customer of such service, excluding the contents of electronic communications and real-time location data, to an investigative or law-enforcement officer only pursuant to:

1. A subpoena issued by a grand jury of a court of the Commonwealth;

2. A search warrant issued by a magistrate, general district court, or circuit court;

3. A court order for such disclosure issued as provided in subsection B; or

4. The consent of the subscriber or customer to such disclosure.

B. A court shall issue an order for disclosure under this section only if the investigative or law-enforcement officer shows that there is reason to believe the records or other information sought are relevant and material to an ongoing criminal investigation, or the investigation of any missing child as defined in § 52–32, missing senior adult as defined in § 52–34.4, or an incapacitated person as defined in § 64.2–2000 who meets the definition of a missing senior adult except for the age requirement. Upon issuance of an order for disclosure under this section, the order and any written application or statement of facts may be sealed by the court for 90 days for good cause shown upon application of the attorney for the Commonwealth in an ex parte proceeding. The order and any written application or statement of facts may be sealed for additional 90–day periods for good cause shown upon subsequent application of the attorney for the Commonwealth in an ex parte proceeding. A court issuing an order pursuant to this section, on a motion made promptly by the service provider, may quash or modify the order, if the information or records requested are unusually voluminous in nature or compliance with such order would otherwise cause an undue burden on such provider.

C. Except as provided in subsection D, a provider of electronic communication service or remote computing service, including a foreign corporation that provides such services, shall disclose the contents of electronic communications or real-time location data to an investigative or law-enforcement officer only pursuant to a search warrant issued by a magistrate, a juvenile and domestic relations district court, a general district court, or a circuit court, based upon complaint on oath supported by an affidavit as required in § 19.2–54, or judicial officer or court of any of the several states of the United States or its territories, or the District of Columbia when the warrant issued by such officer or such court complies with the provisions of subsection G. In the case of a search warrant directed to a foreign corporation, the affidavit shall state that the complainant believes that the records requested are actually or constructively possessed by a foreign corporation that provides electronic communication service or remote computing service within the Commonwealth of Virginia. If satisfied that probable cause has been established for such belief and as required by Chapter 5 (§ 19.2–52 et seq.), the magistrate, the juvenile and domestic relations district court, the general district court, or the circuit court shall issue a warrant identifying those records to be searched for and commanding the person seeking such warrant to properly serve the warrant upon the foreign corporation. A search warrant for real-time location data shall be issued if the magistrate, the juvenile and domestic relations district court, the general district court, or the circuit court is satisfied that probable cause has been established that the real-time location data sought is relevant to a crime that is being committed or has been committed or that an arrest warrant exists for the person whose real-time location data is sought.

D. A provider of electronic communication service or remote computing service, including a foreign corporation that provides such services, shall disclose a record or other information pertaining to a subscriber to or customer of such service, including real-time location data but excluding the contents of electronic communications, to an investigative or law-enforcement officer pursuant to an administrative subpoena issued pursuant to § 19.2–10.2 concerning a violation of § 18.2–374.1 or 18.2–374.1:1, former § 18.2–374.1:2, or § 18.2–374.3 when the information sought is relevant and material to an ongoing criminal investigation.

E. When disclosure of real-time location data is not prohibited by federal law, an investigative or law-enforcement officer may obtain real-time location data without a warrant in the following circumstances:

1. To respond to the user's call for emergency services;

2. With the informed, affirmative consent of the owner or user of the electronic device concerned if (i) the device is in his possession; (ii) the owner or user knows or believes that the device is in the possession of an employee or agent of the owner or user with the owner's or user's consent; or (iii) the owner or user knows or believes that the device has been taken by a third party without the consent of the owner or user;

3. With the informed, affirmative consent of the legal guardian or next of kin of the owner or user, if reasonably available, if the owner or user is reasonably believed to be deceased, is reported missing, or is unable to be contacted; or

4. If the investigative or law-enforcement officer reasonably believes that an emergency involving the immediate danger to a person requires the disclosure, without delay, of real-time location data concerning a specific person and that a warrant cannot be obtained in time to prevent the identified danger, and the possessor of the real-time location data believes, in good faith, that an emergency involving danger to a person requires disclosure without delay.

No later than three business days after seeking disclosure of real-time location data pursuant to this subsection, the investigative or law-enforcement officer seeking the information shall file with the appropriate court a written statement setting forth the facts giving rise to the emergency and the facts as to why the person whose real-time location data was sought is believed to be important in addressing the emergency.

F. In order to comply with the requirements of § 19.2–54, any search of the records of a foreign corporation shall be deemed to have been made in the same place wherein the search warrant was issued.

G. A Virginia corporation or other entity that provides electronic communication services or remote computing services to the general public, when properly served with a search warrant and affidavit in support of the warrant, issued by a judicial officer or court of any of the several states of the United States or its territories, or the District of Columbia with jurisdiction over the matter, to produce a record or other information pertaining to a subscriber to or customer of such service, including real-time location data, or the contents of electronic communications, or both, shall produce the record or other information, including real-time location data, or the contents of electronic communications as if that warrant had been issued by a Virginia court. The provisions of this subsection shall only apply to a record or other information, including real-time location data, or contents of electronic communications relating to the commission of a criminal offense that is substantially similar to (i) a violent felony as defined in § 17.1–805, (ii) an act of violence as defined in § 19.2–297.1, (iii) any offense for which registration is required pursuant to § 9.1–902, (iv) computer fraud pursuant to § 18.2–152.3, or (v) identity theft pursuant to § 18.2–186.3. The search warrant shall be enforced and executed in the Commonwealth as if it were a search warrant described in subsection C.

H. The provider of electronic communication service or remote computing service may verify the authenticity of the written reports or records that it discloses pursuant to this section, excluding the contents of electronic communications, by providing an affidavit from the custodian of those written reports or records or from a person to whom said custodian reports certifying that they are true and complete and that they are prepared in the regular course of business. When so authenticated, the written reports and records are admissible in evidence as a business records exception to the hearsay rule.

I. No cause of action shall lie in any court against a provider of a wire or electronic communication service or remote computing service or such provider's officers, employees, agents, or other specified persons for providing information, facilities, or assistance in accordance with the terms of a court order, warrant, administrative subpoena, or subpoena under this section or the provisions of subsection E.

J. A search warrant or administrative subpoena for the disclosure of real-time location data pursuant to this section shall require the provider to provide ongoing disclosure of such data for a reasonable period of time, not to exceed 30 days. A court may, for good cause shown, grant one or more extensions, not to exceed 30 days each.

K. An investigative or law-enforcement officer shall not use any device to obtain electronic communications or collect real-time location data from an electronic device without first obtaining a search warrant authorizing the use of the device if, in order to obtain the contents of such electronic communications or such real-time location data from the provider of electronic communication service or remote computing service, such officer would be required to obtain a search warrant pursuant to this section. However, an investigative or law-enforcement officer may use such a device without first obtaining a search warrant under the circumstances set forth in subsection E. For purposes of subdivision E 4, the investigative or law-enforcement officer using such a device shall be considered to be the possessor of the real-time location data.

L. For the purposes of this section:

"Electronic device" means a device that enables access to, or use of, an electronic communication service, remote computing service, or location information service, including a global positioning service or other mapping, locational, or directional information service.

"Foreign corporation" means any corporation or other entity, whose primary place of business is located outside of the boundaries of the Commonwealth, that makes a contract or engages in a terms of service agreement with a resident of the Commonwealth to be performed in whole or in part by either party in the Commonwealth, or a corporation that has been issued a certificate of authority pursuant to § 13.1–759 to transact business in the Commonwealth. The making of the contract or terms of service agreement or the issuance of a certificate of authority shall be considered to be the agreement of the foreign corporation or entity that a search warrant or subpoena, which has been properly served on it, has the same legal force and effect as if served personally within the Commonwealth.

"Properly served" means delivery of a search warrant or subpoena by hand, by United States mail, by commercial delivery service, by facsimile or by any other manner to any officer of a corporation or its general manager in the Commonwealth, to any natural person designated by it as agent for the service of process, or if such corporation has designated a corporate agent, to any person named in the latest annual report filed pursuant to § 13.1–775.

"Real-time location data" means any data or information concerning the current location of an electronic device that, in whole or in part, is generated, derived from, or obtained by the operation of the device.

Acts 1988, c. 889. Amended by Acts 2009, c. 378; Acts 2010, c. 319; Acts 2010, c. 473; Acts 2010, c. 582; Acts 2010, c. 720; Acts 2010, c. 721; Acts 2011, c. 392; Acts 2014, c. 388; Acts 2015, c. 43; Acts 2015, c. 634.

CHAPTER 7

ARREST

§ 19.2–71. Who may issue process of arrest

A. Process for the arrest of a person charged with a criminal offense may be issued by the judge, or clerk of any circuit court, any general district court, any juvenile and domestic relations district court, or any magistrate as provided for in Chapter 3 (§ 19.2–26 et seq.) of this title. However, no magistrate may issue an arrest warrant for a felony offense upon the basis of a complaint by a person other than a law-enforcement officer or an animal control officer without prior authorization by the attorney for the Commonwealth or by a law-enforcement agency having jurisdiction over the alleged offense.

B. No law-enforcement officer shall seek issuance of process by any judicial officer, for the arrest of a person for the offense of capital murder as defined in § 18.2–31, without prior authorization by the attorney for the Commonwealth. Failure to comply with the provisions of this subsection shall not be (i) a basis upon which a warrant may be quashed or deemed invalid, (ii) deemed error upon which a conviction or sentence may be reversed or vacated, or (iii) a basis upon which a court may prevent or delay execution of sentence.

Acts 1975, c. 495; Acts 1999, c. 266; Acts 2002, c. 310. Amended by Acts 2009, c. 291; Acts 2009, c. 344; Acts 2010, c. 240; Acts 2011, c. 205; Acts 2011, c. 223.

§ 19.2–72. When it may issue; what to recite and require

On complaint of a criminal offense to any officer authorized to issue criminal warrants he shall examine on oath the complainant and any other witnesses, or when such officer shall suspect that an offense punishable otherwise than by a fine has been committed he may, without formal complaint, issue a summons for witnesses and shall examine such witnesses. A written complaint shall be required if the complainant is not a law-enforcement officer. If upon such examination such officer finds that there is probable cause to believe the accused has committed an offense, such officer shall issue a warrant for his arrest, except that no magistrate may issue an arrest warrant for a felony offense upon the basis of a complaint by a person other than a law-enforcement officer or an animal control officer without prior authorization by the attorney for the Commonwealth or by a law-enforcement agency having jurisdiction over the alleged offense. The warrant shall (i) be directed to an appropriate officer or officers, (ii) name the accused or, if his name is unknown, set forth a description by which he can be identified with reasonable certainty, (iii) describe the offense charged with reasonable certainty, (iv) command that the accused be arrested and brought before a court of appropriate jurisdiction in the county, city or town in which the offense was allegedly committed, and (v) be signed by the issuing officer. The warrant shall require the officer to whom it is directed to summon such witnesses as shall be therein named to appear and give evidence on the examination. But in a city or town having a police force, the warrant shall be directed "To any policeman, sheriff or his deputy sheriff of such city (or town)," and shall be executed by the policeman, sheriff or his deputy sheriff into whose hands it shall come or be delivered. A sheriff or his deputy may execute an arrest warrant throughout the county in which he serves and in any city or town surrounded thereby and effect an arrest in any city or town surrounded thereby as a result of a criminal act committed during the execution of such warrant. A jail officer as defined in § 53.1–1 employed at a regional jail or jail farm is authorized to execute a warrant of arrest upon an accused in his jail. The venue for the prosecution of such criminal act shall be the jurisdiction in which the offense occurred.

Acts 1975, c. 495; Acts 1991, c. 420; Acts 2000, c. 170; Acts 2007, c. 412. Amended by Acts 2009, c. 291; Acts 2009, c. 344; Acts 2010, c. 240; Acts 2011, c. 205; Acts 2011, c. 223; Acts 2013, c. 207.

§ 19.2–73. Issuance of summons instead of warrant in certain cases

A. In any misdemeanor case or in any class of misdemeanor cases, or in any case involving complaints made by any state or local governmental official or employee having responsibility for the enforcement of any statute, ordinance or administrative regulation, the magistrate or other issuing authority having jurisdiction may issue a summons instead of a warrant when there is reason to believe that the person charged will appear in the courts having jurisdiction over the trial of the offense charged.

B. If any person under suspicion for driving while intoxicated has been taken to a medical facility for treatment or evaluation of his medical condition, the officer at the medical facility may issue, on the premises of the medical facility, a summons for a violation of § 18.2–266, 18.2–266.1, 18.2–272 or 46.2–341.24 and for refusal of tests in violation of subsection A of § 18.2–268.3 or subsection A of § 46.2–341.26:3, in lieu of securing a warrant and without having to detain that person, provided that the officer has probable cause to place him under arrest. The issuance of such summons shall be deemed an arrest for purposes of Article 2 (§ 18.2–266 et seq.) of Chapter 7 of Title 18.2.

C. Any person on whom such summons is served shall appear on the date set forth in same, and if such person fails to appear in such court at such time and on such date then he shall be treated in accordance with the provisions of § 19.2–128, regardless of the disposition of, and in addition to, the charge upon which he was originally arrested.

Acts 1975, c. 495; Acts 1978, c. 500; Acts 1981, c. 382; Acts 2005, c. 425. Amended by Acts 2010, c. 840.

§ 19.2–73.1. Notice of issuance of warrant or summons; appearance; failure to appear

In any misdemeanor case or in any class of misdemeanor cases and in a Class 5 or Class 6 felony case, the chief of police of the city or county or his designee, or the sheriff or deputy sheriff of the county, if the county has no police department, in which the case is pending may notify the accused of the issuance of the warrant or summons and direct the accused to appear at the time and place directed for the purpose of the execution of the summons or warrant. However, the issuing judicial officer may direct the execution of such process prior to any such notification. If the accused does not appear, then the warrant or summons shall be executed and returned as provided by § 19.2–76.

Acts 1975, c. 495; Acts 1991, c. 162; Acts 1993, c. 350.

§ 19.2–73.2. Law-enforcement officers to issue subpoenas; penalty

Law-enforcement officers as defined in § 9.1–101 and state police officers, in the course of their duties, in the investigation of any Class 3 or Class 4 misdemeanor or any traffic infraction, may, within seventy-two hours of the time of the offense, issue a subpoena to any witness to appear in court and testify with respect to any such criminal charge or traffic infraction brought against any person as a result of such investigation. The return of service thereof shall be made within seventy-two hours after service to the appropriate court clerk. A subpoena so issued shall have the same force and effect as if issued by the court.

Any person failing to appear in response to a subpoena issued as provided in this section shall be punished as provided by law.

Acts 1995, c. 335.

§ 19.2–74. Issuance and service of summons in place of warrant in misdemeanor case; issuance of summons by special conservators of the peace

A. 1. Whenever any person is detained by or is in the custody of an arresting officer for any violation committed in such officer's presence which offense is a violation of any county, city or town ordinance or of any provision of this Code punishable as a Class 1 or Class 2 misdemeanor or any other misdemeanor for which he may receive a jail sentence, except as otherwise provided in Title 46.2, or for offenses listed in subsection D of § 19.2–81, or an arrest on a warrant charging an offense for which a summons may be issued, and when specifically authorized by the judicial officer issuing the warrant, the arresting officer shall take the name and address of such person and issue a summons or otherwise notify him in writing to appear at a time and place to be specified in such summons or notice. Upon the giving by such person of his written promise to appear at such time and place, the officer shall forthwith release him from custody. However, if any such person shall fail or refuse to discontinue the unlawful act, the officer may proceed according to the provisions of § 19.2–82.

Anything in this section to the contrary notwithstanding, if any person is believed by the arresting officer to be likely to disregard a summons issued under the provisions of this subsection, or if any person is reasonably believed by the arresting officer to be likely to cause harm to himself or to any other person, a magistrate or other issuing authority having jurisdiction shall proceed according to the provisions of § 19.2–82.

2. Whenever any person is detained by or is in the custody of an arresting officer for a violation of any county, city, or town ordinance or of any provision of this Code, punishable as a Class 3 or Class 4 misdemeanor or any other misdemeanor for which he cannot receive a jail sentence, except as otherwise provided in Title 46.2, or to the offense of public drunkenness as defined in § 18.2–388, the arresting officer shall take the name and address of such person and issue a summons or otherwise notify him in writing to appear at a time and place to be specified in such summons or notice. Upon the giving of such person of his written promise to appear at such time and place, the officer shall forthwith release him from custody. However, if any such person shall fail or refuse to discontinue the unlawful act, the officer may proceed according to the provisions of § 19.2–82.

3. Any person so summoned shall not be held in custody after the issuance of such summons for the purpose of complying with the requirements of Chapter 23 (§ 19.2–387 et seq.) of this title. Reports to the Central Criminal Records Exchange concerning such persons shall be made after a disposition of guilt is entered as provided for in § 19.2–390.

Any person refusing to give such written promise to appear under the provisions of this section shall be taken immediately by the arresting or other police officer before a magistrate or other issuing authority having jurisdiction, who shall proceed according to provisions of § 19.2–82.

Any person who willfully violates his written promise to appear, given in accordance with this section, shall be treated in accordance with the provisions of § 19.2–128, regardless of the disposition of, and in addition to, the charge upon which he was originally arrested.

Any person charged with committing any violation of § 18.2–407 may be arrested and immediately brought before a magistrate who shall proceed as provided in § 19.2–82.

B. Conservators of the peace appointed under Chapter 2 (§ 19.2–12 et seq.) may issue summonses pursuant to this section, if such officers are in uniform or displaying a badge of office. On application, the chief law-enforcement officer of the county or city shall supply each officer with a supply of summons forms, for which such officer shall account pursuant to regulation of such chief law-enforcement officer.

C. The summons used by a law-enforcement officer pursuant to this section shall be in form the same as the uniform summons for motor vehicle law violations as prescribed pursuant to § 46.2–388.

Acts 1975, c. 495; Acts 1976, c. 753; Acts 1978, c. 500; Acts 1979, c. 679; Acts 1979, c. 680; Acts 1980, c. 492; Acts 1981, c. 382; Acts 1982, c. 485; Acts 1982, c. 500; Acts 1984, c. 24; Acts 1988, c. 455; Acts 1995, c. 471. Amended by Acts 2010, c. 840; Acts 2014, c. 543.

§ 19.2–74.1. Repealed by Acts 1981, c. 382

§ 19.2–75. Copy of process to be left with accused; exception

Except as provided in § 46.2–936, any process issued against a person charged with a criminal offense shall be in duplicate and the officer serving such process shall leave a copy with the person charged.

Acts 1975, c. 495.

§ 19.2–76. Execution and return of warrant, capias or summons; arrest outside county or city where charge is to be tried

A law-enforcement officer may execute within his jurisdiction a warrant, capias or summons issued anywhere in the Commonwealth. A jail officer as defined in § 53.1–1 employed at a regional jail or jail farm may execute upon a person being held in his jail a warrant, capias or summons issued anywhere in the Commonwealth. A warrant or capias shall be executed by the arrest of the accused, and a summons shall be executed by delivering a copy to the accused personally.

If the accused is a corporation, partnership, unincorporated association or legal entity other than an individual, a summons may be executed by service on the entity in the same manner as provided in Title 8.01 for service of process on that entity in a civil proceeding. However, if the summons is served on the entity by delivery to a registered agent or to any other agent who is not an officer, director, managing agent or employee of the entity, such agent shall not be personally subject to penalty for failure to appear as provided in § 19.2–128, nor shall the agent be subject to punishment for contempt for failure to appear under his summons as provided in § 19.2–129.

The law-enforcement officer or jail officer executing a warrant or capias shall endorse the date of execution thereon and make return thereof to a judicial officer. The law-enforcement officer executing a summons shall endorse the date of execution thereon and make return thereof to the court to which the summons is returnable.

Whenever a person is arrested upon a warrant or capias in a county or city other than that in which the charge is to be tried, the law-enforcement officer or jail officer making the arrest shall either (i) bring the accused forthwith before a judicial officer in the locality where the arrest was made or where the charge is to be tried or (ii) commit the accused to the custody of an officer from the county or city where the charge is to be tried who shall bring the accused forthwith before a judicial officer in the county or city in which the charge is to be tried. The judicial officer before whom the accused is brought shall immediately conduct a bail hearing and either admit the accused to bail or commit him to jail for transfer forthwith to the county or city where the charge is to be tried.

Acts 1975, c. 495; Acts 1979, c. 661; Acts 1993, c. 431; Acts 1994, c. 933; Acts 1997, c. 10; Acts 1998, c. 615. Amended by Acts 2013, c. 207.

§ 19.2–76.1. Submission of quarterly reports concerning unexecuted felony and misdemeanor warrants and other criminal process; destruction; dismissal

It shall be the duty of the chief law-enforcement officer of the police department or sheriff's office, whichever is responsible for such service, in each county, town or city of the Commonwealth to submit quarterly reports to the attorney for the Commonwealth for the county, town or city concerning unexecuted felony and misdemeanor arrest warrants, summonses, capiases or other unexecuted criminal processes as hereinafter provided. The reports shall list those existing felony arrest warrants in his possession that have not been executed within seven years of the date of issuance, those misdemeanor arrest warrants, summonses and capiases and other criminal processes in his possession that have not been executed within three years from the date of issuance, and those unexecuted misdemeanor arrest warrants, summonses and capiases in his possession that were issued for a now deceased person, based on mistaken identity or as a result of any other technical or legal error. The reports shall be submitted in writing no later than the tenth day of April, July, October, and January of each year, together with the unexecuted felony and misdemeanor warrants, or other unexecuted criminal processes listed therein. Upon receipt of the report and the warrants listed therein, the attorney for the Commonwealth shall petition the circuit court of the county or city for the destruction of such unexecuted felony and misdemeanor warrants, summonses, capiases or other unexecuted criminal processes. The attorney for the Commonwealth may petition that certain of the unexecuted warrants, summonses, capiases and other unexecuted criminal processes not be destroyed based upon justifiable continuing, active investigation of the cases. The circuit court shall order the destruction of each such unexecuted felony warrant and each unexecuted misdemeanor warrant, summons, capias and other criminal process except (i) any warrant which charges capital murder and (ii) any unexecuted criminal process whose preservation is deemed justifiable by the court. No arrest shall be made under the authority of any warrant or other process which has been ordered destroyed pursuant to this section. Nothing in this section shall be construed to relate to or affect the time within which a prosecution for a felony or a misdemeanor shall be commenced.

Notwithstanding the foregoing, an attorney for the Commonwealth may at any time move for the dismissal and destruction of any unexecuted warrant or summons issued by a magistrate upon presentation of such warrant or summons to the court in which the warrant or summons would otherwise be returnable. The court shall not order the dismissal and destruction of any warrant which charges capital murder and shall not order the dismissal and destruction of an unexecuted criminal process whose preservation is deemed justifiable by the court. Dismissal of such a warrant or summons shall be without prejudice.

As used herein, the term "chief law-enforcement officer" refers to the chiefs of police of cities, counties and towns and sheriffs of cities and counties, unless a political subdivision has otherwise designated its chief law-enforcement officer by appropriate resolution or ordinance, in which case the local designation shall be controlling.

Acts 1976, c. 252; Acts 1979, c. 34; Acts 1982, c. 608; Acts 1985, c. 199; Acts 1990, c. 626; Acts 1991, c. 542; Acts 1993, c. 550; Acts 2003, c. 147. Amended by Acts 2010, c. 652; Acts 2011, c. 336; Acts 2011, c. 347.

§ 19.2–76.2. Mailing of summons in certain cases

Notwithstanding the provisions of § 19.2–76, whenever a summons for a violation of a county, city or town parking ordinance is served in any county, city or town it may be executed by mailing by first-class mail a copy thereof to the address of the owner of the vehicle as shown on the records of the Department of Motor Vehicles. In addition, whenever a summons for a violation of a county, city or town trash ordinance punishable as a misdemeanor under § 15.2-901 is served in any county, city or town, it may be executed by mailing a copy by first-class mail to the person who occupies the subject premises. If the person fail to appear on the date of return set out in the summons mailed pursuant to this section, the summons shall be executed in the manner set out in § 19.2–76.3 of this Code.

No proceedings for contempt or arrest of a person summoned by mailing shall be instituted for his failure to appear on the return date of the summons.

Acts 1977, c. 232; Acts 1978, c. 781; Acts 1983, c. 254; Acts 1984, c. 119.

§ 19.2–76.3. Failure to appear on return date for summons issued under § 19.2–76.2

A. If any person fails to appear on the date of the return contained in the summons issued in accordance with § 19.2–76.2, then a summons shall be delivered to the sheriff of the county, city or town for service on that person as set out in § 8.01–296.

B. If such person then fails to appear on the date of return as contained in the summons so issued, a summons shall be executed in the manner set out in § 19.2–76.

C. No proceedings for contempt or arrest of any person summoned under the provisions of this section shall be instituted unless such person has been personally served with a summons and has failed to appear on the return date contained therein.

Acts 1983, c. 254; Acts 1994, c. 642.

§ 19.2–77. Escape, flight and pursuit; arrest anywhere in Commonwealth

Whenever a person in the custody of an officer shall escape or whenever a person shall flee from an officer attempting to arrest him, such officer, with or without a warrant, may pursue such person anywhere in the Commonwealth and, when actually in close pursuit, may arrest him wherever he is found. If the arrest is made in a county or city adjoining that from which the accused fled, or in any area of the Commonwealth within one mile of the boundary of the county or city from which he fled, the officer may forthwith return the accused before the proper official of the county or city from which he fled. If the arrest is made beyond the foregoing limits, the officer shall proceed according to the provisions of § 19.2–76, and if such arrest is made without a warrant, the officer shall procure a warrant from the magistrate serving the county or city wherein the arrest was made, charging the accused with the offense committed in the county or city from which he fled.

Acts 1975, c. 495; Acts 1992, c. 881. Amended by Acts 2008, c. 551; Acts 2008, c. 691.

§ 19.2–78. Uniform of officer making arrest

All officers whose duties are to make arrests acting under the authority of any law of this Commonwealth or any subdivision thereof, who shall make any arrest, search or seizure on any public road or highway of this Commonwealth shall be dressed at the time of making any such arrest, search or seizure in such uniform as he may customarily wear in the performance of his duties which will clearly show him to casual observation to be an officer.

Nothing in this section shall render unlawful any arrest, search or seizure by an officer who is not in such customary uniform.

Acts 1975, c. 495.

§ 19.2–79. Arrest by officers of other states of United States

Any member of a duly organized state, county or municipal peace unit of another state of the United States who enters this Commonwealth in close pursuit, and continues within this Commonwealth in such close pursuit, of a person in order to arrest him on the ground that he has committed a felony in such other state shall have the same authority to arrest and hold in custody such person as members of a duly organized state, county or municipal peace unit of this Commonwealth have to arrest and hold in custody a person on the ground that he has committed a felony in this Commonwealth, if the state from which such person has fled extends similar privileges to any member of a duly organized state, county or municipal peace unit of this Commonwealth.

If an arrest is made in this Commonwealth by an officer of another state in accordance with the provisions of the first paragraph of this section, he shall without unnecessary delay take the person arrested before a judge of a general district court, or of the circuit court, of the county or city in which the arrest was made, who shall conduct a hearing for the purpose of determining the lawfulness of the arrest. If the judge determines that the arrest was lawful he shall commit the person arrested to await for a reasonable time the issuance of an extradition warrant by the Governor. If the judge determines that the arrest was unlawful he shall discharge the person arrested.

The first paragraph of this section shall not be construed so as to make unlawful any arrest in this Commonwealth which would otherwise be lawful.

For the purpose of this section the word "State" shall include the District of Columbia.

Acts 1975, c. 495.

§ 19.2–80. Duty of arresting officer; bail

In any case in which an officer does not issue a summons pursuant to § 19.2–74 or § 46.2–936, a law-enforcement officer making an arrest under a warrant or capias shall bring the arrested person without unnecessary delay before a judicial officer. The judicial officer shall immediately conduct a bail hearing and either admit the accused to bail or commit him to jail. However, if (i) the accused is charged with a misdemeanor and is brought before a judge of the court having jurisdiction to try the case and (ii) both the accused and the Commonwealth consent, the judge may proceed to trial instead of conducting a bail hearing.

Acts 1975, c. 495; Acts 1979, c. 679; Acts 1986, c. 327; Acts 1997, c. 10.

§ 19.2–80.1. When arrested person operating motor vehicle; how vehicle removed from scene of arrest

In any case in which a police officer arrests the operator of a motor vehicle and there is no legal cause for the retention of the motor vehicle by the officer, the officer shall allow the person arrested to designate another person who is present at the scene of the arrest and a licensed driver to drive the motor vehicle from the scene to a place designated by the person arrested. If such a designation is not made, the officer may cause the vehicle to be taken to the nearest appropriate place for safekeeping.

Acts 1981, c. 306.

§ 19.2–80.2. Duty of arresting officer; providing magistrate or court with criminal history information

In any case in which an officer proceeds under §§ 19.2–76, 19.2–80 and 19.2–82, such officer shall, to

the extent possible, obtain and provide the magistrate or court with the arrested person's criminal history information prior to any proceeding under Article 1 (§ 19.2–119 et seq.) of Chapter 9 of this title. A pretrial services agency established pursuant to § 19.2–152.2 may, in lieu of the arresting officer, provide the criminal history to the magistrate or court.
Acts 1999, c. 829; Acts 1999, c. 846; Acts 2007, c. 133.

§ 19.2–81. Arrest without warrant authorized in certain cases

A. The following officers shall have the powers of arrest as provided in this section:

1. Members of the State Police force of the Commonwealth;

2. Sheriffs of the various counties and cities, and their deputies;

3. Members of any county police force or any duly constituted police force of any city or town of the Commonwealth;

4. The Commissioner, members and employees of the Marine Resources Commission granted the power of arrest pursuant to § 28.2–900;

5. Regular conservation police officers appointed pursuant to § 29.1–200;

6. United States Coast Guard and United States Coast Guard Reserve commissioned, warrant, and petty officers authorized under § 29.1–205 to make arrests;

7. Conservation officers appointed pursuant to § 10.1–115;

8. Full-time sworn members of the enforcement division of the Department of Motor Vehicles appointed pursuant to § 46.2–217;

Subd. A.9 effective until July 1, 2018

9. Special agents of the Department of Alcoholic Beverage Control; and

Subd. A.9 effective July 1, 2018

9. Special agents of the Virginia Alcoholic Beverage Control Authority; and

10. Campus police officers appointed under Chapter 17 (§ 23–232 et seq.) of Title 23.

B. Such officers may arrest without a warrant any person who commits any crime in the presence of the officer and any person whom he has reasonable grounds or probable cause to suspect of having committed a felony not in his presence.

Such officers may arrest without a warrant any person whom the officer has probable cause to suspect of operating any watercraft or motorboat while (i) intoxicated in violation of subsection B of § 29.1–738 or a substantially similar ordinance of any county, city, or town in the Commonwealth or (ii) in violation of an order issued pursuant to § 29.1–738.4 and may thereafter transfer custody of the person arrested to another officer, who may obtain a warrant based upon statements made to him by the arresting officer.

C. Any such officer may, at the scene of any accident involving a motor vehicle, watercraft as defined in § 29.1–733.2 or motorboat, or at any hospital or medical facility to which any person involved in such accident has been transported, or in the apprehension of any person charged with the theft of any motor vehicle, on any of the highways or waters of the Commonwealth, upon reasonable grounds to believe, based upon personal investigation, including information obtained from eyewitnesses, that a crime has been committed by any person then and there present, apprehend such person without a warrant of arrest. For purposes of this section, "the scene of any accident" shall include a reasonable location where a vehicle or person involved in an accident has been moved at the direction of a law-enforcement officer to facilitate the clearing of the highway or to ensure the safety of the motoring public.

D. Such officers may, within three hours of the alleged offense, arrest without a warrant at any location any person whom the officer has probable cause to suspect of driving or operating a motor vehicle, watercraft or motorboat while intoxicated in violation of § 18.2–266, 18.2–266.1, 46.2–341.24, or subsection B of § 29.1–738; or a substantially similar ordinance of any county, city, or town in the Commonwealth, whether or not the offense was committed in such officer's presence. Such officers may, within three hours of the alleged offense, arrest without a warrant at any location any person whom the officer has probable cause to suspect of operating a watercraft or motorboat in violation of an order issued pursuant to § 29.1–738.4, whether or not the offense was committed in such officer's presence.

E. Such officers may arrest, without a warrant or a capias, persons duly charged with a crime in another jurisdiction upon receipt of a photocopy of a warrant or a capias, telegram, computer printout, facsimile printout, a radio, telephone or teletype message, in which photocopy of a warrant, telegram, computer printout, facsimile printout, radio, telephone or teletype message shall be given the name or a reasonably accurate description of such person wanted and the crime alleged.

F. Such officers may arrest, without a warrant or a capias, for an alleged misdemeanor not committed in his presence when the officer receives a radio message from his department or other law-enforcement agency within the Commonwealth that a warrant or capias for such offense is on file.

G. Such officers may also arrest without a warrant for an alleged misdemeanor not committed in their presence involving (i) shoplifting in violation of § 18.2–96 or 18.2–103 or a similar local ordinance, (ii) carrying a weapon on school property in violation of § 18.2–308.1, (iii) assault and battery, (iv) brandishing a firearm in violation of § 18.2–282, or (v) destruction of property in violation of § 18.2–137, when such property is located on premises used for business or commercial purposes, or a similar local ordinance, when any such arrest is based on probable cause upon reasonable complaint of the person who observed the alleged offense. The arresting officer may issue a summons to any person arrested under this section for a misdemeanor violation involving shoplifting.

Acts 1975, c. 495; Acts 1976, c. 515; Acts 1976, c. 570; Acts 1977, c. 97; Acts 1979, c. 268; Acts 1982, c. 272; Acts 1983, c. 206; Acts 1984, c. 534; Acts 1985, c. 507; Acts 1988, c. 353; Acts 1988, c. 744; Acts 1988, c. 752; Acts 1988, c. 853; Acts 1990, c. 635; Acts 1990, c. 744; Acts 1990, c. 784; Acts 1995, c. 465; Acts 1996, c. 866, eff. July 1, 1997; Acts 1996, c. 929, eff. April 17, 1996; Acts 1996, c. 1015, eff. April 17, 1996; Acts 1998, c. 684; Acts 2004, c. 949; Acts 2005, c. 88; Acts 2005, c. 435. Amended by Acts 2008, c. 460; Acts 2008, c. 737; Acts 2010, c. 840; Acts 2011, c. 510; Acts 2011, c. 643; Acts 2012, c. 776; Acts 2013, c. 787, eff. July 1, 2014; Acts 2014, c. 543; Acts 2015, c. 38, eff. July 1, 2018; Acts 2015, c. 730, eff. July 1, 2018.

§ 19.2–81.1. Arrest without warrant by correctional officers in certain cases

Any correctional officer, as defined in § 53.1–1, may arrest, in the same manner as provided in § 19.2–81, persons for crimes involving:

(a) The escape of an inmate from a correctional institution, as defined in § 53.1–1;

(b) Assisting an inmate to escape from a correctional institution, as defined in § 53.1–1;

(c) The delivery of contraband to an inmate in violation of § 18.2–474 or § 18.2–474.1; and

(d) Any other criminal offense which may contribute to the disruption of the safety, welfare, or security of the population of a correctional institution.

Acts 1976, c. 752.

§ 19.2–81.2. Power of correctional officers and designated noncustodial employees to detain

A. A correctional officer, as defined in § 53.1–1, who has completed the minimum training standards established by the Department of Criminal Justice Services, or other noncustodial employee of the Department of Corrections who has been designated to carry a weapon by the Director of the Department of Corrections pursuant to § 53.1–29 of the Code and who has completed the basic course in detention training as approved by the Department of Criminal Justice Services, may, while on duty in or on the grounds of a correctional institution, or with custody of prisoners without the confines of a correctional institution, detain any person whom he has reasonable suspicion to believe has committed a violation of §§ 18.2–473 through 18.2–475, or of aiding or abetting a prisoner in violating the provisions of § 53.1–203. Such detention shall be for the purpose of summoning a law-enforcement officer in order that the law-enforcement officer can arrest the person who is alleged to have violated any of the above sections.

B. Any employee of the Department of Corrections having the authority to detain any person pursuant to subsection A hereof shall not be held civilly liable for unlawful detention, slander, malicious prosecution, false imprisonment, false arrest, or assault and battery of the person so detained, whether such detention takes place within or without the grounds of a correctional institution, provided that, in causing the detention of such person, the employee had at the time of the detention reasonable suspicion to believe that the person committed a violation for which the detention was undertaken.

C. It is the purpose and intent of this section to ensure that the safety, stability, welfare and security of correctional institutions be preserved insofar as possible.

Acts 1976, c. 740; Acts 1979, c. 642; Acts 1984, c. 720; Acts 1984, c. 779.

§ 19.2–81.3. Arrest without a warrant authorized in cases of assault and battery against a family or household member and stalking and for violations of protective orders; procedure, etc.

A. Any law-enforcement officer with the powers of arrest may arrest without a warrant for an alleged violation of § 18.2–57.2, 18.2–60.4, or 16.1–253.2 regardless of whether such violation was committed in his presence, if such arrest is based on probable cause or upon personal observations or the reasonable complaint of a person who observed the alleged offense or upon personal investigation.

B. A law-enforcement officer having probable cause to believe that a violation of § 18.2–57.2 or 16.1–253.2 has occurred shall arrest and take into custody the person he has probable cause to believe, based on the totality of the circumstances, was the predominant physical aggressor unless there are special circumstances which would dictate a course of action other than an arrest. The standards for determining who is the predominant physical aggressor shall be based on the following considerations: (i) who was the first aggressor, (ii) the protection of the health and safety of family and household members, (iii) prior complaints of family abuse by the allegedly abusing person involving the family or household members, (iv) the relative severity of the injuries inflicted on persons involved in the incident, (v) whether any injuries were inflicted in self-defense, (vi) witness statements, and (vii) other observations.

C. A law-enforcement officer having probable cause to believe that a violation of § 18.2–60.4 has occurred that involves physical aggression shall arrest and take into custody the person he has probable cause to believe, based on the totality of the circumstances, was the predominant physical aggressor unless there are special circumstances which would dictate a course of action other than an arrest. The standards for determining who is the predominant physical aggressor shall be based on the following considerations: (i) who was the first aggressor, (ii) the protection of the health and safety of the person to whom the protective order was issued and the person's family and household members, (iii) prior acts of violence, force, or threat, as defined in § 19.2–152.7:1, by the person against whom the protective order was issued against the person protected by the order or the protected person's family or household members, (iv) the relative severity of the injuries inflicted on persons involved in the incident, (v) whether any injuries were inflicted in self-defense, (vi) witness statements, and (vii) other observations.

D. Regardless of whether an arrest is made, the officer shall file a written report with his department, which shall state whether any arrests were made, and if so, the number of arrests, specifically including any incident in which he has probable cause to believe family abuse has occurred, and, where required, including a complete statement in writing that there are special circumstances that would dictate a course of action other than an arrest. The officer shall provide the allegedly abused person or the person protected by an order issued pursuant to § 19.2–152.8, 19.2–152.9, or 19.2–152.10, both orally and in writing, information regarding the legal and community resources available to the allegedly abused person or person protected by the order. Upon request of the allegedly abused person or person protected by the order, the department shall make a summary of the report available to the allegedly abused person or person protected by the order.

E. In every case in which a law-enforcement officer makes an arrest under this section for a violation of § 18.2–57.2, he shall petition for an emergency protective order as authorized in § 16.1–253.4 when the person arrested and taken into custody is brought before the magistrate, except if the person arrested is a minor, a petition for an emergency protective order shall not be required. Regardless of whether an arrest is made, if the officer has probable cause to believe that a danger of acts of family abuse exists, the law-enforcement officer shall seek an emergency protective order under § 16.1–253.4, except if the suspected abuser is a minor, a petition for an emergency protective order shall not be required.

F. A law-enforcement officer investigating any complaint of family abuse, including but not limited to assault and battery against a family or household member shall, upon request, transport, or arrange for the transportation of an abused person to a hospital or safe shelter, or to appear before a magistrate. Any local law-enforcement agency may adopt a policy requiring an officer to transport or arrange for transportation of an abused person as provided in this subsection.

G. The definition of "family or household member" in § 16.1–228 applies to this section.

H. As used in this section, "law-enforcement officer" means (i) any full-time or part-time employee of a police department or sheriff's office which is part of or administered by the Commonwealth or any political subdivision thereof, and any campus police officer appointed under Chapter 17 (§ 23–232 et seq.) of Title 23, and who is responsible for the prevention and detection of crime and the enforcement of the penal, traffic or highway laws of this Commonwealth; (ii) any member of an auxiliary police force established pursuant to § 15.2–1731; and (iii) any special conservator of the peace who meets the certification requirements for a law-enforcement officer as set forth in § 15.2–1706. Part-time employees are compensated officers who are not full-time employees as defined by the employing police department or sheriff's office.

Acts 1991, c. 715; Acts 1992, c. 886 Acts 1995, c. 413; Acts 1995, c. 433; Acts 1996, c. 866, eff. July 1, 1997; Acts 1997, c. 603; Acts 1998, c. 569; Acts 1999, c. 697; Acts 1999, c. 721; Acts 1999, c. 807; Acts 2002, c. 810; Acts 2002, c. 818; Acts 2004, c. 1016. Amended by Acts 2008, c. 551; Acts 2008, c. 691; Acts 2011, c. 445; Acts 2011, c. 480; Acts 2012, c. 776; Acts 2012, c. 827, eff. April 1, 2012; Acts 2014, c. 779; Acts 2014, c. 797.

§ 19.2–81.4. Repealed by Acts 2008, cc. 600 and 771

§ 19.2–81.5. Cooperation with a law-enforcement officer

Upon receipt of a request and documentation of an indictment or issuance of a warrant from a law-enforcement agency, any public agency within the Commonwealth may disclose to the requesting law-enforcement agency from agency records, to the extent permitted by federal law, the address of an individual who has been indicted or for whom a warrant for arrest for a crime punishable by incarceration has been issued.

Acts 1998, c. 436.

§ 19.2–81.6. Authority of law-enforcement officers to arrest illegal aliens

All law-enforcement officers enumerated in § 19.2–81 shall have the authority to enforce immigration laws of the United States, pursuant to the provisions of this section. Any law-enforcement officer enumerated in § 19.2–81 may, in the course of acting upon reasonable suspicion that an individual has committed or is committing a crime, arrest the individual without a warrant upon receiving confirmation from the Bureau of Immigration and Customs Enforcement of the United States Department of Homeland Security that the individual (i) is an alien illegally present in the United States, and (ii) has previously been convicted of a felony in the United States and deported or left the United States after such conviction. Upon receiving such confirmation, the officer shall take the individual forthwith before a magistrate or other issuing authority and proceed pursuant to § 19.2–82.

Acts 2004, c. 360; Acts 2004, c. 412.

§ 19.2–82. Procedure upon arrest without warrant

A. A person arrested without a warrant shall be brought forthwith before a magistrate or other issuing authority having jurisdiction who shall proceed to examine the officer making the arrest under oath. If the magistrate or other issuing authority having jurisdiction has lawful probable cause upon which to believe that a criminal offense has been committed, and that the person arrested has committed such offense, he shall issue either a warrant under the provisions of § 19.2–72 or a summons under the provisions of § 19.2–73.

As used in this section the term "brought before a magistrate or other issuing authority having jurisdiction" shall include a personal appearance before such authority or any two-way electronic video and audio communication meeting the requirements of § 19.2–3.1, in order that the accused and the arresting officer may simultaneously see and speak to such magistrate or authority. If electronic means are used, any documents filed may be transmitted in accordance with § 19.2–3.1.

If a warrant is issued the case shall thereafter be disposed of under the provisions of §§ 19.2–183 through 19.2–190, if the issuing officer is a judge; under the provisions of §§ 19.2–119 through 19.2–134, if the issuing officer is a magistrate or other issuing officer having jurisdiction.

If such warrant or summons is not issued, the person so arrested shall be released.

B. A warrant may be issued pursuant to this section, where the person has been arrested in accordance with § 19.2–81.6, and the magistrate or other issuing authority examines the officer making the arrest under oath, and finds lawful probable cause to believe the arrested individual meets the conditions of clauses (i) and (ii) of § 19.2–81.6. If such warrant is issued, it shall recite § 19.2–81.6 and the applicable violation of federal criminal law previously confirmed with Immigration and Customs Enforcement. Upon the person being taken into federal custody, such state warrant shall be dismissed. Any warrant issued under this subsection shall expire within 72 hours, or when the person is taken into federal custody, whichever occurs first. Recurrent applications for a warrant under this subsection shall not be permitted within a six-month period except where confirmation has been received from Immigration and Customs Enforcement that the arrested person will be taken into federal custody.

Acts 1975, c. 495; Acts 1981, c. 382; Acts 1983, c. 564; Acts 1984, c. 766; Acts 1991, c. 41; Acts 2002, c. 310; Acts 2004, c. 360; Acts 2004, c. 412. Amended by Acts 2009, c. 669.

§ 19.2–82.1. Giving false identity to law-enforcement officer; penalty

Any person who falsely identifies himself to a law-enforcement officer with the intent to deceive the law-enforcement officer as to his real identity after having been lawfully detained and after being requested to identify himself by a law-enforcement officer, is guilty of a Class 1 misdemeanor.

Acts 2006, c. 387.

§ 19.2–83. Repealed by Acts 1994, c. 273

§ 19.2–83.1. Report of arrest of school employees and adult students for certain offenses

A. Every state official or agency and every sheriff, police officer, or other local law-enforcement officer or conservator of the peace having the power to arrest for a felony, upon arresting a person who is known or discovered by the arresting official to be a full-time, part-time, permanent, or temporary teacher or other employee in any public school division in this Commonwealth for a felony or a Class 1 misdemeanor or an equivalent offense in another state shall file a report of such arrest with the division superintendent of the employing division as soon as practicable. The contents of the report required pursuant to this section shall be utilized by the local school division solely to implement the provisions of subsection B of § 22.1–296.2 and § 22.1–315.

B. Every state official or agency and every sheriff, police officer, or other local law-enforcement officer or conservator of the peace having the power to arrest for a felony, shall file a report, as soon as practicable, with the division superintendent of the school division in which the student is enrolled upon arresting a person who is known or discovered by the arresting official to be a student age 18 or older in any public school division in this Commonwealth for:

1. A firearm offense pursuant to Article 4 (§ 18.2–279 et seq.), 5 (§ 18.2–288 et seq.), 6 (§ 18.2–299 et seq.), 6.1 (§ 18.2–307.1 et seq.), or 7 (§ 18.2–308.1 et seq.) of Chapter 7 of Title 18.2;

2. Homicide, pursuant to Article 1 (§ 18.2–30 et seq.) of Chapter 4 of Title 18.2;

3. Felonious assault and bodily wounding, pursuant to Article 4 (§ 18.2–51 et seq.) of Chapter 4 of Title 18.2;

4. Criminal sexual assault, pursuant to Article 7 (§ 18.2–61 et seq.) of Chapter 4 of Title 18.2;

5. Manufacture, sale, gift, distribution or possession of Schedule I or II controlled substances, pursuant to Article 1 (§ 18.2–247 et seq.) of Chapter 7 of Title 18.2;

6. Manufacture, sale or distribution of marijuana pursuant to Article 1 (§ 18.2–247 et seq.) of Chapter 7 of Title 18.2;

7. Arson and related crimes, pursuant to Article 1 (§ 18.2–77 et seq.) of Chapter 5 of Title 18.2;

8. Burglary and related offenses, pursuant to §§ 18.2–89 through 18.2–93;

9. Robbery pursuant to § 18.2–58;

10. Prohibited criminal street gang activity pursuant to § 18.2–46.2; or

11. Recruitment of juveniles for criminal street gang pursuant to § 18.2–46.3.

Acts 1996, c. 958; Acts 1996, c. 960; Acts 1997, c. 721; Acts 2001, c. 591; Acts 2004, c. 517. Amended by Acts 2011, c. 384, eff. March 23, 2011; Acts 2011, c. 410, eff. March 23, 2011; Acts 2013, c. 746; Acts 2014, c. 674; Acts 2014, c. 719.

§ 19.2–83.2. Jail officer to ascertain citizenship of inmate

Whenever any person is taken into custody at any jail, the sheriff or other officer in charge of such facility shall inquire as to whether the person (i) was born in a country other than the United States, and (ii) is a citizen of a country other than the United States. The sheriff or other officer in charge of such facility shall make an immigration alien query to the Law Enforcement Support Center of the United States Immigration and Customs Enforcement for any person who (i) was born in a country other than the United States, and (ii) is a citizen of a country other than the United States, or for whom the answer to (i) or (ii) is unknown. The sheriff or other officer in charge shall communicate the results of any immigration alien query to the Local Inmate Data System of the State Compensation Board. The State Compensation Board shall communicate, on a monthly basis, the results of any immigration alien query that results in a confirmation that the person is illegally present in the United States to the Central Criminal Records Exchange of the Department of State Police in a format approved by the Exchange. The information received by the Central Criminal Records Exchange concerning the person's immigration status shall be recorded in the person's criminal history record.

Added by Acts 2008, c. 180; Acts 2008, c. 415.

CHAPTER 8

EXTRADITION OF CRIMINALS

ARTICLE 1

FUGITIVES FROM FOREIGN NATIONS

§ 19.2–84. Governor to surrender on requisition of President

The Governor shall whenever required by the executive authority of the United States, pursuant to the Constitution and laws thereof, deliver over to justice any person found within the Commonwealth, who is charged with having committed any crime without the jurisdiction of the United States.

Acts 1975, c. 495.

ARTICLE 2

UNIFORM CRIMINAL EXTRADITION ACT

For text of Uniform Act, and variation notes and annotation materials for adopting jurisdictions, see Uniform Laws Annotated, Master Edition, Volume 11

§ 19.2–85. Definitions

When appearing in this chapter:

(1) The term "Governor" includes any person performing the functions of Governor by authority of the law of this Commonwealth;

(2) The term "executive authority" includes the Governor, and any person performing the functions of Governor in a state other than this Commonwealth;

(3) The term "State," referring to a state other than this Commonwealth, includes any other state or territory, organized or unorganized, of the United States of America, and the District of Columbia; and

(4) The term "judge" means a judge of a court of record having criminal jurisdiction.

Acts 1975, c. 495.

§ 19.2–86. Fugitives from justice; duty of Governor

Subject to the provisions of this chapter, the provisions of the Constitution of the United States controlling, and any and all acts of Congress enacted in pursuance thereof, the Governor shall have arrested and delivered up to the executive authority of any other of the United States any person charged in that state with treason, felony, or other crime, who has fled from justice and is found in this Commonwealth.

Acts 1975, c. 495.

§ 19.2–87. Form of demand

No demand for the extradition of a person charged with, or convicted of, crime in another state shall be recognized by the Governor unless in writing alleging, except in cases arising under § 19.2–91, that the accused was present in the demanding state at the time of the commission of the alleged crime and that thereafter he fled from such state, and accompanied: (1) by a copy of an indictment found, (2) by a copy or an information supported by an affidavit filed in the state having jurisdiction of the crime, (3) by a copy of an affidavit made before a magistrate in such state together with a copy of any warrant which was issued thereupon, or (4) by a copy of a judgment of conviction or of a sentence imposed in execution thereof together with a statement by the executive authority of the demanding state that the person claimed has escaped from confinement or has broken the terms of his bail, probation or parole. The indictment, information or affidavit made before the magistrate must substantially charge the person demanded with having committed a crime under the law of that state; and the copy of the indictment, information, affidavit, judgment of conviction or sentence must be authenticated by the executive authority making the demand.

Acts 1975, c. 495.

§ 19.2–88. Governor may investigate case

When a demand shall be made upon the Governor by the executive authority of another state for the surrender of a person so charged with, or convicted of, crime, the Governor may call upon the Attorney General or any other officer of this Commonwealth to investigate or assist in investigating the demand and to report to him the situation and circumstances of the person so demanded and whether he ought to be surrendered.

Acts 1975, c. 495.

§ 19.2–89. Extradition of persons imprisoned or awaiting trial in another state

When it is desired to have returned to this Commonwealth a person charged in this Commonwealth with a crime and such person is imprisoned or is held under criminal proceedings then pending against him in another state, the Governor may agree with the executive authority of such other state for the extradition of such person before the conclusion of such proceedings or his term of sentence in such other state, upon condition that such person be returned to such other state at the expense of this Commonwealth as soon as the prosecution in this Commonwealth is terminated.

Acts 1975, c. 495.

§ 19.2–90. Extradition of persons who have left demanding state involuntarily

The Governor may also surrender on demand of the executive authority of any other state any person in this Commonwealth who is charged in the manner provided in §§ 19.2–109 to 19.2–111, with having violated the laws of the state whose executive authority is making the demand, even though such person left the demanding state involuntarily.

Acts 1975, c. 495.

§ 19.2–91. Extradition of persons not in demanding state at time of commission of crime

The Governor may also surrender, on demand of the executive authority of any other state, any person in this Commonwealth charged in such other state in the manner provided in § 19.2–87 with committing an act in this Commonwealth, or in a third state, intentionally resulting in a crime in the state whose executive authority is making the demand. The provisions of this chapter not otherwise inconsistent shall apply to such cases, even though the accused was not in that state at the time of the commission of the crime, and has not fled therefrom.

Acts 1975, c. 495.

§ 19.2–92. Issuance of Governor's warrant of arrest; its recitals

If the Governor decides that a demand for the extradition of a person, charged with, or convicted of, crime in another state should be complied with, he shall sign a warrant of arrest, which shall be sealed with the state seal, and be directed to the sheriff or sergeant of any county or city or to any peace officer or other person whom he may think fit to entrust with the execution thereof. The warrant must substantially recite the facts necessary to the validity of its issuance. Any electronically transmitted facsimile of a Governor's warrant shall be treated as an original document, provided the original is received within four working days of receipt of the facsimile.

Acts 1975, c. 495; Acts 2001, c. 214; Acts 2001, c. 226. Amended by Acts 2011, c. 59.

§ 19.2–93. Manner and place of execution of warrant

Such warrant shall authorize the officer or other person to whom it is directed to arrest the accused at any time and at any place where he may be found within the Commonwealth and to command the aid of all peace officers or other persons in the execution of the warrant and to deliver the accused, subject to the provisions of this chapter, to the duly authorized agent of the demanding state.

Acts 1975, c. 495.

§ 19.2–94. Assistance to arresting officer

Every officer or other person empowered to make the arrest, as provided in the preceding section, shall have the same authority, in arresting the accused, to command assistance therein as the sheriffs and sergeants of the several counties and cities of this Commonwealth have by law in the execution of any

criminal process directed to them, with like penalties against those who refuse to render their assistance.
Acts 1975, c. 495.

§ 19.2–95. Rights of accused persons; application for writ of habeas corpus

No person arrested upon such warrant shall be delivered over to the agent whom the executive authority demanding him shall have appointed to receive him unless he shall first be taken forthwith before a judge of a circuit or general district court in the Commonwealth, who shall inform him of the demand made for his surrender and of the crime with which he is charged, and that he has the right to demand and procure legal counsel; and if the prisoner or his counsel shall state that he or they desire to test the legality of his arrest, the judge shall fix a reasonable time to be allowed him within which to apply for a writ of habeas corpus. When such writ is applied for, notice thereof and of the time and place of hearing thereon shall be given to the attorney for the Commonwealth of the county or city in which the arrest is made and in which the accused is in custody, and to the agent of the demanding state.
Acts 1975, c. 495; Acts 2005, c. 839, eff. Oct. 1, 2005.

§ 19.2–96. Penalty for noncompliance with preceding section

Any officer who shall deliver to the agent for extradition of the demanding state a person in his custody under the Governor's warrant in willful disobedience to the last preceding section shall be guilty of a Class 1 misdemeanor.
Acts 1975, c. 495.

§ 19.2–97. Confinement in jail when necessary

The officer or persons executing the Governor's warrant of arrest, or the agent of the demanding state to whom the prisoner may have been delivered, may, when necessary, confine the prisoner in the jail of any county or city through which he may pass; and the keeper of such jail shall receive and safely keep the prisoner until the officer or person having charge of him is ready to proceed on his route, such officer or person being chargeable with the expense of keeping.
Acts 1975, c. 495.

§ 19.2–98. Same; for prisoners being taken through Commonwealth

The officer or agent of a demanding state to whom a prisoner may have been delivered following extradition proceedings in another state or to whom a prisoner may have been delivered after waiving extradition in such other state, and who is passing through this Commonwealth with such prisoner for the purpose of returning immediately such prisoner to the demanding state may, when necessary, confine the prisoner in the jail of any county or city through which he may pass; and the keeper of such jail shall receive and safely keep the prisoner until the officer or agent having charge of him is ready to proceed on his route, such officer or agent, however, being chargeable with the expense of keeping, provided, however, that such officer or agent shall deliver to the jailer the warrant or legal order authorizing custody of the prisoner. Such prisoner shall not be entitled to demand a new requisition while in this Commonwealth.
Acts 1975, c. 495.

§ 19.2–99. Arrest prior to requisition

Whenever: (1) any person within this Commonwealth shall be charged on the oath of any credible person before any judge, magistrate or other officer authorized to issue criminal warrants in this Commonwealth with the commission of any crime in any other state and, except in cases arising under § 19.2–91, (a) with having fled from justice, (b) with having been convicted of a crime in that state and of having escaped from confinement, or (c) of having broken the terms of his bail, probation, or parole, or (2) complaint shall have been made before any such judge, magistrate or other officer in this Commonwealth setting forth on the affidavit of any credible person in another state that a crime has been committed in such other state and that the accused has been charged in such state with the commission of the crime, and, except in cases arising under § 19.2–91, (a) has fled from justice, (b) having been convicted of a crime in that state has escaped from confinement, or (c) broken the terms of his bail, probation or parole, and that the accused is believed to be in this Commonwealth, such judge, magistrate or other officer shall issue a warrant directed to any sheriff or to any peace officer commanding him to apprehend the person named therein, wherever he may be found in this Commonwealth, and to bring him before any judge who may be available in or convenient of access to the place where the arrest may be made, to answer the charge of complaint and affidavit. A certified copy of the sworn charge or complaint and affidavit upon which the warrant is issued shall be attached to the warrant.
Acts 1975, c. 495.

§ 19.2–100. Arrest without warrant

The arrest of a person may be lawfully made also by any peace officer or private person without a warrant upon reasonable information that the accused stands charged in the courts of a state with a crime punishable by death or imprisonment for a term exceeding one year. But when so arrested the accused shall be taken before a judge, magistrate or other officer authorized to issue criminal warrants in this Commonwealth with all practicable speed and complaint made against him under oath setting forth the ground for the arrest as in the preceding section; and thereafter his answer shall be heard as if he had been arrested on a warrant.

Acts 1975, c. 495.

§ 19.2–101. Confinement to await requisition; bail

If from the examination before the judge it appears that the person held pursuant to either of the two preceding sections is the person charged with having committed the crime alleged and, except in cases arising under § 19.2–91, that he has fled from justice, the judge shall, by a warrant reciting the accusation, commit him to jail for such a time, not exceeding thirty days, specified in the warrant as will enable the arrest of the accused to be made under a warrant of the Governor on a requisition of the executive authority of the state having jurisdiction of the offense, unless the accused give bail as provided in the next section, or until he shall be legally discharged.

Acts 1975, c. 495.

§ 19.2–102. In what cases bail allowed; conditions of bond

Unless the offense with which the prisoner is charged is shown to be an offense punishable by death or life imprisonment under the laws of the state in which it was committed, any judge, magistrate or other person authorized by law to admit persons to bail in this Commonwealth may admit the person arrested to bail by bond, with sufficient sureties, and in such sum as he deems proper, conditioned upon his appearance before a judge at a time specified in such bond and upon his surrender for arrest upon the warrant of the Governor of this Commonwealth.

Acts 1975, c. 495.

§ 19.2–103. Discharge, recommitment or renewal of bail

If the accused is not arrested under warrant of the Governor by the expiration of the time specified in the warrant or bond, any judge in this Commonwealth may discharge him or may recommit him for a further period not to exceed sixty days, or such judge may again take bail for his appearance and surrender, as provided in the preceding section, but within a period not to exceed sixty days after the date of such new bond.

Acts 1975, c. 495.

§ 19.2–104. Forfeiture of bail

If the prisoner is admitted to bail and fails to appear and surrender himself according to the conditions of his bond, any judge of a circuit or general district court by proper order, shall declare the bond forfeited and order his immediate arrest without warrant if he be within this Commonwealth. Recovery may be had on such bond in the name of the Commonwealth as in the case of other bonds given by the accused in criminal proceedings within this Commonwealth.

Acts 1975, c. 495.

§ 19.2–105. Persons under criminal prosecution in this Commonwealth at time of requisition

If a criminal prosecution has been instituted against such person under the laws of this Commonwealth and is still pending, the Governor, in his discretion, either may surrender him on demand of the executive authority of another state or hold him until he has been tried and discharged or convicted and punished in this Commonwealth.

Acts 1975, c. 495.

§ 19.2–106. When guilt or innocence of accused inquired into

The guilt or innocence of the accused as to the crime of which he is charged may not be inquired into by the Governor or in any proceeding after the demand for extradition accompanied by a charge of crime in legal form as above provided shall have been presented to the Governor, except as it may be involved in identifying the person held as the person charged with the crime.

Acts 1975, c. 495.

§ 19.2–107. Governor may recall warrant or issue alias

The Governor may recall his warrant of arrest or may issue another warrant whenever he deems it proper.

Acts 1975, c. 495.

§ 19.2–108. Fugitives from this Commonwealth; duty of Governor

Whenever the Governor shall demand a person charged with crime or with escaping from confinement or breaking the terms of his bail, probation or parole in this Commonwealth, from the executive authority of any other state, or from the chief justice or an associate justice of the Supreme Court of the District of Columbia authorized to receive such demand under the laws of the United States, he shall issue a warrant under the seal of this Commonwealth to some agent commanding him to receive the person so charged if delivered to him and convey him to the proper officer of the county or city in this Commonwealth in which the offense was committed. Nothing herein shall prevent the sheriff or police chief of a county or city who has been directed to execute such warrant from authorizing a private prisoner transportation company meeting the minimum qualifications set by the Department of Criminal Justice Services to receive and return the person to the Commonwealth.

Acts 1975, c. 495. Amended by Acts 2009, c. 848.

§ 19.2–109. Application for requisition for return of person charged with crime

When the return to this Commonwealth of a person charged with crime in this Commonwealth is required, the attorney for the Commonwealth shall present to the Governor his written application for a requisition for the return of the person charged, in which application shall be stated the name of the person so charged, the crime charged against him, the approximate time, place and circumstances of its commission, the state in which he is believed to be, including the location of the accused therein at the time the application is made, and certifying that, in the opinion of the attorney for the Commonwealth, the ends of justice require the arrest and return of the accused to this Commonwealth for trial and that the proceeding is not instituted to enforce a private claim.

Acts 1975, c. 495.

§ 19.2–110. Application for requisition for return of escaped convict, etc.

When the return to this Commonwealth is required of a person who has been convicted of a crime in this Commonwealth and has escaped from confinement or broken the terms of his bail, probation or parole, the attorney for the Commonwealth, of the county or city in which the offense was committed, or the warden of the institution or sheriff of the county or city from which the escape was made, shall present to the Governor a written application for a requisition for the return of such person, in which application shall be stated the name of the person, the crime of which he was convicted, the circumstances of his escape from confinement or of the breach of the terms of his bail, probation or parole and the state in which he is believed to be, including the location of the person therein at the time application is made.

Acts 1975, c. 495.

§ 19.2–111. Form of such applications; copies, etc.

The application shall be verified by affidavit, shall be executed in duplicate and shall be accompanied by two certified copies of the indictment returned, or information and affidavit filed, or of the complaint made to the judge of a circuit or general district court or other officer issuing the warrant stating the offense with which the accused is charged, or of the judgment of conviction or of the sentence. The attorney for the Commonwealth, warden or sheriff may also attach such further affidavits and other documents in duplicate as he shall deem proper to be submitted with such application. One copy of the application, with the action of the Governor indicated by endorsement thereon, and one of the certified copies of the indictment, complaint, information, and affidavits, or of the judgment of conviction or of the sentence shall be filed in the office of the Secretary of the Commonwealth, to remain of record in that office. The other copies of all papers shall be forwarded with the Governor's requisition.

Acts 1975, c. 495.

§ 19.2–112. Costs and expenses of extradition

A. The expenses incident to the extradition of any person under the four preceding sections may be paid out of the state treasury, on warrants of the Comptroller issued upon vouchers signed by the Governor, or such other person as may be designated by him for such purpose.

B. If the person extradited is found guilty, or if the person was extradited after illegally leaving the Commonwealth while on parole or on probation, the person extradited, and not the Commonwealth, shall be responsible for the costs and expenses of extradition. The state treasury shall continue to reimburse local jurisdictions for the costs and expenses of extradition. The fugitive shall pay the costs and expenses of his extradition into the state treasury.

Acts 1975, c. 495; Acts 1999, c. 322; Acts 2002, c. 622.

§ 19.2–113. Immunity from service of process in certain civil actions

A person brought into this Commonwealth by, or after waiver of, extradition based on a criminal charge shall not be subject to service of personal process in civil actions arising out of the same facts as the criminal proceeding to answer which he is being or has been returned, until he has been convicted in the criminal proceeding, or, if acquitted, until he has had reasonable opportunity to return to the state from which he was extradited.

Acts 1975, c. 495.

§ 19.2–114. Written waiver of extradition proceedings

Any person arrested in this Commonwealth charged with having committed any crime in another state or alleged to have escaped from confinement, or broken the terms of his bail, probation or parole may waive the issuance and service of the warrant provided for in §§ 19.2–92 and 19.2–93 and all other procedures incidental to extradition proceedings by executing or subscribing in the presence of a judge of a circuit or district court within this Commonwealth a writing which states that he consents to return to the demanding state. However, before the waiver is executed or subscribed by the person, it shall be the duty of the judge to inform the person of his rights to the issuance and service of a warrant of extradition and to obtain a writ of habeas corpus as provided for in § 19.2–95.

If and when such consent has been duly executed, it shall forthwith be forwarded to the office of the Governor and filed therein. The judge shall direct the officer having the person in custody to promptly deliver him to the duly accredited agent of the demanding state, and shall deliver or cause to be delivered to such agent a copy of the consent.

This section shall not be deemed to limit the rights of the accused person to return voluntarily and without formality to the demanding state, nor shall this waiver procedure be deemed to be an executive procedure or to limit the powers, rights or duties of the officers of the demanding state or of this Commonwealth.

Acts 1975, c. 495; Acts 1992, c. 306.

§ 19.2–115. Nonwaiver by this Commonwealth

Nothing in this chapter contained shall be deemed to constitute a waiver by this Commonwealth of its right, power or privilege to try such demanded person for crime committed within this Commonwealth, or of its right, power or privilege to regain custody of such person by extradition proceedings or otherwise for the purpose of trial, sentence or punishment for any crime committed within this Commonwealth, nor shall any proceedings had under this chapter which result in, or fail to result in, extradition be deemed a waiver by this Commonwealth of any of its rights, privileges or jurisdiction in any way whatsoever.

Acts 1975, c. 495.

§ 19.2–116. No right of asylum; no immunity from other criminal prosecutions while in this Commonwealth

After a person has been brought back to this Commonwealth by, or after waiver of, extradition proceedings he may be tried in this Commonwealth for other crimes which he may be charged with having committed here as well as that specified in the requisition for his extradition.

Acts 1975, c. 495.

§ 19.2–117. Interpretation of article

The provisions of this article shall be so interpreted and construed as to effectuate its general purposes to make uniform the law of those states which enact statutes similar thereto.

Acts 1975, c. 495.

§ 19.2–118. Short title

This article may be cited as the Uniform Criminal Extradition Act.

Acts 1975, c. 495.

CHAPTER 9

BAIL AND RECOGNIZANCES

ARTICLE 1

BAIL

§ 19.2–119. Definitions

As used in this chapter:

"Bail" means the pretrial release of a person from custody upon those terms and conditions specified by order of an appropriate judicial officer.

"Bond" means the posting by a person or his surety of a written promise to pay a specific sum, secured or unsecured, ordered by an appropriate judicial officer as a condition of bail to assure performance of the terms and conditions contained in the recognizance.

"Criminal history" means records and data collected by criminal justice agencies or persons consisting of identifiable descriptions and notations of arrests, detentions, indictments, informations or other formal charges, and any deposition arising therefrom.

"Judicial officer" means, unless otherwise indicated, any magistrate serving the jurisdiction, any judge of a district court and the clerk or deputy clerk of any district court or circuit court within their respective cities and counties, any judge of a circuit court, any judge of the Court of Appeals and any justice of the Supreme Court of Virginia.

"Person" means any accused, or any juvenile taken into custody pursuant to § 16.1–246.

"Recognizance" means a signed commitment by a person to appear in court as directed and to adhere to any other terms ordered by an appropriate judicial officer as a condition of bail.

Acts 1975, c. 495; Acts 1984, c. 703; Acts 1991, c. 581; Acts 1993, c. 636; Acts 1999, c. 829; Acts 1999, c. 846. Amended by Acts 2008, c. 551; Acts 2008, c. 691.

§ 19.2–120. Admission to bail

Prior to conducting any hearing on the issue of bail, release or detention, the judicial officer shall, to the extent feasible, obtain the person's criminal history.

A. A person who is held in custody pending trial or hearing for an offense, civil or criminal contempt, or otherwise shall be admitted to bail by a judicial officer, unless there is probable cause to believe that:

1. He will not appear for trial or hearing or at such other time and place as may be directed, or

2. His liberty will constitute an unreasonable danger to himself or the public.

B. The judicial officer shall presume, subject to rebuttal, that no condition or combination of conditions will reasonably assure the appearance of the person or the safety of the public if the person is currently charged with:

1. An act of violence as defined in § 19.2-297.1;

2. An offense for which the maximum sentence is life imprisonment or death;

3. A violation of § 18.2-248, 18.2-248.01, 18.2-255, or 18.2-255.2 involving a Schedule I or II controlled substance if (i) the maximum term of imprisonment is 10 years or more and the person was previously convicted of a like offense or (ii) the person was previously convicted as a "drug kingpin" as defined in § 18.2-248;

4. A violation of § 18.2-308.1, 18.2-308.2, or 18.2-308.4 and which relates to a firearm and provides for a mandatory minimum sentence;

5. Any felony, if the person has been convicted of two or more offenses described in subdivision 1 or 2, whether under the laws of the Commonwealth or substantially similar laws of the United States;

6. Any felony committed while the person is on release pending trial for a prior felony under federal or state law or on release pending imposition or execution of sentence or appeal of sentence or conviction;

7. An offense listed in subsection B of § 18.2-67.5:2 and the person had previously been convicted of an offense listed in § 18.2-67.5:2 or a substantially similar offense under the laws of any state or the United States and the judicial officer finds probable cause to believe that the person who is currently charged with one of these offenses committed the offense charged;

8. A violation of § 18.2-374.1 or 18.2-374.3 where the offender has reason to believe that the solicited person is under 15 years of age and the offender is at least five years older than the solicited person;

9. A violation of § 18.2-46.2, 18.2-46.3, 18.2-46.5, or 18.2-46.7;

10. A violation of § 18.2-36.1, 18.2-51.4, 18.2-266, or 46.2-341.24 and the person has, within the past five years of the instant offense, been convicted three times on different dates of a violation of any combination of these Code sections, or any ordinance of any county, city, or town or the laws of any other state or of the United States substantially similar thereto, and has been at liberty between each conviction;

11. A second or subsequent violation of § 16.1-253.2 or 18.2-60.4 or a substantially similar offense under the laws of any state or the United States;

12. A violation of subsection B of § 18.2-57.2;

13. A violation of subsection C of § 18.2-460 charging the use of threats of bodily harm or force to knowingly attempt to intimidate or impede a witness; or

14. A violation of § 18.2-51.6 if the alleged victim is a family or household member as defined in § 16.1-228.

C. The judicial officer shall presume, subject to rebuttal, that no condition or combination of conditions will reasonably assure the appearance of the person or the safety of the public if the person is being arrested pursuant to § 19.2-81.6.

D. A judicial officer who is a magistrate, clerk, or deputy clerk of a district court or circuit court may not admit to bail, that is not set by a judge, any person who is charged with an offense giving rise to a rebuttable presumption against bail as set out in subsection B or C without the concurrence of an attorney for the Commonwealth. For a person who is charged with an offense giving rise to a rebuttable presumption against bail, any judge may set or admit such person to bail in accordance with this section after notice and an opportunity to be heard has been provided to the attorney for the Commonwealth.

E. The court shall consider the following factors and such others as it deems appropriate in determining, for the purpose of rebuttal of the presumption against bail described in subsection B, whether there are conditions of release that will reasonably assure the appearance of the person as required and the safety of the public:

1. The nature and circumstances of the offense charged;

2. The history and characteristics of the person, including his character, physical and mental condition, family ties, employment, financial resources, length of residence in the community, community ties, past conduct, history relating to drug or alcohol abuse, criminal history, membership in a criminal street gang as defined in § 18.2-46.1, and record concerning appearance at court proceedings; and

3. The nature and seriousness of the danger to any person or the community that would be posed by the person's release.

F. The judicial officer shall inform the person of his right to appeal from the order denying bail or fixing terms of bond or recognizance consistent with § 19.2-124.

G. If the judicial officer sets a secured bond and the person engages the services of a licensed bail bondsman, the magistrate executing recognizance for the accused shall provide the bondsman, upon request, with a copy of the person's Virginia criminal history record, if readily available, to be used by the bondsman only to determine appropriate reporting requirements to impose upon the accused upon his release. The bondsman shall pay a $15 fee payable to the state treasury to be credited to the Literary Fund, upon requesting the defendant's Virginia criminal history record issued pursuant to § 19.2-389. The bondsman shall review the record on the premises and promptly return the record to the magistrate after reviewing it.

Acts 1975, c. 495; Acts 1978, c. 755; Acts 1979, c. 649; Acts 1987, c. 390; Acts 1991, c. 581; Acts 1993, c. 636; Acts 1996, c. 973; Acts 1997, c. 6; Acts 1997, c. 476; Acts 1999, c. 829; Acts 1999, c. 846; Acts 2000, c. 797; Acts 2002, c. 588; Acts 2002, c. 623; Acts 2004, c. 308; Acts 2004, c. 360; Acts 2004, c. 406; Acts 2004, c. 412; Acts 2004, c. 461; Acts 2004, c. 819; Acts 2004, c. 954; Acts 2004, c. 959; Acts 2005, c. 132; Acts 2006, c. 504; Acts 2007, c. 134; Acts 2007, c. 386; Acts 2007, c. 745; Acts 2007, c. 923. Amended by Acts 2008, c. 596; Acts 2010, c. 862; Acts 2011, c. 445; Acts 2011, c. 450; Acts 2011, c. 480; Acts 2012, c. 467; Acts 2015, c. 413.

§ 19.2–120.1. Presumption of no bail for illegal aliens charged with certain crimes

A. In addition to the presumption against the admission to bail under subsection B of § 19.2–120, the judicial officer shall presume, subject to rebuttal, that no condition or combination of conditions will reasonably assure the appearance of the person or the safety of the public if (i) the person is currently charged with an offense listed in subsection A of § 19.2–297.1, subsection C of § 17.1–805, any offense under Chapter 4 (§ 18.2–30 et seq.) of Title 18.2 except any offense under subsection A of § 18.2–57.2, any felony offense under Article 1 (§ 18.2–247 et seq.) of Chapter 7 of Title 18.2, or any offense under Article 2 (§ 18.2–266 et seq.), or any local ordinance substantially similar thereto, 4 (§ 18.2–279 et seq.), 5 (§ 18.2–288 et seq.), 6 (§ 18.2–299 et seq.), 6.1 (§ 18.2–307.1 et seq.), or 7 (§ 18.2–308.1 et seq.) of Chapter 7 of Title 18.2, and (ii) the person has been identified as being illegally present in the United States by United States Immigration and Customs Enforcement.

B. Notwithstanding subsection A, no presumption shall exist under this section as to any misdemeanor offense, or any felony offense under Article 1 (§ 18.2–247 et seq.) of Chapter 7 of Title 18.2, unless United States Immigration and Customs Enforcement has guaranteed that, in all such cases in the Commonwealth, it will issue a detainer for the initiation of removal proceedings and agree to reimburse for the cost of incarceration from the time of the issuance of the detainer.

Added by Acts 2008, c. 469; Acts 2008, c. 834. Amended by Acts 2013, c. 746.

§ 19.2–121. Fixing terms of bail

If the person is admitted to bail, the terms thereof shall be such as, in the judgment of any official granting or reconsidering the same, will be reasonably fixed to assure the appearance of the accused and to assure his good behavior pending trial. The judicial officer shall take into account (i) the nature and circumstances of the offense; (ii) whether a firearm is alleged to have been used in the offense; (iii) the weight of the evidence; (iv) the financial resources of the accused or juvenile and his ability to pay bond; (v) the character of the accused or juvenile including his family ties, employment or involvement in education; (vi) his length of residence in the community; (vii) his record of convictions; (viii) his appearance at court proceedings or flight to avoid prosecution or failure to appear at court proceedings; (ix) whether the person is likely to obstruct or attempt to obstruct justice, or threaten, injure, or intimidate, or attempt to threaten, injure, or intimidate a prospective witness, juror, or victim; and (x) any other information available which the court considers relevant to the determination of whether the accused or juvenile is unlikely to appear for court proceedings.

In any case where the accused has appeared and otherwise met the conditions of bail, no bond therefor shall be used to satisfy fines and costs unless agreed to by the person who posted such bond.

Acts 1975, c. 495; Acts 1978, c. 755; Acts 1980, c. 190; Acts 1991, c. 581; Acts 1992, c. 576; Acts 1993, c. 636; Acts 1999, c. 829; Acts 1999, c. 846.

§ 19.2–122. Repealed by Acts 1986, c. 327

§ 19.2–123. Release of accused on secured or unsecured bond or promise to appear; conditions of release

A. Any person arrested for a felony who has previously been convicted of a felony, or who is presently on bond for an unrelated arrest in any jurisdiction, or who is on probation or parole, may be released only upon a secure bond. This provision may be waived with the approval of the judicial officer and with the concurrence of the attorney for the Commonwealth or the attorney for the county, city or town. Subject to the foregoing, when a person is arrested for either a felony or a misdemeanor, any judicial officer may impose any one or any combination of the following conditions of release:

1. Place the person in the custody and supervision of a designated person, organization or pretrial services agency which, for the purposes of this section, shall not include a court services unit established pursuant to § 16.1–233;

2. Place restrictions on the travel, association or place of abode of the person during the period of release and restrict contacts with household members for a specified period of time;

2a. Require the execution of an unsecured bond;

3. Require the execution of a secure bond which at the option of the accused shall be satisfied with sufficient solvent sureties, or the deposit of cash in lieu thereof. Only the actual value of any interest in real estate or personal property owned by the proposed surety shall be considered in determining solvency and solvency shall be found if the value of the proposed surety's equity in the real estate or personal property equals or exceeds the amount of the bond;

3a. Require that the person do any or all of the following: (i) maintain employment or, if unemployed, actively seek employment; (ii) maintain or commence an educational program; (iii) avoid all contact with an alleged victim of the crime and with any potential witness who may testify concerning the offense; (iv) comply with a specified curfew; (v) refrain from possessing a firearm, destructive device, or other dangerous weapon; (vi) refrain from excessive use of alcohol, or use of any illegal drug or any controlled substance not prescribed by a health care provider; and (vii) submit to testing for drugs and alcohol until the final disposition of his case;

3b. Place a prohibition on a person who holds an elected constitutional office and who is accused of a felony arising from the performance of his duties from physically returning to his constitutional office;

3c. Require the accused to accompany the arresting officer to the jurisdiction's fingerprinting facility and submit to having his photograph and fingerprints taken prior to release; or

4. Impose any other condition deemed reasonably necessary to assure appearance as required, and to assure his good behavior pending trial, including a condition requiring that the person return to custody after specified hours or be placed on home electronic incarceration pursuant to § 53.1–131.2 or, when the person is required to execute a secured bond, be subject to monitoring by a GPS (Global Positioning System) tracking device, or other similar device. The defendant may be ordered by the court to pay the cost of the device.

Upon satisfaction of the terms of recognizance, the accused shall be released forthwith.

In addition, where the accused is an individual receiving services in a state training center for individuals with intellectual disability, the judicial officer may place the individual in the custody of the director of the training center, if the director agrees to accept custody. The director is hereby authorized to take custody of the individual and to maintain him at the training center prior to a trial or hearing under such circumstances as will reasonably assure the appearance of the accused for the trial or hearing.

B. In any jurisdiction served by a pretrial services agency which offers a drug or alcohol screening or testing program approved for the purposes of this subsection by the chief general district court judge, any such person charged with a crime may be requested by such agency to give voluntarily a urine sample, submit to a drug or alcohol screening, or take a breath test for presence of alcohol. A sample may be analyzed for the presence of phencyclidine (PCP), barbiturates, cocaine, opiates or such other drugs as the agency may deem appropriate prior to any hearing to establish bail. The judicial officer and agency shall inform the accused or juvenile being screened or tested that test results shall be used by a judicial officer only at a bail hearing and only to determine appropriate conditions of release or to reconsider the conditions of bail at a subsequent hearing. All screening or test results, and any pretrial investigation report containing the screening or test results, shall be confidential with access thereto limited to judicial officers, the attorney for the Commonwealth, defense counsel, other pretrial service agencies, any criminal justice agency as defined in § 9.1–101 and, in cases where a juvenile is screened or tested, the parents or legal guardian or custodian of such juvenile. However, in no event shall the judicial officer have access to any screening or test result prior to making a bail release determination or to determining the amount of bond, if any. Following this determination, the judicial officer shall consider the screening or test results and the screening or testing agency's report and accompanying recommendations, if any, in setting appropriate conditions of release. In no event shall a decision regarding a release determination be subject to reversal on the sole basis of such screening or test results. Any accused or juvenile whose urine sample has tested positive for such drugs and who is admitted to bail may, as a condition of release, be ordered to refrain from use of alcohol or illegal drugs and may be required to be tested on a periodic basis until final disposition of his case to ensure his compliance with the order. Sanctions for a violation of any condition of release, which violations shall include subsequent positive drug or alcohol test results or failure to report as ordered for testing, may be imposed in the discretion of the judicial officer and may include imposition of more stringent conditions of release, contempt of court proceedings or revocation of release. Any test given under the provisions of this subsection which yields a positive drug or alcohol test result shall be reconfirmed by a second test if the person tested denies or contests the initial drug or alcohol test positive result. The results of any drug or alcohol test conducted pursuant to this subsection shall not be admissible in any judicial proceeding other than for the imposition of sanctions for a violation of a condition of release.

C. Repealed.

D. Nothing in this section shall be construed to prevent an officer taking a juvenile into custody from releasing that juvenile pursuant to § 16.1–247. If any condition of release imposed under the provisions of this section is violated, a judicial officer may issue a capias or order to show cause why the recognizance should not be revoked.

E. Nothing in this section shall be construed to prevent a court from imposing a recognizance or bond designed to secure a spousal or child support obligation pursuant to § 16.1–278.16, Chapter 5 (§ 20–61 et seq.) of Title 20, or § 20–114 in addition to any recognizance or bond imposed pursuant to this chapter.

Acts 1975, c. 495; Acts 1978, c. 500; Acts 1978, c. 755; Acts 1979, c. 518; Acts 1981, c. 528; Acts 1984, c. 707; Acts 1989, c. 369; Acts 1991, c. 483; Acts 1991, c. 512; Acts 1991, c. 581; Acts 1991, c. 585; Acts 1992, c. 576; Acts 1993, c. 636; Acts 1999, c. 829; Acts 1999, c. 846; Acts 2000, c. 885; Acts 2000, c. 1020; Acts 2000, c. 1041; Acts 2001, c. 201; Acts 2006, c. 296. Amended by Acts 2008, c. 129; Acts 2008, c. 884; Acts 2011, c. 799; Acts 2011, c. 837; Acts 2012, c. 476; Acts 2012, c. 507; Acts 2013, c. 614; Acts 2014, c. 466.

§ 19.2–124. Appeal from bail, bond, or recognizance order

A. If a judicial officer denies bail to a person, requires excessive bond, or fixes unreasonable terms of a recognizance under this article, the person may appeal the decision of the judicial officer.

If the initial bail decision on a charge brought by a warrant or district court capias is made by a magistrate, clerk, or deputy clerk, the person shall first appeal to the district court in which the case is pending.

If the initial bail decision on a charge brought by direct indictment or presentment or circuit court capias is made by a magistrate, clerk, or deputy clerk, the person shall first appeal to the circuit court in which the case is pending.

If the appeal of an initial bail decision is taken on any charge originally pending in a district court after that charge has been appealed, certified, or transferred to a circuit court, the person shall first appeal to the circuit court in which the case is pending.

Any bail decision made by a judge of a court may be appealed successively by the person to the next higher court, up to and including the Supreme Court of Virginia, where permitted by law.

B. The attorney for the Commonwealth may appeal a bail, bond, or recognizance decision to the same court to which the accused person is required to appeal under subsection A.

C. The court granting or denying such bail may, upon appeal thereof, and for good cause shown, stay execution of such order for so long as reasonably practicable for the party to obtain an expedited hearing before the next higher court. No such stay may be granted after any person who has been granted bail has been released from custody on such bail.

D. No filing or service fees shall be assessed or collected for any appeal taken pursuant to this section.

Acts 1975, c. 495; Acts 1978, c. 755; Acts 1984, c. 703; Acts 1991, c. 581; Acts 1999, c. 829; Acts 1999, c. 846; Acts 2007, c. 462; Acts 2007, c. 549. Amended by Acts 2010, c. 404; Acts 2010, c. 592; Acts 2013, c. 408; Acts 2013, c. 474.

§ 19.2–125. Release pending appeal from conviction in court not of record

A person who has been convicted of an offense in a district court and who has noted an appeal shall be given credit for any bond that he may have posted in the court from which he appeals and shall be treated in accordance with the provisions of this article.

Acts 1975, c. 495; Acts 1978, c. 755; Acts 1999, c. 829; Acts 1999, c. 846.

§ 19.2–126. Repealed by Acts 1999, cc. 829 and 846

§ 19.2–127. Conditions of release of material witness

If it appears by affidavit that the testimony of a person is material in any criminal proceeding, and it reasonably appears that it will be impossible to secure his presence by a subpoena, a judge shall inquire into the conditions of his release pursuant to this article.

Acts 1975, c. 495; Acts 1999, c. 829; Acts 1999, c. 846.

§ 19.2–128. Penalties for failure to appear

A. Whoever, having been released pursuant to this chapter or § 19.2–319 or on a summons pursuant to § 19.2–73 or § 19.2–74, willfully fails to appear before any court or judicial officer as required, shall, after notice to all interested parties, incur a forfeiture of any security which may have been given or pledged for his release, unless one of the parties can show good cause for excusing the absence, or unless the court, in its sound discretion, shall determine that neither the interests of justice nor the power of the court to conduct orderly proceedings will be served by such forfeiture.

B. Any person (i) charged with a felony offense or (ii) convicted of a felony offense and execution of sentence is suspended pursuant to § 19.2–319 who willfully fails to appear before any court as required shall be guilty of a Class 6 felony.

C. Any person (i) charged with a misdemeanor offense or (ii) convicted of a misdemeanor offense and execution of sentence is suspended pursuant to § 19.2–319 who willfully fails to appear before any court as required shall be guilty of a Class 1 misdemeanor.

Acts 1975, c. 495; Acts 1981, c. 382; Acts 1982, c. 271; Acts 1999, c. 821.

§ 19.2–129. Power of court to punish for contempt

Nothing in this chapter shall interfere with or prevent the exercise by any court of the Commonwealth of its power to punish for contempt, except that a person shall not be sentenced for contempt and under the provisions of § 19.2–128 for the same absence.

Acts 1975, c. 495.

§ 19.2–130. Bail in subsequent proceeding arising out of initial arrest

Any person admitted to bail by a judge or clerk of a district court or by a magistrate shall not be required to be admitted to bail in any subsequent proceeding arising out of the initial arrest unless the court having jurisdiction of such subsequent proceeding deems the initial amount of bond or security taken inadequate. When the court having jurisdiction of the proceeding believes the amount of bond or security inadequate or excessive, it may change the amount of such bond or security, require new and additional sureties, or set other terms of bail as are appropriate to the case, including, but not limited to, drug and alcohol monitoring. The court may, after notice to the parties, initiate a proceeding to alter the terms and conditions of bail on its own motion.

Acts 1975, c. 495; Acts 1978, c. 755; Acts 1991, c. 581. Amended by Acts 2008, c. 363; Acts 2008, c. 812.

§ 19.2–130.1. Bail terms set by court on a capias to be honored by magistrate

A magistrate who is to set the terms of bail of a person arrested and brought before him pursuant to

§ 19.2–234 shall, unless circumstances exist that require him to set more restrictive terms, set the terms of bail in accordance with the order of the court that issued the capias, if such an order is affixed to or made a part of the capias by the court.

Added by Acts 2010, c. 312; Acts 2010, c. 375. Amended by Acts 2011, c. 112.

§ 19.2–131. Bail for person held in jurisdiction other than that of trial

In any case in which a person charged with a misdemeanor or felony, or a juvenile taken into custody pursuant to § 16.1–246 is held in some county, city or town other than that in which he is to be tried upon such charge, he may be admitted to bail by any judicial officer of the county, city or town in which he is so held in accordance with the provisions of law concerning the granting of bail in cases in which persons are so admitted to bail, when held in the county, city or town in which they are to be tried.

In such case, such judicial officer before whom he is brought may, without trial or examination, let him to bail, upon taking a recognizance for his appearance before the court having cognizance of the case. The fact of taking such recognizance shall be certified by the court or officer taking it upon the warrant under which such person was arrested or taken into custody and the warrant and recognizance shall be returned forthwith to the clerk of the court before whom the accused or juvenile taken into custody pursuant to § 16.1–246 is to appear. And to such court, the judicial officer who issued such warrant shall recognize or cause to be summoned such witnesses as he may think proper.

Acts 1975, c. 495; Acts 1978, c. 755; Acts 1992, c. 576.

§ 19.2–132. Motion to increase amount of bond fixed by judicial officer; when bond may be increased

If the amount of any bond fixed by a judicial officer is subsequently deemed insufficient, or the security taken inadequate, or if it appears that bail should have been denied or that the person has violated a term or condition of his release, or has been convicted of or arrested for a felony or misdemeanor, the attorney for the Commonwealth of the county or city in which the person is held for trial may, on reasonable notice to the person and, if such person has been admitted to bail, to any surety on the bond of such person, move the appropriate judicial officer to increase the amount of such bond or to revoke bail. The court may grant such motion and may require new or additional sureties therefor, or both or revoke bail. Any surety in a bond for the appearance of such person may take from his principal collateral or other security to indemnify such surety against liability. The failure to notify the surety will not prohibit the court from proceeding with the bond hearing.

The court ordering any increase in the amount of such bond, ordering new or additional sureties, or revoking such bail may, upon appeal, and for good cause shown, stay execution of such order for so long as reasonably practicable for such person to obtain an expedited hearing before the court to which such order has been appealed.

Acts 1975, c. 495; Acts 1978, c. 755; Acts 1989, c. 519; Acts 1991, c. 581; Acts 1999, c. 829; Acts 1999, c. 846. Amended by Acts 2010, c. 404; Acts 2010, c. 592; Acts 2013, c. 408; Acts 2013, c. 474.

§§ 19.2–132.1, 19.2–133. Repealed by Acts 1991, c. 581

§ 19.2–134. When bail piece to be delivered to accused; form of bail piece

In all cases in which recognizances, at the suit of the Commonwealth, may have been, or shall hereafter be entered into, it shall be the duty of the clerk of the court in which, or in the clerk's office of which, any recognizance is filed, to deliver to the accused and his sureties upon request, a bail piece, in substance, as follows: "A. B. of the county or city of . . ., is delivered to bail, unto C. D. of the county or city of . . ., at the suit of the Commonwealth. Given under my hand, this day of . . ., in the year . . . ."

Acts 1975, c. 495; Acts 1991, c. 581; Acts 1992, c. 576.

Article 2

Recognizances

§ 19.2–135. Commitment for trial; recognizance; notice to attorney for Commonwealth; remand on violation of condition

When a judicial officer considers that there is sufficient cause for charging the accused or juvenile taken into custody pursuant to § 16.1–246 with a felony, unless it be a case wherein it is otherwise specially provided, the commitment shall be for trial or hearing. Any recognizance taken of the accused or juvenile shall be upon the following conditions: (1) that he appear to answer for the offense with which he is charged before the court or judge before whom the case will be tried at such time as may be stated in the recognizance and at any time or times to which the proceedings may be continued and before any court or judge thereafter in which proceedings on the charge are held; (2) that he shall not depart from the Commonwealth unless the judicial officer taking recognizance or a court in a subsequent proceeding specifically waives such requirement; and (3) that he shall keep the peace and be of good behavior until the case is finally disposed of. Every such recognizance shall also include a waiver such as is required by § 49–12 in relation to the bonds therein mentioned and though such waiver be not expressed in the recognizance it shall be deemed to be included therein in like manner and with the same effect as if it was so expressed. The judge shall return to the clerk of the court wherein the accused or juvenile is to be tried, or the case be heard as soon as may be, a certificate of the nature of the offense, showing whether the accused or juvenile was committed to jail or recognized for his appearance; and the clerk, as soon as may be, shall inform the attorney for the Commonwealth of such certificate.

The court may, in its discretion, in the event of a violation of any condition of a recognizance taken pursuant to this section, remand the principal to jail until the case is finally disposed of, and if the principal is remanded to jail, the surety is discharged from liability.

When a recognizance is taken of a witness in a case against an accused or juvenile, the condition thereof shall be that he appear to give evidence in such case and that he shall not depart from the Commonwealth without the leave of such court or judge.

Acts 1975, c. 495; Acts 1977, c. 287; Acts 1978, c. 755; Acts 1979, c. 735; Acts 1988, c. 688; Acts 1992, c. 576.

§ 19.2–136. How bonds in recognizances payable; penalty

Bonds in recognizances in criminal or juvenile cases shall be payable to the county or city in which the case is prosecuted. The treasurer or director of finance of such locality may engage in collection activity regarding the judgment of default rendered pursuant to § 19.2–143. Any responses to the judgment of default rendered pursuant to § 19.2–143 shall be filed with the court, with notice given to such locality. Every bond under this title shall be in such sum as the court or officer requiring it may direct.

Acts 1975, c. 495; Acts 1978, c. 755; Acts 1991, c. 581. Amended by Acts 2011, c. 802; Acts 2012, c. 408.

§ 19.2–137. Order of court on recognizance

When such recognizance is taken by a court of a person to answer a charge or of a witness to give evidence it shall be sufficient for the order of the court taking the recognizance to state that the party or parties recognized were duly recognized upon a bond in such sum as the court may have directed with such surety as the court may have accepted for his or their appearance before such court at such time as may have been prescribed by the court to answer for the offense with which such person is charged or to give evidence, as the case may be.

Acts 1975, c. 495; Acts 1991, c. 581.

§§ 19.2–138 to 19.2–140. Repealed by Acts 1987, c. 670

§ 19.2–141. How recognizance taken for incapacitated or insane person or one under disability

A recognizance which would be taken of a person but for his being a minor, insane or otherwise mentally incapacitated, may be taken of another person and without further surety, if such other person is deemed sufficient, for the performance by such minor, insane or otherwise incapacitated person, of the conditions of the recognizance.

Acts 1975, c. 495; Acts 1997, c. 801, eff. Jan. 1, 1998.

§ 19.2–142. Where recognizance taken out of court to be sent

A person taking a recognizance out of court shall forthwith transmit it to the clerk of the court for appearance before which it is taken; or, if it be not for appearance before a court, to the clerk of the circuit court of the county or city in which it is taken; and it shall remain filed in the clerk's office.

Acts 1975, c. 495.

§ 19.2–143. Where default recorded; process on recognizance; forfeiture on recognizance; when copy may be used; cash bond

When a person, under recognizance in a case, either as party or witness, fails to perform the condition of appearance thereof, if it is to appear before a court of record, or a district court, a hearing shall be held upon reasonable notice to all parties affording them opportunity to show cause why the recognizance or any part thereof should not be forfeited. The show cause notice shall be issued within 45 days of the breach of the condition of appearance.

If the court finds the recognizance or any part thereof should be forfeited, the default shall be recorded therein, unless the defendant or juvenile is brought before the court within 150 days of the findings of default. After 150 days of the finding of default, his default shall be recorded therein, and if it is to appear before a district court, his default shall be entered by the judge of such court, on the case papers unless the defendant or juvenile has been delivered or appeared before the court. The process on any such forfeited recognizance shall be issued from the court before which the appearance was to be, and wherein such forfeiture was recorded or entered. Any such process issued by a judge shall be made returnable before, and tried by, such judge, who shall promptly transmit to the clerk of the circuit court of his county or city wherein deeds are recorded an abstract of such judgment as he may render thereon, which shall be forthwith docketed by the clerk of such court.

If the defendant or juvenile appears before or is delivered to the court within 24 months of the findings of default, the court shall remit any bond previously ordered forfeited by the courts, less such costs as the court may direct.

If it is brought to the attention of the court that the defendant or juvenile is incarcerated in another state or country within 48 months of the finding of default, thereby preventing his delivery or appearance within that period, the court shall remit any bond previously ordered forfeited. If the defendant or juvenile left the Commonwealth with the permission of the court, the bond shall be remitted without deduction of costs; otherwise, the cost of returning him to the Commonwealth shall be deducted from the bond.

Evidence that the defendant or juvenile is incarcerated or subject to court process in another jurisdiction on the day his appearance is required or a medical certificate from a duly licensed physician that the defendant was physically unable to so appear shall be considered evidence of good cause why the recognizance should not be forfeited.

If such recognizance so forfeited is not for such appearance, process thereon shall be issued from the court in which it was taken, or the court to which it was made returnable, and in a proceeding in one court on a recognizance entered in another a copy thereof shall be evidence in like manner as the original would be if it had been entered in the court wherein the proceeding is being had thereon.

However, when any defendant or juvenile who posted a cash bond and failed to appear is tried in his absence and is convicted, the court or judge trying the case shall first apply the cash bond, or so much thereof as may be necessary, to the payment of any fines or costs, or both, adjudged against the defendant or juvenile or imposed by law. Any remaining funds shall be forfeited without further notice. However, if a rehearing is granted, the court may remit part or all of such cash bond not applied ultimately to fines or costs, and order a refund of the same by the State Treasurer, or by the treasurer or director of finance of the locality, if the bond was collected by a locality pursuant to § 19.2-136, but only if good cause is shown.

If the defendant or juvenile posted a cash bond and failed to appear, but is not tried in his absence, the bond shall be forfeited promptly without further notice. However, if the defendant or juvenile appears in court within 60 days after the bond is forfeited, the judge may remit part or all of any bond previously forfeited and order a refund of the same by the State Treasurer, or by the treasurer or director of finance of the locality, if the bond was collected by a locality pursuant to § 19.2-136.

Acts 1975, c. 495; Acts 1978, c. 755; Acts 1979, c. 735; Acts 1987, c. 670; Acts 1988, c. 443; Acts 1990, c. 624; Acts 2000, c. 885; Acts 2003, c. 840; Acts 2005, c. 585; Acts 2006, c. 296; Acts 2006, c. 316. Amended by Acts 2011, c. 802; Acts 2012, c. 408.

§ 19.2-144. Forfeiture of recognizance while in military or naval service

If in any motion, action, suit or other proceeding made or taken in any court of this Commonwealth on a forfeited bail bond or forfeited recognizance, or to enforce the payment of the bond in any manner or any judgment thereon, or to forfeit any bail bond or recognizance, it appears that the person for whose alleged default such bail bond or recognizance was forfeited or judgment rendered, or such motion is made or proceeding taken, was prevented from complying with the condition of such bail bond or recognizance by reason of his having enlisted or been drafted in the army or navy of the United States, then judgment or decree on such motion, action, suit or other proceeding shall be given for the defendant.

Acts 1975, c. 495; Acts 1991, c. 581.

§ 19.2-145. How penalty remitted

When in an action or on a motion to extend the period for enforcement of a judgment on a recognizance the penalty is adjudged to be forfeited the court may on an application of a defendant or juvenile remit the penalty or any part of it and render judgment on such terms and conditions as it deems reasonable.

Acts 1975, c. 495; Acts 1978, c. 755; Acts 1982, c. 153.

§ 19.2-146. Defects in form of recognizance not to defeat action or judgment

No action or judgment on a recognizance shall be defeated or arrested by reason of any defect in the form of the recognizance, if it appear to have been taken by a court or officer authorized to take it and be substantially sufficient.

Acts 1975, c. 495.

§ 19.2-147. Docketing judgment on forfeited recognizance or bond

Whenever a judgment is entered in any court of record in favor of the Commonwealth of Virginia upon a forfeited recognizance or bond, the clerk of the court in which the judgment is rendered shall certify an abstract of the same to the clerk of the circuit court of the county or city wherein the judgment debtor resides or of any city or county in which he may own real property, who shall thereupon enter the abstract of judgment upon his judgment docket.

Acts 1975, c. 495; Acts 1994, c. 432.

§ 19.2-148. Surety discharged on payment of amount, etc., into court

A surety on a bond in a recognizance may, after default, pay into the court from which the process has issued, or may issue thereon, the amount for which he is bound, with such costs as the court may direct, and be thereupon discharged.

Acts 1975, c. 495; Acts 1991, c. 581.

§ 19.2–149. How surety on a bond in recognizance may surrender principal and be discharged from liability

A bail bondsman or his licensed bail enforcement agent on a bond in a recognizance may at any time arrest his principal and surrender him to the court before which the recognizance was taken or before which such principal's appearance is required, or to the sheriff, sergeant or jailer of the county or city wherein the court before which such principal's appearance is required is located; in addition to the above authority, upon the application of the surety, the court, or the clerk thereof, before which the recognizance was taken, or before which such principal's appearance is required, or any magistrate shall issue a capias for the arrest of such principal, and such capias may be executed by such bail bondsman or his licensed bail enforcement agent, or by any sheriff, sergeant or police officer, and the person executing such capias shall deliver such principal and such capias to the sheriff or jailer of the county or the sheriff, sergeant or jailer of the city in which the appearance of such principal is required, and thereupon the surety or the property bail bondsman shall be discharged from liability for any act of the principal subsequent thereto. Such sheriff, sergeant or jailer shall thereafter deliver such capias to the clerk of such court, with his endorsement thereon acknowledging delivery of such principal to his custody. If a magistrate issues a capias pursuant to this section, the magistrate shall transmit a copy of the capias to the court before which such principal's appearance is required by the close of business on the next day that is not a Saturday, Sunday, legal holiday, or day on which the court is lawfully closed.

Acts 1975, c. 495; Acts 1991, c. 581; Acts 2004, c. 460, eff. July 1, 2005. Amended by Acts 2015, c. 622.

§ 19.2–150. Proceeding when surety surrenders principal

If the surrender is to the court, the court shall make such order as it deems proper; if the surrender is to a sheriff or jailer, the officer to whom the accused has been surrendered shall give the surety a certificate of the fact. After such surrender the person shall be treated in accordance with the provisions of Article 1 (§ 19.2–119 et seq.) of Chapter 9 of this title unless the court or judge thereof has reason to believe that no one or more conditions of release will reasonably assure that the person will not flee or pose a danger to any other person or to the community.

Acts 1975, c. 495; Acts 1978, c. 755; Acts 1999, c. 829; Acts 1999, c. 846.

ARTICLE 3

SATISFACTION AND DISCHARGE

§ 19.2–151. Satisfaction and discharge of assault and similar charges

When a person is in jail or under a recognizance to answer a charge of assault and battery or other misdemeanor, or has been indicted for an assault and battery or other misdemeanor for which there is a remedy by civil action, unless the offense was committed (i) by or upon any law-enforcement officer, (ii) riotously in violation of §§ 18.2–404 to 18.2–407, (iii) against a family or household member in violation of § 18.2–57.2, or (iv) with intent to commit a felony, if the person injured appears before the court which made the commitment or took the recognizance, or before the court in which the indictment is pending, and acknowledges in writing that he has received satisfaction for the injury, the court may, in its discretion, by an order, supersede the commitment, discharge the recognizance, or dismiss the prosecution, upon payment by the defendant of costs accrued to the Commonwealth or any of its officers.

Acts 1997, c. 532; Acts 1999, c. 963.

§ 19.2–152. Order discharging recognizance or superseding commitment; judgment for costs

Every order discharging a recognizance shall be filed with the clerk before the session of the court at which the party was to appear. Where a person is held under a commitment, any order superseding a commitment shall be delivered to the jailer, who shall forthwith discharge the witnesses, if any, and the accused or juvenile, and judgment against the accused or juvenile shall be entered in the court for the costs of the prosecution.

Acts 1975, c. 495; Acts 1978, c. 755.

ARTICLE 4

BAIL BONDSMEN

§§ 19.2–152.1 to 19.2–152.1:7. Repealed by Acts 2004, c. 460, eff. July 1, 2005

Article 5

Pretrial Services Act

§ 19.2-152.2. Purpose; establishment of pretrial services and services agencies

It is the purpose of this article to provide more effective protection of society by establishing pretrial services agencies that will assist judicial officers in discharging their duties pursuant to Article 1 (§ 19.2-119 et seq.) of Chapter 9 of this title. Such agencies are intended to provide better information and services for use by judicial officers in determining the risk to public safety and the assurance of appearance of persons age 18 or over or persons under the age of 18 who have been transferred for trial as adults held in custody and charged with an offense, other than an offense punishable by death, who are pending trial or hearing. Any city, county or combination thereof may establish a pretrial services agency and any city, county or combination thereof required to submit a community-based corrections plan pursuant to § 53.1-82.1 shall establish a pretrial services agency.

Acts 1994, Sp.S. II, c. 1, eff. July 1, 1995; Acts 1994, Sp.S. II, c. 2, eff. July 1, 1995; Acts 1999, c. 829; Acts 1999, c. 846; Acts 2004, c. 378; Acts 2007, c. 133.

§ 19.2-152.3. Department of Criminal Justice Services to prescribe standards; biennial plan

The Department of Criminal Justice Services shall prescribe standards for the development, implementation, operation and evaluation of services authorized by this article. The Department of Criminal Justice Services shall develop risk assessment and other instruments to be used by pretrial services agencies in assisting judicial officers in discharging their duties pursuant to Article 1 (§ 19.2-119 et seq.) of Chapter 9 of this title. Any city, county or combination thereof which establishes pretrial services pursuant to this article shall submit a biennial plan to the Department of Criminal Justice Services for review and approval.

Acts 1994, Sp.S. II, c. 1, eff. July 1, 1995; Acts 1994, Sp.S. II, c. 2, eff. July 1, 1995; Acts 1999, c. 829; Acts 1999, c. 846; Acts 2007, c. 133.

§ 19.2-152.4. Mandated services

Any city, county or combination thereof which elects or is required to establish a pretrial services agency shall provide all information and services for use by judicial officers as set forth in Article 1 (§ 19.2-119 et seq.) of Chapter 9 of this title.

Acts 1994, Sp.S. II, c. 1, eff. July 1, 1995; Acts 1994, Sp.S. II, c. 2, eff. July 1, 1995; Acts 1999, c. 829; Acts 1999, c. 846; Acts 2007, c. 133.

§ 19.2-152.4:1. Form of oath of office for local pretrial services officer; authorization to seek capias

Every pretrial services officer who is an employee of a local pretrial services agency established by any city, county or combination thereof or operated pursuant to this article shall take an oath of office as prescribed in § 49-1 and to provide services pursuant to the requirements of this article before entering the duties of his office. The oath of office shall be taken before any general district or circuit court judge in any county or city which has established services for use by judicial officers pursuant to this article.

In addition, any officer of a pretrial services agency established or operated pursuant to this article may seek a capias from any judicial officer for the arrest of any person under the agency's custody and supervision for failure to comply with any conditions of release imposed by a judicial officer, for failure to comply with the conditions of pretrial supervision as established by a pretrial services agency, or when there is reason to believe that the person will fail to appear, will leave, or has left the jurisdiction to avoid prosecution.

Acts 2000, c. 1040; Acts 2007, c. 133.

§ 19.2-152.4:2. Confidentiality of records of and reports on adult persons under investigation by or in the custody or supervision of a local pretrial services agency

A. Any pretrial investigation report prepared by a local pretrial services officer is confidential and is exempt from the Virginia Freedom of Information Act (§ 2.2-3700 et seq.). Such reports shall be filed as a part of the case record. Such reports shall be sealed upon receipt by the court and made available only by court order; except that such reports shall be available upon request to (i) any criminal justice agency, as defined in § 9.1-101, of this or any other state or of the United States; (ii) any agency where the accused is referred for assessment or treatment; or (iii) counsel for the person who is the subject of the report.

B. Any report on the progress of an accused under the supervision or custody of a pretrial services agency and any information relative to the identity of or inferring personal characteristics of an accused, including demographic information, diagnostic summaries, records of office visits, medical, substance abuse, psychiatric or psychological records or information, substance abuse screening, assessment and testing information, and other sensitive information not explicitly classified as criminal history record information, is exempt from the Virginia Freedom of Information Act (§ 2.2-3700 et seq.). However, such information may be disseminated to criminal justice agencies as defined in § 9.1-101 in the discretion of the custodian of these records.

Acts 2002, c. 769; Acts 2007, c. 133.

§ 19.2–152.4:3. Duties and responsibilities of local pretrial services officers

A. Each local pretrial services officer, for the jurisdictions served, shall:

1. Investigate and interview defendants arrested on state and local warrants and who are detained in jails located in jurisdictions served by the agency while awaiting a hearing before any court that is considering or reconsidering bail, at initial appearance, advisement or arraignment, or at other subsequent hearings;

2. Present a pretrial investigation report with recommendations to assist courts in discharging their duties related to granting or reconsidering bail;

3. Supervise and assist all defendants residing within the jurisdictions served and placed on pretrial supervision by any judicial officer within the jurisdictions to ensure compliance with the terms and conditions of bail;

4. Conduct random drug and alcohol tests on any defendant under supervision for whom a judicial officer has ordered testing or who has been required to refrain from excessive use of alcohol or use of any illegal drug or controlled substance or other defendant-specific condition of bail related to alcohol or substance abuse;

5. Seek a capias from any judicial officer pursuant to § 19.2–152.4:1 for any defendant placed under supervision or the custody of the agency who fails to comply with the conditions of bail or supervision, when continued liberty or noncompliance presents a risk of flight, a risk to public safety or risk to the defendant;

6. Seek an order to show cause why the defendant should not be required to appear before the court in those cases requiring a subsequent hearing before the court;

7. Provide defendant-based information to assist any law-enforcement officer with the return to custody of defendants placed on supervision for which a capias has been sought; and

8. Keep such records and make such reports as required by the Commonwealth of Virginia Department of Criminal Justice Services.

B. Each local pretrial services officer, for the jurisdictions served, may provide the following optional services, as appropriate and when available resources permit:

1. Conduct, subject to court approval, drug and alcohol screenings, or tests at investigation pursuant to subsection B of § 19.2–123 or following release to supervision, and conduct or facilitate the preparation of screenings or assessments or both pursuant to state approved protocols;

2. Facilitate placement of defendants in a substance abuse education or treatment program or services or other education or treatment service when ordered as a condition of bail;

3. Sign for the custody of any defendant investigated by a pretrial services officer, and released by a court to pretrial supervision as the sole term and condition of bail or when combined with an unsecured bond;

4. Provide defendant information and investigation services for those who are detained in jails located in jurisdictions served by the agency and are awaiting an initial bail hearing before a magistrate;

5. Supervise defendants placed by any judicial officer on home electronic monitoring as a condition of bail and supervision;

6. Prepare, for defendants investigated, the financial statement-eligibility determination form for indigent defense services; and

7. Subject to approved procedures and if so requested by the court, coordinate for defendants investigated, services for court-appointed counsel and for interpreters for foreign-language speaking and hearing-impaired defendants.

Acts 2003, c. 603; Acts 2007, c. 133. Amended by Acts 2008, c. 551; Acts 2008, c. 691.

§ 19.2–152.5. Community criminal justice boards

Each city, county or combination thereof establishing a pretrial services agency shall also establish a community criminal justice board pursuant to § 9.1–178.

Acts 1994, Sp.S. II, c. 1, eff. July 1, 1995; Acts 1994, Sp.S. II, c. 2, eff. July 1, 1995; Acts 2007, c. 133.

§ 19.2–152.6. Withdrawal from pretrial services

Any participating city or county may, at the beginning of any calendar quarter, by ordinance or resolution of its governing authority, notify the Department of Criminal Justice Services of its intention to withdraw from participation in pretrial services. Such withdrawal shall be effective as of the last day of the quarter in which such notice is given.

Acts 1994, Sp.S. II, c. 1, eff. July 1, 1995; Acts 1994, Sp.S. II, c. 2, eff. July 1, 1995; Acts 2007, c. 133.

§ 19.2–152.7. Funding; failure to comply

Counties and cities shall be required to establish a pretrial services agency only to the extent funded by the Commonwealth through the general appropriation act. The Department of Criminal Justice Services shall periodically review each agency established under this article to determine compliance with the submitted plan and operating standards. If the Department determines that any agency is not in substantial compliance with the submitted plan or standards, the Department may suspend all or any portion of financial aid made available to the locality for purposes of this article until there is compliance.

Acts 1994, Sp.S. II, c. 1, eff. July 1, 1995; Acts 1994, Sp.S. II, c. 2, eff. July 1, 1995; Acts 2007, c. 133.

§ 19.2–152.7:1. Definitions

As used in this chapter:

"Act of violence, force, or threat" means any act involving violence, force, or threat that results in bodily injury or places one in reasonable apprehension of death, sexual assault, or bodily injury. Such act includes, but is not limited to, any forceful detention, stalking, criminal sexual assault in violation of Article 7 (§ 18.2–61 et seq.) of Chapter 4 of Title 18.2, or any criminal offense that results in bodily injury or places one in reasonable apprehension of death, sexual assault, or bodily injury.

Added by Acts 2011, c. 445; Acts 2011, c. 480.

CHAPTER 9.1

PROTECTIVE ORDERS

§ 19.2–152.8. Emergency protective orders authorized

A. Any judge of a circuit court, general district court, juvenile and domestic relations district court or magistrate may issue a written or oral ex parte emergency protective order pursuant to this section in order to protect the health or safety of any person.

B. When a law-enforcement officer or an alleged victim asserts under oath to a judge or magistrate that such person is being or has been subjected to an act of violence, force, or threat and on that assertion or other evidence the judge or magistrate finds that (i) there is probable danger of a further such act being committed by the respondent against the alleged victim or (ii) a petition or warrant for the arrest of the respondent has been issued for any criminal offense resulting from the commission of an act of violence, force, or threat, the judge or magistrate shall issue an ex parte emergency protective order imposing one or more of the following conditions on the respondent:

1. Prohibiting acts of violence, force, or threat or criminal offenses resulting in injury to person or property;

2. Prohibiting such contacts by the respondent with the alleged victim or the alleged victim's family or household members as the judge or magistrate deems necessary to protect the safety of such persons;

3. Such other conditions as the judge or magistrate deems necessary to prevent (i) acts of violence, force, or threat, (ii) criminal offenses resulting in injury to person or property, or (iii) communication or other contact of any kind by the respondent; and

4. Granting the petitioner the possession of any companion animal as defined in § 3.2–6500 if such petitioner meets the definition of owner in § 3.2–6500.

C. An emergency protective order issued pursuant to this section shall expire at 11:59 p.m. on the third day following issuance. If the expiration occurs on a day that the court is not in session, the emergency protective order shall be extended until 11:59 p.m. on the next day that the court which issued the order is in session. The respondent may at any time file a motion with the court requesting a hearing to dissolve or modify the order. The hearing on the motion shall be given precedence on the docket of the court.

D. A law-enforcement officer may request an emergency protective order pursuant to this section and, if the person in need of protection is physically or mentally incapable of filing a petition pursuant to § 19.2–152.9 or 19.2–152.10, may request the extension of an emergency protective order for an additional period of time not to exceed three days after expiration of the original order. The request for an emergency protective order or extension of an order may be made orally, in person or by electronic means, and the judge of a circuit court, general district court, or juvenile and domestic relations district court or a magistrate may issue an oral emergency protective order. An oral emergency protective order issued pursuant to this section shall be reduced to writing, by the law-enforcement officer requesting the order or the magistrate, on a preprinted form approved and provided by the Supreme Court of Virginia. The completed form shall include a statement of the grounds for the order asserted by the officer or the alleged victim of such crime.

E. The court or magistrate shall forthwith, but in all cases no later than the end of the business day on which the order was issued, enter and transfer electronically to the Virginia Criminal Information Network the respondent's identifying information and the name, date of birth, sex, and race of each protected person provided to the court or magistrate. A copy of an emergency protective order issued pursuant to this section containing any such identifying information shall be forwarded forthwith to the primary law-enforcement agency responsible for service and entry of protective orders. Upon receipt of the order by the primary law-enforcement agency, the agency shall forthwith verify and enter any modification as necessary to the identifying information and other appropriate information required by the Department of State Police into the Virginia Criminal Information Network established and maintained by the Department pursuant to Chapter 2 (§ 52–12 et seq.) of Title 52 and the order shall be served forthwith upon the respondent and due return made to the court. However, if the order is issued by the circuit court, the clerk of the circuit court shall forthwith forward an attested copy of the order containing the respondent's identifying information and the name, date of birth, sex, and race of each protected person provided to the court to the primary law-enforcement agency providing service and entry of protective orders and upon receipt of the order, the primary law-enforcement agency shall enter the name of the person subject to the order and other appropriate information required by the Department of State Police into the Virginia Criminal Information Network established and maintained by the Department pursuant to Chapter 2 (§ 52–12 et seq.) of Title 52 and the order shall be served forthwith upon the respondent. Upon service, the agency making service shall enter the date and time of service and other appropriate information required into the Virginia Criminal Information Network and make due return to the court. One copy of the order shall be given to the alleged victim of such crime. The judge or magistrate who issues an oral order pursuant to an electronic request by a law-enforcement officer shall verify the written order to determine whether the officer who reduced it to writing accurately transcribed the contents of the oral order. The original copy shall be filed with the clerk of the appropriate district court within five business days of the issuance of the order. If the order is later dissolved or modified, a copy of the dissolution or modification order shall also be attested, forwarded forthwith to the primary law-enforcement agency responsible for service and entry of protective orders, and upon receipt of the order by the primary law-enforcement agency, the agency shall forthwith verify and enter any modification as necessary to the identifying information and other appropriate information required by the Department of State Police into the Virginia Criminal Information Network as described above and the order shall be served forthwith and due return made to the court. Upon request, the clerk shall provide the alleged victim of such crime with information regarding the date and time of service.

F. The issuance of an emergency protective order shall not be considered evidence of any wrongdoing by the respondent.

G. As used in this section, a "law-enforcement officer" means any (i) person who is a full-time or part-time employee of a police department or sheriff's office which is part of or administered by the Commonwealth or any political subdivision thereof and who is responsible for the prevention and detection of crime and the enforcement of the penal, traffic or highway laws of the Commonwealth and (ii) member of an auxiliary police force established pursuant to § 15.2–1731. Part-time employees are compensated officers who are not full-time employees as defined by the employing police department or sheriff's office.

H. Neither a law-enforcement agency, the attorney for the Commonwealth, a court nor the clerk's office, nor any employee of them, may disclose, except among themselves, the residential address, telephone number, or place of employment of the person protected by the order or that of the family of such person, except to the extent that disclosure is (i) required by law or the Rules of the Supreme Court, (ii) necessary for law-enforcement purposes, or (iii) permitted by the court for good cause.

I. As used in this section, "copy" includes a facsimile copy.

J. No fee shall be charged for filing or serving any petition pursuant to this section.

K. No emergency protective order shall be issued pursuant to this section against a law-enforcement officer for any action arising out of the lawful performance of his duties.

Acts 1997, c. 831; Acts 1998, c. 569; Acts 1998, c. 684; Acts 1999, c. 371; Acts 2001, c. 474; Acts 2002, c. 507; Acts 2002, c. 706; Acts 2002, c. 810; Acts 2002, c. 818; Acts 2003, c. 730. Amended by Acts 2008, c. 73; Acts 2008, c. 246; Acts 2009, c. 341; Acts 2009, c. 732; Acts 2011, c. 445; Acts 2011, c. 480; Acts 2012, c. 146; Acts 2012, c. 637; Acts 2012, c. 827, eff. April 18, 2012; Acts 2014, c. 346.

§ 19.2–152.9. Preliminary protective orders

A. Upon the filing of a petition alleging that (i) the petitioner is or has been, within a reasonable period of time, subjected to an act of violence, force, or threat, or (ii) a petition or warrant has been issued for the arrest of the alleged perpetrator for any criminal offense resulting from the commission of an act of violence, force, or threat, the court may issue a preliminary protective order against the alleged perpetrator in order to protect the health and safety of the petitioner or any family or household member of the petitioner. The order may be issued in an ex parte proceeding upon good cause shown when the petition is supported by an affidavit or sworn testimony before the judge or intake officer. Immediate and present danger of any act of violence, force, or threat or evidence sufficient to establish probable cause that an act of violence, force, or threat has recently occurred shall constitute good cause.

A preliminary protective order may include any one or more of the following conditions to be imposed on the respondent:

1. Prohibiting acts of violence, force, or threat or criminal offenses that may result in injury to person or property;

2. Prohibiting such other contacts by the respondent with the petitioner or the petitioner's family or household members as the court deems necessary for the health and safety of such persons;

3. Such other conditions as the court deems necessary to prevent (i) acts of violence, force, or threat, (ii) criminal offenses that may result in injury to person or property, or (iii) communication or other contact of any kind by the respondent; and

4. Granting the petitioner the possession of any companion animal as defined in § 3.2–6500 if such petitioner meets the definition of owner in § 3.2–6500.

B. The court shall forthwith, but in all cases no later than the end of the business day on which the order was issued, enter and transfer electronically to the Virginia Criminal Information Network the respondent's identifying information and the name, date of birth, sex, and race of each protected person provided to the court. A copy of a preliminary protective order containing any such identifying information shall be forwarded forthwith to the primary law-enforcement agency responsible for service and entry of protective orders. Upon receipt of the order by the primary law-enforcement agency, the agency shall forthwith verify and enter any modification as necessary to the identifying information and other appropriate information required by the Department of State Police into the Virginia Criminal Information Network established and maintained by the Department pursuant to Chapter 2 (§ 52–12 et seq.) of Title 52 and the order shall be served forthwith on the alleged perpetrator in person as provided in § 16.1–264, and due return made to the court. However, if the order is issued by the circuit court, the clerk of the circuit court shall forthwith forward an attested copy of the order containing the respondent's identifying information and the name, date of birth, sex, and race of each protected person provided to the court to the primary law-enforcement agency providing service and entry of protective orders and upon receipt of the order, the primary law-enforcement agency shall enter the name of the person subject to the order and other appropriate information required by the Department of State Police into the Virginia Criminal Information Network established and maintained by the Department pursuant to Chapter 2 (§ 52–12 et seq.) of Title 52 and the order shall be served forthwith on the alleged perpetrator in person as provided in § 16.1–264. Upon service, the agency making service shall enter the date and time of service and other appropriate information required by the Department of State Police into the Virginia Criminal Information Network and make due return to the court. The preliminary order shall specify a date for the full hearing. The hearing shall be held within 15 days of the issuance of the preliminary order. If the respondent fails to appear at this hearing because the respondent was not personally served, the court may extend the protective order for a period not to exceed six months. The extended protective order shall be served as soon as possible on the respondent. However, upon motion of the respondent and for good cause shown, the court may continue the hearing. The preliminary order shall remain in effect until the hearing. Upon request after the order is issued, the clerk shall provide the petitioner with a copy of the order and information regarding the date and time of service. The order shall further specify that either party may at any time file a motion with the court requesting a hearing to dissolve or modify the order. The hearing on the motion shall be given precedence on the docket of the court.

Upon receipt of the return of service or other proof of service pursuant to subsection C of § 16.1–264, the clerk shall forthwith forward an attested copy of the preliminary protective order to primary law-enforcement agency and the agency shall forthwith verify and enter any modification as necessary into the Virginia Criminal Information Network as described above. If the order is later dissolved or modified, a copy of the dissolution or modification order shall also be attested, forwarded forthwith to the primary law-enforcement agency responsible for service and entry of protective orders, and upon receipt of the order by the primary law-enforcement agency, the agency shall forthwith verify and enter any modification as necessary to the identifying information and other appropriate information required by the Department of State Police into the Virginia Criminal Information Network as described above and the order shall be served forthwith and due return made to the court.

C. The preliminary order is effective upon personal service on the alleged perpetrator. Except as otherwise provided, a violation of the order shall constitute contempt of court.

D. At a full hearing on the petition, the court may issue a protective order pursuant to § 19.2–152.10 if the court finds that the petitioner has proven the allegation that the petitioner is or has been, within a reasonable period of time, subjected to an act of violence, force, or threat by a preponderance of the evidence.

E. No fees shall be charged for filing or serving petitions pursuant to this section.

F. Neither a law-enforcement agency, the attorney for the Commonwealth, a court nor the clerk's office, nor any employee of them, may disclose, except among themselves, the residential address, telephone number, or place of employment of the person protected by the order or that of the family of such person, except to the extent that disclosure is (i) required by law or the Rules of the Supreme Court, (ii) necessary for law-enforcement purposes, or (iii) permitted by the court for good cause.

G. As used in this section, "copy" includes a facsimile copy.

Acts 1997, c. 831; Acts 1998, c. 569; Acts 1998, c. 684; Acts 1999, c. 371; Acts 2001, c. 101; Acts 2002, c. 507; Acts 2002, c. 810; Acts 2002, c. 818; Acts 2003, c. 730. Amended by Acts 2008, c. 73; Acts 2008, c. 128; Acts 2008, c. 246; Acts 2009, c. 341; Acts 2009, c. 732; Acts 2011, c. 445; Acts 2011, c. 480; Acts 2014, c. 346.

§ 19.2–152.10. Protective order

A. The court may issue a protective order pursuant to this chapter to protect the health and safety of the petitioner and family or household members of a petitioner upon (i) the issuance of a petition or warrant for, or a conviction of, any criminal offense resulting from the commission of an act of violence, force, or threat or (ii) a hearing held pursuant to subsection D of § 19.2–152.9. A protective order issued under this section may include any one or more of the following conditions to be imposed on the respondent:

1. Prohibiting acts of violence, force, or threat or criminal offenses that may result in injury to person or property;

2. Prohibiting such contacts by the respondent with the petitioner or family or household members of the petitioner as the court deems necessary for the health or safety of such persons;

3. Any other relief necessary to prevent (i) acts of violence, force, or threat, (ii) criminal offenses that may result in injury to person or property, or (iii) communication or other contact of any kind by the respondent; and

4. Granting the petitioner the possession of any companion animal as defined in § 3.2–6500 if such petitioner meets the definition of owner in § 3.2–6500.

B. The protective order may be issued for a specified period of time up to a maximum of two years. The protective order shall expire at 11:59 p.m. on the last day specified or at 11:59 p.m. on the last day of the two-year period if no date is specified. Prior to the expiration of the protective order, a petitioner may file a written motion requesting a hearing to extend the order. Proceedings to extend a protective order shall be given precedence on the docket of the court. The court may extend the protective order for a period not longer than two years to protect the health and safety of the petitioner or persons who are family or household members of the petitioner at the time the request for an extension is made. The extension of the protective order shall expire at 11:59 p.m. on the last day specified or at 11:59 p.m. on the last day of the two-year period if no date is specified. Nothing herein shall limit the number of extensions that may be requested or issued.

C. A copy of the protective order shall be served on the respondent and provided to the petitioner as soon as possible. The court, including a circuit court if the circuit court issued the order, shall forthwith, but in all cases no later than the end of the business day on which the order was issued, enter and transfer electronically to the Virginia Criminal Information Network the respondent's identifying information and the name, date of birth, sex, and race of each protected person provided to the court and shall forthwith forward the attested copy of the protective order and containing any such identifying information to the primary law-enforcement agency responsible for service and entry of protective orders. Upon receipt of the order by the primary law-enforcement agency, the agency shall forthwith verify and enter any modification as necessary to the identifying information and other appropriate information required by the Department of State Police into the Virginia Criminal Information Network established and maintained by the Department pursuant to Chapter 2 (§ 52–12 et seq.) of Title 52 and the order shall be served forthwith upon the respondent and due return made to the court. Upon service, the agency making service shall enter the date and time of service and other appropriate information required into the Virginia Criminal Information Network and make due return to the court. If the order is later dissolved or modified, a copy of the dissolution or modification order shall also be attested, forwarded forthwith to the primary law-enforcement agency responsible for service and entry of protective orders, and upon receipt of the order by the primary law-enforcement agency, the agency shall forthwith verify and enter any modification as necessary to the identifying information and other appropriate information required by the Department of State Police into the Virginia Criminal Information Network as described above and the order shall be served forthwith and due return made to the court.

D. Except as otherwise provided, a violation of a protective order issued under this section shall constitute contempt of court.

E. The court may assess costs and attorneys' fees against either party regardless of whether an order of protection has been issued as a result of a full hearing.

F. Any judgment, order or decree, whether permanent or temporary, issued by a court of appropriate jurisdiction in another state, the United States or any of its territories, possessions or Commonwealths, the District of Columbia or by any tribal court of appropriate jurisdiction for the purpose of preventing violent or threatening acts or harassment against or contact or communication with or physical proximity to another person, including any of the conditions specified in subsection A, shall be accorded full faith and credit and enforced in the Commonwealth as if it were an order of the Commonwealth, provided reasonable notice and opportunity to be heard were given by the issuing jurisdiction to the person against whom the order is sought to be enforced sufficient to protect such person's due process rights and consistent with federal law. A person entitled to protection under such a foreign order may file the order in any appropriate district court by filing with the court, an attested or exemplified copy of the order. Upon such a filing, the clerk shall forthwith forward an attested copy of the order to the primary law-enforcement agency responsible for service and entry of protective orders which shall, upon receipt, enter the name of the person subject to the order and other appropriate information required by the Department of State Police into the Virginia Criminal Information Network established and maintained by the Department pursuant to Chapter 2 (§ 52–12 et seq.) of Title 52. Where practical, the court may transfer information electronically to the Virginia Criminal Information Network.

Upon inquiry by any law-enforcement agency of the Commonwealth, the clerk shall make a copy available of any foreign order filed with that court. A law-enforcement officer may, in the performance of his duties, rely upon a copy of a foreign protective order or other suitable evidence which has been provided to him by any source and may also rely upon the statement of any person protected by the order that the order remains in effect.

G. Either party may at any time file a written motion with the court requesting a hearing to dissolve or modify the order. Proceedings to modify or dissolve a protective order shall be given precedence on the docket of the court.

H. Neither a law-enforcement agency, the attorney for the Commonwealth, a court nor the clerk's office, nor any employee of them, may disclose, except among themselves, the residential address, telephone number, or place of employment of the person protected by the order or that of the family of such person, except to the extent that disclosure is (i) required by law or the Rules of the Supreme Court, (ii) necessary for law-enforcement purposes, or (iii) permitted by the court for good cause.

I. No fees shall be charged for filing or serving petitions pursuant to this section.

J. As used in this section:

"Copy" includes a facsimile copy; and

"Protective order" includes an initial, modified or extended protective order.

Acts 1997, c. 831; Acts 1998, c. 569; Acts 1998, c. 684; Acts 1999, c. 371; Acts 2002, c. 507; Acts 2002, c. 810; Acts 2002, c. 818; Acts 2003, c. 730. Amended by Acts 2008, c. 73; Acts 2008, c. 246; Acts 2009, c. 341; Acts 2009, c. 732; Acts 2010, c. 425; Acts 2010, c. 468; Acts 2011, c. 445; Acts 2011, c. 480; Acts 2012, c. 152; Acts 2012, c. 261; Acts 2014, c. 346.

§ 19.2–152.11. Venue for protective orders

Proceedings in which a protective order is sought pursuant to this chapter shall be commenced where (i) either party has his principal residence; (ii) the act of violence, force, or threat by the respondent against the petitioner occurred; or (iii) a protective order was issued if, at the time the proceeding is commenced, the order is in effect to protect the petitioner or a family or household member of the petitioner.

Added by Acts 2012, c. 637.

§ 19.2–152.12. Compensation for required representation of respondents

Notwithstanding any other provision of law, when, in a proceeding pursuant to this chapter, representation of a respondent by counsel is required under the Servicemembers Civil Relief Act (50 U.S.C. App. § 501 et seq.) or a guardian ad litem is required by law and there is no other provision for the compensation of counsel or a guardian ad litem, the court may order such counsel or guardian ad litem to be compensated for services pursuant to § 19.2–163.

Added by Acts 2015, c. 545; Acts 2015, c. 556.

CHAPTER 10

DISABILITY OF JUDGE OR ATTORNEY FOR COMMONWEALTH; COURT-APPOINTED COUNSEL; INTERPRETERS; TRANSCRIPTS

Article 1

Disability of Judge

§ 19.2–153. When judge cannot sit on trial; how another judge procured to try the case

When the judge of a circuit court in which a prosecution is pending is connected with the accused or party injured, or is so situated in respect to the case as in his opinion to render it improper that he should preside at the trial, or if he has rejected a plea bargain agreement submitted by both parties and the parties do not agree that he may hear the case, he shall enter the fact of record and the clerk of the court shall at once certify this fact to the Chief Justice of the Supreme Court and thereupon another judge shall be appointed, in the manner prescribed by § 17.1–105, to preside at the trial.

Acts 1975, c. 495; Acts 1984, c. 585; Acts 1985, c. 253.

§ 19.2–154. Death or disability of judge during trial; how another judge procured to continue with trial

If by reason of death, sickness or other disability the judge who presided at a criminal jury trial is unable to proceed with and finish the trial, another judge of that court or a judge designated by the Chief Justice of the Supreme Court or by a justice designated by him for that purpose, may proceed with and finish the trial or, in his discretion, may grant and preside at a new trial. If by reason of such disability, the judge who presided at any trial is unable to perform the duties to be performed by the court after a finding of guilty by the jury or the court, another judge of that court, or a judge designated as provided in the preceding sentence, may perform those duties or, in his discretion, may grant and preside at a new trial. Before proceeding with the trial or performing such duties, such judge shall certify that he has familiarized himself with the record of the trial.

Acts 1975, c. 495.

ARTICLE 2

DISABILITY OF ATTORNEY FOR COMMONWEALTH

§ 19.2–155. Disqualification or temporary disability of attorney for Commonwealth; appointment of substitute; powers, duties and compensation of such appointee

If the attorney for the Commonwealth of any county or city is connected by blood or marriage with the accused, or is so situated with respect to such accused as to render it improper, in his opinion, concurred in by the judge, for him to act, or if such attorney for the Commonwealth of any county or city is unable to act, or to attend to his official duties as attorney for the Commonwealth, due to sickness, disability or other reason of a temporary nature, then upon notification by such attorney for the Commonwealth, or upon the certificate of his attending physician, or the clerk of the court, which fact shall be entered of record, the judge of the circuit court shall appoint from another jurisdiction an attorney for the Commonwealth or an assistant attorney for the Commonwealth, with the consent of such attorney for the Commonwealth or assistant, who is not authorized by law to engage in private practice for such case or cases, term or terms of court, or period or periods of time, as may be necessary or desirable, and the same to be forthwith entered of record. However, if the circuit court determines that the appointment of such attorney for the Commonwealth or such assistant attorney for the Commonwealth is not appropriate or that such an attorney or assistant is unavailable, or for other good cause, then the circuit court may appoint an attorney-at-law who shall be compensated pursuant to § 19.2–332. Such appointee shall act in place of, and otherwise perform the duties and exercise the powers of, such disqualified or disabled attorney for the Commonwealth, in regard to such case or cases, for the term or terms of the court, or the period or periods of time, for which the appointment and designation is made, or until the disqualified or disabled attorney for the Commonwealth shall again be able to attend to his duties as such. Nothing herein shall prevent a court from appointing as a special assistant attorney for the Commonwealth, without additional compensation, an attorney employed by a state agency when such appointment is requested by the attorney for the Commonwealth and the court determines such appointment will aid in the prosecution of a particular case or cases.

An attorney for the Commonwealth or assistant attorney for the Commonwealth who is required by law to devote full time to his duties as such shall not receive additional compensation for services rendered on appointment pursuant to this section. However, such attorney for the Commonwealth or assistant may receive reimbursement for actual expenses incurred, as approved by the Compensation Board to be paid by the Compensation Board, provided such expenses are not otherwise reimbursed by the county or city which he is elected or appointed to serve or by the Compensation Board.

Acts 1975, c. 495; Acts 1983, c. 362; Acts 1985, c. 321; Acts 1996, c. 968.

§ 19.2–156. Prolonged absence of attorney for Commonwealth

If it shall be necessary for the attorney for the Commonwealth of any county or city to absent himself for a prolonged period of time from the performance of the duties of his office, then, upon notification by such attorney for the Commonwealth, or by the court on its own motion, and the facts being entered of record, the judge of the circuit court shall appoint an attorney-at-law as acting attorney for the Commonwealth to serve for such length of time as may be necessary. Such acting attorney for the Commonwealth shall act in place of and otherwise perform the duties and exercise the powers of such regular attorney for the Commonwealth, and while so acting shall receive the salary and allowance for expenses fixed by the State Compensation Board for such regular attorney for the Commonwealth, who during such length of time shall not receive any such salary or allowance.

Acts 1975, c. 495.

ARTICLE 3

APPOINTMENT OF ATTORNEY FOR ACCUSED

§ 19.2–157. Duty of court when accused appears without counsel

Except as may otherwise be provided in §§ 16.1–266 through 16.1–268, whenever a person charged with a criminal offense the penalty for which may be death or confinement in the state correctional facility or jail, including charges for revocation of suspension of imposition or execution of sentence or probation, appears before any court without being represented by counsel, the court shall inform him of his right to counsel. The accused shall be allowed a reasonable opportunity to employ counsel or, if appropriate, the statement of indigence provided for in § 19.2–159 may be executed.

Acts 1975, c. 495; Acts 1978, c. 362.

§ 19.2–158. When person not free on bail shall be informed of right to counsel and amount of bail

Every person charged with an offense described in § 19.2–157, who is not free on bail or otherwise, shall be brought before the judge of a court not of record, unless the circuit court issues process commanding the presence of the person, in which case the person shall be brought before the circuit court, on the first day on which such court sits after the person is charged, at which time the judge shall inform the accused of the amount of his bail and his right to counsel. If the court not of record sits on a day prior to the scheduled sitting of the court which issued process, the person shall be brought before the court not of record. The court shall also hear and consider motions by the person or Commonwealth relating to bail or conditions of release pursuant to Article 1 (§ 19.2–119 et seq.) of Chapter 9 of this title. Absent good cause shown, a hearing on bail or conditions of release shall be held as soon as practicable but in no event later than three calendar days, excluding Saturdays, Sundays, and legal holidays, following the making of such motion.

No hearing on the charges against the accused shall be had until the foregoing conditions have been complied with, and the accused shall be allowed a reasonable opportunity to employ counsel of his own choice, or, if appropriate, the statement of indigence provided for in § 19.2–159 may be executed.

Acts 1975, c. 495; Acts 1998, c. 773; Acts 1999, c. 829; Acts 1999, c. 846. Amended by Acts 2014, c. 515.

§ 19.2–159. Determination of indigency; guidelines; statement of indigence; appointment of counsel

A. If the accused shall claim that he is indigent, and the charge against him is a criminal offense which may be punishable by death or confinement in the state correctional facility or jail, subject to the provisions of § 19.2–160, the court shall determine from oral examination of the accused or other competent evidence whether or not the accused is indigent within the contemplation of law pursuant to the guidelines set forth in this section.

B. In making its finding, the court shall determine whether or not the accused is a current recipient of a state or federally funded public assistance program for the indigent. If the accused is a current recipient of such a program and does not waive his right to counsel or retain counsel on his own behalf, he shall be presumed eligible for the appointment of counsel. This presumption shall be rebuttable where the court finds that a more thorough examination of the financial resources of the defendant is necessary. If the accused shall claim to be indigent and is not presumptively eligible under the provisions of this section, then a thorough examination of the financial resources of the accused shall be made with consideration given to the following:

1. The net income of the accused, which shall include his total salary and wages minus deductions required by law. The court also shall take into account income and amenities from other sources including but not limited to social security funds, union funds, veteran's benefits, other regular support from an absent family member, public or private employee pensions, dividends, interests, rents, estates, trusts, or gifts.

2. All assets of the accused which are convertible into cash within a reasonable period of time without causing substantial hardship or jeopardizing the ability of the accused to maintain home and employment. Assets shall include all cash on hand as well as in checking and savings accounts, stocks, bonds, certificates of deposit, and tax refunds. All personal property owned by the accused which is readily convertible into cash shall be considered, except property exempt from attachment. Any real estate owned by the accused shall be considered in terms of the amounts which could be raised by a loan on the property. For purposes of eligibility determination, the income, assets, and expenses of the spouse, if any, who is a member of the accused's household, shall be considered, unless the spouse was the victim of the offense or offenses allegedly committed by the accused.

3. Any exceptional expenses of the accused and his family which would, in all probability, prohibit him from being able to secure private counsel. Such items shall include but not be limited to costs for medical care, family support obligations, and child care payments.

The available funds of the accused shall be calculated as the sum of his total income and assets less the exceptional expenses as provided in paragraph 3 above. If the accused does not waive his right to counsel or retain counsel on his own behalf, counsel shall be appointed for the accused if his available funds are equal to or below 125 percent of the federal poverty income guidelines prescribed for the size of the household of the accused by the federal Department of Health and Human Services. The Supreme Court of Virginia shall be responsible for distributing to all courts the annual updates of the federal poverty income guidelines made by the Department.

If the available funds of the accused exceed 125 percent of the federal poverty income guidelines and the accused fails to employ counsel and does not waive his right to counsel, the court may, in exceptional circumstances, and where the ends of justice so require, appoint an attorney to represent the accused. However, in making such appointments, the court shall state in writing its reasons for so doing. The written statement by the court shall be included in the permanent record of the case.

C. If the court determines that the accused is indigent as contemplated by law pursuant to the guidelines set forth in this section, the court shall provide the accused with a statement which shall contain the following:

> "I have been advised this .... day of ...., 20.., by the (name of court) court of my right to representation by counsel in the trial of the charge pending against me; I certify that I am without means to employ counsel and I hereby request the court to appoint counsel for me."
>
> .... (signature of accused)

The court shall also require the accused to complete a written financial statement to support the claim of indigency and to permit the court to determine whether or not the accused is indigent within the contemplation of law. The accused shall execute the said statements under oath, and the said court shall appoint competent counsel to represent the accused in the proceeding against him, including an appeal, if any, until relieved or replaced by other counsel.

The executed statements by the accused and the order of appointment of counsel shall be filed with and become a part of the record of such proceeding.

All other instances in which the appointment of counsel is required for an indigent shall be made in accordance with the guidelines prescribed in this section.

D. Except in jurisdictions having a public defender, or unless (i) the public defender is unable to represent the defendant by reason of conflict of interest or (ii) the court finds that appointment of other counsel is necessary to attain the ends of justice, counsel appointed by the court for representation of the accused shall be selected by a fair system of rotation among members of the bar practicing before the court whose names are on the list maintained by the Indigent Defense Commission pursuant to § 19.2–163.01. If no attorney who is on the list maintained by the Indigent Defense Commission is reasonably available, the court may appoint as counsel an attorney not on the list who has otherwise demonstrated to the court's satisfaction an appropriate level of training and experience. The court shall provide notice to the Commission of the appointment of the attorney.

Acts 1975, c. 495; Acts 1976, c. 553; Acts 1978, c. 720; Acts 1984, c. 709; Acts 1984, c. 709; Acts 2004, c. 884; Acts 2004, c. 921; Acts 2006, c. 680; Acts 2006, c. 708. Amended by Acts 2008, c. 122; Acts 2008, c. 154.

§ 19.2–159.1. Interrogation by court; filing; change in circumstances; investigation by attorney for Commonwealth

A. The court shall thoroughly interrogate any person making the statement of indigency required in § 19.2–159 and shall further advise such person of the penalty which might result from false swearing, as provided in § 19.2–161.

B. The statement and oath of the defendant shall be filed with the papers in the case, and shall follow and be in effect at all stages of the proceedings against him without further oath. In the event the defendant undergoes a change of circumstances so that he is no longer indigent, the defendant shall thereupon obtain private counsel and shall forthwith advise the court of the change of circumstances. The court shall grant reasonable continuance to allow counsel to be obtained and to prepare for trial. When private counsel has been retained, appointed counsel shall forthwith be relieved of further responsibility and compensated for his services, pro rata, pursuant to § 19.2–163.

C. Upon the request of the court, it shall be the duty of the attorney for the Commonwealth of the county or city in which such statement and oath was made to make an investigation as to the indigency of the defendant, or of any other person making such statement. The attorney for the Commonwealth is authorized to delegate the responsibility for such investigation to any subordinate in his office, or to any agency, state or local, which possesses the facilities to quickly make such investigation. Such investigation shall be reduced to writing and forwarded to the court in which the statement and oath was made within fourteen days after such request by the court is made. Such report shall be placed with the papers in the case.

Acts 1975, c. 495; Acts 1977, c. 6; Acts 1981, c. 289; Acts 1984, c. 709.

§ 19.2–160. Appointment of counsel or waiver of right

If the charge against the accused is a crime the penalty for which may be incarceration, and the accused is not represented by counsel, the court shall ascertain by oral examination of the accused whether or not the accused desires to waive his right to counsel.

In the event the accused desires to waive his right to counsel, and the court ascertains that such waiver is voluntary and intelligently made, then the court shall provide the accused with a statement to be executed by the accused to document his waiver. The statement shall be in a form designed and provided by the Supreme Court. Any executed statement herein provided for shall be filed with and become a part of the record of such proceeding.

In the absence of a waiver of counsel by the accused, and if he shall claim that he is indigent, the court shall proceed in the same manner as is provided in § 19.2–159.

Should the defendant refuse or otherwise fail to sign either of the statements described in this section and § 19.2–159, the court shall note such refusal on the record. Such refusal shall be deemed to be a waiver of the right to counsel, and the court, after so advising the accused and offering him the opportunity to rescind his refusal shall, if such refusal is not rescinded and the accused's signature given, proceed to hear and decide the case. However, if, prior to the commencement of the trial, the court states in writing, either upon the request of the attorney for the Commonwealth or, in the absence of the attorney for the Commonwealth, upon the court's own motion, that a sentence of incarceration will not be imposed if the defendant is convicted, the court may try the case without appointing counsel, and in such event no sentence of incarceration shall be imposed.

Acts 1975, c. 495; Acts 1978, c. 365; Acts 1979, c. 468; Acts 1983, c. 97; Acts 1989, c. 385.

§ 19.2–161. Penalty for false swearing with regard to statement of indigence

Any person charged with a felony who shall falsely swear or who shall execute the statement provided for in § 19.2–159 knowing such statement to be false, shall be guilty of perjury, punishable as a Class 5 felony.

Any person charged with a misdemeanor punishable by confinement in jail who shall falsely swear or who shall execute the statement provided for in § 19.2–159 knowing such statement to be false shall be guilty of a Class 1 misdemeanor.

Acts 1975, c. 495.

§ 19.2–162. Continuances to be granted if necessary

Courts before which criminal proceedings are pending shall afford such continuances and take such other action as is necessary to comply with the provisions of this chapter.

Acts 1975, c. 495.

§ 19.2–163. Compensation of court-appointed counsel

Upon submission to the court, for which appointed representation is provided, of a detailed accounting of the time expended for that representation, made within 30 days of the completion of all proceedings in that court, counsel appointed to represent an indigent accused in a criminal case shall be compensated for his services on an hourly basis at a rate set by the Supreme Court of Virginia in a total amount not to exceed the amounts specified in the following schedule:

1. In a district court, a sum not to exceed $120, provided that, notwithstanding the foregoing limitation, the court in its discretion, and subject to guidelines issued by the Executive Secretary of the Supreme Court of Virginia, may waive the limitation of fees up to (i) an additional $120 when the effort expended, the time reasonably necessary for the particular representation, the novelty and difficulty of the issues, or other circumstances warrant such a waiver; or (ii) an amount up to $650 to defend, in the case of a juvenile, an offense that would be a felony if committed by an adult that may be punishable by confinement in the state correctional facility for a period of more than 20 years, or a charge of violation of probation for such offense, when the effort expended, the time reasonably necessary for the particular representation, the novelty and difficulty of the issues, or other circumstances warrant such a waiver; or (iii) such other amount as may be provided by law. Such amount shall be allowed in any case wherein counsel conducts the defense of a single charge against the indigent through to its conclusion or a charge of violation of probation at any hearing conducted under § 19.2–306; thereafter, compensation for additional charges against the same accused also conducted by the same counsel shall be allowed on the basis of additional time expended as to such additional charges;

2. In a circuit court (i) to defend a felony charge that may be punishable by death an amount deemed reasonable by the court; (ii) to defend a felony charge that may be punishable by confinement in the state correctional facility for a period of more than 20 years, or a charge of violation of probation for such offense, a sum not to exceed $1,235, provided that, notwithstanding the foregoing limitation, the court in its discretion, and subject to guidelines issued by the Executive Secretary of the Supreme Court of Virginia, may waive the limitation of fees up to an additional $850 when the effort expended, the time reasonably necessary for the particular representation, the novelty and difficulty of the issues, or other circumstances warrant such a waiver; (iii) to defend any other felony charge, or a charge of violation of probation for such offense, a sum not to exceed $445, provided that, notwithstanding the foregoing limitation, the court in its discretion, and subject to guidelines issued by the Executive Secretary of the Supreme Court of Virginia, may waive the limitation of fees up to an additional $155 when the effort expended, the time reasonably necessary for the particular representation, the novelty and difficulty of the issues, or other circumstances warrant such a waiver; and (iv) in the circuit court only, to defend any misdemeanor charge punishable by confinement in jail or a charge of violation of probation for such offense, a sum not to exceed $158. In the event any case is required to be retried due to a mistrial for any cause or reversed on appeal, the court may allow an additional fee for each case in an amount not to exceed the amounts allowable in the initial trial. In the event counsel is appointed to defend an indigent charged with a felony that may be punishable by death, such counsel shall continue to receive compensation as provided in this paragraph for defending such a felony, regardless of whether the charge is reduced or amended to a felony that may not be punishable by death, prior to final disposition of the case. In the event counsel is appointed to defend an indigent charged with any other felony, such counsel shall receive compensation as provided in this paragraph for defending such a felony, regardless of whether the charge is reduced or amended to a misdemeanor or lesser felony

prior to final disposition of the case in either the district court or circuit court.

Counsel appointed to represent an indigent accused in a criminal case, who are not public defenders, may request an additional waiver exceeding the amounts provided for in this section. The request for any additional amount shall be submitted to the presiding judge, in writing, with a detailed accounting of the time spent and the justification for the additional amount. The presiding judge shall determine, subject to guidelines issued by the Executive Secretary of the Supreme Court of Virginia, whether the request for an additional amount is justified in whole or in part, by considering the effort expended and the time reasonably necessary for the particular representation, and, if so, shall forward the request as approved to the chief judge of the circuit court or district court for approval.

If at any time the funds appropriated to pay for waivers under this section become insufficient, the Executive Secretary of the Supreme Court of Virginia shall so certify to the courts and no further waivers shall be approved.

The circuit or district court shall direct the payment of such reasonable expenses incurred by such court-appointed counsel as it deems appropriate under the circumstances of the case. Counsel appointed by the court to represent an indigent charged with repeated violations of the same section of the Code of Virginia, with each of such violations arising out of the same incident, occurrence, or transaction, shall be compensated in an amount not to exceed the fee prescribed for the defense of a single charge, if such offenses are tried as part of the same judicial proceeding. The trial judge shall consider any guidelines established by the Supreme Court but shall have the sole discretion to fix the amount of compensation to be paid counsel appointed by the court to defend a felony charge that may be punishable by death.

The circuit or district court shall direct that the foregoing payments shall be paid out by the Commonwealth, if the defendant is charged with a violation of a statute, or by the county, city or town, if the defendant is charged with a violation of a county, city or town ordinance, to the attorney so appointed to defend such person as compensation for such defense.

Counsel representing a defendant charged with a Class 1 felony, or counsel representing an indigent prisoner under sentence of death in a state habeas corpus proceeding, may submit to the court, on a monthly basis, a statement of all costs incurred and fees charged by him in the case during that month. Whenever the total charges as are deemed reasonable by the court for which payment has not previously been made or requested exceed $1,000, the court may direct that payment be made as otherwise provided in this section.

When such directive is entered upon the order book of the court, the Commonwealth, county, city or town, as the case may be, shall provide for the payment out of its treasury of the sum of money so specified. If the defendant is convicted, the amount allowed by the court to the attorney appointed to defend him shall be taxed against the defendant as a part of the costs of prosecution and, if collected, the same shall be paid to the Commonwealth, or the county, city or town, as the case may be. In the event that counsel for the defendant requests a waiver of the limitations on compensation, the court shall assess against the defendant an amount equal to the pre-waiver compensation limit specified in this section for each charge for which the defendant was convicted. An abstract of such costs shall be docketed in the judgment docket and execution lien book maintained by such court.

Any statement submitted by an attorney for payments due him for indigent representation or for representation of a child pursuant to § 16.1–266 shall, after the submission of the statement, be forwarded forthwith by the clerk to the Commonwealth, county, city or town, as the case may be, responsible for payment.

For the purposes of this section, the defense of a case may be considered conducted through to its conclusion and an appointed counsel entitled to compensation for his services in the event an indigent accused fails to appear in court subject to a capias for his arrest or a show cause summons for his failure to appear and remains a fugitive from justice for one year following the issuance of the capias or the summons to show cause, and appointed counsel has appeared at a hearing on behalf of the accused.

Effective July 1, 2007, the Executive Secretary of the Supreme Court of Virginia shall track and report the number and category of offenses charged involving adult and juvenile offenders in cases in which court-appointed counsel is assigned. The Executive Secretary shall also track and report the amounts paid by waiver above the initial cap to court-appointed counsel. The Executive Secretary shall provide these reports to the Governor, members of the House Appropriations Committee, and members of the Senate Finance Committee on a quarterly basis.

Acts 1975, c. 495; Acts 1976, c. 553; Acts 1980, c. 626: Acts 1981, c. 472; Acts 1981, c. 486; Acts 1985, c. 525; Acts 1986, c. 425; Acts 1987, c. 638; Acts 1988, c. 465; Acts 1988, c. 472; Acts 1989, c. 565; Acts 1994, c. 451; Acts 1995, c. 571; Acts 1995, c. 713, eff. April 6, 1995; Acts 1997, c. 492, eff. July 1, 1998; Acts 1998, c. 440; Acts 1998, c. 451; Acts 2000, c. 436; Acts 2000, c. 448; Acts 2001, c. 509; Acts 2006, c. 332; Acts 2007, c. 938; Acts 2007, c. 946. Amended by Acts 2008, c. 760; Acts 2009, c. 284.

ARTICLE 3.1

INDIGENT DEFENSE

§ 19.2–163.01. Virginia Indigent Defense Commission established; powers and duties

A. The Virginia Indigent Defense Commission (hereinafter Indigent Defense Commission or Commission) is established. The Commission shall be supervisory and shall have sole responsibility for the powers, duties, operations, and responsibilities set forth in this section.

The Commission shall have the following powers and duties:

1. To publicize and enforce the qualification standards for attorneys seeking eligibility to serve as court-appointed counsel for indigent defendants pursuant to § 19.2–159.

2. To develop initial training courses for attorneys who wish to begin serving as court-appointed counsel, and to review and certify legal education courses that satisfy the continuing requirements for attorneys to maintain their eligibility for receiving court appointments.

3. To maintain a list of attorneys admitted to practice law in Virginia who are qualified to serve as court-appointed counsel for indigent defendants based upon the official standards and to disseminate the list by July 1 of each year and updates throughout the year to the Office of the Executive Secretary of the Supreme Court for distribution to the courts. In establishing and updating the list, the Commission shall consider all relevant factors, including but not limited to, the attorney's background, experience, and training and the Commission's assessment of whether the attorney is competent to provide quality legal representation.

4. To establish official standards of practice for court-appointed counsel and public defenders to follow in representing their clients, and guidelines for the removal of an attorney from the official list of those qualified to receive court appointments and to notify the Office of the Executive Secretary of the Supreme Court of any attorney whose name has been removed from the list.

5. To develop initial training courses for public defenders and to review and certify legal education courses that satisfy the continuing requirements for public defenders to maintain their eligibility.

6. To periodically review and report to the Virginia State Crime Commission, the House and the Senate Committees for Courts of Justice, the House Committee on Appropriations, and the Senate Committee on Finance on the caseload handled by each public defender office.

7. To maintain all public defender and regional capital defender offices established by the General Assembly.

8. To hire and employ and, at its pleasure, remove an executive director, counsel, and such other persons as it deems necessary, and to authorize the executive director to appoint, after prior notice to the Commission, a deputy director, and for each of the above offices a public defender or capital defender, as the case may be, who shall devote his full time to his duties and not engage in the private practice of law.

9. To authorize the public defender or capital defender to employ such assistants as authorized by the Commission.

10. To authorize the public defender or capital defender to employ such staff, including secretarial and investigative personnel, as may be necessary to carry out the duties imposed upon the public defender office.

11. To authorize the executive director of the Commission, in consultation with the public defender or capital defender to secure such office space as needed, to purchase or rent office equipment, to purchase supplies and to incur such expenses as are necessary to carry out the duties imposed upon him.

12. To approve requests for appropriations and receive and expend moneys appropriated by the General Assembly of Virginia, to receive other moneys as they become available to it and expend the same in order to carry out the duties imposed upon it.

13. To require and ensure that each public defender office collects and maintains caseload data and fields in a case management database on an annual basis.

14. To report annually on or before October 1 to the Virginia State Crime Commission, the House and Senate Committees for Courts of Justice, the House Committee on Appropriations, and the Senate Committee on Finance on the state of indigent criminal defense in the Commonwealth, including Virginia's ranking amongst the 50 states in terms of pay allowed for court-appointed counsel appointed pursuant to § 19.2–159 or subdivision C 2 of § 16.1–266.

B. The Commission shall adopt rules and procedures for the conduct of its business. The Commission may delegate to the executive director or, in the absence of the executive director, the deputy executive director, such powers and duties conferred upon the Commission as it deems appropriate, including powers and duties involving the exercise of discretion. The Commission shall ensure that the executive director complies with all Commission and statutory directives. Such rules and procedures may include the establishment of committees and the delegation of authority to the committees. The Commission shall review and confirm by a vote of the Commission its rules and procedures and any delegation of authority to the executive director at least every three years.

C. The executive director shall, with the approval of the Commission, fix the compensation of each public defender and all other personnel in each public defender office. The executive director shall also exercise and perform such other powers and duties as may be lawfully delegated to him and such powers and duties as may be conferred or imposed upon him by law.

Acts 2004, c. 884; Acts 2004, c. 921; Acts 2005, c. 230; Acts 2006, c. 429; Acts 2006, c. 501; Acts 2007, c. 371. Amended by Acts 2008, c. 536; Acts 2008, c. 815; Acts 2010, c. 314.

§ 19.2–163.01:1. Supplementing compensation of public defender

A. The governing body of any county or city may supplement the compensation of the public defender or any of his deputies or employees above the compensation fixed by the executive director, in such amounts as it may deem expedient. Such additional compensation shall be wholly payable from the funds of any such county or city.

B. Due to the privileged and protected nature of the attorney-client relationship and the statutory scope of representation provided in §§ 19.2–157 and 19.2–163.3, no county or city providing a supplement to compensation under this section shall place any condition or requirement upon the receipt of such funds.

C. Funds provided by any county or city under this section shall be paid directly to the employees with notice to the Indigent Defense Commission of any amount so provided.

Added by Acts 2008, c. 536; Acts 2008, c. 815. Amended by Acts 2010, c. 314.

§ 19.2–163.02. Membership of Indigent Defense Commission; expenses

The Virginia Indigent Defense Commission shall consist of 14 members as follows: the chairmen of the House and Senate Committees for Courts of Justice or their designees who shall be members of the Courts of Justice committees; the chairman of the Virginia State Crime Commission or his designee; the Executive Secretary of the Supreme Court or his designee; two attorneys officially designated by the Virginia State Bar; two persons appointed by the Governor; three persons appointed by the Speaker of the House of Delegates; and three persons appointed by the Senate Committee on Rules. At least one of the appointments made by the Governor, one of the appointments made by the Speaker, and one of the appointments made by the Senate Committee on Rules, shall be an attorney in private practice with a demonstrated interest in indigent defense issues. Persons who are appointed by virtue of their office shall hold terms coincident with their terms of office. If the chairman of the Virginia State Crime Commission is (i) the chairman of the House Committee for Courts of Justice, then the vice-chairman of the Committee shall serve in the position designated for the Committee chairman or (ii) the chairman of the Senate Committee for Courts of Justice, then the Senate Committee on Rules, upon the recommendation of the chairman of the Committee, shall appoint a member of the Committee to serve in the position designated for the Committee chairman. All other members shall be appointed for terms of three years and may be reappointed.

The Commission shall elect a chairman and a vice-chairman from among its membership annually. The chairman or his designee shall preside at all regular and called meetings of the Commission and shall have no additional duties or authority unless set by statute or by resolution of the Commission and annually confirmed by the Commission. A majority of the members shall constitute a quorum. The Commission shall meet at least four times each year. The meetings of the Commission shall be held at the call of the chairman or whenever three of the members so request.

Members shall be paid reasonable and necessary expenses incurred in the performance of their duties. Legislative members shall receive compensation as provided in § 30–19.12 and nonlegislative citizen members shall receive compensation for their services as provided in §§ 2.2–2813 and 2.2–2825.

Acts 2004, c. 884; Acts 2004, c. 921; Acts 2005, c. 176; Acts 2005, c. 758; Acts 2006, c. 429; Acts 2006, c. 501. Amended by Acts 2008, c. 115.

§ 19.2–163.03. Qualifications for court-appointed counsel

A. Initial qualification requirements. An attorney seeking to represent an indigent accused in a criminal case, in addition to being a member in good standing of the Virginia State Bar, shall meet the specific criteria required for each type or level of case. The following criteria shall be met for qualification and subsequent court appointment:

1. Misdemeanor case. To initially qualify to serve as counsel appointed pursuant to § 19.2–159 for an indigent defendant charged with a misdemeanor, the attorney shall:

(i) if an active member of the Virginia State Bar for less than one year, have completed six hours of MCLE-approved continuing legal education developed by the Indigent Defense Commission, or

(ii) if an active member of the Virginia State Bar for one year or more, either complete the six hours of approved continuing legal education developed by the Commission, or certify to the Commission that he has represented, in a district court within the past year, four or more defendants charged with misdemeanors, or

(iii) be qualified pursuant to this section to serve as counsel for an indigent defendant charged with a felony.

2. Felony case.

a. To initially qualify to serve as counsel appointed pursuant to § 19.2–159 for an indigent defendant charged with a felony, the attorney shall (i) have completed the six hours of MCLE-approved continuing legal education developed by the Commission, and (ii) certify that he has participated as either lead counsel or co-counsel in four felony cases from their beginning through to their final resolution, including appeals, if any.

b. If the attorney has been an active member of the Virginia State Bar for more than one year and certifies that he has participated, within the past year, as lead counsel in four felony cases through to their final resolution, including appeals, if any, the requirement to complete six hours of continuing legal education and the requirement to participate as co-counsel shall be waived.

c. If the attorney has been an active member of the Virginia State Bar for more than one year and certifies that he has participated, within the past five years, as lead counsel in five felony cases through to their final resolution, including appeals, if any, the requirement to participate as either lead counsel or co-counsel in four felony cases within the past year shall be waived.

3. Juvenile and domestic relations case.

a. To initially qualify to serve as appointed counsel in a juvenile and domestic relations district court pursuant to subdivision C 2 of § 16.1–266, the attorney shall (i) have completed the six hours of MCLE-approved continuing legal education developed by the Commission, (ii) have completed four additional hours of MCLE-approved continuing legal education on representing juveniles developed by the Commission, and (iii) certify that he has participated as either lead counsel or co-counsel in four cases involving juveniles in a juvenile and domestic relations district court.

b. If the attorney has been an active member of the Virginia State Bar for more than one year and certifies that he has, within the past year, been lead counsel in four cases involving juveniles in juvenile and domestic relations district court, the requirement to complete the 10 hours of continuing legal education shall be waived.

c. If the attorney has been an active member of the Virginia State Bar for more than one year and certifies that he has participated, within the past five years in five cases involving juveniles in a juvenile and domestic relations district court, the requirement to participate as either lead counsel or co-counsel in four juvenile cases shall be waived.

B. Requalification requirements. After initially qualifying as provided in subsection A, an attorney shall maintain his eligibility for certification biennially by notifying the Commission of completion of at least six hours of Commission and MCLE-approved continuing legal education. The Commission shall provide information on continuing legal education programs that have been approved.

In addition, to maintain eligibility to accept court appointments under subdivision C 2 of § 16.1–266, an attorney shall complete biennially thereafter four additional hours of MCLE-approved continuing legal education on representing juveniles, certified by the Commission.

C. Waiver and exceptions. The Commission or the court before which a matter is pending, may, in its discretion, waive the requirements set out in this section for individuals who otherwise demonstrate their level of training and experience. A waiver of such requirements pursuant to this subsection shall not form the basis for a claim of error at trial, on appeal, or in any habeas corpus proceeding.

Acts 2004, c. 884, eff. July 1, 2005; Acts 2004, c. 921, eff. July 1, 2005; Acts 2006, c. 708; Acts 2007, c. 571.

§ 19.2–163.04. Public Defender offices

Public defender offices are established in:

a. The City of Virginia Beach;

b. The City of Petersburg;

c. The Cities of Buena Vista, Lexington, Staunton and Waynesboro and the Counties of Augusta and Rockbridge;

d. The City of Roanoke;

e. The City of Portsmouth;

f. The City of Richmond;

g. The Counties of Clarke, Frederick, Page, Shenandoah and Warren, and the City of Winchester;

h. The City and County of Fairfax;

i. The City of Alexandria;

j. The City of Radford and the Counties of Bland, Pulaski and Wythe;

k. The Counties of Fauquier, Loudoun and Rappahannock;

l. The City of Suffolk;

m. The City of Franklin and the Counties of Isle of Wight and Southampton;

n. The City of Bedford and the County of Bedford;

o. The City of Danville;

p. The Counties of Halifax, Lunenburg and Mecklenburg;

q. The City of Fredericksburg and the Counties of King George, Stafford and Spotsylvania;

r. The City of Lynchburg;

s. The City of Martinsville and the Counties of Henry and Patrick;

t. The City of Charlottesville and the County of Albemarle;

u. The City of Norfolk;

v. The County of Arlington and the City of Falls Church;

w. The City of Newport News;

x. The City of Chesapeake; and

y. The City of Hampton.

Acts 2004, c. 884; Acts 2004, c. 921; Acts 2004, Sp. S. I, c. 4, eff. July 1, 2004; Acts 2005, c. 951, eff. May 4, 2005; Acts 2006, Sp. S. I, c. 2, eff. June 9, 2006.

Article 4

Public Defenders

§§ 19.2–163.1, 19.2–163.2. Repealed by Acts 2004, cc. 884 and 921

§ 19.2–163.3. Duties of public defenders

Public defenders shall carry out the following duties in accordance with the guidance, policies, and authorizations of the Indigent Defense Commission:

(a) To assist the executive director of the Commission in securing office space, to employ a staff, to fix salaries and to do such other things necessary to carry out the duties imposed upon them with the approval of the Commission.

(b) To represent or supervise assistants in representing within their respective jurisdictions as set out in § 19.2–163.04 indigent persons charged with a crime or offense when such persons are entitled to be represented by law by court-appointed counsel in a court of record or a court not of record.

(c) To represent or supervise assistants in representing indigent persons who are entitled to be represented by court-appointed counsel in an appeal of their conviction to the Court of Appeals or the Supreme Court of Virginia.

(d) To submit such reports as required by the Commission.

Acts 1975, c. 495; Acts 1975, c. 495; Acts 1978, c. 698; Acts 1979, c. 194; Acts 1990, c. 734; Acts 1992, c. 80; Acts 2007, c. 680.

§ 19.2–163.4. Inapplicability of §§ 17.1–606 and 19.2–163 where public defender offices established; exception

In counties and cities in which public defender offices are established pursuant to § 19.2–163.04, defense services for indigents charged with jailable offenses shall be provided by the public defenders unless (i) the public defender is unable to represent the defendant or petitioner by reason of conflict of interest or (ii) the court finds that appointment of other counsel is necessary to attain the ends of justice. Except for the provisions of § 19.2–163 relating to reasonable expenses, §§ 17.1–606 and 19.2–163 shall not apply when defense services are provided by the public defenders.

Acts 1975, c. 495; Acts 1975, c. 476; Acts 1975, c. 495; Acts 1992, c. 80; Acts 1994, c. 415.

§ 19.2–163.4:1. Repayment of representation costs by convicted persons

In any case in which an attorney from a public defender or capital defender office represents an indigent person charged with an offense and such person is convicted, the sum that would have been allowed a court-appointed attorney as compensation and as reasonable expenses shall be taxed against the person defended as a part of the costs of the prosecution, and, if collected, shall be paid to the Commonwealth or, if payment was made to the Commonwealth by a locality for defense of a local ordinance violation, to the appropriate county, city or town. An abstract of such costs shall be docketed in the judgment lien docket and execution book of the court.

Acts 2004, c. 884; Acts 2004, c. 921.

§ 19.2–163.5. Legal services to public defenders and/or assistant public defenders

At the request of a public defender, the Attorney General shall provide legal services to such attorney, his assistants, or members of his staff in any proceeding brought against him, his assistants, or staff for money damages, when the cause of action allegedly arises out of the duties of his office.

Any costs chargeable against the defendant or defendants in any such case shall be paid by the Commonwealth from the appropriation for the payment of criminal charges.

Acts 1978, c. 698.

§ 19.2–163.6. Repealed by Acts 2004, cc. 884 and 921

ARTICLE 4.1

COUNSEL IN CAPITAL CASES

§ 19.2–163.7. Counsel in capital cases

In any case in which an indigent defendant is charged with a capital offense, the judge of the circuit court, upon request for the appointment of counsel, shall appoint at least two attorneys from the list or lists established by the Supreme Court and the Indigent Defense Commission or as provided in subsection C of § 19.2–163.8 to represent the defendant at trial and, if the defendant is sentenced to death, on appeal. In all cases where counsel is appointed under this section after July 1, 2004, one of the attorneys appointed shall be from a capital defense unit maintained by the Indigent Defense Commission. This section shall be construed in conformity with the provisions of § 19.2–163.4. If prior to indictment the attorney for the Commonwealth declares in writing that the Commonwealth will not seek the death penalty, the capital defense unit attorney may upon motion before the circuit court seek to withdraw as counsel. The circuit court judge having heard the motion to withdraw shall permit the capital defense unit attorney to withdraw and shall appoint another attorney pursuant to the provisions of § 19.2–159. If the sentence of death is affirmed on appeal, the court shall, within 30 days after the decision of the Supreme Court of Virginia, appoint counsel from the same list, or such other list as the Supreme Court and the Commission may establish, to represent an indigent prisoner under sentence of death in a state habeas corpus proceeding. The Attorney General shall have no standing to object to the appointment of counsel for the petitioner.

Acts 1991, c. 664; Acts 1995, c. 503; Acts 2001, c. 766, eff. Jan. 1, 2002; Acts 2002, c. 614; Acts 2004, c. 329; Acts 2004, c. 884; Acts 2004, c. 921.

§ 19.2–163.8. List of qualified attorneys

A. The Supreme Court and the Indigent Defense Commission, in conjunction with the Virginia State Bar, shall adopt standards for attorneys admitted to practice law in Virginia who are qualified to represent defendants charged with capital murder or sentenced to death, which take into consideration, to the extent practicable, the following criteria: (i) license or permission to practice law in Virginia; (ii) general background in criminal litigation; (iii) demonstrated experience in felony practice at trial and appeal; (iv) experience in death penalty litigation; (v) familiarity with the requisite court system; (vi) current training in death penalty litigation; (vii) current training in the analysis and introduction of forensic evidence, including deoxyribonucleic acid (DNA) testing and the evidence of a DNA profile comparison to prove or disprove the identity of any person; and (viii) demonstrated proficiency and commitment to quality representation.

B. The Supreme Court and the Indigent Defense Commission shall maintain a list of attorneys admitted to practice law in Virginia who are qualified to represent defendants charged with capital murder or sentenced to death. In establishing such a list, the Court and the Commission shall consider all relevant factors, including but not limited to, the attorney's background, experience, and training and the Court's and the Commission's assessment of whether the attorney is competent to provide quality legal representation.

C. Notwithstanding the requirements of § 19.2–163.7, the judge of the circuit court may appoint counsel who is not included on the list, but who otherwise qualifies under the standards established and maintained by the Court and the Commission.

D. Noncompliance with the requirements of this article shall not form the basis for a claim of error at trial, on appeal, or in any habeas corpus proceeding. The performance of habeas corpus counsel appointed pursuant to this article shall not form a basis for relief in any subsequent habeas corpus proceeding.

E. The Supreme Court and the Indigent Defense Commission shall, in conjunction with the Virginia State Bar, promulgate and thereafter maintain standards for the qualifications of counsel who shall be considered eligible to be placed on the list of qualified attorneys.

Acts 1991, c. 664; Acts 2001, c. 766, eff. Jan. 1, 2002; Acts 2004, c. 884; Acts 2004, c. 921.

ARTICLE 5

INTERPRETERS

§ 19.2–164. Interpreters for non-English-speaking persons (Supreme Court Rule 2:507 derived in part from this section)

In any criminal case in which a non-English-speaking person is the accused, an interpreter for the non-English-speaking person shall be appointed. In any criminal case in which a non-English-speaking person is a victim or witness, an interpreter shall be appointed by the judge of the court in which the case is to be heard unless the court finds that the person does not require the services of a court-appointed interpreter. An English-speaking person fluent in the language of the country of the accused, a victim or a witness shall be appointed by the judge of the court in which the case is to be heard, unless such person obtains an interpreter of his own choosing who is approved by the court as being competent. The compensation of an interpreter appointed by the court pursuant to this section shall be fixed by the court in accordance with guidelines set by the Judicial Council of Virginia and shall be paid from the general fund of the state treasury as part of the expense of trial. Such fee shall not be assessed as part of the costs unless (i) an interpreter has been appointed for the defendant, (ii) the defendant fails to appear, (iii) the interpreter appears in the case and no other case on that date, and (iv) the defendant is convicted of a failure to appear on that date the interpreter appeared in the case, then the court, in its discretion, may assess as costs the fee paid to the interpreter. Whenever a person communicates through an interpreter to any person under such circumstances that the communication would be privileged, and such person could not be compelled to testify as to the communications, this privilege shall also apply to the interpreter. The provisions of this section shall apply in both circuit courts and district courts.

Acts 1975, c. 495; Acts 1978, c. 601; Acts 1982, c. 444; Acts 1985, c. 396; Acts 1995, c. 546; Acts 1996, c. 402; Acts 2003, c. 1011; Acts 2007, c. 383.

§ 19.2–164.1. Interpreters for the deaf (Supreme Court Rule 2:507 derived in part from this section)

In any criminal case in which a deaf person is the accused, an interpreter for the deaf person shall be appointed. In any criminal case in which a deaf person is the victim or a witness, an interpreter for the deaf person shall be appointed by the court in which the case is to be heard unless the court finds that the deaf person does not require the services of a court-appointed interpreter and the deaf person waives his rights. Such interpreter shall be procured by the judge of the court in which the case is to be heard through the Department for the Deaf and Hard-of-Hearing.

The compensation of an interpreter appointed by the court pursuant to this section shall be fixed by the court and paid from the general fund of the state treasury as part of the expense of trial. Such fee shall not be assessed as part of the costs.

Any person entitled to the services of an interpreter under this section may waive these services for all or a portion of the proceedings. Such a waiver shall be made by the person upon the record after an opportunity to consult with legal counsel. A judicial officer, utilizing an interpreter obtained in accordance with this section, shall explain to the deaf person the nature and effect of any waiver. Any waiver shall be approved in writing by the deaf person's legal counsel. If the person does not have legal counsel, approval shall be made in writing by a judicial officer. A person who waives his right to an interpreter may provide his own interpreter at his own expense without regard to whether the interpreter is qualified under this section.

The provisions of this section shall apply in both circuit courts and district courts.

Whenever a person communicates through an interpreter to any person under such circumstances that the communication would be privileged, and such person could not be compelled to testify as to the communications, this privilege shall also apply to the interpreter.

In any judicial proceeding, the judge on his own motion or on the motion of a party to the proceeding may order all of the testimony of a deaf person and the interpretation thereof to be visually electronically recorded for use in verification of the official transcript of the proceedings.

Acts 1982, c. 444; Acts 1985, c. 396; Acts 1995, c. 546; Acts 1996, c. 402.

Article 6

Recording Evidence and Incidents of Trial

§ 19.2–165. Recording evidence and incidents of trial in felony cases; cost of recording; cost of transcripts; certified transcript deemed prima facie correct; request for copy of transcript

In all felony cases, the court or judge trying the case shall by order entered of record provide for the recording verbatim of the evidence and incidents of trial either by a court reporter or by mechanical or electronic devices approved by the court. The expense of reporting or recording the trial of criminal cases shall be paid by the Commonwealth out of the appropriation for criminal charges, upon approval of the trial judge. However, if the defendant is convicted, the Commonwealth shall be entitled to receive the amount allocated to the court reporter fund under the fixed felony fee. Localities that maintain mechanical or electronic devices for this purpose shall be entitled to retain their reasonable expenses attributable to the cost of operating and maintaining such equipment. The clerk shall receive the evidence at the time of admission of such evidence by the court and shall maintain control over such evidence until the time such evidence is transferred on appeal, or destroyed or returned in accordance with law.

In all felony cases where it appears to the court from the affidavit of the defendant and other evidence that the defendant intends to seek an appeal and is financially unable to pay such costs or to bear the expense of a copy of the transcript of the evidence for an appeal, the trial court shall, upon the motion of counsel for the defendant, order the evidence transcribed for such appeal and all costs therefor paid by the Commonwealth out of the appropriation for criminal charges. If the conviction is not reversed, all costs paid by the Commonwealth, under the provisions hereof, shall be assessed against the defendant.

The reporter or other individual designated to report and record the trial shall file the original shorthand notes or other original records with the clerk of the circuit court who shall preserve them in the public records of the court for not less than five years if an appeal was taken and a transcript was prepared, or ten years if no appeal was taken. The transcript in any case certified by the reporter or other individual designated to report and record the trial shall be deemed prima facie a correct statement of the evidence and incidents of trial.

Upon the request of any counsel of record, or of any party not represented by counsel, and upon payment of the reasonable cost thereof, the court reporter covering any proceeding shall provide the requesting party with a copy of the transcript of such proceeding or any requested portion thereof.

The court shall not direct the court reporter to cease recording any portion of the proceeding without the consent of all parties or of their counsel of record.

The administration of this section shall be under the direction of the Supreme Court of Virginia.

Acts 1975, c. 495; Acts 1975, c. 640; Acts 1983, c. 505; Acts 1984, c. 752; Acts 1994, c. 497; Acts 1999, c. 9. Amended by Acts 2014, c. 291.

§ 19.2–165.1. Payment of medical fees in certain criminal cases; reimbursement

A. Except as provided in subsection B, all medical fees expended in the gathering of evidence for all criminal cases where medical evidence is necessary to establish a crime has occurred and for cases involving abuse of children under the age of 18 shall be paid by the Commonwealth out of the appropriation for criminal charges, provided that any medical evaluation, examination, or service rendered be performed by a physician or facility specifically designated by the attorney for the Commonwealth in the city or county having jurisdiction of such case for such a purpose. If no such physician or facility is reasonably available in such city or county, then the attorney for the Commonwealth may designate a physician or facility located outside and adjacent to such city or county.

Where there has been no prior designation of such a physician or facility, such medical fees shall be paid out of the appropriation for criminal charges upon authorization by the attorney for the Commonwealth of the city or county having jurisdiction over the case. Such authorization may be granted prior to or within 48 hours after the medical evaluation, examination, or service rendered.

B. All medical fees expended in the gathering of evidence through physical evidence recovery kit examinations conducted on victims complaining of sexual assault under Article 7 (§ 18.2–61 et seq.) of Chapter 4 of Title 18.2 shall be paid by the Commonwealth pursuant to subsection F of § 19.2–368.11:1. Victims complaining of sexual assault shall not be required to participate in the criminal justice system or cooperate with law-enforcement authorities in order to be provided with such forensic medical exams.

C. Upon conviction of the defendant in any case requiring the payment of medical fees authorized by this section, the court shall order that the defendant reimburse the Commonwealth for payment of such fees.

Acts 1976, c. 292; Acts 1982, c. 507; Acts 1987, c. 330; Acts 1997, c. 322; Acts 1999, c. 853; Acts 2000, c. 292; Acts 2003, c. 28; Acts 2003, c. 772. Amended by Acts 2008, c. 203; Acts 2008, c. 251.

§ 19.2–166. Court reporters

Each judge of a court of record having jurisdiction over criminal proceedings shall be authorized, in all felony cases and habeas corpus proceedings to appoint a court reporter to report proceedings or to operate mechanical or electrical devices for recording proceedings, to transcribe the report or record of such proceedings, to perform any stenographic work related to such report, record or transcript including work pertinent to the court's findings of fact and conclusions of law pertinent thereto. Such reporter shall be paid by the Commonwealth on a per diem or work basis as appropriate out of the appropriation for criminal charges.

Acts 1975, c. 495; Acts 2003, c. 140.

CHAPTER 11

PROCEEDINGS ON QUESTION OF INSANITY

§ 19.2–167. Accused not to be tried while insane or feebleminded

No person shall, while he is insane or feebleminded, be tried for a criminal offense.

Acts 1975, c. 495.

§ 19.2–168. Notice to Commonwealth of intention to present evidence of insanity; continuance if notice not given

In any case in which a person charged with a crime intends (i) to put in issue his sanity at the time of the crime charged and (ii) to present testimony of an expert to support his claim on this issue at his trial, he, or his counsel, shall give notice in writing to the attorney for the Commonwealth, at least 60 days prior to his trial, of his intention to present such evidence. However, if the period between indictment and trial is less than 120 days, the person or his counsel shall give such notice no later than 60 days following indictment. In the event that such notice is not given, and the person proffers such evidence at his trial as a defense, then the court may in its discretion, either allow the Commonwealth a continuance or, under appropriate circumstances, bar the defendant from presenting such evidence. The period of any such continuance shall not be counted for speedy trial purposes under § 19.2–243.

Acts 1975, c. 495; Acts 1986, c. 535. Amended by Acts 2008, c. 372.

§ 19.2–168.1. Evaluation on motion of the Commonwealth after notice

A. If the attorney for the defendant gives notice pursuant to § 19.2–168, and the Commonwealth thereafter seeks an evaluation of the defendant's sanity at the time of the offense, the court shall appoint one or more qualified mental health experts to perform such an evaluation. The court shall order the defendant to submit to such an evaluation and advise the defendant on the record in court that a refusal to cooperate with the Commonwealth's expert could result in exclusion of the defendant's expert evidence. The qualification of the experts shall be governed by subsection A of § 19.2–169.5. The location of the evaluation shall be governed by subsection B of § 19.2–169.5. The attorney for the Commonwealth shall be responsible for providing the experts the information specified in subsection C of § 19.2–169.5. After performing their evaluation, the experts shall report their findings and opinions, and provide copies of psychiatric, psychological, medical or other records obtained during the course of the evaluation to the attorneys for the Commonwealth and the defense.

B. If the court finds, after hearing evidence presented by the parties, that the defendant has refused to cooperate with an evaluation requested by the Commonwealth, it may admit evidence of such refusal or, in the discretion of the court, bar the defendant from presenting expert psychiatric or psychological evidence at trial on the issue of his sanity at the time of the offense.

Acts 1982, c. 653; Acts 1986, c. 535.

§ 19.2–169. Repealed by Acts 1982, c. 653

§ 19.2–169.1. Raising question of competency to stand trial or plead; evaluation and determination of competency

A. Raising competency issue; appointment of evaluators.—If, at any time after the attorney for the defendant has been retained or appointed and before the end of trial, the court finds, upon hearing evidence or representations of counsel for the defendant or the attorney for the Commonwealth, that there is probable cause to believe that the defendant, whether a juvenile transferred pursuant to § 16.1–269.1 or adult, lacks substantial capacity to understand the proceedings against him or to assist his attorney in his own defense, the court shall order that a competency evaluation be performed by at least one psychiatrist or clinical psychologist who is qualified by training and experience in forensic evaluation.

B. Location of evaluation.—The evaluation shall be performed on an outpatient basis at a mental health facility or in jail unless the court specifically finds that outpatient evaluation services are unavailable or unless the results of outpatient evaluation indicate that hospitalization of the defendant for evaluation on competency is necessary. If the court finds that hospitalization is necessary, the court, under authority of this subsection, may order the defendant sent to a hospital designated by the Commissioner of Behavioral Health and Developmental Services as appropriate for evaluations of persons under criminal charge. The defendant shall be hospitalized for such time as the director of the hospital deems necessary to perform an adequate evaluation of the defendant's competency, but not to exceed 30 days from the date of admission to the hospital.

C. Provision of information to evaluators.—The court shall require the attorney for the Commonwealth to provide to the evaluators appointed under subsection A any information relevant to the evaluation, including, but not limited to (i) a copy of the warrant or indictment; (ii) the names and addresses of the attorney for the Commonwealth, the attorney for the defendant, and the judge ordering the evaluation; (iii) information about the alleged crime; and (iv) a summary of the reasons for the evaluation request. The court shall require the attorney for the defendant to provide any available psychiatric records and other information that is deemed relevant. The court shall require that information be provided to the evaluator within 96 hours of the issuance of the court order pursuant to this section.

D. The competency report.—Upon completion of the evaluation, the evaluators shall promptly submit a report in writing to the court and the attorneys of record concerning (i) the defendant's capacity to understand the proceedings against him; (ii) his ability to assist his attorney; and (iii) his need for treatment in the event he is found incompetent but restorable, or incompetent for the foreseeable future. If a need for restoration treatment is identified pursuant to clause (iii), the report shall state whether inpatient or outpatient treatment is recommended. No statements of the defendant relating to the time period of the alleged offense shall be included in the report.

E. The competency determination.—After receiving the report described in subsection D, the court shall promptly determine whether the defendant is competent to stand trial. A hearing on the defendant's competency is not required unless one is requested by the attorney for the Commonwealth or the attorney for the defendant, or unless the court has reasonable cause to believe the defendant will be hospitalized under § 19.2–169.2. If a hearing is held, the party alleging that the defendant is incompetent shall bear the burden of proving by a preponderance of the evidence the defendant's incompetency. The defendant shall have the right to notice of the hearing, the right to counsel at the hearing and the right to personally participate in and introduce evidence at the hearing.

The fact that the defendant claims to be unable to remember the time period surrounding the alleged offense shall not, by itself, bar a finding of competency if the defendant otherwise understands the charges against him and can assist in his defense. Nor shall the fact that the defendant is under the influence of medication bar a finding of competency if the defendant is able to understand the charges against him and assist in his defense while medicated.

Acts 1982, c. 653; Acts 1983, c. 373; Acts 1985, c. 307; Acts 2003, c. 735; Acts 2007, c. 781. Amended by Acts 2009, c. 813; Acts 2009, c. 840; Acts 2014, c. 329; Acts 2014, c. 739.

§ 19.2–169.2. Disposition when defendant found incompetent

A. Upon finding pursuant to subsection E of § 19.2–169.1 that the defendant, including a juvenile transferred pursuant to § 16.1–269.1, is incompetent, the court shall order that the defendant receive treatment to restore his competency on an outpatient basis or, if the court specifically finds that the defendant requires inpatient hospital treatment, at a hospital designated by the Commissioner of Behavioral Health and Developmental Services as appropriate for treatment of persons under criminal charge. Any psychiatric records and other information that have been deemed relevant and submitted by the attorney for the defendant pursuant to subsection C of § 19.2–169.1 and any reports submitted pursuant to subsection D of § 19.2–169.1 shall be made available to the director of the community services board or behavioral health authority or his designee or to the director of the treating inpatient facility or his designee within 96 hours of the issuance of the court order requiring treatment to restore the defendant's competency. If the 96–hour period expires on a Saturday, Sunday, or other legal holiday, the 96 hours shall be extended to the next day that is not a Saturday, Sunday, or legal holiday.

B. If, at any time after the defendant is ordered to undergo treatment under subsection A of this section, the director of the community services board or behavioral health authority or his designee or the director of the treating inpatient facility or his designee believes the defendant's competency is restored, the director or his designee shall immediately send a report to the court as prescribed in subsection D of § 19.2–169.1. The court shall make a ruling on the defendant's competency according to the procedures specified in subsection E of § 19.2–169.1.

C. The clerk of court shall certify and forward forthwith to the Central Criminal Records Exchange, on a form provided by the Exchange, a copy of an order for treatment issued pursuant to subsection A.

Acts 1982, c. 653; Acts 2003, c. 735; Acts 2007, c. 781. Amended by Acts 2008, c. 751; Acts 2008, c. 788; Acts 2009, c. 813; Acts 2009, c. 840; Acts 2014, c. 373; Acts 2014, c. 408.

§ 19.2–169.3. Disposition of the unrestorably incompetent defendant; capital murder charge; sexually violent offense charge

A. If, at any time after the defendant is ordered to undergo treatment pursuant to subsection A of § 19.2–169.2, the director of the community services board or behavioral health authority or his designee or the director of the treating inpatient facility or his designee concludes that the defendant is likely to remain incompetent for the foreseeable future, he shall send a report to the court so stating. The report shall also indicate whether, in the board, authority, or inpatient facility director's or his designee's opinion, the defendant should be released, committed pursuant to Article 5 (§ 37.2–814 et seq.) of Chapter 8 of Title 37.2, committed pursuant to Chapter 9 (§ 37.2–900 et seq.) of Title 37.2, or certified pursuant to § 37.2–806 in the event he is found to be unrestorably incompetent. Upon receipt of the report, the court shall make a competency determination according to the procedures specified in subsection E of § 19.2–169.1. If the court finds that the defendant is incompetent and is likely to remain so for the foreseeable future, it shall order that he be (i) released, (ii) committed pursuant to Article 5 (§ 37.2–814 et seq.) of Chapter 8 of Title 37.2, or (iii) certified pursuant to § 37.2–806. However, if the court finds that the defendant is incompetent and is likely to remain so for the foreseeable future and the defendant has been charged with a sexually violent offense, as defined in § 37.2–900, he shall be screened pursuant to the procedures set forth in §§ 37.2–903 and 37.2–904. If the court finds the defendant incompetent but restorable to competency in the foreseeable future, it may order treatment continued until six months have elapsed from the date of the defendant's initial admission under subsection A of § 19.2–169.2.

B. At the end of six months from the date of the defendant's initial admission under subsection A of § 19.2–169.2 if the defendant remains incompetent in the opinion of the board, authority, or inpatient facility director or his designee, the director or his designee shall so notify the court and make recommendations concerning disposition of the defendant as described in subsection A. The court shall hold a hearing according to the procedures specified in subsection E of § 19.2–169.1 and, if it finds the defendant unrestorably incompetent, shall order one of the dispositions described in subsection A. If the court finds the defendant incompetent but restorable to competency, it may order continued treatment under subsection A of § 19.2–169.2 for additional six-month periods, provided a hearing pursuant to subsection E of § 19.2–169.1 is held at the completion of each such period and the defendant continues to be incompetent but restorable to competency in the foreseeable future.

C. If any defendant has been charged with a misdemeanor in violation of Article 3 (§ 18.2–95 et seq.) of Chapter 5 of Title 18.2 or Article 5 (§ 18.2–119 et seq.) of Chapter 5 of Title 18.2, other than a misdemeanor charge pursuant to § 18.2–130 or Article 2 (§ 18.2–415 et seq.) of Chapter 9 of Title 18.2, and is being treated pursuant to subsection A of § 19.2–169.2, and after 45 days has not been restored to competency, the director of the community service board, behavioral health authority, or the director of the treating inpatient facility, or any of their designees, shall send a report indicating the defendant's status to the court. The report shall also indicate whether the defendant should be released or committed pursuant to § 37.2–817 or certified pursuant to § 37.2–806. Upon receipt of the report, if the court determines that the defendant is still incompetent, the court shall order that the defendant be released, committed, or certified, and may dismiss the charges against the defendant.

D. Unless an incompetent defendant is charged with capital murder or the charges against an incompetent criminal defendant have been previously dismissed, charges against an unrestorably incompetent defendant shall be dismissed on the date upon which his sentence would have expired had he been convicted and received the maximum sentence for the crime charged, or on the date five years from the date of his arrest for such charges, whichever is sooner.

E. If the court orders an unrestorably incompetent defendant to be screened pursuant to the procedures set forth in §§ 37.2–903 and 37.2–904, it shall order the attorney for the Commonwealth in the jurisdiction wherein the defendant was charged and the Commissioner of Behavioral Health and Developmental Services to provide the Director of the Department of Corrections with any information relevant to the review, including, but not limited to: (i) a copy of the warrant or indictment, (ii) a copy of the defendant's criminal record, (iii) information about the alleged crime, (iv) a copy of the competency report completed pursuant to § 19.2–169.1, and (v) a copy of the report prepared by the director of the defendant's community services board, behavioral health authority, or treating inpatient facility or his designee pursuant to this section. The court shall further order that the defendant be held in the custody of the Department of Behavioral Health and Developmental Services for secure confinement and treatment until the Commitment Review Committee's and Attorney General's review and any subsequent hearing or trial are completed. If the court receives notice that the Attorney General has declined to file a petition for the commitment of an unrestorably incompetent defendant as a sexually violent predator after conducting a review pursuant to § 37.2–905, the court shall order that the defendant be released, committed pursuant to Article 5 (§ 37.2–814 et seq.) of Chapter 8 of Title 37.2, or certified pursuant to § 37.2–806.

F. In any case when an incompetent defendant is charged with capital murder, notwithstanding any other provision of this section, the charge shall not be dismissed and the court having jurisdiction over the capital murder case may order that the defendant receive continued treatment under subsection A of § 19.2–169.2 for additional six-month periods without limitation, provided that (i) a hearing pursuant to subsection E of § 19.2–169.1 is held at the completion of each such period, (ii) the defendant remains incompetent, (iii) the court finds continued treatment to be medically appropriate, and (iv) the defendant presents a danger to himself or others.

G. The attorney for the Commonwealth may bring charges that have been dismissed against the defendant when he is restored to competency.

Acts 1982, c. 653; Acts 1999, c. 946, eff. April 2, 2003; Acts 1999, c. 985, eff. April 2, 2003; Acts 2003, c. 915; Acts 2003, c. 919; Acts 2006, c. 863; Acts 2006, c. 914; Acts 2007, c. 781; Acts 2007, c. 876. Amended by Acts 2008, c. 406; Acts 2008, c. 796; Acts 2009, c. 813; Acts 2009, c. 840; Acts 2012, c. 668, eff. Jan. 1, 2013; Acts 2012, c. 800, eff. Jan. 1, 2013.

§ 19.2–169.4. Litigating certain issues when the defendant is incompetent

A finding of incompetency does not preclude the adjudication, at any time before trial, of a motion objecting to the sufficiency of the indictment, nor does it preclude the adjudication of similar legal objections which, in the court's opinion, may be undertaken without the personal participation of the defendant.

Acts 1982, c. 653.

§ 19.2–169.5. Evaluation of sanity at the time of the offense; disclosure of evaluation results

A. Raising issue of sanity at the time of offense; appointment of evaluators.—If, at any time before trial, the court finds, upon hearing evidence or representations of counsel for the defendant, that there is probable cause to believe that the defendant's sanity will be a significant factor in his defense and that the defendant is financially unable to pay for expert assistance, the court shall appoint one or more qualified mental health experts to evaluate the defendant's sanity at the time of the offense and, where appropriate, to assist in the development of an insanity defense. Such mental health expert shall be (i) a psychiatrist, a clinical psychologist, or an individual with a doctorate degree in clinical psychology who has successfully completed forensic evaluation training as approved by the Commissioner of Behavioral Health and Developmental Services and (ii) qualified by specialized training and experience to perform forensic evaluations.

The defendant shall not be entitled to a mental health expert of his own choosing or to funds to employ such expert.

B. Location of evaluation.—The evaluation shall be performed on an outpatient basis, at a mental health facility or in jail, unless the court specifically finds that outpatient services are unavailable, or unless the results of the outpatient evaluation indicate that hospitalization of the defendant for further evaluation of his sanity at the time of the offense is necessary. If either finding is made, the court, under authority of this subsection, may order that the defendant be sent to a hospital designated by the Commissioner of Behavioral Health and Developmental Services as appropriate for evaluation of the defendant under criminal charge. The defendant shall be hospitalized for such time as the director of the hospital deems necessary to perform an adequate evaluation of the defendant's sanity at the time of the offense, but not to exceed 30 days from the date of admission to the hospital.

C. Provision of information to evaluator.—The court shall require the party making the motion for the evaluation, and such other parties as the court deems appropriate, to provide to the evaluators appointed under subsection A any information relevant to the evaluation, including, but not limited to (i) copy of the warrant or indictment; (ii) the names and addresses of the attorney for the Commonwealth, the attorney for the defendant and the judge who appointed the expert; (iii) information pertaining to the alleged crime, including statements by the defendant made to the police and transcripts of preliminary hearings, if any; (iv) a summary of the reasons for the evaluation request; (v) any available psychiatric, psychological, medical or social records that are deemed relevant; and (vi) a copy of the defendant's criminal record, to the extent reasonably available.

D. The evaluators shall prepare a full report concerning the defendant's sanity at the time of the offense, including whether he may have had a significant mental disease or defect which rendered him insane at the time of the offense. The report shall be prepared within the time period designated by the court, said period to include the time necessary to obtain and evaluate the information specified in subsection C.

E. Disclosure of evaluation results.—The report described in subsection D shall be sent solely to the attorney for the defendant and shall be deemed to be protected by the lawyer-client privilege. However, the Commonwealth shall be given the report in all felony cases, the results of any other evaluation of the defendant's sanity at the time of the offense, and copies of psychiatric, psychological, medical, or other records obtained during the course of any such evaluation, after the attorney for the defendant gives notice of an intent to present psychiatric or psychological evidence pursuant to § 19.2–168.

F. In any case where the defendant obtains his own expert to evaluate the defendant's sanity at the time of the offense, the provisions of subsections D and E, relating to the disclosure of the evaluation results, shall apply.

Acts 1982, c. 653; Acts 1986, c. 535; Acts 1987, c. 439; Acts 1996, c. 937; Acts 1996, c. 980; Acts 2005, c. 428. Amended by Acts 2009, c. 813; Acts 2009, c. 840.

§ 19.2–169.6. Inpatient psychiatric hospital admission from local correctional facility

A. Any inmate of a local correctional facility who is not subject to the provisions of § 19.2–169.2 may be hospitalized for psychiatric treatment at a hospital designated by the Commissioner of Behavioral Health and Developmental Services as appropriate for treatment of persons under criminal charge if:

1. The court with jurisdiction over the inmate's case, if it is still pending, on the petition of the person having custody over an inmate or on its own motion, holds a hearing at which the inmate is represented by counsel and finds by clear and convincing evidence that (i) the inmate has a mental illness; (ii) there exists a substantial likelihood that, as a result of a mental illness, the inmate will, in the near future, (a) cause serious physical harm to himself or others as evidenced by recent behavior causing, attempting, or threatening harm and any other relevant information or (b) suffer serious harm due to his lack of capacity to protect himself from harm as evidenced by recent behavior and any other relevant information; and (iii) the inmate requires treatment in a hospital rather than the local correctional facility. Prior to making this determination, the court shall consider the examination conducted in accordance with § 37.2–815 and the preadmission screening report prepared in accordance with § 37.2–816 and conducted in-person or by means of a two-way electronic video and audio communication system as authorized in § 37.2–804.1 by an employee or designee of the local community services board or behavioral health authority who is skilled in the assessment and treatment of mental illness, who is not providing treatment to the inmate, and who has completed a certification program approved by the Department of Behavioral Health and Developmental Services as provided in § 37.2–809. The examiner appointed pursuant to § 37.2–815, if not physically present at the hearing, shall be available whenever possible for questioning during the hearing through a two-way electronic video and audio or telephonic communication system as authorized in § 37.2–804.1. Any employee or designee of the local community services board or behavioral health authority, as defined in § 37.2–809, representing the board or authority that prepared the preadmission screening report shall attend the hearing in person or, if physical attendance is not practicable, shall participate in the hearing through a two-way electronic video and audio communication system as authorized in § 37.2–804.1. When the hearing is held outside the

service area of the community services board or behavioral health authority that prepared the preadmission screening report, and it is not practicable for a representative of the board or authority to attend or participate in the hearing, arrangements shall be made by the board or authority for an employee or designee of the board or authority serving the area in which the hearing is held to attend or participate on behalf of the board or authority that prepared the preadmission screening report; or

2. Upon petition by the person having custody over an inmate, a magistrate finds probable cause to believe that (i) the inmate has a mental illness; (ii) there exists a substantial likelihood that, as a result of a mental illness, the inmate will, in the near future, (a) cause serious physical harm to himself or others as evidenced by recent behavior causing, attempting, or threatening harm and any other relevant information or (b) suffer serious harm due to his lack of capacity to protect himself from harm as evidenced by recent behavior and any other relevant information; and (iii) the inmate requires treatment in a hospital rather than a local correctional facility, and the magistrate issues a temporary detention order for the inmate. Prior to the filing of the petition, the person having custody shall arrange for an evaluation of the inmate conducted in-person or by means of a two-way electronic video and audio communication system as authorized in § 37.2–804.1 by an employee or designee of the local community services board or behavioral health authority who is skilled in the assessment and treatment of mental illness and who has completed a certification program approved by the Department as provided in § 37.2–809. After considering the evaluation of the employee or designee of the local community services board or behavioral health authority, and any other information presented, and finding that probable cause exists to meet the criteria, the magistrate may issue a temporary detention order in accordance with the applicable procedures specified in §§ 37.2–809 through 37.2–813. The person having custody over the inmate shall notify the court having jurisdiction over the inmate's case, if it is still pending, and the inmate's attorney prior to the detention pursuant to a temporary detention order or as soon thereafter as is reasonable.

Upon detention pursuant to this subdivision, a hearing shall be held either before the court having jurisdiction over the inmate's case or before a district court judge or a special justice, as defined in § 37.2–100, in accordance with the provisions of §§ 37.2–815 through 37.2–821, in which case the inmate shall be represented by counsel as specified in § 37.2–814. The hearing shall be held within 72 hours of execution of the temporary detention order issued pursuant to this subdivision. If the 72–hour period terminates on a Saturday, Sunday, legal holiday, or day on which the court is lawfully closed, the inmate may be detained until the close of business on the next day that is not a Saturday, Sunday, legal holiday, or day on which the court is lawfully closed. Any employee or designee of the local community services board or behavioral health authority, as defined in § 37.2–809, representing the board or authority that prepared the preadmission screening report shall attend the hearing in person or, if physical attendance is not practicable, shall participate in the hearing through a two-way electronic video and audio communication system as authorized in § 37.2–804.1. When the hearing is held outside the service area of the community services board or behavioral health authority that prepared the preadmission screening report, and it is not practicable for a representative of the board or authority to attend or participate in the hearing, arrangements shall be made by the board or authority for an employee or designee of the board or authority serving the area in which the hearing is held to attend or participate on behalf of the board or authority that prepared the preadmission screening report. The judge or special justice conducting the hearing may order the inmate hospitalized if, after considering the examination conducted in accordance with § 37.2–815, the preadmission screening report prepared in accordance with § 37.2–816, and any other available information as specified in subsection C of § 37.2–817, he finds by clear and convincing evidence that (1) the inmate has a mental illness; (2) there exists a substantial likelihood that, as a result of a mental illness, the inmate will, in the near future, (a) cause serious physical harm to himself or others as evidenced by recent behavior causing, attempting, or threatening harm and any other relevant information or (b) suffer serious harm due to his lack of capacity to protect himself from harm as evidenced by recent behavior and any other relevant information; and (3) the inmate requires treatment in a hospital rather than a local correctional facility. The examiner appointed pursuant to § 37.2–815, if not physically present at the hearing, shall be available whenever possible for questioning during the hearing through a two-way electronic video and audio or telephonic communication system as authorized in § 37.2–804.1. The examination and the preadmission screening report shall be admitted into evidence at the hearing.

B. In no event shall an inmate have the right to make application for voluntary admission as may be otherwise provided in § 37.2–805 or 37.2–814 or be subject to an order for mandatory outpatient treatment as provided in § 37.2–817.

C. If an inmate is hospitalized pursuant to this section and his criminal case is still pending, the court having jurisdiction over the inmate's case may order that the admitting hospital evaluate the inmate's competency to stand trial and his mental state at the time of the offense pursuant to §§ 19.2–169.1 and 19.2–169.5.

D. An inmate may not be hospitalized longer than 30 days under subsection A unless the court which has criminal jurisdiction over him or a district court judge or a special justice, as defined in § 37.2–100, holds a hearing and orders the inmate's continued hospitalization in accordance with the provisions of subdivision A 2. If the inmate's hospitalization is continued under this subsection by a court other than the court which has jurisdiction over his criminal case, the facility at which the inmate is hospitalized shall notify the court with jurisdiction over his criminal case and the inmate's attorney in the criminal case, if the case is still pending.

E. Hospitalization may be extended in accordance with subsection D for periods of 60 days for inmates awaiting trial, but in no event may such hospitalization be continued beyond trial, nor shall such hospitalization act to delay trial, as long as the inmate remains competent to stand trial. Hospitalization may be extended in accordance with subsection D for periods of 180 days for an inmate who has been convicted and not yet sentenced, or for an inmate who has been convicted of a crime and is in the custody of a local correctional facility after sentencing, but in no event may such hospitalization be continued beyond the date upon which his sentence would have expired had he received the maximum sentence for the crime charged. Any inmate who has not completed service of his sentence upon discharge from the hospital shall serve the remainder of his sentence.

F. For any inmate who has been convicted and not yet sentenced, or who has been convicted of a crime and is in the custody of a local correctional facility after sentencing, the time the inmate is confined in a hospital for psychiatric treatment shall be deducted from any term for which he may be sentenced to any penal institution, reformatory or elsewhere.

G. Any health care provider, as defined in § 32.1–127.1:03, or other provider rendering services to an inmate who is the subject of a proceeding under this section, upon request, shall disclose to a magistrate, the court, the inmate's attorney, the inmate's guardian ad litem, the examiner appointed pursuant to § 37.2–815, the community service board or behavioral health authority preparing the preadmission screening pursuant to § 37.2–816, or the sheriff or administrator of the local correctional facility any and all information that is necessary and appropriate to enable each of them to perform his duties under this section. These health care providers and other service providers shall disclose to one another health records and information where necessary to provide care and treatment to the inmate and to monitor that care and treatment. Health records disclosed to a sheriff or administrator of the local correctional facility shall be limited to information necessary to protect the sheriff or administrator of the local correctional facility and his employees, the inmate, or the public from physical injury or to address the health care needs of the inmate. Information disclosed to a law-enforcement officer shall not be used for any other purpose, disclosed to others, or retained.

Any health care provider disclosing records pursuant to this section shall be immune from civil liability for any harm resulting from the disclosure, including any liability under the federal Health Insurance Portability and Accountability Act (42 U.S.C. § 1320d et seq.), as amended, unless the person or provider disclosing such records intended the harm or acted in bad faith.

H. Any order entered where an inmate is the subject of proceedings under this section shall provide for the disclosure of medical records pursuant to subsection G. This subsection shall not preclude any other disclosures as required or permitted by law.

Acts 1975, c. 495; Acts 1986, c. 629; Acts 1987, c. 96; Acts 1990, c. 76; Acts 1995, c. 844; Acts 2005, c. 716, eff. Oct. 1, 2005. Amended by Acts 2008, c. 779; Acts 2008, c. 782; Acts 2008, c. 850; Acts 2008, c. 870; Acts 2010, c. 340; Acts 2010, c. 406; Acts 2012, c. 801; Acts 2014, c. 499; Acts 2014, c. 538; Acts 2014, c. 691.

§ 19.2–169.7. Disclosure by defendant during evaluation or treatment; use at guilt phase of trial

No statement or disclosure by the defendant concerning the alleged offense made during a competency evaluation ordered pursuant to § 19.2–169.1, a mental state at the time of the offense evaluation ordered pursuant to § 19.2–169.5, or treatment ordered pursuant to § 19.2–169.2 or § 19.2–169.6 may be used against the defendant at trial as evidence or as a basis for such evidence, except on the issue of his mental condition at the time of the offense after he raises the issue pursuant to § 19.2–168.

Acts 1982, c. 653.

§§ 19.2–170 to 19.2–174. Repealed by Acts 1982, c. 653

§ 19.2–174.1. Information required prior to admission to a mental health facility

Prior to any person being placed into the custody of the Commissioner for evaluation or treatment pursuant to §§ 19.2–169.2, 19.2–169.3, 19.2–169.6, 19.2–182.2, and 19.2–182.3, and Chapter 9 (§ 37.2–900 et seq.) of Title 37.2, the court or special justice shall provide the Commissioner with the following, if available: (i) the commitment order, (ii) the names and addresses for the attorney for the Commonwealth, the attorney for the person and the judge holding jurisdiction over the person, (iii) a copy of the warrant or indictment, and (iv) a copy of the criminal incident information as defined in § 2.2–3706 or a copy of the arrest report or a summary of the facts relating to the crime. The party requesting the placement into the Commissioner's custody or, in the case of admissions pursuant to §§ 19.2–169.3 and 19.2–169.6, and Chapter 9 (§ 37.2–900 et seq.) of Title 37. 2, the person having custody over the defendant or inmate shall gather the above information for submission to the court at the hearing. If the information is not available at the hearing, it shall be provided by the party requesting placement or the person having custody directly to the Commissioner within 96 hours of the person being placed into the Commissioner's custody. If the 96–hour period expires on a Saturday, Sunday or legal holiday, the 96 hours shall be extended to the next day that is not a Saturday, Sunday or legal holiday.

Acts 1995, c. 645; Acts 1999, c. 946, eff. April 2, 2003; Acts 1999, c. 985, eff. April 2, 2003; Acts 2001, c. 837. Amended by Acts 2010, c. 340; Acts 2010, c. 406.

§ 19.2–175. Compensation of experts

Each psychiatrist, clinical psychologist or other expert appointed by the court to render professional service pursuant to § 19.2–168.1, 19.2–169.1, 19.2–169.5, 19.2–182.8, 19.2–182.9, 19.2–264.3:1, 19.2–264.3:3 or 19.2–301, who is not regularly employed by the Commonwealth of Virginia except by the University of Virginia School of Medicine and the Medical College of Virginia Commonwealth University, shall receive a reasonable fee for such service. For any psychiatrist, clinical psychologist, or other expert appointed by the court to render such professional services who is regularly employed by the Commonwealth of Virginia, except by the University of Virginia School of Medicine or the Medical College of Virginia Commonwealth University, the fee shall be paid only for professional services provided during nonstate hours that have been approved by his employing agency as being beyond the scope of his state employment duties. The fee shall be determined in each instance by the court that appointed the expert, in accordance with guidelines established by the Supreme Court after consultation with the Department of Behavioral Health and Developmental Services. Except in capital murder cases the fee shall not exceed $750, but in addition if any such expert is required to appear as a witness in any hearing held pursuant to such sections, he shall receive mileage and a fee of $100 for each day during which he is required so to serve. An itemized account of expense, duly sworn to, must be presented to the court, and when allowed shall be certified to the Supreme Court for payment out of the state treasury, and be charged against the appropriations made to pay criminal charges. Allowance for the fee and for the per diem authorized shall also be made by order of the court, duly certified to the Supreme Court for payment out of the appropriation to pay criminal charges.

Acts 1975, c. 495; Acts 1976, c. 677; Acts 1978, c. 195; Acts 1978, c. 794; Acts 1979, 516; Acts 1982, c. 653; Acts 1986, c. 535; Acts 1990, c. 697; Acts 1995, c. 645; Acts 2003, c. 1031, eff. April 29, 2003; Acts 2003, c. 1040, eff. May 1, 2003; Acts 2006, c. 114; Acts 2006, c. 170; Acts 2007, c. 829. Amended by Acts 2009, c. 813; Acts 2009, c. 840; Acts 2010, c. 340; Acts 2010, c. 406.

§ 19.2–176. Repealed by Acts 2010, cc. 340 and 406

§ 19.2–177. Repealed by Acts 1988, c. 787; Acts 1988, c. 873

§ 19.2–177.1. Repealed by Acts 2010, cc. 340 and 406

§ 19.2–178. Where prisoner kept when no vacancy in facility or hospital

When a court shall have entered any of the orders provided for in § 19.2–168.1, 19.2–169.1, 19.2–169.5, or 19.2–169.6, the sheriff of the county or city or the proper officer of the penal institution shall immediately proceed to ascertain whether a vacancy exists at the proper facility or hospital and until it is ascertained that there is a vacancy such person shall be kept in the jail of such county or city or in such custody as the court may order, or in the penal institution in which he is confined, until there is room in such facility or hospital. Any person whose care and custody is herein provided for shall be taken to and from the facility or hospital to which he was committed by an officer of the penal institution having custody of him, or by the sheriff of the county or city whose court issued the order of commitment, and the expenses incurred in such removals shall be paid by such penal institution, county or city.

Acts 1975, c. 495; Acts 1995, c. 645. Amended by Acts 2010, c. 340; Acts 2010, c. 406.

§ 19.2–179. Repealed by Acts 1981, c. 310

§ 19.2–180. Sentence or trial of prisoner when restored to sanity

When a prisoner whose trial or sentence was suspended by reason of his being found to be insane or feebleminded, has been found to be mentally competent and is brought from a hospital and committed to jail, if already convicted, he shall be sentenced, and if not, the court shall proceed to try him as if no delay had occurred on account of his insanity or feeblemindedness.

Acts 1975, c. 495.

§ 19.2–181. Repealed by Acts 1991, c. 427

§ 19.2–182. Representation by counsel in proceeding for commitment

A. In any proceeding for commitment under this title, the judge before whom or upon whose order the proceeding is being held, shall ascertain if the person whose commitment is sought is represented by counsel. If the person is not represented by counsel, the judge shall appoint an attorney at law to represent him in the proceeding. The attorney shall receive a fee of twenty-five dollars for his services, to be paid by the Commonwealth.

B. Any attorney representing any person in any proceeding for commitment under this title shall, prior to such proceeding, personally consult with such person.

Acts 1975, c. 495; Acts 1991, c. 427.

§ 19.2–182.1. Repealed by Acts 1982, c. 653

CHAPTER 11.1

DISPOSITION OF PERSONS ACQUITTED BY REASON OF INSANITY

§ 19.2–182.2. Verdict of acquittal by reason of insanity to state the fact; temporary custody and evaluation

When the defense is insanity of the defendant at the time the offense was committed, the jurors shall be instructed, if they acquit him on that ground, to state the fact with their verdict. The court shall place the person so acquitted (the acquittee) in temporary custody of the Commissioner of Behavioral Health and Developmental Services (hereinafter referred to in this chapter as the Commissioner) for evaluation as to whether the acquittee may be released with or without conditions or requires commitment. The evaluation shall be conducted by (i) one psychiatrist and (ii) one clinical psychologist. The psychiatrist or clinical psychologist shall be skilled in the diagnosis of mental illness and intellectual disability and qualified by training and experience to perform such evaluations. The Commissioner shall appoint both evaluators, at least one of whom shall not be employed by the hospital in which the acquittee is primarily confined. The evaluators shall determine whether the acquittee currently has mental illness or intellectual disability and shall assess the acquittee and report on his condition and need for hospitalization with respect to the factors set forth in § 19.2–182. 3. The evaluators shall conduct their examinations and report their findings separately within 45 days of the Commissioner's assumption of custody. Copies of the report shall be sent to the acquittee's attorney, the attorney for the Commonwealth for the jurisdiction where the person was acquitted and the community services board or behavioral health authority as designated by the Commissioner. If either evaluator recommends conditional release or release without conditions of the acquittee, the court shall extend the evaluation period to permit the hospital in which the acquittee is confined and the appropriate community services board or behavioral health authority to jointly prepare a conditional release or discharge plan, as applicable, prior to the hearing.

Acts 1993, c. 295; Acts 1996, c. 937; Acts 1996, c. 980; Acts 2007, c. 485; Acts 2007, c. 565. Amended by Acts 2009, c. 813; Acts 2009, c. 840; Acts 2012, c. 476; Acts 2012, c. 507.

§ 19.2–182.3. Commitment; civil proceedings

Upon receipt of the evaluation report and, if applicable, a conditional release or discharge plan, the court shall schedule the matter for hearing on an expedited basis, giving the matter priority over other civil matters before the court, to determine the appropriate disposition of the acquittee. Except as otherwise ordered by the court, the attorney who represented the defendant at the criminal proceedings shall represent the acquittee through the proceedings pursuant to this section. The matter may be continued on motion of either party for good cause shown. The acquittee shall be provided with adequate notice of the hearing, of the right to be present at the hearing, the right to the assistance of counsel in preparation for and during the hearing, and the right to introduce evidence and cross-examine witnesses at the hearing. The hearing is a civil proceeding.

At the conclusion of the hearing, the court shall commit the acquittee if it finds that he has mental illness or intellectual disability and is in need of inpatient hospitalization. For the purposes of this chapter, mental illness includes any mental illness, as defined in § 37.2–100, in a state of remission when the illness may, with reasonable probability, become active. The decision of the court shall be based upon consideration of the following factors:

1. To what extent the acquittee has mental illness or intellectual disability, as those terms are defined in § 37.2–100;

2. The likelihood that the acquittee will engage in conduct presenting a substantial risk of bodily harm to other persons or to himself in the foreseeable future;

3. The likelihood that the acquittee can be adequately controlled with supervision and treatment on an outpatient basis; and

4. Such other factors as the court deems relevant.

If the court determines that an acquittee does not need inpatient hospitalization solely because of treatment or habilitation he is currently receiving, but the court is not persuaded that the acquittee will continue to receive such treatment or habilitation, it may commit him for inpatient hospitalization. The court shall order the acquittee released with conditions pursuant to §§ 19.2–182.7, 19.2–182.8, and 19.2–182.9 if it finds that he is not in need of inpatient hospitalization but that he meets the criteria for conditional release set forth in § 19.2–182.7. If the court finds that the acquittee does not need inpatient hospitalization nor does he meet the criteria for conditional release, it shall release him without conditions, provided the court has approved a discharge plan prepared by the appropriate community services board or behavioral health authority in consultation with the appropriate hospital staff.

Acts 1991, c. 427; Acts 1993, c. 295; Acts 2005, c. 716, eff. Oct. 1, 2005. Amended by Acts 2012, c. 476; Acts 2012, c. 507.

§ 19.2–182.4. Confinement and treatment; interfacility transfers; out-of-hospital visits; notice of change in treatment

A. Upon commitment of an acquittee for inpatient hospitalization, the Commissioner shall determine the appropriate placement for him, based on his clinical needs and security requirements. The Commissioner may make interfacility transfers and treatment and management decisions regarding acquittees in his custody without obtaining prior approval of or review by the committing court. If the Commissioner is of the opinion that a temporary visit from the hospital would be therapeutic for the acquittee and that such visit would pose no substantial danger to others, the Commissioner may grant such visit not to exceed forty-eight hours.

B. The Commissioner shall give notice of the granting of an unescorted community visit to any victim of a felony offense against the person punishable by more than five years in prison that resulted in the charges on which the acquittee was acquitted or the next-of-kin of the victim at the last known address, provided the person seeking notice submits a written request for such notice to the Commissioner.

C. The Commissioner shall notify the attorney for the Commonwealth for the committing jurisdiction in writing of changes in an acquittee's course of treatment which will involve authorization for the acquittee to leave the grounds of the hospital in which he is confined.

Acts 1991, c. 427; Acts 1993, c. 295; Acts 2006, c. 358.

§ 19.2–182.5. Review of continuation of confinement hearing; procedure and reports; disposition

A. The committing court shall conduct a hearing twelve months after the date of commitment to assess the need for inpatient hospitalization of each acquittee who is acquitted of a felony by reason of insanity. A hearing for assessment shall be conducted at yearly intervals for five years and at biennial intervals thereafter. The court shall schedule the matter for hearing as soon as possible after it becomes due, giving the matter priority over all pending matters before the court.

B. Prior to the hearing, the Commissioner shall provide to the court a report evaluating the acquittee's condition and recommending treatment, to be prepared by a psychiatrist or a psychologist. The psychologist who prepares the report shall be a clinical psychologist and any evaluating psychiatrist or clinical psychologist shall be skilled in the diagnosis of mental illness and qualified by training and experience to perform forensic evaluations. If the examiner recommends release or the acquittee requests release, the acquittee's condition and need for inpatient hospitalization shall be evaluated by a second person with such credentials who is not currently treating the acquittee. A copy of any report submitted pursuant to this subsection shall be sent to the attorney for the Commonwealth for the jurisdiction from which the acquittee was committed.

C. The acquittee shall be provided with adequate notice of the hearing, of the right to be present at the hearing, the right to the assistance of counsel in preparation for and during the hearing, and the right to introduce evidence and cross-examine witnesses at the hearing. Written notice of the hearing shall be provided to the attorney for the Commonwealth for the committing jurisdiction. The hearing is a civil proceeding.

According to the determination of the court following the hearing, and based upon the report and other evidence provided at the hearing, the court shall (i) release the acquittee from confinement if he does not need inpatient hospitalization and does not meet the criteria for conditional release set forth in § 19.2–182.7, provided the court has approved a discharge plan prepared jointly by the hospital staff and the appropriate community services board or behavioral health authority; (ii) place the acquittee on conditional release if he meets the criteria for conditional release, and the court has approved a conditional release plan prepared jointly by the hospital staff and the appropriate community services board or behavioral health authority; or (iii) order that he remain in the custody of the Commissioner if he continues to require inpatient hospitalization based on consideration of the factors set forth in § 19.2–182.3.

D. An acquittee who is found not guilty of a misdemeanor by reason of insanity on or after July 1, 2002, shall remain in the custody of the Commissioner pursuant to this chapter for a period not to exceed one year from the date of acquittal. If, prior to or at the conclusion of one year, the Commissioner determines that the acquittee meets the criteria for conditional release or release without conditions pursuant to § 19.2–182.7, emergency custody pursuant to § 37.2–808, temporary detention pursuant to §§ 37.2–809 to 37.2–813, or involuntary commitment pursuant to Article 5 (§ 37.2–814 et seq.) of Chapter 8 of Title 37.2, he shall petition the committing court. Written notice of an acquittee's scheduled release shall be provided by the Commissioner to the attorney for the Commonwealth for the committing jurisdiction not less than thirty days prior to the scheduled release. The Commissioner's duty to file a petition upon such determination shall not preclude the ability of any other person meeting the requirements of § 37.2–808 to file the petition.

Acts 1991, c. 427; Acts 1993, c. 295; Acts 1996, c. 937; Acts 1996, c. 980; Acts 2002, c. 750; Acts 2007, c. 485; Acts 2007, c. 565.

§ 19.2–182.6. Petition for release; conditional release hearing; notice; disposition

A. The Commissioner may petition the committing court for conditional or unconditional release of the acquittee at any time he believes the acquittee no longer needs hospitalization. The petition shall be accompanied by a report of clinical findings supporting the petition with respect to the factors set forth in § 19.2–182.3 and by a conditional release or discharge plan, as applicable, prepared jointly by the hospital and the appropriate community services board or behavioral health authority. The acquittee may petition the committing court for release only once in each year in which no annual judicial review is required pursuant to § 19.2–182.5. The party petitioning for release shall transmit a copy of the petition to the attorney for the Commonwealth for the committing jurisdiction.

B. 1. When a petition for release is made by the acquittee, the court shall order the Commissioner to appoint two persons in the same manner as set forth in § 19.2–182.2 to assess and report on the acquittee's need for inpatient hospitalization by reviewing his condition with respect to the factors set forth in § 19.2–182.3. The evaluators shall conduct their evaluations and report their finding in accordance with the provisions of § 19.2–182.2, except that the evaluations shall be completed and findings reported within 45 days of issuance of the court's order for evaluation.

2. When a petition for release is made by the Commissioner no further evaluations of the acquittee shall be required unless otherwise deemed necessary by the court. If the court determines that further evaluation is necessary, the court shall order the Commissioner to appoint two persons in the same manner as set forth in § 19.2–182.2 to assess and report on the acquittee's need for inpatient hospitalization by reviewing his condition with respect to the factors set forth in § 19.2–182.3. The evaluators shall conduct their evaluations and report their finding in accordance with the provisions of § 19.2–182.2, except that the evaluations shall be completed and findings reported within 45 days of issuance of the court's order for evaluation.

The Commissioner shall give notice of the hearing to any victim of the act resulting in the charges on which the acquittee was acquitted or the next of kin of the victim at the last known address, provided the person submits a written request for such notification to the Commissioner.

C. Upon receipt of the reports of evaluation, the court shall conduct a hearing on the petition. The hearing shall be scheduled on an expedited basis and given priority over other civil matters before the court. The acquittee shall be provided with adequate notice of the hearing, of the right to be present at the hearing, the right to the assistance of counsel in preparation for and during the hearing, and the right to introduce evidence and cross-examine witnesses. Written notice of the hearing shall be provided to the attorney for the Commonwealth for the committing jurisdiction. The hearing is a civil proceeding.

At the conclusion of the hearing, based upon the report and other evidence provided at the hearing, the court shall order the acquittee (i) released from confinement if he does not need inpatient hospitalization and does not meet the criteria for conditional release set forth in § 19.2–182.3, provided the court has approved a discharge plan prepared jointly by the hospital and the appropriate community services board or behavioral health authority; (ii) placed on conditional release if he meets the criteria for such release as set forth in § 19.2–182.7, and the court has approved a conditional release plan prepared jointly by the hospital and the appropriate community services board or behavioral health authority; or (iii) retained in the custody of the Commissioner if he continues to require inpatient hospitalization based on consideration of the factors set forth in § 19.2–182.3.

D. Persons committed pursuant to this chapter shall be released only in accordance with the procedures set forth governing release and conditional release.

Acts 1991, c. 427; Acts 1993, c. 295; Acts 2007, c. 485; Acts 2007, c. 565; Acts 2007, c. 785.

§ 19.2–182.7. Conditional release; criteria; conditions; reports

At any time the court considers the acquittee's need for inpatient hospitalization pursuant to this chapter, it shall place the acquittee on conditional release if it finds that (i) based on consideration of the factors which the court must consider in its commitment decision, he does not need inpatient hospitalization but needs outpatient treatment or monitoring to prevent his condition from deteriorating to a degree that he would need inpatient hospitalization; (ii) appropriate outpatient supervision and treatment are reasonably available; (iii) there is significant reason to believe that the acquittee, if conditionally released, would comply with the conditions specified; and (iv) conditional release will not present an undue risk to public safety. The court shall subject a conditionally released acquittee to such orders and conditions it deems will best meet the acquittee's need for treatment and supervision and best serve the interests of justice and society.

The community services board or behavioral health authority as designated by the Commissioner shall implement the court's conditional release orders and shall submit written reports to the court on the acquittee's progress and adjustment in the community no less frequently than every six months. An aquittee's conditional release shall not be revoked solely because of his voluntary admission to a state hospital.

After a finding by the court that the acquittee has violated the conditions of his release but does not require inpatient hospitalization pursuant to § 19.2–182.8, the court may hold the acquittee in contempt of court for violation of the conditional release order.

Acts 1991, c. 427; Acts 1999, c. 700; Acts 1999, c. 746; Acts 2007, c. 485; Acts 2007, c. 565. Amended by Acts 2008, c. 810.

§ 19.2–182.8. Revocation of conditional release

If at any time the court that released an acquittee pursuant to § 19.2–182.7 finds reasonable ground to believe that an acquittee on conditional release (i) has violated the conditions of his release or is no longer a proper subject for conditional release based on application of the criteria for conditional release and (ii) requires inpatient hospitalization, it may order an evaluation of the acquittee by a psychiatrist or clinical psychologist, provided the psychiatrist or clinical psychologist is qualified by training and experience to perform forensic evaluations. If the court, based on the evaluation and after hearing evidence on the issue, finds by a preponderance of the evidence that an acquittee on conditional release (a) has violated the conditions of his release or is no longer a proper subject for conditional release based on application of the criteria for conditional release and (b) has mental illness or intellectual disability and requires inpatient hospitalization, the court may revoke the acquittee's conditional release and order him returned to the custody of the Commissioner.

At any hearing pursuant to this section, the acquittee shall be provided with adequate notice of the hearing, of the right to be present at the hearing, the right to the assistance of counsel in preparation for and during the hearing, and the right to introduce evidence and cross-examine witnesses at the hearing. The hearing shall be scheduled on an expedited basis and shall be given priority over other civil matters before the court. Written notice of the hearing shall be provided to the attorney for the Commonwealth for the committing jurisdiction. The hearing is a civil proceeding.

Acts 1991, c. 427; Acts 1993, c. 295; Acts 1996, c. 937; Acts 1996, c. 980; Acts 2006, c. 343; Acts 2006, c. 369; Acts 2006, c. 370. Amended by Acts 2008, c. 810; Acts 2012, c. 476; Acts 2012, c. 507.

§ 19.2–182.9. Emergency custody of conditionally released acquittee

When exigent circumstances do not permit compliance with revocation procedures set forth in § 19.2–182.8, any district court judge or a special justice, as defined in § 37.2–100, or a magistrate may issue an emergency custody order, upon the sworn petition of any responsible person or upon his own motion based upon probable cause to believe that an acquittee on conditional release (i) has violated the conditions of his release or is no longer a proper subject for conditional release and (ii) requires inpatient hospitalization. The emergency custody order shall require the acquittee within his judicial district to be taken into custody and transported to a convenient location where a person designated by the community services board or behavioral health authority who is skilled in the diagnosis and treatment of mental illness shall evaluate such acquittee and assess his need for inpatient hospitalization. A law-enforcement officer who, based on his observation or the reliable reports of others, has probable cause to believe that any acquittee on conditional release has violated the conditions of his release and is no longer a proper subject for conditional release and requires emergency evaluation to assess the need for inpatient hospitalization, may take the acquittee into custody and transport him to an appropriate location to assess the need for hospitalization without prior judicial authorization. The evaluation shall be conducted immediately. The acquittee shall remain in custody until a temporary detention order is issued or until he is released, but in no event shall the period of custody exceed eight hours. If it appears from all evidence readily available (a) that the acquittee has violated the conditions of his release or is no longer a proper subject for conditional release and (b) that he requires emergency evaluation to assess the need for inpatient hospitalization, the district court judge or a special justice, as defined in § 37.2–100, or magistrate, upon the advice of such person skilled in the diagnosis and treatment of mental illness, may issue a temporary detention order authorizing the executing officer to place the acquittee in an appropriate institution for a period not to exceed 72 hours prior to a hearing. If the 72–hour period terminates on a Saturday, Sunday, legal holiday, or day on which the court is lawfully closed, the acquittee may be detained until the next day which is not a Saturday, Sunday, legal holiday, or day on which the court is lawfully closed.

The committing court or any district court judge or a special justice, as defined in § 37.2–100, shall have jurisdiction to hear the matter. Prior to the hearing, the acquittee shall be examined by a psychiatrist or licensed clinical psychologist, provided the psychiatrist or clinical psychologist is skilled in the diagnosis of mental illness, who shall certify whether the person is in need of hospitalization. At the hearing the acquittee shall be provided with adequate notice of the hearing, of the right to be present at the hearing, the right to the assistance of counsel in preparation for and during the hearing, and the right to introduce evidence and cross-examine witnesses at the hearing. Following the hearing, if the court determines, based on a preponderance of the evidence presented at the hearing, that the acquittee (1) has violated the conditions of his release or is no longer a proper subject for conditional release and (2) has mental illness or intellectual disability and is in need of inpatient hospitalization, the court shall revoke the acquittee's conditional release and place him in the custody of the Commissioner.

When an acquittee on conditional release pursuant to this chapter is taken into emergency custody, detained, or hospitalized, such action shall be considered to have been taken pursuant to this section, notwithstanding the fact that his status as an insanity acquittee was not known at the time of custody, detention, or hospitalization. Detention or hospitalization of an acquittee pursuant to provisions of law other than those applicable to insanity acquittees pursuant to this chapter shall not render the detention or hospitalization invalid. If a person's status as an insanity acquittee on conditional release is not recognized at the time of emergency custody or detention, at the time his status as such is verified, the provisions applicable to such persons shall be applied and the court hearing the matter shall notify the committing court of the proceedings.

Acts 1991, c. 427; Acts 1993, c. 295; Acts 1996, c. 937; Acts 1996, c. 980; Acts 2001, c. 837; Acts 2005, c. 716, eff. Oct. 1, 2005; Acts 2006, c. 343; Acts 2006, c. 370. Amended by Acts 2008, c. 810; Acts 2009, c. 21, eff. Feb. 23, 2009; Acts 2009, c. 838, eff. April 8, 2009; Acts 2012, c. 476; Acts 2012, c. 507; Acts 2014, c. 499; Acts 2014, c. 538; Acts 2014, c. 691; Acts 2014, c. 761.

§ 19.2–182.10. Release of person whose conditional release was revoked

If an acquittee is returned to the custody of the Commissioner for inpatient treatment pursuant to revocation proceedings, and his condition improves to the degree that, within 60 days of resumption of custody following the hearing, the acquittee, in the opinion of hospital staff treating the acquittee and the supervising community services board or behavioral health authority, is an appropriate candidate for conditional release, he may be, with the approval of the court, conditionally released as if revocation had not taken place. If treatment is required for longer than 60 days, the acquittee shall be returned to the custody of the Commissioner for a period of hospitalization and treatment which is governed by the provisions of this chapter applicable to committed acquittees.

Acts 1991, c. 427; Acts 1993, c. 295; Acts 2006, c. 199; Acts 2006, c. 225; Acts 2007, c. 485; Acts 2007, c. 565.

§ 19.2–182.11. Modification or removal of conditions; notice; objections; review

A. The committing court may modify conditions of release or remove conditions placed on release pursuant to § 19.2–182.7, upon petition of the supervising community services board or behavioral health authority, the attorney for the Commonwealth, or the acquittee or upon its own motion based on reports of the supervising community services board or behavioral health authority. However, the acquittee may petition only annually commencing six months after the conditional release order is issued. Upon petition, the court shall require the supervising community services board or behavioral health authority to provide a report on the acquittee's progress while on conditional release.

B. As it deems appropriate based on the community services board's or behavioral health authority's report and any other evidence provided to it, the court may issue a proposed order for modification or removal of conditions. The court shall provide notice of the order, and their right to object to it within ten days of its issuance, to the acquittee, the supervising community services board or behavioral health authority and the attorney for the Commonwealth for the committing jurisdiction and for the jurisdiction where the acquittee is residing on conditional release. The proposed order shall become final if no objection is filed within ten days of its issuance. If an objection is so filed, the court shall conduct a hearing at which the acquittee, the attorney for the Commonwealth, and the supervising community services board or behavioral health authority have an opportunity to present evidence challenging the proposed order. At the conclusion of the hearing, the court shall issue an order specifying conditions of release or removing existing conditions of release.

Acts 1991, c. 427; Acts 2007, c. 485; Acts 2007, c. 565.

§ 19.2–182.12. Representation of Commonwealth and acquittee

The attorney for the Commonwealth shall represent the Commonwealth in all proceedings held pursuant to this chapter. The court shall appoint counsel for the acquittee unless the acquittee waives his right to counsel. The court shall consider appointment of the person who represented the acquittee at the last proceeding.

Acts 1991, c. 427; Acts 1993, c. 295.

§ 19.2–182.13. Authority of Commissioner; delegation to board; liability

The Commissioner may delegate any of the duties and powers imposed on or granted to him by this chapter to an administrative board composed of persons with demonstrated expertise in such matters. The Department of Behavioral Health and Developmental Services shall assist the board in its administrative and technical duties. Members of the board shall exercise their powers and duties without compensation and shall be immune from personal liability while acting within the scope of their duties except for intentional misconduct.

Acts 1991, c. 427. Amended by Acts 2009, c. 813; Acts 2009, c. 840.

§ 19.2–182.14. Escape of persons placed or committed; penalty

Any person placed in the temporary custody of the Commissioner pursuant to § 19.2–182.2 or committed to the custody of the Commissioner pursuant to § 19.2–182.3 who escapes from such custody shall be guilty of a Class 6 felony.

Acts 1993, c. 295.

§ 19.2–182.15. Escape of persons placed on conditional release; penalty

Any person placed on conditional release pursuant to § 19.2–182.7 who leaves the Commonwealth without permission from the court which conditionally released the person shall be guilty of a Class 6 felony.

Acts 1993, c. 295.

§ 19.2–182.16. Copies of orders to Commissioner

Copies of all orders and notices issued pursuant to this chapter shall be sent to the Commissioner of the

Department of Behavioral Health and Developmental Services.

Acts 1993, c. 295. Amended by Acts 2009, c. 813; Acts 2009, c. 840.

CHAPTER 12

PRELIMINARY HEARING

§ 19.2-183. Examination of witnesses; assistance of counsel; evidentiary matters and remedies; power to adjourn case

A. The judge before whom any person is brought for an offense shall, as soon as may be practical, in the presence of such person, examine on oath the witnesses for and against him. Before conducting the hearing or accepting a waiver of the hearing, the judge shall advise the accused of his right to counsel and, if the accused is indigent and the offense charged be punishable by confinement in jail or the state correctional facility, the judge shall appoint counsel as provided by law.

B. At the hearing the judge shall, in the presence of the accused, hear testimony presented for and against the accused in accordance with the rules of evidence applicable to criminal trials in this Commonwealth. In felony cases, the accused shall not be called upon to plead, but he may cross-examine any witness who testifies on behalf of the Commonwealth or on behalf of any other defendant, introduce witnesses in his own behalf, and testify in his own behalf.

C. A judge may adjourn a trial, pending before him, not exceeding 10 days at one time, without the consent of the accused.

D. At any preliminary hearing under this section, certificates of analysis and reports prepared pursuant to §§ 19.2-187 and 19.2-188 shall be admissible without the testimony of the person preparing such certificate or report.

Acts 1975, c. 495; Acts 1982, c. 513. Amended by Acts 2010, c. 555.

§ 19.2-183.1. Joint preliminary hearings

Upon motion of the attorney for the Commonwealth, preliminary hearings for persons alleged to have participated in contemporaneous and related acts or occurrences or in a series of such acts or occurrences constituting an offense or offenses may be heard jointly if jurisdiction over each person and offense lies in the same court, unless the court finds that such joint preliminary hearing would constitute prejudice to a defendant. Upon such a finding, the court shall order that the preliminary hearing for that defendant be held separately.

Acts 1993, c. 462; Acts 1993, c. 489.

§ 19.2-184. Witnesses may be separated (Subsection (a) of Supreme Court Rule 2:615 derived in part from this section)

While a witness is under such examination all other witnesses may by order of the judge be excluded from the place of examination and kept separate from each other.

Acts 1975, c. 495.

§ 19.2-185. Testimony may be reduced to writing and subscribed

When the judge deems it proper the testimony of the witnesses may be reduced to writing, and, if required by him, shall be signed by them respectively.

The judge of the court of record to which the case may be or has been certified may order the testimony of the witnesses at the preliminary hearing to be reduced to writing.

Acts 1975, c. 495.

§ 19.2-186. When accused to be discharged, tried, committed or bailed by judge

The judge shall discharge the accused if he considers that there is not sufficient cause for charging him with the offense.

If a judge considers that there is sufficient cause only to charge the accused with an offense which the judge has jurisdiction to try, then he shall try the accused for such offense and convict him if he deems him guilty and pass judgment upon him in accordance with law just as if the accused had first been brought before him on a warrant charging him with such offense.

If a judge considers that there is sufficient cause to charge the accused with an offense that he does not have jurisdiction to try then he shall certify the case to the appropriate court having jurisdiction and shall commit the accused to jail or let him to bail pursuant to the provisions of Article 1 (§ 19.2-119 et seq.) of Chapter 9 of this title.

Acts 1975, c. 495; Acts 1999, c. 829; Acts 1999, c. 846.

§ 19.2-187. Admission into evidence of certain certificates of analysis

In any hearing or trial of any criminal offense or in any proceeding brought pursuant to Chapter 22.1 (§ 19.2-386.1 et seq.), a certificate of analysis of a person performing an analysis or examination, duly attested by such person, shall be admissible in evidence as evidence of the facts therein stated and the results of the analysis or examination referred to therein, provided (i) the certificate of analysis is filed with the clerk of the court hearing the case at least seven days prior to the proceeding if the attorney for the Commonwealth intends to offer it into evidence in a preliminary hearing or the accused intends to offer it into evidence in any hearing or trial, or (ii) the requirements of subsection A of § 19.2–187.1 have been satisfied and the accused has not objected to the admission of the certificate pursuant to subsection B of § 19.2–187.1, when any such analysis or examination is performed in any laboratory operated by the Division of Consolidated Laboratory Services or the Department of Forensic Science or authorized by such Department to conduct such analysis or examination, or performed by a person licensed by the Department of Forensic Science pursuant to § 18.2–268.9 or 46.2–341.26:9 to conduct such analysis or examination, or performed by the Federal Bureau of Investigation, the United States Postal Service, the federal Bureau of Alcohol, Tobacco and Firearms, the Naval Criminal Investigative Service, the National Fish and Wildlife Forensics Laboratory, the federal Drug Enforcement Administration, the Forensic Document Laboratory of the U.S. Department of Homeland Security, or the U.S. Secret Service Laboratory.

In a hearing or trial in which the provisions of subsection A of § 19.2–187.1 do not apply, a copy of such certificate shall be mailed or delivered by the clerk or attorney for the Commonwealth to counsel of record for the accused at no charge at least seven days prior to the hearing or trial upon request made by such counsel to the clerk with notice of the request to the attorney for the Commonwealth. The request to the clerk shall be on a form prescribed by the Supreme Court and filed with the clerk at least 10 days prior to the hearing or trial. In the event that a request for a copy of a certificate is filed with the clerk with respect to a case that is not yet before the court, the clerk shall advise the requester that he must resubmit the request at such time as the case is properly before the court in order for such request to be effective. If, upon proper request made by counsel of record for the accused, a copy of such certificate is not mailed or delivered by the clerk or attorney for the Commonwealth to counsel of record for the accused in a timely manner in accordance with this section, the accused shall be entitled to continue the hearing or trial.

The certificate of analysis of any examination conducted by the Department of Forensic Science relating to a controlled substance or marijuana shall be mailed or forwarded by personnel of the Department of Forensic Science to the attorney for the Commonwealth of the jurisdiction where such offense may be heard. The attorney for the Commonwealth shall acknowledge receipt of the certificate on forms provided by the laboratory.

Any such certificate of analysis purporting to be signed, either by hand or by electronic means, by any such person shall be admissible as evidence in such hearing or trial without any proof of the seal or signature or of the official character of the person whose name is signed to it. The attestation signature of a person performing the analysis or examination may be either hand or electronically signed.

For the purposes of this section and §§ 19.2–187.01, 19.2–187.1, and 19.2–187.2, the term "certificate of analysis" includes reports of analysis and results of laboratory examination.

Acts 1975, c. 495; Acts 1976, c. 245; Acts 1983, c. 178; Acts 1984, c. 607; Acts 1988, c. 494; Acts 1990, c. 737; Acts 1990, c. 825; Acts 1992, c. 56; Acts 1994, c. 41; Acts 1994, c. 375; Acts 1995, c. 437; Acts 1999, c. 296; Acts 2000, c. 336; Acts 2002, c. 832; Acts 2005, c. 868; Acts 2005, c. 881; Acts 2006, c. 294. Amended by Acts 2009, Sp. S. I, c. 1, eff. Aug. 21, 2009; Acts 2009, Sp. S. I, c. 4, eff. Sept. 15, 2009; Acts 2010, c. 656; Acts 2011, c. 384, eff. March 23, 2011; Acts 2011, c. 410, eff. March 23, 2011; Acts 2011, c. 645; Acts 2014, c. 328; Acts 2014, c. 674; Acts 2014, c. 719; Acts 2015, c. 75; Acts 2015, c. 126.

§ 19.2–187.01. Certificate of analysis as evidence of chain of custody of material described therein

A report of analysis duly attested by the person performing such analysis or examination in any laboratory operated by (i) the Division of Consolidated Laboratory Services, the Department of Forensic Science or any of its regional laboratories, or by any laboratory authorized by such Division or Department to conduct such analysis or examination; (ii) the Federal Bureau of Investigation; (iii) the federal Bureau of Alcohol, Tobacco and Firearms; (iv) the Naval Criminal Investigative Service; (v) the federal Drug Enforcement Administration; (vi) the United States Postal Service; (vii) the U.S. Secret Service; or (viii) the Forensic Document Laboratory of the U.S. Department of Homeland Security shall be prima facie evidence in a criminal or civil proceeding as to the custody of the material described therein from the time such material is received by an authorized agent of such laboratory until such material is released subsequent to such analysis or examination. Any such certificate of analysis purporting to be signed by any such person shall be admissible as evidence in such hearing or trial without any proof of the seal or signature or of the official character of the person whose name is signed to it. The signature of the person who received the material for the laboratory on the request for laboratory examination form shall be deemed prima facie evidence that the person receiving the material was an authorized agent and that such receipt constitutes proper receipt by the laboratory for purposes of this section.

Acts 1979, c. 364; Acts 1989, c. 458; Acts 1990, c. 548; Acts 1990, c. 825; Acts 1991, c. 687; Acts 1993, c. 32; Acts 1994, c. 375; Acts 1995, c. 437; Acts 2005, c. 868; Acts 2005, c. 881. Amended by Acts 2011, c. 645; Acts 2015, c. 75; Acts 2015, c. 126.

§ 19.2–187.02. Admissibility of written reports or records of blood alcohol tests conducted in the regular course of providing emergency medical treatment

A. Notwithstanding any other provision of law, the written reports or records of blood alcohol tests conducted upon persons receiving medical treatment in a hospital or emergency room are admissible in evidence as a business records exception to the hearsay rule in prosecutions for any violation of § 18.2–266 (driving while intoxicated) or a substantially similar local ordinance, § 18.2–36.1 (involuntary manslaughter resulting from driving while intoxicated), § 18.2–36.2 (involuntary manslaughter resulting from boating while intoxicated), § 18.2–51.4 (maiming resulting from driving while intoxicated), § 18.2–51.5 (maiming resulting from boating while intoxicated), § 29.1–738 (boating while intoxicated), or § 46.2–341.24 (driving a commercial vehicle while intoxicated).

B. The provisions of law pertaining to confidentiality of medical records and medical treatment shall not be applicable to reports or records of blood alcohol tests sought or admitted as evidence under the provisions of this section in prosecutions as specified in subsection A. Owners or custodians of such reports or records may disclose them, in accordance with regulations concerning patient privacy promulgated by the U.S. Department of Health and Human Services, without obtaining consent or authorization for such disclosure. No person who is involved in taking blood or conducting blood alcohol tests shall be liable for civil damages for breach of confidentiality or unauthorized release of medical records because of the evidentiary use of blood alcohol test results under this section, or as a result of that person's testimony given pursuant to this section.

Acts 2002, c. 749; Acts 2005, c. 801; Acts 2007, c. 379; Acts 2007, c. 679.

§ 19.2–187.1. Procedures for notifying accused of certificate of analysis; waiver; continuances

A. In any trial and in any hearing other than a preliminary hearing, in which the attorney for the Commonwealth intends to offer a certificate of analysis into evidence in lieu of testimony pursuant to § 19.2–187, the attorney for the Commonwealth shall:

1. Provide by mail, delivery, or otherwise, a copy of the certificate to counsel of record for the accused, or to the accused if he is proceeding pro se, at no charge, no later than 28 days prior to the hearing or trial;

2. Provide simultaneously with the copy of the certificate so provided under subdivision 1 a notice to the accused of his right to object to having the certificate admitted without the person who performed the analysis or examination being present and testifying;

2a. When the attorney for the Commonwealth intends to present such testimony through two-way video conferencing, attach to the copy of the certificate provided under subdivision 1 a notice on a page separate from the notice in subdivision 2 specifying that the person who performed the analysis or examination may testify by two-way video conferencing and that the accused has a right to object to such two-way video testimony; and

3. File a copy of the certificate and notice with the clerk of the court hearing the matter (i) on the day that the certificate and notice are provided to the accused or (ii) in the case of a breath test certificate for a violation of any offense listed in subsection E of § 18.2–270, no later than three business days following the day that the certificate and notice are provided to the accused.

B. The accused may object in writing to admission of the certificate of analysis, in lieu of testimony, as evidence of the facts stated therein and of the results of the analysis or examination. Such objection shall be filed with the court hearing the matter, with a copy to the attorney for the Commonwealth, no more than 14 days after the certificate and notice were filed with the clerk by the attorney for the Commonwealth or the objection shall be deemed waived. If timely objection is made, the certificate shall not be admissible into evidence unless (i) the testimony of the person who performed the analysis or examination is admitted into evidence describing the facts and results of the analysis or examination during the Commonwealth's case-in-chief at the hearing or trial and that person is present and subject to cross-examination by the accused, (ii) the objection is waived by the accused or his counsel in writing or before the court, or (iii) the parties stipulate before the court to the admissibility of the certificate. If the accused demands, at hearing or trial, the presence of the person who performed the analysis or examination and he is thereafter found guilty of the charge or charges for which he demanded the presence of such witness, $50 for expenses related to the witness's appearance at hearing or trial shall be charged to the accused as court costs.

B1. When the attorney for the Commonwealth gives notice to the accused of intent to present testimony by two-way video conferencing, the accused may object in writing to the admission of such testimony and may file an objection as provided in subsection B. The provisions of subsection B shall apply to such objection mutatis mutandis.

B2. The two-way video testimony permitted by this section shall comply with the provisions of subsection B of § 19.2–3.1. In addition, unless otherwise agreed by the parties and the court, (i) all orders pertaining to witnesses apply to witnesses testifying by video conferencing; (ii) upon request, all materials read or used by the witness during his testimony shall be identified on the video; and (iii) any witness testifying by video conferencing shall certify at the conclusion of his testimony, under penalty of perjury, that he did not engage in any off-camera communications with any person during his testimony.

C. Where the person who performed the analysis and examination is not available for hearing or trial and the attorney for the Commonwealth has used due diligence to secure the presence of the person, the court shall order a continuance. Any continuances ordered pursuant to this subsection shall total not more than 90 days if the accused has been held continuously in custody and not more than 180 days if the accused has not been held continuously in custody.

D. Any objection by counsel for the accused, or the accused if he is proceeding pro se, to timeliness of the receipt of notice required by subsection A shall be made before hearing or trial upon his receipt of actual notice unless the accused did not receive actual notice prior to hearing or trial. A showing by the Commonwealth that the notice was mailed, delivered, or otherwise provided in compliance with the time requirements of this section shall constitute prima facie evidence that the notice was timely received by the accused. If the court finds upon the accused's objection made pursuant to this subsection, that he did not receive timely notice pursuant to subsection A, the accused's objection shall not be deemed waived and if the objection is made prior to hearing or trial, a continuance shall be ordered if requested by either party. Any continuance ordered pursuant to this subsection shall be subject to the time limitations set forth in subsection C.

E. Nothing in this section shall prohibit the admissibility of a certificate of analysis when the person who performed the analysis and examination testifies at trial or the hearing concerning the facts stated therein and of the results of the analysis or examination.

F. The accused in any hearing or trial in which a certificate of analysis is offered into evidence shall have the right to call the person performing such analysis or examination or involved in the chain of custody as a witness therein, and examine him in the same manner as if he had been called as an adverse witness. Such witness shall be summoned and appear at the cost of the Commonwealth; however, if the accused calls the person performing such analysis or examination as a witness and is found guilty of the charge or charges for which such witness is summoned, $50 for expenses related to that witness's appearance at hearing or trial shall be charged to the accused as court costs.

Acts 1975, c. 495; Acts 1979, c. 364. Amended by Acts 2009, Sp. S. I, c. 1, eff. Aug. 21, 2009; Acts 2009, Sp. S. I, c. 4, eff. Sept. 15, 2009; Acts 2010, c. 555; Acts 2010, c. 656; Acts 2010, c. 800; Acts 2011, c. 32.

§ 19.2–187.2. Procedure for subpoena duces tecum of analysis evidence

No subpoena duces tecum shall issue for the production of writings or documents used to reach the conclusion contained in a certificate of analysis prepared pursuant to § 19.2–187 except upon affidavit that the requested writings or documents are material. Upon a showing by the Commonwealth that the production of such writings and documents would place an undue burden on the Department of Forensic Science, the court may order that the subpoena duces tecum be satisfied by making the writings and documents available for inspection by the requesting party at the laboratory site where the analysis was performed or at the laboratory operated by the Department of Forensic Science which is closest to the court in which the case is pending.

Acts 1993, c. 629; Acts 2005, c. 868; Acts 2005, c. 881.

§ 19.2–188. Reports by Chief Medical Examiner received as evidence

A. Reports of investigations made by the Chief Medical Examiner, his assistants or medical examiners, and the records and certified reports of autopsies made under the authority of Title 32.1, shall be received as evidence in any court or other proceeding, and copies of photographs, laboratory findings and reports in the office of the Chief Medical Examiner or any medical examiner, when duly attested by the Chief Medical Examiner or one of his Assistant Chief Medical Examiners, shall be received as evidence in any court or other proceeding for any purpose for which the original could be received without proof of the official character or the person whose name is signed thereto.

B. Any statement of fact or of opinion in such reports and records concerning the physical or medical cause of death and not alleging any conduct by the accused shall be admissible as competent evidence of the cause of death in any preliminary hearing.

Acts 1975, c. 495; Acts 2003, c. 459. Amended by Acts 2009, c. 640.

§ 19.2–188.1. Testimony regarding identification of controlled substances

A. In any preliminary hearing on a violation of Article 1 (§ 18.2–247 et seq.) of Chapter 7 of Title 18.2 or a violation of subdivision 6 of § 53.1–203, any law-enforcement officer shall be permitted to testify as to the results of field tests that have been approved by the Department of Forensic Science pursuant to regulations adopted in accordance with the Administrative Process Act (§ 2.2–4000 et seq.), regarding whether or not any substance the identity of which is at issue in such hearing is a controlled substance, imitation controlled substance, or marijuana, as defined in § 18.2–247.

B. In any trial for a violation of § 18.2–250.1, any law-enforcement officer shall be permitted to testify as to the results of any marijuana field test approved as accurate and reliable by the Department of Forensic Science pursuant to regulations adopted in accordance with the Administrative Process Act (§ 2.2–4000 et seq.), regarding whether or not any plant material, the identity of which is at issue, is marijuana provided the defendant has been given written notice of his right to request a full chemical analysis. Such notice shall be on a form approved by the Supreme Court and shall be provided to the defendant prior to trial.

In any case in which the person accused of a violation of § 18.2–250.1, or the attorney of record for the accused, desires a full chemical analysis of the alleged plant material, he may, by motion prior to trial before the court in which the charge is pending, request such a chemical analysis. Upon such motion, the court shall order that the analysis be performed by the Department of Forensic Science and shall prescribe in its order the method of custody, transfer, and return of evidence submitted for chemical analysis.

Acts 1991, c. 477; Acts 1993, c. 33; Acts 2005, c. 868; Acts 2005, c. 881; Acts 2006, c. 447. Amended by Acts 2013, c. 60.

§ 19.2–188.2. Certificate of surgeon as evidence

A. In any criminal proceeding, the certificate of a duly qualified surgeon stating that he has removed organs or other body parts from a decedent for transplant in accordance with Chapter 8 (§ 32.1–277 et seq.) of Title 32.1, shall be admissible in evidence as evidence of the facts stated therein. The certificate shall be competent evidence to show that such organs or body parts were functional at the time of recovery and not affected by any injury or illness that caused the decedent's death.

B. A copy of the certificate shall be filed with the attorney for the Commonwealth in the jurisdiction in which the decedent's fatal injury occurred. The certificate shall not be admitted into evidence unless the attorney for the Commonwealth has provided a copy of the certificate to counsel for the defendant at least fourteen days prior to the proceeding in which it is to be offered into evidence.

C. Any such certificate, when properly notarized, purporting to be signed by the surgeon who removed the organs or other body parts shall be admissible in evidence without proof of seal or signature of the person whose name is signed to it. In any hearing or trial the accused shall have the right to call the person signing the certificate and the provisions of § 19.2–187.1 shall apply, mutatis mutandis.

Acts 1997, c. 557.

§ 19.2–188.3. Admissibility of affidavits by government officials regarding a search of government records (Subdivision (10)(b) of Supreme Court Rule 2:803 derived from this section)

In any hearing or trial, an affidavit signed by a government official who is competent to testify, deemed to have custody of an official record, or signed by his designee, stating that after a diligent search, no record or entry of such record is found to exist among the records in his custody, is admissible as evidence that his office has no such record or entry, provided that, if the hearing or trial is a proceeding other than a preliminary hearing, the procedures set forth in subsection G of § 18.2–472.1 for admission of an affidavit have been satisfied, mutatis mutandis, and the accused has not objected to the admission of the affidavit pursuant to the procedures set forth in subsection H of § 18.2–472.1, mutatis mutandis. Nothing in this section shall be construed to affect the admissibility of affidavits in civil cases under § 8.01–390.

Added by Acts 2010, c. 464. Amended by Acts 2011, c. 285.

§ 19.2–189. Commitment of accused for further examination

If the accused be committed, it shall be by an order of the judge stating that he is committed for further examination on a day specified in the order. And on that day he may be brought before such judge by his verbal order to the officer by whom he was committed, or by a written order to a different person.

Acts 1975, c. 495.

§ 19.2–190. To whom, and when, examination and recognizance to be certified

Every examination and recognizance for a felony taken under this chapter, shall, by the person taking it, be certified to the clerk of the circuit court of the county or city in which the party charged is to be tried, or the witness is to appear, on or before the first day of its next term. If he fails he may be compelled to do so by attachment as for a contempt.

Acts 1975, c. 495.

§ 19.2–190.1. Certification of ancillary misdemeanor offenses

Upon certification of any felony offense pursuant to this chapter, the court shall also certify any ancillary misdemeanor offense to the clerk of the circuit court provided that the attorney for the Commonwealth and the accused consent to such certification. Any misdemeanor offense certified pursuant to this section shall proceed in the same manner as a misdemeanor appealed to circuit court pursuant to § 16.1–136.

Added by Acts 2015, c. 548.

CHAPTER 13

GRAND JURIES

ARTICLE 1

IN GENERAL

§ 19.2–191. Functions of a grand jury

The functions of a grand jury are twofold:

(1) To consider bills of indictment prepared by the attorney for the Commonwealth and to determine whether as to each such bill there is sufficient probable cause to return such indictment "a true bill."

(2) To investigate and report on any condition that involves or tends to promote criminal activity, either in the community or by any governmental authority, agency or official thereof. These functions may be exercised by either a special grand jury or a regular grand jury as hereinafter provided.

Acts 1975, c. 495; Acts 1980, c. 517; Acts 2001, c. 4.

§ 19.2–192. Secrecy in grand jury proceedings

Except as otherwise provided in this chapter, every attorney for the Commonwealth, special counsel, sworn investigator, and member of a regular, special, or multi-jurisdiction grand jury shall keep secret all proceedings which occurred during sessions of the grand jury; provided, however, in a prosecution for perjury of a witness examined before a regular grand jury, a regular grand juror may be required by the court to testify as to the testimony given by such witness before the regular grand jury.

Acts 1975, c. 495. Amended by Acts 2014, c. 389.

§ 19.2–192.1. Sealing of indictment

Upon ex parte motion by the Commonwealth and for good cause shown, the circuit court may seal an indictment until such time as the defendant is arrested.

Acts 2002, c. 130.

ARTICLE 2

REGULAR GRAND JURIES

§ 19.2–193. Number of regular grand juries

There shall be a regular grand jury at each term of the circuit court of each county and city, unless the court, on the motion of the attorney for the Commonwealth or with his concurrence, finds that it is unnecessary or impractical to impanel a grand jury for the particular term and enters an order to that effect.

Whenever the number of cases to be considered by the grand jury at a given term is so great as to hamper the intelligent consideration thereof by a single grand jury, the court may order two or more regular grand juries to be impanelled to sit separately at the same or a different time during the term.

Whenever a regular grand jury has been discharged, the court, during the term, may impanel another regular grand jury.

Acts 1975, c. 495.

§ 19.2–194. When and how grand jurors to be selected and summoned; lists to be delivered to clerk

The judge or judges regularly presiding in the circuit court of each county and city shall annually, in the month of June, July, or August, select from citizens of the county or city at least 60 persons and not more than 120 persons 18 years of age or over, of honesty, intelligence, impartiality, and good demeanor and suitable in all respects to serve as grand jurors, who, except as hereinafter provided, shall be the grand jurors for the county or city from which they are selected for the next 12 months. The judge or judges making the selection shall at once furnish to the clerk of the circuit court a list of those selected for that county or city.

The clerk, not more than 20 days before the commencement of each term of his court at which a regular grand jury is required, shall issue a venire facias to the sheriff of his county or city, commanding him to summon not less than five nor more than nine of the persons selected as aforesaid (the number to be designated by the judge of the court by an order entered of record) to be named in the writ to appear on the first day of the court to serve as grand jurors. Those persons who are to be summoned shall be randomly selected but no such person shall be required to appear more than once until all the others have been summoned once, nor more than twice until the others have been twice summoned, and so on. The Circuit Court of James City County, or the judge thereof in vacation, shall select the grand jurors for each court from such county and the City of Williamsburg in such proportion from each as he may think proper.

Any person who has legal custody of and is responsible for a child 16 years of age or younger or a person having a mental or physical impairment requiring continuous care during normal court hours shall be excused from jury service upon his request.

Acts 1975, c. 495; Acts 1991, c. 226; Acts 2003, c. 825; Acts 2004, c. 306. Amended by Acts 2008, c. 644.

§ 19.2–195. Number and qualifications of grand jurors

A regular grand jury shall consist of not less than five nor more than seven persons. Each grand juror shall be a citizen of this Commonwealth, eighteen years of age or over, and shall have been a resident of this Commonwealth one year and of the county or corporation in which the court is to be held six months, and in other respects a qualified juror, and, when the grand juror is for a circuit court of a county, not an inhabitant of a city, except in those cases in which the circuit court of the county has jurisdiction in the city.

Acts 1975, c. 495; Acts 1991, c. 226.

§ 19.2–196. How deficiency of jurors supplied

If a sufficient number of grand jurors do not appear, the court may order the deficiency to be supplied from the bystanders or from a list furnished by the judge to the sheriff or sergeant.

Acts 1975, c. 495.

§ 19.2–197. Foreman of grand jury; oaths of jurors and witnesses

From among the persons summoned who attend the court shall select a foreman who shall be sworn as follows: "You shall diligently inquire, and true presentment make, of all such matters as may be given you in charge, or come to your knowledge, touching the present service. You shall present no person through prejudice or ill-will, nor leave any unpresented through fear or favor, but in all your presentments you shall present the truth, the whole truth, and nothing but the truth. So help you God." The other grand jurors shall afterwards be sworn as follows: "The same oath that your foreman has taken on his part, you and each of you shall observe and keep on your part. So help you God." Any witness testifying before the grand jury may be sworn by the foreman.

Acts 1975, c. 495.

§ 19.2–198. When new foreman or juror may be sworn in

If the foreman or any grand juror, at any time after being sworn, fail or be unable to attend another may be sworn in his stead.

Acts 1975, c. 495.

§ 19.2–199. Judge to charge grand jury

The grand jury, after being sworn, shall be charged by the judge of the court and shall then be sent to their room. In the charge given by the court to a regular grand jury, the court shall instruct it to advise the court after their considerations of the bills of indictment whether it desires to be impanelled as a special grand jury to consider any matters provided for in subdivision (2) of § 19.2–191.

Acts 1975, c. 495.

§ 19.2–200. Duties of grand jury

The grand jury shall inquire of and present all felonies, misdemeanors and violations of penal laws committed within the jurisdiction of the respective courts wherein it is sworn; except that no presentment shall be made of a matter for which there is no corporal punishment, but only a fine, where the fine is limited to an amount not exceeding five dollars. After a regular grand jury has concluded its deliberation on bills of indictment and made its return thereon, the court shall inquire of it whether it recommends that a special grand jury be impanelled to perform any of the functions provided for in subdivision (2) of § 19.2–191. If a majority of the grand jurors responds in the affirmative, the court shall impanel so many of that jury as answer in the affirmative and are also willing to serve thereon, plus any additional members as may be necessary to complete the panel, as a special grand jury and if a minority of the grand jurors responds in the affirmative, the court may impanel a special grand jury in the same manner.

Acts 1975, c. 495; Acts 1978, c. 741; Acts 1980, c. 134.

§ 19.2–201. Officers to give information of violation of penal laws to attorney for Commonwealth

Every commissioner of the revenue, sheriff, constable or other officer shall promptly give information of the violation of any penal law to the attorney for the Commonwealth, who shall forthwith institute and prosecute all necessary and proper proceedings in such case, whether in the name of the Commonwealth or of a county or corporation, and may in such case issue or cause to be issued a summons for any witnesses he may deem material to give evidence before the court or grand jury. Except as otherwise provided in this chapter, no attorney for the Commonwealth shall go before any grand jury except when duly sworn to testify as a witness, but he may advise the foreman of a regular grand jury or any member or members thereof in relation to the discharge of their duties.

Acts 1975, c. 495.

§ 19.2–202. How indictments found and presentment made

At least four of a regular grand jury must concur in finding or making an indictment or presentment. It may make a presentment or find an indictment upon the information of two or more of its own body, or on the testimony of witnesses called on by the grand jury, or sent to it by the court. If only one of their number can testify as to an offense, he shall be sworn as any other witness. When a presentment or indictment is so made or found, the names of the grand jurors giving the information, or of the witnesses, shall be written at the foot of the presentment or indictment.

Acts 1975, c. 495.

§ 19.2–203. Indictments ignored may be sent to another grand jury; what irregularities not to vitiate indictment, etc.

Although a bill of indictment be returned not a true bill the same or another bill of indictment against the same person for the same offense may be sent to, and acted on, by the same or another grand jury. No irregularity in the time or manner of selecting the jurors, or in the writ of venire facias, or in the manner of executing the same, shall vitiate any presentment, indictment or finding of a grand jury.

Acts 1975, c. 495.

§ 19.2–204. Penalties on officers and jurors for failure of duty

A court whose officer fails without good cause, when it is his duty, to summon a grand jury and return a list of its names shall fine him twenty dollars. A person summoned and failing to attend a court as a grand juror shall be fined by the court not less than five dollars nor more than twenty dollars, unless, after being summoned to show cause against the fine, he gives a reasonable excuse for his failure.

Acts 1975, c. 495.

§ 19.2–205. Pay and mileage of grand jurors

Every person who serves upon a grand jury, regular or special, shall receive the same compensation and mileage allowed jurors in civil cases by § 17.1–618 and the same shall be paid out of the county or corporation levy.

Acts 1975, c. 495.

Article 3

Special Grand Juries

§ 19.2–206. When impanelled

A. Special grand juries may be impanelled by a circuit court (i) at any time upon its own motion, (ii) upon recommendation of a minority of the members of a regular grand jury that a special grand jury be impanelled, to perform the functions provided for in subdivision (2) of § 19.2–191, or (iii) upon request of the attorney for the Commonwealth to investigate and report on any condition that involves or tends to promote criminal activity and consider bills of indictment to determine whether there is sufficient probable cause to return each such indictment as a "true bill."

B. A special grand jury shall be impanelled by a circuit court upon the recommendation of a majority of the members of a regular grand jury if the court finds probable cause to believe that a crime has been committed which should be investigated by a special grand jury impanelled to perform the functions provided for in subdivision (2) of § 19.2–191.

Acts 1975, c. 495; Acts 1978, c. 741; Acts 1980, c. 134; Acts 1987, c. 136; Acts 2001, c. 4.

§ 19.2–207. Composition of a special grand jury

Special grand juries shall consist of not less than seven and not more than 11 members, and shall be summoned from a list prepared by the court. Members of a special grand jury shall possess the same qualifications as those prescribed for members of a regular grand jury, including indifferent in the cause to be conducted by the special grand jury. In order to determine a potential juror's qualifications, the presiding judge shall examine each juror individually and under oath. He shall then certify in writing and not under seal that he has examined the members of the special grand jury and has found that they are qualified and are impartial and disinterested in the subject matter and outcome of the investigation. The examination shall be recorded by a court reporter and conducted pursuant to the requirements of secrecy provided for in this chapter. The court shall appoint one of the members as foreman.

Acts 1975, c. 495. Amended by Acts 2008, c. 644.

§ 19.2–208. Subpoena power of special grand jury

The special grand jury may subpoena persons to appear before it to testify and to produce specified records, papers, and documents or other tangible things, but before any witness testifies, he shall be warned by the foreman that he need not answer any questions or produce any evidence that would tend to incriminate him, and that the witness may have counsel of his own procurement present when he appears to testify, and at the same time the foreman also shall warn each witness that he may later be called upon to testify in any case that might grow out of the investigation and report of the special grand jury.

A witness who has been called to testify or produce specified records, papers and documents or other tangible things before a grand jury requested by the attorney for the Commonwealth, and who refuses to testify or produce specified records, papers and documents or other tangible things by expressly invoking his right not to incriminate himself, may be compelled to testify or produce specified records, papers and documents or other tangible things by the presiding judge. Such witness who refuses to testify or produce specified records, papers and documents or other tangible things after being ordered to do so by the presiding judge may be held in contempt and may be incarcerated until the contempt is purged by compliance with the order or the grand jury is discharged. When a witness is compelled to testify or produce specified records, papers and documents or other tangible things after expressly invoking his right not to incriminate himself, and the presiding judge has determined that the assertion of the right is bona fide, the compelled testimony, or any information directly or indirectly derived from such testimony or other information, shall not be used against the witness in any criminal proceeding except a prosecution for perjury.

Notwithstanding the provisions of this section, all provisions of this Code relative to immunity granted to witnesses who testify before a grand jury shall remain applicable.

The foreman shall administer the oath prescribed by law for witnesses, and any member of the special grand jury may examine a witness.

Acts 1975, c. 495; Acts 2001, c. 4; Acts 2003, c. 565.

§ 19.2–209. Presence of counsel for a witness

Any witness appearing before a special grand jury shall have the right to have counsel of his own procurement present when he testifies. Such counsel shall have the right to consult with and advise the witness during his examination, but shall not have the right to conduct an examination of his own of the witness.

Acts 1975, c. 495.

§ 19.2–210. Presence of attorney for the Commonwealth

The attorney for the Commonwealth shall not be present at any time while the special grand jury is in session except that during the investigatory stage of its proceedings he may be present. When the special grand jury is impanelled upon motion of the court or recommendation of a regular grand jury, he may be present during the investigatory stage only when his presence is requested by the special grand jury and may interrogate witnesses provided the special grand jury requests or consents to such interrogation. When the special grand jury was impanelled upon his request, he may examine any witness called to testify or produce evidence, but his examination of a witness shall in no way affect the right of any grand juror to examine the witness.

The attorney for the Commonwealth shall not be present during or after the investigative stage of the proceedings at any time while the special grand jury is discussing, evaluating or considering the testimony of a witness or is deliberating in order to reach decisions or prepare its report, except that he may be present when his legal advice is requested by the special grand jury.

Acts 1975, c. 495; Acts 2001, c. 4.

§ 19.2–211. Provision for special counsel and other personnel

At the request of the special grand jury, the court may designate special counsel to assist it in its work, and may also provide it with appropriate specialized personnel for investigative purposes.

Acts 1975, c. 495.

§ 19.2–212. Provision for court reporter; use and disposition of notes, tapes and transcriptions

A. A court reporter shall be provided for a special grand jury to record, manually or electronically, and transcribe all oral testimony taken before a special grand jury, but such reporter shall not be present during any stage of its deliberations. The notes, tapes and transcriptions of the reporter are for the sole use of the special grand jury, and the contents thereof shall not be divulged by anyone except as hereinafter provided. After the special grand jury has completed its use of the notes, tapes and transcriptions, the foreman shall cause them to be sealed, the container dated, and delivered to the court.

The court shall cause the sealed container to be kept safely. If any witness testifying before the special grand jury is prosecuted subsequently for perjury, the court, on motion of either the attorney for the Commonwealth or the defendant, shall permit them both to have access to the testimony given by the defendant when a witness before the special grand jury, and the testimony shall be admissible in the perjury case.

If no prosecution for perjury is instituted within three years from the date of the report of the special grand jury, the court shall cause the sealed container to be destroyed; however, on motion of the attorney for the Commonwealth, the court may extend the time period for destruction if the grand jury was impanelled at the request of the attorney for the Commonwealth.

B. Upon motion to the presiding judge, the attorney for the Commonwealth shall be permitted to review any evidence that was presented to the special grand jury, and shall be permitted to make notes and to duplicate portions of the evidence as he deems necessary for use in a criminal investigation or proceeding. The attorney for the Commonwealth shall maintain the secrecy of all information obtained from a review or duplication of the evidence presented to the special grand jury. Upon motion to the presiding judge by a person indicted after a special grand jury investigation, similar permission to review, note or duplicate evidence shall be extended if it appears that the permission is consistent with the ends of justice and is necessary to reasonably inform such person of the nature of the evidence to be presented against him, or to adequately prepare his defense.

Acts 1975, c. 495; Acts 2001, c. 4; Acts 2003, c. 96. Amended by Acts 2008, c. 644.

§ 19.2–213. Report by special grand jury; return of true bill

At the conclusion of its investigation and deliberation, a special grand jury impanelled by the court on its own motion or on recommendation of a regular grand jury shall file a report of its findings with the court, including therein any recommendations that it may deem appropriate, after which it shall be discharged. Such report shall be sealed and not open to public inspection, other than by order of the court.

A majority, but not less than five, of the members of a special grand jury convened upon request of the attorney for the Commonwealth must concur in order to return a "true bill" of indictment. A "true bill" may be returned upon the testimony of, or evidence produced by, any witness who was called by the grand jury, upon evidence presented or sent to it.

Acts 1975, c. 495; Acts 1978, c. 638; Acts 2001, c. 4.

§ 19.2–213.1. Discharge of special grand jury

If a special grand jury has not filed a report pursuant to § 19.2–213 within six months of its impanelling, the circuit court appointing it shall discharge it; provided, however, if such court, in its discretion, determines that the special grand jury is making progress in its investigation, the court may direct that special grand jury to continue its investigation pursuant to this article.

Acts 1978, c. 638.

§ 19.2–214. Prosecutions resulting from report

Any bill of indictment for alleged criminal offenses, which may follow as a result of the report of the special grand jury, shall be prepared by the attorney for the Commonwealth for presentation to a regular grand jury.

Acts 1975, c. 495.

§ 19.2–215. Costs of special grand jury

All costs incurred for services provided by the court for a special grand jury shall be paid by the Commonwealth.

Acts 1975, c. 495.

ARTICLE 4

MULTI-JURISDICTION GRAND JURIES

§ 19.2–215.1. Functions of a multijurisdiction grand jury

The functions of a multijurisdiction grand jury are:

1. To investigate any condition that involves or tends to promote criminal violations of:

a. Title 10.1 for which punishment as a felony is authorized;

b. § 13.1–520;

c. §§ 18.2–47 and 18.2–48;

d. §§ 18.2–111 and 18.2–112;

e. Article 6 (§ 18.2–59 et seq.) of Chapter 4 of Title 18.2;

f. Article 7.1 (§ 18.2–152.1 et seq.) of Chapter 5 of Title 18.2;

g. Article 1 (§ 18.2–247 et seq.) and Article 1.1 (§ 18.2–265.1 et seq.) of Chapter 7 of Title 18.2;

h. Article 1 (§ 18.2–325 et seq.) and Article 1.1:1 (§ 18.2–340.15 et seq.) of Chapter 8 of Title 18.2, Chapter 29 (§ 59.1–364 et seq.) of Title 59.1 or any other provision prohibiting, limiting, regulating, or otherwise affecting gaming or gambling activity;

i. § 18.2–434, when violations occur before a multijurisdiction grand jury;

j. Article 2 (§ 18.2–438 et seq.) and Article 3 (§ 18.2–446 et seq.) of Chapter 10 of Title 18.2;

k. § 18.2–460 for which punishment as a felony is authorized;

l. Article 1.1 (§ 18.2–498.1 et seq.) of Chapter 12 of Title 18.2;

m. Article 1 (§ 32.1–310 et seq.) of Chapter 9 of Title 32.1;

n. Chapter 4.2 (§ 59.1–68.6 et seq.) of Title 59.1;

o. Article 9 (§ 3.2–6570 et seq.) of Chapter 65 of Title 3.2;

p. Article 1 (§ 18.2–30 et seq.) of Chapter 4 of Title 18.2;

q. Article 2.1 (§ 18.2–46.1 et seq.) and Article 2.2 (§ 18.2–46.4 et seq.) of Chapter 4 of Title 18.2;

r. Article 5 (§ 18.2–186 et seq.) and Article 6 (§ 18.2–191 et seq.) of Chapter 6 of Title 18.2;

s. Chapter 6.1 (§ 59.1–92.1 et seq.) of Title 59.1;

t. § 18.2–178 where the violation involves insurance fraud;

u. § 18.2–346 for which punishment as a felony is authorized or § 18.2–355, 18.2–356, 18.2–357, or 18.2–357.1;

v. Article 9 (§ 18.2–246.1 et seq.) of Chapter 6 of Title 18.2;

w. Article 2 (§ 18.2–38 et seq.) of Chapter 4 of Title 18.2;

x. Malicious felonious assault and malicious bodily wounding under Article 4 (§ 18.2–51 et seq.) of Chapter 4 of Title 18.2;

y. Article 5 (§ 18.2–58 et seq.) of Chapter 4 of Title 18.2;

z. Felonious sexual assault under Article 7 (§ 18.2–61 et seq.) of Chapter 4 of Title 18.2;

aa. Arson in violation of § 18.2–77 when the structure burned was occupied or a Class 3 felony violation of § 18.2–79;

bb. Chapter 13 (§ 18.2–512 et seq.) of Title 18.2;

cc. § 18.2–246.14 and Chapter 10 (§ 58.1–1000 et seq.) of Title 58.1; and

dd. Any other provision of law when such condition is discovered in the course of an investigation that a multijurisdiction grand jury is otherwise authorized to undertake and to investigate any condition that involves or tends to promote any attempt, solicitation or conspiracy to violate the laws enumerated in this section.

2. To report evidence of any criminal offense enumerated in subdivision 1 and for which a court reporter has recorded all oral testimony as provided by § 19.2–215.9 to the attorney for the Commonwealth or United States attorney of any jurisdiction where such offense could be prosecuted or investigated, or to the chief law-enforcement officer of any jurisdiction where such offense could be prosecuted or investigated, or to a sworn investigator designated pursuant to § 19.2–215.6, or, when appropriate, to the Attorney General.

3. To consider bills of indictment prepared by a special counsel to determine whether there is sufficient probable cause to return each such indictment as a "true bill." Only bills of indictment which allege an offense enumerated in subdivision 1 may be submitted to a multijurisdiction grand jury.

4. The provisions of this section shall not abrogate the authority of an attorney for the Commonwealth in a particular jurisdiction to determine the course of a prosecution in that jurisdiction.

Acts 1983, c. 543; Acts 1991, c. 616; Acts 1995, c. 552; Acts 2000, c. 359; Acts 2002, c. 588; Acts 2002, c. 623; Acts 2004, c. 396; Acts 2004, c. 435. Amended by Acts 2008, c. 704; Acts 2009, c. 491; Acts 2011, c. 504; Acts 2013, c. 83; Acts 2013, c. 314; Acts 2013, c. 459; Acts 2014, c. 389; Acts 2014, c. 422; Acts 2014, c. 534; Acts 2015, c. 690; Acts 2015, c. 691.

§ 19.2–215.2. Application for such grand jury

Provided the Attorney General has approved the application in writing prior to submission, application for a multi-jurisdiction grand jury may be made to the Supreme Court of Virginia by two or more attorneys for the Commonwealth from jurisdictions which would be within the original scope of the investigation. The application shall be in writing and shall state (i) which jurisdictions will be involved in the original scope of the investigation, (ii) in which jurisdiction it is requested that the multi-jurisdiction grand jury be convened, (iii) the name or names of the attorneys for the Commonwealth or their assistants who will serve as special counsel to the grand jury, (iv) the name of the attorney who shall direct the grand jury proceedings. The presiding judge may extend or limit the jurisdictional territory of the investigation, for good cause shown, upon the motion of a grand jury already convened. Notice of every such application shall be given to the attorneys for the Commonwealth in the jurisdictions named in the application and, if the original scope of the investigation is extended into other jurisdictions, notice of such extension shall be given to the attorneys for the Commonwealth in the jurisdictions into which the investigation is extended.

Acts 1983, c. 543.

§ 19.2–215.3. When impaneled; impaneling order

Upon application by two or more attorneys for the Commonwealth, the Chief Justice of the Supreme Court, or any justice designated by the Chief Justice, may within twenty days thereafter order the impaneling of a multi-jurisdiction grand jury for a term of twelve months. The term of such a grand jury may be extended for successive periods of not more than six months by the Chief Justice, or by any justice designated by the Chief Justice, upon the petition of a majority of the members of the grand jury.

The impaneling order shall designate the jurisdiction requested on the application as the jurisdiction where the multi-jurisdiction grand jury shall be convened and shall, unless all judges of that circuit have recused themselves, appoint a judge of the circuit court of that jurisdiction as the presiding judge. The impaneling order shall also designate special counsel and each special counsel who will assist the multi-jurisdiction grand jury as listed in the application. The presiding judge shall substitute or appoint additional special counsel upon motion of special counsel.

Acts 1983, c. 543. Amended by Acts 2010, c. 438.

§ 19.2–215.4. Number and qualifications of jurors; grand jury list; when convened; compensation of jurors

A. A multi-jurisdiction grand jury shall consist of not less than seven nor more than 11 members. Each member of a multi-jurisdiction grand jury shall be a citizen of this Commonwealth, 18 years of age or older, and a resident of this Commonwealth for one year and of one of the jurisdictions named in the application for six months.

B. The presiding judge shall determine the number of grand jurors to be drawn and shall draw them so that, to the extent practicable, each of the jurisdictions named in the application is represented by at least one juror residing in that jurisdiction, but in no event shall said panel have more than 11 members. The grand jurors shall be summoned from a list prepared by the presiding judge. In the preparation of this list, the presiding judge shall select only persons who have been selected as regular grand jurors pursuant to the provisions of § 19.2–194 in the jurisdiction named in the application. Members of a multi-jurisdiction grand jury shall possess the same qualifications as those prescribed for members of a regular grand jury, including indifference in the cause.

C. The provisions of § 19.2–192 dealing with secrecy in grand jury proceedings are incorporated herein by reference.

D. The presiding judge shall determine the time, date and place within the designated jurisdiction where the multi-jurisdiction grand jury is to be convened. The presiding judge shall also appoint one of the grand jurors to serve as foreman. Members of the multi-jurisdiction grand jury shall be compensated according to the provisions of § 19.2–205. The expense of a multi-jurisdiction grand jury shall be borne by the Commonwealth.

Acts 1983, c. 543. Amended by Acts 2008, c. 644.

§ 19.2–215.5. Subpoena power; counsel for witness; oath

A multi-jurisdiction grand jury has statewide subpoena power and, through special counsel, may subpoena persons to appear before it to testify and may subpoena the production of evidence, with or without the custodian of records at the election of special counsel, in the form of specified records, papers, documents, or other tangible things. Such subpoenas shall be returnable for a specific meeting of the multi-jurisdiction grand jury. Mileage and such other reasonable expenses as are approved by the presiding judge shall be paid such persons from funds appropriated for such purpose.

A witness before a multi-jurisdiction grand jury shall be entitled to the presence of counsel in the grand jury room, but he may not participate in the proceedings.

The foreman shall administer the oath required by law for witnesses.

Acts 1983, c. 543. Amended by Acts 2014, c. 389.

§ 19.2–215.6. Role and presence of special counsel; examination of witnesses; sworn investigators

Special counsel may be present during the investigatory stage of a multi-jurisdiction grand jury proceeding and may examine any witness who is called to testify or produce evidence. The examination of a witness by special counsel shall in no way affect the right of any grand juror to examine the witness.

At the request of special counsel, the presiding judge shall designate specialized personnel for investigative purposes. Such personnel shall be designated as a sworn investigator and shall be administered an oath to maintain the secrecy of all proceedings of the multi-jurisdiction grand jury. A sworn investigator is permitted to discuss multi-jurisdiction grand jury proceedings with any other sworn investigator or special counsel and may participate in multi-jurisdiction grand jury proceedings at the request of special counsel or the grand jury. Any specialized personnel who have been administered an oath to maintain the secrecy of all proceedings of the multi-jurisdiction grand jury before July 1, 2014, and who continue to serve in that position are deemed to be sworn investigators under this section.

Special counsel and sworn investigators, however, may not be present at any time during the deliberations of a multi-jurisdiction grand jury except when the grand jury requests the legal advice of special counsel as to specific questions of law.

Acts 1983, c. 543. Amended by Acts 2014, c. 389.

§ 19.2–215.7. Warnings given to witnesses; when witness in contempt; use of testimony compelled after witness invokes right against self-incrimination

A. Every witness testifying before a multi-jurisdiction grand jury shall be warned by special counsel or by the foreman of the grand jury that he need not answer any question that would tend to incriminate him, and that he may later be called upon to testify in any case that may result from the grand jury proceedings.

B. A witness who has been called to testify or produce evidence before a multi-jurisdiction grand jury, and who refuses to testify or produce evidence by expressly invoking his right not to incriminate himself, may be compelled to testify or produce evidence by the presiding judge. A witness who refuses to testify or produce evidence after being ordered to do so by the presiding judge may be held in contempt and may be incarcerated until the contempt is purged by compliance with the order.

C. When a witness is compelled to testify or produce evidence after expressly invoking his right not to incriminate himself, and the presiding judge has determined that the assertion of the right is bona fide, the compelled testimony, or any information directly or indirectly derived from such testimony or other information, shall not be used against the witness in any criminal proceeding except a prosecution for perjury.

Acts 1983, c. 543.

§ 19.2–215.8. Returning a "true bill" of indictment; jurisdiction to be set out

In order to return a "true bill" of indictment, a majority, but in no instance less than five, of the multi-jurisdiction grand jurors must concur in that finding. A multi-jurisdiction grand jury may return a "true bill" of indictment upon the testimony of, or evidence produced by, any witness who was called by the grand jury, upon evidence presented to it by special counsel, or upon evidence sent to it by the presiding judge.

Every "true bill" of indictment returned by a multi-jurisdiction grand jury shall state in which jurisdiction or jurisdictions the offense is alleged to have occurred. Thereafter, when venue is proper in more than one jurisdiction, the presiding judge who directed the grand jury proceeding shall elect in which one of the jurisdictions named in the indictment the indictment is to be prosecuted.

Acts 1983, c. 543.

§ 19.2–215.9. Court reporter provided; safekeeping of transcripts, notes, etc.; when disclosure permitted; access to record of testimony and evidence

A. A court reporter shall be provided for a multi-jurisdiction grand jury to record, manually or electronically, and transcribe all oral testimony taken before a multi-jurisdiction grand jury, but such a reporter shall not be present during any stage of its deliberations. Such transcription shall include the original or copies of all documents, reports, or other evidence presented to the multi-jurisdiction grand jury. The notes, tapes, and transcriptions of the reporter are for the use of the multi-jurisdiction grand jury, and the contents thereof shall not be used or divulged by anyone except as provided in this article. After the multi-jurisdiction grand jury has completed its use of the notes, tapes, and transcriptions, the foreman shall cause them to be delivered to the clerk of the circuit court in whose jurisdiction the multi-jurisdiction grand jury sits, with copies provided to special counsel. Upon motion of special counsel, the presiding judge may order that such notes, tapes, and transcriptions be destroyed at the direction of special counsel by any means the presiding judge deems sufficient, provided that at least seven years have passed from the date of the multi-jurisdiction grand jury proceeding where such notes, tapes, and transcriptions were made.

B. The clerk shall cause the notes, tapes, and transcriptions or other evidence to be kept safely. Upon motion to the presiding judge, special counsel shall be permitted to review any of the evidence which was presented to the multi-jurisdiction grand jury, and shall be permitted to make notes and to duplicate portions of the evidence as he deems necessary for use in a criminal investigation or proceeding. Special counsel shall maintain the secrecy of all information obtained from a review or duplication of the evidence presented to the multi-jurisdiction grand jury, except that this information may be disclosed pursuant to the provisions of subdivision 2 of § 19.2–215.1. Upon motion to the presiding judge by a person indicted by a multi-jurisdiction grand jury, similar permission to review, note, or duplicate evidence shall be extended if it appears that the permission is consistent with the ends of justice and is necessary to reasonably inform such person of the nature of the evidence to be presented against him, or to adequately prepare his defense.

C. If any witness who testified or produced evidence before the multi-jurisdiction grand jury is prosecuted on the basis of his testimony or the evidence he produced, or if any witness is prosecuted for perjury on the basis of his testimony or the evidence he produced before the multi-jurisdiction grand jury, the presiding judge, on motion of either special counsel or the defendant, shall permit the defendant access to the testimony of or evidence produced by the defendant before the multi-jurisdiction grand jury. The testimony and the evidence produced by the defendant before the multi-jurisdiction grand jury shall then be admissible in the trial of the criminal offense with which the defendant is charged (i) to establish a charge of perjury in the Commonwealth's case-in-chief on the basis of his testimony before the multi-jurisdiction grand jury and (ii) for the purpose of impeaching the defendant in the trial of any other criminal matter, provided the testimony or evidence being used for impeachment was produced by the defendant voluntarily before the multi-jurisdiction grand jury.

Acts 1983, c. 543. Amended by Acts 2014, c. 389.

§ 19.2–215.10. Participation by Office of Attorney General; assistance of special counsel permitted in certain prosecutions

Upon request by the applicants or upon motion to the presiding judge by special counsel, the Office of Attorney General may participate as special counsel in the multi-jurisdiction grand jury proceedings and any prosecutions arising therefrom. In any prosecution arising out of the multi-jurisdiction grand jury, the attorney for the Commonwealth may also obtain the assistance of the special counsel to the grand jury as a special assistant attorney for the Commonwealth.

Acts 1983, c. 543.

§ 19.2–215.11. Discharge of grand jury

At any time during the original or extended term of a multi-jurisdiction grand jury, the presiding judge may discharge the grand jury if, in the opinion of the presiding judge, the existence of the multi-jurisdiction grand jury is no longer necessary.

Acts 1983, c. 543.

CHAPTER 14

PRESENTMENTS, INDICTMENTS AND INFORMATIONS

ARTICLE 1

NECESSITY FOR INDICTMENT, ETC.

§ 19.2–216. Definition of indictment, presentment and information

An indictment is a written accusation of crime, prepared by the attorney for the Commonwealth and returned "a true bill" upon the oath or affirmation of a legally impanelled grand jury.

A presentment is a written accusation of crime prepared and returned by a grand jury from their own knowledge or observation, without any bill of indictment laid before them.

An information is a written accusation of crime or a complaint for forfeiture of property or money or for imposition of a penalty, prepared and presented by a competent public official upon his oath of office.

Acts 1975, c. 495.

§ 19.2–217. When information filed; prosecution for felony to be by indictment or presentment; waiver; process to compel appearance of accused

An information may be filed by the attorney for the Commonwealth based upon a complaint in writing verified by the oath of a competent witness; but no person shall be put upon trial for any felony, unless an indictment or presentment shall have first been found or made by a grand jury in a court of competent jurisdiction or unless such person, by writing signed by such person before the court having jurisdiction to try such felony or before the judge of such court shall have waived such indictment or presentment, in which event he may be tried on a warrant or information. If the accused be in custody, or has been recognized or summoned to answer such information, presentment or indictment, no other process shall be necessary; but the court may, in its discretion, issue process to compel the appearance of the accused.

Acts 1975, c. 495.

§ 19.2–217.1. Central file of capital murder indictments

Upon the return by a grand jury of an indictment for capital murder and the arrest of the defendant, the clerk of the circuit court in which such indictment is returned shall forthwith file a certified copy of the indictment with the clerk of the Supreme Court of Virginia. All such indictments shall be maintained in a single place by the clerk of the Supreme Court, and shall be available to members of the public upon request. Failure to comply with the provisions of this section shall not be (i) a basis upon which an indictment may be quashed or deemed invalid; (ii) deemed error upon which a conviction may be reversed or a sentence vacated; or (iii) a basis upon which a court may prevent or delay execution of a sentence.

Acts 1993, c. 319.

§ 19.2–218. Preliminary hearing required for person arrested on charge of felony; waiver

No person who is arrested on a charge of felony shall be denied a preliminary hearing upon the question of whether there is reasonable ground to believe that he committed the offense and no indictment shall be returned in a court of record against any such person prior to such hearing unless such hearing is waived in writing by the accused.

Acts 1975, c. 495.

§ 19.2–218.1. Preliminary hearings involving certain sexual crimes against spouses

A. In any preliminary hearing of a charge for a violation under § 18.2–61, 18.2–67.1, or 18.2–67.2 where the complaining witness is the spouse of the accused, upon a finding of probable cause the court may request that its court services unit, in consultation with any appropriate social services organization, local community services board, or other community mental health services organization, prepare a report analyzing the feasibility of providing counseling or other forms of therapy for the accused and the probability such treatment will be successful. Based upon this report and any other relevant evidence, the court may, with the consent of the accused, the complaining witness and the attorney for the Commonwealth in any case involving a violation of § 18.2–61, 18.2–67.1, or 18.2–67.2, authorize the accused to submit to and complete a designated course of counseling or therapy. In such case, the hearing shall be adjourned until such time as counseling or therapy is completed or terminated. Upon the completion of counseling or therapy by the accused and after consideration of a final evaluation to be furnished to the court by the person responsible for conducting such counseling or therapy and such further report of the court services unit as the court may require, and after consideration of the views of the complaining witness, the court, in its discretion, may discharge the accused if the court finds such action will promote maintenance of the family unit and be in the best interest of the complaining witness.

B. No statement or disclosure by the accused concerning the alleged offense made during counseling or any other form of therapy ordered pursuant to this section or § 18.2–61, 18.2–67.1, 18.2–67.2, or 19.2–218.2 may be used against the accused in any trial as evidence, nor shall any evidence against the accused be admitted which was discovered through such statement or disclosure.

Acts 1986, c. 516; Acts 2005, c. 631. Amended by Acts 2012, c. 476; Acts 2012, c. 507.

§ 19.2–218.2. Hearing before juvenile and domestic relations district court required for persons accused of certain violations against their spouses

A. In any case involving a violation of § 18.2–61, 18.2–67.1, or 18.2–67.2 where the complaining witness is the spouse of the accused, where a preliminary hearing pursuant to § 19.2–218.1 has not been held prior to indictment or trial, the court shall refer the case to the appropriate juvenile and domestic relations district court for a hearing to determine whether counseling or therapy is appropriate prior to further disposition unless the hearing is waived in writing by the accused. The court conducting this hearing may order counseling or therapy for the accused in compliance with the guidelines set forth in § 19.2–218.1.

B. After such hearing pursuant to which the accused has completed counseling or therapy and upon the recommendation of the juvenile and domestic relations district court judge conducting the hearing, the judge of the circuit court may dismiss the charge with the consent of the attorney for the Commonwealth and if the court finds such action will promote maintenance of the family unit and be in the best interest of the complaining witness.

Acts 1986, c. 516; Acts 2005, c. 631.

§ 19.2–219. When capias need not be issued; summons; judgment

No capias need be issued on a presentment or indictment of an offense for which there is no punishment but a fine or forfeiture, limited to an amount not exceeding twenty dollars; but a summons to answer such presentment or indictment may be issued against the accused; and if it be served ten days before the return day thereof, and he does not appear, judgment may be rendered against him for the penalty. If he appear, the court may, unless he demand a jury, hear and determine the matter and give judgment thereon.

Acts 1975, c. 495.

Article 2

Form and Requisites

§ 19.2–220. Contents of indictment in general

The indictment or information shall be a plain, concise and definite written statement, (1) naming the accused, (2) describing the offense charged, (3) identifying the county, city or town in which the accused committed the offense, and (4) reciting that the accused committed the offense on or about a certain date. In describing the offense, the indictment or information may use the name given to the offense by the common law, or the indictment or information may state so much of the common law or statutory definition of the offense as is sufficient to advise what offense is charged.

Acts 1975, c. 495.

§ 19.2–221. Form of prosecutions generally; murder and manslaughter

The prosecutions for offenses against the Commonwealth, unless otherwise provided, shall be by presentment, indictment or information. While any form of presentment, indictment or information which informs the accused of the nature and cause of the accusation against him shall be good the following shall be deemed sufficient for murder and manslaughter:

Commonwealth of Virginia .... county (or city) to-wit: The grand jurors of the Commonwealth of Virginia, in and for the body of the county (or city) of ...., upon their oaths present that A .... B ...., on the ... day of ...., 20..., in the county (or city) of .... feloniously did kill and murder one C .... D .... against the peace and dignity of the Commonwealth.

A grand jury may, in case of homicide, which in their opinion amounts to manslaughter only, and not to murder, find an indictment against the accused for manslaughter and in such case the indictment shall be sufficient if it be in form or effect as follows:

Commonwealth of Virginia .... county (or city) to-wit: The grand jurors of the Commonwealth of Virginia, in and for the body of the county (or city) of ...., upon their oaths present that A .... B ...., on the ... day of ...., 20... in the county (or city) of .... feloniously and unlawfully did kill and slay one C .... D ...., against the peace and dignity of the Commonwealth.

Acts 1975, c. 495.

§ 19.2–222. Repealed by Acts 1996, c. 676

§ 19.2–223. Charging several acts of embezzlement; description of money

In a prosecution against a person accused of embezzling or fraudulently converting to his own use bullion, money, bank notes or other security for money or items of personal property subject to larceny it shall be lawful in the same indictment or accusation to charge and thereon to proceed against the accused for any number of distinct acts of such embezzlements or fraudulent conversions which may have been committed by him within six months from the first to the last of the acts charged in the indictment; and it shall be sufficient to allege the embezzlement or fraudulent conversion to be of money without specifying any particular money, gold, silver, note or security. Such allegation, so far as it regards the description of the property, shall be sustained if the accused be proved to have embezzled any bullion, money, bank note or other security for money or items of personal property subject to larceny although the particular species be not proved.

And in a prosecution for the larceny of United States currency or for obtaining United States currency by a false pretense or token, or for receiving United States currency knowing the same to have been stolen, it shall be sufficient if the accused be proved guilty of the larceny of national bank notes or United States treasury notes, certificates for either gold or silver coin, fractional coin, currency, or any other form of money issued by the United States government, or of obtaining the same by false pretense or token, or of receiving the same knowing it to have been stolen although the particular species be not proved.

Acts 1975, c. 495; Acts 1989, c. 370.

§ 19.2–224. In prosecution for forgery, unnecessary to set forth copy of forged instrument

In a prosecution for forging or altering any instrument or other thing, or attempting to employ as true any forged instrument or other thing, or for any of the offenses mentioned in Article 1 (§ 18.2–168 et seq.) of Chapter 6 of Title 18.2, it shall not be necessary to set forth any copy or facsimile of such instrument or other thing; but it shall be sufficient to describe the same in such manner as would sustain an indictment for stealing such instrument or other thing, supposing it to be the subject of larceny.

Acts 1975, c. 495.

§ 19.2–225. Allegation of intent

Where an intent to injure, defraud or cheat is required to constitute an offense, it shall be sufficient, in an indictment or accusation therefor, to allege generally an intent to injure, defraud or cheat without naming the person intended to be injured, defrauded or cheated; and it shall be sufficient, and not be deemed a variance, if there appear to be an intent to injure, defraud or cheat the United States, or any state, or any county, corporation, officer or person.

Acts 1975, c. 495.

§ 19.2–226. What defects in indictments not to vitiate them

No indictment or other accusation shall be quashed or deemed invalid:

(1) For omitting to set forth that it is upon the oaths of the jurors or upon their oaths and affirmations;

(2) For the insertion of the words "upon their oath," instead of "upon their oaths";

(3) For not in terms alleging that the offense was committed "within the jurisdiction of the court" when the averments show that the case is one of which the court has jurisdiction;

(4) For the omission or misstatement of the title, occupation, estate, or degree of the accused or of the name or place of his residence;

(5) For omitting the words "with force and arms" or the statement of any particular kind of force and arms;

(6) For omitting to state, or stating imperfectly, the time at which the offense was committed when time is not the essence of the offense;

(7) For failing to allege the kind or value of an instrument which caused death or to allege that it was of no value;

(8) For omitting to charge the offense to be "against the form of the statute or statutes";

(9) For the omission or insertion of any other words of mere form or surplusage; or

(10) For omitting or stating incorrectly the Virginia crime code references for the particular offense or offenses covered.

Nor shall it be abated for any misnomer of the accused; but the court may, in case of a misnomer appearing before or in the course of a trial, forthwith cause the indictment or accusation to be amended according to the fact.

Acts 1975, c. 495; Acts 2003, c. 148, eff. Oct. 1, 2004.

§ 19.2–227. When judgment not to be arrested or reversed

Judgment in any criminal case shall not be arrested or reversed upon any exception or objection made after a verdict to the indictment or other accusation, unless it be so defective as to be in violation of the Constitution.

Acts 1975, c. 495.

§ 19.2–228. Name and address of complaining witness to be written on indictment, etc., for misdemeanor

In a prosecution for a misdemeanor the name and address of the complaining witness, if there be one, shall be written at the foot of the presentment, indictment or information when it is made, found or filed. In case the grand jury that brings in such presentment or indictment or the attorney for the Commonwealth who files such information fail to write the name of a complaining witness at the foot of the presentment, indictment or information, then the name of a complaining witness may be entered of record as such by the court on the motion of the defendant or the attorney for the Commonwealth at any time before the judgment.

Acts 1975, c. 495.

§ 19.2-229. When complaining witness required to give security for costs

For good cause the court may require a complaining witness to give security for the costs and if he fails to do so dismiss the prosecution at his costs.

Acts 1975, c. 495.

§ 19.2-230. Bill of particulars

A court of record may direct the filing of a bill of particulars at any time before trial. A motion for a bill of particulars shall be made before a plea is entered and at least seven days before the day fixed for trial and the bill of particulars shall be filed within such time as is fixed by the court.

Acts 1975, c. 495.

Article 3

Amendments

§ 19.2-231. Amendment of indictment, presentment or information

If there be any defect in form in any indictment, presentment or information, or if there shall appear to be any variance between the allegations therein and the evidence offered in proof thereof, the court may permit amendment of such indictment, presentment or information, at any time before the jury returns a verdict or the court finds the accused guilty or not guilty, provided the amendment does not change the nature or character of the offense charged. After any such amendment the accused shall be arraigned on the indictment, presentment or information as amended, and shall be allowed to plead anew thereto, if he so desires, and the trial shall proceed as if no amendment had been made; but if the court finds that such amendment operates as a surprise to the accused, he shall be entitled, upon request, to a continuance of the case for a reasonable time.

Acts 1975, c. 495.

Article 4

Process

§ 19.2-232. What process to be awarded against accused on indictment, etc.

When an indictment or presentment is found or made, or information filed, the court, or the judge thereof, shall award process against the accused to answer the same, if he be not in custody. Such process, if the prosecution be for a felony, shall be a capias; if it be for a misdemeanor, for which imprisonment may be imposed, it may be a capias or summons, in the discretion of the court or judge; in all other cases, it shall be, in the first instance a summons, but if a summons be returned executed and the defendant does not appear, or be returned not found, the court or judge may award a capias. The officer serving the summons or capias shall also serve a copy of the indictment, presentment or information therewith.

Acts 1975, c. 495; Acts 1980, c. 349.

§ 19.2-233. How awarded, directed, returnable and executed

Sections 8.01-292 and 8.01-295 shall apply to process in criminal, as well as in civil cases; and the court may, in the same case against the same person, award at the same time, or different times, several writs of summons or capias directed to officers of different counties or cities. An officer having a capias under which the accused is let to bail shall give a certificate of the fact, which shall protect him against any other capias which may have been issued for the same offense. A summons shall be served by delivering a copy thereof to the party in person and the clerk issuing such summons shall deliver or transmit therewith as many copies thereof as there are persons named therein on whom it is to be served.

Acts 1975, c. 495.

§ 19.2-234. Procedure when person arrested under capias

An officer who, under a capias from any court, arrests a person accused of an offense shall proceed in accordance with § 19.2-80 and Article 1 (§ 19.2-119 et seq.) of Chapter 9 of Title 19.2 regarding bail.

Acts 1975, c. 495; Acts 1986, c. 327.

§ 19.2-235. Clerks to mail process to officers in other counties, etc.

The clerk of every court shall forward, by mail, all process issued for the Commonwealth, directed to the officer of any county or city other than his own.

Acts 1975, c. 495.

§ 19.2–236. Where process of arrest may be executed

When process of arrest in a criminal prosecution is issued from a court, either against a party accused or a witness, the officer to whom it is directed or delivered may execute it in any part of the Commonwealth.
Acts 1975, c. 495.

§ 19.2–237. Process on indictment or presentment for misdemeanor

On any indictment or presentment for a misdemeanor process shall be issued immediately. If the accused appear and plead to the charge, the trial shall proceed without delay, unless good cause for continuance be shown. If, in any misdemeanor case the accused fails to appear and plead, when required the court may either award a capias or proceed to trial in the same manner as if the accused had appeared, plead not guilty and waived trial by jury, provided, that the court shall not in any such case enforce a jail sentence.
Acts 1975, c. 495; Acts 1979, c. 468.

§ 19.2–238. Summons against corporation; proceedings; expense of publication

A summons against a corporation to answer an indictment, presentment or information may be served as provided in §§ 8.01–299 through 8.01–301; and if the defendant after being so served fail to appear, the court may proceed to trial and judgment, without further process, as if the defendant had appeared, plead not guilty and waived trial by jury. And when, in any such case, publication of a copy of the process is required according to such sections, the expense of such publication may be certified by the court to the Comptroller, and shall be paid out of the state treasury; but the same shall be taxed with other costs and collected from the defendant, if judgment be for the Commonwealth, and be paid into the state treasury by the officer collecting the same.
Acts 1975, c. 495.

CHAPTER 15

TRIAL AND ITS INCIDENTS

Article 1

Jurisdiction

§ 19.2–239. Jurisdiction in criminal cases

The circuit courts, except where otherwise provided, shall have exclusive original jurisdiction for the trial of all presentments, indictments and informations for offenses committed within their respective circuits.
Acts 1975, c. 495.

§ 19.2–240. Clerks shall make out criminal docket

Before every term of any court in which criminal cases are to be tried the clerk of the court shall make out a separate docket of criminal cases then pending, in the following order, numbering the same:

1. Felony cases;
2. Misdemeanor cases.

He shall docket all felony cases in the order in which the indictments are found and all misdemeanor cases in the order in which the presentments or indictments are found or informations are filed or appeals are allowed by magistrates and as soon as any presentments or indictments are made at a term of court he shall forthwith docket the same in the order required above.

Traffic infractions shall be docketed with misdemeanor cases.

Cases appealed from the juvenile and domestic relations district court shall not be placed on the criminal docket except for cases involving criminal offenses committed by adults as provided in § 16.1–302. Cases transferred to a circuit court from a juvenile and domestic relations district court pursuant to Article 7 (§ 16.1–269.1 et seq.) of Chapter 11 of Title 16.1 shall be docketed as provided in this section upon return of a true bill of indictment by the grand jury.
Acts 1975, c. 495; Acts 1977, c. 585; Acts 1990, c. 258; Acts 1994, c. 859; Acts 1994, c. 949.

§ 19.2–241. Time within which court to set criminal cases for trial

The judge of each circuit court shall fix a day of his court when the trial of criminal cases will commence, and may make such general or special order in reference thereto, and to the summoning of witnesses, as may seem proper, but all criminal cases shall be disposed of before civil cases, unless the court shall direct otherwise.

When an indictment is found against a person for felony or when an appeal has been perfected from the conviction of a misdemeanor or traffic infraction, the accused, if in custody, or if he appear according to his recognizance, may be tried at the same term and shall be tried within the time limits fixed in § 19.2–243;

provided that no trial shall be held on the first day of the term unless it be with consent of the attorney for the Commonwealth and the accused and his attorney.

Acts 1975, c. 495; Acts 1977, c. 585; Acts 1978, c. 410.

§ 19.2–242. Accused discharged from jail if not indicted in time

A person in jail on a criminal charge shall be discharged from imprisonment if a presentment, indictment or information be not found or filed against him before the end of the second term of the court at which he is held to answer, unless it appear to the court that material witnesses for the Commonwealth have been enticed or kept away or are prevented from attendance by sickness or inevitable accident, and except, also, in the cases provided in §§ 19.2–168.1 and 19.2–169.1. A discharge under the provisions of this section shall not, however, prevent a reincarceration after a presentment or indictment has been found.

Acts 1975, c. 495.

§ 19.2–243. Limitation on prosecution of felony due to lapse of time after finding of probable cause; misdemeanors; exceptions

Where a district court has found that there is probable cause to believe that an adult has committed a felony, the accused, if he is held continuously in custody thereafter, shall be forever discharged from prosecution for such offense if no trial is commenced in the circuit court within five months from the date such probable cause was found by the district court; and if the accused is not held in custody but has been recognized for his appearance in the circuit court to answer for such offense, he shall be forever discharged from prosecution therefor if no trial is commenced in the circuit court within nine months from the date such probable cause was found.

If there was no preliminary hearing in the district court, or if such preliminary hearing was waived by the accused, the commencement of the running of the five and nine months periods, respectively, set forth in this section, shall be from the date an indictment or presentment is found against the accused.

If an indictment or presentment is found against the accused but he has not been arrested for the offense charged therein, the five and nine months periods, respectively, shall commence to run from the date of his arrest thereon.

Where a case is before a circuit court on appeal from a conviction of a misdemeanor or traffic infraction in a district court, the accused shall be forever discharged from prosecution for such offense if the trial de novo in the circuit court is not commenced (i) within five months from the date of the conviction if the accused has been held continuously in custody or (ii) within nine months of the date of the conviction if the accused has been recognized for his appearance in the circuit court to answer for such offense.

The provisions of this section shall not apply to such period of time as the failure to try the accused was caused:

1. By his insanity or by reason of his confinement in a hospital for care and observation;

2. By the witnesses for the Commonwealth being enticed or kept away, or prevented from attending by sickness or accident;

3. By the granting of a separate trial at the request of a person indicted jointly with others for a felony;

4. By continuance granted on the motion of the accused or his counsel, or by concurrence of the accused or his counsel in such a motion by the attorney for the Commonwealth, or by the failure of the accused or his counsel to make a timely objection to such a motion by the attorney for the Commonwealth, or by reason of his escaping from jail or failing to appear according to his recognizance;

5. By continuance ordered pursuant to subsection I or J of § 18.2–472.1 or subsection C or D of § 19.2–187.1;

6. By the inability of the jury to agree in their verdict; or

7. By a natural disaster, civil disorder, or act of God.

But the time during the pendency of any appeal in any appellate court shall not be included as applying to the provisions of this section.

For the purposes of this section, an arrest on an indictment or warrant or information or presentment is deemed to have occurred only when such indictment, warrant, information, or presentment or the summons or capias to answer such process is served or executed upon the accused and a trial is deemed commenced at the point when jeopardy would attach or when a plea of guilty or nolo contendere is tendered by the defendant. The lodging of a detainer or its equivalent shall not constitute an arrest under this section.

Acts 1975, c. 495; Acts 1984, c. 618; Acts 1988, c. 33; Acts 1993, c. 425; Acts 1995, c. 37; Acts 1995, c. 352; Acts 2002, c. 743; Acts 2005, c. 650; Acts 2007, c. 944. Amended by Acts 2009, Sp. S. I, c. 1, eff. Aug. 21, 2009; Acts 2009, Sp. S. I, c. 4, eff. Sept. 15, 2009.

ARTICLE 2

VENUE

§ 19.2–244. Venue in general

A. Except as otherwise provided by law, the prosecution of a criminal case shall be had in the county or city in which the offense was committed. Except as to motions for a change of venue, all other questions of venue must be raised before verdict in cases tried by a jury and before the finding of guilty in cases tried by the court without a jury.

B. If an offense has been committed within the Commonwealth and it cannot readily be determined within which county or city the offense was committed, venue for the prosecution of the offense may be had in the county or city (i) in which the defendant resides; (ii) if the defendant is not a resident of the Commonwealth, in which the defendant is apprehended; or (iii) if the defendant is not a resident of the Commonwealth and is not apprehended in the Commonwealth, in which any related offense was committed.

Acts 1975, c. 495. Amended by Acts 2015, c. 632; Acts 2015, c. 637.

§ 19.2–245. Offenses committed without and made punishable within Commonwealth; embezzlement or larceny committed within Commonwealth; where prosecuted

Prosecution for offenses committed wholly or in part without and made punishable within this Commonwealth may be in any county or city in which the offender is found or to which he is sent by any judge or court; and if any person shall commit larceny or embezzlement beyond the jurisdiction of this Commonwealth and bring the stolen property into the same he shall be liable to prosecution and punishment for larceny or embezzlement in any county or city into which he shall have taken the property as if the same had been wholly committed therein; and if any person shall commit larceny or embezzlement within this Commonwealth and take the stolen property into any county or city other than the county or city within which the same was committed he shall be liable to prosecution and punishment for such larceny or embezzlement in any such county or city into which he shall have taken the property as if the same had been wholly committed therein; provided, that if any person shall commit embezzlement within this Commonwealth he shall be liable as aforesaid or to prosecution and punishment for his offense in the county or city in which he was legally obligated to deliver the embezzled funds or property.

Acts 1975, c. 495; Acts 1977, c. 216.

§ 19.2–245.01. Offenses involving reports or statements concerning cigarette sales or stamping

Any criminal violation of Chapter 42 (§ 3.2–4200 et seq.) of Title 3.2, Article 10 (§ 18.2–246.6 et seq.) of Chapter 6 of Title 18.2, or § 18.2–514 involving reports or statements concerning cigarette sales or stamping may be prosecuted in the City of Richmond.

Added by Acts 2009, c. 847. Amended by Acts 2013, c. 625.

§ 19.2–245.1. Forgery; where prosecuted

If any person commits forgery, that forgery may be prosecuted in any county or city (i) where the writing was forged, or where the same was used or passed, or attempted to be used or passed, or deposited or placed with another person, firm, association, or corporation either for collection or credit for the account of any person, firm, association, or corporation or (ii) where the writing is found in the possession of the defendant.

Acts 1979, c. 30; Acts 2000, c. 327.

§ 19.2–245.2. Tax offenses; where prosecuted

If an offense involving tax, as defined in Title 58.1, is committed, that offense may be prosecuted in either any county or city where a false or fraudulent tax return, document, or statement was filed, or the county or city where the offender resides. However, venue shall not be in the City of Richmond solely because a false or fraudulent tax return, document or statement was filed directly with the Department of Taxation.

Acts 1990, c. 631.

§ 19.2–246. Injury inflicted by person within Commonwealth upon one outside Commonwealth

If a mortal wound or other violence or injury be inflicted by a person within this Commonwealth upon one outside of the same, or upon one in this Commonwealth who afterwards dies from the effect thereof out of the Commonwealth, the offender shall be amenable to prosecution and punishment for the offense in the courts of the county or city in which he was at the time of the commission thereof as if the same had been committed in such county or city.

Acts 1975, c. 495.

§ 19.2–247. Venue in certain homicide cases

Where evidence exists that a homicide has been committed either within or without the Commonwealth, under circumstances that make it unknown where such crime was committed, the homicide and any related offenses shall be amenable to prosecution in the courts of the county or city where the body or any part thereof of the victim may be found or, if the victim was removed from the Commonwealth for medical treatment prior to death and died outside the Commonwealth, in the courts of the county or city from which the victim was removed for medical treatment prior to death, as if the offense has been committed in such

county or city. In a prosecution for capital murder pursuant to subdivision 8 of § 18.2–31, the offense may be prosecuted in any jurisdiction in the Commonwealth in which any one of the killings may be prosecuted.
Acts 1975, c. 495; Acts 1996, c. 959; Acts 2002, c. 503. Amended by Acts 2015, c. 632; Acts 2015, c. 637.

§ 19.2–248. Venue when mortal wound, etc., inflicted in one county and death ensues in another

If a mortal wound, or other violence or injury, be inflicted, or poison administered in one county or city, and death ensues therefrom in another county or city, the offense may be prosecuted in either.
Acts 1975, c. 495.

§ 19.2–249. Offenses committed on boundary of two counties, two cities, or county and city, etc.; where prosecuted

An offense committed on the boundary of two counties, or on the boundary of two cities, or on the boundary of a county and city, or within 300 yards thereof, may be alleged to have been committed, and may be prosecuted and punished, in either county, in either city, or the county or city, and any sheriff, deputy sheriff, or other police officer shall have jurisdiction to make arrests and preserve the peace for a like distance on either side of the boundary line between such counties, such cities, or such county and city.
Acts 1975, c. 495; Acts 1978, c. 354; Acts 2003, c. 116.

§ 19.2–249.1. Offenses committed within towns situated in two or more counties; where prosecuted

An offense or traffic infraction committed within a town situated in two or more counties within the Commonwealth may be alleged to have been committed, and may be prosecuted and punished, in any one of such counties.
Acts 1984, c. 278.

§ 19.2–249.2. Venue for prosecution of computer and other crimes

For the purpose of venue, any violation of the Virginia Computer Crimes Act (§ 18.2–152.1 et seq.) or § 18.2–386.1 shall be considered to have been committed in any county or city:

1. In which any act was performed in furtherance of any course of conduct that violated any provision listed above;

2. In which the owner has his principal place of business in the Commonwealth;

3. In which any offender had control or possession of any proceeds of the violation or of any books, records, documents, property, financial instrument, computer software, computer program, computer data, or other material or objects that were used in furtherance of the violation;

4. From which, to which, or through which any access to a computer or computer network was made whether by wires, electromagnetic waves, microwaves, optics or any other means of communication;

5. In which the offender resides; or

6. In which any computer that is an object or an instrument of the violation is located at the time of the alleged offense.
Acts 2005, c. 746; Acts 2005, c. 761; Acts 2005, c. 827. Amended by Acts 2015, c. 423.

§ 19.2–250. How far jurisdiction of corporate authorities extends

A. Notwithstanding any other provision of this article and except as provided in subsection B hereof, the jurisdiction of the corporate authorities of each town or city, in criminal cases involving offenses against the Commonwealth, shall extend within the Commonwealth one mile beyond the corporate limits of such town or city; except that such jurisdiction of the corporate authorities of towns situated in counties having a density of population in excess of 300 inhabitants per square mile, or in counties adjacent to cities having a population of 170,000 or more, shall extend for 300 yards beyond the corporate limits of such town or, in the case of the criminal jurisdiction of an adjacent county, for 300 yards within such town.

B. Notwithstanding any other provision of this article, the jurisdiction of the authorities of Chesterfield County and Henrico County, in criminal cases involving offenses against the Commonwealth, shall extend one mile beyond the limits of such county into the City of Richmond.
Acts 1975, c. 495; Acts 1978, c. 379; Acts 1998, c. 428; Acts 2007, c. 813.

§ 19.2–251. When and how venue may be changed

A circuit court may, on motion of the accused or of the Commonwealth, for good cause, order the venue for the trial of a criminal case in such court to be changed to some other circuit court. Such motion when made by the accused may be made in his absence upon a petition signed and sworn to by him.

Whenever the mayor of any city, or the sheriff of any county, shall call on the Governor for military force to protect the accused from violence, the judge of the circuit court of the city or county having jurisdiction of the offense shall, upon a petition signed and sworn to by the accused, whether he be present or not, at once order the venue to be changed to the circuit court of a city or county sufficiently remote from the place where the offense was committed to insure the safe and impartial trial of the accused.
Acts 1975, c. 495.

§ 19.2–252. Court ordering change of venue may admit accused to bail and recognize witnesses; remand of accused not admitted to bail

When the venue is so changed, the court making the order may admit the accused to bail and shall recognize the witnesses and the accused if admitted to bail and the bail be given, to appear on some certain day before the court to which the case is removed; if the accused be not admitted to bail or the bail required be not given, the court shall remand him to its own jail and order its officer to remove him thence to the jail of the court to which the case is removed, so that he shall be there before the day for the appearance of the witnesses.

Acts 1975, c. 495.

§ 19.2–253. Procedure upon and after change of venue

The clerk of the court which orders a change of venue shall certify copies of the recognizances aforesaid and of the record of the case to the clerk of the court to which the case is removed, who shall thereupon issue a venire facias, directed to the officer of such court; and such court shall proceed with the case as if the prosecution had been originally therein; and for that purpose the certified copies aforesaid shall be sufficient.

Acts 1975, c. 495.

ARTICLE 3

ARRAIGNMENT; PLEAS; TRIAL WITHOUT JURY

§ 19.2–254. Arraignment; pleas; when court may refuse to accept plea; rejection of plea agreement; recusal

Arraignment shall be conducted in open court. It shall consist of reading to the accused the charge on which he will be tried and calling on him to plead thereto. In a felony case, arraignment is not necessary when waived by the accused. In a misdemeanor case, arraignment is not necessary when waived by the accused or his counsel, or when the accused fails to appear.

An accused may plead not guilty, guilty or nolo contendere. The court may refuse to accept a plea of guilty to any lesser offense included in the charge upon which the accused is arraigned; but, in misdemeanor and felony cases the court shall not refuse to accept a plea of nolo contendere.

With the approval of the court and the consent of the Commonwealth, a defendant may enter a conditional plea of guilty in a misdemeanor or felony case in circuit court, reserving the right, on appeal from the judgment, to a review of the adverse determination of any specified pretrial motion. If the defendant prevails on appeal, he shall be allowed to withdraw his plea.

Upon rejecting a plea agreement in any criminal matter, a judge shall immediately recuse himself from any further proceedings on the same matter unless the parties agree otherwise.

Acts 1975, c. 495; Acts 1987, c. 357. Amended by Acts 2014, c. 52; Acts 2014, c. 165.

§ 19.2–254.1. Procedure in traffic infraction cases

In a traffic infraction case, as defined in § 46.2–100, involving an offense included in the uniform fine schedule established pursuant to § 16.1–69.40:1, a defendant may elect to enter a written appearance and waive court hearing, except in instances in which property damage or personal injury resulted. Arraignment is not necessary when waived by the accused or his counsel, when the accused fails to appear, or when such written appearance has been elected.

An accused may plead not guilty, guilty, or nolo contendere; and the court shall not refuse to accept a plea of nolo contendere. A plea of guilty may be entered in writing without court appearance.

When an accused tenders payment without executing a written waiver of court hearing and entry of guilty plea, such tender of payment shall itself be deemed a waiver of court hearing and entry of guilty plea.

In districts with traffic violations bureaus on July 1, 1977, the chief judge of the district may designate the traffic violations bureau for the receipt of a written appearance, waiver of court hearing and guilty plea.

Acts 1975, c. 495; Acts 1978, c. 605; Acts 1992, c. 54.

§ 19.2–254.2. Procedure in nontraffic offenses for which prepayment is authorized

In any prepayable nontraffic offense case as defined in § 16.1–69.40:2 a defendant may elect to enter a written appearance and waive court hearing. Arraignment is not necessary when waived by the accused or his counsel, when the accused fails to appear, or when such written appearance has been elected.

An accused may plead not guilty, guilty, or nolo contendere; and the court shall not refuse to accept a plea of nolo contendere. A plea of guilty may be entered in writing without court appearance.

When an accused tenders payment without executing a written waiver of court hearing and entry of guilty plea, such tender of payment shall itself be deemed a waiver of court hearing and entry of guilty plea. Likewise when a person charged with a prepayable nontraffic offense fails to enter a written or court appearance, he shall be deemed to have waived court hearing and the case may be heard in his absence. In all other respects prepayable traffic offenses shall be treated as all other misdemeanors.

Acts 1975, c. 495; Acts 1992, c. 54.

§ 19.2–255. Defendant allowed to plead several matters of law or fact

The defendant in any criminal prosecution may plead as many several matters, whether of law or fact, as he shall think necessary, and he may file pleas in bar at the same time with pleas in abatement, or within a reasonable time thereafter; but the issues on the pleas in abatement shall be first tried.

Acts 1975, c. 495.

§ 19.2–256. Approvers

Approvers shall not be admitted in any case.

Acts 1975, c. 495.

§ 19.2–257. Trial without jury in felony cases

Upon a plea of guilty in a felony case, tendered in person by the accused after being advised by counsel, the court shall hear and determine the case without the intervention of a jury; or if the accused plead not guilty, with his consent after being advised by counsel and the concurrence of the attorney for the Commonwealth and of the court entered of record, the court shall hear and determine the case without the intervention of a jury. In such cases the court shall have and exercise all the powers, privileges and duties given to juries by any statute relating to crimes and punishments.

Acts 1975, c. 495.

§ 19.2–258. Trial of misdemeanors by court without jury; failure to appear deemed waiver of jury

In all cases of a misdemeanor upon a plea of guilty, tendered in person by the accused or his counsel, the court shall hear and determine the case without the intervention of a jury. If the accused plead not guilty, in person or by his counsel, the court, in its discretion, with the concurrence of the accused and the attorney for the Commonwealth, may hear and determine the case without the intervention of a jury. In each instance the court shall have and exercise all the powers and duties vested in juries by any statute relating to crimes and punishments.

When a person charged with a misdemeanor has been admitted to bail or released upon his own recognizance for his appearance before a court of record having jurisdiction of the case, for a hearing thereon and fails to appear in accordance with the condition of his bail or recognizance, he shall be deemed to have waived trial by a jury and the case may be heard in his absence as upon a plea of not guilty.

Acts 1975, c. 495.

§ 19.2–258.1. Trial of traffic infractions; measure of proof; failure to appear

For any traffic infraction cases tried in a district court, the court shall hear and determine the case without the intervention of a jury. For any traffic infraction case appealed to a circuit court, the defendant shall have the right to trial by jury. The defendant shall be presumed innocent until proven guilty beyond a reasonable doubt.

When a person charged with a traffic infraction fails to enter a written or court appearance, he shall be deemed to have waived court hearing and the case may be heard in his absence, after which he shall be notified of the court's finding. He shall be advised that if he fails to comply with any order of the court therein, the court may order suspension of his driver's license as provided in § 46.2–395 but the court shall not issue a warrant for his failure to appear pursuant to § 46.2–938.

Acts 1977, c. 585; Acts 1978, c. 605; Acts 1989 c. 705; Acts 2001, c. 414.

§ 19.2–259. On trial for felony, accused to be present; when court may enter plea for him, and trial go on

A person tried for felony shall be personally present during the trial. If when arraigned he will not plead or answer and does not confess his guilt the court shall have the plea of not guilty entered and the trial shall proceed as if the accused had put in that plea. But for the purposes of this section a motion for a continuance, whether made before or after arraignment, shall not be deemed to be part of the trial.

Acts 1975, c. 495.

ARTICLE 4

TRIAL BY JURY

§ 19.2–260. Provisions of Title 8.01 apply except as provided in this article

Except as otherwise provided in this article, trial by jury in criminal cases shall be regulated as provided for in Chapter 11 (§ 8.01–336 et seq.) of Title 8.01.

Acts 1975, c. 495; Acts 1977, c. 624.

§ 19.2–261. Charging grand jury in presence of person selected as juror

The court shall not charge the grand jury in the presence of any person selected as a juror to try any person indicted by the said grand jury. A violation of this provision shall constitute reversible error in any criminal case tried by a jury composed of one or more such veniremen.

Acts 1975, c. 495.

§ 19.2–262. Waiver of jury trial; numbers of jurors in criminal cases; how jurors selected from panel

A. In any criminal case in which trial by jury is dispensed with as provided by law, the whole matter of law and fact shall be heard and judgment given by the court. In appeals from juvenile and domestic relations district courts, the infant, through his guardian ad litem or counsel, may waive a jury.

B. Twelve persons from a panel of not less than 20 shall constitute a jury in a felony case. Seven persons from a panel of not less than 13 shall constitute a jury in a misdemeanor case.

C. The parties or their counsel, beginning with the attorney for the Commonwealth, shall alternately strike off one name from the panel until the number remaining shall be reduced to the number required for a jury.

D. In any case in which persons indicted for felony are tried jointly, if counsel or the accused are unable to agree on the full number to be stricken, or, if for any other reason counsel or the accused fail or refuse to strike off the full number of jurors allowed such party, the clerk shall place in a box ballots bearing the names of the jurors whose names have not been stricken and shall cause to be drawn from the box such number of ballots as may be necessary to complete the number of strikes allowed the party or parties failing or refusing to strike. Thereafter, if the opposing side is entitled to further strikes, they shall be made in the usual manner.

Acts 1975, c. 495; Acts 1975, c. 578; Acts 1979, c. 230; Acts 1997, c. 516; Acts 1997, c. 518; Acts 2005, c. 356.

§ 19.2–262.1. Joinder of defendants

On motion of the Commonwealth, for good cause shown, the court shall order persons charged with participating in contemporaneous and related acts or occurrences or in a series of acts or occurrences constituting an offense or offenses, to be tried jointly unless such joint trial would constitute prejudice to a defendant. If the court finds that a joint trial would constitute prejudice to a defendant, the court shall order severance as to that defendant or provide such other relief justice requires.

Acts 1993, c. 462; Acts 1993, c. 489; Acts 1997, c. 518.

§ 19.2–263. Repealed by Acts 1993, cc. 462 and 489

§ 19.2–263.1. Contact between judge and juror prohibited

No judge shall communicate in any way with a juror in a criminal proceeding concerning the juror's conduct or any aspect of the case during the course of the trial outside the presence of the parties or their counsel.

Acts 1985, c. 176.

§ 19.2–263.2. Jury instructions

A proposed jury instruction submitted by a party, which constitutes an accurate statement of the law applicable to the case, shall not be withheld from the jury solely for its nonconformance with model jury instructions.

Acts 1992, c. 522.

§ 19.2–263.3. Juror information confidential

A. The court may, upon motion of either party or its own motion, and for good cause shown, issue an order regulating the disclosure of the personal information of a juror who has been impaneled in a criminal trial to any person, other than to counsel for either party. Good cause shown includes, but is not limited to, a determination by the court that there is a likelihood of bribery, tampering, or physical injury to or harassment of a juror if his personal information is disclosed. An order regulating the disclosure of information may be modified, and the personal information of the jurors in a criminal case may be disseminated to a person having a legitimate interest or need for the information, with restrictions upon its use and further dissemination as may be deemed appropriate by the court.

B. In addition to the provisions of subsection A, the Supreme Court shall prescribe and publish rules that provide for the protection of the personal information of a juror in a criminal trial.

C. For purposes of this section, "personal information" means any information collected by the court, clerk, or jury commissioner at any time about a person who is selected to sit on a criminal jury and includes, but is not limited to, a juror's name, age, occupation, home and business addresses, telephone numbers, email addresses, and any other identifying information that would assist another in locating or contacting the juror.

Added by Acts 2008, c. 538.

§ 19.2–264. When jury need not be kept together in felony case; sufficient compliance with requirement that jury be kept together

In any case of a felony the jury shall not be kept together unless the court otherwise directs. Whenever a jury is required to be kept together, it shall be deemed sufficient compliance although the court for good cause permits one or more of such jurors to be separated from the others; provided all such jurors, whether separated or not, be kept in charge of officers provided therefor.

Acts 1975, c. 495.

§ 19.2–264.1. Views by juries

The jury in any criminal case may, at the request of either the attorney for the Commonwealth or any defendant, be taken to view the premises or place in question, or any property, matter or thing relating to the case, when it shall appear to the court that such view is necessary to a just decision.

Acts 1977, c. 624.

Article 4.1

Trial of Capital Cases

§ 19.2–264.2. Conditions for imposition of death sentence

In assessing the penalty of any person convicted of an offense for which the death penalty may be imposed, a sentence of death shall not be imposed unless the court or jury shall (1) after consideration of the past criminal record of convictions of the defendant, find that there is a probability that the defendant would commit criminal acts of violence that would constitute a continuing serious threat to society or that his conduct in committing the offense for which he stands charged was outrageously or wantonly vile, horrible or inhuman in that it involved torture, depravity of mind or an aggravated battery to the victim; and (2) recommend that the penalty of death be imposed.

Acts 1977, c. 492.

§ 19.2–264.3. Procedure for trial by jury

A. In any case in which the offense may be punishable by death which is tried before a jury the court shall first submit to the jury the issue of guilt or innocence of the defendant of the offense charged in the indictment, or any other offense supported by the evidence for which a lesser punishment is provided by law and the penalties therefor.

B. If the jury finds the defendant guilty of an offense for which the death penalty may not be imposed, it shall fix the punishment as provided in § 19.2–295.1.

C. If the jury finds the defendant guilty of an offense which may be punishable by death, then a separate proceeding before the same jury shall be held as soon as is practicable on the issue of the penalty, which shall be fixed as is provided in § 19.2–264.4.

If the sentence of death is subsequently set aside or found invalid, and the defendant or the Commonwealth requests a jury for purposes of resentencing, the court shall impanel a different jury on the issue of penalty.

Acts 1977, c. 492; Acts 1983, c. 519; Acts 1994, c. 828; Acts 1994, c. 860; Acts 1994, c. 862; Acts 1994, c. 881.

§ 19.2–264.3:1. Expert assistance when defendant's mental condition relevant to capital sentencing

A. Upon (i) motion of the attorney for a defendant charged with or convicted of capital murder and (ii) a finding by the court that the defendant is financially unable to pay for expert assistance, the court shall appoint one or more qualified mental health experts to evaluate the defendant and to assist the defense in the preparation and presentation of information concerning the defendant's history, character, or mental condition, including (i) whether the defendant acted under extreme mental or emotional disturbance at the time of the offense; (ii) whether the capacity of the defendant to appreciate the criminality of his conduct or to conform his conduct to the requirements of the law was significantly impaired at the time of the offense; and (iii) whether there are any other factors in mitigation relating to the history or character of the defendant or the defendant's mental condition at the time of the offense. The mental health expert appointed pursuant to this section shall be (i) a psychiatrist, a clinical psychologist, or an individual with a doctorate degree in clinical psychology who has successfully completed forensic evaluation training as approved by the Commissioner of Behavioral Health and Developmental Services and (ii) qualified by specialized training and experience to perform forensic evaluations. The defendant shall not be entitled to a mental health expert of the defendant's own choosing or to funds to employ such expert.

B. Evaluations performed pursuant to subsection A may be combined with evaluations performed pursuant to § 19.2–169.5 and shall be governed by subsections B and C of § 19.2–169.5.

C. The expert appointed pursuant to subsection A shall submit to the attorney for the defendant a report concerning the history and character of the defendant and the defendant's mental condition at the time of the offense. The report shall include the expert's opinion as to (i) whether the defendant acted under extreme mental or emotional disturbance at the time of the offense, (ii) whether the capacity of the defendant to appreciate the criminality of his conduct or to conform his conduct to the requirements of the law was significantly impaired, and (iii) whether there are any other factors in mitigation relating to the history or character of the defendant or the defendant's mental condition at the time of the offense.

D. The report described in subsection C shall be sent solely to the attorney for the defendant and shall be protected by the attorney-client privilege. However, the Commonwealth shall be given the report and the results of any other evaluation of the defendant's mental condition conducted relative to the sentencing proceeding and copies of psychiatric, psychological, medical or other records obtained during the course of such evaluation, after the attorney for the defendant gives notice of an intent to present psychiatric or psychological evidence in mitigation pursuant to subsection E.

E. In any case in which a defendant charged with capital murder intends, in the event of conviction, to present testimony of an expert witness to support a claim in mitigation relating to the defendant's history, character or mental condition, he or his attorney shall give notice in writing to the attorney for the Commonwealth, at least 60 days before trial, of his intention to present such testimony. In the event that such notice is not given and the defendant tenders testimony by an expert witness at the sentencing phase of the trial, then the court may, in its discretion, upon objection of the Commonwealth, either allow the Commonwealth a continuance or, under appropriate circumstances, bar the defendant from presenting such evidence.

F. 1. If the attorney for the defendant gives notice pursuant to subsection E and the Commonwealth thereafter seeks an evaluation concerning the existence or absence of mitigating circumstances relating to the defendant's mental condition at the time of the offense, the court shall appoint one or more qualified experts to perform such an evaluation. The court shall order the defendant to submit to such an evaluation, and advise the defendant on the record in court that a refusal to cooperate with the Commonwealth's expert could result in exclusion of the defendant's expert evidence. The qualification of the experts shall be governed by subsection A. The location of the evaluation shall be governed by subsection B of § 19.2–169.5. The attorney for the Commonwealth shall be responsible for providing the experts the information specified in subsection C of § 19.2–169.5. After performing their evaluation, the experts shall report their findings and opinions and provide copies of psychiatric, psychological, medical or other records obtained during the course of the evaluation to the attorneys for the Commonwealth and the defense.

2. If the court finds, after hearing evidence presented by the parties, out of the presence of the jury, that the defendant has refused to cooperate with an evaluation requested by the Commonwealth, the court may admit evidence of such refusal or, in the discretion of the court, bar the defendant from presenting his expert evidence.

G. Repealed.

Acts 1986, c. 535; Acts 1987, c. 439; Acts 1996, c. 937; Acts 1996, c. 980; Acts 2003, c. 1031, eff. April 29, 2003; Acts 2003, c. 1040, eff. May 1, 2003. Amended by Acts 2009, c. 813; Acts 2009, c. 840; Acts 2010, c. 559.

§ 19.2–264.3:1.1. Capital cases; determination of mental retardation

A. As used in this section and § 19.2–264.3:1.2, the following definition applies:

"Mentally retarded" means a disability, originating before the age of 18 years, characterized concurrently by (i) significantly subaverage intellectual functioning as demonstrated by performance on a standardized measure of intellectual functioning administered in conformity with accepted professional practice, that is at least two standard deviations below the mean and (ii) significant limitations in adaptive behavior as expressed in conceptual, social and practical adaptive skills.

B. Assessments of mental retardation under this section and § 19.2–264.3:1.2 shall conform to the following requirements:

1. Assessment of intellectual functioning shall include administration of at least one standardized measure generally accepted by the field of psychological testing and appropriate for administration to the particular defendant being assessed, taking into account cultural, linguistic, sensory, motor, behavioral and other individual factors. All such measures shall be reported as a range of scores calculated by adding and subtracting the standard error of measurement identified by the test publisher to the defendant's earned score. Testing of intellectual functioning shall be carried out in conformity with accepted professional practice, and whenever indicated, the assessment shall include information from multiple sources. The Commissioner of Behavioral Health and Developmental Services shall maintain an exclusive list of standardized measures of intellectual functioning generally accepted by the field of psychological testing.

2. Assessment of adaptive behavior shall be based on multiple sources of information, including clinical interview, psychological testing and educational, correctional and vocational records. The assessment shall

include at least one standardized measure generally accepted by the field of psychological testing for assessing adaptive behavior and appropriate for administration to the particular defendant being assessed, unless not feasible. In reaching a clinical judgment regarding whether the defendant exhibits significant limitations in adaptive behavior, the examiner shall give performance on standardized measures whatever weight is clinically appropriate in light of the defendant's history and characteristics and the context of the assessment.

3. Assessment of developmental origin shall be based on multiple sources of information generally accepted by the field of psychological testing and appropriate for the particular defendant being assessed, including, whenever available, educational, social service, medical records, prior disability assessments, parental or caregiver reports, and other collateral data, recognizing that valid clinical assessment conducted during the defendant's childhood may not have conformed to current practice standards.

C. In any case in which the offense may be punishable by death and is tried before a jury, the issue of mental retardation, if raised by the defendant in accordance with the notice provisions of subsection E of § 19.2–264.3:1.2, shall be determined by the jury as part of the sentencing proceeding required by § 19.2–264.4.

In any case in which the offense may be punishable by death and is tried before a judge, the issue of mental retardation, if raised by the defendant in accordance with the notice provisions of subsection E of § 19.2–264.3:1.2, shall be determined by the judge as part of the sentencing proceeding required by § 19.2–264.4.

The defendant shall bear the burden of proving that he is mentally retarded by a preponderance of the evidence.

D. The verdict of the jury, if the issue of mental retardation is raised, shall be in writing, and, in addition to the forms specified in § 19.2–264.4, shall include one of the following forms:

(1) "We the jury, on the issue joined, having found the defendant guilty of (here set out the statutory language of the offense charged), and that the defendant has proven by a preponderance of the evidence that he is mentally retarded, fix his punishment at (i) imprisonment for life or (ii) imprisonment for life and a fine of $__________.

Signed ____________________
foreman"

or

(2) "We the jury, on the issue joined, having found the defendant guilty of (here set out the statutory language of the offense charged) find that the defendant has not proven by a preponderance of the evidence that he is mentally retarded.

Signed ____________________
foreman"

Acts 2003, c. 1031, eff. April 29, 2003; Acts 2003, c. 1040, eff. May 1, 2003. Amended by Acts 2009, c. 813; Acts 2009, c. 840; Acts 2015, c. 360.

§ 19.2–264.3:1.2. Expert assistance when issue of defendant's mental retardation relevant to capital sentencing

A. Upon (i) motion of the attorney for a defendant charged with or convicted of capital murder and (ii) a finding by the court that the defendant is financially unable to pay for expert assistance, the court shall appoint one or more qualified mental health experts to assess whether or not the defendant is mentally retarded and to assist the defense in the preparation and presentation of information concerning the defendant's mental retardation. The mental health expert appointed pursuant to this section shall be (a) a psychiatrist, a clinical psychologist or an individual with a doctorate degree in clinical psychology, (b) skilled in the administration, scoring and interpretation of intelligence tests and measures of adaptive behavior and (c) qualified by experience and by specialized training, approved by the Commissioner of Behavioral Health and Developmental Services, to perform forensic evaluations. The defendant shall not be entitled to a mental health expert of the defendant's own choosing or to funds to employ such expert.

B. Evaluations performed pursuant to subsection A may be combined with evaluations performed pursuant to § 19.2–169.1, 19.2–169.5, or 19.2–264.3:1.

C. The expert appointed pursuant to subsection A shall submit to the attorney for the defendant a report assessing whether the defendant is mentally retarded. The report shall include the expert's opinion as to whether the defendant is mentally retarded.

D. The report described in subsection C shall be sent solely to the attorney for the defendant and shall be protected by the attorney-client privilege. However, the Commonwealth shall be given a copy of the report, the results of any other evaluation of the defendant's mental retardation and copies of psychiatric, psychological, medical or other records obtained during the course of the evaluation, after the attorney for the defendant gives notice of an intent to present evidence of mental retardation pursuant to subsection E.

E. In any case in which a defendant charged with capital murder intends, in the event of conviction, to present testimony of an expert witness to support a claim that he is mentally retarded, he or his attorney shall give notice in writing to the attorney for the Commonwealth, at least 21 days before trial, of his intention to present such testimony. In the event that such notice is not given and the defendant tenders testimony by an expert witness at the sentencing phase of the trial, then the court may, in its discretion, upon objection of the Commonwealth, either allow the Commonwealth a continuance or, under appropriate circumstances, bar the defendant from presenting such evidence.

F. 1. If the attorney for the defendant gives notice pursuant to subsection E and the Commonwealth thereafter seeks an evaluation concerning the existence or absence of the defendant's mental retardation, the court shall appoint one or more qualified experts to perform such an evaluation. The court shall order the defendant to submit to such an evaluation, and advise the defendant on the record in court that a refusal to cooperate with the Commonwealth's experts could result in exclusion of the defendant's expert evidence. The qualification of the experts shall be governed by subsection A. The attorney for the Commonwealth shall be responsible for providing the experts the information specified in subsection C of § 19.2–169.5. After performing their evaluation, the experts shall report their findings and opinions and provide copies of psychiatric, psychological, medical or other records obtained during the course of the evaluation to the attorneys for the Commonwealth and the defense.

2. If the court finds, after hearing evidence presented by the parties, out of the presence of the jury, that the defendant has refused to cooperate with an evaluation requested by the Commonwealth, the court may admit evidence of such refusal or, in the discretion of the court, bar the defendant from presenting his expert evidence.

Acts 2003, c. 1031, eff. April 29, 2003; Acts 2003, c. 1040, eff. May 1, 2003. Amended by Acts 2009, c. 813; Acts 2009, c. 840.

§ 19.2–264.3:1.3. Expert assistance for indigent defendants in capital cases

A. In any case in which an indigent defendant (i) is charged with a capital offense and (ii) is found by the court to be financially unable to pay for expert assistance, the defendant or his attorney may, upon notice to the Commonwealth, move in circuit court for the court to designate another judge in the same circuit to hear an ex parte request for the appointment of a qualified expert to assist in the preparation of the defendant's defense. No ex parte proceeding, communication, or request may be considered pursuant to this section unless a proper showing is made in an adversarial proceeding before the trial judge demonstrating a particularized need for confidentiality. Any such proceeding, communication, or request shall be transcribed and made part of the record available for appellate review or any other post conviction review.

B. The motion for the appointment of a qualified expert shall be in writing, filed under seal, and shall be heard ex parte as soon as practicable by the designated judge. Upon hearing the ex parte request, the designated judge shall find, by clear and convincing evidence, a particularized need for confidentiality has been demonstrated before considering the request for expert services. After a hearing upon the motion, the court may order the appointment of a qualified expert upon a showing that the provision of the requested expert services would materially assist the defendant in preparing his defense and the lack of such confidential assistance would result in a fundamentally unfair trial. Any expert appointed pursuant to this subsection shall be compensated in accordance with § 19.2–332. The designated judge shall direct requests for scientific investigations to the Department of Forensic Science or Division of Consolidated Laboratory Services whenever practicable.

C. All ex parte hearings conducted under this section shall be on the record, and the record of the hearings, together with all papers filed and orders entered in connection with ex parte requests for expert assistance, shall be kept under seal as part of the record of the case. Following decision on the motion, whether it is granted or denied, the motion shall remain under seal. On motion of any party, and for good cause shown, the court may unseal the record after the trial is concluded. Following final judgment and after all appeals have been exhausted, the court shall unseal all records and other material sealed pursuant to this section. No ex parte ruling by a designated judge pursuant to this section in a proceeding where the Commonwealth is excluded shall be the subject of a claim of error on appeal, or form the basis for relief in any post-conviction litigation on behalf of the defendant.

D. This section does not apply to the appointment of a mental health expert pursuant to § 19.2–264.3:1 or 19.2–264.3:1.2.

Added by Acts 2010, c. 789.

§ 19.2–264.3:2. Notice to the defendant of intention to present evidence of unadjudicated criminal conduct

Upon motion of the defendant, in any case in which the offense for which the defendant is to be tried may be punishable by death, if the attorney for the Commonwealth intends to introduce during a sentencing proceeding held pursuant to § 19.2–264.4 evidence of defendant's unadjudicated criminal conduct, the attorney for the Commonwealth shall give notice in writing to the attorney for the defendant of such intention. The notice shall include a description of the alleged unadjudicated criminal conduct and, to the extent such information is available, the time and place such conduct will be alleged to have occurred.

The court shall specify the time by which such notice shall be given.

Acts 1993, c. 377.

§ 19.2–264.3:3. Limitations on use of statements or disclosure by defendant during evaluations

No statement or disclosure by the defendant made during a competency evaluation performed pursuant to

§ 19.2–169.1, an evaluation performed pursuant to § 19.2–169.5 to determine sanity at the time of the offense, treatment provided pursuant to § 19.2–169.2 or § 19.2–169.6, a mental condition evaluation performed pursuant to § 19.2–264.3:1 or a mental retardation evaluation performed pursuant to § 19.2–264.3:1.2, and no evidence derived from any such statements or disclosures may be introduced against the defendant at the sentencing phase of a capital murder trial for the purpose of proving the aggravating circumstances specified in § 19.2–264.4. Such statements or disclosures shall be admissible in rebuttal only when relevant to issues in mitigation raised by the defense.

Acts 2003, c. 1031, eff. April 29, 2003; Acts 2003, c. 1040, eff. May 1, 2003.

§ 19.2–264.3:4. Notice of expert testimony in capital case

Whenever the defendant, the defendant's attorney, or the attorney for the Commonwealth in a capital case intends to introduce expert opinion testimony at trial, the defendant, defendant's attorney, or attorney for the Commonwealth shall notify the opposing party in writing of such party's intention to present such testimony at least 60 days before the trial. The written notice shall include copies of any written reports of the witness, a summary of the proposed expert testimony that describes the witness's opinions and the basis and reasons for those opinions, and the witness's qualifications and contact information.

Added by Acts 2010, c. 789.

§ 19.2–264.4. Sentence proceeding

A. Upon a finding that the defendant is guilty of an offense which may be punishable by death, a proceeding shall be held which shall be limited to a determination as to whether the defendant shall be sentenced to death or life imprisonment. Upon request of the defendant, a jury shall be instructed that for all Class 1 felony offenses committed after January 1, 1995, a defendant shall not be eligible for parole if sentenced to imprisonment for life. In case of trial by jury, where a sentence of death is not recommended, the defendant shall be sentenced to imprisonment for life.

A1. In any proceeding conducted pursuant to this section, the court shall permit the victim, as defined in § 19.2–11.01, upon the motion of the attorney for the Commonwealth, and with the consent of the victim, to testify in the presence of the accused regarding the impact of the offense upon the victim. The court shall limit the victim's testimony to the factors set forth in clauses (i) through (vi) of subsection A of § 19.2–299.1.

B. In cases of trial by jury, evidence may be presented as to any matter which the court deems relevant to sentence, except that reports under the provisions of § 19.2–299, or under any rule of court, shall not be admitted into evidence.

Evidence which may be admissible, subject to the rules of evidence governing admissibility, may include the circumstances surrounding the offense, the history and background of the defendant, and any other facts in mitigation of the offense. Facts in mitigation may include, but shall not be limited to, the following: (i) the defendant has no significant history of prior criminal activity, (ii) the capital felony was committed while the defendant was under the influence of extreme mental or emotional disturbance, (iii) the victim was a participant in the defendant's conduct or consented to the act, (iv) at the time of the commission of the capital felony, the capacity of the defendant to appreciate the criminality of his conduct or to conform his conduct to the requirements of law was significantly impaired, (v) the age of the defendant at the time of the commission of the capital offense, or (vi) even if § 19.2–264.3:1.1 is inapplicable as a bar to the death penalty, the subaverage intellectual functioning of the defendant.

C. The penalty of death shall not be imposed unless the Commonwealth shall prove beyond a reasonable doubt that there is a probability based upon evidence of the prior history of the defendant or of the circumstances surrounding the commission of the offense of which he is accused that he would commit criminal acts of violence that would constitute a continuing serious threat to society, or that his conduct in committing the offense was outrageously or wantonly vile, horrible or inhuman, in that it involved torture, depravity of mind or aggravated battery to the victim.

D. In the event the jury cannot agree as to the penalty, the court shall dismiss the jury, and impose a sentence of imprisonment for life.

Acts 1977, c. 492; Acts 1980, c. 160; Acts 1990, c. 316; Acts 1990, c. 754; Acts 1998, c. 485; Acts 2000, c. 838; Acts 2003, c. 1031, eff. April 29, 2003; Acts 2003, c. 1040, eff. May 1, 2003. Amended by Acts 2010, c. 658.

§ 19.2–264.5. Post-sentence reports

When the punishment of any person has been fixed at death, the court shall, before imposing sentence, direct a probation officer of the court to thoroughly investigate the history of the defendant and any and all other relevant facts, to the end that the court may be fully advised as to whether the sentence of death is appropriate and just. Reports shall be made, presented and filed as provided in § 19.2–299 except that, notwithstanding any other provision of law, such reports shall in all cases contain a Victim Impact Statement. Such statement shall contain the same information and be prepared in the same manner as Victim Impact Statements prepared pursuant to § 19.2–299.1. After consideration of the report, and upon good cause shown, the court may set aside the sentence of death and impose a sentence of imprisonment for life. Notwithstanding any other provision of law, if the court sets aside the sentence of death and imposes a sentence of imprisonment for life, it shall include in the sentencing order an explanation for the reduction in sentence.

Acts 1977, c. 492; Acts 1993, c. 978; Acts 2004, c. 298.

Article 5

Miscellaneous Provisions

§ 19.2–265. Opening statement of counsel

On the trial of any case of felony or misdemeanor and before any evidence is submitted on either side, the attorney for the Commonwealth and counsel for the accused, respectively, shall have the right to make an opening statement of their case.

Acts 1975, c. 495.

§ 19.2–265.01. Victims, certain members of the family and support persons not to be excluded

During the trial of every criminal case and in all court proceedings attendant to trial, whether before, during or after trial, including any proceedings occurring after an appeal by the defendant or the Commonwealth, at which attendance by the defendant is permitted, whether in a circuit or district court, any victim as defined in § 19.2–11.01 may remain in the courtroom and shall not be excluded unless the court determines, in its discretion, the presence of the victim would impair the conduct of a fair trial. In any case involving a minor victim, the court may permit an adult chosen by the minor to be present in the courtroom during any proceedings in addition to or in lieu of the minor's parent or guardian.

The attorney for the Commonwealth shall give prior notice when practicable of such trial and attendant proceedings and changes in the scheduling thereof to any known victim and to any known adult chosen in accordance with this section by a minor victim, at the address or telephone number, or both, provided in writing by such person.

Acts 1993, c. 447; Acts 1993, c. 452; Acts 1994, c. 361; Acts 1994, c. 598; Acts 1995, c. 687; Acts 1996, c. 546; Acts 1999, c. 844; Acts 2000, c. 339.

§ 19.2–265.1. Exclusion of witnesses (Subsection (a) of Supreme Court Rule 2:615 derived in part from this section and subsection (c) of Supreme Court Rule 2:615 derived from this section)

In the trial of every criminal case, the court, whether a court of record or a court not of record, may upon its own motion and shall upon the motion of either the attorney for the Commonwealth or any defendant, require the exclusion of every witness to be called, including, but not limited to, police officers or other investigators; however, each defendant who is an individual and one officer or agent of each defendant which is a corporation or association shall be exempt from the rule of this section as a matter of right. Additionally, any victim as defined in § 19.2–11.01 who is to be called as a witness shall be exempt from the rule of this section as a matter of law unless, in accordance with the provisions of § 19.2–265.01, his exclusion is otherwise required.

Acts 1975, c. 495; Acts 1990, c. 572; Acts 2004, c. 311.

§ 19.2–265.2. Judicial notice of laws (Supreme Court Rule 2:202 derived in part from this section)

A. Whenever, in any criminal case it becomes necessary to ascertain what the law, statutory or otherwise, of this Commonwealth, of another state, of the United States, of another country, or of any political subdivision or agency of the same is, or was, at any time, the court shall take judicial notice thereof whether specially pleaded or not.

B. The court, in taking such notice, shall consult any book, record, register, journal, or other official document or publication purporting to contain, state, or explain such law, and may consider any evidence or other information or argument that is offered on the subject.

Acts 1978, c. 328.

§ 19.2–265.3. Nolle prosequi; discretion of court upon good cause shown

Nolle prosequi shall be entered only in the discretion of the court, upon motion of the Commonwealth with good cause therefor shown.

Acts 1979, c. 641.

§ 19.2–265.4. Failure to provide discovery

A. In any criminal prosecution for a felony in a circuit court or for a misdemeanor brought on direct indictment, the attorney for the Commonwealth shall have a duty to adequately and fully provide discovery as provided under Rule 3A:11 of the Rules of the Supreme Court. Rule 3A:11 shall be construed to apply to such felony and misdemeanor prosecutions. This duty to disclose shall be continuing and shall apply to any additional evidence or material discovered by the Commonwealth prior to or during trial which is subject to discovery or inspection and has been previously requested by the accused. In any criminal prosecution for a misdemeanor by trial de novo in circuit court, the attorney for the Commonwealth shall have a duty to adequately and fully provide discovery as provided under Rule 7C:5 of the Rules of the Supreme Court.

B. If at any time during the course of the proceedings it is brought to the attention of the court that the attorney for the Commonwealth has failed to comply with this section, the court may order the Commonwealth to permit the discovery or inspection, grant a continuance, or prohibit the Commonwealth from introducing evidence not disclosed, or the court may enter such other order as it deems just under the circumstances.

Acts 1985, c. 538; Acts 1995, c. 504; Acts 2004, c. 348.

§ 19.2–265.5. Prosecuting misdemeanor cases without attorney

Notwithstanding any of the provisions of § 19.2–265.1, whenever in a misdemeanor case neither an attorney for the Commonwealth nor any other attorney for the prosecution is present, the complaining witness may be allowed to remain in court throughout the entire trial if necessary for the orderly presentation of witnesses for the prosecution.

Acts 1987, c. 659.

§ 19.2–265.6. Effect of dismissal of criminal charges

No dismissal of any criminal charge by a court shall bar subsequent prosecution of the charge unless jeopardy attached at the earlier proceeding or unless the dismissal order explicitly states that the dismissal is with prejudice.

Acts 2007, c. 419.

§ 19.2–266. Exclusion of persons from trial; photographs and broadcasting permitted under designated guidelines; exceptions

In the trial of all criminal cases, whether the same be felony or misdemeanor cases, the court may, in its discretion, exclude from the trial any persons whose presence would impair the conduct of a fair trial, provided that the right of the accused to a public trial shall not be violated.

A court may solely in its discretion permit the taking of photographs in the courtroom during the progress of judicial proceedings and the broadcasting of judicial proceedings by radio or television and the use of electronic or photographic means for the perpetuation of the record or parts thereof in criminal and in civil cases, but only in accordance with the rules set forth hereunder. In addition to such rules, the Supreme Court and the Court of Appeals shall have the authority to promulgate any other rules they deem necessary to govern electronic media and still photography coverage in their respective courts. The following rules shall serve as guidelines, and a violation of these rules may be punishable as contempt:

Coverage Allowed.

1. The presiding judge shall at all times have authority to prohibit, interrupt or terminate electronic media and still photography coverage of public judicial proceedings. The presiding judge shall advise the parties of such coverage in advance of the proceedings and shall allow the parties to object thereto. For good cause shown, the presiding judge may prohibit coverage in any case and may restrict coverage as he deems appropriate to meet the ends of justice.

2. Coverage of the following types of judicial proceedings shall be prohibited: adoption proceedings, juvenile proceedings, child custody proceedings, divorce proceedings, temporary and permanent spousal support proceedings, proceedings concerning sexual offenses, proceedings for the hearing of motions to suppress evidence, proceedings involving trade secrets, and in camera proceedings.

3. Coverage of the following categories of witnesses shall be prohibited: police informants, minors, undercover agents and victims and families of victims of sexual offenses.

4. Coverage of jurors shall be prohibited expressly at any stage of a judicial proceeding, including that portion of a proceeding during which a jury is selected. The judge shall inform all potential jurors at the beginning of the jury selection process of this prohibition.

5. To protect the attorney-client privilege and the right to counsel, there shall be no recording or broadcast of sound from such conferences which occur in a court facility between attorneys and their clients, between co-counsel of a client, between adverse counsel, or between counsel and the presiding judge held at the bench or in chambers.

Location of Equipment and Personnel.

1. The location of recording and camera equipment shall be strictly regulated so as not to be intrusive.

2. Media personnel shall not enter or leave the courtroom once the proceedings are in session except during a court recess or adjournment.

3. Electronic media equipment and still photography equipment shall not be taken into the courtroom or removed from the designated media area except at the following times:

a. Prior to the convening of proceedings;

b. During any luncheon recess;

c. During any court recess with the permission of the trial judge; and

d. After adjournment for the day of the proceedings.

Official Representatives of the Media.

The Virginia Association of Broadcasters and the Virginia Press Association may designate one person to represent the television media, one person to represent the radio broadcasters, and one person to represent still photographers in each jurisdiction in which electronic media and still photographic coverage is desired. The names of the persons so designated shall be forwarded to the chief judge of the court in the county or city in which coverage is desired so that arrangements can be made for the "pooling" of equipment and personnel. Such persons shall also be the only persons authorized to speak for the media to the presiding judge concerning the coverage of any judicial proceedings.

Equipment and Personnel.

1. No distracting lights or sounds shall be permitted.

2. Not more than two television cameras shall be permitted in any proceeding.

3. Not more than one still photographer, utilizing not more than two still cameras with not more than two lenses for each camera and related equipment for print purposes, shall be permitted in any proceeding.

4. Not more than one audio system for broadcast purposes shall be permitted in any proceeding.

Audio pickup for all media purposes shall be accomplished with existing audio systems present in the court facility. If no technically suitable audio system exists in the court facility, microphones and related wiring essential for media purposes may be installed and maintained at media expense. The microphones and wiring must be unobtrusive and shall be located in places designated in advance of any proceeding by the chief judge of the court in which coverage is desired.

5. Any "pooling" arrangements among the media required by these limitations on equipment and personnel shall be the sole responsibility of the media without calling upon the presiding judge to mediate any dispute as to the appropriate media representative or equipment authorized to cover a particular proceeding. In the absence of advance media agreement on disputed equipment or personnel issues, the presiding judge may exclude all contesting media personnel from a proceeding.

6. In no event shall the number of personnel in the designated area exceed the number necessary to operate the designated equipment.

7. Only television photographic and audio equipment which does not produce distracting sound or light shall be employed to cover judicial proceedings. No artificial lighting device of any kind shall be employed in connection with the television camera.

8. Only still camera equipment which does not produce distracting sound or light shall be employed to cover judicial proceedings. No artificial lighting device of any kind shall be employed in connection with a still camera.

9. With the concurrence of the chief judge of the court in which coverage is desired, modifications and additions may be made in light sources existing in the facility, provided such modifications or additions are installed and maintained without public expense.

Impermissible Use of Media Material.

None of the film, video tape, still photographs or audio reproductions developed during or by virtue of coverage of a judicial proceeding shall be admissible as evidence (i) in the proceeding out of which it arose, (ii) in any proceeding subsequent and collateral thereto, or (iii) upon any retrial or appeal of such proceedings.

All electronic media and still photography coverage of public judicial proceedings authorized by this section, with the exception of electronic or photographic means authorized for the perpetuation of the record or parts thereof shall be conducted at no cost to the Commonwealth.

Acts 1975, c. 495; Acts 1978, c. 477; Acts 1987, c. 580; Acts 1989, c. 582; Acts 1990, c. 243; Acts 1992, c. 557.

§ 19.2–266.1. Conviction of lesser offense on indictment for homicide

In any trial upon an indictment charging homicide, the jury or the court may find the accused not guilty of the specific offense charged in the indictment, but guilty of any degree of homicide supported by the evidence for which a lesser punishment is provided by law.

Acts 1975, c. 495.

§ 19.2–266.2. Defense objections to be raised before trial; hearing; bill of particulars

A. Defense motions or objections seeking (i) suppression of evidence on the grounds such evidence was obtained in violation of the provisions of the Fourth, Fifth or Sixth Amendments to the Constitution of the United States or Article I, Section 8, 10 or 11 of the Constitution of Virginia proscribing illegal searches and seizures and protecting rights against self-incrimination; (ii) dismissal of a warrant, information, or indictment or any count or charge thereof on the ground that: (a) the defendant would be deprived of a speedy trial in violation of the provisions of the Sixth Amendment to the Constitution of the United States, Article I, Section 8 of the Constitution of Virginia, or § 19.2–243; or (b) the defendant would be twice placed in jeopardy in violation of the provisions of the Fifth Amendment to the Constitution of the United States or Article I, Section 8 of the Constitution of Virginia; or (iii) dismissal of a warrant, information, or indictment or any count or charge thereof on the ground that a statute upon which it was based is unconstitutional shall be raised by motion or objection.

B. Such a motion or objection in a proceeding in circuit court shall be raised in writing, before trial. The motions or objections shall be filed and notice given to opposing counsel not later than seven days before trial in circuit court or, if made under clause (ii) of subsection A, at such time prior to trial in circuit court as the grounds for the motion or objection shall arise, whichever occurs last. A hearing on all such motions or objections shall be held not later than three days prior to trial in circuit court, unless such period is waived by the accused, as set by the trial judge. The circuit court may, however, for good cause shown and in the interest of justice, permit the motions or objections to be raised at a later time.

C. To assist the defense in filing such motions or objections in a timely manner, the circuit court shall, upon motion of the defendant, direct the Commonwealth to file a bill of particulars pursuant to § 19.2–230. The circuit court shall fix the time within which such bill of particulars is to be filed. Upon further motion of the defendant, the circuit court may, upon a showing of good cause, direct the Commonwealth to supplement its bill of particulars. The attorney for the Commonwealth shall certify that the matters stated in the bill of particulars are true and accurate to the best of his knowledge and belief.

D. In a criminal proceeding in district court, any motion or objection as described in subsection A may be raised prior to or at such proceeding. In the event such a motion or objection is raised, the district court shall, upon motion of the Commonwealth grant a continuance for good cause shown.

Acts 1987, c. 710; Acts 2005, c. 622; Acts 2005, c. 694; Acts 2006, c. 578; Acts 2006, c. 862.

§ 19.2–266.3. Continuances; appearances of parties

When the court grants a continuance in advance of the date of a scheduled trial or hearing, if the defendant acknowledges in writing, on a form provided by the Office of the Executive Secretary of the Supreme Court, that he promises to appear in court on the date and time of the newly scheduled trial or hearing, the court shall not require counsel or the defendant to appear on the date when the trial or hearing was originally scheduled. However, if the defendant is in violation of the terms of his pretrial release or has failed to appear at any court proceeding, the court may require the defendant to appear on the date when the trial or hearing was originally scheduled as a condition of any continuance granted.

Added by Acts 2013, c. 154.

CHAPTER 16

EVIDENCE AND WITNESSES

Article 1

In General

§ 19.2–267. Provisions applicable to witnesses in criminal as well as civil cases; obligation to attend; summons

Sections 8.01–396.1, 8.01–402, 8.01–405, 8.01–407, and 8.01–408 to 8.01–410, inclusive, shall apply to a criminal as well as a civil case in all respects, except that a witness in a criminal case shall be obliged to attend, and may be proceeded against for failing to do so, although there may not previously have been any payment, or tender to him of anything for attendance, mileage, or tolls. In a criminal case a summons for a witness may be issued by the attorney for the Commonwealth or other attorney charged with the responsibility for the prosecution of a violation of any ordinance or by the attorney for the defendant; however, any attorney who issues such a summons shall, at the time of the issuance, file with the clerk of the court the names and addresses of such witnesses except to the extent protected under § 19.2–11.2.

Acts 1975, c. 495; Acts 1977, c. 624; Acts 1991, c. 38; Acts 1994, c. 543; Acts 2007, c. 552. Amended by Acts 2008, c. 124; Acts 2014, c. 744.

§ 19.2–267.1. Authority of law-enforcement officer to issue summons to witness; failure to appear

A summons may be issued by a law-enforcement officer during the course of his immediate investigation of an alleged misdemeanor for which an arrest warrant is not required pursuant to § 19.2–81 to any person he reasonably believes was a witness to the offense. The summons shall command the person to appear and testify at the trial of any criminal charge brought against any person as the result of the offense.

A summons issued pursuant to this section shall have the same force as if issued by the court. The failure of any person so summoned to appear after receiving written notice of the date, time and place of the trial at least five days prior to the trial shall be punishable as contempt of the court in accordance with § 18.2–456 (5).

Acts 1983, c. 224.

§ 19.2–267.2. Response to subpoena for information stored in electronic format

When a subpoena has been served pursuant to Rule 3A:12 of the Rules of the Supreme Court on a person who is not a party to the action requiring the production of information that is stored in an electronic format, the person shall produce a tangible copy of the information. If a tangible copy cannot be produced, the person shall permit the parties to review the information on a computer or by electronic means during normal business hours, provided that the information can be accessed and isolated. If a tangible copy cannot reasonably be produced and the information is commingled with information other than that requested in the subpoena and cannot reasonably be isolated, the person may file a motion for a protective order or motion to quash.

Acts 2002, c. 764.

§ 19.2–268. Right of accused to testify

In any case of felony or misdemeanor, the accused may be sworn and examined in his own behalf, and if so sworn and examined, he shall be deemed to have waived his privilege of not giving evidence against himself, and shall be subject to cross-examination as any other witness; but his failure to testify shall create no presumption against him, nor be the subject of any comment before the court or jury by the prosecuting attorney.

Acts 1975, c. 495.

§ 19.2–268.1. Contradiction by prior inconsistent writing (Subdivision (b)(i) of Supreme Court Rule 2:613 derived in part from this section)

A witness in a criminal case may be cross-examined as to previous statements made by him in writing or reduced into writing, relative to the subject matter of the proceeding, without such writing being shown to him; but if it is intended to contradict such witness by the writing, his attention must, before such contradictory proof can be given, be called to the particular occasion on which the writing is supposed to have been made, and he may be asked if he did not make a writing of the purport of the one to be offered to contradict him, and if he denies making it, or does not admit its execution, it shall then be shown to him, and if he admits its genuineness, he shall be allowed to make his own explanation of it; but it shall be competent for the court at any time during the trial to require the production of the writing for its inspection, and the court may thereupon make such use of it for the purpose of the trial as it may think best.

Acts 1977, c. 264.

§ 19.2–268.2. Recent complaint hearsay exception (Subdivision (23) of Supreme Court Rule 2:803 derived from this section)

Notwithstanding any other provision of law, in any prosecution for criminal sexual assault under Article 7 (§ 18.2–61 et seq.) of Chapter 4 of Title 18.2, a violation of §§ 18.2–361, 18.2–366, 18.2–370 or § 18.2–370.1, the fact that the person injured made complaint of the offense recently after commission of the offense is admissible, not as independent evidence of the offense, but for the purpose of corroborating the testimony of the complaining witness.

Acts 1993, c. 592.

§ 19.2–269. Convicts as witnesses (Supreme Court Rule 2:609 derived from this section)

A person convicted of a felony or perjury shall not be incompetent to testify, but the fact of conviction may be shown in evidence to affect his credit.

Acts 1975, c. 495.

§ 19.2–269.1. Inmates as witnesses in criminal cases

Whenever the Commonwealth or a defendant in a criminal prosecution in any circuit court in this Commonwealth requires as a witness in his behalf, an inmate in a state or local correctional facility as defined in § 53.1–1, the court, on the application of such defendant or his attorney, or the attorney for the Commonwealth, shall issue an order to the Director of the Department of Corrections to deliver such witness to the sheriff of the jurisdiction of the court issuing the order. If authorized by the court, the clerk of the circuit court or a deputy clerk may issue these orders on behalf of the court. The sheriff shall go where such witness may then be and carry him to the court to testify as such witness, and after he has testified and been released as such witness, carry him back to the place whence he came, for all of which service the sheriff shall be paid out of the criminal expense funds in the state treasury such compensation as the court in which the case is pending may certify to be reasonable.

Acts 1977, c. 624; Acts 2002, c. 515; Acts 2002, c. 544.

§ 19.2–269.2. Nondisclosure of addresses or telephone numbers of crime victims and witnesses

During any criminal proceeding, upon motion of the defendant or the attorney for the Commonwealth, a judge may prohibit testimony as to the current residential or business address or telephone number of a victim or witness if the judge determines that this information is not material under the circumstances of the case.

Acts 1989, c. 170; Acts 1994, c. 845; Acts 1994, c. 931.

§ 19.2–270. When statement by accused as witness not received as evidence

In a criminal prosecution, other than for perjury, or in an action on a penal statute, evidence shall not be given against the accused of any statement made by him as a witness upon a legal examination, in a criminal or civil action, unless such statement was made when examined as a witness in his own behalf.

Acts 1975, c. 495; Acts 1988, c. 366.

§ 19.2–270.1. Use of photographs as evidence in certain larceny and burglary prosecutions

In any prosecution for larceny under the provisions of §§ 18.2–95, 18.2–96 or § 18.2–98, or for shoplifting under the provisions of § 18.2–103, or for burglary under the provisions of §§ 18.2–89, 18.2–90, 18.2–91 or § 18.2–92, photographs of the goods, merchandise, money or securities alleged to have been taken or converted shall be deemed competent evidence of such goods, merchandise, money or securities and shall be admissible in any proceeding, hearing or trial of the case to the same extent as if such goods, merchandise, money or securities had been introduced as evidence. Such photographs shall bear a written description of the goods, merchandise, money or securities alleged to have been taken or converted, the name of the owner of such goods, merchandise, money or securities and the manner of the identification of same by such owner, or the name of the place wherein the alleged offense occurred, the name of the accused, the name of the arresting or investigating police officer or conservator of the peace, the date of the photograph and the name of the photographer. Such writing shall be made under oath by the arresting or investigating police officer or conservator of the peace, and the photographs identified by the signature of the photographer. Upon the filing of such photograph and writing with the police authority or court holding such goods and merchandise as evidence, such goods or merchandise shall be returned to their owner, or the proprietor or manager of the store or establishment wherein the alleged offense occurred.

Acts 1976, c. 577; Acts 1985, c. 184; Acts 1987, c. 493; Acts 1995, c. 447.

§ 19.2-270.1:1. Computer and electronic data in obscenity, etc. cases; access to defendant

When computer data or electronic data, stored in any form, the possession of which is otherwise unlawful, are seized as evidence in a criminal prosecution of any offense involving obscenity or child pornography, neither the original data nor a copy thereof shall be released to the defendant or his counsel, nor shall a court order the release of such evidence to the defendant or his counsel except as provided herein. The defendant and his counsel shall be allowed the reasonable opportunity to review such evidence in accordance with the rules of discovery. Upon a finding that the production of the original data or a copy thereof to counsel or his designee is necessary and material to the defense of the accused, the court may order such production only under terms that restrict access to specifically identified recipients, prohibit any duplication of the data beyond what is reasonably necessary for the purpose of the production, and require the return of the data to the law-enforcement agency maintaining custody or control of the seized data for appropriate disposition.

Acts 2006, c. 601.

§ 19.2-270.2. Disposition of money, securities or documents seized upon arrest, etc., and pertinent as evidence

A. When in the course of investigation or arrest, the investigating or arresting officer shall seize or come into the possession of moneys, cash, or negotiable or nonnegotiable instruments or securities, hereinafter called "moneys or securities," taken or retained unlawfully from a financial institution or other person, and such moneys or securities, or a portion thereof, shall be pertinent evidence in a pending prosecution or appeal therefrom, the officer or agency having possession thereof, may retain, pending such prosecution or appeal thereof, sufficient of such moneys or securities as shall be necessary to prove the crime of grand larceny or other crimes requiring a specific amount in value. The court upon motion of the attorney for the Commonwealth and for good cause shown may order the release of all moneys or securities, subject to the provisions of this section. The remaining excess moneys or securities, if any, may be released to the owner thereof, upon proper receipt therefor, which release shall be with the consent of the attorney for the Commonwealth. The officer or agency authorizing such release shall make an appropriate record of such moneys or securities released, including designation or copying of serial numbers, and such record or receipt shall be admissible into evidence in any proceeding, hearing or trial of the case to the same extent as if such moneys or securities had been introduced. Such record or receipt shall contain the name of the financial institution or person from whom such moneys or securities were taken, the place from which taken, the name of the accused, and the name of the arresting officer or officers coming into initial possession of such moneys or securities. Pictures shall be taken of any instruments or securities and such pictures shall be attached to the receipt or record above and shall contain further, in the case of such copying, the date of the photograph and the name of the photographer.

B. When in the course of investigation or arrest, the investigating or arresting officer seizes or comes into the possession of moneys or securities under the provisions of this section, and such moneys or securities, or a portion thereof, are introduced as an exhibit in a prosecution or appeal therefrom, the court may, with the consent of the attorney for the Commonwealth, authorize the clerk of the circuit court, upon all appeal rights being exhausted, to deposit such moneys or cash in an interest-bearing account.

Acts 1980, c. 423; Acts 1991, c. 680; Acts 1995, c. 447.

§ 19.2-270.3. Admissible evidence as to identity of party presenting bad check, draft or order

In any prosecution under § 18.2-181 or § 18.2-182 for the presentation of a bad check, draft or order, the following shall be admissible in any proceeding, hearing or trial of the case:

1. The unpaid or dishonored check, draft or order, bearing a notation thereon of the full name, residence address, home telephone number, and either the driver's license, social security or other governmentally issued identification number of the person who delivered such check, draft or order to the payee, the cashing party or its representative, and bearing the initials of the representative of the payee or cashing party to whom the check, draft or order was delivered, as evidence that such information was transcribed on

such check, draft or order at the time of such delivery; or

2. A composite photograph of the check, draft or order, and of the person delivering such check, draft or order, and of other documentation identifying such person, such as a driver's license, social security card, or other governmentally issued identification card, taken together at the time the check, draft or order was delivered by such person to the payee, the cashing party or its representative.

If such evidence is introduced, it may invoke an inference sufficient for the trier of fact to find that the person whose identifying information appears on the check, draft or order was the person who delivered the check, draft or order in question to the payee, cashing party or its representative.

Acts 1981, c. 292; Acts 1991, c. 633.

§ 19.2–270.4. When donation, destruction, or return of exhibits received in evidence authorized

A. Except as provided in § 19.2–270.4:1 and unless objection with sufficient cause is made, the trial court in any criminal case may order the donation or destruction of any or all exhibits received in evidence during the course of the trial (i) in any misdemeanor case, at any time after the expiration of the time for filing an appeal from the final judgment of the court if no appeal is taken or if an appeal is taken, at any time after exhaustion of all appellate remedies and (ii) in any felony case, upon notice in the sentencing order or otherwise to the attorney for the Commonwealth, the defendant at his last known address, and attorney of record for the defendant in the case, after more than one year has expired from exhaustion of all appellate remedies, or, if no appeal is taken, after more than one year from the time for seeking appellate remedies has expired; and in the event the defendant is found not guilty by a court of law, the court may, upon entry of the final order, order the destruction, donation, or return of the exhibits; provided, however, if a petition for writ of habeas corpus is filed within such one-year period, then such order shall not be entered until exhaustion of such habeas corpus proceedings. Notwithstanding the foregoing, in all cases concluded prior to July 1, 2005, the notice requirement in this section shall not apply. The order of donation or destruction may require that photographs be made of all exhibits ordered to be donated or destroyed and that such photographs be appropriately labeled for future identification. In addition, the order shall state the nature of the exhibit subject to donation or destruction, identify the case in which such exhibit was received and from whom such exhibit was received, if known, and the manner by which the exhibit is to be destroyed or to whom donated. However, any money introduced into evidence, unless it is stolen from a third party, shall be subject to forfeiture by law-enforcement officials as otherwise provided by law, and if no forfeiture action is taken or if funds remain after any such forfeiture, the clerk shall escheat such funds as otherwise provided by law. No notice to the defendant shall be required in the case of exhibits the disposal or destruction of which is controlled by § 19.2–386.23 or 19.2–386.24, in any case in which such exhibits may be seized and forfeited to the Commonwealth under Chapter 22.1 (§ 19.2–386.1 et seq.) or Chapter 22.2 (§ 19.2–386.15 et seq.), or any other forfeiture provisions, or in any case where such exhibits are deemed contraband.

B. Except as provided in § 19.2–270.4:1, a circuit court for good cause shown, on notice to the attorney for the Commonwealth and any attorney for a defendant in the case, may order the return of any or all exhibits to the owners thereof, notwithstanding the pendency of any appeal or petition for a writ of habeas corpus. The order may be upon such conditions as the court deems appropriate for future identification and inclusion in the record of a case subject to retrial. In addition, the owner shall acknowledge in a sworn affidavit to be filed with the record of the case, that he has retaken possession of such exhibit or exhibits.

C. Any photographs taken pursuant to an order of donation or destruction or an order returning exhibits to the owners shall be retained with the record in the case and, if necessary, shall be admissible in any subsequent trial of the same cause, subject to all other rules of evidence.

D. Upon petition of any organization which is exempt from taxation under § 501 (c) (3) of the Internal Revenue Code, the court in its sound discretion may order the donation of an exhibit to such charitable organization.

Acts 1984, c. 621; Acts 1989, c. 481; Acts 1994, c. 536; Acts 2001, c. 873, eff. May 2, 2001; Acts 2001, c. 874, eff. May 2, 2001; Acts 2001, c. 875. Amended by Acts 2008, c. 805; Acts 2010, c. 352; Acts 2010, c. 366; Acts 2010, c. 454.

§ 19.2–270.4:1. Storage, preservation and retention of human biological evidence in felony cases

A. Notwithstanding any provision of law or rule of court, upon motion of a person convicted of a felony but not sentenced to death or his attorney of record to the circuit court that entered the judgment for the offense, the court shall order the storage, preservation, and retention of specifically identified human biological evidence or representative samples collected or obtained in the case for a period of up to 15 years from the time of conviction, unless the court determines, in its discretion, that the evidence should be retained for a longer period of time. Upon the filing of such a motion, the defendant may request a hearing for the limited purpose of identifying the human biological evidence or representative samples that are to be stored in accordance with the provisions of this section. Upon the granting of the motion, the court shall order the clerk of the circuit court to transfer all such evidence to the Department of Forensic Science. The

Department of Forensic Science shall store, preserve, and retain such evidence. If the evidence is not within the custody of the clerk at the time the order is entered, the court shall order the governmental entity having custody of the evidence to transfer such evidence to the Department of Forensic Science. Upon the entry of an order under this subsection, the court may upon motion or upon good cause shown, with notice to the convicted person, his attorney of record and the attorney for the Commonwealth, modify the original storage order, as it relates to time of storage of the evidence or samples, for a period of time greater than or less than that specified in the original order.

B. In the case of a person sentenced to death, the court that entered the judgment shall, in all cases, order any human biological evidence or representative samples to be transferred by the governmental entity having custody to the Department of Forensic Science. The Department of Forensic Science shall store, preserve, and retain such evidence until the judgment is executed. If the person sentenced to death has his sentence reduced, then such evidence shall be transferred from the Department to the original investigating law-enforcement agency for storage as provided in this section.

C. Pursuant to standards and guidelines established by the Department of Forensic Science, the order shall state the method of custody, transfer and return of any evidence to insure and protect the Commonwealth's interest in the integrity of the evidence. Pursuant to standards and guidelines established by the Department of Forensic Science, the Department of Forensic Science, local law-enforcement agency or other custodian of the evidence shall take all necessary steps to preserve, store, and retain the evidence and its chain of custody for the period of time specified.

D. In any proceeding under this section, the court, upon a finding that the physical evidence is of such a nature, size or quantity that storage, preservation or retention of all of the evidence is impractical, may order the storage of only representative samples of the evidence. The Department of Forensic Science shall take representative samples, cuttings or swabbings and retain them. The remaining evidence shall be handled according to § 19.2–270.4 or as otherwise provided for in the Code.

E. An action under this section or the performance of any attorney representing the petitioner under this section shall not form the basis for relief in any habeas corpus or appellate proceeding. Nothing in this section shall create any cause of action for damages against the Commonwealth, or any of its political subdivisions or officers, employees or agents of the Commonwealth or its political subdivisions.

Acts 2001, c. 873, eff. May 2, 2001; Acts 2001, c. 874, eff. May 2, 2001; Acts 2001, c. 875; Acts 2002, c. 832; Acts 2005, c. 868; Acts 2005, c. 881.

§ 19.2–270.5. DNA profile admissible in criminal proceeding

In any criminal proceeding, DNA (deoxyribonucleic acid) testing shall be deemed to be a reliable scientific technique and the evidence of a DNA profile comparison may be admitted to prove or disprove the identity of any person. This section shall not otherwise limit the introduction of any relevant evidence bearing upon any question at issue before the court, including the accuracy and reliability of the procedures employed in the collection and analysis of a particular DNA sample. The court shall, regardless of the results of the DNA analysis, if any, consider such other relevant evidence of the identity of the accused as shall be admissible in evidence.

At least twenty-one days prior to commencement of the proceeding in which the results of a DNA analysis will be offered as evidence, the party intending to offer the evidence shall notify the opposing party, in writing, of the intent to offer the analysis and shall provide or make available copies of the profiles and the report or statement to be introduced. In the event that such notice is not given, and the person proffers such evidence, then the court may in its discretion either allow the opposing party a continuance or, under appropriate circumstances, bar the person from presenting such evidence. The period of any such continuance shall not be counted for speedy trial purposes under § 19.2–243. If the opposing party intends to object to the admissibility of such evidence he shall give written notice of that fact and the basis for his objections at least ten days prior to commencement of the proceedings.

Acts 1990, c. 640; Acts 1997, c. 315; Acts 2002, c. 627; Acts 2002, c. 885.

§ 19.2–270.6. Evidence of abuse admissible in certain criminal trials (Supreme Court Rule 2:409 derived from this section)

In any criminal prosecution alleging personal injury or death, or the attempt to cause personal injury or death, relevant evidence of repeated physical and psychological abuse of the accused by the victim shall be admissible, subject to the general rules of evidence.

Acts 1993, c. 5.

§ 19.2–270.7. Determining decibel level of sound with proper equipment; certificate as to accuracy of equipment

A law-enforcement officer may use equipment deemed proper pursuant to subsection C of § 2.2–1112 to determine the decibel level of any sound, including noise. The results of such determinations shall be accepted as prima facie evidence of the decibel level of the sound in any court or legal proceeding where the decibel level of the sound is at issue.

In any court or legal proceeding in which any question arises about the calibration or accuracy of such equipment used to determine the decibel level of sound, a certificate, or a true copy thereof, showing the calibration or testing for accuracy of the equipment, and when and by whom the calibration or test was made, shall be admissible as evidence of the facts therein stated. No calibration or testing of such equipment shall be valid for longer than 12 months.

Added by Acts 2010, c. 558.

§ 19.2–271. Certain judicial officers incompetent to testify under certain circumstances; exceptions (Supreme Court Rule 2:605 derived from this section)

No judge shall be competent to testify in any criminal or civil proceeding as to any matter which came before him in the course of his official duties.

Except as otherwise provided in this section, no clerk of any court, magistrate, or other person having the power to issue warrants, shall be competent to testify in any criminal or civil proceeding as to any matter which came before him in the course of his official duties. Such person shall be competent to testify in any criminal proceeding wherein the defendant is charged with perjury or pursuant to the provisions of § 18.2–460 or in any proceeding authorized pursuant to § 19.2–353.3. Notwithstanding any other provision of this section, any judge, clerk of any court, magistrate, or other person having the power to issue warrants, who is the victim of a crime, shall not be incompetent solely because of his office to testify in any criminal or civil proceeding arising out of the crime.

Acts 1975, c. 495; Acts 1976, c. 269; Acts 1990, c. 602. Amended by Acts 2015, c. 635.

§ 19.2–271.1. Competency of husband and wife to testify

Husband and wife shall be competent witnesses to testify for or against each other in criminal cases, except as otherwise provided.

Acts 1977, c. 624.

§ 19.2–271.2. Testimony of husband and wife in criminal cases (Subsection (b) of Supreme Court Rule 2:504 derived from this section)

In criminal cases husband and wife shall be allowed, and, subject to the rules of evidence governing other witnesses, may be compelled to testify in behalf of each other, but neither shall be compelled to be called as a witness against the other, except (i) in the case of a prosecution for an offense committed by one against the other , against a minor child of either, or against the property of either; (ii) in any case where either is charged with forgery of the name of the other or uttering or attempting to utter a writing bearing the allegedly forged signature of the other; or (iii) in any proceeding relating to a violation of the laws pertaining to criminal sexual assault (§§ 18.2–61 through 18.2–67.10), crimes against nature (§ 18.2–361) involving a minor as a victim and provided the defendant and the victim are not married to each other, incest (§ 18.2–366), or abuse of children (§§ 18.2–370 through 18.2–371). The failure of either husband or wife to testify, however, shall create no presumption against the accused, nor be the subject of any comment before the court or jury by any attorney.

Except in the prosecution for a criminal offense as set forth in (i), (ii) or (iii) above, in any criminal proceeding, a person has a privilege to refuse to disclose, and to prevent anyone else from disclosing, any confidential communication between his spouse and him during their marriage, regardless of whether he is married to that spouse at the time he objects to disclosure. For the purposes of this section, "confidential communication" means a communication made privately by a person to his spouse that is not intended for disclosure to any other person.

Acts 1977, c. 624; Acts 1988, c. 482; Acts 1993, c. 637; Acts 1996, c. 423; Acts 2005, c. 809.

§ 19.2–271.3. Communications between ministers of religion and persons they counsel or advise (Supreme Court Rule 2:503 derived in part from this section)

No regular minister, priest, rabbi or accredited practitioner over the age of eighteen years, of any religious organization or denomination usually referred to as a church, shall be required in giving testimony as a witness in any criminal action to disclose any information communicated to him by the accused in a confidential manner, properly entrusted to him in his professional capacity and necessary to enable him to discharge the functions of his office according to the usual course of his practice or discipline, where such person so communicating such information about himself or another is seeking spiritual counsel and advice relative to and growing out of the information so imparted.

Acts 1985, c. 570.

§ 19.2–271.4. Privileged communications by certain public safety personnel

A. A person who is a member of a critical incident stress management team, established pursuant to subdivision A 13 of § 32.1–111.3, shall not disclose nor be compelled to testify regarding any information communicated to him by emergency medical services or public safety personnel who are the subjects of peer support services regarding a critical incident. Such information shall also be exempt from the Virginia Freedom of Information Act (§ 2.2–3700 et seq.).

B. A person whose communications are privileged under subsection A may waive the privilege.

C. The provisions of this section shall not apply when:

1. Criminal activity is revealed;

2. A member of a critical incident stress management team is a witness or a party to a critical incident that prompted the peer support services;

3. A member of a critical incident stress management team reveals the content of privileged information to prevent a crime against any other person or a threat to public safety;

4. The privileged information reveals intent to defraud or deceive the investigation into the critical incident; or

5. A member of a critical incident stress management team reveals the content of privileged information to the employer of the emergency medical services or public safety personnel regarding criminal acts committed or information that would indicate that the emergency medical services or public safety personnel pose a threat to themselves or others.

Added by Acts 2012, c. 148; Acts 2012, c. 320.

Article 2

Witnesses From or for Another State

§ 19.2-272. Definitions

"Witness" as used in this article shall include a person whose testimony is desired in any proceeding or investigation by a grand jury or in a criminal action, prosecution or proceeding.

The word "state" shall include any territory of the United States and the District of Columbia.

The word "summons" shall include a subpoena (both subpoena ad testificandum and subpoena duces tecum), order or other notice requiring the appearance of a witness or production of documents.

Acts 1975, c. 495; Acts 1988, c. 34.

§ 19.2-273. Certificate that witness is needed in another state; hearing

If a judge of a court of record in any state which by its laws has made provisions for commanding persons within that state to attend and testify in this Commonwealth certifies under the seal of such court (1) that there is a criminal prosecution pending in such court or that a grand jury investigation has commenced or is about to commence, (2) that a person being within this Commonwealth is a material witness in such prosecution or grand jury investigation and (3) that his presence will be required for a specified number of days, upon presentation of such certificate to any judge of a court of record in the county or city in which such person is, such judge shall fix a time and place for hearing and shall make an order directing the witness to appear at a time and place certain for the hearing.

Acts 1975, c. 495.

§ 19.2-274. When court to order witness to attend

If at such hearing the judge determines that the witness is material and necessary, that it will not cause undue hardship to the witness to be compelled to attend and testify in the prosecution or grand jury investigation in the other state and that the laws of the state in which the prosecution is pending, or grand jury investigation has commenced or is about to commence (and of any other state through which the witness may be required to pass by ordinary course of travel) will give to him protection from arrest and the service of civil and criminal process, the judge shall issue a summons, with a copy of the certificate attached, directing the witness to attend and testify in the court where the prosecution is pending, or where a grand jury investigation has commenced or is about to commence at a time and place specified in the summons. In any such hearing the certificate shall be prima facie evidence of all the facts stated therein.

Acts 1975, c. 495.

§ 19.2-275. Arrest of witness

If the certificate recommends that the witness be taken into immediate custody and delivered to an officer of the requesting state to assure his attendance in the requesting state, such judge may, in lieu of notification of the hearing, direct that such witness be forthwith brought before him for the hearing; and the judge at the hearing being satisfied of the desirability of such custody and delivery, for which determination the certificate shall be prima facie proof of such desirability, may, in lieu of issuing subpoena or summons, order that the witness be forthwith taken into custody and delivered to an officer of the requesting state.

Acts 1975, c. 495.

§ 19.2-276. Penalty for failure to attend and testify

If the witness who is summoned as above provided, after being paid or tendered by some properly authorized person reimbursement for reasonable travel and lodging expenses as provided in § 2.2-2823 for each day he is required to travel and attend as a witness, fails without good cause to attend and testify as directed in the summons, he shall be punished in the manner provided for the punishment of any witness who disobeys a Virginia circuit court summons.

Acts 1975, c. 495; Acts 1987, c. 125.

§ 19.2–277. Summoning witnesses in another state to testify in this Commonwealth

If a person in any state which by its laws has made provision for commanding persons within its borders to attend and testify in criminal prosecutions or grand jury investigations commenced or about to commence in this Commonwealth is a material witness in a prosecution pending in a court of record in this Commonwealth, or in a grand jury investigation which has commenced or is about to commence, a judge of such court may issue a certificate under the seal of the court stating these facts and specifying the number of days the witness will be required. The certificate may include a recommendation that the witness be taken into immediate custody and delivered to an officer of this Commonwealth to assure his attendance in this Commonwealth. This certificate shall be presented to a judge of a court of record in the county in which the witness is found.

Acts 1975, c. 495.

§ 19.2–278. Reimbursement for daily mileage to such witnesses; issuance of warrant necessary to make tender

If the witness is summoned to attend and testify in this Commonwealth he shall receive such reimbursement for his daily mileage as prescribed in § 2.2–2823 for each day that he is required to travel and attend as a witness. A witness who has appeared in accordance with the provisions of the summons shall not be required to remain within this Commonwealth a longer period of time than the period mentioned in the certificate, unless otherwise ordered by the court.

The judge issuing the certificate prescribed in § 19.2–277 may, by order, direct the clerk of the court involved to issue such warrant or warrants payable out of the state treasury, as may be necessary to make the tender hereinabove prescribed; and after the entry of such order, such clerk, upon application of the attorney for the Commonwealth of the county or city involved, or of the accused, if certificate for the attendance of witness has been issued by such judge on his behalf as authorized by § 19.2–330, shall issue such warrant or warrants and deliver them to the said attorney for the Commonwealth, who shall, forthwith, cause such tender to be made. Upon issuance of any such warrant or warrants said clerk shall deliver a certified copy of the court's order to the Supreme Court, and the said warrant or warrants shall be paid out of the state treasury upon presentation.

Unless and until appropriate forms shall be obtained, such warrants may be issued on the regular forms provided for the payment of witness fees and allowances, but in such event the clerk issuing the same shall make a notation thereon that they were issued pursuant to the provisions of this section.

Acts 1975, c. 495; Acts 1976, c. 308; Acts 1977, c. 483; Acts 1978, c. 195.

§ 19.2–279. Penalty for failure of such witnesses to testify

If such witness, after coming into this Commonwealth, fails without good cause to attend and testify as directed in the summons, he shall be punished in the manner provided for the punishment of any witness who disobeys a summons issued from a court of record in this Commonwealth.

Acts 1975, c. 495.

§ 19.2–280. Exemption of such witnesses from arrest or service of process

If a person comes into this Commonwealth in obedience to a summons directing him to attend and testify in this Commonwealth he shall not while in this Commonwealth pursuant to such summons be subject to arrest or the service of process, civil or criminal, in connection with matters which arose before his entrance into this Commonwealth under the summons.

If a person passes through this Commonwealth while going to another state in obedience to a summons to attend and testify in that state or while returning therefrom, he shall not while so passing through this Commonwealth be subject to arrest or the service of process, civil or criminal, in connection with matters which arose before his entrance into this Commonwealth under the summons.

Acts 1975, c. 495.

§ 19.2–281. Construction of article

This article shall be so interpreted and construed as to effectuate its general purpose to make uniform the law of the states which enact it.

Acts 1975, c. 495.

§ 19.2–282. How article cited

This article may be cited as the "Uniform Act to Secure the Attendance of Witnesses from without a State in Criminal Proceedings."

Acts 1975, c. 495.

CHAPTER 17

CONVICTIONS; EFFECT THEREOF

ARTICLE 1

PROOF AND VERDICTS

§ 19.2-283. How accused may be convicted of felony

No person shall be convicted of felony, unless by his confession of guilt in court, or by his plea, or by the verdict of a jury, accepted and recorded by the court, or by judgment of the court trying the case without a jury according to law.

Acts 1975, c. 495.

§ 19.2-284. Proof of ownership in offense relating to property

In a prosecution for an offense committed upon, relating to or affecting real estate, or for stealing, embezzling, destroying, injuring or fraudulently receiving or concealing any personal estate it shall be sufficient to prove that when the offense was committed the actual or constructive possession, or a general or special property, in the whole or any part of such estate was in the person or entity alleged in the indictment or other accusation to be the owner thereof.

Acts 1975, c. 495.

§ 19.2-285. Accused guilty of part of offense charged; sentence; on new trial what tried

If a person indicted of a felony be by the jury acquitted of part of the offense charged, he shall be sentenced for such part as he is so convicted of, if the same be substantially charged in the indictment, whether it be felony or misdemeanor. If the verdict be set aside and a new trial granted the accused, he shall not be tried for any higher offense than that of which he was convicted on the last trial.

Acts 1975, c. 495.

§ 19.2-286. Conviction of attempt or as accessory on indictment for felony; effect of general verdict of not guilty

On an indictment for felony the jury may find the accused not guilty of the felony but guilty of an attempt to commit such felony, or of being an accessory thereto; and a general verdict of not guilty, upon such indictment, shall be a bar to a subsequent prosecution for an attempt to commit such felony, or of being an accessory thereto.

Acts 1975, c. 495.

§ 19.2-287. Verdict and judgment, when jury agree as to some and disagree as to others

When two or more persons are charged and tried jointly, the jury may render a verdict as to any of them as to whom they agree. Thereupon judgment shall be entered according to the verdict; and as to the others the case shall be tried by another jury.

Acts 1975, c. 495.

§ 19.2-288. Verdict when accused found guilty of punishable homicide

If a person indicted for murder be found by the jury guilty of any punishable homicide, they shall in their verdict fix the degree thereof and ascertain the extent of the punishment to be inflicted within the bounds prescribed by §§ 18.2-30 to 18.2-36.

Acts 1975, c. 495.

§ 19.2-289. Conviction of petit larceny

In a prosecution for grand larceny, if it be found that the thing stolen is of less value than $200, the jury may find the accused guilty of petit larceny.

Acts 1975, c. 495; Acts 1981, c. 197.

§ 19.2-290. Conviction of petit larceny though thing stolen worth more than $200

In a prosecution for petit larceny, though the thing stolen be of the value of $200 or more, the jury may find the accused guilty; and upon a conviction under this section or § 19.2-289 the accused shall be sentenced for petit larceny.

Acts 1975, c. 495; Acts 1981, c. 197.

§ 19.2-291. Faulty counts; motion to strike; general verdict of guilty

When there are several counts in the indictment one or more of which are faulty, the accused may move to strike the faulty count or counts or move the court to instruct the jury to disregard them. If he does neither and a general verdict of guilty is found, judgment shall be entered against the accused, if any count be good, though others be faulty, unless the court can plainly see that the verdict could not have been found on the good count. If the accused demurs to the faulty count or moves the court to instruct the jury to disregard it and his demurrer or motion is overruled and there is a general verdict of guilty and it cannot be seen on which count the verdict was founded, if the jury has been

discharged, it shall be set aside; but if it is manifest that it could not have been found on the bad count, the verdict shall be allowed to stand.
Acts 1975, c. 495.

§ 19.2–291.1. Report of conviction of school employees for certain offenses

The clerk of any circuit court or any district court in the Commonwealth shall report to the Superintendent of Public Instruction and the division superintendent of any employing school division the conviction of any person, known by such clerk to hold a license issued by the Board of Education, for any felony involving the sexual molestation, physical or sexual abuse, or rape of a child or involving drugs pursuant to Article 1 (§ 18.2–247 et seq.) of Chapter 7 of Title 18.2.
Added by Acts 2008, c. 474; Acts 2008, c. 827.

Article 2

Former Jeopardy

§ 19:2–292. Acquittal by jury on merits bar to further prosecution for same offense

A person acquitted upon the facts and merits on a former trial, may plead such acquittal in bar of a second prosecution for the same offense, notwithstanding any defect in the form or substance of the indictment or accusation on which he was acquitted, unless the case be for a violation of the law relating to the state revenue and the acquittal be reversed on a writ of error on behalf of the Commonwealth.
Acts 1975, c. 495.

§ 19.2–293. When acquittal not a bar to further prosecution for same offense

A person acquitted of an offense on the ground of a variance between the allegations and the proof of the indictment or other accusation, or upon an exception to the form or substance thereof, may be arraigned again on a new indictment or other proper accusation, and tried and convicted for the same offense, notwithstanding such former acquittal.
Acts 1975, c. 495.

§ 19.2–294. Offense against two or more statutes or ordinances

If the same act be a violation of two or more statutes, or of two or more ordinances, or of one or more statutes and also one or more ordinances, conviction under one of such statutes or ordinances shall be a bar to a prosecution or proceeding under the other or others. Furthermore, if the same act be a violation of both a state and a federal statute, a prosecution under the federal statute shall be a bar to a prosecution under the state statute. The provisions of this section shall not apply to any offense involving an act of terrorism as defined in § 18.2–46.4.

For purposes of this section, a prosecution under a federal statute shall be deemed to be commenced once jeopardy has attached.
Acts 1975, c. 495; Acts 1987, c. 241; Acts 2002, c. 588; Acts 2002, c. 623; Acts 2003, c. 736.

§ 19.2–294.1. Dismissal of one of dual charges for driving while intoxicated and reckless driving upon conviction of other charge

Whenever any person is charged with a violation of § 18.2–266 or any similar ordinances of any county, city, or town and with reckless driving in violation of § 46.2–852 or any ordinance of any county, city or town incorporating § 46.2–852, growing out of the same act or acts and is convicted of one of these charges, the court shall dismiss the remaining charge.
Acts 1975, c. 495; Acts 1997, c. 691; Acts 2004, c. 937.

Article 3

Conviction of Aliens

§ 19.2–294.2. Procedure when aliens convicted of certain felonies; duties of probation and parole officer

A. Whenever a person is (i) convicted in a circuit court of any felony and (ii) referred to a probation or parole officer for a report pursuant to § 19.2–299, or for probation supervision, the probation or parole officer shall inquire as to the citizenship of such person. If upon inquiry it is determined that the person may be an alien based upon his failure to produce evidence of United States citizenship, the probation or parole officer shall report this determination to the Central Criminal Records Exchange of the Department of State Police on forms provided by the Exchange.

B. The inquiry required by this section need not be made if it is apparent that a report on alien status has previously been made to the Central Criminal Records Exchange pursuant to this section.

C. It shall be the responsibility of the Central Criminal Records Exchange of the Department of State Police to review arrest reports submitted by law-enforcement agencies and reports of suspected alien-status inquiries made by probation or parole officers, and to report within sixty days of final disposition to the Law Enforcement Support Center of the United States Immigration and Customs Enforcement the identity of all convicted offenders suspected of being an alien.

Acts 1985, c. 247; Acts 1994, c. 579. Amended by Acts 2008, c. 180; Acts 2008, c. 415.

CHAPTER 18

SENTENCE; JUDGMENT; EXECUTION OF SENTENCE

Article 1

General Provisions

§ 19.2–295. Ascertainment of punishment

A. Within the limits prescribed by law, the term of confinement in the state correctional facility or in jail and the amount of fine, if any, of a person convicted of a criminal offense, shall be ascertained by the jury, or by the court in cases tried without a jury.

B. In any case in which a jury has fixed a sentence as provided in this chapter and the sentence is modified by the court pursuant to the authority contained within this chapter, the court shall file with the record of the case a written explanation of such modification including the cause therefor.

Acts 1975, c. 495; Acts 2007, c. 259.

§ 19.2–295.1. Sentencing proceeding by the jury after conviction

In cases of trial by jury, upon a finding that the defendant is guilty of a felony or a Class 1 misdemeanor, or upon a finding in the trial de novo of an appealed misdemeanor conviction that the defendant is guilty of a Class 1 misdemeanor, a separate proceeding limited to the ascertainment of punishment shall be held as soon as practicable before the same jury. At such proceeding, the Commonwealth may present any victim impact testimony pursuant to § 19.2–295.3 and shall present the defendant's prior criminal history, including prior convictions and the punishments imposed, by certified, attested or exemplified copies of the final order, including adult convictions and juvenile convictions and adjudications of delinquency. Prior convictions shall include convictions and adjudications of delinquency under the laws of any state, the District of Columbia, the United States or its territories. The Commonwealth shall provide to the defendant 14 days prior to trial notice of its intention to introduce copies of final orders evidencing the defendant's prior criminal history, including prior convictions and punishments imposed. Such notice shall include (i) the date of each prior conviction, (ii) the name and jurisdiction of the court where each prior conviction was had, (iii) each offense of which he was convicted, and (iv) the punishment imposed. Prior to commencement of the trial, the Commonwealth shall provide to the defendant photocopies of certified copies of the final orders which it intends to introduce at sentencing. After the Commonwealth has introduced in its case-in-chief of the sentencing phase such evidence of prior convictions or victim impact testimony, or both, or if no such evidence is introduced, the defendant may introduce relevant, admissible evidence related to punishment. Nothing in this section shall prevent the Commonwealth or the defendant from introducing relevant, admissible evidence in rebuttal.

If the jury cannot agree on a punishment, the court shall impanel a different jury to ascertain punishment, unless the defendant, the attorney for the Commonwealth, and the court agree, in the manner provided in § 19.2–257, that the court shall fix punishment.

If the sentence imposed pursuant to this section is subsequently set aside or found invalid solely due to an error in the sentencing proceeding, the court shall impanel a different jury to ascertain punishment, unless the defendant, the attorney for the Commonwealth and the court agree, in the manner provided in § 19.2–257, that the court shall fix punishment.

Acts 1994, c. 828; Acts 1994, c. 860; Acts 1994, c. 862; Acts 1994, c. 881; Acts 1995, c. 567; Acts 1996, c. 664; Acts 2001, c. 389; Acts 2007, c. 388; Acts 2007, c. 478. Amended by Acts 2012, c. 134.

§ 19.2–295.2. Postrelease supervision of felons sentenced for offenses committed on and after January 1, 1995, and on and after July 1, 2000

A. At the time the court imposes sentence upon a conviction for any felony offense committed (i) on or after January 1, 1995, the court may, and (ii) on or after July 1, 2000, shall, in addition to any other punishment imposed if such other punishment includes an active term of incarceration in a state or local correctional facility, except in cases in which the court orders a suspended term of confinement of at least six months, impose a term of postrelease supervision of not less than six months nor more than three years, as the court may determine. Such additional term shall be suspended and the defendant placed under postrelease supervision upon release from the active term of incarceration. The period of supervision shall be established by the court; however, such period shall not be less than six months nor more than three years. Periods of postrelease supervision imposed pursuant to this section upon more than one felony conviction may be ordered to run concurrently. Periods of postrelease supervision imposed pursuant to this section may be ordered to run concurrently with any period of probation the defendant may also be subject to serve.

B. The period of postrelease supervision shall be under the supervision and review of the Virginia Parole Board. The Board shall review each felon prior to release and establish conditions of postrelease supervision. Failure to successfully abide by such terms and conditions shall be grounds to terminate the period of postrelease supervision and recommit the defendant to the Department of Corrections or to the local correctional facility from which he was previously released. Procedures for any such termination and recommitment shall be conducted in the same manner as procedures for the revocation of parole.

C. Postrelease supervision programs shall be operated through the probation and parole districts established pursuant to § 53.1–141.

D. Nothing in this section shall be construed to prohibit the court from exercising any authority otherwise granted by law.

Acts 1994, Sp.S. II, c. 1, eff. Oct. 13, 1994; Acts 1994, Sp.S. II, c. 2, eff. Oct. 13, 1994; Acts 1995, c. 502; Acts 1995, c. 574; Acts 2000, c. 767.

§ 19.2–295.2:1. Postrelease supervision of felons sentenced for certain offenses committed on or after July 1, 2006

A. For offenses committed on or after July 1, 2006:

1. At the time the court imposes a sentence upon a conviction for a first violation of subsection A of § 18.2–472.1 the court shall impose an added term of postrelease supervision of six months.

2. For a second or subsequent violation of subsection A of § 18.2–472.1 when both violations occurred after July 1, 2006, or a first violation of subsection B of § 18.2–472.1, the court shall impose an added term of postrelease supervision by the Department of Corrections of two years.

3. For a second or subsequent violation of subsection B of § 18.2–472.1 when both violations occurred after July 1, 2006, the court shall impose an added term of postrelease supervision by the Department of Corrections of five years.

Any terms of postrelease supervision imposed pursuant to this section shall be in addition to any other punishment imposed, including any periods of active incarceration or suspended periods of incarceration, if any.

B. The court shall order that any term of postrelease supervision imposed pursuant to this section be suspended, and the defendant be placed on active supervision under a postrelease supervision program operated by the Department of Corrections. The court shall order that the defendant be subject to electronic monitoring by means of a GPS (Global Positioning System) tracking device, or other similar device during this period of postrelease supervision. Failure to successfully abide by the terms and conditions of the postrelease supervision program shall be grounds to terminate the period of postrelease supervision and recommit the defendant to the Department of Corrections or to a local correctional facility. Procedures for any such termination shall be conducted after a hearing in the court which originally sentenced the defendant, conducted in a manner consistent with a revocation hearing under § 19.2–306, mutatis mutandis.

C. Nothing in this section shall be construed to prohibit the court from exercising any authority otherwise granted by law.

Acts 2006, c. 857; Acts 2006, c. 914.

§ 19.2–295.3. Admission of victim impact testimony

Whether by trial or upon a plea of guilty, upon a finding that the defendant is guilty of a felony, the court shall permit the victim, as defined in § 19.2–11.01, upon motion of the attorney for the Commonwealth, to testify in the presence of the accused regarding the impact of the offense upon the victim. The court shall limit the victim's testimony to the factors set forth in clauses (i) through (vi) of subsection A of § 19.2–299.1. In the case of trial by jury, the court shall permit the victim to testify at the sentencing hearing conducted pursuant to § 19.2–295.1 or in the case of trial by the court or a guilty plea, the court shall permit the victim to testify before the court prior to the imposition of a sentence. Victim impact testimony in all capital murder cases shall be admitted in accordance with § 19.2–264.4.

Acts 1998, c. 485; Acts 2004, c. 310.

§ 19.2–296. Withdrawal of plea of guilty

A motion to withdraw a plea of guilty or nolo contendere may be made only before sentence is imposed or imposition of a sentence is suspended; but to correct manifest injustice, the court within twenty-one days after entry of a final order may set aside the judgment of conviction and permit the defendant to withdraw his plea.

Acts 1975, c. 495.

§ 19.2–297. Repealed by Acts 1994, c. 706

§ 19.2–297.1. Sentence of person twice previously convicted of certain violent felonies

A. Any person convicted of two or more separate acts of violence when such offenses were not part of a common act, transaction or scheme, and who has been at liberty as defined in § 53.1–151 between each conviction, shall, upon conviction of a third or subsequent act of violence, be sentenced to life imprisonment and shall not have all or any portion of the sentence suspended, provided it is admitted, or found by the jury or judge before whom he is tried, that he has been previously convicted of two or more such acts of violence. For the purposes of this section, "act of violence" means (i) any one of the following violations of Chapter 4 (§ 18.2-30 et seq.) of Title 18.2:

a. First and second degree murder and voluntary manslaughter under Article 1 (§ 18.2-30 et seq.);

b. Mob-related felonies under Article 2 (§ 18.2-38 et seq.);

c. Any kidnapping or abduction felony under Article 3 (§ 18.2-47 et seq.);

d. Any malicious felonious assault or malicious bodily wounding under Article 4 (§ 18.2-51 et seq.);

e. Robbery under § 18.2-58 and carjacking under § 18.2-58.1;

f. Except as otherwise provided in § 18.2-67.5:2 or § 18.2-67.5:3, criminal sexual assault punishable as a felony under Article 7 (§ 18.2-61 et seq.); or

g. Arson in violation of § 18.2-77 when the structure burned was occupied or a Class 3 felony violation of § 18.2-79.

(ii) conspiracy to commit any of the violations enumerated in clause (i) of this section; and (iii) violations as a principal in the second degree or accessory before the fact of the provisions enumerated in clause (i) of this section.

B. Prior convictions shall include convictions under the laws of any state or of the United States for any offense substantially similar to those listed under "act of violence" if such offense would be a felony if committed in the Commonwealth.

The Commonwealth shall notify the defendant in writing, at least thirty days prior to trial, of its intention to seek punishment pursuant to this section.

C. Any person sentenced to life imprisonment pursuant to this section shall not be eligible for parole and shall not be eligible for any good conduct allowance or any earned sentence credits under Chapter 6 (§ 53.1-186 et seq.) of Title 53.1. However, any person subject to the provisions of this section, other than a person who was sentenced under subsection A of § 18.2-67.5:3 for criminal sexual assault convictions specified in subdivision f, (i) who has reached the age of sixty-five or older and who has served at least five years of the sentence imposed or (ii) who has reached the age of sixty or older and who has served at least ten years of the sentence imposed may petition the Parole Board for conditional release. The Parole Board shall promulgate regulations to implement the provisions of this subsection.

Acts 1994, c. 828; Acts 1994, c. 860; Acts 1994, c. 862; Acts 1994, c. 881; Acts 1994, Sp. S. II, c. 1, eff. Oct. 13, 1994; Acts 1994, Sp. S. II, c. 2, eff. Oct. 13, 1994; Acts 1995, c. 834; Acts 1996, c. 539.

§ 19.2-298. Pronouncement of sentence

After a finding of guilty, sentence shall be pronounced, or decision to suspend the imposition of sentence shall be announced, without unreasonable delay. Pending pronouncement, the court may commit the accused to jail or may continue or alter the bail except that in those cases where the accused is convicted of a murder in the first degree, the court shall commit him to jail and he shall not be allowed bail pending the pronouncement of sentence. Before pronouncing the sentence, the court shall inquire of the accused if he desires to make a statement and if he desires to advance any reason why judgment should not be pronounced against him.

Whenever any person willfully and knowingly fails to surrender or submit to the custody of a sheriff as ordered by a court, any law-enforcement officer, with or without a warrant, may arrest such person anywhere in the Commonwealth. If the arrest is made in the county or city in which the person was ordered to surrender, or in an adjoining county or city, the officer may forthwith return the accused before the proper court. If the arrest is made beyond the foregoing limits, the officer shall proceed according to the provisions of § 19.2-76, and if such arrest is made without a warrant, the officer shall procure a warrant from the magistrate serving the county or city wherein the arrest was made, charging the accused with contempt of court.

Acts 1975, c. 495; Acts 1976, c. 285. Amended by Acts 2009, c. 192.

§ 19.2-298.01. Use of discretionary sentencing guidelines

A. In all felony cases, other than Class 1 felonies, the court shall (i) have presented to it the appropriate discretionary sentencing guidelines worksheets and (ii) review and consider the suitability of the applicable discretionary sentencing guidelines established pursuant to Chapter 8 (§ 17.1-800 et seq.) of Title 17.1. Before imposing sentence, the court shall state for the record that such review and consideration have been accomplished and shall make the completed worksheets a part of the record of the case and open for inspection. In cases tried by a jury, the jury shall not be presented any information regarding sentencing guidelines.

B. In any felony case, other than Class 1 felonies, in which the court imposes a sentence which is either greater or less than that indicated by the discretionary sentencing guidelines, the court shall file with the record of the case a written explanation of such departure.

C. In felony cases, other than Class 1 felonies, tried by a jury and in felony cases tried by the court without a jury upon a plea of not guilty, the court shall direct a probation officer of such court to prepare the discretionary sentencing guidelines worksheets. In felony cases tried upon a plea of guilty, including cases which are the subject of a plea agreement, the court shall direct a probation officer of such court to prepare the discretionary sentencing guidelines worksheets, or, with the concurrence of the accused, the court and the attorney for the Commonwealth, the worksheets shall be prepared by the attorney for the Commonwealth.

D. Except as provided in subsection E, discretionary sentencing guidelines worksheets prepared pursuant to this section shall be subject to the same distribution as presentence investigation reports prepared pursuant to subsection A of § 19.2–299.

E. Following the entry of a final order of conviction and sentence in a felony case, the clerk of the circuit court in which the case was tried shall cause a copy of such order or orders, the original of the discretionary sentencing guidelines worksheets prepared in the case, and a copy of any departure explanation prepared pursuant to subsection B to be forwarded to the Virginia Criminal Sentencing Commission within five days. Similarly, the statement required by §§ 19.2–295 and 19.2–303 and regarding departure from or modification of a sentence fixed by a jury shall be forwarded to the Virginia Criminal Sentencing Commission.

F. The failure to follow any or all of the provisions of this section or the failure to follow any or all of the provisions of this section in the prescribed manner shall not be reviewable on appeal or the basis of any other post-conviction relief.

G. The provisions of this section shall apply only to felony cases in which the offense is committed on or after January 1, 1995, and for which there are discretionary sentencing guidelines. For purposes of the discretionary sentencing guidelines only, a person sentenced to a boot camp incarceration program pursuant to § 19.2–316.1, a detention center incarceration program pursuant to § 19.2–316.2 or a diversion center incarceration program pursuant to § 19.2–316.3 shall be deemed to be sentenced to a term of incarceration.

Acts 1994, Sp. S. II, c. 1, eff. Oct. 13, 1994; Acts 1994, Sp. S. II, c. 2, eff. Oct. 13, 1994; Acts 1996, c. 552; Acts 1997, c. 345; Acts 1998, c. 200; Acts 1998, c. 353; Acts 1999, c. 286; Acts 2007, c. 259.

§§ 19.2–298.1 to 19.2–298.4. Repealed by Acts 2003, c. 584

§ 19.2–299. Investigations and reports by probation officers in certain cases

A. When a person is tried in a circuit court (i) upon a charge of assault and battery in violation of § 18.2–57 or 18.2–57.2, stalking in violation of § 18.2–60.3, sexual battery in violation of § 18.2–67.4, attempted sexual battery in violation of § 18.2–67.5, or driving while intoxicated in violation of § 18.2–266, and is adjudged guilty of such charge, unless waived by the court and the defendant and the attorney for the Commonwealth, the court may, or on motion of the defendant shall; or (ii) upon a felony charge not set forth in subdivision (iii) below, the court may when there is a plea agreement between the defendant and the Commonwealth and shall when the defendant pleads guilty without a plea agreement or is found guilty by the court after a plea of not guilty; or (iii) the court shall when a person is charged and adjudged guilty of a felony violation, or conspiracy to commit or attempt to commit a felony violation, of § 18.2–46.2, 18.2–46.3, 18.2–48, clause (2) or (3) of § 18.2–49, § 18.2–61, 18.2–63, 18.2–64.1, 18.2–64.2, 18.2–67.1, 18.2–67.2, 18.2–67.3, 18.2–67.4:1, 18.2–67.5, 18.2–67.5:1, 18.2–355, 18.2–356, 18.2–357, 18.2–361, 18.2–362, 18.2–366, 18.2–368, 18.2–370, 18.2–370.1, or 18.2–370.2, or any attempt to commit or conspiracy to commit any felony violation of § 18.2–67.5, 18.2–67.5:2, or 18.2–67.5:3, direct a probation officer of such court to thoroughly investigate and report upon the history of the accused, including a report of the accused's criminal record as an adult and available juvenile court records, any information regarding the accused's participation or membership in a criminal street gang as defined in § 18.2–46.1, and all other relevant facts, to fully advise the court so the court may determine the appropriate sentence to be imposed. Unless the defendant or the attorney for the Commonwealth objects, the court may order that the report contain no more than the defendant's criminal history, any history of substance abuse, any physical or health-related problems as may be pertinent, and any applicable sentencing guideline worksheets. This expedited report shall be subject to all the same procedures as all other sentencing reports and sentencing guidelines worksheets. The probation officer, after having furnished a copy of this report at least five days prior to sentencing to counsel for the accused and the attorney for the Commonwealth for their permanent use, shall submit his report in advance of the sentencing hearing to the judge in chambers, who shall keep such report confidential. Counsel for the accused may provide the accused with a copy of the presentence report. The probation officer shall be available to testify from this report in open court in the presence of the accused, who shall have been provided with a copy of the presentence report by his counsel or advised of its contents and be given the right to cross-examine the investigating officer as to any matter contained therein and to present any additional facts bearing upon the matter. The report of the investigating officer shall at all times be kept confidential by each recipient, and shall be filed as a part of the record in the case. Any report so filed shall be made available only by court order and shall be sealed upon final order by the court, except that such reports or copies thereof shall be available at any time to any criminal justice agency, as defined in § 9.1–101, of this or any other state or of the United States; to any agency where the accused is referred for treatment by the court or by probation and parole services; and to counsel for any person who has been indicted jointly for the same felony as the person subject to the report. Subject to the limitations set forth in § 37.2–901, any report prepared pursuant to the provisions hereof shall without court order be made available to counsel for the person who is the subject of the report if that person (i) is charged with a felony subsequent to the time of the preparation of the report or (ii) has been convicted of the crime or crimes for which the report was prepared and is pursuing a post-conviction remedy. The presentence report shall be in a form prescribed by the Department of Corrections. In all cases where such report is not ordered, a simplified report shall be prepared on a form prescribed by the Department of Corrections. For the purposes of this subsection, information regarding the accused's participation or membership in a criminal street gang may include the characteristics, specific rivalries, common practices, social customs and behavior, terminology, and types of crimes that are likely to be committed by that criminal street gang.

B. As a part of any presentence investigation conducted pursuant to subsection A when the offense for which the defendant was convicted was a felony, the court probation officer shall advise any victim of such offense in writing that he may submit to the Virginia Parole Board a written request (i) to be given the opportunity to submit to the Board a written statement in advance of any parole hearing describing the impact of the offense upon him and his opinion regarding the defendant's release and (ii) to receive copies of such other notifications pertaining to the defendant as the Board may provide pursuant to subsection B of § 53.1-155.

C. As part of any presentence investigation conducted pursuant to subsection A when the offense for which the defendant was convicted was a felony drug offense set forth in Article 1 (§ 18.2-247 et seq.) of Chapter 7 of Title 18.2, the presentence report shall include any known association of the defendant with illicit drug operations or markets.

D. As a part of any presentence investigation conducted pursuant to subsection A, when the offense for which the defendant was convicted was a felony, not a capital offense, committed on or after January 1, 2000, the defendant shall be required to undergo a substance abuse screening pursuant to § 18.2-251.01.

Acts 1975, c. 371; Acts 1975, c. 495; Acts 1979, c. 286; Acts 1980, c. 733; Acts 1981, c. 263; Acts 1983, c. 541; Acts 1987, c. 676; Acts 1989, c. 169; Acts 1991, c. 43; Acts 1991, c. 229; Acts 1992, c. 77; Acts 1993, c. 466; Acts 1993, c. 492; Acts 1994, Sp. S. II, c. 1, eff. July 1, 1995; Acts 1994, Sp. S. II, c. 2, eff. July 1, 1995; Acts 1995, c. 687; Acts 1995, c. 778; Acts 1997, c. 691; Acts 1998, c. 783, eff. July 1, 1999; Acts 1998, c. 840, eff. July 1, 1999; Acts 1999, c. 891; Acts 1999, c. 903; Acts 1999, c. 913; Acts 2001, c. 647; Acts 2003, c. 146; Acts 2003, c. 613; Acts 2004, c. 308; Acts 2004, c. 459; Acts 2004, c. 819; Acts 2005, c. 188; Acts 2005, c. 219; Acts 2005, c. 631; Acts 2006, c. 99; Acts 2006, c. 863; Acts 2006, c. 914; Acts 2006, c. 916. Amended by Acts 2010, c. 223.

§ 19.2-299.1. When Victim Impact Statement required; contents; uses

The presentence report prepared pursuant to § 19.2-299 shall, with the consent of the victim, as defined in § 19.2-11.01, in all cases involving offenses other than capital murder, include a Victim Impact Statement. Victim Impact Statements in all cases involving capital murder shall be prepared and submitted in accordance with the provisions of § 19.2-264.5.

A Victim Impact Statement shall be kept confidential and shall be sealed upon entry of the sentencing order. If prepared by someone other than the victim, it shall (i) identify the victim, (ii) itemize any economic loss suffered by the victim as a result of the offense, (iii) identify the nature and extent of any physical or psychological injury suffered by the victim as a result of the offense, (iv) detail any change in the victim's personal welfare, lifestyle or familial relationships as a result of the offense, (v) identify any request for psychological or medical services initiated by the victim or the victim's family as a result of the offense, and (vi) provide such other information as the court may require related to the impact of the offense upon the victim.

If the court does not order a presentence investigation and report, the attorney for the Commonwealth shall, at the request of the victim, submit a Victim Impact Statement. In any event, a victim shall be advised by the local crime victim and witness assistance program that he may submit in his own words a written Victim Impact Statement prepared by the victim or someone the victim designates in writing.

The Victim Impact Statement may be considered by the court in determining the appropriate sentence. A copy of the statement prepared pursuant to this section shall be made available to the defendant or counsel for the defendant without court order at least five days prior to the sentencing hearing. The statement shall not be admissible in any civil proceeding for damages arising out of the acts upon which the conviction was based. The statement, however, may be utilized by the Virginia Workers' Compensation Commission in its determinations on claims by victims of crimes pursuant to Chapter 21.1 (§ 19.2-368.1 et seq.) of this title.

Acts 1983, c. 541; Acts 1984, c. 282; Acts 1987, c. 676; Acts 1989, c. 374; Acts 1993, c. 436; Acts 1993, c. 569; Acts 1995, c. 687; Acts 1995, c. 720, eff. April 6, 1995; Acts 1996, c. 398.

§ 19.2-299.2. Alcohol and substance abuse screening and assessment for designated Class 1 misdemeanor convictions

A. When a person is convicted of any offense committed on or after January 1, 2000, under Article 1 (§ 18.2-247 et seq.) or Article 1.1 (§ 18.2-265.1 et seq.) of Chapter 7 of Title 18.2, and such offense is punishable as a Class 1 misdemeanor, or when a person is convicted for a second offense of petit larceny, the court shall order the person to undergo a substance abuse screening as part of the sentence if the defendant's sentence includes probation supervision by a local community-based probation services agency established pursuant to Article 9 (§ 9.1-173 et seq.) of Chapter 1 of Title 9.1 or participation in a local alcohol safety action program. Whenever a court requires a person to enter into and successfully complete an alcohol safety action program pursuant to § 18.2–271.1 for a second offense of the type described therein, or orders an evaluation of a person to be conducted by an alcohol safety action program pursuant to any provision of § 46.2–391, the alcohol safety action program shall assess such person's degree of alcohol abuse before determining the appropriate level of treatment to be provided or to be recommended for such person being evaluated pursuant to § 46.2–391.

The court may order such screening upon conviction as part of the sentence of any other Class 1 misdemeanor if the defendant's sentence includes probation supervision by a local community-based probation services agency established pursuant to Article 9 (§ 9.1–173 et seq.) of Chapter 1 of Title 9.1, participation in a local alcohol safety action program or any other sanction and the court has reason to believe the defendant has a substance abuse or dependence problem.

B. A substance abuse screening ordered pursuant to this section shall be conducted by the local alcohol safety action program. When an offender is ordered to enter local community-based probation services established pursuant to Article 9 (§ 9.1–173 et seq.) of Chapter 1 of Title 9.1, rather than the local alcohol safety action program, the local community-based probation services agency shall be responsible for the screening. However, if a local community-based probation services agency has not been established for the locality, the local alcohol safety action program shall conduct the screening as part of the sentence.

C. If the screening indicates that the person has a substance abuse or dependence problem, an assessment shall be completed and if the assessment confirms that the person has a substance abuse or dependence problem, as a condition of a suspended sentence and probation, the court shall order the person to complete the substance abuse education and intervention component, or both as appropriate, of the local alcohol safety action program or such other agency providing treatment programs or services, if available, such as in the opinion of the court would be best suited to the needs of the person. If the referral is to the local alcohol safety action program, the program may charge a fee for the education and intervention component, or both, not to exceed $300, based upon the defendant's ability to pay.

Acts 1998, c. 783, eff. July 1, 1999; Acts 1998, c. 840, eff. July 1, 1999; Acts 1999, c. 891; Acts 1999, c. 913; Acts 2000, c. 958, eff. October 1, 2000; Acts 2000, c. 980, eff. October 1, 2000; Acts 2000, c. 1040; Acts 2007, c. 133. Amended by Acts 2008, c. 762.

§ 19.2–300. Deferring for mental examination sentence of person convicted of offense indicating sexual abnormality

In the case of the conviction in any circuit court of any person for any criminal offense which indicates sexual abnormality, the trial judge may on his own initiative, or shall upon application of the attorney for the Commonwealth, the defendant, or counsel for defendant or other person acting for the defendant, defer sentence until the report of a mental examination conducted as provided in § 19.2–301 of the defendant can be secured to guide the judge in determining what disposition shall be made of the defendant.

Acts 1975, c. 495; Acts 1990, c. 697.

§ 19.2–301. Judge shall require examination under § 19.2–300; by whom made; report; expenses of psychiatrist

The judge shall order the defendant examined by at least one psychiatrist or clinical psychologist who is qualified by specialized training and experience to perform such evaluations. Upon a finding by the court that a psychiatrist or clinical psychologist is not reasonably available for the instant case, the court may appoint a state licensed clinical social worker who has been certified by the Commonwealth as a sex offender treatment provider as defined in § 54.1–3600 and qualified by experience and by specialized training approved by the Commissioner of Behavioral Health and Developmental Services to perform such evaluations. The examination shall be performed on an outpatient basis at a mental health facility or in jail. However, if the court specifically finds that outpatient examination services are unavailable or if the results of outpatient examination indicate that hospitalization of the defendant for further examination is necessary, the court may order the defendant sent to a hospital designated by the Commissioner of Behavioral Health and Developmental Services as appropriate for examination of persons convicted of crimes. The defendant shall then be hospitalized for such time as the director of the hospital deems necessary to perform an adequate examination, but not to exceed 30 days from the date of admission to the hospital. Upon completion of the examination, the examiners shall prepare a written report of their findings and conclusions and shall furnish copies of such report to the defendant, counsel for the defendant, and the attorney for the Commonwealth at least five days prior to sentencing and shall furnish a copy of the report to the judge in advance of the sentencing hearing. The report of the examiners shall at all times be kept confidential by each recipient, except to the extent necessary for the prosecution or defense of any offense, and shall be filed as part of the record in the case and the defendant's copy shall be returned to the court at the conclusion of sentencing. Any report so filed shall be sealed upon the entry of the sentencing order by the court and made available only by court order, except that such report or copies thereof shall be available at any time to the office of the Attorney General for assessment for civil commitment as provided in Chapter 9 (§ 37.2–900 et seq.) of Title 37.2; any criminal justice agency, as defined in § 9.1–101, of this or any other state or of the United States; to any agency where the accused is referred for treatment by the court or by probation and parole services; and to counsel for any person who has been indicted jointly for the same felony as the person who is the subject of the report. Any such report shall without court order be made available to counsel for the person who is the subject of the report if that person is charged with a felony subsequent to the time of the preparation of the report.

Acts 1975, c. 495; Acts 1990, c. 697; Acts 2002, c. 662; Acts 2003, c. 886; Acts 2007, c. 440. Amended by Acts 2009, c. 813; Acts 2009, c. 840.

§ 19.2–302. Construction and administration of §§ 19.2–300 and 19.2–301

Nothing contained in § 19.2–300 or 19.2–301 shall be construed to conflict with or repeal any statute in regard to the Department of Behavioral Health and Developmental Services, and such sections shall be administered with due regard to the authority of, and in cooperation with, the Commissioner of Behavioral Health and Developmental Services.

Acts 1975, c. 495. Amended by Acts 2009, c. 813; Acts 2009, c. 840.

§ 19.2–303. Suspension or modification of sentence; probation; taking of fingerprints and blood, saliva, or tissue sample as condition of probation

After conviction, whether with or without jury, the court may suspend imposition of sentence or suspend the sentence in whole or part and in addition may place the defendant on probation under such conditions as the court shall determine, including monitoring by a GPS (Global Positioning System) tracking device, or other similar device, or may, as a condition of a suspended sentence, require the defendant to make at least partial restitution to the aggrieved party or parties for damages or loss caused by the offense for which convicted, or to perform community service, or both, under terms and conditions which shall be entered in writing by the court. The defendant may be ordered by the court to pay the cost of the GPS tracking device or other similar device. If, however, the court suspends or modifies any sentence fixed by a jury pursuant to § 19.2–295, the court shall file a statement of the reasons for the suspension or modification in the same manner as the statement required pursuant to subsection B of § 19.2–298.01. The judge, after convicting the defendant of a felony, shall determine whether a copy of the defendant's fingerprints are on file at the Central Criminal Records Exchange. In any case where fingerprints are not on file, the judge shall require that fingerprints be taken as a condition of probation. Such fingerprints shall be submitted to the Central Criminal Records Exchange under the provisions of subsection D of § 19.2–390.

In those courts having electronic access to the Local Inmate Data System (LIDS) within the courtroom, prior to or upon sentencing, the clerk of court shall also determine by reviewing LIDS whether a blood, saliva, or tissue sample has been taken for DNA analysis and submitted to the DNA data bank maintained by the Department of Forensic Science pursuant to Article 1.1 (§ 19.2–310.2 et seq.) of Chapter 18 of this title. In any case in which the clerk has determined that a DNA sample or analysis is not stored in the DNA data bank, or in any case in which electronic access to LIDS is not available in the courtroom, the court shall order that the defendant appear within 30 days before the sheriff or probation officer and allow the sheriff or probation officer to take the required sample. The order shall also require that, if the defendant has not appeared and allowed the sheriff or probation officer to take the required sample by the date stated in the order, then the sheriff or probation officer shall report to the court the defendant's failure to appear and provide the required sample.

After conviction and upon sentencing of an active participant or member of a criminal street gang, the court may, as a condition for suspending the imposition of the sentence in whole or in part or for placing the accused on probation, place reasonable restrictions on those persons with whom the accused may have contact. Such restrictions may include prohibiting the accused from having contact with anyone whom he knows to be a member of a criminal street gang, except that contact with a family or household member, as defined in § 16.1–228, shall be permitted unless expressly prohibited by the court.

In any case where a defendant is convicted of a violation of § 18.2–48, 18.2–61, 18.2–63, 18.2–67.1, 18.2–67.2, 18.2–67.3, 18.2–370, or 18.2–370.1, committed on or after July 1, 2006, and some portion of the sentence is suspended, the judge shall order that the period of suspension shall be for a length of time at least equal to the statutory maximum period for which the defendant might originally have been sentenced to be imprisoned, and the defendant shall be placed on probation for that period of suspension subject to revocation by the court. The conditions of probation may include such conditions as the court shall determine, including active supervision. Where the conviction is for a violation of clause (iii) of subsection A of § 18.2–61, subdivision A 1 of § 18.2–67.1, or subdivision A 1 of § 18.2–67.2, the court shall order that at least three years of the probation include active supervision of the defendant under a postrelease supervision program operated by the Department of Corrections, and for at least three years of such active supervision, the defendant shall be subject to electronic monitoring by means of a GPS (Global Positioning System) tracking device, or other similar device.

If a person is sentenced to jail upon conviction of a misdemeanor or a felony, the court may, at any time before the sentence has been completely served, suspend the unserved portion of any such sentence, place the person on probation for such time as the court shall determine, or otherwise modify the sentence imposed.

If a person has been sentenced for a felony to the Department of Corrections but has not actually been

transferred to a receiving unit of the Department, the court which heard the case, if it appears compatible with the public interest and there are circumstances in mitigation of the offense, may, at any time before the person is transferred to the Department, suspend or otherwise modify the unserved portion of such a sentence. The court may place the person on probation for such time as the court shall determine.
Acts 1975, c. 495; Acts 1982, c. 458; Acts 1982, c. 636; Acts 1983, c. 431; Acts 1984, c. 32; Acts 1992, c. 391; Acts 1993, c. 448; Acts 2006, c. 436; Acts 2006, c. 483; Acts 2006, c. 853; Acts 2006, c. 914; Acts 2007, c. 259; Acts 2007, c. 528. Amended by Acts 2011, c. 799; Acts 2011, c. 837.

§ 19.2–303.1. Fixing period of suspension of sentence

In any case where a court suspends the imposition or execution of a sentence, it may fix the period of suspension for a reasonable time, having due regard to the gravity of the offense, without regard to the maximum period for which the defendant might have been sentenced.
Acts 1982, c. 636.

§ 19.2–303.2. Persons charged with first offense may be placed on probation

Whenever any person who has not previously been convicted of any felony pleads guilty to or enters a plea of not guilty to any crime against property constituting a misdemeanor, under Articles 5, 6, 7 and 8 of Chapter 5 (§ 18.2–119 et seq.) of Title 18.2, the court, upon such plea if the facts found by the court would justify a finding of guilt, without entering a judgment of guilt and with the consent of the accused, may defer further proceedings and place him on probation subject to terms and conditions, which may include restitution for losses caused, set by the court. Upon violation of a term or condition, the court may enter an adjudication of guilt and proceed as otherwise provided. Upon fulfillment of the terms and conditions, the court shall discharge the person and dismiss the proceedings against him. Discharge and dismissal under this section shall be without adjudication of guilt and is a conviction only for the purpose of applying this section in subsequent proceedings.
Acts 1985, c. 617.

§ 19.2–303.3. Sentence to local community-based probation services; services agency; requirements for participation; sentencing; and removal from probation; payment of costs towards supervision and services

A. Any offender who is (i) convicted on or after July 1, 1995, of a misdemeanor or a felony that is not a felony act of violence as defined in § 19.2–297.1, and for which the court imposes a total sentence of 12 months or less, and (ii) no younger than 18 years of age or is considered an adult at the time of conviction may be sentenced to a local community-based probation services agency established pursuant to § 9.1–174 by the local governing bodies within that judicial district or circuit.

B. In those courts having electronic access to the Local Inmate Data System (LIDS) within the courtroom, at the time of sentencing, the clerk of court shall determine by reviewing LIDS, in any case where there is a felony conviction, whether a sample of the offender's blood, saliva, or tissue or an analysis of the sample is stored in the DNA data bank maintained by the Department of Forensic Science pursuant to Article 1.1 (§ 19.2–310.2 et seq.) of Chapter 18 of this title. If the clerk has determined that a DNA sample or analysis is not stored in the DNA data bank, or in any case in which electronic access to LIDS is not available in the courtroom, the court shall order that the offender appear within 30 days before the sheriff or community-based probation officer and allow the sheriff or community-based probation officer to take the required sample. The order shall also require that, if the offender has not appeared and allowed the sheriff or community-based probation officer to take the required sample by the date stated in the order, then the sheriff or community-based probation officer shall report to the court the offender's failure to appear and provide the required sample. The court may order the offender placed under local community-based probation services pursuant to § 9.1–174 upon a determination by the court that the offender may benefit from these services and is capable of returning to society as a productive citizen with a reasonable amount of supervision and intervention including services set forth in § 9.1–176. All or part of any sentence imposed that has been suspended, shall be conditioned upon the offender's successful completion of local community-based probation services established pursuant to § 9.1–174.

The court may impose terms and conditions of supervision as it deems appropriate, including that the offender abide by any additional requirements of supervision imposed or established by the local community-based probation services agency during the period of probation supervision.

C. Any sworn officer of a local community-based probation services agency established or operated pursuant to the Comprehensive Community Corrections Act for Local–Responsible Offenders (§ 9.1–173 et seq.) may seek a capias from any judicial officer for the arrest of any person on local community-based probation and under its supervision for (i) intractable behavior; (ii) refusal to comply with the terms and conditions imposed by the court; (iii) refusal to comply with the requirements of local community-based probation supervision established by the agency; or (iv) the commission of a new offense while on local community-based probation and under agency supervision. Upon arrest, the offender shall be brought for a hearing before the court of appropriate jurisdiction. After finding that the offender (a) exhibited intractable behavior as defined herein; (b) refused to comply with terms and conditions imposed by the court; (c) refused to comply with the requirements of local community-based probation supervision established by the agency; or (d) committed a new offense while on local community-based probation and under agency supervision, the court may revoke all or part of the suspended sentence and supervision, and commit the offender to serve whatever sentence was originally imposed or impose such other terms and conditions of probation as it deems appropriate or, in a case where the proceeding has been deferred, enter an adjudication of guilt and proceed as otherwise provided by law.

"Intractable behavior" is that behavior that, in the determination of the court, indicates an offender's unwillingness or inability to conform his behavior to that which is necessary for successful completion of local community-based probation or that the offender's behavior is so disruptive as to threaten the successful completion of the program by other participants.

D. An offender sentenced to or provided a deferred proceeding and placed on community-based probation pursuant to this section may be required to pay an amount towards the costs of his supervision and services received in accordance with subsection D of § 9.1–182.

Acts 1994, Sp. S. II, c. 1, eff. July 1, 1995; Acts 1995, Sp. S. II, c. 2, eff. July 1, 1995; Acts 1995, c. 502; Acts 1995, c. 574; Acts 1999, c. 372; Acts 2000, c. 1040; Acts 2006, c. 883; Acts 2007, c. 133; Acts 2007, c. 528.

§ 19.2–303.4. Payment of costs when proceedings deferred and defendant placed on probation

A circuit or district court, which has deferred further proceedings, without entering a judgment of guilt, and placed a defendant on probation subject to terms and conditions pursuant to § 4.1–305, 16.1–278.8, 16.1–278.9, 18.2–57.3, 18.2–61, 18.2–67.1, 18.2–67.2, 18.2–251 or 19.2–303.2, shall impose upon the defendant costs.

Acts 1995, c. 485; Acts 2000, c. 186; Acts 2002, c. 831, eff. July 1, 2003; Acts 2005, c. 631.

§ 19.2–303.5. Immediate sanction probation programs

There may be established in the Commonwealth up to four immediate sanction probation programs in accordance with the following provisions:

1. As a condition of a sentence suspended pursuant to § 19.2–303, a court may order a defendant convicted of a crime, other than a violent crime as defined in subsection C of § 17.1–805, to participate in an immediate sanction probation program.

2. If a participating offender fails to comply with any term or condition of his probation and the alleged probation violation is not that the offender committed a new crime or infraction, (i) his probation officer shall immediately issue a noncompliance letter pursuant to § 53.1–149 authorizing his arrest at any location in the Commonwealth and (ii) his probation violation hearing shall take priority on the court's docket. The probation officer may, in any event, exercise any other lawful authority he may have with respect to the offender.

3. When a participating offender is arrested pursuant to subdivision 2, the court shall conduct an immediate sanction hearing unless (i) the alleged probation violation is that the offender committed a new crime or infraction; (ii) the alleged probation violation is that the offender absconded for more than seven days; or (iii) the offender, attorney for the Commonwealth, or the court objects to such immediate sanction hearing. If the court conducts an immediate sanction hearing, it shall proceed pursuant to subdivision 4. Otherwise, the court shall proceed pursuant to § 19.2–306.

4. At the immediate sanction hearing, the court shall receive the noncompliance letter, which shall be admissible as evidence, and may receive other evidence. If the court finds good cause to believe that the offender has violated the terms or conditions of his probation, it may (i) revoke no more than 30 days of the previously suspended sentence and (ii) continue or modify any existing terms and conditions of probation. If the court does not modify the terms and conditions of probation or remove the defendant from the program, the previously ordered terms and conditions of probation shall continue to apply. The court may remove the offender from the immediate sanction probation program at any time.

5. The provisions of this section shall expire on July 1, 2016.

Added by Acts 2010, c. 845. Amended by Acts 2014, c. 314.

§ 19.2–304. Increasing or decreasing probation period and modification of conditions

The court may subsequently increase or decrease the probation period and may revoke or modify any condition of probation, but only upon a hearing after reasonable notice to both the defendant and the attorney for the Commonwealth.

Acts 1975, c. 495.

§ 19.2–305. Requiring fines, costs, restitution for damages, support or community services from probationer

A. While on probation the defendant may be required to pay in one or several sums a fine or costs, or both such fine and costs, imposed at the time of being placed on probation as a condition of such probation, and the failure of the defendant to pay such fine or costs, or both such fine and costs, at the prescribed time or times may be deemed a breach of such probation. The provisions of this subsection shall also apply to any person ordered to pay costs pursuant to § 19.2–303.3.

B. A defendant placed on probation following conviction may be required to make at least partial restitution or reparation to the aggrieved party or parties for damages or loss caused by the offense for which conviction was had, or may be required to provide for the support of his wife or others for whose support he may be legally responsible, or may be required to perform community services. The defendant may submit a proposal to the court for making restitution, for providing for support or for performing community services.

C. No defendant shall be kept under supervised probation solely because of his failure to make full payment of fines, fees, or costs, provided that, following notice by the probation and parole officer to each court and attorney for the Commonwealth in whose jurisdiction any fines, fees, or costs are owed by the defendant, no such court or attorney for the Commonwealth objects to his removal from supervised probation.
Acts 1975, c. 495; Acts 1977, c. 682; Acts 1978, c. 716; Acts 1984, c. 32; Acts 1995, c. 485. Amended by Acts 2009, c. 240.

§ 19.2–305.1. Restitution for property damage or loss; community service

A. Notwithstanding any other provision of law, no person convicted of a crime in violation of any provision in Title 18.2, which resulted in property damage or loss, shall be placed on probation or have his sentence suspended unless such person shall make at least partial restitution for such property damage or loss, or shall be compelled to perform community services, or both, or shall submit a plan for doing that which appears to the court to be feasible under the circumstances.

B. Notwithstanding any other provision of law, any person who, on or after July 1, 1995, commits, and is convicted of, a crime in violation of any provision in Title 18.2 shall make at least partial restitution for any property damage or loss caused by the crime or for any medical expenses or expenses directly related to funeral or burial incurred by the victim or his estate as a result of the crime, may be compelled to perform community services and, if the court so orders, shall submit a plan for doing that which appears to be feasible to the court under the circumstances.

B1. Notwithstanding any other provision of law, any person, who on or after July 1, 2005 commits and is convicted of a crime in violation of § 18.2–248 involving the manufacture of any controlled substance, may be ordered, upon presentation of suitable evidence of such costs, by the court to reimburse the Commonwealth or the locality for the costs incurred by the jurisdiction, as the case may be, for the removal and remediation associated with the illegal manufacture of any controlled substance by the defendant.

B2. Notwithstanding any other provision of law, any person who, on or after July 1, 2015, commits and is convicted of a violation of § 18.2–138 for damage to the Capitol or any building, monument, statuary, artwork, or other state property in Capitol Square, or at any other property assigned to the Capitol Police, shall be ordered to pay restitution to the Commonwealth for the full amount of damages. Any person who, on or after July 1, 2015, commits and is convicted of a violation of § 18.2–405, 18.2–407, or 18.2–408 in Capitol Square, or at any other property assigned to the Capitol Police, shall be ordered to pay restitution to the Commonwealth for the full amount of damages to the Capitol or any building, monument, statuary, artwork, or other state property in Capitol Square, or at any other property assigned to the Capitol Police, to which damage is caused during such riot or unlawful assembly. In any prosecution under § 18.2–138, 18.2–405, 18.2–407, or 18.2–408, testimony of the Division of Engineering and Buildings of the Department of General Services or the Division of Risk Management shall be admissible as evidence of value or extent of damages or cost of repairs to the Capitol or any building, monument, statuary, artwork, or other state property in Capitol Square, or at any other property assigned to the Capitol Police. For the purposes of this subsection, "Capitol Square" means the grounds and the interior and exterior of all buildings in that area in the City of Richmond bounded by Bank, Governor, Broad, and Ninth Streets. "Capitol Square" includes the exterior of all state buildings that are at least 50 years old and bordering the boundary streets.

C. At or before the time of sentencing, the court shall receive and consider any plan for making restitution submitted by the defendant. The plan shall include the defendant's home address, place of employment and address, social security number and bank information. If the court finds such plan to be reasonable and practical under the circumstances, it may consider probation or suspension of whatever portion of the sentence that it deems appropriate. By order of the court incorporating the defendant's plan or a reasonable and practical plan devised by the court, the defendant shall make restitution while he is free on probation or work release or following his release from confinement. Additionally, the court may order that the defendant make restitution during his confinement, if feasible, based upon both his earning capacity and net worth as determined by the court at sentencing.

D. At the time of sentencing, the court shall determine the amount to be repaid by the defendant and the terms and conditions thereof. If community service work is ordered, the court shall determine the terms and conditions upon which such work shall be performed. The court shall include such findings in the judgment order. The order shall specify that sums paid under such order shall be paid to the clerk, who shall disburse such sums as the court may, by order, direct. Any court desiring to participate in the Setoff Debt Collection Act (§§ 58.1–520 through 58.1–535) for the purpose of collecting fines or costs or providing restitution shall, at the time of sentencing, obtain the social security number of each defendant.

E. Unreasonable failure to execute the plan by the defendant shall result in revocation of the probation or imposition of the suspended sentence. A hearing shall be held in accordance with the provisions of this Code relating to revocation of probation or imposition of a suspended sentence before either such action is taken.

E1. A defendant convicted of an offense under § 18.2–374.1, 18.2–374.1:1, or 18.2–374.3 shall be ordered to pay mandatory restitution to the victim of the offense in an amount as determined by the court. For purposes of this subsection, "victim" means a person who is depicted in a still or videographic image involved in an offense under § 18.2–374.1, 18.2–374.1:1, or 18.2–374.3.

The Commonwealth shall make reasonable efforts to notify victims of offenses under § 18.2–374.1, 18.2–374.1:1, or 18.2–374.3.

F. If restitution is ordered to be paid by the defendant to the victim of a crime and the victim can no longer be located or identified, the clerk shall deposit any such restitution collected to the Criminal Injuries Compensation Fund for the benefit of crime victims. The administrator shall reserve a sum sufficient in the Fund from which he shall make prompt payment to the victim for any proper claims. Before making the deposit he shall record the name, last known address and amount of restitution due each victim appearing from the clerk's report to be entitled to restitution.

G. If restitution pursuant to § 19.2–305 or this section is ordered to be paid by the defendant to the victim of a crime or other entity, and the Criminal Injuries Compensation Fund has made any payments to or on behalf of the victim for any loss, damage, or expenses included in the restitution order, then upon presentation by the Fund of a written request that sets forth the amount of payments made by the Fund to the victim or on the victim's behalf, the entity collecting restitution shall pay to the Fund as much of the restitution collected as will reimburse the Fund for its payments made to the victim or on the victim's behalf.
Acts 1977, c. 682; Acts 1978, c. 131; Acts 1981, c. 224; Acts 1984, c. 32; Acts 1984, c. 269; Acts 1994, c. 197; Acts 1995, c. 434; Acts 1995, c. 687; Acts 2000, c. 775; Acts 2002, c. 810; Acts 2002, c. 818; Acts 2003, c. 982; Acts 2005, c. 591. Amended by Acts 2011, c. 575; Acts 2011, c. 588; Acts 2013, c. 273; Acts 2015, c. 312; Acts 2015, c. 550.

§ 19.2–305.2. Amount of restitution; enforcement

A. The court, when ordering restitution pursuant to § 19.2–305.1, may require that such defendant, in the case of an offense resulting in damage to or loss or destruction of property of a victim of the offense (i) return the property to the owner or (ii) if return of the property is impractical or impossible, pay an amount equal to the greater of the value of the property at the time of the offense or the value of the property at the time of sentencing.

B. An order of restitution may be docketed as provided in § 8.01–446 when so ordered by the court or upon written request of the victim and may be enforced by a victim named in the order to receive the restitution in the same manner as a judgment in a civil action.
Acts 1988, c. 679; Acts 1989, c. 386.

§ 19.2–305.3. Repealed by Acts 1997, c. 140

§ 19.2–305.4. When interest to be paid on award of restitution

The court, when ordering restitution pursuant to § 19.2–305 or 19.2–305.1, may provide in the order for interest on the restitution. If the court orders the payment of interest, it shall accrue from the date of the loss or damage unless the court specifies a different date in the order, at the rate specified in § 6.2–302.
Acts 1996, c. 544; Acts 2001, c. 122; Acts 2005, c. 14; Acts 2005, c. 79.

§ 19.2–306. Revocation of suspension of sentence and probation

A. In any case in which the court has suspended the execution or imposition of sentence, the court may revoke the suspension of sentence for any cause the court deems sufficient that occurred at any time within the probation period, or within the period of suspension fixed by the court. If neither a probation period nor a period of suspension was fixed by the court, then the court may revoke the suspension for any cause the court deems sufficient that occurred within the maximum period for which the defendant might originally have been sentenced to be imprisoned.

B. The court may not conduct a hearing to revoke the suspension of sentence unless the court, within one year after the expiration of the period of probation or the period of suspension, issues process to notify the accused or to compel his appearance before the court. If neither a probation period nor a period of suspension was fixed by the court, then the court shall issue process within one year after the expiration of the maximum period for which the defendant might originally have been sentenced to be incarcerated. Such notice and service of process may be waived by the defendant, in which case the court may proceed to determine whether the defendant has violated the conditions of suspension.

C. If the court, after hearing, finds good cause to believe that the defendant has violated the terms of suspension, then: (i) if the court originally suspended the imposition of sentence, the court shall revoke the suspension, and the court may pronounce whatever sentence might have been originally imposed or (ii) if the court originally suspended the execution of the sentence, the court shall revoke the suspension and the original sentence shall be in full force and effect. The court may again suspend all or any part of this sentence and may place the defendant upon terms and conditions or probation.

D. If any court has, after hearing, found no cause to impose a sentence that might have been originally imposed, or to revoke a suspended sentence or probation, then any further hearing to impose a sentence or revoke a suspended sentence or probation, based solely on the alleged violation for which the hearing was held, shall be barred.

E. Nothing contained herein shall be construed to deprive any person of his right to appeal in the manner provided by law to the circuit court having criminal jurisdiction from a judgment or order revoking any suspended sentence.

Acts 1975, c. 495; Acts 1978, c. 687; Acts 2002, c. 628.

§ 19.2–307. Contents of judgment order

The judgment order shall set forth the plea, the verdict or findings and the adjudication and sentence, whether or not the case was tried by jury, and if not, whether the consent of the accused was concurred in by the court and the attorney for the Commonwealth. If the accused is found not guilty, or for any other reason is entitled to be discharged, judgment shall be entered accordingly. If an accused is tried at one time for two or more offenses, the court may enter one judgment order respecting all such offenses. The final judgment order shall be entered on a form promulgated by the Supreme Court.

Acts 1975, c. 495; Acts 1996, c. 60, eff. Jan. 1, 1997.

§ 19.2–308. When two or more sentences run concurrently

When any person is convicted of two or more offenses, and sentenced to confinement, such sentences shall not run concurrently, unless expressly ordered by the court.

Acts 1975, c. 495.

§ 19.2–308.1. When sentence may run concurrently with sentence in another jurisdiction

Notwithstanding any other provision of law, in the event that a person is convicted of a criminal offense in any court of this Commonwealth and such person has also been sentenced to imprisonment for a term of one year or more by a court of the United States, or any other state or territory, and, at the time of sentencing in this Commonwealth, is incarcerated in a federal or state penal institution, the court may order the sentence to run concurrently with the sentence imposed by such other court.

Acts 1977, c. 344.

§ 19.2–309. Sentence of confinement for conviction of a combination of felony and misdemeanor offenses

When any person is convicted of a combination of felony and misdemeanor offenses and sentenced to confinement therefor, in determining the sequence of confinement, the felony sentence and commitment shall take precedence and such person shall first be committed to serve the felony sentence.

Acts 1975, c. 495.

§ 19.2–309.1. Sentence of confinement to jail farms maintained by the Cities of Danville, Martinsville and Newport News

§ 19.2–310. Transfer of prisoners to custody of Director of Department of Corrections

Every person sentenced by a court to the Department of Corrections upon conviction of a felony shall be conveyed to an appropriate receiving unit operated by the Department in the manner hereinafter provided. The clerk of the court in which the person is sentenced shall forthwith transmit to the Central Criminal Records Exchange the report of dispositions required by § 19.2–390. The clerk of the court within 30 days from the date of the judgment shall forthwith transmit to the Director of the Department a certified copy or copies of the order of trial and a certified copy of the complete final order, and if he fails to do so shall forfeit $50. The clerk of the court may transmit or make available a copy or copies of such orders electronically. Such copy or copies shall contain, as nearly as ascertainable, the birth date of the person sentenced. The sheriff shall certify to the Director of the Department any jail credits to which the person to be confined is entitled at such time as that person is transferred to the custody of the Director of the Department.

Following receipt of the order of trial and a certified copy of the complete final order, the Director or his designee shall dispatch a correctional officer to the county or city with a warrant directed to the sheriff authorizing him to deliver the prisoner to the correctional officer whose duty it shall be to take charge of the person and convey him to an appropriate receiving unit designated by the Director or his designee. The Director or his designee shall allocate space available in the receiving unit or units by giving first priority to the transportation, as the transportation facilities of the Department may permit, of those persons held in jails who in the opinion of the Director or his designee except as required by § 53.1–20 require immediate transportation to a receiving unit. In making such a determination of priority, the Director shall give due regard to the capacity of local as well as state correctional facilities and, to the extent feasible, shall seek to balance between local and state correctional facilities the excess of prisoners requiring detention.

Acts 1975, c. 495; Acts 1981, c. 529; Acts 1982, c. 476; Acts 1982, c. 636; Acts 1986, c. 606; Acts 1990, c. 676; Acts 1990, c. 768. Amended by Acts 2010, c. 352; Acts 2011, c. 470.

§ 19.2–310.01. Transmission of sentencing documents

Within thirty days of the receipt of a request from the Department of Corrections for certified copies of sentencing documents for any misdemeanor conviction, the clerk of the court receiving such request shall transmit the requested documents to the Director of the Department. In accordance with the provisions of § 17.1–267, the requested documents shall be provided to the Director without the payment of any fee. Acts 1992, c. 498.

§ 19.2–310.1. Repealed by Acts 1982, c. 636

ARTICLE 1.1

DNA ANALYSIS AND DATA BANK

§ 19.2–310.2. Blood, saliva, or tissue sample required for DNA analysis upon conviction of certain crimes; fee

A. Every person convicted of a felony on or after July 1, 1990, every person convicted of a felony offense under Article 7 (§ 18.2–61 et seq.) of Chapter 4 of Title 18.2 who was incarcerated on July 1, 1989, and every person convicted of a misdemeanor violation of § 16.1–253.2, 18.2–60.3, 18.2–60.4, 18.2–67.4, 18.2–67.4:1, 18.2–67.4:2, 18.2–67.5, 18.2–102, 18.2–121, 18.2–130, 18.2–370.6, 18.2–387, 18.2–387.1, or 18.2–479.1 shall have a sample of his blood, saliva or tissue taken for DNA (deoxyribonucleic acid) analysis to determine identification characteristics specific to the person. If a sample has been previously taken from the person as indicated by the Local Inmate Data System (LIDS), no additional sample shall be taken. The Department of Forensic Science shall provide to LIDS the most current information submitted to the DNA data bank on a weekly basis and shall remove from LIDS and the data bank persons no longer eligible to be in the data bank. A fee of $53 shall be charged for the withdrawal of this sample. The fee shall be taxed as part of the costs of the criminal case resulting in the conviction and $15 of the fee shall be paid into the general fund of the locality where the sample was taken and $38 of the fee shall be paid into the general fund of the state treasury. This fee shall only be taxed one time regardless of the number of samples taken. The assessment provided for herein shall be in addition to any other fees prescribed by law. The analysis shall be performed by the Department of Forensic Science or other entity designated by the Department. The identification characteristics of the profile resulting from the DNA analysis shall be stored and maintained by the Department in a DNA data bank and shall be made available only as provided in § 19.2–310.5.

B. After July 1, 1990, the blood, saliva, or tissue sample shall be taken prior to release from custody. Notwithstanding the provisions of § 53.1–159, any person convicted of an offense listed in subsection A who is in custody after July 1, 1990, shall provide a blood, saliva, or tissue sample prior to his release. Every person so convicted after July 1, 1990, who is not sentenced to a term of confinement shall provide a blood, saliva, or tissue sample as a condition of such sentence. A person required under this section to submit a sample for DNA analysis is not relieved from this requirement regardless of whether no blood, saliva, or tissue sample has been taken from the person or, if a sample has been taken, whether the sample or the results from the analysis of a sample cannot be found in the DNA data bank maintained by the Department of Forensic Science.

C. Nothing in this section shall prevent the Department of Forensic Science from including the identification characteristics of an individual's DNA profile in the DNA data bank as ordered by a circuit court pursuant to a lawful plea agreement.

D. A collection or placement of a sample for DNA analysis that was taken or retained in good faith does not invalidate the sample's use in the data bank pursuant to the provisions of this article. The detention, arrest, or conviction of a person based upon a data bank match or data bank information is not invalidated if it is determined that the sample was obtained, placed, or retained in the data bank in good faith, or if the conviction or juvenile adjudication that resulted in the collection of the DNA sample was subsequently vacated or otherwise altered in any future proceeding, including but not limited to post-trial or post-fact-finding motions, appeals, or collateral attacks.

E. The Virginia Department of Corrections and the Department of Forensic Science shall, on a quarterly basis, compare databases of offenders under the custody or supervision of the Department of Corrections with the DNA data bank of the Department of Forensic Science. The Virginia Department of Corrections shall require a DNA sample of those offenders under its custody or supervision if they are not identified in the DNA data bank.

F. The Department of State Police shall verify that a DNA sample required to be taken for the Sex Offender and Crimes Against Minors Registry pursuant to § 9.1–903 has been received by the Department of Forensic Science. In any instance where a DNA sample has not been received, the Department of State Police or its designee shall obtain from the person required to register a sample for DNA analysis.

G. Each community-based probation services agency established pursuant to § 9.1–174 shall determine by reviewing the Local Inmate Data System upon intake and again prior to discharge whether a blood, saliva, or tissue sample has been taken for DNA analysis for each offender required to submit a sample pursuant to this section and, if no sample has been taken, require an offender to submit a sample for DNA analysis.

H. The sheriff or regional jailer shall determine by reviewing the Local Inmate Data System upon intake and again prior to release whether a blood, saliva, or tissue sample has been taken for DNA analysis for each offender required to submit a sample pursuant to this section and, if no sample has been taken, require an offender to submit a sample for DNA analysis.

Acts 1990, c. 669; Acts 1993, c. 33; Acts 1996, c. 154; Acts 1996, c. 952; Acts 1998, c. 280; Acts 2002, c. 54; Acts 2002, c. 753, eff. Jan. 1, 2003; Acts 2002, c. 773, eff. Jan. 1, 2003; Acts 2005, c. 868; Acts 2005, c. 881; Acts 2007, c. 528. Amended by Acts 2011, c. 247; Acts 2015, c. 193; Acts 2015, c. 209; Acts 2015, c. 437.

§ 19.2–310.2:1. Saliva or tissue sample required for DNA analysis after arrest for a violent felony

Every person arrested for the commission or attempted commission of a violent felony as defined in § 19.2–297.1 or a violation or attempt to commit a violation of § 18.2–31, 18.2–89, 18.2–90, 18.2–91, or 18.2–92, shall have a sample of his saliva or tissue taken for DNA (deoxyribonucleic acid) analysis to determine identification characteristics specific to the person. After a determination by a magistrate or a grand jury that probable cause exists for the arrest, a sample shall be taken prior to the person's release from custody. The analysis shall be performed by the Department of Forensic Science or other entity designated by the Department. The identification characteristics of the profile resulting from the DNA analysis shall be stored and maintained by the Department in a DNA data bank and shall be made available as provided in § 19.2–310.5.

The clerk of the court shall notify the Department of final disposition of the criminal proceedings. If the charge for which the sample was taken is dismissed or the defendant is acquitted at trial, the Department shall destroy the sample and all records thereof, provided there is no other pending qualifying warrant or capias for an arrest or felony conviction that would otherwise require that the sample remain in the data bank.

Acts 2002, c. 753, eff. Jan. 1, 2003; Acts 2002, c. 773, eff. Jan. 1, 2003; Acts 2003, c. 150; Acts 2004, c. 445; Acts 2005, c. 868; Acts 2005, c. 881; Acts 2006, c. 182.

§ 19.2–310.3. Procedures for withdrawal of blood, saliva or tissue sample for DNA analysis

Each sample required pursuant to § 19.2–310.2 from persons who are to be incarcerated shall be withdrawn at the receiving unit or at such other place as is designated by the Department of Corrections or, in the case of a juvenile, the Department of Juvenile Justice. The required samples from persons who are not sentenced to a term of confinement shall be withdrawn at a time and place specified by the sentencing court. Only a correctional health nurse technician or a physician, registered nurse, licensed practical nurse, graduate laboratory technician, or phlebotomist shall withdraw any blood sample to be submitted for analysis. No civil liability shall attach to any person authorized to withdraw blood, saliva or tissue as provided herein as a result of the act of withdrawing blood, saliva or tissue from any person submitting thereto, provided the blood, saliva or tissue was withdrawn according to recognized medical procedures. However, no person shall be relieved from liability for negligence in the withdrawing of any blood, saliva or tissue sample.

Chemically clean sterile disposable needles and vacuum draw tubes or swabs shall be used for all samples. The tube or envelope containing the sample shall be sealed and labeled with the subject's name, social security number, date of birth, race and gender; the name of the person collecting the sample; and the date and place of collection. The tubes or envelopes containing the samples shall be secured to prevent tampering with the contents. The steps herein set forth relating to the taking, handling, identification, and disposition of blood, saliva or tissue samples are procedural and not substantive. Substantial compliance therewith shall be deemed to be sufficient. The samples shall be transported to the Department of Forensic Science not more than 15 days following withdrawal and shall be analyzed and stored in the DNA data bank in accordance with §§ 19.2–310.4 and 19.2–310.5.

Acts 1990, c. 669; Acts 1997, c. 862; Acts 1998, c. 280; Acts 2003, c. 150; Acts 2004, c. 440; Acts 2005, c. 868; Acts 2005, c. 881.

§ 19.2–310.3:1. Procedures for taking saliva or tissue sample for DNA analysis

A. Each sample required pursuant to § 19.2–310.2:1 from persons arrested shall be taken before release from custody at such place as is designated by the law-enforcement agency responsible for arrest booking in the jurisdiction. Samples shall be taken in accordance with procedures adopted by the Department of Forensic Science. The sample shall be sealed and labeled with the subject's name, social security number, date of birth, race and gender; the name of the person collecting the sample; the date and place of collection; information identifying the arresting or accompanying officer; and the offense for which the person was arrested. The sample shall be secured to prevent tampering with the contents and be accompanied by a copy of the arrest warrant or capias. The steps herein set forth relating to the taking, handling, identification, and disposition of saliva or tissue samples are procedural and not substantive. The sample shall be transported to the Department of Forensic Science not more than 15 days following withdrawal and shall be analyzed and stored in the DNA data bank in accordance with §§ 19.2–310.4 and 19.2–310.5.

B. Substantial compliance therewith shall be deemed to be sufficient. If a sample has been previously taken from the individual as indicated by the

Local Inmate Data System (LIDS), no additional sample shall be taken. No civil liability shall attach to any person authorized to take saliva or tissue as provided herein as a result of the act of taking saliva or tissue from any person submitting thereto, provided the saliva or tissue was taken according to recognized medical procedures. However, no person shall be relieved from liability for negligence in the taking of any saliva or tissue sample.

Acts 2002, c. 753, eff. Jan. 1, 2003; Acts 2002, c. 773, eff. Jan. 1, 2003; Acts 2003, c. 150; Acts 2005, c. 868; Acts 2005, c. 881.

§ 19.2–310.4. Procedures for conducting DNA analysis of blood, saliva or tissue sample

Whether or not the results of an analysis are to be included in the data bank, the Department shall conduct the DNA analysis in accordance with procedures adopted by the Department to determine identification characteristics specific to the individual whose sample is being analyzed. The Director or his designated representative shall complete and maintain on file a form indicating the name of the person whose sample is to be analyzed, the date and by whom the blood, saliva or tissue sample was received and examined, and a statement that the seal on the tube or envelope containing the sample had not been broken or otherwise tampered with. The remainder of a blood, saliva or tissue sample submitted for analysis and inclusion in the data bank pursuant to § 19.2–310.2 or 19.2–310.2:1 may be divided, labeled as provided for the original sample, and securely stored by the Department in accordance with specific procedures adopted by regulation of the Department to ensure the integrity and confidentiality of the samples. All or part of the remainder of that sample may be used only (i) to create a statistical data base provided no identifying information on the individual whose sample is being analyzed is included or (ii) for retesting by the Department to validate or update the original analysis.

A report of the results of a DNA analysis conducted by the Department as authorized, including the profile and identifying information, shall be made and maintained at the Department. A certificate and the results of the analysis shall be admissible in any court as evidence of the facts therein stated. Except as specifically provided in this section and § 19.2–310.5, the results of the analysis shall be securely stored and shall remain confidential.

Acts 1990, c. 669; Acts 1998, c. 280; Acts 2002, c. 753, eff. Jan. 1, 2003; Acts 2002, c. 773, eff. Jan. 1, 2003; Acts 2003, c. 150; Acts 2005, c. 868; Acts 2005, c. 881.

§ 19.2–310.5. DNA data bank

A. It shall be the duty of the Department to receive samples of human biological evidence and to analyze, classify, and file the results of DNA identification characteristics profiles of samples of human biological evidence submitted pursuant to § 19.2–310.2 or 19.2–310.2:1 and to make such information available as provided in this section. The results of an analysis and comparison of evidence submitted to the Department pursuant to § 9.1–1101 to the identification characteristics of human biological evidence so analyzed, classified, and filed shall be made available directly to duly authorized members of federal, state, and local law-enforcement agencies or private police departments that have been designated as criminal justice agencies by the Department of Criminal Justice Services as defined by § 9.1–101, attorneys for the Commonwealth or attorneys for the United States Department of Justice, or the Office of the Chief Medical Examiner upon request made in furtherance of an official investigation or prosecution of any criminal offense, or to an accused or his attorney pursuant to § 9.1–1104. The Department shall confirm whether or not there is a DNA profile on file for a specific individual if a federal, state or local law-enforcement officer requests that information in furtherance of an official investigation of any criminal offense. The name of the requestor and the purpose for which the information is requested shall be maintained on file with the Department.

B. The Department shall adopt regulations governing (i) the methods of obtaining information from the data bank in accordance with this section and (ii) procedures for verification of the identity and authority of the requestor. The Department shall specify the positions in that agency which require regular access to the data bank and samples submitted as a necessary function of the job.

C. The Department shall create a separate statistical data base comprised of DNA profiles of samples of human biological evidence of persons whose identity is unknown. Nothing in this section or § 19.2–310.6 shall prohibit the Department from sharing or otherwise disseminating the information in the statistical data base with law-enforcement or criminal justice agencies within or without the Commonwealth.

D. The Department may charge a reasonable fee to search and provide a comparative analysis of DNA profiles in the data bank to any authorized law-enforcement agency outside of the Commonwealth.

Acts 1990, c. 669; Acts 1998, c. 280; Acts 2000, c. 284; Acts 2002, c. 753, eff. Jan. 1, 2003; Acts 2002, c. 773, eff. Jan. 1, 2003; Acts 2005, c. 868; Acts 2005, c. 881. Amended by Acts 2010, c. 502; Acts 2011, c. 66; Acts 2011, c. 171; Acts 2011, c. 638.

§ 19.2–310.6. Unauthorized uses of DNA data bank; forensic samples; penalties

Any person who, without authority, disseminates information contained in the data bank shall be guilty of a Class 3 misdemeanor. Any person who disseminates, receives, or otherwise uses or attempts to so use information in the data bank, knowing that such dissemination, receipt, or use is for a purpose other than as authorized by law, shall be guilty of a Class 1 misdemeanor.

Except as authorized by law, any person who, for purposes of having DNA analysis performed, obtains or attempts to obtain any sample submitted to the Department of Forensic Science for analysis shall be guilty of a Class 5 felony.

Acts 1990, c. 669; Acts 2005, c. 868; Acts 2005, c. 881.

§ 19.2–310.7. Expungement when DNA taken for a conviction

A person whose DNA profile has been included in the data bank pursuant to § 19.2–310.2 may request expungement on the grounds that the conviction on which the authority for including his DNA profile was based has been reversed and the case dismissed. Provided that the person's DNA profile is not otherwise required to be included in the data bank pursuant to § 9.1–903, 16.1–299.1, 19.2–310.2, or 19.2–310.2:1, the Department of Forensic Science shall purge all records and identifiable information in the data bank pertaining to the person and destroy all samples from the person upon receipt of (i) a written request for expungement pursuant to this section and (ii) a certified copy of the court order reversing and dismissing the conviction.

Acts 1990, c. 669; Acts 2002, c. 753, eff. Jan. 1, 2003; Acts 2002, c. 773, eff. Jan. 1, 2003; Acts 2005, c. 868; Acts 2005, c. 881. Amended by Acts 2015, c. 209; Acts 2015, c. 437.

Article 2

Indeterminate Commitment

§ 19.2–311. Indeterminate commitment to Department of Corrections in certain cases; duration and character of commitment; concurrence by Department

A. The judge, after a finding of guilt, when fixing punishment in those cases specifically enumerated in subsection B of this section, may, in his discretion, in lieu of imposing any other penalty provided by law and, with consent of the person convicted, commit such person for a period of four years, which commitment shall be indeterminate in character. In addition, the court shall impose a period of confinement which shall be suspended. Subject to the provisions of subsection C hereof, such persons shall be committed to the Department of Corrections for confinement in a state facility for youthful offenders established pursuant to § 53.1–63. Such confinement shall be followed by at least one and one-half years of supervisory parole, conditioned on good behavior. The sentence of indeterminate commitment and eligibility for continuous evaluation and parole under § 19.2–313 shall remain in effect but eligibility for use of programs and facilities established pursuant to § 53.1–63 shall lapse if such person (i) exhibits intractable behavior as defined in § 53.1–66 or (ii) is convicted of a second criminal offense which is a felony. A sentence imposed for any second criminal offense shall run consecutively with the indeterminate sentence.

B. The provisions of subsection A of this section shall be applicable to first convictions in which the person convicted:

1. Committed the offense of which convicted before becoming twenty-one years of age;

2. Was convicted of a felony offense other than any of the following: capital murder, murder in the first degree or murder in the second degree or a violation of §§ 18.2–61, 18.2–67.1, 18.2–67.2 or subdivision A 1 of § 18.2–67.3; and

3. Is considered by the judge to be capable of returning to society as a productive citizen following a reasonable amount of rehabilitation.

C. Subsequent to a finding of guilt and prior to fixing punishment, the Department of Corrections shall, concurrently with the evaluation required by § 19.2–316, review all aspects of the case to determine whether (i) such defendant is physically and emotionally suitable for the program, (ii) such indeterminate sentence of commitment is in the best interest of the Commonwealth and of the person convicted, and (iii) facilities are available for the confinement of such person. After the review such person shall be again brought before the court, which shall review the findings of the Department. The court may impose a sentence as authorized in subsection A, or any other penalty provided by law.

D. Upon the defendant's failure to complete the program established pursuant to § 53.1–63 or to comply with the terms and conditions through no fault of his own, the defendant shall be brought before the court for hearing. Notwithstanding the provisions for pronouncement of sentence as set forth in § 19.2–306, the court, after hearing, may pronounce whatever sentence was originally imposed, pronounce a reduced sentence, or impose such other terms and conditions of probation as it deems appropriate.

Acts 1975, c. 495; Acts 1976, c. 498; Acts 1980, c. 531; Acts 1988, c. 38; Acts 1990, c. 701; Acts 1994, c. 859; Acts 1994, c. 949; Acts 1996, c. 755; Acts 1996, c. 914; Acts 1997, c. 387; Acts 2000, c. 668; Acts 2000, c. 690.

§ 19.2–312. Repealed by Acts 1990, c. 701

§ 19.2–313. Eligibility for release

Any person committed under the provisions of § 19.2–311 shall be eligible for release at the discretion of the Parole Board upon certification by the Director of the Department of Corrections that the person has successfully completed the program established pursuant to § 53.1–63 and a determination that he has demonstrated that such release is compatible with the interests of society and of such person and his successful rehabilitation to that extent. The Department and Parole Board shall make continuous evaluation of his progress to determine his readiness for release. All such persons, in any event, shall be released after four years' confinement. Any person committed under § 19.2–311 who was convicted of a misdemeanor and is determined to be unsuitable for the program established pursuant to § 53.1–63 shall be released after one year of confinement or the maximum confinement for the misdemeanor whichever is less.

Acts 1975, c. 495; Acts 1975, c. 571; Acts 2000, c. 668; Acts 2000, c. 690.

§ 19.2–314. Supervision of persons released

Every person released under § 19.2–313 shall receive intensive parole supervision for a period of at least one and one-half years and may have parole supervision continued for a longer period, if the Parole Board deems it advisable.

Acts 1975, c. 495; Acts 2000, c. 668; Acts 2000, c. 690.

§ 19.2–315. Compliance with terms and conditions of parole; time on parole not counted as part of commitment period

Every person on parole under § 19.2–314 shall comply with such terms and conditions as may be prescribed by the Board according to § 53.1–157 and shall be subject to the penalties imposed by law for a violation of such terms and conditions. Notwithstanding any other provision of the Code, if parole is revoked as a result of any such violation, such person may be returned to the institution established pursuant to § 53.1–63 upon the direction of the Parole Board with the concurrence of the Department of Corrections, provided such person has not been convicted since his release on parole of an offense constituting a felony under the laws of the Commonwealth. Time on parole shall not be counted as part of the four-year period of commitment under this section. In addition, such person may be brought before the sentencing court for imposition of all or part of the suspended sentence.

Acts 1975, c. 495; Acts 1984, c. 33; Acts 2000, c. 668; Acts 2000, c. 690.

§ 19.2–316. Evaluation and report prior to determining punishment

Following conviction and prior to sentencing, the court shall order such defendant committed to the Department of Corrections for a period not to exceed 60 days from the date of referral for evaluation and diagnosis by the Department to determine the person's potential for rehabilitation through confinement and treatment in the facilities and programs established pursuant to § 53.1–63. The evaluation and diagnosis shall include a complete physical and mental examination of the defendant and may be conducted by the Department of Corrections at any state or local facility, probation and parole office, or other location deemed appropriate by the Department. The Department of Corrections shall conduct the evaluation and diagnosis and shall review all aspects of the case within 60 days from the date of conviction or revocation of ordinary probation and shall recommend that the defendant be committed to the facility established pursuant to § 53.1–63 upon finding that (i) such defendant is physically and emotionally suitable for the program, (ii) such commitment is in the best interest of the Commonwealth and the defendant, and (iii) facilities are available for confinement of the defendant.

If the Director of the Department of Corrections determines such person should be confined in a facility other than one established pursuant to § 53. 1–63, a written report giving the reasons for such decision shall be submitted to the sentencing court. The court shall not be bound by such written report in the matter of determining punishment. Additionally, the person may be committed or transferred to a state hospital operated by the Department of Behavioral Health and Developmental Services or other mental health hospital, as provided by law, during such 60–day period.

Acts 1975, c. 495; Acts 1990, c. 701; Acts 2000, c. 668; Acts 2000, c. 690. Amended by Acts 2012, c. 476; Acts 2012, c. 507.

Article 3

Boot Camp Incarceration Program

§ 19.2–316.1. Eligibility for participation; evaluation; sentencing; withdrawal or removal from program

An individual may be eligible to be sentenced as provided herein if he (i) is convicted on or after January 1, 1991, of a nonviolent felony, or is deemed by the court to be nonviolent in character, (ii) is no older than twenty-four at the time of conviction for the offense, (iii) has never before been incarcerated upon a felony conviction in a correctional facility of any state, the District of Columbia, the United States or its territories, and (iv) has not been confined for more than twelve months nor for more than one term of confinement in a local correctional facility of any such jurisdiction; however, confinement for misdemeanor traffic convictions shall not be considered in determining eligibility.

Following conviction and prior to sentencing, upon motion of the defendant, the court may order such defendant committed to the Department of Corrections for a period not to exceed sixty days from the date of referral or the date of revocation of ordinary probation, as the case may be, for evaluation and diagnosis by the Department to determine suitability for participation in the Boot Camp Incarceration Program established pursuant to § 53.1–67.1. The evaluation and diagnosis shall include a complete physical and mental examination of the defendant and may be conducted by the Department of Corrections at any state or local facility, probation and parole office, or other location deemed appropriate by the Department.

The Department of Corrections shall conduct the evaluation and diagnosis and shall review all aspects of the case within sixty days from the date of conviction or revocation of ordinary probation and shall recommend that the defendant be committed to the Boot Camp Incarceration Program upon finding that (i) such defendant is physically and emotionally suitable for the program, (ii) such commitment is in the best interest of the Commonwealth and the defendant, and (iii) facilities are available for confinement of the defendant.

Upon receipt of such a recommendation and written consent of the defendant to participate in the program, and a determination by the court that the defendant will benefit from the program and is capable of returning to society as a productive citizen following a reasonable amount of intensive supervision and rehabilitation including program components set forth in § 53.1–67.1, and the defendant would otherwise be committed to the Department of Corrections for a period of confinement, the court shall impose such sentence of confinement as authorized by law and suspend the sentence and place the defendant on probation. Such probation shall be conditioned upon the defendant's entry into and successful completion of a Boot Camp Incarceration Program established by the Department of Corrections pursuant to § 53.1–67.1. The court may impose such other terms and conditions of probation as it deems appropriate.

Upon the defendant's (i) voluntary withdrawal from the program, (ii) removal from the program by the Department of Corrections for intractable behavior, or (iii) refusal to comply with the terms and conditions of probation imposed by the court, the defendant shall be brought before the court for hearing. Upon a finding that the defendant voluntarily chooses to withdraw from the program, exhibited intractable behavior as defined herein, or refused to comply with terms and conditions of probation, the court may revoke all or part of the suspended sentence and probation. Upon revocation of the suspension and probation, the provisions of §§ 53.1–191, 53.1–196 and 53.1–198 through 53.1–201 shall apply retroactively to the date of sentencing.

Upon the defendant's failure to complete the program or to comply with the terms and conditions of probation imposed by the court through no fault of his own, the defendant shall be brought before the court for hearing. Notwithstanding the provisions for pronouncement of sentence as set forth in § 19.2–306, the court, after hearing, may pronounce whatever sentence was originally imposed, pronounce a reduced sentence, or impose such other terms and conditions of probation as it deems appropriate.

"Intractable behavior" means that behavior which, in the determination of the Department of Corrections, (i) indicates an inmate's unwillingness or inability to conform his behavior to that necessary to his successful completion of the program or (ii) is so disruptive as to threaten the successful completion of the program by other participants.

"Nonviolent felony" means any felony except those considered an "act of violence" pursuant to § 19.2–297.1 or any attempt to commit any of those crimes.

Acts 1990, c. 474; Acts 1992, c. 861; Acts 1994, c. 926; Acts 1995, c. 117; Acts 1996, c. 809; Acts 1996, c. 938; Acts 2000, c. 769.

ARTICLE 4

DETENTION CENTER INCARCERATION PROGRAM

§ 19.2–316.2. Eligibility for participation in detention center incarceration program; evaluation; sentencing; withdrawal or removal from program

A. A defendant who otherwise would have been sentenced to incarceration for a nonviolent felony as defined in § 19.2–316.1 or who has been previously incarcerated for a nonviolent felony as defined in § 19.2–316.1 but otherwise meets the following criteria and (i) who is determined by the court to need more security or supervision than provided by the diversion center incarceration program under § 53.1–67.7, (ii) whose age or physical condition disqualifies him from the Boot Camp Incarceration Program under § 53.1–67.1, and (iii) who can benefit from a regimented environment and structured program, may be considered for commitment to a detention center established under § 53.1–67.8 as follows:

1. Following conviction and prior to imposition of sentence or following a finding that the defendant's probation should be revoked, upon motion of the defendant or the attorney for the Commonwealth or upon the court's own motion, the court may order such defendant committed to the Department of Corrections for a period not to exceed 60 days from the date of commitment for evaluation and diagnosis by the Department to determine suitability for participation in the Detention Center Incarceration Program. The evaluation and diagnosis shall include a complete physical and mental examination of the defendant and may be conducted by the Department at any state or

local correctional facility, probation and parole office, or other location deemed appropriate by the Department. When a defendant who has not been charged with a new criminal offense and who may be subject to a revocation of probation, scores incarceration on the probation violation guidelines and agrees to participate, the probation and parole officer, with the approval of the court, may commit the defendant to the Department for such evaluation, for a period not to exceed 60 days.

2. Upon determination that (i) such defendant is physically and emotionally suited for the program, (ii) such commitment is in the best interest of the Commonwealth and the defendant, and (iii) facilities are available for the confinement of the defendant, the Department shall recommend to the court in writing that the defendant be committed to the Detention Center Incarceration Program.

3. Upon receipt of such a recommendation and a determination by the court that the defendant will benefit from the program and is capable of returning to society as a productive citizen following successful completion of the program, and if the defendant would otherwise be committed to the Department, the court (i) shall impose sentence, suspend the sentence, and place the defendant on probation or (ii) following a finding that the defendant has violated the terms and conditions of his probation previously ordered, shall place the defendant on probation pursuant to this section. Such probation shall be conditioned upon the defendant's entry into and successful completion of the Detention Center Incarceration Program. The court shall order that, upon successful completion of the program, the defendant shall be released from confinement and be under intensive probation supervision for a period to be specified by the court followed by an additional period of regular probation of not less than one year. The court shall further order that the defendant, following release from confinement, shall (a) make reasonable efforts to secure and maintain employment, (b) comply with a plan of restitution or community service, (c) comply with a plan for payment of fines, if any, and costs of court, and (d) undergo appropriate substance abuse treatment, if necessary. The court may impose such other terms and conditions of probation as it deems appropriate. A sentence to the Detention Center Incarceration Program shall not be imposed as an addition to an active sentence to a state correctional facility.

4. Upon the defendant's (i) voluntary withdrawal from the program, (ii) removal from the program by the Department for intractable behavior as defined in § 19.2–316.1, or (iii) failure to comply with the terms and conditions of probation, the court shall cause the defendant to show cause why his probation and suspension of sentence should not be revoked. Upon a finding that the defendant voluntarily withdrew from the program, was removed from the program by the Department for intractable behavior, or failed to comply with the terms and conditions of probation, the court may revoke all or part of the probation and suspended sentence and commit the defendant as otherwise provided in this chapter.

B. Any offender as described in § 19.2–316.1 paroled under § 53.1–155 or mandatorily released under § 53.1–159 and for whom probable cause that a violation of parole or of the terms and conditions of mandatory release, other than for the occurrence of a new felony or Class 1 or Class 2 misdemeanor, has been determined under § 53.1–165, may be considered by the Parole Board for commitment to a detention center as established under § 53.1–67.8 as follows:

1. The Parole Board or its authorized hearing officer, with the violator's consent, may order the violator to be evaluated and diagnosed by the Department of Corrections to determine suitability for participation in the Detention Center Incarceration Program. The evaluation and diagnosis may be conducted by the Department at any state or local correctional facility, probation or parole office, or other location deemed appropriate by the Department.

2. Upon determination that (i) such commitment is in the best interest of the Commonwealth and the violator and (ii) facilities are available for the confinement of the violator, or upon receipt of a defendant's voluntary participation form from the probation and parole officer and a determination that (i) and (ii) have been met, the Department shall recommend to the Parole Board in writing that the violator be committed to the Detention Center Incarceration Program. The Department shall have the final authority to determine an individual's suitability for the program.

3. Upon receipt of such a recommendation and a determination by the Parole Board that the violator will benefit from the program and is capable of returning to society as a productive citizen following successful completion of the program, the violator shall be placed under parole supervision for a period of not less than one year. The Parole Board may impose such other terms and conditions of parole or mandatory release as it deems appropriate.

4. Upon the violator's (i) voluntary withdrawal from the program, (ii) removal from the program for intractable behavior as defined in § 19.2–316.1, or (iii) failure to comply with the terms and conditions of parole or mandatory release, the Department shall conduct a preliminary parole violation hearing to determine if probable cause exists to revoke his parole or mandatory release. Upon a finding that the violator voluntarily withdrew from the program, was removed from the program by the Department for intractable behavior, or failed to comply with the terms and conditions of parole or mandatory release, the Parole Board shall revoke parole or mandatory release and recommit the violator as provided in § 53.1–165.

Acts 1994, Sp. S. II, c. 1, eff. July 1, 1995; Acts 1994, Sp. S. II, c. 2, eff. July 1, 1995; Acts 1995, c. 502; Acts 1995, c. 574; Acts 2000, c. 338; Acts 2002, c. 604; Acts 2005, c. 512; Acts 2005, c. 580. Amended by Acts 2008, c. 362; Acts 2008, c. 761.

ARTICLE 5

DIVERSION CENTER INCARCERATION PROGRAM

§ 19.2–316.3. Eligibility for participation in diversion center incarceration program; evaluation; sentencing; withdrawal or removal from program; payment for costs

A. A defendant (i) who otherwise would have been sentenced to incarceration for a nonviolent felony as defined in § 19.2–316.1 and who the court determines requires more security or supervision than provided by intensive probation supervision or (ii) whose suspension of sentence would otherwise be revoked after a finding that the defendant has violated the terms and conditions of probation for a nonviolent felony as defined in § 19.2–316.1, may be considered for commitment to a diversion center established under § 53.1–67.7 as follows:

1. Following conviction and prior to imposition of sentence or following a finding that the defendant's probation should be revoked, upon motion of the defendant or the attorney for the Commonwealth or upon the court's own motion, the court may order such defendant committed to the Department of Corrections for a period not to exceed 45 days from the date of commitment for evaluation and diagnosis by the Department to determine suitability for participation in the Diversion Center Incarceration Program. The evaluation and diagnosis may be conducted by the Department at any state or local correctional facility, probation and parole office, or other location deemed appropriate by the Department. When a defendant who has not been charged with a new criminal offense and who may be subject to a revocation of probation, scores incarceration on the probation violation guidelines and agrees to participate, the probation and parole officer, with the approval of the court, may commit the defendant to the Department for such evaluation, for a period not to exceed 45 days.

2. Upon determination that (i) such commitment is in the best interest of the Commonwealth and the defendant and (ii) facilities are available for the confinement of the defendant, the Department shall recommend to the court in writing that the defendant be committed to the Diversion Center Incarceration Program.

3. Upon receipt of such a recommendation and a determination by the court that the defendant will benefit from the program and is capable of returning to society as a productive citizen following successful completion of the program, and if the defendant would otherwise be committed to the Department, the court (i) shall impose sentence, suspend the sentence, and place the defendant on probation pursuant to this section or (ii) following a finding that the defendant has violated the terms and conditions of his probation previously ordered, shall place the defendant on probation pursuant to this section. Such probation shall be conditioned upon the defendant's entry into and successful completion of the Diversion Center Incarceration Program. The court shall order that, upon successful completion of the program, the defendant shall be released from confinement and be under intensive probation supervision for a period to be specified by the court followed by an additional period of regular probation of not less than one year. The court shall further order that the defendant, prior to release from confinement, shall (a) make reasonable efforts to secure and maintain employment, (b) comply with a plan of restitution or community service, (c) comply with a plan for payment of fines, if any, and costs of court, and (d) undergo substance abuse treatment, if necessary. The court may impose such other terms and conditions of probation as it deems appropriate. A sentence to the Diversion Center Incarceration Program shall not be imposed in addition to an active sentence to a state correctional facility.

4. Upon the defendant's (i) voluntary withdrawal from the program, (ii) removal from the program by the Department for intractable behavior as defined in § 19.2–316.1, or (iii) failure to comply with the terms and conditions of probation, the court shall cause the defendant to show cause why his probation and suspension of sentence should not be revoked. Upon a finding that the defendant voluntarily withdrew from the program, was removed from the program by the Department for intractable behavior, or failed to comply with the terms and conditions of probation, the court may revoke all or part of the probation and suspended sentence, and commit the defendant as otherwise provided in this chapter.

B. Any offender as described in § 19.2–316.1 paroled under § 53.1–155 or mandatorily released under § 53.1–159 and for whom probable cause that a violation of parole or of the terms and conditions of mandatory release, other than the occurrence of a new felony or Class 1 or Class 2 misdemeanor, has been determined under § 53.1–165, may be considered by the Parole Board for commitment to a diversion center as established under § 53.1–67.7 as follows:

1. The Parole Board or its authorized hearing officer, with the violator's consent or upon receipt of a defendant's written voluntary agreement to participate form from the probation and parole officer, may order the violator to be evaluated and diagnosed by the Department of Corrections to determine suitability for participation in the Diversion Center Incarceration Program. The evaluation and diagnosis may be conducted by the Department at any state or local correctional facility, probation or parole office, or other location deemed appropriate by the Department.

2. Upon determination that (i) such commitment is in the best interest of the Commonwealth and the violator and (ii) facilities are available for the confinement of the violator, the Department shall recommend to the Parole Board in writing that the violator be committed to the Diversion Center Incarceration Program. The Department shall have the final authority to determine an individual's suitability for the program.

3. Upon receipt of such a recommendation and a determination by the Parole Board that the violator will benefit from the program and is capable of returning to society as a productive citizen following successful completion of the program and if the violator would otherwise be committed to the Department, the Parole Board shall restore the violator to parole supervision conditioned upon entry into and successful completion of the Diversion Center Incarceration Program. The Parole Board shall order that, upon successful completion of the program, the violator shall be placed under parole supervision for a period of not less than one year. The Parole Board may impose such other terms and conditions of parole or mandatory release as it deems appropriate. The time spent in the program shall not be counted as service of any part of a term of imprisonment for which he was sentenced upon his conviction.

4. Upon the violator's (i) voluntary withdrawal from the program, (ii) removal from the program by the Department for intractable behavior as defined in § 19.2–316.1, or (iii) failure to comply with the terms and conditions of parole or mandatory release, the Parole Board may revoke parole or mandatory release and recommit the violator as provided in § 53.1–165.

C. A person sentenced pursuant to this article shall be required to pay an amount to be determined by the Board of Corrections pursuant to regulation to defray the cost of his keep.

Acts 1994, Sp. S. II, c. 1, eff. July 1, 1995; Acts 1994, Sp. S. II, c. 2, eff. July 1, 1995; Acts 1995, c. 502; Acts 1995, c. 574; Acts 2000, c. 338; Acts 2002, c. 604; Acts 2005, c. 604. Amended by Acts 2008, c. 384; Acts 2008, c. 757.

CHAPTER 19

EXCEPTIONS AND WRITS OF ERROR

§ 19.2–317. When writ of error lies in criminal case for accused; when for Commonwealth; when for county, city or town

A. A writ of error shall lie in a criminal case to the judgment of a circuit court or the judge thereof, from the Court of Appeals as provided in § 17.1–406. It shall lie in any such case for the accused and if the case is for the violation of any law relating to the state revenue, it shall lie also for the Commonwealth.

B. A writ of error shall also lie for any county, city or town from the Supreme Court to the judgment of any circuit court declaring an ordinance of such county, city or town to be unconstitutional or otherwise invalid, except when the violation of any such ordinance is made a misdemeanor by state statute.

C. A writ of error shall also lie for the Commonwealth from the Supreme Court to a judgment of the Court of Appeals in a criminal case, except where the decision of the Court of Appeals is made final under § 17.1–410 or § 19.2–408.

Acts 1997, c. 358.

§ 19.2–317.1. Repealed by Acts 1990, c. 74

§ 19.2–318. Appeal on writ of error to judgment for contempt

From a judgment for any civil contempt of court an appeal may be taken to the Court of Appeals. A writ of error shall lie from the Court of Appeals to a judgment for criminal contempt of court. This section shall also be construed to authorize an appeal from or writ of error to a judgment of a circuit court rendered on appeal from a judgment of a district court for civil or criminal contempt.

Acts 1975, c. 495; Acts 1979, c. 649; Acts 1984, c. 703.

§ 19.2–319. When execution of sentence to be suspended; bail; appeal from denial

If a person sentenced by a circuit court to death or confinement in the state correctional facility indicates an intention to apply for a writ of error, the circuit court shall postpone the execution of such sentence for such time as it may deem proper.

In any other criminal case wherein judgment is given by any court to which a writ of error lies, and in any case of judgment for any civil or criminal contempt, from which an appeal may be taken or to which a writ of error lies, the court giving such judgment may postpone the execution thereof for such time and on such terms as it deems proper.

In any case after conviction if the sentence, or the execution thereof, is suspended in accordance with this section, or for any other cause, the court, or the judge thereof, may, and in any case of a misdemeanor shall, set bail in such penalty and for appearance at such time as the nature of the case may require; provided that, if the conviction was for a violent felony as defined in § 19.2–297.1 and the defendant was sentenced to serve a period of incarceration not subject to suspension, then the court shall presume, subject to rebuttal, that no condition or combination of conditions of bail will reasonably assure the appearance of the convicted person or the safety of the public.

In any case in which the court denies bail, the reason for such denial shall be stated on the record of the case. A writ of error from the Court of Appeals shall lie to any such judgment refusing bail or requiring excessive bail, except that in any case where a person has been sentenced to death, a writ of error shall lie from the Supreme Court. Upon review by the Court of Appeals or the Supreme Court, if the decision by the trial court to deny bail is overruled, the appellate court shall either set bail or remand the matter to circuit court for such further action regarding bail as the appellate court directs.

Acts 1975, c. 495; Acts 1979, c. 649; Acts 1984, c. 703; Acts 1987, c. 175; Acts 1988, c. 524; Acts 1999, c. 821. Amended by Acts 2008, c. 126; Acts 2008, c. 146.

§ 19.2–320. Petitioner for writ of error to comply with Rules of Court

Any party for whom a writ of error lies may apply therefor by complying with the provisions of the Rules of the Supreme Court of Virginia relative to the appeal of criminal cases to the Court of Appeals, or where an appeal is taken to the Supreme Court, with the Rules of the Supreme Court relative to appeal of criminal cases to the Supreme Court.

Acts 1975, c. 495; Acts 1984, c. 703.

§ 19.2–321. With whom petition for writ of error filed

A. The petition to the Court of Appeals shall be filed with the Clerk of the Court in the manner and within the time provided by law.

B. The petition in a case wherein a writ of error lies from the Supreme Court shall be filed with the Clerk of that Court in the manner and within the time provided by law.

Acts 1975, c. 495; Acts 1976, c. 615; Acts 1984, c. 703.

§ 19.2–321.1. Motion in the Court of Appeals for delayed appeal in criminal cases

A. Filing and content of motion.—When, due to the error, neglect, or fault of counsel representing the appellant, or of the court reporter, or of the circuit court or an officer or employee thereof, an appeal in a criminal case has (i) never been initiated; (ii) been dismissed for failure to adhere to proper form, procedures, or time limits in the perfection of the appeal; or (iii) been denied or the conviction has been affirmed, for failure to file or timely file the indispensible transcript or written statement of facts as required by law or by the Rules of the Supreme Court; then a motion for leave to pursue a delayed appeal may be filed in the Court of Appeals within six months after the appeal has been dismissed or denied, the conviction has been affirmed, or the circuit court judgment sought to be appealed has become final, whichever is later. Such motion shall identify the circuit court and the style, date, and circuit court record number of the judgment sought to be appealed, and, if one was assigned in a prior attempt to appeal the judgment, shall give the Court of Appeals record number in that proceeding, and shall set forth the specific facts establishing the said error, neglect, or fault. If the error, neglect, or fault is alleged to be that of an attorney representing the appellant, the motion shall be accompanied by the affidavit of the attorney whose error, neglect, or fault is alleged, verifying the specific facts alleged in the motion, and certifying that the appellant is not personally responsible, in whole or in part, for the error, neglect, or fault causing loss of the original opportunity for appeal.

B. Service, response, and disposition.—Such motion shall be served on the attorney for the Commonwealth or, if a petition for appeal was granted in the original attempt to appeal, upon the Attorney General, in accordance with the Rules of the Supreme Court. If the Commonwealth disputes the facts alleged in the motion, or contends that those facts do not entitle the appellant to a delayed appeal under this section, the motion shall be denied without prejudice to the appellant's right to seek a delayed appeal by means of petition for a writ of habeas corpus. Otherwise, the Court of Appeals shall, if the motion meets the requirements of this section, grant appellant leave to initiate or re-initiate pursuit of the appeal.

C. Time limits when motion granted.—If the motion is granted, all computations of time under the Rules of the Supreme Court shall run from the date of the order of the Court of Appeals granting the motion, or if the appellant has been determined to be indigent, from the date of the order by the circuit court appointing counsel to represent the appellant in the delayed appeal, whichever is later.

D. Applicability.—The provisions of this section shall not apply to cases in which the appellant is responsible, in whole or in part, for the error, neglect, or fault causing loss of the original opportunity for appeal, nor shall it apply in cases where the claim of error, neglect, or fault has already been alleged and rejected in a prior judicial proceeding.

Acts 2005, c. 836. Amended by Acts 2011, c. 278.

§ 19.2–321.2. Motion in the Supreme Court for delayed appeal in criminal cases

A. Filing and content of motion.—When, due to the error, neglect, or fault of counsel representing the appellant, or of the court reporter, or of the Court of Appeals or the circuit court or an officer or employee of either, an appeal from the Court of Appeals to the Supreme Court in a criminal case has (i) never been initiated; (ii) been dismissed for failure to adhere to proper form, procedures, or time limits in the perfection of the appeal; or (iii) been denied or the conviction has been affirmed, for failure to file or timely file the indispensible transcript or written statement of facts as required by law or by the Rules of the Supreme Court; then a motion for leave to pursue a delayed appeal may be filed in the Supreme Court within six months after the appeal has been dismissed or denied, the conviction has been affirmed, or the Court of Appeals judgment sought to be appealed has become final, whichever is later. Such motion shall identify by the style, date, and Court of Appeals record number of the judgment sought to be appealed, and, if one was assigned in a prior attempt to appeal the judgment to the Supreme Court, shall give the record number assigned in the Supreme Court in that proceeding, and shall set forth the specific facts establishing the said error, neglect, or fault. If the error, neglect, or fault is alleged to be that of an attorney representing the appellant, the motion shall be accompanied by the affidavit of the attorney whose error, neglect, or fault is alleged, verifying the specific facts alleged in the motion, and certifying that the appellant is not personally responsible, in whole or in part, for the error, neglect, or fault causing loss of the original opportunity for appeal.

B. Service, response, and disposition.—Such motion shall be served on the attorney for the Commonwealth or, if a petition for appeal was granted in the Court of Appeals or in the Supreme Court in the original attempt to appeal, upon the Attorney General, in accordance with Rule 5:4 of the Supreme Court. If the Commonwealth disputes the facts alleged in the motion, or contends that those facts do not entitle the appellant to a delayed appeal under this section, the motion shall be denied without prejudice to the appellant's right to seek a delayed appeal by means of petition for a writ of habeas corpus. Otherwise, the Supreme Court shall, if the motion meets the requirements of this section, grant appellant leave to initiate or re-initiate pursuit of the appeal from the Court of Appeals to the Supreme Court.

C. Time limits when motion granted.—If the motion is granted, all computations of time under the Rules of the Supreme Court shall run from the date of the order of the Supreme Court granting the motion, or if the appellant has been determined to be indigent, from the date of the order by the circuit court appointing counsel to represent the appellant in the delayed appeal, whichever is later.

D. Applicability.—The provisions of this section shall not apply to cases in which the appellant is responsible, in whole or in part, for the error, neglect, or fault causing loss of the original opportunity for appeal, nor shall it apply in cases where the claim of error, neglect, or fault has already been alleged and rejected in a prior judicial proceeding, nor shall it apply in cases in which a sentence of death has been imposed.

Acts 2005, c. 836. Amended by Acts 2011, c. 278.

§ 19.2–322. Repealed by Acts 1984, c. 703

§ 19.2–322.1. Suspension of execution of judgment on appeal

Execution of a judgment from which an appeal to the Court of Appeals or the Supreme Court is sought may be suspended during an appeal provided the appeal is timely prosecuted and an appeal bond is filed as provided in § 8.01–676.1.

Acts 1984, c. 703.

§ 19.2–323. Denial by judge or justice no bar to allowance by Court

The denial of a writ of error by a judge or justice of an appellate court, in the vacation of that court, shall not prevent the allowance of the writ by the Court, if by it deemed proper, on presentation of the petition to that Court at its next term.

Acts 1975, c. 495; Acts 1976, c. 615; Acts 1984, c. 703.

§ 19.2–324. Decision of appellate court

The court from which a writ of error lies shall affirm the judgment, if there be no error therein, and reverse the same in whole or in part, if erroneous, and enter such judgment as the court whose error is sought to be corrected ought to have entered; or remand the cause and direct a new trial; affirming in those cases where the voices on both sides are equal.

Acts 1975, c. 495.

§ 19.2–324.1. Erroneously admitted evidence; appeal

In appeals to the Court of Appeals or the Supreme Court, when a challenge to a conviction rests on a claim that the evidence was insufficient because the trial court improperly admitted evidence, the reviewing court shall consider all evidence admitted at trial to determine whether there is sufficient evidence to sustain the conviction. If the reviewing court determines that evidence was erroneously admitted and that such error was not harmless, the case shall be remanded for a new trial if the Commonwealth elects to have a new trial.

Added by Acts 2013, c. 675.

§ 19.2–325. Provisions which apply to criminal as well as civil cases; when plaintiff in error unable to pay printing costs

Sections 8.01–675.1, 8.01–675.2, 8.01–675.3, 8.01–684 and 17.1–328 shall apply as well to criminal cases as to civil cases. In a felony case in the Court of Appeals or the Supreme Court, if the plaintiff in error files with the Clerk of the Court an affidavit that he is unable to pay or secure to be paid the costs of printing the record in the case, together with a certificate of the judge of the trial court to the effect that he has investigated the matter and is of opinion that the plaintiff in error is unable to pay, or secure to be paid, such costs, the printing shall be done as if the costs had been paid and the clerk shall not be required to account for and pay the same into the state treasury. However, if the costs are not paid or secured to be paid and upon the hearing of the case the judgment of the court below is wholly affirmed by the Court of Appeals and no appeal granted by the Supreme Court, or wholly affirmed by the Supreme Court where appeal is granted, the Court in affirming the judgment shall also give judgment in behalf of the Commonwealth against the plaintiff in error for the amount of the costs to be taxed by its clerk.

Acts 1975, c. 495; Acts 1984, c. 703.

§ 19.2–326. Payment of expenses of appeals of indigent defendants

In any felony or misdemeanor case wherein the judge of the circuit court, from the affidavit of the defendant or any other evidence certifies that the defendant is financially unable to pay his attorneys' fees, costs and expenses incident to an appeal, the court to which an appeal is taken shall order the payment of such attorneys' fees in an amount not less than $300, costs or necessary expenses of such attorneys in an amount deemed reasonable by the court, by the Commonwealth out of the appropriation for criminal charges. If the conviction is upheld on appeal, the attorney's fees, costs and necessary expenses of such attorney paid by the Commonwealth under the provisions hereof shall be assessed against the defendant.

Acts 1975, c. 495; Acts 1980, c. 626; Acts 1984, c. 703.

§ 19.2–327. How judgment of appellate court certified and entered

The judgment of the Court of Appeals or of the Supreme Court shall be certified to the court to whose judgment the writ of error was allowed. The court or the clerk thereof shall cause the same to be entered on its order book as its own judgment.

Acts 1975, c. 495; Acts 1984, c. 703.

§ 19.2–327.01. Repealed by Acts 2004, c. 337

CHAPTER 19.1

SCIENTIFIC ANALYSIS OF NEWLY DISCOVERED OR UNTESTED SCIENTIFIC EVIDENCE

§ 19.2–327.1. Motion by a convicted felon or person adjudicated delinquent for scientific analysis of newly discovered or previously untested scientific evidence; procedure

A. Notwithstanding any other provision of law or rule of court, any person convicted of a felony or any person who was adjudicated delinquent by a circuit court of an offense that would be a felony if committed by an adult may, by motion to the circuit court that entered the original conviction or the adjudication of delinquency, apply for a new scientific investigation of any human biological evidence related to the case that resulted in the felony conviction or adjudication of delinquency if: (i) the evidence was not known or available at the time the conviction or adjudication of delinquency became final in the circuit court or the evidence was not previously subjected to testing because the testing procedure was not available at the Department of Forensic Science at the time the conviction or adjudication of delinquency became final in the circuit court; (ii) the evidence is subject to a chain of custody sufficient to establish that the evidence has not been altered, tampered with, or substituted in any way; (iii) the testing is materially relevant, noncumulative, and necessary and may prove the actual innocence of the convicted person or the person adjudicated delinquent; (iv) the testing requested involves a scientific method employed by the Department of Forensic Science; and (v) the person convicted or adjudicated delinquent has not unreasonably delayed the filing of the petition after the evidence or the test for the evidence became available at the Department of Forensic Science.

B. The petitioner shall assert categorically and with specificity, under oath, the facts to support the items enumerated in subsection A and (i) the crime for which the person was convicted or adjudicated delinquent, (ii) the reason or reasons the evidence was not known or tested by the time the conviction or adjudication of delinquency became final in the circuit court, and (iii) the reason or reasons that the newly discovered or untested evidence may prove the actual innocence of the person convicted or adjudicated delinquent. Such motion shall contain all relevant allegations and facts that are known to the petitioner at the time of filing and shall enumerate and include all previous records, applications, petitions, and appeals and their dispositions.

C. The petitioner shall serve a copy of such motion upon the attorney for the Commonwealth. The Commonwealth shall file its response to the motion within 30 days of the receipt of service. The court shall, no sooner than 30 and no later than 90 days after such motion is filed, hear the motion. Motions made by a petitioner under a sentence of death shall be given priority on the docket.

D. The court shall, after a hearing on the motion, set forth its findings specifically as to each of the items enumerated in subsections A and B and either (i) dismiss the motion for failure to comply with the requirements of this section or (ii) dismiss the motion for failure to state a claim upon which relief can be granted or (iii) order that the testing be done by the Department of Forensic Science based on a finding of clear and convincing evidence that the requirements of subsection A have been met.

E. The court shall order the tests to be performed by the Department of Forensic Science and prescribe in its order, pursuant to standards and guidelines established by the Department, the method of custody, transfer, and return of evidence submitted for scientific investigation sufficient to insure and protect the Commonwealth's interest in the integrity of the evidence. The results of any such testing shall be furnished simultaneously to the court, the petitioner and his attorney of record and the attorney for the Commonwealth. The Department of Forensic Science shall give testing priority to cases in which a sentence of death has been imposed. The results of any tests performed and any hearings held pursuant to this section shall become a part of the record.

F. Nothing in this section shall constitute grounds to delay setting an execution date pursuant to § 53.1–232.1 or to grant a stay of execution that has been set pursuant to clause (iii) or (iv) of § 53.1–232.1.

G. An action under this section or the performance of any attorney representing the petitioner under this section shall not form the basis for relief in any habeas corpus proceeding or any other appeal. Nothing in this section shall create any cause of action for damages against the Commonwealth or any of its political subdivisions or any officers, employees or agents of the Commonwealth or its political subdivisions.

H. In any petition filed pursuant to this chapter, the petitioner is entitled to representation by counsel subject to the provisions of Article 3 (§ 19.2–157 et seq.) of Chapter 10.

Acts 2001, c. 873, eff. May 2, 2001; Acts 2001, c. 874, eff. May 2, 2001; Acts 2005, c. 868; Acts 2005, c. 881. Amended by Acts 2013, c. 170.

CHAPTER 19.2

ISSUANCE OF WRIT OF ACTUAL INNOCENCE

§ 19.2–327.2. Issuance of writ of actual innocence based on biological evidence

Notwithstanding any other provision of law or rule of court, upon a petition of a person who was convicted of a felony upon a plea of not guilty or who was adjudicated delinquent upon a plea of not guilty by a circuit court of an offense that would be a felony if committed by an adult, or for any person, regardless of the plea, sentenced to death, or convicted or adjudicated delinquent of (i) a Class 1 felony, (ii) a Class 2 felony, or (iii) any felony for which the maximum penalty is imprisonment for life, the Supreme Court shall have the authority to issue writs of actual innocence under this chapter. The writ shall lie to the circuit court that entered the felony conviction or adjudication of delinquency and that court shall have the authority to conduct hearings, as provided for in § 19.2–327.5, on such a petition as directed by order from the Supreme Court.

Acts 2001, c. 873, eff. Nov. 15, 2002; Acts 2001, c. 874, eff. Nov. 15, 2002. Amended by Acts 2009, c. 139; Acts 2009, c. 320; Acts 2013, c. 170.

§ 19.2–327.2:1. Petition for writ of actual innocence joined by Attorney General; release of prisoner; bond hearing

The Attorney General may join in a petition for a writ of actual innocence made pursuant to § 19.2–327.2. When such petition is so joined, the petitioner may file a copy of the petition and attachments thereto and the Attorney General's answer with the circuit court that entered the felony conviction and move the court for a hearing to consider release of the person on bail pursuant to Chapter 9 (§ 19.2–119 et seq.). Upon hearing and for good cause shown, the court may order the person released from custody subject to the terms and conditions of bail so established, pending a ruling by the Supreme Court on the writ under § 19.2–327.5.

Added by Acts 2015, c. 66.

§ 19.2–327.3. Contents and form of the petition based on previously unknown or untested human biological evidence of actual innocence

A. The petitioner shall allege categorically and with specificity, under oath, the following: (i) the crime for which the petitioner was convicted or the offense for which the petitioner was adjudicated delinquent, and that such conviction or adjudication of delinquency was upon a plea of not guilty or that the person is under a sentence of death or convicted of (a) a Class 1 felony, (b) a Class 2 felony, or (c) any felony for which the maximum penalty is imprisonment for life; (ii) that the petitioner is actually innocent of the crime for which he was convicted or adjudicated delinquent; (iii) an exact description of the human biological evidence and the scientific testing supporting the allegation of innocence; (iv) that the evidence was not previously known or available to the petitioner or his trial attorney of record at the time the conviction or adjudication of delinquency became final in the circuit court, or if known, the reason that the evidence was not subject to the scientific testing set forth in the petition; (v) the date the test results under § 19.2–327.1 became known to the petitioner or any attorney of record; (vi) that the petitioner or his attorney of record has filed the petition within 60 days of obtaining the test results under § 19.2–327.1; (vii) the reason or reasons the evidence will prove that no rational trier of fact would have found proof of guilt or delinquency beyond a reasonable doubt; and (viii) for any conviction or adjudication of delinquency that became final in the circuit court after June 30, 1996, that the evidence was not available for testing under § 9.1–1104. The Supreme Court may issue a stay of execution pending proceedings under the petition. Nothing in this chapter shall constitute grounds to delay setting an execution date pursuant to § 53.1–232.1 or to grant a stay of execution that has been set pursuant to clause (iii) or (iv) of § 53.1–232.1.

B. Such petition shall contain all relevant allegations of facts that are known to the petitioner at the time of filing and shall enumerate and include all previous records, applications, petitions, and appeals and their dispositions. A copy of any test results shall be filed with the petition. The petition shall be filed on a form provided by the Supreme Court. If the petitioner fails to submit a completed form, the Court may dismiss the petition or return the petition to the prisoner pending the completion of such form. The petitioner shall be responsible for all statements contained in the petition. Any false statement in the petition, if such statement is knowingly or willfully made, shall be a ground for prosecution and conviction of perjury as provided for in § 18.2–434.

C. The Supreme Court shall not accept the petition unless it is accompanied by a duly executed return of service in the form of a verification that a copy of the petition and all attachments has been served on the attorney for the Commonwealth of the jurisdiction where the conviction or adjudication of delinquency occurred and the Attorney General or an acceptance of service signed by these officials, or any combination thereof. The Attorney General shall have 30 days after receipt of the record by the clerk of the Supreme Court in which to file a response to the petition. The response may contain a proffer of any evidence pertaining to the guilt or delinquency or innocence of the petitioner that is not included in the record of the case, including evidence that was suppressed at trial.

D. The Supreme Court may, when the case has been before a trial or appellate court, inspect the record of any trial or appellate court action, and the Court may, in any case, award a writ of certiorari to the clerk of the respective court below, and have brought before the Court the whole record or any part of any record.

E. In any petition filed pursuant to this chapter, the petitioner is entitled to representation by counsel subject to the provisions of Article 3 (§ 19.2–157 et seq.) of Chapter 10.

Acts 2001, c. 873, eff. Nov. 15, 2002; Acts 2001, c. 874, eff. Nov. 15, 2002; Acts 2003, c. 131; Acts 2005, c. 868; Acts 2005, c. 881. Amended by Acts 2009, c. 139; Acts 2009, c. 320; Acts 2013, c. 170; Acts 2013, c. 180.

§ 19.2–327.4. Determination by the Supreme Court for findings of fact by the circuit court

If the Supreme Court determines from the petition, from any hearing on the petition, from a review of the records of the case, including the record of any hearing on a motion to test evidence pursuant to § 9.1–1104, or from any response from the Attorney General that a resolution of the case requires further development of the facts under this chapter, the court may order the circuit court to conduct a hearing within 90 days after the order has been issued to certify findings of fact with respect to such issues as the Supreme Court shall direct. The record and certified findings of fact of the circuit court shall be filed in the Supreme Court within 30 days after the hearing is concluded. The petitioner or his attorney of record, the attorney for the Commonwealth and the Attorney General shall be served a copy of the order stating the specific purpose and evidence for which the hearing has been ordered.

Acts 2001, c. 873, eff. Nov. 15, 2002; Acts 2001, c. 874, eff. Nov. 15, 2002; Acts 2005, c. 868; Acts 2005, c. 881.

§ 19.2–327.5. Relief under writ

Upon consideration of the petition, the response by the Commonwealth, previous records of the case, the record of any hearing held under this chapter and the record of any hearings held pursuant to § 19.2–327.1, and if applicable, any findings certified from the circuit court pursuant to § 19.2–327.4, the Supreme Court shall either dismiss the petition for failure to state a claim or assert grounds upon which relief shall be granted; or upon a hearing the Court shall (i) dismiss the petition for failure to establish allegations sufficient to justify the issuance of the writ or (ii) only upon a finding of clear and convincing evidence that the petitioner has proven all of the allegations contained in clauses (iv) through (viii) of subsection A of § 19.2–327.3, and upon a finding that no rational trier of fact would have found proof of guilt or delinquency beyond a reasonable doubt, grant the writ, and vacate the conviction or adjudication of delinquency, or in the event that the Court finds that no rational trier of fact would have found sufficient evidence beyond a reasonable doubt as to one or more elements of the offense for which the petitioner was convicted or adjudicated delinquent, but the Court finds that there remains in the original trial record evidence sufficient to find the petitioner guilty or delinquent beyond a reasonable doubt of a lesser included offense, the Court shall modify the conviction or adjudication of delinquency accordingly and remand the case to the circuit court for resentencing. The burden of proof in a proceeding brought pursuant to this chapter shall be upon the convicted or delinquent person seeking relief. If a writ vacating a conviction or adjudication of delinquency is granted, the Court shall forward a copy of the writ to the circuit court, where an order of expungement shall be immediately granted.

Acts 2001, c. 873, eff. Nov. 15, 2002; Acts 2001, c. 874, eff. Nov. 15, 2002; Acts 2007, c. 465; Acts 2007, c. 824; Acts 2007, c. 883; Acts 2007, c. 905. Amended by Acts 2009, c. 139; Acts 2009, c. 320; Acts 2013, c. 170; Acts 2013, c. 180.

§ 19.2–327.6. Claims of relief

An action under this chapter or the performance of any attorney representing the petitioner under this chapter shall not form the basis for relief in any habeas corpus or appellate proceeding. Nothing in this chapter shall create any cause of action for damages against the Commonwealth or any of its political subdivisions or any officers, employees or agents of the Commonwealth or its political subdivisions.

Acts 2001, c. 873, eff. Nov. 15, 2001; Acts 2001, c. 874, eff. Nov. 15, 2002.

CHAPTER 19.3

ISSUANCE OF WRIT OF ACTUAL INNOCENCE BASED ON NONBIOLOGICAL EVIDENCE

§ 19.2–327.10. Issuance of writ of actual innocence based on nonbiological evidence

Notwithstanding any other provision of law or rule of court, upon a petition of a person who was convicted of a felony upon a plea of not guilty, or the petition of a person who was adjudicated delinquent, upon a plea of not guilty, by a circuit court of an offense that would be a felony if committed by an adult, the Court of Appeals shall have the authority to issue writs of actual innocence under this chapter. Only one such writ based upon such conviction or adjudication of delinquency may be filed by a petitioner. The writ shall lie to the circuit court that entered the conviction or the adjudication of delinquency and that court shall have the authority to conduct hearings, as provided for in this chapter, on such a petition as directed by order from the Court of Appeals. In accordance with §§ 17.1–411 and 19.2–317, either party may appeal a final decision of the Court of Appeals to the Supreme Court of Virginia. Upon an appeal from the Court of Appeals, the Supreme Court of Virginia shall have the authority to issue writs in accordance with the provisions of this chapter.

Acts 2004, c. 1024. Amended by Acts 2013, c. 170.

§ 19.2–327.10:1. Petition for writ of actual innocence joined by Attorney General; release of prisoner; bond hearing

The Attorney General may join in a petition for a writ of actual innocence made pursuant to § 19.2–327.10. When such petition is so joined, the petitioner may file a copy of the petition and attachments thereto and the Attorney General's answer with the circuit court that entered the felony conviction and move the court for a hearing to consider release of the person on bail pursuant to Chapter 9 (§ 19.2–119 et seq.). Upon hearing and for good cause shown, the court may order the person released from custody subject to the terms and conditions of bail so established, pending a ruling by the Court of Appeals on the writ under § 19.2–327.13.

Added by Acts 2015, c. 66.

§ 19.2–327.11. Contents and form of the petition based on previously unknown or unavailable evidence of actual innocence

A. The petitioner shall allege categorically and with specificity, under oath, all of the following: (i) the crime for which the petitioner was convicted or the offense for which the petitioner was adjudicated delinquent, and that such conviction or adjudication of delinquency was upon a plea of not guilty; (ii) that the petitioner is actually innocent of the crime for which he was convicted or the offense for which he was adjudicated delinquent; (iii) an exact description of the previously unknown or unavailable evidence supporting the allegation of innocence; (iv) that such evidence was previously unknown or unavailable to the petitioner or his trial attorney of record at the time the conviction or adjudication of delinquency became final in the circuit court; (v) the date the previously unknown or unavailable evidence became known or available to the petitioner, and the circumstances under which it was discovered; (vi) that the previously unknown or unavailable evidence is such as could not, by the exercise of diligence, have been discovered or obtained before the expiration of 21 days following entry of the final order of conviction or adjudication of delinquency by the circuit court; (vii) the previously unknown or unavailable evidence is material and, when considered with all of the other evidence in the current record, will prove that no rational trier of fact would have found proof of guilt or delinquency beyond a reasonable doubt; and (viii) the previously unknown or unavailable evidence is not merely cumulative, corroborative or collateral. Nothing in this chapter shall constitute grounds to delay setting an execution date pursuant to § 53.1–232.1 or to grant a stay of execution that has been set pursuant to clause (iii) or (iv) of § 53.1–232.1 or to delay or stay any other appeals following conviction or adjudication of delinquency, or petitions to any court. Human biological evidence may not be used as the sole basis for seeking relief under this writ but may be used in conjunction with other evidence.

B. Such petition shall contain all relevant allegations of facts that are known to the petitioner at the time of filing, shall be accompanied by all relevant documents, affidavits and test results, and shall enumerate and include all relevant previous records, applications, petitions, and appeals and their dispositions. The petition shall be filed on a form provided by the Supreme Court. If the petitioner fails to submit a completed form, the Court of Appeals may dismiss the petition or return the petition to the petitioner pending the completion of such form. Any false statement in the petition, if such statement is knowingly or willfully made, shall be a ground for prosecution of perjury as provided for in § 18.2–434.

C. In cases brought by counsel for the petitioner, the Court of Appeals shall not accept the petition unless it is accompanied by a duly executed return of service in the form of a verification that a copy of the petition and all attachments have been served on the attorney for the Commonwealth of the jurisdiction where the conviction or adjudication of delinquency occurred and the Attorney General, or an acceptance of service signed by these officials, or any combination thereof. In cases brought by petitioners pro se, the Court of Appeals shall not accept the petition unless it is accompanied by a certificate that a copy of the petition and all attachments have been sent, by certified mail, to the attorney for the Commonwealth of the jurisdiction where the conviction or adjudication of delinquency occurred and the Attorney General. If the Court of Appeals does not summarily dismiss the petition, it shall so notify in writing the Attorney General, the attorney for the Commonwealth, and the petitioner. The Attorney General shall have 60 days after receipt of such notice in which to file a response to the petition that may be extended for good cause shown; however, nothing shall prevent the Attorney General from filing an earlier response. The response may contain a proffer of any evidence pertaining to the guilt or delinquency or innocence of the petitioner that is not included in the record of the case, including evidence that was suppressed at trial.

D. The Court of Appeals may inspect the record of any trial or appellate court action, and the Court may, in any case, award a writ of certiorari to the clerk of the respective court below, and have brought before the Court the whole record or any part of any record. If, in the judgment of the Court, the petition fails to state a claim, or if the assertions of previously unknown or unavailable evidence, even if true, would fail to qualify for the granting of relief under this chapter, the Court may dismiss the petition summarily, without any hearing or a response from the Attorney General.

E. In any petition filed pursuant to this chapter that is not summarily dismissed, the petitioner is entitled to representation by counsel subject to the provisions of Article 3 (§ 19.2–157 et seq.) and Article 4 (§ 19.2–163.3 et seq.) of Chapter 10. The Court of Appeals may, in its discretion, appoint counsel prior to deciding whether a petition should be summarily dismissed.

Acts 2004, c. 1024. Amended by Acts 2013, c. 170; Acts 2013, c. 180.

§ 19.2–327.12. Determination by Court of Appeals for findings of fact by the circuit court

If the Court of Appeals determines from the petition, from any hearing on the petition, from a review of the records of the case, or from any response from the Attorney General that a resolution of the case requires further development of the facts, the court may order the circuit court in which the order of conviction or the adjudication of delinquency was originally entered to conduct a hearing within 90 days after the order has been issued to certify findings of fact with respect to such issues as the Court of Appeals shall direct. The record and certified findings of fact of the circuit court shall be filed in the Court of Appeals within 30 days after the hearing is concluded. The petitioner or his attorney of record, the attorney for the Commonwealth and the Attorney General shall be served a copy of the order stating the specific purpose and evidence for which the hearing has been ordered.

Acts 2004, c. 1024. Amended by Acts 2013, c. 170.

§ 19.2–327.13. Relief under writ

Upon consideration of the petition, the response by the Commonwealth, previous records of the case, the record of any hearing held under this chapter and, if applicable, any findings certified from the circuit court pursuant to an order issued under this chapter, the Court of Appeals, if it has not already summarily dismissed the petition, shall either dismiss the petition for failure to state a claim or assert grounds upon which relief shall be granted; or the Court shall (i) dismiss the petition for failure to establish previously unknown or unavailable evidence sufficient to justify the issuance of the writ, or (ii) only upon a finding that the petitioner has proven by clear and convincing evidence all of the allegations contained in clauses (iv) through (viii) of subsection A of § 19.2–327.11, and upon a finding that no rational trier of fact would have found proof of guilt or delinquency beyond a reasonable doubt, grant the writ, and vacate the conviction or finding of delinquency, or in the event that the Court finds that no rational trier of fact would have found sufficient evidence beyond a reasonable doubt as to one or more elements of the offense for which the petitioner was convicted or adjudicated delinquent, but the Court finds that there remains in the original trial record evidence sufficient to find the petitioner guilty or delinquent beyond a reasonable doubt of a lesser included offense, the Court shall modify the order of conviction or delinquency accordingly and remand the case to the circuit court that entered the conviction or adjudication of delinquency for resentencing. The burden of proof in a proceeding brought pursuant to this chapter shall be upon the convicted or delinquent person seeking relief. If a writ vacating a conviction or adjudication of delinquency is granted, and no appeal is made to the Supreme Court, or the Supreme Court denies the Commonwealth's petition for appeal or upholds the decision of the Court of Appeals to grant the writ, the Court of Appeals shall forward a copy of the writ to the circuit court, where an order of expungement shall be immediately granted.

Acts 2004, c. 1024; Acts 2007, c. 465; Acts 2007, c. 824; Acts 2007, c. 883; Acts 2007, c. 905. Amended by Acts 2013, c. 170; Acts 2013, c. 180.

§ 19.2–327.14. Claims of relief

An action under this chapter or the actions of any attorney representing the petitioner under this chapter shall not form the basis for relief in any habeas corpus proceeding. Nothing in this chapter shall create any cause of action for damages against the Commonwealth or any of its political subdivisions.

Acts 2004, c. 1024.

CHAPTER 20

TAXATION AND ALLOWANCE OF COSTS

§ 19.2–328. When jailers and sheriffs to summon or employ guards and other persons; allowances therefor

Whenever in the discretion of the court it is necessary for the safekeeping of a prisoner under charge of, or sentence for, crime, whether the prisoner be in jail, hospital, court or elsewhere, the court may order the jailer to summon a sufficient guard, and whenever ordered by the court to do so, the sheriff of any county or city shall summon or employ temporarily such person or persons as may be needed to preserve proper order or otherwise to aid the court in its proper operation and functioning, and for such guard or other service the court may allow therefor so much as it deems proper, not exceeding the hourly equivalent of the minimum annual salary paid a full-time deputy sheriff who performs like services in the same county or city; in addition, mileage and other expenses for rendering the services shall be paid for each person, the same to be paid out of the budget allotted to the sheriff as approved by the Compensation Board, except when payment for such guard is otherwise provided under the provisions of § 53.1–94 of the Code of Virginia.

Acts 1975, c. 495; Acts 1981, c. 386; Acts 1985, c. 321.

§ 19.2–329. Allowance to witnesses

Sections 17.1–612 to 17.1–616, inclusive, shall apply to a person attending as a witness, under a recognizance or summons in a criminal case, as well as to a person attending under a summons in a civil case, except that a person residing out of this Commonwealth, who attends a court therein as a witness, shall be allowed by the court a proper compensation for attendance and travel to and from the place of his abode, the amount of the same to be fixed by the court.

Acts 1975, c. 495; Acts 1977, c. 483.

§ 19.2–330. Compensation to witnesses from out of Commonwealth

Any witness from without the Commonwealth whose attendance is compelled under the provisions of Chapter 16, Article 2 (§ 19.2–272 et seq.) of this title shall be deemed to render a service within the meaning of § 19.2–332 and the compensation and expenses of such witness, whether on behalf of the Commonwealth or the accused, may be paid out of the state treasury in accordance with the provisions of such section. But the compensation and expenses of any witness summoned on behalf of an accused shall not be certified to the state treasury as a compensation under such section except in cases when the court or judge thereof is satisfied that the defendant is without means to pay same and is unable to provide the costs incident thereto.

Acts 1975, c. 495.

§ 19.2–331. When Commonwealth pays witnesses in case of misdemeanor

Payment shall not be made out of the state treasury to a witness attending for the Commonwealth in any prosecution for a misdemeanor unless it appears that the sum to which the witness is entitled cannot be obtained:

(1) If it be a case wherein there is a prosecutor and the defendant is convicted, by reason of the insolvency of the defendant, or

(2) If it be a case in which there is no prosecutor, by reason of the acquittal or insolvency of the defendant or other cause.

Acts 1975, c. 495.

§ 19.2–332. Compensation to officer or other person for services not otherwise compensable

Whenever in a criminal case an officer or other person renders any service required by law for which no specific compensation is provided, or whenever any other service has been rendered pursuant to the request or prior approval of the court, the court shall allow therefor such sum as it deems reasonable, including mileage at a rate provided by law, and such allowance shall be paid out of the state treasury from the appropriation for criminal charges on the certificate of the court stating the nature of the service. This section shall not prevent any payment under § 2.2–816, which could have been made if this section had not been enacted.

This section shall not be construed to authorize the payment of any additional compensation to an officer or other employee of the Commonwealth who is compensated for his services exclusively by salary unless it be otherwise expressly provided by law.

Acts 1975, c. 495.

§ 19.2–333. No state fees to attorney for the Commonwealth

No fee to an attorney for the Commonwealth shall be payable out of the state treasury, unless it be expressly so provided.

Acts 1975, c. 495.

§ 19.2–334. By whom certificate of allowance to be made; vouchers to accompany it; proof of correctness; what entry to state

Any other expense incident to a proceeding in a criminal case which is payable out of the state treasury otherwise than under §§ 2.2–816, 19.2–330 or § 19.2–332 shall be certified by the court. If it be a judge of a district court exercising jurisdiction, it shall be certified by such judge to the Supreme Court. With the certificate of allowance there shall be transmitted to the Supreme Court the vouchers on which it is made. The court, in passing upon any account for fees or expenses required to be certified by it under this section, before certifying the account, may, in its discretion, require proof of the correctness of any item thereof.

The entry of such certificate of allowance shall state how much thereof is on account of each person prosecuted.

Acts 1975, c. 495; Acts 1978, c. 195; Acts 1979, c. 465.

§ 19.2–335. Judge of district court to certify to clerk of circuit court costs of proceedings in criminal cases before him

A judge of a district court before whom there is any proceeding in a criminal case, including any proceeding which has been deferred upon probation of the defendant pursuant to § 16.1–278.8, 16.1–278.9, 18.2–61, 18.2–67.1, 18.2–67.2, 18.2–251 or 19.2–303.2, shall certify to the clerk of the circuit court of his county or city, and a judge or court before whom there is, in a criminal case, any proceeding preliminary to conviction in another court, upon receiving information of the conviction from the clerk of the court wherein it is, shall certify to such clerk, all the expenses incident to such proceedings which are payable out of the state treasury.

Acts 1975, c. 495; Acts 1995, c. 485; Acts 2005, c. 631.

§ 19.2–336. Clerk to make up statement of whole cost, and issue execution therefor

In every criminal case the clerk of the circuit court in which the accused is found guilty or is placed on probation during deferral of the proceedings pursuant to § 16.1–278.8, 16.1–278.9, 18.2–61, 18.2–67.1, 18.2–67.2, 18.2–251 or 19.2–303.2, or, if the conviction is in a district court, the clerk to which the judge thereof certifies as aforesaid, shall, as soon as may be, make up a statement of all the expenses incident to the prosecution, including such as are certified under § 19.2–335, and execution for the amount of such expenses shall be issued and proceeded with. Chapter 21 (§ 19.2–339 et seq.) shall apply thereto in like manner as if, on the day of completing the statement, there was a judgment in such court in favor of the Commonwealth against the accused for such amount as a fine. However, in any case in which an accused waives trial by jury, at least 10 days before trial, but the Commonwealth or the court trying the case refuses to so waive, then the cost of the jury shall not be included in such statement or judgment recorded pursuant to § 17.1–275.5.

Acts 1975, c. 495; Acts 1978, c. 716; Acts 1995, c. 485; Acts 2005, c. 631. Amended by Acts 2012, c. 714.

§ 19.2–337. Claims not presented in time to be disallowed

If by reason of the failure of a person to present his claim in due time a sum be not included in such execution which would have been included if so presented, such claim, unless there be good cause for the failure, shall be disallowed.

Acts 1975, c. 495.

§ 19.2–338. Collection by town of cost of transporting prisoners

(1) Notwithstanding any provision of any charter or any law to the contrary, any town may provide that any person convicted of violating any ordinance of the town may be charged, in addition to all other costs, fines, fees and charges, the costs of transporting such person so convicted to and from a jail or other penal institution outside the corporate limits of such town designated by the town as a place of confinement for persons arrested for violating the ordinances of the town and required to be held in jail pending trial upon such charge. The cost of such transportation shall be taxed as a part of the costs payable by persons convicted of violating such ordinances.

(2) No officer transporting any person convicted of violating any ordinance of the town, as provided in subsection (1) hereof, shall charge or be paid, nor shall such town receive directly or indirectly, more than the cost of transporting such person when more than one person is transported.

Acts 1975, c. 495; Acts 1995, c. 51.

CHAPTER 21

RECOVERY OF FINES AND PENALTIES

ARTICLE 1

PROCEEDINGS TO RECOVER

§ 19.2–339. Word "fine" construed

Whenever the word "fine" is used in this chapter, it shall be construed to refer solely to the pecuniary penalty imposed by a court or jury upon a defendant who has been found guilty of a crime. The word "fine" shall not include other forfeitures, penalties, costs, amercements or the like, even though they follow as a consequence of conviction of crime.

Acts 1975, c. 495.

§ 19.2–340. Fines; how recovered; in what name

When any statute or ordinance prescribes a fine, unless it is otherwise expressly provided or would be inconsistent with the manifest intention of the General Assembly, it shall be paid to the Commonwealth if prescribed by a statute and recoverable by presentment, indictment, information or warrant and paid to the locality if prescribed by an ordinance and recoverable by warrant. Fines imposed and costs taxed in a criminal or traffic prosecution, including a prosecution for a violation of an ordinance adopted pursuant to § 46.2–1220, for committing an offense shall constitute a judgment and, if not paid at the time they are imposed, execution may issue thereon in the same manner as upon any other monetary judgment, subject to the period of limitations provided by § 19.2–341.

Acts 1975, c. 495; Acts 1995, c. 438.

§ 19.2–340.1. Disposition of fines in criminal cases

When a law-enforcement officer of (i) the Department of State Police or (ii) any other division of the state government makes an arrest or issues a summons for a violation of a provision of the Code of Virginia, the person arrested or summoned shall be charged with a violation of that Code provision and shall not be charged with a substantially similar local ordinance. All fines collected upon conviction of any person so arrested or summoned shall be credited to the Literary Fund.

Added by Acts 2012, c. 749.

§ 19.2–341. Penalties other than fines; how recovered; in what name; limitation of actions

When any statute or ordinance prescribes a monetary penalty other than a fine, unless it is otherwise expressly provided or would be inconsistent with the manifest intention of the General Assembly, it shall be paid to the Commonwealth if prescribed by a statute and paid to the locality if prescribed by an ordinance and recoverable by warrant, presentment, indictment, or information. Penalties imposed and costs taxed in any such proceeding shall constitute a judgment and, if not paid at the time they are imposed, execution may issue thereon in the same manner as upon any other monetary judgment. No such proceeding of any nature, however, shall be brought or had for the recovery of such a penalty or costs due the Commonwealth or any political subdivision thereof, unless within twenty years from the date of the offense or delinquency giving rise to imposition of such penalty if imposed by a circuit court, or within ten years if imposed by a general district court.

Acts 1975, c. 495; Acts 1983, c. 499; Acts 1995, c. 438.

§ 19.2–342. Where and in what court proceeding to be

In a proceeding under § 19.2–341, such warrant, presentment, indictment or information shall be in the county or city wherein the offense was committed or the delinquency occurred.

Acts 1975, c. 495.

§§ 19.2–343, 19.2–344. Reserved

ARTICLE 2

REPORTS, ETC., OF FINES AND COSTS

§§ 19.2–345, 19.2–346. Repealed by Acts 1988, c. 509

§ 19.2–347. Repealed by Acts 1983, c. 499

Article 3

Collection and Disposition of Fines

§ 19.2–348. Attorneys for Commonwealth or clerks to superintend issue of executions, etc.

The attorney for the Commonwealth or the clerk of the circuit court shall superintend the issuing of all executions or judgments for fines and penalties going wholly or in part to the Commonwealth or a county, city or town, in the circuit court or appropriate district court of his county or city.

Acts 1975, c. 495; Acts 1983, c. 499; Acts 1992, c. 623; Acts 1994, c. 811.

§ 19.2–349. Responsibility for collections; clerks to report unsatisfied fines, etc.; duty of attorneys for Commonwealth; duties of Department of Taxation

A. The clerk of the circuit court and district court of every county and city shall submit to the judge of his court, the Department of Taxation, the State Compensation Board and the attorney for the Commonwealth of his county or city a monthly report of all fines, costs, forfeitures and penalties which are delinquent more than 30 days, including court-ordered restitution of a sum certain, imposed in his court for a violation of state law or a local ordinance which remain unsatisfied, including those which are delinquent in installment payments. The monthly report shall include the social security number or driver's license number of the defendant, if known, and such other information as the Department of Taxation and the Compensation Board deem appropriate. The Executive Secretary shall make the report required by this subsection on behalf of those clerks who participate in the Supreme Court's automated information system.

B. It shall be the duty of the attorney for the Commonwealth to cause proper proceedings to be instituted for the collection and satisfaction of all fines, costs, forfeitures, penalties and restitution. The attorney for the Commonwealth shall determine whether it would be impractical or uneconomical for such service to be rendered by the office of the attorney for the Commonwealth. If the defendant does not enter into an installment payment agreement under § 19.2–354, the attorney for the Commonwealth and the clerk may agree to a process by which collection activity may be commenced 30 days after judgment.

If the attorney for the Commonwealth does not undertake collection, he shall contract with (i) private attorneys or private collection agencies, (ii) enter into an agreement with a local governing body, (iii) enter into an agreement with the county or city treasurer, or (iv) use the services of the Department of Taxation, upon such terms and conditions as may be established by guidelines promulgated by the Office of the Attorney General, the Executive Secretary of the Supreme Court with the Department of Taxation and the Compensation Board. If the attorney for the Commonwealth undertakes collection, he shall follow the procedures established by the Department of Taxation and the Compensation Board. Such guidelines shall not supersede contracts between attorneys for the Commonwealth and private attorneys and collection agencies when active collection efforts are being undertaken. As part of such contract, private attorneys or collection agencies shall be given access to the social security number of the defendant in order to assist in the collection effort. Any such private attorney shall be subject to the penalties and provisions of § 18.2–186.3.

The fees of any private attorneys or collection agencies shall be paid on a contingency fee basis out of the proceeds of the amounts collected. However, in no event shall such attorney or collection agency receive a fee for amounts collected by the Department of Taxation under the Setoff Debt Collection Act (§ 58.1–520 et seq.). A local treasurer undertaking collection pursuant to an agreement with the attorney for the Commonwealth may collect the administrative fee authorized by § 58.1–3958.

C. The Department of Taxation and the State Compensation Board shall be responsible for the collection of any judgment which remains unsatisfied or does not meet the conditions of § 19.2–354. Persons owing such unsatisfied judgments or failing to comply with installment payment agreements under § 19.2–354 shall be subject to the delinquent tax collection provisions of Title 58.1. The Department of Taxation and the State Compensation Board shall establish procedures to be followed by clerks of courts, attorneys for the Commonwealth, other state agencies and any private attorneys or collection agents and may employ private attorneys or collection agencies, or engage other state agencies to collect the judgment. The Department of Taxation and the Commonwealth shall be entitled to deduct a fee for services from amounts collected for violations of local ordinances.

The Department of Taxation and the State Compensation Board shall annually report to the Governor and the General Assembly the total of fines, costs, forfeitures and penalties assessed, collected, and unpaid and those which remain unsatisfied or do not meet the conditions of § 19.2–354 by each circuit and district court. The report shall include the procedures established by the Department of Taxation and the State Compensation Board pursuant to this section and a plan for increasing the collection of unpaid fines, costs, forfeitures and penalties. The Auditor of Public Accounts shall annually report to the Governor, the

Executive Secretary of the Supreme Court and the General Assembly as to the adherence of clerks of courts, attorneys for the Commonwealth and other state agencies to the procedures established by the Department of Taxation and the State Compensation Board.

Acts 1975, c. 495; Acts 1979, c. 469; Acts 1983, c. 415; Acts 1983, c. 499; Acts 1988, c. 742; Acts 1988, c. 750; Acts 1988, c. 770; Acts 1988, c. 852; Acts 1991, c. 202; Acts 1992, c. 623; Acts 1993, c. 269; Acts 1994, c. 841; Acts 1994, c. 945; Acts 2001, c. 414; Acts 2003, c. 262; Acts 2006, c. 359; Acts 2007, c. 551. Amended by Acts 2012, c. 615.

§ 19.2-349.1. Receipt of unpaid fines, costs, forfeitures, penalties, or restitution by Department of Motor Vehicles

At the direction of the Committee on District Courts or at the request of a circuit court clerk, the Executive Secretary of the Supreme Court may enter into an agreement with the Commissioner of the Department of Motor Vehicles authorizing the Department of Motor Vehicles to receive, on behalf of a district or circuit court, payment of any delinquent fines, costs, forfeitures, and penalties, including any court-ordered restitution of a sum certain, imposed by a court for the violation of a state law or a local ordinance. However, in no case shall the Department of Motor Vehicles be authorized to establish an installment plan for any such payments or to receive partial payment of the full amount imposed by the court for the violation of a state law or a local ordinance.

For each such payment it receives, the Department of Motor Vehicles may impose and collect a processing fee, to be used to defray the costs of the transaction to the Department. Such transaction fee shall be $2, unless payment is made by credit card or debit card and the merchant's fees and other transaction costs imposed by the card issuer are charged to the Department of Motor Vehicles, in which case the processing fee shall be the greater of (i) $2 or (ii) an amount not to exceed four percent of the amount of the payment. The Department may also collect any processing fee charged by a private vendor operating under contract to distribute to the court payments received by the Department. All processing fees imposed and collected by the Department of Motor Vehicles under this section shall be in addition to the other fees specified in this chapter. All such processing fees collected by the Department of Motor Vehicles shall be paid into the state treasury as provided in § 46.2-206 and used to meet the expenses of the Department of Motor Vehicles. The service charge provided under § 46.2-212.1 shall not be added to the processing fee authorized under this section. Other fees specified in this chapter, including those payable pursuant to collections contracts made by attorneys for the Commonwealth, shall not be diminished or offset due to receipt of payments by the Department of Motor Vehicles.

Added by Acts 2015, c. 228.

§ 19.2-350. When sheriff not to receive fines

No sheriff or other law-enforcement officer shall receive any fine, penalty or costs imposed by a court not of record, except under process duly issued.

Acts 1975, c. 495.

§ 19.2-351. How fines disposed of; informer

Although a law may allow an informer or person prosecuting to have part of a fine or penalty, the whole thereof shall go to the Commonwealth, unless the name of such informer or prosecutor be endorsed on, or written at the foot of, the presentment at the time it is made, or of the indictment before it is presented to the grand jury, or of the information before it is filed, or of the writ issued in the action, or the process on the warrant, or the notice of the motion before service of such writ, process, or notice.

Acts 1975, c. 495.

§ 19.2-352. Officers to pay fines to clerks; default; forfeiture, etc.

Every sheriff or other officer receiving money under a writ of fieri facias or capias pro fine shall pay the same to the clerk of the court from which such process issued, on or before the return day of such process; and if such sheriff or other officer fail to pay the money, or fail to return such writ of fieri facias or capias pro fine, he shall, for every such failure, unless good cause be shown therefor, forfeit twenty dollars; and the clerk shall, within ten days from the return day of such process, report the failure to pay such money, or to return such process, to the attorney for the Commonwealth, who shall proceed at once against such officer in default to recover such money and the forfeiture aforesaid.

Acts 1975, c. 495.

§ 19.2-353. Certain fines paid into Literary Fund

The proceeds of all fines and penalties collected for offenses committed against the Commonwealth, and directed by Article VIII, Section 8 of the Constitution of Virginia to be set apart as a part of a perpetual and permanent literary fund, shall be paid and collected only in lawful money of the United States, and shall be paid into the state treasury to the credit of the Literary Fund, and shall be used for no other purpose whatsoever.

Acts 1975, c. 495.

§ 19.2-353.1. Fieri facias and proceedings thereon

Any writ of fieri facias issued under this chapter and the proceedings on the same shall conform to the writ of fieri facias and proceedings thereon under Article 19 (§ 8.01-196 et seq.) of Chapter 3 of Title 8.01.

Acts 1975, c. 495.

§ 19.2–353.2. Repealed by Acts 1988, cc. 770 and 852

§ 19.2–353.3. Acceptance of checks and credit or debit cards in lieu of money; additional fee

Notwithstanding the provisions of § 19.2–353, personal checks and credit or debit cards shall be accepted in lieu of money to collect and secure all fees, fines, restitution, forfeiture, penalties and costs collected for offenses tried in a district court, including motor vehicle violations, committed against the Commonwealth or against any county, city or town. Notwithstanding the provisions of § 19.2–353, personal checks shall be accepted in lieu of money to collect and secure all fees, fines, restitution, forfeiture, penalties and costs collected for offenses tried in a circuit court, including motor vehicle violations, committed against the Commonwealth or against any county, city or town. The clerk of any circuit court shall not be required to but may, in his discretion, accept credit or debit card payment in lieu of money to collect and secure all fees, including filing fees, fines, restitution, forfeitures, penalties, and costs collected. The Committee on District Courts shall devise a procedure for approving and accepting checks and credit or debit cards that shall be accepted by the district courts. Court personnel shall not be held to be guarantors of the payment made in such manner and shall not be personally liable for any sums uncollected. The clerk of the court, in addition to any fees, fines, restitution, forfeiture, penalties or costs, may add to such payment a sum not to exceed four percent of the amount paid for the transaction, or a flat fee not to exceed $2 per transaction, as a reasonable convenience fee for the acceptance of a credit or debit card.

If a check is returned unpaid by the financial institution on which it is drawn or notice is received from the credit or debit card issuer that payment will not be made, for any reason, the fees, fine, restitution, forfeiture, penalty or costs shall be treated as unpaid, and the court may pursue all available remedies to obtain payment. The clerk of the court to whom the dishonored check or credit or debit card was tendered may impose a fee of $50 or 10 percent of the value of the payment, whichever is greater, in addition to the fine and costs already imposed.

The clerk of court may refuse acceptance of checks or credit or debit cards of an individual if (i) he has been convicted of a violation of Chapter 6 (§ 18.2–168 et seq.) of Title 18.2 in which a check, credit or debit card, or credit or debit card information was used to commit the offense, (ii) he has previously tendered to the court a check which was not ultimately honored or a credit or debit card or credit or debit card information which did not ultimately result in payment by the credit or debit card issuer, (iii) authorization of payment is not given by the bank or credit or debit card issuer, (iv) the validity of the check or credit or debit card cannot be verified, or (v) the payee of the check is other than the court.

Acts 1979, c. 525; Acts 1988, c. 770; Acts 1988, c. 852; Acts 1990, c. 899; Acts 1994, c. 432; Acts 1994, c. 841; Acts 1994, c. 945; Acts 1997, c. 819; Acts 1998, c. 720; Acts 1998, c. 731; Acts 2001, c. 481; Acts 2001, c. 501. Amended by Acts 2009, c. 594; Acts 2012, c. 420; Acts 2012, c. 714.

§ 19.2–353.4. Repealed by Acts 1988, cc. 770 and 852

§ 19.2–353.5. Interest on fines and costs

No interest shall accrue on any fine or costs imposed in a criminal case or in a case involving a traffic infraction for a period of forty days from the date of the final judgment imposing such fine or costs or during any period the defendant is incarcerated as a result of that case. In no event shall interest accrue in such cases during any period in which a fine, costs, or both a fine and costs are being paid in deferred or installment payments pursuant to an order of the court. Whenever interest on any unpaid fine or costs accrues, it shall accrue at the judgment rate of interest set forth in § 6.2–302.

Acts 1987, c. 648; Acts 1988, c. 106; Acts 1988, c. 508; Acts 1995, c. 375; Acts 1995, c. 566; Acts 1996, c. 226.

ARTICLE 4

PAYMENT OF FINES AND COSTS ON INSTALLMENT BASIS, ETC.

§ 19.2–354. Authority of court to order payment of fine, costs, forfeitures, penalties or restitution in installments or upon other terms and conditions; community work in lieu of payment

A. Whenever (i) a defendant, convicted of a traffic infraction or a violation of any criminal law of the Commonwealth or of any political subdivision thereof, or found not innocent in the case of a juvenile, is sentenced to pay a fine, restitution, forfeiture or penalty and (ii) the defendant is unable to make payment of the fine, restitution, forfeiture, or penalty and costs within 30 days of sentencing, the court shall order the defendant to pay such fine, restitution, forfeiture or penalty and any costs which the defendant may be required to pay in deferred payments or installments. The court may authorize the clerk to establish and approve the conditions of all deferred or installment payment agreements, pursuant to guidelines established by the court, and such guidelines shall be reduced to writing as well as posted in the clerk's office and on the court's website, if a website is available. As a condition of every such agreement, a defendant who enters into an installment or deferred payment agreement shall promptly inform the court of any change of mailing address during the term of the agreement. If the defendant is unable to make payment within 30 days of sentencing, the court may assess a one-time fee not to exceed $10 to cover the costs of management of the defendant's account until such account is paid in full. This one-time fee shall not apply to cases in which costs are assessed pursuant to § 17.1–275.1, 17.1–275.2, 17.1–275.3, 17.1–275.4, 17.1–275.7, 17.1–275.8, or 17.1–275.9. Installment or deferred payment agreements shall include terms for payment if the defendant participates in a program as provided in subsection B or C. The court, if such sum or sums are not paid in full by the date ordered, shall proceed in accordance with § 19.2–358.

B. When a person sentenced to the Department of Corrections or a local correctional facility owes any fines, costs, forfeitures, restitution or penalties, he shall be required as a condition of participating in any work release, home/electronic incarceration or nonconsecutive days program as set forth in § 53.1–60, 53.1–131, 53.1–131.1, or 53.1–131.2 to either make full payment or make payments in accordance with his installment or deferred payment agreement while participating in such program. If, after the person has an installment or deferred payment agreement, the person fails to pay as ordered, his participation in the program may be terminated until all fines, costs, forfeitures, restitution and penalties are satisfied. The Director of the Department of Corrections and any sheriff or other administrative head of any local correctional facility shall withhold such ordered payments from any amounts due to such person. Distribution of the money collected shall be made in the following order of priority to:

1. Meet the obligation of any judicial or administrative order to provide support and such funds shall be disbursed according to the terms of such order;

2. Pay any fines, restitution or costs as ordered by the court;

3. Pay travel and other such expenses made necessary by his work release employment or participation in an education or rehabilitative program, including the sums specified in § 53.1–150; and

4. Defray the offender's keep.

The balance shall be credited to the offender's account or sent to his family in an amount the offender so chooses.

The Board of Corrections shall promulgate regulations governing the receipt of wages paid to persons participating in such programs, the withholding of payments and the disbursement of appropriate funds.

C. The court shall establish a program and may provide an option to any person upon whom a fine and costs have been imposed to discharge all or part of the fine or costs by earning credits for the performance of community service work before or after imprisonment. The program shall specify the rate at which credits are earned and provide for the manner of applying earned credits against the fine or costs. The court shall have such other authority as is reasonably necessary for or incidental to carrying out this program.

D. When the court has authorized deferred payment or installment payments, the clerk shall give notice to the defendant that upon his failure to pay as ordered he may be fined or imprisoned pursuant to § 19.2–358 and his privilege to operate a motor vehicle will be suspended pursuant to § 46.2–395.

E. The failure of the defendant to enter into a deferred payment or installment payment agreement with the court or the failure of the defendant to make payments as ordered by the agreement shall allow the Tax Commissioner to act in accordance with § 19.2–349 to collect all fines, costs, forfeitures and penalties.

Acts 1975, c. 495; Acts 1977, c. 585; Acts 1982, c. 244; Acts 1984, c. 32; Acts 1986, c. 230; Acts 1988, c. 770; Acts 1988, c. 852; Acts 1994, c. 841; Acts 1994, c. 945; Acts 1995, c. 380; Acts 1995, c. 441; Acts 1996, c. 273; Acts 1998, c. 831; Acts 1999, c. 9; Acts 2001, c. 414; Acts 2002, c. 831, eff. July 1, 2003. Amended by Acts 2009, c. 741; Acts 2012, c. 615; Acts 2015, c. 265.

§ 19.2–355. Petition of defendant

(a) In determining whether the defendant is unable to pay such fine forthwith, the court may require such defendant to file a petition, under oath, with the court, upon a form provided by the court, setting forth the financial condition of the defendant.

(b) Such form shall be a questionnaire, and shall include, but shall not be limited to: the name and residence of the defendant; his occupation, if any; his family status and the number of persons dependent upon him; his monthly income; whether or not his dependents are employed and, if so, their approximate monthly income; his banking accounts, if any; real estate owned by the defendant, or any interest he may have in real estate; income produced therefrom; any independent income accruing to the defendant; tangible and intangible personal property owned by the defendant, or in which he may have an interest; and a statement listing the approximate indebtedness of the defendant to other persons. Such form shall also include a payment plan of the defendant, if the court should exercise its discretion in permitting the payment of such fine and costs in installments or other conditions to be fixed by the court. At the end of such form there shall be printed in bold face type, in a distinctive color the following: THIS STATEMENT IS MADE UNDER OATH, ANY FALSE STATEMENT OF A MATERIAL FACT TO ANY QUESTION CONTAINED HEREIN SHALL CONSTITUTE PERJURY UNDER THE PROVISIONS OF § 18.2–434 OF THE CODE OF VIRGINIA. THE MAXIMUM PENALTY FOR PERJURY IS CONFINEMENT IN THE PENITENTIARY FOR A

PERIOD OF TEN YEARS. A copy of the petition shall be retained by the defendant.

(c) If the defendant is unable to read or write, the court, or the clerk, may assist the defendant in completing the petition and require him to affix his mark thereto. The consequences of the making of a false statement shall be explained to such defendant.

Acts 1975, c. 495.

§ 19.2–356. Payment of fine or costs as condition of probation or suspension of sentence

If a defendant is placed on probation, or imposition or execution of sentence is suspended, or both, the court may make payment of any fine, or costs, or fine and costs, either on a certain date or on an installment basis, a condition of probation or suspension of sentence.

Acts 1975, c. 495; Acts 1987, c. 238.

§ 19.2–357. Requiring that defendant be of peace and good behavior until fine and costs are paid

If a defendant is permitted to pay a fine or fine and costs on an installment basis, or under such other conditions as the court shall fix under the provisions of § 19.2–354, the court may require as a condition that the defendant be of peace and good behavior until the fine and costs are paid.

Acts 1975, c. 495.

§ 19.2–358. Procedure on default in deferred payment or installment payment of fine, costs, forfeiture, restitution or penalty

A. When an individual obligated to pay a fine, costs, forfeiture, restitution or penalty defaults in the payment or any installment payment, the court upon the motion of the Commonwealth in the case of a conviction of a violation of a state law, or attorney for a locality or for the Commonwealth in the event of a conviction of a violation of a local law or ordinance, or upon its own motion, may require him to show cause why he should not be confined in jail or fined for nonpayment. A show cause proceeding shall not be required prior to issuance of a capias if an order to appear on a date certain in the event of nonpayment was issued pursuant to subsection A of § 19.2–354 and the defendant failed to appear.

B. Following the order to show cause or following a capias issued for a defendant's failure to comply with a court order to appear issued pursuant to subsection A of § 19.2–354, unless the defendant shows that his default was not attributable to an intentional refusal to obey the sentence of the court, or not attributable to a failure on his part to make a good faith effort to obtain the necessary funds for payment, or unless the defendant shows that any failure to appear was not attributable to an intentional refusal to obey the order of the court, the court may order the defendant confined as for a contempt for a term not to exceed sixty days or impose a fine not to exceed $500. The court may provide in its order that payment or satisfaction of the amounts in default at any time will entitle the defendant to his release from such confinement or, after entering the order, may at any time reduce the sentence for good cause shown, including payment or satisfaction of such amounts.

C. If it appears that the default is excusable under the standards set forth in subsection B hereof, the court may enter an order allowing the defendant additional time for payment, reducing the amount due or of each installment, or remitting the unpaid portion in whole or in part.

D. Nothing in this section shall be deemed to alter or interfere with the collection of fines by any means authorized for the enforcement of money judgments rendered in favor of the Commonwealth or any locality within the Commonwealth.

Acts 1975, c. 495; Acts 1977, c. 223; Acts 1987, c. 238; Acts 1988, c. 770; Acts 1988, c. 852; Acts 1992, c. 485; Acts 1994, c. 546.

Article 5

Receipts for Fines

§ 19.2–359. Official receipts to be given for fines

Every officer collecting a fine, fine and costs or costs when no fine is imposed shall give an official receipt therefor to the person making the payment, and the clerk of the court shall use the official receipt in receipting to a court not of record for payments made to the clerk; and when the fine, fine and costs or costs are collected by execution, the clerk shall receipt to the officer making payment to him upon the official receipts.

Acts 1975, c. 495.

§ 19.2–360. Forms of receipts; distribution; record of disposition

The Executive Secretary of the Supreme Court shall prescribe and prepare forms of official receipts for fines and distribute them to the clerks of the circuit courts and to the clerks of the district courts for their use. A record of the disposition of each receipt form shall be maintained as prescribed by the Executive Secretary.

Acts 1975, c. 495; Acts 1977, c. 465.

§ 19.2-361. Misuse, misappropriation or willful failure to account for fines is embezzlement

If any officer misuse, misappropriate, or willfully fail to return or account for, a fine collected by him he shall be deemed guilty of embezzlement and shall be punished as for the embezzlement of public funds and the failure, without good cause, to produce or account for any receipt form received by him shall be prima facie evidence of his embezzlement of the amount represented thereby.

Acts 1975, c. 495.

ARTICLE 6

RELIEF FROM FINES AND PENALTIES

§ 19.2-362. Court not to remit fine or penalty, other than fine for contempt, except as provided in § 19.2-358

No court shall remit any fine or penalty, except for a contempt, which the court during the same term may remit either wholly or in part, and except as provided in § 19.2-358. This section shall not impair the judicial power of the court to set aside a verdict or judgment, or to grant a new trial.

Acts 1975, c. 495.

§ 19.2-363. Authority of Governor to grant relief from fines and penalties

The Governor shall have power, in his discretion, to remit, in whole or in part, fines and penalties, in all cases of felony or misdemeanor, after conviction, whether paid into the state treasury or not, except when judgment shall have been rendered against any person for contempt of court, for nonperformance of or disobedience to some order, decree or judgment of such court, or when the fine or penalty has been imposed by the State Corporation Commission, or when the prosecution has been carried on by the House of Delegates. The Governor may, in his discretion, remit, refund or release, in whole or in part, any forfeited recognizance or any judgment rendered thereon, provided, in the opinion of the Governor, the evidence accompanying such application warrants the granting of the relief asked for. But the provisions of the three following sections and § 19.2-368 shall be complied with as a condition precedent to such action by the Governor; provided, that when the party against whom the fine or penalty has been imposed and judgment rendered therefor has departed this life leaving a spouse or children surviving, the Governor may remit such fine or penalty upon the certificate of the judge of the circuit court of the county or city wherein such fine or penalty was imposed and judgment rendered, that to enforce the same against the estate, real or personal, of the decedent, would impose hardship upon the spouse or children. In any case when the Governor remits, in whole or in part, a fine or penalty, if the same has been paid into the state treasury, on the order of the Governor such fine or penalty or so much thereof as is remitted shall be paid by the State Treasurer, on the warrant of the Comptroller, out of the fund into which the fine or penalty was paid.

Acts 1975, c. 495.

§ 19.2-364. Petition for relief; in what court filed; notice to attorney for Commonwealth

Such person or his personal representative, as the case may be, shall file a petition in the clerk's office of the circuit court of the county or city wherein such fine or penalty was imposed, or such liability established, at least fifteen days before the term of the court at which the same is to be heard, and shall set forth the grounds upon which relief is asked. Ten days' notice thereof in writing shall be given to the attorney for the Commonwealth of the county or city.

Acts 1975, c. 495.

§ 19.2-365. Duties of attorney for Commonwealth upon filing of such petition

The attorney for the Commonwealth, at or before the hearing of such petition, shall file an answer to the same. He shall cause to be summoned such witnesses and shall introduce all such testimony as may be necessary and proper to protect the interest of the Commonwealth; and the petitioner may cause to be summoned such witnesses and shall introduce all such testimony as may be necessary and proper to protect his interest.

Acts 1975, c. 495.

§ 19.2-366. Duty of court in which petition filed; certificate and opinion

The court wherein such petition is filed shall hear all such testimony as may be offered, either by the petitioner or attorney for the Commonwealth, and after the evidence has been heard shall cause to be made out by the clerk of the court a certificate of the facts proved, and file with the same an opinion, in writing, as to the propriety of granting the relief prayed for.

Acts 1975, c. 495.

§ 19.2-367. Proceedings to be according to common law

All proceedings had before the court under the provisions of the three preceding sections shall be

according to the course of the common-law practice, except that no formal pleadings shall be necessary.
Acts 1975, c. 495.

§ 19.2–368. Course of proceeding when relief asked of the Governor

Whenever application shall be made to the Governor by or on behalf of any person desiring to be relieved, in whole or in part, of any such fine or penalty, the petition, answer, certificate of facts, and opinion of the court provided for in §§ 19.2–364, 19.2–365 and 19.2–366, duly authenticated by the clerk of the court, shall accompany the application, which shall be in writing. In all cases in which the Governor shall remit a fine or penalty he shall issue his order to the clerk of the court by which such fine or penalty was imposed; or if such fine or penalty was imposed by a court not of record, to the clerk of the circuit court of the county or city in which the judge of such court not of record holds office, and such court shall, at its next term, or immediately, if then in session, cause such order to be spread upon the law order book of its court; and the clerk of such court shall immediately, upon the receipt of such order, mark the judgment for such fine or penalty, and costs, or so much thereof as the person may have been relieved of, "remitted by the Governor," upon the Judgment Lien Docket of the court of the county or city in which it may have been recorded. The Governor shall communicate to the General Assembly at each session the particulars of every case of fine or penalty remitted, with his reason for remitting the same.
Acts 1975, c. 495; Acts 1977, c. 215.

CHAPTER 21.1

COMPENSATING VICTIMS OF CRIME

§ 19.2–368.1. Findings; legislative intent

The General Assembly finds that many innocent persons suffer personal physical injury or death as a result of criminal acts or in their efforts to prevent crime or apprehend persons committing or attempting to commit crimes. Such persons or their dependents may thereby suffer disability, incur financial hardships or become dependent upon public assistance. The General Assembly finds and determines that there is a need for governmental financial assistance for such victims of crime. Therefore, it is the intent of the General Assembly that aid, care and support be provided by the Commonwealth as a matter of moral responsibility for such victims of crime.
Acts 1976, c. 605.

§ 19.2–368.2. Definitions

For the purpose of this chapter:

"Claimant" means the person filing a claim pursuant to this chapter.

"Commission" means the Virginia Workers' Compensation Commission.

"Crime" means an act committed by any person in the Commonwealth of Virginia which would constitute a crime as defined by the Code of Virginia or at common law. However, no act involving the operation of a motor vehicle which results in injury shall constitute a crime for the purpose of this chapter unless the injuries (i) were intentionally inflicted through the use of such vehicle or (ii) resulted from a violation of § 18.2–51.4 or 18.2–266 or from a felony violation of § 46.2–894.

"Family," when used with reference to a person, means (i) any person related to such person within the third degree of consanguinity or affinity, (ii) any person residing in the same household with such person, or (iii) a spouse.

"Sexual abuse" means sexual abuse as defined in subdivision 6 of § 18.2–67.10 and acts constituting rape, sodomy, object sexual penetration or sexual battery as defined in Article 7 (§ 18.2–61 et seq.) of Chapter 4 of Title 18.2.

"Victim" means a person who suffers personal physical injury or death as a direct result of a crime including a person who is injured or killed as a result of foreign terrorism or who suffers personal emotional injury as a direct result of being the subject of a violent felony offense as defined in subsection C of § 17.1–805, or stalking as described in § 18.2–60.3, or attempted robbery or abduction.
Acts 1976, c. 605; Acts 1984, c. 619; Acts 1988, c. 748; Acts 1990, c. 620; Acts 1997, c. 528; Acts 1997, c. 691; Acts 1998, c. 484; Acts 1999, c. 286; Acts 2001, c. 855. Amended by Acts 2008, c. 590; Acts 2012, c. 38.

§ 19.2–368.3. Powers and duties of Commission

The Commission shall have the following powers and duties in the administration of the provisions of this chapter:

1. To adopt, promulgate, amend and rescind suitable rules and regulations to carry out the provisions and purposes of this chapter, to include a distinct policy (i) for the payment of physical evidence recovery kit examinations and (ii) to require each health care provider as defined in § 8.01–581.1 that provides services under this chapter to negotiate with the Commission or its designee to establish prospective agreements relating to rates for payment of claims for such services allowed under § 19.2–368.11:1, such rates to discharge the obligation to the provider in full except where the provider is an agency of the Commonwealth

and the claimant receives a third party recovery in addition to the payment from the Fund.

2. Notwithstanding the provisions of § 2.2–3706, to acquire from the attorneys for the Commonwealth, State Police, local police departments, sheriffs' departments, and the Chief Medical Examiner such investigative results, information and data as will enable the Commission to determine if, in fact, a crime was committed or attempted, and the extent, if any, to which the victim or claimant was responsible for his own injury. These data shall include prior adult arrest records and juvenile court disposition records of the offender. For such purposes and in accordance with § 16.1–305, the Commission may also acquire from the juvenile and domestic relations district courts a copy of the order of disposition relating to the crime. The use of any information received by the Commission pursuant to this subdivision shall be limited to carrying out the purposes set forth in this section, and this information shall be confidential and shall not be disseminated further. The agency from which the information is requested may submit original reports, portions thereof, summaries, or such other configurations of information as will comply with the requirements of this section.

3. To hear and determine all claims for awards filed with the Commission pursuant to this chapter, and to reinvestigate or reopen cases as the Commission deems necessary.

4. To require and direct medical examination of victims.

5. To hold hearings, administer oaths or affirmations, examine any person under oath or affirmation and to issue summonses requiring the attendance and giving of testimony of witnesses and require the production of any books, papers, documentary or other evidence. The powers provided in this subsection may be delegated by the Commission to any member or employee thereof.

6. To take or cause to be taken affidavits or depositions within or without the Commonwealth.

7. To render each year to the Governor and to the General Assembly a written report of its activities.

8. To accept from the government of the United States grants of federal moneys for disbursement under the provisions of this chapter.

Acts 1976, c. 605; Acts 1984, c. 619; Acts 1986, c. 422; Acts 1990, c. 551; Acts 1992, c. 547; Acts 1998, c. 484; Acts 1999, c. 703; Acts 1999, c. 726. Amended by Acts 2008, c. 203; Acts 2008, c. 251; Acts 2010, c. 780.

§ 19.2–368.3:1. Crime victims' ombudsman

A. The Commission shall employ a crime victims' ombudsman and adequate staff to facilitate the prompt review and resolution of crime victim compensation claims and to assure that crime victims' rights are safeguarded and protected during the claims process. The ombudsman shall report directly to the Commission.

B. The ombudsman shall ensure that all parties, including service providers and Criminal Injuries Compensation Fund personnel, are acting in the best interests of the crime victim. The ombudsman shall also provide assistance to crime victims in filling out the necessary forms for compensation and obtaining necessary documentation.

Acts 1998, c. 484.

§ 19.2–368.4. Persons eligible for awards

A. The following persons shall be eligible for awards pursuant to this chapter unless the award would directly and unjustly benefit the person who is criminally responsible:

1. A victim of a crime or the parent or guardian of a minor who is the victim of a crime.

2. A surviving spouse, parent, grandparent, sibling or child, including posthumous children, of a victim of a crime who died as a direct result of such crime.

3. Any person, except a law-enforcement officer engaged in the performance of his duties, who is injured or killed while trying to prevent a crime or an attempted crime from occurring in his presence, or trying to apprehend a person who had committed a crime in his presence or had, in fact, committed a felony.

4. A surviving spouse, parent, grandparent, sibling or child, including posthumous children, of any person who dies as a direct result of trying to prevent a crime or attempted crime from occurring in his presence, or trying to apprehend a person who had committed a crime in his presence or had, in fact, committed a felony.

5. Any other person legally dependent for his principal support upon a victim of crime who dies as a result of such crime, or legally dependent for his principal support upon any person who dies as a direct result of trying to prevent a crime or an attempted crime from occurring in his presence or trying to apprehend a person who had committed a crime in his presence or had, in fact, committed a felony.

B. A person who is criminally responsible for the crime upon which a claim is based, or an accomplice or accessory of such person, shall not be eligible to receive an award with respect to such claim.

C. A resident of Virginia who is the victim of a crime occurring outside Virginia and any other person as defined in subsection A who is injured as a result of a crime occurring outside Virginia shall be eligible for an award pursuant to this chapter if (i) the person would be eligible for benefits had the crime occurred in Virginia and (ii) the state, country or territory in which the crime occurred does not have a crime victims' compensation program deemed eligible pursuant to the provisions of the federal Victims of Crime Act and does not compensate nonresidents.

Acts 1976, c. 605; Acts 1977, c. 215; Acts 1978, c. 210; Acts 1981, c. 592; Acts 1984, c. 747; Acts 1985, c. 446; Acts 1986, c. 422; Acts 1988, c. 406; Acts 1990, c. 550; Acts 1996, c. 86; Acts 2002, c. 665.

§ 19.2–368.5. Filing of claims; deferral of proceedings; restitution

A. A claim may be filed by a person eligible to receive an award, as provided in § 19.2–368.4, or if such person is a minor, by his parent or guardian. In any case in which the person entitled to make a claim is incapacitated, the claim may be filed on his behalf by his guardian, conservator or such other individual authorized to administer his estate.

B. A claim shall be filed by the claimant not later than one year after the occurrence of the crime upon which such claim is based, or not later than one year after the death of the victim. However, (i) in cases involving claims made on behalf of a minor or a person who is incapacitated, the provisions of subsection A of § 8.01–229 shall apply to toll the one-year period; (ii) in cases involving claims made by a victim against profits of crime held in escrow pursuant to Chapter 21.2 (§ 19.2–368.19 et seq.) of this title, the claim shall be filed within five years of the date of the special order of escrow; and (iii) in cases involving claims of sexual abuse of a minor, the claim shall be filed within 10 years after the minor's eighteenth birthday. For good cause shown, the Commission may extend the time for filing for a crime committed on or after July 1, 2001.

In the case of a crime committed on or after July 1, 1977, and before July 1, 2001, for which a claim was not filed in a timely manner, the Commission may, for good cause shown, extend the time for filing if the attorney for the Commonwealth sends written notification to the Commission that the crime is being investigated as a result of newly discovered evidence. For any claim filed pursuant to this paragraph, the Commission shall only consider expenses that the claimant accrues after the date of written notification by the attorney for the Commonwealth.

C. Claims shall be filed in the office of the Commission in person, by mail, or by electronic means in accordance with standards approved by the Commission. The Commission shall accept for filing all claims submitted by persons eligible under subsection A of this section and alleging the jurisdictional requirements set forth in this chapter and meeting the requirements as to form in the rules and regulations of the Commission.

D. Upon filing of a claim pursuant to this chapter, the Commission shall promptly notify the attorney for the Commonwealth of the jurisdiction wherein the crime is alleged to have occurred. If, within 10 days after such notification, the attorney for the Commonwealth so notified advises the Commission that a criminal prosecution is pending upon the same alleged crime, the Commission shall defer all proceedings under this chapter until such time as such criminal prosecution has been concluded in the circuit court unless notification is received from the attorney for the Commonwealth that no objection is made to a continuation of the investigation and determination of the claim. When such criminal prosecution has been concluded in the circuit court the attorney for the Commonwealth shall promptly so notify the Commission. Nothing in this section shall be construed to mean that the Commission is to defer proceedings upon the filing of an appeal, nor shall this section be construed to limit the authority of the Commission to grant emergency awards as hereinafter provided. Upon awarding a claim pursuant to this chapter, the Commission shall promptly notify the attorney for the Commonwealth of the jurisdiction wherein the crime is alleged to have occurred. If a criminal prosecution occurs regarding the same alleged crime, the attorney for the Commonwealth shall request the court to order restitution. However, neither the lack of a restitution order, nor the failure of the attorney for the Commonwealth to request such an order, shall preclude the Fund from exercising its subrogation rights pursuant to § 19.2–368.15. Any such restitution shall be paid over to the Comptroller for deposit into the Criminal Injuries Compensation Fund to the extent of the amount of the award paid from the Fund.

Acts 1976, c. 605; Acts 1977, c. 215; Acts 1978, c. 122; Acts 1986, c. 457; Acts 1992, c. 681; Acts 1997, c. 801, eff. Jan. 1, 1998; Acts 1998, c. 484; Acts 2001, c. 363; Acts 2001, c. 855; Acts 2002, c. 665; Acts 2005, c. 683; Acts 2006, c. 414. Amended by Acts 2009, c. 381; Acts 2014, c. 251; Acts 2014, c. 665.

§ 19.2–368.5:1. Failure to perfect claim; denial

Notwithstanding the provisions of § 19.2–368.5, if, following the initial filing of a claim, a claimant fails to take such further steps to support or perfect the claim as may be required by the Commission within 180 days after written notice of such requirement is sent by the Commission to the claimant, the claimant shall be deemed in default. If the claimant is in default, the Commission shall notify the claimant that the claim is denied and the claimant shall be forever barred from reasserting it; however, the Commission may reopen the proceeding upon a showing by claimant that the failure to do the acts required by the Commission was beyond the control of the claimant.

Acts 1981, c. 302; Acts 1998, c. 484.

§ 19.2–368.5:2. Effect of filing a claim; stay of debt collection activities by health care providers

A. Whenever a person files a claim under this chapter, all health care providers, as defined in § 8.01–581.1 that have been given notice of a pending claim, shall refrain from all debt collection activities relating to medical treatment received by the person in connection with such claim until an award is made on the claim or until a claim is determined to be noncompensable pursuant to § 19.2–368.11:1. The statute of limitations for collection of such debt shall be tolled during the period in which the applicable health care provider is required to refrain from debt collection activities hereunder.

B. For the purpose of this section, "debt collection activities" means repeatedly calling or writing to the claimant and threatening either to turn the matter over to a debt collection agency or to an attorney for collection, enforcement or filing of other process. The term shall not include routine billing or inquiries about the status of the claim.

Acts 2005, c. 683.

§ 19.2–368.6. Assignment of claims; investigation; hearing; confidentiality of records; decisions

A. A claim, when accepted for filing, shall be properly investigated, and, if necessary, assigned by the chairman to a commissioner, deputy commissioner or other proper party for disposition. All claims arising from the death of an individual shall be considered together by the same person.

B. The person to whom such claim is assigned shall examine the papers filed in support of the claim and shall thereupon cause an investigation to be conducted into the validity of the claim. The investigation shall include, but not be limited to, an examination of police, court and official records and reports concerning the crime, and an examination of medical and hospital reports relating to the injury upon which the claim is based. Health care providers, as defined in § 8.01–581.1, shall provide medical and hospital reports relating to the diagnosis and treatment of the injury upon which the claim is based to the Commission, upon request.

C. Claims shall be investigated and determined, regardless of whether the alleged criminal has been apprehended or prosecuted for, or convicted of, any crime based upon the same incident, or has been acquitted, or found not guilty of the crime in question owing to a lack of criminal responsibility or other legal exemption.

D. There shall be a rebuttable presumption that the claimant did not contribute to and was not responsible for the infliction of his injury.

E. The person to whom a claim is assigned may decide the claim in favor of a claimant on the basis of the papers filed in support thereof and the report of the investigation of the claim. If he is unable to decide the claim, upon the basis of the said papers and report, he shall order a hearing. At the hearing any relevant evidence, not legally privileged, shall be admissible. The hearing of any claim involving a claimant or victim who is a juvenile shall be closed. All records, papers, and reports involving such claim shall be confidential except as to the amount of the award and nonidentifying information concerning the claimant or victim.

F. For purposes of this chapter, confidentiality provided for by law applicable to a claimant's or victim's juvenile court records shall not be applicable to the extent that the Commission shall have access to those records only for the purposes set forth in this chapter.

G. After examining the papers filed in support of the claim, and the report of investigation, and after a hearing, if any, a decision shall be made either granting an award pursuant to § 19.2–368.11:1 of this chapter or denying the claim.

H. The person making a decision shall issue a written report setting forth such decision and his reasons therefor, and shall notify the claimant and furnish him a copy of such report.

Acts 1976, c. 605; Acts 1977, c. 215; Acts 1994, c. 834; Acts 1997, c. 528; Acts 1998, c. 484.

§ 19.2–368.7. Review by Commission

A. The claimant may, within forty-five days from the date of the report, apply in writing to the Commission for review of the decision by the full Commission. The Commission may extend the time for filing under this section for good cause shown.

B. Upon receipt of an application pursuant to subsection A of this section, or upon its own motion, the Commission shall review the record and affirm or modify the decision of the person to whom the claim was assigned. The action of the Commission in affirming or modifying such decision shall be final. If the Commission receives no application pursuant to subsection A of this section, or takes no action upon its own motion, the decision of the person to whom the claim was assigned shall become the final decision of the Commission.

C. The Commission shall promptly notify the claimant and the Comptroller of the final decision of the Commission and furnish each with a copy of the report setting forth the decision.

Acts 1976, c. 605; Acts 1977, c. 215; Acts 1986, c. 457; Acts 1989, c. 335; Acts 2000, c. 455; Acts 2001, c. 363.

§ 19.2–368.8. Reinvestigation of decision; reconsideration of award; judicial review

A. The Commission, on its own motion, or upon request of the claimant, may reinvestigate or reopen a decision making or denying an award. Except for claims of sexual abuse that occurred while the victim was a minor, the Commission shall not reopen or reinvestigate a case after the expiration of two years from the date of submission of the original claim. Any claim involving the sexual abuse of a minor that has been denied before July 1, 2001, because it was not timely filed may, upon application filed with the Commission, be reconsidered provided the application for reconsideration is filed within ten years after the minor's eighteenth birthday.

B. The Commission shall reconsider, at least annually, every award upon which periodic payments are being made. An order or reconsideration of an award shall not require refund of amounts previously paid unless the award was obtained by fraud. The right of reconsideration does not affect the finality of a Commission decision for the purposes of judicial review.

C. Within thirty days of the date of the report containing the final decision of the Commission, the claimant may, if in his judgment the award is improper, appeal such decision to the Court of Appeals, as provided in § 65.2–706. The Attorney General may appear in such proceedings as counsel for the Commission.

Acts 1976, c. 605; Acts 1977, c. 215; Acts 1984, c. 703; Acts 2001, c. 855; Acts 2002, c. 665.

§ 19.2–368.9. Emergency awards

Notwithstanding any other provisions of this chapter, if it appears to the Commission, that (1) such claim is one with respect to which an award probably will be made, and (2) undue hardship will result to the claimant if immediate payment is not made, the Commission may make an emergency award to the claimant, pending a final decision in the case, provided that (i) the amount of such emergency award shall not exceed $3,000, (ii) the amount of such emergency award shall be deducted from any final award made to the claimant, and (iii) the excess of the amount of such emergency award over the final award, or the full amount of the emergency award if no final award is made, shall be repaid by the claimant to the Commission.

Acts 1976, c. 605; Acts 1977, c. 215; Acts 1985, c. 446. Amended by Acts 2014, c. 665.

§ 19.2–368.10. When awards to be made; reporting crime and cooperation with law enforcement

No award shall be made unless the Commission finds that:

1. A crime was committed;

2. Such crime directly resulted in an individual becoming a victim as defined in § 19.2–368.2, on whose behalf a claim is filed; and

3. Police records show that such crime was promptly reported to the proper authorities. In no case may an award be made where the police records show that such report was made more than 120 hours after the occurrence of such crime, unless the Commission, for good cause shown, finds the delay to have been justified. The provisions of this subdivision shall not apply to claims of sexual abuse that occurred while the victim was a minor.

The Commission, upon finding that any claimant or award recipient has not fully cooperated with all law-enforcement agencies, may deny, reduce or withdraw any award, as the case may be.

Acts 1976, c. 605; Acts 1977, c. 215; Acts 1985, c. 446; Acts 2001, c. 855; Acts 2005, c. 683.

§ 19.2–368.11. Repealed by Acts 1986, c. 457

§ 19.2–368.11:1. Amount of award

A. Compensation for Total Loss of Earnings: An award made pursuant to this chapter for total loss of earnings which results directly from incapacity incurred by a crime victim shall be payable during total incapacity to the victim or to such other eligible person, at a weekly compensation rate equal to 66 ⅔ percent of the victim's average weekly wages. The total amount of weekly compensation shall not exceed $600. The victim's average weekly wages shall be determined as provided in § 65.2–101.

B. Compensation for Partial Loss of Earnings: An award made pursuant to this chapter for partial loss of earnings which results directly from incapacity incurred by a crime victim shall be payable during incapacity at a weekly rate equal to 66 ⅔ percent of the difference between the victim's average weekly wages before the injury and the weekly wages which the victim is able to earn thereafter. The combined total of actual weekly earnings and compensation for partial loss of earnings shall not exceed $600 per week.

C. Compensation for Loss of Earnings of Parent of Minor Victim: The parent or guardian of a minor crime victim may receive compensation for loss of earnings, calculated as specified in subsections A and B, for time spent obtaining medical treatment for the child and for accompanying the child to, attending or participating in investigative, prosecutorial, judicial, adjudicatory and post-conviction proceedings.

D. Compensation for Dependents of a Victim Who Is Killed: If death results to a victim of crime entitled to benefits, dependents of the victim shall be entitled to compensation in accordance with the provisions of §§ 65.2–512 and 65.2–515 in an amount not to exceed the maximum aggregate payment or the maximum weekly compensation which would have been payable to the deceased victim under this section.

E. Compensation for Unreimbursed Medical Costs, Funeral Expenses, Services, etc.: Awards may also be made on claims or portions of claims based upon the claimant's actual expenses incurred as are determined by the Commission to be appropriate, for (i) unreimbursed medical expenses or indebtedness reasonably incurred for medical expenses; (ii) expenses reasonably incurred in obtaining ordinary and necessary services in lieu of those the victim would have performed, for the benefit of himself and his family, if he had not been a victim of crime; (iii) expenses directly related to funeral or burial, not to exceed $5,000; (iv) expenses attributable to pregnancy resulting from forcible rape; (v) mental health counseling for survivors as defined under subdivisions A 2 and A 4 of

§ 19.2–368.4, not to exceed $3,500 per claim; (vi) reasonable and necessary moving expenses, not to exceed $2,000, incurred by a victim or survivors as defined under subdivisions A 2 and A 4 of § 19.2–368.4; and (vii) any other reasonable and necessary expenses and indebtedness incurred as a direct result of the injury or death upon which such claim is based, not otherwise specifically provided for. Notwithstanding any other provision of law, a person who is not eligible for an award under subsection A of § 19.2–368.4 who pays expenses directly related to funeral or burial is eligible for reimbursement subject to the limitations of this section.

F. Notwithstanding the provisions of subdivision 3 of § 19.2–368.10, §§ 19.2–368.5, 19.2–368.5:1, 19.2–368.6, 19.2–368.7, 19.2–368.8, subsection G of this section, and § 19.2–368.16, the Criminal Injuries Compensation Fund shall pay for physical evidence recovery kit examinations conducted on victims of sexual assault. Any individual that submits to and completes a physical evidence recovery kit examination shall be considered to have met the reporting and cooperation requirements of this chapter. Funds paid for physical evidence recovery kit collection shall not be offset against the Fund's maximum allowable award as provided in subsection H. Payments may be subject to negotiated agreements with the provider. Healthcare providers that complete physical evidence recovery kit examinations may bill the Fund directly subject to the provisions of § 19.2–368.5:2. The Commission shall develop policies for a distinct payment process for physical evidence recovery kit examination expenses as required under subdivision 1 of § 19.2–368.3.

In order for the Fund to consider additional crime-related expenses, victims shall file with the Fund following the provisions of this chapter and Criminal Injuries Compensation Fund policy.

G. Any claim made pursuant to this chapter shall be reduced by the amount of any payments received or to be received as a result of the injury from or on behalf of the person who committed the crime or from any other public or private source, including an emergency award by the Commission pursuant to § 19.2–368.9.

H. To qualify for an award under this chapter, a claim must have a minimum value of $100, and payments for injury or death to a victim of crime, to the victim's dependents or to others entitled to payment for covered expenses, after being reduced as provided in subsection G, shall not exceed $25,000 in the aggregate.

Acts 1986, c. 457; Acts 1988, c. 748; Acts 1989, c. 335; Acts 1990, c. 552; Acts 1992, c. 687; Acts 1996, c. 86; Acts 1998, c. 484; Acts 2000, c. 847; Acts 2002, c. 665; Acts 2005, c. 683; Acts 2007, c. 381. Amended by Acts 2008, c. 203; Acts 2008, c. 251; Acts 2014, c. 665.

§ 19.2–368.12. Awards not subject to execution or attachment; apportionment; reductions

A. No award made pursuant to this chapter shall be subject to execution or attachment other than for expenses resulting from the injury which is the basis for the claim.

B. If there are two or more persons entitled to an award as a result of the death of a person which is the direct result of a crime, the award shall be apportioned among the claimants.

C. In determining the amount of an award, the Commission shall determine whether, because of his conduct, the victim of such crime contributed to the infliction of his injury, and the Commission shall reduce the amount of the award or reject the claim altogether, in accordance with such determination; provided, however, that the Commission may disregard for this purpose the responsibility of the victim for his own injury where the record shows that such responsibility was attributable to efforts by the victim to prevent a crime or an attempted crime from occurring in his presence, or to apprehend a person who had committed a crime in his presence or had, in fact, committed a felony.

Acts 1976, c. 605; Acts 1977, c. 215; Acts 1989, c. 335.

§ 19.2–368.13. Repealed by Acts 1984, c. 619

§ 19.2–368.14. Public record; exception

Except as provided in § 19.2–368.6 concerning juvenile claimants or victims, the record of any proceedings under this chapter shall be a public record; provided, however, that any record or report obtained by the Commission, the confidentiality of which is protected by any other law or regulation, shall remain confidential, subject to such law or regulation.

Acts 1976, c. 605; Acts 1994, c. 834.

§ 19.2–368.15. Subrogation of Commonwealth to claimant's right of action; lien in favor of the Commonwealth; disposition of funds collected

Acceptance of an award made pursuant to this chapter shall subrogate the Commonwealth, to the extent of such award, to any right or right of action accruing to the claimant or the victim to recover payments on account of losses resulting from the crime with respect to which the award is made. However, except as otherwise provided in subsection G of § 19.2–305.1, the Commonwealth shall not institute any proceedings in connection with its right of subrogation under this section within one year from the date of commission of the crime, unless any claimant or victim's right or action shall have been previously terminated. All funds collected by the Commonwealth in a proceeding instituted pursuant to this section shall be paid over to the Comptroller for deposit into the Criminal Injuries Compensation Fund.

Whenever any person receives an award from the Criminal Injuries Compensation Fund, the Commonwealth shall have a lien for the total amount paid by the Fund, or any portion thereof compromised pursuant to the authority granted under § 2.2–514, on the claim of such injured person or his personal representative against the person, firm, or corporation who is alleged to have caused such injuries. The Fund's lien shall be inferior to any lien for payment of reasonable attorney fees and costs, but shall be superior to all other liens created by § 8.01–66.2. The injured person may file a petition or motion to reduce the lien and apportion the recovery pursuant to § 8.01–66.9. The Fund's lien shall become effective when notice is provided pursuant to § 8.01–66.5 and liability shall attach pursuant to § 8.01–66.6.

Acts 1976, c. 605; Acts 1983, c. 227. Amended by Acts 2013, c. 273.

§ 19.2–368.16. Claims to be made under oath

All claims shall be made under oath. Any person who asserts a false claim under the provisions of this chapter shall be guilty of perjury and, in addition, shall be subject to prosecution under the provisions of Article 3 (§ 18.2–95 et seq.) of Chapter 5 of Title 18.2, and shall further forfeit any benefit received and shall reimburse and repay the Commonwealth for payments received or paid on his behalf pursuant to any of the provisions hereunder.

Acts 1976, c. 605.

§ 19.2–368.17. Public information program

The Commission shall establish and conduct a public information program to assure extensive and continuing publicity and public awareness of the provisions of this chapter. The public information program shall include brochures, posters and public service advertisements for television, radio and print media for dissemination to the public of information regarding the right to compensation for innocent victims of crime, including information on the right to file a claim, the scope of coverage, and the procedures to be utilized incident thereto.

Whenever a crime which directly resulted in personal physical injury to, or death of, an individual is reported within the time required by § 19.2–368.10, the law-enforcement agency to which the report is made shall make reasonable efforts, where practicable, to notify the victim or other potential claimant in writing on forms prepared by the Commission of his or her possible right to file a claim under this chapter. In any event, no liability or cause of action shall arise from the failure to so notify a victim of crime or other potential claimant.

Acts 1976, c. 605; Acts 1986, c. 457; Acts 1986, c. 472.

§ 19.2–368.18. Criminal Injuries Compensation Fund

A. There is hereby created a special fund to be administered by the Comptroller, known as the Criminal Injuries Compensation Fund.

B. Whenever the costs provided for in §§ 17.1–275.1, 17.1–275.2, 17.1–275.3, 17.1–275.4, 17.1–275.7, 17.1–275.8, or § 17.1–275.9 or subsections B or C of § 16.1–69.48:1 are assessed, a portion of the costs, as specified in those sections, shall be paid over to the Comptroller to be deposited into the Criminal Injuries Compensation Fund. Under no condition shall a political subdivision be held liable for the payment of this sum.

C. No claim shall be accepted under the provisions of this chapter when the crime that gave rise to such claim occurred prior to July 1, 1977.

D. Sums available in the Criminal Injuries Compensation Fund shall be used for the purpose of payment of the costs and expenses necessary for the administration of this chapter and for the payment of claims pursuant to this chapter.

E. All revenues deposited into the Criminal Injuries Compensation Fund, and appropriated for the purposes of this chapter, shall be immediately available for the payment of claims.

Acts 1976, c. 605; Acts 1978, c. 413; Acts 1980, c. 521; Acts 1985, c. 230; Acts 1988, c. 748; Acts 1993, c. 434; Acts 1996, c. 760; Acts 1996, c. 976; Acts 2002, c. 831, eff. July 1, 2003.

CHAPTER 21.2

PROFITS FROM CRIME

§ 19.2–368.19. Definitions

For purposes of this chapter, the following terms shall have the following meanings unless the context requires otherwise:

"Defendant" means any person who pleads guilty to, is convicted of, or is found not guilty by reason of insanity with respect to a felony resulting in physical injury to or death of another person.

"Division" means the Division of Crime Victims' Compensation.

"Interested party" means the victim, the defendant, and any transferee of proceeds due the defendant under a contract, the person with whom the defendant has contracted, the prosecuting attorney for the Commonwealth, and the Division of Crime Victims' Compensation.

"Victim" means a person who suffers personal, physical, mental, emotional, or pecuniary loss as a direct result of a crime and includes the spouse, parent, child, or sibling of the victim.

Acts 1990, c. 549; Acts 1992, c. 681.

§ 19.2–368.20. Special order of escrow

A. Any proceeds or profits received or to be received directly or indirectly, except property that may be forfeited to the Commonwealth pursuant to §§ 19.2–386.15 through 19.2–386.31, by a defendant or a transferee of that defendant from any source, as a direct or indirect result of his crime or sentence, or the notoriety which such crime or sentence has conferred upon him, shall be subject to a special order of escrow.

B. Income from the defendant's employment in a position unrelated to his crime or the notoriety which such crime has conferred upon him but obtained through the assistance of or rehabilitative training by correctional or mental health programs or personnel shall not be subject to a special order of escrow under this section, and nothing in this section shall be construed to prohibit or hinder the return of property belonging to victims of crime to its rightful owners. Any proceeds from a contract relating to a depiction or discussion of the defendant's crime in a movie, book, newspaper, magazine, radio or television production, or live entertainment or publication of any kind shall not be subject to a special order of escrow unless an integral part of the work is a depiction or discussion of the defendant's crime or an impression of the defendant's thoughts, opinions, or emotions regarding such crime.

C. Upon petition of the attorney for the Commonwealth filed at any time after conviction of such defendant or his acquittal by reason of insanity and after notice to the interested parties, a hearing upon the motion and a finding for the Commonwealth, for good cause shown, any circuit court in which the petition is filed shall order that such proceeds be subject to a special order of escrow.

1. The petition shall be filed in the circuit court of the jurisdiction where the defendant was convicted or acquitted by reason of insanity.

2. The petition shall set forth in general terms the causes for entry of the special order of escrow, and be signed by the attorney for the Commonwealth.

3. Upon the filing of the petition, the clerk shall forthwith issue a warrant directed to the sheriff or other law-enforcement officer of the county or city, commanding him to take the property into his possession and hold the same subject to further proceedings in the cause. If for any cause the warrant was not executed, other like warrants may be successively issued until one is executed. The officer serving the warrant shall take the property into his possession and forthwith return the warrant and report to the clerk in writing.

4. Any person concerned in interest may appear and make defense to the petition, which may be done by answer on oath.

5. When the case is ready for trial, such issues of fact as are made by the pleadings, or as the court may direct, the court shall determine the whole matter of law and fact.

6. Expenses and costs incurred in the proceedings shall be paid as the court, in its discretion, shall determine; except that no costs shall be adjudged against the Commonwealth.

An order issued under this section shall require that the defendant and the person with whom the defendant contracts pay to the Division any proceeds due the defendant under the contract and the proceeds shall be placed in a special escrow account for the victims of the defendant's crime.

Acts 1990, c. 549; Acts 1992, c. 681; Acts 2006, c. 414.

§ 19.2–368.21. Distribution

A. Proceeds paid to the Division under § 19.2–368.20 shall be retained in escrow in the Criminal Injuries Compensation Fund for five years after the date of the order, but during that five-year period may be levied upon to satisfy a money judgment rendered by a court or award of the Workers' Compensation Commission in favor of a victim of an offense for which the defendant has been convicted or acquitted by reason of insanity, or a legal representative of the victim.

B. If ordered by a circuit court in the interest of justice, after motion, notice to all interested parties, and opportunity for hearing, such escrow fund shall be used to:

1. First, satisfy court ordered restitution against a defendant and in favor of a victim;

2. Satisfy a money judgment rendered in the court hearing the matter, in favor of a victim of any offense for which the defendant has been convicted;

3. Pay for legal representation of the defendant in criminal proceedings, including the appeals process, to the extent the defendant's representation was paid for by the Commonwealth or an agency thereof. No more than 25% of the total proceeds in escrow may be used for legal representation; and

4. Pay any fines or costs assessed against the defendant by a court of the Commonwealth.

C. At the end of the five-year period, the remaining proceeds shall be paid into the Literary Fund. However, (i) if a civil action under this section is pending against the defendant, the proceeds shall be held in escrow until completion of the action or (ii) if the defendant has appealed his conviction and the appeals process is not final, the proceeds shall be held in escrow until the appeals process is final, and upon disposition of the charges favorable to the defendant, the Division shall immediately pay any money in the escrow account to the defendant.

Acts 1990, c. 549; Acts 1992, c. 681; Acts 2006, c. 414.

§ 19.2–368.22. Actions to defeat chapter void

Any action taken by any person convicted of a felony, whether by way of execution of a power of attorney, creation of corporate entities, or otherwise, to defeat the purpose of this chapter shall be void.

Acts 1990, c. 549; Acts 1992, c. 59.

CHAPTER 22

ENFORCEMENT OF FORFEITURES

§§ 19.2–369 to 19.2–386. Repealed by Acts 2012, cc. 283 and 756

CHAPTER 22.1

ENFORCEMENT OF FORFEITURES

§ 19.2–386.1. Commencing an action of forfeiture

Except as otherwise specifically provided by law, whenever any property is forfeited to the Commonwealth by reason of the violation of any law, or if any statute provides for the forfeiture of any property or money, or if any property or money be seized as forfeited for a violation of any of the provisions of this Code, the Commonwealth shall follow the procedures set forth in this chapter.

An action against any property subject to seizure under the provisions of Chapter 22.2 (§ 19.2–386.15 et seq.) shall be commenced by the filing of an information in the clerk's office of the circuit court. Any information shall be filed in the name of the Commonwealth by the attorney for the Commonwealth or may be filed by the Attorney General if so requested by the attorney for the Commonwealth. Venue for an action of forfeiture shall lie in the county or city where (i) the property is located, (ii) the property is seized, or (iii) an owner of the property could be prosecuted for the illegal conduct alleged to give rise to the forfeiture. Such information shall (a) name as parties defendant all owners and lienholders then known or of record and the trustees named in any deed of trust securing such lienholder, (b) specifically describe the property, (c) set forth in general terms the grounds for forfeiture of the named property, (d) pray that the same be condemned and sold or otherwise be disposed of according to law, and (e) ask that all persons concerned or interested be notified to appear and show cause why such property should not be forfeited. In all cases, an information shall be filed within three years of the date of actual discovery by the Commonwealth of the last act giving rise to the forfeiture or the action for forfeiture will be barred.

Acts 1989, c. 690; Acts 1991, c. 560; Acts 2002, c. 588; Acts 2002, c. 623; Acts 2004, c. 995. Amended by Acts 2012, c. 283; Acts 2012, c. 756.

§ 19.2–386.2. Seizure of named property

A. When any property subject to seizure under Chapter 22.2 (§ 19.2–386.15 et seq.) or other provision under the Code has not been seized at the time an information naming that property is filed, the clerk of the circuit court or a judge of the circuit court, upon motion of the attorney for the Commonwealth wherein the information is filed, shall issue a warrant to the sheriff or other state or local law-enforcement officer authorized to serve criminal process in the jurisdiction where the property is located, describing the property named in the complaint and authorizing its immediate seizure.

B. In all cases of seizure of real property, a notice of lis pendens shall be filed with the clerk of the circuit court of the county or city wherein the property is located and shall be indexed in the land records in the name or names of those persons whose interests appear to be affected thereby.

C. When any property is seized for the purposes of forfeiture under Chapter 22.2 (§ 19.2–386.15 et seq.) or other forfeiture provision under the Code, the agency seizing the property shall, as soon as practicable after the seizure, conduct an inventory of the seized property and shall, as soon as practicable, provide a copy of the inventory to the owner. An agency's failure to provide a copy of an inventory pursuant to this subsection shall not invalidate any forfeiture.

Acts 1989, c. 690; Acts 2002, c. 588; Acts 2002, c. 623; Acts 2004, c. 995; Acts 2006, c. 766. Amended by Acts 2012, c. 283; Acts 2012, c. 756; Acts 2015, c. 769.

§ 19.2–386.2:1. Notice to Commissioner of Department of Motor Vehicles; duties of Commissioner

If the property seized is a motor vehicle required by the motor vehicle laws of Virginia to be registered, the attorney for the Commonwealth shall forthwith notify the Commissioner of the Department of Motor Vehicles, by certified mail, of such seizure and the motor number of the vehicle so seized, and the Commissioner shall promptly certify to such attorney for the Commonwealth the name and address of the person in whose name such vehicle is registered, together with the name and address of any person holding a lien thereon, and the amount thereof. The Commissioner shall also forthwith notify such registered owner and lienor, in writing, of the reported seizure and the county or city wherein such seizure was made.

The certificate of the Commissioner, concerning such registration and lien, shall be received in evidence in any proceeding, either civil or criminal, under any provision of this chapter, in which such facts may be material to the issue involved.

Added by Acts 2012, c. 283; Acts 2012, c. 756.

§ 19.2–386.3. Notice of seizure for forfeiture and notice of motion for judgment

A. If an information has not been filed, then upon seizure of any property under Chapter 22.2 (§ 19.2–386.15 et seq.) or other provision under the Code, the agency seizing the property shall forthwith notify in writing the attorney for the Commonwealth in the county or city in which the seizure occurred, who shall, within 21 days of receipt of such notice, file a notice of seizure for forfeiture with the clerk of the circuit court. Such notice of seizure for forfeiture shall specifically describe the property seized, set forth in general terms the grounds for seizure, identify the date on which the seizure occurred, and identify all owners and lien holders then known or of record, including the treasurer of the locality in which the seized property is located. The clerk shall forthwith mail by first-class mail notice of seizure for forfeiture to the last known address of all identified owners and lien holders. When property has been seized under Chapter 22.2 (§ 19.2–386.15 et seq.) or other provision under the Code prior to filing an information, then an information against that property shall be filed within 90 days of the date of seizure or the property shall be released to the owner or lien holder.

B. Except as to corporations, all parties defendant shall be served, in accordance with § 8.01–296, with a copy of the information and a notice to appear prior to any motion for default judgment on the information. The notice shall contain a statement warning the party defendant that his interest in the property shall be subject to forfeiture to the Commonwealth unless within 30 days after service on him of the notice, or before the date set forth in the order of publication with respect to the notice, an answer under oath is filed in the proceeding setting forth (i) the nature of the defendant's claim, (ii) the exact right, title or character of the ownership or interest in the property and the evidence thereof, and (iii) the reason, cause, exemption or defense he may have against the forfeiture of his interest in the property, including but not limited to the exemptions set forth in § 19.2–386.8. Service upon corporations shall be made in accordance with § 8.01–299 or subdivision 1 or 2 of § 8.01–301; however, if such service cannot be thus made, it shall be made by publication in accordance with § 8.01–317.

Acts 1989, c. 690; Acts 1991, c. 560; Acts 1996, c. 673; Acts 2002, c. 588; Acts 2002, c. 623; Acts 2004, c. 995. Amended by Acts 2011, c. 83; Acts 2012, c. 283; Acts 2012, c. 756.

§ 19.2–386.4. Records and handling of seized property

Any agency seizing property under § 19.2–386.2, Chapter 22.2 (§ 19.2–386.15 et seq.), or other provision under the Code, pending forfeiture and final disposition, may do any of the following:

1. Place the property under constructive seizure by posting notice of seizure for forfeiture on the property or by filing notice of seizure for forfeiture in any appropriate public record relating to property;

2. Remove the property to a storage area for safekeeping or, if the property is a negotiable instrument or money, deposit it in an interest-bearing account;

3. Remove the property to a place designated by the circuit court in the county or city wherein the property was seized; or

4. Provide for another custodian or agency to take custody of the property and remove it to an appropriate location within or without the jurisdiction of the circuit court in the county or city wherein the property was seized or in which the complaint was filed.

A report regarding the type of property subject to forfeiture and its handling pursuant to this section and § 19.2–386.5, and the final disposition of the property shall be filed by the seizing agency with the Department of Criminal Justice Services in accordance with regulations promulgated by the Board.

Acts 1989, c. 690; Acts 1991, c. 560; Acts 2002, c. 588; Acts 2002, c. 623; Acts 2004, c. 995. Amended by Acts 2012, c. 283; Acts 2012, c. 756.

§ 19.2–386.5. Release of seized property

At any time prior to the filing of an information, the attorney for the Commonwealth in the county or city in which the property has been seized pursuant to Chapter 22.2 (§ 19.2–386.15 et seq.) or other provision under the Code may, in his discretion, upon the payment of costs incident to the custody of the seized property, return the seized property to an owner or lien holder, without requiring that the owner or lien holder post bond as provided in § 19.2–386.6, if he believes the property is properly exempt from forfeiture pursuant to § 19.2–386.8.

Acts 1989, c. 690; Acts 2002, c. 588; Acts 2002, c. 623; Acts 2004, c. 995. Amended by Acts 2012, c. 283; Acts 2012, c. 756.

§ 19.2–386.6. Bond to secure possession

If the owner or lien holder of the named property desires to obtain possession thereof before the hearing on the information filed against the same, such property shall be appraised by the clerk of the court where such information is filed. The clerk shall promptly cause the property to be appraised at its fair cash value, and forthwith make return thereof in writing to the court. Any appraisal fee shall be taxed as costs as provided in § 19.2–386.12. Upon the return of the appraisal, the owner or lien holder may give a bond payable to the Commonwealth, in a penalty of the amount equal to the appraised value of the property plus the court costs which may accrue, with security to be approved by the clerk and conditioned for the performance of the final judgment of the court, on the trial of the information. A further condition shall be that, if upon the hearing on the information, the judgment of the court is that such property, or any part thereof, or such interest and equity as the owner or lien holder may have therein, is forfeited, judgment may thereupon be entered against the obligors on such bond for the penalty thereof, without further or other proceedings against them thereon, to be discharged by the payment of the appraised value of the property so seized and forfeited, and costs. Upon such judgment, execution may issue, on which the clerk shall endorse, "No security to be taken." Upon giving of the bond, the property shall be delivered to the owner or lien holder.

Acts 1989, c. 690.

§ 19.2–386.7. Sale of property liable to deterioration

If the property seized is perishable or liable to deterioration, decay, or injury by being detained in custody pending the proceedings, the circuit court for the county or city in which the information is filed or in which the property is located, may order the same to be sold upon such notice as the court, in its discretion, may deem proper and hold the proceeds of sale pending the final disposition of such proceedings.

Acts 1989, c. 690.

§ 19.2–386.8. Exemptions

The following exemptions shall apply to property otherwise subject to forfeiture:

1. No conveyance used by any person as a lawfully certified common carrier in the transaction of business as a common carrier may be forfeited under the provisions of this section unless the owner of the conveyance was a consenting party or privy to the conduct giving rise to forfeiture or knew or had reason to know of it.

2. No conveyance may be forfeited under the provisions of this section for any conduct committed by a person other than the owner while the conveyance was unlawfully in the possession of a person other than the owner in violation of the criminal laws of this Commonwealth, or any other state, the District of Columbia, the United States or any territory thereof.

3. No owner's interest may be forfeited under this chapter if the court finds that:

a. He did not know and had no reason to know of the conduct giving rise to forfeiture;

b. He was a bona fide purchaser for value without notice;

c. The conduct giving rise to forfeiture occurred without his connivance or consent, express or implied; or

d. The conduct giving rise to forfeiture was committed by a tenant of a residential or commercial property owned by a landlord, and the landlord did not know or have reason to know of the tenant's conduct.

4. No lien holder's interest may be forfeited under this chapter if the court finds that:

a. The lien holder did not know of the conduct giving rise to forfeiture at the time the lien was granted;

b. The lien holder held a bona fide lien on the property subject to forfeiture and had perfected the same in the manner prescribed by law prior to seizure of the property; and

c. The conduct giving rise to forfeiture occurred without his connivance or consent, express or implied.

In the event the interest has been sold to a bona fide purchaser for value in order to avoid the provisions of this chapter, the Commonwealth shall have a right of action against the seller of the property for the proceeds of the sale.

Acts 1989, c. 690; Acts 2005, c. 883.

§ 19.2–386.9. Appearance by owner or lien holder

Any person claiming to be an owner or lien holder of the named property may appear at any time within thirty days after service on him of notice to appear or on or before the date certain set forth in any order of publication under § 8.01–317 or such longer time as the court in its discretion may allow to prevent a miscarriage of justice. Any person without actual or constructive notice of the forfeiture proceedings claiming to be an owner or lienholder may appear at any time before final judgment of the trial court and be made a party to the action. Such appearance shall be by answer, under oath, which shall clearly set forth (i) the nature of the defendant's claim; (ii) the exact right, title or character of the ownership or interest in the property and the evidence thereof; and (iii) the reason, cause, exemption or defense he may have against the forfeiture of the property.

Acts 1989, c. 690; Acts 1991, c. 560.

§ 19.2–386.10. Trial

A. A party defendant who fails to appear as provided in § 19.2–386.9 shall be in default. The forfeiture shall be deemed established as to the interest of any party in default upon entry of judgment as provided in § 19.2–386.11. Within twenty-one days after entry of judgment, any party defendant against whom judgment has been so entered may petition the Department of Criminal Justice Services for remission of his interest in the forfeited property. For good cause shown and upon proof that the party defendant's interest in the property is exempt under subdivision 2, 3 or 4 of § 19.2–386.8, the Department of Criminal Justice Services shall grant the petition and direct the state treasury to either (i) remit to the party defendant an amount not exceeding the party defendant's interest in the proceeds of sale of the forfeited property after deducting expenses incurred and payable pursuant to subsection B of § 19.2–386.12 or (ii) convey clear and absolute title to the forfeited property in extinguishment of such interest.

If any party defendant appears in accordance with § 19.2–386.9, the court shall proceed to trial of the case, unless trial by jury is demanded by the Commonwealth or any party defendant. At trial, the Commonwealth has the burden of proving that the property is subject to forfeiture under this chapter. Upon such a showing by the Commonwealth, the claimant has the burden of proving that the claimant's interest in the property is exempt under subdivision 2, 3 or 4 of § 19.2–386.8. The proof of all issues shall be by a preponderance of the evidence.

B. The information and trial thereon shall be independent of any criminal proceeding against any party or other person for violation of law. However, upon motion and for good cause shown, the court may stay a forfeiture proceeding that is related to any indictment or information.

Acts 1989, c. 690; Acts 1991, c. 560.

§ 19.2–386.11. Judgment of condemnation; destruction

A. If the forfeiture is established, the judgment shall be that the property be condemned as forfeited to the Commonwealth subject to any remission granted under subsection A of § 19.2–386.10 and further that the same be sold, unless (i) a sale thereof has been already made under § 19.2–386.7, (ii) the court determines that the property forfeited is of such minimal value that the sale would not be in the best interest of the Commonwealth or (iii) the court finds that the property may be subject to return to a participating agency. If the court finds that the property may be subject to return to an agency participating in the seizure in accordance with subsection C of § 19.2–386.14, the order shall provide for storage of the property until the determination to return it is made or, if return is not made, for sale of the property as provided in this section and § 19.2–386.12. If sale has been made, the judgment shall be against the proceeds of sale, subject to the rights of any lien holder whose interest is not forfeited. If the property condemned has been delivered to the claimant under § 19.2–386.6, further judgment shall be against the obligors in the bond for the penalty thereof, to be discharged by the payment of the appraised value of the property, upon which judgment, process of execution shall be awarded and the clerk shall endorse thereon, "No security is to be taken."

B. Forfeited cash and negotiable instruments shall be disposed of pursuant to the provisions of § 19.2–386.12.

C. Contraband, the sale or possession of which is unlawful, weapons and property not sold because of the minimal value thereof, may be ordered destroyed by the court.

Acts 1989, c. 690; Acts 1991, c. 560; Acts 1993, c. 484.

§ 19.2–386.12. Sale of forfeited property

A. Any sale of forfeited property shall be made for cash, after due advertisement. The sale shall be by public sale or other commercially feasible means authorized by the court in the order of forfeiture and shall vest in the purchaser a clear and absolute title to the property sold subject to the rights of any lien holder whose interest is not forfeited. The proceeds of sale, and whatever may be realized on any bond given under § 19.2–386.6, and any money forfeited shall be paid over to the state treasury into a special fund of the Department of Criminal Justice Services in accordance with § 19.2–386.14.

B. In all cases of forfeiture under this section, the actual expenses incident to the custody, preservation, and management of the seized property prior to forfeiture, the actual expenses incident to normal legal proceedings to perfect the Commonwealth's interest in the seized property through forfeiture, and the actual expenses incident to the sale thereof, including commissions, shall be taxed as costs and shall be paid to the person or persons who incurred these costs out of the net proceeds from the sale of such property. If there are no proceeds, the actual expenses shall be paid by the Commonwealth from the Criminal Fund. Actual expenses in excess of the available net proceeds shall be paid by the Commonwealth from the Criminal Fund. The party or parties in interest to any forfeiture proceeding commenced under this section shall be entitled to reasonable attorney's fees and costs if the forfeiture proceeding is terminated in favor of such party or parties. Such fees and costs shall be paid by the Commonwealth from the Criminal Fund.

The residue, if any, shall be paid and disbursed as provided in subsection A of § 19.2–386.10 and § 19.2–386.14 and regulations promulgated by the Criminal Justice Services Board.

Acts 1989, c. 690; Acts 1991, c. 560.

§ 19.2–386.13. Writ of error and supersedeas

For the purpose of review on a writ of error or supersedeas, a final judgment or order in the cause shall be deemed a final judgment or order within the meaning of subsection A of § 8.01–670.

Acts 1989, c. 690; Acts 2005, c. 681, eff. Jan. 1, 2006.

§ 19.2–386.14. Sharing of forfeited assets

A. All cash, negotiable instruments, and proceeds from a sale conducted pursuant to § 19.2–386.7 or 19.2–386.12, after deduction of expenses, fees, and costs as provided in § 19.2–386.12, shall, as soon after entry of the forfeiture as is practicable, be distributed in a manner consistent with this chapter and Article VIII, Section 8 of the Constitution of Virginia.

A1. All cash, negotiable instruments and proceeds from a sale conducted pursuant to § 19.2–386.7 or 19.2–386.12, after deduction of expenses, fees and costs as provided in § 19.2–386.12, shall, as soon after entry of the forfeiture as is practicable, be paid over to the state treasury into a special fund of the Department of Criminal Justice Services for distribution in accordance with this section. The forfeited property and proceeds, less 10 percent, shall be made available to federal, state and local agencies to promote law enforcement in accordance with this section and regulations adopted by the Criminal Justice Services Board to implement the asset-sharing program.

The 10 percent retained by the Department shall be held in a nonreverting fund, known as the Asset Sharing Administrative Fund. Administrative costs incurred by the Department to manage and operate the asset-sharing program shall be paid from the Fund. Any amounts remaining in the Fund after payment of these costs shall be used to promote state or local law-enforcement activities. Distributions from the Fund for these activities shall be based upon need and shall be made from time to time in accordance with regulations promulgated by the Board.

B. Any federal, state or local agency or office that directly participated in the investigation or other law-enforcement activity which led, directly or indirectly, to the seizure and forfeiture shall be eligible for, and may petition the Department for, return of the forfeited asset or an equitable share of the net proceeds, based upon the degree of participation in the law-enforcement effort resulting in the forfeiture, taking into account the total value of all property forfeited and the total law-enforcement effort with respect to the violation of law on which the forfeiture is based. Upon finding that the petitioning agency is eligible for distribution and that all participating agencies agree on the equitable share of each, the Department shall distribute each share directly to the appropriate treasury of the participating agency.

If all eligible participating agencies cannot agree on the equitable shares of the net proceeds, the shares shall be determined by the Criminal Justice Services Board in accordance with regulations which shall specify the criteria to be used by the Board in assessing the degree of participation in the law-enforcement effort resulting in the forfeiture.

C. After the order of forfeiture is entered concerning any motor vehicle, boat, aircraft, or other tangible personal property, any seizing agency may (i) petition the Department for return of the property that is not subject to a grant or pending petition for remission or (ii) request the circuit court to order the property destroyed. Where all the participating agencies agree upon the equitable distribution of the tangible personal property, the Department shall return the property to those agencies upon finding that (a) the agency meets the criteria for distribution as set forth in subsection B and (b) the agency has a clear and reasonable law-enforcement need for the forfeited property.

If all eligible participating agencies cannot agree on the distribution of the property, distribution shall be determined by the Criminal Justice Services Board as in subsection B, taking into consideration the clear and reasonable law-enforcement needs for the property which the agencies may have. In order to equitably distribute tangible personal property, the Criminal Justice Services Board may require the agency receiving the property to reimburse the Department in cash for the difference between the fair market value of the forfeited property and the agency's equitable share as determined by the Criminal Justice Services Board.

If a seizing agency has received property for its use pursuant to this section, when the agency disposes of the property (1) by sale, the proceeds shall be distributed as set forth in this section; or (2) by destruction pursuant to a court order, the agency shall do so in a manner consistent with this section.

D. All forfeited property, including its proceeds or cash equivalent, received by a participating state or local agency pursuant to this section shall be used to promote law enforcement but shall not be used to supplant existing programs or funds. The Board shall promulgate regulations establishing an audit procedure to ensure compliance with this section.

E. On or after July 1, 2012, but before July 1, 2014, local seizing agencies may contribute cash funds and proceeds from forfeited property to the Virginia Public Safety Foundation to support the construction of the Commonwealth Public Safety Memorial. Any funds contributed by seizing agencies shall be contributed only after an internal analysis to determine that such contributions will not negatively impact law-enforcement training or operations.

Acts 1991, c. 560. Amended by Acts 2012, c. 126; Acts 2012, c. 283; Acts 2012, c. 373; Acts 2012, c. 756.

CHAPTER 22.2

MISCELLANEOUS FORFEITURE PROVISIONS

§ 19.2–386.15. Seizure of property used in connection with or derived from terrorism

A. The following property shall be subject to lawful seizure by any law-enforcement officer charged with enforcing the provisions of Article 2.2 (§ 18.2–46.4 et seq.) of Chapter 4 of Title 18.2: all moneys or other property, real or personal, together with any interest or profits derived from the investment of such money and used in substantial connection with an act of terrorism as defined in § 18.2–46.4.

B. All seizures and forfeitures under this section shall be governed by the procedures contained in Chapter 22.1 (§ 19.2–386.1 et seq.) of this title.

Acts 2004, c. 995.

§ 19.2–386.16. Forfeiture of motor vehicles used in commission of certain crimes

A. Any vehicle knowingly used by the owner thereof or used by another with his knowledge of and during the commission of, or in an attempt to commit, a second or subsequent offense of § 18.2–346, 18.2–347, 18.2–348, 18.2–349, 18.2–355, 18.2–356 or 18.2–357 or of a similar ordinance of any county, city or town or knowingly used for the transportation of any stolen goods, chattels or other property, when the value of such stolen goods, chattels or other property is $200 or more, or any stolen property obtained as a result of a robbery, without regard to the value of the property, shall be forfeited to the Commonwealth. The vehicle shall be seized by any law-enforcement officer arresting the operator of such vehicle for the criminal offense, and delivered to the sheriff of the county or city in which the offense occurred. The officer shall take a receipt therefor.

B. Any vehicle knowingly used by the owner thereof or used by another with his knowledge of and during the commission of, or in an attempt to commit, a misdemeanor violation of subsection D of § 18.2–47 or a felony violation of (i) Article 3 (§ 18.2–47 et seq.) of Chapter 4 of Title 18.2 or (ii) § 18.2–357 where the prostitute is a minor, shall be forfeited to the Commonwealth. The vehicle shall be seized by any law-enforcement officer arresting the operator of such vehicle for the criminal offense, and delivered to the sheriff of the county or city in which the offense occurred. The officer shall take a receipt therefor.

C. Forfeiture of such vehicle shall be enforced as is provided in Chapter 22.1 (§ 19.2–386.1 et seq.).

Acts 2004, c. 995. Amended by Acts 2010, c. 710; Acts 2011, c. 818; Acts 2011, c. 852; Acts 2012, c. 283; Acts 2012, c. 756.

§ 19.2–386.17. Forfeitures for computer crimes

All moneys and other income, including all proceeds earned but not yet received by a defendant from a third party as a result of the defendant's violations of Article 7.1 (§ 18.2–152.1 et seq.) of Chapter 5 of Title 18.2, and all computer equipment, all computer software, and all personal property used in connection with any violation of such article known by the owner thereof to have been used in violation of such article, shall be subject to lawful seizure by a law-enforcement officer and forfeiture by the Commonwealth in accordance with the procedures set forth in Chapter 22.1 (§ 19.2–386.1 et seq.) of this title, applied mutatis mutandis.

Acts 2004, c. 995.

§ 19.2–386.18. Forfeiture of unlawful electronic communication devices

Any unlawful electronic communication device possessed, manufactured or sold in violation of §§ 18.2–190.2, 18.2–190.3 or § 18.2–190.4 may be seized and forfeited to the Commonwealth, and turned over to the circuit court in the city or county in which it was seized and such property shall be disposed of as provided by law.

Acts 2004, c. 995.

§ 19.2–386.19. Seizure of property used in connection with money laundering

The following property shall be subject to lawful seizure by any officer charged with enforcing the provisions of Article 9 (§ 18.2–246.1 et seq.) of Chapter 6 of Title 18.2: (i) all money, equipment, motor vehicles, and all other personal and real property of any kind or character used in substantial connection with the laundering of proceeds of some form of activity punishable as a felony under the laws of the Commonwealth, another state or territory of the United States, the District of Columbia, or the United States; (ii) all money or other property, real or personal, traceable to the proceeds of some form of activity punishable as a felony under the laws of the Commonwealth, another state or territory of the United States, the District of Columbia, or the United States, together with any interest or profits derived from the investment of such proceeds or other property; and (iii) all money, equipment, motor vehicles, and all other personal and real property of any kind or character used to or intended to be used to promote money laundering. Real property shall not be subject to seizure unless the minimum prescribed punishment for the violation is a term of imprisonment of not less than five years. All seizures and forfeitures under this section shall be governed by Chapter 22.1 (§ 19.2–386.1 et seq.), and the procedures specified therein shall apply, mutatis mutandis, to all forfeitures under Article 9 (§ 18.2–246.1 et seq.) of Chapter 6 of Title 18.2.

Acts 2004, c. 995. Amended by Acts 2012, c. 283; Acts 2012, c. 756.

§ 19.2–386.20. Forfeiture of cigarettes sold or attempted to be sold in an unlawful delivery sale

Any cigarettes sold or attempted to be sold in a delivery sale in violation of Article 10 (§ 18.2–246.6 et seq.) of Chapter 6 of Title 18.2 shall be forfeited to the Commonwealth and destroyed. All fixtures, equipment, materials and personal property used in substantial connection with a delivery sale or attempted delivery sale in a knowing and intentional violation of such article shall be subject to seizure and forfeiture according to the procedures contained in Chapter 22.1 (§ 19.2–386.1 et seq.) of this title, applied mutatis mutandis.

Acts 2004, c. 995.

§ 19.2–386.21. Forfeiture of counterfeit and contraband cigarettes

Section effective until July 1, 2018. See, also, section effective July 1, 2018.

Counterfeit cigarettes possessed in violation of § 18.2–246.14 and cigarettes possessed in violation of § 58.1–1017 or 58.1–1017.1 shall be subject to seizure, forfeiture, and destruction or court-ordered assignment for use by a law-enforcement undercover operation by the Virginia Alcoholic Beverage Control Board or any law-enforcement officer of the Commonwealth. However, any undercover operation that makes use of counterfeit cigarettes shall ensure that the counterfeit cigarettes remain under the control and command of law enforcement and shall not be distributed to a member of the general public who is not the subject of a criminal investigation. All fixtures, equipment, materials, and personal property used in substantial connection with (i) the sale or possession of counterfeit cigarettes in a knowing and intentional violation of Article 10 (§ 18.2–246.6 et seq.) of Chapter 6 of Title 18.2 or (ii) the sale or possession of cigarettes in a knowing and intentional violation of § 58.1–1017 or 58.1–1017.1 shall be subject to seizure and forfeiture according to the procedures contained in Chapter 22.1 (§ 19.2–386.1 et seq.), applied mutatis mutandis.

Acts 2004, c. 995. Amended by Acts 2013, c. 627; Acts 2014, c. 422; Acts 2014, c. 458.

§ 19.2–386.21. Forfeiture of counterfeit and contraband cigarettes

Section effective July 1, 2018. See, also, section effective until July 1, 2018.

Counterfeit cigarettes possessed in violation of § 18.2–246.14 and cigarettes possessed in violation of § 58.1–1017 or 58.1–1017.1 shall be subject to seizure, forfeiture, and destruction or court-ordered assignment for use by a law-enforcement undercover operation by the Virginia Alcoholic Beverage Control Authority or any law-enforcement officer of the Commonwealth. However, any undercover operation that makes use of counterfeit cigarettes shall ensure that the counterfeit cigarettes remain under the control and command of law enforcement and shall not be distributed to a member of the general public who is not the subject of a criminal investigation. All fixtures, equipment, materials, and personal property used in substantial connection with (i) the sale or possession of counterfeit cigarettes in a knowing and intentional violation of Article 10 (§ 18.2–246.6 et seq.) of Chapter 6 of Title 18.2 or (ii) the sale or possession of cigarettes in a knowing and intentional violation of § 58.1–1017 or 58.1–1017.1 shall be subject to seizure and forfeiture according to the procedures contained in Chapter 22.1 (§ 19.2–386.1 et seq.), applied mutatis mutandis.

Acts 2004, c. 995. Amended by Acts 2013, c. 627; Acts 2014, c. 422; Acts 2014, c. 458; Acts 2015, c. 38, eff. July 1, 2018; Acts 2015, c. 730, eff. July 1, 2018.

§ 19.2–386.22. Seizure of property used in connection with or derived from illegal drug transactions

A. The following property shall be subject to lawful seizure by any officer charged with enforcing the provisions of Article 1 (§ 18.2–247 et seq.) of Chapter 7 of Title 18.2: (i) all money, medical equipment, office equipment, laboratory equipment, motor vehicles, and all other personal and real property of any kind or character, used in substantial connection with (a) the illegal manufacture, sale or distribution of controlled substances or possession with intent to sell or distribute controlled substances in violation of § 18.2–248, (b) the sale or distribution of marijuana or possession with intent to distribute marijuana in violation of subdivisions (a) (2), (a) (3) and (c) of § 18.2–248.1, or (c) a drug-related offense in violation of § 18.2–474.1; (ii) everything of value furnished, or intended to be furnished, in exchange for a controlled substance in violation of § 18.2–248 or for marijuana in violation of § 18.2–248.1 or for a controlled substance or marijuana in violation of § 18.2–474.1; and (iii) all moneys or other property, real or personal, traceable to such an exchange, together with any interest or profits derived from the investment of such money or other property. Under the provisions of clause (i), real property shall not be subject to lawful seizure unless the minimum prescribed punishment for the violation is a term of not less than five years.

B. All seizures and forfeitures under this section shall be governed by the procedures contained in Chapter 22.1 (§ 19.2–386.1 et seq.).

Acts 2004, c. 995. Amended by Acts 2011, c. 384, eff. March 23, 2011; Acts 2011, c. 410, eff. March 23, 2011; Acts 2014, c. 674; Acts 2014, c. 719.

§ 19.2–386.23. Disposal of seized controlled substances, marijuana, and paraphernalia

A. All controlled substances, imitation controlled substances, marijuana, or paraphernalia, the lawful possession of which is not established or the title to which cannot be ascertained, which have come into the custody of a peace officer or have been seized in connection with violations of Chapter 7 (§ 18.2–247 et seq.) of Title 18.2, shall be forfeited and disposed of as follows:

1. Upon written application by (i) the Department of Forensic Science, (ii) the Department of State Police, or (iii) any police department or sheriff's office in a locality, the court may order the forfeiture of any such substance or paraphernalia to the Department of Forensic Science, the Department of State Police, or to such police department or sheriff's office for research and training purposes and for destruction pursuant to regulations of the United States Department of Justice Drug Enforcement Administration and of the Board of Pharmacy once these purposes have been fulfilled.

2. In the event no application is made under subdivision 1, the court shall order the destruction of all such substances or paraphernalia, which order shall state the existence and nature of the substance or paraphernalia, the quantity thereof, the location where seized, the person or persons from whom the substance or paraphernalia was seized, if known, and the manner whereby such item shall be destroyed. However, the court may order that paraphernalia identified in subdivision 5 of § 18.2–265.1 not be destroyed and that it be given to a person or entity that makes a showing to the court of sufficient need for the property and an ability to put the property to a lawful and publicly beneficial use. A return under oath, reporting the time, place and manner of destruction shall be made to the court by the officer to whom the order is directed. A copy of the order and affidavit shall be made a part of the record of any criminal prosecution in which the substance or paraphernalia was used as evidence and shall, thereafter, be prima facie evidence of its contents. In the event a law-enforcement agency recovers, seizes, finds, is given or otherwise comes into possession of any such substances or paraphernalia that are not evidence in a trial in the Commonwealth, the chief law-enforcement officer of the agency or his designee may, with the written consent of the appropriate attorney for the Commonwealth, order destruction of same; provided that a statement under oath, reporting a description of the substances and paraphernalia destroyed and the time, place and manner of destruction, is made to the chief law-enforcement officer by the officer to whom the order is directed.

B. No such substance or paraphernalia used or to be used in a criminal prosecution under Chapter 7 (§ 18.2–247 et seq.) of Title 18.2 shall be disposed of as provided by this section until all rights of appeal have been exhausted, except as provided in § 19.2–386.24.

C. The amount of any specific controlled substance, or imitation controlled substance, retained by any law-enforcement agency pursuant to a court order issued under this section shall not exceed five pounds, or 25 pounds in the case of marijuana. Any written application to the court for controlled substances, imitation controlled substances, or marijuana, shall certify that the amount requested shall not result in the requesting agency's exceeding the limits allowed by this subsection.

D. A law-enforcement agency that retains any controlled substance, imitation controlled substance, or marijuana, pursuant to a court order issued under this section shall (i) be required to conduct an inventory of such substance on a monthly basis, which shall include a description and weight of the substance, and (ii) destroy such substance pursuant to subdivision A 1 when no longer needed for research and training purposes. A written report outlining the details of the inventory shall be made to the chief law-enforcement officer of the agency within 10 days of the completion of the inventory, and the agency shall detail the substances that were used for research and training pursuant to a court order in the immediately preceding fiscal year. Destruction of such substance shall be certified to the court along with a statement prepared under oath, reporting a description of the substance destroyed, and the time, place, and manner of destruction.

Acts 2004, c. 995; Acts 2005, c. 868; Acts 2005, c. 881; Acts 2006, c. 107. Amended by Acts 2011, c. 384, eff. March 23, 2011; Acts 2011, c. 410, eff. March 23, 2011; Acts 2014, c. 99; Acts 2014, c. 254; Acts 2014, c. 674; Acts 2014, c. 686; Acts 2014, c. 719; Acts 2015, c. 429.

§ 19.2–386.24. Destruction of seized controlled substances or marijuana prior to trial

Where seizures of controlled substances or marijuana are made in excess of 10 pounds in connection with any prosecution or investigation under Chapter 7 (§ 18.2–247 et seq.) of Title 18.2, the appropriate law-enforcement agency may retain 10 pounds of the substance randomly selected from the seized substance for representative purposes as evidence and destroy the remainder of the seized substance.

Before any destruction is carried out under this section, the law-enforcement agency shall cause the material seized to be photographed with identification case numbers or other means of identification and shall prepare a report identifying the seized material. It shall also notify the accused, or other interested party, if known, or his attorney, at least five days in advance that the photography will take place and that they may be present. Prior to any destruction under this section, the law-enforcement agency shall also notify the accused or other interested party, if known, and his attorney at least seven days prior to the destruction of the time and place the destruction will occur. Any notice required under the provisions of this section shall be by first-class mail to the last known address of the person required to be notified. In addition to the substance retained for representative purposes as evidence, all photographs and records made under this section and properly identified shall be admissible in any court proceeding for any purposes for which the seized substance itself would have been admissible.

Acts 2004, c. 995. Amended by Acts 2011, c. 384, eff. March 23, 2011; Acts 2011, c. 410, eff. March 23, 2011; Acts 2014, c. 674; Acts 2014, c. 719.

§ 19.2–386.25. Judge may order law-enforcement agency to maintain custody of controlled substances, etc.

Upon request of the clerk of any court, a judge of the court may order a law-enforcement agency to take into its custody or to maintain custody of substantial quantities of any controlled substances, imitation controlled substances, chemicals, marijuana, or paraphernalia used or to be used in a criminal prosecution under Chapter 7 (§ 18.2–247 et seq.) of Title 18.2. The court in its order may make provision for ensuring integrity of these items until further order of the court.

Acts 2004, c. 995. Amended by Acts 2011, c. 384, eff. March 23, 2011; Acts 2011, c. 410, eff. March 23, 2011; Acts 2014, c. 674; Acts 2014, c. 719.

§ 19.2–386.26. Seizure and forfeiture of drug paraphernalia

All drug paraphernalia as defined in Article 1.1 (§ 18.2–247 et seq.) of Chapter 7 of Title 18.2 shall be forfeited to the Commonwealth and may be seized and disposed of in the same manner as provided in § 19.2–386.23, subject to the rights of an innocent lienor, to be recognized as under § 19.2–386.8.

Acts 2004, c. 995. Amended by Acts 2012, c. 283; Acts 2012, c. 756.

§ 19.2–386.27. Forfeiture of firearms carried in violation of Article 6.1 (§ 18.2–307.1 et seq.)

Any weapon used in the commission of a violation of Article 6.1 (§ 18.2–307.1 et seq.) of Chapter 7 of Title 18.2 shall be forfeited to the Commonwealth and may be seized by an officer as forfeited, and such as may be needed for police officers, conservators of the peace, and the Department of Forensic Science shall be devoted to that purpose, subject to any registration requirements of federal law, and the remainder shall be disposed of as provided in § 19.2–386.29.

Acts 2004, c. 995; Acts 2005, c. 868; Acts 2005, c. 881. Amended by Acts 2013, c. 746.

§ 19.2–386.28. Forfeiture of weapons that are concealed, possessed, transported or carried in violation of law

Any firearm, stun weapon as defined by § 18.2–308.1, or any weapon concealed, possessed, transported or carried in violation of § 18.2–283.1, 18.2–287.01, 18.2–287.4, 18.2–308.1:2, 18.2–308.1:3, 18.2–308.1:4, 18.2–308.2, 18.2–308.2:01, 18.2–308.2:1, 18.2–308.4, 18.2–308.5, 18.2–308.7, or 18.2–308.8 shall be forfeited to the Commonwealth and disposed of as provided in § 19.2–386.29.

Acts 2004, c. 995; Acts 2007, c. 519. Amended by Acts 2013, c. 746.

§ 19.2–386.29. Forfeiture of certain weapons used in commission of criminal offense

All pistols, shotguns, rifles, dirks, bowie knives, switchblade knives, ballistic knives, razors, slingshots, brass or metal knucks, blackjacks, stun weapons, and other weapons used by any person in the commission of a criminal offense, shall, upon conviction of such person, be forfeited to the Commonwealth by order of the court trying the case. The court shall dispose of such weapons as it deems proper by entry of an order of record. Such disposition may include the destruction of the weapons or, subject to any registration requirements of federal law, sale of the firearms to a licensed dealer in such firearms in accordance with the provisions of Chapter 22.1 (§ 19.2–386.1 et seq.) regarding sale of property forfeited to the Commonwealth.

The court may authorize the seizing law-enforcement agency to use the weapon for a period of time as specified in the order. When the seizing agency ceases to so use the weapon, it shall be disposed of as otherwise provided in this section.

However, upon petition to the court and notice to the attorney for the Commonwealth, the court, upon good cause shown, shall return any such weapon to its lawful owner after conclusion of all relevant proceedings if such owner (i) did not know and had no reason to know of the conduct giving rise to the forfeiture and (ii) is not otherwise prohibited by law from possessing the weapon. The owner shall acknowledge in a sworn affidavit to be filed with the record in the case or cases that he has retaken possession of the weapon involved.

Acts 2004, c. 995; Acts 2007, c. 519. Amended by Acts 2012, c. 283; Acts 2012, c. 756.

§ 19.2–386.30. Forfeiture of money, gambling devices, etc., seized from illegal gambling enterprise; innocent owners or lienors

All money, gambling devices, office equipment and other personal property used in connection with an illegal gambling enterprise or activity, and all money, stakes and things of value received or proposed to be received by a winner in any illegal gambling transaction, which are lawfully seized by any law-enforcement officer or which shall lawfully come into his custody, shall be forfeited to the Commonwealth in accordance with the procedures contained in Chapter 22.1 (§ 19.2–386.1 et seq.).

Acts 2004, c. 995. Amended by Acts 2012, c. 283; Acts 2012, c. 756.

§ 19.2–386.31. Seizure and forfeiture of property used in connection with the exploitation and solicitation of children

All audio and visual equipment, electronic equipment, devices and other personal property used in connection with the possession, production, distribution, publication, sale, possession with intent to distribute or making of child pornography that constitutes a violation of § 18.2–374.1 or 18.2–374.1:1, or in connection with the solicitation of a person less than 18 years of age that constitutes a violation of § 18.2–374.3 shall be subject to lawful seizure by a law-enforcement officer and shall be subject to forfeiture to the Commonwealth pursuant to Chapter 22.1 (§ 19.2–386.1 et seq.). The Commonwealth shall file an information and notice of seizure in accordance with the procedures in Chapter 22.1 (§ 19.2–386.1 et seq.); however, any forfeiture action shall be stayed until conviction of the person whose property is subject to forfeiture. Upon his conviction, the court may dispose of the issue of forfeiture or may continue the civil case allowing the defendant time to answer, at the court's discretion.

Acts 2004, c. 995; Acts 2007, c. 134; Acts 2007, c. 386. Amended by Acts 2012, c. 283; Acts 2012, c. 756.

§ 19.2–386.32. Seizure and forfeiture of property used in connection with the abduction of children

All moneys and other property, real and personal, owned by a person and used to further the abduction of a child in violation of § 18.2–47, 18.2–48, or 18.2–48.1 are subject to lawful seizure by a law-enforcement officer and are subject to forfeiture to the Commonwealth pursuant to Chapter 22.1 (§ 19.2–386.1 et seq.) by order of the court in which a conviction under § 18.2–47, 18.2–48, or 18.2–48.1 is obtained.

Added by Acts 2011, c. 818; Acts 2011, c. 852. Amended by Acts 2012, c. 283; Acts 2012, c. 756.

§ 19.2–386.33. Forfeiture of money, etc., derived from violation of §§ 2.2–3103 through 2.2–3112

In addition to any other fine or penalty provided by law, any money or other thing of value derived by an officer or employee from a violation of §§ 2.2–3103 through 2.2–3112 shall be forfeited, in accordance with the procedures contained in Chapter 22.1 (§ 19.2–386.1 et seq.). If the thing of value received by the officer or employee in violation of §§ 2.2–3103 through 2.2–3112 increases in value between the time of the violation and the time of discovery of the violation, the greater value shall determine the amount of forfeiture.

Added by Acts 2012, c. 283; Acts 2012, c: 756.

§ 19.2–386.34. Forfeiture of vehicle used in a felony violation of § 18.2–266

The vehicle solely owned and operated by the accused during the commission of a felony violation of § 18.2–266 shall be subject to seizure and forfeiture. After an arrest upon a felony violation of § 18.2–266, the vehicle may be forfeited to the Commonwealth pursuant to the procedures set forth in Chapter 22.1 (§ 19.2–386.1 et seq.). Any seizure shall be stayed until conviction and the exhaustion of all appeals at which time, if the information has been filed, the Commonwealth shall give notice of seizure to all appropriate parties pursuant to § 19.2–386.3.

An immediate family member of the owner of any motor vehicle for which an information has been filed under this section who was not the driver at the time of the violation may petition the court in which such information was filed for the release of the motor vehicle. If the immediate family member proves by a preponderance of the evidence that his immediate family has only one motor vehicle and will suffer a substantial hardship if that motor vehicle is seized and forfeited, the court, in its discretion, may release the vehicle.

In the event the vehicle was sold to a bona fide purchaser subsequent to the arrest but prior to seizure in order to avoid seizure and forfeiture, the Commonwealth shall have a right of action against the seller for the proceeds of the sale.

Added by Acts 2012, c. 283; Acts 2012, c. 756.

§ 19.2–386.35. Seizure of property used in connection with certain offenses

All money, equipment, motor vehicles, and other personal and real property of any kind or character together with any interest or profits derived from the investment of such proceeds or other property that (i) was used in connection with the commission of, or in an attempt to commit, a violation of subsection B of § 18.2–47, § 18.2–48 or 18.2–59, subsection B of § 18.2–346, or § 18.2–347, 18.2–348, 18.2–349, 18.2–355, 18.2–356, 18.2–357, 18.2–357.1, 40.1–29, 40.1–100.2, or 40.1–103; (ii) is traceable to the proceeds of some form of activity that violates subsection B of § 18.2–47, § 18.2–48 or 18.2–59, subsection B of § 18.2–346, or § 18.2–347, 18.2–348, 18.2–349, 18.2–355, 18.2–356, 18.2–357, 40.1–29, 40.1–100.2, or 40.1–103; or (iii) was used to or intended to be used to promote some form of activity that violates subsection B of § 18.2–47, § 18.2–48 or 18.2–59, subsection B of § 18.2–346, or § 18.2–347, 18.2–348, 18.2–349, 18.2–355, 18.2–356, 18.2–357, 40.1–29, 40.1–100.2, or 40.1–103 is subject to lawful seizure by a law-enforcement officer and subject to forfeiture to the Commonwealth pursuant to Chapter 22.1 (§ 19.2–386.1 et seq.). Any forfeiture action under this section shall be stayed until conviction, and property eligible for forfeiture pursuant to this section shall be forfeited only upon the entry of a final judgment of conviction for an offense listed in this section; if no such judgment is entered, all property seized pursuant to this section shall be released from seizure.

Real property shall not be subject to seizure unless the minimum prescribed punishment for the violation is a term of imprisonment of not less than five years.

All seizures and forfeitures under this section shall be governed by Chapter 22.1 (§ 19.2–386.1 et seq.), and the procedures specified therein shall apply, mutatis mutandis, to all forfeitures under this section.

Added by Acts 2014, c. 658. Amended by Acts 2015, c. 690; Acts 2015, c. 691.

CHAPTER 23

CENTRAL CRIMINAL RECORDS EXCHANGE

§ 19.2–387. Exchange to operate as a division of Department of State Police; authority of Superintendent of State Police

A. The Central Criminal Records Exchange shall operate as a separate division within the Department of State Police and shall be the sole criminal record-keeping agency of the Commonwealth, except for (i) the Department of Juvenile Justice pursuant to Chapter 10 (§ 16.1–222 et seq.) of Title 16.1, (ii) the Department of Motor Vehicles, (iii) for purposes of the DNA data bank, the Department of Forensic Science and (iv) for the purpose of making parole determinations pursuant to subdivisions 1, 2, 3 and 5 of § 53.1–136, the Virginia Parole Board.

B. The Superintendent of State Police is hereby authorized to employ such personnel, establish such offices, and acquire such equipment as shall be necessary to carry out the purposes of this chapter and is also authorized to enter into agreements with other state agencies for services to be performed for it by employees of such other agencies.

Acts 1975, c. 495; Acts 1988, c. 541; Acts 1990, c. 669; Acts 1993, c. 313; Acts 2001, c. 203; Acts 2001, c. 215; Acts 2003, c. 431; Acts 2005, c. 868; Acts 2005, c. 881.

§ 19.2–387.1. Protective Order Registry; maintenance; access

A. The Department of State Police shall keep and maintain a computerized Protective Order Registry. The purpose of the Registry shall be to assist the efforts of law-enforcement agencies to protect their communities and their citizens. The Department of State Police shall make Registry information available, upon request, to criminal justice agencies, including local law-enforcement agencies, through the Virginia Criminal Information Network (VCIN). Registry information provided under this section shall be used only for the purposes of the administration of criminal justice.

B. No liability shall be imposed upon any law-enforcement official who disseminates information or fails to disseminate information in good faith compliance with the requirements of this section, but this provision shall not be construed to grant immunity for gross negligence or willful misconduct.

Acts 2002, c. 810; Acts 2002, c. 818.

§ 19.2–388. Duties and authority of Exchange

A. It shall be the duty of the Central Criminal Records Exchange to receive, classify and file criminal history record information as defined in § 9.1–101 and other records required to be reported to it by §§ 16.1–299 and 19.2–390. The Exchange is authorized to prepare and furnish to all state and local law-enforcement officials and agencies; to clerks of circuit courts, general district courts, and juvenile and domestic relations district courts; and to corrections and penal officials, forms which shall be used for the making of such reports.

B. Juvenile records received pursuant to § 16.1–299 shall be maintained separately from adult records.

Acts 1975, c. 495; Acts 1976, c. 771; Acts 1982, c. 33; Acts 1993, c. 468; Acts 1993, c. 926; Acts 1996, c. 755; Acts 1996, c. 914.

§ 19.2–389. Dissemination of criminal history record information

A. Criminal history record information shall be disseminated, whether directly or through an intermediary, only to:

1. Authorized officers or employees of criminal justice agencies, as defined by § 9.1–101, for purposes of the administration of criminal justice and the screening of an employment application or review of employment by a criminal justice agency with respect to its own employees or applicants, and dissemination to the Virginia Parole Board, pursuant to this subdivision, of such information on all state-responsible inmates for the purpose of making parole determinations pursuant to subdivisions 1, 2, 3, and 5 of § 53.1–136 shall include collective dissemination by electronic means every 30 days. For purposes of this subdivision, criminal history record information includes information sent to the Central Criminal Records Exchange pursuant to §§ 37.2–819 and 64.2–2014 when disseminated to any full-time or part-time employee of the State Police, a police department or sheriff's office that is a part of or administered by the Commonwealth or any political subdivision thereof, and who is responsible for the prevention and detection of crime and the enforcement of the penal, traffic or highway laws of the Commonwealth for the purposes of the administration of criminal justice;

2. Such other individuals and agencies that require criminal history record information to implement a state or federal statute or executive order of the

President of the United States or Governor that expressly refers to criminal conduct and contains requirements or exclusions expressly based upon such conduct, except that information concerning the arrest of an individual may not be disseminated to a noncriminal justice agency or individual if an interval of one year has elapsed from the date of the arrest and no disposition of the charge has been recorded and no active prosecution of the charge is pending;

3. Individuals and agencies pursuant to a specific agreement with a criminal justice agency to provide services required for the administration of criminal justice pursuant to that agreement which shall specifically authorize access to data, limit the use of data to purposes for which given, and ensure the security and confidentiality of the data;

4. Individuals and agencies for the express purpose of research, evaluative, or statistical activities pursuant to an agreement with a criminal justice agency that shall specifically authorize access to data, limit the use of data to research, evaluative, or statistical purposes, and ensure the confidentiality and security of the data;

5. Agencies of state or federal government that are authorized by state or federal statute or executive order of the President of the United States or Governor to conduct investigations determining employment suitability or eligibility for security clearances allowing access to classified information;

6. Individuals and agencies where authorized by court order or court rule;

7. Agencies of any political subdivision of the Commonwealth, public transportation companies owned, operated or controlled by any political subdivision, and any public service corporation that operates a public transit system owned by a local government for the conduct of investigations of applicants for employment, permit, or license whenever, in the interest of public welfare or safety, it is necessary to determine under a duly enacted ordinance if the past criminal conduct of a person with a conviction record would be compatible with the nature of the employment, permit, or license under consideration;

7a. Commissions created pursuant to the Transportation District Act of 1964 (§ 33.2-1900 et seq.) of Title 33.2 and their contractors, for the conduct of investigations of individuals who have been offered a position of employment whenever, in the interest of public welfare or safety and as authorized in the Transportation District Act of 1964, it is necessary to determine if the past criminal conduct of a person with a conviction record would be compatible with the nature of the employment under consideration;

8. Public or private agencies when authorized or required by federal or state law or interstate compact to investigate (i) applicants for foster or adoptive parenthood or (ii) any individual, and the adult members of that individual's household, with whom the agency is considering placing a child or from whom the agency is considering removing a child due to abuse or neglect, on an emergency, temporary, or permanent basis pursuant to §§ 63.2-901.1 and 63.2-1505, subject to the restriction that the data shall not be further disseminated to any party other than a federal or state authority or court as may be required to comply with an express requirement of law;

9. To the extent permitted by federal law or regulation, public service companies as defined in § 56-1, for the conduct of investigations of applicants for employment when such employment involves personal contact with the public or when past criminal conduct of an applicant would be incompatible with the nature of the employment under consideration;

10. The appropriate authority for purposes of granting citizenship and for purposes of international travel, including, but not limited to, issuing visas and passports;

11. A person requesting a copy of his own criminal history record information as defined in § 9.1-101 at his cost, except that criminal history record information shall be supplied at no charge to a person who has applied to be a volunteer with (i) a Virginia affiliate of Big Brothers/Big Sisters of America; (ii) a volunteer fire company; (iii) the Volunteer Emergency Families for Children; (iv) any affiliate of Prevent Child Abuse, Virginia; (v) any Virginia affiliate of Compeer; or (vi) any board member or any individual who has been offered membership on the board of a Crime Stoppers, Crime Solvers or Crime Line program as defined in § 15.2-1713.1;

12. Administrators and board presidents of and applicants for licensure or registration as a child welfare agency as defined in § 63.2-100 for dissemination to the Commissioner of Social Services' representative pursuant to § 63.2-1702 for the conduct of investigations with respect to employees of and volunteers at such facilities, caretakers, and other adults living in family day homes or homes approved by family day systems, and foster and adoptive parent applicants of private child-placing agencies, pursuant to §§ 63.2-1719, 63.2-1720, 63.2-1720.1, 63.2-1721, and 63.2-1721.1, subject to the restriction that the data shall not be further disseminated by the facility or agency to any party other than the data subject, the Commissioner of Social Services' representative or a federal or state authority or court as may be required to comply with an express requirement of law for such further dissemination;

13. The school boards of the Commonwealth for the purpose of screening individuals who are offered or who accept public school employment and those current school board employees for whom a report of arrest has been made pursuant to § 19.2-83.1;

14. The Virginia Lottery for the conduct of investigations as set forth in the Virginia Lottery Law (§ 58.1-4000 et seq.), and the Department of Agriculture and Consumer Services for the conduct of investi-

gations as set forth in Article 1.1:1 (§ 18.2–340.15 et seq.) of Chapter 8 of Title 18.2;

15. Licensed nursing homes, hospitals and home care organizations for the conduct of investigations of applicants for compensated employment in licensed nursing homes pursuant to § 32.1–126.01, hospital pharmacies pursuant to § 32.1–126.02, and home care organizations pursuant to § 32.1–162.9:1, subject to the limitations set out in subsection E;

16. Licensed assisted living facilities and licensed adult day care centers for the conduct of investigations of applicants for compensated employment in licensed assisted living facilities and licensed adult day care centers pursuant to § 63.2–1720, subject to the limitations set out in subsection F;

Subd. A.17 effective until July 1, 2018

17. The Alcoholic Beverage Control Board for the conduct of investigations as set forth in § 4.1–103.1;

Subd. A.17 effective July 1, 2018

17. The Virginia Alcoholic Beverage Control Authority for the conduct of investigations as set forth in § 4.1–103.1;

18. The State Board of Elections and authorized officers and employees thereof and general registrars appointed pursuant to § 24.2–110 in the course of conducting necessary investigations with respect to voter registration, limited to any record of felony convictions;

19. The Commissioner of Behavioral Health and Developmental Services for those individuals who are committed to the custody of the Commissioner pursuant to §§ 19.2–169.2, 19.2–169.6, 19.2–182.2, 19.2–182.3, 19.2–182.8, and 19.2–182.9 for the purpose of placement, evaluation, and treatment planning;

20. Any alcohol safety action program certified by the Commission on the Virginia Alcohol Safety Action Program for (i) assessments of habitual offenders under § 46.2–360, (ii) interventions with first offenders under § 18.2–251, or (iii) services to offenders under § 18.2–51.4, 18.2–266, or 18.2–266.1;

21. Residential facilities for juveniles regulated or operated by the Department of Social Services, the Department of Education, or the Department of Behavioral Health and Developmental Services for the purpose of determining applicants' fitness for employment or for providing volunteer or contractual services;

22. The Department of Behavioral Health and Developmental Services and facilities operated by the Department for the purpose of determining an individual's fitness for employment pursuant to departmental instructions;

23. Pursuant to § 22.1–296.3, the governing boards or administrators of private or religious elementary or secondary schools which are accredited by a statewide accrediting organization recognized, prior to January 1, 1996, by the State Board of Education or a private organization coordinating such records information on behalf of such governing boards or administrators pursuant to a written agreement with the Department of State Police;

24. Public and nonprofit private colleges and universities for the purpose of screening individuals who are offered or accept employment;

25. Members of a threat assessment team established by a public institution of higher education pursuant to § 23–9.2:10 or by a private nonprofit institution of higher education, for the purpose of assessing or intervening with an individual whose behavior may present a threat to safety; however, no member of a threat assessment team shall redisclose any criminal history record information obtained pursuant to this section or otherwise use any record of an individual beyond the purpose that such disclosure was made to the threat assessment team;

26. Executive directors of community services boards or the personnel director serving the community services board for the purpose of determining an individual's fitness for employment pursuant to §§ 37.2–506 and 37.2–607;

27. Executive directors of behavioral health authorities as defined in § 37.2–600 for the purpose of determining an individual's fitness for employment pursuant to §§ 37.2–506 and 37.2–607;

28. The Commissioner of Social Services for the purpose of locating persons who owe child support or who are alleged in a pending paternity proceeding to be a putative father, provided that only the name, address, demographics and social security number of the data subject shall be released;

29. Authorized officers or directors of agencies licensed pursuant to Article 2 (§ 37.2–403 et seq.) of Chapter 4 of Title 37.2 by the Department of Behavioral Health and Developmental Services for the purpose of determining if any applicant who accepts employment in any direct care position has been convicted of a crime that affects his fitness to have responsibility for the safety and well-being of individuals with mental illness, intellectual disability, or substance abuse pursuant to §§ 37.2–416, 37.2–506, and 37.2–607;

30. The Commissioner of the Department of Motor Vehicles, for the purpose of evaluating applicants for and holders of a motor carrier certificate or license subject to the provisions of Chapters 20 (§ 46.2–2000 et seq.) and 21 (§ 46.2–2100 et seq.) of Title 46.2;

31. The chairmen of the Committees for Courts of Justice of the Senate or the House of Delegates for the purpose of determining if any person being considered for election to any judgeship has been convicted of a crime;

32. Heads of state agencies in which positions have been identified as sensitive for the purpose of determining an individual's fitness for employment in positions designated as sensitive under Department of

Human Resource Management policies developed pursuant to § 2.2–1201.1. Dissemination of criminal history record information to the agencies shall be limited to those positions generally described as directly responsible for the health, safety and welfare of the general populace or protection of critical infrastructures;

33. The Office of the Attorney General, for all criminal justice activities otherwise permitted under subdivision A 1 and for purposes of performing duties required by the Civil Commitment of Sexually Violent Predators Act (§ 37.2–900 et seq.);

34. Shipyards, to the extent permitted by federal law or regulation, engaged in the design, construction, overhaul, or repair of nuclear vessels for the United States Navy, including their subsidiary companies, for the conduct of investigations of applications for employment or for access to facilities, by contractors, leased laborers, and other visitors;

35. Any employer of individuals whose employment requires that they enter the homes of others, for the purpose of screening individuals who apply for, are offered, or have accepted such employment;

36. Public agencies when and as required by federal or state law to investigate (i) applicants as providers of adult foster care and home-based services or (ii) any individual with whom the agency is considering placing an adult on an emergency, temporary, or permanent basis pursuant to § 63.2–1601.1, subject to the restriction that the data shall not be further disseminated by the agency to any party other than a federal or state authority or court as may be required to comply with an express requirement of law for such further dissemination, subject to limitations set out in subsection G;

37. The Department of Medical Assistance Services, or its designee, for the purpose of screening individuals who, through contracts, subcontracts, or direct employment, volunteer, apply for, are offered, or have accepted a position related to the provision of transportation services to enrollees in the Medicaid Program or the Family Access to Medical Insurance Security (FAMIS) Program, or any other program administered by the Department of Medical Assistance Services;

38. The State Corporation Commission for the purpose of investigating individuals who are current or proposed members, senior officers, directors, and principals of an applicant or person licensed under Chapter 16 (§ 6.2–1600 et seq.) or Chapter 19 (§ 6.2–1900 et seq.) of Title 6.2. Notwithstanding any other provision of law, if an application is denied based in whole or in part on information obtained from the Central Criminal Records Exchange pursuant to Chapter 16 or 19 of Title 6.2, the Commissioner of Financial Institutions or his designee may disclose such information to the applicant or its designee;

39. The Department of Professional and Occupational Regulation for the purpose of investigating individuals for initial licensure pursuant to § 54.1–2106.1;

40. The Department for Aging and Rehabilitative Services and the Department for the Blind and Vision Impaired for the purpose of evaluating an individual's fitness for various types of employment and for the purpose of delivering comprehensive vocational rehabilitation services pursuant to Article 11 (§ 51.5–170 et seq.) of Chapter 14 of Title 51.5 that will assist the individual in obtaining employment;

41. Bail bondsmen, in accordance with the provisions of § 19.2–120;

42. The State Treasurer for the purpose of determining whether a person receiving compensation for wrongful incarceration meets the conditions for continued compensation under § 8.01–195.12;

43. The Department of Social Services and directors of local departments of social services for the purpose of screening individuals seeking to enter into a contract with the Department of Social Services or a local department of social services for the provision of child care services for which child care subsidy payments may be provided;

44. The Department of Juvenile Justice to investigate any parent, guardian, or other adult members of a juvenile's household when completing a predispositional or postdispositional report required by § 16.1–273 or a Board of Juvenile Justice regulation promulgated pursuant to § 16.1–233; and

45. Other entities as otherwise provided by law.

Upon an ex parte motion of a defendant in a felony case and upon the showing that the records requested may be relevant to such case, the court shall enter an order requiring the Central Criminal Records Exchange to furnish the defendant, as soon as practicable, copies of any records of persons designated in the order on whom a report has been made under the provisions of this chapter.

Notwithstanding any other provision of this chapter to the contrary, upon a written request sworn to before an officer authorized to take acknowledgments, the Central Criminal Records Exchange, or the criminal justice agency in cases of offenses not required to be reported to the Exchange, shall furnish a copy of conviction data covering the person named in the request to the person making the request; however, such person on whom the data is being obtained shall consent in writing, under oath, to the making of such request. A person receiving a copy of his own conviction data may utilize or further disseminate that data as he deems appropriate. In the event no conviction data is maintained on the data subject, the person making the request shall be furnished at his cost a certification to that effect.

B. Use of criminal history record information disseminated to noncriminal justice agencies under this section shall be limited to the purposes for which it was given and may not be disseminated further.

C. No criminal justice agency or person shall confirm the existence or nonexistence of criminal history record information for employment or licensing inquiries except as provided by law.

D. Criminal justice agencies shall establish procedures to query the Central Criminal Records Exchange prior to dissemination of any criminal history record information on offenses required to be reported to the Central Criminal Records Exchange to ensure that the most up-to-date disposition data is being used. Inquiries of the Exchange shall be made prior to any dissemination except in those cases where time is of the essence and the normal response time of the Exchange would exceed the necessary time period. A criminal justice agency to whom a request has been made for the dissemination of criminal history record information that is required to be reported to the Central Criminal Records Exchange may direct the inquirer to the Central Criminal Records Exchange for such dissemination. Dissemination of information regarding offenses not required to be reported to the Exchange shall be made by the criminal justice agency maintaining the record as required by § 15.2–1722.

E. Criminal history information provided to licensed nursing homes, hospitals and to home care organizations pursuant to subdivision A 15 shall be limited to the convictions on file with the Exchange for any offense specified in §§ 32.1–126.01, 32.1–126.02, and 32.1–162.9:1.

F. Criminal history information provided to licensed assisted living facilities and licensed adult day care centers pursuant to subdivision A 16 shall be limited to the convictions on file with the Exchange for any offense specified in § 63.2–1720.

G. Criminal history information provided to public agencies pursuant to subdivision A 36 shall be limited to the convictions on file with the Exchange for any offense specified in § 63.2–1719.

H. Upon receipt of a written request from an employer or prospective employer, the Central Criminal Records Exchange, or the criminal justice agency in cases of offenses not required to be reported to the Exchange, shall furnish at the employer's cost a copy of conviction data covering the person named in the request to the employer or prospective employer making the request, provided that the person on whom the data is being obtained has consented in writing to the making of such request and has presented a photo-identification to the employer or prospective employer. In the event no conviction data is maintained on the person named in the request, the requesting employer or prospective employer shall be furnished at his cost a certification to that effect. The criminal history record search shall be conducted on forms provided by the Exchange.

Acts 1975, c. 495; Acts 1976, c. 771; Acts 1977, c. 626; Acts 1978, c. 350; Acts 1979, c. 480; Acts 1981, c. 207; Acts 1985, c. 360; Acts 1987, c. 130; Acts 1987, c. 131; Acts 1988, c. 851; Acts 1989, c. 544; Acts 1990, c. 766; Acts 1991, c. 342; Acts 1992, c. 422; Acts 1992, c. 641; Acts 1992, c. 718; Acts 1992, c. 746; Acts 1992, c. 791; Acts 1992, c. 844; Acts 1993, c. 48; Acts 1993, c. 313; Acts 1993, c. 348; Acts 1994, c. 34; Acts 1994, c. 670; Acts 1994, c. 700; Acts 1994, c. 830; Acts 1995, c. 409; Acts 1995, c. 645; Acts 1995, c. 731; Acts 1995, c. 781; Acts 1995, c. 809; Acts 1996, c. 428; Acts 1996, c. 432; Acts 1996, c. 747; Acts 1996, c. 881; Acts 1996, c. 927; Acts 1996, c. 944; Acts 1997, c. 169; Acts 1997, c. 177; Acts 1997, c. 606; Acts 1997, c. 691; Acts 1997, c. 721; Acts 1997, c. 743; Acts 1997, c. 796; Acts 1997, c. 895; Acts 1998, c. 113; Acts 1998, c. 405; Acts 1998, c. 445; Acts 1998, c. 882; Acts 1999, c. 383; Acts 1999, c. 685; Acts 2001, c. 552; Acts 2001, c. 582; Acts 2002, c. 370; Acts 2002, c. 587; Acts 2002, c. 606; Acts 2003, c. 731; Acts 2005, c. 149; Acts 2005, c. 175; Acts 2005, c. 914, eff. April 6, 2005; Acts 2005, c. 928; Acts 2006, c. 257; Acts 2006, c. 277; Acts 2006, c. 644; Acts 2007, c. 12; Acts 2007, c. 361; Acts 2007, c. 495; Acts 2007, c. 572. Amended by Acts 2008, c. 387; Acts 2008, c. 689; Acts 2008, c. 863; Acts 2009, c. 667; Acts 2009, c. 813; Acts 2009, c. 840; Acts 2010, c. 189; Acts 2010, c. 340; Acts 2010, c. 406; Acts 2010, c. 456; Acts 2010, c. 524; Acts 2010, c. 563; Acts 2010, c. 862; Acts 2011, c. 432; Acts 2011, c. 449; Acts 2012, c. 40; Acts 2012, c. 189; Acts 2012, c. 386; Acts 2012, c. 476; Acts 2012, c. 507; Acts 2012, c. 803; Acts 2012, c. 835; Acts 2013, c. 165; Acts 2013, c. 176; Acts 2013, c. 261; Acts 2013, c. 407; Acts 2013, c. 491; Acts 2013, c. 582; Acts 2014, c. 225; Acts 2014, c. 454; Acts 2015, c. 38, eff. July 1, 2018; Acts 2015, c. 343; Acts 2015, c. 540; Acts 2015, c. 730, eff. July 1, 2018; Acts 2015, c. 758; Acts 2015, c. 770.

§ 19.2–389.1. Dissemination of juvenile record information

Record information maintained in the Central Criminal Records Exchange pursuant to the provisions of § 16.1–299 shall be disseminated only (i) to make the determination as provided in §§ 18.2–308.2 and 18.2–308.2:2 of eligibility to possess or purchase a firearm; (ii) to aid in the preparation of a pretrial investigation report prepared by a local pretrial services agency established pursuant to Article 5 (§ 19.2–152.2 et seq.) of Chapter 9, a presentence or post-sentence investigation report pursuant to § 19.2–264.5 or 19.2–299 or in the preparation of the discretionary sentencing guidelines worksheets pursuant to subsection C of § 19.2–298.01; (iii) to aid local community-based probation services agencies established pursuant to the Comprehensive Community Corrections Act for Local–Responsible Offenders (§ 9.1–173 et seq.) with investigating or serving adult local-responsible offenders and all court service units serving juvenile delinquent offenders; (iv) for fingerprint comparison utilizing the fingerprints maintained in the Automated Fingerprint Information System (AFIS) computer; (v) to attorneys for the Commonwealth to secure information incidental to sentencing and to attorneys for the Commonwealth and probation officers to prepare the discretionary sentencing guidelines worksheets pursuant to subsection C of § 19.2–298.01; (vi) to any full-time or part-time employee of the State Police, a police department or sheriff's office that is a part of or administered by the Commonwealth or any political subdivision thereof, and who is responsible for the prevention and detection of crime and the enforcement of the penal, traffic or highway laws of the Commonwealth, for purposes of the administration of criminal justice as defined in § 9.1–101; (vii) to the Department of Forensic Science to verify its authority to maintain the juvenile's sample in the DNA data bank pursuant to § 16.1–299.1; (viii) to the Office of the Attorney General, for all criminal justice activities otherwise permitted and for purposes of performing duties required by the Civil Commitment of Sexually Violent Predators Act (§ 37.2–900 et seq.); (ix) to the Virginia Criminal Sentencing Commission for research purposes; (x) to members of a threat assessment team established by a public institution of higher education pursuant to § 23–9.2:10 or by a private nonprofit institution of higher education, to aid in the assessment or intervention with individuals whose behavior may present a threat to safety; however, no member of a threat assessment team shall redisclose any juvenile record information obtained pursuant to this section or otherwise use any record of an individual beyond the purpose that such disclosure was made to the threat assessment team; and (xi) to any full-time or part-time employee of the State Police or a police department or sheriff's office that is a part of or administered by the Commonwealth or any political subdivision thereof for the purpose of screening any person for full-time or part-time employment with the State Police or a police department or sheriff's office that is a part of or administered by the Commonwealth or any political subdivision thereof.

Acts 1993, c. 468; Acts 1993, c. 926; Acts 1996, c. 755; Acts 1996, c. 870; Acts 1996, c. 914; Acts 2002, c. 701; Acts 2003, c. 107; Acts 2003, c. 432; Acts 2005, c. 868; Acts 2005, c. 881; Acts 2005, c. 914, eff. April 6, 2005; Acts 2006, c. 502; Acts 2007, c. 133. Amended by Acts 2010, c. 456; Acts 2010, c. 524; Acts 2011, c. 622; Acts 2012, c. 386.

§ 19.2–389.2. Background checks of applicants of the Metropolitan Washington Airports Authority

The police department of the Metropolitan Washington Airports Authority as established in Chapter 10 (§ 5.1–152 et seq.) of Title 5.1 may require an applicant, upon conditional offer of employment with the Authority, to submit to fingerprinting and to provide personal descriptive information to be forwarded along with the applicant's fingerprints through the Central Criminal Records Exchange and the Federal Bureau of Investigation for the purpose of obtaining criminal history record information regarding such applicant.

The Central Criminal Records Exchange, upon receipt of an applicant's record or notification that no record exists, shall make a report to the chief of the police department of the Authority or his designee, provided the designee is an employee of the police department of the Authority. In determining whether a criminal conviction directly relates to a position, the Authority shall consider the following criteria: (i) the nature and seriousness of the crime; (ii) the relationship of the crime to the work to be performed in the position applied for; (iii) the extent to which the position applied for might offer an opportunity to engage in further criminal activity of the same type as that in which the applicant had been involved; (iv) the relationship of the crime to the ability, capacity, or fitness required to perform the duties and discharge the responsibilities of the position being sought; (v) the extent and nature of the applicant's past criminal activity; (vi) the age of the applicant at the time of the commission of the crime; (vii) the amount of time that has elapsed since the applicant's last involvement in the commission of a crime; (viii) the conduct and work activity of the applicant prior to and following the criminal activity; and (ix) evidence of the applicant's rehabilitation or rehabilitative effort while incarcerated or following release.

If an applicant is denied employment because of information appearing in his criminal history record, the Authority shall notify the applicant that information obtained from the Central Criminal Records Exchange contributed to such denial. The criminal history record information obtained pursuant to this section shall be used solely to determine an applicant's eligibility for employment by the Authority and access to restricted areas of Ronald Reagan Washington National Airport and Washington Dulles International Airport in compliance with 49 U.S.C. § 44936 and shall otherwise be confidential.

Added by Acts 2014, c. 57.

§ 19.2–390. Reports to be made by local law-enforcement officers, conservators of the peace, clerks of court, Secretary of the Commonwealth and Corrections officials to State Police; material submitted by other agencies

A. 1. Every state official or agency having the power to arrest, the sheriffs of counties, the police officials of cities and towns, and any other local law-enforcement officer or conservator of the peace having the power to arrest for a felony shall make a report to the Central Criminal Records Exchange, on forms provided by it, of any arrest, including those arrests involving the taking into custody of, or service of process upon, any person on charges resulting from an indictment, presentment or information, the arrest on capias or warrant for failure to appear, and the service of a warrant for another jurisdiction, on any of the following charges:

a. Treason;

b. Any felony;

c. Any offense punishable as a misdemeanor under Title 54.1; or

d. Any misdemeanor punishable by confinement in jail (i) under Title 18.2 or 19.2, except an arrest for a violation of § 18.2–119, Article 2 (§ 18.2–415 et seq.) of Chapter 9 of Title 18.2, or any similar ordinance of any county, city or town, (ii) under § 20–61, or (iii) under § 16.1–253.2.

The reports shall contain such information as is required by the Exchange and shall be accompanied by fingerprints of the individual arrested. Effective January 1, 2006, the corresponding photograph of the individual arrested shall accompany the report. Fingerprint cards prepared by a law-enforcement agency for inclusion in a national criminal justice file shall be forwarded to the Exchange for transmittal to the appropriate bureau. Nothing in this section shall preclude each local law-enforcement agency from maintaining its own separate photographic database. Fingerprints and photographs required to be taken pursuant to this subsection or subdivision A 3c of § 19.2–123 may be taken at the facility where the magistrate is located, including a regional jail, even if the accused is not committed to jail.

2. For persons arrested and released on summonses in accordance with § 19.2–74, such report shall not be required until (i) a conviction is entered and no appeal is noted or if an appeal is noted, the conviction is upheld upon appeal or the person convicted withdraws his appeal; (ii) the court dismisses the proceeding pursuant to § 18.2–251; or (iii) an acquittal by reason of insanity pursuant to § 19.2–182.2 is entered. Upon such conviction or acquittal, the court shall remand the individual to the custody of the office of the chief law-enforcement officer of the county or city. It shall be the duty of the chief law-enforcement officer, or his designee who may be the arresting officer, to ensure that such report is completed after a determination of guilt or acquittal by reason of insanity. The court shall require the officer to complete the report immediately following the person's conviction or acquittal, and the individual shall be discharged from custody forthwith, unless the court has imposed a jail sentence to be served by him or ordered him committed to the custody of the Commissioner of Behavioral Health and Developmental Services.

B. Within 72 hours following the receipt of (i) a warrant or capias for the arrest of any person on a charge of a felony or (ii) a Governor's warrant of arrest of a person issued pursuant to § 19.2–92, the law-enforcement agency which received the warrant shall enter the person's name and other appropriate information required by the Department of State Police into the "information systems" known as the Virginia Criminal Information Network (VCIN), established and maintained by the Department pursuant to Chapter 2 (§ 52–12 et seq.) of Title 52 and the National Crime Information Center (NCIC), maintained by the Federal Bureau of Investigation. The report shall include the person's name, date of birth, social security number and such other known information which the State Police or Federal Bureau of Investigation may require. Where feasible and practical, the magistrate or court issuing the warrant or capias may transfer information electronically into VCIN. When the information is electronically transferred to VCIN, the court or magistrate shall forthwith forward the warrant or capias to the local police department or sheriff's office. When criminal process has been ordered destroyed pursuant to § 19.2–76.1, the law-enforcement agency destroying such process shall ensure the removal of any information relating to the destroyed criminal process from the VCIN and NCIC.

B1. Within 72 hours following the receipt of a written statement issued by a parole officer pursuant to § 53.1–149 or 53.1–162 authorizing the arrest of a person who has violated the provisions of his post-release supervision or probation, the law-enforcement agency that received the written statement shall enter, or cause to be entered, the person's name and other appropriate information required by the Department of State Police into the "information systems" known as the Virginia Criminal Information Network (VCIN), established and maintained by the Department pursuant to Chapter 2 (§ 52–12 et seq.) of Title 52.

C. The clerk of each circuit court and district court shall make an electronic report to the Central Criminal Records Exchange of (i) any dismissal, indefinite postponement or continuance, charge still pending due to mental incompetency or incapacity, nolle prosequi, acquittal, or conviction of, including any sentence imposed, or failure of a grand jury to return a true bill as to, any person charged with an offense listed in subsection A, including any action which may have resulted from an indictment, presentment or information, and (ii) any adjudication of delinquency based upon an act which, if committed by an adult, would require fingerprints to be filed pursuant to subsection A. In the case of offenses not required to be reported to the Exchange by subsection A, the reports of any of the foregoing dispositions shall be filed by the law-enforcement agency making the arrest with the arrest record required to be maintained by § 15.2–1722. Upon conviction of any person, including juveniles tried and convicted in the circuit courts pursuant to § 16.1–269.1, whether sentenced as adults or juveniles, for an offense for which registration is required as defined in § 9.1–902, the clerk shall within seven days of sentencing submit a report to the Sex Offender and Crimes Against Minors Registry. The report to the Registry shall include the name of the person convicted and all aliases which he is known to have used, the date and locality of the conviction for which registration is required, his date of birth, social security number, last known address, and specific reference to the offense for which he was convicted. No report of conviction or adjudication in a district court shall be filed unless the period allowed for an appeal has elapsed and no appeal has been perfected. In the event that the records in the office of any clerk show that any conviction or adjudication has been nullified in any manner, he shall also make a report of that fact to the Exchange and, if appropriate, to the Registry. In addition, each clerk of a circuit court, upon receipt of certification thereof from the Supreme Court, shall report to the Exchange or the Registry, or to the law-enforcement agency making the arrest in the case of offenses not required to be reported to the Exchange, on forms provided by the Exchange or Registry, as the case may be, any reversal or other amendment to a prior sentence or disposition previously reported. When criminal process is ordered destroyed pursuant to § 19.2–76.1, the clerk shall report such action to the law-enforcement agency that entered the warrant or capias into the VCIN.

D. In addition to those offenses enumerated in subsection A of this section, the Central Criminal Records Exchange may receive, classify and file any other fingerprints, photographs, and records of arrest or confinement submitted to it by any law-enforcement agency or any correctional institution.

E. Corrections officials, sheriffs, and jail superintendents of regional jails, responsible for maintaining correctional status information, as required by the regulations of the Department of Criminal Justice Services, with respect to individuals about whom reports have been made under the provisions of this chapter shall make reports of changes in correctional status information to the Central Criminal Records Exchange. The reports to the Exchange shall include any commitment to or release or escape from a state or local correctional facility, including commitment to or release from a parole or probation agency.

F. Any pardon, reprieve or executive commutation of sentence by the Governor shall be reported to the Exchange by the office of the Secretary of the Commonwealth.

G. Officials responsible for reporting disposition of charges, and correctional changes of status of individuals under this section, including those reports made to the Registry, shall adopt procedures reasonably designed at a minimum (i) to ensure that such reports are accurately made as soon as feasible by the most expeditious means and in no instance later than 30 days after occurrence of the disposition or correctional change of status and (ii) to report promptly any correction, deletion, or revision of the information.

H. Upon receiving a correction, deletion, or revision of information, the Central Criminal Records Exchange shall notify all criminal justice agencies known to have previously received the information.

As used in this section:

"Chief law-enforcement officer" means the chief of police of cities and towns and sheriffs of counties, unless a political subdivision has otherwise designated its chief law-enforcement officer by appropriate resolution or ordinance, in which case the local designation shall be controlling.

"Electronic report" means a report transmitted to, or otherwise forwarded to, the Central Criminal Records Exchange in an electronic format approved by the Exchange. The report shall contain the name of the person convicted and all aliases which he is known to have used, the date and locality of the conviction, his date of birth, social security number, last known address, and specific reference to the offense including the Virginia Code section and any subsection, the Virginia crime code for the offense, and the offense tracking number for the offense for which he was convicted.

Acts 1975, c. 495; Acts 1976, c. 336; Acts 1976, c. 572; Acts 1976, c. 771; Acts 1978, c. 467; Acts 1978, c. 825; Acts 1979, c. 378; Acts 1981, c. 529; Acts 1982, c. 33; Acts 1982, c. 535; Acts 1990, c. 100; Acts 1990, c. 692; Acts 1992, c. 391; Acts 1993, c. 448; Acts 1993, c. 468; Acts 1993, c. 926; Acts 1994, c. 362; Acts 1994, c. 428; Acts 1994, c. 432; Acts 1996, c. 429; Acts 1996, c. 755; Acts 1996, c. 806; Acts 1996, c. 914; Acts 1997, c. 27; Acts 1997, c. 509; Acts 1997, c. 747; Acts 1997, c. 801, eff. Jan. 1, 1998; Acts 2001, c. 516; Acts 2001, c. 536; Acts 2001, c. 565; Acts 2003, c. 27; Acts 2003, c. 584; Acts 2003, c. 727; Acts 2004, c. 284; Acts 2004, c. 406; Acts 2005, c. 187; Acts 2005, c. 229. Amended by Acts 2008, c. 73; Acts 2008, c. 246; Acts 2009, c. 249; Acts 2009, c. 813; Acts 2009, c. 840; Acts 2010, c. 273; Acts 2013, c. 614.

§ 19.2–390.01. Use of Virginia crime code references required

If any criminal warrant, indictment, information, presentment, petition, summons, charging document issued by a magistrate, or dispositional document from a criminal trial, involves a jailable offense, it shall include the Virginia crime code references for the particular offense or offenses covered. When Virginia crime codes are provided on charging and dispositional documents, the Virginia crime codes shall be recorded and stored for adult offenders in: criminal history computer systems maintained by the State Police; court case management computer systems maintained by the Supreme Court of Virginia; probation and parole case management computer systems maintained by the Department of Corrections and the Virginia Parole Board; pretrial and community-based probation case management computer systems maintained by the Department of Criminal Justice Services; and jail management computer systems maintained by the State Compensation Board. The Department of Juvenile Justice shall record and store Virginia crime codes for particular offenses related to juveniles in case management computer systems.

Virginia crime codes shall only be used to facilitate administration and research, and shall not have any legal standing as they relate to a particular offense or offenses.

Acts 2003, c. 148, eff. Oct. 1, 2004; Acts 2007, c. 133.

§ 19.2–390.02. Policies and procedures for law enforcement to conduct in-person and photo lineups

The Department of State Police and each local police department and sheriff's office shall establish a written policy and procedure for conducting in-person and photographic lineups.

Acts 2005, c. 187; Acts 2005, c. 229.

§ 19.2–390.1. Sex Offender and Crimes Against Minors Registry; maintenance; access

The Department of State Police shall keep and maintain a Sex Offender and Crimes Against Minors Registry, separate and apart from all other records maintained by it.

The Superintendent of State Police shall organize, equip, and staff, within the Department of State Police, the Sex Offender and Crimes Against Minors Registry. The Superintendent shall appoint and designate personnel as he deems necessary to carry out all duties and assignments related to the Sex Offender and Crimes Against Minors Registry as required by Chapter 9 (§ 9.1–900 et seq.) of Title 9.1.

Acts 1994, c. 362; Acts 1996, c. 418; Acts 1996, c. 542; Acts 1996, c. 880; Acts 1997, c. 670; Acts 1997, c. 672; Acts 1997, c. 747; Acts 1998, c. 785; Acts 1998, c. 834; Acts 2000, c. 250; Acts 2003, c. 584; Acts 2006, c. 857; Acts 2006, c. 914.

§ 19.2–390.2. Repealed by Acts 2003, c. 584

§ 19.2–390.3. Child Pornography Images Registry; maintenance; access

A. The Office of the Attorney General, in cooperation with the Department of State Police, shall keep and maintain a Child Pornography Registry to be located within the State Police, separate and apart from all other records maintained by either department. The purpose of the Registry shall be to assist the efforts of law-enforcement agencies statewide to protect their communities from repeat child pornographers and to protect children from becoming victims of criminal offenders by aiding in identifying victims and perpetrators. Criminal justice agencies, including law-enforcement agencies, may request of the State Police a search and comparison of child pornography images contained within the Registry with those images obtained by criminal justice agencies during the course of official investigations.

B. The Registry shall include images of sexually explicit visual material in any form including any picture, photograph, drawing, sculpture, motion picture film, digital image or similar visual representation, presented as evidence and used in any conviction for any offense enumerated in §§ 18.2–374.1 and 18.2–374.1:1.

C. Registry information provided under this section shall be used for the purposes of the administration of criminal justice or for the protection of the public in general and children in particular. Use of the information or the images contained therein for purposes not authorized by this section is prohibited and a willful violation of this section with the intent to harass or intimidate another shall be punished as a Class 6 felony.

D. The Virginia Criminal Information Network and any form or document used by the Department of State Police to disseminate information from the Registry shall provide notice that any unauthorized possession, use or dissemination of the information or images is a crime punishable as a Class 6 felony.

Acts 2003, c. 935; Acts 2003, c. 938.

§ 19.2–391. Records to be made available to Exchange by state officials and agencies; duplication of records

Each state official and agency shall make available to the Central Criminal Records Exchange such of their records as are pertinent to its functions and shall cooperate with the Exchange in the development and use of equipment and facilities on a joint basis, where feasible. No state official or agency shall maintain records which are a duplication of the records on deposit in the Central Criminal Records Exchange, except to the extent necessary for efficient internal administration of such agency. Furthermore, the Virginia Parole Board may receive and use electronically disseminated criminal history record information from the Central Criminal Records Exchange as required to make parole determinations pursuant to subdivisions 1, 2, 3, and 5 of § 53.1–136, provided the data is (i) temporarily stored with the Board solely for operational purposes, (ii) purged within thirty days of receipt of updated data by the Board, and (iii) accessed and viewed solely by Parole Board members and authorized staff pursuant to § 9.1–101 and § 9.1–130.

Acts 1975, c. 495; Acts 1993, c. 313.

§ 19.2–392. Fingerprints and photographs by police authorities

A. All duly constituted police authorities having the power of arrest may take the fingerprints and photographs of: (i) any person arrested by them and charged with a felony or a misdemeanor an arrest for which is to be reported by them to the Central Criminal Records Exchange, or (ii) any person who pleads guilty or is found guilty after being summoned in accordance with § 19.2–74. Such authorities shall make such records available to the Central Criminal Records Exchange. Such authorities are authorized to provide, on the request of duly appointed law-enforcement officers, copies of any fingerprint records they may have, and to furnish services and technical advice in connection with the taking, classifying and preserving of fingerprints and fingerprint records.

B. Such police authorities may establish and collect a reasonable fee not to exceed $10 for the first card and $5 for each successive card for the taking of fingerprints when voluntarily requested by any person for purposes other than criminal violations.

Acts 1975, c. 495; Acts 1978, c. 825; Acts 1985, c. 306; Acts 2005, c. 347.

§ 19.2–392.01. Judges may require taking of fingerprints and photographs in certain misdemeanor cases

The judge of a district court may, in his discretion, on motion of the attorney for the Commonwealth, require the duly constituted police officers of the county, city or town within the territorial jurisdiction of the court to take the fingerprints and photograph of any person who has been arrested and charged with a misdemeanor other than a misdemeanor which is a violation of any provision of Title 46.2.

Acts 1995, c. 407; Acts 1996, c. 755; Acts 1996, c. 914.

§ 19.2–392.02. National criminal background checks by businesses and organizations regarding employees or volunteers providing care to children, or the elderly or disabled

A. For purposes of this section:

"Barrier crime" means any offense set forth in § 63.2–1719 or 63.2–1726.

"Barrier crime information" means the following facts concerning a person who has been arrested for, or has been convicted of, a barrier crime, regardless of whether the person was a juvenile or adult at the time of the arrest or conviction: full name, race, sex, date of birth, height, weight, fingerprints, a brief description of the barrier crime or offenses for which the person has been arrested or has been convicted, the disposition of the charge, and any other information that may be useful in identifying persons arrested for or convicted of a barrier crime.

"Care" means the provision of care, treatment, education, training, instruction, supervision, or recreation to children or the elderly or disabled.

"Department" means the Department of State Police.

"Employed by" means any person who is employed by, volunteers for, seeks to be employed by, or seeks to volunteer for a qualified entity.

"Identification document" means a document made or issued by or under the authority of the United States government, a state, a political subdivision of a state, a foreign government, political subdivision of a foreign government, an international governmental or an international quasi-governmental organization that, when completed with information concerning a particular individual, is of a type intended or commonly accepted for the purpose of identification of individuals.

"Provider" means a person who (i) is employed by a qualified entity and has, seeks to have, or may have unsupervised access to a child or to an elderly or disabled person to whom the qualified entity provides care; (ii) is a volunteer of a qualified entity and has, seeks to have, or may have unsupervised access to a child to whom the qualified entity provides care; or (iii) owns, operates, or seeks to own or operate a qualified entity.

"Qualified entity" means a business or organization that provides care to children or the elderly or disabled, whether governmental, private, for profit, nonprofit or voluntary, except organizations exempt pursuant to subdivision A 10 of § 63.2–1715.

B. A qualified entity may request the Department of State Police to conduct a national criminal background check on any provider who is employed by such entity. No qualified entity may request a national criminal background check on a provider until such provider has:

1. Been fingerprinted; and

2. Completed and signed a statement, furnished by the entity, that includes (i) his name, address, and date of birth as it appears on a valid identification document; (ii) a disclosure of whether or not the provider has ever been convicted of or is the subject of pending charges for a criminal offense within or outside the Commonwealth, and if the provider has been convicted of a crime, a description of the crime and the particulars of the conviction; (iii) a notice to the provider that the entity may request a background check; (iv) a notice to the provider that he is entitled to obtain a copy of any background check report, to challenge the accuracy and completeness of any information contained in any such report, and to obtain a prompt determination as to the validity of such challenge before a final determination is made by the Department; and (v) a notice to the provider that prior to the completion of the background check the qualified entity may choose to deny the provider unsupervised access to children or the elderly or disabled for whom the qualified entity provides care.

C. Upon receipt of (i) a qualified entity's written request to conduct a background check on a provider, (ii) the provider's fingerprints, and (iii) a completed, signed statement as described in subsection B, the Department shall make a determination whether the provider has been convicted of or is the subject of charges of a barrier crime. To conduct its determination regarding the provider's barrier crime information, the Department shall access the national criminal history background check system, which is maintained by the Federal Bureau of Investigation and is based on fingerprints and other methods of identification, and shall access the Central Criminal Records Exchange maintained by the Department. If the Department receives a background report lacking disposition data, the Department shall conduct research in whatever state and local recordkeeping systems are available in order to obtain complete data. The Department shall make reasonable efforts to respond to a qualified entity's inquiry within 15 business days.

D. Any background check conducted pursuant to this section for a provider employed by a private entity shall be screened by the Department of State Police. If the provider has been convicted of or is under indictment for a barrier crime, the qualified entity shall be notified that the provider is not qualified to work or volunteer in a position that involves unsupervised access to children or the elderly or disabled.

E. Any background check conducted pursuant to this section for a provider employed by a governmental entity shall be provided to that entity.

F. In the case of a provider who desires to volunteer at a qualified entity and who is subject to a national criminal background check, the Department and the Federal Bureau of Investigation may each charge the provider the lesser of $18 or the actual cost to the entity of the background check conducted with the fingerprints.

G. The failure to request a criminal background check pursuant to subsection B shall not be considered negligence per se in any civil action.

Acts 2000, c. 860, eff. Jan. 1, 2001; Acts 2001, c. 40; Acts 2001, c. 345; Acts 2005, c. 217. Amended by Acts 2015, c. 758; Acts 2015, c. 770.

CHAPTER 23.1

EXPUNGEMENT OF CRIMINAL RECORDS

§ 19.2–392.1. Statement of policy

The General Assembly finds that arrest records can be a hindrance to an innocent citizen's ability to obtain employment, an education and to obtain credit. It further finds that the police and court records of those of its citizens who have been absolutely pardoned for crimes for which they have been unjustly convicted can also be a hindrance. This chapter is intended to protect such persons from the unwarranted damage which may occur as a result of being arrested and convicted.

Acts 1977, c. 675; Acts 1984, c. 642; Acts 1990, c. 603; Acts 1992, c. 697.

§ 19.2–392.2. Expungement of police and court records

A. If a person is charged with the commission of a crime or any offense defined in Title 18.2, and

1. Is acquitted, or

2. A nolle prosequi is taken or the charge is otherwise dismissed, including dismissal by accord and satisfaction pursuant to § 19.2–151, he may file a petition setting forth the relevant facts and requesting expungement of the police records and the court records relating to the charge.

B. If any person whose name or other identification has been used without his consent or authorization by another person who has been charged or arrested using such name or identification, he may file a petition with the court disposing of the charge for relief pursuant to this section. Such person shall not be required to pay any fees for the filing of a petition under this subsection. A petition filed under this subsection shall include one complete set of the petitioner's fingerprints obtained from a law-enforcement agency.

C. The petition with a copy of the warrant or indictment if reasonably available shall be filed in the circuit court of the county or city in which the case was disposed of by acquittal or being otherwise dismissed and shall contain, except where not reasonably available, the date of arrest and the name of the arresting agency. Where this information is not reasonably available, the petition shall state the reason for such unavailability. The petition shall further state the specific criminal charge to be expunged, the date of final disposition of the charge as set forth in the petition, the petitioner's date of birth, and the full name used by the petitioner at the time of arrest.

D. A copy of the petition shall be served on the attorney for the Commonwealth of the city or county in which the petition is filed. The attorney for the Commonwealth may file an objection or answer to the petition or may give written notice to the court that he does not object to the petition within 21 days after it is served on him.

E. The petitioner shall obtain from a law-enforcement agency one complete set of the petitioner's fingerprints and shall provide that agency with a copy of the petition for expungement. The law-enforcement agency shall submit the set of fingerprints to the Central Criminal Records Exchange (CCRE) with a copy of the petition for expungement attached. The CCRE shall forward under seal to the court a copy of the petitioner's criminal history, a copy of the source documents that resulted in the CCRE entry that the petitioner wishes to expunge, and the set of fingerprints. Upon completion of the hearing, the court shall return the fingerprint card to the petitioner. If no hearing was conducted, upon the entry of an order of expungement or an order denying the petition for expungement, the court shall cause the fingerprint card to be destroyed unless, within 30 days of the date of the entry of the order, the petitioner requests the return of the fingerprint card in person from the clerk of the court or provides the clerk of the court a self-addressed, stamped envelope for the return of the fingerprint card.

F. After receiving the criminal history record information from the CCRE, the court shall conduct a hearing on the petition. If the court finds that the continued existence and possible dissemination of information relating to the arrest of the petitioner causes or may cause circumstances which constitute a manifest injustice to the petitioner, it shall enter an order requiring the expungement of the police and court records, including electronic records, relating to the charge. Otherwise, it shall deny the petition. However, if the petitioner has no prior criminal record and the arrest was for a misdemeanor violation, the petitioner shall be entitled, in the absence of good cause shown to the contrary by the Commonwealth, to expungement of the police and court records relating to the charge, and the court shall enter an order of expungement. If the attorney for the Commonwealth of the county or city in which the petition is filed (i) gives written notice to the court pursuant to subsection D that he does not object to the petition and (ii) when the charge to be expunged is a felony, stipulates in such written notice that the continued existence and possible dissemination of information relating to the arrest of the petitioner causes or may cause circumstances which constitute a manifest injustice to the petitioner, the court may enter an order of expungement without conducting a hearing.

G. The Commonwealth shall be made party defendant to the proceeding. Any party aggrieved by the decision of the court may appeal, as provided by law in civil cases.

H. Notwithstanding any other provision of this section, when the charge is dismissed because the court finds that the person arrested or charged is not the person named in the summons, warrant, indictment or presentment, the court dismissing the charge shall, upon motion of the person improperly arrested or charged, enter an order requiring expungement of the police and court records relating to the charge. Such order shall contain a statement that the dismissal and expungement are ordered pursuant to this subsection and shall be accompanied by the complete set of the petitioner's fingerprints filed with his petition. Upon the entry of such order, it shall be treated as provided in subsection K.

I. Notwithstanding any other provision of this section, when a person has been granted an absolute pardon for the commission of a crime that he did not commit, he may file in the circuit court of the county or city in which the conviction occurred a petition setting forth the relevant facts and requesting expungement of the police records and the court records relating to the charge and conviction, and the court shall enter an order requiring expungement of the police and court records relating to the charge and conviction. Such order shall contain a statement that the expungement is ordered pursuant to this subsection. Upon the entry of such order, it shall be treated as provided in subsection K.

J. Upon receiving a copy of a writ vacating a conviction pursuant to § 19.2–327.5 or 19.2–327.13, the court shall enter an order requiring expungement of the police and court records relating to the charge and conviction. Such order shall contain a statement that the expungement is ordered pursuant to this subsection. Upon the entry of the order, it shall be treated as provided in subsection K.

K. Upon the entry of an order of expungement, the clerk of the court shall cause a copy of such order to be forwarded to the Department of State Police, which shall, pursuant to rules and regulations adopted pursuant to § 9.1–134, direct the manner by which the appropriate expungement or removal of such records shall be effected.

L. Costs shall be as provided by § 17.1–275, but shall not be recoverable against the Commonwealth.

M. Any order entered where (i) the court or parties failed to strictly comply with the procedures set forth in this section or (ii) the court enters an order of expungement contrary to law, shall be voidable upon motion and notice made within three years of the entry of such order.

Acts 1977, c. 675; Acts 1983, c. 394; Acts 1984, c. 642; Acts 1990, c. 603; Acts 1992, c. 697; Acts 2007, c. 465; Acts 2007, c. 824; Acts 2007, c. 883; Acts 2007, c. 905. Amended by Acts 2009, c. 618; Acts 2011, c. 362; Acts 2015, c. 426.

§ 19.2–392.3. Disclosure of expunged records

A. It shall be unlawful for any person having or acquiring access to an expunged court or police record to open or review it or to disclose to another person any information from it without an order from the court which ordered the record expunged.

B. Upon a verified petition filed by the attorney for the Commonwealth alleging that the record is needed by a law-enforcement agency for purposes of employment application as an employee of a law-enforcement agency or for a pending criminal investigation and that the investigation will be jeopardized or that life or property will be endangered without immediate access to the record, the court may enter an ex parte order, without notice to the person, permitting such access. An ex parte order may permit a review of the record, but may not permit a copy to be made of it.

C. Any person who willfully violates this section is guilty of a Class 1 misdemeanor.

Acts 1977, c. 675; Acts 1978, c. 713.

§ 19.2–392.4. Prohibited practices by employers, educational institutions, agencies, etc., of state and local governments

A. An employer or educational institution shall not, in any application, interview, or otherwise, require an applicant for employment or admission to disclose information concerning any arrest or criminal charge against him that has been expunged. An applicant need not, in answer to any question concerning any arrest or criminal charge that has not resulted in a conviction, include a reference to or information concerning arrests or charges that have been expunged.

B. Agencies, officials, and employees of the state and local governments shall not, in any application, interview, or otherwise, require an applicant for a license, permit, registration, or governmental service to disclose information concerning any arrest or criminal charge against him that has been expunged. An applicant need not, in answer to any question concerning any arrest or criminal charge that has not resulted in a conviction, include a reference to or information concerning charges that have been expunged. Such an application may not be denied solely because of the applicant's refusal to disclose information concerning any arrest or criminal charge against him that has been expunged.

C. A person who willfully violates this section is guilty of a Class 1 misdemeanor for each violation.

Acts 1977, c. 675.

CHAPTER 24

INSPECTION WARRANTS

§ 19.2–393. Definitions

An "inspection warrant" is an order in writing, made in the name of the Commonwealth, signed by any judge of the circuit court whose territorial jurisdiction encompasses the property or premises to be inspected or entered, and directed to a state or local official, commanding him to enter and to conduct any inspection, testing or collection of samples for testing required or authorized by state or local law or regulation in connection with the manufacturing, emitting or presence of a toxic substance, and which describes, either directly or by reference to any accompanying or attached supporting affidavit, the property or premises where the inspection, testing or collection of samples for testing is to occur. Such warrant shall be sufficiently accurate in description so that the official executing the warrant and the owner or custodian of the property or premises can reasonably determine from the warrant the activity, condition, circumstance, object or property of which inspection, testing or collection of samples for testing is authorized.

For the purposes of this chapter, "manufacturing" means producing, formulating, packaging, or diluting any substance for commercial sale or resale; "emitting" means the release of any substance, whether or not intentional or avoidable, into the work environment, into the air, into the water, or otherwise into the human environment; and "toxic substance" means any substance, including (i) any raw material, intermediate product, catalyst, final product and by-product of any operation conducted in a commercial establishment and (ii) any biological organism, that has the capacity, through its physical, chemical, or biological properties, to pose a substantial risk to humans, aquatic organisms or any other animal of illness, death or impairment of normal functions, either immediately or over a period of time.

Acts 1976, c. 625; Acts 1979, c. 122.

§ 19.2–394. Issuance of warrant

An inspection warrant may be issued for any inspection, testing or collection of samples for testing or for any administrative search authorized by state or local law or regulation in connection with the presence, manufacturing or emitting of toxic substances, whether or not such warrant be constitutionally required. Nothing in this chapter shall be construed to require issuance of an inspection warrant where a warrant is not constitutionally required or to exclude any other lawful means of search, inspection, testing or collection of samples for testing, whether without warrant or pursuant to a search warrant issued under any other provision of the Code of Virginia. No inspection warrant shall be issued pursuant to this chapter except upon probable cause, supported by affidavit, particularly describing the place, things or persons to be inspected or tested and the purpose for which the inspection, testing or collection of samples for testing is to be made. Probable cause shall be deemed to exist if either reasonable legislative or administrative standards for conducting such inspection, testing or collection of samples for testing are satisfied with respect to the particular place, things or persons or there exists probable cause to believe that there is a condition, object, activity or circumstance which legally justifies such inspection, testing or collection of samples for testing. The supporting affidavit shall contain either a statement that consent to inspect, test or collect samples for testing has been sought and refused or facts or circumstances reasonably justifying the failure to seek such consent in order to enforce effectively the state or local law or regulation which authorizes such inspection, testing or collection of samples for testing. The issuing judge may examine the affiant under oath or affirmation to verify the accuracy of any matter indicated by the statement in the affidavit. After issuing a warrant under this section, the judge shall file the affidavit in the manner prescribed by § 19.2–54.

Acts 1976, c. 625; Acts 1979, c. 122. Amended by Acts 2014, c. 354.

§ 19.2–395. Duration of warrant

An inspection warrant shall be effective for the time specified therein, for a period of not more than ten days, unless extended or renewed by the judicial officer who signed and issued the original warrant, upon satisfying himself that such extension or renewal is in the public interest. Such warrant shall be executed and returned to the clerk of the circuit court of the city or county wherein the inspection was made within the time specified in the warrant or within the extended or renewed time. After the expiration of such time, the warrant, unless executed shall be void.

Acts 1976, c. 625. Amended by Acts 2014, c. 354.

§ 19.2–396. Conduct of inspection, testing or collection of samples for testing; special procedure for dwelling

An inspection, testing or collection of samples for testing pursuant to such warrant may not be made in the absence of the owner, custodian or possessor of the particular place, things or persons unless specifically authorized by the issuing judge upon a showing that such authority is reasonably necessary to effectuate the purpose of the law or regulation being enforced. An entry pursuant to this warrant shall not be made forcibly, except that the issuing judge may expressly authorize a forcible entry where facts are shown sufficient to create a reasonable suspicion of an immediate threat to public health or safety, or where facts are shown establishing that reasonable attempts to serve a previous warrant have been unsuccessful. In the case of entry into a dwelling, prior consent must be sought and refused and notice that a warrant has been issued must be given at least twenty-four hours before the warrant is executed, unless the issuing judge finds that failure to seek consent is justified and that there is a reasonable suspicion of an immediate threat to public health or safety.

Acts 1976, c. 625; Acts 1979, c. 122.

§ 19.2-397. Refusal to permit authorized inspection; penalty

Any person who willfully refuses to permit an inspection, testing or collection of samples for testing lawfully authorized by warrant issued pursuant to this chapter shall be guilty of a Class 3 misdemeanor.

Acts 1976, c. 625; Acts 1979, c. 122.

CHAPTER 25

APPEALS BY THE COMMONWEALTH

§ 19.2-398. When appeal by the Commonwealth allowed

A. In a felony case a pretrial appeal from a circuit court may be taken by the Commonwealth from:

1. An order of a circuit court dismissing a warrant, information or indictment, or any count or charge thereof on the ground that (i) the defendant was deprived of a speedy trial in violation of the provisions of the Sixth Amendment to the Constitution of the United States, Article I, Section 8 of the Constitution of Virginia, or § 19.2-243; or (ii) the defendant would be twice placed in jeopardy in violation of the provisions of the Fifth Amendment to the Constitution of the United States or Article I, Section 8 of the Constitution of Virginia; or

2. An order of a circuit court prohibiting the use of certain evidence at trial on the grounds such evidence was obtained in violation of the provisions of the Fourth, Fifth or Sixth Amendments to the Constitution of the United States or Article I, Section 8, 10 or 11 of the Constitution of Virginia prohibiting illegal searches and seizures and protecting rights against self-incrimination, provided the Commonwealth certifies that the appeal is not taken for purpose of delay and that the evidence is substantial proof of a fact material in the proceeding.

B. A petition for appeal may be taken by the Commonwealth in a felony case from any order of release on conditions pursuant to Article 1 (§ 19.2-119 et seq.) of Chapter 9 of this title.

C. A petition for appeal may be taken by the Commonwealth in a felony case after conviction where the sentence imposed by the circuit court is contrary to mandatory sentencing or restitution terms required by statute.

D. Nothing in this chapter shall affect the Commonwealth's right to appeal in civil matters or cases involving a violation of law relating to the state revenue or appeals pursuant to § 17.1-411 or subsection C of § 19.2-317.

E. A pretrial appeal may be taken in any criminal case from an order of a circuit court dismissing a warrant, information, summons, delinquency petition, or indictment, or any count or charge thereof, on the ground that a statute or local ordinance on which the order is based is unconstitutional.

Acts 1985, c. 510; Acts 1987, c. 710; Acts 1998, c. 251; Acts 1999, c. 829; Acts 1999, c. 846; Acts 2002, c. 611; Acts 2002, c. 692; Acts 2003, c. 109; Acts 2005, c. 622; Acts 2005, c. 694; Acts 2006, c. 571; Acts 2006, c. 876.

§ 19.2-399. Renumbered as § 19.2-266.2

§ 19.2-400. Appeal lies to the Court of Appeals; time for filing notice

An appeal taken pursuant to § 19.2-398, including such an appeal in a capital murder case, shall lie to the Court of Appeals of Virginia.

No appeal shall be allowed the Commonwealth pursuant to subsection A of § 19.2-398 unless within seven days after entry of the order of the circuit court from which the appeal is taken, and before a jury is impaneled and sworn if there is to be trial by jury or, in cases to be tried without a jury, before the court begins to hear or receive evidence or the first witness is sworn, whichever occurs first, the Commonwealth files a notice of appeal with the clerk of the trial court. If the appeal relates to suppressed evidence, the attorney for the Commonwealth shall certify in the notice of appeal that the appeal is not taken for the purpose of delay and that the evidence is substantial proof of a fact material to the proceeding. All other requirements related to the notice of appeal shall be governed by Part Five A of the Rules of the Supreme Court. Upon the filing of a timely notice of appeal, the order from which the pretrial appeal is taken and further trial proceedings in the circuit court, except for a bail hearing, shall thereby be suspended pending disposition of the appeal.

An appeal by the Commonwealth pursuant to subsection C of § 19.2–398 shall be governed by Part Five A of the Rules of the Supreme Court.

Acts 1987, c. 710; Acts 2003, c. 109.

§ 19.2–401. Cross appeal; when allowed; time for filing

The defendant shall have no independent right of appeal pursuant to § 19.2–398. If the Commonwealth appeals, the defendant may cross appeal from any orders from which the Commonwealth may appeal, pursuant to § 19.2–398. The defendant shall be under no obligation to defend an appeal filed by the Commonwealth. However, when an appeal is taken by the Commonwealth, and the defendant wishes to defend or cross appeal, the circuit court shall, where the defendant is indigent, appoint counsel to represent the defendant on appeal. The remuneration to be awarded appointed counsel shall be governed by § 19.2–326.

In pretrial appeals, the defendant shall file a notice of cross appeal with the clerk of the circuit court within seven days following the notice of appeal filed by the Commonwealth.

Any brief on cross appeal shall be consolidated with the defendant's brief as appellee, if any.

Acts 1987, c. 710; Acts 2003, c. 109.

§ 19.2–402. Petition for appeal; brief in opposition; time for filing

A. When a notice of appeal has been filed pursuant to § 19.2–400, the Commonwealth may petition the Court of Appeals for an appeal pursuant to § 19.2–398. The Commonwealth shall be represented by the attorney for the Commonwealth prosecuting the case.

B. The provisions of this subsection apply only to pretrial appeals. The petition for a pretrial appeal shall be filed with the clerk of the Court of Appeals not more than 14 days after the notice of transcript or written statement of facts required by § 19.2–405 is filed or, if there are objections thereto, within 14 days after the judge signs the transcript or written statement of facts. The accused may file a brief in opposition with the clerk of the Court of Appeals within 14 days after the filing of the petition for pretrial appeal. If the accused has filed a notice of cross appeal, he shall file a petition for cross appeal to be consolidated with, and filed within the same time period as, his brief in opposition. The Commonwealth may file a brief in opposition to any petition for cross appeal within 10 days after the petition for cross appeal is filed. Except as specifically provided in this section, all other requirements for the petition for pretrial appeal and brief in opposition shall conform as nearly as practicable to Part Five A of the Rules of the Supreme Court of Virginia.

Acts 1987, c. 710; Acts 2003, c. 109. Amended by Acts 2014, c. 33; Acts 2014, c. 294.

§ 19.2–403. Procedures on petition for pretrial appeal

The procedures on a pretrial appeal to the Court of Appeals by the Commonwealth pursuant to § 19.2–398, and on a cross appeal of a pretrial appeal by the accused pursuant to § 19.2–401, shall be governed by the provisions of subsections C and D of § 17.1–407. The Court of Appeals, however, shall grant or deny the petition for a pretrial appeal, and the petition for cross appeal, if any, not later than 30 days after the brief in opposition is timely filed or the time for such filing has expired.

No petition for rehearing may be filed in any pretrial appeal pursuant to this chapter. If the petition for a pretrial appeal pursuant to this chapter is denied, the Court's mandate shall immediately issue and the clerk of the Court of Appeals shall return the record forthwith to the clerk of the trial court.

Acts 1987, c. 710; Acts 2003, c. 109.

§ 19.2–404. Procedures on awarded pretrial appeal

This section applies only to pretrial appeals. If the Court of Appeals grants the Commonwealth's petition for a pretrial appeal, the Attorney General shall thereafter represent the Commonwealth during that appeal.

The Commonwealth shall file its opening brief in the office of the clerk of the Court of Appeals within 25 days after the date of the certificate awarding the appeal. The brief of the appellee shall be filed in the office of the clerk of the Court of Appeals within 25 days after the filing of the Commonwealth's opening brief. The Commonwealth may then file a reply brief, including its response to any cross appeal, in the office of the clerk of the Court of Appeals within 15 days after the filing of the brief of the accused. With the permission of a judge of the Court of Appeals, the time for filing any brief may be extended for good cause shown. Four copies of each brief shall be filed and three copies shall be mailed or delivered to opposing counsel on or before the date of filing. Except as specifically provided in this section, all other requirements of the brief shall conform as nearly as practicable to Part Five A of the Rules of the Supreme Court of Virginia. The Court of Appeals shall accelerate the appeal on its docket and render its decision not later than 60 days after the filing of the appellee's brief or after the time for filing such brief has expired.

When the opinion is rendered by the Court of Appeals, the mandate shall immediately issue and the clerk of the Court of Appeals shall return the record forthwith to the clerk of the trial court. No petition for rehearing may be filed.

Acts 1987, c. 710; Acts 2003, c. 109.

§ 19.2–405. Pretrial appeals; record on appeal; transcript; written statement of facts; time for filing

This section applies only to pretrial appeals. The record on appeal shall conform, as nearly as practicable, to the requirements of Part Five A of the Rules of the Supreme Court for the record on appeal, except as hereinafter provided. The transcript or written statement of facts shall be filed with the clerk of the circuit court from which the appeal is being taken, no later than 25 days following entry of the order of the circuit court. Upon motion of the Commonwealth, the Court of Appeals may grant an extension of up to 45 days for filing the transcript or written statement of facts for good cause shown. If a transcript or written statement of facts is filed, the Commonwealth shall file with the clerk of the circuit court a notice, signed by the attorney for the Commonwealth, who is counsel for the appellant, identifying the transcript or written statement of facts and reciting its filing with the clerk. There shall be appended to the notice a certificate by the attorney for the Commonwealth that a copy of the notice has been mailed or delivered to opposing counsel. The notice of filing of the transcript or written statement of facts shall be filed within three days of the filing of the transcript or written statement of facts or within 14 days of the order of the circuit court, whichever is later.

Any party may object to the transcript or written statement of facts on the ground that it is erroneous or incomplete. Notice of the objection specifying the errors alleged or deficiencies asserted shall be tendered to the trial judge within 10 days after the notice of filing of the transcript or written statement of facts is filed in the office of the clerk. The trial judge shall, within three days after the filing of such objection, either overrule the objection, or take steps deemed necessary to make the record complete or certify the respect in which the record is incomplete, and sign the transcript or written statement of facts to verify its accuracy. The clerk of the trial court shall forthwith transmit the record to the clerk of the Court of Appeals.

Acts 1987, c. 710; Acts 2003, c. 109. Amended by Acts 2014, c. 33; Acts 2014, c. 294.

§ 19.2–406. Bail pending pretrial appeal

This section applies only to pretrial appeals. Upon a pretrial appeal being taken by the Commonwealth pursuant to § 19.2–398, if the defendant moves the trial court for release on bail, that court shall promptly, but in no event later than three days after the Commonwealth's notice of appeal is filed, hold a hearing to determine the issue of bail. The burden shall be upon the Commonwealth to show good cause why the bail should not be reduced or the accused released on his own recognizance. If it is determined that the accused shall be released on bail, bail shall be set and determined in accordance with Article 1 (§ 19.2–119 et seq.) of Chapter 9 of this title.

Acts 1987, c. 710; Acts 1999, c. 829; Acts 1999, c. 846; Acts 2003, c. 109.

§ 19.2–407. Review by the Supreme Court

Pursuant to § 17.1–409, the Supreme Court in its discretion may certify an appeal taken pursuant to § 19.2–398, or a cross appeal taken pursuant to § 19.2–401, for expedited review by the Supreme Court before it has been determined by the Court of Appeals. Such certification may be made only when the Supreme Court determines that at least one of the conditions set forth in subsection B of § 17.1–409 exists.

Acts 1987, c. 710.

§ 19.2–408. Finality of decision of the Court of Appeals in pretrial appeals

The decision of the Court of Appeals shall be final for purposes of a pretrial appeal pursuant to § 19.2–398, or a cross appeal of a pretrial appeal taken pursuant to § 19.2–401, and no further pretrial appeal shall lie to the Supreme Court.

Acts 1987, c. 710; Acts 2003, c. 109.

§ 19.2–409. Exclusion of pretrial appeal period from time within which accused must be tried; reconsideration of issues after conviction

This section applies only to pretrial appeals. The provisions of § 19.2–243 shall not apply to the period of time commencing when the Commonwealth's notice of pretrial appeal is filed pursuant to this chapter and ending 60 days after the Court of Appeals or Supreme Court issues its mandate disposing of the pretrial appeal. Such finality of the Court of Appeals' decision shall not preclude a defendant, if he is convicted, from requesting the Court of Appeals or Supreme Court on direct appeal to reconsider an issue which was the subject of the pretrial appeal.

Acts 1987, c. 710; Acts 2003, c. 109; Acts 2007, c. 414.

INDEX TO CRIMINAL PROCEDURE

ABDUCTION
Kidnapping, generally, this index

ABORTION
Crimes and offenses, limitation of prosecutions, **19.2–8**
Limitation of prosecutions, **19.2–8**

ABSENCE AND ABSENTEES
Prosecuting attorneys, **19.2–156**

ABUSE
Child Abuse, generally, this index
Domestic Violence, generally, this index

ABUSE OF CHILDREN
Child Abuse, generally, this index

ABUSE OF SUBSTANCES
Chemically Dependent Persons, generally, this index

ACCIDENTS
Personal Injuries, generally, this index

ACCOMPLICES AND ACCESSORIES
Conviction of crime, **19.2–286**

ACTIONS AND PROCEEDINGS
Adoption, generally, this index
Appeal and Review, generally, this index
Appeals in Criminal Prosecutions, generally, this index
Commencement of actions. Limitation of Actions, generally, this index
Costs, generally, this index
Damages, generally, this index
Decrees. Judgments and Decrees, generally, this index
District Courts, generally, this index
Evidence, generally, this index
Executions, generally, this index
Forfeitures, generally, this index
Habeas Corpus, generally, this index
Judgments and Decrees, generally, this index
Jury, generally, this index
Limitation of Actions, generally, this index
Process, generally, this index
Production of Books and Papers, generally, this index
Statute of limitations. Limitation of Actions, generally, this index
Stay. Supersedeas or Stay, generally, this index
Subpoenas, generally, this index
Summons, generally, this index

ACTIONS AND PROCEEDINGS—Cont'd
Supersedeas or Stay, generally, this index
Suppression, searches and seizures, **19.2–60**
Time. Limitation of Actions, generally, this index
Trial, generally, this index
Venue, generally, this index
Wiretapping, damages, **19.2–69**
Witnesses, generally, this index

ACTS OF GOD
Limitation of prosecutions, **19.2–243**

ACTUAL INNOCENCE
Writs, **19.2–327.2 et seq.**
Nonbiological evidence, **19.2–327.10 et seq.**

AD VALOREM TAXES
Real Property Taxation, generally, this index

ADDICTS
Chemically Dependent Persons, generally, this index

ADDRESS
Protective orders, confidential or privileged information, **19.2–152.8 et seq.**
Stalking, protective orders, confidential or privileged information, **19.2–152.8 et seq.**

ADOPTION
Crimes and offenses, limitation of prosecutions, **19.2–8**
Criminal history record information, disclosure, **19.2–389**
Exemptions, television and radio, **19.2–266**
Limitation of prosecutions, **19.2–8**
Television and radio, exclusion, **19.2–266**

ADULT DAY CARE CENTERS
Criminal history record information, disclosure, **19.2–389**

ADVERSE OR PECUNIARY INTEREST
Attorney for the commonwealth, disqualification, **19.2–155**
Magistrates, **19.2–37**

ADVERTISEMENTS
Crime victims, compensation and salaries, **19.2–368.17**
Legal advertisements. Notice, generally, this index
Wiretapping, **19.2–63**

ADVOCATES
Attorneys, generally, this index

AFFIDAVITS
Extradition, applications, **19.2–111**

AFFIDAVITS—Cont'd
Searches and seizures, warrants, **19.2–52, 19.2–54**

AFFIRMATIONS
Oaths and Affirmations, generally, this index

AGE
Grand jury, **19.2–194, 19.2–195**
Multijurisdiction grand juries, **19.2–215.4**

AIR FORCE
Military Forces, generally, this index

AIRCRAFT
Drones, unmanned aircraft, searches and seizures, warrants, **19.2–60.1**
Unmanned aircraft, searches and seizures, warrants, evidence, **19.2–60.1**

AIRPORTS AND LANDING FIELDS
Bonds (officers and fiduciaries), conservators of the peace, **19.2–15**
Conservators of the peace, **19.2–15**

ALCOHOLIC BEVERAGES
Boats and boating, driving under influence of alcohol or drugs, arrest, **19.2–81**
Driving under influence of alcohol or drugs. Traffic Rules and Regulations, this index
Tests and testing, pretrial services, officers and employees, powers and duties, **19.2–152.4:3**

ALCOHOLICS AND INTOXICATED PERSONS
See, also, Chemically Dependent Persons, generally, this index
Crimes and offenses, pretrial services, officers and employees, powers and duties, **19.2–152.4:3**
Criminal history record information, disclosure, **19.2–389**
Driving under influence of alcohol or drugs. Traffic Rules and Regulations, this index

ALIENS
Arrest, law enforcement officers, powers and duties, **19.2–81.6, 19.2–82**
Bail, **19.2–120**
Presumptions, **19.2–120.1**
Conviction of crimes, **19.2–294.2**
Jails, reports, **19.2–83.2**
Law enforcement officers, arrest, powers and duties, **19.2–81.6, 19.2–82**

ALTERATION OF INSTRUMENTS
Forgery, generally, this index

AMBULANCES
Emergency Medical Services, generally, this index

ANIMALS
Fish and Game, generally, this index
Game. Fish and Game, generally, this index
Protective orders, companion animals, possession, **19.2–152.8 et seq.**
Wild animals and birds. Fish and Game, generally, this index

APPEAL AND REVIEW
Bail, **19.2–24, 19.2–25**
Bonds (officers and fiduciaries), **19.2–322.1**
Certificates and certification, **19.2–327**
Contempt, **19.2–318**
Crime victims, compensation and salaries, **19.2–368.7, 19.2–368.8**
Criminal prosecutions. Appeals in Criminal Prosecutions, generally, this index
Indigent persons, transcripts, **19.2–325**
Rules and regulations, **19.2–320**
Stay of proceedings. Supersedeas or Stay, generally, this index
Supersedeas or Stay, generally, this index

APPEALS IN CRIMINAL PROSECUTIONS
Generally, **19.2–317 et seq.**
Actual innocence, writs, **19.2–327.2 et seq.**
Nonbiological evidence, **19.2–327.10 et seq.**
Affirmance, **19.2–324**
Attorney fees, indigent persons, **19.2–326**
Attorneys, delayed appeals, motions, **19.2–321.1, 19.2–321.2**
Bail, this index
Biological evidence, **19.2–327.1 et seq.**
Briefs, state, **19.2–402, 19.2–403**
Certificates and certification, judgments and decrees, **19.2–327**
Costs, indigent persons, **19.2–326**
Crime victims,
Names, sex offenses, confidential or privileged information, **19.2–11.2**
Notice, **19.2–11.01**
Criminal history record information, expungement, **19.2–392.2**
Orders of court, **19.2–327.5, 19.2–327.13**
Cross appeals, state, **19.2–401**
Decisions, appellate courts, **19.2–324**
Delayed appeals, motions, **19.2–321.1, 19.2–321.2**
Dismissal and nonsuit, state, **19.2–398 et seq.**
DNA,
Application of law, samples, **19.2–303**
Testing, **19.2–327.1 et seq.**
Dockets and docketing, **19.2–240**
Double jeopardy, state, **19.2–398**
Errors, delayed appeals, motions, **19.2–321.1, 19.2–321.2**
Evidence, sufficiency, erroneously admitted, consideration, **19.2–324.1**
Execution, sentence, supersedeas or stay, **19.2–322.1**
Capital punishment, **19.2–319**
Fault, delayed appeals, motions, **19.2–321.1, 19.2–321.2**
Filing, petitions, **19.2–321**
Indigent persons, **19.2–326**
State, cross appeals, **19.2–401**
Transcripts, **19.2–165, 19.2–325**
Limitation of actions, state, **19.2–400**
Mandatory sentences, state, **19.2–398**

APPEALS IN CRIMINAL PROSECUTIONS —Cont'd
Neglect, delayed appeals, motions, **19.2–321.1, 19.2–321.2**
New trial, **19.2–324**
Evidence, erroneously admitted, sufficiency, **19.2–324.1**
Petitions, **19.2–320, 19.2–321**
State, **19.2–398**
Presentence investigations, reports, confidential or privileged information, **19.2–299**
Pretrial appeals, **19.2–398**
Public defenders, **19.2–163.3**
Restitution, state, **19.2–398**
Reversal, **19.2–324**
Sex offenses, crime victims, names, confidential or privileged information, **19.2–11.2**
Speedy trial, state, **19.2–398**
State, **19.2–398 et seq.**
Supersedeas or Stay, generally, this index
Suspended sentences, **19.2–306**
Time, delayed appeals, motions, **19.2–321.1, 19.2–321.2**
Transcripts, **19.2–165**
Indigent persons, **19.2–325**
State, **19.2–405**
Trial de novo, **19.2–324**
Evidence, erroneously admitted, sufficiency, **19.2–324.1**
Twenty one day rule, actual innocence, writs, nonbiological evidence, **19.2–327.10 et seq.**
Venue, state, **19.2–400**

APPEARANCE
Bail, generally, this index
Crimes and Offenses, this index
Subpoenas, generally, this index
Summons, generally, this index

ARMED FORCES
Military Forces, generally, this index

ARMS
Weapons, generally, this index

ARMY
Military Forces, generally, this index

ARRAIGNMENT
Generally, **19.2–254 et seq.**
Approvers, **19.2–256**
Pleas, **19.2–254 et seq.**
Presence of defendant, **19.2–259**
Pretrial services, officers and employees, powers and duties, **19.2–152.4:3**
Traffic rules and regulations, **19.2–254.1**
Trial, without jury, **19.2–257 et seq.**
Waiver, **19.2–254 et seq.**

ARREST
Generally, **19.2–71 et seq.**
Address, state agencies, **19.2–81.5**

ARREST—Cont'd
Agents and agency, executions, **19.2–76**
Aliens, law enforcement officers, powers and duties, **19.2–81.6, 19.2–82**
Appearance, warrantless arrest, **19.2–82**
Assault and battery, warrantless arrest, **19.2–81**
Bail, this index
Close pursuit, **19.2–77**
Foreign states, **19.2–79**
Conservators of the peace, **19.2–18**
Contents, warrants, **19.2–72**
Conviction of crime, surrender, failure, **19.2–298**
Corporations, executions, **19.2–76**
Correctional institutions, **19.2–81.1**
Accomplices and accessories, **19.2–81.2**
Criminal history record information, bail, **19.2–80.2**
Destruction, warrants, **19.2–76.1**
DNA, violent felonies, samples, **19.2–310.2:1, 19.2–310.3:1**
Domestic violence, **19.2–81.3**
Escape, **19.2–77, 19.2–81.1**
Executions, **19.2–76**
Warrants, **19.2–72**
Extradition, close pursuit, **19.2–79**
Flight, **19.2–77**
Foreign states, **19.2–79**
Habeas Corpus, generally, this index
Homicide, this index
Indictment and information, **19.2–236**
Investigations and investigators, subpoenas, **19.2–73.2**
Magistrates, **19.2–45**
Notice,
DNA, violent felonies, samples, **19.2–310.2:1**
Warrants, **19.2–73.1**
Oaths and affirmations, **19.2–72**
Partnerships, executions, **19.2–76**
Protective orders, violations, **19.2–81.3**
Pursuit, **19.2–77**
Foreign states, **19.2–79**
Release, summons, **19.2–74**
Reports, executions, **19.2–76.1**
Saliva samples, DNA, violent felonies, **19.2–310.2:1, 19.2–310.3:1**
School officers and employees, reports, **19.2–83.1**
Schools and school districts,
Reports, **19.2–83.1**
Weapons, **19.2–81**
Schoolteachers, reports, **19.2–83.1**
Searches and Seizures, generally, this index
Shoplifting, **19.2–81**
Stalking, **19.2–81.3**
Standards, domestic violence, **19.2–81.3**
State agencies, address, **19.2–81.5**
Summons, release, **19.2–74**
Tissue samples, DNA, violent felonies, **19.2–310.2:1, 19.2–310.3:1**
Unexecuted warrants, reports, **19.2–76.1**
Uniforms, law enforcement officers, **19.2–78**

ARREST—Cont'd
Venue, warrants, **19.2–72**
Warrantless arrest, **19.2–81, 19.2–82**
Aliens, law enforcement officers, powers and duties, **19.2–81.6, 19.2–82**
Correctional institutions, **19.2–81.1**
Extradition, **19.2–100**
Warrants,
Bail, **19.2–20**
Contents, **19.2–72**
Destruction, unexecuted warrants, **19.2–76.1**
Dismissal and nonsuit, unexecuted, **19.2–76.1**
Executions, **19.2–76**
Issuance, **19.2–72**
Unexecuted warrants, reports, **19.2–76.1**
Virginia Crime Code references, **19.2–390.01**
Weapons, warrantless arrest, **19.2–81**
Witnesses, foreign states, **19.2–275**

ARSON
Arrest, DNA, violent felonies, samples, **19.2–310.2:1, 19.2–310.3:1**
DNA, violent felonies, samples, **19.2–310.2:1, 19.2–310.3:1**
Second and subsequent offenses, sentencing, **19.2–297.1**
Three strikes, sentencing, **19.2–297.1**

ASSAULT AND BATTERY
Arrest, **19.2–81**
DNA, violent felonies, samples, **19.2–310.2:1, 19.2–310.3:1**
Bail, satisfaction and discharge, **19.2–151**
Children and minors. Child Abuse, generally, this index
Criminal history record information, sentencing, **19.2–299**
DNA, violent felonies, samples, **19.2–310.2:1, 19.2–310.3:1**
Domestic Violence, generally, this index
Evidence, prior abuse, **19.2–270.6**
Husband and wife. Domestic Violence, generally, this index
Investigations and investigators, presentence investigations, **19.2–299**
Life imprisonment, three strikes, **19.2–297.1**
Marriage. Domestic Violence, generally, this index
Presentence investigations, **19.2–299**
Prior abuse, evidence, **19.2–270.6**
Protective orders, **19.2–152.7:1 et seq.**
Second and subsequent offenses, sentencing, **19.2–297.1**
Sex Offenses, generally, this index
Three strikes, sentencing, **19.2–297.1**
Venue, **19.2–246**

ASSIGNATION
Prostitution, generally, this index

ASSISTANCE
Social Services, generally, this index

ASSISTED LIVING FACILITIES
Criminal history record information, disclosure, **19.2–389**

ASSOCIATIONS AND SOCIETIES
Corporations, generally, this index

ATTESTATION
Oaths and Affirmations, generally, this index

ATTORNEY FEES
Appointment, court appointment, crimes and offenses, **19.2–163**
Capital punishment, indigent persons, **19.2–163**
Court appointment, crimes and offenses, **19.2–163**
Crimes and offenses, indigent persons, **19.2–163**
Criminal injuries compensation fund, liens and incumbrances, priorities and preferences, **19.2–368.15**
Indigent persons, crimes and offenses, **19.2–163**
Liens and incumbrances, criminal injuries compensation fund, priorities and preferences, **19.2–368.15**
Limitation, crimes and offenses, court appointment, waiver, **19.2–163**
Protective orders, **19.2–152.10**
Respondent, **19.2–152.12**
Reports, indigent defense, appointments, **19.2–163.01**
Stalking, protective orders, **19.2–152.10**
Waiver, crimes and offenses, court appointment, limitation, **19.2–163**
Wiretapping, **19.2–69**

ATTORNEY FOR THE COMMONWEALTH
Prosecuting Attorneys, generally, this index

ATTORNEY GENERAL
Actual innocence, writs, petitions, joining, **19.2–327.2:1, 19.2–327.10:1**
Public defenders, legal services, **19.2–163.5**

ATTORNEYS
Appeals in criminal prosecutions, delayed appeals, motions, **19.2–321.1, 19.2–321.2**
Boards and commissions, indigent defense commission, **19.2–163.01 et seq.**
Capital Punishment, this index
Compensation and salaries. Attorney Fees, generally, this index
Continuing education, indigent defense, appointment, **19.2–163.01, 19.2–163.03**
Court appointments, crimes and offenses, **19.2–157 et seq.**
Crimes and offenses,
Continuance, appearance, **19.2–266.3**
Delayed appeals, motions, **19.2–321.1, 19.2–321.2**
Electronic video and audio communications, representation, determination, **19.2–3.1**
Indigent defense commission, **19.2–163.01 et seq.**
Prosecuting Attorneys, generally, this index
Public Defenders, generally, this index

ATTORNEYS—Cont'd
Crimes and offenses—Cont'd
Trial, opening statements, **19.2–265**
Errors, delayed appeals, motions, **19.2–321.1, 19.2–321.2**
Extradition, **19.2–95**
Fault, delayed appeals, motions, **19.2–321.1, 19.2–321.2**
Fees. Attorney Fees, generally, this index
Felonies, indigent defense, appointment, qualifications, **19.2–163.03**
Grand Jury, this index
Indigent defense commission, **19.2–163.01 et seq.**
Licenses and permits, crimes and offenses, limitation of prosecutions, **19.2–8**
Limitation of prosecutions, licenses and permits, crimes and offenses, **19.2–8**
Lists, indigent defense, appointment, **19.2–163.01**
Magistrates,
Chief magistrates, appointments, **19.2–36**
Eligibility, **19.2–37**
Misdemeanors, indigent defense, appointment, qualifications, **19.2–163.03**
Motions, generally, this index
Negligence, delayed appeals, motions, **19.2–321.1, 19.2–321.2**
Privileges and immunities, public defenders, compensation and salaries, supplementing, **19.2–163.01:1**
Prosecuting Attorneys, generally, this index
Public Defenders, generally, this index
Qualifications, indigent defense, appointment, **19.2–163.01, 19.2–163.03**
Reports, indigent defense, appointments, **19.2–163.01**
Right to counsel, **19.2–157 et seq., 19.2–163.01 et seq.**
Appeals in criminal prosecutions, **19.2–326**
Capital punishment, **19.2–163.7, 19.2–163.8**
Delayed appeals, motions, **19.2–321.1, 19.2–321.2**
DNA testing, **19.2–327.1 et seq.**
Indigent defense commission, **19.2–163.01 et seq.**
Pretrial services, officers and employees, powers and duties, **19.2–152.4:3**
Public Defenders, generally, this index
Special grand juries, **19.2–208**
Rules and regulations, indigent defense commission, **19.2–163.01**
Searches and seizures, warrants, **19.2–56.1**
Standards, indigent defense, appointment, **19.2–163.01, 19.2–163.03**
State,
Attorney General, generally, this index
Prosecuting Attorneys, generally, this index
Training, indigent defense, appointment, **19.2–163.01, 19.2–163.03**
Waiver, indigent persons, **19.2–160**
Wiretapping, damages, **19.2–69**
Withdrawal, capital punishment, **19.2–163.7**

ATTORNEYS FOR THE COMMONWEALTH
Prosecuting Attorneys, generally, this index

AUDITS AND AUDITORS
Magistrates, **19.2–48**

AUTOMOBILES
Motor Vehicles, generally, this index

AUTOPSIES
Evidence, crimes and offenses, **19.2–188**

BABIES
Children and Minors, generally, this index

BACKGROUND INVESTIGATIONS
Criminal History Record Information, generally, this index

BADGES, EMBLEMS AND INSIGNIA
Conservators of the peace, **19.2–13**

BAIL
Generally, **19.2–119 et seq.**
Actual innocence, writs, **19.2–327.2:1, 19.2–327.10:1**
Aliens, **19.2–120**
Presumptions, **19.2–120.1**
Appeals in criminal prosecutions, **19.2–24, 19.2–25, 19.2–120, 19.2–124, 19.2–319**
Capital punishment, **19.2–319**
Release, pending appeal, **19.2–125, 19.2–319**
Arrest, **19.2–80**
Criminal history record information, **19.2–80.2**
Discharge, surety, **19.2–149, 19.2–150**
Assault and battery, satisfaction, discharge, **19.2–151**
Bondspersons,
Criminal history record information, **19.2–389**
Fees, **19.2–120**
Discharge, **19.2–149**
Breath tests, second and subsequent offenses, **19.2–123**
Capias, terms, **19.2–130.1**
Capital punishment,
Appeals in criminal prosecutions, **19.2–319**
Presumptions, **19.2–120**
Certificates and certification, **19.2–190**
Change of venue, **19.2–252**
Child abuse, protective orders, second and subsequent offenses, **19.2–120**
Community criminal justice boards, pretrial services, **19.2–152.5**
Complaints, keeping the peace, **19.2–20**
Conditions, **19.2–135**
Second and subsequent offenses, **19.2–123**
Constitutional officers, release, conditions, **19.2–123**
Contempt, **19.2–129**
Controlled substances, presumptions, **19.2–120**
Crime victims, notice, **19.2–11.01**
Criminal history record information, **19.2–80.2, 19.2–120, 19.2–121**

BAIL—Cont'd
Defects, **19.2–146**
Discharge,
  Assault and battery, **19.2–151**
  Forfeitures, surety, **19.2–148 et seq.**
  Orders of court, **19.2–152**
Dockets and docketing, forfeitures, **19.2–147**
Domestic violence, protective orders, second and subsequent offenses, **19.2–120**
Driving under influence of alcohol or drugs, presumptions, **19.2–120**
Electronic monitoring, second and subsequent offenses, **19.2–123**
Electronic video and audio communications, appearance, **19.2–3.1**
Evidence, **19.2–121**
Extradition, **19.2–102 et seq.**
Fees,
  Criminal history record information, **19.2–120**
  Filing, service of process, appeals in criminal prosecutions, **19.2–124**
Filing, **19.2–142**
  Fees, appeals in criminal prosecutions, **19.2–124**
Fingerprints and fingerprinting, release, second and subsequent offenses, conditions, **19.2–123**
First appearance, motions, **19.2–158**
Force and violence, presumptions, **19.2–120**
Foreign jurisdictions, **19.2–131**
Forfeitures, **19.2–128, 19.2–143 et seq.**
  Discharge, surety, **19.2–148 et seq.**
  Dockets and docketing, **19.2–147**
  Extradition, **19.2–104**
  Military forces, **19.2–144**
Gangs, presumptions, **19.2–120**
Global positioning systems, second and subsequent offenses, **19.2–123**
Hearings, time, **19.2–158**
Increase, **19.2–132**
Keeping the peace, **19.2–19 et seq.**
Labor and employment, second and subsequent offenses, **19.2–123**
Mentally ill persons, **19.2–141**
Mentally retarded and developmentally disabled persons, **19.2–141**
  Second and subsequent offenses, **19.2–123**
Motions, **19.2–158**
Motor vehicles, driving under influence of alcohol or drugs, presumptions, **19.2–120**
Notice,
  Forfeitures, **19.2–128**
  Increase, **19.2–132**
  Presumptions, **19.2–120**
Obscenity, children and minors, **19.2–120**
Orders of court, **19.2–137**
  Discharge, **19.2–152**
Payment, **19.2–136**
Photography and pictures, release, second and subsequent offenses, conditions, **19.2–123**
Presumptions, **19.2–120**
  Aliens, **19.2–120.1**

BAIL—Cont'd
Pretrial services, officers and employees, powers and duties, **19.2–152.4:3**
Revocation or suspension, **19.2–132**
Screening, alcohol or drugs, second and subsequent offenses, **19.2–123**
Second and subsequent offenses, **19.2–123**
Service of process, fees, appeals in criminal prosecutions, **19.2–124**
Show cause, forfeitures, **19.2–143**
Stay, appeals in criminal prosecutions, **19.2–124, 19.2–132**
Strangulation, **19.2–120**
Subsequent proceedings, **19.2–130**
Supersedeas or stay, appeals in criminal prosecutions, **19.2–124, 19.2–132**
Surrender, defendants, discharge, surety, **19.2–149, 19.2–150**
Terms, **19.2–121**
  Capias, **19.2–130.1**
Terrorism, **19.2–120**
Tests and testing, controlled substances, second and subsequent offenses, **19.2–123**
Threats, **19.2–19 et seq.**
Time, **19.2–3**
  Hearings, **19.2–158**
Traffic rules and regulations, driving under influence of alcohol or drugs, presumptions, **19.2–120**
Trespass, keeping the peace, **19.2–19 et seq.**
Urine tests, second and subsequent offenses, **19.2–123**
Venue, change of venue, **19.2–252**
Weapons, this index

BANK DEPOSITS AND COLLECTIONS
Production of books and papers, records and recordation, **19.2–10.1**
Records and recordation, production of books and papers, **19.2–10.1**

BANKS AND BANKING
Production of books and papers, records and recordation, **19.2–10.1**
Records and recordation, production of books and papers, **19.2–10.1**

BAR
Attorneys, generally, this index

BARRISTER
Attorneys, generally, this index

BATTERY
Assault and Battery, generally, this index

BETTING
Gambling, generally, this index

BILLS OF PARTICULARS
Crimes and offenses, **19.2–266.2**

BINGO AND RAFFLES
Criminal history record information, **19.2–389**

BIOLOGICAL EVIDENCE
DNA, generally, this index

BIOTERRORISM
Terrorism, generally, this index

BIRDS
Fish and Game, generally, this index

BLIND PERSONS
Criminal history record information, disclosure, **19.2–389**

BLOOD
Samples, searches and seizures, warrants, privileges and immunities, **19.2–53.1**

BLOOD TESTS
Boats and boating, driving under influence of alcohol or drugs, **19.2–187.02**
DNA, generally, this index
Emergency medical services, evidence, admissibility, **19.2–187.02**
Samples, searches and seizures, warrants, privileges and immunities, **19.2–53.1**

BLUE SKY LAW
Securities, generally, this index

BOARDS AND COMMISSIONS
Attorneys, indigent defense commission, **19.2–163.01 et seq.**
Indigent defense commission, **19.2–163.01 et seq.**

BOATS AND BOATING
See, also, Ships and Shipping, generally, this index
Arrest, **19.2–81**
Blood tests, driving under influence of alcohol or drugs, **19.2–187.02**
Boarding, probable cause, searches and seizures, **19.2–10.3**
Driving under influence of alcohol or drugs,
  Arrest, **19.2–81**
  Blood tests, **19.2–187.02**
Inspection and inspectors, probable cause, searches and seizures, **19.2–10.3**
Probable cause, searches and seizures, **19.2–10.3**
Searches and seizures, probable cause, **19.2–10.3**

BOMBS
Arson, generally, this index

BONDS
Securities, generally, this index

BONDS (OFFICERS AND FIDUCIARIES)
Bail, generally, this index
Conservators of the peace, **19.2–13**
Magistrates, **19.2–39**
Special conservators of the peace, registration, **19.2–13**

BONDSPERSONS
Bail, this index

BOOKMAKING
Gambling, generally, this index

BOOKS AND PAPERS
Evidence, generally, this index
Forgery, generally, this index
Lewdness and obscenity. Obscenity, generally, this index
Obscenity, generally, this index
Pornography. Obscenity, generally, this index
Production of Books and Papers, generally, this index
Records and Recordation, generally, this index
Searches and Seizures, generally, this index
Subpoena duces tecum. Production of Books and Papers, generally, this index

BOOT CAMPS
Crimes and offenses, **19.2–316.1**

BOUNDARIES
Venue, crimes and offenses, **19.2–249 et seq.**

BRASS KNUCKLES
Weapons, generally, this index

BREAKING AND ENTERING
DNA, violent felonies, samples, **19.2–310.2:1, 19.2–310.3:1**

BRIBERY AND CORRUPTION
Forfeitures, public office, **19.2–386.33**

BUILDING CODES
Limitation of prosecutions, **19.2–8**

BUILDINGS
Arson, generally, this index
Limitation of prosecutions, **19.2–8**
Searches and Seizures, generally, this index

BURGLARY
DNA, violent felonies, samples, **19.2–310.2:1, 19.2–310.3:1**

BURNING
Arson, generally, this index

BUSINESS AND COMMERCE
Corporations, generally, this index
Real Property Taxation, generally, this index

BUSINESS CORPORATIONS
Corporations, generally, this index

CAMERAS
Photography and Pictures, generally, this index

CAPITAL PUNISHMENT
Generally, **19.2–264.2 et seq.**
Actual innocence, writs, DNA testing, **19.2–327.2 et seq.**
Age, mitigation, **19.2–264.4**
Aggravating circumstances, **19.2–264.4**
Appeals in criminal prosecutions, **19.2–319**

CAPITAL PUNISHMENT—Cont'd
Assessments, mentally retarded and developmentally disabled persons, **19.2–264.3:1.1, 19.2–264.3:1.2**
Attorney fees, indigent persons, **19.2–163**
Attorneys, indigent persons, **19.2–163.01 et seq., 19.2–163.7, 19.2–163.8**
Bail,
  Appeals in criminal prosecutions, **19.2–319**
  Presumptions, **19.2–120**
Burden of proof, mentally retarded and developmentally disabled persons, **19.2–264.3:1.1**
Confidential or privileged information, mentally retarded and developmentally disabled persons, evaluations, **19.2–264.3:3**
Continuances,
  Mentally ill persons, **19.2–264.3:1**
  Mentally retarded and developmentally disabled persons, evaluations, **19.2–264.3:1.2**
Crime victims, impact statements, **19.2–264.4, 19.2–264.5, 19.2–299.1**
Criminal history record information, notice, **19.2–264.3:2**
Criminal insanity, evaluations, **19.2–264.3:1**
  Disclosure, **19.2–264.3:3**
Disclosure, mental examinations, **19.2–264.3:3**
DNA testing, **19.2–327.1 et seq.**
Evaluations,
  Mentally ill persons, **19.2–264.3:1**
    Mentally retarded and developmentally disabled persons, disclosure, **19.2–264.3:3**
  Mentally retarded and developmentally disabled persons, **19.2–264.3:1.1, 19.2–264.3:1.2**
Evidence,
  Criminal history record information, **19.2–264.3:2**
  DNA testing, **19.2–327.1 et seq.**
  Evaluations, disclosure, **19.2–264.3:3**
  Mentally retarded and developmentally disabled persons, **19.2–264.3:1.2**
    Burden of proof, **19.2–264.3:1.1**
  Sentencing, **19.2–264.4**
Ex parte proceedings, experts, assisting in defense, appointments, **19.2–264.3:1.3**
Expert testimony, evidence, notice, **19.2–264.3:4**
Experts, assisting in defense, appointments, **19.2–264.3:1.3**
Forms, mentally retarded and developmentally disabled persons, verdicts, **19.2–264.3:1.1**
Impact statements, crime victims, **19.2–264.4, 19.2–264.5, 19.2–299.1**
Indictment and information, **19.2–217.1**
Indigent persons,
  Attorneys, **19.2–163.01 et seq., 19.2–163.7, 19.2–163.8**
  Experts, assisting in defense, appointments, **19.2–264.3:1.3**
  Mentally ill persons, evaluations, **19.2–264.3:1**
  Mentally retarded and developmentally disabled persons, evaluations, **19.2–264.3:1.2**

CAPITAL PUNISHMENT—Cont'd
Investigations and investigators, postsentence reports, **19.2–264.5**
Jury, **19.2–264.2, 19.2–264.3**
  Mentally retarded and developmentally disabled persons, **19.2–264.3:1.1**
Lists, attorneys, indigent persons, **19.2–163.8**
Mentally ill persons,
  Evaluations, **19.2–264.3:1**
    Disclosure, **19.2–264.3:3**
  Mitigation, **19.2–264.4**
Mentally retarded and developmentally disabled persons,
  Assessments, **19.2–264.3:1.1, 19.2–264.3:1.2**
  Mitigation, **19.2–264.4**
Mitigating circumstances, **19.2–264.4**
Motions, experts, assisting in defense, appointments, **19.2–264.3:1.3**
Notice,
  Criminal history record information, **19.2–264.3:2**
  Mental examinations, **19.2–264.3:1**
    Mentally retarded and developmentally disabled persons, **19.2–264.3:1.2**
  Opinions or expert testimony, evidence, **19.2–264.3:4**
Opinions or expert testimony, evidence, notice, **19.2–264.3:4**
Postsentence investigations, **19.2–264.5**
Presumptions, bail, **19.2–120**
Records and recordation, experts, assisting in defense, appointments, **19.2–264.3:1.3**
Reports,
  Mentally retarded and developmentally disabled persons, evaluations, **19.2–264.3:1.2**
  Postsentence investigations, **19.2–264.5**
Setting aside, **19.2–264.5**
Supersedeas or stay, appeals in criminal prosecutions, **19.2–319**
Trial, **19.2–264.2 et seq.**
Unadjudicated crimes and offenses, notice, **19.2–264.3:2**
Verdicts, **19.2–264.4**
  Mentally retarded and developmentally disabled persons, forms, **19.2–264.3:1.1**
  Setting aside, **19.2–264.5**
Withdrawal, attorneys, **19.2–163.7**
Witnesses, opinions or expert testimony, evidence, notice, **19.2–264.3:4**
Writs, actual innocence, DNA testing, **19.2–327.2 et seq.**

CAPITOL SQUARE
Damages, restitution, evidence, **19.2–305.1**

CARJACKING
Second and subsequent offenses, sentencing, **19.2–297.1**

CARRIERS
Ships and Shipping, generally, this index

CARS
Motor Vehicles, generally, this index

CEMETERIES
Conservators of the peace, **19.2–14**

CENTRAL CRIMINAL RECORDS EXCHANGE
Generally, **19.2–387 et seq.**

CERTIFICATES AND CERTIFICATION
Grand jury, examinations and examiners, **19.2–207**
Magistrates, **19.2–38**

CHEATING
Fraud, generally, this index

CHEMICALLY DEPENDENT PERSONS
See, also, Mentally Ill Persons, generally, this index
Crimes and offenses, pretrial services, officers and employees, powers and duties, **19.2–152.4:3**
Criminal history record information, disclosure, **19.2–389**
Screening, crimes and offenses, sentencing, **19.2–299**

CHEMICALS, CHEMISTRY AND CHEMISTS
Blood Tests, generally, this index
Hazardous Substances and Waste, generally, this index

CHILD ABUSE
Bail, protective orders, second and subsequent offenses, **19.2–120**
Criminal history record information, disclosure, investigations and investigators, **19.2–389**
Investigations and investigators, criminal history record information, disclosure, **19.2–389**
Second and subsequent offenses, protective orders, bail, **19.2–120**
Witnesses, husband and wife, **19.2–271.2**

CHILD CARE FACILITIES
Criminal history record information, contracts, social services department, disclosure, **19.2–389**

CHILD CARING INSTITUTIONS
Criminal history record information, contracts, social services department, disclosure, **19.2–389**

CHILD PORNOGRAPHY
Children and minors. Obscenity, this index

CHILDREN AND MINORS
Abuse. Child Abuse, generally, this index
Adoption, generally, this index
Crime victims,
  Compensation and salaries, claims, **19.2–368.4, 19.2–368.5**
  Sex offenses, **19.2–11.01**
Crimes and offenses,
  Delinquent Children, generally, this index
  Obscenity, this index
  Registration, postrelease supervision, **19.2–295.2:1**
Delinquent Children, generally, this index

CHILDREN AND MINORS—Cont'd
Forfeitures, kidnapping, **19.2–386.32**
Juvenile delinquents. Delinquent Children, generally, this index
Photography and pictures, privacy, crimes and offenses, venue, **19.2–249.2**
Pornography. Obscenity, this index
Schools and School Districts, generally, this index
Searches and seizures, kidnapping, forfeitures, **19.2–386.32**
Video tapes, privacy, crimes and offenses, venue, **19.2–249.2**

CHIROPRACTORS
Health Care Professionals, generally, this index

CIGARETTE TAX
Collection,
  Delivery,
    Crimes and offenses, venue, **19.2–245.01**
    Forfeitures, **19.2–386.20**
  Transportation, forfeitures, **19.2–386.20**
Forfeitures,
  Contraband, tax paid cigarettes, **19.2–386.21**
  Delivery, collection, **19.2–386.20**
  Stamps, unstamped cigarettes, **19.2–386.21**
Stamps, counterfeiting, forfeitures, **19.2–386.21**

CIGARETTES AND CIGARS
Brands, marks and labels, counterfeiting, forfeitures, **19.2–386.21**
Certificates and certification, delivery, crimes and offenses, **19.2–245.01**
Counterfeiting, forfeitures, **19.2–386.21**
Crimes and offenses,
  Delivery, venue, **19.2–245.01**
  Venue, **19.2–245.01**
Forfeitures,
  Contraband, counterfeiting, **19.2–386.21**
  Delivery, violations, **19.2–386.20**
Fraud, certificates and certification, delivery, crimes and offenses, **19.2–245.01**
Taxation. Cigarette Tax, generally, this index
Venue, crimes and offenses, **19.2–245.01**

CIRCUIT COURTS
Adverse or pecuniary interest, judges, **19.2–153**
Appointments, **19.2–6**
  Conservators of the peace, **19.2–13**
Conservators of the peace, appointments, **19.2–13**
Crimes and offenses,
  Ancillary misdemeanors, certificates and certification, **19.2–190.1**
  Jurisdiction, **19.2–239**
  Motions, pretrial proceedings, **19.2–266.2**
  Objections and exceptions, pretrial proceedings, **19.2–266.2**
  Trial, judges, disability or death, **19.2–154**
Disqualification, judges, **19.2–153**
Executions, generally, this index
Judges,
  Adverse or pecuniary interest, **19.2–153**

CIRCUIT COURTS—Cont'd
Judges—Cont'd
Death, **19.2–154**
Disability, **19.2–154**
Disqualification, **19.2–153**
Multijurisdiction grand juries, **19.2–215.3**
Powers and duties, appointments, **19.2–6**
Magistrates, generally, this index

CITIES AND TOWNS
Municipalities, generally, this index

CITIZENS AND CITIZENSHIP
Jails, reports, **19.2–83.2**
Magistrates, appointments, **19.2–37**

CIVIL DEFENSE
Terrorism, generally, this index

CIVIL PENALTIES
Fines and Penalties, generally, this index

CIVIL PROCESS
Process, generally, this index

CLERGY
Confidential or privileged information, witnesses, **19.2–271.3**
Privileges and immunities, witnesses, **19.2–271.3**
Wiretapping, damages, **19.2–69**
Witnesses, **19.2–271.3**

COAST GUARD
Military Forces, generally, this index

COINS
Money, generally, this index

COLLEGES AND UNIVERSITIES
Criminal history record information,
Disclosure, **19.2–389**
Threats, teams, assessments, **19.2–389, 19.2–389.1**
Sex offenses, registration, proof, nonresidents, **19.2–298**
Threats, assessments, criminal history record information, **19.2–389, 19.2–389.1**

COLLUSION
Fraud, generally, this index

COMMERCIAL PAPER
Negotiable Instruments, generally, this index

COMMITMENT
Mentally Ill Persons, this index

COMMONWEALTH
State, generally, this index

COMMONWEALTH ATTORNEYS
Prosecuting Attorneys, generally, this index

COMMUNICATIONS
Confidential or Privileged Information, generally, this index

COMMUNICATIONS—Cont'd
Telecommunications, generally, this index

COMMUNITY CORRECTIONS
Generally, **19.2–303.3**
Screening, substance abuse, **19.2–299.2**

COMMUNITY SERVICE
Generally, **19.2–305, 19.2–305.1**

COMPANIES
Corporations, generally, this index

COMPENSATION AND SALARIES
Attorney Fees, generally, this index
Crime victims, **19.2–368.1 et seq.**
Criminal Injuries Compensation Fund, generally, this index
Indigent defense commission, **19.2–163.02**
Magistrates, **19.2–38, 19.2–46, 19.2–46.1**
Public defenders, supplementing, **19.2–163.01:1**

COMPUTERS
Confidential or privileged information, real time location data, records and recordation, **19.2–70.3**
Crimes and offenses,
Limitation of prosecutions, **19.2–8**
Subpoenas, information, **19.2–267.2**
Venue, **19.2–249.2**
Electronic Mail, generally, this index
Evidence, remote computing services, hearsay, exceptions, **19.2–70.3**
Foreign states, remote computing services, records and recordation, search warrants, **19.2–70.3**
Forfeitures, crimes and offenses, **19.2–386.17**
Internet, generally, this index
Limitation of prosecutions, **19.2–8**
Real time location data, records and recordation, disclosure, **19.2–70.3**
Remote computing services,
Records and recordation, disclosure, **19.2–70.3**
Searches and seizures, warrants, **19.2–56**
Subpoenas, crimes and offenses, investigations and investigators, **19.2–10.2**
Searches and seizures, **19.2–53**
Real time location data, records and recordation, **19.2–70.3**
Subpoenas,
Crimes and offenses, records and recordation, investigations and investigators, **19.2–10.2**
Real time location data, records and recordation, disclosure, **19.2–70.3**
Venue, crimes and offenses, **19.2–249.2**
Warrants, searches and seizures, real time location data, records and recordation, **19.2–70.3**

CONCEALMENT
Shoplifting, generally, this index
Theft, generally, this index

CONCURRENT SENTENCES
Crimes and offenses, **19.2–308.1**

CONFIDENTIAL OR PRIVILEGED INFORMATION
See, also, Disclosure, generally, this index
Capital punishment, mentally retarded and developmentally disabled persons, evaluations, **19.2–264.3:3**
Clergy, witnesses, **19.2–271.3**
Computers, real time location data, records and recordation, **19.2–70.3**
Crime Victims, this index
Crimes and Offenses, this index
Criminal history record information, **19.2–389**
Critical incident stress management teams, emergency medical services, **19.2–271.4**
DNA testing, convicted felons, **19.2–310.5, 19.2–310.6**
Grand jury, **19.2–192**
Multijurisdiction grand juries, **19.2–215.4**
Husband and wife, crimes and offenses, witnesses, **19.2–271.2**
Internet, real time location data, records and recordation, **19.2–70.3**
Jury, orders, **19.2–263.3**
Protective orders, **19.2–152.8 et seq.**
Stalking, protective orders, **19.2–152.8 et seq.**
Wiretapping, generally, this index
Witnesses, this index

CONSERVATION
Fish and Game, generally, this index

CONSERVATORS OF THE PEACE
Generally, **19.2–12 et seq.**
Special conservators of the peace, registration, **19.2–13**

CONSTITUTION OF THE UNITED STATES
Double Jeopardy, generally, this index
Speedy Trial, generally, this index

CONSTITUTION OF VIRGINIA
Double Jeopardy, generally, this index
Speedy Trial, generally, this index

CONSTITUTIONAL OFFICERS
Attorney General, generally, this index
Bail, release, conditions, **19.2–123**

CONTEMPT
Appeal and review, **19.2–318**
Bail, **19.2–129**
Grand jury, special grand juries, **19.2–208**
Show cause hearings, **19.2–11**

CONTINUANCE
Crimes and Offenses, this index

CONTINUING EDUCATION
Attorneys, indigent defense, appointment, **19.2–163.01, 19.2–163.03**
Public defenders, **19.2–163.01**

CONTRABAND
Correctional institutions, arrest, without warrants, **19.2–81.1**

CONTROLLED SUBSTANCES
See, also, Drugs and Medicine, generally, this index
Addicts. Chemically Dependent Persons, generally, this index
Bail, presumptions, **19.2–120**
Boats and boating, driving under influence of alcohol or drugs, crimes and offenses, arrest, **19.2–81**
Certificates of analysis, **19.2–187**
Chemically Dependent Persons, generally, this index
Destruction, forfeitures, **19.2–386.23**
Pretrial, **19.2–386.24**
Driving under influence of alcohol or drugs. Traffic Rules and Regulations, this index
Drug addicts. Chemically Dependent Persons, generally, this index
Evidence, field tests, **19.2–188.1**
Fines and penalties, forfeitures, **19.2–386.1 et seq.**
Forfeitures, **19.2–386.1 et seq., 19.2–386.22 et seq.**
Destruction, **19.2–386.23**
Pretrial, **19.2–386.24**
Hazardous substances and waste, manufacturers and manufacturing, cleanup, restitution, **19.2–305.1**
Health care providers, falsifying patient records, limitation of prosecutions, **19.2–8**
Inventories, searches and seizures, law enforcement agencies, reports, **19.2–386.23**
Limitation of prosecutions, falsifying patient records, health care providers, **19.2–8**
Manufacturers and manufacturing, restitution, hazardous substances and waste, cleanup, **19.2–305.1**
Marijuana,
Field tests, **19.2–188.1**
Inventories, searches and seizures, law enforcement agencies, **19.2–386.23**
Notice, forfeitures, destruction, **19.2–386.24**
Orders of court, custody, law enforcement agencies, **19.2–386.25**
Presentence investigations, **19.2–299**
Records and recordation, falsifying patient records, crimes and offenses, limitation of prosecutions, **19.2–8**
Reports, searches and seizures, inventories, law enforcement agencies, **19.2–386.23**
Restitution, manufacturers and manufacturing, hazardous substances and waste, cleanup, **19.2–305.1**
Searches and seizures, **19.2–386.22 et seq.**
Forfeitures, **19.2–386.1 et seq.**
Destruction, **19.2–386.23, 19.2–386.24**
Synthetic cannabinoids, inventories, searches and seizures, law enforcement agencies, **19.2–386.23**

CONVERSION
See, also, Theft, generally, this index

CONVERSION—Cont'd
Embezzlement, generally, this index

CONVICTION OF CRIME
Crimes and Offenses, this index

CONVICTS
Correctional Institutions, generally, this index
Jails, generally, this index

CORPORATIONS
Arrest, executions, **19.2–76**
Indictment and information, **19.2–238**
Summons, indictment and information, **19.2–238**

CORRECTIONAL INSTITUTIONS
See, also, Jails, generally, this index
Arrest,
Accomplices and accessories, **19.2–81.2**
Warrantless arrest, **19.2–81.1**
Boot camps, **19.2–316.1**
Capital Punishment, generally, this index
Contraband, arrest, **19.2–81.1**
Crimes and offenses, arrest, **19.2–81.1**
Death penalty. Capital Punishment, generally, this index
Detention, accomplices and accessories, **19.2–81.2**
Detention centers, **19.2–316.2**
Diversion centers, **19.2–316.3**
Escape, generally, this index
Executions. Capital Punishment, generally, this index
Habeas Corpus, generally, this index
Indeterminate commitment, **19.2–311 et seq.**
Officers and employees, arrest, accomplices and accessories, **19.2–81.2**
Parole, generally, this index
Postrelease supervision. Probation, generally, this index
Priorities and preferences, transportation, **19.2–310**
Probation, generally, this index
Release,
Actual innocence, writs, **19.2–327.2:1, 19.2–327.10:1**
Habeas Corpus, generally, this index
Parole, generally, this index
Probation, generally, this index
Strip searches, **19.2–59.1**
Time, terms, imprisonment, **19.2–295 et seq.**
Transportation, **19.2–310**
Witnesses, processing, **19.2–269.1**
Work release, costs, failure to pay, **19.2–354**

COSTS
Crimes and Offenses, this index
Criminal injuries compensation fund, liens and incumbrances, priorities and preferences, **19.2–368.15**
Extradition, **19.2–112**
Probation, this index
Protective orders, **19.2–152.10**
Stalking, protective orders, **19.2–152.10**

COSTS—Cont'd
Wiretapping, **19.2–69**

COUNSEL
Attorneys, generally, this index

COUNSELORS AND COUNSELING
Crime victims, compensation and salaries, **19.2–368.11:1**
Indictment and information, domestic violence, **19.2–218.1, 19.2–218.2**
Psychiatrists and Psychiatry, generally, this index
Psychologists and Psychology, generally, this index
Wiretapping, damages, **19.2–69**

COUNTERFEITING
Forgery, generally, this index

COUNTIES
Circuit Courts, generally, this index
Commonwealth attorneys. Prosecuting Attorneys, generally, this index
Correctional institutions. Jails, generally, this index
Delinquent Children, generally, this index
District Courts, generally, this index
Jails, generally, this index
Licenses and permits, professions and occupations, limitation of prosecutions, **19.2–8**
Limitation of prosecutions, professions and occupations, licenses and permits, **19.2–8**
Prisons and prisoners. Jails, generally, this index
Professions and occupations, licenses and permits, limitation of prosecutions, **19.2–8**
Public Defenders, generally, this index
Real Property Taxation, generally, this index
Sheriffs, generally, this index
Taxation. Real Property Taxation, generally, this index
Venue, crimes and offenses, **19.2–249 et seq.**

COUNTY JAILS
Jails, generally, this index

COURT COSTS
Costs, generally, this index

COURT OF APPEALS
Appeals in Criminal Prosecutions, generally, this index
Crimes and offenses. Appeals in Criminal Prosecutions, generally, this index
Delayed appeals, appeals in criminal prosecutions, motions, **19.2–321.1**

COURT OFFICERS AND EMPLOYEES
Attorneys, generally, this index

COURT REPORTERS
Crimes and offenses, **19.2–166**
Habeas corpus, **19.2–166**
Multijurisdiction grand juries, **19.2–215.9**
Special grand juries, **19.2–212**

COURTHOUSES
Security, **19.2–328**

COURTS
Appeal and Review, generally, this index
Attorneys, generally, this index
Circuit Courts, generally, this index
Contempt, generally, this index
Costs, generally, this index
Courts not of record. District Courts, generally, this index
District Courts, generally, this index
Guards, costs, **19.2–328**
Habeas Corpus, generally, this index
Judges, generally, this index
Judgments and Decrees, generally, this index
Jury, generally, this index
Not of record. District Courts, generally, this index
Officers and employees, witnesses, **19.2–271**
Parole, generally, this index
Probation, revocation, **19.2–306**
Records and recordation, expungement, **19.2–327.5, 19.2–327.13, 19.2–392.2**
Reporters. Court Reporters, generally, this index
Revocation,
  Probation, **19.2–306**
  Suspended sentences, **19.2–306**
Security, **19.2–328**
Suspended sentences, revocation, **19.2–306**
Witnesses, officers and employees, **19.2–271**

COURTS NOT OF RECORD
District Courts, generally, this index

COURTS OF RECORD
Courts, generally, this index

CREDIT
History, records and recordation, production of books and papers, **19.2–10.1**
Reports, records and recordation, production of books and papers, **19.2–10.1**

CREDIT CARDS
Fines and penalties, **19.2–353.3**
Records and recordation, production of books and papers, **19.2–10.1**

CREDIT UNIONS
Production of books and papers, records and recordation, **19.2–10.1**
Records and recordation, production of books and papers, **19.2–10.1**

CRIME INJURIES COMPENSATION FUND
Generally, **19.2–368.18**

CRIME VICTIM AND WITNESS FUND
Generally, **19.2–11.3**

CRIME VICTIMS
Address, confidential or privileged information, **19.2–269.2**
Advertisements, compensation and salaries, **19.2–368.17**
Amount, compensation and salaries, **19.2–368.11:1**

CRIME VICTIMS—Cont'd
Appeal and review, compensation and salaries, **19.2–368.7, 19.2–368.8**
Attachment, compensation and salaries, **19.2–368.12**
Bail and recognizance, notice, **19.2–11.01**
Capital punishment, impact statements, **19.2–264.4, 19.2–264.5, 19.2–299.1**
Children and Minors, this index
Claims, compensation and salaries, **19.2–368.5 et seq.**
Compensation and salaries, **19.2–368.1 et seq.**
  Profits from crime, **19.2–368.21**
Confidential or privileged information, **19.2–11.2, 19.2–269.2**
  Compensation and salaries, **19.2–368.3**
Counselors and counseling, compensation and salaries, **19.2–368.11:1**
Criminal injuries compensation fund, **19.2–368.1 et seq.**
Deferral, compensation and salaries, claims, **19.2–368.5**
Denial, compensation and salaries, claims, **19.2–368.5:1**
Depositions, compensation and salaries, **19.2–368.3**
Disposition, notice, **19.2–11.01**
Duress or coercion, **19.2–11.01**
Eligibility, compensation and salaries, **19.2–368.4**
Emergencies, awards, **19.2–368.9**
Escape, notice, **19.2–11.01**
Evidence,
  Compensation and salaries, hearings, **19.2–368.3**
  Impact statements, **19.2–295.3, 19.2–299.1**
Exclusion, trial, **19.2–265.01**
Executions, compensation and salaries, **19.2–368.12**
Exemptions, compensation and salaries, **19.2–368.12**
Forms, rights, **19.2–11.01**
Funds,
  Crime injuries compensation fund, **19.2–368.18**
  Crime victim and witness fund, **19.2–11.3**
Funeral expenses, compensation and salaries, **19.2–368.11:1**
Guardian and ward, compensation and salaries, claims, **19.2–368.5**
Habeas corpus, notice, **19.2–11.01**
Hearings, compensation and salaries, **19.2–368.3**
Impact statements, **19.2–295.3, 19.2–299.1**
  Capital punishment, **19.2–264.4, 19.2–264.5, 19.2–299.1**
Interpreters, hearing impaired persons, **19.2–164.1**
Investigations and investigators, compensation and salaries, claims, **19.2–368.3, 19.2–368.6**
  Reinvestigation, **19.2–368.8**
Limitation of actions, compensation and salaries,
  Claims, **19.2–368.5**
  Medical care and treatment, collections, **19.2–368.5:2**
Medical care and treatment, compensation and salaries, **19.2–368.11:1**
  Rates and charges, **19.2–368.3**

CRIME VICTIMS—Cont'd
Moving expenses, compensation and salaries, **19.2–368.11:1**
Names, appeals in criminal prosecutions, sex offenses, confidential or privileged information, **19.2–11.2**
New trial, notice, **19.2–11.01**
Notice, **19.2–11.01**
Oaths and affirmations, compensation and salaries, claims, **19.2–368.16**
Ombudsman, compensation and salaries, **19.2–368.3:1**
Posttrial assistance, **19.2–11.01**
Pregnancy, compensation and salaries, **19.2–368.11:1**
Presumptions, compensation and salaries, claims, **19.2–368.6**
Privacy, **19.2–11.01**
Production of books and papers, compensation and salaries, **19.2–368.3**
Profits from crime, **19.2–368.21**
Protection, **19.2–11.01**
Reconciliation, **19.2–11.4**
Reconsideration, compensation and salaries, **19.2–368.8**
Records and recordation, compensation and salaries, **19.2–368.14**
Release, notice, **19.2–11.01**
Restitution, **19.2–11.01**
  Criminal injuries compensation fund, **19.2–368.1 et seq.**
Sentencing, impact statements, **19.2–295.3, 19.2–299.1**
Sex Offenses, this index
Stay, compensation and salaries, medical care and treatment, collections, **19.2–368.5:2**
Subrogation, compensation and salaries, **19.2–368.15**
Supersedeas or stay, compensation and salaries, medical care and treatment, collections, **19.2–368.5:2**
Time, awards, **19.2–368.9**
Trial, exclusion, **19.2–265.01**
Witnesses,
  Compensation and salaries, **19.2–368.3**
  Exclusion, **19.2–265.1**

CRIMES AND OFFENSES
  Generally, **19.2–295 et seq.**
Acquittal,
  Criminal insanity, **19.2–182.2 et seq.**
  Double jeopardy, **19.2–292**
Affidavits, evidence, official records, searches and seizures, **19.2–188.3**
Aliens, conviction of crimes, **19.2–294.2**
Ancillary misdemeanors, certificates and certification, **19.2–190.1**
Appeals in Criminal Prosecutions, generally, this index
Appearance,
  Continuance, **19.2–266.3**

CRIMES AND OFFENSES—Cont'd
Appearance—Cont'd
  Electronic communications, **19.2–3.1**
  Facsimile transmissions, **19.2–3.1**
  Failure to appear, **19.2–76.3**
  Pretrial services, officers and employees, powers and duties, **19.2–152.4:3**
  Video and audio communications, **19.2–3.1**
  Warrantless arrest, **19.2–82**
Application of law, **19.2–5**
  Witnesses, **19.2–267**
Arraignment, generally, this index
Arrest, generally, this index
Arson, generally, this index
Assault and Battery, generally, this index
Assignation. Prostitution, generally, this index
Attempts,
  Conviction of crime, **19.2–286**
  DNA, violent felonies, samples, **19.2–310.2:1**
Attorneys, this index
Attorneys for the commonwealth. Prosecuting Attorneys, generally, this index
Bail, generally, this index
Battery. Assault and Battery, generally, this index
Bill of particulars, **19.2–266.2**
Biological evidence,
  Actual innocence, writs, **19.2–327.2 et seq.**
  Storage, retention, **19.2–270.4:1**
Blood tests, **19.2–327.1 et seq.**
Boot camps, **19.2–316.1**
Capital Punishment, generally, this index
Carjacking, second and subsequent offenses, sentencing, **19.2–297.1**
Certificates and certification,
  Ancillary misdemeanors, **19.2–190.1**
  Costs, **19.2–334, 19.2–335**
Certificates of analysis, evidence, **19.2–187 et seq.**
Chain of custody, certificates of analysis, **19.2–187.1, 19.2–187.01**
Change of venue, **19.2–251 et seq.**
Circuit Courts, this index
Computers, this index
Concurrent sentences, **19.2–308.1**
Confidential or privileged information,
  Clergy, **19.2–271.3**
  DNA testing, convicted felons, **19.2–310.5, 19.2–310.6**
  Husband and wife, **19.2–271.2**
Consecutive sentences, **19.2–308**
Construction of laws, **19.2–5**
Contempt, generally, this index
Continuance, **19.2–162**
  Appearance, **19.2–266.3**
  Certificates of analysis, evidence, **19.2–187.1**
  Motions, objections and exceptions, defense, **19.2–266.2**
Conviction of crime, **19.2–283**
  Accomplices and accessories, **19.2–286**
  Aliens, **19.2–294.2**

CRIMES AND OFFENSES—Cont'd
Conviction of crime—Cont'd
Appeals in Criminal Prosecutions, generally, this index
Arrest, surrender, failure, **19.2–298**
Attempts, **19.2–286**
Boot camps, **19.2–316.1**
Costs, public defenders, attorney fees, **19.2–163.4:1**
Detention center incarceration program, **19.2–316.2**
Diversion center incarceration program, **19.2–316.3**
DNA,
Testing, **19.2–327.1 et seq.**
Vacating or setting aside, application of law, **19.2–303**
Homicide, **19.2–288**
Lesser included offenses, **19.2–266.1**
Indeterminate commitment, **19.2–311 et seq.**
Judgment order, **19.2–307**
Lesser included offenses, **19.2–285**
Homicide, **19.2–266.1**
Multiple convictions, **19.2–294**
Presentence investigations, **19.2–299**
Indeterminate commitment, **19.2–316**
Pronouncement, sentencing, **19.2–298**
Public defenders, attorney fees, costs, **19.2–163.4:1**
Reversal, **19.2–324**
Rewards, **19.2–7**
Surrender, failure, arrest, **19.2–298**
Theft, **19.2–289, 19.2–290**
Twenty one day rule, actual innocence, writs, nonbiological evidence, **19.2–327.10 et seq.**
Costs, **19.2–328 et seq.**
Appeal and review, **19.2–325**
Default, **19.2–358**
Delinquencies, **19.2–354 et seq.**
DNA testing, convicted felons, fees, **19.2–310.2**
Evidence, medical care and treatment, **19.2–165.1**
Installments, **19.2–354 et seq.**
Interest, **19.2–353.5**
County jails. Jails, generally, this index
Court reporters, **19.2–166**
Crime Victims, generally, this index
Criminal Injuries Compensation Fund, generally, this index
Critical incident stress management teams, emergency medical services, privileges and immunities, **19.2–271.4**
Death penalty. Capital Punishment, generally, this index
Defenses, **19.2–266.2**
Criminal Insanity, generally, this index
Delayed appeals, motions, **19.2–321.1, 19.2–321.2**
Delinquent Children, generally, this index
Detention center incarceration program, **19.2–316.2**
Discovery, **19.2–265.4**

CRIMES AND OFFENSES—Cont'd
Dismissal and nonsuit,
DNA testing, **19.2–327.1 et seq.**
Mentally ill persons, **19.2–169.3**
Nolle prosequi, **19.2–265.3**
Preliminary hearings, **19.2–186**
State, appeals in criminal prosecutions, **19.2–398 et seq.**
Subsequent prosecution, **19.2–265.6**
Summons, warrants, unexecuted, **19.2–76.1**
District Courts, this index
Diversion centers, **19.2–316.3**
Dockets and docketing, **19.2–240**
Domestic Violence, generally, this index
Double jeopardy, **19.2–292 et seq.**
Appeals in criminal prosecutions, state, **19.2–398**
Defenses, motions, time, **19.2–266.2**
Dismissal and nonsuit, **19.2–265.6**
Driving under influence of alcohol or drugs. Traffic Rules and Regulations, this index
Eavesdropping. Wiretapping, generally, this index
Electronic communications, appearance, **19.2–3.1**
Electronic incarceration, costs, failure to pay, **19.2–354**
Embezzlement, generally, this index
Escape, generally, this index
Escrows and escrow agents, profits, **19.2–368.20**
Evidence,
Abuse, **19.2–270.6**
Accused, testimony, **19.2–268, 19.2–270**
Actual innocence, writs,
DNA testing, **19.2–327.2 et seq.**
Nonbiological evidence, **19.2–327.10 et seq.**
Affidavits, official records, searches and seizures, **19.2–188.3**
Analysis, certificates of analysis, **19.2–187 et seq.**
Autopsies, **19.2–188**
Bad checks, **19.2–270.3**
Blood tests, **19.2–327.1 et seq.**
Certificates of analysis, **19.2–187 et seq.**
Chain of custody, certificates of analysis, **19.2–187.1, 19.2–187.01**
Discovery, **19.2–265.4**
Disposition, **19.2–270.4**
DNA, generally, this index
Husband and wife, witnesses, **19.2–271.1, 19.2–271.2**
Impeachment, witnesses, previous statements, **19.2–268.1**
Judicial notice, **19.2–265.2**
Laboratories, certificates of analysis, **19.2–187 et seq.**
Medical care and treatment, costs, **19.2–165.1**
Medical examiners, **19.2–188**
Money, disposition, **19.2–270.2, 19.2–270.4**
Official records, searches and seizures, affidavits, **19.2–188.3**
Photography and pictures, theft, **19.2–270.1**

CRIMES AND OFFENSES—Cont'd
Evidence—Cont'd
Physicians and surgeons, transplants, **19.2–188.2**
Presumptions, self incrimination, **19.2–268**
Records and recordation, **19.2–165**
Searches and seizures, affidavits, **19.2–188.3**
Return, **19.2–270.4**
Securities, disposition, **19.2–270.2**
Self Incrimination, generally, this index
Suppression,
Motions, **19.2–266.2**
State, appeal and review, **19.2–398**
Examinations and examiners, certificates and certification, **19.2–190**
Exclusion, media coverage, **19.2–266**
Execution. Capital Punishment, generally, this index
Expenses and expenditures, **19.2–328 et seq.**
Delinquencies, **19.2–354 et seq.**
Expungement, records and recordation, **19.2–392.1 et seq.**
Extradition, generally, this index
False pretenses. Fraud, generally, this index
Fees, DNA testing, convicted felons, **19.2–310.2**
Fines and Penalties, generally, this index
Force and Violence, generally, this index
Forensic science, DNA testing, **19.2–270.5**
Convicted felons, **19.2–310.2 et seq.**
Forgery, generally, this index
Fraud, generally, this index
Funds,
Crime injuries compensation fund, **19.2–368.18**
Crime victim and witness fund, **19.2–11.3**
Criminal Injuries Compensation Fund, generally, this index
Profits, **19.2–368.19 et seq.**
Gangs, generally, this index
Global positioning systems, sentences, suspension, modification, **19.2–303**
Grand Jury, generally, this index
Guilty Pleas, generally, this index
Habeas Corpus, generally, this index
Hearings,
Motions, **19.2–266.2**
Preliminary hearings, **19.2–183 et seq., 19.2–218**
Sexual offenses, spouses, **19.2–218.1**
History record information. Criminal History Record Information, generally, this index
Home electronic incarceration,
Costs, failure to pay, **19.2–354**
Pretrial services, officers and employees, powers and duties, **19.2–152.4:3**
Homicide, generally, this index
Immediate sanction probation program, suspension, sentences, **19.2–303.5**
Indeterminate commitment, **19.2–311 et seq.**
Indictment and Information, generally, this index
Indigent Persons, this index
Infractions. Traffic Rules and Regulations, this index

CRIMES AND OFFENSES—Cont'd
Insanity. Criminal Insanity, generally, this index
Instructions to jury, **19.2–263.2**
Interpreters, **19.2–164, 19.2–164.1**
Jails, generally, this index
Joinder, **19.2–262.1**
Verdicts, **19.2–287**
Judgments and decrees, **19.2–307**
Judicial notice, **19.2–265.2**
Jurisdiction, **19.2–239**
Jury, this index
Kidnapping, generally, this index
Laboratories,
DNA testing, **19.2–270.5**
Convicted felons, **19.2–310.2 et seq.**
Evidence, certificates of analysis, **19.2–187 et seq.**
Larceny. Theft, generally, this index
Lesser included offenses, conviction of crime, **19.2–285**
Life imprisonment, three strikes, **19.2–297.1**
Limitation of Prosecutions, generally, this index
Lineups, policies, writing, **19.2–390.02**
Literary fund, fines and penalties, credits, **19.2–340.1**
Mandatory sentences, appeals in criminal prosecutions, state, **19.2–398**
Media coverage, trial, **19.2–266**
Medical examiners, evidence, **19.2–188**
Mental examinations,
Capital punishment, **19.2–264.3:1, 19.2–264.3:1.2**
Competency, **19.2–169.1 et seq.**
Criminal insanity, **19.2–168.1, 19.2–169.5**
Sex offenses, sentencing, **19.2–300 et seq.**
Mentally Ill Persons, this index
Mentally Retarded and Developmentally Disabled Persons, this index
Modification, sentencing, records and recordation, **19.2–295, 19.2–303**
Motions,
Change of venue, **19.2–251 et seq.**
Continuance, defense, **19.2–266.2**
Delayed appeals, **19.2–321.1, 19.2–321.2**
DNA testing, **19.2–327.1 et seq.**
Guilty pleas, withdrawal, **19.2–296**
Indictment and information, sealing, **19.2–192.1**
Nolle prosequi, **19.2–265.3**
Pretrial proceedings, **19.2–266.2**
Suppression, evidence, **19.2–266.2**
Time, **19.2–266.2**
Multiple convictions, **19.2–294**
Murder. Homicide, generally, this index
Nolle prosequi, **19.2–265.3**
Nonbiological evidence, actual innocence, writs, **19.2–327.10 et seq.**
Not guilty pleas,
Criminal Insanity, generally, this index
Refusal to plead, **19.2–259**
Notice,
Certificates of analysis, evidence, **19.2–187.1**

CRIMES AND OFFENSES—Cont'd
Notice—Cont'd
Child pornography, registers and registries, **19.2–390.3**
Criminal insanity, defense, **19.2–168**
DNA tests, **19.2–270.5**
Violent felonies, samples, **19.2–310.2:1**
Motions, **19.2–266.2**
Right to counsel, **19.2–157, 19.2–158**
Second and subsequent offenses, sentencing, **19.2–297.1**
Summons, **19.2–73.1**
Time, **19.2–3**
Objections and exceptions, **19.2–266.2**
Certificates of analysis, evidence, **19.2–187.1**
Continuance, defense, **19.2–266.2**
DNA tests, **19.2–270.5**
Indictment and information, **19.2–227**
Time, **19.2–266.2**
Obscenity, generally, this index
Opening statements, attorneys, **19.2–265**
Outlawry, abolishment, **19.2–10**
Parole, generally, this index
Penal institutions. Correctional Institutions, generally, this index
Penalties. Fines and Penalties, generally, this index
Petitions,
Actual innocence, writs, nonbiological evidence, **19.2–327.10 et seq.**
DNA testing, **19.2–327.1 et seq.**
State, appeals in criminal prosecutions, **19.2–398**
Plea agreements, rejection, judges, recusal, **19.2–254**
Pleas,
Agreements, rejection, judges recusal, **19.2–254**
Arraignment, **19.2–254 et seq.**
Competency, **19.2–169.1 et seq.**
Guilty Pleas, generally, this index
Refusal to plead, **19.2–259**
Withdrawal, guilty pleas, **19.2–296**
Pornography. Obscenity, generally, this index
Postrelease supervision. Parole, generally, this index
Preliminary hearings, **19.2–183 et seq., 19.2–218**
Sexual offenses, spouses, **19.2–218.1**
Presentence investigations, **19.2–299**
Indeterminate commitment, **19.2–316**
Pretrial services,
Officers and employees, powers and duties, **19.2–152.4:3**
Virginia Crime Code references, records and recordation, **19.2–390.01**
Priorities and preferences,
Sentencing, **19.2–309**
Trial, **19.2–241 et seq.**
Prisons and prisoners. Correctional Institutions, generally, this index
Privileges and immunities,
Clergy, **19.2–271.3**

CRIMES AND OFFENSES—Cont'd
Privileges and immunities—Cont'd
DNA testing, **19.2–327.1 et seq.**
Husband and wife, **19.2–271.2**
Self Incrimination, generally, this index
Probable Cause, generally, this index
Probation, generally, this index
Profits, **19.2–368.19 et seq.**
Prosecuting Attorneys, generally, this index
Prostitution, generally, this index
Protective Orders, generally, this index
Public Defenders, generally, this index
Rape. Sex Offenses, generally, this index
Records and recordation,
Central criminal records exchange, **19.2–387 et seq.**
Criminal History Record Information, generally, this index
DNA testing, convicted felons, **19.2–310.2 et seq.**
Evidence, **19.2–165**
Searches and seizures, affidavits, **19.2–188.3**
Expungement, **19.2–392.1 et seq.**
Pretrial services, officers and employees, powers and duties, **19.2–152.4:3**
Sentencing, suspension, modification, **19.2–295, 19.2–303**
Transcripts, **19.2–165**
Virginia Crime Code references, **19.2–390.01**
Registers and registries, child pornography, **19.2–390.3**
Release,
Bail, generally, this index
Criminal insanity, commitment, **19.2–182.6 et seq.**
Hearings, time, **19.2–158**
Pretrial services, officers and employees, powers and duties, **19.2–152.4:3**
Removal or transfer of causes, federal courts, **19.2–9**
Reports,
Criminal insanity, evaluations, **19.2–169.5**
Presentence investigations, **19.2–299**
Pretrial services, officers and employees, powers and duties, **19.2–152.4:3**
Summons, unexecuted summons, **19.2–76.1**
Restitution, generally, this index
Reversal, conviction, **19.2–324**
Rewards, **19.2–7**
Right to counsel,
Attorneys, this index
Public Defenders, generally, this index
Robbery, generally, this index
Screening, chemically dependent persons, **19.2–299.2**
Sealing, indictment and information, **19.2–192.1**
Searches and Seizures, generally, this index
Second and subsequent offenses,
Photography and pictures, privacy, venue, **19.2–249.2**
Sentencing, **19.2–297.1**

CRIMES AND OFFENSES—Cont'd
Second and subsequent offenses—Cont'd
Three strikes, life imprisonment, **19.2–297.1**
Video tapes, privacy, venue, **19.2–249.2**
Self Incrimination, generally, this index
Sex Offenses, generally, this index
Shoplifting, generally, this index
Special conservators of the peace, registration, **19.2–13**
Speedy Trial, generally, this index
Stalking, generally, this index
Statistical data base, DNA testing, convicted felons, **19.2–310.2 et seq.**
Statute of limitations. Limitation of Prosecutions, generally, this index
Stolen property. Theft, generally, this index
Subpoenas, **19.2–73.2**
Electronic format, computers, information, **19.2–267.2**
Summons, **19.2–73**
Execution, **19.2–76**
Failure to appear, **19.2–76.3**
Mail and mailing, **19.2–76.2**
Notice, **19.2–73.1**
Release, **19.2–74**
Unexecuted summons, reports, **19.2–76.1**
Virginia Crime Code references, **19.2–390.01**
Witnesses, **19.2–267, 19.2–267.1**
Foreign states, **19.2–274, 19.2–277**
Supersedeas or Stay, generally, this index
Supervision, commitment, **19.2–314**
Suppression, evidence,
Motions, **19.2–266.2**
State, appeal and review, **19.2–398**
Suspension, sentences, **19.2–303 et seq.**
Boot camps, **19.2–316.1**
Immediate sanction probation program, **19.2–303.5**
Television and radio, trial, **19.2–266**
Terrorism, generally, this index
Theft, generally, this index
Three strikes, sentencing, **19.2–297.1**
Time,
Defenses, **19.2–266.2**
Delayed appeals, motions, **19.2–321.1, 19.2–321.2**
Limitation of Prosecutions, generally, this index
Motions, pretrial proceedings, **19.2–266.2**
Trial, **19.2–241 et seq.**
Tracking devices, searches and seizures, warrants, confidential or privileged information, **19.2–56.2**
Traffic Rules and Regulations, this index
Transcripts, **19.2–165**
Appeals in criminal prosecutions,
Indigent persons, **19.2–325**
State, **19.2–405**
Court reporters, **19.2–166**
Multijurisdiction grand juries, **19.2–215.9**
Preliminary hearings, **19.2–185**

CRIMES AND OFFENSES—Cont'd
Transcripts—Cont'd
Special grand juries, **19.2–212**
Trial, **19.2–239 et seq., 19.2–260 et seq.**
Change of venue, **19.2–251 et seq.**
Competency, **19.2–167, 19.2–169.1 et seq.**
Exclusion,
Crime victims, **19.2–265.01**
Witnesses, **19.2–265.1, 19.2–265.5**
Judges, disability or death, **19.2–154**
Jury, **19.2–260 et seq.**
Limitation of Prosecutions, generally, this index
Media coverage, **19.2–266**
Opening statements, **19.2–265**
Speedy Trial, generally, this index
Television and radio, media coverage, **19.2–266**
Venue, **19.2–244 et seq.**
Without jury, **19.2–257 et seq.**
Trial de novo,
Appeals in criminal prosecutions, **19.2–324**
Evidence, erroneously admitted, **19.2–324.1**
Crime victims, notice, **19.2–11.01**
Discovery, **19.2–265.4**
Twenty one day rule, actual innocence, writs, nonbiological evidence, **19.2–327.10 et seq.**
Vacating or setting aside, DNA, application of law, samples, **19.2–303**
Venue, **19.2–244 et seq.**
Change of venue, **19.2–251 et seq.**
Verdicts, **19.2–283 et seq.**
Homicide, **19.2–288**
Joinder, **19.2–287**
Victims. Crime Victims, generally, this index
Virginia Crime Code references, records and recordation, **19.2–390.01**
Waiver,
Arraignment, **19.2–254 et seq.**
Indictment and information, **19.2–217**
Jury, **19.2–257, 19.2–258**
Self incrimination, **19.2–268**
Warrants,
Arrest, this index
Virginia Crime Code references, **19.2–390.01**
Wiretapping, generally, this index
With prejudice, dismissal and nonsuit, subsequent prosecution, **19.2–265.6**
Withdrawal,
Guilty pleas, **19.2–296**
Nolle prosequi, **19.2–265.3**
Witnesses, **19.2–267 et seq.**
Accused, testimony, **19.2–268, 19.2–270**
Clergy, **19.2–271.3**
Compensation and salaries, **19.2–329 et seq.**
Confidential or privileged information, **19.2–269.2**
Clergy, **19.2–271.3**
Husband and wife, **19.2–271.2**
Correctional institutions, **19.2–269.1**
Court officers and employees, **19.2–271**

CRIMES AND OFFENSES—Cont'd
Witnesses—Cont'd
Criminal insanity, opinion and expert testimony, **19.2–175**
Capital punishment, **19.2–264.3:1**
Cross examination,
Accused, **19.2–268, 19.2–270**
Previous statements, **19.2–268.1**
Prior convictions, **19.2–269**
Exclusion, trial, **19.2–265.1, 19.2–265.5**
Exemptions, foreign states, process, **19.2–280**
Fees, **19.2–329 et seq.**
Fines and penalties, foreign states, **19.2–276, 19.2–279**
Foreign states,
Attendance, **19.2–272 et seq.**
Fees, **19.2–330**
Husband and wife, **19.2–271.1, 19.2–271.2**
Impeachment,
Previous statements, **19.2–268.1**
Prior convictions, **19.2–269**
Judges, **19.2–271**
Media coverage, **19.2–266**
Mentally retarded and developmentally disabled persons, opinion and expert testimony, capital punishment, **19.2–264.3:1.2**
Opinion and expert testimony,
Criminal insanity, **19.2–175**
Capital punishment, **19.2–264.3:1**
Mentally retarded and developmentally disabled persons, capital punishment, **19.2–264.3:1.2**
Preliminary hearings, **19.2–183 et seq.**
Previous statements, impeachment, **19.2–268.1**
Privileges and immunities,
Accused, prior statements, **19.2–270**
Clergy, **19.2–271.3**
Husband and wife, **19.2–271.2**
Separation, **19.2–184**
Subpoenas, **19.2–73.2**
Summons, **19.2–267, 19.2–267.1**
Foreign states, **19.2–274, 19.2–277**
Transcripts, preliminary hearings, **19.2–185**
Trial, exclusion, **19.2–265.1, 19.2–265.5**
Writ of error. Appeals in Criminal Prosecutions, generally, this index

CRIMINAL APPEALS
Appeals in Criminal Prosecutions, generally, this index

CRIMINAL EXTRADITION ACT
Generally, **19.2–85 et seq.**

CRIMINAL HISTORY RECORD INFORMATION
Adult care services, disclosure, **19.2–389**
Adult day care centers, disclosure, **19.2–389**
Aliens, **19.2–294.2**
Jails, reports, **19.2–83.2**
Appeal and review, expungement, **19.2–392.2**

CRIMINAL HISTORY RECORD INFORMATION—Cont'd
Appeals in criminal prosecutions, expungement, **19.2–392.2**
Orders of court, **19.2–327.5, 19.2–327.13**
Arrest, bail, **19.2–80.2**
Assault and battery, sentencing, **19.2–299**
Bail, this index
Bingo and raffles, **19.2–389**
Blind persons, disclosure, **19.2–389**
Central criminal records exchange, **19.2–387 et seq.**
Citizens and citizenship, jails, reports, **19.2–83.2**
Colleges and universities, threats, teams, assessments, **19.2–389, 19.2–389.1**
Commutation of sentence, **19.2–390**
Confidential or privileged information, **19.2–389**
Conservators of the peace, **19.2–13**
Costs, expungement, **19.2–392.2**
Delinquent Children, this index
Disclosure, **19.2–389**
Expunged records, **19.2–392.3**
Driving under influence of alcohol or drugs, sentencing, **19.2–299**
Escape, **19.2–390**
Exchange, central criminal records exchange, **19.2–387 et seq.**
Expungement, **19.2–327.5, 19.2–327.13, 19.2–392.1 et seq.**
Fees, bail, bondspersons, **19.2–120**
Fingerprints and Fingerprinting, this index
Hearings, expungement, **19.2–392.2**
Home based services, adults, disclosure, **19.2–389**
Identity and identification, expungement, **19.2–392.2**
Jails, citizens and citizenship, reports, **19.2–83.2**
Law enforcement agencies, reports, **19.2–390**
Magistrates, appointment, **19.2–35**
Mass transportation, officers and employees, **19.2–389**
Medical assistance, transportation, screening, disclosure, **19.2–389**
Metropolitan Washington airports authority, labor and employment, reports, notice, **19.2–389.2**
Money transmitters, money orders, sales, investigations and investigators, **19.2–389**
Motions,
Disclosure, **19.2–389**
Expungement, orders, voidable, **19.2–392.2**
National criminal background checks, **19.2–392.02**
Notice, expungement, orders, voidable, **19.2–392.2**
Pardons, **19.2–390**
Expungement, **19.2–392.1 et seq.**
Parole, postrelease supervision, violations, reports, **19.2–390**
Petitions, expungement, **19.2–392.2**
Photography and pictures, **19.2–390, 19.2–392, 19.2–392.01**
Presentence investigations, **19.2–299**
Probation, violations, reports, **19.2–390**

CRIMINAL HISTORY RECORD INFORMATION—Cont'd
Real estate brokers and salespersons, licenses and permits, **19.2–389**
Registration, sex offenses, **19.2–390, 19.2–390.1**
Reports, **19.2–390**
Reprieves, **19.2–390**
School officers and employees, disclosure, **19.2–389**
Sex Offenses, this index
Sheriffs, reports, **19.2–390**
Social services, disclosure, **19.2–389**
Special conservators of the peace, **19.2–13**
State agencies, **19.2–391**
  Labor and employment, **19.2–389**
Virginia Crime Code references, **19.2–390.01**
Vocational rehabilitation, disclosure, **19.2–389**
Wrongful incarceration, disclosure, **19.2–389**

CRIMINAL INJURIES COMPENSATION FUND
  Generally, **19.2–368.1 et seq.**
Liens and incumbrances, **19.2–368.15**
Restitution, **19.2–305.1**

CRIMINAL INSANITY
  Generally, **19.2–167 et seq.**
Acquittal, **19.2–182.2 et seq.**
Attorneys, commitment, **19.2–182, 19.2–182.12**
Capital punishment, evaluations, **19.2–264.3:1, 19.2–264.3:3**
Commitment, **19.2–169.6**
  Acquittal, **19.2–182.2 et seq.**
Compensation and salaries, expert witnesses, **19.2–175**
Conditional release, **19.2–182.6 et seq.**
Disclosure, evaluations, **19.2–169.5**
  Capital punishment, **19.2–264.3:3**
Emergencies, commitment, released defendant, **19.2–182.9**
Escape, commitment, **19.2–182.14, 19.2–182.15**
Evaluations, **19.2–168.1, 19.2–169.1**
  Acquittal, commitment, **19.2–182.2 et seq.**
  Capital punishment, **19.2–264.3:1, 19.2–264.3:3**
Expert witnesses, compensation and salaries, **19.2–175**
Extension, commitment, emergencies, released defendant, **19.2–182.9**
Hearings, commitment, acquittal, **19.2–182.3**
Hospitals, **19.2–169.6, 19.2–174.1**
Motions, **19.2–169.4**
Notice, release, **19.2–182.5**
Objections and exceptions, **19.2–169.4**
Petitions, commitment, release, **19.2–182.6**
Priorities and preferences, commitment, acquittal, **19.2–182.3, 19.2–182.5**
Release, commitment, **19.2–182.6 et seq.**
Reports,
  Commitment, **19.2–182.5**
  Evaluations, **19.2–169.5**
    Capital punishment, **19.2–264.3:1**
      Disclosure, **19.2–264.3:3**

CRIMINAL INSANITY—Cont'd
Revocation or suspension, conditional release, **19.2–182.8**
Self incrimination, treatment, **19.2–169.7**
Treatment, **19.2–169.6, 19.2–174.1**
Trial, **19.2–167**
Visitation, commitment, **19.2–182.4**
Witnesses, compensation and salaries, **19.2–175**

CRIMINAL JUSTICE
Crimes and Offenses, generally, this index

CRITICAL INCIDENT STRESS MANAGEMENT TEAMS
Privileges and immunities, emergency medical services, **19.2–271.4**

CURRENCY
Money, generally, this index

DAMAGES
Capitol square, restitution, evidence, **19.2–305.1**
Liquidated damages, wiretapping, **19.2–69**
Searches and seizures, warrantless searches, **19.2–59**
Wiretapping, **19.2–69**

DANGEROUS WEAPONS
Weapons, generally, this index

DATA PROCESSING
Computers, generally, this index

DEAF AND MUTE PERSONS
Hearing Impaired Persons, generally, this index

DEATH
Capital Punishment, generally, this index
Homicide, generally, this index
Judges, criminal trial, **19.2–154**

DEATH PENALTY
Capital Punishment, generally, this index

DECEIT
Fraud, generally, this index

DECEPTION
Fraud, generally, this index

DECISIONS
Judgments and Decrees, generally, this index

DECREES
Judgments and Decrees, generally, this index

DEFINITIONS
Words and Phrases, generally, this index

DELINQUENCIES
Fines and Penalties, this index

DELINQUENT CHILDREN
Actual innocence, writs, **19.2–327.1 et seq.**
Appeal and review,
  Actual innocence, writs, **19.2–327.1 et seq.**

DELINQUENT CHILDREN—Cont'd
Appeal and review—Cont'd
Jury, waiver, **19.2–262**
Attorney fees, **19.2–163**
Attorneys,
Appointment, **19.2–163 et seq.**
Qualifications, appointment, **19.2–163.03**
Bail, **19.2–123, 19.2–135 et seq.**
Biological evidence, actual innocence, writs, **19.2–327.1 et seq.**
Boot camps, **19.2–316.1**
Central criminal records exchange, **19.2–387 et seq.**
Commitment, indeterminate commitment, **19.2–311 et seq.**
Competency, trial, **19.2–169.1, 19.2–169.2**
Confidential or privileged information, media coverage, exclusion, **19.2–266**
Conviction of crime, actual innocence, writs, **19.2–327.1 et seq.**
Criminal history record information,
Central criminal records exchange, **19.2–387 et seq.**
Disclosure, **19.2–389, 19.2–389.1**
Expunging records, actual innocence, writs, **19.2–327.5, 19.2–327.13**
Detention center incarceration program, **19.2–316.2**
Disclosure, criminal history record information, **19.2–389, 19.2–389.1**
Dismissal and nonsuit, actual innocence, writs, **19.2–327.1 et seq.**
Evaluations, indeterminate commitment, **19.2–316**
Evidence, actual innocence, writs, **19.2–327.1 et seq.**
Expunging records, actual innocence, writs, **19.2–327.5, 19.2–327.13**
Gangs, generally, this index
Indeterminate commitment, **19.2–311 et seq.**
Indigent persons, attorneys, appointment, **19.2–163 et seq.**
Jury, waiver, **19.2–262**
Media coverage, exclusion, **19.2–266**
Nonbiological evidence, actual innocence, writs, **19.2–327.10 et seq.**
Petitions, actual innocence, writs, nonbiological evidence, **19.2–327.10 et seq.**
Photography and pictures, exclusion, **19.2–266**
Records and recordation,
Expunging records, actual innocence, writs, **19.2–327.5, 19.2–327.13**
Virginia Crime Code references, **19.2–390.01**
Release, indeterminate commitment, **19.2–311 et seq.**
Supervision, commitment, **19.2–314**
Television and radio, exclusion, **19.2–266**
Trial, competency, **19.2–169.1, 19.2–169.2**
Virginia Crime Code references, records and recordation, **19.2–390.01**
Waiver, jury, **19.2–262**
Writs, actual innocence, **19.2–327.1 et seq.**

DELINQUENT CHILDREN—Cont'd
Youth gangs. Gangs, generally, this index

DEPENDENT OR NEGLECTED CHILDREN
See, also, Delinquent Children, generally, this index
Abuse of children. Child Abuse, generally, this index
Child Abuse, generally, this index
Juvenile delinquents. Delinquent Children, generally, this index

DEPOSITIONS
Crime victims, compensation and salaries, **19.2–368.3**

DESTITUTE PERSONS
Indigent Persons, generally, this index

DETENTION
Arrest, generally, this index
Jails, generally, this index

DETENTION FACILITIES
Correctional Institutions, generally, this index
Detention center incarceration program, **19.2–316.2**
Jails, generally, this index

DEVELOPMENTALLY DISABLED PERSONS
Mentally Retarded and Developmentally Disabled Persons, generally, this index

DISASTERS
Limitation of prosecutions, **19.2–243**

DISCHARGE
Bail, this index

DISCLOSURE
See, also, Confidential or Privileged Information, generally, this index
Capital punishment, mental examinations, **19.2–264.3:3**
Criminal insanity, evaluations, **19.2–169.5**
Wiretapping, investigations and investigators, **19.2–67**

DISCOVERY
Production of Books and Papers, generally, this index

DISMISSAL AND NONSUIT
Crimes and Offenses, this index
Mentally ill persons, crimes and offenses, **19.2–169.3**
With prejudice, subsequent prosecution, **19.2–265.6**

DISORDERLY HOUSES
Prostitution, generally, this index

DISTRICT COURTS
Bail, hearings, time, **19.2–158**
Crimes and offenses,
Motions, pretrial proceedings, **19.2–266.2**
Objections and exceptions, pretrial proceedings, **19.2–266.2**

DISTRICT COURTS—Cont'd
Crimes and offenses—Cont'd
Trial, judges, disability or death, **19.2–154**
Executions, generally, this index
Judgments and Decrees, generally, this index
Release, hearings, time, **19.2–158**
Trial, generally, this index

DISTRICTS
Real Property Taxation, generally, this index

DIVERSION CENTER INCARCERATION PROGRAM
Crimes and offenses, **19.2–316.3**

DNA
Generally, **19.2–270.5, 19.2–327.1 et seq.**
Appeals in criminal prosecutions, application of law, samples, **19.2–303**
Convicted felons, **19.2–310.2 et seq.**
Actual innocence, writs, **19.2–327.2 et seq.**
Storage, retention, **19.2–270.4:1**
Vacating or setting aside, application of law, samples, **19.2–303**
Violent felonies, samples, **19.2–310.2:1, 19.2–310.3:1**

DOCKETS AND DOCKETING
Crimes and offenses, **19.2–240**

DOMESTIC ABUSE
Domestic Violence, generally, this index

DOMESTIC CORPORATIONS
Corporations, generally, this index

DOMESTIC VIOLENCE
See, also, Child Abuse, generally, this index
Arrest, **19.2–81.3**
Bail, protective orders, second and subsequent offenses, **19.2–120**
Child Abuse, generally, this index
Confidential or privileged information, crime victims, **19.2–11.2**
Counselors and counseling, indictment and information, **19.2–218.1, 19.2–218.2**
Crime victims, confidential or privileged information, **19.2–11.2**
Indictment and information, counselors and counseling, **19.2–218.1, 19.2–218.2**
Predominant physical aggressor, arrest, **19.2–81.3**
Preliminary hearings, **19.2–218.1, 19.2–218.2**
Protective orders, **19.2–152.7:1 et seq.**
Registry, **19.2–387.1**
Second and subsequent offenses, protective orders, bail, **19.2–120**
Standards, arrest, **19.2–81.3**

DOMICILE AND RESIDENCE
Grand Jury, this index
Magistrates, **19.2–37**
Venue, generally, this index

DOUBLE JEOPARDY
Generally, **19.2–292 et seq.**

DOUBLE JEOPARDY—Cont'd
Appeals in criminal prosecutions, state, **19.2–398**
Defenses, motions, time, **19.2–266.2**
Dismissal and nonsuit, **19.2–265.6**

DRIVING UNDER INFLUENCE OF ALCOHOL OR DRUGS
Traffic Rules and Regulations, this index

DRONES
Unmanned aircraft, searches and seizures, warrants, **19.2–60.1**

DRUG ABUSE
Chemically Dependent Persons, generally, this index

DRUG ADDICTS
Chemically Dependent Persons, generally, this index

DRUG PARAPHERNALIA
Forfeitures, **19.2–386.23, 19.2–386.26**

DRUGS AND MEDICINE
See, also, Controlled Substances, generally, this index
Addicts. Chemically Dependent Persons, generally, this index
Chemically Dependent Persons, generally, this index
Driving under influence of alcohol or drugs. Traffic Rules and Regulations, this index
Hazardous substances and waste, manufacturers and manufacturing, cleanup, restitution, **19.2–305.1**
Manufacturers and manufacturing, restitution, hazardous substances and waste, cleanup, **19.2–305.1**
Narcotics. Controlled Substances, generally, this index
Restitution, manufacturers and manufacturing, hazardous substances and waste, cleanup, **19.2–305.1**
Tests and testing, pretrial services, officers and employees, powers and duties, **19.2–152.4:3**

DRUNKEN DRIVING
Driving under influence of alcohol or drugs. Traffic Rules and Regulations, this index

DURESS OR COERCION
Crime victims, **19.2–11.01**
Terrorism, generally, this index
Witnesses, **19.2–11.01**

DWI
Driving under influence of alcohol or drugs. Traffic Rules and Regulations, this index

E MAIL
Electronic Mail, generally, this index

EARNINGS
Compensation and Salaries, generally, this index

EAVESDROPPING
Wiretapping, generally, this index

EDUCATION
Colleges and Universities, generally, this index
Continuing Education, generally, this index
Magistrates, **19.2–37**
Schools and School Districts, generally, this index
Schoolteachers, generally, this index

EDUCATIONAL INSTITUTIONS
Colleges and Universities, generally, this index
Schools and School Districts, generally, this index

ELECTION OFFENSES
Campaign contributions and expenditures, limitation of prosecutions, **19.2–8**
Limitation of prosecutions, campaign contributions and expenditures, **19.2–8**

ELECTIONS
Campaign contributions and expenditures, limitation of prosecutions, **19.2–8**
Registration of voters, criminal history record information, disclosure, **19.2–389**

ELECTRONIC DATA PROCESSING
Computers, generally, this index

ELECTRONIC MAIL
Crimes and offenses,
  Interception, disclosure, **19.2–62**
  Subpoenas, records and recordation, investigations and investigators, **19.2–10.2**
Disclosure, interception, **19.2–62**
Financial institutions, production of books and papers, records and recordation, **19.2–10.1**
Forfeitures, crimes and offenses, **19.2–386.17**
Interception, crimes and offenses, **19.2–62**
Obscenity, crimes and offenses, **19.2–386.17**
Searches and seizures, warrants, **19.2–56, 19.2–70.3**
  Affidavits, **19.2–54**
Subpoenas, crimes and offenses, records and recordation, investigations and investigators, **19.2–10.2**

ELECTRONIC SURVEILLANCE
Wiretapping, generally, this index

ELECTRONIC TRANSACTIONS
Searches and seizures, warrants, affidavits, **19.2–54**

ELEMENTARY SCHOOLS
Schools and School Districts, generally, this index

EMBEZZLEMENT
  See, also, Theft, generally, this index
Evidence, moneys or securities, disposition, **19.2–270.2**
Fines and penalties, **19.2–361**
Indictment and information, **19.2–223**
Venue, **19.2–245**

EMERGENCIES
Crime victims, awards, **19.2–368.9**

EMERGENCIES—Cont'd
Criminal insanity, commitment, released defendant, **19.2–182.9**

EMERGENCY MEDICAL SERVICES
Blood alcohol tests, evidence, admissibility, **19.2–187.02**
Medical records, blood alcohol tests, evidence, admissibility, **19.2–187.02**
Motor vehicles, blood alcohol tests, evidence, admissibility, **19.2–187.02**
Privileges and immunities,
  Blood alcohol tests, evidence, admissibility, **19.2–187.02**
  Critical incident stress management teams, **19.2–271.4**
Reports, blood alcohol tests, evidence, admissibility, **19.2–187.02**

EMPLOYMENT
Labor and Employment, generally, this index

ENLISTED MEN
Military Forces, generally, this index

ENTRY OF JUDGMENT
Executions, generally, this index

ENVIRONMENTAL PROTECTION
Hazardous Substances and Waste, generally, this index

EQUITY
Supersedeas or Stay, generally, this index

ERRORS AND APPEALS
Appeal and Review, generally, this index

ESCAPE
Arrest, **19.2–81.1**
Crime victims, notice, **19.2–11.01**
Criminal history record information, **19.2–390**
Criminal insanity, commitment, **19.2–182.14, 19.2–182.15**
Rewards, **19.2–7**

ESCROWS AND ESCROW AGENTS
Crimes and offenses, profits, **19.2–368.20**

EVIDENCE
Affidavits, generally, this index
Appeals in criminal prosecutions, sufficiency, erroneously admitted, consideration, **19.2–324.1**
Autopsies, crimes and offenses, **19.2–188**
Bad checks, **19.2–270.3**
Bail, **19.2–121**
Blood Tests, generally, this index
Burden of proof, capital punishment, mentally retarded and developmentally disabled persons, **19.2–264.3:1.1**
Capital Punishment, this index
Capitol square, damages, restitution, **19.2–305.1**
Chain of custody, DNA, **19.2–270.4:1**

EVIDENCE—Cont'd
Computers, remote computing services, hearsay, exceptions, **19.2–70.3**
Confidential or Privileged Information, generally, this index
Crime victims, compensation and salaries, hearings, **19.2–368.3**
Crimes and Offenses, this index
Destruction, crimes and offenses, **19.2–270.4**
Disposition, crimes and offenses, **19.2–270.4**
DNA, generally, this index
Drones, unmanned aircraft, searches and seizures, suppression, **19.2–60.1**
Emergency medical services, blood alcohol tests, admissibility, **19.2–187.02**
Erroneously admitted, appeals in criminal prosecutions, sufficiency, consideration, **19.2–324.1**
Forfeitures, money, **19.2–270.4**
Habeas corpus, disposition, crimes and offenses, **19.2–270.4**
Hearsay, exceptions,
  Blood alcohol tests, emergency medical services, **19.2–187.02**
  Telecommunications, remote computing services, **19.2–70.3**
Identity and identification, crimes and offenses, DNA tests, **19.2–270.5**
Interest, moneys or securities, **19.2–270.2**
Interpreters, generally, this index
Medical examiners, crimes and offenses, **19.2–188**
Money, disposition, **19.2–270.2, 19.2–270.4**
New trial, erroneously admitted, appeals in criminal prosecutions, sufficiency, **19.2–324.1**
Noise, machinery and equipment, weights and measures, certificates and certification, **19.2–270.7**
Notice, disposition, crimes and offenses, **19.2–270.4**
Objections and exceptions,
  Crimes and Offenses, this index
  DNA tests, **19.2–270.5**
Opinions and expert testimony. Witnesses, this index
Photography and pictures,
  Destruction, **19.2–270.4**
  Theft, **19.2–270.1**
Presumptions,
  Bad checks, **19.2–270.3**
  Bail, generally, this index
  Husband and wife, witnesses, **19.2–271.2**
  Self incrimination, **19.2–268**
Privileged communications. Confidential or Privileged Information, generally, this index
Production of Books and Papers, generally, this index
Records and recordation, searches and seizures, affidavits, **19.2–188.3**
Remote computing services, hearsay, exceptions, **19.2–70.3**
Return, crimes and offenses, **19.2–270.4**
Searches and Seizures, this index

EVIDENCE—Cont'd
Securities, disposition, **19.2–270.2**
Sex Offenses, this index
Suppression,
  Searches and seizures, **19.2–60**
    Unmanned aircraft, warrants, **19.2–60.1**
  Wiretapping, **19.2–68**
Telecommunications, hearsay, exceptions, **19.2–70.3**
Theft, this index
Time, destruction, **19.2–270.4**
Unmanned aircraft, searches and seizures, warrants, suppression, **19.2–60.1**
Wiretapping, **19.2–65**
  Suppression, **19.2–68**
Witnesses, generally, this index

EVIDENCES OF INDEBTEDNESS
Securities, generally, this index

EX PARTE PROCEEDINGS
Capital punishment, experts, assisting in defense, appointments, **19.2–264.3:1.3**

EXCHANGE, BILLS OF
Negotiable Instruments, generally, this index

EXECUTIONS
Crime victims, compensation and salaries, **19.2–368.12**
Fines and penalties, **19.2–340, 19.2–341**

EXECUTIVE DIRECTORS
Indigent defense commission, **19.2–163.01**

EXPERT WITNESSES
Opinions and expert testimony. Witnesses, this index

EXPUNGEMENT
Criminal History Record Information, this index

EXTORTION
Searches and seizures, forfeitures, **19.2–386.35**

EXTRADITION
Affidavits, applications, **19.2–111**
Applications, **19.2–109 et seq.**
Arrest, **19.2–99**
  Without warrants, **19.2–100**
Attorneys, **19.2–95**
Bail, **19.2–102 et seq.**
Confinement, **19.2–97 et seq.**
Consent, **19.2–114**
Expenses and expenditures, **19.2–112**
Foreign countries, **19.2–84**
Forfeitures, bail, **19.2–104**
Forms, **19.2–87**
  Applications, **19.2–111**
Habeas corpus, **19.2–95**
Indictment and information, demands, **19.2–87**
Investigations and investigators, **19.2–88**
Jails, **19.2–97, 19.2–98**

EXTRADITION—Cont'd
Notice, habeas corpus, **19.2–95**
Recall, arrest warrant, **19.2–107**
Transportation, jails, **19.2–97, 19.2–98**
Waiver, **19.2–114**
Warrants, **19.2–92**

EXTRAORDINARY WRITS
Habeas Corpus, generally, this index

FACSIMILE TRANSMISSIONS
Appearance, crimes and offenses, **19.2–3.1**
Searches and seizures, warrants, affidavits, **19.2–54**

FAIRS OR EXPOSITIONS
Conservators of the peace, **19.2–14**

FALSE IMPRISONMENT
Habeas Corpus, generally, this index
Kidnapping, generally, this index

FALSE STATEMENTS
Fraud, generally, this index

FEDERAL LAWS
Double jeopardy, **19.2–294**

FEEBLE MINDED PERSONS
Mentally Retarded and Developmentally Disabled Persons, generally, this index

FELONIES
Crimes and Offenses, generally, this index

FIDELITY BONDS
Bonds (Officers and Fiduciaries), generally, this index

FIDUCIARIES
Attorneys, generally, this index
Bonds (Officers and Fiduciaries), generally, this index

FIERI FACIAS
Executions, generally, this index

FILMS
Video Images, generally, this index

FINAL PROCESS
Executions, generally, this index

FINANCIAL INSTITUTIONS
Electronic communications, production of books and papers, records and recordation, **19.2–10.1**
Production of books and papers, records and recordation, **19.2–10.1**
Records and recordation, production of books and papers, **19.2–10.1**
Software and electronic data, production of books and papers, records and recordation, **19.2–10.1**

FINANCIAL STATEMENTS AND REPORTS
Indigent persons, statement of indigency, right to counsel, **19.2–159, 19.2–159.1**

FINES AND PENALTIES
See, also, Crimes and Offenses, generally, this index
Generally, **19.2–295 et seq., 19.2–339 et seq.**
Actions and proceedings, collection, **19.2–349**
Attorney fees, collection, **19.2–349**
Bad checks, **19.2–353.3**
Boot camps, **19.2–316.1**
Capital Punishment, generally, this index
Checks, **19.2–353.3**
Collections, **19.2–348 et seq.**
Community work in lieu of payment, **19.2–354**
Death sentence. Capital Punishment, generally, this index
Default, **19.2–358**
Delinquencies,
- Community work in lieu of payment, **19.2–354**
- Installments, **19.2–354 et seq.**
- Reports, **19.2–349**

Detention center incarceration program, **19.2–316.2**
Disposition, **19.2–351 et seq.**
Diversion centers, **19.2–316.3**
Electronic incarceration, costs, failure to pay, **19.2–354**
Embezzlement, **19.2–361**
Forfeitures, generally, this index
Forms, receipts, **19.2–360**
Governor, relief, **19.2–363, 19.2–368**
Grand jury, **19.2–204**
Guilty Pleas, generally, this index
Highway patrol, literary fund, credits, **19.2–340.1**
Home electronic incarceration, costs, failure to pay, **19.2–354**
Indeterminate commitment, **19.2–311 et seq.**
Indigent persons, petitions, **19.2–355**
Installments, **19.2–354 et seq.**
Interest, **19.2–353.5**
Law enforcement officers, state officers and employees, literary fund, credits, **19.2–340.1**
Limitation of actions, **19.2–341**
Literary fund, **19.2–353**
Payment, **19.2–353.3**
- Community work in lieu of payment, **19.2–354**
- Default, **19.2–358**
- Embezzlement, **19.2–361**
- Installments, **19.2–354 et seq.**
- Receipts, **19.2–359, 19.2–360**
- Relief, **19.2–362 et seq.**

Petitions, relief, **19.2–364**
Probation,
- Conditions, **19.2–305, 19.2–356**
- Revocation, **19.2–306**

Receipts, **19.2–359, 19.2–360**
Records and recordation, receipts, **19.2–359, 19.2–360**
Relief, **19.2–362 et seq.**
Reports, **19.2–349**
Restitution, crime victims, **19.2–368.5**
Searches and seizures, warrantless searches, **19.2–59**

FINES AND PENALTIES—Cont'd
Venue, **19.2–342**
Wiretapping, **19.2–62**
  Forfeitures, **19.2–64**

FINGERPRINTS AND FINGERPRINTING
Criminal history record information, **19.2–390, 19.2–392, 19.2–392.01**
  Expungement, orders, **19.2–392.2**
Magistrates, appointment, **19.2–35**
Metropolitan Washington airports authority, labor and employment, reports, notice, **19.2–389.2**
Special conservators of the peace, **19.2–13**

FIREARMS
Weapons, generally, this index

FIREFIGHTERS AND FIRE DEPARTMENTS
Emergency Medical Services, generally, this index

FIRES AND FIRE PROTECTION
Arson, generally, this index
Crimes and offenses. Arson, generally, this index

FIRST AID
Emergency Medical Services, generally, this index

FISH AND GAME
Crimes and offenses, limitation of prosecutions, **19.2–8**
Limitation of prosecutions, **19.2–8**
Searches and seizures, **19.2–59**

FOOD
Fish and Game, generally, this index

FORCE AND VIOLENCE
Assault and Battery, generally, this index
DNA, violent felonies, samples, **19.2–310.2:1, 19.2–310.3:1**
Domestic Violence, generally, this index
Presumptions, bail, **19.2–120**
Terrorism, generally, this index

FOREIGN CORPORATIONS
Corporations, generally, this index

FOREIGN COUNTRIES
Aliens, generally, this index
Crimes and offenses, extradition, **19.2–84**
Immigration. Aliens, generally, this index

FOREIGN STATES
Arrest, witnesses, **19.2–275**
Certificates and certification, witnesses, **19.2–273, 19.2–277**
Computers, remote computing services, records and recordation, search warrants, **19.2–70.3**
Crimes and offenses,
  Extradition, generally, this index
  Witnesses,
    Attendance, **19.2–272 et seq.**
    Fees, **19.2–330**
Exemptions, witnesses, process, **19.2–280**

FOREIGN STATES—Cont'd
Extradition, generally, this index
Fines and penalties, witnesses, **19.2–276, 19.2–279**
Summons, witnesses, crimes and offenses, **19.2–274, 19.2–277**

FOREIGNERS
Aliens, generally, this index

FORFEITURES
  Generally, **19.2–386.1 et seq.**
Appeal and review, **19.2–386.13**
Appraisal and appraisers, **19.2–386.6**
Bail, this index
Bonds (officers and fiduciaries), possession, **19.2–386.6**
Bribery and corruption, public office, **19.2–386.33**
Cigarette Tax, this index
Computers, crimes and offenses, **19.2–386.17**
Controlled Substances, this index
Costs, **19.2–386.12**
Custodians, **19.2–386.4**
Default, **19.2–386.10**
Distribution, sales, proceeds, **19.2–386.14**
Driving under influence of alcohol or drugs, **19.2–386.34**
Drug paraphernalia, **19.2–386.23, 19.2–386.26**
Electronic communications devices, crimes and offenses, **19.2–386.18**
Electronic mail, crimes and offenses, **19.2–386.17**
Enforcement, **19.2–386.1 et seq.**
Evidence, money, **19.2–270.4**
Exemptions, **19.2–386.8**
Extortion, **19.2–386.35**
Gambling, **19.2–386.30**
Internet, crimes and offenses, **19.2–386.17**
Inventories, terrorism, **19.2–386.2**
Jury, **19.2–386.10**
Kidnapping, **19.2–386.35**
Landlord and tenant, exemptions, **19.2–386.8**
Liens and incumbrances, **19.2–386.9**
Money laundering, **19.2–386.19**
Motor Vehicles, this index
Motor vehicles department, collection, fees, **19.2–349.1**
Notice, **19.2–386.3**
  Motor vehicles, **19.2–386.2:1**
Obscenity, sexually explicit items involving children, **19.2–386.31**
Perishable property, sales, **19.2–386.7**
Prostitution, **19.2–386.35**
Release, **19.2–386.5**
Reports, **19.2–386.4**
Sales, **19.2–386.11, 19.2–386.12**
  Perishable property, **19.2–386.7**
  Proceeds, **19.2–386.14**
Service of process, **19.2–386.3**
Sex offenses, **19.2–386.35**
Storage, **19.2–386.4**
Stun weapons, **19.2–386.28**

FORFEITURES—Cont'd
Supersedeas or stay, **19.2–386.10**
Tasers, **19.2–386.28**
Telecommunications, devices, **19.2–386.18**
Terrorism, **19.2–386.15**
  Inventories, **19.2–386.2**
Title to property, **19.2–386.9**
  Sales, **19.2–386.12**
Trial, **19.2–386.10**
Venue, **19.2–386.1**
Warrants, **19.2–386.2**

FORGERY
Indictment and information, **19.2–224**
Venue, **19.2–245.1**
Witnesses, husband and wife, **19.2–271.2**

FORMER JEOPARDY
Double jeopardy. Crimes and Offenses, this index

FORMS
Capital punishment, mentally retarded and developmentally disabled persons, verdicts, **19.2–264.3:1.1**
Extradition, **19.2–87**
  Applications, **19.2–111**
Indictment and information, **19.2–220**
  Homicide, **19.2–220**

FOSTER CARE
Adults, criminal history record information, disclosure, **19.2–389**
Criminal history record information, disclosure, **19.2–389**

FRAUD
  See, also, Forgery, generally, this index
Critical incident stress management teams, emergency medical services, privileges and immunities, **19.2–271.4**
Embezzlement, generally, this index
Law enforcement officers, identity and identification, **19.2–82.1**
Limitation of prosecutions, **19.2–8**

FREEDOM OF INFORMATION
Critical incident stress management teams, emergency medical services, application of law, **19.2–271.4**

FUGITIVES FROM JUSTICE
Extradition, generally, this index

FUNDS
Crimes and Offenses, this index
Criminal Injuries Compensation Fund, generally, this index

GAMBLING
Devices, forfeitures, **19.2–386.30**
Forfeitures, **19.2–386.30**
Money, forfeitures, **19.2–386.30**
Property, forfeitures, **19.2–386.30**

GAME
Fish and Game, generally, this index

GAMING
Gambling, generally, this index

GANGS
Bail, presumptions, **19.2–120**
Presentence investigations, **19.2–299**
Probation, **19.2–303**
Witnesses, crimes and offenses, confidential or privileged information, **19.2–11.2**

GENERAL DISTRICT COURTS
District Courts, generally, this index

GENETICS
DNA, generally, this index

GLOBAL POSITIONING SYSTEMS
Bail, second and subsequent offenses, **19.2–123**
Sentences, suspension, modification, **19.2–303**
Tracking devices, searches and seizures, warrants, **19.2–56.2**

GOODS, WARES AND MERCHANDISE
Shoplifting, generally, this index

GOVERNOR
Powers and duties, fines and penalties, relief, **19.2–363, 19.2–368**

GPS
Global Positioning Systems, generally, this index

GRAND JURY
  Generally, **19.2–191 et seq.**
Age, **19.2–194, 19.2–195**
  Multijurisdiction grand juries, **19.2–215.4**
Attorneys,
  Multijurisdiction grand juries, **19.2–215.3, 19.2–215.6**
  Special counsel,
    Multijurisdiction grand juries, **19.2–215.3, 19.2–215.6**
    Special grand juries, **19.2–211**
  Special grand juries, **19.2–208**
Certificates and certification, examinations and examiners, **19.2–207**
Charge, **19.2–199, 19.2–261**
Charging, presence of juror, **19.2–261**
Compensation and salaries, **19.2–205**
  Multijurisdiction grand juries, **19.2–215.4**
Confidential or privileged information, **19.2–192**
  Multijurisdiction grand juries, **19.2–215.4**
Contempt, special grand juries, **19.2–208**
Court reporters,
  Multijurisdiction grand juries, **19.2–215.9**
  Special grand juries, **19.2–212**
Discharge, special grand juries, **19.2–213.1**
Domicile and residence, **19.2–194, 19.2–195**
  Multijurisdiction grand juries, **19.2–215.4**
Examinations and examiners, **19.2–207**
Expenses and expenditures,
  Multijurisdiction grand juries, **19.2–215.4**
  Special grand juries, **19.2–215**

GRAND JURY—Cont'd
Experts, special grand juries, **19.2–211**
Fines and penalties, **19.2–204**
Forepersons, **19.2–197, 19.2–198**
Handicapped persons, **19.2–194**
Indictment and Information, generally, this index
Investigations and investigators, **19.2–191**
  Multijurisdiction grand juries, **19.2–215.6**
Judges, multijurisdiction grand juries, **19.2–215.3**
Mentally ill persons, **19.2–194**
Multijurisdiction grand juries, **19.2–192, 19.2–215.1 et seq.**
Numbers and numbering, **19.2–195**
  Multijurisdiction grand juries, **19.2–215.4**
  Special grand juries, **19.2–207**
Powers and duties, **19.2–191, 19.2–200**
  Multijurisdiction grand juries, **19.2–215.1**
Privileges and immunities, special grand juries, **19.2–208**
Probable cause, **19.2–191**
Production of books and papers,
  Multijurisdiction grand juries, **19.2–215.5**
  Special grand juries, **19.2–208**
Prosecuting attorneys,
  Multijurisdiction grand juries, **19.2–215.10**
  Special grand juries, **19.2–210**
Records and recordation, examinations and examiners, **19.2–207**
Reports, special grand juries, **19.2–213**
Secrecy, **19.2–192**
  Special grand juries, **19.2–212**
Selection, **19.2–194**
Self incrimination, multijurisdiction grand juries, **19.2–215.7**
Special counsel,
  Multijurisdiction grand juries, **19.2–215.3, 19.2–215.6**
  Special grand juries, **19.2–211**
Special grand juries, **19.2–191, 19.2–206 et seq.**
  Multijurisdiction grand juries, **19.2–215.5**
  Special grand juries, **19.2–208**
Summons, **19.2–194**
Transcripts,
  Multijurisdiction grand juries, **19.2–215.9**
  Special grand juries, **19.2–212**
Travel expenses, **19.2–205**
Witnesses,
  Multijurisdiction grand juries, **19.2–215.5**
  Oaths and affirmations, **19.2–197**
  Special grand juries, **19.2–208**
  Testimony, sealed, special grand juries, **19.2–212**

GUARDIAN AD LITEM
Protective orders, compensation and salaries, **19.2–152.12**

GUARDIAN AND WARD
Crime victims, compensation and salaries, claims, **19.2–368.5**

GUILTY PLEAS
Courts, powers and duties, **19.2–257, 19.2–258**

GUILTY PLEAS—Cont'd
Judges, powers and duties, **19.2–257, 19.2–258**
Notice, crime victims, **19.2–11.01**
Trial, without jury, **19.2–257, 19.2–258**
Withdrawal, **19.2–296**

GUNS
Weapons, generally, this index

HABEAS CORPUS
Court reporters, **19.2–166**
DNA testing, **19.2–327.1 et seq.**
Evidence, disposition, crimes and offenses, **19.2–270.4**
Extradition, **19.2–95**
Transcripts, **19.2–166**

HABITUAL OFFENDERS
Second and subsequent offenses. Crimes and Offenses, this index

HANDGUNS
Weapons, generally, this index

HANDICAPPED PERSONS
Deaf and mute persons. Hearing Impaired Persons, generally, this index
Grand jury, **19.2–194**
Hearing Impaired Persons, generally, this index
Interpreters, generally, this index
Mentally Ill Persons, generally, this index
Mentally Retarded and Developmentally Disabled Persons, generally, this index

HARASSMENT
Child pornography, **19.2–390.3**
Stalking, generally, this index

HATE CRIMES
Terrorism, generally, this index

HAZARDOUS MATERIALS
Hazardous Substances and Waste, generally, this index

HAZARDOUS SUBSTANCES AND WASTE
Affidavits, inspection and inspectors, warrants, **19.2–394**
Controlled substances, manufacturers and manufacturing, cleanup, restitution, **19.2–305.1**
Crimes and offenses, limitation of prosecutions, **19.2–8**
Drugs and medicine, manufacturers and manufacturing, cleanup, restitution, **19.2–305.1**
Entry on property, inspection warrants, **19.2–393 et seq.**
Inspection and inspectors, warrants, **19.2–393 et seq.**
Limitation of prosecutions, **19.2–8**
Notice, inspection and inspectors, warrants, **19.2–396**
Warrants, inspection and inspectors, **19.2–393 et seq.**

HAZARDOUS WASTE
Hazardous Substances and Waste, generally, this index

HEALTH
Medical Care and Treatment, generally, this index

HEALTH AND SANITATION
Drugs and Medicine, generally, this index
Medical Care and Treatment, generally, this index

HEALTH CARE AND TREATMENT
Medical Care and Treatment, generally, this index

HEALTH CARE PROFESSIONALS
Controlled substances, falsifying patient records, limitation of prosecutions, **19.2–8**
Limitation of prosecutions, controlled substances, falsifying patient records, **19.2–8**
Records and recordation, falsifying patient records, limitation of prosecutions, **19.2–8**

HEARING IMPAIRED PERSONS
Crimes and offenses, interpreters, **19.2–164.1**
Interpreters, crimes and offenses, **19.2–164.1**
Witnesses, interpreters, crimes and offenses, **19.2–164.1**

HIGH SCHOOLS OR SECONDARY SCHOOLS
Schools and School Districts, generally, this index

HIGHER EDUCATION
Colleges and Universities, generally, this index

HIGHWAY PATROL
Close pursuit, fleeing or attempting to elude, **19.2–77**
Escape, arrest, **19.2–77**
Fines and penalties, literary fund, credits, **19.2–340.1**
Fleeing or attempting to elude, pursuit, **19.2–77**
Lineups, policies, writing, **19.2–390.02**
Pursuit, fleeing or attempting to elude, **19.2–77**

HIGHWAYS AND ROADS
Highway Patrol, generally, this index
Police. Highway Patrol, generally, this index
State patrol. Highway Patrol, generally, this index
Traffic Rules and Regulations, generally, this index

HOME AND COMMUNITY BASED SERVICES
Criminal history record information, disclosure, **19.2–389**

HOMELAND SECURITY
Terrorism, generally, this index

HOMICIDE
Arrest, **19.2–71**
  DNA, violent felonies, samples, **19.2–310.2:1, 19.2–310.3:1**
Capital murder, arrest, warrants, destruction, **19.2–76.1**
Conviction of crime, **19.2–288**
Indictment and information, forms, **19.2–221**

HOMICIDE—Cont'd
Lesser included offenses, conviction, **19.2–266.1**
Limitation of prosecutions, **19.2–8.1**
Manslaughter, limitation of prosecutions, **19.2–8.1**
Mentally ill persons, treatment, charges, dismissal and nonsuit, **19.2–169.3**
Second and subsequent offenses, sentencing, **19.2–297.1**
Three strikes, sentencing, **19.2–297.1**
Venue, **19.2–247, 19.2–248**
Verdicts, **19.2–288**

HOSPITALS
Criminal history record information, officers and employees, **19.2–389**
Officers and employees, criminal history record information, **19.2–389**

HOSTAGES
Kidnapping, generally, this index

HOUSING
Real Property Taxation, generally, this index
Searches and Seizures, generally, this index

HUNTING
Fish and Game, generally, this index

HUSBAND AND WIFE
Abuse. Domestic Violence, generally, this index
Assault and battery. Domestic Violence, generally, this index
Confidential or privileged information, crimes and offenses, witnesses, **19.2–271.1, 19.2–271.2**
Crimes and offenses,
  Domestic Violence, generally, this index
  Witnesses, **19.2–271.1, 19.2–271.2**
Domestic Violence, generally, this index
Evidence, witnesses, crimes and offenses, **19.2–271.1, 19.2–271.2**
Privileges and immunities, witnesses, crimes and offenses, **19.2–271.2**
Sex offenses,
  Counselors and counseling, indictment and information, **19.2–218.2**
  Indictment and information, counselors and counseling, **19.2–218.2**
  Preliminary hearings, **19.2–218.1**
  Witnesses, **19.2–271.2**
Violence. Domestic Violence, generally, this index
Wiretapping, damages, **19.2–69**
Witnesses, crimes and offenses, **19.2–271.1, 19.2–271.2**

IDENTITY AND IDENTIFICATION
DNA, generally, this index
Fingerprints and Fingerprinting, generally, this index

IDENTITY THEFT
Limitation of prosecutions, **19.2–8**

ILLNESS
Mentally Ill Persons, generally, this index

IMMEDIATE SANCTION PROBATION PROGRAM
Crimes and offenses, suspension, sentences, **19.2–303.5**

IMMIGRATION
Aliens, generally, this index

IMMORALITY
Obscenity, generally, this index

IMMUNITIES
Privileges and Immunities, generally, this index

IMPRISONMENT
Correctional Institutions, generally, this index
Jails, generally, this index

INCEST
Witnesses, husband and wife, **19.2–271.2**

INCOME
Compensation and Salaries, generally, this index

INDECENCY
Obscenity, generally, this index

INDICTMENT AND INFORMATION
Generally, **19.2–202, 19.2–216 et seq.**
Amendments, **19.2–226, 19.2–231**
Arrest, **19.2–236**
Bill of particulars, **19.2–230**
Bonds (officers and fiduciaries), complaints, **19.2–229**
Capias, **19.2–219, 19.2–232 et seq.**
Capital punishment, **19.2–217.1**
Complaints, witnesses, **19.2–228**
Bonds (officers and fiduciaries), **19.2–229**
Contents, **19.2–220**
Corporations, **19.2–238**
Counselors and counseling, domestic violence, **19.2–218.1, 19.2–218.2**
Defects, **19.2–226**
Amendments, **19.2–231**
Striking, **19.2–291**
Discharge, time, **19.2–242**
Dismissal and nonsuit, domestic violence, counselors and counseling, **19.2–218.2**
Embezzlement, **19.2–223**
Extradition, **19.2–87**
Forgery, **19.2–224**
Forms, **19.2–220**
Homicide, forms, **19.2–221**
Intent, **19.2–225**
Judgments and decrees, objections or exceptions, **19.2–227**
Jurisdiction, **19.2–239**
Limitations of prosecutions, discharge, **19.2–242**
Mail and mailing, process, **19.2–235**
Motions, sealing, **19.2–192.1**
Multijurisdiction grand juries, **19.2–215.1 et seq.**
Objections or exceptions, **19.2–227**
Omissions, **19.2–226**
Amendments, **19.2–231**

INDICTMENT AND INFORMATION—Cont'd
Preliminary hearings, **19.2–218**
Presentment, **19.2–216**
Process, **19.2–217, 19.2–232 et seq.**
Records and recordation, capital offenses, **19.2–217.1**
Resubmitting evidence, **19.2–203**
Sealing, **19.2–192.1**
Self incrimination, counselors and counseling, domestic violence, **19.2–218.1**
Service of process, **19.2–232 et seq.**
Striking, defective counts, **19.2–291**
Summons, **19.2–219, 19.2–232 et seq.**
Corporations, **19.2–238**
Theft, **19.2–223**
Time, discharge, **19.2–242**
Virginia Crime Code references, **19.2–226, 19.2–390.01**
Waiver, **19.2–217**
Witnesses, complaints, **19.2–228**
Bonds (officers and fiduciaries), **19.2–229**

INDIGENT DEFENSE COMMISSION
Generally, **19.2–163.01 et seq.**

INDIGENT PERSONS
Appeal and review, transcripts, **19.2–325**
Appeals in Criminal Prosecutions, this index
Attorney fees,
Appeals in criminal prosecutions, **19.2–326**
Crimes and offenses, **19.2–163**
Attorneys,
Public Defenders, generally, this index
Right to counsel. Attorneys, this index
Boards and commissions, attorneys, appointment, **19.2–163.01 et seq.**
Capital Punishment, this index
Costs,
Appeals in criminal prosecutions, **19.2–326**
Petitions, **19.2–355**
Court appointed attorneys, crimes and offenses, **19.2–157 et seq.**
Crimes and offenses,
Appeals in Criminal Prosecutions, this index
Attorneys, **19.2–157 et seq.**
Capital punishment, mental examinations, **19.2–264.3:1, 19.2–264.3:1.2**
Pretrial services, officers and employees, powers and duties, **19.2–152.4:3**
Public Defenders, generally, this index
Transcripts, **19.2–165, 19.2–325**
Examinations and examiners, statement of indigency, right to counsel, **19.2–159, 19.2–159.1**
Financial statements and reports, statement of indigency, right to counsel, **19.2–159, 19.2–159.1**
Fines and penalties, petitions, **19.2–355**
Investigations and investigators, statement of indigency, right to counsel, **19.2–159, 19.2–159.1**

INDIGENT PERSONS—Cont'd
Perjury, statement of indigency, **19.2–161**
Public Defenders, generally, this index
Restitution, **19.2–355**
Right to counsel. Attorneys, this index
Social Services, generally, this index
Statement of indigency, right to counsel, **19.2–159, 19.2–159.1**
Transcripts, **19.2–325**
Crimes and offenses, **19.2–165**
Waiver, right to counsel, crimes and offenses, **19.2–160**

INFANTS
Children and Minors, generally, this index

INFORMATION
Confidential or Privileged Information, generally, this index
Criminal History Record Information, generally, this index
Disclosure, generally, this index
Indictment and Information, generally, this index

INFORMATION SUPERHIGHWAY
Internet, generally, this index

INFRACTIONS
Traffic Rules and Regulations, this index

INJURIES
Personal Injuries, generally, this index

INSANITY
Mentally Ill Persons, generally, this index

INSANITY DEFENSE
Criminal Insanity, generally, this index

INSPECTION AND INSPECTORS
Ships and shipping, searches and seizures, noncommercial vessels, **19.2–10.3**

INSTALLMENTS
Fines and penalties, **19.2–354 et seq.**
Restitution, **19.2–354 et seq.**

INSTRUCTIONAL STAFF
Schoolteachers, generally, this index

INSTRUCTORS
Schoolteachers, generally, this index

INTELLECTUAL DISABILITIES
Mentally Retarded and Developmentally Disabled Persons, generally, this index

INTEREST
Fines and penalties, **19.2–353.5**
Restitution, **19.2–305.4**

INTERNATIONAL COMPUTER NETWORK
Internet, generally, this index

INTERNET
Confidential or privileged information, real time location data, records and recordation, **19.2–70.3**

INTERNET—Cont'd
Forfeitures, crimes and offenses, **19.2–386.17**
Real time location data, records and recordation, confidential or privileged information, **19.2–70.3**
Searches and seizures, real time location data, records and recordation, confidential or privileged information, **19.2–70.3**
Subpoenas, real time location data, records and recordation, **19.2–70.3**
Warrants, searches and seizures, real time location data, records and recordation, **19.2–70.3**

INTERPRETERS
Confidential or privileged information, crimes and offenses, **19.2–164, 19.2–164.1**
Crime victims, **19.2–164**
Crimes and offenses, **19.2–164, 19.2–164.1**
Witnesses, **19.2–11.01, 19.2–164**
Crimes and offenses, **19.2–164**

INTERSTATE EXTRADITION
Extradition, generally, this index

INTRASTATE TELECOMMUNICATIONS
Telecommunications, generally, this index

INVENTORIES
Controlled substances, searches and seizures, law enforcement agencies, reports, **19.2–386.23**
Searches and seizures,
Terrorism, **19.2–386.2**
Warrants, **19.2–56 et seq.**

INVESTMENT CONTRACTS
Securities, generally, this index

INVESTMENT SECURITIES
Securities, generally, this index

INVESTMENTS
Securities, generally, this index

INVOLUNTARY COMMITMENT
Commitment. Mentally Ill Persons, this index

ISSUE
Children and Minors, generally, this index

ISSUES, PROOF AND VARIANCE
Evidence, generally, this index

JAILS
See, also, Correctional Institutions, generally, this index
Aliens, reports, **19.2–83.2**
Citizens and citizenship, reports, **19.2–83.2**
Criminal history record information, citizens and citizenship, reports, **19.2–83.2**
Detention center incarceration program, **19.2–316.2**
Escape, generally, this index
Extradition, **19.2–97, 19.2–98**
Habeas Corpus, generally, this index
Officers and employees, courthouses, security, **19.2–328**

JAILS—Cont'd
Release, pretrial services, officers and employees, powers and duties, **19.2–152.4:3**
Reports, citizens and citizenship, **19.2–83.2**
Strip searches, **19.2–59.1**
Transportation, costs, **19.2–338**
Work release, costs, failure to pay, **19.2–354**

JEOPARDY
Double jeopardy. Crimes and Offenses, this index

JOINDER
Crimes and offenses, **19.2–262.1**

JUDGES
Circuit Courts, this index
Conservators of the peace, **19.2–12 et seq.**
Death, criminal trial, **19.2–154**
Disability, criminal trial, **19.2–154**
Grand jury, multijurisdiction grand juries, **19.2–215.3**
Jury, contact, crimes and offenses, **19.2–263.1**
Multijurisdiction grand juries, **19.2–215.3**
Plea agreements, rejection, recusal, **19.2–254**
Recusal, plea agreements, rejection, **19.2–254**
Witnesses, **19.2–271**

JUDGMENTS AND DECREES
Appeal and Review, generally, this index
Damages, generally, this index
Entry of judgment. Executions, generally, this index
Executions, generally, this index
Fines and Penalties, generally, this index
Probation, revocation, **19.2–306**
Restitution, **19.2–305.2**
Review. Appeal and Review, generally, this index
Supersedeas or Stay, generally, this index
Suspended sentences, revocation, **19.2–306**

JUDICIAL DEPARTMENT
Courts, generally, this index
Judges, generally, this index

JUDICIAL NOTICE
Crimes and offenses, **19.2–265.2**

JUDICIAL REVIEW
Appeal and Review, generally, this index

JUDICIAL SALES
Executions, generally, this index

JURISDICTION
Indictment and information, **19.2–239**
Magistrates, **19.2–44**
Venue, generally, this index

JURY
Capital Punishment, this index
Communications, judges, crimes and offenses, **19.2–263.1**
Confidential or privileged information, orders, **19.2–263.3**

JURY—Cont'd
Contact, judges, crimes and offenses, **19.2–263.1**
Contempt, show cause hearings, **19.2–11**
Crimes and offenses, **19.2–260 et seq.**
  Capital punishment, **19.2–264.2, 19.2–264.3**
  Communications, judges, **19.2–263.1**
  Instructions to jury, **19.2–263.2**
  Media coverage, **19.2–266**
  Numbers and numbering, **19.2–262**
  Preemptory strikes, **19.2–262**
  Sentencing, **19.2–295, 19.2–295.1**
  Sequestration, **19.2–264**
  Striking, **19.2–262**
  Views, **19.2–264.1**
  Waiver, **19.2–257, 19.2–258, 19.2–262**
Delinquent children, waiver, **19.2–262**
Fines and penalties, sentencing, **19.2–295, 19.2–295.1**
Grand Jury, generally, this index
Impaneling, sentencing, **19.2–295.1**
Instructions to jury, crimes and offenses, **19.2–263.2**
Judges, communications, crimes and offenses, **19.2–263.1**
Media coverage, **19.2–266**
Numbers and numbering, crimes and offenses, **19.2–262**
Photography and pictures, **19.2–266**
Preemptory strikes, crimes and offenses, **19.2–262**
Sentencing, crimes and offenses, **19.2–295, 19.2–295.1**
Sequestration, crimes and offenses, **19.2–264**
Striking, crimes and offenses, **19.2–262**
Television and radio, media coverage, **19.2–266**
Traffic rules and regulations, trial, **19.2–258.1**
Views, crimes and offenses, **19.2–264.1**
Waiver, crimes and offenses, **19.2–257, 19.2–258, 19.2–262**

JUSTICES
Judges, generally, this index

JUVENILE AND DOMESTIC RELATIONS DISTRICT COURTS
  See, also, District Courts, generally, this index
Attorneys, qualifications, appointment, **19.2–163.03**

JUVENILE DELINQUENTS AND DEPENDENTS
Delinquent Children, generally, this index

KIDNAPPING
Children and minors, searches and seizures, forfeitures, **19.2–386.32**
Forfeitures,
  Children and minors, searches and seizures, **19.2–386.32**
  Searches and seizures, **19.2–386.35**
Searches and seizures,
  Children and minors, forfeitures, **19.2–386.32**
  Forfeitures, **19.2–386.35**

KIDNAPPING—Cont'd
Second and subsequent offenses, sentencing, **19.2–297.1**

KNIVES
Weapons, generally, this index

KNOWLEDGE
Notice, generally, this index

KNUCKLES
Metallic knuckles. Weapons, generally, this index

LABOR AND EMPLOYMENT
Compensation and Salaries, generally, this index
Criminal history record information,
Disclosure, **19.2–389**
State agencies, **19.2–389**
Professions and Occupations, generally, this index
Protective orders, confidential or privileged information, **19.2–152.8 et seq.**
Salaries. Compensation and Salaries, generally, this index
Sex offenses, registration, proof, nonresidents, **19.2–298**
Stalking, protective orders, confidential or privileged information, **19.2–152.8 et seq.**

LABORATORIES
Crimes and Offenses, this index

LACHES
Limitation of Actions, generally, this index

LAKES AND PONDS
Fish and Game, generally, this index

LANDLORD AND TENANT
Forfeitures, exemptions, **19.2–386.8**
Wiretapping, orders of court, **19.2–68**

LARCENY
Theft, generally, this index

LASCIVIOUS BEHAVIOR
Obscenity, generally, this index

LAW ENFORCEMENT AGENCIES
Criminal history record information, reports, **19.2–390**
Reports, criminal history record information, **19.2–390**

LAW ENFORCEMENT OFFICERS
See, also, Police, generally, this index
Aliens, arrest, powers and duties, **19.2–81.6, 19.2–82**
Arrest, generally, this index
Close pursuit, fleeing or attempting to elude, **19.2–77**
Foreign states, **19.2–79**
Crimes and offenses, identity and identification, **19.2–82.1**
Escape, arrest, **19.2–77**
Fleeing or attempting to elude, pursuit, **19.2–77, 19.2–79**

LAW ENFORCEMENT OFFICERS—Cont'd
Foreign states, pursuit, **19.2–79**
Fraud, identity and identification, **19.2–82.1**
Highway Patrol, generally, this index
Identity and identification, fraud, **19.2–82.1**
Powers and duties, aliens, arrest, **19.2–81.6, 19.2–82**
Privileges and immunities, protective orders, registry, **19.2–387.1**
Protective orders, issuance, **19.2–152.8**
Pursuit, fleeing or attempting to elude, **19.2–77**
Foreign states, **19.2–79**
Special conservators of the peace, registration, **19.2–13**
State officers and employees, fines and penalties, literary fund, credits, **19.2–340.1**
State police. Highway Patrol, generally, this index
Subpoenas, issuance, **19.2–73.2**

LAW OF THE ROAD
Traffic Rules and Regulations, generally, this index

LAWYERS
Attorneys, generally, this index

LEAD
Hazardous Substances and Waste, generally, this index

LEVY
Executions, generally, this index

LEWDNESS AND OBSCENITY
Obscenity, generally, this index

LICENSES AND PERMITS
Limitation of prosecutions, **19.2–8**

LIENS AND INCUMBRANCES
Criminal injuries compensation fund, **19.2–368.15**

LIMITATION OF ACTIONS
Appeals in criminal prosecutions, state, **19.2–400**
Crime victims, compensation and salaries,
Claims, **19.2–368.5**
Medical care and treatment, collections, **19.2–368.5:2**
Crimes and offenses. Limitation of Prosecutions, generally, this index
Fines and penalties, **19.2–341**
Probation, revocation, **19.2–306**
Suspended sentences, revocation, **19.2–306**

LIMITATION OF PROSECUTIONS
Generally, **19.2–8, 19.2–243**
Attorneys, licenses and permits, crimes and offenses, **19.2–8**
Computers, **19.2–8**
Controlled substances, falsifying patient records, health care providers, **19.2–8**
Double jeopardy, **19.2–292 et seq.**
Health care professionals, controlled substances, falsifying patient records, **19.2–8**
Indictment and information, discharge, **19.2–242**

LIMITATION OF PROSECUTIONS—Cont'd
Manslaughter, **19.2–8.1**
Multiple convictions, **19.2–294**
Murder, **19.2–8.1**

LINEUPS
Crimes and offenses, policies, writing, **19.2–390.02**

LISTS
Attorneys, indigent defense, appointment, **19.2–163.01**

LITERARY FUND
Fines and penalties, **19.2–353**

LOCAL DETENTION FACILITIES
Jails, generally, this index

LOW INCOME PERSONS
Indigent Persons, generally, this index

MACHINERY AND EQUIPMENT
Noise, weights and measures, certificates and certification, evidence, **19.2–270.7**
Wiretapping, **19.2–63**

MAGAZINES
Lewdness and obscenity. Obscenity, generally, this index
Obscenity, generally, this index

MAGISTRATES
Generally, **19.2–26 et seq.**
Acknowledgments, **19.2–45**
Adverse or pecuniary interest, **19.2–37**
Appointments, **19.2–35 et seq.**
Arrest, **19.2–45**
Attorneys,
Chief magistrates, appointments, **19.2–36**
Eligibility, **19.2–37**
Audits and auditors, **19.2–48**
Bail, **19.2–45**
Bonds (officers and fiduciaries), **19.2–39**
Certificates and certification, **19.2–38**
Retirement and pensions, **19.2–46.2**
Chief magistrates, **19.2–36**
Citizens and citizenship, appointments, **19.2–37**
Compensation and salaries, **19.2–38, 19.2–46, 19.2–46.1**
Conservators of the peace, **19.2–12 et seq., 19.2–45**
Criminal history record information, appointment, **19.2–35**
Domicile and residence, **19.2–37**
Education, **19.2–37**
Examinations and examiners, **19.2–38**
Fingerprints and fingerprinting, appointment, **19.2–35**
Jurisdiction, **19.2–44**
Numbers and numbering, **19.2–34**
Oaths and affirmations, **19.2–45**
Offices, **19.2–48.1**
Powers and duties, **19.2–33, 19.2–45**
Probation, **19.2–38**

MAGISTRATES—Cont'd
Retirement and pensions, state officers and employees, **19.2–46.2**
Searches and seizures, warrants, **19.2–45**
Standards, training, **19.2–38.1**
Subpoenas, **19.2–45**
Supervision, **19.2–35**
Terms of office, **19.2–38**
Training, **19.2–38, 19.2–38.1**
Travel expenses, **19.2–46.1**

MAIL AND MAILING
Certified or registered mail, searches and seizures, warrants, affidavits, **19.2–54**
Electronic Mail, generally, this index

MAIMING
Protective orders, **19.2–152.7:1 et seq.**

MAMMALS
Fish and Game, generally, this index

MAPS AND PLATS
Global Positioning Systems, generally, this index

MARINE CORPS
Military Forces, generally, this index

MARRIAGE
See, also, Husband and Wife, generally, this index
Assault and battery. Domestic Violence, generally, this index
Crimes and offenses. Domestic Violence, generally, this index
Domestic Violence, generally, this index
Violence. Domestic Violence, generally, this index

MARRIAGE AND FAMILY THERAPISTS
Wiretapping, damages, **19.2–69**

MASS MEDIA AND COMMUNICATIONS
Telecommunications, generally, this index

MASS TRANSPORTATION
Officers and employees, criminal history record information, fingerprints and fingerprinting, **19.2–389**

MASTER AND SERVANT
Labor and Employment, generally, this index

MEDICAL CARE AND TREATMENT
Blood alcohol tests, evidence, admissibility, **19.2–187.02**
Crime victims, compensation and salaries, **19.2–368.11:1**
Crimes and offenses, evidence, costs, **19.2–165.1**
Emergency Medical Services, generally, this index
Evidence,
Blood alcohol tests, emergency medical services, admissibility, **19.2–187.02**
Crimes and offenses, costs, **19.2–165.1**
Health Care Professionals, generally, this index

MEDICAL CARE AND TREATMENT—Cont'd
Privileges and immunities, blood alcohol tests, emergency medical services, evidence, **19.2–187.02**
Sex Offenses, this index

MEDICAL EXAMINERS
Evidence, crimes and offenses, **19.2–188**
Opinions and expert testimony, evidence, **19.2–188**
Reports, opinions and expert testimony, evidence, **19.2–188**
Witnesses, reports, opinions and expert testimony, evidence, **19.2–188**

MEDICAL RECORDS
Blood alcohol tests, evidence, admissibility, **19.2–187.02**
Privileges and immunities, blood alcohol tests, evidence, admissibility, **19.2–187.02**

MEDICAL TREATMENT
Medical Care and Treatment, generally, this index

MEDICINE
Drugs and Medicine, generally, this index

MENTAL CONDITION OR CAPACITY
Mentally Ill Persons, generally, this index
Mentally Retarded and Developmentally Disabled Persons, generally, this index

MENTAL EXAMINATIONS
Crimes and Offenses, this index
Sex offenses, sentencing, **19.2–300 et seq.**

MENTALLY ILL PERSONS
See, also, Mentally Retarded and Developmentally Disabled Persons, generally, this index
Bail, **19.2–141**
Capital Punishment, this index
Commitment,
Crimes and offenses, **19.2–169.6, 19.2–174.1**
Acquittal, criminal insanity, **19.2–182.2 et seq.**
Criminal insanity, release, **19.2–182.6 et seq.**
Escape, criminal insanity, **19.2–182.14, 19.2–182.15**
Medical records, disclosure, **19.2–169.6**
Privileges and immunities, records and recordation, **19.2–169.6**
Records and recordation, disclosure, **19.2–169.6**
Sexually violent predators, **19.2–169.3**
Conviction of crime, evaluation, sentencing, capital punishment, **19.2–264.3:1**
Crimes and offenses,
See, also, Criminal Insanity, generally, this index
Acquittal, criminal insanity, **19.2–182.2 et seq.**
Conviction of crime, evaluation, sentencing, capital punishment, **19.2–264.3:1**
Dismissal and nonsuit, **19.2–169.3**
Evaluations,
Acquittal, commitment, **19.2–182.2 et seq.**

MENTALLY ILL PERSONS—Cont'd
Crimes and offenses—Cont'd
Evaluations—Cont'd
Competency to proceed, **19.2–167, 19.2–169.1 et seq.**
Conviction of crime, sentencing, capital punishment, **19.2–264.3:1**
Criminal insanity, capital punishment, **19.2–264.3:1**
Insanity. Criminal Insanity, generally, this index
Motions, **19.2–169.4**
Criminal Insanity, generally, this index
Discharge, crimes and offenses, criminal insanity, **19.2–182.6 et seq.**
Dismissal and nonsuit, crimes and offenses, **19.2–169.3**
Escape, criminal insanity, commitment, **19.2–182.14, 19.2–182.15**
Facilities, officers and employees, criminal history record information, **19.2–389**
Grand jury, **19.2–194**
Homicide, treatment, charges, dismissal and nonsuit, **19.2–169.3**
Medical care and treatment, crimes and offenses, restoration to competency, **19.2–169.2, 19.2–180**
Medical records, disclosure, **19.2–169.6**
Psychiatrists and Psychiatry, generally, this index
Psychologists and Psychology, generally, this index
Screening, sexually violent predators, **19.2–169.3**
Trial, crimes and offenses, **19.2–167, 19.2–169.1 et seq.**

MENTALLY RETARDED AND DEVELOPMENTALLY DISABLED PERSONS
See, also, Mentally Ill Persons, generally, this index
Bail, **19.2–141**
Second and subsequent offenses, **19.2–123**
Capital Punishment, this index
Conviction of crime, evaluation, sentencing, capital punishment, **19.2–264.3:1, 19.2–264.3:1.2**
Crimes and offenses,
Conviction of crime, evaluation, sentencing, capital punishment, **19.2–264.3:1.2**
Evaluations,
Competency to proceed, **19.2–167, 19.2–169.1 et seq.**
Conviction of crime, sentencing, capital punishment, **19.2–264.3:1.2**
Trial, **19.2–167, 19.2–169.1 et seq.**
Definitions, capital punishment, **19.2–264.3:1.1**
Facilities, officers and employees, criminal history record information, **19.2–389**
Trial, crimes and offenses, **19.2–167, 19.2–169.1 et seq.**

METROPOLITAN WASHINGTON AIRPORTS AUTHORITY
Fingerprints and fingerprinting, criminal history record information, labor and employment, **19.2–389.2**

MILITARY FORCES
Bail, forfeitures, **19.2–144**
Change of venue, **19.2–251**
Crimes and offenses,
  Bail, failure to appear, **19.2–144**
  Change of venue, **19.2–251**
Venue, change of venue, **19.2–251**

MINISTERS
Clergy, generally, this index

MINORS
Children and Minors, generally, this index

MISAPPROPRIATION OF FUNDS
Embezzlement, generally, this index

MISDEMEANORS
Crimes and Offenses, generally, this index

MISREPRESENTATION
Fraud, generally, this index

MONEY
Embezzlement, generally, this index
Evidence, disposition, **19.2–270.2, 19.2–270.4**
Gambling, forfeitures, **19.2–386.30**

MONEY TRANSMITTERS
Records and recordation, production of books and papers, **19.2–10.1**

MORTGAGE BROKERS AND LENDERS
Criminal history record information, disclosure, **19.2–389**

MOTION PICTURES
Lewdness and obscenity. Obscenity, generally, this index
Obscenity, generally, this index
Pornography. Obscenity, generally, this index

MOTIONS
Bail, **19.2–158**
Crimes and Offenses, this index
Criminal history record information, disclosure, **19.2–389**
Searches and seizures, suppression, **19.2–60**

MOTOR VEHICLES
  See, also, Traffic Rules and Regulations, generally, this index
Alcoholic beverages, driving under influence of alcohol or drugs. Traffic Rules and Regulations, this index
Arrest, **19.2–81**
  Impoundment, **19.2–80.1**
Crimes and offenses, forfeitures, **19.2–386.16**
Driving under influence of alcohol or drugs. Traffic Rules and Regulations, this index
Forfeitures,
  Crimes and offenses, **19.2–386.16**
  Driving under influence of alcohol or drugs, **19.2–386.34**

MOTOR VEHICLES—Cont'd
Forfeitures—Cont'd
  Notice, **19.2–386.2:1**
Impoundment, arrest, **19.2–80.1**
Notice, forfeitures, **19.2–386.2:1**
Prostitution, children and minors, forfeitures, **19.2–386.16**
Searches and seizures,
  Forfeitures, **19.2–386.16**
  Tracking devices, warrants, **19.2–56.2**
Tracking devices, searches and seizures, warrants, **19.2–56.2**
Traffic Rules and Regulations, generally, this index

MOTOR VEHICLES DEPARTMENT
Costs, collection, **19.2–349.1**
Fees, fines and penalties, collection, **19.2–349.1**
Fines and penalties, collection, **19.2–349.1**
Forfeitures, collection, fees, **19.2–349.1**
Restitution, collection, fees, **19.2–349.1**

MOTORBOATS
Boats and Boating, generally, this index

MOTORCYCLES
Rules of the road. Traffic Rules and Regulations, generally, this index

MUNICIPALITIES
Courts. District Courts, generally, this index
District Courts, generally, this index
Jails, generally, this index
Law enforcement officers. Police, generally, this index
Licenses and permits, professions and occupations, limitation of prosecutions, **19.2–8**
Limitation of prosecutions, professions and occupations, licenses and permits, **19.2–8**
Police, generally, this index
Professions and occupations, licenses and permits, limitation of prosecutions, **19.2–8**
Public Defenders, generally, this index
Real Property Taxation, generally, this index
Schools and School Districts, generally, this index
Taxation. Real Property Taxation, generally, this index
Venue, crimes and offenses, **19.2–249 et seq.**

MURDER
Homicide, generally, this index

MUTE PERSONS
Hearing Impaired Persons, generally, this index

NAMES
Crime victims, appeals in criminal prosecutions, sex offenses, confidential or privileged information, **19.2–11.2**
Sex offenses, crime victims, appeals in criminal prosecutions, confidential or privileged information, **19.2–11.2**

NARCOTICS
Controlled Substances, generally, this index

NATURAL RESOURCES
Fish and Game, generally, this index

NAVY
Military Forces, generally, this index

NEGOTIABLE INSTRUMENTS
Bad checks,
Evidence, **19.2–270.3**
Fines and penalties, **19.2–353.3**
Checks, fines and penalties, **19.2–353.3**
Crimes and offenses, evidence, **19.2–270.2**
Evidence, disposition, **19.2–270.2**
Presumptions, bad checks, **19.2–270.3**

NETWORK (COMPUTERS)
Internet, generally, this index

NEWSPAPERS
Legal advertising. Notice, generally, this index
Notice, generally, this index

NOISE
Machinery and equipment, weights and measures, certificates and certification, evidence, **19.2–270.7**

NOLLE PROSEQUI
Crimes and offenses, **19.2–265.3**

NOLO CONTENDERE
Guilty Pleas, generally, this index

NON COMPOS MENTIS
Mentally Ill Persons, generally, this index

NONCRIMINAL VIOLATIONS
Fines and Penalties, generally, this index

NONRESIDENTS
Foreign States, generally, this index
Sex offenses, registration, **19.2–298**

NONSTOCK CORPORATIONS
Corporations, generally, this index

NORTH CAROLINA
Foreign States, generally, this index

NOT GUILTY BY REASON OF INSANITY
Criminal Insanity, generally, this index

NOTICE
Bail, this index
Capital Punishment, this index
Crimes and Offenses, this index
DNA, violent felonies, samples, **19.2–310.3:1**
Probation, revocation, **19.2–306**
Special conservators of the peace, labor and employment, **19.2–13**
Suspended sentences, revocation, **19.2–306**

NURSING HOMES
Criminal history record information, officers and employees, **19.2–389**
Officers and employees, criminal history record information, **19.2–389**

OATHS AND AFFIRMATIONS
Affidavits, generally, this index
Crime victims, compensation and salaries, claims, **19.2–368.16**
Grand jury, **19.2–197**
Magistrates, **19.2–45**
Searches and seizures, warrants, **19.2–52**

OBSCENITY
Bail, children and minors, **19.2–120**
Children and minors,
Computers, **19.2–270.1:1**
Registers and registries, child pornography, **19.2–390.3**
Restitution, **19.2–305.1**
Electronic mail, crimes and offenses, **19.2–386.17**
Forfeitures, sexually explicit items involving children, **19.2–386.31**
Internet,
Children and minors, **19.2–270.1:1**
Crimes and offenses, **19.2–386.17**
Notice, child pornography, registers and registries, **19.2–390.3**
Registers and registries, child pornography, **19.2–390.3**
Searches and seizures, sexually explicit items involving children, **19.2–386.31**

OCCUPATIONS
Professions and Occupations, generally, this index

OFFENSES
Crimes and Offenses, generally, this index

OFFICIAL BONDS
Bonds (Officers and Fiduciaries), generally, this index

OMBUDSMAN
Crime victims, compensation and salaries, **19.2–368.3:1**

OPINIONS AND EXPERT TESTIMONY
Witnesses, this index

ORDERS
Judgments and Decrees, generally, this index

ORDERS OF COURT
See, also, Judgments and Decrees, generally, this index
Controlled substances, custody, law enforcement agencies, **19.2–386.25**
Protective Orders, generally, this index
Subpoenas, generally, this index
Summons, generally, this index
Wiretapping, this index

OTHER STATES
Foreign States, generally, this index

PANEL TRUCKS
Motor Vehicles, generally, this index

PAPERS
Production of Books and Papers, generally, this index

PARAMEDICS
Emergency Medical Services, generally, this index

PARENT AND CHILD
Children and Minors, generally, this index

PAROLE
See, also, Probation, generally, this index
Boot camps, **19.2–316.1**
Criminal history record information, postrelease supervision, violations, reports, **19.2–390**
Detention center incarceration program, **19.2–316.2**
Diversion centers, **19.2–316.3**
Indeterminate commitment, **19.2–311 et seq.**
Records and recordation, Virginia Crime Code references, **19.2–390.01**
Reports, criminal history record information, postrelease supervision, violations, **19.2–390**
Supervision, criminal history record information, violations, **19.2–390**

PARTIES
Costs, generally, this index
Process, generally, this index
Service of process. Process, this index
Summons, generally, this index

PARTNERSHIPS
Arrest, executions, **19.2–76**

PASSPORTS
Criminal history record information, disclosure, **19.2–389**

PASTORS
Clergy, generally, this index

PATENT MEDICINES
Drugs and Medicine, generally, this index

PATHOLOGISTS
Medical Examiners, generally, this index

PATROL
Highway Patrol, generally, this index

PAUPERS
Indigent Persons, generally, this index

PAY
Compensation and Salaries, generally, this index

PAYMENT
Fines and Penalties, this index

PAYROLLS
Compensation and Salaries, generally, this index

PEACE OFFICERS
Law Enforcement Officers, generally, this index
Police, generally, this index

PEN REGISTERS
Wiretapping, **19.2–62, 19.2–70.1, 19.2–70.2**

PENAL INSTITUTIONS
Correctional Institutions, generally, this index

PENALTIES
Fines and Penalties, generally, this index

PENITENTIARIES
Correctional Institutions, generally, this index

PER DIEM
Compensation and Salaries, generally, this index

PERFORMANCE BONDS
Bonds (Officers and Fiduciaries), generally, this index

PERSONAL INJURIES
Bail, keeping the peace, **19.2–19 et seq.**
Crimes and offenses,
  Protective orders, **19.2–152.7:1 et seq.**
  Venue, **19.2–246**
Criminal Injuries Compensation Fund, generally, this index
Keeping the peace, bail, **19.2–19 et seq.**
Protective orders, **19.2–152.7:1 et seq.**

PERSONAL PROPERTY
Executions, generally, this index
Forfeitures, generally, this index
Levy of execution. Executions, generally, this index
Searches and Seizures, generally, this index
Theft, generally, this index
Warrants. Searches and Seizures, this index

PERSONAL SERVICE
Service of process. Process, this index

PERSONNEL
Labor and Employment, generally, this index

PETITIONS
Crimes and Offenses, this index

PHARMACISTS
Controlled Substances, generally, this index

PHOTOGRAPHY AND PICTURES
Bail, release, second and subsequent offenses, conditions, **19.2–123**
Crimes and offenses,
  Obscenity, generally, this index
  Trial, **19.2–266**
Criminal History Record Information, this index
Evidence, theft, **19.2–270.1**
Lewdness and obscenity. Obscenity, generally, this index
Obscenity, generally, this index
Pornography. Obscenity, generally, this index
Shoplifting, evidence, **19.2–270.1**
Theft, evidence, **19.2–270.1**
Trial, crimes and offenses, **19.2–266**
Video Images, generally, this index

PHRASES
Words and Phrases, generally, this index

PHYSICIANS AND SURGEONS
Controlled Substances, generally, this index
Drugs and Medicine, generally, this index
Evidence, crimes and offenses, transplants, **19.2–188.2**
Psychiatrists and Psychiatry, generally, this index
Psychologists and Psychology, generally, this index
Wiretapping, damages, **19.2–69**

PICKUP TRUCKS
Motor Vehicles, generally, this index

PICTURES
Photography and Pictures, generally, this index

PISTOLS
Weapons, generally, this index

PLEADINGS
Motions, generally, this index

PLEAS
Crimes and Offenses, this index
Guilty Pleas, generally, this index

POLES AND WIRES
Wiretapping, generally, this index

POLICE
See, also, Law Enforcement Officers, generally, this index
Aliens, arrest, powers and duties, **19.2–81.6, 19.2–82**
Arrest, generally, this index
Close pursuit, fleeing or attempting to elude, **19.2–77**
Foreign states, **19.2–79**
Criminal history record information, reports, **19.2–390**
Escape, arrest, **19.2–77**
Extradition, generally, this index
Fleeing or attempting to elude, pursuit, **19.2–77**
Foreign states, **19.2–79**
Foreign states, pursuit, **19.2–79**
Highway Patrol, generally, this index
Lineups, policies, writing, **19.2–390.02**
Powers and duties, aliens, arrest, **19.2–81.6, 19.2–82**
Pursuit, fleeing or attempting to elude, **19.2–77**
Foreign states, **19.2–79**
Records and recordation, expungement, **19.2–327.5, 19.2–327.13, 19.2–392.2**
Reports, criminal history record information, **19.2–390**
Searches and Seizures, generally, this index
Sheriffs, generally, this index
State police. Highway Patrol, generally, this index
Subpoenas, issuance, **19.2–73.2**
Traffic Rules and Regulations, generally, this index

POLITICAL SUBDIVISIONS
Counties, generally, this index
Municipalities, generally, this index

POLITICAL SUBDIVISIONS—Cont'd
Real Property Taxation, generally, this index
Taxation. Real Property Taxation, generally, this index

POLLUTION
Hazardous Substances and Waste, generally, this index

POLYGRAPH TESTS
Witnesses, crime victims, notice, **19.2–9.1**

POOR PERSONS
Indigent Persons, generally, this index

POPULAR NAME LAWS
Criminal Extradition Act, **19.2–85 et seq.**
Megans Law, sex offender registration, **19.2–390.1**
Twenty one day rule, actual innocence, writs, nonbiological evidence, **19.2–327.10 et seq.**
Uniform Act to Secure the Attendance of Witnesses from Without a State in Criminal Proceedings, **19.2–272 et seq.**

PORNOGRAPHY
Obscenity, generally, this index

POSTRELEASE SUPERVISION
Parole, generally, this index

POSTSECONDARY EDUCATION
Colleges and Universities, generally, this index

PRACTICE OF LAW
Attorneys, generally, this index

PREACHERS
Clergy, generally, this index

PRESUMPTIONS
Evidence, this index

PRETRIAL RELEASE
Bail, generally, this index

PRIESTS
Clergy, generally, this index

PRIMA FACIE EVIDENCE
Evidence, generally, this index

PRIORITIES AND PREFERENCES
Criminal insanity, commitment, acquittal, **19.2–182.3, 19.2–182.5**

PRISONS AND PRISONERS
Correctional Institutions, generally, this index
Jails, generally, this index

PRIVACY
Confidential or Privileged Information, generally, this index

PRIVILEGED COMMUNICATIONS
Confidential or Privileged Information, generally, this index

PRIVILEGED INFORMATION
Confidential or Privileged Information, generally, this index

PRIVILEGES AND IMMUNITIES
Blood, samples, searches and seizures, warrants, **19.2–53.1**
Clergy, witnesses, **19.2–271.3**
Confidential or Privileged Information, generally, this index
Conservators of the peace, **19.2–13**
Crimes and Offenses, this index
Critical incident stress management teams, emergency medical services, **19.2–271.4**
Protective orders, registry, **19.2–387.1**

PROBABLE CAUSE
Boats and boating, searches and seizures, **19.2–10.3**
Protective orders, violations, arrest, **19.2–81.3**
Real time location data entry, searches and seizures, warrants, **19.2–70.3**
Searches and Seizures, this index
Ships and shipping, searches and seizures, noncommercial vessels, **19.2–10.3**

PROBATION
See, also, Parole, generally, this index
Generally, **19.2–303 et seq.**
Boot camps, **19.2–316.1**
Community service, **19.2–305, 19.2–305.1**
Conditions, **19.2–305 et seq.**
Community based probation, **19.2–303.3**
Fines and penalties, **19.2–356**
Costs, **19.2–303.3, 19.2–303.4**
Condition, supervision, **19.2–305**
Criminal history record information,
Disclosure, **19.2–389**
Violations, reports, **19.2–390**
Detention center incarceration program, **19.2–316.2**
Disclosure, criminal history record information, **19.2–389**
Diversion centers, **19.2–316.3**
Evidence, immediate sanction probation program, noncompliance letters, **19.2–303.5**
Expenses and expenditures, **19.2–303.3, 19.2–303.4**
Fees, condition, supervision, **19.2–305**
Fines and penalties, conditions, **19.2–356**
Supervision, **19.2–305**
Gangs, **19.2–303**
Hearings,
Immediate sanction probation program, **19.2–303.5**
Revocation or suspension, **19.2–304, 19.2–306**
Immediate sanction probation program, **19.2–303.5**
Indeterminate commitment, **19.2–311 et seq.**
Installments, fines and penalties, **19.2–356**
Intractable behavior, revocation or suspension, **19.2–303.3**
Investigations and investigators, **19.2–299**
Noncompliance letters, immediate sanction probation program, evidence, **19.2–303.5**

PROBATION—Cont'd
Records and recordation, Virginia Crime Code references, **19.2–390.01**
Reports,
Criminal history record information, violations, **19.2–390**
Investigations and investigators, **19.2–299**
Restitution, conditions, **19.2–305 et seq., 19.2–356**
Revocation or suspension, **19.2–304, 19.2–306**
Community based probation, **19.2–303.3**
Immediate sanction probation program, **19.2–303.5**
Intractable behavior, **19.2–303.3**
Screening, community based probation, substance abuse, **19.2–299.2**
Supervision, **19.2–295.2**
Indeterminate commitment, **19.2–314**
Support, conditions, **19.2–305**
Suspended sentences, **19.2–303 et seq.**
Immediate sanction probation program, **19.2–303.5**
Time, **19.2–295.2**

PROBATION OFFICERS
Presentence investigations, **19.2–299**
Reports, presentence investigations, **19.2–299**

PROCESS
Executions, generally, this index
Indictment and information, **19.2–217, 19.2–232 et seq.**
Probation, revocation, **19.2–306**
Service of process,
Extradition, **19.2–113**
Indictment and information, **19.2–232 et seq.**
Probation, revocation, **19.2–306**
Suspended sentence, revocation, **19.2–306**
Subpoenas, generally, this index
Summons, generally, this index

PRODUCTION OF BOOKS AND PAPERS
Banks and banking, records and recordation, **19.2–10.1**
Credit, reports, records and recordation, **19.2–10.1**
Credit cards, records and recordation, **19.2–10.1**
Credit unions, records and recordation, **19.2–10.1**
Crime victims, compensation and salaries, **19.2–368.3**
Financial institutions, records and recordation, **19.2–10.1**
Grand jury,
Multijurisdiction grand juries, **19.2–215.5**
Special grand juries, **19.2–208**
Money, transmitters, **19.2–10.1**
Trust companies, records and recordation, **19.2–10.1**

PROFANITY
Obscenity, generally, this index

PROFESSIONS AND OCCUPATIONS
Attorneys, generally, this index

PROFESSIONS AND OCCUPATIONS—Cont'd
Counselors and Counseling, generally, this index
Crimes and offenses, limitation of prosecutions, **19.2–8**
Health Care Professionals, generally, this index
Licenses and permits, limitation of prosecutions, **19.2–8**
Limitation of prosecutions, **19.2–8**
Police, generally, this index
Psychiatrists and Psychiatry, generally, this index
Psychologists and Psychology, generally, this index

PROMISSORY NOTES
Negotiable Instruments, generally, this index

PROOF
Evidence, generally, this index

PROPERTY
Executions, generally, this index

PROSECUTING ATTORNEYS
Absence and absentees, **19.2–156**
Adverse or pecuniary interest, disqualification, **19.2–155**
Conservators of the peace, **19.2–12 et seq.**
Disability, disqualification, **19.2–155**
Discovery, powers and duties, **19.2–265.4**
Disqualification, **19.2–155**
Federal courts, removal or transfer of causes, **19.2–9**
Fees, **19.2–333**
Fines and penalties, collection, **19.2–349**
Grand juries,
  Multijurisdiction grand juries, **19.2–215.10**
  Special grand juries, **19.2–210**
Multijurisdiction grand juries, **19.2–215.10**
Special grand juries, **19.2–210**
Substitution, temporary disability, **19.2–155**
Wiretapping, applications, **19.2–66**

PROSECUTION
Crimes and Offenses, generally, this index

PROSTITUTION
Forfeitures, searches and seizures, **19.2–386.35**
Motor vehicles, children and minors, forfeitures, **19.2–386.16**
Searches and seizures, forfeitures, **19.2–386.35**

PROTECTIVE ORDERS
  Generally, **19.2–152.7:1 et seq.**
Arrest, violations, **19.2–81.3**
Assault and battery, **19.2–152.7:1 et seq.**
Attorney fees, respondent, **19.2–152.12**
Guardian ad litem, compensation and salaries, **19.2–152.12**
Maiming, **19.2–152.7:1 et seq.**
Personal injuries, **19.2–152.7:1 et seq.**
Privileges and immunities, registry, **19.2–387.1**
Probable cause, violations, arrest, **19.2–81.3**
Registry, **19.2–387.1**

PROTECTIVE ORDERS—Cont'd
Sex offenses, **19.2–152.7:1 et seq.**
Stalking, **19.2–152.7:1 et seq.**
Venue, **19.2–152.11**

PSYCHIATRISTS AND PSYCHIATRY
Capital punishment, opinion and expert testimony, **19.2–264.3:1**
  Mentally retarded and developmentally disabled persons, **19.2–264.3:1.2**
Criminal insanity, opinion and expert testimony, **19.2–175**

PSYCHOLOGISTS AND PSYCHOLOGY
Capital punishment, opinion and expert testimony, **19.2–264.3:1**
  Mentally retarded and developmentally disabled persons, **19.2–264.3:1.2**
Criminal insanity, opinion and expert testimony, **19.2–175**
Wiretapping, damages, **19.2–69**

PUBLIC ASSISTANCE
Social Services, generally, this index

PUBLIC DEFENDERS
  Generally, **19.2–163.01 et seq., 19.2–163.3 et seq.**
Appeals in criminal prosecutions, **19.2–163.3**
Attorney fees, conviction of crime, costs, taxation, **19.2–163.4:1**
Attorney general, legal services, **19.2–163.5**
Capital punishment, **19.2–163.7**
Compensation and salaries, supplementing, **19.2–163.01:1**
Continuing education, **19.2–163.01**
Lists, capital punishment, **19.2–163.8**
Offices, **19.2–163.04**
Powers and duties, **19.2–163.3**
Right to counsel, pretrial services, officers and employees, powers and duties, **19.2–152.4:3**
Standards, capital punishment, **19.2–163.8**
Training, **19.2–163.01**

PUBLIC OFFICERS AND EMPLOYEES
Bonds (Officers and Fiduciaries), generally, this index
Police, generally, this index
School Officers and Employees, generally, this index

PUBLIC RECORDS
Records and Recordation, generally, this index

PUBLIC SCHOOLS
Schools and School Districts, generally, this index

PUBLIC UTILITIES
Telecommunications, generally, this index

PUBLIC WELFARE
Social Services, generally, this index

PUPILS
Schools and School Districts, generally, this index

QUESTIONS OF LAW AND FACT
Jury, generally, this index
Trial, generally, this index

RABBIS
Clergy, generally, this index

RAILROADS
Taxation. Real Property Taxation, generally, this index

RAPE
Sex Offenses, generally, this index

REAL ESTATE
Crimes and offenses, burden of proof, **19.2–284**
Money laundering, forfeitures, **19.2–386.19**
Taxation. Real Property Taxation, generally, this index

REAL ESTATE BROKERS AND SALESPERSONS
Criminal history record information, licenses and permits, **19.2–389**
Licenses and permits, criminal history record information, **19.2–389**

REAL PROPERTY TAXATION
Crimes and offenses,
  Limitation of prosecutions, **19.2–8**
  Venue, **19.2–245.2**
Limitation of prosecutions, **19.2–8**
Venue, crimes and offenses, **19.2–245.2**

REAL TIME LOCATION DATA
Telecommunications, records and recordation, disclosure, **19.2–70.3**

RECOGNIZANCE
Bail, generally, this index

RECORDINGS
Video Images, generally, this index

RECORDS AND RECORDATION
Central criminal records exchange, **19.2–387 et seq.**
Confidential or Privileged Information, generally, this index
Courts, this index
Crime victims, compensation and salaries, **19.2–368.14**
Crimes and Offenses, this index
Criminal History Record Information, generally, this index
Delinquent Children, this index
Documentary evidence. Evidence, generally, this index
Falsifying patient records, crimes and offenses, limitation of prosecutions, **19.2–8**
Grand jury, examinations and examiners, **19.2–207**
Police, this index
Production of Books and Papers, generally, this index

RECORDS AND RECORDATION—Cont'd
Searches and seizures, warrants, **19.2–53**
Telecommunications, this index
Transcripts, generally, this index

RECREATION AND RECREATIONAL AREAS
Fish and Game, generally, this index

REFORMATORIES
Correctional Institutions, generally, this index

REGISTERS AND REGISTRIES
Child pornography, **19.2–390.3**
Criminal history record information, **19.2–390**
Obscenity, child pornography, **19.2–390.3**
Protective orders, **19.2–387.1**

REGISTRATION
Special conservators of the peace, **19.2–13**

REGISTRIES
Registers and Registries, generally, this index

RELEASE
Bail, generally, this index
Crimes and Offenses, this index
Parole, generally, this index

RELIGION
Clergy, generally, this index

RELIGIOUS ORGANIZATIONS AND SOCIETIES
Clergy, generally, this index

REMOTE COMPUTING SERVICES
Computers, this index

REMOVAL OR TRANSFER OF CAUSES
  See, also, Venue, generally, this index
Crimes and offenses, federal courts, **19.2–9**

REMUNERATION
Compensation and Salaries, generally, this index

REPARATION
Restitution, generally, this index

REPORTS
Capital punishment,
  Mentally ill persons, evaluations, **19.2–264.3:1**
  Mentally retarded and developmentally disabled persons, evaluations, **19.2–264.3:1.2**
Crimes and Offenses, this index
Criminal history record information, **19.2–390**
Criminal Insanity, this index
Indigent defense commission, **19.2–163.01**

RESCUE SQUADS
Emergency Medical Services, generally, this index

RESIDENT ALIENS
Aliens, generally, this index

RESTITUTION
  Generally, **19.2–305 et seq.**

RESTITUTION—Cont'd
Appeals in criminal prosecutions, state, **19.2–398**
Capitol square, damages, **19.2–305.1**
Criminal injuries compensation fund, **19.2–305.1**
Default, **19.2–358**
Delinquencies,
  Installments, **19.2–354 et seq.**
  Reports, **19.2–349**
Dockets and docketing, **19.2–305.2**
Indigent persons, **19.2–355**
Installments, **19.2–354 et seq.**
Interest, **19.2–305.4**
Judgments and decrees, **19.2–305.2**
Motor vehicles department, collection, fees, **19.2–349.1**
Payment, installments, **19.2–354 et seq.**
Probation, conditions, **19.2–305 et seq., 19.2–356**
Suspended sentences, **19.2–303**

RETARDED PERSONS
Mentally Retarded and Developmentally Disabled Persons, generally, this index

REVIEW
Appeal and Review, generally, this index

REWARDS
Crimes and offenses, **19.2–7**

RIFLES
Weapons, generally, this index

RIGHT TO COUNSEL
Attorneys, this index

RIOTS AND MOBS
Limitation of prosecutions, **19.2–243**

RIVERS AND STREAMS
Fish and Game, generally, this index

ROBBERY
Life imprisonment, three strikes, **19.2–297.1**
Second and subsequent offenses, sentencing, **19.2–297.1**
Three strikes, sentencing, **19.2–297.1**

SAILBOATS
Boats and Boating, generally, this index

SAILORS
Military Forces, generally, this index

SALARIES
Compensation and Salaries, generally, this index

SALES
Crimes and offenses. Fraud, generally, this index
Forfeitures, this index

SATELLITE TRACKING
Global Positioning Systems, generally, this index

SAVINGS AND LOAN ASSOCIATIONS
Production of books and papers, **19.2–10.1**

SAVINGS AND LOAN ASSOCIATIONS—Cont'd
Records and recordation, production of books and papers, **19.2–10.1**

SAVINGS BANKS
Production of books and papers, **19.2–10.1**

SCHEMES
Fraud, generally, this index

SCHOOL OFFICERS AND EMPLOYEES
Arrest, reports, **19.2–83.1**
Crimes and offenses, arrest, reports, **19.2–83.1**
Criminal history record information, disclosure, **19.2–389**
Instructional personnel. Schoolteachers, generally, this index
Reports, arrest, **19.2–83.1**
Schoolteachers, generally, this index
Teachers. Schoolteachers, generally, this index

SCHOOLS AND SCHOOL DISTRICTS
Adults, arrest, reports, **19.2–83.1**
Age, arrest, reports, **19.2–83.1**
Arrest,
  Reports, **19.2–83.1**
  Weapons, **19.2–81**
Colleges and Universities, generally, this index
Continuing Education, generally, this index
Employees. School Officers and Employees, generally, this index
Instructional personnel. Schoolteachers, generally, this index
Labor and employment. School Officers and Employees, generally, this index
Officers and employees. School Officers and Employees, generally, this index
Reports, arrest, **19.2–83.1**
Schoolteachers, generally, this index
Sex offenses, registration, proof, nonresidents, **19.2–298**
Teachers. Schoolteachers, generally, this index
Weapons, arrest, **19.2–81**

SCHOOLTEACHERS
Arrest, reports, **19.2–83.1**
Crimes and offenses, arrest, reports, **19.2–83.1**
Reports,
  Arrest, **19.2–83.1**
  Sex offenses, **19.2–291.1**
Sex offenses, reports, **19.2–291.1**

SEARCHES AND SEIZURES
Affidavits, warrants, **19.2–52, 19.2–54**
  Tracking devices, **19.2–56.2**
Appeals in criminal prosecutions, state, **19.2–398**
Attorneys, warrants, **19.2–56.1**
Blood, samples, warrants, privileges and immunities, **19.2–53.1**
Boats and boating, probable cause, **19.2–10.3**
Body cavity searches, **19.2–59.1**
Body fluids, warrants, **19.2–53**

SEARCHES AND SEIZURES—Cont'd
Bonds (officers and fiduciaries), possession, **19.2–386.6**
Certificates and certification, warrants, affidavits, **19.2–54**
  Tracking devices, **19.2–56.2**
Complaints, warrants, **19.2–52**
Computers, **19.2–53**
  Real time location data, records and recordation, **19.2–70.3**
Confidential or privileged information, warrants, attorneys, **19.2–56.1**
Controlled Substances, this index
Damages, warrantless searches, **19.2–59**
Description, warrants, **19.2–54**
Disposition, personal property, **19.2–58**
Drones, unmanned aircraft, warrants, **19.2–60.1**
Drug paraphernalia, **19.2–386.23, 19.2–386.26**
Electronic communications, warrants, **19.2–56, 19.2–70.3**
  Affidavits, **19.2–54**
Evidence,
  Official records, affidavits, **19.2–188.3**
  Suppression, **19.2–60**
    Unmanned aircraft, warrants, **19.2–60.1**
  Warrants, **19.2–54**
Executions, warrants, **19.2–57**
Exemptions, **19.2–386.8**
Extortion, forfeitures, **19.2–386.35**
Facsimile transmissions, warrants, affidavits, **19.2–54**
Fines and penalties, warrantless searches, **19.2–59**
Gender, strip searches, **19.2–59.1**
Global positioning systems,
  Tracking devices, warrants, **19.2–56.2**
  Warrants, **19.2–70.3**
Health and sanitation, body cavity searches, **19.2–59.1**
In camera proceedings, warrants, attorneys, **19.2–56.1**
Internet, real time location data, records and recordation, confidential or privileged information, **19.2–70.3**
Inventories,
  Terrorism, **19.2–386.2**
  Warrants, **19.2–56 et seq.**
Kidnapping, forfeitures, **19.2–386.35**
Liens and incumbrances, **19.2–386.9**
Magistrates, warrants, **19.2–45**
Mail and mailing, warrants, affidavits, **19.2–54**
Money, disposition, **19.2–270.2**
Money laundering, **19.2–386.19**
Motions, suppression, **19.2–60**
Notice, **19.2–386.3**
Oaths and affirmations, warrants, **19.2–52**
Obscenity, sexually explicit items involving children, **19.2–386.31**
Perishable property, sales, **19.2–386.7**
Probable cause,
  Real time location data entry, warrants, **19.2–70.3**

SEARCHES AND SEIZURES—Cont'd
Probable cause—Cont'd
  Tracking devices, warrants, **19.2–56.2**
  Warrants, **19.2–52**
Prostitution, forfeitures, **19.2–386.35**
Real time location data, telecommunications, records and recordation, disclosure, **19.2–70.3**
Records and recordation, warrants, **19.2–53**
Release, **19.2–386.5**
Remote computing services, warrants, **19.2–56**
Reports, **19.2–386.4**
Return, seized property, **19.2–60**
Sales, **19.2–386.11, 19.2–386.12**
  Perishable property, **19.2–386.7**
Securities, disposition, **19.2–270.2**
Service of process, **19.2–386.3**
Sex offenses, forfeitures, **19.2–386.35**
Ships and shipping, probable cause, noncommercial vessels, **19.2–10.3**
Software and electronic data, **19.2–53**
State, appeal and review, **19.2–398**
Stolen property, warrants, **19.2–53**
Strip searches, **19.2–59.1**
Suppression, **19.2–60**
  State, appeal and review, **19.2–398**
  Unmanned aircraft, warrants, **19.2–60.1**
Time, warrants, **19.2–56**
Title to property, **19.2–386.9**
Tracking devices, warrants, **19.2–56.2**
Unmanned aircraft, warrants, **19.2–60.1**
Warrantless searches, **19.2–59**
Warrants, **19.2–52 et seq., 19.2–386.2**
  Affidavits, **19.2–52, 19.2–54**
    Tracking devices, **19.2–56.2**
  Blood, samples, privileges and immunities, **19.2–53.1**
  Books and papers, **19.2–53**
  Drones, unmanned aircraft, **19.2–60.1**
  Execution, **19.2–57**
  Magistrates, **19.2–45**
  Real time location data, records and recordation, telecommunications, **19.2–70.3**
  Remote computing services, foreign states, records and recordation, **19.2–70.3**
  Telecommunications, foreign states, records and recordation, **19.2–70.3**
  Tracking devices, **19.2–56.2**
  Unmanned aircraft, **19.2–60.1**
Wiretapping, devices, **19.2–64**

SECOND AND SUBSEQUENT OFFENSES
Crimes and Offenses, this index

SECRETS AND SECRECY
Confidential or Privileged Information, generally, this index

SECURE THE ATTENDANCE OF WITNESSES FROM WITHOUT A STATE IN CRIMINAL PROCEEDINGS ACT
Generally, **19.2–272 et seq.**

SECURITIES
Crimes and offenses, evidence, disposition, **19.2–270.2**
Evidence, disposition, **19.2–270.2**
Searches and seizures, disposition, **19.2–270.2**

SECURITY
See, also, Bonds (Officers and Fiduciaries), generally, this index
Bail, generally, this index

SEIZURES
Searches and Seizures, generally, this index

SELF INCRIMINATION
Criminal insanity, treatment, **19.2–169.7**
Grand jury, multijurisdiction grand juries, **19.2–215.7**
Presumptions, **19.2–268**
Waiver, **19.2–268**

SENTENCE AND PUNISHMENT
Crimes and Offenses, generally, this index

SEPTEMBER 11 TERRORIST ATTACK
Terrorism, generally, this index

SERVICE OF PROCESS
Process, this index

SEX OFFENDERS AND CRIMES AGAINST MINORS REGISTRY
See, also, Sex Offenses, generally, this index
Generally, **19.2–390.1**

SEX OFFENSES
Appeals in criminal prosecutions, crime victims, names, confidential or privileged information, **19.2–11.2**
Arrest, DNA, violent felonies, samples, **19.2–310.2:1, 19.2–310.3:1**
Children and minors,
Conviction of crime, registration, **19.2–390.1**
Obscenity, this index
Complaints, corroborating testimony, **19.2–268.2**
Confidential or privileged information, crime victims, **19.2–11.2**
Corroborating testimony, complaints, **19.2–268.2**
Crime victims, **19.2–11.01**
Compensation and salaries,
Limitation of actions, **19.2–368.5**
Reconsideration, **19.2–368.8**
Confidential or privileged information, **19.2–11.2**
Medical care and treatment, evidence, expenses and expenditures, **19.2–165.1**
Polygraph examinations, notice, **19.2–9.1**
Criminal history record information,
Registration, **19.2–390, 19.2–390.1**
Sentencing, **19.2–299**
DNA, violent felonies, samples, **19.2–310.2:1, 19.2–310.3:1**
Domicile and residence, proof, nonresidents, **19.2–298**

SEX OFFENSES—Cont'd
Evidence, medical care and treatment, expenses and expenditures, **19.2–165.1, 19.2–368.11:1**
Rates and charges, **19.2–368.3**
Examinations and examiners, mentally ill persons, sentencing, **19.2–300 et seq.**
Extension, protective orders, **19.2–152.10**
Forfeitures, searches and seizures, **19.2–386.35**
Guidelines, sentencing, **19.2–298.01**
Husband and Wife, this index
Identity and identification, crime victims, **19.2–11.2**
Investigations and investigators, sentencing, **19.2–299**
Life imprisonment, three strikes, **19.2–297.1**
Limitation of actions, crime victims, compensation and salaries, **19.2–368.5**
Reconsideration, **19.2–368.8**
Medical care and treatment, evidence, expenses and expenditures, **19.2–165.1, 19.2–368.11:1**
Rates and charges, **19.2–368.3**
Mental examinations, sentencing, **19.2–300 et seq.**
Mentally ill persons, examinations and examiners, sentencing, **19.2–300 et seq.**
Names, crime victims, appeals in criminal prosecutions, confidential or privileged information, **19.2–11.2**
Nonresidents, registration, **19.2–298**
Notice, registration, **19.2–390.1**
Obscenity, generally, this index
Polygraph examinations, crime victims, notice, **19.2–9.1**
Pornography. Obscenity, generally, this index
Presentence investigations, **19.2–299**
Prostitution, generally, this index
Protective orders, **19.2–152.7:1 et seq.**
Psychiatrists and psychiatry, tests and testing, confidential or privileged information, **19.2–301**
Registration, **19.2–390.1**
Postrelease supervision, **19.2–295.2:1**
Searches and seizures, forfeitures, **19.2–386.35**
Second and subsequent offenses, sentencing, **19.2–297.1**
Sentencing,
Guidelines, **19.2–298.01**
Mental examinations, **19.2–300 et seq.**
Social workers, tests and testing, confidential or privileged information, **19.2–301**
Supervision, registration, postrelease supervision, **19.2–295.2:1**
Three strikes, sentencing, **19.2–297.1**
Time, complaints, corroborating testimony, **19.2–268.2**
Witnesses, husband and wife, **19.2–271.2**

SHARES AND SHAREHOLDERS
Securities, generally, this index

SHERIFFS
Arrest, generally, this index
Close pursuit, fleeing or attempting to elude, **19.2–77**

SHERIFFS—Cont'd
Criminal history record information, reports, **19.2–390**
Escape, arrest, **19.2–77**
Executions, generally, this index
Fines and penalties,
Failure to pay, **19.2–352**
Process, **19.2–350**
Fleeing or attempting to elude, pursuit, **19.2–77**
Jails, generally, this index
Process, generally, this index
Pursuit, fleeing or attempting to elude, **19.2–77**
Reports, criminal history record information, **19.2–390**
Searches and Seizures, generally, this index
Service of process. Process, this index

SHIPS AND SHIPPING
See, also, Boats and Boating, generally, this index
Boarding, searches and seizures, noncommercial vessels, **19.2–10.3**
Criminal history record information, shipyards, disclosure, **19.2–389**
Inspection and inspectors, searches and seizures, noncommercial vessels, **19.2–10.3**
Probable cause, searches and seizures, noncommercial vessels, **19.2–10.3**
Searches and seizures, probable cause, noncommercial vessels, **19.2–10.3**

SHIPYARDS
Criminal history record information, disclosure, **19.2–389**

SHOPLIFTING
See, also, Theft, generally, this index
Arrest, **19.2–81**
Evidence, photography and pictures, **19.2–270.1**
Photography and pictures, evidence, **19.2–270.1**

SHORT TITLES
Popular Name Laws, generally, this index

SHOTGUNS
Weapons, generally, this index

SIGNATURES
Forgery, generally, this index

SLINGSHOTS
Weapons, generally, this index

SOCIAL MEDIA
Internet, generally, this index
Telecommunications, generally, this index

SOCIAL SERVICES
Abuse. Child Abuse, generally, this index
Adoption, generally, this index
Adult services, criminal history record information, disclosure, **19.2–389**
Child Abuse, generally, this index
Children and minors. Adoption, generally, this index

SOCIAL SERVICES—Cont'd
Crime victims, **19.2–11.01**
Criminal history record information, officers and employees, **19.2–389**
Home based services, criminal history record information, disclosure, **19.2–389**
Medical assistance, transportation, criminal history record information, disclosure, **19.2–389**
Officers and employees, criminal history record information, **19.2–389**
Witnesses, **19.2–11.01**

SOCIAL WORKERS
Wiretapping, damages, **19.2–69**

SOFTWARE AND ELECTRONIC DATA
See, also,
Internet, generally, this index
Computers, generally, this index
Financial institutions, production of books and papers, records and recordation, **19.2–10.1**
Searches and seizures, **19.2–53**

SOLDIERS AND SAILORS
Military Forces, generally, this index

SOLICITATION
Prostitution, generally, this index

SOLICITORS
Attorneys, generally, this index

SOLID WASTE
Hazardous Substances and Waste, generally, this index

SPECIAL CONSERVATORS OF THE PEACE
Registration, **19.2–13**

SPEEDY TRIAL
Generally, **19.2–241 et seq.**
Appeals in criminal prosecutions, state, **19.2–398**
Defenses, motions, time, **19.2–266.2**

SPOUSE ABUSE
Domestic Violence, generally, this index

SPOUSES
Domestic Violence, generally, this index
Husband and Wife, generally, this index

STALKING
Arrest, **19.2–81.3**
Attorney fees, protective orders, **19.2–152.10**
Criminal history record information, sentencing, **19.2–299**
Presentence investigations, **19.2–299**
Protective orders, **19.2–152.8 et seq.**

STANDARDS
Attorneys, indigent defense, appointment, **19.2–163.01, 19.2–163.03**

STATE
Appeals in criminal prosecutions, **19.2–398 et seq.**

STATE—Cont'd
Attorney General, generally, this index
Attorneys,
  Attorney General, generally, this index
  Prosecuting Attorneys, generally, this index
Briefs, appeals in criminal prosecutions, **19.2–402, 19.2–403**
Correctional Institutions, generally, this index
Crimes and offenses, appeals in criminal prosecutions, **19.2–398 et seq.**
Foreign States, generally, this index
Highway Patrol, generally, this index
Limitation of actions,
  Appeal and review, **19.2–400**
  Appeals in criminal prosecutions, **19.2–400**
Police. Highway Patrol, generally, this index
Prosecuting Attorneys, generally, this index
Social Services, generally, this index
Transcripts, appeals in criminal prosecutions, **19.2–405**
Venue, appeals in criminal prosecutions, **19.2–400**

STATE AGENCIES
Criminal history record information, labor and employment, **19.2–389**
Labor and employment, criminal history record information, **19.2–389**
Motor Vehicles Department, generally, this index

STATE CAPITOL
Capitol square, damages, restitution, evidence, **19.2–305.1**

STATE DEPARTMENTS
Motor Vehicles Department, generally, this index

STATE OFFICERS AND EMPLOYEES
Attorney General, generally, this index
Criminal history record information, disclosure, **19.2–389**
Highway Patrol, generally, this index
Law enforcement officers, fines and penalties, literary fund, credits, **19.2–340.1**
Police. Highway Patrol, generally, this index

STATE POLICE
Highway Patrol, generally, this index

STATUTE OF LIMITATIONS
Limitation of Actions, generally, this index
Limitation of Prosecutions, generally, this index

STATUTES
Popular Name Laws, generally, this index

STAY
Supersedeas or Stay, generally, this index

STEALING
Embezzlement, generally, this index
Robbery, generally, this index
Theft, generally, this index

STOLEN PROPERTY
Robbery, generally, this index

STOLEN PROPERTY—Cont'd
Searches and seizures, warrants, **19.2–53**

STORAGE
Searches and seizures, **19.2–386.4**
  Personal property, **19.2–58**

STORES
Shoplifting, generally, this index

STRANGULATION
Bail, **19.2–120**

STREET GANGS
Gangs, generally, this index

STREETS AND ALLEYS
Traffic Rules and Regulations, generally, this index

STRIP SEARCHES
Generally, **19.2–59.1**

STUDENTS
Colleges and Universities, generally, this index
Schools and School Districts, generally, this index

STUN WEAPONS
Forfeitures, **19.2–386.28**

SUBPOENA DUCES TECUM
Production of Books and Papers, generally, this index

SUBPOENAS
Books and papers. Production of Books and Papers, generally, this index
Computers, crimes and offenses, records and recordation, investigations and investigators, **19.2–10.2**
Crimes and offenses, **19.2–73.2**
  Electronic format, information, **19.2–267.2**
Documents. Production of Books and Papers, generally, this index
Electronic mail, crimes and offenses, records and recordation, investigations and investigators, **19.2–10.2**
Grand jury,
  Multijurisdiction grand juries, **19.2–215.5**
  Special grand juries, **19.2–208**
Police, issuance, **19.2–73.2**
Production of Books and Papers, generally, this index
Real time location data, telecommunications, records and recordation, disclosure, **19.2–70.3**
Remote computing services, crimes and offenses, records and recordation, investigations and investigators, **19.2–10.2**

SUBROGATION
Crime victims, compensation and salaries, **19.2–368.15**

SUBSTANCE ABUSE
Chemically Dependent Persons, generally, this index

SUBSTANCE ABUSE—Cont'd
Controlled Substances, generally, this index

SUMMONS
Arrest, release, **19.2–74**
Crimes and Offenses, this index
Grand jury, **19.2–194**
Indictment and information, **19.2–219, 19.2–232 et seq.**
  Corporations, **19.2–238**
Witnesses, this index

SUPERSEDEAS OR STAY
  Generally, **19.2–322.1**
Bail, appeals in criminal prosecutions, **19.2–124, 19.2–132**
Capital punishment, appeals in criminal prosecutions, **19.2–319**
Crime victims, compensation and salaries, medical care and treatment, collections, **19.2–368.5:2**

SUPPORT
Probation, conditions, **19.2–305**

SUPPRESSION
Evidence, this index

SUPREME COURT
Appeals in criminal prosecutions, delayed appeals, motions, **19.2–321.2**

SURETIES AND SURETYSHIP
Bail, generally, this index
Bonds (Officers and Fiduciaries), generally, this index
Official bonds. Bonds (Officers and Fiduciaries), generally, this index

SURETY BAIL BONDSPERSONS
  See, also, Bail, this index
Discharge, **19.2–149**

SURVEILLANCE
Wiretapping, generally, this index

SWEARING
Oaths and Affirmations, generally, this index

SWINDLING
Embezzlement, generally, this index
Fraud, generally, this index
Theft, generally, this index

SWORN STATEMENTS
Oaths and Affirmations, generally, this index

SYNTHETIC CANNABINOIDS
Inventories, searches and seizures, law enforcement agencies, **19.2–386.23**

TAKING
Fish and Game, generally, this index

TAPE AND SOUND RECORDINGS
Appearance, crimes and offenses, **19.2–3.1**
Video Images, generally, this index

TAXATION
Cigarette Tax, generally, this index
Crimes and offenses, venue, **19.2–245.2**
Real Property Taxation, generally, this index
Venue, crimes and offenses, **19.2–245.2**

TEACHERS
Schoolteachers, generally, this index

TEAR GAS
Weapons, generally, this index

TELECOMMUNICATIONS
Computers, generally, this index
Confidential or privileged information. Wiretapping, generally, this index
Crimes and offenses,
  Appearance, video and audio communications, **19.2–3.1**
  Records and recordation, subpoenas, investigations and investigators, **19.2–10.2**
Disclosure, records and recordation, **19.2–70.3**
Eavesdropping. Wiretapping, generally, this index
Evidence, hearsay, exceptions, **19.2–70.3**
Foreign corporations, records and recordation, disclosure, **19.2–70.3**
Foreign states, records and recordation, searches and seizures, warrants, **19.2–70.3**
Forfeitures, devices, **19.2–386.18**
Interception of private communications. Wiretapping, generally, this index
Internet, generally, this index
Numbers and numbering, stalking, protective orders, confidential or privileged information, **19.2–152.8 et seq.**
Privileges and immunities, records and recordation, disclosure, **19.2–70.3**
Protective orders, confidential or privileged information, **19.2–152.8 et seq.**
Real time location data, records and recordation, disclosure, **19.2–70.3**
Records and recordation,
  Crimes and offenses, subpoenas, investigations and investigators, **19.2–10.2**
  Disclosure, **19.2–70.3**
  Subpoenas, **19.2–70.3**
Remote computing services, records and recordation, disclosure, **19.2–70.3**
Searches and seizures,
  Records and recordation, **19.2–70.3**
  Warrants, **19.2–56**
Subpoenas,
  Crimes and offenses, investigations and investigators, **19.2–10.2**
  Records and recordation, **19.2–70.3**
Warrants, searches and seizures, real time location data, records and recordation, **19.2–70.3**
Wiretapping, generally, this index

TELEPHONES
Telecommunications, generally, this index

TELEVISION AND RADIO
Crimes and offenses, trial, **19.2–266**

TELEVISION AND RADIO—Cont'd
Trial, crimes and offenses, **19.2–266**
Video Images, generally, this index

TERRORISM
Bail, **19.2–120**
Forfeitures, **19.2–386.15**
 Inventories, **19.2–386.2**
Searches and seizures, **19.2–386.15**
 Inventories, **19.2–386.2**

TESTIMONY
Evidence, generally, this index
Witnesses, generally, this index

TESTS AND TESTING
Blood Tests, generally, this index

THEFT
Arrest, DNA, violent felonies, samples, **19.2–310.2:1, 19.2–310.3:1**
Burden of proof, **19.2–284**
Conviction of crime, **19.2–289, 19.2–290**
DNA, violent felonies, samples, **19.2–310.2:1, 19.2–310.3:1**
Embezzlement, generally, this index
Evidence,
 Burden of proof, **19.2–284**
 Moneys or securities, disposition, **19.2–270.2**
 Photography and pictures, **19.2–270.1**
Fraud, generally, this index
Indictment and information, **19.2–223**
Lesser included offenses, **19.2–289**
Money, evidence, disposition, **19.2–270.2**
Robbery, generally, this index
Searches and seizures, warrants, **19.2–53**
Securities, evidence, disposition, **19.2–270.2**
Shoplifting, generally, this index
Venue, **19.2–245**
Verdicts, **19.2–289, 19.2–290**

THERAPISTS
Counselors and Counseling, generally, this index
Psychiatrists and Psychiatry, generally, this index
Psychologists and Psychology, generally, this index

THREATS
Bail, **19.2–19 et seq.**
Keeping the peace, bail, **19.2–19 et seq.**
Stalking, generally, this index
Terrorism, generally, this index

TITLES OF ACTS
Popular Name Laws, generally, this index

TOBACCO AND TOBACCO PRODUCTS
 See, also, Cigarettes and Cigars, generally, this index
Taxation. Cigarette Tax, generally, this index

TORTS
Personal Injuries, generally, this index

TOWNS
Municipalities, generally, this index

TOXIC SUBSTANCES
Hazardous Substances and Waste, generally, this index

TRACKING DEVICES
Searches and seizures, warrants, **19.2–56.2**

TRAFFIC RULES AND REGULATIONS
 See, also, Motor Vehicles, generally, this index
Accidents, arrest, **19.2–81**
Arraignment, **19.2–254.1**
Arrest, **19.2–81**
Crimes and offenses,
 Arraignment, **19.2–254.1**
 Dockets and docketing, **19.2–240**
 Jury, **19.2–258.1**
Dockets and docketing, **19.2–240**
Driving under influence of alcohol or drugs,
 Arrest, **19.2–81**
 Bail, presumptions, **19.2–120**
 Blood tests,
  Emergency medical services, evidence, **19.2–187.02**
  Evidence, emergency medical services, **19.2–187.02**
 Double jeopardy, **19.2–294.1**
 Emergency medical services, blood tests, evidence, **19.2–187.02**
 Evidence, blood tests, emergency medical services, **19.2–187.02**
 Forfeitures, **19.2–386.34**
 Medical care and treatment, summons, **19.2–73**
 Motor carriers, blood tests, emergency medical services, **19.2–187.02**
 Presentence investigations, **19.2–299**
 Summons, medical care and treatment, **19.2–73**
Infractions,
 Arraignment, **19.2–254.1**
 Dockets and docketing, **19.2–240**
 Jury, **19.2–258.1**
Jury, trial, **19.2–258.1**
Reckless driving, double jeopardy, **19.2–294.1**
Trial, jury, **19.2–258.1**
Waiver, jury, **19.2–258.1**

TRAINING
Magistrates, **19.2–38, 19.2–38.1**
Public defenders, **19.2–163.01**

TRANSCRIPTS
Appeals in Criminal Prosecutions, this index
Court reporters, crimes and offenses, **19.2–166**
Crimes and Offenses, this index
Grand jury,
 Multijurisdiction grand juries, **19.2–215.9**
 Special grand juries, **19.2–212**
Habeas corpus, **19.2–166**
Indigent persons, **19.2–325**
 Crimes and offenses, **19.2–165**
Multijurisdiction grand juries, **19.2–215.9**
Special grand juries, **19.2–212**

TRANSCRIPTS—Cont'd
State, appeals in criminal prosecutions, **19.2–405**

TRANSPORTATION
Extradition, jails, **19.2–97, 19.2–98**

TRAVELING EXPENSES
Conservators of the peace, **19.2–23**
Indigent defense commission, **19.2–163.02**

TREATMENT
Medical Care and Treatment, generally, this index

TRESPASS
Bail, keeping the peace, **19.2–19 et seq.**

TRIAL
Bail, generally, this index
Capital punishment, **19.2–264.2 et seq.**
Competency, crimes and offenses, **19.2–167, 19.2–169.1 et seq.**
Contempt, generally, this index
Costs, generally, this index
Crimes and Offenses, this index
Evidence, generally, this index
Exclusion, television and radio, **19.2–266**
Forfeitures, **19.2–386.10**
Guilty pleas, without jury, **19.2–257, 19.2–258**
Judgments and Decrees, generally, this index
Jury, generally, this index
Media coverage, **19.2–266**
Motions, generally, this index
Photography and pictures, **19.2–266**
Place of trial. Venue, generally, this index
Process, generally, this index
Records and recordation,
  Crimes and offenses, **19.2–165**
  Transcripts, generally, this index
Speedy Trial, generally, this index
Supersedeas or Stay, generally, this index
Television and radio, **19.2–266**
Traffic rules and regulations, jury, **19.2–258.1**
Venue, generally, this index
Waiver of jury trial. Jury, this index
Witnesses, generally, this index

TRIAL DE NOVO
Crimes and Offenses, this index

TRICK
Fraud, generally, this index

TRUST COMPANIES
Production of books and papers, records and recordation, **19.2–10.1**
Records and recordation, production of books and papers, **19.2–10.1**

TWENTY ONE DAY RULE
Actual innocence, writs, nonbiological evidence, **19.2–327.10 et seq.**

UNDERTAKINGS
Bail, generally, this index

UNDERTAKINGS—Cont'd
Bonds (Officers and Fiduciaries), generally, this index

UNIFORM COMMERCIAL CODE
Negotiable Instruments, generally, this index

UNIFORM LAWS
Criminal Extradition Act, **19.2–85 et seq.**
Extradition, **19.2–85 et seq.**

UNIVERSITIES
Colleges and Universities, generally, this index

UNMANNED AIRCRAFT
Searches and seizures, warrants, **19.2–60.1**

UNSOUND MIND
Mentally Ill Persons, generally, this index

UTTERING
Forgery, generally, this index

VACATING OR SETTING ASIDE
DNA, application of law, samples, **19.2–303**

VANS
Motor Vehicles, generally, this index

VEHICLES
Motor Vehicles, generally, this index

VENUE
Arrest, warrants, **19.2–72**
Assault and battery, **19.2–246**
Bail, change of venue, **19.2–252**
Change of venue, crimes and offenses, **19.2–251 et seq.**
Cigarettes and cigars, crimes and offenses, **19.2–245.01**
Computers, crimes and offenses, **19.2–249.2**
Counties, crimes and offenses, **19.2–249 et seq.**
Embezzlement, **19.2–245**
Fines and penalties, **19.2–342**
Forgery, **19.2–245.1**
Homicide, **19.2–247, 19.2–248**
Military forces, change of venue, **19.2–251**
Motions, crimes and offenses, **19.2–244**
Municipalities, crimes and offenses, **19.2–249 et seq.**
Personal injuries, crimes and offenses, **19.2–246**
Protective orders, **19.2–152.11**
State, appeals in criminal prosecutions, **19.2–400**
Taxation, crimes and offenses, **19.2–245.2**
Theft, **19.2–245**
Wiretapping, applications, **19.2–66, 19.2–70.2**

VERDICTS
Capital Punishment, this index

VESSELS
Boats and Boating, generally, this index
Ships and Shipping, generally, this index

VICTIMS
Crime Victims, generally, this index

VIDEO IMAGES
Appearance, crimes and offenses, **19.2–3.1**
Children and minors, privacy, crimes and offenses, venue, **19.2–249.2**
Crimes and offenses,
Appearance, **19.2–3.1**
Privacy, persons in state of undress, venue, **19.2–249.2**
Obscenity, generally, this index
Pornography. Obscenity, generally, this index

VILLAGES
Municipalities, generally, this index

VIOLENCE
Force and Violence, generally, this index

VIOLENT CRIMES
Crimes and Offenses, generally, this index

VOCATIONAL REHABILITATION
Criminal history record information, disclosure, **19.2–389**

VOLUNTEERS
Criminal history record information, disclosure, **19.2–389**

VULNERABLE ADULTS
Mentally Ill Persons, generally, this index
Mentally Retarded and Developmentally Disabled Persons, generally, this index

WAGERING
Gambling, generally, this index

WAGES
Compensation and Salaries, generally, this index

WARRANTS
Arrest, this index
Extradition, **19.2–92**
Hazardous substances and waste, inspection and inspectors, **19.2–393 et seq.**
Searches and Seizures, this index

WASTE
Hazardous Substances and Waste, generally, this index

WATERCRAFT
Boats and Boating, generally, this index
Ships and Shipping, generally, this index

WATERS AND WATERCOURSES
Fish and Game, generally, this index

WEAPONS
Arrest, **19.2–81**
Bail, **19.2–121**
Presumptions, **19.2–120**
Second and subsequent offenses, **19.2–123**
Concealed weapons, forfeitures, **19.2–386.27 et seq.**
Conservators of the peace, **19.2–13**

WEAPONS—Cont'd
Destruction, used in crime, **19.2–386.29**
Drones, unmanned aircraft, deployment, **19.2–60.1**
Forfeitures, **19.2–386.27 et seq.**
Searches and seizures, **19.2–386.27 et seq.**
Warrants, **19.2–53**
Second and subsequent offenses, bail, **19.2–123**
Unmanned aircraft, deployment, **19.2–60.1**

WEIGHTS AND MEASURES
Noise, machinery and equipment, certificates and certification, evidence, **19.2–270.7**

WELFARE
Social Services, generally, this index

WIFE
Husband and Wife, generally, this index

WILD ANIMALS AND BIRDS
Fish and Game, generally, this index

WILDLIFE
Fish and Game, generally, this index

WIRETAPPING
Generally, **19.2–61 et seq.**
Actions and proceedings, damages, **19.2–69**
Advertisements, **19.2–63**
Applications, **19.2–66**
Orders of court, **19.2–68**
Pen registers, **19.2–70.2**
Attorney fees, **19.2–69**
Consent, **19.2–62**
Contempt, **19.2–68**
Costs, **19.2–69**
Damages, **19.2–69**
Defenses, **19.2–69**
Pen registers, **19.2–70.2**
Devices, **19.2–63 et seq.**
Disclosure, investigations and investigators, **19.2–67**
Evidence, **19.2–65**
Suppression, **19.2–68**
Exemptions, **19.2–62**
Fines and penalties, **19.2–62**
Forfeitures, **19.2–64**
Forfeitures, devices, **19.2–64**
Investigations and investigators,
Disclosure, **19.2–67**
Pen registers, **19.2–70.2**
Landlord and tenant,
Orders of court, **19.2–68**
Pen registers, **19.2–70.2**
Machinery and equipment, **19.2–63 et seq.**
Monitoring, locations, **19.2–68**
Oaths and affirmations, applications, orders of court, **19.2–68**
Orders of court, **19.2–68**
Pen registers, **19.2–70.1, 19.2–70.2**
Pen registers, **19.2–62, 19.2–70.1, 19.2–70.2**
Possession, devices, **19.2–63**

WIRETAPPING—Cont'd
Privileges and immunities,
Pen registers, **19.2–70.2**
Records and recordation, disclosure, **19.2–70.3**
Prosecuting attorneys, applications, **19.2–66**
Records and recordation, **19.2–68**
Disclosure, **19.2–70.3**
Reports, **19.2–70**
Orders of court, **19.2–68**
Searches and seizures, devices, **19.2–64**
Suppression, **19.2–68**
Switchboards, exemptions, **19.2–62**
Time,
Orders of court, **19.2–68**
Pen registers, **19.2–70.2**
Trap and trace devices, **19.2–62, 19.2–70.1, 19.2–70.2**
Venue, applications, **19.2–66, 19.2–70.2**
Witnesses, **19.2–67**

WITNESSES
Generally, **19.2–11.01 et seq., 19.2–267 et seq.**
Abuse of children, husband and wife, **19.2–271.2**
Address, confidential or privileged information, **19.2–269.2**
Appearance. Subpoenas, generally, this index
Application of law, **19.2–267**
Arrest, foreign states, **19.2–275**
Bail,
Duress or coercion, presumptions, **19.2–120**
Release, **19.2–127**
Capital punishment, opinions or expert testimony, evidence, notice, **19.2–264.3:4**
Certificates and certification, foreign states, **19.2–273, 19.2–277**
Clergy, **19.2–271.3**
Confidential or privileged information, **19.2–269.2**
Clergy, **19.2–271.3**
Husband and wife, crimes and offenses, **19.2–271.2**
Contempt,
Crimes and offenses, summons, **19.2–267.1**
Show cause hearings, **19.2–11**
Court officers and employees, **19.2–271**
Crime victims,
Compensation and salaries, **19.2–368.3**
Exclusion, **19.2–265.1**
Crimes and Offenses, this index
Criminal insanity, opinion and expert testimony, **19.2–175**
Critical incident stress management teams, emergency medical services, privileges and immunities, **19.2–271.4**
Cross examination. Crimes and Offenses, this index
Custody, foreign states, **19.2–275**
Duress or coercion, **19.2–11.01**
Exclusion, crimes and offenses, **19.2–265.1, 19.2–265.5**
Exemptions,
Foreign states, process, **19.2–280**

WITNESSES—Cont'd
Exemptions—Cont'd
Media coverage, **19.2–266**
Fees,
Crimes and offenses, **19.2–329 et seq.**
Opinion and expert testimony, criminal insanity, **19.2–175**
Fines and penalties, foreign states, **19.2–276, 19.2–279**
Foreign states, crimes and offenses, **19.2–272 et seq.**
Fees, **19.2–330**
Forms, rights, **19.2–11.01**
Funds, crime victim and witness fund, **19.2–11.3**
Gangs, crimes and offenses, confidential or privileged information, **19.2–11.2**
Grand Jury, this index
Hearing impaired persons, interpreters, **19.2–164.1**
Incest, husband and wife, **19.2–271.2**
Interpreters, this index
Judges, **19.2–271**
Media coverage, crimes and offenses, **19.2–266**
Medical examiners, reports, opinions and expert testimony, evidence, **19.2–188**
Notice, **19.2–11.01**
Opinions and expert testimony,
Capital punishment,
Evidence, notice, **19.2–264.3:4**
Mental examinations, **19.2–264.3:1, 19.2–264.3:1.2**
Criminal insanity, **19.2–175**
Medical examiners, reports, evidence, **19.2–188**
Photography and pictures, crimes and offenses, **19.2–266**
Polygraph examinations, crimes and offenses, **19.2–9.1**
Presumptions, husband and wife, **19.2–271.2**
Privacy, **19.2–11.01**
Privileges and immunities, clergy, **19.2–271.3**
Process, foreign states, exemptions, **19.2–280**
Protection, **19.2–11.01**
Restitution, **19.2–11.01**
Rights, **19.2–11.01 et seq.**
Self Incrimination, generally, this index
Sex offenses, husband and wife, **19.2–271.2**
Subpoenas, generally, this index
Summons,
Crimes and offenses, **19.2–267, 19.2–267.1**
Foreign states, **19.2–274, 19.2–277**
Telecommunications, confidential or privileged information, **19.2–269.2**
Television and radio, crimes and offenses, **19.2–266**
Transportation, correctional institutions, **19.2–269.1**
Traveling expenses, foreign states, **19.2–278**

WIVES
Husband and Wife, generally, this index

WOMEN
Husband and Wife, generally, this index

WORDS AND PHRASES
Act of violence, sentencing, **19.2–297.1**
Act of violence force or threat, protective orders, **19.2–152.7:1**
Aggrieved person, wiretapping, **19.2–61**
Aural transfer, wiretapping, **19.2–61**
Bail, **19.2–119**
Barrier crime, criminal history record information, **19.2–392.02**
Barrier crime information, criminal history record information, **19.2–392.02**
Bonds, bail, **19.2–119**
Care, criminal history record information, **19.2–392.02**
Certificates of analysis, crimes and offenses, laboratories, evidence, **19.2–187**
Chief law enforcement officers, criminal history record information, **19.2–390**
Claimant, crime victims, compensation and salaries, **19.2–368.2**
Commission, crime victims, compensation and salaries, **19.2–368.2**
Confidential communications, husband and wife, privileges and immunities, crimes and offenses, **19.2–271.2**
Content, wiretapping, **19.2–61**
Copy, protective orders, **19.2–152.8**
Court, crimes and offenses, **19.2–5**
Courts not of record, crimes and offenses, **19.2–5**
Crime, crime victims, compensation and salaries, **19.2–368.2**
Criminal history, bail, **19.2–119**
Debt collection activities, crime victims, medical care and treatment, limitation of actions, **19.2–368.5:2**
Defendant, crimes and offenses, profits, **19.2–368.19**
Departments, criminal history record information, **19.2–392.02**
District court, crimes and offenses, **19.2–5**
Division, crimes and offenses, profits, **19.2–368.19**
Electronic, mechanical or other device, wiretapping, **19.2–61**
Electronic communication, interception, **19.2–61**
Electronic communication system, interception, **19.2–61**
Electronic communications service, interception, **19.2–61**
Electronic reports, criminal history record information, **19.2–390**
Electronic storage, wiretapping, **19.2–61**
Emitting, hazardous substances and waste, inspection and inspectors, **19.2–393**
Employed by, criminal history record information, **19.2–392.02**
Executive authority, extradition, **19.2–85**
Family, crime victims, compensation and salaries, **19.2–368.2**
Fine, **19.2–339**
Foreign corporation,
  Searches and seizures, warrants, **19.2–56**

WORDS AND PHRASES—Cont'd
Foreign corporation—Cont'd
  Telecommunications, records and recordation, disclosure, **19.2–70.3**
Governor, extradition, **19.2–85**
Identification documents, criminal history record information, **19.2–392.02**
Indictment, **19.2–216**
Information, **19.2–216**
Inspection warrant, hazardous substances and waste, **19.2–393**
Intercept, communications, **19.2–61**
Interested party, crimes and offenses, profits, **19.2–368.19**
Intractable behavior,
  Boot camps, **19.2–316.1**
  Parole and probation, revocation or suspension, **19.2–303.3**
Investigative or law enforcement officer, wiretapping, **19.2–61**
Judge,
  Crimes and offenses, **19.2–5**
  Extradition, **19.2–85**
Judge of competent jurisdiction, wiretapping, **19.2–61**
Judicial officers,
  Bail, **19.2–119**
  Tracking devices, searches and seizures, warrants, **19.2–56.2**
Law enforcement officer,
  Protective orders, **19.2–152.8**
  Tracking devices, searches and seizures, warrants, **19.2–56.2**
Manufacturing, hazardous substances and waste, inspection and inspectors, **19.2–393**
Mentally retarded, capital punishment, **19.2–264.3:1.1**
Monitor, wiretapping, **19.2–61**
Nonviolent felony, boot camps, **19.2–316.1**
Oral communication, interception, **19.2–61**
Pen register, wiretapping, **19.2–61**
Person,
  Bail, **19.2–119**
  Wiretapping, **19.2–61**
Personal information, jury, confidential or privileged information, orders, **19.2–263.3**
Presentment, **19.2–216 et seq.**
Properly served,
  Searches and seizures, warrants, **19.2–56**
  Telecommunications, records and recordation, disclosure, **19.2–70.3**
Protective orders, **19.2–152.10**
Provider, criminal history record information, **19.2–392.02**
Qualified entities, criminal history record information, **19.2–392.02**
Readily accessible to the general public, wiretapping, **19.2–61**
Real time location data, telecommunications, records and recordation, disclosure, **19.2–70.3**

WORDS AND PHRASES—Cont'd
Recognizance, **19.2–119**
Remote computing service, wiretapping, **19.2–61**
Scene of any accident, arrest, **19.2–81**
Sex offenses, crime victims, polygraph examinations, notice, **19.2–9.1**
Sexual abuse, crime victims, compensation and salaries, **19.2–368.2**
State,
  Extradition, **19.2–85**
  Witnesses, foreign states, **19.2–272**
Strip searches, **19.2–59.1**
Summons, witnesses, foreign states, **19.2–272**
Toxic substance, inspection and inspectors, **19.2–393**
Tracking devices, searches and seizures, warrants, **19.2–56.2**
Trap and trace device, wiretapping, **19.2–61**
Unmanned aircraft, searches and seizures, **19.2–60.1**
Unmanned aircraft systems, searches and seizures, **19.2–60.1**
Use of a tracking device, searches and seizures, warrants, **19.2–56.2**
User, wiretapping, **19.2–61**

WORDS AND PHRASES—Cont'd
Victim,
  Compensation and salaries, **19.2–368.2**
  Crimes and offenses, **19.2–11.01**
    Profits, **19.2–368.19**
  Restitution, **19.2–305.1**
Wire communication, interception, **19.2–61**
Witness, foreign states, **19.2–272**

WORK
Labor and Employment, generally, this index

WORLD WIDE WEB
Internet, generally, this index

WRITS
Actual innocence,
  DNA, evidence, crimes and offenses, **19.2–327.2 et seq.**
  Nonbiological evidence, **19.2–327.10 et seq.**
Executions, generally, this index
Fieri facias. Executions, generally, this index
Habeas Corpus, generally, this index

YOUTH GANGS
Gangs, generally, this index

MEDICAL MALPRACTICE RULES OF PRACTICE

Including Amendments Received Through October 15, 2015

Table of Rules

Rule	
ONE.	Applicability; Definitions.
TWO.	Request for Medical Malpractice Review Panel.
THREE.	Designation of Panel; Certificate of Parties.
FOUR.	Convening of Panel.
FIVE.	Request for Ore Tenus Hearing.
SIX.	Conduct of an Ore Tenus Hearing.
SEVEN.	Expenses and Costs.

APPENDIX OF FORMS

Form
Subpoena.
Subpoena Duces Tecum.

RULE ONE. APPLICABILITY; DEFINITIONS

(a) These Rules are promulgated in accordance with Section 8.01–581.11 of the Code of Virginia and shall govern all formal proceedings instituted pursuant to the provisions of Chapter 21.1 of Title 8.01 with respect to the activities of a duly constituted Medical Malpractice Review Panel. The Rules shall not apply to any cause of action which arose prior to July 1, 1976, the effective date of Chapter 21.1 of Title 8.01 unless the claimant has filed notice under § 8.01–581.2 and such filing occurred prior to the expiration of any applicable statute of limitation.

(b) References herein to "it" and "its" shall apply equally to "him," "his," or "her." The singular shall include the plural. Terms used in this part that are defined in Chapter 21.1 of Title 8.01 are used with the definitions therein contained.

[Effective August 15, 1979. Amended effective September 24, 1993.]

RULE TWO. REQUEST FOR MEDICAL MALPRACTICE REVIEW PANEL

(a) Request for Panel. The plaintiff or any defendant health care provider may, within thirty days from the filing of the responsive pleading in any action brought for malpractice against a health care provider, file a written request for a review by a panel with the clerk of the Supreme Court of Virginia. The request for review of such claim by a panel shall be deemed to be filed when delivered or mailed by registered or certified mail to the clerk of the Supreme Court of Virginia. The request shall include a copy of the complaint and a copy of all responsive pleadings. A copy of the request shall be filed with the clerk of the circuit court wherein the malpractice action has been filed, and a copy of such request shall be mailed to the opposing party and its counsel, if known. The request shall include the name of the judge to whom the case is assigned. Upon receipt of the request the circuit court clerk shall immediately advise the judge to whom the case has been assigned.

(b) Contents of Request. The request for the appointment of a medical review panel shall contain the following (to the extent known):

(1) The name, address and telephone number of the plaintiff.

(2) The name, address and telephone number of the attorney of record for the plaintiff.

(3) The name, address and telephone number of the defendant health care provider(s).

(4) The name, address and telephone number of the attorney of record for the health care provider.

(5) A statement specifying the classification of the health care provider in accordance with Section 8.01–581.1 of the Code and, in the case of a physician, his specialty or subspecialty.

(6) A certification that a copy of the request for a review panel has been mailed to all other parties and their counsel, if known.

(7) The name of the judge to whom the case is assigned.

(c) Multiple Parties. Any health care provider named as a defendant shall have the right to request a panel and, in that event, shall mail copies of its request to the other health care providers named in the complaint as well as to the plaintiff and his counsel of record. When a request for a panel is made by any party, a single panel shall be designated and all health care providers against whom a claim is asserted shall be subject to the jurisdiction of such panel.

[Effective August 15, 1979. Amended effective September 24, 1993; February 1, 1997; July 1, 2000; February 28, 2006.]

RULE THREE. DESIGNATION OF PANEL; CERTIFICATE OF PARTIES

(a) Designation of Panel. Upon receipt of a request for the appointment of a medical review panel, the Supreme Court of Virginia shall designate the panel within sixty days after receipt of the request.

(b) Composition. The panel so designated shall consist of two impartial attorneys and two impartial health care providers, licensed and actively practicing their professions and a circuit court judge of the court in which the action was filed who shall preside over the panel but need not attend or participate in the deliberations of the panel.

(c) Attorney Members. The Supreme Court of Virginia shall select the attorney members of each panel from a list provided by the Virginia State Bar. The Virginia State Bar shall provide to the Executive Secretary of the Supreme Court of Virginia a list of two hundred forty actively practicing attorneys. Such list shall include the office address and telephone number of each attorney. One third of such list shall be replaced each year but members may be reappointed to the list without limit in time.

(d) Health Care Provider Members. The Supreme Court of Virginia shall select the health care provider members of the panel from a list provided by the State Board of Medicine. The State Board of Medicine shall provide to the Executive Secretary of the Supreme Court of Virginia a list of nine hundred fifteen health care providers. Such a list shall include the office address and telephone number of each health care provider. The list furnished by the State Board of Medicine shall be by classification, as stated in Section 8.01–581.1 of the Code, and, where practical, by specialty as follows:

(1) *Physicians (605).* Seventy-five in General Practice; sixty in Surgery; fifty in Internal Medicine; thirty in Orthopedic Surgery; sixty in Obstetrics and Gynecology; thirty in Anesthesiology; forty in Emergency Medicine; and twenty in each of the following: Dermatology, Neurology, Neurosurgery, Ophthalmology, Otorhinolaryngology, Pediatrics, Pathology, Physical Medicine, Plastic Surgery, Radiology, Urology, Psychiatry and Osteopathy.

(2) *Hospitals (40).* Forty hospital administrators.

(3) *Dentists (60).* Twenty in General Practice. Ten in each of the following specialties: Oral Surgery, Endodontics, Orthodontics and Periodontics.

(4) *Pharmacists (40).* Twenty each in community pharmacy and hospital pharmacy.

(5) *Registered or Licensed Practical Nurses or Nurse Practitioners (40).*

(6) *Optometrists (20).*

(7) *Podiatrists (20).*

(8) *Chiropractors (10).*

(9) *Physical Therapists (10).*

(10) *Physical Therapy Assistants (10).*

(11) *Clinical Psychologists (10).*

(12) *Nursing Homes (20).* Twenty nursing home administrators.

(13) *Clinical Social Workers (10).*

(14) *Professional Counselors (10).*

(15) *Dental Hygienists (10).*

It shall be the responsibility of the State Board of Medicine to coordinate with the State Board of Health, State Board of Dentistry, State Board of Pharmacy, State Board of Nursing, State Board of Optometry, and such other regulatory boards as may be necessary to compile this list. A new list shall be provided every three years but members may be reappointed to the list without limit in time.

(e) Withdrawal From List.

(1) An individual whose name is included on any list may have his or her name withdrawn from the list by notifying the Virginia State Bar or the State Board of Medicine. Upon receipt of such notification, the Virginia State Bar or the State Board of Medicine shall advise the Executive Secretary of the Supreme Court of Virginia of this change and submit a replacement.

(2) Any person subject to disciplinary action by his or her profession shall be automatically removed from the list by the appropriate regulatory body and a replacement submitted to the Executive Secretary of the Supreme Court.

(3) Any person who is unable through sickness, disability, or for any other reason to serve regularly on a panel shall be removed from the list and a replacement submitted to the Executive Secretary of the Supreme Court.

(4) The Executive Secretary of the Supreme Court may request that a name be removed from the list because of constant refusal to serve.

(f) Manner of Selection.

(1) Selection from the lists by the Supreme Court of Virginia will be rotated based on availability with due regard to the nature of the claim.

(2) Unless it shall prove impracticable, one health care provider on the panel shall represent the medical specialty involved in the claim.

(3) Any member of the panel may disqualify himself if he believes that his presence constitutes a conflict of interest or gives the appearance of impropriety. A party may move for such disqualification for cause within ten days after receiving notice of designation of the panel. The motion shall be in writing addressed to the judge presiding over the panel and served by mail on the opposing party or its counsel. The judge shall act on the motion unless the panel member in question disqualifies himself. In the event of such disqualifica-

tion, the Supreme Court of Virginia shall designate a new panel member.

(g) Rescission. A party may rescind a request for review by a panel at any time prior to the selection of the panel, in which event, if no other party had also requested the panel, the presiding judge shall dismiss the panel. After the selection of the members of the review panel, the requesting party may rescind a request for review by the panel only with the consent of all parties or with leave of the judge presiding over the panel. The Executive Secretary of the Supreme Court of Virginia shall be notified of any dismissal. [Amended effective July 1, 1984; August 1, 1985; July 1, 1986; July 1, 1988; October 1, 1992; September 24, 1993; September 1, 1994; December 1, 1994; July 1, 2000; January 1, 2002.]

RULE FOUR. CONVENING OF PANEL

(a) Notice of Appointment. Upon selection of the panel members by the Supreme Court, the Executive Secretary shall mail a letter to the panel members advising them of their selection to the panel and of the names and addresses of the parties and attorneys involved in this proceeding. A brief description of the claim shall be included in this letter. The panelists, within ten days thereafter, shall advise the Executive Secretary if they will be unable to serve. Upon expiration of the ten days, the Supreme Court will issue an official designation specifying the style of the proceeding and each panel member. A copy of this designation shall be mailed together with the names, addresses and professional practice of each panel member to the plaintiff and the health care provider and their counsel. This designation shall recite that the date, time, and place for the convening of the panel shall be fixed by the judge presiding over the panel in consultation with the members of the panel.

(b) Additional Parties. Upon request, the judge of the circuit court hearing the case may grant leave to amend the request for a review panel to add additional parties or causes of action in furtherance of the ends of justice except where (i) the request for leave to amend is made less than ten days before the date set for the review panel to convene or (ii) the judge finds that the request for leave to amend is without merit. If leave to amend is granted, the judge may, upon motion of either party, stay the review panel proceedings, extend the time for completion of discovery, filing of submissions and other procedural limitation periods, or enter such orders as are appropriate to avoid prejudice to the parties and to avoid unnecessary delay and duplication in the proceedings. Leave to add additional parties shall not be granted if the judge finds that the applicable statute of limitations has expired with respect to the new or additional parties or causes of action.

(c) Notification. At the time the panel is designated the Supreme Court shall advise the clerk of the circuit court in which the matter is filed of the names of the panel members. The Supreme Court shall also notify the parties of the name, address and professional practice of each panel member and shall also notify the panel members, in writing, of their appointment.

(d) Completion of Discovery. Within ten days of receipt of the request for the panel the judge shall advise the parties of the date set for the completion of discovery. Except for good cause shown, the date for completion of discovery shall not be set beyond one hundred twenty days from the date on which the panel was requested. Procedures for the taking of depositions shall be governed by Part Four of the Rules of the Supreme Court and the provisions of Section 8.01–581.4 of the Code of Virginia, 1950, as amended.

(e) Submission by Plaintiff. The plaintiff within ten days after the date set for completion of discovery, shall submit to each member of the panel, including the judge, a statement of facts together with all documentary evidence he or she desires to introduce. The plaintiff shall submit to the panel members only those portions of deposition transcripts, medical records, treatises and other documents which are relevant to the claim. However, upon request of the judge, the plaintiff shall produce all or part of any such document submitted. These materials shall be accompanied by a certificate stating that a copy of all such materials has been mailed to the health care provider and its counsel. All costs attendant to the submission of these materials shall be borne by the plaintiff. If the plaintiff fails to comply with this subsection, the judge shall prescribe a time within which the health care provider may submit evidence and shall order that the matter be considered solely upon the evidence. If the health care provider fails to comply with such order, the judge shall order the panel discharged.

(f) Submission by Health Care Provider. Within ten days after receipt of the materials filed by the plaintiff, the health care provider shall submit to each panel member, including the judge, a counter statement of facts and all materials that it desires to introduce. The health care provider shall submit to the panel members only those portions of deposition transcripts, medical records, treatises and other documents which are relevant to the claim. However, upon request of the judge, the health care provider shall produce all or part of any such document submitted. These materials shall be accompanied by a certificate stating that a copy of all such materials has been mailed to the plaintiff and his counsel. All costs attendant to the submission of these materials shall be borne by the health care provider.

(g) Extension of Time. The time periods stated in Rules Four (e) and Four (f) above may be extended by the judge for good cause shown.

(h) Convening of Panel. The circuit judge presiding over the panel, within the period set for the taking of discovery and upon consultation with the panel members, shall notify all parties of the date, time and place for a hearing by the review panel, if any, or the date on which the panel will convene, having given due regard to the location of the other panel members and the parties involved and the time periods granted the parties to file their submissions. Such date shall not be set sooner than ten days after the date set for filing of the submission by the health care provider.

(i) Oath. Upon convening of the panel, the judge shall swear in each panel member as follows:

> I do solemnly swear (or affirm) that I have no past or present relationship with the parties nor am I aware of anything that would prevent me from being impartial in my deliberations. I further swear (or affirm) that I will render an opinion faithfully and fairly on the basis of the evidence presented, applying any professional expertise I may have, giving due regard to the nature of the claim and the nature of the practice of the health care provider.

[Amended effective August 31, 1981; August 1, 1985; July 1, 1988; September 24, 1993.]

RULE FIVE. REQUEST FOR ORE TENUS HEARING

Either party may request the panel to conduct an ore tenus hearing and, when such a hearing is requested, it shall be held. Such a request shall be made in writing to the judge within ten days after the receipt of the designation of a panel. A copy of the request for an ore tenus hearing shall be sent to each panel member, the opposing party and its counsel. The panel may, in the absence of a request from either party, determine that an ore tenus hearing shall be held. If an ore tenus hearing is held, the judge shall notify all parties and panel members of the date, time and place for such a hearing. If no ore tenus hearing is held, the judge may, on the request of any party, extend the time for the submission of evidence in order to permit the parties to take and file depositions, and, in any such case, the panel shall convene at the direction of the judge in executive session for the purpose of conducting its review of the written evidence; provided, however, that when the panel chooses to act only in executive session, counsel for all parties shall be notified of the date, time and place of that session.

[Amended effective September 24, 1993.]

RULE SIX. CONDUCT OF AN ORE TENUS HEARING

(a) Subpoenas. The judge, upon the oral or written request of any party, without notice, or upon motion of the panel, may issue subpoenas for the attendance of witnesses and for the production of books, records, documents, and other evidence. When so issued, such subpoenas and subpoenas duces tecum shall be in the form prescribed in the Appendix of Forms attached hereto and shall be returnable to the office of the Clerk of the Circuit Court where the action was filed. Any expense incurred in the service of such subpoenas shall be borne by the requesting party except in the case of subpoenas requested by the panel in which case the expense will be distributed as costs.

(b) [Reserved].

(c) Copies. Any party may obtain from the clerk of the court to which subpoenas are returnable copies of any books, records or documents and other tangible evidence, upon paying to the clerk the reasonable cost of the copy.

(d) Assembly of Record. The judge shall see to the transportation to the panel's meeting place of such books, records and documents as have been lodged in such clerk's office. The judge, upon request of any party, shall, for the purpose of depositions, permit such books, records and documents to be transported by counsel for such party to the place for the taking of depositions after such counsel has given an appropriate receipt to the clerk, and such counsel shall be responsible for the return of such materials to the clerk's office. Upon conclusion of deliberations and rendering of an opinion by the panel, all documentary evidence submitted to the panel, a transcript of the ore tenus hearing, if any, and a copy of the written opinion of the panel shall be filed in the office of the clerk in which the action was filed. The clerk shall mail a copy of the written opinion to the plaintiff and the defendant within five days of the date of rendering. A copy of such opinion shall also be mailed to the Executive Secretary of the Supreme Court of Virginia together with the apportionment of the costs as may be determined by the judge.

(e) Quorum. All members of the panel must be present at a hearing unless waived by both parties.

(f) Decision. A majority vote of the panel members may decide any question and determine the ultimate opinion. The judge shall have no vote.

(g) Evidence. The judge shall rule upon the admissibility of all evidence, but strict rules of evidence need not be observed. Caution should be taken to insure that an opinion is not based entirely on hearsay evidence. Evidence should be material, but should be excluded only when it does not contribute to the development of a fair record.

(h) Exclusion of Witnesses. Witnesses other than the parties or one representative of each may be excluded at the discretion of the judge.

(i) Reporter. Upon application of either party, a court reporter may be present to prepare a transcript of the proceeding. The cost of such reporter shall be borne by the party or parties using the services of the court reporter.

(j) Procedure at Hearing. The following general procedure shall be followed at an ore tenus hearing:

(1) The judge shall convene the hearing, state the style of the case, and state any general rules adopted by the panel.

(2) The judge shall swear in all panel members as provided in Rule Four (i).

(3) Preliminary motions may be made except that no demurrers, motions to dismiss or motions to strike will be permitted.

(4) All testimony shall be taken under oath.

(5) The counsel for the plaintiff may make an opening statement giving a chronological account of events, stating the acts or omissions that he believes constitute the professional negligence and specifying the evidence that he expects to produce.

(6) The counsel for the health care provider may make an opening statement setting forth his statement of facts and the evidence that he expects to produce.

(7) The counsel for the plaintiff shall then produce his evidence. All witnesses are subject to cross-examination and may be questioned by the panel.

(8) The counsel for the health care provider shall then produce his evidence. All witnesses are subject to cross-examination and may be questioned by the panel.

(9) The panel may call any witnesses that it desires to hear including expert witnesses. Any expense incurred by the panel in the calling of expert witnesses shall be apportioned as costs.

(10) Counsel for the plaintiff may present oral argument.

(11) Counsel for the health care provider may present oral argument.

(12) If oral argument is presented by the health care provider, counsel for the plaintiff shall be allowed rebuttal.

(13) At the conclusion of the hearing, the panel will deliberate in executive session and render its decision pursuant to Section 8.01–581.7 of the Code. The judge presiding over the panel need not attend or participate in the deliberations.

[Amended effective July 1, 1984; July 1, 1988; September 24, 1993; September 1, 1994.]

RULE SEVEN. EXPENSES AND COSTS

(a) Expenses. Each member of the panel including the judge shall be reimbursed for his actual and necessary expenses.

(b) Compensation. Each member of the panel except the judge shall be paid at a rate of fifty dollars per day for service as a member of the panel.

(c) Claims. The Executive Secretary of the Supreme Court of Virginia shall provide a form of voucher to each member of the panel for reimbursement and compensation. All vouchers shall be submitted by panel members to the Executive Secretary not later than thirty days after the rendering of the decision by the panel.

(d) Costs. The judge shall apportion to the parties the expenses of conducting the panel in such proportions as may be determined by the judge in his discretion. When apportioning the costs, the judge shall add to the per diem and other expenses of the panel a fee of twenty-five dollars to cover administrative costs incurred by the Commonwealth with respect to proceedings under Chapter 21.1 of Title 8.01 of the Code of Virginia.

(e) Expert Witness. The charges of any expert witness called by any party shall be paid by such party.

(f) Payment. The Executive Secretary shall invoice the costs as apportioned by the judge. Within thirty days after the date of the invoice, each party shall send to the Executive Secretary of the Supreme Court of Virginia a check or money order payable to the Treasurer of Virginia in payment of all sums due and owing as that party's respective share of the costs. It shall be the duty of the counsel of record to insure that such payments are forwarded to the Executive Secretary.

[Amended effective September 24, 1993.]

APPENDIX OF FORMS

SUBPOENA

COMMONWEALTH OF VIRGINIA

COUNTY OF (OR CITY OF) ...., to-wit:

To the Sheriff of said City/County Greeting:

We command you in the name of the Commonwealth of Virginia at the instance of a Medical Malpractice Review Panel duly constituted in accordance with §§ 8.01-581.2 and 8.01-581.3 of the Virginia Code to summon...

....

to appear before the Medical Malpractice Review Panel, at...

............., Virginia, at .... a.m./p.m. on ...., 20..., to give evidence in connection with a claim pending before the Medical Malpractice Review Panel brought by................

....

against...
and make return how you have executed this subpoena.

Given under my hand this .... day of ...., 20 ......

Medical Malpractice Review Panel

By ....

Judge or Clerk

[Amended effective September 2012.]

SUBPOENA DUCES TECUM

COMMONWEALTH OF VIRGINIA

COUNTY OF (OR CITY OF) ...., to-wit:

To the Sheriff of said City/County Greeting:

We command you in the name of the Commonwealth of Virginia at the instance of a Medical Malpractice Review Panel duly constituted in accordance with §§ 8.01-581.2 and 8.01-581.3 of the Virginia Code to summon..

....

to produce on or before ...., 20 ...., at the office of the Clerk of the Circuit Court of

....

the following written material, to-wit:

....

....

....

such material to remain in such office until further ordered and to be available for review and copy, and make return how you have executed this subpoena.

Medical Malpractice Review Panel

By ....

Judge or Clerk

[Amended effective September 2012.]

RULES OF THE JUDICIAL INQUIRY AND REVIEW COMMISSION

Effective February 14, 2006

Including Amendments Received Through October 15, 2015

Table of Rules

Rule
1. General.
2. Definitions.
3. Procedures for Handling Complaints/Inquiries.
4. Informal Conferences.
5. Formal Specification of Pleadings.
6. General Requirements as to Pleadings.
7. Filing of Documents.
8. Service.
9. Time for Filing Documents.
10. Computation of Time.
11. Preliminary Matters.
12. Subpoenas.
13. Hearings.
14. Waiver of Procedural Rules.
15. Disposition of Charges.
16. Preservation of Files.
17. Effective Date.

RULE 1. GENERAL

A. Applicability. These rules shall govern proceedings before the Judicial Inquiry and Review Commission.

B. Gender. The words "he", "him", "his", or similar words as used in these Rules are intended to include both the feminine and the masculine.

C. Exceptions. When the interests of justice require and for good cause shown, the Commission may waive the requirements of any rule.

[Effective February 14, 2006.]

RULE 2. DEFINITIONS

A. "Commission" shall mean the Judicial Inquiry and Review Commission.

B. "Member or Members" shall mean members of the Judicial Inquiry and Review Commission and substitute members appointed pursuant to Va. Code § 17.1–901.

C. "Judge" shall mean the person who is under investigation by the Commission.

D. "Formal hearing" shall mean an investigative hearing to determine whether a judge has violated the Canons of Judicial Conduct and, if so, what sanctions should be imposed. A formal proceeding is initiated by a Notice of Hearing. Formal hearings may be conducted at such times and places in the Commonwealth as the Commission shall determine.

E. "Informal Conference" is a meeting between the judge and the Commission or one or more of its members to discuss alleged improper conduct by the judge.

F. "Document" shall mean any writing, including but not limited to a pleading, exhibit, chart, table or photograph.

G. "Presiding member" shall mean the Chairman or the commission member who presides at a prehearing conference or at any meeting, conference or formal hearing conducted by the Commission.

H. "Investigation" shall mean the process by which the Commission investigates charges coming before it pursuant to Va. Code § 17.1–902. An investigation may or may not include a formal hearing or informal conference. The Commission or the chairman may order an investigation to be made in such manner as is deemed appropriate. The judge may or may not be notified of the investigation.

I. "Complaint" shall mean information alleging any misconduct by a judge whether or not the alleged misconduct violates the Canons of Judicial Conduct.

J. "Inquiry" shall mean any complaint alleging misconduct which is in violation of the Canons of Judicial Conduct or which would be the basis for retirement, censure, or removal of a judge.

K. "Evidence" shall mean the findings of fact contained in the Commission's order that support the determination that the judge has violated the Canons of Judicial Conduct or that the judge's conduct would be the basis for retirement, censure, or removal.

L. "Charge" shall mean an Inquiry that the Commission determines, after a preliminary investigation by counsel and upon the recommendation of counsel, could be a violation of the Canons of Judicial Conduct or the basis for retirement, censure, or removal of a judge.

M. "Well Founded" shall mean that the Commission has found based upon clear and convincing evidence and supported by facts and sound judgment that the misconduct has occurred.

[Effective February 14, 2006.]

RULE 3. PROCEDURES FOR HANDLING COMPLAINTS/INQUIRIES

A. Receipt of Complaints:

(1) The Commission requests that all Complaints be submitted in writing to the Commission Office by mail at Post Office Box 367, Richmond, Virginia 23218–0367. Verbal complaints may be considered.

(2) Counsel for the Commission shall promptly acknowledge receipt of initial letters of Complaint.

(3) Any Complaint not stating a violation of the Canons of Judicial Conduct or which would not be the basis for retirement, censure, or removal of a judge need not be presented to the Commission and the sender will be notified by Commission Counsel.

(4) Any Complaint, which Commission Counsel believes to allege a violation of the Canons of Judicial Conduct, or which would be the basis for retirement, censure or removal of a judge, shall be presented to the Commission as an Inquiry.

(5) Each inquiry presented to the Commission shall be numbered and considered by the Commission, along with Commission Counsel's findings and recommendation after a preliminary investigation.

(6) If the Commission determines that the Inquiry has no merit, the Inquiry shall be dismissed and Commission Counsel will notify the sender.

B. Establishment of Charges:

(1) If the Commission determines that the Inquiry may have merit, it shall establish the Inquiry as a charge and the Commission may direct further investigation or propose an informal conference with the judge.

(2) Upon determination that the charge, if well founded, would be the basis for retirement, censure, or removal of a judge, the Commission may proceed with a formal hearing.

(3) Disposition of charges shall be as provided in Rule 15 of the Rules of the Commission, or as may be provided by statute.

C. Temporary Suspension/Mental and Physical Examination:

(1) In any pending investigation or formal hearing, the Commission may suspend a judge with pay pursuant to Va. Code § 17.1–911.

(2) Whenever the Commission has probable cause to believe that a judge is unable to perform his duties because of excessive use of alcohol or drugs or physical or mental illness, the Commission may direct a physical or mental examination pursuant to Va. Code § 17.1–912.

D. Termination of Charges:

(1) The Commission may terminate the charge or charges at any time when it determines that the investigation is complete and the charge or charges are without merit or not sufficient to constitute the basis of retirement, censure or removal.

(2) The charge or charges against a judge shall be terminated with a finding and an order, signed by the Commission Chairperson and Commission Counsel, and a copy of the finding and order shall be forwarded to the judge if the judge has been made aware of the charge.

(3) The finding shall state whether the charge was well-founded and whether of sufficient gravity to constitute the basis for retirement, censure or removal, or whether the charge was well-founded and, with the consent of the judge, an agreement for supervision was reached under terms and conditions approved by the Commission.

(4) The order shall state the action taken by the Commission, including the status of the charge on the Commission's docket.

(5) Commission Counsel shall notify the complainant when the charge is terminated.

[Effective February 14, 2006.]

RULE 4. INFORMAL CONFERENCES

In the discretion of the Commission, a judge who is alleged to have violated the Canons of Judicial Conduct may be invited to meet with the Commission or a member or members to discuss informally the allegations and possible solutions. Counsel may represent the judge but no witnesses will be permitted to testify. If the judge and the Commission do not resolve the matter at such an informal conference, the Commission may remove the matter from the Commission's docket or give the judge notice of a formal proceeding. The Commission may proceed directly to a formal proceeding without first holding an informal conference. Informal conferences shall not be governed by these rules.

[Effective February 14, 2006.]

RULE 5. FORMAL SPECIFICATION OF PLEADINGS

A. Number of Copies. Unless otherwise specified, an executed original and eight (8) true copies of each document required or permitted to be filed under these rules shall be filed with the Commission. The copies need not be signed but the name of the person signing the document, as distinguished from the firm he represents, shall also be typed or printed on all copies below the space provided for signature.

B. Facsimile Transmission. Pleadings may not be filed by facsimile transmission.

[Effective February 14, 2006.]

RULE 6. GENERAL REQUIREMENTS AS TO PLEADINGS

A. Contents. All pleadings shall contain a proper identification of the case and a concise but complete statement of the facts relied upon and the relief sought.

B. Subscription. Every pleading submitted to the Commission shall be signed by the judge filing same and his attorney. The signature of an attorney or party constitutes a certificate by him that (i) he has read the pleading, motion, or other paper, (ii) to the best of his knowledge, information and belief, formed after reasonable inquiry, it is well grounded in fact and is warranted by existing law or a good faith argument for the extension, modification, or reversal of existing law, and (iii) it is not interposed for any improper purpose, such as to harass or to cause unnecessary delay or needless increase in the cost of litigation. If a pleading, written motion, or other paper is not signed, it shall be stricken unless it is signed promptly after the omission is called to the attention of the pleader or movant. An oral motion made by an attorney or party before the Commission constitutes a representation by him that (i) to the best of his knowledge, information and belief formed after reasonable inquiry it is well grounded in fact and is warranted by existing law or a good faith argument for the extension, modification or reversal of existing law, and (ii) it is not interposed for any improper purpose, such as to harass or to cause unnecessary delay or needless increase in the cost of litigation.

C. Answers. A judge who receives a Notice of Hearing shall file his answer within 21 days of service. For good cause the Commission or the Presiding Member may shorten or extend the time in which the Answer must be filed. The Answer shall fully and completely state the nature of the defense and shall admit or deny specifically and in detail each allegation of the Notice of Hearing unless the judge is without knowledge, in which case, his Answer shall so state and the statement shall operate as a denial. Matters alleged as affirmative defenses shall be separately stated and numbered.

[Effective February 14, 2006.]

RULE 7. FILING OF DOCUMENTS

A. Where Filed. All documents shall be filed with the Commission either by personal delivery at 100 North Ninth Street, Suite 661, Richmond, Virginia 23219 or by mail at Post Office Box 367, Richmond, Virginia 23218–0367. Documents shall be deemed filed on the date of actual receipt by the Commission.

B. Name of Person Filing. Every document shall include the name, address, telephone number and signature of the person filing same.

[Effective February 14, 2006.]

RULE 8. SERVICE

A. Persons To Be Served. The Commission shall serve its Notice by personal delivery upon the judge. Thereafter documents will be served upon the judge unless he is represented by an attorney in which case succeeding documents shall be served upon his attorney. Documents shall be served upon the Commission by delivering such documents to the Commission's Counsel.

B. Where Served. The Notice shall be served upon the judge at his home, if possible, in order to protect the confidentiality of the proceeding. If the judge cannot be served at his home, he may be served at any place where he may be found.

C. Proof of Service. Proof of service shall accompany all documents when they are filed and shall consist of a certificate of mailing executed by the person mailing the document, an acknowledgement of service, or a certificate of service.

[Effective February 14, 2006.]

RULE 9. TIME FOR FILING DOCUMENTS

A. Amendments. An amendment to any pleading may be made prior to the filing of answers thereto, or if no answer be filed, prior to its hearing date. The Commission may permit amendments to the pleadings prior to the close of the hearing for the sole purpose of insuring that the pleadings conform to the evidence.

B. Other Documents. All other documents shall be filed within the period established by the Commission or its Presiding Member.

[Effective February 14, 2006.]

RULE 10. COMPUTATION OF TIME

A. Effect of Holidays. When any period of time fixed by these rules shall expire on a Saturday, Sunday or legal holiday, it shall be extended to the next day not a Saturday, Sunday or legal holiday.

B. Extensions of Time. Upon good cause shown the Commission or its Presiding Member may grant extensions of time. Motions to continue hearings are regarded with disfavor and will be granted only for extraordinary reasons.

[Effective February 14, 2006.]

RULE 11. PRELIMINARY MATTERS

A. Motions. At least fourteen (14) days before the hearing, preliminary motions must be filed. If a prehearing conference is held, such motions must be filed at least fourteen (14) days before the prehearing conference.

B. Prehearing Conference. The Commission or the Presiding Member may on its own motion, the motion of the Commission's Counsel, or the judge's motion, hold prehearing conferences to consider:

(1) The simplification of the issues.

(2) The necessity or desirability of amendments to the pleadings.

(3) The possibility of obtaining admissions of fact and of documents which will avoid unnecessary proof.

(4) The limitation of the number of witnesses.

(5) Lists of witnesses.

(6) Stipulations of evidence.

(7) Admissibility of evidence.

(8) Any preliminary motion filed.

(9) Any other procedural matters, which will expedite the hearing, process.

The prehearing conference will be held at a specified place and date before the Presiding Member after notice or at the beginning of the hearing, as the Presiding Member shall determine. An official reporter may record prehearing conferences.

C. Prehearing Conference Order. The Presiding Member shall prepare a written order which recited the action taken at the prehearing conference, the amendments allowed to the pleadings, and the agreements made by counsel as to any of the matters considered, and any ruling made by the Presiding Member. Such order when entered controls the subsequent course of the action unless modified by the Commission to prevent manifest injustice. The official transcript, if any, of the prehearing conference may serve as the order to the extent that it includes rulings and agreements on material questions raised at the prehearing conference.

D. Discovery. When a judge is formally charged with a violation of the Canons, once the judge obtains the services of an attorney, Commission Counsel promptly will contact the judge's attorney and offer to meet in order to discuss the case. Upon request by the judge's attorney, Commission Counsel will meet with the judge's attorney, outline the Commission's case, summarize what each of the Commission's witnesses is expected to say, and provide copies of all documents that the Commission intends to present at the hearing. It is the intent of the Commission that the judge and the judge's attorney have a clear understanding of the Commission's case in advance of the hearing and that they not be surprised by any of the Commission's evidence presented at the hearing. Any testimony or documents to be presented that come to the attention of Commission Counsel after the initial meeting with the judge's attorney will be disclosed promptly to the judge's attorney.

[Effective February 14, 2006.]

RULE 12. SUBPOENAS

A. Application for Subpoenas. An application for a subpoena shall be made at least fourteen (14) days before the hearing.

B. Issuance of Subpoenas. The Commission's Counsel shall issue the subpoenas requested if the application complies with these rules.

C. Service of Subpoenas; Motions to Quash. Subpoenas issued under this section shall be served upon the person to whom directed. Within seven (7) days after service of a subpoena, a motion to quash or modify the subpoena may be filed with the Commission.

[Effective February 14, 2006.]

RULE 13. HEARINGS

A. Order of Presentation. The Commission's Counsel shall present the case in chief against the judge, which shall be followed by the case on behalf of the judge. The judge shall be required to attend unless the Commission excuses his appearance.

B. Evidence. Evidence must be material and relevant to the issues. Hearsay evidence is admissible so long as it is material, relevant, and probative. Irrelevant, immaterial, insubstantial, and repetitive evidence shall not be permitted.

C. Objections. Objections to the admission or exclusion of evidence shall be in short form, stating the grounds relied upon. Objections may be stated in writing before the hearing commences. When the hearing is convened, all objections may be orally stated.

D. Exhibits. When written exhibits are offered in evidence, the original and eight (8) copies shall be presented. If the Commission or Presiding Member has not fixed a time for the exchange of exhibits, each party shall exchange copies of exhibits not later than fourteen (14) days before the hearing convenes.

E. Substitution of Copies for Originals. In its discretion, the Commission may permit the withdrawal of original documents offered in evidence and the substitution of true copies.

F. Records in Other Proceedings. If any portion of the record in any other proceeding is offered in evidence, a true copy of the same shall become an exhibit.

G. Transcript. An official reporter shall record hearings.

[Effective February 14, 2006.]

RULE 14. WAIVER OF PROCEDURAL RULES

A. Waivers of any procedural rules shall be in writing and signed by the judge and his attorney and by the Commission's Counsel. If the hearing has been convened, such waivers may be stated on the record rather than in writing.

[Effective February 14, 2006.]

RULE 15. DISPOSITION OF CHARGES

A. After an investigation has been concluded, the Commission may take any of the following actions:

(1) Remove the charges from the Commission's docket.

(2) If the Commission finds the charges against the judge to be well founded and of sufficient gravity to constitute the basis for retirement, censure or removal, it shall file a complaint against the judge in the Supreme Court of Virginia.

(3) If the Commission finds the charges against the judge to be well founded but not of sufficient gravity to constitute the basis for retirement, censure or removal, it may summon the judge before the Commission or designated Commission members, and advise the judge of its findings. The charges shall then be removed from Commission's the docket but may, nevertheless, be considered with any other future charges against the judge.

(4) If the Commission finds the charges against the judge to be well founded, the Commission may, with the consent of the judge, place the judge on a period of supervision under such terms and conditions as the Commission shall determine. Violation of such terms and conditions shall be grounds for a new charge of failure to cooperate with the Commission.

(5) If the Commission finds the charges against the judge to be well founded under 15 A(2), (3), or (4), the Commission shall transmit its findings and final order to the legislature in accordance with Va. Code § 17.1–918 and such information shall be sent to the judge.

B. The Commission may take any of the actions listed in the foregoing sections of this Rule after an informal conference with the judge, provided that the judge consents to such actions.

[Effective February 14, 2006.]

RULE 16. PRESERVATION OF FILES

A. It shall be the responsibility of Counsel to maintain the records of the Commission in the following manner:

B. Proceedings that are disposed of by Counsel or the Commission without an adverse finding by the Commission against a judge.

C. All records related to such proceedings shall be maintained in the Commission's confidential files. Counsel shall destroy such records upon the judge's death, resignation, or retirement not subject to recall.

D. Proceedings that are disposed of by the Commission after an adverse finding by the Commission against a judge.

E. All records related to such proceedings shall be maintained in the Commission's confidential files. Any adverse finding by the Commission against a judge shall be reported by Counsel to the General Assembly pursuant to Rule 15A(5), but shall not be re-reported upon any subsequent election or re-election of the judge. Counsel shall destroy all records relating to an adverse finding by the Commission against a judge upon the judge's death, resignation, or retirement not subject to recall.

F. Proceedings that are disposed of by filing a formal complaint in the Supreme Court of Virginia.

G. All records related to such proceedings shall be maintained in the Commission's confidential files. Counsel shall destroy such records upon the judge's death, resignation, or retirement not subject to recall. A copy of the record and briefs filed in the Supreme Court of Virginia, however, and any order issued by that Court in such proceedings, shall be retained permanently in the Commission's files.

H. All agendas and annotated agendas of the Commission's meetings shall be retained in the Commission's confidential files.

I. Counsel shall report to the Commission on an annual basis as to any records destroyed pursuant to this Rule.

[Effective February 14, 2006.]

RULE 17. EFFECTIVE DATE

These rules shall be effective February 14, 2006.

[Effective February 14, 2006.]

RULES OF THE VIRGINIA WORKERS' COMPENSATION COMMISSION

Effective January 1, 1994

Including Amendments Received Through October 15, 2015

Table of Rules

Definitions.

RULE 1. PREHEARING PROCEDURES

Rule

1.1. Employee's Original Claim for Benefits.
1.2. Employee's Claim on the Ground of Change in Condition or Other Relief.
1.3. Dismissal Upon Failure to File Supporting Evidence.
1.4. Employer's Application for Hearing.
1.5. Acceptance or Rejection of Claim or Application.
1.6. Review of Decision Accepting or Rejecting Claim or Application.
1.7. Compromise Settlement; Lump Sum Payment.
1.8. Discovery.
1.9. Informal Dispute Resolution.
1.10. Willful Misconduct.
1.11. Prehearing Statement.
1.12. Enforcement of the Act and Rules of the Commission; Sanctions.

RULE 2. HEARING PROCEDURES

2.1. Decision on the Record.
2.2. Evidentiary Hearing.
2.3. Expedited Hearing.

RULE 3. POSTHEARING PROCEDURES

3.1. Request for Review.
3.2. Written Statements.
3.3. Additional Testimony.
3.4. Oral Argument.

RULE 4. FILING DOCUMENTS

4.1. Agreements.
4.2. Medical Reports.

Rule

RULE 5. COST OF MEDICAL SERVICES

RULE 6. AWARD OF ATTORNEY'S FEES UNDER § 65.2–714 OF THE CODE OF VIRGINIA

6.1. Agreement Between Parties as to a Fee.
6.2. Parties Fail to Agree on a Fee.

RULE 7. EMPLOYER RESPONSIBILITIES

7.1. Proof of Insurance Coverage.
7.2. Posting Notices.

RULE 8. SELF–INSURANCE

8.1. The Commonwealth of Virginia, Its Municipalities and Political Subdivisions.
8.2. Confidentiality of Self–Insurer Information.

RULE 9. PAYMENT OF COMPENSATION

9.1. Waiting Period.
9.2. Direct Payment.

RULE 10. X–RAY EVIDENCE FOR COAL WORKERS' PNEUMOCONIOSIS CLAIMS

10.1. Limitation on X–Ray Submissions.
10.2. Reading by Pulmonary Committee.
10.3. Appointment of Pulmonary Committee.

RULE 11. PNEUMOCONIOSIS TABLE

RULE 12. HEARING LOSS TABLE

RULE 13. TABLE OF PERCENTAGE OF LOSS OF VISUAL ACUITY

RULE 14. DEFINITION OF COMMUNITY

DEFINITIONS

These rules are issued to provide procedures to identify and resolve disputed issues promptly through informal dispute resolution or hearing.

The following words and terms, when used in these rules, shall have the following meaning, unless the context clearly indicates otherwise:

"Act" means the Virginia Workers' Compensation Act.

"Commission" means the Virginia Workers' Compensation Commission.

"Employer" includes the employer's insurance carrier unless the context otherwise requires.

[Effective January 1, 1994.]

RULE 1. PREHEARING PROCEDURES

RULE 1.1. EMPLOYEE'S ORIGINAL CLAIM FOR BENEFITS

An employee's original claim for benefits shall be filed within the applicable statutes of limitation.

A. An original claim for benefits shall be in writing, signed and should set forth:

1. Employee's name and address;
2. Employer's name and address;
3. Date of accident or date of communication of occupational disease;
4. Nature of injury or occupational disease;
5. Benefits sought: temporary total, temporary partial, permanent total, permanent partial or medical benefits;
6. Periods of disability, if appropriate.

[Effective January 1, 1994. Amended effective March 12, 2009.]

RULE 1.2. EMPLOYEE'S CLAIM ON THE GROUND OF CHANGE IN CONDITION OR OTHER RELIEF

A. A change in condition claim must be in writing and state the change in condition relied upon. A copy of the claim should be sent to the employer.

B. Additional compensation may not be awarded more than 90 days before the filing of the claim with the Commission. Requests for cost of living supplements are not subject to this limitation.

[Effective January 1, 1994. Amended effective March 12, 2009.]

RULE 1.3. DISMISSAL UPON FAILURE TO FILE SUPPORTING EVIDENCE

If supporting evidence is not filed within 90 days after an employee's claim is filed, it may be dismissed upon motion of the employer after notice by the Commission to the parties.

[Effective January 1, 1994. Amended effective March 12, 2009.]

RULE 1.4. EMPLOYER'S APPLICATION FOR HEARING

A. An employer's application for hearing shall be in writing and shall state the grounds and the relief sought. At the time the application is filed with the Commission, a copy of the application and supporting documentation shall be sent to the employee and a copy to the employee's attorney, if represented.

B. Each change in condition application filed by an employer under § 65.2–708 of the Code of Virginia shall:

1. Be in writing;
2. Be under oath;
3. State the grounds for relief; and
4. State the date for which compensation was last paid.

C. Compensation shall be paid through the date the application was filed, unless:

1. The application alleges the employee returned to work, in which case payment shall be made to the date of the return.

2. The application alleges a refusal of selective employment or medical attention or examination, in which case payment shall be made to the date of the refusal or 14 days before filing, whichever is later.

3. The application alleges a failure to cooperate with vocational rehabilitation, in which case payment must be made through the date the application is filed.

4. An employer files successive applications, in which case compensation shall be paid through the date required by the first application. If the first application is rejected, payment shall be made through the date required by the second application.

5. The same application asserts multiple allegations, in which case payment is determined by the allegation that allows the earliest termination date.

D. An employer may file a change in condition application while an award is suspended.

E. No change in condition application under § 65.2–708 of the Code of Virginia shall be accepted unless filed within two years from the date compensation was last paid pursuant to an award.

F. A change in condition application may be accepted and docketed when payment of compensation continues.

[Effective January 1, 1994. Amended effective March 12, 2009.]

RULE 1.5. ACCEPTANCE OR REJECTION OF CLAIM OR APPLICATION

A. After receipt the Commission shall review the claim or application for compliance with the Workers' Compensation Act and Rules of the Commission.

B. The Commission may order the employer to advise whether the employee's claim is accepted or to provide reasons for denial.

1. Response to the order shall be considered a required report pursuant to § 65.2–902 of the Code of Virginia.

2. The employer's response to this order shall not be considered part of the hearing record.

C. If the employer's application is technically acceptable, the opposing party shall be permitted up to 15 days from the date the application was filed to present evidence in opposition to the application.

1. Pending acceptance or rejection of the application, the employer may suspend or modify compensation payments as of the date for which compensation was last paid.

2. If rejected, the Commission shall advise the employer of the reason for rejection and compensation shall be reinstated immediately.

3. If accepted, the application shall be referred:

a. For dispute resolution,

b. For decision on the record, or

c. For an evidentiary hearing.

[Effective January 1, 1994. Amended effective March 12, 2009.]

RULE 1.6. REVIEW OF DECISION ACCEPTING OR REJECTING CLAIM OR APPLICATION

A. A request for review of a decision accepting or rejecting a change in condition claim or application shall be filed within thirty (30) days from date of the decision. No oral argument is permitted.

B. The letter requesting a review should specify each determination of fact and law to which exception is taken. A copy of the request shall be sent to the opposing party.

C. The opposing party shall have 10 days from the date the review request is filed to provide a written response to the Commission.

D. Only information contained in the file at the time of the original decision along with the review request and any response from the opposing party will be considered. Additional evidence will not be accepted.

E. If rejection of a claim or application is affirmed on review, the penalty and interest provisions of §§ 65.2–524 and 65.2–707 of the Code of Virginia shall apply from the date the application was initially rejected.

[Effective January 1, 1994. Amended effective March 12, 2009; July 13, 2010.]

RULE 1.7. COMPROMISE SETTLEMENT; LUMP SUM PAYMENT

A. A proposed compromise settlement shall be submitted to the Commission in the form of a petition setting forth:

1. The matters in controversy;

2. The proposed terms of settlement;

3. The total of medical and indemnity payments made to date of submission and the date through which all medical expenses will be paid;

4. The proposed method of payment;

5. Such other facts as will enable the Commission to determine if approval serves the best interests of the claimant or the dependents.

B. The petition shall be signed by the claimant and, if represented, an attorney and by the other parties or their attorneys. An endorsing attorney must be licensed to practice in Virginia.

C. The petition shall be accompanied by:

1. A medical report stating the claimant's current condition and whether the injuries have stabilized;

2. An informational letter from the claimant or counsel stating whether the claimant is competent to manage the proceeds of the settlement and describing the plan for managing the proceeds;

3. A notarized affidavit attesting the claimant's understanding of and voluntary compliance with the terms of the settlement; and

4. A fee statement endorsed by the claimant and the claimant's attorney.

D. If the proposed settlement contemplates payment in a lump sum, the petition shall set forth in detail the facts relied upon to show that the best interests of the employee or the dependents will be served thereby.

If the proposed settlement contemplates an annuity, the petition shall state that the company issuing the annuity is authorized by the State Corporation Commission to transact the business of insurance in the Commonwealth and that, in case of default, the employer or carrier shall remain responsible for payment.

E. The parties shall submit an original proposed order, properly endorsed.

F. Payment shall be due within 10 days after entry of the order approving the compromise.

[Effective January 1, 1994. Amended effective March 12, 2009.]

RULE 1.8. DISCOVERY

A. Scope and Method. The scope of discovery shall extend only to matters which are relevant to issues pending before the Commission and which are not privileged. It is not ground for objection that the information sought will be inadmissible at the trial if the information sought appears reasonably calculated to lead to the discovery of admissible evidence. Discovery may be obtained by oral or written deposition, interrogatories to parties, production of documents or things, requests for admission, inspection of premises or other means of inquiry approved by the Commission.

B. Limiting Discovery. The Commission may limit the frequency or extent of discovery if it is unreasonably cumulative, duplicative, expensive or if the request was not timely made. The Commission will consider the nature and importance of the contested issues, limitations on the parties' resources and whether the information may be obtained more conveniently and economically from another source.

C. Stipulation to Discovery. Except as specifically provided by these rules, the parties may by written stipulation agree to other methods of discovery or provide that depositions may be taken before any person, at any time or place, upon any notice and in any manner and when so taken may be used like other depositions.

D. Supplementation of Responses. A party who has responded to a request for discovery with a response that was complete when made is under no duty to supplement a response to include information thereafter acquired unless such information materially affects a prior response.

E. Protective Order. Upon good cause shown, the Commission may enter an order limiting discovery to protect a party, a witness, or other person from embarrassment, oppression, or undue burden or expense.

F. Subpoenas. A party requesting a subpoena for witness or subpoena duces tecum shall prepare the subpoena and submit it to the Commission for insertion of return date and Clerk certification; a check or money order for service fee, payable to the appropriate sheriff's office, shall accompany the request. The Commission shall forward the subpoena and service fee to the designated sheriff's office, unless requested to do otherwise.

Subpoenaed records may be made returnable to the requesting party or, at the direction of the Commission, to the Clerk of the Commission or to a regional office. If subpoenaed records contain medical reports they must be filed with the Commission pursuant to Rule 4.2.

Requests for subpoenas may be filed with the Commission at Richmond or in the regional office assigned to hear the case.

1. *Subpoenas for Witnesses.* Requests should be filed at least 10 days prior to hearing.

2. *Subpoenas Duces Tecum.* Requests should be filed at least 15 days before hearing and the subpoena shall describe with particularity the materiality of the documents or articles to be produced.

All requests for subpoenas duces tecum shall be served on each counsel of record, or the unrepresented party, by delivering or mailing a copy to each on or before the day of filing. Each request shall have appended either acceptance of service or a certificate that copies were served in accordance with the law, showing the date of delivery or mailing.

G. Depositions. After a claim or application has been filed, any party may take the testimony of any person, including a party, by deposition upon oral examination or upon written questions.

The attendance of witnesses may be compelled by subpoena. The deposition of a party or physician may be taken without permission of the Commission. Leave of the Commission shall be obtained to take the deposition of any other persons. Depositions shall be taken in accordance with the requirements and limitations of the Rules of the Supreme Court of Virginia governing actions at law unless the parties stipulate to discovery as set forth in Rule 1.8(C), supra.

For good cause shown the deposition of an attending panel physician may be ordered to be taken at the expense of the employer if the physician has not prepared and completed an Attending Physician's Report (Form 6) or has not otherwise prepared written reports which are sufficient to answer questions concerning injury, diagnosis, causation, disability and other matters not stipulated and deemed by the Commission to be material to a claim or to a defense. The expenses of such depositions are subject to the approval of the Commission. Depositions shall be filed with the Commission and be made a part of the record.

H. Interrogatories to Parties. After a claim or application has been filed, interrogatories limited to contested issues may be served by one party on another party, more than 21 days before hearing without prior Commission approval.

Answers under oath to each interrogatory are to be filed within 21 days after service. Objections must be included with answers. If there is objection to an interrogatory and the party serving the interrogatory moves the Commission for relief, the hearing officer shall enter an order resolving the issue, after giving the parties an opportunity to state their positions in writing.

No party shall serve upon any other party, at one time or cumulatively, more than 15 interrogatories, including all parts and subparts, without leave of the Commission for good cause shown. Leave shall be timely requested in writing. Relevant interrogatories should be served promptly upon commencement of a contested claim.

It is not necessary to file interrogatories or answers with the Commission unless they are the subject of a motion.

I. Request for Admission. After a claim or application has been filed, a party may serve upon any other party a written request for the admission of the truth of any material matter.

Each request must be numbered and set forth separately. Copies of documents shall be served with the request unless they have been furnished or made available for inspection and copying.

An admission under this rule may be used only for providing evidence in the proceeding for which the request was made and shall not have force or effect with respect to any other claim or proceeding. An admission or denial must be offered in evidence to be made part of the record. A party is required to respond within 30 days or be subject to compliance under Rule 1.8(K) or sanctions under Rule 1.12.

J. Production of Wage Information. If the average weekly wage is contested, the employer shall timely file a wage chart showing all wages earned by an employee in its employment for the term of employment, not to exceed one year before the date of injury.

If an employee has earned wages in more than one employment, the employee shall have responsibility for filing information concerning wages earned in an employment other than the one in which claim for injury is made.

K. Failure to Make Discovery; to Produce Documentary Evidence; to Comply With Request for Admission. A party, upon reasonable notice to other parties and all persons affected thereby, may request an order compelling discovery as follows:

A timely request in writing in the form of a motion to compel discovery may be made to the Commission or to such regional office of the Commission where an application is assigned to be heard.

Failure of a deponent to appear or to testify; failure of a party on whom interrogatories have been served to answer; failure of a party or other person to respond to a subpoena for production of documents or other materials; or failure to respond to a request for admission shall be the basis for an order addressing a request to compel compliance or for sanctions, or both.

L. Disposition of Discovery Material. Any discovery material not admitted in evidence and filed in the Commission may be destroyed by the Clerk of the Commission after one year from entry of a final decision of the Commission or appellate court.

[Effective January 1, 1994. Amended effective March 12, 2009.]

RULE 1.9. INFORMAL DISPUTE RESOLUTION

At the request of either party, or at the Commission's direction, contested claims and applications for hearing will be evaluated and may be referred for informal dispute resolution. When it appears that a claim may be resolved by informal dispute resolution, the Commission will refer the case to a Commission representative who may schedule the parties for personal appearance or telephone conference. The Commission will attempt to identify disputed issues and to bring about resolution through agreement. Parties need not be represented by counsel. If agreement is reached it shall be reduced to writing and shall be binding.

Examples of limited issues often subject to prompt resolution are:

A. Average weekly wage;

B. Closed periods of disability;

C. Change in treating physician;

D. Contested medical issues including bills;

E. Permanent disability ratings;

F. Return to work;

G. Failure to report incarceration, change in address or return to work;

H. Attorney fee disputes.

If there is no agreement between the parties and there is no material fact in dispute, issues may be referred for decision on the record. If it is determined that material issues of fact are in dispute or that oral testimony will be required, the case will be referred to the docket for evidentiary hearing.

[Effective January 1, 1994. Amended effective March 12, 2009.]

RULE 1.10. WILLFUL MISCONDUCT

If the employer intends to rely upon a defense under § 65.2–306 of the Act, it shall give to the employee and file with the Commission no less than 15 days prior to the hearing, a notice of its intent to make such defense together with a statement of the particular act relied upon as showing willful misconduct.

[Effective January 1, 1994. Amended effective March 12, 2009.]

RULE 1.11. PREHEARING STATEMENT

The Commission may require a prehearing statement by the parties as to the particulars of a claim and the grounds of defense.

[Effective January 1, 1994. Amended effective March 12, 2009.]

RULE 1.12. ENFORCEMENT OF THE ACT AND RULES OF THE COMMISSION; SANCTIONS

In addition to the statutory authority of the Commission to levy fines, to assess attorney fees and punish contempt, the Commission may enforce its rules and the provisions of the Workers' Compensation Act upon motion of a party, or upon its own motion, after giving a party or other interested person the opportunity to be heard, by imposition of the following sanctions:

A. Rejection of a pleading including, but not limited to, all or part of a claim and grounds of defense;

B. Exclusion of evidence from the record;

C. Dismissal of a claim or application.

[Effective January 1, 1994. Amended effective March 12, 2009.]

RULE 2. HEARING PROCEDURES

At the request of either party, or at the Commission's direction, contested issues not resolved informally through prehearing procedures will be referred for decision on the record or evidentiary hearing.

[Effective January 1, 1994. Amended effective March 12, 2009.]

RULE 2.1. DECISION ON THE RECORD

When it appears that there is no material fact in dispute as to any contested issue, determination will proceed on the record. After each party has been given the opportunity to file a written statement of the evidence supporting a claim or defense, the Commission shall enter a decision on the record.

A. Written Statements. When the Commission determines that decision on the record is appropriate, the parties shall be given 20 days to submit written statements and evidence. Ten additional days shall be given to respond. For good cause shown additional time may be allowed. Copies of all written statements and evidence shall be furnished to the Commission and all parties.

B. Review. Request for review of decision on the record shall proceed under § 65.2–705 of the Code of Virginia and Rule 3.

[Effective January 1, 1994. Amended effective March 12, 2009.]

RULE 2.2. EVIDENTIARY HEARING

An evidentiary hearing by the Commission shall be conducted as a judicial proceeding. All witnesses shall testify under oath and a record of the proceeding shall be made. Except for rules which the Commission promulgates, it is not bound by statutory or common law rules of pleading or evidence nor by technical rules of practice.

The Commission will take evidence at hearing and make inquiry into the questions at issue to determine the substantial rights of the parties, and to this end hearsay evidence may be received. The party having the burden of proof shall have the right to open and close. Each party shall be allowed 20 minutes in which to present evidence unless prior arrangement is made through the Commission to extend hearing time.

A. Continuances. The parties should be prepared to present evidence at the time and place scheduled for hearing. A motion to continue will be granted only when it appears that material or irreparable harm may result if not granted.

B. Evidence.

1. Stipulations to agreed facts shall be included in the record. Each exhibit offered shall be marked and identified, and the record shall show whether it was admitted in evidence.

2. Reports and records of physicians and reports of medical care directed by physicians may be admitted in evidence as testimony by physicians or medical care providers. Upon timely motion, any party shall have the right to cross-examine the source of a medical document offered for admission in evidence.

3. The parties shall specifically designate, by author, deponent and date, medical reports, records or depositions to be received in evidence. Those portions of a deposition to be included in the record must be specifically identified by page and line.

4. Medical reports, records or deposition portions designated by the parties or included by the Commission will be admitted into evidence.

[Effective January 1, 1994. Amended effective March 12, 2009.]

RULE 2.3. EXPEDITED HEARING

An employee may request an expedited hearing before the Commission when the employer has submitted an Application for Hearing pursuant to Rule 1.4 and probable cause has been found to suspend benefits pending a hearing on the matter. An employee may also seek expedited determination of any disputed claim arising after the initial compensability of the accident has been determined by the Commission.

A. Written Request. An employee seeking an expedited hearing must file a written request with the Clerk's office, and a copy of the request shall be sent to the employer. The request must include, by way of description, attachment or enclosure, evidence sufficient to find that, without an expedited proceeding to determine the merits of the dispute, the employee will be caused to suffer severe economic hardship. What constitutes severe economic hardship will be determined by the Commission on a case-by-case basis. A copy of the employee's accepted request will be sent to the employer's counsel of record, the designated third-party administrator and the carrier, along with a Notice of Request For Expedited Hearing.

B. Loss of Income. When the employee alleges that he/she is not receiving compensation benefits, and is unemployed, unable to work, or only partially employed because of an injury compensable under the Act, the employee must establish that failure to grant an expedited hearing will result in severe, immediate economic hardship. In this regard, the Commission will consider, but is not limited in considering the following evidence:

1. Whether, and to what extent, the employee is presently employed, and what other sources of income are available to support the employee;

2. Whether the employee has dependents for whom the employee's wages, salary and/or other income were the sole or primary source of financial support;

3. Whether the employee has received notices of imminent or threatened foreclosure or eviction actions, or the employee is in a state of homelessness;

4. Whether the employee has received notices of imminent repossession of personal vehicles necessary for employment or medical treatment visits;

5. Whether the employee's financial difficulties were caused by the termination of workers' compensation benefits by prior adjudication, caused by other circumstances, or both; and

6. Any other evidence demonstrating that the employee's immediate ability to provide food, clothing and shelter will be threatened by failure to grant an expedited hearing.

C. Medical Expenses. When the employee seeks an expedited hearing, asserting that authorization of, or payment for recommended medical treatment has been denied by the employer or insurer, the employee must establish that failure to grant an expedited hearing will result in severe economic hardship. In this regard, the Commission will consider, but is not limited in considering the following evidence:

1. The general nature of the employee's injuries;

2. Whether, if authorization is being sought for recommended treatment not already obtained, the employee's physician has stated that the procedure must be performed on an emergent basis, and failure to do so will threaten the employee's life or result in immediate and severe deterioration of the employee's physical or mental condition;

3. Whether, if payment or reimbursement for medical expenses already incurred is being sought, reasonable and necessary ongoing medical treatment will be withheld for failure to pay for prior medical treatment, and that the withholding of such treatment will threaten the employee's life or result in immediate and severe deterioration of the employee's physical or mental condition;

4. The cost of the medical treatment in dispute, and the employee's ability to pay for it; and

5. Any other evidence demonstrating that failure to grant an expedited hearing on this issue will result in severe economic hardship.

D. Employer Response. Upon issuance of the Commission's Notice of Request for Expedited Hearing, the employer shall have fourteen (14) days to investigate the basis for the employee's expedited hearing request. Prior to, or at the expiration of the fourteenth day, the employer shall file with the Commission, by hand-delivery, electronic filing or certified mail, a written statement indicating whether the employer will or will not agree to the employee's request for expedited hearing. If the employer will not agree to proceed on an expedited basis, it must state, with specificity, the basis for its inability to proceed pursuant to an expedited hearing schedule. Filing shall be effective upon receipt by the Commission or its agent, or by placing the statement in certified mail.

E. Informal Conference. Once the Commission has received the employer's response statement, or fourteen (14) days pass without a filed response from the employer, the Commission shall schedule, as expeditiously as possible, an informal conference with the parties, whether in person, by teleconference or by other electronic transmission. With regard to expedited claims for payment of medical expenses pursuant to Rule 2.2(D), no informal conference will be scheduled until the employee submits medical evidence to the employer and the Commission supporting both the underlying claim and the necessity of expedited proceedings. During the informal conference, the Commission will discuss issues relevant to the grant or denial of an expedited hearing including, but not limited to, discovery between the parties, the timing and scheduling of depositions and the parties' ability to secure other relevant evidence in an expedited manner. The Commission will discuss the issues raised by the claim, and try to limit the scope of any matter ultimately referred to the expedited hearing docket by facilitating agreements between the parties. The Commission will confer with the parties about scheduling a hearing date at the informal conference, or by teleconference after the informal conference.

F. Grant or Denial of Expedited Hearing. During the informal conference, or within seven (7) days of its completion, the Commission will determine whether the claim underlying the request for expedited hearing is appropriate for the expedited hearing docket. If the request for an expedited hearing is granted, the Commission will advise the parties of this decision during the informal conference, or in writing within seven (7) days. If the Commission determines that the matter is not appropriate for the expedited docket, the parties will be advised of the Commission's determination, and the matter will be referred for regular processing.

G. Scheduling and Continuances. The matter will be set for a hearing no less than ten (10) days, and no more than twenty-eight (28) days after the expedited hearing was granted. Ordinarily, once the matter is set down for an expedited hearing, neither party will be granted a continuance. A continuance will be granted only for good cause shown, involving exceptional circumstances beyond the control of the party, or the party's attorney. Any claim pending on the expedited docket that is continued or non-suited at the request of the employee will be removed from the expedited docket, and shall not be reinstated for expedited proceedings.

H. Closing the Record. The record shall close at the end of the expedited hearing unless, for good cause shown, one or both parties are unable to present necessary medical or factual evidence.

I. Decision. The Deputy Commissioner hearing the case will issue an opinion within fourteen (14) days after the record closes in an expedited hearing proceeding.

J. Expedited Review. Either party may seek an expedited Review of the decision to grant or deny an expedited hearing. Parties seeking expedited Review must file a written request within seven (7) days of the date of the decision to grant or deny an expedited hearing. The written request must include a statement explaining the grounds for review, and must enclose all information the party believes is necessary for consideration of the request. A copy of the Request for Expedited Review shall be furnished to the opposing party. The Commission shall provide Notice of the request for expedited review within three (3) days of its receipt. The opposing party shall have seven (7) days from the date of the Commission's Notice to file a written statement addressing the merits of the review request, and enclosing all information it believes is necessary for consideration on review. The Commission shall review the decision to grant or deny an expedited hearing, and will issue a decision by Order within seven (7) days.

K. Review After Expedited Hearing. Review of a Deputy Commissioner's decision following an expedit-

ed hearing shall proceed according to the provisions of Rule 3.1 and § 65.2–705 of the Code of Virginia.
[Effective July 1, 2003. Amended effective March 12, 2009; July 13, 2010.]

RULE 3. POSTHEARING PROCEDURES

RULE 3.1. REQUEST FOR REVIEW

A request for review of a decision, order or award of the Commission shall be filed by a party in writing with the Clerk of the Commission within thirty (30) days of the date of such decision, order or award.

A request for review should assign as error specific findings of fact and conclusions of law. Failure of a party to assign any specific error in its request for review may be deemed by the Commission to be a waiver of the party's right to consideration of that error. The Commission may, however, on its own motion, address any error and correct any decision on review if such action is considered to be necessary for just determination of the issues.

A copy of the request for review shall be furnished to the opposing party. Upon request to the Clerk, a party may obtain a copy of the hearing transcript subject to an appropriate charge.
[Effective January 1, 1994. Amended effective March 12, 2009; July 13, 2010.]

RULE 3.2. WRITTEN STATEMENTS

The Commission will advise the parties of the schedule for filing brief written statements supporting their respective positions. The statements shall address all errors assigned, with particular reference to those portions of the record which support a party's position. No schedules for written statements shall be issued in connection with interlocutory appeals, appeals of award orders issued pursuant to agreements or appeals of decisions accepting or rejecting a change in condition claim or application. However, where a decision accepting or rejecting a change in condition claim or application has been appealed, the non-appealing party shall have ten days from the date the Request for Review was filed to provide a written response.
[Effective January 1, 1994. Amended effective March 12, 2009; July 13, 2010.]

RULE 3.3. ADDITIONAL TESTIMONY

No new evidence may be introduced by a party at the time of review except upon agreement of the parties. A petition to reopen or receive after-discovered evidence may be considered only upon request for review.

A petition to reopen the record for additional evidence will be favorably acted upon by the full Commission only when it appears to the Commission that such course is absolutely necessary and advisable and also when the party requesting the same is able to conform to the rules prevailing in the courts of this State for the introduction of after-discovered evidence.
[Effective January 1, 1994. Amended effective March 12, 2009.]

RULE 3.4. ORAL ARGUMENT

A party may request oral argument at the time of application for review. Otherwise, the review shall proceed on the record.

If oral argument is requested and the Commission considers it necessary or of probable benefit to the parties or to the Commission in adjudicating the issues, the parties will be scheduled to present oral argument.

Any party may request the Commission to schedule argument by telephone conference by giving notice to the Clerk of the Commission and to opposing counsel at least five days before the scheduled date for argument.

Each side will be limited to no more than 15 minutes for presentation of oral argument.

If oral argument is requested and the requesting party fails to appear in person or by scheduled telephone conference, the Commission may impose sanctions in the absence of good cause shown.
[Effective January 1, 1994. Amended effective March 12, 2009.]

RULE 4. FILING DOCUMENTS

RULE 4.1. AGREEMENTS

All agreements as to payment of compensation shall be reduced to writing by the employer and promptly filed with the Commission. If the claim is denied the employer shall notify the employee and the Commission promptly in writing.
[Effective January 1, 1994. Amended effective March 12, 2009.]

RULE 4.2. MEDICAL REPORTS

Each party shall promptly provide the other parties with copies of any medical records they receive as they receive them. Unless otherwise directed by the Commission or these Rules, the parties shall not file medical records with the Commission until a hearing request is filed. The requesting party shall promptly file medical records supporting the request, if applicable. After a hearing request has been filed, the parties shall file with the Commission only medical records that are related to the hearing request. These records shall be filed upon receipt by the party filing them, and are required reports subject to the provisions of 65.2–902. A party is not required to file copies of medical records that another party has already filed.

A medical care provider attending an injured employee shall, upon request from an employer or an employee, furnish a copy of required reports, at no cost except for a nominal copying charge.

A medical care provider is entitled to a reasonable fee for preparation of a narrative report written in response to a request from a party if the report requires significant professional research or preparation.

[Effective January 1, 1994. Amended effective March 12, 2009.]

RULE 5. COST OF MEDICAL SERVICES

A claimant under an award shall not be liable for the cost of medical services payable under the Act.

[Effective January 1, 1994. Amended effective March 12, 2009.]

RULE 6. AWARD OF ATTORNEY'S FEES UNDER § 65.2–714 OF THE CODE OF VIRGINIA

RULE 6.1. AGREEMENT BETWEEN PARTIES AS TO A FEE

An attorney's fee shall be awarded from sums recovered for the benefit of a third-party insurance carrier or a health care provider pursuant to § 65.2–714 of the Code of Virginia, if agreement is reached and an order, endorsed by counsel and the carrier or provider, identifying the amount of medical charges recovered and the agreed fee, is submitted to the Commission.

[Effective January 1, 1994. Amended effective March 12, 2009.]

RULE 6.2. PARTIES FAIL TO AGREE ON A FEE

A. An Attorney's fee shall be awarded from sums recovered for the benefit of a third-party insurance carrier or a health care provider pursuant to § 65.2–714 of the Code of Virginia, if the parties cannot agree, upon filing of a statement including the name and address of each carrier or provider from whom the fee is requested, the amount of the medical charge recovered for each carrier or provider and the amount of the fee requested, and certification that:

1. The claim was contested or that the defense was abandoned;

2. Prior to the filing of a request with the Commission the attorney and carrier or provider made a reasonable good faith effort to resolve the matter;

3. The insurance carrier or health care provider was given reasonable notice that a motion for an award of such fee would be made;

4. A copy of the motion has been sent to each carrier and health care provider identified.

B. If the request is referred to the evidentiary hearing docket, counsel must provide notice of the hearing to each carrier or provider. The notice must state the amount of the medical charge recovered for the carrier or provider, the amount of the attorney's fee requested and the time and place of the hearing.

[Effective January 1, 1994. Amended effective March 12, 2009.]

RULE 7. EMPLOYER RESPONSIBILITIES

RULE 7.1. PROOF OF INSURANCE COVERAGE

Every employer subject to the Act shall file with the Commission proof of compliance with the insurance provisions (§§ 65.2–800 and 65.2–801) of the Act. A notice from the insurer (Form No. 45F) certifying this fact will be received as acceptable proof.

[Effective January 1, 1994. Amended effective March 12, 2009.]

RULE 7.2. POSTING NOTICES

Every employer subject to the Act shall post and keep posted, conspicuously, in the plant, shop or place of business at a location frequented by employees, notice of compliance with the provisions of the Act. Such notice shall follow substantially the form prescribed by the Commission. The Commission will supply employers with printed notices upon request. Failure by an employer to give such notice to an employee may constitute waiver of the notice defense pursuant to § 65.2–600 of the Code of Virginia.

[Effective January 1, 1994. Amended effective March 12, 2009.]

RULE 8. SELF–INSURANCE

RULE 8.1. THE COMMONWEALTH OF VIRGINIA, ITS MUNICIPALITIES AND POLITICAL SUBDIVISIONS

Permission for self-insurance will be granted by the Commission to the Commonwealth and its political subdivisions and to Virginia municipalities upon application for certification, without submission of proof of financial ability and without deposit of bond or other security. However, the premium tax provided for in § 65.2–1006 of the Act shall be paid.

[Effective January 1, 1994. Amended effective March 12, 2009.]

RULE 8.2. CONFIDENTIALITY OF SELF–INSURER INFORMATION

No record of any information concerning the solvency and financial ability of any employer acquired by a Commissioner or his agent by virtue of his powers under the Act shall be subject to inspection; nor shall any information in any way acquired for such purposes by virtue of such powers be divulged by a Commissioner or his agent, unless by order of the court, so long as said employer shall continue solvent and the compensation legally due from him, in accordance with provisions of the Act, shall continue to be paid.

[Effective January 1, 1994. Amended effective March 12, 2009.]

RULE 9. PAYMENT OF COMPENSATION

RULE 9.1. WAITING PERIOD

If the employee is not paid wages for the entire day on which the injury occurred, the seven-day waiting period prescribed by the Act shall include the day of injury regardless of the hour of the injury.

All days or parts of days when the injured employee is unable to earn a full day's wages, or is not paid a full day's wages, due to injury, shall be counted in computing the waiting period even though the days may not be consecutive.

[Effective January 1, 1994. Amended effective March 12, 2009.]

RULE 9.2. DIRECT PAYMENT

All compensation due an injured employee or compensation awarded on account of death under the Act must be paid directly to the beneficiary in accordance with the award. This ruling applies whether or not the employee is represented.

Compensation awarded shall be paid promptly and in strict accordance with the award issued by the Commission. When an award provides for an attorney fee, the employer shall pay the fee directly to the attorney unless there is alternative provision in the award.

[Effective January 1, 1994. Amended effective March 12, 2009.]

RULE 10. X–RAY EVIDENCE FOR COAL WORKERS' PNEUMOCONIOSIS CLAIMS

RULE 10.1. LIMITATION ON X–RAY SUBMISSIONS

In any claim for first, second, or third stage pneumoconiosis under § 65.2–504 of the Code of Virginia, the employer and the employee each shall be limited to submission of not more than three medical interpretations (readings) of x-ray evidence without regard to the number of x-rays. For good cause shown, additional interpretations may be received as evidence if deemed necessary by the Commission.

[Effective January 1, 1994. Amended effective March 12, 2009.]

RULE 10.2. READING BY PULMONARY COMMITTEE

Any party to a contested claim, or the parties upon agreement, may submit the x-ray evidence to the Commission for interpretation by the Pulmonary Committee. If a party agrees to accept the x-ray reading of the Pulmonary Committee as the binding classification, the costs of evaluation shall be borne by the Commission.

[Effective January 1, 1994. Amended effective March 12, 2009.]

RULE 10.3. APPOINTMENT OF PULMONARY COMMITTEE

The Commission shall appoint a Pulmonary Committee to be composed of at least three qualified physicians certified as B readers under standards promulgated by the International Labour Organization (ILO).[1]

[Effective January 1, 1994. Amended effective March 12, 2009; July 13, 2010.]

[1]The General Assembly amended section 65.2–504 of the Virginia Code, effective July 1, 2000, to add subsection (E), which provides that "All members of any panel or committee required to interpret or classify a chest roentgenogram for the purposes of diagnosing a coal worker's pneumoconiosis shall be B-readers approved by the National Institute for Occupational Safety and Health."

RULE 11. PNEUMOCONIOSIS TABLE

A table for conversion of medically-classified categories of pneumoconiosis (under ILO standards) into stages of pneumoconiosis shall be promulgated by the Commission and information from the table shall be the basis for determining the amount of compensation due, if any, under § 65.2–504 of the Code of Virginia for coal workers' pneumoconiosis and under § 65.2–503 of the Code of Virginia for other pneumoconioses.

TABLE

Medical interpretations of radiographic evidence, for the purpose of conversion to stages under this table, shall be based upon the ILO 1980 International Classification of Radiographs of the Pneumoconioses.

First Stage:	Category	1 and 2 p,s
	"	1 q,t
Second Stage:	Category	3 p,s
	"	2 and 3 q,t
	"	1, 2 and 3 r,u
Third Stage:	Category	A, B and C

[Effective January 1, 1994. Amended effective March 12, 2009.]

RULE 12. HEARING LOSS TABLE

A table for determining compensable percentage of hearing loss shall be promulgated by the Commission.

All determinations are to be made (i) without the use of a hearing aid; and (ii) with a pure-tone audiometer by air conduction alone.

Hearing loss in decibels is to be recorded at 500, 1,000, 2,000 and 3,000 cycles per second. The audiometer must be calibrated to the ANSI 1969 standard.

The average decibel loss is to be translated into percentage of compensable hearing loss of each ear according to the following table:

Average Decibel Loss	Percent of Compensable Hearing Loss	Average Decibel Loss	Percent of Compensable Hearing Loss
27	0.8	60	55.0
28	2.2	61	56.7
29	3.6	62	58.3
30	5.0	63	60.0
31	6.7	64	61.7
32	8.3	65	63.3
33	10.0	66	65.0
34	11.7	67	66.7
35	13.3	68	68.3
36	15.0	69	70.0
37	16.7	70	71.7
38	18.3	71	73.3
39	20.0	72	75.0
40	21.7	73	76.4
41	23.3	74	77.8
42	25.0	75	79.2
43	26.7	76	80.6
44	28.3	77	82.0
45	30.0	78	83.4
46	31.7	79	84.8
47	33.3	80	86.2
48	35.0	81	87.6
49	36.7	82	89.0
50	38.3	83	90.4
51	40.0	84	91.8
52	41.7	85	93.2
53	43.3	86	94.6
54	45.0	87	96.0
55	46.7	88	97.4

Average Decibel Loss	Percent of Compensable Hearing Loss	Average Decibel Loss	Percent of Compensable Hearing Loss
56	48.3	89	98.8
57	50.0	90	
58	51.7	and	
59	53.3	over	100

No allowance for presbycusis is to be made

[Effective January 1, 1994. Amended effective March 12, 2009.]

RULE 13. TABLE OF PERCENTAGE OF LOSS OF VISUAL ACUITY

SNELLEN'S CHART

Snellen's Chart Readings	Percentage of Loss of Visual Acuity
20/20	0
20/25	5
20/30	10
20/40	20
20/50	25
20/60	33_2
20/70	40
20/80	50
20/90	62_2
20/100	75
20/110	80
20/120	85
20/130	87
20/140	89
20/150	91
20/160	93
20/170	95
20/180	97
20/190	99
20/200	100

Any other deviation from normal vision caused by the injury shall be considered.

[Effective January 1, 1994. Amended effective March 12, 2009.]

RULE 14. DEFINITION OF COMMUNITY

For the purpose of Code of Virginia Section 65.2–605, the word "community" shall mean one or more planning districts as set forth below:

Community	Planning District(s)
1	Districts 1 & 2
2	District 3
3	District 4
4	District 5
5	District 11 & 13
6	District 12
7	District 6
8	District 7
9	District 16
10	District 9 & 10
11	District 8
12	District 17 & 18
13	District 22 & 23
14	District 14 & 15
15	District 19

Virginia Planning District Map

Whenever an employee receives treatment outside of the Commonwealth, the Commission will determine the appropriate community in the state or territory where the treatment is rendered upon application of either the employee, employer (or its representative), or medical provider.

When the commission deems appropriate, it may consider additional data to determine the prevailing community rate.

(Effective July 1, 1996.)

[Effective July 1, 1996. Amended effective March 12, 2009.]

BYLAWS OF THE VIRGINIA STATE BAR AND COUNCIL

Including Amendments Received Through
October 15, 2015

Table of Articles

PART I. BYLAWS OF THE VIRGINIA STATE BAR

Article
I. Members.
II. Officers.
III. Election of President–Elect.
IV. Meetings.
V. Committees.

PART II. BYLAWS OF THE COUNCIL

I. Members.
II. Election of Council.
III. Secretary–Treasurer [Executive Director].

Article
IV. Notices of Meetings.
V. Meetings.
VI. Executive Committee.
VII. District Committees and the Disciplinary Board.
VIII. Standing Committees.
IX. Votes by Mail or Telephone.
X. Vacancies in Committees.
XI. Sections.

PART III. MISCELLANEOUS

Amending Bylaws.

PART I. BYLAWS OF THE VIRGINIA STATE BAR

ARTICLE I. MEMBERS

The Virginia State Bar is comprised of all attorneys licensed to practice law in Virginia.

[Amended effective October 24, 2014.]

ARTICLE II. OFFICERS

The officers of the Virginia State Bar shall be a President, a President–Elect, an Immediate Past President and a Secretary–Treasurer.

[Amended effective October 24, 2014.]

ARTICLE III. ELECTION OF PRESIDENT–ELECT

Sec. 1. Nominations. In order to qualify for election to the office of president-elect for the ensuing bar year, a candidate must be duly qualified as set forth in Paragraph 4 of the Rules of Court, Part Six, Section IV and must file a nominating petition with the executive director.

Sec. 2. Petition. The nominating petition shall be signed by at least 50 members of the Virginia State Bar and shall be signed by the candidate, who shall certify that he or she is qualified to run for the office. The nominating petition must be received by the executive director on or before October 1 of each year.

Sec. 3. Method of Election. In the event only one nominating petition is received by the executive director on or before October 1 of any year, the election for the office of president-elect shall be held at the next annual meeting in accordance with the provisions of Article IV, below.

In the event two or more nominating petitions are received by the executive director on or before October 1 of any year, the election of the president-elect will be in accordance with the provisions of Sections 4 and 5, below.

Sec. 4. Ballots. In the event nominating petitions for two or more candidates are received by the executive director, then:

(a) The executive director shall prepare a ballot which shall list in alphabetical order the names of those persons nominated to the office of president-elect.

(b) The ballot shall be distributed by mail or made available by electronic means to all members on or before November 5. The form of the ballot and the procedure for distribution, collection and tabulation of ballots shall be determined by the executive director.

(c) If any member fails to receive a ballot within ten (10) days of distribution, or by November 15, whichever is later, the intended recipient shall be given a replacement ballot upon executing an affidavit, in a form to be prescribed by the Executive Committee, averring (i) that no ballot has been received and (ii) that in the event the original ballot is subsequently received, it will promptly be returned unmarked to the executive director. The affidavit and request for a replacement ballot must be received by the executive director not later than November 22, and the replacement ballot must be returned to the executive director by December 1.

(d) If any member receives more than one ballot, he or she shall return the excess ballot or ballots, unmarked, to the executive director in the same envelope provided for return of his or her marked ballot.

Sec. 5. Ballot Elections. The ballots shall be collected and counted in a manner which assures the confidentiality of the members' votes. A plurality of the votes cast by all members shall elect. No ballot received by the executive director after December 1 shall be counted. Write–in votes shall be permitted, but the executive director may exclude illegible write-in votes and shall exclude write-in votes for any candidate ineligible to serve pursuant to these bylaws, if elected.

Sec. 6. General Provisions. The following provisions shall be applicable to any election of the president-elect under this Article III.

(a) For purposes of these provisions, a "member" is an active member in good standing of the Virginia State Bar. Only such person may nominate, be nominated, vote or be elected in any election for the office of president-elect.

(b) Records maintained by the executive director as to membership and good-standing status shall be controlling.

(c) The failure to comply with the dates designated for the occurrence or completion of certain acts shall not invalidate any election, unless substantial prejudice can be shown to have resulted therefrom.

(d) For purposes of determining voter and candidate eligibility, the membership list maintained by the executive director as of October 1 shall be controlling. Except to correct clerical errors in records maintained as of that date, no revisions or additions to the membership list for purposes of the election shall be made after October 1.

(e) The executive director shall announce to the bar the results of the election for the office of president-elect.

(f) Any responsibility assigned herein to be discharged by the executive director may be assumed and discharged by the Executive Committee, at its discretion.

(g) Any challenge to an election shall be resolved by a committee which shall be chaired by the president and shall include the president-elect, the immediate past president and two members of Council appointed by the president who shall not be current members of the Executive Committee.

[Amended effective February 19, 2005; October 19, 2012; October 24, 2014.]

ARTICLE IV. MEETINGS

Sec. 1. The Secretary shall give thirty days' notice of annual meetings of the bar, and such notice of special meetings of the bar as the Executive Committee shall prescribe in its call. Meetings of the organization shall be held at such times and places and after such notices as may be prescribed by the appropriate provisions of Section IV, Rules of the Supreme Court for the Integration of the Virginia State Bar and Council Bylaws.

Sec. 2. A quorum at any such meeting shall be as set forth in the Court Rules.

Sec. 3. The program and order of business at any meeting of the Virginia State Bar, unless otherwise ordered by the Council, shall be determined by the president in consultation with the president-elect and the executive director.

Sec. 4. Proceedings at any such meeting shall be governed by Roberts Rules of Order, except that no member shall without unanimous consent speak more than twice on any one subject nor more than five minutes at any one time.

Sec. 5. Voting at any such meeting shall be viva voce with each active member present entitled to vote, unless at least ten active members shall either before or immediately after such vote demand a vote by judicial circuits on a roll called in numerical order. In the latter event, each circuit shall be entitled to one vote for each twenty-five active members or fraction of twenty-five registered in that circuit. When a vote by circuits is ordered, the active members present from each circuit shall cast the entire vote to which such circuit is entitled. If there be a division among the active members present from any circuit as to how the vote of such circuit shall be cast, the vote of such circuit shall be divided and cast in proportion to the vote on such division, unless such circuit at a meeting of its members shall have adopted and caused to be certified to the Secretary a resolution providing that the entire vote of such circuit shall be cast as a majority of the active members from that circuit present and voting shall determine.

Provided, however, that in any election for the office of president-elect, voting shall be viva voce unless more than one candidate shall be duly nominated, in which event voting shall be by ballot as provided in Article III above.

Sec. 6. An active member shall be deemed to be registered in the circuit where he or she is entitled to vote for a member of Council provided that for the purpose of this section, no member may change his or her registration within five days preceding a meeting of the organization. At the opening of the meeting the Secretary shall post in a conspicuous place a list showing the number of votes to which each circuit is entitled and shall, upon the request of a member of any circuit, also post a list of the active members officially registered in that circuit. The lists so posted shall be conclusive as to the number of votes to which each circuit is entitled and as to the active members registered in each circuit, provided that any interested active member challenging the correctness of any such list, either as to the number of votes to which a circuit is entitled or as to the circuit in which an active member is registered, may appeal to the floor; but the circuits or members affected shall not vote on such appeal.

[Amended effective October 24, 2014.]

ARTICLE V. COMMITTEES

Sec. 1. Unless otherwise provided in the Supreme Court Rules, by action of Council, or elsewhere in these by-laws or the by-laws of Council, all committees shall be appointed by the president, who shall have power to determine the size and composition of the committee and to designate the chair thereof and to fill any vacancy therein.

Sec. 2. A majority of any committee shall constitute a quorum.

Sec. 3. In addition to the Executive Committee, district committees, and standing committees specified in the by-laws of Council, there shall be special committees to carry out the other ongoing work of the bar, and study committees, where appropriate in the judgment of the president, to examine and make recommendations on specific proposals or programs within a reasonably brief and discrete period of time.

Sec. 4. Members of special committees shall be appointed to three-year terms, with the exception of the Special Committee on Lawyer Malpractice Insurance whose members shall be appointed to five-year terms. No member shall serve more than two consecutive terms on such a committee. A member appointed to fill an unexpired term shall be eligible to serve two additional full terms. An eligible member wishing to be reappointed to a special committee shall be required to reapply in writing prior to the end of his or her current term under procedures established by Council and administered by the executive director. If any member of a committee fails to attend either three meetings during any bar year or two successive meetings of the committee without providing an explanation satisfactory to the committee chair, or in the case of a lawyer member, is declared not in good standing with the Virginia State Bar, such person's position shall automatically be considered vacated and filled as in the case of other vacancies.

Sec. 5. In making initial appointments to new special committees, the president shall appoint members to one, two and three-year terms so as to allow for the retirement or reappointment of one-third of the membership of each special committee at the end of each bar year.

Sec. 6. Effective July 1, 1996, the size of special committees shall be as specified by Council. A list of the committees and their respective sizes shall be maintained by the executive director. Changes in the size of special committees may be approved by the Executive Committee.

[Amended effective February 24, 1996; November 1, 2002; October 24, 2014.]

PART II. BYLAWS OF THE COUNCIL

ARTICLE I. MEMBERS

The Council is comprised of attorneys elected or appointed in accordance with applicable provisions of Section IV, Rules of the Supreme Court for the Organization and Government of the Virginia State Bar.

[Amended effective October 24, 2014.]

ARTICLE II. ELECTION OF COUNCIL

The election of members of Council for each circuit shall be by one of the two following methods.

Sec. 1. Circuit Bar Meeting. Prior to March 1 of any year in which a Council member from the circuit is to be elected, the executive director shall notify the Chief Judge of the circuit of the need for a meeting of the bar of the circuit and the number of vacancies to be filled. The executive director shall obtain from the Chief Judge the date and location for a meeting of the members of the circuit which shall be held prior to May 1. The executive director shall give at least fourteen days notice to the members of the meeting.

All members whose Virginia State Bar membership mailing addresses are maintained in the circuit may attend and vote at the meeting. A quorum shall consist of those members who vote at the meeting. No member shall vote by proxy. Prior to the meeting, the executive director shall transmit to the Chief Judge or the designated presiding officer a list of the members whose names appear on the membership roster for such circuit. The Chief Judge shall either preside at the meeting, designate another active or retired judge of the circuit to preside, or designate an attorney to preside who is neither a candidate for election to Council nor associated in the practice of law with a candidate nominated for election.

At the circuit meeting, any member eligible to vote in the circuit who is not then serving a second successive full term on Council shall be eligible for election. Nominations may be made at the circuit meeting or by any member eligible to vote in the circuit. No supporting petition or second for such nomination will be required. After the nominations are closed, an election by written ballot shall be conducted. In the event of a tie vote, the winner shall be chosen by lot drawn by the presiding judge or his designee.

Within ten days after the meeting, the presiding officer or the Chief Judge shall communicate the names of the person or persons elected to the executive director.

Sec. 2. Ballot. On or about March 1, the executive director shall cause to be distributed by mail or electronic means to every member eligible to vote in the circuit a notice of any vacancy or vacancies on Council, and a brief description of the method of nomination and voting. All members whose Virginia State Bar membership mailing addresses are maintained in the circuit are eligible to vote.

Nominations for election to Council shall be by petition filed by the candidate with the executive director. Such petition shall be signed by not fewer than ten other members eligible to vote in the circuit, and shall be accompanied by a statement of qualifications not exceeding one hundred and fifty words. Nominations must be filed in the office of the executive director on or before April 1. Any petition failing to comply with these requirements shall be rejected.

On or before April 15, the executive director shall distribute by mail or electronic means to all eligible members of the circuit a ballot containing the names of all persons nominated, along with each nominee's statement of qualifications.

The form of the ballot and the procedure for distribution, collection and tabulation of ballots shall be determined by the executive director. In the event of a tie vote, the executive director shall pick the winner by lot. No ballot received by the executive director after May 1 shall be counted.

Write-in votes shall be permitted, but the executive director may exclude illegible write-in votes and shall exclude write-in votes for any candidate ineligible to serve pursuant to these bylaws, if elected. In those instances where there are more candidates for Council positions than there are positions to be filled from the circuit, the ballot will contain instructions to vote only for the same number of persons or fewer person(s) as there are positions to be filled; ballots which do not conform to this requirement will not be counted.

Sec. 3. General Provisions. The following provisions shall be applicable to both methods of election:

(a) The timeline for special elections to fill vacancies on Council shall be determined by the executive director.

(b) For purposes of these provisions, a "member" is an active member in good standing of the Virginia State Bar. Only such person may nominate, be nominated, vote or be elected in any Council election.

(c) Records maintained by the executive director as to membership, good-standing status and assignment of a member to a particular circuit shall be controlling.

(d) The failure to comply with the dates designated for the occurrence or completion of certain acts shall not invalidate any election unless substantial prejudice can be shown to have resulted therefrom.

(e)

1) In all elections the candidate receiving the highest number of votes shall be elected.

2) In the event that more than one full term is to be filled by a circuit at any single election, the candidates receiving the highest number of votes shall be elected.

3) In the event that a regular election and special election to fill an unexpired term are held simultaneously in the same circuit, they shall be conducted as a single election and the successful candidate receiving the highest number of votes shall be entitled to choose either a regular term or the unexpired term, with the choice passing down in order until the unexpired term is selected. The successful candidate(s) receiving the lower number of votes shall be elected to fill the term(s) not chosen. In the event two or more unexpired terms are to be filled in the same election, the longer unexpired term(s) shall go to the successful candidate(s) receiving the highest number of votes who choose(s) to fill an unexpired term.

4) As a part of the election process in each circuit under these bylaws, the voting members of the circuit shall prescribe the method for that circuit's next election and, in the event of a meeting, shall determine the length of time during which ballots may be cast in the next election, not to exceed one business day. A vote to change the method of election shall be by majority of votes cast. The ballot in each circuit's election shall provide a space for the voting member to indicate a preference for one of the two election methods described by these bylaws. For the meeting method, the ballot shall also provide a space to indicate whether voting shall be allowed all day, half day or only during the meeting. No quorum call shall be required for any meeting.

5) For purposes of determining voter and candidate eligibility, the membership list maintained by the executive director as of March 15 shall be controlling. Except to correct clerical errors in records maintained as of that date, no changes in circuit membership, revisions or additions to the membership list for purposes of the election shall be made after March 15.

6) The executive director shall announce to the bar the results of the election for the office of Council.

7) Any challenge to an election shall be resolved by a committee which shall be chaired by the president and shall include the president-elect, the immediate past president, and two members of Council appointed by the president who shall not be current members of the Executive Committee.

8) Should a member of Council change his or her address of record from the circuit he or she represents, his or her seat shall be declared vacant. A vacancy among the elected members of Council shall

be cause for a special election to occur for the unexpired term of the vacant seat.

[Amended effective October 24, 2014.]

ARTICLE III. SECRETARY–TREASURER [EXECUTIVE DIRECTOR]

Sec. 1. The Secretary–Treasurer [Executive Director] shall perform all duties prescribed by the Rules and these by-laws, and in addition such other duties as may be delegated to him from time to time by the Council or Executive Committee. He or she shall act as Secretary of the Bar, of the Council and of the Executive Committee.

Sec. 2. The Secretary–Treasurer [Executive Director] shall give bond of $250,000 with corporate surety conditioned for the faithful performance of his or her duties, the premium of which shall be paid by the bar.

[Amended effective October 24, 2014.]

ARTICLE IV. NOTICES OF MEETINGS

The Secretary shall give twenty days' notice by mail of all meetings of the Council, and five days' notice by mail of all meetings of the Executive Committee. Notice of mailing shall commence on the date of mailing.

[Amended effective October 24, 2014.]

ARTICLE V. MEETINGS

Sec. 1. In the absence of specific action by the Council, the Executive Committee shall fix the time and place of the annual meeting of the bar, and may call any special meetings of the bar at such time and place as it shall designate.

Sec. 2. In the absence of specific action by the Council, the Executive Committee shall fix the time and place of all meetings of the Council. There shall be at least two meetings annually. Special meetings of the Council may be called at any time by the Executive Committee. The Executive Committee shall call a special meeting at the written request of twelve members of the Council.

Sec. 3. The Executive Committee shall meet on the call of the president or of the president-elect and a meeting shall be called at the written request of three members of the committee.

Sec. 4. Proceedings at all meetings shall be governed by Roberts Rules of Order, except that no member shall without unanimous consent speak more than twice on any one subject or more than five minutes at any one time.

[Amended effective October 24, 2014.]

ARTICLE VI. EXECUTIVE COMMITTEE

Sec. 1. There shall be an Executive Committee consisting of thirteen members, six of whom shall be elected annually by and from the Council, with the president, president-elect, immediate past president, President of the Young Lawyers Conference, Chair of the Senior Lawyers Conference, Chair of the Conference of Local Bar Associations, and Chair of the Diversity Conference serving as ex officio members.

Sec. 2. A quorum of the Executive Committee shall consist of six members thereof.

Sec. 3. The Executive Committee shall have authority to:

(a) Allocate funds as required for authorized bar purposes and functions within amounts available to the bar;

(b) Employ such staff as it deems necessary and fix the duties and compensation of such staff;

(c) Cause proper books and records of account to be kept and audited annually, and cause proper financial statements of receipts and expenditures to be prepared and regularly presented to Council;

(d) Review annually the performance of the Executive Director, Deputy Executive Director and Bar Counsel and set the compensation of each;

(e) Review matters which are placed on the agenda for Council meetings and make recommendations to Council when appropriate; and

(f) Between meetings of Council, perform any other duties and powers prescribed for Council under any of the rules of the Supreme Court of Virginia, except such duties and powers as Council may reserve to itself or delegate to other committees.

[Amended effective July 1, 1998. Approved after November 21, 2002. Amended effective February 21, 2004; June 13, 2013; October 24, 2014.]

ARTICLE VII. DISTRICT COMMITTEES AND THE DISCIPLINARY BOARD

Sec. 1. District Committees. The several district committees provided for by Part 6, Section IV, Paragraph 13 of the Rules of Court and elected by the Council shall be known as District Committees under numerical designation of the respective districts, for example, First District Committee, etc. A district committee shall consist of ten or, in the discretion of Council, twenty, thirty or forty members. Three members of a ten-member district committee, six members of a twenty-member district committee, nine members of a thirty member district committee, and twelve members of a forty member district committee shall be non-lawyers. All other district committee members shall be active members of the bar. No member of the Council shall be a member of a district committee. All potential district committee appointees shall fulfill the qualification requirements provided for in Paragraph 13 before appointment.

Effective July 1, 1992, the District Committees shall be comprised of the following judicial circuits:

First District Committee: Circuits 1, 3, 5, 7 and 8

Second District Committee: Circuits 2 and 4 (2 sections)

Third District Committee: Circuits 6, 11, 12, 13 and 14 (3 sections)

Fourth District Committee: Circuits 17 and 18 (2 sections)

Fifth District Committee: Circuits 19 and 31 (3 sections)

Sixth District Committee: Circuits 9 and 15

Seventh District Committee: Circuits 16, 20 and 26

Eighth District Committee: Circuits 23 and 25

Ninth District Committee: Circuits 10, 21, 22 and 24

Tenth District Committee: Circuits 27, 28, 29 and 30 (2 sections)

The Secretary shall notify the members of each district committee of their appointments and each district committee shall meet within forty (40) days thereafter and shall elect from their attorney members a Chair, Vice–Chair, and Secretary and such other officers as they deem necessary.

Sec. 2. Disciplinary Board. The Council shall recommend persons to the Court for appointment as members of the Disciplinary Board. The Disciplinary Board shall consist of twenty members, four of whom shall be non-lawyers and sixteen of whom shall be active members of the bar. The Council shall also recommend attorney members of the Disciplinary Board to the Court to serve as Chair and two Vice Chairs. All potential Disciplinary Board appointees shall fulfill the qualification requirements provided for in Paragraph 13 before appointment.

[Amended effective October 21, 2005; October 24, 2014.]

ARTICLE VIII. STANDING COMMITTEES

Sec. 1. Committee on Legal Ethics. There shall be a standing committee to be appointed by the president and to be known as the Committee on Legal Ethics. The committee shall consist of nine active members of the bar, at least two of whom shall be members of the Council. All powers and duties of the Council with respect to legal ethics, not otherwise delegated or reserved, shall be exercised and discharged by the committee.

Members shall be appointed to three-year terms. No member shall serve more than two consecutive three-year terms. A member appointed to fill an unexpired term shall be eligible to serve two additional full three-year terms. An eligible member wishing to be reappointed shall be required to reapply in writing prior to the end of his or her current term under procedures established by Council and administered by the executive director.

Sec. 2. Committee on Unauthorized Practice of Law. There shall be a standing committee to be appointed by the president and to be known as the Committee on the Unauthorized Practice of Law. The committee shall consist of nine members. Seven of the members shall be active members of the bar, at least two of whom shall be members of the Council. Two of the members shall be non-lawyers. All powers and duties of the Council with respect to the unauthorized practice of the law, not otherwise delegated or reserved, shall be exercised and discharged by the committee.

Members shall be appointed to three-year terms. No member shall serve more than two consecutive three-year terms. A member appointed to fill an unexpired term shall be eligible to serve two additional full three-year terms. An eligible member wishing to be reappointed shall be required to reapply in writing prior to the end of his or her current term under procedures established by Council and administered by the executive director.

Sec. 3. Committee on Lawyer Discipline. There shall be a standing committee to be appointed by the president and to be known as the Committee on Lawyer Discipline. The committee shall consist of twelve persons, ten of whom shall be active members of the bar and two shall be non-lawyers. In addition, the vicechairman of the Virginia State Bar Disciplinary Board shall be an ex-officio, non-voting member of the committee. At least two of the lawyers who are members shall be members of the Council. All members shall serve a three-year term and the president shall appoint members to the committee so as to allow for the retirement from the committee of one third of its membership at the end of each fiscal year. No member shall serve more than two consecutive three-year terms. A member appointed to fill an unexpired term shall be eligible to serve two additional full three-year terms. An eligible member wishing to be reappointed shall be required to reapply in writing under procedures established by Council and administered by the executive director. All powers and duties of the Council with respect to operation of the bar's disciplinary system, not otherwise delegated or reserved, shall be exercised and discharged by the committee.

Sec. 4. Committee on Professionalism. There shall be a standing committee to be appointed by the president and to be known as the Committee on Professionalism. The committee shall consist of fifteen members, each of whom shall be an active or judicial member of the bar. At least two of the committee members shall be members of the Council, at least three shall be current or former members of the faculty of the mandatory course on professionalism, and at least one shall, when initially appointed, be an officer or member of the board of governors of the Young Lawyers Conference. In addition, the Virginia State Bar Counsel shall be an ex officio member of the committee. All members shall serve for a three-year term. No member may serve more than two consecutive three-year terms. A member appointed to fill an unexpired term shall be eligible to serve two additional full three-year terms. An eligible member wishing to be reappointed shall be required to reapply in writing under procedures established by Council and administered by the executive director. All powers and duties of Council with respect to the implementation of Paragraph 13.1 of Part Six, Section IV of the Rules of the Supreme Court of Virginia, and with respect to professionalism in the practice of law in Virginia, not otherwise delegated or reserved, shall be exercised and discharged by the Committee.

Sec. 5. Budget and Finance Committee. There shall be a standing committee to be appointed by the president and to be known as the Budget and Finance Committee. The committee shall consist of nine active members of the bar, three of whom shall be elected members of the Executive Committee and three of whom shall be other members of Council. In addition, the president-elect shall serve as an ex officio member.

All members, other than the president-elect, shall serve three-year terms. No member shall serve more than two consecutive three-year terms. A member appointed to fill an unexpired term shall be eligible to serve two additional full three-year terms. An eligible member wishing to be reappointed shall be required to reapply in writing under procedures established by Council and administered by the Executive Director.

The committee shall perform such tasks as are delegated or assigned by the Executive Committee and/or the Bar Council. The committee shall work with appropriate members of the bar staff to develop the bar's annual budget and present the budget to the Executive Committee and Council for approval. The committee shall also be responsible for reviewing and making recommendations with respect to the bar's appropriation requests prior to their submission to the Commonwealth of Virginia, Department of Planning and Budget. The committee shall also be responsible for assessing and making recommendations to the Executive Committee and Council regarding other budget matters, including personnel issues which are budget-related or budget-driven.

[Amended effective July 1, 1995; February 24, 1996; June 19, 1997; July 1, 1998; October 1, 2000; June 16, 2011; October 24, 2014.]

ARTICLE IX. VOTES BY MAIL OR TELEPHONE

By unanimous consent of the members of any committee, all questions before such committee may be settled by mail ballot or telephone call.

[Amended effective October 24, 2014.]

ARTICLE X. VACANCIES IN COMMITTEES

All vacancies in committees appointed by the president shall be filled by him. Vacancies in other committees shall be temporarily filled by the president, his or her appointees to act until the next meeting of the Council.

[Amended effective October 24, 2014.]

ARTICLE XI. SECTIONS

The Council may create and abolish sections as it may consider necessary or desirable to accomplish the purposes and serve the interests of the Virginia State Bar and of the sections and shall prescribe the powers and duties of the sections. The bylaws of any section shall be subject to approval of Council.

[Amended effective October 24, 2014.]

PART III. MISCELLANEOUS

AMENDING BYLAWS

Upon motion of a Council member, the bylaws contained in either Part I or Part II may be amended at any regular meeting of the Bar Council provided there has been at least 30 days' notice of the proposed amendment to all Virginia State Bar members. Amendment of the bylaws must be by a two-thirds vote of the Council members present and voting at that regular meeting.

[Adopted effective June 12, 2014. Amended effective October 24, 2014.]

MANDATORY CONTINUING LEGAL EDUCATION REGULATIONS

Effective July 1, 1991

Including Amendments Received Through October 15, 2015

Table of Regulations

Purpose.

Regulation

101. Definitions.
102. Requirements and Computations.
103. Standards for Approval of Programs.
104. Procedure for Approval of Programs.
105. Procedure for Accreditation of Sponsors.
106. Delegation.
107. Board's Determination and Review.
108. Reporting of Certification Procedures.

Regulation

109. Noncompliance, Restoration and Reinstatement.
110. Exemptions.
111. Waivers, Extensions and Deferrals.
112. Representations by Members.

Form

2. Certification of Attendance.
3. Certification of Teaching.
4. Attorney Application for CLE Course Approval.
4. Law Firm Sponsor Application for CLE Approval.
4. Sponsor Application for CLE Course Approval.

PURPOSE

The Virginia Supreme Court has established, by Rule of Court, a mandatory continuing legal education program in the Commonwealth of Virginia, which requires each active member of the Virginia State Bar annually to complete a minimum of twelve (12) hours of approved continuing legal education courses, of which at least two (2) hours shall be in the area of legal ethics or professionalism, unless expressly exempted from such requirement.

The Virginia Supreme Court has established a Continuing Legal Education Board to administer the program and has given to it those general administrative and supervisory powers necessary to effectuate the purposes of the Rule, including the power to adopt reasonable and necessary regulations consistent with the Rule.

Pursuant to this authority, these regulations have been adopted by the Continuing Legal Education Board.

[Amended effective November 1, 2011.]

REGULATION 101. DEFINITIONS

As used in these regulations, the following definitions shall apply:

(a) The "Rule" shall mean the provisions of the Mandatory Continuing Legal Education (also referred to as "MCLE") Rule established by Paragraph 17 of Section IV, Part Six, Rules of Virginia Supreme Court.

(b) The "Board" shall mean the Virginia State Bar Mandatory Continuing Legal Education Board established by Paragraph B of the Rule.

(c) A "Member" as defined by Paragraph 2 of Section IV, Part Six, Rules of Virginia Supreme Court, shall comprise all attorneys-at-law in this commonwealth.

(d) An "Active Member," shall mean an Active or Emeritus Member as defined by Paragraph 3 of Section IV, Part Six, Rules of Virginia Supreme Court.

(e) A "newly-admitted member" shall mean a person first admitted to practice during the current completion period.

(f) A "program sponsor" or "sponsor" is any person or entity presenting or offering to present one or more continuing legal education programs.

(g) The terms "course" and "program" mean a discrete continuing legal education (also referred to as "CLE") offering, regardless of length or daily schedule, provided that the course or program is a minimum of 30 minutes in length.

(h) An "accredited sponsor" shall mean an organization which, based on a history of providing approved courses and pursuant to Regulation 105, has been granted approval for its programs. The programs must meet the approval standards of Regulation 103 and are not subject to the individual course application procedures of Regulation 104(a).

(i) An "approved course" means a course expressly approved by the Board for the relevant completion period or a course offered by an accredited sponsor during the completion period for which the sponsor is accredited and meets the approval standards of Regulation 103.

(j) A "pre-recorded course" means a program where a live presentation has been recorded and presented via any electronic media (e.g., videotaped, DVD or CD–ROM presentations, audiotaped or CD presentations, pre-recorded telephone seminars or webcasts, on-demand online courses, etc.) that does not include simultaneous, live interaction with the presenter.

(k) A "specially approved course or program" means a course which does not meet the standards of regulation 103(b) and (c) but which, because of its significant value to the practice of a member who has sought approval, has been approved by the Board for such member. As to such member, the term "approved course" includes a specially approved course or program.

(*l*) The term "panel(s)" shall mean a committee or committees organized by the Board for the purpose of expeditiously considering and deciding matters arising under the Rule and these regulations.

(m) The term "Director of MCLE" or "MCLE Director" shall mean the head of the Mandatory Continuing Legal Education Department of the Virginia State Bar who acts as the liaison and administrative staff for the Board.

(n) A course or program offered "in-house" means one sponsored by a single private law firm, a single corporate law department or a single federal, state or local governmental agency or military branch for lawyers who are members or employees of the firm, department, agency or branch.

(*o*) The term "completion period" shall mean a period of one year beginning on November 1, of one year and ending on October 31 of the next year; provided, however, that the next completion period following June 30, 2001, shall be July 1, 2001, to October 31, 2002.

(p) The term "faculty member" shall mean a person qualified by practical or academic experiences to teach the subject he or she covers.

(q) "Credit hours" (also referred to in context as "hours," "credits," and "hours credit") are the 60–minute units used for measuring completion of Mandatory Continuing Legal Education as required by the Rule.

(r) "Ethics credits" are credit hours which apply toward Mandatory Continuing Legal Education in the area of legal ethics or professionalism as required by the Rule.

(s) A "qualified ethics course or component" is a clearly identified segment of a course or program which meets the requirements of Regulation 103(d) and is devoted to one or more topics embraced in recognized formulations of rules of professional conduct or codes of professional responsibility applicable to attorneys and/or to the systems and procedures which have been established for enforcement and interpretation of those rules or codes. An ethics component in a course or program involving a substantive area of law may constitute a "clearly identified segment" if the integration of the substantive material is necessary to understand the ethical topic, and if the ethical topic is the primary focus of the segment. Such a segment must be appropriately described or entitled in the course materials and must have a defined duration in the course or program schedule.

(t) A "qualified professionalism course or component" is a clearly identified segment of a course or program which meets the requirements of Regulation 103(d) and is devoted to one or more topics designed to educate and encourage attorneys to aspire to and achieve higher and more noble standards of professional conduct than the minimum standards set forth in recognized formulations of rules of professional conduct or codes of professional responsibility. All or part of a malpractice program may qualify as a professionalism course or component if it is devoted to one or more topics designed to educate and encourage attorneys to take measures in the conduct of the practice of law to serve the interests of the client, consistent with the attorney's fiduciary duty to the client, and to endeavor to maintain an appropriate standard of care in the practice of the profession. Such a course or component will not be approved if the primary focus is malpractice litigation tactics or strategy. A professionalism component in a course or program involving a substantive area of law may constitute a "clearly identified segment" if the integration of the substantive material is necessary to understand the professionalism topic, and if the professionalism topic is the primary focus of the segment. Such a segment must be appropriately described or entitled in the course materials and must have a defined duration in the course or program schedule.

(u) A "course presented by distance learning methods" includes any course in which the participant seeking credit received the instruction at a location different from the location from which the instruction was presented or at a time different from the time when the instruction was presented. Thus, all courses presented to participants from pre-recorded media (e.g., videotape, DVD or CD–ROM presentations, audiotape or CD presentations, pre-recorded telephone seminars or webcasts, on-demand online courses, etc.) are "courses presented by distance learning methods." Similarly, any course taken by a participant at a location separate from the instructor (e.g., live telephone seminars, live webcasts, live videoconferences, etc.) are "courses presented by distance learning methods." (Comment: See MCLE Board Opinion 16.)

(v) The term "online MCLE record" shall mean the electronic access to the individual attorney's MCLE record maintained by the MCLE Department of the Virginia State Bar.

[Amended September 1, 1998; August 7, 2000; July 1, 2001; November 1, 2004; November 1, 2011.]

REGULATION 102. REQUIREMENTS AND COMPUTATIONS

(a) Each active member, other than a newly-admitted member as defined in Regulation 101, shall complete, during each completion period in which he or she is an active member for any part thereof, a minimum of twelve (12) credit hours of approved continuing legal education (also referred to as CLE) courses, of which at least two (2) hours shall be in the area of legal ethics or professionalism. Of the twelve credit hours required, no more than eight (8) may be earned from prerecorded courses. Credit must be obtained in the manner hereinafter provided, unless expressly exempted therefrom pursuant to the provisions of Regulation 110 or waived pursuant to Regulation 111.

(b) Credit will be given to a member who personally attends an approved course and to a member who prepares written materials for an approved course and to a member who personally participates as an instructor for such course. Credit in the area of legal ethics or professionalism will be given a member who attends a course approved for credit in such area and to a member who personally prepares materials for a qualified ethics or professionalism component of such course and to a member who personally participates as an instructor for such a component.

(c) Credits for attendance will be awarded on the basis of time spent in personal attendance at an approved course which meets the standards of these regulations. Credits for teaching will be awarded on the basis of time spent in personal participation as an instructor at an approved course. However, no credit will be awarded for teaching and preparation of a "specially approved course or program." Credit hours will be computed by calculating the total instructional minutes attended or taught for the course, rounded to the nearest half hour. Credit will not be given for time spent in meal or coffee breaks. Credit will not be given for keynote speeches or introductory remarks or time spent on any subject matter which is not directly related to instruction pertinent to that course.

EXAMPLES:

(1) A member attends a one-day course or seminar with seven (7) segments, each lasting 50 minutes. Two of the segments are in the area of legal ethics or professionalism under the standards set forth in Regulation 103. Credit hours will be computed by calculating the total instructional minutes rounded to the nearest half hour. Since there are 350 total instructional minutes (5 hours, 50 minutes) the Board will round this time to the nearest half hour and the member will receive six (6) hours credit, not seven (7). Of such six (6) hours credit, one and one-half (11/2) hours (100 minutes rounded to the nearest half hour) will be in the area of legal ethics or professionalism.

(2) A member attends a course or program which is presented all day Friday and on Saturday morning. The member attends a 3 hour, 15 minute Friday morning session; a 2 hour, 15 minute Friday afternoon session; and a 3 hour, 10 minute Saturday morning session. Since the total instruction time is eight (8) hours and 40 minutes for the two-day program, the Board will round this time to the nearest half hour and the member will receive 8 1/2 hours of credit.

(3) A member attends a course or program which is advertised as having been "approved by the Virginia Mandatory Continuing Legal Education Board" for six (6) credit hours, of which one and one-half (1 1/2) apply in the area of legal ethics or professionalism. No further computation need be made by the member if he attends the entire course or program.

(4) A member personally teaches any of the courses in the previous examples. The teaching member will receive credit hours for teaching time computed in the same fashion as the credit hours are computed for the attending member.

(5) A member is a teacher at a one-day course or program with seven (7) segments, each lasting 50 minutes. Application forms are filed certifying that the member taught one segment and also attended one segment. The member did not attend or teach the other five segments. Since the member attended or taught 100 total instructional minutes for the course, the Board will round this time to the nearest half hour and the member will receive 1 1/2 hours of credit. The member does not receive one credit hour for 50 minutes teaching plus one credit hour for the other 50 minutes attending.

(d) Credits for preparation will be awarded on the basis of time spent by a member (i) in preparing written materials which meet the standards of these regulations for use in the presentation of an approved course; and (ii) in preparing a personal presentation as an instructor for an approved course. The number of preparation minutes eligible for credit shall not exceed four times the number of instructional minutes in the presentation which is being prepared. Credit hours will be computed by calculating the total minutes spent in preparation for the course, rounded to the nearest half hour. In no event shall more than eight (8) hours of credit be awarded for preparing a single course or program.

EXAMPLES:

(1) A member prepares thorough, high-quality instructional written materials which appropriately cover the subject matter for an approved program which lasts 120 minutes. The member certifies that eight (8) hours or more was spent preparing the written materials. The Board will award eight (8) credit hours for preparation time. This does not exceed the maximum limit of four times the presentation time of the program and is consistent with the maximum limit of eight (8) hours of credit for preparing a single course or program.

(2) Same as example 1 above except the member also taught the entire program and certifies that an

additional eight (8) hours or more was spent preparing for the presentation as an instructor. This is a total preparation time of sixteen (16) hours. The Board will still award eight (8) credit hours for preparation time because this is the maximum limit of four times the presentation time and also because this is the maximum limit of credit for preparing a single course or program. However, the member will be awarded two (2) credit hours for teaching time and will therefore receive a total of ten (10) credit hours for the activities in preparing and teaching the program.

(3) A member teaches at a course approved for five (5) credits including one (1) ethics credit. The member certifies that he taught the morning ethics segment of twenty (20) minutes. The member further certifies that one hour and twenty minutes was spent preparing for the presentation. Since the member taught twenty (20) minutes eighty (80) minutes (four (4) times the presentation time) of the member's preparation time is eligible for credit. The Board will total the minutes and round this time to the nearest half hour and the member will therefore receive a total of one and one half (1.5) hours CLE credit including one and one half (1.5) hours ethics credit for teaching and preparing the ethics segment.

(e) A one-year carryover of credit hours will be permitted, so that accrued credit hours in excess of one year's requirement may be carried forward to meet the requirement of the following year. A member may carry forward a maximum of twelve (12) credit hours, not more than two (2) of which, if earned in the area of legal ethics or professionalism, may be counted toward credit hours required in such area. No more than eight (8) credit hours, of which not more than two (2) ethics or professionalism credit hours, may be carried forward from pre-recorded programs.

(f) A member shall not receive credit for any course attended in preparation for admission to practice law in any state. A member shall not receive credit for teaching that is directed primarily to persons preparing for admission to practice law. Regular full time, part-time and adjunct academic faculty shall not receive credit for teaching any law school courses (undergraduate or graduate) or bar review courses. A member attending law classes, for a purpose other than preparing for admission to practice law, may receive credit in accordance with the manner described in Regulation 102(c). A member may not receive credit for any course which is not materially different in substance from a course for which the same member received credit during the same completion period or the completion period immediately prior to the one for which credit is sought.

(g) A member may receive credit for attending a course delivered by distance learning methods which otherwise satisfies the requirements of these Regulations. No more than eight (8) credit hours may be earned in any twelve hour period attending pre-recorded courses. (Comment: See MCLE Board Opinion 16.)

[Amended effective July 1, 2001; November 1, 2004; November 1, 2011.]

REGULATION 103. STANDARDS FOR APPROVAL OF PROGRAMS

(a) Subject to the provisions of Regulation 105(d), a course is approved for credit if it has been specifically approved by the Board or is presented by an accredited sponsor previously designated by the Board under the provisions of Regulation 105. A course is approved for credit in the area of legal ethics or professionalism if and to the extent specifically approved by the Board. Subject to the provisions of Regulation 105(d), a course presented by an accredited sponsor is also approved for credit in the area of legal ethics or professionalism if and to the extent so represented by such sponsor.

(b) The course must have significant intellectual or practical content. Its primary objective must be to increase the attendee's professional competence and skills as an attorney, and to improve the quality of legal services rendered to the public.

(c) The course must pertain to a recognized legal subject or other subject matter which integrally relates to the practice of law, or to the professional responsibility or ethical obligations of the participants.

(1) A course which addresses law practice management may be approved so as to promote the efficient, economical and competent delivery of legal services. The course must cover topics that teach attorneys how to organize and manage their law practices and other law practice issues, which if improperly handled, could result in malpractice, disciplinary complaints or client dissatisfaction. A course which primarily focuses on marketing techniques, client development or other general business topics applicable to any business shall not be approved. (Comment: See MCLE Board Opinion 17.)

(2) A course which addresses substance abuse, stress management, or work/life balance issues may be approved if the topics relate to the practice of law and the quality of legal services rendered to the public. (Comment: See MCLE Board Opinion 19.)

(3) A course which addresses general skills topics such as time management, writing, communication or presentation skills may be approved provided the topics are specifically directed to an attorney audience and are covered in the context of the practice of law.

(d) A course may be approved for credit in the area of legal ethics or professionalism only to the extent that the course constitutes or contains one or more qualified ethics or professionalism components as defined in Regulation 101. Topics which will not generally be approved for ethics credit include ethics standards of conduct applicable to other professions such as government employees, government contractors, accountants and businesses including corporate compliance. Also, rules of procedure, rules of evidence and litigation tactics will not generally be approved for ethics credit. (Comment: See MCLE Board Opinion 13.) A minimum scheduling of thirty (30) minutes in the aggregate of one or more qualified ethics or professionalism components is required before an approved course can be approved for credit in the area of legal ethics or professionalism.

EXAMPLES:

(1) A sponsor's application for approval of a one-day program comprising seven 50 minute segments states in relevant part "each speaker will devote ten minutes of allotted time to ethical considerations." The program does not contain a qualified ethics component and is not eligible for approval for credit in the area of legal ethics. The requirement that a qualified component be a "clearly defined segment" is not met. Such segment must be capable of identification on the schedule and have a defined beginning and end.

(2) A sponsor's application for approval of a one-day program reveals in relevant part that the opening 30 minute morning segment is clearly identified as devoted to ethical considerations and that the concluding 20 minutes of the afternoon session is also clearly identified as devoted to ethical considerations. Assuming that other requirements for course approval are met, the Board will approve the program for one (1) hour credit in the area of legal ethics or professionalism. (See Regulation 102.)

(e) Courses must be conducted in a setting physically suitable to the educational course or program, free from distractions and conducive to learning.

(f) No credit will be allowed (or "be granted") for any course or part thereof taken simultaneously with any other course or part thereof.

(g) Thorough, high quality instructional written materials which appropriately cover the subject matter must be distributed to all attendees at or before the time the course is presented. A mere agenda or topical outline will not be sufficient. (Comment: See MCLE Board Opinion 14.)

(h) Each course shall be presented by a faculty member or members qualified by academic or practical experience to teach the subjects covered. Consistent with Virginia State Bar policy, course sponsors should exercise care to ensure that faculty members, where possible, reflect the racial and gender diversity of the State Bar as a whole.

(i) A course presented by distance learning methods which otherwise satisfies the requirements of these Regulations may be approved provided the speakers and attendees are participating simultaneously. Pre-recorded courses in any electronic form which otherwise satisfy the requirements of these regulations may be approved however no other form of self-study will be approved. (Comment: See MCLE Board Opinion 16.)

(j) A program offered "in-house" may be approved by the Board provided the subject matter of the program does not primarily focus on internal policies, practices and procedures. An in-house program will be approved if it otherwise meets the standards of these regulations and if the approval procedures prescribed by these regulations are followed. (Comment: See MCLE Board Opinion 17.)

(k) Participation in deliberative groups concerned with political activism, law reform, judicial administration, or regulation of the profession generally will not be approved for credit. Activities associated with membership or attendance at committee meetings, business meetings or work sessions will generally not be approved for credit.

(*l*) To be accredited, a course must have no attendance restrictions based on race, color, national origin, religion, creed, gender, age, disability, sexual orientation or marital status.

(m) No credit will be given for any course primarily focused on marketing a particular product or service. (Comment: See MCLE Board Opinion 15.)

(n) A course that does not meet the requirements of subsections (b) and (c) of this Regulation may, on application of a member, be approved as a "specially approved course or program" for the applicant where the Board is satisfied that the course has significant value to the applicant's practice. Thus, for example, in appropriate cases courses on engineering, accounting or medical topics may be approved for a particular member.

[Amended effective November 1, 2004; November 1, 2011.]

REGULATION 104. PROCEDURE FOR APPROVAL OF PROGRAMS

(a) A member or course sponsor desiring approval of a course or program shall submit to the Board all information called for by the "Application for Approval of a Continuing Legal Education Course." The content of this application has been promulgated by the Board and may be changed from time to time. A member seeking approval of a course as a "specially approved course or program" should include on the Application for Approval of a Continuing Legal Education Course, or as an attachment thereto, a statement of why the course has significant value to the member's practice. The Board shall then determine whether or not the course or program satisfies the requirements of Regulation 103. If the course or program is approved, the Board also shall determine the number of credit hours to be awarded. The Board shall notify the requesting member or sponsor of its decision within 90 days after receipt of the completed application. The Board shall maintain and make available a list of all approved courses and programs for each completion period. An approved course or program is accredited only for the completion period for which it is approved. A "specially approved course or program" is accredited only for the member for whom approved.

(b) The sponsor of an approved course or program should include in its brochures or course descriptions the information contained in the following illustrative statement: "This course or program has been approved by the Virginia Mandatory Continuing Legal Education Board for ___ hours of credit, of which ___ hours will also apply in the area of legal ethics or professionalism." An announcement is permissible only after the course or program has been specifically approved pursuant to an application submitted directly by the sponsor.

(c) The sponsor of an approvable course or program that has not yet been approved after application should announce: "Application for approval for this course or program is pending with the Virginia Mandatory Continuing Legal Education Board."

(d) At each presentation of an approved course or program or one for which approval is pending, the sponsor shall make available copies of the Board's Certification of Attendance for completion by the attendees and the Board's Certification of Teaching for completion by the instructors, copies of which will be provided by the Board with the course approval notification. The content of these certifications has been promulgated by the Board and may change from time to time. Where some portion of the program has not been approved for CLE or ethics credit, the sponsor shall provide that information to the attendees with the certification of attendance.

(e) In the instance of a course or program presented while an application for approval is pending, it will be the responsibility of the sponsor to provide the attendees with the Board's Certification of Attendance or Teaching as required in Regulation 104(d) immediately upon receipt of the approval notification. If such course or program is not approved, the sponsor shall immediately notify the attendees that credit for the course has been denied. Under certain circumstances a member may seek approval for a specially approved course or program as defined in Regulation 101(k) in the manner specified in Regulation 104(f).

(f) Any member seeking credit for attendance at a course or program shall submit to the Board immediately following such attendance all information called for on the Application for Approval of a Continuing Legal Education Course. The Board will then determine whether the program qualifies under these Regulations and, if so, how many credit hours are approved. The Board will promptly notify the applicant of its decision. Applications received more than 90 days following the date of the program shall be subject to a late application fee.

(g) Any sponsor seeking approval after presenting a course or program, shall submit to the Board within 30 days after the date of the program all information called for on the Application for Approval of a Continuing Legal Education Course. The Board will then determine whether the program qualifies under these Regulations and, if so, how many credit hours are approved. The Board will promptly notify the applicant of its decision.

(h) Failure to comply with the sponsor requirements of Regulation 104 or Regulation 105 may result in fines; revocation of course approval; denial of future course credit; suspension or revocation of accreditation; or any other sanction deemed fit by and in the discretion of the Board.

[Amended effective November 1, 2011.]

REGULATION 105. PROCEDURE FOR ACCREDITATION OF SPONSORS

(a) Any sponsor may apply for approval of individual courses by complying with the criteria of Regulation 103 and the procedures of Regulation 104.

(b) If the Board determines that a sponsor regularly provides a significant volume of continuing legal education courses, that these courses uniformly meet the approval criteria of Regulation 103, and that the sponsor will maintain and submit the records directed by these Regulations, the Board may designate such a course provider as an "accredited sponsor" under the Rule. Such designation shall be effective for a period of no more than two years unless renewed.

(c) A sponsor applying for status as an accredited sponsor shall submit to the Board all information called for on the Application for Status as Accredited Sponsor of Continuing Legal Education.

(d) An accredited sponsor shall be subject to and governed by the applicable provisions of the Rule and these regulations, including the quality standards of Regulation 103 and the record-keeping and reporting requirements of this Regulation 105. The Board may at any time review an accredited sponsor program and reserves the right to deny CLE or ethics credit when the standards for approval are not met. Accordingly, for example, an accredited sponsor may represent in its descriptive literature that a course or program generates credits in the area of legal ethics or professionalism only to the extent the course contains one or more qualified ethics components as provided in Regulation 103.

(e) The approval procedure of Regulation 104 does not apply to accredited sponsors. An accredited sponsor shall provide the Board at least thirty days in advance of a program with a descriptive course agenda or brochure which includes the name, date, location and credit hours requested for a particular course pursuant to the approval standards of Regulation 103, including, where appropriate, credit hours requested in the area of legal ethics or professionalism and a description of the content of the ethics session(s). The Board may request additional information regarding a course or program. The Board will provide the sponsor with copies of the Board's Certification of Attendance and

Certification of Teaching for each course or program and the sponsor shall make available, collect and transmit such forms in accordance with the requirements of Regulation 104(d).

(f) The Board may at any time reevaluate and revoke the status of an accredited sponsor. If the Board finds there is a basis for revocation of the accreditation granted to an accredited sponsor, the Board shall send notice by certified mail to that sponsor of the revocation within thirty (30) days of the Board's decision.

(g) Law firms, professional corporations, and corporate law departments are not eligible to become accredited sponsors.

[Amended effective April 8, 1996; November 1, 2011.]

REGULATION 106. DELEGATION

(a) The Board may organize itself into panels to facilitate course approval, sponsor accreditation, interpretation of these regulations and to consider and decide matters arising under the Rule and under these regulations.

(b) To facilitate the orderly and prompt administration of the Rule and these regulations, and to expedite the processes of course approval the Board may, under its supervision and direction, delegate to the Director of MCLE (hereafter referred to as the MCLE Director) general authority to act on behalf of the Board to review applications and approve or deny programs for credit pursuant to the approval standards of Regulation 103.

[Amended effective November 1, 2011.]

REGULATION 107. BOARD'S DETERMINATION AND REVIEW

(a) Pursuant to directions established by the Board, a panel or the MCLE Director on behalf of the Board shall, in response to written requests for approval of courses or programs or for awarding of credit for the attendance at or teaching in approved courses, waivers, extensions of time deadlines and interpretations of these regulations, make a written response describing the action taken. A Panel or the MCLE Director may seek a determination of the Board before taking action. Upon request of the Board, the panel or MCLE Director shall report on all determinations made since the last meeting of the Board.

(b) An aggrieved party may file with the Board a written appeal of an adverse decision by a panel or the MCLE Director within thirty (30) days after notice of the adverse decision has been mailed to him or her. No form of appeal is required but the affected person or program sponsor shall state in narrative form the action complained of and all of the reasons he or she believes the decision is erroneous.

(c) The Board shall review any adverse determination of a panel or the MCLE Director which has been appealed to it pursuant to Regulation 107(b). The aggrieved party may present information to the Board in writing or in person, and at such time and place as the Board may direct. If the Board finds that a panel or the MCLE Director has incorrectly interpreted the facts, the provisions of the Rule or the provisions of these regulations, it may take such action as may be appropriate. The Board shall advise the affected party or program sponsor of its findings and any action taken.

(d) Pursuant to Paragraph 17 of Section IV, Part Six, Rules of the Virginia Supreme Court, the Virginia State Bar may from time to time establish fees for processing applications, approving courses and accrediting sponsors; the remittance of any of these may be required before action is taken by the Board.

(e) All decisions of the Board under this Regulation 107 and any other of these regulations shall be final and binding on all persons affected thereby and no appeal or other relief therefrom shall lie, except as specifically provided in Regulation 109.

[Amended effective November 1, 2011.]

REGULATION 108. REPORTING OF CERTIFICATION PROCEDURES

(a) Where a sponsor makes copies of the Certification of Attendance and the Certification of Teaching available at a course or program, each active member who wishes credit may certify attendance electronically as instructed on the MCLE attendance reporting site of the Virginia State Bar's internet website.

(b) Where a member attends a course or program, and for any reason the member is unable to certify his or her attendance or teaching credit electronically, the member who wishes the Board to record credit may obtain a copy of the Certification of Attendance or Certification of Teaching from the sponsor, complete it and forward it to the Board.

(c) On or before October 31 of each year each active member shall certify attendance online or submit the Certification of Attendance or Certification of Teaching for the minimum educational requirement.

(d) The MCLE Board shall provide ongoing access to each individual attorney's MCLE record for the current compliance year on the Virginia State Bar's internet website. The record shall include carryover hours from the previous reporting period, identifying course information including the number of hours reported for each course and the total hours of CLE, including the totals for those CLE hours designated as ethics or professionalism and those hours for prerecorded courses which are limited to eight (8) hours per reporting period. Attorneys shall periodically review this online MCLE record to ensure accuracy and timely compliance.

(e) Following the end of each completion period, the Board shall advise each active member of his or her status respecting completion of the annual educational requirements. This notice shall be entitled the "MCLE END OF YEAR REPORT" and shall include the information reflected on the individual attorney's MCLE record as of October 31 and instructions for completion and timely compliance.

(f) If the active member accepts the MCLE END OF YEAR REPORT as accurately reflecting his or her credit hours for the period, including any carryover hours from the previous reporting period, and the form lists 12.0 or more CLE credits of which 2.0 or more are ethics or professionalism credits, the member does not need to file his form with the MCLE Board. If a member believes that the information reflected on the Board's records is erroneous or incomplete, then additions and corrections to the MCLE END OF YEAR REPORT must be filed as instructed and received by the MCLE office no later than close of business on December 15 of the year in which the credit is sought.

(g) To the extent not completed online, the MCLE End of Year Report must accompany any request for credit or corrections submitted after October 31.

(h) Delinquency fees for failure to timely complete the MCLE requirements are set forth in Paragraph 19 of Section IV, Part Six, Rules of Virginia Supreme Court. Members who have attended an insufficient number of required credits by the October 31 deadline shall remit a delinquency fee hereto referred to as a "noncompliance fee." Members who certify attendance after the December 15 certification deadline shall remit the appropriate delinquency fee hereto referred to as a "late filing fee." The late filing fee amount shall be doubled for members who fail to comply with the certification requirements by February 1 following the completion period.

(i) After December 15, a member who wishes to receive credit for credit hours earned during the previous completion period whether for compliance or additional carryover credit may forward to the Board a certification on the appropriate forms together with remittance of the late filing fee. Any credits approved shall be recorded for the previous completion period and shall be eligible for the one year carryover into the current completion period in the same fashion as other credits. A member may not apply for credits earned earlier than the next preceding completion period.
[Amended effective July 1, 2001; November 1, 2011.]

REGULATION 109. NONCOMPLIANCE, RESTORATION AND REINSTATEMENT

(a) Noncompliance.

(1) An active member who fails to comply with the educational and certification requirements of the Rule and these regulations, including payment of any required fees, and has not obtained a waiver or extension for good cause shown by December 15 of each year, shall be subject to suspension of such active member's license to practice law as is provided by Paragraph 13.2 of Section IV, Part Six, Rules of Virginia Supreme Court.

(2) Pursuant to Paragraph 13.2 of Section IV, Part Six, Rules of Virginia Supreme Court, whenever the Board determines that an active member has failed to (i) complete the mandatory continuing legal education requirements as required by Regulation 102 and/or (ii) failed to certify attendance and pay any required fees as required by Regulation 108 without first obtaining a waiver or extension in accordance with Regulation 111, the member shall be deemed to be delinquent.

(b) Restoration and Reinstatement.

(1) A delinquent member may be restored to good standing only following (i) his or her certifying to the Secretary–Treasurer of the Virginia State Bar of compliance with the requirements of the Rule in the manner provided by Regulation 108 and as instructed in the notice of impending suspension provided pursuant to Paragraph 19 of Section IV, Part Six, Rules of Virginia Supreme Court, and a determination by the Board that he or she has completed the mandatory continuing legal education requirements of the Rule and paying any required fees, or (ii) the obtaining of a waiver or extension in accordance with Regulation 111.

(2) A delinquent member who is suspended pursuant to Paragraph 13.2 shall not further engage in the active practice of law until he or she has been reinstated. A suspended member may be reinstated only after paying any required fees and certifying compliance with the Rule as provided in Paragraph 13.2 and these regulations.

(3) Where a default in compliance is cured by earning credit hours in a subsequent completion period, credit hours applied to correct the default shall not be applied to satisfy the requirements of any other period.

(4) A member suspended for an entire completion period must show attendance at 12.0 CLE credit hours including 2.0 ethics credits earned within the previous 12 months. This member cannot rely on credits earned through carryover in the previous completion period or credits used to satisfy the requirement of any previous compliance year.
[Amended effective July 1, 2001; November 1, 2011.]

REGULATION 110. EXEMPTIONS

The Rule exempts from the certification requirement a newly admitted member for the completion period in which he or she is first admitted to practice in Virginia. A newly admitted member will not receive credit under these regulations for attending or teaching any course prior to his or her admission to the Virginia State Bar.

EXAMPLE:

Attorney A is first licensed to practice law in October 2009. Attorney A is not required to comply with the minimum continuing legal education requirement of the Rule and these regulations by taking or teaching approved courses until on and after November 1, 2009. Attorney A also shall not be required to file the certification required by Regulation 108 until December 15, 2010. If Attorney A attends or teaches approved courses between October 2009 and November 1, 2009, he may "carry over" to the next completion period credits in accordance with Regulation 102. Attorney A, beginning on November 1, 2009, will be subject to said requirement as long as he or she is an active member of the Virginia State Bar.

[Amended effective August 7, 2000; July 1, 2001; November 1, 2011.]

REGULATION 111. WAIVERS, EXTENSIONS AND DEFERRALS

(a) Waivers.

(1) A waiver of the MCLE requirement or of any fees associated with MCLE noncompliance may be sought by filing a request with the Board, together with any appropriate or required supporting material or documentation (e.g. doctors' letters, medical records). The filing of any waiver request does not toll the running of any time limit set forth in these regulations or the Rule regarding suspension.

(2) A waiver shall be valid for a single completion period, unless renewed or extended by the Board. A waiver will be granted only for good cause.

(3) If the waiver is based on medical reason, condition, illness or hospitalization, then the application for waiver shall be a completed form entitled "Request for Waiver Based on Hospitalization, Illness or Medical Reason." It must be completed and signed by the admitting, family or attending health care provider and it must set forth the medical condition, hospitalization or illness which prevents the member from completing the required MCLE courses for the period for which the Waiver is being requested and have attached to it any appropriate supporting material or documentation.

(4) If the waiver is based on non-medical reasons, then the grounds shall be stated in a letter to the Board and any appropriate supporting material or documentation shall be attached.

(5) A member who is unable to satisfy the MCLE requirement due to extraordinary or extenuating circumstances beyond the control of the member may apply as prescribed in Regulation 111(a)(1) to have all or part of the eight-hour limitation on pre-recorded courses waived.

(6) All waiver requests should be promptly submitted when the grounds for the waiver request become known to the applicant or applicant's representative. Failure to file a waiver request in a timely manner may be considered by the Board in determining whether to grant a waiver. A prudent lawyer will use the carryover of credits provision of the Rule to avoid most non-medical based waiver requests.

(b) Extensions.

(1) An extension may be sought by filing with the Board a request, together with any appropriate or required supporting material or documentation (e.g. physicians' letters, medical records, military deployment orders). The filing of an extension request does not toll the running of any time limit set forth in these regulations or the Rule regarding suspension.

(2) An extension shall be valid for the specific time period granted by the Board unless renewed or extended. An extension will be granted only for good cause.

(3) If the extension is based on medical reason, condition, illness or hospitalization, then the application for extension shall be a completed form entitled "Request for an Extension Based on Hospitalization, Illness or Medical Reason." It must be completed and signed by the admitting, family or attending health care provider and it must set forth the medical condition, hospitalization or illness which prevents the member from completing the required MCLE courses for the period for which an extension is being requested and have attached to it any appropriate supporting material or documentation.

(4) If the extension is based on non-medical reasons, then the grounds should be stated in a letter to the Board and any appropriate supporting material or documentation should be attached.

(5) All extension requests should be promptly submitted when the grounds for the extension request become known to the applicant or the applicant's representative. Failure to file an extension request in a timely manner may be considered by the Board in determining whether to grant an extension. A prudent lawyer will use the carryover of credits provision of the Rule to avoid most non-medical based extension requests.

(c) Deferrals.

(1) Members who change their class of membership from Active or Emeritus Member to any other class of membership, as defined in Paragraph 3 of Section IV, Part Six, Rules of Virginia Supreme Court, during the course of the compliance year may defer the completion of any remaining MCLE requirements (including payment of any outstanding MCLE delinquency fee obligations) for that compliance year including any MCLE deficiencies for any previous year(s). Prior to reactivation of their membership status, members shall satisfy all deferred MCLE requirements in addition to the requirement for the current compliance year. Credit hours reported for compliance with the current year's requirement must have been completed within the previous twelve months prior to reactivation.

[Amended effective November 1, 2011.]

REGULATION 112. REPRESENTATIONS BY MEMBERS

A member who makes a materially false statement in any document filed with the Board shall be subject to appropriate disciplinary action.

[Amended effective November 1, 2011.]

FORM 2. CERTIFICATION OF ATTENDANCE

Virginia MCLE Board
Virginia State Bar
707 East Main Street, 15th Floor
Richmond, VA 23219-2800
(804) 775-0577 · (804) 775-0544 · Web site: www.vsb.org

CERTIFICATION OF ATTENDANCE (FORM 2)

Pursuant to Paragraph 17B, C and D of Section IV, Part Six, Rules of the Supreme Court of Virginia. The information provided will be available for inspection by the public under the Freedom of Information Act. Complete all requested information and sign certification.

Contact the Sponsor First for Virginia Approval Information and Form.

When provided, also attach any sponsor generated attendance form. The Virginia certification of attendance and/or Virginia course approval ID# has been provided to the sponsor for all Virginia approved programs.

Member Name: ______________________ VSB Member Number: ______________

Official Address of Record: ______________________

______________________ Daytime Phone (   ) ______________

______________________ E-Mail Address: ______________

City State Zip

Course ID Number:

Sponsor:

Course/Program Title:

CLE (Ethics) Credits: (   ) Ethics

CERTIFICATION

Date(s) Attended: ______________________ Location(s): ______________________

Delivery method: _____Live or Group Video _____*Live Telephone or live Webcast _____*Videoconference or Satellite
_____* Internet on-demand _____*CD-rom _____♦ Video/DVD _____♦Audio/CD _____Other____________

Setting: _____Group (with other attendees) _____* Individual attendance at my location

Distance Learning Programs Require Attendance Form Verified and Provided by the Course Sponsor when done in an Individual Setting.
♦Video and Audio programs require at least 2 attorneys in attendance

By my signature below I certify

___ I attended a total of ____________ (hrs/mins) of **approved CLE**, of which (________) (hrs/mins) were in **approved Ethics**.

___ The sessions I am claiming had written instructional materials to cover the subject.

___ I participated in this program in a setting physically suitable to the course and a suitable writing surface was available.

___ I was given the opportunity to participate in discussions with other attendees and/or the presenter.

___ I understand I may not receive credit for any course/segment which is not materially different in substance than a course/segment for which credit has been previously given during the same completion period or the completion period immediately prior.

___ I understand that a materially false statement shall be subject to appropriate disciplinary action.

NOTE: Credit is awarded for actual time in attendance rounded to the nearest half hour.

______________________ ______________________

Date Signature

You may certify your MCLE attendance online at www.vsb.org

MCLE Completion Deadline - October 31
Deadline to Certify MCLE Approved Hours - December 15
A $100 fee will be charged for failure to comply with either deadline
Fax transmissions are subject to receipt by the MCLE office of complete and legible forms.

[Amended effective September 1, 2012.]

FORM 3. CERTIFICATION OF TEACHING

Virginia MCLE Board

CERTIFICATION OF TEACHING (FORM 3)

MCLE requirement pursuant to Paragraph 17, of Section IV, Part Six, Rules of the Supreme Court of Virginia and the MCLE Board Regulations.

INSTRUCTIONS

E-mail this form to mymcle@vsb.org

Complete this Certification to Include Both Teaching and Attendance hours. Retain copy for two years.

MCLE Compliance Deadline - October 31. MCLE Reporting Deadline - December 15.

A $100 fee will be assessed for failure to comply with either deadline.

Member Name: ____________________ **VSB Member Number:** ____________

Address: ____________________ **Daytime Phone:** ____________

____________________ **E-mail Address:** ____________

____

City State Zip

Course ID Number:

Sponsor:

Course/Program Title:

CLE (Ethics) Credits: ______ (______) Ethics

Date(s) of Teaching: ____________ Location(s): ____________

ONLY SESSIONS WITH WRITTEN INSTRUCTIONAL MATERIALS ARE APPROVABLE FOR CREDIT

- My teaching segment was ______ (hrs/mins) of CLE, of which (______) (hrs/mins) were in Ethics.
- In addition, I attended *other* segments totaling ______ (hrs/mins) of CLE, of which (______) (hrs/mins) were in Ethics.
- I spent ______ hours preparing for teaching my segment of the course.
- No more than four (4) hours of preparation credit may be claimed per one hour of instructional time in your presentation, and no more than eight (8) hours total for any one course. Total credit is awarded for actual time spent teaching, attendance and preparation rounded to the nearest half hour. (Example: 1hr 15min = 1.5hr)
- A materially false statement shall be subject to appropriate disciplinary action.

____________ ____________________

Date **Signature**

Questions? Contact the MCLE Department at (804) 775-0577 or E-mail questions to mcle@vsb.org

If not e-mailed, this form may be mailed or faxed (fax disabled Nov 2-Dec 31)
Virginia MCLE Board
Virginia State Bar
707 East Main Street, 15th Floor
Richmond, VA 23219-2800
Web site: www.vsb.org Fax: (804) 775-0544

[Amended effective September 1, 2012.]

FORM 4. ATTORNEY APPLICATION FOR CLE COURSE APPROVAL

Virginia MCLE Board
Virginia State Bar
1111 East Main Street, Suite 700
Richmond, VA 23219-3565
(804) 775-0577 Website: www.vsb.org

BOARD USE ONLY
Course ID# ____________ **Decision:** ____________
CLE hours: ____________
Ethics hours ____________ **Reason:** ____________

ATTORNEY APPLICATION FOR CLE COURSE APPROVAL (FORM 4)

MCLE Deadline October 31

1. Applicant: VSB ID Number:____________ Course Sponsor:____________
   Name:____________ Sponsor Representative*____________
   Address:____________ Address:____________
   Daytime phone:(______)____________ Phone:(______)____________
   FAX #: (______)____________ FAX #:(______)____________
   E-Mail Address:____________ E-Mail Address:____________
2. Title of Program: ____________
3. Total CLE hours: ______ including (______) Ethics hours (Only sessions with written materials are approvable)

   To qualify for credit <u>Ethics components must be clearly identified on the course schedule</u> and total a minimum of 30 minutes. ***A SAMPLE OF THE ETHICS MATERIAL DISTRIBUTED MUST BE ATTACHED.***
4. Check ALL that apply to this presentation:
   <u>TYPE</u>: ___LIVE **<u>DELIVERY METHOD</u>**: ___Speaker in Room ___*Videoconference ___*Telephone ___*Webcast
   ___PRE-RECORDED **<u>DELIVERY METHOD</u>**: ___*Internet ___*CD-Rom ___*Video ___*Audio ___ Other____________
   SETTING: ____Group Setting ___*Delivered to Individuals ___In-house **ATTENDANCE**:___OPEN ___CLOSED
   See Opinion 16 and complete page 2 for pre-recorded and distance learning courses.
5. Date(s):____________
   Location (City & Venue):____________
6. Course Registration Fee: $______ **Target audience:** CLIENTS____ ATTORNEYS____ OTHER____
7. **<u>REQUIRED ATTACHMENTS</u>: MCLE Board will only consider applications with required attachments.**
   a. **Program Time Schedule or Agenda (times are required to compute approvable credit hours)**
   b. **Table of Contents AND a sample of materials from each session (5 pages each)**
   c. **Course provider must complete page 2 for all pre-recorded and distance learning courses. See Opin.16**
8. Description of materials: **Total pages** ______ Printed ______ Other____________
   Materials are distributed: Before program ______ At program ______ Other____________
   I am only requesting credit for sessions which had substantive written materials YES ____ Unknown ______
9. Physical Facilities: Conference room____ Theater style____ Writing surface? ____________
10. Number of attorneys present or anticipated:______ (Clients:______) Number of non-attorneys: ______
11. If the program does not cover a recognized legal topic, attach a statement of how this course relates to your practice.
12. **Attendance Certification:**
    I certify that I attended ______ CLE hours, including (____) Ethics hours, of the above-named course.
    Sponsor provided certification of attendance must be provided for all distance learning programs.
13. **$50 LATE APPLICATION FEE required for applications received or that remain incomplete 90 days following the program. $50 fee required for in-house audio/video or CD-ROM applications.**
    Make payable to Treasurer of Virginia.

Signature____________
(VSB Member Applicant)
A materially false statement shall be subject to appropriate disciplinary action.

FAX & EMAIL TRANSMISSIONS NOT ACCEPTED.

Please allow 90 days for board decision on all applications

MCLE Opinion 16 Compliance Information
This information must be completed by course provider for all distance learning courses.

1. The course must afford interaction between attendees and the presenter or other subject matter expert with respect to the subject matter of the course. Please describe how interaction is achieved for your program.

____

____

____

2. The provider must have a system which allows certification of attendance to be controlled by the provider which permits the provider to verify the date and time of attendance. How do you accomplish this?

____

____

____

3. Do you provide information on the original recording date?_______________

4. Is the program provided in audio or audiovisual format?__________ Text based?__________

5. Do you provide written instructional materials to cover the subject matter of the program?______
How and when are the materials provided?_______________

____

6. You must provide the attorney with a certification of attendance once you have verified actual time in attendance.

____
Course Provider

____
Contact Name

____
Signature

Attendance at pre-recorded programs is limited to 8.0 hours per compliance year. Pre-recorded programs that include an appropriate simultaneous, live interactive component may be considered for live interactive approval and not be subject to the 8.0 hours limitation.

Request for Special Live Interactive Approval of a Pre-recorded Program (See Opinion 16)

Please respond to the following questions and provide attachments:

1. Will this recorded program be held in a group setting? _______ If so, estimated number in attendance__________

2. How will "simultaneous, live interaction" be achieved? ______________________________

   ____

   ____

3. Will the live interaction be with the original presenter? ________ If not, please provide name(s) and attach the resume/credentials for the discussion facilitator or panel members.

   ____

4. Attach agenda showing times devoted to recorded presentation and live interaction.

DEFINITION OF COURSE TYPES AND EXPLANATION OF VIRGINIA CRITERIA FOR APPROVAL

OPEN - Course advertised and open to all attorneys
CLOSED - Course open only to law firm, in-house law department, government agency or members of a professional organization.
LIVE - Instructor and attendees participate simultaneously
IN-HOUSE - Program offered to attorneys within a firm, corporation or government agency
GROUP SETTING - Program offered in group of 2 or more attorneys. (Where individual attendees are conferenced into a program the sponsor must meet Opinion 16 standards)
TELECONFERENCE, SATELLITE, VIDEOCONFERENCE, OR LIVE WEBCAST- To meet Virginia regulations the course must
(1) have a means to connect audience with faculty and/or other attendees to allow for live interaction and discussion.
(2) written materials must be available to participants prior to the broadcast.
(3) have attendance tracking - See OPINION 16
VIDEO, AUDIO, CD-ROM - To meet Virginia regulations the course must
(1) have ability to interact with the presenter or other subject matter expert. (E-mail contact information is sufficient)
(1) have at least 2 attorney participants or be proctored (not restricted to only VA attorneys)
(2) be conducted in an educational setting
(3) have written materials provided to each participant prior to the presentation.
INTERNET, CD-ROM ON-DEMAND programming (SELF STUDY NOT APPROVABLE) - To meet Virginia regulations the course must
(1) be in audio or audio/video format. Text based courses are not approvable
(2) allow the participant to interact with the presenter and/or other attendees
(3) have written materials available to participants for reference during and subsequent to program
(4) have attendance tracking - See OPINION 16

For additional information see MCLE Regulation 103 and MCLE Board Opinions available at **http://www.vsb.org/site/members/mcle-courses**

INSTRUCTIONS FOR COMPLETING APPLICATION FOR CLE APPROVAL (FORM 4)

1. Complete attorney information on left hand side. Complete identifying sponsor information on right hand side of application.

2. Give Title of Program

3. **Total CLE hours** are the number of 60 minute hours of course presentation excluding introductory remarks, breaks, meals, closing remarks. **ONLY SESSIONS WITH WRITTEN INSTRUCTIONAL MATERIALS ARE APPROVABLE.** Keynote, mealtime speakers, judicial presentations or roundtable discussions are given CLE credit only when written handout materials are given to appropriately cover the topic. **Total Ethics hours** are the number of 60-minute hours devoted to Ethics as it applies to Attorneys. Ethics relating to other professions, government employees, business professionals or general ethics are not approvable for Ethics credit. The Ethics time segment must be clearly defined on the course schedule and be accompanied by specific ethics materials. A sample of the ethics material must be included with this application. (See Opinion #13 for approvable ethics topics)

4. **Indicate type of course, setting and delivery method** specific to the course you attended. ***All distance learning courses require a statement from the sponsor on how their programs meet Opinion 16 standards.*** Presentations resulting from the rental or purchase of video or audio programs require 2 or more attorneys in attendance and accompanied by appropriate written instructional materials. **Please contact the MCLE office for special instructions and forms.**

5. Give the dates and locations of your attendance. The MCLE reporting year runs from November 1 - October 31. Courses are approved for the reporting year they are presented and **must be reported during that period.**

6. Enter the price you paid for course attendance. **Target audience**: Courses must be directed primarily to attorneys and address a legal topic to be approved. Special approval may be given for non-legal courses if pertinent to the attorney's practice. (See #11 below)

7. **Warning!** Application must include the following attachments:
a. Program time schedule or agenda (TIMES ARE NEEDED TO COMPUTE APPROVABLE CREDIT HOURS)
b. Table of contents, if available **AND** a sample of the written materials for each session (2-3 pages) distributed to the attendees at the program. Ethics materials must be submitted to receive ethics credit. (See Opinion #14 on Written Materials) The MCLE Board reserves the right to request a complete set of materials.

8. **Description of materials** - Give approximate total pages and check type of materials and when distributed. **Only sessions with written materials are approvable.**

9. Physical Facilities - select applicable type. A writing surface should be provided where appropriate.

10. Enter approximate number of attorneys and non-attorneys present or anticipated.

11. Attach a statement of how a non-legal course relates to your practice if applicable.

12. Complete certification of attendance. For teaching credit please use the Form #3 Certification of Teaching.

13. **IN-HOUSE AUDIO/VIDEO or CD-ROM programs require a $50 application fee.** Make payable to Treasurer of Virginia.

[Amended effective September 1, 2012.]

FORM 4. LAW FIRM SPONSOR APPLICATION FOR CLE APPROVAL

Virginia MCLE Board
Virginia State Bar
1111 East Main Street, Suite 700
Richmond, VA 23219-3565
(804) 775-0577
Website: www.vsb.org

BOARD USE ONLY

Course ID# ____________ Letter# ____________
CLE hours ____________ Decision: ____________
Ethics hours ____________ Reason: ____________

LAW FIRM SPONSOR APPLICATION FOR CLE COURSE APPROVAL (FORM 4)

(MCLE Annual Completion Deadline October 31)

1. Course Sponsor: ____________
   Sponsor Representative* ____________
   Address: ____________
   Phone: ( ) ____________ REGISTRATION phone:( ) ____________
   E-mail address ____________ Web address ____________
2. Title of Program: ____________
   ____
   (Course ID# of any prior VA approval of this program content : ____________)
3. Total CLE hours: ______ including (______) Ethics hours Only sessions with written materials are approvable
4. CHECK ALL that apply to this presentation:
   TYPE: __LIVE DELIVERY METHOD: __Speaker in Room __*Videoconference __*Telephone __*Webcast
   __PRE-RECORDED DELIVERY METHOD: __*Internet __*CD-Rom __*Video __*Audio
   Other ____________
   SETTING: __Group Setting __*Delivered to Individuals __In-house ATTENDANCE: __OPEN __CLOSED
   ****See Opinion 16 and complete page 2 for all pre-recorded and distance learning courses.***
5. Date(s): ____________ Times: (Begin/End) ____________
   Venue/Location(s): ____________
6. Course Registration Fee: $______ **Target audience:** CLIENTS____ ATTORNEYS____
   OTHER ____________
7. **REQUIRED ATTACHMENTS: MCLE Board will only consider applications with required attachments.**
   a. Program Time Schedule or Agenda (times are required to compute approvable credit hours)
   b. Complete set of written materials provided to attendees
   c. Faculty name(s) and credentials
   d. Complete page 2 for all pre-recorded and distance learning courses. See Opinion 16
8. Description of materials: **Total pages** ______ Printed ______ Other ____________
   Materials are distributed: Before program ______ At program ______ Other ____________
9. Physical Facilities: Conference room______ Theater style ______ Writing surface? ____________
10. Number of attorneys present or anticipated: ____/____/____ (Firm Clients Other) Number of non-attorneys: ____/____ (Staff Clients)
11. Do you monitor time in attendance? ____________ How? ____________
12. SPONSOR agrees to provide Certification of Attendance forms (Form #2) and Certification of Teaching forms (Form #3) to Virginia attorneys attending or teaching the program. (Course attendance lists are not acceptable)
13. **SPONSORS MUST FILE A $50 FEE WITH THIS APPLICATION.** Fee is double ($100) for applications received more than 30 days after program. Make payable to Treasurer of Virginia.

Signature ____________
(Sponsor Representative)
A materially false statement may jeopardize approval of this and future programs

Check # ____________
Fax & Email Transmissions not accepted.
Please allow 90 days for board decision on all applications

MCLE Opinion 16 Compliance Information

This information is required for all pre-recorded and distance learning courses.
See Opinion 16 at http://www.vsb.org/site/members/mcle-opinion-16

1. The course must afford interaction between attendees and the presenter or other subject matter expert with respect to the subject matter of the course. Please describe how interaction is achieved for your program.

____

____

____

2. The provider must have a system which allows certification of attendance to be controlled by the provider and which permits the provider to verify the date and time of attendance. How do you accomplish this?

____

____

____

3. Please provide a copy of your certification of attendance if you do not plan to use the Virginia certification of attendance which we will provide.

Request for Live Interactive Approval of a Pre-recorded Program (See Opinion 16)

Pre-recorded programs that include an appropriate simultaneous, live interactive component may be considered for live interactive approval and not be subject to the 8.0 hours limitation.

Please respond to the following questions and provide attachments:

1. Will this recorded program be held in a group setting? _______ If so, estimated number in attendance__________

2. How will "simultaneous, live interaction" be achieved? ____

____

____

3. Will the live interaction be with the original presenter? _______ If not, please provide name(s) and attach the resume/credentials for the discussion facilitator or panel members.

____

4. Attach agenda showing times devoted to recorded presentation and live interaction.

COURSE TYPES AND EXPLANATION OF VIRGINIA CRITERIA FOR APPROVAL

OPEN - Course advertised and open to all attorneys

CLOSED - Course open only to firm or government agency, members of professional organization.

LIVE - Instructor and attendees participate simultaneously

PRE-RECORDED – Recorded version of an original live CLE presentation. Attendance at pre-recorded programs is limited to 8.0 hours per compliance year.

IN-HOUSE - Program offered to attorneys within a firm, corporation or government agency.

GROUP SETTING - Program offered in group of 2 or more attorneys. (Where individual attendees are conferenced into a program you must meet Opinion 16 standards and submit a separate application and fee)

DISTANCE LEARNING – See examples and requirements below

TELECONFERENCE, SATELLITE, VIDEOCONFERENCE, OR LIVE WEBCAST- To meet Virginia regulations the course must

(1) attendees must be given the opportunity to participate in discussions with other attendees and/or the presenter
(2) written materials must be available to participants prior to the broad cast.
(3) have attendance tracking - See OPINION 16

VIDEO, AUDIO, CD-ROM - To meet Virginia regulations the course must

(1) have interactivity with the presenter or other subject matter expert. (E-mail contact information is sufficient)
(2) have at least 2 attorney participants or be proctored (not restricted to only VA attorneys)
(3) be conducted in an educational setting
(4) have written materials provided to each participant prior to the presentation.

INTERNET ON-DEMAND- To meet Virginia regulations the course must

(1) be in audio or audio/video format. Text based courses are not approvable
(2) allow the participant to interact with the presenter
(3) have written materials available to participants for reference during and subsequent to program
(4) have attendance tracking - See OPINION 16

For additional information see MCLE Regulation 103 and MCLE Board Opinions available at

http://www.vsb.org/site/members/mcle-courses

INSTRUCTIONS FOR COMPLETING APPLICATION FOR CLE APPROVAL (FORM 4)

Please allow 4 to 6 weeks for board decision on all applications

1. **Complete identifying sponsor information**

2. **Give Title of Program (Include VA course ID# of any prior approval)**

3. **Total CLE hours** are the number of ***60-minute hours*** of course presentation excluding introductory remarks, breaks, meals, closing remarks. **ONLY SESSIONS WITH WRITTEN INSTRUCTIONAL MATERIALS ARE APPROVABLE.** Keynote, mealtime speakers, judicial presentations or roundtable discussions are given CLE credit only when written handout materials are given to appropriately cover the topic.

   Total Ethics hours are the number of ***60-minute hours*** devoted to Ethics as it applies to Attorneys. Ethics relating to other professions, government employees, business professionals or general ethics are not approvable for Ethics credit. The Ethics time segment must be clearly defined on the course schedule and be accompanied by specific ethics materials. A sample of the ethics material must be included with this application (See Opinion #13 for approvable ethics topics.)

4. **Circle type of course, setting and delivery method** of the course you are presenting. Live presentations and subsequent video, audio or distance learning presentations of the live program require separate applications and application fees.

5. **Give all dates and locations**. The MCLE reporting year runs from November 1 - October 31. Courses are approved for the reporting year they are presented.

6. Enter the price you charge for course attendance. **Target audience**: Courses must be directed primarily to attorneys and address a legal topic to be approved.

7. **REQUIRED ATTACHMENTS: THE MCLE BOARD WILL ONLY CONSIDER APPLICATIONS WITH REQUIRED ATTACHMENTS!**
   a. Program time schedule or agenda (TIMES ARE NEEDED TO COMPUTE APPROVABLE CREDIT HOURS)
   b. Complete set of written materials distributed to the attendees at the program. Ethics materials must be submitted to receive ethics credit. (See Opinion #14 on Written Materials)
   c. Faculty name(s) and bio

8. **Description of materials** - Give approximate total pages and check type of materials and when distributed. ***Written materials are required for all sessions***.

9. Physical Facilities - select applicable type.

10. Enter approximate number of attorneys and non-attorneys present or anticipated.

11. Explain if and how you track attendance. This information is required for all distance learning programs.

12. After the course is approved the MCLE Board will send you certifications of attendance and teaching forms for your course. These forms are to be given to the Virginia attorneys attending or teaching the program.

13. Sponsors must pay a $50 Application fee for each course. $50 late fee for applications received more than 30 days after program.

[Added effective September 1, 2012.]

FORM 4. SPONSOR APPLICATION FOR CLE COURSE APPROVAL

Virginia MCLE Board
Virginia State Bar
1111 East Main Street, Suite 700
Richmond, VA 23219-3565
(804) 775-0577
Website: www.vsb.org

BOARD USE ONLY

Course ID#: ______		Letter#: ______	
CLE hours: ______		Decision: ______	
Ethics hours: ______		Reason: ______	

SPONSOR APPLICATION FOR APPROVAL OF A CLE COURSE (FORM 4)

(MCLE Annual Completion Deadline October 31)

1. Course Sponsor: ______
   Sponsor Representative* ______
   Address: ______
   Phone:(____) ______ REGISTRATION phone:(____) ______
   E-mail address ______ Web address: ______
2. Title of Program: ______
   (Course ID# of any prior VA approval of this program content: ______)
3. Total CLE hours: ______ including (______) Ethics hours Only sessions with written materials are approvable
4. CHECK ALL that apply to this presentation:
   TYPE: __LIVE **DELIVERY METHOD**: __Speaker in Room __*Videoconference __*Telephone __*Webcast
   __PRE-RECORDED **DELIVERY METHOD**: __*Internet __*CD-Rom __*Video __*Audio
   __ Other ______
   SETTING: __Group Setting __*Delivered to Individuals __In-house **ATTENDANCE**: __OPEN __CLOSED
   See Opinion 16 and complete page 2 for pre-recorded and distance learning courses.
5. Date(s): ______
   Location(s): ______
6. Course Registration Fee: $______ **Target audience:** CLIENTS____ ATTORNEYS____
   OTHER ______
7. **REQUIRED ATTACHMENTS: MCLE Board will only consider applications with required attachments.**
   a. **Program Time Schedule or Agenda (times are required to compute approvable credit hours)**
   b. **Table of Contents AND a sample of materials from each session (5 pages each)**
   c. **Faculty name(s) and credentials**
   d. **Complete page 2 for all pre-recorded and distance learning courses. See Opinion 16**
8. Description of materials: **Total pages** ______ Printed ______ Other ______
   Materials are distributed: Before program ______ At program ______ Other ______
9. Physical Facilities: Conference room____ Theater style____ Writing surface? ______
10. Number of attorneys present or anticipated: ______ (Clients: ____) Number of non-attorneys: ______
11. Do you monitor time in attendance? ______ How? ______ (attach statement)
12. SPONSOR agrees to provide Certification of Attendance forms (Form #2) and Certification of Teaching forms (Form #3) to Virginia attorneys attending or teaching the program. (Course attendance lists are not acceptable)
13. **SPONSORS MUST FILE A $50 FEE WITH THIS APPLICATION.** Fee is double ($100) for applications received more than 30 days after program. Make payable to Treasurer of Virginia.

Signature ______
(Sponsor Representative)

Email and Fax Transmissions not accepted.
Please allow 90 days for board decision on all complete applications

A materially false statement may jeopardize approval of this and future programs

MCLE Opinion 16 Compliance Information

This information is required for all pre-recorded and distance learning courses.
See Opinion 16 at http://www.vsb.org/site/members/mcle-opinion-16

1. The course must afford interaction between attendees and the presenter or other subject matter expert with respect to the subject matter of the course. Please describe how interaction is achieved for your program.

____

____

____

2. The provider must have a system which allows certification of attendance to be controlled by the provider and which permits the provider to verify the date and time of attendance. How do you accomplish this?

____

____

____

3. Please provide a copy of your certification of attendance if you do not plan to use the Virginia certification of attendance which we will provide.

Request for Live Interactive Approval of a Pre-recorded Program (See Opinion 16)

Pre-recorded programs that include an appropriate simultaneous, live interactive component may be considered for live interactive approval and not be subject to the 8.0 hours limitation.

Please respond to the following questions and provide attachments:

1. Will this recorded program be held in a group setting? ________ If so, estimated number in attendance__________

2. How will "simultaneous, live interaction" be achieved? ______________________________

____

____

3. Will the live interaction be with the original presenter? ________ If not, please provide name(s) and attach the resume/credentials for the discussion facilitator or panel members.

____

4. Attach agenda showing times devoted to recorded presentation and live interaction.

Keep The Following Pages For Your Information

COURSE TYPES AND EXPLANATION OF VIRGINIA CRITERIA FOR APPROVAL

OPEN - Course advertised and open to all attorneys

CLOSED - Course open only to firm or government agency, members of professional organization.

LIVE - Instructor and attendees participate simultaneously

PRE-RECORDED – Recorded version of an original live CLE presentation. Attendance at pre-recorded programs is limited to 8.0 hours per compliance year.

IN-HOUSE - Program offered to attorneys within a firm, corporation or government agency.

GROUP SETTING - Program offered in group of 2 or more attorneys. (Where individual attendees are conferenced into a program you must meet Opinion 16 standards and submit a separate application and fee)

DISTANCE LEARNING – See examples and requirements below

TELECONFERENCE, SATELLITE, VIDEOCONFERENCE, OR LIVE WEBCAST - To meet Virginia regulations the course must

(1) attendees must be given the opportunity to participate in discussions with other attendees and/or the presenter
(2) written materials must be available to participants prior to the broad cast.
(3) have attendance tracking - See OPINION 16

VIDEO, AUDIO, CD-ROM - To meet Virginia regulations the course must

(1) have interactivity with the presenter or other subject matter expert. (E-mail contact information is sufficient)
(2) have at least 2 attorney participants or be proctored (not restricted to only VA attorneys)
(3) be conducted in an educational setting
(4) have written materials provided to each participant prior to the presentation.

INTERNET ON-DEMAND- To meet Virginia regulations the course must

(1) be in audio or audio/video format. Text based courses are not approvable
(2) allow the participant to interact with the presenter
(3) have written materials available to participants for reference during and subsequent to program
(4) have attendance tracking - See OPINION 16

For additional information see MCLE Regulation 103 and MCLE Board Opinions related to course standards at **http://www.vsb.org/site/members/mcle-courses**

INSTRUCTIONS FOR COMPLETING APPLICATION FOR CLE APPROVAL (FORM 4)

Please allow up to 90 days for board decision on all applications

1. Complete identifying sponsor information

2. Give Title of Program

3. **Total CLE hours** are the number of 60-minute hours of course presentation excluding introductory remarks, breaks, meals, closing remarks. **ONLY SESSIONS WITH WRITTEN INSTRUCTIONAL MATERIALS ARE APPROVABLE.** Keynote, mealtime speakers, judicial presentations or roundtable discussions are given CLE credit only when written handout materials are given to appropriately cover the topic.

   Total Ethics hours are the number of 60-minute hours devoted to Ethics as it applies to Attorneys. Ethics relating to other professions, government employees, business professionals or general ethics are not approvable for Ethics credit. The Ethics time segment must be clearly defined on the course•schedule and be accompanied by specific ethics materials. A sample of the ethics material must be included with this application.(See Opinion #13 for approvable ethics topics)

4. Check type of course, setting and delivery method of the course you are presenting. Live presentations and subsequent recorded or distance learning presentations of the live program require separate applications and application fees.

5. Give all dates and locations. The MCLE reporting year runs from November 1 - October 31. Courses are approved for the reporting year they are presented.

6. Enter the price you charge for course attendance. Target audience: Courses must be directed primarily to attorneys and address a legal topic to be approved.

7. **REQUIRED ATTACHMENTS: THE MCLE BOARD WILL ONLY CONSIDER APPLICATIONS WITH REQUIRED ATTACHMENTS!**
   a. Program time schedule or agenda (Times Are Needed To Compute Approvable Credit Hours)
   b. Table of contents, if available and a sample of the written materials for each session (2-3 pages) distributed to the attendees at the program. Ethics materials must be submitted to receive ethics credit.(See Opinion #14 on Written Materials)
   c. Faculty name(s) and bios
   d. Complete page 2 for all pre-recorded and distance learning courses. See Opinion 16

8. Description of materials - Give approximate total pages and check type of materials and when distributed. ***Written materials are required for all sessions.***

9. Physical Facilities - select applicable type.

10. Enter approximate number of attorneys and non-attorneys present or anticipated.

11. Explain if and how you track attendance. This information is required for all distance learning programs.

12. After the course is approved the MCLE Board will send you certifications of attendance and teaching forms for your course. These forms are to be given to the Virginia attorneys attending or teaching the program.

13. Sponsors must pay a $50 Application fee for each course. $50 late fee for applications received more than 30 days after program.

REGULATION 103
STANDARDS FOR APPROVAL OF PROGRAMS

(a) Subject to the provisions of Regulation 105(d), a course is approved for credit if it has been specifically approved by the Board or is presented by an accredited sponsor previously designated by the Board under the provisions of Regulation 105. A course is approved for credit in the area of legal ethics or professionalism if and to the extent specifically approved by the Board. Subject to the provisions of Regulation 105(d), a course presented by an accredited sponsor is also approved for credit in the area of legal ethics or professionalism if and to the extent so represented by such sponsor.

(b) The course must have significant intellectual or practical content. Its primary objective must be to increase the attendee's professional competence and skills as an attorney, and to improve the quality of legal services rendered to the public.

(c) The course must pertain to a recognized legal subject or other subject matter which integrally relates to the practice of law, or to the professional responsibility or ethical obligations of the participants.

(1) A course which addresses law practice management may be approved so as to promote the efficient, economical and competent delivery of legal services. The course must cover topics that teach attorneys how to organize and manage their law practices and other law practice issues, which if improperly handled, could result in malpractice, disciplinary complaints or client dissatisfaction. A course which primarily focuses on marketing techniques, client development or other general business topics applicable to any business shall not be approved. (Comment: See MCLE Board Opinion 17.)

(2) A course which addresses substance abuse, stress management, or work/life balance issues may be approved if the topics relate to the practice of law and the quality of legal services rendered to the public. (Comment: See MCLE Board Opinion 19.)

(3) A course which addresses general skills topics such as time management, writing, communication or presentation skills may be approved provided the topics are specifically directed to an attorney audience and are covered in the context of the practice of law.

(d) A course may be approved for credit in the area of legal ethics or professionalism only to the extent that the course constitutes or contains one or more qualified ethics or professionalism components as defined in Regulation 101. Topics which will not generally be approved for ethics credit include ethics standards of conduct applicable to other professions such as government employees, government contractors, accountants and businesses including corporate compliance. Also, rules of procedure, rules of evidence and litigation tactics will not generally be approved for ethics credit. (Comment: See MCLE Board Opinion 13.) A minimum scheduling of thirty (30) minutes in the aggregate of one or more qualified ethics or professionalism components is required before an approved course can be approved for credit in the area of legal ethics or professionalism.

EXAMPLES:

(1) A sponsor's application for approval of a one-day program comprising seven 50 minute segments states in relevant part "each speaker will devote ten minutes of allotted time to ethical considerations." The program does not contain a qualified ethics component and is not eligible for approval for credit in the area of legal ethics. The requirement that a qualified component be a "clearly defined segment" is not met. Such segment must be capable of identification on the schedule and have a defined beginning and end.

(2) A sponsor's application for approval of a one-day program reveals in relevant part that the opening 30 minute morning segment is clearly identified as devoted to ethical considerations and that the concluding 20 minutes of the afternoon session is also clearly identified as devoted to ethical considerations. Assuming that other requirements for course approval are met, the Board will approve the program for one (1) hour credit in the area of legal ethics or professionalism. (See Regulation 102.)

(e) Courses must be conducted in a setting physically suitable to the educational course or program, free from distractions and conducive to learning.

(f) No credit will be allowed (or "be granted") for any course or part thereof taken simultaneously with any other course or part thereof.

(g) Thorough, high quality instructional written materials which appropriately cover the subject matter must be distributed to all attendees at or before the time the course is presented. A mere agenda or topical outline will not be sufficient. (Comment: See MCLE Board Opinion 14.)

(h) Each course shall be presented by a faculty member or members qualified by academic or practical experience to teach the subjects covered. Consistent with Virginia State Bar policy, course sponsors should exercise care to ensure that faculty members, where possible, reflect the racial and gender diversity of the State Bar as a whole.

(i) A course presented by distance learning methods which otherwise satisfies the requirements of these Regulations may be approved provided the speakers and attendees are participating simultaneously. Pre-recorded courses in any electronic form which otherwise satisfy the requirements of these regulations may be approved however no other form of self-study will be approved. (Comment: See MCLE Board Opinion 16.)

(j) A program offered "in-house" may be approved by the Board provided the subject matter of the program does not primarily focus on internal policies, practices and procedures. An in-house program will be approved if it otherwise meets the standards of these regulations and if the approval procedures prescribed by these regulations are followed. (Comment: See MCLE Board Opinion 17.)

(k) Participation in deliberative groups concerned with political activism, law reform, judicial administration, or regulation of the profession generally will not be approved for credit. Activities associated with membership or attendance at committee meetings, business meetings or work sessions will generally not be approved for credit.

(l) To be accredited, a course must have no attendance restrictions based on race, color, national origin, religion, creed, gender, age, disability, sexual orientation or marital status.

(m) No credit will be given for any course primarily focused on marketing a particular product or service. (Comment: See MCLE Board Opinion 15.)

[Added effective September 1, 2012.]

CLIENTS' PROTECTION FUND RULES

Including Amendments Received Through October 1, 2015

Table of Rules and Regulations

Resolution of the Council of the Virginia State Bar.

RULES OF PROCEDURE OF THE CLIENTS' PROTECTION FUND OF THE VIRGINIA STATE BAR

Rule

I. Definitions.

Rule

II. Application for Reimbursement.
III. Processing Petitions.
IV. Assignment When Payment Made.
V. Payment of Receivership Costs.
VI. Meeting of the Board.
VII. General Purposes.
VIII. Authorized Investments.
IX. Amendments.

RESOLUTION OF THE COUNCIL OF THE VIRGINIA STATE BAR

Establishing a Clients' Protection Fund

WHEREAS, it is the desire of the lawyers of Virginia acting through the State Bar to preserve and protect the honor and integrity of the profession, and;

WHEREAS, it is recognized that despite the high standards of ethical conduct required of and generally maintained by the Virginia State Bar, a member of the Virginia State Bar may engage in dishonest conduct and that such conduct may result in losses to clients, and;

WHEREAS, it is the desire of the Virginia State Bar to alleviate the injury to persons so sustaining loss or damage in certain cases.

NOW, THEREFORE, BE IT RESOLVED BY THE VIRGINIA STATE BAR:

1. That there is hereby established a special Board of the Virginia State Bar to be known as the Clients' Protection Fund Board (hereinafter called the "Board") whose function it shall be to receive, hold, manage and distribute, pursuant to the terms herein contained, such funds as may from time to time be appropriated to it by the Council of the Virginia State Bar or through voluntary contribution or otherwise for the purpose of maintaining the integrity and protecting the good name of the legal profession by reimbursing to the extent deemed proper and feasible by the Board losses caused by the dishonest conduct of members of the Virginia State Bar.

2. The Board shall consist of fourteen members, one of whom shall be a nonlawyer, appointed by the Council. One member shall be from each of the ten (10) Disciplinary Districts in Virginia, and four (4) shall be appointed from the State at large. All appointments shall be for a term of three years. No appointees shall serve more than two consecutive full terms until after the expiration of at least one year. Vacancies shall be filled by appointment by the President of the Virginia State Bar for the unexpired term.

3. The Board shall be authorized to consider petitions for reimbursement of losses arising after January 1, 1976 and caused by the dishonest conduct of a member of the Virginia State Bar, acting either as a lawyer or as a fiduciary in the matter in which the loss arose except to the extent to which they are bonded or to the extent such losses are otherwise covered, provided such member has been disbarred or suspended from the practice of law pursuant to any provision of Paragraph 13 of Part 6, Section IV of the Rules of the Supreme Court of Virginia, has voluntarily resigned from the practice of law in Virginia, has died, has been adjudicated incompetent, has been the subject of a bankruptcy case that would stay, reduce or discharge the claims of the lawyer's past or present clients, or whose whereabouts is unknown to the Virginia State Bar. The Board shall be authorized and empowered to admit or reject such petitions in whole or in part, and the Board shall have complete discretion in determining the order, extent, and manner of payment. On establishing the Clients' Protection Fund, the Virginia State Bar does not create or acknowledge any legal responsibility for the acts of individual lawyers in the practice of law. All reimbursements of losses from the Clients' Protection Fund shall be in the sole discretion of the Board and not as a matter of right. No client or member of the public shall have any right in the Clients' Protection Fund as a third party beneficiary or otherwise. No attorney shall be compensated for presenting a petition except as authorized by the Board.

4. The Board shall operate pursuant to rules of procedure approved by the Council of the Virginia State Bar for the management of the Board's funds

and affairs, for the presentation of petitions, and the processing and payment thereof.

5. All sums appropriated by the Council of the Virginia State Bar for the use of the Board shall be held and invested as a separate account known as Clients' Protection Fund, subject to the written direction of the Board under written Board rules approved by the Council of the Virginia State Bar; the interest or other income thereby received to be added to and automatically become a part of the Fund.

6. The Board may use or employ the Clients' Protection Fund for any of the following purposes within the scope of the Board's objectives, as heretofore outlined:

(a) To make payments or reimbursements on approved petitions as herein provided to clients and members of the public;

(b) To purchase insurance to cover such losses in whole or in part, provided that such insurance is obtainable at reasonable costs and is deemed appropriate and provided that the purchase of such insurance is approved by the Council of the Virginia State Bar;

(c) To reimburse to the Virginia State Bar those costs of receiverships initiated by the Virginia State Bar occasioned by the need for the receiver to administer, pursue or defend assets, the recovery or preservation of which would inure to the benefit of one or more clients or other members of the public who have suffered losses as a result of the dishonest conduct of the Virginia State Bar member who is the subject of the receivership, acting as either a lawyer or as a fiduciary in the matter or matters in which the loss or losses occurred.

7. The administrative expenses of the Board shall be paid out of the general fund of the Virginia State Bar in accordance with policies established by the Council. However, the board annually at its discretion may contribute to the cost of administration by designating a sum to be paid out of the Clients' Protection Fund to the Virginia State Bar.

8. The Board shall provide a full report of its activities at least yearly to the Council of the Virginia State Bar, and it shall make such other report of its activities and give only such publicity to same as the Council may deem advisable.

9. The Council at any time may abolish the Board and the Fund. In the event of such abolition, all assets of the Fund shall be and remain the property of the Virginia State Bar to be used for its general purposes, as determined by the Council.

10. The financial condition of the Clients' Protection Fund shall be reviewed annually in conjunction with the State Bar's annual budgeting process. The Council of the Virginia State Bar shall make appropriations adequate to maintain the funding of the Clients' Protection Fund at a reasonable level, provided, however, that no appropriation may be made which will increase the assets of the fund to an amount in excess of $5,000,000.00.

11. Payment shall be made from the Fund only upon condition that the Virginia State Bar receive a pro tanto assignment from the payee of the payee's assignable rights against the lawyer or others involved, their personal representatives, heirs, devisees and assigns, and upon condition that the Fund shall be entitled to reimbursement on such terms as the Board may deem proper under the circumstances, including reimbursement of costs incurred in prosecuting a claim against said lawyer, his personal representatives, etc. The net proceeds collected by reason of such assignment shall be for the sole benefit of the Fund and applied thereto, and enforcement of this right shall be within the sole discretion of the Board.

12. The Board may give such publicity to awards made or to the work, procedures, and existence of the Clients' Protection Fund as it shall deem proper, except that in no case shall the name of the payee be stated in any release to the media. Copies of all releases shall be sent to the Executive Director of the Virginia State Bar to ensure conformity with this rule. No publicity shall be given to pending claims without the express approval of the Council of the Virginia State Bar.

[Amended effective February 24, 1996; June 17, 1999; February 22, 2003; March 3, 2006; October 24, 2014.]

RULES OF PROCEDURE OF THE CLIENTS' PROTECTION FUND OF THE VIRGINIA STATE BAR

RULE I. DEFINITIONS

For the purpose of these Rules of Procedure, the following definitions shall apply:

1. The "Board" shall mean the Clients' Protection Fund Board.

2. The "Fund" shall mean the Clients' Protection Fund of the Virginia State Bar.

3. A "Lawyer," "Attorney" or "Respondent" shall mean one who, at the time of the act complained of, was a member of the Virginia State Bar, was domiciled in Virginia, and was actually engaged in the practice of law in Virginia. The fact that the act complained of took place outside of the Commonwealth of Virginia does not necessarily mean that the Lawyer was not engaged in the practice of law in Virginia.

4. A "Petitioner" or "Claimant" shall mean a person or entity that applies to the Clients' Protection Fund Board for payment pursuant to the rules applicable to the Fund.

5. "Reimbursable Losses" are limited to actual, out-of-pocket or quantifiable losses, supported by documentation, of money or other property that meet the following tests:

(a) The conduct which occasioned the loss occurred on or after January 1, 1976.

(b) The loss must be caused by the dishonest conduct of the Lawyer and shall have arisen out of and by reason of a lawyer-client relationship or a fiduciary relationship between the Lawyer and the Claimant.

(c) The Lawyer has been disbarred or suspended from the practice of law pursuant to any provision of Paragraph 13 of Part 6, Section IV of the Rules of the Supreme Court of Virginia, has voluntarily resigned from the practice of law in Virginia, has died, has been adjudicated incompetent, has been the subject of a bankruptcy case that would stay, reduce or discharge the claims of the Lawyer's past or present clients, or whose whereabouts is unknown to the Virginia State Bar.

5.1 The following shall be excluded from "Reimbursable Losses":

(a) Losses of spouses, other close relatives, partners, associates and employees of Lawyers causing the losses;

(b) Losses covered by any bond, surety agreement, or insurance contract to the extent covered thereby, including any loss to which any bonding agent, surety or insurer is subrogated;

(c) Losses of any financial institution which are recoverable under a "banker's blanket bond" or similar commonly available insurance or surety contract;

(d) Losses by any business entity controlled by the Lawyer;

(e) Losses incurred by any governmental entity or agency;

(f) Losses occasioned by a loan or an investment transaction with a Lawyer, unless it arose out of and in the course of the attorney-client relationship and but for the fact that the dishonest attorney enjoyed an attorney-client relationship with the Claimant such loss could not have occurred. In considering whether that standard has been met, the following factors will be considered:

1. The disparity in bargaining power between the attorney and the client and their respective educational backgrounds and business sophistication.

2. The extent to which the attorney-client relationship overcame the normal prudence of the applicant.

3. The extent to which the attorney, by virtue of the attorney-client relationship with the applicant, became privy to information as to the applicant's financial affairs.

4. Whether a principal part of the service arose out of a relationship requiring a license to practice law.

(g) Claims by a Petitioner for damages for a cause of action in which a Lawyer represented a Petitioner and that never resulted in a settlement or judgment;

(h) Claims for interest, late fees, penalties, surcharges or other consequential damages, even if such damages arise out of Reimbursable Losses.

6. "Dishonest Conduct" may include, but is not necessarily limited to

(a) Any act committed by a Lawyer in the nature of theft, conversion embezzlement or withholding of money or property from its rightful owner, recipient or person entitled to receive such money or property;

(b) Any act committed by a Lawyer in the nature of failure, refusal or inability to refund unearned fees received in advance where the Lawyer performed no legal services or such an insignificant service that the failure, refusal or inability to refund the unearned fees constitutes a wrongful taking or conversion. Where the Board finds that the legal services performed by the Lawyer are more than insignificant, but the Lawyer has not fully earned the entire fee, the failure, refusal or inability to refund the unearned fees may still constitute a wrongful taking or conversion, and the Board may reimburse fifty percent of the total fees paid by the Petitioner.

6.1 The Board shall exercise its discretion in deciding whether a Lawyer committed Dishonest Conduct. In making its determination, the Board may consider as compelling evidence of such Dishonest Conduct, in addition to other factors:

(a) an order from any court or disciplinary tribunal disciplining a Lawyer for the same act or conduct alleged in a Petition or otherwise finding that a Lawyer committed Dishonest Conduct; or

(b) a final judgment imposing civil or criminal liability upon a Lawyer for such conduct.

[Amended effective February 22, 2003; October 17, 2003; March 3, 2006; February 23, 2013; October 24, 2014.]

RULE II. APPLICATION FOR REIMBURSEMENT

0. The Board shall prepare a form of Petition for reimbursement; in its discretion the Board may waive a requirement that a Petition be filed on such form.

1. At a minimum, the form shall require the Petitioner to state:

(a) The name, address and telephone number of the Petitioner.

(b) The name and last known address of the Lawyer allegedly responsible for the claimed loss.

(c) The amount of the loss claimed

(d) Documentation supporting the loss, including proof of payment for monies the Petitioner or anyone on his behalf paid directly to the Lawyer.

(e) The date or period of time the alleged loss occurred.

(f) A description of the efforts by the Petitioner to recover the alleged loss from the Lawyer or from other sources of payment besides the Virginia State Bar.

(g) The notarized signature of the Petitioner.

2. The Petition shall contain the following statement in bold type:

"IN ESTABLISHING THE CLIENTS' PROTECTION FUND, THE VIRGINIA STATE BAR DID NOT CREATE OR ACKNOWLEDGE ANY LEGAL RESPONSIBILITY FOR THE ACTS OF INDIVIDUAL LAWYERS IN THE PRACTICE OF LAW. ALL REIMBURSEMENTS OF LOSSES FROM THE CLIENTS' PROTECTION FUND SHALL BE IN THE SOLE DISCRETION OF THE BOARD ADMINISTERING THE FUND AND NOT AS A MATTER OF RIGHT. NO CLIENT OR MEMBER OF THE PUBLIC SHALL HAVE ANY RIGHT IN THE CLIENTS' PROTECTION FUND AS A THIRD PARTY BENEFICIARY OR OTHERWISE."

3. Petitions shall be submitted to the central office of the Virginia State Bar in Richmond, Virginia. If the staff of the Virginia State Bar determines that the Petition complies with the minimum requirements of these Rules, the Petition shall be investigated and approved or denied by the Board.

[Amended effective February 22, 2003; March 3, 2006; February, 23, 2013; October 24, 2014.]

RULE III. PROCESSING PETITIONS

0. The Chair of the Board or such bar staff as the Chair designates shall cause each Petition to be sent to a member of the Board or other member of the Virginia State Bar for investigation and report. A copy shall be sent to the Lawyer at his address of record maintained by the membership department of the bar. The Lawyer or his representative may respond to the Petition within thirty (30) days of the date of the letter or letters transmitting the Petition to him.

Petitions shall be assigned considering the workload of each Board member, and, when possible, by giving preference for assignment to a Board member who works or lives in the jurisdiction in which the Lawyer maintained his office, place of employment, or address of record with the Virginia State Bar.

1. A member to whom a Petition is referred for investigation shall conduct such investigation as to him seems necessary and desirable in order to determine whether the same is for a Reimbursable Loss and in order to guide the Board in determining the extent, if any, to which the loss should be reimbursed from the Fund.

2. When, in the opinion of the member to whom the Petition has been referred, the Petition is clearly not for a reimbursable loss, no further investigation need be conducted, but a report with respect to such Petition shall be made by the member to whom the Petitioner was referred, as hereinafter specified.

3. The Board member who investigates a Petition shall prepare a written report and recommendation as to whether the Petition should be paid or denied. Such report shall be available for inspection by the Board members attending the meeting at which the Petition is reviewed.

4. No Petition with respect to which an inadequate opportunity for investigation has been afforded need be considered by the Board for reimbursement in the year in which such claim is presented.

5. In those instances where the reporting member in his report suggests or any other member of the Board, after studying the reports of Petitions to be processed, requests that the Board hear evidence, the Board shall hear the Petitioner, the Lawyer and such other evidence as may be presented. Absent such recommendation or request, Petitions may be processed on the basis of information contained therein and in the report of the member who investigated each Petition. The Lawyer or his personal representative, or the Petitioner or his personal representative, may request to address the Board at a meeting at which the Board is considering the claim. Any such request must be made to the Chair or his designee, and the Chair may place restrictions and/or limitations on the length or subject matter of any statements allowed.

6. The Board shall, in its sole discretion and by a majority vote, determine the amount of loss, if any, for which any Petitioner shall be reimbursed from the Fund. Although only a majority vote is required to approve or deny a Petition, the Board should aspire to come to a consensus on every Petition. In making such determination, the Board shall consider *inter alia*, the following:

(a) Any conduct of the Petitioner which contributed to the loss.

(b) The loss to be paid to any one Petitioner shall not exceed $75,000 for losses incurred on or after July 1, 2015, or $50,000 for losses incurred on or after July 1, 2000, and prior to July 1, 2015, or $25,000 for losses incurred prior to July 1, 2000. For purposes of this provision, the Board may regard two or more persons, firms or entities as one Petitioner with respect to a Lawyer's dishonest conduct in handling a given matter where the facts and entities are found to justify such a conclusion.

(c) The total amount of losses reimbursable hereunder on account of the misconduct of any one lawyer or association of lawyers (including, without limitation, a law firm, professional corporation, or an office-sharing arrangement among lawyers) shall be limited to fifteen percent (15%) of the net worth of the Clients' Protection Fund at the time the first claim is made. In the event of multiple claims on account of the misconduct of any one lawyer or association of lawyers, claims may be considered in any order or grouping which the Board, in its discretion, finds appropriate, taking into account the equities and timeliness of each claim, and no further payment shall be made in respect to misconduct of any one lawyer or association of lawyers once the fifteen percent limit has been reached.

(d) The total amount of Reimbursable Losses in previous years for which payment has not been made and the total assets of the Fund.

(e) The Board may, in its sole discretion, allow further payment in any year on account of a reimbursable loss allowed by it in prior years which has not been fully paid; provided such further payment would not be inconsistent or in conflict with any previous determination with respect to such loss.

(f) No payment shall be made upon any Petition, a summary of which has not been submitted to the members in accordance with these Rules of Procedure. No payment shall be made to any Petitioner unless said payment is duly approved by the Board.

(g) No claim shall be considered by the Board unless the same shall have been filed within seven years from the time the Claimant knew or should have known of the Lawyer's Dishonest Conduct, or within one year after the first occurrence of one of the following events, whichever date is later:

i. the Lawyer has been disbarred or suspended from the practice of law pursuant to any provision of Part 6, Section IV, Paragraph 13 of the Rules of the Supreme Court of Virginia;

ii. the Lawyer has voluntarily resigned from the practice of law in Virginia;

iii. the Lawyer has died;

iv. the Lawyer has been adjudicated incompetent;

v. the Lawyer has been the subject of a bankruptcy that would stay, reduce or discharge the claims of the Lawyer's past or present clients; or

vi. the whereabouts of the Lawyer is unknown to the Virginia State Bar.

(h) The Board may make a finding of Dishonest Conduct for purposes of adjudicating a claim. Such a determination is not a finding of Dishonest Conduct for purposes of professional discipline.

7. A member who has or has had a lawyer-client relationship or financial relationship with a Claimant or Lawyer who is the subject of a claim shall not participate in the investigation or adjudication of a claim involving that Claimant or Lawyer. A member with any other past or present relationship with a Claimant or the Lawyer whose alleged conduct is the subject of the claim, shall disclose such relationship to the Board and, if the Board deems appropriate, that member shall not participate in any proceeding relating to such claim.

8. The Claimant or Respondent may request reconsideration in writing within 30 days of the denial or determination of the amount of a claim. If the Claimant or Respondent fails to make a request or the request is denied, the decision of the Board is final. There shall be no appeal from a decision of the Board.

9. A Lawyer whose Dishonest Conduct has resulted in reimbursement to a Claimant shall make restitution to the Fund including interest and the expense incurred by the Fund in processing the claim.

[Amended effective July 1, 1995; February 22, 2003; October 17, 2003; March 3, 2006; February, 23, 2013; October 24, 2014.]

RULE IV. ASSIGNMENT WHEN PAYMENT MADE

In the event payment is made from the Fund to a Petitioner, the Fund shall require an assignment from the Petitioner of such claim as he may have against the Lawyer complained of and may bring such action thereon in the name of the Petitioner as is deemed advisable against the Lawyer, his assets or his estate. The Petitioner shall be required to execute such an assignment. Prior to the commencement of an action by the Board, it shall advise the Petitioner thereof at his last known address. The Petitioner may then join in such action to press a claim for his loss in excess of the amount of the payment made by the Fund or for any other claims. The Board may impose such other conditions and requirements as it may deem appropriate in connection with payment to any Petitioner. [Amended effective February 22, 2003; March 3, 2006; February, 23, 2013; October 24, 2014.]

RULE V. PAYMENT OF RECEIVERSHIP COSTS

Costs of any Virginia State Bar receivership occasioned by the need for the receiver to administer, pursue or defend assets, the recovery or preservation of which would inure to the benefit of one or more clients or other members of the public who have suffered losses as a result of the dishonest conduct of the Virginia State Bar member who is the subject of the receivership, acting as either a lawyer or as a fiduciary in the matter or matters in which the loss or losses occurred, shall be documented and certified to the Board by the Virginia State Bar staff for consideration of payment from the Fund by the Board as an agenda item at a meeting of the Board.

[Adopted effective June 17, 1999. Amended effective March 3, 2006; February, 23, 2013; October 24, 2014.]

RULE VI. MEETING OF THE BOARD

0. The Board shall meet at least one time during each fiscal year. The first meeting of any fiscal year shall be designated the "Annual Meeting." The Annual Meeting shall take place after the beginning of the fiscal year, but not later than September 30. In addition, the Board shall meet from time to time upon call of the Chair or any two members of the Board.

1. The members shall be given not less than 15 days' written notice of the time and place of the annual meeting and not less than 5 days' written notice of each special meeting. Notice of any meeting may be waived by a member either before or after the meeting.

2. A quorum at any meeting of the Board shall be six (6) members. No action shall be taken by the Board in the absence of a quorum; except that any action which might be taken at a meeting may be taken without a meeting if a consent in writing, setting forth the action so to be taken, shall be signed before such action by all the members of the Board.

3. Written minutes of each meeting shall be prepared and permanently maintained.

4. The Chair and Vice Chair of the Board shall be elected by a majority of the Board at the last meeting of the fiscal year. Their terms shall extend until the last meeting of the next fiscal year and until their successors are elected and qualified. Should a vacancy occur in the office of Chair or Vice Chair, such vacancy shall be filled by majority vote of the members of the Board at the meeting next following the occurrence of the vacancy.

[Former Rule V renumbered as Rule VI June 17, 1999. Amended effective March 3, 2006; February, 23, 2013; October 24, 2014.]

RULE VII. GENERAL PURPOSES

These Rules of Procedure shall be liberally interpreted and, in any given case, the Board may waive technical adherence to these Rules of Procedure in order to achieve the objectives of the Fund, as contained in the enabling Resolution establishing the Fund.

[Former Rule VI renumbered as Rule VII June 17, 1999. Amended effective March 3, 2006; February, 23, 2013; October 24, 2014.]

RULE VIII. AUTHORIZED INVESTMENTS

Investment of monies of the Clients' Protection Fund shall be restricted to the following:

(a) Interest-bearing deposits (including as well certificates of deposit) in federally insured banks and savings institutions located in the state of Virginia.

(b) Direct obligations of the Commonwealth of Virginia and the United States Government, and securities of entities created by Congress and authorized to issue such securities; provided that no such deposit, certificate or obligation shall have a maturity beyond ten years from the date of the investment; and provided further that the interest, discount or other gain or income realized from any such investment, net of any bank or brokerage charges incurred in connection therewith, shall automatically become a part of the Fund.

[Former Rule VII renumbered as Rule VIII June 17, 1999. Amended effective March 3, 2006; February, 23, 2013; October 24, 2014.]

RULE IX. AMENDMENTS

These Rules may be changed at any time by a majority vote of the Board at a duly held meeting at which a quorum is present, and subject to the approval of the Council of the Virginia State Bar.

[Former Rule VIII renumbered as Rule IX June 17, 1999. Amended effective March 3, 2006; February, 23, 2013; October 24, 2014.]